핸디 한영사전

민중서림 편집국 편

[제6판]

사서전문
민중서림

머 리 말
— 개정판을 내면서 —

 이 "신한영소사전(新韓英小辭典)"의 초판을 펴낸 것은 1961년이었다. 그 이후 독자들의 끊임없는 격려와 호평 속에서 여러 번 개정을 거듭하며 중쇄(重刷)를 되풀이해 오다가, 1992년에 제5 개정판을 내었고, 1996년 8월에는 휴대에 편리하면서도 활자와 지면을 기존의 소사전보다 크게 키운 같은 내용의 '포켓판' 초판을 내어 각계각층의 독자들로부터 분에 넘치는 격려와 사랑을 듬뿍 받아왔다.

 이제 우리는 동서의 냉전 구조가 붕괴되고, 국제화·정보화가 빠른 속도로 이루어지는 국경 없는 무한 경쟁 시대인 21세기의 문턱에 서게 되었다. 이에 따른 정치·경제·사회 등 각 분야에 걸친 큰 변화, 첨단 과학 기술과 산업의 급속한 발전, 환경 문제, 국제 교류의 활발한 진전 등은 수많은 새로운 낱말들을 만들어내고 종래의 어휘에 새로운 의미를 부가시키는 결과를 낳기도 하였다.

 해외로 넓고 크게 뻗어나가야 하는 우리들에게 세계 공통어인 영어의 필요성은 더욱더 그 비중이 높아져, "한영 사전"의 요긴함이 날로 증폭되어 가고 있는 실정이다.

 이 개정판은, 이러한 시대적 요구에 부응하는 쓸모있고 알찬 사전을 만들어야 한다는 사명감으로, 기존 내용을 하나하나 검토하면서 보다 새로운 표현으로 다듬어 보완하고 수집된 새로운 자료들을 실용 위주로 선별 보충하는 대폭적인 전면 개정 작업으로 이루어지게 되었다.

 특히, 이번 개정에서 역점을 둔 점은 아래와 같다.

1. 새로 나온 과학·경제·정치·사회·환경·일상 생활 등에 관련된 중요한 신어들을 대폭 보충하였다.
2. 실무 영작문에 필요한 예문, 일상 생활·업무 관계 등으로 외국인과 대화할 때 그대로 활용할 수 있는 실용적인 예문을 많이 실었다.
3. 한 표제어에 대응하는 여러 개의 역어가 있어 그 쓰임에 혼동이 될 염려가 있는 낱말에는 그 용법·뜻의 차이를 알 수 있도록 가능한 한 《 》, 또는 ( )안에 그 뜻이나 용도를 명기하였다.
4. 표제어 하나만으로 관련 사항을 폭넓게 파악할 수 없는 주요 사항에 대하여는 별도의 박스난을 설정하여 충분한 지식을 접할 수 있도록 하였다.
5. 실용성이 높은 다양한 내용을 부록으로 실었다.

개정 작업을 마치고 나니, 언제나처럼 "좀더 알차고 완벽한 사전을 만들었어야 했는데…" 하는 아쉬움이 남는다. 최선을 다했지만, 예상하지 못한 미비한 점도 있으리라 생각된다. 독자 여러분의 교시와 비판을 바라면서, 앞으로 더욱더 노력하여 보다 실용적이고 알찬 사전을 만드는 일에 헌신할 것을 약속 드리는 바이다.

1998년 5월 일

민중서림 편집국

일러두기

이 사전의 구성

이 사전은 현재 널리 쓰이고 있는 우리말과 외래어, 학술 용어 및 시사어 등을 가나다순으로 배열하였다.

A. 표제어

(1) 표제어는 고딕 활자로 보였고 한문에서 온 말은 괄호 속에 한자를 병기하였으며 일부가 우리말이고 다른 일부가 한자어인 것은 —과 한자를 붙여 병기하였다.
   보기 가난, 상임(常任), 도도하다(滔滔—)
(2) 접두사, 접미사 및 어미(語尾)로 쓰이는 표제어는 각기 그 앞뒤에 …을 붙였다.
   보기 가…(假), …강(强), …도록
(3) 낱말은 각각 독립 표제어로 내놓는 것을 원칙으로 하되, 지면 절약을 위하여 경우에 따라서는 다음과 같은 방법을 쓰기도 하였다.
   a) 표제어를 어간(語幹)으로 한 낱말은 표제어가 길지 않을 때 독립 표제어로 내세우지 않고 어간인 표제어의 역어 다음에 병기해 주었다.
   보기 ㄱ. **억지** unreasonableness; obstinacy; compulsion. ¶ ~부리다〔쓰다〕 insist on having *one's* own way; persist stubbornly.
   ㄴ. **엄살** ~하다 pretend pain〔hardship〕.
   b) 동의어 및 원말과 준말 등은 병기해 준 것도 있다.
   보기 **덕적덕적, 덕지덕지 가마(니)**

B. 역어와 용례

(1) 역어와 용례는 현대 영어를 표준으로 하였으며, 속어·전문어 및 속담 등도 필요에 따라 적적히 곁들였다.
(2) 영어의 철자는 미식을 위주로 하되, 특히 주의를 요하는 말은 영식을 아울러 보인 것도 있다. 단, 이 때에는 역어 뒤에《英》을 보임으로써 그 구별을 나타냈다.
   보기 **수표**(手票) a check; a cheque《英》.
(3) 역어에 있어 미식·영식이 각기 그 표현을 달리할 때에는 다음처럼 표시했다.
   보기 **왕복**(往復) … ‖ ~차표 a round-trip ticket《美》; a return ticket《英》.
(4) 외래어(外來語)로서 아직 영어에 완전히 동화되지 않은 것은 이탤릭체(體)로 표시했다.
   보기 **사후**(事後) ¶ ~의 *ex post facto*〔라〕.
(5) 표제어가 형용사일 때에는 (be)를 역어 앞에 붙여 형용사임을 나타냈다. 단, 동사로 밖에 표현되지 않는 경우에, 그 구분을 명백히 할 필요가 있을 때는 역어 앞에《서술적》, 역어 뒤에는 (서술적)이라고 표시했다.
   보기 **어리둥절하다** (be) dazed〔stunned〕; bewildered;《서술적》be 〔get〕 confused; be puzzled.
(6) *one* (*oneself*), *a person*: 이것들은 일반적으로 「사람」을 가리키는 명사·대명사임을 나타낸다. *one*은 주어와 같은 사람을, *a person*은 주어와 다른 사람임을 나타낸다.

보기 **가로막다** interrupt 《*a person*》.
　　　생활(生活) ～ 하다 support *oneself*.
(7) 마찬가지로, *a thing*은 「물건」을, *a matter*는 「일」을, *a place*는 「장소」를 가리킨다.
(8) *do*는 일반적인 동사를 대표하며, *to do*는 부정사, *doing*은 동명사를 표시한다.
보기 **떳떳하다**... ¶ …을 떳떳하지 않게 여기다 be too proud 《*to do*》; be above 《*doing*》.

C. 기호의 용법

(1) 〖 〗의 용법
　학술어와 기타 전문 용어 및 그 약어를 표시할 때
　보기 **양서류**(兩棲類) 〖動〗 Amphibia.
(2) 《 》의 용법
　표제어 또는 용례의 뜻을 설명하거나 어법·용법상의 설명을 가할 때
　보기 **양여**(讓與) 《영토의》 cession.
　　　가게... ¶ ～를 닫다 close the store; 《폐업》 shut 〔close〕 up store.
　　　가곡(歌曲) 《노래》 a song; 《곡조》 a melody.
(3) 《 》의 용법
 a) 역어의 각국별 용법 및 어원 등을 표시할 때
　　보기 **감옥**(監獄) a jail 《美》; a gaol 《英》.
　　　　마티네 a *matinée* 《프》.
 b) 그 역어가 취하는 관련 전치사·형용사·동사 및 보충 설명적인 목적어 등을 보인다.
　　보기 **거처**(居處)... ¶ ～를 정하다 take up *one's* residence 〔quarters〕 《*at, in*》.
　　　　개진(開陳) ～ 하다…: express 《*one's* opinion》.
　　　　반소(反訴) 《bring》 a cross action.
(4) ( )의 용법
 a) 생략이 가능한 말을 쌀 때
　　보기 **프로그램** a program(me)
　　　　　　　|＝ a program
　　　　　　　|＝ a programme
　　　　데이트... ～ 하다 date (with) 《*a girl*》.
　　　　　　　|＝ date 《*a girl*》
　　　　　　　|＝ date with 《*a girl*》.
 b) 역어의 보충 설명 및 그 생략어·기호 따위
　　보기 **붕사**(硼砂) borax; tincal (천연의).
　　　　붕소(硼素) 〖化〗 boron (기호 B).
　　　　삼월(三月) March (생략 Mar.).
 c) 복합어에 곁달린 말들을 보였다.
　　보기 **양도**(讓渡)... ¶ ～인 a grantor; a transferer(피～인 a transferee).
 d) 머리글자로 만들어진 생략형 역어의 원어를 표시할 때
　　보기 **아이오시** IOC. (◀ the International Olympic Committee)
 e) 표제어가 형용사임을 보이기 위해 be를 사용할 때
　　보기 **아름답다** (be) beautiful: pretty.
(5) 〔 〕의 용법
　그 부분이 대치될 수 있음을 표시할 때
　보기 **양원**(兩院) both 〔the two〕 Houses.
　　　　　　|＝ both Houses
　　　　　　|＝ the two Houses
(6) 〚 〛의 용법
　그 역어의 복수형을 보였다.

보기 **용매**(溶媒) a menstruum [*pl.* ~ s. -strua]
(7) ~는 표제어와 일치한다.
보기 **가속**(加速)···. ¶ ~적으로 with increasing speed.
(8) ☞는 「다음의 항을 보라」, =은 「다음 것과 같다」의 뜻임.
(9) ∥이하는 복합어, 연어를 보인다.
보기 **양심**(良心)···. ∥ ~선언 a declaration of conscience.
(10) 「=」는 본래의 하이픈이 행말(行末)에 왔을 때 표시했다.
보기 **양화**(洋畫) ① 《서양화》 a Western=
 style painting.

약 어 풀 이

(자명한 것은 생략)

《美》	美國用法	《獨》	獨逸語
《英》	英國用法	《그》	그리스語
《러》	러시아語	《라》	라틴語
《이》	이탈리아語	《梵》	梵語
《中》	中國語	《口》	口語
《프》	프랑스語	《俗》	俗語
[建]	建築	[野]	野球
[經]	經濟	[藥]	藥學
[工]	工業	[魚]	魚類
[鑛]	鑛物・鑛山	[言]	言語學
[敎]	敎育	[倫]	倫理學
[軍]	軍事	[衣]	衣服
[基]	基督敎	[醫]	醫學
[幾]	幾何	[理]	物理學
[氣]	氣象	[印]	印刷
[倫]	論理學	[電]	電氣
[農]	農業・農學	[鳥]	鳥類
[動]	動物學	[宗]	宗敎
[文]	文法	[證]	證券
[法]	法律	[地]	地質・地理學
[寫]	寫眞	[天]	天文學
[商]	商業	[哲]	哲學
[生]	生理學・生物學	[鐵]	鐵道
[船]	造船	[蟲]	昆蟲
[聖]	聖經	[컴]	컴퓨터
[數]	數學	[土]	土木
[植]	植物學	[韓醫], [漢醫]	韓醫學・漢醫學
[心]	心理學	[海]	航海・海事
[樂]	音樂	[解]	解剖學
[冶]	冶金	[化]	化學

박스 기사 색인

한·미군 계급	142
우리나라 내각 명칭	179
동물의 울음소리	241
날짜·요일의 표시	303
배수(倍數)의 표현 방법	375
사과의 표현	471
여행	614
자동차	730
친인척 계보표	778
컴퓨터	787
만화에 나오는 의성어·의음어	814
병명(病名)·병원(病院)	842
회사의 조직과 직위의 영어명	905

신한영 소사전 부록 차례

Ⅰ. 이력서 쓰기	907
Ⅱ. 편지 쓰기	907
Ⅲ. 기호 읽기	909
Ⅳ. 수	909
Ⅴ. 미·영 철자의 차이	910
Ⅵ. 도량형표	911
Ⅶ. 국어의 로마자 표기법	912
Ⅷ. 지방 행정 단위의 영어 표기	914
Ⅸ. 한국 전통 식품의 영어명 표기 방법	915
Ⅹ. 우리식 표현의 영어 낱말들	917
Ⅺ. 국제 전화 거는 법	918
Ⅻ. 세계 주요도시 표준시 대조표	919
XIII. 우리 나라 행정 구역의 로마자 표기	920
XIV. 미국의 주명	923
XV. 불규칙동사표	924

KOREAN-ENGLISH
DICTIONARY

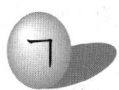

ㄱ

가 《가장자리》 an edge; a border; a margin; a brink; a verge; 《옆》 a side.

가(可) 《성적》 fairly good; 《좋음》 good; right. ¶ ~히 (may) well; fairly well; (might) well / ~히 짐작할 수 있다 It can readily be imagined that ....

가(假) 《임시의》 temporary; provisional; 《잠시의》 transient; 《비공식의》 informal. ¶ ~계약 provisional contract / ~계정(計定) temporary account / ~입학(入學) admission (of students) on probation / ~처분 (make) provisional disposition.

…가(街) a street; St. (고유명사에). ¶ 3~ the 3rd St.

가가대소(呵呵大笑) ~하다 have a good laugh; laugh heartily.

가가호호(家家戶戶) each (every) house (door); from door to door.

가감(加減) ~하다 add and deduct; moderate, adjust (조절). ‖ ~ 승제(乘除) addition, subtraction, multiplication and division: the four rules of arithmetic. 「rary building (house).」

가건물(假建物) (build) a temporary

가게 a shop; a store (美); a booth (노점). ¶ ~를 보다 tend [keep] a shop / ~를 내다 open [start] a shop / ~를 닫다 close the store; 《폐업》 shut [close] up store; wind up business.

가격(價格) worth; value; 《값》 price. ¶ 일정한 ~으로 at a fixed price / ~을 유지하다 hold the price line / ~을 조작 [동결] 하다 manipulate [freeze] the price. ‖ ~인상 a price advance / ~인하 a price reduction; discount / ~차 a price margin / ~파괴 a price destruction [slash] / ~표 a price list.

가결(可決) approval; adoption; passage. ~하다 adopt 《a bill》; carry 《a motion》; approve; vote. ¶ 원안대로 ~하다 pass a bill as drafted / 거수로 ~하다 decide 《on a bill》 by (a) show of hands.

가결의(假決議) a temporary decision; a provisional resolution.

가경(佳景) fine scenery; a picturesque scene; a wonderful view.

가경(佳境) ① 《고비》 the most interesting [exciting] part 《of a story》; the climax 《of a story》. ¶ 얘기는 ~에 들어간다 Now we come to the most interesting part of the story. ② =가경(佳景).

가계(家系) a family line; lineage; pedigree. ‖ ~도 a family tree.

가계(家計) a family budget; household economy; 《생계》 livelihood; living (expense). ‖ ~부 a household account book; a petty cashbook (~부를 적다 keep household accounts) / ~비 household expenses.

가곡(歌曲) 《노래》 a song; 《곡조》 a melody; a tune. ‖ ~집 a collection of songs.

가공(加工) processing. ~하다 process; manufacture. ¶ 우유를 ~하다 process milk / ~공장 a processing plant / ~무역 processing trade / ~식품 processed foods / ~업 processing industries / ~업자 a processor / ~품 processed [manufactured] goods.

가공(可恐) ¶ ~할 fearful; fearsome; terrible; dreadful / ~할 만한 적 a terrible foe.

가공(架空) ① 《허구적》 ¶ ~의 unreal; imaginary; fictitious / ~의 인물 an unreal person. ② 《공중 가설》 ~의 overhead; aerial. ‖ ~삭도(索道) an aerial ropeway (cableway) / ~전선 an overhead power line.

가공사(假工事) provisional construction work.

가관(可觀) ¶ ~이다 《볼 만하다》 be well worth seeing; 《꼴이 좋다》 be a sight / 경치가 ~이다 have a beautiful outlook; command a fine

가교(架橋) ~하다 (build a) bridge; span (*a river*) with a bridge. ¶ ~공사 bridging works.

가교(假橋) a temporary bridge.

가구(家口) a household; a house (집). ¶ ~수 the number of households; ~주 a householder; the head of a family.

가구(家具) (household) furniture; upholstery. ¶ ~한 점[세트] a piece [set] of furniture. ¶ ~상 a furniture store; a furniture dealer (상인); ~장이 a furniture maker.

가규(家規) rules of the house.

가극(歌劇) a musical drama; an opera; an operetta (소가극). ¶ ~단(장, 배우) an opera company (house, singer); 'poultry.

가금(家禽) a domestic fowl; (총칭)

가급적(可及的) as ... as possible; as ... as *one* can. ¶ ~ 빨리 as soon as possible / ~이면 if possible.

가까스로 with difficulty; narrowly; barely. ¶ ~ 도망치다 have a narrow escape / ~ 제시간에 대다 be barely in time for (*the train*).

가까워지다 (때·거리가) approach; draw (get) near; be near [close] at hand; (사이가) become friendly; make friends with. ¶ 완성에 ~ be near completion / 종말에(이) ~ draw to a close (an end).

가까이 near; nearby; close by; (친밀하게) intimately; ~하다 make friends (*with*); keep company (*with*). ¶ ~ 가다 approach; draw (come) near / 술을 ~하다 take wine habitually / 나쁜 벗들을 ~하지 마라 Keep away from bad company.

가깝다 (거리) (be) near; close(near by; (시간) (be) near; immediate; (관계) (be) familiar; friendly; near; (근사) (be) akin to; close upon; allied to. ¶ 가까운 친구 (close, best) friend / 가까운 친척 a near relative / 가까운 예(例) a familiar example / 가깝다 be very close to; be near at hand / 가까이하다 be on good [intimate] terms (*with*) / 원숭이는 사람에 ~ The ape is closely allied to man.

가꾸다 (식물을) grow; cultivate; raise; (치장하다) dress *oneself* up (옷으로); make *oneself* up(얼굴을); decorate (꾸미다).

가끔 occasionally; once in a while; from time to time. ¶ ~ 들르다 drop in from time to time.

가나다 the Korean alphabet. ¶ ~순으로 하다 alphabetize; arrange in alphabetical order.

가나오나 wherever *one* may go (be); always; all the time; constantly. ¶ 그는 말썽을 일으킨다 He is a constant troublemaker.

가난 poverty; want; indigence (극빈); destitution(결핍); penury (빈궁). ~하다 (be) poor; destitute; needy; in want. ¶ 몹시 ~한 사람 a poverty-stricken man / ~한 집에 태어나다 be born poor / ~이 들다 be (run) short of 《something》; suffer a dearth (shortage, need) of 《talent》 / 찢어지게 ~하다 be extremely poor / ~하게 살다 live in poverty (want) / ~해지다 become poor; be reduced to poverty.

가난뱅이 a poor man; a pauper (극빈자); the poor (총칭).

가납(嘉納) acceptance; approval; appreciation. ~하다 accept (*a present*) with pleasure; approve; appreciate.

가내(家內) (가족들) a family; a household; ¶ ~공업 home (domestic) industry.

가냘프다 (be) slender; slim; (목소리가) (be) feeble; faint. ¶ 가냘픈 팔 a thin and weak arm / 몸이 ~ be a slender build.

가누다 keep under control; keep steady. ¶ 고개를 ~ hold up *one's* head / 몸을 ~ keep *one's* balance.

가늘다 (be) thin; slender; fine (실 따위). ¶ 가는 목소리 a thin voice / 가는 다리 slender legs / 가는 실 a fine thread / 가는 막대기 a thin rod.

가늠 (헤아림) guess; (겨냥) aim; sight; (식별·어림) discernment; estimate. ~하다 ~보다 (take) aim (*at*); sight (*on*); guess; weigh; estimate. ¶ ~의 the bead; the foresight / ~자 the sight(s) / a gun sight.

가능(可能) ~하다 (be) possible. ¶ ~하면 if (it) is possible / ~한 빨리 as soon as possible / ~한 범위 내에서 as far as possible / ~한 계획 a practicable (feasible, workable) plan / 나는 ~하다고 생각한다 I think it's possible. ‖ ~성 possibility; potential (잠재적인).

가다 ① (일반적) go; come (상대방 본위로); (방문) visit; call on 《*a person*》; (출석) attend; go to 《*church*》 (떠나다) go away (*to*); leave. ¶ ...을 타고 ~ go by

《*train, bus*》/ 걸어 ~ walk; go on foot / 미국에 ~ go over to America / 2등을 타고 ~ travel [go] second class / 여수까지 ~ go as far as *Yeosu* / 하루 20마일을 ~ make [cover] twenty miles a day / 집에 가는 도중에 on one's way home. ② 《시간이》 pass (by); go by; elapse; fly. ¶ 얼마 안 가서 before long / 시간이 ~ time passes / 세월이 가는 줄도 모르다 be unconscious of the flight [elapse] of time. ③ 《죽다》 die; pass away. ④ 《꺼지다》 go [die] out. ¶ 전깃불이 ~ electric light fails. ⑤ 《지탱하다》 wear; last; hold; be durable. ¶ 구두가 오래 ~ shoes wear well. ⑥ 《변하다》 go bad; rot; turn sour [시어지다]; get stale (생선 따위). ¶ 맥주 맛이 ~ beer gets flat. ⑦ 《들다》 take; need; be required [needed]. ¶ 품이 많이 가는 일 a work that requires much labor. ⑧ 《값어치》 be worth. ¶ 백만원 가는 책 a book worth a million *won* today. ⑨ 《짐작이》 이해가 가는 처사 an understandable measure [step].
가다가 (때때로) at times; now and then; once in a while.
가다듬다 《마음을》 brace oneself (up); collect oneself; 《목소리를》 put one's voice in tune.
가닥 a ply; a strand. ¶ 실 한 ~ a piece of string / 세 ~으로 꼰 밧줄 a rope of three strands / 한 ~의 희망 a ray of hope.
가단성 (可鍛性) malleability. ¶ ~이 있는 malleable.
가담 (加擔)《원조》 assistance; support; 《참여》 participation; 《공모》 conspiracy; ~하다 《돕다》 assist; aid; take side with; 《참여하다》 take part [participate] in; be a party to; be involved in. ¶ 음모에 ~하다 take part in the plot. ¶ ~자 an accomplice; a conspirator.
가당 (加糖) ¶ ~한 sweetened. ‖ ~분유 sugared powder [pulverized] milk / ~연유 (練乳) sweetened condensed milk.
가당찮다 (一) be unreasonable, unjust, improper(온당찮다); excessive, extravagant (엄청나다); tough, hard(난감하다). ¶ 가당찮은 요구 [값] an excessive demand [an unreasonable price].
가당하다 (可當一) 《합당하다》 (be) reasonable; proper; right; 《감당할 수 있다》 be able to cope with.
가도 (街道) a highway; a main road. ¶ 경인 (京仁) ~ the *Gyeongin* Highway.
가동 (稼動) operation; work. ~하다 operate; run. ¶ ~을 시작(중단)하다 start [stop] operation / ~중이다 be working; be in operation; be at work. ‖ ~률 (率) the rate of operation; the capacity utilization rate / ~시간 the hours of operation / ~일수 the number of workdays / 완전~ full (-scale) operation / 주야 ~ around-the-clock [24-hour] operation.
가동성 (可動性) mobility; movability.
가두 (街頭) a street corner; 《십자로》 a crossing; 《가로》 a street. ‖ ~데모 [시위] a street demonstration / ~모금 street fund raising / ~선전 [wayside] propaganda [advertising] / ~연설 a street [wayside, stump] speech / ~인터뷰 a curbside interview / ~풍경 a street scene. 《*a person*》
가두다 shut [lock] in [up]; confine
가두리 《모자・그릇의》 a brim; a rim; 《천・옷 따위의》 a fringe; a hem; 《장식》 a frill. ‖ ~양식 fish farming.
가드 a guard, a watchman(경비원); a guard(농구의).
가드락거리다 swagger; be elated.
가득 full; crowded. ~하다 be full (*of*). ¶ 한 잔 ~ a glassful / ~채우다 [차다] fill be filled up / 컵에 ~ 붓다 fill a cup to the brim / 사람들로 ~ 차 있다 be crowded with people.
가뜩이나 to add to; in addition to; moreover. ¶ ~ 곤란한데 to add to one's misery; to make matters worse.
가뜬하다 (be) light; nimble; 《심신이》 feel light [good]. ¶ 가뜬히 lightly; nimbly; 《쉽게》 without difficulty [trouble].
가라사대 say. ¶ 공자 ~ Confucius said...; 성경에 ~ The Bible says ....
가라앉다 ① 《밑으로》 sink; go down; go to the bottom; fall [cave] in (지반이). ¶ 가라앉은 배 a sunken ship [boat] / 물속으로 ~ sink [be submerged] under water. ② 《고요해지다》 become quiet; calm [quiet] down; 《풍파가》 go [die] down; subside. ¶ 바람이 ~ the wind dies down. ③ 《마음・성질이》 recover one's composure; restore the presence of mind; become calm; calm down. ④ 《부기・고통 등이》 abate; subside; go down. ¶ 부기가 가라앉았다 The swelling has gone down. ⑤ 《진압되다》 be put down; be suppressed; be quelled; 《분쟁이》 be settled.
가라앉히다 ① 《물속에》 sink; send

가락 ① 《음조》 a key; a pitch; a tune; tone. ② 《박자·장단》 time; (a) rhythm. ¶ ~에 맞추어 to the time of《the music》.

가락² ① 《방추》 a spindle. ② 《가늘고 긴 물건》 a stick. ¶ 엿 한 ~ a stick of 《gluten candy》.

가락국수 wheat vermicelli; Korean noodle; noodles. ¶ ~집 a 《Korean》 noodle shop.

가락지 a set of twin rings.

가람 (伽藍) a Buddhist temple; a cathedral.

가랑눈 powdery 〔light〕 snow.

가랑머리 hair braided in two plaits. ┌~가 내리다 drizzle.

가랑비 a drizzle; a light rain.¶

가랑이 a crotch; a fork. ¶ ~를 벌리다 set *one's* legs apart.

가랑잎 dead 〔withered〕 leaves.

가래¹ 《농기구》 a spade. ‖ ~질 spading. ¶ ~질하다 plow; spade; do spadework.

가래² 《담 (痰)》 phlegm; sputum 〔*pl.* sputa〕. ¶ ~를 뱉다 spit phlegm out. ‖ ~침 spittle.

가래³ 《열매》 a kind of walnut.

가래⁴ 《긴 토막》 a piece; a stick. ¶ ~떡 bar rice cake / 떡 한 ~ a stick of rice cake.

가래톳 a bubo 《*pl.* -es》.

가량 (假量) 《쯤》 about; some; more or less; or so; approximately. ¶ 30명 ~ some thirty people / 2개월 ~ some two months / 1 마일 ~ a mile or so / 예순살 ~의 노인 an old man of about sixty / 두 시간 ~ 지나면 in about two hours / ~없다 〔어림없다〕 be poor at guessing; 《당찮다》 be wide of the mark.

가련하다 (可憐─) (be) poor; pitiful; pathetic; sad; wretched; miserable. ¶ 가련한 처지 a sad plight / 가련히 여기다 take pity on 《*a person*》 / 가련한 친구로군 What a poor fellow he is!

가렴주구 (苛斂誅求) extortion (exaction) of taxes; laying 〔imposing〕 heavy taxes 《*on*》.

가렵다 (be) itchy; itching; itchy. ¶ 가려운 데를 긁다 scratch an itchy spot / 온 몸이 ~ I feel itchy all over.

가령 (假令) (even) if; though; although; supposing that; granted that. ¶ ~ 그것이 그렇다 치더라도 admitting that it is so / ~ 그가 그렇게 말했다 치〔하〕더라도 even if he did say so.

가로 (幅) width; breadth; 《부사적》 across; sideways; horizontally; from side to side《좌우로》. ¶ ~의 sidelong; horizontal / ~ 2피트 two feet wide 〔in width〕 / ~ 쓰다 write sideways / 줄을 ~ 치다 draw a horizontal line / ~ 놓다 lay 〔put〕 《*a thing*》 sideways / ~ 놓이다 lie across 〔sideways〕 / 배는 ~ 흔들렸다 The ship rolled from side to side.

가로 a street; a road; an avenue (美); a boulevard. ‖ ~등 a street lamp / ~수 street 〔roadside〕 trees.

가로닫이 a sliding door 〔window〕.

가로되 say. ¶ 옛말에 ~ An old saying has it that ….

가로막다 interrupt 《*a person*》; obstruct 《*the view*》; block 〔bar〕《*the way*》. ¶ 입구〔도로〕를 ~ block 〔obstruct〕 the entrance 〔road〕 / 그녀의 말을 ~ interrupt her; cut her short.

가로막히다 (get) obstructed; be blocked 〔up〕; be barred.

가로맡다 take over; take upon *oneself*.

가로새다 sneak away from; slip away 〔off〕; get 〔go〕 away unobserved.

가로세로 《명사적》 breadth and length; 《부사적》 breadthwise and lengthwise; horizontally and vertically.

가로쓰기 writing in a lateral line; writing from left to right.

가로지르다 《건너지름》 put 《*a bar*》 across; 《가로긋다》 draw 《*a line*》 across; 《건너감》 cross; go across.

가로채다 seize 《*a thing*》 by; snatch 〔away〕 《*from, off*》; intercept.

가로퍼지다 grow broad; 《뚱뚱하다》 be thickset 〔stout〕. ┌ment.

가료 (加療) (be under) medical treat-

가루 (분말) powder; dust; 《곡식가루》 flour; meal. ¶ ~로 만들다〔빻다〕 reduce to 〔grind into〕 powder. ‖ ~비누 soap powder 〔flakes〕 / ~약 powdered medicine / ~우유 powder(ed) milk; evaporated milk / ~음식 flour food.

가르다 ① 《분할·분배》 divide; part; sever; split; distribute. ¶ 다섯으로 ~ divide into five parts / 이익을 반반으로 ~ split the profit

half-and-half 머리를 한가운데서 [오른쪽에서] ~ part one's hair in the middle [on the right] / 부부의 의를 ~ sever a husband and wife; cut a husband from his wife. ② 《분류》 sort (out); group; classify; assort. ¶ 크게 둘로 ~ classify into two large groups. ③ 《구별》 discriminate; distinguish; know (tell) (A) from (B); judge. ¶ 좋은 책과 나쁜 책을 ~ discriminate good and bad books.

가르랑거리다 ☞ 그렁거리다.

가르마, 가리마 ¶ ~을 타다 part one's hair (on the left).

가르치다 《지식을》 teach; instruct; give lessons (in); educate (in); coach (지도); enlighten (계몽); 《알아듣게》 show; tell. ¶ 수학을 ~ teach (a person) mathematics / 수영을 ~ teach (show) (a person) how to swim / 피아노를 ~ give lessons in piano / 길을 가르쳐 주다 tell (show) (a person) the way to a place.

가르침 《교훈》 teachings; an instruction; 《교리》 a doctrine; 《계율》 a precept; 《신조》 a creed. ¶ 소크라테스의 ~ the teachings of Socrates / ~을 받다 receive one's instruction; be taught (by).

가름하다 divide (up); separate; discriminate; 《대신하다》 substitute (one thing for another).

가리 《더미》 a stack; a pile; a rick. ¶ 노적~ 노적가리.

가리가리 to (in) pieces; into (to, in) shreds. ¶ 편지를 ~ 찢다 tear a letter into pieces.

가리개 a cover; a shade (over); a two-fold screen (병풍).

가리나무 tinder of pine needles and twigs.

가리다¹ ① 《고르다》 choose; select; make a choice of; prefer; pick out. ¶ 날을 ~ choose (select) a day / 때와 장소를 가리지 않고 disregarding the time and place / 물불을 가리지 않는다 be willing to take any risk; dare the dangers of. ② 《까다롭다》 be fastidious (particular) (about). ¶ 음식을 ~ be fastidious about food. ③ 《분별》 distinguish (between); tell (discern) (A) from (B); have the sense (to do). ¶ 시비를 ~ tell right from wrong. ④ 《셈을》 square (settle) accounts (with a person). ¶ 빚을 ~ clear off (up) one's debts. ⑤ 《낯을》 be shy of (strangers); 《머리를 빗다》 comb [tidy] one's hair. [heap (up)].

가리다² 《쌓다》 pile up; stack; rick;

가리다³ 《막다》 shield; screen; shelter; cover; shade (눈을); hide; conceal. ¶ 눈을 ~ blindfold / 얼굴을 ~ have one's face masked; cover one's face with his hands (두 손으로).

가리키다 point to (at); indicate; show. ¶ 방향을 ~ point the direction.

가리틀다 ① 《방해하다》 prevent (a person from doing); counteract. ② 《요구하다》 demand a share of (a person's) unexpected gain.

가마¹ 《머리의》 the whirl of hair on the head; a hair whirl.

가마² ① 가마솥. ② 《기와·질그릇 을 굽는》 a kiln; a stove; 《빵굽는》 an oven.

가마³ 《탈것》 a palanquin; a sedan chair (주로 유럽의). ‖ ~꾼 a palanquin bearer.

가마(니)⁴ a straw-bag(-sack).

가마리 an object; a target; a focus; a butt. ¶ 욕~ the butt of abuse / 조소~ a laughingstock; the butt of derision.

가마솥 a cauldron; a large iron pot; 《기관(汽罐)》 a boiler.

가마우지 〔動〕 a cormorant.

가막조개 〔貝〕 a corbicula.

가만가만 stealthily; quietly; gently; softly; lightly.

가만있자 well; let me see.

가만히 《넌지시》 covertly; tacitly; stealthily; imperceptibly; 《몰래》 in secret (private); privately; secretly. ¶ ~ 남의 얼굴을 살피다 scan a person covertly / ~ 집을 빠져나오다 slip out of the house. ② 《조용히》 still; calmly; quietly; silently; motionlessly. ¶ ~ 놓다 put (place) (a thing) cautiously / ~ 있다 keep still; remain quiet / ~ 누워 있다 lie motionless / 그런 모욕을 잠자코 않겠다 I would not stand such a humiliation.

가망(可望) hope; promise; chance; probability, possibility (가능성); a prospect (전망). ¶ ~없는 hopeless / 성공할 ~이 있다 have a good chance of success.

가맣다 ☞ 까맣다.

가매장(假埋葬) temporary interment (burial). ~하다 bury temporarily; be provisionally buried.

가맹(加盟) joining; participation; alliance; affiliation. ~하다 join; take part in. ‖ ~국 a member nation (of the UN); a signatory (조약의) / ~단체 a member (affiliated) organization / ~자 a member / ~점 a member store (of a chain store association).

가면(假面) a mask. ¶ …의 ~하에 under the mask of; under

가면허 a temporary license.
가명(家名) the family name; honor of *one's* family. ¶ ~을 더럽히다 disgrace (stain) the family name.
가명(假名) an assumed (a false) name; a fictitious name; an alias. ¶ ~으로 under an assumed name; incognito ¶ ~을 쓰다 use a false (fictitious) name. ‖ ~계좌 a deposit (bank account) in a fictitious name.
가묘(家廟) a family shrine.
가무(歌舞) singing and dancing; all musical and other entertainments. ¶ ~음곡 일체를 중지 시키다 order a suspension of all public performances in music and dancing.
가무러지다 faint; be dazed; be stunned.
가무스름하다 ☞ 거무스름하다.
가무잡잡하다 (be) darkish; dingy; dusky.
가문(家門) *one's* family (clan). ¶ ~의 영예 an honor (a credit) to *one's* family / ~이 좋은 (나쁜) of a good (bad) stock; of high (low) descent / 좋은 ~에 태어나다 come of a good stock (family).
가문비 [植] a spruce; a silver fir.
가물거리다 ① (불빛이) flicker; glimmer; blink. ¶ 가물거리는 불빛 a flickering light. ② (희미하게) be dim (misty). ¶ (정신이) have a dim consciousness (memory, *etc.*). ¶ 가물거리는 기억을 더듬다 trace back a vague memory.
가물다 (날씨) be droughty (dry); have a spell of dry weather.
가물들다 ① (농작물) suffer from a drought; (부족) be in short supply.
가물치 [魚] a snakehead.
가물타다 be easily affected by dry weather.
가뭄 dry weather; a drought.
가미(加味) (맛) seasoning; flavoring; (부가) an addition; an additive. ~하다 season (flavor) (*something*) with (*another*); add (*something*) with (*another*) (부가). ¶ 법에 인정을 ~하다 temper justice with mercy.
가발(假髮) (wear) a wig; false hair; (부분적인) a hair piece; a toupee.
가방 a bag; a satchel; a trunk (대형의); a suitcase(소형의). ¶

~에 넣다 put (*things*) in a bag.
가법(家法) family rules (traditions); household etiquette.
가벼이, 가볍게 lightly; rashly ¶ ~ 보아 넘기다 overlook (*a person's fault*) / ~ 행동하다 act rashly / ~ 나무라다 give a light scolding / 형량을 ~ 하다 reduce a sentence.
가변(可變) variableness; (형용사적) variable. ‖ ~비용 variable expenses / ~익(翼) variable wings / ~자본 variable capital / ~저항기 a variable resistor / ~전압발전기 a variable voltage generator.
가볍다 ① (무게가) (be) light; not heavy. ¶ 가벼이 ~ be as light as a feather / 가벼운 짐 a light load; a light baggage / 체중이 ~ be light in weight. ② (경미) (be) slight; not serious; trifling. ¶ 가벼운 두통 a slight headache / 가벼운 범죄 minor offenses. ③ (수월함) (be) simple; easy; light. ¶ 가벼운 일 a light (an easy) work / 가벼운 기분으로 with a light heart. ④ (식사 등) (be) light; not heavy; plain. ¶ 가벼운 식사 a light meal; a snack. ⑤ (사람이) (be) rash; imprudent; indiscreet; thoughtless. ¶ 입이 ~ be glib tongued; be too talkative.
가보(家寶) a family treasure; an heirloom.
가봉(加俸) an extra (additional) allowance.
가봉(假縫) a fitting; basting; tacking ~하다 baste; tack; try (fit) (*a coat*) on. ¶ 새 양복을 ~하러 양복점에 가다 go to the tailor for a fitting of a new suit.
가부(可否) (옳고 그름) right or wrong; (적부) suitableness; propriety; (찬부) ayes and noes; pros and cons; for and against; yes or no. ¶ ~간 right or wrong (옳고 그름); for or against (찬부) / ~를 논하다 argue for and against (*a matter*); discuss whether (it) is appropriate or not / 부표로 ~를 결정하다 decide (*a matter*) by vote; put (*a matter*) to vote.
가부장(家父長) a patriarch. ‖ ~정치 patriarchal government / ~제도 patriarchy; patriarchal system.
가불(假拂) an advance; advance payment. ~하다 pay in advance; make an advance. ¶ ~받다 receive (draw, borrow) *one's* wages in advance; get an advance. ‖ ~금 an advance.
가뿐하다 (be) light; not heavy.
가쁘다 (숨소리) pant (gasp) (for breath); be out of breath.

가사(家事) household affairs [chores]; domestic duties; housework; housekeeping. ¶ ~를 처리하다 manage the household tasks [affairs] / ~에 얽매여 있다 be occupied with household cares.

가사(假死) apparent death; syncope; suspended animation. ¶ ~상태에 있다 be in a syncopic state.

가사(袈裟) a (Buddhist priest's) stole; a surplice; a cope.

가사(歌詞) the text [words] of a song; the (song) lyrics.

가산(加算) addition. ¶ ~하다 add; include. ¶ 이자를 ~하다 include interest; add interest to principal(원금에). / ~금 additional dues / ~기 an adding machine / ~세 an additional tax / 중~세 a heavy additional tax.

가산(家産) family property (estate); one's fortune. ¶ ~을 탕진하다 go through one's (inherited) fortune.

가상(假想) imagination; supposition. ¶ ~하다 imagine; suppose. ¶ ~적인 imaginary; hypothetical / ~의 적(敵) a hypothetical [potential, supposed] enemy. ¶ ~현실 (컴퓨터) virtual reality.

가상(假像) a false image; a ghost; [鑛] a pseudomorph.

가상하다(嘉尙―) ¶ ~여기다 applaud 《a person for his deed》.

가내지르다 cross 《A and B》; place 《things》 crosswise.

가새풀 [植] a milfoil; a yarrow.

가석방(假釋放) release on parole. ~하다 put [release] 《a person》 on parole. ¶ ~되다 be paroled. ‖ ~자 a paroleer; a criminal on parole.

가선(架線) wiring(공사); a wire(선). ‖ ~ 공사 wiring works.

가설(架設) construction; building; installation. ¶ ~하다 construct [build] 《a bridge, a railroad》; install 《a telephone》. ‖ ~공사 building [construction] work / ~비 the installation [building] cost.

가설(假設) temporary construction. ¶ ~의 temporary; transient. ¶ ~무대 (put up) a makeshift stage / ~주택 a temporary dwelling; temporary housing(총칭).

가설(假說) [論] a hypothesis; assumption; supposition (가정). ¶ ~적인 hypothetical.

가성(苛性) causticity. ‖ ~석회(石灰) quicklime / ~소다(알칼리) caustic soda (alkali).

가성(假性) ¶ ~의 false; pseud(o)-. ‖ ~ 근시 pseudomyopia / ~콜레라 pseudocholera.

가성(假聲) a feigned voice. ¶ ~을 내다 disguise one's voice.

가세(加勢) ~하다 (조력) help; aid; assist; (지지) support; take sides 《with》. ¶ ~하러 가다 (오다) go [come] to 《a person's》 assistance.

가세(家勢) the fortunes of a family. ¶ ~가 기울었다 The family is down on its luck.

가소(可塑) ¶ ~의 plastic. ‖ ~물 plastics; plastic material / ~성 plasticity / ~제 a plasticizer.

가소롭다(可笑―) (be) laughable; ridiculous; nonsensical. ¶ 가소롭기 짝이 없다 be highly ridiculous; be quite absurd.

가속(加速) acceleration. ~하다 accelerate; speed up. ¶ ~적으로 with increasing speed. ‖ ~계 an accelerometer / ~도 (degree of) acceleration / ~력 an accelerating force / ~운동 an accelerated motion / ~장치 an accelerator.

가솔린(揮發油) gasoline.

가수(歌手) a singer; a vocalist(성악가). ¶ 대중~ a popular (pop) singer.

가수금(假受金) a suspense receipt.

가수분해(加水分解) [化] hydrolysis.

가수요(假需要) fictitious [disguised, speculative] demand.

가스 gas. ¶ ~를 켜다 (잠그다) turn on (off) the gas / ~불을 올리다 (내리다) turn the gas up (down) / 뱃~이 차다 have gas [wind] in the bowels / 셋집: ~ 수도 완비 (게시) House for Rent: with all main services. ‖ ~검침원 a gas-meter reader / ~계량기 a gas meter / ~관(管) a gas pipe / ~난로 a gas heater / ~레인지 (오븐) a gas range (oven) / ~수금원 a gas-bill collector / ~요금 a gas rate / ~전(栓) a gas tap / ~중독 gas-poisoning / ~탱크 a gas tank; a gasholder / ~폭발 a gas explosion / ~회사 a gas company / 도시 (천연, 프로판) ~ city (natural, propane) gas.

가슬가슬하다 (be) rough; peevish.

가슴 the breast; the chest(흉곽); the bosom(품); heart, mind (마음). ¶ ~의 병 chest troubles / ~속 깊이 간직한 생각 an idea cherished deep in one's heart / ~이 뭉클해지다 have a lump in one's throat / ~이 뛰다 one's heart throbs 《with》 / ~이 설레다 feel excited (elated); 《사물이 주어》 cause in 《a person》 a lift of the heart / ~이 후련해지다 feel

가슴앓이 [醫] heartburn. [relieved.

가습(加濕) humidification. ~하다

가시 (갈퀴 따위의) a thorn; (풀잎 등의) a prickle; (밤송이의) a bramble; (밤송이의) a bur; (나무·대·뼈 따위의) a splinter; (물고기의) a spine. ¶ ~ 돋은 thorny; spiny / ~가 목에 걸리다 have a bone stuck in *one's* throat / 손에 ~가 박이다 get a sticker in *one's* finger. ‖ ~나무 a thorn (bush); a bramble / ~나무 울타리 a hedge of thorn / ~덤불〔밭〕 a thorny thicket / ~밭길 a thorny path.
가시 (구더기) a worm; a maggot.
가시광선 (可視光線) visible rays.
가시다 ① (씻어내다) rinse; wash out. ¶ 병을 ~ rinse out a bottle. ② (뒷맛을) take off (away); get rid of. ¶ 입안의 쓴 맛을 ~ take the bitter taste out of *one's* mouth. ③ (없어지다) disappear; leave; pass (*off*); (누그러지다) soften; lessen; calm down. ¶ 두통이 가셨다 Headaches passed off.
가시세다 (완고) (be) stubborn; wilful; obstinate; headstrong.
가시철(―鐵) barbed wire. ‖ ~망 (barbed-)wire entanglements.
가식(假飾) affectation; hypocrisy. ~하다 affect; pretend; play the hypocrite; (be) pathetic; false; affected / ~이 없는 unaffected; unpretentious; frank(솔직한) / ~ 없이 행동하다 behave in a unaffected manner.
가심 a rinse; a wash(ing). ~하다 wash out.   〔column.
가십 gossip. ‖ ~난 a gossip
가압(加壓) pressurization. ~하다 pressurize; apply (*give*) pressure (*to*). ‖ ~장치 a pressure device.
가압류(假押留) provisional seizure. ~하다 seize (*another's*) property provisionally.
가야금(伽倻琴) a *gayageum*; a Korean harp.
가약(佳約) the pledge of eternal love; a deep pledge. ☞ 백년가약.
가언(假言) 【論】 a conditional (word). ¶ ~적 conditional; hypothetic(al). ‖ ~명제 a hypothetical proposition.
가업(家業) *one's* family trade (business). ¶ ~을 잇다 succeed to *one's* father's business.
가없다 (be) boundless; endless. ¶ 가없는 바다 a boundless ocean.
가연(可燃) ~성 inflammability; combustibility / ~성의 combustible; inflammable. ‖ ~물 combustibles; inflammables.
가열(加熱) heating. ~하다 heat. ¶ ~ 살균하다 sterilize (*milk*) by heating. ‖ ~기 a heater; a heating apparatus / ~ 분해 decomposition by heating / ~시험 a heat(ing) test.
가엾다 (불쌍하다) (be) pitiable; pitiful; poor; sad; miserable; (애틋하다) (be) pathetic; touching. ¶ 가엾게 여기다 feel pity (sorry) for; take pity on; pity (*a person*); sympathize with / 가 엾어라 What a pity!; Alas, poor 〔thing〕!
가오리 〔魚〕 a stingray.
가옥(家屋) a house; a building; 〔法〕 a messuage. ‖ ~관리비 the managing expense of a house / ~대장 a house register (ledger) / ~세 a house tax.
가외(加外) ~의 extra; spare; excessive / 가외일을 하다 do extra work; work extra time. ‖ ~수입 extra income.
가요(歌謠) a song; a melody. ‖ ~곡 a popular song.
가용(可溶) ~성 a soluble body; ~성 solubility (~성의 soluble).
가용(可融) ~물 a fusible body / ~성 fusibility (~성의 fusible).
가용(家用) 《비용》 cost of household; household expenses; 《자가용》 domestic use; family use.
가운(家運) retrieve *one's* family fortune.   〔academic gown.
가운 a gown. ¶ 대학생의 ~ an
가운데 ① (중간) the middle; the midway; the center, the heart(복판); (안쪽) the inside. ¶ ~에 가르마를 타다 part *one's* hair in the middle / ~를 잡다 hold (*a thing*) in the middle / ~로 들어가 주십시오 (버스 등에서) Step forward, please. ② (중에서) between(둘); among(셋 이상); out of. ¶ 이 일곱 개 ~서 어느 것이든 다섯 개만 골라라 Choose any five 〔out of (from among)〕 these seven. ③ (…하는 중) in; amid(st).
가운뎃손가락 the middle finger.
가웃 a half. ¶ 석 말 ~ three *mal* and a half.
가위 scissors; shears; clippers (털 베는). ¶ ~ 한 자루 a pair of scissors. ‖ ~질 scissoring / 가 윗말 cuttings.
가위(可謂) literally; exactly; truly; practically; in a sense; so to speak.
가위놀리다 have a nightmare.
가윗날 추석.   〔(fall).
가을내 throughout the autumn
가을 autumn; fall 《美》. ¶ ~의 autumn(al); fall. ‖ ~갈이 autumn plowing / ~경치 autumnal scenery / ~바람 autumn wind / ~보리 autumn-sown barley / 늦~ late autumn (fall) / 초~ early autumn (fall).

가이던스 guidance 《*in the course of one's studies*》.
가이드 a 《*tour*》 guide (사람); a guide book (안내서).
가인(佳人) a beautiful woman; a beauty. ¶ ~ 박명(薄命) Beauties die young.
가일(佳日) an auspicious day.
가일층(加一層) (the) more; still 〔much〕 more; all the more. ¶ ~ 노력하다 make still more efforts.
가입(加入) joining; admission; subscription (전화 따위의). ~하다 join 《*an association*》; become a member of 《*a club*》. ¶ 야구부에 ~하다 join the baseball club. ~금 an entrance 〔admission〕 fee; ~신청 application for admission; subscription(전화 따위의). ~자 a member; a (telephone) subscriber.
가자미〔魚〕a flatfish; a flounder.
가작(佳作) a fine piece 〔work〕 of work; a work of merit.
가장(家長) the head of a family; a patriarch (남자); a matriarch (여자); *one's* husband (남편).
가장(假葬) temporary burial. ~하다 bury temporarily.
가장(假裝) ① 〔변장〕 disguise; fancy dress. ~하다 disguise *oneself* 《*as*》; dress up (be disguised) 《*as*》. ¶ ~하여 in disguise / 여자로 ~하다 dress up as a woman. ¶ ~무도회 a fancy 〔dress〕 ball; a masquerade / ~ 행렬 a fancy dress parade. ② 〔거짓〕 pretence; semblance; camouflage. ~하다 feign; pretend; affect; assume; make believe. ¶ ~을 ~하여 under pretense of the cloak) of / 우정을 ~하다 pretend to be a friend.
가장 most; least(적을 때). ¶ ~ 쉬운 방법 the easiest method.
가장귀 a crotch 〔fork〕 of a tree.
가장이 a branch; a twig.
가장자리 the edge; the verge; the brink; the margin.
가장집물(家藏什物) household furnishings.
가재〔動〕a crawfish; a crayfish 《*英*》; ~ 걸음하다 crawfish; walk (crawl) backward; make very slow progress / ~는 게 편이다 〔俗談〕 Like attracts like.
가재(家財) household belongings 〔goods〕; furniture and effects.
가전(家傳) ~의 hereditary; proprietary / ~의 보물 a family heirloom.
가전(家電) ‖ ~메이커 a household 〔home〕 appliance manufacturer / ~산업 a home appliance industry / ~제품 electric home appliances.
가절(佳節) an auspicious occasion.
가정(家政) household management; housekeeping. ‖ ~과 (the) domestic economics (course) (학문); the department of domestic science(대학의) / ~부 a housekeeper; a lady-help.
가정(家庭) home; a family. ¶ ~의 home; domestic; family / ~용으로 for domestic use / ~을 갖다 start a home; get married and settle down. ‖ ~경제 household(domestic) economy / ~교사 a private teacher; a tutor(~교사를 두다 engage a tutor / ~교사를 하다 teach 《*a boy*》 at his house) / ~교육 home education / ~내 폭력 violence in the home / ~란 a domestic column / ~문제 home problems / ~방문 a home visit (~방문하다 pay a home visit) / ~부인 a housewife / ~불화 family trouble (discord); friction between man and wife(부부의) / ~생활 home life / ~의(醫) *one's* family doctor / ~의례 family rite / ~의례준칙 the Simplified Family Rite (Ritual) Standards / ~쟁의 a family dispute; a domestic trouble / ~환경 *one's* family background: home environment.
가정(假定) (a) supposition; (an) assumption; a hypothesis; 〔法〕(legal) fiction. ~하다 suppose; assume. ¶ ~적인 hypothetic(al); imaginary; assumptive …이라 ~하여 on the assumption that …. ‖ ~법 〔文〕 the subjunctive mood.
가정법원(家庭法院) a family (domestic relations) court.
가제 (cotton, antiseptic) gauze. ‖ 소독 ~ sterilized gauze.
가져가다 take (carry) away; take 《*a thing*》 along 《*with one*》; walk off with(훔치다). ¶ 누군가가 우산을 가져갔다 Someone has walked off with my umbrella.
가져오다 ① 〔지참〕 bring (over); get; fetch. ¶ 가서 책을 가져오너라 Go and get (bring) me a book. / 내 책상에서 책을 가져오너라 Please fetch a book from my desk. ② 〔초래〕 invite; cause; result 〔end〕 in; bring about. ¶ 그는 나에게 온갖 걱정거리를 가져왔다 He caused all sorts of trouble to me.
가조(一調)〔樂〕 the tone A.
가조약(假條約) a provisional treaty. ¶ ~을 맺다 conclude (make up, enter into) a provisional treaty 《*with another country*》.

가조인(假調印) a preliminary (provisional) signature; an initial signature. ~하다 sign provisionally; initial. ‖ ~식 an initialing ceremony.
가족(家族) a family; one's folks (people) 《美》. ¶ 6인 ~ a family of six / ~동반의 여행 a family trip / ~이 몇입니까 How large (big) is your family? ‖ ~계획 family planning / ~구성 a family structure / ~묘지 a family burial ground / ~수당 the family allowance / ~제도 the family system / ~회사 a family firm (concern) / ~회의 (have, hold) a family council.
가주거(假住居) a temporary residence (abode).
가주소(假住所) one's temporary residence (address).
가죽(표피) the skin; a hide(주로 마소의); 《무두질한》 (tanned) leather; tanned (dressed) skin; chamois leather (양·사슴의); 《모피》 (a) fur. ~으로 만든 leather (*belt*); ~을 벗기다 skin. ‖ ~공장 a tannery / ~부대 a leather bag / ~세공 leather work / ~장갑 leather gloves / ~제품 leather goods (products) / ~표지 a leather cover.
가죽나무 〖植〗 a tree of heaven.
가중(加重) ① 《무겁게 함》 weighting. ~하다 weight. ‖ ~평균 weighted average. ② 《형벌》 ~하다 aggravate. ‖ ~형(刑) 을 ~하다 raise (aggravate) the penalty.
가증서(假證書) a provisional certificate; an interim bond.
가증하다(可憎―) (be) hateful; disgusting; detestable.
가지¹ a branch; a bough(큰); a twig, a sprig(작은); a spray(꽃 있는). ¶ ~를 뻗다 spread branches / ~를 꺾다 break (off) a branch / ~를 치다 cut (lop) off branches; prune (trim) (*a tree*).
가지² 〖植〗 an eggplant; an egg apple (열매).
가지³ (종류) a kind; a variety. ¶ ~각색의 various; sundry; all sorts of / 세 ~ three kinds / ~~의 경험 a varied experience / ~~ 이유로 for various reasons.
가지다 ① 《손에 쥐다》 have; take; hold; 《휴대·운반》 carry; have (*something*) with one. ¶ 나는 돈을 가지고 있지 않다 I have no money with me now. / 여행에 사진기를 가지고 가다 carry a camera on a trip. ② 《소유》 own; possess; keep; 《마음에》 have; cherish; harbor; hold. ¶ 확실한 인생관을 ~ have a clear view of life / 그에게 적의를 ~ hold malice toward him / 가게 를 가지고 있다 keep (own) a shop. ③ 《임신》 conceive; become pregnant. ¶ 아이를 가지고 있다 be pregnant.
가지런하다 (be) neat and trim; even; be of equal (uniform) size (height, *etc*.); be in order. ¶ 가지런히 trimly; evenly / 키가 ~ be of the same height.
가집행(假執行) 〖法〗 provisional execution. ~하다 execute provisionally.
가짜(假―) 《모조품》 an imitation; a sham; a spurious article; 《위조품》 a forgery; a counterfeit; a fake; a bogus. ~의 false; sham; bogus; fake(d); forged. ‖ ~다이아 a faked (sham) diamond / ~대령 a pretended colonel / ~돈 counterfeit money; false money / ~박사학위 a faked doctoral degree / ~수표 a bogus check / ~편지 a forged letter / ~학생 a bogus student / ~형사 a phony detective.
가차없다(假借―) (be) merciless; relentless; ruthless. ¶ 가차없이 without mercy; relentlessly; unscrupulously.
가책(呵責) blame; rebuke; censure; pangs(양심의). ¶ 양심의 ~을 받다 feel the pangs of conscience.
가처분(假處分) provisional disposition. ~하다 make provisional disposition (*of*). ‖ ~ 신청을 하다 apply for an injunction. ‖ ~소득 a disposable income.
가청(可聽) 《형용사적》 audible; audio. ‖ ~거리 (within) earshot / ~범위 the audible range / ~음 audible sounds.
가축(家畜) domestic animals; livestock(총칭). ¶ ~을 치다 raise livestock. ‖ ~병원 a veterinary hospital; a pet's hospital 《애완 동물의》 / ~사료 stock feed.
가출(家出) ~하다 run (go) away from home; leave home. ‖ ~소녀 [소년] a runaway girl (boy) / ~인 a runaway; an absconder.
가출옥(假出獄) 〖法〗 가석방.
가치(價値) value; worth; merit. ¶ ~ 있는 valuable; worthy / ~ 없는 worthless; of no value. ‖ ~관 one's sense of values / ~기준 (척도) a standard (measure) of value / ~ 판단 valuation; evaluation / ~실용~ utility value.
가친(家親) my father.
가칭(假稱) 《잠정의》 a provisional (tentative) name; 《사칭》 impersonation; false assumption. ~하다 call tentatively; assume a

가탁하다 false name (사칭하다).
가탄하다(可歎─) be lamentable(deplorable, regrettable). ¶ 가탄할 일 a matter worthy of grief; a deplorable affair.
가탈부리다 make trouble; raise problems; hinder.
가탈지다 go wrong; run into problems (hindrances).
가택(家宅) a house; a residence. ‖ ~ 수색 a house search(~ 수색하다 search a house; ~ 수색을 당하다 have one's house searched) / ~ 수색영장 a search warrant / ~ 침입 (the charge of) housebreaking; (a) trespass(~ 침입하다 trespass (a person's house)).
가톨릭교(─敎) Catholicism; the Roman Catholic Church. ¶ ~ 의 Catholic. ‖ ~ 도 (a) Roman Catholic.
가트 (관세와 무역에 관한 일반 협정) GATT. (《General Agreement on Tariffs and Trade》)
가파르다(傾斜─) (be) steep; precipitous. ¶ 가파른 언덕 (비탈) a steep hill (slope).
가표(加標) a plus (sign)(+); the sign of addition.
가표(可票) an affirmative vote. ¶ ~ 를 던지다 cast an aye vote for (a bill); vote in favor of (a bill).
가풍(家風) the family tradition (custom); the ways of a family.
가필(加筆) ─ 하다 correct; revise; retouch; touch up.
가하다(可─) (옳다) (be) right; rightful; reasonable; (좋다) (be) good; fair; nice.
가하다(加─) ① (가산) add (up); sum up; (부가) add. ¶ 원금에 이자를 ~ add interest to the principal / (주다) give; inflict (on). ¶ 압력을 ~ pressure (a person) / 일격을 ~ deal (a person) a blow / 열을 ~ apply heat. ③ (증가) increase. ¶ 속도를 ~ speed up.
가학(加虐) maltreatment; cruelty. ─ 하다 be cruel to (a person).
가해(加害) ① (손해를) doing harm; causing damage (losses). ~ 다 damage; do harm (to); inflict a loss (on). (상해를) inflicting injury; violence; an assault. ─ 하다 commit a violence (on); assault. ‖ ~ 자 an assaulter; an assailant.
가호(加護) divine protection; providence; guardianship. ¶ 신명의 ~ 로 by the grace of God / 신의 ~ 를 빌다 pray to God for help.
가혹(苛酷) (무참) cruelty; (잔인) brutality; (엄) severity; harshness. ─ 하다 (be) merciless; severe; cruel; hard; harsh. ¶ ~

하게 cruelly; harshly; severely; brutally / ─ 한 근로조건 severe working conditions / ~ 한 벌 a severe punishment / ~ 한 비평 severe (harsh) criticism / ~ 한 운명 a cruel fate / ~ 한 짓 a cruel act / ~ 한 처우 cruel treatment.
가훈(家訓) (observe) family precepts (mottos).
가희(歌姬) a songstress; a chantress; a female singer.

각(各) each; every. ¶ ~ 자 each one; everybody.
각(角) ① 〖動〗〖뿔〗 a horn; an antler(사슴의). ‖ ~ 도장 a seal made of horn. ② (모퉁이) a corner; a turn(ing) (돌아가는). ③ 〈사각〉 square. ④ 〖數〗《각도》 an angle.
각가지(各─) various kinds; all sorts. ¶ ~ 의 various kinds (all sorts) of.
각각(各各) 《따로따로》 separately; 《각기》 respectively; each; every. ¶ ~ 의 respective; individual.
각각으로(刻刻─) every moment; moment by moment.
각개(各個) each; every one; one by one. ‖ ~ 격파 defeating one by one / ~ 교련 individual drill.
각개인(各個人) each; each (every) individual; each person. ¶ ~ 의 소유물 the belongings of each person.
각계(各界) every field (sphere, walk) of life; various circles (quarters). ¶ ~ 각층의 명사 notables representing various departments of society.
각고(刻苦) hard work; arduous labor; indefatigable industry. ~ 하다 work hard; apply oneself closely to. ¶ ~ 정려하여 by dint of industry.
각골난망(刻骨難忘) ─ 하다 indelibly engrave on one's memory.
각광(脚光) footlights. ¶ ~ 을 받다 (사람·일이) be in the limelight; be highlighted (spotlighted).
각국(各國) every country; each nation; (여러 나라) various countries. ¶ 세계 ~ all countries of the world / ~ 의 무역 사정을 시찰하러 가다 go to various countries to observe trade affairs.
각기(脚氣) beriberi. ¶ ~ 에 걸리다 have an attack of beriberi.
각기(各其) each; respectively; apiece. ¶ ~ 제 ~ respectively; in one's own way.
각기둥(角─) 〖數〗 a prism.
각도(角度) an angle; (관점) a viewpoint; a point of view; a standpoint. ¶ 45도의 ~ 에서 at an angle of 45 degrees / ~ 를 재다

각등 (角燈) a square hand-lantern; a bull's-eye 《렌즈가 달린》.

각뜨다(脚-) cut up a carcass in parts; butcher.

각론(各論) an itemized discussion; particulars; details. ¶ ~으로 들어가다 go into the details (particulars) 《of a subject》.

각료(閣僚) a cabinet member (minister); a member of the Cabinet. ∥ ~급 회담 a minister-level conference / ~회의 a Cabinet meeting / 주요 ~ key ministers of the Cabinet.

각막(角膜) 【解】 the cornea. ∥ ~염 keratitis / ~은행 an eye bank / ~이식 corneal transplant(ation). 「[stick].

각목(角木) a square wooden club」

각박(刻薄) ~하다 (be) hard; severe; harsh; stern; heartless; stingy(인색한). ¶ ~한 세상 a hard (tough) world / 참 ~한 세상이로군 What a hard (cold) world we live in!

각반(脚絆) (wear) leggings; gaiters.

각방(各方), **각방면**(各方面) every direction; all directions. ¶ ~으로 in every direction / 사회 ~의 사람들 all classes of people; people in all walks of life.

각별하다(各別—) ① 《특별》(be) special; particular; exceptional(파격적). ¶ 각별한 사랑(호의) special love(favor) / 각별히 especially; particularly; exceptionally / 각별히 주의하다 pay special attention / 더운 날에는 생맥주 맛은 ~ Draft beer tastes especially good on a hot day. ② 《깍듯하다》(be) polite; courteous. ¶ 각별히 politely; civilly; courteously / 각별한 환영 give a warm reception.

각본(脚本) 《연극의》 a play(book); a drama; 《영화의》 a (film) script; a scenario; a screenplay. ∥ ~작가 a playwright; a dramatist; a scenario writer.

각부(各部) each (every) part (section); every department (ministry)(정부의). ∥ ~장관 the minister of each department.

각부분(各部分) each (every) part; all (various) parts.

각살림(各一) ~하다 live separately(apart) 《from》. ¶ ~나다 set up one's own home.

각색(各色) ① 《종류》 every kind; all sorts. ¶ 각양 ~ various; of every kind; of all sorts. ② 《빛깔》 various (all) colors; each color.

각색(脚色) dramatization. ~하다 dramatize 《a story》; adapt 《a novel》 for a play. ∥ ~가 a dramatizer; an adapter.

각서(覺書) a memorandum; a memo; 《외교상》 a note; 《의정서》 a protocol. ¶ 양국은 외교상의 ~를 교환했다 The two countries exchanged diplomatic notes with each other.

각선미(脚線美) the beauty of leg lines. ¶ ~있는 여자 a woman with nice (shapely) legs.

각설(却說) ① 《화제를 돌림》 ~하다 resume 《one's story》; return to the subject. ② 《부사적》 now; now to resume our story.

각설이(却說―) 《민요》 a singing beggar (at the marketplace).

각설탕(角雪糖) cube (lump) sugar. ¶ ~한 개 a lump of sugar.

각섬석(角閃石) 【鑛】 amphibole.

각성(覺醒) awakening. ~하다 awake 《from》; wake up 《to》; be disillusioned(미몽에서). ¶ ~시키다 awaken; open 《a person's》 eyes; bring 《a person》 to 《his》 senses. ∥ ~제 a stimulant; a pep pill 《美俗》.

각시(一) a doll bride; 《새색시》 a bride. ¶ ~놀음하다 play with dolls.

각양(各樣) ~ 《각색》의 various; all sorts of; a variety of / 사람의 마음은 ~ 각색이다 So many men, so many minds (ways).

각오(覺悟) 《마음 준비》 preparedness; readiness; 《결심》 (a) resolution; 《체념》 resignation. ~하다 be prepared (ready) 《for》; be resolved 《to do》; be determined; be resigned. ¶ 노여움 살 것을 ~하고 말하다 dare a person's anger and say / 그쯤은 ~한 바다 I have expected as much. or I am prepared for it. / 나는 최선을 다할 ~이다 I am determined to do my best.

각운(脚韻) a rhyme. 「best.」

각위(各位) every one (of you); 《편지에서》 Gentlemen; Sirs. ¶ 관계자 ~ 《서한에서》 To whom it may concern / 회원 ~에게 to the members.

각의(閣議) a Cabinet council. ∥ 정례〔임시〕 ~ an ordinary (extraordinary) session of the Cabinet council.

각인(各人) each person; every one; 《모두》 everybody.

각자(各自) each; each (every) one; ~에 each; respective; one's own / ~ 도시락을 지참할 것 Everyone to bring his own lunch.

각재(角材) square lumber.
각적(角笛) a horn; a bugle.
각종(各種) every kind; various kinds; all kinds (sorts) *of*. ∥ ~동물 all kinds of animal / ~학교 (one of the) miscellaneous schools.
각주(角柱) a square pillar.
각주(脚註) footnotes. ¶ ~를 달다 give footnotes (*to*).
각지(各地) every (each) place; [여러 지방] various places [quarters]; [전 지방] all parts of the country. ~에서 ~로부터 from every corner [all parts] of the world.
각질(角質) horniness; [生·化] keratin; chitin (곤충 등의). ~층 horny layer; stratum corneum.
각처(各處) ☞ 각지.
각추(角錐) [數] a pyramid.
각추렴(各-) an equal split (of the expenses); a Dutch treat. ~하다 collect from each; split the cost (account); go Dutch
각축(角逐) (a) competition; rivalry; contest. ¶ ~(전)을 벌이다 compete (*with*); contend (*with*); vie (*with*) / ~장 the arena of competition.
각층(各層) each class (of society). ¶ 각계~ of all social standings / 각계~의 명사 notables in (of) all walks of life.
각파(各派) each party; all political parties [groups] (정당); each faction (파벌); all sects (종파); all schools (유파, 학파).
각필(閣筆·擱筆) ~하다 lay down *one's* pen; leave off (stop) writing.
각하(閣下) (2인칭) Your Excellency; (3인칭) His [Her] Excellency; Their Excellencies (복수).
가항(街巷) each item [paragraph]; every clause.
각형(角形) [모난 형상] a square shape; [사각형] a quadrangle.
간 (전 정도 · 맛) seasoning (with salt); a salty taste. ¶ ~을 치다 apply salt (*to*); season with salt / ~보다 taste (*a thing*) to see how it is seasoned / ~이 맞다 be well (properly) seasoned / ~이 싱겁다 be not salty enough; be not well salted.
간(肝) ① [解] the liver. ∥ ~경변(증) cirrhosis of the liver. ② [배짱] pluck; courage; guts (口). ∥ ~이 큰 daring; bold; plucky / ~이 콩알만 하다 be amazed; be scared stiff; be terrified.
간(間) ① [길이] a *kan* (= 5.965ft). ② [면적] ☞ 칸. ☞ 칸살.
...간(間) [기간] for; during; a period; [사이] from ... to ...; between; among; [간격] an interval; [관계] relation(ship). ¶ 형제~ brotherly relation / 형제~의 싸움 a quarrel between brothers / 3일~ in three days / 친구~에 among *one's* friends.
간간이(間間-) occasionally; at times; (every) now and then; once in a while; at intervals; from time to time. ¶ ~ 소나기가 오겠습니다 There will be showers from time to time.
간간짭짤하다 (be) pleasantly salty; good and salty.
간간하다 (맛이) be somewhat salty.
간거르다 be alternate; skip (*a thing*) every other.
간격(間隔) [시간·공간] a space; an interval. ¶ 5미터의 ~을 두고 at five-meter intervals; at intervals of five meters.
간결(簡潔) brevity; conciseness. ~하다 be brief; concise; succinct. ¶ ~히 briefly; concisely / ~한 설명 a brief explanation.
간계(奸計) a trick; an evil design; a vicious plan; a sly artifice.
간고(艱苦) hardships; suffering; privations.
간곡(懇曲) ~하다 (be) polite; courteous; [친절] (be) kind; cordial. ¶ ~한 권고 kind advice / ~한 부탁 a polite request.
간과(干戈) arms; weapons (of war).
간과(看過) ~하다 fail to notice; overlook; pass over; connive at (묵인).
간교(奸巧) ~하다 (be) cunning; wily; sly; crafty; artful.
간국 salt (brine) water. ¶ ~에 절이다 soak in brine; pickle [salt] (*vegetables*).
간균(桿菌) [生] a bacillus (*pl*. -il); a bacterium (*pl*. -ria).
간극(間隙) a gap; an opening.
간기능검사(肝機能檢査) [醫] a liver-function exam(ination).
간난(艱難) hardship; privations. ¶ ~신고(辛苦)하다 undergo (suffer, go through) hardships.
간단(間斷) ~ 없는 continual; incessant; continuous / ~없이 incessantly; ceaselessly; continuously.
간단(簡單) brevity; simplicity. ~하다 (be) brief; simple; short; light(식사 따위가). ¶ ~한 편지 a brief letter / ~한 수속 a simple procedure / ~한 식사 a light meal / ~히 simply; briefly; in brief; easily; with ease (손쉽게) / ~히 말하면 to put it simply; in brief; to be brief / ~명료한 simple and plain (clear) / ~히 말하다 give a short account (*of*);

explain briefly.
간담(肝膽) ① 《간과 쓸개》 liver and gall. ②《속마음》 one's innermost heart. ¶ ~을 서늘케 하다 strike chill into *a person's* heart; curdle *a person's* blood / ~이 서늘해지다 be extremely frightened; *one's* blood runs cold.
간담(懇談) a chat; a familiar talk. ~하다 have a familiar talk *(with)*; chat *(with)*. ‖ ~회 a social gathering (meeting); a get-together for friendly talk.
간당거리다 dangle; tremble. ¶ 간당간당 danglingly.
간데족족 everywhere; wherever *one* goes. 「(지름길).
간도(間道) a bypath; a short cut
간동그리다 arrange neatly; bundle *something* up.
간두지세(竿頭之勢) the most critical situation. 「gle.
간드랑거리다 swing gently; dan-
간드러지다 (be) charming; coquettish; fascinating. ¶간드러지게 웃다 laugh coquettishly.
간들간들 《태도》 charmingly; in fascinating manners; 《바람》 gently; lightly; 《물체》 rockingly; unsteadily.
간들거리다 ①《태도》 act coquettishly; put on coquettish air. ②《바람》 blow gently; breeze. ③《물체》 shake; rock; totter.
간디스토마 〔醫〕 distoma hepaticum; a liver fluke.
간략(簡略) simplicity; brevity. ¶ ~한 simple; brief; informal (약식) / ~히 simply; briefly; succinctly / ~한 기사 a short account / ~한 보고〔설명〕 a brief report (explanation) / ~하게 하다 make simple (brief); simplify; shorten / 출원 수속을 ~화하다 simplify an application procedure.
간막이(間―) ☞ 칸막이.
간만(干滿) ebb and flow; flux and reflux; tide. ¶ ~의 차 the range of tide; a tidal range.
간망(懇望) an entreaty; an earnest request. ~하다 entreat *(a person)* to *(do)*; beg earnestly.
간명(簡明) ☞ 간결. ¶ ~한 brief and to the point / ~하게 설명하다 explain briefly and to the point.
간물 salt(y) water; brine. 「point.
간물(乾物) ☞ 건물(乾物).
간밤 last night.
간병(看病) nursing. ☞ 병구완.
간부(姦婦) a wicked woman.
간부(姦夫) an adulterer.
간부(姦婦) an adulteress.
간부(幹部) the leading members; the (managing) staff; the executives; the management. ‖ ~ 요원 a staff in a responsible post / ~회 an executive council; a staff meeting / ~ 후보생 a military cadet.
간사(奸邪・奸詐) cunningness; wickedness. ~하다 〔스럽다〕 (be) wicked; cunning; sly; crafty. ¶ ~한 사람 a wicked person.
간사(幹事) 《사람》 a manager; a secretary. ‖ ~장 a chief secretary / 원내~ the whip 《英》; an executive secretary 《美》.
간살(間―) ☞ 칸살.
간살부리다 flatter; adulate; fawn upon; curry favor with *(a person)*. ¶ 간살부리는 사람 a flatterer.
간상(奸商) a dishonest merchant; a fraudulent dealer. ‖ ~배 (a group of) dishonest [crooked] merchants.
간상균(桿狀菌) a bacillus 〔*pl*. -li〕.
간색(間色) a compound (secondary) color.
간석지(干潟地) a dry beach; a tideland; a beach at ebb tide.
간선(幹線) a trunk (main) line. ‖ ~도로 a highway; a main (trunk) road; an arterial road.
간섭(干涉) interference; intervention; meddling. ~하다 interfere *(in, with)*; meddle *(in, with)*; put *one's* nose into (口). ~을 받다 be interfered with / 내정에 ~하다 intervene (interfere) in the internal affairs of a country / 내일에 ~하지 마라 Leave me alone. ‖ 무력~ armed intervention.
간소(簡素) simplicity. ¶ ~한 simple; plain (and simple) / ~한 식사를 a homely (plain) meal / ~한 생활을 하다 lead a simple life. ‖ ~화 simplification (~화하다 simplify).
간수(一水) ☞ 간물.
간수(看守) ☞ 교도관(矯導官).
간수하다 keep; have *(a thing)* in *one's* keeping; take custody (charge) *(of)*. ¶ 그것은 내가 간수하고 있다 I have it in my custody.
간식(間食) eating between meals; a snack. ~하다 eat *(something)* between meals; have a snack.
간신(奸臣) a treacherous (unfaithful) retainer; a traitor.
간신(諫臣) a faithful advisor to the king; a devoted retainer.
간신히(艱辛―) narrowly; barely; with difficulty (힘겹게). ¶ ~ 살아 가다 make (earn) a bare living; barely make a living / ~ 도망치다 have a narrow escape; escape narrowly / ~ 시험에 합격하다 pass an examination with difficulty.
간악(奸惡) wickedness; treachery. ~하다 (be) wicked; villainous.

간암(肝癌) cancer of the liver.
간언(諫言) admonition; advice. ~하다 advise; admonish.
간염(肝炎) [醫] hepatitis. ¶ ~예방접종 the anti-hepatitis inoculation / 바이러스성 ~ viral hepatitis / A형[B형] ~ hepatitis A[B] / 전염성 ~ infectious hepatitis.
간원(懇願) ☞ 간청.
간유(肝油) cod-liver oil. ∥ ~드롭스 cod-liver oil drops.
간음(姦淫) adultery; misconduct; illicit intercourse. ~하다 commit adultery 《with》; have illicit intercourse 《with》. ∥ ~죄 adultery.
간이(簡易) simplicity; handiness; easiness. ~하다 be simple; easy; handy. ¶ ~화 생활의 simplification of living. ∥ ~법원 a summary court / ~수도 a provisional water supply system / ~숙박소 a cheap lodging house; a flophouse 《美俗》 / ~식당 a quick-lunch room; a snack bar / ~주택 a simple frame house.
간작(間作) catch cropping. ~하다 intercrop; grow 《beans》 as a catch crop. ~물 a catch crop.
간장(一醬) soy (sauce).
간장(肝腸) 《간과 창자》 the liver and intestines; 《마음》 (the) heart; the seat of emotion 《sorrow》. ¶ ~을 태우다 torture with anxiety / ~을 녹이다 《매료하다》 charm; captivate.
간장(肝臟) [醫] the liver. ∥ ~병 liver trouble / ~염 ☞ 간염.
간절(懇切) ~하다 (be) earnest; eager; fervent. ¶ ~한 부탁 one's earnest request / ~한 소원 one's fervent desire / ~히 earnestly; eagerly; sincerely / ~히 부탁하다 entreat / ~히 권하다 urge 《a person》 strongly; strongly advise.
간접(間接) indirectness. ¶ ~의 indirect; roundabout; secondhand / ~적인 영향 an indirect influence / ~적으로 indirectly; at second hand / ~으로 듣다 have the news at second hand; learn 《about something》 indirectly / 그 사건에 ~적인 관계가 있다 be indirectly concerned in the affair. ∥ ~목적어 an indirect object / ~무역 indirect trade / ~선거 indirect election / ~세 an indirect tax / ~조명 indirect (concealed) lighting / ~촬영 《흉부 의》 fluoroscopy; radiography / ~화법 indirect narration [speech] / ~흡연 indirect smoke pollution; secondhand smoke.
간조(干潮) ebb tide; low water.
간주(看做) ~하다 consider [regard, look upon] 《as》; take 《for》. ¶ 해결된 것으로 ~하다 look upon 《a matter》 as settled / 침묵을 승낙으로 ~하다 regard silence as consent.
간주곡(間奏曲) [樂] an interlude; an intermezzo.
간지(干支) the sexagenary cycle.
간지(奸智) cunning; craft; guile; wiles; subtlety.
간지럼 a ticklish sensation. ¶ ~타다 be ticklish; be sensitive to tickling / ~태우다 tickle; titillate.
간지럽다 ① 《몸이》 (be) ticklish. ¶ 간지러워하다 feel ticklish / 발이 ~ My foot tickles. ② 《마음이》 be[feel] abashed; be pricked.
간직하다 keep; store; put away; harbor, hoard 《가슴속에》. ¶ 가슴속에 깊이 간직해 두다 keep in one's heart.
간질(癎疾) [醫] epilepsy; an epileptic fit《발작》. ∥ ~환자 an epileptic.
간질세포(間質細胞) [解] interstitial cells.
간질이다 tickle; titillate. ¶ 겨드랑 밑을 ~ tickle 《a person》 under his arm.
간책(奸策) a dirty 《shrewd》 trick; a crafty design. ~을 부리다 play a dirty trick 《on》.
간척(干拓) land reclamation by drainage. ~하다 reclaim 《land》 by drainage. ∥ ~사업[공사] reclamation works / ~지(地) reclaimed land.
간첩(間諜) a spy; a secret agent. ¶ ~노릇을 하다 spy 《into, on》; act as spy / ~단 a spy ring / ~망 espionage chain; a spy network / ~활동 espionage (action) 《do, have》 espionage activities / 고정 ~ a resident spy; a sleeper agent 《美》 / 이중 ~ a double agent.
간청(懇請) entreaty; solicitation; an earnest request. ~하다 entreat; implore; solicit 《a person for》; earnestly request; ask; beg. ¶ ~에 의하여 at 《a person's》 earnest request.
간추리다 sum up; summarize; epitomize; abridge; brief 《美》. ¶ 간추린 summarized; abridged / 이 이론을 간추리면 이러하다 This is a summary of the theory.
간친(懇親) ∥ ~회 a social meeting 《gathering》; a social; a get-together 《美》.
간통(姦通) adultery; illicit intercourse. ~하다 have (illicit) intercourse 《with》; commit adultery 《with》. ∥ ~죄 adultery.
간파(看破) ~하다 see through 《a fraud》; read 《a person's thought》;

간판(看板) ① 《상점 따위의》 a sign (-board); a billboard; 《사무소·병원 등의》 a doorplate; a shingle 《美》. 《옥상의》 a roof (sky) sign / ~을 내걸다 set up (hang out) a signboard. ‖ ~장이 a sign maker (painter). ② 《학벌·경력 따위의》 a draw; a chief attraction; 《허울》 a (false) front; a figurehead. ¶ 그녀는 이 술집의 손님을 끄는 ~이다 She is what draws customers into this bar. or She is the chief attraction in this bar.

간편(簡便) ~하다 (be) simple; easy; handy; convenient. ¶ ~한 방법 an easy (a simple) method.

간하다(諫—) advise 《a person》 not to do; remonstrate 《with a person》; admonish 《a person against》.

간행(刊行) publication. ~하다 publish; issue; bring out. ‖ ~물 a publication.

간헐(間歇) intermittence. ¶ ~적 (으로) intermittent(ly). ‖ ~열 an intermittent fever / ~천 a geyser; an intermittent spring.

간호(看護) nursing; tending. ~하다 nurse; care for; attend on 《a sick person》; ~를 해야할 환자가 있다 have sick people to look after / 그녀는 그를 헌신적으로 ~했다 She nursed him devotedly. ‖ ~보조원 a nurse's aide / ~인 a person tending the sick; a (sick) nurse / ~학 the science (study) of nursing / ~학교 a nurses' school.

간호사(看護師) a (sick) nurse. ‖ 병원 ~ a hospital nurse / 수 ~ a head (chief, staff) nurse / 정 ~ a registered nurse 《美》 (생략 RN) / 준~ a practical nurse 《美》 / 파출 ~ a visiting (hired) nurse.

간혹(間或) occasionally; sometimes; once in a while. ¶ ~있는 occasional; infrequent / ~오는 손님 a casual visitor / ~찾아오다 show up once in a while.

간힘쓰다 hold *one's* breath in an effort to endure (stand) pain.

갇히다 be confined; be shut up; be locked up in; be imprisoned 《감옥에》. 《fined》 water.

갇힌물 standing (stagnant, con-

갈가마귀 a jackdaw.

갈거미 〖蟲〗 a long-legged spider.

갈겨쓰다 scrawl; scribble 《a letter》. ¶ 갈겨 쓴 메모 a scribbled note.

갈고랑쇠 ① 《쇠》 an iron hook; a fluke. ② 《사람》 perverse (cross minded) person.

갈고랑이 a hook; a gaff 《작살의》.

갈고쟁이 a hook.

갈구하다(渴求—) crave (long, yearn, thirst) for; be thirsty after (for); desire eagerly. 《root.》

갈기(髻) the root of an arrow

갈기(鬣) a mane. ¶ ~있는 짐승 a maned beast.

갈기갈기 to pieces; (in)to shreds. ¶ ~ 찢다 tear to pieces; tear into strips.

갈기다 (때리다) beat; strike; hit; knock; thrash; (베다) cut; slash; prune. ¶ 따귀를 ~ slap 《a person's》 cheeks (face) / 채찍으로 ~ lash; whip / 호되게 ~ hit 《a person》 hard.

갈길 *one's* way; *one's* path; 《목적지》 designation.

갈다¹ 《땅을》 till; plow; plough 《英》; cultivate; get 《the soil》 turned over.

갈다² 《바꾸다》 renew; change; replace; alter; fix anew. ¶ 구두의 뒤축을 ~ reheel a shoe / 이름을 ~ change *one's* name.

갈다³ ① 《숫돌에》 whet; sharpen; grind. ¶ 칼을 ~ sharpen a knife. ② 《광이 나게》 polish; burnish; cut (광석을). ¶ 금강석을 ~ cut (polish) a diamond. ③ 《문지르다》 rub; file (줄로). ¶ 먹을 ~ rub (down) an ink stick. ④ 《가루로》 grind (down); rub fine; reduce to powder. ¶ 옥수수를 ~ grind corn into flour. ⑤ 《이를》 grind (grit) *one's* teeth. ¶ 이를 갈며 분해하다 grind *one's* teeth with vexation 《at》.

갈대 〖植〗 a reed. ¶ ~많은 reedy / 여자의 마음은 ~와 같다 Woman is as fickle as a reed. ‖ ~같이 눈 먼 reed blind (screen) / ~밭 a field of reeds.

갈등(葛藤) trouble; discord; 《마음의》 mental (emotional) conflict. ¶ ~을 일으키다 cause; trouble; breed discord; give rise to complications.

갈라서다 break (off relations) 《with》; separate; divorce *oneself* (from); be divorced 《from》 (이혼). ¶ 아내와 ~ be parted from *one's* wife.

갈라지다 ① 《물체가》 split; be split; crack; be cracked; break; cleave. ¶ 두 조각으로 ~ be split into two pieces / 벽의 갈라진 틈 a crack in the wall. ② 《사람 사이가》 split (break) 《with a person》; be divided. ¶

그 점에 관해 의견이 갈라졌다 The opinions were divided on the points.
갈래《분기》 a fork; a divergence; 《분파》 a branch; a sect. ¶두~길의 crossroad(s) / ~진 three-forked / ~지다 fork; be forked; diverge 《from, into》.
갈륨《化》 gallium.
갈리다¹ ① 《갈게 하다》 get 《a person》 to change; have 《get》 《something》 replaced. ¶구두창을 ~ have one's shoes resoled. ② 《바뀌다》 be replaced (changed).
갈리다² 《칼 따위를》 have 《a knife》 sharpened 《갈게 하다》; be sharpened; be whetted.
갈리다³ 《가루로》 make 《a person》 grind (up); have 《grain》 ground 《갈게 하다》; be ground to powder (갈아지다).
갈리다⁴ 《분리》 be divided 《into》; break into; branch off 《from》; fork. ¶두 패로 ~ be divided into two groups / 여기서 길이 갈린다 At this point the road branches.
갈리다⁵ 《논밭을》 make 《a person》 plow (plough 《英》); have 《land》 cultivated (갈게 함); be cultivated.
갈림길 a forked (branch) road; a fork (in the road); a crossroad(s) (십자로); a turning point (전환점). ¶생의 ~에 서다 stand at the crossroads of one's life.
갈마(羯磨) karma 《梵》.
갈마들다 take turns; take by spells; alternate 《with another》.
갈망(渴望) ~하다 long (yearn, thirst, crave) 《for》; be anxious 《for, to do》. ¶지적(知的) ~ an intellectual thirst (desire).
갈망하다 《수습·처리하다》 deal (cope) with; manage 《a matter》; set 《matters》 right; square away.
갈매《植》 Chinese green; lokato. ~나무 《植》 a kind of buckthorn.
갈매기《鳥》 a sea gull.
갈무리하다 put 《a thing》 away in order; finish 《a thing》 up.
갈미《動》 a sea cucumber.
갈보 a harlot; a prostitute; a street walker. ¶~ 노릇을 하다 go(live) on the streets; walk the streets. ‖ ~집 a brothel; a whorehouse.
갈분(葛粉) arrowroot starch.
갈비 the ribs; a rib (요리). ‖ ~구이 roasted ribs / ~찜 beef-rib stew / ~탕 beef-rib soup / 갈빗대 a rib / 쇠~ ribs of beef.
갈색(褐色) brown. ¶~의 brown. ‖ ~인종 the brown races.
갈수(渴水) a shortage of water; a water famine. ‖ ~기 the drought (dry) season.

갈수록 more and more; as time goes on (시간이). ¶날이 ~ as days go by / ~ 태산이다 things get worse and worse.
갈씬거리다 be close to almost reach (touch).
갈아내다 change; replace 《an old thing with a new one》; renew. ¶묵은 기왓장을 ~ replace an old tile.
갈아대다 replace; change; substitute; put in 《something》 new 《for replacement》. ¶우산대를 ~ put a new stem to an umbrella.
갈아들다 supplant; supersede; take the place of.
갈아들이다 replace 《A》 with 《B》; substitute 《B》 for 《A》.
갈아입다 change 《one's》 clothes. ¶갈아입을 옷 spare clothes; a change of clothes.
갈아타다 change cars (trains) 《at》; transfer 《to another train》; transship (배를). ¶갈아타는 역 a transfer station; a junction / 목포행으로 ~ change for Mokpo.
갈이 ① 《논밭의》 plowing; ploughing 《英》; tillage; cultivating. ¶~질 farming. ② 《넓이》 the acreage that can be plowed by 《a person》 (in a day).
갈잎(枯葉) fallen (dead) leaves; (떡갈잎) leaves of an oak.
갈증(渴症) 《목마름》 thirst. ¶~이 나다 feel thirsty / ~을 풀다 appease one's thirst.
갈채(喝采) cheers; applause. ~하다 applaud; cheer; give 《a person》 a cheer. ¶우뢰 같은 ~ a storm (thunder) of applause / ~를 받다 receive (win) applause.
갈철광(褐鐵鑛) 《鑛》 limonite.
갈취(喝取) ~하다 extort 《money from a person》 by threats. [fish
갈치《魚》 a hairtail; a scabbard
갈퀴 a rake. ¶~로 긁어모으다 rake together (up).
갈탄(褐炭) brown coal; lignite.
갈파(喝破) ~하다 outshout; declare; proclaim.
갈팡질팡 confusedly; in a flurry; waveringly; this way and that. ~하다 be confused (perplexed) get flurried; do not know what to do; be at a loss.
갈포(葛布) hemp cloth.
갈피 a space between folds (layers); 《요점》 the point; the sense; the gist. ¶책 ~속에 사진을 끼워 두다 keep a picture between the leaves of a book / ~를 잡을 수 없다 cannot make head or tail 《of》; cannot catch (grasp) the meaning 《of》.
갉다《쏠다》 gnaw; nibble 《at》;

갉아먹다 ① 《이로》 gnaw; nibble 《at》. ② 《재물을》 squeeze; extort.
감¹ 〔植〕 a persimmon. ‖ ~나무 a persimmon tree.
감² 《재료》 material; stuff; 《옷감》 texture; 《비유적》 a suitable person 《for》; good material 《for》. ¶ ~이 좋은 of fine texture / 기둥 ~ wood for a pillar / 사윗 ~ a likely son-in-law / ~이 좋다 That's good material. [☞ 감하다.
감(減) a decrease; (a) deduction.
감(感) (느낌) feeling; sense; touch (촉감) an impression. ¶ 5 ~ the five senses / 공복의 ~ a sense of hunger / …(한) ~을 주다 impress 《strike》 《a person》; give the impression that … / 이 천은 거칠거칠한 ~이 있다 This cloth is rough to the touch.
감가(減價) reduction of price; depreciation; a discount. ~하다 reduce (discount) the price 《of》. ‖ ~상각 depreciation / ~상각 준비 적립금 a depreciation reserve.
감각(感覺) sense; feeling; sensation (감성). ¶ 미적(美的) ~ one's sense of beauty / ~적 sensible; sensual / ~이 없는 senseless; numb / ~을 잃다 become senseless / ~이 날카롭다 (둔하다) have keen (dull) senses. ‖ ~기관 a sense organ / ~력 sensibility / ~론 sensationalism; sensualism / ~마비 sensory paralysis / ~신경 a sensory nerve / ~주의 sensualism / ~중추 a sensory center.
감감하다 ① 《소식이》 hear nothing of; learn no news of 《a person》. ¶ 그 후 소식이 ~ 《감감소식이다》 I have not heard from him ever since. ② 《차이·시간 등이》 (be) far above; long 《before》. ¶ 내가 그의 학식을 따라 가려면 아직 ~ It will be long before I get as much knowledge as he has. ③ 《기억을》 forget entirely.
감개(感慨) deep emotion. ¶ ~무량하다 be deeply moved; be filled with deep emotion.
감격(感激) strong (deep) emotion. ~하다 be deeply moved (impressed, touched) 《by, with》. ¶ 《사람을》 ~케 하는 연설 an inspiring (a touching) speech / ~적인 장면 a dramatic (touching) scene / ~시키다 inspire; impress; give a deep impression 《to a person》 / ~의 눈물을 흘리다 be moved to tears / 그녀의 친절에 ~했다 I was deeply moved (touched) by her kindness.

감광(感光) 《사진의》 exposure (to light); sensitization. ~시키다 expose 《the film》 to light. ‖ ~계 a sensitometer / ~도 photosensitivity / ~막 〔膜〕 sensitive film / ~색소 light-sensitive pigments / ~제 〔劑〕 a sensitizer / ~지 sensitive paper / ~판 〔板〕 a sensitive plate.
감국(甘菊) 〔植〕 a winter chrysanthemum.
감군(減軍) a military manpower reduction; arms (armament) reduction. ~하다 cut (reduce) armed forces.
감금(監禁) confinement; imprisonment. ~하다 confine; imprison; detain; lock up. ¶ 자택에 ~하다 place 《a person》 under house arrest.
감기(感氣) a cold. ¶ 심한 ~ a bad cold / ~에 걸리다 catch (take) (a) cold; have a cold / ~로 누워 있다 be laid up (in bed) with a cold. ‖ ~약 medicine for a cold; a cold remedy.
감기다¹ ① 《넝쿨 따위가》 twine (coil) around; wind itself round; entwine / 《덩쿨 따위가》 be wound / 《거치적거리다》 cling to; 《걸리다》 be caught in. ② 《감게 하다》 let (make) 《a person》 wind.
감기다² 《눈》 《one's eyes》 be closed (shut) of their own accord; 《감게 하다》 let 《a person》 close (shut) 《his eyes》.
감기다³ 《씻기다》 wash (bathe) 《a baby》. ¶ 아기의 머리를 ~ wash a baby's hair / 멱을 ~ give a bath 《to》.
감내(堪耐) ~하다 bear; endure; stand; put up with. ¶ 불행을 ~하다 bear up under misfortune.
감다¹ 《눈》 shut (close) 《one's eyes》. ¶ 눈을 꼭 감고 with one's eyes shut tight.
감다² 《씻다》 wash; bathe; have a bath. ¶ 머리를 ~ wash one's hair.
감다³ 《실 따위를》 wind; coil; twine; bind round. ¶ 시계 태엽을 ~ wind a clock / 목에 붕대를 ~ tie a bandage round the neck.
감당(堪當) ~하다 be equal to 《a task》; be capable of 《doing》; cope (deal) with; be competent for. ¶ 일을 ~해 내다 cope with the enemy / ~하지 못하다 be unequal to; be incompetent for; be beyond one's power.
감도(感度) sensitivity; reception. ¶ ~가 좋다 be highly sensitive 《to》 / 이 부근은 라디오 ~가 나쁘다 Radio reception is not good around here.

감독(監督) superintendence; supervision; control; 《사람》 a supervisor; a superintendent; a manager(운동의); a director (영화의); a foreman(현장 근로자의). ~하다 superintend; supervise; control; oversee; direct; be in charge of. ¶ …의 ~하에 under the supervision [direction] of 《a person》 / 김 ~의 영화 a film directed by Mr. Kim / ~을 엄히 할 것 Strict supervision should be executed. / 시험 ~을 하다 proctor an examination. ‖ ~관 an inspector / ~관청 the supervisory [competent] authorities.

감돌다 《둘레를》 go [turn] round; 《급이》 wind; meander; curve; 《…기운이》 linger; hang low.

감동(感動) impression; deep emotion. ~되다 be moved [touched, affected] 《by》. ~시키다 impress; move; affect; appeal to 《a person》 / 크게 ~하다 be deeply moved.

감득(感得) ~하다 become awake 《of》; take a hint 《of》; 《깨닫다》 realize; perceive.

감등(減等) ~하다 《등급을》 lower the grade; 《형을》 demote; commute; reduce.

감람(橄欖) an olive. ‖ ~나무 〔植〕 an olive tree / ~빛 olive color [green] / ~석 〔鑛〕 olivine; peridot.

감량(減量) a loss in weight [quantity]. ~하다 《양을》 reduce the quantity 《of》; 《체중을》 reduce [lower] one's weight. ¶ ~에 먹다 have a hard time losing weight; have difficulty reducing one's weight. ‖ ~경영 belt-tightening management(~경영하다 streamline management) / ~식품 diet (low-calorized) food.

감로(甘露) nectar; honeydew. ‖ ~주 sweet liquor.

감루(感淚) tears of gratitude.

감리(監理) supervision; superintendence. ~하다 supervise.

감리교(監理敎) Methodism. ‖ ~신자 a Methodist / ~회 the Methodist Church.

감마선(-線) 〔理〕 gamma rays.

감면(減免) 《세금의》 reduction and exemption; 《형벌의》 mitigation and remission. ~하다 exempt; remit. ¶ 세금의 ~ reduction of and exemption from taxes / 여행자는 소비세가 ~된다 Tourists are exempt from paying the consumption tax. ‖ ~조건 conditions of reduction and exemption.

감명(感銘) (deep) impression. ~하다 be (deeply) impressed [moved, touched] 《by》. ¶ ~시키다 impress 《a person》; make an impression on 《a person》.

감미(甘味) sweetness; a sweet taste. ~롭다 (be) sweet. ‖ ~료 sweetener / 인공~료 an artificial sweetener.

감방(監房) a cell; a ward. ¶ ~에 처넣다 throw 《a person》 into a cell.

감배(減配) a reduction in a dividend. ~하다 reduce the dividend 《to 10 %》; reduce [cut] the ration(배당).

감법(減法) 〔數〕 subtraction.

감별(鑑別) discrimination; discernment. ~하다 discriminate; discern. ¶ 병아리를 ~하다 sex a chicken; discern the sex of a fowl.

감복(感服) admiration. ~하다 admire; be struck with admiration 《at》; wonder 《at》. ¶ ~할 만한 업적 admirable results; praiseworthy achievements / ~시키다 excite 《a person's》 admiration; strike 《a person》 with admiration.

감봉(減俸) a pay [salary] cut. ~하다 reduce 《a person's》 salary 《from 300,000 won to 200,000 won》. ¶ ~당하다 have one's pay cut down.

감사(感謝) thanks; gratitude; appreciation; 《신에의》 thanksgiving. ~하다 thank; be thankful [grateful] 《for》; feel grateful; express one's gratitude. ¶ ~의 표시로서 as a token of gratitude / 친절에 ~드립니다 I am very grateful for your kindness. or I appreciate your kindness. ‖ ~장 a letter of thanks 〔appreciation〕 / ~제 Thanksgiving Day (美) / ~패 an appreciation plaque.

감사(監事) 《사람》 an inspector; a supervisor; an auditor (회계의).

감사(監査) 《검사》 (an) inspection; audit (회계의). ~하다 inspect; audit 《accounts》 (회계의). ‖ ~보고 an audit report / ~역 an auditor / ~원(장) (the Chairman of) the Board of Audit and Inspection / ~증명 an audit certificate.

감산(減算) 〔數〕 subtraction.

감산(減産) 《자연적인》 a decrease [drop] in production [output]; 《인위적》 a reduction of production; a (20 percent) production cut. ~하다 reduce [cut] production 《by 20 percent》. ¶ 불경기로 자동차를 10% ~하다 reduce production of cars by 10 percent due to the recession. ‖ ~체제

감상(感傷) sentimentality. ¶ ~적인 sentimental; emotional / ~적으로 되다 become sentimental. ‖ ~주의 sentimentalism / ~주의자 a sentimentalist.

감상(感想) feelings; thoughts; impression(s). ¶ ~을 말하다 (give) one's impressions (of) / 한국에 대해 느끼신 ~는 어떻습니까 What is your impression of Korea? or How does Korea strike you? ‖ ~담 comments; expression of one's feeling / ~문 a description of one's impressions.

감상(鑑賞) appreciation. ~하다 appreciate; enjoy. ¶ 음악을 ~하다 listen [enjoy listening] to music. ‖ ~력 an appreciative power; an eye (for beauty) / 명화 ~회 a special show of noted [well-known] films.

감색(紺色) dark navy blue; indigo.

감성(感性) sensitivity; sensibility; susceptibility (감수성).

감세(減稅) reduction of taxes; a tax cut. ~하다 reduce [cut, lower] taxes. ¶ 대폭적인 ~를 하다 make a drastic cut in taxes. ‖ ~법안 a tax reduction bill / ~안 a tax cut program.

감소(減少) (a) decrease; (a) reduction. ~하다 decrease; fall off; drop; lessen; be reduced. ¶ 인구 [수입]의 ~ a decrease in population [one's income] / ~하고 있다 be on the decrease / 출생율이 10% ~했다 The birth rate has decreased [dropped] by ten percent.

감속(減速) speed reduction. ~하다 reduce the speed (of); slow down; decelerate. ¶ 교차점 앞에서 ~하다 slow down before the crossroads. ‖ ~경제 decelerated economy / ~장치 reduction gear.

감손(減損) decrease; diminution; loss (손해); wear (마손).

감쇄(減殺) ~하다 lessen; diminish; reduce; attenuate; deaden (force).

감수(甘受) ~하다 be resigned to; submit (to); put up with. ¶ 비난을 ~하다 submit to reproach / 모욕을 ~하다 swallow [put up with] an insult / 자기의 운명을 ~하다 accept one's lot without complaining.

감수(減水) the receding [subsiding] of water. ~하다 fall; subside; go down. ¶ 강물이 ~하기 시작했다 The level of the river has begun to fall [subside].

감수(減收) 《suffer》 a decrease in income [harvest, production].

감수(減壽) ~하다 shorten one's life; one's life is shortened.

감수(監修) 〔editorial〕 supervision. ~하다 supervise. ¶ 영한 사전을 ~하다 supervise the compilation of an English-Korean dictionary / 양 박사 ~ compiled under the supervision of Dr. Yang. ‖ ~자 an editorial supervisor.

감수성(感受性) sensibility; susceptibility; sensitivity. ¶ ~이 강한 sensitive (to); susceptible (to, of) / ~이 예민한 아이 a boy who has a high degree of sensibility.

감시(監視) 《파수》 watch; lookout; observation; surveillance. ~하다 watch; observe; keep watch (on, over). ¶ ~하에 두다 put 《a person》 under observation 〔police surveillance〕 / 엄중하게 ~되어 있다 be closely watched; be kept under close observation. ‖ ~기구 a supervisory organization / ~망 〔system〕 a surveillance network 〔system〕 / ~병 a guard / ~선 a patrol boat / ~소 a lookout; an observation post / ~원 a watchman.

감식(減食) reduction of one's diet; dieting. ~하다 go [be] on a diet; eat less. ‖ ~요법 a reduced diet cure.

감식(鑑識) judgment; discernment; 《범죄의》 (criminal) identification. ~하다 judge; discern; discriminate. ¶ 보석에 대한 ~안이 있다 have an eye for jewelry. ‖ ~가 a judge; a connoisseur (of) 《미술품의》 / 범죄 〔지문〕 ~ criminal 〔fingerprint〕 identification / 시경 ~과 the Identification Section of the Metropolitan Police Bureau.

감실거리다 flicker; glimmer.

감싸다 《감아 싸다》 wrap (in); wind 《something》 round; 《비호》 protect; shield; take 《a person》 under one's wings. ¶ 죄인을 ~ shelter 〔harbor〕 a culprit.

감안(勘案) consideration. ~하다 take 《something》 into consideration 〔account〕. ¶ 잘 ~해서 after more mature consideration.

감액(減額) a reduction; a cut; a curtailment. ~하다 reduce; curtail; cut down.

감언(甘言) sweet talk; honeyed 〔sweet〕 words; flattery; cajolery. ¶ ~으로 속이다 coax 《a person》 into; deceive 《a person》 with honeyed words / ~에 넘어가다 be taken in by honeyed words. ‖ ~이설 soft and seductive language; flattery.

감연히 (敢然—) boldly; daringly; fearlessly; resolutely. ¶ ~ 일어나다 stand up bravely《*against*》.

감염 (感染) infection;《간접의》contagion. ~하다, ~되다《병·악습이》infect;《사람이 병에》get infected《*with*》; catch. ¶ ~성의 infectious; contagious / 병에 ~된 사람 an infected person / 콜레라에 ~되다 be infected with cholera / 이 병은 ~된다 This disease is infectious (contagious). ‖ ~경로 an infection route / ~원 the source of infection.

감염식 (減鹽食) a low-salt diet.

감옥 (監獄) a prison;《美》a gaol《英》. ¶ ~살이 imprisonment; a prison life; servitude (~살이하다 be in prison; serve a prison term).

감우 (甘雨) a welcome〔seasonable〕rain. ☞ 단비.

감원 (減員) reduction of the staff; a personnel cut. ~하다 lay off; reduce the personnel《*of*》. ‖ ~선풍 a sweeping reduction of the personnel.

감은 (感恩) gratitude《*for kindness*》.

감읍 (感泣) ~하다 be moved to tears; shed tears of gratitude《*for*》.

감응 (感應)《전기의》induction; influence;《공감》sympathy;《영감》inspiration;《신명의》(divine) response; answer. ~하다 induce; sympathize《*with*》; respond《*to*》. ‖ ~전기 induced electric current / ~코일 an induction coil.

감자 (柑) a (white) potato.

감자 (減資) a reduction of capital; capital reduction. ~하다 reduce the capital《*from...to...*》.

감작 (減作) a short crop.

감전 (感電) (receiving) an electric shock. ~하다 get shocked; be struck by electricity. ¶ ~되어 죽다 be killed by an electric shock; be electrocuted. ‖ ~사 electrocution.

감점 (減點) a demerit mark. ~하다 give《*a person*》a demerit mark; take (off) (deduct) points. ¶ ~을 당하다 receive a cut in marks. ‖ ~법《스포츠의》the bad-mark system; a penalty count system.

감정 (感情) feeling(s); (an) emotion;《정서》(a) passion《격정》; (a) sentiment. ¶ ~적인〔으로〕sentimental(ly); emotional(ly) / ~적인 사람 an emotional 〔a passionate〕person / ~을 자극하다 stir〔excite〕《*a person's*》emotion / ~을 해치다 hurt《*a person's*》feelings; offend《*a person*》/ ~에 흐르다 give way to *one's* feelings / 일시적인 ~에 이끌려 on the impulse of the moment / ~을 나타내다〔억제하다〕express〔control〕*one's* feeling / 인간은 ~의 동물이다 Man is a creature of feelings. ‖ ~론 an emotionally-charged argument / ~이입〔心〕empathy.

감정 (鑑定) ① 《판단》judgment; an expert opinion《전문가의》. ~하다 judge; give an (expert) opinion. ¶ 필적을 ~하다 give an expert opinion on handwriting / 술맛을 ~하다 taste liquor. ② 《가격의》(an) appraisal. ~하다 appraise; estimate. ¶ 허위 ~을 하다 give a false appraisal. ‖ ~가격 an appraisal; the estimated value / 한국~원 the Korea Appraisal Board. ③ 《소송의》legal advice. ~하다 give legal advice.

감정인 (鑑定人) a judge;《미술품의》a connoisseur;《술 따위의》a taster;《자산의》an appraiser;《법정의》an expert witness.

감죄 (減罪) ☞ 감형.

감주 (甘酒) rice nectar.

감지 (感知) perception. ~하다 perceive; sense; become aware of. ¶ 지진〔위험〕을 ~하다 sense an earthquake (danger). ‖ ~장치〔電子〕a sensor; a detector.

감지덕지하다 (感之德之—) be〔feel〕very thankful (grateful)《*for*》.

감질나다 (疳疾—) feel insatiable; never feel satisfied; feel〔be〕dying for more.

감쪽같다 ~ (be) as good as new (before); just as it was;《꾸민 일이》(be) successful. ¶ 감쪽같이 nicely; successfully; artfully / 감쪽같이 속다 be nicely〔completely〕taken in; fall an easy victim to a trick.

감찰 (監察) inspection;《사람》an inspector; a supervisor. ~하다 inspect; supervise. ‖ ~감《軍》an inspector general.

감찰 (鑑札) a license. ¶ ~을 내주다〔내다〕grant〔take (out)〕a license. ‖ ~료 a license fee / 영업 ~ a business〔trade〕license.

감채 (減債) partial payment of a debt. ¶ ~기금 a sinking fund; an amortization fund.

감청 (紺青) deep〔ultramarine〕blue; navy〔dark〕blue.

감초 (甘草)〔植〕a licorice (root). ¶ 약방의 ~ an indispensable man; a key person; a person active in all sorts of affairs.

감촉 (感觸) the (sense of) touch; the feel; feeling. ~하다 touch; feel; perceive through the senses. ¶ 이 부드럽다 feel soft; be soft to the touch; be pleasant to the taste (혀에).

감추다 《숨겨두다》 hide; conceal; put out of sight; keep secret; 《드러나지 않게》 cover; veil; cloak; disguise. ¶ 몸을 ~ hide *oneself* / 나이를 〔감정을〕 ~ conceal *one's* age (feelings) / 행방을 ~ disappear; conceal *oneself* / 눈물을 ~ stifle *one's* tears.

감축(減縮) reduction; diminution; retrenchment. ~하다 reduce; diminish; retrench; curtail; cut down. ¶ 군비의 ~ the reduction of armaments / 경비를 ~하다 cut down the expenses.

감축(感祝) celebrate ~하다 congratulate enthusiastically; thank heartily.

감치다 《잊히지 않다》 linger (haunt) (in *one's* mind); be haunted (by); 《꿰매다》 hem; sew up.

감칠맛 《맛》 good flavor; savory taste; 《끄는 힘》 charm; attraction.

감탄(感歎) admiration; wonder; marvel. ~하다 admire; be struck with admiration; marvel (at). ¶ ~할 만한 admirable; wonderful. ‖ ~문 an exclamatory sentence / ~부호 an exclamation mark / ~사 an interjection; an exclamation.

감퇴(減退) (a) decline; (a) decrease; (a) loss. ~하다 decline; lose; decrease; fall off. ¶ 기억력의 ~ failing of memory / 식욕의 ~ loss of appetite / 정력의 ~ a decline in energy / 수요는 전반적으로 ~되어 있다 The demand remains generally in a slump.

감투 ① 《모자》 a horsehair cap formerly worn by the common people. ② 《벼슬》 a high office; a distinguished post. ¶ ~를 쓰다 assume office; hold a prominent post. ‖ ~싸움 a struggle for an influential post.

감투(敢鬪) ~하다 fight courageously (bravely). ‖ ~상 a prize for fighting-spirit / ~정신 a fighting spirit.

감하다(減—) subtract; deduct (*from*); 《줄이다》 decrease; lessen; reduce; diminish; 《경감》 mitigate. ¶ 값을 ~ cut down a price / 형(刑)을 ~ reduce a penalty (on).

감행(敢行) ~하다 venture [dare] (*to do*); carry out; risk. ¶ 적에게 야습을 ~하다 risk a night attack on the enemy.

감형(減刑) reduction of penalty; commutation of a sentence. ~하다 commute (mitigate) (*a sentence*).

감호처분(監護處分) preventive custody.

감화(感化) influence; reform (교정). ~하다 influence; inspire; reform. ¶ ~를 받다 be influenced (affected) (*by*) / …의 ~를 받다 under the influence of ... . ‖ ~교육 reformatory instruction (training) / ~력 power to influence / ~사업 reformatory work / ~원 a reformatory; a reform school.

감회(感懷) deep emotion; impressions; sentiments; reminiscences. ¶ ~에 젖다 be overcome by deep emotion / ~를 표현 express (give) *one's* feelings (sentiments) (*about*).

감흥(感興) interest; fun. ¶ ~을 자아내다 arouse (stimulate) *one's* interest.

감히(敢—) boldly; daringly; positively. ¶ ~ …하다 dare (venture) to (*do*).

갑(甲) 《위의 것》 the former; the one; 《등급》 grade "A". ¶ ~과 을(乙) the former and the latter; the one and the other / ~에게 주다 give (*a student*) A.

갑(匣) a case; a box; a pack (담배 따위의). ¶ 담배 한 ~ a pack of cigarettes.

갑(岬) a cape.

갑각(甲殼) a shell; a crust; a carapace. ‖ ~류 〔動〕 Crustacea.

갑갑증(—症) tedium; boredom.

갑갑하다 《지루하다》 (be) bored; tedious; 《답답하다》 (be) stuffy; stifling; suffocating; heavy. ¶ 가슴이 ~ feel heavy in the chest / 갑갑해 죽겠다 be bored to death.

갑골문자(甲骨文字) inscriptions on bones and tortoise carapaces.

갑근세(甲勤稅) the earned income tax (of Grade A). ¶ 월급에서 ~를 공제하다 deduct the earned income tax from *one's* salary.

갑론을박(甲論乙駁) the pros and cons. ~하다 argue for and against (*a matter*); argue pro and con.

갑문(閘門) a lock gate; a sluice (gate); a floodgate.

갑부(甲富) the richest man; the wealthiest; a millionaire.

갑상선(甲狀腺) 〔醫〕 the thyroid gland. ‖ ~비대 hypertrophied thyroid gland / ~염 thyroiditis / ~호르몬 thyroid hormone.

갑옷(甲—) (a suit of) armor.

갑자기(별안간) suddenly; all of a sudden; all at once; 《뜻밖에》 unexpectedly. ¶ ~ 병에 걸리다 be suddenly taken ill / ~ 해고하다 dismiss (*a person*) without notice.

갑작스럽다 (be) sudden; abrupt; unexpected. ¶ 갑작스러운 일 an

갑절 ☞ 배(倍).
갑종(甲種) grade A; first grade; top-grade. ¶ ~합격자 a first grade conscript 《*in physical check-up*》.
갑충(甲蟲) 【蟲】 a beetle.
갑판(甲板) a deck. ¶ ~에 나가다 go on deck. / ~사관 a deck officer / ~선원 a deck hand / ~승강구 a hatchway / ~실 a deckhouse / ~장 a boatswain.
값 (가격) price; cost; 《가치》 value; worth. ¶ 엄청난 ~ an unreasonable price / 알맞은 ~ a reasonable price / 비싼 ~ 나가는 expensive; dear / ~(이) 싼 lowpriced; cheap / ~치다 be valuable / ~을 올리다 [내리다] raise [lower] the price / ~을 치르다 pay for 《*an article*》 / ~을 더 [덜] 먹다 [적게 먹다] / ~을 좀더 깎아주세요 Come down just a little more.
값어치 《가치》 value; worth. ¶ 한 푼의 ~도 없다 be not worth a penny.
갓¹ (쓰는) a Korean top hat (made of horsehair).
갓² (방금) fresh from; just (now); newly. ¶ ~ 지은 밥 rice hot from the pot / ~ 구운 빵 bread fresh from the oven / ~ 결혼한 부부 a newly wedded couple; newlyweds / ~스물이다 be just twenty years old. [baby.
갓나아이, 갓난애 a (newborn)
강(江) a river. ¶ ~ 건너(에) across the river / ~을 따라 along the river / ~을 건너다 cross the river / ~을 거슬러 올라 [내려] 가다 go up [down] the river. ‖ ~가 (기슭) a riverside / ~둑 a river embankment; a levee / ~바닥 the bottom of a river; a riverbed / ~바람 breeze from the river / ~어귀 이기 the mouth of a river / ~줄기 the course of a river.
…강(強) a little over (more). ¶ 5할 ~ a little over 50 percent.
강간(強姦) (a) rape. ~하다 rape; commit rape 《*upon*》; violate. ‖ ~미수 an attempted rape / ~범 a rapist(사람) / ~죄 rape; criminal assault.
강강술래, 강강수월래 a Korean circle dance (under the bright full moon).
강건(強健) robust health. ¶ 한 ~한 robust; healthy; strong.
강경(強硬) ~하다 (be) strong; firm; resolute. ¶ ~한 결의문 a strongly-worded resolution / ~한 태도를 취하다 take a firm attitude 《*toward*》 / ~히 반대하다 oppose 《*something*》 strongly. ‖ ~노선 a hard [tough] line / ~수단 a drastic measure; a resolute step / ~파 the hardliners; the hawks.
강관(鋼管) a steel pipe [tube].
강구(講究) ~하다 study; consider; contrive; take measures [steps].
강국(強國) a great [strong] power; a strong nation [country]. ¶ 세계의 ~ the powers of the world / 7대 ~ the Big Seven.
강권(強勸) ~하다 press; urge; recommend against 《*a person's*》 will. ¶ 사직을 ~하다 urge 《*someone*》 to resign.
강권(強權) authority; state power. ¶ ~을 발동하다 take forcible [strong] measures; appeal to legal action. ‖ ~발동 the invocation of the state power / ~정치 power [a high-handed] politics.
강남(江南) 《서울의》 the south of the Han River. ‖ ~지역 the areas south of the Han River.
강낭콩 【植】 a kidney bean.
강다짐하다 ① (마른밥을) eat boiled rice without water or soup. ② (까닭 없이 꾸짖음) scold 《*a person*》 without listening to *his* story. ③ (부림) force 《*a person*》 to work without pay.
강단(講壇) a (lecture) platform(학술의); a pulpit(설교단); a rostrum (연단). ¶ ~에 서다 stand on a platform; (비유적) teach school.
강당(講堂) a (lecture) hall; an auditorium; an assembly hall.
강대(強大) ~하다 (be) mighty; powerful; strong. ‖ ~국 a powerful country; a big power.
강도(強度) strength; intensity; tenacity(질김); solidity(단단함). ¶ ~시험 a strength test 《*on a sample of steel*》.
강도(強盜) a burglar; a robber. ‖ ~질 burglary; robbery / ~질하다 commit burglary [robbery].
강동거리다 leap lightly; skip.
강동하다 be rather [too] short.
강등(降等) demotion; degradation. ~하다 demote; reduce [degrade] to a lower rank.
강력(強力) ~하다 (be) strong; powerful; mighty. ‖ ~범 a violent crime(죄); a criminal of violence(사람) / ~비타민제 a high-potency vitamin preparation / ~접착제 a high-strength adhesive.
강렬(強烈) ~한 severe; intense; strong / ~한 색채 a loud color / ~한 냄새 a powerful odor / ~한 인상 a strong impression.
강령(綱領) general principles; 《정당의》 a platform 《美》; a pro-

강론(講論) a lecture. ~하다 lecture 《*on*》.

강림(降臨) descent from Heaven; advent. ~하다 descend (from Heaven). ¶ 성령이 ~하셨습니다 The Holy spirit descended upon them. ‖ ~절 the Advent.

강매(强賣) ~하다 force a sale 《*on*》; force [press] 《*a person*》 to buy 《*a thing*》. ¶ ~하는 판매원 a pushy salesman / ~사절《게시》 No Soliciting (Peddling) / 나는 그것을 ~당했다 I was forced to buy it. *or* They sold it to me by force.

강모(剛毛) 〖動·植〗 a bristle; a seta.

강물(江—) a river; a stream; river water. ¶ ~이 붇다 The river rises.

강박(强迫) coercion; compulsion. ~하다 compel; coerce; force. ‖ ~관념 an obsession / ~관념에 사로잡히다 suffer from an obsession).

강변(江邊) a riverside. ‖ ~도로 a riverside road / ~도시고속도로 the riverside urban expressway.

강변하다(强辯—) reason against reason; insist obstinately 《*on doing, that* ...》; quibble.

강병(强兵) 〖군사〗 a strong soldier; 〖병력〗 a powerful [strong] army.

강보(襁褓) swaddling clothes. ¶ 아기를 ~에 싸다 wrap a baby in swaddling clothes.

강보합세(强保合勢) ¶ ~의 〖證〗 (be) firm (steady) with an upward tendency.

강북(江北) the north of a river; 《서울의》 the north of the Han River. ‖ ~지역 the areas north of the Han River.

강사(講士) a speaker.

강사(講師) a lecturer; an instructor; 《직》 lectureship. ¶ 서울대학교 ~ a lecturer at [of] Seoul National University.

강산(江山) 《강과 산》 rivers and mountains. ¶ 《강토》 one's native land. ¶ 삼천리 금수 ~ the beautiful land of Korea, far and wide.

강새암 ☞ 강쌈.

강생(降生) incarnation. ~하다 be incarnated.

강선(鋼線) a steel wire.

강설(降雪) snowing; a snowfall. ‖ ~량 the (amount of) snowfall.

강성(强盛) ~하다 (be) powerful; thriving; flourishing.

강세(强勢) 《음의》 (a) stress; emphasis; 《시세의》 a strong [firm] tone. ¶ ~를 두다 emphasize [lay [put] emphasis [stress] 《*on*》.

강속구(强速球) 〖野〗 fast [speed] ball. ¶ ~를 던지다 throw a fast [speed] ball. ‖ ~투수 a strong-armed pitcher; a speed ball hurler.

강쇠바람 the east wind in early autumn.

강수(降水) precipitation. ☞ 강우. ‖ ~량 (a) precipitation.

강술 ~을 마시다 drink liquor without snack (food).

강습(强襲) ~하다 storm 《*into*》; assault 《*on*》; take 《*a fort*》 by storm.

강습(講習) (a short) course; a class. ¶ ~을 받다 [행하다] take [give] a course 《*in first aid*》. ‖ ~생 a student / ~소 a training school / 여름(겨울) ~ a summer [winter] school.

강시(僵屍) the body of a person frozen to death.

강신술(降神術) spiritualism.

강심(江心) the center of a river.

강심제(强心劑) a heart stimulant (medicine); a cardiotonic drug.

강아지 a pup; a puppy.

강아지풀 〖植〗 a foxtail.

강압(强壓) pressure; oppression. ~하다 coerce; oppress; put pressure 《*on*》. ¶ ~적 high-handed; coercive. ‖ ~수단 a high-handed (coercive) measure / ~ 정책 a high-handed policy; a big-stick policy《美俗》.

강약(强弱) strength and weakness; the strong and the weak; stress《음의》.

강연(講演) a lecture; an address. ~하다 (give) a lecture 《*on*》; address 《*a meeting*》. ¶ 라디오 (TV)로 ~하다 give a lecture on the radio (TV). ‖ ~자 a lecturer; a speaker / ~회 a lecture meeting.

강온(强穩) toughness and moderateness. ¶ ~양면정책 a carrot-and-stick policy / ~ 양파 the hawks and the doves.

강요(强要) forcible demand; coercion. ~하다 force; coerce; demand; compel. ¶ 아무에게 …을 ~하다 force (compel) 《*a person*》 to 《*do*》.

강우(降雨) rain; a rainfall. ‖ ~기 the wet [rainy] season / ~량 the (amount of) rainfall [rain] / ~전선 a rain front / ~량 the annual rainfall 《*in Seoul*》.

강의(講義) a lecture; an explanation (설명); an exposition (해설). ~하다 lecture; give a lecture; explain 《*a book*》. ¶ ~를 빼먹다《학생이》 cut (quit) a lecture. ‖ ~록 a transcript of lectures.

강인(强靭) ~하다 (be) tough; stiff; tenacious; unyielding. ¶ ~ 한

강자 의지 a tough spirit; an iron will. ‖ ~성 strength; toughness; solidarity.

강자(強者) a strong man; the powerful, the strong (총칭). ¶ ~와 약자 the strong and the weak.

강장(強壯) ¶ ~한 strong; robust; sturdy; sound; stout. ‖ ~제 a tonic; a bracer 《美口》.

강장동물(腔腸動物) a coelenterate.

강재(鋼材) steel (materials); rolled steel(압연강).

강적(強敵) a powerful enemy; a formidable rival (foe).

강점(強占) ~하다 occupy (possess) 《a person's house》 by force.

강점(強點) (이점) a strong point; an advantage; one's strength. ¶ 그의 ~은 …다는 점이다 His strength lies in….

강정 a glutinous cake coated with rice (sesame, etc.).

강정제(強精劑) a tonic.

강제(強制) compulsion; coercion; enforcement. ~하다 compel; enforce; force; coerce. ¶ ~적인 compulsory; forced / ~적으로 by force (compulsion); forcibly / ~적으로 …하게 하다 compel (force) 《a person》 to do / ~로 계약서에 서명하다 sign the contract under compulsion. ‖ ~노동 forced labor / ~송환 enforced repatriation / ~수단 a coercive measure / ~수용소 a concentration camp / ~조정 (집행) compulsory mediation (execution) / ~착륙 a forced landing / ~처분 disposition by legal force.

강조(強調) stress; emphasis. ~하다 stress; emphasize; put (lay) stress on. ¶ 지나치게 ~하다 overemphasize / 저축의 필요성을 ~하다 stress the need of savings.

강좌(講座) a (professional) chair; 《강의》 a lecture 《on music》; a course. ¶ ~를 개설하다 establish (create) a chair 《of》 / 라디오 영어 ~ a radio English course.

강주정(一酒酊) feigned drunkenness. ~하다 pretend to be drunk.

강직(剛直) ~하다 (be) upright; incorruptible. ¶ ~한 사람 a man of integrity.

강직(強直) ☞ 경직.

강진(強震) a violent (severe) earthquake.

강짜 (unreasonable) jealousy (complaint). ¶ ~ 부리다 show unreasonable jealousy; burn with unreasonable complaints.

강쳘(鋼鐵) ~같은 의지 an iron will. ‖ ~판 a steel plate.

강청(強請) exaction; persistent demand. ~하다 extort 《money》.

강촌(江村) a riverside village.

강추위 severe (dry) cold weather.

강타(強打) a hard (heavy) blow; 《야구의》 a heavy hit; a blast; 《골프·테니스의》 a (powerful) drive. ~하다 hit hard. ¶ ~를 퍼붓다 rain hard blows 《on》 / 가슴을 ~당하다 get (receive) a hard blow on the chest. ‖ ~자 (野) a heavy hitter; a slugger.

강탈(強奪) seizure; robbery; hijacking 《美口》. ~하다 seize; rob 《a person》 of 《a thing》; hijack. ‖ ~품 plunder; spoils; booty / ~자 a plunderer; a robber; a hijacker.

강태공(姜太公) an angler.

강토(疆土) a territory; a realm.

강판(鋼板) a steel plate(두꺼운); a steel sheet(얇은).

강판(薑板) a grater. ¶ ~에 갈다 grate 《a radish》.

강평(講評) a comment; (a) review; (a) criticism. ~하다 comment on 《papers》; make comments on; review.

강풍(強風) a strong (high) wind; a gale. ‖ ~주의보 a strong-wind warning.

강하(降下) (a) descent; a fall; a drop. ~하다 descend; fall; drop. ¶ 기온의 ~ a drop in temperature. ‖ ~물 (radioactive) fallout / 급 ~ a sudden (steep) descent; a nose dive.

강하다(強一) (be) strong; 《힘이》 powerful; mighty; 《정도·작용이》 intense; hard; 《능력·지식이》 competent; good 《at》. ¶ 강하게 hard; severely; strongly; powerfully / 강해지다 grow strong / 강하게 하다 make strong; strengthen / 씨서가 멍린 시깁 ~ a man of strong will / 강한 빛 strong (intense) light / 그는 수학에 ~ He is good at mathematics. / 오늘은 바람이 ~ It is blowing hard today.

강행(強行) ~하다 enforce; force. ¶ 저물가 정책을 ~하다 enforce a low-price policy.

강행군(強行軍) a forced march; 《비유적》 a very vigorous (tight) schedule. ~하다 make a forced march.

강호(江湖) 《세상》 the (reading) public. ‖ ~제현 the general public; people at large.

강호(強豪) a veteran (player); ¶ 전국에서 선발한 ~ 팀 powerful teams selected from all over the country.

강화(強化) ~하다 strengthen; toughen (산업 따위); enforce;

tighten(단속함); **reinforce**(세력·구조 따위); **consolidate**(지위 따위); **intensify**(훈련 따위). ¶국방을 ~하다 strengthen the national defense. ‖ ~식품 enriched foods / ~유리 tempered glass.

강화(講和) peace; reconciliation. ~하다 make peace 《*with*》. ¶굴욕적인 ~ a humiliating peace. ‖ ~조건 conditions [terms] of peace / ~조약 (conclude) a peace treaty / ~협상 [제의] peace negotiations [proposals].

갖…《가죽》 leather; fur. ‖ ~바치 a shoemaker / ~신 leather shoes / ~옷 clothes lined with fur.

갖은 all (sorts of); every (possible). ¶~ 고생 (go through) all sorts [kinds] of hardships / ~ 수단 (try) every means available [conceivable]; every possible means.

갖추다《구비하다》have; possess; be endowed with 《*talents*》; prepare 《*for*》; make preparations 《*for*》; make [get] 《*a thing*》 ready. ¶위엄을 ~ have 〔a certain〕 dignity / 음악적 재능을 갖추다 be endowed with genius in music / 전쟁 준비를 ~ prepare for the war.

같다 ① 《동일》 be (one and) the same; (be) identical. ¶똑~ be the very same; be just the same as; be much 〔about, almost〕 ~ be the same 《*as*》 / 그것은 내 가방과 ~ That is the same bag as mine. ② 《동등》 (be) equal 《*to*》; uniform; equivalent 《*to*》. ¶같은 액수 a like sum / 같은 자격으로 협상하다 negotiate on equal terms / 자네와 나는 키가 거의 ~ You are about as tall as I. ③ 《같은 모양》 (be) similar; like; alike; such ... as. ¶그 같은 자 a man like him / 생게 이나 ~ be as good as new / 꼭 ~ be exactly alike / 샛별 같은 눈 eyes like stars / 사형 선고와 ~ be same as a death sentence / 같은 입장에 있다 face the same situation; stand on same ground; be in the same boat. ④ 《공통》 (be) common. ¶기원이 ~ have a common origin 《*with*》. 《불변》 be changeless; 《서술적》 be (remain) unchanged; be the same. ¶성미는 설없을 때와 ~ He remains the same in disposition as when he was young. ⑥ 《생각되다》 seem; 《보이다》 look 〔like〕; appear; seem; 《될 것 같다》 be likely 《*to*》; probably. ¶참말 같은 거짓말을 하다 lie like the truth / 장사꾼 ~ look like a merchant / 비가 올 것 ~ It looks like rain. *or* It is likely to rain. ⑦ 《가정》 if it were. ¶나 같으면 if it were me; if I were you / 옛날 같으면 if these were the old days.

같은 값이면 if... at all; if possible. ¶~ 잘해라 If you do it at all, do it well.

같이 ① 《같게》 like; as; likewise; similarly; (in) the same (way); equally 《동등하게》. ¶여느 때와 ~ as usual / 말씀하시는 바와 ~ as you say / 이와 ~ 하여 in this manner [way] / 의견을 ~ 하다 share the same view. ② 《함께》 (along, together) with; in company with. ¶~ 살다 live together / ~ 자다 share the same bed / 자리를 ~ 하다 sit together / 행동을 ~ 하다 cooperate with / 운명 (기쁨)을 ~ 하다 share *one's* fate [joy] / 식사를 ~ 하다 dine together.

같잖다 (be) trivial; worthless. ¶같잖은 물건 a no-good thing / 같잖은 인간 a worthless [good-for-nothing] fellow.

갚다 ①《돈을》 repay; pay back; refund. ¶빚을 ~ pay *one's* debts; pay the money back. ②《물어주다》 indemnify; compensate 《*for*》; requite. ¶손해본 것을 갚아주다 compensate 〔indemnify〕 《*a person*》 for the loss. 《죄를》 atone [expiate] for. ¶죄를 ~ expiate for an offense. 《은혜를》 return; repay; requite. ¶공을 ~ reward 《*a person*》 for his service / 은혜를 원수로 ~ return evil for good. ⑤《원수를》 revenge (자신의); avenge (타인의); requite; take vengeance 《*upon*》. ¶아버지를 죽인 원수를 ~ avenge *one's* father's murder.

개《견》 a dog; a puppy 《강아지》; a hound 《사냥개》; a spy 《앞잡이》. ¶~ 같은 doggish; doglike / ~를 기르다 keep a dog.

개《箇》 a piece. ¶사과 세 ~ three apples / 비누 두 ~ two pieces [cakes] of soap.

개가《改嫁》 remarriage (of a woman). ~하다 marry again; remarry. ¶~를 권하다 advise 《a woman》 to remarry / ~한 여자 a woman married second time.

개가《凱歌》 a triumphant [victory] song. ¶현대 과학의 ~ a triumph of modern science / ~를 올리다 sing in triumph; win a victory 《*over*》.

개각《改閣》 a cabinet shake-up [reshuffle]. ~하다 reorganize [reshuffle] the Cabinet. ¶~을 단행하다 effect a cabinet reshuf-

개간(改刊) revision. ~하다 reprint; issue a revised edition.

개간(開墾) cultivation; reclamation. ~하다 bring under cultivation; clear (*the land*); reclaim (*wasteland*). ‖ ~사업 reclamation (work) / ~지 a reclaimed land / 미~지 a virgin soil.

개값 ¶ ~으로 at a sacrifice (low price) / ~으로 팔다 sell dirt-cheap.

개강(開講) ~하다 begin *one's* first lecture (*on*); open a course.

개개(箇箇) ¶ ~의 individual; each one of.

개개풀어지다 ① (국수 등이) lose (*its*) stickiness; come loose. ② (눈이) get bleary; be bleary-eyed (heavy-eyed).

개고(改稿) rewriting *one's* manuscript; 《원고》 a rewritten manuscript. ~하다 rewrite *one's* manuscript.

개고기 ① (고기) dog meat. ② (사람) a rude and bad-tempered person.

개골창 a drain; a gutter; a ditch.

개과(改過) ~하다 repent; mend *oneself*; turn over a new leaf.

개관(開館) the opening. ~하다 open (*a hall*). ‖ ~식 (hold) an opening ceremony.

개관(概觀) a general survey (view); an outline. ~하다 survey; take a bird's-eye (general) view (*of*).

개괄(槪括) a summary. ~하다 summarize; sum up. ¶ ~적인 general / ~해서 말하면 on the whole; generally (speaking).

개교(開校) ~하다 open (found) a school. ‖ ~기념일 the anniversary of the founding of a school / ~식 the opening ceremony of a school.

개구리 a frog. ¶ 우물 안 ~ a man of narrow views. ‖ ~헤엄 평영.

개구리밥 〔植〕 a great duckweed.

개구멍 a doghole. ‖ ~받이 a foundling; an abandoned child (found on a doorstep).

개구쟁이 a naughty (mischievous) boy; a brat.

개국(開國) ~하다 《건국》 found a state; 《개방》 open the country to the world. ‖ ~주의 an open-door policy. [gangster.

개그 a gag. ‖ ~맨 a gagman; a

개근(皆勤) perfect attendance. ~하다 do not miss a single day. ‖ ~상 a reward for perfect attendance (*for two years*) / ~수당 an allowance for nonabsence service / ~자 one who has not missed a day (*at work*).

개기(皆旣) 〔天〕 a total eclipse. ‖ ~일(皆旣日)식 a total solar (lunar) eclipse. [face.

개기름 (natural) grease on *one's*

개꿈 a wild (silly) dream.

개나리 〔植〕 a forsythia; the golden bell.

개념(槪念) a general idea; a concept. ¶ ~적인 conceptional; notional / 행복의 ~ the concept (idea) of happiness. ‖ ~론 conceptualism / 기본~ fundamental notions.

개다¹ (날씨·안개 따위가) clear up (away, off); 《it가 주어》 be fine.

개다² (물에) knead (*flour*); mix up. ¶ 진흙을 ~ knead clay.

개다³ (접어서) fold (up). ¶ 옷을 ~ fold (up) clothes / 이부자리를 ~ put away the bedding; fold up quilts.

개돼지 ¶ ~ 같은 사람 a brute (of a man); a man no better than a beast.

개떡 a bran cake; steamed bread of rough flour.

개떡같다 (be) worthless; rubbish. ¶ 개떡같이 여기다 don't care a bit (*about*).

개똥밭(犬糞~) a fertile land; 《더러운 곳》 a place all dirty with dog droppings. ¶ ~에도 이슬 내릴 날이 있다 《俗談》 Every dog has his day. [worm.

개똥벌레 〔蟲〕 a firefly; a glow-

개략(槪略) (give) an outline (*of*); a summary.

개량(改良) (an) improvement; (a) reform; betterment. ~하다 improve; reform; better. ¶ ~의 여지 room for improvement / ~품질을 ~하다 improve the quality (*of*). ‖ ~종 an improved breed / ~형 an improved model.

개런티 a guarantee.

개론(槪論) an introduction; an outline. ~하다 outline; survey. ¶ 영문학~ an introduction to English literature.

개막(開幕) ~하다 raise the curtain; begin the performance; open; start. ‖ ~식 (전) the opening ceremony (*game*).

개머루 〔植〕 a wild grape.

개머리(銃) a gunstock; a butt. ‖ ~판 the butt of a rifle.

개명(改名) ~하다 change *one's* name; rename.

개문(開門) opening a gate. ¶ ~ 발차 starting with doors open.

개미 〔蟲〕 an ant. ¶ ~떼 a swarm of ants / ~집 an ant nest; an anthill (독).

개미핥기 〔動〕 an anteater.

개미허리 a slender (slim) waist.

개발(開發) development; exploitation(자원 등의); cultivation(능력 의). ~하다 develop; exploit; cultivate. ¶ 새로운 시스템을 ~하다 develop a new system / ~중인 기계 a machine in the development stage / 잠재적 능력을 ~하다 develop *one's* latent ability. ‖ ~계획 a development project (program, plan) / ~규제 《carry out》 development control / ~금융 development credit / ~도상국 a developing country / 저~국 an underdeveloped country.

개발코 a snub nose. ¶ ~에 도토리다 be an outcast of *one's* associates.

개밥바라기 〖저녁의 금성〗 morning star; Vesper; Hesperus; Venus.

개방(開放) ~하다 open. ¶ ~(인) 분위기 a frank and easy atmosphere / …에 대하여 문호를 ~하다 open doors to … / 도서관은 일반에게 ~되어 있다 The library is open to the public. / ~금지 《게시》 Don't leave the door open. ‖ 〈문호〉~주의 the open-door policy.

개벽(開闢) the Creation. ¶ ~ 이래 since the beginning of the world.

개변(改變) 〖고침〗 change; alteration. ~하다 change; alter.

개별(個別) ~적(으로) individual(ly); separate(ly) ¶ 문제를 ~적으로 검토하다 discuss the problems separately. ‖ ~심사 individual screening / ~절충 a separate negotiation 《with individuals》. 〔scription system.

개병 제도(皆兵制度) a universal conscription system.

개복 수술(開腹手術) 〖醫〗 an abdominal operation; laparotomy.

개봉(開封) unsealing; (a) release (영화의). ~하다 release 《a film》; open 《a letter》; break a seal. ¶ ~관 a firstrunner; a first-run theater / ~영화 a first-run 《a newly released》 film.

개비 a piece of (split wood); a stick. ¶ 성냥 ~ a matchstick.

개비(改備) ~하다 renew; refurnish; replace 《A with B》.

개산(概算) a rough calculation. ~하다 make a rough estimate 《of》.

개살구 〖植〗 a wild apricot. ¶ 빛좋은 ~다 be not so good as it looks; be deceptive.

개새끼 〖강아지〗 a pup; a puppy; 〖개자식〗 a "son-of-a-bitch".

개서(改書) 〖다시 씀〗 rewriting; 《어음·증서 등의》 (a) renewal. ~하다 《어음 등을》 renew 《a bill》. ‖ ~어음 a renewed bill.

개선(改善) improvement; betterment; reformation. ~하다 improve; reform; better; make 《*something*》 better. ¶ 생활 ~ the betterment of living / 노동 조건의 ~을 외치다 cry for better working conditions / 그 제도에는 ~의 여지가 많다 That system leaves much room for improvement. ‖ ~책 a reform measure; a remedy. 〔elect.

개선(改選) reelection. ~하다 re-

개선(疥癬) the itch. 〔음.

개선(凱旋) a triumphal return. ~하다 return in triumph. ¶ ~가〈문〉 a triumphal song 〈arch〉 / ~군〈장군〉 a victorious army (general).

개설(開設) opening; establishment. ~하다 open; establish; set up. ¶ 신용장을 ~하다 open 〈establish〉 an L/C / 전화를 ~하다 have a telephone installed / 연구소를 ~하다 set up a research institute.

개설(概說) a summary; an outline. ~하다 give an outline 《of》.

개성(個性) individuality; personality. ~하다 ~을 존중하다 respect 《*one's*》 personality / ~을 계발하다 〖발전시키다〗 display 〈develop〉 *one's* personality.

개소(個所) 《곳》 a place; a spot. 《부분》 a part; a portion.

개소리 silly talk; nonsense.

개수(改修) repair; improvement. ~하다 repair; improve. ‖ ~공사 river improvement 〈conservation〉 works.

개수작(-酬酌) silly talk; nonsense; a foolish remark.

개술(槪述) ~하다 summarize; give an outline 《of》.

개시(開市) ① 〖시장을 엶〗 ~하다 open a market. ② 〖마수걸이〗 ~하다 make the first sale of the day.

개시(開始) start; opening; beginning. ~하다 open; start; begin. ¶ ~부터 from the outset / 교섭을 ~하다 open negotiations / 영업을 ~하다 start business / 공격을 ~하다 launch 〈open〉 an attack 《on, against》.

개신(改新) reformation; renovation. ~하다 reform; renew.

개심(改心) ~하다 reform *oneself*; turn over a new leaf.

개악(改惡) a change for the worse. ~하다 change for the worse. ¶ 헌법의 ~ an undesirable amendment to the constitution.

개안(開眼) opening *one's* eyes; gaining eyesight. ~하다 ~수술 an eyesight recovery operation.

개암(-열매) a hazelnut.

개업(開業) ~하다 start (a) business; open a store; start practice(의사·변호사의). ‖ ~대매출 an opening sale. ‖ ~비 the initial cost of business / ~의 a general [medical] practitioner(일반〔내과〕의).

개역(改譯) a revision of a translation. ~하다 revise [correct] a translation. ‖ ~판 a revised [corrected] version.

개연성(蓋然性) probability. ¶ ~이 높다 be highly probable.

개오(開悟) spiritual awakening. ~하다 be spiritually awakened.

개요(概要) an outline; a summary.

개운하다(기분이) feel refreshed [relieved]; (맛이) (be) plain; simple. ¶ 맛이 개운한 음식 plain food.

개울을 a brook; a streamlet.

개원(開院) ~하다 open the House (의회의); open a hospital [an institution] (병원·기관의). ¶ ~식(국회의) the opening ceremony of the House [Diet, National Assembly].

개의(介意) ~하다 mind; care about; pay regard to. ¶ ~치 않다 do not care about; pay no attention (to).

개인(個人) an individual; a private person. ¶ ~의, ~적인 individual; personal; private / ~적으로 individually; personally; privately / ~ 자격으로 in one's private capacity / 내 ~ 의견으로는 in my personal opinion / ~ 용의 for private [personal] use / ~ 주택 a private residence. ‖ ~감정 personal feelings / ~ 교수 private lessons / ~기업 a private enterprise / ~문제 a private affair / ~소득 a personal income / ~숭배 a personality cult / ~ 컴퓨터 a personal computer / ~전(展) a private exhibition / ~전(戰) an individual match / ~주의 individualism / ~주의자 an individualist / ~ 택시(기사) an owner-driven taxi (driver).

개입(介入) intervention. ~하다 intervene (in); meddle (in). ¶ 남의 일에 ~하다 intervene in another's affairs / 무력 ~ armed intervention.

개자리[植] a snail clover.

개작(改作) (an) adaptation 《from》. ~하다 adapt. ¶ 이야기를 연극으로 ~하다 adapt a story for the stage. ‖ ~자 an adapter.

개장(改裝) remodeling; redecoration. ~하다 remodel. ¶ 거실을 서재로 ~하다 remodel the living room into a study.

개장(開場) ~하다 open (the doors). ¶ 오후 1시 ~ The doors open at 1 p.m. ‖ ~식 the opening ceremony.

개장(국) (-醬) (-) dog-meat broth.

개재(介在) ~하다 lie [stand] between.

개전(改悛) repentance; penitence; reform. ~하다 repent [be penitent] 《of》. ¶ ~의 빛이 뚜렷하다 show sincere repentance.

개전(開戰) the outbreak of war. ~하다 start [open, begin] war 《on, against》.

개점(開店) ~하다 open [set up] a store. ¶ ~은 9시입니다 This store opens at nine. / 그 상점은 ~ 휴업 상태였다 The store was opened but there were few customers.

개정(改正) 《수정》 revision; amendment; 《변경》 alteration. ~하다 revise; amend; alter. ¶ ~된 세율 revised tax rates / ~안 a bill [proposal] to revise; a reform bill / ~된 정가 the revised price.

개정(改定) a reform; a revision. ~하다 reform; revise 《the tariff》. ¶ 운임의 ~ a revision of fares.

개정(改訂) revision. ~하다 revise. ‖ ~증보판 a revised and enlarged edition.

개정(開廷) ~하다 open [hold] a court; give a hearing. ¶ ~중이다 The court is sitting.

개조(改造) remodeling; reconstruction; reorganization. ~하다 remodel; reconstruct; reorganize. ¶ 사회를 ~하다 reconstruct society.

개종(改宗) conversion. ~하다 get [be] converted; change one's religion (sect). ‖ ~자 a convert.

개죽음 useless death. ~하다 die to no purpose; die in vain.

개중(個中) ¶ ~에는 among them [the rest] / ~에는 반대자도 있었다 Some of them objected it.

개진(開陳) ~하다 state 《express, give》 《one's opinion》.

개집 a doghouse; a kennel.

개차반 the filthy scum (of the earth).

개착(開鑿) excavation. ~하다 excavate; cut; dig.

개선(改善) correction; revision (of writing). ~하다 correct; revise.

개찰(改札) ~하다 examine [punch] tickets. ‖ ~구 a ticket barrier (gate).

개척(開拓) 《토지의》 cultivation; reclamation; 《개발》 exploitation. ~하다 reclaim 《wasteland》; bring 《land》 into cultivation(개간); open up(새로 열다); exploit.

¶ 시장을 ~하다 open up (find) a new market / 자원을 ~하다 exploit (develop) natural resources. ∥ ~사업 reclamation work / ~자 a pioneer; a frontiersman / ~자 정신 the pioneer (frontier) spirit / ~지 reclaimed land / ~지 undeveloped land.

개천(開川) an open sewer (ditch). ¶ ~에서 용난다 (俗談) It's really a case of a kite breeding a hawk.

개천절(開天節) the National Foundation Day (of Korea).

개체(個體) an individual. ∥ ~발생 (生) ontogeny.

개최(開催) ~하다 hold; open. ¶ ~중이다 be open; be in session (회의가). ∥ ~국 the host country (for) / ~일 the date(s) (for (of) the exhibition) / ~지 the site (of (for) a meeting).

개축(改築) rebuilding; reconstruction. ~하다 rebuild; reconstruct. ∥ ~공사 reconstruction works.

개칭(改稱) ~하다 change the name (title) (of); rename.

개키다 fold (up). ¶ 옷을 ~ fold the clothes up (neatly).

개탄(慨歎) ~하다 deplore; lament; regret. ¶ ~할 만한 deplorable; lamentable; regrettable.

개통(開通) ~하다 be opened to (for) traffic; (복구) be reopened (for service). ∥ ~식 the opening ceremony (of a railroad).

개판(改版) 〔印〕 revision; (개정판) a revised edition. ~하다 revise; issue a revised edition.

개펄 a tidal (mud) flat.

개편(改編) reorganization. ~하다 reorganize.

개평 the winner's tip. ¶ ~을 떼다 (주다) take (give) away the winner's tip. ∥ ~꾼 onlookers expecting for the winner's tip.

개폐(改廢) ~하다 reorganize; make a change (in).

개폐(開閉) opening and shutting (closing). ~하다 open and shut. ∥ ~교 a drawbridge / ~기 a circuit breaker / ~기 a switch.

개표(開票) ballot counting. ~하다 open (count) the ballots (votes). ∥ ~소 a ballot counting office / ~속보 up-to-the-minute (election) returns / ~참관인 a ballot counting witness.

개피떡 a rice-cake stuffed with bean jam.

개학(開學) the beginning of school. ~하다 school begins.

개함(開函) opening of a ballot box. ~하다 open the ballot boxes.

개항(開港) ~하다 open a port (an airport) (to foreign trade).

개헌(改憲) a constitutional amendment (revision). ~하다 amend (revise) a constitution. ∥ ~론자 (지지자) an advocate of constitutional amendment / ~안 a bill for amending the constitution.

개혁(改革) reform(ation); innovation. ~하다 reform; innovate. ¶ ~에 착수하다 start a reform. ∥ ~안 a reform bill / ~자 a reformer.

개화(開化) civilization; enlightenment. ~하다 be civilized (enlightened). ∥ ~된 국민 civilized people.

개화(開花) flowering; efflorescence. ~하다 flower; bloom. ∥ ~기 the flowering (blooming) season (time).

개황(槪況) a general condition; an outlook.

개회(開會) a meeting. ¶ ~를 선언하다 declare 《the meeting》 open; call 《the meeting》 to order 〔美〕. ∥ ~사 an opening address / ~식 the opening ceremony.

개흙 slime (mud) on the bank of an inlet; silt.

객고(客苦) discomfort suffered in a strange land; weariness from travel. ¶ ~에 지치다 be travel-worn.

객관(客觀) 〔哲〕 the object; (객관성) objectivity. ¶ ~적인 objective / ~화하다 objectify / 사물을 ~적으로 보다 look at a thing objectively. ∥ ~식 테스트 〔문제〕 an objective test (question).

객기(客氣) ill-advised bravery; blind daring.

객담(客談) (an) idle (empty) talk.

객담(喀痰) expectorating; spitting. ∥ ~검사 the examination of one's sputum.

객사(客死) ~하다 die abroad. ¶ 런던에서 ~하다 die abroad in London.

객석(客席) a seat (for a guest).

객선(客船) a passenger boat.

객소리(客-) idle (useless) talk. ~하다 say useless things.

객식구(客食口) a dependent; a hanger-on.

객실(客室) a guest room(여관 등의); a passenger cabin(배·비행기의).

객원(客員) a guest (non-regular) member. ∥ ~교수 a guest (visiting) professor.

객주(客主) 〈거간〉 a commission merchant (agency); 《객줏집》 a peddler's inn; a commission

객지 (客地) a strange (an alien) land; *one's* staying place on a journey.
객쩍다 (be) unnecessary; useless. ¶ ~적은 소리를 하다 talk nonsense.
객차 (客車) a passenger car (coach).
객토 (客土) soil brought from another place (to improve the soil).
객향 (客鄉) a foreign land (town).
객혈 (喀血) hemoptysis. ~하다 expectorate blood; spit (cough out) blood.
갤런 a gallon.
갯가재 [動] a squilla.
갯지렁이 [動] a lugworm; a lobworm; a nereid.
갱 (坑) a (mining) pit; a shaft.
갱 (強盜) a gangster; a gang (집합적). ‖ ~단 (團) a gang of robbers / ~영화 a gangster movie (film).
갱내 (坑內) (in) the pit (shaft). ‖ ~근로자 an underground (a pit) worker / ~사고 an underground mine accident / ~수 mine water / ~출수 mine-flooding.
갱년기 (更年期) the turn (change) of *one's* life; a Critical Period; the menopause (여성). ‖ ~장애 a menopausal disorder.
갱도 (坑道) a (mining) gallery (a drift (가로); a shaft, a pit (세로). ¶ ~를 파다 mine. ‖ pillar (post).
갱목 (坑木) a pit prop; a mine
갱부 (坑夫) a miner; a mine worker; a pitman; a digger.
갱생 (更生) rebirth; revival; regeneration. ~하다 be born again; start *one's* life afresh; be regenerated. ¶ ~시키다 rehabilitate (a person). ‖ ~원 a rehabilitation center.
갱신 (更新) renewal; renovation. ~하다 renew; renovate. ¶ ~하다 renew a contract.
갱지 (更紙) (거친 종이) pulp paper; rough (printing) paper.
갱충쩍다 (be) loose and stupid; imprudent; careless.
가륵하다 (be) praiseworthy; laudable; admirable; commendable. ¶ 가륵한 정신 a commendable spirit / 가륵한 행실 exemplary behavior; good conduct.
가름하다 (be) pleasantly oval; nicely slender. ¶ ~ 기름하다.
갹금 (醵金) (기부금) a contribution; (모금) a collection. ~하다 contribute; raise money; collect funds. ¶ 유족을 위해 100만원을 ~하다 contribute a million *won* for a bereaved family.
갹출 (醵出) ~하다 contribute; chip in; donate 《to》.
거간 (居間) (행위) brokerage; (사람) a broker. ~하다 do (the) brokerage; act as a broker. ‖ ~꾼 a broker; a middleman.
거구 (巨軀) a gigantic (massive) figure; a big frame.
거국 (擧國) the whole country (nation). ¶ ~적(인) nationwide / ~적으로 on a nationwide scale. ‖ ~일치내각 a cabinet supported by the whole nation.
거금 (巨金) big money; a large sum of money. ¶ ~을 벌다 make a lot of money.
거기 ① 《장소》 that place; there. ¶ ~서 (기다려라) (Wait) there. ② 《그것》 that; (범위) so far; to that extent. ¶ ~까지는 좋았으나… So far so good, but… / ~까지는 인정한다 I admit as that much.
거꾸러뜨리다 (사람・물체를) throw (bring, knock, push) down; (패배・망하게 하다) overthrow; topple; defeat; ruin; (죽임) kill. ¶ 폭군을 ~ bring down a tyrant / 부패한 정부를 ~ overthrow the corrupt government.
거꾸러지다 fall (down); collapse; tumble down; 《죽다》 die. ¶ 앞으로 ~ fall forward.
거꾸로 reversely; (in) the wrong way; (안팎을) inside out; (아래위를) upside down; wrong side (end) up. ¶ ~하다 invert; turn (a thing) upside down / 빗자루를 ~ 세우다 stand a broom the wrong end up / ~ 떨어지다 fall head over heels.
…거나 whether … or. ¶ 너야 하 말~ whether you do it or not.
거나하다 (be) half-tipsy; slightly drunk (intoxicated).
거느리다 (인솔하다) be accompanied (followed) by 《a person》; lead (head) 《a party》; (지휘하다) be in command (of an army); (부양하다) have a family (to support). ¶ 친선 사절단을 거느리고 도미하다 go to America, leading a goodwill mission / 그는 부하들을 거느리고 왔다 He came, followed by his men. / 김 장군이 거느리는 군대 the army under the command of General Kim.
…거늘 much (still) more; much (still) less; while. ¶ 개조차 주인에게 충실하거늘 하물며 사람에 있어서랴 If a dog is so faithful to its master, how much more should we human beings be!
…거니와 not only … but also …; as well as; admitting that … ¶ 얼굴은 곱거니와 마음씨도 곱다 have not only a pretty face but also

거닐다 take a walk (stroll). ¶ 공원을 ~ take a walk in the park.
거담(去痰) the discharge of phlegm. ‖ ~제 an expectorant.
거당(擧黨) the whole party.
거대(巨大) ¶ ~한 huge; gigantic; enormous; colossal / ~한 배 a mammoth ship / ~한 도시 a megalopolis.
거덕거덕하다 (be) shaky; unsteady; rickety.
거덜나다 be ruined; become (go) bankrupt; fail; go broke.
거동(擧動) 〈처신〉 conduct; behavior; 〈행동〉 action; movement. ¶ ~이 수상하다는 이유로 on account of one's suspicious behavior.
거두(巨頭) a leader; a prominent figure. ¶ 정계〔재계〕의 ~ a leading politician〔financier〕. ‖ ~회담 a top-level〔summit〕 talk〔conference〕.
거두다 ①《모으다》 gather (in); collect〈돈을〉; harvest〈곡식을〉. ¶ 세금을 ~ collect taxes / 곡식을 ~ harvest crops. ②《성과를》 gain; obtain. ¶ 승리를 ~ gain〔win〕 the victory / 좋은 성과를 ~ obtain excellent results. ③〈돌보다〉 take care of; look after. ¶ 아이들을 ~ take care of the children. ④〈숨을〉 die; breathe one's last.
거두절미(去頭截尾) ①〈자르기〉 ~하다 cut off the head and tail〔of it〕. ②〈요약〉 ~하다 summarize; leave out details; make a long story short.
거드럭거리다 assume an air of importance; swagger.
거드름 a haughty attitude; an air of importance. ¶ ~스러운 haughty / ~ 피우며 haughtily / ~ 부리다 give oneself airs; act with an important air; behave haughtily.
…거든 ①〈가정〉 if; when. ¶ 그를 만나~ 오라고 전해라 If you meet him, tell him to come here. ②〈더구나〉 much (still). ¶ 네가 그토록 공부해야 하~ 하물며 나는 어떠랴 If you must study so hard, how much more must I?
거들다 help; assist; aid; give〔lend〕 a helping hand 《to》.
거들떠보다 pay attention 《to》; take notice 《of》. ¶ 거들떠보지도 않다 take no notice 《of》; ignore completely / 그는 나를 거들떠보지도 않았다 He took no notice of me. or He ignored me completely.
거듭 (over) again; repeatedly. ~하다 repeat 《mistakes》; do 《a thing》 over again. ¶ ~되는 실패 repeated failures / ~되는 불운 a series of misfortunes / ~나다 be born again; resuscitate / ~ 말하지만, 그는 죄가 없다 I repeat, he is innocent.
거래(去來) transactions; dealings; business; trade. ~하다 do〔transact〕 business 《with》; deal〔have dealings〕 《with》; trade 《in silk with a person》. ¶ ~를 개시하다〔중지하다〕 open〔close〕 an account in 《tea》 《with》 / 돈 ~ lending and borrowing money. ‖ ~관계 business relations〔connections〕 / ~소 an exchange / ~액〔고〕 the volume〔amount〕 of business; a turnover / ~은행 one's bank / ~처〔선〕 a customer; a client; a business connection 〔총칭〕.
거론(擧論) ~하다 take up a problem〔subject〕 for discussion; make 《it》 a subject of discussion.
거룩하다 (be) divine; sublime; sacred; holy.
거룻배 a barge; a lighter; a sampan.
거류(居留) residence. ~하다 live〔reside〕 《in》. ‖ ~민《Korean》 residents 《in, at》 / ~지 a 《foreign》 settlement〔concession〕 《in Korea》.
거르다¹〈여과〉 filter; strain; percolate.
거르다²〈차례를〉 skip 《over》; omit. ¶ 하루〔이틀〕 걸러 every other〔third〕 day / 점심을 ~ go without lunch.
거름〈비료〉 manure; muck; a fertilizer. ¶ ~ 주다 manure; fertilize.
거리¹ a street; an avenue; a road. ¶ ~의 여자 a street girl.
거리²〈재료〉 material; matter; stuff;〈대상〉 the cause; a butt. ¶ 국 ~ soup makings / 웃음 ~ a laughingstock / 걱정 ~ the cause of one's anxiety.
거리(距離) (a) distance; an interval〈간격〉; a range;〈차이〉 a gap; (a) difference. ¶ ~가 있다 be distant;〈차이〉 be different 《from》 / ~감 a sense of distance / 직선 ~ distance in a straight line.
거리끼다 be afraid 《of doing》; hesitate 《to do》; refrain from 《doing》. ¶ 거리낌없이 openly; without hesitation〔reserve〕.
거마비(車馬費) traffic expenses; a carfare; a car〔taxi, bus, train〕 fare.
거만(倨慢) ¶ ~의 부를 쌓다 amass a vast fortune; become a millionaire.

거만(倨慢) ~하다 (be) arrogant; haughty; insolent. ¶ ~을 떼다 give *oneself* airs; act haughtily; take an overbearing attitude.

거머리 ① [動] a leech. ②〈사람〉a bur. 「chubby.

거머무트름하다 (be) dark and

거머삼키다 swallow; gulp (down).

거머쥐다 take hold of; seize (on, upon); grasp.

거멀못 a clamp; a cramp.

거멓다 (be) deep black; jet-black.

거메지다 turn black; get tanned (볕에 타서).

거목(巨木) a great (big, monster) tree. 「ish; swarthy.

거무스름하다 (be) dark(ish); black-

거문고 a *gŏmungo*; a Korean harp.

거물(巨物)《사람》a leading (prominent) figure; a bigwig (口). ¶ 당대의 ~ the lion of the day / 재계의 ~ a financial magnate / 정계의 ~ a leading figure in politics.

거미 a spider. ∥ ~줄 a spider's thread / ~집 a spider's web; a cobweb.

거미줄치다 ① spin (weave) a web. ②〈굶주리다〉go hungry; starve.

거병하다(擧兵) rise in arms; raise an army; take up arms.

거보(巨步) ¶ ~를 내딛다 make a giant step (*toward*).

거부(巨富) a man of great wealth; a (multi)millionaire.

거부(拒否) (a) refusal; denial. ~하다 deny; refuse; reject; veto (*on*). ¶ 아무의 제안을 ~하다 turn down (reject) *a person's* proposal. / ~권 (exercise) a veto / ~반응 a rejection symptom; an immune response (항원 항체 반응).

거북 a tortoise; a (sea) turtle.

거북선(-船) the "Turtle Boat"; an ironclad battleship shaped like a turtle.

거북하다 〈몸이〉feel (be) unwell; 〈형편이〉(be) awkward; uncomfortable; ill at ease. ¶ 입장이 ~ be in an awkward position.

거비(巨費) an enormous expenditure; a great cost.

거사(擧事) ~하다〈반란·거병하다〉rise in revolt (arms); raise an army; 〈큰 사업을〉start (launch) a big enterprise.

거상(巨商) a wealthy merchant; a merchant prince; a business magnate.

거상(巨像) a colossus; a gigantic statue.

거상(居喪) ~하다 be in mourning (*for*). ¶ ~을 입다 go into mourning (*for two weeks*).

거석(巨石) a huge stone; a megalith (기념물). ∥ ~문화 megalithic culture.

거성(巨星) a giant star; 〈비유적〉a great man; a big shot (口). ¶ 문단의 ~ a great writer.

거세(去勢) ①〈불을 깜〉castration; emasculation. ~하다 castrate; emasculate; geld; sterilize (단종). ¶ ~한 소 〔말〕 a bullock (gelding). ②〈세력 제거〉a purge (숙청); weakening (약화); exclusion (배제); eradication (근절). ~하다 purge; weaken; exclude.

거세다 (be) rough; wild; violent. ¶ 거센 바람과 the storms of life / 거센 여자 an unruly woman. 「abode (residence).

거소(居所) a dwelling place; *one's*

거수(擧手) ~하다 raise *one's* hand; show *one's* hand (표결에). ∥ ~경례 a military salute (~경례 하다 salute; give (make) a salute) / ~표결 voting by show of hands.

거스러미 〈손톱의〉an agnail; a hangnail; 〈나무의〉a splinter.

거스러지다 ①〈성질이〉grow wild; become rough (rude). ②〈털이〉bristle; get ruffled.

거스르다 ①〈거역〉oppose; go (act) against; disobey (*one's parents*); resist (반항하다); contradict (반론하다). ¶ 아무의 뜻을 ~ act against *a person's* wishes / 거슬러 올라가다〈강을〉go upstream; 〈과거로〉go (date) back to; retroact (소급) / 시대의 조류을 ~ go against the current (tide) of the times. ②〈잔돈을〉give the change. ¶ 거슬러 받다 get the change.

거스름돈 change. ¶ ~을 받다〔주다〕get (give) the change / "여기 ~ 있습니다." / "그냥 두세요." "Here is your change." — "Please keep the change."

거슬리다 offend; be offensive; displease; get on *one's* nerves. ¶ 귀에 ~ be harsh (unpleasant) to the ear / 눈에 ~ offend the eye; be an eyesore / 그 소리가 〔신경에〕거슬린다 The noise gets on my nerves.

거슴츠레하다 〈눈이〉(be) sleepy; drowsy; dull; fishy.

거시(巨視) ∥ ~적인 macroscopic / ~적으로 보다 take a broad view (*of*). ∥ ~경제학 macroeconomics / ~이론 a macroscopic theory.

거실(居室) a living (sitting (英)) room. ∥ ~겸 침실 a bedroom-cum-living room.

거액(巨額) big〔great, large, enormous〕sum〔amount〕(of money). ¶ ~의 부채 a large debt / ~에 달하는 amount to a great sum.

거역목(植) a (snail) clover.

거역(拒逆) ~하다 disobey; oppose; go against; contradict; offend.

거울 ① (모양을 보는) a mirror; a looking glass. ¶ ~을 보다 look in a glass. ② (모범) a mirror; a pattern; a model; an example. ¶ …을 ~로 삼다 model〔pattern〕after《a person》; follow the example of《a person》/ 신문은 사회의 ~이다 The press is the mirror of society.

거웃 pubic hair; pubes.

거위¹〔鳥〕a goose〔pl. geese〕 / (수컷) a gander.

거위²〔蛔虫〕a roundworm.

거유(巨儒) a great scholar (of Confucianism).

거의 (대체로) practically; nearly; (부정) little; hardly; scarcely. ¶ ~ 다 almost all; mostly; the greater part《of》/ ~ 불가능하다 be next to impossible / 그것을 믿는 사람은 ~ 없다 Scarcely anybody believes that.

거인(巨人) a giant; a great man (위인). ¶ 재계의 ~ a leading figure in financial circles; a financial magnate.

거장(巨匠) a (great) master; a *maestro*. ¶ 화단〔문단〕의 ~ a great painter〔writer〕.

거재(巨財) an enormous〔a huge〕fortune. ¶ ~을 투입하다 invest millions (in an enterprise).

거저 free (of charge); for nothing. ¶ ~ 일하다 work for nothing.

거저먹기 an easy task〔job〕; a cinch (美俗). ¶ 그것은 ~다 That's an easy job. *or* That's nothing.

거적 (a straw) mat. ¶ ~을 깔다 spread a mat.

거절(拒絶) (a) refusal; (a) rejection; (a) denial. ~하다 refuse; reject; turn down. ¶ 딱 ~하다 give a flat refusal; refuse pointblank / 제안을 ~하다 turn down *a person's* offer. ‖ (인수·지불의) ~증서〔法〕a protest for nonacceptance〔nonpayment〕.

거점(據點) a position; a foothold; a base(기지).

거족(巨族) a powerful family; a mighty clan.

거족(擧族) ~적 nationwide; national / ~적으로 throughout the nation; on a national scale.

거주(居住) residence; dwelling. ~하다 live〔dwell, reside〕《at, in》; inhabit《a place》. ‖ ~권 the right of residence / ~자 a resident / ~증명서 a certificate of residence / ~지 *one's* place of residence.

거죽 (표면) the face; the surface; (외면부) the exterior; (외관) the appearance.

거중조정(居中調停) (inter)mediation; intervention; arbitration. ¶ ~에 나서다 undertake mediation.

거증(擧證) ~하다 establish a fact (by evidence). ‖ ~책임 the burden of proof.

거지 a beggar; a mendicant. ‖ ~근성 a mean spirit.

거지반(半) ☞ 거의.

거짓 fraud; falsehood; untruth; a lie(거짓말). ¶ ~의 false; untrue; unreal / 이 광고에는 ~이 있다 There is something untrue in this advertisement. ‖ ~울음 sham〔crocodile〕tears / ~웃음 a feigned smile / ~증언 false testimony.

거짓말 a lie. ~하다 (tell) a lie. ¶ ~의 false / ~ 같은 이야기 an incredible story / 새빨간 ~ 를 여다붙이는, 그럴듯한 ~ a downright〔transparent, plausible〕lie. ‖ ~쟁이 a liar; a storyteller / ~탐지기 a lie detector.

거짓이름 (가명) a false〔an assumed〕name.

거찰(巨刹) a big Buddhist temple.

거창(巨創) ¶ ~한 great; huge; gigantic; colossal / ~한 계획 a mammoth enterprise.

거처(居處) *one's* (place of) residence; *one's* abode (address). ~하다 reside; live. ¶ ~를 정하다 take up *one's* residence〔quarters〕(*at, in*). ‖ 임시 ~ a temporary abode〔residence〕.

거추장스럽다 (거북함) be burdensome; cumbersome; troublesome. ¶ 거추장스러운 짐 a piece of burdensome baggage.

거충거충 cursorily; roughly.

거취(去就) (행동) *one's* course of action; (태도) *one's* attitude. ¶ ~를 정하다 define〔decide〕*one's* attitude / ~를 망설이다 be at a loss how to act / ~를 분명히 하다 make it clear where *one* stands.

거치(據置) (지금 등의) deferment. ~하다 leave unredeemed. ¶ ~의 unredeemable; deferred / 5년 ~의 대부 a loan unredeemable for five years / 3년 ~의 be unredeemable for three years. ‖ ~기간 a period of deferment / ~예금 deferred savings.

거치다 pass〔go〕through; go by way《of》; stop〔call〕at *one's*

way. ¶ …을 거쳐 through; by way of: via / 런던을 거쳐 파리에 가다 go to Paris via (by way of) London.
거치적거리다 cause hindrance to; be a drag (burden) on (to) 《*a person*》.
거칠다 (be) coarse; rough; harsh; violent. ¶ 바닥이 거친 천 coarse cloth / 거친 바다 the rough sea / 성질이 거친 사람 a rough-natured (quick-tempered) person / 거친 살결 a rough skin / 숨결이 ~ breathe hard / 거칠게 다루다 work 《*a person*》 too hard; handle roughly (물건을) / 말씨가 ~ be rough on *one*'s speech; use harsh (violent) language.
거칠하다 (be) haggard; 《서술적》 look emaciated. ¶ ~ 까칠하다.
거침 ¶ ~없이 without a hitch; without hesitation (서슴지 않고) / ~없는 대답 a ready answer / ~없이 말하다 say without reserve (hesitation).
거탄(巨彈) ① 《탄환》 a heavy (huge) shell. ② 《비유적》 a hit; a feature (영화의).
거포(巨砲) a big (huge) gun; 《강타자》 a slugger 《口》.
거푸 again and again; over again; repeatedly.
거푸집 《주형》 a mold; a cast.
거품 a bubble; foam; froth. ¶ ~이 이는 foamy; frothy / ~이 일다 foam; froth; bubble / 물~이 되다 come to nothing.
거한(巨漢) a giant; a big (large-built) fellow (man).
거함(巨艦) a big warship.
거행(擧行) performance; celebration. ~하다 hold (give) 《*a reception*》; perform 《*a ceremony*》. ¶ 결혼식을 ~하다 hold a wedding.
걱정 ① 《근심》 apprehensions; anxiety; concern; 《불안》 uneasiness; fear; 《신경 씀》 care; worry; trouble. ~하다 feel anxiey; be anxious 《*about*》; be concerned; be worried 《*about*》 (걱정). ¶ ~스러운 듯이 with a concerned air / ~스러운 나머지 in an excess of anxiety / ~을 끼치다 give 《*a person*》 trouble / ~으로 병이 되다 worry *oneself* ill. ǁ ~거리 a cause for anxiety; cares; worries; troubles / ~꾸러기 a (natural) worrier. ② 《꾸중》 scolding; lecture; reproach. ~하다 scold; reprove; reprimand. ¶ ~듣다 receive a reprimand; be reproved.
건(巾) ① 《두건》. ② a hood.
건(件) a matter; a case; an affair. ¶ 예(例)의 ~ the matter in question.
건(腱)〔解〕 a tendon.
건(鍵)〔樂〕 a key.
건…(乾) dried. ǁ ~ 대구 a dried cod.
건각(健脚) strong legs.
건강(健康) health. ~하다 (be) well; healthy; sound; 《서술적》 be in good health. ¶ ~에 좋은 (나쁜) (un)healthful; good (bad) for the health / ~에 조심하다 take (good) care of *oneself* / ~을 회복하다 get *one*'s health back; regain *one*'s health / ~을 잃다 ruin (injure) *one*'s health. ǁ ~관리 health care 《*for the aged*》 / ~미 health beauty / ~상태 the condition of *one*'s health / ~식품 health food / ~식품점 a health food store / ~진단 (undergo) a medical examination; a physical checkup 《美》 / ~체 a healthy body.
건건하다 (be) salty; brackish.
건곤일척(乾坤一擲) ~하다 stake all upon the cast.
건국(建國) the founding of a country (state). ~하다 found a state (nation). ǁ ~공로훈장 the Order of Merit for National Foundation / ~기념일 National Foundation Day.
건너 the opposite (other) side. ¶ ~편에 on the opposite (other) side / 저 ~ 숲 속에 in the wood(s) over there / 강 ~에 살다 live across the river / ~뛰다 jump across; skip (over) (읽을 때) / 미국으로 ~가다 go over to America.
건너다 cross 《*a bridge*》; walk (run, ride) across; sail (swim, wade) across 《*a river*》; go (pass) over (to).
건널목 (railroad) crossing. ǁ ~지기 a watchman; a flagman 《美》 ~차단기 a crossing barrier.
건네다 ① 《건너게 하다》 pass (set) 《*a person*》 over (across); take (ferry) over (배로). ② 《주다》 hand (over); deliver; transfer.
건달(乾達) a good-for-nothing; a libertine; a scamp.
건답(乾畓) a rice field that dries easily; a dry paddy field.
…건대 when; if; according to. ¶듣~ as I hear; according to what people say.
건더기 《국의》 solid stuff in soup; 《내용》 a ground; substance.
건드러지다 ¶ 간드러지다.
건드레하다 (be) mellow; tipsy; 《서술적》 be a bit high.
건드리다 《손대다》 touch; jog; 《감정을》 provoke; fret; tease (집적대

건들거리다 다); 《여자를》 become intimate (with). ¶ 비위를 ~ get (jar) on (a person's) nerve.
건들거리다 《바람이》 blow gently; 《물체가》 sway; dangle; 《사람이》 idle (dawdle) one's time away.
건류(乾溜) dry distillation; carbonization. ~하다 dry (up) by distillation; carbonize.
건립(建立) ~하다 build; erect.
…건마는 but; though; although; still; while. ¶ 생각은 있으나 돈이 없네 I want it, but I don't have the money to get it.
건망(健忘) forgetfulness; a short memory. ¶ ~증 amnesia / ~증이 심하다 be forgetful; have a short (poor) memory.
건목치다 《일을》 do a cursory (rough) job of (it).
건물달다 get all heated up for nothing; run madly about to no purpose.
건물(建物) a building; a structure; an edifice (큰). ¶ 부속 ~ an attached building.
건반(鍵盤) a keyboard. ‖ ~악기 keyboard instruments.
건방지다 《젠체하다》 (be) (self-)conceited; affected; 《주제넘다》 (be) cheeky; saucy; impudent; forward; impertinent; haughty; freshy (口). ¶ 건방진 태도 an impudent manner / 건방지게 굴다 behave oneself haughtily / 건방진 소리 마라 None of your cheek. or Don't be so fresh. or Don't be smart with me.
건배 a toast. ▷ 축배(祝杯)
건백(建白) ~하다 memorialize. ‖ ~서 a written memorial.
건빵 a cracker; hardtack; a (hard) biscuit 《英》.
건사하다 ① 《일거리를》 provide work (for). ② 《수습》 manage; control; deal (cope) with. ③ 《간수》 keep; preserve; 《보살피다》 take care of.
건선거(乾船渠) a dry dock.
건설(建設) construction; erection; building. ~하다 construct; build; erect; establish. ¶ ~적 constructive / 복지 국가를 ~하다 establish (build up) a welfare state. ‖ ~공사 construction works / ~교통부 the Ministry of Construction and Transportation / ~용지 a building lot (site) / ~현장 a construction site / ~협회 the Construction Association of Korea.
건성(乾性) ~의 dry. ‖ ~유 drying oil / ~피부 dry skin.
건성 《목적없이》 aimlessly; 《정신없이》 absent-mindedly; halfheartedly. ¶ ~(으로) 듣다 listen to

건지다 《a person》 in an absent sort of way / ~으로 대답하다 give a vague answer. 「cases of theft.
건수(件數) 도난 ~ the number of
건습(乾濕) ‖ ~계 a psychrometer.
건시(乾柿) a dried persimmon.
건실(健實) ~하다 (be) steady; solid; sound; reliable; safe. ¶ ~하게 steadily; soundly / ~한 사상 sound ideas / ~한 사람 a steady (reliable) person.
건아(健兒) a healthy young man.
건어(乾魚) dried fish. (mitment.
건옥(建玉) 【証】 engagement; a com-
건울음 make-believe crying. ¶ ~을 울다 shed crocodile tears.
건위(健胃) ‖ ~제 a peptic; a stomachic; a digestive.
건으로(乾―) without reason (cause); to no purpose (avail).
건의(建議) 《제의》 a proposal; a suggestion. ~하다 propose; suggest; move. ¶ ~서 a memorial / ~안 a proposition; a motion / ~자 a proposer.
건장(健壯) ¶ ~한 strong; stout; robust; sturdy / ~한 체격 a tough (robust) constitution.
건재(建材) building (construction) materials. ¶ 새로운 ~ (a) newly developed building materials. ‖ ~상 a building materials shop (dealer 《상인》).
건재(健在) ~하다 be well; be in good health (shape).
건재(乾材) dried medicinal herbs. ‖ ~약국 a wholesale medicinal-herb store.
건전(健全) ~하다 (be) healthy; sound; wholesome. ¶ ~한 사상 wholesome ideas / ~한 신체에 ~한 정신 A sound mind in a sound body.
건전지(乾電池) a dry cell (battery).
건조(建造) building; construction. ~하다 build; construct. ¶ ~중이다 be under construction. ‖ ~물 a building; a structure.
건조(乾燥) ¶ ~한 dry; dried; arid / 무미 ~한 dry; tasteless; dull / ~시키다 dry (up). ‖ ~기(期) the dry season / ~기(機) a dryer; a desiccator / ~실(室) a drying room / ~제(劑) a desiccant.
건주정(乾酒酊) ~하다 pretend to be drunk.
건지다 ① 《물에서》 take (bring) 《a thing》 out of water; pick up. ② 《구명·구제》 save (rescue) 《a person from》; help 《a person》 out of; relieve 《a person from》. ¶ 간신히 목숨을 ~ escape death by a hair's breadth. ③ 《손해에서》 save 《from》; retrieve. ¶ 밑천

건초 을 ~ recoup one's capital.
건초(乾草) dry grass; hay.
건축(建築) construction; building; erection. ㅎ다 build; construct; erect. ¶ ~중이다 be under construction. ¶ ~가 an architect / ~ 공사 construction work / ~ 기술 building-construction techniques / ~물 a building / ~법규 the building code / ~비[재료] building expenses [materials] / ~ 사 a qualified [registered] architect / ~ 양식 a style of architecture / ~업자 a builder; a building contractor.
건투(健鬪) a good fight; strenuous efforts(노력). ㅎ다 put up a good fight; exert oneself hard. ¶ ~를 빕니다 Good luck to you! or We wish you good luck.
건판(乾版) 〖寫〗 a dry plate.
건평(建坪) a floor space.
건폐율(建蔽率) building coverage; the building-to-land ratio.
건포(乾脯) dried slices of meat
건포도(乾葡萄) raisins. [fish].
건필(健筆) a ready [facile, powerful] pen. ¶ ~을 휘두르다 wield a facile pen.
건함(建艦) naval construction.
걷다 ①(걷어올리다) tuck [roll] up 《one's sleeves》; gather up 《curtain》; fold up (카키다). ②(치우다) take away; remove. ¶ 빨래를 ~ remove the laundry 《from》 / 천막을 ~ strike a tent.
걷다 (발로) walk; go on foot; stroll; trudge(터벅터벅). ¶ 걷기 시작하다 (아기가) begin to toddle.
걷어차다 kick hard; give 《a person》 a hard kick.
걷어치우다 ①(치우다) put [take] away; clear off; remove. ②(그만둠) stop; quit; shut [close] up (정포를). ¶ 하던 일을 ~ stop doing a job; leave off one's work.
걷잡다 hold; stay; stop; (막다) check; keep 《a danger》 at bay. ¶ 걷잡을 새 없이 swiftly; quickly; before you can say any word / 걷잡을 수 없는 혼란에 빠지다 get into uncontrollable confusion.
걷히다 ①(비·안개 등이) clear up [away, off]; lift. ¶ 안개가 ~ a fog lifts. ②(돈 따위가) be collected; be gathered.
걸걸하다(傑傑―) (be) openhearted; free and easy; (쾌활) cheerful; sprightly.
걸근거리다 ①(욕심내다) covet; be greedy 《for, of》. ②(목구멍이) be scratchy.
걸다[1] ①(땅이) (be) rich; fertile.

②(액체가) (be) thick; heavy; turbid. ③(식성이) (be) not particular; not fastidious. ④(언사가) (be) foulmouthed; abusive.
걸다[2] ①(매달다) hang; suspend 《from》; put 《a cloth》 on [over]. ¶ 간판을 ~ put up a signboard / 못에 ~ hang 《a thing》 on a peg. ②(올가미를) lay 《a snare》; set 《a trap》. ③(시비를) pick; provoke; fasten; force. ¶ 싸움을 ~ pick a quarrel 《with a person》. ④(돈을) pay; advance; bet(노름에서). ¶ 계약금 ~ advance money on a contract; pay earnest money. ⑤(목숨을) stake; risk 《one's life》. ¶ 목숨을 걸고 싸우다 fight at the risk of one's life. ⑥(말을) talk [speak] to 《a person》; address 《a person》. ⑦(전화를) call (up); ring 《a person》 up; telephone 《a person》; make a (phone) call to 《a person》. ⑧(문고리를) fasten; lock(자물쇠를). ⑨(발동을) start 《a machine》 going; start 《an engine》.
걸러 at intervals of. ¶ 하루[이틀] ~ every other [third] day / 5피트 ~ at intervals of five feet. ☞ 거르다[2].
걸레 a dustcloth; a floor cloth; a mop(자루 달린). ¶ ~질하다 wipe with a wet [damp] cloth; mop 《the floor》.
걸리다 ①(매달린) hang 《from, on》; be suspended 《from》. ¶ 벽에 걸려 있는 풍경화 a landscape hanging on the wall. ②(걸려 안 떨어지다) catch 《on a nail》; stick in one's throat. ¶ 목에 걸린 생선가시 a fish bone caught in one's throat. ③(병에) fall [be taken] ill; catch. ¶ 감기에 ~ catch [get] a cold. ④(갇히다) be [get] caught; be pinched 《俗》. ¶ 교통순경에게 ~ be pinched by a traffic cop / 법망에 ~ be caught by the law. ⑤(빠지다) fall 《into》; (말려듦) be involved 《in》; get entangled 《with》. ¶ 나쁜 여자에게 ~ get entangled with a bad girl. ⑥(시간이) take; require. ¶ 학교까지 10분 걸린다 It takes ten minutes to get to school. ⑦(마음에) worry; weigh on one's mind. ¶ 그것이 마음에 걸린다 That worries me. ⑧(작동) work; run. ¶ 시동이 걸리지 않다 cannot get the engine to start.
걸리다[2] (걷게 하다) make 《a person》 walk [go on foot]; walk 《a person》; 〖野〗 walk a batter.
걸림돌 a stumbling block; an obstacle.

걸맞다 (be) suitable 《*for, to*》; becoming 《*to*》. ¶ 걸맞은 becoming; suitable 《*for*》; well-matched; 《정도가 알맞게》 well-balanced [-proportioned] / 사회적 지위에 걸맞는 수입 income appropriate to one's social position.

걸머잡다 catch hold of; clutch at.

걸머지다 ① 《등에》 carry 《*a thing*》 on one's shoulder; 《책임을》 bear; take upon oneself. ② 《빚을》 be saddled with 《*a debt*》; get [run] into 《*debt*》. 「man.

걸물(傑物) a great [remarkable]

걸상(一床) 《sit on [in]》 a chair; a seat; a bench; a stool.

걸쇠 a catch; a latch.

걸식(乞食) ~하다 go begging; beg one's bread.

걸신(乞神) ¶ ~들리다 have a voracious appetite; have a wolf in one's stomach / ~들린 듯이 hungrily; greedily. 「arms」

걸어총(一銃) 《구령》 Stack [Pile]

걸음 walking; a step; pace(보조). ¶ ~이 빠른 [느린] swift- [slow-] footed / 한 ~ 한 ~ step by step; by degrees / ~이 빠르다 [느리다] be quick [slow] of foot / ~을 재촉하다 quicken one's pace. ‖ ~걸이 one's manner of walking. 「feet.

걸음마 ~를 하다 toddle; find its

...걸이(거는 제구) a peg; a rack; 《얹는 것》 a rest. ¶ 모자~ a hat-rack / 옷~ a clothes hanger.

걸작(傑作) a masterpiece; one's best work. 「for anything.

걸쩍거리다 be active; be ready

걸차다 (be) fertile; fruitful. ¶ 걸찬 땅 a fertile land; rich soil.

걸출(傑出) ~하다 be outstanding [distinguished, prominent] 《*at, in*》. ¶ ~한 인물 a distinguished character.

걸치다 ① 《건너 걸치다》 lay [place, build] over [across]; 《기대어 놓다》 place [set up] 《*a thing against*》; put up 《*against*》. ¶ 강에 다리가 걸쳐 있다 A bridge is laid across the river. ② 《얹어 놓다》 put [drape] 《*a thing*》 over. ¶ 어깨에 손을 ~ put [lay] one's hand on 《*a person's*》 shoulder. ③ 《옷을》 slip [throw] on. ¶ 외투를 ~ slip on one's overcoat. ④ 《범위가》 cover 《*a wide field*》; range 《*from ... to*》; 《시간·거리》 extend 《*over*》. ¶ 여러 해에 ~ extend over so many years.

걸타앉다 sit 《*on, in*》; sit astride.

걸터타다 mount; straddle.

걸프[地] the Gulf. ¶ ~전쟁 the war in the Gulf / ~협력회의 the Gulf Cooperation Council (생략 GCC).

걸핏하면 too often; readily; without reason. ¶ ~ ...하다 be apt [liable] to 《*do*》 / ~ 울다 tend to cry over nothing.

검(劍) a sword; a saber(군도); a bayonet(총검); a dagger(단검).

검객(劍客) a swordsman.

검거(檢擧) an arrest; 《일제히》 a roundup. ~하다 arrest; 《일제히》 round up. ¶ ~된 사람 a person in custody / 일제히 ~하다 make a wholesale arrest 《*of*》; round up 《*narcotic traffickers*》 / 마약 소지 혐의로 ~되다 be arrested for having drugs.

검경판(檢鏡板) 《현미경의》 an object plate; a slide.

검뇨(檢尿) a urine test. ¶ ~를 받다 have one's urine examined. ‖ ~기 a urinometer.

검누렇다 (be) dark yellow.

검다 (be) black; dark; swarthy; sooty(그을린). ¶ 검디 ~ be jet-black / 속검은 사람 a black-hearted person.

검댕 soot. ¶ ~투성이의 sooty; sooted / ~이 앉다 become sooty; be stained with soot.

검도(劍道) the art of fencing.

검동이(살검은 이) a dark-skinned person; 《흑인》 a black [colored] person.

검량(檢量) measuring; weighing; 《적하의》 metage. ¶ ~기 a gauging rod / ~료 a weighing charge. 「ter; a galvanoscope.

검류계(檢流計) 《電》 a galvanometer.

검무(劍舞) a sword dance.

검문(檢問) an inspection; a check; a search. ~하다 inspect; check up 《*passers-by*》. ¶ 차를 ~하다 check up on [search] a car. ‖ ~소 a checkpoint.

검버섯 dark spots (on the skin of an old man); a blotch.

검변(檢便) a stool test; scatoscopy. 「grass [leaves].

검부러기 remnants [bits] of dry

검불 dry grass; dead leaves.

검붉다 (be) dark-red.

검사(檢事) a public prosecutor; a district attorney(美).

검사(檢査) an inspection; 《undergo》 an examination; a test; an overhaul(기계의). ~하다 inspect; examine; test; overhaul. ¶ ~를 받다 go through an inspection [examination]; be examined [inspected] / 기계의 정기 ~ a periodical [regular] overhaul. ‖ ~관 an inspector [examiner] / ~소 an inspecting office / ~필(畢) Examined. 「accounts.

검산(檢算) ~하다 verify [check]

검색(檢索) reference 《*to*》. ~하다

검소(儉素) frugality; simplicity. ~한 (be) frugal; simple; plain. ¶ ~한 옷차림을 하다 be plainly dressed / ~하게 살다 live in a small way.

검속(檢束) (an) arrest. ~하다 arrest; take 《a person》 into custody.

검술(劍術) fencing; swordsmanship. ¶ ~의 달인 a master swordsman.

검시(檢屍) 〔hold〕 an inquest 〔autopsy〕 《over》. ~하다 examine a corpse. ¶ ~관 a coroner.

검안(檢眼) an eye examination. ~하다 examine 〔test〕 《a person's》 eyes 〔eyesight〕. ¶ ~을 받다 have one's eyes examined. ‖ ~경 an ophthalmoscope.

검약(儉約) thrift; economy. ~하다 economize 《on a thing》; be thrifty 〔frugal〕. ¶ ~가 a thrifty person.

검역(檢疫) quarantine; medical inspection. ~하다 quarantine. ‖ ~관〔소〕 a quarantine officer 〔station〕.

검열(檢閱) censorship (간행물의); (an) inspection. ~하다 censor; inspect; examine. ¶ ~을 받다 be censored 〔inspected〕; be submitted for censorship. ‖ ~관 an inspector; a film censor(영화의) / ~필《게시》 Censored. / 사전 ~ pre-censorship / 신문 ~ press censorship.

검온기(檢溫器) a clinical thermometer.

검이경(檢耳鏡) an auriscope.

검인(檢印) a seal 〔stamp〕 (of approval).

검전기(檢電器) an electroscope; a detector(누전의).

검정 black (color).

검정(檢定) 〔give〕 official approval 〔sanction〕 《to》. ~하다 approve; authorize. ¶ ~고시《시험》 a qualifying 〔license〕 examination / ~교과서 an authorized textbook / ~료 an authorization fee / 교육부 ~필 Approved by the Ministry of Education.

검증(檢證) verification; an inspection. ~하다 verify; inspect; probate (유언을). ¶ 살인 현장을 ~하다 inspect the scene of the murder.

검진(檢診) a medical examination; a physical checkup. ~하다 examine; check up. ¶ ~을 위해 병원에 가다 go to the doctor's for a checkup. ‖ 정기~ a regular health checkup / 집단 ~ a group checkup.

검질기다 (be) persistent; tenacious.

검찰(檢察) (investigation and) prosecution. ¶ ~측의 증인 a witness for the prosecution. ‖ ~관 a public prosecutor; a prosecuting attorney 《美》 / ~당국 the prosecution / ~청 the Public Prosecutor's Office / ~총장 the Public Prosecutor-General; the Attorney General 《美》 / 대~청 the Supreme Public Prosecutor's Office.

검출(檢出) 〔化〕 detection. ~하다 detect; find. ¶ 그의 피에서 비소가 ~되었다 Arsenic was detected in his blood. ‖ ~기 a detector.

검침(檢針) meter-reading. ~하다 check 〔read〕 《gas》 meter. ‖ ~원 a 《gas-》meter reader.

검토(檢討) (an) examination; (an) investigation. ~하다 examine; investigate; study; think over. ¶ ~할 여지가 있다 need more consideration / ~할 가치가 있다 be worth considering / 노동 문제는 지금 ~중이다 The labor problem is under examination. ‖ 재~ re-examination; review.

검푸르다 (be) dark-blue.

겁(怯) 〔소심〕 cowardice; timidity; 〔공포〕 fear; fright. ¶ ~ 많은 cowardly; timid; weak-kneed / ~결에 in the excess of fear; driven by horror / ~(이) 나다 be seized with fear / ~내다 fear; dread; be afraid of / ~을 집어먹다 be frightened; be scared / ~을 주다 threaten; frighten; terrify; scare. ‖ ~쟁이 a coward; a chicken.

겁탈(劫奪) 〔약탈〕 plunderage; (a) robbery; 〔강간〕 rape. ~하다 plunder; rape (violate 《a woman》).

것 〔사람·물건〕 a one; the one; a thing; an object; 〔…것〕 the one that…; 〔소유〕 the one of; -'s. ¶ 새 ~ a new one / 이 ~ this; this one / 저 ~ that; that one / 볼 ~ the one to see / 내 ~ mine.

것둥하다 (be) rather short.

것성드룻하다 (be) sparse; thin; scattered. 〔strides.

것정거리다 walk with rapid

겉 〔표면〕 the face; the surface; the right side(옷의); 〔외면〕 the outside; the exterior; outward appearance(외관). ¶ ~으로는 outwardly; on the surface / ~만 보고 판단하다 judge by appearance / ~을 꾸미다 make outward show; put on a show. ‖ ~모양 outward appearance; show; look.

겉… 〔외부의〕 outer. ¶ ~꺼풀 an outer covering; a husk; a

걷가량 　　　　　　　　　　46　　　　　　　　　　**겨레**

crust / ~대 《푸성귀의》 the outer stalk / ~싸개 an outer covering; a cover; a wrapper / ~잎 an outer leaf.

걷가량(-假量) 《make》 a rough estimate; eye measure (눈대중).

걷날리다 scamp 《one's work》.

걷놀다 ① 《못·나사 따위가》 slip; do not fit. ② ☞ 겉돌다.

걷늙다 look older than one's age; look old for one's age.

겉돌다 《바퀴·기계가》 spin free; run idle; race; 《물체가》 do not mix freely; 《사람이》 do not get along well; be left alone; be left out of 《the class》.

겉말 mere talk; lip service [homage].

겉바르다 gloss over; smooth over; temporize. [exterior.

겉면(-面) the surface; the face;

겉보리 unhulled barley. [ingly.

겉보기 ¶ ~에는 outwardly; seemingly.

겉봉(-封) 《봉투》 an envelope; 《겉에 쓴 것》 an address (주소 성명). ‖ ~을 쓰다 address 《a letter》.

겉약다 《be》 clever in a superficial way; smart merely in appearance.

걷어림 ☞ 겉가량.

걷잡다 《걷어림》 make a rough estimate 《calculation》; measure 《something》 by 《the》 eye 《헤아림》 guess; get a rough idea 《of》.

겉장(-張) 《일면》 the first [front] page; 《표지》 the cover of a book.

겉짐작 a rough estimate.

겉치레 outward show; ostensible display; a show; 《a》 pretense. ~하다 dress up; make outward show; show a good front; show off; cut a dash. ¶ ~의 apparent; make-believe; pretended / 그의 친절은 ~였다 His kindness was all pretense.

걷치장(-治粧) an outward show; ostensible decoration. ~하다 put on a fair show; dress up.

게 《動》 a crab. ¶ ~의 집게발 claws; nippers. ‖ ~거품 foam; froth / ~걸음 a sidewise crawl of a crab (~걸음 치다 walk sideways) / ~딱지 the crust of a crab.

게걸 greed for food. ¶ ~스럽다 《be》 greedy 《for food》; voracious / ~을(를)나다 get an insatiable appetite; get gluttonous.

게놈 《유전》 a genome(e). ¶ 인간 ~ 분석 the human genome analysis.

게다가 moreover; besides; what is more; in addition 《to that》. ¶그녀는 지적이고 ~ 매우 아름답기도 하다 She is intelligent and, what is more, very beautiful.

게르만 ¶ ~의 Germanic. ‖ ~민족 the Germanic race.

게릴라 a guerilla. ‖ ~대원 a guerilla / ~전 guerilla war(fare) / ~전술 《use》 guerilla tactics.

게시(掲示) a notice; a bulletin. ~하다 post [put up] a notice 《on the wall》; notify. ‖ ~판 a notice [bulletin] board.

게양(掲揚) hoisting; raising. ~하다 hoist; raise 《a flag》.

게우다 vomit; throw [fetch] up. ¶먹은 것을 ~ vomit [throw up] what one has eaten.

게으르다 《be》 idle; lazy; tardy; indolent. ¶게을러 빠지다 be intolerably lazy.

게으름 idleness; laziness; indolence. ¶ ~부리다 [피우다] be idle [lazy]; loaf. ‖ ~뱅이 an idle [lazy] fellow; a lazybones.

게을리하다 neglect 《one's work》; be negligent 《of duty》.

게이지 a gauge.

게임 a game; a match (경기). ¶ ~을 하다 play a game. ‖ ~세트 《테니스》 game and set; 《일반적》 Game (is) over.

게장(-醬) 《간장》 soy sauce in which crabs are preserved.

게재(揭載) ~하다 publish; print; carry 《the news》; insert; run 《美》. ¶신문에 광고를 ~하다 run an ad in the paper / 신문에 ~되다 appear [be printed] in a newspaper / 그 논문이 ~된 잡지 the magazine which carries the article. ‖ ~금지 a press ban.

게저분하다 be laden with unwanted 《dirty》 things; be untidy.

게젓 pickled crabs; crabs preserved in soy sauce. [ner.

게트림하다 belch in haughty manner.

겨 chaff; hulls [husks] of grain; bran. ‖ ~죽 rice-bran gruel.

겨냥 ① 《조준》 an aim; aiming. ~하다 《take》 aim 《at》; aim one's gun 《at》. ¶잘 ~해서 쏘다 take good aim and fire / ~이 빗나가다 miss one's aim [the mark]. ② 《치수》 measure; size. ~하다 measure; take measure of. ‖ ~도 a 《rough》 sketch.

겨누다 ① 《겨냥하다》 《take》 aim at; level 《a gun》 at. ¶권총을 가슴에 ~ point [level] a pistol at the breast. ② 《대보다》 compare 《A with B》; measure. ¶길이를 겨누어 보다 compare lengths.

겨드랑(이) ① 《몸의》 the armpit. ¶ ~에 끼다 carry [hold] 《a thing》 under one's arm. ‖ ~털 hair of the armpit. ② 《옷의》 the armhole.

겨레 《한 조상의》 offspring of the same forefather; 《동포》 a fellow countryman; a compatriot; brethren; 《민족》 a race; a people; a nation. ‖ ~붙이 members of a people / 한 ~ one and the same

겨루다 compete (contend, vie) with 《*a person for a thing*》; pit 《*one's skill against*》. ¶ 상을 놓고 서로 ~ compete with each other for the prize / 1위를 ~ contend for first place.

겨를 leisure; spare moments; time to spare. ¶ 책을 읽을 겨를이 없다 have no time to read; be too busy to read a book.

겨우 barely; narrowly; with difficulty; only 《*fifty won*》. ¶ ~ 스무살 된 여자 a girl just out of her teens / ~ 살아가다 make a bare living; eke out a scanty livelihood.

겨우내 throughout the winter; all winter through.

겨우살이 [植] a mistletoe; a parasite.

겨울 winter. ¶ ~의 winter; wintry / ~을 보내다 pass the winter 《*at a place*》 / ~ 준비를 하다 prepare for the winter. ǁ ~날 a winter day / ~날씨 winter weather / ~방학 the winter vacation (holidays) / ~옷 winter clothes (wear) / ~철 the winter season.

겨워하다 feel 《*something*》 to be too much 《*for one*》; feel 《*something*》 to be beyond *one's* control.

겨자 (양념) mustard; (풀) a mustard (plant). ǁ ~채 mustard salad.

격 (格) (지위·등급) rank; status; standing; class; capacity (자격); [文] the case. ¶ ~이 다르다 belong to a different class / ~이 오르다 [내리다] rise (fall) in rank / ~을 올리다 raise 《*a person*》 to higher status; upgrade.

격감 (激減) a sharp decrease. ~하다 decrease sharply; show a marked decrease.

격나다 (隔—) break up with; break relations 《*with*》; become alienated (estranged) 《*from*》.

격납고 (格納庫) a hangar; an airplane (aviation) shed.

격년 (隔年) ¶ ~으로 every other (second) year.

격노 (激怒) wild rage; fury. ~하다 rage; be enraged 《*with a person*》. 《*into, against*》.

격돌 (激突) a crash. ~하다 crash

격동 (激動) turbulence; excitement (인심의); agitation (동요). ~하다 shake violently; be thrown into turmoil. ¶ ~의 시대 turbulent times / ~하는 사회 정세 a rapidly changing social situation / ~의 한해 a year of violent 《*political*》 change.

격랑 (激浪) raging (stormy) waves; heavy seas.

격려 (激勵) encouragement. ~하다 encourage; urge 《*a person to do*》; cheer 《*a person*》 up. ¶ ~의 말 words of encouragement; stirring remarks.

격렬 (激烈) ~한 (하게) violent(ly); severe(ly); vehement(ly); keen(ly) ǁ ~한 경쟁 a keen competition; a hot contest.

격론 (激論) (have) a heated discussion 《*with*》; a hot argument. ~하다 argue hotly.

격류 (激流) a rapid (swift) current; a torrent. ¶ ~에 휩쓸리다 be swept away by a torrent.

격리 (隔離) isolation; segregation. ~하다 isolate; segregate 《*A from B*》. ¶ 환자를 ~하다 isolate a patient; keep a patient in isolation. ǁ ~병실 [병동] an isolation room (ward).

격막 (隔膜) the diaphragm.

격멸 (擊滅) destruction; annihilation. ~하다 destroy; exterminate; annihilate.

격무 (激務) a busy office (post); hard (pressing) work. ¶ ~로 쓰러지다 break down under the strain of hard work / ~를 맡다 undertake a difficult task / ~에 쫓기다 feel hard pressed.

격문 (檄文) (issue) manifesto; an appeal; a declaration.

격발 (激發) an outburst 《*of emotion*》. ~하다 burst (out); explode.

격발신관 (激發信管) a percussion fuse / ~장치 percussion lock.

격벽 (隔壁) a partition. ¶ 방화용 ~ a fire wall.

격변 (激變) a sudden change; revulsion (감정의). ~하다 undergo a sudden change; change violently (suddenly). ¶ 사회의 ~ an upheaval in society; rapid changes of society.

격분 (激忿) wild rage; vehement; indignation. ~하다 be enraged; fly into a fury; blow up.

격상 (格上) ~하다 raise (promote) 《*a person*》 to higher status (to a higher rank); upgrade 《*a person*》. ¶ 판매부장으로 ~되다 be promoted to sales manager.

격세 (隔世) a (quite) different age. ¶ ~지감이 있다 feel as if *one* were living in a quite different 《*age*》. ǁ ~유전 [生] atavism; reversion; (a) throwback.

격식 (格式) (a) formality; established formalities; social rules. ¶ ~을 차리다 stick (adhere) to formalities / ~을 차리는 formal; ceremonious.

격심하다 (激甚—) (be) extreme; in-

격앙 tense; severe; fierce; keen. ¶ 격심한 추위 severe cold / 격심한 경쟁 keen competition / 격심한 타격 devastating damage.

격앙(激昂) (in) excitement; rage; fury. ~하다 get excited; be enraged.

격언(格言) a proverb; a maxim; (a wise) saying.

격원하다(隔遠─) (be) a long way off; far away.

격월(隔月) every other month. ‖ ~간행물 a bimonthly.

격의(隔意) ¶ ~없는 unreserved; frank; ~없이 이야기하다 talk frankly; have a frank talk; talk without reserve.

격일(隔日) a day's interval. ¶ ~로 every other day; on alternate days / ~제로 근무하다 shift once in two days. ‖ ~열[熱] a tertian (fever).

격자(格子) [무늬] a lattice; latticework; [그릴] a grille (금속성의). ‖ ~무늬 cross stripes; a checkered pattern / ~창 a lattice window.

격전(激戰) hot fighting; a fierce (severe) battle; a hot contest (선거 등의). ~하다 have a fierce battle. ‖ ~지 a hard-fought field; [선거의] a closely contested constituency.

격정(激情) a violent emotion; (in a fit of) passion.

격조(格調) 《작품의》 style; gusto; tone; 《사람의》 character; personality. ¶ ~ 높은 sonorous; refined; high-toned / ~ 높은 문장 writing in fine (noble) style.

격조(隔阻) long silence; neglect to write (call). ~하다 be remiss in writing (calling). ¶ ~함을 사과하다 apologize for *one's* long silence.

격주(隔週) a weekly interval. ¶ ~의 fortnightly; biweekly / ~로 every two weeks; every other week.

격증(激增) a sudden (rapid) increase (in). ~하다 increase suddenly (markedly); 《수량이》 (swell) rise rapidly.

격지다(隔─) get estranged; be at odds (outs) 《with》.

격진(激震) a severe earthquake.

격차(格差·隔差) a gap; a difference; a disparity; a differential. ¶ 임금의 ~ a wage differential / 양국간 경제력의 ~ a disparity in economic power between the two countries / 소득의 ~를 없애다 abolish pay (earnings) differentials.

격찬(激讚) (win) high praise. ~하다 praise highly; extol; speak highly of.

격추(擊墜) ~하다 shoot (bring) down; down 《a plane》.

격침(擊沈) ~하다 (attack and) sink 《a ship》; send 《a ship》 to the bottom.

격통(激痛) an acute (a sharp) pain.

격퇴(擊退) ~하다 repulse; repel; drive back; beat off.

격투(格鬪) a grapple; (a hand-to-hand) fight. ~하다 grapple (fight) 《with》. [smash (up).

격파(擊破) ~하다 defeat; crush;

격하(格下) degradation; demotion《美》. ~하다 degrade; demote《美》; lower the status 《of》. ¶ 평사원으로 ~되다 be demoted to the status of an ordinary employee.

격하다(隔─) 《시간·공간의》 leave an interval; [사이에 두다] interpose; [막다] screen. ¶ 강을 격하다 《a village》 across (over) the river / 벽 하나를 격하여 on the other side of the wall.

격하다(激─) be (get) excited; be enraged. ¶ 격하기 쉬운 성질의 사람 a hot-blooded (hot-tempered) person / 격한 감정 an intense feeling / 격한 어조 a violent tone.

격화(激化) ~하다 grow more intense (violent); intensify. ¶ ~일로에 있다 be increasingly intensified.

격화소양(隔靴搔癢) scratching through the sole of *one's* shoes; feeling irritated (impatient); (have) an itch *one* can't scratch.

겪다 ① [경험] experience; go through; undergo; suffer. ¶ 어려움을 ~ experience hardships / 갖은 고초를 ~ undergo all sorts of hardships. ② 《치르다》 receive; entertain; treat hospitably. ¶ 손님을 ~ receive (entertain) guests.

견(絹) silk. ‖ ~방적 silk spinning / ~방직 silk weaving.

견갑(肩胛) the shoulder. ‖ ~골 the shoulder blade.

견강부회(牽強附會) a far-fetched interpretation; distortion. ~하다 force (wrench) the meaning; draw a forced inference. ¶ ~의 forced (views); far-fetched《opinions》.

견고(堅固) ¶ ~한 strong; solid; stout; firm / ~한 진지 a strong position; a stronghold / ~히 하다 solidify; strengthen.

견과(堅果) [植] a nut. ¶ ~상(狀)의 glandiform.

견디다 ① [참다] bear; endure; put up with; stand; tolerate. ¶ 견딜 수 있는 bearable; endurable; tolerable / 견디기 어려운 unbearable; intolerable / 견딜 수 없다 be unable to bear; cannot stand; be unbearable / 시련을

견딜성 ~ bear a trial / 어려움을 ~ endure hardships / 더워 견딜 수 없다 be unbearably hot / 걱정이 돼 견딜 수 없다 be oppressed with anxiety. ② 《일·사용 등에》 wear; last; endure; keep; hold (on); be good for. ¶ 불에 ~ 이다 be proof against fire; be fireproof / 10년간 사용에 ~ 이다 be good for ten years.

견딜성(-性) endurance; perseverance; patience.

견마지로(犬馬之勞) ¶ ~을 다하다 do one's best 《for a person》.

견문(見聞) information; knowledge; experience(경험). ¶ ~이 넓다 (좁다) be well-informed (poorly informed) / ~을 넓히다 add to one's information (knowledge); see more of life (the world).

견물생심(見物生心) Seeing is wanting.

견본(見本) a sample; a specimen (표본); a pattern (무늬, 천의). ¶ ~ 대로 as per sample / 이것은 ~ 과 같다 This meets the specifications. or This comes up to the sample. / 이것은 ~ 만 못하다 This is below the sample. ‖ ~ 시 a trade sample fair.

견사(絹絲) silk thread (yarn).

견사(繭絲) raw silk.

견습(見習) apprenticeship; probation; 《사람》 an apprentice 《to》. ¶ ~ 중이다 be now on probation. ‖ ~ 수습(修習)

견식(見識) 《의견》 a view; an opinion; judgment (판단력); insight (통찰력). ¶ ~ 이 있는 사람 a man of insight (judgment) / ~이 넓다 have a broad vision.

견실하다(堅實-) (be) steady; reliable; sound; solid. ¶ 견실하게 steadily; reliably; soundly / 견실한 사람 a steady (reliable) person / 견실한 투자 a sound investment.

견우성(牽牛星) 〖天〗 Altair.

견원(犬猿) ¶ ~ 지간이다 lead a cat-and-dog life(특히 부부가); be on bad terms 《with》.

견인(牽引) traction; hauling. ~ 하다 pull; draw; drag; haul. ‖ ~력 pulling (traction) capacity / ~차 a tow truck; a tractor.

견인(堅忍) perseverance. ¶ ~ 불발(不拔)의 indomitable; persevering.

견장(肩章) a shoulder strap; an epaulet(te).

견적(見積) an estimate; estimation; a quotation. ~ 하다 make an estimate 《of》; estimate 《at》. ¶ 과대 (과소)~ 하다 overestimate (underestimate) / 비싸게 (싸게) ~ 하다 estimate the cost high (low) / 아무리 싸게 ~ 하여도 at the lowest estimate. ‖ ~ 가격 an estimated cost / ~ 서 a written estimate / ~ 액 an estimated amount (sum).

견제(牽制) ~ 하다 (hold in) check; restrain; 〖軍〗 Contain. ¶ 서로 ~ 하다 hold each other in check / 주자를 ~ 하다 〖野〗 check (peg) a runner. ‖ ~ 공격 a containing attack / ~ 구 (make) a feint ball; a pick-off throw.

견제품(絹製品) silk manufactures; silk goods(견직물).

견주다(비교) compare 《A》 with 《B》; 《겨루다》 compete (contend, vie) 《with》.

견지 a fishing troll (reel, spool). ¶ ~ 질하다 fish with a reel.

견지(見地) a standpoint; a viewpoint; a point of view; an angle. ¶ 소비자의 ~ 에서 보면 from the consumer's point of view.

견지(堅持) ~ 하다 stick (hold fast) 《to》; maintain firmly. ¶ 방침을 ~ 하다 hold fast (adhere) to policy. 《goods; silks》.

견직물(絹織物) silk fabrics; silk

견진(堅振) 〖카톨릭〗 confirmation. ‖ ~ 성사 the sacrament of confirmation.

견책(譴責) (a) reprimand; (a) reproof. ~ 하다 reprimand; reprove. ¶ ~ 을 당하다 be reprimanded. ‖ ~ 처분 an official reprimand.

견치(犬齒) a canine; an eyetooth.

견학(見學) study by observation (inspection). ~ 하다 visit 《a place》 for study; make a field trip to 《a museum》. ¶ 신문사를 ~ 하다 visit a newspaper office for study. ‖ ~ 여행 a tour study / 실지~ a field trip.

견해(見解) an opinion; (give) one's view 《on a subject》. ¶ ~ 를 같이(달리)하다 agree (differ) in opinion; have the same (a different) opinion. ‖ ~ 차 divergence of opinion.

결고들다 persist (hold out) to the end; struggle over.

결 ① 《나무·피부 따위의》 grain; texture. ¶ ~ 이 고운 fine-grained (-textured); delicate 《skin》. ② 《물결》 a wave; 《숨결》 breathing. ③ 《마음의》 disposition; temper. ④ 《…하는 겨를》 a while; an occasion; a chance; 《때》 a time (moment). ¶ 아침 ~ 에 in the morning / 지나는 ~ 에 잠시 들르다 drop in on one's way.

결가부좌(結跏趺坐) 〖佛〗 sitting with legs crossed (as in Buddhist statues).

결강(缺講) ~ 하다 《교수가》 do not

결격 (缺格) disqualification. ‖ ~자 a person disqualified 《for》.

결과 (結果) (a) result; (a) consequence; an outcome; an effect; (good, bad) fruit (성과). ¶ 원인과 ~ cause and effect / …의 ~로서 as a result of; in consequence of; …한 ~가 되다 result in; come (turn) out / 좋은 ~를 얻다 (낳다) obtain (produce) good results / 수술 ~가 좋았다 (나빴다) The surgical operation resulted in success (failure).

결국 (結局) in the end; in the long run; finally; eventually; after all. ¶ ~ 내가 옳았다 I was right after all.

결근 (缺勤) absence 《from》. ~하다 be absent [absent *oneself*] 《*from work*》. ‖ ~계 (tender) a report of absence / ~자 an absentee / 무단~ absence without notice.

결기 (一氣) impetuosity; vehemence; hot temper. ¶ ~ 있는 사람 a man of impetuous temper; a hotheaded man.

결단 (決斷) decision; determination; resolution. ~하다 decide; determine; resolve. ¶ ~력이 강한 사람 a man of decision / ~성이 있다 (없다) be resolute (irresolute) / ~을 내리다 reach (come to) a definite decision.

결단 (結團) ~하다 form a group (team). ‖ ~식 an inaugural meeting (rally).

결당 (結黨) formation of a party. ~하다 form a party. ‖ ~식 the inaugural ceremony of a party.

결딴 ruin; collapse; destruction. ¶ ~나다 be spoilt (ruined); fail; come to nothing; go wrong / ~내다 spoil; mar; ruin; destroy; make a mess of.

결렬 (決裂) a rupture; a breakdown. ~하다 come to a rupture; break down; be broken off. ¶ ~시키다 break off; rupture / 교섭은 ~되었다 The negotiations were broken off (broke down).

결례 (缺禮) failure to pay *one's* compliments. ~하다 fail (omit) to pay *one's* compliments (to offer *one's* greetings).

결론 (結論) a conclusion; a concluding remark. ~하다 conclude; close; ~으로서 in conclusion; to conclude / ~에 도달하다 reach (come to) a conclusion.

결리다 feel a stitch (have a crick) 《*in*》; get stiff. ¶ 옆구리가 ~ have a stitch in the side.

결막 (結膜) the conjunctiva. ‖ ~염 〖醫〗 conjunctivitis.

결말 (結末) an end; a close; a conclusion; settlement (낙착); 《결과》 a result; an outcome. ¶ ~나다 be settled; come to a conclusion (an end) / ~이 안 나다 remain unsettled / ~내다 (짓다) settle; bring 《*a matter*》 to a conclusion (close); put an end to.

결박 (結縛) ~하다 bind; tie (up); pinion. ¶ 범인을 ~짓다 tie a criminal with cords; pinion a criminal.

결백 (潔白) purity (순결); 《prove *one's*》 innocence (무죄); integrity (청렴). ~하다 be pure; innocent; cleanhanded. ¶ 그는 자기의 ~을 주장했다 He insisted that he was innocent.

결번 (缺番) a missing number. ¶ 4번은 ~이다 The number four is blank on the roll.

결벽 (潔癖) ~하다 (be) fastidious; dainty; overnice. ¶ ~증이 있는 사람 a person who is fastidious about cleanness / 옷에 대해 ~증이 있다 be too fastidious (particular) in (about) *one's* clothes.

결별 (訣別) ~하다 part from; bid farewell 《*to*》.

결부 (結付) ~하다 connect 《*A*》 with 《*B*》; link (tie) together. ¶ 양자를 밀접히 ~시키다 link the two into closer relations with each other / …와 ~시켜 생각하다 consider 《*A*》 in relation to 《*B*》.

결빙 (結氷) freezing. ~하다 freeze (be frozen) over. ¶ ~을 방지하다 prevent freezing. ‖ ~기 the freezing season (time).

결사 (決死) ¶ ~적인 desperate / ~의 각오로 with desperate courage; with a "do-or-die" spirit / ~투쟁하다 struggle desperately. ‖ ~대 a suicide corps.

결사 (結社) (form) an association. ¶ ~의 자유 the freedom of association.

결삭다 soften; become mild; be mollified.

결산 (決算) settlement (closing) (of accounts). ~하다 settle (balance) an account. ‖ ~기 a settlement term / ~보고 a statement of accounts / ~일 a settling day.

결석 (缺席) absence; nonattendance. ~하다 be absent 《*from*》; absent *oneself* 《*from*》; fail to attend. ¶ 무단으로 ~하다 be absent without notice. ‖ ~계 a report of absence / ~률 (the rate of) absenteeism / ~자 an

결석 (結石) [醫] a ⟨renal⟩ calculus; a stone ⟨in the bladder⟩.

결선 (決選) a final vote (election). ¶ ~투표 (take) the final vote [ballot] ⟨on⟩.

결성 (結成) ~하다 organize; form. ¶ 신당을 ~하다 form a new political party. ‖ ~식 an inaugural ceremony (meeting).

결속 (結束) union; unity. ~하다 unite; band together. ¶ ~이 안 되다 fail to present a united front / ~을 강화하다 strengthen the unity ⟨of⟩.

결손 (缺損) ⟨손실⟩ a loss; ⟨적자⟩ deficit. ¶ ~이 생기다 ⟨나다⟩ have a deficit of ⟨one million won⟩; suffer a loss / ~을 메우다 cover ⟨make up⟩ the loss. ‖ ~액 the amount of loss; a deficit / ~처분 deficits disposal.

결승 (決勝) a final match [game]; the finals. ‖ ~전 the final round [game, match]; the final(s) (~에 진출하다 go into the finals) / ~점 (reach) the finishing line; the goal.

결식 (缺食) ~하다 go without a meal; skip (miss) a meal. ‖ ~아동 undernourished [poorly-fed] children.

결실 (結實) ~하다 bear fruit; 《비유적》 produce good results. ‖ ~기 the fruiting season.

결심 (決心) determination; resolution. ~하다 make up one's mind; determine; resolve ⟨to do, that⟩; decide ⟨to do, on a matter, that⟩. ¶ ~이 서지 않다 be in two minds; be undecided ⟨whether, about⟩ / ~을 굳히다 make a firm resolution / 나는 이 일을 끝까지 해내려고 ~했다 I am determined to carry out this task.

결심 (結審) the conclusion of a hearing [trial]. ~하다 close ⟨a hearing⟩.

결여 (缺如) (a) lack; (a) want. ~하다 lack; be lacking [wanting] ⟨in⟩. ¶ 상식 ⟨경험, 자제심⟩의 ~ a lack of common sense ⟨experience, self-control⟩.

결연 (結緣) ~하다 form ⟨establish⟩ a relationship ⟨with⟩.

결연하다 (決然—) (be) determined; firm; resolute; decisive. ¶ 결연히 resolutely; firmly; in a decisive manner / 결연한 태도 a determined attitude.

결원 (缺員) a vacancy; a vacant post; an opening. ¶ ~을 보충하다 fill (up) a vacancy.

결의 (決意) resolution; determination (☞ 결심). ¶ ~를 새로이 하다 make a fresh determination / 나는 금연의 ~를 굳혔다 I determined (made up my mind) to stop smoking.

결의 (決議) a resolution ⟨안⟩; a decision. ~하다 resolve; pass a resolution; decide. ¶ 그 계획에 찬성 ⟨반대⟩을 ~하다 decide [pass a resolution] for ⟨against⟩ the plan. ‖ ~기관 a voting organ / ~사항 resolutions / ~안⟨문⟩ a resolution (~안을 제출⟨채택⟩하다 offer [adopt] a resolution).

결의 (結義) ~하다 swear ⟨to be brothers⟩; take an oath ⟨of⟩. ‖ ~형제 sworn brothers.

결장 (結腸) [解] the colon.

결재 (決裁) decision; approval. ~하다 decide ⟨on⟩; make a decision ⟨on, about⟩. ¶ ~를 맡다 obtain ⟨a person's⟩ approval [sanction]. ‖ ~권 the right of decision.

결전 (決戰) a decisive battle ⟨전쟁⟩; 《경기의》 a final game; finals. ~하다 fight a decisive battle; fight to a ⟨the⟩ finish.

결점 (缺點) a fault; a defect; a flaw; a shortcoming; a weak point ⟨약점⟩. ¶ ~이 있는 defective; faulty / ~이 없는 flawless; faultless / 남의 ~을 찾다 find fault with a person / 성마른 것이 그의 유일한 ~이다 His only defect is that he is short-tempered.

결정 (決定) (a) decision; (a) determination; (a) conclusion; (a) settlement. ~하다 decide; determine; settle; fix⟨날짜 따위의⟩. ¶ ~적 (으로) definite (ly); decisive (ly) / ~적인 순간 a crucial moment / 그 건에 대한 중대한 ~을 내리다 make an important decision on that matter / 결혼 날짜를 ~하다 fix the date for the wedding. ‖ ~권 the decisive power / ~타 [野] a game-winning hit; a decisive blow / ~판 a definitive edition / ~표 a deciding [casting] vote.

결정 (結晶) crystallization; a crystal⟨결정체⟩. ~하다 crystallize ⟨into⟩. ¶ 노력의 ~ the fruit of one's labor / 눈의 ~ a snow crystal. ‖ ~학 crystallography.

결제 (決濟) ~하다 settlement. ~하다 settle [square] accounts. ‖ ~자금 a settlement fund.

결집 (結集) ~하다 concentrate; gather together. ¶ 총력을 ~하여 그 계획 수행에 임하다 concentrate our efforts on carrying out the plan.

결초보은 (結草報恩) ~하다 carry

결코(決−) never; by means; not... in the least; on no account; not... at all. ¶ ~ 약속을 어기지 않다 never break *one's* promise / ~ 해결은 ~ 쉽지 않다 The solution is not at all easy. *or* The solution is by no means easy.

결탁(結託) ~하다 conspire 《with》. ¶ ...과 ~하여 in conspiracy (collusion) with.

결투(決鬪) a duel. ~하다 duel 《with》. ¶ ~을 신청하다 challenge 《a person》 to a duel.

결판(決判) ¶ ~ 내다 bring 《a matter》 to an end; settle 《a quarrel》 / ~ 나다 be settled (brought to an end).

결핍(缺乏) want; lack; (부족) shortage; scarcity; deficiency. ~하다 lack; want; be wanting (lacking) 《in》; run short 《of》. ¶ 북한은 심각한 식량 ~으로 고통받고 있다 North Korea is suffering from a desperate shortage of food. / ~증 a 《vitamin》 deficiency disease.

결하다(決−) decide [resolve] 《to do, on》; determine. ¶ 승부를 ~ fight it out; decide a contest.

결함(缺陷) a defect; a fault; shortcomings. ¶ ~이 있는 defective; faulty / 성격의 ~ a defect in *one's* character / ~을 드러내다 betray *one's* weakness / ~을 지적하다 point out defects 《in a machine》. ǁ ~제품 a faulty (defective) product / ~차 a defective car.

결합(結合) union; combination. ~하다 unite; combine. ¶ A와 B를 ~하다 unite (combine) A with B.

결항(缺航) the cancellation of a sailing (flight). ~하다 cancel. ¶ 폭우로 모든 항공편이 ~되었다 Due to the heavy rain, all flights have been canceled.

결핵(結核) tuberculosis(생략 TB; T.B.). ¶ ~성의 tubercular; tuberculous. / ~균 tubercle bacilli / ~예방 prevention of tuberculosis / ~요양소 a sanatorium for T.B. patients / ~환자 a T.B. patient.

결행(決行) ~하다 carry out resolutely; take a resolute step. ¶ 소풍은 우천 불구하고 내일 ~한다 The excursion will be held as scheduled tomorrow even if it rains.

결혼(結婚) marriage. ~하다 marry; get married 《to a person》. ¶ ~을 신청하다 propose 《to》; make a proposal of marriage / ~을 승낙 [거절]하다 accept [reject] a proposal of marriage / 딸을 부자와 ~시키다 marry *one's* daughter to a rich man. ǁ ~상담소 a matrimonial agency / ~상대 a marriage partner; *one's* fiancé (남자); *one's* fiancée(여자) / ~생활 a married life / ~선물 a wedding present [gift] / ~식 a wedding (ceremony) / ~적령기 [연령] (a) marriageable age / ~피로연 a wedding reception.

결혼사기(結婚詐欺) a matrimonial [marriage] fraud; a false [fake] marriage. ǁ ~꾼 a matrimonial swindler.

겸(兼) and; in addition; concurrently; at the same time. ¶ 수상 ~ 외상 the Premier and concurrently Foreign Minister / 거실 ~ 침실 a bed-cum-living room / 사업도 할 ~ 관광도 할 ~ with a double purpose of business and sightseeing.

겸무(兼務) ~하다 serve (hold) the post concurrently 《as》.

겸비(兼備) ~하다 have 《two things》 at the same time. ¶ 재색 ~의 여성 a woman with both beauty and intelligence.

겸사(謙辭) (말) humble speech; (사양) declining humbly.

겸사겸사 for a double purpose; partly ... and partly .... ¶ 일도 보고 구경도 할 겸 ~ 서울에 가다 go to Seoul partly on business and partly for sightseeing.

겸상(兼床) a table for two; (식사) a tête-à-tête dinner. ~하다 sit at the same dinner table; take a tête-à-tête dinner.

겸손(謙遜) modesty; humility. ~하다 (be) modest; humble. ¶ ~하게 with modesty; in a modest way.

겸양(謙讓) modesty; humility. ǁ ~지덕 the virtue of modesty.

겸업(兼業) a side job; a sideline. ~하다 take up a side job; pursue 《another trade》 as a side job. ¶ 저 상점은 제과점과 다방을 ~하고 있다 The store is both a confectionery and coffee shop. / ~농부 a farmer with a side job.

겸연쩍다(慊然−) (서술적) be embarrassed; be abashed; feel awkward.

겸용(兼用) combined use. ~하다 use 《a thing》 both as... and.... ¶ 거실과 서재 ~의 방 a living room which also serves as a study / 이 방은 거실과 서재 ~이다 This room is used both as a living room and a study.

겸유(兼有) ~하다 have [possess,

겸임(兼任) ~하다 hold an additional post; serve concurrently (as). ¶교육부 장관을 ~하다 hold concurrently the portfolio of Education.

겸직(兼職) ~하다 have (hold) more than one job. ¶공무원은 ~이 금지되어 있다 Civil servants are not allowed to have other jobs.

겸하다(兼一) ① combine (A with B); serve both as (A and B). ②겸임, 겸직.

겸행(兼行) ¶주야 ~으로 일하다 work day and night.

겸허(謙虛) ~한 humble; modest; ~하게 in a humble way; with modesty.

겹 fold; a layer; a ply. ¶두 ~ twofold / 여러 ~ many folds.

겹겹이 ply on ply; in many folds; one upon another. ¶~ 쌓여 있다 be piled thick one over another.

겹다 (be) uncontrollable; (be) beyond one's capacity (power); too much for (one). ¶힘겨운 일 work beyond one's power / 설움에 겨워 in a passion of grief.

겹옷 lined clothes.

겹질리다 be sprained.

겹창(一窓) a double window.

겹치다 ① (…을) put one upon another; pile up. ② (…이) be piled up; overlap (each other); (날짜가) fall on (Sunday). ¶불행에 불행이 ~ have a series of misfortunes.

경(更) one of the five watches of the night. ¶삼~ midnight.

경(卿) (호칭) Lord; Sir.

경(經) (불경) a sutra; the Buddhist scriptures. ¶~을 읽다 chant a sutra.

경―(輕) light; light-weight.

…경(頃) about; around. ¶3시 ~ about three o'clock / 월말~에 around the end of month.

경각(頃刻) a moment; an instant. ¶~에 in a moment.

경각심(警覺心) (self-) consciousness; (self-) awakening. ¶~을 불러일으키다 arouse (a person's) attention.

경감(輕減) ~하다 reduce (lighten) (the tax); mitigate; alleviate.

경감(警監) a senior inspector.

경거(輕擧) a rash (hasty) act; rashness. ¶~망동 rash and thoughtless act.

경건(敬虔) piety; devotion. ~하다 be pious; devout. ¶~한 기도를 올리다 pray devoutly (before).

경계(境界) a boundary; a border; a frontier (국경). ¶~선 a border line (between) / ~표 a landmark; a boundary stone.

경계(警戒) (pre)caution; lookout (감시); guard (경비). ~하다 take precautions (against); look out (watch) (for); guard (against). ¶~ 태세를 취하다 be on the alert / 적에 대한 ~를 엄중히 하다 keep strict watch (guard) against an enemy. ¶~경보 a preliminary alert / ~망 a police cordon (~을 펴다 throw (draw) a police cordon) / ~색 sematic coloration.

경고(警告) (a) warning; (a) caution. ~하다 warn (a person against, of); give warning (to).

경골(脛骨) 【解】 the shinbone; the tibia.

경골(硬骨) ① (굳은 뼈) hard bone. ② (기골참) inflexibility; a firm character. ¶~한(漢) a man of firm character.

경골(頸骨) 【解】 the neck bone.

경공업(輕工業) light industries.

경과(經過) ① (일의) progress; a development; course. ~하다 progress; develop ¶수술 후의 ~ progress after an operation / 사건의 ~ the development of an affair / 사태의 ~를 지켜보다 watch the course of the events / (환자의) ~가 양호하다 be doing well (fine); be making satisfactory progress. ¶~조치 a temporary measure. ② (기한의) lapse (of time); expiration (기한의). ~하다 elapse; pass; go by. ¶시간의 ~에 따라 as time goes by; in course (process) of time.

경관(景觀) a scene; a spectacle; a view. ¶일대 ~ a grand sight.

경관(警官) a police officer; a policeman (남); a policewoman (여); a constable (英); a cop (俗); the police (총칭). ¶~대 a police squad (force).

경구(硬球) a hard (regulation) ball.

경구(經口) ~의 oral. ¶~감염 oral infection / ~피임약 an oral contraceptive pill. [gram.

경구(警句) an aphorism; an epi-

경구개(硬口蓋) the hard palate.

경국(傾國) ¶~지색 a woman of matchless (peerless) beauty; a Helen of Troy.

경국(經國) ¶~지사 a statesman / ~지재 the capacity of a states-

경금속(輕金屬) light metals. [man.

경기(景氣) ① (시황) business (conditions); market. ¶~의 회복 business recovery / ~의 후퇴 (a) business recession / ~의 순환 a business cycle / ~가 서서히 좋아지다 (나빠지다) ~ Business is looking up (declining) slowly. / ~가 좋다 (나쁘다) Busi-

ness is brisk (dull). ¶ ~변동 business fluctuations / ~부양책 measures to boost the economy / ~상승 a business upturn / ~예측 business forecasting / ~지표 a business barometer. ② 《세상 전반의》 the times; things.
경기(競技) a game; a match; a contest; an event(종목). ~하다 have a game (match); play a game (match). ¶ ~에 이기다(지다) win (lose) a game (match). ‖ ~대회 an athletic meet(ing) / ~장 a ground; a field(육상) / ~종목 sporting events.
경기관총(輕機關銃) a light machine gun.
경기구(輕氣球) a balloon.
경내(境內) (in) the grounds (precincts); the premises.
경단(瓊團) a rice cake dumpling (covered with powdered bean).
경대(鏡臺) a dressing table; a mirror stand.
경도(硬度) hardness; solidity. ‖ ~계 a durometer.
경도(經度)¹ 《월경》 the menses.
경도(經度)² 《지구상의》 longitude.
경도(傾度) gradient; inclination.
경도(傾倒) ~하다 devote *oneself 〈to literature〉*; be devoted 〈*to*〉.
경동맥(頸動脈) 〖解〗 the carotid artery.
경락(經絡) 〖韓醫〗 special nerve parts around the body which shows the signs of illness for acupuncture.
경량(輕量) light weight. ‖ ~급 (권투선수) a lightweight (boxer).
경력(經歷) a career; *one's* (personal) history. ¶ ~이 좋다 〈나쁘다〉 have a good (bad) career / 그는 어떤 ~의 사람이냐 What is his past career (background)? / 무대 ~ *one's* stage career.
경련(痙攣) convulsions; (a) cramp (근육의); a spasm. ¶ ~성의 spasmodic; convulsive / ~을 일으키다 have a convulsive fit (a cramp).
경례(敬禮) (make) a bow; a salute. ~하다 salute; bow 〈*to*〉. ¶ ~에 답하다 return (acknowledge) 《*a person's*》 salute.
경로(敬老) respect for the old. ‖ ~잔치 a feast in honor of the aged / ~회 a respect-for-the-aged party.
경로(經路) a course; a route; a channel(정보·전달의); a process (과정). ¶ 발달의 ~ the processes of growth / 비밀 ~를 통해 through secret channels / 같은 ~를 밟다 follow the same course.
경륜(經綸) statesmanship; statecraft. ¶ ~을 펴다 administer state affairs.
경륜(競輪) a cycle race. ‖ ~선수 a cycle racer.

경리(經理) accounting. ¶ ~에 밝다 be expert in accounting / 회사에서 ~를 맡고 있다 be in charge of accounting for *one's* company. ‖ ~과(부) the accounting section (department).
경마 a rein; a bridle. ¶ ~ 잡다 hold a horse by the bridle / ~ 잡히다 have a groom lead a horse / 말타면 ~ 잡히고 싶다 《俗談》 Avarice knows no bounds.
경마(競馬) horse racing; a horse race. ‖ ~말 a race horse / ~장 a race horse track.
경망(輕妄) ~하다 (be) thoughtless; rash; imprudent. ¶ ~한 짓 a rash act.
경매(競賣) auction; public sale. ~하다 sell by (at) auction; put 《*an article*》 at auction. ¶ ~에 부쳐지다 come under (go to) the hammer. ‖ ~인 an auctioneer / ~장 an auction room.
경멸(輕蔑) contempt; disdain; scorn. ~하다 despise; scorn; look down on; make light of. ¶ ~할 만한 contemptible; despicable / ~하는 scornful; contemptuous. 「general.
경무관(警務官) a superintendent
경미하다(輕微—) (be) slight; trifling. ¶ 경미한 손해 a slight damage.
경박하다(輕薄—) (be) frivolous; flippant; fickle. ¶ 경박한 사람 a frivolous character.
경범죄(輕犯罪) a minor offense; misdemeanor. ‖ ~처벌법(위반) (a violation of) the Minor Offense Law.
경변증(硬變症) 〖醫〗 cirrhosis.
경보(競步) 《스포츠》 a walking race. ‖ ~선수 a walker.
경보(警報) an alarm; a warning. ¶ ~를 발하다 give a warning; raise an alarm. ‖ ~기 an alarm (signal) / ~해제 All Clear.
경부(京釜) Seoul and Pusan. ‖ ~고속도로 the Seoul-Pusan expressway (speedway 《美》) / ~(선) the Seoul-Pusan line.
경부(頸部) the neck (area).
경비(經費) 《비용》 expenses; cost; 《지출》 expenditure; an outlay. ¶ ~ 관계로 for financial reasons / ~를 줄이다 cut down the expenses / 차를 유지하는 데 많은 ~가 든다 It costs a lot to maintain a car. ‖ ~절약(절감) curtailment of expenditure / 제(諸)~ overhead expenses.
경비(警備) defense; guard. ~하다 defend; guard. ‖ ~대 a garrison / ~병 〖원〗 a guard / ~정 a patrol boat / ~회사 a security company.

경사(傾斜) (an) inclination; a slant; a slope(비탈). ¶ ~지다 incline; slant; slope / 가파른 [완만한] ~ a steep [gentle] slant [slope]. ‖ ~도 a gradient / ~면 an incline; a slope.

경사(慶事) a happy event; a matter for congratulation. ¶ ~스러운 날 a happy day.

경사(警査) an assitant inspector.

경상(經常) ~의 ordinary; current; working. ‖ ~비 working [running] expenses / ~ 세입[세출] ordinary revenue [outlay] / ~수지 a current balance / 예산 the working [ordinary] budget / ~이익[손실] (an) ordinary profit [loss].

경상(輕傷) a slight injury [wound]. ¶ ~을 입다 be slightly injured; suffer a slight injury. ‖ ~자 the slightly injured [wounded].

경색(梗塞) stoppage; blocking; tightness (핍박); [醫] infarction. ‖ 금융~ monetary [financial] stringency; tight money(시장의).

경서(經書) Chinese classics.

경선(頸腺) [解] cervical gland.

경성(硬性) hardness. ‖ ~하감 [醫] chancre.

경세(經世) administration; statesmanship. ‖ ~가 a statesman.

경솔(輕率) rashness; carelessness. ¶ ~하다 (be) rash; hasty; careless. ‖ ~히 rashly; hastily; thoughtlessly / ~한 짓을 하다 commit a rash act; act [behave] rashly; do something rash.

경수(硬水) hard water.

경수(輕水) light water. ‖ ~로 a light-water reactor.

경승(景勝) picturesque scenery. ‖ ~지 a scenic spot.

경시(輕視) ~하다 slight; neglect; make light [little] of. ¶ 문제를 ~하다 treat a matter lightly.

경식(硬式) ~하다 hard; rigid; regulation-ball / ~ 테니스 tennis.

경신(更新) renewal. ¶ ~하다 renew; renovate. ¶ 계약[세계기록]을 ~하다 renew a contract [a world record]. [God.

경신(敬神) piety; reverence for

경악(驚愕) astonishment; amazement. ¶ ~하다 be astonished [amazed] (at, by).

경애(敬愛) respect and affection. ¶ ~하다 love and respect. ¶ ~하는 dear; venerable.

경야(經夜) 《지냄》 passing a night; 《새움》 staying awake for a night. ¶ ~하다 stay [sit] up all night.

경어(敬語) a term of respect; an honorific.

경연(競演) a contest. ~하다 compete (on the stage). ‖ 음악 ~회 (hold) a music contest.

경영(經營) management; administration; operation(운영). ~하다 manage (a bank); run (a hotel); keep (a store); operate (a railroad). ¶ 사업을 ~하다 run (carry on, operate) a business / ~난에 빠지다 fall into financial difficulties. ¶ ~방침 management [business] policy / ~자 a manager / ~진 management(새로운 ~진 밑에서 under new management) / ~학 business administration [management] / ~합리화 business rationalization / 다각~ multiple management.

경영(競泳) a swimming race (contest). ‖ ~대회 a swimming meet.

경옥(硬玉) [鑛] a jade; a jadeite.

경우(境遇) 《때》 an occasion; a time; 《사정》 circumstances; a case. ¶ …한 ~에는 in case of … / 그런 ~에는 in that (such a) case / 어떤 ~에도 under any circumstances / ~에 따라서는 according to circumstances.

경운기(耕耘機) (drive, run) a cultivator (farm tractor).

경원(敬遠) ~하다 keep (a person) at a respectful distance; give (a person) a wide berth.

경위(經緯) ① 《경위도》 longitude and latitude. ¶ ~선 lines of longitude and latitude. ② 《날과 씨》 warp and woof. ③ 《사건 따위의 전말》 the sequence of events; details; particulars; 《사정》 the circumstance. ¶ 사고의 ~ the details of an accident / 나는 그가 파산하게 된 ~를 모른다 I don't know how he came to be bankrupt. ④ 《시비의 구별》 discernment; judgment. ¶ ~에 어긋난 짓 an improper act; unreasonable doings / ~를 모르다 be unreasonable; don't know what is right and wrong.

경위(警衛) 《직위》 an Inspector; a (police) lieutenant 《美》; 《경호》 guard; escort.

경유(經由) ~하다 go by way of; pass (go) through. ¶ …을 ~하여 via; by way of / 시베리아~ 파리에 가다 go to Paris via Siberia.

경유(輕油) light oil; diesel oil.

경유(鯨油) whale oil; train oil.

경음(硬音) a fortis (consonant).

경음악(輕音樂) light music. ¶ ~작곡가 a light composer.

경의(敬意) respect; regard; homage. ¶ ~를 표하다 pay one's respects [regards] (to); do [pay, offer] homage (to); defer (to).

경이(驚異) (a) wonder; a marvel. ¶ ~적 wonderful; marvelous /

~의 눈으로 보다 stare in wonder.

경인(京仁) Seoul and Inchŏn. ‖ ~고속도로 the *Gyeongin* Expressway / ~지방 the Seoul-Inchŏn area; the *Gyeongin* district(s).

경작(耕作) cultivation; farming. ~하다 cultivate; farm. ‖ ~(부)적합한 (un)arable. ‖ ~물 farm products / ~자 a farmer / ~지 cultivated land. 「reform.

경장(更張) a reform. ~하다

경장(警長) a senior policeman.

경쟁(競爭) competition; a contest. ~하다 compete; contest. ‖ 격심한 ~ keen [severe] competition / ~에 이기다 defeat *one's* competitor / 가격 인하 ~을 하고 있다 compete in price reduction / 학문에 있어서는 그와 경쟁할 수가 없다 I'm not match for him as a scholar. ‖ ~가격 a competitive price / ~상품 competitive goods / ~시험 a competitive examination / ~심 a competitive spirit / ~율 the competitive rate / ~자 a rival; a competitor / ~터 an arena of competition / 판매~ sales competition.

경쟁력(競爭力) competitive power. ‖ ~을 약화시키다(가르다) weaken *one's* competitiveness / 수출 가격의 상승은 세계 시장에서 우리의 ~을 약화시킨다 Higher export prices will weaken our competitive position in world markets.

경적(警笛) an alarm whistle; a (warning) horn. ‖ ~을 울리다 give an alarm whistle; sound a horn(자동차 따위의).

경전(經典) sacred books; the *Sutra*(불교의); the *Koran*(회교의).

경정(更正) correction; revision. ~하다 correct; revise; rectify.

경정(警正) a superintendent.

경정맥(頸靜脈) the jugular vein.

경제(經濟) ① 《일반적》 economy; finance(재정). ‖ ~의 economic / ~적(으로) economical(ly) / ~적 난국 an economic deadlock / 전후 한국 ~는 눈부신 발전을 이룩했다 Korea's economy has made a remarkable development since the Korean war. ‖ ~각료 Cabinet ministers in charge of economic affairs; economic ministers / ~개발 economic development / ~개발 5개년계획 a five-year plan for economic development / ~관념 a sense of economy / ~기반 the economic infrastructure 《*of a country*》/ ~문제 an economic problem / ~봉쇄 an economic blockade / ~부양책 an economic stimulus package / ~상태 economic conditions; the state of *one's* finances(개인의) / ~성장(률)(the rate of) economic growth / ~수역 (the exclusive 200-mile) economic waters [zone] / ~지표 an (economic) indicator / ~학 economics / ~활동 [행위] economic activities [actions]. ② 《절약》 thrift; frugality; economy. ‖ ~적인 economical / ~적인 차 an economical car.

경제계(經濟界) financial circles; the economic world. 「sis.

경제공황(經濟恐慌) a financial cri-

경제권(經濟圈) an economic bloc.

경제대국(經濟大國) a great economic nation [power].

경제란(經濟欄) financial columns.

경제력(經濟力) economic strength; financial power.

경제면(經濟面) 《신문 따위의》 the financial page [columns].

경제백서(經濟白書) an economic white paper.

경제사범(經濟事犯) 《죄》 an economic offense; 《사람》 an economic criminal; an offender of economic law. 「soft landing.

경제연착륙(經濟軟着陸) an economic

경제원조(經濟援助) financial support [aid, help]. ‖ ~계획 an economic aid program.

경제위기(經濟危機) an economic [financial] crisis.

경제윤리(經濟倫理) economic [business] ethics. ‖ ~강령 the Economic Ethics Charter [Code] / ~위원회 the Economic Ethics Commission. 「a businessman.

경제인(經濟人) an economic man;

경제전(經濟戰) an economic war; a white war.

경제정책(經濟政策) (an) economic policy. 「tions.

경제제재(經濟制裁) economic sanc-

경제질서(經濟秩序) the economic order. 「cial] figures.

경제통계(經濟統計) economic [finan-

경제특구(經濟特區) 《중국 등지의》 a special economic zone.

경제협력(經濟協力) economic co-operation. ‖ ~개발기구 the Organization for Economic Cooperation and Development 《생략 OECD》. 「very.

경제회복(經濟回復) economic reco-

경조(競漕) a boat race.

경조부박(輕佻浮薄) frivolity; levity. ‖ ~한 fickle and frivolous.

경조비(慶弔費) expenses for congratulations and condolences.

경종(警鐘) an alarm [a fire] bell; a warning(경고). ‖ ~을 울리다 ring [sound] an alarm bell; 《경

경죄(輕罪) 경범죄.

경주(傾注) ~하다 devote *oneself* 〔*to*〕; concentrate 《*on*》. ¶ …에 정력을 ~하다 concentrate *one's* energies on.

경주(競走) 《run》 a race; a sprint (단거리의). ¶ ~에 이기다 〔지다〕 win 〔lose〕 a race.

경중(輕重) 《중요도》 importance; value; gravity; 《무게》 weight. ¶ 상황의 ~ the gravity of the situation / 병의 ~ the relative seriousness of an illness.

경증(輕症) a slight illness; a mild case. ¶ ~의 우울증 a touch 〔slight attack〕 of depression. ‖ ~환자 a mild case 《*of pneumonia*》.

경지(耕地) a cultivated field 〔area〕; arable land. ‖ ~면적 acreage under cultivation / ~정리 readjustment of arable lands.

경지(境地) ① 《상태》 a state; a condition; a stage. ¶ …에 이르다 reach 〔attain〕 a stage of. ② 《분야·영역》 a sphere; territory; ground. ¶ 새로운 ~를 개척하다 break new 〔fresh〕 ground; open up a new field 《*in literature*》.

경직(硬直) ~하다 stiffen; get 〔become〕 stiff.

경질(更迭) a change; a reshuffle. ~하다 〔make〕 a change; reshuffle; switch. ¶ 내각의 ~ a reshuffle of the Cabinet.

경질(硬質) ¶ ~의 hard. ‖ ~유리 〔고무〕 hard glass 〔rubber〕.

경찰(警察) the police 〔force〕; a police station (경찰서). ¶ ~의 조사 a police inquiry / ~에 알리다 〔고발하다〕 report 〔inform〕 to the police / ~에 자수하다 give *oneself* up to the police / ~의 보호를 받다 get 〔receive〕 police protection / ~을 부르다 call the police / ~은 지금 그 범인의 행방을 쫓고 있다 The police are now searching for the criminal. ‖ ~견 a police dog / ~관 a police officer; a policeman / ~국가 a police state / ~대학 the National Police College / ~봉 a police officer's club / ~서장 the chief of a police station / ~청 the National Police Agency / 서울지방~청 the Seoul Metropolitan Police Agency.

경천동지(驚天動地) ~하다 astound 〔startle〕 the world; take the world by surprise.

경첩 a hinge. ¶ ~이 빠지다 be off the hinges.

경청(傾聽) ~하다 listen 〔intently〕 《*to*》. ¶ ~할 만하다 be worth listening to.

경축(慶祝) congratulation; celebration. ~하다 congratulate; celebrate. ¶ ~일 a national holiday; a festival 〔feast〕 day / ~ 행사 festivities.

경치(景致) scenery; a landscape; a scene. ¶ ~좋은 곳 a scenic spot. ‖ 시골~ rural scenery; a country scene.

경치다 《벌을 받다》 suffer torture; be heavily punished; 《혼나다》 have a hard 〔rough〕 time 〔of it〕.

경칭(敬稱) a title of honor; a term of respect.

경쾌(輕快) ~하다 〔be〕 light; nimble; light-hearted (마음이). ¶ ~ 하게 lightly; with a light heart.

경탄(驚歎) wonder; admiration. ~하다 wonder 〔marvel〕 《*at*》; admire. ¶ ~할 만한 wonderful; admirable; marvelous.

경편(輕便) ~하다 〔be〕 convenient; handy; portable; light (간이).

경품(景品) a gift; a premium; a giveaway 《美》. ¶ ~을 내놓다 offer gifts (giveaways). ‖ ~권 a premium ticket; a gift coupon / ~부 대매출 a sale with gifts.

경풍(驚風) (children's) fits; convulsions.

경하(慶賀) congratulation. ~하다 congratulate 《*a person on his success*》. ¶ …은 ~할 만한 일이다 It is a matter of congratulation that ….

경합(競合) concurrence; rivalry; competition. ~하다 compete 〔conflict〕 《*with*》. ¶ 심한 ~ keen 〔hot〕 competition; a tight 《*election*》race. ‖ ~범 concurrent offenses.

경합금(輕合金) a light alloy.

경향(京鄕) the capital and the rest of the country.

경향(傾向) a tendency; a trend; an inclination (성격상의). ¶ …하는 ~이 있다 have a tendency to *do*; be apt to *do*; tend to *do* / 유행의 최근 ~ the latest trends in fashion / 한국인의 평균 수명은 해마다 늘어나는 ~이 있다 The average life span of the Koreans tends to increase from year to year.

경험(經驗) (an) experience. ~하다 experience; go through. ¶ ~이 있는 〔없는〕 사람 an experienced 〔inexperienced〕 person / ~으로 알다 know 《*something*》 from *one's* experience / 내 ~으로는 from my own experience / …에 ~이 있다 have experience in 《*teaching English*》 / ~을 쌓다 gain experience / ~을 살리다 make good use of *one's* experi-

ence. ‖ ~과학 empiric science / ~담 a story of *one's* experience / ~론 empiricism / ~자 a person of experience; an expert (~자를 구함〔광고〕 Wanted: experienced hands (*in trade*)) / ~불문 experience not required.

경혈(經穴)〔韓醫〕 spots on the body suitable for acupuncture.

경호(警護) guard; escort. ~하다 guard; escort. ¶ ~하에 under guard (escort) of... / ~을 맡다 act as escort; stand (keep) guard (*over*). ‖ ~원 a (body-)guard; a security guard.

경화(硬化) hardening; stiffening. ~하다 become hard (stiff); harden; stiffen. ¶ 태도를 ~시키다 stiffen *one's* attitude. 〔a coin.

경화(硬貨) hard money (currency)〕

경화기(輕火器)〔軍〕light firearms.

경황(景況) ¶ ~없다 have no mind (time) for; have no interest in; be too busy for.

곁 ‖ ~에 by (the side of); at *one's* side / ~에 두다 keep (*a thing*) at hand / ~에 앉다 sit by (*a person*).

곁가지 a side branch.

곁눈 a side glance. ¶ ~으로 보다 cast a side glance (*at*) / ~을 주다 give a side glance (*at*); give a suggestion with a look / ~질하다 look aside (sideways) / ~질하지 않고 without looking aside; wholeheartedly. 〔work.

곁두리 snacks for farmhands at

곁들이다 《음식을》 assist (help) (*a person*) in lifting 《something》;《돕다》help; lend (give) a helping hand (*to*). 《일을》 do 《something》along with. ¶ 요리에 파슬리를 ~ garnish a dish with parsley / 선물에 곁들여 보낸 명함 a calling card attached to a gift. 〔key.

곁쇠 a passkey; a duplicate

계(戒) ① 〔훈계〕 a precept. ② 〔계율〕 a Buddhist commandment.

계(計) ① 〔총계〕 the total; 〔합계해서〕 in total; in all; all told. ② 〔계기〕 a meter; a gauge. ③ 〔계략〕 a scheme.

계(係) 〔기구〕 a section (*in an office*); 〔담당〕 charge; 〔담당자〕 a person (clerk) in charge. ¶ 접수~ a reception clerk.

계(契) a (mutual) loan club; a credit union; a mutual financing (assistance) association (society). ¶ ~에 들다 (를 모으다) join (found) a loan club.

…계(系) 〔조직〕 a system; 〔혈통〕 a family line; lineage; 〔당파〕 a faction; a clique; a party; 《수학의》 a corollary. ¶ 한국~ 미국인 a Korean-American.

…계(界) circles; a community; a world; a kingdom.

계간(季刊) (a) quarterly publication. ‖ ~지 a quarterly (magazine).

계간(鷄姦) sodomy; buggery.

계고(戒告) ~하다 give a warning to; caution; warn.

계곡(溪谷) a valley; a dale.

계관(桂冠) a laurel. ‖ ~시인 a poet laureate.

계궁역진(計窮力盡) ~하다 come to the end of *one's* tether.

계급(階級) 〔신분〕 a class; 〔지위〕 a rank; 〔등급〕 a grade. ¶ ~이 다르다 belong to different classes / ~이 상위이다 be senior to 《a person》 in rank / ~없는 사회 a classless society / ~의 차별을 철폐(타파)하다 abolish (break down) class distinction. ‖ ~장《군인의》a badge of rank / ~투쟁〔의 의식〕 class strife (consciousness).

계기(計器) a gauge; a meter; an instrument. ‖ ~비행〔착륙〕an instrument flight (landing) / ~판 an instrument board 〔비행기의〕; a dashboard 〔자동차의〕.

계기(契機) a chance; an opportunity. ¶ 이것을 ~로 taking this opportunity; with this as a turning point.

계단(階段) a flight of stairs (steps); 〔현관의〕 doorsteps. ¶ ~을 오르다〔내리다〕 go up (down) the stairs. 〔family tree.

계도(系圖) genealogy; lineage; a

계도(啓導) guidance; leading; instruction; teaching; enlightenment. ~하다 guide; lead; instruct; teach; enlighten.

계란(鷄卵) a hen's egg; an egg. ‖ ~지〔紙〕 albumenized paper.

계략(計略) a scheme; a design; a plot; a trick. ¶ ~에 넘어가다 fall into (*a person's*) trap / ~에 빠뜨리다 entrap; ensnare / ~을 꾸미다 lay a plan; think out a scheme.

계량(計量) ~하다 measure; weigh. ‖ ~경제학 econometrics / ~기 a meter; a gauge 《가스 등의》; a scale.

계류(溪流) a mountain stream.

계류(繫留) mooring. ~하다 moor 《at, to》. ‖ ~기구(氣球) a captive balloon / ~탑 a mooring mast.

계리사(計理士) 公認 회계사.

계면(界面) 〔物〕 the interface (*between two liquids*). ‖ ~장력 interfacial tension / ~활성제 a surfactant; an interface activator.

계명(戒名) (a posthumous) Buddhist name.

계명(誡命) 〔宗〕 commandments.
계모(繼母) a stepmother.
계몽(啓蒙) enlightenment. ~하다 enlighten; educate. ‖ ~적인 lightening 《books》. ‖ ~운동 an enlightening movement / 〔史〕 the Enlightenment / 농촌 ~운동 a rural enlightenment drive.
계보(系譜) pedigree; genealogy; lineage. ¶ 한국문학의 ~ genealogy of Korean literature.
계부(季父) an uncle.
계부(繼父) a stepfather.
계사(鷄舎) a henhouse; a poultry 〔fowl〕 house. ¶ 닭을 ~에 넣다 house chickens 〔fowls〕.
계산(計算) calculation; counting; computation. ~하다 calculate; count; compute; do sums. ¶ ~이 느리다 〔빠르다〕 be slow 〔quick〕 at figures / ~에 넣다 take 《a thing》 into account / ~을 잘못하다 make an error in one's calculations; miscalculate. ‖ ~서 a bill; an account.
계상(計上) ~하다 〔합계〕 add up; sum 〔count〕 up; 《충당》 appropriate 《a sum》. ¶ 예산 중 장학금을 ~하다 appropriate 《20 million won》 for the scholarship in the budget.
계선(繋船) mooring; 《배》 a laid-up 〔an idle〕 ship. ~하다 moor 〔lay up〕 a ship. ‖ ~료 a mooring fee.
계속(繼續) continuance; continuation; renewal 《갱신》. ~하다 continue; go on with; last. ¶ ~적인 continuous; continual / 30년~ 사업 a thirty-year program / 《신문의》 구독을 ~하다 renew one's subscription 《for》. ‖ ~기간 period of duration / ~범(犯) a continuing crime / ~심의 continuous deliberation / ~예산 a rolling budget.
계수(季嫂) a sister-in-law.
계수(計數) calculation; computation. ~하다 count; calculate; compute. ‖ ~기 a calculating machine.
계수(係數) 〔數〕 a coefficient.
계수나무(桂樹─) 〔植〕 a 《Chinese》 cinnamon; a cassia 《bark》.
계승(繼承) succession. ~하다 succeed to; accede to; inherit. ‖ ~자 a successor 《to the throne》; an inheritor.
계시(計時) clocking. ~하다 《경기 따위에서》 〔check〕 time. ‖ ~원(員) a timekeeper.
계시(啓示) revelation; apocalypse. ~하다 reveal. ¶ 신의 ~ a revelation of God. ‖ ~록 〔聖〕 the Book of Revelation; the Apocalypse《요한 계시록》.

계시다 be; stay. ¶ 김 선생은 어디 계신가요 Where is Mr. Kim?
계약(契約) a contract; an agreement. ~하다 contract; make a contract 《with》; enter into an agreement 《with》. ¶ ~을 이행하다 fulfill 〔carry out〕 a contract / ~을 취소〔파기〕하다 cancel 〔break off〕 a contract / ~을 갱신하다 renew a contract. ‖ ~고〔액〕 contract amount / ~금 a contract money / ~기한 the term of contract / ~서 a 《written》 contract / ~위반 (a) breach of contract / ~자 a contractor《개인》; the parties to the contract《단체》 / ~조건 the terms 〔conditions〕 of a contract / ~수의 a private contract.
계엄(戒嚴) ‖ ~령 martial law 《시내 전역에 ~령을 펴다 place the whole city under martial law / ~령을 해제하다 lift martial law》 / ~사령관 the Martial Law Commander / ~사령부 the Martial Law Command.
계열(系列) a series; a group《회사 따위의》; a chain《상점·호텔의》; a category 《유파 따위의》. ¶ 기업의 ~화 the grouping of enterprises. ‖ ~거래 transactions through business affiliation / ~점 a chain store / ~회사 an affiliated company.
계원(係員) a clerk.
계원(契員) a member of a credit union 〔loan club, mutual aid association〕.
계율(戒律) commandments; religious law; Buddhist precepts.
계인(契印) a tally impression; a joint seal. ~하다 put 〔affix〕 a seal over two edges.
계장(係長) a subsection head 〔chief〕; a chief clerk.
계쟁(係爭) a dispute; a lawsuit. ¶ ~ 중이다 be in dispute / ~중인 문제 a question at issue; a pending point. ‖ ~당사자 a litigant / ~점 a point at issue; a disputed point.
계절(季節) a season. ¶ ~의 seasonal. ‖ ~노동자 a seasonal worker / ~풍 the monsoon.
계정(計定) an account《a/c》. ¶ …의 ~에 넣다 place 〔pass〕 to the account of….
계제(階梯) ① 《순서》 steps; stages; the course 《of things》. ② 《기회》 an opportunity; a chance; an occasion. ¶ 이 ~에 taking this opportunity.
계좌(計座) 《open》 an account 《with a bank》.
계주(契主) the organizer of a mutual finance association 〔credit union〕.

계주경기(繼走競技) a relay (race).

계집 ① 《여자》 a female; the fair sex. ¶ ~아이 a girl; ~종 a maid(-servant); a servant girl. ② 《아내》 a wife; 《정부》 a mistress. ¶ ~질 keeping a mistress (첩질); whoring (오입); debauchery(난봉).

계책(計策) a stratagem; a scheme; a plot. ¶ ~을 쓰다 adopt [use] a stratagem.

계체량(計體量) 《체중검사》 a weigh-in. ¶ ~통과에 실패하다 fail to pass the weight-in.

계측(計測) ~하다 measure; 《토지 따위를》 survey. ¶ 공학 instrumentation engineering / ~기학(器學) instrumentology.

계층(階層) a class; a social stratum. ¶ 모든 ~의 사람 people from all classes of society; people of all walks of life / ~사회 a stratified society.

계통(系統) 《조직》 a system; 《계도》 a family line; lineage; 《당파》 a party. ¶ ~적인 systematic; ~적으로 systematically; methodically / ~을 세우다 systematize. ¶ 소화기~ the digestive system.

계투(繼投) 《야구에서》 a relief. ~하다 pitch in relief.

계표(界標) a boundary mark.

계피(桂皮) cinnamon bark. ǁ ~가루 cinnamon (powder).

계획(計劃) a plan; a project; a scheme; a program. ~하다 plan; make [form] a plan; project; scheme. ¶ ~적인 intentional(고의의); deliberate (숙고한); premeditated(사전 고려된) / ~적으로 intentionally; deliberately / ~적인 거짓말 a deliberate lie / ~적인 범죄 a premeditated crime / 사막을 비옥하게 하는 ~ a project for making the desert fertile / ~을 실행하다 carry out a plan / 환영회를 ~하다 plan to hold a welcome party. ǁ ~경제 (a) planned economy / ~안 a draft / 5개년~ a five-year plan.

곗돈(契-) money for [from] the mutual financing association.

고(끈 따위의) a loop (of a string).

고(故) the late. ¶ ~ A씨 the late Mr. A.

고가(古家) an old house. [Mr. A.

고가(高架) ~의 elevated; overhead; high-level. ¶ ~도로 a high-level road / ~선 overhead wires / ~철도 an elevated railroad.

고가(高價) a high price. ¶ ~의 expensive; costly; high-priced / ~로 팔다 sell (a thing) at a high price. ǁ ~품 a costly (high-priced) article.

고갈(枯渴) drying up; running dry. ~하다 be dried up; run dry; be drained (exhausted). ¶ 나라의 자원을 ~시키다 exhaust the resources of the country.

고개 ① 《목의》 the nape; the scruff (of the neck); the head (머리). ¶ ~를 가로 젓다 say "no" / ~를 들다 raise (hold up) one's head / ~를 들지 못하다 cannot hold up one's head (for shame). ② 《산·언덕의》 a slope; (a mountain) pass. ¶ ~를 넘다 cross over a pass / ~턱 the head of a pass (slope) / 고갯길an uphill (ascending) pass. ③ 《절정》 the crest; the height; the summit. ¶ 50~를 넘다 be on the shady side of fifty / 물가가 ~를 숙였다 The prices are falling.

고객(顧客) a customer; a patron; a client; custom (총칭). ¶ ~이 많다 have a large custom. ǁ ~명단 a list of customers.

고갱이 〖植〗 the heart of a plant; the pith.

고견(高見) ① 《남의 의견》 your opinion (view, idea). ② 《뛰어난 의견》 an excellent opinion; a fine idea.

고결(高潔) ~하다 (be) noble; lofty; noble-minded. ¶ ~한 사람 a man of noble character.

고경(苦境) adverse circumstances; a difficult position; a fix. ¶ ~에 처하다 be in a fix; be in great difficulties.

고계(苦界) the bitter world; the world of mortals.

고고학(考古學) archeology. ¶ ~의 archeological / ~상으로 archeologically. ǁ ~자 an archeologist.

고공(高空) a high in the sky; high altitude. ¶ ~을 날다 fly high up in the air. ǁ ~비행 high-altitude flying (flight).

고과(考課) evaluation of (a person's) merits. ǁ ~표 (사람의) a personnel record / (회사의) a business record / 인사~ (a) merit (efficiency) rating.

고관(高官) a high official (officer); a dignitary; 《직위》 a high office.

고교(高校) a high school. ǁ ~내신성적 high school records / ~평준화 the academic standardization of high schools.

고구마 a sweet potato.

고국(故國) one's native country; (leave) one's homeland. ǁ ~방문계획 a 'Homeland Visit' program.

고군(孤軍) an isolated force. ¶ ~분투하다 fight alone (unsupport-

고궁 ed); put up a solitary struggle.
고궁(古宮) an old palace.
고귀하다(高貴一) be noble; highborn; exalted. ¶그녀는 고귀한 집안 출신이다 She comes from a noble family.
고금(古今) ancient and modern ages; all ages. ¶ ～에 없는 unprecedented / ～을 통하여 through (in) all ages.
고급(高級) ¶ ～의 high-class (-grade); higher. ‖ ～공무원 higher (government) officials / ～장교 a high-ranking officer; the brass (집합적) / ～차 a high-class (deluxe) car / ～품 goods of superior quality; high-grade articles.
고급(高給) a high (big) salary. ‖ ～사원 high-salaried employees.
고기 ①《동물의》meat; beef(소의); pork(돼지의). ¶～한 점 a piece of meat / 다진 ～ minced (hashed) meat. ②《물고기》fish. ‖ ～잡이 fishing, fishery(어업) / ～잡이배 a fisher(어부).
고기밥 ①《미끼》a bait. ②《먹이》feed.
고기압(高氣壓) high atmospheric pressure. ‖ 대륙성 ～ the continental high pressure.
고기전골(一煎一) a hot beef casserole.
고깔 a cowl; a monk's hood.
고깝다 (be) vexing; disgusting; disagreeable; unpleasant.
고난(苦難) distress; suffering; hardship; affliction. ¶ ～을 겪다 undergo hardships / ～을 극복하다 overcome difficulties.
고뇌(苦惱) suffering; distress; affliction; anguish.
고니〖鳥〗a swan.
고다 ①《끓이다》boil hard; boil down. ¶쇠고기를 흐무러지게 ～ boil beef to a pulp. ②《양조》brew; distil. ¶소주를 ～ distil *soju*.
고단하다 (be) tired; fatigued. ¶고단해 보이다 look tired.
고달이 a loop (of a string).
고달프다 (be) exhausted; fatigued; tired out; done up. ¶고달픈 인생 a weary (hard) life.
고담(古談) an old tale; folklore.
고답(高踏) ¶ ～적인 highbrow; hightoned / ～적인 사람들 the highbrows / ～적 문학 highbrow literature.
고대(古代) ancient (old) times; the remote past. ¶ ～의 ancient / ～로부터 from ancient times / ～의 유물 antiquities; ancient relics. ‖ ～사 ancient history / ～인 the ancients; ancient people.
고대(苦待) ～하다 wait eagerly for; eagerly look forward to.

¶ ～하던 소식 the long-awaited news. 「ago.
고대(막) just now; a moment
고대광실(高大廣室) a grand house; a lordly mansion.
고도(古都) an ancient city.
고도(孤島) a solitary (an isolated) island.
고도(高度) ①《높이》altitude; height. ¶600미터의 ～를 유지하다 keep (maintain) the altitude (height) of 600 meters. / ～계 an altimeter / ～비행 an altitude flight. ②《정도》a high power(degree). ¶ ～의 high; powerful; high-degree(-grade); advanced 《*civilization*》 / ～로 발달된 기술 highly-developed technology / 경제의 ～ 성장 high growth of the 《*Korean*》 economy / ～ 성장기 a high-growth period / 이것은 ～의 정밀도가 필요하다 This requires a high order of accuracy. ‖ ～정보통신망 시스템 the Information Network System(생략 INS).
고도리〖魚〗a young mackerel.
고독(孤獨) solitude; loneliness. ～하다 (be) solitary; lonely. ¶ ～한 생활을 하다 lead a solitary life; live in solitude.
고동 ①《장치》a starter; a switch; a stopcock (수도 등의); a handle. ¶ ～을 틀다 (잠그다) turn on (off) 《*the water*》. ②《기적》a steam whistle; a siren. ¶ ～을 울리다 blow a whistle.
고동(鼓動) beat(ing); pulsation; palpitation. ～하다 beat; palpitate; throb. ¶심장의 ～ (a) heartbeat.
고되다 (be) hard (to bear); painful. ¶고된 일 hard work.
고두밥 rice cooked hard.
고둥〖貝〗a conch; a spiral.
고드름 an icicle. 「hard.
고들고들 ～하다 (be) dry and
고등(高等) ¶ ～의 high; higher; advanced; high-class(-grade). ‖ ～교육 《a man with》higher education / ～군사법원 a general court-martial / ～기술 (a) high technique / ～동물 a higher animal / ～법원 a high court (of justice) / ～생물 higher forms of life / ～학교 a (senior) high school.
고등어〖魚〗a mackerel.
고딕 Gothic. ‖ ～식 건축 Gothic architecture / ～체《활자의》Gothic
고라니〖動〗an elk. 「type.
고락(苦樂) pleasure and pain; joys and sorrows. ¶ ～을 같이하다 share *one's* joys and sorrows 《*one's fortunes*》.
고랑[1] (수갑) handcuffs; mana-

고랑 cles. ¶ ~을 채우다 handcuff 《*a person*》; put handcuffs on 《*a person*》.

고랑¹ (두둑 사이) a furrow. ¶ ~을 짓다 make furrows.

고랑창 a narrow deep furrow; a ditch.

고래 [動] a whale. ‖ ~기름 whale oil / ~ 수염 a whale fin.

고래(古來) ¶ ~로 from ancient [old] times / ~의 old; time-honored / 이것은 한국 ~의 습관이다 This is a time-honored custom in Korea.

고래고래 loudly; snarlingly. ¶ ~ 소리지르다 roar; brawl.

고량(高粱) [植] kaoliang; African [Indian] millet. ‖ ~주 kaoliang wine.

고량진미(膏粱珍味) rich and delicious food; all sorts of delicacies.

고려(考慮) consideration; deliberation. ~하다 consider; think《*a matter*》over; take《*a matter*》into account (consideration). ¶ 충분히 ~하여 after due consideration / ~하지〔에 넣지〕않다 disregard; leave《*a matter*》out of consideration / 새로운 계획을 ~ 중이다 A new project is under consideration. / 이 문제는 다소 ~의 여지가 있다 There is some room for further consideration regarding this matter.

고려자기(高麗磁器) *Koryŏ* ceramics (porcelain, pottery)

고령(高齡) an advanced age. ¶ ~으로 죽다 die at the old age《*of ninety*》. ‖ ~자 the aged; the elderly; a person of advanced age / ~출산 late childbearing / ~화 사회 an aging society.

고령토(高嶺土) kaolin(e). ety.

고로(高爐) a blast furnace.

고로(故一) and so; accordingly; therefore. ☞ 그러므로.

고로롱거리다 be troubled with a lingering disease.

고료(稿料) fee for a manuscript (an article); a manuscript fee.

고루 equally; evenly; fairly. ¶ ~ 나누다 divide《*a pie*》equally.

고루(高樓) a lofty building.

고루하다(固陋一) be bigoted; narrow-minded; conservative.

고르다¹ ① be even; equal; uniform. ¶ 고르지 않은 uneven; unequal; rugged / 고르게 evenly; equally. ② (평평하게) level; make even; roll (롤러로). ¶ 땅을 ~ level the ground.

고르다² (선택) choose; select. ¶ 골라내다 pick out; select / 잘〔잘못〕 ~ make a good (bad) choice.

고름 pus; purulent matter. ¶ 상처에 ~이 생겼다 The wound has formed pus. / ~을 짜다 press〔squeeze〕out the pus.

고리 (둥근 것) a ring; a link; a loop (실 따위의). ¶ ~를 만들다 form a ring; make a loop.

고리(高利) high interest; usury. ¶ ~로 돈을 빌리다〔빌려 주다〕borrow (lend) money at high interest. ‖ ~대금업 usury / ~대금업자 a usurer; a loan shark《美》/ ~채 a usurious loan.

고리다 ① (냄새가) (be) rancid; stink; rank; fetid. ② (행동이) (be) illiberal; small; mean.

고리버들 [植] an osier; a red osier.

고리짝 a wicker trunk; (짐) luggage; baggage《美》.

고리타분하다 ① (냄새가) (be) stinking; rancid; fetid; rank. ② (성질이) (be) narrow-minded; small; stingy; hackneyed (진부한). ¶ 고리타분한 소리 a trite remark.

고린내 a bad smell; an offensive odor; a stench.

고릴라 [動] a gorilla.

고립(孤立) isolation. ~하다 be isolated; stand alone. ¶ ~한 isolated; solitary / ~된 무원이다 be alone and unaided / 국제적인 ~ international isolation. ‖ ~정책 an isolationist policy / ~주의 isolationism.

고마움 (감사) gratitude; thankfulness; (가치) value; blessing《*of health*》. ¶ 건강의 ~을 알다 know the value of good health / 돈의 ~을 알다 know what it means to have money / 그는 돈의 ~을 모른다 He is a stranger to the value of money. / 부모님에 대한 ~을 잊지 마라 Don't forget how much you owe to your parents.

고막 [貝] an ark shell.

고막(鼓膜) [解] the eardrum. ¶ ~이 찢어질 것 같은 소리 a deafening noise / ~이 터지다 have *one's* eardrum ruptured〔split〕.

고맙다 (감사한) (be) thankful; grateful; obliged; appreciative; (환영할 만한) (be) welcome; 《친절한》 (be) kind. ¶ 고마우신 말씀 your kind words / 고맙게〔도〕 gratefully; thankfully; fortunately; luckily / 선물을 고맙게 받다 accept a gift gratefully / 고맙지 않은 손님 an unwelcome guest / 대단히 고맙습니다 Thank you very much. *or* Thanks ever so much. / 고맙게도 곧 날씨가 좋아졌다 Fortunately it soon cleared up.

고매하다(高邁一) (be) lofty; noble; high-minded. ¶ 고매한 이상 a lofty ideal.

고명(양념) a garnish; a relish; a condiment.

고명(高名) a famous name. ~하다 (be) famous. ¶ 그는 익히 들어 알고 있습니다 I have heard a lot about you. ‖ ~s many sons.

고명딸 the only daughter among sons.

고모(姑母) one's father's sister; a paternal aunt. ‖ ~부 the husband of one's paternal aunt; an uncle.

고목(古木) an old tree.

고목(枯木) a dead tree.

고무(鼓舞) encouragement. ~하다 cheer up; encourage; inspire; stir up. ¶ 군인들의 사기를 ~하다 stir up the morale of the troops.

고무(India) rubber; gum. ‖ ~지우개 an eraser. ¶ ~창을 댄 rubber-soled 《shoes》/ ~공 a rubber ball / ~나무 a rubber tree 〔plant〕/ ~신 rubber shoes / ~제품 rubber goods / ~줄 an elastic cord 〔string〕/ ~풀 gum arabic.

고무래 a wood rake.

고문(古文) ancient 〔archaic〕 writing; classics(고전).

고문(拷問) torture; the third degree(美). ~하다 torture; give 《a person》 the third degree. ‖ ~대 a rack.

고문(顧問) an adviser; a counselor; a consultant. ‖ ~변호사 a consulting lawyer.

고물[komul] ground grain for coating rice-cakes.

고물[배의] the stern.

고물(古物) ① ☞ 골동품. ②〔낡은 것〕an old article; a second-hand 〔used〕 article. ‖ ~상 a secondhand dealer(사람); a secondhand store(가게).

고물딱지 worn-out articles 〔furniture〕.

고미(苦味) a bitter taste.

고미다락 a kind of attic; a garret.

고민(苦悶) agony; anguish. ~하다 be in agony 〔anguish〕; writhe in agony. ¶ 사랑의 ~ agony of ardent love / ~에 찬 표정 an agonized look / ~ 끝에 병들다 worry *oneself* sick.

고발(告發) accusation; charge. ~하다 accuse 《a person》 of 《a crime》; bring a charge against 《a person》. ¶ 그는 수뢰죄로 ~되었다 He was accused of taking bribes. ‖ ~자 an accuser; an informant / ~장 a bill of indictment.

고배(苦杯) a bitter cup. ¶ ~를 마시다 drink a bitter cup; go through an ordeal; be miserably defeated(승부에서).

고백(告白) confession. ~하다 confess; own up; admit. ¶ 죄상을 ~하다 confess *one's* guilt 〔fault〕/ 사랑을 ~하다 declare *one's* love 《for a girl》.

고별(告別) leave-taking; parting. ~하다 take *one's* leave 《of》; say good-bye 《to》; bid adieu 〔farewell〕《to》. ‖ ~사 a farewell address / ~식 a farewell ceremony; a farewell 〔funeral〕 service(사자에 대한).

고병(古兵) 노병(老兵).

고본(古本) a secondhand book; an old book. ‖ ~상 a secondhand book store; a secondhand bookseller(사람).

고봉(高峰) a lofty peak; a high mountain. ‖ ~준령 high mountains and steep peaks.

고부(姑婦) mother-in-law and daughter-in-law.

고분(古墳) an old mound 〔tomb〕; a tumulus. ¶ ~을 발굴하다 unearth 〔dig up〕 an old tomb.

고분고분 gently; meekly; obediently. ~하다 (be) gentle; meek; mild; obedient.

고분자(高分子)〔化〕 a high molecule 〔polymer〕. ‖ ~화합물 a high-molecular compound; a high polymer.

고비¹〔절정〕 the climax; the crest; the height; 〔위기〕 the brink; the verge; a critical moment; a crisis. ¶ ~를 넘다 pass the critical moment 〔위기〕; pass the peak 《of》 (물가 따위) / 생사의 ~를 넘나들고 있다 be on the verge of death.

고비²〔植〕 a flowering fern.

고비사막(―沙漠) the Gobi desert.

고뿔 a cold. ☞ 감기.

고삐 reins; a bridle. ¶ ~를 당기다 tighten 〔pull up〕 the reins / ~를 늦추다 slacken the reins; give the reins 《to the horse》.

고사(古史) ancient history.

고사(考査) an examination; a test. ~하다 examine; test. ‖ ~장 a test 〔an examination〕 site / 고입 선발 ~ the qualifying examination for high school entrance.

고사(告祀) a traditional practice 〔rite〕 appeasing household gods; *kosa*. ¶ ~를 지내다 hold 〔perform〕 the *kosa* rites; make offerings to household gods.

고사(固辭) ~하다 refuse 〔decline〕 positively.

고사(枯死) withering to death. ~하다 wither and die; be dead.

고사(故事)〔유래〕 an origin; a historical fact; an ancient event; 《구비(口碑)》 (a) tradition; folklore. ¶ ~를 인용하다 allude to historical event.

고사(高射) ‖ ~기관총 an anti-aircraft machine gun / ~포 an anti-aircraft gun; an A.A. gun / ~포 부대 an anti-aircraft battery.

고사리 [植] a bracken.

고사하다(姑捨—) apart from; setting aside; 《말할 것도 없고》 to say nothing 《of》; not to mention; 《커녕》 anything but; far from; not at all.

고산(高山) a high 〔lofty〕 mountain. ‖ ~병 [醫] mountain sickness / ~식물 [植] an alpine plant; alpine flora (총칭).

고상하다(高尙—) (be) lofty; refined; elegant. ¶ 고상한 취미 an elegant taste / 고상한 인격 noble character.

고색(古色) an antique look. ¶ ~ 창연한 antique-looking; time-worn / 그 절은 ~이 창연하다 The temple looks very old.

고생(苦生) 《곤란》 trouble(s); hardship(s); difficulties; sufferings; 《수고》 labor; pains; toil. ~하다 have a hard time; suffer hardships; have difficulty 〔trouble〕 《in doing》; take pains. ¶ 가난으로 ~하다 suffer from poverty / ~을 같이하다 share in a person's hardship / ~을 시키다 give 〔cause〕 《a person》 trouble / 그녀의 얼굴에는 ~한 흔적이 역력했다 Hardship had left traces upon her features. / ~살이 a hard life; a life full of hardships.

고생대(古生代) [地] the Paleozoic (era). ‖ ~의 Paleozoic.

고생물(古生物) extinct animals and plants. ‖ ~학 paleontology.

고서(古書) an old book; rare books; 〔진귀본〕; a secondhand book (헌 책).

고성(古城) an old 〔ancient〕 castle.

고성(高聲) a loud voice. ¶ ~으로 loudly; aloud / ~ 방가하다 sing with a loud voice.

고성능(高性能) high performance 〔efficiency〕. ¶ ~의 highly efficient; high-performance 〔-powered〕 / 그 배는 ~ 엔진을 장착하고 있다 The boat is equipped with a high-powered engine. ‖ ~수신기 a high-fidelity receiver / ~증식로(增殖爐) a fast breeder reactor (생략 FBR).

고소(告訴) [法] an accusation; a complaint; a legal action. ~하다 accuse 《a person of a crime》; bring a charge 〔suit〕 《against》; sue 《a person》 《for a crime》. ¶ ~를 수리(기각, 취하)하다 accept 〔reject, withdraw〕 a complaint / 사기로 ~ 당하다 be accused of fraud. ‖ ~인 an accuser; a complainant / ~장 a letter of complaint.

고소(苦笑) bitter 〔grim, forced〕 smile. ~하다 smile bitterly 〔grimly〕; force a smile.

고소(高所) a high place 〔ground〕; a height. ‖ ~공포증 acrophobia.

고소득(高所得) a high 〔large〕 income.

고소하다 《맛·냄새가》 taste 〔smell〕 like sesame; (be) tasty; savory; nice-smelling. ¶ 깨를 볶는 고소한 냄새 the aroma of sesame being toasted. ② 《남의 일이》 be pleased 《to see other's fault》. ¶ 고소하게 여기다 gloat over 《another's misfortunes》; take an unholy pleasure 《in》 / 아이 (고것) 고소해 Serve(s) you right!

고속(高速) high speed; super-speed. ¶ ~으로 달리다 run at high 〔full〕 speed. ‖ ~도로 a freeway; an expressway; a motorway 《英》(경부~도로 the Seoul-Pusan Expressway) / ~버스 an express bus / ~증식로 a fast breeder reactor (생략 FBR) / ~철도 a high-speed railway / ~화 도로 a semi-expressway.

고수(固守) ~하다 adhere 〔stick〕 to. ¶ 자기 입장을 ~하다 stick 〔hold fast〕 to one's position.

고수(鼓手) a drummer.

고수머리 〔머리〕 curly 〔frizzled〕 hair; 《사람》 a curly-pate; a curly-pated person.

고수부지(高水敷地) the riverside highlands; the terrace land on the river.

고스란히 all; altogether; wholely; untouched; intact. ¶ ~ (그대로) 있다 remain as it was; remain intact; be left untouched.

고슬고슬하다 〔밥이〕 be cooked just right (설슬밥).

고슴도치 [動] a hedgehog.

고승(高僧) a high priest.

고시(告示) a notice; a bulletin; an announcement. ~하다 notify; give notice 《of》. ‖ ~가격 an officially fixed price / ~판 a bulletin board; a message board.

고시(考試) (an) examination. ‖ 고등~ the higher civil service examination / 국가~ a state examination.

고식(姑息) ¶ ~적인 temporizing; makeshift / ~적 수단을 쓰다 take half measures; resort to makeshifts.

고실(鼓室) [解] the eardrum.

고심(苦心) 〈노력〉 pains; hard work. ~하다 work hard; take

고아 pains; make every possible effort. ¶ ~의 작품 the fruit (result) of immense effort / ~한 흔적이 보이다 bear traces of efforts. ‖ ~담 an account of one's hard experience.

고아(孤兒) an orphan. ¶ ~가 되다 be orphaned; be left an orphan. ‖ ~원 an orphanage.

고아하다(古雅—) (be) antique and elegant; quaint; classical.

고안(考案) an idea; a design. ~하다 devise; contrive; design; work out. ¶ 이 상품은 학생이 ~한 것이다 These commodities were devised by a student. ‖ ~자 a designer; an originator.

고압(高壓) high pressure; 《전기의》 high voltage. ¶ ~적인 high-handed; oppressive / ~적인 공무원 a high-handed official. ‖ ~선 a high-voltage cable / ~수단 a high-handed action (measure) / ~전류 a high-voltage current.

고액(高額) a large sum (of money). ‖ ~권 a bill of high denomination / ~납세자 a high (an upper-bracket) taxpayer / ~소득자 a large-income earner.

고약(膏藥) a plaster; an ointment.

고약하다 《생김새가》 (be) bad-looking; 《성미가》 (be) ill-natured; crooked; wicked; 《냄새·맛·날씨 따위가》 (be) bad; nasty; foul; disgusting; offensive. ¶ 고약한 놈 an ill-natured (a nasty) fellow / 고약한 냄새 a nasty (foul) smell / 고약한 성미 an ugly temper.

고양이 a cat; a puss(y) 《애칭》. ‖ ~새끼 a kitten.

고어(古語) an archaic word.

고언(苦言) bitter counsel; candid (outspoken) advice. ¶ ~을 하다 give candid advice 《to》.

고역(苦役) hard work; a tough job; toil; drudgery. ¶ ~을 치르다 have a hard time of it; sweat.

고열(高熱) a high fever (temperature). ¶ ~이 있다 have (get) a high fever 《of 39 degrees》/ ~에 시달리다 suffer from a high fever / ~로 헛소리를 하다 mutter (babble) deliriously in a high fever.

고엽(枯葉) a dead (withered) leaf. ‖ ~작전 defoliation tactics / ~제 a defoliant; Agent Orange 《월남전에서 사용했던》.

고옥(古屋) an old house.

고온(高溫) a high temperature. ‖ ~계(計) a pyrometer.

고요하다 (be) quiet; silent; still; calm; placid; tranquil. ¶ 고요한 밤 a silent night / 고요한 바다 a calm sea.

고용(雇用) employment; hire. ~하다 employ; hire. ‖ ~주 an employer.

고용(雇傭) 《피고용》 employment; engagement. ~하다 be employed (hired). ‖ ~계약 an employment contract / ~관계 an employment relationship / ~살이 service as an employee; domestic service 《머슴의》/ ~인 《피고용》 an employee / ~조건 employment conditions (terms) / ~조정 the adjustment of employment.

고원(高原) a plateau; a highland. ‖ ~지대 plateau area.

고위(高位) a high rank. ‖ ~관리 a ranking government official / ~급 회담 a high-level talk / ~성직자 a religious dignitary.

고위도(高緯度) a high latitude.

고유(固有) ¶ ~의 peculiar (unique, proper) 《to》; characteristic 《of》; of one's own 《독특한》; native 《자국의》/ ~의 동양 ~의 풍속 a custom peculiar to the Orient / 한국 ~의 동식물 plants and animals indigenous (native) to Korea. ‖ ~명사 a proper noun / ~성 peculiarity.

고육지계(苦肉之計) ¶ ~를 쓰다 have recourse to the last resort; take a desperate measure 《under the circumstances》.

고율(高率) a high rate. ¶ ~의 이자 a high (rate of) interest. ‖ ~관세 a high tariff / ~배당 a high rate dividend.

고을 a county; a district.

고음(高音) a high-pitched tone; a high key. ‖ ~부 《樂》 the soprano; the treble.

고의(故意) ¶ ~의 intentional; deliberate; willful 《法》. ~로 intentionally; on purpose; deliberately / ~가 아닌 unintentional / 미필적 ~ 《法》 willful negligence / ~인지 우연인지 intentionally or accidentally / 결코 ~가 아니었습니다 I certainly didn't do it on purpose.

고이 ① 《곱게》 beautifully; finely; gracefully. ② 《조용히》 peacefully; gently; quietly; carefully. ¶ ~ 잠들다 fall gently to sleep; pass away peacefully 《죽다》/ ~ 다루다 handle carefully / 영령이여 ~ 잠드소서 May your noble soul rest in peace!

고인(故人) the deceased (departed); the dead 《총칭》. ¶ ~이 되다 die; pass away.

고인돌 a dolmen.

고자(鼓子) a man with underdeveloped genital organs.

…고자 (in order) to; wishing to. ¶ ~ 하 ― 하다 intend (to); plan.
고자세(高姿勢) a high-handed attitude. ¶ ~로 나오다 take a high-handed (an aggressive) attitude.
고자쟁이(告者 ―) a taleteller.
고자질(告者 ―) ~ 하다 tell on (a person); tell(bring) tales (about). ¶ 엄마에게 나에 대해 ~ 하지 마라 Don't tell mother on me.
고작 at (the) most; at best; no more than; only. ¶ 그는 ~ 20세밖에 안 된다 He is twenty at the most.
고장 (지방) locality; (산물의) the place of production; (동식물의) the home; the best place (for). ¶ 말의 ~ a horse-breeding district / 사과의 ~ the home of the apple / 그 ~ 팀 the home team.
고장(故障) (기계 따위의) a breakdown; a fault; trouble. ¶ ~ 나다 get out of order; break down; go wrong / 기관의 ~ engine trouble / 전기의 ~ (a) power failure / ~이 난 차 a disabled (broken-down) car / 이 TV는 어딘가 ~이 나 있다 There is something wrong with this TV set. / 이 시계는 ~이다 This watch is out of order.
고쟁이 a woman's drawers (panty).
고저(高低) (기복) undulations; (시세의) fluctuations; height (높이); pitch; modulation (음성의). ¶ ~ 있는 undulating; uneven; fluctuating.
고적(古蹟) historic remains; a place of historical interest.
고적(孤寂) solitude; loneliness. ~ 하다 (be) solitary; lonely.
고적대(鼓笛隊) a drum and fife band.
고적운(高積雲) an altocumulus.
고전(古典) the classics. ¶ ~ 적인 classic(al). ‖ ~ 미 classical beauty / ~ 주의 classicism.
고전(古錢) an ancient (old) coin. ‖ ~ 수집가 a collector of old coins.
고전(苦戰) a hard fight (battle); (경기의) a close game; a tight (tough) game. ~ 하다 fight hard (desperately); have a close contest / 그는 선거에서 ~ 하고 있다 He is facing a tough game in the election.
고정(固定) ~ 하다 fix; settle. ¶ ~ 된 fixed; regular; stationary / 장대를 땅에 ~ 시키다 fix a pole in the ground. ‖ ~ 관념 a fixed idea / ~ 급 a regular pay / ~ 손님 a regular customer / ~ 수입 a fixed income / ~ 자산 fixed property (assets) / ~ 표 solid (loyal) votes / ~ 환율제 a

fixed-exchange rate system.
고제(古制) old systems; ancient institutions.
고조(高潮) (조수의) the high tide; flood tide; (고비) the climax. ¶ ~ 된 장면 a thrilling scene / 최 ~ 에 달하다 reach the climax.
고조모(高祖母) one's great-great-grandmother. [grandfather.
고조부(高祖父) one's great-great-
고종 사촌(姑從四寸) a cousin; a child of one's father's sister.
고주망태 (dead) drunkenness. ¶ ~ 가 되다 get dead drunk.
고주파(高周波) high-frequency.
고증(考證) (a) historical research (investigation, study). ~ 하다 study (ascertain) the historical evidence (for). ‖ ~ 학 the methodology of historical researches.
고지 (호박 따위의) chopped and dried pumpkins, eggplant, etc.
고지(告知) a notice; a notification. ~ 하다 notify (a person) of (a matter). ¶ (납세) ~ 서 a tax bill; tax papers.
고지(高地) highlands; (고원) heights; a plateau. ‖ ~ 훈련 high altitude training.
고지대(高地帶) the hilly sections (of a city). ¶ ~ 의 주민 hillside residents. [grosbeak.
고지새 (鳥) a migratory Chinese
고지식하다 (be) simple and honest; simple-minded; tactless.
고진감래(苦盡甘來) Sweet after bitter. or Pleasure follows pain.
고질(痼疾) a chronic disease.
고집(固執) stubbornness; persistence; adherence. ~ 하다 persist in; adhere (stick) to; hold fast to; insist on. ¶ ~ 센 stubborn; headstrong / 자기 견해를 ~ 하다 stick (hold fast) to one's view. ‖ ~ 불통 extreme stubbornness (persistence) / ~ 쟁이 a headstrong person; a stubborn one.
고착(固着) ~ 하다 adhere(stick) to. ‖ ~ 관념 a fixed idea.
고찰(古刹) an old (ancient) temple.
고찰(考察) consideration; (a) study. ~ 하다 consider; study; examine. ¶ 사회 문제에 관한 ~ a study of the social problem / 사건의 역사적 의의를 ~ 하다 consider the historical significance of an event.
고참(古參) a senior; a veteran; an old-timer. ‖ ~ 의 senior; veteran / ~ 병 a veteran soldier; a senior comrade.
고철(古鐵) scrap iron; steel scraps. ‖ ~ 상 a junk dealer.
고체(古體) archaic style; archaism.
고체(固體) (理) a solid (body). ¶ ~

고초 (苦楚) hardships; sufferings; troubles; trials. ¶ ~를 겪다 suffer hardships. 「ancient tomb.
고총 (古塚) an old mound; an
고추 (椒) a red pepper. ¶ ~바람 a cutting (biting) wind; ~잠자리 a red dragonfly; ~장 Korean hot pepper paste; 고춧가루 powdered red pepper.
고충 (苦衷) a painful position; a dilemma; a predicament. ¶ ~을 알아주다 appreciate (a person's) painful position; sympathize with (a person) in a predicament. 「fidelity (생략 hi-fi).
고충실도 (高忠實度) [전축 따위의] high-
고취 (鼓吹) ~하다 inspire (a person) with an idea; put (an idea) into (a person's) mind; advocate (nationalism). ¶ 애국심을 ~하다 inspire (infuse) patriotism into the hearts of (the people).
고층 (高層) 《건물의》 higher stories; upper floors; 《대기의》 a high layer. ¶ ~건(축)물 a high (tall) building; a skyscraper; ~기류 the upper air (current); ~단지 a high-rise housing (apartment) complex.
고치 (silk) cocoon. ¶ 빈 ~ a pierced cocoon; ~에서 실을 잣다 reel silk off cocoons.
고치다 ① 《치료》 cure; heal; remedy. ¶ 병을 ~ cure a disease; 두통을 고치는 약 a medicine for headache. ② 《수리》 mend; repair; fix (up). ¶ 기계를 ~ repair a machine. ③ 《교정》 remedy; reform; correct. ¶ 나쁜 버릇을 ~ correct (get rid of; get over) a bad habit. ④ 《정정》 correct; amend. ¶ 틀린 데를 ~ correct errors (mistakes); 작문을 ~ correct (improve) a composition. ⑤ 《변경》 alter; change; shift. ¶ 예정표를 ~ change the schedule. ⑥ 《조정》 set right; put in order; adjust. ¶ 복장을 ~ adjust one's dress; tidy oneself.
고토 (故土) one's native land (place).
고토 (苦土) [化] magnesia. ǁ ~운모 (雲母) [鑛] biotitie.
고통 (苦痛) pain; suffering; agony; anguish. ¶ ~스러운 painful; afflicting; tormenting; ~을 느끼다 feel a pain (suffer); ~중에 있다 be in pain; ~을 참다 endure (bear) the pain; ~을 주다 give (a person) pain; hurt (a person); ~을 덜다 relieve (ease) the pain.
고패 a pulley. ǁ 고팻줄 a pulley cord (rope).
고풍 (古風) an antique style; an old fashion. ¶ ~스런 옷 old-fashioned dress. 「feel hungry.
고프다 (be) hungry. ¶ 배가 ~
고하 (高下) 《지위의》 rank; 《품질의》 quality; 《시세의》 fluctuations. ¶ 지위의 ~에 관계없이 irrespective [regardless] of rank.
고하다 (告—) tell; inform; announce. ¶ 사실을 ~ tell (reveal) the truth; …에게 작별을 ~ bid farewell to …; 일반에게 ~ announce to the public.
고학 (苦學) study under adversity; work one's way through school (college). ¶ 그는 ~으로 대학을 나와 변호사가 되었다 He worked his way through university and into the legal profession. ǁ ~생 a self-supporting (working) student.
고함 (高喊) a shout; a roar; a yell. ¶ ~ 지르다 shout; yell; roar.
고해 (苦海) this (bitter human) world. ¶ 인생은 ~ Life is full of rubs and worries.
고행 (苦行) asceticism; penance. ~하다 practice asceticism; do penance. ¶ ~자 an ascetic.
고향 (故鄕) one's home; one's native place; one's birthplace. ¶ 제2의 ~ one's second home; one's land of adoption; ~을 그리워하다 long for home; be homesick ; ~에 돌아가다 return to one's native place; go home. ǁ ~방문 home visits.
고혈 (膏血) sweat and blood. ¶ 백성의 ~을 빨다 exploit [sweat] the people.
고혈압 (高血壓) [醫] high blood pressure; hypertension. ǁ ~환자 a hypertensive.
고형 (固形) solidity. ¶ ~의 solid; ~화하다 solidify. ¶ ~물[체] a solid body; a solid.
고혼 (孤魂) a solitary spirit. ¶ 수중 ~이 되다 die at sea.
고화 (古畫) an ancient picture; an old painting.
고환 (睾丸) [解] the testicles. ǁ ~염 orchitis.
고희 (古稀) threescore and ten. ¶ 연세가 ~에 이르다 obtain one's 70th year of age.
곡 (曲) 《음악의》 a tune; an air; a piece of music. ¶ 바이올린으로 한 ~ 연주하다 play a tune on the violin / 한 ~ 부르다 sing an air.
곡 (哭) wailing; lamentation. ~하다 lament; weep; bewail.
곡가 (穀價) the price of grain.
곡괭이 a pick; a pickax.
곡구 (曲球) [野] a curve (ball); a bender; [撞] a fancy shot.

곡기(穀氣) food. ¶ ~를 끊다 go without meals.

곡류(穀類) cereals; grain 《美》; corn 《英》.

곡률(曲率) curvature. ‖ 공간 ~ a space curvature.

곡마(曲馬) a circus (show). ¶ ~단 a circus (troupe).

곡목(曲目) a program; a selection (*for a concert*); a number.

곡물(穀物) cereals; grain 《美》; corn 《英》. ¶ ~가격 (cereal) prices / ~시장 the grain market / ~창고 a granary.

곡사(曲射) high-angle fire. ¶ ~포 a howitzer; a high-angle gun.

곡선(曲線) a curve; a curved line. ¶ ~을 그리다 curve; describe a curve. ‖ ~미 the beauty of *one's* curves; curvaceousness (~미의 여인 a woman with a beautiful figure; a curvaceous woman) / ~운동 movement along a curve.

곡성(哭聲) a cry; a wail.

곡식(穀一) cereals; corn 《英》; grain 《美》.

곡예(曲藝) a (an acrobatic) feat; a stunt; a trick. ¶ ~를 하다 do stunts (*on horseback*). ‖ ~사 an acrobat; a tumbler / 공중 ~ an aerial stunt performance (서커스의); stunt flying, aerobatics (항공기의).

곡절(曲折) ① 《까닭》 reasons; the whys and hows. ¶ 무슨 ~인지 for some unknown reason / 여러 가지 ~이 있어서 for many reasons combined. ② 《복잡》 complications; vicissitudes; ups and downs (부침). ¶ 인생의 우여 ~을 겪다 experience the vicissitudes (the ups and downs) of life.

곡조(曲調) a tune; an air; a melody. ¶ ~에 안 맞는 노래 a song out of tune / 한 ~ 부르다 sing a tune.

곡창(穀倉) a granary; a grain elevator 《美》. ‖ ~지대 a granary.

곡해(曲解) misconstruction; (willful) distortion; interpret wrongly; distort. ¶ 그녀는 내 말을 ~ 했다 She has misconstrued my words. / 자네는 그녀의 뜻을 ~ 해서는 안되네 You shouldn't pervert (distort, twist) what she meant.

곤경(困境) an awkward position; a predicament; a fix. ¶ ~에 빠지다 be thrown into a fix.

곤궁(困窮) poverty; destitution. ¶ ~한 poor; needy; destitute / ~한 사람들 the poor; the needy.

곤돌라 a gondola.

곤두박이치다 fall headlong; fall head over heels. ¶ 술 취한 사람이 시궁창으로 곤두박이쳤다 The drunkard fell head first into the ditch.

곤두서다 stand on end; 《머리칼이》 bristle up. ¶ 그 얘기에 머리칼이 곤두서는 것 같았다 The story almost made my hair bristled (stand on end).

곤두세우다 set on end; erect; bristle up(머리칼을); ruffle up(깃털을).

곤드라지다 drop off to sleep; sink into a slumber. ¶ 술에 취해 ~ drink *oneself* to sleep.

곤드레만드레 dead-drunk. ¶ ~가 되다 get dead-drunk.

곤란(困難) difficulty; trouble; 《곤궁》 distress; 《고난》 hardships. ¶ ~한 difficult; hard; troublesome / ~한 처지 a difficult (tight) situation / ~을 극복하다 overcome difficulties / 생활이 ~ 하다 be hard up; be in needy circumstances / 호흡을 ~ 느끼다 have difficulty in breathing / 이 문제는 해결이 ~ 하다 This problem is difficult to solve.

곤룡포(袞龍袍) an Imperial (a Royal) robe.

곤봉(棍棒) a club; a cudgel; 《경찰봉》 a billy 《美》; a truncheon 《英》. ¶ ~으로 때리다 hit (beat) (*a person*) with a club.

곤약(菎蒻) paste made from the arum root.

곤욕(困辱) bitter insult; extreme affront. ¶ ~을 당하다 suffer a bitter insult.

곤장(棍杖) a club (for beating criminals). ¶ ~을 안기다 flog.

곤쟁이 《魚》 a kind of tiny shrimp. ‖ ~젓 the shrimps preserved in brine.

곤죽 ① 《진창》 sludge; quagmire. ② 《뒤범벅》 a mess. [mouse.

곤줄박이 《鳥》 a varied tit; a tit-

곤지 the red spot on a bride's brow. ¶ ~ 찍다 put a rouge spot on *one's* forehead.

곤충(昆蟲) an insect. ¶ ~을 채집하다 collect insects. ‖ ~망 an insect net / ~채집 insect collecting / ~학 entomology / ~학자 an entomologist.

곤하다(困―) (be) exhausted; weary; fatigued; dog-tired. ¶ 몸시 ~ be tired to death / 곤히 자다 sleep soundly.

곧 ① 《바로》 at once; immediately; directly; without delay; 《머지않아》 soon; before long. ¶ 지금 ~ this very instant; right now / 식사가 끝나는 ~ right after dinner / ~ 오너라 Come at once. *or* Come as soon as possible. / 그녀는 ~ 여기 올 것이다 She will be here before long. / 나는 ~

끝다 돌아오겠다 I'll be back soon. ② 《쉽게》 easily; readily; straight off. ¶ ~ 배울 수 있다 be easy to learn. ③ 《즉》 namely; that is (to say). ¶ 가장 어린 소녀, 낸시 the youngest girl, Nancy by name.

곧다 ① 《물건이》 (be) straight; upright. ¶ 곧은 길 a straight road. ② 《마음이》 (be) honest; upright. ¶ 곧은 사람 an honest man; a man of upright character.

곧바로 straight; at once. ¶ ~ 집에 돌아가다 go home straight.

곧이곧대로 honestly; straightforwardly. ¶ ~ 말하다 tell it straight; speak out in a straightforward manner.

곧이듣다 take 《*a person's*》 words seriously; believe 《*what a person says*》; accept 《*a thing*》 as true. ¶ 농담을 ~ take a joke seriously.

곧잘 《꽤 잘》 fairly [pretty] well; readily. ¶ ~ 읽다 read pretty well.

곧장 directly; straight; without delay. ¶ ~ 집으로 돌아가다 go straight home / 그 길로 ~ 떠나다 leave without delay.

골¹ 【解】《골수》 the (bone) marrow; 《머릿골》 the brain.

골² 《틀》 a block; a mold. ¶ 구둣 ~ a shoe last / 모자의 ~ a hat block.

골³ 《성》 anger; rage. ¶ ~이 나다 be angry / ~나게 하다 make 《*a person*》 angry; provoke 《*a person*》 to anger / ~내다 get [become] angry 《with, at》 / lose *one's* temper / 좀처럼 ~을 안 내다 be slow to anger.

골⁴ the goal. ∥ ~라인(포스트) a goal line (post) / ~키퍼 a goalkeeper.

골간(骨幹) 《뼈대》 physique; framework; 《골자》 essentials; the basis; the fundamentals. ¶ 조정안의 ~ the basis of a mediation plan.

골갱이 ① 《심》 a core; the heart. ② 《골자》 the gist; the pith.

골격(骨格) 《체격》 frame; build; 《건물의》 a framework. ¶ 이 건장한 사람 a man of sturdy [stout] build.

골골하다 suffer from a chronic disease; suffer constantly from weak health. ¶ 골골하는 사람 a confirmed invalid.

골다 《코를》 snore. ¶ 드르렁드르렁 코를 ~ snore heavily.

골동품(骨董品) a curio; an antique. ∥ ~상 a curio [antique] store; an antique dealer(사람) / ~ 애호가 a virtuoso; a curioso.

골든아워(at) the prime time; the peak listening [viewing] hour.

골똘하다 (be) absorbed (engrossed, lost) 《*in*》; intent 《*on*》; given 《*to*》. ¶ 골똘히 intently; absorbedly / 골똘히 생각에 잠기다 be lost in thought.

골라잡다 choose; take *one's* choice. ¶ 골라잡아 100원. 100 *won* a piece at your choice.

골마루 a rear veranda(h).

골막(骨膜) 【解】 the periosteum. ∥ ~염 【醫】 periostitis.

골머리 the brain; the head. ¶ ~를 앓다 be troubled; be annoyed.

골목 an alley; a side street [road]; a byway. ¶ 막다른 ~ a blind alley; the dead end. ∥ ~대장 the cock of the walk; the boss of youngsters.

골몰하다(汨沒—) be immersed [absorbed, engrossed] 《*in*》. ¶ 사업에 ~ be engrossed in business.

골무 a thimble.

골반(骨盤) 【解】 the pelvis.

골방(—房) a back room; a closet.

골병들다(—病—) get injured internally.

골분(骨粉) powdered bones; bone dust. ∥ ~비료 bone manure.

골상(骨相) physiognomy; *one's* features. ∥ ~학 phrenology / ~학자 a phrenologist.

골생원(—生員) 《옹졸한》 a narrow-minded person; 《허약한》 a weak [sickly] man.

골수(骨髓) 【解】 the (bone) marrow; the medulla. ¶ ~에 사무치다 cut [go] deep into *one's* heart / 나는 그에게 ~에 사무친 원한이 있다 I bear him a bitter grudge. ∥ ~기증자 a bone-marrow donor / ~눈사 a hard core / ~염 【醫】 osteomyelitis / ~이식 a marrow transplant / ~종 a myeloma.

골육(骨肉) *one's* own flesh and blood; kindred; blood relations. ¶ ~상잔 a strife among flesh and blood; an internecine feud / ~종(腫) an osteosarcoma.

골자(骨子) the gist; the essence; the main point. ¶ 문제의 ~ the gist of the question.

골저리다(骨—) be chilled to the bone.

골절(骨折) a fracture (of a bone). ¶ ~하다 break a bone; suffer a fracture.

골질(骨質) bony [osseous] tissue.

골짜기 a valley; a gorge; a ravine; a dale.

골초(—草) 《담배》 poor-quality tobacco; 《사람》 a heavy smoker.

골치 the head. ¶ ~ 아픈 문제 a troublesome question / ~ 앓다 be troubled (annoyed, worried) / ~가 아프다 have a headache. ‖ 골칫거리 a pain in the neck; a hard nut to crack (그는 골칫거리야 He is a hard nut to crack).
골탄(骨炭) animal (bone) charcoal; boneblack.
골탕(-湯) great injury (insult). ¶ ~ 먹다 suffer a big loss; have a hard (rough) time of it.
골통대 a tobacco pipe.
골패(骨牌) domino(e)s.
골품(-稟) a rush.
골프 golf. ¶ ~ 를 치다 play golf. ‖ ~연습장 a driving range / ~ 장 golf links; a golf course / ~ 채(-) a golf club (ball).
골학(骨學) [解] osteology.
골회(骨灰) bone ashes.
곪다 ① (상처가) form pus; fester; gather. ¶ 종기가 ~ a boil festers (comes to a head). ② (사물이) come to a head; ripen.
곪다² (덜 차다) remain unfilled; be still not full; be a little short of full. ② go hungry. ¶ 곪은 배를 채우다 satisfy one's hunger.
곪다³ (썩다) rot; go bad; spoil; get stale. ¶ 곪은 달걀 bad eggs. ② (언걸들어) suffer (receive) damage (a loss); get injured internally (골병).
곪리다 ① (그릇을) fill short of the full measure. ② (배를) underfeed; let (a person) go hungry.
곪리다² (썩이다) rot; spoil; (해롭게 하다) inflict injury (damage) upon (a person); do harm to; cause damage to; (약자를) bully; play trick on.
곯아떨어지다 (술에) lie with liquor; drink oneself to sleep; (잠에) be dead asleep.
곰 ① [動] a bear. ¶ ~ 가죽 bearskin / ~ 새끼 a bear's cub. ② (사람) a fathead; a slow-witted person; a simpleton.
곰곰(이) carefully; deeply; deliberately. ¶ ~ 생각하다 think it over; mull (the matter) over.
곰국 thick soup of meat; beef broth.
곰방대 a short tobacco pipe.
곰배팔이 a person with a deformed (mutilated) arm.
곰보 a pockmarked person.
곰살갑다 (너그럽다) (be) generous, broad-minded; (다정스럽다) (be) tender; kind; gentle.
곰살굿다 (be) gentle; meek; kind.
곰탕(-湯) ② (밥을 넣은) meat and rice soup.
곰팡(이) mold; mildew; must. ¶ ~내 나는 musty; fusty; moldy / ~ 나다 (슬다) get (become) moldy (musty); be covered with mold. ‖ ~균 a mold (fungus).
곱(곱절) times; (배) double.
곱다 ① (모습·소리 따위가) (be) beautiful; pretty; lovely; fine; (마음씨가) (be) tender; kindly; gentle. ¶ 곱게 beautifully; prettily; charmingly / 고운 목소리 a sweet voice / 고운 마음씨 a tender heart / 곱게 차려 입다 dress oneself beautifully; be finely dressed.
곱다² (손때가) (be) numb; be numbed (with cold). ¶ 추위서 손 발이 ~ one's limbs are numb with cold.
곱똥 mucous feces (stools).
곱빼기 ① (음식의) a double-measure of (liquor); a double-the-ordinary dish (요리). ② (겹침) double; two times. (back.
곱사등이 a humpback; a hunch-
곱살끼다 fret; be fretful.
곱살스럽다 (be) pretty(얼굴이); gentle (마음씨가).
곱새기다 (오해) misunderstand; misconstrue; (곡해) misinterpret; (고깝게 여기다) think ill of; (거듭 생각하다) think (a matter) over and over.
곱셈 multiplication. ~하다 multiply; do multiplication.
곱슬곱슬하다 (be) curled; curly; wavy.
곱자 a square.
곱쟁이 double.
곱절(배倍) times; double. ~하다 double (it). ¶ ~ twice; two times / 두 ~ 의 양 twice as much (many) as.
곱창 the small intestines of cattle.
곱치다 ① (곱절하다) double. ② (둘로 접다) double; fold up.
곱하다 multiply. ¶ 3에 2를 ~ multiply 3 by 2. ‖ 곱하기 multiplication.
곳(장소) a place; a spot (좁은); a scene(현장); (사는 곳) one's home (address). ¶ 안전한 ~ a place of safety / 사고가 일어난 ~ the spot of the accident / 이~ 저~ here and there / 가는 ~마다 everywhere; wherever one goes / ~에 따라 다르다 be different in localities / 사는 ~을 알리다 give (tell) one's address.
곳간(庫間) a warehouse; a storehouse. ‖ ~차 a box waggon (英); a boxcar (美). (house.
곳집(庫 -) a warehouse; a store-
공을 차다 (던지다) kick (throw) a ball / ~을 튀기다 bounce a ball.
공(公) (공사) public matters; public affairs. ¶ ~과 사를 구별하

공 draw the line between public and private matters. ② 《공작》 a duke 《영국의》. ¶ 에든버러 ~ the Duke of Edinburgh.

공(功) a meritorious service; merits. ¶ 특히 ~이 있는 사람 a person of exceptional merit / ~을 세우다 render meritorious services 《for the country》 / ~을 들이다 elaborate; exert oneself 《to do》; work hard.

공(空) 《영》 zero; 《무》 naught; nothing (허사); 《빔》 emptiness; 《원》 a circle; an 'O'.

공 a gong. ¶ ~이 울렸다 《권투》 There is the bell.

공가(空家) an empty (an unoccupied, a vacant) house.

공간(空間) room. ¶ ~의 spacial; spatial / 무한한 ~ infinite space / 시간과 ~을 초월하다 neglect time and space / 이 세상은 시간과 ~ 속에 존재한다 This world exists in time and space. ‖ ~감각 a sense of space / ~예술 spatial arts.

공갈(恐喝) a threat; a menace; blackmail. ~하다 threat; blackmail; menace. ¶ ~하여 돈을 빼앗다 blackmail 《a person》 for money. ‖ ~자 a blackmailer / ~죄 the crime of blackmail / ~취재(取財) extortion by threats.

공감(共感) sympathy. ~하다 sympathize 《with》. ¶ ~을 불러일으키다 sympathize 《from》 / ~을 얻다 win (get) 《a person's》 sympathy.

공개(公開) ~하다 open 《a thing》 to the public; exhibit. ¶ ~된 open (to the public) / 주식의 ~ public offering of stocks; a public sale of shares / ~석상에서 in public / 정보의 ~를 요청하다 require that the information be made public / 그 궁전은 일반에게 ~되어 있다 The palace is open to the public. ‖ ~강좌 an open class; an extension course / ~수사 an open investigation / ~청문회 a public hearing / ~토론회 an open forum.

공개념(公槪念) the public concept. ¶ 토지의 ~ the public concept of land ownership.

공개방송(公開放送) open broadcasting. ~입찰 [open] bidding.

공개입찰(公開入札) a public [an open] bidding.

공것(空一) a thing that can be had for nothing; a thing got for nothing; something free.

공격(攻擊) an attack; an assault; an offense; 《비난》 a charge; (a) censure. ~하다 attack; assault; 《비난》 charge; criticize. ¶ ~적인 태도를 취하다 adopt an offensive attitude 《toward》 / ~은 최대의 방어이다 A good offense is the best defense. / 미사일 ~을 개시하다 launch a missile attack / 시장의 무능을 ~하다 charge the mayor with incompetence. ‖ ~개시(예정)시간 H-hour; zero hour / ~군 an attacking force / ~력 striking (offensive) power / ~용무기 offensive weapons (arms) / ~정신 [자세] an offensive spirit (posture) / ~측 《야구의》 the team at bat / 기습 ~ a surprise attack.

공경(恭敬) respect; reverence. ~하다 respect 《one's teacher》; revere. ¶ ~할 만한 respectable; venerable.

공고(工高) a technical high school.

공고(公告) a public (an official) announcement (notice). ~하다 notify publicly; announce.

공고하다(鞏固—) (be) firm; solid; strong. ¶ 공고한 유대 strong ties.

공공(公共) ~의 public; common / ~의 이익을 도모하다 promote the public interests (good); work for the public benefit. ‖ ~기관 a public institution / ~기업체 a public corporation / ~단체 a public body / ~복지 public welfare / ~사업 a public enterprise / ~생활 communal life / ~심 public spirit / ~요금 public utility charges / ~위생 (시설, 재산) public health (facilities, property).

공공(空公) 《형용사적》 undisclosed; a certain; unidentified. ¶ ~기지 an undisclosed base / ~부대 an unnamed unit / ~사건 a certain affair.

공공연하다(公公然—) (be) open; public. ¶ 공공연히 openly; publicly; in public / 공공연한 비밀 an open secret / 공공연한 사실 a matter of common knowledge.

공과(工科) the engineering department. ‖ ~대학 an engineering college; an institute of technology.

공과(功過) merits and demerits.

공과금(公課金) public imposts (charges); taxes.

공관(公館) an official residence; Government establishments. ‖ ~장 회의 a conference of the heads of diplomatic mission abroad.

공교롭다(工巧—) 《뜻밖》 (be) unexpected; coincidental; (in)opportune; casual; accidental. ¶ 공교로운 때 an (in)opportune time (occasion) / 공교롭게 by chance (우연히); unluckily; unfortunate-

ly 〔재수없게〕; unexpectedly 〔의외로〕/ 공교롭게도 그날은 비가 왔다 The day happened to be rainy.
공구(工具) a tool; an implement. ¶ ~ 한 벌 a set of tools. ∥ ~상자 a toolbox / 기계~ a machine tool / 정밀~ a precision tool.
공구(工區) a section of works.
공국(公國) a dukedom.
공군(空軍) an air force. ∥ ~기지 an air base / ~력 air power / ~사관학교 an air-force academy / ~작전〔부대〕 an air operation 〔unit〕 / 한국~ the Republic of Korea Air Force (ROKAF).
공권(公權) ① 〔국가의〕 = ~력. ② 〔개인의〕 civil rights; citizenship. ¶ ~을 박탈당하다 be deprived of *one's* civil rights. ∥ ~력 governmental authority; public power (~력의 행사 the exercise of governmental authority) / ~박탈〔정지〕 deprivation 〔suspension〕 of civil rights.
공권(空拳) a bare hand. ¶ 〔적수〕~으로 with *one's* naked 〔bare〕 hands.
공극(空隙) an opening; a gap.
공금(公金) public funds 〔money〕. ¶ ~을 횡령하다 embezzle public money.
공급(供給) supply; provision. ~하다 supply 〔furnish, provide〕 《*a person*》with. ¶ ~을 받다 be supplied 《*with*》; get a supply 《*of*》. ∥ ~원(源) a source of supply / ~자 a supplier.
공기(工期) 〔建〕 a term of works.
공기(公器) a public organ (institution).
공기(空氣) air; atmosphere〔분위기〕. ¶ 탁한〔신선한〕~ foul 〔fresh〕 air / ~ 유통이 좋은〔나쁜〕 well- 〔poorly-〕ventilated; airy 〔stuffy〕/ 좌중의 ~〔분위기〕 the atmosphere of a meeting. ∥ ~냉각기 an air cooler / ~오염 air pollution; atmospheric pollution / ~전염 infection by air / ~청정기 an air purifier / ~제동기〔압착기〕 a pneumatic brake 〔compressor〕 / ~총 an air gun.
공기업(公企業) public enterprise; a government project.
공납금(公納金) 〔부과금〕 public imposts; 〔학교의〕 regular school payments.
공단(工團) an industrial complex.
공단(公團) a public corporation.
공대(恭待) ~하다 receive 《*a person*》cordially 〔대접〕; address with respect〔존대〕.
공대공(空對空) ~미사일 《*missile*》.
공대지(空對地) air-to-surface 《*missile*》.
공대함(空對艦) air-to-ship 《*missile*》.

공덕(公德) public morality. ∥ ~심 sense of public morality; public spirit.
공덕(功德) charity; a pious act. ¶ ~을 쌓다 do an act of charity; do charitable acts 〔deeds〕.
공도(公道) 〔도로〕 a highway; a public way; 〔정의〕 equity. ¶ ~를 밟다〔걸어가다〕 take the path of justice.
공돈(空-) easy money; unearned 〔easily gained〕 money. ¶ ~은 오래 못 간다 Lightly come, lightly go. *or* Easy come, easy go.
공동(共同) cooperation; collaboration. ~하다 cooperate with; work together. ¶ ~으로 in cooperation with / ~의 이익을 위하여 for common benefit / ~의 적 a common enemy. ∥ ~개발 joint development / ~경영 joint operation / ~기자회견 a joint press conference / ~묘지 a joint cemetery / ~성명〔issue〕a joint communiqué 〔statement〕 / ~연구 joint 〔group〕 researches; a joint study / ~작업 group work / ~작전 concerted operations / ~재산 joint 〔common〕 property / ~제작 joint production / ~주최〔under〕the joint auspices 《*of*》 / ~출자 joint investment.
공동(空洞) a cave; a cavern. ¶ ~화하다 become hollow; lose substance / 산업의 ~화 deindustrialization.
공동가입(共同加入) 〔전화〕joint subscription. ∥ ~선 a party line / ~자 a joint subscriber.
공동생활(共同生活) community 〔communal〕 life. ¶ ~하다 live together.
공동체(共同體) a community; a communal society.
공들다(功-) require 〔take〕 much labor; cost strenuous effort. ¶ 공드는 일 hard 〔laborious〕 work.
공들이다(功-) elaborate; do elaborate 〔careful〕 work; exert *oneself*; apply *oneself* to. ¶ 공들인 준비 elaborate preparations.
공략(攻略) take 《*a castle*》; capture 《*a fort*》.
공란(空欄) a blank; a blank space 〔column〕. ¶ ~에 기입하다 fill up the blanks in the sheet.
공람(供覽) ~하다 submit 《*things*》to public inspection; exhibit 《*things*》before the public.
공랭(空冷) air cooling. ¶ ~의 air-cooled 《*engine*》.
공략(攻略) capture; invasion〔침략〕. ~하다 capture; invade.
공로(功勞) meritorious services; merits. ¶ ~에 의하여 in recognition of *one's* services / ~를

공로 세우다 render distinguished service. ‖ ~자 a person (man) of merits / ~장 a distinguished service medal / ~주(株) [商] a bonus stock.

공로(空路) an air route (lane); an airway. ¶ ~로 by plane (air) / 김포를 출발, ~로 하와이에 가다 fly from Kimp'o toward Hawaii.

공론(公論) public opinion; the consensus (of opinion).

공론(空論) an empty theory; a futile argument; an academic argument (discussion). ‖ ~가 a doctrinaire / 탁상 ~ an armchair theory (plan).

공룡(恐龍) a dinosaur. 「power.

공률(工率) rate of production; [理]

공리(公利) public welfare (interests).

공리(功利) utility. ¶ ~적인 utilitarian / 사물을 ~적으로 생각하다 take a utilitarian view of things; view things in a practical way. ‖ ~주의 utilitarianism / ~주의자 a utilitarian.

공립(公立) ~의 public; municipal (시립의). ‖ ~학교 a public school.

공매(公賣) public auction (sale). ~하다 sell by auction; sell at auction《美》. ¶ ~에 부치다 put 《a thing》 to public sale; sell 《a thing》 by (at) public auction. ‖ ~처분 disposition by public sale.

공명(公明) fairness; justice; openness. ¶ ~정대한 fair; just; open / ~정대하게 하자 Let's play fair. ‖ ~선거 a clean (corruption-free) election.

공명(功名) a great exploit (achievement); a glorious deed; a feat of arms(무공). ¶ ~심 aspiration; ambition / ~심에 불타다 be very thirsty (eager) for fame.

공명(共鳴) [理] resonance; 《공감》 sympathy; response. ~하다 《물체가》 be resonant with; 《마음이》 sympathize (feel) with; respond to. ‖ ~기 a resonator.

공모(公募) a public appeal 《for contribution》; an offer for public subscription (주식) ; public advertisement (of a post). ~하다 offer shares for public subscription(주식을); raise 《a fund》 by subscription (기부를). ¶ 비서를 ~하다 advertise for a secretary / 소설의 ~는 내일로 마감이다 Tomorrow is the deadline for public contribution for novels.

공모(共謀) conspiracy. ~하다 conspire (plot) together; conspire (plot) with 《a person》. ‖ ~자 a conspirator; an accomplice.

공무(公務) official business (duties); government affairs. ¶ ~로 여행하다 travel on official business / ~중의 재해보상 compensation for accidents in the line of duty. ‖ ~방해 interference with a government official in the exercise of his duties.

공무원(公務員) an official; a public official; a civil servant. ¶ ~이 되다 enter into public service. ‖ ~정년제 the age limit system for civil servants.

공문(公文) 《문서》 an official document (paper). ¶ ~서를 위조하다 forge official documents. ‖ ~서 위조 forgery of an official document.

공문(空文) a dead letter. ¶ ~화하다 turn out a dead letter.

공물(供物) an offering 《to the spirits of one's ancestors》; a tribute.

공민(公民) a citizen. ‖ ~ 교육 civic education / ~권 citizenship; civil rights (~권을 박탈하다 disfranchise 《a person》; deprive 《a person》 of his civil rights).

공박(攻駁) refutation; attack. ~하다 refute; confute; argue against.

공방(攻防) offense and defense. ¶ ~전 an offensive and defensive battle.

공배수(公倍數) [數] a common multiple.

공백(空白) a blank; blank (unfilled) space; 《비유적》 a vacuum. ¶ ~을 메우다 fill (in) the blank 《with》. 「accomplice.

공범(共犯) conspiracy. ‖ ~자 an

공법(工法) a method of construction. ‖ 실드~ [建] the shield method.

공법(公法) public law. ‖ 국제~ international law.

공병(工兵) a military engineer. ‖ ~대 a military engineer corps.

공보(公報) an official report (bulletin). ‖ ~선거 an election bulletin. ‖ ~실 [국] the Office (Bureau) of Public Information / 미국 ~원 the U.S. Information Service (생략 USIS).

공복(公僕) a public servant.

공복(空腹) hunger; an empty stomach. ¶ ~에 on an empty stomach; before meal / ~을 느끼다 feel hungry.

공부(工夫) study. ~하다 study. ¶ ~를 잘하다 (못하다) be good (poor) at one's studies. ‖ 시험 ~ study for an examination.

공분(公憤) righteous indignation. ¶ ~을 느끼다 be morally indignant 《at, over something》.

공비(工費) the cost of construc-

공비 (工費) public expense.

공비 (共匪) red [communist] guerrillas. ¶ 무장 ~ armed red guerrillas.

공사 (工事) (construction) works; construction. ~하다 construct; do construction work 《at, on》. ¶ ~중이다 be under construction. ‖ ~비 the cost of construction / 입찰 a bid for construction work / 현장 [판] a site of construction / 수리 [증축] ~ repair [extension] works / 토목 ~ civil engineering works; public works.

공사 (公司) a company; a firm.

공사 (公私) official [public] and private matters. ¶ ~ 간에 both in public and private / ~를 구별한다 draw the line between public and private matters.

공사 (公社) a public corporation.

공사 (公使) a minister. ¶ 주한 프랑스 ~ the French Minister to Korea / 대리 ~ a chargé d'affaires / 특명전권 ~ an envoy extraordinary and minister plenipotentiary. ‖ ~관 a legation / ~관원 the personnel [staff] of a legation (총칭).

공사 (公事) public [official] affairs.

공사채 (公社債) bonds; (public) bonds and coporate debentures. ‖ ~시장 the bond market / ~형 투자신탁 a bond investment trust.

공산 (公算) probability. ¶ …할 ~이 크다 There is a strong probability that....

공산 (共産) ¶ ~화하다 communize 《a country》/ 북한~집단 the band of Communists in North Korea. ‖ ~권 the Communist bloc / ~당 the Communist Party / ~당원 a Communist (party member) / ~주의 communism 《~주의자 communist(ic)》/ ~진영 the Communist camp / ~화 communization.

공산명월 (空山明月) ① the moon shining on a lone mountain. ② 《대머리》 a bald head. 「ucts.」

공산품 (工産品) industrial products.

공상 (空想) an idle fancy; a daydream; imagination. ~하다 fancy; imagine; daydream. ¶ ~적인 fanciful; imaginary / ~에 잠기다 be lost [indulge] in fantasy; be given to daydreaming / 아이들은 ~의 세계를 좋아한다 Children like a fantacy world. ‖ ~가 a (day)dreamer / ~과학소설 science fiction (생략 SF).

공생 (共生) [生] symbiosis. ‖ ~관계 a symbiotic relationship.

공서양속 (公序良俗) [法] good public order and customs.

공석 (公席) ① 《공식 석상》 a public occasion; the meeting. ¶ ~에서 on a public occasion. ② 《공무보는 자리》 an official post.

공석 (空席) a vacant seat; a vacancy. ¶ ~을 채우다 fill (up) a vacancy.

공설 (公設) ¶ ~의 public; municipal. ‖ ~시장 a public market.

공세 (攻勢) the offensive [aggressive]. ¶ ~를 취하다 take the offensive 《against》 / ~로 전환하다 change [switch] to the offensive. ‖ 외교 ~ a diplomatic offensive.

공소 (公訴) [法] arraignment; prosecution; public action. ~하다 arraign; prosecute. ¶ ~사실 a charge / ~장 a written arraignment.

공손 (恭遜) ¶ ~한 polite; civil; courteous / ~히 politely; civilly; humbly; courteously.

공수 (攻守) offense and defense; [野] batting and fielding. ‖ ~동맹 an offensive and defensive alliance.

공수 (空輸) air transport; airlift. ~하다 transport 《a thing》 by air; airlift. ¶ 구호물자를 ~하다 transport relief goods by air. ‖ ~부대 an airborne unit (corps); an airlift troop / ~작전 an airlift operation / ~화물 air cargo (freight).

공수병 (恐水病) ☞ 광견병.

공수표 (空手票) a fictitious bill; a bad check; 《비유적》 an empty promise. ¶ ~를 떼다 make an empty promise (비유). 「uor.」

공술 (空─) a free drink; free liquor.

공술 (供述) a statement; a deposition (법정에서의). ~하다 depose; state; testify. ‖ ~서 a written statement / ~자 a deponent.

공습 (空襲) an air raid (attack). ~하다 make an air raid 《on》. ‖ ~경보 《give》 an air-raid alarm [warning] 《~경보를 내리다 put out [sound] an air-raid warning / ~경보를 해제하다 sound the "all clear"》.

공시 (公示) public announcement [notice]. ~하다 announce publicly. ¶ ~가격 a posted price; the publicly assessed value 《of land》 / ~최고 [法] a public summons.

공식 (公式) [수학의] a formula; 《정식》 formality. ¶ ~의 formal; official; state / ~을 적용하다 apply a formula 《to a problem》 / ~적인 사고방식 a stereotyped way of thinking / ~으로 발표하다 an-

공신 (功臣) a meritorious retainer.

공신력 (公信力) (lose) public confidence [trust].

공안 (公安) public peace (and order); public security [safety]. ¶ ~을 유지하다 [해치다] keep (disturb) public peace. ‖ ~위원회 a public safety commission.

공알 (음핵) the clitoris.

공약 (公約) a public pledge (promise); a commitment. ~하다 pledge [commit] oneself. ¶ 선거 ~을 지키다 keep election [campaign] promises.

공약수 (公約數) 【數】 a common measure (divisor). ‖ 최대~ greatest common measure (생략 G.C.M.).

공양 (供養) ~하다 provide (one's elders) with food; hold a mass [memorial service] for (the dead). ‖ ~미 rice offered to Buddha.

공언 (公言) (open) declaration. ~하다 declare (openly); profess.

공업 (工業) (manufacturing) industry. ¶ ~의 industrial; manufacturing; technical / ~용의 for industrial use [purpose] / ~의 발전을 촉진하다 spur (the country's) industrial growth. ‖ ~가 an industrialist / ~계 industrial circles / ~고등학교 a technical high school / ~국 an industrial nation / ~규격 ☞ 산업규격 / ~기술 industrial technology / ~단지 an industrial complex / ~도시 an industrial city / ~용수 water for industrial use / ~용지 an industrial site / ~지내 an industrial area (district) / ~화 industrialization / ~화하다 industrialize / 석유화학~ the petrochemical industry.

공여 (供與) giving; a grant. ~하다 give; grant; make a grant (of).

공역 (共譯) joint translation.

공연 (公演) a public performance. ~하다 perform; play. ‖ 위문~ a consolation performance.

공연 (共演) ~하다 coact; play together. ‖ ~자 a costar; a coactor.

공연 (空然) ¶ ~한 useless; futile; needless; unnecessary / ~히 to no purpose; uselessly; unnecessarily; in vain.

공염불 (空念佛) a fair but empty phrase. ¶ ~에 그치다 end in an empty talk.

공영 (公營) public management. ~하다 place (an undertaking) under public management. ‖ ~주택 public [municipal] housing (집합적).

공영 (共榮) mutual prosperity.

공영 (共營) joint management. ~하다 operate jointly (with).

공예 (工藝) industrial arts; a craft. ¶ 미술~ arts and crafts. ‖ ~가 a craftsman / ~기술 craftmanship / ~미술 applied fine arts / ~품 an art work.

공용 (公用) public use; official [public] business. ¶ ~으로 on official business [duty]. ‖ ~어 an official language / ~차 an official vehicle.

공용 (共用) common use. ~하다 use (a thing) in common; share (a thing) with (another). ¶ 이 수도전(栓)은 ~이다 This tap (water faucet) is for common use. / 나는 그와 이 방을 ~하고 있다 I use this room in common with him.

공원 (工員) a (factory) worker.

공원 (公園) a park. ‖ 국립~ a national park.

공유 (公有) public ownership. ¶ ~의 public; public(ly) owned. ‖ ~물 (재산) public property / ~지 public land.

공유 (共有) joint [common] ownership. ~하다 hold (a thing) in common; own (a thing) jointly. ‖ ~자 a joint owner / ~재산 common property / ~지 a common land.

공으로 (空—) free (of charge); for nothing; gratis. ¶ ~얻다 [일하다] get [work] for nothing.

공의 (公醫) a community doctor.

공이 a pestle; a pounder; a firing pin (총의). ¶ ~로 찧다 pestle. ‖ ~ (총의) a hammer.

공이치기 (총의) a hammer.

공익 (公益) the public benefit [interest, good]; the common good. ¶ ~을 도모하다 work for the public good. ‖ ~단체 [사업] a public corporation (utility works) / ~법인 a public service corporation / ~우선 public interests first.

공인 (公人) a public man [figure]. ¶ ~으로서의 생활 one's public life / ~으로서 발언하다 express one's opinion in one's official capacity.

공인 (公認) authorization; official approval [recognition]. ~하다 recognize officially; authorize. ¶ ~의 authorized; official / ~을 받다 gain official approval. ‖ ~기록 an official record / ~중개사 a licensed real estate agent / ~후보자 a recognized [an authorized] candidate.

공일(空―)〖거저일〗~하다 work for nothing. 〖일〗a holiday.
공일(空日)〖일요일〗Sunday; 《공휴》
공임(工賃) a wage; wages; pay. ¶ ~을 올리다〔줄이다〕raise〔cut down〕the wages.
공자(公子) a little prince.
공자(孔子) Confucius.
공작(工作) handicraft; 《행동》maneuvering. ~하다《제작》work; make;《책동》maneuver. ¶ 준비 ~을 하다 pave the way (*for*) / 화평 ~을 하다 make a peace move. ‖ ~금 operational funds / ~기계 a machine tool / ~대 a worktable / ~물 a structure; a building / ~실 a workshop / ~원 an agent; an operative / ~품 handicrafts / 정치 ~ political maneuvering / 지하 ~ underground activities.
공작(孔雀)〖鳥〗a peacock; a peahen(암컷).
공작(公爵) a prince; a duke《英》. ‖ ~부인 a princess; a duchess.
공장(工匠) a craftsman; an artisan.
공장(工場) a factory; a plant; a workshop; a mill(종이·목제의). ‖ ~관리 factory management / ~용지 a factory site / ~장 a plant manager / ~지대 a factory district〔area〕/ ~폐쇄 a lockout (파업에 의한); a (factory) closure(불경기에 의한) / ~폐수 factory effluent〔waste water〕; industrial sewage.
공장도(工場渡)〖商〗ex factory. ‖ ~가격 the factory price.
공저(共著) collaboration; a joint work (책). ‖ ~자 a joint author; a coauthor.
공적(公的) public; formal; official. ¶ ~으로 officially; publicly; formally / ~생활 public life / ~성격을 띠다 be of〔have, assume〕 a public character.
공적(公敵) a public (common) enemy. ¶ 인류의 ~ an enemy of mankind.
공적(功績) a meritorious deed; merits; services. ¶ ~을 세우다 render distinguished services to 《*the country*》.
공전(公轉)〖天〗revolution. ~하다 revolve; move around the sun.
공전(空前) ¶ ~의 unprecedented; unheard-of; record-breaking. ¶ ~절후의 명화 the greatest film of all time / 그것은 ~절후의 폐가이다 It is the first and probably the last brilliant achievement.
공전하다(空轉―)〖기계 따위가〗race; run idle;〖논의 따위가〗argue in a circle;〖국회 따위〗stall; remain idle (*since*). ¶ 국회는 개회 첫날부터 공전하고 있다 The National Assembly has remained idle since the first day of the session.
공정(工程) the progress of work; a (manufacturing) process. ¶ ~은 약 70퍼센트이다 The work is about 70 percent finished. ‖ ~관리 process control / ~안전관리 Processing Safety Management (생략 PSM) / ~표 a work schedule.
공정(公正) justice; fairness; impartiality. ¶ ~한 just; impartial; fair / ~한 처리 a fair〔square〕deal / ~한 가격 just price. ‖ ~거래위원회 the Fair Trade Commission / ~증서〖法〗a notarial deed.
공정(公定) ¶ ~의 official; legal; (officially) fixed. ‖ ~가격 an official price / ~환율 an official exchange rate.
공정(부) **대**(空挺(部)隊)〖軍〗airborne troops; paratroops.
공제(共濟) mutual aid (relief). ‖ ~사업 a mutual aid〔aid〕 project / ~조합 a mutual-aid association; a (mutual) benefit society.
공제(控除) subtraction; deduction. ~하다 subtract; deduct (*from*). ¶ 보험료 ~를 신청하다 apply for an insurance premium tax exemption. ‖ ~액 an amount deducted.
공존(共存) coexistence. ~하다 coexist; live together. ¶ 번영과 빈곤과 ~한다 Prosperity coexists with poverty. ‖ ~공영 coexistence and coprosperity / 평화적 ~ peaceful coexistence.
공죄(功罪) merits and demerits.
공주(公主) a princess.
공중(公衆) the (general) public. ¶ ~의 public; common / ~앞에서 in public / ~의 이익 the public interest; the general good. ‖ ~도덕 public morality / ~목욕탕 a public bath / ~변소 a public lavatory / ~위생 public health〔hygiene〕/ ~전화 a public telephone;〔전화 박스〕a telephone booth 《美》/ 카드식 ~전화 a cardphone.
공중(空中) the air. ¶ ~의 aerial; in the air / ~에 뜨다 float in the air. ‖ ~급유(-to-air) refueling / ~보급 an airlift / ~분해 a midair disintegration / ~수송 air transportation / ~전 an air battle / ~조기경보 관제시스템 Airborne Warning and Control System (생략 AWACS) / 조기경보(기) an Airborne Early

공중감시(空中監視) (an) air surveillance; aerial inspection.

공중납치(空中拉致) hijacking of an airplane; skyjacking. ~하다 highjack (hijack) a (passenger) plane. ‖ ~범 a hijacker.

공중누각(空中樓閣) a castle in the air; an air castle; a dream. ¶ ~을 짓다 build castles in the air / 마음속으로 ~을 그리는 사람 a daydreamer; a visionary.

공중제비(空中—) a somersault; a tumble. ¶ ~를 하다 turn a somersault; turn head over heels.

공증인(公證人) a notary (public).

공지(空地) vacant ground (land); a vacant lot.

공지(公知) common (universal) knowledge. ¶ ~의 known to all; widely known; well-known / ~ 사항 the official announcement.

공직(公職) (a) public office. ¶ ~에 있다 hold (be in) a public office; ~을 떠나다 leave public life; resign from public office. ‖ ~생활 a public career (life) / ~ 추방 purge from public office.

공직자(公職者) a public (government) official; a holder of (public) office; an officeholder. ¶ ~들의 무사 안일주의와 수동적인 자세 the easygoing and passive attitude on the part of government officials. ‖ ~사회 the bureaucratic society / ~윤리법 the Public Servants' Ethics Law.

공짜(空—) an article got for nothing. ¶ ~로 for free (nothing); gratis.

공차(空車) 〈빈차〉 an empty car; 《무료 승차》 a free (stolen) ride. ¶ ~를 타다 steal a ride; get a free ride.

공창(工廠) an arsenal.

공창(公娼) a licensed prostitute (사람); licensed prostitution (제도).

공채(公債) 〈채무〉 a public loan (debt); 〈증권〉 a public (loan) bond. ¶ ~를 발행하다 issue bonds / ~를 상환하다 redeem a loan. ‖ ~시장 the bond market / 장기~ a long-term government bond.

공처가(恐妻家) a henpecked (submissive) husband.

공천(公薦) public nomination. ~하다 nominate publicly. ¶ 후보자를 ~하다 officially adopt a candidate; nominate a candidate.

공청회(公聽會) (hold) a public (an open) hearing.

공출(供出) delivery; offering. ~하다 tender; offer; turn in. ‖ ~미 rice tendered (to the government) / ~할당 allocation of delivery quotas.

공치다(空—) 〈허탕〉 be unsuccessful (fruitless); 《동그라미》 draw a circle.

공치사(功致辭) self-praise; admiration of *one's* own merit. ~하다 praise *one's* own service; brag of *one's* merit.

공칭(公稱) ~의 nominal; official. ‖ ~자본금 nominal (authorized) capital.

공탁(供託) a deposit; a trust. ~하다 deposit 《money》 in (with); give 《a thing》 in trust. ‖ ~금 deposit money / ~물 a deposit; a deposited article / ~소 a depository / ~자 a depositor.

공터(空—) a vacant lot; an open space.

공통(共通) ¶ ~의 common 《to》 / ~의 이해 common interests / ~되는 점이 하나도 (없다) have something (nothing) in common / 두 사람은 ~된 취미가 있다 The two share the same interests. / ~분모(分母) 〔數〕 a common denominator / ~어 a common language / ~점 a point in common 《between》; something *they* have in common.

공판(公判) a (public) trial (hearing). ¶ 사건을 ~에 부치다 bring a case to trial; put a case on trial / ~을 열다 hold (a) court / ~ 중이다 be on trial. ‖ ~정 the court (of trial).

공판장(共販場) a joint market.

공편(共編) coeditorship.

공평(公平) impartiality; justice. ¶ ~한 fair; just; impartial / ~히 impartially; fairly; equally / ~무사한 fair and disinterested / ~한 판단 a fair judgment / ~한 태도로 학생들을 대하다 deal with students with an impartial attitude.

공포(公布) promulgation; proclamation. ~하다 promulgate; proclaim.

공포(空砲) a blank shot. ¶ ~를 쏘다 fire a blank shot.

공포(恐怖) fear; terror; horror. ¶ ~에 사로잡히다 be seized with fear; be terror-stricken / ~의 빛을 보이다 look scared (frightened) / ~에 떨다 tremble with fear. ‖ ~감 (a sensation of) fear / ~영화 a horror film / ~증 a phobia; a morbid fear.

공폭(空爆) an air bombardment.

공표(公表) 《공포》 official (public) announcement; 《발표》 publication. ~하다 announce official-

공학 ly; publish; make public. ¶ 의견을 ~하다 make *one's* opinion known / 그 사건의 관련자 명단은 ~되지 않았다 The names of people concerned in the affair have never been made public. / …라고 ~되었다 It was officially announced that…..

공학(工學) engineering (science). ‖ ~부 the department of technology / ~사 [박사] a bachelor [doctor] of engineering.

공학(共學) coeducation. ¶ 남녀 ~의 학교 a coeducational (co-ed) school.

공한(公翰) an official letter.

공한지(空閑地) idle land.

공항(空港) an airport. ¶ (비행기가) ~을 이륙하다 take off from the airport / ~에 착륙하다 land at an airport. ‖ ~출입국 관리소 (세관) the airport immigration office (customs house) / 국제 ~ an international airport.

공해(公海) the open sea; the high seas; international waters. ¶ ~ 상에서 핵실험을 하다 conduct nuclear tests over international waters / ~의 자유 freedom of the open sea. ‖ ~어업 high sea fishery.

공해(公害) environmental pollution. ¶ 무~의 non-polluting; pollution-free (*cars*) / ~ 를 제거 [방지]하다 remove (prevent) environmental pollution / ~를 일으키다 cause harm to the public. ‖ ~기업 the industries causing environmental pollution / ~대책 antipollution measures / ~문제 a pollution problem / ~방지산업 antipollution industry / ~방지조례 pollution control ordinance / ~병 a pollution-caused disease / ~병 환자 victims of pollution-caused disease / 산업 ~ industrial pollution / 소음 ~ noise pollution / 식품 ~ food contamination / 원자력 ~ atomic pollution.

공허(空虛) emptiness. ¶ ~한 empty; vacant / ~한 느낌이 들다 feel hollow / ~감 a sense of emptiness; a hollow feeling.

공헌(貢獻) (a) contribution; service. ¶ ~하다 contribute (*to*); make a contribution (*to*) / 시 발전에 크게 ~하다 make a great contribution to the development of the city.

공화(共和) ¶ ~의 republican. ‖ ~국 a republic / ~당 (미국의) the Republican Party; the Grand Old Party (~ 의원 a Republican) / ~정치 republican government / ~제 republican-

과년하다

ism.

공황(恐慌) a panic; consternation. ¶ ~을 가져오다 bring on (cause) a panic / ~을 이겨내다 get over a crisis. ‖ 금융 ~ a financial panic.

공회전(空回轉) 《엔진의》 the idling of an engine. ¶ ~시키다 《엔진의》 keep an engine idling.

공훈(功勳) merits; an exploit. ¶ ~을 세우다 perform meritorious deeds.

공휴일(公休日) 《법정의》a (legal) holiday; a red-letter day (일반적인). …곶 a cape; a headland.

곶감 a dried persimmon.

과(科) 《학과의》a department; 《과정》a course / 《동식물의》 a family. ¶ 고양이 ~의 동물 an animal in the cat family. ‖ 문~ the literature [science] course / 영어 ~ the English Department.

과(課) 《학과》a lesson; 《분과》 a section. ¶ 제2~ Lesson 2 (two) / ~원 the staff of a section / ~ 장 the head of a section / 인사~ the personnel section.

과 and; 《함께·대항·분리·비교》 with; against; from. ¶ 손 ~ 발 hand and foot / 그 사람 ~ 같이 가다 go with him / 남 ~ 관계를 끊다 break with *a person*.

과감(果敢) ¶ ~한 daring; bold.

과객(過客) a passer-by; a foot passenger.

과거(科擧) *kwagŏ*, the state examination to recruit ranking officials during the *Chosŏn* Dynasty.

과거(過去) the past (days); 《과거 생활》 *one's* past; 《시제의》 the past tense. ¶ ~가 있는 남자 a man with a (shady) past / ~를 묻지 마라 Let bygones be bygones. ‖ ~분사 a past participle / ~완료 the past perfect / ~지사 past events; bygones.

과격(過激) ¶ ~한 excessive; violent; radical; extreme / ~한 수단 a drastic measure / ~한 사상 a radical idea. ‖ ~분자 a radical element / ~주의 extremism; radicalism / ~파 the radicals; the extremists.

과꽃 [榴] A China aster.

과납(過納) ¶ ~하다 pay in excess. ‖ ~액 an amount paid in excess.

과녁 a target; a mark. ¶ ~을 맞히다 [못 맞히다] hit (miss) the target.

과년도(過年度) last (the previous) year; 《회계상의》 the past financial (fiscal) year.

과년하다(過年 —) (be) past the marriageable age. ¶ 과년한 처녀 an old maid.

과념(過念) ~하다 mind excessively; worry too much.
과다(過多) excess; overplus. ¶~한 excessive; superabundant. ‖ ~청구 overcharge / 공급~ an excess of supply; oversupply / 영양~ an excess of nutrition.
과단(果斷) ¶~한 decisive; resolute. / ~성 decisiveness; promptness in decision 《~성 있는 사람 a man of decision / ~성이 없다 lack decision》.
과당(果糖) fruit sugar; fructose.
과당경쟁(過當競爭) excessive (cutthroat) competition.
과대(過大) ¶~한 [하게] excessive(-ly); too much 《나에게 ~한 요구를 마라 make an excessive demand / 그에게 ~한 기대를 걸지 마라 Don't expect too much of him. / ~시 overrating / ~평가 overestimation 《능력을 ~평가하다 overestimate *one's* ability》.
과대(誇大) ~ 과장(誇張). ‖ ~광고 an extravagant advertisement 《口》 a puff / ~망상 megalomania / ~망상환자 a megalomaniac.
과도(果刀) a fruit knife.
과도(過度) excess. ¶~한 excessive; immoderate; too much / ~하게 excessively; immoderately; too much 《~하게 먹다 eat too much / ~한 노동 excessive work.
과도(過渡) ¶~내각 [정부] an interim [a caretaker] cabinet (government).
과도기(過渡期) a transitional period (stage); an age [a period] of transition. ¶한국의 경제는 지금 ~에 있다 Korea's economy is now in a period of transition. ‖ ~현상 a transient phenomenon.
과두정치(寡頭政治) oligarchy. [non.
과람하다(過濫—) be more than *one* deserves.
과로(過勞) excessive labor; overwork. ¶~하다 work too hard; overwork *oneself*.
과료(科料) a fine. ¶~에 처하다 fine; impose a fine 《upon》.
과립(顆粒) a granule. ¶~모양의 granular.
과목(科目) a subject; a lesson; a course 《과정》; a curriculum 《전과목》; items 《항목》.
과묵(寡默) taciturnity. ¶~한 reserved; taciturn; reticent.
과문하다(寡聞—) be ill-informed 《as to》; have little knowledge
과물(果物) ☞ 과일. [《of》.
과민(過敏) ¶~한 nervous; too sensitive; oversensitive; keen. ¶그는 신경 ~이다 He is too (all) nervous. ‖ ~증 《醫》 hypersensitivity 《to》.
과밀(過密) overcrowding; overpopulation 《인구의》. ‖ ~도시 an overpopulated 《overcrowed》 city.
과반수(過半數) the majority; 《대부분》 the greater part 《number》 《of》. ¶~를 얻다 get 《win, obtain》 a majority / ~를 차지하다 hold a majority 《*in the Assembly*》.
과보(果報) 《佛》 retribution.
과부(寡婦) a widow. ¶~로 사는 여자 a woman living in widowhood / ~가 되다 be widowed; lose *one's* husband.
과부족(過不足) overs and shorts. ¶~없이 neither too much nor too less / 분량은 ~이 없다 The quantity is just enough.
과분(過分) ¶~한 excessive; undue; undeserved / ~한 영광 an undeserved honor.
과산화(過酸化) ‖ ~망간 manganese dioxide / ~물 peroxides / ~수소 hydrogen peroxide.
과세(過歲) ~하다 greet 《celebrate》 the New Year.
과세(課稅) taxation. ~하다 tax; impose a tax 《on》. ¶ 수입품에 ~하다 tax imported goods. ‖ ~율 the tax rate / ~품 an article subject to taxation; a customable goods 《美》 누진~ progressive taxation / 인정~ optional taxation / 중~ heavy taxation.
과소(過小) ¶~한 too small.
과소(過少) ¶~한 too little 《small》. ‖ ~평가 underestimation 《~평가하다 underrate; underestimate》.
과소(過疎) 《인구의》 depopulation. ¶~된 depopulated 《*areas*》 / 인구 ~된 지역 a sparsely populated area; a depopulated area.
과소비(過消費) overconsumption; conspicuous consumption.
과속(過速) overspeed. ¶~으로 달리다 overspeed. ‖ ~차량 an overspeeding vehicle.
과수(果樹) a fruit tree. ‖ ~원 an orchard / ~재배 fruit culture.
과시(誇示) ~하다 display; show off; make a display of. ¶권력을 ~하다 show off *one's* authority.
과식(過食) ~하다 overeat *oneself*; eat too much. ¶그는 ~해서 배탈이 났다 He overeat and had a stomach upset.
과신(過信) overconfidence. ~하다 put 《place》 too much confidence 《*in*》; be overconfident 《*of*》. ¶자기 실력을 ~하다 overestimate *one's* own ability; have too much confidence in *oneself*.
과실(果實) ☞ 과일. ¶법정~ legal fruits / ~주 fruit wine.
과실(過失) ① 《과오》 a fault; a

과언(過言) 《지나친 말》 saying too much; 《과장》 exaggeration. ¶ …이라 해도 ~이 아니다 It is not too much (no exaggeration) to say that…

과업(課業) ① 《학업》 a lesson; schoolwork; a task. ② 《임무》 a task; a duty. ~을 맡기다 assign 《a person》 to a task / ~을 완수하다 perform (carry out) one's duties.

과연(果然) as expected; just as one thought; sure enough; really 《정말》. ¶ ~ 그는 거기 있었다 Sure enough, there he was.

과열(過熱) ~하다 overheat. ¶ ~된 경제 an overheated economy / 한국 경제는 ~되어 있다 The Korean economy is overheating.

과오(過誤) a fault; an error; a mistake. ¶ ~를 깨닫다 see the error of one's ways / ~를 저지르다 commit a fault; make a mistake.

과외(課外) ¶ ~의 extracurricular; extraclassroom. ‖ ~공부 out-of-school studies / ~수업 an extracurricular lesson / ~활동 extracurricular (after-school) activities.

과욕(過慾) avarice; greed. ¶ ~을 부리다 be greedy (avaricious, covetous) 《of》; expect too much.

과욕(寡慾) ¶ ~한 unselfish; disinterested / ~한 사람 a man of few wants.

과용하다(過用-) spend 《money》 too much (in excess); take an overdose of 《heroin》.

과원(課員) a member of the section staff; a staff of a section.

과유불급(過猶不及) Too much is as bad as too little.

과음(過飮) excessive drinking. ~하다 drink too much; drink to excess; overdrink oneself.

과인산(過燐酸) 【化】 perphosphoric acid. ¶ ~비료 a superphosphate.

과일 a fruit; fruit(age) 《총칭》. ¶ ~을 따다 pick fruit / ~을 맺다 bear fruit. ‖ ~상 a fruit shop (store) 《가게》; a fruit dealer (seller) 《사람》.

과잉(過剩) an excess; a surplus. ¶ ~의 surplus; superfluous.

과자(菓子) 《총칭》 confectionery; 《생과자》 cake; 《파이 따위》 pastry; cookie; biscuit; cracker. ¶ ~점 a confectionery; a candy store 《美》.

과장(誇張) exaggeration. ~하다 exaggerate; overstate. ¶ ~된 사실을 ~하는 버릇이 있다 He is given to exaggeration. / 나는 전혀 ~해서 말하는 것이 아니다 I'm not exaggerating (stretching it) at all.

과장(課長) a section(al) chief.

과정(過程) a process; a course. ¶ 생산(진화, 심의)의 ~ the process of production (evolution, discussion).

과정(課程) a course; a curriculum. ¶ 중학 ~를 마치다 finish the course of junior high school.

과제(課題) a subject; a theme; 《임무》 a task; an assignment; 《숙제》 homework; 《문제》 a problem. ¶ 논문의 ~ the subject of one's thesis / 여름방학 ~ summer homework; a summer assignment / 연구 ~ a study assignment / 우리는 당면 ~ 해결에 최선을 다해야 한다 We must do our best to solve the problems which confront us now.

과줄 a fried cake made of flour, honey and oil.

과중(過重) ¶ ~한 too heavy; burdensome / ~한 노동 overwork / ~한 부담(책임) too heavy a burden (responsibility).

과즙(果汁) fruit juice.

과찬(過讚) ~하다 praise excessively; overpraise.

과태료(過怠料) a fine for default; a negligence fine.

과표(課標) 《과세표준》 a standard of assessment. ¶ ~액 the taxable amount.

과하다(過-) (be) too much; excessive; undue. ¶ 과하게 to excess; excessively; unduly / 술을 과하게 마시다 drink too much; drink to excess / 과한 부담을 지우다 overtask; impose a heavy burden 《on》 / 농담이 ~ carry a joke too far.

과하다(課-) impose; assign. ¶ 무거운 세금을 ~ impose a heavy tax / 과해진 임무를 다하다 perform the duty that has been assigned 《you》.

과학(科學) science. ¶ ~화하다 make scientific / ~적(으로) scientific(ally) / ~적인 조사 결과, 사고 원인이 밝혀졌다 A scientific investigation cleared up the cause of the accident. ‖ ~기술 science technique / ~기술처 the Ministry of Science and Technology / ~용어 a scientific term /

과학 ~자 a scientist / ~전[무기] scientific warfare [weapon] / 한국~ 기술연구원 the Korea Institute of Science and Technology (생략 KIST) / 한국 ~기술원 the Korea Advanced Institute for Science and Technology (생략 KAIST).

과히(過一) 《너무》 too (much); excessively; overly; to excess; 《부정과 함께》 (not) very (quite); (not) so much. ¶ ~ 걱정 마라 Take it easy! / ~ 좋지 않다 be not very (so) good.

관(棺) a coffin. ¶ 꽃으로 장식된 ~ a flower-decked coffin.

관(管) a pipe; a tube. 「rant.

관(館) a Korean-style restau-

관(貫) 《무게》 a kwan (=3.75kg).

…관(觀) a view; an outlook. ¶ 사회~ one's view of social life / 세계~ an outlook on the world.

관개(灌漑) irrigation; watering. ~하다 irrigate; water. ¶ ~공사 irrigation works / ~용수 irrigation water. 「ence (총칭).

관객(觀客) a spectator; the audi-

관건(關鍵) 《핵심》 a key (pivotal) point. ¶ 문제의 ~를 쥐다 hold the key to the question / …해결의 ~을 쥐다 hold the key to the solution of.

관계(官界) the official world; official circles; officialdom. ¶ ~에 있다 (들어가다) be in (go into) government service.

관계(關係) ① 《관련》 relation; (a) connection; (a) relationship (연고). ~하다 be related (to); be connected (with); have 《something》 to do with. ¶ 친자 ~ a parent-child relationship / ~가 없다 have no relation (to); have nothing to do with; be cut off 《with》 / ~를 끊다 sever (cut off) one's connection 《with》 / ~를 수립하다 establish 《trade》 relations 《with》 / 우호~를 유지하나 maintain friendly relations 《with a country》 / 수요는 공급과 ~가 있다 Demand bears a relation to supply. ¶ ~대명사 a relative pronoun / ~법규 the related laws and regulations / ~서류 the related (relevant) documents / 외교~ diplomatic relations / 인과~ the relation between cause and effect / 한미~ Korea-U.S. relations. ② 《관여》 (a) participation; concern; 《연루》 involvement. ~하다 participate (take part) in 《a plot》; be concerned (in); be involved (in). ¶ 경영에 ~하다 participate in the management / 나는 그 추문과 ~가 없다 I'm not concerned with the scandal. or The scandal doesn't concern me. ∥ ~기관[당국] the organiza-

tions [authorities] concerned / ~자 a person [party] concerned; an interested party (이해의). ③ 《영향》 influence; effect. ~하다 affect; have influence on. ¶ 물가 상승은 국민 생활에 직접 ~된다 A rise in prices has a direct influence on people's way of life.

관공(官公) ∥ ~리 public officials [servants] / ~서 government and municipal offices.

관광(觀光) sightseeing; tourism. ~하다 go sightseeing; do [see] the sights 《of》. ¶ ~의 계절 a tourist season / ~의 명소 tourist attractions / 경주로 ~하러 가다 go to Kyŏngju to see the sights. ∥ ~객 a sightseer; a tourist / ~버스 a sightseeing bus / ~사업 the tourist industry; tourism / ~시설 tourist facilities / ~여행을 하다 take a sightseeing trip / ~지 (단, 호텔, 선) a tourist resort (party, hotel, ship) / ~코스 a tourist route.

관구(管區) a district (under jurisdiction); a jurisdiction.

관군(官軍) the government forces [troops]. 「[power].

관권(官權) government authority

관급(官給) government supply [issue]. ∥ ~품 government issue articles (美).

관기(官紀) official discipline. ∥ ~문란 a laxity in official discipline.

관내(管內) (an area) within the jurisdiction 《of》. ¶ ~를 순시하다 make a tour of inspection through one's (area of) jurisdiction.

관념(觀念) ① 《의식》 a sense. ¶ 시간 ~이 없다 have no sense of time. ∥ 도의 ~ a moral sense / 의무 ~ a sense of duty [responsibility]. ② 《철학·심리학의》 an idea; a conception (개념). ¶ ~적인 ideal / 추상적 ~ an abstract idea / ~의 유희 a mere abstraction. ∥ ~론 idealism.

관능(官能) sense. ¶ ~적인 sensuous (감각적); sensual (육감적) / ~적인 쾌락 sensual pleasure / ~적 ~ a sensual dance. ∥ ~주의 sensualism.

관대(寬大) broad-mindedness; generosity; tolerance. ¶ ~한 broad-minded; generous; liberal; tolerant / ~히 generously; liberally; tolerantly / ~한 태도 a generous attitude / ~한 처분 lenient dealing 《~한 처분을 탄원하다 plead for leniency》.

관등(官等) official rank. ∥ ~성명

관등 *one's* official rank and name.

관등(觀燈) the celebration of the birthday of *Buddha*; the Lantern Festival.

관람(觀覽) inspection; viewing. ¶ ~하다 see; view; watch. ¶ ~이 자유롭다 be open to visitors (the public). ‖ ~객 a spectator; a visitor / ~권 an admission ticket / ~료 admission fee / ~석 《극장의》 a seat; a box; 《야구장 따위의》 a stand.

관련(關聯) relation; connection. ~하다 relate 《to》; be related 《to》; be connected 《with》. ¶ ~와 ~하여 in connection with...; in relation to.... ‖ ~성 relevance.

관례(冠禮) a ceremony to celebrate 《*a person's*》 coming of age.

관례(慣例) a custom; a usage; a usual practice; a precedent (선례). ¶ 사회의 ~ a social custom (code) / ~에 따라 in accordance with the custom / ~을 따르다 (를 깨다) follow (break) custom / ...하는 것이 ~이다 It is customary with us to *do*....

관록(官祿) a stipend; a salary.

관록(貫祿) dignity; weight. ¶ ~이 붙다 gain in dignity.

관료(官僚) bureaucracy; officialdom; 《사람》 a bureaucrat. ~적인 bureaucratic. ‖ ~주의 bureaucratism.

관류하다(貫流一) run (flow) through.

관리(官吏) a government official; a public servant. ¶ ~가 되다 enter government service.

관리(管理) 《경영·운영》 management; administration; control; 《보관》 charge; care. ~하다 administer; manage; control; take charge of. ¶ 정부 ~하에 있다 be under government control. ‖ ~가격 an administered price / ~인 〔자〕 a manager; an administrator; a superintendant; a custodian(공공시설의); a caretaker(집); an executor(유산의) / ~직 an administrative post; the managerial class(집합적) / 생산 〔노무〕~ production (labor) management / 품질~ quality control.

관립(官立) ¶ ~의 government(al).

관망(觀望) ~하다 observe; watch; 《형세를》 wait and see; sit on the fence. ¶ 사태의 추이를 ~하다 watch the course of events / ~적 태도를 취하다 take a wait-and-see attitude.

관명(官名) an official title. ¶ ~을 사칭하다 assume an official title.

관명(官命) (by) official (government) orders.

관모(冠毛) [植] a pappus; [動] a crest.

관목(灌木) a shrub; a bush.

관문(關門) a barrier; a gateway 《to》; a difficulty (어려움). ¶ 최후의 ~을 통과하다 get through the entrance exam 《and enter S University》.

관물(官物) government property; article supplied by the government.

관민(官民) officials and people; the government and the people. ¶ ~이 협력하여 by the united efforts of government and people. ⌜cial quarters.

관변(官邊) government circles; offi-

관보(官報) the official gazette. ¶ ~로 발표하다 gazette; announce in the official gazette / ~에 실리다 be published in the official gazette.

관복(官服) an official outfit.

관비(官費) government expense(s). ¶ ~로 유학하다 study abroad at government expense. ‖ ~유학생 a student sent abroad by the government.

관사(官舍) an official residence.

관사(冠詞) an article. ‖ 정 [부정]~ a definite (an indefinite) article.

관상(冠狀) ¶ ~의 coronary; coronal; crown-shaped. ‖ ~동맥〔정맥〕 the coronary arteries (veins).

관상(管狀) ¶ ~의 tubular; tubulous; tube-shaped.

관상(觀相) phrenological interpretation. ¶ ~을 보다 tell 《*a person's*》 fortune by physiognomy (남의); get 《*a person*》 to tell one's fortune by physiognomy (자기의). ‖ ~술 physiognomy; phrenology / ~쟁이 a physiognomist; a phrenologist.

관상(觀象) meteorological observation. ‖ ~대 a weather station; a meteorological observatory.

관상(觀賞) ~하다 admire; enjoy. ‖ ~식물 a decorative plant / ~어 an aquarium fish.

관서(官署) a government office.

관선(官選) ¶ ~의 chosen (appointed) by the government. ‖ ~이사 a government-appointed trustee. ⌜the government.

관설(官設) ¶ ~의 established by

관성(慣性) [理] inertia. ‖ ~의 법칙 the law of inertia. / ~유도 inertial guidance.

관세(關稅) customs (duties); a (customs) tariff; a duty. ¶ ~를 부과하다 impose (levy) a duty 《on》 / ~를 물지 않는 duty-free / ~를 무는 dutiable / 「이 제

관세음보살(觀世音菩薩) the Buddhist Goddess of Mercy.

관수(官需) an official demand. ‖ ~물자 supplies for government use.

관습(慣習) a custom; a convention (인습). ‖ ~을 깨다 (지키다) break (keep up) an old custom. ‖ ~법 the customary (common) law.

관심(關心) concern; interest. ¶…에 ~을 갖다 be interested in (concerned with); take interest in / …에 ~이 없다 be indifferent to; take no interest in / 그는 UFO에 ~이 있다 He is interested in UFO's. ‖ ~사 a matter of concern.

관악(管樂) pipe-music; wind music. ‖ ~기 a wind instrument.

관업(官業) a government enterprise.

관여(關與) participation. ~하다 participate (take part, have a share) 《in》.

관영(官營) ☞ 국영(國營).

관용(官用) 《용무》 government (official) business (duty); 《사용》 official use. ¶ ~으로 on official business (use). ‖ ~차 an official vehicle.

관용(寬容) tolerance; generosity. ~하다 tolerate; be generous. ¶ ~의 정신 the spirit of tolerance.

관용(慣用) usage; common use. ¶ ~이 common; usual; idiomatic (이구나). ‖ ~어구 an idiomatic expression; an idiom.

관위(官位) official rank.

관인(官印) an official (a government) seal. ¶ ~을 찍다 affix an official seal.   [one's head.

관자놀이(貫子 ~) the temple of

관작(官爵) an office and rank; official rank. ¶ ~을 주다 grant 《a person》 official rank.

관장(管掌) management; charge; control. ~하다 manage; take charge of; have 《a matter》 in charge. ¶ ~업무 the business in one's charge.

관장(館長) a director; a (chief) librarian (도서관의); a curator (박물관의).

관장(灌腸) (an) enema. ~하다 give an enema to 《a person》. ‖ ~기 an enema.

관재(管財) administration of property. ~하다 manage (administer) property. ‖ ~국 the bureau of property custody (a trustee (공공물의); an administrator (유산의); a receiver (청산시의); a property custodian (정부 등의).

관저(官邸) an official residence. ¶ 대통령 ~ the Presidential residence.

관전(觀戰) ~하다 witness a battle; watch a game (경기를). ‖ ~기 a witness's account 《of a chess match》.

관절(關節) 【解】 a joint; an articulation. ¶ ~의 articular / ~을 삐다 dislocate a joint. ‖ ~류머티즘 articular (joint) rheumatism / ~염 arthritis / ~통 arthralgia.

관점(觀點) a point of view; a viewpoint; a standpoint. ¶ 이 ~에서 from this viewpoint / ~이 다르다 have a different point of view; differ in opinion 《from》.

관제(官製) ~의 government-made; manufactured by the government. ¶ ~데모 a government-inspired demonstration / ~엽서 a postal card 《美》; a postcard 《英》.

관제(管制) control; controlling. ‖ ~사 a controller / ~장치 a controlling gear / ~탑 a control tower (공항의).

관조(觀照) 【佛】 contemplation; meditation. ~하다 contemplate. ¶ 미의 ~ contemplation of beauty.

관존민비(官尊民卑) the preponderance of official power. ¶ ~의 습관 custom of putting the Government above the people.

관중(觀衆) spectators; an audience; onlookers.

관직(官職) government service; an official post. ¶ ~에 있다 be in the government service.

관찰(觀察) observation. ~하다 observe; watch closely; 《사물을 정확히》 ~하다 observe things accurately / ~기록을 쓰다 write one's observations 《on birds》. ‖ ~력 the power of observation / ~안 an observing eye / ~자 an observer.   [governor.

관찰사(觀察使) 【史】 a (provincial)

관철(貫徹) accomplishment; realization. ~하다 accomplish; realize; carry out. ¶ 목적을 ~하다 attain one's object / 초지를 ~하다 realize (carry out) one's original purpose.

관청(官廳) a government office (agency). ‖ ~가 a government office quarter / ~스타일 [식] officialism; red-tapism / ~용어 offi-

cialese.
관측(觀測) observation. ~하다 observe; survey. ¶ 회망적 ~ wishful thinking. ‖ ~기구 an observation balloon; (비유적) a trial balloon / ~소 an observatory / ~자 an observer.
관통(貫通; 뚫음) penetration. ~하다 pierce; penetrate; pass through; shoot through (탄알이). ~총상 a piercing bullet wound / 가슴에 ~상을 입다 be shot through the chest / 터널이 ~되었다 The tunnel was completed.
관포지교(管鮑之交) 《중국 고사에서》 an intimate (inseparable) friendship.
관하(管下) ¶ ~의〔에〕 under the jurisdiction (control) of.
관하다(關一) ① 《관계》 be connected (concerned) with; concern; be related to. …에 관하여〔는〕 about; on; regarding; concerning / …에 관한 about; on; relating to / …에 관한 한 as (so) far as (it is) concerned / 그 점에 관해서 on that point; in that connection / 철학에 관한 책 a book on philosophy / 그 건에 관하여는 아무 정보도 없다 We have no information on (about) the matter. ② 《영향》 affect; concern. ¶ 명예에 관한 문제 a question affecting one's honor.
관할(管轄) jurisdiction; control. ~하다 have (exercise) jurisdiction (over); control. ¶ …의 ~하에 있다 be (fall) under the jurisdiction (control) of…. ‖ ~관청 the competent (proper) authorities / ~구역 the district (sphere) of jurisdiction / ~권 jurisdiction / ~다툼 a jurisdictional dispute / ~서 the police station concerned.
관함식(觀艦式) a naval review.
관행(慣行) (a) habitual practice; a custom; a practice. ¶ ~적 customary / 국제적 ~ an international practice.
관향(貫鄕) one's ancestral home.
관허(官許) government permission. ¶ ~의 licensed. ~요금 (government)-licensed charge.
관헌(官憲) the authorities; the officials.
관현악(管絃樂) orchestral music. ¶ ~의 반주 an orchestral accompaniment / ~단 an orchestra.
관혼상제(冠婚喪祭) ceremonial occasions.
괄괄하다 《성질이》 (be) brisk; spirited; fiery; impetuous; hot-tempered.
괄다 《화력이》 (be) strong; high.

괄시(恝視) ~하다 《박대》 treat 《a person》 coldly; 《경멸》 hold 《a person》 in contempt; make light of.
괄약근(括約筋) a sphincter (muscle). ¶ 항문의 ~ the anal sphincter.
괄태충(括胎蟲) 〖動〗 a slug.
괄호(括弧) 《둥근》 parenthesis / 《각》 brackets; 《긴》 a brace. ‖ ~ 속에 넣다 put 《a word》 in parentheses.
광(光) light; brightness. ☞ 빛, 광택. ‖ ~메모리 (an) optical memory. 〔width; breadth.〕
광(廣; 넓이) area; extent; 《너비》
광(鑛) 《경》 a pit; a mine; 《덩어리》 a (mineral) ore.
…광(狂) a fan; a maniac; a fanatic; an addict. ¶ 댄스 ~ a dance maniac / 영화〔야구〕~ a movie〔baseball〕fan.
광각(光角) 〖理〗 an optic angle.
광각렌즈(廣角—) a wide-angle lens.
광갱(鑛坑) a mine (shaft); a pit.
광견(狂犬) a mad dog. ‖ ~병 rabies; hydrophobia.
광경(光景) a sight; a view; a scene. ¶ 아름다운 ~ a beautiful sight / 참담한 ~ a miserable (sad) scene.
광고(廣告) an advertisement; an ad (口); publicity (선전); 《고지》 an announcement; a notice. ¶ ~하다 advertise; announce. ¶ 전면에 걸친 ~《흔히 신문의》a full-page advertisement / 3행 ~ classified ads / H신문에 ~를 내다 put (run) an advertisement in the H / 그것은 우리 회사의 좋은 ~가 된다 That will make our firm better known to the public. ‖ ~대리점 an advertising agent / ~란 an ad column / ~료 advertisement rates / ~매체 the advertising media / ~맨 an adperson / ~방송 a commercial broadcast / ~전단 a (show) bill; a handbill / ~탑 a poster column; an advertising tower (pillar)(옥외).
광공업(鑛工業) the mining and manufacturing industries.
광구(鑛區) 〖鑛〗 a mining area.
광궤(廣軌) a broad gauge. ‖ ~철도 a broad-gauge railroad.
광기(狂氣) madness; insanity. ¶ ~의 insane; mad; crazy / ~를 일으키다 become mad (insane).
광나다(光—) (be) glossy; lustrous; polished. 〔glossy.〕
광내다(光—) polish up; make
광년(光年) 〖天〗 a light-year.
광대 a feat actor (actress); an acrobatic (a stunt) performer (곡예); a mask performer (탈춤).
광대(廣大) ¶ ~한 immense; vast; extensive / ~무변한 (vast and)

광대뼈 (光大뼈) the cheekbones; the malar bone. ¶ ~가 나온 사람 a person with high cheekbones.
광도 (光度) 【理】 luminous intensity; luminosity; (the degree of) brightness. ¶ 별의 ~ the brightness of a star. ‖ ~계 a photometer.
광독 (鑛毒) mineral pollution; copper poisoning. ¶ ~의 피해 damage from mine pollution.
광란 (狂亂) madness; craziness. ~하다 go mad (crazy) 《with grief》; become frantic. ¶ 반~의 half-mad; half-crazy.
광막 (廣漠) ¶ ~한 vast; wide; boundless / ~한 땅 a wide spread of land / ~한 평원 a vast expanse of plains.
광맥 (鑛脈) a vein (of ore); a lode. ¶ ~을 찾아내다 strike a vein of gold.
광명 (光明)(光) light; (희망) hope; a bright future. ¶ 삶에서 한 가닥의 ~을 보다 find a ray (gleam) of hope in life / 그녀의 앞날에는 ~이 있다 She has a bright future before her.
광목 (廣木) cotton cloth.
광물 (鑛物) a mineral. ¶ ~계 the mineral kingdom / ~자원 mineral resources / ~질 mineral matter / ~학 mineralogy.
광범 (廣範) ¶ ~한 extensive; wide; broad; far-reaching / ~한 지식 extensive knowledge / ~한 영향을 미치다 exert a far-reaching influence 《on, over》.
광범위 (廣範圍) 〔지역〕 a large (wide) area; 〔넓은 범위〕 a large extent; a wide range. ¶ ~한 파괴 widespread destruction / ~에 걸치다 cover (extend over) a wide area.
광복 (光復) the restoration of independence. ~하다 regain 《a country's》 independence. ‖ ~절 Independence (Liberation) Day of Korea.
광부 (鑛夫) a miner; a mineworker.
광분 (狂奔) ~하다 make desperate (frantic) efforts 《to do》; be very busy 《in doing》; busy oneself about 《something》.
광산 (鑛山) a mine. ¶ ~을 채굴하다 work a mine. ‖ ~공학 mining engineering / ~기사 a mining engineer / ~노동자 a miner; a mineworker / ~물 mineral products / ~업 the mining industry / ~채굴권 mining concessions.
광상 (鑛床) (mineral) deposits.
광상곡 (狂想曲) a rhapsody.
광석 (鑛石) a mineral; an ore; a crystal (라디오의). ‖ ~검파기 〔수신기〕 a crystal detector (set).

광선 (光線) light; a ray; a beam. ‖ ~분석 spectrum analysis / ~요법 phototherapy.
광섬유 (光纖維) optical fiber.
광속 (光束) 【理】 luminous flux.
광속 (光速) the velocity of light; light speed.
광신 (狂信) fanaticism. ¶ ~적인 fanatic(al). ‖ ~자 a fanatic.
광야 (曠野) a wild (desolate) plain; a wilderness; the wilds.
광양자 (光量子), **광자** (光子) 【理】 a photon; light quantum. 〔marks.
광언 (狂言) mad talk; crazy re-
광업 (鑛業) mining (industry). ‖ ~권 a mining right / ~소 a mining station (office) / ~주(가) a mine owner (operator).
광역 (廣域) a wide (large) area. ‖ ~경제 great-sphere economy / ~도시 a metropolitan city / ~수사 a search 《for a criminal》 conducted over a wide area / ~지방의회선거 a large-unit local election / ~행정 integrated administration of a large region.
광열 (光熱) light and heat. ‖ ~비 lighting and heating expenses.
광영 (光榮) honor; glory. ☞ 영광.
광우리 ☞ 광주리.
광원 (光源) a source of light; a luminous source; an illuminant.
광의 (廣義) a broad sense. ¶ ~로 해석하다 interpret 《it》 in a broad sense. 〔lunatic.
광인 (狂人) an insane person; a
광장 (廣場) an open space; a plaza; a (public) square. ‖ ~공포증 agoraphobia.
광재 (鑛滓) slag; dross.
광적 (狂的) mad; insane; lunatic; wild; frantic.
광전 (光電) 【電】 photoelectricity. ¶ ~관 a phototube; a cathode-ray tube(TV의) / ~자 a photoelectron / ~지 a photovoltaic cell; a photocell.
광주리 a round wicker (bamboo) basket. ¶ ~장수 a peddler carrying her wares in a basket
광증 (狂症) ☞ 광기. 〔on her head.
광차 (鑛車) a mine car.
광채 (光彩) luster; brilliancy. ¶ ~가 나다 be brilliant (lustrous); show luster; shine / ~를 발하다 shed luster; shine.
광천 (鑛泉) a mineral spring; mineral water (광수).
광체 (光體) a luminous body.
광치다 〜해버리다. 〔puter.
광컴퓨터 (光—) an optical com-
광태 (狂態) shameful (crazy) conduct. ¶ ~를 부리다 behave disgracefully; make a scene; get wild in drink(취해서).

광택(光澤) luster; gross; shine. ¶ ~ 있는 lustrous; glossy / ~을 내다 polish; burnish; shine.
광통신(光通信) optical communication.
광파(光波)【理】a light wave.
광포(狂暴) ~한 furious; frenzied; outrageous; violent.
광풍(狂風) a raging wind.
광학(光學) optics; optical science. ‖ ~기계 an optical instrument / ~병기 optical weapon.
광합성(光合成)【植】photosynthesis. ‖ ~세균 photosynthetic bacteria.
광활(廣闊) spaciousness; extensiveness. ¶ ~한 spacious; extensive; wide.
광휘(光輝) brilliance; glory; splendor. ¶ ~ 있는 brilliant; splendid.
광희(狂喜) wild joy; (a) rapture; (an) ecstasy. ~하다 go (be) mad with joy; be in raptures.
괘념(掛念) ~하다 mind; care; worry about.
괘도(掛圖) a wall map (chart) (지도); a hanging scroll (건축).
괘력(掛曆) a wall calendar.
괘선(罫線) a ruled line; a rule mark. ‖ ~지 ruled (lined) paper.
괘씸하다 (be) rude; impertinent; unpardonable; ungrateful; outrageous. ¶ 괘씸한 짓 an improper act; an offensive deed; outrageous doings / 괘씸하게 굴다 behave impertinently.
괘종(掛鐘) a (wall) clock.
괜찮다 ① (쓸만하다) (be) passable; not so bad; good; will do. ¶ 맛이 ~ taste quite good. ② (상관없다) do not care (mind); may; can; be all right. ¶ 괜찮으시다면 if you don't mind...; if it is convenient to you / 비가 와도 ~ I don't care if it rains. or I am all right. or I don't mind.
괭이(농기구) a hoe; a mattock.
괴경(塊莖)【植】a tuber. ‖ ~식물 a tuber plant.
괴괴하다 (be) quiet; calm; deserted.
괴근(塊根)【植】a tuberous root.
괴금(塊金) a nugget.
괴나리봇짐 a traveller's back bundle.
괴다¹ (물이) gather; form a puddle; collect; stagnate; stay. ¶ 빗물이 웅덩이에 ~ rain water collects (forms a puddle) in a hollow.
괴다² (받치다) support; prop; (쌓다) pile up (*nuts*) on the plate.
괴담(怪談) a ghost (weird) story.
괴도(怪盜) a mysterious (phantom) thief.
괴력(怪力) superhuman strength.
괴로움(오뇌) agony; trouble; (곤고) sufferings; distress; hardship;《고통》pain. ¶ 삶의 ~ worries (troubles) of life / 마음의 ~ anguish of heart; mental affliction / 무슨 ~이 있느냐 What's bothering (troubling) you?
괴로워하다 be troubled (*with*); be worried (*about*); suffer (*from*); be sick at heart; be cursed with. ¶ 그 문제로 ~ be troubled (worried) about the matter / 무엇으로 괴로워하고 있느냐 What are you worried about?
괴롭다 (고통) (be) painful; distressing; trying; tormenting; (곤란) (be) hard; difficult; (경제적으로) be straitened; needy; (거북하다) (be) awkward; embarrassing. ¶ 괴로운 입장 a painful (an awkward) position / 괴로운 마음 a troubled heart / 괴로운 나머지 driven by pain; in *one's* distress.
괴롭히다 trouble; annoy; worry; bother; harass;《고통으로》afflict; give《*a person*》pain. ¶ 적을 ~ harass the enemy / 마음을 ~ worry *oneself* about; be concerned about《*a matter*》/ 기묘한 질문으로 선생님을 ~ trouble (bother) teachers with strange questions.
괴뢰(傀儡)《꼭두각시》a puppet. ‖ ~정부 a puppet government.
괴멸(壞滅) distruction; annihilation (전멸). ~하다 be destroyed (ruined, annihilated). ¶ ~시키다 destroy; annihilate.
괴물(怪物) a monster; (사람) a mysterious person.
괴변(怪變) a strange accident; a curious affair.
괴상(怪常) ~한 일 a strange (queer) thing; an oddity / ~하게 여기다 think it strange that...
괴상(塊狀) ~의 massive. ‖ ~암(巖) a massive rock / ~용암 block lava.
괴수(怪獸) a monster; a monstrous animal.
괴수(魁首) the ringleader.
괴승아(怪勝兒) a wood sorrel; an oxalis.
괴이하다(怪異-) (be) mysterious; strange; odd; funny.
괴질(怪疾) a mystery disease; an unidentified disease.
괴짜 an odd (eccentric) person; a queer sort of fellow.
괴팍하다 fastidious; finicky; fussy; perverse; eccentric. ¶ 괴팍한 사람 a fastidious (finicky) person / 괴팍한 성미 a fussy temperament.
괴한(怪漢) a suspicious fellow.
괴혈병(壞血病)【醫】scurvy.
괴화(怪火) a mysterious fire; a fire of unknown origin.
굄돌 a stone prop (support).
굉굉하다(轟轟—) (be) thunderous;

굉음(轟音) a roaring sound; a deafening roar; an earsplitting sound. ¶ ~을 내다 make (produce) a thundering noise.

굉장하다(宏壯-) 〔넓고 큰〕 (be) grand; magnificent; imposing; 〔엄청난〕 (be) terrible; awful; tremendous. ¶ 굉장히 magnificently; awfully / 굉장한 저택 a magnificent residence; a stately mansion / 굉장한 부자 an awfully rich man / 굉장히 가난하다 be deadly poor / 굉장히 덥다 be awfully hot / 굉장히 아름답다 be strikingly beautiful.

교가(校歌) a school (college) song.

교각(橋脚) a (bridge) pier; a bent.

교각살우(矯角殺牛) a deadly effect of a good intention; "The remedy is worse than the disease."

교감(校監) a head teacher; an assistant (acting) principal.

교감신경(交感神經) the sympathetic nerve.

교갑(膠匣) a capsule.

교골(交骨) 〔解〕 치골(恥骨).

교과(教科) a course of study; the curriculum; a subject. ‖ ~서 a textbook; a schoolbook / ~서 검정 the screening of school textbooks 《by the Education Ministry》. ~ing staff〔전체〕.

교관(教官) an instructor; the teacher.

교교하다(皎皎-) (be) bright; brilliant. ¶ 교교히 bright(ly).

교구(教具) teaching tools.

교구(教區) 《교회의》 a parish. ‖ ~민 a parishioner.

교권(教權) 《종교상의》 ecclesiastical authority; 《교육상의》 educational authority. ‖ ~ 확립 the establishment of the educational authority.

교규(校規) school regulations.

교근(咬筋) the masticatory muscle.

교기(校紀) school discipline.

교기(校旗) a school banner.

교기(驕氣) a proud air; haughtiness. ¶ ~ 부리다 behave haughtily (arrogantly).

교내(校內) the school grounds; the campus. ¶ ~의 interclass; intramural / ~에(서) in the school grounds; on campus. ‖ ~ 운동대회 an interclass athletic meet / ~ 폭력 school violence; violence in the classroom.

교단(教團) a religious body; an order; a brotherhood.

교단(教壇) 《학교의》 the platform. ¶ ~에 서다 teach at school; be a teacher. ‖ ~생활 a teaching career.

교당(教堂) a church; a temple; a cathedral; a mosque (회교의).

교대(交代) change; a shift. ~하다 take turns; take 《a person's》 place; relieve 《each other》; change places 《with》. ¶ ~로 by turns; in shifts; alternately / ~ 주야 ~로 일하다 work in shifts day and night / 8시간씩 3~로 일하다 work in three shifts of eight hours / 1일 3~제로 on a three-shift-a-day basis / 다음 ~ 시간까지 나는 여기서 꼼짝 못한다 I'm tied down here until I'm relieved. ‖ ~시간 the changing time; a shift / ~원 a relief; a next shift / ~ 조업 shift operation; working in shift / 2~제 a double shift; a two-shift system.

교도(教徒) a believer; a follower 《of》. ‖ 이슬람 ~ a Muslim / 불교 ~ a Buddhist / 기독 ~ a Christian.

교도(教導) instruction; teaching; guidance. ~하다 instruct; teach; guide. ‖ ~민주주의 guided democracy.

교도(矯導) ‖ ~관 a prison officer; a (prison) guard; a warder / ~소 a prison; a jail; a penitentiary / ~소에 들어가다 be put in prison; be sent to jail.

교두보(橋頭堡) 〔軍〕 a bridgehead; a beachhead (해안의). ¶ ~를 구축하다 establish a bridgehead.

교란(攪亂) disturbance; derangement. ~하다 disturb; derange; stir up; throw into confusion.

교량(橋梁) a bridge. ¶ ~을 놓다 construct (build) a bridge 《over》 / ~ 역할을 하다 play a bridge role 《for》.

교련(教鍊) (a) military drill. ~하다 drill. ‖ ~교관 a drill instructor.

교료(校了) 《부호》 O.K. ~하다 finish proofreading; be OK'd. ‖ ~쇄 an OK'd proof.

교류(交流) interchange; exchange; 〔電〕 alternating current 〔AC〕. ¶ 한미 간의 문화 ~ cultural exchange between Korea and America / 학자의 ~ an exchange of scholars. ‖ ~발전기 an AC generator.

교리(教理) a doctrine; a dogma; a tenet. ‖ ~문답 catechism.

교린(交隣) relations of neighboring countries. ‖ ~정책 a good-neighbor policy.

교만(驕慢) haughtiness; arrogance. ¶ ~한 haughty; arrogant; insolent / ~한 태도를 취하다 take an arrogant attitude 《to me》. ¶ arbor.

교목(喬木) a tall (forest) tree; an

교묘(巧妙) ~하다 be clever; skillful; dexterous; deft; tactful. ¶ ~하게 cleverly; skillfully; deftly;

교무 / ~한 솜씨 a deft performance; exquisite workmanship / ~한 수단 a subtle (clever, shrewd) trick / ~하게 속이다 play a clever (neat) trick (on a person).

교무(教務) ① 《학교》 school (academic) affairs (administration). ‖ ~과 the educational affairs section / ~주임 a curriculum coordinator. ② 《교회》 religious affairs.

교문(校門) a school gate. ¶ ~을 나서다 leave the school gates; (졸업하다) leave school.

교미(交尾) copulation; mating. ~하다 copulate; mate. ‖ ~기 the mating season.

교배(交配) crossbreeding; hybridization. ~하다 crossbreed; cross; hybridize. ‖ ~종 a crossbreed; a hybrid.

교복(校服) a school uniform.

교부(交付) delivery; grant. ~하다 deliver; issue; grant. ¶ 허가증을 ~하다 grant a license (permit) / 보조금을 ~하다 grant a subsidy (to). ‖ ~금 a grant; a subsidy / ~자 a deliverer.

교분(交分) friendship. ¶ ~이 두텁다 be good friends with; enjoy a close intimacy with. 「building.

교사(校舍) a schoolhouse; a schoolbuilding.

교사(教師) a teacher; an instructor; a schoolteacher; a master (무용 따위의). ¶ 여~ a woman (lady) teacher / 무용~ a dancing master (teacher) / 가정~ a private teacher; a tutor / 영어(어학)~ an English (a language) teacher. ‖ ~용 지도서 a teacher's manual / ~자격증 a teacher's license; a teaching certificate.

교사(教唆) incitement; instigation. ~하다 incite; instigate. ‖ ~자 an instigator / ~죄 the crime of instigation.

교살(絞殺) strangulation. ~하다 strangle; hang.

교생(教生) a student teacher.

교서(教書) a message.

교섭(交涉) negotiations; bargaining; (관계) connection. ~하다 negotiate with (a person) about (a matter); bargain with (a person) about (a matter) (값을). ¶ ~을 시작하다 begin (start) negotiation / ~중에 있다 be in (under) negotiation / ~은 합의를 이루지 못했다 The negotiations have fallen through. / ~을 중단하다 break off negotiations (with) / 남북한간의 평화~ the peace negotiations between South and North Korea / …와 ~이 없다 have no connection with (a person). ‖ ~단체 a bargaining (negotiating) body.

교수(教授) 《가르치기》 teaching; instruction; tuition; 《사람》 a professor; the faculty (전체). ~하다 teach; instruct; give lesson (in French). ¶ H대학의 김 ~ Professor Kim at H University. ‖ ~법 a teaching method / ~진 the faculty; the professors / ~회 a faculty meeting.

교수(絞首) hanging; strangulation. ~하다 hang; strangle. ‖ ~대 the gallows / ~형 hanging / ~형에 처하다 put to death by hanging.

교습(教習) ~하다 give (a person) lessons (in); instruct. ¶ 피아노 개인~을 하다 (받다) give (take) private piano lessons. ‖ ~소 a training school.

교시(教示) teaching; instruction. ~하다 instruct; teach.

교신(交信) exchanges of communications. ~하다 communicate (with); conduct a correspondence (with). ¶ ~와 무전~중에 있다 be in radio communication with….

교실(教室) a classroom; a schoolroom; a lecture room.

교안(教案) a teaching (lesson) plan. ¶ ~을 짜다 work out a teaching plan.

교양(教養) culture; education. ¶ ~(이) 있는 cultured; (well-)educated; refined / ~이 없는 uneducated / ~을 높이다 elevate the level of one's culture; cultivate oneself. ‖ ~과목 liberal arts / ~과정 the liberal arts course / ~프로 an educational program / ~학부 the department of liberal arts and sciences; the college of general education.

교역(交易) trade; commerce; barter(교환). ~하다 trade (barter) with. ¶ 최근 한중간의 ~이 활발하다 The Korea-China trade has become active recently.

교역자(教役者) a religious worker.

교열(校閱) reading and correcting (a person's) manuscript; review. ~하다 read and correct; review. ‖ ~자 a reviewer; a person who checks the accuracy of (another's) manuscripts.

교외(郊外) the suburbs; the outskirts. ¶ 그 도시 ~에서 살다 live in the suburbs of the town. ‖ ~거주자 a suburban resident / ~생활 a suburban life / ~전동차 a suburban train.

교외(校外) ~의 (에) outside the school; out of school. ‖ ~활동 extramural activities.

교우(交友) 《사귐》 making friends

교우 《with》; 《관계》 association; 《친구》 a friend; a companion; an acquaintance. ¶ ~ 범위가 넓다 have a large circle of friends (acquaintances). ∥ ~관계 one's associates (company).

교우(校友) a schoolfellow; a schoolmate;《동창생》a graduate (of the same school);《미》an alumnus(남); an alumna(여). ∥ ~회 a students' association.

교우(敎友) a fellow believer (Christian, Buddhist); a brother in the same faith.

교원(敎員) a teacher; an instructor; the (teaching) staff (총칭). ¶ ~이 되다 take up teaching. ∥ ~ 검정시험 a certificate examination for teachers / ~ 양성소 a teachers' training school.

교유(交遊) companionship; friendship. ~하다 associate 《with》; keep company 《with》.

교육(敎育) education; schooling (교양); teaching; instruction;《훈련》training. ~하다 educate; instruct; train. ¶ ~ 받은 educated; cultured / ~ 받지 못한 uneducated; illiterate / ~을 잘 받은 well-educated〔-trained〕/ ~의 기회 균등 equal educational opportunity / ~을 받다 be educated; have〔get, receive〕education / 최고의 ~을 받은 사람 a man of the highest education / 자식 ~에 극성스런 어머니 an education-minded mother; a mother who is obsessed with her children's education. ∥ ~감 the superintendent of education / ~개혁 educational reform / ~계 the educational world / ~공무원 an educational public service employee / ~과정 a curriculum; a course of study / ~기관 an educational institution / ~대학 a college of education; a teachers' college / ~비 educational 〔educational〕expenses / ~산업 the education industry〔business〕/ ~시설〔행정〕educational facilities〔administration〕/ ~영화 an educational film / ~위원회 the Board of Education; a school board《미》/ ~자 an educator; a teacher / ~제도 a school〔an educational〕system / ~기술 ~ technical education.

교육부(敎育部) the Ministry of Education.

교의(交誼) friendship; friendly relationship.

교의(校醫) a school physician〔doctor〕.

교의(敎義) a doctrine; a creed; dogma.

교인(敎人) a believer; a follower.

교자상(交子床) a large (dining) table.

교장(校長) a director (고교의); a principal (중학의); a headmaster (초등학교의).

교장(校葬) a school funeral.

교장(敎場) a drill ground〔field〕.

교재(敎材) teaching materials; training aids.

교전(交戰) war; hostilities;《전투》a battle; an action. ~하다 fight《with, against》; engage in a battle; wage war. ¶ 비무장 지대에서 산발적인 ~이 있었다 Sporadic skirmishes are reported in the demilitarized zone. ∥ ~국 a belligerent; warring nations / ~상태 (be in) a state of war.

교접(交接)《성교》sexual intercourse. ∥ ~기관〔解〕a copulatory organ.

교정(校正) proofreading. ~하다 read proofs; proofread《an article》. ∥ ~쇄 a proof sheet; proofs / ~원 a proofreader / ~필 a corrected proof;《기호》Corrected. O.K.

교정(校訂) revision. ~하다 revise. ∥ ~본〔판〕a revised edition / ~자 a revisor.

교정(校庭) a schoolyard;《초·중등학교 운동장》a (school) playground;《대학 구내》the campus.

교정(矯正) reform; correction; remedy. ~하다 correct; reform; remedy; cure. ¶ 나쁜 버릇을 ~하다 break《a person》of a bad habit / 치열을 ~하다 straighten one's teeth / 말더듬이를 ~하다 cure《a person》of stammering. ∥ ~시력 corrected sight.

교제(交際) association; company; friendship; acquaintance; relations. ~하다 associate with; keep company with. ¶ ~상 as a matter of social courtesy / ~가 넓다 know a lot of people; have a large〔wide〕circle of friends〔acquaintances〕/ ~를 넓히다 extend one's acquaintance / ~를 끊다 break off relations with / ~를 맺다 form a friendship《with》; get acquainted《with》/ 그녀와는 고교때부터 ~하고 있다 I have been keeping company with her since my high school days. ∥ ~가 a sociable person / ~범위 a circle of acquaintance / ~비 social expenses;《기업의》an expense account.

교조주의(敎條主義) doctrinism. ∥ ~자 a doctrinist.

교주(敎主) the proprietor of a religion; the head of a sect.

교직(交織) a mixed〔combined〕

교직(教職) 《학교의》 the teaching profession. ~에 몸을 담다 become a teacher; enter the teaching profession / ~에 종사하다 be engaged in teaching. ‖ ~과정 a course of study for the teaching profession / ~원 the teaching staff; the faculty / ~원조합 a teachers' union.

교질(膠質) stickiness; a colloid.

교차(交叉) intersection; crossing. ~하다 cross (intersect) 《each other》. ¶ 직각으로 ~하다 intersect at right angle. ‖ ~로 (a) crossroads; an intersection / ~승인 cross-recognition / ~점 a cross(ing); a junction.

교착(交錯) complication; intricacy; blending; mixture. ~하다 be complicated (intricated, entangled); cross (mingle with) each other. ¶ 명암(明暗)의 ~ a mixture of light and shade.

교착(膠着) agglutination; 《시세 따위의》 stalemate. ~하다 stick 《to》; adhere 《to》; agglutinate. ¶ ~상태에 있다 《사물이》 be deadlocked; be at a standstill / ~상태에 빠지다 come to a standstill; become deadlocked.

교체(交替) replacement; a change; a switch《투수의》. ~하다 change; replace. ¶ 내각 ~ a cabinet reshuffle.

교칙(校則) school regulations.

교탁(教卓) a teacher's desk.

교태(嬌態) coquetry. ¶ ~를 부리다 put on coquettish airs; play the coquetry.

교통(交通) 《왕래》 traffic; 《연락》 communication; 《운수》 transport; transportation. ¶ ~이 번잡한 거리 a busy street / ~이 편리한 집 a house conveniently situated / ~을 차단하다 shut off traffic; block the street / ~을 완화하다 relieve (ease) traffic / 그 곳은 ~편이 좋다 (나쁘다) The place is easy (hard) to reach. ‖ ~규칙 traffic regulations (rules) / ~기관 a means of transportation / ~난 (정체, 지옥) a traffic congestion (jam, mess) / ~도덕 traffic morals / ~량 traffic (volume) (이 도로는 ~량이 많다 There is a lot of traffic in this road.) / ~마비 traffic paralysis / ~망 a traffic network / ~방해 obstruction of traffic / ~비 traffic expenses; carfare / ~사고 a traffic accident(~사고를 일으키다 cause a traffic accident) / ~순경 a traffic policeman / ~신호 a traffic signal / ~안전 traffic safety / ~안전 운동 a traffic safety campaign / ~안전 주간 Traffic Safety Week / ~위반 a traffic offense / ~위반자 a traffic offender (violator) / ~정리 traffic control / ~체증 a traffic backup (holdup) / ~표지 a traffic sign / 건설一부 the Ministry of Construction & Transportation. (ligious) sect.

교파(教派) a denomination; a (re-

교편(教鞭) ¶ ~을 잡다 be a teacher; teach at a school.

교포(僑胞) a Korean resident abroad; overseas Koreans(총칭).

교풍(校風) school traditions.

교합(交合) sexual union.

교향(交響) ~곡 a symphony(베토벤 제9 ~곡 Beethoven's Ninth Symphony) / ~악단 a symphony orchestra.

교화(教化) enlightenment. ~하다 educate; enlighten; civilize. ‖ ~사업 educational work.

교환(交換) (an) exchange; (an) interchange; barter 《물품의》;《어음의》 clearing. ~하다 exchange; interchange; barter; clear 《어음을》. ¶ …과 ~으로 in exchange (return) for… / 중고차에 웃돈을 얹어 새차와 ~하다 trade a used car in for a new model / 우리는 솔직히 의견을 ~했다 We exchanged our views frankly. ‖ ~가격 (가치) the exchange price (value) / ~고 exchanges 《어음의》 / ~교수 (학생) an exchange professor (student) / ~대 a switchboard / ~소 a clearing house《어음의》 / ~수 a telephone operator / ~업무 clearance operation《어음의》 / ~용 부품 replacement (units and) parts / ~조건 a bargaining point.

교환(交歡·交驩) an exchange of courtesies. ~하다 exchange courtesies (greetings); fraternize 《with》. ¶ ~경기 a good-will match.

교활(狡猾) ~한 cunning; sly; crafty / ~하게 굴다 act craftily / ~한 수단을 쓰다 use cunning measures (a sharp practice).

교황(教皇) the Pope. ¶ ~의 papal. ‖ ~청 the Vatican.

교회(教會) a church; a chapel. ¶ 일요일마다 ~에 가다 go to church every Sunday / ~에서 결혼하다 be married in church.

교훈(校訓) school precepts; a motto for school discipline.

교훈(教訓) a lesson; teachings; a moral(우화). ~적인 instructive; edifying / ~을 얻다 learn (get) a lesson 《from》 / 그 경험은 나에게 좋은 ~이 되었다 That experience

taught me a good lesson.
구(句) 〖어구〗 a phrase; 〖표현〗 an expression. ¶ 관용~를 쓰다 use an idiomatic phrase.
구(球) 〖數〗 a globe; a sphere; 〖공〗 a ball.
구(區) 《도시의》 a ward; 《구역》 a section; a district. ¶ 그녀는 시의회에서 어느 ~를 대표하느냐 Which ward does she represent on the city council?
구(九) nine; 《아홉째》 the ninth. ¶ 9분의 1, a ninth.
구~(舊) former, ex-(전); old(낡은). ¶ ~사상 an old fashioned idea / ~소련 the former Soviet Union / ~정치인 an expolitician.
구가(謳歌) ~하다 glorify; eulogize; sing the praises 〖joys〗 of 《life》. ¶ 청춘을 ~하다 openly enjoy the joys of youth.
구각(舊殼) ¶ ~을 벗다 break with 〖discard〗 the tradition.
구간(區間) the section (between A and B). ¶ ~ 버스요금 the bus fare for a section.
구강(口腔) the mouth; the oral cavity. ‖ ~외과 oral surgery / ~위생 oral 〖dental〗 hygiene.
구개(口蓋) 〖解〗 the palate; the roof of the mouth. ‖ ~음 a palatal 〖sound〗.
구걸(求乞) begging. ~하다 beg; ask charity; go 〖about〗 begging. ¶ 집집마다 ~하며 다니다 beg from door to door.
구경 a visit; sightseeing. ~하다 see; see 〖do〗 the sights of 《a city》; visit. ¶ ~스럽다 be worth seeing / 연극을(영화를) ~하다 see a play(movie) / 시장을 ~하다 look round the market / 서울은 ~할 곳이 많다 There are lots of sights to see in Seoul. ‖ ~가마리 a laughingstock; an object of ridicule / ~거리 a sight; a spectacle; an object of interest / ~꾼 a spectator; a sightseer; a visitor; an onlooker(방관자).
구경(口徑) caliber; calibre 《英》. ¶ 16인치 포 a 16-inch gun.
구곡(舊穀) grain produced in the previous year; long-stored grain.
구관(舊館) the old(er) building.
구관조(九官鳥) 〖鳥〗 a (hill) myna.
구교(舊交) 《오랜 정분》 old friendship 《acquaintance》.
구구(九九) the rules of multiplication. ‖ ~표 the multiplication table.
구구하다(區區─) 《변변찮음》 (be) petty; small; insignificant; minor; trivial; 《각각》 (be) various; diverse; divided. ¶ 구구한 변명 a lame [poor] excuse / 의견이 ~

be divided in opinion.
구국(救國) national salvation. ‖ ~운동 the save-the-nation movement / ~지사 a patriot who is devoted to the salvation of his country.
구균(球菌) a microccus 〖pl. -ci〗.
구근(球根) 〖植〗 a bulb. ‖ ~식물 a bulbous plant.
구금(拘禁) detention; confinement; custody. ~하다 detain; confine; imprison; keep 《a person》 in custody. ¶ 3일간 구치소에 ~되다 be detained 〖confined〗 in a prison for three days.
구급(救急) ~의 emergency; first-aid. ‖ ~상자 〖약, 치료〗 a first-aid kit 〖medicine, treatment〗 / ~차 an ambulance.
구기(球技) a ball game. ‖ ~장 a ball 〖playing〗 ground.
구기다 crumple; wrinkle; rumple; crush. ¶ 구겨지다 be crumpled 〖wrinkled〗; get mussed.
구기자(枸杞子) 〖植〗 a Chinese matrimony vine.
구김살 wrinkles; creases; rumples; folds. ¶ ~을 펴다 smooth out wrinkles; smooth 《the dress》.
구깃구깃하다 (be) creasy; crumpled; wrinkled.
구난(救難) rescue; salvage. ‖ ~선 a rescue 〖salvage〗 ship / ~작업 rescue 〖salvage〗 work.
구내(構內) premises; a compound; an enclosure; the yard. ¶ 학교 ~ school grounds; the campus 《美》/ 역 ~에서 in the station yard. ‖ ~식당 a refectory(美 등의); a refreshment room(역 따위의).
구내염(口內炎) 〖醫〗 stomatitis.
구년(舊年) the old 〖past〗 year; last year.
구더기 a maggot. ¶ ~가 들끓다 be infested with maggots.
구덩이 a hollow; a cavity; a pit; a sunken place.
구도(求道) seeking after truth. ‖ ~자 a seeker after truth.
구도(構圖) composition. ¶ ~가 좋다 〖나쁘다〗 be well(poorly) composed 〖designed, planned〗.
구도(舊都) an old city; a former capital.
구독(購讀) subscription. ~하다 subscribe to 《a newspaper》; take 《a newspaper》. ¶ ~을 계속하다 renew one's subscription 《to, for》. ‖ ~자 a subscriber.
구두 《a pair of》 shoes; boots(장화). ¶ ~를 신다 〖벗다〗 put on 〖take off〗 one's shoes / ~를 닦다 shine 〖polish〗 one's shoes; give one's shoes shine / ~를

수선케 했다 I had my shoes mended (repaired). / 이 ~는 내게 너무 작다 (크다) These shoes are too small (big) for me. / ~골 a shoetree / ~끈 a shoelace; a shoestring 《美》 / ~닦이 shoe polishing; a shoeshiner (사람) / ~수선 shoe mending / ~수선인 a shoe repairer / ~약 shoe (boot) polish / ~장이 a shoemaker / ~주걱 a shoehorn; a shoe lifter / ~창 the sole of a shoe / 구둣방 a shoe store / 구둣솔 a shoe brush.

구두 (口頭) ~의 oral; verbal; spoken / ~로 orally; verbally / ~로 전달하다 give a verbal message. ‖ ~계약 a verbal contract / ~변론 [法] oral proceedings / ~선 empty slogan (한낱 ~선에 그치다 become more empty slogan) / ~시험 an oral test.

구두 (句讀) punctuation. ‖ ~점 punctuation marks (points) (~점을 찍다 punctuate 《a sentence》).

구두쇠 a miser; a stingy person; a closefisted person. 「dry up.

구드러지다 become hard and dry.

구들장 flat pieces of stone used for flooring a Korean 《ondol》 room. 「end of last year.

구랍 (舊臘) last December; the

구렁 (패인 곳) a dent; a hollow; a cavity; a pit; 《비유적》 a chasem; an abyss; the depths. ¶ 가난의 ~ (텅이) the depths of poverty / 절망의 ~ (텅이) (be down in) the depths of despair.

구렁이 ① 《뱀》 a large snake; a serpent. ¶ ~ 담 넘어가듯 하다 realize *one's* aim in an unnoticed way. ② 《사람》 a crafty (blackhearted) fellow.

구레나룻 whiskers. 「dar.

구력 (舊曆) the old (lunar) calen-

구령 (口令) a word of command. ~하다 give (shout) an order.

구루 (佝僂) a hunchback. ‖ ~병 [醫] rickets.

구류 (拘留) detention; custody. ~하다 detain; keep (hold) 《a person》 in custody. ¶ 10일간의 ~처분을 받다 be sentenced to ten days' detention.

구르다¹ (데굴데굴) roll (over). ¶ 굴러 떨어지다 roll in; fall into *one's* hands (유산 등이).

구르다² (발을) stamp *one's* feet; stamp with impatience (vexation).

구름 a cloud; the clouds (총칭). ¶ ~ 없는 cloudless / ~이 낀 cloudy / ~ 사이의 break (rift) in the clouds / ~을 잡는 듯한 이야기 a vague story / ~에 덮이다 be covered with clouds; be clouded over / ~ 위에 솟다 soar to the sky; rise above the clouds / 하늘에는 ~ 한 점 없다 There is not a speck of cloud in the sky.

구름다리 an overpass; a footbridge; a viaduct.

구릉 (丘陵) a hill; a hillock. ‖ ~지대 hilly districts.

구리 copper. ¶ 구릿빛의 coppercolored / ~를 입히다 copper; plate 《a thing》 with copper. ‖ ~철사 copper wire.

구리다 ① 《냄새가》 smell bad; stink; foul-smelling. ¶ 구린내 a bad (or, an offensive) smell. ② 《행동이》 (be) suspicious; shady; nasty. ¶ 제 맘이 ~ have something on *one's* conscience / 무언가 구린 짓을 하고 있다 be engaged in something shady.

구매 (購買) purchase; buying. ~하다 purchase; buy. ¶ 이 상품은 소비자의 ~욕을 돋굴 것이다 This product should whet the consumer's appetite. ‖ ~력 purchasing (buying) power (~력이 늘고 (줄고) 있다 Purchasing power is increasing (decreasing).) / ~자 a buyer / ~조합 a purchasing guild (association); a cooperative.

구멍 ① a hole; an opening (개구부); a gap; crack (갈라진 틈); a hollow (공동). ¶ 깊이 (크게, 주위) 2미터의 ~ a hole two meters deep (across, around) / 벽의 ~ an opening in the wall / 도로상의 ~ a hole in the road / ~을 막다 stop (fill) up a hole / 지면에 ~을 파다 dig a hole in the ground / 판자에 ~을 뚫다 bore a hole through the plank. ② (결점·결함) a fault; a defect; a loss; a deficit (결손). ¶ 장부에 100만원의 ~이 나 있다 There is a deficit of one million *won* in the account. / 그 이야기는 앞뒤가 ~투성이다 The story leaves a lot of loose ends.

구멍가게 a small store; a mom-and-pop store; a penny candy store.

구메농사 (~農事) 《소농》 small-scale farming. 「face.

구면 (球面) [數] a spherical sur-

구면 (舊面) an old acquaintance. ¶ 그와 나는 ~이다 He is an old acquaintance of mine.

구명 (究明) ~하다 study; investigate; look (inquire) into 《a matter》; bring 《a matter》 to light. ¶ 사고 원인을 ~하다 clear up (inquire into) the cause of the accident.

구명 (救命) life saving. ¶ ~용 life-

saving. ‖ ~구 a life preserver; a life jacket (vest) (재킷); a life belt (벨트형의) / ~정 a lifeboat.
구명(舊名) an old name.
구물러거리다 be slow (tardy); move slowly; hesitate.
구문(口文) ☞ 구전.
구문(構文) sentence structure; construction of a sentence. ‖ ~법 syntax.
구문(舊聞) old (stale) news.
구미(口味) appetite; taste; (흥미) one's interest. ‖ ~가 당기다 appeal to one's appetite (interest) / ~에 맞다 be pleasant to one's taste; suite one's taste.
구미(歐美) Europe and America; the West. ‖ ~의 European and American; Western. ‖ ~인 Europeans and Americans; Westerners / ~제국 Western countries.
구박(驅迫) cold (harsh, cruel) treatment; maltreatment. ~하다 maltreat; treat (a person) badly; be hard upon (a person).
구변(口辯) ‖ ~이 좋다 have a fluent (ready) tongue / ~이 좋은 사람 a good speaker; a glib talker.
구별(區別) distinction; discrimination; (a) difference. ~하다 distinguish (discriminate) (A from B, between A and B); tell (know) (A from B). ‖ 남녀의 ~없이 without (any) distinction of sex; irrespective (regardless) of sex / 정치가는 공사를 엄중히 ~해야 한다 Politician have to draw a sharp line between public and private affairs.
구보(驅步) a run; (말의) a canter; a gallop. ‖ ~로 가다 go at a run (gallop) / (군인의) march at the double / ~로 가 (구령) "At the double. March !"
구부리다 ① (몸을) stoop; bend forward; bow; crouch. ‖ 허리가 구부러진 노인 a man bent (down) with age / 앞으로 구부리고 걷다 walk with a stoop / 몸을 구부려 꽃을 꺾다 stoop (bend) (down) to pick up a flower. ② (물건을) bend; curve. ‖ 철산을 직각으로 구부리다 bend an iron bar into a right angle / 철사를 구부려 고리를 만들다 bend an iron wire into a ring.
구부정하다 (be) somewhat bent.
구분(區分) (분할) division; (구획) a section; (분류) classification. ~하다 divide (into); sort; section; classify. ‖ 그것을을 네 개의 큰 그룹으로 ~하다 classify (devide) them into four large divisions / 우체국에서는 번호로 우편물을 ~한다 At the post office they sort mails by zip number.

구불구불 ‖ ~한 winding; meandering; curved.
구비(口碑) oral tradition; a legend; folklore. ‖ ~로 전해지다 be handed down by tradition (orally).
구비(具備) ~하다 have; be possessed of; be furnished (equipped) (with). ‖ 모든 조건을 ~하다 fulfil all the conditions; satisfy all the requisites. ‖ ~서류 required documents.
구사(驅使) ~하다 (사람·동물을 부리다) have (a person) at one's beck and call; keep (a person) on the trot; (기계·기능을 활용하다) use freely; have a good command of. ‖ 영어를 능숙하게 ~하다 have a good command of English / 컴퓨터를 ~하여 정보를 처리했다 We made full use of a computer to process the information.
구사일생(九死一生) a narrow escape from death. ‖ 나는 ~으로 살아났다 I had a narrow escape.
구상(求償) ‖ ~무역 compensation trade.
구상(具象) ‖ ~적인 concrete; figurative / ~화하다 exteriorize; reify. ‖ ~개념 a concrete concept / ~화 a representational painting.
구상(球狀) a spherical shape. ‖ ~의 spherical; globular.
구상(鉤狀) ‖ ~의 hook-shaped. ‖ ~골(骨) an unciform bone.
구상(構想) an idea; a plan; (a) conception; a plot. ‖ 소설의 ~ the plot of a novel / ~을 짜다 work over one's idea / ~이 떠오르다 conceive an idea (a plan).
구색(具色) an assortment (of goods). ‖ ~을 갖추다 assort; provide an assortment of (goods). ‖ ~이 갖추어져 있다 have all well-assorted stock / 저 상점은 각종 초콜릿의 ~을 갖춰놓고 있다 All kinds of chocolates are assorted at that store.
구석 a corner. ‖ ~에 in a corner / ~~에 in every nook and corner; in every corner (of). ‖ ~자리 a corner seat.
구석기(舊石器) a paleolith. ‖ ~시대 the Old Stone Age.
구석지다 (be) secluded; inmost; sequestered. ‖ 숲의 가장 구석진 곳 the most secluded part of a forest / 빌딩의 가장 구석진 방 the innermost room of the building.
구설(口舌) public censure; malicious gossip. ‖ ~을 듣다 suffer from malicious gossip. ‖ ~수 the bad luck to be verbally abused.
구성(構成) constitution; composi-

구세(救世) salvation (of the world). ‖ ~군 the Salvation Army / ~주 the Savior; the Messiah.

구세계(舊世界) the Old World.

구세대(舊世代) the old generation.

구속(拘束) restriction; restraint; 《감금》 confinement; custody. ~하다 restrict; bind; confine. ¶용의자의 신병을 ~하다 detain the suspect; hold the suspect in custody / 집회의 자유를 ~하다 restrict the freedom of assembly. ‖ ~력 《have》 binding force 《for a person》 / ~시간 《노동의》 actual working hours / ~영장 a warrant of arrest.

구속(球速) 〖野〗 (a pitcher's) pace; the speed of a pitched ball. ¶~이 있다 pitch a very swift ball / ~을 바꾸다 change one's pace.

구수하다 《맛·냄새가》 (be) tasty; pleasant; good; 《이야기 따위가》 (be) interesting; humorous; delightful. ¶구수한 a delicious 〔savory〕 smell / 구수한 이야기 an interesting 〔a humorous〕 story.

구수회의(鳩首會議) a conference. ~하다 counsel together; lay 〔put〕 《their》 heads together.

구술(口述) an oral statement; a dictation. ~하다 state orally; dictate. ¶~의 oral; verbal. ‖ ~서 a verbal note.

구슬 glass beads; 《보옥》 a gem; a jewel; 《진주》 a pearl. ‖ ~백 a beaded bag.

구슬땀 beads of sweat. ¶~을 흘리며 일하다 work with sweat running down in beads.

구슬리다 coax 〔cajole, wheedle〕 《a person into...》.

구슬프다 (be) sad; touching; sorrowful; mournful; plaintive. ¶구슬픈 노래 a sad song.

구습(舊習) old (time-honored) customs. ¶~을 고수하다 stick to old customs 〔practices〕.

구승(口承) (an) oral tradition. ~하다 hand down orally; pass 《a story》 down from generation to generation by oral tradition. ‖ ~문학 oral literature.

구시대(舊時代) the old era. ¶~의 정치인 an old-school politician.

구시렁거리다 keep grumbling 《at, over, about》; nag 《at》.

구식(舊式) an old style 〔fashion, school〕. ¶~ 사람 an old-fashioned person / 그 옷은 ~이다 The clothes are out of date.

구신(具申) ~하다 report 《to》; make a representation to 《a superior》. ‖ ~서 a (detailed) report.

구실(역할·직무) one's function; a role; a duty; one's business; a part; one's share 《몫》. ¶~을 하다 do 〔discharge〕 one's duties; play a role / 제 ~을 하다 do one's share of duty / 영어의 부사 중에는 형용사 ~을 하는 것도 있다 Some English adverbs function as adjectives.

구실(口實) an excuse; a pretext; a pretence. ¶…을 ~로 하여 on the pretext 〔pretence〕 of / ~을 만들다 make up an excuse.

구심(求心) ~적 (으로) centripetal(ly). ‖ ~력 centripetal force.

구심(球審) 〖野〗 a ball (chief) umpire.

구십(九十) ninety. ¶제 ~ the ninetieth.

구악(舊惡) one's past crime (misdeed); the old evils (사회 등의). ¶~을 들추다 expose 《a person's》 past misdeed / ~을 일소하다 make a clean sweep of the old evil. 〔~하다 woo〕 court.

구애(求愛) courting; courtship.

구애(拘礙) adhesion. ~하다 stick 〔adhere〕 to; keep to. ¶~하지 않고 freely; irrespective of / 사소한 일에 ~하다 be particular about trifles / 형식에 ~하다 stick to formality. ‖ ~ment.

구약성서(舊約聖書) the Old Testament.

구어(口語) (the) spoken 〔colloquial〕 language. ¶~의 spoken; colloquial / ~로 in spoken language; colloquially / ~적 표현 a colloquial expression. ‖ ~체 a colloquial 〔conversational〕 style.

구역(區域) a zone; an area; a district; the limits. ¶자기 담당 ~을 도는 경찰관 a policeman walking his round / …의 ~내에서 within the limits of; inside the boundary of / 서울의 인구 밀집 ~ a thickly populated district in Seoul / 위험 〔안전〕 ~ 안에 있다 be in danger 〔safety〕 zone.

구역(嘔逆) nausea. ~나다 feel sick 〔nausea〕. ‖ ~질 nausea (~ 질 나는 sickening; nauseating). 「하다 recite; tell 《a story》.

구연(口演) an oral narration. ~」

구연(舊緣) old relationship (ties).

구연산(枸櫞酸) 〖化〗 citric acid.

구우일모(九牛一毛) a mere frac-

구워지다 《빵 따위가》 be baked; be toasted《토스트》 be grilled; 《고기가》 be roasted; 《생선이》 be broiled. ¶ 설~ be underdone / 잘 ~ be well-done.

구원(救援) relief; rescue; aid《국제적인》. ~하다 rescue; relieve; aid. ¶ 난민에게 ~의 손길을 뻗어야 한다 We should provide aid (relief) for refugees. ‖ ~대 a relief (rescue) party / ~물자 relief goods / ~투수《野》 a relief pitcher / ~활동 a rescue operation.

구원(舊怨) an old grudge.

구월(九月) September (생략 Sept.).

구유 a manger; a trough.

구의(舊誼) old friendship.

구이 roast meat《고기》; broiled fish《생선》. ¶ 돼지고기~ roast pork / 생선~ fish broiled with salt / 통닭~ a roast chicken.

구인(求人) a job offer; the offer of a position; 《게시》 Help Wanted. ~하다 offer a job; seek help. ¶ ~의 요구 조건 hiring requirements (terms). ‖ ~광고 a help-wanted advertisement [ad 《美》] / ~난(難) a labor shortage / ~란(欄) the help-wanted column.

구일(九日) ① 《초아흐레》 the ninth (day) of a month. ② 《9일간》 nine days.

구입(購入) purchase; buying. ~하다 purchase; buy; get. ‖ ~가격 the purchase price / ~도서 books purchased / ~자 a purchaser.

구장(球場) a baseball ground (stadium)《야구》 a soccer ground《축구》.

구적법(求積法)《數》stereometry (체적의); planimetry (면적의).

구전(口傳) oral tradition (instruction). ~하다 instruct (teach) orally; hand down by word of mouth.

구전(口錢) a commission; brokerage. ¶ 매출에 대해 5%의 ~을 받다 take (a) 5 percent commission on the sale of《books》.

구절(句節) a phrase and a clause;《문장》a paragraph.

구절양장(九折羊腸) a meandering path; a winding road.

구절초(九節草)《植》the Siberian chrysanthemum.

구절판(九折坂)《饌盒》a nine sectioned lacquer ware serving plate.

구접스럽다 (be) dirty; filthy; nasty; mean; untidy.

구정(舊正) the Lunar New Year.

구정(舊情) old friendship. ¶ ~을 새로이 하다 renew one's old friendship.

구정물 filthy [dirty] water; sewage《하수》.

구제(救濟) relief; help; aid; salvation(영혼의). ~하다 relieve; give relief《to》; help; save. ¶ 정부는 난민을 ~했다 The government gave relief to the refugees. ‖ ~금융 (조치)《經濟學》a bailout / ~기금 relief funds / ~사업 relief work / ~책 a relief measure; a remedy.

구제(驅除) extermination. ~하다 exterminate; get rid of; stamp out. ¶ 해충을 ~하다 stamp out noxious insects / 집안의 쥐를 ~하다 get rid of rats in the house.

구제도(舊制度) the old (former) system.

구조(救助) rescue; aid; relief; help. ~하다 rescue; save; help. ¶ 인명을 ~하다 save a life / ~를 청하russian call for help. ‖ ~대 a rescue team (party) / ~선 a lifeboat; a rescue boat / ~신호 a Mayday (call) / ~원 a rescue man / ~작업 a rescue operation / ~책 relief measures.

구조(構造) structure; organization (조직). ¶ ~상의 structural / 사회의 ~ the organization of society / 문장의 ~ sentence structure / 이 기계에는 ~상의 결함이 있다 There is a structural defect in this machine. ‖ ~개혁 structural reform / ~식 [化] a structural formula / ~언어학 structural linguistics.

구좌(口座) an account. ☞ 계좌.

구주(舊株)《證》an old stock (share).

구중궁궐(九重宮闕) the Royal Palace; the Court.

구중중하다 (be) damp; moist; wet; nasty.

구지레하다 (be) dirty; unclean; untidy. ¶ 그는 언제나 구지레한 옷차림을 하고 있다 He always wears dirty clothes.

구직(求職) job hunting. ~하다 seek (hunt for) a job. ¶ ~신청이 쇄도하다 have a flood of applications for vacancies. ‖ ~광고 a situation-wanted advertisement (~광고를 내다 advertise for a position) / ~광고란 a situation-wanted column / ~자 a job seeker.

구질구질하다 ① ☞ 구중중하다. ②《지저분》(be) dirty; filthy; untidy; sordid. ③《언행이》(be) mean; base.

구차하다《苟且─》《가난하다》(be) very poor; destitute; needy; miserable; be badly off; be hard up;《구구함》(be) ignoble; humiliating; unworthy; clumsy (변명 따위). ¶ 구차한 목숨 a

humiliating life / 구차한 변명 a clumsy (poor) excuse / 살림이 ~ be in poverty; be in needy circumstances / 남에게 구차한 소리를 하다 beg *another's* favor; ask for *another's* sympathy.

구척장신(九尺長身) a person of extraordinary stature; a giant.

구천(九泉) Hades; the nether world; the grave.

구청(區廳) a ward (district) office. ‖ ~장 the chief of a ward / ~직원 a ward official.

구체(具體) concreteness. ¶ ~적인 concrete; definite / ~적으로 concretely; definitely / ~적으로 말하면 to put it concretely / ~적인 예를 몇 개 들겠다 Let me give you some concrete examples. / ~화 embodiment; materialization (계획을 ~화하다 give shape to a plan / 그는 자기 생각을 ~하였다 He put his ideas into action.)

구체제(舊體制) an old structure (system); the old order.

구축(驅逐) ~하다 drive away; expel; oust. ¶ ~함 a destroyer.

구축하다(構築—) build; construct.

구출(救出) rescue. ~하다 rescue; save. ¶ 부상자를 ~하다 rescue the injured person from 《under rubble》. ‖ ~작업 a rescue operation.

구충(驅蟲) ‖ ~약 〖제〗 an insecticide; a vermifuge (회충약).

구취(口臭) 〖have〗 (a) bad (foul) breath.

구치(臼齒) 〖解〗 a molar (tooth).

구치(拘置) confinement. ~하다 confine; detain; keep 《a person》 in custody. ‖ ~소 a prison; a jail.

구칭(舊稱) an old name; a former title.

구타(毆打) beating; 〖法〗 battery. ~하다 beat 〔strike, hit〕 《a person》 on 《the head》.

구태(舊態) the old (former) state of things. ¶ ~의연한 사고 방식 the obsolete way of thinking / ~의연하다 remain unchanged (as it was).

구태여《일부러》purposely; deliberately; intentionally; daringly (감히); knowingly(알면서). ¶ ~ 할 필요는 없다 You need not take the trouble to do./~ 반대하지 않는다 I dare not oppose it.

구토(嘔吐) vomiting. ~하다 vomit; throw (bring) up 《one's food》. ¶ ~를 일으키는 고약한 냄새 a sickening smell. ‖ ~설사 vomiting and diarrhea / ~제 an emetic.

구파(舊派) an old school (유파); the conservatives (보수파).

구판(舊版) an old (a former) edition; an old book.

구푸리다 ☞ 구부리다.

구하다(求—) ① 〔얻다〕 get; obtain; gain; acquire; 〔사다〕 buy; purchase. ¶ 구하기 힘든 hard (rare) to get / 서울에서 구한 물건 a thing bought in Seoul. ② 〔찾다〕 seek; search for (after); look for; pursue; 〔요구하다〕 ask for; request; demand. ¶ 셋집을 ~ look for a house to let / 행복을 ~ pursue happiness / 조언을 ~ ask 《a person》 for advice / P의 값을 구하라 Find the value of P. / 그 회사는 숙련공을 구하고 있다 The company is looking for skilled workers.

구하다(救—) relieve (rescue) 《a person》 from 《danger》; help 《a person》 out of 《fire》; save. ¶ 인명을 ~ save a man's life / 가난한 사람들을 ~ relieve (help) the poor / 아무를 구하러 가다 go to 《a person's》 rescue.

구현(具現) embodiment. ~하다 embody. ¶ 말은 사상을 ~한다 Words embody thoughts.

구형(求刑) prosecution. ~하다 prosecute; demand a penalty 《for》. ¶ 피고에게 징역 2년을 ~하다 demand a sentence of two years' imprisonment for the accused.

구형(球形) a globular (spherical) shape. ¶ ~의 spherical; globular; globe-shaped.

구형(舊型) an old model (type, style). ¶ ~의 old-fashioned; outmoded; out-of-date.

구호(口號) 〔표어〕 a slogan; a motto; a catchword; a rallying word. ¶ …이란 ~를 내걸고 under the slogan of…. / 선거 ~ an election slogan.

구호(救護) relief; rescue; aid; help. ~하다 relieve; rescue; aid; help. ¶ ~금 (a) relief fund (money) / ~물자 relief goods / ~미 relief (emergency) rice / ~반 a relief squad / ~소 a first-aid station.

구혼(求婚) a proposal (an offer) of marriage; courtship. ~하다 court; propose 《to》. ¶ ~을 승낙 (거절)하다 accept (decline) 《a man's》 hand. ‖ ~광고 a matrimonial advertisement / ~자 a suitor; a wooer.

구황(救荒) ~하다 relieve (the sufferers from) famine.

구획(區劃) 〔구분〕 a division; a section; a lot (토지의). ~하다 divide; partition; mark off. ¶ 그 토지는 넷으로 ~되어 분양되었다 The land was divided into four lots for sale. ‖ ~정리 land readjustment. 〔하다 relieve; aid.

구휼(救恤) relief (of the poor). ~

국 soup; broth. ¶진한(맑은) ～ thick (clear) soup / ～을 먹다 eat soup. ‖ ～거리 material for soup / ～그릇 a soup bowl / ～말이 soup containing boiled rice.

국(局) ① 《관서》 a government office; a bureau; a department 《英》. ¶ 전화～ a telephone office; the central 《美》 / 다이얼을 듣고 싶은 방송～에 맞추다 tune in to the broadcasting station. ② 《바둑 따위의 승부》 a game.

국가(國家) a state; a country; a nation. ¶ ～의 national; state / ～적인 행사 a national event / ～의 번영을 위해 열심히 일하다 work hard for national prosperity. ‖ ～경제 the national economy / ～공무원 a government official; a national public service personnel(총칭) / ～관리 state (government) control / ～권력 state power / ～기관 a state organ / ～대표팀 the 《Korea》 national team / ～보안법 the National Security Law / ～비상사태 (declare) a state of national emergency / ～사업 a national enterprise / ～시험 a state examination / ～안보회의 the National Security Meeting / ～안전기획부 the Agency for National Security Planning / ～재정 the finances of the state / ～주의 nationalism / ～총동원 a national mobilization.

국가(國歌) the national anthem. ¶ ～를 부르다 [연주하다] sing (play) the national anthem.

국경(國境) the frontier; the border; the boundaries (of a country). ¶ 사랑엔 ～이 없다 Love knows no frontier. ‖ ～경비대 (분쟁, 선) a border garrison (dispute, line).

국경일(國慶日) a national holiday.

국고(國庫) the (National) Treasury. ¶ 비용은 ～ 부담으로 되어 있다 The expenses are supposed to be paid from the national treasury. ‖ ～금 national funds / ～보조 a state (government) subsidy / ～부담 state liability / ～수입 national revenues / ～채권 《美》 a treasury bond (bill).

국교(國交) diplomatic relations. ¶ ～를 맺다 enter into diplomatic relations 《with》. ‖ ～단절 (회복) a severance (restoration) of diplomatic relations / ～정상화 normalization of diplomatic relations. [～회 의 성공회.

국교(國敎) a state religion.
국군(國軍) 《일반적인》 the armed forces of a nation; 《한국 군대》 the Korean army; ROK Army (Armed Forces). ¶ ～의 날 the (ROK) Armed Forces Day.

국권(國權) national (state) power (rights); sovereign rights(통치권). ¶ ～을 발동하다 exercise the right of the state / ～을 신장하다 expand national power.

국기(國技) a national sport (game).

국기(國旗) the national flag. ¶ ～를 게양하다 hoist (put up) a national flag. ‖ ～게양식 a flag hoisting ceremony.

국난(國難) a national crisis. ¶ ～을 구하다 save the nation in a great crisis.

국내(國內) the interior; internal; domestic; home / ～에(서) in the country; within a country / ～의 수요 the domestic demand 《for a product》. ‖ ～문제 〔사정〕 internal (domestic) affairs / ～법 municipal (civil) law / ～산업 domestic industries / ～선 a domestic line (flight) / ～시장 the domestic market / ～우편 a domestic mail.

국도(國道) a national road (highway). ¶ ～ 2호선 National highway 2; Route 2.

국란(國亂) a civil war; an internal disturbance.

국력(國力) national strength (power); 《자원·부》 national resources (wealth). ¶ ～의 확장 (쇠퇴) the expansion (decline) of national power / ～을 기르다 (증진하다) build up (increase) national power.

국록(國祿) a government salary. ¶ ～을 먹다 be in government service.

국론(國論) national (public) opinion. ¶ ～을 통일하다 unify public opinion; create (achieve) a national consensus / ～이 비등하고 있다 There is a heated public discussion. or Public opinion is greatly agitated.

국리(國利) ¶ ～민복을 도모하다 promote national interests and the welfare of the people.

국립(國立) ¶ ～의 national; state; government. ‖ ～경기장 the National Athletic Stadium / ～국악원 the National Classical Music Institute / ～극장 a national theater / ～대학 a national university / ～묘지 the National Cemetery / ～박물관 the National Museum / ～병원 a national hospital.

국면(局面) 《판국》 the situation; the aspect of affairs; a phase. ¶ ～을 타개하다 break the deadlock; find the way out of the situation / ～이 일변하다 enter into

국명(國名) [無電] a call sign; call letters;《방송국의》the name of a station.

국명(國名) the name of a country.

국모(國母)《황후》an empress;《왕후》a queen.

국무(國務) state affairs; the affairs of state. ¶ ~를 관장하다 administer [conduct] the affairs of state. ∥ ~부 the Department of State《美》/ ~위원 a minister of state; a minister without portfolio (무임소장관) / ~장관 [차관, 차관보] the Secretary [Undersecretary, Assistant Undersecretary] of State《美》/ ~총리 the Prime Minister; the Premier / ~회의 a Cabinet council [meeting].

국문(國文)《문학》national [Korean] literature;《국어》the national [Korean] language;《문자》the Korean alphabet. ¶ ~법 Korean grammar / ~학과 the Korean literature course / ~학자 a scholar of Korean literature.

국민(國民) a nation; a people;《개인》a citizen; a national. ¶ ~의 national. ∥ ~가요 national folk songs / ~감정 [정신] national sentiment [spirit] / ~개병 (의) universal conscription (system) / ~개(皆)보험 medical services and pension insurance for the whole nation / ~건강보험 national health insurance / ~경제 the national economy / ~군 the militia / ~병 a militiaman / ~복지연금 the citizen's welfare pension / ~성 the national character [traits] / ~소득 the national income / ~연금 national pension / ~운동 a national campaign [movement] / ~의례 national ceremony / ~장 a people's [public] funeral / ~총생산 gross national product (생략 GNP) / ~투표 a plebiscite; a (national) referendum / ~화합 the national harmony [reconciliation].

국밥 rice-and-meat soup.

국방(國防) national defense. ¶ ~부 [장관] the Ministry [Minister] of National Defense / ~비 national defense expenditure / ~성《美》the Department of Defense; the Pentagon / ~자원 national defense resources.

국번(局番) an exchange number. ¶ 시내 [시외] ~ a local [an out-of-town] telephone exchange number.

국법(國法) the national law; the laws of the country. ¶ ~을 따르다 [위반하다] obey [break, violate] the laws of the country.

국별무역장벽보고서(國別貿易障壁報告書) National Trade Estimate Report on Foreign Trade Barriers.

국보(國寶) a national treasure. ¶ ~적 존재 a national asset / ~지정을 받다 be designated a national treasure.

국부(局部)《일부》a part; a section;《국지》a local area;《환부》the affected part;《음부》the private parts. ¶ ~적 (으로) local (·ly), sectional(ly); partial(ly) / ~화하다 localize. ∥ ~마취 local an(a)esthesia.

국부(國父) the father of the country.

국부(國富) [經] national wealth.

국비(國費) the national expenditure [expenses]. ¶ ~로 유학하다 study abroad at government [national] expense. ∥ ~유학생 a government student abroad / ~장학생 a holder of a scholarship from the government.

국빈(國賓) a guest of the state; a national guest. ¶ ~대우를 받다 be treated as a state guest.

국사(國史) the national history;《한국의》the history of Korea; Korean history. ∥ ~연표 a historical calendar of Korea.

국사(國事) a national affair; the affairs of state. ¶ ~를 논하다 discuss the affairs of a nation. ∥ ~범 a political offense [crime]; a political offender(사람).

국산(國産) domestic production. ¶ ~의 homemade; domestic. ∥ ~자동차 a homemade car; a motorcar made in Korea / ~품 home products; homemade articles / ~품 장려 encouragement of the use of home products; "Buy-Korean" campaign (운동) / 순~품 an all-Korean product.

국상(國喪) national mourning.

국새(國璽) the Seal of the State.

국선변호인(國選辯護人) a court-appointed lawyer. ¶ ~을 대다 assign a defense counsel (to a defendant).

국세(國稅) a national tax. ∥ ~청 the Office of National Tax Administration; the Internal Revenue Service《美》.

국세(國勢) the state of a country. ∥ ~조사 a (national) census; ~조사를 행하다 take a national census) / ~조사원 a census taker.

국수 noodles; spaghetti; vermicelli. ¶ 국숫집 a noodle shop / 손〔수타〕~ hand-made noodles.

국수(國手) ¶ 바둑·장기의 ~ a national champion (master player) of 《paduk, etc》; 《명의》 a noted physician.

국수주의(國粹主義) ultranationalism; extreme patriotism.

국시(國是) 《fix》 a national 《state》 policy.

국악(國樂) (traditional) Korean music.

국어(國語) the national 〔Korean〕 language; one's mother tongue. ¶ 2개 ~의 bilingual. ‖ ~ 교사 a teacher of Korean.

국영(國營) state 〔government〕 operation; nationalization. ¶ ~화의 state-operated; state-〔government〕-owned; state-run / 광산을 ~화하다 nationalize the mines. ‖ ~기업 a state 〔national〕 enterprise; a government-run corporation.

국왕(國王) a king; a monarch; a sovereign.

국외(局外) the outside; an independent position. ¶ ~의 outside; external / ~에 서다 stand outside; keep aloof 《from》. ‖ ~자 an outsider; a looker-on / ~중립 neutrality (~중립을 지키다 observe neutrality; stand neutral) / ~중립국 a neutral country.

국외(國外) ¶ ~에서〔로〕 abroad; overseas / ~ outside the country / ~로 추방하다 expel 《a person》 from the country; expatriate / ~퇴거명령 a deportation order.

국운(國運) national fortunes; the destiny 〔fate〕 of a country. ¶ ~의 성쇠 the prosperity and decline of a country / ~을 걸다 stake the national destiny.

국위(國威) national prestige 〔dignity〕. ¶ ~를 선양하다 〔손상시키다〕 enhance 〔damage〕 the national prestige.

국유(國有) ¶ ~의 state-〔government〕-owned; national(ized). ‖ ~림 〔철도〕 a national 〔state〕 forest 〔railway〕 / ~재산 national 〔state〕 property 〔assets〕 / ~지 state 〔national〕 land / ~화 nationalization (~화하다 nationalize).

국으로 within bounds 《one's limitations》. ¶ ~ 가만히 있다 keep within bounds; keep 《know》 one's place.

국은(國恩) one's debt to his country.

국자 a (large) ladle; a dipper.

국장(局長) the director 〔chief〕 of a bureau; a postmaster (우체국의).

국장(國葬) a state 〔national〕 funeral.

국장(國章) a national emblem.

국적(國籍) nationality; citizenship 《美》. ¶ ~ 불명의 배 〔비행기〕 a ship 〔plane〕 of unknown nationality / ~을 취득〔상실〕하다 acquire 〔lose〕 citizenship. ‖ ~상실 loss of nationality / 이중 ~ dual 〔double〕 nationality / ~취득 acquisition.

국전(國展) the National Art Exhibition.

국정(國政) (national) administration; 《국무》 state affairs. ¶ ~에 참여하다 participate in the (national) administration / ~을 담당〔관장〕하다 administer the affairs of the state. ‖ ~감사 〔parliamentary〕 inspection on state administration / ~조사권 《국회의》 the right to conduct investigations in relation to government.

국정(國定) ¶ ~의 state; national. ‖ ~교과서 a state textbook; a government-designated textbook; a school textbook compiled by the state.

국정(國情) the state of affairs in a country; the social 〔political〕 conditions of a country.

국제(國際) ¶ ~적(인) international / ~적으로 internationally; universally / ~적인 견지에서 from the international point of view / ~적으로 알려져 있다 be known the world over; be internationally famous. ‖ ~견본시 an international trade fair / ~결제은행 the Bank of International Settlement / ~결혼 intermarriage; international marriage / ~공항 an international airport / ~관계 international relations / ~노동기구 《생략 ILO》 the International Labor Organization / ~도시 a cosmopolitan city / ~법 international law / ~부흥개발은행 the International Bank for Reconstruction and Development 《생략 IBRD》 / ~분쟁 international disputes / ~선 an international flight / ~수지 the balance of international payment / ~어 〔문제, 정세〕 an international language 〔problem, situation〕 / ~연합 the United Nations 《생략 UN》 / ~연합 안전보장 이사회 the United Nations Security Council / ~의원연맹 the Inter-Parliamentary Union 《생략 IPU》 / ~인 a cosmopolitan; a citizen of the world / ~전화 the international telephone service / ~친선 international amity / ~통화 〔通貨〕 international currency / ~통화기금 the International Monetary Fund 《생략 IMF》 / ~해사 위성지구국 an inter-

국지(局地) a locality. ¶ ~적(인) local; regional / ~화하다 localize. ¶ ~전쟁 a local war; a limited warfare.

국채(國債) a (government) bond; (공채) a government loan. ¶ ~를 모집(상환)하다 raise (redeem, sink) a government loan. ‖ ~의존도 percentage of bond sale in total budget revenue.

국책(國策) a national (state) policy. ¶ ~을 따르다 (수행하다) follow (carry out) the national policy. ‖ ~은행 a government-run bank / ~회사 a national policy concern (company).

국체(國體) national constitution; national structure.

국치(國恥) ~일 the National Humiliation Day; a day of national infamy.

국태민안(國泰民安) national prosperity and the welfare of the people.

국토(國土) a country; a territory; a domain. ¶ ~를 개척하다 cultivate (reform) the national land / 한국은 좁은 ~에 인구가 너무 많다 Korea has too many people for its limited land space. / ~개발 national land development / ~계획 national land planning / ~방위 national defense / ~보전 territorial integrity / ~분단 territorial division.

국판(菊判) a small octavo; a medium octavo《美》. ¶ ~ 300 페이지의 책 a 300-page octavo volume.

국학(國學) Korean (classical) literature. ‖ ~자 a Korean (classical) scholar.

국한(局限) localization; limitation. ~하다 localize; limit; set limits (*to*). ¶ 전염병은 그 지역에~되어 있다 The epidemic was limited to that area.

국헌(國憲) the national constitution. ¶ ~을 준수하다 respect (observe) the national constitution.　　　　　　　〔try.

국호(國號) the name of a coun-

국화(國花) the national flower.

국화(菊花) a chrysanthemum.

국회(國會) the National Assembly (한국, 프랑스); Parliament(영국); the (National) Diet(일본, 덴마크, 스웨덴 따위); Congress(미국). ¶ ~는 개회(폐회) 중이다 The National Assembly is now in (out of) session. / ~가 소집(해산) 되었다 The National Assembly was convened (dissolved). ‖ ~도서관 (법) the National Assembly Library (Law) / ~사무처 the Secretariat of the National Assembly / ~의사당 the Assembly Hall; the Capitol 《美》 / ~의원 an Assemblyman; a member of parliament(생략 an M.P.); a Congressman (미국의) / ~청문회 a parliamentary hearing (*on the Hanbo corruption scandal*) / 정기 (특별, 임시) ~ an ordinary (a special, an extraordinary) session of the National Assembly.

군(君) 〔자네〕 you; 〔이름에〕 Mister; Mr. 《Kim》.

군(軍) (군대) an army; a force; troops. ¶ 제1야전~ the First Field Army.

군(郡) a district; a county.

군 extra (가외); superfluous; unnecessary. ¶ ~비용 extra expenses / ~식구 a freeloader; a sponger; a defendent / ~것 unnecessary things / ~사람 an extra person.

군가(軍歌) a war (military) song.

군거(群居) gregarious life. ~하다 live gregariously (in flocks). ‖ ~본능 the herd instinct / ~성 gregariousness; sociability.

군것질 a snack; between-meals refreshments. ~하다 spend *one*'s pocket money on candy (sweets).

군경(軍警) the military and the police.

군계(群鷄) ‖ ~일학(一鶴) a jewel on a dunghill; a Triton among the minnows.

군관구(軍管區) a military district.

군국(軍國) ~주의 militarism / ~주의자 a militarist.

군기(軍紀) military discipline; troop morals. ¶ ~를 유지 [문란하게]하다 maintain (break) military discipline.

군기(軍旗) the (*regimental*) colors; a battle flag; an ensign; a standard.

군기(軍機) a military secret. ¶ ~를 누설하다 disclose a military secret. ‖ ~누설 leakage of military secrets.

군납(軍納) supply of goods and services to the military. ~하다 provide supplies or services for an army; purvey for an army. ‖ ~업자 a military goods supplier(물품의) / ~회사 service contractors for the army (용역의) / ~계약 military supply contract firm.

군내 an unpleasant (unwanted) smell.

군단(軍團) an army corps; a corps. ¶ 제2 ~ the 2nd Corps. ‖ ~사령부 the corps headquarters.

군대(軍隊) an army; troops; forces; the military. ¶ ~에 입대하다 join (enlist in) the army / ~생활을 하다 serve in the army / ~식으로 in military way (fashion). ‖ ~생활 army life.

군더더기 a superfluity.

군데(곳) a place; a spot; a point(지점); 《부분》 a part. ¶ 군데 ~에 in places; here and there; sporadically / 한 ~에 머물다 stay in a place.

군도(軍刀) a saber; a sword.

군도(群島) an archipelago; a group of islands. ‖ 말레이 ~ the Malay Archipelago.

군란(軍亂) an army insurrection (rebellion); a *coup d'état*.

군략(軍略) a stratagem; tactics. ‖ ~가 a strategist; a tactician.

군량(軍糧) military provisions.

군령(軍令) a military command.

군림(君臨) reigning. ~하다 reign (rule) 《over》. ¶ 영화계에 ~하다 dominate (lord it over) the film world.

군말 idle talk; an unnecessary (uncalled-for) remark; prattle. ~하다 say useless (irrelevant) things; talk nonsense.

군모(軍帽) a military cap.

군목(軍牧) 『軍』 a chaplain.

군무(軍務) military affairs (service, duty).

군문(軍門) a military camp; an army. ¶ ~에 들어가다 enlist in the army.

군민(軍民) soldiers and civilians.

군번(軍番) (a soldier's) serial number; service number (생략 SN).

군벌(軍閥) the military clique. ‖ ~ 정치 militaristic government.

군법(軍法) martial (military) law.

군복(軍服) a military (naval) uniform. ¶ ~을 입고 있다 be in military uniform.

군부(軍部) the military authorities; the military. ¶ 그 나라에서는 최근 ~ 세력이 대두하고 있다 Recently the military authorities have been gaining power in the country.

군불 ¶ ~(을) 때다 heat the floor (of a Korean *ondol*).

군비(軍備) armaments; military preparedness 《美》. ¶ ~경쟁 an armament race / ~철폐 disarmament / ~축소《확장》reduction (expansion) of armaments.

군비(軍費) war expenditure.

군사(軍事) military affairs. ¶ ~상의 military; strategic (작전상의) ~상의 목적으로 for military (strategic) purposes / 이 섬은 ~상 매우 중요하다 This island is very important for military reason. / ~제재를 가하다 impose military sanctions 《*on*》. ‖ ~개입 (a) military intervention / ~거점 a strategic position / ~고문단 the Military Advisory Group / ~기지 a military base / ~대국 a major military power / ~동맹 a military alliance / ~력 military (armed) strength (capacity) / ~법원 a court-martial / ~분계선 the Military Demarcation Line / ~시설 military establishments (installations) / ~원조 (우편) military aid (mail) / ~위성 a military satellite / ~재판 court-martial / ~재판에 회부하다 try 《*a soldier*》by court-martial / ~재판을 소집하다 call a court-martial) / ~정권 a military regime / ~행동 military movements (action) / ~훈련 military drill (training).

군사령관(軍司令官) an army commander.

군사령부(軍司令部) the army headquarters.

군사설(― 辭說) a long and uncalled-for speech.

군살(궂은살) proud flesh; granulation; 《손발에 생기는》 a callus; a corn; 《군더더기 살》 superfluous flesh; fat (지방). ~이 붙다 put on extra flesh / 엄지발가락에 ~이 배기다 get callus on *one's* big toe.

군상(群像) ① 《조각》 a sculptured group. ② 《많은 사람들》 a large group of people.

군색하다(窘塞―) 《구차》(be) indigent; poor; needy; 《어렵게 보임》 (be) lame; clumsy; be in a fix. ¶ 군색한 변명 a clumsy excuse.

군서(群棲) gregarious life. ~하다 live gregariously.

군세(軍勢) 《병력》 the number of soldiers; troops; forces; 《형세》 the military situation 《*of a country*》.

군소(群小) minor; petty; lesser. ‖ ~ 정당 minor political parties.

군소리 ① 《군말》 superfluous words; an uncalled-for remark; nonsense. ~하다 talk nonsense. ② ~ 헛소리.

군속(軍屬) a civilian employee of the army (navy).

군수(軍需) ~공장 a munitions factory / ~산업 the munitions (war) industry / ~품 (물자) war supplies; munitions.

군수(郡守) the magistrate of a county; a county headman.

군식구(―食口) ☞ 군.

군신(君臣) sovereign and subject; lord and vassal.
군신(軍神) the god of war; Mars (로마 신화); Ares(그리스 신화).
군악(軍樂) military music. ǁ ~대 a military band.
군영(軍營) a military camp (base).
군용(軍用) (for) military use (purpose). ǁ ~견 a war (military) dog / ~기 a warplane / ~도로 a military road / ~열차 a troop train.
군웅(群雄) a number of rival leaders. ǁ ~할거 rivalry between warlords / ~할거의 시대 the age of rival chiefs (warlords)).
군원(軍援) military aid (assistance).
군율(軍律)(軍紀) martial law; (군기) military discipline.
군음식(-飮食) a between-meals snack; a snack.
군의(軍醫) an army (a naval) doctor (surgeon). ǁ ~관 a medical officer.
군인(軍人) a serviceman; a soldier (육군); a sailor(해군); an airman (공군). ¶ ~을 soldierly; soldierlike. ǁ ~부양 가족 dependents of military personnel / ~사회 military circles / ~생활 military life / ~연금 a soldier's pension / ~정신 the military spirit / ~출신 an ex-soldier.
군자(君子) a man of virtue (noble character); a wise man.
군자금(軍資金) war funds; campaign funds (선거 자금 등).
군장(軍裝) (평시의) military uniform; (전시의) war outfit (attire).
군장(軍葬) a military funeral.
군적(軍籍) the military register; (신분) military status (position).
군정(軍政) (establish, be under) military administration. ǁ ~청 the Military Government Office.
군제(軍制) a military system.
군주(君主) a monarch; a sovereign; a ruler. ǁ ~국 a monarchy / ~정체 monarchism.
군중(群衆) a crowd (throng) (of people); the masses (대중). ǁ ~을 헤치고 나아가다 push *one's* way through a crowd. ǁ ~심리 mob (mass) psychology.
군진(軍陣) a military camp; an encampment.
군집(群集) ~하다 gather; throng; crowd together.
군짓 doing unnecessary (useless) things; things done unnecessarily (in vain). ~하다 do unnecessary (useless) things.
군청(郡廳) a county office.
군축(軍縮) disarmament; arm reduction. ~하다 disarmament. ǁ ~회담 disarmament talks / ~회의 a disarmament conference.
군침 slaver; saliva; slobber; drool. ¶ ~을 흘리다 drivel; slaver; run at the mouth; 《육심이 나다》 lust 《for》; be envious 《of》 / 그 파이를 보니 ~이 돈다 The pies make my mouth water.
군턱 a double chin.
군함(軍艦) a warship; a vessel of war; a battleship. ǁ ~기 a naval ensign.
군항(軍港) a naval port (station).
군호(軍號) a password; a watchword.
군화(軍靴) military shoes; combat (army) boots; GI shoes 《美》.
군후(軍侯) a (feudal) lord.
굳건하다 (be) strong and steady; firm; solid.
굳다¹ 《물체가》 (be) hard; solid; 《정신·태도가》 (be) firm; strong; adamant; 《인색하다》 (be) frugal; tight-fisted; stingy; 《표정·몸이》 (be) stiff. ¶ 굳게 strongly; firmly; solidly / 굳은 결심 a firm resolution / 굳은 의지 strong (iron) will / 굳게 약속하다 give a firm promise / 굳은 표정으로 입구에 서 있다 stand at the entrance with a stern look.
굳다² 《동사》 become stiff (hard); harden; stiffen; set. ¶ 젤리가 굳었다 The jelly has set.
굳세다 (be) firm; strong; stout; adamant. ¶ 굳세게 stoutly; undauntedly; firmly / 굳센 신념 a firm (strong) conviction.
굳이 positively; firmly; solidly; obstinately. ¶ ~ 사양하다 decline persistently.
굳히다 make 《*something*》 hard; harden; stiffen; 《공고히》 strengthen; consolidate. ¶ 결심을 ~ make a firm determination.
굴(蠣) 《패》 an oyster. ǁ ~껍질 an oyster shell / ~양식장 an oyster bed (farm).
굴(窟) ① 《짐승의》 a lair; a den; a burrow (토끼 따위); an earth (여우의). ② 《동혈》 a cave; a cavern. ③ 《터널》 a tunnel.
굴곡(屈曲) bending; winding; (해안의) indentation. ~하다 bend; wind; be crooked. ¶ ~이 진 winding; meandering (강이); (도로가) zigzagging; crooked. ǁ ~부 a bent; a turn.
굴다 《행동하다》 act; behave; conduct *oneself* 《*like a gentleman*》. ¶ 난폭하게 ~ behave (conduct) *oneself* rudely 《*to another*》 / 공명정대하게 ~ play fair with 《*somebody*》 / 예교있게 ~ behave amiably.

굴다리 an overpass; a viaduct.
굴대 an axle; an axis; a shaft.
굴도리 a round (cylindrical) beam.
굴뚝 a chimney; a (smoke) stack; a funnel(기선의); a (stove) pipe (난로의). ‖ ~청소 chimney sweeping.
굴뚝새 〔鳥〕 a wren. 〔Ling.〕
굴렁쇠 a hoop.
굴레 a bridle. ¶ ~를 씌우다 bridle; 《속박》 restrain; curb / ~를 벗다 take off a bridle; get released.
굴리다 ① 《굴러가게》 roll 《a ball》. ② 《한구석에》 throw 《a thing》 to one side; leave 《a thing》 negligently. ③ 《돈을》 lend out 《money》. ④ 《운영》 run. ¶ 버스를 ~ have a bus running for business purposes.
굴복(屈服) surrender; submission. ~하다 yield; submit; surrender; give in 《to》. ¶ ~시키다 bring 《a person》 to his knees; make 《a person》 give in / 적에게 ~하다 surrender to the enemy.
굴비 a dried yellow corvina.
굴신(屈伸) extension and flexion. ~하다 bend and stretch; extend and contract. ¶ ~이 자유자재한 elastic; flexible / 무릎의 ~ 운동을 하다 do knee-bends.
굴욕(屈辱) humiliation; disgrace; an insult. ¶ ~적인 humiliating; disgraceful / ~을 주다 humiliate; insult; put 《a person》 to shame / ~을 참다 swallow an insult. / ~감 a sense of humiliation / ~외교 a submissive foreign policy.
굴절(屈折) bending; winding; 〔理〕 refraction. ~하다 refract; bend. ‖ ~광선 a refracted light (ray) / ~렌즈 a refracting lens; a refractor / ~율 a refractive index / ~어 〔言〕 an inflectional language.
굴젓 salted (pickled) oysters.
굴종(屈從) submission. ~하다 submit; yield; succumb 《to》.
굴지(屈指) ¶ ~의 leading; prominent; outstanding / ~의 실업가 a leading businessman / 포항은 한국 ~의 산업도시이다 Pohang is one of the leading industrial cities in Korea. 「into, under」.
굴진(掘進) ~하다 dig through
굴착(掘鑿) digging; excavation. ~하다 excavate; dig out. ‖ ~기 an excavator.
굴하다(屈一) ① ~굽히다 ①. ② 《복종》 yield (submit) 《to》; give in; bow 《to》. ¶ 역경에 굴하지 않다 bear up well under difficult 《adverse》 circumstances / 어떤 일에도 굴하지 않을 용기가 있다 have the courage never to submit (yield) to anything.

굵다 (be) big; thick; deep(음성이); bold (활자가). ¶ 굵은 목소리로 in a thick voice / 굵은 눈썹 heavy (brushy) eyebrows / 굵은 팔 a big arm / 굵은 실 (나뭇가지) a thick thread (branch) / 굵은 글씨로 쓰다 write in bold strokes.
굶기다 starve; let (make) 《a person》 go hungry. ¶ 굶겨 죽이다 starve 《a person》 to death.
굶다 go without food (eating); go hungry; starve; famish. ¶ 굶어 죽다 die of hunger; starve to death / 지금도 북한에서는 많은 사람들이 굶어 죽고 있다 Many people starve to death in North Korea even today.
굶주리다 (못 먹다) starve; be (go) hungry; be starving (갈망하다); hanker 《after》; be hungry (thirsty) for; starve for. ¶ 굶주린 많은 사람들을 a mass of hungry (starving) people / 사랑에 ~ hanker after love / 지식에 굶주려 있다 have a thirst for knowledge.
굼뜨다 (be) slow; tardy; sluggish. ¶ 일하는 것이 ~ be slow at the job.
굼벵이 ① (벌레) a white grub; a maggot. ② (사람) a laggard; a sluggard.
굼틀거리다 writhe; wriggle; twist; wiggle. ¶ 굼틀거리며 나아가다 wriggle along.
굽 ① (마소의) a hoof. ¶ 갈라진 ~ cloven hoofs / 말발 ~ 소리 the sound of a horse's hoofs. ② (신발의) a heel. ¶ ~이 높은 (낮은) 구두 high-(low-)heeled shoes. ③ (그릇의) a foot (of a glass).
굽다¹ (휘다) (be) bent; curved; crooked; winding; stooped. ¶ 굽은 나무 a crooked tree / 나이가 들어 허리가 ~ be stooped (bent) with age / 도로는 해안선을 따라 굽어 있다 The road curves along the coastline.
굽다² (음식을) roast 《meat》; broil 《fish》; barbecue 《fish or meat》; grill 《a steak, a chicken》; toast 《a slice of bread》; bake 《potatoes》; (벽돌 등을) make (burn, bake) 《bricks》. ¶ 덜 구워지게 be underdone; be half-done / "스테이크를 어떻게 구울까요?" "잘 구워 (중간 정도로; 설구워) 주세요." "How would you like your steak?" "Well-done (Medium, Rare), please." 「of a room.
굽도리 the lower parts of walls
굽실거리다 cringe (kowtow, crawl) 《to》; be obsequious 《to》. ¶ 굽실 굽실 obsequiously / 상사에게 ~ cringe to one's superiors / 그에게 그렇게 굽실거릴 필요는 없다 You

굽어보다 《내려다보다》 look down; overlook; 《굽어 살피다》 condescend to help. ¶ 골짜기를 ~ look down into a valley.

굽이 a turn; a curve; a bend. ¶ ~마다 at every turn〔bend〕. ¶ ~굽이치며 흐르는 개울 a meandering stream.

굽히다 ① 《무릎·허리를》 bend; bow; stoop. ¶ 무릎을 ~ bend *one's* knees / 몸을 앞뒤로 ~ bend *one's* body forward and backward. ② 《뜻을》 yield; submit; give in. ¶ 주의를 ~ depart from *one's* principles / 압력에 못이겨 의지를 ~ yield under pressure.

굿 《무당의》 an exorcism; a shaman ritual. *Gut*. 《구경거리》 a spectacle; a show. ¶ ~을 하다 exorcise; perform an exorcism / ~뒤에 낫장구 useless talks on a matter which has already been decided; crying over spilt milk / ~들은 무당 a person who is only too happy to be of service.

굿바이히트 〔野〕 a game ending hit.

궁(宮) a palace.

궁경(窮境) ① 《가난》 poverty; needy circumstances; destitution. ② ☞ 궁지.

궁궐(宮闕) the royal palace.

궁극(窮極) extremity; finality. ¶ ~의 final; ultimate; eventual / ~의 목적 *one's* ultimate purpose〔object〕 / ~에 가서는 finally; eventually; in the end; in the long run / ~에 가서 그는 성공할 것이다 He will succeed eventually.

궁금하다 (be) anxious; worried; concerned 《about, for》; interested 《in》. ¶ 《아무의》 소식이 ~ be anxious to hear from 《a person》 / 딸의 안부를 궁금해하다 be concerned〔anxious〕 about their daughter's safety.

궁녀(宮女) a court lady〔maid〕.

궁노루 〔動〕 a musk deer.

궁도(弓道) archery; bowmanship.

궁도련님(宮 一) a green youth 《of noble birth》.

궁둥이 the hips; the buttocks; the behinds; the backside; the butt 《口》; the ass 《俗》; the rump(동물의). ¶ ~가 무겁다 be lazy〔sluggish〕 / ~가 질기다 have a habit of overstaying / 여자 ~를 쫓아다니다 chase after a girl.

궁리(窮理) 《생각》 deliberation; consideration; meditation; 《연구》 study〔research〕 of the state of affairs〔things〕. ~하다 ponder 《on》; think〔mull〕 over. ¶ …할 ~를 하다 mull over ways of *doing*... / ~에 잠기다 be lost in thought; be absorbed in *one's* thought.

궁벽하다(窮僻 一) (be) out-of-the-way; remote; secluded. ¶ 궁벽한 곳 an out-of-the-way place.

궁상(弓狀) arch. ¶ ~의 arched; bow-shaped; curved.

궁상(窮狀) a sad plight; straitened circumstances; wretched condition. ¶ ~스럽다〔맞다〕 (be) miserable looking; wretched; have a look of poverty / ~떨다 behave like a poor person; pretend poverty.

궁상(窮相) a meager face.

궁수(弓手) an archer; a bowman.

궁술(弓術) archery; bowmanship. ¶ ~대회 an archery match.

궁시(弓矢) bow and arrow.

궁여지책(窮餘之策) (a plan as) a last resort; a desperate shift 〔measure〕. ¶ ~으로서 as a (means of) last resort.

궁전(宮殿) a (royal) palace. ¶ 버킹엄 ~ Buckingham Palace.

궁정(宮廷) the Court. ‖ ~문학〔생활〕 court literature〔life〕 / ~화가 a court painter.

궁중(宮中) the (Royal) Court. ¶ ~에서 at Court. ‖ ~요리 the (Korean) royal cuisine.

궁지(窮地) a predicament; an awkward position; a difficult situation; a dilemma. ¶ ~를 벗어나다 get out of difficulty / ~로 몰아 넣다 drive 《a person》 into a corner / 그녀는 ~에 빠져 있다 She is caught in a dilemma. *or* She is in a fix〔tight corner〕.

궁핍(窮乏) poverty; destitution. ~하다 (be) poor; be in needy circumstances; be badly off. ¶ ~해지다 become poor; be reduced to poverty; 궁핍한 생활 a life of distress〔want〕.

궁하다(窮 一) 《살림이》 be in distress〔want〕; (be) destitute; needy; 《입장이》 be in an awkward position; be in a dilemma; be at a loss. ¶ 돈에 ~ be pressed for money / 그녀는 대답에 궁했다 She didn't know what to answer. / 궁하면 통한다 《俗談》 There is always some way out of a difficulty if you really look for one.

궁합(宮合) 〔民俗〕 marital harmony predicted by a fortune-teller. ¶ ~을 보다 predict marital harmony / ~을 보게 하다 have 《*their*》 marital harmony predicted 《*by*》 / ~이 맞는〔안 맞는〕 부부 a well-matched〔an ill-matched〕 couple.

궁형(弓形) a crescent (form); 《數》 a segment of a circle; a lune.
굳다 ① 〔얹짢다〕 (be) cross; bad; undesirable. ¶ 굳은 일 an ungrateful affair; a disaster / 심술 ~ 하다 be bad-natured; be cross-minded. ② 〔날씨가〕 (be) bad; foul; nasty; rainy; wet. ¶ 굳은 날씨 nasty weather / 굳은 비 a long and nasty rain.
권(卷) ① 〔책 한 권의〕 a volume; a book; 〔영화의〕 a reel. ¶ 제1~ the first volume; vol. I. ② 〔종이의〕 twenty sheets of Korean paper; a Korean quire.
권고(勸告) (a piece of) advice; counsel; recommendation. ~ 하다 advise; counsel; give advice (counsel); recommend. ¶ 의사의 ~를 따르다 follow one's doctor's advice / 사직을 ~하다 advise (urge) (a person) to resign. ‖ ~서 a written advice /. ~안 a recommendation.
권내(圈內) (be) within the range (sphere) (of influence). ¶ 당선 권 ~에 있다 have a good chance of being elected (passing the exam) / 폭풍 ~에 들다 enter the range of a violent storm.
권농(勸農) ~ 하다 encourage (promote) agriculture.
권두(卷頭) the beginning (opening page) of a book. ‖ ~논문 the opening article (of a journal) / ~사 a foreword; a preface.
권력(權力) power; authority; influence (세력). ¶ ~ 있는 powerful; influential / ~을 얻다 (잃다) get (lose) power / ~을 행사하다 wield (exercise) authority (power) / ~을 잡다 seize power / ~에 굶주려 있다 be hungry for power. ‖ ~가 a man of power (influence) / ~욕 the desire for power / 평치 power politics / ~주의 authoritarianism / ~투쟁 a struggle for power.
권리(權利) a right; a claim (요구); a title (소유권); a privilege (특권). ¶ ~를 행사 (남용)하다 exercise (abuse) one's rights / ~이 있다 have a right (to do); be entitled (authorized) (to do) / ~를 침해하다 infringe on another's rights / ~을 주장하다 insist (assert) a right / ~를 포기하다 give up a right / 나에게는 발언 (투표) 할 ~가 있다 I have a right to speak (the right to vote). ‖ ~ 금 a premium; key (concession) money / ~의식 a sense of entitlement (~의식에 눈뜨다 become aware of one's right) / ~이전 a transfer of rights / ~증서 a certificate of title.

권말(卷末) the end of a book.
권모술수(權謀術數) trickery; scheming; machinations. ¶ ~에 능한 사람 a schemer; an expert in cunning plots / ~를 쓰다 resort to trickery. family.
권문세가(權門勢家) an influential
권불십년(權不十年) Every flow has its ebb. or Pride goes before a fall. or Pride will have a fall.
권선(捲線) a coil; winding. ‖ ~ 기 a (coil) winding machine.
권선징악(勸善懲惡) encouraging the good and punishing the evil; poetic justice. ¶ ~의 극 a play with a moral purpose; a morality play.
권세(權勢) power. ¶ 권력. ¶ ~를 부리다 wield (exert) power 《over》 / ~를 독차지하다 monopolize the power. / ~욕 a lust for power.
권속(眷屬) ① 〔식구〕 one's family (dependents); 〔영화의〕 a whole family. ② 〔아내〕 my wife.
권솔(眷率) one's family (dependents). [powerful courtier.
권신(權臣) an influential vassal; a
권업(勸業) ~ 하다 promote (encourage) industry.
권외(圈外) be outside of the range (circle); out of range. ¶ 레이더 ~ out of radar range / 〔선거에서〕 당선 ~에 있다 have no chance of getting elected.
권위(權威) authority; power; 《위엄》 dignity; 《대가》 an authority. ¶ ~ 있는 authoritative; authentic / 부모의 ~ parental authority / 세계적인 ~ a world authority 《on》 / ~를 잃다 (회복하다) lose (reassert) one's authority.
권유(勸誘) invitation; solicitation; persuasion; canvass. ~ 하다 invite; solicit; canvass; persuade. ¶ 가입을 ~하다 canvass for subscription / 가입을 ~하다 invite 《a person》 to join 《a club》. ‖ ~원 a canvasser; an agent; a solicitor.
권익(權益) (protect one's) rights and interests.
권장(勸奬) ~ 하다 encourage; urge; promote; recommend. ¶ 회사에서 ~하는 조기〔명예〕퇴직 early retirement at the suggestion of the company.
권좌(權座) (the seat of) power. ¶ ~에 오르다 come (rise) to power.
권총(拳銃) a pistol; a revolver(회전식); a gun (美); a handgun (美). ¶ ~을 겨누다 point (aim) a gun at 《a person》 ‖ ~강도 a burglar armed with a pistol / 6연발~ a six-shooter (美).
권태(倦怠) boredom; weariness; fatigue. ¶ ~를 느끼다 feel tired;

권토중래(捲土重來) ~하다 make another attempt with redoubled efforts; resume *one's* activities with redoubled energies.

권투(拳鬪) boxing; pugilism. ~하다 box《with》. ¶ ~계 the boxing world / ~선수 a boxer;《프로의》a prizefighter / ~시합 a boxing match〔bout〕/ ~장 a boxing ring.

권하다(勸─) ① 《추천》 recommend. 책을 ~ recommend a book to《a person》. ② 《권고》ask; advise; suggest; persuade. ¶ 금연하라고 ~ advise《a person》not to smoke; advise against smoking / 모임에 들라고 ~ ask《a person》to join a society. ③ 《권유》invite;《강권》press on《a person》; urge;《내놓다》offer. ¶ 담배를〔술을〕 ~ offer a cigarette〔a glass of wine〕.

권한(權限) authority; power; competence(법령에 근거한). ¶ ~이 있는 사람 a person in authority / ~을 행사하다 exercise *one's* authority /《~을 부여하다 authorize《a person》《to do》; give《a person》authority《to do》/ 나에게는 그것을 행할 ~이 없다 I have no authority to do it. / ~을 넘다 exceed *one's* authority〔competence〕/ ~을 지키다 observe the limits of competence / 그의 행위는 ~밖의 짓이었다 His act was unauthorized〔unwarranted〕. ‖ ~ 대행 the acting《*President*》.

권화(權化) incarnation; embodiment; avatar. 化신(化身).

궐기(蹶起) ~하다 rise〔to action〕; rouse *oneself* to action. ‖ ~대회 a rally.

궐내(闕內)〈within〉the royal palace.

궐위(闕位)《왕위의》the interregnum.

궤(櫃) a chest; a coffer; a box.

궤도(軌道)《천체의》an orbit;《철도의》a(railroad) track《美》; a railway. ¶ 지구를 도는 인공위성의 ~ the orbit of a satellite around the earth /《열차가》~를 벗어나다 run off the track / 인공위성이 ~에 진입했다〔~를 벗어났다〕 The satellite has gone into〔out of〕 orbit. / 사업이 마침내 ~에 올라섰다 Business finally got on the right track. ‖ ~비행 an orbital flight / 단선〔복선〕~ a single(double) track〔철도의〕.

궤멸(潰滅) a rout; a collapse; annihilation(전멸). ~하다 be defeated; be routed; destroy.

궤변(詭辯) sophism; sophistry. ¶ ~을 부리다 quibble; sophisticate. ¶ ~가 a sophist; a quibbler.

궤양(潰瘍)《醫》an ulcer. bler.

궤적(軌跡)《數》a locus; 《바퀴자국》the trace of wheels. ¶ ~을 구하다 find a locus.

궤주(潰走) a rout. ~하다 be routed; be put to rout〔flight〕.

궤짝(櫃─)《상자》a box; a chest.

귀《듣는》an ear;《청각》hearing;《가장자리》an edge(물건의); a selvage(직물의). ¶ ~에 손을 대고 with *one's* hand cupped behind *one's* ear / ~가 밝다〔밝다〕 be hard(quick) of hearing / ~에 익다 be familiar / ~가 안 들리다 be deaf(of one ear) / 어머님의 말씀이 아직도 ~에 쟁쟁하다 My mother's words still ring in my ears. ¶ ~뿌리 the root of *one's* ear / ~앓이 an earache / ~약 an ear remedy; eardrops.

귀…(貴)《당신의》your esteemed. your. ¶ ~국 your(esteemed) country / ~사(社) your company / ~서(書) your(esteemed) letter / ~정부 your government / ~지(紙) your(esteemed) column; your(valued) paper (5월 10일자 ~지 보도와 같이 as stated in your paper dated May 10).

귀가(歸家) return(ing) home. ~하다 return(come, go) home. ¶ ~가 늦다 be late in coming home.

귀감(龜鑑) a model; a pattern; a mirror. ¶ 군인의 ~ a model soldier; a pattern of soldiery.

귀갑(龜甲) a tortoise shell.

귀거슬리다 be unpleasant(disagreeable) to hear; be bitter to hear.

귀걸이(귓식용) earmuffs; an earcap;《장식용》an earring; a pendant.

귀결(歸結) a conclusion; an end;《결과》a result; a consequence. ¶ 당연한 ~로서 as a natural consequence / ~짓다 bring to a conclusion.

귀경(歸京) ~하다 return to Seoul.

귀고리 an earring; an eardrop.

귀골(貴骨)《사람》people of noble birth;《골격》noble features.

귀공자(貴公子) a young noble(-man). ¶ ~다운 noble-looking; princely.

귀국(歸國) ~하다 return(come back) to *one's* country; go(come, get) home. ¶ ~ 길에 오르다 leave for home.

귀금속(貴金屬) precious metals. ¶ ~상 a dealer in jewelry; a jeweler《美》; a jewelery store.

귀납(歸納) induction. ~하다 induce 《*A* from *B*》; make an induction 《*from the facts*》. ‖ ~적(으로) inductive(ly) / ~적 추리 inductive reasoning. ‖ ~법 induction; the inductive method.

귀농(歸農) ~하다 return to the farm (farming). ‖ ~운동 a "back-to-the-earth" movement. (fully).

귀담아듣다 listen willingly (care

귀동냥 knowledge picked up by listening to others; learning by the ear without real study. ~하다 learn by listening to others carefully.

귀동자(貴童子) one's dear (son).

귀두(龜頭) 〖解〗 the glans (of the penis). ‖ ~염 〖醫〗 balanitis.

귀때 a spout; a tap (술통 따위의).

귀뚜라미 〖蟲〗 a cricket. ¶ ~가 울다 a cricket chirps.

귀뜨다 《a baby》 start to hear for the first time.

귀띔 a tip; a hint; a suggestion. ~하다 give a tip; hint 《*at*》; whisper 《*something*》 into 《*a person's*》 ear. ¶ 사의를 ~하다 hint at one's resignation.

귀로(歸路) one's way home (back); 《여행길의》 one's return journey (trip). ¶ ~에 오르다 start on one's way home; leave (start) for home / 호주에서 ~에 홍콩에서 일박했다 I stopped over in Hong-kong for a night on my way home from Australia.

귀리 〖植〗 oats.

귀머거리 a deaf person.

귀먹다 become deaf; be deafened (일시적으로).

귀물(貴物) a rare (precious) thing; a treasure. 〔to hear.

귀밝다 (be) sharp-eared; be quick

귀부인(貴婦人) a (titled) lady; a noblewoman. ‖ ~다운 ladylike.

귀빈(貴賓) a guest of honor; a distinguished (an honored) guest. ‖ ~석 (실) seats (a room) reserved for distinguished guests (VIPs).

귀설다 (be) unfamiliar (unaccustomed, strange) to one's ear.

귀성(歸省) home-coming. ~하다 return (go, come) home; go back to one's hometown (village). ¶ 정거장은 ~객으로 혼잡했다 The station was crowded with passengers going home. ‖ ~객 homecoming people / ~열차 a train for home-coming passengers. 〔stinct.

귀소본능(歸巢本能) the homing in-

귀속(歸屬) reversion; return. ~하다 revert 《*to*》; be restored 《*to*》. ¶ T섬의 ~문제 the question of the title to T Island. ‖ ~의식 (a feeling of) identification 《*with*》;

a sense of belonging.

귀순(歸順) submission; surrender. ~하다 submit 《*to*》; (항명하다) defect 《*to*》. ~을 맹세하다 swear (pledge) allegiance 《*to the ruler*》 / ~자 a defecting soldier / ~자 a defector.

귀신(鬼神) a departed soul; a ghost; (악령) a demon; a fierce god. ¶ ~ 같다 be supernatural / ~도 모른다 No one knows. / ~도 울리다 make even the gods weep.

귀아프다 be fed up with; have heard enough; be harsh (offensive) to the ear. ¶ 귀아픈 잡음 a jarring noise / 귀아프도록 들어왔네 I have heard enough of it.

귀양(史) exile; banishment. ¶ ~살다 live in exile / ~가다 be sent into exile; be banished (exiled) 《*to a remote province*》 / ~보내다 condemn 《*a person*》 to exile; banish. ‖ ~살이 living in exile; an exile(사람).

귀엣말 a whisper; whispering. ~하다 whisper (speak) in 《*a person's*》 ear; talk in whispers.

귀여겨듣다 listen attentively 《*to*》; be all ears.

귀여리다 (be) credulous; gullible; be easily convinced.

귀염 love; favor; affection. ¶ ~받다 be loved; be liked; enjoy a person's favor. ‖ ~성 charm; attractiveness; lovableness.

귀엽다 (be) lovely; charming; attractive; lovable; sweet. ¶ 귀여운 얼굴 a lovely (sweet) face / 귀여운 여자 아이 a lovely little girl / 귀여워하다 love; pet; be affectionate 《*to*》; fondle; caress.

귀영(歸營) ~하다 return to one's barracks. ‖ ~시간 the hour for returning to barracks.

귀의(歸依) devotion; (개종) conversion. ~하다 become a devout believer 《*in Buddhism*》; embrace 《*Christianity*》. ¶ 기독교에 ~하다 be converted to Christianity. ‖ ~자 a believer; an adherent; (개종자) a convert.

귀이개 an earpick.

귀인(貴人) a nobleman; a dignitary. ‖ ~상 (相) a noble face (visage).

귀일(歸一) ~하다 be united (unified) into one; be reduced to one.

귀임(歸任) ~하다 return (come back, go back) to one's post.

귀잠 a sound (deep) sleep. ¶ ~들다 fall into a deep sleep.

귀재(鬼才) (사람) a genius; an outstandingly talented person; a wizard; (재주) remarkable tal-

ent; unusual ability.
귀접스럽다 ① 《더럽다》 (be) dirty; filthy. ② 《천하다》 (be) mean; base; low; nasty.
귀접이하다 round the edges off.
귀족(貴族) 《총칭》 the nobility; nobles; the peerage; 《개인》 a noble(man); a peer; an aristocrat. ¶ ~의, ~적인 noble; aristocratic. ‖ ~계급 the aristocratic class / ~ 정치 aristocracy.
귀중(貴中) Messrs. ¶ 스미스 상회 ~ Messrs. Smith & Co.
귀중(貴重) ~하다 (be) precious; valuable. ¶ ~한 시간 valuable time. ‖ ~품 a valuable; valuables (총칭).
귀지 ear wax.
귀질기다 (be) unresponsive; insensitive; be slow to understand.
귀착(歸着) ~하다 《돌아오다》 return; come back; 《귀결되다》 arrive at 《a conclusion》; result (end) in. ¶ 토론의 ~점 the logical conclusion of an argument / 그것은 결국 돈 문제로 ~된다 In the end it comes down to a question of money.
귀찮다 (be) troublesome; annoying; bothering; irksome. ¶ 귀찮은 사람 an annoying(a troublesome) person / …하는 것이 귀찮아지다 get (grow, become) tired (weary) of doing / 매우 귀찮아하다 think (it) very troublesome (to do); grudge the trouble of (doing) / 《아무에게》 굳다 trouble 《a person》; bother; annoy; give 《a person》 trouble / 그녀는 귀찮아하지 않고 길을 가르쳐 주었다 She took the trouble to show me the way.
귀천(貴賤) high and low; the noble and the mean. ¶ ~의 차별없이 irrespective of rank; high and low alike.
귀청(貴聽)〔解〕 the eardrum. ¶ ~이 터질 듯한 deafening; ear-splitting.
귀추(歸趨) a trend; a tendency 《결과》 an issue; a consequence. ¶ 당연한 ~로서 as a natural course of events.
귀퉁이 a corner; an angle.
귀틀집 a log hut (cabin).
귀하(貴下) Mr. (남성); Mrs. (기혼여성); M(d)me(부인); Miss(미혼여성); you(당신).
귀하(貴一) ① 《드물다》 (be) rare; uncommon; 《귀중》 (be) precious; valuable. ¶ 귀한 물건 a rarity; a valuable thing / 귀한 손님 a welcome visitor. ② 《고귀》 (be) noble; august; honorable. ¶ 귀하신 분 a person of noble birth.
귀함(歸艦) ~하다 return to one's warship.
귀항(歸航) a return passage; a homeward voyage(trip). ~하다 sail for home; make a homeward voyage(trip).
귀항(歸港) ~하다 return to port.
귀향(歸鄕) home-coming. ~하다 go (come, return) home. ‖ ~활동 activity at one's constituency.
귀화(歸化) naturalization. ~하다 be naturalized 《as a Korean citizen》. ‖ ~식물 a naturalized plant / ~인 a naturalized citizen.
귀환(歸還) a return. ~하다 return. ¶ 우주선은 지구에 무사히 ~했다 The space shuttle returned to the earth safely. ‖ ~병 a returned soldier / ~자 a repatriate; a returnee.
귀휴(歸休) 《근로자의》 (a) layoff. ¶ ~되다 be on leave from 《(the) service》 / ~중이다 be home on leave. ‖ ~병 a soldier on (terminal) leave / 《노동》 / ~제도〔經〕 the layoff system.
귓결 ~에 듣다 just happen to hear 《a story》.
귓구멍 an ear-hole; the ear.
귓등 ~으로 듣다 do not listen carefully.
귓바퀴 a pinna; an auricle.
귓밥 (the thickness of) an ear-lobe.
귓불 an earlobe.
귓속말 a whisper. ¶ 아무에게 ~하다 whisper 《a matter》 in 《a person's》 ear. 「in 《a person's》 ear.
귓전 ~에 대고 속삭이다 whisper
귓집 earmuffs.
규격(規格) a standard. ¶ ~외 《미달》의 non-standardized; substandard / ~화(化)하다 standardize / 그 상품은 ~에 안 맞는다 The goods are not up to the standards. ‖ ~통일〔화〕 standardization / ~판 a standard size / ~품 a standardized article 《~품의 구두를 팔다 sell standard sizes of shoes》.
규명(糾明) a close examination. ~하다 examine closely; look into 《a matter》 minutely (to light); investigate; study. ¶ 그 사건은 아직 충분히 ~되어 있지 않다 The case has not yet been properly investigated.
규모(規模) a scale; 《범위》 a scope; 《구조》 structure. ¶ 대 《소》 ~로 on a large (small) scale; in a large (small) way / ~를 확대〔축소〕하다 enlarge (reduce) the scale (of) / 전국적인 ~로 on a nation-wide scale. 「quarters.
규방(閨房) a boudoir; women's
규범(規範) 《모범》 a rule; a pattern; 《표준》 a standard; a criterion; a norm. ¶ ~적 법칙〔문법〕 normative law (grammar).

규사(硅砂)〖鑛〗silica.
규산(硅酸)〖化〗silicic acid. ‖ ~염 a silicate.
규석(硅石)〖鑛〗silex; silica.
규소(硅素)〖化〗silicon(기호 Si). ‖ ~수지 silicone resins.
규수(閨秀) ① 〈처녀〉 a young unmarried woman; a maiden. ② 《학예에 뛰어난 여자》 a literary woman; a bluestocking. ‖ ~시인 a female poet; a poetess / ~작가 a lady[woman] writer / ~화가 a lady[woman] painter.
규약(規約) 《규정》 a rule; 《협약》 an agreement; 《정관》 the article; a statute. ¶ ~을 정하다 lay down [make] rules / ~을 지키다[깨다] keep[break] the rules.
규율(規律) discipline; order; 《규칙》 rules; regulations. ¶ ~있는 well-diciplined; orderly / ~없는 disorderly; undisciplined / ~을 지키다[어기다] observe[break] the rules / ~있는 생활을 하다 lead an orderly life / ~에 맞게 행동하다 Act in an orderly manner.
규정(規定) 《규칙》 rules; regulations; 《조항》 provisions; stipulations(계약의). ~하다 prescribe; provide; stipulate 《for》. ¶ ~된 서식을 이용하다 use the prescribed form / 제3조 ~에 따라 처벌되다 be punished in Accordance with the provisions of Article 3. ‖ ~요금 the regulation charge / ~종목 《제조 동의》 compulsory exercises / ~통행 the traffic regulations. ‖ ~inner rules; a bylaw.
규정(規程) official regulations.
규제(規制) regulation; control; restriction. ~하다 regulate; control; restrict. ¶ 법적 ~를 가하다 impose legal controls 《on》 / ~를 해제하다 remove the controls on 《the price of oil》. ¶ 교통 traffic control / 자기 ~ voluntary control[restrictions] 《on her car exports to the U.S.》.
규조(硅藻)〖植〗a diatom. ‖ ~토 diatom earth.
규칙(規則) a rule; a regulation. ¶ ~적인 regular; methodical; systematic / ~에 따라 according to the rule / 학교 ~을 지키다[어기다] obey[break] the school rules / 실내 금연은 하나의 ~이다 It is the rule that you should not smoke in the room. / 그것은 교통 ~ 위반이다 It is against the traffic regulations. ‖ ~동사 a regular verb / ~서 a prospectus / ~위반 violation of regulations; a breach of the rules.
규탄(糾彈) censure; impeachment. ~하다 censure; impeach; denounce; accuse. ¶ 부정을 ~하다 impeach[denounce] 《a person》 for an injustice.
규토(硅土)〖化〗silica; silex.
규폐(증)(硅肺(症))〖醫〗silicosis. ‖ ~환자 a silicosis sufferer[victim].
규합(糾合) ~하다 rally; muster; call together. ¶ 동지를 ~하다 rally likeminded people 《around a person》.
균(菌) 《세균》 a bacillus [pl. bacilli]; a bacterium [pl. -ria]; a germ. ¶ ~류 a fungus [pl. -es, -gi] / ~류학 fungelogy / ~배양 germiculture; cultivation of bacteria.
균등(均等) equality. ¶ ~한 equal; even / 이익을 ~히 나누다 distribute the profit equally / 기회 ~의 원칙 the principle of equal opportunity. ‖ ~분배 equal division(~분배하다 divide equally; equalize).
균분(均分) equal division. ~하다 divide equally; equalize. ‖ ~상속 equalized inheritance.
균열(龜裂) a crack; a fissure. ¶ ~이 생기다 《벽 따위에》 be cracked; crack; split.
균일(均一) uniformity. ¶ ~한 uniform; equal; flat / ~하게 하다 unify; make 《a thing》 uniform / 백 원 ~ a uniform rate of 100 won. ‖ ~요금 a uniform [flat] rate.
균점(均霑) equal allotment of profits. ~하다 get[share] an equal allotment of profit.
균질(均質) homogeneity. ¶ ~의 homogeneous / ~화 하다 homogenize.
균형(均衡) balance; equilibrium. ¶ 세력의 ~ the balance of power / ~이 잡힌 well-balanced / ~을 잃지아니[잃지] keep[lose] the balance. ‖ ~예산 a balanced budget / ~재정 balanced[sound] finance.
귤(橘)〖植〗a tangerine. ¶ ~ 껍질을 벗기다 peel a tangerine. ‖ ~밭 a tangerine orchard(plantation).
그¹ 《사람》 that[the] man; he; that[the] woman; she. ¶ ~의 his; her.
그² 《형용적으로》 that; those; its. ¶ ~날 that[the] day / ~때 then; that time / ~같이 thus; so; like that; in that manner.
그건그렇고 by the way; well; now. ¶ ~, 자네에게 할 말이 있네 By the Way I have something 그것 it; that (one). to tell you.
그곳 there; that place.
그글피 three days after tomorrow; four days hence.

그까짓 such; so trivial (trifling). ¶ ~ 일로 걱정 마라 Don't worry yourself over such a trifle.

그끄저께 three days ago; two days before yesterday.

그나마 even that; and (at) that. ¶ ~ 없다 Even that one is gone.

그냥 (그대로) as it is (stands); as you find it; with no change; (내쳐) all the way; continuously; (…않고) without doing anything; just as one is; (무료로) free of charge. ¶ 의자를 있는 그대로 ~ 놔 둬라 Leave the chairs as they are. / ~ 울고만 있다 do nothing but cry / 사신 물건은 ~ 배달해 드립니다 Articles bought here will be delivered free of charge.

그네 a swing. ¶ ~를 타다 get on a swing. ‖ 그넷줄 the swing rope(s).

그녀 she. ¶ ~의(를, 에게) her.

그늘 ① (응달) shade. ¶ 나무 ~ the shade of a tree. ② (남의 비호) protection; patronage. ¶ ~의 under the patronage of / 부모 ~에서 자라다 grow up under one's parents' wings. ③ (배후) the back (behind). ¶ 차 ~에 숨다 hide oneself behind a car / 남의 ~에 숨어서 behind (a person's) back. ‖ 그늘진 shady.

그늘지다 get (be) shaded; be in the shade.

그다지 (not) so much; so; very. ¶ ~ 좋아하지 않다 do not care much for / ~ 춥지 않다 be not so cold.

그대 you; thou. ¶ ~들 you; all of you; you people.

그대로 as it is (stands); intact; just like that. ¶ ~ 내버려 두다 leave (a matter) as it is / ~ 있다 remain intact (as it was); be left untouched.

그동안 the while; during that time; these (those) days. ¶ ~ 안녕하셨는지요 Have you been well all these days?

그따위 such a one; that kind (sort) of. ¶ ~ 모자 such a hat.

그랑프리 a grand prix 《프》; a grand prize.

그래 ① (동료·아랫사람에 대한 대답) yes; all right; So it is. ¶ ~ That's right. ② 그래서. ¶ ~ 어떻단 말인가 So what?

그래도 but; still; and yet.

그래서 (and) then; and (so); so; therefore. ¶ ~ 그녀는 보이는 모습이 안 보이게 되었다 And then she went out of sight. / ~ 어떻게 되었느냐 Then, what happened? / ~ 어딜 갔느냐 And then where did you go?

그래야 ~ 사나이다 That's worthy of a man. / ~ 그답다 That's just like him. or That's typical of him.

그래프 a graph; a graphic chart. ‖ ~ 용지 graph (section) paper.

그랜드 ‖ ~ 오페라 a grand opera / ~ 피아노 a grand piano.

그램 a gram 《m》.

그러구러 (manage to do) somehow (or other); in someway or other; barely. ¶ 학교 과정을 ~ 마치다 go through one's school course somehow or other.

그러나 but; still; however.

그러나저러나 anyway; anyhow; in any case; either way.

그러니까 so; thus; for that reason; therefore; accordingly.

그러담다 gather (rake) up (something) into. ¶ 낙엽을 가마니에 ~ rake up fallen leaves into a straw bag.

그러면 then; if so; in that case. ¶ ~ 내일 오겠다 Well then, I'll come tomorrow. / ~ 이렇게 하도록 하자 In that case let's do it this way. / ~ 그에게 전화를 하지 요 If so I'll call him now.

그러모으다 rake (scrape) up (together). ¶ 낙엽을 ~ rake up fallen leaves.

그러므로 so; therefore; accordingly; hence. ¶ ~ 그는 친구가 많다 That is why he has so many friends.

그러잡다 clasp; grasp; take (get) hold of.

그러저러하다 (be) so and so; such and such. ¶ 그러저러해서 for such and such reasons.

그러하다 (be) so; such; like that. ¶ 그러한 사람 such a person; a man of that kind / 그러한 경우엔 in such a case; in case like that / 그런 까닭으로 such being the case.

그럭저럭 somehow (or other); one way or another.

그런고로 ☞ 그러므로.

그런데 but; however; and yet.

그런즉 therefore; so; then.

그럴싸(듯)하다 (be) plausible; likely specious. ¶ 그럴싸하게 들리다 sound plausible / 그럴싸한 거짓말을 하다 tell a plausible lie / 너의 설명은 그럴싸하게 들린다 Your explanation sounds plausible.

그럼 (긍정의 대답) yes; certainly; (그러면) then; well.

그렁그렁하다 (눈물이) be almost tearful; be suffused with tears. ¶ 눈물이 그렁그렁한 눈 eyes suffused (filled) with tears.

그렇게 so (much); to that extent; (부정어와 함께) (not) very (so); (그런 식으로) in that manner (way); like that. ¶ ~까지 so

그렇고말고 far (much); to such an extent / ~ 심한 병도 아니다 It is not a very serious illness. / ~ 말을 하지만 You may be right in saying so, but….

그렇고말고 indeed; of course; certainly; You're right.

그렇다 《그러하다》 (be) so; (be) like that; 《대답》 That's right.; You're right.; Yes; No. ¶ ~고 생각한다 I think so. / 「나는 행복하다.」—「나도 ~.」 "I am happy." — "So do I." 《잠시 차 한 잔 할까?》 "Shall we have a coffee break?" — "Yes, let's." / 「어제 그녀를 만나지 못했지」 — 「예, 그렇습니다.」 "Couldn't you meet her yesterday?" — "No, I couldn't." / 「이 계획은 불가능할 것 같애.」—「나도 그렇게 생각 해.」 "I'm afraid this plan is almost impossible." — "I think so, too."

그렇지 yes; So it is.; That's right.; You are right. ¶ 그도 ~만…. That's all very well, but…; You are right in a way, but….

그로기 groggy. ¶ ~ 상태가 되다 become groggy 《with a punch》; be punch-drunk.

그로스 a gross (=12 dozen).

그로테스크 ¶ ~ 한 grotesque.

그루 《나무의》 a stump (베고난 것); 《셀 때》 a plant; a tree. ¶ 한 ~의 소나무 one pine tree.

그룹 a group. ¶ ~을 이루다 form a group / 학생들을 ~으로 나누다 divide the students into groups / 작은 ~으로 나뉘어 출발하다 set out in small groups. ‖ ~ 활동 group activities / 삼성 ~ the Samsung Business Group.

그르다 ① 《옳지 않다》 (be) wrong; bad; blamable; be to blame; be in the wrong. ¶ 그런 짓을 ~ a wrong; an evil deed / 마음이 그른 사람 a bad (ill-natured) person / 네가 글렀다 You are to blame. ② 《가망이 없다》 (be) no good; hopeless; go wrong. ¶ 일이 글렀다 The matter is hopeless. / 그 애 사람되기는 글렀다 The boy will never become a good man.

그르렁거리다 《소리가》 wheeze; be wheezy; 《소리를》 make wheeze; gurgle. ¶ 《사람이》 목을 ~ make a gurgling sound.

그르치다 spoil; ruin; err; make a failure of. ¶ 계획을 ~ spoil (ruin) a plan / 판단을 ~ make an error of judgment / 일생을 ~ make a failure of one's life.

그릇 ① 《용기》 a vessel; a container. ¶ 빈 ~이 큰 소리를 낸다 An empty vessel makes the greatest sound. ② 《기량》 caliber; capacity; ability. ¶ ~이 크다(작다) be a man of large (small) caliber.

그릇되다 go wrong (amiss); be mistaken; fail; be ruined (다). ¶ 그릇된 wrong; mistaken / 그릇된 길 the wrong way; an evil course / 그릇된 짓을 하다 misconduct oneself; do wrong.

그리니치 Greenwich. ‖ ~ 표준시 Greenwich (mean) time 《생략 G.M.T.》.

그리다¹ 《그림을》 draw (무채색); paint (채색화); portray (인물화); sketch (약도를); picture (마음에); 《표현하다》 describe; depict. ¶ 산수(山水)를 ~ paint a landscape / 마음에 ~ picture to oneself / 지도를 ~ draw a map / 오늘의 미국인 생활을 ~ describe (depict) today's American life.

그리다² 《사모·동경》 long (yearn) for. ☞ 그리워하다.

그리스 Greece. ¶ ~의 Greek; Grecian. ‖ ~ 말 Greek / ~ 문명 Greek civilization / ~ 사람 a Greek; the Greeks (총칭).

그리스도 《Jesus》 Christ. ‖ ~ 교 Christianity.

그리움 yearning; longing; nostalgia; a dear feeling. ¶ ~에 사무치다 feel an irresistable yearning for (after).

그리워하다 yearn for (after) 《a person》; miss 《a friend》; long for 《one's home》; think fondly of 《a person》. ¶ 그는 학생 시절을 그리워했다 She longed for her school days.

그린란드 Greenland.

그릴 a grill (room).

그림 a picture (일반적); a painting (채색화); a drawing (무채색); a sketch (사생·약도); an illustration (삽화). ¶ ~을 그리다 paint (draw) a picture / ~ 처럼 아름다운 풍경 a picturesque view / 피카소의 ~ a 《picture by》 Picasso / ~의 떡 (비유적) (be nothing but) pie in the sky / 이것은 무슨 ~이냐 What is this a picture of? ‖ ~물감 pigments; paints; oil (water) colors / ~엽서 a picture (post) card / ~책 a picture book.

그림자 《투영》 a shadow; a silhouette; 《영상》 a reflection; an image; 《모습》 a figure. ¶ 장지에 비친 사람 ~ the shadow of a man falling on the paper sliding door / 호수에 비친 산의 ~ the reflection (image) of the mountain on the lake / ~를 던지다 cast 《throw》 《its》 shadow 《on, over》 / ~를 감추다 conceal oneself; disappear.

그립다 《동사적》 feel yearning for;

그만 long for; yearn after (for). ¶그리운 dear; dearest; beloved / 그리운 사람 *one's* beloved / 그리운 고향 *one's* dear old home / 옛날이 ~ I long for the old days.

그만 (그 정도로) to that extent; so much (many); that much (and no more). ¶이제 ~하면 됐다 We have had quite enough of it. / ~한 일에 울다니 우습다 It is silly of you to cry over such a trifle.

그만그만하다 be much (almost) the same. ¶어느 쪽이건 ~ There is not much to choose between them.

그만두다 ① (중단) stop; cease; discontinue; give up; quit. ¶장사를 ~ quit *one's* business / 학교를 ~ leave (give up) school. ② (사직) resign (*one's* post); quit; leave. ¶회사를 ~ leave the job of company.

그만저만하다 (be) so-so; not too good and not too bad; about the same.

그만큼 as much (as that); so (that) much; to that extent. ¶나는 ~밖에 모른다 I only know that much.

그만하다 ① (정도) be nearly (about) the same; be neither better nor worse. ② (크기·수량 등이) be about (much) the same; be as much (many) as; be neither more nor less. ③ (중지하다) stop; cease; leave off.

그맘때 about (around) that time; about the age (나이).

그물 a net; a dragnet (끄는); a casting net (팽이); netting (총칭). ¶~에 걸리다 be trapped (caught) in a net / ~을 치다 pitch (set) a net. ¶~코 a net knot / a netting loop / 새 ~ a sparrow net.

그믐 the end (last day) of the month. ¶이 달 ~에 at the end of this month. ¶~께 around the end of the month / ~밤 the last night of the (lunar) month / 설달~ (on) New Year's Eve.

그밖 the rest; the others. ¶~의 other; further / ~에 besides; moreover; on top of that.

그스르다 smoke; scorch; sear; fumigate.

그슬리다 ① ☞ 그스르다. ② (피동) get smoked (scorched). ¶새까맣게 ~ be scorched black / 그슬린 burnt (*wood*); scorched (*linen*); singed (*hair*).

그악스럽다 (장난이 심하다) be mischievous; naughty; (부지런하다) (be) hardworking; industrious.

그야말로 really; quite; indeed.

그예 at last; finally; in the end; ultimately; after all.

그윽하다 ① (고요하다) (be) deep and quiet; secluded; still; silent. ② (생각이) (be) deep; profound.

그을다 (햇볕에) get sunburned; get a tan; (연기에) be sooted (up); be stained with soot.

그을음 soot. ¶~이 앉다 (끼다) be sooted; become sooty; be soot-covered.

그저 ① (줄곧) still; without ceasing (stopping). ¶비가 ~ 오고 있다 It is still raining. ② (이유없이) without any reason; (목적없이) casually; recklessly; aimlessly. ¶~ 빚을 마구 지다 go into debt recklessly / 왠지 모르지만, 나는 그녀가 ~ 싫다 I don't like her, I don't know why. *or* For some obscure reason I dislike her. ③ (그런대로) so and so; not so (good). ④ (단지) only; just (제발) please. ¶~ 재미로 just for fun / 그 영화는 ~ 그렇더라 The movie was so-so. / ~ 살려만 주십시오 Please save my life.

그저께 the day before yesterday. ¶~ 밤 the night before last

그전(-前) before that; previous (prior) to that time; former times (days); the past. ¶~에는 formerly; before; in old days / ~같이 as before.

그제야 only then; not ... until; only when. ¶건강을 잃게 되면 ~ 그 고마움을 알게 된다 You don't realize the blessing of health until you have lose it.

그중(-中) ① (그것 중) among the rest (others); of them. ¶나도 ~의 하나다 I am one of them. ② (제일) most; best. ¶~ 좋다 (나쁘다) be the best (worst).

그지없다 (한이 없다) (be) endless; boundless; eternal; (be) beyond description (expression). ¶그지없는 사랑 eternal love / 그지없는 기쁨 an everlasting joy / 불쌍하기 ~ be too pitiful for words.

그치다 stop; cease; end; be over. ¶그칠새없이 without cease; continuously.

그후(-後) (이후) after that; thereafter; (이래) (ever) since; since then.

극(極) ① (지구·자석의) a pole; the poles (양극). ¶~지방 the polar regions. ② (절정·극도) the height; the extreme; the climax; the zenith. ¶영화(榮華)의 ~ the height of glory / …의 ~에 달하다 reach the height

극(劇) a drama; a play. ¶ ~적(으로) dramatic(ally) / ~을 공연하다 perform[stage] a play / ~을 연출하다 render a play / ~화(化)하다 dramatize; adapt [turn] 《a novel》 into a play; make a dramatic version of 《a story》. ‖ ~영화 a film [feature] play / ~화(畫) a story comic; a comic strip with a dramatic story.

극광(極光) [地] the aurora; the polar lights.

극구(極口) ¶ ~ 칭찬하다 speak highly of 《a person》 / ~ 변명하다 spare no points to justify *oneself*.

극기(克己) self-control [-denial]. ~하다 deny *oneself*; exercise self-denial. ‖ ~심 a spirit of self-denial [self-control].

극단(極端) an extreme; extremity. ¶ ~적인[으로] extreme; excessive(ly) / ~적으로 말하면 speaking in the extreme / 희망과 절망의 양~ the extremes of hope and despair / ~으로 흐르다 go too far; go to extremes. ‖ ~론 an extreme view [opinion] / ~론자 an extremist.

극단(劇團) a theatrical company; a troupe. ‖ 순회~ a traveling troupe. 「the maximum value.

극대(極大) the maximum. ‖ ~치

극도(極度) ~의 utmost; extreme; maximum / ~로 extremely; to the utmost / ~에 달하다 reach an extreme / ~로 비관하다 be in extreme grief / ~의 신경쇠약에 걸리다 have a nervous breakdown of the worst kind.

극동(極東) the Far East. ~의 Far Eastern. ‖ ~문제 Far Eastern problems.

극락(極樂) 【佛】 (the Buddhist) paradise; the home of the happy dead. ¶ ~왕생하다 die a peaceful death. / ~정도 the land of Perfect Bliss / ~조 a bird of paradise

극력(極力) to the utmost; to the best of *one's* ability; strenuously. ¶ ~ 부인(반대)하다 deny [oppose] stubbornly [to the last].

극렬분자(極烈分子) a radical; an extremist.

극론(極論) ~하다 make an extreme argument. ¶ ~하면 to state an extreme case; to exaggerate.

극미(極微) ¶ ~한 microscopic; infinitesimal / ~한 세계 a microscopic world.

극복(克服) conquest. ~하다 conquer; overcome; get [tide] over. ¶ 병을 ~하다 get over an illness / 많은 어려움을 ~하다 overcome a lot of difficulties.

극비(極秘) strict secrecy; a top secret. ¶ ~의 top-secret; strictly confidential / 사고를 ~로 하다 keep an accident in absolute secrecy. ‖ ~문서 a classified [top-secret] document.

극빈(極貧) extreme poverty. ¶ ~한 extremely poor; destitute. ‖ ~자 a needy [destitute] person.

극상(極上) ¶ ~의 the best; first-rate; the highest quality; of the finest quality / ~의 치즈 cheese of the highest quality. ‖ ~품 a choice article; the best *of its kind*.

극성(極盛) ¶ ~스러운 extreme; overeager; impetuous / ~부리다 run to extremes / 극성스러운 사람 an impetuous person / ~스럽게 work like mad; work frantically.

극소(極小) minimum. ¶ ~한 smallest; minimum; infinitesimal. ‖ ~랑 the minimum / ~수 the minimum number; a small minority / ~치 the minimum value.

극심(極甚) ¶ ~한 extreme; excessive; intense; severe; fierce; keen / ~한 경쟁 a keen [tough] competition / ~한 더위 an intense heat / ~한 손해 devastating damage.

극악(極惡) ¶ ~한 heinous; atrocious; extremely wicked; villainous / ~무도한 사람 an utter villain. ‖ ~(이ce) a poison.

극약(劇藥) a powerful [drastic] medicine.

극언(極言) ~하다 be bold enough to say 《that...》; go so far as to say 《that...》. ¶ ~하면 to put it strongly [at its most extreme].

극영화(劇映畫) a dramatic movie.

극우(極右) an ultra-rightist; the extreme right. ¶ ~의 ultranationalistic / ~파 the extreme right; an extreme right wing.

극작(劇作) playwriting. ~하다 write a play [drama]. ‖ ~가 a dramatist; a playwright.

극장(劇場) a theater; a playhouse. ‖ ~가(街) a theater district.

극점(極點) 《한도》 the extreme point; a climax; 《북극·남극》 the North (South) pole.

극좌(極左) the extreme left. ¶ ~의 ultraleftist. ‖ ~파 extreme leftist.

극지(極地) the pole; the polar regions. ‖ ~탐험 a polar expedition.

극진(極盡) ¶ ~한 very kind (cor-

극초단파(極超短波) microwave.
극치(極致) the perfection; the zenith; the acme; the culmination. ¶ 미의 ~ the perfect beauty / 예술의 ~ the highest reach of art / ~에 달하다 attain the highest perfection.
극피동물(棘皮動物) [動] an echinoderm.
극한(極限) the limit; an extremity; the bounds. ¶ ~에 달하다 reach the limit (*of*). ‖ ~ 상황 (be placed in) an extreme situation / ~치 [數] a limiting value / ~투쟁 struggle to the extremes.
극한(極寒) severe [intense] cold.
극형(極刑) capital punishment; the death penalty. ¶ ~에 처하다 condemn (*a person*) to capital punishment.
극히(極一) (심히) very; highly; (가장) most; (아주) quite.
근(斤) a *kun* (=0.6 kilogram).
근(根) (증기의) the core (of a boil); [數] a root; [化] a radical.
근간(近刊) a recent [forthcoming] publication. ¶ ~의 책 forthcoming books / ~예고 an announcement of books in preparation.
근간(近間) one of these days. ☞ 요새.
근간(根幹) (뿌리와 줄기) root and trunk; (근본) the basis; the root; (기본) the keynote. ¶ ~을 이루다 form the keynote of / 농업은 나라의 ~이다 Agriculture is the basis of a nation.
근거(根據) a basis; a foundation; ground(s); authority (전거). ¶ ~가 있는 well-grounded [-founded] / ~가 없는 groundless; unfounded / 믿을 만한 합리적 ~가 없다 have no reasonable ground for believing. ‖ ~지 a base (of operations).
근거리(近距離) a short distance. ¶ ~에 있다 be a little way off.
근검(勤儉) thrift and diligence. ¶ ~한 thrifty; frugal. ‖ ~저축 thrift and saving / ~지대 [zome.
근경(根莖) [植] a rootstock; a rhi-
근계(謹啓) Dear...; Dear Sir [Sirs] (회사・단체 앞); Gentlemen (美); My dear...; Dear Mr. [Miss, Mrs.,] Ms. (여성에게).
근골(筋骨) bones and sinews; (체격) build; physique. ¶ ~이 억센 muscular; sinewy.
근교(近郊) the suburbs; the outskirts. ¶ ~의 suburban; neighboring / ~에 in the suburbs (*of*) / ~의 주택지 a suburban residential area.
근근(僅僅ー) barely; narrowly; with difficulty (☞ 간신히). ¶ ~ 살아가다 eke out [barely make] a living; live from hand to mouth.
근기(根氣) perseverance; patience; endurance; energy (정력). ¶ ~ 있게 patiently; with perseverance (patience) / ~가 없다 lack patience; soon get tired.
근년(近年) recent [late] years. ¶ ~에 in recent [of late] years / ~ 없던 심한 추위 the coldest weather we have had in recent
근농(勤農) diligent farming. [years.
근대(根) a (red) beet; a chard.
근대(近代) the modern age; recent [modern] times. ¶ ~의 modern / ~적인 modern(istic); up-to-date (최신의). ‖ ~국가 a modern nation / ~사 (영어) modern history [English] / ~화 modernization (~화하다 modernize / 한국은 지난 40년 사이에 급속히 ~화했다 Korea has rapidly modernized itself for the last forty years.)
근동(近東) [地] the Near East.
근들거리다 sway (rock) slightly.
근래(近來) these days; recently; lately. ¶ ~의 recent; late / ~에 보기 드문 인물 the greatest man in recent years.
근력(筋力) muscular strength (power); 기력(氣力).
근로(勤勞) labor; service. ‖ ~기준법 the Labor Standard Law / ~대중 the working masses / ~봉사 a labor service / ~소득 an earned income / ~의욕 the will to work / ~자 a worker; a laborer; a workman; a workingman; labor (총칭) / ~조건 working conditions.
근린(近隣) a neighborhood. ¶ ~의 이웃나라 the neighboring countries. ‖ ~소음 noises from the surrounding neighborhood.
근면(勤勉) diligence; industry. ¶ ~한 industrious; diligent; hard-working.
근무(勤務) service; duty; work. ¶ ~하다 serve; work; be on duty. ¶ 은행에서 ~하다 work in [for] a bank. ‖ ~능률 service efficiency / ~성적 *one's* service record / ~시간 office [working, business] hours / ~연한 the length of *one's* service / ~자 a man on duty [in service] / ~수당 an area allowance / ~처 *one's* place of employment [work] / ~태도 assiduity / ~평

근묵자흑(近墨者黑) He who touches pitch shall be defiled therewith.

근배(謹拜) 《편지의 맺음말》 Yours truly (sincerely, respectfully).

근본(根本) 《기초》 the foundation; the basis; 《근원》 the root; the source; the origin. ¶ ~적인 fundamental; basic; radical / ~적으로 fundamentally; radically; completely / ~적인 문제 a fundamental (basic) problem / 문제를 ~적으로 해결하다 settle 《*a problem*》 completely / ~을 거슬러 캐다 trace 《*something*》 to its origin. ∥ ~원리 fundamental (basic) principles / ~원인 the root cause / ~정신 the fundamental principle.

근사(近似) ¶ ~한 《비슷한》 approximate; closely resembled; 《멋진》 fine, nice. ∥ ~치 approximate quantity (value).

근성(根性) 《근본성질》 disposition; nature; 《기질》 temper; spirit (정신); 《부지》 will power; guts. ¶ ~이 나쁜 ill-natured / 비뚤어진 ~ a crooked nature / ~이 있는 사나이 a man with (a lot of) guts.

근세(近世) 《史》 modern times. ☞ 근대. ∥ ~사 modern history.

근소(僅少) ¶ ~한 a few (수); a little (양); small; trifling / ~한 차로 이기다 win by a narrow margin.

근속(勤續) continuous (long) service. ¶ ~10년의 사원 an office clerk with ten years of continuous service / 30년 ~하다 serve (work) 《*in a firm*》 for thirty years. ∥ ~수당 a long-service allowance / ~연한 the length of *one's* service. 「kun.

근수(斤數) the weight expressed in

근시(近視) nearsightedness 《美》; shortsightedness 《英》; near (short) sight. ¶ ~의 near-(short-)sighted / ~의 사람 a near-sighted person / ~안적인 정책 a near-sighted policy. ∥ ~안경 spectacles for shortsightedness.

근신(近臣) *one's* trusted vassal; a close court attendant.

근신(謹愼) ~하다 《언행을 조심하다》 be on *one's* good behavior; behave *oneself*; 《과오를 반성하다》 be penitent; be confined at home (자택에서). ¶ ~을 명받다 be ordered to be on *one's* best behavior. 「ous.

근실(勤實) ¶ ~한 diligent; assidu-

근실거리다 itch; feel itchy.

근심 anxiety; concern; worry; cares; trouble. ~하다 be anxious (concerned) about; be worried (troubled) about; feel uneasy; care; worry. ¶ ~에 쌓이다 be full of cares (worries) / 뭘 그리 ~하느냐 What are you worrying about? / ~이 떠날 날이 없다 I always have one trouble or another.

근엄(謹嚴) sobriety. ¶ ~한 serious; grave; stern / ~한 태도 a dignified mien.

근원(根源) 《시초》 the origin; the source; 《원인》 the cause; 《근본》 the root. ¶ 모든 사회악의 ~ the root of all social evils / ~을 캐다 trace 《*something*》 to its origin.

근위대(近衛隊) the Royal Guards.

근육(筋肉) muscles; sinews. ¶ ~의 운동 muscular movement (motion). ∥ ~노동 physical (muscular) labor / ~노동자 a laborer; a manual worker / ~조직 muscular tissue / ~주사 an intramuscular injection.

근인(近因) an immediate cause.

근일(近日) 《부사적》 soon; shortly; at an early date.

근자(近者) these days; 《부사적》 lately; recently.

근작(近作), **근저**(近著) *one's* latest (recent) work.

근저당(根抵當) fixed collateral.

근절(根絶) extermination; eradication. ~하다 exterminate; eradicate; root (stamp) out. ¶ 사회악을 ~하다 root (stamp) out social evils.

근접(近接) approach; proximity. ~하다 draw near; come (go) close (to); approach. ¶ ~한 neighboring; adjacent / ~해 있다 be (stand) close (adjacent

근정(謹呈) presentation; 《저자가 책에 서명할 때》 With the Compliments of the Author. ~하다 present; make a present of 《*a thing*》.

근제(謹製) carefully produced 《by》. ~하다 make (prepare) carefully.

근지점(近地點) 《天》 the perigee.

근질거리다 feel ticklish itchy.

근착(近着) recent (new) arrivals. ¶ ~의 양서 newly arrived Western books.

근처(近處) the neighborhood; the vicinity. ¶ ~의 사람 a neighbor / ~의 아이들 the neighborhood children / ~의 절 a nearby temple.

근청(謹聽) ~하다 listen to 《*a person*》 with attention.

근치(根治) complete cure. ~하다 cure completely. ¶ 암을 ~하다

근천(近親) a near [close] relation (relative); a kin (집합적). ¶ 우리는 ~간이다 We are closely related to each other. ∥ ~결혼 an intermarriage / ~상간(相姦) incest.

근태(勤怠) diligence and/or indolence.

근하신년(謹賀新年) (I wish you) a Happy New Year.

근해(近海) the neighboring [home] waters; the nearby seas. ∥ ~어 shore fish / ~어업 inshore fishery [fishing] / ~항로 a coastal route.

근황(近況) the present condition. ¶ ~이 어떠신지요 Let me know how you are getting along.

글 writings; a composition; prose (산문); an article; a sentence (문장); letters (문학); a letter [character] (문자); learning (학문). ¶ 좋은 [나쁜] ~ good (bad) writing / 쉬운 ~로 쓰다 write in an easy style / ~을 모르다 be unlettered (illiterate) / ~을 좋아하다 love learning / ~을 배우다 learn; study. ∥ ~짓기 composition.

글귀 words; a phrase (구), a clause (절); 《인용절》 a passage; an expression. ¶ ~를 외다 memorize a passage.

글동무 a schoolmate.

글라디올러스 [植] a gladiolus.

글라스 《잔》 a glass.

글라이더 a glider.

글래머걸 a glamor girl.

글러브 [野] a glove; [拳] gloves.

글러지다 go amiss [wrong]; 《악화》 get (grow) worse. ¶ 계획이 ~ a plan goes wrong.

글루탐산(―酸) glutamic acid. ∥ ~나트륨 monosodium glutamate.

글리세린 [化] glycerin(e).

글리코겐 [化] glycogen.

글방(―房) a private school for Chinese classics.

글썽글썽 with tearful eyes. ∥ ~하다 be in tears; be moved to tears. ¶ 눈물이 ~한 눈 tearful eyes; eyes filled with tears.

글쎄 well; let me see; I say (단정). ¶ ~ 하란 말이야 I say you do it. / ~ 갈 생각이 없는 걸 Well, I don't feel like going. / ~ 그걸 어디다 놓았더라 Let me see — where did I put it?

글씨 a letter; a character; 《글씨 쓰기》 writing; handwriting. ¶ ~ 쓰는 법 penmanship / ~를 잘 [못] 쓰다 write a good (poor) hand / ~를 가르치다 teach how to write. ∥ ~체 a style of handwriting. 「(편지).

글월 a sentence (문장); a letter

글자(―字) a letter; a character.

글재주 literary talent [ability, genius]. ¶ ~가 있다 have a talent for writing.

글제(―題) a subject [title, theme] of an article.

글피 two days after tomorrow.

긁다 ① scratch; scrape. ¶ 머리를 ~ scratch one's head. ② 《그러모으다》 rake. ¶ 낙엽을 ~ rake (up) fallen leaves. ③ 《감정·비위를》 provoke; nag. ¶ 그의 아내는 늘 바가지를 긁는다 His wife nags him constantly.

긁어먹다 ① 《이 따위로》 scrape (out) and eat. ¶ 참외를 숟가락으로 ~ scrape out the meat of melon with a spoon and eat it. ② 《재물을》 extort; squeeze. ☞ 착취.

긁적거리다 scratch and scratch; scrape and scrape.

긁히다 be scratched [scraped].

금¹ 《값》 a price. ¶ 적당한 ~ a moderate [reasonable] price / ~보다. ~을 놓다 bid [name] a price (for); make an offer / ~이 나가다 cost much; be high in price.

금² ① 《줄》 a line. ¶ ~을 긋다 draw a line. ② 《균열》 a cleft; a crack. ¶ ~이 가다 crack; be cracked.

금(金) ① gold (기호 Au). ¶ ~의 gold; golden / 18 ~의 시계 an 18-karat gold watch / ~을 입히다 plate (a thing) with gold / ~ 반지 a gold ring. ② 《금액》 money. ¶ 일 ~ 10만원 the sum of 100,000 won.

금강사(金剛砂) emery (powder).

금강산(金剛山) *Kumgangsan*, the Diamond Mountains. ¶ ~도 식후경이라 《俗談》 Bread is better than the song of the birds.

금강석(金剛石) a diamond. ¶ ~을 갈다 cut [polish] a diamond.

금계(禁界) the forbidden ground.

금계랍(金鷄蠟) [藥] quinine.

금고(金庫) a safe; a strongbox; a vault (은행의 금고실). ¶ 돈을 ~에 넣다 put away money in a safe. ∥ ~털이 《행위》 safebreaking, safecracking / 《사람》 a safebreaker, a safecracker / 대여 ~ a safe-deposit box.

금고(禁錮) [法] confinement; imprisonment. ¶ ~ 3개월에 처해지다 be sentenced to three months' imprisonment.

금과옥조(金科玉條) a golden rule. ¶ ~로 삼다 adhere strictly (to).

금관(金冠) a gold crown.

금관악기(金管樂器) [樂] (a) brass.

금광(金鑛) a gold mine; 《광석》 gold ore. ¶ ~ 덩이 a gold bar.

금괴(金塊) a nugget; a gold ingot.

금권(金權) the power of money;

금궤(金櫃) a money chest (box).
금귤(金橘) 〖植〗 a kumquat.
금기(禁忌) taboo; 〖醫〗 contraindication. ¶ 배합 ∼의 약품 incompatible drugs.
금난초(金蘭草) 〖植〗 a helleborine.
금남(禁男) 〖揭示〗 No men admitted. ¶ ∼의 집 a house(dormitory) closed to men.
금낭화(錦囊花) 〖植〗 a dicentra.
금년(今年) this year. ¶ ∼ 올해.
금니(金—) a gold tooth. ¶ ∼ 박이 a man with gold teeth.
금단(禁斷) ∼하다 prohibit; forbid. ¶ ∼의 prohibited; forbidden / ∼의 열매 the forbidden fruit. ¶ ∼중상 (suffer from) withdrawal symptoms; an abstinence syndrome(증후군).
금도금(金鍍金) gilding; gold plating. ∼하다 plate (*a thing*) with gold; gild. ¶ ∼한 시계 a gold-plated watch / ∼이 벗겨지다 The gilt comes off.
금란지계(金蘭之契) close friendship.
금력(金力) the power of money (wealth). ¶ ∼으로 by employing *one's* financial power; through the influence of money / 그는 ∼으로 좌우될 수 있는 인간이 아니다 He is the last man to be influenced by money.
금렵(禁獵) prohibition of hunting. ¶ ∼기 the off-season; the closed season / ∼지구 a (game) preserve; a no-hunting area(이 주변은 ∼지구이다 These districts are preserved).
금령(禁令) a prohibition; a ban. ¶ ∼을 내리다 issue a ban (*on*) / ∼을 풀다 lift the ban (*on*).
금리(金利) interest (on money); a rate of interest. ¶ ∼를 올리다(내리다) raise (lower) the rate of interest / ∼가 높다(낮다) Interest rates are high (low). ¶ 고 ∼ 불황 a high-interest recession.
금맥(金脈) a vein of gold; 《자금주》 (shady) sources of funds.
금메달(金—) a gold medal. ¶ ∼을 따다 win (be awarded) a gold medal. ¶ ∼ 수상자 a gold medal winner; a gold medalist.
금명간(今明間) today or tomorrow; in a couple of days.
금물(金—) gold braid (lace). ¶ ∼의 gold-braided.
금물(禁物) (a) taboo; a prohibited (forbidden) thing. ¶ 담배는 환자에게 ∼ Smoking is bad for the patient.
금박(金箔) gold foil; gold leaf. ¶ ∼ 입히기(박기) gold pressing; gilding in the press.
금발(金髮) golden (fair) hair. ¶ ∼의 blonde(여자); blond(남자).
금방(金房) a goldsmith's shop.
금보다 〖평가하다〗 make an appraisal (estimate, evaluation); put a value (*on a thing*); value (*a thing*).
금본위(金本位) (제도(制度)) the gold standard (system). ¶ ∼를 폐지하다 go off the gold standard.
금분(金粉) gold dust.
금불(金佛) a gold image of Buddha.
금붕어(金—) goldfish.
금붙이(金—) things made of gold.
금비(金肥) (a) chemical fertilizer.
금빛(金—) golden color. ¶ ∼이 찬란하다 glitter with golden colors. 「statue.
금상(金像) a gold statue; a gilt
금상첨화(錦上添花) ¶ ∼이다 add luster to what is already brilliant; add something more to the beauty (honor) (*of*).
금새 price. 「book.
금서(禁書) a banned (forbidden)
금석(今昔) past and present. ¶ ∼지감을 금할 수 없다 be struck by the change (effects) of times.
금석(金石) minerals and rocks. ¶ ∼지약(之約) a firm promise / ∼학 epigraphy. 「star.
금성(金星) 〖天〗 Venus; the day-
금성철벽(金城鐵壁) a citadel; an impregnable fortress.
금세공(金細工) goldwork. ¶ ∼장이 a goldsmith.
금속(金屬) 〖化〗 (a) metal. ¶ ∼(제)의 metal; metallic / ∼성의 소리 a metallic sound. ¶ ∼가공 (加工) the processing of a metal / ∼공 a metal worker / ∼공업 the metal industry / ∼공학 metal engineering / ∼광택 metallic luster / ∼성(性) metallic character / ∼원소 a metallic element / ∼제품 metal goods; hardware(집합적) / 반∼ semimetal; a metalloid(반∼의 semimetallic; metalloid).
금수(禁輸) an embargo on the export (import) of. ∼하다 embargo; ban the export (import) (*of*). ¶ ∼품 articles under an embargo; contraband (goods).
금수(禽獸) birds and beasts; animals. ¶ ∼와 같은 행위 beastly conduct / ∼와 다를 바 없다 be no better than a beast.
금수(錦繡) ¶ ∼강산 the land of beautiful scenery; Korea (별칭).
금슬(쯧뚱) ¶ ∼이 좋다 live in conjugal harmony; lead a happy married life.

금시(今始) ¶ ~ 초문이다 have never heard of before; be news to one. ¶ ~ 초견(初見) seeing for the first time.

금시계(金時計) a gold watch.

금식(禁食) fasting. ~하다 fast; go without food. ‖ ~일 a fast day.

금실(金一) gold thread; spun 〔gold〕.

금싸라기(金一) a thing of great value. ‖ ~땅 an exceedingly high-priced plot of land.

금액(金額) an amount 〔a sum〕 of money. ¶ 큰〔적은〕~ a large 〔small〕 amount of money.

금어(禁漁) a ban on fishing; 《게시》 No Fishing. ¶ ~구(역) a marine preserve / ~기 the closed season for fishing.

금언(金言) a golden 〔wise〕 saying; a proverb; a maxim.

금연(禁煙) 《게시》 No Smoking; Smoking prohibited. ~하다 prohibit smoking(못 피우게); stop 〔give up〕 smoking (끊음). ¶ 차내에서는 ~입니다 Smoking is prohibited in cars. ‖ ~일 No-Smoking Day.

금요일(金曜日) Friday.

금욕(禁慾) abstinence; continence(성욕의). ~하다 control the passions; be ascetic (continent). ‖ ~생활 (lead) an ascetic life / ~주의 stoicism / ~주의자 a stoic.

금융(金融) finance; the money market. ¶ ~을 긴축하다 tighten the money market (situation). ‖ ~계 the financial circles / ~공황 a financial crisis 〔panic〕 / ~기관 a banking 〔financial〕 institution / ~긴축〔완화〕정책 a tight-money 〔an easy-money〕 policy / ~시장 the money 〔financial〕 market / ~업 financial business / ~업자 a moneylender; a financier / ~자본 financial capital / ~자유화 financial liberalization / ~정책 a financial policy.

금융거래실명제(金融去來實名制) the real-name financial transaction system.

금융경색(金融梗塞) money (monetary) stringency; a tight-money market (situation).

금융부조리(金融不條理) malpractices at banks; bank-related irregularities.

금융사고(金融事故) a banking incident; a loan fraud.

금융조작(金融造作) money market manipulation.

금융특혜(金融特惠) privileged loans 〔to〕.

금은(金銀) gold and silver. ‖ ~보배 money and valuables.

금의환향(錦衣還鄕) ~하다 go 〔come〕 home in glory.

금일봉(金一封) a gift of money. ¶ ~을 주다 grant 〔give〕 《a person》 money (in appreciation of his services).

금자탑(金字塔) 《업적》 a monumental achievement. ¶ ~을 세우다 accomplish a monumental work.

금작화(金雀花) 〔植〕 a genista; a common broom.

금잔(金盞) a gold cup 〔goblet〕.

금잔디(金一) (golden) turf.

금잔화(金盞花) 〔植〕 a common marigold; a yellow oxeye.

금장식(金粧飾) gold decoration.

금전(金錢) money; cash. ¶ ~상의 문제 a money matter; a financial problem. ‖ ~출납기 a cash register / ~출납계원 a cashier / ~출납부 a cashbook.

금제(禁制) prohibition; a ban. ¶ 여인 ~의 《a place》 closed to women / ~를 풀다 lift a ban (on). ‖ ~품 contraband (prohibited) goods.

금족(禁足) 〔佛〕 prohibition against entrance; 《외출금지》 confinement. ¶ ~을 명하다 order 《a person》 to stay in one place (at home) (for five days).

금주(今週) this week. ¶ ~중에 some time this week.

금주(禁酒) temperance; 《절대적인》 total abstinence. ~하다 stop 〔give up; abstain from〕 drinking(개인적으로); go dry (제도적으로). ‖ ~법 the prohibition (dry) law / ~운동 a temperance movement; a dry campaign / ~자 an abstainer / ~주의 teetotalism / ~주의자 a teetotaler; an anti-alcoholist.

금준비(金準備) the gold reserve.

금지(禁止) prohibition; a ban; an embargo (수출입의). ~하다 forbid 《a person to do》(사적으로); prohibit 《a person from doing》(공적으로); ban (법적으로). ¶ 전면적인 ~ the total ban / ~를 해제하다 remove the prohibition; lift the ban / 과격한 운동을 ~시키다 prohibit 《a person》 taking too much exercise. ‖ ~법 the prohibition law / ~조항 a forbidden clause / ~처분 prohibitive measures / 상연 ~ a ban on performance / 수출 ~ an embargo / 수출입 ~품목 items on the contraband list / 정차 ~ 《게시》 No waiting (standing). / 판매 ~ prohibition of sale.

금지옥엽(金枝玉葉) 《임금님의》 a person of royal birth; 《귀하게 자란》 precious 〔beloved〕 child. ¶ ~으로 자라다 be brought up like a prince 〔princess〕.

금지환(金指環) a gold ring.
금치산(禁治産) 〖法〗 incompetency. ∥~자 an incompetent / 준~자 a quasi-incompetent.
금침(衾枕) bedclothes and a pillow; bedding.
금테(金 —) gold rims(안경의); a gilded frame (사진틀의). ∥~ 안경 gold-rimmed spectacles.
금품(金品) money and goods. ¶~을 주다 make a gift of money and other valuables.
금하다(禁—) ① 『금지하다. ②『억제』 suppress; repress; restrain; 『절제』 refrain [abstain] 《from》. ¶웃음을 금할 수가 없다 cannot help laughing / 술을 ~ abstain from drinking.
금형(型型) a mold; a matrix; a cast.
금혼식(金婚式) a golden wedding.
금화(金貨) a gold coin; gold currency (총칭).
금환식(金環蝕) 〖天〗 an annular eclipse of the sun.
금후(今後) after this; hereafter; in (the) future; from now (on). ¶~의 계획 the future plan / ~ 5년 내지 10년은 for five or ten years from now.
급(急) ①『위급』 (an) emergency; a crisis; 『긴급』 urgency. ¶~을 하는 urgent; pressing / ~을 고하다 give [raise] the alarm / ~을 요함 〖指示〗 Urgent. ②『형용사적』 emergent; critical(위급한); steep (급경사의); sudden (돌발적인). ¶~경사 a steep slope / ~변 a sudden change / ~한 경우 an emergency case.
급(級) 〖등급·학년〗 a class; a grade. ¶대사 ~ 회담 an ambassador-level conference / 일~ 품 first class goods; an article of the highest quality / 헤비~ 선수 a heavyweight / 그는 나보다 한 ~ 위 [아래]이다 He is one grade above [below] me.
급각도(急角度) an acute angle. ¶~로 돌다 make a sudden turn.
급감(急減) a sudden decrease. ~하다 decrease suddenly (rapidly).
급강하(急降下) 《항공기의》 a (steep) dive; a nose-dive. ~하다 nosedive; zoom down. ¶~폭격 dive bombing / ~폭격기 a dive bomber.
급거(急遽) in haste; in a hurry; hastily; hurriedly. ¶~ 상경하다 hurry up [rush] to Seoul.
급격(急激) ¶~한 sudden; abrupt; rapid (급속한); radical (과격~) / ~히 suddenly; rapidly / ~한 변화 a sudden [radical] change.

급경사(急傾斜) a steep slope(물매); a steep ascent (치받이); a steep descent (내리받이).
급고(急告) an urgent notice. ~하다 give an urgent notice.
급급하다(汲汲一) be eager 《to please one's employer》; be intent 《on making money》. ¶책임 전가에 ~ be busy trying to shift the responsibility to others.
급기야(及其也) at last; finally; in the end.
급등(急騰) a sudden [sharp] rise; a jump. ~하다 rise suddenly; skyrocket; jump 《to 800 won》.
급락(及落) success or failure 《in an exam》; examination results.
급락(急落) a sudden drop; a sharp decline; a slump. ~하다 decline heavily; slump; fall suddenly. ¶주식 시세가 ~했다 The stock market suffered a sharp decline.
급료(給料) 급여, 봉급, 임금. ∥~ 생활자 a wage earner.
급류(急流) a rapid stream (current); 《격류》 a torrent; rapids.
급무(急務) urgent business; a pressing need. ¶우리가 해야 할 ~는 경제 재건이다 The first thing [urgent business] we must do is to reconstruct the economy.
급박하다(急迫一) (be) imminent; urgent; pressing. ¶급박해지다 become [grow] tense (critical, acute) / 북한에서는 식량 문제가 ~ The food problem is acute in North Korea.
급변(急變) a sudden change [turn]; 《변고》 an emergency; an accident. ~하다 change suddenly. ¶~하는 세계 정세 the rapidly changing world situation / 날씨가 ~하다 the weather suddenly changes.
급보(急報) an urgent message [report, dispatch]. ~하다 send an urgent message 《to》; report promptly. ¶~에 접하다 receive the urgent news 《of》.
급부(給付) presentation; a benefit (급부금); delivery(교부); payment(지급). ~하다 deliver 《a thing》; pay 《a benefit》. ∥반대 ~ a consideration.
급사(急死) a sudden death. ~하다 die suddenly. ¶그녀는 열병으로 ~했다 She died suddenly of a fever.
급사(急使) an express messenger; a courier.
급사(給仕) 《사무실의》 an office boy; 《호텔의》 a page 《英》; a bellboy 《美》; 《식당의》 a waiter; waitress(여자); 《배의》 a cabin boy; 《열차의》 a boy; a porter 《美》.

급살맞다 (急煞—) meet a sudden death; die suddenly.

급상승 (急上昇) a sudden rise; a zoom (비행기의). ~하다 rise suddenly; zoom.

급선무 (急先務) the most urgent business; a pressing need.

급성 (急性) ¶ ~의 질병 an acute disease / ~이 되다 run an acute course. ‖ ~ 맹장염(폐렴) acute appendicitis (pneumonia).

급성장 (急成長) a rapid growth. ~하다 grow rapidly; achieve a rapid growth. ¶ ~하는 시장 the big emerging market.

급소 (急所) a vital point (part) (몸의); a vulnerable (weak) spot (약점); a tender (sore) spot (아픈 곳); a key point (요점). ¶ ~를 얻어맞다 be hit in the vitals / ~를 찌른 질문 a question to the point / ~를 찌르다 hit (a person) on a vital spot.

급속 (急速) rapidity. ¶ ~한 rapid; swift; sudden / ~히 rapidly; swiftly; promptly / ~한 진전을 이루다 make rapid progress (advance) / 기온이 ~히 상승했다 The temperature rose suddenly (sharply). ‖ ~냉동 quick freezing (~냉동하다 quick-freeze).

급송 (急送) ~하다 send (ship) (a thing) by express (in haste); dispatch (a message); express (the goods) (美).

급수 (級數) (數) (일련의 수) a series. ‖ 산술(기하) ~ arithmetical (geometrical) series.

급수 (給水) water supply (service). ~하다 supply (a town) with water. ‖ ~관 a water pipe / ~ 설비 water-supply facilities / ~전(栓) a hydrant / ~제한 restriction on water supply / ~차 a water supply truck / ~탑 a water tower / ~탱크 a water tank.

급습 (急襲) a sudden (surprise) attack; a raid. ~하다 make a surprise attack (on); raid; storm.

급식 (給食) meal service; 《학교의》 a school lunch. ~하다 provide meals (lunch) (for). ‖ ~비 the charge for a meal / ~시설 facilities for providing meals.

급여 (給與) 《수당》 an allowance; 《봉급》 pay; a salary; wages; 《물품》 supply; grant. ~하다 grant; allow; supply (provide) (a person) with; pay. ¶ ~소득 an earned income / ~수준 a pay (wage) level / ~체계 a wage system (structure).

급우 (級友) a classmate.

급유 (給油) oil supply; 《연료의》 refu-

eling. ~하다 fill (a tank); refill (a car) with gas; refuel (an airplane). ‖ ~기 a tanker plane / ~소 a filling (gas; petrol 英) station.

급전 (急轉) ~하다 change suddenly; take a sudden turn. ¶ ~직하로 all at once; abruptly / 사태가 ~했다 Things changed suddenly.

급전 (急錢) urgently needed money for immediate use.

급정주 (急停車) a sudden stop. ~하다 stop suddenly (short); bring (a car) to a sudden stop; stamp (slam) on the brakes (구어). ¶ 버스를 불의의 사태로 ~하는 경우가 있다 Something unexpected brings a bus to a sudden stop.

급제 (及第) ~하다 pass (an examination); make the grade.

급조 (急造) ~하다 construct in haste; build hurriedly. ¶ ~의 hurriedly (hastily) built.

급증 (急增) a sudden (rapid) increase. ~하다 increase suddenly (rapidly). ¶ ~하는 교통량 rapidly increasing traffic / 그 나라에서는 흉악 범죄가 ~하고 있다 Dreadful crimes are increasing rapidly in the country.

급진 (急進) ¶ ~적인 radical (과격한); extreme (극단적인) / 그의 사상은 ~적이다 He has radical ideas. ‖ ~주의 radicalism / ~파 the radicals (extremists).

급템포 (急—) (로) rapid(ly); double-quick / 복구 공사는 ~로 진전되었다 The restoration work progressed rapidly.

급파 (急派) ~하다 dispatch; rush. ¶ 사고 현장에 구급차를 ~하다 dispatch an ambulance to the scene of the accident.

급하다 (急—) 《일·사태가》 (be) urgent; pressing; imminent; 《성질이》 (be) impatient; quick-(short-) tempered; 《병이》 (be) critical; serious; 《경사가》 (be) steep; sharp (커브가). ¶ 급한 볼일 urgent business / 급한 병 a critical illness / 성미가 급한 사람 a quick-tempered person; a hothead / 경사가 급한 언덕 a steep hill (slope) / 시간이 ~ be pressed for time / 급한 볼일이 생겼다 Some urgent business has turned up.

급행 (急行) 《급히 감》 a rush; a hurry; 《열차》 an express (train). ~하다 hasten; rush; hurry (to). ¶ 6시 30분의 ~ the 6:30 express / ~으로(열차로) 가다 take an express (to); travel (hurry) (to a place) by express / 현장으로 ~하

다 rush to the scene 《*of an accident*》. ∥ ~권 an express ticket / ~버스 an express bus / ~요금 an express charge.

급환(急患) an emergency case; a sudden illness.

굿다 《줄을》 draw; 《성냥을》 strike 《*a match*》. ¶ 선을 ~ draw a line.

긍정(肯定) affirmation. ~하다 affirm; answer "yes"; acknowledge. ¶ ~적인 affirmative / ~도 부정도 않다 make no commitment either way. ∥ ~명제 an affirmative 《proposition》 / ~문 an affirmative sentence.

긍지(矜持) pride; dignity; self-respect. ¶ 그녀는 자기 일에 ~를 가지고 있다 She has 《takes》 pride in her work.

기(忌) 《a period of》 mourning; an anniversary of 《*a person's*》 death.

기(氣) ① 《만물의 기》 the spirit of all creation. ② 《기력》 energy; vigor. ¶ ~가 넘치는 be full of energy 《life》 / ~를 되찾다 regain *one's* energy 《vigor》. ③ 《의기・기세》 spirits; heart; ardor. ¶ ~가 나서 exultantly / ~가 죽다 be dispirited 《discouraged》; be in low spirits / ~를 못 펴다 feel constrained. ④ 《숨・호흡》 breath; wind. ☞ 기막히다. ⑤ 《온 힘》 all *one's* energy; all-out effort. ☞ 기쓰다. ⑥ 《기미》 a touch 《*of*》; a dash; a shade; a tinge. ¶ 익살 ~ a touch of humor / 감기 ~가 있다 have a touch of cold / 그녀의 머리색은 붉은 ~를 띠고 있다 Her hair may have a tinge of red.

기(旗) a flag; a pennant 《가느다란 3각기》; 《군기》 a standard; a banner; an ensign 《함선의》. ¶ ~를 올리다〔내리다〕 hoist〔lower〕 a flag; run up〔take down〕 a flag / ~가 바람에 펄럭이고 있다 A flag is streaming〔flying〕 in the wind.

기…(幾) some; several. ¶ ~천의 thousands of.

…기(期) 《기일・기간》 a date; a time; a term 《기간》; 《시대》 a period; an age; 《계절》 a season; 《병의》 a stage. ¶ 제1학 ~ the first term / 우〔건〕 ~ the rainy 〔dry〕 season / 제1~의 폐병 tuberculosis in its first stage.

기각(棄却) 《각하》 rejection; 《法》 dismissal. ~하다 turn down; reject; dismiss. ¶ 소(訴)를 ~하다 dismiss a suit.

기간(基幹) a mainstay; a nucleus. ∥ ~산업 key〔basic〕 industries.

기간(旣刊) ¶ ~의 already 《previously》 published〔issued〕.

기간(期間) a term; a period. ¶ 일정한 ~ 내에 within a certain period of time.

기갈(飢渴) starvation; hunger and thirst.

기갑부대(機甲部隊) a panzer unit; armored troops 〔forces 《美》〕.

기강(紀綱) 《관기》 official discipline; 《질서》 public order; law and order. ¶ ~을 바로잡다 improve the moral fiber 《*of*》; tighten discipline 《*among*》.

기개(氣槪) spirit; backbone; mettle; guts 《구어》. ¶ ~ 있는 《high-》 spirited / ~를 보이다 show *one's* mettle / ~가 없다 have no spirit 〔backbone〕.

기거(起居) 《일상 생활》 *one's* daily life. ¶ ~를 같이하다 live together 《*with a person*》.

기결(旣決) ¶ ~의 decided; settled. ∥ ~수 a convict; a convicted prisoner.

기계(奇計) a cunning plan; a clever scheme.

기계(器械) an instrument; an apparatus; an appliance. ∥ ~체조 apparatus gymnastics / 의료~ medical appliances 〔instruments〕.

기계(機械) a machine; machinery 《총칭》; works《시계의》. ¶ ~적인〔으로〕 mechanical〔ly〕 / ~적인 동작 mechanical movements / ~와 같은 machinelike / ~를 움직이다 start a machine; set a machine in motion; operate 〔run〕 a machine《조작하다》 / ~로 움직이는 장난감 a mechanical toy / ~로 읽을 수 있는 machine-readable 《*input texts*》 / 이 ~는 가동 중이다〔고장이 나 있다〕 This machine is running〔out of order〕. ∥ ~공 a mechanic / ~공업 the machine industry / ~공장 a machine shop《factory》 / ~공학 mechanical engineering / ~과(科) 《학교의》 a course in mechanical engineering / ~기사 a mechanical engineer / ~력 machine power / ~문명 machine civilization / ~번역 machine translation / ~언어 (a) machine code《language》 / ~장치 mechanism.

기계화(機械化) mechanization. ~하다 mechanize. ¶ 그 작업은 모두 ~되어 있다 All the work is done by machines. ∥ ~농업 mechanized farming / ~부대 a mechanized unit.

기고(寄稿) (a) contribution. ~하다 contribute 《*to*》; write 《*for*》. ¶ 과학 잡지에 ~하다 write for 〔contribute to〕 a scientific journal.

기고만장(氣高萬丈) ~하다 《의기양양》 (be) elated; be in high spirits; be big with pride.

기골(氣骨) 《골격》 a build; a frame; 《기개》 spirit; mettle; pluck. ¶ ~이 장대한 사람 a sturdily built man; a man of sturdy build / ~이 있는 사내 a man of spirit (mettle).

기공(起工) ~하다 set to work; begin (start) the construction (of a bridge); break ground (for) (건축·토목공사의); lay down (a keel) (배·철도의). ¶ ~식 《일반적으로》 a commencement ceremony; 《건축의》 the ceremony of laying the cornerstone; 《토목공사의》 the ground-breaking ceremony.

기공(技工) a craftsman; a technician. ¶ 치과~사 a dental technician. 「動」 a stigma.

기공(氣孔) a pore; 「植」 a stoma;

기관(汽罐) a (steam) boiler. ¶ ~사 a boiler man / ~실 a boiler room; a stokehole (기선의).

기관(氣管) 「解」 the trachea; the windpipe. ¶ ~의 tracheal.

기관(器官) an organ. ¶ 생명 유지에 중요한 ~ a vital organ. ¶ 감각 〔소화〕 ~ sense (digestive) organs.

기관(機關) ① 《기계의》 an engine; a machine. ¶ ~고 an engine shed / ~단총 a submachine (burp) gun / ~사 an engineer; an engineman / ~실 a machinery room / ~차 a locomotive; an engine / ~총 a machine gun; a heavy machine gun(기관포) / 내연~ an internal-combustion engine / 보조~ an auxiliary engine / 전기〔증기, 디젤〕~ an electric (a steam, a diesel) engine. ② 《수단·기구·설비》 means; an institution; a system; an organ; facilities. ¶ 통신~ means of communication / 교육~ educational institutions / 금융~ banking facilities / 교통~ means of transport; transporting facilities / 보도~ information media / 행정~ an administrative organ / 정부~ a government agency / 집행~ an executive organ.

기관지(氣管支) 「解」 a bronchus; bronchial tube. ¶ ~염 「醫」 bronchitis.

기괴(奇怪) ~한 strange; mysterious; queer.

기교(技巧) art; technique; technical skill; 《책략》 a trick. ¶ ~를 부리다 use a trick.

기구(氣球) a balloon. ¶ ~를 띄우다 (raise) a balloon. ¶ 계류〔관측〕~ a captive (an observation) balloon.

기구(器具) 《가정용의》 a utensil; 《특정 목적의》 an implement; 《특히 한 벌의》 an apparatus; 《정밀·정확한》 an instrument; fixtures (설비된). ¶ 난방~ a heating apparatus.

기구(機構) 《구조》 a structure; 《조직》 organization; 《제도》 a system; 《운영상의》 a mechanism; machinery. ¶ 국제 연합의 복잡한 ~ the complex mechanism of the United Nations / ~를 개편하다 reorganize the system. ¶ ~개편 the reorganization of the system; a structural reform; restructuring / 경제~ the economic structure / 국제~ an international organization / 당(黨)~ party apparatus / 행정~ the machinery of government.

기구하다(崎嶇—) 《불행·불우한》 (be) unhappy; unfortunate; ill-fated; checkered; 《험한》 be rugged. ¶ 기구한 생애 a checkered life / 기구한 일생을 보내다 lead an unhappy (unstable) life.

기권(棄權) 《투표에서》 abstention (from voting); 《권리의》 the renunciation of one's right; 《경기의》 default. ~하다 abstain (from voting); give up (abandon) one's right; withdraw one's entry. ¶ ~율 the abstention rate / ~자 an abstentionist; an absentee; a nonvoter.

기근(飢饉) (a) famine; crop failure; 《결핍》 scarcity. ¶ ~구제자금 a famine-relief fund / 물~ a water shortage.

기금(基金) a fund; a foundation (재단). ¶ ~을 설립하다 establish a fund / ~을 모집하다 collect (raise) a fund. ¶ ~모집 the collection of a fund.

기급하다(氣急—) be aghast; be frightened out of one's wits; cry out in surprise.

기기(器機) machinery and tools.

기기묘묘(奇奇妙妙) ~하다 (be) wonderful and beautiful; marvellous; fabulous.

기꺼이 willingly; with pleasure; readily (선뜻). ¶ ~ 승낙하다 consent with pleasure / ~ …하다 be ready (willing) to do; be delighted to do.

기껏 ① 《헴껏》 to the utmost; as hard as possible. ¶ ~ 애쓰다 do one's best; exert oneself to the utmost. ② 《고작》 at (the) most; at (the) best. ¶ ~해야 1마일 a mile at the outside / ~해야 10일 ten days at the longest.

기낭(氣囊) an air bladder (sac).

기네스북 the Guinness Book of Records.

기념(記念) commemoration; memory. ~하다 commemorate. ¶ ~의 commemorative; mem

기능 / ~으로 in memory [commemoration] of...; as a souvenir [token] of... / ~으로 사진을 찍읍시다 Let's have our photograph taken to commemorate this occasion. ¶ ~물[품] a souvenir; a memento; a keepsake / ~비 a monument / ~사진 a souvenir picture / ~우표 a commemoration stamp / ~일 a memorial day; 《년 1회의》 an anniversary (결혼 ~일 a wedding anniversary) / ~제 a commemoration; 《매년의》 an anniversary / ~행사 a memorial event.
기능(技能) (technical) ability. ¶ ~이 뛰어나다 be highly skilled 《in》 / ~공[자] a technician / ~교육[훈련] technical education [training] / ~올림픽 the International Vocational Training Competition.
기능(機能) faculty; function. ¶ ~을 하다 function; work / ~적인 functional / ~을 발휘하다 fulfill one's function. / ~검사 a functional test / ~장애 a functional disorder / ~저하 (a) malfunction / 소화 ~ digestive functions.
기다 crawl; creep; grovel(배를 깔고). ¶ 기어 가다 go on all fours / 기어 다니다 crawl about [along] / 기어 오르다 climb [crawl] up.
기다랗다 rather long; lengthy.
기다리다 wait 《for》; await; 《기대》 look forward to; expect; anticipate. ¶ 차례를 ~ wait for one's turn / 기다리게 하다 keep 《a person》 waiting / 기회를 ~ watch [wait] for an opportunity.
기담(奇談) a strange story [tale].
기대(期待) expectation; anticipation; hope. ~하다 expect; look forward to; hope for; count on. ¶ ~을 ~하고 in anticipation [expectation, hopes] of / ~에 반하여 contrary to [against] one's expectation(s) / ~에 부응하다 [어긋나다] meet [fall short of] one's expectation(s).
기대다 ① 《몸을》 lean on [against]; rest [stand] against. ② 《의뢰》 rely [depend, lean] on. ¶ 자식에게 ~ depend on one's son for support; lean on one's son.
기도(企圖) 《계획》 a plan; a scheme; a plot; 《시도》 an attempt. ~하다 plot; design; try; attempt; scheme. ¶ 반란의 ~는 실패했다 An attempt to start a revolt ended in failure. / 우리 회사는 해외 진출을 ~하고 있다 Our firm is planning [designing] to expand its business overseas.
기도(新禱) prayer; grace (식사 때의). ~하다 pray; offer [give] prayers; say grace. ¶ ~서 a prayer book. 「ry tract.
기도(氣道) the airway; respirato-
기독교(基督敎) Christianity. ¶ ~의 Christian / ~를 믿다 believe in Christianity; be a Christian. ‖ ~교회 a Christian church / ~도 a Christian / ~여자 청년회 the Young Women's Christian Association(생략 Y.W.C.A.) / ~청년회 the Young Men's Christian Association(생략 Y.M.C.A.).
기동(起動) 《시동》 starting; 《운신》 one's movement. ~하다 move about; stir; get started. ¶ ~력 motive power.
기동(機動) 《경찰대》 the riot police; a riot squad / ~력 mobile power / ~부대 mobile troops; a task force / ~성 mobility; maneuverability / ~연습 a maneuver / ~작전 mobile operations / ~타격대 a special strike [task] force.
기둥 ① 《건축의》 a pillar; a pole; a column(둥근). ¶ ~을 세우다 erect [set up] a pillar. ② 《버팀목》 a prop; a support; a post. ③ 《사람》 a pillar; a support. ¶ 나라 [집안]의 ~ the pillar of the state [family]. 「a pimp.
기둥서방 a kept man; a gigolo;
기득(既得) ¶ ~의 already acquired; vested. ‖ ~권 vested rights (~권의 침해 infringement of 《a person's》 vested rights).
기라성(綺羅星) ¶ ~ 같은 고관들 a galaxy of dignitaries.
기량(技倆) ability; skill; competence. ¶ ~을 기르다 improve one's skill / ~을 충분히 발휘하다 give full play to one's abilities
기러기 《鳥》 a wild goose 《pl. wild geese》 / ~아빠 a lonely wild goose father (separated from his family staying abroad).
기러기발 《현악기의》 the bridge (on a string instrument).
기력(氣力) ① 《힘》 energy; spirit; vigor; vitality. ¶ ~이 왕성한 energetic; vigorous; full of vitality. ② 《理》 air pressure.
기로(岐路) 《갈림길》 a forked road; a crossroad. ¶ 인생의 ~에 서다 stand [be] at the crossroads of one's life.
기록(記錄) 《적음》 recording; 《문서의》 a record; a document; archives(관청의); minutes(의사록의); a chronicle (연대기의); 《경기의》 a 《world》 record. ~하다 record; register; write down; put 《a thing》 on record. ¶ 정확한 ~ an accurate record / 최고 [공식] ~ the best [an official] record / ~

기리 에 남다 be on record; be recorded / ~에서 삭제하다 strike (*some words*) from the record / ~을 깨다 《경기 따위에서》 break (beat) the record / ~을 경신하다 better the record / ~을 깨는 record-breaking / 〈신〉~을 세우다 make (establish) a (new) record (*in*) / 득점을 ~하다 keep (the) score. ∥ ~보유자 a record (title) holder / ~영화 a documentary film / ~원 a recorder; a scorer / ~적 저온 the record-low temperature.

기뢰(機雷) 〖軍〗 an underwater (submarine) mine; a mine. ∥ ~를 부설하다 lay (place) mines.

기류(氣流) an air (aerial) current; a current (stream) of air. ¶상승 ~를 타다 ride an ascending air current.

기르다 ①《양육》bring up; rear; raise. ¶모유〔유아〕로 ~ raise (*a child*) at the breast (on the bottle). ②《사육·재배》breed; raise; keep; grow; cultivate(재배). ¶가축을 ~ raise livestock. ③《양성》cultivate; develop; build up(세력 따위를). ¶도의심을 ~ cultivate moral sense / 국력을 ~ build up national power. ④《버릇을》form (*a habit*). ⑤《머리·수염을》grow (*a mustache*).

기름 oil(액체); 《지방》fat; lard; grease(윤활용). ¶기계에 ~을 치다 oil a machine / ~을 짜다 press oil (*from*) / 이 고기는 ~이 많다 This meat has a lot of fat. / 생선을 ~에 튀기다 fry fish in oil / ~이 묻다 become oily (greasy) / 불에 ~을 붓다 add fuel to the flames / ~기가 없는 oil-free.

기름지다 ① 《기름기》 (be) greasy; fatty; oily; fat(살찐). ¶기름진 음식 greasy (fatty; rich) food. ② 《땅이》 (be) fertile; rich; productive. ¶기름진 밭 fertile (rich) field.

기름틀 an oil press.

기름하다 (be) somewhat (rather) long; longish. 〔praise to.

기리다 praise; admire; give high

기린(麒麟) 〖動〗a giraffe. ∥ ~아 a (child) prodigy; a wonder child.

기립(起立) Rise!; Stand up! ~하다 stand up; rise. ¶~ 투표 a rising (standing) vote.

기마(騎馬)《말타기》(horse) riding; 《타는 말》a riding horse. ∥ ~경찰 a mounted policeman / ~민족 a nomadic (equestrian) people / ~전 (play) a mock cavalry battle.

기막히다(氣─)《숨막히다》stifle; feel stifled (suffocated, choked); 《어이 없다》(be) amazed; stunned; aghast; dumbfounded; 《엄청남》 (be) breathtaking; amazing. ¶기막힌 소식 stunning (amazing) news / 기막힌 부자 an amazingly rich man / 기막힌 일 a horribly (disgusting) thing / 기막히게 예쁜 be stunningly beautiful / 기가 막혀서 말이 안 나오다 be dumbfounded.

기만(欺瞞) deception; (a) deceit. ~하다 deceive; cheat. ¶~적인 deceptive; tricky / ~적인 행위 a deceitful (fraudulent) act.

기맥(氣脈) 〖양〗 통하다 conspire (*with*); be in collusion (*with*).

기명(記名)《서명》signature. ~하다 sign *one's* name. ¶~날인하다 sign and seal. ∥ ~《무~》투표 an open (secret) vote.

기묘(奇妙) ¶~한 strange; queer; odd; curious; funny.

기물(器物) 《그릇》a vessel; household dishes; 《기구》a utensil; 《가구》furniture.

기미(얼굴의) freckles. ¶~가 낀 얼굴 a freckled face / ~가 끼다 freckle.

기미(氣味) ① 《냄새와 맛》 smell and taste. ② 《듯싶은 기분》 a touch; a smack; a tinge; 《징후》 a sign; an indication. ¶감기 ~가 있다 have a touch of a cold.

기민(機敏) ¶~한 prompt; smart; sharp; shrewd / ~한 동작 quick action (movement) / ~하게 행동하다 act smartly / ~한 조치를 취해야 한다 It is necessary to take prompt measures.

기밀(氣密) ¶~의 airtight. ∥ ~복 a pressured suit / ~성 airtightness / ~실 an airtight chamber.

기밀(機密) secrecy(상태); a secret (일). ¶~의 secret; confidential / 군사(외교)상의 ~ a military (diplomatic) secret / ~을 누설하다 let (leak) out a secret. ∥ ~누설 a leak of secret information / ~비 secret (service) funds / ~사항 confidential matters / ~서류 a confidential document.

기박(奇薄) ¶~한 unfortunate; hapless; unlucky; ill-fated / ~한 팔자를 타고 나다 be born under an unlucky star.

기반(基盤) a base; a basis; a foundation; foothold(발판). ¶~을 이루다 form the basis (foundation) of / ~을 굳히다 solidify *one's* footing.

기반(羈絆) bonds; ties; fetters. ¶~을 벗어나다 set *oneself* free (*from*); shake off the fetters.

기발(奇拔) ¶~한 original; novel; eccentric; fanciful (*patterns*) / ~한 생각 a novel idea.

기백(氣魄) spirit; vigor; soul.

기범선(機帆船) a motor-powered sailing boat.

기법(技法) a technique. ¶ ~상의 문제 a technical problem / ~을 익히다 acquire (master) the technique (*of*).

기벽(奇癖) an eccentric (a strange) habit; an eccentricity.

기별(奇別) information; a notice. ~하다 inform (notify) (*a person*) of; give information; report.

기병(起兵) ~하다 raise an army; rise in arms (*against*).

기병(騎兵) a cavalryman; cavalry (총칭). 〔of *paduk*〕

기보(棋譜) the record of a game

기보(旣報) a previous report. ¶ ~한 바와 같이 as previously (already) reported.

기복(起伏) ups and downs; undulation. ~하다 rise and fall; roll; undulate. ¶ ~이 있는 평야 an undulating (a rolling) plain.

기본(基本) 《기초》 a foundation; a basis; 《기초적 사항》 basics; fundamentals; 《기준》 a standard. ¶ ~적인 fundamental; basic; standard / 영어의 ~ the ABC's of English / ~적인 인권 fundamental human rights / 영어를 ~부터 시작하다 study English from the basics. ‖ ~급 *one's* basic (regular) pay (wages, salary); *one's* base pay(퇴직금 계산시) 기초가 되는 / ~단위 a standard unit / ~방침 a basic policy / ~어휘 a basic vocabulary / ~요금 a basic rate; the basic (base) fare (택시의); the basic charge (사용료의) / ~원리 a fundamental (basic) principle / ~형 a basic pattern.

기부(寄附) (a) contribution; 《기증》 a donation; (a) subscription. ~하다 donate; contribute; subscribe. ¶ ~금을 모으다 raise subscriptions; collect contributions / 그녀는 적십자사에 많은 돈을 ~했다 She donated a large amount (of money) to the Red Cross. ‖ ~금 a contribution; a subscription; a donation / ~자 a contributor; a subscriber; a donor / ~행위 an act of endowment (donation).

기분(氣分) a feeling; a mood; frame of mind; sentiment; atmosphere(분위기). ¶ ~이 좋다 feel well (good, all right) / ~이 좋지 않다 do not feel well (good) / ~이 나쁘다 feel ill (bad) / 아무의 ~을 상하게 하다 hurt *a person's* feelings / 즐거운 ~에 잠겨 있다 be in a happy state of mind / 공부할 ~이 나지 않는다 I'm in no mood for study (work). / 두통으로 ~이 좋지 않다 I don't feel well because I have a headache. /「(환자에게) 오늘 ~이 어떠십니까?」—「많이 좋아졌습니다.」"How are you feeling today?" *or* "How do you feel today?"—"Much better, thanks." ‖ ~파 a moody person; a man of moods.

기분전환(氣分轉換) ~으로 for recreation; for a change / ~으로 산책이나 하자 Let's take a walk for a change. / 오늘 저녁에는 ~으로 외식이나 하러 나가자 How (What) about eating out this evening for a change?

기뻐하다 be glad (pleased, delighted); rejoice; take delight (*in*). ¶ 그녀는 그 소식을 듣고 기뻐했다 She was glad to hear the news.

기쁘다 (be) glad; delightful; happy; pleasant(유쾌). ¶ 기쁜 날 a happy day / 기쁜 소식 glad (happy) news / 기쁜 일 a happy event / 기쁘게 하다 please; delight; make (*a person*) happy; give pleasure (*to*); gladden / 집 안 일을 도와 어머니를 기쁘게 했다 I made my mother happy by helping her with the domestic chores.

기쁨 joy; happiness; delight; rejoice; pleasure. ¶ 인생의 ~ joys of life / 성공의 ~ the pleasure of success / 커다란 ~ great pleasure / ~을 참을 수 없다 be unable to contain *one's* delight / 그녀의 얼굴에는 ~이 넘쳐 있었다 Her face beamed with joy.

기사(技師) an engineer. ‖ 건축~ an architectural engineer.

기사(記事) 《신문의》 a news story (item); a report; news; an article. ¶ ~를 쓰다 write a report (an article) (*on*) / 오늘 아침 「한남 일보」에 그 화재 ~가 나와 있다 The fire is reported in this morning's Hannam Ilbo. ‖ ~금지 a press ban / 3면~ city news / 특종~ a scoop; a beat (美).

기사(騎士) a knight. ‖ ~도 knighthood; chivalry.

기사회생(起死回生) revival (resuscitation) (from serious illness). ~하다 revive; resuscitate. ¶ ~의 묘약 a miracle (wonder) drug / ~을 위해 홈런을 날리다 hit a homer to pull the game out of the fire / ~의 만루 홈런 a table-turning grand slam.

기산(起算) ~하다 reckon (count) from (*a date*); measure from (*a point*). ‖ ~일 the initial date (in reckoning).

기상(起床) ~하다 rise; get up. ¶ ~나팔 the reveille; the morning bugle / ~시각 the rising hour; the hour of rising.

기상(氣象) weather; atmospheric phenomena; a climate(기후). ¶ ~을 관측하다 make meteorological (weather) observation / ~의 변화 a change in the weather. ‖ ~경보 a weather warning / ~대 a weather station; a meteorological observatory / ~도(圖) a weather map (chart) / ~레이더 a weather radar / ~위성 a weather satellite / ~재해(주의보, 통보) a weather disaster(warning, report) / ~정보 weather information / ~청 the Meteorological Administration / ~학 meteorology.

기색(氣色) 〔안색〕 a complexion; 〔표정〕 a look; a countenance; an expression; 〔태도〕 manner; bearing; 〔기미〕 signs. ¶ 노한 ~ an angry look / 아무의 ~을 살피다 try to judge *a person's* state of mind (from *his* expression); read *a person's* expression (face) / 조금도 두려워하는 ~ 없이 without showing the slightest sign of fear. 「a *kisaeng's* house.

기생(妓生) a *kisaeng*. ‖ ~집 〔방〕

기생(寄生) parasitism. ~하다 be parasitic on 《*a tree*》; live on (with) 《*its host*》. ‖ ~동물 〔식물〕 a parasite; a parasitic animal (plant) / ~충 a parasite; a parasitic worm / ~충 구충제 a parasiticide.

기선(汽船) a steamship; a steamer. ¶ ~으로 가다 go 《*to London*》 by steamer. ‖ ~정기 ~ a regular liner.

기선(機先) ¶ 우리는 적의 ~을 잡았다 We got a head start on the enemy. *or* We stole a march on the enemy.

기설(旣設) ¶ ~의 established; existing.

기성(奇聲) ¶ ~을 발하다 give 《utter》 a strange sound; squeal.

기성(旣成) ¶ ~의 accomplished; existing; established; ready-made (옷 따위). ‖ ~개념 a stereotype (~개념에 사로잡히다 adhere to *one's* stereotype) / ~복 ready-made clothes; a ready-to-wear suit 〔dress〕 / ~사실 an accomplished 〔established〕 fact / ~세대 the older generation / ~정당 the existing political parties / ~품 ready-made goods 〔articles〕.

기성(棋聖) a great master of *paduk* (chess).

기성회(期成會) 〔학교의〕 a school supporting organization. ‖ ~비 dues for school supporting organization.

기세(氣勢) spirit; vigor; ador. ¶ ~가 오르다 be in high spirits / ~를 올리다 get elated; arouse *one's* enthusiasm / ~를 껶다 dispirit; discourage.

기소(起訴) 〔행사〕 prosecution; indictment. ~하다 prosecute (indict) 《*a person*》 for a crime; charge 《*a person*》 with a crime. ¶ ~를 유예하다 suspend an indictment; leave a charge on the file / 불 ~ 처분하다 drop a case. ‖ ~장 an indictment.

기수(基數) a cardinal number.

기수(旗手) a standard-bearer; a flag-bearer.

기수(機首) the nose of an airplane. ¶ ~를 남으로 돌리다 head for the south; turn southward / ~를 내리다 〔올리다〕 nose up (down); lower 〔pull up〕 the nose.

기수(騎手) a rider; a horseman; a jockey(경마의).

기수범(旣遂犯) a crime that has already been committed.

기숙(寄宿) ~하다 lodge 〔board〕 《*at, with a person*》. ‖ ~사 a dormitory / ~생 a boarding (resident) student; a boarder / ~학교 a boarding school.

기술(技術) an art(기예); technique (전문적 기교); technology (과학기술); a skill. ¶ ~적인 technical / ~상 technically / ~상의 어려움 a technical difficulty / ~의 진보 technological 〔technical〕 advance / 외국~의 도입 introduction 〔importation〕 of foreign techniques. ‖ ~개발 technical development / ~격차 disparity in technique / ~고문 a technical adviser / ~마찰 friction over technology (exchange) / ~수출 technology export / ~원조 technical assistance / ~이전 the transfer of technical knowhow / ~자 a technical expert; a technician / ~제휴 (join in) a technical tie-up / ~혁신 a technological innovation / ~협력 technical cooperation / 핵심~ core technology.

기술(記述) a description; an account(설명). ~하다 describe; give an account 《*of*》. ¶ ~적인 descriptive; narrative.

기술인력(技術人力) skilled technical hands; (highly) skilled technical manpower. ¶ 될 수 있는 대로 많은 ~을 양성하다 foster as much excellent skilled manpower as possible.

기술집약산업(技術集約産業) a technology-intensive industry.

기술축적(技術蓄積) the accumulation of technology (industrial know-how).

기슭 the foot (base); the edge. ¶산~에 at the foot of a mountain / 강~에 on the edge (brink) of a river.

기습(奇習) a strange custom.

기습(奇襲) a surprise (attack); a sudden attack. ~하다 make a surprise attack (on); take (*the enemy*) by surprise. ¶배후에서 ~을 시도하다 attempt a surprise attack from behind.

기승(氣勝) an unyielding spirit. ¶~스러운 여자 a woman of spirit; a strong-minded (-spirited) woman.

기승전결(起承轉結) the four steps in composition (*i.e.* the introduction, the development of the theme, conversion, and summing up).

기식(寄食) ~하다 sponge (live) on (*one's relative*); be a parasite (*on, to*). ‖~자 a hanger-on; a parasite.

기신호(旗信號) flag signaling.

기실(其實) the truth (reality). ¶~은 in reality (fact); as a matter of fact / ~은 그는 해고 당했다 The truth is that he has been dismissed.

기쓰다(氣—) do *one's* utmost; make every possible effort; spare no labor. ¶기쓰고 일하다 work with all *one's* might.

기아(棄兒)(아이) an abandoned child; a foundling. ~하다 desert (abandon) *one's* child.

기아(飢餓) hunger; starvation. ¶~에 직면하다 face starvation / ~선상에 있다 be starving; be on the brink (verge) of starvation / 이들 외국의 원조가 없다면, 그들은 ~상태를 면치 못할 것이다 Without this aid from foreign countries, they would be reduced to near starvation. ‖ ~임금(賃金) starvation wages.

기악(器樂) instrumental music.

기안(起案) drafting. ~하다 prepare a draft; draw up a plan.

기암괴석(奇岩怪石) rocks of fantastic shape.

기압(氣壓) atmospheric (air) pressure. ‖ ~계 a barometer / ~골 a trough of low atmospheric pressure. 「다 promise; pledge.

기약(期約) promise; pledge. ~하

기어이(期於—) by all means; at any cost; under any circumstances.

기억(記憶) memory; remembrance; recollection. ~하다 remember; remain in *one's* memory; 《상기》 recall; recollect; 《잊지 않도록》 bear (*a thing*) in mind; 《암기》 lean by heart; memorize. ¶~할 만한 날 a memorable day / 내 ~으로는 as far as I can remember / ~을 더듬어가며 tracing back in memory / 어린 시절의 희미한 ~ dim memories of *one's* childhood / 또렷이 ~하다 have a clear memory (*of*) / ~에 새롭다 be fresh in *one's* memory. ‖ ~력 memorial power; memory / ~력이 좋다(나쁘다) have a good (poor) memory / ~상실증(症) amnesia / ~술 mnemonics; the art of memory / 주~장치 a main storage (memory).

기업(企業) an enterprise; an undertaking; 《a》 business. ¶한국의 해외~ Korea's overseas enterprises / ~의 비밀 an industrial (a company) secret / ~의 합리화 rationalization of enterprises / ~의 계열화 the grouping of enterprises / 민간~ a private enterprise / ~을 일으키다 plan (embark in) an enterprise / 인플레로 ~이 재정난에 직면됐다 Business has encountered financial difficulties because of inflation. ‖ ~가 an *entrepreneur* 《프》; a man of enterprise / ~연합 a cartel / ~윤리 business ethics / ~진단 industrial readjustment / ~활동 management consulting / ~합동 a trust / ~화 commercialization (commercialize).

기업공개(企業公開) a corporation's public offering (sale) of stocks (shares); going public. ~를 권장하다 encourage (a corporation) to go public

기여(寄與)(a) contribution. ~하나 contribute; be conducive. ¶세계평화에 ~하다 make a contribution to world peace.

기연(奇緣) a strange turn of fate; a curious coincidence.

기연가미연가하다 not be sure.

기염(氣焰) tall (big) talk; bombast. ¶~을 토하다 talk big; speak with great vehemence.

기예(技藝) arts and crafts.

기예(氣銳) (a) spirited; energetic / 신진~의 예술가 a young and energetic artist.

기온(氣溫) (atmospheric) temperature. ¶~의 변화 a change of (in the) temperature.

기와 a tile. ¶~로 지붕을 이다 tile a roof; roof (*a house*) with tiles. ‖ ~공장 a tilery / ~지붕 a tiled roof / ~집 a tile-roofed house / 기왓가마 a tile-kiln.

기왕(既往) the past; bygone days. ¶ ~에 since it is done / ~이면 if it is done: 《선택》 if I must take 〔choose〕 / ~증 the medical history of a patient.

기용(起用) appointment. ~하다 appoint; employ the service 《of》. ¶ 새 부서로 ~되다 be appointed to the new position.

기우(杞憂) unnecessary anxiety; needless 〔imaginary〕 fears; groundless apprehension. ¶ 자네 걱정은 ~에 불과하다 Your fears are groundless.

기우(祈雨) praying for rain. ~하다 offer prayers for rain. ‖ ~제 a rite to pray for rain.

기우듬하다 (be) somewhat slanted. ¶ 기우듬한 기둥 a slanting pillar / 왼쪽으로 ~ have a tilt to the left.

기우뚱거리다 sway from side to side; shake; totter. ¶《불안정하다》 be unsteady 〔shaky〕. ¶ 기우뚱거리는 의자 a rickety chair / 몸을 ~ sway *one's* body 《from one side to the other》.

기운 ① 《체력》 (physical) strength; energy; force; might. ¶ ~이 있다 〔세다〕 be strong 〔mighty〕 / ~이 없다 〔약하다〕 be weak 〔feeble〕; do not have much strength / ~을 얻다 gain strength / ~이 빠지다 lose *one's* strength / ~을 내다 put forth 〔out〕 *one's* strength. ② 《기력·활력》 vigor; energy; spirits; vitality. ¶ ~이 찬 vigorous; energetic / ~을 내다 brace *oneself* up / ~을 북돋우다 cheer up; invigorate. ③ 《기미》 a touch; a dash; a shade; a tinge. ¶ 감기 ~ a touch of cold / 술 ~이 있다 be under the influence of liquor; be tipsy / 붉은 ~이 돌다 be tinged with red / 〔약 따위가〕 ~이 빨리 퍼지다 take effect rapidly.

기운(氣運) a tendency; a trend. ¶ 화해〔혁명〕의 ~이 감돌고 있다 There is a growing tendency toward reconciliation 〔revolution〕.

기운(機運) 《운수》 fortune; luck; 《기회》 an opportunity; a chance. ¶ ~이 무르익기를 기다리다 wait for a ripe opportunity.

기울 《밀 따위의》 bran.

기울다 ① 《경사지다》 incline; tilt; slant; slope 《밑으로》; list 《배가》; bank 《선회시에》; lurch 《급하게》. ¶ 좌로 ~ lean to the left / 〔건물이〕 한쪽으로 기울고 있다 be leaning to one side. ② 《쇠하다》 decline; wane; sink. ¶ 그의 운세도 기울고 있다 His fortune is waning 〔on the wane〕. ③ 《해·달이》 decline; go down; sink. ④ 《경향》 be inclined; lean; incline 《to》. ¶ 정치적으로 극우에 ~ be politically inclined to the extreme right / 그녀 마음은 나에게 기울었다 Her heart inclined to me.

기울어뜨리다 incline; lean; tip.

기울어지다 ① 《경사》 incline; lean; tilt; slant; list 《배가》; bank 《비행기가》. ¶ 50도로 ~ be inclined at fifty degrees / 한쪽으로 ~ lean to one side. ② 《해·달이》 decline 《toward》; be going down. ③ 《경향》 tend 《to》; be inclined 《to》. ¶ 숙명론에 ~ lean towards fatalism.

기울이다 《경사지게 하다》 incline; bend; lean; tilt; 《기구 등을》 tip; slant. ¶ 고개를 ~ incline *one's* head / 술잔을 ~ have a drink / 책상을 ~ tilt a desk. 《마음을 집중하다》 devote *oneself* to; concentrate 《*one's* attention》 on. ¶ 공부에 전력을 ~ devote *one's* energy to *one's* studies / 남의 말에 귀를 ~ listen 〔lend an ear〕 to what *one* says / 애정을 ~ fix 〔set〕 *one's* heart 《on》.

기웃거리다 《고개를》 stretch 〔crane〕 *one's* neck to see 《*something*》; 《엿보다》 look 《in, into》; peep 《into; through》; snoop 《around, about》. ¶ 창문으로 안을 ~ look in at the window / 기웃거리는 사람 a snooper; a peeping Tom.

기원(祈願) a prayer. ~하다 pray. ¶ ~을 an optative sentence / 필승 ~ a prayer for victory.

기원(紀元) an era; an epoch. ¶ ~전 500년, 500 B.C. (=Before Christ). ☞ 서기·신기원.

기원(起源) origin; beginning. ~하다 originate 《in》; have *its* origin 〔roots〕 《in》. ¶ ~을 더듬다 trace 《*something*》 to *its* origin 〔source〕 / 그 ~은 불명이다 Its origin is unknown.

기원(棋院) a *paduk* club 〔house〕.

기음문자(記音文字) phonetic letters.

기이하다(奇異─) (be) strange; curious; queer; odd.

기인(奇人) an eccentric (person); an odd 〔strange〕 fellow.

기인(起因) ~하다 be due to; be caused by; originate in. ¶ 그 병은 과로와 수면 부족에 ~한다 The disease is caused by overwork and lack of sleep.

기일(忌日) an anniversary of *one's* death; a deathday.

기일(期日) a (fixed) date; an appointed day; 《기한》 a due date; a time limit. ¶ ~을 지키다 keep to the schedule 〔the appointed day〕; meet the deadline

기입 entry. ~하다 enter; make an entry 《*in*》; fill out [in] 《*the form*》. ¶ 장부에 금액을 ~하다 enter a sum in a ledger / 신청서에 필요 사항을 ~하다 fill out the application / 이곳에 주소·성명을 ~하시오 Please fill in your name and address here. ∥ ~누락 an omission / ~필 Entered.

기자(記者) 《신문의》 a newspaperman; a (newspaper) reporter; a pressman 《英》 《보도관계자 전반》 a journalist. ¶ 그는 H신문~이다 He is a reporter for the H. / 여성~ a woman reporter / 스포츠~ a sports writer / 경제~ a financial reporter. ∥ ~단〔클럽〕 a press corps (club) / ~석 a press gallery(의회의); a press stand [box] (경기장의) / ~회견〔hold〕 a press [news] conference.

기장¹〔稷〕 (Chinese) millet.
기장²〔옷의〕 the length of a suit; the dress length.
기장(記章) a badge; a medal.
기장(機長) a captain; a pilot.
기재(奇才) 《사람》 a genius; a prodigy; 《재주》 remarkable talent.
기재(記載) mention; 〔簿記〕 entry. ~하다 state; record; mention. ¶ 별항(위)에 ~한 바와 같이 as stated elsewhere (above). ∥ ~사항 mentioned items / 허위~ a false entry. [materials.
기재(器材) 《기구와 재료》 tools and
기재(機材) 《기계의 재료》 machine parts; materials for making machinery.
기저(基底) a base; a foundation.
기저귀 a diaper 《美》; a baby's napkin; a nappy 《英》. ¶ ~를 채우다 diaper 《*a baby*》; put a diaper on 《*a baby*》. [siren 《美》.
기적(汽笛) a (steam) whistle; a
기적(奇蹟) a miracle; a wonder. ¶ ~적(으로) miraculous(ly) / 한강의 ~ the 'miracle' on the Han river / ~적으로 살아나다 escape death by a miracle.
기전(起電) generation of electricity. ∥ ~기 an electric motor / ~력 electromotive force.
기절(氣絶) fainting. ~하다 faint; lose consciousness; lose *one's* senses.
기점(起點) a starting point.
기정(旣定) an established fact. ∥ ~ 방침에 따라 according to a prearranged program (plan).
기제(忌祭) a memorial service held on the anniversary of 《*a person's*》 death.
기조(基調) the keynote; the underlying tone; the basis. ¶ 한국 경제의 ~ the basic economic condition 《*of Korea*》 / …의 ~를 이루다 form the keynote of…. ∥ ~연설 a keynote speech [address] / ~연설자 a keynote speaker. [facilities.
기존(旣存) ~의 시설 the existing
기종(氣腫) 〔醫〕 emphysema.
기준(基準) a standard; a yardstick; a basis 《이론 등의 근거》. ¶ ~이 되는 standard; basic / ~설정하다 set 〔establish〕 a standard / 안전~에 맞다 meet safety standards. ∥ ~가격 a standard price / ~량 a norm / ~시세 the basic rate / ~임금 standard wages / ~점 a base point; a reference point (측량의).
기중(忌中) (in) mourning.
기중기(起重機) a crane; a derrick (배의). ¶ ~로 들어올리다 [hoist] 《*a thing*》 with a crane.
기증(寄贈) presentation; donation. ~하다 present; donate. ∥ ~본 a presentation copy / ~자 a donator; a donor / ~품 a gift; a present.
기지(基地) a base. ∥ ~촌 a military campside town / 관측~ an observation base / 작전~ a base of operations / 항공~ an air base.
기지(旣知) ~의 already-known. ∥ ~수 a known quantity.
기지개 a stretch. ¶ 그녀는 침대에서 일어나 크게 ~를 켰다 She got out of bed and had a good stretch.
기진(氣盡) ¶ ~맥진하다 be utterly exhausted; be really worn out; be dead tired.
기질(氣質) disposition; nature; temper; temperament. ¶ 지기 싫어하는 ~ an unyielding nature [spirit] / 예술가적인 〔온화한〕 ~ an artistic 〔a gentle〕 temperament.
기차(汽車) 〔열차〕 a (railroad) train. ¶ 목포행(발) ~ a train for 〔from〕 *Mokp'o* / ~를 타다 take [board] a train / ~로 여행하다 travel by train / ~ 창문에서 보이는 경치 a scene viewed from a train window. ∥ ~놀이 〔兒語〕 a choochoo 《美》; a puff-puff 《英》 / ~시간표 a railroad schedule 《美》 / ~운임 a train 〔railroad〕 fare 《美》 / ~표 a (railroad) ticket.
기차다(氣 —) 〔어이없다〕 be dumbfounded 《*at*》; be disgusted 《*at*》.
기착(寄着) a stopover. ~하다 stop over 《*at Honolulu*》.

기채(起債) flotation of a loan. ~하다 float (raise) a loan; issue bonds. ‖ ~시장 the bond (capital) market.

기척 a sign; an indication. ¶ 누군가가 다가오는 ~이 있었다 I sensed someone approaching.

기체(氣體) gas; vapor(증기). ¶ ~의 gaseous ~가 되다 become (turn into) a gas. ‖ ~연료 gaseous fuel.

기체(機體) the body (of a plane); an airframe; a fuselage(동체).

기초(起草) drafting. ~하다 draft (a bill); draw up (a plan). ‖ ~위원(회) a drafting committee / ~자 a draftsman.

기초(基礎) (lay) the foundation (of); the basis; the base. ¶ ~적인 fundamental; basic; elementary / 영어의 ~ 강좌 elementary lessons in English / ~부터 배우다 learn (English) from the beginning / ~를 만들다 (쌓다) lay the foundation (of); lay the groundwork (for) / ~를 굳히다 put (the project) on a firm basis; consolidate the foundation (of). ‖ ~공사 foundation work / ~공제 the basic deduction (from taxable income) / ~과학 (a) basic science / ~산업 (a) key(basic) industry / ~지식 an elementary (a basic) knowledge (of English) / ~학과 primary subjects (of study) / ~훈련 a basic training.

기총(機銃) a machine gun. ¶ ~소사하다 machine-gun; strafe.

기축통화(基軸通貨) key currency.

기치(旗幟) a flag; a banner; (깃발) one's attitude (stand). ¶ ~를 선명히 하다 make clear one's attitude.

기침 a cough; coughing. ~하다 cough; have a cough. ¶ 잔~ a slight cough / 헛~을 하다 clear one's throat; give a cough. ‖ 감기로 ~ a cold on the chest / ~약 a cough medicine.

기타(其他) the others; the rest; and others; and so forth (on); et cetera(생략 etc.). ¶ ~는 모두 가짜다 All the others are fakes.

기타 (play) a guitar. ‖ ~연주가 a guitarist.

기탁(寄託) deposit(ion); [法] bailment. ~하다 deposit (a thing with a person); entrust (a person with a thing). ‖ ~금 trust money / ~자 a depositor; [法] a bailor / ~증서 a deposit certificate.

기탄(忌憚) reserve. ¶ ~없는 frank; outspoken; unreserved / ~없이 without reserve; frankly / ~없이 말하면 to be frank (with you); frankly speaking.

기통(汽筒) a cylinder. ¶ 6~ 엔진 a six-cylinder(ed) engine.

기특(奇特) ¶ ~한 laudable; praiseworthy; commendable / ~한 행동 a commendable deed.

기틀 the crux (of a matter); the key (pivotal) point.

기포(氣泡) a bubble.

기포(氣胞) an air bladder.

기폭(起爆) detonation. ¶ 혁명의 ~제가 되다 (사물이 주어) trigger a revolution. ‖ ~장치 a detonator; a triggering device.

기표(記票) balloting. ~하다 fill in a ballot. ‖ ~소 a polling booth.

기품(氣品) elegance; grace; dignity. ¶ ~있는 dignified; graceful; elegant.

기풍(氣風) (개인의) character; disposition; (사회의) (an) ethos; spirit(경향·정신); trait(특성); 《단체의》 tone. ¶ 국민의 ~ the ethos of a nation / 그 지역의 보수적인 ~ the conservative traits of the locality.

기피(忌避) (징집 등의) evasion; (법률상의) a challenge. ~하다 evade; avoid; challenge. ¶ 징병을 ~하다 evade military service; dodge the draft / 배심원에 대한 ~ a challenge to jurors. ‖ ~신청 a motion for challenge / ~인물 (외자) an unwelcome (unacceptable) person / ~자 an evader (of service); a shirker.

기필코(期必一) certainly; by all means; without fail.

기하(幾何) geometry. ¶ ~학적(으로) geometrical(ly).

기하다(期一) ① 《일시를 미리 정하다》 fix the date; set a term (time limit) (for). ¶ 월말을 기해 전화요금을 지불하다 pay one's phone bill at the end of the month. ② 《기약하다》 make up one's mind; promise; be determined (resolved) (to). ¶ 재회를 ~ promise to meet again / 우승을 기하고 열심히 연습하다 be resolved to win and practice hard.

기한(期限) a term; a period; a time limit; a deadline (美). ¶ 일정한 ~ 내에 within a definite period of time / ~부의 (로) with a (one-year) time limit / ~이 되다 (fall) due / ~을 연장하다 extend the term / 최종 ~을 정하다 set a deadline (for) / ~이 넘다 be over due / 이 어음은 지불 ~이 내일이다 This bill is due tomorrow. ‖ ~경과 (만료) the expiration of a period (term) / 지

불 ~ the time of payment.
기함(旗艦) a flagship.
기함(氣合) 《정신 집중》 concentration of spirit; 《소리》 a shout; a yell; 〖軍〗 disciplinary punishment (*upon a group*). ¶ ~을 넣다 show (display) *one's* spirit with a yell / ~을 주다 〖軍〗 chastise; discipline. ¶ ~술 the art of mesmerizing by *one's* willpower.
기항(寄港) a call (stop) at a port. ~하다 call (stop) at a port. ~지 a port of call.
기행(奇行) eccentric conduct.
기행(紀行) an account of travels; a record of *one's* travel. ‖ ~문 travel notes.
기형(畸形) deformity; malformation. ¶ ~아 a deformed (malformed) child.
기호(記號) a mark; a sign; a symbol; a clef(음악의). ¶ ~를 붙이다 put a mark (*on*).
기호(嗜好) a taste; liking. ¶ ~에 맞다 suit *one's* taste; suit *one's* taste(s). ‖ ~품 《식품》 *one's* favorite food; a table luxury (술·커피 따위).
기혼(既婚) ¶ ~의 married. ‖ ~자 a married (wo)man.
기화(奇貨) ¶ …을 ~로 삼다 take advantage of / 아무의 약점을 ~로 삼다 presume on *a person's* weakness.
기화(氣化) 〖理〗 vaporization. ~하다 vaporize; evaporate. ‖ ~기 a carburetor / ~열 evaporation heat.
기회(機會) 《seize, miss》 an opportunity; a chance; an occasion. ¶ 절호의 ~ a golden opportunity / ~균등주의 the principle of equal opportunity / ~주의 opportunism / ~주의자 an opportunist; a timeserver.
기획(企劃) planning; a plan; a project. ~하다 make (form) a plan; draw up a project. ‖ ~관리 planning and management / ~관리실 the Planning and Management Office / ~력 planning ability / ~부 the planning department / ~성 the ability to make plans / ~조정실 the Office of Planning and Coordination.
기후(氣候) climate; weather. ¶ 온화한(험악한, 해양성, 대륙성, 열대성) ~ a mild (severe, maritime, continental, tropical) climate / ~변화에 주의하다 be careful about changes in the weather.
긴급(緊急) emergency; urgency. ¶ ~한 pressing; urgent / ~시에는 in an emergency / ~ 용무로 on urgent (pressing) business / ~히 회의를 열 필요가 있다 We must hold an urgent meeting. ‖ ~동의(make) an urgent motion / ~명령 an emergency order / ~사태 (declare) a state of emergency / ~용직통전화 a hot line / ~조치(대책) emergency measures; urgent countermeasures.
긴밀(緊密) ¶ ~한 close; intimate / ~한 연락을 취하다 《제휴을》 be in close contact (cooperation) with.
긴박(緊迫) tension; strain. ¶ ~한 정세 a tense (an acute) situation / ~한 국제관계 a tense international relationship / ~해지다 become tense (acute); grow strained.
긴요(緊要) ¶ ~한 vital; important; essential; indispensable.
긴장(緊張) tension; strain. ~하다 get (become) tense; be strained; be on edge. ¶ ~한 strained; tense / 국제간의 ~ international tension / ~된 분위기 a tense atmosphere / ~을 완화하다 relieve (ease) the tension / 냉전의 ~이 고조되었다 Cold-war tension has mounted (built up). ‖ ~완화 《국제간의》 détente.
긴축(緊縮) 《경제적》 (strict) economy; retrenchment; deflation(통화의); austerity(생활의). ~하다 economize; retrench; cut down (삭감). ‖ ~생활 (lead) an austere life; (practice) austerity / ~예산〖재정〗 a reduced budget / ~정책 (adopt) a belt-tightening policy.
긴하다(緊—) 《긴요하다》 (be) important; vital; essential; (유용하다) (be) useful; necessary; (급하다) (be) urgent; pressing. ¶ 긴한 사람 a very important person / 긴한 일 urgent (pressing) business / 긴한 청 a vital request / 긴히 쓰다 make good use of / 긴한 물건 a useful article.
긷다《물을》 draw; dip (scoop) up. ¶ 갓 길어온 우물물 water fresh from the well / 우물물을 ~ draw water from a well (*with a bucket*).
길 《깊이》 a fathom.
길 ① 《도로》 a way; a road; a street(가로); 《국도·공도》 a highway; 《좁은 길》 a path; a lane; 《통로》 passage. ¶ 시골 ~ a country lane / 산 ~ a mountain path; a pass / 가까운 ~ a shorter way / 돌아오는 ~ *one's* way back / ~을 만들다 build a road / ~을 잃다 lose (miss) *one's* way; get lost / ~을 잘못 들다 take the wrong way / ~을 묻다 ask (*a person*) the way (*to*);

ask (*a person*) how to get (*to*) ~을 막다 block (*a person's*) passage; stand in (*a person's*) way / 동물원 가는 ~을 가르쳐 주십시오 Please tell me the way to the zoo. ② 《가야 할 길》 a way; a journey; a distance(거리). ¶ 하룻 ~ a day's distance / 길을 떠나다 start (set out) on a journey. ③ 《진로·수단·방법》 a course; a route; a way; a means; 《올바른 길》 the path; a way. ¶ 성공으로의 ~ the way (road) to success / 학자가 되는 유일한 ~ the only way to become a scholar / 인간의 바른 ~을 설교하다 preach the right way of life / 아무에게 ~을 잘못 들게 하다 lead *a person* astray / 후진을 위해 ~을 트다 make way for *one's* junior / 우리가 취해야 할 ~은 이것뿐이다 This is the only way left open to us.

길² 《등급》 a class; a grade. ¶ 상 (핫)~ a superior (an inferior) grade.

길거리 a street. ¶ ~를 쏘다니다 roam about the streets.

길길이 ① 《높이》 high; tall. ¶ ~ 쌓다 pile up high. ② 《몹시》 very; extremely; exceedingly. ¶ 성이 나서 ~ 뛰다 be very angry.

길년(吉年) an auspicious year.

길눈 《방향 감각》 a sense of direction. ¶ ~이 밝다(어둡다) have a good (poor) sense of direction.

길다 be long; lengthy. ¶ 길게 (be) long; lengthy, lengthily.

길드 a guild.

길들다 ① 《동물이》 grow (become) domesticated (tame). ¶ 길든 고양이 a tame cat. ② 《윤나다》 get (become) polished (glossy). ③ 《익숙》 get (be) accustomed (used) to; grow familiar with.

길들이다 ① 《동물을》 tame; domesticate; train (*a dog*). ② 《윤나게》 give a polish to; polish up; make (*it*) glossy. ③ 《익숙해지게》 get (make) (*a person*) used (accustomed) to; accustom (*a person*) to. ¶ 명령에 복종하도록 길들여진 국민 a people accustomed to accepting orders (from above).

길마 《안장》 a packsaddle. ¶ 두 ~ 보기 sit on the fence.

길목 ① 《길모퉁이》 a street corner. ② 《요소》 an important (key) position (on the road).

길몽(吉夢) a lucky dream.

길보(吉報) good news.

길손 a wayfarer; a traveler.

길쌈 weaving (*by hand*). ¶ ~하다 weave (*on a hand loom*). ¶ ~의 homewoven; homespun. ¶ ~꾼 a weaver.

길운(吉運) luck; good fortune.

길¹ 《거리》 length. ¶ 무릎 ~의 코트 an overcoat of knee length / ~가 2미터이다 be 2 meters long.

길이² 《오래》 long; forever.

길일(吉日) a lucky day.

길조(吉兆) a good (lucky) omen.

길쭉하다 (be) longish; rather long.

길차다 《수목이 우거지다》 be densely (thickly) wooded; 《미끈하게 길다》 be neatly tall (long). ¶ 길찬 숲 a thickly wooded forest.

길하다(吉—) (be) auspicious; lucky; fortunate; good.

길흉(吉凶) good or ill luck; fortune. ¶ ~을 점치다 tell *a person's* fortune.

김¹ 《먹는》 laver; dried laver(말린). ¶ ~양식 laver farming.

김² 《수증기》 steam; vapor; 《입·코의》 breath; 《냄새·맛》 smell; scent; aroma; flavor. ¶ ~이 무럭무럭 나다 be steaming hot / 냄새나는 입 ~ bad (foul) breath / 빠진 맥주 flat (vapid) (*beer*).

김³ 《잡초》 weeds. ¶ ~ 매다 weed.

김⁴ 《…하는 ~에》 while; when; as / 온 ~에 while I am here / 생각난 ~에 as I am reminded of (*the matter*) / 지나는 ~에 인사 드리려고 잠시 들렀습니다 As I passing this way, I've just dropped in to say hello. ② 《홧 ~에》 in a fit of anger / 술 ~에 under the influence of drink.

김장 《담근 것》 kimchi prepared for the winter; 《담그기》 kimchi-making (preparing kimchi) for the winter. ¶ ~하다 make (prepare) kimchi for the winter. ∥ ~독 a kimchi (pickle) jar / ~철 the time (season) for preparing kimchi for the winter.

김치 kimchi; pickled vegetables (by traditional Korean style); pickles; spicy pickled vegetables. ¶ ~를 담그다 prepare (make) kimchi. ∥ ~찌개 kimchi stew / 배추(무청, 나박, 갓)~ cabbage (radish leaf, watery, mustard leaf) kimchi.

깁다 sew (together) (꿰매다); stitch; mend; patch up(헝겊을 대고); darn(양말 따위를). ¶ 옷을 ~ patch up clothes / 헤진 곳을 ~ mend (sew up) a rip.

깁스 [醫] a plaster cast. ¶ ~를 하다 wear a plaster cast.

깃¹ 《옷의》 a collar; a lapel(접는). ¶ 코트의 ~을 세우다 turn up *one's* coat collar / 그녀의 옷 ~은 너무 깊이 파져 있다 The neckline of her dress is cut much too low.

깃² ① 《날개털》 a feather; a plume. ¶ 《새가》 ~을 다듬다

깃대 〖旗〗 a flagstaff〔flagpole〕.

깃들이다 《새가》 (build a) nest; 《비유적》 lodge; dwell. ¶ 건전한 정신은 건전한 신체에 깃들인다 A sound mind (dwells) in a sound body.

깃발 〖旗〗 a flag; a banner.

깊다 ① 《물·산 따위가》 (be) deep. ¶ 한없이 깊은 bottomless; fathomless / 깊은 구멍〔계곡〕 a deep hole〔gorge〕 / 깊은 바다 the deep sea / 이 호수는 여기가 가장 ~ This lake is deepest here. ② 《정도·생각 따위가》 (be) deep; profound (심원한). ¶ 깊은 슬픔〔애정〕 deep sorrow〔affections〕 / 깊은 잠 (a) deep〔sound〕 sleep / 깊은 상처 a deep wound / 깊은 사상 profound religious thought / 깊은 지식 profound knowledge 《of》 / 그의 이야기에 깊은 감명을 받았다 I was deeply impressed by his story. ③ 《관계가》 (be) close; intimate. ¶ 깊은 관계 a close relation〔connection〕 / 남녀간의 깊은 사이 an intimate relationship. ④ 《밤이》 (be) late. ¶ 밤이 깊어지다 grow late; advance; wear on.

깊숙하다 (be) deep; secluded. ¶ 깊숙한 골짜기 a deep valley / 외지고 깊숙한 시골 마을 a secluded village.

깊이 ① 《명사적》 depth; deepness. ¶ ~ 6피트(이다) (It is) six feet deep〔in depth〕 / ~를 재다 sound the depth 《of》. ② 《부사적》 deep(ly); intensely; strongly. ¶ ~ 파다 dig deep / ~ 생각하다 think deeply / ~ 사랑하다 love deeply〔intensely〕.

까뀌 a hatchet.

까끄라기 〖이삭의〗 an awn; an arista.

까놓다 〖털어놓다〗 unbosom oneself to; open one's heart; confide 《to》. ¶ 까놓고 말하면 frankly speaking.

까다 ① 《껍질을》 peel 《an orange》; rind; pare 《an apple》; shell 《a chestnut》; hull. ¶ 호두를 ~ crack a nut. ② 《새끼를》 hatch; incubate. ¶ 병아리를 ~ hatch out chickens.

까다² 〖비난·공격하다〗 criticize (severely); speak〔write〕 against; denounce; censure; attack; 《俗》 〖차다〗 kick 《at》; hack〔축구에서〕.

까다³ 〖제하다〗 deduct; subduct; subtract. ¶ 그 비용은 내 월급에서 깠다 The cost was taken away 〔deducted〕 from my pay.

까다롭다 ① 《성미가》 (be) hard to please; difficult; fastidious; particular(음식·옷 따위에). ¶ 까다로운 노부인 a difficult old lady / 까다롭게 굴다 be particular〔fastidious〕 《about one's food》. ② 《일·문제가》 (be) troublesome; complicated; difficult; ¶ 까다로운 문제 a delicate matter; a ticklish question.

까닥거리다 nod 《one's head》.

까닭 〖이유〗 reason; a cause(원인); ground(근거); a motive(동기); 〖구실〗 an excuse; a pretext. ¶ 무슨 ~으로 why; for what reason / ~ 없이 without any reason / 무슨 ~인지 for some reason or other; somehow or other / ~을 묻다 demand (inquire) the reason / 아무런 ~없이 나를 의심하다 hold a groundless suspicion against me.

까딱하면 very nearly(자칫하면); easily(쉽사리). ¶ ~ 화를 내다 be easily offended / ~ 차에 치일 뻔했다 I was nearly run over by a car. / 그는 ~으로 죽을 뻔했다 He was within a hairsbreadth of death.

까마귀 〖鳥〗 a crow; a raven(갈가마귀). ¶ ~ 는 bird of ill omen(별명).

까마득하다 (be) far(away); far distant; far-off; remote. ¶ 까마득한 옛날 a long long time ago.

까막눈이 an illiterate.

까맣다 《빛깔이》 (be) black; deep-black; coal-black; 〖아득하다〗 far off(away). ¶ 까맣게 타다 be scorched black.

까먹다 ① 《까서 먹다》 peel〔shell, crack〕 and eat. ② 《재산을》 spend all one's money〔fortune〕 《on》; squander; run through 《one's fortune》. ③ 〖잊다〗 forget.

까무러뜨리다 make 《a person》 insensible; stun(깨뜨리).

까무러치다 faint; lose consciousness; fall unconscious; fall into a swoon. ¶ 놀라서 ~ faint with surprise.

까발리다 《속의 것을》 pod〔shuck, shell〕 《a thing》 out; 〖폭로〗 expose; disclose 《a secret》.

까부르다 winnow; fan. ¶ 까불리다 get(be) winnowed. ¶ 까불림 winnowing.

까불다 ① 〖행동을〗 act frivolously; be flippant. ¶ 까불까불 flippantly. ② 《물건을》 jolt.

까불이 a sportive〔jocose〕 boy; a frivolous person.

까지 ①《때》 till; until; (up) to; before(…이전까지); by(기한). ¶ 아침부터 저녁 ~ from morning till night / 다음달 ~ till next month / 그때 ~ till then; up to that time / 칠십 ~ 살다 live to (be) seventy / 출발 ~ 5분이 남다 have five minutes before we start / 일은 8시 ~ 끝날 것이다 The work will be finished by 8 o'clock. ② 《장소》 (up) to; as far as. ¶ 서울~가다 go to [as far as] Seoul / 제5장 ~ 읽다 read to Chapter 5. ③ 《범위·정도》 to (the extent of); so (as) far as; even; up to. ¶ 빚 ~ 지다 go to the extent of incurring a debt / 도둑질 ~ 하다 go so far as to commit a theft / 물은 무릎 ~ 올라왔다 The water came up to the knees.

까치 《鳥》 a magpie.
까치발 《建》 a bracket; a tripod.
까치설날 New Year's Eve.
까칠하다 (be) haggard; thin; emaciated; be worn out. ¶ 까칠한 모습 a haggard look / 근심으로 ~ be careworn / 과로로 인해 몹시 ~ be worn out with overwork.
까투리 a hen pheasant. ¶ croak.
깍깍 cawing. ¶ ~ 울다 caw;
깍두기 Radish roots kimchi.
깍듯하다 (be) courteous; civil; polite; well-mannered. ¶ 인사가 깍듯한 사람 a courteous man; a man of polite greetings / 깍듯이 인사하다 greet 《a person》 politely; make a low bow.
깍쟁이 《인색한》 a shrewd 《stingy》 person; a niggard; a miser. ¶ 서울~ the shrewd Seoulite; a city slicker (큰 도시의).
깍지¹ 《껍질》 a pod; a shell; a husk.
깍지² 《활 쏠 때의》 an archer's thimble. ¶ ~ 끼다 lock 《interlace, knot》 one's fingers; clasp one's hands.
깎다 ① 《값을》 beat down 《the price》; haggle over 《the price》; knock 《the price》 down; bargain. ¶ 값을 몹시 ~ drive a hard bargain 《with a merchant》. ② 《머리를》 cut; trim; 《수염을》 shave; 《양털을》 shear 《a sheep》 ¶ 머리를 짧게 ~ cut one's hair short 《close》. ③ 《껍질을》 peel; pare; skin; 《연필 등을》 sharpen. ¶ 사과를 ~ pare an apple. ④ 《낯·체면을》 make 《a person》 lose face; disgrace; put to shame; hurt 《harm, injure》 《a person's reputation》. ⑤ 《삭감》 cut (down); reduce 《the budget》. ¶ steep.
깎아지르다 (be) precipitous; very steep.
깎이다 ① 《사동》 have 《one's hair》 cut; let 《a person》 cut 《shave, shear, etc.》. ② 《피동》 be hurt; be reduced. ¶ 낯이 ~ lose face.
깐깐하다 《까다롭다》 (be) particular; fastidious; 《꼼꼼하다》 (be) cautious; scrupulous; exact.

깔개 a cushion; matting.
깔기다 let off; discharge. ¶ 《aloud》.
깔깔 ¶ ~ 웃다《대다》 laugh loudly
깔깔하다 《감촉이》 (feel) rough; be sandy. ¶ 깔깔한 촉감 a rough 《sandy》 feel.
깔끔하다 《외양·태도가》 (be) neat and tidy; sleek and clean; 《성격이》 (be) tidy; sharp; sensitive. ¶ 옷 맵시가 ~ be neatly dressed / 깔끔한 성질 a sharp 《sensitive》 temper.
깔다 ① spread; lay; pave. ¶ 요를 ~ lay out the bedding; make a bed / 마루에 융단을 ~ lay a carpet on the floor / 돗자리를 ~ spread a mat / 철도를 ~ lay a railway. ② 《깔고 앉다》 sit 《seat oneself》 on 《a cushion》. ③ 《군림하다》 dominate; get 《a person》 under. ¶ 남편을 깔고 뭉개다 dominate one's husband. ④ 《돈·상품을》 lend out 《money》 widely; invest in. ¶ 빚을 여기저기 깔아 놓다 lend one's money out near and far.
깔때기 a funnel.
깔리다 ① 《널리》 be spread 〔covered〕 all over. ¶ 얼음이 ~ be frozen all over. ② 《밑에》 get 《be caught, be pinned》 under. ¶ 큰 곰인형 밑에 ~ be pinned under a big teddy bear.
깔보다 make light of 《a person》; look down upon 《a person》; hold 《a person》 in contempt; despise.
깔축없다 show no loss of weight 《volume, value, size, etc.》.
깜깜하다 《어둠》 (be) pitch-dark; 《모름》 (be) ignorant. ¶ 그 일에는 전혀 ~ be utterly ignorant of the matter.
깜박거리다 《명멸》 twinkle (별이); flicker; glitter; blink; 《눈을》 blink 《one's eyes》; wink. ¶ 깜박이는 신호 a blinking signal / 깜박거리는 등불 a blink of 《flickering》 light.
깜부기 a smutted ear 《of barley》. ¶ ~ 병 smut; bunt (밀의).
깜빡 《잠시》 for the moment. ¶ ~ 잊다 forget for the moment.
깜작 ¶ ~ 거리다(이다, 하다) blink; wink.
깜짝 ¶ ~ 놀라다 be surprised 《startled》 / 아이구 ~ 이야 What a surprise!
깜찍스럽다 be (too) clever (for one's age); precocious.
깝신거리다 behave frivolously; be flippant.
깡그리 all; wholly; altogether; entirely; without exception.
깡똥하다 (be) unbecomingly 《awkwardly》 short. ¶ steps.
깡쫑거리다 walk with hopping

깡통 a can 《美》; a tin 《英》. ¶ ~차다 be reduced to begging. ¶ ~따개 a can (tin) opener.

깡패 a hoodlum; a hooligan; a gangster; gang of racketeers (폭력단). ¶ ~생활에서 손을 씻다 quit the life of a gangster.

깨 ① 《식물》 a sesame. ☞ 참깨, 들깨. ② 《씨》 sesame seeds. ∥ ~소금 salt and sesame.

깨끗이 ① 《청결》 clean(ly); 《정연》 neatly; tidily. ~하다 (make) clean; make neat (tidy). ② 《결백》 clean(ly); innocently; 《공정》 fairly. ¶ ~지다 be fairly beaten / ~살다 lead an honest (a pure) life. ③ 《완전히》 completely; thoroughly; 《미련없이》 ungrudgingly; with good grace. ¶ 빚을 ~ 갚다 pay one's debt in full; clear of (up) one's debts / ~ 잘못을 인정하다 admit one's fault with good grace.

깨끗하다 ① 《청결한》 (be) clean, cleanly; pure; 《맑다》 (be) clear; 《정연》 (be) tidy; neat. ¶ 깨끗한 물(공기) clear (pure) water (air) / 옷차림이 깨끗한 neatly-dressed. ② 《결백》 (be) pure; clean; innocent; noble(고상); chaste (순결); 《공정》 (be) fair; clean. ¶ 깨끗한 일생 a career with a clean record / 깨끗한 사랑(남녀의) platonic (pure) love / 깨끗한 정치 clean politics / 깨끗한 투표 corruption-free balloting / 깨끗한 한 표 (cast) an (an honest) vote. ③ 《심신이》 (be) well; refreshed. ¶몸이 깨끗지 않다 be unwell.

깨다¹ ① ☞ 깨어나다. ② 《개화》 become civilized. ③ 《잠을》 wake up; awake; rouse (arouse) 《a person》 from sleep; 《술기운을》 sober 《a person》 up; make 《a person》 sober; 《미몽에서》 awaken, 《깨어 있다》 be (wide) awake; lie awake in bed〔잠자리에서〕/ 술기운을 깨기 위해 옥외로 나가다 go outdoors to sober up / 아버님 말씀이 나를 깨웠다 My father's words awakend me. ④ ☞ 깨우다.

깨다² ① 《부수다》 break; crush; smash. ¶ 그릇(침묵)을 ~ break a dish (the silence). ② 《일을》 bring to a rupture; break off 《negotiations》. ¶ 혼담을 ~ break off a proposed marriage / 흥을 ~ spoil the fun 《of》; cast a chill 《upon, over》.

깨닫다 see; perceive; realize; understand; sense; be aware of; be convinced of. ¶ 진리를 ~ perceive a truth / 제 잘못을 ~ be convinced of one's error (fault) / 사태의 중대성을 ~ realize (become aware of) the seriousness of the situation / …을 깨닫게 하다 make 《a person》 realize 《something》; open 《a person's》 eyes to 《a thing》.

깨뜨리다 break. ☞ 깨다².

깨물다 bite; gnaw. ¶혀를 ~ bite one's tongue.

깨어나다 《잠에서》 wake up; awake; 《미몽에서》 come (be brought) to one's senses; be disillusioned; 《술·마취 등에서》 sober up; get (become) sober; regain consciousness; come to life again. ¶망상에서 ~ be awakened from one's illusions.

깨우다 《잠을》 wake up; awake; (a)rouse; call〔아침에〕.

깨우치다 awaken; disillusion; enlighten〔계몽〕.

깨지다 ① 《부서지다》 break; be broken〔smashed, damaged〕. ¶ 깨지기 쉬운 brittle; easily breaking; fragile / 산산조각이 이 유리는 깨지기 쉽다 This glass breaks easily. ② 《일이》 fall through; be broken off; be ruptured. ¶ 그 혼담은 깨졌다 The match was broken off. ③ 《흥 따위》 be dampened〔spoiled〕.

깨지락거리다 do (perform) sluggishly.

깨치다 《해득》 master; learn; understand; comprehend. ¶한글을 ~ learn (master) Korean language.

꽥 ¶ ~ 소리치다 scream; shout; roar; bawl.

깻묵 oil cake; sesame dregs.

꽹 ¶ ~ 울다 yap; yip.

꺼내다 《속에서》 take (bring, draw, put) out. ¶ 주머니에서 …을 ~ take (draw) 《a thing》 out of one's pocket; introduce; broach. ¶ 이야기를 ~ broach a matter; introduce a topic (subject).

꺼머꺼머 ¶ ~하다 be dryish; be damp-dry.

꺼리다 《싫어하다》 dislike; hate; be unwilling to 《do》; 《금기》 taboo. ② 《피하다》 avoid; shun; 《두려워하다》 be afraid of. ¶ 남의 눈을 ~ be afraid of being seen. ③ 《주저》 hesitate 《to do》.

꺼림(칙)하다 feel somewhat uneasy 《about》; be rather unwilling 《to》; 《양심 등에》 have pricks of conscience.

꺼멓다 (be) black.

꺼지다 ① 《불이》 go (die) out; 《화재가》 be put out; be extinguished. ¶ 꺼져가는 불 a dying fire. ② 《거품이》 break; burst. ③ 《지반이》 cave (fall) in; sink; subside. ¶ 지반이 푹 꺼졌다 The

꺼풀 skin; film; coat; skim; outer layer.

꺽다리 a tall person.

꺾다 ① 《부러뜨리다》 break (off); snap. ¶나뭇가지를 ~ break off a twig of the tree / 꽃을 ~ pick [pluck] a flower / 지팡이를 반으로 뚝 ~ snap the stick in half. ② 《접다》 fold (*a thing*) over. ③ 《방향을》 take [make] a turn (*to*); turn. ¶자동차 핸들을 ~ turn the wheel. ④ 《기운을》 break (down); crush; discourage; damp(en). ¶아무의 기를 ~ dampen (*a person's*) spirits / 용기를 ~ shake (*a person's*) courage / 적의 사기를 ~ break down the enemy's morale / 적의 예봉을 ~ break the brunt of the enemy. ⑤ 《고집을》 yield (*to*); concede (*to*); give in (*to*). ¶그는 고집을 꺾고 어머니 의견을 따랐다 He gave in to his mother's opinion. ⑥ 《지우다》 defeat; beat. ¶상대방을 ~ beat a person 《*at a game*》.

꺾쇠 (fasten with) a clamp; a cramp (iron); a staple.

꺾이다 ① 《부러지다》 break; be broken; snap. ② 《접히다》 be folded [doubled]. ③ 《방향이》 bend; turn. ④ 《기세가》 break (down); be discouraged; 《굴복》 bend [bow] (*to*); yield (*to*). ¶금력에 ~ bow to money / 한번의 작은 실수로 의기가 꺾여서는 안 된다 You should not be discouraged by one little failure.

껄껄 ¶ ~ 웃다 laugh aloud.

껄껄하다 (be) rough; coarse; harsh.

껄끔거리다 be [feel] rough.

껄떡껄떡 gulpingly 《삼킴》; gasping(ly) 《숨이》.

껄렁하다 (be) worthless; insignificant; trashy; useless. ¶껄렁한 학교 a third-rate school.

껌 chewing gum. ¶ ~ 을 씹다 chew gum.

껌껌하다 《어둡다》 (be) very dark; 《마음이》 (be) black-hearted; wicked.

껍데기 a shell. ☞ 껍질.

껍질 (나무의) bark; (과실의) skin; rind; peel; (깎기) husk; a shell (견과의); (얇은 껍질) film. ¶바나나 ~ a banana skin / ~을 벗기다 bark (*a tree*); rind; peel (*an orange*); skin; shell.

…껏 as... as possible; to the utmost 《full extent》 of.... ¶힘 ~ 일하다 work as hard as *one* can; work to the utmost of *one's* power / 정성 ~ 대접하다 treat 《*a person*》 as well as one can / 양 ~ 먹다 eat *one's* full.

껑충 with a jump 《leap》.

께 《에게》 to; for 《*a person*》. ☞ 에게. ¶어머님 ~ 전화하다 call mother on the phone / 하느님 ~ 기도하다 pray to God.

…께 《경(頃)》 about; toward 《*a time*》; around 《때》; 《곳》 around; near 《*a place*》. ¶그믐 ~ toward the end of 《near, around》 the month / 정거장 ~ near the station.

께끄름하다 feel uneasy 《about》; 《사람이 주어》 weigh on *one's* mind; get on *one's* nerves.

께죽거리다 grumble (*at*); keep complaining 《*of, about*》.

께지럭거리다 (일을) do 《*something*》 half-heartedly; (음식을) pick at *one's* food; chew dryly at 《*one's* food》.

껴들다 hold 《*a thing*》 between *one's* arms 《hands》.

껴안다 embrace [hug] (each other); hold 《*a baby*》 in *one's* arms. ¶꼭 ~ hug 《*a person*》 tightly.

껴입다 wear 《*a coat*》 over another; wear 《*two undershirts*》 one over another.

꼬다 ① 《끈 따위를》 twist (together); twine. ¶새끼를 ~ twist [make] a rope with straw. ② 《몸을》 twist *oneself*; writhe.

꼬드기다 ① 《부추김》 stir up; incite; urge; push 《*a person*》 up 《*to commit a crime*》. ② 《연을》 tug at a kite line.

꼬들꼬들 ¶ ~ 한 dry and hard; hard-boiled 《*rice*》.

꼬락서니 ☞ 꼴.

꼬리 a tail (일반적); a brush (여우 따위); a scut (토끼 따위); a train (공작 따위). ¶ ~ 를 물고 (잇달아) one after another; in rapid succession / ~ 를 흔들다 wag its tail / ~ 가 길다 (짧다) have a long [short] tail / ~ 가 잡히다 《비유적》 give a clue 《*to the police*》 / ~ 곰탕 oxtail soup / ~ 지느러미 a caudal fin.

꼬리표 (一票) a tag; a label. ¶ ~ 를 달다 put on a tag; tag [label] 《*a trunk*》.

꼬마 (소년) a boy; a (little) kid; a shorty; (물건) a tiny thing; midget; miniature. ¶ ~ 자동차 a midget car; a minicar / ~ 전구 a miniature (electric) bulb.

꼬박, 꼬박 whole; full(y). ¶ ~ 이틀 two full days; a full two days / ~ 뜬눈으로 밤을 새우다 do not sleep a wink all night.

꼬박꼬박 without fail 《어김없이》; to the letter (정확히). ¶세금을 ~ 내다 pay *one's* taxes regularly.

꼬부라지다 bend; curve; be bent; be crooked. ¶ 꼬부라진 소나무 a crooked pine / 늙어 허리가 ~ be bent with age.

꼬부랑하다 (be) bent; crooked. ¶ 꼬부랑 글자 alphabetic letters / 꼬부랑 늙은이 a bent (stooped) old man.

꼬부리다 stoop; bend; curve; crook.

꼬불꼬불하다 (be) winding; meandering. ¶ 꼬불꼬불한 길 a winding road.

꼬이다 ① 〈실·끈 등이〉 get twisted; be entangled. ② 〈일이〉 be upset (frustrated); go wrong (amiss). ¶ 그로 인해 모든 일이 꼬였다 Everything went wrong because of him. ③ 〈마음이〉 become crooked (peevish). ¶ 성격이 꼬여 있다 have a crook in one's character.

꼬장꼬장하다 〈노인이〉 (be) hale and hearty; 〈성미가〉 (be) stern; unbending; upright; incorruptible. ¶ 성미가 ~ have a stern character.

꼬집다 ① 〈살을〉 (give a) pinch; nip. ② 〈비꼼〉 make cynical remarks about; say spiteful things.

꼬챙이 a spit; a skewer. ¶ ~에 꿰다 spit; skewer / 꼬치구이 ~에 꿰어 굽다 broil (grill) a fish on a skewer.

꼬치 skewered stuff; food on a skewer. ¶ ~구이 〈행위〉 spit-roasting; 〈고기〉 (lamb) roasted on a spit.

꼬치꼬치 ① ~ 마르다 be worn (reduced) to a shadow (skeleton) / ~ 캐묻다 be inquisitive (about); ask inquisitively.

꼬투리 ① 〈깍지〉 a pod; a shell; a hull; a shuck. ② 〈꽁초〉 a cigaret(te) butt. ③ 〈발단〉 the cause; reason. ¶ 아무~도 없이 without any reason.

꼭 ① 〈단단히〉 tight(ly); firmly; (hold) fast. ¶ 문을 ~ 닫다 shut the door tight / ~ 쥐다 grasp firmly / ~ 묶다 bind (tie) (a thing) tightly. ② 〈꼭 맞거나 끼게〉 tight(ly); closely; to a T; exactly. ¶ ~ 끼는 모자 a tight cap / ~ 맞는 뚜껑 a close lid / 〈옷 등이〉 ~ 맞다 fit like a glove. ③ 〈정확하게〉 exactly; just. ¶ ~ 세 시간 exactly (full) three hours; three hours to minute / ~ 같다 be just the same (as). ④ 〈틀림없이〉 surely; certainly; by all means; without fail. ¶ ~ 출석하다 attend without fail / ~ 하다 be sure to (do). ⑤ 〈마치〉 just like; as if. ¶ ~ 마치.

꼭대기 the top; the summit.

꼭두각시 a puppet; a dummy.

꼭두새벽 the peep of dawn. ¶ ~에 before dawn.

꼭두서니 〈植〉 a (Bengal) madder.

꼭뒤지르다 forestall; get ahead of (a person).

꼭지 ① 〈수도 따위의〉 a cock; a tap; a faucet. ¶ 수도 ~를 틀다 (잠그다) turn on (off) the water. ② 〈뚜껑의〉 a knob; a nipple (우유병의). ③ 〈식물의〉 a stalk; a stem.

꼴 〈모양〉 shape; form; 〈외양〉 appearance; 〈상태〉 a state; a condition; a situation; 〈광경〉 a sight; a spectacle; a scene. ¶ ~이 사나운 unsightly; ungainly; indecent; shabby. ∥ 세모~ a triangle.

…꼴 rate; proportion; ratio. ¶ 한 근 (하루) 5백원 ~로 at the rate of 500 won a kun (a day).

꼴꼴꼴꼴 gurgling(ly).

꼴뚜기 〈動〉 an octopus.

꼴불견 〈不見〉 (be) unbecoming (indecent); be unsightly.

꼴찌 the last; the bottom; the tail (end); the tail ender (사람·팀). ¶ ~ 에서 둘째 the last but (save) one / 반에서 ~이다 be at the end (bottom) of the class.

꼼꼼하다 be scrupulous; meticulous; methodical. ¶ 꼼꼼한 사람 a methodical man; a man of method / 꼼꼼히 exactly; methodically; punctually.

꼼짝 ¶ ~도 않다 remain motionless; do not stir (budge) an inch; stand firm / ~ 못하다 cannot move (stir) an inch / 〈상대에게〉 ~ 못하다 be under (a person's) thumb / ~ 못하게 하다 beat (a person) hollow; talk (argue) (a person) down (말로).

꼽다 count (on one's fingers). ¶ 날짜를 ~ count (reckon) the days.

꼽추 ☞ 곱사등이.

꼿꼿하다 (be) erect; straight; upright. ¶ 꼿꼿이 서다 stand upright.

꽁무니 the rear (end); 〈궁둥이〉 the buttocks; 〈끝〉 the tail (end); the bottom; the last. ¶ ~ 빼다 flinch (from one's duty); try to escape / 여자 ~를 따라다니다 chase (run) after a woman.

꽁보리밥 unmixed boiled barley.

꽁지 a tail; a train (공작 따위의).

꽁지벌레 a maggot.

꽁초 〈一草〉 a cigar(ette) butt.

꽁치 〈魚〉 a mackerel pike.

꽁하다 (be) introvert and narrow-minded; reserved and unsociable; hidebound.

꽂다 stick (in (to)); put (fix) (in (to)); drive into; 〈끼우다〉 insert; put into. ¶ 장식핀을 머리에 ~ stick an ornamental pin in the hair / 병에 꽃을 ~ put flowers

꽃을대 (총포용) a cleaning rod.
꽂히다 be driven in; be fixed; get inserted; be stuck; be put in. ¶ 화살이 과녁에 꽂힌다 An arrow is stuck (fixed) in the target. / 칼이 땅에 꽂혔다 The knife stuck in the ground.
꽃 ① (초목의) a flower; a blossom (과수의); bloom (총칭). ¶ ~의 floral / ~다운 소녀 a girl (as) pretty as a flower / ~을 심다 plant flowers / 꽃병에 ~을 꽂다 put flowers in a vase / 현관에 ~을 장식하다 arrange flowers in the hall / ~이 피다 flowers come out (open) / 정원에 ~을 물을 주다 water flowers in the garden. ‖ ~가루 pollen / ~구경 flower-viewing / ~나무 a flower tree / ~놀이 a flower-viewing excursion / ~다발 a bouquet; a bunch of flowers / ~무늬 a floral pattern / ~밭 a flower garden (bed) / ~봉오리 a (flower) bud / ~송이 a blossom; an open flower / ~재배 floriculture; flower gardening. ② (미인·명물) flower; pride; a belle (사교계의); 《정화(精華)》 the essence.
꽃꽂이 flower arrangement. ‖ ~회 a flower (floral) arrangement club.
꽃샘 (추위) a cold snap in the flowering season; a spring cold.
꽈리 (植) a ground cherry.
꽉 ① (단단히) 꼭. ② (가득히) close(ly); tight(ly); full(y); crammed (packed) with. ¶ ~찬 스케줄 a full (crammed, tight) schedule / ~차다 be packed to the full; be crammed (with); be full (of) / 냉장고는 식품으로 ~차 있다 The refrigerator is filled up (crammed) with food. ③ ☞ 꾹.
꽐꽐 gurglingly; gushing.
꽝 with a bang (boom, slam). ¶ 문을 ~ 닫다 bang a door.
꽤 fairly; considerably; pretty; quite. ¶ ~ 잘 하다 do fairly well / ~ 좋다 (힘들다) be pretty good (hard).
꽥 ~ 소리지르다 give a shout (yell); shout (yell, roar) (at).
꽹과리 a small hand gong.
꾀 (슬기) resources; resourcefulness; wit; (계략) a trick; an artifice; a ruse; a trap. ¶ ~가 많은 사람 a resourceful (witty) man; a man of wit (resources) / 일에 ~를 부리다 spare oneself; shirk (one's duty) with a phony excuse / ~ 바르다 be crafty (shrewd, clever) / 제 ~에 제가 넘어가다 outwit oneself; be outwitted by one's own cleverness.
꾀꼬리 (鳥) an oriole; a (Korean) nightingale. ¶ ~ 같은 목소리 a beautiful voice. 〔er〕 flock.
꾀다 (모이다) swarm; crowd; gather.
꾀다 (유혹) tempt; (미)lure; entice; seduce (나쁜 길로). ¶ 감언이설로 그녀를 집에서 꾀어내다 entice her away from home by using honeyed words.
꾀병 (一病) feigned (pretended) illness. ¶ ~ 부리다 pretend (feign) illness; pretend to be ill (sick).
꾀보 a tricky (wily) person.
꾀이다 《꾐을 당하다》 be lured (enticed, tempted); be seduced.
꾀잠 sham (pretended) sleep; make-believe sleep. ¶ ~ 자다 pretend (feign) to be asleep.
꾀죄(죄)하다 (be) untidy; shabby; slovenly; poor-looking.
꾀하다 ① (계획) plan; contrive; attempt (suicide); scheme; (나쁜 짓을)plot; conspire. ¶ 반란을 ~ conspire to rise in revolt. ② (추구) seek; intend (to do). ¶ 사리를 ~ seek one's own interests.
꾐 temptation; allurement; enticement. ¶ ~에 빠지다 yield to (fall into) temptation / 악우들에게 ~을 당해 나쁜 길로 빠지다 be tempted (enticed) into wrong ways by the wrong company.
꾸기적거리다 crumple (up); wrinkle; rumple; crush.
꾸다 (빌리다) borrow 《money from a person》; have (money) on loan; have a loan of 《5 million won》.
꾸드러지다 be dried and hardened.
꾸들꾸들 ¶ ~한 dry and hard.
···꾸러기 one who is given to; a glutton for···. ¶ 잠~ a late riser / 욕심~ a greedy person.
꾸러미 a bundle (in a wrapper); a parcel. ¶ 옷 ~ a bundle of clothes.
꾸르륵 ¶ ~거리다 (give a) rumble.
꾸리다 ① (짐을) pack (up); wrap (tie) up. ¶ 짐을 다시 ~ repack baggage. ② (일을) manage; arrange. ¶ 살림을 ~ manage household affairs / 그녀는 혼자손으로 그 상점을 꾸려 나가고 있다 She is managing the store entirely by herself.
꾸무럭거리다, 꾸물거리다 be slow (long, tardy); waste time; dawdle (over); linger. ¶ 꾸무럭거리지 마라 Don't be slow (long). / 꾸물거릴 시간이 없다 There is no time to lose.
꾸미다 ① (치장) decorate 《a room》; ornament; adorn; dress 《a shop-window》; (화장) make up; 《말을》 embellish. ¶ 얼굴을 곱게 ~

꾸밈 ¶ ~ 없는 simple; plain; frank (솔직한) / ~ 없이 talk frankly; speak plainly. ‖ ~새 (모양) a shape; a form; (양식) a style; (구조) make.

꾸미다 make up *one's* face beautifully / 꽃으로 식탁을 ~ decorate the table with flowers. ② (가장) feign; affect; pretend. ¶ 꾸민 태도 an affected attitude. ③ (조작) invent; fabricate; (계획) plot (음모를); design (설계). ¶ 꾸며낸 얘기 a made-up [an invented] story / 어린이들을 위해 꾸며진 동물원 a zoo designed especially for children. ④ (조직) form; organize. ¶ 새 내각을 ~ form a new cabinet / 가정을 ~ make a home. ⑤ (작성) make; draw up. ¶ (계약서를) 두 통 ~ make out (a contract) in duplicate.

꾸벅거리다 ① (졸다) doze (off); fall into a doze; feel drowsy. ¶ 그는 신문을 읽으며 꾸벅거렸다 He was dozing over the newspaper. ¶ 꾸벅거리면서, 나는 열차가 움직이기 시작하는 것을 느꼈다 Half asleep, I felt the train start moving. ② (절하다) make repeated bows; kow(t)ow (to). ¶ 저 녀석은 상사에게 늘 꾸벅거린다 He is always kowtowing to his superiors.

꾸역꾸역 in great numbers; in a crowd; in a steady stream.

꾸준하다 (be) untiring; steady; assiduous. ¶ 꾸준히 untiringly; steadily; assiduously.

꾸지람 a scolding; a reprimand. ~하다 scold; reprove; rebuke. ¶ ~ 듣다 be scolded [reproved]; get a scolding.

꾸짖다 scold; rebuke; reprove; reproach; (口) tell off. ¶ 심하게 [가볍게] ~ scold severely [mildly]; give (*a person*) a good (mild) scolding.

꾹 ① (참는 모양) patiently. ¶ ~ 참다 bear (*the pain*) patiently. ② (누르는 모양) tightly; firmly; hard. ¶ ~ 누르다 press hard.

꿀 honey. ¶ ~처럼 달다 be sweet as honey. ‖ ~떡 a honey cake / ~물 honeyed water / 벌 a honey bee; a bee.

꿀꺽 (삼키는 모양) at a gulp; (참는 모양) holding [keeping] back (*one's* anger); patiently. ¶ 약을 한 입에 ~ 삼키다 swallow the dose at one gulp / 울컥 솟는 분함을 ~ 참다 gulp down *one's* resentment patiently.

꿀꿀 (돼지 울음소리) oink. ¶ ~거리다 grunt; oink.

꿀떡 ~ 삼키다 gulp (down); swallow at a gulp.

꿀리다 ① (형편이) be hard up ((for money)); be in straitened circumstances. ② (켕기다) be guilty; feel small; be overwhelmed. ¶ 꿀리지 않고 without flinching; undaunted (by).

꿇다 kneel (down); fall (drop) on *one's* knees. ¶ ~앞에 무릎을 ~ bow the knee to (before) ((*a person*)).

꿇어앉다 sit on *one's* knees.

꿈 (수면 중의) a dream; a nightmare (악몽); (이상) a vision; a dream; (환상) an illusion. ¶ 들어맞는 (개) a true [false] dream / 불길한 ~ an evil dream / ~의 세계 a dreamland; a dream world / ~ 같은 dreamlike; dreamy / 젊은 시절의 ~ the romantic vision of youth / ~에서 깨어나다 awake from a dream; be disillusioned (망상에서) / ~자리가 좋다 (사납다) have a good (bad) dream / ~에 ~보다 see ((*something*)) in a dream; dream of ((about))…

꿈결 ¶ ~에 half awake (and asleep); between asleep and awake / ~같다 be like a dream / ~에 듣다 listen half asleep.

꿈꾸다 ① (잠을 자면서) dream; have a dream. ② (바라다) dream of ((*success*)); have an ambition ((to…)). ¶ 미래의 작가를 ~ have a dream of be coming a writer.

꿈실거리다 (벌레 따위가) creep about ((over one's body)); stir restlessly.

꿈지럭거리다 stir [move] sluggishly (slowly, clumsily). ¶daunted.

꿈쩍없다 remain unmoved; be undaunted. **꿈틀거리다** 굼틀거리다.

꿋꿋하다 (be) firm; strong; unyielding; inflexible. ¶ 꿋꿋한 의지 a strong [an iron] will.

꿍꿍 (신음) ¶ 부상자의 ~거리는 소리 the groans of the injured / ~ 앓다 groan; moan.

꿍꿍이셈. 꿍꿍이속 a secret design ((intention)); calculation concealed in *one's* heart. ¶ 틀림없이 ~이 있다 ☞ There must be something secret behind the scene.

꿩 (鳥) a pheasant.

꿰다 (구멍에) run (pass) ((*a thing*)) through. ¶ 바늘에 실을 ~ run a thread through a needle; thread a needle.

꿰뚫다 ① (관통하다) pierce; pass (run) through; penetrate; shoot through (탄환 따위가). ② (정통) be well versed in; have a thorough knowledge of; (통찰) penetrate; see through.

꿰매다 (바늘로) sew; stitch. ¶ 해진[터진] 데를 ~ sew up a rip /

께지다 상처를 두 바늘 ~ put two stitches in the wound. ②《깁다》 patch up.

꿰지다 ①《미어지다》 be torn; tear; rip; 《해지다》 be worn out. ②《터지다》 break; be broken; burst; be punctured.

꿰뚫다 thrust (run) through.

꿱 ¶ ~ 소리 지르다 give a shout (yell). 「gas; fart《俗》

뀌다《방귀를》 break (pass) wind; pass

끄나풀 ①《끈》 a piece of string. ②《앞잡이》 a tool; a cat's-paw; an agent; a pawn. ¶ 아무를 ~로 쓰다 use *a person* as a tool / 그들은 경찰의 ~이다 They are pawns of the police.

끄느름하다 (be) gloomy; cloudy; dreary; dim.

끄다 ①《덩어리를》 break (*a thing*) (into pieces); crack; crush. ¶ 얼음을 ~ crack (break) ice. ②《불을》 put out; extinguish; blow out(불어서). ¶ 불을 ~ extinguish (put out) a fire / 촛불을 ~ blow out a candle. ③《전기·가스 등을》 switch (turn) off (*the light*); put off (out). ¶ 엔진을 ~ stop (kill) an engine.

끄덕이다, 끄덕거리다 nod (at, to). ¶ 말없이 ~ nod without a word / 가볍게 ~ give a slight nod / 승낙의 뜻으로 ~ nod *one's* agreement.

끄들다 ¶《머리》를 잡다 seize (grab) (*a person's*) hair; seize (*a person*) by the hair.

끄떡없다, 끄떡않다 do not budge an inch(움직이지 않다); remain composed (unmoved)(태연); be all right (safe)(안전). ¶ 끄떡없이 dauntlessly; without flinching (wincing) / 그는 어떤 일에도 끄떡않는다 Nothing flinches him. *or* Nothing makes him wince.

끄르다 untie (*a knot*); undo; unfasten; unbind; loose. ¶ 단추를 ~ undo a button; unbutton / 문의 자물쇠를 ~ unlock the door.

끄무레하다 (be) cloudy; overcast.

끄물거리다《날씨가》 become cloudy off and on; be unsettled.

끄집다 hold and pull; draw; take. ¶ 끄집어내다 pull (draw) (*a thing*) out; take (get) (*a thing*) out / 끄집어내리다 take (pull, bring, carry) down / 끄집어올리다 take (pull) up.

끄트러기 odd ends (pieces); a (broken) piece; a fragment; a cut.

끄트머리 ①《맨 끝》 an end; a tip; (stand at) the tail end. ②《실마리》 a clue.

끈《줄》 (tie) a string; a cord; 《끈 것》 a braid; a lace; 《가죽 끈》 a strap; a thong.

끈기(一氣) ①《끈끈함》 stickiness; viscosity; glutinousness. ②《견디는 정신》 tenacity; patience; perseverance. ¶ ~ 있게 patiently; perseveringly / 공부는 ~가 필요하다 Study requires a lot of patience.

끈끈이 birdlime.

끈끈하다《끈적임》 (be) sticky; adhesive; viscous.

끈덕거리다 become shaky.

끈덕지다, 끈질기다 (be) tenacious; persevering; 《口》 stick-to-itive. ¶ 끈덕진 노력 a strenuous effort / 그는 끈덕지게 그 일을 해냈다 He carried through the work tenaciously.

끈적거리다 be sticky.

끊다 ①《자르다》 cut (off); sever; disconnect; break. ¶ 밧줄을 ~ cut (break) a rope. ②《중단·차단》 cut off; interrupt; stop(교통을); pause; 《전화를》 hang up off. ¶ 적의 퇴로를 ~ cut off the enemy's retreat. ③《인연·관계를》 sever; break off; break with (*a person*). ¶ 교제(交際)를 ~ sever acquaintance with. ④《그만두다》 abstain from; quit; give up. ¶ 술을 ~ stop (give up) drinking; abstain from alcohol. ⑤《목숨을》 kill *oneself*. ⑥《사다》 buy (*a ticket*). ⑦《발행》 issue (draw) (*a check*).

끊어지다《절단》 be cut; break; come apart; snap(뚝하며). ¶ 밧줄이 끊어졌다 The rope has broken. ②《중단·차단》 be stopped; be cut off; be interrupted (discontinued, ceased). ¶《사람이 주어》 be cut off from supplies (the supply) (*of*) / 교통이 ~ traffic is stopped (interrupted). ③《관계 등이》 break (off) with; come to an end; be cut (severed); be through (done) with. ¶ 서로의 인연이 ~ be separated; be through with each other. ④《목숨이》 expire; die.

끊임없다 (be) ceaseless; incessant; continual; constant. ¶ 끊임없는 노력 ceaseless (constant) efforts / 끊임없는 걱정 endless worries / 손님이 ~ have a constant stream of visitors / 끊임없이 ceaselessly; incessantly; continually; constantly.

끌 a chisel.

끌다 ①《당기다》 draw; pull; tug (배를); 《질질》 drag; trail(늘어뜨려 옴). ¶ 아무의 소매를 ~ pull (*a person*) by the sleeve. ②《지연》 delay; prolong; protract; drag on. ¶ 오래 끄는 병 a long illness / 오래 끌어온 협상 long-pending negotiations / 회답을 ~ a delay in answering. ③《이끌다》 attract;

끌러지다 draw; catch. ¶ 손님을 ~ draw customers / 주의를 ~ attract (draw) (a person's) attention / 인기를 ~ catch (win, gain) popularity. ④ (인도) lead. ¶ 노인의 손을 ~ lead an old man by the hand. ⑤ (끌어들이다) conduct (water into); draw (water off a river); admit; (가설) lay on (수도, 가스 따위를); install (전등, 전화 등를). [untied (undone).
끌러지다 come (get) loose; get
끌리다 ① (당겨지다) be drawn (pulled, dragged); be tugged; be trailed (질질). ¶ 치마가 ~ one's skirt trails (on). ② (연행) be taken (to) (the police). ③ (마음이) be attracted (drawn, caught); be charmed; be touched.
끌어내다 take (pull) out; drag (a thing) out (of); lure (a person) out (from) (꾀어냄). [down.
끌어내리다 take (pull, drag, draw)
끌어당기다 draw (a thing) near (toward); pull up. ☞ 끌다
끌어대다 ① (돈을) borrow money for (a business); finance. ② (인용) cite; quote. ¶ 전례를 ~ cite precedents.
끌어들이다 ① (안으로) draw (take) in (into); pull in. ② (자기편에) gain (win) (a person) over (to one's side). ¶ 사업에 자본가를 ~ interest capitalists in an enterprise.
끌어안다 embrace; hug; hold (a person) in one's arms (to one's breast). ¶ ~ salvage (배를).
끌어올리다 pull (draw, drag) up;
끓다 ① (물이) boil; seethe; grow hot. ¶ 끓는 물 boiling water / 끓어 넘치다 boil over. ② (마음이) seethe (boil) with (rage); be in a ferment; fret; fume; be excited. ¶ 나는 분함에 속이 부글부글 끓었다 My blood boiled (seethed) with anger (indignation). ③ (배가) rumble. ④ (가래가) make a gurgling sound. ⑤ (우글거리다) swarm; be crowded with. ¶ 파리가 ~ be infested with flies.
끓이다 ① (뜨겁게 하다) boil (water); heat. ② (익히다) cook. ¶ 밥을 ~ cook (boil) rice / 국을 ~ make soup. ③ (속태우다) worry; bother; fret one's nerves.
끔찍하다 ① (참혹하다) (be) awful; terrible; horrible. ¶ 끔찍한 광경 a horrible sight. ② (극진하다) (be) very hearty (kind); warm; very thoughtful. ¶ 끔찍이 awfully; horribly; terribly / (극진히) warmly; whole-heartedly; cordially; deeply / 끔찍이 사랑하다 love deeply.
끙끙 ¶ ~ 앓다 groan; moan.

끝 ① (첨단) the point (of a pencil); the tip (of a finger); the end (top) (of a pole). ¶ 혀 ~ the tip of one's tongue. / ~에서 ~까지 from end to end. ② (한도) the end; the limit. ¶ ~없는 endless; boundless; everlasting. ③ (마지막) an end; a close; a conclusion (결말). ¶ ~의 last; final; concluding / ~으로 finally; in the end; in conclusion. ④ (행렬·차례의) the last; the tail end. ¶ 행렬의 ~ the tail end of a procession.
끝끝내 to the last; to the (bitter) end. ¶ ~ 반대하다 persist in one's opposition; be dead set against; oppose stoutly.
끝나다 (come to an) end; close; be over (up); be finished; expire (기한이); result in. ¶ 실패로 ~ end (result) in failure.
끝내다 end; finish; complete; get (go) through (with); conclude; settle (an account). ¶ 대학 과정을 ~ complete (pass through) one's university course.
끝마감 closing; conclusion. ~하다 close; conclude.
끝물 the last (farm) products of the season. ¶ ~ 수박 late watermelons.
끝수 (一數) a fraction; an odd sum; odds. ¶ ~를 버리다 omit (ignore, round off) fractions.
끝장 (마지막) an end; a conclusion; (낙착) settlement. ¶ ~이 나다 be ended; be over (settled); come to an end / ~내다 settle; finish; bring (something) to an end / 일을 ~ 내다 finish one's work / 싸움을 ~ 내다 put an end to a quarrel; settle a quarrel.
끝판 the end; the last stage (of); (승부의) the last round (of).
끼니 a meal; a repast. ¶ ~때 a mealtime / ~를 거르다 (굶다) miss (skip) a meal; go hungry.
끼다 ① (안개·연기 등이) gather; hang over; envelop; be veiled (wrapped). ¶ 아침 안개가 자욱이 낀 마을 the village veiled (enveloped) in a morning mist. ② (때·먼지 등이) be soiled (stained, smeared); become (get) dirty. ¶ 때가 낀 옷가지 soiled (dirty, unclean) clothes.
끼다 ① ☞ 끼이다. ② ☞ 끼우다. ③ (착용) put (pull) on; wear. ¶ 장갑을 ~ draw (pull) on one's gloves. ④ (팔짱을) fold (one's arms). ¶ 팔짱을 끼고 있다 with one's arms folded / (남과) arm in arm (with). ⑤ (옆구리에) hold (a thing) under one's arm. ¶ 책을

몇 권 끼고 with some books under one's arm. ⑥ 《참가》 join; participate in; be a party to. ¶일행에 ~ join the party. ⑦ 《따라서》 ¶…을 끼고 along; by / 강을 끼고 along the river. ⑧ 《배경》 be backed by. ¶권력을 ~ have an influential person at one's back.

…끼리 among (by, between) themselves. ¶~ 싸우다 quarrel (fight) among themselves.

끼리끼리 each in a group; group by group; in separate groups. ¶~ 식사하다 dine together in separate parties.

끼얹다 《물 따위를》 pour (shower, throw) 《water》 on (over) 《a person》. ¶등에 물을 ~ dash water on one's back.

끼우다 《사이·속·틈에》 put (hold) 《a thing》 between; get (put, let) in; insert 《in》; fix (fit) into (맞춰 넣다). ¶창에 유리를 ~ fix glass in a window.

끼워팔기 a tie-in sale.

끼이다 《사이에》 get between; be caught in; be sandwiched between; be tight (구두 따위).

끼적거리다 scribble; scrawl.

끼치다 ① 《두려움 따위로 소름이》 ¶소름이 끼치는 hair-raising; blood-curdling; frightful / 소름이 ~ get goose flesh. ② 《불편·걱정 따위》 give (cause) 《a person》 trouble; trouble; annoy; bother; be a nuisance 《to》. ¶폐를 ~ trouble 《a person》; give 《a person》 trouble; cause inconvenience 《to》.

끽소리 ¶~ 못하다 be completely (utterly) silenced (defeated); can't say a thing.

낄낄 ¶~ 거리다 giggle; titter.

낌새 《기미》 a sign; an indication; a delicate turn of the situation. ¶~를 전혀 보이지 않다 show not the slightest sign (hint) of ….

한·미군 계급 (ROK - US Military ranks)				
한 국 (공통)	미 국			
	육 군	공 군	해 군	해 병
대 장	General	General	Admiral	General
중 장	Lieutenant General	Lieutenant General	Vice Admiral	Lieutenant General
소 장	Major General	Major General	Rear Admiral	Major General
준 장	Brigadier General	Brigadier General	Commodore	Brigadier General
대 령	Colonel	Colonel	Captain	Colonel
중 령	Lieutenant Colonel	Lieutenant Colonel	Commander	Lieutenant Colonel
소 령	Major	Major	Lieutenant Commander	Major
대 위	Captain	Captain	Lieutenant	Captain
중 위	1st Lieutenant	1st Lieutenant	Lieutenant Junior Grade	1st Lieutenant
소 위	2nd Lieutenant	2nd Lieutenant	Ensign	2nd Lieutenant
준 위	Warrant Officer	Warrant Officer	Warrant Officer	Warrant Officer
원 사	Sergeant Major	Chief Master Sergeant	Master Chief Petty Officer	Sergeant Major
상 사	Master Sergeant	Senior Master Sergeant	Senior Chief Petty Officer	Master Gunnery Sergeant
중 사	Sergeant 1st Class	Master Sergeant	Chief Petty Officer	Gunnery Sergeant
하 사	Staff Sergeant	Technical Sergeant	Petty Officer 1st Class	Staff Sergeant
병 장	Sergeant	Staff Sergeant	Petty Officer 2nd Class	Sergeant
상 병	Corporal	Airman 1st Class	Petty Officer 3rd Class	Corporal
일 병	Private 1st Class	Airman 2nd Class	Seaman	Lance Corporal
이 병	Private	Airman 3rd Class	Seaman Apprentice	Private 1st Class
훈 병	Recruit	Airman Basic	Seaman Recruit	Private

나 I; myself. ¶ ~의 my / ~에게(를) me / ~의 것 mine / ~로서는 as for me; for my part.

나가다 ① 《밖으로》 go (out, step) out. ¶ 뜰로 ~ go out into the garden / 방에서 ~ go out of a room. ② 《출석》 attend; be present 《at》. ¶ 강의에 ~ attend a lecture. ③ 《근무》 work 《in, at, for》. ¶ 신문사에 ~ work in a newspaper office / 회사에 ~ be employed in a company. ④ 《참가》 join; participate in; take part in. ¶ 올림픽에 ~ take part in the Olympic games. ⑤ 《입후보》 run 《for》. ¶ 대통령 선거에 ~ run for the presidency. ⑥ 《팔리다》 sell; get sold. ¶ 잘 ~ sell well. ⑦ 《지출》 be paid out; be disbursed. ¶ 나가는 돈 expenditure; outlay. ⑧ 《비용·가치 등이》 cost; be worth. 《무게가》 weigh. ¶ 5만원 나가는 물건 an article worth fifty thousand won / 무게가 60킬로 ~ weigh 60 kilograms; be 60 kilograms in weight. ⑨ 《떠남》 leave; go away. ¶ 집을 ~ leave home. ⑩ 《진출》 launch (out); enter 〔advance〕 《into, to》; forth ahead. ¶ 정계에 ~ enter into politics; enter the political world / 결승전에 ~ advance to the finals. ⑪ 《닮으·꺼짐》 be out; be broken; be worn out. ¶ 불이 ~ the (electric) light is out / 구두 뒤축이 ~ the heel of one's shoe is worn out.

나가자빠지다 ① 《뒤로 넘어지다》 be knocked down; be thrown off; fall flat on one's back. ¶ 한 방에 ~ be knocked down at a single blow. ② 《녹초가 되다》 be worn (tired) out; be done up (in) 《일》.

나가자빠지다 ① ☞ 나가떨어지다. ② 《회피·불이행》 evade 〔dodge, shirk〕 one's responsibilities 〔duty, tasks, etc.〕; withdraw oneself 《from》; back out; do not pay 〔welsh on〕 《one's debt》. ¶ 불경기로 ~ go bankrupt owing to the depression / 그는 계약을 이행하지 않고 나가자빠지려 했다 He tried to back out of the contract.

나귀 an ass; a donkey.

나그네 a traveler; a stranger; a wanderer; a visitor (손).

나긋나긋하다 (be) tender; soft.

나날이 daily; every day; day by day. ¶ 정세는 ~ 악화되어 갔다 Things grew worse with each passing day.

나누다 ① 《분할》 divide; part; split 《into》; separate(분리). ¶ 나눌 수 없는 indivisible; inseparable / 둘로 ~ divide 《a thing》 into two. ② 《분배》 distribute 《among》; share 《something》 out 《among》. ¶ 과자를 아이들에게 나누어 주다 distribute cookies among the children. ③ 《구별》 sort out; classify. ¶ 세 항목으로 ~ classify into three items / 선인과 악인을 ~ sort out the good men from bad men. ④ 《함께 하다》 share 《something》 with; spare. ¶ 음식을 나누어 먹다 share food with a person / 기름을 ~ share one's joy / 휘발유를 좀 나눠주다 spare a little gasoline to a person.

나누이다 be (get) divided.

나눗셈 (a) division. ~하다 divide.

나다 ① 《출생》 be born. ¶ 어디(에)서 났는가 Where were you born? ② 《싹이 나다》 spring up; sprout; 《자라다》 grow; come out(돋아나다); 《치아가》 cut one's teeth. ¶ 아기가 ~ grow wings / 아기의 이가 났다 The baby has cut its teeth. ③ 《산출·발생》 produce; yield. ¶ 쌀이 나는 지방 a rice-producing district / 이익이 ~ yield profits. ④ 《살림을》 set up a separate family; live apart 《from》. ⑤ 《별장이》 come to an end; be finished. ⑥ 《기타》 smell / 맛이 ~ taste / 이름이 ~ become famous / 병이 ~ sick; become ill / 성이 ~ get angry / 눈물이 ~ tears flow / 땀이 ~ sweat / 신문에 ~ appear in the newspaper / 탄로(綻露) ~ get discovered / 새 길이 ~ a new road is opened / 소문이 ~ a rumor gets abroad 〔about〕.

나다니다 go out; wander 〔gad〕.

나들이 going out; an outing. ~하다 go out; go on a visit. ¶ ~ 가다〔오다〕 go 〔come〕 on a visit. ‖ ~옷 one's sunday clothes; one's best dress〔suit〕.

나라 ① 《국토》 a country; a land; 《국가》 a state; a nation. ¶ ~를 위하여 《lay down one's life》 for one's country. ‖ ~님 the king; his sovereign. ② 《특수세계》 a world; a realm. ‖ 꿈 ~ a dreamland.

나락(奈落) hell; an abyss. ¶ ~으로 떨어지다 fall into the bottomless pit.

나란히 in a row (line); side by side. ¶ ~서다 stand in a row / ~앉다 sit side by side / 우로 ~《구령》Right dress!

나래(농기구) soil leveler (grader).

나루 a ferry. ¶ ~터 a ferry / 나룻배 a ferry(boat) / 나룻배 사공 a ferryman / 나룻targeted ferriage.

나룻 whiskers; a beard; a mustache. ¶ ~이 석자라도 먹어야 샌님《俗談》Long beards alone cannot make a gentleman.

나르다 carry; convey; transport.

나르시시즘《心》narcissism.

나른하다 feel languid (weary, tired); be dull (heavy). ¶ 나른한 오후 a slack afternoon / 몸이 ~ I feel lazy (languid).

나름 ¶ 자기(그) ~대로 in one's (its) own way / 값은 물건 ~ The price varies with the quality. / 그것은 사람 ~이다 That depends on the person.

나리(尊稱) sir; gentleman; your honor.

나리《植》a lily.

…나마 though; even. ¶ 그만한 비~와 주니 다행이다 Even that much of rain is of great help.

나막신 (wooden) clogs.

나머지 ① (남은 것) the rest; the remainder; the balance (잔금); leftovers (음식물의). ¶ ~의 remaining / ~는 가지고 가도 된다 You may take the rest. ② 《…든 끝에》excess. ¶ 기쁜 ~ in the excess of one's joy; elated by joy.

나무 ① (수목) a tree; a plant. ¶ ~그늘 the shade of a tree / 나뭇결 the grain / ~등걸 a stump / 나뭇잎 a leaf; foliage(총칭) / ~의 줄기 the trunk of a tree / ~에 오르다 climb (up) a tree / ~를 심다 plant a tree (in the park) / ~는 보되 숲을 못 본다 You cannot see the forest for the trees. ② (재목) lumber (美); timber (英). ¶ ~로 만든 책상 a wooden desk; a desk made of wood / ~토막 a chunk (piece) of wood / ~상자 a wooden box. ③ (땔나무) firewood. ~하다 gather firewood; cut wood for fuel. ¶ ~꾼 a woodman; a woodcutter; a timberjack; a lumberjack.

나무라다 reprove; reproach; reprimand; scold. ¶ 나무랄 데 없다 have no fault to find with; be without blemish.

나무람 reproof; reproach; reprimand; scolding.

나무아미타불(南無阿彌陀佛) Save us, merciful Buddha!; (명복을 빌 때) May his soul rest in peace!

나물 wild greens; vegetables; herbs. ¶ ~국 soup with greens in it / ~을 무치다 season boiled greens / 산에 ~ 캐러 가다 go to pick herbs (greens) in the mountain.

나방《蟲》a moth.

나병(癩病)《醫》leprosy. ¶ ~에 걸려 있다 be leprous. ¶ ~원 a leper house / ~환자 a leper.

나신(裸身) a woman in the nude.

나부끼다 fly; flutter; flap; wave. ¶ 깃발이 바람에 ~ a flag flutters (waves) in the wind.

나부랭이 a scrap; a piece; odds and ends.

나불거리다 (입을) wag one's tongue; chatter.

나비 a butterfly. ¶ ~ 넥타이 a bow (tie) ~매듭 a bowknot.

나쁘다 ① (도덕상) (be) bad; (옳지 않은) (be) wrong; (사악한) (be) evil; wicked. ¶ 나쁜 짓을 하다 do (something) wrong; commit a crime (sin). ② (해롭다) (be) bad; harmful (to); injurious. ¶ ~ be bad for the eyes / 담배는 건강에 ~ Smoking is bad for your health. ③ (과실·잘못) (be) wrong; be to blame. ¶ 그건 네가 나빴다 It was your fault. or It was you that were to blame. ④ (몸·건강이) (be) sick; ill; unwell. ¶ 위가 ~ have (suffer from) stomach trouble / 안색이 ~ look pale / 몸의 컨디션이 ~ feel ill (unwell). ⑤ (품질 등이) (be) bad; poor; coarse; inferior. ¶ 이 제품은 질이 ~ This product is of poor quality. / 값싼 물건이 언제나 나쁘지만은 않다 Cheap goods are not always bad. ⑥ 《머리·기억력이》(be) poor; weak. ¶ 머리가 ~ be weak-headed (dull, stupid) / 기억력이 ~ have a poor memory. ⑦ (날씨가) (be) bad; nasty; foul. ¶ 나쁜 날씨 foul (bad, nasty) weather. ⑧ (평판이) (be) bad; ill. ¶ 그는 학생들에게 평판이 ~ He has a bad reputation among students. / 평판이 나쁜 사내 a man of ill fame. ⑨ 《도로 따위가》(be) bad; rough; muddy. ¶ 도로가 나쁘기로 유명하다 be notorious for its bad roads. ⑩ (성질이) (be) ill; wicked; malicious. ¶ 성질이 ~ be ill-natured. ⑪ (불운) (be) bad; unlucky; ominous. ¶ 나쁜 소식 a bad (sad) news / 나쁜 징조 a bad omen / 일진이 ~ be an evil (unlucky) day. ⑫ (기분이) feel bad (unwell, uncomfortable); be out of sorts. ⑬ (고장) (be) wrong; bad; be out of order. ¶ 엔진의 상태가 ~ Something is wrong with the engine. ⑭ 《관용적 표현》¶ 나쁘게 안 할테니 나를 믿어라 (내게

나쁘다 맡겨라) You can trust me. *or* You can safely leave it to me. / 나쁜 때에 그녀가 나타났다 She came at an unfortunate moment.

나쁘(나쁘게) badly; ill; (부족하게) not enough; unsatisfactorily. ¶ ~ 여기지 말게 Don't take it ill, please.

나사(螺絲) (못) a screw. ¶ ~로 죄다 screw up / ~를 돌리다 (늦추다) turn (loosen) a screw / ~를 뽑다 unscrew. ‖ ~돌리개 a screw-driver.

나사(羅紗) woollen cloth.

나사(미국 항공 우주국) NASA. (◀ the National Aeronautics and Space Administration).

나상(裸像) a nude figure (statue).

나서다 ① (앞으로) come (step) forward; (나타나다) come out (forth); appear; present *oneself*. ¶ 한 발 앞으로 ~ make a step forward / 대중 앞에 ~ step forward in front of the crowd. ② (떠나다) leave; go out; set out (*off*); start. ¶ 교문을 ~ get out of the campus; leave the school. ③ (진출하다) enter upon; go into. ¶ 실업계에 ~ go into business / 정계에 ~ enter upon a political career. ④ (간섭) intrude; obtrude; interfere. ¶ 남의 일에 나서기를 싫어하다 be unobtrusive / 네가 나설 자리가 아니다 This is none of your business. ⑤ (구하는 것이) turn up; present *itself*. ¶ 일자리가 ~ find a job / 희망자가 하나도 나서지 않았다 No one applied for it. ⑥ (출마하다) run [stand] for. ¶ 대통령 후보로 ~ run in the presidency / …의 후보자로 ~ stand [run] as a candidate for ….

나선(螺旋) a screw; a spiral. ¶ ~상(狀)의 spiral. ‖ ~계단 a spiral stairs.

나스닥(證) National Association of Securities Dealers Automated Quotations(생각 NASDAQ;(거래되는 증권류의 가격 등을 알리는 전미(全美) 증권업협회의 온라인 서비스).

나아가다 ① (전진) advance; move [step] forward; go [step] ahead; proceed; make *one's* way. ¶ 한 걸음 ~ make [take] a step forward / 사람을 헤치고 ~ push [elbow] *one's* way through the crowd. ② (진보하다) (make) progress; improve; (진전하다) advance; get on with (*one's studies*). ¶ 시대와 함께 ~ keep up with the times / 시대보다 앞서 ~ get ahead of the times. ③ (좋아지다) change for the better; take a favorable turn.

나아지다 become [get] better; improve; make a good progress; change for the better.

나약(懦弱) effeminacy. ~하다 (be) weak; effeminate; soft and spiritless; weak-minded. ¶ ~한 국민 a soft and spiritless people.

나열(羅列) enumeration. ~하다 marshal; arrange in a row; enumerate. ¶ 숫자를 ~하다 enumerate (marshall) figures / 예를 ~하다 cite one example after another.

나오다 ① (나타나다) appear; emerge (*from*); show *oneself*; haunt (유령이), (무대에) ~ appear on the stage / 나쁜 버릇이 ~ *one's* bad habit peeps out / 저 집에는 유령이 나온다 A ghost haunts that house. ② (밖으로 떠나다) leave; get out of; go (come) out of. ¶ 정원으로 ~ go out into the garden / 방에서 ~ come out of a room / 집을 ~ leave the house. ③ (음식이) be brought; be served. ¶ 곧 요리가 나왔다 Presently dinner was served. ④ (태도) take (*a move*); assume (*an attitude*). ¶ 강경한 태도로 ~ take a firm attitude / 그가 어떻게 나올지 볼 만하다 Let's wait and see what move he will take. ⑤ (유래하다) come from; be derived from(말이); originate from(소문이). ¶ 이 말은 라틴어에서 나왔다 This word comes (is derived) from Latin. ⑥ (실리다) appear; be in. ¶ 그 기사는 오늘 신문에 나와 있다 The news is in today's paper. / 그 단어는 내 사전에 나와 있지 않다 The word is not found in my dictionary. ⑦ (출판되다) be published (issued); come out. ¶ 그의 새 저서는 다음 달에 나온다 His new book will come out next month. ⑧ (흘러 나오다) come out; flow (stream) out; bleed(피가); sweat (땀이). ¶ 물이 ~ water comes out / 피가 많이 ~ bleed a lot. ⑨ (졸업) graduate (*from*). ¶ 대학을 ~ graduate from (a) university. ⑩ (싹이) shoot; sprout; bud. ⑪ (돌출) stick (jut) out. ¶ 판자에서 못이 나와 있다 A nail sticks out from the board. ⑫ (문제가) be given; be brought up. ¶ 모임에서는 교육에 관한 문제가 나왔다 An educational issue was brought up at the meeting. ⑬ (노출) be exposed (*to*). ⑭ (산출) produce. ⑮ (통하다) lead to. ¶ 이 길로 가면 어디다 나옵니까 Where does this road lead to? ⑯ (참가) join; take part in; enter; launch into. ¶ 정계에 ~ enter upon a political career. ⑰ (석방) be released (*from the prison*). ⑱ (말이) be spoken (said, uttered). ¶ 볼멘소리가 ~ angry words are spo-

나왕 ken[uttered]. ⑲《관용적 표현》 ¶ (통화하실) 전화가 나왔습니다《교환원의 말》Your party is on the line. / 이 차는 200km 이상의 시속이 나온다 This car can go as fast as 200km an hour. 〔목〕.

나왕(羅王)〖植〗a lauan; lauan(재목).

나위 ¶ 말할 ~ 없다 be needless to say; be not worth mentioning / 더할 ~ 없는 물건 a first-rate article.

나이 age; years. ¶ ~ 지긋한 elderly; well advanced in age / ~ 탓으로 due to〔because of〕one's age / ~ 순으로 according to age / ~에 비해 젊어 보이다 look young for one's age / ~ 를 먹다 grow old; become older. ‖ ~배기 a person older than he looks.

나이테(나무의) an annual ring.

나이트(밤) a night. ‖ ~가운 a night gown / ~클럽 a night club.

나이프 a knife.

나인 a court lady.

나일론 nylon.

나잇값 behavior appropriate to one's age.

나전(螺鈿) mother-of-pearl〔光〕; nacre. ‖ ~세공 mother-of-pearl work / ~칠기 lacquer ware inlaid with mother-of-pearl.

나절 half a day. ¶ 아침 ~ the morning / 반~ a quarter day.

나조(一調)〖樂〗B. ¶ 나장조〔단조〕B major〔minor〕.

나중 ¶ ~에 later (on); afterwards; some time later / ~에 가겠다 I'll come later. / 그가 맨 ~에 왔다 He was the last to come.

나지리 ¶ ~ 보다〔여기다〕make light of; hold 《a person》cheap.

나지막하다(be) somewhat low. ‖ 나지막한 소리 a low voice.

나체(裸體) a naked〔nude〕body; the nude. ‖ ~의 naked; nude. ‖ ~모델 a nude model / ~주의 nudism / ~화 a nude (picture).

나치스 a Nazi; Nazis(총칭). ¶ ~의 Nazi.

나침반(羅針盤) a compass.

나타나다 ① 《출현》appear; show up; present〔show〕oneself; emerge. ¶ 현장에 ~ appear on the scene / 그는 늦게야 나타났다 He turned up late. ② (표면에) show (itself); be expressed (revealed, exposed); be found (out). ¶ 술을 마시면 본성이 나타난다 Liquor reveals one's true self. / 그녀의 말투에는 인품이 잘 나타나 있다 Her way of speaking clearly shows her personality. / 세상에 나타나지 않고 숨어서 살다 live in obscurity. ③ 《언급됨》mention. ¶ 미국 문헌에 나타난 한국 Korea mentioned in American literature. ④ (약효·사실 따위가) ¶ 이 약의 효력은 즉시 나타났다 This medicine had an immediate effect. / 새로운 사실이 나타났다 Many new facts have 「come〔been brought〕to light.

나타내다 ① (표시) show; indicate; manifest; (증명) prove; speak for. ¶ 성격을 ~ show the character / 그 사실은 그녀의 결백을 나타낸다 The fact indicates〔proves〕her innocence. ② 《드러내다》disclose; reveal; betray. ¶ 정체를 ~ betray oneself. ③ (표현) express; describe. ¶ 말로 나타낼 수 없다 be beyond expression〔description〕. ④ (상징·의미하다) represent; stand for. ¶ 붉은 색은 위험을 나타낸다 Red represents danger. / UN은 국제 연합을 나타낸다 UN stands for "United Nations." ⑤ 《뚜렷이》distinguish. ¶ 두각을 ~ distinguish oneself; cut a figure.

나태(懶怠) idleness; laziness; indolence. ¶ ~한 lazy; idle; indolent; slothful; sluggish.

나토 NATO. (◀ the North Atlantic Treaty Organization)

나트륨 natrium; sodium (기호 Na).

나팔(喇叭) a trumpet; a bugle. ¶ ~을 불다 blow a trumpet. ‖ ~수 a trumpeter; a bugler.

나팔관(喇叭管)〖解〗the oviduct.

나포(拿捕) capture; seizure. ~하다 capture; seize. ‖ ~선 a captured ship.

나폴리 Naples.

나풀거리다 flutter; wave; flap.

나프타 naphtha. ¶ ~ 분해 naphtha cracking.

나프탈렌〖化〗naphthalene.

나흗날 the fourth (day) of the month.

나흘 ① (넷날) four days. ☞ ☞ ② 〔흗날.

낙(樂)《즐거움·기쁨》pleasure; enjoyment; delight; joy; amusement(오락); a hobby(취미); (기대) expectation; hope. ¶ 인생의 ~ the joy〔pleasure〕of life / 노후의 ~ pleasures of one's old age / 독서의 ~ the pleasure of reading / …을 ~으로 삼다 delight in; take pleasure in / 자식의 장래를 ~으로 살고 있다 live for the (great) future of one's child.

낙관(落款) 《서명·날인》a writer's〔painter's〕signature (and seal). ~ 하다 sign and seal.

낙관(樂觀) optimism; an optimistic view. ~하다 be optimistic 《about》; take an optimistic view 《of》; look on the bright side 《of things》; take things easy. ¶ ~적 optimistic / 사태는 ~을

낙농 불허한다 The situation does not warrant any optimism. ‖ ~론 optimism / ~론자 an optimist.
낙농(酪農) dairy farming. ‖ ~가 a dairy farmer / ~장 a dairy (farm) / ~제품 dairy products.
낙담(落膽) discouragement; disappointment. ~하다 be discouraged (disappointed); lose heart. ¶ ~시키다 discourage / 그 소식에 크게 ~하다 be very (greatly) disappointed at the news.
낙도(落島) a remote (deserted) island.
낙뢰(落雷) 벼락. ~하다 weep.
낙루(落淚) ~하다 shed tears.
낙마(落馬) a fall from one's horse. ~하다 fall (be thrown) off from a horseback.
낙반(落磐) a cave-in; a roof-fall. ¶ ~사고로 광부 3명이 죽었다 The mine caved in and three miners were killed. ‖ ~사고 a roof-fall (cave-in) accident.
낙방하다(落榜 —) fail in an examination.
낙상(落傷) a hurt from a fall. ~하다 get hurt from a fall.
낙서(落書) a scribble; a scrawl; graffiti (공공장소의). ~하다 scribble; scrawl. ¶ 벽에 ~하다 scribble on the wall. ‖ ~금지 (게시) Graffiti forbidden.
낙석(落石) a falling stone (rock). ‖ ~주의 (게시) Warning: Falling or fallen rocks.
낙선(落選) 《선거의》 defeat (failure) in an election; 《작품 응모의》 rejection. ~하다 be defeated (unsuccessful) in an election; be rejected (작품이). ‖ ~자 an unsuccessful candidate / ~작 a rejected work.
낙성(落成) completion. ~하다 be completed; be finished. ‖ ~식 a completion ceremony (of a building).
낙수물(落水 —) raindrops (from the eaves); eavesdrips. ‖ ~소리 pattering of raindrops.
낙승(樂勝) an easy victory (win). ~하다 win easily; have an easy win (over the team).
낙심(落心) ☞ 낙담.
낙엽(落葉) fallen leaves. ¶ ~이 지다 shed (cast) its leaves (나뭇가). ‖ ~수 a deciduous tree.
낙오(落伍) ~하다 drop (fall) out; drop (lag, be left) behind (the others). ¶ 행군 중에 ~하다 fall (drop) out during the march. ‖ ~자 a straggler; a dropout; a failure (인생의).
낙원(樂園) a paradise; Eden. ¶ 지상의 ~ an earthly paradise.

낙인(烙印) a brand (mark). ¶ ~을 찍다 brand / 그는 거짓말쟁이라는 ~이 찍혔다 He was branded (as) a liar.
낙장(落張) a missing leaf (page).
낙제(落第) failure (in an examination). ~하다 fail; flunk (an exam); be (get) flunked; 《유급하다》 repeat the same class; be rejected (검사에). ¶ 화학 시험에 ~하다 flunk (fail) chemistry / 겨우 ~를 면하다 just manage to get passing grades. ‖ ~생 a failure; a flunked student; a repeater / ~점 a failing grade (mark).
낙조(落照) the setting sun.
낙지 【動】 an octopus.
낙진(落塵) fallout.
낙차(落差) 【物】 the difference in elevation (between); 【電】 a head. ¶ 고(저)위 ~ a high (low) head.
낙착(落着) a settlement. ~하다 be settled; come to a settlement. ¶ ~되다 be settled; be brought to an end.
낙찰(落札) a successful bid. ~다 (사람이 주어) make a successful bid. ¶ 그 계약은 그에게 ~되었다 The contract was awarded to him. ‖ ~가격 the price of the highest bid; the contract price / ~자(인) a successful bidder.
낙천(樂天) ~적인 optimistic ~적으로 optimistically. ‖ ~가 an optimist / ~주의 optimism.
낙천자(落薦者) an unsuccessful applicant for nomination.
낙타(駱駝) 【動】 a camel. ¶ ~의 혹 a camel's hump / ~의 털 camel's hair. ‖ 단봉(쌍봉) ~ an Arabian (a Bactrian) camel.
낙태(落胎) (an) abortion. ~하다 have an abortion. ‖ ~수술 a surgical abortion.
낙토(樂土) a paradise; Heaven.
낙하(落下) falling; a fall. ~하다 fall; come down; drop; descend. ¶ ~지점 《미사일 등의》 an impact point.
낙하산(落下傘) a parachute; a chute. ¶ ~으로 내리다 parachute (down); descend (come down) by parachute. ‖ ~병 a parachutist; a paratrooper / ~부대 a parachute troop; paratroops.
낙향(落鄕) rustication. ~하다 rusticate; move to (retire into) the country.
낙화(落花) 《꽃이 짐》 the falling of blossoms (flowers); 《진 꽃》 fallen blossoms. 〔others〕.
낙후(落後) ~하다 fall behind (the others).
낚다 《물고기를》 fish (trout); angle for (carp); catch (a fish);

낚시 다) allure; entice; take in. ¶ 강에서 고기를 ~ fish (in) the river.

낚시〔낚시질〕 fishing; angling. ~하다 fish; angle for (*carp*). ¶ ~하러 가다 go fishing / ~를 잘〔못〕하다 be a good (poor) angler / 강~ river fishing / 밤~ night fishing / ~를 드리우다 drop (cast) *one's* line in a river. ¶ ~꾼 an angler / ~도구 fishing tackle / ~바늘 a fishing hook / ~찌 a float / ~터 a fishing place〔낚싯대 fishing rod / 낚시밥 a bait / 낚시봉 a sink(er) / 낚싯줄 a fishing line.

난(蘭) ☞ 난리.

난(欄)〔신문 등의〕 a column; a section;〔여백〕 a space; a blank (공란). ¶ 광고란 the advertisement column / 스포츠~ the sports section / 이 ~에는 기입하지 마시오 Do not write in this space.

난(難)〔겹미어〕 hardship; trouble; difficulty; shortage;〔형용사〕 difficult; troublesome. ¶ 식량~ a shortage of food / ~문제 a difficult problem.

난간(欄干) a railing; a rail; a handrail; a balustrade (계단의).

난감(難堪) ~하다〔견디기 어려움〕 (be) unbearable; intolerable; insufferable; be hard to bear;〔힘겨움〕 (be) beyond *one's* ability 〔power〕;〔딱함〕 be quite at a loss.

난공불락(難攻不落) impregnability. ¶ ~의 impregnable / ~의 요새 an impregnable fortress.

난공사(難工事) a difficult construction work.

난관(難關) a barrier; an obstacle; a difficulty(곤란). ¶ ~을 돌파하다 overcome a difficulty.

난국(難局) a difficult〔serious〕 situation; a crisis(위기). ¶ ~에 봉착하다 be in a fix / ~를 타개하다 break the deadlock; get over a crisis. ~의 turbulent air.

난기류(亂氣流)〔氣〕(air) turbulence.

난다긴다하다 have an outstanding talent〔*for*〕; excell all others〔*at, in*〕; be by far the best 〔*speaker of English*〕. ¶ 난다긴다하는 사람 a man of great ability.

난대(暖帶) the subtropical zone.

난데없이 to *one's* surprise; all of a sudden; unexpectedly.

난도질(亂刀一) ~하다 hack〔chop〕 (*something*) to pieces; mince; hash.

난독(亂讀) random〔unsystematic, desultory〕 reading. ~하다 read at random〔without system〕.

난동(暖冬) a mild winter.

난동(亂動)《문란》 confusion; disorder;《난폭한 행동》 violence; an outrage;〔폭동〕 a riot. ¶ ~을 부리다 do violence〔*to*〕; commit an outrage〔*on*〕; raise〔create〕 a disturbance; start a riot / ~을 가라앉히다 suppress a riot 〔trouble〕.

난로(媛爐) a heater; a stove. ¶ ~를 켜다〔끄다〕 turn on〔off〕 a heater / ~를 쬐다 warm *oneself* at a stove.

난류(暖流) a warm current.

난리(亂離)〔전쟁〕 a war; a revolt (반란); a rebellion (모반);〔혼란〕 a confusion; commotion. ¶ 그 소식에 온 집안이 ~가 났다 The news threw the whole house into confusion.

난립(亂立) ¶ 각종 고층 빌딩이 ~하여 있다 be crowded with every sort of tall buildings / 이번 선거에는 많은 후보자가 ~하고 있다 Too many candidates are running in the coming election.

난만(爛漫) ~한 splendid; glorious; blooming in profusion / ~하게 in full bloom; in all (*their*) glory.

난맥(亂脈) disorder; confusion; chaos. ¶ ~상을 나타내다 be thrown into disorder; fall into chaos.

난무(亂舞) ~하다 dance boisterously〔wildly〕; be rampant.

난문제(難問題) a difficult〔hard, knotty〕 problem; a poser;〔口〕 a hard nut to crack; a hot potato.

난민(難民) sufferers (이재민);〔피난민〕 refugees; displaced persons (조국을 쫓겨난). ¶ ~수용소〔피난민의〕 a refugee camp / 경제~ an economic refugee.

난바다 a far-off sea; an offing.

난반사(亂反射)〔理〕 diffused reflection.

난발(亂髮) disheveled〔ruffled〕 hair.

난방(煖房) heating. ¶ ~용 기름 heating oil / ~용 기구 a heating apparatus; a heater. ‖ ~비 heating expenses / ~설비 heating facilities / ~장치 a heating system; a heater / 집중〔증기〕~ central〔steam〕 heating.

난백(卵白) ☞ 흰자위 ②.

난봉 dissipation; debauchery; prodigality. ¶ ~부리다 lead a dissipated life. ‖ ~꾼 a libertine; a prodigal;《口》 a loose fish.

난사(亂射) a random firing〔shot〕. ~하다 fire blindly〔at random〕.

난사(難事) a difficult thing〔matter〕; a difficulty.

난사람 an outstanding〔a distinguished〕 person.

난산(難産) a difficult delivery. ~하다 have a difficult delivery.
난삽하다(難澁一) (be) hard; difficult.
난색(難色) disapproval; reluctance. ¶ 그는 나의 계획에 ~을 보였다 He 「was opposed to〔showed disapproval for〕my plan.
난생(卵生) ¶ ~의 oviparous. ‖ ~동물 an oviparous 〔egg-laying〕 animal.
난생처음 (for) the first time in one's life.
난세(亂世) (the) troubled 〔disturbed〕 times; a turbulent period 〔age〕. ¶ ~의 영웅 a hero in a turbulent age.
난세포(卵細胞) 〖生〗 an egg cell; an ovum.
난센스 a nonsense. ‖ ~ 소설 a nonsense novel.
난소(卵巢) 〖解〗 an ovary. ‖ ~호르몬 ovarian hormones.
난수표(亂數表) the table of random numbers 〔digits〕.
난숙(爛熟) ~하다 (be) overripe; overmature; reach 〔come to〕 full maturity. ‖ ~기〔문화의〕 the age of matured culture.
난시(亂視) 〖醫〗 astigmatism. ‖ ~의 astigmatic.
난외(欄外) a margin. ¶ ~의 주(註) a note in the margin; a marginal note / ~여백 marginal space.
난이(難易) hardness (or ease); relative difficulty. ‖ ~도 the degree of difficulty.
난입(亂入) ~하다 force one's way into; break 〔burst〕 into. ‖ ~자 an intruder.
난자(卵子) 〖生〗 an ovum 〔pl. ova〕.
난잡(亂雜)〈혼잡〉disorder; confusion. ¶ ~한 disorderly; confused; untidy / 책을 ~하게 겹집이 쌓아 놓다 pile books up in a disorderly fashion.
난장판 a scene of disorder; a chaotic scene; a mess. ¶ ~이 되다 fall into utter confusion / 그녀의 방은 ~이다 Her room is in a terrible mess.
난쟁이 a dwarf; a pigmy.
난전(亂戰) confused fighting; a dogfight; a melee.
난점(難點) a difficult 〔knotty〕 point; the crux of a matter.
난제(難題) a difficult problem; a knotty subject;《무리한 요구》an unreasonable demand 〔request〕. ¶ 이것은 하나의 ~다 This will be difficult to solve. / ~를 끄집어 내다 make an unreasonable demand 《of a person》.
난조(亂調)《음악》discord; a lack of harmony;《혼란》confusion; disorder;《시세》violent fluctuations. ¶ ~를 보이다《투수가》lose control / ~에 빠지다 be thrown into disorder; be out of tune / 주가가 ~를 보이고 있다 Stock prices are fluctuating violently.
난중(亂中) the midst of turmoil 〔commotion〕; time of war; a tumultuous period. ¶ ~에 during a war; in the midst of turmoil. ‖ ~일기〔책 이름〕 A War Diary.
난중지난(難中之難) the most difficult of all things. ‖ ~사 the hardest thing to do.
난처하다(難處一) (be) hard to deal with; awkward; embarrassing. ¶ 난처한 일 a matter hard to deal with / 난처한 입장에 있다 be in an awkward position.
난청(難聽) difficulty in hearing. ¶ ~의 hard of hearing. ‖ ~자 a person who is hard of hearing / ~지역〔라디오의〕 a blanket area; a fringe area (where reception is bad).
난초(蘭草) 〖植〗 an orchid.
난층운(亂層雲) 〖氣〗 nimbo-stratus.
난치(難治) ~의 hard to cure; almost incurable; fatal.
난타(亂打) pommeling; repeated knocking 〔blows〕. ~하다 strike 〔knock〕 violently; beat 〔hit〕《a person》repeatedly. ¶ 경고의 종을 ~하다 strike an alarm bell wildly. ‖ ~전〖拳·野〗a slugfest〖美口〗.
난투(亂鬪) a free 〔confused〕 fight; a scuffle; a free-for-all. ¶ 피아가 뒤섞인 ~가 벌어졌다 A free fight developed between the two sides 〔teams〕. ‖ ~ 국회 a disorderly 〔roughhouse〕 session of the National Assembly / ~극 a scene of violence and confusion.
난파(難破) a (ship)wreck. ~하다 be (ship)wrecked. ‖ ~선 a wrecked ship 〔vessel〕.
난폭(亂暴) violence; an outrage; roughness. ~하다 (be) violent; rude; rough; wild. ¶ ~한 언사 (use) violent 〔wild〕 language / ~한 행위 outrageous behavior / ~하게 다루다 handle《a thing》roughly / ~하게 굴다 behave rudely 〔roughly〕; use 〔resort to〕 violence. ‖ ~자 a wild 〔rowdy〕 fellow; a roughneck《美》.
난필(亂筆) hasty handwriting; scribble. ¶ ~을 용서하십시오 Please excuse my hasty writing.
난하다(亂一) (be) gaudy; showy; loud. ¶ ~색이 너무 ~ The colors are too loud. / 옷을 난하게 차려입다 be showily 〔flashily〕 dressed.
난항(難航) ① 《배·비행기의》a difficult voyage 〔flight〕. ~하다 have a rough passage. ② 《일 따위가》

난해 ~하다 have[face] hard[rough] going. ¶ 그 사고의 조사는 ~하고 있다 The investigation of the accident has hardly progressed.

난해(難解) ¶ ~한 difficult[hard] (to understand); knotty (*problems*).

난형난제(難兄難弟) ¶ ~다 There is little to choose between them. *or* They are nearly all alike.

난황(卵黃) the yolk; the yellow of an egg.

낟가리 a stack of grain stalks.

낟알 a grain (of rice).

날¹ ① 《달력상의》 a day; a date (날짜); time (시일). ¶ 어느 ~ one day / 매일 ~ every day; daily / 초하루 ~ the first day of the month / ~을 보내다 pass *one's* days / ~을 정하다 fix a date (*for a meeting*) / ~이 밝다 the day breaks (dawns). ② 《경우·때》 when; in case of; in the event of. ¶ 성공하는 ~에는 when *one* succeeds / 완성하는 ~에 on the completion of the work. ③ ☞ 날씨.

날² 《칼 따위의》 an edge; a blade. ¶ ~을 세우다 put an edge (*on*); sharpen / ~이 서다 be edged

날³ 《피륙의》 warp. ¶ [sharpened].

날⁴ 《안 익은》 uncooked; raw. ¶ ~것 raw[uncooked] food / ~계란[고기] a raw egg[meat].

날강도(一强盗) a barefaced[shameless] robber.

날개 a wing. ¶ ~가 달린 winged / 《새가》 ~를 펴다[접다] spread[fold] *its* wings / ~를 퍼덕이다 flap the wings / ~ 돋친듯 팔리다 sell like hot cakes.

날다 ① 《하늘을》 fly; flutter. ¶ 날고 있는 새 a bird flying in the air; a flying bird / 높이[낮게] ~ fly high[low]. ② 《빨리 가다》 fly; rush (*to*). ¶ 현장으로 날아가다 [나는 듯이 달려가다] rush to the scene.

날다² ① 《색이》 fade; discolor. ¶ 색이 날지 않는 cloth of fast colors / 색이 난 바지 a pair of faded jeans. ② 《냄새가》 lose odor.

날들다 clear (up). ☞ 개다.

날뛰다 jump[leap] up; 《사람이》 behave[act] violently; rush about wildly; rage. ¶ 좋아 ~ leap for joy / 날뛰기 시작하다 start acting violently.

날래다 (be) quick; swift; nimble.

날려보내다 《놓아주다》 fly; let fly; set free. ¶ 비둘기를 ~ fly[let loose] a pigeon / 잡은 새를 ~ set a bird free.

날렵하다 (be) sharp; acute; agile.

날로 ① 《나날이》 daily; day by day. ¶ ~ 나아지다 get better day by day. 《날것으로》 raw. ¶ ~ 먹다 eat (*fish*) raw.

날로 quickly; swiftly.

날름거리다 《혀 따위를》 let (*a tongue*) dart in and out. ¶ 뱀이 혀를 ~ a snake's tongue darts in and out. ② 《탐내다》 be greedy for; be covetous of.

날리다 ① 《날게 하다》 fly; let fly; blow off (바람이). ② 연을 ~ fly a kite / 바람에 모자를 ~ have *one's* hat blown off / 타자는 왼쪽 필드로 장타를 날렸다 The batter hit a long drive to left field. ② 《잃다》 lose; waste; squander (dissipate) (*a fortune*). ¶ 하룻밤에 모든 재산을 ~ squander *a* fortune in a single night / 그는 그 사건으로 좋은 기회를 날렸다 He lost his good opportunity because of the trouble. ③ 《이름을》 win fame; become famous. ¶ 명성을 온 세계에 ~ become known all over the world; win[achieve] global fame. ④ 《일을》 scamp (*one's work*); do (*a thing*) in a half-hearted[careless] manner. ¶ 일을 ~ scamp *one's* work; do a slipshod[careless, hasty] job; do *one's* work in a rough-and-ready way.

날림 (일) slipshod work; rough and hurried work; 《물건》 a thing made carelessly. ¶ ~공사 rough and hurried construction; a slipshod construction work / ~집[건물] a jerry-built house[building]. 「(night).

날밤새우다 sit up all (through

날벼락 (야단) an unreasonable scolding; (재앙) a sudden calamity; a thunderbolt from a clear sky. 「per day.

날변(一邊) daily interest; interest

날불한당(一不汗黨) a barefaced [shameless] swindlers [crooks].

날붙이 blade implements; bladeware; cutlery.

날쌔다 (be) quick; swift; nimble. ¶ 날쌔게 nimbly; quickly; swiftly.

날삯 daily wages. ¶ ~꾼 a day

날실 warp threads. [laborer.

날씨 the weather; weather condition. ¶ 좋은 ~ fair[fine] weather / 궂은 ~ bad[nasty] weather / ~가 좋으면 if it is fine...; if weather permits....

날씬하다 (be) slender; slim. ¶ 날씬한 여자 a slim[slender] woman.

날염(捺染) (textile) printing. ~하다 print.

날인(捺印) seal. ~하다 seal; affix *one's* seal (*to a document*). ¶ ~자 a sealer.

날조(捏造) fabrication; invention. ~하다 fabricate; invent; forge;

날짐승 fowls; birds.
날짜 a date. ¶ ~가 없는 undated. / ~를 매기다 date 《a letter》.
날짝지근하다 (be) very languid; much weary; very dull.
날치 〖魚〗 a flying fish.
날치기 〖行爲〗 snatching; 《사람》 a snatcher. ¶ ~하다 snatch. ¶ ~를 당하다 have 《a thing》 snatched.
날카롭다 《날의 끝이》 (be) sharp; keen; pointed (뾰족하다); 《감각·두뇌가》 (be) smart; shrewd; sharp; 《비평·기계 따위가》 biting; cutting; caustic; sharp. ¶ 날카로운 비판 cutting (biting) criticism / 날카로운 질문 a sharp question / 날카로운 통증 a sharp (acute) pain / 신경이 날카로워지다 get (become) nervous.
날탕 a person with no means; a good-for-nothing.
날품 daywork; day labor. ¶ ~을 팔다 work (be hired) by the day. / ~삯 daily wages / ~팔이꾼 a day laborer.
낡다 《오래되다》 (be) old; aged; 《오래 써서》 (be) used; worn-out; 《구식》 (be) old-fashioned; outdated (시대에 뒤진); out of date. ¶ 낡은 옷 old (worn-out) clothes / 낡은 생각 an old-fashioned idea.
남 《타인》 another person; others; 《친척 아닌》 an unrelated person. ¶ 아무런 관계가 없는 ~ an utter stranger / ~ 모르는 secret; hidden 《sorrow》 / ~몰래 만나다 have a secret meeting 《with》 / ~모르는 고생 hardships unknown to others / ~모르게 secretly; in secret (private) / ~같이 대하다 treat 《a person》 like a stranger / ~의 눈을 피하다 shun the public eye; avoid public notice / ~보다야 일가가 낫다 Blood is thicker than water.
남(男) 〖사내〗 a man; a male.
남(南) the south. ¶ ~으로 가다 go south.
남(藍) 《쪽》 indigo; 《남빛》 deep blue.
남가일몽(南柯一夢) an empty (a vain) dream.
남계(男系) the male line. ¶ ~의 on the male side (only) / ~의 친척 an agnate (relative).
남국(南國) a southern country.
남극(南極) the South Pole. ¶ ~의 antarctic. ¶ ~광 an aurora australis; the southern lights / ~대륙 (권, 해) the Antarctic Continent (Circle, Ocean) / ~성 the south polestar / ~탐험 an antarctic expedition.
남근(男根) a penis.
남기다 ① 《뒤에》 leave (behind); 《예비로》 save; set aside; reserve; 《…하지 않고》 leave 《something》 undone. ¶ 발자국을 ~ leave footmarks / 이름을 후세에 ~ leave one's name to posterity / 처자를 남기고 죽다 leave a widow and children / 일을 끝내지 않고 ~ leave one's work unfinished (half-done) / 뒤에 남겨진 가족 the bereaved family / 돈을 좀 남겨 두어야 한다 You should save some money, you know. / 그는 많은 재산을 남기고 죽었다 He died leaving a fortune. ② 《이를 보다》 make (get, obtain) a profit (of). ¶ 천원 ~ get (realize) a profit of 1,000 원 / 이를 많이 ~ make a large profit.
남김없이 all; entirely; without exception. ¶ 한 사람 ~ to the last man / 그는 ~ 다 먹었다 He ate it all up. / 아는 것을 ~ 다 말해라 Tell me all you know about it. / ~east (생략 SSE).
남남동(南南東) the south-south-east.
남남북녀(南男北女) South for manly qualities and North for womanly beauty.
남남서(南南西) the south-south-west (생략 SSW).
남녀(男女) man and woman; both sexes. ¶ ~노소 할 것 없이 regardless of sex or age / ~ 간의 격차 a gender gap (가치관의) / (a) disparity between the sexes (임금·기회 등의) / ~공용의 옷 unisex clothes. ¶ ~고용평등법 the Equal Employment Opportunity Law / ~공학 coeducation / ~동권 (평등) equal rights for 'both sexes [men and women]; sexual equality / ~유별 distinction between the sexes / ~차별 sex discrimination.
남녘(南─) the south. ¶ ~의 south; southern.
남다 ① 《여분으로》 be left (over); 《잔류하다》 remain; stay; 《잔존하다》 linger; be left alive. ¶ 《쓰고》 남은 돈 the money left over / 고스란히 남아 있다 be left untouched / 끝까지 ~ remain (stay) to the last / 늦게까지 회사에 ~ remain (stay) late at the office / 기억에 오래 ~ linger long in one's memory / 최후까지 살아 ~ survive to the last / 사후에 처자가 ~ be survived by one's wife and children / 그 향기가 한참 동안 남아 있었다 The fragrance hung around for a while. / 10에서 3을 빼면 7이 남는다 Three from ten leaves seven. / 그의 악명은 영구히 남을 것이다 His notoriety will live on forever. / 시골에는 아직 그 풍습이

남다르다 152 **남위**

남아 있다 The custom still lingers on in the countryside. ② 《이익이》《a business》 yield a profit. ¶ 남는 장사 a profitable (paying) business.

남다르다 (be) peculiar; uncommon; be different from others.

남단(南端) the southern end (tip).

남달리 extraordinarily; unusually; exceptionally. ¶ ~ 노력하다 work harder than others / ~ 키가 크다 be exceptionally tall.

남대문(南大門) the South Gate (of Seoul).

남동(南東) the southeast. ‖ ~ 풍 a southeastern wind.

남동생(男同生) a younger brother; *one's* little brother.

남루(襤褸) 《누더기》 rags; shreds; ragged (tattered) clothes. ~ 하다 (be) ragged; tattered; shabby. ¶ ~ 한 옷을 입은 사람 a person in rags.

남매(男妹) brother and sister. ¶ 그들은 ~ 간이다 They are brother and sister.

남미(南美) South (Latin) America. ¶ ~ 의 South American. ¶ ~ 대륙 the South American Continent.

남반구(南半球) the Southern Hemisphere.

남발(濫發) an overissue; an excessive issue. ~ 하다 issue recklessly; overissue. ¶ 지폐의 ~ an overissue of bank notes.

남방(南方) the south. ¶ ~ 의 southern. ¶ ~ 셔츠 an aloha shirt.

남벌(濫伐) reckless (indiscriminate) deforestation. ~ 하다 cut down (fell) 《trees》 recklessly; deforest indiscriminately.

남부(南部) the southern part; the South.

남부끄럽다 be (feel) shameful; be ashamed 《of》. ¶ 남부끄러운 일 a shameful thing; a shame / 못난 아들을 두어 남부끄럽다 I am ashamed of my son.

남부럽다 be envious of others. ¶ 남부럽잖게 살다 be well off; live no need to envy others.

남부여대(男負女戴) ~ 하다 (a family) set out on a vagabond (wandering) life.

남북(南北) south and north; 《남북한》 South and North Korea; Seoul and Pyongyang. ~ 으로 뻗어 있는 간선도로 a north-south highway. ¶ ~ 경제회담 a South-North Korean economic conference; the Inter-Korean economic talks / ~ 대화 the South-North dialog(ue); 《한국의》 Inter-Korean dialogue 〔talks〕 / 《빈국과 부국간의》 the North-South problem; the problem of disparity in income level between developed and developing countries; 《한국의》 Inter-Korean problems / ~ 적십자회담 the South-North Red Cross talks 〔conference〕 / ~ 전쟁 《미국의》 the Civil War / ~ 조절위원회 the South-North Coordinating Committee / ~ 체육회담 the inter-Korean sports talks / ~ 통일 reunification of North and South 〔Korea〕; the national reunification / ~ 한교차 승인 a cross recognition of South and North Korea / ~ 한 정상회담 (the) South-North Korean summit talks / ~ 한직통전화 the Seoul-Pyongyang hot line / ~ 협력 South-North cooperation.

남빙양(南氷洋) 〔地〕 the Antarctic Ocean.

남사당(男一) 〔民俗〕 a wayfaring male entertainer; a troupe of strolling entertainers. ~ 패 a troupe of players.

남산골샌님(南山一) a penniless (poor) scholar.

남상(男相) a woman's face having masculine features; an unwomanly face.

남새 vegetables. ‖ ~ 밭 a vegetable garden.

남색(男色) sodomy; buggery; pederasty.

남색(藍色) 《남빛》 indigo; dark blue.

남생이 〔動〕 a terrapin.

남서(南西) (the) southwest. ‖ ~ 풍 a southwestern wind.

남성(男性) 《남자》 a man; 《생물의》 the male (sex); 《문법에서》 the masculine gender. ¶ ~ 적 manly; masculine / ~ 의 male / 그에겐 ~ 다운 데가 없다 He lacks manliness. / ~ 미 masculine beauty / ~ 호르몬 male (sex) hormone.

남성(男聲) a male voice. ¶ ~ 4중창 a male quartet / ~ 합창 a male chorus. 〔Cross; the Crux.

남십자성(南十字星) the Southern

남아(男兒) 《아이》 a boy; a son; 《대장부》 a manly one. ¶ 일언 중천금 A man's word is as good as a bond. ¶ ~ 선호사상 a notion of preferring a son to a daughter.

남아메리카(南一) South America.

남아프리카(南一) South Africa. ‖ ~ 공화국 the Republic of South Africa.

남양(南洋) the South Seas. ‖ ~ 군도 the South Sea Islands.

남용(濫用) misuse; abuse; improper (unlawful) use. ~ 하다 misuse; abuse; use improperly. ¶ 직권을 ~ 하다 abuse *one's* official authority.

남우(男優) an actor.

남위(南緯) the south latitude. ¶ ~ 20도 30분 상에 in lat. 20°30′S

남유럽 (=latitude 20 degrees 30 minutes south).
남유럽(南—) Southern Europe.
남의집살다 work (be employed) as a domestic servant of a household.
남자(男子) a man; a male. ¶ 다운 manly / ~만의 세계 the male-only world / ~는 배짱, 여자는 절개 In a man courage, in a woman chastity. ‖ ~옷 men's wear.
남작(男爵) a baron. ¶ M~ Baron M. ‖ ~부인 a baroness.
남작(濫作) overproduction; excessive production. ~하다 overproduce; produce (write) too much.
남장(男裝) male attire. ~하다 be dressed like a man; wear men's clothes.
남정네(男丁—) 〈남자들〉 the menfolk; 〈남편들〉 the husbands.
남조(濫造) overproduction; shoddy (careless) manufacture. ~하다 produce in (to) excess; overproduce; manufacture carelessly. ‖ ~조제품의 ~ excessive production of poor-quality articles.
남존여비(男尊女卑) predominance of man over woman. ¶ ~의 사회 a male-dominated society.
남중국해(南中國海) the South China Sea.
남진(南進) southward advance. ~하다 advance southward. ‖ ~정책 the southward expansion policy.
남짓하다 (be) slightly over (above). ¶ 1년 ~ be a little over a year.
남쪽(南—) the south. ☞ 남(南).
남침(南侵) ~하다 invade the south. ¶ 북괴의 ~ a north Korean invasion of the south.
남탕(男湯) the men's section of a public bath.
남태평양(南太平洋) the South Pacific.
남파(南派) ~하다 send《a spy》into the South. ‖ ~간첩 an espionage agent sent (by the North) to the South.
남편(男便) a husband. ¶ ~있는 역자 a married woman.
남포(등) a lamp; an oil lamp. ¶ ~의 등피〔심지, 갓〕 a lamp chimney (wick, shade).
남풍(南風) the south wind; a wind from the south.
남하(南下) ~하다 go (come, advance) south(ward). ¶ 자유을 찾아 ~하다 come to the south seeking for freedom / 사단은 ~를 계속했다 The division kept moving south.
남한(南韓) South Korea.
남해(南海) the southern sea.
남해안(南海岸) the south coast.

남행(南行) ~하다 go (down to the) south. ‖ ~열차 a south-bound train.
남향(南向) facing (looking) south. ‖ ~집 a house facing south; a house looking toward the south.
남회귀선(南回歸線) the Tropic of Capricorn.
남획(濫獲) reckless (indiscriminate) fishing (hunting). ~하다 fish (hunt) recklessly (excessively).
납《연(鉛)》 lead (기호 Pb).
납(蠟) wax. ¶ ~세공 waxwork / ~인형 a wax doll (figure).
납골(納骨) ~하다 lay *one's* ashes to rest. ‖ ~단지 a cinerary urn / ~당 a charnel house.
납금(納金) payment of money (지불); the money due (지불할); the money paid (지불한). ~하다 pay《money》.
납기(納期) 〈돈의〉 the date (time) of payment; 〈물품의〉 the date (time) of delivery. ¶ 세금의 ~ the date of tax payment.
납길(納吉) ~하다 notify the bride's family of the date set for the wedding.
납득(納得) understanding. ~하다 understand. ¶ ~하기 어려운 unconvincing; hard to understand / ~시키다 convince《a person》of; persuade《a person》to do.
납땜(鑞—) soldering. ~하다 solder《a leaky pot》. ‖ ~인두 a soldering iron.
납량(納凉) ~하다 enjoy the cool air. ‖ ~특집(프로) a special summer evening program.
납본(納本) ~하다 present a specimen copy for censorship.
납부(納付)〈세금 등의〉 payment; 〈물품의〉 delivery. ~하다 pay; deliver. ¶ 기일까지 반드시 ~할 것 Be sure to complete the payment by the due date. ‖ ~기 한 the deadline for payment / ~서 a statement of payment (delivery) / ~액 the amount of payment / ~자 a payer / 분할 ~ divided payments.
납북(拉北) kidnaping to the north. ~되다 be kidnaped to the north. ‖ ~어부 a fisherman kidnaped to North Korea.
납석(蠟石) 〔鑞〕 agalmatolite.
납세(納稅) payment of taxes; tax payment. ~하다 pay *one's* taxes. ¶ ~의 의무 a legal obligation to pay *one's* taxes. ‖ 고지서 a tax notice / ~기일 the due date; the date on which taxes are due (for payment); the tax day / ~신고 income tax returns (declaration) / ~신고 용지 tax forms /

납신거리다

~액 the amount of taxes / ~필 Tax (Duty) paid / ~필증 a certificate of tax (duty) payment.

납신거리다 chatter; prattle; jabber.

납입(納入) ~하다 pay 《*a tax*》; deliver 《*goods*》. ∥ ~금 (지불된) money paid; (지불할) money due / ~품 supplies; goods for supply.

납작(모양) flat; low; (빨리) with quick motion. ¶ ~ 엎드리다 lie down flat (with quick motion). ∥ ~보리 pressed (rolled) barley / ~코 a flat nose.

납작하다 (be) flat; low. ¶ 납작한 집 a low house / 납작하게 찌부러지다 be crushed flat / 코가 납작해지다 (비유적) behumbled; lose face.

납지(蠟紙) wax paper.

납지(鑞紙) tin foil; silver paper.

납질(蠟質) waxy substance.

납채(納采) betrothal presents (to the bride's house).

납치(拉致) kidnaping; hijacking (배·비행기의). ~하다 kidnap; hijack 《*a passenger plane*》; take 《*a person*》 away. ¶항공기의 ~ skyjacking / ~된 여객기의 승객을 passengers from the hijacked airbus / 이북으로 ~되다 be kidnaped to North Korea. ∥ ~범 a kidnaper; a hijacker.

납품(納品) delivery of goods. ~하다 deliver goods 《*to*》. ∥ ~업자 a supplier / ~(증명)서 a statement of delivery.

납회(納會) the last meeting of the year; (證) the closing session of the month.

낫 a sickle; a scythe (큰 낫). ¶ ~ 놓고 기역자도 모르다 do not know A from B.

낫다¹ 《좋다·잘하다》 be better 《*than*》; be preferable 《*to*》; outdo; surpass. ¶ 나아지다 become better; be improved / 아버지보다 ~ surpass (outdo) *one's* father.

낫다² 《병이》 recover from 《*illness*》; get well (better); be cured of 《*a disease*》; heal (up) (상처가). ¶ 감기가 ~ get over *one's* cold / 이 약을 먹으면 감기가 낫는다 This medicine will cure a cold.

낭군(郞君) (my) dear husband.

낭독(朗讀) reading; recitation (암송). ~하다 read (aloud); recite. ¶ 시를 ~하다 read (recite) poems.

낭떠러지 a precipice. ¶ ~에서 떨어지다 fall over a precipice.

낭랑하다(朗朗─) (be) ringing; clear; sonorous; resonant.

낭만(浪漫) ¶ ~적인 romantic / ~적인 생각에 잠기다 indulge in romantic dreaming (thought). ∥

낯참

~주의 romanticism / ~주의자 a romanticist.

낭보(朗報) good (happy) news.

낭비(浪費) waste; wasteful expenditure; extravagance. ~하다 waste; squander; throw 《*one's money*》 away. ¶ ~적인 wasteful; extravagant / 그것은 시간의 ~이다 It's a waste of time. / 정말 우리는 연료를 ~하지 않고 있는가 Aren't we wasteful with oil? ∥ ~벽 a wasteful habit (~벽이 있다 have the habit of wasting money) / ~자 a waster; a spendthrift.

낭설(浪說) a groundless rumor; false rumors. ¶ ~을 퍼뜨리다 circulate (set) a false rumor / ~을 믿다 take a rumor as it is.

낭송(朗誦) ☞ 낭독.

낭자(娘子) a maiden; a girl.

낭자(狼藉) disorder; confusion. ~하다 (be) in wild disorder; in a terrible mess; scattered all over. ¶ 유혈이 ~하다 be all covered with blood.

낭패(狼狽) failure; frustration; a fiasco; a blunder. ~하다 fail 《*in*》; be frustrated; make (commit) a blunder. ¶ 이거 참 ~로군 What a most awkward case this is!

낭하(廊下) a corridor; a passage. ☞ 복도.

낮 day; daytime. ¶ ~에 in (during) the daytime; by day / ~일 day work / 밤 ~으로 day and night / ~말은 새가 듣고 밤말은 쥐가 듣는다 (俗談) Pitchers (Walls) have ears.

낮다 ① 《높이·정도·값·소리 등이》 (be) low. ¶ 낮은 산 (산) 값 a low hill (price) / 낮은 수입으로 살다 live on a low (small) income / 낮은 목소리로 말하다 speak in a low voice; talk in whispers / 10년 전의 우리들 생활 수준은 지금보다 훨씬 낮았다 Our standard of living ten years ago was far lower than now. ② 《지위·신분이》 (be) low; humble; mean. ¶ 신분이 ~(지위)가 have low status; be low in social standing; (태생이) have (be of) humble origin; come from a humble background. [tard.

낮도깨비 《사람》 a shameless bas-

낯도둑 a sneak (noonday) thief.

낮은음자리표 (樂) bass (F) clef.

낮잠 a (midday) nap; a siesta. ¶ ~자다 take a nap (siesta).

낮잡다 estimate (rate) low; underestimate. ¶ 집값을 ~ rate the price of a house low.

낮차(─車) a day train.

낮참(점심) a midday meal; lunch; (쉬는 시간) a noon recess; a lunch break.

낮추다 lower; bring down; drop (목소리 따위를). ¶ 값을 ~ lower (bring down) the price / 텔레비전 소리를 ~ turn (tone) down the TV / 말씀 낮추시지요 Drop your honorifics, please.

낮추보다 look down on; despise; hold (a person) in contempt. ¶ 남의 능력을 ~ look down on another's ability.

낮춤말 familiar (plain) terms.

낯 ① (얼굴) a face; (표정) a look. ¶ ~을 붉히다 (become) red in the face; blush / 서로 ~ 대하다 face each other / 웃는 ~으로 손님을 맞다 welcome a guest with a smile / 불쾌한 ~으로 나오다 come out with a displeased look / …때문에 자네 볼 ~이 없네 I am ashamed to face (see) you because…. ② (체면) face; honor; credit; dignity. ¶ ~을 세워주다 save (a person's) face (honor) / ~이 서다 (깎이다) win (lose) one's face (honor, dignity) / ~을 세우는 분쟁의 해결책 a face-saving solution to the dispute.

낯가리다 be shy of strangers; be bashful in front of strangers. ¶ 낯가리어 울다 cry at the sight of a stranger / 이 애는 낯가리지 않는다 This baby takes to strangers.

낯가죽 ¶ ~이 두껍다 be thick-skinned, brazen-faced, impudent, shameless / 참 ~ 두꺼운 녀석이군 What a brazen-faced fellow he is! 〔abashed.

낯간지럽다 (be) bashful; shy; feel

낯나다 get credit (for); reflect credit (honor) on (a person); gain (win) honor.

낯내다 do honor to oneself; do oneself proud (credit); reflect credit on oneself. ¶ 낯내느라고 기부하다 make a donation just to reflect (credit) honor on oneself.

낯두껍다 ☞ 낯가죽.

낯붉히다 (성이 나서) get angry; be red with anger; (부끄러워) blush for shame.

낯설다 (be) unfamiliar; strange. ¶ 낯선 사람 a stranger / 낯선 곳 a strange (an unfamiliar) place.

낯익다 be familiar (to). ¶ 낯익은 얼굴 a familiar face / 그녀에게 낯익게 보이려고 애쓰다 try hard to be a familiar figure to her.

낯짝 ☞ 얼굴, 낯.

낱개 a piece; each piece. ¶ ~로 팔다 sell by the piece.

낱낱이 one by one; separately; each; without omission. ¶ ~ 캐묻다 ask questions in detail / ~ 이름을 들다 mention each by name.

낱말 a word; a vocabulary.

낳다 ①《출산》have a baby; give birth to (be delivered of) (a baby); breed(동물이); 도 (알(낳). ¶ 사내 아이를 ~ give birth to a boy. ②《생기다》produce; bring forth; give rise to; yield(이자를). ¶ 좋은 결과를 ~ produce good results / ~ 이자를 yield (bear) interest (at 10 percent) / 한국이 낳은 최고의 피아니스트 the greatest pianist (that) Korea has ever produced.

내¹ (나의) my; (내가) I; myself. ¶ ~ 것 mine.

내² (개울) a stream; a brook.

내³ (연기) smoke;《냄새》smell.

내…(來) next; coming. ¶ ~ 주 next week.

…내(내내)all through; throughout. ¶ 하룻밤 ~ all night through / 일년 ~ all the year round. 〔in the period (of).

…내(內) within. ¶ 기한 ~ within.

내가다 take (bring) out (away).

내각(內角)〔幾〕an interior angle.

내각(內閣) a cabinet; a ministry (英); the government(정부); the administration (美). ¶ ~을 조직하다 form a Cabinet / 현재의 ~ the present Cabinet / K~ the K Cabinet / 초당파 ~ a non-party cabinet. ‖ ~개편 a reshuffle of the Cabinet / ~수반 the Premier; the Prime Minister / ~책임제 the parliamentary cabinet system; the cabinet-responsible system / ~ 총사직 a general resignation of the Cabinet.

내갈기다 hit; (글씨를) dash off; scribble; scrawl.

내강(內剛) ¶ ~한 stout-hearted; strong-minded(-willed) / 그는 외유 ~한 사람이다 He looks gentle but is tough inside. 〔guest.

내객(來客) a visitor; a caller; a

내걸다 ① (밖에) hoist (a flag); put up; hang out. ¶ 간판을 ~ hang out a sign (board) / 문패를 ~ put up one's name plate. ② (주의·주장을) hold up. ¶ 이상을 ~ hold up an ideal / 슬로건을 내걸고 under the slogan (of). ③ (목숨 등을) risk; stake; bet. ¶ 생명을 ~ risk (stake) one's life.

내경(內徑) the inside diameter.

내공(耐空) ¶ ~하다 stay up (in the air); make an endurance flight. ‖ ~비행(기록) an endurance flight (record).

내과(內科)(의학) internal medicine; (병원의) the internal medicine department. ¶ ~질환 an internal disease. ‖ ~의 a physi-

내구(耐久) endurance; durability. ¶ ~소비재 durable consumer goods / ~시험 an endurance test.

내구력(耐久力) 《물건의》 durability; 《사람의》 power of endurance; staying power; stamina. ¶ ~이 있는 durable; lasting; persistent / 그에겐 ~이 없다 He has no endurance in him.

내국(內國) home; the home country. ¶ ~의 home; domestic; internal. ¶ ~세 an internal tax / ~우편 domestic mail / ~인 a native / ~채(債) domestic loans / ~항로 a domestic line / ~환(換) domestic exchange.

내규(內規) bylaws; a private regulation; rules. ¶ …라고 ~에 규정되어 있다 be provided in the rules 《of the company》 that…

내근(內勤) indoor service; office (desk) work. ~하다 work inside (in the office). ‖ ~기자 a deskman / ~사원 an office inner service employee; an office worker.

내기 a bet; a wager; 《도박》 betting; gambling. ~하다 bet (on); lay a wager (on); gamble. ¶ ~에 이기다(지다) win (lose) a wager (bet) / ~ 바둑을 두다 play paduk for money.

내내 from start to finish; all the time (way); all along. ¶ 1년 ~ throughout the year; all the year round.

내내년(來來年) the year after next.

내내월(來來月) the month after next.

내년(來年) next year; the coming year. ¶ ~ 이맘 때 about this time next year.

내놓다 ① 《밖으로 꺼내놓다》 take (put, bring, carry) out. ¶ 방 밖으로 책상을 ~ take a desk out of a room / 가방에서 수첩을 ~ take a notebook out of one's bag. ② 《드러내다》 expose; show; bare. ¶ 의사에게 젖가슴을 ~ bare one's breasts for the doctor. ③ 《가둔 것을》 let out; turn 《drive, put》 out. ¶ 고양이를 방 밖으로 ~ let a cat out of the room / 소를 들판에 ~ turn the cattle out to the fields. ④ 《출품·출간·팔려고》 exhibit; publish; put out; put 《a thing》 on sale. ¶ 전람회에 그림을 ~ exhibit a picture at a show / 집을 팔려고 ~ put a house on sale / 몇 가지 신제품을 시장에 ~ put out a number of new products to the market / 그녀는 회상록을 내놓았다 She published her memoirs. ⑤ 《제출》 present; send (hand) in; 《기부·투자》 give; contribute; invest. ¶ 의안을 ~ present a bill / 사표를 ~ hand in one's resignation / 명함을 ~ present one's card (to) / 교회 짓는 데 돈을 ~ contribute money for building a church / 사업에 돈을 ~ invest money in an enterprise. 《음식 따위를》 offer; serve. ¶ 손님에게 음식을 ~ serve food and drink to the guest. ⑦ 《포기》 give (throw) up; discard. ¶ 목숨을 ~ lay down one's life / 직위를 ~ throw up one's office.

내다〔연기가〕 smoke; smolder; be smoky. ¶불이 낸다 The fire is smoking.

내다 ① 《밖으로》 take 《a thing》 out 《of》. ¶ 상자들을 밖으로 ~ take boxes out of 《the room》. ② 《발휘하다》 ¶힘을 ~ exert (put forth) one's strength / 용기를 ~ pluck up one's courage / 기운을 ~ cheer up; pluck up. ③ 《소리를》 utter; let out; give; 《빛·열 따위를》 emit (give out) 《light, heat》; 《속도를》 put on (get up) 《speed》; 《먼지를》 raise 《the dust》; 《불을》 cause (start) 《a fire》. ¶ 이상한 소리를 ~ make a strange noise / 큰 소리를 ~ utter (give) a loud cry / 그 열차는 전속력을 냈다 The train 「got up (put on) full speed. ④ 《제출》 give (send) in; present; 《발행》 publish; issue; 《게재》 run; print; 《발송》 mail; post; send out. ¶ 답안을 ~ give (hand) in one's paper / 편지를 ~ mail (post) a letter / 원서를 ~ present an application / 신문에 광고를 ~ run an ad in the paper / 특종 기사를 ~ publish an exclusive story 《on》 / 책을 ~ publish a book / 초대장을 ~ send out an invitation. ⑤ 《개설》 open; set up. ¶ 가게를 ~ open (set up) a shop / 길을 ~ open a road / 길을 내어 주다 make way 《for》. ⑥ 《음식을》 serve; offer; treat. ¶ 차를 ~ offer 《a person》 tea / 한턱 ~ give 《a person》 a treat. ⑦ 《산출·발생》 produce; turn out; 《소문》 set 《a rumor》 afloat; spread. ¶ 인재(人材)를 ~ turn out men of ability / 사상자를 ~ suffer casualties. ⑧ 《지불》 pay; give; 《자금을》 invest; contribute 《기부》. ¶ 수업료를 ~ pay a school fee / 자선 사업에 많은 돈을 ~ contribute (give) a large sum of money to charities. ⑨ 《시간을》 make; arrange. ¶ 시간을 내서 참석하다 make (find) time to be present

내다보다 at a meeting. ⑩《얻다》take out; get. ¶빚을 ~ get〔get out〕a loan / 여권을〔여가를〕 ~ get a passport〔permission〕《from》. ⑪《팔다》sell. ¶곡식을 ~ sell grain; put grain on the market. ⑫《과하다》give; set 《a question》. ¶선생님은 많은 숙제를 내신다 Our teacher gives (us) a lot of homework.

내다보다 look out 《밖을》; look forward 《앞을》; foresee, anticipate 《앞일을》. ¶창 밖을 ~ look out of a window / 앞일을 ~ foresee the future. 「ward〕.

내닫다 run 〔dash, rush〕 out 〔for-

내달(來―) next month.

내담(來談) ― 하다 visit 《for a talk》; pay 《a person》 a visit. ¶본인 직접 ~ 할 것《광고에서》 Apply in person.

내던지다 ①《밖으로》throw 〔cast〕 away. ¶빈 강통을 차 밖으로 ~ throw away empty cans out of〔from〕a car. ②《내리다》give 〔throw〕 up; abandon. ¶지위를 ~ throw up one's office / 사표를 ~ thrust one's resignation at 《the employer》. 「come 〔to〕.

내도(來到) ―하다 arrive 《at, in》;

내돌리다 hand 〔pass〕 《a thing》 round 〔on〕 recklessly 《without reason》.

내두르다 ①《흔들다》wave 〔swing〕 《something》 about; brandish; wield 《a club》. ¶손을 ~ wave one's hand about. ②《사람을》 have 《a person》 under one's thumb; lead 《a person》 by the nose.

내둘리다 ① 《남에게》 be led by the nose; be at the mercy of 《a person》. ②《어찔해지다》 be shaky; feel dizzy.

내딛다 (take a) step forward; advance. ¶한 걸음 ~ take a step forward / 새로운 인생을 ~ embark on a new career〔life〕/ 인생의 첫발을 잘못 ~ make a wrong start in life.

내락(內諾) consent 〔an informal 〔a private〕 agreement〕. ~ 하다 give an informal consent. ¶ ~ 을 얻다 obtain 《a person's》 private consent.

내란(內亂) a civil war; internal disturbances; rebellion 《반란》. ¶ ~ 을 일으키다 〔진정시키다〕 raise 〔suppress〕 a rebellion / ~ 이 일어났다 A civil war broke out.

내려가다 〔아래로 가다〕 go 〔come, get〕 down; descend; fall 《기온 등이》. ¶언덕을 ~ go down a hill / 기온이 영하로 ~ fall down below zero.

내려놓다 put 〔take〕 down; take 《a thing》 off. ¶선반에서 꽃병을 ~ take a vase down from the shelf / 냄비를 ~ take a pot off the fire. 「《a cup》.

내려다보다 ①《밑을》overlook; look down. ②《앝보다》look down upon; despise.

내려뜨리다 let 《a thing》 fall; drop

내려앉다 《자리를》 take a lower seat; 《무너져》 fall〔break〕 down; collapse. ¶건물이 쿵하며 내려 앉았다 The building fell down with a crash.

내려오다 come down; descend.

내려치다 give a downright blow. ¶책상을 주먹으로 ~ hit the table with one's fist.

내력(來歷) ① 〔경력〕 a history; a career; 〔유래〕 an origin; a history. ¶ ~ 을 캐다 trace 《a history》 to its origin. ②《내림》 inheritance; heredity; blood relationship. ¶책을 좋아하는 것은 우리집 안의 ~ 이다 A love of books is in my blood. 「area.

내륙(內陸) inland. ‖ ~ 지방 inland

내리 ①《아래로》downward. ¶지붕에서 ~ 구르다 fall down from the roof. ②《잇달아》 continuously; through; without a break. ¶ ~ 사흘을 for three successive days / 비가 ~ 오다 keep on raining.

내리긋다 draw 《a line》 down. 「ing.

내리깎다 knock 〔beat〕 down the price.

내리깔다 drop 〔lower, cast down〕 one's eyes. ¶눈을 내리깔고 with downcast eyes.

내리다[1] 〔자동사〕 ①《높은 데서》 come 〔go, get, step〕 down; descend; 《하강》 get off; drop; 《차에서》 alight from; get〔step〕 off; get out 《of》. ¶ 연단에서 ~ descend from the platform / 택시에서 ~ get out of a taxi / 물가가 ~ the price 《of something》 falls 〔goes down〕. ②《먹은 것이》 be digested. ③《부기 따위가》 subside; go down; 《살이》 lose flesh; become leaner. ④《신이》 be possessed 《by a spirit》. ⑤《뿌리를》 take root 《in the ground》.

내리다[2] 〔타동사〕 ①《내려뜨리다》 take down; lower; bring 〔put, pull〕 down; drop. ¶선반에서 책을 ~ take down a book from a shelf / 커튼을 ~ drop the curtain / 차에서 짐을 ~ get a bundle off a car / 불에서 냄비를 ~ take the pot off the fire / 가게 앞에서 내려 주시오 Drop me before the shop. ②《판결·명령·허가 등을》 give; pass; issue; grant. ¶사건에 판결을 ~ pass〔give〕 a judgement on a case / 명령을 ~ give〔issue〕 an order. ③《값·계급·정도를》 lower; bring down;

demote (지위를). ¶ 값을 ~ lower (bring down) the price / 계급을 ~ demote (*a person*) to a lower rank. ④ 〖짐을〗 unload. ¶ 트럭에서 짐을 ~ unload goods from the truck.

내리닫이 (창) a sash window; 〖옷〗 children's overalls with a slit in the seat.

내리뜨다 ☞ 내리깔다.

내리막 ① 〖길의〗 a downward slope; a downhill; a descent. ¶ ~길이 되다 slope (go) down; run (go) downhill. ② 〖쇠퇴〗 a decline; an ebb. ¶ 인생의 ~ the downhill of life / ~이 되다 be on the decline; decline; be in decline / 그녀의 인기는 이미 ~ 이다 Her popularity is already in decline.

내리사랑 parental love (affection) toward *one's* children.

내리쬐다 shine (blaze, beat) down (*on*). ¶ 내리쬐는 태양 a burning (scorching) sun / 태양은 지붕을 내리쬐고 있었다 The sun was blazing down on the roofs.

내림 (來臨) (*one's* esteemed) attendance (presence). ~하다 attend; be present at.

내림세 (一勢) a downward trend; a falling (declining) tendency.

내막 (內幕) the inside facts (information); the low-down (*on*) 〖美口〗. ¶ ~ 이야기 an inside story / 사건의 ~을 밝히다 expose the inside facts about the affair / ~을 알다 〖살피다〗 see (peep) behind the scene.

내맡기다 leave (*a matter*) (entirely) to (*a person*); leave (*a thing*) in (*a person's*) hands; entrust. ¶ 사업을 고용인에게 ~ leave *one's* business in the charge (hands) of *one's* employee.

내면 (內面) the inside; the interior. ~적(으로) internal(ly) / ~적 관찰 introspection / ~ 생활 *one's* inner life / ~ 세계 the inner world.

내명 (內命) informal (secret) orders. ¶ ~을 받다 receive secret orders.

내몰다 turn (send, drive) out.

내몰리다 be expelled (turned out).

내무 (內務) home (domestic) affairs. ‖ ~반 〖軍〗 (living) quarters; barracks / ~부 〖省〗 the Department of the Interior 〖美〗; the Home Office 〖英〗 / ~장관 〖美〗 the Secretary of the Interior 〖英〗.

내밀 (內密) ¶ ~한 secret; private; confidential / ~한 이야기 a private (confidential) talk / ~한 일 a private matter (affair) / ~히 secretly; in secret; privately.

내밀다 push (thrust, put, stick) out. ¶ 창문으로 머리를 ~ stick *one's* head out of the window.

내밀리다 be pushed (forced) out.

내방 (來訪) a visit; a call. ~하다 visit; call on (*a person*).

내배다 ooze (seep) out; exude.

내뱉다 〖침·말 따위를〗 spit out.

내버려두다 〖그냥두다〗 leave (*a thing*) as it is; leave (*a person*, *a thing*) alone. ¶ 제 마음대로 하게 ~ let (*a person*) do what he wants / 일을 하지 않고 ~ leave *one's* work undone.

내버리다 〖던져서〗 throw (cast) away; abandon (버리다).

내보내다 ① 〖나가게 하다〗 turn (put, drive, force) out (강제로); send out (축무릎). ¶ 고양이를 방에서 ~ let a cat out of the room / 척후를 ~ send out scouts. ② 〖해고〗 dismiss; fire. ¶ 하인을 ~ dismiss (fire) a servant.

내복 (內服) ~ 속용. 〖醫〗 internal use. ‖ ~약 an internal medicine.

내부 (內部) the inside; the interior; the inner part. ¶ ~의 inside; internal; inner / ~에 within / ~의 사정 the internal affairs; the inside story / ~의 사람 an insider. ‖ ~고발 whistle-blowing from the inside / ~구조 inner (interior) structure / ~분열 an internal disunion.

내분 (內紛) an internal trouble (conflict); domestic discord.

내분비 (內分泌) 〖生〗 internal secretion. ‖ ~선 an internal gland.

내빈 (來賓) a guest; a visitor. ‖ ~석 the visitors' seats; 〖게시〗 For Guests. / ~실 a guest room.

내빼다 fly; flee; run away.

내뿜다 spout (out); gush (spurt) out (물·피 따위가); blow up (out) (가스·증기 따위가); belch out; shoot up (연기·화염 따위가).

내사 (內査) a secret investigation; an internal probe. ~하다 investigate secretly.

내산 (耐酸) resistance to acids; acid-resistance. ‖ ~성의 물질 acid-resistance substance / ~성의 금속 a metal resistant to acids.

내색 (-色) *one's* facial expression; (a revealing) look. ~하다 betray *one's* emotions; give expression to *one's* feelings. ¶ ~도 않다 do not show (betray) any hint of *one's* emotions in his look (manners).

내선 (內線) 〖전기의〗 interior wiring; 〖전화의〗 an extension. ‖ ~전화 an interphone.

내성 (內省) introspection; reflec-

내성 tion. ~하다 introspect; reflect on *oneself*. ¶ ~적인 성격 an introspective nature.
내성(耐性) tolerance. ¶ ~이 있다 be tolerant 〔*of, to*〕 / ~이 있다 tolerate. ¶ ~항생물질 ~균 antibiotic-resistant bacteria.
내세(來世) the life after death〔to come〕; the next world. ¶ 현세와 ~ this world and the next. ¶ ~ 신앙 belief in the life after death.
내세우다 ① 〔앞·전면에〕 put up; put forward; make 〔*a person*〕 stand in the front; make 〔let〕 〔*a person*〕 represent. ¶ 간판을 ~ put up a signboard / 그를 후보자로 ~ put him forward for a candidate / 아무로 회사 대표로 ~ have 〔make〕 *a person* represent the company. ② 〔권리·조건·의견 등을〕 insist 〔*on*〕; put forward; state; stand on; advocate; single out 〔*for praise*〕. ¶ 이유를 ~ state 〔give〕 *one's* reasons / 자기의 권리를 ~ insist 〔stand〕 on *one's* right / 이의(異議)를 ~ raise 〔lodge〕 an objection 〔*against*〕 / 그에게는 내세울 만한 재주가 없다 He has no talent to speak of.
내소박(內疎薄) mistreating *one's* husband. ~하다 mistreat *one's* husband.
내수(內需) domestic demand. ¶ ~ 를 확대하다 expand 〔boost〕 domestic demand. ¶ ~용 원자재 raw materials for domestic demand 〔consumption〕.
내수(耐水) ¶ ~의 waterproof; watertight. ¶ ~성 waterproofing; water-resisting qualities.
내수면(內水面) inland waters. ¶ ~어업 fresh-water fishery.
내숭스럽다 (be) wicked; treacherous.
내쉬다 breathe out.
내습(來襲) an attack; a raid. ~하다 attack; raid; assault; invade.
내습(耐濕) ¶ ~의 wetproof; dampproof; moisture-resistant.
내시(內示) unofficial announcement. ~하다 announce unofficially.
내시(內侍) a eunuch.
내시경(內視鏡) an endoscope. ‖ ~ 검사(법) endoscopy.
내식성(耐蝕性) corrosion resistance. ¶ ~의 corrosion-resistant; corrosion-proof.
내신(內申) an unofficial report. ~하다 report unofficially. ¶ ~ 성적 (고교의) the high school records; the academic reports 〔from high schools to universities〕.
내신(來信) a letter received.
내실(內室) 〔안방〕 women's quarters; 〔남의 아내〕 your 〔his〕 wife.
내실(內實) substantiality. ¶ ~을 기하다 insure substantiality / ~ 화하다 make 〔*something*〕 substantial 〔solid〕.
내심(內心) *one's* inmost heart; *one's* real intention. ¶ ~으로(는) at heart; inwardly. ¶ ~는 …하고 싶어하다 have a secret desire to do.
내야(內野) 〔野〕 the infield. ‖ ~수 an infielder / ~안타 〔플라이〕 an infield hit 〔fly〕.
내약(內約) ~하다 make a private agreement 〔contract〕 〔*with*〕.
내역(內譯) items; details. ¶ ~을 밝히다 state the items 〔*of an account*〕. ¶ ~명세서 an itemized statement.
내연(內緣) ¶ ~의 처 a common-law wife; a wife not legally married / ~의 관계를 맺다 make a common-law marriage 〔*with*〕.
내연(內燃) internal combustion. ‖ ~기관 an internal-combustion engine.
내열(耐熱) ¶ ~의 heatproof; heat-resistant. ‖ ~복(服) a heatproof suit / ~시험 a heat-resistance test / ~유리 heat-resistant glass.
내오다 bring 〔take, carry〕 out.
내왕(來往) 〔왕래〕 comings and goings; traffic〔차의〕; communication〔편지의〕; 〔교제〕 association. ~하다 come and go; intercommunicate 〔*with*〕; associate 〔*with*〕.
내외(內外)¹ 〔부부〕 husband and wife; a 〔married〕 couple.
내외(內外)² ① 〔안팎〕 the inside and outside. ¶ ~의 internal and external; 〔나라의〕 home 〔domestic〕 and foreign. ¶ 국~에 알려져 있다 be known both at home and abroad. ¶ ~ 동포 *one's* countrymen both at home and abroad / ~정세 the internal and external state of affairs. ② 〔대략〕 some; about; around; or so. ¶ 일주일 ~ a week or so.
내외하다(內外—) 〔the sexes〕 keep their distance 〔from each other〕; avoid society with the opposite sex.
내용(內用) internal use. ¶ ~복.
내용(內容) contents; substance〔실질〕; details. ¶ 편지〔사건〕의 ~ the contents of a letter 〔the details of a case〕 / 형식과 ~ form and matter. ¶ ~증명 certification of contents ~ 증명우편 contents-certified mail.
내용연수(耐用年數) durable years.
내우(內憂) internal troubles. ¶ ~외환 domestic troubles and external threats / ~외환에 시달리다 be beset with troubles both

내원(來援) help; aid; assistance. ¶ ~을 요청하다 ask 《a person》 to come and help.

내월(來月) next month; proximo

내의(內衣) ☞ 속옷. 〔(생략 prox.).

내의(來意) ¶ ~를 알리다 tell 《a person》 what *one* has come for; state the purpose of *one's* visit.

내이(內耳) 【生】 the internal (inner) ear.

내일(來日) tomorrow. ¶ ~ 아침(밤) tomorrow morning (night) / ~의 한국 Korea's tomorrow.

내자(內子) my wife.

내자(內資) domestic capital (fund). ‖ ~동원 the mobilization of local capital.

내장(內粧) interior decoration. ‖ ~공사 【建】 interior finish work.

내장(內障) 【醫】 amaurosis (흑내장); cataract (백내장).

내장(內藏) ~하다 have 《something》 built-in. ¶ 거리계가 ~된 사진기 a camera with a built-in range finder.

내장(內臟) 【生】 the internal organs; the intestines. ¶ ~의 visceral. ‖ ~질환 an internal disease / ~파열 a visceral cleft.

내재(內在) 【哲】 immanence. ~하다 be inherent (immanent) 《in》. ¶ ~적인 immanent; inner; indwelling.

내적(內的) ~인 internal; mental(마음의). ‖ ~생활 *one's* inner life.

내전(內戰) a civil (an internal) war.

내접(內接) 【數】 ~하다 be inscribed. ‖ ~원(圓) an inscribed circle.

내정(內定) informal (unofficial) decision. ~하다 decide informally (unofficially). ¶ ~되다 be informally arranged (decided).

내정(內政) domestic (home) administration. ‖ ~간섭 (불간섭) intervention (non-intervention) on domestic affairs 《of another country》.

내정(內情) (내부사정) inside affairs; (실정) the real state of affairs. ¶ ~에 밝다 be familiar with the inside affairs.

내조(內助) *one's* wife's help. ~하다 help *one's* husband. ¶ ~의 공으로 *through the assistance* (thanks to the support) of *one's* wife.　　　　　　　〔aunt.

내종(內從) cousins by a paternal

내주(來週) next week. ¶ ~의 오늘 this day (next) week.

내주(內主) ① 《돈·재산·물건 등을》 hand (turn) over; give; give out (away); deliver 《goods》; pay(지불). ¶ 월급을 ~ pay *one's* salary / 재산을 조카에게 ~ hand *one's* estate over to his nephew / 서랍에서 서류를 ~ hand over documents out of *one's* drawer / 쌀을 ~ give rice out (away) / 현금과 교환으로 물품을 ~ deliver the goods in exchange for cash. ② 《자리·길을》 give (way to); yield; 《권리 등을》 give; hand (turn, make) over. ¶ 길을 ~ make way for 《a person》; give the road to 《a person》 / 왕위를 ~ turn the throne over 《to》 / 후진에게 자리를 ~ resign *one's* post in favor of a junior. ③ 《허가·면허 등을》 grant; issue. ¶ 면허장을 ~ grant (issue) a license.

내주장(內主張) pettycoat government. ~하다 henpeck *one's* husband. ¶ 그 집은 ~이다 The wife is the ruler in that house.

내지(內地) the interior (of a country); inland. ‖ ~인 inlanders.

내지(乃至) from…to…; between… and…; or(또는).

내직(內職) a side job; side work; a sideline; 《부녀의》 a job (work) for housewives. ¶ ~을 하다 do a side job.

내진(內診) an internal examination. ~하다 make an internal examination.　　　　　　　〔doctor.

내진(來診) ¶ ~을 청하다 send for a

내진(耐震) ¶ ~성의 earthquake-proof (-resistant). ‖ ~건물 (구조) an earthquake-proof building (construction).

내쫓기다 《밖으로》 be expelled; be turned out; 《해고》 be dismissed; be fired.

내쫓다 ① 《밖으로》 expel; turn (send, drive) out. ②《해고》 dismiss; fire; 《아내를》 divorce.

내착(來着) arrival. ~하다 reach; arrive 《at, in》.　　　　〔tic) loan.

내채(內債) an internal 《a domes-

내처《잇달아》 continuously; without a pause (break); 《단숨에 끝까지》 at a stretch (breath). ¶ 여섯 시간 ~ 일하다 work for six hours without a break / 읽던 책을 ~ 끝까지 다 읽다 read a book at one sitting.

내출혈(內出血) 【醫】 internal bleeding (hemorrhage). ¶ ~을 하다 bleed internally.

내치(內治) ① 《내정》 home administration. ② 《내과 치료》 internal treatment.

내치다《요구를》 reject; turn down; 《물리치》 drive back (out, away).

내친걸음 ¶ ~이다 We are already in it with both feet. *or* We have gone too far to retreat.

내키다 《마음이》 feel inclined; feel like 《doing》; have a mind to

내탐(內探) a private inquiry; a secret investigation. ∥ ~하다 make private inquiries.

내통(內通) secret communication; betrayal. ∥ ~하다 communicate secretly with 《a person》; betray 《a person》 to 《the enemy》; 《남녀가》 have improper relations 《with》. ∥ ~자 a betrayer.

내포(內包) 【論】 connotation. ∥ ~하다 involve; connote.

내핍(耐乏) austerity. ∥ ~하다 practice austerities; lead [bear] a hard life. ∥ ~생활 a life of austerity; belt-tightening.

내한(來韓) a visit to Korea; arrival in Korea. ∥ ~하다 visit 〔come to〕 Korea. ¶ ~중인 넬슨 씨 Mr. Nelson now visiting Korea.

내한(耐寒) ¶ ~의 coldproof 〔-성의 cold-resistant 〔-tolerant〕 《plants》; (winter-)hardy 《grasses》. ∥ ~훈련 training for endurance in low temperatures.

내항(內港) the inner harbor.

내항(內項) 【數】 internal terms.

내항(內航) coastal service. ∥ ~로(路) a coasting line 〔route〕 / ~선 a coasting liner / ~해운사업 coastal shipping.

내항(來航) a visit 《to Korea》. ~하다 《a ship》 come on a visit. ¶ 엘리자베스호의 ~을 환영하다 welcome a visit of the Elizabeth to Korea.

내향(內向) ¶ ~하다 turn in upon *oneself*. ¶ ~적인 사람 an introvert. ∥ ~성 【心】 introversion.

내화(內貨) 【經】 local currency.

내화(耐火) fireproofing. ¶ ~의 fireproof / ~성이 있다 be able to resist fire. ∥ ~건물 a fireproof building / ~벽돌 a firebrick / ~재 fireproof material.

내환(內患) the sickness of *one's* wife. ② ☞ 내우.

내후년(來後年) three years hence.

냄비 a pan (얕은); a pot (깊은). ∥ ~국수 pot-boiled noodles / ~뚜껑 a pot lid / ~요리 a dish served in the pot.

냄새 ① 《일반적인》 smell; odor; scent; 《향내》 fragrance; perfume; 《악취》 stench; stink 《of oil》; reek 《of garlic》. ¶ ~나다 smell; have a smell 《of tobacco》 / ~가 좋다(나쁘다) smell sweet(bad) / ~맡다 smell 《flowers》 / ~를 피우다 send forth 〔emit〕 a smell. ② 《느낌·낌새》 ¶ 범죄 행위의 ~ a sign 〔an indication〕 of a foul play / 일상 생활의 ~가 물씬 나는 수필 an essay which captures the mood of daily life.

냅다[1] 《연기가》 (be) smoky. ¶ 아이, 내워 Oh, how smoky!

냅다[2] 《몹시》 violently; severely; 《빨리》 at full speed; in all haste. ¶ ~ 달아나다 flee in all haste.

냇가 a riverside; the bank 〔edge〕 of a river 〔stream〕.

냇내 the smell of smoke; smoky 〔scent〕.

냉(冷) 《대하증》 leucorrhea; 《몸·배의》 a body 〔stomach〕 chill.

냉…(冷) cold; iced. ∥ ~국 soup prepared cold / ~육 cold meat / ~커피 iced coffee.

냉각(冷却) cooling; refrigeration. ~하다 refrigerate; cool (down). ∥ ~기(器) a freezer; a refrigerator / ~기간 a cooling-off period / ~수(액) (a) coolant / ~장치 a cooling device 〔apparatus〕 / ~1차수 the primary cooling water.

냉간(冷間) ∥ ~압연공장 a cold strip iron mill.

냉기(冷氣) cold; chill. ¶ 아침의 ~를 느끼다 feel the morning chill.

냉난방(冷暖房) air conditioning; an air conditioner. ∥ ~완비《게시》 Air-conditioned.

냉담(冷淡) coolness; indifference. ~하다 (be) cool; cold; indifferent; half-hearted / ~하게 coolly; coldly; indifferently; half-heartedly.

냉대(冷待) ☞ 푸대접. 〔-ledly.

냉동(冷凍) freezing; refrigeration. ~하다 freeze; refrigerate. ¶ ~보존하다 keep 《something》 in a freezer / 급속 ~하다 freeze 《food》 quickly; quick-freeze. ∥ ~고(庫) a freezer / ~기(機) a freezing machine; a refrigerator / ~냉장고 a refrigerator with a deep freezer / ~마취 refrigeration anesthesia; cryoanesthesia / ~선(車) a refrigerator boat 〔car〕 / ~식품〔생선〕 frozen food〔fish〕.

냉랭하다(冷冷—) 《한랭》 (be) very cold; chilly; 《냉담》 (be) cold; unfriendly; cold-hearted.

냉면(冷麵) buckwheat vermicelli served in cold soup; *naengmyŏn*.

냉방(冷房) 《찬 방》 an unheated room; 《행위》 air conditioning. ~하다 air-condition 《a room》. ∥ ~병 a cooling disorder / ~장치 air-conditioning; an air-conditioner / ~차 an air-conditioned car.

냉소(冷笑) a cold 〔sardonic〕 smile; a sneer; a derision. ~하다 smile derisively; sneer 《at》.

냉수(冷水) cold water. ∥ ~마찰 a cold-water rubbing 《~마찰을 하다 rub *oneself* with a cold wet towel》 / ~욕 a cold-water bathing 《~욕을 하다 take a cold bath》.

냉습(冷濕) ~하다 (be) cold and moist [damp].

냉엄(冷嚴) ~하다 (be) grim; stern. ¶ ~한 현실 grim realities of life.

냉이 〖植〗 a shepherd's-purse.

냉장(冷藏) cold storage. ~하다 keep (*a thing*) in cold storage; refrigerate. ‖ ~고 a refrigerator; an icebox 《美》.

냉전(冷戰) a cold war.

냉정(冷情) ~한 cold(-hearted); pitiless; heartless.

냉정(冷靜) calmness; coolness. ~하다 (be) calm; cool. ¶ ~한 사람 a cool-headed person / ~히 calmly; coolly / ~을 잃다 lose *one's* temper; be (get) excited.

냉차(冷茶) iced tea; ice (cold) tea.

냉철(冷徹) ~한 (be) cool-headed; hardheaded (빈틈없는).

냉큼 promptly; instantly; at once.

냉해(冷害) ~(suffer much) damage from (by) cold weather.

냉혈(冷血) 〖온혈에 대한〗 cold-bloodedness; 〖무정〗 cold-heartedness; heartlessness. ~의 cold-blooded(-hearted); heartless. ‖ ~동물 a cold-blooded animal / ~한(漢) a cold-hearted fellow.

냉혹(冷酷) cruelty; heartlessness. ¶ ~한 cruel; unfeeling; heartless; cold-hearted.

냠냠 Yum-yum! ~하다 〖먹고 싶어〗 want to eat; 〖갖고 싶어〗 have an itch (*for a thing*). ¶ ~거리다 go yum-yum; smack *one's* lips. ‖ ~이 dainty food; a delicacy.

냥(兩) 〖단위〗 a *nyang*. ¶ 엽전 열 ~ ten copper *nyang*.

너 〖2인칭〗 you. ¶ ~의 your 〖에게〗 you.

너구리 〖動〗 a raccoon dog.

너그러이 leniently; generously; liberally. ¶ ~ 용서하다 forgive generously.

너그럽다 (be) lenient; liberal. ¶ 너그러운 태도 generous attitude / 너그러운 관대 a lenient sentence.

너나없이 ~ 모두 all (both) (*of us*); everyone; everybody.

너더분하다 (be) disorderly; untidy; messy; confused; tedious (상황). ¶ ~분하게 늘어놓아있다 be in an untidy state; be in a mess.

너더너더 ~기운 patchy; full of patches 〖옷〗 ~ 깁다 put up *one's* clothes all over.

너덜거리다 flutter; dangle in tatters. ¶ 바람에 너덜거리는 찢어진 커튼 the torn curtain fluttering in the wind. 〖tered〗; ragged.

너덜너덜 ~한 worn-out; tattered.

너덧 about four (*people*).

너르다 (be) wide; vast; extensive;

spacious; roomy (집이).

너머 the opposite (other) side (*of*); across. ¶ 산 ~에 across (beyond) a mountain / 어깨 ~로 over *one's* shoulder / 그 마을은 언덕 ~에 있다 The village lies beyond the hill.

너무 too (much); over; excessively. ¶ ~ 젊다 (크다) be too young (large); ~ 먹다 eat too much.

너부죽이 flat; pronely. ¶ ~ 엎드리다 lay *oneself* flat. 〖broad.

너부죽하다 (be) somewhat flat and

너불거리다 flutter; flap; wave.

너비 width; breadth. ¶ ~가 넓 (좁)다 be wide (narrow)(in width) / ~가 5피트다 be five feet wide.

너새 ① 〖鳥〗 a great bustard. ② 〖建〗 a hip. ¶ ~지붕 a hip(ped) roof.

너스레 ① 〖걸치는 것〗 a frame of crosspieces (put over an opening). ② 〖허튼 수작〗 a sly remark; a practical joke. ¶ ~를 떨다 make a sly remark; play a practical joke (*on*).

너울 a lady's (black) veil.

너울거리다 〖물결이〗 wave; roll; 〖나무·풀이〗 flutter; undulate; waver.

너울너울 waving; swaying. ¶ ~ 춤을 추다 dance with swaying arms. 〖disorderly.

너저분하다 (be) untidy; shabby;

너절하다 〖추접하다〗 (be) mean; vulgar; disgusting; 〖허름하다〗 (be) shabby; poor looking; seedy; 〖시시하다〗 (be) worthless; rubbishy. ¶ 너절한 옷 shabby clothes / 너절한 이야기 a disgusting story.

너털거리다 ☞ 너털거리다.

너털웃음 a good (hearty) laugh; loud laughter; a guffaw.

너펄거리다 flutter (flap, sway, wave) in the wind.

너희 you; you people (folks).

넉가래 a wooden shovel; a snow shovel. ¶ ~질하다 shovel (*grain*, *snow*).

넉넉하다 (be) enough; sufficient. ¶ 넉넉히 enough; sufficiently; fully; well / 살림이 ~ be well off / 시간이 ~ have plenty of time / 치수가 ~ have ample measure.

넉살좋다 (be) impudent (cheeky) 〖서술적〗 have (a lot of) nerve. ¶ 너 참 넉살좋구나 What a nerve you've got!

넋 a soul; a spirit (정신). ¶ ~을 잃고 beside *oneself*; vacantly; absent-mindedly / ~을 잃다 lose *one's* senses; become (get) absent-minded / ~을 위로하다 pray for the repose of the departed soul.

넋두리 〖무당의〗 spiritualism; 〖푸

넌더리 a complaint; a grumble. ~하다 make complaints; grumble 〈at, over〉; bewail one's lot.
넌더리 ¶ ~ 나다 be sick of; be fed up 〈with〉; get weary of / ~ 나게 하다 make 《a person》 sick; weary 《with》.
넌센스 ☞ 난센스.
넌지시 tacitly; allusively; implicitly; indirectly; in a casual way. ¶ ~ 말하다 hint 〈at〉; / ~ 경고하다 give a veiled warning / ~ 돈을 요구하다 make a tacit demand for money.
널 ① 《널빤지》 a board; a plank. ¶ ~ 을 깔다 lay boards 〈on〉; board 〈over〉 / 두께 2센치의 ~ a board two centimeters thick. ② 《관》 a coffin; a casket. ¶ ~ 에 넣다 lay in a coffin. ③ 《널뛰기의》 a seesaw board.
널다 《볕·바람에》 spread 《grains》 out; air 《clothes, mats》; hang 《something》 out to dry; dry up 〈off〉. ¶ 젖은 옷을 ~ hang wet clothes 〈out〉 to dry.
널따랗다 (be) wide; extensive; spacious; roomy.
널뛰기 〈play〉 seesaw; teeter-totter.
널리 widely; far and wide; generally (일반적으로). ¶ ~ 세상에 알려지다 be widely known / 세계를 여행하다 travel far and wide in the world.
널리다 ① ☞ 넓히다. ② 《흩어져 있다》 be spread 〈scattered〉 《over, around》. ¶ 간선 도로변에 널려 있는 농가들 farm houses scattered along the highway.
널빤지 a board; a plank.
널찍하다 ☞ 널따랗다. ¶ 널찍이 widely; spaciously.
넓다 ① 《폭·넓이가》 (be) broad; wide; large; extensive; spacious; roomy. ¶넓은 의미로 in a broad sense / 시야가 넓다 have a broad outlook 〈on〉. ② 《마음이》 (be) broadminded; generous.
넓이 《폭》 width; breadth; 《면적》 area; floor space(건물의); extent (범위). ¶ 정원의 ~ the area of the garden / 지식의 ~ the extent of one's knowledge.
넓이뛰기 the broad jump. ¶ 제자리 ~ the standing broad jump.
넓적다리 the thigh.
넓적하다 (be) flat (and wide).
넓죽 ① 《입을》 with one's mouth wide open; 《주저없이》 without hesitation. ② 《몸을》 flat. ¶ ~ 엎드리다 prostrate oneself.
넓히다 widen; enlarge; broaden; extend. ¶ 운동장을 ~ enlarge the playground / 지식〈견문〉을 ~ broaden 〈extend〉 one's knowledge.
넘겨다보다 look over(넘어다보다); 「covet (탐내다).
넘겨씌우다 put [fix] 《a blame》 on another; lay 《a fault》 at another's door; impute 《the accident》 〈to〉.
넘겨잡다 guess 〈out〉; suppose; conjecture.
넘겨짚다 make a random guess; speculate 〈on, about〉; guess; make a shot 〈at〉. ¶ 남의 의도를 ~ guess a person's intention / 넘겨 짚어 말해 보다 try a shot in the dark.
넘고처지다 be either too long or too short; be not in proportion to; be not suitable.
넘기다 ① 《인도》 hand 〈over〉; turn over; transfer; pass. ¶ 범인을 경찰에 ~ hand over a criminal to the police / 다음 사람에게 ~ pass 《a thing》 to the next person. ② 《넘어뜨리다》 throw down; overthrow. ③ 《기한 등을》 pass. ¶ 기한을 ~ pass a fixed term. ④ 《이월》 carry over 〈forward〉. ¶ 남은 회비를 내년으로 ~ carry forward the remaining dues to next year. ⑤ 《극복해내다》 get over 〈through〉; overcome; ride out 《the trouble》. ¶ 그의 도움으로 경제적 위기를 ~ get through the financial crisis with his help. ⑥ 《젖히다》 turn over 《the pages of a book》.
넘나다 behave out of keeping with one's station; get out of line.
넘나들다 frequent; make frequent access 〈to〉. ¶ 문턱이 닳도록 ~ frequent a 《person's》 house.
넘다 ① 《넘어》 cross; go over; go [get] beyond; clear. ¶ 산을 넘어 나아가다 go on over the mountain. ② 《초과》 exceed; pass; be over 〈above, more than〉. ¶ 마흔이 넘었다 he be over forty. ③ 《범람》 overflow; flow over. ¶ 강물이 둑을 넘었다 The river has overflowed its banks.
넘버 a number; 《자동차 번호판》 a license (number) plate. ‖ ~링머신 a numbering machine / ~ 원 No. 1; number one; A-1.
넘보다 hold 《a person》 cheap; make light of 《a person》; look down on; underestimate. ¶ 그를 단순한 어린애라고 ~ make light of him as a mere child.
넘성거리다 《탐이 나서》 stretch 《crane》 one's neck with envy.
넘실거리다 surge; roll; swell. ¶ 파도가 크게 넘실거리고 있었다 The waves were surging heavily.
넘어가다 ① 《때·시간이》 expire; be over; overdue. ¶ 기한이 ~ the term expires. ② 《해·달이》 sink; set; go down. ¶ 해가 ~ the sun

넘어뜨리다 164 **노그라지다**

sets [sinks]. ③ 《쓰러지다》 fall (down); come down; collapse. ¶ 앞으로 [뒤로] ~ 잇달아 fall forward [backward]. ④ 《망하다》 go [become] bankrupt(회사가); go to ruin; be overthrown [ruined]. ¶ 정부가 ~ a government is overthrown / 기업이 잇따라 넘어갔다 Businesses have gone bankrupt one after another (*this month*). ⑤ 《남의 손으로》 pass into (*another's*) hands [possession]; change hands. ¶ 토지는 그 회사로 넘어갔다 The land passed into the hands of the firm. ⑥ 《속다》 be cheated [deceived]. ¶ 너는 그의 얌전한 듯한 태도에 넘어갔다 You are deceived by his quiet manner. ⑦ 《음식물이》 be swallowed.

넘어뜨리다 ① 《넘어지게 하다》 throw [tumble] down; knock over; overthrow; fell. ¶ 바람이 나무들을 넘어뜨렸다 The wind blew down several trees. ② 《지우다》 defeat; beat. ③ 《전복》 overthrow.

넘어서다 pass [get] over. ¶ 어려운 고비를 ~ get over the hump [the hard period].

넘어오다 ① 《넘어서 이쪽으로》 come over [across]. ¶ 국경을 ~ come over [across] the border line (*to*). ② 《제 차지로》 come into *one's* hand; be turned over.

넘어지다 fall (down); come down; drop; tumble down. ¶ 《돌에》 걸려 ~ stumble [trip, fall] over (a stone).

넘치다 ① 《범람》 overflow; flow [run, brim] over (*with*); flood; be full of. ¶ 기쁨에 ~ be full of joy. ② 《초과》 exceed; be above [beyond]. ¶ 분에 넘치는 영광 an undeserved honor.

넙치 [魚] a flatfish; a halibut.

넝마 old clothes; rags. ¶ ~ 장수 a ragman; a junkman / ~ 주이 a ragpicker.

넣다 ① 《속에》 put in [into]; set [let] in; stuff (속에). ¶ 커피에 우유를 ~ put milk into coffee / 주머니에 손을 ~ put *one's* hand in [into] *one's* pocket / 이불에 솜을 ~ stuff bedclothes with cotton (wool). ② 《학교 등에》 send [put] (*to*); 《입장》 admit. ¶ 학교에 ~ put [send] (*a child*) to school. ③ 《포함》 include. ¶ 이자를 넣어서 [넣지 않고] 2만 원 twenty thousand *won*, inclusive [exclusive] of interest.

네¹ ① 《너》 you. ¶ ~가 잘못했다 You are to blame. ② 《너의》 your. ¶ ~ 아들 your son.

네² 《넷》 four. ¶ ~ 사람 four people. ¶ 낸시~ Nancy's family.

…네 《들》 ¶ 우리~ we / 낸시~

네가 《필름》 negative (film).
네거리 a crossroads; a crossing.
네글리제 a negligee.
네까짓 ¶ ~ 놈[년] such a creature [a wench] as you / ~ 것 the likes of you.
네댓 four or five; several. ¶ ~ 새 a few days.
네덜란드 the Netherlands. ¶ ~ 의 Dutch / ~ 말 Dutch / ~ 사람 a Dutchman.
네모 a square. ¶ ~ 난 four-cornered; square. ¶ ~ 꼴 a quadrilateral; a tetragon.
네발짐승 a quadruped.
네쌍둥이(一雙童一) quadruplets.
네온 [化] neon (기호 Ne). ¶ ~ 사인 neon lights [signs].
네이블 [植] a navel orange.
네이팜 [軍] napalm. ¶ ~ 탄 a napalm bomb. 「fourth place.
네째 the fourth; No. 4; the
네커치프 a neckerchief.
네크리스 a necklace.
네트 a net. ¶ ~ 워크 a network.
네티즌 [컴] a netizen; a user of the internet. (◀ *network*+*citizen*)
네팔 Nepal. ¶ ~ 의 Nepalese / ~ 말 Nepali / ~ 사람 a Nepalese.
네활개 ¶ ~ 치다 strut; swagger; 《비유적》 behave triumphantly [in high spirits].
넥타이 a necktie; a tie. ¶ ~ 핀 a tiepin; a stickpin (美). 「four.
넷 four. ¶ ~ 으로 자르다 cut in
녀석 a fellow; a guy; a chap.
년 a woman; a bitch; a wench.
년(年) a year.
녘 toward(s). ¶ 해뜰 ~ toward daylight / 동 ~ (the) east.
노(櫓) an oar; a paddle; a scull. ¶ ~ 를 젓다 pull an oar; row; scull (*a boat*).
노…(老) old; aged. ¶ ~ 신사 an old gentleman.
노구(老軀) *one's* old bones (body).
노간주나무 [植] a juniper tree.
노경(老境) old [advanced] age; *one's* declining years. ¶ ~ 에 들다 be in *one's* old age.
노고(勞苦) labor; pains; toil. ¶ ~ 를 아끼지 않다 spare no pains.
노곤하다(勞困一) (be) tired; exhausted; weary; languid.
노골(露骨) ¶ ~ 적인 《솔직한》 plain; outspoken; frank; open; 《음란한》 indecent / ~ 적으로 plainly; outspokenly; openly / ~ 적인 표현을 피하다 avoid frank expression / 그 그림은 너무 ~ 적이다 The picture is too suggestive.
노구라지다 ① 《지치다》 be tired out; be exhausted; be dead tired. ¶ 노구라져 깊이 잠들다 fall asleep dog-tired. ② 《빠지다》 be infatuated (*with, by*); give *one*-

노기 165 **노릇**

노기(怒氣) anger; wrath; indignation. ¶ ~등등하다 be in a black rage; be furious / ~충천하다 boil with rage.

노끈 a string; a cord.

노년 old [advanced] age. ‖ ~기 senescence; old age / ~성 치매 senile dementia / ~의학 geriatirics.

노느매기 distribution; sharing; division. ~하다 share 《with》; distribute 《among》; divide 《between》; allot 《to》.

노닐다 stroll [ramble] about; saunter [lounge] around 《about》.

노다지 a rich mine; a bonanza. ¶ ~를 캐다 strike a bonanza.

노닥거리다 keep chatting [joking]; be bantering away.

노대(露臺) [建] a balcony; an open-air platform [stage].

노대가(老大家) an old [a great] master; a veteran [venerable] authority [in].

노도(怒濤) raging billows; angry waves; a high sea.

노독(路毒) (sickness from) the fatigue of travel. ¶ ~을 풀다 take a good rest after one's journey.

노동(勞動) labor; toil; work. ~하다 labor; work; toil. ¶ 하루 8시간 ~제 daily eight-hour working system / 주 5일 [40시간] ~ a 5-day (40-hour) (working) week / 하루 8시간 ~하다 work eight hours a day. ‖ ~계약 a labor contract / ~관계 조정법 the Labor Relations Adjustment Act / ~당(黨) the Labor Party / ~ 당원 a Laborite / ~력 labor-power; labor (power) / ~문제 a labor problem / ~법 labor law / ~부 the Ministry of Labor / ~생산성 labor productivity / ~시간 working hours / ~시장 the labor market / ~운동 a labor movement / ~인구 working population; labor force / ~자 a laborer ☞ 근로자 / ~재해 an industrial accident / ~재해보상 compensation for workmen's accident / ~쟁의 labor troubles [disputes] / ~절 May Day; Labor Day (美) / ~조건 working [labor] conditions / ~조합 a labor union (美); a trade union (英) / ~환경 labor environment / 정신 ~ mental work.

노랑 yellow; yellow dyes(물감).

노랑이 ① (노란 것) a yellow thing [one]. ② (인색한 이) a miser; a stingy person.

노랗다 (be) yellow.

노래 a song; a ballad; singing (창가). ~하다 sing (a song). ¶ ~를 잘하다 be a good singer / 피아노에 맞춰 ~하다 sing to the piano / 곡 (가락)에 맞게 [틀리게] ~하다 sing in (out of) tune. ‖ ~자랑 an amateurs' singing contest / ~랫소리 a singing voice.

노래기 (一蟲) a millipede; a myriapod.

노래방(一房) a Noraebang; a Korean commercial singing establishment (where one can sing a song to musical accompaniment while reading the lyrics on a video monitor).

노략질(擄掠一) plunder(ing); pillage. ~하다 pillage; despoil; plunder; loot. [other].

노려보다 glare (stare) at 《each

노력(努力) (an) endeavor; (an) effort; exertion. ~하다 endeavor; strive for; make efforts; exert oneself. ¶ 온갖 ~을 다하다 make all possible efforts; do one's best / 그의 ~은 보답되었다 His efforts were rewarded. / 모든 ~은 수포로 돌아갔다 All my efforts were in vain. / ~한 보람으로 thanks to one's efforts. ‖ ~가 a hard worker / ~상 a prize (awarded) for effort.

노력(勞力) 《수고》 trouble; pains; effort; (노동) labor. ¶ ~이 드는 일 laborious work / ~을 제공하다 offer personal labor / 회사 재건에 ~을 아끼지 않겠다 I'll spare no effort (pains) to reconstruct the company.

노련(老鍊) ¶ ~한 experienced; veteran; expert; skilled / ~한 선수 a veteran player / ~한 솜씨 masterly skill (dexterity) / ~한 교사 an experienced teacher / ~한 사람 an expert; a veteran.

노령(老齡) old [advanced] age. ¶ ~의 신사 an old gentleman. ‖ ~화 사회 an aging society.

노루 〔動〕 a roe (deer). ‖ ~잠 a light sleep; a catnap.

노루발장도리 a claw hammer.

노르스름하다 (be) yellowish.

노르웨이 Norway. ‖ ~의 Norwegian / ~사람 (a) Norwegian.

노른자(위) the yolk (of an egg) / (비유적) the most valuable (important) part of a place.

노름 gambling; gaming; betting (내기). ~(질)하다 gamble; play for stakes (money). ¶ ~꾼 a gambler; a gamester / ~판 a gambling place (house).

노릇 (역할) a part; a role; (일) a job; work; (기능) function. ¶ 선생~ a teaching job; teaching / 바보 ~을 하다 act (play) the fool / 사람 ~을 다하다 discharge

노리개 (장신구) a pendent trinket; (장난감) a plaything; a toy.
노리다¹ ① (냄새가) (be) stinking; fetid; (서술적) smell like burning hair(타는); smell like a skunk (동물의). ‖ 노린내 a stench; the smell of a skunk. ② (다랍다) (be) mean; stingy.
노리다² (목표·기회 등을) (take) aim 《at》; have an eye 《to》; watch 《for》 (기회를); aspire 《to, after》. ¶ 기회를 ~ watch for a chance / 목숨을 ~ seek 《a person's》 life / 높은 지위를 ~ aspire to a high position.
노망(老妄) dotage; senility. ~하다 be in one's dotage; become [get] senile.
노면(路面) the road surface. ¶ ~ 재포장 공사가 여기저기서 진행 중이다 Resurfacing work is being carried out here and there. ‖ ~동결 《게시》 Icy [Frozen] road. / ~전차 a surface [street] car / ~포장 road surfacing.
노모(老母) one's old [aged] mother.
노목(老木) an old [aged] tree.
노무(勞務) labor; work. ‖ ~과(課) the labor section / ~관리 personnel [labor] management / ~자 a worker; a laborer.
노반(路盤) a roadbed.
노발대발(怒發大發) ~하다 be furious; be in a towering rage.
노방(路傍) the road [路邊] the roadside (wayside). ‖ 노방초 grass at [by] the roadside.
노벨 (스웨덴의 화학자) Alfred Bernhard Nobel(1833-96). ‖ ~상 a Nobel prize / ~상 수상자 a Nobel prize winner / ~평화상 the Nobel prize for peace. [fireside chat.
노변(爐邊) the fireside. ‖ ~집담
노병(老兵) an old soldier; a war veteran. ¶ ~은 죽지 않고 사라질 뿐이다 Old soldiers never die, they only fade away.
노복(奴僕) a manservant.
노부(老父) one's old [aged] father.
노부모(老父母) one's aged [old] parents. [vants; domestics.
노비(奴婢) male and female ser-
노비(路費) traveling expenses.
노사(勞使) capital and labor; labor and management. ‖ ~관계 the relations between labor and capital / ~분쟁 a labor management dispute / ~불일(不一) the amicable labor-management relations / ~정(政)위원회 the labor-management-government commission / ~협의회 a joint labor-management conference / ~협조 cooperation [harmonization] of capital and labor.

노산(老産) delivery in one's old age. ~하다 deliver a child in one's old age.
노상(늘) always; all the time; habitually (버릇으로).
노상(路上) ¶ ~에서 by the roadside; on the street. ‖ ~강도 a highwayman; a holdup (man) / ~강도짓을 하다 commit highway [動] a mule. [robbery).
노새
노색(怒色) anger; an angry look.
노선(路線) a route; a line; a course. ¶버스 ~ a bus service route / 정치 ~ (one's) political
노성(怒聲) an angry voice. [line.
노소(老少) young and old; age and youth. ¶ ~를 막론하고 without distinction of age.
노송(老松) an old pine tree.
노쇠(老衰) infirmity of old age; decrepitude; senility. ~하다 be old and infirm; grow senile. ¶ ~하여 죽다 die of old age. ‖ ~기 senescence.
노숙(老熟) ☞ 노련. ~하다 attain maturity; mature; mellow.
노숙(露宿) camping (out). ~하다 sleep in the open air; camp out. [ness.
노스탤지어 nostalgia; homesick-
노심초사(勞心焦思) ~하다 be consumed with worry; exert one's mind; be worried.
노아(聖) Noah. ¶ ~의 홍수 the Flood; Noah's flood; the Deluge / ~의 방주 Noah's ark.
노아웃(野) no out. ¶ ~에 만루다 The bases are loaded with no outs.
노안(老眼) 〔醫〕 presbyopia; farsightedness due to old age. ¶ 나이를 먹을수록 ~ 증상이 심해졌다 My eyesight has got dimmer and dimmer with age. ‖ ~경 spectacles for the aged.
노약자(老弱者) the old and the weak. [language.
노어(露語) Russian; the Russian
노여움 anger; rage; indignation; displeasure. ¶ ~을 사다 arouse [excite] 《a person's》 anger; incur [provoke] 《a person's》 anger [wrath, displeasure].
노여워하다 be offended [displeased] 《at》; feel hurt; get angry 《with, at, about》.
노역(勞役) work; labor; toil. ~하다 labor; work.
노염 ☞ 노여움.
노엽다 feel bitter 《about, at》; be [feel] vexed 《at, with》; be offended 《with》; feel hurt. ¶ 그의 말이 ~ I'm offended at his remark.
노예(奴隷) a slave (사람); slavery (신세). ¶ ~ 같은 slavish; servile / ~처럼 일하다 work like a slave /

그는 돈의 ~다 He is a slave to [of] money. ‖ ~근성 a servile spirit / ~제도 slavery / ~폐지운동 an anti-slavery movement / ~해방 emancipation of slaves.
노유(老幼) the young and the old.
노이로제 【醫】 neurosis; (a) nervous breakdown. ¶ ~에 걸리다 become neurotic; have a nervous breakdown. ‖ ~환자 a neurotic.
노익장(老益壯) a vigorous old age. ¶ ~을 자랑하며 enjoy a green old age.
노인(老人) an old [aged] man; (총칭) the aged [old]; a senior citizen. ¶ ~의 집 (양로기관) a home for the aged; an old people's home. ‖ ~병 a disease of the aged / ~복지 old people's welfare; welfare for the aged / ~성 치매증 senile dementia; Alzheimer's disease / ~학 gerontology.
노임(勞賃) wages; pay. ☞ 임금. ¶ ~을 받다 (지불하다) receive [pay] wages.
노자(老子) Lao-tzu. ‖ ~사상 Taoism(도교).
노자(路資) traveling expenses.
노작(勞作) a laborious work. ¶ 다년간의 ~ the product of *one's* many years' labor.
노장(老將) a veteran (general); an old-timer. ‖ ~선수 a veteran player.
노적가리(露積一) a stack [rick] of grain in the open air.
노점(露店) a street stall; a booth; a roadside stand. ¶ ~을 내다 [하고 있다] open [keep] a street stall. ‖ ~가 open-air stall quarters / ~상(人) a stallkeeper; a street vendor.
노정(路程) (이수·거리) distance; mileage; the distance to be covered; (여정) an itinerary; the plan [schedule] for *one's* journey. ‖ ~표 a table of itinerary.
노정(露呈) exposure; disclosure. ~하다 expose; disclose.
노조(勞組) ☞ 노동 조합. ‖ ~간부 a union leader / ~원 a unionist; a union man. 「spinster.
노처녀(老處女) an old maid; a
노천(露天) the open air. ‖ ~의 open-air; outdoor. ‖ ~굴(堀) strip [opencut] mining / ~극장 an open-air theater.
노총(勞總) ¶ 한국 ~ the Federation of Korean Trade Unions / 민주 ~ The Korean Confederation of Trade Unions.
노총각(老總角) an old bachelor.
노출(露出) (an) exposure. ~하다 expose; bare; crop out (광맥이). ¶ ~된 exposed; bare; naked / 이 사진은 ~과다 [부족]이다 This picture is overexposed [underexposed]. ‖ ~계 【寫】 an exposure (a light) meter / ~광(狂) an exhibitionist / ~시간 exposure time / ~증 exhibitionism.
노친(老親) *one's* old parents.
노크 a knock; knocking. ~하다 knock (*at, on*).
노타이(셔츠) an open-necked shirt.
노트¹ 【海】 a knot. ¶ 20~를 내다 do [log] 20 knots.
노트² (필기) a note; (필기장) a notebook. ~하다 note [jot] down; take notes of [on] (*a lecture*).
노티(老一) signs of (old) age; looking old. ¶ ~가 나다 look old for *one's* age.
노파(老婆) an old woman.
노파심(老婆心) (지나친 친절) excessive (grandmotherly) kindness; (지나친 배려) excessive consideration [concern]. ¶ ~에서 한마디 충고하겠다 Let me give you a piece of advice though I know it's none of my business.
노폐물(老廢物) wastes. ‖ ~처리센터 a wastes treatment center.
노폭(路幅) the width of a street.
노하다(怒一) get angry; be offended; get mad (美).
노하우 know-how.
노형(老兄) 《당신》 you.
노호(怒號) a roar; a bellow. ~하다 roar; bellow.
노화(老化) aging. ~하다 age. ¶ ~는 다리부터 시작된다 Aging starts with one's legs. ‖ ~현상 the symptoms of aging.
노환(老患) the infirmities [diseases] of old age; senility. ¶ ~으로 죽다 die of old age.
노회(老獪) ~한 crafty; cunning; foxy / ~한 사내 an old fox.
노획(鹵獲) capture; seizer. ~하다 capture; seize; plunder. ‖ ~물 booty; spoil(s).
노후(老朽) superannuation. ¶ ~한 wornout; timeworn; superannuated; decrepit / ~화하다 become too old for work [use]; become superannuated. ‖ ~한 배 a superannuated vessel / ~시설 an outworn equipment.
노후(老後) *one's* old age. ¶ ~에 대비하다 provide for [against] *one's* old age / 마음 편히 ~를 보내다 spend *one's* remaining years in peace and quiet.
녹(祿) a fief; a stipend; an allowance. ¶ ~을 먹다 receive a stipend.
녹(綠) (금속의) rust. ¶ ~슬다 rust; get [become] rusty / ~슨 검

녹각 (鹿角) a deer's horn; an antler.

녹나무 [植] a camphor tree.

녹내장 (綠內障) [醫] glaucoma.

녹다 ① 〖열에 의해〗 melt; fuse 〖금속이〗; thaw 〖눈·얼음이〗; 〖액체에 의해〗 dissolve. ¶ 잘 녹는 easily soluble / 잘 녹지 않는 nearly insoluble / 얼음이 햇볕에 녹았다 The ice melted 〖thawed〗 in the sun. / 설탕은 물에 녹는다 Sugar dissolves in water. / 구리와 아연은 녹아서 놋쇠가 된다 Copper and zinc fuse into brass. ② 〖따뜻해지다〗 be warmed; get 〖become〗 warm. ¶ 달렸더니 몸이 녹았다 I got 〖became〗 warm after running. ③ 〖주색에〗 ruin *one*'s health 《*with dissipation*》; be infatuated 《enchanted》 with 《a girl》. ④ 〖혼나다〗 have a terrible experience; have a rough time (of it).

녹다운 a knock-down. ¶ ~시키다 knock 《a person》 down; floor (美).

녹두 (綠豆) [植] green 〖mung〗 beans. ‖ ~묵 mung-bean jelly.

녹로 (轆轤) a lathe; a potter's wheel; 〖고패〗 a pulley. ‖ ~세공 turnery.

녹록하다 (碌碌―) (be) useless; of little value; trivial; of no importance.

녹말 (綠末) starch; farina. ¶ ~질 (質)의 starchy; farinaceous.

녹변 (綠便) green shit 〖stool〗.

녹비 (鹿―) deerskin; buckskin.

녹비 (綠肥) green manure.

녹색 (綠色) green. ‖ ~신고(서) a green return.

녹신녹신하다 (be) very soft and flexible; tender; elastic; pliant.

녹아웃 a knockout (생략 K.O.). ¶ ~시키다 knock out.

녹엽 (綠葉) green leaves; green foliage 〖집합적〗.

녹용 (鹿茸) [韓醫] a young antler.

녹음 (綠陰) the shade of trees.

녹음 (綠音) recording. ¶ ~하다 record 《a speech》; make a recording 《of》; tape 〖테이프에〗; transcribe 《a program》. ¶ 강연을 테이프에 ~해도 좋습니까 May I record your lecture on tape? ‖ ~기 a (tape) recorder / ~기사 a recording engineer / ~방송 (electrical) transcription broadcasting / ~실 a recording room / ~장치 recording equipment / ~테이프 a recording tape.

녹이다 ① 〖녹게 함〗 melt 《ice》; fuse; smelt 《ore》; thaw 《frozen food》; dissolve 《salt in water》. ② 〖녹해하다〗 fascinate; enchant; charm; bewitch. ¶ 마음을 녹일 듯한 시선을 주다 give 〖cast〗 《him》 a melting glance. ③ 〖몸을〗 warm *oneself* 《*at*》; make 《*it*》 warm.

녹지 (綠地) a green tract of land. ‖ ~대 a green belt 〖zone〗.

녹진녹진하다 (be) soft and sticky.

녹차 (綠茶) green tea.

녹초 ¶ ~가 되다 be (utterly) exhausted 〖done up〗; be worn out; be dead tired.

녹화 (綠化) tree planting; afforestation. ~하다 plant trees 《*in an area*》; plant 《*an area*》 with trees. ¶ 도시의 ~ the greening of cities. ‖ ~운동 a tree-planting campaign.

녹화 (錄畵) videotape recording. ~하다 record 《a scene》 on videotape; videotape. ¶ 럭비 경기를 ~하다 record a rugby game on videotape / ~방송하다 broadcast a program recorded on videotape. ‖ ~방송 a filmed TV broadcast.

논 a rice 〖paddy〗 field. ¶ ~에 물을 대다 irrigate a rice field. ‖ ~도랑 a ditch around a rice paddy / ~두렁 a ridge between rice fields / ~두렁길 a footpath between rice paddies.

논 (論) ☞ ···론(論), 논하다.

논갈이 plowing a rice field. ~하다 plow 〖till〗 a rice field.

논객 (論客) a controversialist; a debater; a disputant.

논거 (論據) the basis of 〖grounds for〗 an argument. ¶ ~가 확실하다 《one's argument》 be well grounded / ···의 ~가 되다 supply argument for···.

논고 (論告) the prosecutor's final (concluding) speech.

논공행상 (論功行賞) the official recognition of distinguished services. ~하다 confer rewards 《honors》 according to the merits 《of》.

논구하다 (論究―) discuss thoroughly; make a full discussion.

논급하다 (論及―) 언급하다.

논고 a rice-field sluice gate.

논농사 (―農事) rice farming; rice cultivation. ~하다 do rice farming; cultivate rice.

논다니 a harlot; a prostitute.

논단 (論壇) the world of criticism; 〖언론계〗 the press; the world of journalism.

논란 (論難) (adverse) criticism; a charge; denunciation. ~하다 criticize; denounce; refute.

논리 (論理) logic. ¶ ~적인 logical / ~적으로 logically / ~적으로 설명

논문(論文) 〖일반적인〗 a paper 〖학회 등의〗; an essay 〖평론 등〗; 〖학술의〗 a treatise 〖졸업·학위의〗 a thesis; a dissertation 〖신문 등의〗 an article. ¶ ~을 쓰다 write a paper (thesis) (*on a subject*) / ~을 제출하다 submit (present) a thesis (*to*). ‖ ~ 심사 examination of theses / ~집 a collection of treatises. / ~답 a paddy field.
논문서(一文書) the title (deed) of
논박(論駁) refutation; confutation. ~하다 argue against; refute; confute.
논법(論法) logic; reasoning.
논봉(論鋒) the force of an argument. ¶ 예리한 ~ an incisive (a keen) argument.
논설(論說) 〖사설〗 a leading article; a leader 〖주로 英〗; an editorial 〖美〗; 〖논평〗 a comment. ‖ ~란 the editorial column / ~위원 an editorial (a leader) writer; an editorialist.
논술(論述) (a) statement. ~하다 state; set forth. ‖ ~식 시험 an essay-type examination (test).
논어(論語) the Analects of Confucius.
논외(論外) ~의 〖문제 안 되는〗 out of the question; 〖본제를 떠난〗 beside the question.
논의(論議) a discussion; an argument; a debate. ~하다 argue; dispute; discuss; debate. ¶ ~할 문제 a matter of argument (debate) / ~ 중이다 be under discussion / ~할 여지가 없다 be indisputable (inarguable).
논자(論者) a disputant; 〖논객〗 the writer 〖필자〗; an advocate (*of*) 〖주창자〗. ¶ 개혁론자 an advocate of reform.
논쟁(論爭) a dispute; (a) controversy. ~하다 argue (dispute) (*about, with*); take issue (*with a person on a matter*). ¶ ~의 여지가 있다 be debatable (open to argument (dispute)).
논전(論戰) wordy warfare; a battle of words; a controversy.
논점(論點) the point at issue (in question; under discussion).
논제(論題) a subject (theme, topic) for discussion. ¶ ~에서 벗어나다 stray (digress) from *one's* theme (topic).
논조(論調) the tone (tenor) of an argument. ¶ 신문의 ~ the tone of the press.
논죄(論罪) ~하다 rule; find.
논증(論證) proof; (a) demonstration. ~하다 demonstrate; prove.
논지(論旨) the drift (point) of an argument. ¶ ~를 명백히 하다 make *one's* point (of argument) clear.
논파(論破) ~하다 refute; confute; argue (talk) (*a person*) down.
논평(論評) (a) criticism; a comment; (a) review. ~하다 criticize; review; comment (*on*). ¶ 이 문제에 대한 신문의 ~ press (newspaper) comments on this subject / ~을 삼가다 reserve comment (*on*). ‖ ~가 fictioneer.
논픽션 nonfiction. ‖ ~작가 a nonfictioneer.
논하다(論─) discuss; argue; treat (*of*); deal with; talk (*about*). ¶ 정치를 ~ dicuss politics / 유전 공학의 위험성을 논하는 책 a book dealing with the hazards of genetic engineering / 이 논문은 공해 문제를 논하고 있다 This paper treats the problem of pollution.
놀¹ 〖하늘의〗 a glow in the sky. ¶ 저녁 ~ an evening glow; a red sunset.
놀² 〖파도〗 wild (raging) waves; billows; a heavy sea. ¶ ~이 치다 have a heavy sea.
놀다 ① 〖유희〗 play; 〖즐기다〗 amuse (enjoy) *oneself*; 〖행락〗 make a (pleasure) trip (*to*); go on an excursion; 〖유흥〗 make merry; have a spree. ¶ 숨바꼭질을 하며 ~ play hide-and-seek / 카드를 가지고 ~ play cards / 강에서 헤엄을 치고 ~ enjoy (*oneself*) swimming in the river. ② 〖휴식·무위〗 relax; idle (away); be idle; do nothing; loaf (*around*). ¶ 놀고 있는 사람 an idle man; an idler; an unemployed person 〖실직자〗 / 노는 날 a holiday / 놀고 지내다 live in idleness; live a life of ease 〖안락하게〗 / 놀고 있다 be out of work 〖무직〗. ③ 〖유휴〗 (lie) idle; be not in use. ¶ 노는 돈 idle money / 노는 기계 a machine not in use / 놀고 있는 땅 land lying idle. ④ 〖나사 따위가〗 be loose (unsteady). ¶ 나사가 논다 The screw is loose. / 이가 ~ have a loose tooth.
놀라다 ① 〖경악〗 be surprised (astonished, amazed, startled) (*at, to hear*); 〖공포·질겁〗 be frightened (scared) (*at*). ¶ 놀랄 만한 surprising; astounding; amazing / 놀라게 하다 startle; surprise. ② 〖경이〗 wonder (marvel) (*at*). ¶ 놀랄 만한 wonderful; marvellous / 아무의 용기에 ~ marvel at *a person's* courage.
놀라움 〖경이〗 wonder; 〖경악〗 surprise; astonishment; amazement; 〖공포〗 fright.
놀랍다 (be) wonderful; marvellous; surprising; amazing.

놀래다 surprise; astonish; amaze; startle; frighten(무섭게 하다); create a sensation(화제를 일으키다).

놀리다 ① 《조롱》 banter; ridicule; tease; play a joke on; make fun (sport) of 《*a person*》. ② 《놀게 하다》 let [have] 《*a boy*》 play; 《쉬게 하다》 give a holiday(휴일을 주다); leave 《*a person, a thing*》 idle (안 부리다). ¶ 공장을 ~ leave a factory idle. ③ 《움직이다》 move; set [put] in motion; operate; 《조종하다》 manipulate; work 《*puppets*》. ¶ 손발을 ~ move [work] one's arms and legs. ④ 《돈을》 lend out money; loan; lend money at interest. ¶ 2푼 이자로 돈을 ~ lend money at two percent interest.

놀림 banter; teasing; ridicule. ¶ 반 ~조로 partly for fun. ∥ ~감 (거리) an object of ridicule.

놀아나다 《남의 장단에》 play into another's hands; 《바람 피우다》 have an affair with 《*a person*》; play around 《미인》.

놀아먹다 lead a dissipated life.

놀이 《유희》 play; 《경기》 a game; a sport (야외의); 《오락》 amusement; pastime; a recreation; 《행락》 an outing; a picnic. ∥ ~터 a playground; a pleasure resort (유원지 등) / 꽃 ~ flower viewing.

놈 a fellow; a chap; a guy.

놈팡이 a disreputable (dissolute) fellow; 《건달》 a bum; a loafer.

놋 brass. ¶ ~쇠로 만든 brazen. ∥ ~그릇 brassware / ~세공 brasswork / ~점 a brassware shop.

놋쇠 ☞ 놋.

놋좆 (檻一) a rowlock; a thole (pin).

농 (弄) sport; a joke; a jest; fun; a pleasantry. ¶ 《반》 ~으로 (half) for fun (in joke, in jest).

농 (膿) pus. ☞ 고름.

농 (欌) 《장농》 a chest; a bureau 《美》; 《옷상자》 a trunk; a clothbox.

농가 (農家) a farmhouse.

농간 (弄奸) machination; a trick; an artifice; a wicked design; the techniques. ¶ ~을 부리다 play [use] tricks on 《*another*》; carry out a wicked design.

농경 (農耕) tillage; farming. ∥ ~민족 an agricultural tribe [people] / ~시대 the Agricultural Age.

농공 (農工) agriculture and industry.

농과 (農科) the agricultural department(학부); an agricultural course(과정). ∥ ~대학 an agricultural college.

농구 (農具) farm (agricultural) implements; farming tools.

농구 (籠球) basketball. ∥ ~선수 a basketball player.

농군 (農軍) a farmer [farmhand].

농기 (農期) the farming season.

농기구 (農機具) farming machines and implements; agricultural machinery(집합적).

농노 (農奴) a serf; serfdom (신분).

농단 (壟斷) monopolization; ~하다 monopolize; have 《*a thing*》 to oneself.

농담 (弄談) a joke; a jest; a prank. ~하다 crack [make] a joke; joke; jest. ¶ ~으로 for fun; for a joke / ~은 그만하고 joking (jesting) apart [aside] / ~을 진담으로 받아들이다 take a joke seriously.

농담 (濃淡) light and shade (명암); shade 《*of color*》. ¶ ~을 나타내다 shade 《*a painting*》.

농도 (濃度) thickness; density; 〖化〗 concentration. ¶ 바닷물의 염분 ~를 측정하다 measure the concentration of salt in sea water.

농뗑이 a lazybones; an idler.

농락 (籠絡) ~하다 trifle [toy] with; make sport of. ¶ 여자를 ~하다 make sport of a woman / 남자에게 ~당하다 fall a prey to a man's lust.

농림 (農林) agriculture and forestry. ∥ ~부 the Ministry of Agriculture and Forestry.

농막 (農幕) a farm(er)'s hut.

농무 (農務) agricultural affairs.

농무 (濃霧) a dense fog. ∥ ~주의보 a dense fog warning.

농민 (農民) a farmer; a farmhand. [for farmers.

농번기 (農繁期) the busiest season

농본주의 (農本主義) physiocracy; the "agriculture-first" principle.

농부 (農夫) a farmer; a peasant.

농사 (農事) agriculture; farming. ¶ ~ 짓다 engage in agriculture; do farming; farm. ∥ ~시험장 an agricultural experiment station / ~철 the farming season.

농산물 (農産物) farm products (produce); the crops. ∥ ~가격 farm prices.

농성 (籠城) 《성을 지킴》 holding a castle; 《농성투쟁》 a sit-in; a sit-down (strike). ~하다 hold a castle; be besieged; be shut up; go on a sit-down (strike).

농수산 (農水産) agriculture and fisheries. ∥ ~물 agricultural and marine products.

농아 (聾啞) a deaf-and-dumb person; a deaf-mute. ∥ ~학교 a school for the deaf and dumb.

농악 (農樂) instrumental music of peasants. ∥ ~대 a farm band.

농약 (農藥) agricultural chemicals.

농어 ¶ ~을 뿌리다 spray 《*vegetables*》 with agricultural chemicals. ∥ 무야채 chemical-free vegetables; organic vegetables.

농어 〔魚〕 a sea bass; a perch.

농어촌(農漁村) farming and fishing villages 〔communities〕.

농업(農業) agriculture; farming. ¶ ~의 agricultural / ~에 종사하다 be engaged in agriculture / ~ 관련 산업 agribusiness. ∥ ~국 〔정책〕 an agricultural country 〔policy〕 / ~기술 agricultural techniques / ~인구 the farming population / ~학교 an agricultural school / ~협동조합 an agricultural cooperative (association) / ~협동조합 중앙회 the National Agricultural Cooperative Federation(생략 NACF).

농예(農藝) 〈농업기술〉 agricultural technology; 〈농업과 원예〉 agriculture and horticulture; farming and gardening. ∥ ~화학 agricultural chemistry.

농우(農牛) a plow ox; farming cattle.

농원(農園) a farm; a plantation.

농작(農作) farming. ∥ ~물 the crops; farm produce.

농장(農場) a farm; a plantation; a ranch 《美》. ∥ ~경영자 a farmer.

농정(農政) agricultural administration.

농지(農地) farmland; agricultural land. ∥ ~개량 improvement of farmland / ~개혁 an agrarian reform.

농지거리(弄―) joking; jesting.

농촌(農村) a farm village; a rural community; an agricultural district. ¶ ~의 rural; agrarian. ∥ ~문제 a rural 〔an agrarian〕 problem / ~지대 an agricultural region; a farm area / ~진흥청 the Rural Development Administration.

농축(濃縮) concentration. ~하다 concentrate; condense; enrich. ∥ ~세제 a concentrated detergent / ~우라늄 enriched uranium.

농토(農土) farmland; agricultural land.

농학(農學) agriculture. ∥ ~과 the department of agriculture.

농한기(農閑期) the farmer's slack 〔leisure〕 season; the off-season for farmers.

농후(濃厚) ~하다 (be) thick; dense; rich; heavy; strong. ¶ 전쟁이 일어날 가능성이 ~하다 There is a strong possibility of war.

높낮이 〈고저〉 high and low; 〈기복〉 unevenness; undulations.

높다 ① 〈장소·높이〉 (be) high; tall; lofty; elevated. ¶ 높은 산 a high mountain / 높은 건물 a tall 〔high〕 building. ② 〈지위·희망〉 (be) high; lofty; noble. ¶ 높은 사람 a dignitary; a high official / 높은 이상 a lofty ideal. ③ 〈음성〉 (be) loud; high-pitched. ¶ 높은 소리로 loudly; in a loud voice. ④ 〈값이〉 (be) high; expensive; costly. ¶ 높은 생활비 a high cost of living / 물가가 ~ Prices are high. ⑤ 〈비율·도수가〉 (be) high; strong. ¶ 도수 높은 안경 strong 〔powerful〕 glasses / 높은 이자 at a high interest.

높다랗다 (be) very high.

높이 〈명사〉 height; altitude〈고도〉; loudness〈소리의〉; pitch〈가락〉; 〈부사〉 high; aloft. ¶ ~가 5미터이다 It is five meters high 〔in height〕. / 하늘 ~ (fly) high up in the air / ~ 쳐들다 raise 《*a thing*》 high.

높이다 raise; elevate; enhance 《*the value*》; improve. ¶ 담을 ~ make a wall higher; raise a wall / 질을 ~ raise 〔improve〕 the quality.

높이뛰기 the high jump.

높직하다 (be) rather high.

놓다 ① 〈물건을〉 put; place; lay; set. ¶ 책상 위에 ~ put 《*a book*》 on the table / 덫을 ~ lay 〔set〕 a trap 《*for*》. ② 〈방면·방치〉 let go; set free; release; unloose. ¶ 잡은 손을 ~ let go one's hold. ③ 〈가설〉 build; construct; lay; install. ¶ 전화를 ~ install a telephone / 강에 다리를 ~ build 〔lay〕 a bridge over a river. ④ 〈총포를〉 fire (discharge, shoot) 《*a gun*》. ⑤ 〈불을〉 set fire to 《*a house*》. ⑥ 〈마음을〉 ease; set 《one's mind》 at ease; 〈방심〉 relax 《*one's attention*》. ⑦ 〈셈을〉 calculate; reckon; estimate. ¶ 주판으로 ~ reckon 〔count〕 on the abacus / 비용을 놓아보다 estimate the expense. ⑧ 〈주사·침을〉 inject; apply; give 《*injections*》. ¶ 침을 ~ needle; apply acupuncture. ⑨ 〈자수를〉 do embroidery 《*on*》; embroider 《*figures on*》. ⑩ 〈중간에 사람을〉 put in 《*as an intermediary*》; send 《*a person*》. ¶ 사람을 놓아 수소문하다 send a person for information. ⑪ 〈ㅡ해 두다〉 keep; have; leave. ¶ 문을 열어 ~ leave 〔keep〕 the door open. ⑫ 〈기타〉 ¶ 엄포를 ~ make a threat / 말을 ~ talk plainly / 돈을 4푼 이자로 ~ lend money at 4 percent interest / 속력을 ~ increase speed; speed up.

놓아두다 〈가만두다〉 let 《*a thing, a person*》 alone; leave 《*a matter*》 as it is.

놓아먹이다 pasture; graze 《cattle》.
놓아주다 let go; set 《a bird》 free; release 《a prisoner》.
놓이다 ① (얹히다) be put(set, laid, placed). ② (마음이) feel easy(at ease); feel(be) relieved.
놓치다 (쥔 것을) miss one's hold (of); drop; let slip; fail to catch (못 잡다); 《사람을》 let 《a person》 go; let 《a thief》 escape; (기회를) miss(lose) 《a chance》. ¶ 그릇을 ~ drop a dish; let a dish fall / 2시 부산행 항공편을 ~ miss the two o'clock flight to Pusan.
뇌(腦) [解] the brain. ¶ ~의 cerebral / ~의 손상 brain damage. ‖ ~경색 (a) cerebral infarction / ~성마비 cerebral palsy / ~세포 a brain cell / ~외과 brain surgery / ~졸중(卒中) a stroke; (cerebral) apoplexy 《~졸중에 걸리다 have a stroke》.
뇌격(雷擊) ~하다 attack with torpedoes; torpedo. ‖ ~기 a torpedo bomber(plane).
뇌관(雷管) a percussion cap; a detonator. ‖ ~장치 a percussion lock.
뇌까리다 repeat; harp on(upon).
뇌다 (말을) repeat; reiterate.
뇌리(腦裡) ¶ ~에 떠오르다 flash across one's mind; occur to one / ~에서 떠나지 않다 haunt one's memory / ~에 새겨지다 make a deep impression (on).
뇌막(腦膜) [醫] the meninges. ‖ ~염 meningitis; brain fever.
뇌명(雷鳴) ⇒ 뇌성.
뇌문(雷文) a fret. ‖ ~세공 fretwork.
뇌물(賂物) 《금품》 a bribe. ¶ ~이 통하는(통하지 않는) bribable(unbribable); corruptible(incorruptible) / ~을 주다 offer(give) a bribe / ~을 먹다 take(receive) a bribe; be bribed (by) / 그는 공직자에게 ~을 주어 그것을 하게 했다 He bribed the officials into doing it.
뇌병(腦病) a brain disease.
뇌빈혈(腦貧血) [醫] (have an attack of) cerebral anemia.
뇌사(腦死) [醫] brain (cerebral) death. ¶ ~상태의 brain-dead / ~를 선고하다 pronounce 《a person》 brain dead.
뇌성(雷聲) thunder; a roar(clap) of thunder. ‖ ~벽력 a thunderbolt.
뇌쇄(惱殺) ~하다 fascinate; enchant; charm; bewitch. ¶ 《사람을》 ~시키는 매력 (an) irresistible charm.
뇌수(腦髓) the brain.
뇌수술(腦手術) [醫] brain surgery. ~하다 perform an operation on the brain.
뇌신경(腦神經) [解] a cranial(cerebral) nerve. ‖ ~세포 a brain cell.
뇌염(腦炎) [醫] encephalitis. ‖ ~경보 a warning against the outbreak of encephalitis / ~모기 a culex mosquito; an encephalitis-bearing mosquito / ~증세 symptoms of encephalitis / ~환자 an encephalitis patient.
뇌우(雷雨) a thunderstorm.
뇌일혈(腦溢血) [醫] cerebral hemorrhage. ¶ ~을 일으키다 be stricken with cerebral hemorrhage.
뇌장(腦漿) [解] the fluid in the brain.
뇌장애(腦障碍) [醫] a brain injury; brain trouble. ¶ ~를 일으키다 suffer from brain trouble; get (be) injured in the brain.
뇌전(雷電) a thunderbolt.
뇌조(雷鳥) [鳥] a snow grouse; a ptarmigan.
뇌종양(腦腫瘍) brain tumor.
뇌진탕(腦震蕩) [醫] brain concussion.
뇌척수(腦脊髓) ‖ ~막염 [醫] cerebrospinal meningitis / ~액 [解] cerebrospinal fluid.
뇌출혈(腦出血) [醫] cerebral hemorrhage.
뇌충혈(腦充血) [醫] congestion of the brain; cerebral hyperemia.
뇌파(腦波) [醫] brain waves. ‖ ~검사 a brain wave test.
뇌하수체(腦下垂體) [解] the pituitary body(gland). [bosis.
뇌혈전(腦血栓) [醫] cerebral thrombosis.
누(累) trouble; implication; an evil influence(effect); involvement. ¶ 남에게 ~를 끼치다 get (involve) others in trouble; cause troubles to others; have a harmful (damaging) effect 《on》.
누(樓) a tower; a turret; a lookout (망루).
누(壘) a base. [out (망루).
누가(累加) cumulation. ~하다 increase cumulatively; accumulate.
누가복음(-福音) [聖] (the Gospel of) Luke.
누각(樓閣) a tower; a turret; a belvedere. ‖ 공중~ a castle in the air.
누계(累計) the (sum) total; the aggregate. ~하다 sum up; total. ¶ 어제 현재의 ~는 100만원이다 The aggregate comes to one million won as of yesterday.
누관(淚管) [解] a tear (lachrymal) duct.
누구 ① (의문) who (누가); whose (누구의); whom (누구에게, 누구를). ② (부정(不定)) anyone; anybody; any; some(one); whoever (누구든지, 누구나, 누구라도)

누그러뜨리다 soften; 《고통 따위를》 ease; lessen; relieve; 《감정을》 calm; appease; pacify; 《목소리를》 tone down; 《알맞게》 moderate. ¶ 진통제로 아픔을 ~ take some painkillers to relieve the pain / 목소리[태도]를 ~ soften one's voice (attitude).

누그러지다 soften; be softened; 《고통이》 be relieved [eased]; 《마음이》 be soothed; be pacified; be appeased; calm down; 《날씨가》 go down; get milder; subside; abate. ¶ 그의 말에 그녀의 태도가 누그러졌다 His words softened her attitude. / 바람이 누그러졌다 The wind has abated [gone down].

누글누글하다 (be) tender; soft; flexible; pliant.

누긋하다 (be) soft; placid; calm. ¶ 누긋한 성질 a placid temper.

누기(漏氣) moisture; dampness. ¶ ~ 찬 damp; humid; moist / ~가 없는 dry; free from moisture.

누나 one's elder sister.

누년(累年) successive years.

누누이(屢屢─) repeatedly; over and over (again); many times.

누다 《오줌을》 urinate; make [pass] water; 《똥을》 have a bowel movement; empty one's bowel; relieve oneself.

누대(累代) successive generations. ¶ ~에 걸쳐 from generation to generation.

누더기 rags; tatters; patched [tattered] clothes. ¶ ~를 걸친 사람 a person in rags.

누덕누덕 in patches. ¶ ~ 기운 옷 clothes covered in patches / ~ 집다 patch 「up [and dam].

누드 (the) nude. ¶ ~의 nude; naked / ~로 in the nude. ‖ ~ 모델 a nude model / ~ 사진 a nude photo(picture).

누락(漏落) an omission. ~하다 《…이》 omit; leave out; 《…이》 be omitted [left out]. ¶ ~ 없이 기입하여 fill up without omission.

누란(累卵) 위의 위기에 처해 있다 be in a most dangerous situation; be in imminent peril (danger). 「be a golden yellow.

누렇다 (be) deep [quite] yellow;」

누룩 malt; malted rice 《효모 yeast; leaven.

누룽지 scorched rice from the bottom of the pot.

누르다 《빛이》 (be) yellowish; sallow(얼굴이 병적으로).

누르다 ① 《내리 누름》 press [hold, push] (down); weigh on; stamp 《a seal》. ¶ 초인종을 ~ press the bell button / 아래로 ~ push [press] down / 사다리를 안 미끄러지도록 단단히 눌러라 Hold the ladder firmly. / 돌로 ~ place[put] a stone as a weight on 《something》. ② 《억제하다》 restrain; keep down; control; check(저지하다); 《진압하다》 put down; suppress. ¶ 자기 감정을 ~ control [restrain, keep down] one's emotion / 노여움을 ~ hold back [keep down, suppress, repress] one's anger; control one's temper / 물가상승을 5% 이하로 ~ prevent prices from rising more than five percent. ③ 《제압》 beat 《a person, a team》; defeat; 《야구에서 투수가》 hold 《the opposing team》. ¶ 그 투수는 상대팀을 3안타로 눌렀다 The pitcher held [limited] the opposing team to three (scattered) hits.

누르락붉으락하다 《서술적》 change one's countenance with anger; flare up.

누르스름하다 (be) yellowish; 《서술적》 be tinged with yellow.

누릇누릇하다 (be) yellowy; yellow-「누리(세상) the world. 「spotted.

누린내 《생선의》 smell of fat [grease]. ¶ 누린내 unpleasant smell of fat [grease].

누리다 《복을》 enjoy. ¶ 건강을 ~ enjoy good health / 장수를 ~ live a long life.

누명(陋名) ~을 쓰다 [suffer] disgrace 《for》; be falsely [unjustly] accused 《of》; be falsely charged 《with》 / ~을 씻다 clear one's name.

누범(累犯) repeated offenses. ~자 a repeated offender.

누비 quilting. ‖ ~ 옷 quilted clothes / ~ 이불 a quilt.

누비다 《옷 등을》 quilt 《clothes》; 《혼잡한 속을》 thread; weave. ¶ 군중 속을 누비며 가다 thread one's way through the crowd.

누선(淚腺) 〖解〗 the lachrymal gland.

누설(漏泄) leakage; a leak. ~하다 leak out; be divulged (disclosed). ¶ 비밀을 ~하다 let out [leak] a secret. ‖ 군기 ~ a leakage of military secrets.

누수(漏水) leakage of water; a water leak.

누습(陋習) an evil custom [practice]. ¶ ~을 타파하다 do away with an evil custom.

누승(累乘) 〖數〗 involution. 「cape.

누실(漏失) ~하다 leak (out); es-」

누심(壘審) 〖野〗 a base umpire.

누에 a silkworm. ¶ ~를 치다 rear [raise] silkworms. ‖ ~고치 a cocoon / ~나방 a silkworm moth / ~씨 silkworm eggs.

누옥(陋屋) a humble house [cottage].

누워떡먹기 《be》 an easy task; a piece of cake.

누워먹기 live an idle life; eat the bread of idleness.

누이 a sister; 《손위》 an elder sister; 《손아래》 a younger sister.

누이다 ① ☞ 눕히다. ②《대소변을》 make 〔let〕《a child》 urinate 〔defecate〕.

누적(累積) accumulation. ¶ ~된 서류 accumulated papers 《on the table》.

누전(漏電) a leakage of electricity; a short circuit. ¶ ~되다 short-circuit / ~에 의한 화재 a fire caused by a short circuit.

누정(漏精) spermatorrhea.

누지다 《be》 damp; wettish.

누진(累進) successive promotion. ~하다 be promoted from one position to another; rise step by step. ¶ ~적(으로) progressive(ly); gradual(ly). ‖ ~《과》세 progressive 〔gradual〕 tax《ation》 / ~세율 progressive tax rates.

누차(屢次) repeatedly; over and over 《again》; time and again. ¶ ~ 말하다 speak repeatedly.

누추(陋醜) ¶ ~한 dirty; filthy; humble; shabby《옷차림이》/ 옷이 ~하다 be shabbily dressed.

누출(漏出) ¶ ~되다 leak 〔out〕; escape / 가스가 ~되다 the gas escapes.

눅눅하다 《be》 damp; humid. ¶ 눅 눅한 빵 soggy bread.

눅다¹ 《값이》 fall 〔drop, decline〕 in price; 《날씨가》 become mild(er); warm up.

눅다² 《반죽이》 《be》 soft; limp; 《눅눅하다》 《be》 damp; soft 《with wet》; 《성질의》 《be》 genial; placid.

눅신눅신하다 《be》 soft; supple; pliant; elastic; flaccid.

눅이다 ①《부드럽게》 soften; make soft 〔tender〕. ②《마음을》 soften; appease; calm; quiet 《one's anger》. ③《촉촉이》 damp; moisten; make 《a thing》 damp.

눅지다 《날씨가》 become genial 〔mild〕.

눅진눅진하다 《be》 soft and sticky.

눈 ① 《시각 기관》 an eye. ¶ ~이 큰〔푸른〕 big-〔blue-〕eyed / ~ 깜 짝할 사이에 in the twinkling of an eye; in an instant 《a moment》 / ~이 아프다 have sore eyes; 《안질》 have eye trouble / ~을 뜨다 《감다》 open 〔close〕 one's eyes / ~에 티가 들어가다 have a mote 〔get something〕 in one's eyes / ~에 거슬리다 offend the eye / ~에 선하다 be clear in one's memory; linger before one's eye / 돈에 ~이 멀다 be blinded by money; be lured by gain / ~에 들다 be in 《a person's》 favor; find favor 《with a person》 / ~ 밖에 나다 be out of favor 《with a person》 / ~은 ~으로, 이는 이로《구약 성서》 an eye for an eye, a tooth for a tooth. ②《눈길》 a look; an eye. 부러운 ~으로 보다 see with an envious eye. ③《시력》 eyesight; sight; eyes. ¶ ~이 좋다 〔나쁘다〕 have good 〔bad〕 sight. ④《주의》 notice; attention; surveillance 《감시》~에 띄지 않는 곳 a secret corner / ~을 끌다 draw 《a person's》 attention; attract notice; catch the eyes 《of》. ⑤《견지》 a point of view; a viewpoint. ¶ 서양 사람의 ~으로 보면 from a Westerner's point of view. ⑥《안식》 an eye; judgment 《판단력》. ¶ 전문가의 ~ an expert's eye / ~이 높은 appreciative / 사람을 보는 ~이 있다 have an eye for character. ⑦《기타》 ¶ 태풍의 ~ the eye of a typhoon / ~이 뒤집히다 lose control of oneself; behave irrationally / ~을 감다 《죽다》 die; breathe one's last / 성(性)에 ~을 뜨다 be aware of one's sexual feelings.

눈² ① 《자·저울의》 a graduation; a scale. ¶ 저울 ~을 속이다 give short weight. ②《나무의 싹》 a sprout; a germ; a bud. ¶ ~을 뜨다 bud; shoot; sprout. ③《그물의》 a mesh. ¶ 그물의 ~ the mesh(es) of a net / ~이 촘촘한 〔성긴〕 철망 a fine 〔coarse〕 wire mesh.

눈³ 《내리는》 snow; a snowfall《강설》; snows《쌓인 눈》. ¶ 큰 ~ a heavy snow / 함박~ large snowflakes / 싸락~ powdery snow / 첫~ the first snow of the year / ~길 a snowy 〔snow-covered〕 road / ~처럼 희고 흰 살갗 snow-white skin / ~을 치다 rake 〔shovel〕 away snow; clear 《a street》 of snow / ~으로 덮이다 be covered with 〔in〕 snow / ~에 갇히다 be snowbound 〔snowed in〕 / ~이 온다 It snows. or Snow falls. / ~이 내리기 시작했다 It began to snow. / ~이 올 것 같다 It looks like snow. / ~으로 교통이 마비되었다 All traffic stopped owing to snow. or The snow stopped all traffic.

눈가개 an eye bandage; blinders《말의》. ¶ ~를 하다 blindfold 《a person》.

눈가림 a false front; (a) sham; (a) pretense; deception. ~하다 make a show of; pretend; feign; make 《a thing》 look like

눈감다 〈*the genuine article*〉; deceive. ¶ ~의 deceptive; make-believe; false / 그의 친절은 ~ 일 뿐이다 His kindness is a mere show [pretense].

눈감다 ① 〈눈을〉 close [shut] *one's* eyes. ¶ 본능적으로 ~ instinctively shut *one's* eyes. ② 〈죽다〉 die; breathe *one's* last.

눈감아주다 overlook; pass over; connive at; turn a blind eye to. ¶ 이번만은 눈감아 주겠다 I will let the matter pass for this once.

눈거칠다 (be) offensive to the eye.

눈겨룸 (play) a staring game.

눈결 (at) a glance [glimpse].

눈곱 〈눈의〉 eye mucus [discharges, matter]; 〈극소의 양〉 a grain of *truth*; a very small quantity. ¶ ~이 잔뜩 낀 눈 eyes blurred with mucus / ~이 끼다 *one's* eyes are gummy [mattery] / 양심이라곤 ~ 만큼도 없다 haven't got an ounce of conscience.

눈구멍 〔解〕 the eye socket.

눈구석 the corner of the eye.

눈금 a scale; graduations. ¶ ~을 매기다 graduate; mark 〈*a thing*〉 with degrees / ~을 10에 맞추다 set the scale [dial] at 10.

눈깜작이 a blinkard.

눈꺼풀 an eyelid.

눈꼴사납다 ① 〈아니꼽다〉 be an offense to the eye; be hateful to see; be an eyesore; be unsightly. ¶ 그 녀석이 거드럭거리는 품은 정말 ~ It is really hateful to see him swaggering. ② 〈눈이 부드럽지 않다〉 (be) hard-featured; villainous-looking.

눈꼴틀리다 hate to see; be sick of; be disgusting.

눈높다 〈좋은 것만 찾다〉 be desirous of things beyond *one's* means; aim high; 〈안목이 있다〉 have an expert eye 〈*for*〉; be discerning.

눈대중 eye measure; a rough estimate. ~하다 measure by the eye. ¶ ~으로 재다 measure with *one's* eye.

눈독 ¶ ~들이다 have [keep] *one's* eye 〈*on*〉; mark 〈*something, someone*〉 out [down]; fix on 〈*somebody*〉 as *one's* choice / 재산에 ~을 들이다 have an eye on 〈*a person's*〉 property. [the eye].

눈동자 〈―瞳子〉 〔解〕 the pupil (of

눈두덩 〔解〕 the upper eyelid. ¶ ~이 붓다 have swollen eyes.

눈퉁부리 〈눈〉 a pop eye 〈*사람*〉 a bug-eyed person.

눈뜨다 ① 〈눈을〉 open *one's* eyes; wake (up) 〈깨다〉. ② 〈깨닫다〉 awake [be awakened] 〈*to*〉; come to *one's* senses. ¶ 엄한 현실에 ~ have *one's* eyes opened to the stern realities of life.

눈뜬장님 〈문맹〉 an illiterate (person); a blind fool.

눈망울 〔解〕 an eyeball. [other].

눈맞다 fall in love with each

눈맞추다 〈마주 보다〉 look at each other; 〈남녀가〉 make eyes at each other; make silent love to each other.

눈매, 눈맵시 the shape of *one's* eyes. ¶ 사랑스러운 ~ (have) charming eyes.

눈멀다 become blind; lose *one's* sight; 〈현혹〉 be dazzled [blinded].

눈물 ① 〈일반적〉 tears. ¶ 겨운 이야기 a pathetic [touching] story / ~에 젖은 얼굴 a tear-stained face / 어린 눈 watery [tearful] eyes / ~짓다 be moved to tears / ~을 흘리다 cry; shed [drop] tears / ~을 닦다 dry *one's* eyes / ~을 보이다 show weak eyes / ~을 자아내다 call [draw] tears / ~을 참다 keep back *one's* tears / 연기로 인해 ~이 나왔다 The smoke made my eyes water. ② 〈인정〉 tender heart; sympathy. ¶ ~ 있는 사람 a sympathetic person / 피도 ~도 없는 cold-hearted. [ble]; sore eyes.

눈병〈―病〉 an eye disease [trou-

눈보라 〈have〉 a snowstorm.

눈부시다 ① 〈부시다〉 (be) dazzling; glaring; blinding; radiant. ¶ 눈부시게 희다 be dazzling white. ② 〈빛나다〉 (be) bright; brilliant; remarkable. ¶ 눈부신 업적 brilliant achievements.

눈빛 eye color; the cast of *one's* eyes; the expression in *one's* eyes. ¶ 애원하는 듯한 ~ a look of appeal.

눈사람 (make) a snowman.

눈사태〈―沙汰〉 an avalanche; snowslide. [brows; frown.

눈살 ¶ ~을 찌푸리다 knit *one's*

눈석임 thawing. ~하다 thaw. ¶ ~물 snow water.

눈설다 (be) unfamiliar; strange.

눈속이다 cheat; deceive; trick.

눈속임 deception; trickery.

눈송이 a snowflake.

눈시울 ¶ ~이 뜨거워지다 be moved to tears / ~을 적시는 광경 a deeply moving [touching] scene.

눈싸움 (have) a snowball fight.

눈썰미 ¶ ~가 있다 [없다] have a quick [dull] eye for learning things.

눈썹 an eyebrow. ¶ ~을 그리다 pencil *one's* eyebrows / ~ 하나 까딱 않고 똑바로 보다 look straight without batting an eye.

눈알 an eyeball.

눈앞 ¶ ~에 just in front of *one*;

눈어림 ☞ 눈대중.

눈에 띄다 〈눈을 끌다〉 attract 〈draw〉 *(a person's)* attention; 〈두드러지다〉 be conspicuous 〈*by, for*〉; stand out.

눈엣가시 an eyesore; a pain in the neck. ¶ ~로 여기다 regard *(a person)* as an eyesore.

눈여겨보다 take a good look 〈*at*〉; observe closely 〈carefully〉.

눈요기(-療飢) ~하다 feast *one's* eyes 〈*on*〉. ¶ ~가 되다 be a feast 〔joy〕 to the eye.

눈웃음 a smile with *one's* eyes. ¶ ~을 치다 smile with *one's* eyes; make eyes at; cast amorous glances at〈추파〉.

눈익다 〈사물이 주어〉 (be) familiar 〈*to*〉; 〈사람이 주어〉 get 〈become〉 used to seeing 〈*a thing*〉.

눈인사(-人事) a nod; nodding. ~하다 nod 〈*to*〉; greet with *one's* eyes.

눈자위 the rim of the eyes.

눈정기(-精氣) the glitter 〔keenness〕 of *one's* eyes.

눈주다 give *(a person)* the eye; wink 〈*at*〉.

눈짓 a wink; winking. ~하다 wink 〈*at*〉; make a sign with *one's* eyes.

눈초리 the corner 〔tail〕 of the eye.

눈총 a glare; a sharp look. ¶ ~을 맞다 be glared at; be hated 〔detested〕 〈*by*〉; 〈뭇사람의〉 be a common eyesore.

눈총기(-聰氣) ¶ ~가 좋다 have acute observation; be quick at learning.

눈치 ① 〈센스〉 quick wit; tact; sense. ¶ ~가 빠르다 be quick-witted; have the sense enough to *do* / ~가 없다 be dull-witted; lack the sense to *do*. ② 〈마음의 기미〉 *one's* mind 〔inclination, intention〕; *one's* mental attitude toward *(a person)*; 〈기색〉 a sign; an indication; a look. ¶ ~를 채다 become aware of *(a person's)* intention / ~채이다 arouse 〔excite〕 *(a person's)* suspicion; be smelled out / 남의 ~를 보다 try to read *a person's* mind 〔face〕 / 좋아하는 〔싫어하는〕 ~를 보이다 give 〔show〕 signs of pleasure 〔displeasure〕 / 그의 ~가 좀 이상하다 He is somewhat strange in his manners.

눈치레 mere show. ¶ ~로 for show; for appearance sake.

눈칫밥 food given perfunctorily 〔unwillingly, coldly〕. ¶ ~ 먹다 be treated coldly; be a hanger on 〔dependent〕.

눈코뜰새없다 (be) very busy; be in a whirl of business.

눋다 scorch; get scorched; burn. ¶ 눋은 밥 scorched rice.

눌러(계속) in succession; consecutively. ¶ ~앉다 stay on; remain in office〈유임〉.

눌러보다 overlook; connive at.

눌리다¹ be pressed down; 〈압도〉 be overwhelmed 〔overpowered〕. ¶ 다수에 ~ be overwhelmed by the majority.

눌리다² 〈눋게 하다〉 burn; scorch.

눌변(訥辯) slowness of speech.

눌어붙다 ① 〈타서〉 scorch and stick to. ② 〈한군데에〉 stick to; stay on.

눕다 lie down; lay *oneself* down. ¶ 쭉 뻗고 ~ lie at full length; stretch *oneself* at ease / 자리에 ~ lie in *one's* bed / 병으로 누워 있다 be laid up; keep *one's* bed with illness.

눕히다 lay down; make 〔have〕 *(a person)* lie down. ¶ 자리에 ~ put *(a person)* to bed.

뭉치다 soothe 〔appease〕 with nice words. 〔rice.

뉘 〈쌀의〉 a grain of unhulled

뉘앙스 nuance. ¶ 말의 ~ a shade of difference in meaning 〔expression〕.

뉘엿거리다 ① 〈해가〉 be about to set 〔sink〕. ② 〈뱃 속이〉 feel sick 〔nausea, queasy〕.

뉘우치다 regret; be sorry 〈*for*〉; repent 〈*of one's past error*〉. ¶ 뉘우치는 빛도 없이 without any repentance / 자기가 한 것을 깊이 ~ deeply repent what *he* has done.

뉴스 news. ¶ 해외 〔국내〕 ~ foreign 〔home, domestic〕 news / 〈라디오·TV의〉 ~시간 the news hour / 지금 들어온 ~에 의하면 according to the latest news 〈*from Taipei*〉 / ~〈거리〉가 되다 make 〔become〕 news. ¶ ~가치 news value / ~방송 a newscast / ~속보 a news flash / ~영화 a newsreel; a news film / ~해설 a news commentary / ~해설자 a news commentator. 〔Yorker.

뉴욕 New York. ¶ ~ 사람 a New

뉴질랜드 New Zealand. ¶ ~ 사람 a New Zealander.

뉴트론(理) neutron.

뉴페이스 a new face.

느글거리다 feel sick 〔nausea〕.

느긋하다 〈서술적〉 be well pleased 〔satisfied 〈*with*〉〕; be 〔feel〕 relaxed 〔relieved〕.

느끼다 ① 〈지각〉 feel; sense; be

느끼하다 aware〔conscious〕《of》. ¶ 고통〔공복〕을 ～ feel pain〔hungry〕 / 불편을 ～ find it inconvenient《to do》; experience〔suffer〕inconvenience / 어려움을 ～ find difficulty《in doing》 / 위험을 ～ sense danger / …을 느끼지 않다 be insensitive《to pain》; be dead《to all sense of shame》. ② 《감동》 be impressed《with, by》; be moved〔touched〕《by》. ¶ 아무의 친절을 고맙게 ～ be moved by a person's kindness / 깊이 느끼게 하다 touch《a person》to the heart; move〔impress〕《a person》profoundly.

느끼하다 (be) too fatty〔greasy, rich〕. ¶ 느끼한 음식 fatty〔greasy, rich〕food.

느낌 〔인상〕 an impression; an effect 〔그림 따위가 주는〕; 《감정》 (a) feeling; a sense 〔촉감〕 touch. ¶ 좋은〔나쁜〕～을 주다 impress《a person》 favorably〔unfavorably〕; make a favorable〔an unfavorable〕impression on 《a person》/ 거칠거칠한〔매끈매끈한〕～을 주다 feel rough〔smooth〕; be rough〔smooth〕to the touch〔feel〕/ 뭔가 묘한 ～이 들었다 Somehow I felt strange. ‖ ～표 an exclamation mark.

느닷없이 suddenly; all of a sudden; unexpectedly; without notice. ¶ ～ 덤벼들다 make a sudden spring at《a person》.

느루 ¶ ～ 먹다 eat《food》sparingly; make《food》last 〔long〕.

느른하다 (be) languid. ☞ 나른하다.

느릅나무 〔植〕 an elm 〔tree〕.

느리광이 a sluggard; an idler.

느리다 ① 《움직임이》 (be) slow; tardy; sluggish. ¶ 느리게 slowly; tardily / 일손이 ～ be slow in one's work. ② 《짜임새가》 loose.

느림 〔장식용의〕 a tassel. ┌loose.

느릿느릿 《동작이》 slowly; tardily; sluggishly/《성기게》loose; slack. ¶

느물거리다 act craftily; talk〔behave〕insidiously.

느슨하다 〔헐겁다〕 (be) loose; lax; slack; relaxed〔마음이〕. ¶ 느슨하게 loose〔ly〕 느슨해지다 loosen.

느즈러지다 ① 〔느슨해지다〕 loosen; slacken; become loose; relax 〔마음이〕. ② 〔기한이〕 be put off; be postponed.

느지감치 rather late. ¶ 아침 ～ 일어나다 get up rather late in the morning.

느지막하다 (be) rather late.

느타리 〔植〕 〔버섯의〕 an agaric.

느티나무 〔植〕 a zelkova 〔tree〕.

늑간 〔肋間〕〔解〕 ‖ ～ 신경 the intercostal nerve / ～ 신경통 intercostal neuralgia. ┌frame.

늑골 〔肋骨〕 a rib; 《선박의》 the

늑대 〔動〕 a wolf.

늑막 〔肋膜〕〔解〕 the pleura. ‖ ～염 〔dry, moist〕 pleurisy.

늑장부리다 be slow; dawdle《over》; linger; tarry 〔away〕; be tardy. ¶ ～가 기회를 놓치다 dally away one's opportunity.

는적거리다 feel squashy〔flabby〕; be decomposed〔고기가〕.

는 ☞ 언제나.

는그막 ¶ ～에 in one's old age; in one's declining years.

늘다 ① 《증가》 increase; be on the increase〔rise〕; gain 〔힘·무게가〕; rise; multiply〔배가하다〕. ¶ 30퍼센트 ～ increase by 30 percent / 장서가 2년 사이에 배로 늘었다 My library has doubled in the last two years. / 회원이 ～ have an increased membership / 체중이 (2킬로) ～ gain (two kilograms) in weight / 차량의 수가 속 늘고 있다 The number of cars 〔goes on increasing〔is on the increase〕. / 실업자〔의 수〕가 늘고 있다 Unemployment is 「up〔on the rise〕. ② 《향상》 progress《in》; advance《in》; be improved. ¶ 영어가 ～ make progress in one's English.

늘리다 〔수·양을〕 increase; add to; raise 〔증액〕; multiply〔배가〕;《면적을》enlarge; extend. ¶ 인원을 ～ increase the number of men; add to the staff / 재산을 ～ increase〔add to〕one's fortune. ┌〔spread out〕.

늘비하다 〔서술적〕 be 「arrayed

늘씬하다 (be) slender; slim. ¶ 늘씬한 미인 a beautiful girl, slender as a lily.

늘어가다 go on increasing; be on the increase.

늘어나다 ① 〔길이가〕 lengthen; extend; grow longer; stretch. ¶ 고무줄이 ～ a rubber band stretches. ② 《많아지다》 increase 《in number》.

늘어놓다 ① 《배열》 arrange; place《things》in order; 〔진열〕 display; lay out. ② 〔어지럽게〕 scatter《about》; leave《things》lying about. ③ 〔말을〕 mention; 〔열거〕 enumerate; list. ④ 〔배치〕 post; station; 《사업을》 carry on 《various enterprises》.

늘어뜨리다 〔아래로〕 hang down; suspend; droop. ¶ 머리를 등에 늘어뜨리고 있다 have one's hair hanging down on one's back.

늘어서다 stand in a row; form in a line; stand abreast〔옆으로〕. ¶ 두 줄로 ～ form〔stand in〕two rows / 배급을 타려고 죽 ～ make a queue waiting for the ration.

늘어지다 ① 〔길어지다〕 extend; lengthen; grow longer. ② 〔처지다〕 hang (down); dangle; droop. ③ 〔몸이〕 droop: be languid 〔exhausted〕. ④ 〔팔자가〕 live in comfort; be on easy street.
늘이다 ① ☞ 늘어뜨리다. ② 〔길게〕 lengthen; make (something) longer; stretch; extend. ¶ 고무줄을 ～ stretch a rubber band.
늘쩍지근하다 feel tired 〔weary〕.
늘컹거리다 be squashy 〔flabby〕.
늙다 grow old; age; advance in age. ¶ 늙은 old; aged / 나이보다 늙어 보이다 look old for one's age.
늙다리 (사람) a dotard; a silly old man; 〔짐승〕 an old animal.
늙수그레하다 (be) fairly old; oldish.   〔old; the aged.
늙은이 an old man. ¶ 〔총칭〕
늙히다 make (a person) old. ¶ 처녀로 ～ let (a girl) become an old maid.
늠름하다(凜凜—) (be) gallant; imposing; commanding; dignified. ¶ 늠름한 태도 an imposing 〔awe-inspiring〕 attitude.   〔leum.
능(陵) a royal tomb; a mausoeum.
능가(凌駕) ～하다 be superior to; surpass; exceed; override; outstrip. ¶ 젊은이를 ～하다 outdo 〔surpass〕 the young / …을 훨씬 ～해 있다 be far superior to…; be head and shoulders above….
능구렁이 ① 〔뱀〕 a yellow-spotted serpent. ② 〔사람〕 an old fox; a insidious person.
능글능글하다 (be) sly; cunning; sneaky; insidious.
능금 a crab apple.
능동(能動) ¶ ～적인 voluntary; active. ‖ ～태〔文〕 the active voice.
능란하다(能爛—) (be) skillful; dexterous; deft; expert. ¶ 능란하게 well; skillfully; with skill; tactfully / 말솜씨가 ～ have an oily tongue.
능력(能力) ability; capacity; competence. ¶ ～ 있는 able; capable; …할 수 있는 (competent) to do; be capable of (doing). ‖ ～급(給) pay according to ability / ～자 a competent (capable) person / ～ 테스트 a competence test / 생산 ～ productive capacity / 지불 ～ solvency.
능률(能率) efficiency. ¶ ～적인 efficient / 비～적인 inefficient / ～을 올리다 〔떨어뜨리다〕 improve 〔lower〕 the efficiency. ‖ ～곡선 an efficiency curve / ～급 an efficiency wages / ～저하〔증진〕 lowering 〔increase, improvement〕 of efficiency / ～제 승진제 도 the proficiency salary raise system.   〔dain.
능멸(凌蔑) ～하다 despise; disdain.
능변(能辯) eloquence. ¶ ～의 eloquent / ～가 an eloquent speaker.
능사(能事) a suitable work 〔적당한〕; something in one's line〔잘 하는〕. ¶ …을 ～로 삼다 make it one's business to (do) / 돈을 모으는 것만이 ～가 아니다 It is not everything to accumulate money.
능선(稜線) a ridgeline.
능소능대하다(能小能大—) (be) good at everything; able and adaptable; versatile.
능수(能手) (숙씨) capability; capacity; 〔사람〕 an able man 〔hand〕; an expert; a veteran.
능수버들 a weeping willow.
능숙(能熟) skill. ¶ ～된 skilled; skillful; proficient; experienced / ～해지다 become skillful; attain proficiency.
능욕(凌辱) 〔강간〕 a rape; 〔모욕〕 (an) insult; (an) indignity. ～하다 rape; insult. ¶ ～당하다 be raped 〔insulted, violated〕.
능지기(陵—) the caretaker of a royal tomb.
능지처참(陵遲處斬) ～하다 behead and dismember (a criminal).
능청 dissimulation; feigning; false pretense. ¶ ～ 떨다〔부리다〕 dissimulate; feign ignorance; pretend not to know; play the innocent.
능청거리다 be pliable 〔pliant〕.
능청스럽다 (be) dissembling; insidious; deceitful.
능통하다(能通—) (be) proficient (in); well-acquainted (with); well-versed (in); good (at); skilled; expert. ¶ 영어에 ～ be at home in English; be well-versed in English / 사무에 ～ be proficient in office work.
능한(能—) (be) good (at); proficient 〔versed, expert〕 (in). ¶ 영어에 ～ be good at English.
능히(能—) well; easily; ably. ¶ ～ 할 수 있다 can easily do; be able to do; be equal to; be capable of (doing). ‖ ～ (서슴지 않다) make no scruple of (doing); be capable of any (crime).
늦… late. ¶ ～ 가을 late autumn.
늦다 ① 〔시간적으로〕 (be) late; behind time; 〔속도가〕 (be) slow. ¶ 늦게 late / 늦어도 at (the latest) / 밤늦게 (까지) (until) late at night / 열차에 ～ be late for the train / 약속 시간에 ～ be one hour late for one's appointed time / 늦게 떠나다 make a belated start / 5분 ～ be five minutes slow / 때는 이미 늦었다 It is too late now. ② 〔느슨하다〕 (be)

loose; slack.
늦더위 the lingering summer heat; the heat of late summer.
늦되다 mature late; be slow to mature. ¶ 늦되는 과일 late fruit.
늦둥이 a child *one* had late in *one's* life.
늦바람 ① 《바람》 an evening breeze. ② 《방탕》 dissipation in *one's* later years. ¶ ~ 나다 take pleasure-seeking life late in *one's* years.
늦벼 late rice (plants).
늦복(—福) happiness in *one's* later days.
늦잠 late rising; oversleeping. ¶ ~ 자다 rise [get up] late; sleep late in the morning. ‖ ~ 꾸러기 a late riser.
늦장마 the rainy spell in late [summer.
늦추다 ① 《느슨히》 loosen; unfasten; relax《정신을》; slow down《속도를》. ¶ 고삐를 ~ slack the rein; let the rein go / 경계를 ~ relax *one's* guard《against》. ② 《시일

을》 postpone; put off. ¶ 마감 날짜를 이틀 ~ put the deadline off two days. 「afterwinter cold.
늦추위 the lingering cold; the
늪 a swamp; a marsh; a bog.
니스 varnish. ¶ ~ 칠하다 varnish.
니카라과 Nicaragua.
니켈 《化》 nickel (기호 Ni).
니코틴 《化》 nicotine. ‖ ~ 중독 nicotinism.
니크롬선(—線) (a) nichrome wire.
니트로글리세린 《化》 nitroglycerine.
니트웨어 knitwear.
니힐 nihil. ¶ ~ 리스트 a nihilist / ~ 리즘 nihilism.
님 《경칭》 Mister, Mr.; Esq. (남자); Miss(미혼 여자); Mrs.(부인). ¶ 사장 ~ Mr. President; 《여자》 Madam President / 선생 ~ Sir !; Mr. [Miss] 《*Brown*》 / 임금 ~ His Majesty; 《호칭》 Your Majesty !
님비현상(—現象) the NIMBY phenomena《NIMBY=Not In My Back Yard》.
닢 a piece 《of coin [copper]》.

우리나라 행정 각부 명칭	
※ 2013년 9월. 관사 the는 편의상 생략.	
국무총리	Prime Minister
기획재정부	Ministry of Strategy and Finance
~장관	Minister of Strategy and Finance
통일부	Ministry of Unification
~장관	Minister of Unification
외교부	Ministry of Foreign Affairs
~장관	Minister of Foreign Affairs
법무부	Ministry of Justice
~장관	Minister of Justice
국방부	Ministry of National Defense
~장관	Minister of National Defense
안전행정부	Ministry of Security and Public Administration
~장관	Minister of Security and Public Administration
교육부	Ministry of Education
~장관	Minister of Education
미래창조과학부	Ministry of Science, ICT and Future Planning
~장관	Minister of Science, ICT and Future Planning
문화체육관광부	Ministry of Culture, Sports and Tourism
~장관	Minister of Culture, Sports and Tourism
농림축산식품부	Ministry of Agriculture, Food and Rural Affairs
~장관	Minister of Agriculture, Food and Rural Affairs
산업통상자원부	Ministry of Trade, Industry & Energy
~장관	Minister of Trade, Industry & Energy
보건복지부	Ministry of Health & Welfare
~장관	Minister of Health & Welfare
환경부	Ministry of Environment
~장관	Minister of Environment
고용노동부	Ministry of Employment and Labor
~장관	Minister of Employment and Labor
국토교통부	Ministry of Land, Infrastructure and Transport
~장관	Minister of Land, Infrastructure and Transport
해양수산부	Ministry of Oceans and Fisheries
~장관	Minister of Oceans and Fisheries
감사원	Board of Audit and Inspection of Korea
~장	Chairman of the Board of Audit and Inspection of Korea

다 (모두) all; everything; everyone; utterly; completely. ¶ 둘 ~ both together; both (of us) / ~ 먹다 eat up / ~ 알다 know thoroughly. [closer.
다가놓다 bring near; put (place)
다가붙다 stick nearer (to).
다가서다 step (come) up to; approach closer; come (go) nearer.
다가앉다 sit close.
다가오다 approach; draw (come) near; draw close (to). ¶ 종말이 ~ draw to a close / 시험이 다가온다 The examination is drawing on (near).
다각(多角) ¶ ~적인 many-sided (tastes); versatile (genius). ‖ ~경영 diversified (multiple) management / ~ 무역 multilateral trade / ~ 형(形)[數] polygon (~형의 polygonal).
다갈색(茶褐色) (yellowish) brown; liver-color. ‖ ~의 brown; liver-colored.
다감(多感) ¶ ~한 emotional; sensitive; sentimental / ~한 시인 a passionate poet.
다과(多寡) many and (or) few; (a) quantity (양); (an) amount (액); (a) number (수).
다과(茶菓) tea and cake; (light) refreshments. ‖ ~회 a tea party.
다관(茶罐) a teakettle; a teapot.
다구(茶具) tea-things; tea utensils; a tea set (한 벌의).
다국적(多國籍) ‖ ~군 the multinational (coalition) forces / ~기업 a multinational corporation (enterprise).
다그다 bring (up) near; draw close; (기일을) advance; set ahead (the date of).
다그치다 ① ☞ 다그다. ② (감정·행동) press; urge; impel. ¶ 다그쳐 묻다 press (a person) (hard) for an answer.
다급하다 (be) imminent; impending; pressing; urgent. ¶ 다급한 용무로 on an urgent business.
다기지다(多氣~) (be) courageous; bold; plucky; daring.
다난(多難) ¶ ~하다 be full of troubles; (be) eventful. ¶ ~한 해 a tumultuous year / 국가 ~한 때(에) in a national crisis.
다녀가다 drop in for a short visit; call at (a house); look (a person) up; stop by (in).
다녀오다 get (come) back (from visiting); be (back) home.
다년(多年) many years. ¶ ~간 for many years. ‖ ~생 식물 a perennial (plant).
다뇨증(多尿症) [醫] polyuria.
다능(多能) ¶ ~한 many-talented; many-sided; versatile.
다니다 (왕래) come and go; go (walk) about (around); (왕복) go and return; go to (a place) and back; (매가) ply (between, from...to..); (기차 따위가) run between; (통근·통학) attend (a college); go to; commute (to the office) (통근); (들르다) visit. ¶ 자주 ~ frequent; visit frequently / 학교에 ~ attend school / 회사에 ~ work for a company / 경인간을 다니는 버스 a bus running between Seoul and Inch'ŏn.
다다르다 arrive (at, in, on); reach; get to (at); come (to).
다다미 a Japanese mat; matting. ¶ ~를 깔다 lay mats; mat (a room).
다다이즘 Dadaism; Dada.
다다익선(多多益善) The more, the better.
다닥다닥 in clusters.
다닥치다 run against (into); come across; (절박) come (round); draw near; be imminent.
다달이 every month; monthly.
다대하다(多大~) (be) much; huge; great; heavy; considerable; serious. ¶ 다대한 손실 a heavy loss.
다도(茶道) the tea ceremony.
다도해(多島海) an archipelago [pl. -es, -s].
다독(多讀) extensive reading. ~하다 read much (widely). ‖ ~가 an extensive reader / ~ 주의 the principle of extensive reading.
다듬다 ① (매만짐) arrange; smooth; finish (up); do up; (단장) adorn; face (색채 등을); plume (깃 따위를), trim (나무 따위를); plane (대패로). ¶ 머리를 ~ [arrange] one's hair. ② (부성귀를) trim; nip (off). ③ (땅바닥을) (make) even; level off (out); smooth. ④ (천을) full (cloth); smooth clothes by pounding with round sticks.
다듬이 ‖ ~질 smoothing cloth / 다듬잇돌 stone (wooden) block for pounding cloth / 다듬잇방망이 a round wooden-stick for pounding cloth with.
다듬질 ① finishing touches.

다락 a loft; garret.
다람쥐 [動] a squirrel.
다랍다 ① ☞ 더럽다. ②《인색》(be) stingy; niggardly; mean.
다랑어(―魚) a tunny; a tuna (美).
다래끼 《바구니》 a fish basket; a creel; 《눈병》 a sty(e).
다량(多量) ¶ ~의 much; a lot of; plenty of; a large quantity of; a great deal of / ~으로 abundantly; in great quantities.
다루다 ①《처리·대우》handle; manage; deal with; treat. ¶ 다루기 힘든 unmanageable; hard to deal with. ②《가죽을》tan; dress 《leather》. ¶ 다루지 않은 untanned; raw 《hide》.
다르다 《상위》(be) different from; 《서술적》vary; differ from; 《닮지 않음》(be) unlike; 《불일치》do not agree 《with》; do not correspond 《with, to》. ┌ more [less] than.
다름아닌 (be) nothing but; no
다름없다 《같다》be not different 《from》, be similiar 《to》; be alike《서술적》;《변치 않음》(be) constant; as ever; 《매한가지》be as good as《dead, new》《서술적》.
다리¹ 《사람·동물의》a leg; a limb; 《물건의》a leg.
다리²《교량》a bridge; ~를 놓다 build [construct] a bridge 《across》. ¶ 다릿목 the approach to a bridge / 홍예~ an arch bridge.
다리³《머리의》a hairpiece; (a tress of) false [artificial] hair.
다리다 iron (out); press; do the ironing.
다리미 a flatiron; an iron. ¶ ~질 하다 iron《clothes》; do the ironing / 증기~ a steam iron.
다리쇠 a trivet; a tripod.
다림《수직의》plumbing;《수평의》levelling. ¶ ~ 보다 plumb;《이해를》keep alert to one's own interest. ¶ ~줄 a plumbing line / ~추 a plummet; a plumb / ~판 a levelling plate.
다림질 ironing. ~ 하다 iron (out); press; do the ironing.
다딧돌 a stepping stone.
다만《오직》only; merely; simply; 《그러나》but; still; however; provided that.
다망(多忙) pressure of work. ~ 하다 be busy; have a lot of work. ¶ 공무~ 하여 owing to pressure of official business.
다모작(多毛作) multiple cropping.
다목적(多目的) ¶ ~의 multipurpose; ~으로 사용할 수 있는 기구 a multipurpose gadget. ‖ ~댐 a multipurpose dam / ~차량 a multi-purpose vehicle《생략 MPV》.
다문(多聞) ‖ ~박식 much information and wide knowledge.
다물다 shut; close. ¶ 입을 꼭 ~ keep one's lips tight; keep silent. ┌ kempt whiskers.
다박나룻 a bushy beard; un-
다발 a bundle; a bunch. ¶ 꽃 한 ~ a bunch of flowers.
다방(茶房) a teahouse; a tearoom; a coffee shop 《호텔 따위의》. ‖ ~레지 a teahouse waitress / ~마담 the manageress of a tearoom.

다방면(多方面) ¶ ~의 varied; various; many-sided; versatile / ~으로 in many fields [directions] / ~에 교우관계가 있다 have a wide circle of acquaintances.
다변(多邊) ¶ ~적인 multilateral / 수출 시장의 ~화 diversification of export markets. ‖ ~외교 a multilateral diplomacy / ~형 a polygon. ┌ talkative; garrulous.
다변(多辯) talkativeness. ¶ ~의
다병(多病) ~ 하다 (be) weak; infirm; sickly; of delicate health.
다복(多福) ~ 하다 (be) happy; lucky; blessed.
다부일처(多夫一妻) polyandry.
다부지다 《사람이》 staunch; firm; determined. ¶ 다부진 사람 a stout-hearted person.
다분(多分)히 much; greatly; in large measure; quite a lot.
다붓하다 (be) close; dense; be at short intervals. ¶ 다붓이 close(ly); dense(ly).
다비(茶毘) [佛] cremation. ~ 하다 cremate 《the remains》.
다사(多事) ~ 하다 (be) eventful; busy. ¶ ~스러운 officious; meddlesome; nosy / ~ 다난(多難)한 생애 an eventful life / 이런 ~ 다난한 시대에 in these eventful and critical times / 지난 5년이란 세월은 정말 ~ 다난했다 I have encountered one difficulty after another these last five years.
다산(多産) ¶ ~의 productive; prolific. ‖ ~부 a prolific woman.
다섯 five; fivefold: quintuple.
다소(多少) ①《수·양의》 (the) number(수); (the) quantity(양); (the) amount(액). ¶ …의 ~에 따라 according to the number [amount, quantity] of…. ②《다소의》 a few; some; 《다소의 양》 a little; some. ¶ ~의 돈 some money. ③《얼마간》 a little; somewhat; to some extent [degree]; in a way. ¶ ~ 모자라는 점이 있다 It leaves something to be desired. / ~ 사실과 다르다 be not quite faithful

다소곳하다 (be) modest and quiet with *one's* head lowered; obedient. ¶ 다소곳이 gently; obediently.

…다손치더라도 (even) though; even if; no matter how(what, who); Admitting(Granting) that …. ¶ 그럴 ~ Admitting that it is so…. / 설사 무슨 일이 ~ no matter what may happen; come what may.

다수(多數) a large (great) number; many; a majority. ¶ ~의 (a great) many; a large number of; numerous / ~를 믿고 by (relying on) force of numbers / 압도적 ~로 by an overwhelming majority. ¶ ~결 decision by majority (~결로 정하다 decide by majority) / ~당 the majority party / ~안 a majority proposal / ~의견 a majority opinion.

다수확(多收穫) ¶ ~의 high-yielding *(wheat)*. ‖ ~품종 a high-yield variety *(of grain)*.

다스 a dozen. ¶ 5 ~ five dozen *(pencils)* / ~로 팔다 sell by the dozen.

다스리다 ① 〈통치〉 rule (reign) over; govern *(the people)*; manage *(one's household)* (관리). ② 〈바로 잡다〉 put *(things)* in order; set *(things)* to right. ③ 〈통제〉 control; keep under control; regulate *(rivers)* (진압) put down; supress. ¶ 폭동을 ~ put down a revolt. ④ 〈병을〉 treat; cure; heal. ⑤ 〈죄를〉 punish; bring *(a person)* to justice.

다습하다(多濕-) (be) damp; humid. ¶ 다습한 기후 humid weather.

다시 (또) again; (all) over again; once more (again); (겨듭) repeatedly; again and again; (새로이) anew; afresh. ¶ ~ 보다 look at *(it)* again / 같은 잘못을 ~ 되풀이하지 마라 Don't repeat the same

다시마 〔植〕 a (sea) tangle. 〔error.

다시없다 (견줄 곳 없다) (be) unique; matchless; unequaled; (두 번 없다) be never to happen again. ¶ 다시없는 기회 a golden opportunity / 이렇게 좋은 사전은 ~ This dictionary has no equal.

…다시피 (마찬가지로) as; like; (같은 정도로) almost; nearly. ¶ 보시〔아시〕 ~ as you see〔know〕/ 멸망하 ~ 되다 be almost ruined.

다식(多食) ¶ ~하다 eat much; eat to excess; overeat. ‖ ~가 a great eater / ~증 polyphagia; bulimia.

다식(多識) wide knowledge.

다신교(多神教) polytheism. ‖ ~도 a polytheist. 〔amount〕 of.

다액(多額) ¶ ~의 a large sum

다양(多樣) ¶ ~하다 (be) various; diverse; a great variety of. ¶ 매우 ~한 의견 a very wide diversity〔variety〕 of opinions. ‖ ~성 diversity; variety / ~화 diversification (~하다 diversify).

다언(多言) 〈다변〉 talkativeness; 〔여러 말〕 many words. 〔acid.

다염기산(多鹽基酸) 〔化〕 polybasic

다우존스〔證〕 ~산식〔式〕 the Dow-Jones formula / ~평균주가 the Dow-Jones average price of stocks.

다운〔拳〕 a knock-down. ¶ ~되다 be knocked down / ~시키다 knock down; floor.

다원(多元) pluralism. ¶ ~적인 plural. ‖ ~론 pluralism / ~방송 a broadcast from multiple origination.

다위니즘 〈진화론〉 Darwinism.

다육(多肉) ¶ ~의 fleshy; pulpy. ‖ ~식물 a fleshy plant.

다음 the next; the second (두번째). ¶ ~의 next; following; coming / ~날 the next (following) day / ~달 the next month / ~해〔년〕 the following month 〔year〕/ ~에 next; secondly; in the second place / ~주 월요일 next Monday / ~ ~ 일요일 (오늘부터) on Sunday after next / (과거·미래의 어떤 날부터) two Sundays later (after that) / 이 도시는 한국에서 서울 ~으로 크다 This city is the largest next to Seoul in Korea.

다음절(多音節) ¶ ~자 a polyphone / ~절 a polysyllable.

다의(多義) polysemy. ¶ ~의 polysemous. ‖ ~어 a word of many meanings.

다이너마이트 dynamite. ¶ ~로 폭파하다 dynamite *(a rock)*.

다이빙 diving.

다이아 ① → 다이아몬드. ② 〈운행표〉 a railway schedule〔timetable〕.

다이아나 〔로神〕 Diana.

다이아몬드 a diamond.

다이아진 〔藥〕 (sulfa)diazine.

다이어트 a diet. ¶ ~ 중이다 be on a diet; be dieting / ~를 하다 go on a diet; diet *oneself*.

다이얼 a dial. ¶ ~을 돌리다 turn a dial / ~113번을 돌리다 dial 113. / ~통화 direct-dialing.

다이얼로그 a dialog(ue).

다이오드 〔電子〕 diode.

다작(多作) ¶ ~하다 be prolific in writing; write many works. ¶ ~의 prolific. ‖ ~가 a prolific writer〔author〕.

다잡다 《사람을》 closely supervise; exercise strict; control *(over)*;

다재 urge; 《마음을》 brace *oneself* up 《for a task》.
다재(多才) versatile talents. ¶ ~ 한 versatile; multi-talented; many-sided / ~ 한 사람 a many-sided man.
다정(多情) ¶ ~ 한 warm(-hearted); tender; affectionate; kind / ~ 다감한 emotional; sentimental; passionate / ~ 히 warmly; kindly; affectionately / ~ 한 친구 a close friend / ~ 하게 지내다 be on good (friendly) terms 《with》 / ~ 다한 (多情) 한 일생을 보내다 live a life full of tears and regrets.
다조(一調) [樂] C. 《명》.
다족류(多足類) [動] *Myriapoda*(학
다중(多重) ~ 의 multiplex; multiple. ‖ ~ 방송 multiplex broadcasting; ~ 방송 a multiplex broadcast / ~ 방식 a multiplex system / ~ 인격 a multiple character / ~ 회로 a multiple circuit.
다지다 ① 《단단하게》 ram; harden 《the ground》. ¶ 땅을 평탄하게 ~ ram the soil flat. ② 《고기를》 mince; hash; chop (up). ③ 《다짐받다》 press 《a person》 for a definite answer, make sure 《of》.
다짐(확약) a definite answer (promise); a pledge; an oath; 《보증》 reassurance; guarantee. ~ 하다 assure; (give) *one's* pledge; (make a) vow; take an oath. ¶ ~ 받다 make sure 《of》; get an assurance from 《a person》; secure a definite answer.
다짜고짜로 without warning (notice); abruptly. ¶ ~ 사람을 치다 hit *a person* abruptly.
다채(多彩) ¶ ~ 롭다 (be) colorful; variegated / ~ 로운 행사 colorful events.
다처(多妻) a plurality of wives. ¶ 일부 ~ polygyny; polygamy.
다치다 get (be) hurt; be wounded (injured). ¶ 다리를 ~ get hurt in the leg / 자동차 사고로 ~ be injured in an auto accident.
다큐멘터리 ~ 영화 a documentary film.
다크호스 a dark horse; a doc(口).
다투다 fight; quarrel 《about a matter with a person》; dispute 《with a person》 (논쟁); be at variance 《with》 (불화); 《겨루다》 contest; compete; vie 《with》; struggle. ¶ 사소한 일로 ~ quarrel over trifles / 우승을 ~ compete for the championship / 주도권 ~ 의석을 ~ struggle for leadership / 의석을 ~ contend for a seat.
다툼(논쟁) a dispute; an argument; a quarrel (경쟁); a contest; a competition 《for a position》. ¶ 주도권 ~ 에 말

려들다 be dragged into a struggle for leadership.
다하다 《없어지다》 be exhausted; run out; be all gone; 《끝나다》 (come to an) end; be out (up, over).
다하다 ① 《다 들이다》 exhaust; use up; run through. ¶ 최선을 ~ do *one's* best / 힘을 ~ put forth all *one's* strength. ② 《끝내다》 finish; get done; go through; be through 《with》; 《완수》 accomplish; carry out; 《이행》 fulfill; perform. ¶ 일을 ~ finish *one's* work / 본분을 ~ perform *one's* duty / 사명을 ~ accomplish (carry out) *one's* mission.
다항식(多項式) [數] a polynominal (multinominal) expression.
다행(多幸) good fortune (luck). ~ 하다 (be) happy; lucky; blessed; fortunate. ¶ ~ 히 happily; fortunately; luckily; by good luck / ~ 히도 …하다 be lucky enough to 《do》; have the luck to 《do》 / ~ 스럽다 =다행하다.
다혈질(多血質) a sanguine (hot) temperament. ¶ ~ 인 사람 a man of sanguine temperament; a hot-blooded man.
다홍(一紅) deep red; crimson. ‖ ~ 치마 a red skirt.
닥나무 [植] a paper mulberry.
닥뜨리다 encounter; meet with; face; be confronted by.
닥치는 대로 at random; haphazardly; indiscreetly; rashly. ¶ ~ 무엇이나 whatever (anything that) comes handy 《along *one's* way》 / ~ 읽다 read at random.
닥치다 approach; draw near; be (close) at hand; be imminent. ¶ 눈 앞에 닥친 위험 an impending (a pressing) danger / 죽음이 눈 앞에 ~ be on the verge of death.
닥터 a doctor; a doc(口).

닦다 ① 《윤내다》 polish; burnish; shine; brighten. ¶ 구두를 ~ shine (polish) *one's* shoes. ② 《씻다》 clean; wash; brush; 《훔치다》 wipe; mop; scrub. ¶ 이를 ~ brush (clean) *one's* teeth / 걸레로 ~ wipe 《*the floor*》 with a floorcloth / 눈물을 ~ dry *one's* eyes. ③ 《단련·연마》 cultivate; train; improve. ¶ 기술을 ~ improve *one's* skill / 지덕을 ~ cultivate wisdom and virtue / 무예를 ~ train *oneself* in military arts. ④ 《고루다》 level; make even. ¶ 터를 ~ level the ground. ⑤ 《토대·기반을》 prepare the ground; pave the way 《for》.
닦달질하다 scold; rebuke; give 《a person》 a good talking-to; take 《a person》 to task 《for》; teach

닦아세우다 ☞ 닦달질하다.

닦음질 cleaning; wiping.

닦이다 ① 《닦음을 당하다》 be wiped [polished, shined, cleaned, washed, brushed]. ② 《뒤닦이다》 be strongly rebuked; have a good scolding; catch it.

단 《묶음》 a bundle; a bunch; a sheaf (볏 따위); a faggot (장작 따위). ¶ ~ 짓다 bundle; tie up in a bundle; sheave.

단(段) ① 《지적 단위》 a *dan*(=about 0.245 acres). ② 《인쇄용의》 a column. ¶ 삼~ 표제 a three-column heading. ③ 《등급의》 a grade; a class; a rank. ¶ 바둑 9~ a ninth grader in *paduk* / ~ 수가 틀리다 be not in a class with; stand on different levels. ④ 《층계》 a step; a stair.

단(壇) a platform; a raised floor; a rostrum; a stage (무대); a pulpit (교회의 연단); an altar (제단).

단(斷) decision; resolution; judgment. ¶ ~을 내리다 make a final decision.

단(單) only (one). ¶ ~ 한 번 only once.

단(但) but; however; provided that (조건).

단(團) a body; a corps; a group; a party; a team (경기단); a troupe (극단); a gang (악한 따위의). ¶ 외교~ a diplomatic corps / 관광~ a tourist party. 「rean ode.

단가(短歌) a *dan-ga*(poem); a Ko-

단가(單價) a unit cost [price]. ¶ ~ 50원으로 한 개에 50 *won* a piece. ‖ 생산~ the unit cost of production. 「association.

단가(團歌) the (official) song of an

단가(檀家) 《佛》 a parishioner; a supporter of a Buddhist temple.

단강(鍛鋼) forged steel.

단거리(短距離) a short distance; a short range (사정(射程)의). ‖ ~ 경주 a short-distance race; a sprint (race) / ~ 선수 a sprinter / ~이착륙기 a short takeoff and landing plane [aircraft] (생략 STOL) / ~전략핵병기 a short-range strategic nuclear weapon / ~탄도미사일 a short-range ballistic missile (생략 SRBM).

단검(短劍) a short sword; a dagger (비수).

단견(短見) short-sightedness; a narrow view [opinion].

단결(團結) unity; union; solidarity. ~하다 unite; hold [get] together. ‖ ~권 the right of organization (근로자의) / ~력 power of combination / ~심 cooperative spirit; *esprit de corps* (프).

단결에, 단김에 while it is hot; before the chance slips away.

¶ 쇠뿔도 ~ 빼랬다《俗談》 Strike while the iron is hot.

단경(短徑) 《機》 the minor axis.

단경(斷經) 《韓醫》 menopause: natural cessation of menstruation. ~하다 go through menopause. ‖ ~기 (the time of) menopause.

단경기(端境期) an off-crop (a pre-harvest) season.

단계(段階) a stage; a step; a phase. ¶ ~적인 해소 [폐지] a phaseout 《of the old system》 / ~적인 도입 a phase-in 《of the new policy》 / 병력의 ~적인 철수 phased withdrawals of troops / 그 계획은 아직 실험 ~에 있다 The project is still in an experimental stage. ‖ 최종~ (be in) the final stage.

단골(관계) custom; connection; patronage; 《사람》 a regular customer; a patron; a client. ¶ 오랜 ~ an old customer / ~이 많다 have a large custom (connection).

단과대학(單科大學) a college.

단교(斷交) a rupture; a break of relations; a severance. ~하다 break off relations 《with》. ‖ 경제~ a rupture of economic relations.

단구(段丘) 《地》 a terrace. ‖ 해안 (하안)~ a marine [river] terrace.

단구(短軀) (be) of short stature.

단궤(單軌) a monorail. ‖ ~철도 a monorail [centripetal] railway.

단근질 torturing with a red-hot iron. ~하다 torture 《a criminal》 with a red-hot iron.

단기(單記) single entry. ‖ ~투표 single voting.

단기(短期) a short term [time]. ¶ ~의 short-term; short-dated. ‖ ~강습 a short(-term) course 《in English》 / ~계약 a short-term contract / ~대부 [융자] a short-term loan / ~유학 a short period of study abroad / ~자금 short-term funds.

단기(單騎) a single horseman.

단기(團旗) an association banner.

단내 a burnt [scorched] smell. ¶ ~가 난다 I can smell something burning.

단념(斷念) abandonment. ~하다 give up 《an idea》; abandon; quit. ¶ ~시키다 persuade 《a person》 to give up 《the idea of doing》; dissuade 《a person》 from 《doing》 / 그 계획을 아직 ~하지 않았다 I still have hope for that project.

단단하다 (be) hard; solid; strong (세다); firm (굳다); tight (매듭이). ¶ 단단히 hard; solidly (튼튼히); tightly (꽉); fast (안 움직이게); firmly (굳게); strongly (세게); strict-

단대목

ly(엄중히); severely(되게); greatly (크게); 단단한 기초 a solid foundation / 단단한 결속 strong solidarity / 단단히 결심하다 be firmly resolved / 단단히 약속하다 make a solemn promise / 단단히 이르다 give strict orders.

단도(單─) the high tide《of》; an important opportunity(positon》 / 단도 a dagger. [tion].

단도직입(單刀直入) ¶ ~적(으로) point-blank; straightforward(ly); direct(ly); frank(ly) / ~적인 질문 a point-blank question / ~적으로 말하다 speak plainly[bluntly] / ~적으로 말하라 Come straight (right) to the point.

단독(丹毒)〖醫〗erysipelas.

단독(單獨) ¶ ~의 single; sole; individual(개인의); independent (독립의); separate(개개의); single-handed(혼자 힘으로); ~으로 alone; by *oneself*; independently / ~으로 산에 오르다 climb the mountain alone(by *oneself*) / ~행동을 취하다 take independent action; act independently. ∥ ~강화《conclude》a separate peace 《treaty》/ ~내각 a one-party cabinet / ~범 a one-man(single-handed》crime; a crime committed without accomplices; a sole offender(범인) / ~비행 a solo flight / ~회견 an exclusive interview.

단두대(斷頭臺) a guillotine. ¶ 마침내 ~의 이슬로 사라지다 be finally sent to the guillotine.

단락(段落)《문장의》(the end of) a paragraph;《일·사건의 구획》an end; a close; conclusion; settlement. ☞ 일단락. ¶ ~을 짓다 bring 《a matter》to a conclusion.

단락(短絡)〖電〗a short (circuit).

단란(團欒) ~ 하다 (be) happy; harmonious; sit in a happy circle. ¶ ~ 한 가정 생활 a happy home life.

단련(鍛鍊) ①《금속》temper; forging. ~ 하다 temper《iron》; forge. ②《심신》training; discipline. ~하다 train; discipline. ¶심신을 ~하다 train *one's* body and mind.

단리(單利)〖經〗simple interest.

단막(單幕) one act. ∥ ~극 a one act drama(play).

단말마(斷末魔) *one's* last moments. ¶ ~의 고통 death agony; the throes of death. [taste.

단맛 sweetness;《have》a sweet

단면(斷面) ¶ ~의 sectional《cross》. ¶ ~도 a cross section《of》;

185

단색

a sectional drawing / 부분~도 a partial cross section.

단명(短命) a short life. ¶ ~한 short-lived / ~한 정권 a short-lived administration / 재사(才士) ~ Men of talent die young.

단모음(單母音) a single vowel.

단무지 pickled《yellow》radish.

단문(短文) a short sentence.

단문(單文)〖文〗a simple sentence.

단물 ①《담수》fresh water. ②《맛이 단 물》sweet water. ③《알속》the cream;《take》the lion's share. ¶ ~을 빨아먹다 take the lion's share; skim the cream off. / ~《연수》soft water.

단박 instantly; immediately; right away; promptly; at once. ¶일을 ~에 해치우다 finish up *one's* work right away.

단발(單發) ①《한 발》a shot. ¶ ~에 at a shot. / ~총 a single-loader. ②《발동기》a single engine. / ~기 a single-engined plane.

단발(短髮) short hair.

단발(斷髮) bobbed hair; a bob. ~하다 bob *one's* hair. / ~미인 a beautiful woman with bobbed hair.

단백(蛋白) albumen. ∥ ~뇨증(尿症) albuminuria / ~석〖鑛〗opal.

단백질(蛋白質) protein; albumin. ¶ ~이 풍부한(적은) 식품 high=(low-)protein foods / protein=rich (-poor) foods / 고급 ~을 포함한 식품 high-quality protein foods / 동물성(식물성) ~ animal (vegetable) protein.

단번(單番) ¶ ~에 at a stroke (stretch); at one coup (try); by one effort; at once / ~에 결정 짓다 decide《a matter》by one effort.

단벌(單─)《옷》*one's* only suit. ¶ ~ 나들이옷 *one's* sole Sunday best. / ~신사 a poor gentleman who has no spare suit.

단본위제(本本位制)〖經〗monometallism; a single standard system (base).

단봉낙타(單峰駱駝)〖動〗an arabian (a single-hump) camel.

단비 a welcome(timely) rain. ¶ 오랜 가뭄 끝의 ~ long-awaited rain after a long spell of dry weather.

단비(單比)〖數〗simple ratio. [er.

단비례(單比例)〖數〗simple proportion.

단사(丹砂)〖鑛〗cinnabar. [tion.

단산(斷産) ~ 하다《자연적》pass the age of bearing;《인위로》stop childbearing.

단상(壇上) ¶ ~에 서다 stand on (take) the platform.

단상(單相)〖電〗single phase. ∥ ~전동기 a single-phase motor.

단색(單色) ¶ ~의 unicolored; mo-

단서(但書) a proviso; a conditional [provisory] clause. ¶ ~가 붙은 conditional / …라는 ~를 붙여 with the proviso that….

단서(端緒) (처음) the beginning; the start; (제일보) the first step; (실마리) a clue [key] (to). ¶문제 해결의 ~ the first step toward the solution of a question / ~를 잡다 have [get, gain] a clue [key] for solving a problem / ~를 잡다 have [get, gain] a clue.

단선(單線) ① (한 줄) a single line. ② (단궤) a single track. ~철도 a single-track railway.

단선(斷線) the snapping [breaking down] of a wire; disconnection. ¶ ~되다 be disconnected; be cut; (a wire) break; snap / 지진으로 전선이 ~되었다 The power lines have been cut by the earthquake.

단성(單性) [生] unisexuality. ‖ ~생식 monogenesis / ~화 a unisexual flower.

단세포(單細胞) [生] a single cell. ‖ ~동물[식물] a unicellular animal [plant].

단소하다(短小━) (be) small and [short.

단속(團束) (규제) control; regulation; management; (감독) supervision; (규율) discipline. ~하다 (keep under) control; keep in order; regulate; manage; supervise; maintain 《*discipline*》; oversee. ¶폭력에 대한 ~ regulations against violence / 주차 위반의 일제 ~ a crackdown on illegal parking / ~이 잘 되어 있다 be well controlled [supervised] / ~을 엄중히 하다 tighten (the) control 《*of, over*》. ‖ ~법규 regulations / ~집중 an intensive control squad.

단속(斷續) ¶ ~적인 intermittent; sporadic / ~적으로 on and off; intermittently; sporadically. ‖ ~기 an interrupter.

단속곳 a slip; an underskirt.

단수(斷水) (a) suspension of water supply. ~하다 cut off the water supply. ¶내일은 ~된다 The water supply will be cut off tomorrow.

단수(單數) [文] the singular number. ‖ ~의 singular.

단순(端數) ☞ 끝수, 우수리.

단순(單純) simplicity. ~하다 (be) simple; plain; simple-minded [-hearted] 《사람이》 / ~히 simply; merely / ~하게[화]하다 simplify. ‖ ~개념 a simple concept.

단순호치(丹脣皓齒) red lips and white teeth; 《용모》 a lovely face; 《미인》 a beauty.

단술 a sweet rice drink.

단숨에(單━) at a stretch [stroke]; at [in] a breath; at one effort. ¶ ~ 마시다 drink 《*a mug of beer*》 in one gulf.

단시(短詩) a sonnet; a short poem [verse]. ‖ ~작가 a sonneteer.

단시간(短時間) (in) a short (space of) time.

단시일(短時日) ~에 in a short (period of) time; in a few days.

단식(單式) [數] a simple expression; 《부기》 single entry; 《테니스·탁구》 singles.

단식(斷食) a fast; fasting. ~하다 fast. ‖ ~일 [요법] a fasting day [cure] / ~투쟁 (go on) a hunger strike.

단신(單身) 《부사적》 alone; by *oneself*; single-handed; singly; unattended. ¶ ~ 여행하다 travel alone / ~ 부임하다 take up a post 《*in London*》 without *one's* family. ‖ ~부임자 a business bachelor.　　　　[sage, news).

단신(短信) a brief letter [note, message].

단심제(單審制) single-trial system.

단아(端雅) ~한 elegant; graceful.

단안(斷案) a decision (결정); a conclusion (결론). ¶ ~을 내리다 make a (final) decision.

단애(斷崖) a precipice; a cliff. ‖ ~절벽 a precipitous [an overhanging] cliff.

단어(單語) a word; a vocabulary (어휘). ‖ ~집 a collection of words / ~기본 a basic word.

단언(斷言) an affirmation; an assertion; a positive [definite] statement. ~하다 affirm; assert; state positively.

단역(端役) 《play》 a minor part [role]; ~ an extra 《사람》.

단연(斷然) 《단호히》 firmly; resolutely; positively; decidedly; 《훨씬》 by far 《*the best*》. ¶ ~ 제일이다 be by far the best of all / ~ 유리하다 have a decided advantage / ~ 다른 것을 리드하다 hold the unquestioned lead.

단연(斷煙) ~하다 〔give up〕 [quit〕 smoking.

단열(斷熱) insulation. ~하다 insulate. ¶불완전한 ~ inadequate insulation. ‖ ~재 insulating material; a heat shield [insulator].

단엽(單葉) [植] single-leaf; unifoliate. ‖ ~비행기 a monoplane.

단오절(端午節) the *Dano* Festival (on the 5th of the fifth lunar month).

단원(單元) 《학습 단위》 a unit.

단원(團員) a member 《*of a group*》.

단원제(單院制) the unicameral

[single-chamber] system.
단위(單位) a unit; a denomination. ¶ ~를 틀리다 get the unit wrong; mistake the unit / ~면적[질량]당 per unit area [mass].
단음(短音) a short sound. ‖ ~[樂] the minor scale.
단음(單音) a single sound; [樂] a monotone.
단일(單一) ¶ ~의 singular; single; unique; simple; sole / ~화하다 simplify. ‖ ~환율 a single exchange rate / ~후보 a single[single] candidate. [monad.
단자(單子) a list of gifts; [哲]
단자(短資) a short-term loan. ‖ ~거래 call loan transaction / ~시장 the short-loan market / ~회사 a short-loan financing company.
단자(端子) [電] a terminal.
단작(單作) a single crop. ‖ ~지대 a one-crop area [belt].
단작스럽다 (be) mean; base; stingy. [sleep.
단잠 (sleep) a sweet [sound]
단장(丹粧) 《꾸밈》 decoration; colorful painting 《색칠》; 《화장》 makeup; (a) toilet; dressing 《옷치장》. ~하다 《꾸미다》 decorate; adorn; paint 《화장하다》 make (oneself) up; 《옷치장하다》 dress (oneself); dress up. ‖ ~새로 ~된 강당 the refurbished auditorium / 곱게 ~하고 나서서 go out beautifully dressed up. [cane.
단장(短杖) a walking stick; a
단장(團長) a head [leader] (of a party); ‖ ...을 ~으로 하여 headed [led] by...
단장(斷腸) ¶ ~의 heartrending; heartbreaking / ~의 비애 heartbreaking grief / ~의 비애를 느끼다 feel as if one's heart would break.
단적(端的) ¶ ~으로 말하다 speak frankly [plainly]; go right to the point / ~으로 말하면 plainly speaking; to be frank with you.
단전(丹田) the hypogastric region; the abdomen. ¶ ~에 힘을 주다 strain the abdomen.
단전(斷電) power failure; 《중단》 suspension of power supply. ~하다 suspend power supply 《to》; cut off electricity. ‖ ~일 a non-power-supply day; a no power day.
단절(斷絶) rupture; break 《결렬》; extinction 《소멸》; interruption 《중단》; a gap 《격차》. ~하다 《끊음》 sever; cut [break] off. ¶ ~되다 become extinct 《소멸》; 《결렬》 be broken off; come to a rupture; be severed / 세대간의 ~ a generation gap. ‖ ~감 a sense of alienation.

단점(短點) a weak point; a defect; a fault; a shortcoming.
단정(短艇) a boat.
단정(端正) ~하다 (be) right; upright; decent; handsome 《face》. ¶ ~히 properly; neatly; tidily / ~치 못한 slovenly; loose; untidy; disorderly.
단정(斷定) ~하다 draw [come to] a conclusion; conclude; decide; judge.
단조(單調) monotony; dullness. ¶ ~롭다 (be) monotonous; dull / ~로운 빛깔 a dull [flat] color / ~로운 생활을 하다 lead a monotonous life.
단조(短調) [樂] a minor (key).
단종(斷種) castration 《거세》; sterilization. ~하다 sterilize; castrate.
단좌(單坐) ¶ ~식의 single-seated. ‖ ~식 전투기 a single-seated fighter (plane).
단죄(斷罪) conviction. ~하다 convict; find (a person) guilty.
단주(端株) [證] a broken [an odd] lot.
단주(斷酒) ~하다 abstain from wine; give up drinking.
단지 a jar; a pot; a crock.
단지(團地) ¶ ~주택 a housing development [complex]; a collective [public] housing area / ~공업 an industrial complex.
단지(斷指) ~하다 cut off one's finger.
단지(但只) simply; merely; only.
단짝 a devoted [great] friend; a chum.
단청(丹青) a picture [painting] of many colors and designs.
단체(單體) [化] a simple substance.
단체(團體) a body; a group; a party; 《조직체》 an organization. ¶ ~를 조직[해산]하다 form [dissolve] an organization / ~경기 a team event; team competition / ~교섭(권) collective bargaining (right) / ~생활 a group life / ~손님 party travelers / ~여행 (make) a group tour / ~정신 a group [corporate] spirit / ~할인 a group discount [reduction] / ~행동 collective action; teamwork / ~협약 a collective agreement.
단총(短銃) a pistol; a revolver. ‖ ~기관 a submachine gun.
단추 a button; a stud 《장식 단추》. ¶ ~를 채우다 button (up) / ~를 끄르다 unbutton; undo a button / ~를 달다 sew a button 《on a coat》. ‖ 단추구멍 a buttonhole.
단축(短軸) [鑛·機] the minor axis.
단축(短縮) shortening; reduction;

단출하다 curtailment. ~하다 shorten; reduce; cut (down); curtail. ¶시간을 ~하다 reduce the time / 휴가를 5일간 ~하다 shorten (cut down) the vacation by five days. ‖ ~수업 shortened school hours.

단출하다 《식구가》 be a family of small members; 《간편》 be simple; handy; convenient. ¶단출한 살림 a simple ménage (household) / 단출한 식구 a small family.

단층(單層) ¶ ~의 one-storied. ‖ ~집 a one-storied house.

단층(斷層) [地] a fault; a dislocation.

단침(短針) the short (hour) hand.

단칸(單一) a single room. ‖ ~살림 living in a single room.

단칼(單一) with one stroke of the sword.

단타(單打) [野] single 《to right field》. ¶ ~를 치다 single 《to right field》.

단타(短打) [野] a short-distance ball. ¶ ~로 큰 것을 치다 chop 《the ball》.

단파(短波) a shortwave. ‖ ~방송 shortwave broadcasting / ~수신 〔송신기〕 a shortwave receiver (transmitter).

단판(單一) a single round. ‖ ~에 in a single round. ¶ ~승부 a game of single round.

단팥죽 sweet red-bean broth.

단편(短篇) a short piece; a sketch. ‖ ~소설 a short story / ~소설집 a collection of short stories / ~영화 a short film.

단편(斷片) a piece; a fragment; a scrap. ¶ ~적인 fragmentary / ~적인 지식 scraps of information.

단평(短評) a short criticism (comment). ¶ ~을 하다 make a brief comment 《on》. ¶시사~ a brief comment on current events.

단풍(丹楓) ① 《나무》 a maple (tree). ② 《잎》 fall foliage; red (yellow) leaves; autumnal tints. ¶ ~ 들다 turn red (yellow, crimson). ‖ ~놀이 (go on) an excursion for viewing autumnal tints; a maple-viewing.

단합(團合) ⇒ 단결. ‖ ~대회 a rally to strengthen the unity.

단항식(單項式) [數] a monomial (expression).

단행(單行) ‖ ~범 [法] a single offense / ~법 a special law / ~본 a book; a separate volume.

단행(斷行) ~하다 carry out 《one's *plan*》 resolutely; take a resolute step. ¶소신대로 ~하다 act according to *one's* convictions.

단호(斷乎) ¶ ~한 firm; decisive; resolute; drastic / ~히 firmly; decisively; resolutely / ~한 조처를 취하다 take decisive (drastic measures; take strong action.

단화(短靴) shoes.

닫다 《열린 것을》 shut; close. ¶ 쾅 ~ slam, bang 《*the door*》 / 닫아 걸다 lock 《a door》.

닫히다 be shut; get closed. ¶문이 저절로 닫혔다 The door shut (closed) by itself. / 창문이 잘 닫히지 않는다 The window will not close (shut). / 학교 문은 닫혀 있었다 The school gate was closed (shut).

달 ① 《하늘의》 the moon. ¶ ~의 여신 Diana / ~ 없는 밤 a moonless night / ~의 표면 〔궤도〕 the lunar surface (orbit) / ~이 차다 [이지러지다] the moon waxes (wanes). ‖ ~착륙 a lunar (moon) landing / ~착륙선 a lunar module 《생략 LM》. ②《달력의》 a month. ¶윤~ an intercalary month / 전전~ the month before last / ~마다 every month; monthly / 큰 〔작은〕 ~ an odd (even) month / 임신 다섯 ~째다 be five month pregnant.

달가닥거리다 rattle; clatter.

달가당거리다 jingle; clang; clink.

달갑다 (be) satisfactory; desirable. ¶달갑지 않은 손 an unwelcome guest / 달갑지 않은 친절 misplaced kindness; an unwelcome favor.

달개(집) a penthouse; a lean-to.

달걀 an egg. ‖ ~모양의 egg-shaped / ~의 흰자위 〔노른자〕 the white (yolk) of an egg / ~껍데기 an eggshell / 반숙 〔날, 갓 낳은〕 ~ a soft-boiled (raw, new-laid) egg / ~을 깨다 break an egg.

달견(達見) a far-sighted (an excellent) view; a fine idea.

달관(達觀) ~하다 take a long-term (philosophic) view 《of》. ¶장래를 ~하다 see far into the future 《of》 / 그는 모든 것을 ~한 사람이다 He is a philosopher.

달구 a ground rammer. ‖ ~질 ramming earth 《~질하다 ram; harden the ground》.

달구다 heat 《a piece of iron》.

달구지 a large cart; an oxcart.

달그락거리다 rattle; rumble.

달그랑거리다 jingle; clank; clink.

달다¹ ① 《맛이》 (be) sweet; sugary. ¶단것 sweet things; sweets / 맛이 ~ taste sweet; have a sweet taste / 인생의 쓴맛 단맛 the sweets and bitters of life. ② 《입맛이》 (be) tasty; palatable; pleasant to taste; 《서술적》 have a good appetite. ¶달게 먹다 eat with gusto.

달다² ① 《뜨거워지다》 become (get) heated; become hot; burn. ¶쇠가 ~ iron is heated / 빨갛게 be-

달다¹ come red-hot / 그녀의 붉은 부끄러워서 빨갛게 달아 있었다 Her cheeks were burning with shame. ② 〈마음 타다〉 fret; be anxious (impatient, nervous). ¶애인이 보고 싶어 몸이 ~ be anxious to see one's sweetheart.

달다³ ① 〈붙이다〉 attach; affix; fasten; 〈가설〉 install; fix; set up. ¶문에 종을 ~ fix a bell on the door / 셔츠에 단추를 ~ sew a button on a shirt / 전화를 ~ install [set up] a telephone; have a telephone installed. ② 〈걸다〉 put up [hang out] (a sign). ③ 〈착용〉 put on; wear. ¶메달을 ~ put on [wear] a medal. ④ 〈매달다〉 hoist; fly (a national flag). ⑤ 〈기입〉 give; enter; put (down); 〈주(註)〉 annotate; annex (make) (notes). ¶외상을 ~ put down (charges) to one's credit account.

달다⁴ 〈무게를〉 weigh. ¶저울로 ~ weigh (a thing) in the balance.

달다⁵ ask [beg] for (a thing); request; demand.

달라붙다 stick (cling, adhere) to.

달라지다 (undergo a) change; be changed (altered); turn; vary; become different. ¶마음이 ~ change one's mind / 달라지지 않다 be (remain) unchanged / 지금은 옛날과 사정이 달라졌다 Things are not what they used to be. / 크게 달라진 게 없다 It doesn't make much difference.

달랑거리다 〈방울이〉 jingle; tinkle.

달래 〈植〉 a wild rocambole.

달래다 appease; soothe; coax; calm (a person) (down). ¶우는 어린애를 ~ soothe a crying child / 시름을 술로 ~ drown one's sorrows in drink.

달러 a dollar (기호 $); a buck 〈美俗〉. ¶5~ 50센트 five dollars and fifty cents / ~로 지불해 주십시오 I'd like to be paid in dollars, please. ‖ ~박스 a source of big profits; a moneymaker / ~시세 the exchange rates of the dollar / ~지역 a dollar area.

달려들다 go at; pounce on; fly at; jump [leap] (at) on. ¶개가 사람에게 ~ a dog jumps [leaps] at a person.

달력(—曆) a calendar; an almanac (책력).

달로켓 a lunar (moon) rocket.

달리 differently; in a different way; separately (따로). ~ 하다 differ (be different) (from). ¶생각했던 것과는 ~ contrary to one's expectations / ~ 견해를 ~ 하다 have a different opinion.

달리기 a run; a race (경주). ¶~에서 이기다 win a race. ‖ ~선수 a runner; a racer.

달리다¹ 〈부족〉 떨리다.

달리다² 〈기운이〉 sag; be languid (tired). ¶기운이 ~ lose one's energy (vigor); become enervated.

달리다³ 〈질주〉 run; dash; hurry; sail (배가); drive (a car) (with speed); gallop (a horse). ¶달려서 run (hasten) to / 달려오다 come running; run up to / 현장으로 달려가다 rush to the scene (of).

달리다⁴ ① 〈매달리다〉 hang (on, from); dangle; be suspended (from); be hung. ② 〈붙어 있다〉 be attached (fixed). ¶큰 거울이 달린 화장대 a dressing table with a large mirror / 꼬리표가 달린 트렁크 a trunk with a tag attached (fixed). ③ 〈여하에〉 depend on. ¶그것은 사정 여하에 달렸다 It depends on the (respective) circumstances.

달마(達磨) Dharma 〈梵〉.

달맞이 ~ 하다 view [welcome] the first full moon.

달무리 a halo; a ring around the moon.

달밤 a moonlight (moonlit) night.

달변(達辯) eloquence; fluency. ¶~의 eloquent; fluent.

달빛 moonlight. ¶~을 받고 in the moonlight.

달성(達成) achievement. ~ 하다 accomplish; achieve; attain; carry through. ¶목적을 ~ 하다 attain one's purpose.

달아나다 ① 〈도망〉 run (get) away; flee; take to flight; escape; make off. ¶…을 가지고 ~ run away (make off) with (public money) / 적을 달아나게 하다 put the enemy to flight. ② 〈달리다〉 run; dash; speed. ¶차는 쏜살같이 달아났다 The car sped away.

달아매다 hang; suspend; dangle.

달아보다 〈무게를〉 weigh. ② 〈사람을〉 test (out); put [bring] to the test.

달아오르다 〈뜨거워지다〉 become red-hot; 〈얼굴·몸이〉 feel hot; burn.

달음(박)질 running; a run. ~ 하다 run.

달이다 boil down. ¶약을 ~ make a medical decoction / 시럽을 알맞은 농도로 ~ boil syrup down to a proper consistency.

달인(達人) an expert (at, in); a master (of).

달짝지근하다 (be) sweetish.

달창나다 〈해지다〉 wear out; be worn out; 〈바닥나다〉 run out; be used up; be all gone. 「rattle.

달카닥거리다 〈소리〉 clang; clatter;

달콤하다 (be) sweet; sugary. ¶달콤한 말 honeyed (sugared) words.

달통(達通) ~하다 be a master 《of》.

달팽이 [動] a snail. ¶ ~처럼 느린 걸음으로 [walk] at a snail's pace.

달포 a month odd.

달품 work paid for by the month.

달필(達筆) a skillful hand(솜씨); a good (running) hand(글씨); ~이다 write a good hand.

달하다 (達一) ① 《목적 등을》 attain 《one's aim》; accomplish; achieve; realize 《one's hopes》. ② 《도달》 reach; arrive in[at]; get to [at]; come up to 《the standard》. ¶ 수준에 ~ reach the level. ③ 《수량이》 reach; amount to; come (up) to. ¶ 5백만원에 ~ reach [amount to] five million won.

닭 a hen(암탉); a cock (rooster) (수탉); a chicken. ¶ ~을 치다 keep hens; raise chickens / ~이 "꼬끼오"하고 울었다 "Cock-a-doodle-doo", crowed the rooster. ‖ ~고기 chicken / ~고집 a bigot; a stiff-necked fellow / ~똥집 a gizzard / ~싸움 a cockfight / ~장 a henhouse.

닮다 resemble; be alike; look like; take after. ¶ 많이 ~ resemble 《a person》 closely.

닳다 ① 《마멸》 wear [be worn] out; be rubbed [down]. 《해지다》 get [become] threadbare. ② 《세파에》 lose one's simplicity (naïveté, modesty); get sophisticated. ¶ 닳고 단 worldly-wise; sophisticated / 닳고 닳은 여자 a saucy wench. ③ 《살갗이》 be flushed with cold.

닳리다 (해드리다) wear away [down]; rub off [down]. ¶ 구두 뒤축을 ~ wear down the heels of one's shoes.

담 (집의) a wall; a fence (울타리). ¶ ~을 두르다 set up a wall; fence round 《a house》.

담(痰) phlegm; sputum. ¶ ~을 뱉다 cough out [bring up] phlegm; spit phlegm out.

담(膽) (쓸개) gall(bladder); 《담력》 courage; pluck; nerves. ¶ ~이 작은 timid; faint-hearted.

담갈색(淡褐色) light brown.

담결석 (痰結石) 담석(膽石).

담그다 ① (물에) soak [steep] 《in》; dip 《into》. ② (김치 등) prepare (kimchi) / ③ 《절이다》 salt; preserve with salt. ③ (술을) ferment; brew (sul).

담기다 be filled [put in]; hold; be served (음식이); be bottled (병에).

담낭(膽囊) [解] the gall(bladder). ‖ ~관 the cystic duct / ~염 [醫] cholecystitis.

담다 ① 《그릇에》 put in; fill; 《음식을》 fill; serve. ¶ 밥그릇에 밥을 가득 ~ fill a rice bowl with rice / 광주리에 ~ put into a basket. ② 《입에》 speak of; talk about; mention. ¶ 입에 담지 못할 이야기 a topic that should not be mentioned / 그런 것은 입에 담지도 마라 Don't talk about such a thing. ③ ☞ 담그다.

담담하다(淡淡―) 《마음이》 (be) indifferent; disinterested; serene; 《빛·맛이》 (be) plain; light. ¶ 담담한 심경 a serene state of mind / 담담한 맛 plain taste.

담당(擔當) charge. ~하다 take charge of; be in charge 《of》 / 담당시키다 put [place] 《a person》 in charge 《of》. ¶ ~검사 the prosecutor in charge / ~구역 a district assigned to one; one's round (beat) / ~업무 the business in one's charge / ~자 a person in charge 《of》.

담대(膽大) ¶ ~한 bold; daring; fearless; plucky. ~성 fulness.

담략(膽略) courage and resource.

담력(膽力) courage; pluck; nerve; guts. ¶ ~있는 bold; courageous; plucky / ~이 없는 timid; cowardly / ~을 기르다 cultivate [foster] courage.

담록색(淡綠色) light [pale] green.

담론(談論) (a) (lively) conversation; (a) talk; a discussion. ~하다 talk over; discuss.

담배 tobacco(살담배); a cigaret(te) (궐련), ~씹는 ~ chewing tobacco / ~를 피우다 smoke (a cigaret); smoke [have] a pipe. ‖ ~가게 a cigar store (美); a tobacconist's (shop) / ~꽁초 a cigarette butt / ~쌈지 a tobacco pouch / ~설대 the bamboo stem of a pipe / 담뱃갑 a cigarette case / 담뱃값 money for tobacco / 담뱃대 a tobacco pipe / 파이프 ~ pipe tobacco.

담백(淡白) ¶ ~한 《마음이》 indifferent; candid; frank; 《맛·빛이》 light; plain; ~한 사람 a man of few wants (욕심 없는); an open-hearted person (솔직한).

담벼락 the surface of a wall.

담보(擔保) ① (보증) guarantee; assurance. ~하다 guarantee; assure. ② 《채무의》 security; mortgage(부동산의). ¶ ~로 넣다 (잡히다) give (offer) 《a thing》 as a security 《for》 / ~를 잡다 take security / …을 ~로 잡고 … 집을 ~로 하고 돈을 빌리다 borrow money on the security of 《something》. ‖ ~권 a security right / ~금 a security / ~대부 loan

담비 [動] a marten; a sable.
담뿍 ☞ 듬뿍.
담색(淡色) a light color.
담석(膽石) [醫] a gallstone. ‖ ~증 cholelithiasis.
담세(擔稅) ‖ ~력 tax-bearing capacity / ~자 a tax-payer.
담소(談笑) ~하다 chat 《with》; have a pleasant talk 《with》.
담소하다(膽小─) (be) timid; cowardly; chicken-hearted.
담수(淡水) fresh water. ‖ ~어〔魚〕 a fresh-water fish〔lake〕.
담쌓다 ①〔두르다〕 surround 《a house》 with a wall〔fence〕; build〔set up〕 a wall 《around》. ②〔관계를 끊다〕 break off relation with 《a person》; be through with. ¶ 이제 그녀와는 담을 쌓았다 I am through with her now.
담요(毯─) a blanket.
담임(擔任) charge. ~하다 be in〔take〕 charge of; take 《a class》 under one's charge. ¶2학년 영어를 ~하다 teach English in the second-year class. ‖ ~교사 a class〔homeroom 《美》〕 teacher; a teacher in charge 《of a class》 / ~반 a class under one's charge.
담쟁이 [植] an ivy.
담즙(膽汁) bile; gall. ‖ ~질 bilious temperament.
담차다(膽─) (be) stout-hearted; daring; bold; plucky.
담청색(淡靑色) light blue.
담판(談判) (a) negotiation; a parley; talks. ~하다 negotiate 《with》; have talks 《with》; bargain 《with》.
담합(談合) ①〔의논〕 consultation; conference. ~하다 consult 〔confer〕 with. ¶ ~에 의해 by mutual consent. ②〔입찰에서의〕 artful prebidding arrangement; an illegal〔improper〕 agreement 《to fix prices》; 〔口〕 bid rigging. ~하다 consult before bidding; conspire 〔collude〕 to fix prices before tendering. ¶ ~입찰에 put in 〔make〕 a rigged bid〔collusive tender〕 《for the contract》.
담홍색(淡紅色) (rose) pink.
담화(談話) a talk; a conversation; a statement (성명). ~하다 talk〔converse〕 《with》; have a talk 《with》. ‖ ~문 an official statement.
담황색(淡黃色) lemon yellow.
답(答) an answer; a reply; a response; a solution〔解答〕. ~을 내다 get〔work out〕 an answer / ~을 하지 않다 make no answer〔reply〕.

…답다 (be) -ly; -like; worthy of. ¶ 남자〔여자〕다운 manly 〔womanly, ladylike〕 / 신사답지 못한 행위 a conduct unworthy of a gentleman.
답답하다(沓沓─) ①《장소가》 (be) stuffy; suffocating; stifling; 〔숨이〕 have difficulty; breathe with difficulty; 〔날씨·분위기 등이〕 (be) oppressive; gloomy; heavy. ¶ 회의의 답답한 분위기 the stuffy〔oppressive〕 atmosphere of the meeting / 답답한 날씨 a gloomy〔sullen〕 sky / 가슴이 ~ feel heavy in the chest. ②《사람됨이》 (be) hidebound; unadaptable; lack versatility. ¶ 답답한 사람 an unadaptable man. ③《안타깝게》 (be) irritating; vexing; impatient. ¶ 자네 하는 짓이 참말 답답하군 I'm losing my patience with you. / 너무 꾸물거려 정말 ~ You are so slow that it really gets on my nerves.
답례(答禮) a return courtesy (인사에 대한); a return call (방문에 대한); a return present (선물에 대한). ~하다 salute in return; return a call; make a return 《for》; give 《a person a present》 in return.
답변(答辯) an answer; a reply; an explanation; a defense (변호). ~하다 reply; answer; explain; defend oneself.
답보(踏步) a standstill; (정체) stagnation; delay; stalemate. ~하다 step; mark time; be at a standstill; (비유적) make no progress〔headway〕.
답사(答辭) an address in reply; a response. ~하다 make a formal reply 《to》.
답사(踏査) a survey; (an) exploration; a field investigation. ~하다 explore; survey; investigate. ‖ ~대 an exploring party / 현지 ~ (make) a field investigation.
답습(踏襲) ~하다 follow〔tread〕 in 《a person's》 footsteps; follow 《the policy of…》.
답신(答申) ~하다 submit a report 《to》. ‖ ~서 a report.
답안(答案) (답) an answer; a paper; an examination paper (답안 용지). ¶ ~을 내다 hand in one's (answer) paper.
답장(答狀) an answer; a reply. ~하다 answer〔reply to〕 a letter.
답전(答電) a reply telegram. ~하다 answer 〔reply to〕 a telegram; wire back.
답지(遝至) ~하다 rush〔pour〕 in; throng〔rush〕 to 《a place》. ¶ 주문이 ~하다 have a rush of orders.

답파(踏破) ~하다 travel on foot; tramp; traverse.

답하다(答-) answer 《a question》; reply 《to》; give an answer; respond 《to》; solve (풀다).

닷… five. ¶ ~ 말 five *mal*.

닷새 ① (초닷새) the fifth day of the month. ② (다섯날) five days.

당(黨) (단체) a party; a faction (당파); a clique (도당). ¶ ~을 조직하다 form a party. ‖ ~간부 a party officer / ~권 party hegemony / ~규 party regulations / ~기 party discipline / ~기관 a party apparatus / ~대회 a (party) convention.

당(糖) sugar. ¶ 혈액 중의 ~ blood sugar. ‖ ~도 saccharinity.

당…(當) (이) this; the present, the current (현재의); (그) that; the said; 《문제의》in question; at issue. ‖ ~역(驛) this station / ~20세 be 20 years old. 그는 ~20세이다 He is 20 years old.

당고모(堂姑母) one's grandfather's niece on his brother's side.

당과(糖菓) sweets; candy.

당구(撞球) billiards. ¶ ~를 하다 play billiards. ‖ ~대 a billiard table / ~봉 a cue / ~장 a billiard room.

당국(當局) 《관계》the authorities (concerned). ¶ ~의 명에 의하여 by order of the authorities. ‖ ~자 a person in authority (한 사람).

당근(植) a carrot.

당기(當期) (this) (the current, the present) term (period). ¶ ~의 결산 the settlement of accounts for this term. ‖ ~손익 the profits and losses for this term.

당기다 〔끌다〕 draw; pull; tug; haul; 〔앞당기다〕 advance; move 《a date》up 〔forward〕.

당기다 〔입맛이〕 stimulate 〔whet〕 one's appetite; make one's mouth water.

당나귀 an ass; a donkey.

당년(當年) 《금년》 this 〔the current〕 year; 《왕년》 those years 〔days〕.

당뇨병(糖尿病) 〔醫〕 diabetes. ‖ ~환자 a diabetic.

당닭(唐-) a bantam.

당당(堂堂) ¶ ~한 grand; stately; dignified; fair / ~히 in a dignified 〔grand〕 manner; fair and square / ~한 풍채 a stately 〔dignified〕 appearance / ~히 싸우다 play fair.

당대(當代) 《한평생》 one's lifetime; 《시대》 the present generation 〔age〕; those days.

당도(當到) ~하다 arrive 《at, in》; reach; gain; get to.

당돌(唐突) ¶ ~한 bold; plucky; fearless; 《주제넘은》forward; rude / ~히 abruptly; rudely.

당락(當落) the result of an election; success (or defeat) in an election. ‖ ~정책 party policy.

당략(黨略) party politics; a party policy.

당량(當量) 〔理·化〕 equivalent.

당론(黨論) a party opinion.

당류(糖類) 〔化〕 a saccharide.

당리(黨利) the party interests. ¶ ~를 도모하다 promote 〔advance〕 party interests. ‖ ~당략 party interests and politics.

당면(唐麵) Chinese noodles; starchy 〔farinaceous〕 noodles.

당면(當面) ~하다 face; confront. ¶ ~한 문제 the matter 《question》 in hand; an urgent problem.

당무(黨務) party affairs. ‖ ~자(英).

당밀(糖蜜) syrup; molasses; treacle.

당번(當番) duty(의무): (a) turn(차례); watch; 《사람》 the person on duty(watch). ~하다 be on duty.

당부(當否) right or wrong; justice; 《적부》 propriety; fitness.

당부하다(當付—) ask 〔tell, request〕《a person》to do 《something》; entrust 《a person》with.

당분(糖分) (the amount of) sugar. ¶ ~을 함유하다 contain sugar. ‖ ~측정기 a saccharometer.

당분간(當分間) 〔현재〕 for the present 〔time being〕; 〔얼마 동안〕 for some time (to come).

당비(黨費) party expenditure 〔expenses〕.

당사(當事) ~국 the countries concerned 〔involved〕 / ~자 the person concerned; an interested party.

당선(當選) 〔선거에서의〕 (success in an) election; 〔현상에서의〕 winning a prize. ~하다 〔선거에서〕 be elected; win a seat in 《the Senate》; 〔현상에서〕 win a prize; be accepted. ¶ 그는 ~이 확실하다 He has a good chance of being elected. / 현상의 논문이 1등으로 ~되다 win the first prize in the prize essay contest. ‖ ~소설 a prize novel / ~자 a successful candidate; an elected; a prize winner (현상의).

당세(當世) the present day 〔time〕.

당세(黨勢) the strength 〔size〕 of a party. ¶ ~를 확장하다 expand the party strength; enhance the party prestige.

당수(黨首) the party leader; the leader 〔head〕 of a political party. ¶ 3당 ~회담 a conference 〔talk〕 among the heads of three political parties.

당숙(堂叔) a male cousin of one's father.

당시(唐詩) the poems of *Tang* age.

당시(當時)《그때》(in) those days; (at) that time; then. ¶ ~의 of those days; then / ~의 총리 the then Prime Minister / ~의 대학생 university students of those days.

당신(當身)《2인칭》you;《애인·부부 호칭》(my) dear, (my) darling.

당아욱(唐一)〖植〗a mallow.

당연(當然) ~한 reasonable; right; proper; natural / ~히 justly; properly; naturally; as a matter of course / ~한 결과 a natural[an expected] result / ~한 권리 an undoubted right / ~한 의무 an inevitable duty / ~한 일 a matter of course / 이치(사리)상 ~하다 be in the nature of things / …하는 것은 ~하다 It is proper[natural] that one should…. / ~히 …하다고 생각하다 take it for granted that….

당원(黨員) a member of a party; a party man. ¶ ~이 되다 join a party. ‖ ~명부 the list of party members.

당월(當月) ① ☞ 이달. ②《그달》 (that) month.

당의(糖衣) sugar-coat(ing). ‖ ~정 a sugar-coated tablet [pill].

당의(黨議)《회의》a party council;《결의》a party decision.

당일(當日) the [that] day; the appointed day.

당일치기(當日一) ~로 여행을 하다 make a day's trip《to》.

당자(當者) ☞ 당사자.

당장(當場)《즉시》at once; right away [now]; immediately;《그 자리에서》on the spot; then and there. ¶ ~ 필요한 것 an immediate need / ~ 돌아가거라 Go back at once.

당쟁(黨爭) party strife. ¶ ~을 일삼다 be given to party squabbles.

당적(黨籍) the party register.

당정협의(黨政協議) a government-ruling party session; a special cabinet and ruling party consultative session.

당조짐하다 put《a person》under strict discipline; supervise strictly.

당좌(當座) ¶ ~를 트다 open a current account. ‖ ~계정 a current account / ~대부 a call loan / ~대월 an overdraft / ~수표 a check 〖美〗; a cheque 〖英〗 / ~예금 a current [checking 〖美〗] account [deposit].

당직(當直) being on duty [watch]. ~하다 be on duty [watch]. ‖ ~원 a person on duty / ~의사 a duty doctor / ~장교 an officer of the day [guard].

당직(黨職) a party post. ‖ ~개편 reorganization of a party's hierarchy / ~자 a party executive; the party leadership (총칭).

당질(堂姪) a son of male cousin.

당집(堂一) a temple; a shrine.

당차다 be small but sturdy built.

당착(撞着) contradiction; conflict. ~하다 be contradictory《to》; be inconsistent《with》; clash [conflict]《with》. ☞ 자가 당착.

당찮다(當一) (be) unreasonable; absurd; unjust; improper.

당첨(當籤) prize winning. ~하다 win a prize; draw a lucky number. ‖ ~번호 a lucky number / ~자 a prize winner.

당초(當初) the beginning. ¶ ~에 is at first; at the beginning / ~부터 from the first [start] / ~의 계획 the original plan.

당초문(唐草紋) an arabesque pattern [design].

당파(黨派) a party; a faction; a clique. ¶ ~를 만들다 form a faction [clique] / ~로 갈라지다 split into factions. ‖ ~심 partisan spirit / ~싸움 a party dispute.

당하다(當一) ①《사리에》(be) reasonable; sensible; right. ②《겪다》 encounter; experience; meet with. ¶ 불행을 ~ experience [encounter] a disaster / 사고를 ~ meet with an accident. ③《감당하다》 match; cope《with》; be equal to; be faced [confronted] 《직면》. ¶ …에는 당할 수 없다 be no match for; be too much for / 나로선 그녀를 당할 수가 없다 She is too much for me.

…당하다(當一)《입다》receive; suffer; get; be …ed. ¶ 도난 ~ be stolen; have《a thing》stolen.

당해(當該) ¶ ~의 proper; concerned; competent. ‖ ~관청 the competent [proper] authorities; the authorities concerned.

당혹(當惑) perplexity; embarrassment. ~하다 be perplexed; be embarrassed; be puzzled.

당화(糖化)〖化〗saccharification. ‖ ~효소 diastatic enzyme.

당황하다(唐慌一) be confused [upset, flustered]; lose *one's* head; panic. ¶ 당황하여 in a fluster; in confusion / 당황케 하다 confuse; upset / 당황하지 마라 Don't panic. *or* Don't get excited.

닻 an anchor. ¶ ~을 내리다 cast anchor / ~을 감다 weigh anchor. ‖ ~줄 an anchor cable.

닿다《도착하다》arrive《at, in》; get to; reach;《접하다》touch; reach (미치다). ¶ 손 닿는 [닿지 않는] 곳에 within [beyond, out of]*one's* reach / 이 방은 천장이 낮아 머리가

닿다 The ceiling of this room is so low that our heads touch **닿소리** ☞ 자음. 【reach】 것.

대[竹] (a) bamboo. ¶ 〈성격이〉 ~쪽 같은 사람 a man of frank [straightforward] disposition. ¶ ~나무세공 bamboo work / ~마디 a bamboo joint / ~바구니 a bamboo basket / ~발 a bamboo blind [screen] / ~숲 a clump of bamboo / ~울 a bamboo fence.

대 ①〈줄기〉 a stem; a stalk;〈막대〉 a pole; a staff; a holder (붓·펜의). ¶ ~가 약하다〈비유〉 be weak-kneed [fainthearted]. ②〈담뱃대〉 a (tobacco) pipe. ¶〈피우는 도수〉 a smoke; a fill(양). ¶ ~ 피우다 have a smoke [pipe]. ③〈주먹 따위의〉 a blow; a stroke. ¶ 한 ~에 at a stroke [blow].

대(大)〈greatness; largeness;〈크기〉 large size;〈커다란〉 big; large; great; grand; heavy (손해 따위). ¶ ~서울 Great Seoul / ~손해 a great loss / 실물~의 동상 a life-sized statue.

대(代)〈시대〉 a time; an age; a generation(세대); a reign (치세);〈생존대〉 one's lifetime. ¶ 10~의 소녀들 girls in their teens; teen-age girls / 제2~ 왕 the second king / ~를 잇다 carry on a family line / 미국의 제16~ 대통령 the sixteenth President of the United States.

대(隊)〈일행〉 a company; a party;〈군대의〉 a body (of troops); a corps; a unit; a squad(소수의);〈악대의〉 a band.

대(對) ①〈짝〉 a pair; a counterpart; a couple. ②《A 대 B》(A) versus (B) (생략 v.、vs.);〈…에 대한〉 against; to; toward; with. ¶ 서울 ~ 부산 경기 Seoul vs. Busan game / 4 ~ 2의 스코어 a score of 4 to 2 / 한국의 ~미 정책 Korea's policy toward the United States / ~미 교섭 negotiations with the United States / 근로자 ~ 자본가의 투쟁 a struggle of labor against capital.

대(臺) ①〈받침·걸이〉 a stand; a rest; a holder; a table(탁자); a support(지주); a pedestal(동상 등의); foundation(토대). ¶ 악보~ a music stand / 작업~ a work-table. ②〈대수〉 ¶ 5~의 자동차 five cars / 발동기 3~ three motors. ③〈액수〉 a level. ¶ 만원 ~에 달하다 touch [rise to] the level of 10,000 won.

…대(帶) a zone; a belt. ¶ 한(寒)~ the frigid zone / 화산~ a volcanic zone.

대가(大家) ①〈권위〉 an authority; a great master. ¶ 음악의 ~ a great musician / 문단의 ~ a distinguished writer [author]. ②〈큰 집안〉 a great [distinguished] family.

대가(代價) price; cost; (a) charge. ¶ ~를 치르다 pay the price; pay for《an article》/ 어떤 ~를 치르더라도 at any price [cost] / 값비싼 ~를 치르다 pay heavily [a painful price] 《for》.

대가(貸家) a house to let.

대가다 get《somewhere》on time; be in time《for》. ¶ 약속 시간에 ~ present oneself at the appointed time.

대가리 the head; the top.

대가족(大家族) a large [big] family. ¶ ~제도 an extended family system.

대각(大覺) ~하다 attain spiritual enlightenment; perceive absolute truth.

대각(對角) [數] the opposite angle. ¶ ~선 a diagonal line.

대각거리다 crackle; clatter; rattle.

대간첩(對間諜) counterespionage. ¶ ~작전 (conduct) a counterespionage operation.

대갈(大喝) ~하다 yell 《at》; thunder [roar] 《at》.

대강(大綱) 〈대강령〉 general principles;〈대략〉 an outline;〈부사적〉 generally; roughly. ¶ ~ 설명하다 (give an) outline; give a short sketch 《of》 / ~ 끝나다 be almost finished.

대강(代講) ~하다 teach [give a lecture] for [in place of《another》].

대갚음(對 ―) revenge; retaliation. ~하다 revenge; revenge oneself 《on》; give [pay] tit for tat;〈口〉 get even with《somebody》.

대개(大槪)〈개요〉 an outline;〈대략〉 mostly; generally; in general; for the most part; mainly;〈거의〉 practically; almost; nearly. ¶ ~의 경우에 most / ~의 경우 in most cases; generally.

대개념(大槪念) [論] a major concept.

대거(大擧)〈부사적〉 in a body; en masse; in great [full] force; in large [great] numbers.

대거리(對 ―) ~하다 talk [answer] back; retort.

대검(帶劍) ① wearing a sword; a sword at one's side. ② [軍] a bayonet.

대검찰청(大檢察廳) the Supreme Public Prosecutor's Office.

대견하다 (be) satisfactory; gratified; helpful. ¶ 대견하게 여기다 feel satisfactorily; take《it》laudable.

대결(對決) confrontation; a showdown. ~하다 confront oneself

대경 《with》. ¶ ~시키다 bring 《a person》face to face 《with》; confront《a person》with《another》.
대경(大驚) ~하다 be greatly surprised; be astounded (consternated). ¶ ~실색하다 lose color with astonishment.
대계(大系) an outline.
대계(大計) a far-sighted〔reaching〕policy. ¶국가의 백년 ~ a far-reaching state policy.
대고모(大姑母) a grand-aunt on one's father's side.
대공 【建】 a king post.
대공(大功) a great merit; distinguished services; a signal deed. ¶ ~을 세우다 render meritorious services; achieve great things.
대공(對空) anti-air. ¶ ~ 미사일〔포〕 anti-aircraft missile〔fire〕/ ~사격 shooting at an aircraft (from the ground).
대과(大科) the higher civil service examination.
대과(大過) a serious error; a grave〔gross〕mistake; a blunder.
대과거(大過去) 《文》 the past perfect tense.
대관(大官) a high official; a dignitary.
대관(大觀) a general〔comprehensive〕view.
대관(戴冠) coronation. ‖ ~식 a coronation〔ceremony〕.
대관절(大關節) 《부사적》 on earth; in the world; in the name of God.
대교(大橋) a grand bridge.
대구(對句) 【魚】 a codfish; a cod.
대구루루 ¶ ~굴리다 roll 《a coin》over 《the table》.
대국(大局) the general situation. ¶ ~적으로는 on the whole / ~적 견지에서 보면 on a broad survey.
대국(大國) a large country; a big power; the great powers (총칭).
대국(對局) a game《of baduk》. ~하다 play (a game of) chess〔baduk〕《with》.
대군(大君) a (Royal) prince.
대군(大軍) a large army〔force〕.
대굴대굴 ¶ ~굴르다 roll over and over.
대권(大圈) a great circle. ‖ ~항로 the great circle route.
대권(大權) sovereignty; the supreme〔governing〕power.
대궐(大闕) the royal palace. ¶ ~같은 집 a palatial mansion.
대규모(大規模) a large scale. ¶ ~의 large-scale / ~로 on a large scale; in a big〔large〕way.
대그락거리다 keep clattering〔rattling〕; clatter.
대금(大金) a large sum (of money).
대금(代金) (a) price; the (purchase) money; (a) charge; (a) cost(비용). ¶ ~을 치르다 pay the price[bill]; pay for《a thing》/ ~을 거두다 collect bills; ~ 상환으로 in exchange for the money; cash〔collect《美》〕on delivery (생략 C.O.D.). ‖ ~선불 advance payment / ~후불 deferred payment.
대금(貸金) a loan. ‖ ~업 money-lending business; usury(고리대금).
대기(大氣) the air; the atmosphere. ‖ ~권 the atmosphere《~권 밖으로 into outer space》/ ~압[력] atmospheric pressure / ~오염 (atmospheric) pollution.

대기(大器) (그릇) a large vessel; (인재) a great talent〔genius〕. ‖ ~만성 Great talents mature late.
대기(待機) stand by; waiting for a chance. ~하다 watch and wait 《for》; stand ready for. ¶ 항상 ~하고 있다 be on constant alert. ‖ ~궤도 a parking orbit / ~명령 an order to leave one's post and to wait for further action; being placed on the waiting list / ~상태 stand-by status.
대기업(大企業) a large enterprise〔corporation〕; a conglomerate; big business.
대길(大吉) excellent luck; a great stroke of luck.
대난(大難) a great misfortune; crisis.
대남(對南) ‖ ~간첩 an espionage agent against the South / ~공작 operations against the South.
대납(代納) payment by proxy. ~하다 pay for 《another》.
대낮(백주) broad daylight; the daytime; high noon; midday.
대내(對內) ¶ ~적인 domestic; internal; home. ‖ ~정책 a domestic policy.
대농(大農) large-scale farming (부농); a wealthy farmer.
대뇌(大腦) the cerebrum〔pl. -s, -bra〕; the brain proper. ‖ ~막 the cerebral membrane / ~피질 the cerebral cortex.
대다¹ ① (접촉) put《a thing》on〔over〕; place; lay; apply《a thing》to〔on〕; touch. ¶손을 ~ touch; put one's hand to; 손대지 마시오 Hands off. ② (비교) compare with; make a comparison with. ¶길이를 보다와 compare the length / …에 댈 것이 못되다 be no match for; cannot stand comparison with. ③ (착수·관여) set one's hand 《to》; have a hand 《in》; concern oneself 《with》; start〔attempt〕《a new business》; meddle with〔in〕. ¶ 정

치에 손을 ~ meddle in politics / 투기에 손을 ~ dabble in (go in for) speculation / 어디서부터 손을 대야할 지 모르겠다 I don't know where to begin. ④ 《공급》 furnish (supply, provide) 《a person》 with. ¶ 학비를 ~ supply a student with his school expenses. ⑤ 《도착》 bring to; pull. ¶ 배를 해안에 ~ bring a boat to the shore. ⑥ 《알리다》 tell; inform; confess (고백); make (평계를). ¶ 증거를 ~ give evidence / 평계를 ~ make an excuse for *oneself*. ⑦ 《관개》 water; irrigate. ¶ 논에 물을 ~ water a rice field. ⑧ 《연결·대면》 bring into contact; connect; link; get 《a person》 on the telephone (전화에). ¶ 살 사람과 팔 사람을 ~ bring a buyer into contact with a seller / 김군 좀 대주시오 Get me Mr. Kim, please.
대다 《행동·동작》 ~ 를 떠들어나 noise about / 먹어 ~ gluttonize (바람이) 불어 ~ blow hard.
대다수(大多數) a large majority; the greater part 《of》. ¶ ~ 를 점하다 hold a large majority.
대단(大端) ~ 한 《수가》 a great (large) number of; 《양이》 much; a great (good) deal of; 《엄청남》 innumerable; enormous; 《놀라운》 horrible; tremendous; wonderful; 《중대·심각》 serious; grave; 《뛰어난》 great / ~ 히 very; awfully; seriously; exceedingly; greatly / ~ 찮은 of little (no) importance (value); insignificant; slight; trivial; worthless.
대단원(大團圓) the end; the (grand) finale; the finis.
대담(大膽) ~ 한 bold; daring / ~ 하게 boldly; daringly; fearlessly / ~ 하게도 … 하다 be bold enough (have the nerve) to 《do》.
대담(對談) a talk; a conversation; an interview. ¶ ~ 하다 talk; converse 《*with*》; have a talk 《*with*》.
대답(對答) an answer; a reply; a response. ¶ ~ 하다 answer; reply; give an answer.
대대(大隊) a battalion. ‖ ~ 장 a battalion commander.
대대(代代) ¶ ~ 로 for generations; from generation to generation; from father to son.
대대적(大大的) ¶ ~ 으로 extensively; on a large scale / 신제품을 ~ 으로 선전하다 advertise *one's* new product in a big way.
대도(大道) ① ☞ 대로(大路). ② 倫 the right way; a great moral principle. ‖ ~ 무문(無門) A great way has no door.
대도시(大都市) a large city. ‖ ~ 권 the metropolitan area.

대독(代讀) reading by proxy. ~ 하다 read for 《*another*》.
대동(大同) ¶ ~ 소이하다 be practically (just about) the same; be much alike. ‖ ~ 단결 unity; (grand) union; solidarity.
대동(帶同) ~ 하다 take 《a person》 (along) 《*with one*》; be accompanied 《*by*》. ‖ ~ 맥[解] the main artery; the aorta.
대두(大豆) a soybean. ☞ 콩.
대두(擡頭) rise 《of》. ~ 하다 raise 《*its*》 head; gain power; become conspicuous. ¶ 민족주의의 ~ the rise of nationalism.
대들다 fall on (upon); defy; challenge; fly at; retort (말대꾸).
대들보(大-) a girder; a crossbeam.
대등(對等) equality. ¶ ~ 한 equal; even / ~ 하게 on equal terms; on an equal footing.   [right.
대뜸 at once; immediately; outright.
대란(大亂) a great disturbance.
대략(大略) 《개요》 an outline; 《적요》 a summary; 《발췌》 an abstract; 《약》 about; roughly; 《거의》 mostly; nearly. ¶ ~ 를 말하다 give an outline (a summary) 《*of*》 / ~ 다음과 같다 It summarized as follows.
대량(大量) a large quantity 《*of*》; a large amount. ‖ ~ 생산 mass production 《~ 생산하다 mass-produce》 / ~ 소비 mass consumption 《~ 주문 a bulk order》 / ~ 학살 mass murder; massacre / ~ 해고 (a) mass discharge (dismissal).
대령 ~ 하다 await orders.
대령(大領) 《육군》 a colonel 《생략 Col.》; 《해군》 a captain 《생략 Capt.》; 《공군》 a group captain 《英》; a (flight) colonel 《美》.
대례(大禮) 《결혼》 a marriage (wedding) ceremony.
대로(大怒) wild rage; violent (great) anger. ~ 하다 be enraged 《*with*, *at*》; be (grow) furious.
대로(大路) a broad street; a highway.
대로 ① 《같이》 like; as; as it is; 《…에 따라》 as; according to [as]; in accordance with. ¶ 예상한 ~ as was expected / 규칙 ~ according to the rule / 법률 ~ in accordance with the law. ② 《곧》 as soon as; immediately; directly. ¶ 도착하는 ~ as soon as *one* arrives; on *one's* arrival / 형편 닿는 ~ at *one's* earliest opportunity.
대롱 (a bamboo) tube. [venience.
대롱거리다 dangle; swing.
대류(對流) a convection (current).
대륙(大陸) a continent. ¶ ~ 의 [적인] continental / 아시아 [유럽] ~

대리 the Continent of Asia (Europe). ‖ ~간 탄도탄 an intercontinental ballistic missile (생략 ICBM) / ~붕 a continental shelf / ~성 기후 a continental climate / ~이 동설 the continental-drift theory / ~횡단철도 a transcontinental railroad (railway).

대리(代理) 《행위》 representation; 《대리인》 an agent; a representative; a proxy; a deputy; attorney(변정의). ~하다 act for (in behalf of) 《a person》; represent; act as 《a person's》 proxy. ¶ …의 ~로 in (on) behalf of…; ~로 by proxy / 내가 남편의 ~노릇을 하겠다 I'll act for my husband. ¶ ~공사 (대사) a *chargé d'affaires* / ~모 a surrogate mother / ~전생 a war by proxy; a proxy war / ~점 an agency.

대리석(大理石) marble.

대립(對立) opposition; confrontation; antagonism; rivalry (대항). ~하다 be opposed 《to》; confront 《each other》. ¶ 서로 ~하는 의견 an opposing (a rival) opinion / ~와 ~하여 in opposition to…; in rivalry with….

대마(大麻) 《植》 hemp. ¶ ~로 만든 hempen. ‖ ~초 marijuana; hemp; a hemp cigarette.

대만(臺灣) Taiwan. ¶ ~의 Taiwanese / ~사람 a Taiwanese / ~해협 the Taiwan Strait.

대만원(大滿員) 만원. ¶ ~의 filled to overflowing / ~의 관중 an overflowing audience.

대망(大望) (an) ambition; (an) aspiration. ~하다 ~을 가진 ambitious; aspiring / ~을 품다 have (harbor) an ambition 《to do》.

대망(待望) ~하다 wait for; expect; look forward to. ¶ ~의 hoped-for; long-awaited (-expected) / ~의 사내아이가 태어났다 The long-awaited baby boy was born.

대매출(大賣出) a special big sale. ‖ 반액(싼) ~ a half-price (thankyou) big sale.

대맥(大麥) barley. ☞ 보리.

대머리(머리) a bald head; 《사람》 a bald-headed person. ¶ ~가 되다 become bald-headed.

대면(面面) an interview. ~하다 interview; meet; see. ¶ 첫 ~ the first meeting / 20년만에 ~하다 meet after twenty years' separation.

대명(待命) awaiting orders; pending appointment. ~하다 be ordered to await further instructions.

대명사(代名詞) a pronoun. ‖ 관계 (지시, 인칭, 의문) ~ the relative (demonstrative, personal, interrogative) pronoun.

대모(代母) a godmother.

대모집(大募集) a wholesale employment; an extensive employment.

대목 《시기》 the busiest (highest) occasion; the most important time; a rush period (상인의); 《부분》 a part; a passage. ¶ 설달 ~ the rush period of the year-end / 어려운 ~ a difficult passage.

대목(臺木) 《접목의》 a stock. ☞ sage.

대문(大門) the front (main) gate.

대문자(大文字) a capital (letter). ¶ ~로 쓰다 write in capitals.

대문장(大文章) 《잘된 글》 masterful writing; 《사람》 a great master of (literary) style.

대물(對物) ~의 real; objective. ‖ ~렌즈 an object glass (lens) / ~배상책임보험 property damage liability insurance.

대물(代物) a substitute. ‖ ~변제 payment in substitutes.

대물리다(代一) hand down (leave, transmit) to *one's* posterity. ¶ 손자에게 재산을 ~ bequeath *one's* property to *one's* grandson.

대미(對美) ¶ 한국인의 ~ 감정 the Korean sentiments toward the Americans / ~ 의존 reliance upon (on) the U.S. ‖ ~무역 trade with the U.S. / ~수출 export to the U.S. / ~수출자주 규제 voluntary restriction (curtailment) of exports to the U.S. / ~정책 a policy toward the U.S.

대민(對民) ¶ ~봉사활동 service for public welfare / ~사업 a project for the people.

대박(反駁) retort; contradict.

대받다(代一) succeed to; inherit.

대번에 (곧) at once; immediately; in a moment; easily(쉽게).

대범(大汎) ~한 liberal; broadminded; large-hearted.

대법관(大法官) a justice of the Supreme Court.

대법원(大法院) the Supreme Court. ‖ ~장 the Chief Justice.

대법회(大法會) 《佛》 a (Buddhist) high mass; a great memorial service.

대변(大便) excrement; feces; stools. ¶ ~을 보다 defecate; empty (evacuate) *one's* bowels; relieve *oneself*; have a bowel movement.

대변(代辯) ~하다 speak for 《another》; act as spokesman 《of》. ‖ ~자(인) a spokesman; a mouthpiece; a spokesperson.

대변(貸邊) 《장부의》 the credit side. ¶ ~에 기입하다 enter on the credit side. ‖ ~계정 a credit account.

대변(對邊) [數] the opposite side.
대별(大別) ~하다 classify [divide] roughly 《*into*》; make a general classification 《*of*》.
대보다 compare 《*A with B*》; make a comparison 《*between*》.
대보름(大一) the 15th of January by the lunar calendar.
대본(大本) the foundation; the basic principle. [rental book.
대본(貸本) a book for rent; ⌐
대본(臺本) 《연극의》 a (play) script; 《영화의》 a (film) script, a scenario; 《가극의》 a libretto.
대본산(大本山) the main temple of a Buddhist sect.
대부(代父) a godfather.
대부(貸付) loan(ing). ~하다 lend; loan. ‖ ~계(원) a loan teller / ~계정 a loan account / ~금 a loan; an advance / 신용~ a loan on personal pledge; an open credit.
대부분(大部分) most 《*of*》; the major (greater) part 《*of*》; 《부사적으로》 mostly; largely; for the most part. [mother.
대부인(大夫人) your (his) (esteemed)⌐
대북방송(對北放送) broadcasting toward the North. [dha.
대불(大佛) a big statue of Bud-⌐
대비(大妃) a Queen Dowager; a Queen Mother.
대비(對比) 《對照》 contrast; comparison. ~하다 contrast (compare) 《*two things, A and B*》.
대비(對備) provision 《*for, against*》; preparation 《*for*》. ~하다 prepare for; provide against (for). ¶ 만일에 ~하다 provide against emergency (a rainy day) / 적의 습격에 ~하다 provide (guard *oneself*) against an enemy attack.
대사(大事) 《중대사》 a matter of grave concern; 《大禮》 a marriage ceremony.
대사(大使) an ambassador; an envoy (특사). ¶ 주영 ~ an ambassador to Great Britain / ~급 회담을 열다 hold a meeting at ambassadorial level; hold an ambassadorial-level meeting.
대사(大師) a saint; a great Buddhist priest.
대사(大赦) ☞ 일반 사면.
대사(臺詞) speech; *one's* lines; words. ¶ ~를 말하다 speak *one's* part; deliver *one's* lines / ~를 잊다 forget *one's* lines.
대사관(大使館) an embassy. ‖ ~원 (a member of) the embassy staff / ~참사관 a councilor of an embassy / 미국~ the American Embassy / 주미한국~ the Korean Embassy in Washington, D.C.

대사업(大事業) a great undertaking; a great enterprise.
대상(大祥) the second anniversary of 《*a person's*》 death.
대상(代償) compensation; a price. ¶ …의 ~으로 in compensation (return) for / ~을 요구 (지불)하다 demand (pay) compensation 《*for*》. ‖ ~수입 compensatory imports.
대상(隊商) a caravan.
대상(對象) the object 《*of study*》; a target 《*of criticism*》. ¶ 고교생을 ~으로 하는 사전 a dictionary for highschool students.
대생(對生) [植] ~의 opposite. ‖ ~엽 opposite leaves.
대서(大書) ~특필하다 write in large (golden) letters; mention specially; make special mention 《*of*》; 《신문 따위가》 lay special stress on. [for another.
대서(代書) ~하다 write 《*a letter*》⌐
대서다 ① 《뒤따라서다》 stand close behind 《*a person*》; follow. ② 《대들다》 stand against 《*a person*》; turn against (upon) 《*a person*》; defy.
대서양(大西洋) [地] the Atlantic (Ocean). ¶ ~의 Atlantic. ‖ ~헌장 the Atlantic Charter / ~횡단 비행 a transatlantic flight.
대석(臺石) a pedestal (stone).
대선거구제(大選擧區制) a major constituency system.
대설(大雪) 《눈》 a heavy snow; 《절후》 the 21st of the 24 seasonal divisions of the year.
대성(大成) ~하다 《사람이》 attain (come to) greatness; be crowned with success.
대성(大聖) a great sage.
대성(大聲) a loud voice (tone). ¶ ~질호하다 address vehemently; thunder; vociferate / ~통곡하다 weep loudly (bitterly).
대성황(大盛況) prosperity; a great success. ¶ ~을 이루다 be prosperous (a great success).
대세(大勢) 《形勢》 the general situation (trend); the main current. ¶ 세계의 ~ the international situation / ~에 따르다 (역행하다) go with (against) the tide.
대소(大小) great and small sizes; size (크기). ¶ ~의 large and (or) small; of all (various) sizes / ~에 따라 according to size.
대소(大笑) ~하다 roar with laughter; laugh (out) aloud.
대소(代訴) litigation by proxy. ~하다 sue on behalf of 《*another*》; sue by proxy.
대소동(大騷動) an uproar; (a) fuss; a great disturbance. ☞ 소동. ¶ 하찮은 일로 ~을 일으키다 make a

대소변(大小便) urine and feces; (용변) urination and defecation. ¶ 혼자서는 ~도 못 가린다 be unable to defecate or urinate by oneself.

대속(代贖) redemption (atonement) on behalf of another. ~하다 redeem; atone for 《a person》.

대손(貸損) a bad debt; an irrecoverable debt. ~준비금 a bad debt reserve.

대수(大數) ① 《큰 수》 a great 〔large〕 number. ② 《대운》 a good luck; great fortune.

대수(代數) 〖數〗 algebra. ~식 an algebraical expression / ~학자 an algebraist.

대수(對數) 〖數〗 a logarithm. ~표 a table of logarithms.

대수롭다 (be) important; valuable; significant; serious. ¶ 대수롭지 않은 trifle; trivial; of little 〔no〕 importance; insignificant / 대수롭게 여기지 않다 slight; ignore; pay little attention 《to》 / 대수롭지 않은 일에 화를 내다 lose one's temper on a slight provocation.

대수술(大手術) a major operation.

대숲 a bamboo thicket 〔grove〕.

대승(大乘) ¶ ~적 견지 a broader viewpoint. ‖ ~불교 Mahayanist Buddhism.

대승(大勝) ~하다 win 〔gain〕 a great victory; win a landslide 〔over〕 (선거에서).

대식(大食) gluttony. ~하다 eat a lot 〔a great deal〕. ~的 gluttonous. ‖ ~가 a great 〔big〕 eater; a glutton.

대신(大臣) a minister 〔of state〕; a State 〔Cabinet〕 minister.

대신(代身) 《부사적》 instead of; in place of; on 〔in〕 behalf of; (as a substitute) for; while (반면에); in return (exchange, compensation) 〔for〕 (대상으로). ~하다 take the place of; take 《a person's》 place; be substituted for. ¶ 가스 ~ 전기를 쓰다 use electricity instead of gas / 자기 사람을 보내다 send a deputy / 비싼 ~ 오래 간다 While a bit expensive, it wears long. / 그 ~ 내일은 자네가 한턱 내야 해 In return, you should treat me tomorrow.

대실(貸室) a room to 〔for〕 hire.

대심(對審) a trial (공판); confrontation (대질). ~하다 confront 《the accused with the accuser》.

대아(大我) absolute ego; the higher self.

대안(代案) an alternative 〔plan〕. ~을 제시하다 make an alternative plan 〔measure〕.

대안(對岸) the other side 《of a river》; the opposite bank 〔shore〕. ~의 불구경하듯하다 look on 《a trouble》 unconcernedly.

대안(對案) a counterproposal.

대액(大厄) 〈재난〉 a great misfortune (calamity, disaster).

대야 a basin; a washbowl.

대양(大洋) the ocean. ¶ ~의 oceanic; ocean. ‖ ~주 Oceania.

대어(大魚) a large 〔big〕 fish. ¶ ~를 놓치다 (비유적) narrowly miss a great chance of obtaining success. 〔good haul.

대어(大漁) a large 〔good〕 catch; a

대언(大言) big talk; boasting; bragging. ¶ ~장담하다 talk big 〔tall〕; brag; boast 《of, about》.

대업(大業) a great achievement 〔enterprise〕.

대여(貸與) lending; a loan. ~하다 loan; lend. ‖ ~금 a loan / ~장학금 a loan scholarship.

대여섯 five or six; several.

대역(大役) an important task 〔duty, mission〕; an important part (role). ¶ ~을 맡다 be charged with an important part 〔duty〕 / ~을 완수하다 accomplish one's important mission.

대역(代役) a substitute; (연극의) an understudy; (영화의) a stand-in. ¶ ~을 하다 act in 《a person's》 place; play the part for 《another》.

대역(對譯) a translation printed side by side with the original text.

대역죄(大逆罪) high treason.

대열(隊列) a line; the ranks formation. ~을 짓다 form ranks / ~을 지어 in line 〔procession〕 / ~ in formation. 〔days.

대엿새 five or six days; several

대오(大悟) spiritual awakening. ~하다 attain spiritual awakening; be enlightened. 〔for〕.

대오다 come 〔arrive〕 on time

대왕(大王) a (great) king. ¶ 세종 ~ Sejong the Great.

대외(對外) ~의 foreign; external; outside (외부). ¶ ~경제협력 기구 EDCF (◀ Economic Development Cooperation Fund) / ~관계 international relations / ~무역 foreign 〔overseas〕 trade / ~방송 a broadcasting abroad / ~원조 a foreign aid / ~정책 a foreign policy.

대요(大要) 〈개략〉 an outline; a summary; a résumé (프.). ¶ 국사 ~ an outline of Korean history / ~를 설명하다 give the outline 《of》.

대용(代用) substitution. ~하다 substitute 《A for B》; use 《one

thing) as a substitute for 《*another*》. ¶ 빈 깡통을 재떨이 ~으로 이용하다 use the empty can as an ashtray / 이것은 화병의 ~이 된다 This serves as a vase. ‖ ~품 a substitute (article).

대용(貸用) ~하다 take 〔use〕 on loan; borrow.

대우(待遇) treatment(처우); reception(접대); pay(급료). ~하다 treat; receive; pay. ¶ ~가 좋다 〔나쁘다〕 be treated well 〔badly〕; meet with a friendly 〔cold〕 reception; 《급료》 be well 〔poorly〕 paid / 이사 ~의 부장 a department chief with board-member status / 신사 ~를 하다 treat 《*a person*》 as a gentleman. ‖ ~개선 《근로조건의》 improvement of working conditions; 《급료 인상》 increase of wages.

대운(大運) great fortune; good luck. ‖ ~ary (of a temple).

대웅전(大雄殿) the main sanctuary.

대원(大願) one's cherished desire.

대원수(大元帥) the generalissimo.

대원칙(大原則) the broad principle.

대월(貸越) an overdraft; an outstanding account.

대위(大尉) 《육군》 a captain; 《공군》 a captain; a flight lieutenant 《英》; 《해군》 a lieutenant.

대위법(對位法) 〔樂〕 counterpoint.

대유(大儒) a great Confucianist (유학의); a great scholar.

대응(對應) ~하다 correspond with 《to》; 《맞먹다》 be equivalent to; 《대항·대처》 cope with; deal with. ‖ ~책 a countermeasure.

대의(大意) 《요지》 the gist; the substance; 《개략》 a general idea; an outline.

대의(大義) 《목적》 a (great) cause; 《충의》 loyalty; 《정의》 justice; righteousness. ¶ 평화라는 ~를 위하여 in 〔for〕 the noble cause of peace / ~ 명분이 서지 않다 cannot be justified; be not justifiable / …라는 ~ 명분으로 in the cause of…; on the pretext of….

대의(代議) ‖ ~원 a delegate; a representative / ~제도 a representative 〔parliamentary〕 system.

대인(大人) ①《남의 아버지》 your 〔his〕 (esteemed) father. ②《어른》 a grown-up; an adult. ‖ ~용 for adults. ③《위인》 a great man.

대인(代印) signing per procuration. ~하다 sign 〔set a seal〕 by proxy.

대인(對人) ‖ ~관계 〔신용, 담보〕 personal relations 〔credit, security〕/ ~방어 man-to-man defense.

대인기(大人氣) a big hit; great popularity; a great success. ¶ ~다 be very popular 《*with, among*》; make a great hit.

대인물(大人物) a great man (character, figure).

대일(對日) ‖ ~감정 the sentiment toward Japan / ~관계 〔무역〕 relations 〔trade〕 with Japan.

대임(大任) a great task; an important charge (mission). ¶ ~을 맡다 undertake a great task / ~을 맡기다 entrust 《*a person*》 with an important duty.

대입준비학원(大入準備學院) a college entrance test preparation institute.

대입학력고사(大入學力考査) the national 〔state-run〕 scholastic achievement test for the college entrance.

대자대비(大慈大悲) great mercy and compassion.

대자보(大字報) a big-character paper; a wall poster.

대자연(大自然) nature; creation; Mother Nature; 《Mighty》 Nature.

대작(大作) a great work; a masterpiece (걸작); a voluminous work (방대한).

대작(代作) 《글의》 ghostwriting. ~하다 ghostwrite; write for 《*a person*》. ¶ ~자 a ghostwriter.

대작(對酌) drink together; exchange cups 《*between*》; hobnob 《*with*》.

대장(大將) a general (육군, 공군); an admiral (해군).

대장(大腸) the large intestine. ‖ ~균 a colon bacillus / ~염 colitis / ~카타르 catarrh of the large intestine.

대장(隊長) a (troop) commander; a captain; a leader.

대장(臺帳) a ledger (회계부); a register (登錄部). ¶ ~에 기입하다 make an entry (of an item) in the ledger. ‖ ~간 a smithy; a forge.

대장간(一間) a blacksmith's shop.

대장경(大藏經) 〔佛〕 the complete collection of Buddhist Scriptures 《Sutras》.

대장부(大丈夫) a (brave) man; a manly (great) man. ¶ ~답게 굴라 Be a man! *or* Play the man!

대장장이(一匠一) a blacksmith.

대저(大抵) generally 〔speaking〕; on the whole; as a rule.

대적(大敵) a powerful 〔formidable〕 enemy; a formidable rival (경쟁자).

대적(對敵) ~하다 turn 〔fight, face〕 against; 《겨루다》 vie 〔contend〕 《*with*》; compete 《*with*》.

대전(大典) 《의식》 a state ceremony; 《법전》 a code of laws.

대전(大戰) a great war 〔battle〕. ‖

대전 구라파 ~ the great European war / 제2차 세계 ~ World War II; the Second World War.

대전(帶電) [理] electrification. ¶ ~ 하다 take an electrical charge. ¶ ~ 방지용 스프레이 an anti-static spray. ‖ ~ 체 a charged body.

대전(對戰) ~ 하다 encounter 《the enemy》; fight 《with》; play a match 《against》 / ~ 시키다 match 《a person》 against 《another》. ¶ ~ 료 a fight money / ~ 상대 an opponent / ~ 성적 the win-lose records 《between》.

대전제(大前提) [論] the major premise.

대전차(對戰車) anti-tank. ‖ ~ 포(미사일) an anti-tank gun (missile).

대절(貸切) ¶ ~ 의 chartered; reserved; booked 《英》 / 이 차량은(차는) ~ 이다 This carriage (car) is reserved. / ~ 버스(비행기) a chartered bus (plane).

대접(그릇) a (soup) bowl.

대접(待接) treatment; reception; entertainment. ~ 하다 treat; receive; entertain. ¶ 극진히 ~ 하다 give 《a person》 warm hospitality; entertain 《a person》 cordially. 〔venae cavae〕.

대정맥(大靜脈) the vena cava 〔pl.

대제(大帝) a great emperor. ¶ 피터 ~ Peter the Great.

대제(大祭) a grand festival.

대조(大潮) the flood (major) tide.

대조(對照) (a) contrast; (a) comparison. ~ 하다 contrast (compare) 《A with B》. ¶ ~ 를 이루다 form (present) a contrast 《with》 / …와 ~ 적으로 in contrast to….

대졸(大卒) a college (university) graduate.

대종(大宗) (系統) the main stock; 《주요품》 the main items. ¶ 수출의 ~ the staple items for export. ‖ ~ 가 a head (main) family.

대좌(對坐) ~ 하다 sit opposite 《to》; sit face to face 《with》.

대죄(大罪) a heinous (high) crime; a grave offense; a felony.

대죄(待罪) ~ 하다 await the official decision on one's punishment.

대주(貸主) the lender; the creditor; the lessor (부동산의).

대주교(大主敎) an archbishop.

대주다 supply (provide, furnish) 《a person with》.   〔runner.

대주자(代走者) 《야구의》 a pinch

대중 《걸어림》 a rough estimate (calculation); 《추측》 guess; 《표준》 a standard. ~ 을 잡다 〔겉어림하다〕 make a rough estimate 《of》; 〔기준을 세우다〕 set up a standard / ~ 없다 be hard to foresee; be uncertain (irregular); be without a fixed principle(주견 없다).

대중(大衆) the masses; the populace; 《일반 대중》 the (general) public. ¶ ~ 의 지지를 얻다 have the support of the public; have mass support / ~ 화하다 popularize; make a thing popular. ‖ ~ 매체 the mass media / ~ 문학(문화) popular literature (culture) / ~ 성 popular appeal; popularity / ~ 식당 a cheap restaurant / ~ 운동 a mass movement / ~ 지(잡지) a popular writer (magazine).

대증(對症) ‖ ~ 요법 symptomatic treatment.

대지(大地) the earth; the ground.

대지(垈地) a (building) site (lot); (a plot of) ground.

대지(臺紙) (paste)board; ground paper; a mount (사진의).

대지(臺地) 《고지》 a height; 《고원》 a tableland; a plateau.

대지(貸地) land (a lot) to let (for rent).

대지(對地) ¶ ~ 의 ground to ground. ‖ ~ 공격 a ground attack; an air raid.

대지주(大地主) a great landowner.

대진(代診) a locum 《for》. ~ 하다 examine (diagnose) 《a patient》 in behalf of 《another doctor》. ‖ ~ 의사 a locum.

대진(對陣) ~ 하다 be encamped facing each other; play a match 《against》.

대질(對質) confrontation. ¶ ~ 시키다 confront 《a person》 with 《another》. ‖ ~ 심문 (a) cross-examination.

대짜(大-) a big one.

대차(大差) a great (wide, big) difference. ¶ ~ 가 있다 be very different 《from》; differ a great deal 《from》 / …와 ~ 없다 do not make much difference; be much the same.

대차(貸借) (a) loan; debit and credit. ¶ 나는 그와 아무런 ~ 관계가 없다 I have no accounts to settle with him. ‖ ~ 결제 the settlement of accounts / ~ 계정 a debtor and creditor account / ~ 대조표 a balance sheet.

대찰(大刹) a grand temple.

대책(對策) a measure; a countermeasure. ¶ 인플레 ~ 을 강구하다 take an antiinflation measure.

대처(帶妻) ‖ ~ 승 a married Buddhist priest.

대처(對處) ~ 하다 meet; deal (cope) with. ¶ 어떻게 ~ 할 방도가 없다 There is nothing that can be done about it.

대첩(大捷) a great victory. ~ 하다 win a sweeping victory.

대청(大廳) the main floored room.
대체(大體) 《개요》 an outline; a summary; 《요정》 the principal parts; 《도대체》 on earth. ¶ ~적인 general; main; rough / ~로 generally; as a whole / ~로 말하여 generally [broadly] speaking / ~넌 누구냐 What on earth are you?
대체(代替) ~하다 substitute 《A for B》; replace 《A》 with 《B》; alternate 《with》. ¶ ~물 《法》 a substitute; a fungible / ~식품 substitute food 《for rice》 / ~에너지 자원 alternative energy resources.
대체(對替) 《商》 transfer. ¶ ~로 송금하다 send money by postal transfer. / ~계정 a transfer account / ~전표 a transfer slip.
대추(植) 《나무》 a jujube tree; 《열매》 a jujube.
대출(貸出) lending; a loan. ~하다 lend; loan out; make a loan 《to》. ¶ ~금 loaned money / 부당~ an illegal advance.
대충 roughly; approximately; 《거의》 about; nearly, almost. ¶ ~설명하다 explain briefly / ~훑어보다 glance [run one's eyes] over; run over 《a morning paper》.
대충자금(對充資金) 《經》 the counterpart fund.
대치(對峙) ~하다 stand face to face 《with》; confront; face. ¶ 서로 ~하다 face with each other.
대칭(對稱) 《數》 symmetry. ¶ ~대명사 a 2nd-person pronoun / ~점 a symmetrical point.
대타(代打) 《野》 pinch-hitting. ¶ ~자 a pinch hitter.
대통(大統) the Royal line.
대통령(大統領) the Chief Executive; the President. ¶ ~의 presidential / ~클린턴 President Clinton. / ~관저 the presidential residence; the White House / 《미국의》 ~교서 a Presidential message / ~보좌관 a presidential aid / 《美》 ~부인 the First Lady / 《美》 ~선거 〔입후보자〕 a presidential election 〔candidate〕 / 예비선거 《미국의》 the presidential primary / ~제 a presidential government. 〔acting President.
대통령권한대행(大統領權限代行) the
대퇴(大腿) 《解》 the thigh. ¶ ~골 a thighbone / ~부 the femur.
대파(大破) ~하다 be greatly 〔badly〕 damaged; be ruined 〔smashed〕. 〔tion 《for》.
대파(代播) ~하다 sow in substitu=
대판(大一) ~ 싸우다 have a 「violent quarrel [big fight]《with》.
대판(大版) large size 〔edition〕.
대패 《공구》 a plane. ¶ ~질하다 plane 《a board》. / ~대팻날 a plane iron / 대팻밥 wood shavings.
대패(大敗) crushing 〔complete〕 defeat. ~하다 suffer 〔meet with〕 a crushing defeat; be severely defeated; be routed.
대폿 drinking from a bowl. ¶ 대폿값 drink money / 대폿집 a groggery; a pub.
대포(大砲) ① 《軍》 a cannon. ¶ ~를 쏘다 fire a gun. ② 《거짓말》 a 〔big〕 lie. ¶ ~를 놓다 tell a lie.
대폭(大幅) 《부사적》 largely; sharply; steeply. ¶ ~적인 가격 하락 a big fall in prices / ~적인 임금 인상 a big 〔substantial〕 raise in pay / ~적인 삭감 a sharp cut; a drastic retrenchment.
대표(代表) representation; 《대표자》 a delegation〔단체〕; a delegate 〔representative〕〔개인〕. ~하다 represent; stand 〔act〕 for. ¶ ~적인 representative; typical 〔전형적 인〕 ... 을 ~하여 on 〔in〕 behalf of.... ¶ ~번호 《전화의》 the key 〔main〕 number / ~사원 a representative partner. 〔wind.
대풍(大風) a strong 〔violent, big〕
대풍(大豊) an abundant harvest; a bumper 〔record〕 crop.
대피(待避) ~하다 take shelter 《in, under》. ¶ ~선 《철도》 a siding; a sidetrack / ~소 《좁은 도로상의》 a turnout 《美》; a passing= place 《英》 / ~호 a dugout; a 〔bomb〕 shelter.
대하(大河) a large river. ¶ ~소설 a saga 〔long〕 novel.
대하(大蝦) 《動》 a lobster.
대하다(對一) ① 《마주보다》 face; confront; 《대항하다》 oppose; 《응대하다》 receive; treat. ¶ 서로 얼굴을 ~ face each other / 친절하게 ~ receive 《a person》 warmly / 예로써 ~ treat 《a person》 with due courtesy / 힘에는 힘으로 대하라 Oppose force with force. ② 《...에 대한》 toward; to; for; 《...에 대항하여》 against. ¶ 물음에 대한 답 an answer to a question / 부모에 대한 의무 one's duty to one's parents / 문학에 대한 취미 interest in literature / 노후에 대한 충분한 대비 ample provision against one's old age / 시험에 대한 준비 preparations for an examination.
대하증(帶下症) 《醫》 leucorrhea.
대학(大學) a university 〔종합〕; a college 〔단과〕. ¶ ~ 1 〔2, 3, 4〕학년생 a freshman 〔sophomore, junior, senior〕 / ~에 가다 〔다니다〕 go to 〔be in〕 college 〔university〕 / ~을 졸업하다 graduate from

대학자 (大學者) a great scholar.
대한 (大寒) midwinter; the coldest season; (절후) the last of the 24 seasonal divisions of the year.
대한 (大韓) Korea. ‖ ~무역투자진흥공사 the Korea Trade-Investment Promotion Agency (생략 KOTRA) / ~무역협회 the Korean Foreign Trade Association (생략 KFTA) / ~민국 the Republic of Korea (생략 ROK) / ~상공회의소 the Korea Chamber of Commerce and Industry / ~적십자사 the Korea National Red Cross / ~해협 the Straits of Korea.
대합 (大蛤) a large clam. ‖ ~구이 (貝) grilled clam meat in shell / ~찜 steamed clam meat in shell.
대합실 (待合室) a waiting room.
대항 (對抗)~하다 stand against; oppose; cope with; meet. ¶ ~시키다 pit (set up) 《a person》 against 《another》. ‖ ~경기 a match; a tournament / ~책 (take) a countermeasure.
대해 (大害) great harm.
대해 (大海) the ocean; the sea. ¶ ~의 일속(一粟) a drop in the bucket (ocean).
대행 (代行)~하다 deputize 《for》; execute as proxy; act for 《another》. ¶ 아버지를 ~하다 act for one's father; act on one's father's behalf. ‖ ~기관 an agency / ~업무 agency business / ~사 an agent / ~수출 [수입] ~업자 an export [import] agent.
대헌장 (大憲章) Magna Carta.
대형 (大形) a large size. ¶ ~의 a large (-sized).
대형 (隊形) (a) formation; order. ¶ ~을 정리하다 put the formation in good order / ~을 흩뜨리다 break ranks.
대화 (對話) (a) conversation; a dialogue. ~하다 talk (converse) 《with》; have a conversation (talk) 《with》. ¶ ~형식으로 쓰인 written in dialogue.

대회 (大會) a mass [large] meeting; a rally; a general meeting; a convention; a meet [tournament] (경기의). ¶ ~를 열다 hold a mass meeting.
대흉 (大凶) worst luck; the worst of ill fortune. ¶ 흉년.
댁 (宅) (집) a house; a residence; (자택) one's house [home]; (당신) Mrs. ....
댁내 (宅內) your (his) family.
댁대구루루 ‖ ~ 구르다 roll over and over.
댄서 a dancer; a dancing girl.
댄스 a dance; dancing. ‖ ~교습소 [교사] a dancing school (instructor) / ~파티 a dance; a ball / ~홀 a dance hall.
댐 (제방) a dam. ¶ ~을 만들다 build a dam. ‖ 다섯 번 five times. 대략 다섯 번. over about five. ¶ ~번 about 댓... terrace stones.
댓바람 at a stroke [blow]; at once; quickly. ¶ 일을 ~에 해치우다 finish one's work at a stroke.
댓진 (一津) nicotine; tar.
댕그랑거리다 tinkle; jingle; clang.
댕기 a pigtail ribbon.
댕기다 (불을) light; kindle; ignite; (불이) catch fire.
댕댕 jingling; dingdong; tinkling.
댕댕하다 ① (팽팽하다) (be) tight; taut; tense. ② (옹골차다) (be) stuffed; firm; solid.
댕돌같다 (be) as hard as a rock.
더 more; longer (시간); farther (거리); further (더욱). ¶ ~ 한층 more and more; still more / 그만큼 ~ as many [much] more / 조금만 ~ a little (few) more / ~ 많이 more (a lot) more (양); (a good) many more 《?》.
더군다나 besides; moreover; further (more); in addition; what is more (worse).
더껑이 scum; cream; film. 「dirt.
더께 encrusted dirt; a layer of
더덕 〔植〕 Codonopsis lanceolata.
더덕더덕 in clusters; in bunches.
더듬거리다 ① (눈으로 보지 않고) grope (fumble, feel) 《for, after》. ¶ 더듬거리며 가다 feel (grope) one's way 《in the dark》 / 열쇠를 더듬거리며 찾다 feel (grope) for a key. ② (말을) stammer; stutter. ¶ 더듬더듬 stammering / 더듬거리며 사과하다 stammer (stutter) out an apology.
더듬다 ① ☞ 더듬거리다. ② (기억·근원 따위를) trace; follow up 《a clue》. ¶ 근원을 더듬어 올라가다 trace 《something》 back to its origin / ~ 보다 try to recall.
더듬이 〔蟲〕 a tentacle; a feeler.
더디다 (be) slow; tardy 《at》. ¶ 일손이 ~ be slow in one's work.

…더라도 if; even if; (even) though; admitting that. ¶ 아무리 적 ~ no matter how small it may be / 설령 그렇 ~ admitting (granting) that it is so; even if it were so.

더러 《다소》 some; somewhat; a little; 《이따금》 occasionally; at times; once in a while.

더러워지다 《때문다》 become dirty; be soiled; be stained.

더럭 all of a sudden; suddenly. ¶ 겁이 ~ 나다 be struck with horror.

더럽다 (be) unclean; dirty; filthy; mean(비열); indecent(추잡); stingy(인색). ¶ 더러운 옷 dirty [soiled] clothes / 돈 문제에서 ~ 굴다 be mean over money matters / 더러운 수를 쓰다 use [play] a mean [dirty] trick.

더럽히다 《때묻히다》 make dirty; soil; stain; 《명예 따위를》 disgrace; dishonor; 《오염시키다》 pollute; contaminate. ¶ 커피로 옷을 ~ stain one's dress with coffee / 하수로 강물을 ~ foul [contaminate] a river with sewage.

더미 a pile; a heap; a stack. ¶ 쓰레기 ~ a rubbish heap.

더미씌우다 shift the burden of responsibility (on a person); lay the blame at (a person's) door.

더벅머리 《머리》 disheveled [unkempt] hair. ¶ ~ 소년 a boy [lad] (who still has busy hair).

더부룩하다 《머리·수염이》 (be) bushy; shaggy. ¶ 수염이 ~ have a shaggy growth of whiskers.

더부살이 a living-in [resident] servant.

더불어 《함께》 together; with. ¶ 그녀와 ~ 기쁨을 나누다 share one's joy with her.

더블 double. ¶ ~베드 a double bed / ~플레이 [野] a double play / ~헤더 [野] a doubleheader.

더블유 W.C.; a water closet.

더블유에이치오 《세계보건기구》 WHO. (◀ the World Health Organization).

더블유티오 《세계무역기구》 WTO. (◀ the World Trade Organization).

더빙 [映·TV] dubbing.

더벅거리다 act [behave] rashly.

더없이 most of all; extremely. ¶ ~ 행복하다 be as happy as can be / ~ 기뻐하다 be delighted beyond measure.

더욱 more; more and more; still more. ¶ ~ 중대한 것은 what is more important / ~ (더) 적어지다 grow less and less / ~ 좋다 [나쁘다] be so much the better [worse].

더욱이 besides; moreover; what is more; in addition (to that).

더위 the heat; hot weather. ¶ ~를 식히다 beat the heat / ~먹다 be affected by the heat; suffer from hot weather / ~를 타다 be sensitive to the heat.

더치다 《병세가》 become [grow] worse; take a bad turn.

더킹 《拳》 ducking. ~ 하다 duck (to avoid blows).

더펄거리다 《머리털 따위가》 bounce up and down; 《사람이》 act frivolously.

더펄머리 bouncing hair.

더하다¹ 《보태다》 add (to); add [sum] up; 《증가》 increase; gain; grow; add (to); 《심해지다》 get [grow] worse (serious). ¶ 3에 4를 ~ add 4 to 3 / 두통이 ~ one's headache becomes worse / 수량이 더해지다 increase [grow] in number(s) [volume] / 인기가 더해지다 gain in popularity / 병세가 ~ one's illness take a turn for the worse.

더하다² 《비교해》 (be) more…; -er. ¶ 크기가 ~ be bigger.

더할 나위 없다 (be) perfect; leave nothing to be desired; (be) the finest [greatest]. ¶ 더할 나위 없이 기쁘다 feel the greatest joy / 아버님의 기쁨은 더할 나위 없었다 Father's joy knew no bounds.

덕 《德》 《미덕》 (a) virtue; goodness; a merit; 《덕택》 indebtedness; favor. ¶ ~이 높은 사람 a man of high virtue / …의 ~으로 by virtue [dint] of…; thanks to… [ing.

덕대 《鑛》 a subcontractor of min-

덕망 《德望》 moral influence. ¶ ~ 있는 a man of high (moral) repute.

덕분 《德分》 ☞ 덕택.

덕성 《德性》 moral character; moral nature. ¶ ~스럽다 be virtuous.

덕업 《德業》 virtuous deeds.

덕육 《德育》 moral training [education]; character-building.

덕지덕지, 덕지덕지 in a thick layer; thickly. ¶ 때가 ~ 끼다 be thickly covered with dirt.

덕택 《德澤》 《은혜》 indebtedness; favor; 《후원》 support. ¶ …의 ~으로 thanks to (a person); by a person's favor [help]; 《원인·이유》 due (owing) to.

덕행 《德行》 virtuous [moral] conduct; virtue; goodness.

덕화 《德化》 《감화》 moral influence [reform].

던적스럽다 《비열》 (be) mean; base; sordid; 《추잡》 (be) indecent; obscene; filthy.

던지다 《내던지다》 throw; hurl; fling; cast. ¶ 공을 ~ throw [pitch]

덜 less; incompletely. ¶ ~ 마른 half-dried / ~ 익은 스테이크 half-cooked (underdone) steak / ~ 익은 과일 unripe fruit.

덜거덕거리다 rattle; clatter.

덜다 ① 《경감·완화》 lessen; ease; mitigate; relieve; alleviate; lighten; 《결약》 save; spare. ¶ 수고를 ~ save (a person) trouble; save labor / 고통을 ~ ease the pain. ② 《빼다》 subtract; deduct 《from》; take off; 《적게 하다》 decrease; lessen; abate; reduce. ¶ 세 개를 ~ remove three; take three from.

덜덜 ¶ ~ 떨다 tremble (for fear); quiver; shiver; tremble all over.

덜되다 ① 《미완성》 (be) incomplete; unfinished; 《덜 익다》 be not ripe. ¶ 덜된 원고 an unfinished manuscript. ② 《사람이》 be no good; be not up to the mark; be half-witted.

덜렁거리다 《소리》 jingle; tinkle; clink; 《행동》 behave oneself flippantly.

덜렁하다 《소리가》 jingle; 《가슴이》 feel a shock; get startled.

덜리다 (be) reduced (deducted, removed).

덜미 ☞ 뒷덜미. ¶ ~ 잡이하다 take [seize] (a person) by the scruff of the neck.

덜커덕거리다 rattle; clatter.

덜컥 ① 《갑자기》 suddenly; unexpectedly. ¶ ~ 죽다 die suddenly; drop dead. ② 《소리》 with a click (clatter, bump).

덤 《더 얹어 주는 것》 an extra; something thrown in; a throw-in; an addition; a free gift. ¶ ~을 주다 throw in something (for good measure).

덤덤탄[-彈]【軍】 a dumdum [soft-nosed] bullet.

덤덤하다 (be) speechless; remain silent.

덤받이 a child by one's former marriage.

덤벙거리다 《행동을》 act frivolously (rashly); 《물에서》 splash; splatter.

덤벨 a dumbbell.

덤불 a thicket; a bush.

덤비다 ① 《달려들다》 turn (fall) on (a person); pick a quarrel with; spring (leap) on; fly at. ¶ 맹호같이 덤벼들다 spring at with tiger-like ferocity. ② 《서둘다》 be hasty; hurry; make undue haste. ¶ 덤비지 말라 Don't be so hasty. or Take easy.

덤프카 a dump truck (lorry 《英》).

덤핑[經] dumping. ~하다 dump (goods). ¶ 해외 시장에서 ~ 공세를 취하다 conduct offensive dumping in overseas markets. ‖ ~방지 관세 antidumping duties / ~시장 a dumping market / 반~법 Anti-Dumping Act.

덥다 hot; warm; feel hot. ¶ 더운 날씨 hot weather / 더운 물 hot water / 몸이 ~ have a fever.

덥석 quickly; suddenly; tightly (단단히). ¶ 손을 ~ 쥐다 suddenly clasp [grasp] (a person's) hand; ~ 물다 snap (at).

덧 a short time (while); a brief span of time. ¶ 어느 ~ before one knows; without one's knowledge.

덧나다 ① 《병이》 grow worse; get [become] inflamed. ② 《성나다》 be offended (at).

덧내다 《병을》 cause to take a bad turn; make (a boil) worse.

덧니 a snaggletooth; a double tooth (겹니). ¶ ~가 나다 cut a snaggletooth. ‖ ~박이 a person with a snaggletooth.

덧문(-門) an outer door; a shutter.

덧붙이다 add [attach, stick] 《one thing to another》; 《말을》 add; make an additional remark.

덧셈 addition. ~하다 add up figures. ‖ ~표 plus sign.

덧신 overshoes; rubbers 《美》.

덧없다 (be) transient; vain; uncertain; short-lived; fleeting. ¶ 덧없는 인생 a transient (an ephemeral) life / 덧없는 세월 fleeting (quick-passing) time.

덩굴[植] a vine. ¶ ~손 a tendril; a runner / 포도~ grape vines.

덩그렇다 《헌거롭다》(be) high and big; imposing; 《텅비다》 look hollow (empty).

덩달다 imitate [follow] (a person) blindly; follow suit. ¶ 내가 그 안(案)에 찬성하자 모두가 덩달아 찬성했다 I consented to the plan and all the rest chimed in.

덩실거리다 dance lively (sprightly).

덩어리 a lump; a mass. ¶ ~지다 lump; (form a) mass / 얼음 ~ a lump of ice / 흙~ a clod of earth.

덩치 a body; a frame. ¶ ~가 큰 bulky; hulking / 그는 ~가 크다 He is big.

덫 a snare; a trap. ¶ ~을 놓다 set [lay] a trap (snare) (for) / ~에 걸리다 be caught in a trap.

덮개 a cover; a covering; a lid (뚜껑); a coverlet (침구).

덮다 《씌우다》 cover (with); put (a thing) on; veil; overspread; 《은폐》 hide; cover up; cloak; 《닫다》 shut; close. ¶ 책을 ~ close [shut] a book.

덮어놓고 without asking [giving]

덮어두다 any reason; causelessly. ¶ ~때리다 hit 《a person》 without giving any explanation.
덮어두다 shut one's eyes 《to》; overlook; pass 《a person's sin》 over; ignore; take no heed of.
덮어씌우다 ① 《가림》 cover 《a thing with…》; put 《a thing》 over 〔on〕. ② 《죄를》 accuse 《a person》 of 《theft》 falsely 〔unjustly〕; make a false charge of espionage》; put 〔lay〕 《the blame》 on 《a person》.
덮이다 be covered 〔veiled, hidden, wrapped〕.
덮치다 ① 《망 따위로 ~》 throw 〔cast〕 《a net》 over 《birds》; 《파도·홍수 따위가》 surge 〔rush〕 《on》; 《a storm》 overtake 《a ship》; 《군중 따위가》 swarm in 《on somebody》. ② 《엄습하다》 attack; raid; fall on; assail. ¶ 적을 배후에서 ~ attack the enemy from the rear / 마약의 아지트를 ~ raid the dope den. ③ 《여러 가지 일이 한꺼번에》 have several things at a time. ¶ 불행이 한꺼번에 ~ have a series of misfortune at a time / 엎친 데 덮친 격이다 Misfortune never comes singly.
데 a place; a spot; a point; 《경우》 an occasion; a case.
데구루루, 데굴데굴 ¶ ~ 구르다 roll over and over.
데꺽 at once 〔곧〕; easily 〔쉽게〕.
데꺽거리다 clatter; rattle.
데다 ① 《불에》 get burnt; have a burn; scald oneself; get scalded. ¶ 손을 ~ get burnt in the hand; burn one's hand. ② 《혼나다》 have a bitter experience.
데드라인 a deadline. ¶ 논문 제출의 ~ the deadline for handing in the essay.
데드볼 〔野〕 a pitch which hits the batter.
데려가다 take 《a person》 along; take 《a person》 with one.
데려오다 bring 《a person》 along; bring 《a person》 with one.
데리다 take 〔bring〕 《a person》 with one; be accompanied by. ¶ 데리고 나오다 take 〔bring〕 out / 데리러 오다 call for; come to claim 《a person》 / 데리러 가다 go for; go and bring 《a person》 / 데리고 놀다 amuse; take care of 《아이를》.
데릴사위 a son-in-law taken into the family. ¶ 데릴사윗감 a model youth.
데마 《고기》 circulate》 a false rumor; demagogy.
데면데면하다 《be》 careless; negligent.
데모 《stage》 a demonstration. ~하다 demonstrate 《against》. ¶ ~대 《a group of》 demonstrators / ~행진 a demonstration parade.
데모크라시 democracy.

데뷔 a début(프). ~하다 make one's début.
데삶다 parboil; boil 《an egg》 soft 〔lightly〕. ¶ 데삶기다 be half-done 〔-boiled〕. ┌《rough》 sketch.
데생 〔美術〕 a dessin 《프》; a 데설궂다 《be》 rough; rude.
데시… deci-. ¶ ~미터 a deciliter 《생략 dl》 / ~미터 a decimeter 《생략 dm》 / ~벨 a decibel 《생략 dB, db》. ┌《대워 먹다 eat hot.
데우다 make warm; heat 《up》. ¶
데이비스컵 〔테니스〕 the Davis cup.
데이터 《gather》 data 《on》. ¶ ~처리장치 a data processing machine. ┌《a girl》.
데이트 a date. ~하다 date 《with》
데익다 be half-cooked 〔-done〕.
데치다 scald; parboil 《vegetables》.
데카당 a decadent.
데카당스 decadence.
데탕트 détente 《프》.
데퉁스럽다 《be》 clumsy; gawky.
덴마크 Denmark. ¶ ~의 Danish / ~ 사람 a Dane.
델리키트 《be》 delicate.
델린저현상(—現象) 〔物〕 Dellinger phenomena.
델타 〔地〕 a delta. ¶ ~지대 〔평야〕 a delta land 〔plain〕.
뎅그렁거리다 jangle; clang.
도(度) ① 《온도·각도》 a degree. ¶ 60~ sixty degrees. ② 《정도》 a degree; 《an》 extent; 《a》 measure. ¶ ~를 지나치다 go too far; carry to excess; be intemperate.
도(道)¹ 〔행정 구획〕 a province. ¶ 경기~ Kyŏnggi Province / ~ (립)의 provincial.
도(道)² 《도리》 teachings 〔가르침〕; doctrines 〔교리〕; truth 〔진리〕; morality 〔도의〕; one's duty 〔지켜야 할〕; 〔술〕 an art. ¶ ~를 닦다 cultivate one's moral 〔religious〕 sense / ~를 깨닫다 perceive a truth.
도 〔樂〕 do.
도 ① 《및, …도 …도》 and; as well 《as》; both… and 〔긍정〕; neither … nor 〔부정〕; 《역시》 too; also; not… either 〔부정〕. ② 《조차》 ① even; not so much as. ¶ 지금 ~ even now / 작별 인사 ~ 없이 without so much as saying good-bye. ③ 《비록 …이라도》 even if; 〔al〕though.
도가니 a melting pot; a crucible. ¶ 흥분의 ~로 화하다 turn into a scene of wild excitement.
도가머리 a crest 《of a bird》.
도감(圖鑑) a pictorial 〔an illustrate〕 book. ‖ 동물 〔식물〕 ~ an illustrated animal 〔plant〕 book.
도강(渡江) ~하다 cross a river. ¶ ~작전을 강행하다 force river-crossing operations.

도개교(跳開橋) a bascule bridge.
도거리 ¶ ~로 in a lump [the gross]; in bulk.
도검(刀劍) a sword; swords (도검류).
도계(道界) a provincial border.
도공(刀工) a swordsmith.
도공(陶工) a ceramist.
도관(導管) a conduit (pipe); pipe.
도괴(倒壞) collapse. ~하다 collapse; fall down; crumble.
도교(道敎) Taoism.
도구(道具) ① (공구) a tool; an implement; a utensil; (용구일체) an outfit. ② (수단·방편) a means; a tool. ¶ 사람을 ~로 사용하다 use 《a person》 as a tool.
도굴(盜掘) ~하다 rob a grave [tomb]. ‖ ~범 a grave robber.
도금(鍍金) gilding; plating. ~하다 plate; gild. ¶ 은 ~한 숟가락 a silver-plated spoon / 구리를 은으로 ~하다 plate copper with silver.
도급(都給) a contract 《for work》. ¶ ~ 맡다 contract 《for》; undertake; get 《receive》 a contract 《for》 / ~주다 give 《a person》 a contract 《for》; let a contract 《to somebody》. ‖ 일괄~계약 a contract on the turnkey basis / 일괄~(수출) (export) by turnkey system.
도기(陶器) earthen(ware); earthenware; pottery. ‖ ~상 a china shop; a china-dealer.
도깨비 a bogy; a ghost. ¶ ~가 나오는 집 a haunted house.
도깨비불 a will-o'-the-wisp; a jack-o'-lantern.
도끼 an ax; a hatchet (손도끼); a chopper. ¶ ~질하다 wield an ax. ‖ ~자루 an ax haft [handle].
도난(盜難) 《a case of》 robbery (burglary, theft). ¶ ~당하다 be robbed 《of one's money》; have 《one's money》 stolen; have 《물건이 주어》. ‖ ~경보기 a burglar alarm / ~품 stolen goods.
도내(道內) ¶ ~의[에] in 《within》 the province.
도넛 a doughnut. ‖ ~화 현상 《도심부의》 the hollowing-out effect; the doughnut phenomenon.
도달(到達) arrival. ~하다 arrive in 《at》; reach; get to. ¶ 결론에 ~하다 arrive at a conclusion.
도당(徒黨) a faction; a clique. ¶ ~을 짓다 band together; form a league (faction, clique).
도대체(都大體) on earth; in the world.
도덕(道德) morality; virtue; morals. ¶ ~상(적)으로 morally; from the moral point of view / ~의식의 결여 lack of moral sense. ‖ ~가 a moralist; a virtuous man / ~교육 moral education / ~률 a moral law; an ethical code / ~심 a moral sense; a sense of morality / ~재무장운동 a moral rearmament movement.
도도하다《거만》 (be) proud [arrogant, haughty]. ¶ 도도하게 proudly; arrogantly / 도도한 태도 a haughty attitude.
도도하다(滔滔—) ① (변설이) (be) eloquent; fluent. ¶ 도도한 변설 a flood of eloquence. ② (흐름이) ¶ 도도히 흐르다 flow with a rush; run [flow] in a large stream.
도둑 ¶ ~맞다 《사람이 주어》 have 《a thing》 stolen; be robbed of 《one's purse》; (물건이 주어) be stolen. ¶ ~고양이 a stray cat / ~놈 a thief; a burglar. ‖ ~ 자 theft; burglary; stealing 《~질하다 commit theft; steal; rob》.
도드라지다 ① (형용사적) (be) swollen; protuberant; (현저하다) be salient; prominent. ② (자동사적) swell; protrude; heave.
도떼기시장(―市場) an open-air 《flea》 market.
도라지 ① 〔植〕 a Chinese balloon flower; a broad bellflower. ② 《뿌리》 platycodon.
도락(道樂) a hobby; a pleasure. ¶ …을 ~으로 삼다 do 《something》 as a hobby [for pleasure].
도란거리다 ☞ 두런거리다.
도랑 a drain; a gutter. ¶ ~을 치다 clear out a ditch. ‖ ~창 a gutter; a drain.
도래(到來) arrival; advent. ~하다 arrive; come.
도래(渡來) ~하다 visit; come from abroad; be introduced 《into》. ¶ 기독교의 ~ the introduction of Christianity 《into Korea》.
도량(度量) 〔마음〕 magnanimity; liberality; generosity ¶ ~이 큰 magnanimous; generous; liberal; broad-minded / ~이 좁은 narrow-minded; illiberal; ungenerous; dominant; prevail.
도량(跳梁) ~하다 be rampant; be dominant; prevail.
도량(道場) 〔佛〕 a Buddhist seminary.
도량형(度量衡) weights and measures. ‖ ~기 measuring instruments / ~표 tables of weights and measures.
도려내다 scoop [gouge] out; bore 《a hole through》; hollow out.
도련님 a young gentleman; an unmarried boy (as addressed by servants); (호칭) Master; Darling; (시동생) a young brother-in-law.
도령 (총각) an unmarried man; a boy.
도로(徒勞) ¶ ~에 그치다 come to

도로(道路) a road; a street; a highway 《공도》. ∥ ~공사 road repairing 〔construction〕; road works; street improvement / ~교통법 the Road Traffic (Control) Law / ~교통정보 a road traffic report 〔information〕 / ~망 a network of roads; a road system / ~보수 road repairs / ~작업la roadman / ~지도 a road 〔highway〕 map / ~청소 street cleaning / ~표지 a road sign; a signpost / 한국~공사 the Korea Highway Corporation.

도로 (다시) back; (over) again; 《전처럼》 as (it was) before. ¶ ~주다 give back / ~ 가다 〔오다〕 go 〔come〕 back / 제자리에 ~ 놓다 leave *a thing* as it was.

도로아미타불(―阿彌陀佛) a relapse; a setback. ¶ ~이 되다 lose all that *one* has gained; be back where *one* started.

…도록 ① 《목적》 to; so as to; in order to 〔that〕; so that *one* may…. ¶ ~지 않다 (so as) not to; that… may not; lest… 나에게 …하~ 그가 말했다 He suggested to me that I might…. ② 《…때까지》 till; until. ¶ 밤 늦~ till late at night. ③ 《되도록…》 as… as possible. ¶ 되~ 빨리 as soon as possible.

도롱뇽 〔動〕 a salamander.

도롱이 a straw raincoat.

도료(塗料) paints. ∥ ~분무기 a paint sprayer.

도루(盜壘) 〔野〕 a stolen base; a steal. ~하다 steal a base.

도루묵 〔魚〕 a kind of sandfish.

도륙(屠戮) ~하다 massacre; butcher; slaughter.

도르다¹ 《분배》 distribute; pass out; deal out; serve round; deliver 《배달》. ¶ 신문을 ~ deliver newspapers / 초대장을 ~ send out invitations.

도르다² 《융통》 raise; procure. ¶ 돈을 ~ raise money; secure a loan; borrow money.

도르래 《장난감》 a pinwheel top; 《돌돌》 rolling. 〔활차〕 a pulley.

도리 〔建〕 a beam; a crossbeam.

도리(道理) ① 《사리》 (事理). ② 《방도》 a way; a means; a measure. ¶ ~가 없다 have no alternative / 기다릴 수 밖에 다른 ~가 없다 We have nothing to do but wait. ③ 《의리》 duty; obligation. ¶ 자식의 ~ filial duty.

도리깨 (thresh with) a flail.

도리다 cut (out) round; scoop out; 《구멍을》 hollow out; bore.

도리도리 《아기에게》 Shake-shake!

도리어 《반대로》 instead; on the contrary; 《오히려》 rather; (all the) more.

도리질 ①《아기의》 ~하다 《a child》 shake *one's* head for fun (from side to side). ②《거절》 ~하다 shake *one's* head in denial; say "No."

도립(倒立) a handstand; a headstand. ~하다 stand on *one's* 〔head and〕hands.

도립(道立) ¶ ~의 provincial. ∥ ~병원 a provincial hospital.

도마 a chopping board 〔block〕. ¶ ~ 위에 오른 고기 be resigned to *one's* fate.

도마뱀 〔動〕 a lizard.

도망(逃亡) escape; flight. ~하다 《치다》 run away; flee; fly; escape 《from》. ¶ ~치게 하다 put 《*a person*》 to flight / 무사히 ~하다 make good *one's* escape 《to》; run away to 《*a safe distance*》. ∥ ~범죄인 인도조약 an extradition treaty / ~병 a runaway soldier; a deserter / ~자 a runaway; a fugitive.

도말다 undertake alone; take all upon *oneself*; 《책임을》 answer for; take responsibility for. ¶ 모든 책임을 혼자서 ~ take the whole responsibility alone.

도매(都賣) wholesale. ~하다 sell wholesale. ∥ ~물가(지수) wholesale price (index) 《carry on》 a wholesale trade 〔business〕 《영업》; a wholesale dealer 《사람》; a wholesale store 《상점》 / ~시세 (값) 《at》 a wholesale price / ~시장 a wholesale market.

도면(圖面) a drawing; a sketch; a plan. ¶ 건축~ a blueprint.

도모(圖謀) ~하다 ☞ 꾀하다.

도무지 quite; entirely; utterly; (not) at all; (not) in the least. ¶ ~ 개의치 않다 do not care at all / ~ 알 수 없다 can hardly understand.

도미 〔魚〕 a sea bream.

도미(渡美) ~하다 visit (go to) the States. ∥ ~유학 going to the U.S. for further study.

도미노 dominoes. ∥ ~이론 the "domino" theory.

도민(島民) an islander; the inhabitants of an island. 《vince.

도민(道民) the residents of a pro-

도박(賭博) gambling. ~하다 gamble. ∥ ~꾼 a gambler / ~상습자 a confirmed 〔habitual〕 gambler / ~장 a gambling house; a casino / ~사기 fraudulent gambling.

도발(挑發) provocation. ~하다 arouse; provoke. ¶ ~적인 provocative; suggestive 《성적으로》 / 전쟁을 ~하다 provoke a war / ~

도배(塗褙) papering 《*walls and ceiling*》. ~하다 paper 《*walls and ceiling*》; wallpaper. ‖ ~장이 a paperhanger / ~지 wallpaper.

도버해협(一海峽) the Strait of Dover.

도벌(盜伐) ~하다 fell trees in secret; cut down trees without (a) license.

도범(盜犯) robbery; theft.

도법(圖法) drawing. ‖ 투영~ projection.

도벽(盜癖) a thieving habit; kleptomania. ‖ ~이 있다 be larcenous; be kleptomaniac.

도벽(塗壁) plastering. ~하다 plaster a wall.

도별(道別) ~의 by province. ‖ ~ 인구표 a population chart by province.

도보(徒步) walking. ‖ ~로 (go) on foot. ‖ ~ 경주 a walking [foot] race / ~ 여행 (go on) a walking tour.

도부(到付) ~ 치다 peddle; hawk. ‖ 도붓장사 peddling; hawking / 도붓장수 a peddler; a hawker.

도불(渡佛) a visit to France. ~하다 visit [go to] France.

도사(道士) 《도교의》 a Taoist; 《불교의》 an enlightened Buddhist.

도사리다 (앉다) sit cross-legged; sit with *one's* legs crossed; 《마음을》 calm 《*one's* mind》; 《뱀 따위가》 coil itself 《up》.

도산(倒産) ① bankruptcy. ~하다 go [become] bankrupt (insolvent); go under. ‖ 그 회사는 ~했다 The firm went bankrupt. ② 『醫』 a cross birth. 〔tail.

도산매(都散賣) wholesale and re-
도살(屠殺) slaughter; butchery. ~하다 slaughter; butcher. ‖ ~ 자 a butcher / ~장 a slaughterhouse.

도상(圖上) ~작전 a war game; tactics on the map(s).

도색(桃色) rose (color); pink. ‖ ~의 rosy; pink. ‖ ~ 영화 a sex [blue] film / ~ 유희 an amorous [a love] affair / ~ 잡지 a yellow journal.

도서(島嶼) islands.
도서(圖書) books. ‖ ~관 a library / ~관장 the chief librarian / ~관학 library science / ~목록 a catalog of books / ~실 a reading room / 국립중앙~관 the National Central Library / 대학 [학교, 순회] ~관 a university [school, mobil] library / 신간 ~ a new book.

도선(渡船) a ferry (boat). ‖ ~장 a ferry (station).

도선(導船) pilotage; piloting. ~하다 pilot (a boat). 〔ing〕w.
도선(導線) the leading [conduct-
도수(度數) ① (횟수) the number (of) times; frequency. ‖ 〈전화의〉 ~ 요금 message rates / ~제 the message-[call-]rate system. ② 《각도·안경 등의》 the degree. ‖ ~ 가 높은 안경 strong [thick] glasses; powerful spectacles. ③ 《알코올분의》 proof. ‖ ~가 높은 위스키 high-proof whisky.

도수(徒手) an empty hand. ‖ ~ 공권(空拳)으로 with bare hands; with no capital to start on.

도스르다 brace *oneself* (up); tighten *one's* nerves.

도승(道僧) an enlightened Buddhist monk [priest].

도시(都市) a city; a town; a metropolis (대도시). ‖ ~의 발달 the growth of cities; urban growth / 대~ a large [big] city / 중소~ small towns. ‖ ~가스 city [town] gas / ~ 게릴라 urban guerrillas / ~ 계획 city [town] planning / ~ 교통 urban transport / ~ 국가 a city-state / ~ 문제 an urban problem / ~ 생활 a city [urban] life / ~ 생활자 a city dweller; city people / ~위생 urban sanitation / ~ 재개발 urban renewal [redevelopment] / ~화 urbanization 《~화하다 urbanize; be urbanized》. 〔trate.
도시(圖示) illustration. ~하다 illus-
도시락 a lunch box(그릇); 《점심》 a lunch; a box [packed] lunch. ‖ ~을 먹다 eat [take] *one's* lunch / ~을 싸다 make [prepare, fix] a lunch / ~ 편지 a letter (letter).

도식(倒食) 〔印〕 a reversed character.
도식(圖式) a diagram; a graph; a schema. ‖ ~으로 나타내다 show [display] in diagram / ~화하다 diagrammatize.

도식하다(徒食一) 《무위도식》 lead an idle life; live in idleness.

도심(都心) the heart [center] of a city; the downtown area. ‖ ~의 호텔 a midtown hotel / 서울 ~에 살다 live in downtown Seoul.

도안(圖案) a design [sketch, plan]. ‖ ~을 만들다 design / ~화하다 make a design 《of》. / ~가 a designer.

도야(陶冶) cultivation. ~하다 cultivate; train; build (up). ‖ 인격 ~ character building.

도약(跳躍) a jump; jumping. ~하다 jump. ‖ ~운동 a jumping exercise / ~판 a springboard.

도열(堵列) ~하다 line up; form a line.

도열병(稻熱病) 『植』 rice blight.
도영(渡英) a visit to England.

~하다 go (over) to England.
도예(陶藝) ceramic art. ‖ ~가 a potter / ~술 ceramics; pottery.
도와주다 (조력) aid; help; assist; (구제) relieve 《the poor》; give a relief to 《a person》.
도외시(度外視) ~하다 ignore; disregard; overlook.
도요새 [鳥] a snipe; a longbill.
도용(盜用) (문장·아이디어의) plagiarism; theft; illegal use; (돈·사물 등의) embezzlement. ~하다 plagiarize 《a person's book》; (금전·사물을) steal; embezzle; appropriate.
도움 help; assistance; aid; support(부조). ‖ ~을 청하다 call [ask, cry] for help / ~이 되다 be helpful [a help] 《to》; be of help 《to》; be useful.
도원경(桃源境) Shangri-La, Shangri-la.
도읍(都邑) a capital; (도읍지) the seat of government; (도시) a city[town].
도의(道義) morality; morals. ‖ ~적 책임 a moral obligation. ‖ ~심 the moral sense.
도이치 Germany. ☞ 독일.
도입(導入) introduction. ~하다 introduce 《new technology》.
도자기(陶磁器) pottery; ceramic ware. ‖ ~공 a ceramist.
도장(道場) an exercise[a training] hall.
도장(塗裝) painting; coating. ~하다 coat with paint; paint 《a wall》. ‖ ~공 a painter / ~재료 coating materials.
도장(圖章) a seal; a stamp (소인) a postmark (우편의). ‖ ~을 찍다 seal; affix a seal 《to》; stamp / ~을 파다 engrave a seal.
도저히(到底―) 《(cannot) possibly》; (not) at all; utterly; absolutely. ‖ 나는 ~ 갈 수 없다 I cannot possibly go. /기일 내에 그 일을 마치는 것은 ~ 불가능하다 It is utterly impossible for me to complete the work by the set date.
도전(挑戰) a challenge; defiance. ~하다 challenge; make[give] a challenge; defy. ‖ ~적 challenging; defiant / ~에 응하다 accept a challenge / ~적인 태도를 취하다 take [assume] a defiant attitude. ‖ ~자 a challenger / ~장 a (written) challenge.
도전(導電) electric conduction. ‖ ~체 an electric conductor.
도정(道程) distance; itinerary.
도제(徒弟) an apprentice.
도조(賭租) rice paid as land tax.
도주(逃走) ☞ 도망.
도중(途中) ‖ ~에 on one's way 《to, from》; (give up) halfway (중도에); in the middle of 《one's talk》 / ~ 일박하다 stop overnight 《at》 / ~ 하차하다 stop over 《at》.
도지다 (병의 악화) grow (get); get complicated; worse; (재발) (병이 주어) return; recur; (사람이 주어) relapse 《into》; have a lapse 《of》. [nor.
도지사(道知事) a provincial gover-
도착(到着) arrival. ~하다 arrive 《at, in》; reach; get to. ‖ ~순으로 in order of arrival / ~하는 대로 upon[immediately on one's] arrival. ‖ ~불 payment on delivery / ~역(항) an arrival station [harbor] / ~항구도 (무역의) free port of destination.
도착(倒錯) perversion. ‖ 성 ~자 a sexual pervert.
도처(到處) ‖ ~에(서) everywhere; throughout [all over] 《the country》; wherever 《one goes》.
도청(盜聽) wire tapping. ~하다 tap[wiretap] 《the telephone》; bug (俗). ‖ ~기 a concealed microphone(대화의) a wiretap; a secret listening apparatus; a bug (俗) / ~사건 a wiretap scandal / ~자 a wiretapper; a pirate listener.
도청(道廳) a provincial office. ‖ ~소재지 the seat of a provincial government.
도체(導體) [理] a medium [매개물]; a conductor (전기, 열의).
도축(屠畜) ☞ 도살(屠殺).
도취(陶醉) intoxication; fascination. ~하다 be intoxicated [fascinated, enraptured].
도치(倒置) ~하다 invert; reverse. ‖ ~법 inversion.
도킹 docking; linking-up. ‖ ~시키다 dock 《spacecraft》; link up (in space).
도탄(塗炭) misery; distress. ‖ ~에 빠지다 fall into extreme distress. [weed [comb] out.
도태(陶汰) selection. ~하다 select;
도토(陶土) potter's clay.
도토리 an acorn. ‖ 개밥에 ~ an outcast; an ostracized person. / ~묵 acorn jelly.
도통(都統) (도합) in all; all together; (전혀) (not) at all. [enment.
도통(道通) ~하다 attain enlight-
도포(塗布) ~하다 spread; apply 《an ointment to》.
도포(道袍) Korean robe.
도표(道標) a guidepost; signpost.
도표(圖表) a chart; a diagram; a graph. ‖ ~로 나타내다 put 《figures》 into the form of a diagram; diagramatice.
도품(盜品) stolen goods.
도피(逃避) a flight 《of capital》; an escape. ~하다 flee; escape.

도핑 doping; drug use. ¶ ~ 테스트 a drug check; a dope test.
도하(都下) ¶ ~의(에) in the capital (metropolis).
도하(渡河) ☞ 도강(渡江). ¶ ~작전 a river-crossing operations.
도학(道學) ethics; moral philosophy. ¶ ~자 a moralist.
도합(都合) (총계) the (grand) total; (부사적) in all; all told; altogether.
도항(渡航) a passage; a voyage. ~하다 make a voyage (passage) (to); go over (to). ¶ ~자 a passenger (to); ~증 a passport (for a foreign voyage).
도해(圖解) a diagram; an illustration. ~하다 illustrate (by a diagram); show in a graphic form.
도형(圖形) a figure; a device; a diagram. ‖입체~ a solid figure.
도화(桃花) a peach-blossom.
도화(圖畵) (a) drawing; a picture. ‖~지 drawing paper.
도화선(導火線) a fuse; a (powder) train. ~이 되다 cause; give rise to; touch off.
독(독) a jar; a jug; a pot. ¶~ 안에 든 쥐다 be like a rat in a trap / 밑 빠진 ~에 물 붓기 be like throwing water on thirsty soil.
독(船渠) a dock; a dockyard (조선·수리용). ¶배를 ~에 넣다 dock a ship; put a ship into dock. 부(浮)~ a floating (dry) dock.
독(毒) poison; venom (독사의); virus (병독); harm (해독). ¶~이 있는 poisonous; venomous; harmful; ~을 넣은 음료 a poisoned drink (치다) poison *a person* (*a person's* food); ~을 없애다 neutralize a poison.
독가스(毒—) poison gas; asphyxiating gas. ‖~공격 a gas attack / ~탄 a poison-gas shell (bomb).
독감(毒感) influenza; flu; a bad cold. ¶~에 걸리다 be attacked by influenza.
독거(獨居) solitary life. ~하다 live alone; lead a solitary life.
독경(讀經) sutra-chanting. ~하다 chant Buddhist sutra.
독과점(獨寡占) monopoly and oligopoly. ‖~품목 monopolistic and oligopolistic items.
독극물(毒劇物) toxic chemicals. ¶ 식품회사 ~ 협박범을 엄단하다 deal sternly with extortionists threatening food companies with poison-lacing.
독기(毒氣) (독기운) noxious air (gas); (독성) poisonous character; (악의) malice; acrimony. ¶~있는 poisonous; malicious.
독나방(毒—) [蟲] a brown-tailed moth.
독농가(篤農家) a diligent farmer.
독단(獨斷) arbitrary decision; dogmatism. ¶~적인 arbitrary; dogmatic / ~(적)으로 on *one's* own judgment (responsibility).
독도(獨島) *Tokdo* Island.
독려(督勵) encouragement. ~하다 encourage; stimulate; urge.
독력(獨力) ¶~으로 by *one's* own efforts; for (by) *oneself*; unaided.
독립(獨立) independence; self-reliance; self-supporting (자활). ~하다 become independent (*of*); be self-supporting. ¶ ~의 independent; self-supporting ¶ ~된 가옥 a separate house. ¶ ~국 an independent country (state) / ~국가연합 the Commonwealth of Independent States (생략 CIS) / ~기념일 (미국의) Independence Day (7월 4일) / ~심 the spirit of independence / ~운동 an independence movement / ~자영 independent management / ~자존 independence and self-existence / ~자활 independence and self-support / ~전쟁 the war of independence; (미국의) the Revolutionary War / ~채산제 a self-supporting accounting system / ~투사 a fighter for national independence.
독무대(獨舞臺) ¶ ~를 이루다 have the stage all to *oneself*; be (stand) without a rival.
독물(毒物) poisonous substance.
독방(獨房) a single room; a room to *oneself*; a solitary cell (감옥의). ‖ ~감금 solitary confinement.
독백(獨白) a soliloquy; a monologue. ~하다 say to *oneself*; soliloquize.
독보(獨步) ¶ ~적인 unique; matchless; peerless; unequalled.
독본(讀本) a reader. ¶영어~ an English reader. [woman.
독부(毒婦) a vamp; a wicked
독불(獨佛) ¶ ~의 Franco-German; French-German ‖ ~전쟁 Franco-German (relations).
독불장군(獨不將軍) (싫도는) a person who is left out; an outcast; (고집쟁이) a stubborn fellow; a man of self-assertion; a self-conceited fellow.
독사(毒蛇) a venomous snake.
독살(毒殺) poisoning. ~하다 poison; kill (murder) by poison. ‖

독살부리다 ~자 a poisoner.
독살부리다 (毒殺−) give vent to one's spite; act spitefully; act wickedly.
독살스럽다 (毒−) (be) venomous; virulent; malignant; bitter.
독생자 (獨生者) (Jesus Christ,) the only begotten son (of God).
독서 (讀書) reading. ~하다 read (books). ¶ ~가 좋아하다 be fond of reading. ‖ ~가 a reader; a great reader(다독가) / ~계 the reading public[world] / ~력 reading ability; power of reading / ~주간 a book week / ~회 a reading circle.
독선 (獨善) self-righteousness. ¶ ~적인 self-righteous. ‖ ~관료 bureaucratic self-righteousness.
독설 (毒舌) a bitter [spiteful, malicious] tongue. ¶ ~을 퍼붓다 speak bitterly (of); give one's spiteful tongue; give (a person) a tongue-lashing / 그는 ~가이다 He has a bitter [spiteful] tongue.
독성 (毒性) virulent; poisonous. ¶ ~의 virulent; poisonous.
독소 (毒素) poisonous matter; a toxin.
독수 (毒手) a vicious means; a dirty trick. ~에 걸리다 fall a victim to; fall into the claws of.
독수공방 (獨守空房) ~하다 live in solitude with one's husband away from home.
독수리 (禿−) [鳥] an eagle.
독순술 (讀脣術) lip-reading.
독식 (獨食) ~하다 monopolize.
독신 (獨身) ~의 single; unmarried. ~이다 be single / ~으로 살다 remain single. ¶ ~생활을 하다 live a single life / ~자 an unmarried person; a bachelor(남자); a spinster(여자) / ~ 아파트 (live in) a bachelor apartment.
독신 (篤信) ~하다 believe in (Buddhism) earnestly.
독실 (篤實) ~하다 (be) sincere; faithful; earnest.
독심술 (讀心術) mind reading.
독아 (毒牙) ¶ ~에 걸리다 fall a victim (to).
독액 (毒液) venom (독사의); poisonous liquid (juice, sap).
독약 (毒藥) a poison. ¶ ~을 먹다 take poison / ~을 먹이다 poison (a person).
독연 (獨演) ((give)) a solo performance (a recital (음악)).
독염 (毒焰) a poisonous flame.
독영 (獨英) ¶ ~의 Anglo-German; England-Germany (relations).
독일 (獨逸) Germany. ¶ ~의 German / ~어 (the) German (language) / ~인 a German; the Germans (총칭).
독자 (獨子) the only son(외아들); the only child(자식).
독자 (獨自) ¶ ~의(개인의) personal; individual; (독특한) original; characteristic; unique / ~적인 견지에서 from an independent standpoint. ‖ ~성 individuality; originality.
독자 (讀者) a reader; a subscriber (구독자); the reading public(독서계). ¶ ~가 많다 (신문·잡지 따위가) have (enjoy) a large circulation; (책이) be widely read. ‖ ~란 the reader's column / ~층 a class of readers.
독장수셈 an unreliable account.
독장치다 (獨場−) stand without rivals; stand unchallenged.
독재 (獨裁) dictatorship. ¶ ~적인 dictatorial; autocratic. ‖ ~자 an autocrat; a dictator / ~정치 dictatorship; dictatorial government(~정치를 펴다 impose one-man rule (on)) / ~주의 dictatorism; despotism.
독전 (督戰) ~하다 urge the soldiers to fight vigorously.
독점 (獨占) monopoly; exclusive possession. ~하다 monopolize; have (something) to oneself. ¶ ~적인 monopolistic; exclusive. ‖ ~가격 a monopoly price / ~권 the right to a monopoly; an exclusive right / ~금지법 the Antimonopoly [Antitrust] Law [Act] / ~기업 a monopolistic enterprise [undertaking] / ~욕 a desire to have entire possession (of) / ~인터뷰 an exclusive interview (with) / ~자 a monopolizer [monopolist]; a sole owner / ~판매 an exclusive sale.
독종 (毒種) 《사람》 a person of fierce character; 《짐승》 fierce animal.
독주 (毒酒) ① (독한) strong liquor. ② (독을 탄) poisoned liquor.
독주 (獨走) (앞서 달리다) leave (all the other runners) far behind; (낙승하다) walk away from; (제멋대로 하다) do as one likes; have one's own way.
독주 (獨奏) a recital; a solo (performance). ~하다 play a solo. ‖ ~곡 a solo / ~자 a soloist / ~회 (give, have) a recital.
독지 (篤志) charity; benevolence. ¶ ~가 a charitable person; a volunteer.
독직 (瀆職) corruption; bribery; (a) graft. ¶ ~을 적발하다 expose corruption. ‖ ~공무원 a corrupt official / ~사건 a corruption scandal [case].
독차지 (獨−) ~하다 take all to

독창 (獨唱) a (vocal) solo. ~하다 sing (give) a solo. ‖ ~자 a soloist / ~회 a vocal recital.
독창 (獨創) originality. ~적인 original; creative. ‖ ~력 (develop) originality; creative talent / ~성 originality. 「(rate) house.
독채 (獨一) an unshared (a separate)
독초 (毒草) a poisonous plant (herb); a noxious weed.
독촉 (督促) pressing; urging. ~하다 press (*a person*) for; urge. ‖ ~장 a letter of reminder.
독충 (毒蟲) a poisonous insect.
독침 (毒針) 《곤충 따위의》 a poison sting(er); 《독을 바른 바늘》 a poisoned needle.
독탕 (獨湯) a private bath. ~하다 take a bath in a private bathroom.
독특 (獨特) ~한 peculiar 《*to*》; characteristic; special; unique.
독파 (讀破) ~하다 read through.
독하다 (毒一) ① 《유독》 (be) poisonous; virulent. ② 《술·담배가》 (be) strong. ¶독한 담배(술) strong tobacco (liquor). ③ 《모질다》 (be) wicked; harsh; hardhearted; hard. ¶독한 여자 a wicked woman / 마음을 ~ 먹다 harden oneself 《*against*》.
독학 (獨學) self-study (-education). ~하다 teach *oneself*; study (learn) by *oneself*. ‖ ~한 사람 a self-educated(-taught) person.
독항선 (獨航船) an independent fishing boat.
독해 (讀解) reading comprehension. ¶ ~력 ability to read and understand / ~력을 테스트하다 give 《*students*》 a reading comprehension test. 「charity.
독행 (篤行) a good deed; an act of
독행 (獨行) ~하다 go alone; act independently 《자립》.
독혈 (毒血) 〔韓醫〕 bad blood. ‖ ~증(症) toxemia.
독회 (讀會) a reading. ‖ 제 1〔2〕 ~ the first (second) reading.
독후감 (讀後感) *one's* impressions of a book 《an article, *etc.*》.
돈 (金錢) money; gold; cash; 《재산》 wealth; riches. ¶큰 (적은) ~ a large (small) sum of money / 부정한 ~ ill-gotten money / ~ 있는 rich; wealthy / ~으로 살 수 없는 priceless / ~이 많이 들다 be expensive; be costly / ~을 벌다 make money / ~을 내다 pay for 〔지불〕; contribute money to 〔기부〕; invest in 〔투자〕 / ~에 눈이 어둡다 be blinded by money / ~을 물쓰듯하다 squander money like water / ~지랄하다 spend money in a crazy way / ~이면 안 되는 일이 없다 Money governs (Gold rules) the world.
돈구멍 (돈孔) a source of income (money). ¶ ~을 찾다 find a supplier of funds. 「strongbox.
돈궤 (一櫃) a money-chest; a
돈꿰미 (꿰) a string for threading coins; 《돈》 a string of coppers.
돈냥 (一兩) ¶ ~까나 벌다 amass a small fortune.
돈놀이 moneylending. ~하다 run moneylending business; practice usury.
돈독 (敦篤) sincerity. ~하다 (be) sincere; simple and honest; friendly. ¶ ~한 관계를 ~히 하다 promote friendly relations 《*between*》.
돈맛 ¶ ~을 알다〔들이다〕 know what money is; learn the value (taste) of money; come to realize the use of money.
돈벌이 moneymaking. ~하다 make (earn) money. ‖ ~가 되는 일 a lucrative (profitable) job / ~를 잘 하다 be clever at making money.
돈복 (一福) luck with money.
돈세탁 (一洗濯) money laundering.
돈수 (頓首) ①《절》a bow; obeisance. ②《편지의》 Yours truly.
돈아 (豚兒) my son.
돈육 (豚肉) pork.
돈절 (頓絶) ~하다 cease suddenly; be cut off once and all.
돈주머니 a purse; a moneybag.
돈줄 a line of credit; a source of money. ‖ ~이 떨어지다 lose *one's* financial backing.
돈지갑 (一紙匣) a purse; a wallet; a pocketbook.
돈쭝 《무게의 단위》 a ton(=3.7565 grams).
돈치기 (play) chuck-farthing.
돈키호테 (a) Don Quixote. ¶ ~식의 quixotic(al).
돈푼 a small sum of money. ‖ ~깨나 있다 have a pretty fortune; be rich. 「honest; naive.
돈후 (敦厚) ~하다 (be) simple and
돋구다 raise; make higher; 《자극하다》 excite; arouse; tempt; stimulate. ¶ 미각〔식욕〕을 ~ tempt 〔whet, stimulate〕 *one's* appetite.
돋다 ①《해가》 rise. ②《싹이》 bud (out); sprout; shoot (forth); come out. ③《종기 따위가》 form; break (come) out.
돋보기 (老眼鏡) spectacles for the aged;《확대경》a magnifying glass.
돋보이다 look better; be set off (to advantage). ¶ 돋보이게 하다 set 《*a thing*》 off (to advantage).
돋우다 ①《심지를》 turn up 《*the*》

wick. ② (높이다) raise; elevate; make higher. ¶ 목청을 ~ raise one's voice. ③ (화를) offend; provoke; aggravate (더욱). ¶ 남의 부아를 ~ offend *a person*; aggravate *a person's* anger. ④ (일으키다) excite *(curiosity)*; stimulate. ⑤ (고무) encourage; cheer up. ¶ 사기를 ~ heighten the morale *(of troops)*. ⑥ (충동이다) instigate; incite; stir up. 〔in relief.

돋을새김 relief. ¶ ~으로 하다 carve
돋치다 (내밀다) grow; come out; rise (sprout) up. ¶ 날개가 ~ grow wings / 날개돋친 듯이 팔리다 sell like hot cakes.

돌¹ ① a baby's first birthday. ¶ ~잔치를 하다 celebrate *one's* first birthday. ② a full day (year); an anniversary. ¶ 해방 열 ~ 기념식 the 10th anniversary of the Liberation.

돌² (a) stone; a pebble(조약돌); (라이터의) a flint (for the lighter). ¶ ~을 깐 paved with stone / ~이 많은 stony.

돌개바람 a whirlwind.
돌격(突擊) a dash; a rush; a charge. ~하다 dash at; charge; rush. ‖ ~대 shock troops; a storming party.
돌계단(─階段) ☞ 돌층계.
돌고드름 [鑛] a stalactite.
돌고래 [動] a dolphin.
돌관(突貫) ‖ ~공사 rush work.
돌기(突起) a projection; a protuberance. ~하다 protrude; project.
돌다 ① (회전) go around; turn; spin; revolve, rotate. ¶ 오른쪽으로 ~ turn to the right / 뱅뱅 ~ turn round and round / 지구는 태양의 주위를 돈다 The earth moves (revolves) round the sun. ② (순회) make a round; go one's round; (회유(回遊)) tour; make a tour. ¶ 호남 지방을 ~ make a tour of the Honam area. ③ (우회) go (come) round. ¶ 곶을 ~ (배가) (go) round a cape. ④ (약·술 따위가) take effect. ¶ 독이 전신에 돌았다 The poison has passed into his system. ⑤ (소문이) circulate; be afloat; get about; spread. ¶ 내각 사직의 소문이 돌고 있다 Rumors are afloat that Cabinet will step out. ⑥ (통용) circulate. ¶ 불경기로 인해서 돈이 잘 안 돈다 Money is tight owing to the trade depression. ⑦ (눈이) feel dizzy; get giddy. ¶ 눈이 ~ go off *one's* head (chump 《英》). ⑨ (전염병이) prevail; be prevalent.
돌다리 a stone bridge. ¶ ~도 두드려보고 건너다 be extremely prudent (cautious).
돌담 a stone wall. 〔son.
돌대가리 a stupid (bigoted) per-
돌덩이 a stone; a piece of rock.
돌도끼 a stone ax.
돌돌 rolling up; with a twirl. ¶ 종이를 ~ 말다 roll up a sheet of paper. 〔round.
돌라주다 distribute; share; serve
돌려내다 ① (사람을) win (*a person*) over (*to*); lure (*a person*) out of (*a place*). ② (따돌리다) leave (*a person*) out (in the cold); exclude; ostracize. 〔(around).
돌려놓다 change direction; turn
돌려보내다 (반환) return; give back; (원래의 자리로) put back; restore; (반송) send back.
돌려보다 circulate (*a letter*); send round (*a notice*).
돌려쓰다 borrow (*money, things*).
돌려주다 ① (반환) return; give (*something*) back; send (*something*) back(반송); pay back (돈을). ② (융통) lend; let out; lend (*one's money*) out (*at 10 per cent interest*).
돌리다¹ ① (고비를 넘기다) turn the corner; ease (get over) a crisis. ② (회생) come to *oneself*; recover. ③ (돈을) borrow money (*from*); get a loan.
돌리다² (방향을) turn; change; divert; convert. ¶ 눈을 ~ avert (turn away) *one's* eyes from / 마음을 ~ change *one's* mind; divert *oneself* from care / 화제를 ~ change the subject. ①) turn (round); roll; spin; revolve. ¶ 핸들을 ~ turn a handle / 팽이를 ~ spin a top. ③ (차례로 건네다) pass (send, hand) (*a thing*) around (on); (전송(轉送)하다) forward (*a letter*); (회부하다) transmit; send round (*the papers*) to (*the section in charge*). ¶ 술잔을 ~ pass a glass of wine round / 다음으로 ~ pass on to the next / 편지를 옮겨 준 주소로 ~ forward a letter to *a person's* new address. ④ (운전시키다) set in motion; run; drive; work. ¶ 기계를 ~ run (work) a machine. ⑤ (기타) 농담으로 ~ treat (*a matter*) as a joke / 신문을 ~ deliver newspapers / 마음을 ~ change *one's* mind / 초대장을 ~ send out invitation / 일반의 관심을 국내 문제로부터 외부 세계로 ~ divert the public attention from its domestic trouble to the outside world.
돌리다³ (원인 따위를) attribute (ascribe) (*a matter*) to. ¶ 성공을 행운으로 ~ attribute (credit) *one's* success to luck.
돌림감기(─感氣) influenza; flu 《俗》;

돌림병(―病) a contagious disease; an epidemic.

돌림자(―字) a part of name which is common to the same generation of a family.

돌림쟁이 a person left out; an outcast; a person hated [shunned] by everybody.

돌멘 『考古』 a dolmen.

돌멩이 a small stone; a piece of stone; a pebble. ¶ ~질하다 throw a stone at 《a dog》.

돌무더기 a pile of stones.

돌발(突發) a burst; an outbreak. ~하다 break [burst] out; occur suddenly. ¶ ~적(으로) sudden(-ly); unexpected(ly). ¶ ~사건 an unforeseen accident [incident].

돌변(突變) ~하다 change suddenly; undergo a sudden change.

돌보다(보살피다) take care of; care for; look [see] after 《a person》; attend to. ¶ 환자를 ~ look after [tend to] a patient.

돌부리 a jagged edge of a rock. ¶ ~에 채여 넘어지다 stumble over a stone.

돌부처 a stone (image of) Buddha.

돌비(―碑) a stone monument.

돌비늘 『鑛』 mica; isinglass.

돌솜 『鑛』 asbestos.

돌아가다 ① 《본디의 장소로》 go [get] back; return; be back; 《집으로》 go home; return home; 《본디의 것으로》 return to; turn back; 《떠나다》 leave; take one's leave. ¶ 제자리로 ~ go back to one's seat / 서둘러 집에 ~ hurry home / 그는 어젯밤 늦게 집에 돌아갔다 He went home late last night. / 자네 이제 돌아가도 좋네 You can leave now. / 내가 어제 말한 이야기로 ~ return to the subject I spoke of yesterday. ② 《우회》 take a roundabout way; go a long way round. ③ 《회복·복구되다》 return 《to》; be restored to; resume. ¶ 이전의 상태로 ~ return to the former state / 본디 몸으로 ~ be restored to one's health. ④ 《귀착》 come [to]; result in; end in. ¶ 수포로 ~ come to naught. ⑤ 《책임 따위가》 fall 《upon》; attribute 《to》; ascribe 《to》. ⑥ 《죽다》 die; be dead. ⑦ 《되어가다》 turn out; develop (발전하다). ¶ 사태가 어떻게 돌아가는지 두고 보다 wait and see how the matter develops.

돌아눕다 turn (over) in bed; lie the other way round.

돌아다니다 (다니다) walk [gad, wander] about; go around; 《순회하다》 make a round (on) one's round; patrol; 《회유하다》 make a tour 《of Europe》. ¶ 하는 일 없이 ~ gad about idly / 연설하며 ~ go around making speeches / 학교들을 시찰하며 ~ go round inspecting schools / 이리저리 ~ wander from place to place / 경찰관들이 돌아다니고 있다 The police officers are on patrolling. ② 《퍼지다》 go round; be abroad; be prevalent(among). ¶ 소문이 ~ a rumor goes round.

돌아(다)보다 ① 《뒤를》 look [turn] round; look back 《at》. ¶ 그녀가 지나가자 모두가 뒤를 돌아다보았다 When she passed, everybody turned around to look at her. ② 《회상》 look back upon 《one's past》.

돌아서다 ① 《뒤로》 turn one's back; turn on one's heels. ② 《동지를》 break up with; fall out with; be alienated. ③ 《병세가》 take a favorable turn.

돌아앉다 sit the other way round.

돌아오다 ① 《귀환》 return; come back [home]; be back. ¶ 회사에서 ~ come home from the office. ② 《차례·때가》 come; come round. ¶ 차례가 ~ one's turn comes (round). ③ 《책임 따위가》 fall on; be brought upon. ¶ 나에게 욕이 ~ disgrace is brought upon me. ④ 《정신이》 제정신이 ~ recover one's senses; come to oneself.

돌연(突然) suddenly; on [all of] a sudden; unexpectedly; all at once. ~한 sudden; abrupt; unexpected; unlooked-for. ¶ ~한 방문 an unexpected [a surprise] visit. ~변이 mutation.

돌이키다 ① 《고개를》 look back. **돌아다보다**. ② 《회상·반성하다》 look back on [to] something 《in the past》; reminisce; think back on 《something》; reflect on 《one's past conduct》. ¶ 청춘 시절을 돌이켜 보다 reminisce about one's youth / 과거를 돌이켜 보다 think back to the past days. ③ 《마음을》 change one's mind 》; 《재고하다》 reconsider; think 《something》 over; think better of 《something》. ¶ 돌이켜 생각컨대 on second thought 《英》. ④ 《원 상태로》 get back; recover; regain. ¶ 돌이킬 수 없는 과거 the irrevocable past / 돌이킬 수 없는 손실 the irreparable loss.

돌입(突入) ~하다 dash in 〔into〕; rush into; charge into. ¶ 파업에 ~ rush into a strike.

돌잔치 the celebration of a baby's first birthday.

돌절구 a stone mortar.

돌진(突進) a rush; a dash; a charge. ~하다 rush [dash] 《at》;

돌쩌귀 216 **동기**

돌쩌귀 charge. ¶ 적을 향해 ~하다 charge [rush] at the enemy.
돌쩌귀 a hinge.
돌출(突出) protrusion; projection. ~하다 stand [jut] out; protrude. ‖ ~부 a projection part.
돌층계(—層階) 〖계단〗 a stone step; (a flight of) stone steps.
돌파(突破) ~하다 break [smash] through 《the enemy's line》; pass 《a difficult examination》; exceed, be over〖넘다〗; overcome〖극복〗. ¶ 천원대를 ~하다 break the 1,000 won level / 난관을 ~하다 overcome the difficulties / 지원자는 1,000명을 ~했다 The number of applicants exceeded 1,000. ‖ ~구 a breakthrough.
돌팔매 a throwing stone. ¶ ~질하다 throw stones.
돌팔이 a wandering tradesman (semiprofessional). ‖ ~선생 an inferior teacher / ~의사 a traveling healer; a quack doctor.
돌풍(突風) a (sudden) gust of wind.
돌피 〖植〗 a barnyard grass (millet).
돕다 ① 〖조력〗 help; aid; assist; 〖지지〗 support; back up. ② 〖구조〗 save; rescue; relieve 〖구제〗. ③ 〖이바지〗 contribute to; help.
돗바늘 a big needle.
돗자리 a (rush) mat; matting 〖총칭〗. ¶ ~를 깔다 spread a mat.
동 〖묶음〗 a bundle.
동(東) the east. ¶ ~의 east; eastern / ~에 [으로] in [to, on] the east.
동(洞) 〖촌〗 a village; a hamlet; 〖행정구역〗 a sub-district; a *dong*. ‖ ~사무소 a *dong* (village) office.
동(胴) 〖몸의〗 the trunk; the body.
동(銅) copper (기호 Cu).
동(同) the same; the said 〖상기의〗; corresponding 〖상당한〗. ¶ ~시대 the same generation.
동가식서가숙(東家食西家宿) ~하다 lead a vagabond [wandering] life; live as a tramp.
동감(同感) the same opinion [sentiment]; sympathy. ¶ ~이다 〖동의〗 agree 《with a person》; 〖동감〗 be of the same opinion 《with a person》; 〖공감〗 feel the same way.
동갑(同甲) ¶ ~이다 be (of) the same age.
동강 a (broken) piece. ¶ ~ 나다 break into pieces [parts] / ~ 치다 cut 《a thing》 into pieces. ¶ ~치마 a short skirt.
동거(同居) ~하다 live together; live [stay] with 《a family》. ‖ ~인 a housemate 〖동거인〗; a roommate; 〖하숙인〗 a lodger.
동격(同格) the same rank; 〖文〗 apposition. ¶ ~이다 rank [be on a level] 《with a person》; 〖文〗 be in apposition 《with》.
동결(凍結) a freeze. ~하다 freeze. ¶ 자산의 ~ a freeze on assets / 임금의 ~ a wage freeze / ~을 해제하다 unfreeze. ‖ ~방지제 (an) antifreeze / 임금 ~정책 a wage freezing policy.
동경(東經) east longitude. ¶ ~ 20도 40분, 20 degrees 40 minutes east longitude: Long. 20°40′ E.
동경(憧憬) longing; yearning. ~하다 long (sigh) 《for》; aspire 《to》; yearn [hanker] 《after》.
동계(冬季) winter season; wintertime. ‖ ~방학 [휴가] a winter vacation / ~올림픽 the Winter Olympic Games.
동계(同系) ¶ ~의 of the same stock; affiliated 《concerns》 / ~ 의 색 a similar color. ‖ ~회사 an allied (affiliated) company.
동계(動悸) heartbeat; palpitation; throbbing. ~하다 beat; palpitate; throb.
동고동락(同苦同樂) ~하다 share *one*'s joys and sorrows 《with》.
동고비 〖鳥〗 a nuthatch.
동공(瞳孔) the pupil; the apple of the eye. ‖ ~반사 a pupillary reflex / ~확대 [수축] the dilatation (contraction) of the pupil.
동광(銅鑛) copper ore; crude copper; 〖광산〗 a copper mine.
동구(東歐) Eastern Europe.
동구(洞口) ¶ ~ 밖 (on) the outskirts of a village.
동국(同國) a fellow (said) country. ‖ ~인 a fellow countryman.
동굴(洞窟) a cavern; a cave; a grotto. ‖ ~벽화 a wall painting in a cave / ~ 탐험 spelunking.
동궁(東宮) 〖왕세자〗 the Crown Prince; 〖세자궁〗 the Palace of the Crown Prince.
동권(同權) equality; equal rights.
동그라미 〖원형〗 a circle; a ring; a loop (실, 끈으로 만든). ¶ ~를 그리다 [만들다] describe (make, draw) a circle. ‖ ~표 the circle symbol.
동그라지다 tumble 《down, over》; fall 《down, over》.
동그랗다 (be) round; circular; globular 〖구형〗.
동그스름하다 (be) roundish. ☞ 동 글스름하다.
동급(同級) the same class. ‖ ~ 생 a classmate; a classfellow.
동기(冬期) the winter (season).
동기(同氣) brothers (남자); sisters (여자). ‖ ~간 sibling relationship 《~ 간의 우애 fraternal love》.
동기(同期) (corresponding) period. ¶ 작년의 ~와 비교하여 compared with the same period of last year / 그와 나는 ~이다 He

동기(動機) a motive 《of, for》; an inducement 《to do》. ¶ 범죄의 ~ the motive of a crime; 불순한 ~ 《from》 an ulterior motive / 이 ~ 되어 motivated by.... / ~ 부여가 강할수록 외국어 학습은 효과가 오른다 The stronger the motivation, the more quickly a person will learn a foreign language. ∥ ~론 〖倫〗 motivism.

동기(銅器) a copper 〔bronze〕 vessel; copper ware. ¶ ~시대 the Copper Age.

동나다 run out 《of stock》; be all gone. ¶ 석유가 ~ be 〔run〕 out of kerosene.

동남(東南) the southeast. ¶ ~의 southeast(ern); southeasterly. ∥ ~아시아 Southeast Asia / ~풍 the southeast wind.

동냥 ~하다 beg 《food, rice, money》; beg one's bread; beg 〔ask〕 for alms(중이); ∥ ~아치 a beggar / ~질 begging.

동네(洞─) a village (마을); the neighborhood (사는 근처). ∥ ~사람 a villager; village folk (복수).

동년(同年) the same year; the same age (동갑).

동녘(東─) the east.

동단(東端) the eastern end.

동닿다 ① 《조리가 맞다》 be consistent 〔logical〕. ∥ ~ 닿지 않는 inconsistent; incoherent. ② 《이어지다》 come 〔follow〕 in succession.

동댕이치다 throw 〔cast〕 《something》 at; 《그만둠》 abandon.

동동¹ 《북소리》 tom-tom. ☞ 둥둥.

동동² ① 《물위에》 ¶ ~ 뜨다 float; drift; be adrift. ② 《발을》 ¶ ~ 구르다 stamp 《one's feet》 on 《the floor》.

동등(同等) equality; parity. ~하다 (be) equal; equivalent. ¶ ~히 equally; on the same level / ~히 다루다 treat 《them》 equally; do not discriminate 《between》 / ~한 입장에서 이야기하다 talk with 《someone》 on equal terms / ~ 졸업 또는 ~한 학력을 가진 사람 college graduates or the equivalent.

동떨어지다 be far apart; be far from; be quite different 《from》.

동란(動亂) agitation; disturbance; upheaval; a riot; a war. ¶ ~중의 중동 the strife-torn Middle East. / ~을 일으키다 rise in riot.

동량(棟梁) ∥ ~지재(之材) the pillar 《of the state》.

동력(動力) (motive) power. ¶ ~에 ~을 공급하다 supply power 《to》; power 《a factory》 / ~으로 작동되는 공구 a power-driven tool. / ~선 a power line / ~원 a source of power; a power source.

동렬(同列) the same rank (file).

동료(同僚) one's colleague; a fellow worker; an associate; a co-worker. ¶ 직장의 ~ a colleague in one's office (at work).

동류(同類) 《동종류》 〔belong to〕 the same class 〔category, kind〕; an accomplice (공모자).

동리(洞里) a village. ☞ 동네.

동마루(棟─) the ridge of a tiled roof.

동맥(動脈) 〖解〗 an artery. ¶ ~의 arterial. ∥ ~경화증 the hardening of arteries; arteriosclerosis / ~류 an aneurysm.

동맹(同盟) an alliance; a league; a union (연합). ~하다 ally with; be allied 〔leagued〕 with; unite; combine. ∥ ~국 an ally; an allied power / ~군 allied forces 〔armies〕 / ~파업 a strike / ~휴학 a school strike.

동메달(銅─) a copper medal.

동면(冬眠) winter sleep; hibernation. ~하다 hibernate. ¶ ~ 동물 a hibernating animal.

동명(同名) the same name. ∥ ~이인 a different person of the same name.

동명사(動名詞) 〖文〗 a gerund.

동무 a friend; a companion; a comrade; a pal (口). ∥ 길~ a fellow traveler; a traveling companion.

동문(同文) the same (common) script. ¶ 이하 ~ and so forth; and so on.

동문(同門) 《동창》 a fellow student 〔disciple〕; 《졸업생》 an alumnus 〔pl. -ni〕; an alumna 〔pl. -nae〕 (여자). ∥ ~회 an alumni association.

동문서답(東問西答) an irrelevant answer. ~하다 give an irrelevant 〔incoherent〕 answer to a question.

동문수학(同門修學) ~하다 study under the same teacher 《with a person》.

동물(動物) an animal. ¶ ~적 〔성의〕 animal / ~적인 본능 (an) animal instinct / 인간은 사회적 ~이다 Man is a social animal. ∥ ~계 the animal kingdom / ~병원 a veterinary hospital / ~실험 experiments using 〔on〕 animals / ~애호협회 the Society for Prevention of Cruelty to Animals (생략 SPCA) / ~원 a zoological garden; a zoo / ~학 zoology / ~학자 a zoologist / ~행동학 ethology. 〔folk.

동민(洞民) a villager; the village

동박새 [鳥] a white-[silver-]eye.
동반(同伴) ~하다 go with; accompany; take 《*a person*》with. ¶ ~자 one's companion. 〔sphere.
동반구(東半球) the Eastern hemi-
동반자살(同伴自殺) 〔남녀의〕 a lovers' suicide; a double suicide; 〔한 집안의〕 a (whole) family suicide.
동방(東方) the east; the Orient. ¶ ~의 eastern.
동방(洞房) ‖ ~화촉 sharing bed on the bridal night.
동배(同輩) one's equal; a fellow; a comrade; a colleague (동료).
동백(冬柏) camellia seeds. ¶ ~기름 camellia oil / ~꽃 a camellia (blossom) / ~나무 a camellia.
동병(同病) the same sickness (disease). ¶ ~상련(相憐)하다 Fellow sufferers pity one another.
동병(動兵) ~하다 mobilize 《*an army*》.
동복(冬服) winter clothes (clothing); winter wear.
동복(同腹) ‖ ~의 uterine. ¶ ~형제〔자매〕 brothers (sisters) of the same mother; uterine brothers (sisters).
동봉(同封) ~하다 enclose 《*a letter*》. ¶ ~한 서류 the enclosed papers / ~해 보내다 send under the same cover. ‖ ~서류 enclosures.
동부(東部) the eastern part.
동부인(同夫人) ~하다 go out with one's wife; take one's wife along 《*with*》; accompany one's wife.
동북(東北) 〔동북간〕 the northeast. ¶ ~의 northeast(ern). ‖ ~동 east-northeast(생략 E.N.E.) / ~풍 the northeast wind.
동분서주(東奔西走) ~하다 bustle about; busy oneself about 《*a thing*》.
동사(凍死) ~하다 be frozen to death; die of (from) cold.
동사(動詞) a verb. ¶ ~의 verbal. ‖ ~규칙 (불규칙) ~ a regular (an irregular) verb / 완전 (불완전) ~ a complete (an incomplete) verb.

동생(同生) a (younger) brother (sister); one's little brother (sister).
동생공사(同生共死) ~하다 share the fate with others. ¶ 모두 ~의 운명이다 be all in the same boat.
동서(同書) ① 〔같은 책〕 the same book. ② 〔그 책〕 the said book. ‖ ~에서〔출처 표시로〕 ibidem (생략 ib., ibid).
동서(同壻) ① 〔자매간의 남편〕 the husband of one's wife's sister; a brother-in-law. ② 〔형제간의 아내〕 the wife of one's husband's brother; a sister-in-law.
동서(同棲) cohabitation. ~하다 cohabit (live together) 《*with*》. ¶ ~하는 사람 a cohabitant.
동서(東西) east and west; 〔동서양〕 the East and the West. ‖ ~고금 all ages and countries / ~남북 the (four) cardinal points.
동석(同席) ~하다 sit with 《*a person*》; share a table with 《*a person*》 (식당 등에서). ‖ ~자 those present; the (present) company.
동석(凍石) 〔鑛〕 steatite; soapstone.
동선(同船) 〔같은 배〕 the same (said) ship. ~하다 take the same ship; sail on the same ship (vessel). ‖ ~자 a fellow passenger.
동선(銅線) copper wire (wiring).
동선(動線) the line of flow.
동설(同說) the same opinion (view).
동성(同性) ① 〔남녀의〕 the same sex; homosexuality. ¶ ~의 of the same sex; homosexual. ‖ ~애 homosexual love; homosexuality; lesbianism (여자간의) / ~애자 a homosexual; a homo (俗); a gay (남성); lesbian (여성). ② 〔성질의〕 homogeneity; congeniality. ¶ ~의 homogeneous; congenial.
동성(同姓) the same surname. ‖ ~동명인 a person of the same family and personal name / ~동본 the same surname and the same family origin / ~인 (人) a namesake; a person of the same surname as oneself.
동소체(同素體) 〔化〕 allotrope.
동수(同數) the same number. ¶ ~의 as many 《*…as*》; of the same number / 찬부 ~의 투표 (30—30) tie vote / 가부 ~인 경우에는 in case of a tie.
동숙(同宿) ~하다 stay at the same hotel; lodge in the same house. ‖ ~자 a fellow lodger (boarder).
동승(同乘) ~하다 ride together; ride with 《*another*》 in 《*the same car*》; share a car 《*with*》. ‖ ~자 a fellow passenger.

동사(東死) ~하다 be frozen to death; die of (from) cold.

동상(同上) ~의 be same as (the) above; ditto (생략 do.).
동상(凍傷) a frostbite; chilblains. ¶ ~에 걸리다 be (get) frostbitten. ‖ ~자 a frostbitten person.
동상(銅像) a bronze statue; a copper image. ¶ ~을 세우다 erect (set up) a statue.
동색(同色) the same color. ¶ 초록은 ~이다 《俗談》 Like attracts like.

동시(同時) the same time. ¶ ~의 simultaneous; concurrent / ~에 at the same time, simultaneously [concurrently] 《with》; at a time, at once(일시에); while, on the other hand(한편으로는). ‖ ~ 녹음 synchronous recording /~녹음하다 synchronize / ~ 발표 a simultaneous announcement / ~ 상영 a double feature; a two-picture program / ~ 선거 a double election / ~성 simultaneity / ~ 통역 《make》 simultaneous interpretation / ~ 통역사 a simultaneous interprete.

동시(同視) ① ☞ 동일시. ② 「같은 대우」~하다 treat alike; treat without discrimination.

동시(童詩) children's verse; nursery rhymes.

동시대(同時代) the same age. ¶ ~ 의 contemporary 《with》; in the same age (period) / ~에 in the same age (period) / ~의 사람 a contemporary.

동식물(動植物) animals and plants; fauna and flora.

동실동실 ☞ 둥실둥실.

동심(同心) ① 「같은 마음」the same mind. ¶ 두 사람은 ~ 일체다 The two are practically of a mind. ‖ ~ 협력 harmonious cooperation. ② 「幾」「같은 중심」concentricity. ‖ ~ 원 a concentric circle.

동심(童心) the child [childish, juvenile] mind. ¶ ~으로 돌아가다 become children again / ~을 좀먹다 destroy the innocence of a child's mind.

동아(東亞) East Asia.

동아리 (부분) a part; (무리) confederates; companions; a group.

동아줄 a thick and durable rope.

동안 ① (간격) an interval. ¶ 일정한 ~을 두고 at regular intervals. ② (기간) time; a space; a period; (부사적) for; during; while. ¶ 오랫 ~ for a long time / 잠깐 ~ for a little while.

동안(東岸) the east coast.

동안(童顔) a boyish face. ¶ ~의 boyish-looking.

동안뜨다 have an interval [a space] between; have a longer interval than usual.

동액(同額) the same amount 《of money》; the same price. ¶ ~의 of the same amount.

동양(東洋) the East; the Orient. ¶ ~의 Eastern; Oriental. ‖ ~ 문명 [文明] Oriental civilization [culture] / ~ 사람 an Oriental / ~ 사상 Orientalism / ~학 Oriental studies / ~ 학자 an Orientalist / ~화 an Oriental painting.

동업(同業) ① 「같은 업」the same trade [profession]. ¶ ~ 동아일보 the Dong-a Ilbo, our contemporary. ‖ ~자 men of the same industry [trade, profession] / ~ 조합 a trade association. ② 「공동」~하다 do [engage in] business in partnership; run business together. ‖ ~자 a partner.

동여매다 bind; tie; fasten. ‖ ~ 매다 《a thing》 to a post / 나무에 밧줄을 ~ fasten a rope to a tree.

동역학(動力學)「理」kinetics.

동요(動搖)「진동」tremble; quake; shake;「마음·사회의」agitation; disturbance; unrest;「차의」jolting. ~하다「진동하다」tremble; quake; shake; jolt(차가);「소란해지다」be agitated; be disturbed;「불안해지다」become restless. ¶ 사상의 ~ an agitation of thought / 정계의 ~ political disturbance / 전국적으로 민심이 ~하고 있다 There is public unrest throughtout the country.

동요(童謠) a children's song; a nursery rhyme.

동우(同友) a colleague; a fellow member.

동원(動員) mobilization. ~하다 mobilize 《troops》; set in motion. ¶ 많은 관객을 ~하다 draw a large audience. ‖ ~ 계획 a mobilization plan / ~령 《issue》mobilization orders / 강제 ~ compulsory mobilization 《of students》.

동월(同月) the same month.

동위(同位) co-ordinate. ‖ ~ 각 corresponding angles / ~ 원소 an isotope.

동유(桐油) tung oil.

동음(同音) the same sound; homophony. ‖ ~어 a homophone / ~ 이의어 [異義語] a homonym.

동의(同意) agreement; consent; approval(승인). ~하다 agree with 《a person》; agree on 《a point》; agree to do; approve of 《a proposal》; consent to 《a proposal》. ¶ ~을 얻다 obtain 《a person's》 consent [approval].

동의(同義) synonymy; the same meaning. ¶ ~의 synonymous. ‖ ~어 a synonym.

동의(動議) a motion. ~하다 make [bring in] a motion. ¶ ~를 철회하다 withdraw a motion / ~를 가결하다 adopt a motion.

동이 a jar. ‖ 물 ~ a water jar.

동이다 bind (up); tie (up); fasten. ¶ 상처를 ~ bind (up) a wound / 끈으로 짐을 ~ tie up a bundle with string.

동인(同人) ① 「회원」a member; a coterie 「문예상의」. ‖ ~ 잡지 a literary coterie magazine. ② 「같은 사람」the same [said] person.

동인(動因) a motive; motivation; a cause. ¶ 이 범죄의 ~ the motive for this crime.

동인도(제도)(東印度(諸島)) the East Indies.

동일(同一) identity; sameness. ~하다 (be) the same; identical. ¶ ~ 수준에 있다 be on the same level 《with》. ¶ ~성 identity; oneness; sameness / ~인물 the same person.

동일(同日) the same [said] day.

동일시(同一視) ~하다 put in the same category; identify [equate] 《(A) with (B)》 (A를 B로). ¶ 저런 사람들과 ~되는 것을 원치 않는다 I don't like to be classed with them.

동자(童子) a child; a boy. ‖ ~중 a young [boy] monk.

동작(動作) action; movement(s); manners. ¶ ~이 빠르다 [느리다] be quick [slow] in action.

동장(洞長) a dong headman; the chief of a dong office.

동장군(冬將軍) a severe [hard] winter.

동적(動的) dynamic; kinetic.

동전(銅錢) a copper (coin). ¶ ~ 한푼 없다 haven't a penny [cent].

동절(冬節) the winter (season).

동점(同點) ¶ ~이 되다 tie [draw] 《with》 / ~으로 끝나다 finish in a tie.

동정(同情) sympathy; pity. ~하다 sympathize 《with》; pity; feel pity 《for》. ¶ ~적인 sympathetic / ~하여 out of sympathy 《with, for》 / ~의 뜻을 표하다 express one's sympathy 《for》. ¶ ~심 a sympathetic feeling; sympathy / ~자 a sympathizer / ~표(票) a sympathy vote.

동정(童貞) chastity; a virginity. ¶ ~을 지키다 [잃다] keep [lose] one's chastity [virginity]. ‖ ~녀 a virgin; 《성모》 the Virgin (Mary).

동정(動靜) movements; a state of things; one's doings. ¶ 정계의 ~ development of political affairs / 적의 ~을 살피다 feel out the movements of the enemy.

동제(銅製) ¶ ~의 copper(y); made of copper. ‖ ~품 copper manufactures.

동조(同調) ~하다 side [sympathize] 《with》; come into line 《with》; follow suit. ‖ ~자 a sympathizer.

동족(同族) the same family [race, tribe]. ¶ ~상잔(相殘)의 비극을 겪다 experience the tragedy of fratricidal war. ‖ ~결혼 endogamy / ~목적어 〖文〗 a cognate object / ~애 fraternal love / ~회사 〈가족의〉 a family concern [firm]; 《관계의》 an affiliated concern.

동종(同宗) the same blood [family]; the same sect (종파).

동종(同種) ~(of) the same kind [sort].

동지(冬至) the winter solstice. ‖ 동짓달 the 11th lunar month.

동지(同志) a comrade; a fellow member. ¶ ~를 모으다 rally like-minded people.

동진(東進) ~하다 move [march] eastward; proceed east.

동질(同質) the same quality; homogeneity. ¶ ~의 homogeneous; of the same quality.

동쪽(東-) the east. ¶ ~의 east; eastern; easterly / ~으로 to the east 《of》; in the direction of the east.

동차(同次) 〖數〗 ¶ ~식 (방정식) homogeneous expression [equation].

동창(同窓) a schoolmate; a fellow student (학우, 동급생). ¶ 우리는 ~이다 We attended the same school. or We were at school together. ¶ ~생 〈졸업생〉 a graduate; an old boy; 《美》 alumnus [pl. -ni]; alumna [pl. -nae] 《여》 / ~회 an old boys' association; an alumni association; an alumni reunion (모임).

동체(胴體) the body [trunk]; the hull (배의); the fuselage (비행기의). ¶ ~착륙 (make) a belly landing; belly-landing.

동체(動體) 〖理〗 a body in motion (움직이는); a fluid (유동체).

동치(同値) 〖數〗 the equivalent.

동치다 bind [tie] up.

동치미 watery radish kimchi.

동침(-鍼) 〖韓醫〗 a fine and long needle.

동침(同寢) ~하다 sleep with 《a person》; share the (same) bed 《with》.

동태(凍太) a (frozen) pollack.

동태(動態) the movement (of population). ‖ ~통계 vital statistics (인구의).

동통(疼痛) a pain; an ache.

동트다(東-) dawn; day breaks. ¶ 동틀녘에 at daybreak (dawn).

동티나다 ① 〈앙얼 입다〉 suffer the wrath of the earth gods. ② 〈잘못되다〉 get into trouble; incur trouble.

동판(銅版) a copperplate; sheet copper. ‖ ~인쇄 a copperplate print.

동편(東便) the east(ern) side.

동포(同胞) 〈같은 겨레〉 brethren; a fellow countryman [citizen]; a compatriot. ‖ ~애 brotherly love.

동풍(東風) the east wind. ¶ 마이~이다 turn a deaf ear to 《a

동하다(動—) ① 《움직이다》 move; stir. ② 《마음이 움직이다》 be moved (감동); be touched [shaken] (동정 따위가); be [feel] inclined to 《*to do*》 (…하고 싶다); have an itch [desire] 《*for, to do*》 (욕심이 나다). ¶ 구미가 동하다 feel an appetite 《*for*》 / 마음이 동하지 않다 be unperturbed; remain firm / 그녀 이야기에 마음이 ~ be moved by her story.

동학(同學) a fellow scholar [student, researcher].

동해(東海) the East Sea (of Korea).

동해(凍害) frost damage.

동해안(東海岸) the east coast.

동행(同行) ‖ ~ 하다 go [come] (along) with; accompany 《*a person*》; travel together. ¶ 경찰서로 ~ 하기를 요구받다 be asked to come to the police station. ‖ ~ 자[인] a fellow traveler; a (traveling) companion.

동향(同鄕) ‖ ~ 인 a person from the same town [village, district].

동향(東向) facing east; eastward. ‖ ~ 집 a house facing east.

동향(動向) a trend; a tendency; a movement. ¶ 여론의 ~ 을 주시하다 watch the trend of public opinion / 경제의 ~ economic trends.

동굴(洞窟) a cave; a cavern.

동형(同型) the same type [pattern].

동호(同好) ‖ ~ 인 people having [sharing] the same taste [interest] / 낚시~ 회 an (amateur) anglers' club / 영화~ 회 a movie lovers' society.

동화(同化) assimilation. ~ 하다 assimilate. ¶ ~ 작용 assimilation.

동화(童畫) an animation; an animated film.

동화(童話) a nursery tale [story]; a fairy tale. ‖ ~ 극 a juvenile play.

동활자(銅活字) a copper type.

동활차(動滑車) a movable pulley.

동회(洞會) ☞ 동사무소.

돛 a sail. ¶ ~ 을 올리다 [내리다] hoist [lower] a sail. ‖ ~ 단 배 a sailboat; a sailing ship [boat, vessel] / ~ 대 a mast.

돼지 ① 《가축》 a pig; a hog. ¶ 식용의 ~ a pork pig / ~ 를 치다 raise [breed] hogs. ‖ ~ 고기 pork / ~ 우리 a pigsty. ② 《사람》 a piggish person.

되 《계량 단위》 a (dry, liquid) measure; a doe. ¶ ~ 를 속이다 give short measure.

되— 《도로》 back. ¶ ~ 찾다 regain; get back / ~ 묻다 inquire again.

되넘기다 resell.

되놈 a Chinaman; a Chink 《俗》.

되는대로 《마구》 at random; 《거칠게》 roughly; carelessly; slovenly; slapdash. ¶ ~ 지껄이다 talk at random / ~ 살다 live in a happy-go-lucky way.

되다¹ ① 《질지 않다》 (be) thick; hard (밥 따위). ② 《벅차다》 (be) hard; laborious. ③ 《심하다》 (be) hard; heavy; severe; intense. ¶ 되게 severely; hard; heavily / 되게 꾸짖다 scold severely. ④ 《켕기다》 (be) tight; taut; tense. ¶ 되게 tightly; tautly.

되다² 《되질》 measure.

되다³ ① 《신분·상태가》 become; get; be; grow; turn; develop. ¶ 부자가 ~ become rich / 어른이 ~ grow up (to be a man) / 버릇이 ~ grow into habit / 빨갛게 ~ turn red / 기독교 신자가 ~ become a Christian; turn Christian. ② 《…하게 되다》 begin [come] to 《*do*》; get to 《*do*》. ¶ 좋아하게 ~ begin [get, come] to like 《*a thing, a person*》. ③ 《성립·구성》 consist of; be composed of; be made 《*up*》 of. ¶ 물은 산소와 수소로 돼 있다 Water consists [is composed] of oxygen and hydrogen. / 배심원은 12명으로 되어 있다 A jurry is made up of twelve men. ④ 《생육·흥성》 grow; thrive; prosper. ¶ 이 땅에서는 채소가 잘 된다 Vegetables grow well in this soil. / 장사가 잘 ~ do good [prosperous] business. ⑤ 《성취》 succeed; be accomplished; be attained. ¶ 일이 뜻대로 ~ succeed in *one*'s attempt / 어려운 댐 공사가 마침내 다 되었다 The tough dam construction has finally been completed. ⑥ 《결과가》 result [end] 《*in*》; turn out; prove. ¶ 거짓말이 ~ turn out false / 치명상이 ~ prove fatal / 만사가 그녀 소망대로 되었다 Everything turned out as she had hoped. ⑦ 《수량·금액이》 come to; amount to; run up to; make. ¶ 6에 3을 더하면 아홉이 된다 Six and three make nine. / 총액은 3만원이 됩니다 The total comes [amounts] to 30,000 won. ⑧ 《역할·소용》 act as; serve as. ¶ 이 소파는 침대도 된다 This sofa serves as a bed. / 알코올은 소독약이 된다 Alcohol acts as a disinfectant. ⑨ 《나이·계절·시간 등이》 ¶ 나는 곧 20세가 된다 I'll very soon be twenty. / 봄이 되었다 Spring has come. / 그를 만난지 3년이 되었다 It's going on three years since I saw him last. ⑩ 《가능》 can; be able to; be possible. ¶ 될 수 있으면 if possible; if *one* can / 될 수 있으면 빚을 지고 싶지 않다 I will not borrow

되도록 as... as possible; as... as *one* can. ¶ ~ 많이 as much [many] as possible.
되돌아가다 turn [go] back; return. ¶ 중간에서 ~ turn back halfway.
되돌아오다 return; come back.
되돌리다 dangle; sway; swing.
되묻다 《다시 묻다》 ask again; 《반문》 ask back; ask a question in return.
되바라지다 ① 《그릇 따위》 (be) open; shallow. ② 《사람이》 (be) precocious; pert; saucy. ¶ 되바라진 아이 a precocious child / 되바라진 소리를 하다 say pert things.
되살다 ☞ 소생하다.
되새기다 《음식을》 chew over and over again (because of poor appetite); 《소 등이》 ruminate; chew the cud; 《비유적》 ruminate (*about, on, over*); think over again; relive. ¶ 고통스러웠던 6·25의 역사를 ~ relive the painful history of the Korean war.
되씌우다 《잘못 따위를》 put a blame on another.
되씹다 《말을》 repeat; harp on the same string; dwell (*on*).
되어가다 ① 《일이》 go (*on*); work; get along. ¶ 잘 ~ go well [all right]; work well. ② 《물건이》 be getting finished [completed].
되지못하다 《하찮다》 (be) worthless; trivial; be no good 《서술적》; 《건방지다》 (be) impertinent; saucy. ¶ ~ bit too hard.
되직하다 (be) somewhat thick; **되질** measuring with a *toe*. ~ 하다 measure with a *toe*.
되짚어 back; turning right away. ¶ ~ 가다 go [turn] back right away.
되풀이하다 repeat; reiterate. ¶ 되풀이하여 over again; repeatedly.
된밥 hard-boiled rice.
된서리 a heavy frost; a severe frost. ¶ ~ 맞다 《비유적》 receive a bitter blow; suffer heavily.
된서방(-書房) a hard 《severe, harsh》 husband. ¶ ~ 맞다 get married to a harsh husband.
된소리 a strong sound; a fortis.
된장(-醬) 《醬》 (soy)bean paste; *doenjang*. ¶ ~국 beanpaste soup.
된장찌개(-醬-) 《醬》(soy)bean paste stew; *doenjang jjigae*.
될성부르다 ¶ 될성부른 나무는 떡잎부터 알아본다 《俗談》 Genius displays itself even in childhood.
됨됨이 《사람》 one's nature 《본성》; character 《성격》; personality 《인품》; 《물건》 make; structure.
됫박 a *toe*(되) used as a measure.
됫박질 ~ 하다 measure (*rice*) with a gourd bowl; 《조금씩 사다》 buy (*rice*) in small quantities.
두(頭) ¶ 소 70 ~ seventy head of cattle.
두(둘) two; a couple (*of*). ¶ ~ 가지 two kinds (*of*)《종류》; two ways《방법》 / ~ 배 double; two times / ~ 번 twice; two times.
두각(頭角) ¶ ~을 나타내다 cut a conspicuous 《brilliant》 figure (*in*); distinguish *oneself*.
두개골(頭蓋骨) 《解》 the skull.
두건(頭巾) a mourner's hempen hood.
두견(-鵑) 《鳥》 a cuckoo. ② ☞ 진달래.
두고두고 for a long time; over and over again. ¶ ~ 생각하다 think over and over again / ~ 쓸 수 있다 can be used for a long time.
두근거리다 《one's heart》 throb; beat 《fast》; palpitate; feel uneasy 《nervous》; go pit-a-pat. ¶ 가슴을 두근거리며 발표를 기다리다 wait for the announcement with a beating heart.
두길마보다 straddle; sit on the fence; see how the wind blows.
두꺼비 《動》 a toad. ¶ ~ 파리 잡아먹듯 be ready to eat anything. ‖ ~집《電》 a fuse box.
두껍다 (be) thick; heavy; bulky. ¶ 두꺼운 책 a thick book / 두껍게 하다 thicken; make thicker.
두께 thickness. ¶ ~ 가 5인치다 be five inches thick 《in thickness》.
두뇌(頭腦) brains; a head. ¶ 치밀〔산만〕한 ~ a close 〔loose〕 head / ~가 명석한 사람 a clear-headed person / ~ 집약적인 brain-intensive. ‖ ~노동 brainwork / ~노동자 a brainworker / ~유출 brain drain / ~집단 a think tank 《factory》.
두다 ① 《놓다》 put; place; set 《세워서》; lay 《뉘어서》; 《보존》 keep; store 《저장》. ¶ 돈을 금고에 ~ keep money in a safe. ② 《사람을》 keep; take in 《하숙인을》; hire; employ 《고용》. ¶ 첩을 ~ keep a mistress / 하숙인을 ~ take in boarders / 가정 교사를 ~ keep 〔hire〕 a (private) tutor. ③ 《배치》 put; station. ¶ 보초를 ~ post a guard. ④ 《사이를》 leave. ¶ 간격을 두지 않다 leave no space. ⑤ 《마음을》 have a mind to; set *one's* mind on; 《마음에》 bear; hold; keep. ¶ 염두에 ~ bear (*a thing*) in mind. ⑥ 《넣다》 stuff. ¶ 이불에 솜을 ~ stuff a quilt with cotton. ⑦ 《바둑·장기를》 play. ⑧ 《설치》 set up; establish. ¶ 각 대학에 도서관을 ~ set up a library at each university. ⑨ 《뒤에 남김》 leave (behind). ¶ 두고 온 물건

a thing left behind.
두더지 [動] a mole.
두덩 a bank; a levee.
두둑하다 《두껍다》 (be) thick; heavy; 《풍부하다》 (be) plenty; ample; 《솟다》 be swollen [bulged] (*out*). ¶두둑한 보수 an ample reward.
두둔하다 side (*with*); take sides (*with*); support; back up. ¶그 녀만을 두둔하지 마라 Don't always take sides with her.
두드러기 nettle rash. ¶~가 돋다 [나다] get nettle rash.
두드러지다 ① 《내밀다》 bulge out. ② 《뚜렷함》 (be) noticeable; conspicuous; outstanding; striking; stand out (동사적). ¶두드러진 차이 a striking difference.
두드리다 strike; beat; knock. ¶문을 ~ knock at the door / 가볍게 ~ tap / 세게 ~ rap; bang.
두런거리다 exchange whispers; murmur together.
두렁 a ridge between fields; a levee. ¶논~길 a path between rice fields.
두레박 a well bucket. ¶~질하다 draw water with a well bucket / ~우물 a draw well.
두려움 《공포》 fear; dread; terror; 《염려》 anxiety; apprehension; 《외경》 awe; reverence. ¶~으로 [때문에] out of fear; from [with] fear.
두려워하다 《무서워하다》 be afraid of; fear; dread; be terrified (*of*, *at*); have a fear of. ¶병 날까 ~ be afraid [in fear] of falling ill / 아무 것도 두려워할 것 없다 You have nothing to be afraid of.
두렵다 ① 《무섭다》 (be) fearful [terrible, horrible]; ② 《염려》 (be) feared (*of*, *that*...). ¶…이 두려워서 for fear (*of*, *that*...). ¶주려워서 고개를 못 들다 be too much awed to raise *one's* head.
두령 (頭領) a leader; a boss.
두루 《일반적》 generally; 《전체적으로》 all over; all around; 《골고루》 equally; evenly; 《예외 없이》 without exception; 《일반》 for general [popular] use / ~ 살피다 look all around carefully / 전국을 ~ 돌아다니다 go around all over the country.
두루마기 a Korean overcoat.
두루마리 a roll (*of paper*); a scroll.
두루뭉수리 《사물》 an unshapely thing; a mess; 《사람》 a nondescript person; a good-for-nothing (fellow).
두루뭉실하다 ① 《모양이》 (be) somewhat roundish; neither edged nor round. ② 《언행이》 (be) indistinct [uncertain; noncommital

(*in one's manner*). 두루뭉실한 태도를 취하다 take an uncertain attitude (*on a matter*) / 두루뭉실 한 대답을 하다 give a noncommittal [vague] answer.
두루미 [鳥] a crane. ¶재~ a white-neck crane / 흑~ a hooded crane.
두루치기 《둘러쓰기》 using a thing for various purposes.
두르다 ① 《둘러싸다》 enclose (*with*, *in*); surround (*with*, *by*); encircle; 《입다》 put on; wear. ¶돌담을 ~ enclose (*a house*) with a stone wall / 치마를 ~ put on [wear] *one's* skirt. ② 《변통하다》 make shift; contrive; manage to (*do*). ¶돈을 ~ manage to raise 두름 a string (*of fish*). [money.
두름성 resourcefulness; management; versatility (융통성). ¶~이 있다 be versatile [resourceful].
두리반 (一盤) a large round dining table.
두리번거리다 look around (about).
두마음 double-heartedness; double-dealing. ¶~이 있는 double-hearted; treacherous; 《두 얼굴을 가진》 have two faces; play (a) double game.
두말 ¶~할 것 없이 of course; needless to say / ~ 않다 do not raise objection (반대 않다); do not complain (불평 않다); do not mention again (재론 않다).
두메 an out-of-the-way mountain village; a remote village in the country. ¶~에 살다 live in the remote countryside.
두목 (頭目) a chief; a head; a leader; a boss; a ringleader (*of robbers*).
두문불출 (杜門不出) ~하다 keep [stay] indoors; be confined to *one's* home.
두문자 (頭文字) the first letter of a word; a capital letter (대문자); 《이름의》 an initial. [one's hair.
두발 (頭髮) the hair (of the head).
두벌갈이 [農] a second sowing [plowing]. ~하다 till [plow] a second time.
두부 (豆腐) bean curd. ¶~ 한 모 a piece [cake] of bean curd / ~튀김 fried bean curd.
두부 (頭部) the head. ¶~에 부상 을 입다 be wounded in [on] the head.
두서 (頭書) ¶~의 the foregoing; the above-mentioned.
두서 (頭緒) ¶~ 있는 rambling; incoherent; illogical / ~ 없는 이야 기를 하다 talk incoherently; make pointless [disjointed] remarks.
두서너, 두서넛 two or three; a few.

두엄(거름) compost. ¶ ~을 주다 manure (compost) (a field).
두유(豆乳) soymilk.
두절(杜絶) ~하다 be stopped; be interrupted (cut off); be held (held) up. ¶ 소식은 ~되다 hear nothing from / 눈보라로 교통이 ~되었다 Traffic was paralyzed (held up) by the snowstorm.
두주(斗酒) ¶ ~도 불사하다 be ready to drink kegs (gallons) of wine.
두주(頭註) marginal notes.
두텁다 be close; cordial; warm. ¶ 두터운 우정 a close friendship.
두통(頭痛) (have) a headache. ¶ ~거리 a headache, a trouble; a nuisance.   (rough.
두툴두툴하다 (be) uneven; rugged;
두툼하다 be somewhat thick. ¶ 두툼한 책 a thick book.
둑 a bank; a dike; an embankment. ¶ ~을 쌓다 build a dike; embank.
둔각(鈍角) [幾] an obtuse angle.
둔감(鈍感) ¶ ~한 dull; insensible / ~ 소리에 ~하다 be dull to sound.
둔갑(遁甲) ~하다 change (transform) oneself (into).
둔기(鈍器) a dull (blunt) weapon.
둔덕 an elevated land; a mound.
둔부(臀部) the buttocks; the rump; the hip.
둔재(鈍才) (사람) a dull (dull-witted) person; a stupid.
둔전(屯田) [史] a farm cultivated by stationary troops.
둔탁(鈍濁) ~하다 (소리가) (be) dull; thick; dead. ¶ ~한 소리 a dead sound.
둔하다(鈍一) (머리·동작이) (be) dull; slow; stupid. ¶ 둔한 사람 a dull man / 동작이 ~ move clumsily; be slow-moving / 센스가 ~ have a slow perception.
둘 two. ¶ ~도 없는 unique; only; matchless / ~ 다 both / ~씩 two at a time; by twos.
둘둘 ¶ ~ 감다 twine (coil) around; wind up (a cord) in a coil.
둘러대다 ① (꾸며대다) give an evasive answer; make an excuse (for). ¶ 그럴 듯한 이유를 ~ cook up a good reason. ② (변통) make shift (with); manage somehow.
둘러막다 ☞ 두르다, 둘러치다.
둘러보다 look (a)round (about).
둘러서다 stand in a circle.
둘러싸다 (포위) besiege; lay siege to; (에워싸다) surround; enclose. ¶ 적에게 둘러싸이다 be besieged (surrounded) by the enemy / 삼면이 바다로 둘러싸여 있다 be surrounded by the sea on three sides / 난로를 둘러싸고 앉다 sit around a stove.
둘러쌓다 pile (things) up in a circle.
둘러쓰다 뒤집어쓰다.
둘러앉다 sit in a circle.
둘러치다 ① (두르다) surround; enclose. ¶ 담을 ~ surround with walls. ② (내던지다) throw hard; hurl.
둘레(주위) circumference. ¶ ~에 round; round; about / ~ 3피트 three feet round.
둘레둘레 ¶ ~ 둘러보다 look around; stare around (about).
둘리다 (둘러 막히다) be enclosed (surrounded, encircled).
둘째 the second; number two. ¶ ~로 secondly; in the second place / ~형 one's second eldest brother.
둥 (하는 듯 마는 듯) ¶ 자는 ~ 마는 ~ 하다 be half asleep.
둥개다 (사람이 주이) cannot manage; do not know what to do with; (사물이 주이) be too much (for). ¶ 일이 많아서 ~ have more work than one can manage.
둥그스름하다 (be) somewhat round.
둥근톱 a circular saw.
둥글다 (be) round; circular; globular (구상의). ¶ 얼굴이 둥근 round faced / 둥글둥글하게 만들다 make (something) round.
둥글대 (평미레) a round strickle.
둥글리다 round; make (a thing) round. ¶ 식탁 모서리를 ~ round off the edge of the table.
둥덩거리다 keep beating (a drum); beat boom-boom.
둥둥 (북소리) rub-a-dub; rataplan; boom-boom.
둥실둥실 float slowly floating.
둥실거리다 move slowly (sluggishly); waddle.
둥우리 a basket.
둥지 a nest.
뒤 ① (배후·후방) the back; the rear. ¶ ~의 back; behind; rear / ~에(로) behind; back; after; backward / ~에서 in the rear; at the back; behind one's back(배후에서); in secret(몰래) / ~로부터 from behind / ~로 물러나다 step back / ~에 남다 stay (remain) behind / ~로 돌아 가(구령) About face! ② (장래) future. ③ (나중·다음) ¶ ~에 after; later / 사오일 ~에 a few days later. ④ (종적) ¶ ~를 따르다 (밟다) follow; trail (a person); shadow (a person). ⑤ (뒤쪽) ¶ ~를 잇다 succeed. ⑥ (대변) feces; excrement; stools. ¶ ~를 보다 relieve oneself / ~ 마렵다 want to relieve oneself. ⑦ (돌봄) support; backing. ¶ ~를 밀어 주다 give support to; back

뒤꼍 a rear garden; a back yard
뒤꿈치 a heel. [lot).
뒤끓다 (혼잡하다) be in confusion; be crowded; thronged (with); swarm (with). ¶시장에 사람이 뒤끓었다 The market place was crowded with people.
뒤끝 (종말) the end (of an affair); a close. ¶일의 ~을 맺다 wind [end] up an affair; bring (a matter) to an end. [tumble.
뒤넘다 fall backward; overturn;
뒤늦다 (be) late; belated.
뒤대다 (공급) supply (a person with); provide (a person with).
뒤덮다 cover; overspread; veil.
뒤덮이다 be covered (all over) (with). [look) round.
뒤돌아보다 look back (at); turn
뒤틀어지다 ① (뒤틀리다) be distorted (twisted). ② (생각이) grow crooked (perverse).
뒤떨어지다 fall (drop) behind; be left behind (the times); be backward (in) (후진적); be inferior to. ¶경주에서 ~ fall behind in a race / 문화가 ~ be backward in civilization / 유행에 뒤떨어지지 않도록 keep pace with the fashion / 이 외투는 품질면에서 내 것에 뒤떨어진다 This overcoat is inferior to mine in quality.
뒤뚱거리다 be shaky (unsteady); totter; stagger; falter. ¶뒤뚱뒤뚱 falteringly; unsteadily / 뒤뚱거리며 걷다 walk with faltering steps.
뒤뜰 a back garden (yard).
뒤룩거리다 roll (goggle) (one's eyes); sway (one's body); waddle (성이 나서) jerk with anger.
뒤미처 soon (shortly) after.
뒤바꾸다 invert; reverse. ¶순서를 ~ reverse the order.
뒤바뀌다 be inverted (reversed); get out of order; be mixed up. ¶순서가 뒤바뀌었다 The order went wrong.
뒤밟다 track (a person); follow; shadow; tail. ¶아무를 뒤밟게 하다 put a shadow (tail) on a person. [er.
뒤버무리다 mix up; mix together;
뒤범벅 ~이 되다 be mixed up; be jumbled together; ~을 만들다 jumble (up) together; mix up. [(ease) oneself.
뒤보다 (용변) go to stool; relieve
뒤서다 fall behind.
뒤섞다 mix up; mingle together.
뒤섞이다 be mixed (mingled, up); be jumbled (together, up).
뒤숭숭하다 (be) confused; disorderly; restless; nervous; ill at ease. ¶마음이 ~ feel restless (nervous).
뒤엉키다 get entangled; get confused (mixed).
뒤엎다 upset; overturn; overthrow.
뒤웅박 a gourd. [throw.
뒤적이다 make search; rummage; ransack. ¶서랍을 뒤적여 그녀의 편지를 찾다 rummage the drawer for her letter.
뒤져내다 rummage out; hunt (seek, search) out.
뒤주 a wooden rice chest (bin).
뒤죽박죽 a mess; mix-up; confusion. ¶ ~ 의 confused; mixed-up / ~ 으로 in disorder (confusion); in a mess / ~ 이 되다 get mixed up (confused) / ~ 을 만들다 make (mess) up; throw (a room) into confusion (disorder).
뒤쥐 [動] a shrewmouse.
뒤지 (-紙) toilet paper.
뒤지다¹ (찾다) search; ransack; rummage; fumble. ¶열쇠를 찾기 위해 모든 사람을 ~ search all the drawers for the key.
뒤지다² (뒤처지다) fall (lag, be) behind; be backward (in). ¶유행에 ~ be behind the fashion / 일이 다른 사람보다 ~ be behind the others in one's work / 시류에 ~ fall (be) behind the times.
뒤집다 ① (겉을) turn inside out; turn (it) over. ② (엎다) upset; overturn; reverse; invert. ¶판결을 ~ reverse a sentence. ③ (혼란시키다) throw into confusion. ¶그 소식은 온 시내를 발칵 뒤집어 놓았다 The news threw the whole city into utter confusion.
뒤집어쓰다 ① (온몸에) pour (water) on oneself; be covered with (dust). ② (이불 따위를) draw (pull) over. ¶머리에 담요를 ~ pull the blanket over one's head. ③ (죄・책임을) take (another's fault) upon oneself. ¶죄를 뒤집어 씌우다 lay the blame on (a person) for something / 부하의 죄를 뒤집어 쓰고 사직하다 resign one's post taking the responsibility for his subordinate's mistake.
뒤집어엎다 upset; overturn; overthrow; turn over. ¶정권을 ~ overthrow the government.
뒤집히다 ① (안팎이) be turned inside out; be turned over. ¶ (우산 따위가) 바람에 ~ be blown inside out. ② (순서・판결 따위가) be reversed; be overruled. ③ (뒤집어지다) overturn; be upset; be overturned (overthrown); be toppled. ¶배가 뒤집혔다 The boat overturned (was capsized). / 그 이론은 새로운 발견에 의해 뒤집혔다

뒤쫓다 / 226 / **뒷자리**

The theory was overthrown by the new discovery. ④ 《속·정신이》 feel sick (nausea); go (run) mad. ¶ 눈알이 ~ lose one's head; be beside oneself.

뒤쫓다 pursue; chase; run after 《a person》; track; trail.

뒤채 a backhouse; the back wing.

뒤처리(―處理) settlement 《of an affair》. ~하다 settle 《an affair》; put 《things》 in order. ¶ 파산한 회사의 ~를 하다 clear up the affairs of a bankrupt company.

뒤축 the heel. ¶ ~이 높은 (낮은) 구두 high-(low-)heeled shoes.

뒤치다꺼리 ① 《돌봄》 care. ~하다 look after; take care of. ¶ 애들 ~를 하다 take care of one's children. ☞ 뒤처리, 뒷수습.

뒤탈 later trouble. ¶ ~이 두려워서 for fear of later troubles / ~이 없도록 so as to prevent any trouble that might occur in future / ~이 없도록 하다 leave no seeds of future troubles.

뒤통수 the back of the head.

뒤통스럽다 (be) clumsy; bungling; thick-headed. ¶ 뒤통스러운 사람 a clumsy fellow; a bungler.

뒤틀다 ① 《비틀다》 twist; wrench; distort; wring. ¶ 팔을 ~ twist [wrench] a person's arm. ② 《방해하다》 thwart; frustrate; foil; baffle. ¶ 아무의 계획을 ~ thwart a person's plan.

뒤틀리다 ① 《비틀어지다》 be distorted [twisted]; be warped; be cross-grained(마음이). ¶ 뒤틀린 distorted; twisted; wry; crooked / 뒤틀린 성질 a twisted [crooked] personality / 뒤틀린 견해 a distorted view. ② 《일이》 go wrong; go amiss.

뒤흔들다 ① 《사물을》 shake violently; sway hard. ¶ 《파문을 일으키다》 disturb; stir. ¶ 경제계를 ~ create [cause] a stir in the economic world.

뒷간 a washroom [toilet]; a latrine.

뒷갈이 ☞ 그루갈이.

뒷감당(―堪當) dealing with the aftermath 《of an affair》; setting 《matters》 right; settlement; winding up 《an affair》. ~하다 deal with the aftermath; straighten (out) the rest 《of an affair》.

뒷거래(―去來) backdoor [illegal] dealing [business].

뒷걸음치다 move [step] backwards; 《무서워서》 flinch; shrink back [away] 《from》; hesitate 《at》. ¶ 불을 보고 ~ shrink back [away] from the fire.

뒷골목 a back street; an alley; a bystreet.

뒷공론(―公論) backbiting (험담);

gossip. ~하다 backbite; speak ill of [talk about] 《a person》 behind his back.

뒷구멍 the back [rear] door; backstairs (channel). ¶ ~에서 영업을 하다 do [conduct] under-the-counter business. ∥ ~거래 backdoor deals [transactions] / ~입학 obtain, get) a backdoor admission to a school.

뒷굽 《동물의》 the back hoof of an animal; 《신의》 the heel of a shoe.

뒷길 a back street. [shoe.

뒷날 days to come; another day (후일); future (장래).

뒷다리 a hind [rear] leg.

뒷당그(―擔―) taking charge [care] of the rest [aftermath] 《of an affair》.

뒷덜미 the nape; the back of the neck. ¶ ~를 잡다 seize [grab] 《a person》 by the scruff of his neck.

뒷돈 capital; funds. ¶ 장사 ~을 대다 supply 《a person》 with funds for business / 노름 ~을 대다 supply 《a person》 with gambling stakes [money].

뒷동산 a hill at the back 《of》.

뒷말 backbiting; bad gossip.

뒷맛 aftertaste. ¶ ~이 좋다 [나쁘다] have a pleasant [an unpleasant] aftertaste.

뒷모양(―模樣) the sight of one's back; the figure [appearance] from behind.

뒷문(―門) a back [rear] gate.

뒷물 ¶ ~하다 bathe one's private parts; take a sitz bath.

뒷바라지 looking after; taking care of. ~하다 look after; take care of; care for.

뒷바퀴 a rear [back] wheel.

뒷받침 backing; backup. ~하다 back up; support.

뒷발(―) a hind [rear] leg [foot].

뒷발질 ¶ ~하다 kick with one's heel.

뒷북치다 rush [fuss] around fruitlessly after the event.

뒷소문(―所聞) gossip [rumor] about something happened before; after-talk.

뒷손가락질 ~하다 point after 《a person》. ¶ ~받다 be an object of people's contempt.

뒷손없다 be careless [loose] about finishing things up.

뒷수습(―收拾) settlement 《of an affair》. ¶ 사건의 ~을 하다 settle an affair.

뒷이야기 a sequel to the story.

뒷일 (나중일) the aftermath of an event; the rest; 《장래·사후의》 future affairs; affairs after one's death.

뒷자리 《take》 a back seat.

뒷조사(一調査) a secret investigation [inquiry]. ~하다 investigate secretly [in private].
뒷짐 ¶ ~지다 cross [fold] *one's* hands behind *his* back; ~결박을 하다 tie *a person's* hands behind *his* back.
뒹굴다 ① (누워서) roll (about); tumble about. ② (놀다) idle away; roll about.
듀스 (테니스) deuce. ¶ ~가 되다 go to deuce.
듀엣 〔樂〕 a duet.
드나들다 (출입하다) go in and out; (방문) visit; frequent. ¶ 드나드는 상인 *one's* regular salesman / 자로이 드나들 수 있다 have free access to 《a house》.
드넓다 (be) wide; spacious; large.
드높다 (높이가) (be) high; tall; lofty; eminent.
드디어 at last [length]; finally.
드라마 (연극) a drama; a play.
드라이 dry. ¶ ~밀크 dry [dried, powdered] milk / ~아이스 dry ice / ~진 dry gin / ~클리닝 dry cleaning.
드라이버 a driver.
드라이브 a drive. ~하다 take [have] a drive 《to》. ~하러 가다 go for a drive.
드러나다 ① (표면에) appear on the surface; be revealed; show *itself*; be exposed; become known [famous]. ¶ 죄가 ~ *one's* crime is exposed / 이름이 세상에 ~ become famous [known] in the world / 술을 마시면 본성이 드러난다 Liquor reveals *one's* true self. ② (감춘 것이) come to light; be found (out); be discovered. ¶ 음모가 드러났다 The plot came to light. / 비밀이 곧 드러났다 The secret soon came [leaked] out.
드러내다 ① (나타내다) indicate; display. ② (노출시키다) disclose; reveal; bare; expose. ¶ 비밀을 ~ disclose a secret / 자신의 무지를 ~ reveal *one's* ignorance / 넓적다리를 ~ bare *one's* thigh.
드러눕다 lie 《throw *oneself*》 down. ¶ 드러누워 책을 보다 read a book lying down 《in bed》.
드러쌓이다 be piled [heaped] up; accumulate.
드럼 a drum. [ily [loudly].
드렁드렁 ¶ ~코를 끌다 snore heav-
드레스 a dress. ¶ ~메이커 a dressmaker.
드레지하다 try 《*a person's*》 prudence; size up 《*a person*》.
드로잉 drawing. ¶ ~페이퍼 drawing paper.
드롭스 (사탕) a drop.
드르렁거리다 snore loudly.
드르르 ① (미끄럽게) slipperily;

smoothly. ② (떠는 모양) trembling; shivering. ③ (막힘없이) smoothly; without a hitch.
드리다¹ 《주다》 give; present; offer. ¶ 선생님께 선물을 ~ give a present to *one's* teacher / 기도를 ~ offer *one's* prayers.
드리다² 《방·마루 따위를》 make; set; construct; add [attach] 《*two rooms*》 to 《*one's house*》.
드리블 〔競〕 a dribble.
드리우다 ① (늘어뜨림) hang down; let 《*something*》 down; suspend. ¶ 막을 ~ let a curtain down. ② (이름을 후세에 남김) leave one's name to posterity.
드릴 (송곳) a drill.
드림 (기(旗)드림) a pennant; a streamer; (장막) a curtain; hangings.
드림제(一劑) an invigorating drink; a health [pep-up] drink.
드문드문 ① (시간적) once in a while; at 《rare, long》 intervals; occasionally. ¶ ~찾아오다 come once in a while. ② (공간적) at intervals; sparsely; thinly; here and there. ¶ 나무를 ~ 심다 plant trees sparsely [thinly].
드물다 (be) rare; scarce; unusual; uncommon. ¶ 드물게 rarely; seldom / 드문 일 an unusual thing; a rarity / 드문 일 a rare occurrence.
드새다 pass the night 《at an inn》. ¶ 하룻밤 ~ stay overnight; stop for the night.
드세다 (be) violent; very strong; (집터 따위가) be ominous; unlucky; ill-omened.
드잡이 《싸움》 a scuffle; a grapple. ~하다 scuffle; grapple 《*with*》. ② (압류) attachment; seizure. ~하다 attach; seize.
드티다 ① (자리·날짜가) be extended [stretched out]. ② (자리·날짜를) extend; stretch out.
득(得) (이익) profit; gain; advantage; benefit. ¶ ~보다 profit; gain 《*from*》 / ~이 되다 be profitable [advantageous]; benefit 《*a person*》.
득남(得男) ~하다 give birth to a son. ¶ ~턱 celebration of the birth of *one's* son.
득녀(得女) ~하다 give birth to a daughter. [become famous.
득명(得名) ~하다 win [gain] fame;
득세(得勢) ~하다 obtain [gain, acquire] influence; become influential.
득승(得勝) ~하다 win 《a victory》.
득시글득시글하다 be swarming [crowded, teeming] 《*with*》. ¶ 득시글거리다 swarm; teem 《*with*》 / 거기는 구더기가 득시글거렸다 The place

득실(得失) merits and demerits; gain and loss. ¶ ~은 엇비슷하다 The gains and losses are about on a par.

득의(得意) pride; exultation; triumph; elation. ¶ ~만면하여 proudly; triumphantly; in triumph.

득인심(得人心) ~하다 win the hearts of the people.

득점(得點) marks; a point; a score. ~하다 score (a point). ‖ ~표 a scoreboard; scoreboard.

득책(得策) a good policy; the best policy; a wise way. ¶ ~이다 be wise; be advisable.

득표(得票) the number of votes obtained (polled). ~하다 get (gain) votes. ¶ 법정 ~수 the legal number of votes / 그의 ~수는 다른 후보자를 훨씬 웃돌았다 His polling score was far larger than that of any other candidate. / 500표로 ~차로 이기다 win by a majority of five hundred votes.

든 ① (들판) a field; a plain (평원). ② (야생의) wild. ¶ ~장미 wild roses.

든 (따위) and so forth [on]; and [or] the like. ☞ 따위.

...든 (복수) -s. ¶ 여학생~ schoolgirls / 농민~ farmers.

든것 a stretcher.

든거지난부자(─富者) a person who looks rich but is really poor.

든든하다 ① (굳세다) (be) firm; solid; strong; (견실한) (be) steady; sound. ¶ 든든히 firmly; fast; solidly / 든든한 기초[구조] a firm (solid) foundation (structure) / 든든하게 만든 strongly-(solidly-)built / 든든한 회사 a sound business firm / 방비가 ~ be strongly (heavily) fortified. ② (미덥다) (be) reassuring; safe; reliable; trustworthy. ¶ 든든한 사람 a reliable man / 마음 든든히 여기다 feel reassured (secure). ③ (배부른) (be) stomachful. ¶ 든든히 먹다 eat one's fill.

든부자난거지(─富者─) a person who looks poor but is really rich.

...든지 either...or; whether... or. ¶ 좋~ 나쁘~ good or bad / 너~ 나~ either you or I.

든직하다 (be) dignified imposing; composed. ¶ 든직한 태도 a dignified manner / 그는 든직하니 믿음직스럽게 보인다 He looks dignified (composed) and reliable.

든침모(─針母) a resident seamstress (needlewoman).

듣다¹ ① (소리를) hear; (전해) hear (learn) from others; learn by hearsay; be told (informed) (of); (경청) listen (give ear) to. ¶ 듣는 사람 a hearer; a listener / 듣자니 I hear (am told, learn) that; from what I hear / 연설을 ~ hear (listen to) a speech / 잘 못 ~ hear (something) wrong; mishear / 우연코 ~ hear casually (by chance) / 강의를 ~ attend a lecture / 듣기 좋은 sound well / 듣기 싫다 be offensive to the ear. ② (칭찬·꾸지람을) receive; suffer. ¶ 꾸지람을 ~ be scolded; catch a scolding. ③ (따르다·들어주다) obey; take; follow; listen to. ¶ 충고를 ~ take (follow) one's advice / 부모의 말을 ~ obey one's parents. ④ (효험있다) be efficacious; take [have] effect (on); be good (for); (기계 등이) act; work. ¶ 잘 듣는 약 a very effective medicine / 브레이크가 안 듣는다 The brake refuses to act (work).

듣다² (물방울이) drip; drop; trickle.

들 ① (들판) a field; a plain (평원). ② (야생의) wild. ¶ ~장미 wild roses.

들 (따위) and so forth [on]; and [or] the like. ☞ 따위.

...들 (복수) -s. ¶ 여학생~ schoolgirls / 농민~ farmers.

들것 a stretcher.

들고나다 ① (간섭) interfere (in, with); meddle (in); poke one's nose (into). ② (집안 물건을) carry out (household articles) for sale to raise money.

들국화(─菊花) [植] a wild chrysanthemum.

들기름 perilla oil.

들까부르다 ① (키질하다) fan (winnow) briskly; (흔들다) move up and down; (자동차가) jolt; (배가) pitch and roll; rock. ¶ 무릎 위에서 갓난 아기를 ~ rock a baby on one's knees.

들깨 [植] a perilla; *Perilla frutescens* (L.).

들끓다 ① (메지어) crowd; swarm (with flies). ② (소란) get excited; be in an uproar. ¶ 들끓는 군중 a boiling (an excited) crowd.

들날리다 (이름·세력 등을) enjoy a great popularity (prosperity).

들녘 a plain; an open field.

들놀이 a picnic; an outing. ¶ ~ 가다 go on a picnic; have an outing.

들다¹ (날씨가) clear (up); become clear. ¶ 정오경에 날이 들기 시작했다 It began to clear up around noon.

들다² (칼날이) cut (well). ¶ 잘 드는 [안 드는] 칼 a sharp (blunt) knife.

들다³ (나이가) grow (get) older. ¶ 나이가 듦에 따라 as one grows old(er).

들다⁴ ① (손에) take (have, carry) in one's hand; hold. ¶ 펜을 ~ take a pen in hand; write / 손에 무엇을 들고 있니 What do you

들다 have in your hand? / 잠시 이것을 들고 있어요 Just hold this for me, will you? 《사실·예를》 give 《*an example*》; mention 《*a fact*》; cite. ¶ 이유를 ~ give a reason / 증거를 ~ give (bring forward, produce) evidence 《*to*》. ③ 《올리다》 raise; lift (up); hold up. ¶ 손을 ~ hold (lift) up *one's* hand; raise *one's* hand. ④ 《음식을》 ~ take 《*a meal*》; have; eat; drink (마시다).

들다² ① 《들어가다》 go (get, come) in 《*to*》; enter; 《살다》 settle 《*at, in*》. ¶ 자리에 ~ go to bed / 새집에 ~ settle in a new house. ② 《가입·참여》 join 《*a club*》; go into; enter. ③ 《풍흉·절기 등이》 set in; begin; come. ¶ 풍년(흉년)이 ~ have a good (bad) harvest / 장마가 ~ the rainy season sets in. ④ 《물이》 be dyed 《*black*》; take color. ⑤ 《버릇 등이》 take to 《*a habit*》; fall into 《*the habit of doing*》. ⑥ 《마음에》 be satisfied (pleased) 《*with*》; suit *one's* fancy; like. ¶ 마음에 드는 집 a house to *one's* taste; a house *one* likes / 나는 그것이 마음에 든다 I like it. *or* It suits me. ⑦ 《포함》 contain; hold; 《들어 있다》 be included; be among. ⑧ 《소요》 take; need; require; cost 《*much*》. ⑨ 《병이》 suffer from; catch 《*cold*》. ⑩ 《침입》 break in. ¶ 도둑이 ~ a burglar breaks in 《into a house》. ⑪ 《햇빛이》 shine in. ⑫ 《정신이》 ~ come (be brought) to *one's* senses.

들들 ¶ ~ 볶다 parch 《*beans*》; nag 《at》 《*a person*》 constantly.

들떼놓고 indirectly; in a roundabout way.

들뜨다 ① 《붙은 것이》 become loose; come off. ¶ 벽지가 ~ the wallpaper comes off from the wall. ② 《마음이》 be unsteady; grow restless. ③ 《얼굴이》 누렇게 들뜬 얼굴 a yellow and swollen face.

들락날락하다 go in and out frequently.

들러리 《신랑의》 a best man; 《신부의》 a bridesmaid. ¶ ~ 서다 serve as a bridesmaid (best man).

들러붙다 adhere (stick, cling) 《*to*》. ¶ 찰싹 ~ stick fast to.

들려주다 let 《*a person*》 know 《*of*》; tell (말해); read to (읽어); play for (연주해); sing for (노래해).

들르다 《도중에》 drop in 《*at*》; stop by 《*in*》; call 《*at, on*》.

들리다¹ ① 《소리가》 be audible; be heard; hear; 《울리다》 sound; ring 《*true*》. ¶ 들리지 않는 inaudible / 부르면 들리는 데서 within call (earshot, hearing) / 이상하게 들릴지 모르지만 strange as it may sound. ② 《소문이》 be said (rumored); come to *one's* ears. ¶ 들리는 바에 의하면 according to a report (rumor); it is said that...; I hear (am told) that....

들리다² ① 《병이》 suffer from; be attacked 《*by*》; catch. ② 《귀신이》 be possessed (obsessed) 《*by*》. ¶ 귀신들린 것처럼 like *one* possessed.

들리다³ ① 《올려지다》 be lifted (raised). ② 《들게 하다》 let 《*a person*》 raise (lift).

들먹거리다 《움직이다》 move up and down; shake. ¶ 어깨가 ~ *one's* shoulders move up and down. ② 《마음을 흔들리게 하다》 make 《*a person*》 restless; instigate; stir up. ¶ 근로자를 들먹거려 파업을 일으키다 instigate workers to go on strike. ③ 《말하다》 mention; refer to. ¶ 그 사람까지 들먹거릴 필요야 없지 You don't have to mention his name.

들먹이다 ☞ 들먹거리다.

들보 〖建〗 a crossbeam; a girder.

들볶다 annoy; torment; be hard on 《*a person*》; be cruel to. ¶ 들볶이다 be tormented 《annoyed, molested》 / 며느리를 ~ be cruel to *one's* daughter-in-law.

들부수다 break 《*a thing*》 to pieces; smash up; crush.

들새 wild fowl(총칭); a wild (field) bird.

들소 〖動〗 a wild ox; a bison.

들손 a handle; a bail.

들쑤시다 ☞ 들먹이다.

들쓰다 《덮어쓰다》 put 《*something*》 on all over *oneself*; 《머리에》 put on; cover. ③ 《물 따위를》 pour 《*water*》 on *oneself*; be covered with 《*dust*》. ④ 《허물 따위를》 take 《*blame, responsibility*》 upon *oneself*.

들씌우다 ① 《덮다》 cover 《*with*》; put on. ② 《들어붓다》 pour 《*on*》. ③ 《죄 따위를》 impute 《*a fault*》 to 《*another*》; lay 《*a fault*》 on 《*a person*》; shift 《*a blame*》 on 《*someone*》.

들어가다 《안으로》 enter; go (get, walk, step) in (into). ¶ 몰래 ~ sneak into 《*a room*》 / 앞 문으로 ~ enter at the front door. ② 《가입·참가함》 join 《*a club*》; take part in 《*a campaign*》. ¶ 학교(회사)에 ~ enter a school (company) / 실업계에 ~ go into business. ③ 《틈·속·사이에》 go through; be inserted. ¶ 뚫고 ~ penetrate in. ④ 《비용이》 be spent; cost. ¶ 100달러가 ~ cost 100 dollars. ⑤ 《쑥 들어간 눈 sunken (hollow) eyes / 배가 고파

들어내다 그의 눈이 쑥 들어갔다 His eyes hollowed with hunger.
들어내다 ① 《내놓다》 take [bring, carry] out; remove. ② 《내쫓다》 turn [drive] out.
들어맞다 《적중》 hit (the mark); 《꿈·예언 등이》 come true; be [prove] correct; 《알맞다》 fit; suit; 《일치하다》 be in accord with. ¶ 옷이 몸에 꼭 들어맞는다 The clothes fit perfectly. / 꿈 [예언]이 들어맞았다 A dream [prophesy] came true. / 《의견이》 딱 ~ be in perfect accord (with).
들어먹다 《탕진하다》 squander; run through; dissipate 《one's fortune》. ¶ 도박으로 [술로] 재산을 ~ gamble [drink] away one's fortune / 하룻밤에 재산을 ~ squander one's fortune in a single night.
들어박히다 ① 《촘촘히》 be packed; be stuffed. ② 《칩거》 confine oneself to 《a room》; shut [lock] oneself up (in); stay indoors. ¶ 종일 방에 ~ keep to one's room all day long.
들어서다 ① 《안으로》 step in; enter; go [come] into. ② 《꽉 차다》 be full 《of》; be filled 《with》; be crowded 《with houses》. ③ 《자리에》 succeed 《a person》; accede to; take a position 《as》. ¶ 후임으로 ~ succeed 《a person》 at a post. ④ 《접어들다》 begin; set in. ¶ 장마철에 ~ the rainy season sets in.
들어앉다 ① 《안쪽으로》 sit nearer to the inside. ② 《은퇴》 retire from 《work》; 《자리에》 settle down; become. ¶ 본처로 ~ become a spouse
들어오다 ① 《안으로》 enter; come [get] in; walk in [into]. ② 《수입이》 have 《an income of》; get; receive. ③ 《입사·입회》 join [enter] 《a company》; be employed 《by》.
들어주다 grant; hear; answer 《a person's prayer》. ¶ 소원을 ~ grant one's wishes / 청을 들어주지 않다 turn a deaf ear to 《a person's》 request.
들어차다 be packed; be crowded. ¶ 꽉 ~ be packed to the full.
들여가다 ① 《안으로》 take [bring, carry] in. ② 《사다》 buy; get.
들여놓다 ① 《안으로》 bring [take] in. ¶ 비가 오기 전에 빨래를 ~ take the washing in before it begins to rain. ② 《사들이다》 buy [lay] in 《a stock of》 《goods》. ③ 들여놓은 가격은 the cost [buying] price / 식량을 ~ lay in provisions.
들여다보다 ① 《안을》 look 《in》; peep 《into, through》. ¶ 열쇠구멍으로 ~ look [peep] through a keyhole. ② 《자세히》 look into; examine carefully. ¶ 아무의 얼굴을 ~ look 《a person》 in the face. ③ 《들르다》 look [drop] in 《on, at》. ¶ 잠시 상점을 ~ look in at a store.
들여다보이다 《속이》 be transparent; be seen through. ¶ 뻔히 들여다뵈는 거짓말 a transparent [an obvious] lie.
들여보내다 send in; let [allow] in;
들여앉히다 《여자를》 have [make, let] a woman settle down in one's home.
들여오다 ① 《안으로》 take [bring, carry] in. ② 《사들이다》 buy (in); purchase; import《수입》. ¶ 여름옷을 대량으로 ~ buy a large stock of summer wear.
들은풍월 (一風月) knowledge picked up by listening to others.
…들이 (capable of) holding; containing. ¶ 두 말 ~ 자루 a sack holding two mal / 10갑 ~ 한 포 a 10-pack carton / 2리터 ~ 한 병 a two-liter bottle.
들이다 ① 《안으로》 let [allow] in; admit. ② 《비용을》 spend 《on》; invest; 《힘을》 take 《troubles》; make 《efforts》. ¶ 큰 돈을 들여서 ~ at a great cost / 힘들여서 with great efforts. ③ 《고용》 engage; employ; hire. ¶ 가정 교사를 ~ have [engage] a tutor 《for one's child》. ④ 《맛을》 get [acquire] a taste for; take to 《gambling》. ¶ 돈에 맛을 ~ get a taste for money. ⑤ 《물감을》 dye 《black》.
들이닥치다 come with a rush; storm 《a place》; 《사람이》 be visited suddenly; 《위험 등이》 be impending [imminent].
들이대다 ① 《대들다》 defy; oppose; protest. ② 《흉기 등을》 thrust [put] 《a thing》 before [under] one's nose; point 《a revolver》 at 《a person》. ③ 《제시》 produce. ¶ 증거를 ~ thrust evidence at 《a person》.
들이덤비다 《덤벼들다》 fall [turn] upon 《a person》; defy; 《서둘다》 busy oneself with; bustle 《up, about》; be in great haste.
들이마시다 《기체를》 inhale; breathe in 《fresh air》; 《액체를》 drink (in); suck in; gulp down.
들이몰다 drive in; 《마구》 drive fast [violently].
들이밀다 push [thrust, shove] in.
들이밀리다 《안으로》 be pushed [thrust] in; 《한 곳으로》 crowd; swarm; gather [flock] (together).
들이받다 run [bump] into; collide with; knock [strike, run] against. ¶ 차가 전주를 들이받았다 The car ran into an electric pole. / 트럭이 소형차를 들이받았다

들이쉬다 《숨을》 breathe in; inhale; inspire; draw 《a breath》.
들이치다 《비·눈이》 come into 《a room》; drive 〔be driven〕 into. ¶ 비가 들이치지 않도록 창문을 닫아라 Shut the windows so that the rain can't come in.
들이닥치다 《습격》 attack; assault; 〔일〕 farm work; work in the fields.
들쥐 《動》 a field rat.
들짐승 a wild animal.
들적지근하다 (be) sweetish.
들쭉나무 《植》 a blueberry.
들쭉날쭉하다 (be) uneven; indented; jagged.
들창(一窓) a small window.
들창코(一窓一) a turned-up 〔an upturned〕 nose.
들추다 ① 《뒤지다》 search; ransack; rummage. ② 《폭로》 reveal; disclose; expose.
들추어내다 disclose; lay bare; bring to light; dig into 〔up〕; rake up 《an old scandal》. ¶ 아무의 불미스런 과거를 ~ dig up *a person's* ugly past.
들치기 《행위》 shoplifting; 《사람》 a shoplifter. ~하다 shoplift. ¶ ~ 상습범 a habitual shoplifter.
들키다 be found out; be detected; be caught 《*doing*》.
들통(一筒) a pail; a bucket. ¶ ~나다 be detected 〔disclosed〕; get found out.
들판 a field; a plain.
듬뿍 much; plenty; brimfully; fully; generously. ¶ 돈이 ~ 있다 have plenty of money / 팁을 ~ 주다 tip 《a porter》 generously.
듬성듬성 sparsely; thinly.
듯이 like; as 《...as》; as if 〔though〕. ¶ 자기 아들 사랑하~ 사랑하다 love 《a child》 like *one's* own.
듯하다 look like; seem; appear. ¶ 비가 올 ~ It looks like rain.
등 《사람·동물의》 the back; 《산의》 the ridge; 《책의》 a back; the spine 《*of a book*》. ¶ 의자의 ~ the back of a chair / 적에게 ~을 보이다 turn *one's* back to the enemy.
등(等) 《등수》 a grade. ¶ 1~ first class 〔grade〕. ☞ 등급. ② 《따위》.
등(燈) a lamp; a lantern; a light. ¶ 30 와트짜리 ~ a 30-watt lamp.
등(藤) 《植》 a rattan; a cane; 《등나무》 a wisteria. ¶ ~꽃 〔덩굴〕 wisteria flower 〔vines〕.
등가(等價) 《化》 equivalence. ∥ ~량 an equivalent.
등각(等角) 《幾》 equal angles. ∥ ~3각형 an equiangular triangle.
등갓(燈一) a 〔lamp〕 shade.
등거리 a sleeveless shirt.
등거리(等距離) an equal distance; equidistance. ∥ ~외교 an even-handed 〔equidistant〕 foreign policy.
등걸 a stump; a stub.
등걸잠자다 sleep with *one's* clothes on (without any covering).
등겨 rice chaff.
등고선(等高線) a contour 〔line〕.
등골 the line of the backbone. ¶ ~이 오싹하다 feel a chill run down *one's* spine.
등과(登科) ~하다 pass the higher civil service examination.
등교(登校) ~하다 attend 〔go to〕 school. ¶ ~거부 (a) refusal to attend school / ~거부 아동 a school hater 〔rejecter〕.
등귀(騰貴) a rise 《*in prices*》; an advance; 《화폐가치의》 (an) appreciation. ~하다 rise; advance; go 〔run〕 up; appreciate. ¶ 달러의 ~ the appreciation of the dollar.
등극(登極) ~하다 ascend 〔come〕 to the throne.
등급(等級) a class; a grade; a rank. ¶ ~을 매기다 classify; grade / 품질에 따라 A, B, C로 ~이 매겨지다 be graded A, B and C according to quality.
등기(登記) registration; registry. ~하다 register; have 《a thing》 registered. ¶ ~우편으로 by registerd mail / 미~의 unregistered. ∥ ~료 a registration fee / ~부 a register 〔book〕 / ~소 a registry 〔office〕 / ~필 〔표시〕 Registered / ~필증 a registration certificate / 가~ provisional registration.
등단(登壇) ~하다 go on the platform; take 〔mount〕 the rostrum.
등달다 be in a stew 〔fret〕 《*about*》; be impatient 〔irritated〕.
등대(燈臺) a lighthouse. ∥ ~선 a light ship /~지기 a lighthouse keeper / 등불을 a beacon lamp; lights.
등대다 lean 〔depend〕 on; rely 〔upon〕.
등덜미 the upper part of the back.
등등(等等) etc.; and so on; others.
등등하다(騰騰—) be in high spirits; be on a high horse. ¶ 그의 참가로 팀의 기세가 등등해졌다 His participation put our team in high spirits.
등락(騰落) rise and fall; ups and downs; fluctuations. ¶ 주가의 ~ the fluctuations of stock prices.
등록(登錄) registration; entry. ~하다 register 《a trademark》; make registration 《*for*》; make an entry; enrole. ¶ 유권자의 ~ the

등반(登攀) climbing. ~하다 climb (up). ‖ ~대 a climbing party / ~자 a climber.
등변(等邊) 〖幾〗 equal sides. ‖ ~삼각형 an equilateral triangle.
등본(謄本) a (certified) copy; a transcript; a duplicate. ¶ ~을 신청하다 apply for a copy.
등분(等分) ~하다 divide equally [in equal parts]; share equally. ¶ 2~하다 bisect; divide (a thing) into two. ‖ 2~ bisection.
등불(燈―) a light; a lamp.
등비(等比) 〖數〗 equal ratio.
등뼈 the backbone; the spine.
등사(謄寫) copy; transcription. ~하다 copy; make a copy (of); mimeograph. ‖ ~원지 stencil paper / ~판 a mimeograph.
등산(登山) mountaineering; mountain climbing. ~하다 climb (ascend, go up) a mountain. ‖ ~가 a mountaineer; an alpinist / ~대 a mountaineering (climbing) party / ~지팡이 an alpenstock / ~화 (a pair of) mountaineering boots.
등색(橙色) orange (color).
등성이 the ridge of a mountain.
등세공(藤細工) rattanwork; canework.
등속(等速) equal speed; 〖理〗 uniform velocity. ‖ ~운동 uniform motion.
등수(等數) a grade; a rank; (같은 수) an equal number.
등식(等式) 〖數〗 an equality.
등신(等身) (실물 크기) life-size; full-length. ‖ ~상 a life-size statue.
등신(等神) a fool; a stupid; a blockhead. ¶ ~같은 짓을 하다 do something foolish [stupid]; play [act] the fool.
등심(燈心) a (lamp) wick.
등쌀 annoyance; harassing; bothering; molesting. ¶ ~대다 harass; bother; pester; annoy; play the bully / 모기 ~에 잠을 잘 수 없다 The mosquitoes are so annoying that I can't sleep. / 이 애 ~에 못견디겠다 I can't suffer any more the ill nature of this child.
등압선(等壓線) an isobar; an isobaric line.
등에 〖蟲〗 a horsefly; a gadfly.
등온(等溫) 의 isothermal. ¶ ~선 〖地〗 an isothermal (line).
등외(等外) a failure; (경주에서) an also-ran. ¶ ~의 unplaced(경기에서); offgrade; substandard(품질이) / ~가 되다 fail to win the prize; fall under the regular grades (품평회 따위에서). ~품 an offgrade article.
등용(登用) 〖任用〗 appointment. ~하다 appoint (assign) (a person to a position). ¶ 인재를 ~하다 engage (employ) men of ability / 인재의 ~의 길을 열다 make all careers open to talent; open the offices to talent / 조직을 활성화하기 위해 유망한 신인을 ~하기로 하였다 It was decided to make full use of promising new recruits in order to breathe new life into the organization.
등용문(登龍門) the gateway to success (in life). 〔House.
등원(登院) ~하다 attend the
등유(燈油) lamp oil; kerosene.
등자(橙子) 〖植〗 a bitter orange.
등잔(燈盞) a lamp-oil container. ¶ ~ 밑이 어둡다 (俗談) It's darkest at the foot of the lampstand. or Sometimes one doesn't see what is right under one's nose. ‖ ~불 a lamplight.
등장(登場) ① 〔劇〕 entrance on the stage; entry. ~하다 enter [appear] on the stage. ② (나타남) advent; appearance. ¶ 신무기의 ~ the advent of new weapons. ‖ ~인물 the characters (in a play).
등재(登載) registration; record. ~하다 register; record.
등정(登頂) ~하다 reach the top (summit) of a mountain.
등정(登程) departure. ~하다 start [set] out on a journey; depart.
등줄기 the line of the backbone.
등지(等地) (and) like places. ¶ 서울·부산 ~ Seoul, Pusan and like cities (places).
등지다 ① (사이가) break [fall out, split] with; be estranged [alienated] (from). ¶ 두 사람은 오랫동안 서로 등져 있다 The couple has been on bad terms [at odds] for a long time. ② (등 뒤에 두다) lean one's back against (a wall). ③ (저버리다) turn against; turn one's back (on); leave; forsake. ¶ 나라를 ~ turn against one's country / 고향을 ~ leave one's hometown / 세상을 ~ forsake the world.
등짐 a pack carried on one's back. ‖ ~장수 a pack-peddler.
등차(等差) ‖ ~급수 〖數〗 arithmetical progression. 〔the office.
등청(登廳) ~하다 attend (go to)
등치다 ① (때리다) slap (a person) on the back. ② (빼앗다) rack-

등쳐먹고 살다 eteer; extort 《*money*》; blackmail. ¶ 등쳐먹고 살다 live by racketeering.

등판 (登板) ~하다 [野] take the 등판.

등피 (燈皮) a lamp chimney.

등하불명 (燈下不明) One has to go abroad to get news of home. ☞ 등잔.

등한 (等閑) ~하다 (be) negligent; careless. ¶ ~히 하다 neglect 《*one's duties*》; give no heed to.

등화 (燈火) a light; a lamplight. ¶ ~ 가친지절 (可親之節) a good season for reading / ~관제 a blackout (~관제하다 black out).

디데이 (the) D-day.

디디다 step on. ¶ 외국 땅을 ~ step on foreign soil.

디딜방아 a treadmill (pestle); a mortar (worked by treading).

디딤돌 a stepstone; (수단) a stepping stone.

디럭스 deluxe 《*cars*》. ¶ ~판 an edition deluxe; a deluxe edition / ~호텔 a hotel deluxe.

디렉터 a director.

디스카운트 discount 《*sale*》; price cutting. ‖ ~스토어 a discount store.

디스코 a disco. ‖ ~뮤직 disco music / ~테크 a discotheque.

디스크 a disk. ‖ ~자키 a disk jockey(생략 D.J.).

디스토마 (편충) a distoma; (병) distomiasis. [bonucleic Acid]

디엔에이 [生·化] DNA. (◀Deoxyri-

디자이너 a designer; a stylist (美). ‖ ~공업 an industrial designer.

디자인 a design; designing. ~하다 design 《*a dress*》.

디저트 (a) dessert. ¶ ~는 뭘로 하시겠습니까 What will you have for dessert?

디젤 diesel. ‖ ~기관차 a diesel locomotive / ~기관 a Diesel [diesel] engine.

디지털 ~식의 digital. ‖ ~시계 a digital clock [watch] / ~신호 a digital signal / ~컴퓨터 a digital computer / ~통신 digital communications / ~화 digitization.

디프테리아 [醫] diphtheria. ‖ ~혈청 antidiphtheria serum.

디플레이션 deflation. ‖ ~정책 a deflationary policy.

딜레마 (fall into) a dilemma. ¶ ~에 빠뜨리다 force 《*a person*》 into a dilemma.

딩딩하다 ① (힘이 셈) (be) strong; stout; robust. ② (팽팽하다) (be) tense; taut. ③ (기반이) (be) stable; secure; solid.

따갑다 (뜨겁다) (be) unbearably hot; (쑤시듯이) (be) prickly; tin-

gling; pricking; smart.

따귀 ¶ ~를 때리다 slap 《*a person*》 on the cheek [in the face].

따끈따끈 ¶ ~한 hot; heated

따끔하다 ① (쑤시다) (be) prickly; pricking. ② (호되다) (be) sharp; severe. ¶ 따끔한 맛을 보이다 teach [give] 《*a person*》 a lesson.

따다 ① (잠아떼다) pick; pluck; nip (off). ¶ 꽃을 ~ pluck [pick] a flower. ② (종기를) open 《*an abscess*》; (강통을) open 《*a can*》; uncork (마개를). ~ 곪은 데를 ~ open a boil. ③ (발췌) quote; pick out. ¶ 밀턴의 시에서 한 절을 ~ quote a passage from Milton. ④ (얻다) get; gain; take; obtain; win. ¶ 만점을 ~ get a full mark 《*in*》 / 학위를 ~ take [get] a degree / 돈을 ~ win money 《*in gambling*》.

따돌리다 leave 《*a person*》 out (in the cold); exclude; boycott; ostracize (사회적으로). ¶ 그는 그룹에서 따돌림을 받았다 The group left him out in the cold. *or* He was excluded from the group.

따뜻하다 (온도가) (be) warm; mild; (정이) (be) kindly; cordial; warm (-hearted). ¶ 따뜻이 warmly; kindly / 따뜻한 겨울 a mild [soft] winter / 따뜻한 마음씨 a warm [kindly] heart / 따뜻이 대접하다 give 《*a person*》 a hearty reception.

따라가다 (동행) go along with; (뒤를) follow 《*a person*》; (놓치지 않고) keep [catch] up with.

따라붙다 overtake; catch [come] up with.

따라서 ① (…에 준하여) in accordance [conformity] with; according to. ¶ 국내법에 ~ in accordance with the national law / 관습에 ~ according to custom / in obedience to 《*a person's*》 orders. ② (비례하여) in proportion to 《*as*》 with; as. ¶ 세상이 진보함에 ~ with the progress of the world / 문명이 발달함에 ~ as civilization progresses. ③ (~을 끼고) along; by; parallel to [with]. ¶ 강둑을 ~ 걷다 walk along the river bank / (길로 따위가) 강을 ~ 이어져 오다 run parallel to a river. ④ (…을 모방하여) after (the example [model] of). ¶ …에 ~ 만들다 make 《*a thing*》 after the model of…. ⑤ (그러므로) accordingly; consequently; therefore; so that. ¶ 나는 존재한다, 나는 존재한다 I think, therefore I am.

따라오다 (수행) come with; accompany; follow; (쫓아온) keep up with; (남 하는 대로) follow; catch up. ☞ 따르다¹ ①, ③.

따라잡다 ⇨ 따라붙다.
따라죽음 a wretched life.
따로 (별개로) apart; separately; (추가로) additionally; besides; in addition; (특별히) especially; in particular; particularly. ¶ ~ 두다 keep [lay] aside / ~ 10만원 수입이 있다 have additional income of 100,000 *won* / ~ 살다 live separately / ~ 할 말이 없다 have nothing particular to mention.
따르다[1] ① (따라가다) go along with; follow; accompany; go after. ¶ 남의 뒤를 ~ go after *a person* / 유행을 ~ follow the fashion. ② (수반하다) accompany; go with; be followed [attended] by. ¶ 여러 곤란이 ~ be attended by various difficulties / 특권에는 책임이 따른다 Responsibilities go with privileges. / 번개에는 벼락이 따른다 Thunder is accompanied by lightning. ③ (본뜨다) follow; model (*after*). ¶ 남의 예에 ~ follow another's example. ④ (복종·준수) obey; follow; comply with (*a request*); abide by (*the rule*). ¶ 충고에 ~ follow (*a person's*) advice / 강제로 따르게 하다 compel (*a person*) to obey. ⑤ (겨루다) equal; be a match for. ¶ 따를 사람이 없다 be peerless. ⑥ (좋아하다) be attached to (*a person*); love (*a person*); be tamed (동물). ¶ 그녀를 친엄마처럼 ~ love her like a real mother.
따르다[2] (붓다) pour (*out, in*).
따르르 ¶ ~ 구르다 roll fast / ~ 울리다 tinkle; ring clamorously.
따름 just; only; merely; alone. ¶ …일 [할] ~이다 it is just that ….
따리 flattery; cajolery. ¶ ~ 붙이다 flattery; fawn (up)on.
따분하다 ① (느른함) be languid; dull. ② (지루함·맥빠짐) be boring; tedious; wearisome. ¶ 따분한 세상 wearisome life / 따분한 이야기 a boring tale.
따오기 [鳥] a crested ibis.
따옴표 (—標) quotation marks.
따위 ① (…와 같은) … and such like; such (*a thing*) like [as] …; the like (of). ¶ 너 ~ 네 ~는 likes of you / 예를 들면 … ~ such as; for example. ② (등등) and so on (forth); et cetera (생략 etc.); and [or] the like.
따지다 ① (셈을) calculate; count; compute (*interest*). ② (시비) inquire into; distinguish (*between*); discriminate (*one from another*); demand an explanation of.
딱 ① (벌린 꼴) wide. ¶ 입을 ~ 벌리고 with *one's* mouth wide open. ② (정확히) exactly; just; to a T;

sharp; (들어맞게) perfectly; (꽉) tight(ly); closely. ¶ ~ 맞는 옷 a perfectly fitting coat. ③ (꼭) 버티는 꼴) firmly; stiffly. ¶ ~ 버티고 서다 stand firmly against (*a person*). ④ (단호히) positively; flatly. ¶ ~ 거절하다 refuse flatly; decline positively. ⑤ (꼭) only; just. ¶ ~ 한 번 only [but] once. ⑥ (소리) with a snap (crack).
딱따구리 [鳥] a woodpecker.
딱따기 (나무) wooden clappers; (사람) a night watchman.
딱 with claps [cracks, raps]; with snaps.
딱딱거리다 snap (*at*); nag (*at*); speak harshly [roughly].
딱딱하다 (단단하다) (be) hard; solid; (굳어서) (be) stiff; rigid; tough; (엄격) (be) strict; rigid; (학문이) (be) academic; (문장이) (be) bookish; stiff; (형식이) (be) formal; stiff.
딱바라지다 (사람이) (be) thickset; stocky; (물건이) (be) wide and shallow. 「람」.
딱부리 a lobster-eyed person (사람).
딱새 [鳥] a redstart (bird).
딱성냥 a friction match.
딱장대 a harsh person.
딱장받다 torture (*a thief*); make (*a suspect*) confess *his* crime.
딱정벌레 ① (갑옷) a beetle. ② [蟲] a ground beetle.
딱지[1] (부스럼의) a scab; (게·소라의) a shell; a carapace; (시계의) a case. ¶ ~가 앉다 scab; a scab forms over (*a boil*).
딱지[2] (라벨) a label; (우표) a (postage) stamp; (꼬리표) a tag; (스티커) a sticker. ¶ 짐에 ~를 붙이다 put labels [tags] on *one's* luggage / ~가 붙은 (비유적으로) marked (주의를 끌게); notorious (나쁘게). ② (놀이 딱지) a card; a pasteboard dump. ③ (주차 위반의) a (traffic) ticket. ¶ (교통 순경이) ~를 떼다 give (*a driver*) a ticket; ticket a traffic offender.
딱지[3] (거절) rejection; a rebuff (퇴짜). ¶ ~를 놓다 refuse [reject] bluntly; give (*a suitor*) the mitten / ~ 맞다 be rejected; get snubbed; get the mitten (구혼자에게). 「er (푹죽).
딱총 (—銃) a popgun; a firecrack-
딱하다 ① (가엾다) (be) pitiable; pitiful; sad; (안되다) (be) sorry; regrettable. ¶ 딱한 처지 a pitiable circumstances / 딱하게 여기다 pity; take pity on; sympathize with; (feel) regret. ② (난처) (be) awkward; embarrassing. ¶ 딱한 입장 an awkward [a painful] position.
딴 other; another; different. ¶ ~ 것 other things; another; the

딴딴하다 (be) hard; solid.
딴마음 《다른 생각》 any other intention; 《연략》 a secret intention; 《반심》 duplicity, treachery. ¶ ~이 있는 double-faced; treacherous / ~이 있다 (없다) have (don't have) a secret intention.
딴말 《무관한 말》 irrelevant remarks; 《뒤바꿈 말》 a double tongue(일구이언).
딴머리 a false hair; a wig.
딴사람 《다른 사람》 a different person; another person; 《새사람》 a new being; a changed man. ¶ 그는 아주 ~이 되었다 He is quite another man now.
딴살림하다 live separately.
딴생각 a different intention; another motive(idea); an ulterior motive(속다른).
딴소리 irrelevant remarks. ☞ 딴말.
딴은 ① 《하기는》 really; indeed; I see. ¶ ~ 그는 말이오 Indeed you are right. ② 《…으로는》 as. ¶ 내 ~ as for me; for(on) my part.
딴전부리다 make irrelevant remarks(딴말로); pretend (feign) ignorance(시치미떼다).
딴판 아주 ~이다 be quite different; ~이 되다 change completely.
딸 a daughter.
딸가닥거리다 clatter; rattle.
딸기 《植》 a strawberry. ∥ ~밭 a strawberry bed(patch).
딸꾹질 a hiccup; a hiccough. ~하다 hiccough; have hiccups.
딸랑거리다 tinkle; jingle.
딸리다 ① 《부속》 belong to; be attached to; 《딸려 있다》 be relied (depended) on. ¶ 가구 딸린 셋집 a furnished house to let / 딸린 식구 dependants / 딸린 가족이 많다 have a large family who are dependent on 《me》; have many dependants. ② 《시중》 let 《a person》 attend (accompany). ③ 《부치다》 be inferior to; be no equal for; 《부족》 be (fall, run) short 《of》. ¶ 돈이 ~ run short of funds / 역량이 ~ be beyond one's capacity.
땀 sweat; perspiration. ¶ ~ 나는 sweaty; perspiring / ~ 홀려 번 돈 money earned by the sweat of one's brow; honestly earned money / ~의 결정(結晶) the fruits of one's labor (hard work) / ~을 흘리다 sweat; be sweaty / 이마에서 ~이 뚝뚝 떨어졌다 Sweat dripped from my forehead. / 손에 ~을 쥐고 경기를 보다 watch the game breathlessly / 얼굴의 ~을 닦다 wipe the sweat off one's face.
땀내 the smell (stink) of sweat. ¶ ~ 나는 옷 garments stinking with sweat.
땀띠 (have) prickly heat; (a) heat rash. ¶ ~약 prickly heat powder.
땀받이 a sweat shirt. 「(汗腺).
땀샘 《生》 a sweat gland. ☞ 한선
땅 ① 《대지·지면》 the earth; the ground. ¶ ~을 파다 dig in the ground / ~에 떨어지다 fall to the ground. ② 《영토》 territory; land; 《토양》 soil; earth; 《토지》 land; a lot; an estate. ¶ ~을 갈다 cultivate land / ~을 사다 (팔다) buy (sell) a piece of land / 한국 ~을 밟다 set foot on Korean soil / 이국 ~에서 죽다 die in a foreign land / 이 ~은 장미 재배에 알맞다 This soil is suited to the cultivation of roses. ∥ ~임자 a land owner.
땅² 《총소리》 (with a) bang.
땅가뢰 《蟲》 a blister beetle.
땅강아지 《蟲》 a mole cricket.
땅거미 《動》 a ground spider.
땅거미 《저녁어스름》 (at) twilight; dusk. ¶ ~질 무렵 at dusk; toward evening / ~가 내리다 grow dark.
땅기다 《음이》 be cramped; have the cramp (in one's leg); 《가까이》 draw (near); pull.
땅꾼 a snake-catcher.
땅덩이 land; the earth (지구); territory(국토).
땅딸막하다 (be) thickset; chunky.
땅딸보 a stocky person.
땅땅거리다 ① 《큰소리치다》 talk big (high-handedly). ② ☞ 땅땅거리
땅뙈기 a patch of land. 「다.
땅마지기 a few acres of field.
땅바닥 the (bare) ground. ¶ ~에 앉다 squat on the (bare) ground.
땅버들 《植》 a sallow; a goat willow.
땅벌레 a grub; a ground beetle.
땅별이 《野》 a grounder; a bounder.
땅사기꾼 a land swindler; a fake land broker.
땅울림 earth tremor; a rumbling of the earth.
땅콩 a groundnut; a peanut.
땅투기 land speculation.
땋다 plait; braid.
때¹ ① 《시각·시간》 time; hour; moment. ¶ 점심 ~ lunch time / ~를 어기지 않고 punctually; on time / ~늦은 《늦게》 late / 《매일》 이맘~에 at this time of day / 이제 잘 ~이다 It's time for you to go to bed. ② 《경우》 a case; an occasion; (a) time. ¶ ~한 ~에는 in time (case) of / 위험한 ~와 경우에 따라서는 according to the time

때 ① 《더러운》 dirt; filth; grime; 《얼룩》 a stain; a spot; a blot. ¶ ~(가) 묻다 become dirty[filthy, soiled]; be stained with dirt / ~를 빼다(씻다) wash off the dirt; remove stain《*from*》. ② 《시골티 따위》 ¶ ~를 벗은 refined; elegant; smart / ~를 벗지 못한 unpolished; rustic.

때구루루 ¶ ~ 구르다 roll over.

때굴때굴 ¶ ~ 굴리다 roll 《*a thing*》 over and over.

때까치 〖鳥〗 a bull-headed shrike.

때깔 the shape and color (of cloth).

때다¹ 《불을》 burn; make a fire. ¶ 불을 ~ make a fire / 석탄(장작)을 ~ burn coal (wood). 〔tune〕

때다² 《액(厄)을》 overcome 《*evil for-*

때때로 occasionally; now and then; from time to time; at times; sometimes. ¶ ~ 방문하다 call on 《*a person*》 from time to time. 〔dren.

때때옷 a colorful dress for chil-

때리다 strike; beat; hit; slap 《손바닥으로》. ¶ 때려 눕히다 knock 《*a person*》down / 때려 부수다 knock 《*a thing*》to pieces; break up; smash up / 때려 죽이다 strike [beat] to death / 얼굴을 ~ hit [slap]《*a person*》in the face.

때마침 opportunely; seasonably; timely; at the right moment.

때문 ¶ ~에 because of; due to; owing to; on account of / 전쟁 ~에 due to the war / 그 ~에 because of that / 부주의 ~에 because of carelessness.

때물벗다 be refined; be polished.

때우다 ① 《깁다》patch up;《땜질》solder; tinker up. ②《넘기다》 make shift 《*with*》; manage 《*with*》; do with(out); substitute 《doughnuts for lunch》.

땔나무 firewood.

땜장이 a tinker.

땜질 tinkering; soldering. ~하다 tinker (up); solder; patch up.

땡감 an unripe and astringent persimmon.

땡그랑거리다 clink; clang; jingle.

땡땡 ding-dong; clang-clang.

땡땡하다 (be) full; taut.

땡잡다 make a lucky hit; hit the jackpot 〖美〗.

떠꺼머리 ¶ ~ 처녀 〖총각〗 a pigtailed old maid (bachelor).

떠나다 ①《출발함》leave; start 《*from*》; set out; depart 《*from*》. ¶ 서울을 ~ leave Seoul for / ~ start for [set off to] Pusan / 세상을 ~ depart this life; die; pass away. ②《물러나다》leave; quit; resign 《*from*》;《떨어지다》separate; part from《with》. ¶ 직을 ~ quit *one's* post / 멀리 떠나 살 live far apart.

떠내다 dip [scoop] up.

떠다니다 drift (wander) about.

떠돌다 《표류》drift about; float; 《방랑》wander (roam) about.

떠돌이 a wanderer; a Bohemian. ¶ ~별 〖天〗 a planet.

떠들다 ①《큰소리로》make a noise; be noisy clamour 《*for*》. ②《술렁거리다》kick up a row; make much ado.

떠들썩하다 (be) noisy; clamorous. ¶ 떠들썩하게 noisily; clamorously.

떠들어대다 raise a clamor; make an uproar; set up a cry; make a fuss 《*about*》.

떠름하다 ①《맛이》(be) slightly astringent. ②《내키지 않다》(be) indisposed; feel (be) creepy;《꺼림하다》feel (be) leery.

떠맡기다 leave 《*a matter*》 to others; saddle 《*a person*》 with. ¶ 억지로 ~ force on; pass [impose] upon.

떠맡다 undertake; assume; take 《*a task*》 upon *oneself*; be saddled with; take over. ¶ 빚을 ~ hold *oneself* liable for a debt / 책임을 ~ assume the responsibility.

떠받들다 ①《쳐들다》hold up; lift; raise; push up. ②《공경》revere; hold 《*a person*》 in esteem;《추대》set 《*a person*》 up 《*as*》; exalt; support. ③《소중히》make much of.

떠받치다 support; prop up.

떠버리 a braggart; a chatterbox.

떠벌리다 ①《과장》talk big; brag; 《떠들어댐》wag *one's* tongue. ②《크게 차리다》set up 《*a thing*》 in a large scale.

떠보다 ①《무게를》weigh. ②《속을》sound; feel. ③《인품을》 size up 《*a person*》.

떠오르다 ① 《물위에》 be afloat; rise (come up) to the surface; 《공중에》 rise; fly aloft; soar. ¶ 잠수함이 해면 위로 떠올랐다 The submarine came (up) to the surface of the sea. ② 《생각이》 occur to 〔strike〕 one; come across 〔into〕 one's mind. ¶ 좋은 생각이 떠올랐다 A bright 〔good〕 idea occured (came to, struck) me. ③ 《표면에 나타나다》 appear; loom up (emerge) 《as a suspect》. ¶ 만족의 빛이 그녀의 얼굴에 떠올랐다 A look of contentment appeared on her face. / 피해자의 조카가 용의자로 떠올랐다 The victim's nephew has emerged as a suspect.

떡¹ rice cake. ¶ 그림의 ∼ pie in the sky / 누워서 ∼ 먹기다 《俗談》 Nothing is easier. ¶ ∼ 가래 a stick (bar) of rice cake / ∼국 rice-cake soup / ∼메 a rice-cake mallet / ∼볶이 a broiled dish of rice-cake bars (sticks).

떡² 《버티는 모양》 firmly; 《벌린 모양》 widely. ¶ ∼ 버티다 stand firmly against / 입을 ∼ 벌리고 with one's mouth wide open. ¶ 〔목〕 oak.

떡갈나무 〔植〕 an oak (tree); 〔재〕 oak.

떡밥 〔낚시미끼〕 (a) paste bait.

떡방아 a rice-flour mill. ¶ ∼를 찧다 pound rice into flour.

떡잎 a seed leaf. ¶ 될성부른 나무는 ∼부터 알아본다 《俗談》 Genius will assert itself at an early age.

떨거덕거리다 clatter; rattle.

떨거지 one's folk; one's relatives.

떨기 a cluster; a bunch; a plant. ¶ 한 ∼ 꽃 a bunch of flowers.

떨다¹ ① 《붙은 것을》 remove; beat 〔shake, brush〕 off. ¶ 먼지를 ∼ shake the dust off. ② 《곡식을》 thrash. ③ 《비우다》 clear off; empty 《one's purse》. ④ 《팔다 남은 것을》 sell off; clear out 《remaining stocks》. ⑤ 《부리다》 show; display. ¶ 애교를 ∼ be profuse of one's smiles; turn on the charm / 수다를 ∼ wag one's tongue / 아프다고 엄살 ∼ pretend to be in pain.

떨다² 《몸을》 shake; tremble 《for fear》; shiver 《with cold》; quiver; shudder 《with terror》.

떨리다¹ ① 《떨어지다》 be shaken (swept, brushed) off; be thrown off. ② 《쫓겨나다》 get fired; be dismissed.

떨리다² 《몸이》 shake; tremble; shiver; quiver; chatter(이가); shudder(무서워). ¶ 떨리는 목소리 a trembling voice.

떨어뜨리다 ① 《아래로》 drop; let fall; throw 《something》 down; 《공을》 miss. ¶ 컵을 ∼ drop a cup. ② 《줄이다》 decrease; reduce; lessen. ¶ 값〔속력〕을 ∼ reduce the price (speed). ③ 《지위·명성을》 debase; detract; degrade; lower. ¶ 〔일〕의 인기를 ∼ detract from one's popularity / 계급을 ∼ demote; reduce to a lower rank. ④ 《질을》 debase; lower; deteriorate. ¶ 품질을 ∼ lower in quality; deteriorate. ⑤ 《함락》 capture; take. ⑥ 《해뜨리다》 wear out (down). ⑦ 《재고 등을》 exhaust; run out; use up. ¶ 재고를 ∼ use the rice up. ⑧ 《불합격》 reject 《a candidate》; fail.

떨어지다 ① 《낙하》 fall; drop; come down; crash (비행기가). ¶ 쿵 ∼ fall with a thud / 나무에서 ∼ fall down from a tree. ② 《묻거나 붙은 것이》 come (fall) off. ¶ 단추가 ∼ a button comes off / 얼룩이 안 떨어진다 The stain won't come out. ③ 《남다》 be left (over). ¶ 이문이 많이 ∼ yield much profit. ④ 《뒤지다》 fall off; drop behind; lag behind. ¶ 경주에서 다른 선수에게 ∼ fall behind another runner in a race / 비행술이 서양에 ∼ lag behind the West in the art of flying. ⑤ 《값이》 fall; go down; decline. ¶ 값이 ∼ go down in price; decline (fall) in price. ⑥ 《감퇴》 decrease; diminish; go down; fall. ¶ 가치가 ∼ decrease (diminish) in value / 인기가 ∼ lose one's popularity; fall in popularity. ⑦ 《못하다》 be inferior (to); be worse (than). ¶ 품질이 ∼ be inferior in quality. ⑧ 《해지다》 be worn out. ¶ 떨어진 ragged; threadbare; worn-out / 구두가 ∼ one's shoes are worn out. ⑨ 《바닥나다》 run (get) out of; be (run) short of; be all gone; be out of stock (상품이). ¶ 용돈이 ∼ run out of pocket money / 식량이 ∼ run out of food. ⑩ 《숨이》 breathe one's last; die; expire. ⑪ 《병·습관이》 be shaken off; be got rid of. ¶ 감기가 ∼ shake off one's cold. ¶ 《거리·간격》 be 《a long way》 off; be away 《from》. ¶ 멀리 떨어진 far-off; distant / …에서 4마일 떨어져 있다 be four miles away from. ⑬ 《갈라짐》 separate; part from 〔with〕; leave (떠나). ¶ 떨어질 수 없는 inseparable / 떨어져 나오다 break off 《with》. ⑭ 《함락》 fall. ⑮ 《실패》 fail; be unsuccessful. ¶ 시험에 ∼ fail (flunk) an examination / 선거에서 ∼ be defeated in an election. ⑯ 《수중·술책에》 fall into 《another's snare》.

떨이 goods for clearance sale.
떨치다 ① 《명성을》 become (get) well known; 《타동사적》 make well known in the world; 《힘을》 wield 《*power*》. ¶ 이름을 ~ win fame. ② 《흔들어서》 shake off; whisk off.
떫다 (be) astringent; sour. ¶ 떫은 감 an astringent persimmon / 떫은 포도주 rough wine.
떳떳하다 (be) just; fair; right; have a clear conscience. ¶ 떳떳이 fairly; openly; with a clear conscience / 떳떳한 요구 〔처사〕 a fair demand 〔deal〕 / 떳떳이 행동하다 act fair and square / …을 떳떳하지 않게 여기다 be ashamed 《*to do*》; be too proud 《*to do*》; be above 《*doing*》 / 떳떳하게 지다 be a good loser; accept defeat 「cheerfully 〔with a good grace〕 / 떳떳한 부부가 되다 become a legitimate couple.
떵떵거리다 live in great splendor 〔style〕; live like a prince.
떼¹ 《무리》 a group; a crowd; a throng 〔사람〕; a herd 〔마소〕; a flock 〔양, 새〕; a shoal 〔어유〕; a swarm 〔벌레〕. ¶ ~를 지어 〔서〕 in crowds 〔flocks, shoals, swarms〕; in a group / 떼지어 덤비다 attack all in a bunch.
떼² 《잔디》 sod; turf. ¶ ~를 뜨다 cut out sod / ~을 입히다 sod; turf. ¶ 떼장 a turf; a piece of sod.
떼³ 《억지》 perversity; an unreasonable demand 〔claim〕. ¶ ~ 쓰다 ask for the impossible; fret; be fretful; pester 〔nag〕 《*a person*》 to *do* / 인형을 사달라고 엄마에게 ~를 쓰다 keep nagging *one's* mother for the doll. 「over.
떼굴떼굴 ¶ ~ 구르다 roll over and
떼다 ① 《붙은 것을》 remove 《*a sign*》; take off 《*away*》. ② 《분리》 part; separate; pull apart; pluck 〔tear〕 off; 《사이를》 keep apart; leave 《*space*》. ¶ 행간을 ~ leave spaces between lines. ③ 《봉한 것을》 break 〔open〕 the seal; cut 《*a letter*》. ④ 《공제》 deduct 〔detract〕 《*from*》 / 봉급에서 ~ deduct 《*a sum*》 from *one's* pay; take 《*a sum*》 off *one's* pay. ⑤ 《절연》 cut 〔sever〕 connections with 《*a person*》; break 〔off〕 with 《*a person*》 / 맬래야 맬 수 없는 사이다 be inseparably bound up with each other. ⑥ 《수표 따위를》 draw 〔issue〕 《*a check*》.
떼새 ① 〔鳥〕 a plover. ② 《새의 떼》 a flock of birds.
떼어놓다 《분리》 pull apart 《*persons*, *things*》 apart; separate 〔part〕 《*things*》; estrange 〔이간〕.
떼어먹다 《가로채다》 appropriate; embezzle; 《안 갚다》 bilk; fail to pay 〔return〕; leave 《*a bill*》 unpaid; be welshed on 《*one's debt*》. ¶ 그에게 빌려 준 100만원을 떼였다 The one million *won* which I lent him was never paid back.
떼이다 《빚 따위를》 become irrecoverable; have a loan 〔bill, debt〕 unpaid; be welshed on 《*one's debt*》. ☞ 떼어버리다 ①, ⑤. 「paid.
떼치다 《붙는 것을》 shake *oneself* loose 〔free〕 from; break loose 《*from*》; 《거절》 refuse; reject; turn down. 「man.
뗏목 (一木) a raft. ∥ ~꾼 a rafts-
뗑그렁거리다 clang; jingle; tinkle.
또 ① 《또다시》 again; once more. 《거듭》 repeatedly. ¶ 한번 ~ once again 〔more〕 / ~ 하나의 the other; another 〔딴〕. ② 《또한》 too; also; as well. ¶ 나도 ~ 가지고 있다 I have it, too. ③ 《그 위에》 and; moreover; besides.
또는 (either…) or; 《아마》 perhaps; probably; maybe.
또다시 again; once more 〔again〕. ¶ ~하다 do over again.
또닥거리다 tap; pat; rap.
또랑또랑 ¶ ~한 clear; bright; distinct.
또래 (of) about the same age; 《물건》 (of) the (same) size 〔shape〕.
또렷하다 (be) clear. ☞ 뚜렷하다.
또한 《한가지로》 too; also; as well; 《그 위에》 besides; moreover; at the same time. 「flop).
똑¹ 《소리》 with a snap 〔crack,
똑² 《틀림없이》 just; exactly. ¶ ~같다 be just the same 《*as*》; be just like; be identical 〔~같이 just like; alike; likewise; equally; impartially.
똑딱거리다 click; clack; 《시계가》 tic(k)-toc(k); ¶ 똑딱똑딱 clicking; tick(-tack). 「boat.
똑딱선 (一船) a (small) steam-
똑똑 ① 《두드리는 소리》 rapping; knocking. ¶ 문을 ~ 두드리다 knock 〔tap〕 at the door. ② 《부러지는》 with a snap. ③ 《액체가》 dripping; trickling; drop by drop.
똑똑하다 ① 《영리》 (be) clever; sharp; intelligent; bright; smart. ¶ 똑똑한 아이 a bright child. ② 《분명》 (be) clear; distinct; vivid; plain. ¶ 똑똑한 발음 clear 〔articulate〕.
똑똑히 《명료하게》 clearly; distinctly; plainly; definitely; 《영리하게》 wisely; smartly. ¶ ~ 굴다 act wisely.
똑바로 《바르게》 in a straight line; straight; 《곧추》 upright; erect; 《바른대로》 honestly; frankly; 《정

똑똑 확하게 correctly; exactly; 《옳게》 right(ly); 《정면으로》 to (in) one's face; directly (직격).

똑똑 ¶ ~ 말다 roll up (a sheet of paper). ¶ 《sharp》 smart.

똑똑하다 (be) clever; bright.

똥 feces; stool; excrement; dung (동물의). ¶ ~을 푸다 dip up night soil / ~ 푸는 사람 a night-soil man / ~ 마렵다 have a call of nature; want to relieve oneself; be taken short (급히) / 얼굴에 ~ 칠하다 disgrace one's name.

똥값 a giveaway (dirt-cheap) price. ¶ ~으로 팔다 sell dirt-cheap; sell at a sacrifice.

똥거름 night soil; dung-manure.

똥구멍 the anus; the back passage. ¶ ~이 찢어지게 가난하다 be extremely poor; be as poor as a church mouse. 《very much.

똥끝타다 feel anxious (worried)

똥누다 evacuate (move) the bowels; ease nature; relieve oneself.

똥똥하다 (be) thick-set; pudgy; plump.

똥싸개 a pants-soiler; a baby.

똥싸다 ① 《혼나다》 have a hard time (of it); be put to it. ② 《a》 washer.

똬리 a head pad. ‖ ~쇠 a (met-

뙈기 《논밭의》 a patch; a plot (lot).

뙤약볕 the burning (scorching) sun; strong sunshine. ¶ ~을 쬐다 expose oneself to scorching sunshine; be under the full sun.

뚜 《소리》 with a toot (hoot, honk).

뚜껑 a lid (솥, 상자의); a cover (덮개); a cap (병, 만년필의); a shield (붓 따위의); a flap (호주머니의). ¶ ~을 덮다 put on the lid; cover up / ~을 열다 open; uncover; take off (lift) the lid (cover).

뚜뚜 《소리》 toot-toot; hoot-hoot.

뚜렷하다 (be) clear; plain; vivid; distinct; obvious; evident; manifest; 《현저》 (be) striking; remarkable; brilliant. ¶ 뚜렷이 clearly; distinctly; strikingly; remarkably.

뚜벅거리다 swagger (strut) (along).

뚜쟁이 a pander; a pimp.

뚝 ① 《갑자기》 suddenly. ¶ ~ 그치다 come to a dead stop; stop suddenly. ② 《떨어지는 소리》 with a thud (thump). ③ 《꺾는 소리》 with a snap.

뚝딱거리다 clatter; rattle. ② 《가슴이》 go pitapat; palpitate; throb.

뚝뚝 ① 《물방울 소리》 dripping; trickling; drop by drop. ② 《부러짐》 with snaps; snappingly.

뚝뚝하다 ① 《애교가 없다》 (be) un-

뛰어오르다 sociable; unaffable; blunt; brusque. ¶ 뚝뚝하게 bluntly; curtly; surlily. ② 《굳다》 (be) stiff; rigid.

뚝배기 an earthen(ware) bowl.

뚝별나다 (be) quick-tempered; peevish; touchy.

뚝심 staying power; endurance.

뚫다 《구멍을》 bore; punch; make (drill) 《a hole》; 《판통》 pierce; cut (pass, run) through; shoot through (관통하여). ¶ 뚫고 나아가다 《사람들·곤란을》 force (cut) one's way through; get through.

뚫리다 be opened; be bored through; be drilled; be pierced; be run through. ¶ 길이 ~ a road is made (open) / 구멍이 ~ a hole is made; 《비유적》 a way is found.

뚫어지다 ☞ 뚫리다.

뚱딴지 ① 《사람》 a log; a blockhead. ② 《같은》 wild; preposterous; absurd. ② 《전기의》 an insulator.

뚱기적거리다 keep drumming and twanging. ¶ 뚱기적거리고 놀다 make merry.

뚱뚱보 a fatty (plump) person.

뚱뚱하다 (be) fat; corpulent; plump. 《person. ¶☞ 뚱뚱보.

뚱보 《뚱한 사람》 a dull (taciturn)

뚱하다 (be) taciturn.

뛰놀다 jump (frisk, gambol) (about); romp (about); be frisky.

뛰다 ① 《도약》 leap; spring; jump; 《튀다》 bound; 《가슴이》 throb; palpitate; 《달리다》 run; 《시계가》 rise; jump (to). ¶ 뛰는 가슴으로 with beating heart / 좋아서 정중정중 ~ jump for (dance with) joy. ¶ ~ 《거르다》 skip (over); jump 《a chapter》. ③ 《그네·널을》 swing; seesaw. ¶ 널을 ~ play Korean seasaw. 《for》.

뛰어가다 go at a run (to); rush

뛰어나가다 run out; rush out; start forward (out).

뛰어나다 《남보다》 be superior (to); excel (in); surpass; stand (tower) high above 《the others》. ¶ 뛰어난 eminent; prominent; superior; distinguished.

뛰어내리다 jump (leap, spring) down (off). ¶ 달리는 차에서 ~ jump off a running car.

뛰어넘다 ① 《숫구체》 leap (jump, spring, vault) over. ¶ 담장을 ~ leap (jump over) a fence. ② ☞ 뛰다 ②.

뛰어다니다 《깡총깡충》 jump (romp) about; frisk; frolic; 《바쁘게》 run about; busy oneself (about).

뛰어들다 jump (leap, plunge) in(to); dive into (물 속으로).

뛰어오다 run; come running (up.

뛰어오르다 jump on; leap (spring)

뜀 《도약》 a jump; a leap; a spring; 《달림》 a run. ¶ ~박질 jumping《도약》; running《달리기》.

뜀뛰기 [競] jumping. ¶ ~선수 a jumper / ~운동 a jumping exercise / ~판 a springboard; a leaping board.

뜀틀 《체조》 a buck; a vaulting horse. ¶ ~을 뛰어넘다 vault over a buck.

뜨개질 knitting; knitwork. ¶ ~하다 do knitting; knit. ¶ ~바늘 a knitting pin(stick, needle); a crochet hook 《코바늘》.

뜨겁다 (be) hot; burning; passionate.

뜨끈뜨끈 (burning) hot. ~하다 (be) piping(burning) hot.

뜨끔거리다 ☞ 뜨끔하다.

뜨끔하다 (be) stinging; prickly; 《서술적》 prick; sting.

뜨내기 ① 《사람》 a tramp; a vagabond. ¶ ~손님 a chance(casual) customer / ~장사 a casual business. ② 《일》 an odd job; casual labor.

뜨다¹ ① 《느리다》 (be) slow; 《둔하다》 (be) dull; slow-witted. ¶ 걸음이 ~ be slow-paced / 눈치가 ~ be slow at sensing a situation. ② 《입이》 (be) taciturn; reticent. ¶ 입이 뜬 사람 a man of few words. ③ 《칼날이》 (be) dull; blunt. ④ 《비탈이》 (be) easy; gentle. ¶ 경사가 뜬 비탈 a gentle slope.

뜨다² ① 《물·하늘이》 float 《on the water, in the air》. ② 《해·달이》 rise; come up. ③ 《사이가》 be distant(apart) 《from》; get separated; be estranged 《관계가》. ¶ 사이를 뜨게 하다 leave a space; space out / 십리나 사이가 ~ be ten ri away. ④ 《빌려준 것 따위》 ☞ 떼이다.

뜨다³ ① 《썩다》 become stale; grow moldy(musty); undergo fermentation 《발효》. ② 《얼굴이》 become sallow. ¶ 누렇게 뜬 얼굴 a sallow face.「with moxa.

뜨다⁴ 《뜸을》 cauterize 《the skin》⌐

뜨다⁵ 《있던 곳을》 leave; go away 《from》; 《옮기다》 move; remove. ¶ 고향을 ~ leave one's hometown / 세상을 ~ depart (from) this life; pass away; die.

뜨다⁶ 《물 따위를》 scoop up; ladle 《국자로》; 《떠내다》 cut out 《out》; 《뗏장을》 shovel off 《고기를》; slice; cut into slices; 《각뜨다》 cut up; 《종이를》 make; shape; 《옷감을》 cut up 《buy》 a piece of cloth.

뜨다⁷ 《눈을》 open 《one's eyes》; wake up; awake.

뜨다⁸ 《실로》 knit; crochet 《코바늘로》; darn, stitch 《깁다》; 《그물을》 net; weave.

뜨다⁹ 《본을》 copy (out); imitate; follow suit 《남을》.

뜨뜻하다 (be) warm; hot. 「been washed.

뜨물 water in which rice has⌐

뜨음하다 ☞ 뜸하다.

뜨이다 ① 《눈이》 (come) open; be opened; awake; 《비유적》 come to one's senses; have one's eyes opened. ¶ 현실에 눈이 ~ awake to the realities of life. ② 《발견》 be seen; catch one's eye; attract the attention; come to one's notice; be striking. ¶ 흡연자의 수가 눈에 뜨이게 줄었다 The number of smokers has decreased noticeably.

뜬구름 ¶ ~ 같은 인생 transient life / 인생이란 ~이다 Life is an empty dream.

뜬눈 ¶ ~으로 밤을 새우다 sit up all night; pass a sleepless night.

뜬소문(一所聞) a wild(groundless) rumor.

뜬숯 used charcoal; cinders.

뜯기다 ① 《빼앗기다》 be extorted (squeezed, exploited) 《by》. ¶ 돈을 ~ have one's money taken (squeezed, extorted); be fleeced of money. ② 《물리다》 get bitten. ¶ 벼룩에게 뜯긴 자리 a fleabite. ③ 《마소에 풀을 먹임》 graze 《cattle》.

뜯다 ① 《분리·분해》 take down 《off》; tear 《tear apart》; break up; 《풀·털 따위를》 pluck; pull; tear (off); pick. ② 《악기를》 play 《on》. ③ 《얻다》 ask 《a person》 for 《money》; extort; squeeze.

뜯어내다 ① 《붙은 것을》 take down 《off》; remove; pick (pluck) off. ② 《분해》 take 《a thing》 to pieces; take 《a machine》 apart; dismantle. ③ 《금품을》 extort; fleece.

뜯어말리다 《싸움 등을》 pull (draw) apart.

뜯어먹다 ① 《붙은 것을》 take 《a thing》 off and eat; eat at(on); gnaw(bite) off. ② 《졸라대서》 squeeze; exploit 《a person》; sponge 《off a person》.

뜯어벌이다 ① 《벌여 놓다》 take 《a machine》 apart; pull (take) to pieces. ② 《이야기를》 give a long talk.

뜯어보다 ① 《살펴보다》 examine carefully; study closely; scrutinize. ¶ 아무의 얼굴을 자세히 ~ scrutinize a person's face carefully. ② 《봉한 것을》 open 《a letter》 and read it.

뜰 《정원》 a garden; 《울안》 a yard;

뜸 [韓醫] moxa; moxibustion. ¶ ~ 뜨다 cauterize 《the skin》 with moxa; apply moxa 《to》.

뜸부기 [鳥] a moorhen; a water cock.

뜸직하다 (be) dignified; reserved.

뜸질 〖뜸뜨기〗 moxa cautery.

뜸하다 (be) infrequent; have a rather long interval. ¶ 뜸해지다 come to (a state of) lull; hold (let) up.

뜻 ① 〖의지〗 (a) will; mind; 〖의향〗 (an) intention; a motive; 〖목적〗 an object; an aim; (a) purpose; 〖지망〗 an aspiration; (an) ambition; 〖희망〗 desire(s); wish(es). ¶ 큰 ~ a high ambition (aspiration) / ~대로 as *one* expects (wishes) / ~을 두다 intend; aim at; aspire to; have an ambition to / ~을 이루다 attain *one's* aim; realize *one's* aspirations. ② 〖의미〗 (a) meaning; a sense; 〖취지〗 effect; the intent; the import. ¶ ~이 통하지 않는 말 senseless talk / ~있는 눈짓 a significant (meaningful) glance.

뜻맞다 〖의기상통〗 be of a mind; be like-minded; 〖마음에 들다〗 be after *one's* fancy; suit *one's* fancy (taste).

뜻밖 ¶ ~의 unexpected; unlooked-for; surprising / ~에 unexpectedly / ~하게 되다 happen (chance) to 《*do*》.

뜻하다 〖의도〗 intend to *do*; aim at 《*doing something*》; have 《*it*》 in mind; 〖의미〗 mean; signify; imply. ¶ 뜻하지 않은 unexpected.

띄다 〖눈에〗 catch the eye; attract *one's* attention.

띄어쓰다 write leaving a space between words.

띄엄띄엄 〖단속적〗 intermittently; 〖드문문〗 sparsely; here and there; sporadically; 〖새를 두고〗 at intervals.

띄우다 ① 〖물위에〗 float; set 《*a ship*》 afloat; sail 《*a toy boat*》; 〖공중에〗 (let) fly; float in the air. ② 〖얼굴에〗 show; express; wear. ¶ 웃음을 ~ (wear a) smile / 입가에 미소를 띄우고 with a smile about *one's* lips. ③ 〖훈김으로〗 ferment; mold. ¶ 누룩 〖메주〗을 ~ ferment malt [steamed soybean lumps]. ④ 〖사이를〗 leave a space 《*between*》; space 《*the lines*》. ⑤ 〖편지 따위를〗 send; dispatch.

띠 a belt; a (waist) band; a sash 〖여자의〗. ¶ 가죽~ a leather belt / ~를 매다 tie a belt (sash) / ~를 끄르다 undo a belt.

띠다 ① 〖두르다〗 put on; do up; wear. ¶ 띠를 ~ do up a belt; wear a belt (girdle). ② 〖지니다〗 wear; carry; be armed with. ③ 〖용무 따위를〗 be charged (entrusted) 《*with*》. ¶ 중요한 사명을 ~ be charged with some important mission. ④ 〖빛·기색 따위를〗 have; wear; be tinged with. ¶ 붉은 빛을 띤 tinged with red / 걱정하는 빛을 ~ look worried; have a worried look.

띠지(-紙) a strip of paper; a money band 〖돈다발 묶는〗.

띵하다 〖머리가〗 (be) dull; have a dull pain. ¶ 머리가 ~ have a dull headache.

동물의 울음소리

1. 의성어(擬聲語)에 의한 표현:
   개 — bowwow / 고양이 — mew; meow / 돼지 — wee-wee-wee / 당나귀 — hee-haw / 소 — moo / 암탉 — cock-a-doodle-doo / 피꼬리 — jug-jug-jug-pee-yew / 백설조(또는 지빠귀) — Did he do it? He did, he did, he did / 오리 — quack, quack.

2. 동사에 의한 표현: 동물의 울음소리 위에 열거한 의성어를 사용하지 않고 해당 동물의 우는 모양이나 울음소리 등을 본따서 만들어진 동사를 사용하여 나타내는 방식이 있다. 이 중에는 위에 열거한 mew, moo, quack 따위 의성어가 그대로 동사로 전용되는 경우도 있다.

개 (dog) — bark (멍멍); growl (으르렁); whine (낑낑); yap; yelp (깽깽, 왕왕); howl (멀리서 짖는); snarl (이를 드러내고 달려들며 내는 소리)
소 (bull, cow, ox) — moo; low (음매); bellow (수소의 큰 울음소리)
말 (horse) — neigh; whinny (히힝); snort (코를 벌룽거리며)
고양이 (cat) — mew; meow (야옹); purr (가르릉)
쥐 (mouse) — squeak (찍찍)
호랑이 (tiger) — growl (으르렁); roar (어흥)
양 (sheep) — baa; bleat (메헤)
돼지 (pig) — grunt (꿀꿀); squeal (꾁꾁)
작은새 (bird) — sing; chirp; twitter (지저귀는 소리)
오리 (duck) — quack
수탉 (rooster) — crow (꼬끼요)
암탉 (hen) — crackle; cluck
병아리 (chick) — peep; cheep
비둘기 (dove) — coo
개구리 (frog) — croak (개굴개굴)
여치 (grasshopper) — chirp
귀뚜라미 (cricket) — chirp
뱀 (snake) — hiss
벌 (bee) — hum; buzz

ㄹ

…ㄹ 것같다 ① 《추측》 look (like); seem; appear (to be). ¶비가 올 것 같다 It looks like rain, or It is likely to rain. ② 《막…할 것 같다》 threaten [be ready] (to do). ¶곧 울음을 터뜨릴 것 같다 be ready to cry; be almost in tears.

…ㄹ망정 though; even if (though); however; but. ¶비록 그는 늙었을 망정 though he is old; old as he is / 몸은 약할망정 의지는 굳다 He may be weakly but has a strong will. / 빌어먹을망정 신세는 안 지겠다 Even if I were brought to begging, I would never ask a favor of him.

…ㄹ바에 if… at all; if (only) one is to do. ¶이왕 할 바에(는) if you do it at all / 이왕 싸울 바에는 끝까지 싸우리라 If you do fight, fight it out.

…ㄹ뿐더러 not only [merely]… but (also); as well as. ¶걷는 것은 경제적일뿐더러 몸에도 좋다 Walking is not merely economical but also good for the health.

…ㄹ수록 《비교》 the more…, the more [the less…, the less] (덜). ¶자식은 어릴수록 귀엽다 The younger the child, the dearer it is to you.

…ㄹ지 whether (…or not); if. ¶올지 안 올지 whether one will come or not.

…ㄹ지도 모르다 may [might] (be, do); maybe; perhaps; possible. ¶그는 가버렸을지도 모른다 He may have gone away. / 그럴지도 모른다 It may be so.

…ㄹ지라도 but; (al)though; however; even (if); no matter (how, who, what). ¶아무리 가난할지라도 however poor one may be / 결과가 어찌 될지라도 whatever the consequence may be.

…ㄹ지어다 should; ought to (do). ¶도둑질하지 말지어다 Thou shalt not steal.

…ㄹ지언정 even if (though); rather (sooner) (than). ¶죽을지언정 항복은 않겠다 I would rather die than surrender.

…ㄹ진대 if; in case (of); provided that (조건). ¶그럴진대 if (it be) so; in that case.

라 《계명》 la; 《음명》 re; D.

…라고 to. ¶들어오~ 해라 Tell him to come in. 「온이 낮아지는 현상」.

라니냐(현상) 《氣》 La Niña 《해면수

…라도 even; any; either …or. ¶어린애 ~ even a child / 어느 것이 ~ either one / 어디 ~ anywhere / 이제 ~ even now.

라돈 《化》 radon (기호 Rn).

라듐 《化》 radium (기호 Ra). ‖ ~광천 《요업》 a radium spring [treatment] / ~방사능 radioactivity.

라드 lard. ‖ ~유 lard oil.

라디에이터 a radiator.

라디오 (a) radio; (a) wireless 《英》. ¶ ~를 듣다 [틀다] turn [switch] on [off] the radio / ~를 듣다 listen (in) to the radio / ~를 listen to 《a musical performance》 [over] the radio / ~를 KBS에 맞추다 tune in to KBS. ‖ ~강좌 a radio 《English》course / ~드라마 a radio drama [play] / ~방송 radio broadcasting / ~방송국 a radio (broadcasting) station / ~좌담회 a radio forum / ~중계 hookup; relay / ~청취자 a radio listener / ~체조 radio exercises [gymnastics] / ~프로 a radio program / ~해설자 a radio commentator.

라르고 《樂》 largo.

라마 (라마승) a lama. ‖ ~교도 a Lamaist; a Lamaite / ~사원 a lamasery.

라면 《국수》 *ramyon*; instant (Chinese) noodles.

라벨 a label. ¶ ~을 붙이다 label 《a bottle》; put a label on 《a bottle》.

라스베이거스 《미국의 도시》 Las Vegas.

라야(만) only; alone. ¶너 ~ you alone [only you] 《can do it》.

라오스 Laos. ¶ ~의 Laotian / ~사람 a Laotian.

라운드 《拳》 a round. ¶10 ~의 권투 시합 a boxing-match of ten rounds.

라운지 《호텔 등의》 a lounge.

라이너 ① 《野》 《타구의》 a liner; a line drive. ② 《안감》 a liner.

라이노타이프 《印》 a linotype.

라이닝 《機》 lining.

라이덴(병)《(瓶)》《理》 a Leyden jar.

라이벌 a rival. ¶ ~의 rival. ‖ ~의식 the spirit of rivalry / ~회사 a rival company [firm].

라이선스 a license 《美》; a licence 《英》. ¶A급 ~ a class A license. ‖ ~생산 production under license; licensed production.

라이스카레 curry and rice; curried rice.

라이온 《動》 a lion; a lioness (암

라이온스클럽 243 **레지**

컷. ¶ ~의 새끼 a lion cub.
라이온스클럽 the Lions Club.
라이터 a lighter. ¶ ~기름 lighter oil (fluid) / ~돌 a lighter flint.
라이트 (car) light. ¶ ~를 켜다 (끄다) switch on (off) a light.
라이트급〖拳〗 the light weight class. ¶ ~선수 a light-weight (boxer).
라이트윙〖蹴〗 the right wing.
라이트필더〖野〗 a right fielder.
라이트필드〖野〗 the right field.
라이프〖生命·人生〗 life. ¶ ~보트 a lifeboat / ~사이언스 life science / ~재킷 a life jacket. ¶ ~사이클 a life cycle / ~스타일 a life-style.
라이플(총)〖銃〗 a rifle.
라인 a line. ¶ ~을 긋다 draw a line.
라인강〖江〗 the Rhine.
라인업〖野구·축구 등의〗 the (starting) line-up 《of a team》.
라일락〖植〗 a lilac.
라임라이트 (the) limelight.
라조(一調)〖樂〗 D. ¶ **라장**(단)조 D major (minor).
라켓 a racket; 〖탁구의〗 a paddle;
라틴 Latin. ¶ ~민족 the Latin races / ~어 Latin.
라틴아메리카 Latin America. ¶ ~음악 Latin American music.
…락말락 on the brink of; (be)
란제리 lingerie. 「about to.
랑데부 a rendezvous; a date. ¶ ~하다 have a rendezvous (date) 《with》. ¶ 궤도상에서 ~하다 rendezvous in orbit 《with》; have an orbital rendezvous 《with》.
래커 lacquer.
랜턴 a lantern.
램〖컴〗〖임의접근 기억장치〗 RAM. (◀ Random Access Memory)
램프 a lamp.
램프〖입체 교차로의 진입로〗 a ramp.
랩소디〖樂〗 a rhapsody.
랩타임(the 500 *meter*) lap time.
랩톱〖컴〗 ~형의 lap-top. ¶ ~형 컴퓨터 a lap-top computer.
랭크 a rank. ¶ 이 노래는 인기 차트 제1위에 ~되었다 This song is ranked No.1 in the hit chart.
랭킹 ranking. ¶ ~1위를 차지하다 take the first ranking.
러너〖野〗 a runner. ¶ ~를 일소하다 empty (clear) the bases (of runners).
러닝〖경주〗 a running (race). ¶ 공원에서 한 시간씩 ~하다 do an hour's running in the park. ¶ ~메이트 a running mate / ~셔츠 a (sleeveless) undershirt.
러버〖고무〗 rubber; 〖애인〗 a lover.
러브〖연애〗 love. ¶ ~레터 a love letter / ~신 a love scene / ~호텔 a love hotel.

러시아 Russia. ¶ ~의 Russian / ~말 Russian / ~사람 a Russian / ~황제 a czar; a tzar.
러시아워 the rush hour(s).
러키 lucky. ¶ ~세븐〖野〗 the lucky seventh inning.
럭비 Rugby (football); a rugger.
럭스〖조명도의 단위〗 a lux.
런던 London. ¶ ~사람 a Londoner; a Cockney / ~탑 the Tower of London / ~식 사투리 〔억양〕 a Cockney accent.
런치〖점심식사〗 lunch. ¶ ~타임 lunchtime.
럼(주)(―酒) rum.
레귤러〖정식의〗 regular;《정식 선수》 a regular player. ¶ ~멤버 a regular member.
레그혼〖鷄〗 a leghorn.
레디메이드 ¶ ~의 ready-to-wear; ready-made.
레모네이드 lemonade.
레몬 a lemon. ¶ ~수 lemonade / ~즙〔주스〕 lemon juice.
레벨 a level. ¶ ~이 높다〔낮다〕 be on a high (low) level.
레스토랑 a restaurant. ¶ ~경영자 a restaurateur.
레슨 a lesson. ¶ 피아노 ~ (have, take) a piano lesson. 「tler.
레슬링 wrestling. ¶ ~선수 a wres-
레이〖하와이의 화환〗 a lei. ¶ ~를 목에 걸다 put a lei around one's neck.
레이더 a radar (◀ radio detecting and ranging). ¶ ~기지 a radar base (station) / ~망 a radar fence (screen, network) / ~유도 미사일 a radar-guided missile / ~장치 a radar system (device).
레이디 a lady. ¶ ~퍼스트 Ladies first. ¶ 퍼스트 ~ the First lady (대통령 부인).
레이스〖경주〗 a race.
레이스〖끈장식〗 lace. ¶ ~를 달다 trim with lace.
레이온 rayon; artificial silk.
레이저 (a) laser. ¶ ~광선 laser beams (rays) / ~디스크 a laser disk / ~메스 a laser surgical knife / ~병기 a laser(-beam) weapon / ~수술 (conduct) laser surgery / ~폭탄〔銃〕 a laser bomb (gun).
레인지 a range; an oven. ¶ 가스 ~ a gas range (stove) / 전자~ a microwave oven.
레인코트 a raincoat.
레일 a rail; a track 〖선로〗〖美〗. ¶ ~을 깔다 lay rails.
레저 leisure. ¶ ~붐 a leisure boom / ~산업 the leisure industry / ~시설 leisure facilities / ~용 차량 Recreational Vehicle (생략 RV) / ~웨어 a leisure wear.
레즈비언 a lesbian.   「waitress.
레지〖다방의〗 a tearoom (cafe

레지스탕스 resistance (activity). ‖ ~운동 a resistance movement.
레지스터 (금전 등록기) a (cash) register.
레커차(—車) (구난차) a wrecker; a tow truck. ‖ ~에 끌려가다 be towed by a wrecker.
레코드 ① (기록) a record. ‖ ~보지자 a record holder. ② (축음기의) a phonograph record; a disk. ‖ ~를 틀다 play a record. / 콘서트 ~ a record (disc) concert / 플레이어 a record player.
레크리에이션 recreation. ‖ 낚시는 좋은 ~이다 Fishing is a good recreation. / ~센터 a recreation center.
레테르 ☞ 라벨.
레퍼리 (심판) a referee.
레퍼토리 (상연목록) repertory; repertoire. ‖ 그 곡은 ~에 없다 The music isn't in *our* repertory.
렌즈 a lens. ‖ ~를 맞추다 train the lens (on).
렌치 (공구) a wrench.
렌터카 a rental car; a rent-a-car (美). ‖ ~를 빌리다 rent a car. / ~회사 (업자) a car-rental company (agent).
…려고 (in order) to. ‖ ~식사하러 리에 앉다 sit down to dinner / 늦지 않으~ 일찍 출발하다 leave early in order not to be late.
…로 ① (원인) with; from; due to; through; for. ‖ 감기~ 누워 있다 be in bed with a cold / 부주의~ through (one's) carelessness. ② (단위) by. ‖ 다스~ 팔다 sell by the dozen / 26을 둘~ 나누다 divide 26 by 2. ③ (원료) from; of. ‖ 벽돌~ 지은 집 a house (built) of brick / 맥주는 보리~ 만든다 Beer is made from barley. ④ (수단) by; with; on; in; through; by means of. ‖ 기차~ by train / 도보~ on foot / 영어~ in English. ⑤ (추정·근거) by; from. ‖ 목소리~ 알다 recognize by voice. ⑥ (방향) to; in; at; for; toward. ‖ 여수~ 향하다 leave for Yeosu / 프랑스~ 가다 go to France. ⑦ (지위·신분) as; for. ‖ 대표~ as a representative / 맏이 (첫째) ~ 태어나다 be born eldest (a genius).
로고스 (哲) logos.
로그 (數) a log(arithm).
로드맵 (운전자용 지도) a road map.
로드쇼 (映) a road show (美).
로드워크 (운동선수의) a roadwork.
로마 Rome. ‖ ~는 하루 아침에 이루어진 것이 아니다 Rome was not built in a day. / ~가톨릭교 Roman Catholicism / ~가톨릭교회 the Roman Catholic Church / ~교황청 the Vatican / ~자 (숫자) Roman letters (numerals).
로마네스크 Romanesque (*style*).
로맨스 a romance; a love affair. ‖ ~그레이 a gentleman with gray hair.
로맨티시즘 romanticism.
로맨틱 romantic. ~하다 (be) romantic. ‖ ~한 생각에 잠기다 indulge in romantic dreaming (thoughts).
로봇 a robot; (허수아비 같은 사람) a figurehead. ‖ 산업용 ~ an industrial robot / ~조종의 비행기 a robot-controlled (*airplane*).
로비 a lobby; a lounge. ‖ ~활동 a lobbying activity.
…로서 (지위·신분·자격) as; for; in the capacity of. ‖ 학자~ as a scholar / 나~는 as for me.
로션 (a) lotion. ‖ 스킨~ skin lotion / 헤어~ hair lotion.
로스트 (불고기) roast beef (pork).
로열 ‖ ~박스 a royal box / ~젤리 royal jelly.
로열티 a royalty. ‖ 소설의 ~로 2천 달러를 받다 receive two thousand dollars in royalties from (on) one's novel.
로이터 Reuters. ‖ ~통신사 the Reuters News Agency.
로커빌리 (樂) rock-a-billy.
로컬 local. ‖ ~뉴스 local news.
로케 (이션) location. ‖ ~중이다 be on location (*in*) / 제주도로 ~가다 go over to Cheju island on location.
로켓 a rocket. ‖ ~을 발사하다 launch a rocket / ~으로 인공위성을 궤도에 올리다 rocket a satellite into orbit / ~으로 비행하다 fly by rocket (*to*). / ~발사대 a rocket launching pad / ~발사장치 a rocket launcher / ~엔진 a rocket engine / ~추진 rocket propulsion / ~포 (탄, 비행기) a rocket gun (bomb, plane) / 3 (다) 단식 ~ a three-stage (multistage) rocket. (ture).
로코코식 (—式) rococo (*architec*-
로큰롤 (樂) rock-'n'-roll (music); rock-and-roll. ‖ ~춤에 푹 빠져 있는 청년들 youngsters rock-'n'-rolling frantically.
로터리 a rotary. ‖ ~클럽 the Rotary Club.
로테이션 rotation. ‖ ~으로 (do something) in (by) rotation.
로프 a rope; a cable. ‖ ~웨이 a ropeway; an aerial cableway.
로힐 low-heeled shoes. (rea)
록 ROK. (◀the Republic of Ko-
론 (經) (대부금) a loan. ‖ 뱅크 ~ a bank loan.
…론 (論) a theory (이론); an opinion (의견); an essay (*on*) (논설). ‖ 문학~ an essay on literature / 한자 제한~ the question of limiting the use of Chinese

롤러 a roller. ¶ ~스케이트 roller skates.
롤링 (배의) rolling; a roll. ~하다 roll. (only memory)
롬 [컴] (늘기억 장치) ROM. (◀ read-)
롱런 a long run (of a film).
뢴트겐 [理] X-rays; Roentgen rays. ¶ ~검사 an X-ray examination / ~사진 a radiograph; an X-ray photograph (~ 사진을 찍다 take an X-ray photograph (of)). (Museum).
루브르 (파리의 박물관) the Louvre
루블 (러시아 화폐) a r(o)uble.
루비 a ruby (ring).
루주 rouge; lipstick(입술 연지). ¶ ~를 바르다 rouge.
루트 (경로) a route; a channel.
루피 (인도 화폐) a rupee.
룩색 a rucksack.
룰 (규칙) a rule. ¶ ~에 어긋나다 be against the rules. (wheel).
룰렛 (도박) roulette; a roulette
룸바 [樂] (춤·곡) rumba.
룸펜 (부랑자) a loafer; a tramp; a hobo (美); (실직자) a jobless man. ¶ ~생활 hoboism (美).
류머티즘 [醫] rheumatism.
르네상스 the Renaissance.
르완다 Rwanda. ¶ ~의 Rwandese; Rwandan / ~ 공화국 the Rwandese Republic / ~ 사람 a Rwandan. (port (on)).
르포 (르타주) reportage (프); a re-
리골레토 [樂] rigoletto (이).
리그 a (baseball) league. ¶ ~전 a league game.
리넨 linen.
리더 (지도자) a leader.
리드 (앞섬) a lead. ~하다 (경기에서) lead; have a lead; (지도하다) lead. ¶ 3점 ~하고 있다 have a lead (the opposing team) by three points [runs] / ~ 근소하게 ~하고 있다 have [hold] a slight [narrow] lead (over) / ~를 빼앗기다 lose the lead (to) / 댄스에서 상대를 ~하다 lead one's partner in a dance / 우리 팀은 4대 2로 ~하고 있다 Our team leads by 4 to 2 lead. or Our team leads by 4 to 2.
리듬 rhythm. ¶ ~에 맞추어 to the rhythm. (lire).
리라 (이탈리아의 화폐) a lira [pl.
리모트컨트롤 (원격조작) remote control. ~로 조종하다 operate (a machine) by remote control. ¶ ~ 장치 a remote-control device.
리무진 (자동차) a limousine.
리바운드 (농구) a rebound.
리바이벌 revival (boom).
리버럴 ¶ ~한 liberal. / ~리스트 a liberalist / ~리즘 liberalism.
리베이트 (환불금) a rebate; (수수료) a commission; (수뢰) (수뢰) give (a person) a commission [kickback].

리벳 a rivet. ¶ ~을 박다 rivet; fasten (something) with rivets.
리보핵산 (一核酸) ribonucleic acid (생략 RNA).
리본 a ribbon; a band(모자의).
리볼버 (연발 권총) a revolver.
리사이클 (재활용) recycling. ~하다 recycle (aluminum cans); reuse.
리사이틀 [樂] a recital. ¶ ~을 열다 give [have] a (piano) recital.
리셉션 a reception. ¶ ~을 열다 hold [give] a reception.
리스트 ¶ ~를 작성하다 make [draw] a list (of) / ~에 올리다 put (a person) on the list.
리시버 a receiver.
리어카 a cart; a handcart.
리얼 ¶ ~한 real; realistic / ~하게 realistically / ~한 초상화 a realistic portrait. ¶ ~리즘 realism / ~타임 [컴] real time ~ 타임처리 real-time processing.
리조트 (행락지) a resort. ¶ 여름 ~ a summer resort / ~호텔 a resort hotel / ~웨어 resort wear; a holiday outfit.
리치 (권투의) reach. ¶ ~가 길다 have a long reach.
리콜 (상품·해임·결함상품의 회수) (a) recall. ~하다 recall. ¶ 시민은 시장을 ~했다 The citizen recalled the mayor. / 500대의 차가 안전성에 결함이 있어 ~되었다 Five hundred cars were recalled for safety reasons. ¶ ~제 the recall system.
리터 a liter.
리턴매치 a return match (game).
리트머스 ¶ ~ 시험지 litmus paper.
리포트 (보고) a report; (학교의) (term) paper. ¶ ~를 쓰다 write a paper on (a subject).
리프트 a lift; a ski (chair) lift.
리허설 (하다) a rehearsal.
린치 lynch (law); lynching. ¶ ~를 inflict illegal punishment using violence (on) / ~를 가해 아무를 죽이다 lynch a person.
릴 (낚싯대의) a (fishing) reel; (필름의) a spool. ¶ ~낚싯대 a (fishing) rod and reel.
릴레이 a (400-meter) relay (race). ~하다 relay (a message); pass (a bucket) from one person to another. ¶ ~방송 a relay broadcast.
립스틱 a lipstick. (cast).
링 ① [拳] the ring. ¶ ~사이드 (sit at) the ringside. ② (반지) a ring.
링거 [醫] ¶ ~주사 (give) an injection of Ringer's solution.
링크¹ [經] link. ¶ ~제 a link system (~제로 하다 place (something) in a link system).
링크² (스케이트장) a rink.
링크스 (골프장) a links.

마 [植] a yam.

마(魔) a demon; a devil; an evil spirit. ¶ ~의 건널목 a fatal (railroad) crossing / ~가 끼다 be possessed [tempted] by an evil spirit; be jinxed 《俗》.

마(碼) a yard (생략 yd.). ¶ ~로 팔다 sell by the yard.

…마(魔) devilish; diabolic; fiendish. ¶ 살인~ a devilish murderer.

마가린 margarine; marge 《英口》. ¶ 빵에 ~을 바르다 spread margarine on bread.

마가목 [植] a mountain ash.

마가복음(─福音) [聖] the (Gospel of) Mark.

마각(馬脚) ¶ ~을 드러내다 show the cloven hoof; show *one*'s true colors.

마감 closing. ~하다 close. ¶ ~날 the closing day; the deadline / ~시간 the closing hour.

마개 a stopper(병 따위의); a bung(통 따위의); a cork(코르크의); a (stop)cock(수도 따위의); a plug. ¶ ~를 뽑다 uncork; unstop / ~를 하다 cork; put a stopper 《on》. ¶ ~뽑이 a bottle opener; a corkscrew(코르크의).

마고자 a traditional Korean jacket worn by men over their vest.

마구(馬具) harness; horse (riding) gear. ¶ ~를 채우다 [풀다] harness [unharness] 《a horse》.

마구 carelessly; recklessly; at random; immoderately. ¶ ~ 지껄이다 talk at random / 비가 ~ 쏟아진다 It rains cats and dogs. / 돈을 ~ 쓰다 squander [lavish] money.

마구간(馬廏間) a stable; a barn. ¶ ~에 넣다 stable 《a horse》.

마구잡이 a blind [reckless] act; 《남획》 indiscriminate fishing [hunting].

마굴(魔窟) ① 《마귀의》 a lair of devils. ② 《악한의》 a den of rascals. 《창녀의》 a brothel.

마권(馬券) a betting ticket 《on a horse》. ¶ ~을 사다 buy a betting ticket / ~ 매표구 a betting booth [window]; a ticket window.

마귀(魔鬼) a devil; a demon; an evil spirit. ¶ ~ 할멈 a witch; a hag; a harridan.

마그나카르타 the Magna Carta; the Great Charter.

마그네사이트 [鑛] magnesite.

마그네슘 [化] magnesium (기호 Mg); 《사진의》 flash powder.

마그네시아 [化] magnesia. ‖ 황산 ~ sulfate of magnesia.

마나님 an elderly lady; an old woman; 《호칭》 madam; your (good) lady.

마냥 ① 《실컷》 to the full; as much as *one* wishes. ¶ ~ 즐기다 enjoy *one*'s heart's contents. ② 《오직》 solely; only; but; intently; single-mindedly; 《끝없이》 endlessly; ceaselessly. ¶ 그녀는 ~ 울기만 했다 She did nothing but cry. / 물가는 ~ 올라가기만 한다 Prices go [keep] on rising. / ~ 남편만을 그리워하다 miss *one*'s husband single-mindedly.

마네킹 a mannequin; a manikin. ¶ ~걸 a manikin girl.

마녀(魔女) a witch; a sorceress. ‖ ~사냥 witch-hunting / ~재판 a witch trial.

마노(瑪瑙) [鑛] agate.

마누라 《아내》 a wife; 《노파》 an old woman.

마늘 [植] a garlic. ¶ ~ 냄새가 나는 garlicky; smelling of garlic.

마니교(魔尼敎) Manich(a)eism.

마닐라 Manila. ‖ ~삼[紙] Manila hemp [paper].

마님 (부인) a lady; 《호칭》 my lady; madam.

마다 every; each; at intervals of; whenever 《…할 때마다》. ¶ 5분 ~ every five minutes; at intervals of five minutes / 해 ~ every year.

마담 a madam; *madame* (프); 《술집 등의》 a hostess; a bar madam.

마당 (뜰) a garden; a yard; a court(안뜰). ¶ 뒷~ a backyard. ‖ ~발 a flatfoot; a splayfoot / ~질 threshing; flailing.

마대(麻袋) a gunny bag [sack]; a jute bag.

마도로스 a sailor. ‖ ~파이프 a pipe.

마돈나 (성모) the Madonna.

마드무아젤 *mademoiselle* 《프》.

마들가리 《나무의》 twigs; sticks; dead branches; 《해진 옷의》 seams of a worn-out garment.

마디 ① (뼈의) a joint; a knuckle (손가락, 무릎의); 《생긴 마디》 a knot; a knob(혹). ② 《말·노래의》 a word; a phrase; a tune.

마디다 (be) durable; enduring; long-lasting.

마땅하다 ① 《적합》 (be) becoming;

마라톤 a marathon (race). ‖ ~ 선수 a marathoner.
마량(馬糧) fodder; forage.
마력(馬力) horsepower(생략 h.p.). ¶ 50 ~의 발동기 a 50-horsepower motor; a motor of 50 h.p. / 10 ~을 내다 produce〔deliver〕10 horsepower〔h.p.〕.
마력(魔力) magical〔magic〕power; magic. ¶ 숫자의 ~ the magic of numbers.
마련(磨鍊) ~ 하다 manage《to do》; arrange; prepare; make shift《to do》; raise《money》. ¶ 돈을 ~ 하다 manage to raise money.
마렵다《오줌〔똥〕이》feel an urge to urinate〔defecate〕; want to relieve oneself.
마로니에〔植〕a marronnier《프》; a horse chestnut (tree).
마루 ① 《집의》 a floor. ¶ ~ 방 a floored room / ~ 를 놓은 floor《a house》; lay a floor. ‖ ~면적 floorage; floor space / ~ 운동 floor exercises / ~ 청 a floorboard; flooring《~ 청을 깔다 board the floor》. ② 《산·지붕의》 a ridge.
마루터기, **마루턱** the ridge.
마르다 ① 《건조》 (be) dry (up); get dry; run dry 《물이》; wither 《시들다》. ¶ 마른 가지 a dead〔withered〕branch / 우물이 ~ well dries up. ② 《여위다》 become〔grow〕 thin〔lean〕; lose flesh. ¶ 마른 사람 a thin〔lean, skinny〕person. ③ 《목이》 be〔feel〕 thirsty.
마르다《재단》cut out 《a garment》; cut《a suit, etc.》. ¶ 마르는 법 a cut; cutting.
마르크《독일 화폐》 a mark.
마르크스《Karl》Marx. ‖ ~ 주의 Marxism / ~ 주의자 a Marxist.
마른걸레 a dry cloth〔mop〕.
마른기침 a dry〔hacking〕cough.
마른반찬 dried meat〔fish〕 eaten with rice.
마른버짐〔醫〕psoriasis.
마른안주 a relish of dried meat and fish taken with wine.
마른하늘 a clear (blue) sky. ¶ ~ 에 날벼락 "a bolt from the blue." 〔美〕.
마른행주 a dishtowel; a dishcloth
마름모꼴 a lozenge; a diamond shape; 〔數〕a rhombus.
마름쇠 a caltrap; a caltrop.
마름질 cutting (out). ~ 하다 cut out 《lumber, clothes》.
마리 a head. ¶ 강아지 다섯 ~ five puppies / 소 두 ~ two head of cattle / 물고기 세 ~ three fish.
마리아(聖母) the Virgin Mary.
마리화나 marihuana; marijuana. ¶ ~ 를 피우다 smoke marijuana.
마마(媽媽) ① 《존칭》 Your〔His, Her〕Highness〔Majesty〕. ② 《천연두》 smallpox. ‖ 마맛자국 a pockmark; a pit.
마멸(磨滅) wear (and tear); abrasion. ~ 하다 wear out〔away〕; be worn out〔away〕.
마무르다 ① 《일을》 finish 《something》 up〔off〕; complete; get through with 《one's work》. ② 《가장자리를》 hem; fringe; border.
마무리 finishing; finishing touches〔strokes〕. ~ 하다 give the finishing〔last〕touches 《to》; touch up. ¶ 이 보석상자는 ~ 가 잘 되어 있다 This jewel case has a good finish. ‖ ~공 a finisher / ~기계 a finishing machine.
마바리《말》a pack-horse;《짐》 a horse load. ‖ ~꾼 a pack-horse man〔driver〕.
마법(魔法) ☞ 마술(魔術).
마부(馬夫) a (pack-horse) driver; a horseman; a coachman.
마분(馬糞) horse dung; stable manure. ‖ ~ 지 millboard; strawboard.
마비(痲痺) paralysis; palsy; numbness. ~ 성의 paralytic / ~ 되다 be paralyzed; be 〔become〕 numbed / ~ 시키다 paralyze / 한쪽 팔이 ~ 되다 be paralyzed on one arm / 추위로 발의 감각이 ~ 되었다 My feet are numbed with〔by〕cold. / 교통이 ~ 되어 있다 Traffic is at a complete standstill. / 그는 정의감이 완전히 ~ 되어 있다 He has no sense of justice at all. ‖ ~ 증상 paralytic symptoms / 뇌성 ~ cerebral paralysis.
마사지 massage. ~ 하다 massage 《a person on the arm》. ‖ ~사 a massagist / ~요법 massotherapy.
마사회(馬事會) ¶ 한국 ~ the Korea Racing Authority.
마상이 a canoe; a skiff.
마성(魔性) devilishness.
마손(磨損) friction loss; wear and tear; abrasion《기계 따위의》. ¶ ~ 되다 wear (away).
마수(魔手) an evil hand; evil power. ¶ ~ 를 뻗치다 attempt to victimize《a person》/ ~ 에 걸리다 fall a victim 《to》.
마수걸다 sell for the first time.
마수걸이 the first sale of the day; the first transaction at the beginning of a business. ~ 하다 make the first sale of the day.

마술(馬術) horsemanship. ¶ ~경기 an equestrian event.

마술(魔術) magic; black art. ¶ ~을 쓰다 use (practice) magic / ~로 모자에서 토끼를 꺼내다 use magic to produce a rabbit from a hat. ‖ ~사 a magician.

마스카라 mascara.

마스코트 a (good-luck) mascot.

마스크 a mask; a respirator. ¶ 산소 ~ an oxygen mask / ~을 쓰다 wear a mask.

마스터 master. ~하다 master (*English*). ‖ ~키 a master key / ~플랜 a master plan.

마스트 a mast.

마시다 ① 《액체를》 drink; take; have; swallow. ¶ 물(술)을 ~ drink water (wine) / 차를 ~ take (sip) tea. ② 《기체를》 breathe in; inhale.

마약(痲藥) a narcotic; a drug; a dope 《美俗》. ¶ ~을 맞다 (흡입하다) inject (inhale) a narcotic / ~에 중독되다 become addicted to narcotics. ‖ ~거래 traffic in drugs / ~근절캠페인 a Campaign to Uproot Drug Abuse / ~단속 a dope check; narcotics control / ~단속법 Narcotics Control Law / ~밀매자 a narcotic trafficker; a drug dealer (peddler) / ~범죄 narcotics crimes / ~상용자 a drug addict; a junkie 《俗》 / ~중독 drug addiction.

마왕(魔王) Satan; the Devil.

마요네즈 mayonnaise.

마우스피스 a mouthpiece.

마운드 《野》 the mound. ¶ ~에 서다 take the mound; be on the mound.

마을 《동리》 a village; a hamlet (촌락). ¶ ~ 사람들 villagers; village people / ~ 가다 visit one's neighborhood (*for a chat*). ‖ ~금고 a village fund / ~문고 a village library.

마음 ① 《정신》 mind; spirit; mentality (심성); 《생각》 idea; thought. ¶ ~의 양식 〔자세〕 mental food (attitude) / ~이 넓은 generous; liberal; large- (broad-)minded / ~이 좁은 ungenerous; illiberal; narrow-minded / ~에 걸리다 weigh upon one's mind / ~을 합치다 be united; act in concert with / ~이 맞다 be like-minded; get along very well. ② 《심정》 heart; feeling. ¶ 불안한 ~ a feeling of uneasiness / ~이 변하다 be unfaithful; grow out of love 《*with*》 (남녀) / ~을 끌다 attract; appeal to. ③ 《사려》 thought; 《인정》 consideration; sympathy; 《마음씨》 (a) nature. ¶ ~을 쓰다 be sympathetic; be considerate / ~이 좋다 be gentle-hearted; be good-natured / ~이 나쁘다 be ill-natured. ④ 《주의》 mind; attention. ¶ ~에 두다 bear (*something*) in mind; be mindful (*of*) / …에 ~을 집중하다 concentrate one's attention on …. ⑤ 《의사》 will; mind; intention. ¶ ~이 있다 have a mind to (*do*); be interested (*in*) / ~ 먹어서 안 되는 일 없다 Where there is a will, there is a way. ⑥ 《기분》 a mood; (a) feeling; humor; 《취미·기호》 fancy; taste; liking; mind. ¶ ~에 드는 집 a house to one's mind (fancy) / ~을 상하게 하다 hurt (*a person's*) feelings / ~에 들다 be to one's liking; suit one's taste; be in one's favor / ~에 들지 않다 be disagreeable to (*a person*); be not to one's liking.

마음가짐 《마음태도》 one's mental attitude; 《결심》 one's state of mind; determination; resolution.

마음결 a cast of mind; disposition; nature.

마음껏 to the full; as much as one likes (pleases); to one's heart's content; freely. ¶ ~ 즐기다 enjoy oneself to the full.

마음내키다 feel inclined to (*do*); be interested in (*something*); feel like (*doing*). ¶ 마음이 내키지 않다 be reluctant to (*do*); be in no mood to (*do*); do not take interest (*in*).

마음놓다 feel [be] relieved. ¶ 마음놓고 free from care (fear); without anxiety (worry).

마음대로 as one pleases (likes, wishes); of one's own accord; at one's convenience; arbitrarily; 《자유로이》 freely. ¶ …을 ~하다 have one's (own) way (*in everything*); do what one pleases / ~해라 Do as you please!

마음먹다 ① 《결심》 resolve; determine; be determined; make up one's mind. ¶ 굳게 ~ be firmly determined. ② 《의도》 intend to; 《계획》 plan; have a mind to; think; 《희망》 wish; hope. ¶ …하려고 ~ intend to (*do*).

마음보 disposition; nature. ¶ ~ 고약한 ill-natured; bad.

마음속 one's mind; (the bottom of) one's heart. ¶ ~ 깊이 deep down in the heart of / ~에 묻어두다 keep (*the story*) to oneself / ~을 떠보다 sound (*a person's*) views.

마음씨 disposition; nature. ¶ ~ 고운 good-natured; tender-hearted.

마음졸이다 worry (*oneself*) (*about*); be concerned (*about*); be anx-

마이너스 minus; 《불리》 a disadvantage; a handicap. ¶ ~가 되다 lose; suffer a loss / 그것은 이 계획의 ~가 된다 That is the disadvantage of this plan. ‖ ~ 부호 a minus sign / ~성장 negative (economic) growth.

마이동풍(馬耳東風) ~으로 들어넘기다 turn a deaf ear [pay no attention] to 《a person's advice》.

마이신(黴生素) streptomycin.

마이크로…《극히 작은》 micro-. ¶ ~버스 a microbus; a minibus / ~컴퓨터 a microcomputer / ~프로세서 a microprocessor / 필름 a microfilm.

마이크(로폰) a microphone; a mike. ‖ ~공포증 mike fright.

마일 a mile. ¶ 1시간에 4~ 가다 cover [make] four miles in an hour / 시속 60~ 로 달리다 run at (the rate of) sixty miles per hour. ‖ ~수 mileage.

마작(麻雀) mah-jong. ~하다 play mah-jong.

마장(馬場) 《방목장》 a grazing land for horse; 《경마장》 a racecourse.

마저 《남김없이》 with all the rest; all (together); 《까지도》 even; too; so much as; so far as.

마적(馬賊) mounted bandits.

마전(漂白) bleaching. ~하다 bleach. ‖ ~장이 a bleacher; ~터 a bleaching establishment.

마조(一調) 《樂》 the tone E.

마조히즘(醫) masochism.

마주 《directly》 opposite; face to face. ¶ ~ 대하다 face each other / ~ 앉다 sit face to face with 《a person》 / ~ 놓다 set 《things》 opposite each other.

마주치다 ① ☞ 부딪치다. ② 《조우하다》 come across; encounter; meet with.

마중 meeting; reception. ~하다 go [come] out to meet 《a person》 at a place; greet. ¶ 역으로 ~나가다 go to meet 《a person》 at the station.

마중물 《펌프의》 priming water. ¶ ~을 붓다 prime [fetch] 《a pump》.

마지기 a patch of field requiring one *mal* of seed; a *majigi* (= 500 m²). ¶ 논 한 ~ a patch of rice paddy.

마지막 the last; the end; the conclusion (결말); 《형용사적》 last; final; terminal. ¶ ~으로 finally; at the end / ~까지 to the end (last) / ~ 수단 the last resort.

마지못하다 be compelled [forced, obliged] to 《do》; have no choice but to 《do》. ¶ 마지못하여 unwillingly; reluctantly; against one's will / 마지못해 그와 동행하다 go with him reluctantly.

마지않다 can never 《thank》 enough. ¶ 감사해 ~ can never thank 《a person》 enough; offer one's heartful thanks.

마진 a margin 《of profit》. ¶ 근소한 ~ a slim [narrow] margin / 약장사는 ~이 크다 The profit margin is wide in the drug business. ‖ ~ 카트 (장마진).

마차(馬車) a coach; a carriage; a cart.

마찬가지 ¶ ~의 the same; similar 《to》; like / ~로 similarly; likewise; equally.

마찰(摩擦) friction; 《비벼댐》 rubbing; 《불화》 a trouble; friction; discord. ~하다 rub 《against》; chafe 《the skin》. ¶ ~을 낳다 [피하다] cause [avoid] friction. ‖ ~열 frictional heat / ~음 a fricative (sound).

마천루(摩天樓) a skyscraper.

마취(麻醉) anesthesia; narcotism. ~하다 put 《a person》 under an anesthetic; anesthetize. ¶ ~약 an anesthetic; a narcotic / ~전문의 an anesthetist.

마치¹ 《장도리》 a small hammer. ‖ ~질 hammering.

마치² 《흡사》 as if [though]; just (like). ¶ ~ 미친 사람 같다 look as if *one* were mad.

마치다 《끝내다》 finish; end; be [go] through; complete. ¶ 학업을 ~ complete a school course.

마침 《기회 좋게》 luckily; fortunately; opportunely; just in time. ¶ ~ 그 때 just then.

마침내 (at) long last; at length; in the end; in the long run; finally.

마침표(一標) a period; a full stop.

마카로니 macaroni. ¶ ~웨스턴 《이탈리아 영화》 a Spaghetti Western.

마케팅 marketing. ‖ ~ 리서치 marketing research.

마켓 a market. ¶ 새로운 ~을 개척하다 develop a new market. ‖ ~ 셰어 *one's* market share.

마크(표) a mark; 《레터러》 a label.

마키아벨리즘 Machiavellism.

마태복음(一福音) 《聖》 the (Gospel of) Matthew.

마티네 a matinée 《프》. 「southerly.

마파람 the south wind; a

마포(麻布) hemp cloth (삼베).

마피아 《범죄결사》 the Mafia.

마하(理) Mach (number) 《略 M》. ¶ ~3으로 날다 fly at Mach 3.

마호가니 mahogany.

마호메트교 ☞ 이슬람교.

마흔 forty.

막(幕) ① 《위장》 a curtain; a hang-

ing screen. ¶ ~을 올리다 raise a curtain(위로); draw a curtain (aside)(옆으로) / ~이 오르다 (내리다) the curtain rises (drops). ② (극의) an act. ¶ 제2막 제3장 Act 2, Scene 3. ③ (작은 집) a cottage; a hut; a shack. ④ (끝장) an end; a close. ¶ 전쟁의 ~을 내리다 put an end to the war.
막(膜)〔解〕 a membrane.
막(방금) just (now); a moment ago. ¶ ~하려 하다 be on the point of 〈*do*〉; be on the point of 〈*doing*〉.
막² = 마구.
막간(幕間) an interval (between acts); an intermission 〖美〗. ‖ ~극 an interlude.
막강(莫強) ¶ ~한 mighty; enormously powerful. 〖*makkŏli*〗
막걸리 unrefined (raw) rice wine;
막내 the youngest (child). ‖ ~아들 the last (youngest) son.
막노동(—勞動) ☞ 막일.
막다 ① (구멍 등을) stop (up); plug. ¶ 쥐구멍을 ~ stop up a rathole. ② (차단·방해) intercept; block; obstruct. ¶ 길을 ~ block the way; stand in the way / 바람을 ~ shelter 〈*a person*〉 from the wind. ③ (방어) defend; keep off (away); 〈저지〉 check; stop; 〈예방〉 prevent; 〈금지〉 prohibit; forbid. ¶ 적을 ~ keep off the enemy / 전염을 ~ prevent infection. ④ (구획) screen off; compart. ¶ 칸을 ~ partition a room.
막다르다 come to the end of the road; come to a deadlock (사태가). ¶ 막다른 골목 a blind alley / 막다른 지경에 이르다 run into a blind alley; be driven into a corner; come to a deadlock.
막대(莫大) ¶ ~한 vast; huge; enormous; immense / ~한 비용 an enormous expense.
막대기 a stick; a staff; a rod.
막도장(—圖章) an unofficial (small-sized) seal.
막되다 (be) rude; unmannerly.
막둥이 (막내) the youngest son.
막론(莫論) ¶ ~을 ~하고 not to speak of…; to say nothing of….
막료(幕僚) the staff (전체); a staff 〈officer〉(한 사람).
막막하다(寞寞—) (be) lonely; lonesome; dreary; desolate.
막막하다(漠漠—) (be) vast; boundless; limitless.
막말 rude (rough) talk. ~하다 speak roughly (thoughtlessly).
막무가내(莫無可奈) ¶ ~로 obstinately; stubbornly; firmly.
막바지 the very (dead) end; the top (of a hill); a climax (절정); the last moment (고비).

막벌이 earning wages as a day laborer. ~하다 earn wages as a day laborer. ‖ ~꾼 a day laborer; an odd-jobber.
막사(幕舍) a camp; a barracks.
막상 actually (really) (in the end); when it comes down to it. ¶ ~ 때가 닥치면 if the time comes; at the last moment / ~ 해보면 어려운 법이다 When you come down to doing it, you will find it rather difficult.
막상막하(莫上莫下) ¶ ~의 equal; even; equally-matched / ~의 경기 a close (seesaw) game.
막심하다(莫甚—) (be) tremendous; enormous; heavy. ¶ 후회가 ~ I regret it very much.
막역(莫逆) ¶ ~한 intimate; close / ~한 친구 a close friend.
막연하다(漠然—) (be) vague; obscure; ambiguous. ¶ 막연한 대답을 하다 give a vague answer.
막일 hard manual labor; heavy (rough) work. ~하다 be engaged in rough work. ‖ ~꾼 a manual (physical) laborer.
막자 a medicine pestle; a muller. ‖ ~사발 a mortar.
막장(鑛) a coal (working) face; a face. ¶ ~에서 일하다 work at the face.
막중(莫重) ¶ ~한 (be) very important; invaluable.
막차(—車) the last bus (train).
막판(마지막판) the last round; the final scene; 〖고비〗 the last (critical) moment.
막후(幕後) ¶ ~공작 behind-the-scene maneuvering / ~ 교섭〔흥정〕 behind-the-scenes negotiations (dealings) / ~인물 a man behind the curtain (scene); wire-puller.
막히다 be closed; be clogged; be stopped (stuffed) (up); be blocked (up) (길 따위); be chocked (숨이). ¶ 말이 ~ be stuck for a word / 길이 ~ the road is blocked / 하수도가 ~ a drain is stopped up.
만(卍)〔표지〕 the Buddhist emblem; 〖글자〗 a fylfot; a swastika.
만(滿) just; full(y); whole. ¶ ~ 5일 동안 (for) a full five days.
만(灣) a bay (작은); a gulf (큰).
만(萬) ten thousand; a myriad. ¶ 수십 ~ hundreds of thousands 〈*of*〉.
만¹ (경과) after. ¶ 닷새 ~에 on the fifth day; after five days.
만² ① (단지) only; merely; just. ¶ 한 번 ~ only once / 한 번 ~ 더 just once again / 이 번 ~은 for this once / 밥 ~ 먹다

eat only rice / 그것은 못 하겠다 I will do anything but that. ② (비교) as... as. 나는 너키가 너와 ~하다 I am as tall as you (are). ③ (겨우 그 정도) so trifling; such a small. ¶그~ 일로 성낼 것은 없네 Don't be offended at such a trifle.

만가 (輓歌) an elegy; a dirge; a lament; a funeral song.

만감 (萬感) a flood of emotions.

만강 (滿腔) ~의 hearty; heart-felt (*thanks*).

만경 (萬頃) ¶ ~창파 the boundless expanse of water.

만고 (萬古) ~불변의 eternal; immutable (*truths*) / ~불후의 immortal; everlasting; eternal / ~풍상(을 다 겪다) (undergo) all kinds of hardships / ~의 영웅 a hero for all ages.

만곡 (灣曲) ~하다 curve; bend.

만국 (萬國) world nations; all countries on earth. ¶ ~기 the flags of all nations / ~박람회 a world's fair; an international exposition / ~우편연합 the Universal Postal Union (생략 UPU) / ~저작권 조약 the Universal Copyright Convention.

만금 (萬金) an immense sum of money.

만기 (滿期) expiration (*of a term*); maturity (*of a bill*). ¶ ~가 되다 expire; mature; serve out *one's* time / 보험~가 되다 the term of *one's* insurance expires (*on April 5*) / 어음은 다음 달로 ~가 된다 The bill falls due in a month. ‖ ~상환 redemption on maturity / ~어음 a matured bill / ~일 the day of maturity; the due date / ~제대 an honorable discharge.

만끽 (滿喫) ~하다 enjoy fully [to the full]; have enough (*of*).

만나다 ① (사람을) see; meet; interview (면회). ② 우연히 ~ come across [upon] (*a person*). ② (당하다) meet with (*an accident*); suffer. ¶ 화를 ~ suffer a calamity / 소나기를 ~ be caught in a shower.

만난 (萬難) ¶ ~을 무릅쓰고 at any cost; at all costs (*risks*).

만년 (晩年) ¶ ~에 in *one's* last (later) years; late in life.

만년 (萬年) eternity; ten thousand years. ¶ ~설 perpetual (eternal) snow / ~필 a fountain pen.

만능 (萬能) ~의 almighty; omnipotent. ‖ ~선수 an all-(a)round player / ~후보 an ever unsuccessful candidate.

만단 (萬端) ~의 준비가 되었다 Everything [All] is ready.

만담 (漫談) have a comic chat. ~하다 have a comic chat. ‖ ~가 a comic-chat artiste; a comedian.

만대 (萬代) all ages. ¶ ~에 for all ages; forever.

만돌린 (樂) a mandolin.

만두 (饅頭) a dumpling stuffed with minced meat.

만득 (晩得) ~하다 beget a child in *one's* later years.

만들다 ① (제조) make; manufacture; produce (*cars*); (양조) brew (*beer*); distill (*whisky*). 진흙으로 인형을 ~ make a doll out of clay / 쌀로 술을 ~ make wine from rice. ② (작성) make (out); draw up. ¶서류[계약서]를 ~ draw up a document (contract). ③ (건설) make; build. 길을 ~ build a road. ④ (조직·창설) set up; establish; organize; form. ¶회사를 ~ set up a company / 클럽을 ~ organize a club. ⑤ (조작) make-up; invent. ¶ 꾸며 낸 이야기 a made-up (an invented) story. ⑥ (요리) make; prepare; fix (음식); cook (불을 사용해서). ¶ 저녁 식사를 ~ prepare (fix) supper / 케이크를 ~ make (bake) a cake. ⑦ (마련) make; get; raise (*money*). ¶ 재산을 ~ make (amass) a fortune / 기금을 ~ raise a fund.

만듦새 make; workmanship; craftsmanship; cut (옷 따위의). ¶ (물품의) ~가 좋은 (나쁜) well-(poorly-)made; of fine (poor) make.

만료 (滿了) expiration; expiry. ~하다 expire. ¶ 임기가 ~되는 날 the day *one's* term of office expires. ‖ 임기~ the termination of office.

만루 (滿壘) [野] a full base. ‖ ~홈런 a base-loaded homer; a grand slam (美) / 일사 (一死) ~ one out bases loaded.

만류 (挽留) ~하다 (try to) prevent (*a person*) from (*leaving*); (제지하다) detain; keep (hold) back; check. ¶ 소매를 잡고 ~하다 detain (*a person*) by the sleeve / 싸우지 말라고 ~하다 hold (*a person*) back from wrangling.

만류 (滿流) the Gulf Stream.

만리 (萬里) ¶ ~장성 the Great Wall (of China).

만만 (滿滿) ~하다 (be) full (*of*). ¶ 패기 (자신) ~하다 be full of ambition (self-confidence).

만만하다 ① (보드랍다) (be) soft; tender. ② (다루기가) (be) easy (*to deal with*); negligible; not formidable (두렵지 않다). ¶ 만만히

만면(滿面) the whole face. ¶ ~에 미소를 띠우고 smiling *a* ; *all* with *one's face*; 희색이 ~하여 with *one's face beaming with joy*.

만무(萬無) ~하다 cannot be; be most unlikely. ¶ 그럴 리가 ~하다 It is next to impossible. *or* It's most unlikely.

만물(萬物) all things (under the sun); all creation. ¶ 사람은 ~의 영장이다 Man is the lord of creation. ¶ ~박사 a walking dictionary; a jack-of-all-trades / ~상 a general store.

만민(萬民) the whole nation; all the people. ¶ ~법 *jus gentium* (라).

만반(萬般) ~의: all; every; ~의 준비를 갖추다 make full (thorough) preparations (*for*).

만발(滿發) ~하다 bloom all over; come into full bloom; be in full bloom (blossom).

만방(萬方) all directions; every way.

만방(萬邦) nations of the world.

만백성(萬百姓) all the people.

만병(萬病) all kinds of diseases. ¶ ~통치약 a panacea; a cure-all.

만보(漫步) a ramble; a stroll.

만복(萬福) lots of good fortunes. ¶ 소문~래 Fortune comes to a merry home. *or* Laugh and be (grow) fat.

만복(滿腹) satiety; a full stomach.

만부당(萬不當) ~하다 (be) utterly unjust; upright; unlawful; unreasonable; inappropriate.

만분지일(萬分之一) one in ten thousand; a ten-thousandth.

만사(萬事) all (things); everything. ¶ ~에 all things / ~가 여의(형통)하다 Everything turns out as *one* wishes. *or* All goes well. / 이제 난 ~가 끝장이다 It's all over for me now.

만삭(滿朔) (the month of) parturiency. ~하다 be in the last month of pregnancy; be parturient. ¶ ~의 부인 a parturient woman.

만상(萬象) the visible world; the *universe*; all (things in) nature.

만생종(晩生種) a variety of late ripening.

만석꾼(萬石─) a rich landlord; a millionaire.

만성(晩成) ~하다 mature late; be slow to develop.

만성(慢性) 〔醫〕 chronicity. ¶ ~의 (적인) chronic; deep-seated / ~이 되다 pass into a chronic state; become chronic (*with*) / ~인 실업 chronic unemployment. ¶ ~병 a chronic disease / ~병 환자 a chronic invalid / 위장병 inveterate (chronic) dyspepsia / ~인플레 chronic inflation.

만세(萬世) ☞ 만세(萬世). ¶ ~ eternity.

만세(萬歲) ① ☞ 만세(萬歲). ¶ ~력 a perpetual almanac. ② (외치는) cheers; hurrah; hurray. ¶ ~ 삼창하다 give three cheers (*for a person*).

만수(萬壽) longevity. ¶ ~무강(無疆) a long life; longevity / ~하다 live long; enjoy longevity.

만시(晩時) ¶ ~지탄 a belated regret.

만신(滿身) the whole body. ¶ ~창이다 be covered all over with wounds.

만심(慢心) pride; self-conceit. ~하다 be proud; be conceited; be puffed up (*with*); be bloated (inflated) with pride. ¶ ~케 하다 make (*a person*) conceited.

만약(萬若) if; in case (*of*). ¶ 그것이 사실이라면 if it is true.

만연(漫然) ~한 random; rambling; desultory / ~히 aimlessly; at random; desultorily.

만연(蔓延) ~하다 spread; be prevalent. ¶ 질병이 ~한 난민 수용소 a disease-ridden refugee camp.

만용(蠻勇) recklessness. ¶ ~을 부리다 show reckless valor.

만우절(萬愚節) April Fools' Day.

만원(滿員) (게시) House full; Full house; Sold out (매진); (전차 따위의) Car full. ¶ ~의 관객 a capacity audience (crowd) / 초~이다 be more than full; be filled to bursting / ~이 된 청중에게 연설하다 deliver a speech to a packed house. ¶ ~버스 a jam-packed bus / ~사례 (게시) Thank you for giving us a full house today.

만월(滿月) a full moon.

만유인력(萬有引力) 〔理〕 universal gravitation. ¶ ~의 법칙 the law of universal gravitation.

만인(萬人) every man; all people.

만인(蠻人) a savage; a barbarian.

만일(萬一) by any means; if; in case (*of. that*). ¶ ~의 경우에는 if anything should happen; in case of emergency.

만자(卍字) a swastika; a fylfot. ¶ ~ 모양의 swastika-shaped (*frame*).

만장(萬丈) ¶ ~의 기염을 토하다 talk big; make a grand splurge.

만장(輓章) a funeral ode; an elegy.

만장(滿場) the entire audience (전

만재(滿載) ~하다 be fully loaded 《with》; carry a full cargo; be loaded to capacity. 《승객을 ~하다》 carry a full load of passengers. ∥ ~흘수선(吃水線) the load line 《load draft》.

만전(萬全) ¶ ~의 sure; secure / ~을 기하다 make assurance doubly sure / ~의 대책을 강구하다 adopt a prudent 《the safest》 policy; take all possible measures to ensure 《the success of a project》.

만점(滿點) a full mark. ¶ ~을 따다 get full marks / ~이다 《완전》 be perfect; be satisfactory.

만져보다 touch; feel; finger.

만조(滿潮) a high 《full》 tide; high water. ¶ ~시에 at high tide / ~는 오후 1시다 The tide is full at 1 p.m.

만족(滿足) satisfaction; gratification(욕망의); contentment. ~하다 be satisfied 《gratified》 《with》; be content 《pleased》 《with》. ~할 만한 satisfactory; sufficient 《충분한》/ ~시키다 satisfy; gratify; give 《a person》 satisfaction / 미소로 ~의 뜻을 나타내다 express one's satisfaction with a smile / 그 결과에 ~하다 be happy 《pleased》 with the result / 이것으로 ~할 만한 설명이 되었다고 생각한다 I believe this is a sufficient explanation. ∥ ~감 a feeling of satisfaction.

만종(晚鐘) the curfew.

만좌(滿座) the whole company 《assembly》. ¶ ~중에 in public; before the whole company.

만주(滿洲) Manchuria. ¶ ~의 Manchurian.

만지다 finger; handle; touch; feel. ¶ 손으로 ~ touch 《a thing》 with the hand / 만지지 마시오 《게시》 Hands off.

만지작거리다 keep fingering; fumble with; tamper with.

만찬(晚餐) dinner; supper. ¶ ~에 초대하다 ask 《invite》 《a person》 to dinner. ∥ ~회 《give》 a dinner party.

만천하(滿天下) ¶ ~에 in the whole country; throughout the country; 《announce》 publicly.

만추(晚秋) late autumn 《fall》.

만춘(晚春) late spring.

만취(漫醉·滿醉) ~하다 get dead drunk; be beastly drunk.

만큼 《비교》 as...as 《긍정》; not as 〔so〕...as 《부정》 / 《정도》 so much that; enough; 《…이므로》 since;

in view of. ¶ 그~ as 《so that》 much / 얼마~ how much; to what extent / 때가 때인~ in view of the times.

만태(萬態) various phases. ∥ 인생 ~ various phases of life.

만판 《마음껏》 to the full; to one's heart's content; as much as one pleases; 《마냥》 at all times; all the time; constantly. ¶ ~ 먹다〔마시다〕 eat 〔drink〕 one's fill / ~ 인생을 즐기다 enjoy life to the full / ~ 놀기만하다 spend all one's time loafing.

만평(漫評) a satire; a satiric comic; a rambling criticism(비평). ∥ 시사~ rambling comments on current events.

만필(漫筆) lightehearted 《carefree》 jottings.

만하(晚夏) late summer.

만하다 ① 《족하다》 be enough(sufficient) 《to do》. ¶ 나이가 일하기 좋을~ be old enough to work efficiently. ② 《가치·힘이》 be worth 《doing》; be worthy of…; deserve. ¶ 칭찬할~ deserve praise.

…만하다 《정도》 be to the extent of; be as...as. ¶ 크기가 네 것~ be as big as yours.

만학(晚學) ~하다 study 《begin to learn》 late in life. ∥ ~자 a late learner.

만행(蠻行) savagery; a brutality; an atrocity. ¶ ~을 저지르다 commit an act of brutality.

만혼(晚婚) a late marriage. ~하다 marry late 《in life》.

만화(漫畵) a caricature(인물의); a cartoon 《풍자적》; 《연재의》 a comic strip; comics. ∥ ~가 a caricaturist; a cartoonist; a comic stripper / ~ 영화 an animated cartoon; a cartoon film / ~책 a comic book / 불량 ~ substandard comic books.

만화경(萬華鏡) a kaleidoscope.

만화방창(萬化方暢) luxuriant growth of all things in spring. ~하다 all things grow luxuriantly 《in spring》.

만회(挽回) recovery; retrieval(명예 동의); restoration(복구). ~하다 recover 《one's losses》; restore 《one's reputation》; retrieve 《one's fortunes》. ¶ ~할 수 없는 irrecoverable; irretrievable. ∥ ~책 measures for retrieving 《one's lost credit》.

많다 《수》 be many; numerous; 《양》 (be) much; (be) a lot of; plenty of; 《풍부》 (be) abundant 《plentiful》; abound in; 《충분》 (be) enough; sufficient; 《잦다》 (be) frequent; often; prevalent. ¶ 많이 《다수·수량》

말 much; lots; plenty; a great deal; in a large amount (number); in large quantities (large 책 many books / 많은 돈 much money / 많은 사람 a great crowd of people / 볼일이 ~ have many things to do / 강에는 잉어가 ~ The river abounds in carp. / 많을수록 좋다 The more, the better. / 일본에는 지진이 ~ Japan has frequent earthquakes.

말 firstborn; the eldest. ‖ ~ 아들 the eldest son / ~형 the eldest brother.

맏물 the first product (crop) of the season; the first fruits.

맏배 the firstborn (of animals); the first batch (hatch, litter). ‖ ~돼지 the first litter of pigs / ~병아리 chickens of the first hatch.

맏사위 the husband of one's firstborn daughter.

맏상제 (-喪制) the chief mourner; the eldest son of the deceased.

맏손자 (-孫子) the eldest (first) grandson (grandchild).

맏이 the firstborn (eldest) son.

말¹ 《타는》 a horse. ‖ 마차 ~ a carriage horse / 수~ a stallion (종마) / 암~ a mare / 조랑 ~ a pony / 짐 싣는 ~ a pack-horse / ~을 타다 (mount) a horse / ~을 타고 가다 go on horseback.

말² 〔斗〕 a *mal* (≒18 liters).

말³ ①《언어》 language; speech; a word (낱말); a language (국어). ‖ 서울 ~ Seoul speech. ②《인사》 a talk; a speech; a conversation; a chat; a remark; a statement. ‖ ~ 없이 without a word / ~이 많다 be talkative (loquacious) / ~이 적다 be taciturn; be a man of few words / ~이 서투르다 be a poor speaker / ~을 걸다 speak to (*a person*) / ~을 놓다 don't mister (*a person*) / ~을 잘 하다 be eloquent (fluent).

말⁴ 〔浮萍〕 duckweed.

말⁵ 《장기·윷의》 a marker in chess; a piece; a chessman.

…말 (末) 《끝》 the end (*of May*); the close (*of the century*).

말갈기 a mane.

말갛다 (be) clear; clean; limpid.

말경 (末境) 《끝판》 the end; the close; 《말년》 the declining years of one's life.

말고삐 reins; a bridle.

말공대 (-恭待) addressing in honorifics. ‖ ~ 하다 address in honorifics.

말괄량이 a romp; a tomboy; a hussy; a minx; a flapper.

말구종 (-驅從) a footman; a groom.

말굴레 a bridle; a headgear.

말굽 a horse's hoof; a horseshoe (편자). ‖ ~ 소리 the clattering of a horse's hoofs.

말귀 《말뜻》 the meaning of what *one* says; 《이해력》 understanding; apprehension; an ear (for words). ‖ ~를 못 알아 듣다 can't make out what (*a person*) says.

말기 (末期) the last stage (years, days); the end; the close. ‖ ~적 증상이다 show signs of a downfall.

말꼬리 ~를 잡다 catch (*a person*) in *his* own words; take up (*a person*) on a slip of the tongue.

말끔 completely; thoroughly; all; entirely; wholly; totally. ‖ 빚을 ~ 청산하다 clear off one's debts.

말끔하다 (be) clean; neat; tidy. ‖ 말끔히 clean(ly); neatly; tidily.

말끝 ~을 흐리다 leave one's statement vague; prevaricate / 그는 ~ 마다 그런 소리를 한다 He never opens his mouth without saying it.

말내다 ① 《얘기삼아》 bring into the conversation; begin to talk about. ②《비밀을》 disclose; divulge; reveal; expose.

말년 (末年) ① 《일생의》 one's later years. ② 《말엽》 the last years.

말다¹ 《둘둘》 roll (*paper*). ⌊(days).

말다² 《몸에》 put (*rice*) into water; mix (*food*) with (*soup*).

말다³ 《그만두다》 give up; quit; stop; cease. ‖ 하다가 만 일 an unfinished work.

말다⁴ ①《금지》 don't; not; never; avoid. ‖ 잊지 마라 Don't forget. ②《필경 …되다》 end up (*doing*); finally (*do*). ‖ 그는 마침내 술로 죽고 말았다 Drink ended him.

말다툼 a dispute; a quarrel; a wrangle; a squabble; an argument. ‖ ~ 하다 have a quarrel (an argument, a dispute) with; quarrel (argue) with.

말단 (末端) the end; the tip. ‖ 행정기구의 ~ the smallest unit of the administrative organization; a government office in direct contact with the public. ‖ ~공무원 a petty official / ~사원 a minor clerk.

말대꾸 a reply; a response; an answer. ‖ ~ 하다 make a reply.

말대답 (- 對答) back talk; a retort; a comeback (口). ‖ ~ 하다 talk back (*to a person*); answer back; retort; give (*a person*) back talk. ‖ 어른한테 ~ 해서는 못 쓴다 You shouldn't talk back to your elders.

말더듬다 ☞ 더듬다, 더듬거리다.

말더듬이 a stammerer; a stutterer. ¶ ~ 교정ىل an articulator.
말똥말똥 with vacant fixed eyes. ~ 하다 be wide-awake.
말뚝 a pile; a stake; a post.
말라깽이 a living skeleton; a bag of bones. 「malarial fever.
말라리아 [醫] malaria. ‖ ~
말라빠지다 be(come) thin (lean); grow gaunt; lose flesh. 「elastic.
말랑말랑하다 (be) soft; tender;
말레이 Malay. ‖ ~어 Malay / ~사람 a Malay(an) / ~반도 the Malay Peninsula.
말레이시아 (the Federation of) Malaysia. ‖ ~의 Malaysian / ~사람 a Malaysian.
말려들다 be dragged (in); be involved (entangled) (in). ¶ 전쟁 [분쟁]에 ~ be involved in a war (trouble).
말로 (末路) the last days; the (final) fate; the end (of one's career). ¶ 영웅의 ~ the last days of a hero.
말리 (茉莉) a jasmine. 「up.
말리다¹ 《둘둘》 be rolled (curled)
말리다² 《건조》 (make) dry; desiccate (저장용); season (재목을); drain (고랑). ¶ 불에 ~ dry (a thing) over the fire.
말리다³ 《만류》 dissuade (a person from doing); get (a person) not to; stop. ¶ 싸움을 ~ stop a quarrel.
말마디 a phrase; a speech; a talk. ¶ 그 사람 ~깨나 할 줄 안다 He is quite a good speaker.
말막음 ¶ ~ 하다 hush up; shut (a person) up; stop (a person's) mouth.
말리다 ¶ ~ 말 돌리다 change the subject of one's speech.
말먹이 fodder; hay; forage.
말몰이꾼 a pack-horse driver.
말문 (一門) ¶ ~이 막히다 be struck dumb; be at a loss for words.
말미 leave (of absence); furlough. ¶ ~를 얻다 get (be granted) a leave of absence / ~를 주다 give (grant) leave (of absence).
말미 (末尾) the end; the close. ¶ 보고서 ~에 at the end of the report.
말미암다 《유래》 come (arise) from; be derived (from); 《원인》 be due to; be caused by. ¶ 부주의로 말미암은 사고 an accident due to carelessness / 말미암아 owing to; because of; on account of.
말미잘 [動] a sea anemone.
말버릇 one's manner of speaking; one's way of talking.
말버짐 psoriasis.
말벌 [蟲] a wasp; a hornet.

말벗 a companion; someone to talk to (with). ¶ ~이 되다 keep (a person) company.
말복 (末伏) the third of the three periods of summer doldrums; the last of the dog days.
말본 grammar. ☞ 문법.
말살 (抹殺) ① 《숙청·살해》 purge; liquidation; erasure. ~ 하다 purge; liquidate; get rid of; kill (the existence of). ② ☞ 말소.
말상 (一相) a long face. ¶ ~이다 be long-(horse-)faced.
말석 (末席) the lowest seat; the bottom. ¶ ~을 더럽히다 be humbly present (at a meeting).
말세 (末世) a degenerate age; the end of the world.
말소 (抹消) erase; efface; strike (cross) out. ¶ 등기의 ~ cancellation of registration.
말소리 a voice. ¶ ~가 들리다 hear (a person) talking.
말솜씨 one's ability to speak (talk); eloquence. ¶ ~가 좋다 be good at speaking; be eloquent. 「turn; reticent.
말수 (一數) ¶ ~가 적은 silent; tac-
말승냥이 ① 《이리》 a wolf. ② 《키 큰 사람》 a tall man.
말실수 (一失手) a slip of the tongue. ~ 하다 make a slip of the tongue.
말썽 trouble; complaint; a dispute (분쟁). ¶ ~을 부리다 complain; cause trouble; lead to a dispute. ¶ ~거리 a cause (source) of trouble; a matter for complaint / ~꾸러기 (꾼) a troublemaker; a grumbler. 「nice.
말쑥하다 be clean; neat; smart;
말씨 the use of words; one's way of speaking; the language. ¶ 점잖은 ~ refined diction / ~가 상스럽다 be rough in speech.
말아니다 ① 《언어도단》 (be) unreasonable; absurd; nonsensical. ② 《형편이》 be in very bad shape; (be) extremely poor (miserable; wretched).
말안되다 (be) absurd; unreasonable; contrary to logic.
말없이 《묵묵히》 in silence; silently; without comment; without saying anything; 《선뜻》 without a word; readily; 《무단으로》 without notice.
말엽 (末葉) the end; the close. ¶ 20세기 ~ toward the end of the 20th century.
말오줌나무 [植] an elderberry.
말일 (末日) the last day; the end (of May). ¶ 응모는 이 달 ~ 까지이다 The deadline for the application is the end of this month.
말장난 a play on words; a word-

말재주 (a) talent for speaking; eloquence. ¶ ~ 있는 eloquent; glib-tongued.

말조심 (一操心) ~하다 be careful of *one's* speech.

말주변 the gift of gab. ¶ ~이 있는 glib-tongued / ~이 좋다 have a ready tongue / ~이 없다 be a poor talker.

말직 (末職) a small post; a petty office; the lowest position.

말질 tale-telling; gossiping; 《말다툼》 a quarrel. ~하다 tell tales about others; gossip; quarrel.

말짱하다 《온전》 (be) perfect; whole; flawless; sound; free from blemish; 《안 취함》 remain sober 《서술적》. ¶ 정신이 ~ have a clear mind; be sound in mind.

말참견 (一參見) interfering; meddling. ~하다 put in words; poke *one's* nose into; interfere 《in》.

말채찍 a horsewhip.

말초 (末梢) ¶ ~적인 unimportant; trifling; trivial; [解] peripheral. ‖ ~신경 a peripheral nerve.

말총 horsehair.

말치레 ~하다 use fine [fair, honeyed] words; say nice [pretty] things.

말캉말캉하다 ☞ 물렁물렁하다.

말투 *one's* way of talking; the way *one* talks. ¶ 야비한 ~ a mean [low] expression / ~가 거칠다 use harsh language; be rough in *one's* speech.

말판 a game [dice] board.

말편자 a horseshoe.

말하다 《얘기》 talk 《about》; speak; converse; relate; have a talk [chat] with; 《알리다》 tell; say; speak of; state; mention; narrate; set forth; 《표현》 express; touch upon; refer to. ¶ 말할 수 없는 unspeakable; indescribable / …은 말할 것도 없거니와 / 말하자면 so to speak; as it were / 한마디로 말하면 in short; in a word / 간단히 [자세히] ~ state briefly [in detail] / 좋게 [나쁘게] ~ speak well [ill] of 《*a person*》 / ~은 말할 것도 없다 It is needless to say 《that…》 / …이라 말해도 좋다 It may safely be said that….

맑다 ① 《물이》 (be) clear; clean; limpid; pure; 《소리가》 resonant. ② 《날씨가》 (be) fine; clear. ¶ 맑은 하늘 clear sky. ③ 《마음이》 (be) clear; pure; fresh. ④ 《청빈》 (be) poor (but honest).

맑은장국 (一醬一) clear meat soup; *consommé* 《프》. ‖ ~바지 pipe trousers.

맘보 a mambo. ¶ ~바지 drainpipes.

맙소사 Oh, no!; Good God!; Good gracious [heaven]!

맛 ① 《음식의》 (a) taste; (a) flavor; savor. ¶ 매운 [신, 쓴] ~ a hot [sour, salty] taste / ~이 좋은 nice; tasty; palatable; delicious / ~ 없는 untasty; ill-tasting; unpalatable / 아무 ~도 없는 tasteless / ~이 변하다 turn sour [stale]. ② 《사물의》 relish; taste; interest. ¶ ~을 알다 know the taste 《of》 / ~을 보다 taste; try [have] a taste of 《*food*》 / 돈~ a taste for money / 여자 ~ an interest in women / …에 ~을 들이다 get [acquire] a taste for; take a liking for [to] / 성공의 ~을 알다 taste the benefits of success / 가난의 ~을 아직 모르다 don't know the taste of poverty yet. ③ 《관용적》 ¶ 따가운 ~을 보여 주다 teach 《*a person*》 a lesson / 오늘 꼭 가야 ~이냐 Why do you have to choose to go today necessarily?

맛깔스럽다 《맛이》 (be) tasty; palatable; agreeable. ¶ 맛깔스러운 음식 an agreeable food.

맛나다 ① 《맛있다》 (be) delicious; nice; tasty. ② 《맛이 나다》 taste good [nice]; have a flavor of.

맛난이 《조미료》 flavoring; seasoning; a spice 《香料》.

맛들다 pick up flavor; become tasty; grow ripe.

맛들이다 ① 《재미 붙이다》 acquire [get] a taste 《of》. ② 《맛들게 하다》 season (flavor) with; make tasty.

맛맛으로 according to *one's* pleasure [taste, desire]. ¶ ~ 골라 먹어라 Help yourself according to your taste.

맛배기 《특제》 a special order.

맛보다 《맛을》 taste; try the flavor of; 《경험》 experience; suffer; undergo. ¶ 인생의 쓰라림을 ~ experience hardships of life.

맛부리다 behave in an insipid manner [way].

맛없다 ① 《맛이 없다》 (be) untasty; tasteless; unpalatable; unsavory. ② 《재미 없다》 (be) dry; flat; dull; insipid.

맛있다 (be) nice; tasty; delicious; palatable; dainty. ¶ 맛있어 보이는 tempting; delicious-looking / 맛있게 먹다 eat with relish.

맛적다 《맛이》 lack flavor; (be) flat; dull; tasteless; 《재미가》 lack charm; (be) unpleasant; unenjoyable.

망 (望) 《살핌》 watch; lookout; guard; vigilance. ¶ ~을 보다 keep a watch; stand guard; look out for.

망 (網) ① 《그물》 a net; netting

망각(忘却) ~하다 forget; be forgetful (oblivious) (of 《one's responsibilities》).

망간(化) manganese (기호 Mn).

망건(網巾) a headband made of horsehair.

망고(植) a mango [pl. -(e)s].

망국(亡國) the ruin of one's country; national ruin (decay). ¶ ~적(인) ruinous to one's country / ~지한(之恨) lamentation (grief) over the national ruin.

망그뜨리다 break down; damage; ruin; disable; destroy.

망그지다 break; be put out of shape; be damaged (broken, destroyed, ruined); get out of order.

망극(罔極) ~하다 《은혜가》 (be) immeasurable; great; immense; 《슬픔》 (be) grievous; be deeply in sorrow(서적으). ¶ 성은이 ~ 하나이다 Immeasurable are the King's favors.

망나니 ① 《사형 집행인》 an executioner. ② 《못된 사람》 a wretch; a rogue; a villain; a scoundrel.

망년회(忘年會) a year-end party.

망동(妄動) a rash (reckless) act. ~하다 act blindly; commit a rash act.

망둥이(魚) a goby fish.

망라(網羅) ~하다 《포함》 include; comprise; contain; comprehend; 《모으다》 bring together; collect. ¶ 총~ exhaustive; comprehensive; (thorough) and complete.

망령(亡靈) a departed spirit (soul).

망령(妄靈) dotage; senility. ¶ ~되다 be childish; foolish; silly; absurd; unreasonable / ~ 들다 be in one's dotage; be in one's second childhood; be senile / ~ 부리다 behave like a child; commit an absurd act.

망루(望樓) a watchtower; an observation tower; a lookout.

망막(網膜) 〔解〕 the retina. ‖ ~ 검시경 a retinoscope; a skiascope / ~염 〔醫〕 retinitis.

망망(茫茫) ~하다 (be) vast; extensive; boundless. ‖ ~대해 an immense expanse of water.

망명(亡命) exile(국외로); (적국으로의). ~하다 exile oneself; seek (take) refuge 《in》; flee (defect) from one's own country 《for political reasons》. ¶ 미국으로 ~하다 seek (take) refuge (asylum) in America / ~을 요청 하다 ask for political asylum 《in France》. ‖ ~객〔자〕 an exile; a (political) refugee; a defector / ~ 정권 an exiled government 《regime》.

망발(妄發) thoughtless words; a reckless remark. ~하다 make an absurd (thoughtless, disgraceful) remark. ‖ ~ 풀이 a treat given to make up for one's thoughtless remarks.

망부(亡父) one's deceased father.

망부(亡夫) one's deceased husband.

망사(網紗) gauze. [band.

망상(妄想) a wild fancy; a fantastic idea; a delusion. ¶ ~에 빠지다 be lost in wild fancies / ~에 시달리다 suffer from delusions / ~을 품다 hold delusions in the mind.

망상(網狀) reticulation. ¶ ~의 netlike; reticular; net-shaped. ‖ ~섬유 a reticulum / ~조직 a retiform tissue; a network 《of tiny vessels》.

망상스럽다 (be) frivolous; saucy; impertinent. [marionette.

망석중이 《꼭두각시》 a puppet; a

망설이다 hesitate; scruple; waver; be irresolute. ¶ 망설이면 hesitatingly / 망설이지 않고 without hesitation; unhesitatingly / 갈까 말 까 ~ can't make up one's mind whether to go or not.

망신(亡身) a disgrace; a shame; humiliation. ~하다 disgrace oneself; be disgraced. ~시키다 disgrace; bring shame on; put 《a person》 out of countenance.

망실(亡失) loss. ~하다 lose.

망아지 a pony; a foal; a colt(수 컷); a filly(암컷).

망양지탄(望洋之歎) lamenting one's inability (to cope with a situation); a feeling of hopelessness (total incapacity).

망언(妄言) thoughtless words; reckless remarks. ~하다 make an absurd remark.

망연(茫然) ① 《정신없음》 ¶ ~ 히 vacantly; blankly; absentmindedly; in dumb surprise / ~자 실하다 be stunned (stupefied) 《at, by》; be dumbfounded; be struck dumb with surprise. ② ☞ 아득하다.

망울 ① 《덩어리》 a (hard) lump; a bud 《꽃망울》. ② 〔醫〕 an enlarged lymph node; lymphadenoma. [ic sight.

망원가능자(望遠 —) 〔理〕 a telescopic

망원경(望遠鏡) a telescope; a spyglass; field glasses(쌍안경). ¶ ~ 으로 보다 look at 《a star》 through a telescope. / 유료~ a pay telescope.

망원렌즈(望遠 —) a telephoto lens.

망원사진(望遠寫眞) a telephoto-

망월(望月) 〔보름달〕 a full moon.
망인(亡人) the deceased.
망일(望日) a full-moon day.
망조(亡兆) an omen of ruin. ¶ ~가 들다 show signs of ruin; be doomed to ruin.
망주석(望柱石) a pair of stone posts in front of a tomb.
망중한(忙中閑) a moment of relief from busy hours; a break. ¶ ~을 즐기다 enjoy some leisure in the intervals of one's work.
망처(亡妻) one's deceased wife.
망측하다(罔測-) (be) absurd; (상스러움) (be) low; mean; indecent; nasty; (꼴사나움) (be) ugly; unsightly; unshapely.
망치 a hammer; a sledge(hammer). ¶ ~질 hammering (~질하다 hammer).
망치다 spoil; ruin; destroy; frustrate; make a mess (of). ¶ 신세를 ~ ruin oneself; make a failure of one's life.
망태기(網-) a mesh bag.
망토 a mantle; a cloak.
망판(網版) [印·寫] a halftone; a halftone plate (block).
망하다(亡-) ① 〔멸망〕 fall; perish; die out; 〔영락〕 be ruined; go to ruin; fall (sink) low; go in reduced circumstance; 〔파산〕 go (become) bankrupt; fail. ¶ 망할 위험에 처해 있다 be in danger of perishing / 망해 (할) be ruined) together / 망해서 거지가 되다 be reduced to beggary / 그 나라는 3,000년 전에 망했다 The country perished 3,000 years ago. / 그 회사는 망했다 The company went 「bankrupt 〔under〕. ② 〔어렵다〕 be hard to deal with. ¶ 그 책은 읽기가 ~ The book is hard to read.
망향(望鄕) homesickness; nostalgia. ¶ ~병에 걸리다 become (get) homesick. 「each other.
맞... 마주. ¶ ~보다 look at
맞고소(-告訴) a cross (counter) action. ~하다 counterclaim (against).
맞다¹ ① 〔정확〕 be right (correct); keep good time (시계가). ¶ 꼭 ~ be perfectly correct (계산이). ② 〔어울림〕 become; suit; match well; go well (with). ¶ 복장을 장소에 맞도록 하다 suit one's clothes to the occasion / 그 넥타이는 옷과 잘 맞는다 The tie goes well with your coat. ③ 〔옷·크기 등이〕 fit; suit; be fitted (to); 〔알맞다〕 be suitable; suit; serve (the purpose). ¶ 잘 맞는 옷 well fitting clothes; a good fit / 쐐기가 구멍에 ~ a wedge fits in a hole / 체질에 맞는 음식 food suitable to one's constitution / 마음에 ~ suit (a person's) taste (fancy). ④ 〔일치〕 agree (with); be in accord (with). ¶ 서로 의견이 ~ agree with each other / 이 사본은 원본과 맞지 않는다 This copy does not agree with the original. ⑤ 〔적중〕 hit; come true (예상이); 〔대비·복권이〕 draw; win. ¶ 화살이 과녁에 ~ an arrow hits the mark / 복권이 ~ draw (get) a lottery prize. ⑥ 〔수지가〕 pay. ¶ 수지 맞는 장사 a paying business.
맞다² ① 〔영접〕 meet; receive. ¶ ~를 반가이 welcome (a person); receive (a person) with delight / 정거장에서 ~ meet (a person) at the station. ② 〔맞아들임〕 invite; engage. ¶ 아내를 ~ take a wife; get married / 새 비서를 ~ engage a new secretary. ③ 〔맞이〕 새해를 ~ greet the New Year / 생일을 ~ meet one's (53rd) birthday. ④ 〔비바람 등〕 be exposed to (rain); expose oneself to. ⑤ 〔매를〕 get a blow; be struck; be shot (총탄을). ¶ 머리에 ~ be struck on the head. ⑥ 〔당하다〕 meet with; come across; suffer. ¶ 도둑을 ~ have (a thing) stolen; be stolen (금품이 주어) / 단단히 ~ get (have) a scolding / 퇴짜를 ~ get rejected. ⑦ 〔주사를〕 get (have) (an injection); 〔침을〕 get acupunctured.
맞닥뜨리다 be faced with; be confronted with; encounter.
맞담배 ¶ ~질을 하다 smoke to (a person's) face.
맞당기다 draw (pull) each other.
맞닿다 touch each other; meet.
맞대다 bring (a person) face to face with (another); confront (a person) with (another); bring (join) (something) together. ¶ 아무와 얼굴을 ~ come face to face with a person / 얼굴을 맞대고 앉았다 We sat facing each other. / 그에 관해 무릎을 맞대고 이야기하다 (비유적) have a heart-to-heart talk about (it).
맞대하다(-對-) face (confront) each other.
맞돈 cash payment; payment in cash; cash (down). ¶ ~으로 사다 〔팔다〕 buy (sell) (a thing) for cash. 「thing) together.
맞들다 lift together; hold up (a
맞먹다 〔필적하다〕 be equal (to); be a match for; be equivalent to. ¶ 월급 2개월분과 맞먹는 보너스 a bonus equivalent to two month's pay.
맞물다 bite each other; gear (into,

맞바꾸다 *with*》; engage 《*with*》. ¶ 맞물리다 be [go] in gear 《*with*》.
맞바꾸다 exchange 《*a watch for a camera*》; barter. ¶ 〜 《*of paduk*》.
맞바둑 an unhandicapped match
맞바람 a head wind.
맞받다 《정면으로》 receive [face] directly; 《들이받다》 run [clash] against [into]; collide head-on 《*with*》; 《응수》 give 《*a person*》 tit for tat; (make a) retort.
맞벌이 ¶ 〜하다 earn a livelihood together; work [run] in double harness. ‖ 〜가정 [생활] a double-income [two-income] family [living] / 〜부부 a working couple.
맞부딪치다 run [crash] into; run [collide, hit] against. ☞ 충돌.
맞붙다 《싸움 따위》 wrestle [grapple] 《*with*》; be matched against; tackle 《*a difficult problem*》.
맞붙이다 《물건을》 stick [paste, fix, join] 《*things*》 together; 《사람을》 bring 《*them*》 together [into contact]; match 《*A*》 with [against] 《*B*》.
맞상대(―相對) direct confrontation.
맞서다 《마주서다》 stand face to face 《*with*》; face each other; confront; 《대항하다》 stand [fight] 《*against*》; oppose; defy.
맞선 an arranged meeting with a view to marriage. ¶ 〜보다 meet [see] each other with a view to marriage / 〜보고 하는 결혼 an arranged marriage.
맞소송(―訴訟) a cross action; a counterclaim.
맞수(―手) a (good) match.
맞아떨어지다 tally; be correct.
맞은편(―便) the opposite side. ¶ 〜에 opposite; on the opposite side of.
맞잡다 《잡다》 take [hold] together [each other]; 《드잡이》 grapple with each other; 《협력》 cooperate 《*with*》; collaborate 《*with*》; work together. ¶ 손에 손을 맞잡고 hand in hand 《*with*》.
맞잡이 an equal; a match.
맞장구치다 chime in 《*with*》.
맞장기(―將棋) even-match chess. ¶ 〜를 두다 play chess on even terms.
맞절하다 bow to each other.
맞추다 ① 《짜맞춤》 put together; assemble; fit into (끼워). ② 《맞게끔》 set [fit, suit] 《*a thing to another*》; adjust 《*a radio dial*》. ¶ 시계를 〜 set *one's* watch 《*by the radio*》. ③ 《대조》 compare 《*with*》; check (up). ¶ 계산을 맞추어 보다 check accounts. ¶ 《주문》 order; give an order. ¶ 양복을 〜 order a suit; have a suit made / 특별히 맞춘 구두 shoes specially made to order.
맞춤 《주문》 an order; 《물건》 the order; the article ordered. ‖ 〜옷 a custom-made suit; a suit made to order.
맞춤법(―法) the rules of spelling; orthography. ‖ 〜통일안 a draft for unified [standardized] spelling system.
맞흥정 a direct [face-to-face] deal. 〜하다 make a direct bargain [deal].
맞히다 ① 《알아 맞히다》 guess right; give a right answer. ¶ 잘못 〜 guess wrong. ② 《명중》 hit; strike. ¶ 맞히지 못하다 miss the mark. ③ 《눈·비 따위》 expose 《*to*》. ¶ 비를 〜 expose to the rain; put out in the rain.
맡기다 ① 《보관》 leave [deposit] 《*a thing with a person*》; entrust 《*a person with a thing*》. ¶ 돈을 은행에 〜 put money in a bank / 짐을 〜 check *one's* baggage. ② 《위임》 entrust [leave] 《*a matter*》 to 《*a person*》. ¶ 임무를 〜 charge 《*a person*》 with a duty / 운을 하늘에 〜 trust to chance [luck]; leave 《*a thing*》 to chance.

맡다¹ ① 《보관》 be entrusted with 《*money*》; keep; receive 《*a thing*》 in trust. ¶ 이 돈을 맡아 주시오 Please keep this money for me. ② 《담임·감독》 take (be in) charge of; take care of; 《떠맡기》 take 《*a task*》 upon *oneself*; 《역할을》 play (the role of). ¶ 5학년을 〜 have charge of the fifth-year class. ③ 《허가를》 get; receive; secure; obtain 《*permission*》. ¶ 허가 맡고 영업하다 do business under license.
맡다² ① 《냄새를》 smell; sniff 《*at*》; scent. ¶ 맡아 보다 give a sniff to; sniff at; have [take] a smell at. ② 《낌새를》 sense; get wind 《*scent of a plot*》; smell out 《*the secret*》.
매 《때리는》 a whip; a cane; whipping (때림). ¶ 〜를 때리다 whip; flog; beat; give 《*a person*》 a blow / 〜를 맞다 be whipped [flogged]; be beaten [struck, hit].
매² 《맷돌》 a millstone.
매³ 《鳥》 a goshawk; a hawk; a falcon. ¶ 〜사냥 hawking; falconry. 〜 every Sunday.
매…(毎) every; each. ¶ 〜일요일
매가(買價) a purchase price.
매가(賣家) a house for sale.
매가(賣價) a sale [labeled] price. ¶ 이것을 〜의 반으로 드리죠 I offer this at half the sale price.
매각(賣却) disposal by sale. 〜하다 sell (off); dispose of. ‖ 〜공고 a public notice of sale.

매개(媒介) mediation. ~하다 mediate 《between two parties》; carry 《germs》. ¶ …의 ~로 through the medium 《good offices》 of. ‖ ~물 a medium; a carrier 《병균의》/ ~자 a mediator; a middleman. 〔cept: the mean term.
매개념(媒概念) 〖論〗 the middle con-
매거(枚擧) 낱낱이 말함; 하나하나 enumerate; mention one by one. ¶ 이루 다 ~할 수 없다 be too many to mention 〔enumerate〕.
매관매직(賣官賣職) ~하다 traffic in government posts.
매국(賣國) betrayal of 《selling》 one's country. ‖ ~노 a traitor to one's country; a betrayer of one's country. 〔od〕.
매기(每期) each 〔every〕 term 〔peri-
매기(買氣) a buying tendency; 〔證〕 a bullish sentiment.
매기다 값을 put 《a price》 on; fix; bid; 〔등급을〕 grade; classify; give 《marks》 《점수를》; 〔번호를〕 number.   〔pery.
매끄럽다 〔be〕 smooth; slimy; slip-
매끈하다 ☞ 미끈하다.
매나니 〔맨손〕 an empty 〔a bare〕 hand. ¶ ~로 with empty hands; empty-handed / ~로 사업을 시작하다 start a business with no capital.
매너 (have good) manners.
매너리즘 (fall into) mannerism.
매년(每年) every 〔each〕 year; 〔부사적〕 annually. ¶ ~의 yearly.
매니저 a manager.   〔annual.
매니큐어 (a) manicure. ¶ ~를 칠하다 paint one's nails.
매다¹ 〔동이다〕 tie (up); bind; fasten; 〔목을〕 hang oneself. ¶ 구두 끈을 ~ tie a shoestring.
매다² 〔김을〕 weed out. 〔monthly.
매달(每月) every month. ¶ ~의
매달다 ① 〔달아맴〕 hang; suspend; attach 〔fasten〕 《to》 《부착》. ② 〔일·직장에〕 tie oneself down 《bind oneself to》. ¶ 회사에 목숨을 ~ be tied hand and soul to the company.
매달리다 ① 〔늘어짐〕 hang 〔be suspended〕 《from》; dangle 《from》. ② 〔붙잡다〕 cling 〔hold on〕 《to a rope》; hang 《on》; 〔애원〕 entreat; implore. ③ 〔의지〕 depend 〔rely, lean〕 《up》on.
매대기¹ ~치다 smear 〔daub〕 all over.
매도(罵倒) denunciation. ~하다 abuse; denounce.
매도(賣渡) ~하다 sell 《a thing》 over to 《a person》; deliver; negotiate 〔어음을〕. ‖ ~가격 the sale 〔selling〕 price / ~계약 a contract for selling / ~인 a seller / ~증서 a bill of sale.
매독(梅毒) (get, contract) syphilis.

¶ ~성의 syphilitic. ‖ ~환자 a syphilitic.
매듭 a knot; a tie. ¶ ~을 맺다 〔풀다〕 make 〔untie〕 a knot.
매듭짓다 settle; conclude; complete; put an end to. ¶ 일을 ~ conclude one's work / 연구를 ~ round off one's researches / 협상을 ~ bring the negotiations to a successful close.
매력(魅力) (a) charm; (a) fascination. ¶ ~있는 charming; attractive / 성적 ~ a sex appeal.
매료(魅了) ~하다 charm; fascinate; enchant.
매립(埋立) (land) reclamation. ~하다 fill up; reclaim. ¶ 신공항 건설을 위해 바다를 ~하다 reclaim land from the sea to build a new airport. ‖ ~공사 reclamation work / ~지 a reclaimed land.
매만지다 smooth down 《one's hair》; trim; adjust one's dress.
매매(賣買) buying and selling; purchase and sale; 《거래》 trade; dealing; a bargain. ~하다 buy and sell; deal 〔trade〕 《in》. ¶ ~계약을 맺다 make a sales contract 《with》. ‖ ~가격 the sale 〔selling〕 price / ~조건 terms of sale / 견본 ~ a sale by sample.
매머드 《거대한》 mammoth. ¶ ~기업 a mammoth enterprise.
매명(賣名) self-advertisement. ~하다 advertise oneself; seek publicity. ‖ ~가 a self-advertiser; a publicity seeker / ~행위 an act of self-advertisement; publicity stunts.
매몰(埋沒) ~하다 bury 《under, in》. ~되다 be 〔lie〕 buried 《in》.
매몰스럽다 〔be〕 heartless; cold; unkind.
매무시 primping. ~하다 primp 《oneself》. ¶ ~가 단정하다 keep oneself neat and trim; be careful about one's personal appearance.
매문(賣文) literary hackwork.
매물(賣物) an article for 〔on〕 sale; "For Sale" 《게시》. ¶ ~로 내놓다 offer 《a thing》 for sale.
매미 〖蟲〗 a cicada; a locust 《美》. ¶ ~소리 the shrill chirrup of a cicada. 〔time; 《자주》 very often.
매번(每番) 《때마다》 each 〔every〕
매복(埋伏) ~하다 lie in ambush 〔wait〕 《for》; waylay.
매부(妹夫) one's brother-in-law; one's sister's husband.
매부리 《매 부리는 사람》 a hawker; a falconer; 《매의 주둥이》 a hawk's beak. ‖ ~코 a hooked 〔a Roman〕 nose.
매사(每事) every business 〔mat-

매상(買上) ~하다 a purchase; buy. ‖ ~가격 the (government's) purchasing price.

매상(賣上) sales; receipts. ¶ 그날의 ~을 계산하다 count the receipts for the day / ~이 크게 늘었다〔줄었다〕 Sales have picked up (fallen off) considerably. ‖ ~고 sales (volume) / ~금 proceeds; takings〔학교축제 ~금 the proceeds from the school festival〕/ ~세(稅) VAT (◀ *value-added tax*) / ~장부〔전표〕a sales book (slip).

매석(賣惜) an indisposition to sell. ~하다 be indisposed to sell; be unwilling to sell.

매설(埋設) ~하다 lay (*cables*) under the ground.

매섭다 (be) fierce; sharp; severe.

매수(買收) ~하다 purchase; buy up (out); (뇌물로) bribe (buy over) (*a person*). ‖ ~합병 mergers and acquisition (생략 M & A).

매수(買受) ~하다 buy (take) over; acquire (*a thing*) by purchase. ‖ ~인 a buyer; a purchaser.

매스게임 a mass (group) game.

매스미디어 the mass media.

매스커뮤니케이션 mass communications.

매시(每時) every hour; per hour.

매식(買食) ~하다 eat out; take (have) a meal at a restaurant.

매실(梅實) a *maesil*; a Japanese apricot. ‖ ~주 *maesil* liquor; spirits flavored with *maesil*.

매씨(妹氏) your (his) sister.

매암돌다 spin oneself round; whirl. 「round.

매암돌리다 spin (turn) (*a person*)

매약(賣藥) a patent medicine; a drug. ~하다 sell patent medicines. 「time.

매양(每-) always; every (all the)

매연(煤煙) soot and smoke. ¶ ~이 많은〔적은〕도시 a smoky (smokeless) city. / ~공해 smoke pollution / ~차량 harmful-gas emitting vehicles.

매염(媒染) mordanting. ‖ ~료〔제〕(劑) a mordant; a fixative.

매우 very (much); greatly; awfully. ¶ ~ 덥다 be very hot.

매운탕(-湯) a pepper-pot soup.

매월(每月) every (each) month.

매음(賣淫) prostitution. ~하다 practice prostitution; walk the streets. ¶ ~굴 a brothel / ~녀〔부〕a prostitute; a streetwalker; a call girl / ~방지법 the Anti-Prostitution Law.

매이다 (끈으로) be tied (*to*); be fastened; (일에) be fettered (*to one's task*); be tied down (*to*);

be bound (*by a rule*). ¶ 매인 데 없는 free.

매인(每人) each man; every one. ‖ ~당 per head (capita) for each person.

매일(每日) every day; daily. ¶ ~의 daily; everyday / ~의 일 daily works / ~ 같이 almost every day.

매일반(一一般) ☞ 매한가지.

매입(買入) buying; purchase. ~하다 purchase; buy in; lay in; take in. ‖ ~원가 the purchase price (cost).

매장(埋葬) ①(시체의) (a) burial; (an) internment. ~하다 bury. ‖ ~비 cost of burial / ~식 (perform) the burial service / ~지 a burial place (ground) / ~허가증 a burial certificate (permit). ②(사회적) social ostracism. ~하다 ostracize; oust (*a person*) from society.

매장(埋藏) ~하다 (묻다) hide underground; bury in the ground; (땅이 자원을) have (*oil*) deposits underground. ‖ ~량 reserves / 석탄 ~량 the estimated amount of coal deposits. 「shop; a store.

매장(賣場) a counter; (점포) a

매절(賣切) being sold out. 「~매진.

매점(買占) a corner; cornering. ~하다 corner the market (*in wheat*); buy up (*all the coffee in the market*); corner (*the soybean market*); hoard.

매점(賣店) a stand; a stall; a booth. ¶ 역의 ~ a station stall / ~을 내다 install a booth; set up a stand (stall).

매정스럽다 (be) cold; icy; heartless; unfeeling. ¶ 매정스럽다 be hard on (*a person*); treat coldly / 매정스럽게 거절하다 give a point-blank refusal.

매제(妹弟) a younger sister's husband; a brother-in-law.

매주(每週) every week; weekly; per week (1주일마다).

매주(買主) a buyer (purchaser).

매주(賣主) a seller (dealer).

매직 magic. ‖ ~아이 a magic eye / ~유리 one-way glass / ~잉크 Magic ink (상표).

매진(賣盡) (다 팔림) a sellout; (게시) Sold Out (today). ~하다 be sold out; run out of stock.

매진(邁進) ~하다 go forward (on) (undaunted); strive (*for*).

매질 thrashing; whipping. ~하다 whip; flog; beat.

매체(媒體) a medium [*pl.* media, ~s]. ¶ 공기는 소리를 전하는 ~의 하나다 Air is one of the mediums of sound.

매축(埋築) reclamation; filling-up. ~하다 reclaim (*land from*

매춘(賣春) ☞ 매음.
매출(賣出) a sale; selling. ¶ ~하다 sell off [out]; put 《a thing》 on sale. ¶ ~가격 an offering price.
매치(競技) a match.
매캐하다(연기가) (be) smoky; (곰팡내가) (be) musty; moldy.
매콤하다 (be) hot; pungent.
매트 (spread) a mat.
매트리스 a mattress.
매파(一派) a hawk; a hard-liner.
매판자본(買辦資本) comprador capital.
매팔자(一八字) a free and easy mode of life. ¶ ~다 lead an easy life; be comfortably off.
매표(賣票) ¶ ~구(口) a ticket window / ~소 a ticket [booking 《英》] office; a box office.
매품(賣品) goods for sale; merchandise; "For sale." (게시).
매한가지 all the same; (much) the same. ¶ …는 ~다 be as good as 《dead, new》; be little [no] better than 《a beggar》; might as well 《throw money away》 as 《spend it on bicycle races》.
매형(妹兄) one's elder sister's husband; a brother-in-law.
매호(每戶) every house(hold).
매혹(魅惑) fascination; captivation. ¶ ~하다 fascinate; charm; enchant. ¶ ~시키는 charming; captivating; fascinating; ~되다 be charmed [fascinated].
매화(梅花) 〔植〕 a maehwa (Japanese apricot) tree(나무); a maehwa blossom(꽃).
맥(脈)〔맥박〕 the pulse. ¶ ~을 짚어 보고 feel the pulse / ~이 뛰다 pulsate; the pulse beats.
맥고모자(麥藁帽子) a straw hat.
맥관(脈管) ①〔혈맥〕 (the system of) veins. ②〔사물의〕 (a thread of) connection; coherence; the intricacies (내용).
맥류(麥類) barley, wheat, etc.
맥막하다 ①(코가) (be) stuffy; be stuffed up (서술적). ②〔생각이〕 be stuck 《for an idea》; be at a loss (서술적).
맥박(脈搏) pulsation; (the stroke of) the pulse. ¶ ~계(計) a pulsimeter; a sphygmometer / ~수 pulse frequency; pulse rate.
맥보다(脈一) ①〔맥박을〕 feel [take] the pulse. ②〔남의 의중을〕 sound 《a person on a subject》; sound out 《a person's view》.
맥빠지다(脈一) ①〔기운 없다〕 be worn out [spent up]. ②〔낙심〕 be disappointed [damped].
맥아(麥芽) ☞ 엿기름. ¶ ~당 maltose; malt sugar.
맥없다(脈一) ①〔기운 없다〕 (be) enervated; feeble; 〔서술적〕 be exhausted [spent up]; feel depressed; be dispirited (풀없다).
맥없이 feebly; spiritlessly; helplessly; easily(무르게). ¶ ~이 없이 다〕 맥없이 without any reason; for no reason.
맥작(麥作) barley culture [crop].
맥적다 ①〔따분하다〕 be tedious; dull. ②〔낯없다〕 be ashamed of oneself; be put out of countenance.
맥주(麥酒) beer; ale. ¶ 김빠진 ~ stale [flat] beer / ~ 한 잔 하다 have (a glass) of beer. ¶ ~거품 froth (foam) of beer / ~집 [홀] a beer hall.
맨 (오로지) nothing but [else]; just; full of; (가장) (ut)most; extreme. ¶ ~ 꼴찌 the very last [bottom] / ~ 먼저 at the very first; first of all / ~ 거짓말이다 be full of falsehood.
맨…(안 섞인) just; bare; naked; unadulterated. ¶ ~바닥 the bare floor / ~손 an empty [bare] hand.
맨나중 the very last [end]. ¶ ~의 final; terminal / ~에 finally; at the very last(end); lastly.
맨드라미 〔植〕 a cockscomb.
맨땅 (sit on) the bare ground.
맨머리 a bare head; a hatless head.
맨먼저 the beginning(최초); at the very first [beginning] (최초의); first of all (우선).
맨몸 ①〔알몸〕 a naked body; a nude. ②〔무일푼〕 being penniless; an empty hand.
맨발 bare feet. ¶ ~의 barefoot(ed) / ~로 (walk) barefoot.
맨밥 boiled rice served without any side dishes. (class of)
맨션 an apartment of better class.
맨손 an empty [a bare] hand. ¶ ~체조 free gymnastics.
맨숭맨숭하다 (be) hairless (털 없다); bare; bald(민둥민둥하다); sober (술이 취하지 않다).
맨아래 the very bottom. ¶ ~의 the lowest; the undermost.
맨앞 the foremost; the (very) front; the head. ¶ ~의 foremost / ~에 at the head (of).
맨위 the (very) top; the summit; the peak. ¶ ~의 topmost; highest; uppermost / ~에 on (the) top (of).
맨입 (start) with empty stomach.
맨주먹 a naked fist; an empty [bare] hand. ¶ ~으로 큰 돈을 모으다 make a fortune starting with nothing.

맨투맨 ‖ ~ 방어 a man-to-man defense.
맨틀피스 a mantelpiece.
맨홀 a manhole. ¶ ~ 뚜껑 a manhole cover.
맬서스 Malthus. ‖ ~ 주의 Malthusianism.
맴돌다 ☞ 매암돌다.
맵다 (맛이) (be) hot; pungent; 《혹독》 (be) intense; severe; strict. ¶ 매운 추위 the intense cold.
맵시 figure; shapeliness. ¶ ~ 있는 smart; shapely; well-formed. ¶ 옷~ the cut of one's clothes.
맷돌 a hand mill; a millstone. ¶ ~ 질하다 grind grain in a stone mill.
맹격(猛擊) (strike) a hard blow 《at, on》; (make) a violent attack 《on》.
맹견(猛犬) a fierce [ferocious] dog. ¶ ~ 주의 "Beware of the Dog!" (게시).
맹공격(猛攻擊) a fierce attack; a violent assault. ~ 하다 make a vigorous attack 《on》.
맹금(猛禽) ‖ ~ 류 birds of prey.
맹꽁이 〔動〕 a kind of small round frog; 〔멍청〕 a bird-brain; a simpleton; a blockhead. ¶ ~ 자물쇠 a padlock.
맹도견(盲導犬) a seeing-eye [guide] dog.
맹독(猛毒) (a) deadly poison. ¶ ~ 을 가진 뱀 a highly poisonous snake.
맹랑하다(孟浪―) (허망) (be) false; untrue; (믿을 수 없다) (be) incredible; (터무니없다) (be) groundless; absurd; nonsensical; (만만찮다) (be) no small; not negligible. ¶ 맹랑한 설 groundless [unreliable] views / 맹랑한 소문을 퍼뜨리다 set wild rumors afloat.
맹렬(猛烈) ~ 하다 (be) violent; furious; fierce. ~ 히 violently; furiously; fiercely / ~ 한 반대 strong opposition.
맹목(盲目) ¶ ~ 적(으로) blind(ly); reckless(ly) / ~ 적인 사랑 [모방] blind love [imitation].
맹물 ① 〔물〕 fresh [plain] water. ② 〔사람〕 a spineless [dull] person; a jellyfish.
맹방(盟邦) an ally; an allied nation.
맹성(猛省) serious reflection. ~ 하다 reflect on 《something》 seriously. ¶ ~ 을 촉구하다 urge 《a person》 to reflect seriously.
맹세 an oath; a pledge; a vow. ~ 하다 swear; vow; take an oath; give one's pledge. ¶ ~ 코 upon my honor [word]; by God / ~ 을 지키다 [어기다] keep [break] one's vow [oath, pledge].
맹수(猛獸) a fierce animal. ‖ ~ 사냥 《go》 a big-game hunting.
맹습(猛襲) a vigorous [fierce]

attack. ~ 하다 make a fierce attack 《on》.
맹신(盲信) blind [unquestioning] acceptance 《of a theory》; blind faith. ~ 하다 give hasty credit 《to》; believe blindly.
맹아(盲啞) the blind and dumb. ‖ ~ 학교 a blind and dumb school.
맹약(盟約) 〔서약〕 a pledge; a covenant; a pact; 〔동맹〕 alliance; a league. ~ 하다 make [form] a pact 《with》; form an alliance.
맹연습(猛練習) ~ 하다 do hard training; train hard; carry out vigorous practice.
맹위(猛威) fierceness; ferocity; fury. ¶ ~ 를 떨치다 《사물이》 rage; be rampant; 《사람이》 exercise overwhelming influence 《over》.
맹인(盲人) a blind person; the blind(층칭).
맹자(孟子) Mencius.
맹장(盲腸) the blind gut; the appendix. ¶ ~ 수술을 받다 have an operation for appendicitis. ‖ ~ 염 appendicitis.
맹장(猛將) a brave general; a veteran fighter.
맹점(盲點) a blind spot. ¶ 법의 ~ a loophole [blind spot] in the law / ~ 을 찌르다 pinpoint a weak point.
맹종(盲從) blind [unquestioning] obedience. ~ 하다 follow [obey] blindly.
맹주(盟主) a leader of a confederation. ¶ ~ 가 되다 become the leader of.
맹진(猛進) ~ 하다 dash forward.
맹추 a stupid [thickheaded] person.〔hit〕.
맹타(猛打) 《give》 a heavy blow
맹탕(국물) insipid [watery] soup; 《사람》 a dull [flat] person.
맹폭(盲爆) blind [indiscriminate] bombing. ~ 하다 bomb blindly.
맹폭(猛爆) heavy bombing. ~ 하다 bomb [bombard] heavily.
맹호(猛虎) a fierce tiger.
맹활동(猛活動) vigorous activity. ~ 하다 be in full activity 《swing》.
맹휴(盟休) a strike; a school strike. ☞ 동맹휴교.
맺다 ① (끈·매듭을) (make) a knot; tie (up). ② (끝을) finish; complete; conclude. ¶ ~ 에 대한 전망을 말하며 강연을 ~ conclude one's speech by giving one's own view on. ③ (계약·관계를) make 《a contract》; conclude 《a treaty》; form 《a connection with》; enter (into) 《a relation with》. ¶ 교우 관계를 ~ form a friendship 《with》 / 동맹을 ~ enter into an alliance

맺히다 〈with a nation〉. ④ 〈열매를〉 bear 〈fruit〉. ⑤ 〈원한을〉 bear; harbor 〈an enmity toward〉.

맺히다 ① 〈매듭이〉 be tied; be knotted. ② 〈열매가〉 come into bearing; fruit; 〈go to〉 seed. ③ 〈원한이〉 be pent up; smolder. ¶ 원한이 ~ have a long smoldering grudge. ④ 〈눈물·이슬이〉 form. ¶ 이슬이 ~ dew forms; be dewy.

머금다 ① 〈입에〉 keep 〈hold〉 〈water〉 in one's mouth. ② 〈마음에〉 bear in mind; bear 〈malice to〉. ③ 〈기타〉 눈물을 ~ have tears in one's eyes / 이슬을 ~ have dew on 〈it〉; be dewy / 웃음을 ~ wear a smile.

머루 〖植〗 wild grapes 〔grapevines〕.

머리 ① 〈두부〉 the head. ¶ ~가 아프다 have a headache / ~ 에 at one's bedside. ② 〈두뇌·기억력〉 a brain; a head; mind. ¶ ~를 쓰다 use one's head / ~ 가 좋다 have a clear head / ~ 회전이 빠르다 〔더디다〕 have a quick 〔slow〕 mind; be quick-witted 〔slow-witted〕. ③ 〈머리털〉 hair. ¶ ~를 감다 wash one's hair; shampoo one's hair / ~를 깎다 have 〔get〕 one's hair cut / ~를 묶다 dress 〔fix, do up〕 one's hair / 긴 〔짧은〕 ~ 모양을 하고 있다 wear one's hair long 〔short〕. ¶ ~채 a long tress of hair / ~핀 a hairpin. ④ 〈사물의 머리·끝〉 the top 〔head〕 〈of〉. ¶ 기둥 ~ the top of a pillar / 못의 ~ the head of a nail.

머리끝 ¶ ~에서 발끝까지 from top 〔head〕 to toe / ~이 쭈뼛해지다 one's hair stands on end.

머리띠 a headband.

머리말 a preface; a foreword.

머리카락 ☞ 머리털.

머리털 one's hair; the hair on the head. ¶ ~이 자꾸 빠지다 one's hair is thinning / ~의 색깔 the color of one's hair.

머릿기름 hair oil; pomade.

머릿수 (─數) the number of persons; a head 〔nose〕 count.

머무르다 〈묵다〉 stay; stop; put up 〈at an inn〉; 〈남다〉 remain. ¶ 현직에 ~ remain in one's present office.

머무적거리다 hesitate; waver; linger; 〈말을〉 mumble; falter. ¶ 머무적거리며 hesitatingly / 머무적머무적 hesitantly; diffidently / 대답을 못하고 ~ be hesitant to make an answer.

머슴 a farmhand; a farmer's man. ¶ ~살이 the life of a farmhand.

머쓱하다 ① 〈키가〉 (be) lanky. ② 〈기가 죽다〉 (be) in low spirits.

머위 〖植〗 a butterbur.

머줍다 (be) dull; slow; sluggish.

머츰하다 stop 〔cease〕 for a while; break; lull; hold up.

머큐로크롬 mercurochrome.

머플러 a muffler.

먹 an ink stick. ¶ ~을 갈다 rub down an ink stick.

먹구름 dark 〔black〕 clouds.

먹다 ① 〈음식 따위를〉 eat; take; have 〈one's meal〉. ¶ 먹어보다 try 〈the dish〉; taste / 다 ~ eat up all / 쌀을 먹고 살다 live on rice / 약을 ~ take medicine〈s〉. ② 〈생활하다〉 live on; 〈부양하다〉 support. ¶ 붓을 먹고 살다 live by one's pen / 가족을 먹여 살리다 support 〔provide for〕 one's family / 먹고 살기 어렵다 find it hard to make one's living. ③ 〈남의 재물을〉 seize; appropriate; embezzle. ¶ 뇌물을 ~ take 〔accept〕 a bribe. ④ 〈욕을〉 get 〈a scolding〉; be abused; be scolded. ⑤ 〈마음을〉 fix; set 〈one's mind on〉; make up one's mind 〈to〉. ⑥ 〈겁을〉 be scared; be frightened. ⑦ 〈나이를〉 grow 〔become, get〕 old〔er〕. ⑧ 〈벌레가〉 eat into; be worm-eaten. ⑨ 〈이문〉 get 〈a commission〉; receive; have. ⑩ 〈더위를〉 be affected by the heat. ⑪ 〈판돈·상금을〉 win 〔take〕 〈the prize〕. ⑫ 〈한대〉 be given a blow 〈맞음〉. ⑬ 〈녹을〉 receive 〈a stipend〉.

먹다 ① 〈귀가〉 lose the hearing; become deaf. ② 〈날이 잘 들다〉 bite 〔cut〕 well. ¶ 톱이 잘 ~ a saw bites 〔cuts〕 well. ③ 〈물감·풀이〉 dye 〈well〉; soak in 〈well〉. ④ 〈비용이〉 cost; be spent. ¶ 돈이 많이 ~ be costly 〔expensive〕.

먹먹하다 〈귀가〉 (be) deaf; deafened; stunned. ¶ 먹먹해지다 deaf.

먹물 Indian 〔Chinese〕 ink. 〔en.

먹성 ¶ ~이 좋다 have a good appetite; be omnivorous.

먹실 a string stained with ink; 〈문신〉 tattooing. ¶ ~넣다 tattoo 〈a flower on one's arm〉.

먹음새 the way of eating; table manners.

먹음직스럽다 (be) delicious-looking; appetizing; tempting.

먹이 〈양식〉 food; 〈사료〉 feed; fodder. ¶ ~의 ~ 가 되다 become food 〈for〉; become the prey of 〈야수〉 / ~를 찾다 〈야수가〉 seek for prey; forage for food.

먹이다 ① 〈음식을〉 let someone eat 〔drink〕; feed 〈cattle on grass〉. ¶ 젖을 ~ give the breast 〈to a baby〉. ② 〈가축을〉 keep; raise; rear. ③ 〈부양〉 support 〈one's fami-

먹자판 a scene of riotous eating; a big feast; a spree.

먹줄 an inking line; an inked string.

먹칠 ~하다 smear with (Chinese) ink; 《명예 따위에》 injure; disgrace; impair 《one's dignity》; mar.

먹통(一桶) ① 《목수의》 a carpenter's ink-pad. ② 《바보》 a fool.

먹히다 be eaten up 《by》; be devoured 《by》; 《먹을 수 있다》 can be eaten; be edible; 《빼앗기다》 be cheated of; be taken for; 《든 이》 require; cost. ¶ 먹느냐 먹히느냐의 싸움 a life-and-death struggle.

먼나라 a far-off land; a remote country.

먼눈 ① a blind eye. ② a distant view.

먼데 a distant place; a long way.

먼동 the dawning sky. ¶ ~ 트다 dawn; daybreak / ~이 트기 전에 before dawn (daybreak).

먼발치(기) somewhat distant place; far away.

먼빛으로 《view》 from afar; from a distance.

먼저 ① 《앞서》 go first (ahead). ② 《우선》 first (of all); above all; before anything (else). ¶ 《미리》 earlier (than); beforehand. ¶ 돈을 ~ 치르다 pay in advance. ④ 《전에》 previously; formerly. ¶ ~ 말한 바와 같이 as previously stated.

먼지 dust. ¶ ~ 투성이의 dusty / ~를 털다 dust 《one's coat》. ‖ ~ 떨이 a duster.

멀거니 vacantly; absent-mindedly; with a blank look.

멀겋다 《흐릿하다》 (be) dull; be a bit clear; 《묽다》 (be) wishy-washy; watery; sloppy.

말끔하다 be clean; cleanly; tidy.

멀다 ① 《거리가》 be far(-off); far-away; distant; 《…에서가》 a long way off; 《…까지》 (be) a long way to. ¶ 멀리 떨어지다 keep far away / 멀리 풀리나다. ② 《시간적으로》 remote. ¶ 머지 않아 soon; shortly; before long; in the near future / 먼 옛날에 in the far-off days. ③ 《관계가》 (be) distant. ¶ 먼 친척 a distant relative.

멀다 ② 《눈이》 go blind; lose one's sight; be blinded 《by》 《욕심에》. ¶ 돈에 눈이 멀어지다 be blinded by money.

멀떠구니 [鳥] a crop; a craw.

멀뚱멀뚱 《눈이》 vacantly; absent-mindedly. ¶ ~ 바라보다 gaze at 《a thing》 vacantly.

멀리 far away; in the (at a) distance. ¶ ~에서 from afar; from a distance / ~하다 keep away 《from》; drive off (물리치다); estrange (소원); abstain 《from》 (절제).

멀미 ① 《배·차의》 sickness; sea-sickness (배의); airsickness (비행기); carsickness (차). ~하다 get sick; feel nausea. ② 《진저리》 being fed up 《with》. ~하다 《나다》 get sick and tired 《of》; be fed up 《with》; become disgusted 《with》.

멀쑥하다 ① 《키가》 (be) lanky; lean and tall. ② 《묽다》 (be) watery; thin. ③ ☞ 말쑥하다.

멀어지다 go away 《from》; recede 《from view》; die away (소리 등이); be(come) alienated (estranged) 《from》 (관계가); come less frequently, fall away 《from》 (발길이).

멀쩡하다 ① 《온전》 (be) flawless; spotless; free from blemish; perfect; 《다친 데 없다》 (be) unhurt; unwounded; 《정신이》 (be) sane; sober. ② 《뻔뻔하다》 (be) impudent; shameless. ¶ 멀쩡한 거짓말 a barefaced lie / 멀쩡한 놈 a brazenfaced fellow. ③ 《부당》 (be) absurd; groundless (무근). ¶ 멀쩡한 소문 a groundless rumor.

멀찍막하다 (be) pretty far; rather distant.

멀찍하다 ☞ 멀찍막하다. ¶ 멀찍이 pretty far; far apart; away from; at a distance / 멀찍이 사이를 두다 leave a pretty long interval 《between》.

멈추다 《…이》 cease; halt; come to a stop; be interrupted; 《…을》 stop; break [lay] off; bring 《a thing》 to a stop; put a stop 《to》. ¶ 비가 멈주었다 It stopped raining. / 차를 ~ bring a car to a stop.

멈춧거리다 hesitate 《at; over》; shrink [hold] back; flinch 《from》.

멈칫하다 stop abruptly (for a moment); flinch 《from》; wince 《at》. ¶ 멈칫멈칫 hesitatingly; lingeringly / 하던 말을 ~ suddenly stop talking for a moment.

멋 《세련미》 dandyism; foppery. ¶ ~ 있는 smart(-looking); stylish; chic / ~으로 《wear glasses》 for show [appearance' sake] / ~을 부리다 [내다] dress stylishly [smartly]; dress oneself up; be foppish. ② 《풍치》 relish; flavor; taste; zest; pleasure; de-

멋대로 as *one* likes; at pleasure (will); willfully; waywardly. ¶ ~ 굴다 (하다) have *one's* own way (*in*).

멋들어지다 (be) nice; smart; stylish. ¶ 멋들어지게 smartly; nicely; fascinatingly; with zest.

멋없다 (be) not smart (stylish); tasteless; insipid; dull.

멋쟁이 (남자) a dandy; a fop; (여자) a dressy (chic) woman.

멋쩍다 (be) awkward.

멋지다 (be) stylish; smart; dandyish; refined; chic; splendid. ¶ 멋진 솜씨 great (wonderful) skill; excellent workmanship.

멍 ① (피부의) a bruise; a contusion. ¶ ~들다 bruise; turn black and blue; be bruised / ~들도록 때리다 beat (*a person*) black and blue / 눈이 ~들다 have a black eye / 그의 말이 그녀의 마음을 멍들게 했다 His words bruised her feelings. ② (일의 탈) a serious hitch (setback). ¶ ~들다 suffer a serious hitch (heavy blow); be severely hit / 화재로 인해 그의 사업은 크게 멍들었다 His business suffered a heavy blow from the fire.

멍석 a straw mat.

멍에 (put) a yoke (*upon*).

멍울 = 망울.

멍청이 a fool; a dullard.

멍청하다 (be) stupid; dull.

멍텅구리 a fool; an idiot (ass).

멍하다 (be) absent-minded; blank; vacant. ¶ 멍하니 absent-mindedly; vacantly; blankly.

메(방망이) a mallet (목제), a hammer(철제).

메가톤 a megaton. ¶ ~ 급의 (a hydrogen bomb) in the megaton range.

메가폰 a megaphone. ¶ ~을 잡다 direct the production of a motion picture.

메가헤르츠 [理] a megahertz (MHz).

메기 [魚] a catfish.

메기다 (화살을) fix; put. ¶ 화살을 ~ fix an arrow in *one's* bow.

메뉴 a menu; a bill of fare.

메다¹ (막히다) be stopped (stuffed, blocked, choked) (up); be clogged. ¶ 목이 ~ feel choked / 코가 메었다 My nose is stuffed up.

메다² shoulder (*a gun*); carry (*a load*) on *one's* shoulder (back).

메달 (win) a medal. ¶ ~리스트 a medalist.

메들리 a medley. ¶ ~ 릴레이 a medley relay (race) / 크리스마스 곡의 ~ a medley of Christmas songs.

메뚜기 [蟲] a grasshopper; a locust.

메리야스 knitted (cotton) goods; knitwear. ¶ ~내의 a knit(ted) undershirt. ¶ ~공장 a knitting mill / ~기계 a knitting machine; a knitter.

메마르다 (땅이) (be) dry; arid; (볼모) (be) poor; barren; sterile; (마음이) (be) harsh. ¶ 메마른 땅 dry (sterile) land / 메마른 생활을 하다 lead a prosaic (drab) life.

메모 a memo; a memorandum. ¶ ~를 하다 take a memo; make notes (*of*). ¶ ~장 a note pad / ~지 scratch paper.

메밀 buckwheat. ¶ ~국수 buckwheat noodles / ~묵 buckwheat jelly.

메부수수하다 (be) boorish; rustic.

메스 [醫] a surgical knife; a scalpel. ¶ ~를 가하다 (비유) probe (*into a matter*).

메스껍다 ① (역겹다) feel sick (nausea). ② ☞ 아니꼽다

메슥거리다 feel sick (nausea); feel like vomiting.

메시아 Messiah.

메시지 (send) a message. ¶ 축하 ~ a congratulatory message / ~를 남기다 leave a message.

메신저 a messenger.

메아리 an echo. ¶ ~ 치다 echo; be echoed; resound.

메어치다 throw (*a person*) over *one's* shoulder.

메우다 ① (빈곳・구멍을) fill up (in) (*cracks*); stop (*a gap*); plug (up) (*a hole*); (매립하다) reclaim (*land from the sea*). ¶ 틈을 ~ make (stop) up a gap / 여백을 ~ fill in the blank spaces / 결원을 ~ fill up a vacancy. ② (부족을) make up for; compensate for. ¶ 결손을 ~ cover (make up) a loss. ③ (통을) hoop; fix. ¶ 통에 테를 ~ hoop a barrel.

메이저리그 the Major Leagues.

메이커 a maker; a manufacturer. (일류) ~ 제품 articles manufactured by well-known makers; name brands.

메이크업 make-up. ¶ ~ 하다 make up.

메조소프라노 [樂] mezzo-soprano.

메주 soybean malt; fermented soybeans. ¶ ~콩 malt soybeans / ~콩으로 ~ 쑨대도 곧이 안 듣다 do not believe a story to be true.

메지다 (be) nonglutinous.

메질 ~하다 hammer; strike with

메추라기 a mallet; pound 《on》.
메추리, 메추라기 [鳥] a quail.
메카 Mecca 《동경의 땅》.
메커니즘 (a) mechanism.
메탄 [化] methane. ¶ ~ 가스 methane (gas).
메탄올 [化] methanol.
메틸알코올 methyl alcohol.
멕시코 Mexico. ¶ ~의 Mexican / ~ 사람 a Mexican.
멘델 ∥ ~ 법칙 Mendel's laws; Mendel's the menses. ☞ 월경.
멘탈테스트 (give) a mental test.
멜대 a carrying pole.
멜로드라마 a melodrama.
멜로디 [樂] a melody.
멜론 a melon.
멜빵 a shoulder strap; a sling (총의); (양복바지의) suspenders; braces (英).
멤버 a member. ¶ 베스트 ~ (of the best members [players] / 정규 ~ a regular member.
멥쌀 nonglutinous rice.
멧닭 a black grouse; a blackcock (수컷); a gray hen (암컷).
멧돼지 [動] a wild boar.
멧새 [鳥] a meadow bunting.
멧参다리 [鳥] a mountain hedgesparrow.
며느리 a daughter-in-law. ¶ ~를 보다 get a wife for *one's* son.
며느리발톱 [動・鳥] a spur; a calcar.
며칠 (그달의) what day; (날수) how many days; how long; a few days. ¶ ~ 동안 for days / 오늘이 ~인가 What's the date today?
멱 a throat; a gullet. ¶ ~을 따다 cut (*a fowl's*) gullet [throat].
멱 (冪) [數] a power. ¶ ~수 an exponent.
멱살 the throat. ¶ ~ 잡다 [들다] seize (*a person*) by the collar [coat lapels]; grab (*a person's*) throat.
멱서리 a straw-bag.
면 (面) ① (얼굴) a face. ② 체면. ③ (표면) the (sur)face; (측면) a side; (다면체의) a facet; a face. ④ (방면) an aspect; a phase; a field; a side. ¶ 재정 ~에서 in every respect. ⑤ (지면(紙面)) a page. ⑥ (행정 구역) a *myŏn* (as a subdivision of a *gun*); a township; a subcounty.
면 (綿) cotton. ☞ 무명.
…면 if; when; in case. ¶ 비가 오~ if it rains.
면경 (面鏡) a hand [small] mirror.
면구스럽다 (面灸 -) (be) shamefaced; abashed; feel awkward [nervous, embarrassed] (서술적). ¶ 그런 일로 표창을 받게 되어 ~ I feel embarrassed to be officially commended for such a thing.
면담 (面談) an interview; a talk. ¶ ~ 하다 have an interview 《with》; talk personally 《with》.
면대 (面對) ∥ ~하다 meet face to face 《with》; face (each other). ¶ ~ 하여 face to face.
면도 (面刀) shaving. ∥ ~하다 shave *oneself*; (남을 시켜) have *one's* face shaved; get a shave. ∥ ~ 날 a razor blade / ~칼 a razor.
면류 (麵類) noodles; vermicelli.
면류관 (冕旒冠) a (royal) crown.
면면 (綿綿) ∥ ~한 unbroken; continuous; endless / ~히 without a break; ceaselessly.
면모 (面貌) a countenance; looks; features; (an) appearance (일의). ¶ ~를 일신하다 put on quite a new aspect; undergo a complete change / ~를 되찾다 return to (*its*) former conditions.
면목 (面目) (체면) face; honor; credit; dignity; (모양) an appearance; an aspect. ¶ ~을 잃다 lose *one's* face / ~을 유지하다 [세우다] save *one's* face [honor] / ~ 없다 be ashamed of *oneself* / ~을 일신하다 change the appearance (*of*); undergo a complete change.
면밀 (綿密) ∥ ~한 (세밀한) detailed; minute; close; (빈틈없는) careful; scrupulous / ~히 minutely; carefully; scrupulously / ~한 검사 a close examination / ~한 관찰 minute observation.
면바르다 (面 -) (be) even; level; clean-cut; well-formed.
면박 (面駁) ∥ ~하다 refute to *one's* face; reprove [blame] (*a person*) to *his* face.
면방적 (綿紡績) cotton spinning. ∥ ~기 a cotton spinning machine.
면벽 (面壁) [佛] (sit in) meditation facing the wall (*of a cave*).
면부득 (免不得) ~하다 be unavoidable [inevitable].
면사 (免死) ~하다 escape [be saved from] death.
면사 (綿絲) cotton yarn (직조용); cotton thread (마느질용).
면사무소 (面事務所) a *myeon* office.
면사포 (面紗布) a wedding [bridal] veil. ¶ ~를 쓰다 marry; get married.
면상 (面上) *one's* face.
면상 (面相) a countenance; looks.
…면서 ① (동작의 진행) …ing; (동시에) as; while; over; during. ¶ 웃으~ with a smile; smiling / 책을 읽으~ 걷다 read as *one* walks. ② (불구하고) (al)though; and yet; still; in spite of; for all that. ¶ 나쁜 일일 줄 알~ though I knew it was wrong / 큰 부자이~도 그의 욕심은 한이 없다 Although he is rich [With all

면서기(面書記) a *myeon* official; an official of township office.

면세(免稅) tax exemption. ~하다 exempt《*a person*》from taxes; free《*goods*》from (customs) duty. ¶ ~가 되어 있다 be free of tax / ~로 사다 buy《*something*》duty-free. ∥ ~소득 tax-free income / ~점(店) a duty-free shop / ~점(點)(raise, lower) the tax exemption limit / ~품 tax-exempt [-free] articles.

면소(免訴) dismissal《*of a case*》; discharge《*of a prisoner*》. ~하다 dismiss《*a case*》; acquit [release]《*a prisoner*》. ¶ ~되다 have one's case dismissed; be acquitted《*of*》.

면식(面識) acquaintance. ¶ ~이 있다 be acquainted《*with*》; know / ~이 없는 사람 a stranger / ~이 있는 사람 an acquaintance.

면양(緬羊) a (wool) sheep.

면역(免役) exemption from public labor [military service].

면역(免疫)〖生理〗immunity《*from a disease*》. ¶ ~이 되다 become [be] immune《*to*》/ ~이 되게 하다 immunize《*a person against*》/ ~이 되어 있다 be immune《*to, against, from*》/ (비유적)be hardened [impervious]《*to*》《*public criticism*》/ ~성이 생기다 develop proper immunity《*to, against, from*》/ ~성이 없는 nonimmune. ∥ ~기간 a period of immunity / ~반응 (an) immune reaction / ~주사 (a protective) inoculation / ~체 an immune body / ~학 immunology.

면장(免狀) a license; a certificate. ¶ 수입~ an import license.

면장(面長) the chief of a *myeon* [township].

면적(面積) (an) area; square measure; size《*of land*》. ¶ ~을 차지하다 cover an area《*of ten acres*》.

면전(面前) ¶ ~에서 before [in the presence of]《*a person*》/ 내 ~에서 in my presence.

면접(面接) an interview. ~하다 (have) an interview. ¶ 개인 ~ an individual interview. ∥ ~시험 an oral test (구술의); a personal interview (사원 등의).

면제(免除) (an) exemption《*from*》. ~하다 exempt《*a person*》from《*tax*》; release [excuse]《*a person*》from《*a duty*》. ¶ 징집[병역]이 ~되다 be exempted from draft [military service]. ∥ 일부[전부] ~ partial [total] exemption / 입학금 ~ exemption of the entrance fee.

면제품(綿製品) cotton goods.

면종복배(面從腹背) false [pretended, treacherous] obedience; (a) Judas kiss.

면지(面紙)《책의》the inside of a book cover; a flyleaf.

면직(免職) dismissal [removal] from office; discharge. ~하다 dismiss [discharge, remove]《*a person*》(from office); fire (口). ¶ ~되다 be dismissed [fired]. [tiles].

면직물(綿織物) cotton fabrics [tex-

면책(免責)(have, receive) exemption from responsibility [obligation]. ∥ ~조항 exemption [escape] clause / ~특권《외교관의》diplomatic immunity;《국회의원의》the privilege of exemption from liability.

면책(面責) personal reproof. ~하다 reprove《*a person*》to his face.

면치레(面——) ~하다 keep up appearances; put up a good front; assume the appearance《*of*》.

면포(綿布) cotton cloth [stuff].

면하다(免一) ① 《모면하다》escape《*danger*》; be saved [rescued] from《*drowning*》;《피하다》avoid; evade. ¶ 가까스로 죽음 고비를 ~ get through a crisis / 욕을 ~ avoid dishonor; save one's face / 면하기 어려운 unavoidable; inevitable. ② 《면제》be exempt[ed] [free]《*from*》; be immune《*from*》. ¶ 병역을 ~ be exempted from military service.

면하다(面—) face (on); front; look out《*on, onto*》. ¶ 바다에 면한 집 a house facing the sea / 바다에 ~ front the sea / 이 방은 호수에 면해 있다 This room looks out on the lake.

면학(勉學) study; academic pursuit. ~하다 study; pursue one's studies. ¶ ~분위기를 조성하다 create an academic atmosphere.

면허(免許) a permission; a license. ¶ ~ 있는 [없는] (un)licensed / ~를 얻다 obtain [take] a license. ∥ ~료 a license fee / ~제 a license system / ~증《*driving*》a license; a certificate.

면화(棉花) a cotton. ☞ 목화(木花).

면회(面會) an interview; a meeting. ~하다 meet; see; have an interview《*with*》. ¶ ~를 청하다 ask《*a person*》to see 《*one*》; ask for [request] an interview《*with*》/ ~를 사절하다 refuse to see a visitor. ∥ ~시간 visiting hours / ~실 a visiting room / ~일 a visiting [receiving] day / (작업 중) ~사절 (게시) Interview Declined (During Working Hours).

멸공(滅共) crushing communism; rooting up communists. ‖ ~ 정신 the spirit to crush [exterminate] communism. 「hopper.
멸구(蟲) a rice insect; a leaf
멸균(滅菌) 살균(殺菌)
멸망(滅亡) a (down)fall; ruin; destruction; collapse. ‖ ~ 되다 be ruined [destroyed]; perish.
멸문(滅門) ‖ ~ 지화(之禍) a disaster that wipes out 《*a person's*》 whole family.
멸사봉공(滅私奉公) selfless devotion to *one's* country.
멸시(蔑視) contempt; disdain; disregard 《~ 경멸》. ‖ ~ 하다 despise; disdain; hold 《*a person*》 in contempt. ‖ ~ 받다 be held in contempt.
멸족(滅族) ‖ ~ 하다 《타동사》 exterminate (eradicate) 《*a person's*》 whole family; 《자동사》 《*a family*》 be exterminated.
멸종(滅種) ‖ ~ 하다 《타동사》 exterminate (eradicate) a stock; 《자동사》 《*a stock*》 be exterminated (eradicated). 「ed anchovies.
멸치[魚] an anchovy; ‖ ~ 젓 salt-
멸하다(滅一) ruin; destroy 《*an enemy*》; exterminate. 「목화」
면(무명) cotton cloth; a cotton
명(命) ① ☞ 명령. ② 당국의 ~에 의하여 by order of the authorities. ② 《수명》 *one's* (span of) life; *one's* destiny (운명). ‖ 제 ~에 죽다 die a natural death.
명(銘) 《기념비》 an inscription; 《묘비》 an epitaph; 《칼의》 a signature; 《스스로의 계율》 a precept; a motto. ‖ 좌우 ~ *one's* (favorite) motto. 「twenty persons.
명(名) 《사람수》 persons. ‖ 20 ~
명…(名) great; noted; celebrated; excellent; famous. ‖ ~ 배우 a star actor / ~ 연주 an excellent performance.
명가(名家) 《명문》a distinguished (prestigious) family. ‖ 그는 ~ 의 출신이다 He comes of a distinguished family. 「singer.
명가수(名歌手) a great (famous)
명검(名劍) a noted sword; an excellent blade.
명경(明鏡) a stainless (clear) mirror. ‖ ~ 지수(止水) a mind as serene as a polished mirror; a mind undisturbed by evil thoughts.
명곡(名曲) (appreciate) a famous (an excellent) piece of music.
명공(名工) a skillful craftsman; an expert artisan.
명관(名官) a celebrated governor; a wise magistrate.
명구(名句) 《구(句)》 a famous phrase 《명답》 a wise saying. 「arch.
명군(明君) an enlightened mon-
명궁(名弓) 《사람》 an expert archer; 《활》 a noted bow.
명금(鳴禽) a songbird.
명기(明記) ‖ ~ 하다 state (write) clearly; specify.
명년(明年) next year.
명단(名單) a list (roll, register) of names. ‖ 초대자의 ~ a list of guests invited.
명단(明斷) ‖ ~ 을 내리다 pass a fair judgment 《*on*》.
명답(名答) a clever (right) answer. ~ 하다 answer brilliantly (correctly).
명답(明答) a definite answer. ‖ ~ 을 피하다 avoid giving a definite answer.
명당(明堂) ① 《대궐의》 the king's audience hall. ② 《묏자리》 a propitious site for a grave.
명도(明度) luminosity; brightness.
명도(明渡) evacuation. ‖ ~ 인도(引 ~ 하다 vacate 《*a house*》. ‖ ~ 를 요구하다 ask 《*a person*》 to vacate 《*the house*》. ‖ 《가옥의》 ~ 소송 an eviction suit.
명도(冥途) Hades; the other world; the underworld.
명동(鳴動) ‖ ~ 하다 rumble. ‖ 태산 ~ 에 서일필(鼠一匹) 《俗談》 Much cry and little wool.
명란(明卵) pollack roe. ‖ ~ 젓 salted pollack roe.
명랑(明朗) ‖ ~ 한 clear / ~ 한 목 소리로 in a clear voice / ~ 한 가 정 a merry home / ~ 한 청년 a bright and cheerful young man.
명령(命令) an order; a command; a direction; instruction (훈령). ‖ ~ 하다 order (command, instruct 《*a person*》 to *do*); give orders. ‖ ~ 조로 (speak) in a commanding (an authoritative) tone / ~ 에 따르다 obey (carry out) an order / ~ 대로 하다 do as *one* is told. ‖ ~ 계통 a line of command: a command system / ~ 문 《文》 an imperative sentence / ~ 법 《文》 the imperative (mood) / ~ 위반 violation of an order.
명론(名論) an excellent opinion; a sound (convincing) argument; a well-founded theory. ‖ ~ 탁설 (卓說) excellent arguments and eminent views.
명료(明瞭) ‖ ~ 한(하게) clear(ly); distinct(ly); plain(ly) / ~ 하게 하 다 make clear. ‖ ~ 도 《通信》 clarity; articulation.
명리(名利) (run after) fame and fortune (wealth). ‖ ~ 를 좇다 strive after fame and wealth / ~ 에 뜻이 없다 be above (indifferent to) riches and fame.

명마(名馬) a good (fine) horse.
명망(名望) (a) reputation; popularity (인망). ‖ ~가 a man of high reputation.
명맥(命脈) life; the thread of life; existence. ¶ ~을 유지하다 《사람이》 remain (keep) alive; 《풍습 따위가》 remain (stay) in existence.
명멸(明滅) ~하다 《불이》 flicker; glimmer; blink; come and go. ¶ ~하는 불빛 a flickering light. ‖ ~신호 a blinking signal.
명명(命名) naming; christening. ~하다 christen; name. ¶ ~식 a naming (christening) ceremony.
명명백백(明明白白) ¶ ~한 (as) clear as day; quite obvious.
명목(名目) 《명칭》 a name; 《구실》 a pretext. ¶ ~상의 nominal; in name only / ~에 지나지 않다 be in name only / ~상의 사장 a nominal (figurehead) president / ~상의 이유 the ostensible reason / 정치헌금이라는 ~으로 정치인에게 뇌물을 주다 offer a bribe to a politician under the pretext of giving a political donation. ‖ ~가격 a nominal price / ~임금 nominal wages.
명문(名文) a literary gem; a beautiful passage (composition). ‖ ~가 a fine writer; a stylist.
명문(名門) a distinguished (noble) family. ‖ ~교 a distinguished (prestige) school.
명문(明文) an express provision (statement). ¶ ~화하다 stipulate expressly in the text; put 《something》 in the statutory form / 법률에 ~화되어 있다 be expressly stated in the law / 제외한다는 ~이 없으면 if it is not expressly excluded. ‖ ~규정 (a) substantive enactment.
명물(名物) 《산물》 a special (famous, well-known) product; a specialty; 《저명한 것》 a feature; an attraction; a popular figure 《in town》 (사람). ¶ 지방의 ~ a local specialty.
명미하다(明媚—) (be) beautiful; of scenic beauty. ¶ 풍광 명미한 땅 a place of scenic beauty.
명민하다(明敏—) (be) sagacious; intelligent; clear; sharp.
명반(明礬) alum.
명백하다(明白—) (be) clear; evident; plain; obvious. ¶ 명백한 사실 an obvious fact / 명백히 clearly; obviously.
명복(冥福) happiness in the other world; heavenly bliss. ¶ ~을 빌다 pray for the repose of 《a person's》 soul.
명부(名簿) a list (roll) of names. ¶ 선거인 ~ a pollbook / ~를 만들다 make (prepare) a list 《of》.
명부(冥府) Hades; the other world.
명분(名分) 《본분》 one's moral obligations (duty); 《정당성》 (moral) justification. ¶ ~이 서는 is justifiable / ~이 안 서는 행동 unjustifiable act / ~을 세우다 justify oneself 《one's conduct》.
명사(名士) a man of distinction (note); a distinguished (noted) person; a celebrity.
명사(名詞) 〖文〗 a noun.
명산(名山) a noted mountain.
명산(名産) a special (noted) product; a specialty.
명상(瞑想) meditation. ~하다 meditate 《on》; contemplate. ¶ ~적인 meditative / ~에 잠기다 be lost in meditation.
명색(名色) a title; a name; an appellation. ☞ 명복.
명석(明晳) ~하다 (be) clear; bright. ¶ 두뇌 ~하다 be clearheaded.
명성(名聲) fame; reputation; renown. ¶ 세계적인 ~ world-wide fame / ~을 얻다 gain (win) fame (a reputation) / ~을 높이다 (더 럽히다) enhance (injure) one's reputation.
명세(明細) details; particulars; specifies. ¶ 지출의 ~ an account of payments / 선적 ~서 shipping specifications. ‖ ~서 a detailed account (statement) (계산서); specifications (설명서); ~ 서 an itemized account.
명소(名所) a noted place; a beauty (scenic) spot. ¶ ~를 구경하다 see (do) the sights 《of Seoul》.
명수(名手) a master-hand 《at》; an expert 《at, in》. ¶ 사격의 ~ a good (an expert) marksman; a sharpshooter.
명수(命數) ☞ 명(命) ②.
명승(名勝) ¶ ~고적 places of scenic beauty and historic interest / ~지 a beautiful place.
명승(名僧) a great priest.
명시(明示) ~하다 point out (state) clearly; clarify. ¶ ~적(으로) explicit(ly).
명실(名實) ¶ ~공히 both in name and reality / ~상부하다 be true to the name; be up to 《its》 reputation.
명심(銘心) ~하다 bear (keep) 《a matter》 in mind; take 《the advice》 to heart.
명아주 〖植〗 a goosefoot.
명안(名案) a good (wonderful, great) idea (plan); a splendid suggestion. ¶ ~이 떠오르다 hit on (have) a good idea.
명암(明暗) light and darkness (shade). ¶ 인생의 ~ the bright

명약관화(明若觀火) ~하다 《서술적》 be as clear as day [daylight]; quite obvious.
명언(名言) a wise [golden] saying; a witty remark.
명언(明言) ~하다 declare; say definitely; state explicitly.
명역(名譯) an excellent [admirable] translation.
명연기(名演技) good acting; a fine [an excellent] performance.
명예(名譽) honor; credit. ¶ ~로운 honorable (*position*) / ~를 걸고 on *one's* honor / ~를 얻다 win [gain] honor / ~를 잃다 lose *one's* honor / ~에 관계되다 affect *one's* honor [reputation] / ~가 되다 be an honor [a credit] to (*a person*) / ~를 더럽히다 bring disgrace (*on a person*); stain (*a person's*) honor. ‖ ~ 교수 an honorary professor; a professor emeritus / ~ 시민 [직, 회장] an honorary citizen [post, president] / ~심 a desire for fame; aspiration after fame / ~퇴직 ☞ 퇴직 / ~회복 restoration of reputation / ~훼손죄 defamation of character; a libel(문서로) ; (a) slander(말로).
명왕성(冥王星) Pluto.
명우(名優) a great actor [actress]; a (famous) star.
명운(命運) *one's* fate [destiny]. ¶ ~이 다하다 go to *one's* fate.
명월(明月) a bright [full] moon. ‖ 중추의 ~ the harvest moon.
명의(名義) a name. ¶ ~상의 nominal / ~의 ~로 in (*a person's*) name / 집을 아내의 ~로 바꾸다 transfer a house to my wife's name. ‖ ~도용 an illegal use of other's name / ~변경 title transfer / ~인 the holder *of a title deed*; a registered owner.
명의(名醫) a noted [great] doctor; a skilled physician.
명인(名人) an expert (*at, in*); a (past) master (*in, of*). ¶ 피아노의 ~ an accomplished [excellent] pianist / 바둑의 ~ a master of *baduk* / 바둑 대회에서 ~ 자리를 차지하다 win the championship in the *baduk* tournament. ‖ ~기질 the spirit of a master artist / ~전 (바둑의) the professional *baduk* players' championship series.
명일(名日) a national holiday; a festive [fete] day.
명일(明日) tomorrow.
명작(名作) a masterpiece; a fine piece (*of literature*); a fine work (*of art*).

명장(名匠) a master-hand; a master-craftsman.
명장(名將) a famous general; a great commander.
명저(名著) a fine [great] book; a masterpiece(결작).
명절(名節) a gala day; a fete (day); a national holiday. ¶ ~ 기분 festive mood.
명제(命題) [論] a proposition.
명조(明朝) ① tomorrow morning. ②(活字) ~체 Ming-style type.
명주(明紬) [絹織物] silk fabric; silks. ‖ ~실 silk thread.
명주(銘酒) high-quality liquor; liquor of a famous brand.
명중(命中) a hit. ~하다 hit (*the mark*); strike home. ~하지 않다 miss (*the mark*). ‖ ~률 an accuracy rate / ~탄 a (direct) hit; a telling shot.
명찰(名札) a name plate (tag).
명찰(明察) keen insight; clear discernment. ~하다 see through.
명창(名唱) a great [noted] singer (사람); a famous song (노래).
명철(明哲) sagacity; intelligence. ~하다 be(a) sagacious; intelligent.
명추(明秋) next autumn [fall].
명춘(明春) next spring.
명치 the pit (of the stomach).
명칭(名稱) (give) a name; a title; a designation.
명콤비(名 —) (form) an ideal combination; (make) a good pair.
명쾌(明快) ~한 plain; clear; lucid.
명태(明太) [魚] a Alaska pollack.
명필(名筆) a fine handwriting [calligraphy]; (사람) a noted calligrapher.
명하다(命 —) ① ☞ 명령하다. ②《임명》 appoint; nominate.
명함(名銜) a (name) card; a calling card(사교용); a business card(영업용). ¶ ~을 내다 give *one's* card (*to*) / ~을 교환하다 exchange cards. ‖ ~판 (사진의) a *carte de visite* (프).
명현(名賢) a man of great wisdom; a noted sage.
명화(名畫) a famous [great] picture; a masterpiece; a good [an excellent] film (영화).
명확(明確) ¶ ~한 clear; precise; accurate; definite / ~하게 clearly; precisely; accurately / ~한 답변을 요구하다 demand a definite answer / 이 점을 ~히 해주면 좋겠다 I want you to make this point clear.
몇 (얼마) how many(수); how much(양, 금액); how far(거리); how long(시간); some. ¶ ~년 how many; some (긍정) / ~년

몇몇 how many years / ~ 번 how many times; how often; what number(번호) / ~ 사람 how many people (persons); some people (약간) / ~ 시 what time; when / ~ 이냐 How old are you? / ~ 시입니까 What time is it?

몇몇 some; several (persons).

모¹ ①《각》 an angle. ¶ ~가 난 angular; angled. ②《모서리》. ③《언행의》 angularity; harshness. ¶ ~가 있는 angular; stiff; unsociable / ~지 않는 사람 a smooth-mannered person / ~난 소리를 하다 speak harshly. ‖ ~ 난 편의 the side. ¶ 여러 ~로 in various (many) ways; in every respect / ~로 눕다 lie on *one's* side.

모²《벼의》 a (rice) seedling; (묘목) a sapling (☞ 모내다). ¶ ~를 심다 transplant rice seedlings.

모³《두부 따위의》 a cake《of bean curd》; a piece《of》.

모⁴《某》《모씨》 a certain person; Mr. So-and-so; (어떤) a; one; certain. ¶ ~처 a certain place / 김~(金某) a certain Kim.

모가치 one's share. ☞ 모개.

모개 ‖ ~로 altogether; all taken together; in bulk (mass); in a lump / ~로 사다 buy《things》in bulk (mass). ‖ ~ 흥정 a package deal / 모갯돈 a sizable sum of money.

모계(母系)《on》the maternal line (mother's side). ‖ ~사회 a matrilineal society.

모계(謀計) a trick; a scheme; a plot; a stratagem.

모골(毛骨) ¶ ~이 송연하다 shudder; feel *one's* hair stand on end.

모공(毛孔) pores (of the skin).

모과〔植〕 a Chinese quince.

모관(毛管) ☞ 모세관.

모교(母校) *one's* old school; *one's* Alma Mater (라).

모국(母國) *one's* mother country; *one's* homeland. ‖ ~어 *one's* mother tongue (스페인어를 ~어처 럼 말하다 speak Spanish like a native speaker).

모국(某國) a certain state (nation); an undisclosed country.

모권(母權) mother's authority; maternal rights. ‖ ~제 사회 a matriarchal society.

모근(毛根) the root of a hair; a hair root. ‖ ~이식 implantation of hair.

모금(募金) fund raising; collection of subscriptions (contributions). ~하다 raise a fund《for》; collect contributions. ‖ ~운동 a fund-raising campaign; a drive to raise fund《for》.

모금 a mouthful《of》; a draft; a puff (담배의); a sip (차 따위). ¶ 물을 한 ~ 마시다 drink a draft of water.

모기 a mosquito. ¶ ~ 소리로 in a very faint voice / ~에 물리다 be bitten (stung) by a mosquito. ‖ ~장 (put up) a mosquito net (curtain) / ~향 a mosquito (-repellent) stick (coil).

모깃불 a smudge; a mosquito smoker (fumigator).

모나다 ① (물건이) be angular; be edged (angled, pointed). ¶ 모난 기둥 a square pillar / 모나게 깎다 sharpen the edges. ②《성행이》 be angular (stiff, harsh); be unsociable. ¶모나게 굴다 act (behave) harshly (unsociably). ③《두드러지게》 be conspicuous; be odd. ¶ 모난 행동 odd behavior. ④《쓰임새가》 be useful (effective). ¶ 돈을 모나게 쓰다 spend money well (to good cause).

모나코 Monaco. ¶ ~공국(公國) the Principality of Monaco.

모내기 rice planting. ~하다 transplant rice seedlings; plant rice. ‖ ~철 the rice-planting season.

모내다 ① ☞ 모내기하다. ②《각지게 하다》 make angular.

모녀(母女) mother and daughter.

모노레일 a monorail.

모노타이프 a monotype.

모놀로그 a monologue.

모니터 a monitor. ‖ ~제 a monitor system (방송).

모닝코트 a morning coat (dress).

모닥불 a fire in the open air; a bonfire. ¶ ~을 피우다 build up a fire.

모더니즘 modernism.

모던 modern. ‖ ~아트 (재즈) modern art (jazz).

모데라토〔樂〕*moderato*《이》.

모델 a model. ¶ ~이 되다 pose (sit, stand) for an artist. ‖ ~케이스 a model case / ~하우스 a model house. 〔장치〕.

모뎀〔컴〕a modem (변복조 (變復調) 장치).

모독(冒瀆) profanation. ~하다 profane; blaspheme.

모두(冒頭) (at) the beginning; the opening; the outset.

모두뜀 hopping on both feet.

모든 all; whole; every. ¶ ~ 점에 서 in all points; in every re-

모란(牡丹) 〖植〗 a (tree) peony.
모랄 moral sense; morals; ethics; *morale* 〖프〗.
모래 sand; grit (굵은). ¶ ~바람 a sand-laden wind / ~가 많은 sandy / ~장난을 하다 play with sand / ~가 눈에 들어가다 get some sand in *one's* eyes. ‖ ~땅 sandy soil / ~밭 the sands; ~벌판 a sandy plain / ~사장 a sandy beach / ~시계 a sandglass; an hourglass / ~주머니 a sandbag / ~찜질 a sand bath / ~채취장 a sandpit / ~폭풍 a sandstorm.
모래무지 〖魚〗 a false (goby) minnow gudgeon.
모래집 the amnion. ‖ ~물 amniotic fluid.
모략(謀略) a plot; a trick; stratagem. ¶ ~을 꾸미다 form a plot; plan a stratagem / ~에 걸리다 be caught in a trap. ‖ ~선전 strategical propaganda.
모레 the day after tomorrow.
모로 (비스듬히) diagonally; obliquely; (옆으로) sideways. ¶ ~ 걷다 (walk) sideways.
모로코 Morocco. ¶ ~의 Moroccan. / ~인 a Moroccan.
모루 an anvil. ‖ ~채 a hammer.
모르다 ① (일반적) do not know; be ignorant 《of》; (생소함) be not acquainted 《with》; be unfamiliar; (추측 못하다) cannot tell. ¶ 모르는 곳 an unfamiliar place / 모르는 말 a language *one* doesn't know / 글을 ~ be ignorant (illiterate) / 어찌 할 바를 ~ do not know what to do / 전혀 ~ know nothing 《about》. ② (이해 못함) do not understand; have no idea 《of》; (인식 못함) do not recognize (appreciate). ¶ 시를 ~ have no relish for poetry / 중요성을 ~ do not recognize the importance 《of》 / 돈을 ~ be indifferent to money. ③ (깨닫지 못함) be unaware 《of》; be unconscious 《of》; (못느낌) do not feel; be insensible 《of, to》. ¶ 모르는 사이에 before *one* knows / 창피를 ~ be shameless. ④ (기억 못함) do not remember. ⑤ (무관계) have no relation 《with》; have nothing to do 《with》; (무경험) have no experience; be ignorant 《with》. ¶ 세상을 ~ be ignorant of the world / 난 모르는 일이다 I have nothing to do with it.
모르모트 〖動〗 a guinea pig.
모르몬교(—敎) Mormonism. ‖ ~도 a Mormon.
모르쇠 know-nothingism; playing dumb. ¶ ~ 잠다 play dumb; pretend not to know.

모르타르 mortar.
모르핀 morphia; morphine. ‖ ~중독 morphinism / ~중독자 a morphine addict.
모른체하다 (시치미떼다) pretend not to know; feign ignorance; (무관심) be indifferent 《to》; (아무 안만났을 때) look the other way; cut 《a person》. ¶ 모른 체하고 with an unconcerned air; as if *one* knew nothing about it.
모름지기 by all means; necessarily; it is proper that *one* should 〔ought〕 to 《do》.
모리(謀利) profiteering. ¶ ~하다 make (plan) undue profits 《on》; profiteer. ‖ ~자 a profiteer.
모리타니 Mauritania. ‖ ~사람 a Mauritanian.
모면(謀免) ~하다 escape 《danger》; be rescued (saved) from; avoid; evade; shirk. ¶ ~할 수 없는 unavoidable 《disasters》; inevitable 〔conclusions〕 / 간신히 ~하다 have a narrow escape / 책임을 ~하다 evade *one's* responsibility.
모멸(侮蔑) contempt. ☞ 경멸.
모모(某某) certain (such and such) persons; Mr. So-and-sos.
모모한(某某) worthy of mentioning; notable; well-known. ¶ ~ 인사 a man of distinction; a celebrity; a notable.
모반(母斑) a nevus; a birthmark.
모반(謀叛) a rebellion; a revolt. ~하다 plot a rebellion (treason); rise (rebel) 《against》. ‖ ~자 a rebel; a traitor / ~죄 treason.
모발(毛髮) hair. ‖ ~영양제 a hair tonic.
모방(模倣) imitation; copy; mimicry. ~하다 imitate; copy 《from, after》; model after 《on》. ¶ ~적인 imitative / 유명 작가의 문체를 교묘히 ~하다 write well in imitation of the famous writer's style. ‖ ~본능 the instinct of imitation / ~예술 imitative arts / ~자 an imitator; a copier.
모범(模範) a model; an example; a pattern (귀감). ¶ ~적인 exemplary; model; typical / ~을 ~으로 삼다 model after; follow the example 《of》 / ~을 보이다 set (give) an example. ‖ ~생 a model student / ~수 a trusty 〔trustee〕 〖美〗; a well-behaved prisoner / ~시민 an exemplary citizen / ~운전사(공무원) an exemplary driver 〔official〕.
모병(募兵) recruiting; conscription. ~하다 recruit; draft 〖美〗.
모사(毛絲) ☞ 털실.
모사(模寫) (일) copying; (물건) a copy. ~하다 copy (out); trace; reproduce.

모사(謀士) a strategist; a tactician; a schemer.

모사(謀事) ~하다 plan; devise (*a stratagem*); plot (*against*).

모살(謀殺) ~하다 murder; kill (*a person*) of malice prepense.

모새 fine sand.

모색(摸索) ~하다 grope (*for*). ¶ 암중 ~하다 grope (blindly) in the dark / 평화적 통일을 ~하다 explore ways toward peaceful unification.

모서리 an angle; an edge; a corner. ¶ ~를 훑다 round off the angles.

모선(母船) a mother ship (vessel); 《우주선의》 a mother craft; a command module.

모성(母性) motherhood; maternity. ‖ ~본능 maternal instinct / ~애 maternal affection (love).

모세(聖) Moses.

모세관(毛細管) a capillary tube. ‖ ~현상 a capillary action (phenomenon); 〈vessel〉.

모세혈관(毛細血管)《解》a capillary

모순(矛盾) contradiction; inconsistency; conflict. ¶ ~되다 be inconsistent [incompatible] (*with*); be contradictory (*to*); 《論》 a contradiction in terms / ~된 말을 하다 contradict *oneself*; make a contradictory statement.

모스 ‖ ~부호 the Morse code.

모스크(회교의) a mosque.

모스크바 Moscow; Moskva.

모슬린 muslin.

모습(몸매·모양) a figure; a shape; a form; 《용모·외관》 looks; features; appearance; a guise; 《영상》 an image; 《사물의 상태》 a state; a condition; an aspect. ¶ 날씬한 ~ a slender figure / 한라산의 아름다운 ~ the beautiful shape of Mt. *Halla* / ~을 나타내다 appear; show up; come in sight / ~을 바꾸다 disguise *oneself* / 한국의 참 ~ Korea as she really is / 어릴적 ~을 찾아볼 수 없다 His infant features are gone.

모시 ramie cloth. ‖ ~옷 clothes [of ramie cloth].

모시다 ① 《섬기다》 attend [wait] upon (*a person*); serve. ¶ 부모를 ~ have *one's* parents with *one*; serve *one's* parents. ② 《인도》 show (*a person*) in [into]; 《함께 가다》 go with (*a person*); accompany (*a person*). ¶ 손님을 방으로 ~ show a caller into the room / 주인을 모시고 가다 escort *one's* master. ③ 《받들다》 set (*a person*) up (*as*); deify; worship (신으로); enshrine (사당에). ¶ 조상을 ~ worship *one's* ancestors / 그를 사장으로 ~ set him up as president.

모시조개(貝)《황합》a short-necked clam; 《가막조개》a corbicula.

모시풀(苧) a Chinese silk plant; a ramie.

모씨(某氏) a certain person; an unnamed person; Mr. X.

모양(模樣) 《생김새》 shape; form; 《자태》 《personal》 appearance; figure; look; 《태도》 air; manner; bearing; 《상태》 the state (of affairs); the condition. ~이 좋은 shapely; well-shaped [-formed] / ~ 사나운 unshapely; ill-formed; unsightly; disgraceful(점잖잖은); …은 ~이다 seem to be … / …할 ~이다 seem about to be [do] … / …하는 ~이다 seem to be *do*ing.

모어(母語) *one's* mother tongue.

모여들다 gather; come [get] together; crowd (flock) in.

모옥(茅屋) a straw-thatched cottage; a hovel.

모욕(侮辱) insult; contempt. ~하다 insult; treat (*a person*) with contempt; affront. ¶ ~ 적인 언사 (make) an insulting remark / ~을 당하다 be insulted; suffer an affront / ~을 참다 bear [brook] an insult.

모유(母乳) mother's milk. ¶ ~로 자란 아이 a breast-fed child / ~로 기르다 feed (*a baby*) on mother's milk.

모으다 ①《한데 모으다》 gather; collect; get (bring) together; get in (*subscriptions*). ¶ 자금을 ~ raise the funds / 재료를 ~ gather materials. ②《집중》 focus on; concentrate; 《끌다》 draw; attract; absorb. ¶ …에 주의를 ~ concentrate *one's* attention on…. ③ 《저축》 save; lay by; put aside; store; lay up; amass. ¶ 돈을 ~ save (accumulate) money.

모음(母音) a vowel (sound). ¶ ~변화 (조회) vowel gradation (harmony) / 기본~ a cardinal vowel / 반~ a semivowel / 이중~ a diphthong.

모의(模擬) ~의 imitation; sham; mock; simulated. ‖ ~국회 a model parliament / ~시험 a practice (trial) examination / ~재판 (戱) a mock trial (battle).

모의(謀議) a conspiracy 《음모》; (a) conference 《상의》. ~하다 conspire [plot] together (*against*); consult together (*about*).

모이 feed; food. ¶ 닭~ chicken feed / ~를 주다 feed (*chickens*) / 이 새의 ~는 무엇인가 What does this bird feed on ?

모이다 ① 《몰려들》 gather [flock] (together); come [get] together;

모인 swarm; line up (정렬). ②《회동》meet; assemble. ¶ 다 ~ meet all together. 《집중》center 《on, in, at》; concentrate 《on》; focus 《on》. ④《축적》be saved 〔accumulated〕. ⑤《검렴》be collected.

모인(某人) a certain person; Mr. So-and-so.

모일(某日) a certain day.

모임 〔have 〔hold〕〕 a meeting; a gathering; an assembly; a reception; a party (사교적).

모자(母子) mother and son.

모자(帽子) a hat(테 있는); a cap (테 없는); headgear (총칭). ¶ ~ 를 쓰다 〔벗다〕 put on 〔take off〕 a 《one's》 hat. ‖ ~걸이 a hatrack.

모자라다 ①《부족》be not enough; be insufficient 〔deficient〕; be short of; want. ¶ 원기가 ~ lack energy / 식량이 ~ be short of hands 〔provisions〕 / 역량이 ~ be wanting in ability. ②《우둔》be dull 〔stupid〕; be half-witted.

모자이크 a mosaic.

모정(母情) maternal affection.

모정(慕情) longing; love.

모조(模造) imitation. ~하다 imitate; make an imitation 《of》. ~의 imitation; artificial; counterfeit; faked. ‖ ~가죽 imitation leather / ~지 vellum paper / ~지폐 a forged 〔counterfeit〕 (bank) note / ~진주 〔보석〕 an imitation pearl 〔gem〕 / ~품 an imitation.

모조리 all; wholly; entirely; all together; without (an) exception. ¶ ~ 가져가다 take away everything / ~ 검거하다 make a wholesale arrest 〔sweeping roundup〕 / 전답을 ~ 팔아 치우다 sell all one's estate.

모종 a seedling; a sapling(묘목). ~하다 〔내다〕 plant 〔transplant〕 a seedling; bed out. ‖ ~삽 a (garden) trowel.

모종(某種) a certain kind. ¶ ~의 a certain; unnamed; some / ~ 의 이유로 for a certain reason / ~의 혐의를 받다 be under some suspicion.

모주 a drunkard; a sot. ‖ ~꾼

모주(母酒) crude liquor; raw spirits. ‖ ~ 모나다.

모지다 《모양・성품이》(be) angular.

모지라지다 wear out 〔away〕; be worn out; become blunt.

모지랑비 a worn-out broom.

모직(毛織) woolen fabric 〔cloth〕. ¶ ~의 woolen; worsted (꼰 털실의) / ~공장 a woolen mill / ~물 woolen goods 〔fabrics, textiles〕 / ~상 a woolen merchant / ~업 the woolen textile industry.

모진목숨 one's damned 〔contemptible, wretched〕 life; one's hard lot.

모진바람 a hard 〔strong, violent〕 wind.

모질다 ①《독함》(be) harsh; ruthless; hardhearted. ¶ 사람에 대하다 treat 《a person》 harshly / 마음을 모질게 먹다 harden oneself 《against》. ②《배거넘》(be) hard; tough; die-hard. ¶ 《힘든 일을》 모질게 이겨내는 사람 a die-hard; a tough guy. ③《날씨 따위》(be) hard; severe; bitter. ¶ 모진 추위 a severe cold.

모집(募集) ①《회원・병사 따위의》recruitment; 《지원자의》invitation. ~하다 recruit; enlist; invite; advertise (광고로). ¶ 새 회원을 ~하다 recruit new members / 군인을 ~하다 enlist 〔recruit〕 men for the army / 현상 논문을 학생으로부터 ~하다 invite students to enter a prize essay contest / 신문 광고로 가수를 ~하다 advertise for singers in the newspaper. ②《기부금 따위의》raising; collection. ~하다 raise; collect; appeal 〔call〕 for. ¶ 기금 ~ 운동 a drive to raise funds / 새로운 병원의 건설 자금을 ~하다 raise a fund for a new hospital. ‖ ~광고 an advertisement for subscription; a want ad / ~액 the amount of money to be raised / ~요항 the list of entrance requirements / ~인원 the number 《of persons》 to be admitted / 점원 ~《게시》 Clerks Wanted.

모채(募債) loan floatation. ~하다 float 〔raise, issue〕 a loan.

모처(某處) a certain place. ¶ 시내 ~에서 somewhere in town.

모처럼 ①《오랜만에》after a long time〔interval, silence, separation〕;《고대한》long-awaited. ¶ ~의 좋은 날씨 fine weather after a long spell 《of rain》/ ~의 여행이 비로 인해 엉망이 되었다 Our long-awaited journey was completely ruined by rain. ②《친절한 게》kindly; with special kindness. ¶ ~ 권하시는 것이기에 as 〔since〕 you so kindly recommend it. ③《부른 끝에》¶ ~ 박물관에 갔더니 실망스럽게 휴관이었다 Though I came all the way to visit the museum, to my great disappointment, it was closed.

모체(母體) the mother's body); 《주체・중심》the parent body; a base; a nucleus. ¶ ~보호를 위해서 for the health of the mother / 조직의 ~ the nucleus of the organization / …을 ~로 하다 stem 〔branch〕 from. ‖ ~전염 heredi-

모춤 a bunch of rice seedlings.
모친(母親) one's mother. ¶ ~상 the death of one's mother.
모태(母胎) the mother's womb.
모택동(毛澤東) Mao Tse-tung(1893-1976).
모터 a motor; an engine. ‖ ~보트 a motorboat / ~사이클 a motorcycle.
모텔〈자동차 여행자용 호텔〉 a motel.
모토 a motto. ¶ ~로 하다 make it one's motto 《to do》.
모퉁이 〈turn〉 a corner; a turning. ¶ ~집 a house at the corner.
모티브 a motive.
모판(―板) 〖農〗 a nursery; a seedbed; a seed plot.
모포(毛布) a blanket; a rug.
모표(帽標) a cap badge.
모피(毛皮) a fur 〈부드러운〉; a skin 〈거친〉. ‖ ~상 a furrier / ~외투 a fur(-lined) overcoat.
모필(毛筆) a writing brush; a hair pencil. ‖ ~화 a hair pencil picture. 「~画 ☞ 이슬람교.
모하메드 Mohammed; Mahomet.
모함(母艦) a mother ship.
모함(謀陷) ~하다 intrigue against; slander; speak ill 《of》.
모항(母港) a home port.
모해(謀害) ~하다 harm 《a person》 of malice aforethought.
모험(冒險) an adventure; a risky attempt; a venture; run a risk; take chances. ¶ ~적인 adventurous; risky / 목숨을 건 ~을 하다 stake (venture) one's life. ‖ ~가 an adventurer / ~담 an adventure story / ~심 an adventurous spirit / ~주의 adventurism.
모형(母型) 〖印〗 a matrix.
모형(模型) a model; a pattern 〈기계의〉; a dummy. ¶ 실물 크기의 ~ a life-size model 《of》 / 축척된 ~ a scale model / ~을 만들다 make a model 《of》 / ~비행기 a model airplane / ~지도 a relief map.
모호(模糊) ¶ ~한 vague; obscure; uncertain; ambiguous.
모회사(母會社) a parent company; a holding company.
목 ①〈모가지〉 a neck. ¶ ~이 굵은 〈가는〉 thick-(thin-)necked / ~을 길게 늘이다 crane one's neck / ~을 조르다 strangle 《a person》 to death. ☞ 목구멍. ②〈길 등의〉 a neck; a key position (on the road).
목(目)〈항목〉 an item; 〈분류상의〉 an order; 〈동식물의〉 a piece; 〈돌〉 a cross 〈관의〉.
목가(牧歌)〈노래〉 a pastoral (song); 〈시가〉 an idyll; a pastoral poem. ¶ ~적 pastoral; bucolic.

목각(木刻) wood carving. ‖ ~술 woodcraft / ~인형 a wooden doll.
목간(沐間)〈목욕간〉 a bathhouse; a bath.
목걸이 a necklace; a collar〈개의〉. ¶ 진주 ~를 하다 wear a pearl necklace / 개에게 ~를 끼우다 put a collar on a dog.
목검(木劍) a wooden sword.
목격(目擊) ~하다 witness; observe; see with one's own eyes. ‖ ~자 an eyewitness 《~자의 이야기 an eyewitness account; a first-hand account》.
목공(木工) a woodworker; a carpenter〈목수〉; woodworking〈일〉. ‖ ~소 a woodworking (carpentry) shop (plant).
목관(木管) a wooden pipe. ‖ ~악기 a woodwind (instrument); the woodwinds〈총칭〉.
목구멍 a throat; a gullet〈식도〉; a windpipe〈기관〉. ¶ ~이 아프다 have a sore throat / ~에 포도청〈俗談〉The belly has no ears.
목금(木琴) 〖樂〗 a xylophone.
목기(木器) woodenware.
목다리(木―)〈a pair of〉 crutches. ¶ ~로 걷다 walk on crutches.
목덜미 the nape (back, scruff) of the neck. ¶ ~를 잡다 take (seize) 《a person》 by the scruff of his neck.
목도 a pole (for shouldering). ‖ ~꾼 a shoulder-pole carrier.
목도리 a neckcloth; a comforter〈털로 된 것〉; 〈wear〉 a muffler (scarf); a neckerchief.
목돈 a (good) round sum; a sizable sum 《of money》.
목동(牧童) a shepherd boy; a cowboy.
목련(木蓮) 〖植〗 a magnolia.
목례(目禮) a nod. ~하다 nod 《to》; greet with a nod. ¶ ~를 나누다 exchange nods.
목로(木壚) a drinking stall. ‖ ~주점 a stand-up bar; a public house〈英〉; a pub〈英口〉.
목록(目錄) ①〈상품·장서의〉 a list 《of articles》; a catalog(ue). ¶ ~을 만들다 make a list / ~에 올리다 put 《an item》 on (in) the catalog / ~에 올라 있다 be (listed) in the catalog. ‖ 상품 ~ a commercial catalog. ② 〈차례〉〈a table〉 of contents.
목마(木馬) a wooden horse; a rocking horse〈장난감〉; a (vaulting) horse〈체조용의〉. ¶ ~를 뛰어넘다 vault a horse. ‖ 회전 ~ a merry-go-round.
목마르다 ①〈갈증〉 be (feel) thirsty〈서술적〉. ②〈갈망〉 have a thirst for 《money, knowledge》; hanker

목말 for 〔after〕 《*affection*》 (서술적).

목말 ¶ ~ 타다 ride a pickaback; ride on another's shoulders.

목매달다 〔남을〕 hang 《*a person*》; 〔스스로〕 hang oneself 《*on a tree*》.

목메다 〔슬퍼서〕 be choked 〔suffocated〕 《*with*》; be stifled 《*by*》. ¶ 목메어 울다 be choked with tears.

목면(木棉·木綿) ① 〔植〕 a cotton plant. ② 〔목화〕 raw cotton. ③ 〔무명〕 cotton (cloth).

목목이 at every turn of a road; at all important points 〔positions〕. ¶ ~ 지키다 stand guard at every turn of the way.

목민(牧民) ~하다 govern the people. ‖ ~관 a governor; a magistrate.

목발(木一) ☞ 목다리.

목불인견(目不忍見) ¶ ~이다 cannot bear to see; be unable to stand the sight of.

목사(牧師) a pastor; a minister; a clergyman; 〔교구의〕 a rector; a parson. ¶ 김 ~님 the Reverend 〔Rev.〕 Kim / ~가 되다 become a clergyman; take (holy) orders. ‖ ~직(職) ministry.

목상(木像) a wooden image 〔statue〕.

목석(木石) trees and stones; 〔무감각물〕 inanimate objects. ¶ ~ 같은 heartless / ~이 아니다 be made of flesh and blood.

목선(木船) a wooden vessel.

목성(木星) 〔天〕 Jupiter.

목세공(木細工) woodwork.

목소리 a voice. ¶ 큰〔작은, 굵은, 가는〕 ~ a loud 〔low, deep, thin〕 voice / 떠는 ~로 with a quivering voice / ~를 높이다〔낮추다〕 raise 〔lower〕 one's voice.

목수(木手) a 《*ship*》 carpenter. ‖ ~일 《*do*》 carpentering.

목숨 life. ¶ ~이 있는 한 as long as one lives / ~을 건 《a matter》 of life and death / ~을 건지다 save one's life.

목쉬다 get hoarse 〔husky〕. ¶ 목쉰 소리로 in a hoarse 〔husky〕 voice.

목양(牧羊) sheep farming. ‖ ~자 a sheep-raiser; a shepherd.

목양말(木洋襪) cotton socks.

목요일(木曜日) Thursday.

목욕(沐浴) bathing; a bath. ~하다 bathe 《*oneself*》 《*in*》; take 〔have〕 a bath. ¶ ~시키다 give 《a child》 a bath / ~재계하다 have a ceremonial cleaning 〔wash〕 of mind and body; purify oneself. ‖ ~물 (hot) water for a bath: bath water / ~실 a bathroom / ~탕 a bathhouse; a public bath / ~통 a bathtub; a bath.

목자(牧者) ① 《목양자》 a shepherd; a herdsman. ② 〔성직자〕 a shepherd; a clergyman.

목자르다 ① 〔목베다〕 cut off the head 《*of*》; behead. ② 〔해고〕 dismiss; discharge; fire 《口》.

목잠기다 get 〔become〕 hoarse 〔husky〕; be too hoarse to speak.

목장(牧場) a pasture; a stock-farm; a meadow; a ranch 《美》. ¶ ~을 경영하다 run a ranch. ‖ ~주인 a rancher; a ranchman.

목장갑(木掌匣) (a pair of) cotton work gloves.

목재(木材) wood; 〔건축용〕 timber; lumber 《美》. ‖ ~상 a timber 〔lumber〕 dealer.

목적(目的) a purpose; an aim; an object; an end. ~하다 intend 《*to do*》; aim 《*at*》. ¶ ~과 수단 ends and means / …할 ~으로 with the object of 《*doing*》; with a view to 《*doing*》; for the purpose of 《*doing*》 / ~을 정하다 set a purpose / ~을 달성하다 attain one's object. ‖ ~격 〔文〕 the objective (case) / ~론 〔哲〕 teleology / ~물 the object / ~어 〔文〕 an object / ~의식 a sense of purpose / ~지 one's destination.

목전(目前) ~의 imminent; immediate / …에서 in the presence of; under one's very nose / ~에 닥치다 be near 〔close〕 at hand / ~의 이익을 좇다 be after immediate gain; seek immediate gain.

목정(木精) 메틸알코올.

목젖 the uvula 《*pl*. -s, -lae》.

목제(木製) ~의 wooden; made of wood. ‖ ~품 wooden goods; woodenware.

목조(木造) ~의 wooden; built 〔made〕 of wood. ‖ ~건물 a wooden building.

목질(木質) ~의 woody; ligneous. ‖ ~부 the woody parts 《*of a plant*》 / ~섬유 woody fiber / ~소(素) 〔化〕 lignin / ~조직 woody tissue.

목차(目次) (a table of) contents.

목책(木柵) a wooden fence (barricade).

목청(성대) the vocal chords; 《목소리》 one's voice. ¶ ~껏 at the top of one's voice / ~을 돋우다 raise 〔lift〕 one's voice.

목초(牧草) grass; pasturage. ‖ ~지 a meadow; grass land.

목축(牧畜) cattle breeding; stock raising. ~하다 raise 〔rear〕 cattle. ‖ ~업 stock-farming / ~업자 a livestock raiser; a rancher 《美》 / ~지대 cattle land.

목측(目測) eye measurement. ~

목침 하다 measure with the eye. ‖ ~거리 distance measured with the eye.
목침(木枕) a wooden pillow.
목타르(木—) wood tar; pine tar.
목탁(木鐸) 【佛】 a wood block; a wooden bell; 《선도자》 a guide of the public. ¶ 사회의 ~ a leader of society / 사회의 ~이어야 할 신문 the press that should lead the public.
목탄(木炭) 《美》 charcoal. ‖ ~화 a fusain; a charcoal drawing.
목판(木板) a wooden tray.
목판(木版) a wood printing plate; a woodblock. ¶ ~본 a book printed from wood blocks / ~술 wood engraving; woodblock printing / ~화(畫) a woodblock; a woodcut.
목표(目標) a mark; a target (표적); an object; an aim. ~하다 aim at; have...as an object; set the goal at. ¶ ~에 달하다 reach (attain) the goal. ‖ ~시간 target time / ~연도 the goal year / ~지점 an objective point / 공격 ~ the target for an attack.
목피(木皮) bark (of a tree).
목하(目下) now; at present.
목형(木型) a wooden pattern.
목화(木花) 【植】 a cotton (plant); cotton wool. ¶ ~에서 씨를 빼다 gin cotton. ‖ ~송이 a cotton ball / ~씨 a cottonseed.
몫 a share; a portion; a quota; a split 《俗》. ¶ 내 ~ my share / 한 ~ 끼다 (have a) share 《in》/ 한 ~ 주다 give a share 《to》/ ~을 공평히 나누다 divide into equal shares.
몬순 【氣】 a monsoon.
몰각(沒却) ~하다 ignore; forget.
몰골 unshapeliness; shapelessness. ¶ ~ 사나운 짓 unseemly (mean) behavior / ~ 사납다 be ill-shaped; be offensive to the eye / ~ 사나운 복장을 하다 be shabbily dressed (in).
몰교섭(沒交涉) ~하다 have no relation (friendship) with 《a person》.
몰년(歿年) the year of 《a person's》 death; 《a person's》 age at death.
몰다 ① 《차·말 등을》 drive 《a car》; urge 《a horse》 on. ② 《뒤쫓다》 pursue; go (run) after; hunt out. ③ 《궁지에》 corner; drive. ¶ 궁지에 ~ drive 《a person》 into a corner. ④ 《죄인 따위로》 charge 《a person with a crime》; denounce 《as a traitor》.
몰두(沒頭) ~하다 be absorbed (engrossed) in; devote oneself to. ¶ 그는 연구에 ~하고 있었다 He was absorbed in his research.

몰라보다 cannot (fail to) recognize 《a person》.
몰락(沒落) 《파멸》 ruin; downfall; 《파산》 bankruptcy. ~하다 go to ruin; fall; be ruined.
몰래 secretly; stealthily; in secret; privately. ¶ ~ 도망하다 steal away; slip off / ~ 뒤를 밟다 shadow 《a person》 stealthily.
몰려가다 ① 《떼지어》 go in force (groups, crowds, flocks); crowd (throng, swarm) toward. ② 《쫓기어》 be driven (pushed) away.
몰려나다 ① 《쫓겨나다》 be driven (put, expelled) out; be ousted. ② 《떼지어 나가다》 go out in crowds (groups).
몰려다니다 ① 《떼지어》 go (move) about in crowds (groups). ② 《쫓겨》 be driven (chased) round (about); run after.
몰려들다 ① 《쫓기어》 be driven (chased) into. ② 《떼지어》 come in crowds (flocks, swarms); crowd (flock, swarm) in.
몰려오다 《떼지어》 come in flocks (crowds, en masse); crowd in (on). ¶ 사방에서 ~ flock from quarters / 피난민들이 몰려온다 Refugees come pouring in.
몰리다 ① 《쫓기다》 be pursued after; be chased. ② 《일에》 be pressed 《with work》; be driven 《by business》. ③ 《돈에》 be pressed (hard up) for 《money》; be driven to a corner; be cornered. ④ 《한군데로》 gather (flock, swarm) together; surge (in); throng. ¶ 많은 군중이 경기장으로 몰렸다 A big crowd surged in the stadium.
몰리브덴 【化】 molybdenum (기호 Mo).
몰매 ☞ 뭇매.
몰사(沒死) ~하다 be annihilated; be extinct; die to the last man.
몰살(沒殺) massacre; annihilation. ~하다 massacre; annihilate; wipe out. ¶ 온 가족을 ~하다 murder the whole family.
몰상식(沒常識) lack of (common) sense. ~하다 have no common sense; (be) senseless; absurd.
몰수(沒收) confiscation; forfeiture. ~하다 confiscate; forfeit. ¶ ~당하다 be confiscated. ‖ ~물 a confiscated article; a forfeit(ure).
몰식자(沒食子) 【韓醫】 a gallnut. ‖ ~산 gallic acid.
몰아 (all) in all; altogether; in a lump; in one lot. ¶ ~ 지불하다 pay in a lump sum / ~ 사다 buy 《things》 in a mass.
몰아(沒我) self-effacement. ¶ ~의 경지에 이르다 rise above self; at-

몰아가다 tain a state transcending self.
몰아가다 drive (away); sweep away (휩쓸어).
몰아내다 expel; drive out; eject; oust (지위에서).
몰아넣다 drive (안으로); push, force) in(to); (휩쓸어서) press (jam, put) all into. ¶궁지에 ~ corner 《a person》; drive (get) 《a person》 into a corner.
몰아대다 (막 해댐) give 《a person》 a setdown; take 《a person》 to task; (재촉) spur 《a horse》 on; urge on; press.
몰아들이다 (넣다) drive (chase) in; (휩쓸어) take in all together; take all in a mass; buy (up) in a lot (사들이다).
몰아받다 (한꺼번에) get 《it》 at a time (in a lump); (대표해서) receive all the shares on behalf of a group. [one side.
몰아붙이다 put (push) 《it》 all to
몰아세우다 rebuke (blame) 《a person》 severely; take 《a person》 roundly to task.
몰아주다 give 《it》 all at once; pay up the whole amount.
몰아치다 ① (비바람이) storm; blow violently (hard). ② (한곳으로) put all to one side; drive to 《a place》. ③ (일을) do 《one's work》 all at a time (dash).
몰염치 (沒廉恥) ☞ 파렴치.
몰이 (사냥의) chasing; hunting. ~하다 chase; beat; hunt out. ¶~꾼 a beater.
몰이해 (沒理解) lack of understanding. ~한 unfeeling; heartless; unsympathizing.
몰인정 (沒人情) want of sympathy; heartlessness. ¶~한 inhuman; cruel; hard-(cold-)hearted.
몰입 (沒入) ~하다 be absorbed (immersed) 《in》; devote oneself 《to》.
몰지각 (沒知覺) lack of discretion. ¶~한 indiscreet; thoughtless.
몰취미 (沒趣味) lack of taste. ¶~한 tasteless; dry; vulgar.
몰하다 (歿—) die; pass away.
몸¹ ① (신체) the body; (체격) build; physique; constitution; frame; (덩치) stature; size. ¶~의 bodily; physical / ~이 큰 (작은) large-(small-)sized / ~이 튼튼한 사람 a man of sturdy (solid) build; a well-built man / ~을 단련하다 build up one's physique / ~이 감당 못 하다 be not physically strong enough 《to do》. ② (건강) health; (체질) constitution. ¶~의 상태가 좋다 (나쁘다) be in good (poor) health / ~이 약한 사람 a person with a weak constitution; a person who is in delicate health / 담배는 ~

에 나쁘다 Smoking is bad for your health. ③ (신분) one's (social) status; one's position. ¶종의 ~ one's status as a servant / 귀한 ~ a person of noble birth. ④ (관용적 표현) give herself to 《a man》 (여자가); go all the way with 《a man》 / ~을 사리다 spare oneself / ~을 팔다 sell herself / 일이 ~에 익다 be accustomed to a job / ~을 맡기다 give oneself up 《to》 / ~을 바치다 devote oneself to.
몸² (월경) menses. ~하다 be in the flowers; have one's periods.
몸가짐 (품행) behavior; conduct; (태도) an attitude. ¶~이 얌전하다 behave well 《oneself》 / ~을 조심하다 be prudent in one's conduct.
몸값 price of redemption; (a) ransom; money paid for prostitution.
몸나다 grow fat; get stout.
몸단속 (—團束) ~하다 (경계) arm oneself against 《danger》; be on one's guard.
몸단장 (—丹粧) ~하다 dress (equip) oneself. ¶리셉션을 위해 ~하다 get oneself ready for the reception.
몸달다 fidget; be eager (anxious).
몸둘 ¶~ 곳이 없다 have no place to live (stay) in.
몸동이 body; frame. ¶~가 크다 have a bulky frame.
몸매 one's 《graceful, slender》 figure.
몸부림 ¶~치다 struggle; writhe; wriggle; flounder.
몸살 ¶~나다 suffer from fatigue.
몸서리 ¶~치다 shiver; shudder 《at》; tremble 《at》; feel repugnance to / ~쳐지는 horrible; shocking / 그것을 생각만 해도 ~쳐진다 shudder at the mere thought of it.
몸소 oneself; in person; personally. ¶~ 방문하다 make a personal call 《on, at》.
몸수색 (—搜索) a body search; a frisk(ing). ~하다 frisk; search 《a person for weapons》.
몸져눕다 take to one's bed; be bedridden; be confined to bed with a serious illness.
몸조리 (—調理) ~하다 take good care of one's health.
몸조심 (—操心) ~하다 take care of oneself; behave oneself.
몸종 a maid in attendance; a lady's (chamber) maid.
몸집 the body; the frame; one's build. ¶~이 큰 large-built; of large build.

몸짓 a gesture; (a) motion. ~하다 make gestures; motion. 과장된 ~으로 with exaggerated (dramatic) gestures.
몸채 〈집의〉 the main part of a house.
몸치장(─治粧) dressing (oneself) up. ~하다 dress (trim) oneself up.
몸통 the trunk; the body. ∥up.
몸풀다 ① 〈분만〉 give birth to 《a baby》; be delivered of 《a boy》. ② 〈피로를〉 relieve one's fatigue.
몹시 very (much); hard; greatly; awfully; extremely. ¶ ~ 서두르다 be in a great hurry / ~ 피로하다 be very tired.
몹쓸 bad; evil; wicked; ill-natured. ¶ ~ 놈 a wicked man; a rascal / ~ 짓 an evil deed; a misdeed; a vice.
못¹ 〈연못〉 a pond; a pool 〈작은〉; 〈저수지〉 a reservoir.
못² 〈박는〉 a nail; a peg 〈나무못〉. ¶ ~을 박다 〈빼다〉 drive in (pull out) a nail.
못³ 〈살가죽의〉 a callosity; a corn. ¶ 발바닥에 ~이 생기다 have (get) a corn on the sole / 귀에 ~이 박히다 be sick (tired) of hearing 《something》.
못⁴ 〈불가·불능〉 (can)not; unable 《to do》; won't. ¶ ~ 보다 cannot (fail to) see / ~ 가겠다 I won't (can't) go.
못걸이 a clothes rack; a peg.
못나다 ① 〈용모가〉 (be) ugly; bad-looking. ② 〈어리석다〉 (be) stupid; foolish; silly. ¶ 못난 짓을 하다 play the fool.
못내 〈늘〉 always; constantly; ever. ¶ ~ 그리워하다 retain a lingering love 《for》 / ~ 잊지 못하다 never forget; hold a person's memory ever dear.
못되다 ① 〈미달〉 (be) under; short of; less than 《2 years》. ② 〈악하다〉 (be) bad; evil; wrong; wicked. ¶ 못된 짓을 an evil deed; a misdeed. ③ 〈모양·상태가〉 look poor; be in bad shape; get worse. ¶ 앓고 나서 얼굴이 ~ look poor (thin) after one's illness.
못마땅하다 (be) unsatisfactory; distasteful; disagreeable; displeased. ¶ 못마땅한 말 distasteful (disagreeable) remarks.
못박이다 ① 〈손·발에〉 get (have) a corn (callus). ② 〈가슴에〉 cut deep 《into one's heart》; feel a deep rancor (grudge). ③ 〈그 자리에〉 stand transfixed (riveted) (on the spot).
못본체하다 pretend not to see; 〈묵인〉 overlook; connive 《at》; 〈방치〉 neglect.
못뽑이 pincers; a nail puller.
못살게굴다 be hard on 《a person》;

be cruel to 《a dog》; bully 〈약한 자를〉. ¶ 약한 자를 못살게 구는 풍조 a tendency of bullying the weak / 나를 못살게 굴지 마라 Don't be so mean to me 〈hard on me〉.

못생기다 〈생김새〉 (be) plain; ugly; ill-favored; homely.
못쓰다 be useless 〈worthless〉bad; 〈금지〉 must (shall) not (do). ¶ 〈물건이〉 못쓰게 되다 become useless / 너 그러면 못쓴다 You shouldn't do that.
못자리 a rice seedbed.
못지않다 be just as good as; be not inferior 《to》; be no less 《than》. ¶ 누구 ~ be second to none / 오락은 일 못지않게 필요하다 Recreation is no less necessary than work.
못질 nailing. ~하다 nail.
못하다¹ 〈질·양이〉 (be) inferior to; worse than; not as good as. ¶ 보기에 …만 ~ compare unfavorably with… / 짐승만도 ~ be worse than a beast.
못하다² 〈불능〉 cannot (do); fail; be unable to (do). ¶ 가지 ~ fail to (cannot) go.
몽고(蒙古) ☞ 몽골. ∥ ~반(斑) a Mongol(ian) spot.
몽골 Mongolia. ¶ ~의 Mongol; Mongolian. ∥ ~어 Mongolian / ~인 a Mongol; a Mongolian.
몽구리 a close-cut head; 〈중〉 a Buddhist monk.
몽글다 (be) beardless; awnless.
몽글리다 ① 〈낟알을〉 remove awns from 《grains》; clear 《grains》. ② 〈단련〉 make 《a person》 accustomed 《to》; inure. ③ 〈맵시를〉 trim (spruce) up; preen oneself.
몽당비 a wornout broom.
몽당치마 a short skirt.
몽둥이 a stick; a club; a cudgel 〈짧고 굵은〉. ∥ ~찜질 〈세례〉 clubbing; cudgeling; drubbing.
몽땅 all; wholly; entirely; altogether; in full.
몽롱(朦朧) ¶ ~한 dim; indistinct; vague / ~하게 dimly; indistinctly; vaguely / 의식이 ~해지다 get fuzzy.
몽매(蒙昧) ~하다 (be) unenlightened; ignorant; uncivilized.
몽매(夢寐) ¶ ~간에도 잊지 못하다 do not forget even in sleep.
몽상(夢想) a (day)dream; visions; a fancy. ~하다 dream 《of》; fancy. ¶ ~가 a (day)dreamer.
몽설(夢泄) a wet dream; nocturnal emission.
몽실몽실 plump; fleshily; round. ~하다 (be) lumpy; plump.
몽유병(夢遊病) sleepwalking; somnambulism. ∥ ~자 a sleepwalker; a somnambulist.

몽진(蒙塵) ~하다 flee from the Royal Palace (the capital).
몽치 a club; a bar; a cudgel.
몽타주 (a) *montage* 《프》. ‖ ~ 사진 a photomontage 《chunks》.
몽탕몽탕 ‖ ~ 자르다 cut in lumps
뫼 《무덤》 a tomb; a grave; a sepulcher. ‖ ~선산에 ~를 쓰다 bury in the family ground / 묏자리 《designate》 a grave site.
묘(卯) the Hare. ‖ ~년 the year of the Hare.
묘(妙) 《현묘》 a mystery; a wonder; 《교묘》 skill; cleverness. ‖ ~를 터득하고 있다 be skillful 《in》; have the knack 《of》.
묘(墓) ☞ 뫼, 무덤.
묘계(妙計) ☞ 묘책.
묘기(妙技) exquisite skill; a wonderful performance. ‖ ~를 보이다 exhibit 〔display〕 one's feats. ‖ 공중 ~ an aerial stunt.
묘령(妙齡) youth; blooming age. ‖ ~의 여인 a young 〔blooming〕 lady.
묘리(妙理) an abstruse principle.
묘막(墓幕) a hut nearby a grave.
묘목(苗木) a sapling; a seedling; a young tree.
묘미(妙味) charms; 〔exquisite〕 beauty. ‖ ~를 맛보다 appreciate the charm 〔beauty〕 《of》.
묘방(妙方) 《약의》 an excellent prescription.
묘법(妙法) an excellent method; a secret 《비법》.
묘비(墓碑) a tombstone; a gravestone.
묘사(描寫) description; depiction. ~하다 《그림으로》 draw; sketch; paint; 《글로》 describe; depict; portray. ‖ 등장 인물을 생생하게 ~하다 describe 〔portray〕 the character vividly. ‖ ~력 the power of description.
묘상(苗床) a nursery; a seedbed.
묘수(妙手) 《솜씨》 excellent skill; 《바둑 등의》 a nice 〔clever〕 move; 《사람》 a skillful person.
묘안(妙案) a good 〔bright〕 idea; an excellent plan 〔scheme〕. ‖ ~을 생각해 내다 hit on a bright idea.
묘안석(猫眼石) 〔鑛〕 a cat's-eye.
묘약(妙藥) a wonder drug; a golden remedy. ‖ 두통의 ~ an excellent remedy for headache.
묘역(墓域) a graveyard.
묘연하다(杳然—) 《거리가》 (be) far away; remote; 《소식이》 (be) unknown; missing. ‖ 그의 행방은 아직도 ~ His whereabouts are still unknown.
묘지(墓地) a graveyard; a burial ground; a cemetery 《공동 묘지》. ‖ 공원 ~ a cemetery park.
묘지기(墓—) a grave keeper.

묘책(妙策) a clever scheme; a capital plan.
묘판(苗板) ☞ 못자리.
묘포(苗圃) a nursery 〔garden〕.
묘하다(妙—) (be) strange; queer; curious; mysterious. ‖ 묘한 말을 하다 say strange things / 묘하게 들리다 sound strange 〔funny〕.
묘혈(墓穴) a grave. ‖ 스스로 ~을 파다 dig one's own grave; bring about one's own ruin.
무(蕪) a radish. ‖ ~김치 radish *kimchi* / ~채 radish shreds 〔strips〕.
무(武) 《무예》 military 〔martial〕 arts; 《군사》 military affairs.
무(無) nothing; naught; nil; zero.
무가내(無可奈), 무가내하(無可奈何) ‖ ~다 be at one's wit's end; be helpless 〔uncontrollable〕 《다룰 수 없다》; be at a loss what to do 《with》 《어찌할 바를 모르다》.
무가치(無價値) ‖ ~한 worthless; valueless; of no value.
무간(無間) ‖ ~한 intimate; close / ~하게 지내다 be on an intimate footing with 《a person》.
무간섭(無干涉) nonintervention. ‖ ~주의 a laissez-faire policy; a policy of noninterference.
무감각(無感覺) ‖ ~한 insensible; senseless; numb; apathetic.
무강(無疆) ‖ ~한 infinite; eternal; immortal; endless.
무개(無蓋) ‖ ~의 open; uncovered. ‖ ~자동차 an open car / ~화차 an open freightcar.
무겁다 ① 《무게가》 (be) heavy; weighty. ‖ 무거운 짐〔부담〕 a heavy 〔weighty〕 burden. ② 《중대하다》 (be) important; weighty; serious; grave. ‖ 무거운 사명 an important mission / 무거운 죄 a serious 〔grave〕 crime. ③ 《병·벌 따위가》 (be) severe; critical; serious. ‖ 무거운 병 a serious 〔severe〕 illness / 무거운 벌 a severe 〔heavy〕 punishment. ④ 《기분이》 (be) heavy; depressed. ‖ 머리가 ~ one's head feels heavy; feel heavy in the head / 마음이 ~ be depressed in spirits. ⑤ 《입이》 (be) taciturn; 《행동이》 (be) grave and quiet. ‖ 입이 무거운 사람 a close-mouthed person.
무게 ① 《중량》 weight. ‖ ~를 달다 weigh 《a thing》 / 엄청난 ~ a heavy weight / ~가 늘다 gain 〔pick up〕 in weight / ~가 60 킬로이다 weigh sixty kilograms; be sixty kilograms in weight. ② 《중요》 importance; 《관록》 weight; dignity. ‖ ~가 붙다 gain 〔grow〕 in importance 〔weight〕 / ~를 두다 lay 〔put, place〕 stress 〔emphasis〕 on; attach importance to / ~가 있는 《an idea》 of weight;

무결근(無缺勤) perfect attendance; dignified (관록 있는) / …를 ~로 더두다 give added weight to 《*the opinion*》. [regular attendance.
무경쟁(無競爭) ¶ ~의 (으로) without competition 〔a rival〕.
무경험(無經驗) ¶ ~의 inexperienced; green; untrained.
무계획(無計劃) ¶ ~한 planless; unplanned; haphazard.
무고(無故) ~하다 (be) safe; well; have no trouble.
무고(無辜) ¶ ~한 innocent; guiltless / ~한 백성 innocent people.
무고(誣告) a false charge (accusation); a libel (문서의); a slander; a calumny (구두의). ~하다 accuse 《*a person*》 falsely; make a false accusation; slander. ∥ ~자 a false accuser; a calumniator / ~죄 a calumny.
무곡(舞曲) dance music.
무골충(無骨蟲) ① 〖動〗 boneless worms. ② 〈사람〉 a spineless fellow.
무골호인(無骨好人) an excessively good-natured person.
무공(武功) military merits 〔exploits〕. ¶ ~을 세우다 render distinguished military services; distinguish *oneself* in a war 〔battle〕. [sponsibility.
무과실책임(無過失責任) no-fault re-
무관(武官) a military officer (육군); a naval officer (해군). ∥ 대사관부~ a military 〔naval〕 *attaché* to an embassy.
무관(無冠) ¶ ~의 제왕 an uncrowned king; a journalist.
무관(無關) ☞ 무관계.
무관계(無關係) ~하다 have no connection 〔relation〕 《*with*》; have nothing to do 《*with*》; be irrelevant 《*to*》.
무관심(無關心) indifference; unconcern. ~하다 be indifferent 《*to*》; unconcerned 《*about*》; have no interest 《*in*》 (서술적).
무교육(無敎育) ¶ ~의 uneducated; uncultured; illiterate. ∥ ~자 uneducated people; an illiterate (person).
무구(無垢) ¶ ~한 pure; spotless; innocent; immaculate.
무국적(無國籍) statelessness. ¶ ~의 stateless 《*refugees*》. ∥ ~자 a stateless person.
무궁(無窮) ¶ ~한 infinite; eternal; immortal; endless / ~무진한 infinite; unlimited.
무궁화(無窮花) 〖植〗 the rose of Sharon; hibiscus flowers.
무궤도(無軌道) ¶ ~의 railless; trackless; reckless (행동이) / ~한 생활 a reckless 〔dissipated〕 life. / ~전차 a trolly bus.

무균(無菌) 〖醫〗 asepsis. ¶ ~의 germ-free; sterilized (살균의). ∥ ~우유 sterilized milk.
무극(無極) 〖化〗 ∥ ~분자 〔결합〕 non-polar molecule (union).
무근(無根) ¶ ~의 groundless; unfounded. ∥ ~지설 a groundless 〔wild〕 rumor.
무급(無給) ¶ ~의 unpaid / ~으로 일하다 work without pay. ∥ ~휴가 unpaid holidays.
무기(武器) arms; a weapon. ¶ ~를 들다 take up arms; rise in arms 《*against*》 / ~를 버리다 give up 〔lay down〕 *one's* arms. ∥ ~고 an armory; an arsenal.
무기(無期) ¶ ~의 unlimited; indefinite; 《징역의》 for life. ∥ ~연기 indefinite postponement / ~징역 life imprisonment; a life term / ~징역수 a life-timer.
무기(無機) 〖化〗 ¶ ~의 inorganic; mineral. ∥ ~물 〖화학〗 inorganic substance 〔chemistry〕 / ~산 a mineral acid / ~화합물 an inorganic compound.
무기력(無氣力) ¶ ~한 spiritless; enervate; nerveless.
무기명(無記名) ¶ ~의 unregistered; unsigned; uninscribed / ~식의 blank 《*endorsement*》. / ~예금 an uninscribed deposit / ~증권 a bearer bond 〔debenture〕 / ~투표 secret voting.
무기한(無期限) ¶ ~으로 indefinitely; for an indefinite period.
무꾸리(질) 〖民俗〗 a shaman's rites 〔divination〕. ~하다 have a shaman perform a *mukkuri*.
무난(無難) ¶ ~한 《쉬운》 easy; 《안전》 safe; secure; 《무난한》 passable; acceptable / ~히 easily; without difficulty 〔trouble〕 / ~히 이기다 win an easy victory 《*over*》. [daughter.
무남독녀(無男獨女) an 〔the〕 only
무너뜨리다 break 〔pull〕 down; bring down; destroy.
무너지다 crumble; collapse; go 〔fall〕 to pieces; break; be destroyed.
무념무상(無念無想) 〖佛〗 freedom from all worldly thoughts. ~하다 be free from distraction.
무능(無能) incompetency; lack of talent. ¶ ~한 incapable; incompetent; good-for-nothing.
무능력(無能力) incompetence; disability; incapacity. ∥ ~자 an incompetent person; a person without legal capacity.
무늬 a pattern; a design; a figure. ¶ ~ 없는 plain; unadorned; unfigured.
무단(武斷) ¶ ~정치 military government / ~주의 militarism.

무단(無斷) ¶ ~히 without notice; without leave [permission] (허가 없이). ‖ ~거주자 a squatter / ~결석 absence without notice [leave] / ~사용 illegal use / ~횡단 jaywalking / ~횡단자 a jaywalker.

무담보(無擔保) ¶ ~의 unsecured; without collateral ‖ ~로 돈을 빌려주다 grant (*a person*) a loan without collateral. ‖ ~대부금 an unsecured loan / ~사채 an unsecured [a naked] debenture.

무당(巫堂) 《民俗》 a (female) shaman; an exorcist. ‖ ~이 제 굿 못하고 소경이 저 죽을 날 모른다 《俗談》 The fortuneteller cannot tell his own fortune. ‖ ~서방 (남편) a shaman's husband; (꿩만 바라는 사람) a man who likes things which are free; a drone.

무당벌레 《蟲》 a ladybird (ladybug).

무대(舞臺) 《연극의》 the stage; 《활동의》 one's sphere [field] (*of activity*). ¶ ~인이 되다 go on the stage / 첫 ~를 밟다 make *one's début*. ‖ ~극 [감독] a stage drama (director) / ~장치 (stage) setting; the set(s) / ~효과 stage effect.

무더기 a heap; a pile; a mound. ¶ ~ 해고 a mass discharge [layoff] / ~로 쌓이다 be piled up.

무더위 sultriness; sweltering heat; hot and humid weather.

무던하다 ① 《사람이》 (be) generous; broad-minded; liberal. ② 《정도가》 (be) quite good [nice]; satisfactory.

무던히 quite; fairly; considerably; quite nicely (잘). ¶ ~ 애를 쓰다 make considerable efforts.

무덤 a grave; a tomb.

무덥다 (be) sultry; sweltering; hot and damp; muggy.

무도(無道) ¶ ~한 inhuman; brutal; cruel; heartless / ~한 짓을 하다 act brutally toward (*a person*); be cruel (*to*).

무도(舞蹈) ¶ ~ a dance; dancing. ~하다 dance. ‖ ~곡 dance music / ~병 《醫》 St. Vitus's dance; chorea / ~장 a dance hall; a ballroom / ~회 a dancing party; a ball.

무독(無毒) ¶ ~한 innoxious; poisonless; nontoxic; harmless.

무두질 tanning. ~하다 tan; dress.

무득점(無得點) ¶ ~의 scoreless / ~으로 끝나다 end scoreless.

무디다 ① 《우둔하다》 (be) dull; slow. ¶ 눈치가 무딘 사람 a dull person. ② 《말씨가》 blunt; curt; brusque. ¶ 말을 무디게 하다 talk bluntly. ③ 《칼날이》 (be) blunt; dull. ¶ 무딘 면도날 a dull razor blade. [unaffable.

무뚝뚝하다 (be) curt; brusque;]

무람없다 (be) impolite; rude.

무량(無量) ¶ ~하다 (be) infinite; inestimable; immeasurable. ‖ ~수전(壽殿) 《佛》 the Hall of Eternal Life; the *Muryangsujeon*.

무럭무럭 ① 《빨리》 (grow up) rapidly; well. ② 《김 따위가》 ¶ 김이 ~ 나는 수프 steaming [piping hot] soup.

무려(無慮) about; some; as many as; no less than (*3,000*).

무력(武力) military power. ¶ ~으로 by force (of arms) / ~에 호소하다 appeal [resort] to arms; use force. ‖ ~개입 an armed intervention / ~외교 power diplomacy / ~충돌 (avoid) an armed clash.

무력(無力) ¶ ~한 powerless; helpless; impotent; incompetent.

무렵(때) time; 《즈음》 about; around; toward(s); (…살 무렵) about the time when…. ¶ 꽃 필 ~ the flower season / 해질 ~에 toward evening / 그 ~에 in those days; at that time; then.

무례(無禮) ¶ ~한 rude; impolite; discourteous; uncivil; insolent / ~하게는 ~하다 be rude enough to (*do*).

무뢰한(無賴漢) a rogue; a rascal; a scoundrel; a hooligan.

무료(無料) ¶ ~의 [로] free (of charge); gratis; for nothing; without a fee / ~로 제공하다 be offered free [for nothing]. ‖ ~관람 [입장] 권 a free ticket [pass] / ~배달 free delivery / ~봉사 free service / ~수하물 허용량 《여객기 등의》 free baggage allowance / ~숙박소 a free lodging house / ~승차권 a (free) pass / ~입장자 a free visitor.

무료(無聊) tedium; boredom; ennui. ¶ ~한 tedious / ~함을 달래다 beguile the tedium; while away the time.

무루(無漏) without omission [exception]; to everybody; all.

무르녹다 ① 《익다》 get [become] ripe; ripen; mellow. ② 《녹음이》 deepen; become deeper.

무르다 ① 《물건이》 (be) soft; tender; limp; squashy. ② 《사람이》 (be) weak; soft (*on, with*); tender-hearted(정에); weak-kneed (대가). ¶ 여자에게 ~ have a soft spot for women / 아이에게 ~ be soft on *one's* child.

무르다 《산 것을》 return (*a thing*) and get the money back; cancel a purchase (and take back the money).

무르익다 ① (익다) ripen; mellow. ¶무르익은 감 a fully ripened persimmon. ② (때가) be ripe (*for*); mature. ¶때가 무르익기를 기다리다 wait till the time is ripe (*for*).

무릅쓰다 (곤란 등을) risk; brave; venture to do. ¶위험을 ~ brave danger; run the risk (of being killed) / 폭풍우를 무릅쓰고 in spite of the storm / 생명의 위험을 무릅쓰고 아이를 구하다 rescue a child at the risk of *one's* life.

무릇[植] a squill.

무릇[副] generally (speaking); as a (general) rule; on the whole; in general. ¶~ 사람이란 것 a man in general. 「Utopia.

무릉도원(武陵桃源) an Arcadia;

무릎 a knee; a lap. ¶~ 깊이의 knee-deep / ~을 꿇다 kneel down; fall on *one's* knees (*before*). ‖ ~ 관절 the knee joint.

무리 ① (사람의) a group; a throng; a crowd (군중); a mob (폭도); (짐승의) a flock (*of sheep*); a herd (*of cattle*); a pack (*of wolves*). ② (해·달의) a halo; a ring; a corona.

무리(無理) ① (부조리) unreasonableness. ¶~ 한 unreasonable; unjust; unnatural / ~ 없는 reasonable; natural; justifiable / ~ 하게 unreasonably; unjustly / 그것은 ~ 한 주문이다 That's asking too much. / ~ 없는 자세가 natural posture. ② (불가능) impossibility. ¶~ 한 impossible; ~ 한 짓을 하다 attempt the impossible / 그 일은 나에게 ~ 이다 I am not equal to the task. ③ (지나침) excessiveness; (과로) overwork; overstrain. ¶~ 한 excessive; immoderate / ~ 를 하다 overwork (overstrain) *oneself* / ~ 하지 마라 Take it easy. ④ (강제) compulsion. ¶~ 한 forcible; forced; compulsory / ~ 하게 by force; against *one's* will / ~ 하게 …하도록 하다 compel (force) (*a person*) *to do*. ‖ ~ 수(식, 방정식) an irrational number (expression, equation).

무마(撫摩) ① (손으로) ~ 하다 pat; stroke. ② (달램) ~ 하다 appease; pacify; sooth; quiet.

무면허(無免許) ~ 의 unlicensed. (drive a car) without a license. ‖ ~ 운전사 (의사) unlicensed driver (practitioner).

무명(무명) cotton; cotton cloth. ‖ ~ 옷 cotton clothes.

무명(無名) ¶~ 의 nameless; unnamed; anonymous (익명의); obscure (알려지지 않은) / ~ 용사의 묘 the Tomb of the Unknown Soldiers. ‖ ~ 씨 an anonymous person / ~ 작가 an obscure writer.

무명조개[貝] a clam.

무명지(無名指) a ringfinger.

무모(無毛) ~ 의 hairless. ‖ ~ 증[醫] atrichosis.

무모(無謀) ~ 하다 (be) reckless; thoughtless; rash; imprudent. ¶~ 하게 recklessly; rashly. 「cle.

무문근(無紋筋)[解] a smooth mus-

무미(無味) ~ 한 (맛없는) tasteless; flat; vapid; flavorless / ~ 건조한 dry; insipid; uninteresting; prosaic (*life*). 「rifle.

무반동총(無反動銃)[軍] a recoilless

무반주(無伴奏) ¶~ 의 unaccompanied (*cello sonata*).

무방비(無防備) ¶~ 의 defenseless; unfortified; open. ‖ ~ 도시 an open city.

무방하다(無妨--) do no harm; do not matter; (…해도 좋다) may; can; be all right. ¶그렇게 해도 ~ You may do so. / 약간의 산책은 ~ A little walk will do you no harm.

무배당(無配當)[經] ¶~ 의 without dividend. ‖ ~ 주 a non-dividend stock.

무벌점(無罰點) ¶~ 이다 be clean of penalty marks.

무법(無法) ¶~ 한 unlawful; unjust. ‖ ~ 자 a ruffian; an outlaw / ~ 천지 a lawless world (state); anarchy.

무변(無邊) ~ 의 boundless; limitless; infinite. ‖ ~ 대해(大海) a boundless ocean.

무변화(無變化) changelessness; monotony (단조로움).

무병(無病) ~ 하다 (be) in good health; healthy.

무보수(無報酬) ~ 의 gratuitous / ~ 로 without pay (recompense, reward); (무료의) free of charge; for nothing.

무분별(無分別) thoughtlessness; indiscretion. ~ 하다 (be) thoughtless; indiscreet; imprudent.

무불간섭(無不干涉) indiscreet meddling in everything; indiscreet interference. ~ 하다 always nose into; meddle constantly.

무비(無比) ¶~ 한 peerless; unparalleled; unique / 당대 ~ 의 unparalleled by *one's* contemporaries.

무비판(無批判) ¶~ 적 (으로) uncritical(ly); indiscriminate (ly).

무사(武士) a warrior; a soldier; a knight.

무사(無私) ¶~ 한 unselfish; disinterested / 공평 ~ 한 just and fair.

무사(無事) (안전) safety; security; (평온) peace; (건강) good health. ~ 하다 (be) safe; well; peaceful;

무사(無死) ∥ ~ 만루 full bases with no outs.

무사고(無事故) without an accident. ∥ ~ 비행(운전) accident-free flying(driving).

무사마귀 a wart; a verruca.

무사분주(無事奔走) ~하다 (be) very busy about nothing.

무사안일(無事安逸) ~주의 an easy-at-any-price principle; an easygoing attitude.

무사태평(無事泰平) ~하다 (be) peaceful; easygoing; carefree.

무산(無産) ~의 propertyless; unpropertied. ∥ ~계급 the proletariat / ~자 a proletarian; a man without property.

무산(霧散) ~하다 disperse; be dispelled; dissipate.

무상(無上) ~의 the highest; the greatest; supreme; the best / ~의 영광 the supreme honor.

무상(無常) uncertainty; mutability; transiency. ~한 uncertain; mutable; transient / 인생의 transient affairs of (this) life; the frailty of life / 인생은 ~하다 Nothing is certain in this world.

무상(無償) ~(으로) gratis; for nothing; free (of charge). ∥ ~ 교부(證) delivery without compensation / ~ 대부 a free loan / ~ 배급 free distribution / ~ 원조 a grant; grant-type aid / ~ 주 a stock dividend.

무상출입(無常出入) ~하다 go in and out constantly; visit freely; have free access to.

무색(-色) dyed color. ∥ ~옷 clothes made of colored cloth.

무색(無色) ① 《빛깔》 ~의 colorless; achromatic 《lens》 / ~ 투명의 액체 a colorless transparent liquid. ②《무안》 ~하다 be ashamed; feel shame. ∥ ~케 하다 put 《a person》 to shame; put 《a person》 in the shade; outshine 《eclipse》 《a person》.

무생물(無生物) an inanimate object (being); a lifeless (nonliving) thing. ∥ ~계 inanimate nature.

무서리 the first frost of the year; an early frost.

무서움 fear; fright; terror. ¶ ~을 타다 be easily frightened / ~을 모르다 have no fear; be fearless; fear nothing / ~을 참다 bear one's fear.

무서워하다 fear; be fearful 《of》; be afraid 《of a thing, to do》; be frightened 《at》; be scared 《at》.

무선(無線) ~(by) wireless (radio). ∥ ~공학 radio engineering / ~사진전송 radiophotography / ~송신 wireless transmission / ~전신 a wireless (telegraphy) / ~전신(전화)국 a radio (wireless) station / ~전화 a radiotelephone; a radiophone; cellular phone; a walkie-talkie / ~제어(조종) radio control / ~주파수 radio frequency / ~중계 radio relay / ~통신 radio (wireless) communication / ~표지 a radio beacon / ~호출기 a pager (beeper); a radio beeper.

무섭다 ①《두렵다》(be) fearful; terrible; dreadful; horrible; frightful. ¶ 무서운 병 a horrible disease / 무서운 구두쇠 an awful miser / 무섭게 하다 frighten; terrify; scare. ②《사납다》(be) ferocious; fierce; formidable.

무성(茂盛) ~한 thick; dense; luxuriant / 나무가 무성한 산 a thickly-wooded hill / 풀이 ~하다 be densely covered with grass.

무성(無性) ~의 《生》 nonsexual; asexual; 《植》 neutral 《flowers》. ∥ ~생식 asexual reproduction.

무성(無聲) ~의 silent; voiceless. ~영화 a silent picture / ~음 a voiceless sound.

무성의(無誠意) insincerity. ~하다 (be) insincere; unfaithful.

무세(無稅) ~의 free 《imports》; tax-(duty-)free / ~로 free of duty; duty-free.

무소(動) a rhinoceros.

무소(無所) omni-. ¶ ~부재(부지, 불능) omnipresent (omniscient, omnipotent).

무소득(無所得) ~하다 gain nothing (little) 《from, by》.

무소속(無所屬) ~의 independent; unattached; neutral; nonpartisan(정당의) / ~으로 입후보하다 run for an election independent of any party. ∥ ~의원 an independent (member); nonaffiliated members.

무소식(無消息) ¶ ~이다 hear nothing from 《a person》 / ~이 희소식 No news is good news.

무쇠 (cast) iron.

무수(無水) 《化》 ~의 anhydrous. ∥ ~(化合)물 an anhydrous compound; anhydride.

무수(無數) ~한 numberless; innumerable; countless / ~히 innumerably; without number.

무수리[鳥] an adjutant (bird).

무숙자(無宿者) a tramp; a vagabond; a vagrant.

무순(無順) irregularity; disorder; (단서로) "Not in order." ¶ ~으로 without order.

무술(武術) military (martial) arts.
무슨 what 《*book*》: what sort (kind) of 《*a man*》. ¶ ~ 일로 on what business / ~ 까닭에: for what reason / ~ 일이 있더라도 above all things; at any cost; by all means.
무승부(無勝負) a draw; a drawn game; a tie. ¶ ~가 되다 draw (tie) with 《*a person*》; end in a draw (tie).
무시(無視) ~하다 ignore; disregard; pay no attention (heed) (to); take no notice (of). ¶ ~을 ~하고 in disregard of / 남의 기분을 ~하다 pay no attention to other's feelings. 「all times.
무시로(無時로) at any time; at
무시무시하다 (be) terrible; horrible; dreadful; awful; frightful.
무시험(無試驗) ¶ ~으로 (be admitted) without examination.
무식(無識) ignorance; illiteracy. ¶ ~한 ignorant; illiterate; uneducated. ‖ ~쟁이 an ignorant man; a sheer illiterate.
무신경(無神經) ¶ ~한 insensitive; thick-skinned; inconsiderate.
무신고(無申告) ¶ ~로 without notice (leave). ‖ ~데모 an unsanctioned demonstration / ~집회 a meeting held without previous notice.
무신론(無神論) 〔哲〕 atheism. ¶ ~의 atheistic. ‖ ~자 an atheist.
무실점(無失點) ¶ ~으로 without losing a point.
무심(無心) ① ~하다 〔무관심〕 be indifferent 《*in*》: do not care 《*about*》: 〔순진〕 (be) innocent 《*의도 없음*》: unintentional; casual. ¶ ~코 unintentionally; inadvertently; casually; incidentally; carelessly / ~코 한 말 a casual remark. ② 〔佛〕 mindlessness; no-mindedness.
무쌍(無雙) ~하다 (be) peerless; matchless; unparalleled.
무아(無我) self-effacement; selflessness. ¶ ~의 경지에 달하다 attain a spiritual state of perfect selflessness; rise above self. ‖ ~경 ecstasy; transports; absorption.
무안(無顔) ~하다 be ashamed of 《*oneself*》; feel shame; lose face. ¶ ~을 주다 put 《*a person*》 to shame; put 《*a person*》 out of countenance; make 《*a person*》 blush.
무안타(無安打) 〔野〕 no hits. ‖ ~ 무득점경기 a no-hit, no-run game.
무어라 ¶ ~ 하든 whatever one may say; after all 〔결국〕 / ~ 말할 수 없다 be unspeakable; One cannot tell.

무언(無言) silence. ¶ ~의 silent; mute / ~ 중(에) in silence; without uttering a word / ~의 용사 silent (dead) war heroes. ‖ ~극 a dumb show; a pantomime.
무엄(無嚴) ¶ ~한 rude; audacious; impudent; indiscreet / ~하게도 …하다 have the indiscretion (impudence) to 《*do*》; be impertinent enough to 《*do*》.
무엇(대명사) 〔의문〕 what: 〔부정〕 something. ¶ ~이든 anything; whatever / ~보다도 above all 〔things〕: first of all / ~하러 what for.
무역(貿易) 〔foreign〕 trade; commerce. ~하다 trade 《*with*》: have trade relations 《*with*》. ¶ ~을 진흥(확대)하다 promote (expand) foreign trade / 한국의 대미 ~ Korea's trade with the United States / 한중 간의 ~ trade between Korea and China; Korea-China trade / 점증하는 ~의 불균형 the growing trade imbalance / ~의 자유화 liberalization of trade. ‖ ~격차 a trade gap / ~경쟁국 a trade rival / ~관리 (foreign) trade control (management) / ~규모 the volume of trade / ~마찰 trade friction (conflicts) 《*between*》 / ~박람회 a trade fair / ~상 a trader / ~상대국 a trading partner / ~수지 the trade balance (~수지의 적자 trade loss) / ~액 the amount of trade / ~외 수지 the invisible trade balance / ~장벽 a trade barrier / ~적자(흑자) a trade deficit (surplus) / ~정책 a trade policy / ~품 trade goods / ~항 a trading port / ~협정 a trade agreement / ~회사 a trading firm (company).
무역역조(貿易逆調) adverse trade balance of payments; trade imbalance.
무연(無煙) ¶ ~의 smokeless. ‖ ~탄 anthracite; hard coal 《*美*》 / ~화약 smokeless powder.
무연(無鉛) ‖ ~가솔린 lead-free (unleaded) gasoline.
무연고(無緣故) ¶ ~의 without relations; unrelated. ‖ ~분묘 a grave having no surviving relatives; a neglected (forlorn) grave.
무예(武藝) ⇨ 무술.
무욕(無慾) ¶ ~의 (be) free from avarice; unselfish.
무용(武勇) bravery; valor. ‖ ~담 a tale of heroism.
무용(無用) ¶ ~의 useless; of no use. ‖ ~지물 a useless thing; a good-for-nothing.
무용(舞踊) dancing; a dance. ~하다 dance; perform a dance.

무운(舞−)단 a ballet troupe; a *corps de ballet* (프).

무운(武運) the fortune(s) of war. ¶ ~을 장구를 빌다 pray for *(a person's)* good fortune in battle.

무운(無韻) ¶ ~의 unrhymed; blank *(verse).* 「(glory).

무위(武威) (raise) military prestige

무위(無爲) idleness; inactivity. ¶ ~의 생활 an idle life / ~ 무책의 정부 a do-nothing government / ~도식하며 live [lead] an idle life; eat the bread of idleness.

무의무탁(無依無托) ~하다 (be) homeless; 《서술적》 have no one to depend [rely] on.

무의미(無意味) ¶ ~한 meaningless; senseless; insignificant.

무의식(無意識) unconsciousness. ¶ ~적(으로) unconscious(ly); involuntar(il)y; mechanical(ly).

무의촌(無醫村) a doctorless village.

무이자(無利子) ¶ ~의 [로] without [free of] interest. ‖ ~ 공채 flat [passive] bonds.

무익(無益) ~하다 (be) useless; futile. ¶ ~한 살생 (the) wanton destruction of life / ~한 논쟁 a futile dispute / 유해~하다 do more harm than good.

무인(武人) a warrior; a soldier.

무인(拇印) a thumbmark.

무인(無人) ¶ ~건널목 an unattended (railroad) crossing / ~ 비행기 a pilotless [radio-controlled] plane / ~위성 an unmanned satellite / ~판매기 a vending machine.

무인도(無人島) a desert [an uninhabited] island.

무인지경(無人之境) an uninhabited region. ¶ ~을 가듯하다 carry everything before one. 「niless.

무일푼(無一−) ¶ ~이다 be pen-

무임(無賃) ¶ ~으로 free of charge; ~ 승차를 하다 ride free (of charge); have a free ride. ‖ ~승차권 a free pass.

무임소(無任所) ¶ ~의 unattached; unassigned; without portfolio. ‖ ~장관 a Minister (of State) without portfolio.

무자각(無自覺) ¶ ~의 insensible *(of)*; unconscious *(of)*.

무자격(無資格) disqualification; incapacity. ¶ ~의 disqualified; 《무면허의》 unlicensed / ~교원 an unlicensed teacher / ~자 a disqualified person.

무자력(無資力) lack of funds.

무자맥질 diving; ducking. ~하다 dive into [in, under] water; duck *down*.

무자본(無資本) ¶ ~으로 without capital [funds].

무자비(無慈悲) ¶ ~한 merciless; cruel; ruthless / ~한 짓을 하다 do a cruel thing.

무자식(無子息) ~하다 (be) childless; heirless.

무자위 a water pump.

무작위(無作爲) ¶ ~의 random / ~로 randomly; at random / ~로 샘플을 뽑다 choose samples at random / ~(표본) 추출(법) random sampling.

무작정(無酌定) lack of any definite plan. ¶ ~하고 recklessly; with no particular object in mind; ~ 돈을 쓰다 spend money recklessly / ~ 상경하다 go up to Seoul with no particular object [plan] in mind.

무장(武將) a general; a warlord.

무장(武裝) 《나라의》 armaments; 《병사의》 equipments. ~하다 arm; bear arms; be under arms. ¶ ~한 armed *(bandits)* / ~을 풀다 disarm. ‖ ~간첩 an armed spy / ~간첩선 an armed espionage ship / ~강도 an armed robber / ~봉기 rising in arms; an armed uprising / ~중립 armed neutrality / ~해제 disarmament; demilitarization / ~화 militarization. 「army.

무장지졸(無將之卒) a leaderless

무저항(無抵抗) nonresistance. ¶ ~으로 without resistance. ‖ ~주의 the principle of nonresistance.

무적(無敵) ¶ ~의 invincible; unconquerable. ‖ ~함대 《史》 《스페인의》 the Invincible Armada.

무적자(無籍者) a person without a registered domicile.

무전(無電) (by) radio; wireless. ‖ ~실 a radioroom / ~장치 a radio [wireless] apparatus.

무전(無錢) ¶ ~ 취식하다 leave a restaurant without paying the bill / ~ 여행하다 travel without money.

무절제(無節制) ~하다 (be) intemperate; immoderate; incontinent.

무절조(無節操) ¶ ~한 inconstant; unchaste; unprincipled.

무정(無情) ¶ ~한 heartless; hardhearted; cold-hearted.

무정견(無定見) ¶ ~한 inconstant; unprincipled; fickle; wavering.

무정란(無精卵) an unfertilized [wind] egg.

무정부(無政府) anarchy. ¶ ~의 anarchic(al) / ~ 상태에 있다 be in a state of anarchy. ‖ ~주의 anarchism / ~주의자 an anarchist.

무정형(無定形) ¶ ~의 formless;

무제(無題) 《작품에서》 no title. ¶ ~의 titleless; without a title.

무제한(無制限) ¶ ~의 limitless; unrestricted; free / ~으로 without any restriction; with no restriction; freely.

무조건(無條件) ¶ ~의 unconditional; unqualified / ~으로 unconditionally; unqualifiedly. ¶ ~반사 an unconditional reflex / ~항복 unconditional surrender.

무좀 〖醫〗 athlete's foot.

무종교(無宗敎) ¶ ~의 irreligious; atheistic. ¶ ~자 an atheist; an unbeliever.

무죄(無罪) innocence. ¶ ~의 not guilty; innocent; guiltless / ~를 선고하다 declare 《*a person*》 not guilty / ~석방 acquittal (and discharge).

무주의(無主義) ¶ ~한 without any (fixed) purpose; unprincipled.

무주정(無酒精) ¶ ~음료 a nonalcoholic beverage; a soft drink.

무주택(無住宅) ¶ ~서민(층) the homeless masses / ~자 a houseless 〔homeless〕 person / ~증명서 a certificate verifying 《*a person's*》 homeless status.

무중력(無重力) (a state of) weightlessness 〔nongravitation〕.

무증거(無證據) lack of evidence 〔proof〕; no evidence 〔witness〕.

무지(無知) ignorant; illiteracy. ~하다 (be) ignorant; stupid. ¶ ~한 백성 unenlightened people.

무지개 a rainbow. ‖ ~빛 rainbow color.

무지근하다 feel heavy 〔dull〕.

무지렁이 a fool; an ignoramus.

무지막지하다(無知莫知一) (be) ignorant and uncouth; rough; heartless.

무지몰각하다(無知沒覺一) be utterly ignorant; know nothing.

무직(無職) ¶ ~의 unemployed; jobless; out of work / 그는 ~이다 He has no job. *or* He is out of work. / ~자 a jobless man; the unemployed.

무진(無盡) ☞ **무한**(無限).

무진장(無盡藏) ¶ ~한 inexhaustible; abundant / ~한 천연자원 inexhaustible natural resources.

무질서(無秩序) disorder; confu*sion*; chaos. ¶ ~한 *disordered*; confused; chaotic; lawless / ~한 상태에 있다 be in disorder.

무찌르다 defeat; crush; smash; attack; mow down 《*the enemy*》.

무차별(無差別) indiscrimination. ¶ ~의 indiscriminate / ~한 대우 (give them) equal treatment / ~하게 indiscriminately; without distinction 《*of sex*》.

무착륙(無着陸) ¶ ~의 nonstop / ~ 비행을 하다 make a nonstop flight; fly nonstop 《*to*》.

무참(無慘) ¶ ~한 merciless; cruel; pitiless.

무책(無策) lack of policy 〔plan〕.

무책임(無責任) irresponsibility. ¶ ~한 irresponsible / ~하게 irresponsibly / 그는 ~한 사내다 He has no sense of responsibility.

무척 very 《much》; quite; highly; extremely; exceedingly.

무척추동물(無脊椎動物) an invertebrate animal. 〔less.

무취(無臭) ¶ ~의 odorless; scent-

무취미(無趣味) ☞ 몰취미.

무치다 season; dress. ¶ 나물을 ~ season 〔dress〕 vegetables.

무턱대고 《무모하게》 recklessly; blindly; rashly; 《이유 없이》 without reason; 《준비 없이》 with no preparation; 《수단·능력 없이》 with no resources 〔capability〕.

무테(無一) brimless; rimless. ¶ ~안경 (a pair of) rimless spectacles.

무통(無痛) ¶ ~의 painless. ¶ ~분만 〖醫〗 painless delivery.

무투표(無投票) ¶ ~로 without voting. ¶ ~당선 being chosen without voting / ~당선지구 a district uncontested in election.

무표정(無表情) ¶ ~한 expressionless; blank; deadpan 《美俗》.

무풍(無風) ¶ ~의 windless; calm. ‖ ~대 〖地〗 the calm latitudes; the doldrums / ~상태 a (dead) calm; a peaceful condition 《비유》.

무학(無學) ignorance. ¶ ~의 ignorant; illiterate; uneducated.

무한(無限) infinity. ~하다 (be) limitless; endless; infinite; boundless; eternal 《영구》. ¶ ~의 infinitely; boundlessly; eternally / ~대 《소》의 infinite 〔infinitesimal〕. ‖ ~궤도(차) a caterpillar (tractor) / ~급수 〖數〗 an infinite series / ~책임(사원) (a member with) unlimited liability / ~책임회사 an unlimited (liability) company.

무해(無害) ¶ ~의 harmless 《*to*》 / ~ 무익한 neither harmful nor useful.

무허가(無許可) ¶ ~의 unlicensed; nonlicensed. ¶ ~건물 〔판자집〕 an unlicensed building 〔shack〕.

무혈(無血) ¶ ~혁명 〔점령〕 a bloodless revolution 〔occupation〕.

무협(武俠) chivalry; heroism.

무형(無形) ¶ ~의 《비물질적》 immaterial; 《추상적》 abstract; 《정신적》 moral; spiritual; 《안 보이는》 invisible; 《형체 없는》 formless; intangible. ‖ ~문화재 an intan-

무화과(無花果) 〖植〗 ~ a fig (tree).

무환(無換) ∥ ~수입[수출] no-draft import [export].

무효(無效) invalidity; ineffectiveness. ¶ ~의 invalid; unavailable; ineffectual; fruitless; futile / ~가 되다 become null [void, invalid]; come to nothing / ~로 하다 annul; invalidate 《a contract》; make (null and) void. ∥ ~투표 an invalid vote.

무훈(武勳) a distinguished military service. ☞ 무공(武功).

무휴(無休) ¶ ~이다 have no holiday.

무희(舞姬) a dancer; a dancing girl; a ballet girl.

묵 젤리 ~ buckwheat jelly.

묵객(墨客) a calligrapher; an artist; a painter.

묵계(默契) a tacit understanding [agreement] 《with, between》. ~하다 agree tacitly; make a tacit agreement.

묵과(默過) connivance. ~하다 overlook; connive 《at》.

묵낙(默諾) a tacit consent. ~하다 consent tacitly 《to》.

묵념(默念) ① 《묵도(默禱)》 a silent [tacit] prayer. ~하다 pray silently 《for》. ② ☞ 묵상.

묵다 ① (숙박) stay [stop, put up] 《at》. ¶ 호텔에 ~ put up [stop] at a hotel. ② (오래되다) become old; be timeworn (stale). ¶ 묵은 잡지 a back number magazine / 묵은 사상 an old-fashioned idea.

묵독(默讀) ~하다 read silently.

묵례(默禮) ~하다 a nod. ~하다 (make a) bow 《to》; bow in silence.

묵묵(默默) ~하다 (be) silent; mute. ¶ ~히 silently; in silence; mutely / ~히 부답하다 be silent and make no response.

묵비권(默秘權) 〖法〗 (use) the right of silence; (take) the Fifth (Amendment) 《美》.

묵살(默殺) ~하다 take no notice 《of》; ignore. ¶ 반대 의견을 ~하다 ignore objections / 항의를 ~하다 turn a deaf ear to protests.

묵상(默想) (a) meditation. ~하다 meditate 《on》; muse 《on》.

묵시(默示) ① 《신의》 a revelation. ~하다 reveal. ∥ ~록 〖聖〗 ☞ 계시록. ② 《명시에 대한》 implication. ~하다 imply. ¶ ~적 implicit; implied.

묵시(默視) ~하다 overlook; pass over; connive 《at》.

묵은해 the old year; last year.

묵인(默認) a tacit [silent] approval; connivance. ~하다 permit tacitly; give a tacit consent; wink 〔connive〕 《at》.

묵정밭 a fallow field that has gone to waste.

묵정이 an old thing; old stuff.

묵종(默從) acquiescence. ~하다 acquiesce 《in》.

묵주(默珠) 〖가톨릭〗 a rosary.

묵직하다 《무게가》 (be) massive; heavy; 《언행이》 (be) rather grave; dignified. ¶ 묵직이 heavily; gravely.

묵화(墨畫) an India-ink drawing.

묵히다 leave unused [wasted]; let 《goods》 lie idle; keep 《money》 idle.

묶다 bind; tie; fasten. ¶ 손발이 묶이다 be tied [bound] hand and foot.

묶음 a bundle; a bunch; a sheaf 《벼·서류 등의》. ¶ ~을 짓다 bundle; tie up in a bundle.

문(文) ① 〖文〗 a sentence. ② 《학문》 literature; the pen. ¶ ~은 무보다 강하다 The pen is mightier than the sword.

문(門) ①《대문》 a gate; 《출입구》 a door. ¶ ~을 닫다 [열다] close [open] the door. ②《분류상의》 a phylum 《동물》; a division《식물》.

문(問) ☞ 문제. ¶ 제1~ the first question.

문간(門間) a door; an entrance; a doorway; the gate section.

문갑(文匣) a stationery chest.

문경지교(刎頸之交) lifelong friendship; 《친구》 a sworn friend.

문고(文庫) a library. ∥ ~본 a pocket edition; a paperback(ed) book.

문고리 a door ring; a door pull.

문과(文科) 〖人文科〗 the department of liberal arts; 〖史〗 《과거》 the higher civil service examination. ∥ ~대학 a college of liberal arts.

문관(文官) a civil official; the civil service (총칭).

문교(文敎) education. ¶ ~ 업무를 관장하다 be in charge of educational affairs. ∥ ~ 당국 educational authorities concerned / ~예산 the education budget / ~정책 an educational policy / ~행정 educational administration.

문구(文句) words; phrases; an expression.

문기둥(門─) a gatepost.

문단(文壇) the literary world [circles]; the world of letters.

문단속(門團束) ~하다 lock a door securely; secure a door.

문답(問答) questions and answers; a dialog(ue) (대화). ~하다 hold a dialogue; exchange questions and answers. ¶ ~식

으로 in the form of questions and answers. ‖ ~식 교수 catechism.

문대다 rub; scrub. ☞ 문지르다.

문덕(문덕) in lumps; into pieces. ~하다 fall apart 《from decay》.

문둥병(-病) leprosy; lepra; Hansen's disease.

문둥이 a leper; a leprous patient.

문드러지다 ulcerate; fester; decompose; disintegrate.

문득, 문뜩 suddenly; unexpectedly; by chance; casually.

문란(紊亂) disorder; confusion. ~하다 be in disorder. ‖ 풍기 ~ corruption of public morals; an offense against public decency.

문례(文例) a model sentence; an example.

문리(文理) ① 《문맥》 the context; the line of thought. ② 《문과와 이과》 liberal arts and sciences. ‖ ~과 대학 the College of Liberal Arts and Science(s).

문맥(文脈) the context 《of a passage》. ¶ ~상의 contextual.

문맹(文盲) ignorance; illiteracy. ‖ ~률 〔lower〕 the illiteracy rate / ~자 an unlettered person; an illiterate / ~퇴치운동 a crusade against illiteracy.

문면(文面) the contents 〔wording〕 of a letter. ¶ ~에 의하면 according to the letter.

문명(文名) literary fame. ¶ ~을 날리다 win literary fame.

문명(文明) civilization. ¶ ~한 civilized; enlightened / ~의 이기 modern conveniences / ~이 발달함에 따라 with the advance of civilization. ‖ ~국〔사회〕 a civilized country〔society〕 / ~시대 the age of civilization; an enlightened age / ~인 a cultured person.

문묘(文廟) 《공자 사당》 a Confucian shrine 〔temple〕.

문무(文武) civil and military arts; the pen and the sword. ¶ ~겸전(兼全)하다 be well up in both literary and military arts. ‖ ~백관 civil and military functionaries 〔officials〕.

문물(文物) civilization 〔명물〕; culture 〔문화〕. ¶서양의 ~ Occidental civilization 〔culture〕.

문민(文民) a civilian. ‖ ~시대 a civilian's era / ~정부 a civilian government / ~통제 civilian control.

문밖(門-) ① 《문의 밖》 the outside of a house; outdoors. ¶ ~의 outdoor; outside the door 〔door〕 / ~에서 out of doors; in the open 〔air〕. ② 《성밖》 the outside of a castle; 《교외》 the outskirts 《of a city》; suburbs. ‖ ~에 살다 live in the suburbs.

문방구(文房具) stationery; writing materials. ‖ ~점 a stationery store; a stationer's.

문벌(門閥) 《가문》 lineage; 《명문》 good lineage; a distinguished family.

문법(文法) grammar. ¶ ~적(으로) grammatical(ly) / ~강의 a lecture on grammar. ‖ ~학자 a grammarian.

문병(問病) a visit to a sick person. ~하다 visit 《a person》 in hospital 〔one's sickbed〕.

문빗장(門-) a gate bar; a latch.

문사(文士) a literary man; a writer; a man of letters.

문살(門-) the frame of a paper sliding door.

문상(問-) ☞ 조상(弔喪).

문서(文書) 《서류》 a document; 《통신문》 correspondence; 《기록》 a record. ¶ 공 ~ official documents / ~로 in writing / ~로 하다 put 《an agreement》 in writing; commit 《an agreement》 to writing / 회답은 ~로 하여 주십시오 You are requested to answer in writing 〔in written form〕. ‖ ~과 the section of archives / ~위조 forgery of documents.

문선(文選) an anthology; 〔印〕 type picking. ~하다 pick types. ‖ ~공 a type-picker.

문설주(門-) a doorjamb.

문소리(門-) a sound 〔noise〕 made by opening or shutting a door.

문수(文數) the size of shoes.

문신(文臣) a civil minister 〔vassal〕. 「too.

문신(文身) a tattoo. ~하다 tat-

문안(門-) ① 《문의 안》 indoors. ② 《성내》 inside the city gate 〔walls〕; within the castle.

문안(文案) a draft. ¶ ~을 작성하다 make 〔prepare〕 a draft 《of, for》; draft. ‖ ~작성자 a drafter.

문안(問安) an inquiry; paying one's respects to 《a person》. ~하다 inquire after another's health; pay the compliments of the season; pay a sympathy visit 《to》; go and comfort 《a person》.

문약(文弱) effeminacy; imbecility 〔나약〕. ‖ ~으로 흐르다 become effeminate.

문어(文魚) 〔動〕 an octopus.

문어(文語) written 〔literary〕 language. ¶ ~체 literary style.

문예(文藝) 〔art and〕 literature; literary art. ‖ ~기자〔란〕 a literary writer〔column〕 / ~부흥 the Renaissance / ~작품〔영화〕 literary works〔films〕 / ~잡지 a lit-

erary magazine / ~평론 literary criticism. 「man (비전문가).
문외한(門外漢) an outsider; a layman.
문우(文友) one's pen pal [friend].
문의(文義) the meaning of a passage.
문의(問議) an inquiry; a reference(신원 따위의). ─하다 inquire 《of a person》 about 《a matter》; make inquiries 《about》; refer 《to a person about a matter》. ¶ 전화로 ─하다 make inquiries by telephone. ‖ ~서 a letter of inquiry / ~처 a reference.
문인(文人) a literary man; a man of letters. ‖ ~협회 the Literary Men's Association. 「follower.
문인(門人) a pupil; a disciple; a
문자(文字) ① 《글자》 a letter; a character (한문 따위). ¶ ─대로 해석하다 interpret 《a passage》 literally 《to the letter》; ~를 모르다 be illiterate [unlettered] / 대[소]~ a capital [small] letter / 표의~ an ideograph / 음표~ a phonogram / ~ 다중방송 a teletext / ~반 《시계의》 a dial [plate]. ② 《한문 문구 따위》 a phrase; an idiomatic phrase from the Chinese classics.
문장(文章) a sentence; a composition; a writing; an article (논문); a style; ¶ ~이 능하다 [서툴다] be a good [bad] writer.
문재(文才) literary talent [ability].
문전(門前) ¶ ~ 앞에 before [in front of] the gate; at the door / ~ 걸식하다 go out begging / ~성시를 이루다 have a constant stream of visitors.
문제(問題) ① 《시험 따위의》 a question; a problem; 《화제·연구의 대상》 a subject; a topic. ¶ 영어 ~ a question in English / ~에 답하다 answer a question / ~를 풀다 solve [work out] a problem / 이 ~에 관한 저서 works on this subject / 환경 보호는 오늘날 가장 중요한 ~의 하나이다 Environmental protection is one of the most crucial topics today. ② 《논의의 대상》 a question; an issue; a problem. ¶ 당면한 ~ the question at issue / 긴급한 ~ a pressing [burning] question; an urgent problem. ③ 《사건·사항》 a matter; an affair; 《골칫거리》 a trouble. ¶ ~를 일으키다 cause trouble / 금전상의 ~ a matter of money / 생사에 관한 ~ a matter of life and death. ¶ ~극 [소설] a problem play [novel] / ~아 a problem child / ~영역 a problem area / ~외 out of the question / ~의식 a critical mind; an awareness of issues / ~점

the point at issue / ~집 a collection of problems.
문제화(問題化) ─하다 become an issue; (표면화) come to a head [the fore]; 《말썽》 cause 《give rise to》 trouble. ¶ 정치 ─하다 make a political issue 《of a matter》.
문조(文鳥) 〔鳥〕 a Java sparrow; a paddybird. 「son》 of a crime.
문죄(問罪) ─하다 accuse 《a per-
문중(門中) a family; a clan.
문지기(門─) a gatekeeper; a gateman; a doorman; a janitor (美).
문지르다 rub; scour; scrub. ¶ 문질러 없애다 rub off [out].
문지방(門地枋) the threshold; a doorsill(문의).
문진(文鎭) a (paper) weight.
문집(文集) a collection of works; an anthology; analects.
문짝(門─) a leaf [flap] of a door.
문책(文責) the responsibility for the wording of an article.
문책(問責) ─하다 reprehend; censure; reprove; rebuke.
문체(文體) a literary style. ¶ 간결 [화려]한 ~ a concise [florid] style / 쉬운 ~로 in an easy [a plain] style.
문초(問招) investigation. ─하다 investigate; inquire 《into》. ¶ ~를 받다 be examined 《by the police》.
문치(文治) civil administration.
문치(門齒) the incisor.
문턱(門─) the threshold; a doorsill. ¶ ~이 닳도록 (visit) frequently / ~을 넘어서다 cross [step over] the threshold.
문틀(門─) a doorframe. 「plate.
문패(門牌) a nameplate; a door-
문풍지(門風紙) a weather strip.
문필(文筆) literary art; writing. ¶ ~로 먹고 살다 live by one's pen. ‖ ~가 a writer; a literary man.
문하(門下) ¶ ~생 one's pupil [disciple, follower].
문학(文學) literature. ¶ ~의 〔적〕 literary. ‖ ~가 a literary man / ~계 the literary world [circles] / ~박사 a Doctor of Literature (생략 Litt. D.) / ~사 a Bachelor of Art (생략 B.A.) / ~작품 literary works / ~청년 a literary youth / 대중 ~ popular literature.
문헌(文獻) literature; documentary records; documents. ¶ 이 문제에 관한 ~ the literature on the subjects / ~을 조사하다 refer to documents. ‖ 참고 ~ a bibliography; references.
문형(文型) a sentence pattern.
문호(文豪) a master [great] writer.
문호(門戶) the door. ¶ ~를 개방 [폐쇄]하다 open [close] the door

문화 (to). ¶ ~개방주의 the open-door principle [policy].

문화(文化) culture; civilization. ¶ ~적 cultural. ¶ ~교류 cultural exchange / ~권 a cultural [culture] area [zone] / ~사 cultural history / ~생활 cultural life / ~수준 a cultural level / ~영화 a cultural [an educational] film / ~유산 a cultural inheritance / ~인 a man of culture; a cultured man / ~인류학 cultural anthropology / ~재 cultural assets [properties] / ~재 관리국 the Cultural Property Preservation Bureau / ~주택 a modern [an up-to-date] house / ~체육관광부 the Ministry of Culture, Sports and Tourism / ~축제 [행사] a cultural festival / ~협정 a cultural agreement / ~훈장 an Order of Cultural Merits; a Cultural Medal.

문후(問候) ~하다 inquire after; pay *one's* respect *(to)*.

묻다¹ 《땅에》 bury 《in, under》; inter 《매장》.

묻다² 《칠 따위가》 be stained 《with》; be smeared 《with》. ¶ 피 묻은 옷 bloodstained clothes.

묻다³ 《문의》 ask; inquire; question.

묻히다¹ 《칠 따위를》 smear; stain; apply 《바르다》. ¶ 옷에 흙을 ~ soil *one's* clothes / 신발에 흙을 ~ get mud on *one's* shoes.

묻히다² 《덮이다》 be buried [under]; be covered with.

물¹ ①《일반적》 water. ¶ 화초에 ~을 주다 water flowers [plants] / ~을 타다 dilute; mix 《wine》 with water / ~에 빠져 죽다 be drowned (to death). ②《홍수》 a flood; (an) inundation. ¶ ~이 나다 be flooded [inundated].

물² 《빛깔》 dyed color (☞ 물들다, 물들이다). ¶ 검정 ~을 들이다 dye black / ~이 날다 the color fades.

물³ ①《신선도》 freshness. ¶ ~이 좋은 생선 a fresh fish. ②《차례》 첫물.

물가 the water's edge; the waterside; the beach.

물가(物價) prices (of commodities). ¶ ~의 움직임 price movement / 저~ 정책 a low-price policy / ~의 급등 a rapid (galloping) rise in prices / ~가 오르다 prices rise (go up) / ~가 내리다 prices fall (come down). ¶ ~고 대책 [정책] a (commodity) price policy / ~상승 [하락] a rise (fall) in prices / ~수준 the price level / ~인상 a price hike / ~지수 a price index / ~체계 a price structure [system] / ~통제 price control / ~파동 the fluctuations of prices.

물가안정(物價安定) price stabilization; stability of commodities prices. ¶ 건실한 ~에 바탕을 둔 지속적인 경제 성장을 추구하다 pursue sustained economic growth based on the firm foundation of price stabilization. ¶ ~선 a price stabilization zone.

물갈퀴 a webfoot.

물감 dyes; dyestuffs; color.

물개 [動] a fur seal.

물거미 [蟲] a water spider.

물거품 a foam; froth; a bubble. ¶ ~이 되다 end [go up] in smoke; come to naught.

물건(物件) an article; goods; a thing; an object.

물걸레 a wet floorcloth. ¶ ~질하다 wipe [mop] with a damp [wet] cloth.

물것 biting insects.

물결 a wave; billow (큰 물결); a ripple (잔 물결); a swell (너울거리는); a surf (밀려오는); a breaker (흰 물결); a wash (물가를 씻어 내리는); a stream (사람·차 따위의). ¶ 속세의 거친 ~ rough dealings of the world / ~을 헤치고 나아가다 plough the waves / ~에 떠다니다 drift on the waves / ~에 휩쓸리다 be swallowed up [carried away] by the waves.

물결치다 move in waves; wave; roll; undulate. ¶ 물결치는 벼이삭 waving heads of rice.

물경(勿驚) to *one's* surprise. ¶ 빚이 ~ 500만 원이다 The debt adds up to a surprising amount of five million *won*.

물고(物故) death. ¶ ~자 the deceased / ~나다 die; pass away.

물고기 a fish.

물고늘어지다 ①《이빨로》 bite at *something* and hang on to *it*. ②《약점·자리 따위를》 hold [hang] on to; cling [stick] to. ¶ 끝까지 ~ stick to *one's* last / 말꼬리를 ~ catch 《a person》 in *his* own words; cavil at 《a person's》 words.

물고동 a stopcock; a faucet. ¶ ~을 틀다 [잠그다] turn on [off] a faucet.

물곬 (도랑) (make) a drain.

물구나무서다 stand on *one's* head and hands.

물구덩이 a pool; a (mud) puddle.

물굽이 a bend [curve] of a stream.

물권(物權) a real right; a right *in rem*. ¶ ~의 설정 the creation of a real right. ¶ ~법 the law of realty.

물귀신(一 鬼神) a water demon. ¶ ~이 되다 be drowned (to death).

물굿하다 《묽다》 (be) somewhat thin [washy, watery].

물기(一 氣) moisture. ¶ ~가 있는

물기름 moist; damp; wet; watery; humid.
물기름 〔머릿기름〕 hair oil.
물길 a waterway; a watercourse.
물꼬 a sluice (gate).
물끄러미 (look) fixedly; steadily. ¶얼굴을 ~ 쳐다보다 look blankly [vacantly] at *a person's* face; stare *(a person)* in the face.
물난리(一亂離) ¶《수해》a flood disaster. ¶~를 겪다 suffer from a flood. ②《수난》the shortage of water supply.
물납(物納) payment in kind. ‖ ~세 a tax in kind.
물놀이 〔물가 놀이〕 a waterside vacation. ¶~ 가다 go swimming 《to the seaside》《for》.
물다¹ 〔지불〕pay; 〔배상〕compensate 《for》.
물다² ① 〔깨물다〕 bite. ② 〔입에〕 put [hold] *(a thing)* in *one's* mouth. ③ 〔벌레가〕 sting 〔모기가〕. ④ 《뮤니바퀴 등이》 engage with.
물독 a water jar [pot].
물두부(一豆腐) bean curds cooked in water.
물들다 ① 〔빛깔이〕 dye; be [get] dyed 《black》; take color. ②〔사상·행실 등이〕 be infected [stained, tainted] with 《vices》; be influenced by. ¶ 아이들을 사회악에 물들지 않도록 하다 prevent children from being infected with the evils of society.
물들이다 dye; color; tint. ¶검게 ~ dye *(a thing)* black; get *(a thing)* dyed black.
물딱총(一銃) a water pistol; a squirt (gun); a syringe.
물때¹ 〔물의〕 fur; incrustation; scale. ¶~를 벗기다 scrub off the scale 《of》.
물때² 〔조수의〕 the tidal hour; 《만조시》 the high tide.
물량(物量) the amount [quantity] of materials [resources]. ¶~ 작전으로 on the strength of material superiority.
물러가다 〔떠나다〕leave; retire; go off [away] 《from》; withdraw 《from》; 〔뒤로〕move backwards; draw [step] back; 〔끝나다〕 pass; be gone; leave. ¶ 한 마디도 없이 ~ leave [go off] from the place without saying a word / 한 걸음 뒤로 ~ take a step backward / 추위가 물러갔다 The cold weather is over [gone].
물러나다 withdraw; retire; resign. ¶식탁에서 ~ withdraw from the table / 공직을 ~ retire [resign] from public life.
물러서다 〔후퇴〕 move backward; draw back; recede; 〔은퇴〕 retire; resign 《*position*》; leave.
물러앉다 ① 〔뒤에 앉다〕 move *one's* seat backward. ②《지위에서》 retire; resign.
물러지다 soften; become tender.
물렁물렁하다 (be) soft; tender.
물렁하다 ¶〔푹 익어서〕(be) overripe; mellow; soft. ②〔성질이〕 (be) flabby; weak-hearted.
물레 a spinning wheel.
물레방아 a water mill.
물려받다 inherit 《*from*》; take over; obtain by transfer. ¶부모에게서 물려받은 inherited from [handed down by] *one's* parents; hereditary.
물려주다 〔양도〕 hand [turn] over; transfer; 《지위를》 abdicate; 《동산을》 bequeath; 《부동산을》 devise. ¶아들에게 사업을 ~ turn the business over to *one's* son.
물론(勿論) (as a matter) of course; to be sure; to say nothing of; naturally. ¶그는 영어는 ~이고 프랑스말도 한다 He knows English, not to speak of French.
물류(物流) 〔經〕 physical distribution. ¶높은 ~비용을 절감하기 위해 산업 기반을 확장하다 expand infrastructure to pare down high distribution costs. ‖ ~관리 (the) administrative control of physical distribution / ~비 distribution costs / ~산업 the distribution industry.
물리(物理) ①〔이치〕 the law of nature. ② ☞ 물리학. ③ ~적인 physical. ‖ ~요법 physiotherapy / ~화학 physical chemistry.
물리다¹ 〔실증나다〕 get sick of; lose interest in; be fed up with.
물리다² ① 〔연기하다〕 postpone; put off; defer. ② 〔옮기다〕 move; shift; get around; 〔뒤로〕 move back[ward]; put back. ③ ☞ 물려주다.
물리다³ 〔치우다〕 clear away; put [take] away.
물리다⁴ 〔푹 익힘〕 cook soft [tender].
물리다⁵ 〔동물·벌레에〕 get bitten by 《fleas》; 〔재갈을〕 bridle 《a horse》; gag 《a person with》.
물리다⁶ 〔돈을〕 make *(a person)* pay [compensate].
물리치다 〔거절하다〕 reject; refuse; turn down; 〔퇴〕 repulse; drive away; beat back.
물리학(物理學) physics. ¶ ~(상)의 physical. ‖ ~자 a physicist / 응용 ~ applied physics / 핵 ~ nuclear physics.
물마루 the crest (of waves); a wave crest.
물만두(一饅頭) boiled ravioli 〔dumplings〕.
물망(物望) popular expectation. ¶ ~에 오르다 be popularly expected; rise in popularity.
물망초(勿忘草) 〔植〕 a forget-me-not.

물매¹ 《경사》 a slope; a slant; an incline; a pitch. ¶ ~가 싼 지붕 a steeply pitched roof.
물매² 《매질》 hard flogging (whipping). ¶ ~ 맞다 be flogged hard.
물목(物目) a list of articles; a catalogue (목록).
물문(一門) a sluice; a floodgate.
물물교환(物物交換) barter. ~하다 barter 《A for B》.
물밀다 《만조가 되다》 rise; flow; 《밀려오다》 surge; rush 《to》.
물방앗간 a (water) mill. 물방앗간 a (water) mill.
물방울 a drop of water; a waterdrop.
물뱀 a sea (water) snake.
물베개 a (rubber) water-pillow (-cushion).
물벼락 ¶ ~ 맞다 get doused.
물벼룩 《動》 a water flea.
물병(一甁) a water bottle (flask).
물보라 a spray (of water).
물부리 《담뱃대의》 the mouthpiece; 《궐련의》 a cigarette holder.
물분(一粉) a liquid face-paint.
물불 ¶ ~을 안 가리고 go through fire and water 《for》; be ready to face any hardship.
물비누 liquid soap; soft soap.
물산(物産) a product; produce (총칭). ¶ ~의 집산지 a product distributing center / 한국의 중요 ~ the staple products of Korea / ~이 풍부하다 be rich in products.
물살 the current of water. ¶ ~이 세다 A current is swift.
물상(物象) 《사물》 an object. ② 《현상》 material phenomena. ③ 《교과》 the science of inanimate nature. [fowl. ②☞물총새.
물새 《鳥》 a water bird; water-
물색하다(物色一) 《찾다》 look for; search for; hunt (up);《고르다》 select; pick.
물샐틈없다 ① 《틈이 없다》 (be) watertight. ② 《완벽》 (be) strict; watertight; airtight. ¶물샐틈없는 경계망을 펴다 throw a tight cordon around. [☞물락.
물세례(一洗禮) ① 《宗》 baptism. ②
물소 《動》 a buffalo.
물수건(一手巾) a wet towel; a steamed (hot) towel.
물수제비뜨다 skip stones; play ducks and drakes.
물시계(一時計) ① 《시계》 a water clock. ② 《계량기》 a water gauge.
물심(一心) ~ 양면으로 both materially and morally.
물싸움 《논물의》 an irrigation (a water-rights) dispute. ~하다 dispute about (over) the water rights.
물써다 ebb; be on the ebb.
물쑥 《植》 an artemisia.
물쓰듯하다 spend money or goods like water.
물씬하다 《물체가》 (be) soft; tender; 《물의》 smell strong; stink 《of fish》 (악취가).
물안경(一眼鏡) swimming goggles.
물약(一藥) a liquid medicine.
물어내다 《변상》 pay for; compensate.
물어떼다 bite (gnaw) off [sate.
물어뜯다 bite off; tear off with one's teeth.
물어보다 《묻다》 ask; inquire; question; 《조회》 make inquiries.
물어주다 ☞ 물어내다.
물억새 《植》 a common reed.
물역(物役) construction (building) materials.
물엿 millet jelly.
물오르다 《초목이》 (sap) rise; 《셈퍼이다》 emerge from poverty; get better off than before. [lard.
물오리 《鳥》 a wild duck; a mal-
물욕(物慾) worldly desires; love of gain. ¶ ~이 강하다 be greedy.
물유리(一琉璃) 《化》 water glass.
물음 a question. ¶ ~표 a question mark.
물의(物議) public censure; trouble. ¶ ~를 자아내다 (일으키다) cause public discussion; give rise to scandal (hot criticism).
물자(物資) goods; commodities; (raw) materials (원료); resources (자원). ¶ ~의 결핍 a scarcity of materials / ~의 공급을 받다 get a supply of commodities / 구호 ~가 그 나라에 보내졌다 Relief supplies were sent to the country.
물자동차(一自動車) ① 《살수차》 a street sprinkler. ② ☞ 급수차(給水車).
물장구 the thrash; the flutter kick. ¶ ~ 치다 make flutters; swim with the thrash.
물장난 ¶ ~ 치다 dabble in the water; play with water.
물적(物的) material; physical. ‖ ~ 자원 material (physical) resources / ~ 증거 real (material) evidence.
물정(物情) 《사물의》 the state of things; the conditions of affairs; 《세태의》 public feeling; the world. ¶ 세상 ~을 모르다 be ignorant of the world.
물주(物主) 《자본주》 a financier; 《노름판의》 a banker.
물줄기 a watercourse; a flow; 《분출하는》 a spout (jet) of water.
물지게 an A-framed yoke for carrying water.
물질(物質) matter; substance. ¶ ~적(인) material; physical / 그는 ~적으로 혜택받고 있다 He is blessed with material comforts. ‖ ~계 the material world / ~ 대사 《生》 metabolism / ~ 명사 a

물집 (피부의) a (water) blister. ¶ ~이 생기다 get a blister (on).

물쩨등 liquid (loose) stool.

물차 (一車) a street sprinkler(살수차); a water carrier(물 공급차).

물체 (物體) a body; an object.

물총새 [鳥] a kingfisher.

물컥 with a strong stink [stench]; stinkingly.

물컹이 (사람) a softy; a weakling; (물건) soft stuff.

물컹하다 (be) soft; squashy.

물크러지다 be reduced to pulp; decompose (썩어).

물통 a water bucket [tank].

물표 (物標) a tally; a (baggage) check.

물푸레 (나무) [植] an ash tree.

물품 (物品) articles; things; goods; commodities. ǁ ~목록 a list of goods / ~세 a commodity tax.

물화 (物貨) goods; commodities (일용품); merchandise (상품).

묽다 ① (농도) thin; watery; washy. ② 묽게 하다 thin; dilute. ③ (사람이) (be) weak(-hearted).

뭇¹ (묶음) a bundle; a faggot; a sheaf (볏단).

뭇² (여러) many; numerous. ¶ ~ 사람 people of all sorts; the people; the public.

뭇매 beating in a group; sound thrashing. ¶ ~맞다 get [be under] a pelting rain of kicks and blows. 「kicks.

뭇매질(get) a pelting rain of

뭇소리 many voices. 「lic gaze.

뭇시선 (~視線) everyone's eyes; pub-

뭇입 public rebuke; criticism from all [many] people.

뭉개다 ① (으깨다) crush; smash; squash; mash. ② (일을) do not know what to do [how to deal with]; find (*a thing*) unmanageable; make a mess of.

뭉게구름 a cumulus.

뭉게뭉게 thickly; in thick clouds.

뭉그러뜨리다 crumble; throw down. 「(down); collapse.

뭉그러지다 crumble; fall [come]

뭉글뭉글하다 (be) clotty; lumpy.

뭉긋하다 (기울기) (be) gently sloped; (휘어짐) (be) slightly bent.

뭉때리다 ☞ 시치미떼다.

뭉때하다 (할 일을) deliberately shirk *one*'s duty.

뭉툭하다 (be) dull; blunt; stubby; stumpy.

뭉뚱그리다 wrap up in a slipshod way; bundle up crudely.

뭉실뭉실하다 (be) plump; portly.

뭉치 a bundle; a bunch.

뭉치다 ① (덩이지다) lump; mass. ② (합치다) put [bind, gather] together; 「한데 뭉쳐 in a lump [bunch] / 짚을 뭉쳐 단을 짓다 bind straw together into a bundle. ③ (덩이짓다) make a lump. ¶ 눈을 ~ make snowball. ④ (완결하다) unite; be united; stand together; combine. ¶ 굳게 ~ be strongly united.

뭉클하다 ① (먹은 것이) feel heavy on *one*'s stomach. ② (가슴이) be filled with (*sorrow*); have a lump in *one*'s throat; be very touching. ¶ 가슴이 뭉클해서 아무 말도 못했다 My heart was too full for words. *or* I was too moved to say anything.

뭉키다 lump; mass; cake. ¶ 단단히 ~ form a hard mass.

뭉텅이 a lump; a bundle; a mass.

뭉툭하다 ☞ 뭉뚝하다.

뭍 land; the shore (배에서 본).

뮤지컬 a musical. ~드라마 (코미디) a musical drama (comedy).

뭐 ① 무엇. ② (감탄·놀람의 표시) What?!; huh?! ¶ ~ 그 사람이 죽었다고 have a keen sense of taste. ǁ ~기관 a taste organ / ~신경 the gustatory nerve.

미 (美) beauty; the beautiful. ¶ 자연의 ~ natural beauty; beauties of nature.

미가 (米價) the price of rice. ǁ ~정책 the rice price policy / ~조절 control (regulation) of the rice price. 「ished; unprocessed.

미가공 (未加工) ¶ ~의 raw; unfin-

미각 (味覺) the palate; the (sense of) taste. ¶ ~을 돋우다 tempt the appetite; make *one*'s mouth water / ~이 예민하다 have a keen sense of taste. ǁ ~기관 a taste organ / ~신경 the gustatory nerve.

미간 (未刊) ¶ ~의 unpublished.

미간 (眉間) the middle of the forehead (the brow). ¶ ~을 찌푸리다 knit *one*'s brows.

미간지 (未墾地) uncultivated land.

미개 (未開) ¶ ~의 uncivilized; savage; primitive (원시적인); undeveloped(미개발의). ǁ ~사회 a primitive society / ~인 a primitive man; a barbarian / ~지 a savage (barbaric) land (만지); (미개발지) a backward region.

미개간 (未開墾) ¶ ~의 uncultivated.

미개발 (未開發) ¶ ~의 undeveloped; uncultivated; underdeveloped.

미개척 (未開拓) ¶ ~의 undeveloped; unexploited; wild, ǁ ~분야 an unexplored field / ~지 undeveloped land; virgin soil.

미거 (美擧) a commendable act; a praiseworthy undertaking.

미결 (未決) ¶ ~의 undecided; pending; unsettled; unconvicted /

미결산 (未決算) ¶ ~의 unsettled (*debt*); outstanding.
미결제 (未決濟) ¶ ~의 unsettled (*bills*); outstanding; unpaid.
미경험 (未經驗) inexperience. ¶ ~의 inexperienced. ‖ ~자 an inexperienced person; a green hand.
미곡 (米穀) rice. ‖ ~보유량 rice in stock / ~상 a rice dealer / ~연도 the rice [crop] year.
미골 (尾骨) [解] the coccyx.
미공인 (未公認) ¶ ~의 not yet officially recognized; unofficial. ☞ 비공인 (非公認).
미관 (美觀) a fine [beautiful] sight [view]. ¶ ~을 이루다 present a fine spectacle / ~을 해치다 spoil the beauty (*of*).
미관 (味官) the taste organs.
미관 (微官) a low office; a low official (사람).
미구 (未久) ¶ ~에 before long; shortly; in the near future.
미국 (美國) the United States (of America) (생략 U.S.; U.S.A.). ¶ ~의 American; U.S. / ~화하다 Americanize. ‖ ~국기 the American flag; the Stars and Stripes; the Star-Spangled Banner(성조기) / ~문화원 the U.S. Cultural Center / ~본토 (the) stateside / ~식품 및 의약품국 the U.S. Food and Drug Administration(생략 U.S.FDA) / ~어 American English / ~인 an American; the Americans(총칭) / ~정부 the U.S. Government.
미군 (美軍) the U.S. Armed Forces; (병사) an American soldier; a GI.
미궁 (迷宮) mystery; a maze; a labyrinth. ¶ ~에 빠지다 become shrouded in mystery.
미그 (러시아제 전투기) a MIG; a Mig jet fighter.
미급 (未及) ¶ ~하다 《미달》 fall short (*of*); be not up to standard; 《영웅》 be inferior (*to*); be no match (*for*).
미기 (美技) a fine play.
미꾸라지 [魚] a loach; a mudfish.
미끄러지다 slide; glide; slip; (실패) fail (in) an examination.
미끄럼 sliding. ¶ ~(을) 타다 slide [play] on a slide; slide [skate] on the ice; slide over the snow (눈 위에서). ‖ ~대 a slide.

미끄럽다 (be) slippery; slimy; (반드럽다) (be) smooth; sleek.
미끈거리다 be slippery [slimy].
미끈미끈 ¶ ~한 slippery; slimy.
미끈하다 (be) sleek; clearcut; handsome; fine-looking.
미끼 ① 《낚시의》 a fish bait. ¶ 낚시에 ~를 달다 bait a fishhook. ② 《유혹물》 a bait; a decoy; a lure. ¶ ~에 걸려들다 be lured; get decoyed. ‖ ~떡밥 (a) paste
미나리 [植] a dropwort. [(bait).
미남 (美男) a handsome man; a good-looking man; an Adonis.
미납 (未納) ¶ ~의 unpaid; in arrears; back (*rent*) / ~의 회비 unpaid membership fees. ‖ ~금 (the amount in) arrears / ~자 a person in arrears; a (*tax*) defaulter / ~처분 punishment for failure to pay.
미네랄 (a) mineral. ‖ ~워터 mineral water; minerals(英).
미녀 (美女) a beauty; a belle; a beautiful woman [girl]. ¶ 절세의 ~ a rare beauty; a woman of matchless beauty.
미뉴에트 [樂] a minuet(te).
미늘 《낚시의》 a barb (of a fishhook); 《갑옷의》 metal scales. ‖ ~창(槍) a halberd; a forked spear.
미니 a mini. ‖ ~스커트 a miniskirt / ~카메라 a minicam(era).
미니어처 miniature. ‖ ~세트 a miniature set.
미닫이 a sliding door [window].
미달 (未達) shortage; lack; insufficiency. ¶ ~하다 be short (*of*); be less than. ‖ ~연령 ~의 underage / 정원 ~로 for want [in the absence] of quorum.
미담 (美談) a beautiful [a noble, an inspiring] story; a fine episode.
미덕 (美德) a virtue. ¶ 겸양의 ~ the virtue of modesty / ~을 쌓다 keep on doing good deeds; accumulate virtues.
미덥다 (be) trustworthy; reliable; dependable. ¶ 미덥지 못한 unreliable; untrustworthy; not to be depended upon.
미동 (微動) a slight shock; a tremor. ¶ ~도 않다 do not move an inch; stand as firm as a rock.
미들 ¶ ~급의 middleweight. ‖ ~급 선수 a middleweight (boxer).
미등 (尾燈) 《자동차의》 a taillight [tail lamp]; a rear light(英).
미디 a midi; a midi-skirt; a midi-dress.
미라 a mummy. ¶ ~로 만들다 mummify; mummy.
미래 (未來) 《장래》 (the) future; time

미량(微量) a very small quantity (amount) 《*of*》. ¶ ~ 분석 microanalysis / ~ 측정기 a microdetector. ‖ ~ 한 ful; fine; lovely.

미려(美麗) beauty. ¶ ~ 한 beautiful.

미력(微力) 〔능력〕 poor ability; 〔자본력〕 slender means; 〔세력〕 little influence. ¶ ~ 을 다하다 do one's bit 〔best〕; do what 〔little〕 one can.

미련 stupidity. ¶ ~ 한 stupid; dull; thickheaded. ‖ ~ 둥이 〔잠이〕 a dullard; a stupid person.

미련(未練) lingering attachment; regret. ¶ ~ 이 있다 be still attached to; have a lingering regret 《*for*》.

미로(迷路) a maze; a labyrinth.

미루다 ① 〔연기〕 postpone; put off; adjourn; defer; delay 〔지연〕. ¶ 뒤로 ~ let 《*a matter*》 wait / 하루하루 ~ put off from day to day / 오늘 할 수 있는 일을 내일로 미루지 마라 Never put off till tomorrow what you can do today. ② 〔전가〕 lay 〔throw〕 《*the blame*》 onto 《*a person*》; shift 〔shuffle off〕 《*the responsibility*》 onto 《*a person*》. ¶ 남에게 책임을 미루지 마라 Don't shift the responsibility onto others. ③ 〔헤아리다〕 infer 〔gather〕 《*from*》; guess; judge 《*by, from*》. ¶ 이것으로 미루어 보아 judging from this.

미루적거리다 prolong; protract; delay; drag out. ¶ 일을 ~ delay one's work.

미륵보살(彌勒菩薩) Maitreya 〔梵〕; a stone statue of Buddha.

미리 beforehand; in advance; previously; in anticipation.

미립자(微粒子) a minute particle; a fine grain; 〔理〕 a corpuscle. ¶ ~ 의 corpuscular. ‖ ~ 필름 a fine grained film.

미만(未滿) 〔이하〕 under; less than.

미망(迷妄) an illusion; a delusion.

미망인(未亡人) a widow. ¶ ~ 이 되다 be widowed; lose one's husband / 아이가 딸린 ~ a widowed mother. ‖ ~ break; at dawn.

미명(未明) ~ 에 before 〔at〕 daybreak.

미명(美名) ¶ …의 ~ 아래 under the pretense 〔veil〕 of 《*charity*》.

미모(美貌) beauty; good (attractive) looks. ¶ ~ 의 beautiful; good-looking / 보기 드문 ~ 의 여인 a woman of rare personal beauty.

미목(眉目) features; looks. ¶ ~ 이 수려하다 have a handsome face (clean-cut features).

미몽(迷夢) an illusion; a delusion. ¶ ~ 에서 깨어나다 be disillusioned; come to one's senses.

미묘(微妙) ¶ ~ 한 delicate; subtle; nice; fine / ~ 한 뜻의 차이 delicate (subtle) shades of meaning.

미문(美文) elegant prose 〔style〕.

미물(微物) ① 〔하찮은 것〕 a trifle. ② 〔미생물〕 a microorganism; a microbe.

미미(美味) 〔맛〕 a good flavor; relish; deliciousness. ¶ ~ 의 tasty; delicious.

미미(微微) ¶ ~ 한 slight; tiny; petty; minute; insignificant.

미발표(未發表) ¶ ~ 의 unpublished; not yet made public.

미복(微服) shabby (tattered) clothes for disguise. ¶ ~ 을 잠행하다 go in (under) the disguise 《*of a salesman*》.

미봉(彌縫) ~ 하다 temporize; patch up; make shift. ‖ ~ 책 a makeshift; a stop-gap policy measure.

미부(尾部) the tail (part). 〔sure〕.

미분(微分) 〔數〕 differential calculus. ~ 하다 differentiate. ‖ ~ 방정식 a differential equation.

미분자(微分子) an atom; a molecule.

미불(未拂) ¶ ~ 의 unpaid; outstanding / ~ 임금 back pay. ‖ ~ 금 an amount not yet paid; an unpaid (outstanding) account / ~ 잔고 an outstanding balance.

미불(美弗) the U.S. dollar.

미불입(未拂入) ¶ ~ 주 〔자본금〕 unpaid (-up). / ~ 주 〔자본금〕 unpaid stocks (capital).

미비(未備) ¶ ~ 의 insufficient; imperfect; defective; not up to the mark / 위생 시설의 ~ lack of proper sanitation / ~ 한 점 a fault; something unsatisfactory; a defect.

미사(美辭) flowery words (language). ¶ ~ 여구를 늘어놓으 use all sorts of flowery words.

미사(가톨릭의) a mass; missa 〔라〕. ¶ ~ 를 올리다 say (read) mass. ‖ 진혼 (추도) ~ a requiem (memorial) mass.

미사일 a missile. ¶ 공대공 ~ an air-to-air missile / 공대지 ~ an air-to-surface missile / 지대공 ~ a surface-to-air missile / 대륙간 탄도 ~ an intercontinental ballistic missile (생략 ICBM) / 전략 〔전술〕 용 ~ a strategic (tactical)

미삼(尾蔘) rootlets of ginseng.

미상(未詳) ¶ ~한(의) unknown; unidentified: not exactly known / 작자 ~ anonymous; unidentified.

미상불(未嘗不) really; indeed.

미상환(未償還) ¶ ~의 outstanding; unredeemed.

미색(米色) light (pale) yellow.

미색(美色) a beautiful woman; a beauty.

미생물(微生物) a microorganism; a microbe. ‖ ~학 microbiology / ~학자 a microbiologist.

미성(美聲) a sweet (beautiful) voice.

미성년(未成年) minority; 《法》 nonage. ¶ ~이다 be under age; be not yet of age. ‖ ~죄 juvenile delinquency / ~자 a minor; 《法》 an infant / ~자 출입금지 《게시》 No minors.

미세(微細) ¶ ~한 minute; detailed; delicate; nice; subtle.

미세스 a married woman; Mrs.

미션스쿨 a mission school.

미소(微小) ¶ ~한 very small; minute; microscopic.

미소(微少) ¶ ~한 very little; a very small amount 《of》.

미소(微笑) a smile. ¶ ~짓다 smile 《at》; beam / 입가에 ~를 띄우고 with a smile on *one's* lips / ~로 찬성의 뜻을 나타내다 smile *one's* approval.

미소년(美少年) a handsome youth; a good-looking boy; an Adonis.

미송(美松) 《植》 an Oregon pine.

미수 a cold drink of roast-grain powder. ‖ 미숫가루 powder of roast grain (rice, barley).

미수(未收) ¶ ~의 uncollected 《*revenue*》; accrued 《*interest*》; receivable 《*bills*》. ‖ ~금 an outstanding amount; an amount receivable.

미수(未遂) ¶ ~의 attempted / ~로 그치다 fail (end) in the attempt. ‖ ~범 an attempted crime; a would-be criminal 《사람》.

미수교국(未修交國) a nation with which it has no diplomatic ties.

미숙(未熟) ① ¶ ~한 unripe; green; immature. ② 《익숙지 못함》 ¶ ~한 (be) inexperienced; unskilled; raw; green.

미숙련(未熟練) ¶ ~의 unskilled; unskilled. ‖ ~공 an unskilled worker (laborer).

미술(美術) art; the fine arts. ¶ ~적인 artistic / 공업(근대) ~ industrial (modern) art / 상업(조형) ~ commercial (plastic) art / 장식 ~ decorative art. ‖ ~가 an artist / ~공예 arts and crafts; fine and applied arts / ~관 an art museum (gallery) / ~대학 a college of fine arts / ~애호가 an art lover / ~전람회 an art exhibition / ~품 a work of art.

미스¹(호칭) Miss 《*Kim*》; (미혼녀) an unmarried woman. ¶ ~유니버스 Miss Universe / 그녀는 아직 ~이다 She is still single (not married yet).

미스²(틀림·잘못) a mistake; an error. ¶ ~를 저지르다 make a mistake / 이 원고에는 교정 ~가 많다 There are plenty of proofreading errors in this manuscript. ‖ ~프린트 a misprint.

미스터 Mister: Mr. 《*pl.* Messrs》.

미스터리 《소설 따위》 a mystery 《novel, *etc.*》.

미식(米食) rice diet. ~하다 eat (live on) rice. ¶ ~인종 rice-eating people.

미식(美食) dainty (delicious) food. ~하다 live on dainty food. ‖ ~가 an epicure; a gourmet.

미식축구(美式蹴球) American football.

미신(迷信) (a) superstition. ¶ ~적인 superstitious / ~을 타파하다 do away with a superstition. ‖ ~가 a superstitious person.

미심(未審) ¶ ~스럽다 (쩍다) (be) doubtful; suspicious; questionable / ~스러운 점 a suspicious (doubtful) point / ~쩍은 듯이 suspiciously; with a doubtful air.

미아(迷兒) a missing (lost) child. ¶ ~가 되다 be missing; be (get) lost 《*in the crowd*》. ‖ ~보호소 a home for missing children.

미안(未安) ¶ ~하다 (be) sorry; regrettable; have no excuse 《*for*》. ¶ ~한 생각이 들다 feel sorry; regret / ~합니다마는 Excuse me. but...; (I am) sorry to trouble you but...

미안(美顔) ‖ ~수 a beauty wash (lotion) / ~술 facial treatment; beauty culture.

미약(微弱) ¶ ~한 weak; feeble.

미얀마 Myanmar; 《공식명》 the Union of Myanmar.

미양(微恙) a slight illness.

미어뜨리다 tear a hole in; rend.

미어지다 get torn; tear; be worn out.

미역¹ 《植》 brown seaweed.

미역²《목욕》 a bath; a swim; swimming. ~감다 swim; bathe in water.

미역국 (國) brown-seaweed soup. ¶ ~ 먹다 《비유적》 fail an exam; be dismissed (discharged); get the sack; be fired.

미연 (未然) ¶ ~에 before 《*it*》 happens; previously / ~에 방지하다 prevent 《*a war*》; nip 《*a plot*》 in the bud.

미열 (微熱) 《have》 a slight fever.

미온 (微溫) ¶ ~적인 lukewarm; half-hearted 《태도가》.

미완 (未完), **미완성** (未完成) ¶ ~인 채로 있다 be left unfinished. ‖ 미완성교향곡 the "Unfinished Symphony."

미용 (美容) beauty; beautiful features. ¶ ~을 위해 식사를 제한하다 diet for beauty; go on a beauty diet. ¶ ~사 a beautician; a hairdresser / ~술 cosmetology; the art of cosmetic treatment / ~식 food for beauty / ~실〔원〕 a beauty parlor 〔shop, salon〕 / ~체조 shape-up exercises; calisthenics / ~학교 a beauty school.

미욱하다 (be) stupid; dull.

미움 hatred; hate; enmity. ¶ ~을 받다 be hated 〔detested〕.

미워하다 hate; detest; have a spite against. ¶ …을 미워하는 나머지 out of hatred for…

미음 (米飮) thin rice gruel; water gruel; rice water.

미의식 (美意識) an (a)esthetic sense.

미익 (尾翼) 《비행기의》 the tail.

미인 (美人) a beautiful woman 〔girl〕; a beauty. ‖ ~계 a badger game / ~계를 쓰다 pull a badger game / ~선발대회 a beauty contest. ②《미국인》 an American.

미작 (米作) a rice crop 〔harvest〕 《수확》; rice culture 《재배》. ‖ ~지대 a rice-producing district.

미장 (美粧) beauty culture 〔treatment〕. ‖ ~원 a beauty shop 〔parlor〕.

미장 (美裝) a fine dress. ~하다 be finely 〔well〕 dressed.

미장이 (―匠―) a plasterer. ¶ ~일 plastering; plaster work.

미저골 (尾骶骨) 〔解〕 the coccyx.

미적 (美的) (a)esthetic. ¶ ~ 감각 an esthetic sense.

미적거리다 ① 《밀다》 push 〔shove〕 forward little by little. ②《연기》 put off from day to day; delay; procrastinate. 「lus.

미적분 (微積分) infinitesimal calcu-

미적지근하다 (be) tepid; lukewarm; half-hearted.

미전 (美展) ☞ 미술 전람회. 「ity.

미점 (美點) a merit; a good qual-

미정 (未定) ¶ ~의 undecided; unsettled; unfixed; uncertain / 날짜는 아직 ~이다 The date is not fixed yet. *or* The date is still undecided. 「standing; unpaid.

미제 (未濟) ¶ ~의 unfinished; out-

미제 (美製) ¶ ~의 American-made; made in U.S.A.

미조 (美爪) ¶ ~사 a manicurist / ~ 술 manicure; pedicure 《발톱의》.

미주 (美洲) the Americas.

미주신경 (迷走神經) 〔解〕 a vagus; the pneumogastric nerves.

미주알고주알 inquisitively; minutely. ¶ ~ 캐묻다 ask inquisitively.

미증유 (未曾有) ¶ ~의 unheard-of; unprecedented.

미지 (未知) ¶ ~의 unknown. ‖ ~수 an unknown quantity.

미지근하다 ☞ 미적지근하다.

미진 (未盡) ¶ ~하다 (be) incomplete; unfinished; 《미흡》 (be) unsatisfied. ¶ 마음에 ~한 데가 있다 have an unsatisfied feeling.

미진 (微震) a faint earth tremor; a slight shock 《of an earthquake》.

미착 (未着) ¶ ~의 not yet arrived 〔delivered〕 / ~의 물품 goods to arrive 〔not yet delivered〕. 「ed.

미착수 (未着手) ¶ ~의 not yet start-

미채 (迷彩) camouflage; dazzle paint.

미처 (as) yet; up to now; so far; before; (not) up to that; far enough. ¶ ~ 손도 쓰기 전에 《die》 before we come to 《*a person's*》 rescue / 그것까지는 ~ 생각 못했다 I was not far-sighted enough to think of that.

미천 (微賤) ¶ ~한 humble; obscure; ignoble.

미취학 (未就學) ¶ ~의 not (yet) attending school. ‖ ~아동 a preschool child.

미치광이 (美致狂―) a madman; a lunatic; 《열광자》 a maniac; a fan. ¶ ~의 mad; insane; crazy.

미치다[1] 《정신이》 go 〔run〕 mad; go 〔become〕 insane; go 〔become〕 crazy; lose *one*'s mind 〔senses〕. ¶ 미친 mad; insane; crazy / 미치게 되다 be insane / 미치게 하다 drive 《*a person*》 mad 〔crazy〕; 《열광》 be crazy 〔mad〕 《about》; lose *one*'s head 《over》. ¶ 여자에 ~ be infatuated with 〔be crazy about〕 a woman / 놀음에 ~ have a mania for gambling.

미치다[2] ① 《이르다》 reach; come 〔up〕 to 《*standard*》; amount to 《액수가》; 《뻗치다》 extend 《to, over》; range 《over》. ¶ 미치지 않다 do not reach; fall short 《of》; 《겨룰 수 없다》 be inferior 《to》; be no match 《for》 / 힘이 미치는 한 무엇이든 다 하다 do everything in

one's power. ②《영향을》 exert influence 《on》; affect.
미크론 a micron (기호 μ). ‖밀리 ~ a millimicron (기호 mμ).
미터 ① meter. ‖ ~법 the metric system. ②《계량기》 a meter; a gauge. ¶ 2개월에 한 번 ~ 검사를 하다 read the meter once every two months. ¶ 가스[수도]~ a gas(water) meter / 택시 ~ a taxi.
미투리 hemp shoes.
미트 《야구 장갑》 a mitt.   [meter.
미풍(美風) a fine [good] custom. ‖ ~양속 good morals and manners.
미풍(微風) a breeze; a gentle wind.
미필(未畢) ¶ ~의 unfinished; unfulfilled.
미필적 고의(未必的故意)〔법〕 willful [conscious] negligence.
미학(美學) (a)esthetics. ¶ ~상의 esthetic. ‖ ~자 an esthetician.
미해결(未解決) ¶ ~의 unsolved; unsettled; pending.
미행(尾行) ~하다 follow; track 《a person》; shadow. ¶ ~을 당하다 be shadowed 《by》. ‖ ~자 a shadow(er); a tail.
미행(美行) a praiseworthy [good] conduct; a good deed.
미행(微行) incognito traveling. ~하다 travel incognito; pay a private visit; go in disguise.
미혹(迷惑) 《미망》 a delusion; an illusion; 《당혹》 perplexity; bewilderment. ~하다 be perplexed [bewildered]; be seduced; be infatuated [captivated] 《with, by》.
미혼(未婚) ¶ ~의 unmarried; single. ‖ ~모 an unmarried mother / ~자 an unmarried person.
미화(美化) beautification. ~하다 beautify 《a city》; make 《the look of the town》 beautiful. ¶ 교내 ~운동 a campaign to beautify the school / 전쟁을 ~하다 glorify [romanticize] war / 죽음을 ~하는 것은 잘못이다 It is wrong to beautify death. ‖ 도시 ~운동 a city beautification [keep-the-city-beautiful] movement.
미화(美貨) American money [currency]; the U.S. dollar.
미확인(未確認) ¶ ~의 not yet confirmed; unconfirmed. ¶ ~보도 news from an unconfirmed source / ~비행물체 an unidentified flying object(생략 UFO).
미흡(未洽) ¶ ~한 insufficient; unsatisfactory; imperfect; defective / ~한 점이 있다[없다] leave something [nothing] to be desired.
미희(美姬) a beautiful girl.
믹서 a [an electric] mixer.
민가(民家) a private house.

민간(民間) ¶ ~의 private; nonofficial; civil; civilian / ~에서 among the people. ‖ ~기업 a private enterprise [business] / ~단체 a nongovernment organization; an NGO / ~방송 a commercial [private] broadcasting / ~설화 [전승] folklore: a folktale: (a) legend / ~신앙 a folk belief / ~의료 people-to-people diplomacy / ~요법 an old wives' remedy: a folk remedy / ~인 a private citizen; a civilian / ~항공 civil aviation / ~회사 a private company.
민감(敏感) ¶ ~한 sensitive 《to》; susceptible 《to》.
민권(民權) the people's rights; civil rights. ‖ ~을 옹호 [신장] 하다 defend [extend] the people's rights.
민단(民團) a foreign settlement group. ‖ 재일본 대한민국~ the Korean Residents Union in Japan.
민도(民度) the living [cultural] standard of the people.
민둥둥하다 (be) bald; bare; treeless.   [tain.
민둥산(一山) a bald [bare] mountain.
민들레 [槿] a dandelion.
민란(民亂) a riot; an insurrection; a revolt; an uprising.
민망(憫惘) ~하다 (be) embarrassed; sorry; pitiful; sad.
민머리 a bald [bare] head; 《쪽 안 찐》 undone hair.
민며느리 a girl brought up in one's home as a future wife for one's son.
민물 fresh water. ‖ ~고기 a fresh-water fish.   [vate house.
민박(民泊) ~하다 lodge at a private house.
민방위(民防衛) civil defense. ‖ ~대 a Civil Defense Corps / ~훈련 Civil Defense training [drill].
민법(民法) the civil law. ‖ ~학자 a scholar of the civil law.
민병(民兵) a militiaman; the militia(부대). ‖ ~단 a militia corps.
민복(民福) well-being of the people; national welfare.
민본주의(民本主義) democracy.
민사(民事) civil affairs. ¶ ~사건 a civil case / ~소송 a civil suit [action] / ~재판 a civil trial.
민생(民生) the public welfare; the people's livelihood. ¶ ~의 안정 the stabilization of the people's livelihood.
민선(民選) ¶ ~의 elected [chosen] by the people. ‖ ~의원 a representative elected by the people [by popular vote].
민속(民俗) folk customs; folkways. ‖ ~무용 folk dance /

민수(民需) private (civilian) demands (requirements). ‖ ~산업 civilian industry / ~품 civilian goods; consumer's goods.

민숭민숭하다 (be) bare; treeless; bald; hairless.

민심(民心) public sentiment; popular feelings. ¶ ~의 동요 popular unrest / ~을 거역하다 go against public sentiment / ~을 얻다 win the confidence of the people. ~contract.

민약설(民約說) the theory of social

민어(民魚) 【魚】 a croaker.

민영(民營) private management (operation). ¶ ~의 private; privately-operated [-managed] / ~으로 하다 privatize; put 《something》 under private management. ‖ ~사업 a private business [enterprise] / ~화 privatization.

민예(民藝) folkcraft; folk art. ‖ ~관 a folkcraft museum / ~품 a folkcraft.

민완(敏腕) ¶ ~의 able; capable; shrewd. ‖ ~가 an able man; a man of ability / ~형사 a shrewd police detective.

민요(民謠) a folk song; a (folk) ballad. ¶ ~가수 a folk singer.

민원(民怨) public resentment (grievance). ¶ ~을 사다 incur the enmity of the people.

민원(民願) a civil appeal. ‖ ~봉사실 a civil petition section / ~사무 civil affairs administration / ~서류 civil affair documents / ~실 the Public Service Center / ~안내(실) the Civil Service Information (Room) / 청구 a window for civil petitions.

민유(民有) ¶ ~의 privately-owned; private. ‖ ~지 private land.

민의(民意) the will of the people; public opinion (consensus). ¶ ~를 존중〔반영〕하다 respect (reflect) the will of the people / ~를 묻다 seek the judgment of the people; consult the will of the people.

민정(民政) 《군정에 대한》 civil administration (government). ¶ ~을 펴다 place 《the country》 under civil administration.

민정(民情) the realities of the people's lives. ¶ ~을 시찰하다 see how the people are living.

민족(民族) a race; a people; a nation. ¶ 한~ the Korean people / 소수~ an ethnic minority / ~적 우월감 racism; ethnocentrism. ‖ ~감정 a national sentiment / ~문제 a racial problem / ~문화 national culture / ~성 racial [national] characteristics (traits) / ~운동 a nationalist movement / ~의식 ethnic [national] consciousness / ~자결 racial self-determination / ~자본 national capital / ~정신 the national spirit / ~주의 racialism; nationalism / ~통일연구원 the Research Institute for National Unification / ~학 ethnology / ~해방 national liberation.

민주(民主) democracy. ‖ ~적인 democratic / 비~적인 undemocratic / ~적으로 in a democratic way / ~화하다 democratize. ‖ ~공화국 a democratic republic / ~국가 a democratic nation (country) / ~당 (美) the Democratic Party; the Democrats / ~정치 a democratic form of government / ~제도 a democratic system / ~주의 democracy / ~주의자 a democrat.

민중(民衆) the people; the masses. ¶ ~화하다 popularize. ‖ ~예술 popular arts / ~오락 popular amusements / ~운동 a popular movement.

민첩(敏捷) ¶ ~한 quick; nimble; prompt; agile / 행동이 ~하다 be quick in action.

민통선(民統線) the farming restriction line (in Korea); the Civilian Control Line (생략 CCL).

민틋하다 (be) smoothly aslant.

민폐(民弊) an abuse suffered by the public; a public nuisance. ¶ ~를 끼치다 cause a nuisance to the people.

민활(敏活) ¶ ~한 prompt; quick.

믿다 ① 《경말로》 believe; accept 《a report》 as true; place credence 《in》; be convinced 《of》; 《신용·신뢰》 trust; credit; have faith in; believe in 《a person》; rely [depend] on 《a person》. 믿을 수 있는 believable / 믿을 만한 reliable 《source》; trustworthy; credible / 남의 말을 그대로 ~ take 《a person》 at his word / …을 굳게 믿고 있다 firmly believe that…; have a firm belief that (in)…; be sure convinced that (of)…. ② 《신을》 believe in 《God》.

믿음 faith; belief. ¶ ~이 두터운 pious; devout / ~이 없는 unbelieving; impious.

믿음성(-性) reliability; dependability. ¶ ~ 있는 trustworthy;

믿음직하다 (be) reliable; trustworthy; dependable; (유망) hopeful; promising.
밀(소맥) wheat.
밀(밀랍) beeswax; (yellow) wax. ¶ ~로 만든 wax; waxen. 「dough.
밀가루 wheat flour. 「~반죽
밀감(蜜柑) 〔橘〕 a mandarin orange.
밀계(密計) a secret scheme; a plot. ¶ ~를 꾸미다 plot secretly.
밀고(密告) (secret) information 《against》; betrayal. ~하다 inform (report, tell) 《the police》 against (on) 《a person》; betray. ¶ 친구를 경찰에 ~하다 inform on (against) one's friend to the police. ‖ ~자 an informer.
밀국수 wheat vermicelli; noodles.
밀기울 (wheat) bran.
밀다 ① (떠밀다) push; shove; thrust. ¶ 밀어내다 push out / 밀어젖히다 push aside / 밀고 들어가다 force oneself into. ② shave (면도로); plane (대패로). ¶ 수염을 ~ shave oneself; have a shave / 대패로 판자를 ~ plane a board. ③ (때를) rub (wash) off 《the dirt》; scrub. ④ (후원·추천하다) support; recommend. ¶ ☞ 밀다⑤.
밀담(密談) (have) a secret (private) talk 《with》.
밀도(密度) density. ‖ ~측정 densimetry / 인구~ density of population.
밀도살(密屠殺) illegal butchery. ~하다 slaughter 《cattle》 in secret.
밀랍(蜜蠟) beeswax.
밀레니엄 (1천년의) a millennium. ‖ ~버그 〔컴〕 a millennium bug.
밀렵(密獵) poaching. ~하다 poach; steal game. ‖ ~자 a poacher.
밀리 millimeter; milli-. ¶ 그램 a milligram (생략 mg) / ~리터 a milliliter (생략 ml) / ~미터 a millimeter (생략 mm).
밀리다 ① (일이) be delayed (belated); be behind with 《one's work》; be left undone. ¶ 밀린 사무를 정리하다 clear up belated business / 일이 산더미처럼 밀려있다 There is a good deal of work left undone. ② (지불이) be left unpaid; fall into (be in) arrears 《with the rent》; be overdue. ¶ 밀린 집세 arrears of rent; back rent. ③ (떠밀리다) be pushed (thrust, jostled); be pushed (forced) out / 인파에 ~ be swept along in the crowd. 「a jungle.
밀림(密林) a dense (thick) forest;
밀매(密賣) an illicit sale 〔trade〕. ¶ ~하다 sell 《liquor》 illicitly; smuggle. ¶ 마약의 ~를 적발하다 expose the illegal drug trade / 마약 ~인 a pusher. ‖ ~자 an illicit dealer 〔seller〕.
밀매매(密賣買) ~하다 traffic in 《drugs》; engage in illicit traffic 《in》.
밀매음(密賣淫) illegal prostitution. ~하다 prostitute illegally.
밀무역(密貿易) smuggling; contraband trade 《with》. ~하다 smuggle. ‖ ~업자 a smuggler.
밀물 the flowing (high) tide.
밀보리 rye (쌀보리); wheat and barley (밀과 보리).
밀봉(密封) ~하다 seal up 《a letter》; seal 《a container》 hermetically. ‖ ~교육 secret 〔clandestine〕 training.
밀봉(蜜蜂) a honeybee.
밀사(密使) a secret messenger 〔envoy〕; an emissary.
밀생(密生) ~하다 grow thick(ly).
밀서(密書) a secret (confidential) letter 〔message, papers〕.
밀수(密輸) smuggling. ~하다 smuggle. ¶ 마약을 국내(국외)로 ~하다 smuggle drugs in (abroad). ‖ ~단 a smuggling ring / ~선 a smuggling boat / ~자 a smuggler / ~품 smuggled goods.
밀수입(密輸入) ~하다 smuggle 《a thing》 (into the country); import 《something》 through illegal channels. 「thing》 abroad.
밀수출(密輸出) ~하다 smuggle 《a
밀실(密室) a secret room 〔chamber〕; a closed room.
밀약(密約) a secret promise 〔agreement, treaty〕. ~하다 make a secret promise. ¶ ~을 맺다 conclude 〔enter into〕 a secret agreement 《with》.
밀월(蜜月) a honeymoon. ¶ 두 나라 사이의 ~시대 a honeymoon (period) between the two countries. ‖ ~여행 the honeymoon.
밀의(密議) (have) a secret conference.
밀입국(密入國) ~하다 make an illegal entry 《into a country》. ‖ ~자 an illegal entrant 〔immigrant〕.
밀전병(—煎餠) a grilled wheat cake.
밀접(密接) ¶ ~한 close; intimate / ~한 관계가 있다 be closely related 〔connected〕 《with》.
밀정(密偵) a spy; a secret agent.
밀조(密造) illicit manufacture; illicit brewing (술의). ~하다 manufacture (brew) illicitly 〔illegally〕.
밀주(密酒) home-brew; moonshine (美俗); bootleg. ‖ ~업자 a moonshiner; a home-brewer.
밀집(密集) ~하다 gather 〔stand〕 close together; crowd; swarm; mass. ¶ 가옥의 ~지대 a densely built-up area / ~부대 massed

밀짚 wheat (barley) straw. ¶ ~ troops. 「모자 a straw hat.
밀짚 wheat (barley) straw. ¶ ~ a wax candle.
밀착(密着) ~하다 adhere closely to; stick fast to. ¶사건을 ~ 취재하다 keep up *one's* close coverage of a case. ‖ ~ 인화 a contact print.
밀초 a wax candle.
밀치다 push; shove; thrust.
밀크 ① 우유. ‖ ~ 셰이크 a milk shake / ~ 커피 café au lait (프).
밀탐(密探) ~하다 spy 《*on a person, into a secret*》; investigate secretly (in secret).
밀통(密通) ① ~하다 내통. ② (남녀의) illicit intercourse; adultery. ~하다 commit adultery 《*with*》.
밀폐(密閉) ~하다 shut (close) up tight; make (keep) 《*a box*》 airtight. ‖ ~ 용기 an airtight container.
밀항(密航) ~하다 a secret passage; stowing away. ~하다 stow away 《*on a boat*》; steal a passage 《*to*》. ‖ ~자 a stowaway.
밀행(密行) ~하다 prowl 《*about*》; go secretly 《*to*》.
밀회(密會) a clandestine (secret) meeting; a rendezvous. ~하다 meet 《*a person*》 in secret. ‖ ~ 장소 the place of a secret meeting.
밉다 (be) hateful; abominable; detestable; spiteful. ¶미운 녀석 a hateful fellow / 미운 짓 spiteful conduct.
밉살스럽다 (be) hateful; disgusting; detestable; repulsive. ¶밉살스러운 얼굴 a repulsive countenance; a hateful look.
밋밋하다 (be) long and slender; straight and smooth.
밍밍하다 (맛이) (be) tasteless; insipid; thin; washy; weak.
밍크 〖動〗 a mink. ¶ ~ 코트 a mink coat; 《wear》 a mink.
밎 (both…) and; as well (as).
밑 ① (아래쪽) the lower part; the bottom; the foot. ¶ ~의 lower; under / 책상의 오른쪽 ~의 서랍 the lower right drawer of a desk / ~에서 받치다 support 《*a thing*》 from below. ¶ ~의 lower; subordinate / 그는 나보다 두 살 ~이다 He is two years younger than I. ③ (근본) the root; the origin. ¶ ~도 같도 없는 소문 a groundless rumor. ④ (음부) the private parts; the secrets. ⑤ (바닥) the bottom. ¶ 바다 ~ the bottom of the sea.
밑각(一角) 〖數〗 a base angle.
밑거름 〖農〗 manure given at sowing (planting) time; initial (base) manure. ¶ ~이 되다 (비유적) sacrifice *oneself* for.
밑그림 (그림의) a rough sketch; a draft.
밑돌다 be lower (less) than; fall below.
밑동 the root; the base.
밑면(一面) the base.
밑바닥 the bottom (base).
밑바탕 (근저) the foundation; the ground; the base; (본성) nature; one's true colors.
밑받침 an underlay; a desk pad (책상 위의); a board.
밑변(一邊) the base.
밑줄 an underline. ¶ ~친 부분 an underlined part / ~을 치다 underline; underscore (a line).
밑지다 lose (money) 《*over*》; suffer (incur) a loss; cannot cover the cost. ¶밑지고 팔다 sell 《*a thing*》 at a loss (below cost).
밑창 the sole 《*of a shoe*》.
밑천 《자본》 capital; funds; principal(원금). ¶ ~ 장사 ~을 대다 provide 《*a person*》 with capital.

날짜·요일의 표시	
1. 날짜의 표시 방법: 1998년 10월 1일을 표시할 때, 다음 두 가지 방법이 있다. • 미국식: 월→일→연도 October 1, 1998 (October first nineteen ninety=eight) 간략형: 10/1/98 • 영국식: 일→월→연도 1st October, 1998 (the first of October, nineteen ninety-eight) 간략형: 1/10/98 • 월명의 생략형 1월 Jan. 2월 Feb. 3월 Mar. 4월 Apr. 5월 May 6월 Jun. 7월 Jul. 8월 Aug. 9월 Sep(t).	10월 Oct. 11월 Nov. 12월 Dec. 2. 요일의 표시 방법: • 요일의 생략형 일 Sun. 월 Mon. 화 Tue. 수 Wed. 목 Thur(s). 금 Fri. 토 Sat. • 관련된 표현 금요일에 on Friday 다음 수요일에 next Wednesday 지난 월요일에 last Monday 어느 (한, 일요일) on a Sunday 9월 5일, 월요일 아침에 on the morning of Monday, September 5.

…ㅂ시다 let's. ¶ 갑시다 Let's go.
바¹ (밧줄) a rope; a hawser(동아줄); (끈) a cord; a string.
바² (술집) a bar; a saloon (美); a pub (英). ¶ ~걸 a barmaid.
바³ [꽃] bar. ¶ 밀리~ millibar.
바⁴ (일) a thing; what; (방법) way; means; (범위) extend. ¶ 그가 말하는 ~ what he says / 할 ~를 모르다 don't know what to do / 내가 아는 ~로는 as far as I know.
바가지 ① (그릇) a gourd (dipper). ② (요금 등의) the overcharge. ¶ ~를 쓰다 pay exorbitantly / ~ 씌우다 overcharge (a person) for (the fur coat) / ~ 요금 an exorbitant prices. ③ (아웅거림) nagging. ¶ ~를 긁다 nag (yap) (at one's husband) / ~ 긁는 아내 a nagging wife.
바각거리다 make scraping sounds.
바겐세일 a bargain sale.
바구니 a basket. ‖ 장~ a market (shopping) basket.
바구미 [蟲] a rice weevil.
바글바글 (끓이) boiling (hot); (거품이) bubbling. ¶ 물을 ~ 끓이다 boil water; keep the water boiling (hot).
바깥 the outside(외부); the exterior (외면); out-of-doors (야외). ¶ ~의 outside; outdoor; outer; external / ~에서 in the open (air); out of doors; outside. ‖ ~양반 my [your] husband.
바께쓰 ☞ 버킷.
바꾸다 ① (교환) exchange; change; barter(물물교환); (대체) replace; (갱신) renew. ¶ 돈을 ~ change money / 수표를 현찰로 ~ cash a check / 생명은 돈과 바꿀 수 없다 Life cannot be bartered for gold. ② (변경) change; alter; shift; convert. ¶ 바꾸어 말하면 in other words / 방향을 ~ change the direction / 코스를 ~ alter the course.
바뀌다 change [turn] (into); be changed [altered, varied]; (개정되다) be revised. ¶ 변하다.
바나나 (peel) a banana. ¶ ~ 껍질 a banana skin [peel].
바느질 sewing; needlework. ~하다 sew; do needlework. ¶ ~품을 팔다 earn one's living by needlework.
바늘 a needle; a pin(핀); a hook(낚시 등의); a hand(시계의). ¶ ~ 방석에 앉은 것 같다 feel very nervous / ~에 실을 꿰다 thread a needle / ~여섯 ~ 꿰매다 have six stitches (on one's cut). ‖ ~겨레 a needle pad; a pincushion / ~귀 a needle's eye.
바다 the sea; the ocean(대양). ¶ ~로 나가다 go (sail) out to sea.
바다표범 [動] a seal.
바닥 ① (평면) the floor; the ground. ¶ 마룻 ~에서 자다 lie on the bare floor. ② (밑부분) the bottom; the bed (of a river); the sole (of a shoe). ③ (끝) the end (of the resources). ¶ ~이 나다 be exhausted; run out; be all gone; be out of stock. ④ (번잡한 곳) a congested area. ¶ 장~ a marketplace. ⑤ (짜임새) texture. ¶ ~이 고운 [거친] fine [coarse] in texture. ‖ ~시세 the bottom price / ~짐 (배의) ballast.
바닷가 the shore (seashore); the beach.
바닷물 sea water. ¶ ~ 고기 a sea fish.
바닷새 a seabird; a seafowl.
바동거리다 (kick and) struggle; writhe; wriggle.
바둑 baduk. ¶ ~을 두다 play [have a game of] baduk. ‖ ~돌 a baduk stone / ~판 a baduk board / ~판 무늬 checkers; a check pattern. [and white.
바둑이 a dog spotted with black
바득바득 doggedly; perversely.
바디 a reed; a yarn guide.
바라다 ① (예기·기대) expect; hope for; count on; look forward to. ¶ …을 바라고 in the hope (that…); in expectation of…. ② (소원함) want; wish; desire; hope. ¶ 행복을 ~ wish for happiness. ③ (간원·부탁) beg; request; entreat. ¶ 파티에 참석해 주기를 ~ request the pleasure of one's company at the party.
바라보다 see; look (at); watch; gaze (at, on) (응시); look (on) (방관); (관망하다) view; take (get) a view of. ¶ 한참동안 ~ take a long look (at).
바라보이다 be looked over; command; overlook.
바라지 care; looking after. ~하다 take care (of); look after.
바라지다 ① (몸이) (be) stumpy;

바라지다 have a stocky build. ② 《그릇이》 (be) shallow. ③ 《마음이》 get too smart 《for *one's* age》; be precocious 〔saucy〕.
바라지다 《갈라지다》 split off; 《열리다》 open out; be wide open.
바라크 a barrack; a shack.
바락바락 desperately; doggedly. ¶ ~ 를 쓰다 make desperate efforts.
바람¹ ① 《공기의 흐름》a wind; a current of air; a breeze 〈미풍〉; a gale 〈강풍〉; a draft 〈밖에서 들어오는〉. ¶ 살을 에는 듯한 찬 ~ a cutting 〔biting〕 wind / ~ 이 있는 〔없는〕 windy 〔windless〕 / ~ 이 불다 the wind blows; it is windy / ~ 이 잘 통한다be well ventilated / ~ 에 쐬다 expose *oneself* to the wind / ~ 이 일다〔자다〕 the wind rises 〔drops〕 / 선풍기 ~ 쐬다 sit in the current of an electric fan / …을 ~ 곁에 들었다 It has come to my ear that…; The wind brought the news that…. ② 《들뜬 마음》ficklekness; inconstancy. ¶ ~ 난 fickle; inconstant; wanton; ~ 을 피우다 have an affair with 《a person》; be unfaithful to *one's* husband 〔wife〕; play around 《美口》. ¶ ~ 둥이 a playboy〈남자〉; a flirt〈여자〉. ③ 《중풍》 palsy; paralysis.
바람² ① 《계유・기회》¶ ~ 에 in conjunction 《with》; in the process 《of》; as a consequence 《of》 일어나는 ~ 에 in the act of rising / 출동하는 ~ 에 by the force of impact. ② 《차림》¶ 셔츠 ~ 으로 in shirt sleeves; without *one's* coat on.
바람개비 a weathercock.
바람들다 ① 《푸성귀가》 get pulpy; get soft inside; get soggy. ¶ 바람든 무 a pulpy radish. ② 《바람나다》 become indiscreet; go wild; take up a gay life. ③ 《일・계획이》 be upset; fail; be spoiled 〔hindered〕; go wrong.
바람막이 a windscreen; a shelter from the wind.
바람맞다 ① 《속다》 be fooled 〔deceived〕; be stood up by 《a person》〈기다리다〉. ¶ 바람맞히다 stand 《a person》 up. ② 《풍병이》 be stricken with paralysis. 「wind.
바람받이 a place exposed to the
바람잡다 《허왕된 짓을 도모하다》 conceive a wild hope 〔scheme〕; take a shot in the dark.
바람잡이 〈허풍선이〉 a braggart; an empty boaster; a gasbag; 〈소매치기의〉 a pickpocket's mate.
바람직하다 (be) desirable; advisable. ¶ 바람직한 일 a matter to be desired / 바람직하지 않다 (be) undesirable.
바랑 a Buddhist's pack-sack.
바래다¹ ① 《변색》fade; discolor. ¶ 바래지 않는 fade-proof; color-fast; standing. ② 《표백》bleach 《cotton》.
바래다² ① 《배웅》see 《a person》 off; give 《a person》 a send-off.
바로 ① 《정당하게》 rightly; justly; properly; 《틀림없게》 correctly; accurately; 《합법하게》 lawfully; legally; 《진실하게》 honestly; truly. ¶ ~ 대답하다 give a correct answer / ~ 말하다 tell the truth / 외국어를 ~ 발음하다 pronounce a foreign language correctly. ② 《곧》 right away; 《똑바로》 straight; 《막》 just; right; exactly. ¶ ~ 앉다 sit straight / ~ 눈앞에 right under *one's* nose / ~ 집으로 가다 go straight home / ~ 알아맞추다 guess right / ~ 이웃에 살다 live close by / ~ 그 곳에서 그를 보았다 I saw him just about here. ③ 《구멍》 Eyes front !
바로미터 a barometer. 「front !
바로잡다 ① 《굽은 것을》 straighten; make straight 〔right〕. ② 《교정》 correct; redress; remedy; reform; set right.
바로크 ¶ ~ 시대 the baroque age / ~ 음악 baroque music.
바륨 [化] barium〈기호 Ba〉.
바르다¹ ① 《곧다》(be) straight; straight forward; upright〈직립〉. ② 《정당》(be) right; righteous; just; 〈참되다〉(be) honest; upright; 〈적절〉(be) proper; 〈합법〉(be) lawful; 〈정확〉(be) correct; accurate.
바르다² ① 《붙이다》 stick; paste; plaster; 《종이를》 paper. ② 《칠하다》 paint; coat 《칠 따위를》; plaster 《회반죽을》; apply 《연고 등을》; 《분 따위를》 powder; put on. ¶ 버터를 바른 빵 bread and butter / 연고를 ~ apply an ointment 《to》.
바르다³ ☞ 발라내다.

바르르 ¶ ~ 끓다 come to a bubbling boil; be hissing hot / 화나서 ~ 떨다 flare up in anger / 추위에 ~ 떨다 shiver with cold.
바르샤바 Warsaw〈폴란드의 수도〉. ¶ ~ 조약 the Warsaw Pact.
바른길 《곧은 길》a straight way; 《옳은 길》 the right path 〔track〕.
바른말 《옳은 말》a reasonable 〔right〕 word; 《직언》 plain speaking; a straight talk. ~ 하다 speak reasonably 〔plainly〕.
바리 《짐》a pack 〔load〕 《of firewood》; 《나뭇짓》 a brass 〔wooden〕 rice bowl.
바리케이드 a barricade. ¶ ~ 를 치다 set up a barricade; barri-

바리케이드 (*a place*) / ~를 돌파하다 break through a barricade.
바리톤 [樂] baritone; a baritone (가수); baritone voice.
바림 [美術] shadings [gradations] of a color; shading off.
바바리(코트) a Burberry (coat) (상표명); a trench coat. 「Babel.
바벨 [聖] ‖ ~ 탑 the tower of
바보 a fool; a stupid; an ass; an idiot; a simpleton. ¶ ~ 같은 silly; foolish; stupid / ~ 같은 소리를 하다 talk nonsense (silly) / ~ 같은 짓을 하다 do a foolish (silly) thing.
바비큐 barbecue. 「Babylonian.
바빌로니아 Babylonia. ‖ ~ 사람 a
바쁘다 (be) busy (*in, with*); (급하다) be pressing; urgent. ¶ ~게 busily; hurriedly / 바쁜 걸음으로 at a quick pace / 시험 준비에 ~ be busy preparing for the examination / 바빠서 이리뛰고 저리뛰다 run (bustle) about busily.
바빼 (바쁘게) busily; (급히) hurriedly; in haste; in a hurry; (즉시) at once; immediately. ¶ 한시 ~ without a moment's delay.
바삭거리다, **바스락거리다** (make a) rustle. ¶ 바삭바삭 rustlingly; with a rustle.   「(into pieces).
바스러뜨리다 crush; smash; break
바스러지다 be broken (crushed, smashed); fall to pieces.
바싹 ① (바삭) rustlingly; with a rustle. ② (물기가 없게) (dried up) completely; as dry as a bone; (몸이 마른) thinly, haggardly. ¶ ~ 말라붙은 우물 a dried-up well / 마른 입술 parched lips / 몸이 마르다 be reduced to a skeleton. ③ (죄는 모양) fast; tightly; closely. ¶ 나사를 ~ 죄다 screw tightly / ~ 다가 앉다 sit closer to (*a person*).
바야흐로 막 ···하려 하다 be going (about) to (*do*); be on the point of (*doing*).
···바에야 (이왕 ···이면) at all; (차라리) rather (than); as soon as. ¶ 이왕 그만둘 ~ if you give it up at all / 항복할 ~ 죽겠다 I would rather die than surrender.
바위 a rock; a crag. ¶ 흔들 ~ a rocking stone / ~가 많은 rocky.
바위옷 [植] rock moss; lichen.
바이러스 [醫] a virus. ¶ ~성의 viral / ~에 기인하는 virus-caused (*tumors*) / B형 ~성 간염 viral hepatitis type B / 에이즈 ~ the AIDS virus.
바이블 (swear on) the Bible.
바이스 (공구) a vise; a vice.
바이올린 a violin. ‖ ~ 주자 a violinist.
바이트 [컴] a byte(기억 용량 단위).

바자¹ (울타리) ‖ ~을 a roughly-wooven (bamboo) fence.
바자² (자선시) a (charity) baza(a)r; a fancy fair. ¶ ~를 열다 open (hold) a bazaar.
바작바작 (소리) with a crackling (sizzling); (초조) fretfully; in a state of anxiety.
바제도병 [病] Basedow's disease.
바조 (一調) [樂] F major(장조); F minor (단조).
바주카포 [軍] a bazooka.
바지 (a pair of trousers); pants (美). ¶ 헐렁한 (꽉 끼는) ~ full (narrow) trousers. ‖ ~멜빵 suspenders (美).
바지락(조개) a short-necked clam.
바지랑대 a laundry pole.
바지저고리 jacket (coat) and trousers; (비유적) a good-for-nothing; a figurehead(무실권자).
바지직 sissling; hissing.
바치다¹ (드리다) give; offer; present; consecrate (신에게); devote (노력·심신을); sacrifice (헌신). ¶ 일생을 ~ devote *one's* life to / 나라를 위해 목숨을 ~ give *one's* life for *one's* country.
바치다² (지나치게 즐기다) have an excessive liking for; be addicted to.
바캉스 (a) vacation; holidays; *vacances* (프). ‖ ~ 웨어 holiday clothes.
바코드 a bar code. ¶ ~를 달다 (붙이다) bar-code (*the books*).
바퀴¹ [蟲] a cockroach.
바퀴² (수레의) a wheel; (일주) a round (turn). ¶ 한 ~ 돌다 take a turn; go *one's* rounds(담당 구역을). ‖ ~살 a spoke / ~ 자국 ruts; tracks / 앞 (뒷) ~ the front (back) wheel.
바탕 (기초) foundation; basis; (성질) nature; character; (a) disposition; (소질) the makings; (체질) the constitution; (재료) a ground; texture(직물의). ¶ 이 지역 경제의 ~이 되다 form the basis of economy in this area / ~이 좋다 (나쁘다) be good-natured (ill-natured) / 노란 ~에 푸른 무늬 a blue design on a yellow ground / 옷감의 ~이 곱다 be of fine texture.
바탕² for some (a) time. ¶ 소나기가 한 ~ 내렸다 There was a shower for some time.
바터 barter. ‖ ~무역 barter trade / ~제 the barter system (basis).
바텐더 a bartender.
바통 a baton. ¶ ~을 넘기다 hand over the baton (*to*) / ~을 받다 receive the baton (*from*) / (비유적) take over (*a task*).
바투 close; closely.

바특하다 《국물이》 (be) thick.
바티칸 (로마 敎皇廳) the Vatican.
박 [植] a gourd; a calabash.
박(箔) foil(두꺼운); leaf (얇은).
박격포(迫擊砲) [軍] a mortar.
박공(牔栱) [建] a gable.
박다¹ (못 따위를) drive (strike) 《*in, into*》; hammer 《*in*》 (못 못을); (상감) set; inlay; fix.
박다² (사진을) take 《*a picture*》; 《인쇄》 print; get 《*a thing*》 printed. ¶ 재봉틀로 ~ sew 《*something*》 with a sewing machine.
박달[植] a birch.
박대(薄待) ¶ ~하다 냉대.
박덕(薄德) want [lack] of virtue.
박두(迫頭) ¶ ~하다 draw [come] near; approach; be at hand; be imminent. ¶ 눈앞에 ~한 위험 an impending [imminent] danger / 시험이 ~했다 The Examination is near at hand.
박람회(博覽會) an exhibition; a fair. ‖ ~장 the exhibition [fair] grounds.
박력(迫力) force; power; intensity. ¶ ~이 있다 be powerful; be moving; appeal strongly 《*to*》; ~이 없다 be weak; lack power; have little appeal to.
박리(薄利) small profits. ¶ ~로 팔다 sell at small profits. ‖ ~다매 small profits and quick returns / ~다매주의 a quick-returns policy.
박막(薄膜) a thin film. ‖ ~집적회로 a thin-film integrated circuit.
박멸(撲滅) ¶ ~하다 eradicate; exterminate; stamp [wipe] out.
박명(薄命) ¶ ~한 unfortunate; unlucky; ill-fated. ¶ 가인(佳人) ~ Beauty and long life seldom go hand in hand.
박물(博物) ‖ ~관 a museum / ~군자 a man of erudition / ~학 natural history / ~학자 a naturalist.
박박 ① 《긁거나 찢는 모양》¶ ~ 소리를 내다 make [produce] a rasping [scratching] noise / 모기가 문 곳을 ~ 긁다 scratch a mosquito bite / 편지를 ~ 찢다 tear the letter to pieces. ②《얽은 모양》. ¶ ~ 얽은 얼굴 a face pockmarked [pitted] all over. ③《짧게》 ¶ ~ 머리를 깎다 have a close crop haircut.
박복(薄福) misfortune; sad fate. ¶ ~하다 (be) unlucky; unfortunate.
박봉(薄俸) a small [low] salary; small pay. ¶ ~으로 생활하다 live on small pay.
박사(博士) a doctor(생략 Dr.). ‖

~논문 a doctoral thesis / ~위 a doctor's degree (~학위를 따다 take a doctorate).
박살 ¶ ~ 내다 shatter; knock 《*a thing*》 to pieces.
박살(撲殺) ¶ ~하다 beat 《*a person*》 to death.
박색(薄色) an ugly look; a plain woman.
박수 a male diviner [shaman].
박수 hand clapping. ¶ ~하다 clap one's hands. ¶ 우뢰 같은 ~ a thunderous clapping of hands. ¶ ~갈채 cheers; applause (~ 갈채하다 give 《*a person*》 a clap and cheers) / ~부대 《극장 등의》 *claque* (프) (總稱).
박식(博識) erudition. ¶ ~한 erudite; well-informed.
박애(博愛) philanthropy. ¶ ~의 philanthropic; charitable. ‖ ~주의 philanthropism.
박약(薄弱) ¶ ~한 feeble; weak / 의지 ~의 weak-minded.
박음질 sewing; sewing-machine stitches.
박이다 ① 《속에》 stick; run into; get stuck [embedded] in; 《마음에》 sink deep in 《*one's heart*》. ¶ 손가락에 가시가 박였다 A splinter ran into[stuck in] my finger. ② 《몸에 배다》 become a habit; fall into a habit 《*of*》. ¶ 담배에 인이 ~ fall into the habit of smoking.
박자(拍子) time; rhythm; beat. ¶ ~를 맞추다 keep (good) time with(to) 《*the music*》; beat time / ~를 맞추어 in (measured) time.
박장대소(拍掌大笑) applause mingled with laughter. ¶ ~하다 laugh aloud clapping one's hands.
박절(迫切) ¶ ~한 (薄情).
박정(薄情) ¶ ~한 cold-hearted; heartless; unfeeling; cruel / ~한 말을 하다 speak cruelly [heartlessly]; say a harsh thing.
박제(剝製) a stuffed bird [animal]. ¶ ~하다 stuff 《*a bird*》. ¶ ~한 stuffed; mounted. ‖ ~사 a taxidermist / ~술 taxidermy.
박주(薄酒) untasty liquor; unpalatable *sul*.
박쥐 [動] a bat. ‖ ~구실 opportunism; wait-and-see policy / ~우산 an umbrella.
박진(迫眞) truthfulness to life. ¶ ~감 있는 true to life / ~감 있다 be true to nature; be realistic.
박차(拍車) a spur. ¶ ~를 가하다 《말에》 spur (on) one's horse; 《비유적》 spur on; give impetus to.
박차다 kick away [off] (《뿌리치다》) kick 《*a person's proposal*》; reject; snub.
박처(薄妻) ¶ ~하다 treat one's wife

박치기 butting. ~하다 butt (*at*, *against*); give a butt to (*a person*).
박탈하다(剝奪一) ~ 빼앗다.
박테리아 a bacterium [*pl.* -ria].
박토(薄土) barren [sterile] soil.
박하(薄荷) [植] peppermint. ¶ ~ 담배 a mentholated cigaret / ~사탕 a peppermint candy / ~유 (pepper)mint oil.
박하다(薄一) (be) little; (인색) (be) illiberal; stingy; severe (점수가) (인정이) (be) heartless; unfeeling; hard. ¶ 인심이 ~ be inhospitable / 점수가 ~ be strict [severe] in marking.
박학(博學) erudition; great learning. ¶ ~한 erudite; learned.
박해(迫害) persecution. ~하다 persecute; oppress. ¶ ~자 a persecutor; an oppressor.
박히다 (들어가다) get stuck; be driven (*in*); (인쇄물이) be printed; (사진이) be taken.
밖 ① 바깥 the rest; the others; and so on (forth); and the like; (…뿐) only; but. ¶ 그 ~에 besides; in addition (*to*) / 그 ~의 사람들 the rest; the others / 하나 ~에 없는 몸 the only body we have.
반(半) ① (절반) a half. ¶ 1다스 ~ a dozen and a half / 3시 ~ half past three / 1시간 ~ an hour and a half / ~마일 half a mile; a mile / ~으로 가르다 divide (*a thing*) into halves; cut in half / …의 ~쯤 half as many [much] as…. ② (반쯤) partial; half. ¶ ~은 농으로 half in jest.
반(班) (학급) a class; (동네의) a neighborhood association; (집단) a party; a team; (군대의) a section; a squad.
반…(反) anti-. ¶ ~제국주의 anti-imperialism / ~세 [tured goods.
반가공품(半加工品) semimanufac-
반가부좌(半跏趺坐) sitting with *one's* legs half-crossed as in Buddhist statues.
반가워하다 be glad [pleased, delighted] (*at, about*); rejoice in.
반가이 gladly; delightedly; with joy; with pleasure.
반감(反感) antipathy; ill-feeling. ¶ ~을 사다 offend (*a person*); provoke (*a person's*) antipathy / ~을 품다 harbor ill-feeling (*towards*).
반감(半減) ~하다 reduce [cut] (*the price*) by half; halve.
반갑다 (be) glad; joyful; happy; delightful; pleasant. ¶ 반가운 소식 glad [happy] news / 반갑잖은 손님 an unwelcome guest.
반값(半一) half (the) price. ¶ ~으로 at half-price; at half the (usual) price / ~으로 팔다 take off half the price.
반격(反擊) a counterattack. ~하다 counterattack; strike back.
반경(半徑) a radius. ¶ 학교에서 ~ 2마일 이내에 within a 2=mile radius from the school.
반공(反共) anti-Communism. ¶ ~의 anti-Communist. ¶ ~운동 an anti-Communist drive [movement] / ~정신 anti-Communist spirit / ~포로 the anti-Communist prisoners of war.
반공일(半空日) a half-holiday; Saturday.
반관반민(半官半民) a semi-governmental organization.
반구(半球) a hemisphere.
반국가적(反國家的) antinational; anti-[state.
반군(叛軍) a rebel army.
반기(反旗) a standard [banner] of revolt. ¶ ~를 들다 rise in revolt (*against*); take up arms (*against*).
반기(半期) ¶ ~의 half-yearly; semiannual / 상(하)~ the first [second] half of the year. ¶ ~결산 the half-yearly account / ~배당 a semiannual dividend.
반기(半旗) a flag at half-mast. ¶ ~를 달다 fly [hoist] a flag at half-mast.
반기다 be glad [happy]; be pleased [delighted]; rejoice (*over*). ¶ 손님을 ~ be delighted to see a guest. [half the morning.
반나절(半一) a quarter of a day;
반나체(半裸體) semi-nudity. ¶ ~의 half-naked; seminude.
반납(返納) ~하다 return (*a book*); give back (*a thing*).
반년(半年) half a year; a half year. ¶ ~마다 half-yearly.
반닫이(半一) (a cedar) chest with a hinged front flap.
반달(半一) ① (반개월) half a month. ② (달의) a half moon. ¶ ~형의 semicircular.
반대(反對) ① (반항) opposition; (이의) (an) objection. ~하다 oppose; be opposed (*to*); be [stand] against; object (*to*). ¶ ~의사를 표명하다 declare *oneself* (to be) against (*a policy*) / ~를 당하다 meet with [run into] opposition / 너는 그것에 대해 찬성이냐 ~냐 Are you for it or against it? ¶ ~당 an opposition (party) / ~세력 counter force / ~신문 [法] a cross-examination / ~운동 a counter [an opposition] movement; a movement [campaign] against (*the war*) / ~자 an opponent

반도(半島) a peninsula. ¶ ~의 반도 rebels; insurgents.
반도체(半導體) a semiconductor.
반독(反獨) ¶ ~의 anti-German.
반동(反動) (a) reaction; recoil (총 따위의). ~하다 react; rebound; kick; recoil. ~적(的) reactionary. ‖ ~분자 reactionary elements / ~주의자 a reactionary.
반드럽다 (be) smooth; glossy; slippery.
반드르르 ¶ ~한 smooth; glossy.
반드시 《확실히》 certainly; surely; without fail (틀림없이); 《꼭》 by all means; 《항상》 always; invariably; 《필연》 necessarily; inevitably. ¶ ~ …하다 be sure to 《do》 / ~은 아니다 be not necessarily [always]… / 그는 ~ 온다 He will certainly come.
반들거리다 《윤나다》 glisten; shine; have a gloss; 《게으름피우다》 be idle; play truant.
반듯이 straight; upright; even.
반듯하다 (be) straight; upright; erect; even; 《용모가》 (be) comely; good-looking; neat.
반등(反騰) a reactionary rise; a rebound; a rally. ~하다 rally; rebound. ¶ 주가의 ~ a sharp rebound in stock prices.
반딧불 the glow of a firefly.
반락(反落) a reactionary fall 《in stock prices》. ~하다 fall [drop] in reaction; fall [slip] back. ¶ ~급 a sharp setback.
반란(反亂) a revolt; (a) rebellion. ¶ ~을 일으키다 rise in revolt; rebel [rise] 《against》. ‖ ~군 a rebel [an insurgent] army / ~자 a rebel.
반려(伴侶) a companion; a partner.
반려(返戾) ~하다 give back; return.
반론(反論) a counterargument; a refutation. ~하다 argue against; refute.
반말(半一) the informal speech level; crude language; rough talk. ~하다 talk roughly; speak impolitely.
반면(反面) the other side; the reverse. ¶ ~에 on the other hand.
반면(半面) one side; 《사물의》 half the face. ‖ ~상 a profile; a silhouette.
반모음(半母音) a semivowel.

반목(反目) antagonism; hostility. ~하다 be hostile [antagonistic] to 《a person》; be at odds with 《a person》; feud 《with》.
반문(反問) ~하다 ask in return.
반문(斑紋) a spot; a speckle.
반미(反美) ¶ ~의 anti-American.
반미치광이(半一) a slightly mad [crazy] person. [(trousers).
반바지(半一) shorts; knee pants
반박(反駁) confutation; refutation. ~하다 refute; retort 《on, against》.
반반(半半) ¶ ~ (으로) 《mix》 half-and-half; fifty-fifty 《주로 美》.
반반하다 ①《바닥이》 (be) smooth; even. ②《인물이》 (be) nice-looking; fine. ¶ 얼굴이 ~ have a handsome [beautiful] face. ③《지체가》 (be) decent; respectable.
반발(反撥) repulsion. ~하다 repel; repulse; resist. ‖ ~력 repulsion power; repulsive force.
반백(半白) ¶ ~의 gray-haired; grizzled. [mumbler.
반벙어리(半一) a half-mute;
반병신(半病身) a partially disabled person; a half-cripple; a half-wit(반편).
반복(反復) ~하다 repeat. ¶ ~하여 repeatedly; over again.
반분(半分) ~하다 halve; divide into halves; cut in half.
반비(反比) 【數】 reciprocal ratio.
반비례(反比例) 【數】 ~하다 be in inverse proportion 《to》.
반사(反射) 《열·빛의》 reflection; 《생리적 반응》 reflex. ~하다 reflect 《light》. ‖ ~경 a reflex mirror / ~광[열] reflected light [heat] / ~운동 a reflex movement / ~작용 a reflex action.
반사회적(反社會的) antisocial. ‖ ~집단[행위] an antisocial group [action].
반삭(半朔) half a month; a half month.
반상(기)(飯床(器)) a table service; a set of tableware.
반상회(班常會) a neighborhood meeting; a monthly neighbors' meeting.
반색하다 show great joy; rejoice; be delighted.
반생(半生) half one's life; half a lifetime.
반석(盤石) a rock; a crag. ¶ ~같은[같이] as firm as a rock.
반성(反省) self-examination; reflection. ~하다 reflect on; reconsider. ¶ ~을 촉구하다 urge [ask] 《a person》 to reconsider [reflect on] 《one's conduct》.
반세기(半世紀) half a century.
반소(反訴) (bring) a cross action.
반소매(半一) a half(-length) sleeve.

반송(返送) ~하다 return; send back. ‖ ~료 〖우편의〗 return postage / ~화물 〖운임〗 return cargo 〔freight〕.

반송장(半一) a half-dead person; a person who is as good as dead.

반수(半數) half the number.

반숙(半熟) ~의 half-cooked; half-boiled; half-done / ~한 달걀 a half-boiled egg.

반시간(半時間) half an hour; a half hour 〖美〗.

반식민지(半植民地) ‖ ~국가 a semi-colonial state.

반신(半身) half the body 〖상하의〗; one side of the body 〖좌우의〗. ¶ 왼쪽 ~이 마비되다 be paralyzed on the left side of the body. ‖ ~상 a half-length statue 〔portrait〕 / ~불수 hemiplegia.

반신(返信) a reply; an answer. ‖ ~료 return postage / ~용 엽서 a reply 〔postal〕 card.

반신반의(半信半疑) ~하다 be dubious 〔doubtful〕 《about, of》; be half in doubt.

반심(叛心) treacherous mind.

반암(斑岩) 〖地〗 porphyry.

반액(半額) half the amount 〔sum, price, fare〕. ‖ ~으로 at half the price 〔fare〕; at half-price / ~으로 하다 reduce the price by half.

반양자(反陽子) 〖理〗 an antiproton.

반어(反語) irony. ~적(으로) ironical(ly).

반역(叛逆) treason; a rebellion. ~하다 rebel 〔revolt〕 《against》; rise in revolt. ‖ ~자 a traitor; a rebel.

반영(反映) reflection. ~하다 reflect; be reflected 《in》.

반영(反英) ¶ ~의 anti-British.

반영구적(半永久的) semipermanent.

반올림 ¶ ~하다 round off; round 《a figure》 off.

반원(半圓) 〖幾〗 a semicircle. ¶ ~형의 semicircular.

반월(半月) a half moon. ¶ ~(형)의 crescent(-shaped).

반유대(反一) ¶ ~의 anti-Semitic.

반유동체(半流動體) 〖理〗 (a) semifluid; (a) semiliquid.

반음(半音) 〖樂〗 semitone; half step. ¶ ~하다 〖낮추다〗 sharp 〔flat〕 《the tone》.

반응(反應) (a) reaction; (a) response; 〖효과〗 an effect. ~하다 react 《to, on》; respond 《to》 〖반향하다〗. ¶ ~이 없다 show no reaction; have no effect 《on》 / ~이 둔하다 be slow to react 〔respond〕 / ~을 일으키다 produce a response.

반의반(半一半) a quarter; one fourth.

반의식(半意識) 〖心〗 subconsciousness. ¶ ~적 subconscious; half-conscious.

반의어(反意語) an antonym.

반일(反日) ¶ ~의 anti-Japanese.

반입(搬入) ~하다 carry 〔bring, take〕 in.

반자 a ceiling. ‖ ~널 a ceiling board 〔pannel〕 / ~지 ceiling paper. 「다 react 《on, to》.

반작용(反作用) (a) reaction. ~하-

반장(班長) a monitor 〔학급의〕; a foreman 〔직공의〕; the head of a neighborhood association 〔동네

반장화(半長靴) half boots. 「의〕.

반전(反戰) ¶ ~의 antiwar; pacifistic. ‖ ~론 〖주의〗 pacifism / ~론 〖주의〕자 a pacifist / ~운동 an antiwar movement.

반전(反轉) ~하다 turn 〔roll〕 over.

반절(半折) folding in half. ~하다 fold in half 〔two〕. ‖ ~지 a piece of paper folded in half.

반점(斑點) a spot; a speck. ¶ ~ 이 있는 spotted; speckled. 「ment.

반정부(反政府) ¶ ~의 antigovern-

반제국주의(反帝國主義) anti-imperialism. ¶ ~적 anti-imperialistic.

반제품(半製品) half-finished goods.

반주(伴奏) an accompaniment. ~하다 accompany 《a person on the piano》. ¶ 피아노 ~로 노래하 다 sing to a piano accompaniment. ‖ ~자 an accompanist.

반주(飯酒) liquor taken at meal time; liquor with one's meals.

반죽 kneading; dough. ~하다 knead 《dough》; work 《clay》.

반죽음(半一) being half-dead. ~하다 be nearly 〔all but〕 killed.

반증(反證) (a) disproof; (an) evidence to the contrary. ¶ ~을 들다 disprove; prove the contrary.

반지(斑指) a (finger) ring. ¶ 금 〔다이아몬드〕 ~ a gold 〔diamond〕 ring / ~를 끼다 〔끼고 있다〕 put 〔wear〕 a ring on 《one's finger》 / ~를 빼다 take a ring off 《one's finger》. ‖ 결혼 〔약혼〕 ~ a wedding 〔an engagement〕 ring.

반지르르 ~하다 glossily; sleekly.

반지름(半一) ☞ 반경(半徑).

반지빠르다 〔어중되다〕 be unsuitable either way; not quite satisfactory; awkward. ¶ 무언가 반지빠른 느낌이 든다 feel that something is missing. 「al.

반직업적(半職業的) semiprofession-

반짇고리 a workbox; a needle case; a housewife 〔házif〕.

반질거리다 ① 〔매끄럽다〕 be glossy 〔smooth, slippery〕. ② 〔교활하 다〕 be sly 〔saucy, cunning〕.

반질반질 ¶ ~한 glossy; smooth; slippery.

반짝거리다 shine; glitter; sparkle; twinkle (별이); glimmer (깜박임).

반쪽 (半—) (a) half.

반찬 (飯饌) a side dish; dishes to go with rice. ∥ 고기 ~ a meat dish / 생선 ~ 으로 먹다 eat rice with fish. ¶ ~ 가게 a grocer's (shop); a grocery / ~ 거리 groceries.

반창고 (絆瘡膏) a sticking [an adhesive] plaster. ¶ ~ 를 붙이다 apply an adhesive plaster 〈*to the wound*〉.

반체제 (反體制) anti-Establishment. ∥ ~ 운동 an anti-Establishment / ~ 인사 a dissident; an anti-Establishmentarian.

반추 (反芻) rumination. ~ 하다 ruminate; chew the cud. ∥ ~ 동물 a ruminant.

반출 (搬出) ~ 하다 carry [take] out.

반취 (半醉) ~ 하다 get half-drunk.

반칙 (反則) (경기의) a foul; violation of the rules [law] (범규의). ~ 하다 (play) foul; break (violate) the rule / ~ 이다 be against the rule / ~ 패하다 lose a game on a foul.

반타작 (半打作) [農] sharing a tenant crop fifty-fifty with the landowner. ~ 하다 share the crop equally.

반투명 (半透明) ¶ ~ 의 semitransparent *(body)*; translucent.

반편 (이) (半偏—) a half-wit (simpleton); a fool. ¶ ~ 노릇 [짓] 하다 play the fool; make a fool of *oneself*.

반포 (頒布) ~ 하다 promulgate; circulate.

반품 (返品) returned goods. ~ 하다 return *(goods)*. ∥ ~ 사절 [게시] All Sales Final; No Refund.

반하다 (매혹) fall [be] in love 〈*with*〉; take a fancy 〈*to*〉; lose *one's* heart 〈*to*〉.

반하다 (反—) be contrary to *(one's interests)*; go [be] against; violate (break) *(a rule)*. ¶ 의사에 반하여 against *one's* will / 에 반하여 on the contrary; on the other hand.

반합 (飯盒) a messtin; a mess kit.

반항 (反抗) resistance; opposition; defiance. ~ 하다 resist; oppose; defy. ¶ ~ 적인 defiant *(attitude)*; rebellious *(spirit)*.

반핵 (反核) ¶ ~ 의 antinuclear. ∥ ~ 데모 [집회] an antinuclear demonstration (meeting) / ~ 운동 an antinuclear campaign / ~ 운동가 an antinuker; a nukenik.

반향 (反響) an echo; reverberation(s); a response; influence. ~ 하다 echo; resound. ¶ ~ 을 일으키다 create a sensation / ~ 이 있다 be echoed; have [meet with] a public response.

반혁명 (反革命) a counterrevolution. ~ 적 anti-revolutionary.

반환 (返還) return. ~ 하다 return; give back; restore.

받다 ① (수령) receive; accept; be given (granted, presented); have; take; get. ∥ 교육을 ~ receive education; be educated 〈*at*〉 / 환영을 ~ receive [meet with] a welcome. ② (당하다) receive; suffer; sustain. ∥ 손해를 ~ suffer (sustain) a loss / 혐의를 ~ fall (come) under suspicion. (겪다) undergo; go through. ¶ 치료를 ~ undergo medical treatment / 문초를 ~ undergo an examination. ④ (던진 공 따위를) catch (stop) *(a ball)*; receive. ∥ 빗물을 ~ catch rainwater *(in the bucket)*. ⑤ (우산을) put up *(an umbrella)*; hold. ⑥ (뿔·머리로) butt; horn; toss. ∥ 황소에게 ~ be gored by a bull. ⑦ (별·바람 따위를) bask; be bathed *(in)*. ∥ 햇볕을 ~ be bathed in the sunlight. ⑧ (아기) deliver *(a woman of a child)*. ⑨ (응답) answer. ¶ 전화를 ~ answer a telephone call; have a call from *(a person)*.

받들다 ① (추대) have *(a person)* as (over). ¶ 왕을 회장으로 ~ have the King as *its* president. ② (지지) hold up; support; 《보좌》 assist; help; 《순복하다》 obey. ¶ ~ 의 명령을 받들어 in obedience to *a person's* order. ③ (공경) respect; honor. ¶ 윗사람을 ~ honor *one's* superiors. ④ (받쳐들) lift (up); hold up.

받들어총 (구령) Present arms!

받아들이다 accept [agree to] 〈*a proposal*〉; receive; grant 〈*a request*〉.

받아쓰기 (a) dictation.

받아쓰다 write (take, put) down; take dictation. ¶ 받아쓰게 하다 dictate 〈*to a person*〉.

받을어음 [商] bills receivable (생략 B/R, b.r.).

받치다 ① (괴다) prop; bolster (up); support; hold. ② (먹은 것이) lie heavy on the stomach. ∥ 우산 따위를 hold *(an umbrella)* over *one's* head; put up.

받침대 a prop; a support; a stay; a strut.

받히다 be butted (gored).

발¹ a foot; a leg (다리); a paw (개·고양이의); tentacles; arms (문어의). ¶ ~ 을 멈추다 stop; halt / ~ 을 맞추다 keep pace 〈*with*〉 / ~ 을 헛디디다 miss *one's* footing / ~ 이 빠르다 [느리다] be quick [slow] on *one's* feet /

발 을 끊다 《비유적》 cease to visit / ~을 빼다 《비유적》 wash one's hands of 《the shady business》; sever one's connection 《with》; break 《with》.

발(치는) a (bamboo) blind.

발(깊이·길이의 단위) a fathom.

발(發) ①《출발》¶오전 10시 ~ 열차 the 10 a.m. train 《for Pusan》/ 6월 10일 목포 ~의 배 a boat leaving Mokpo on June 10. ②《탄알 수》a round; a shot《소총의》; a shell《대포의》¶ ~ 탄알 1만 ~ 10,000 rounds of ammunition.

발가락 a toe.

발각(發覺) ¶ ~되다 be found out; be detected; be brought to light.

발간(發刊) publication; issue. ~ 하다 publish; issue; start 《a magazine》.

발갛다 《b》 light red. *lazine]*.

발개지다 turn bright-red; redden. ¶얼굴이 ~ blush; flush.

발걸음 a pace; a step. ¶ ~을 재촉하다 quicken one's pace.

발견(發見) (a) discovery. ~ 하다 find 《out》; make a discovery; discover. ‖ ~자 a finder; a discoverer.

발광(發光) radiation. ~하다 radiate; emit; give light. ‖ ~도료 luminous paint / ~체 a luminous body.

발광(發狂) ~하다 go 《run》 mad; become insane 《lunatic》. ¶ ~케 하다 drive 《a person》 mad.

발구르다 stamp one's feet; stamp with vexation.

발군(拔群) ¶ ~의 distinguished; outstanding; unparalleled.

발굴(發掘) excavation. ~하다 dig up 《out》; excavate; exhume.

발굽 a hoof; an unguis [*pl.* -gues].

발그레하다 (be) reddish.

발그림자 a footmark; a trail.

발급(發給) ~하다 issue. ¶ 여권을 ~ 하다 issue a passport. 「spots.

발긋발긋 ¶ ~ 한 dotted with red

발기(勃起)《근육의》erection. ~하다 stand erect; become rigid 《stiff》. ¶ ~가 되다 be impotent / ~력 감퇴 impotency.

발기(發起)《사업의》 promotion;《계획》 a projection;《제의》 a suggestion; a proposal. ~하다 promote; project; suggest; propose. ¶ ~의 ~로 at a person's suggestion. ‖ ~인 projector; a promoter.

발기다 open up; tear to pieces.

발길 ¶ ~이 잦다 make frequent calls 《on, at》/ ~을 돌리다 turn back. ‖ ~질 a kick.

발꿈치 the heel.

발끝 the tips of the toes; a tiptoe; a toe 《구두·양말 따위의》.

발단(發端) the origin; the opening; the beginning. ¶ 사건의 ~ the origin of an affair.

발달(發達) development; growth;《진보》 progress; advance《ment》. ~하다 develop; grow; make progress. ¶ 심신의 ~ the growth of mind and body / 공업의 ~ the development of industry / 도시의 급속한 ~ the rapid growth of cities.

발돋움 ~하다 stand on tiptoe; stretch oneself;《비유적》 overstretch oneself; try to do what is beyond one's power.

발동(發動) operation; exercise 《법·권력의》. ~하다 move; put 《a law》 into operation; exercise.

발동기(發動機) a motor; an engine. ‖ ~선 a motorboat.

발뒤꿈치. 발뒤축 the heel. ¶ ~도 못 따라가다 be no match 《for a person》/ ~등 the instep.

발라내다 tear [peel, strip] off; clean; pare. ¶ 생선 뼈를 ~ bone a fish. 「favor with.

발라맞추다 flatter; cajole; curry

발랄(潑剌) ¶ ~ 한 fresh; lively; 「brisk.

발레 a ballet.

발레리나 a ballerina.

발령(發令) an (official) announcement. ~하다 announce 《one's appointment》 officially; issue 《a warning》. ¶ 인사 이동을 ~하다 announce personnel changes.

발로(發露) expression.

발론(發論) a proposal; a motion. ~하다 propose; move. ‖ ~자 a proposer; a mover.

발맞다 fall into step. ¶ 발맞지 않은 out of step.

발맞추다 keep pace 《with》; fall [get] into step 《with》; act in concert 《with》《행동상》.

발매(發賣) ~하다 sell; put 《a thing》 on sale [the market]. ¶ ~중이다 be on sale. ‖ ~금지 prohibition of sale / ~처 a sales agent.

발명(發明) (an) invention. ~하다 invent. ¶ ~의 newly-invented / ~의 재능이 있다 have a genius for invention. ‖ ~가 an inventor / ~품 an invention.

발목 an ankle. ¶ ~ 잡히다 《일에》 be chained 《tied》 to one's business;《약점을》 give a handle to the enemy.

발밑 ¶ ~에 at one's feet.

발바닥 the sole of a foot.

발바리 a spaniel 《dog》.

발발(勃發) an outbreak; an outburst. ~하다 break 《burst》 out; occur suddenly.

발버둥이치다 flutter one's feet;

발병(發病) ~하다 be taken ill; fall ill [sick]; get sick.
발본(拔本) eradication. ~하다 root out [up]; eradicate. ¶ 악을 ~색원하다 eradicate the root of evil / ~적 조치를 취하다 adopt drastic measures.
발부리 tiptoe; a toe. ~를 돌에 채다 tip on [stumble over] a stone.
발분(發憤) ~하다 be inspired [stimulated; roused] 《by》. ¶ ~망식(忘食)하다 give *oneself* up entirely to.
발뺌(회피) an evasion; 《구실》an excuse; a way out. ~하다 excuse *oneself*; talk *oneself* out of a difficulty.
발사(發射) firing; discharge; launching(로켓의); liftoff(우주선의). ~하다 fire; shoot; discharge; launch. ∥ ~[장] a launching pad [site] / ~장치 a launcher.
발산(發散) 《증기·냄새의》emission; 《빛·열의》emanation; radiation; 《정력의》 explosion. ~하다 give [send] out [forth]; radiate; emit; let off. ¶ 향기를 ~하다 emit a sweet fragrance / 격정을 ~ let off steam / 젊음을 ~하다 radiate youthfulness.
발상(發想) an idea; a way of thinking. ¶ 한국적인 ~ the Korean way of thinking. ∥ ~기호 an expression mark.
발상지(發祥地) the place of origin; the cradle 《of》; the birthplace 《of》.
발생(發生) 《사건의》occurrence; 《나쁜 일의》an outbreak. ~하다 happen; occur; break out. ¶ 전쟁(화제)의 ~ an outbreak of a war (fire). ∥ ~학 embryology.
발생률(發生率) a rate of incidence. ¶ 위암의 높은 ~ the high incidence of stomach cancer / 범죄의 ~ the crime rate.
발설(發說) ~하다 divulge; make public; disclose.
발성(發聲) utterance. ~하다 utter [produce] a sound. ∥ ~기관 the vocal organs / ~법 vocalization / ~연습 vocal exercises.
발소리 the sound of footsteps. ~를 죽이고 with stealthy steps.
발송(發送) 《물품》dispatch; forward; ship off. ¶ 우편물을 ~하다 mail letters / 화물을 ~하다 ship a cargo. ∥ ~역 a forwarding station / ~인 a sender; a consignor(출하주) / ~항 a port of dispatch.
발신(發信) ~하다 send 《a telegram》; dispatch 《a message》. ∥ ~국 the sending office / ~음 《전화의》 a dial tone / ~인 the sender / ~지 the place of dispatch.
발싸개 feet wraps. [patch.
발아(發芽) ~하다 germinate; bud; sprout. ¶ ~기 a germinating period.
발악(發惡) ~하다 revile; curse and swear; abuse. ¶ 최후의 ~ the last-ditch struggling.
발안(發案) (a) suggestion; an idea. ~하다 suggest; propose 《a bill》; move; originate. ∥ ~권 the right to submit a bill to the Congress / ~자 a proposer; an originator.
발암(發癌) ~성의 carcinogenic; cancer-causing. ∥ ~물질 a carcinogen; a carcinogenic substance / ~섬유유전자 an oncogene.
발언(發言) a remark; a speech; (an) utterance. ~하다 speak; utter. ¶ ~을 취소하다 retract *one's* words. ∥ ~권 the right to speak; a voice 《in》 / ~자 a speaker.
발열(發熱) ① 《기계의》 generation of heat. ~하다 generate heat. ∥ ~량 calorific value. ② 《몸의》 (an attack of) fever. ~하다 run [have] a fever.
발원(發源) ~하다 originate 《in》; rise; spring 《from》.
발원(發願) ~하다 offer a prayer 《to a deity》.
발육(發育) growth; development. ~하다 grow; develop. ¶ ~이 불완전한 underdeveloped; undergrown / ~이 빠르다 [늦다] grow rapidly [slowly]. ∥ ~기 the period of growth (development).
발음(發音) pronunciation. ~하다 pronounce. ¶ 잘못 ~하다 mispronounce. ∥ ~기관 a vocal organ / ~기호 a phonetic symbol [sign] / ~학 phonetics.
발의(發議) a suggestion; a proposal; a motion(동의). ~하다 propose; suggest; move. ¶ …의 ~로 at 《a person's》suggestion. ∥ ~권 the initiative.
발인(發靷) ~하다 carry a coffin out of the house.
발자국 a footprint; a footmark; a track. ¶ ~을 남기다 leave *one's* footprints.
발자취 《종적》 a trace; a course. ¶ 지난 5년간의 ~를 더듬어 think of the course one has followed for five years.
발작(發作) a fit; a spasm. ~하다 have a fit [spasm]. ¶ ~적(으로) spasmodic(ally); fitful(ly).
발장단(-長短) ¶ ~ 치다 beat time 《to the music》 with *one's* foot.

발전(發展) 《발달》 development; growth; 《융성》 prosperity. ~하다 develop; expand; prosper. 《공업의 ~ industrial growth / 사업을 ~시키다 develop one's business. ‖ ~도상국 a developing country / ~성 possibilities.

발전(發電) 〖電〗 generation of electric power. ~하다 generate electricity. ‖ ~기 a generator; a dynamo / ~소 a power plant (station) / 수력(원자력, 화력) ~소 a water (nuclear, thermal) power plant.

발정(發情) 〖動〗 sexual excitement; estrus (동물의). ~하다 go (come) into rut (수놈이); go (come) into beat (암놈이). ‖ ~기 the mating season.

발족(發足) inauguration. ~하다 (make a) start; be inaugurated. 〔(give an) order.

발주(發注) ordering. ~하다 order;

발진(發疹) 〖醫〗 eruption; rash. ~하다 break out (in a rash); effloresce. ‖ ~성의 eruptive. ~티푸스 eruptive typhus.

발진(發進) 《비행기의》 departure; takeoff; lift-off(헬리콥터의). ~하다 leave; take off; depart 《from》.

발진기(發振器) 〖電〗 an oscillator.

발차(發車) departure. ~하다 start; leave; depart 《at 6 p.m.》. ‖ ~계원 a starter / ~시간 the time for departure / ~신호 a starting signal.

발착(發着) departure and arrival. ~하다 arrive and depart. ‖ ~시간표 a timetable; a 《*railroad*》 schedule 《美》.

발췌(拔萃) 《행위》 extraction; selection; 《사물》 an extract; an excerpt; summary; a selection. ~하다 extract; select 《from》. ‖ ~곡 a selection.

발치 the foot 《*of one's bed*》.

발칙하다 ① 《무례》 (be) ill-mannered; rude. ② 《괘씸》 (be) insolent; unpardonable.

발칵 all of a sudden; suddenly.

발칸(發) ‖ ~반도 the Balkan peninsula.

발코니 a balcony.

발탁(拔擢) ~하다 select; single (pick) out; choose.

발톱 toenails(사람); a claw(짐승); a talon(맹금); a nail(고양이).

발틱해(— 海) the Baltic Sea.

발파(發破) ~하다 blast; set a dynamite. ‖ ~공 a blaster.

발판(—板) ① a footboard; a footstool; a step (비계) a scaffold. ② 《기반·거점》 a footing; a foothold. ~을 얻다 gain 《secure》 a footing 《*in society*》. ③ 《수단》 a stepping-stone.

발포(發布) promulgation. ~하다 promulgate; proclaim; issue.

발포(發泡) foaming. ~하다 foam; froth. ‖ ~스티롤 styrol foam; 《상표》 Styrofoam / ~제 a blowing (foaming) agent.

발포(發砲) ~하다 fire 《*on*》; open fire 《*on*》; discharge 《*a gun*》. ‖ ~사건 a shooting incident.

발표(發表) announcement; expression; publication. ~하다 announce 《*a statement*》; make known (public); release 《*the news*》; express 《*one's opinion*》. ¶ 연구를 ~하다 《출판물로》 publish the results of one's research. ‖ 미~작품 an unpublished work.

발하다(發—) ① 《빛·열 등을》 emit; emanate; radiate; give forth (out); shed (향기 등을). ② 《명령 등을》 issue; publish; promulgate 《*a decree*》. ¶ 명령을 ~ issue an order. ③ 《출발》 leave; start. ④ 《기원》 originate 《*in*》.

발한(發汗) ~하다 sweat; perspire. ‖ ~제 a diaphoretic.

발행(發行) ① 《도서의》 publication; issue. ~하다 publish; issue. ¶ 매월《월 2회》 잠지 a monthly (semi-monthly) (magazine). ‖ ~금지〔정지〕 prohibition〔suspension〕 of publication / ~부수 《신문·잡지의》 a circulation 《단행본의》 copies printed / ~처 a publishing office. ② 《어음 등의》 drawing; issue. ~하다 draw 《*a bill upon a person*》. ‖ ~인 a drawer / ~일 the date of issue. ③ 《지폐·채권 등의》 flo(a)tation. ~하다 float 《*a bond*》; issue. ‖ ~고 issue amount.

발호(跋扈) ~하다 be rampant.

발화(發火) ~하다 catch fire; ignite. ‖ ~장치 an ignition device / ~점 the ignition [firing] point.

발효(發效) effectuation. ~하다 become effective; come into effect.

발효(醱酵) fermentation. ~하다 ferment. ‖ ~시키다 ferment. ‖ ~소 yeast; a ferment.

발휘(發揮) ~하다 show; display; exhibit. ¶ 수완을 ~하다 display (show) one's ability.

발흥(勃興) ~하다 rise suddenly (into power); make a sudden rise. ¶ 인도의 ~ the rise of India.

밝기(明度) luminosity.   〔India.

밝다[¹] ① 《환하다》 (be) light; bright. ¶ 밝은 데 a light place / 밝게 하다 lighten; light up. ② 《정통하다》 (be) familiar with; well versed in; conversant with. ¶ 미국 사정에 ~ be conversant with American affairs. ③ 《귀·눈이》 (be) sharp; keen; quick. ¶ 귀가 ~ have a sharp ear; be quick of hearing. ④ 《성격·사정

이) (be) cheerful; bright. ¶밝은 표정 a cheerful (bright) look / 밝은 미래(전망) a bright future (prospect). ⑤ 《공명하다》 (be) clear; clean. ¶밝은 정치 clean politics.
밝다² 《날이》 dawn; 《day》 break. ¶밝아 오는 하늘 the dawning sky / 날이 밝기 전에 before light.
밝을녘 daybreak; dawn; break of day.
밝히다 ① 《불을》 brighten; lighten; light up; make brighter. ② 《증명하다》 make (*a matter*) clear; clear (up); clarify; bring (*a matter*) to light. ¶신분을 ~ prove *one's* identity. ③ 《밤새움》 sit (stay) up all night.
밟다 ① 《발로》 step (tread) on. ¶보리를 ~ step (tread) on the seedling of barley. ② 《가다》 set foot on. ¶이국 땅을 ~ set foot on foreign soil. ③ 《경험》 무대를 ~ tread the stage. ④ 《절차 등을》 go through (*formalities*); complete. ¶정규 과정을 ~ complete (go through) a regular course. ⑤ 《뒤를》 follow; shadow; trail; dog (*a person's steps*).
밟히다 be stepped (trampled) on; be trod upon.
밤¹ 《야간》 night; evening. ¶~에 at night; in the evening / ~의 서울 Seoul by night / ~거리의 여인 a street girl / ~마다 every night; night after night / ~늦게(까지) (till) late at night / 한 ~중에 in the dead of night / ~이 되다 night falls (closes in) / 애기로 ~을 새우다 talk the night away. ¶~거리 night streets / ~경치 a night scene. ② 《행사》 an evening. ¶음악의 ~ (have) a musical evening.
밤² 《栗》 a chestnut. ¶~나무 a chestnut tree / ~색(의) chestnut; nut-brown.
밤길 a walk at night; a night trip.
밤낚시 night fishing (angling). ¶~하다 go fishing by night. ¶~꾼 a night angler. 「the time 《날.
밤낮 day and night; always, all
밤눈 night vision. ¶~이 어둡다 be blind at night.
밤바람 a night wind (breeze).
밤비 rain in the night.
밤사이 during the night.
밤새도록 all night (long); overnight; all the night through.
밤새(우)다 sit (stay) up all night.
밤새움하다 sit up all night.
밤소경 a night-blind person.
밤소일 (─消日) a night out. ~하다 go out in the evening for pleasure.
밤손님 a night thief (prowler); a burglar; a nightbird 《俗》.
밤송이 a chestnut bur.
밤안개 a night fog (mist).
밤알 a chestnut.
밤이슬 the night dew.
밤일 night-work. 「night.
밤잠 night sleep; sleeping at
밤중(─中) midnight. ¶~에 at (mid)night.
밤차(─車) a night train.
밤톨 ¶~만하다 be as big as a chestnut.
밤하늘 a night sky. 「chestnut.
밥 《쌀밥》 boiled (cooked) rice. ¶~을 짓다 cook (boil) rice. ② 《식사》 a meal; food; 《생계》 *one's* living. ¶~을 먹다 take (have) a meal; make a living; earn *one's* bread. ③ 《먹이》 feed; food; bait 《낚시용》. ¶돼지 ~ hog feed / …의 ~이 되다 fall a prey (victim) to.
밥값 food expenses (costs); board 《하숙비》.
밥그릇 a rice bowl. 「《입맛》.
밥맛 the flavor of rice; appetite
밥벌레 a do-nothing; a useless mouth; a good-for-nothing.
밥벌이 breadwinning. ~하다 make a living; earn *one's* daily bread.
밥상(─床) a dining (an eating) table. ¶~을 차리다 (치우다) set (clear) the table.
밥솥 a kettle for cooking rice.
밥솥전기 an electric rice cooker.
밥술 a few spoonfuls of boiled rice; a rice spoon 《숟가락》.
밥알 a grain of cooked rice.
밥장사하다 sell meals; run an eating house. 「house.
밥장수 one who runs an eating
밥주걱 a (wooden) paddle for serving rice.
밥줄 *one's* means of livelihood. ¶~이 끊어지다 lose *one's* job; be out of job(work). 「house.
밥집 an eating house; a chophouse.
밥통(─桶) ① a boiled-rice container. ② ☞위《胃》. ③ ☞밥벌레, 바보.
밥투정하다 grumble over meals.
밥풀 ① 《풀》 rice paste. ② 《밥알》 grains of boiled rice.
밧줄 a rope; a line. ¶생명의 ~ a lifeline / ~을 당기다 draw(pull) the rope; haul at(upon) a rope / ~을 타고 내려 오다 climb down a rope.
방(房) a room; a chamber. ¶자기 ~ *one's* (own) room / 양지 바른 ~ a sunny room / ~이 셋 있는 집 a three-room(ed) house / ~을 빌리다 《세놓다》 hire (rent) a room.
방(榜) 《방문》 a placard; a public (an official) notice.
방(放) 《탄환의》 a shot; a round.

¶ 한~의 포성 a roar of cannon.
…방(方) 《우편 등에서》 care of《생략 c/o》. ¶ 김씨 ~ 유씨 Mr. Yu, care of (c/o) Mr. Kim.
방갈로 a bungalow.
방값《방세》 room rent;《호텔 등의》 room charge.
방계(傍系) ~의 collateral; subsidiary. ‖ ~회사 a subsidiary (an affiliated) company.
방공(防空) air defense. ‖ ~연습(훈련) an anti-air-raid (air defense) drill / ~호 air-raid (a bomb) shelter; a dugout / 한국 ~식별구역 Korean Air Defense Identification Zone《생략 KADIZ》.
방과(放課) dismissal of a class. ¶ ~후 after school (hours).
방관(傍觀) ~하다 remain (sit as) a spectator; stand by idly; look on (unconcernedly). ¶ ~적 태도를 취하다 assume the attitude of an onlooker. ‖ ~자 an onlooker; a bystander.
방광(膀胱) the bladder. ‖ ~염 〖醫〗 inflammation of the bladder; cystitis.
방귀 wind; a fart《俗》. ¶ ~ 뀌다 break wind; fart.
방글레 ~ 웃다 smile; beam.
방글(방긋)거리다 smile; beam. ¶ 방글방글(방긋방긋) with a gentle (bland) smile; smilingly; beamingly.
방금(方今) just now; only a moment ago.
방긋하다 (be) ajar; slightly open.
방년(芳年) the sweet age《of a young lady》. ¶ ~ 20세의 처녀 a girl of sweet twenty.
방놓다(房一) build a room.
방뇨(放尿) urination; pissing《俗》. ¶ ~하다 pass urine; urinate; make (pass) water; piss《俗》.〔talk〕.
방담(放談) a random (free) speech
방대(尨大) ~한 bulky; massive; huge; enormous; vast / ~한 계획 a huge-scale plan. 「a way.
방도(方道) a means; a measure;
방독(防毒) ‖ ~마스크 〖면〗 an anti-gas mask; a gas mask; a respirator《英》.
방랑(放浪) ~하다 wander (roam) about; rove. ‖ ~객(자) a wanderer; a vagabond / ~벽 vagrant habits / ~생활 a vagabond (wandering) life.
방류(放流) ~하다《물을》 discharge;《물고기를》 stock (plant)《a river》with《fish》.
방망이 a club; a stick; a billy (club); a cudgel. 「offer for sale.
방매(放賣) selling; sale. ¶ ~하다
방면(方面)《방향》 a direction;《지방》 a quarter; a district. ¶ 제주~ the *Cheju* districts. ② 《분야》 a line; a field.

방면(放免) ~하다 set《a person》 free; acquit; release; liberate. ‖ 훈계~ release after admonition.
방명(芳名) your (honored) name. ‖ ~록 a list of names; a visitor's register (list).
방목(放牧) ~하다 pasture; graze; put (cattle) out to grass. ‖ ~지 a grazing land; a pasture.
방문(房門) a door (of a room).
방문(訪問) a call; a visit. ¶ ~하다 (pay a) visit; (make a) call on 《a person》; call at《a house》; go and see《a person》. ¶ ~을 받다 receive a call (visit) / 인사차 ~ 하다 pay a courtesy call《on》. ‖ ~간호사 a visiting nurse / ~객 a caller; a visitor / ~단 a group (team) of visitors / ~외교 diplomacy by visit / ~판매 door-to-door selling.
방물장수 a peddler of fancy goods.
방미(訪美) a visit to the United States. ¶ ~길에 오르다 leave for America.
방바닥(房一) the floor of a room.
방방곡곡(坊坊曲曲) ¶ ~에서 throughout the length and breadth of the land; all over the country.
방범(防犯) crime prevention. ‖ ~대원 a (night) watchman / ~주간 Crime Prevention Week.
방법(方法)《방식》 a way; a method;《과정》 a process;《수단》 a means;《방책》 a plan; a system;《조치》 a step; a measure. ¶ 최선의 ~ the best method (way) / ~을 강구하다 take steps (measures) *to do* / 소금 만드는 새로운 ~ a new process for making salt. ‖ ~론 methodology.
방벽(防壁) a protective (defensive) wall; a barrier.
방부(防腐) preservation from decay; antisepsis. ¶ …에 ~ 처리를 하다 apply antiseptic treatment 《to》. ‖ ~제 an antiseptic; a preservative.
방불(彷彿) ~하다 resemble closely. ¶ ~케 하다 remind *one* of《a thing》.
방비(防備) defense; defensive preparations. ~하다 defend; guard. ‖ 무~도시 an open city / ~를 강화하다 strengthen the defense 《of a country》.
방사(房事) sexual intercourse. ¶ ~를 삼가다 be continent.
방사(放射) radiation; emission. ~하다 radiate; emit. ¶ X선을 ~ 하다 radiate X-rays. ‖ ~상도로 a radial road / ~에너지 radiant energy / ~열 radiant heat.
방사능(放射能) radioactivity. ¶ ~의 radioactive / ~의 강도 intensi-

방사선(放射線) radiation; radial rays. ¶ ~치료를 받다 receive radiation treatment. ǁ ~과 the department of radiology / ~요법 radiotherapy / ~의학 radiology.

방사성(放射性) ~의 radioactive. ǁ ~낙진 radioactive fallout / ~동위원소 radioisotope / ~물질 radioactive substance / ~폐기물 radioactive waste.

방생(放生)〖佛〗 the release of captive animals.

방석(方席) a cushion.

방성통곡(放聲痛哭) ~하다 cry loudly and bitterly.

방세(房貰) a room rent. ¶ ~를 올리다 raise the (room) rent.

방세간(房─) room furniture.

방송(放送) broadcasting; a broadcast(일회의); go on the air; send 《news》 on the air. ¶ 2개 국어 ~ a bilingual broadcast / ~중이다 be on the air. ǁ ~국 a broadcasting (radio, TV) station / ~극 a radio (television) drama / ~기자 a radio (TV) reporter / ~망 a radio (TV) network / ~방해 jamming / ~사업 the broadcasting industry / ~실 a radio (TV) studio / ~위성 a broadcasting satellite / ~통신대학 the University of the Air and Correspondence / ~프로 a radio (TV) program.

방수(防水) waterproofing. ~하다 make 《cloth》 waterproof; waterproof 《cloth》. ¶ ~의 waterproof; watertight. ǁ ~격벽 watertight bulkhead / ~제(포) waterproof cloth / ~처리 (가공) waterproofing / ~화 a pair of overshoes / ~전 a sluiceway.

방수로(放水路) a drainage canal.

방습(防濕) damproofing. ¶ ~의 damproofing. ǁ ~제 a desiccant.

방식(方式) 〖형식〗 a formula; a form; 〖양식〗 a mode; 〖방법〗 a method; 〖체계〗 a system. ¶ 새로운 분류 ~ a new system of classification.

방식제(防蝕劑)〖化〗 an anticorrosive.

방실거리다 smile (sweetly); beam.

방심(放心) ~하다 be off one's guard; be careless; be unwatchful. ¶ ~하고 있는 틈에 in an unguarded moment.

방아 a (grinding) mill. ǁ 방앗간 a flour(ing) mill.

방아깨비〖蟲〗 a kind of grasshopper; a locust.

방아쇠 a trigger. ¶ ~를 당기다 pull the trigger; trigger 《a rifle》.

방안(方案) a plan; a device; a scheme; a program. ¶ ~을 세우다 draw up a plan.

방안지(方眼紙) graph paper.

방약무인(傍若無人) ~한 arrogant; overbearing; audacious; outrageous.

방어(防禦) defense; protection. ~하다 defend; protect. ¶ 선수권을 ~하다 defend the title. ǁ ~율 (야구에서) earned run average(생략 ERA) / ~전 a defensive war (fight) / ~지역〖籠〗 zone defense.

방어(魴魚)〖魚〗 a yellowtail.

방언(方言) a dialect; a provincialism.

방역(防疫) prevention of epidemics. ~하다 take preventive measures against epidemics. ǁ ~대책 anti-epidemic measure.

방열(防熱) ~의 heatproof. ǁ ~복 heatproof clothes.

방영(放映) televising 《a movie》. ~하다 televise; telecast. ¶ ~권 the televising right.

방울 ① 〖쇠방울〗 a bell. ¶ ~소리 the tinkling of a bell. ② 〖물의〗 a drop. ¶ ~~ (떨어지다) (fall) in drops.

방울새〖鳥〗 a greenfinch.

방위(方位) a direction. ǁ ~각 an azimuth (angle); a declination.

방위(防衛) defense. ~하다 defend; protect; safeguard. ¶ 자기 ~를 위해 in self-defense. ǁ ~계획 a defense plan / ~산업 《develop》 the defense industry / ~성금 (contribution) to the national defense fund / ~세 a defense tax / ~소집 the defense call-up; the defensive mobilization / ~예산 a national defense budget.

방음(防音) ¶ ~의 soundproof. ǁ ~실 a soundproof room / ~장치 soundproofing; 《음향장치》 a sound arrester; a silencer.

방임(放任) ~하다 let (leave) 《a person》 alone. ǁ ~주의 a let-alone (noninterference) policy; a laissez-faire principle.

방자 ~하다 curse; execrate; wish ill of 《a person》.

방자하다(스럽다)(放恣─) (be) self-indulgent; licentious; willful.

방적(紡績) spinning. ǁ ~견사 spun silk / ~공 a spinner / ~공업 (the cotton) spinning industry / ~공장 (기계, 회사) a spinning mill (machine, company).

방전(放電) electric discharge. ~하다 discharge electricity. ǁ 공중 ~ atmospheric electricity.

방점(傍點) a side point [mark].
방정 ¶ ~ 맞다 be flighty [rash] / ~ 떨다 behave rashly.
방정(方正) ~하다 (be) good; upright; correct. ¶ 품행이 ~한 사람 a man of good conduct.
방정식(方程式) an equation. ‖ 1[2, 3]차~ a simple [quadratic, cubic] equation.
방제(防除) 《해충 등의》 prevention and extermination 《of flies》; control of insect pests》.
방조(幇助) assistance; aiding and abetting 《범죄의》. ~하다 assist; aid; help; aid and abet 《suicide, etc.》. ‖ ~자 an abettor 《범죄의》.
방조제(防潮堤) a tide embankment; a seawall.
방종(放縱) self-indulgence; dissoluteness; licentiousness. ~한 self-indulgent; licentious; dissolute; loose.
방주(方舟) an ark. ¶ 노아의 ~ Noah's ark.
방주(旁註) marginal notes; foot notes 《각주(脚註)》.
방증(傍證) circumstantial evidence.
방지(防止) prevention. ~하다 prevent; check. ¶ 전쟁의 위험을 ~하다 prevent the danger of war. ‖ ~책 a preventive measure / 인플레~책 an anti-inflation policy.
방직(紡織) spinning and weaving. ‖ ~(공)업 the textile industry / ~공장 a spinning mill.
방책(方策) 《방안》 a plan; a scheme; 《방침》 a policy; 《수단》 a measure. ¶ 최선의 ~ the best policy / 현명한 ~ a wise plan.
방책(防柵) a palisade; a barricade; a stockade.
방첩(防諜) anti-[counter-]espionage; counter-intelligence 《美》. ‖ ~부대 Counter-Intelligence Corps 《생략 C.I.C.》.
방청(傍聽) hearing; attendance. ~하다 hear; listen to; attend. ‖ ~권 an admission ticket / ~석 seats for the public; the (visitor's) gallery 《의회·법정 등의》 / ~인 a hearer; an auditor; an auditor (청중).
방추(方錐) a square drill. ¶ ~형의 pyramidal.
방추(紡錘) a spindle. ¶ ~형(의) spindle-shape(d).
방축(防縮) ¶ ~의 shrink-proof. ~가공을 한 천 shrink-resistant [preshrunk] fabrics.
방출(放出) release 《of goods》; discharge (배출). ~하다 release; discharge. ¶ 정부(보유)미의 ~ the release of government rice. ‖ ~물자 released goods [commodities]. 【약】 a mothball.
방충제(防蟲劑) an insecticide; 《좀

방취(防臭) ‖ ~제 a deodorizer; a deodorant.
방치(放置) ~하다 let 《a thing》 alone; leave 《a matter》 as it is; neglect(등한시).
방침(方針) 《방향》 a course; a line; 《정책》 a policy; 《원칙》 a principle; 《계획》 a plan. ¶ ~을 세우다 map out one's course; lay down the lines 《of》 / ~을 실행하다 carry out one's plan.
방탄(防彈) ¶ ~의 bulletproof; bombproof. ¶ ~조끼 [유리] a bulletproof jacket [glass].
방탕(放蕩) dissipation; debauchery. ~하다 (be) dissipated; prodigal; 《서술적》 lead a dissipated [dissolute] life. ‖ ~생활 a fast life; fast living / ~자 a libertine; a debauchee.
방파제(防波堤) a breakwater.
방패(防牌) a shield; a buckler(원형의). ¶ ⋯을 ~ 삼다 use 《something》 as a shield 《against》; shield oneself behind 《something》. ¶ 인간 ~ human shields.
방편(方便) 《수단》 expediency; an expedient; a means; 《도구》 an instrument; 《일시적》 a temporary expedient; a makeshift.
방풍(防風) ‖ ~림 a shelter belt; a windbreak (forest).
방학(放學) school holidays; a vacation. ~하다 close the school; go on vacation.
방한(防寒) protection against the cold. ‖ ~모 a winter cap / ~복 (special) winter clothes / ~화 winter shoes; arctic boots; arctics 《美》.
방한(訪韓) a visit to Korea. ~하다 visit Korea. ¶ ~중인 K씨 Mr. K who is on a visit to Korea.
방해(妨害) obstruction; disturbance; a hindrance; 《간섭》 interference. ~하다 obstruct; disturb; interrupt; interfere with. ¶ 계획을 ~하다 block [obstruct] a plan / 작업을 ~하다 hinder 《a person》 in his work; hinder 《a person's》 work. ‖ ~공작 sabotage / ~물 an obstacle; an obstructive tactics; a filibuster 《美》.
방향(方向) 《방위》 direction; bearings; 《진로》 a course. ¶ ~을 전환하다 change one's course. ‖ ~감각 a sense of direction / ~탐지기 a direction finder.
방향(芳香) a sweet smell; perfume; fragrance. ‖ ~제 an aromatic.
방형(方形) a square. ¶ ~의 square.
방호(防護) protection. ~하다 protect; guard.
방화(防火) fire prevention [fight-

방화 ¶ ~의 fireproof. ‖ ~벽〔셔터, 연창〕 a fire wall〔shutter, drill〕/ ~설비 fire-protection equipment / ~주간 Fire Prevention Week.

방화(邦畫)(영화) a Korean film〔movie, motion picture〕.

방화(放火)(행위) arson; incendiarism;(불) an incendiary fire. ~하다 set fire to(*a house*). ‖ ~광 a pyromaniac / ~범 an arsonist; an incendiary; a firebug《美俗》/ ~죄 arson.

방황(彷徨) wandering. ~하다 wander〔roam〕 about; rove.

밭 a field; a farm. ‖ 배추~ a cabbage patch / 옥수수~ a corn field / 채소~ a vegetable〔kitchen〕 garden.

밭갈이 plowing; cultivating. ~하다 cultivate; plow; till.

밭고랑 a furrow.

밭곡식(一穀一) dry-field grain〔corn〕.

밭농사(一農事) dry-field farming.

밭다① (시간·공간적으로) be very〔too〕close〔near〕. ② (기침이) be dry; hacking. ¶ 밭은 기침을 하다 have a dry〔hacking〕 cough.

밭다(거르다) filter; strain; percolate.

밭도랑 a ditch in a dry field.

밭두둑 a ridge between fields.

밭벼 a dry-field rice plant.

밭이랑 a ridge in a field.

밭일 farming; farm work. ~하다 work in the fields.

배① 《복부》 the belly; the abdomen; 《창자》 the bowels; 《위》 the stomach. ¶ ~가 나온 potbellied; big-bellied / ~가 아프다 have a stomachache / 제 ~만 불리다 enrich *one's* own pocket; feather *one's own* nest. ② (맘속) a heart; a mind. ¶ 뱃속 검은 blackhearted; wicked; evil-minded. ③ (시샘) ¶ ~가 아프다 be green with envy. ④ (밴) a womb. ¶ ~가 부르다 be large with a child.

배²(타는) a ship; a boat; a vessel; a steamer (기선). ¶ ~로 (go) by ship / ~를 타다 go〔get, on board〕 (a ship); embark / ~에서 내리다 get off〔leave〕 a ship; disembark.

배³(과일) a pear.

배(胚)〔植〕an embryo. 〔動〕a fetus.

배(倍)①(2배) double. ② double; twice; two times《美》; twofold / ~로 하다〔되다〕 double (*the profit*); be doubled. ②(곱절) times; -fold. ¶ 한 ~ 반 one and a half times / …의 3 ~ 하다 thrice as much as… / 3 ~ three times; treble; thrice; threefold / 4 ~ quadruple / 5 ~ quintuple / 6 ~ sextuple / 7 ~ septuple / 8 ~ octuple / 9 ~ nonuple / 10 ~ decuple / 백 ~ centuple.

배가(倍加) ~하다 (make) double; increase markedly. ¶ 노력을 ~하다 redouble *one's* efforts / 매력을 ~하다 make《*something*》 doubly attractive.

배갈 a strong Chinese liquor.

배겨나다 bear up《*under*》; put up《*with*》; suffer patiently《*through*》.〔ject; drive out.

배격(排擊) ~하다 denounce; re-

배경(背景)①(후면) a background;(무대의) scenery; setting;(배후 사정) the background.¶ ~ 사건의 background of an affair. ¶ ~음악 background music. ②(후원) backing; support; pull《美俗》;(사람) a backer; a supporter. ¶ 유력한 ~ strong backing; a strong backer / 정치적 ~ political backing / ~이 없다 have no "pull" behind *one*.

배고프다 (be) hungry. ¶ 배고파 죽겠다 be dying with hunger.

배곯다 have an empty stomach.

배관(配管) plumbing. ‖ ~공 a plumber; a pipe fitter / ~공사 piping work; plumbing.

배교(背敎) apostasy. ‖ ~자 an apostate.〔수 a volleyball player.

배구(排球)〔競〕volleyball. ‖ ~선

배금(拜金) ‖ ~주의 mammonism / ~주의자 a mammonist.

배급(配給) distribution; rationing. ~하다 distribute; supply; ration (식량을). ‖ ~소 a distributing station〔center〕/ ~쌀〔품〕 rationed rice〔goods〕/ ~제〔도〕 distributing〔rationing〕 system / ~통장〔표〕 a ration book〔ticket〕.

배기(排氣) exhaust; ventilation. ‖ ~가스 exhaust gas〔fumes〕/ ~관 an exhaust pipe / ~량 engine displacement / ~장치 an exhauster / ~구 an air escape.

배기다 endure; bear with; suffer. ¶ 배길 수 있는 bearable; endurable / 배길 수 없는 unbearable; unendurable.

배기다(받치다) be hard on(*one's back*); pinch; squeeze.

배꼽 the navel. ¶ ~이 빠지도록 웃다 laugh like anything; die with laughing.

배낭(背囊)〔植〕an embryo sac.

배낭(背囊) a knapsack; a rucksack; a backpack.〔baby.

배내옷 clothes for a newborn

배냇니 a milk tooth.〔ple.

배냇병신(一病身) a congenital crip-

배뇨(排尿) urination. ~하다 urinate; pass〔make〕 water.

배다¹ 《촘촘하다》 (be) close; fine.

배다² 《잉태》 conceive; become (get) pregnant. ¶ 애를 ~ conceive a child; be pregnant / 새끼를 ~ be big with young.

배다³ ① 《스미다》 sink 《into》; soak through; permeate. ¶ 피가 밴 붕대 a bandage saturated with blood. ② 《익숙》 get used 《to》; become accustomed 《to》. ¶ 몸에 밴 일 a familiar job [work] / one's accustomed work / 일이 손에 ~ get skilled 《in》.

배다르다 be born of a different mother; be half-blooded. ¶ 배다른 형제[자매] one's half brother [sister].

배다리 《가교》 a pontoon bridge.
배달(倍達) ‖ ~민족 the Korean race.
배달(配達) delivery. ~하다 deliver; distribute. ‖ ~료 the delivery charge / ~원 a deliveryman; a mailman (우편); a milkman(우유); a newsboy(신문) / ~증명서 a delivery receipt / ~처 the destination / 무료~ free delivery / 시내~ local delivery / 특별~ special delivery.
배당(配當) allotment; a dividend. ~하다 allot; pay a dividend(배당금을). ¶ 이익의 ~을 받다 share in the profits. ‖ ~금 a dividend; a share / ~락 ex dividend; dividend off / ~률 dividend rate / ~부(附) cum dividend; dividend on.
배드민턴 badminton.
배란(排卵) ovulation. ~하다 ovulate. ‖ ~기 an ovulatory phase / ~억제제 (an) anovulant / ~억제제 (an) anovulatory medication / ~유발제 an ovulatory (ovulation-inducing) drug.
배럴 《용량 단위》 a barrel.
배려(配慮) 《마음씀》 care; consideration. ~하다 consider. ¶ 세심한 ~ thoughtful consideration.
배례(拜禮) ~하다 bow; salute.
배맞다 make an illicit intercourse.
배면(背面) the rear; the back. ‖ ~공격 a rear attack.
배밀이 ¶ ~하다 crawl; creep.
배반(背反, 背叛) betrayal. ~하다 betray; turn (rebel) 《against》. ¶ 친구를 ~하다 turn against a friend / 남자를 ~하다 jilt a man / 나라를 ~하다 turn traitor to one's country. ‖ ~자 a betrayer; a traitor.
배반(胚盤) 《動》 the germinal disk.
배변(排便) evacuation. ~하다 evacuate [open] the bowels.
배본(配本) distribution of books. ~하다 distribute books.
배부(配付) distribution. ~하다 distribute (among, to); deliver.

배부르다 have a full stomach; be large with child (임신해서). ¶ 배부른 흥정 a take-it-or-leave-it deal (sale).
배분(配分) distribution. ~하다 distribute; allot.
배불뚝이 a person with a potbelly.
배사(背斜) 《地》 anticline. ‖ ~의 anticlinal. ‖ ~구조 an anticline.
배상(賠償) reparation; indemnity; compensation. ~하다 compensate; indemnify; make reparation 《for》. ¶ ~을 요구하다 demand reparation; claim for compensation. ‖ ~금 an indemnity; reparations(전쟁의) / 현물(現物)~ reparation in kind (cash).
배색(配色) a color scheme; coloring.
배서(背書) ~하다 (an) endorsement. ~하다 endorse 《a check》; back 《a bill》. ‖ ~인 an endorser / 피~인 an endorsee.
배석(陪席) ~하다 sit with 《one's superior》. ‖ ~자 an attendant / ~판사 an associate judge; an assessor. ¶ ~석 《on a line》.
배선(配船) ~하다 place 《assign》 a ship.
배선(配線) wiring. ~하다 wire 《a house》. ¶ ~처 electric wiring.
배설(排泄) excretion; discharge. ~하다 excrete; evacuate; discharge. ‖ ~기관 the excretory organs / ~물 excrements; body waste.
배속(配屬) assignment. ~하다 assign; attach. ¶ 영업부에 ~되다 be assigned to the sales department. ‖ ~장교 a military officer attached to a school.
배수(拜受) ~하다 receive; accept.
배수(配水) ~하다 supply water 《to》. ‖ ~관 a conduit 〔water〕 pipe / ~지(池) a distributing reservoir.
배수(倍數) 《數》 a multiple. ¶ 공~ a common multiple.
배수(排水) draining; drainage. ~하다 drain; pump out. ‖ ~관 a drainpipe / ~구 a drain 〔ditch〕 / ~량 displacement (이 배의 ~량은 2만 톤이다 This ship displaces twenty thousand tons.) / 펌프 a drainage pump.
배수진(背水陣) ¶ ~을 치다 fight with one's back to the wall (sea); burn one's boats; burn the bridges behind one.
배신(背信) betrayal; a breach of faith. ~하다 betray 《a person's》 confidence; break faith. ‖ ~자 a betrayer; a traitor; a turncoat(변절자) / ~행위 a breach of faith 〔trust〕.
배심(陪審) jury. ‖ ~원 a jury

배아 (胚芽) a germ; an embryo bud. ‖ ~미(米) rice with germs.
배알 entrails; guts. ☞ 창자.
배알(拜謁) an audience 《with the king, etc.》. ~하다 have an audience with 《the king》.
배앓이 stomach trouble; colic; the gripes.
배액(倍額) double the amount 〔price〕; a double sum.
배양(培養) culture; cultivation. ~하다 cultivate; nurture; breed. ¶ 세균을 ~ cultivate 〔culture〕 bacteria. ‖ ~기 (culture) medium / ~액 a culture fluid / 인공~ artificial culture / 조직~ tissue culture.
배역(配役) the cast 《of a play》. ¶ ~을 정하다 cast 《an actor》 for a part; cast a part 《to an actor》.
배열(排列) arrangement; disposition. ~하다 arrange; dispose; put 《things》 in order.
배엽(胚葉) 〔動〕 a germ(inal) layer.
배영(背泳) the backstroke.
배외(排外) ¶ ~의 anti-foreign. ‖ ~사상 anti-foreign ideas; anti-foreignism; anti-alienism.
배우(俳優) a player; an actor (남자); an actress (여자). ¶ ~가 되다 become an actor 〔actress〕; go on the stage. ‖ ~학교 a school of acting / 영화〔연극〕 ~ a film 〔stage〕 actor / 인기 ~ a star.
배우다 learn; study; be taught; take lessons 《in, on》 《연습》 practice; be trained in. ¶ 철저히 ~ learn thoroughly / 피아노를 ~ take lessons on the piano / 차 운전을 ~ learn how to drive a motorcar.
배우체(配偶體) 〔生〕 a gamete.
배우자(配偶子) a spouse; one's mate (husband, wife). ‖ ~공제 tax exemption for one's spouse.
배움 study; learning. ‖ ~의 길 the pursuit of studies; learning. ¶ ~터 a school; a place for learning.
배웅 send-off. ~하다 show 《a person》 out; see 〔send〕 《a person》 off. ¶ ~나가다 go 《to the station》 to see 《a person》 off.
배유(胚乳) 〔植〕 an albumen; an endosperm.
배율(倍率) magnification.
배은망덕(背恩忘德) ingratitude. ~하다 be ungrateful; lose one's gratitude. ¶ ~한 사람 an ungrateful person. 「an overtone.
배음(倍音) 〔樂〕 a harmonic 〔tone〕

배일(排日) ¶ ~의 anti-Japanese 《feeling, movement》. 「pism.
배일성(背日性) 〔植〕 negative heliotro-
배임(背任) breach of trust; misappropriation (부정 유용). ‖ ~행위 an act in violation of one's duty. 「than ever.
배전(倍前) ~ ~ redoubled; more
배전(配電) ~하다 supply electricity; distribute power. ‖ ~반 a switchboard / ~선 an electrcity main; a service wire / ~소 a power distribution station.
배점(配點) ~하다 allot 《20 points》 to 《a question》.
배정(配定) assignment. ~하다 assign; allot.
배제(排除) exclusion; removal. ~하다 exclude; remove; eliminate. ¶ 정실을 ~하다 eliminate favoritism. 「a badge.
배지 a badge. ¶ ~를 달다 wear
배짱 boldness; pluck; courage; guts. ‖ ~센 daring; bold; plucky; courageous / ~ 없는 timid; faint-(chicken-)hearted.
배차(配車) allocation of cars. ~하다 allocate 〔dispatch〕 cars 〔buses〕. ‖ ~계(員) a dispatcher.
배척(排斥) expulsion; a boycott. ~하다 drive out; oust; expel. ¶ 일본 상품에 대한 ~ a boycott of Japanese good. ‖ ~운동 a boycott movement 〔campaign〕.
배추 a Chinese cabbage. ‖ ~김치 cabbage *kimchi*; pickled cabbage.
배출(排出) discharge. ~하다 discharge; excrete. ¶ 가스〔연기〕를 ~하다 discharge gas 〔smoke〕 / 노폐물을 ~하다 excrete waste matter from the body. ‖ ~관 an exhaust 〔a discharge〕 pipe / ~구 an outlet / ~물 waste matter; industrial waste (공장의).
배출(輩出) ~하다 produce a large number of 《scholars》; appear in great numbers.
배치(背馳) ~하다 be contrary 《to》; run counter 《to》; contradict 《each other》.
배치(配置) arrangement; disposition. ~하다 arrange; 〔부서에〕 post; station; dispose. ¶ 군대를 ~하다 place 〔station〕 troops 《in the province》. ‖ ~계획 block 〔plot〕 planning / ~도〔圖〕 an arrangement plan; 〔建〕 a plot plan / 인원 ~ disposition of men.
배치 batch. ‖ ~생산 batch production / ~처리 〔컴〕 batch processing / ~플랜트 a batch plant.
배타(排他) exclusion. ‖ ~적인 exclusive. ‖ ~주의 exclusivism; exclusionism;

배탈(一頃) (have) a stomach trouble (upset, disorder).
배태(胚胎) 하다 originate 《*in*》; have 《*its*》 origin 《*in*》.
배터리 a battery.
배터박스 〖野〗 a batter's box.
배트 〖野〗 a bat.
배팅 〖野〗 batting. ¶ ～오더 the batting order.
배편(一便) shipping service. ¶ ～으로 by ship (water, sea).
배포(配布) distribution. ～하다 distribute 《*among, to*》.
배포(排布) a plan (scheme) (in *one's* mind). ¶ ～가 크다 be magnanimous; think on a large scale.
배필(配匹) a partner for life; a spouse; a mate. ¶ 천생～ a well-matched couple (pair).
배합(配合) 〔결합〕 combination; 〔조화〕 harmony; match; 〔혼합〕 mixture. ～하다 combine; match; harmonize; mix. ¶ ～색의 color scheme (harmony) / ～비료 compound fertilizer / ～사료 assorted feed.
배화교(拜火敎) fire worship; Zoroastrianism.
배회(徘徊) 하다 wander (roam, loiter) about; hang about (around).
배후(背後) the back; the rear. ¶ ～에서 조종하다 pull the wires (strings) from behind. ¶ ～인물 a wirepuller; a man behind the scenes.
백(白) white.
백(百) a (one) hundred. ¶ ～번 a hundred times / 백번(의) the hundredth / 수～ 명 hundreds of men.
백계(白系) ¶ ～러시아인 a Russian émigré.
백계(百計) all (every) means. ¶ ～ 무책 helplessness.
백곡(百穀) all kinds of grain.
백골(白骨) a bleached white bone. ¶ ～난망이다 be very grateful; be unforgettable.
백곰(白─) a white (polar) bear.
백과사전(百科事典) an encyclopa(e)dia. ¶ ～적(인) encyclopedic (*knowledge*).
백관(百官) all the government officials. ¶ 문무～ civil and military officials.
백구(白鷗) 〖鳥〗 a white gull.
백군(白軍) 〔경기의〕 the white team; the white(s).
백금(白金) white gold; 〖化〗 platinum (기호 Pt).
백기(白旗) a white flag; a flag of truce (surrender). ¶ ～를 들다 hang out a white flag.
백납(白─) 〖醫〗 vitiligo; leucoderma. ¶ ～먹다 have a leucoderma.
백내장(白內障) 〖醫〗 cataract.
백넘버 〔운동복의〕 a player's (uniform) number; a jersey number.
백네트 〖野〗 the backstop.
백년(百年) a (one) hundred years; a century. ¶ ～하청을 기다리다 wait one hundred years for the waters in the Yellow River to clear. ¶ ～제 a centennial (anniversary) / 〔국가〕 ～대계 a far-sighted (national) policy (program).
백년가약(百年佳約) a marriage bond; conjugal tie. ¶ ～을 맺다 tie the nuptial knot.
백년해로(百年偕老) ～하다 grow old together in wedded life.
백대하(白帶下) 〖醫〗 leucorrhea; whites 〔俗〕.
백랍(白蠟) white (refined) wax.
백로(白鷺) 〖鳥〗 an egret; a snowy heron.
백마(白馬) a white horse.
백만(百萬) a million. ¶ ～분의 1 a millionth / ～분의 1 지도 a map on a scale of one to a million. ‖ ～장자 a millionaire.
백면서생(白面書生) a stripling; a greenhorn; a novice.
백모(伯母) an aunt; an auntie 〔애칭〕.
백문불여일견(百聞不如一見) Seeing is believing.
백미(白米) polished rice.
백미(白眉) the best 《*of*》; a masterpiece 〔결작〕.
백미러 a rearview mirror.
백반(白飯) boiled (cooked) rice.
백반(白礬) 〖化〗 alum.
백발(白髮) white (gray, snowy) hair. ¶ ～의 white-haired; gray-haired / ～이 되다 〔머리가〕 turn gray / 〔사람이〕 grow gray. ‖ ～노인 a white-haired (-headed) old man.
백발백중(百發百中) ～하다 never miss the target; never fail.
백방(百方) all (every) means. ¶ ～으로 노력하다 make every effort.
백배(百拜) ～사죄하다 bow a hundred apologies.
백배(百倍) a hundred times. ～하다 increase 《*a number*》 a hundredfold; centuple. ¶ ～의 centuple; hundredfold.
백병전(白兵戰) a hand-to-hand fight; a close combat. ¶ ～을 벌이다 fight hand to hand 《*with*》.
백부(伯父) an uncle.
백분(白粉) face (toilet) powder.
백분(百分) ～하다 divide into a hundred parts. ¶ ～의 1, one hundredth; one percent. ‖ ～율 〔비〕 (a) percentage.
백사(白沙) white sand. ‖ ～장 a sandy beach; the sands.
백삼(白蔘) white ginseng.
백색(白色) white. ¶ ～인종 the white race(s); Caucasians / ～테러 the White Terror.
백서(白書) (issue, publish) a

백선 (白癬) 【醫】 ringworm; favus.
백설 (白雪) snow. ¶ ～ 같은 a snowy; snow-white / ～로 덮인 산 a snow-capped mountain.
백설탕 (白雪糖) white (refined) sugar.
백성 (百姓) the people; the populace; the nation《국민》; beasts.
백수 (白髮) 【髮】 ～ 의 왕 the king of
백수건달 (白手乾達) a penniless bum (tramp); a good-for-nothing.
백숙 (白熟) a dish of fish or meat boiled in plain water.
백신 (白身) vaccine. ‖ ～ 주사 (a) vaccine injection; (a) vaccination / 생～ a live vaccine.
백씨 (伯氏) your (his) esteemed elder brother.
백악 (白堊) chalk. ‖ ～관 the White House / ～기 【地】 the Cretaceous period.
백안시 (白眼視) ～ 하다 frown upon; look coldly on; look askance at; take a prejudiced view of. ¶ 세상을 ～ 하다 take refuge in cynicism. 「night sun.
백야 (白夜) nights under the midnight.
백약 (百藥) all sorts of medicine. ¶ ～ 이 무효하다 All medicines prove useless.
백양 (白羊) a white sheep (goat). ‖ ～ 궁 【天】 the Aries; the Ram.
백양 (白楊) 【植】 a (white) poplar; a white aspen. 「up.
백업 (背業) backup. ～ 하다 back
백연 (白鉛) white lead; ceruse《분 만드는》; ～ 광 【鑛】 cerusite.
백열 (白熱) incandescence; white heat. ～ 하다 become white-hot; be incandescent. ‖ ～ 하는 heated; exciting. ‖ ～ 등 an incandescent (glow) lamp / ～ 전 a close contest; a blistering race.
백옥 (白玉) a white gem.
백운 (白雲) a white cloud.
백운모 (白雲母) 【鑛】 white mica.
백의 (白衣) a white dress (robe). ‖ ～ 민족 the white-clad (Korean) people / ～ 천사 an angel in white; a white-clad nurse (간호사).
백인 (白人) a white man (woman). ¶ ～ 에 의한 지배 white domination《in Africa》. ‖ ～ 종 the white races; the whites.
백일 (白日) broad daylight. ¶ ～ 하에 드러나다 be brought to light; be exposed to the light of day (the public eye).
백일 (百日) 《백날》 the hundredth day of a newborn baby; 《백일 간》 one hundred days. ‖ ～ 기도 a prayer for a hundred days / ～ 잔치 the feast (celebration) of a hundred-day-old baby / ～ 재 【佛】 a Buddhist memorial service on the hundredth day after 《a person's》 death.
백일몽 (白日夢) a daydream; a daydreaming; a fantasy.
백일장 (白日場) a composition (literary) contest. ‖ 주부～ a literary contest for housewives.
백일초 (百日草) 【植】 a zinnia.
백일해 (百日咳) pertussis; whooping cough.
백일홍 (百日紅) 【植】 a crape myrtle.
백작 (伯爵) a count; an earl 《英》. ‖ ～ 부인 a countess.
백장 (도살자) a butcher.
백전노장 (百戰老將) a veteran; an old campaigner; an old-timer.
백전백승 (百戰百勝) ～ 하다 win every battle (that is fought); be ever victorious.
백절불굴 (百折不屈) ～ 의 indefatigable; indomitable / ～ 의 정신 an indomitable spirit.
백점 (百點) one (a) hundred points; 《만점》 full marks. ¶ 영어에서 ～ 받다 get full marks for English.
백조 (白鳥) a swan.
백주 (白晝) ～ 에 in broad daylight; in the daytime.
백중 (伯仲) ～ 하다 be equal 《to》; match 《each other》; be even 《with》; be well contested.
백중(날) (百中(一)) the Buddhist All Souls' Day (mid July by the lunar calendar).
백지 (白紙) a (blank) sheet of paper; white paper (흰종이). ¶ ～ 답안을 내다 give (hand) in a blank paper / ～ (상태)로 돌리다 start afresh; start with a clean slate. ‖ ～ 위임장 a blank power of attorney; a *carte blanche* 《프》.
백차 (白車) a (police) patrol car; a squad car 《美》.
백척간두 (百尺竿頭) ¶ ～ 에 서다 be in a dire extremity; be driven (reduced) to the last extremity.
백청 (白淸) white honey of fine quality.
백출 (百出) ～ 하다 arise in great numbers. ¶ 의견이 ～ 하다 become the subject of heated discussion.
백치 (白痴) 《상태》 idiocy; 《사람》 an idiot; an imbecile.
백탄 (白炭) hard charcoal. 「gue).
백테 (白毛) 【醫】 fur (on the ton-
백토 (白土) white clay. (el coin).
백통 (白 一) nickel. ‖ ～ 전 a nick-
백팔번뇌 (百八煩惱) 【佛】 the 108 passions. ¶ ～ 은 man is subject to.
백팔십도 (百八十度) ¶ ～ 전환하다 do a complete about-face; make a complete change 《*in one's policy*》.
백퍼센트 (百 一) 100% 《percent》. ¶ ～ 효과 ～ 의 100% efficacious.

백포도주(白葡萄酒) white wine.
백합(百合) 〖植〗 a lily.
백해무익(百害無益) 〜하다 be very harmful. ¶흡연은 〜하다 Smoking has innumerable harmful effects without doing any good at all.
백핸드(테니스) backhand; a backhand drive.
백혈(白血) ‖ 〜구 a white blood corpuscle / 〜병 leukemia.
백형(伯兄) one's eldest brother.
백호(白濠) 〜주의 the White Australia principle [policy].
백화(百花) all sorts of flowers. ¶〜만발한 (The field is) ablaze with all sorts of flowers.
백화점(百貨店) a department store. ¶〜으로 쇼핑 가다 go shopping at a department store.
밴댕이〖魚〗 a large-eyed herring.
밴드 ① (혁대) a belt; (띠·건) a band (strap). ② (악대) a band. ‖ 〜마스터 a bandmaster / 〜맨 a bandman.
밴텀급(一級) the bantamweight class. ‖ 〜선수 a bantamweighter.
밸런스 balance. ☞ 균형. ¶〜가 잡힌 well-balanced.
밸브(안전판) a valve. ‖ 〜장치 valve gear / 〜꼭지 a valve cock.
뱀 a snake; a serpent (구렁이). ‖ 〜가죽 snakeskin / 〜허물 the slough of a snake.
뱀딸기〖植〗 an Indian strawberry.
뱀뱀이 upbringing; breeding; discipline. ¶〜가 없다 be ill-bred.
뱀장어(一長魚)〖魚〗 an eel.
뱁새〖鳥〗 a Korean crow-tit. ‖ 〜눈이 a person with slitted [narrow] eyes.
뱃고동 a boat whistle.
뱃길 a (ship's) course; a waterway. ¶〜로 가다 go by ship [water].
뱃노래 a boatman's song.
뱃놀이 a boating (excursion); a boat ride (美). 〜하다 enjoy boating [a boat ride]. ¶〜 가다 go boating.
뱃대끈(마소의) a bellyband.
뱃머리 the bow [prow, head]. ¶〜를 돌리다 put a ship about; head (for).
뱃멀미 seasickness. 〜하다 get seasick. ¶〜를 하는[안 하는] 사람 a bad [good] sailor.
뱃밥 oakum; calking.
뱃사공(一沙工) a boatman.
뱃사람 a seaman; a sailor; a mariner.
뱃삯(승선료) passage (fare); boat fare; (나룻배의) ferriage; (화물의) freight (rates).
뱃살 〜 잡다 shake one's sides with laughter; split one's sides.
뱃속 ① (복부) the stomach. ②

(속마음) mind; heart; intention. ¶〜이 검은 evil-hearted; black-hearted.
뱃심 〜이 좋다 be shameless and greedy; be impudent.
뱃전 the side of a boat; a gunwale.
뱃짐 a (ship's) cargo; a freight.
뱅뱅 (go, turn) round and round (about).
뱅어〖魚〗〖魚〗 a whitebait.
뱅충맞다 (be) shy; clumsy; self-conscious; weak-headed. ‖ 뱅충맞이 a clumsy fellow; a dull and bashful person.
뱉다 ① (입밖으로) spew; spit (out); cough up. ¶가래를 〜 cough out phlegm / 얼굴에 침을 〜 spit in a person's face. ② (비유적으로) surrender; disgorge. ¶착복한 돈을 뱉아내다 surrender the embezzled money.
버걱거리다 rattle; clatter.
버겁다 (be) too big [bulky] to handle; unmanageable.
버글버글 〜 끓다 seethe; boil.
버금 〜 가다 be in the second place; rank (come) next to.
버긋하다 (be) split; open; ajar.
버너 a burner. ¶가스〜 a gas burner. [struggle; flounder.
버둥거리다 wriggle; (kick and)
버드나무 a willow.
버드러지다 ① (밖으로) protrude (이 따위가). ② (뻣뻣해지다) stiffen; get stiff; become rigid.
버들 a willow. ‖ 〜개지 willow catkins / 〜고리 a wicker trunk.
버들옻〖植〗 an euphorbia.
버라이어티쇼 a variety show; a vaudeville (美).
버럭 suddenly. ¶〜 소리를 지르다 shout [cry] suddenly / 〜 화를 내다 explode with anger. [gle.
버르적거리다 struggle; writhe; wrig-
버름하다 (틈이) (be) slightly open; loosely fitted; (마음이) (be) discordant.
버릇 ① (습관) a habit; a way. ¶나쁜 〜 a bad habit / 좀처럼 떼기 힘든 〜 an inveterate habit / 〜이 되다 become [grow into] a habit / 〜이 붙다 get [fall] into a habit (of) / 〜을 고치다 cure (a person) of a habit (남의); cure [break] oneself of a habit (자기의) / …하는 〜이 있다 have a habit [way] of doing. ② (특징) a peculiarity; a (one's) way. ¶말 〜 one's peculiar way of speaking. ③ (예의) manners; etiquette; breeding (품행); behavior (행실). ¶〜 없게 be badly brought up; be ill-mannered / 〜 없이 rudely / 〜 없는 아이 a ill-bred [spoilt] child / 〜을 가르

버릇하다 《바르다》 (be) straight;

치다 teach 《a person》 manners; give 《a person》 a lesson.
버릇하다 (get) used to 《doing》; form a habit. ¶ 술을 먹어 ~ get used to drinking / 일찍 일어나~ accustom *oneself* to early rising.
버리다¹ ① 《내던지다》 throw 《cast, fling》 away. ¶ 음식을 〔쓰레기를〕 ~ throw away food〔waste〕. ② 《포기·유기》 abandon; forsake; desert; give up. ¶ 버림받다 be abandoned〔forsaken, deserted〕/ 지위를 ~ give up *one's* position / 처자를 ~ desert *one's* wife and children. ③ 《망치다》 ruin; spoil. ¶ 애를 ~ spoil a child / 위를 ~ injure the stomach.
버리다² 《끝내다》 up; through. ¶ 다 읽어 ~ read through 《a book》/ 다 써 ~ use up 《*money*》/ 다 먹어 ~ eat up 《*the food*》.
버마 《Myanmar의 구칭》 Burma.
버무리다 mix (up). ¶ 나물을 ~ mix a salad.
버뮤다 《북대서양의 섬》 Bermuda Island. ¶ ~3각 수역 the Bermuda 〔Devil's〕 Triangle.
버석거리다 rustle; make a rustle. ¶ 버석버석 rustlingly.
버선 Korean socks.
버섯 【植】 a mushroom; a fungus. ¶ ~을 따다 gather〔pick up〕 mushrooms. ¶ ~ 구름 a mushroom cloud(핵폭발의) / ~ 재배자 a mushroom grower.
버성기다 ① 《틈이》 (be) loose; have gaps between. ② 《사이가》 be estranged〔alienated〕.
버스 a bus. ¶ ~로 가다 go by bus; take a bus. ¶ ~ 노선 a bus route / ~ 여행 a bus tour / ~ 운전사 a bus driver / ~ 요금 a bus fare / ~ 정류장, 종점〕 a bus fare〔stop, terminal〕/ ~ 전용차로 (제도) the bus-only lanes (system) / ~ 회사 a bus company.
버스러지다 ① 《뭉그러지다》 crumble. ② 《벗겨짐》 peel〔scale〕 off; exfoliate; be worn off; get skinned. ③ 《벗나가다》 go beyond; exceed.
버스름하다 be slightly open(틈이); be estranged〔alienated〕(관계가).
버스트 a bust.
버저 a buzzer. ¶ ~를 누르다 buzz; press a buzzer.
버적버적 crackling; with a crunching sound.
버젓하다 《당당하다》 (be) fair and square; 《떳떳하다》 (be) respectable; decent. ¶ 버젓이 fairly; openly; decently / 버젓한 인물 〔직업〕 a respectable person 〔occupation〕.
버지다 ① 《베어지다·긁히다》 be cut 〔scratched〕. ② 《찢어지다》 fray; be worn out.

버짐 ringworm; psoriasis.
버찌 a cherry (bob). ¶ ~씨 a cherry stone.
버캐 an incrustation; crust. ¶ 소금(오줌) ~ salt〔urine〕 incrustations.
버클 a (belt) buckle.
버킷 a bucket; a pail.
버터 butter. ¶ 빵에 ~를 바르다 butter *one's* bread; spread butter on *one's* bread.
버터플라이 《수영법》 the butterfly stroke.
버티다 ① 《괴다》 support; prop (up); bolster up. ¶ 기둥으로 ~ support 《*a wall*》 with a post. ② 《맞서다》 stand up to; contend〔compete〕 with. ¶ 끝까지 ~ 《주장을》 persist to the end; hold out to the end. ③ 《견디다》 bear up 《under》; sustain; endure; hold (out). ¶ 버티어 나가다 endure through; persevere.
버팀목(-木) a support; a prop; a stay.
벅적거리다 be crowded〔thronged〕 《with》; be in a bustle; swarm.
벅차다 ① 《힘에》 be beyond *one's* power〔ability〕; be too much for 《*a person*》. ¶ 이 일은 내게 ~ I am not equal to this task. ② 《가슴이》 be too full. ¶ 벅찬 기쁨 an ineffable joy / 가슴이 벅차서 말이 안 나온다 My heart is too full for words.
번(番) ① 《당번》 watch; guard; (night) duty. ¶ ~을 서다 keep watch 《over》; watch〔guard〕 《over》. ② 《횟수》 a time; 《번호》 number. ¶ 여러 ~ many times / 2~ number two.
번각(飜刻) reprinting; a reprint. ~하다 reprint. ¶ ~자 a reprinter / ~판 a reprinted edition.
번갈아(番-) alternately; by turns; one after another; in turn.
번개 (a flash of) lightning. ¶ ~같이 as swiftly as lightning; in a flash / ~가 번쩍하다 lightning flashes. ¶ 번갯불 a bolt of lightning.
번거롭다 《복잡》 (be) troublesome; annoying; complicated.
번뇌(煩惱) agony; 【佛】 worldly desires; the lusts of the flesh(육욕). ¶ ~에 시달리다 be harassed by (worldly) passions.
번다(煩多) ~한 troublesome; onerous.
번데기 【蟲】 a chrysalis; a pupa.
번득거리다, 번득이다 《광채가》 flash; glitter; sparkle.
번들거리다 be smooth〔slippery, glossy〕. ¶ 번들번들한 smooth; slippery; glossy.
번들다(番-) be on duty; go on guard〔watch〕.
번듯하다 《바르다》 (be) straight;

번롱(飜弄) ~하다 trifle 〔play〕 with; make fun of. ¶ ~당하다 be trifled with; be made a fool of / 풍파에 ~당하다 be tossed about by the wind and waves.

번문욕례(繁文縟禮) red tape; red-tapery〔-tapism〕; officialism.

번민(煩悶) worry; agony; anguish. ~하다 worry; agonize; be in anguish〔agony〕.

번복(飜覆) ~하다 change; reverse; 「turn.

번서다(番 ─) stand guard.

번성(蕃盛) ~하다 flourish; thrive;《수목이》grow thick.

번성(繁盛) prosperity. ~하다 prosper; flourish; thrive.

번식(繁殖) breeding; propagation. ~하다 breed; increase; propagate *itself*. ‖ ~기 a breeding season〔time〕/ ~력 ability to breed; propagating power (~력이 있는 fertile 〔~력이 왕성한 prolific〕) / ~지 breeding grounds / 인공 ~ artificial fecundation.

번안(飜案) ①《안건의》change. ~하다 change; reverse《a former plan》. ②《작품의》(an) adaptation. ~하다 adapt; rehash. ‖ ~소설 an adapted story.

번역(飜譯) (a) translation. ~하다 translate〔put, render〕《English》into《Korean》/ ~틀린 ~ a mistranslation / ~을 잘하다〔이 서투르다〕 be a good〔poor〕 translator. ‖ ~권 the right of translation / ~서 a translation; a translated version / ~자 a translator.

번영(繁榮) prosperity. ~하다 prosper; flourish; thrive. ¶ 국가의 ~ national prosperity.

번의(飜意) ~하다 change *one's* mind〔decision〕; go back on *one's* resolution.

번잡(煩雜) ~하다 (be) complicated; troublesome; intricate. ¶ ~한 거리 crowded streets.

번지(番地) a house〔lot〕 number; an address. ¶ 정동 48 ~, 48 *Chŏngdong*.

번지다 ①《잉크 등이》 blot; spread; run. ②《확대》 spread; extend. ③《옮다》 spread; affect(병이).

번지르르 ¶ ~ 한 glossy; lustrous; smooth.

번지점프 bungee jumping.

번쩍 ①《거뜬히》lightly; easily;《높이》high; aloft.¶큰 돌을 ~ 들어 올리다 lift up a huge stone lightly / 상대를 ~ 들어올리다 hold *one's* opponent high. ②《빛이》 with a flash. ~하다 (give out

a) flash. ③《감각》 suddenly; with a start. ¶ (눈에) ~ 뜨이지 않는 unattractive; obscure / 귀가 ~ 뜨이다 strike〔catch〕 *one's* ears / 정신이 ~ 들다 come to *oneself* with a start. 「twinkle; flash.

번쩍거리다, 번쩍이다 glitter; glare;

번창(繁昌) prosperity. ¶ ~ 한 prosperous; flourishing; thriving.

번철(燔鐵) a frying pan.

번트 〔野〕 a bunt. ~하다 bunt.

번호(番號) a number; a mark (부호);《구령》Number ! ¶ ~ 순(으로) (in) numerical order / ~ 를 매기다〔달다〕 number. ‖ ~ 표〔패〕 a number ticket〔plate〕.

번화(繁華) ¶ ~ 한 도시 a flourishing〔thriving〕 town / ~ 한 거리 a bustling〔busy〕 street / ~ 해지다 grow prosperous. ‖ ~ 가《상가》 shopping quarters; a downtown area /《유흥가》 an amusement center.

벋가다 go astray; stray《from》.

벋서다 resist; oppose.

벌〔벌판〕 an open field; a plain. ¶ 황량한 ~ a wilderness.

벌[蜂] a bee; a wasp(땅벌). ¶ ~떼 a swarm of bees / ~에 쏘이다 be stung by a bee.

벌《옷·그릇 등》 a suit《of clothes》; a pair(바지의); a set《of dishes》; a suite《of furniture》. ¶ 찻잔 한 ~ a tea set〔service〕.

벌(罰) punishment; (a) penalty. ~하다〔주다〕 punish; discipline; give a punishment〔for *crime*〕. ¶ ~로서 as a penalty〔for〕/ ~을 받다 be punished; suffer punishment / ~을 면하다 escape punishment.

벌거벗다 become naked; strip *oneself* naked. ¶ 벌거벗기다 unclothe; strip《*a person*》naked.

벌거숭이 a nude; a naked body. ¶ ~의 naked; undressed / ~산 a bare〔naked, treeless〕 mountain. 「ruddy (얼굴 따위가).

벌겋다 (be) crimson;

벌게지다 turn red; blush (얼굴이).

벌그스름하다 (be) reddish.

벌금(罰金) a fine; a penalty; a forfeit(위약금). ¶ ~을 과하다〔물리다〕 punish《*a person*》with a fine / ~을 물다 be fined; pay a penalty. ‖ ~형 〔法〕 amercement.

벌꺽 suddenly; in a rage(성나).

벌다 ①《이익》 earn〔make〕《*money*》; make a profit; gain. ¶ 힘들여 번 돈 hard-earned money / 돈을〔잘〕 ~ make〔good〕 money / 생활비를 〔용돈을〕 ~ earn *one's* living〔pocket money〕/ 작년에 천만 원을 벌었다 I gained〔made a profit of〕 ten million *won* last year.

벌떡 suddenly; quickly.

벌떡거리다 ① (가슴이) throb; beat; go pit-a-pat; palpitate. ② (들이마시는 모양) gulp 《one's beer》 down; take a big gulp 《of》.

벌렁 ¶ ~ 드러눕다 lie on one's back / ~ 뒤집히다 be overturned.

벌레 ① (곤충) an insect; a bug; (구더기 등) a worm; (나방·좀 등) a moth; (해충) vermin. ¶ ~ 먹은 이 a decayed tooth / ~ 먹은 worm-(moth-)eaten; wormy / ~ 먹은 사과 a wormy apple / ~ 가 먹다 be eaten by worms. ② (비유적). ¶ 공부~ a diligent student; a dig 《美俗》/ 책~ a bookworm; a great booklover.

벌룩거리다, 벌름거리다 inflate and deflate (swell and subside) alternately; quiver 《one's nostrils》.

벌리다 ① (열다) open. ¶ 입을 ~ open one's mouth wide; gape. ② (늘이다) leave 《space》; widen; spread. ¶ 다리를 ~ set one's legs apart / 팔을 ~ open one's arms.

벌린춤 a situation (thing) that cannot be halted or rejected. ~ 이다 Having set about it, there is no turning back.

벌목 (伐木) felling; cutting; logging. ~ 하다 cut (hew) down trees; fell; lumber 《a forest》. ‖ ~ 기(期) [작업] a felling season (operation) / ~ 꾼 a feller; a wood cutter; a lumberjack.

벌벌 ¶ ~ 떨다 tremble; shake; shiver.

벌써 ① (이미) already; yet(의문문에); (지금은) by now. ② (오래 전) long ago; a long time ago.

벌어먹다 earn one's bread; make a living. ¶ 가족을 벌어먹이다 support one's family.

벌어지다 ① (사이가) split; crack; open; be separated. ¶ 틈이 ~ a gap widens. ② (몸이) grow stout (firm). ¶ 어깨가 딱 ~ have broad shoulders. ③ (일 등이) occur; come about; take place.

벌이 (돈벌이) moneymaking; earning money; (일) work; (번 돈) earnings; income(수입). ~ 하다 work for one's living; earn one's bread. ¶ ~ 하러 가다 go to (for) work / ~ 가 좋다 (나쁘다) have a good (poor) income.

벌이다 ① (시작하다) begin; start; set about; embark on; open 《a shop》; establish. ¶ 사업을 ~ start an enterprise / 전쟁을 ~ enter into a war. ② (늘어놓다) arrange; display 《goods》; spread. ③ (모임 등을) hold; give. ¶ 잔치를 ~ hold a banquet; give a feast.

벌잇줄 a source of earning; a means to earn one's bread. ¶ ~ 이 끊기다 lose one's job.

벌점 (罰點) (give) a black (demerit) mark 《for》.

벌주 (罰酒) liquor one is forced to drink as a penalty.

벌집 a beehive; a honeycomb. ¶ ~ 을 건드리지 마라 Let sleeping dogs lie.

벌채 (伐採) felling. ~ 하다 cut (hew) down; fell 《trees》; lumber 《美》. ¶ ~ 한 면적 a cutover area / 산림을 ~ 하다 cut down a forest.

벌초 (伐草) ~ 하다 weed a grave; tidy up a grave.

벌충하다 supplement; make up 《for》; cover (make good) 《the loss》.

벌칙 (罰則) penal regulations (clauses); punitive rules. ‖ ~ 규정 penal provisions.

벌통 (─桶) a beehive; a hive.

벌판 a field; fields; a plain (평야); a wilderness(황야).

범 [動] a tiger; a tigress(암컷). ¶ 새끼 ~ a tiger kitten; a cub / 자는 ~ 코침 주기 《俗談》 Let a sleeping dog lie. ~ 을 잡는다 《俗談》 Nothing venture, nothing gain.

범… (汎) Pan-. ¶ ~ 민족대회 a pan-national rally / ~ 아시아 Pan-Asiatic / ~ 아시아주의 Pan-Asianism / ~ 유럽 Pan-Europe.

…**범** (犯) offense. ¶ 파렴치~ an infamous criminal(사람).

범국민 (汎國民) ~ 적인 pan-national; nation-wide. ‖ ~ 운동 (conduct) a pan-national (nationwide) campaign(movement, drive) 《for, against》.

범람 (氾濫) ~ 하다 overflow; flow (run) over 《the banks》; flood. ¶ ~ 하기 쉬운 강 a river prone to rampage.

범례 (凡例) introductory remarks; explanatory notes; a legend(지도·도표의).

범미 (凡美) Pan-American. ‖ ~ 주의 Pan-Americanism.

범백 (凡百) ① (사물이) all things (matters). ② (언행) manners; etiquette; breeding; behavior.

범벅 ① (뒤복박죽) a pell-mell; a mess; a hotchpotch. ¶ ~ (이) 되다 go to pie; be jumbled (mixed) up. ② (음식) a thick mixed-grain porridge.

범법 (犯法) violation of the law. ~ 하다 break (violate) the law; commit an offense. ‖ ~ 자 a lawbreaker / ~ 행위 an illegal act. 「son; a layman.

범부 (凡夫) (속인) an ordinary per-

범사 (凡事) ① (모든 일) all mat-

범상 ters; everything. ② 《평범한 일》 an ordinary matter (affair).
범상(凡常) ¶ ~한 commonplace; ordinary; usual; average / ~치 않은 extraordinary; out of the common; uncommon.
범서(梵書) Sanskrit literature; 《불경》 the Buddhist scriptures.
범선(帆船) a sailing ship (boat).
범속(凡俗) vulgarity. ¶ ~한 vulgar; common; vulgar.
범신론(汎神論) 〖哲〗 pantheism.
범어(梵語) Sanscrit; Sanskrit.
범연(泛然) ¶ ~한 careless; indifferent; inattentive. 〖mon(place)〗
범용(凡庸) ¶ ~한 mediocre; com-
범위(範圍) an extent; a scope; a sphere; a range; 《제한》 limits; bounds. ¶ ~ 내〔외〕에서 within [beyond] the limits 《of》/ 내가 아는 ~로는 as far as I know / 활동 〔세력〕 ~ one's sphere of activity (influence).
범의(犯意) a criminal intent. ¶ ~를 인정하다 recognize one's criminal intent.
범인(凡人) ☞ 범부(凡夫).
범인(犯人) a criminal; an offender; a culprit. ¶ ~을 은닉하다 harbor a criminal. / ~수색 man [criminal] hunt / ~인도 협정 the bilateral agreement on extradition of criminals.
범재(凡才) (a man of) common (ordinary) ability.
범절(凡節) manners; etiquette.
범죄(犯罪) a crime; a criminal act(행위). ¶ ~의 criminal / ~를 저지르다 commit a crime / ~와의 전쟁 a war against crime. ‖ ~기록 criminal records / ~발생률 a crime rate / ~사실 facts constituting an offense / ~수사 (a) criminal investigation / ~ 예방 crime prevention / ~용의자 a suspect; a suspected criminal / ~유형 a crime type / ~자 a criminal / ~조직 a criminal syndicate / ~현장 the scene of a crime.
범주(範疇) a category. ¶ ~에 들다 come within (fall under) the category 《of》.
범천(왕)(梵天(王)) Brahma.
범칙(犯則) violation. ¶ ~물자 illegal materials [goods] / ~(밀수)품 a smuggled article. 〖ular name.〗
범칭(汎稱) a general title; a pop-
범타(凡打) 〖野〗 (hit) an easy fly.
범태평양(汎太平洋) Pan-Pacific.
범퇴(凡退) 〖野〗 ~하다 be easily put out / ~시키다 retire 《a batter》/ 삼자 ~하다 All the three go out in quick order.
범퍼 a bumper.

범포(帆布) canvas; sailcloth.
범하다(犯一) 《죄를》 commit; 《법률 등을》 violate; infringe; break; 《여자를》 rape; assault; violate. ¶ 죄를 ~ commit a crime / 과오을 ~ make an error.
범행(犯行) a crime; an offense. ¶ ~을 자백 〔부인〕하다 confess [deny] one's crime. ‖ ~현장 the scene of an offense.
법(法) ① 《법률》 the law; 《법칙·규칙》 a rule; a regulation. ¶ ~의 정신 the spirit of the law / ~에 어긋난 unlawful; illegal / ~을 지키다 〔어기다〕 observe [break] the law / ~에 호소하다 appeal to the law / ~을 확대 해석하다 stretch the law. ¶ 특별 ~ a special law. ② 《방법》 a method; a way. ¶ 학습 ~ a learning method / 수학의 효과적인 교수 ~ an effective method of teaching mathematics. ③ 《도리》 reason. ¶ 그런 ~은 없다 That's unreasonable. ④ 〖文〗 mood. ¶ 가정 ~ the subjunctive mood.
법과(法科) the law department; a law course(과정). ‖ ~대학 a law college; a school of law 《美》/ ~출신 a graduate of the law department [school] / ~학생 a law student.
법관(法官) a judicial officer; a judge; 《총칭》 the judiciary.
법규(法規) laws and regulations. ¶ 상거래에 관한 ~ regulations regarding business transactions / ~를 지키다 〔어기다〕 obey [violate] regulations / ~상의 수속을 마치다 go through legal formalities. ‖ 현행 ~ the law in force.
법당(法堂) the main hall (of the Buddhist temple).
법도(法度) a law; a rule.
법등(法燈) the light of Buddhism.
법랑(琺瑯) 《porcelain》 enamel. ¶ ~을 입힌 enameled. ‖ ~철기 enameled ironware.
법령(法令) a law; laws and ordinances; a statute. ‖ ~집 a statute book.
법례(法例) the law governing the application of laws.
법률(法律) a law; (the) law(총칭). ¶ ~의 legal; juridical / ~상 legally / …을 금하는 ~ a law prohibiting 《gambling》 / ~을 제정하다 enact a law / ~을 시행 〔집행〕하다 enforce [administer] a law. ‖ ~가 a lawyer(변호사); a jurist(학자) / ~고문 a legal adviser / ~문제 a legal problem / ~사무소 a law office / ~상담 legal advice / ~용어 a legal (law) term / ~위반 a breach [violation] of the law.

법리(法理) a principle of law. ‖ ~학 jurisprudence / ~학자 a jurist.

법망(法網) the net (clutches) of the law. ¶ ~에 걸리다 come into grip of the law / ~을 피하여 evade (elude) the law.

법명(法名) 《佛》 one's Buddhist name.

법무(法務) judicial affairs. ‖ ~관 a law officer / ~부 the Ministry (Minister) of Justice / ~사 a judicial scrivener.

법문(法門) ~에 들다 embrace Buddhism; become a Buddhist.

법복(法服) a (judge's) robe; a gown; 《승려의》 the robe of a Buddhist priest.

법사(法師) a Buddhist priest (monk); a bonze.

법사위원회(法司委員會) the Legislation-Judiciary Committee.

법석 a noisy (boisterous, clamorous) way; fuss; ado. ~하다 be noisy; raise a clamor; make a fuss; fuss 《about》. ¶ ~ 떨다 make a lot of noise (fuss).

법식(法式) 《법도와 양식》 rules and forms; formalities. ¶ ~에 따르다 〔어긋나다〕 follow (run counter to) the formalities.

법안(法案) a bill. ¶ ~을 제출〔가결, 부결〕하다 introduce (pass, reject) a bill.

법어(法語) 《설교》 a Buddhist sermon; Buddhist literature; 《용어》 a Buddhist term.

법열(法悅) ① 《즐거움》 (an) ecstasy; rapture. ② 《종교적》 religious ecstasy (exultation).

법원(法院) a court of justice; a law court. ‖ 가정 ~ a domestic (family) court / 관할 ~ the competent court / 민사 〔형사〕 ~ a civil (criminal) court.

법의학(法醫學) medical jurisprudence; legal medicine. ¶ ~의 medicolegal. ‖ ~자 a doctor of forensic medicine.

법인(法人) a juridical (legal) person; a corporation. ¶ ~ 조직으로 하다 incorporate 《a firm》. ‖ ~세 the corporation tax / ~소득 the income of a corporation.

법적(法的) legal(istic). ¶ ~ 근거 a legal basis / ~으로 legally (speaking) / ~ 조치를 취하다 take legal steps (action) / ~ 하자 a legal flaw.

법전(法典) a code (of laws).

법정(法廷) a (law) court; a court of justice. ¶ ~에서 in court / ~에 서다 stand at the bar. ‖ ~모욕죄 contempt of court / ~투쟁 court struggle.

법정(法定) ~의 legal; statutory. ¶ ~가격 a legal price / ~대리인 a legal representative / ~상속인 an heir-at-law / ~화폐 legal tender / ~휴일 a legal holiday.

법제(法制) laws; legislation. ‖ ~처 the Office of Legal Affairs.

법조(法曹) the legal profession. ¶ ~계 legal circles; the judicial world / ~계의 거물들 leaders of the law.

법치(法治) constitutional government. ‖ ~국가 a constitutional state; a law-governed country / ~사회 a law-abiding society.

법칙(法則) a law; a rule. ¶ 수요 공급의 ~ the law of supply and demand. ‖ 자연 ~ the law of nature; a natural law.

법통(法統) a religious tradition. ¶ ~을 잇다 receive the mantle 《of the preceding abbot》.

법하다 be likely 《to》; may. ¶ 그가 올 법하다 He might come. / 그런 일도 있을 ~ It's possible.

법학(法學) law; jurisprudence 《법률학》. ¶ ~을 배우다 study law. ‖ ~개론 an outline of law / ~도 a law student / ~박사 Doctor of Laws《생략 LL.D.》 / ~부 the law department / ~사 Bachelor of Laws《생략 LL.B.》.

법화(法貨) legal tender. 〔vice〕.

법회(法會) a Buddhist mass (service).

벗(親구) a friend; a companion 《반려》; a pal 《口》. ☞ 친구. ¶ 오랜 〔진실한〕 ~ an old (a true) friend / 평생의 ~ a lifelong friend / …을 ~ 삼다 make a companion (friend) of; keep friends with; have 《books》 for companions.

벗겨지다 《wear, fall, peel》 off; be taken (stripped) off.

벗기다 ① 《껍질 따위를》 peel; rind; pare; skin; strip. ② 《옷을》 strip 《a person》 of 《his clothes》; take off 《a person's clothes》. ¶ 옷을 ~ unclothe; undress / 외투를 벗겨 주다 help 《a person》 out of his overcoat. ③ 《덮은 것을》 remove; take off 《a lid》. ¶ 위선자의 가면을 ~ unmask a hypocrite.

벗나가다 deviate (swerve) 《from》; go astray.

벗다 take (put) off; slip (fling) off 《급히》. ¶ 모자를 〔안경을〕 ~ take off one's hat (glasses) / 옷을 ~ take off one's clothes / 장갑을 ~ pull off one's gloves.

벗어나다 《헤어나다》 get out of 《difficulties》; escape from; free oneself from 《a bondage》. ¶ 가난에서 ~ overcome poverty / 질곡에서 ~ shake off fetters; cast off the yoke 《of》. ② 《어긋나다》 be contrary to; be against 《the rules》; deviate 《from》. ¶ 예의에 ~ get against etiquette. ③ 《눈

벗어버리다 take off; throw (cast, fling) off; kick off (신을).

벗어지다 ① (옷·신 따위가) come off; be taken (stripped) off; peel (off) (거죽이). ② (머리가) become (grow) bald.

벗하다 make friends with; associate with; keep company with. ¶ 자연을 ~ commune (live) with nature.

벙거지 a felt hat; a hat.

벙글거리다. 벙긋거리다 smile; beam.

벙굿하다 ☞ 방굿하다.

벙벙하다 《서술적》 be puzzled; be dumbfounded; be at a loss. ¶ 어안이 ~ be quite at a loss; be amazed.

벙실거리다 smile; beam.

벙어리 ① (사람) a (deaf-)mute; a dumb person; the dumb (총칭). ¶ ~의 dumb. ¶ ~ 장갑 a mitten. ② 《저금통》 bank 《미》; a piggy bank.

벚꽃 cherry blossoms [flowers]. ¶ ~ 놀이 가다 go to see the cherry blossoms.

벚나무 [植] a cherry tree.

베 hemp cloth (삼베).

베개 a pillow. ¶ 팔~를 베다 make a pillow of one's arm / 베갯머리에 앉다 sit up by 《a person's》 bedside. ¶ 베갯속 the stuffing of a pillow / 베갯잇 a pillowcase; a pillow slip.

베고니아 [植] a begonia.

베끼다 copy; transcribe; take a copy 《of》. ¶ (공)책을 ~ copy a (note)book.

베네룩스 Benelux. (◀ Belgium, the Netherlands and Luxemburg)

베네수엘라 Venezuela. ¶ ~의 Venezuelan.

베니스 Venice. ¶ ~의 상인 "The Merchant of Venice".

베니어판(一板) a veneer board; a plywood(합판). 「on 《a pillow》.

베다 (베개를) rest [lay] one's head

베다 (자르다) cut; chop; saw(톱으로); shear(가위로); slice(얇게); (베어넘기다) hew; cut down; (곡물을) reap; gather in; harvest; (풀을) mow; cut down. ¶ 손가락을 ~ cut one's finger 《on a knife》 / 목을 ~ cut off 《a person's》 head; behead.

베드 a bed. ¶ ~ 신《장면》 a bedroom scene.

베들레헴 Bethlehem.

베란다 a veranda; a porch 《미》.

베레모(一帽) a beret.

베를린 Berlin. ¶ ~봉쇄 《장벽》 the Berlin Blockade (Wall). 「(Strait).

베링해 ¶ ~해 (海) the Bering Sea

베물다 bite off (away). 「seller.

베스트 best. ¶ ~ 셀러 a best [top]

베슬거리다 shirk 《from》.

베실 hemp yarn (thread).

베어내다 cut off (out, away).

베어링 a bearing. ¶ 볼~ a ball bearing.

베어먹다 cut off and eat; take a bite out of 《an apple》. ¶ 케이크를 ~ slice a cake to eat.

베어버리다 cut; cut down.

베(헴)(프) hemp(en) clothes.

베이비 a baby. ¶ ~ 붐 a baby boom (~ 붐 때 태어난 사람 a baby boomer) / ~ 시터 《사람》 a baby-sitter / ~ 카메라 a baby (midget) camera.

베이스¹ [樂] bass.

베이스² [野] a base. ¶ ~를 밟다 tread on the base. ¶ ~ 볼 baseball. ② (기준) a base. ¶ 임금 ~ the wage base.

베이스캠프 [登山] a base camp.

베이식 [컴] BASIC (규격화된 일상어를 사용하는 초급의 프로그래밍 언어). (◀ Beginner's All-purpose Symbolic Instruction Code)

베이지 beige. ¶ ~색 beige.

베이컨 bacon.

베이킹파우더 baking powder.

베일 a veil. ¶ ~을 올리다 lift a veil / ~을 쓰다 veil one's face.

베짱이 [蟲] a grasshopper.

베타 beta; B, β. ¶ ~선 (입자) beta rays (particles).

베테랑 a veteran; an expert; an old hand.

베트남 Vietnam. ¶ ~의 Vietnamese. ¶ ~사람 a Vietnamese / ~어 Vietnamese.

베틀 a (hemp-cloth) loom.

베풀다 ① (주다) give; bestow; show 《kindness》; grant. ¶ 은혜를 ~ bestow a favor 《on a person》 / 자선을 ~ give alms 《to》. ② (잔치 등을) give (hold) 《a party》.

벤젠 [化] benzene; benzol.

벤진 [化] benzine.

벤처 [經] a venture. ¶ ~기업 a venture business / ~ 캐피털 venture capital.

벤치 a bench.

벨 a bell; a doorbell(현관의). ¶ ~을 울리다 (누르다) ring (press, push) the bell. 「an.

벨기에 Belgium. ¶ ~사람 a Belgi-

벨로드롬 (경륜장) a velodrome.

벨벳 velvet.

벨트 a belt. ¶ ~를 매다 fasten a belt. ¶ 컨베이어 ~ a belt conveyor / 그린~ a green belt.

벼 a rice plant; a paddy; an unhulled rice(낟알). ¶ ~를 심다 plant rice. ¶ ~베기 rice reaping.

벼농사(一農事) (농사) rice farming; (작황) a rice crop. ~하다 do (engage in) rice farming.

벼락 a thunderbolt; a stroke of lightning. ¶ ~ 같은 thunderous /

벼락감투 331 **변모**

벼락 ~치다 a thunderbolt falls / ~맞다 be struck by lightning.
벼락감투 a government position given as a political favor; a patronage appointment. ¶ ~를 쓰다 become a government official overnight.
벼락공부(一工夫) ~하다 cram up 《for an exam》.
벼락부자(一富者) a mushroom 《an overnight》 millionaire; an upstart; the newly rich. ¶ ~가 되다 become 〔get〕 rich suddenly.
벼락치기 hasty preparation. ¶ ~의 hastily prepared / ~공사로 지은 집 a hurriedly constructed building; a jerry-built house.
벼랑 a cliff; a precipice; a bluff.
벼루 an inkstone. ‖ 벼룻집 an inkstone case.
벼룩 a flea. ‖ ~에 물리다 [시달리다] be bitten [tormented] by fleas. ¶ ~시장 a flea market.
벼르다 ① 《분배》 divide 〔distribute, share〕 equally. ② 《꾀하여 《do》be firmly determined to 《do》; plan; design; intend. ¶ 기회를 ~ watch for a chance.
벼리 the border ropes of a fishing net.
벼리다 sharpen; forge a blade 〔on〕.
벼슬 《관직》 a government post service. ~하다 enter the government service. ¶ ~살이하다 be in government service. ¶ ~아치 a government official.
벼훑이 a rice-thresher.
벽(壁) a wall; a partition (wall) 〔칸막이〕. ¶ ~을 바르다 plaster a wall / ~에 부딪치다 《비유적》 be deadlocked. ‖ ~걸이 a wall tapestry / ~난로 a fireplace / ~시계 a wall clock.
벽공(碧空) the blue 〔azure〕 sky.
벽돌(甓一) (a) brick. ¶ ~을 굽다 burn [bake, make] bricks / ~을 쌓다 lay bricks. ¶ ~공 a brickmaker(제조공); a bricklayer(쌓는 사람); ~공장 a brickyard / ~집 〔담〕 a brick house [wall].
벽두(劈頭) the outset. ¶ ~에 at the very beginning; at the outset / ~부터 from the start.
벽력(霹靂) ☞ 벼락.
벽보(壁報) a wall newspaper; a bill; a poster. ¶ ~를 붙이다 put up a bill [poster]. 〔surname〕.
벽성(僻姓) an unusual 〔a rare〕
벽안(碧眼) the blue-eyed.
벽오동(碧梧桐) 〔植〕 a sultan's parasol.
벽옥(碧玉) jasper. 〔sol.
벽자(僻字) a rare 〔an odd〕 character.
벽장(壁欌) a (wall) closet.
벽지(僻地) an out-of-the-way place; a remote corner of the country. ¶ ~ 학교의 교육 school education in remote rural areas.
벽지(壁紙) wallpaper.
벽창호(碧昌―) an obstinate person; a blockhead (바보).
벽촌(僻村) a remote village.
벽토(壁土) plaster; wall mud.
벽해(碧海) the blue sea.
벽화(壁畵) a mural (wall) painting; a fresco. ‖ ~가 a muralist. 〔cant; a lingo.
변 《곁말》 a jargon; an argot; a
변(便) 《대변》 motions; feces. ¶ 된 〔묽은〕 ~ hard [loose] feces.
변(邊)¹ ① 〔數〕 a side. ② 《가장자리》 a side; an edge.
변(邊)² 《연리》 (rate of) interest.
변(變) 《재앙》 an accident; a disaster; a disturbance. ¶ ~을 당하다 have a mishap; meet with an accident.
변격(變格) ① 〔文〕 《변격 활용》 irregular conjugation. ② ☞ 변칙.
변경(邊境) a frontier district; a border(land).
변경(變更) change; alteration; modification; transfer (명의의). ~하다 change; alter; modify; transfer. 〔hap; a disaster.
변고(變故) an accident; a mishap; a disaster.
변광성(變光星) 〔天〕 a variable star.
변기(便器) a toilet (seat); a (chamber) pot; a urinal(소변용); a bedpan(환자용).
변덕(變德) caprice; whim; fickleness; ~스러운 fickle; capricious; whimsical / ~ 부리다 behave capriciously. ¶ ~쟁이 a man of moods; a fickle [capricious] person. 〔est; a loan.
변돈(邊―) money lent at inter-
변동(變動) change; alteration; fluctuation. ~하다 change; fluctuate(시세가). ¶ 물가의 ~ fluctuations in prices. ¶ ~환율제 a floating exchange rate system / 대~ a violent radical change; a cataclysm(사회의).
변두리(邊―) ① 《교외》 the outskirts; a suburb. ¶ 서울 ~에 살다 live in a suburb / ~에 on the outskirts of Seoul / ② 《가장자리》 a brim; an edge; a border.
변란(變亂) a (social) disturbance, a civil war; an uprising (반란).
변론(辯論) discussion; argument; debate (토론); pleading (법정의). ~하다 discuss; argue; debate; plead 《in court》. ¶ ~ 자 a debater / 최종~ the final argument.
변리사(辯理士) a patent attorney.
변명(辯明) an explanation; an excuse. ~하다 explain *oneself*; apologize 《for one's fault》.
변모(變貌) transfiguration. ~하다 undergo a (complete) change.

변모없다 ① 《무뚝뚝하다》 (be) un-affable; blunt. ② 《변통성 없다》 (be) unadaptable; hidebound.

변박(辯駁) refutation; confutation. ~하다 refute; argue against.

변방(邊方) ☞ 변경(邊境).

변변하다 《생김새가》 (be) fairly good-looking; handsome; 《나무랄 데 없다》 (be) fairly good; fair. ¶ 변변치 않은 worthless; insignificant; trifling / 변변치 못한 사람 a good-for-nothing; a stupid person / 변변치 않은 선물 a small (humble) present.

변복(變服) (a) disguise. ~하다 disguise (dress) oneself 《as》; be disguised 《as》; incognito. ¶ ~으로 in disguise.

변비(便秘) constipation. ¶ ~에 걸리다 be constipated.

변사(辯士) ① 《연설하는》 a speaker; an orator. ② 《무성영화의》 a film interpreter.

변사(變死) an unnatural death. ~하다 die an unnatural 〔a violent〕 death. ‖ ~자 a person accidentally killed.

변상(辨償) compensation. ~하다 compensate; indemnify. ‖ ~금 a compensation; an indemnity.

변색(變色) discoloration. ~하다 change color; discolor; fade.

변설(辯舌) eloquence. ¶ ~가 있는 an eloquent speaker; an orator.

변성(變成) regeneration. ~하다 regenerate. ‖ ~암〔地〕 a metamorphic rock.

변성(變性) degeneration. ~하다 degenerate(바꾸다); denaturalize, denature(바꾸다).

변성(變聲) ~하다 one's voice changes. ‖ ~기 the age at which one's voice changes; puberty.

변성명(變姓名) ~하다 change one's name.

변소(便所) a toilet (room); a water closet 《略 W.C.》; a lavatory; a rest room(극장 등의); 《美》 《개인주택의》 a bathroom; a washroom. ¶ ~에 가다 go to the toilet; go to wash one's hands. ‖ 옥외~ an outhouse.

변속(變速) a change of speed. ‖ ~기 《자동차의》 a gearbox; a transmission / ~기어 《자전거의》 a (ten-speed) derailleur; a bicycle gearshift.

변수(變數) 〔數〕 a variable.

변신(變身) ~하다 《변장》 disguise oneself 《as a monk》; 《변태》 change 《into》.

변심(變心) a change of mind; fickleness. ~하다 change one's mind; 《배반》 betray 《a person》.

변압(變壓) 〔電〕 transformation. ~하다 transform 《current》. ‖ ~기 a (current) transformer.

변온동물(變溫動物) 〔動〕 a cold-blooded (poikilothermal) animal.

변위(變位) 〔理〕 displacement. ‖ ~전류(電流) a displacement current.

변이(變異) 〔生〕 (a) variation.

변장(變裝) disguise. ~하다 disguise oneself 《as》; 《…으로》 ~하고 in (under) the disguise of 《a merchant》.

변재(辯才) oratorical talent (skill); eloquence(능변). ¶ ~가 있는 eloquent; fluent / ~가 없다 be awkward in speaking; be a poor speaker.

변전(變轉) mutation; change. ~하다 change; transmute.

변전소(變電所) a (transformer) substation.

변절(變節) (an) apostasy; (a) betrayal; (a) treachery. ~하다 apostatize; change one's coat. ‖ ~자 an apostate; a turncoat.

변제(辨濟) (re)payment. ~하다 pay back; repay 《one's debt》.

변조(變造) 《개조》 alteration (위조) falsification; forgery. ~하다 alter; forge; falsify; counterfeit. ‖ ~어음 a forged check / ~자 a forger / ~지폐 a counterfeit note.

변조(變調) 〔樂〕 (a) variation; 〔無〕 modulation; 《언행의》 irregularity. ¶ 주파수~ frequency modulation(생략 FM) / 진폭~ amplitude modulation(생략 AM).

변종(變種) 〔生〕 a variety; a sport; a mutation.

변주곡(變奏曲) 〔樂〕 a variation.

변죽(邊~) ① a brim; an edge. ¶ ~을 울리다 hint 《at》; intimate; allude to 《a fact》; give a hint.

변증법(辨證法) dialectic(s). ¶ ~적 dialectic(al) / ~적 유물론 dialectic(al) materialism.

변지(邊地) a remote region; a frontier district. ☞ 벽지(僻地).

변질(變質) ~하다 change in quality; degenerate; go bad(음식이). ‖ ~자 a degenerate.

변차(變差) 〔天〕 (a) variation.

변천(變遷) a change; transition; vicissitudes. ~하다 change; undergo (suffer) changes. ¶ 시대의 ~ the change of times.

변칙(變則) irregularity; an anomaly. ¶ ~적인 irregular; abnormal. ‖ ~국회 an abnormal National Assembly session.

변태(變態) ① 《이상》 (an) anomaly; abnormality. ¶ ~적인 abnormal; anomalous. ‖ ~심리(성욕) abnormal mentality (sexuality); mental (sexual) perversion. ② 〔生〕 a metamorphosis; 《변형》 (a) trans-

변통(便通) a passage; the action [motion] of the bowels. ¶ ~약 a laxative; a purgative.

변통(變通) (융통성) versatility; adaptability; flexibility; (임기응변) a makeshift; management; arrangement. ~하다 manage 《with (without) something》; make shift 《with, without》; arrange [manage] 《to do》; raise 《money》. ¶ 어떻게든 ~해 보겠다 I'll see to it, somehow or other. ¶ ~성 adaptability; flexibility.

변하다(變一) change; undergo a change; be altered; turn into; 《달라지다》 vary. ¶ 변하기 쉬운 changeable / 변하지 않는 unchanging; constant / 마음이 ~ change one's mind / 그의 기분은 매일 변한다 His mood varies from day to day.

변함없다(變一) be [remain] unchanged; show no change. ¶ 변함없는 unchangeable; constant; steady / 변함없이 without a change; (전과 같이) as usual; as ever / 올해도 변함없이 애호해 주십시오 I beg you will continue to favor me this year.

변혁(變革) a change; a reform(개혁); a revolution(혁명). ~하다 change; reform; revolutionize.

변형(變形) (a) transformation; (a) deformation. ~하다 change the shape 《of》; turn [change] 《into》; be transformed 《into》; spoil the form 《of》. ¶ 열에 의해 플라스틱 장난감이 ~됐다 Heat spoiled the plastic toy.

변호(辯護) defense; pleading. ~하다 plead; defend 《a person》; stand [speak] for. ¶ ~의뢰인 a client / ~인 a counsel; a pleader / ~인단 defense counsel.

변호사(辯護士) a lawyer; (법정의) a counsel 《美》 (사무의) an attorney (at law)《美》. ¶ ~ 자격을 얻다 be admitted to the bar / ~ 개업을 하다 practice law / ~를 대다 engage a lawyer. ¶ ~사무소 a law office / ~ 수임료 a lawyer's fee / ~회 a bar association.

변화(變化) (a) change; (a) variation; 《변경》 alteration; 《다양》 variety; 《변형》 (a) transformation; 《동사의》 conjugation. ~하다 change 《into》; make [undergo a] change; turn 《from, into》; alter; vary; be transformed 《into》; conjugate. ¶ ~ 없는 changeless; lacking in variety; monotonous (단조) / ~가 많은 full of variety; varied; diverse / 정세 [일기] 의 ~ a change in situation [the weather]. ¶ ~구 [野] a slow [curve] ball. 「divert.

변환(變換) ~하다 change; convert;」
별(星) a star; the stars. ¶ ~빛 starlight / ~ 같은 starlike; starry / ~이 반짝이다 the stars twinkle.

별갑(鱉甲) tortoiseshell. ¶ ~세공 tortoiseshell work.

별개(別個) ¶ ~의 separate; another; different; special.

별거(別居) separation; limited divorce. ~하다 live apart [separately] 《from》; live in a separate house. ¶ ~중인 아내 a separated wife; a grass widow. ¶ ~수당 alimony; a separate allowance.

별것(別一) something peculiar; a rarity; a different [another] thing(다른 것).

별고(別故) 《이상》 a trouble; an untoward event; something wrong. ¶ ~ 없다 be well; be all right; there is nothing wrong 《with》 / ~ 없이 지내다 get along well.

별과(別科) a special course.

별관(別館) an annex 《to a building》; an extension.

별궁(別宮) a detached palace.

별기(別記) ¶ ~와 같이 as stated elsewhere [in a separate paragraph].

별꼴(別一) obnoxious thing [person]. ¶ ~ 다 보겠다 What a sight!

별꽃 [植] a chickweed. 「[mess]!

별나다(別一) (be) strange; queer; peculiar. ¶ 별나게 strangely; peculiarly / 별나게 굴다 behave eccentrically.

별납(別納) seperate payment [delivery]. ~하다 pay [deliver] separately.

별다르다(別一) 《이상》 (be) uncommon; extraordinary; (특별) be of a particular kind. ¶ 별다른 것이 아니다 It is nothing peculiar.

별당(別堂) a separate house.

별도(別途) ¶ ~의 special. ¶ ~지출 a special outlay.

별도리(別道理) a better way; an alternative; a choice. ¶ ~ 없다 have no choice but to 《do》; there is no alternative but to 《do》. 「detached force.

별동대(別動隊) a flying party;」
별똥(별) a meteor; a shooting star.

별로(別一) in particular; especially; particularly. ¶ ~ 할 일도 없다 I have nothing particular to do.

별말(別一) (make) a preposterous [an absurd] remark. ¶ ~ 다 한다 You talk nonsense.

별말씀(別一) ¶ ~ 다 하십니다 Don't mention it. *or* Not at all.

별명(別名) another name; a nickname; a byname; a pseudonym. ¶ ~을 붙이다 nickname (*a person*); give (*a person*) a nickname / 스미스란 ~으로 통하다 go by the alias of Smith.

별문제(別問題) another (a different) question; another thing [matter]. ¶ …은 ~로 하고 apart [aside] from… / 그것은 ~이다 That's a different story.

별미(別味) (맛) peculiar taste; an exquisite flavor; (음식) a dainty; a delicacy.

별별(別別) of various and unusual sorts. ¶ ~ 사람 all sorts of people / ~일 unusual things of all sorts.

별봉(別封) ~으로 (보내다) (send) under separate cover.

별사람(別―) an eccentric; a queer bird; an odd duck; a mess. ¶ ~ 다 보겠다 I have never seen such a mess of a man.

별석(別席) another [a special] seat.

별세(別世) death. ~하다 die; decease; pass away.

별세계(別世界) another [a different] world.

별소리(別―) ☞ 별말. [ent].

별수(別數) special luck (운수); a special (peculiar) way [means] (방법); the magic formula [법]. ¶ 너도 ~ 없구나 You don't have any magic formula, either.

별식(別食) specially-prepared food; a rare dish. [er room.

별실(別室) (withdraw into) another

별안간(瞥眼間) suddenly; all at once; all of a sudden; abruptly. ¶ ~ 죽다 die suddenly.

별일(別―) a strange [an odd] thing; (특별한 일) something particular. ¶ ~ 없이 safely; without any accident.

별자리(〖天〗) a constellation.

별장(別莊) a villa; a country house; a cottage (〖美〗).

별정직 ‖ ~공무원 officials in special government service.

별종(別種) a special kind; a different kind.

별지(別紙) ☞ 별표. [ent kind.

별찬(別饌) a rare dish; a dainty.

별책(別冊) a separate volume; (잡지 따위의) an extra number. ‖ ~부록 a separate-volume supplement.

별천지(別天地) ☞ 별세계.

별첨(別添) an annexed [attached] paper; an accompanying [a separate] sheet. ¶ ~의 enclosed herewith / ~과 같이 as per enclosure. [name.

별칭(別稱) a byname; another

별표(一標) (별모양의) a star; an asterisk (기호).

별표(別表) an attached [annexed] table [list, sheet]. ‖ ~양식 an attached form.

별항(別項) another [a separate] paragraph [section, clause].

별행(別行) another [a new] line.

별호(別號) a pen name; 《별명》 a nickname.

볍씨 rice seed. [crown.

볏 a cockscomb; a crest; a

볏가리 a rick; a stack of rice.

볏단 a rice sheaf.

볏섬 a sack of rice.

볏짚 rice straw.

병(丙) the third grade [class]; C.

병(病) (an) illness; (a) sickness (〖美〗); a disease; an ailment (가벼운); (국부적) a trouble; a disorder. ¶ ~난 il; sick; unwell; diseased / ~ 때문에 on account of illness; owing to ill health / 가벼운 [물치의] ~ a slight [incurable, a fatal] illness / ~의 자각 [의식] consciousness of disease / ~들다 [에 걸리다] get [fall, become, be taken] ill / ~에 걸리기 쉽다 be liable to illness (a disease) / ~이 낫다 get well; recover from *one's* illness / ~으로 죽다 die of illness [a disease] / ~을 치료하다 cure a disease. ‖ ~문안 a visit to a sick person.

병 (a) bottle. ¶ 아가리가 넓은 ~ a jar / 목이 가는 ~ a decanter / ~목 the neck of a bottle / 맥주 한 ~ a bottle of beer / ~에 담긴 bottle (*milk*) / ~에 담은 bottled. [strategist.

병가(兵家) 《병법가》 a tactician;

병가(病暇) sick leave.

병결(病缺) absence due to illness.

병고(病苦) suffering [pain] from sickness. ¶ ~에 시달리다 labor under *one's* disease.

병과(兵科) a branch of the service [army]; an arm. ‖ ~장교 a combatant officer / 보병 ~ the infantry branch [arm].

병구(病軀) a sick body; ill health. ¶ ~를 무릅쓰고 in spite of *one's* sickness.

병구완(病―) nursing; care (for the sick). ~하다 nurse; care for; tend; attend on (*a person*).

병권(兵權) (seize, hold) military power [authority].

병균(病菌) pathogenic [disease-causing] germs [bacteria]; a virus. ¶ …의 ~을 분리하다 isolate the virus of….

병기(兵器) arms; weapons of war; weaponry. ‖ ~고 an armory / ~창 an arsenal; an ordnance department [depot (〖美〗)].

병나다(病―) ① ☞ 병들다. ② (탈나다) get out of order; go wrong;

병내다(病―) ① 〖병을〗 cause (bring about) illness; make (a person) sick. ② 〖탈을 내다〗 bring (put) (a thing) out of order.
병단(兵團) an army corps.
병독(病毒) disease germs; a virus.
병동(病棟) a ward. ‖ 격리〖일반〗~ an isolation (a general) ward.
병들다(病―) get sick 《美》; fall (be taken) ill. ¶ 병든 sick.
병란(兵亂) a war; a military disturbance.
병략(兵略) strategy; tactics.
병력(兵力) force of arms; military power (strength); troop strength. ¶ 10만의 ~ a force 100,000 strong / ~을 삭감〖증강〗하다 reduce (build up) its troop strength.
병렬(竝列) ~하다 stand in a row. ‖ ~회로 a parallel (circuit).
병리(病理) ‖ ~학 pathology (~상의 pathological) / ~학자 a pathologist / ~해부학 pathological anatomy.
병립(竝立) ~하다 stand abreast (side by side); coexist.
병마(兵馬) military affairs (군사); war (전쟁); troops (군대).
병마(病魔) ¶ ~가 덮치다 get (fall) ill; be attacked by a disease / ~에 시달리다 be afflicted with a disease.
병마개(甁―) a bottle cap; a stopper; a cork (코르크). ¶ ~를 뽑다 open (uncork) a bottle / ~로 막다 put a cap on a bottle.
병명(病名) the name of a disease.
병무(兵務) military (conscription) affairs. ‖ ~소집 a call for reserve training / ~청 the Office of Military Manpower.
병발(竝發) concurrence; a complication (병의). ~하다 concur; develop (accompany) 《another disease》. ‖ ~증 《develop》 a complication.
병법(兵法) tactics; strategy. ‖ ~가 a strategist; a tactician.
병사(兵士) a soldier; a serviceman; a private; troops.
병사(兵舍) (a) barracks.
병사(兵事) military affairs. ‖ ~계원 a clerk in charge of military affairs.
병사(病死) death from sickness. ~하다 die of (from) a disease; die in one's bed.
병살(倂殺) 〖野〗(make) a double play (killing).
병상(病床) a sickbed. ‖ ~일지 a clinical diary; a sickbed record.
병상(病狀) the condition of a patient (disease).
병색(病色) ¶ ~이 보이다 look sickly. 〖strategy〗
병서(兵書) a book on tactics.
병석(病席) a sickbed. ¶ ~에 있다 be ill in bed; be confined to bed.
병선(兵船) a warship.
병세(病勢) the condition of a disease (patient). ¶ ~가 악화〖호전〗되다 take a turn for the worse (better).
병술(甁―) bottled sul (liquor); liquor sold by the bottle.
병신(病身) ① 〖불구자〗a deformed (maimed) person; a cripple; 《병자》an (a chronic) invalid. ¶ ~을 만들다 deform; maim; cripple / ~이 되다 be crippled (disabled). ② 〖물건〗a defective thing; an odd set. ③ 〖바보〗a stupid person; a fool. ¶ ~ 노릇을 하다 act the fool.
병실(病室) a sickroom; a (sick) ward (병원); a sick bay (군함).
병아리 a chicken; a chick. ¶ ~를 까다 hatch chickens. ‖ ~감별사 a (chick) sexer.
병약(病弱) ¶ ~한 (constitutionally) weak; sickly; invalid; infirm.
병어 〖魚〗a pomfret; a butterfish.
병역(兵役) military service. ‖ ~기피자 a draft evader (dodger) / ~면제 exemption from (military) service / ~미필자 a person who has not yet completed his military duty / ~의무 obligatory (compulsory) military service.
병영(兵營) (a) barracks.
병용(倂用) ~하다 use (a thing) together (with); use (two things) at the same time.
병원(兵員) military personnel; strength (of a troop).
병원(病院) a hospital; a clinic (진료소); a doctor's office 《美》. ¶ ~에 입원하다 enter (go into) a hospital; be hospitalized / ~에 다니다 go to (attend a) hospital. ‖ ~선 a hospital ship / ~장 the superintendent (director) of a hospital.
병원(病原) the cause of a disease. ‖ ~균 a (disease) germ; a bacillus; a virus / ~체 pathogenic organ.
병인(病因) the cause of a disease. ‖ ~학 etiology.
병자(病者) a sick person; an invalid; a patient; the sick (총칭).
병장(兵長) a sergeant.
병적(兵籍) one's military records (registers); one's military status (신분). ‖ ~부 a muster roll.
병적(病的) morbid; diseased; abnormal. ¶ ~으로 morbidly; abnormally.

병조림(瓶—) bottling. ~하다 bottle 《a thing》; seal 《a thing》 in a bottle.

병존(並存) coexistence. ~하다 coexist 《with》; be coexistent 《with》; exist together.

병졸(兵卒) a soldier; a private; an enlisted man 《美》: the rank and file(총칭).

병종(兵種) the third class 《grade》.

병중(病中) during one's illness; while one is ill. ¶ ~이다 be ill in bed. 「ease.

병증(病症) the nature of a disease.

병진(竝進) ~하다 advance together; keep abreast of; keep pace with. 「flaw.

병집(病—) a fault; a defect; a

병참(兵站) communications. ‖ ~감 the quartermaster general / ~기지 a supply base / ~부 the commissariat; the quartermaster depot / ~사령부 the Logistic Support Command / ~선 a line of communications; a supply line / ~장교 a quartermaster. 「(in chorus).

병창(並唱) ~하다 sing together

병충해(病蟲害) damages by blight and harmful insects.

병칭(並稱) ~하다 rank [class] 《A》 with 《B》.

병탄(倂呑) ~하다 annex 《A to B》; absorb 《into》; swallow up.

병폐(病弊) an evil; a vice; a morbid practice.

병풍(屛風) a folding screen. ¶ 여 섯폭 ~(을 치다) (set up) a sixfold screen.

병합(倂合) ☞ 합병.

병행(竝行) ~하다 go side by side 《with》; do 《carry out, try》 《two things》 simultaneously.

병화(兵火) ¶ ~에 파괴되다 be destroyed by fire in a battle.

병환(病患) illness; sickness.

병후(病後) ¶ ~의 convalescent / ~의 몸조리 aftercare.

볕 sunshine; sunlight. ¶ ~이 들다 the sun comes in 《a window》 / ~에 말리다 dry 《a thing》 in the sun / ~에 타다 be sunburnt / ~에 쬐다 expose 《a thing》 to the sun / ~을 쬐다 bask [bathe] in the sun.

보(保) 《보증》 a guarantee; security; 《보증인》 a guarantor. ¶ ~서 다 stand guaranty 《for》 / ~를 세우다 find surety 《for》.

보(洑) 《저수지》 a reservoir; an irrigation pond.

보(褓) ☞ 보자기.

보(步) a [one] step; a pace.

…보(補) assistant; probationary. ¶ 서기~ an assistant clerk / 차관~ an assistant secretary 《美》.

보각(補角) 〖數〗 a supplementary angle; a supplement. 「book.

보감(寶鑑) a thesaurus; a hand-

보강(補強) ~하다 strengthen; reinforce; invigorate. ‖ ~공사 reinforcement work.

보강(補講) a supplementary lecture; a make-up lesson. ~하 다 make up for missing lecture.

보건(保健) (preservation of) health; 《위생》 sanitation; hygienics. ‖ ~ 복지부 the Ministry of Health and Welfare / ~소 a health center.

보검(寶劍) a treasured sword.

보결(補缺) 《일》 a supplement; 《사 람》 a substitute; an alternate 《美》. ~의 supplementary; substituted. ‖ ~모집 an invitation for filling vacancies / ~생 a standby student.

보고(報告) a report. ~하다 report; inform 《a person of an event》. ‖ ~서 a (written) report / ~자 a reporter. 「house.

보고(寶庫) a treasury; a treasure

보관(保管) custody; (safe)keeping; charge. ~하다 keep; take custody [charge] of; have 《a thing》 in one's keeping. ‖ ~료 custody fee / ~물 an article in custody / ~인 a custodian; a keeper. 「patriotism.

보국(報國) patriotic service 《by》.

보결(補缺) a special election 《美》; a by-election 《英》.

보균자(保菌者) a germ carrier; an infected person. 「steadily.

보글보글 ¶ ~ 끓다 simmer; boil

보금자리 a nest; a roost. ¶ 사랑 의 ~ a love nest.

보급(普及) diffusion; spread; popularization (대중화). ~하다 diffuse; spread; propagate; popularize. ‖ ~률 the diffusion 《of TV sets》 / ~소 a distributing agency / ~판 a popular (cheap) edition.

보급(補給) a supply. ~하다 supply; replenish 《coal, fuel》. ‖ ~ 관 [감] a quartermaster / ~기 지 (로, 선) a supply base 《route, ship》.

보기1 an example; an instance.

보기2 《보는 각도》 a way of looking at 《things》. ¶ 내가 ~ in my eyes 《opinion》 / ~에 따라서 는 in a 《certain》 sense.

보까다 suffer from indigestion.

보내다 ① 《물품을》 send; forward; dispatch; ship(배·화물로); remit (돈을). ¶ 편지 [상품, 전보, 서류]를 ~ send 《dispatch》 a letter 《goods, a telegram, documents》 to 《a person》 / 상품을 화물열차로 ~ ship the goods by freight train / 찬

보너스

사를 ~ pay (*a person*) a compliment. ② (사람을) send; dispatch. ¶심부름 ~ send (*a person*) on errand / 부르러 ~ send for (*a doctor*). ③ (이별) see (*a person*) off; give (*a person*) a send-off. ④ (세월을) pass; spend; lead. ¶행복한 나날을 ~ lead (live) a happy life / 시골에서 노후를 ~ spend *one's* remaining years in the country / 헛되이 세월 [시간] 을 ~ idle away *one's* time.

보너스 a bonus.

보다 ① (눈으로) see; look (*at*); 《목격》 witness. ¶본 일이 없는 unfamiliar; strange / …을 보고 있는 at the sight of / 보는 데서 in *one's* sight / 보기 좋게 beautifully, finely (아름답게); excellently; skillfully (멋지게) / 보시는 바와 같이 as you see / 흘낏 ~ catch a glimpse of; glance at / 뚫어지게 ~ stare [gaze] (*at*) / 잘 ~ have a good look (*at*) / 몰래 ~ steal a glance at; cast a furtive glance at / 차마 볼 수 없다 cannot bear to see; be unable to bear the sight of (*a thing*). ② (관찰) observe; look at; view; see; 《시찰》 inspect; visit; 《간주》 look upon (*as*); regard (*as*); consider; take (*a thing*) for [to do]. ¶내가 본 바로는 from my point of view; in my opinion / 어느 모로 보나 in every respect; from every point of view / 보는 바가 다르다 view a matter differently. ③ (구경) see (*the sights*); do (*the town*); visit (*a theater*). ¶텔레비전을 ~ watch television / 볼 만하다 be worth seeing [visiting] / 박물관을 보러 가다 visit a museum. ④ (읽다) read; see; (훑어 보다) look through [over]. ¶신문을 ~ read [see] the papers. ⑤ (조사) look over; look into; examine; (참고) refer to; consult (*dictionary*). ¶답안을 ~ look over the examination papers / 환자를 ~ (의사가) examine a patient. ⑥ (판단) judge; read; tell (*fortune*). ¶손금을 ~ read (*a person's*) palm. ⑦ (견적) estimate (*at*); offer (*a price*); bid; value; put. ¶손해를 만 원으로 ~ estimate the loss at 10,000 *won*. ⑧ (보살피다) look [see] after; take charge [care] (*of*); watch over (*a child*); attend to; manage. ¶아기를 ~ nurse a baby; baby-sit (美) / 집을 ~ watch over a house / 사무를 ~ attend to business. ⑨ (…ување 보다) try; have a try (*at*); test. ¶양복을 입어 ~ try on a new suit / 자전거를 타 ~ try a ride

보디

on a bicycle. ⑩ (시험을) take [sit for] (*an examination*). ⑪ (대소변을) do (*one's*) needs; relieve [ease] (*nature*). ⑫ (자손 등) take; get (*a child*). ¶사위를 ~ take a husband for *one's* daughter. ⑬ (이해를) get; experience; undergo; go through; suffer. ¶손해를 ~ suffer (sustain) a loss / 이익을 ~ make a profit / 재미를 ~ enjoy *oneself*. ⑭ (전의(轉義)) 두고 보아라 You shall soon see. / 두고 보자 I'll soon be even with you. *or* You shall smart for this.

보다² (…인 것 같다) look like; seem; it seems (to me) that …; I guess. ¶그 사람이 아픈가 ~ He seems to be ill. / 그가 벌써 왔는가 ~ I guess he is here already.

보다³ (비교) (more, better) than; rather than; 《superior, inferior》 to. ¶~ 정확하게 말하면 to be more exact; to speak more precisely / 낫다(못하다) be superior (inferior) to; be better (worse) than / 목숨~ 이름을 중히 여기다 value honor above life.

보다못해 being unable to remain a mere spectator.

보답(報答) 《보상》 recompense; a reward. ~하다 return (repay) (*a person's kindness*); reward; recompense. ¶노력에 ~하다 recompense (*a person*) for *his* labor.

보도(步道) a sidewalk (美); a pavement (英); a footpath.

보도(報道) a report; news; information; intelligence. ~하다 report; inform (*a person*) of (*a fact*); publish the news. ¶신문 ~에 의하면 according to the paper [the newspaper reports] / 단편적으로 ~하다 make a fragmentary report (*of*). ∥ ~관제 (newspaper) blackout; news censorship / ~기관 the press; a medium of information; a news medium / ~기사 a news story / ~사진 a news photograph / ~진 reporters; the press (corps); a news front / ~프로 a news program.

보도(輔導) guidance; direction. ~하다 lead; guide; direct. ∥ ~과 the guidance section / 학생~ student guidance.

보도독거리다 creak; graze; grind.

보동보동 ~한 plump; chubby.

보드랍다 ☞ 부드럽다.

보드카 vodka.

보들보들하다 (be) soft; pliant; supple; lithe.

보디 a body. ∥ ~가드 a body-

guard / ~랭귀지 (a) body language / ~ 블로 (拳) (deliver) a body blow / ~빌딩 body-building / ~체크 a body search.
보따리(褓─) a package; a bundle. ¶ ~장수 a peddler.
보람(효력) worth; effect; result. ¶ ~있는 fruitful; effective / ~없는 useless; vain; fruitless; ineffective / ~있는 생활 a life worth while to live / ~없이 in vain; to no purpose; uselessly / ~있다 be worth while 《to do》; be worth 《doing》.
보랏빛 light purple color; violet; lavender. ¶ 연~ lilac.
보료 a decorated mattress used as cushion.
보루(堡壘) a battery; a bulwark; a fort; a rampart.
보류(保留) reservation. ~하다 reserve; withhold; defer. ¶ 그 문제에 대한 태도를 ~하다 reserve one's attitude on the problem. ¶ ~조건 reservations.
보르네오 Borneo. ¶ ~의 Bornean.
보름 ① (15일) fifteen days; half a month. ② (보름날) the fifteenth day of a lunar month. ¶ ~달 a full moon.
보리(大麥) barley. ¶ ~ 타작하다 thresh barley. ¶ ~농사 the barley raising (farming) / ~밥 boiled barley (and rice) / ~밭 a barley field / ~차 a barley water (tea) / 보릿고개 the spring famine (just before the barley harvest) / 보릿짚 barley straw.
보리(菩提) Bodhi (梵); the Supreme Enlightenment.
보모(保姆) a nurse. ¶ 유치원의 ~ a kindergarten teacher.
보무(步武) ¶ ~ 당당히 《march》 in fine array.
보무라지, 보풀 tiny scraps of paper (cloth). ¶ 실~ tiny bits of thread; lint.
보물(寶物) a treasure; a treasured article; valuables. ¶ ~선 (섬) a treasure ship (island) / ~찾기 treasure hunting.
보배 a treasure; precious (valuable) things.
보병(步兵) infantry (총칭); (병사) an infantryman; a foot soldier. ¶ ~연대 (학교) an infantry regiment (school).
보복(報復) retaliation; revenge; (a) reprisal. ~하다 retaliate 《against》; take revenge 《on》; take reprisal 《against》. ¶ ~적인 retaliatory; revengeful ¶ 동일한 수단으로 ~하다 retaliate in kind.
보부상(褓負商) a peddler; a packman. ¶ ~을 하다 peddle; hawk.
보사위원회(保社委員會) the Health & Social Affairs Committee of the National Assembly.
보살(菩薩) [佛] *Bodhisattva*(梵); a Buddhist saint.
보살피다 look after; take care of; care for; attend to 《the sick》.
보상(補償) compensation; remuneration. ~하다 recompense; remunerate; reward.
보상(報償) (a) compensation; indemnity. ~하다 compensate; indemnify; make good 《the loss》. ¶ ~ 손해를 ~을 약속하다 promise to compensate for the loss / 전면 ~을 요구하다 demand full compensation. ¶ ~금 an indemnity; compensation (money) / ~안 compensation plan. 「col.
보색(補色) a complement(ary)
보석(保釋) bail. ~하다 let 《a prisoner》 out on bail; bail 《a person》 out. ¶ ~중이다 be out on bail / ~되다 be released on bail. ¶ ~금 bail (money) 《~금을 내다 put up (furnish) bail》 / ~보증인 a bailsman / ~신청 an application for bail / 병~ sick bail.
보석(寶石) a jewel; a gem; a precious stone. ¶ ~류 (세공) jewelry / ~상 a jeweler; (상점) a jeweler's (shop).
보선(保線) maintenance of tracks. ¶ ~공 a trackman (美); a lineman (美) / ~공사 track work.
보세(保稅) bond. ¶ ~가공 (무역) bonded processing (trade) / ~공장 (창고) a bonded factory (warehouse) / ~화물 bonded goods.
보송보송하다 (be) dry; parched.
보수(保守) conservatism. ¶ ~적 conservative. ¶ ~당 the Conservative Party / ~세력 conservative force / ~주의 conservatism / ~진영 the conservative camp.
보수(報酬) a reward; remuneration; a fee(의사 등의); pay(급료). ¶ …의 ~로 in reward (return, recompense) for / 무~로 without pay (fee) / ~를 기대하다 expect (demand, receive) a reward / 그에게 ~를 주다 give (offer) a reward 《*of* 5,000 *won*》 to him.
보수(補修) repair; mending. ~하다 mend; repair; fix. ¶ ~중이다 be under repair. ¶ ~공사 repair work.
보수계(步數計) a pedometer.
보스 a boss. ¶ 정계 (암흑가)의 ~ a political (an underworld) boss.
보슬보슬 《fall》 gently; softly; drizzly.
보슬비 a drizzle; a drizzling rain.
보습 a share; a plowshare.
보습(補習) a supplementary les-

보시 son; refresher training; an extra lecture. ~하다 supplement. ¶수학의 ~을 받다 receive a supplementary lesson in math.

보시(布施) an offering; alms; charity.

보시기 a small bowl.

보신(保身) keeping *oneself* from harm; self-defense. ‖ ~술 the art of self-protection.

보신(補身) ~하다 build *oneself* up by taking tonics. ‖ ~탕 soup of dog's meat.

보쌈김치(褓—) *Kimchi* wrapped in a large cabbage leaf like a bundle.

보아란듯이 ostentatiously; showily; for show [display].

보아주다 take care of; take trouble; look after; help.

보안(保安) the preservation (maintenance) of public peace; security. ¶ ~과 the (public) security section / ~관 a sheriff / ~당국 the security authorities / ~림 a reserved forest / ~처분 an order for preserving public peace; compulsory hospitalization 《of the mentally ill》 《정신질환자에 대한》.

보안사범(保安事犯) national security violators; a public security offender.

보안요원(保安要員)《탄광 등의》 the maintenance personnel.

보약(補藥) a tonic; a restorative; an invigorator.

보양(保養) preservation of health; 《병후의》 recuperation. ~하다 take care of *one's* health; recuperate. ‖ ~소 a convalescent hospital; a rest home; a sanatorium / ~지 a health resort.

보양(補陽) ~하다 strengthen the virile power; invigorate *oneself*.

보얗다 ① 《빛깔이》 (be) whitish; milky. ¶ 살결이 ~ have a pearly skin. ② 《연기·안개가》 (be) hazy; misty.

보어(補語) 〖文〗 a complement. ‖목적격~ an objective complement.

보여주다 let 《*a person*》 see; show.

보온(保溫) ~하다 keep warm. ‖ ~병 a thermos (bottle); a vacuum flask / ~재 lagging materials.

보완(補完) ~하다 complement. ¶상호 ~적이다 be complementary to each other.

보우(保佑) ~하다 protect; aid.

보위(保位) the throne; the crown.

보유(保有) possession. ~하다 possess; hold; keep; retain. ‖ ~자 a holder; a possessor / 금~고 gold holdings / 정부 미~ government-stocked rice.

보유스름하다 (be) whitish; milky.

보육(保育) ~하다 bring up; nurse; nurture; rear; foster. ‖ ~기《미숙아용의》 an incubator / ~원 a nursery school.

보은(報恩) requital 〔repayment〕 of kindness; gratitude. ~하다 requite 〔repay〕 another's kindness.

보이 a boy; a waiter《식당의》; a bellboy《기차·호텔의》. ¶ ~장 a head waiter; a bell captain《호텔의》.

보이다[1]《보게 하다》 show; let《*a person*》see〔look at〕;《전시하다》 exhibit; display. ¶ 실력을 ~ show〔display〕 *one's* ability.

보이다[2] ①《눈에》 see; catch sight of;《사물이》 be seen (visible); be in sight; appear; show up (나타나다). ¶ 보이지 않게 되다 go out of sight / 보이게 되다 come in sight (into view). ②《…같다》 seem; appear; look (like). ¶ 슬퍼 ~ look sad / 그녀는 서른쯤 되어 보인다 She looks about thirty.

보이스카우트 the Boy Scouts; a boy scout《한 사람》.

보이콧 a boycott (movement). ~하다 boycott《*a shop, goods*》.

보일러〖機〗 a boiler.

보자기 (a cloth) wrapper.

보잘것없다 ~하다.

보장(保障) guarantee; security. ~하다 guarantee; secure. ¶평화의 ~ a guarantee of peace. ‖ ~제도 a security system / 상호 안전 ~조약 a mutual security treaty / 집단안전~ collective security.

보전(保全) integrity; preservation. ~하다 preserve; maintain (safeguard) the integrity《*of*》. ¶환경을 ~하다 preserve the environment. ‖ 영토~ maintenance of the territorial integrity.

보전(寶典) a handbook; a thesaurus.

보조(步調) a step; a pace. ¶ ~를 맞추다 keep pace〔step〕《*with*》; act in concert《*with*》. ¶ ~가 맞지 않다 walk out of step; break step.

보조(補助)《원조》 assistance; help; support; aid;《보족(補足)》 a supplement. ~하다 assist; help; aid. ¶생활비를 ~하다 help《*a person*》with living expenses / 재정적으로 ~하다 give financial assistance《*to*》. ‖ ~금 a subsidy; a grant-in-aid / ~엔진 an auxiliary engine / ~원 an assistant; a helper / ~의자 a spare chair; a jump seat《버스의》 / ~탱크 a spare tank / ~화폐 subsidiary coins.

보조개 a dimple.

보족(補足) ~하다 complement; supplement; make good 《a deficiency》. ¶ ~설명 a supplementary explanation.

보존(保存) preservation; conservation. ~하다 preserve; keep; conserve. ¶ 유적의 ~ preservation of historic spots.

보좌(補佐) aid; assistance. ~하다 aid; assist; help; advise. ¶ 시장을 ~하다 assist a mayor. ‖ ~관 an aide.

보증(保證) a guarantee; a security; an assurance; a warrant. ~하다 guarantee; warrant; assure; vouch (answer) for. ¶ ~부(付)의 guaranteed; warranted; secured / ~을 서다 stand surety 〔guarantee〕 for 《a person》 / 신원을 ~하다 vouch for 《a person》 / 품질을 ~하다 guarantee (warrant) the quality 《of an article》 / 2년 ~의 자동차 a car guaranteed for two years; a car with a two-year guarantee. ‖ ~금 security money; a deposit / ~서 a (written) guarantee / ~ 수표 a certified check / ~인 a guarantor; a surety.

보지 [解] the vulva.

보지(保持) ~하다 maintain; hold; retain.

보직(補職) assignment to a position. ¶ ~되다 be assigned (appointed) 《to the post of》.

보채다 fret; be peevish. ¶ 보채는 아이 a fretful child.

보철(補綴) (치과의) (a) dental prosthesis. ¶ 부분~ a partial denture.

보청기(補聽器) a hearing aid; 《상 표명》 an Acousticon.

보초(步哨) a sentry. ¶ ~를 서다 stand sentry; be on sentry duty / ~를 세우다 post 《a soldier》 on sentry / ~를 교대시키다 relieve a sentry. ‖ ~병 a guard; a sentry / ~선 a sentry line.

보충(補充) supplement; replacement. ~하다 supplement; replenish; fill up; replace. ¶ 결원을 ~하다 fill (up) a vacancy. ‖ ~계획 a replacement program / ~대 drafts; reserves / ~병 a reservist / ~수업 supplementary lessons / ~역 reservist duty.

보칙(補則) supplementary rules.

보컬리스트 [樂] a vocalist.

보컬음악 vocal music.

보크사이트 [鑛] bauxite.

보태다 ① (보충) supply 《a lack》; make up 《for》; supplement. ¶ 모자람을 ~ make up a deficiency / 보탬이 되다 go towards; be an aid 《to》. ② (가산) add (up); sum up.

보통(普通) 《부사적》 usually; ordinarily; commonly; generally. ¶ ~의 《통상의》 usual; general; ordinary; common; 《정상적인》 normal; ordinal; 《평균의》 average / ~ 사람들 ordinary people / ~ 이상 (이하) 이다 be above (below) the average / ~의 경우에(는) in ordinary circumstances; usually / 이 추위는 ~이 아니다 The cold weather is rather unusual. ‖ ~교육 general education / ~명사 a common noun / ~선거 universal (popular) suffrage / ~열차 an accommodation train / ~예금 an ordinary deposit / ~우편 ordinary mail.

보통내기(普通—) (not) an ordinary person; (not) a mediocrity.

보퉁이(褓—) a bundle; a package; a parcel.

보트 a boat. ¶ ~를 젓다 row a boat / ~타러 가다 go boating. ‖ ~레이스 a boat race / ~선수 an oarsman.

보편(普遍) 《보편성》 universality. ¶ ~적인 universal; general / ~적 진리 universal truth. ‖ ~타당성 universal validity.

보폭(步幅) a stride; a pace.

보표(譜表) [樂] a staff; a score; a stave.

보풀 shag; nap 《of cloth》; flue; fuzz 《of paper》. ¶ ~이 인 shaggy; nappy 《silk》.

보풀다 become nappy; have fuzz.

보풀리다 raise a nap on; nap.

보풀보풀 ~하다 have a nap; be nappy 《downy, fuzzy》.

보필(輔弼) ~하다 assist; counsel; give advice.

보하다(補—) 《보직》 appoint; assign; 《원기를》 tone up; build up 《one's health》.

보학(譜學) genealogy.

보합(保合) [經] steadiness. ~하다 (keep) balance; remain the same (steady). ¶ 시세는 ~ 상태이다 Prices are steady.

보행(步行) ~하다 walk; go on foot. ‖ ~자 a walker; a pedestrian.

보험(保險) insurance; assurance 《英》. ¶ ~에 들다 insure 《one's house against fire》 / ~에 들어 있다 be insured 《against》 / ~을 ~ 계약하다 buy (take) an insurance policy / ~을 해약하다 cancel (surrender) one's insurance policy. ‖ ~계약 an insurance contract / ~계약자 a policyholder / ~금 insurance money / ~금 수취인 a beneficiary / ~료 insurance due; a premium /

~업자 an insurer; an underwriter / ~증서 an insurance policy / 실업~ unemployment insurance.
보혈(補血) ‖ ~제 a hematic.
보호(保護) protection; protective custody; 《보존》 conservation. ~하다 protect; defend; guard; 《돌보다》 take care (of); look after 《a person》; 《보존하다》 preserve; conserve. ¶ 문화재 ~ (the) preservation of cultural assets / 삼림 ~ conservation of forests / …의 ~하에 under the protection [care] of… / 경찰에 ~를 요청하다 apply to the police for protection / ~관세 a protective tariff 《place an offender on》 probation / ~구 a sanctuary 《for wild animal》 / ~무역 protective trade / ~색 protective coloring / ~수역 protected waters / ~자 a protector; a guardian; a patron.
보훈(報勳) ‖ ~병원 Korea Veterans Hospital; the Patriots and Veterans Hospital / 국가 ~처 the Ministry of Patriots and Veterans Affairs.
복 [魚] a swellfish; a blowfish; a globefish; a puffer. [mer.
복(伏) the dog days; midsum-
복(福) good luck; fortune; happiness; a blessing. ¶ ~된 happy; blessed / ~을 받다 be blessed / ~많이 받으십시오 Happy New Year!
복간(復刊) reissue; revived publication. ~하다 republish; reissue.
복강(腹腔) the abdominal cavity. ‖ ~임신 abdominal pregnancy.
복걸(伏乞) ~하다 prostrate *oneself* and beg.
복고(復古) restoration; revival. ¶ ~조(調) (of) a revival mood / ~주의 reactionism.
복교(復校) ~하다 return to school.
복구(復舊) restoration. ~하다 be restored to normal conditions. ‖ ~공사 repair [restoration] works.
복권(復權) restoration (of rights). ~하다 be restored to *one's* rights.
복권(福券) a lottery ticket. ¶ ~에 당첨되다 win (a prize) in a lottery; get [draw] a lottery prize. / ~추첨 a lottery.
복귀(復歸) ~하다 return (to); come back (to); 〖法〗 revert to 《재산 등의》 / 직장에 ~하다 return to work.
복대기 slag; dross.
복대기다 be noisy [boisterous; in a bustle]; be tossed about; be jostled around.
복더위(伏-) a heat wave during the dog days.
복덕방(福德房) a real estate agent; a realtor 《美》.
복도(複道) a corridor; a passage; a gallery; a lobby 《극장의》.
복리(福利) ☞ 복지.
복리(複利) compound interest. ~로 계산하다 calculate at compound interest.
복마전(伏魔殿) a hotbed of corruption; a pandemonium.
복막(腹膜) the peritonium. ‖ ~염 peritonitis.
복망(伏望) ~하다 desire earnestly.
복면(覆面) a veil; a mask. ~하다 wear a mask. ¶ ~을 한 masked / ~을 벗다 unmask (*oneself*). ‖ ~강도 a masked robber.
복명(復命) ~하다 report on *one's* mission. ‖ ~서 a report.
복모음(複母音) 〖音聲〗 a diphthong.
복무(服務) service. ~하다 serve; be in (public) service. ‖ ~규정 the service regulations; standing orders / ~연한 the term of office.
복문(複文) a complex sentence.
복받치다 be filled 《with emotion》; have a fit 《of》; well up《추구침》; fill one's heart《사물이 주어》.
복배(腹背) the back and front.
복병(伏兵) an ambush; men [troops] in ambush. ¶ ~을 두다《만나다》 lay [fall into] an ambush.
복본위제(複本位制) the double standard system; bimetallism.
복부(腹部) the abdomen; the belly. ‖ ~수술 an abdominal operation.
복부인(福夫人) a wealthy housewife chasing after the speculative benefit; women speculators swarming to a place of bidding.
복비례(複比例) 〖數〗 portion.
복사(複寫) reproduction; duplication; reprint; 《복사물》 a copy; a reproduction. ~하다 reproduce; copy. ‖ ~기 a duplicator; a copying machine; a copier / ~사진 a photocopy / ~용잉크 [종이] copying ink [paper].
복사(輻射) radiation. ~하다 radiate. ‖ ~선 a radiant ray / ~열 radiant heat / ~체 a radiator.
복사뼈 the ankle (bone); the talus. [ing 《for》.
복상(服喪) ~하다 go into mourn-
복색(服色) the color and style of a uniform; 《의상》 clothes; attire.
복서(伏線) a boxer.
복선(伏線) a covert reference. ¶ ~을 치다 lay an underplot; drop a hint as to what is to

복선(複線) a double track [line]. ¶ ~으로 하다 double-track. ‖ ~공사 double-tracking.

복성스럽다 (be) happy-looking.

복수(復讐) revenge; vengeance; retaliation〔報復〕. ~하다 revenge oneself (on a person); take revenge (for, on). ‖ ~심(에 불타다) (burn with) revengeful thought / ~자 a revenger / ~전(競技의) a return match [game].

복수(腹水) 〔醫〕 abdominal dropsy.

복수(複數) the plural. ¶ ~의 plural. ‖ ~명사 a plural noun / ~여권 a multiple passport.

복술(卜術) the art of divination.

복숭아 a peach. [calf.

복스(상자·좌석) a box;〔가죽〕box

복스럽다(福一) (be) happy-looking; prosperous-looking.

복슬복슬하다 (be) fat and shaggy.

복습(復習) review. ~하다 review [repeat] one's lessons.

복시(複視) 〔醫〕 diplopia; double vision. ¶ ~의 diplotic. [ments.

복식(服飾) dress and its orna-

복식(複式) ¶ ~의 double-entry (부기); plural(투표의); compound (기계의). ‖ ~부기 bookkeeping by double entry / ~투표 plural voting. [ing.

복식호흡(腹式呼吸) abdominal breath-

복싱 boxing. ¶ 섀도~ shadow-boxing.

복안(腹案) a plan [scheme] in one's mind; an idea.

복약(服藥) ~하다 take medicine.

복어(一魚) ☞ 복.

복역(服役) 〔penal〕 servitude. ~하다 serve one's term [sentence]. ‖ ~기간 a term of sentence.

복엽(複葉)〔植〕a compound leaf. ‖ ~기 a biplane.

복용(服用)〔약의〕internal use; dosage. ~하다 take 《medicine》; use internally. ‖ ~량 dosage; a dose.

복원(復元) restoration. ~하다 restore to the original state; revert. ‖ ~력 〔機〕 stability.

복원(復員) demobilization. ~하다 be demobilized.

복위(復位) restoration; reinstatement. ~하다 be restored 《to the throne》.

복음(福音) ¶ ~의 gospel; 〔좋은 소식〕good [welcome] news. ‖ ~교회 the Evangelical Church / (사)~서 the (four) Gospels.

복음(複音) a compound sound.

복자(覆字) a turn (in set type); a reversal of type in printing.

복잡(複雜) ~하다 (be) complicated; complex; intricate. ¶ ~한 기계 an intricate piece of machinery / ~한 수속 a complicated 〔troublesome〕 procedure / ~한 표정〔wear〕 an expression showing one's mixed feelings. ‖ ~골절 a compound fracture.

복장(服裝) dress; costume; attire; clothes. ¶ ~은 자유 Dress optional(초대장 등에서). ‖ ~검사 a dress inspection.

복적(復籍) ~하다 return to one's original domicile [family].

복제(服制) dress regulation〔system〕; costume.

복제(複製) reproduction;《복제품》a reproduction; a duplicate; a replica. ~하다 reproduce; reprint(책의). ‖ ~불허 All rights reserved. or Reprinting prohibited / ~화 a reproduced picture.

복종(服從) obedience; submission. ~하다 obey 《one's parents》; be obedient to; submit 〔yield〕《to》.

복죄(服罪) ~하다 plead guilty (to); enter a plea of guilty. ¶ ~하지 않다 plead not guilty.

복지(福祉) 〔public〕welfare; well-being. ¶ 국민의 ~를 증진하다 promote the welfare of the people. ‖ ~국가 a welfare state / ~사업 welfare work / ~시설 welfare facilities.

복직(復職) reinstatement; reappointment. ~하다 be reinstated in 〔come back to〕 one's former post 〔position〕. ‖ ~명령 the back-to-work order.

복창(復唱) ~하다 repeat 《one's senior's order》.

복채(卜債) a fortune-teller's fee.

복첨(福籤) a lottery. ¶ ~을 뽑다 hold a lottery.

복통(腹痛) 〔have〕 a stomachache.

복판 the middle [center, heart]. ¶ ~에 right [just] in the middle [center] 《of》 / 길 ~을 걷다 walk in the middle of the road 《of》.

복합(複合) ¶ ~의 compound; complex. / ~개념 a complex concept / ~기업 a conglomerate / ~렌즈 a compound lens / ~비료 compound fertilizer / ~빌딩 a multiple-purpose building / ~어 a compound 〔word〕 / ~영농 combined agriculture / ~오염 multiple pollution / ~체 a complex / ~형 컴퓨터 a hybrid computer.

복화술(腹話術) ventriloquy.

복활차(複滑車) a tackle; a compound pulley.

볶다 ① 〔분에〕parch; roast; fry (기름에). ② 〔들볶다〕ill-treat; treat 《a person》harshly; be hard on 《a person》; annoy; bully.

북아대다 keep bothering (annoying, pestering).

북아치다 hurry (up); urge; press; hasten. ¶ 빨리 준비하라고 ~ urge 《a person》 to prepare more quickly.

북음 ① 《부기》 panbroiling; roasting; parching. ② 《음식》 any panbroiled (roasted) food; a roast; a broil. ¶ ~밥 fried rice / 닭~ broiled chopped kicken / 미나리~ broiled parsley (dropwort).

본(本) ① 《본보기》 an example; a model. ¶ ~을 보이다 set a good example 《to students》. ② 《옷 따위의》 a pattern. ¶ 종이로 ~을 뜨다 make a pattern out of paper 《for a dress》. ③ 《본관》 family origin.

본…(本) 《이, 현재의》 this; the present 《meeting》; 《주요한》 the main 《store》; principal; 《진짜의》 real 《name》; regular.

본가(本家) ① 《본집》 the main family; 《친정》 one's old home. ② 《원조》 the originator; the original maker.

본값(本─) the cost price; the prime cost. ¶ ~에 팔다 sell 《something》 at cost (price) / ~을 건지다 cover the cost.

본거(本據) the headquarters; a base; a stronghold. ¶ 생활의 ~ the base and center of one's life / 종파의 ~ the headquarters of a religious sect.

본건(本件) this affair (item); the case in question.

본격(本格) ¶ ~적인 regular; real; ~적으로 in earnest / ~적인 여름 a real summer.

본견(本絹) pure silk.

본고장(本─) 《원산지》 the home 《of tobacco》; a habitat 《서식지》; 《중심지》 the center; 《고향》 one's native place. ¶ 사과의 ~ the home of the apple.

본과(本科) the regular course. ‖ ~생 a regular student.

본관(本官) 《자칭》 the present official; I.

본관(本貫) family origin; one's ancestral home.

본관(本管) a main (pipe). ¶ 가스(수도)~ a gas (water) main.

본관(本館) the main building.

본교(本校) this 《our》 school; the principal school 《분교에 대한》.

본국(本局) the main (head) office; 《전화의》 a central 《美》.

본국(本國) one's home (native, mother) country. ‖ ~정부 the home government.

본남편(本男便) one's ex-husband; 《법적인》 one's legal husband.

본능(本能) (an) instinct. ¶ ~적(으로) instinctive(ly).

본대(本隊) the main body (force).

본댁(本宅) one's home.

본데 discipline; education; good manners 《범절》. ¶ ~ 있다 (없다) be well-(ill-)bred; have good (no) manners.

본드 bond, adhesives. ‖ ~흡입 glue-(bond-) sniffing.

본디(本─) originally; from the first; by nature.

본보기(本─) ① 《본보기》 an example; a model. ¶ ~ 있다 be exemplary (splendid). ② 《교훈》 a lesson; a warning. ¶ ~을 보이다 make a lesson 《of》; punish.

본뜨다(本─) follow 《an example》; model after; copy from a model.

본뜻(本─) 《본심》 one's real intention; will; 《본의》 the original meaning.

본래(本來) 《원래》 originally; primarily; from the beginning (부터). ¶ ~의 original; primary / 이 말 ~의 뜻 the original meaning of this word.

본론(本論) the main subject (issue). ¶ ~으로 들어가다 go on the main issue.

본루(本壘) 《野》 the home base (plate). ‖ ~타 a home run; a homer.

본류(本流) the main stream.

본말(本末) ¶ ~을 전도하다 mistake the means for the end; put the cart before the horse.

본명(本名) one's real name.

본무대(本舞臺) the main stage.

본문(本文) the body 《of a letter》; the text 《of a treaty》.

본밀천(本─) capital; funds.

본바닥(本─) ⇒ 본고장.

본바탕(本─) essence; (real) substance; one's true color. ¶ ~이 정직한 honest by nature.

본받다(本─) follow 《a person's》 example; imitate 《a person》; model (copy) 《after》.

본보기(本─) 《모범》 an example; 《본뜨는 자료》 a model; a pattern. ¶ ~으로 삼다 make an example 《of a person》.

본봉(本俸) the regular salary; a basic pay; base pay.

본부(本部) the headquarters; the head (main) office; an administrative building 《대학 따위의》.

본분(本分) one's duty (part, role); function. ¶ ~을 다하다 do (perform, fulfill) one's duty (part).

본사(本社) 《본점》 the main (head) office; 《자기 회사》 our firm; this company; we.

본산(本山) the head temple.

본새(本─) 《생김새》 the original

본색(本色) looks; features; 《바탕》 the nature; basic quality. ¶ ~가 곱다 be nice-looking; have good features.

본색(本色) *one's* real character [nature]; *one's* true colors. ¶ ~을 드러내다 reveal *one's* true character; show *one's* true colors; betray [unmask] *oneself*.

본서(本署) the chief police station.

본선(本船) 《이 배》 this [our] ship; 《모선》 a mother [depot] ship. ‖ ~인도 free on board(생략 F.O.B., f.o.b.).

본선(本線) the main [trunk] line.

본성(本性) ⇨ 본색.

본시(本是)《부사적》 originally; primarily; from the first.

본심(本心) 《진심》 *one's* real intention; 《마음》 *one's* right [true] mind; *one's* heart; *one's* senses. ¶ ~으로는 at heart.

본안(本案) 《이 안건》 this proposal [bill]; 《원안》 the original proposal [bill, motion].

본업(本業) *one's* main occupation; *one's* regular business [work]; [ent; proper.

본연(本然) ¶ ~의 natural; inher-

본위(本位) standard(기준); principle(주의); a basis(기초). ¶ 자기 ~의 self-centered; selfish. ‖ 화폐 ~ a standard money [coin] / 금 ~ the gold standard.

본의(本意) *one's* will; *one's* real intention; *one's* original purpose. ¶ ~아니게 against *one's* will; unwillingly; reluctantly.

본인(本人) the person himself [herself]; the principal(대리인에 대한); 《문제의》 the said person; the person in question; 《나 자신》 I; me; myself. ¶ ~ 자신이 in person; personally / ~이 출석하다 present *oneself* 《at a court》.

본적(本籍) 《permanent》 domicile; *one's* family register.

본전(本錢) ① principal 《sum》; capital(밑천). ② ⇨ 본금.

본점(本店) 《the》 head [main] office [store]; 《이》 this store; our shop.

본제(本題) the original topic [subject]. ¶ ~로 돌아가서 to return to our subject.

본지(本旨) 《참목적》 the true aim; the object in view; 《본래의 취지》 the main [principal] object.

본지(本紙) this [our] paper.

본지(本誌) this [our] journal (magazine).

본직(本職) ① 《본업》 *one's* (regular) occupation [job]; *one's* principal profession [trade]. ② 《관리의 자칭》 I; me; myself.

본질(本質) essence; essential qualities; true nature; substance(실질). ¶ ~적인 essential; substantial / ~적으로 essentially; substantially; in essence.

본처(本妻) a lawful [legal] wife.

본체(本體) the true form; 《실체》 substance; 《실재》 reality. ‖ ~론 ontology.

본초(本草) 《한약재》 medical herbs. ¶ ~가(家) a herbalist / ~학 Chinese medical botany.

본초자오선(本初子午線) the prime [first] meridian.

본토(本土) the mainland. ¶ ~박이 aborigines; natives / 중국 ~ the Chinese mainland.

본담회(本會談) a full-dress talk; the main conference.

본회의(本會議) a plenary session; a general [regular] meeting.

볼 ① 《뺨》 a cheek. ② 《넓이》 width; breadth.

볼 《공》 a ball.

볼가심 ~하다 eat [have] just a bite of food to appease *one's* hunger.

볼기 the buttocks; the ass. ¶ ~를 때리다 spank; beat on the buttocks / ~ 맞다 be spanked.

볼꼴사납다 (be) ugly; mean; unseemly; unsightly.

볼되다 ① 《벅차다》 be a strain on one; (be) too hard. ② 《세다》 (be) intense; very tight.

볼레로 a bolero.

볼록 ~거리다 swell and subside; palpitate / ~하다 be bulgy. ‖ ~거울 [렌즈, 면] a convex mirror (lens, surface).

볼륨 volume. ¶ ~이 있는 voluminous; bulky / ~을 높이다 turn up the volume on.

볼리비아 Bolivia. ‖ ~의 Bolivian. ¶ ~ 사람 a Bolivian. [alley.

볼링 bowling. ‖ ~장 a bowling

볼만하다 《볼 가치가 있다》 be worth seeing.

볼멘소리 sullen [grouchy] words. ¶ ~로 in angry tone / ~로 대답하다 give a sullen answer.

볼모 ① 《담보》 a pawn. ② 《사람》 a hostage. ¶ ~로 잡다 take 《a person》 as hostage / ~로 잡히다 be held [taken] as a hostage.

볼셰비즘 Bolshevism.

볼셰비키 a Bolshevik.

볼썽사납다 (be) awkward; unsightly; unseemly; indecent.

볼일 business; an engagement; things [work] to do. ¶ ~이 있다 be engaged 《in》; have something to do / ~이 없다 be free; have nothing to do / ~ 보다 on business / ~을 다 마치다 finish [carry out] *one's* work.

불장 ¶ ~다 보다 be all up with…; All is over with…; have done with 《*a thing*》. ¶ 저 녀석도 ~다 봤다 The game is up for him. *or* He's done for.
볼트¹ [電] a volt; voltage. ‖ ~미터 a voltmeter.
볼트² [機] a bolt.
볼펜 a ballpoint (pen).
볼품 appearance; show; looks. ¶ ~있다 be attractive; make a good show / ~없다 have a bad appearance; be unattractive.
볼호령(一號令) a howl; an angry roar. ~하다 roar; bellow; howl.
봄 ① [계절] spring (time). ¶ ~의 spring; vernal / 이른 [늦은] ~ in the early [late] spring. ‖ ~농사 a spring crop / ~누에 spring silkworms / ~바람 a spring breeze [wind] / ~보리 spring-sown barley / ~비 a spring rain / ~빛 spring scenery [view] / ~아지랑이 spring haze / ~옷 spring wear. ② [청춘] the prime 《*of life*》.
봄갈이(do) the spring plowing.
봄나물 young greens [herbs]. ¶ ~을 캐다 pick young herbs.
봄날 (l) a spring day; [날씨] spring weather.
봄맞이꽃 [植] a rock jasmine.
봄추위 the lingering cold in spring.
봄타다 suffer from spring fever.
봅슬레이 a bobsleigh.
봇도랑(洑一) an irrigation ditch.
봇물(洑一) reservoir water.
봇짐(褓一) a bundle; a package; a packet. ‖ ~장수 a packman; a peddler.
봉(封) a paper package. ¶ 약 한 ~ a packet of medicine.
봉(鳳) ① ☞ 봉황. ② [만만한] a dupe; an easy mark [victim]; a pigeon; a sucker (俗). ¶ ~이 되다 fall an easy victim [prey] to 《*a person's trick*》.
봉건(封建) [制度] feudalism; the feudal system. ~ 적인 feudal; feudalistic. ‖ ~국가 a feudal state / ~사상 a feudalistic idea / ~사회 a feudal society / ~시대 the feudal age [times]; the era of feudalism / ~영주 a feudal lord / ~주의 feudalism; feudality.
봉급(俸給) a salary; pay; wages. ¶ 높은 [낮은] ~ a good [poor] salary / ~이 오르다 [내리다] get a raise [cut] in one's pay / ~이 많다 [적다] be well [ill, poorly] paid / ~을 타다 draw [get] a pay 《*of 800,000 won a month*》 / ~을 올리다 raise 《*a person's*》 pay / 낮은 ~으로 일하다 work for low pay. ‖ ~생활자 a salaried person [worker] / ~일 a payday.
봉기(蜂起) an uprising. ~하다 rise in revolt [arms]; rise 《*against*》.
봉납(奉納) ~하다 offer; dedicate; present; consecrate.
봉놋방(一房) the lodging room in an inn [a tavern] where a guest sleeps with his fellow lodgers; the inn dormitory.
봉당(封堂) the unfloored area [space] between two rooms.
봉돌 [낚싯줄의] a sink(er).
봉두난발(蓬頭亂髮) disheveled [unkempt, shaggy] hair.
봉랍(封蠟) sealing wax.
봉박다 [구멍을] patch a hole; stop up a hole.
봉변(逢變) ① [모욕당함] ~하다 be insulted [humiliated]; be shamed. ② [변을 당함] ~하다 meet with an accident [a mishap].
봉분(封墳) ~하다 mound 《*a grave*》; build a mound over a grave.
봉사(奉仕) service. ~하다 serve; give one's service. ¶ 지역 사회에 ~하다 serve one's community. ‖ ~가격 a bargain price / ~료 a tip / ~사회 a social [public] service.
봉살(封殺) [野] a force-out. ¶ 주자를 ~하다 force a runner out.
봉서(封書) a sealed letter.
봉선화(鳳仙花) [植] a balsam; a touch-me-not (flower).
봉쇄(封鎖) a blockade; blocking up; freezing (동결). ~하다 blockade; block up; freeze 《*funds*》. ¶ ~를 풀다 lift the blockade; unfreeze 《*the enemy's assets*》. ‖ ~구역 a blockade zone / ~선 a blockade line.
봉양(奉養) ~하다 support [serve] one's parents (faithfully).
봉오리 a bud (☞ 꽃봉오리). ¶ ~가 지다 have [bear] buds.
봉우리 a peak; a top; a summit.
봉인(封印) a seal; sealing. ~하다 seal up. ¶ ~된 be sealed.
봉제(縫製) needlework; sewing. ~하다 sew. ‖ ~공 a seamster (남자) / ~공녀 a seamstress(여자) / ~공장 a sewing factory / ~품 needlework products; sewing (총칭).
봉지(封紙) a paper bag. ¶ 약 한 ~ a pack of medicinal herbs.
봉직(奉職) ~하다 serve 《*at, in*》; be in the service 《*of*》; work 《*for*》; hold a position 《*in*》.
봉착(逢着) ~하다 encounter; face; come upon; meet 《*with*》; be faced [confronted] 《*with*》. ¶ 난관에 ~하다 be confronted with a difficulty.

봉창 ~하다 make up for 《*one's loss*》(변충); lay aside stealthily(감추어 둠). ‖ ~질 hoarding things.

봉천(封窓) ① 《봉한 창》 a sealed window; sealing (up) a window (봉하기). ② 《구멍만 낸》 an opening in the wall.

봉토(封土) a fief; a feud.

봉투(封套) an envelope; a paper bag (sack). ‖ 반신용~ a return envelope.

봉하다(封一) ① 《붙이다》 seal 《*a letter*》; seal up 《*a window*》; 《봉해 넣다》 enclose; confine. ② 《다물다》 shut 〔close〕 《*one's mouth*》. ③ 《봉토를》 invest 《*a person*》 with a fief; enfeoff. ④ 《작위를》 confer a peerage.

봉함(封緘) a seal; sealing. ~하다 seal 《*a letter*》. ‖ ~엽서 a letter card.

봉합(縫合) 〔醫〕 suture. ~하다 suture; stitch (together).

봉화(烽火) a signal 〔beacon〕 fire; a rocket. ‖ ~를 올리다 light a signal fire. ‖ ~대 a beacon lighthouse.

봉황(鳳凰) a Chinese phoenix.

봐하니 so far as my observation goes; to all appearances; apparently.

뵙다 humbly see 〔meet〕 《*one's elders*》; have an audience with 《*the King*》.

부(否) no; nay(s); negation.

부(部) ① 《부분》 a part; a portion. ② 《부과》 a department; a bureau; a division; a section; 《내각의》 a department; a ministry. ③ 《서적의》 a copy 《*of a book*》; a volume.

부(富) wealth; riches; opulence.

부(賦) poetical prose; an ode.

부…(副) assistant; deputy; vice-; sub-. ‖ ~교수 an associate professor / ~시장 a deputy mayor / ~영사 a vice-consul / ~지배인 an assistant manager / ~지사 a deputy 〔lieutenant〕 governor / ~통령〔회장, 총재〕 a vice-president.

…부(附) ① 《날짜》 dated 《*Aug. 3rd*》; under the date of 《*the 5th inst.*》. ② 《부속》 attached to; belonging to. ‖ 대사관~ 육〔군〕 무관 a military 〔naval〕 *attaché* to an embassy.

부가(附加) ~하다 add 《*to*》; supplement; 《첨부》 annex; append. ‖ ~적인 additional; supplementary. ‖ ~가치세 a tax on value added; a value-added tax / ~물 an addition; an appendage / ~세 an additional tax; a surtax.

부각(浮刻) ~하다 emboss; raise; 《새기다》 carve in relief. ‖ ~되다 stand out in bold relief / ~시키다 bring 《*a thing*》 into relief.

부감(俯瞰) ~하다 overlook; command a bird's-eye view 《*of*》. ‖ ~도 a bird's-eye view 《*of*》; an aerial view. ☞ 조감도.

부강(富强) wealth and power. ~하다 be rich and powerful.

부걱거리다 bubble up; foam; pop.

부결(否決) rejection; voting down. ~하다 reject; vote down; decide 《*against a bill*》.

부계(父系) the father's side; the paternal line.

부고(訃告) an announcement of 《*a person's*》 death; an obituary 〔notice〕.

부과(賦課) ~하다 levy 〔impose, assess〕 《*a tax on land*》. ‖ ~금 dues; taxes / ~액 the amount imposed / ~징수 assessment and collection / 자동~제 taxation-by-schedule system.

부관(副官) an adjutant. ‖ 고급~ a senior adjutant / 전속~ an *aid-de-camp* 〔프〕; an aide.

부교(浮橋) a pontoon 〔floating〕 bridge.

부교재(副敎材) an auxiliary textbook.

부국(富國) a rich country; a prosperous nation. ‖ ~강병 a rich country with powerful armed forces / ~강병책 measures to enrich and strengthen the country.

부군(夫君) one's husband.

부권(父權) paternal rights.

부권(夫權) husband's 〔marital〕 rights.

부귀(富貴) wealth and fame. ‖ ~영화 wealth and prosperity 《~영화를 누리다 live in splendor》.

부그르르 ~ 끓다 sizzle / ~ 일다 bubble up.

부근(附近) neighborhood; vicinity. ‖ ~의 neighboring; nearby; adjacent / ~에 near; in the neighborhood 〔vicinity〕 of.

부글거리다 《끓어서》 simmer; 《거품이》 bubble up.

부금(賦金) an installment; a premium 《보험의》.

부기(附記) an addition; an additional remark 〔note〕. ~하다 add 《*that…*》; append 《*a note*》; write in addition.

부기(浮氣) swelling 《of the skin》. ‖ ~가 빠지다 the swelling subsides 〔goes down〕.

부기(簿記) bookkeeping. ‖ ~법 rules of bookkeeping / 단식〔복식〕~ bookkeeping by single 〔double〕 entry.

부끄럼 ① 《창피》 shame; disgrace.

부끄럽다 ¶ ~을 알다〔모르다〕 have a〔no〕 sense of shame. ② 《수줍음》 shyness; bashfulness. ¶ ~을 타다 be shy〔bashful〕.

부끄럽다 《창피하다》(be) shameful; disgraceful; 《수줍다》(be) shy〔abashed〕; bashful. ¶ 부끄러운 듯이 bashfully; shyly ¶ 부끄러워하다 be〔feel〕shy; feel shame〔at〕; be ashamed〔of〕; 말하기 부끄럽지만 … I am ashamed to say that….

부나비 〔虫〕 a tiger moth.
부녀(父女) father and daughter.
부녀자(婦女子) 《부인》 a woman; 《총칭》 womenfolk; the fair sex.
부농(富農) a rich farmer.
부닥치다 《만나다》 come upon〔across〕; encounter; meet with; 《직면하다》face; be confronted by. ¶ 난관에 ~ face〔be confronted by〕a difficulty / 그 제안은 반대에 부닥쳤다 The proposal met with opposition.

부단(不斷) ~하다 (be) constant; continual; ceaseless; incessant. ¶ ~한 노력 constant efforts.

부담(負擔) a burden; a load; a charge《지불의》; a responsibility《책임》; ~하다 bear《the expenses》; shoulder《a burden》; share《in》《일부를》; 《비용을》be charged with. ¶ 주 20시간의 수업 ~ a teaching load of twenty hours a week / ~을 주다 impose a burden on《a person》 / …의 ~을 덜어주다 lighten the burden imposed on《a person》 / ~액 one's share《in the expenses》.

부당하다(不當一) (be) unjust; unfair; unreasonable; exorbitant《과도의》. ¶ 부당한 값.. unreasonable price / 부당한 요구 an unreasonable demand / 부당한 판결 an unjust decision. ‖ 부당노동행위 an unfair labor practice / 부당이득 an undue profit / 부당해고 unfair dismissal.

부대(附帶) ~의 incidental《expenses》; supplementary《items》; subsidiary《enterprises》; attendant《circumstances》 / …에 ~하다 incidental to…; accompanying…. ¶ ~결의 a supplementary〔an additional〕resolution / ~공사 appurtenant work / ~사업 a subsidiary enterprise / ~설비 incidental facilities / ~조건 a collateral〔an incidental〕condition.

부대(負袋) a burlap bag; a sack. ¶ 밀가루 한 ~ a sack of flour.
부대(部隊) a《military》unit; a corps; a force; a detachment. ‖ ~배치 troop disposition / ~장 a commander; a commanding officer《생략 C.O.》.

부대끼다 be troubled〔tormented〕《by, with》; be pestered《by》. ¶ 밤새도록 모기에 ~ be annoyed by mosquitoes all night long / 심한 두통에 ~ be tormented with a violent headache.

부덕(不德) want〔lack〕of virtue. ¶ 모두 내 ~의 소치이다 I am solely to blame for it.

부덕(婦德) womanly〔female〕virtue. ¶ ~의 귀감 a symbol of female virtue.

부도(不渡) failure to honor《a check》; dishonor. ¶ ~ 나다 be dishonored / ~를 내다 dishonor a bill〔check〕. ‖ ~어음〔수표〕 a dishonored bill〔check〕.

부도(婦道) womanhood; the duty of a woman.

부도덕(不道德) immorality. ¶ ~한 immoral / ~한 행동 immoral conduct.

부도체(不導體) a nonconductor.
부동(不動) ¶ ~의 firm; immovable; solid; motionless; fixed / ~의 신념 firm〔unshakable〕faith / ~의 자세를 취하다 stand at attention.

부동(浮動) ~하다 float《in the air》; waft《향기 따위가》; fluctuate《변동》. ‖ ~기뢰 a floating mine / ~주《株》floating stocks / ~표 a floating vote.

부동산(不動産) real《immovable》 estate; fixed property; immovables. ¶ ~감정사 a real estate appraiser / ~등기 real-estate registration / ~소득 〔an〕income from real estate / ~실명 제 the real-name property ownership system; the real-name system for real estate trading / ~업자 a real estate agent; a realtor《美》 / ~취득세 real estate acquisition tax / ~투기 speculation in real estate; land speculation.

부동액(不凍液) antifreeze.
부동일(不同一) unequal; uneven; be lacking in uniformity.
부동항(不凍港) an ice-free port.
부두(埠頭) a quay; a pier; a wharf. ‖ ~인부 a stevedore; a longshoreman.

부둥키다 embrace; hug; hold〔take〕《a person》in one's arms.
부드럽다 (be) soft; tender; gentle; mild. ¶ 부드럽게 softly; mildly; tenderly / 부드러운 목소리〔빛〕a soft〔gentle〕voice〔light〕 / 마음씨가 ~ have a tender heart.

부득부득 stubbornly; obstinately; persistently; importunately.
부득불(不得不) ☞ 부득이.
부득이(不得已) against one's will;

부들 a cattail; a reed mace.

부들부들 ¶ ~ 떨다 quiver 《with emotion》; tremble 《with rage》; shiver 《with cold》.

부듯하다 ① 《꼭 맞다》 (be) tight; close. ② 《꽉 뽀다》 (be) full; close. ③ 《가슴이》 feel a lump in one's throat.

부등(不等) disparity; inequality. ¶ ~의 unequal. ‖ ~식 an inequality.

부등변(不等邊) ¶ ~의 inequilateral; scalene 《triangles》.

부디 ① 《꼭》 by all means; without fail; in any case. ¶ ~ 오십시오 Come, by all means. ② 《바라건대》 (if you please); (will you) kindly.

부딪치다 《충돌》 run [knock, clash] against; collide with; 《봉착》 meet with; come across; encounter. [run] into.

부딪히다 be bumped [crashed].

뚜막 a kitchen [cooking] range; a kitchen furnace.

부라리다 glare [stare] 《at》; look with glaring eyes.

부락(部落) a village; a hamlet. ‖ ~민 villagers; village folk.

부란(孵卵) incubation; hatching. ‖ ~기(器) an incubator.

부랑자(浮浪者) a vagabond; a vagrant; a tramp.

부랴부랴 in a great hurry; in deadly haste; hurriedly. ¶ ~ 달려가다 rush to 《the scene》.

부러 purposely; on purpose; intentionally; deliberately; knowingly (알면서).

부러뜨리다 break; snap 《딱 소리를 내며》; fracture (뼈를).

부러워하다 envy 《a person》; be envious 《of》; feel envy 《at》.

부러지다 break; be broken; snap; give way.

부럽다 (be) enviable; envious 《of》. ¶ ~ 듯이 enviously; (glance) with envy; 부럽게 하다 make 《others》 envy [envious]; excite 《a person's》 envy.

부레 an air bladder.

부려먹다 ~ 부리다. ¶ 막 ~ work [drive] 《a person》 hard.

부력(浮力) 【理】 buoyancy; floatage; lift (비행기의). ‖ ~계(計) a buoyancy gauge.

부령(部令) an order [a decree] from a government ministry.

부록(附錄) an appendix; a supplement 《to the magazine》.

부루퉁하다 《부어서》 (be) swollen; bulging; 《성나서》 (be) sulky. ¶ 부루퉁한 얼굴 a sullen face.

부류(部類) 《종류》 a class; a kind; 《종속》 a species; a category; a head. ¶ …의 ~에 들다 come under the category [head] of.

부르다¹ ① (배가) (be) full. ¶ 배 부르게 먹다 eat one's fill. ② 《임신하여》 (be) pregnant.

부르다² ① call; call (out) to 《a person》. ¶ 부르면 들릴 곳에 within call / 이름을 ~ call 《a person》 by name / 의사를 부르러 보내다 send for a doctor / 불러내다 (들이다) call 《a person》 out (in). ② 《일컫다》 call; name; term; designate. ¶ …라고 ~ be called…. ③ 《청하다》 invite [ask] 《a person》 to 《dinner》; 《소환》 summon 《a person by letter》. ④ 《값을》 bid 《a price》; offer; set. ¶ 부르는 값에 사다 buy 《an article》 at the price asked / 값을 싸게 ~ (a seller) set the price low; (a buyer) offer a low price. ⑤ 《노래를》 sing 《a song》. ⑥ 《외치다》 cry; shout. ¶ 만세를 ~ cry "Hurrah!"

부르르 ~ 떨다 tremble 《with fear》; shiver 《with cold》; quiver.

부르주아 a bourgeois (사람); the bourgeoisie (계급).

부르쥐다 clench 《one's fist》.

부르짖다 ① 《외치다》 shout; cry; utter [give] a cry; exclaim; 《비명》 shriek; scream. ② 《창도(唱導)》 cry 《for》; clamor 《for》; advocate. ¶ 개혁을 ~ cry (loudly) for a reform.

부르트다 ① 《물집이》 blister; get a blister; have a corn 《on the sole》; ② 《물려서》 swell up.

부릅뜨다 open 《one's eyes》 wide; make one's eyes glare; glare fiercely. ¶ 눈을 부릅뜨고 with angry (glaring) eyes.

부리¹ ①《새의》 a bill (평평한); a beak (매의). ② 《물건의》 a pointed end (head); a tip.

부리나케 in a hurry; in haste; hurriedly. ¶ ~ 도망가다 flee in all haste.

부리다¹ ① 《일시키다》 keep 《a person, a horse》 at work; work; set [put] 《a person》 to work; use; hire; employ (고용). ¶ 사람을 심하게 ~ work [drive] a person hard; be a hard master. ② 《조종하다》 manage; work; handle; run; operate. ¶ 기계를 ~ operate a machine. ③ 《행사》 exercise; use; wield; exert 《one's》 power. ¶ 권력을 ~ exercise one's power. ④ 《재주·말썽을》 play 《a trick》; show 《one's ability》; start 《trouble》.

부리다² 《짐을》 unload 《a truck》; discharge; get off.
부리망(─網) a muzzle 《for cattle》.
부리부리하다 (be) big and bright.
부마(駙馬) a princess' husband; a king's son-in-law.
부메랑 《throw》 a boomerang. ¶ ～ 효과 a boomerang effect.
부모(父母) one's parents. ¶ ～의 parental 《love, affection》.
부목(副木) a splint. ¶ ～을 대다 splint 《one's arm》; apply splints 《to》.
부문(部門) a class; a group; a department; a category; a section; a branch; a line. ¶ ～으로 나누다 divide 《things》 into classes; classify / …의 ～에 넣다 classify 《things》 under; bring 《place》 《things》 under the division 〔category〕.
부박(浮薄)~한 frivolous; fickle;
부복(俯伏)~하다 lie prostrate.
부본(副本) a copy; a duplicate.
부부(夫婦) man 〔husband〕 and wife; a 〔married〕 couple. ¶ ～의 conjugal; matrimonial / ～가 되다 become man and wife; be married. ～싸움 a quarrel between husband and wife / ～ 씨 Mr. and Mrs. Kim.
부분(部分) a part; a portion; a section. ¶ ～적인 partial; sectional. ‖ ～식(蝕) a partial eclipse 《of the sun》.
부빙(浮氷) floating ice. 「delegate.
부사(副使) a vice-envoy; a deputy
부사(副詞) 〔文〕 an adverb. ¶ ～ 적(으로) adverbial(ly). ‖ ～구 an adverbial phrase.
부산물(副産物) a by-product 《of》; (a) spin-off 《from》《대규모 사업 의》. ¶ 연구의 ～ a by-product of research.
부산하다 《떠들썩하다》 (be) noisy; boisterous; uproarious; 《바쁘다》 (be) busy; bustling.
부삽(─ 鋪) a fire shovel.
부상(負傷) an injury; a wound; a hurt. ¶ ～하다 get (be) injured; be wounded; get hurt. ‖ 충격으로 팔에 ～을 입다 be wounded in the arm by a shot. ‖ ～자 a wounded person; the wounded (총칭).
부상(浮上)~하다 surface; come 〔rise〕 to the surface; 《비유적》 rise 〔emerge〕 from obscurity 《무명에서》. ¶ 잠수함이 ～하다 a submarine surfaces 〔rise to the surface〕 / 인기가 다시 ～하다 regain one's popularity.
부상(副賞) an extra 〔a supplementary〕 prize.
부서(部署) one's post 〔place〕. ¶ ～를 지키다 keep one's post.

부서(副署) countersignature. ～하다 countersign; endorse.
부서지다 break; be smashed 〔broken, wrecked〕; go 〔fall〕 to pieces; be damaged. ¶ 부서지기 쉬운 fragile; easy to break; delicate / 부서진 의자 a broken chair.
부석부석 ¶ ～한 somewhat 〔slightly〕 swollen 〔tumid〕.
부선거(浮船渠) a floating dock.
부설(附設)~하다 attach; annex. ¶ 대학에 연구소를 ～하다 establish a research center attached to a university. ‖ ～기관 an auxiliary organ / ～도서관 a library attached 《to》; an annex library.
부설(敷設) construction; laying. ～하다 lay; build; construct. ¶ 철도를 ～하다 lay 〔build〕 a railroad. ‖ ～권 a right of construction.
부성애(父性愛) a paternal love.
부속(附屬)~하다 belong 《to》; be attached 《to》. ¶ ～의 attached; accessory(보조적인) / …에 ～되어 있다 be attached to… / H 대학 ～병원 the H University Hospital. ‖ ～품 〔물〕 accessories / ～학교 an attached school.
부수(附隨)~하다 accompany; be attended. ¶ ～적인 accompanying; incidental 《to》; attendant 《on》 / 전쟁에 ～되는 재해 the evils accompanying war.
부수(部數) the number of copies; the circulation (발행 부수).
부수다 break; destroy; smash.
부수수하다 (be) in disorder; disheveled; untidy; loose.
부수입(副收入) an additional 〔a side〕 income; the income from a side 〔part-time〕 job.
부스러기 a bit; a fragment; scraps 《of meat》; odds and ends; crumbs 《of bread》; chips 《of wood》.
부스러뜨리다 break; smash; crush.
부스러지다 be smashed; be broken; go to pieces.
부스럭거리다 rustle. ¶ 부스럭부스럭 rustlingly; with a rustle.
부스럼 a swelling; a boil; an abscess. ¶ ～이 나다 have a boil 《on》. 「zles.
부슬부슬 ¶ 《비가》 ～ 내린다 It drizzles.
부싯돌 a metal piece (for striking fire). ‖ 부싯돌 a flint.
부시다¹ 《눈이》 (be) dazzling; glaring. ¶ 눈이 부시도록 아름다운 여자 a lady of dazzling beauty / 눈이 부시게 빛나다 dazzle; glare.
부시다² 《그릇을》 wash 〔out〕; rinse 〔out〕. ¶ 병을 ～ wash 〔rinse〕 out a bottle.
부시장(副市長) a deputy mayor.
부식(扶植)~하다 plant; implant;

부식(腐植) ☞ 부식물(腐植物).

부식(腐蝕) corrosion; erosion. ~하다 corrode; erode (산에 의해); rust (녹슬다). ‖ ~방지제 a corrosive inhibitor; an anticorrosive / ~작용 corrosion.

부식물(副食物) a side dish; dishes to go with the rice.

부식토(腐植土) humus soil.

부신(副腎) [解] adrenal glands. ‖ ~피질 the adrenal cortex.

부실(不實) ~하다 ① (불성실) (be) faithless; unfaithful; insincere; (믿음성이) (be) unreliable; untrustworthy. ¶ ~한 아내 an undeserving [faithless] wife. / ~ 공사 (행위) illegal [faithless] construction practices / ~기업 an insolvent enterprise. ② (부족·불충실) (be) short; incomplete; insufficient. ③ (몸이) (be) feeble; weak; delicate. ¶ 몸이 부실한 편이다 be in poor health.

부심(副審) a subumpire (야구); referee.

부심(腐心) ~하다 take great pains 《to do》; be at pains 《to do》; rack one's brains.

부아 ① (허파) the lungs. ② (분함) anger; temper. ¶ ~가 나다 be [feel] offended [vexed] 《with, at》 / 그는 그녀의 말을 듣고 ~가 났다 He was offended [vexed] at [by] her remarks.

부양(扶養) support; maintenance. ~하다 maintain; support. ¶ 가족을 ~할 의무가 있다 have a duty to support one's family. / ~가족 a dependent / ~가족공제 exemption for dependents / ~가족수당 a family allowance / ~자 a supporter; the breadwinner (of a family).

부양(浮揚) ~하다 float 《in the air》; (경기를) pick up. ¶ 경기를 ~시키다 stimulate the economy. ‖ ~력 buoyancy.

부언(附言) an additional remark; a postscript (생략 P.S.). ~하다 add 《that...》; say in addition.

부업(副業) a side job; a sideline. ~으로(서) as a sideline.

부엉이 [鳥] a horned owl.

부엌 a kitchen. ¶ ~에서 일하다 work in the kitchen. ‖ ~세간 kitchen utensils; kitchenware / ~일 kitchen work.

부여(附與) ~하다 give; grant; allow. ¶ 권한을 ~하다 give 《a person》 an authority 《to do》.

부여(賦與) ~하다 endow [bless] 《a person》 with.

부역(賦役) compulsory labor [ser-

부연(敷衍) ~하다 explain... more fully; amplify 《the subject》; expatiate [elaborate] on 《a subject》.

부영사(副領事) a vice-consul.

부옇다 (be) whitish; grayish.

부예지다 get misty [hazy]; 《눈이》 dim; be blurred.

부용(芙蓉) ① 《연꽃》 a lotus. ② 《목부용》 a cotton rose.

부원(部員) a staff member; the staff (전체).

부유(浮遊) ~하다 float; drift. ¶ ~기뢰 a floating mine / ~물 floating matters / ~생물 plankton.

부유(富裕) ~하다 (be) wealthy; (rich); opulent.

부유스름하다 somewhat pearly (milky); frosty.

부음(訃音) an obituary notice; an announcement of death. ¶ ~에 접하다 be informed of 《a person's》 death.

부응하다(副應—) 《필요·요구에》 meet; satisfy; 《반응하다》 answer; 《적응하다》 be suited 《to》. ¶ 시대의 요구에 ~ meet the demand of the times.

부의(附議) ~하다 refer 《a matter》 to 《a committee》.

부의(賻儀) a condolence [an obituary] gift. ‖ ~금 condolence [incense] money.

부의장(副議長) a vice-president [= chairman]; a deputy speaker.

부익부빈익빈(富益富貧益貧) the rich-get-richer and the poor-get-poorer.

부인(夫人) a wife; a married lady; 《경칭》 Mrs.; Madam.

부인(否認) (a) denial; negation; nonrecognition. ~하다 deny; refuse to admit; say no 《to》. ¶ 기소 사실을 전면 ~하다 deny all the indicted facts.

부인(婦人) a married woman. ‖ ~과 gynecology / ~과 의사 a gynecologist / ~병 women's diseases / ~회 a women's club [society].

부임(赴任) ~하다 leave [start] for one's new post. ‖ ~지 the place of appointment; one's new post.

부자(父子) father and son. ¶ ~가정 a family consisting of father and children.

부자(富者) a rich [wealthy] man; a man of wealth [property, means]; the rich (총칭). ¶ ~가 되다 become rich; make a fortune.

부자연(不自然) ~한 unnatural; artificial (인위적); forced (무리한); affected (꾸민). ¶ ~스러운 웃음 a forced smile / ~스러운 자세로 서 있다 stand in an unnatural posture.

부자유(不自由) lack of freedom; 《불편》 (an) inconvenience. ~하

부작용(副作用) a side effect. ¶ ~을 일으키다 produce [have] side effects 《on》 / ~이 없다 have no [be free from] side effects.

부장(部長) the head [chief, director] (of a department). ¶ ~검사 a chief public prosecutor.

부장품(副葬品) grave goods; tomb furnishings.

부재(不在) absence. ~하다 be absent; be out; be 「not at [away from] home. ¶ ~중에 during [in] one's absence. ¶ ~자 an absentee / ~자투표 absentee ballot / ~지주 an absentee landowner.

부적(符籍) an amulet; a talisman; a charm.

부적격(不適格) ☞ 부적임.

부적임(不適任) ¶ ~한 inadequate; unqualified; unfit; unsuitable 《for》 / 그 자리에 ~이다 be unfit [not the right man] for the positon. ¶ ~자 an unqualified [incompetent] person.

부적절(不適切) ¶ ~한 unsuitable 《for》; inappropriate 《to》; inadequate 《for》; ill-suited 《for, to》; unfit 《for, to》 / 장소에 ~한 표현 an unsuitable [inappropriate] expression for the occasion.

부전(附箋) a slip; a tag; a label. ¶ ~을 붙이다 tag; label; attach a tag.

부전승(不戰勝) an unearned win. ~하다 win without fighting [playing].

부전자전(父傳子傳) transmission from father to son. ¶ ~이다 Like father, like son.

부전조약(不戰條約) an antiwar pact [treaty].

부전패(不戰敗) ~하다 lose a game by default [without fighting].

부절제(不節制) excess; intemperance. ~하다 be intemperate.

부젓가락 fire tongs.

부정(不正) (an) injustice; dishonesty; illegality (위법); (a) wrong (비행). ¶ ~한 unjust; unfair; dishonest; illegal; wrong / ~한 일을 하다 do something dishonest; behave unfairly / ~을 밝히다 expose injustice / ~을 바로잡다 redress [remedy] injustice / ~입학하다 enter 《a university》 through the back door. ¶ ~공무원 a corrupt[ed] official / ~대부[융자] fraudulent loans / ~사건 [공무원의] a bribery [graft] case / ~선거 a rigged election / ~축재자 an illicit fortune maker / ~행위 a dishonest act; an unfair practice.

부정(不定) ¶ ~의 indefinite; unfixed; unsettled. ¶ ~관사 an indefinite article / ~사 an infinitive.

부정(不貞) unchastity; unfaithfulness. ¶ ~한 아내 an unfaithful wife.

부정(不淨) ¶ ~한 unclean; dirty; impure / ~한 돈 [재물] ill-gotten gains / ~타다 suffer an evil.

부정(否定) (a) denial. ~하다 deny; negate. ¶ ~할 수 없는 undeniable / ~적인 견해 a negative point of view. ¶ ~문 a negative sentence / ~어 a negative.

부정기(不定期) ¶ ~의 irregular / ~적인 수입 an irreguler income. ¶ ~편(비행기의) a non-scheduled flight.

부정맥(不整脈) [醫] arrhythmia; an irregular pulse. ¶ ~한 dishonest.

부정직(不正直) dishonesty.

부정확(不正確) inaccuracy; incorrectness. ¶ ~한 inaccurate; incorrect.

부조(不調) bad condition; irregularity. ~하다 be irregular; be in disorder; 《운동선수가》 be in a bad condition.

부조(扶助) ① 《도움》 help; aid; assistance; support. ~하다 aid; assist; help. ¶ 상호~ mutual aid. ② 《금품》 a congratulatory gift [money] (축의금); condolence money [goods] (조의금).

부조(浮彫) relief; a relief sculpture (carving). ¶ ~로 하다 work [carve] in relief. ¶ ~세공 relief work.

부조리(不條理) irrationality; absurdity; unreasonableness. ¶ 온갖 ~를 제거하다 do away with all kinds of irregularities.

부조화(不調和) disharmony; discord (·ance). ¶ ~의 inharmonious; discordant.

부족(不足) 《모자람》 shortage; deficiency (금전의); 《결핍》 want; lack; 《불충분》 insufficiency; 《불만족》 dissatisfaction; discontent. ¶ ~한 (be) insufficient; scanty; scarce; 《서술적》 be short (of); be in want (of); be lacking (in). ¶ 천 원 ~하다 be one thousand won short / ~한 점이 없다 leave nothing to be desired. ¶ ~액 shortage; a deficit; a difference (차액) / 수면 ~ want [lack] of sleep / 식량 ~ a food shortage / 체중 ~ short weight.

부족(部族) a tribe. ¶ ~의 tribal.

부존(賦存) ~하다 be blessed [favored] 《with》. ¶ ~자원 natural

부주의(不注意) carelessness; heedlessness; negligence. ~하다 be careless 《in, about》; be inattentive 《to》; be heedless (negligent). ¶ ~하게 carelessly; heedlessly / ~로 due to one's carelessness.

부지(扶支) ~하다 bear; endure; stand; hold out. ¶ ~하다 maintain (sustain) one's life.

부지(敷地) a site; a lot; the ground. ¶ ~를 선정하다 [찾다] select (look for) a site 《for》.

부지기수(不知其數) being numberless (countless).

부지깽이 a poker.

부지런하다 (be) diligent; assiduous; industrious. ¶ 부지런히 diligently; industriously; assiduously; hard / 부지런한 사람 a hard worker.

부지불식간(不知不識間) ☞ 부지중.

부지중(不知中) ~에 unknowingly; unconsciously; all awares; in spite of oneself / ~에 눈물을 흘리다 be moved to tears in spite of oneself / ~에 눈을 감다 shut one's eyes instinctively.

부지하세월(不知何歲月) ~이다 Nobody can tell when it will be done (completed).

부진(不振) dullness; inactivity; depression (불경기); a slump (선수의). ~하다 be dull; inactive; depressed; stagnant; slack; be in slump(서울적).

부진(不盡) poor progress. ~하다 make poor (little) progress.

부질없다 (be) vain; useless; futile; worthless; insignificant; trivial. ¶ 부질없는 생각 a useless [an idle] thought / 부질없는 시도 a vain attempt 《to do》.

부집게 (a pair of) iron tongs.

부쩍 (우기는 모양) persistently; stubbornly; (급격히) rapidly; (현저히) remarkably. ¶ ~ …이 향상되다 make a remarkable improvement 《in》.

부차적(副次的) secondary.

부착(附着) ~하다 adhere (stick, cling) to. ‖ ~력 adhesive power.

부창부수(夫唱婦隨) a way of life in which the wife follows the lead set by her husband.

부채 a 《folding》 fan. ¶ ~질하다 (use a) fan; fan oneself 《선동》 instigate; excite; stir up ¶ ~에 ~ 질하는 격이다 It is like adding oil to the fire.

부채(負債) a debt (빚); liabilities (채무). ¶ ~를 갚다 pay off one's debts / 그에게 5백원의 ~가 있다 I owe him 500 won. ‖ ~자 a debtor.

부처 (불타) Buddha; (불상) an image of Buddha. ¶ ~ 같은 사람 a saint of a man; a merciful person.

부처(夫妻) husband and wife; a couple. ¶ ~ Mr. and Mrs. Kim.

부총리(副總理) the deputy Prime Minister; the vice-premier.

부추(植) a leek.

부추기다 stir up; incite; instigate. ¶ 부추겨서 …하게 하다 incite (instigate) 《a person》 to do.

부축하다 help 《a person》; give one's arm to. ¶ 노부인을 부축해 내리다 help an old lady off (out of) the car.

부치다¹ (힘에) be beyond one's power (capacity); be too much for 《one》.

부치다² ① (보내다) send; forward; ship (배·차로); mail (우송); remit (돈을). ¶ 편지를 ~ send a letter 《to》 / 기차로 물건을 ~ ship goods by rail / 돈을 수표로 ~ remit money by a check. ② 《관용적 표현》 ¶ 불문에 ~ overlook; pass over 《a small offense》 / 토의에 ~ put 《a question》 to debate / 재판에 ~ commit 《a case》 for trial.   (grow.

부치다³ (논밭을) cultivate; farm;

부치다⁴ (번철에) griddle; cook on a griddle; fry 《eggs》.

부칙(附則) 《규칙》 an additional rule (clause).

부침(浮沈) ups and downs 《of life》; rise and fall; vicissitudes 《of life》.

부탁(付託) a request; a favor. ~하다 (make a) request; ask 《a person to do》; beg; solicit. ¶ ~을 들어주다 《거절하다》 comply (decline) 《a person's》 request / ~이 있다 I have a favor to ask of you. / …의 ~으로 at the request of...

부탄 (化) butane.

부터 (사람) from; through. ¶ 친구로 ~ 온 편지 a letter from a friend. (장소) from; out of; off. ¶ 서울로 ~ 인천까지 from Seoul to Inch'ŏn. 《시간》 from; since (이래); after (이후). ¶ 세시 ~ 다섯시까지 from three to five / 그 때 ~ since then / 지금 ~ from now on. ④ 《판단의 기준》 from; by. ¶ 이러한 사실로 ~ 판단하면 judging from these facts. ⑤ (범위) from. ¶ 값은 10달러 ~ 20달러까지이다 The prices range (vary) from ten to twenty dollars. ⑥ (순서) beginning with; first; starting from. ¶ 무엇 ~ 할 까 What shall I begin with? / 너 ~ 해라 You begin.

부통령(副統領) the Vice-President

부패(腐敗) 《물질의》 decay; rot; spoiling; decomposition; 《정신의》 corruption; degeneration. ~하다 《물질이》 go 〔become〕 bad; rot; spoil; decay; 《정신이》 rot; corrupt; degenerate; become corrupted. ¶ ~한 rotten; spoiled; decayed; corrupt 《officials》 / 하기 쉬운 perishable; corruptible / 지금의 정치가들은 형편없이 ~되어 있다 Politicians today are hopelessly corrupt. / ~공무원 a tainted 〔corrupt〕 official.

부평초(浮萍草) 〔植〕 a duckweed.

부표(否票) a "nay" vote; a vote "no". ¶ ~를 던지다 vote against 〔in opposition to〕….

부표(浮標) a 〔marker〕 buoy. ¶ ~등 a buoy light.

부풀다 《팽창하다》 be bulky; swell 《up, with》; bulge; rise 《빵이》; expand 《팽창하다》. ¶ 빵이 ~ bread rises / 희망으로 가슴이 부풀었다 My breast swelled with hope.

부풀리다 《팽창시키다》 swell 〔out〕; bulge 《one's pocket with candies》; inflate 《a balloon with gas》; puff out 《one's cheeks》.

부품(部品) parts 《of a machine》; 《car》 components. ¶ ~을 교환하다 replace a part. / ~판매업자 a parts supplier.

부피 bulk; volume; size. ¶ ~있는 bulky; voluminous.

부하(負荷) ① 《짐》 a burden; a load. ② 〔電〕 load. ‖ ~전류 〔을, 시험〕 a load current 〔factor, test〕.

부하(部下) one's men; a subordinate; a follower 《추종자》. ¶ ~사병 the soldiers under one's command / …의 ~로 3년간 일하다 work 〔serve〕 under 《a person》 for three years / 그에겐 우수한 ~가 몇명 있다 He has some able men under him.

부합(符合) ~하다 agree 〔tally, coincide〕 with. ¶ 그의 증언은 사실과 ~한다 His statement tallies 〔fits in〕 with the facts.

부형(父兄) parents and brothers.

부호(符號) a mark; a sign; a symbol; a code 《전신》. ¶ ~화하다 〔convert〕 《information》 into code; encode; code.

부호(富豪) a rich man; a man of wealth; a millionaire 《백만장자》; a billionaire 《억만장자》.

부화(孵化) hatching; incubation. ~하다 hatch 〔incubate〕 《chickens》. ‖ 인공 ~ artificial incubation / 인공 ~기 an artificial incubator.

부화뇌동(附和雷同) blind following. ~하다 follow 《another》 blindly; echo 《another's views》.

부활(復活) revival 《회복》; restoration 《재홍》; 《예수의》 the Resurrection 《of Christ》. ~하다 revive; restore; resurrect. ¶ 그 나라에서는 군주제가 ~했다 The monarchy was restored in the country. ‖ ~절 Easter.

부흥(復興) revival; reconstruction; rehabilitation. ~하다 be reconstructed; be revived. ¶ 한국의 전후 ~ Korean's postwar rehabilitation. ‖ ~사업 reconstruction 〔rehabilitation〕 work / 경제 ~ economic rehabilitation.

북[1] 〔樂〕 a drum. ¶ ~을 치다 beat a drum / ~치는 사람 a drummer.

북[2] 《베틀의》 a spindle; a shuttle.

북(北) the north. ☞ 북쪽. ¶ ~의 north; northern / ~으로 〔to the〕 north; northward(s).

북경(北京) 《중국의》 Peking; Beijing.

북괴(北傀) the North Korean puppet regime. ‖ ~의 Scandinavian.

북구(北歐) Northern Europe.

북극(北極) the North 〔Arctic〕 Pole. ¶ ~의 arctic; polar; pole. ‖ ~곰 a polar bear / ~광 the nothern lights; the aurora borealis / ~권 the Arctic Circle / ~성 the polestar / ~양 the Arctic Ocean / ~지방 the Arctic region / ~탐험 an Arctic 〔polar〕 expedition. ‖ ~지방 〔northern part.

북녘(北-) the north(ward); the

북단(北端) the north(ern) end.

북대서양(北大西洋) the North Atlantic 〔Ocean〕. ‖ ~조약기구 the North Atlantic Treaty Organization 《생략 NATO》.

북데기 waste straw.

북돋우다 ① 《북주다》 heap earth around 《a plant》. ② 《원기·힘을》 cheer up; stimulate; encourage. ¶ 사기를 ~ stimulate the morale 《of troops》.

북동(北東) northeast 《생략 N.E.》. ‖ ~풍 a northeasterly wind.

북두칠성(北斗七星) the Great Bear 〔Dipper〕; the Plow 《英》.

북미(北美) North America. ¶ ~의 North American / ~대륙 the North American Continent. ‖ ~자유무역협정 the North America Free Trade Agreement 《생략 NAFTA》.

북반구(北半球) the Northern Hemisphere.

북방(北方) the north; the northward. ¶ ~의 northern; northerly / ~에 〔으로〕 to 〔on〕 the north; in the direction of the north; northward(s). ‖ ~한계선 the Northern Boundary Line 《생략 NBL》.

북부(北部) the north(ern part).

북북 《세게》《scrape, scratch》

북북동(北北東) north-northeast.
북북서(北北西) north-northwest.
북빙양(北氷洋) the Arctic Ocean.
북상(北上) ~하다 go (up) north; proceed northward.
북새 hustle; bustle; commotion; hubbub. ¶ ~를 놓다 hustle and bustle / ~통에 in the confusion; during the commotion.
북서(北西) northwest 《생략 N.W.》. ∥ ~풍 a northwesterly wind.
북슬개 a shaggy dog; a poodle.
북슬북슬 ~하다 (be) bushy; shaggy.
북안(北岸) the northern coast.
북양(北洋) the northern sea.
북어(北魚) a dried pollack.
북위(北緯)〖地〗the north latitude 《생략 N.L.》. ¶ ~37도 30분 lat. 37°30´N.
북적거리다 bustle; be crowded 〔jammed〕 《with people》; be thronged 《with》. ¶ 거리는 구경꾼으로 북적거렸다 The streets were thronged with onlookers.
북적북적 in a bustle; full of stir; bustling.
북주다 hill 《potatoes》; heap soil around 《a plant》; earth up.
북진(北進) ~하다 march 〔go〕 north; sail northward.
북쪽(北一) the north《☞ 북》. ¶ ~의 north; northern; northerly / ~으로 northward 《ward》.
북채〖樂〗a drumstick.
북풍(北風) the north(erly) wind. ¶ 살을 에는 ~ a biting 〔freezing〕 north wind.
북한(北韓) North Korea.
북해(北海) the North Sea.
북향(北向) a northern aspect 〔exposure〕. ~하다 face (the) north. ∥ ~집 a house facing north.
북회귀선(北回歸線)〖地〗the Tropic of Cancer.
분(分) ①《시간・각도의》a minute 《of an hour, of a degree》. ¶ 15 ~ a quarter 《of an hour》; fifteen minutes. ②(1/10) one-tenth; a tenth. ¶ 1할 5~ fifteen percent.
분(憤・忿)《분함》vexation; chagrin; mortification;《분개》resentment; indignation; wrath; anger. ¶ 아, 분하다 How vexing! / How disappointing! / 너무 ~해서 책상을 두들기다 pound the table in a fit of anger.
분(盆) a flower pot.
분(粉)(face) powder. ¶ ~을 바르다 powder *one*'s face. ∥ ~내 the smell of powder.
…분(分) ①《부분》a part. ¶ 3~ 의 1 one (a) third / 5만~의 1 지도 a one-to-fifty-thousand map.
② 《분량》 ¶ 2일~의 양식 food for two days / 식사 5인~ dinner for five people / 5인~의 일을 하다 do the work of five men. ③《함유량》a percentage; content. ¶ 알코올~이 많은 술 liquor containing a high percentage of alcohol. ④《성분》an ingredient; a component. ¶ 주성~ the main ingredient.
분가(分家) a branch family. ~하다 establish 〔set up〕 a branch 〔separate〕 family.
분간(分揀)《분별》distinction; discrimination. ~하다 distinguish 《between A and B, A from B》; tell 〔know〕《A from B》; discriminate 《between》. ¶ ~하기 어려운 indistinguishable; unrecognizable.
분갑(粉匣) a compact.
분개(分介)〖簿〗journalizing. ~하다 journalize. ∥ ~장 a journal.
분개(憤慨) indignation; resentment. ~하다 be (get) very angry; be indignant 《at》. ¶ ~하여 in resentment 〔a rage〕 / ~시키다 enrage; infuriate.
분격(奮激)☞ 분기(奮起).
분견(分遣) detachment. ~하다 detach. ∥ ~대 a detachment; a contingent.
분결같다(粉一) (be) clear 〔smooth〕 and spotless; fair-skinned. ¶ 얼굴이 ~ have a fair-skinned face.
분계(分界) a boundary; a border; 《한계》 demarcation. ~하다 demarcate; delimit. ∥ ~선 a boundary (demarcation) line.
분골쇄신(粉骨碎身) ~하다 do *one*'s very best; exert *oneself* to the utmost.
분과(分科) a branch; a section; a department. ¶ 과학의 한 ~ a branch of science. ∥ ~위원회 a subcommittee.
분관(分館) an annex; a detached building.
분광(分光) spectrum. ∥ ~기 a spectroscope / ~사진 a spectrogram / ~학 spectroscopy.
분교(分校) a branch school.
분국(分局) a branch (office).
분권(分權) decentralization (of authority 〔power〕)《지방분권》. ∥ ~제 decentralism.
분규(紛糾) a complication; confusion; a trouble; a dispute. ¶ ~를 일으키다 cause 〔arouse, make〕 trouble / ~를 거듭하다 grow more and more confused.
분극(分極)〖電〗polarization.
분기(分岐) ~하다 branch off; diverge; be ramified. ∥ ~선 a branch (line) / ~점 a turning point; a crossroads.
분기(分期) a quarter (of the year); a quarter term; one fourth of a

fiscal year. ¶ 제1[2]~ the first [second] quarter of the year / 나는 집세를 ~로 낸다 I pay my rent by the quarter. / 그 회사는 제1~에 이익이 11퍼센트 증가했다 The company's profits rose by 11 percent in the first quarter.

분기(奮起) ~하다 rouse *oneself* ⦅*to action*⦆; be inspired. ¶ ~시키다 inspire ⦅*a person*⦆; stir ⦅*a person*⦆ up; rouse ⦅*a person*⦆ into activity.

분꽃(粉—) [植] a four-o'clock; a marvel-of-Peru.

분납(分納) an installment payment. ~하다 pay ⦅*one's school fees*⦆ by [in] installments.

분노(憤怒) (a) fury; rage; indignation. ~하다 be [get] angry ⦅*at, with*⦆; be enraged.

분뇨(糞尿) excreta; excrement and urine; night soil. ¶ ~차 a honey wagon [truck]; a dung cart / ~ 처리 sewage disposal.

분단(分斷) dividing into parts. ~하다 divide into parts; cut in halves. ∥ ~국 a divided [partitioned] country / ~책 a divide and rule policy [strategy].

분담(分擔) ⦅책임의⦆ partial responsibility; ⦅할당된 일·의무⦆ assignment; ⦅비용·일의 부담⦆ one's share. ~하다 share ⦅*with, between, among*⦆; take *one's* share of ⦅*the responsibility*⦆. ¶ 비용을 ~하다 share the expenses with ⦅*a person*⦆ / 일을 ~시키다 allot a portion of the work to each. ∥ ~금 a share of the expenses / ~액 an alloted amount; an allotment.

분당(分黨) ~하다 secede ⦅*from a political party*⦆; split up ⦅*into two parties*⦆.

분대(分隊) a squad⦅육군⦆; a division⦅해군⦆. ∥ ~장 a squad leader⦅육군⦆; a divisional officer⦅해군⦆.

분란(紛亂) ⦅혼란⦆ disorder; confusion; ⦅말썽⦆ trouble. ¶ ~을 일으키다 cause [raise] trouble; throw ⦅*something*⦆ into confusion.

분량(分量) quantity; amount; a dose⦅약의⦆. ¶ 많은[적은] ~ a large [small] quantity / ~이 늘다[줄다] gain [diminish] in quantity.

분류(分溜) [化] fractional distillation; fractionation. ~하다 fractionate.

분류(分類) (a) classification; grouping; assortment; arrangement ⦅정리⦆. ~하다 classify; divide ⦅*things*⦆ into classes; group; sort. ¶ 상품을 색에 따라 ~하다 classify goods according to colors / 같은 종류의 것으로 ~하다 class *one* with *another*. ∥ ~번호 a class number / ~법 classification system / ~표 a classified list [table] / ~학 taxonomy.

분류(奔流) a rapid stream; a torrent.

분리(分離) (a) separation; segregation; secession⦅이탈⦆. ~하다 ⦅떼다⦆ separate ⦅*a thing*⦆ from; segregate ⦅*A from B*⦆; secede ⦅*from a party*⦆. ¶ ~할 수 없는 inseparable / 정치와 종교의 ~ separation of politics and religion / 물과 기름을 ~하다 separate oil from water. ∥ ~과세 separate taxation / ~대(帶) ⦅도로 중앙의⦆ a median [strip] ⦅美⦆.

분리수거(分離收去) separate collection. ¶ 쓰레기 ~ separate garbage collection.

분립(分立) ~하다 separate (segregate, secede) ⦅*from*⦆; become independent ⦅*of*⦆.

분만(分娩) childbirth; delivery. ~하다 give birth to ⦅*a boy*⦆. ∥ ~비 childbirth expenses / ~실 a delivery room / 자연 ~ natural childbirth.

분말(粉末) powder; dust. ¶ ~ 모양의 powdered / ~로 하다 powder; reduce ⦅*something*⦆ to powder.

분망(奔忙) being busy. ~하다 (be) very busy; be fully occupied [heavily engaged] ⦅*with work*⦆.

분매(分賣) ~하다 sell ⦅*parts of a set*⦆ singly [separately].

분명(分明) clearness. ~하다 (be) clear; distinct; plain; evident; obvious; unquestionable. ¶ ~히 clearly; plainly; apparently / ~한 증거 a positive proof / ~히 하다 make clear; clarify / ~해 지다 become clear [plain].

분모(分母) [數] a denominator.

분묘(墳墓) a tomb; a grave.

분무(噴霧) ~하다 atomize; spray. ∥ ~기 a spray(er); a vaporizer; an atomizer⦅살충제를 ~기로 뿌리다 spray insecticide on ⦅over⦆ ⦅*plants*⦆.

분발(奮發) ~하다 put a lot of effort ⦅*into*⦆; exert *oneself* ⦅*to do*⦆; make strenuous efforts ⦅*to do*⦆.

분방(奔放) ~하다 (be) free; unrestrained. ¶ ~하게 freely; without restraint / 자유 ~하게 행동하다 have *one's* own way; behave as *one* pleases.

분배(分配) distribution; share; division. ~하다 distribute ⦅*among*⦆; divide ⦅*among, between*⦆; share ⦅*with, between*⦆ / ...의 ~를 받다 have [get] a share ⦅*of*⦆; share in ⦅*the profit*⦆. ∥ ~액[금] a

분별 share of profit; a dividend.
분별(分別) ① 〖사려분별〗 discretion; sense; 〖양식〗 wisdom; common sense. 〖판단〗 judgment. ~하다 judge; discern; use discretion. ¶ ~이 있는 sensible; discreet; prudent / ~이 없는 indiscreet; imprudent; thoughtless / 그는 ~이 있는 사내다 He is a man of sense. ② 〖구별〗 distinction; difference; discrimination. ~하다 tell 〖know〗 (*A from B*); distinguish (*between A and B*).
분봉(分蜂) ~하다 hive off.
분부(分付·吩咐) the bidding of a superior; an order; 〖지시〗 directions. ~하다 bid; tell; order; give directions. ¶ ~대로 하다 do as one is bidden; act according to orders.
분분하다(紛紛―) ¶ 제설(諸說)이 ~ There are diversities of opinions.
분비(分泌) secretion. ~하다 secrete, produce. ‖ ~기관 a secretory organ / ~물 a secretion / ~선(腺) a secreting gland.
분사(分詞) 〖文〗 a participle. ‖ ~ 구문 a participial construction / 현재〖과거〗~ a present 〖past〗 participle.
분사(噴射) a jet. ~하다 emit a jet (*of liquid fuel*); jet (out). ¶ 엔진이 화염을 ~하고 있다 The engine is jetting flames. / 추진기붙이 ~ 제트기 a jet-engined plane / ~ 추진엔진 a jet engine.
분산(分散) dispersion; (a) breakup 〖이산〗. ~하다 break up; scatter; disperse. ¶ 인구를 ~하다 disperse the population / 프리즘은 빛을 ~한다 A prism breaks up light. / 공장을 교외로 ~시키다 decentralize industries into the suburbs.
분석(分析) (an) analysis; an assay (광석의). ~하다 analyze; assay. ¶ ~적인 analytic(al). ‖ ~학 analytics / ~학자 an analyst (assayer) / ~화학 analytical chemistry. 〖a branch (of).〗
분설(分設) ~하다 establish 〖set up〗
분성(分性) 〖理〗 divisibility.
분손(分損) 〖經〗 a partial loss.
분쇄(粉碎) ~하다 (be) reduce to powder; pulverize; 〖가루로〗 shatter 〖smash〗 to pieces; 〖격파〗 crush; smash; annihilate. ‖ ~기 a pulverizer; a grinder; a crusher.
분수(分數) ① 〖분별〗 discretion; propriety; good sense; prudence. ¶ ~없다 lack prudence. ② 〖처지〗 one's lot (status, place); one's means; one's social standing. ¶ ~에 맞게〖안 맞게〗(live) within 〖above〗 one's means /

분외 ~를 지키다 keep to one's sphere in life; keep within one's bounds / ~를 모르다 fail to know oneself; get oneself above. ③ 〖數〗 fraction; a fractional number. ¶ ~의 fractional. ‖ ~식 a fractional expression.
분수(噴水) a fountain; a jet (*of water*). ‖ ~기 a waterspout.
분수령(分水嶺) 〖form〗 a watershed 〖英〗; a divide 〖美〗.
분승(分乘) ~하다 ride separately.
분식(扮飾) (an) embellishment; (a) decoration; adornment. ~하다 embellish; adorn; decorate. ‖ ~결산 fraudulent 〖rigged〗 accounts; window-dressed accounts; window dressing.
분식(粉食) (have) food made from flour. ¶ ~을 장려하다 encourage the use of flour for food.
분신(分身) ① 〖佛〗 an incarnation of the Buddha. ② 〖제2의 나〗 the other self; the alter ego; one's child.
분신(焚身) ~하다 burn oneself to death. ¶ ~자살 burning oneself to death; self-burning.
분실(分室) a detached 〖branch〗 office.
분실(紛失) loss. ~하다 lose; be lost 〖missing〗. ‖ ~물 a lost 〖missing〗 article / ~신고 a report of the loss (*of an article*).
분야(分野) a field; an area; a branch. ¶ 과학의 각 ~ various fields 〖spheres〗 of science / ~가 다르다 be off (out of) one's line. ‖ 연구~ a field (an area) of study (research).
분양(分讓) ~하다 sell 〖land〗 in lots. ¶ 이 아파트는 지금 ~중이다 The apartment house is being sold in lots. ‖ ~주택〖지〗 houses 〖land〗 offered for sale in lots (*by a real estate corporation*).
분업(分業) division of labor; specialization. ~하다 divide work (*among*); specialize (*in*).
분연(憤然) ¶ ~히 indignantly; in a rage.
분연(奮然) ¶ ~히 resolutely; courageously; vigorously.
분열(分列) ~하다 (be) file off. ¶ ~행진하다 march in file. ‖ ~식 a march-past (~식을 행하다 march in review; march past).
분열(分裂) a split; division; breakup. ~하다 (be) split (*in, into*); break up; divide. ¶ 정당의 ~ a split in a political party. ‖ ~생식 reproduction by fission.
분외(分外) 〖과분한〗 beyond one's lot (status); undeserved; undue / ~의 영광 an undeserved honor.

분요(紛擾) ☞ 분란.
분원(分院) a detached building; a branch hospital (institute).
분위기(雰圍氣) (produce, create) an atmosphere. ¶ 자유로운 ~에서 in an atmosphere of freedom / ~를 조성하다 (깨뜨리다) create (destroy) an atmosphere.
분유(粉乳) powdered milk. ¶ 탈지~ nonfat dry milk.
분자(分子) ① [化] a molecule; [數] a numerator. ∥ ~식 molecular weight / ~식 a molecular formular. ② 《사람》 an element. ¶ 불평~ discontented elements / 정계의 부패~를 일소해야 한다 We must purge corrupt elements from the political world.
분장(分掌) division of duties. ¶ 사무를 ~하다 divide (office) duties 《among》.
분장(扮裝) make-up; disguise (변장). ~하다 make *oneself* up 《as》; be dressed 《as》; disguise *oneself* 《as》. ¶ 여자로 ~하다 be dressed (disguised) as a woman. ∥ ~실 a dressing room.
분재(分財) ~하다 distribute *one's* property 《among》.
분재(盆栽) a bonsai; a dwarf tree in a pot; a potted plant; 《행위》 raising dwarf tree. ~하다 raise plants in pots.
분쟁(紛爭) a trouble; a dispute; (a) strife. ¶ ~의 씨 an apple of dispute / 국제~ an international dispute / ~중에 있다 be in conflict (dispute) 《with》 / ~에 휘말려 들다 get entangled (involved) in a dispute. ∥ 민족~ ethnic strife.
분전(奮戰) a desperate fight; hard (hot) fighting. ~하다 fight desperately (hard).
분점(分店) a branch store (shop).
분주(奔走) ~하다 (be) busy; engaged; occupied. ¶ ~하게 busily; in hurried manner.
분지(盆地) a basin. [ture(백률).
분지르다 break; snap (딱하다); frac-
분책(分冊) a separate volume.
분첩(粉貼) (a powder) puff.
분초(分秒) a minute and a second; a moment. ¶ ~를 다투다 There isn't a moment to lose.
분출(噴出) ~하다 (액체를) gush out; spurt; spout; 《연기·가스·화염이》 belch (out); shoot up (공중으로); jet; emit. ¶ 석유가 유전에서 ~하다 the well spouts oil / 화산이 용암을 ~하다 volcanoes spew out lava. ∥ ~물 jet; ejecta; eruptions (화산의).
분침(分針) the minute (long) hand.
분탄(粉炭) slack; dust coal.
분탕질(焚蕩―) ~하다 squander;

run through; dissipate.
분통(憤痛) resentment; vexation. ¶ ~이 터지다 be greatly vexed; be mortified; resent 《at》.
분투(奮鬪) a hard struggle; strenuous efforts. ~하다 struggle; (hard); strive; exert *oneself* 《to do》; make strenuous efforts 《to do》.
분파(分派) a sect; a faction. ∥ ~활동 factional activities.
분패(憤敗) ☞ 석패 (惜敗).
분포(分布) (a) distribution. ~하다 be distributed; range 《from a place to another》. ¶ ~도 a distribution chart / ~지역 an area of distribution.
분풀이(憤―) ~하다 vent [give vent to] *one's* anger 《on》; get back at 《a person》; revenge *oneself* on 《a person》 for 《something》. ¶ ~로 out of spite; by way of revenge.
분필(粉筆) a piece of chalk.
분하다(憤―) ① 《원통》 (be) mortifying; vexing. ¶ 분해서 못 견디다 be out of vexation / 분해하다 be [feel] vexed [mortified] 《at》; resent. ② 《아깝다》 (be) regrettable; sorry. ¶ 분해하다 regret; be regretful.
분할(分割) division; partition. ~하다 divide 《a thing into》; partition; cut [split] up. ¶ 토지를 ~하여 팔다 sell *one's* land in lots / ~지불로 차를 사다 buy 《a car》 on the installment (easy payment) plan; 《美》 buy 《a car》 on time. ∥ ~상환 redemption by installments.
분할(分轄) ~하다 divide for administrative purposes.
분해(分解) 《분석》 analysis; [化] resolution; decomposition; 《해체》 dismantling; disassembly. ~하다 《분석》 analyze; decompose; resolve; 《해체》 break up; take 《a machine》 to pieces. ¶ 물을 수소와 산소로 ~하다 decompose water into hydrogen and oxygen. ∥ ~수리 an overhaul / ~작용 disintegration / ~효소 breakdown enzyme.
분향(焚香) ~하다 burn incense.
분홍(粉紅) pink (color).
분화(分化) differentiation; specialization. ~하다 differentiate; specialize; branch into.
분화(噴火) an eruption; volcanic activity. ~하다 erupt; burst (go) into eruption. ∥ ~구 a crater / ~산 a volcano. [chapter.
분회(分會) a branch; a (local)
붇다 ① 《물에》 swell (up); become sodden; get soaked. ② 《늘다》 increase; gain; grow bulky (부피); swell. ¶ 강물이

the river rises.
불 ① 《일반적》 fire; 《화염》 flame; blaze. ¶ ~ 붙기 쉬운 easily set on fire; easy to catch fire; inflammable / ~(이) 붙다 catch [take] fire / ~을 붙이다 [놓다] set fire 《to》; set 《a house》 on fire / ~을 일으키다 make a fire / ~을 끄다 put out a fire. ② 《등화》 a light; a lamp; an electric light. ¶ ~을 켜다 (make a) light; light a lamp; switch [turn] on the light(s) / ~을 끄다 put out [turn off] the light (a lamp). ③ 《화재》 a fire. ¶ ~을 내다 start [cause] a fire / ~이 나다 a fire breaks out / ~을 조심하다 look out for fire; take precautions against fire. ‖ ~ 바다 a sea of flame.
불(佛) a dollar. ☞ 달러.
불(佛) 《부처님》 Buddha. ② 《프랑스》 France.
불…(不) not; un-; in-; non-.
불가(不可) ~하다 (be) wrong; not right; bad; improper; unadvisable.
불가(佛家) ① 《불문》 (Buddhist) priesthood; a Buddhist《신자》. ② 《절》 a Buddhist temple.
불가결(不可缺) ~하다 (be) indispensable 《to》; essential 《to》.
불가능(不可能) impossibility. ~하다 (be) impossible; unattainable; impracticable. ¶ ~한 일 an impossibility.
불가리아 Bulgaria. ¶ ~의 Bulgarian / ~ 사람 a Bulgarian.
불가분(不可分) indivisibility. ¶ ~의 inseparable; indivisible / ~의 관계에 있다 be inseparably related 《to each other》.
불가결(不可抗) inevitably; whether willing or not; willy-nilly. ¶ ~ 해야(만) 하다 have no choice but to do.
불가사리 [動] a starfish; an asteroid.
불가사의(不可思議) (a) mystery; a wonder; a miracle《기적》. ~하다 (be) incomprehensible; mysterious; strange; marvelous.
불가시(不可視) invisibility. ‖ ~광선 invisible) rays.
불가역(不可逆) ~적인 irreversible《changes》. ‖ ~성(性) irreversibility / ~현상 an irreversible phenomenon.
불가침(不可侵) nonaggression; inviolability《신성》. ¶ ~의 inviolable; sacred. ‖ ~권 an inviolable right / ~조약 a nonaggression pact [treaty]《with》.
불가피(不可避) ~의 inevitable; unavoidable.
불가항력(不可抗力) an irresistible force; *force majeure*《프》; an act of God. ¶ ~의 unavoidable; inevitable; beyond human control / ~이다 be inevitable; beyond our control.
불가해(不可解) ~한 mysterious; incomprehensible; strange / ~한 일 a mystery; an enigma.
불간섭(不干涉) nonintervention; noninterference. ~하다 do not interfere [meddle]《in, with》. ‖ ~주의 a nonintervention [laissez-faire] policy.
불감증(不感症) [醫] frigidity. ¶ ~의 여자 a frigid woman / ~이 되다 grow insensible 《to》.
불개미 [蟲] a red ant.
불개입(不介入) nonintervention; noninvolvement. ‖ ~정책 [주의] a nonintervention policy.
불거지다 ① 《속에 있는 것이》 protrude; jut out; bulge out; swell out. ② 《숨겼던 것이》 appear; come out.
불건전(不健全) ¶ ~한 unsound; unwholesome; unhealthy.
불겅거리다 be chewy 〔lumpy, leathery〕.
불결(不潔) ~하다 (be) dirty; unclean; filthy; foul; unsanitary. ‖ ~한 물 foul 〔dirty〕 water.
불경(不敬) ~한 disrespectful; irreverent. ‖ ~죄 lese majesty.
불경(佛經) the Buddhist scriptures; the sutras.
불경기(不景氣) 《일반의》 hard 〔bad〕 times; dullness; 《상업의》 (business) depression; slump. ¶ 심각한 ~ a serious depression.
불경제(不經濟) bad economy; a waste《of time, energy, money》. ¶ ~의 uneconomical; expensive.
불계승(不計勝) 《바둑》 a one-sided game. ~하다 win《a game》 by a wide margin.
불고(不顧) ~하다 neglect; disregard; ignore; be indifferent《about》; pay no attention《to》.
불고기 *bulgogi*; thin-sliced grilled meat.
불공(不恭) ¶ ~한 insolent; impolite.
불공(佛供) (offer) a Buddhist mass.
불공대천지수(不共戴天之讎) a mortal foe; a sworn enemy.
불공정(不公正) ~하다 (be) unfair; unjust. ¶ ~거래 unfair trade.
불공평(不公平) ~하다 (be) partial; unequal; unfair; unjust. ¶ ~한 세무 행정 the unfair tax system / ~ 하게 다루다 treat《a person》 unfairly.
불과(不過) only; mere(ly)《지나지 않는》 nothing but…; no more than…. ¶ 그것은 구실에 ~하다 It

불과 is nothing but an excuse.
불과(佛果)〖佛〗 Buddhahood; Nirvana〖梵〗.
불교(佛敎) Buddhism. ¶ ~의 Buddhist(ic). ‖ ~도(徒) a Buddhist: a follower of Buddhism / ~문화 Buddhist civilization〔culture〕.
불구(不具) deformity; being deformed; maimed; crippled(절름발이); disabled. ¶ ~자 a disabled person; a (physically) handicapped person.
불구(不拘) ¶ ~하고 in spite of; despite (of); notwithstanding; 《상관 없이》 regardless〔irrespective〕 《of》 / 비가 오는데도 ~하고 in spite of〔notwithstanding〕 the rain / 연령〔성별〕 ~하고 irrespective of age〔sex〕.
불구속(不拘束) nonrestraint. ¶ ~으로 without physical restraint. ‖ ~입건 booking without detention.
불굴(不屈) ¶ ~의 indomitable; dauntless / ~의 정신 an indomitable spirit.
불귀(不歸)《죽음》 ¶ ~의 객이 되다 pass away; go on *one's* last journey.
불규칙(不規則) irregularity. ~하다 (be) irregular; unsystematic; unsteady. ¶ ~하게 irregularly; unsystematically / ~한 생활을 하다 live an irregular life.
불균형(不均衡) lack of balance; imbalance; inequality; disproportion. ~하다 (be) out of balance; ill-balanced; disproportionate. ¶ 경제적인 ~을 시정하다 redress〔reduce〕 the economic imbalance〔dish.
불그데데하다 (be) somberly red.
불그레하다 (be) reddish.
불급(不急) ¶ ~한 not urgent〔pressing〕. 〔red.
불긋불긋 ~하다 be dotted with
불기(一氣) heat〔a sign〕 of fire. ¶ ~ 없는 방 an unheated room.
불기둥 a pillar of fire〔flames〕.
불기소(不起訴) non-prosecution. ¶ ~로 ~하다 drop a case / ~가 되다 be not indicted. ‖ ~처분 a disposition not to institute a public action.
불길 a fire〔flame, blaze〕. ¶ ~에 휩싸이다 be wrapped in flames / ~을 잡다 put out a fire; bring 〔get〕 a fire under control.
불길(不吉) ¶ ~한 unlucky; ominous; ill-omened / ~한 예감 an ominous presentiment / ~한 전조 an ill omen.
불김 《in》 the warmth of a fire.
불까다 castrate; emasculate; geld.
불꽃 《화염》 a flame; a blaze; 《불똥》 a spark. 《꽃불》 fireworks.

¶ ~ 튀는 논전(論戰)《have》 a hot〔heated〕 discussion / ~이 튀다 spark / ~을 쏴 올리다 display〔set off〕 fireworks. ‖ ~놀이 a fireworks display.
불끈《갑자기》 suddenly; 《단단히》 firmly; fast; tightly. ¶ ~ 화내다 flare up; fly into a passion / 주먹을 ~ 쥐다 clench *one's* fist.
불나방 a tiger moth.
불난리(一亂離) 《in》 the confusion of a fire.
불놀이(불장난) playing with fire. ~하다 play with fire.
불능(不能) impossibility(불가능); inability(무능); impotence(성적인). ¶ 해결 ~의 문제 an insoluble problem. ¶ 지급 ~ insolvency; *one's* inability to pay / 통행 ~《게시》 No road, *or* No passing.
불다¹《바람이》 blow; breathe. ¶ 바람이 세게 분다 It blows hard.
불다² ① 《입으로》 blow; breathe out (숨을). ◇ 촛불을 불어 끄다 blow out a candle. ② 《악기를》 play 《a flute》; sound 《a trumpet》; blow 《a whistle》. ③ 《죄를》 confess 《*one's* guilt》.
불단(佛壇) a Buddhist altar.
불당(佛堂) a Buddhist shrine〔temple〕.   〔fever.
불덩어리 a fireball; 《고열》 a high
불도(佛徒) a Buddhist; a believer in Buddhism. 〔Buddhism.
불도(佛道) Buddhist doctrines.
불도저 a bulldozer. ¶ ~로 땅을 밀다 bulldoze land.
불독《개》 a bulldog.
불두덩 the pubic region.
불똥 a spark (of fire). ¶ ~을 튀기다 spark; give out sparks.
불뚱거리다 take〔get into〕 a huff; swell up with anger.
불뚱이 a passion; a fit of temper; a short-〔hot-〕tempered person(사람). ¶ ~ 내다〔누르다〕 lose 〔control〕 *one's* temper; fly into a 〔keep down *one's*〕 passion.
불란서(佛蘭西) France. 〖프랑스.
불량(不良) ¶ ~의 《상태·품질이》 (be) bad; inferior; 《행실이》 (be) wicked; depraved; delinquent / ~해지다 go wrong〔to the bad〕; be degraded; become delinquent. ‖ ~도제 a nonconductor / ~배 a scoundrel; a hoodlum / ~소년소녀 a juvenile delinquent / ~약품 illegal〔fraudulent〕 drugs / ~채권 a bad debt / ~품 a substandard〔rejected〕 article / ~학생 a disorderly〔bad〕 student.
불러내다 call 《a person》; 《전화통에》 call 《a person》 up 《on the phone》; 《꾀어내다》 lure 《a person》 out of 《from》.

불러오다 call 《a person》 to one's presence; summon; 《사람을 보내》 send for 《a person》.

불러일으키다 arouse; rouse; stir up. ¶ 여론을 ~ arouse [stir up] public opinion / 주의를 ~ call 《a person's》 attention 《to》.

불려가다 be summoned to 《the police》. ¶ 사장에게 ~ be called before the president.

불로(不老) eternal youth. ‖ ~불사 eternal youth and immortality / ~장생 eternal youth and long life / ~초 an elixir of life.

불로소득(不勞所得) an unearned income; a windfall income. ‖ ~생활자 a person living on unearned incomes; a *rentier* (프).

불룩하다 (be) swollen; baggy; fat; bulgy.

불륜(不倫) immorality. ¶ ~의 immoral 《conduct》; illicit 《love》.

불리(不利) a disadvantage; a handicap. ¶ ~한 disadvantageous; unfavorable / ~한 입장에 서다 be at a disadvantage; be handicapped / …에게 ~한 증언을 하다 testify against 《the accused》.

불리다¹ 《배를》 fill 《one's stomach》; 《사복을》 enrich oneself 《with public fund》; feather one's nest.

불리다² ① 《쇠를》 forge; temper. ② 《곡식을》 까부르다.

불리다³ 《바람에》 be blown; blow.

불리다⁴ ① 《물에》 soak 《dip, steep》 《a thing》 in water; sodden; soften. ② 《늘리다》 increase 《one's fortune》; add 《to》.

불림 《쇠붙이의》 tempering.

불만(不滿), **불만족**(不滿足) dissatisfaction; discontent. ¶ ~스럽다 (be) unsatisfactory; dissatisfied / ~의 dissatisfied; discontented; unsatisfactory / ~으로 여기다 be not satisfied 《with》.

불매운동(不買運動) a consumer buyers'] strike [boycott]; a civic campaign to boycott some products. 「day and night.

불면불휴(不眠不休) ¶ ~의

불면증(不眠症) (suffer from) insomnia. ‖ ~환자 an insomniac.

불멸(不滅) 《정신적이》 immortality; 《물질의》 indestructibility. ¶ ~의 immortal; eternal.

불명(不明) 《사리에》 lack of brightness; 《불명료》 indistinctness; ~하다 (be) unwise; indistinct; obscure. ¶ ~원인 ~인 화재 a fire of unknown origin.

불명료(不明瞭) ~하다 (be) indistinct; obscure; not clear; vague.

불명예(不名譽) (a) dishonor; (a) disgrace; (a) shame. ¶ ~스러운 dishonorable; shameful; disgraceful. ‖ ~제대 dishonorable

discharge.

불모(不毛) ¶ ~의 barren; sterile. ‖ ~지 barren [waste] land.

불문(不問) ¶ ~하고 without regard to; regardless of 《sex》 / ~에 부치다 pass over 《a matter》; connive at 《a matter》.

불문(佛門) priesthood; Buddhism. ¶ ~에 들다 become a Buddhist.

불문가지(不問可知) ¶ ~이다 be obvious; be self-evident.

불문곡직(不問曲直) ~하다 do not inquire into the rights and wrongs 《of a case》; do not care the propriety 《of》.

불문율(不文律) an unwritten law; *lex non scripta* (라).

불미(不美) ¶ ~한 〔스러운〕 ugly; unsavory; unworthy; scandalous; shameful / ~스러운 일 a scandal; an ugly case.

불민(不敏) lack of sagacity; stupidity. ¶ ~한 incompetent; dull.

불발(不發) ~하다 misfire; fail to explode 《go off》; 《계획 등이》 fall through; miscarry. ¶ 계획은 ~로 끝났다 The plan fell through. ‖ ~탄 an unexploded shell [bomb] / ~탄 처리반 a bomb disposal squad [unit].

불법(不法) illegality; ¶ ~의 unlawful; unjust; illegal; wrongful. ‖ ~거래 illegal transactions / ~루트 illegal channels / ~소지 illegal possession 《of firearms》 / ~외국인 근로자 an illegal foreign worker / ~입국 illegal entry [immigration] / ~입국자 an illegal entrant / ~점거 unlawful [illegal] occupation; squatting / ~집회 an illegal assembly / ~행위 〔감금〕 an illegal action [confinement].

불법(佛法) Buddhism; 《finement》.

불벼락 ① 《번갯불》 a bolt of lightning. ② 《비유적》 《issue》 a tyrannical decree [order].

불변(不變) ¶ ~의 unchangeable; immutable; invariable; constant. ‖ ~색(色) a permanent [fast] color / ~성 immutability / ~수 [數] a constant; an invariable.

불볕 a burning [scorching] sun.

불복(不服)《불복종함》 disobedience 《to》; 《불복죄》 a denial of 《one's guilt》; 《의의》 an objection; a protest. ~하다 disobey; be disobedient; deny one's guilt; object to; protest against 「(order).

불복종(不服從) disobedience 《to an order》.

불분명(不分明) ¶ ~한 not clear; obscure; vague; indistinct; ambiguous; dim.

불붙다 catch [take] fire; burn. ¶ 쉽사리 불붙지 않다 do not kindle [catch fire] easily; be slow

불붙이다 to catch fire.
불붙이다 set 《*a thing*》 alight; kindle; light; ignite.
불비(不備) ¶ ~의 defective; deficient; incomplete. ‖ 미비.
불빛 light. ¶ ~이 어둡다 the light is dim.
불사(不死) ¶ ~의 immortal; eternal. ‖ ~조 a phoenix. [vice.
불사(佛事) 《hold》 a Buddhist ser-
불사르다 burn (up); set 《*a thing*》 on fire; put 《*a thing*》 into the flames.
불사신(不死身) ¶ ~ 의 invulnerable.
불사하다(不辭-) fail to 《do (not) decline. ¶ …하기를 ~ be (quite) willing to 《*do*》; be ready to 《*do*》.
불상(佛像) an image of Buddha; a Buddhist image [statue]. ¶ 청동 ~ a bronze statue of Buddha.
불상사(不祥事) an unpleasant [a disgraceful] affair.
불서(佛書) the Buddhist scriptures; Buddhist literature.
불선명(不鮮明) unclearness. ~하다 (be) indistinct; obscure; blurred.
불성립(不成立) ~하다 fail; end in failure; fall through.
불성실(不誠實) insincerity. ¶ ~한 insincere; unfaithful.
불성인사(不省人事) ~하다 lose consciousness 《*one's* senses》.
불세지재(不世之才) a man of rare talent; a prodigy; an extraordinary talent [gift].
불세출(不世出) ¶ ~의 rare; uncommon; unparalleled; matchless / ~의 위인 a great man with few parallels in history.
불소(不少) ~하다 be not a little; be much 《indebted to》.
불소(弗素) 《化》 fluorine (기호 F). ¶ ~수지 fluoric resin / ~첨가 fluoridation.
불손(不遜) insolence. ~하다 (be) insolent; haughty; arrogant.
불수(不隨) paralysis. ¶ 반신 [전신] ~ partial [total] paralysis.
불수의(不隨意) ¶ ~근(筋) an involuntary muscle / ~운동[작용] an involuntary movement [action].
불순(不純) impurity. ~하다 (be) impure; foul; mixed. ¶ ~한 동기 a dishonest [selfish] motive. ‖ ~물 impurities / ~분자 an impure element.
불순(不順) ~하다 《일기가》 (be) unseasonable; changeable; irregular; unsettled. ‖ 생리 ~ irregular menstruation.
불승인(不承認) disapproval; nonrecognition [신청권 등의].
불시(不時) ¶ ~의 《때 아닌》 untimely; [뜻밖의] unexpected; 《우연의》 accidental / ~에 unexpectedly;

without notice [warning] / ~ 공격 a surprise attack / ~의 변 an (unforeseen) accident / ~에 방문하다 pay 《*a person*》 a surprise visit / ~의 재난을 당하다 suffer an unexpected calamity; meet with an accident.
불시착(不時着) 《make》 an emergency [unscheduled] landing.
불식(拂拭) ~하다 wipe out 《*a disgrace*》; sweep off; clean.
불신(不信) distrust; discredit. ~하다 discredit; distrust. ¶ 국민의 정치에 대한 ~ the nation's distrust of politics. ‖ ~ 풍조 a trend of mutual distrust / ~ 행위 a breach of faith.
불신감(不信感) (a) distrust; (a) suspicion. ¶ ~을 품다 be distrustful of; have a (deep) distrust 《*of*》.
불신임(不信任) nonconfidence. ~하다 have no [do not place] confidence 《*in*》; distrust. ¶ ~ 안을 제출[결의]하다 move [pass] a nonconfidence bill [vote]. ‖ ~ 결의 a nonconfidence resolution; a vote of censure / ~투표 a vote of nonconfidence; a nonconfidence vote.
불심(不審) doubt; suspicion. ¶ ~ 검문을 받다 be questioned 《by a policeman》.
불쌍하다 (be) poor; pitiful; pitiable; pathetic; miserable. ¶ 불쌍해서 out of pity [sympathy] / 불쌍히 여기다 pity 《*a person*》; feel pity [sorry] for 《*a person*》.
불쏘시개 kindlings.
불쑥 abruptly; all of a sudden.
불쑥하다 (be) protruding; bulgy.
불씨 live charcoal to make a fire; [원인의] a cause. ¶ 분쟁의 ~ an apple of discord.
불안(不安) uneasiness; anxiety; unrest. ~하다 (be) uneasy; anxious. ¶ ~하게 여기다 feel 《*be*》 uneasy 《about》; feel anxious 《about》.
불안정(不安定) instability; unrest. ¶ ~한 unstable; unsteady; precarious; insecure / ~한 사회정세 social unrest.
불알 the testicles; the balls 《俗》.
불야성(不夜城) a nightless quarters [city]. [French language.
불어(佛語) 《프랑스말》 French; the
불어나다 increase; grow. ¶ 강물이 ~ the river rises.
불여의(不如意) ~하다 《일이》 go contrary to 《*one's* wishes》; go wrong [amiss]. [else; if not so.
불연(不然) ¶ ~이면 otherwise; or
불연성(不燃性) incombustibility. ¶ ~의 incombustible; nonflammable; fireproof. ‖ ~물질 in-

불연속선 (不連續線) [氣] a line of discontinuity.

불온 (不穩) unrest; disquiet. ¶ ~한 threatening; disquieting. ‖ ~문서 a seditious circular [document] / ~분자 dissidents; disturbing elements / ~사상 a threatening [riotous] idea.

불완전 (不完全) imperfection; incompleteness. ¶ ~한 imperfect; incomplete; defective. ‖ ~고용 underemployment / ~자(동)사 an incomplete intransitive [transitive] verb.

불요불굴 (不撓不屈) ¶ ~의 unyielding; indomitable; inflexible; dauntless.

불요불급 (不要不急) ¶ ~한 not urgent [pressing] / ~한 사업 non-essential enterprises.

불용 (不用) disuse. ¶ ~의 useless; of no use; unnecessary; disused. ‖ ~품 a discarded [an unwanted] article.

불용성 (不溶性) insolubility. ¶ ~의 insoluble 《*matter*》; infusible.

불우 (不遇) ill fate; misfortune (불행); adversity (역경); obscurity (영락). ¶ ~한 unfortunate; adverse / ~하게 지내다 lead an obscure life / 불우한 처지에 있다 be in adverse circumstances. ‖ ~이웃 돕기 운동 a "Let's help needy neighbors" campaign.

불운 (不運) (a) misfortune; ill luck. ¶ ~한 unfortunate; unlucky; ill-fated / ~하게도 unfortunately; unluckily.

불원 (不遠) 《거리》 not far 《off》; 《시간》 before too long; in the near future. ¶ ~천리하고 despite the long way / ~한 장래에 in the not-too-distant future.

불응 (不應) ¶ ~하다 do not comply with [consent to].

불의 (不意) ¶ ~의 unexpected; sudden; unlooked-for. ☞ 불시.

불의 (不義) 《부도덕》 immorality; 《부정》 injustice; 《밀통》 adultery. ¶ ~의 immoral; illicit; unjust / ~의 씨 an illegitimate child / ~의 사랑 illicit love.

불이익 (不利益) disadvantage. ☞ 불리.

불이행 (不履行) nonfulfillment; nonobservance. ¶ ~계약의 ~ nonfulfillment of a contract / 약속의 ~ failure to keep *one's* promise / 채무의 ~ failure to pay *one's* financial debt; default. ‖ ~자 a defaulter.

불인가 (不認可) disapproval; refusal; rejection.

불일내 (不日內) ¶ ~에 at an early date; shortly; before long.

불일듯하다 (be) prosperous; thriving; flourishing. ¶ 장사가 ~ *one's* business is spreading [growing] like wildfire.

불일치 (不一致) disagreement; discord; disharmony (부조화); 《성격의》 incompatibility of temperament / 《언행의》 the inconsistency of *one's* words with *one's* actions.

불임증 (不姙症) sterility.

불입 (拂入) payment. ~하다 pay in; pay up. ¶ ~금 money due; 《불입된》 money paid / ~자본(금) paid-up [paid-in] capital.

불잉걸 live [burning] charcoal.

불자동차 (一自動車) a fire engine.

불잡다 《진화》 quench [put out] a fire; get a fire under control.

불재 (佛齋) a Buddhist funeral.

불장난 ~하다 play with fire; 《남녀간의》 play with fire; have an idle love affair. ¶ 사랑의 ~ an amorous adventure.

불전 (佛典) the Buddhist scripture.

불전 (佛殿) a Buddhist sanctum.

불제 (祓除) ~하다 exorcise; purify.

불조심 (一操心) 《take》 precautions against fire. ~하다 look out for fire.

불좌 (佛座) the seat of a Buddhist idol.

불지피다 make [build up] a fire.

불질하다 《불때다》 make a fire 《*for cooking*》; 《발포》 fire 《*a gun*》; shoot.

불집 ¶ ~을 건드리다 arouse a nest of hornets; stir up a hornets' nest.

불쬐다 《사람이》 warm *oneself* at the fire; 《사물을》 put 《*a thing*》 over the fire.

불착 (不着) nonarrival; nondelivery.

불찬성 (不贊成) disagreement; disapproval; objection. ~하다 be against 《*a plan*》; do not agree 《*to a thing, with a person*》; object 《*to*》; disapprove 《*of*》.

불찰 (不察) negligence; carelessness; mistake; a blunder.

불참 (不參) absence; nonattendance. ~하다 be absent 《*from*》; fail to attend; do not appear. ‖ ~자 an absentee.

불철저 (不徹底) ~하다 (be) inconclusive; be not thorough (going); 《논지 등이》 (be) inconsistent.

불철주야 (不撤晝夜) ¶ ~로 《work》 day and night.

불청객 (不請客) an uninvited guest.

불체포특권 (不逮捕特權) immunity from arrest; the privilege of exemption from apprehension.

불초 (不肖) ¶ ~의 unworthy 《*of*》; incapable (무능한) / ~자식 a son unworthy of *one's* father.

불출(不出) 《사람》 a stupid person; a fool.
불충(不忠) disloyalty; infidelity. ¶ ~의 disloyal; unfaithful.
불충분(不充分) insufficiency; inadequacy. ¶ ~한 insufficient; not enough; inadequate / 증거 ~으로 무죄가 되다 be acquitted for lack of evidence.
불충실(不充實) disloyalty; infidelity. ¶ ~한 disloyal; unfaithful.
불측(不測) ~하다 (be) immeasurable; unforeseeable; 《흉악》 (be) bad; wicked. ‖ ~지변 an unforeseen accident; an unexpected calamity.
불치(不治) ¶ ~의 incurable; fatal / ~의 환자 a hopeless case. ‖ ~병 an incurable disease.
불친소 a bullock; a steer.
불친절(不親切) unkindness. ¶ ~한 unkind; unfriendly.
불침번(不寢番) 《직킴》 night watch; vigil; all-night watch; a night watchman 《사람》. ¶ ~을 서다 keep watch during the night.
불켜다 light (up) 《a lamp》; turn (put, switch) on a light.
불쾌(不快) unpleasantness; displeasure; (a) discomfort. ~하다 《서술적》 feel unpleasant (uncomfortable, displeased). ‖ ~지수 a discomfort index 《생략 DI》; the temperature-humidity index 《생략 T-H index》.
불타(佛陀) Buddha.
불타다 burn; blaze; be on fire (in flames).
불통(不通) ① 《교통・통신의》 (an) interruption; a stoppage 《of traffic》; a tie-up. ~하다 be cut off; be interrupted; be tied up. ¶ ~되는 곳 a break 《on the line》. ② 《모르다》 no understanding; unfamiliarity; ignorance. ~하다 have no understanding; be unfamiliar 《with》; be ignorant 《of》. ‖ 언어 ~ (have) language difficulty.
불퇴전(不退轉) ¶ ~의 indomitable 《resolve》; determined.
불투명(不透明) opacity. ¶ ~한 opaque 《glass》; cloudy 《liquid》.
불퉁불퉁 ① 《표면》 ruggedly; knottily. ¶ ~한 uneven; rough; knotty. ② 《퉁명스럽게》 bluntly; curtly. ~하다 (be) curt; blunt.
불퉁하다 (be) bulgy; protuberant.
불티 embers; flying sparks; fireflakes. ¶ ~나게 팔리다 sell like hot cakes.
불편(不便) ①《몸 따위가》 discomfort; sickness. ~하다 (be) uncomfortable; 《서술적》 be not well; feel unwell. ②《편리하지 않음》 inconvenience. ~하다 (be) inconvenient. ¶ ~을 느끼다 feel inconvenience / ~을 끼치다 cause inconvenience 《to》.
불편부당(不偏不黨) impartiality. ¶ ~한 impartial; fair.
불평(不平) 《불만》 discontent; dissatisfaction;《투덜댐》 a complaint; a grievance. ~하다 grumble 《at, about》; complain 《about, of》. ¶ ~이다 be dissatisfied 《with》. ‖ ~가〔객〕 a grumbler / ~분자 a discontent.
불평등(不平等) inequality. ¶ ~한 unequal; unfair. ‖ ~조약 an unequal treaty.
불포화(不飽和) (being) unsaturated. ‖ ~화합물 an unsaturated compound.
불피우다 make (build) a fire.
불필요(不必要) ¶ ~한 unnecessary; needless; unessential.
불하(拂下) a sale 《of government property》; disposal. ~하다 sell; dispose of. ¶ ~품 articles disposed of by the government.
불학무식(不學無識) illiteracy. ¶ ~한 illiterate; utterly ignorant.
불한당(不汗黨) a gang of bandits 《robbers》; hooligans; gangsters.
불합격(不合格) failure; rejection. ~하다 fail 《in the examination》; be rejected (eliminated); come short of the standard. ‖ ~자 an unsuccessful candidate / ~품 rejected goods.
불합리(不合理) irrational; illogical; unreasonable; absurd.
불행(不幸) unhappiness; misery; 《불운》 (a) misfortune; ill luck; a disaster 《재난》. ¶ ~한 unhappy; unfortunate; unlucky; wretched / ~히(도) unfortunately; unluckily; unhappily / ~중 다행 a stroke of good luck in the midst of misfortune; one consolation in sadness.
불허(不許) ~하다 do not permit (allow); disapprove. ¶ 《복제(複製)》 ~ "Reprint prohibited."
불현듯이 suddenly; all at once.
불협화(不協和) discord; disharmony. ¶ ~의 dissonant; discordant. ‖ ~음 a discord; a dissonance.
불호령(一號令) ¶ ~을 내리다 issue a fiery order; give a strict command.
불혹(不惑) the age of forty.
불화(不和) a trouble; a quarrel; (a) discord. ~하다 be on bad terms 《with》; be in discord 《with》. ¶ ~하게 되다 fall out 《with》.
불화(弗化) 〔化〕 fluoridation. ‖ ~수소〔칼슘〕 hydrogen (calcium) flu-

oride.
불화(弗貨) a dollar. [picture].
불화(佛畫) a Buddhist painting
불확대(不擴大) ~방침 a nonexpansion policy; a localization policy (국지화).
불확실(不確實) ǁ ~한 uncertain; unreliable. ☞ 확실.
불확정(不確定) ǁ ~한 indefinite; uncertain; undecided. ☞ 확정.
불환지폐(不換紙幣) inconvertible note; flat money. [(-es).
불황성(不活性) ǁ ~가스 inert gas
불황(不況) a business [trade] depression; dull business; a slump; a recession. ǁ ~의 inactive; dull; stagnant / ~을 극복하다 get over [out of] the recession; overcome the recession. ǁ ~대책 an anti-recession policy [measures] / ~시대 depression days; hard times / ~카르텔 an anti-recession cartel.
불효(不孝) lack [want] of filial piety. ǁ ~한 undutiful; unfilial. ǁ ~자 an undutiful [a bad] son [daughter].
붉다 red; crimson(심홍); scarlet (주홍); 《사상이》 be communist(ic). ǁ 붉은 사상 Communism / 붉어지다 turn red; redden; blush (볼 따위가); blush(부끄러워서); be flushed 《with anger》.
붉은물 a muddy stream.
붉히다 turn red; blush (with shame); blaze (with fury).
붐 a boom 《in shipbuilding》.
붐비다 (be) crowded; congested; packed; jammed; thronged (with people). ǁ 붐비는 시간 the rush hour (출퇴근시).
붓 《모필》 a (writing) brush; 《펜》 a pen. ǁ ~을 들다 take up one's pen [brush]; write / ~을 놓다 lay down one's pen [brush]; cease to write. ǁ ~집 a brush [pen] case / ~통 a brush [pen] stand.
붓꽃 《植》 an iris; a blue flag.
붓끝 ① 《붓의》 the tip of a (writing) brush. ② 《필봉》 a stroke of the pen [brush].
붓다¹ ① 《살이》 swell up; become swollen. ǁ 얼굴이 ~ have a swollen face. ② 《성나서》 get [be] sulky. ǁ 부은 얼굴 a sullen face.
붓다² ① 《쏟다》 pour 《in, out》; fill 《a cup with tea》; put 《water in a bowl》. ② 《돈을》 pay in [by] installments. pay one's share by installments. [brush].
붓대 the stem of a writing
붓질 drawing; painting. ~하다 stroke; make strokes with a brush; paint.

붕괴(崩壞) collapse; a breakdown. ~하다 collapse; crumble; break [fall] down; give way.
붕굿하다 ① 《솟다》 (be) a little high; 《서술적》 form a little hill (bump). ② 《들뜨다》 (be) a bit loose. ③ 《배가》 (be) bulgy; big.
붕당(朋黨) a faction; a clique.
붕대(繃帶) a bandage; dressing. ǁ ~를 감다 bandage; apply a bandage 《to》; dress 《a wound》.
붕붕거리다 hum; buzz.
붕사(硼砂) borax; tincal (천연의).
붕산(硼酸) 《化》 boric acid.
붕소(硼素) 《化》 boron (기호 B).
붕어 《魚》 a crucian carp.
붕어(崩御) demise; death.
붕장어(一長魚) 《魚》 a sea eel.
붙다 ① 《부착》 stick 《to》; adhere (cling); 《접하다》 adjoin; be adjacent 《to》; 《바짝》 keep [stand] close 《to》. ǁ 붙어 앉다 sit closely together. ② 《딸리다》 be joined (with); be attached 《to》. ③ 《생기다·늘다》 ǁ 이자가 ~ bear (yield) interest / 버릇이 ~ get (fall) into a habit 《of》 / 별명이 ~ be nicknamed / 살이 ~ gain flesh / 취미가 ~ acquire a taste (for); take an interest 《in》 / 영어 실력이 ~ become proficient in English. ④ 《편들다》 take sides with; attach oneself to; join (가담); 《수발들다》 attend [wait] 《on》. ǁ 간호사가 붙어 있다 be attended by a nurse / 적에게 ~ go over to the enemy. ⑤ 《의지하다》 depend (rely) on. ǁ ~ 붙어 살다 live [sponge] on 《a person》. ⑥ 《불이》 catch 《fire》; be ignited. ⑦ 《시험에》 pass 《an examination》. ⑧ 《싸움이》 start; be started; develop 《into》. ⑨ 《마각이》 be possessed (obsessed) 《by, with》. ⑩ ☞ 간동하다.
붙들다 ① 《잡다》 ☞ ②. ②《만류》 detain; hold. ③ 《도와 주다》 help; assist; aid.
붙들리다 《잡히다》 be caught [arrested; seized]; 《만류》 be detained; be made to stay.
붙박이 a fixture; a fixed article. ǁ ~의 fixed: built-in.
붙박이다 be fixed; be fastened immovably; 《집에》 be confined [closeted] in 《one's room》.
…붙이 ① 《일가·친척》 kith and kin. ǁ 가까운 ~ one's near relatives. ② 《같은 종류》 things made of.... ǁ 쇠~ ironware.
붙이다 ① 《부착》 put (fix, affix, stick) 《to, on, together》; attach (fasten) 《to》; paste(풀로); glue (아교로); 《고약 등을》 apply 《to》. ǁ 우표를 ~ put a stamp on /

붙임성 꼬리표를 ~ attach a tag to (*a parcel*) / 책상을 벽에 ~ place a desk close to the wall. ② (첨부) add; attach (*to*); give (set) (*to*). ¶ 의견을 ~ make an additional comment / 조건을 ~ attach a condition (*to*). ③ (몸을) rely on (*a person*) for (*one's care*); hang (sponge) on (*one's relations*). ④ (불을) light; kindle. ⑤ (흥정·싸움 따위를) act as intermediary (go-between); mediate (*between*); bring two parties together for (*a negotiation*); arrange. ¶ 싸움을 ~ make (*persons*) quarrel / 흥정을 ~ arrange a bargain. ⑥ (이름 따위를) give (a name) (*to*); name; entitle (제목을). ⑦ (사람을) have (*a person*) in attendance; let (*a person*) be attended (waited upon). ¶ 감시를 ~ keep (place) (*a person*) under guard. ⑧ (때리다) (give a) slap. ¶ 따귀를 ~ box (*a person's*) ears. ⑨ (교미) mate (*a dog*); pair (*animals*). ⑩ (구미 타) 재미를 ~ take (an) interest (*in*); find pleasure (*in*) / 재미를 ~ acquire a taste (*for*) (an interest (*in*)).

붙임성 (-性) amiability; affability. ¶ ~ 있는 사람 an affable (sociable) person / ~이 있다 be sociable; be easy to approach.

붙잡다 ① (잡다) seize; grasp. ¶ 붙잡다 ①, ②, ④. ③ (일자리를) get (obtain) a job. ③ (돕다) ¶ 붙잡아 주다 help; aid (*a person*).

붙잡히다 be seized (caught); be arrested.

뷰티파러(살롱) a beauty parlor (salon); a beauty shop.

브라스밴드 a brass band.

브라우닝(자동권총) a Browning (revolver).

브라운관(-管) a TV (picture) tube; a cathode-ray tube. ¶ ~에 모습을 나타내다 make an appearance on television.

브라질 Brazil. ¶ ~의 (사람) a Brazilian.

브래지어 a *brassière* (프); a bra (美社). ¶ ~슬립 a bra-slip.

브래킷 (까치발) a bracket (괄호) (square brackets).

브랜드 a brand. ¶ ~제품 a brand-name item.

브랜디 (양주) brandy.

브러시 a brush.

브레이크¹ a brake. ¶ ~를 걸다 apply (put on) the brake.

브레이크² (拳) a break.

브레인트러스트 a brain trust.

브로마이드 a bromide; bromide paper (감광지).

브로치 a brooch; a breastpin.

브로커 (act as) a broker.

브롬 [化] bromine. ¶ ~칼리 potassium bromide / ~화 bromination (~화하다 brominate).

브리지 ① (다리) a bridge. ② (트럼프놀이) (play) bridge.

브리튼 (Great) Britain. ¶ ~사람 a Briton; a British; a Britisher.

브이티아르 a VTR (◀videotape recorder). ¶ ~를 보다 watch videotaped programs.

블라우스 a blouse.

블랙리스트 a black list.

블록 (동맹·거리의 구획) a bloc. ‖ ~경제 bloc economy / 달러(금) ~ the dollar (gold) bloc.

블루진 blue jeans.

비¹ (내리는) rain; (한 번의 강우) a rainfall; a shower (소나기). ¶ ~가 많은 rainy / ~가 많이 오는 계절 a rainy (wet) season / ~가 오다(멎다) (It) rains (stops raining).

비² (쓰는) a broom.

비 (比) (비율) ratio; proportion; (비교) comparison; (대조) contrast; (필적) an equal; a match.

비 (妃) (왕비) a queen (consort); (왕세자비) a crown princess.

비 (碑) (묘비) a gravestone; (기념비) a monument.

비… (非) (반대의) non-; un-; in-; anti-.

비가 (悲歌) an elegy; a dirge.

비각 (碑閣) a monument house.

비감 (悲感) sad feeling; grief; sorrow.

비강 (鼻腔) [解] the nasal cavity.

비겁 (卑怯) ¶ ~한 cowardly; mean (비열한); foul (부정한) / ~한 자 a coward / ~한 짓을 하다 play (*a person*) foul (상대에게).

비견 (比肩) (나란히 함) ~하다 rank (*with*); equal; be comparable (*with*); be on a par (*with*).

비결 (秘訣) a secret; a key (*to*). ¶ 성공의 ~ the secret of (a key to) success.

비경 (秘境) an unexplored (untrodden) region; one of the most secluded regions.

비경 (悲境) a sad (miserable) condition; distressing (adverse) circumstances. ¶ ~에 빠지다 be reduced to poor circumstances.

비계¹ fat; lard (돼지의).

비계² [建] a scaffold; scaffolding.

비계 (秘計) a secret plan; *one's* trump card.

비고 (備考) a note; a remark; a reference. ¶ ~란 a reference (remarks) column.

비곡 (悲曲) a plaintive melody.

비공개 (非公開) ¶ ~의 not open to the public; private; informal; closed (*meeting*) / ~입출 a closed tender.

비공식 (非公式) ¶ ~적(으로) unoffi-

비공인(非公認) unofficial(ly); informal(ly) / ~ 견해 an unofficial view〔opinion〕.
비공인(非公認) ¶ ~의 unofficial; unauthorized; unrecognized / ~ 세계기록 an as-yet-unratified〔a pending〕world record.
비과세(非課稅) tax exemption. ‖ ~ 품 a tax-free article.
비과학적(非科學的) unscientific.
비관(悲觀) pessimism; disappointment. ~하다 be pessimistic〔of, about〕; take a gloomy view〔of〕; be disappointed. ¶ ~적(인) pessimistic. ‖ ~론자 a pessimist.
비관세(非關稅) ¶ ~장벽 a non-tariff barrier〔생략 NTB〕.
비교(比較) (a) comparison. ~하다 compare〔two things, A with B〕. ¶ ~적(으로) comparative(ly) / ~와 ~ 하면 (as) compared with ... / ~ 가 안 되다(낫다) be more than a match〔for〕(못하다) cannot be compared〔with〕. ‖ ~급〔文〕the comparative (degree) / ~문학 comparative literature / ~연구 a comparative study.
비구(飛球) a fly〔ball〕.
비구니(比丘尼) a priestess; a nun.
비구승(比丘僧) a bhikku〔梵〕; a Buddhist monk.
비국민(非國民) an unpatriotic person.
비군사(非軍事) ¶ ~적(인) nonmilitary. ‖ ~화 demilitarization.
비굴(卑屈) ¶ ~한 mean; servile.
비극(悲劇) 《end in》 a tragedy. ¶ ~적(인) tragic / 가정의 ~ a domestic tragedy. ‖ ~배우 a tragedian; a tragic actor〔actress〕.
비근(卑近) ¶ ~한 familiar; common. ¶ ~한 예를 들다 give〔cite〕a familiar example.
비근거리다 be shaky〔rickety〕.
비금속(非金屬) a nonmetal; a metalloid.
비금속(卑金屬) a base metal.
비기다 ①〔무승부〕end in a draw; tie〔draw〕〔with〕. ②〔상쇄〕offset〔cancel〕each other.
비기다〔비유·견줌〕liken《to》; compare《to》. ¶ ~비길 데 없는 incomparable; indescribable.
비꼬다 ①〔끈을〕twist; entwist; twine. ②〔말을〕make cynical remarks; give a sarcastic twist to one's words.
비꼬이다 ①〔끈·실이〕get twisted; ②〔일이〕get (en)tangled; 〔마음이〕get peevish; become crooked〔distorted〕.
비끗거리다 ①〔잘 안 되다〕go wrong〔amiss〕. ②〔어긋나다〕work loose; be not firmly fixed.
비난(非難) blame; (a) censure. ~하다 blame〔censure〕《a person for》; accuse《a person of》; criticize. ¶ ~의 대상이 되다 become the focus〔target〕of criticism.
비너스 Venus.
비녀〔wear〕an ornamental hairpin. ‖ ~장 a linchpin.
비논리적(非論理的) illogical.
비뇨기(泌尿器) the urinary organs. ‖ ~과 urology / ~과 의사 a urologist.
비누《a cake of》soap. ¶ 가루 ~ soap powder / 세숫〔빨랫〕~ toilet〔washing, laundering〕soap / ~로 씻다 wash with soap and water / 얼굴에 ~ 칠을 하다 lather one's face. ‖ ~거품 soap bubbles; lather / 비눗갑 soap case.
비늘 a scale. ¶ ~이 있다 be covered with scales / ~을 벗기다 scale《a fish》/ ~구름 a cirrocumulus.
비능률(非能率) inefficiency. ¶ ~적(인) inefficient.
비닐 vinyl. ‖ ~ 수지 vinyl resin / ~하우스 a vinyl plastic hothouse.
비닐론〔상표명〕Vinylon.
비다 (be) empty; vacant. ¶ 빈 집 a vacant house / 뱃속이 ~ be hungry / 손이 ~ be free.
비단(緋緞) silk fabric; silks. ¶ ~ 결 같이 be soft as velvet.
비단(非但) merely; simply; only. ¶ ~ ... 뿐만 아니라 ... not only ... but (also) ....
비당파적(非黨派的) (being) nonpartisan; nonparty.
비대(肥大) ¶ ~한 fat; enlarged. ‖ ~ 심장 ~ enlargement of the heart.
비데 a bidet〔프〕.
비동맹(非同盟) ¶ ~국 a nonaligned nation / ~국 회의 the nonaligned conference.
비둘기 a dove; a pigeon. ‖ ~장 a dovecot(e); a pigeon house / ~파 the doves; a soft-liner.
비듬 dandruff; scurf. ¶ ~투성이의 머리 a scurfy〔dandruffy〕head. ‖ ~ 약 a hair lotion.
비등(比等) ~하다 be on a par; be about the same; be equal to.
비등(沸騰) ~하다〔끓다〕boil (up); seethe;〔여론 따위가〕get〔become〕heated〔excited〕. ‖ ~점 the boiling point.
비디오 a video. ‖ ~게임 a video game / ~디스크 a videodisc / ~카메라 a video camera / ~카세트 a video cassette〔cartridge〕/ ~테이프 녹화 a videotape recording 〔생략 VTR〕.
비뚜로 obliquely; aslant; slantwise.
비뚜름하다 be somewhat crooked〔askew, oblique〕.

비뚝거리다 《흔들거리다》 wobble; be shaky〔rickety〕; 《절다》 limp 〔along〕. 「ing.
비뚤다 (be) crooked; tilted; slant-
비뚤어지다 ① 《사물이》 get crooked; slant; incline; be tilted. ¶ 비뚤어진 코 a crooked nose. ② 《마음》 be perverse 〔crooked, twisted, warped〕.
비래(飛來) ~하다 come flying; come by air(비행기로). 「ging.
비럭질 begging. ~하다 go beg-
비련(悲戀) tragic〔blighted〕 love.
비례(比例) proportion; a ratio(비율). ~하다 be in proportion 《to》. ¶ …에 정〔반〕~ 하다 be directly〔inversely〕 proportional to. ‖ ~대표(제) (the) proportional representation〔quotal〕 / ~배분 proportional〔quotal〕 allotment / ~식 a proportional expression.
비례(非禮) discourtesy; impoliteness; rudeness.
비로소 for the first time; not…until〔till〕…. 「cord〕.
비록(秘錄) a (secret) memoir〔re-
비록(雖) (al)though; if; even if. ¶ ~ 비가 오더라도 even if it should rain.
비롯하다 begin; commence; originate; initiate. ¶ …을 비롯하여 including…; …and; as well as…; beginning with….
비료(肥料) manure; fertilizer. ‖ ~ 화학 chemical fertilizer〔manure〕 / ~를 주다 manure; fertilize. ‖ ~공장 a fertilizer plant.
비루(獸醫) mange. ~먹다 suffer from mange. 「base.
비루(鄙陋) ~한 vulgar; mean;
비리(非理) irrationality; unreasonableness; absurdities and irregularities.
비리다 《생선이》 (be) fishy; 《피가》 (be) bloody; 《아니꼽다》 (be) disgusting.
비린내 a fishy smell; a bloody smell(피의). ¶ ~나다 smell fishy〔bloody〕.
비릿하다 be slightly fishy.
비만(肥滿) obesity; fatness. ~하다 (be) fat; corpulent; plump. ¶ ~해지다 get fat; become stout. ‖ ~아 an overweight〔obese〕 child / ~증 obesity / ~형 a pyknic〔pycnic〕 type.
비말(飛沫) a splash; a spray.
비망록(備忘錄) a memorandum 〔pl. -da〕; a memo.
비매품(非賣品) an article not for sale; 《게시》 "Not for Sale."
비명(非命) ¶ ~에 죽다〔가다〕 die 〔meet with〕 an unnatural death.
비명(悲鳴) a scream; a shriek. ¶ ~을 지르다 scream; shriek 《for help》.
비명(碑銘) an epitaph; an inscription (on a monument).
비몽사몽(非夢似夢) ¶ ~간에 between asleep and awake.
비무장(非武裝) ~의 demilitarized; unarmed / 도시를 ~화하다 demilitarize a city. ‖ ~도시 an open city / ~중립 unarmed neutrality / ~지대 a demilitarized zone (생략 DMZ).
비문(碑文) an epitaph; an inscription. 「nondemocratic.
비민주적(非民主的) undemocratic;
비밀(秘密) secrecy; a secret; a mystery(신비). ¶ ~의〔히〕 secret (-ly); confidential(ly); private (-ly) / 다 아는 ~ an open secret / ~로 하다 keep 《a matter》 secret / ~을 지키다 keep a secret / ~을 밝히다 disclose a secret 《to》. ‖ ~결사〔단체, 조약〕 a secret so-ciety〔organization, treaty〕 / ~번호 a personal code number / ~서류 a confidential document / ~회의 a closed-door session.
비바람 rain and wind; a storm. ¶ ~을 무릎쓰고 가다 go through the raging storm.
비바리 a girl diver.
비방(秘方) a secret method〔recipe〕; a secret formula(약의).
비방(誹謗) slander; abuse. ~하다 slander; abuse; speak ill of.
비번(非番) ~이다 be off duty / ~날에 on one's day off / 오늘은 ~이다 I am off duty today. or This is my day off.
비범(非凡) ~한 extraordinary; unusual; uncommon; rare.
비법(秘法) a secret method.
비법인(非法人) ~의 unincorporated.
비보(悲報) sad〔heavy〕 news.
비복(婢僕) (domestic) servants.
비본(秘本) a treasured book.
비분(悲憤) resentment; indignation. ~ 강개하다 deplore; be indignant 《at, over》.
비브라폰(악기) a vibraphone.
비브리오(菌)(의) a vibrio.
비비(狒狒)(動) a baboon.
비비꼬다 ① (en)twist over and over again. ② ☞ 비꼬다.
비비꼬이다 (be) get〕twisted many times; 《일이》 go wrong 《amiss》.
비비다 ① 《문지르다》 rub. ② 《둥글게》 (make a) roll. ③ 《뒤섞어》 mix. ④ 《송곳을》 twist 《a gimlet into a plank》; drill.
비비대기치다 《붐빔》 hustle and jostle; push and shove; 《부산떨다》 move about busily; bustle about.
비비적거리다 rub 〔chafe〕 《against》.

비비틀다 twist (wrench, turn) hard.
비빈(妃嬪) ˹royal concubine.
비빔국수 the queen and the boiled noodle with assorted mixtures.
비빔밥 boiled rice with assorted mixtures.
비사(秘史) a secret history.
비사교적(非社交的) unsociable.
비산(飛散) ¶ ~하다 scatter; disperse; fly.
비상(非常) ① (보통이 아님) unusualness; extraordinariness. ~하다 (be) unusual; uncommon; extraordinary; exceptional. ¶ ~한 인물 an uncommon being / ~한 솜씨 unusual skill. ② (사태의) an emergency; a contingency; a disaster (재해). ¶ ~시에는 in (case of) emergency. ¶ ~경보 an alarm (signal, bell) / ~계단 an emergency staircase / ~구 a fire exit (escape); an emergency exit / ~시대 (declare) a state of emergency / ~소집 an emergency call / ~수단 (adopt) an emergency measure / ~시 an emergency; a crisis / ~식량 emergency provisions.
비상(砒霜) arsenic poison.
비상(飛翔) ¶ ~하다 fly; soar (up).
비상근(非常勤) ¶ ~의 part-time / ~의 일 a part-time job / ~으로 일하다 work part time. ‖ ~직원 a part-time worker; a part-timer.
비상선(非常線) a (police) cordon; a fire line (화재의). ¶ ~을 펴다 form a (police) cordon / ~을 돌파하다 break through a cordon.
비상장주(非上場株)〔證〕an unlisted stock (share).
비생산적(非生産的) unproductive; nonproductive. ¶ ~인 사고방식 a far from constructive idea.
비서(秘書) (비서역) a private secretary. ‖ ~실 a secretariat.
비석(碑石) a stone monument; 〔묘비〕a tombstone.
비소(砒素)〔化〕arsenic (기호 As).
비속(卑俗) vulgar; low.
비수(匕首) a dirk; a dagger.
비술(秘術) a secret (art).
비스듬하다 (be) slant; skew; oblique. ¶ 비스듬하게 obliquely; aslant; diagonally.
비스름하다 be somewhat similar.
비스코스〔化〕viscose. ˹(英).
비스킷 a cracker (美); a biscuit
비스타비전〔電〕Vista Vision.
비슥거리다 dawdle (one's work); (빼돌다) keep to oneself; hang back.
비슬거리다 totter; reel; stagger.
비슷비슷하다 be all much the same; be of the same sort.
비슷하다 (닮다) (be) like; similar; look like (서슷이); (비스듬하다) lean a bit to one side. ¶ 비슷한 데가 있다 have certain points of likeness.
비시지〔醫〕BCG (vaccine). (◀ Bacillus Calmette-Guérin) ‖ ~접종 inoculation by BCG.
비신사적(非紳士的) ungentlemanly; ungentlemanlike.
비실제적(非實際的) unpractical.
비싸다 (be) dear; expensive; costly; high. ¶ 비싸게 사다 buy at a high price; pay dear.
비아냥거리다 make sarcastic remarks; be cynical (about).
비애(悲哀) sorrow; grief; sadness; pathos. ¶ ~를 느끼다 feel sad.
비애국적(非愛國的) unpatriotic.
비약(祕藥) a secret remedy (medicine); a nostrum.
비약(飛躍) a leap; a jump. ¶ 논리의 ~ a leap in argument / ~적인 발전을 하다 make rapid progress; take long strides.
비양(飛揚) ¶ ~하다 make a flight; fly; soar (up) (높이).
비어(卑語) a slang; a vulgar word.
비어(麥酒) beer; ale. ‖ ~홀 beer hall.
비업무용(非業務用)(of) non-business purpose. ¶ ~ 토지를 백만 평이나 소유하다 possess one million p'yong of non-business idle land. ‖ ~부동산 real estate held for non-business purpose; idle land.
비엔날레〔美術〕the Biennale. ¶ ~전(展) a biennial exhibition.
비역(鷄姦) sodomy; buggery. ~하다 practice sodomy.
비열(比熱)〔理〕specific heat.
비열(卑劣) ¶ ~한 mean; base; dirty; low; sordid / ~한 수단 a dirty (nasty) trick / ~한 놈 a sneak; a mean fellow.
비영리(非營利) nonprofit. ¶ ~법인 (단체, 사업) a nonprofit corporation (organization, undertaking).
비예술적(非藝術的) inartistic.
비오리 a merganser.
비옥(肥沃) ¶ ~한 fertile; rich.
비옷 a raincoat; rainwear.
비올라〔樂〕a viola.
비용(費用) cost; expense(s). ¶ 결혼식 ~ wedding expenses / ~이 드는 expensive; costly / ~에 관계없이 regardless of expense / ~이 얼마나 드나 How much does it cost (to do)? ¶ ~절감운동 a cost-saving move.
비우다 empty (a box); clear (a room); vacate (quit) (a house); absent (stay away) from (home).
비우호적(非友好的) unfriendly.

비운(悲運) misfortune; ill luck.
비웃다 laugh(sneer) at; ridicule; deride. ¶ 남을 ~ sneer at others.
비웃음 a sneer; ridicule; scorn.
비원(秘苑) a palace garden; 〈창덕궁의〉 the Secret Garden.
비위(脾胃) ①〈기호〉 taste; palate; liking. ¶ ~에 맞다 suit one's taste. ②〈기분〉 humor; temper. ¶ ~를 거스르다 〔건드리다〕 rub *(a person)* the wrong way; put *(a person)* in a bad humor / ~를 맞추다 put *(a person)* in a good humor; curry favor with / ~(가) 상하다 be offended; be〔feel〕disgusted 《at, by, with》/ ~가 좋다 〈뻔뻔하다〉 have a nerve.
비위생적(非衛生的) unwholesome; unsanitary.
비유(比喩, 譬喩) a figure of speech; a simile〈직유〉; a metaphor〈은유〉. ~하다 compare 《to》; speak figuratively; use a metaphor. ¶ ~적(ly) figurative(ly); metaphorical(ly).
비육우(肥肉牛) beef cattle.
비율(比率) proportion; rate; ratio; percentage. ¶ …의 ~로 at the rate〔ratio〕of.
비음(鼻音) a nasal (sound).
비인간적(非人間的) inhuman; impersonal. 〔brutal.
비인도(非人道) ¶ ~적인 inhumane.
비인칭(非人稱) ¶ ~의 impersonal.
비일비재(非一非再) ~하다 (be) very common; frequent; there are many such cases.
비자 a visa. ¶ 여권에 ~를 받다 have one's passport visaed / 미국 가는 ~를 신청하다 apply for a visa to the United States. ¶ 관광 ~ a tourist visa / 입국〔출국〕 ~ an entrance〔exit〕visa / 취업 및 관광 겸용 ~ (the issuance of) working holiday visas.
비자금(秘資金) slush fund.
비잔틴 Byzantine.
비장(秘藏) ~하다 treasure; keep *(a thing)* with great care. ¶ ~의 treasured; precious; favorite. ¶ ~품 a treasure.
비장(悲壯) ¶ ~한 touching; tragic; grim; heroic〈장렬〉.
비장(脾臟) 〖解〗 the spleen.
비재(菲才) lack of ability; incapacity. ¶ 이제 저는 incapable as I am. 〔mysteries.
비전(秘傳) a secret; a recipe; the ~이 있는 사람 a man of vision. 〔goods.
비전략물자(非戰略物資) nonstrategic
비전투원(非戰鬪員) a noncombatant; a civilian. 〔heartless; cruel.
비정(非情) ¶ ~한 cold-hearted;
비정(秕政) maladministration; misgovernment; misrule.

비정규군(非正規軍) irregular troops.
비정상(非正常) anything unusual; abnormality; irregularity. ¶ ~의 abnormal; unusual; exceptional; singular. ¶ ~아〔兒〕 an abnormal child / ~자〔者〕a deviate.
비좁다 (be) narrow and close〔confined〕; cramped. ¶ 비좁은 곳 a confined place.
비종교적(非宗敎的) nonreligious.
비주룩하다 (be) sticking out a bit.
비주류(非主流) non(-)mainstreamers; the non(-)mainstream faction〔group〕. 〔(up) a lip.
비죽거리다 pout *(one's lips)*; make
비준(批准) ratification. ~하다 ratify *(a treaty)*. ¶ ~서 an instrument of ratification.
비중(比重) 〖理〗 specific gravity. ¶ ~계 a gravimeter; a hydrometer.
비지 bean-curd dregs.
비지땀 ¶ ~을 흘리다 drip with perspiration; have heavy sweating.
비질 sweeping (with a broom). ~하다 sweep with a broom.
비집다 ①〈틈을〉 split open; push〔force〕open. ②〈눈을〉 rub one's eyes open.
비쭉 ~ 내밀다 pout *(one's lips)*.
비쭉거리다 pout *(one's lips)*; make up a lip.
비참(悲慘) ¶ ~한 miserable; wretched; tragic(al); pitiable; sad / ~한 생활 a miserable〔wretched〕life; (lead) a dog's life.
비책(秘策) a secret plan〔scheme〕; a subtle stratagem. ¶ ~을 짜다 elaborate〔work out〕a secret
비책으로하다 ㅁ 비틀거리다. 〔plan.
비천(卑賤) ¶ ~한 humble(-born); low(ly); obscure / ~한 몸 a man of low birth. 〔al.
비철금속(非鐵金屬) nonferrous met-
비추다 ①〈빛이〉 shine *(on)*; shed light *(on)*; light (up); illuminate. ②〈그림자를〉reflect *(a mountain)*. ③〈비교·참조〉 compare with; collate. ¶ …에 비추어 보아 in the light of; in view of. ④〈암시〉 hint; suggest; allude to. ¶ 사직할 뜻을 ~ hint at resignation.
비축(備蓄) a stockpile. ¶ ~하다 save for emergency; stockpile. ¶ ~미 reserved rice.
비취(翡翠) ①〖鳥〗 a kingfisher. ②〖鑛〗 nephrite; green jadeite; jade. ¶ ~색 jade green.
비치(備置) ~하다 equip〔furnish〕with; provide with; keep〔have〕*(a thing)* ready.
비치다 ①〈빛이〉 shine. ②〈그림자가〉 be reflected〔mirrored〕《in》. ③

《통해 보이다》 show 《*through*》.
비칭(卑稱) a humble title.
비켜나다 draw back; move aside; step aside. 「out of the way.
비켜서다 step 〔move〕 aside; get
비키니 a bikini. ¶ ~스타일로 in (a) bikini. ‖ ~수영복 a bikini.
비키다 move out; step aside; remove.
비타민 vitamin(e). ¶ ~결핍증 a vitaminosis / 종합~ multivitamin.
비타협적(非妥協的) ~인 unyielding; uncompromising; intransigent / ~태도 intransigence; intransigency.
비탄(悲嘆) grief; sorrow; lamentation. ~하다 grieve; mourn; sorrow 《*over, on*》; lament.
비탈 a slope; an incline; a hill.
비통(悲痛) grief; sorrow. ¶ ~한 sad; pathetic; touching; sorrowful.
비트족(一族) the beat generation.
비틀거리다 stagger; totter; falter; reel. ¶ 비틀걸음 unsteady〔reeling〕steps; tottering / 비틀비틀 totteringly.
비틀다 twist; twirl; wrench; distort. ¶ 팔을 ~ wrench 〔twist〕 《*a person's*》 arm.
비틀어지다 be twisted 〔distorted〕.
비파(琵琶) a Korean mandolin.
비판(批判) criticism; a comment. ~하다 criticize; comment 《*on*》. ¶ ~적(으로) critical(ly). ‖ ~력 critical power 〔ability〕 / ~자 a critic.
비평(批評) criticism; a comment; (a) review〔논평〕. ~하다 criticize; comment on; review 《*a book*》. ‖ ~가 a critic; a commentator; a reviewer / 문예~ a literary criticism.
비폭력(非暴力) nonviolence; ahimsa. ¶ ~의 nonviolent.
비품(備品) furniture; furnishings; fixtures; fitting.
비프스테이크 beefsteak.
비하(卑下) ~하다 humble 〔depreciate〕 oneself. 「*with B*》.
비하다(比一) compare 《*the two, A*
비학술적(非學術的) unscientific; unacademic. 「ful.
비합법적(非合法的) illegal; unlaw-
비핵(非核) ~의 nonnuclear; anti-nuclear. ‖ ~국 a nonnuclear country〔nation〕 / ~무장 nonnuclear armament / ~지대 the nuclear-free zone / ~3원칙 the three nonnuclear principles / ~화(化) denuclearization 《~하다 denuclearize 《*an area, a nation*》》.
비행(非行) delinquency; a misdeed; misconduct. ¶ 청소년 ~ juvenile delinquency. ‖ ~소년 a juvenile delinquent.
비행(飛行) flying; flight.〔항공술〕aviation. ~하다 fly; make a flight; travel by air. ¶ 저공~ a low-altitude flight / 시험 ~하다 make a test flight. ‖ ~경로 a flight path / ~복 a flying suit; a G-suit / ~사 an aviator; a flier; an airman; a pilot〔조종사〕 / ~속도 (an) air speed / ~시간 flight time(비행기의); flying hours(조종사의) / ~장 an airfield, an airport / ~장교 a flight officer / ~세계일주〔연습〕 ~ a round-the-world〔training〕 flight / 정기 ~ a regular air service.
비행기(飛行機) an airplane〔美〕; a plane; aircraft〔총칭〕. ¶ ~를 타다 board 〔take, get on board〕 a plane / ~에서 내리다 leave 〔get off〕 a plane / ~로 가다 go by plane; fly 《*to Europe*》 / ~로 보내다 send 《*something*》 by air / 여객〔화물〕용 ~ a passenger〔cargo〕 plane. ‖ ~사고 a plane accident; a plane crash(추락) / ~운(雲) a contrail; a vapor trail.
비행선(飛行船) an airship.
비현실적(非現實的) unreal; impractical; fantastic. ¶ ~인 생각(사람) an impractical idea〔person〕 / ~인 이야기 a fantastic story.
비호(庇護) protection; patronage. ~하다 protect; shelter; cover. ¶ …의 ~하에 under the patronage〔protection〕 of….
비호(飛虎) a flying tiger. ¶ ~같이 like a shot; as quick as lightning.
비화(秘話) a secret story; a behind-the-scenes story.
비화(飛火) flying sparks; leaping flames. ~하다 flames leap 《*to, across*》; 《사건이》 come to involve 《*a person*》. ¶ 독직 사건은 정계의 거물급에게까지 될 것이다 The bribery case will come to involve a great political figure.
비화(悲話) a sad〔pathetic〕 story.
빅딜 〔큰 거래〕 a big deal.
빅뱅〔우주 대폭발·큰 규모의 근본적 제도 개혁〕 the big bang.
빅수(一手) a move to end 《*a game*》 in a draw.
빈 Vienna. ¶ ~사람 a Viennese.
빈객(賓客) a guest (of honor); an honored guest.
빈곤(貧困), **빈궁**(貧窮) poverty; indigence; need. ¶ ~한 poor; needy; destitute / ~에서 벗어나다 emerge from poverty.〔ant〕.
빈농(貧農) a poor farmer〔peas-
빈대 a bedbug; a housebug.
빈대떡 a mung-bean pancake.

빈도(頻度) frequency. ¶ 높은[낮은] ~수 high [low] frequency.

빈둥거리다 idle away; loaf around; loiter about. ¶ 빈둥빈둥[빈들빈들] idly; indolently.

빈말 an idle talk; empty words; an empty promise. ~하다 talk idly; make idle promise.

빈민(貧民) the poor; the needy. ‖ ~구제 the relief of the poor / ~굴 the slums.

빈발(頻發) frequent occurrence. ~하다 occur frequently.

빈방(一房) a vacant room.

빈번(頻繁) ¶ ~한 frequent; incessant; ~히 frequently.

빈병(一瓶) an empty bottle.

빈부(貧富) wealth and poverty; rich and poor (사람). ¶ ~의 차 disparity in wealth; the gap between (the) rich and (the) poor / ~의 차별 없이 rich and poor alike.

빈사(瀕死) ¶ ~상태의 환자 a dying patient / ~상태에 있다 be on the verge of death.

빈소(殯所) the place where a coffin is kept until the funeral day.

빈속 (drink on) an empty stomach.

빈손 an empty hand. ¶ ~으로 empty-handed.

빈약(貧弱) ¶ ~한 poor; scanty; meager.

빈자(貧者) a poor man; the poor (총칭). ¶ ~의 일등(一燈) the widow's mite.

빈자리(결원) a vacancy; an opening; (공석) a vacant seat.

빈정거리다 be sarcastic; make sarcastic remarks; be cynical.

빈집 a vacant [an unoccupied, an empty] house.

빈차(一車) an empty car; (택시) a disengaged taxi; 《택시의 게시》 For hire; Vacant.

빈천(貧賤) poverty (and lowliness). ¶ ~한 poor and lowly.

빈촌(貧村) a poor village.

빈축(嚬蹙) ~하다 frown upon; be scandalized at; (남의) ~을 사다 be frowned at [on] (by).

빈탕 emptiness; vacancy; 《과실의》 an empty nut.

빈털터리 a penniless person. ¶ ~가 되다 become penniless.

빈틈 ①《간격》 an opening; an aperture; a gap; a chink. ¶ ~없이 closely; compactly. ②《불비》 unpreparedness; an opening. ¶ ~없는 사람 a shrewd [sharp] fellow.

빈혈(貧血) 〖醫〗 anemia. ¶ ~을 일으키다 have an attack of anemia.

빌다 ①《구걸》 beg; solicit. ②《간청》 ask; request; beg; appeal; sue for; entreat. ③《기원》 pray (to God); wish (소원). ④《사죄》 beg (a person's) pardon; beg another's forgiveness.

빌딩(建物) an office building.

빌려주다 (사용케 하다) let (a person) use (a thing). ☞ 빌리다.

빌로도 velvet.

빌리다 ① 《금품을 빌려주다》 lend; loan (out) (美); advance. ¶ 2부 이자로 돈을 빌려주다 lend [loan] money at 2 percent interest / 책을 빌려주다 lend a book. ② 《임대하다》 rent (a room) to (a person); lease (land); let (英); rent [hire (英)] out. ¶ 집을 월 10만원에 ~ rent out a house at hundred thousand won a month. ③ 《차용하다》 borrow; rent (a house); hire (a boat); rent (a house); lease (land). ¶ 친구에게서 책을 [돈을] ~ borrow a book [some money] from a friend. ④ 《힘을》 get (a person's) aid [help]. ¶ …의 힘을 빌려 by the aid of…; with the help of…

빌미 the cause of evil [disease]. ¶ ~붙다 inflict an evil [a curse] (on); curse; haunt (원귀가) ~잡다 attribute (a calamity) to.

빌붙다 curry favor (with); win one's favor by flattery; flatter.

빌어먹다 beg one's bread; go begging. ¶ 빌어먹을 Damn it!; Hell!

빗 a comb. ‖ ~살 the teeth of a comb / ~솔 a comb-brush.

빗각(一角) 〖數〗 an oblique angle.

빗나가다 turn away [aside]; deviate; wander (from); (빗맞다) miss; go astray.

빗대다 ①《비교》 insinuate (that); hint at. ②《틀리게》 make a false statement; perjure.

빗듣다 《잘못 듣다》 hear (it, him) wrong (amiss); mishear.

빗맞다 ①《빗나가다》 miss (the mark); go wide (of the mark). ②《뜻한 일이》 fail; go wrong.

빗먹다 (톱이) veer off-line; go off.

빗물 rainwater.

빗발 ¶ ~치듯하다 (탄알이) fall in showers; shower like hail; come thick and fast / ~같이 쏟아지는 총알 a shower of bullets.

빗방울 a raindrop. ‖ ~소리 the drip of rain.

빗변(一邊) 〖幾〗 the hypotenuse.

빗장 a bolt; a (cross)bar. ¶ ~을 걸다 bar the gate.

빗질하다 comb (one's hair).

빗치개 an instrument for parting hair and cleaning combs.

빙(一) ¶ ~돌다 circle [turn] round; swing.

빙고(氷庫) an icehouse.

빙과(氷菓) an ice; a popsicle.

빙괴(氷塊) a lump [block] of ice.

빙그레 ¶ ~웃다 beam 《*upon a person*》; smile 《*at a person*》.
빙그르르 《go, turn》 round and round.
빙글거리다 smile 《*at a person*》; beam 《*upon a person*》.
빙벽(氷壁) an ice ridge.
빙부(聘父) 장인. ☞ round; circle.
빙빙 ~돌다 turn round and round.
빙산(氷山) an iceberg; an ice floe. ¶ ~의 일각 a tip of an iceberg / 이 사건은 ~의 일각에 지나지 않다 This case is nothing but a small part of the whole. *or* This incident is only the tip of the iceberg.
빙상(氷上) ¶ ~에서 on the ice. ‖ ~경기 ice sports.
빙설(氷雪) ice and snow.
빙수(氷水) shaved ice; iced water.
빙원(氷原) an ice field.
빙자(憑藉) ~하다 make a pretext 〔plea〕 of; make an excuse of. ¶ …을 ~하여 under the pretense 〔pretext〕 of.
빙점(氷點) the freezing point.
빙초산(氷醋酸) 〖化〗glacial acetic acid.
빙충맞다 (be) clumsy; stupid.
빙충맞이, 빙충이 a clumsy 〔stupid〕 person.
빙탄(氷炭) ¶ ~불상용(不相容)이다 be as irreconcilable as oil and water; agree like cats and dogs; be antagonistic to each other.
빙그러지다 go wrong; 《성질이》 have a perverse 〔crooked〕 temper.
빙판(氷板) a frozen 〔an icy〕 road.
빙하(氷河) 〖地〗a glacier. ‖ ~시대 the glacial 〔ice〕 age / ~작용 glaciation.
빚 a debt; a loan. ¶ ~을 지다 run 〔get〕 into debt; incur debt / ~을 갚다 pay off a debt.
빚거간(一周旋) ~하다 act as a loan agent. 〔a loan.
빚내다 borrow money 《*from*》; get
빚놀이 lending money; making a loan.
빚다 ① 《술을》 brew 《wine》; 《만두·송편 따위를》 shape dough for; make dumplings. ② ☞ 빚어내다.
빚돈 a debt; a loan; liabilities; borrowings.
빚물이하다 pay *another*'s debts.
빚받이하다 collect 〔debts〕.
빚어내다 bring about 〔on〕; give rise to; cause; engender. ¶ 분쟁을 ~ bring about trouble; give rise to dispute.
빚쟁이 a moneylender; a usurer (고리 대금업자); a dun (받으로 온).
빚주다 lend 〔loan〕 《*a person*》 money; 〔contract〕 a debt; owe.
빚지다 run 〔get〕 into debt; incur
빛 ① 《광명》light; 《광선》rays 〔of light〕; a beam; a flash(섬광); a gleam(어둠 속의); a twinkle(별의); a glimmer(미광); 《광휘》glow; shine; brightness; brilliancy. ② 《색세》a color; a hue; a tint; a tinge(빛깔). ③ 《안색 따위》 complexion; color; 《표정》a countenance; a look; an air(표시) a sign. ¶ 피곤한 ~을 나타내다 show signs of fatigue.
빛깔 color(ing); hue. ☞ 색채.
빛나다 ① 《광선이》give forth light; radiate. ② 《광차가》shine; glitter(금 따위가); be bright; glisten(반사로); glimmer(어슴푸레); gleam(어둠 속에); flash(번쩍); twinkle(별이); sparkle(보석이); be lustrous(윤이). ③ 《영광스럽게》 be bright 〔brilliant〕. ¶ 빛나는 장래 a bright 〔promising〕 future / 빛나는 업적 a brilliant achievement.
빛나다 light up; brighten; make 《*a thing*》 shine. ¶ 이름을 ~ win fame.
빛살 rays of light.
빠개다 split; cleave; rip. ¶ 장작을 ~ split firewood.
빠개지다 split 〔apart〕; cleave; be split 〔broken〕; 《일이》get spoilt; be ruined; come to nothing.
빠드득거리다 creak; grate; rasp.
…빠듯 a bit less than; just under; a little short of. ¶ 두 자 ~ just under two feet 〔long〕.
빠듯하다 ① 《겨우 미침》(be) barely enough. ¶ ~빠듯이 barely; narrowly. ② 《꼭 껴》be tight; close fitting. ¶ 빠듯한 구두 tight shoes.
빠트리다 ① 《누락》omit; miss 〔out〕; pass over; leave out. ② 《잃다》 lose; drop. ③ 《물속 따위에》drop; throw into 《*a river*》; 《함정에》entrap; ensnare; 《유혹 등에》lead into 《*temptation*》; allure.
빠르다 ① 《속도가》(be) quick; fast; swift; speedy; rapid. ¶ 발이 ~ be swift of foot / 진보가 ~ make rapid progress. ② 《시간이》(be) early; premature(시기 상조). ¶ 빠르면 빠를수록 좋다 The sooner, the better.
빠이빠이 bye-bye (주로 아이들 말).
빠지다 ① 《허방 따위에》 fall 〔get〕 into; 《물에》sink; go down. ¶ 물 속에 ~ sink under the water. ② 《탐닉》indulge in; be given 〔up〕 to; abandon *oneself* to; 《어떤 상태에》fall 〔get, run〕 into; be led into. ¶ 주색에 ~ be addicted to sensual desires; indulge in wine and women / 위험 상태에 ~ run into danger.

③ 《탈락》 come (fall, slip) off (out). ¶ 털이 ~ one's hair falls out; one's hair thins out. ④ 《빠다》 be left out; be omitted. ⑤ 《없다》 be wanting; be missing. ⑤ 《살이》 become thin; lose flesh (병으로). ⑥ 《물 등이》 drain; flow off; run out. ⑦ 《빛·힘·김 따위가》 come out (out); be removed; be taken out(얼룩 등이). ⑧ 《지나가다》 go (through); pass through. ⑨ 《골목으로》 go by a lane. ⑨ 《탈출》 escape; slip out; get away; 《피하다》 evade; excuse oneself from. ¶ 위기를 빠져나가다 escape danger. ⑩ 《탈퇴하다》 leave; quit; withdraw 《from》; secede from. ⑪ 《…만 못하다》 be inferior (to); fall behind. ⑫ 빠지지 않다 be as good as 《anyone else》. ⑫ 《제비에 뽑히다》 draw; win 《in a lottery》; fall 《to one's lot》.

빠짐없이 without omission; one and all; in full; exhaustively; thoroughly. ¶ ~ 투표하다 vote without exception.

빡빡 ① 《얽은 모양》 ¶ ~ 얽은 pitted all over one's face. ② 《머리깎은 모양》 ¶ ~ 깎다 crop the hair; have one's hair cut close.

빡빡하다 ① 《꽉차다》 (be) close; closely packed; chock-full. ② 《두름성이》 (be) unadaptable; rigid; strait-laced. ③ 《음식 따위가》 (be) dry and hard.

빤드르르 ~ 한 smooth; glassy; 《glossily》.

빤들거리다 《매끄럽다》 be smooth; 《약게만 굴다》 be too smart.

빤들빤들 smoothly; glossily; lustrously; shiningly; 《빈들빈들》 idly; lazily; slothfully.

빤작거리다 glitter; sparkle; twinkle.

빤하다 《분명하다》 (be) transparent; clear; obvious. ¶ 빤한 사실 an obvious fact / 빤한 거짓말 a transparent lie.

빤히 ① 《분명히》 clearly; plainly; obviously; undoubtedly. ② 《뚫어지게》 staringly; with a searching look.

빨간 downright; utter. ¶ ~ 거짓말 a downright lie(barefaced) lie.

빨강 red (color); crimson (심홍색).

빨강이 《물건》 a red-colored thing.

빨갛다 (be) crimson; deep red.

빨개지다 turn bright-red; redden.

빨갱이 《공산주의자》 a Red; a Commie 《俗》; a Communist.

빨그스름하다 be reddish; reddy.

빨다[1] 《입으로》 suck; sip; smoke, puff at 《담배를》; 《습수》 absorb; suck in.

빨다[2] 《세탁》 wash; launder.

빨다[3] 《뾰족함》 (be) pointed; sharp.

빨대 a straw; a sipper(종이의).

빨딱거리다 《가슴이》 go pit-a-pat; throb; palpitate; 《맥이》 pulsate.

빨랑빨랑 quickly; promptly; in a hurry.

빨래 washing; the laundry(세탁물). ~하다 wash. ¶ ~ 집게 a clothespin / ~터 a wash place / ~통 a washtub / ~판 a washboard / 빨랫감 washing; laundry / 빨랫줄 a clothesline.

빨리 《일찍》 early; 《바로》 soon; immediately; instantly; 《신속》 fast; rapidly; quickly; in haste(급히); promptly(기민하게). ¶ 걸음을 ~하다 quicken one's steps / ~해라 Go at once ! / ~해라 Make haste! or Hurry up!

빨리다 ① 《흡수되다》 be absorbed; be sucked (soaked) up. ② 《착취당하다》 be squeezed (extorted). ③ 《빨아먹이다》 let 《a person》 suck; suckle 《a child》.

빨병 (-瓶) 《수통》 a canteen; a flask; a water bottle 《英》.

빨아내다 suck (soak) up; absorb; 《醫》 aspirate (고름 따위를).

빨아들이다 《기체를》 inhale; breathe (draw) in; 《액체를》 suck in; absorb. ¶ 연기를 ~ inhale the smoke.

빨아먹다 ① 《음식을》 suck; imbibe. ② 《우려내다》 squeeze; exploit.

빨치산 a partisan; a guerrilla.

빨판 《吸》 a sucker.

빳빳하다 (be) rigid; stiff; straight and stiff. ¶ 풀기 ~ 뻣뻣한 stiffly starched.

빵[1] bread; 《버터 〔잼〕 바른》 ~ bread and butter (jam) / ~ 한 조각 a slice (piece) of bread / ~을 굽다 bake (toast) bread.

빵[2] 《소리》 pop; bang.

빵꾸 puncture. ¶ ~나다 be punctured; have a blowout; have (suffer) a flat tire.

빵집 a bakery; a bakeshop《美》.

빻다 pound; pulverize; grind into powder(갈아서).

빼기 《數》 subtraction. ¶ ~를 하다 subtract; take away 《a number from another》.

빼내다 ① 《골라내다》 pick (single) out; select; 《뽑아내다》 draw (pull) out; extract. ② 《훔쳐내다》 pilfer; steal. ③ 《매인 몸을》 ransom; redeem; bail out.

빼놓다 ① 《빼어 놓다》 drop; omit; leave out. ② 《뽑아 놓다》 draw (pull) out; extract. ③ 《골라 놓다》 pick (single) out; select.

빼다 ① 《빼어 놓다》 take (pull) out; draw 《a sword》; extract 《a tooth》. ② 《얼룩을》 remove 《an inkblot》; wash off; take out.

빼먹다 ③ 《생략》 omit; exclude; take off; leave out. ④ 《감산》 subtract 《from》; deduct 《from》. ¶10에서 5를 ~ subtract five from ten. ⑤ 《회피하다》 evade; shirk; avoid. ¶꽁무니를 ~ shirk one's responsibility. ⑥ 《차려 입다》 dress (doll) up.

빼먹다 ① 《빠뜨리다》 omit; leave (miss) out; skip over(건너뛰다). ② 《훔쳐내다》 pilfer; steal. ③ 《수업을》 학교를 ~ play truant (hooky 《美俗》).

빼물다 《거만하게》 be haughty; pout one's lips (화가 나서).

빼쏘다 be exactly alike.

빼앗기다 ① 《탈취》 be deprived (robbed) of 《something》; have 《something》 taken away. ② 《정신을》 be absorbed (engrossed) 《in》; 《매혹되다》 be fascinated (captivated).

빼앗다 ① 《탈취》 take 《a thing》 away from 《a person》; snatch 《a thing》 from; 《약탈》 rob 《a person》 of 《a thing》; plunder; pillage; 《찬탈》 usurp 《the throne》; 《박탈》 divest (deprive) 《a person》 of 《a thing》; 《함락》 capture 《a castle》. ② 《정신을》 absorb 《one's attention》; engross 《one's mind》; 《매혹하다》 fascinate; charm; captivate.

빼어나다 excel 《in》; surpass; be superior 《to》; be excellent.

백¹ 《후원자》 a backer; a supporter; a patron; 《연출·배경》 patronage; backing; pull 《美》.

백² 《소리》 ¶~ 소리 지르다 shout; cry out; brawl. [closely.

빽빽이 compactly; tightly; thickly;

빽빽하다 《좁촘하다》 (be) close; 《촘밀》 (be) dense; thick; 《가득하다》 (be) packed (to the) full; chock-full; 《막히다》 (be) clogged stuffy.

뺀들거리다 idle one's time away.

뺄셈 subtraction. ~하다 subtract.

뺑 round; around. ¶~ 둘러싸다 surround completely.

뺑소니 flight. ¶~치다 《도망》 run away; take 《to》 flight; 《자동차가》 make a hit and run. ∥~차 《운전사, 사고》 a hit-and-run car (driver, accident).

뺨 a cheek. ¶~을 때리다 slap 《a person》 in the cheek / ~ 맞다 get slapped in the cheek / ~을 비비다 rub one's cheek(손으로); press (nestle) one's cheek against another's (남의 뺨에).

뺨치다 ① 《때리다》 give 《a person》 a slap in the cheek. ② 《무색케하다》 outdo; outshine. ¶전문가를 뺨치는 솜씨다 (almost) outdo a professional.

뻐근하다 feel heavy; have a dull pain.

뻐기다 boast; be proud(haughty); give oneself airs; talk big(말로).

뻐꾸기 《鳥》 a cuckoo. [apart.

뻐끔하다 (be) (wide) open; split

뻐드렁니 a projecting front tooth; a bucktooth.

뻐꺽 ¶담배를 ~ 피우다 puff at a cigarette 《one's pipe》.

뻐적지근하다 feel stiff and sore. ¶어깨가 ~ feel stiff in the shoulders.

뻔뻔하다 (be) shameless; impudent; audacious; unabashed. ¶뻔뻔하게 impudently; shamelessly; brazen-facedly; saucily.

뻔하다 ☞ 빤하다.

뻔² 《까딱하면…》 be (come, go) near 《doing》; almost; nearly (do); just barely escape 《doing》. ¶ (하마터면) 죽을 ~ come near being dead (killed).

뻔히 ☞ 빤히.

뻗다 ① 《가지·뿌리 등이》 extend; spread; stretch. ¶뿌리가 (를) ~ spread the root. ② 《연이음》 extend; stretch; run. ¶동서로 ~ run east and west / …까지 뻗어 있다 extend to (as far as)…. ③ 《팔다리를》 extend; stretch (out). ¶손을 ~ reach out 《one's hand》 《to, for》. ④ 《발전》 make progress; develop; expand. ⑤ 《죽다》 collapse; pass out.

뻗대다 hold out 《against》; take a stand 《against》; hold one's own 《against》; do not yield 《to》.

뻗다 《관계》 ¶조카 ~이다 stand 《to one》 in the relation of nephew.

뻣뻣하다 《억세다》 (be) stiff; hard; 《태도가》 (be) tough; unyielding. ¶목이 ~ have a stiff neck.

뻥 ① 《소리》 pop. ¶~하고 with a pop. ② 《구멍이》 ¶~ 뚫어지다 break open. ③ ☞ 거짓말.

뻥굿거리다 smile 《at》; beam.

뻥하다 be at a loss; (be) puzzled.

뻥실거리다 beam; smile gently.

뼈 ① 《골격》 a bone; 《유골》 ashes; remains. ¶생선 ~를 바르다 bone a fish / ~가 부러지다 break a bone. ② 《숨은 뜻》 a hidden meaning. ¶~있는 말 words full of hidden (latent) meaning; suggestive words.

뼈다귀 a bone.

뼈대 《골격》 frame; build; physique; 《구조물의》 skeleton; framework; structure. ¶~가 단단한 stoutly-built.

뼈물다 plan to do 《something》.

뼈저리다 feel (go) deep into one's heart; sting (cut, touch) 《one》 to the quick. ¶뼈저린 keen; severe; acute / 뼈저리게 keenly;

뼈지다 severely; acutely; bitterly.
뼈지다 《옹골차다》 (be) solid; firm; 《딱딱》 (be) sharp; pungent; harsh.
뼘 a span. ¶ ~으로 재다 span.
뽀얗다 (be) grayish; whitish.
뽐내다 boast; be proud; be haughty; give *oneself* airs.
뽑다 ① 《박힌 것을》 pull (take) out; draw 《*a sword, lots*》; extract 《*a tooth*》; root up 《*a tree*》. ② 《선발》 select; pick (single) out; 《선거》 elect. ③ 《모집》 enlist; enroll; recruit.
뽕 the mulberry leaf. ‖ ~나무 mulberry (tree).
뽕빠지다 suffer a heavy loss; go bankrupt; fail; be broken.
뾰로통하다 (be) sullen; sulky; 《서술적》 look sullen.
뾰롱뾰롱하다 (be) ill-tempered; cross-grained.
뾰루지 an eruption; a boil. ¶ ~가 나다 A boil forms.
뾰조록하다 《서술적》 stick out a bit.
뾰족탑(-塔) a steeple; a spire; a pinnacle.
뾰족하다 (be) pointed; sharp(-pointed). ¶ 뾰족하게 하다 sharpen.
뿌리 a root. ¶ ~ 깊은 deep-rooted 《*evil*》 / ~를 박다 take (strike) root; root / ~를 빼다 root up.
뿌리다 《껴얹다》 sprinkle 《물 따위》; spray 《*an insecticide*》; strew 《꽃 따위》; 《흩뜨리다》 scatter; diffuse; disperse. ¶ 씨를 ~ sow seed.
뿌리치다 shake off; reject; refuse; discard. ¶ 손목을 ~ shake off 《*a person's*》 hand.
뿌옇다 (be) whitish; grayish; hazy 《안개같이》.

뿐 merely; alone; only; but. ¶ …할 ~만 아니라 not only… but (also).
뿔 a horn; an antler 《사슴의》. ¶ ~로 받다 horn; gore. ‖ ~세공 a hornwork.
뿔뿔이 scatteredly; in all directions; separately; dispersedly. ¶ ~ 흩어지다 be scattered; scatter; disperse; break up.
뿜다 belch; emit; spout; spurt; gush out. ¶ 연기를 ~ belch smoke / 용암을 ~ spout lava.
뿡뿡 ¶ ~ 소리내다 honk; hoot.
삐거덕거리다 creak; squeak; grate.
삐다¹ 《수족을》 sprain; dislocate; wrench; twist.
삐다² 《물이》 subside; go down; sink.
삐대다 make a nuisance of *oneself*; outstay (wear out) *one's* welcome.
삐딱거리다 wobble; be shaky 《rickety》.
삐딱하다 (be) slant; inclined.
삐라 (hand)bill; a leaflet. ¶ ~를 뿌리다 distribute handbills (leaflets). 《치다 beep; page》.
삐삐 a beeper; a pager.
삐죽거리다 pout 《*one's*》 lips; make a lip. ¶ 울려고 ~ sulk (pout) almost to tears.
삐죽하다 (be) protruding.
삑 《기적식》 with a whistle. ¶ ~ 울리다 whistle.
뺑 round; around 《美》; completely 《완전히》. ¶ ~ 둘러싸다 surround 《*a person, a thing*》.
삥땅 pocketing; a kickback 《美》; a rake-off. ¶ ~ 하다 take off; pocket a rake-off 《*of*》.

배수(倍數)의 표현 방법

1. …의 ×배《크기·길이 따위》
   (1) ×times as + 형용사 + as…
   그녀의 방은 내 방보다 두 배나 크다
   Her room is *twice* as large as mine.
   이 다리는 저 다리의 3배나 길다
   This bridge is *three times* as long as that one.
   (2) ×times as + 부사 + as…
   그는 적어도 나보다 배나 공부한다
   He studies at least *twice* as hard as I do.
   (3) ×times the + 명사 + of…; ×times + 인칭대명사의 소유격 + 명사
   그 나라의 면적은 한국의 5배나 된다
   The country is *five times* the size of Korea. / 그는 나의 2배의 급료를 받고 있다 He gets *twice* your salary.
2. …의 ×배《의 수》
   ×times as many(much) + 복수명사(단수명사) + as…
   그녀는 나의 배나 되는 책을 갖고 있다

   She has *twice* as many books *as* I do. / 너는 적어도 나의 3배의 돈을 갖고 있다 You have at least *three times as much* money *as* I do.
3. …의 몇배《몇십배나(부른, 되는)》…
   many times(dozens of times) + 형용사(부사)+as…; many times(dozens of times) as much + 단수명사 + as…
   그녀는 나보다 몇배나 빠르게 헤엄칠 수 있다 She can swim *many times as fast* as I can. / 한국은 지금 20년전의 몇십배나 되는 기름을 소비하고 있다 Korea consumes *dozens of times as much* oil as she did 20 years ago.
4. …의 절반의《크기, 길이, 돈, 책 따위》
   half as + 형용사(부사) + as…; half as many(much) + 복수명사(단수명사) + as…
   이 정원은 저것의 약 절반 크기이다
   This garden is about *half* as large *as* that.

入

사¹ 《단춧구멍의》 a buttonhole stitch. ☞ 사뜨다.
사² 《樂》 G; sol 《이》. [snake.
사(巳) the zodiacal sign of the
사(四) four; the fourth (제 4). ‖ ~차원의 the fourth dimension.
사(私) privateness; privacy; self 《자기》; self-interest 《사리》. ‖ ~가 있는 selfish; self-interested / ~가 없는 unselfish; disinterested.
사(邪) wrong; injustice; unrighteousness; 《사악》 evil; vice.
사(社) 《회사》 a company; a corporation 《美》; a firm.
사(紗) (silk) gauze; gossamer.
…사(史) history. ‖ 국(世界)~ Korean (world) history.
…사(辭) a message. ‖ 환영~ an address of welcome.
사가(史家) a historian.
사가(私家) a private residence 《집》; one's (private) home 《가정》.
사각(四角) a square. ‖ ~의 four-cornered; square. ‖ ~형 a quadrilateral; a tetragon.
사각(死角) the dead angle (ground).
사각(射角) an angle of fire.
사각(斜角) 《數》 an oblique angle.
사각사각 ‖ ~ 먹다 munch; crunch.
사감(私憾) a personal spite (grudge, resentment); a bitter feeling; malice.
사감(舍監) a dormitory inspector (superintendent, dean); 《여자》 a house mistress; a dormitory matron.
사개 a dovetail (joint).
사거리(四―) a crossroads; a cross.
사거리(射距離) a range.   Ling.
사건(事件) an event; an incident; a happening; 《일》 an affair; a matter; 《법률상의》 a case. ‖ 생사가 걸린 ~ a matter of life and death / 역사상 획기적인 ~ the epoch-making events of history / ~를 흐지부지 해버리다 hush (cover) up an affair / ~를 떠맡다 take up a case in hand. ‖ ~기자 a news reporter on the police beat / 간통~ an adultery scandal.
사격(射擊) firing; shooting. ‖ ~하다 shoot; fire at. ‖ ~대회 a shooting match / ~ 술 marksmanship / ~ 연습 shooting practice / ~장 a firing range / ~전을 벌이다 fight a gun battle 《with》; exchange (shots) 《with》.
사견(私見) one's personal (private) opinion (view). ‖ ~으로는 in my opinion.
사경(死境) a deadly situation; the brink of death; 《궁경》 a sad plight. ‖ ~을 헤매다 hover (hang) between life and death / ~을 벗어나다 escape from the jaws of death.
사경제(私經濟) 《경제》 private (individual) economy.   [sons.
사계(四季) 《사철》 the four seasons
사계(斯界) this circle (world, field); the line; the subject. ‖ ~의 권위 an authority on the subject; an expert in the line.
사고(社告) an announcement (a notice) of a company.
사고(事故) an incident 《예측 못한》; an accident; 《고장》 a hitch; a trouble. ‖ ~로 죽다 be killed in an accident / ~를 일으키다 cause an accident. ‖ ~다발지점 a 〔an accident〕 black spot / ~뭉치 a trouble maker / ~방지운동 a "Safety First" movement / ~사 an accidental death / 《교통》~ a railway 〔traffic〕 accident.
사고(思考) thought; consideration. ‖ ~하다 think; consider; regard 《a thing》 as. ‖ ~력 ability to think; thinking power / ~방식 a way of thinking.
사고무친(四顧無親) ~하다 have no one to turn to for help; be without kith and kin.   [man
사공(沙工) a boatman; a ferryman
사과(沙果) an apple. ‖ ~나무 an apple tree / ~산(酸) malic acid / ~ 사이다 cider; apple wine.
사과(謝過) an apology. ‖ ~하다 apologize 《for》; make 〔offer〕 an apology; beg one's pardon. ‖ ~문(狀) a written apology; a letter of apology.
사관(士官) an officer. ‖ 육군〔해군〕~ a military 〔naval〕 officer. ‖ ~학교 a military academy / ~후보생 a cadet.
사관(史觀) a historical view.
사교(邪敎) a heretical 〔false〕 religion. ‖ ~도 a heretic.
사교(社交) social relationships; society. ‖ ~적인 sociable / ~상의 social. ‖ ~가 a sociable person; a good mixer 《美口》 / ~계 fashionable society 〔circles〕 (~계의 여왕 the queen 〔belle〕 of

사구(四球)〖野〗《give》four balls; walk. ¶ ~로 나가다 walk.
사구(死球)〖野〗 a pitch which hits the batter.
사구(砂丘) a sandhill; a dune.
사군자(四君子)〖美術〗 the Four Gracious Plants(=plum, orchid, chrysanthemum and bamboo).
사권(私權)〖法〗 a private right.
사귀(邪鬼) an evil spirit; a devil.
사귀다 make friends 《with》; associate 《keep company》 with; mix with; go around 《about》 with. ¶ 좋은 [나쁜] 친구와 ~ keep good [bad] company / …와 친하게 ~ be on friendly terms with; get along with 《a person》.
사귐성(-性) affability; sociability. ¶ ~있는 sociable; congenial.
사그라지다 go down; subside; decompose(썩어); melt away (녹아서); be resolved (종기 등이).
사극(史劇) a historical play (drama).
사근사근하다(성질이) (be) amiable; affable; pleasant; (먹기에) (be) crisp; fresh.
사글세(-貰) monthly rent (rental). ‖ ~방 a rented room / 사글셋집 a rented house.
사금(砂金) gold dust; alluvial gold. ‖ ~채집 alluvial mining.
사금융(私金融) private loan.
사금파리 a piece of broken glass [ceramics].
사기(士氣) morale; fighting spirit. ¶ ~가 떨어지다 be demoralized / ~를 고무하다 raise the morale / ~왕성하다 have high morale.
사기(史記) a historical book [work]; a chronicle.
사기(沙器) chinaware; porcelain.
사기(詐欺) (a) fraud; fraudulence; a swindle. ~하다 (치다) swindle; commit a fraud. ‖ ~를 당하다 get [be] swindled. ‖ ~꾼 a swindler; an impostor / ~혐의자 a fraudulence suspect.
사기업(私企業) a private enterprise; an individual enterprise.
사나이 ①(남자) a man; a male. ②(남성) manhood; the male sex. ③(사내다움) manliness. ¶ ~다운 manly; manlike; manful / ~답게 like a man; in a manly manner.
사날¹ three or four days; several days.
사날² ¶ ~좋다 be self-indulgent; be arbitrary; have one's own way / ~좋게 as one pleases [likes]; arbitrarily.
사납금(社納金) (택시 기사의) money which taxi drivers have to turn over to the company out of their daily earning.
사납다 (be) fierce; wild; violent; rude; rough; ferocious; (운수가) (be) unlucky. ¶ 사나운 짐승 a wild animal; a fierce beast / 사납게 생긴 rough-[fierce-]looking.
사낭(砂囊) a sandbag; (날짐승의) a gizzard.
사내 ① ☞ 사나이. ‖ ~아이 a boy / ~ 종 a man servant. ②(남편) a husband.
사내(社內) ¶ ~의[에] in the firm [office]. ‖ ~결혼 an intra-office marriage / ~보(報) a house organ [journal] / ~연수(研修) in-house training / ~유보 internal reserves.
사냥 hunting; a hunt. ~하다 hunt; shoot. ¶ 여우 ~ fox hunting / ~가다 go hunting. ‖ ~감 game; a game animal / ~개 a hound; a hunting dog / ~꾼 a hunter / ~터 a hunting ground.
사념(邪念) an evil thought [mind, desire].
사농공상(士農工商) the traditional Four Classes of society (i.e. aristocrats, farmers, artisans and tradesmen).
사다 ①(구매) buy; purchase. ¶ 싸게 [비싸게] ~ buy cheap [dear]; make a good [bad] bargain / 외상[현금]으로 ~ buy 《a thing》 on credit [for cash]. ②(가져오다) incur; invite; bring 《upon》 / 환심을 ~ win [gain] 《a person's》 favor / 미움을 ~ incur hatred. ③(인정하다) appreciate 《a person's effort》; think highly of 《a person's ability》.
사다리 ☞ 사다리꼴. ‖ ~꼴〖數〗 a trapezoid / ~소방차 a fire engine with ladder; a hook-and-ladder.
사다새〖鳥〗 a pelican. ‖ ~ truck.
사다리차(climb, go up) a ladder; (소방용) an extension ladder. ¶ ~를 놓다 place [set up] a ladder 《against》.
사단(社團) a corporation. ‖ ~법인 a corporation; a corporate body.
사단(事端) the origin [cause] of an affair; the beginning. ¶ ~을 일으키다 stir up troubles.
사단(師團) a [an army] division. ‖ ~사령부 the division[all] headquarters (생략 D.H.Q.) / ~장 a division[al] commander.
사담(私談) a private talk. ~하다 have a private talk with.
사당(私黨) a faction; a private party.
사당(祠堂) a shrine; a sanctuary.
사대(事大) ‖ ~근성 slavish sub-

mission to power / ～사상 [주의]
flunkeyism; toadyism / ～주의자
a toady; a flunkey.
사대부(士大夫) a man of a high birth.
사도(私道) a private road [path].
사도(邪道) an evil way [course]; vice.
사도(使徒) an apostle 《of peace》. ‖ ～행전 [聖] the Acts of the Apostles / 십이(十二)～ the (Twelve) Apostles.
사도(斯道) the line (방면); the art (기술). ¶ ～의 대가 an authority in the line; a master of the art.
사돈(査頓) a member of the family of 《one's》 daughter-(son-)in-law; in-laws (美口). ¶ ～의 팔촌 distant relatives. ‖ ～집 the house of in-laws.
사동(使童) an office (errand) boy.
사두마차(四頭馬車) a coach-and-four; a four-horse coach.
사들이다 lay in 《goods》; stock 《a shop with goods》; purchase.
사디스트 a sadist.
사디즘 sadism.
사뜨다 buttonhole; hemstitch. 「cross-stitch.
사라사 printed cotton; chintz; calico (美); print.
사라지다 vanish; disappear; fade away; go out of sight; (소멸) die away [out]; (어둠 속으로 ～ disappear in the darkness / 연기처럼 ～ vanish like smoke.
사람 ① (인류) man (kind); (개인) a man; a person; a human being. ¶ 김이라는 ～ a man called Kim; a Mr. Kim / ～의 떼 a crowd; a throng / ～의 일생 a human life / ～을 보내다 send a messenger / ～은 만물의 영장 Man is the soul of the universe. ② (인재) a man of talent; a capable man; (성격·인물) character; nature; personality. ¶ ～이 좋은 [나쁜] good-(ill-)natured / ～을 잘[잘못] 보다 be a good (bad) judge of character / ～ 구실을 하다 worth 《one's》 salt / ～들 앞에서 울다 cry in the presence of others.
사람답다 (be) truly human; decent; modest.
사람멀미하다 feel sick from the jostling of a crowd.
사랑 love; affection; attachment (애착); tender passion. ～하다 love; be fond of; be attached to. ¶ ～는 beloved; dear / ～스러운 lovable; lovely / 정신적 ～ platonic love / 불의의 ～ illicit love / ～하는 《one's》 sweetheart; a lover (남자); a lover (여자) / ～의 보금자리 a love nest / ～의 표시 a love token; a token of affection / ～에 번민하다 be love-

sick [lovelorn] / ～을 고백하다 confess 《one's》 love 《to》 / ～에 빠지다 fall in love 《with》. ‖ ～싸움 a matrimonial [love] quarrel.
사랑(舍廊) a detached room used as man's quarters. ‖ ～양반 your husband / ～채 a detached
사랑니 a wisdom tooth. 「house.
사래질 winnowing. ～하다 winnow.
사레 ¶ ～ 들리다 swallow the wrong way; be choked 《by, with》.
사려(思慮) thought; consideration; discretion; sense; prudence(분별). ¶ ～ 깊은 thoughtful; prudent; discreet; sensible.
사력(死力) ¶ ～을 다하다 make desperate [frantic] efforts.
사력(社歷) (회사의) the history of a company; (개인의) 《one's》 career with 〔in〕 a company.
사련(邪戀) illicit 〔immoral〕 love.
사령(司令) command. ‖ ～관 a commander; a commandant / ～부 the headquarters / ～선 a command module (우주선의) / ～탑 a conning tower / 연합군 최고 ～관 the Supreme Commander for the Allied Powers (생략 SCAP).
사령(辭令) ① (응대의 말) diction; wording. ¶ 외교～ diplomatic language. ② (사령장) a written appointment [order].
사례(事例) an instance; an example; a case; a precedent (선례). ¶ ～연구 a case study.
사례(謝禮) (감사) thanks; (보수) a remuneration. ～하다 reward; remunerate; recompense 《a person for》; pay a fee. ¶ ～금 a reward; a recompense.
사로자다 have a restless sleep.
사로잠그다 lock [bolt] 《a door》 halfway.
사로잡다 catch 《an animal》 alive; capture [take] 《a person》 (생포); (매혹) captivate; charm.
사로잡히다 be captured (alive); be taken prisoner; (매혹) be captivated; (얽매이다) be seized with 《fear》; be a slave of 《honor and gain》. 「tise).
사론(史論) a historical essay (treatise).
사론(私論) 《one's》 personal opinion.
사뢰다 tell; relate; inform; report 《to a high personage》.
사료(史料) historical materials.
사료(思料) ～하다 consider; regard.
사료(飼料) fodder; feed; forage.
사륙배판(四六倍判) a large octavo.
사륙판(四六判) duodecimo; 12mo.
사르다¹ (불을) set fire 《to》; make a fire; (피우다) kindle; burn(태우다); set 《a thing》 on fire.

사르다[2] (곡식을) winnow.
사르르 gently; lightly; softly.
사리 (국수·새끼 등의) a coil.
사리 (私利) one's own interest; self-interest; personal gain (profit). ¶ ~를 꾀하다 look after one's own interests.
사리 (송利) *sarira* (梵); ashes (화장한). ‖ ~탑 a *sarira* stupa / ~함 a *sarira* casket.
사리 (事理) reason. ¶ ~에 닿다 stand to reason; be reasonable; be logical / ~에 밝다 be sensible; have good sense.
사리다 ① (말다) coil (up); wind (*rope*, etc.) round. ② (몸을 아끼다) spare *oneself*; take care of *oneself*; shrink from danger.
사린 (四隣) the surrounding countries; the whole neighborhood.
사립 (私立) ¶ ~의 private. ‖ ~탐정 a private detective / ~학교 (대학) a private school (college, university).
사립문(一門) a gate made of twigs.
사마귀 a mole; 《무사마귀》 a wart.
사막(沙漠) a desert. ¶ 사하라 ~ the Sahara (Desert). ‖ ~화 desertification.
사망(死亡) death; decease. ~하다 die; pass away. ¶ ~률을 mortality; the death rate / ~신고서 a notice of death / ~자 the dead; the deceased / ~자 명단 a death roll (list) / ~진단서 a certificate of death / ~추정시각 the estimated time of death.
사면(四面) the four sides; all directions. ¶ ~팔방에 on all sides. ‖ ~체 a tetrahedron.
사면(赦免) (a) pardon; (an) amnesty(대사). ~하다 pardon; remit (*somebody*) off (*a punishment*); let (*somebody*) off (*a penalty*); discharge. ¶ 일반~ a general pardon / 특별~ a particular pardon; a special amnesty.
사면(斜面) a slope; a slant; an inclined plane. ¶ 급(완)~ a steep (an easy) slope.
사면(辭免) ~하다 resign; retire from office.
사면초가(四面楚歌) ¶ ~이다 be surrounded by foes (on all sides); be forsaken by everybody.
사멸(死滅) ~하다 die out; become extinct; be annihilated; perish.
사명(社命) an order of the company.
사명(使命) a mission. ¶ ~을 띠다 be entrusted with a mission. ‖ ~감 a sense of mission.
사모(思慕) ~하다 be attached to; long for; yearn after.
사모(師母) one's teacher's wife. ‖ ~님 Madam; Mrs.

사무(事務) business; affairs; office (clerical) work. ¶ ~적인 businesslike; practical / ~적으로 in a businesslike manner; perfunctorily / ~를 보다 attend to one's business (official duties); do office work / ~를 처리하다 manage (execute) the business / ~에 쫓기다 be pressed (kept busy) with business. ‖ ~관 a secretary; an administrative official / ~관리 office administration / ~당국 the authorities in charge / ~소 an office / ~실 an office (room) / ~용품 office supplies; stationery / ~원 (직원) a clerk; an office worker / ~인계 taking over the work (the management of an office) (*from one's predecessor*) / ~장 a head official / 차관 an undersecretary (美) / ~총장 a secretary-general.
사무자동화(事務自動化) office automation. ¶ ~기기 the office automated machine.
사무치다 touch the heart deeply; sink deeply into one's mind; penetrate (*through*); pierce. ¶ 원한이 골수에 사무쳤다 Resentment has stung (cut, hurt) me to the quick.
사문(死文) ¶ ~화되다 proved (to be) a dead letter.
사문(沙門) (중) a Buddhist monk.
사문(査問) inquiry; inquisition. ~하다 interrogate; examine; inquire (*into a matter*). ‖ ~위원회 an inquiry committee.
사문서(私文書) a private document. ‖ ~위조 forgery of a private document.
사문석(蛇紋石) [鑛] serpentine; ophite (大理석).
사물(死物) a dead (lifeless) thing; an inanimate object.
사물(私物) one's private thing; personal effects.
사물(事物) things; affairs. ¶ 한국의 ~ things Korean.
사물놀이(四物一) (the Korean) traditional percussion quartet; *Samulnori*.
사뭇 (몹시) very much; quite; 《거리낌없이》 as *one* pleases (likes); willfully.
사바사바하다 bribe (buy off) an official.
사바세계(娑婆世界) *Sabha* (梵); this world; the world of suffering; 《이 세상》 earthly; worldly; mundane.
사박거리다 crunch softly.
사박스럽다 (be) rude; rough.
사반(四半) a quarter; one fourth. ‖ ~기 a quarter / ~세기 a quarter of a century.
사반(死斑) a death spot.

사발(沙鉢) a (porcelain) bowl. ¶ ~농하다 live as a beggar. ‖ ~시계 a bowl-shaped clock.
사방(四方) four sides; all directions (quarters); on all sides; on every side; in all directions; all round / ~ 2피트 two feet square / 삼지 ~ 으로 in all directions; far and wide.
사방(砂防) erosion control; sand-bank fixing. ¶ ~공사 sand arrestation work; sand guards.
사방침(四方枕) an armrest; an elbow rest.
사방형(斜方形) a rhomb(us). ¶ ~의 rhombic.
사배(四倍) four times; quadruple. ¶ ~하다 multiply by four; quadruple. ¶ ~의 fourfold.
사범(事犯) an offense; a crime. ¶ 경제~ an economic offense / 선거~ election illegalities.
사범(師範) a teacher; a master; a coach. ‖ ~대학 a college of education / ~학교 a normal school / 검도~ a fencing master.
사법(司法) administration of justice; the judicature. ‖ ~의 judicial; judiciary. ‖ ~경찰 the judicial police / ~관 a judicial officer (official) / ~관 시보 a probationary judicial officer / ~권 judicial power (rights) / ~당국 the judiciary (authorities) / ~ 연수생 a judicial apprentice / ~ 연수원 the Judicial Research and Training Institute / ~제도 the judicial system / ~행정 judicial administration / 국제~ 재판소 the International Court of Justice.
사법(死法) a dead law.
사법(私法) [法] private law.
사법시험(司法試驗) a judicial examination; the State Law Examination.
사변(四邊) ‖ ~형 a quadrilateral.
사변(事變) an incident; a trouble; a disturbance.
사변(思辨) speculation; ~하다 speculate 《about, on》.
사변(斜邊) ㅅ 빗변.
사별(死別) ~하다 be bereaved of 《a son》; lose 《one's husband》.
사병(士兵) a soldier; an enlisted man (美); the rank and file.
사보타주 sabotage. ¶ ~하다 go on a sabotage; go slow.
사복(私服) plain (civilian) clothes. ‖ ~형사 (경찰관) a plainclothes man (policeman).
사복(私腹) ¶ ~을 채우다 fill one's own pocket; enrich oneself.
사본(寫本) a copy; a manuscript; a duplicate (부본). ¶ ~을 만들다 (make a) copy.

사부(四部) ‖ ~작 a tetralogy / ~합주 a quartet / ~합창 a chorus in four parts.
사부(師父) (스승) a fatherly master; an esteemed teacher.
사분(四分) ~하다 divide in four; quarter. ¶ ~의 일 one fourth; a quarter. ‖ ~ [數] a quadrant / ~음표 [樂] a quarter note (美); a crotchet (英). 「amiable.
사분사분하다 ¶ be kindly; gentle;
사분오열(四分五裂) ~하다 be torn apart (asunder, into pieces); be disrupted; become totally disorganized.
사비(私費) private expenses. ¶ ~로 at one's own expense (cost); at private expense.
사분사분 softly; lightly.
사사(私事) personal affairs; private matters.
사사(師事) ~하다 become a person's pupil; study 《under》.
사사건건(事事件件) in everything; each and every event (matter, case, affair).
사사롭다(私私—) (be) personal; private. ¶ 사사로이 personally; privately; in private.
사사오입(四捨五入) ~하다 round 《a number to》; raise 《to a unit》.
사산(死産) a stillbirth. ~하다 give birth to a dead child.
사살(射殺) ~하다 shoot 《a person》 dead (to death).
사상(史上) in history. ¶ ~ 유례가 없는 unparalleled in history.
사상(死傷) ¶ ~자 the killed and wounded; the dead and injured; casualties.
사상(思想) thought; an idea. ¶ 근대~ modern thought / 신~ a new idea / 자유~ a liberal thought / 정치~ political ideas / 진보 (혁명) ~ a progressive (revolutionary) idea. ‖ ~가 a (great) thinker / ~범 political offense; a political offender(사람) / ~전 ideological warfare.
사상(絲狀) ¶ ~의 filiform; thready / ~균 a filamentous fungus.
사색(四色) 《빛깔》 four color; [史] the Four Factions (of the Yi Dynasty); ~ 당쟁 strife among the Four Factions. 「look.
사색(死色) deadly (ghastly) pale
사색(思索) thinking; contemplation; meditation. ~하다 think; contemplate; speculate. ¶ ~적 인 speculative; meditative / ~ 에 잠기다 be given to speculation; be lost in meditation. ‖ ~가 a thinker.
사생(死生) life and (or) death. ¶ ~ 결단하고 at the risk of one's life.

사생(寫生) sketching; a sketch (작품). ~하다 sketch; sketch from nature[life]. ‖ ~대회 a sketch contest.

사생아(私生兒) an illegitimate child; 《경멸적》 a bastard. ¶ ~로 태어나다 be of illegitimate birth; be born out of wedlock.

사생활(私生活) one's private life. ¶ ~에 참견하다 dig (nose) into 《a person's》 private life.

사서(四書) ~삼경(三經) the Four Books and the Three Classics.

사서(司書) a librarian.

사서(史書) a history book.

사서(私書) a private document; 《사신》a private letter. ‖ ~함 a post-office box(생략 P.O.B.).

사서(辭書) ☞ 사전(辭典).

사석(私席) an unofficial [an informal, a private] occasion. ¶ ~에서 at a private meeting.

사선(死線) 《죽음 고비》 a life-or-death crisis. ¶ ~을 넘다 survive a life-or-death crisis.

사선(射線) a trajectory; 《사격선》 firing line.

사선(斜線) an oblique line. 「way」.

사설(私設) ~의 private 《railway》.

사설(邪說) a heretical doctrine.

사설(社說) an editorial (article); a leading article 《英》. ‖ ~란 the editorial column. 「of the world」.

사성(四聖) the four greatest sages

사세(社勢) the influence [strength] of a company. ¶ ~를 확장하다 extend [broaden] the strength of a company.

사세(事勢) the situation; the state of things [affairs]. ¶ ~부득이 unavoidably; out of sheer necessity.

사소(些少) ~한 trifling; trivial; small; slight / ~한 일 a (mere) trifle; a trifling matter; a little thing; (a) triviality.

사수(死守) ~하다 defend 《a position》 to the death [last]; maintain desperately.

사수(射手) a shooter; a marksman; a gunner(포수). ¶명 ~ a crack [master] shot.

사숙(私淑) ~하다 adore 《a person》 in one's heart; take 《a person》 for a model.

사숙(私塾) a private school.

사순절(四旬節) 〖基〗 Lent.

사슬 a chain. ¶ ~을 벗기다 unchain; undo the chain / ~로 매다 chain 《a dog》 / ~에 매인 개 a dog on a chain. ‖ ~고리 a link.

사슴 a deer; a stag (수컷); a hind (암컷). ‖ ~가죽 deer skin / ~고기 venison / ~뿔 an antler / ~사육장 a deer garden.

¶ ~ 내내 all the year round; throughout the year.

사시(斜視) a squint; 〖醫〗 strabismus. ¶ ~의 squint-[cross-] eyed / ~이다 be squint-eyed. / ~수술 〖醫〗 strabotomy / 내[외] ~ cross-eyed [wall-eyed] strabismus.

사시나무 〖植〗 a poplar; an aspen. ¶ ~ 떨듯하다 tremble like an aspen leaf.

사시장춘(四時長春) 《늘 봄》 everlasting spring; 《늘 잘 지냄》 an easy life; a comfortable living.

사식(私食) food privately offered to a prisoner. 「sage」.

사신(私信) a private letter [message].

사신(使臣) an envoy; an ambassador. ¶ ~을 파견하다 dispatch an envoy 《to》.

사실(史實) a historical fact.

사실(私室) a private room.

사실(事實) a fact; the truth(진실); a reality(현실); the case(실정). ¶ ~상 in fact; actually; really; as a matter of fact / ~상의 actual; virtual; practical / 무근의 unfounded; groundless / 움직일 수 없는 ~ an established [accomplished] fact / ~에 반하다 be contrary to the fact / ~을 왜곡하다 falsify the facts; pervert the truth / ~ 그대로 말하다 tell the whole truth; tell it like it is. ‖ ~오인 〖法〗 a mistake of fact / ~조사 fact-finding 《美》.

사실(寫實) ¶ ~적(으로) realistic(-ally); graphic(ally). ‖ ~주의 realism / ~주의자 a realist.

사심(私心) selfishness; self-interest; a selfish motive. ¶ ~이 없는 unselfish; disinterested.

사심(邪心) evil mind; malicious intention.

사십(四十) forty. ¶제 ~ the fortieth / ~대의 사람 a person in his forties. / ~견(肩) shoulder pain one often suffers from around forty years of age.

사십구재(四十九齋) the memorial services on the forty-ninth day after 《a person's》 death.

사악(邪惡) wickedness; evil; vice. ¶ ~한 wicked; vicious; evil / ~한 사람 a wicked man.

사안(私案) one's private plan.

사암(砂岩) 〖地〗 sandstone.

사약(賜藥) ~을 내리다 bestow poison upon 《a person》 as a death penalty.

사양(斜陽) (be in) the setting sun. ¶ ~산업 a declining industry / ~족(族) the new poor; the declining upper class.

사양(辭讓) ~하다 decline; excuse

사어(死語) a dead language; an obsolete word.

사업(事業) 〖일〗 work; a task; 〖기업〗 an enterprise; an undertaking; a project; 《상업·실업》 business; an industry(산업). ¶ 국가적 ～ a state (national) undertaking / ～을 하다 run (carry on) a business; engage in business / ～을 시작하다 start an enterprise / ～에 성공(실패) 하다 succeed (fail) in business / 교육 ～ educational work / 정부(민간) ～ a government (private) enterprise. ‖ ～가 an entrepreneur(기업가); an industrialist(경영가); a businessman(실업가) / ～비 working expense / ～소득 an income from an enterprise / ～소득세 the business tax / ～연도 a business year / ～자금 business funds / ～채 (債) industrial bonds.

사에이치클럽(四─) (a member of) a Four-H [4-H] club.

사역(使役) ～하다 set 《somebody》 to work 《on》; use; employ. ‖ ～동사 〖文〗 a causative verb.

사연(事緣) the origin and circumstances of a case; the (full) story; matters (as they stand). ¶ 「어찌 된 ～이냐」What's the story? / ～은 이러하다 This is how it is. 「the gist.

사연(辭緣) contents (of a letter).

사열(四列) four lines (rows). ¶ ～로 행진하다 go (march) by fours.

사열(査閱) inspection. ～하다 inspect; examine. ‖ ～관 an examiner; an inspector; an inspecting officer / ～식 (hold) a military review; a parade.

사염화(四鹽化) ‖ ～물 〖化〗 tetrachloride.

사영(私營) ～하다 run (operate) privately.

사영(射影) 〖數〗 projection. 「pany).

사옥(社屋) the building (of a company).

사옥(沙浴) a (hot) sand bath.

사욕(私慾) self-interest. ¶ ～ 있는 selfish / ～ 없는 unselfish / ～을 채우다 satisfy one's selfish desires.

사욕(邪慾) an evil passion; a carnal (wicked, vicious) desire.

사용(私用) private (personal) use; (on) private (personal) business (용무). ～하다 turn to private use; appropriate to oneself. ¶ ～ 전화는 삼가하여 주시오 Please refrain from using the telephone for private business.

사용(使用) use; employment. ～하다 use; make use of(이용); employ; apply. ¶ ～을 제한하다 limit the use (of) / ～ 가능한 usable; available; workable. ‖ ～권 the right to use 《something》 / ～료 a rental fee / ～법 how to use; directions for use / ～인 an employee; a hired person 〖美〗 / ～자 a user; an employer(고용주); a consumer (소비자). 「business.

사용(社用) ¶ ～으로 on (company)

사우 a colleague; a friend of a firm.

사우나 ¶ ～탕 a sauna (bath).

사우디아라비아 Saudi Arabia. ¶ ～의 Saudi Arabian. ‖ ～사람 a Saudi; a Saudi Arabian.

사우스포 〖野〗 a southpaw.

사운(社運) ¶ ～을 걸다 stake the fate (future) of a company on 《a project》. 「box.

사운드 sound. ‖ ～박스 a sound

사원(寺院) a Buddhist temple.

사원(私怨) a personal (private) grudge (spite, enmity). ¶ ～을 품다 have a grudge against 《a person》 / ～을 풀다 satisfy one's grudge.

사원(社員) a staff member; an employee (of a company); the staff(총칭). ¶ ～이 되다 join the staff (of a company) / 그는 이 회사의 ～이다 He is on the staff of this company. or He works for this company. ‖ ～식당 the staff canteen / 신입 (퇴직) ～ an incoming (outgoing) employee / 임시 ～ a temporary employee.

사월(四月) April.

사위 a son-in-law. ‖ 사윗감 a suitable person for a son-in-law. 「ing.

사위다 burn up; burn to noth-

사위스럽다 (be) abominable; loathsome; abhorrent; ominous.

사유(私有) ‖ ～의 private (-owned). ‖ ～물 〖재산, 지〗 private possessions (property, land).

사유(事由) a reason; a cause; a ground; conditions. ¶ 다음과 같은 ～로 for the reason(s) given below.

사유(思惟) thinking. ～하다 think; speculate; consider.

사육(飼育) raising; breeding. ～하다 raise; rear; breed; keep 《animals》 in captivity. ‖ ～자 a breeder; a raiser / ～장 a (cat-tle-)breeding farm.

사육제(謝肉祭) the carnival.

사은(謝恩) ‖ ～(대매출) thank-you sales / ～회 a thank-you party; a testimonial dinner.

사의(私意) self-will; a selfish motive; one's own will.

사의(謝意)《감사》thanks; gratitude; appreciation. ¶ ~를 표하다 express one's gratitude.
사의(辭意) one's intention to resign. ¶ ~를 내비치다 hint at resignation / ~를 밝히다 reveal [make known] one's intention to resign.
사이 ① 《거리》(a) distance; 《간격》an interval; 《공간》a space. ¶ ~에 between (둘의); among (셋 이상의); through (통하여); amidst (한 가운데) / 10미터 ~를 두고 at intervals of 10 meters / ~를 두다 leave a space (for). ② 《시간》an interval; time. ¶ ~에 in (for) (a week); during (the lesson); between (중간); while (…동안) / 외출한 ~에 while one is out / 어느 ~에 before one knows. ③ 《관계》relations; terms. ¶ 정다운 ~ harmonious relations / ~가 벌어지다 be estranged from each other / ~를 중재하다 mediate between (two parties); act as go-between / ~를 가르다 estrange / ~가 좋다 (나쁘다) be on good (bad) terms (with).
사이다 (a) soda pop. ‖ ~병 a pop bottle.
사이드카 a sidecar.
사이렌 a siren; a whistle. ¶ ~을 울리다 sound (blow) a siren.
사이비(似而非)《행동·사적으로》false; pseudo; sham; pretended; mock; make-believe. ‖ ~ 학자 a pretended scholar; a charlatan.
사이사이 ① 《공간》spaces; intervals. ② 《시간》(every) now and then.
사이언스 science.
사이언티스트 a scientist.
사이즈 size. ¶ ~가 (안) 맞다 be (out of) one's size / ~를 재다 take the size (of).
사이참(一站)《휴식》a rest; an intermission; a break; 《음식》a snack; a light meal between regular meals. ‖ ~ 사이클 a cycle.
사이클로트론 [理] cyclotron.
사이클링 cycling. ¶ ~ 가다 go cycling (bike-riding).
사이펀 a syphon; a siphon.
사인(死因) 《inquire into》the cause of (a person's) death.
사인(私人) ¶ ~의 자격으로 in one's private (individual) capacity.
사인(私印) a private seal.
사인 [數] a sine (생략 sin).
사인² ①《부호·암호》a signal; a sign. ②《서명》a signature; an autograph. ~하다 sign; autograph. ¶ ~을 받다 get a person's autograph / ~ 좀 부탁합니다 Will you oblige me with your autograph? / ~북 an autograph book.
사일로 [農] a silo.

사임(辭任) resignation. ☞ 사직. ~하다 resign (one's post).
사자(死者) a dead person; the deceased; the dead (총칭); 《사고에의한》fatalities; loss of life.
사자(使者) a messenger.
사자(獅子) a lion; a lioness (암컷).
사자(嗣子) an heir; an heiress.
사자코(獅子-) a pug (snub) nose.
사자후(獅子吼) 《열변》harangue; fiery eloquence. ¶ ~를 토하다 make an impassioned speech.
사장(死藏) ~하다 hoard; keep (a thing) idle; keep idle on stock.
사장(社長) the president (of a company); a managing director (英). ¶ ~실 the president's office / 부~ a vice-president.
사재(私財) private means (funds, property). ¶ ~를 털어 out of one's own pocket (purse); at one's own expense / ~를 투자하다 expend (use) one's funds (on).
사저(私邸) one's private residence.
사적(史的) historic(al). ¶ ~ 고찰 historical researches.
사적(史蹟) a historic spot (site); a place of historic interest. ¶ ~이 많다 be rich in historic remains.

사적(史籍) historical books.
사적(私的) personal; private. ‖ ~ 감정 personal feeling / ~생활 one's private life.
사전(事前) ¶ ~에 before the fact; beforehand; in advance / ~에 알리다 inform (a person) in advance. / ~검열 precensorship / ~선거운동 preelection campaign / ~통고 an advance (previous) notice / ~협의 prior consultation.
사전(辭典) a dictionary. ¶ 인명[지명]~ a biographical (geographical) dictionary / ~을 찾다 look (a word) up in a dictionary; consult (refer to) a dictionary. / ~편집자 a lexicographer / ~학 lexicography.
사절(四折) ¶ ~의 fourfold; folded in four. ¶ ~판 a quarto edition.
사절(使節) an envoy; an ambassador; a delegate. ¶ ~로 가다 go on a (trade) mission (to the U.S.). ‖ ~단 a (military) mission; a delegation / 《방한》문화 ~단 a cultural mission (to Korea).
사절(謝絶) refusal. ~하다 refuse; decline; turn down. ¶ 면회를 ~하다 decline to see a visitor / 외상 ~ 《게시》No credit allowed.
사정(司正) audit and inspection.
사정(私情) personal feelings (re-

사정 (事情) ① 〖처지·곡절〗 circumstances; conditions; reasons; 〖형세〗 the state of things (matters, affairs). ¶ 자세한 ~ the whole details; the whole circumstances / ~이 허락하는 한 as far as circumstances permit / 부득이한 ~이 있어 for some unavoidable reasons; under unavoidable circumstances. ¶ ~식량 ~ food situation. ② 〖하소연〗 ~하다 beg 《a person's》 consideration(s); ask a favor. ¶ ~ 없다 be merciless [relentless].

사정 (査定) assessment. ~하다 assess 《one's property》. ¶ ~가격 an assessed value [price] / ~액 an assessed amount / 세액 ~ the assessment of taxes.

사정 (射程) a range. ¶ ~ 안 [밖]에 within [out of] range. ‖ 유효 ~ the effective range.

사정 (射精) ejaculation. ~하다 emit semen; ejaculate.

사제 (司祭) a priest; a pastor. ‖ ~관 a parsonage.

사제 (私製) ~의 private; unofficial. ¶ ~엽서 an unofficial postcard / ~품 privately made goods; an article of private manufacture.

사제 (師弟) master and pupil; teacher and student. ‖ ~관계 the relation of [between] teacher and student.

사조 (思潮) the trend of thought; the drift of public opinion. ¶ 문예 ~ the trend of literature.

사족 (四足) ¶ ~의 four-footed; quadruped / ~ 못쓰다 be spellbound; be crazy 《about》; be helplessly fond 《of》.

사족 (蛇足) superfluity; redundancy. ¶ ~을 달다 make an unnecessary addition.

사죄 (死罪) a capital offense.

사죄 (赦罪) ~하다 pardon; remit 《a punishment》.

사죄 (謝罪) apology. ~하다 apologize 《to a person for》; make an apology 《for》; express one's regret 《for》.

사주 (四柱) ~쟁이 a fortune-teller / ~ 팔자 one's lot (fate).

사주 (社主) the proprietor 《of a firm》.

사주 (使嗾) instigation. ~하다 instigate; incite; egg 《a person》 on 《to do》. ¶ …의 ~로 instigated by 《a person》; at 《a person's》 instigation.

사주 (砂洲) a sand bar; a delta.

사중 (四重) ‖ ~주〖창〗 a quartet(te).

사증 (査證) a visa; a visé. ¶ 입국 [출국] ~ an entry [exit] visa.

사지 (四肢) the limbs; the legs and arms.

사지 (死地) the jaws of death; a fatal position. ¶ ~로 들어가다 [를 벗어나다] go into [escape from] the jaws of death.

사직 (司直) the judicial authorities; the court. ¶ ~의 손이 뻗치다 the arm of the law reaches 《somebody》. ‖ ~당국 =사직(司直).

사직 (社稷) the guardian deities of the State; 〖국가〗 the State.

사직 (辭職) resignation. ~하다 resign; resign (from) one's office; step down from office. ¶ ~을 권고하다 advise [urge] 《a person》 to resign. ‖ ~서(를 내다) (tender, hand in) one's resignation / ~자 a resigner / 권고 ~ a resignation urged by one's senior.

사진 (寫塵) dust.

사진 (寫眞) a photograph; a photo; a picture; photography 〖사진술〗. ¶ ~을 찍다 (take a) photograph 《of》; have a picture taken 《남이 찍어 주다》 / ~을 인화(印畫) [확대]하다 print [enlarge] a photograph / ~을 현상하다 develop a film / 컬러 ~ a color photograph [picture] / 흑백 ~ a black and white photograph. ‖ ~관 a photo studio / ~기 a camera / ~ 모델 a photographic model / ~식자기 a photocomposer / ~전송 facsimile / ~첩 an album / 반신 ~ a half-length photograph.

사차 (四次) ~의 biquadratic 《equation》. ‖ ~원 the fourth dimension. ‖ ~로 road [highway].

사차선도로 (四車線道路) a four-lane road.

사찰 (寺刹) ☞ 절.

사찰 (査察) inspection. ~하다 inspect; make an inspection 《of》. ¶ 공중 [현지] ~ an aerial [on-site] inspection / 세무 ~ tax investigation.

사창 (私娼) 〖업〗 unlicensed prostitution; 〖사람〗 an unlicensed prostitute; a street-walker. ¶ ~굴 a house of ill fame; a brothel.

사채 (私債) a personal debt [loan]; private liabilities. ‖ ~놀이 private loan business / ~시장 the private money market / ~업자 a private moneylender.

사채 (社債) a corporate bond [debenture]. ‖ ~권(券) a debenture (certificate) / ~발행 debenture issue / ~상환 debenture redemption / ~보증 ~ a guaranteed debenture / 장기[단기] ~ a long- [short-]term debenture.

사천왕 (四天王) the Four Devas.

사철(四─) the four seasons; seasons of the year; 《부사적》 throughout the year; all the year round.
사철길(鐵) 《사설 철도》 a private railway.
사철나무 〖植〗 a spindle tree.
사체(死體) ☞ 주검.
사초(莎草) ① ☞ 잔디. ②〈잔디입히기〉 ~하다 turf〈sod〉 a tomb.
사촌(四寸) a 〈first〉 cousin. ‖ ~형 an elder cousin.
사춘기(思春期) adolescence; 〈the age of〉 puberty. ‖ ~의 pubescent; adolescent / ~의 남녀 boys and girls at puberty / ~에 달하다 attain 〈reach〉 puberty.
사출(射出) ~하다 shoot out 《flames》; emit 《light》; fire 《bullets》; eject 《the pilot》. ‖ ~좌석 《항공》 an ejection seat.
사취(詐取) ~하다 obtain 《money》 by fraud; swindle 《money from》; defraud 《a person of a thing》.
사치(奢侈) luxury; extravagance. ~하다 be extravagant 《in food》; indulge in luxury. ‖ ~스러운 luxurious; extravagant / ~에 빠지다 indulge in luxury; fall into luxurious habits. ‖ ~세 luxury tax / ~품 a luxury, a luxurious article / ~풍조 luxurious trends; extravagance tendency.
사칙(社則) the 〈company's〉 regulations.
사친회(師親會) a Parent-Teacher Association〈생략 P. T. A.〉.
사칭(詐稱) false assumption. ~하다 assume another's 〈a false〉 name. ‖ ~라고 ~하여 under the feigned name of ... / ~학력 ~ a false statement of one's academic career.
사카린 〖化〗 saccharin.
사커 〖蹴〗 soccer; association football.
사타구니 the groin. 〖ball. ☞ 축구.
사탄 Satan; the devil.
사탕(砂糖) ① 〈설탕〉 sugar. ¶ 모~ lump 〈cube〉 sugar / 얼음 ~ rock 〈sugar〉 candy. ‖ ~무 white 〈sugar〉 beet / ~수수 the sugar cane. ②〈과자〉 sweets; candy.
사탕발림(砂糖─) cajolery; flattery; honeyed words. ~하다 sweet-talk; sugar 〈butter〉 〈up〉; soft-soap; flatter; cajole; coax.
사태(沙汰) ① 〈산의〉 a landslip; a landslide; an avalanche〈눈의〉. ②〈많음〉 a flood; lots 《of》; a multitude 《of》. ¶ 사람 ~ a flood of overflowing people; crowds.
사태(事態) a situation; the state 〈position〉 of affairs 〈things〉. ¶ 비상~ a state of emergency.
사택(私宅) a private residence.
사택(社宅) a company〈-owned〉 house 《for its employees》.
사토(沙土) sandy soil.
사통(私通) intimacy; illicit intercourse; 〈illicit〉 liaisons. ~하다 misconduct oneself with.
사통오달(四通五達) ~하다 run 〈radiate, stretch〉 in all directions.
사퇴(辭退) ① 〈사양〉 declination〈美〉; refusal. ~하다 decline 《an offer》; refuse to accept. ② 〈사직〉 resignation. ~하다 resign 《one's post》. ¶ 자진 ~ voluntary resignation.
사투(死鬪) a 〈life or death〉 struggle. ~하다 fight 〈struggle〉 desperately.
사투리 a dialect; an accent; a provincialism.
사특(邪慝) ~한 wicked; vicious.
사파리 a safari.
사파이어 〖鑛〗 a sapphire.
사팔눈 a squint〈-eye〉; cross-eyes. ¶ ~의 squint-〈cross-〉eyed / ~son; a squinter.
사팔뜨기 a cross-〈squint-〉eyed person.
사포(砂布) sandpaper.
사표(師表) a model; a pattern; an example; a paragon.
사표(辭表) a written resignation; a letter of resignation. ¶ ~를 제출하다 tender 〈give in〉 one's resignation / ~를 반려 〈철회〉하다 turn down 〈withdraw〉 one's resignation.
사뿐사뿐 softly; lightly. 〖ignation.
사프란 〖植〗 a saffron.
사필귀정(事必歸正) a matter of course; a corollary. ~하다 Right will prevail in the end. or Truth wins out in the long run.
사하다(赦─) pardon; forgive.
사하중(死荷重) the deadweight; the dead load 《of a wagon》.
사학(史學) history 〈as science〉; historical science. ‖ ~자 a historian. 〖lege, university.
사학(私學) a private school〈college, university〉.
사학(斯學) this study; this field; the subject. ¶ ~의 권위 an authority on the subject.
사할린 Sakhalin.
사항(事項) matters; facts〈사실〉; 〈항목〉 items; articles; particulars. ¶ 조사 ~ matters for investigation / 주요 ~ an essential particular; a main point.
사해(四海) the four seas; 〈천하〉 the whole world. ‖ ~동포 the brotherhood of mankind; universal fraternity.
사해(死海) the Dead Sea.
사행(射倖) speculation; adventure. ‖ ~심 a speculative 〈gambling〉 spirit.
사향(麝香) musk. ‖ ~노루 a musk deer / ~수 musk water / ~초 a wild thyme.

사혈(瀉血) phlebotomy. ~하다 phlebotomize; bleed.
사형(死刑) death penalty (sentence); capital punishment. ¶ ~에 처하다 put to death; execute; condemn to death. / ~선고 sentence of death / a capital sentence / ~수 a criminal under sentence of death / ~장 the execution ground / ~집행인 an executioner.
사형(私刑) lynch; lynching. ~을 가하다 lynch 《a person》.
사형(舍兄) my elder (big) brother.
사화(士禍) the massacre (purge) of scholars; the calamity of the literati.
사화(史話) a historical tale (story).
사화(私和) reconciliation. ~하다 become (be) reconciled 《with》.
사화산(死火山) an extinct volcano.
사환(使喚) an errand boy; a boy [an office boy (girl)].
사활(死活) life and death. ~문제 a matter of life and (or) death.
사회(司會) chairmanship. ~하다 preside at (over) 《a meeting》; take the chair. ¶ ~봉 a gavel / ~자 the chairman; the toastmaster (연회의); the master (mistress (여자); of ceremonies (생략 m.c., M.C.) (TV 의).
사회(社會) a society; the world (세상); a community (지역사회). ¶ ~적인 social / 반~적인 antisocial / 이슬람 ~ Islamic society / ~적 지위가 있는 사람 a person in a public position / ~ 풍조 (동향)에 따르다 go with the trend of society / ~에 나가다 go out into the world / 인간은 ~적 동물이다 Man is a social animal. / 원시 (봉건) ~ primitive (feudal) society / 일반 ~ the general public. ‖ ~개량 (도덕, 질서) social improve (morality, order) / ~과학 social science / ~문제 (면) a social problem (column, page (신문의)) / ~보장 (제도) social security (system) / ~복귀 rehabilitation in society (the community) / ~복귀시키다 rehabilitate 《a person》 in society) / ~사업 social work (service) / ~사업가 a social worker / ~상 social phenomenon / ~악 (불안) social evils (unrest) / ~인 a member of society / ~장 (葬) a public funeral / ~주의 socialism / ~통념 a socially accepted idea / ~학 sociology / ~학자 a sociologist.
사회간접자본(社會間接資本) [經] (the) social overhead capital (생략 SOC).
사회기강(社會紀綱) social discipline.
사회복지(社會福祉) social welfare. ¶ ~를 피하다 take a measure with a view to social welfare / ~를 증진하다 promote social welfare.
사회정화(社會淨化) social purification. ‖ ~운동 a social purification drive / ~위원회 the Social Reform Commission.
사회현상(社會現狀) a social phenomenon (phase).
사회환경(社會環境) social environment.
사후(死後) posthumous. ¶ ~에 after one's death; posthumously / ~세계 the world after death. ‖ ~강직 stiffening after death; *rigor mortis* 《라》.
사후(事後) ~의 after the fact; *ex post facto* 《라》 / ~에 after the fact; *post factum* 《라》. ¶ ~승낙 *ex post facto* approval (consent).
사흗날(3일) the third (day of the month).
사흘 ① 《세 날》 three days. ¶ ~째 the third day. ☞ 사흗날.
삭(朔) 《달》 a month.
삭감(削減) a cut; curtailment. ~하다 cut (down); curtail; slash; retrench. ¶ 예산의 ~ a budgetary cut (cutback) / 경비를 ~하다 cut down expenses; curtail (retrench) expenditures.
삭과(蒴果) [植] a capsule.
삭다 ① 《먹은 것이》 be digested; digest. ② 《옷 따위가》 wear thin (threadbare); 《부식되다》 get rotten; decay; rust. ③ 《종기가》 get resolved. ④ 《마음이》 calm down; be appeased (alleviated); 《울이》 be burnt out. ⑤ 《익다》 acquire (develop, absorb) flavor; ferment (술 따위). ⑥ 《묽어지다》 become watery; turn bad.
삭도(索道) a cableway; a ropeway.
삭막(索莫) ¶ ~한 dim (in one's memory); 《황야 등이》 dreary; bleak; desolate.
삭망(朔望) the first and fifteenth days of the lunar month.
삭발(削髮) ~하다 have one's hair cut.
삭월세(朔月貰) ¶ ~ 사글세. [cut.
삭이다 digest.
삭정이 dead twigs (branches).
삭제(削除) ~하다 strike (cross) out; delete; cancel. ¶ 명부에서 ~하다 strike 《a person's name》 off the list. [erase.
삭치다(削 —) cancel; strike out.
삭탈관직(削奪官職) removing a government official from office. ~하다 deprive (strip) 《a person》 of his office.
삭풍(朔風) the north wind of winter.
삭히다 digest (소화); make 《something》 ripe; mellow; (cause to)

삯 《요금》 charge; 《찻삯》 fare; 《운송》 carriage; freight; 《품삯》 wages; pay. ¶ ~전 wages; pay; ~품 wage labor.
삯바느질 needlework for pay.
산(山) a mountain; a hill《동산》. ¶ ~이 많은 mountainous; hilly.
산(酸) an acid. ¶ ~의 acid.
…산(産) a product 《of》. ¶ 외국~ foreign-made / 외국《국내》~의 밀 foreign-[home-]grown wheat.
산가지(算—) primitive counting sticks; 《점치는》 a divining stick.
산간(山間) ¶ ~의《에》 among [in] the mountains [hills]. ¶ ~벽지 a secluded place in the mountains.
산개(散開) 【軍】 deployment. ~하다 deploy; spread out. ~되어 있다 be dispersed 《in the field》 / ~시키다 get 《the men》 into open order. 「[range, system].
산계(山系) 《줄기》 a mountain chain
산고(産苦) birth pangs; labor pains. 「 a secluded place.
산골(山—) a mountain district;
산골짜기(山—) a ravine; a gorge.
산과(産科) obstetrics. ¶ ~병원 a maternity hospital [ward] / ~의사 an obstetrician / ~학 obstetrics. 「light.
산광(散光) 【理】 scattered [diffused]
산금(産金) gold mining. ¶ ~량 gold output / ~지대 a gold field.
산기(産氣) labor pains; pangs of childbirth. ¶ ~가 돌다 [있다] begin labor; labor starts. 「delivery.
산기(産期) the expected time of
산기슭(山—) the foot [base] of a mountain.
산길(山—) a mountain path.
산꼭대기(山—) the top [summit] of a mountain; the mountain-top.
산나물(山—) wild edible greens.
산놓다(算—) calculate with sticks.
산더미(山—) a heap 《of》; a large pile 《of》. ¶ ~같이 쌓인 a mountain of; lots [heaps] of.
산도(酸度) 【化】 acidity. ¶ ~계 an acidimeter / ~측정 acidimetry.
산돼지(山—) 【動】 a wild boar.
산들거리다 blow cool and gentle.
산들바람 a gentle [light] breeze.
산들산들 gently; softly.
산등성이(山—) a (mountain) ridge.
산뜻하다 《선명》 (be) clear; fresh; vivid; bright; 《보기 좋다》 (be) neat; tidy; trim; clear; smart; nice. ¶ 산뜻한 옷 a neat dress.
산란(産卵) ~하다 lay egg(s); spawn 《물고기가》. ¶ ~기 a breeding season; spawning-time / ~장 a spawning ground / ~회유 (回遊) spawning migration.

산란(散亂) ~하다 be scattered about; lie about in disorder. ¶ 마음이 ~해지다 be distracted.
산록(山麓) (at) the foot [base] of a mountain.
산림(山林) a forest; woodlands. ¶ ~을 조성하다 afforest a mountain. / ~보호 forest conservancy / ~업 the forestry industry / ~청 the Forest Service; the Forest Service / ~학 forestry.
산마루(山—) a mountain ridge. ‖ ~터기 산마루. 「desultory;
산만(散漫) ¶ ~한 loose; vague; / ~소매(小賣).
산맥(山脈) a mountain range [chain]. ¶ 알프스~ the Alps; the Alpine range.
산모(産母) a woman in childbed.
산모퉁이(山—) the spur [corner] of a mountain (skirts).
산목숨 one's life.
산문(散文) prose (writings). ¶ ~적인 prosaic. ¶ ~시 a prose poem / ~체 prose style; prosaism.
산물(産物) a product; production; produce《총칭》; 《성과》 a product; a result; (the) fruit(s). ¶ 주요 ~ staple products.
산미(酸味) acidity; sourness.
산밑(山—) the foot [base] of a mountain.
산발(散發) ~하다 occur sporadically. ¶ ~적인 sporadic(al). ‖ ~안타 scattered hits.
산발(散髮) disheveled hair. ~하다 have [wear] one's hair disheveled. ¶ ~한 모양 a horrible experience.
산벼락 ¶ ~ 맞다 undergo a hor-
산병(散兵) a skirmisher; 《산개》 loose [extended] order. ¶ ~선 a skirmish(ing) line / ~호 a fire [firing, shelter] trench.
산복(山腹) (on) a mountainside; a hillside.
산봉우리(山—) a (mountain) peak; a summit [top] of a mountain.
산부(産婦) ☞ 산모(産母).
산부인과(産婦人科) obstetrics and gynecology. ¶ ~의사 an obstetrician《산과》; a gynecologist《부인과》.
산불(山—) a forest fire.
산비둘기(山—) a ringdove; a turtledove. 「slope.
산비탈(山—) a steep mountain
산뽕나무(山—) 【植】 a wild mulberry tree. 「a May tree.
산사나무(山査—) 【植】 a hawthorn;
산사람(山—) a mountain man; a wood(s)man; a hillbilly 《美》.
산사태(山沙汰) a landslide; a landslip 《英》; a landfall. 「tion.
산삭(産朔) the month of parturi-
산산이(散散—) to [in] pieces; scatteringly.

산산조각(散散—) ¶ ~이 나다 be broken to pieces; be smashed to fragments.
산삼(山蔘) a wild ginseng.
산상(山上) ¶ ~의[에] on the top [summit] of a mountain (hill). ∥ ~ 수훈(垂訓) 〖聖〗 the Sermon on the Mount.
산새(山—) a mountain bird.
산색(山色) mountain scenery.
산성(山城) a castle on a hill.
산성(酸性) 〖化〗 acidity. ¶ ~의 acid / ~화하다 acidify / ~ (an) acid reaction / ~산화물 an acid oxide / 토양의 ~ soil acidity. ∥ ~비 acid rain / ~식품 acid foods / ~염료 acid dyes.
산세(山勢) the physical aspect [geographical features] of a mountain.
산소(山所) a grave; a tomb; an ancestral graveyard(묘소).
산소(酸素) 〖化〗 oxygen. ∥ ~결핍 deficiency of oxygen / ~요법 oxygen treatment / ~용접 oxyacetylene welding / ~통(봄베) an oxygen cylinder / ~화합물 an oxide / ~흡입 oxygen inhalation.
산소리하다 do not yield《to》; do not give in; talk big.
산속(山—) the recesses [heart] of a mountain.
산송장 a living corpse. ¶ ~이다 be as good as a living corpse.
산수(山水) a landscape; scenery. ∥ ~화 a landscape (painting) / ~화가 a landscape painter.
산수(算數) ① ~ 산술. ②《계산》 calculation.
산수소(酸水素) oxyhydrogen. ∥ ~용접 oxyhydrogen welding.
산술(算術) arithmetic. ¶ ~의 arithmetical.
산스크리트 Sanskrit; Sanscrit.
산식(算式) 〖數〗 an arithmetic expression; a formula.
산신령(山神靈) the god of a mountain.
산실(産室) a lying-in [delivery] room; a maternity ward.
산아(産兒) 《해산》 childbirth; 《아이》 a new-born baby. ∥ ~제한 [조절] 《practice》 birth control.
산악(山岳) mountains. ∥ ~병(病) mountain sickness / ~부 a mountaineering [an alpine] club / ~전 *mountain* warfare / ~지대 a mountainous region.
산액(産額) the yield 《of rice》; the output 《of gold》.
산야(山野) fields and mountains.
산양(山羊) ① 《염소》 a goat. ② 《영양》 an antelope.
산업(産業) (an) industry. ¶ ~의 industrial. ∥ ~을 장려하다 encourage industry. ∥ ~개발 industrial development / ~계 the industrial world / ~구조 industrial structure / ~규격 industrial standards(한국~규격 Korean (Industrial) Standards(생략 KS)) / ~금융채권 industrial finance debenture / ~도시 an industrial city / ~별 노조 an industrial union / ~사회 industrial society / ~사회학 industrial sociology / ~스파이 an industrial spy / ~용 로봇 an industrial robot / ~자본 [자금] industrial capital (funds) / ~재해 ☞ 산재(産災) / ~재해보험 the Workmen's Accident Compensation Insurance / ~폐기물 industrial wastes / ~합리화 the rationalization of industry / ~혁명 〖史〗 the Industrial Revolution / 제1 [2, 3]차~ the primary [secondary, tertiary] industries.
산욕(産褥) childbed; confinement. ¶ ~열 puerperal fever.
산울림(山—) ☞ 메아리.
산울타리 a hedge.
산원(産院) a maternity [lying-in] hospital.
산월(産月) ☞ 산삭(産朔).
산유국(産油國) an oil-producing country [nation].
산입(算入) ~하다 include in; count [reckon] in.
산자수명(山紫水明) beautiful scenery; scenic beauty.
산장(山莊) a mountain retreat [villa].
산재(散在) ~하다 be [lie] scattered; 《장소가 주어》 be dotted 《with》.

산재(散財) ~하다 spend [squander] money; run through *one's* fortune.
산재(産災) an injury incurred while on duty [at work].
산적(山賊) a bandit; a brigand.
산적(山積) ~하다 lie in piles; accumulate; make a pile; have a mountain of 《work to do》.
산적(散炙) skewered slices of seasoned meat.
산전(産前) ¶ ~에 before childbirth / ~산후의 휴가 a maternity leave.
산전수전(山戰水戰) ¶ ~ 다 겪다 taste the sweets and bitters of life; go through hell and high water.
산정(山頂) the summit [top] 《of a mountain》.
산정(算定) ~하다 compute; work out; 《추정》 estimate; appraise.
산줄기(山—) a mountain range; a chain of mountains.
산중(山中) ¶ ~에〈-에서〉 in the mountain(s).
산증(疝症) 〖醫〗 lumbago. ¶ ~ 앓다 suffer from lumbago.
산지(山地) a mountainous district.
산지(産地) a place of production

산지기 [origin]; 《동식물의》 the home; the habitat. ¶ ~ 직송의 감자 potatoes direct from the farm.

산지기(山 一) a (forest) ranger; a grave keeper(묘지의).

산책(散策) a walk; a stroll. ~다 take a walk; stroll. ¶ ~길 / ~ 나가다 go (out) for a walk.

산천(山川) mountains and rivers. ‖ ~초목 nature; landscape.

산촌(山村) a mountain village.

산출(産出) ~하다 produce; yield; bring forth. ‖ ~고(高) production; output.

산출(算出) ~하다 compute 《at》; calculate; reckon.

산탄(散彈) a shot; a buckshot. ‖ ~총 a shotgun.

산토끼(山一) 《動》 a hare.

산토닌 [藥] santonin; santonic acid.

산통(算筒) ¶ ~ 깨뜨리다 spoil (ruin) 《a scheme》; put a spoke in 《a person's》 wheel.

산파(産婆) a midwife (☞ 조산사). ¶ ~역을 맡다 serve as a midwife to 《assist in》 《the formation of a cabinet》.

산패(酸敗) 《맛이 시어짐》 acidification. ~하다 acidify; turn sour.

산표(散票) scattered votes.

산하(山河) mountains and rivers.

산하(傘下) ~의 under the influence 《of》. ‖ ~기업 (조합) an affiliated enterprise (union).

산학협동(産學協同) industrial-educational cooperation. ‖ ~체 an educational-industrial complex.

산해진미(山海珍味) all sorts of delicacies; a sumptuous feast.

산허리(山一) 《on》 a mountainside; a hillside.

산호(珊瑚) coral. ‖ ~섬 a coral island / ~수(樹) a coral / ~초 (礁) a coral reef (insect).

산화(散華) a heroic death in battle (action). ~하다 die a glorious death.

산화(酸化) [化] oxid(iz)ation. ~다 oxidize; be oxidized. ‖ ~물 an oxide / ~철 iron oxide.

산회(散會) adjournment. ~하다 break up; adjourn; close.

산후(産後) ¶ ~의 [에] after childbirth / ~가 좋다 [나쁘다] be doing well [badly] after childbirth.

살[1] 《몸의》 flesh; muscles(근육); the skin(살결); 《과실의》 flesh. ¶ ~이 많은 fleshy / ~이 오르다 [빠지다] gain [lose] flesh.

살[2] 《창대》 《장기 따위의》 a rib(우산, 부채 따위의); a tooth(빗살); a spoke(바퀴의).

살[3] 《어살》 a weir; 《화살》 an arrow.

살[4] 《나이》 age; years.

살(煞) ① 《나쁜 기운》 an evil spirit; baleful influence; an ill-fated (unlucky) touch. ¶ ~이 낀 날 an ill-starred 《a fateful》 day. ② 《나쁜 정의》 bad blood; poor relations within a family.

살가죽 the skin.

살갑다 ① 《속이》 (be) broad-minded. ② 《313정함》 (be) warm-(heart ed); kind.

살결 the skin; complexion. ¶ ~이 곱다 have a fair complexion.

살거리 fleshiness.

살결 the (texture of) skin. ¶ ~이 고운 of close (delicate) texture.

살구 an apricot.

살균(殺菌) sterilization. ~하다 sterilize; pasteurize 《milk》. ‖ ~력 sterilizing power / ~제 a sterilizer; a disinfectant.

살그머니 secretly; stealthily; quietly; by stealth.

살금살금 softly; with stealthy steps; stealthily; noiselessly.

살긋하다 be tilted; slanting.

살기(殺氣) a look (an atmosphere) of menace; a highly-charged atmosphere. ¶ ~를 띤 wildly excited; bloodthirsty; ferocious / ~를 띠다 grow (get) excited; be bloodthirsty; look menacing.

살길 a means to live. ¶ ~을 찾다 seek a way to make living.

살깃 the feathers of an arrow.

살내리다 lose flesh; get thin.

살다 ① 《생존》 live; be alive. ¶ ~을 먹고 ~ live on 《rice》. ② 《생활》 live; make a living; get along. ¶ 이럭저럭 살아가다 manage to live / 잘 ~ be well-off. ③ 《거주》 live; reside; inhabit. ④ 《생동》 be enlivened. ¶ 살아 있는 듯한 초상화 a portrait full of life. ⑤ [野] be safe.

살담배 cut (pipe) tobacco.

살대 《화살대》 an arrow-shaft.

살뜰하다 (be) frugal; thrifty. ☞ 알뜰하다.

살랑거리다 《바람이》 blow gently

살래살래 ¶ 머리를 ~ 흔들다 shake (wag) one's head.

살려주다 save (rescue) 《a person》 from; spare.

살롱 a salon (프); a saloon (술집).

살리다 ① 《목숨을》 save; spare 《a person's》 life; keep 《a fish》 alive(살려 두다); bring (restore) 《a person》 to life(소생). ② 《활용》 make good use of 《one's money》. ③ 《생기를 주다》 give life

살리실산(-酸) salicylic acid.

살림(殺生) 《생계》 living; livelihood; 《살림살이》 housekeeping. ~하다 run the house; manage a household. ¶ ~이 넉넉하다 [넉넉지 못하다] be well (badly) off / ~에 쩌들다 be worn out with the cares

살림꾼 of housekeeping / 새~을 차리다 make a new home; set up house / 한 집안의 ~을 꾸려가다 maintain (support) one's family / 신분에 어울리는(안 어울리는) ~을 하다 live within (beyond) one's means.

살림꾼 (맡은 이) the mistress of a house; 《잘 하는 이》 a good housewife; 《household》.

살림말다 take charge (care) of a household.

살며시 ☞ 슬며시.

살몽혼 (一朦昏) local anesthesia. ~하다 anesthetize locally.

살무사 (蝮) a viper; an adder.

살바르산 (藥) salvarsan.

살벌 (殺伐) ~하다 (be) bloody; bloodthirsty; brutal; savage; violent.

살별 〖天〗 a comet.

살붙이 one's kith and kin.

살빛 the color of the skin; flesh color. ¶ ~의 flesh-colored.

살사리 a wily (tricky) person; a back scratcher; a boot-licker.

살살 softly; gently; stealthily.

살상 (殺傷) bloodshed(ding). ~하다 shed blood.

살생 (殺生) the taking of life. ~하다 kill; take life. ¶ 무익한 ~ wanton destruction of life; useless (pointless) cruelty.

살수 (撒水) ~하다 water 《a street》; sprinkle with water. ¶ ~기 (장치) a sprinkler / ~차 a water-sprinkler.

살신성인 (殺身成仁) ~하다 become a martyr to humanity.

살아나다 ① 《소생》 revive; be resuscitated; be restored to life. ② 《구명》 be saved (rescued); survive (조난의 경우). ③ 《곤경에서》 escape 《death, danger》.

살아생전 (一生前) ¶ ~에 during one's lifetime.

살얼음 thin ice; a thin coat of ice. ¶ ~을 밟는 것 같다 feel as if one were treading on thin ice.

살육 (殺戮) ~하다 massacre; butcher; slaughter. ¶ ~을 자행하다 kill recklessly; massacre brutally.

살의 (殺意) 《conceive》 murderous intent; 《with》 intent to kill.

살인 (殺人) homicide; murder. ~하다 commit murder; kill 《a person》. ¶ ~적인 deadly; hectic. ‖ ~광선 a death ray / ~미수 an attempted murder / ~범 a homicide; a murderer / ~사건 a murder case.

살점 (一點) a piece of meat; a cut.

살집 fleshiness. ¶ ~이 좋다 be fleshy (plump, stout).

살찌다 grow (get) fat; gain (put on) flesh; 《땅이》 grow fertile (rich).

살찌우다 make 《a pig》 fat; fatten up.

살촉 (一鏃) an arrowhead; a pile.

살충제 (殺蟲劑) an insecticide; an insect powder (가루).

살코기 lean meat; red meat.

살쾡이 a wildcat; a lynx.

살팍지다 (be) muscular; brawny.

살판나다 come into a fortune; strike it rich.

살펴보다 look around (about); look into; examine; see.

살포 (撒布) ~하다 scatter; sprinkle; spread.

살풍경 (殺風景) ¶ ~한 inelegant; prosaic; tasteless; vulgar; 《정취 없는》 dreary; bleak.

살피다 ① ☞ 살펴보다. ② 《헤아리다》 judge; gather (판단); sympathize with; feel for (동정).

살해 (殺害) ~하다 murder; kill; put 《a person》 to death; slay. ¶ ~자 a murderer; a murderess (여자). ‖ lead a life; live.

삶 life; living. ¶ ~을 영위하다

삶다 ① 《끓이다》 boil; cook. ¶ 달걀을 ~ boil an egg / 삶아지다 be boiled. ② ☞ 구슬리다.

삼[1] flax (아마); hemp (대마); ramie (저마); jute (황마).

삼[2] (胎아이) the amnion and placenta.

삼[3] 《눈동자의》 a white speck; a leucoma.

삼 (三) three. ¶ 제 ~ (의) the third.

삼 (蔘) ginseng. ☞ 인삼.

삼가 respectfully; humbly. ¶ ~ 말씀드립니다 I beg to inform you.

삼가다 ① 《조심》 be discreet (prudent, careful). ¶ 언행을 ~ be discreet in word and deed. ② 《억제》 abstain (keep, refrain) from; 《절제》 be moderate 《in》. ¶ 술을 ~ abstain (keep) from drinking.

삼각 (三角) a triangle. ¶ ~의 triangular; three-cornered / ~(형)으로 하다 triangulate. ‖ ~건 a triangle (bandage) / ~관계 the eternal triangle; a love triangle / ~근 a deltoid muscle / ~기 a triangular pennant; a pennon / ~법 trigonometry / ~익 (翼) a delta wing / ~자 a set square / ~점 (測) a triangulation point / ~주 a delta / ~파 chopping waves / ~함수 trigonometric function.

삼각 (三脚) a tripod. ¶ ~의 three-legged; tripodal. ‖ ~가 (架) a tripod.

삼각형 (三角形) a triangle. ¶ ~의 triangular; triangle-shaped.

삼강오륜 (三綱五倫) the three fundamental principles and the five moral disciplines in human relations.

삼거리 (三一) a junction (inter-

section) of three roads; a three-forked road.
삼계사(三─) three-ply thread.
삼경(三更) midnight.
삼계탕(蔘鷄湯) *samgyet'ang*, young chicken soup with ginseng (and other fruits).
삼국(三國) ‖ ~ 동맹 a triple alliance / ~유사(遺事) *Samguk Yusa* Legends and History of the Three Kingdoms / 제~ a third power (country).
삼군(三軍) the armed forces; the whole army. ¶ ~을 지휘하다 command the whole army. ‖ ~의 장대 the tri-service honor guard.
삼권분립(三權分立) the separation of the three powers.
삼남(三南) three southern provinces of Korea.
삼년(三年) three years. ¶ ~생(학생) a third-year student.
삼다 ①《…을 …으로》make; set up 《a person》as; use [have] 《a thing》as. ¶ 그녀를 며느리로 ~ make her one's daughter-in-law. ②《생각》¶ 책을 벗 ~ have books for companion / 장난삼아 half in fun. ③《짚신을》make 《straw shoes》.
삼단 a bunch of hemp. ¶ ~ 같은 머리 long thick hair.
삼단논법(三段論法) a syllogism.
삼대(三代) three generations.
삼동(三冬) ①《겨울의 석달》the three months of winter. ②《세 겨울》three winters.
삼두정치(三頭政治) triumvirate.
삼등(三等) the third class [rate]; the third place. ‖ ~차표 [석] a third-class ticket [seat].
삼등분(三等分) ~ 하다 cut [divide] into three equal parts; trisect.
삼라만상(森羅萬象) all things in nature; the whole of creation.
삼루(三壘) 【野】 the 3rd base. ¶ ~수 a third-baseman / ~타 a three-base hit; a triple. 「class.
삼류(三流) ¶ ~의 third-rate; low-
삼륜차(三輪車) (ride) a three-wheeler.
삼림(森林) 산림.
삼매(三昧) absorption; concentration; *samâdhi*《梵》. ¶ ~경에 들다 attain the perfect state of spiritual concentration.
삼면(三面) three sides [faces];《신문의》the third page. ‖ ~기사 city [local] news. 「a year.
삼모작(三毛作)(raise) three crops
삼목(三木) a cedar.
삼민주의(三民主義) the Three Principles of the People.
삼박자(三拍子) 【樂】 triple time.
삼발이 a tripod; a trivet.
삼배(三倍) three times; thrice. ~하다 treble; multiply by three.

¶ ~의 threefold; treble; triple /…의 ~나 되는 three times as many [much, large] as….
삼베 hemp cloth.
삼복(三伏) the hottest period of summer; midsummer. ‖ ~더위 the midsummer heat.
삼부(三部) three parts [sections]; three copies (서류 따위); three volumes (서적); three departments(부처). ‖ ~작 a trilogy / ~합창 a (vocal) trio.
삼분(三分) ~ 하다 divide 《a thing》 into three parts; trisect. ~ 의 일, one [a] third.
삼분오열(三分五裂) ~ 하다 break [tear] asunder; be broken [torn] asunder; be disrupted.
삼산염기(三酸鹽基) a triacid base.
삼산화물(三酸化物)【化】 a triox-ide.
삼삼오오(三三五五) ¶ ~로 by twos and threes; in groups.
삼삼하다 ①《기억이》be vivid; haunt 《a person》②《음식이》be tasty with slight touch of saltiness.
삼색(三色) three (primary) colors. ¶ ~의 three-color; tricolored. / ~기 the tricolor.
삼승(三乘) 『數』 세제곱.
삼시(三時) three daily meals;《때》morning, noon and evening.
삼십(三十) thirty. ¶ 제 ~(의) the thirtieth / ~대이다 be in one's thirties.
삼십육계(三十六計) running away. ¶ ~를 놓다 beat a retreat; take to one's heels.
삼엄(森嚴) ~ 하다 (be) solemn; sublime; awe-inspiring; grave.
삼오야(三五夜) a night of full moon.
삼용(蔘茸) ginseng and antler.
삼원색(三原色) the three primary colors.
삼월(三月) March (생략 Mar.).
삼위일체(三位一體) the Trinity. ‖ ~론 Trinitarianism.
삼인조(三人組) a trio; a triad.
삼인칭(三人稱) the third person.
삼일(三一) ‖ ~운동 the 1919 Independence Movement (of Korea) / ~절 Anniversary of the *Samil Independence Movement*.
삼일(三日) three days; the third (day) (셋째날). ¶ ~ 동안 for three days. ¶ ~ 천하 short-lived ruler.
삼자(三者) ~ 범퇴 『野』 three up and three down / ~회담 a tripartite meeting [conference].
삼중(三重) ¶ ~의 threefold; treble; triple. ‖ ~주[창] a trio.
삼지사방(-四方) ¶ ~으로 in all directions.
삼진(三振) 【野】 a strike-out. ¶ ~ 당하다 be struck out.
삼차(三次) the third; cubic (수학

삼차신경(三叉神經)〖解〗the trigeminal; the trigeminus.
삼창(三唱)〖만세의〗three cheers. ¶～하다 give three cheers.
삼척동자(三尺童子) a mere child.
삼촌(三寸)〖숙부〗an uncle.
삼총사(三銃士) a trio.
삼추(三秋) ① 〖가을의 석 달〗the three autumn months. ②〖세 가을〗three autumns.
삼출(渗出) ～하다 ooze out; exude. ‖ ～액 an exudate; a percolate.
삼층(三層) three stories; the third floor (story) 〖美〗. ‖ ～집 a three-storied (-story) house.
삼치〖魚〗a Spanish mackerel.
삼칠일(三七日) the 21st day after (a baby's birth).
삼키다 ①〖입으로〗swallow; gulp down (떡). 〖통째〗swallow (a biscuit) whole. ②〖참다〗suppress. ¶눈물을 ～ keep back one's tears. ③〖횡령〗make (a thing) one's own; appropriate.
삼태기 a carrier's basket.
삼투(滲透) saturation; infiltration; permeation;〖化・生理〗osmosis. ～하다 saturate; permeate; infiltrate; pass into. ‖ ～성 osmosis; permeability.
삼파전(三巴戰) a three-cornered (-sided) contest (fight). ¶～을 벌이다 break out a three-way struggle.
삼팔육세대(386世代) the so-called '386 generation' means those who are in their 30s, attended collge in the 80s, and born in the 60s.
삼팔선(三八線) the 38th parallel.
삼포(蔘圃) a ginseng field.
삼한사온(三寒四溫) a cycle of three cold days and four warm days.
삼항식(三項式)〖數〗a trinomial (expression). ¶질하다 shovel.
삽 a shovel; a scoop. ¶～
삽사리, 삽살개 a shaggy dog.
삽시간(霎時間) ¶～에 in a twinkling; in an instant; in less than no time.
삽입(挿入) ～하다 insert; put (a thing) in (between). ‖ ～구 a parenthesis.
삽화(挿話) an episode.
삽화(挿畵) an illustration; a cut. ‖ ～가 an illustrator.
삿갓 a conical bamboo hat.
삿자리 a reed mat.
상(上)〖윗부분〗upper;〖등급〗the first (class, grade); the superior;〖상권〗the first volume.
상(床) a (dining) table; a small table. ¶밥 한 ～ a meal set on

a table / ～을 차리다 set the table (for dinner) / ～을 치우다 clear the table.
상(相)〖상태〗an aspect; a phase; 〖인상〗physiognomy;〖얼굴〗countenance; a face, a look(표정). ¶～을 찌푸리고 with a frown.
상(喪) mourning (for). ¶～을 입다〖벗다〗go into (out of) mourning /～중이다 be in mourning (for).
상(像) a figure; a statue; an image;〖화상〗a picture.
상(賞) a prize; a reward (보수). ¶1등～ the first prize; first honors / ～을 타다 win (get) a prize.〖ness section (quarters).
상가(商街) a downtown; the busi-
상가(喪家) a house of mourning; a family in mourning.
상각(償却) ～하다 repay; refund; redeem; pay (clear) off. ‖ ～자금 a redemption (sinking) fund.
상감(上監) His Majesty.
상감(象嵌) inlaying; inlaid work. ～하다 inlay (a thing with).
상갑판(上甲板) an upper deck.
상객(上客) the guest of honor; a chief guest; a guest of high rank.
상객(常客) a regular customer (patron); a frequenter.
상거래(商去來) a commercial transaction; a business deal.
상견(相見) ～하다 meet (see) each other; interview; exchange looks.
상경(上京) ～하다 come (go) (up) to Seoul (the capital).
상고(上古) ancient times. ¶～의 ancient; of remote antiquity. ‖ ～사 an ancient history.
상고(上告)〖法〗an appeal (to). ～하다 appeal (to a higher court); petition for revision. ¶～를 기각하다 reject an appeal. ‖ ～인 an appellant.〖crew cut.
상고머리 a square-cut hair; a
상공(上空) the upper air; the sky; the skies (of Seoul). ¶서울～을 날다 fly over Seoul.
상공(商工)〖상공업〗commerce and industry. ¶중소～업자 small and medium merchants and industrialists.
상과(商科) a commercial course. ‖ ～대학 a commercial college.
상관(上官)〖superior〗officer; a senior officer.
상관(相關)〖상호 관계〗correlation; mutual relation(s). ～하다 correlate; be mutually related (to). ¶…와 밀접한 ～ 관계가 있다 correlate closely with. ②〖관련〗relation; connection;〖관여〗participation; involvement;〖관심・개의〗concern; care. ～하다 take part (in); concern oneself (in);

상관습 be involved 《in》 (연루). ¶ ~ 않다 do not mind《개의》; be indifferent 《to》 / ~ 없다《무관계》 have nothing to do with; It does not matter. / 네가 ~ 할 게 아니다 It's none of your business. ③《남녀의》(sexual) relations. ~하다 have connection [relations] 《with》.

상관습(商慣習) commercial practice; business usage.

상궁(尙宮) a court lady.

상권(上卷) the first volume; Vol. 1.

상권(商權) 《acquire》 commercial supremacy; commercial rights.

상궤(常軌) the normal course. ¶ ~을 벗어나다 go off the track; be abnormal 《eccentric》.

상규(常規) established rules.

상그레 ¶ ~ 웃다 beam; smile blandly.

상극(相剋) (a) conflict; (a) rivalry; a friction. ¶ ~이다 be mutually exclusive; be conflicted 《with》.

상근(常勤) full-time 《lecturer》. ‖ ~자 a full-timer.

상글거리다 beam; smile blandly.

상금(賞金) a reward; a prize; prize money. ¶ ~을 타다[내걸다] win [offer] a prize.

상급(上級) a high rank; an upper [a higher] grade [class]. ¶ ~의 upper; higher; superior; senior. ‖ ~관청 superior offices [authorities] / ~생 an upper-class student / ~직 a senior post / ~학교 a school of higher grade.

상긋거리다 smile blandly; beam.

상기(上記) ¶ ~의 the above-mentioned; the said.

상기(上氣) ~하다 have a rush of blood to the head. ¶ ~된 빰 flushed cheeks.

상기(想起) ~하다 remember; recollect; call 《something》 to mind. ¶ ~을 ~시키다 remind 《a person》 《of a thing》.

상기(詳記) ~하다 describe minutely; state in detail; give a full account 《of》.

상길(上一) the highest quality.

상납(上納) ~하다 pay to the authorities [government]; offer a (regular) bribe 《to》.

상냥하다 (be) gentle; kind; sweet; affectionate; amiable; affable. ¶ 상냥하게 대하다 be kind 《good, nice》 《to a person》.

상념(想念) a notion; conception.

상놈(常—) a mean [vulgar] fellow; an ill-bred fellow.

상단(上端) the top; the upper end.

상담(相談) a consultation. ¶ ~에 응하다 give counsel [advice] 《to》. ‖ ~란《신문·잡지의》 the advice column / ~소 information [a consultation] office.

상담(商談) 《have》a business talk. ¶ ~을 매듭짓다 strike a bargain.

상당(相當) ~하다 ①《알맞다》be proper; fit; suitable; appropriate;《상응하다》(be) equal 《to》; correspond 《to》; equivalent 《to》;《타당하다》(be) reasonable. ¶ 2만원 ~의 선물 a gift worth twenty thousand won / 2개월 급료에 ~한 보너스 a bonus equivalent to two months' pay / 지위에 ~한 수입 an income befitting one's rank. ②《어지간하다》(be) considerable; fair; decent. ¶ ~히 pretty; fairly; considerably / ~한 금액 a considerable sum of money / ~한 집안 a decent family / ~한 교육[수입] a good education [income] / 그는 회사에서 ~한 지위에 있다 He holds a considerably high position in his company.

상대(相對) ①《마주 대함》facing each other. ¶ ~하다 face [confront] each other / ~하여 앉다 sit face to face 《with》. ②《친구·짝》(one's) companion [mate, partner]. ~하다 make a companion of; keep company 《with》. ¶ ~하다 keep 《a person》 company; entertain 《one's guest》 / ~하지 않다 refuse to deal with 《a person》; ignore. ③《상대방》 the other party;《승부의》an opponent; a rival. ~하다 deal with; contend with; play 《against》. ¶ ~가 안 되다 be no match 《for》. ④《哲》《상대성》 relativity. ¶ ~적 (으로) relative(ly). ‖ ~개념 a relative concept / ~성 이론 [원리] the theory (principle) of relativity / ~습도 relative humidity / ~평가 relative evaluation.

상대역(相對役) the player of an opposite role;《춤의》a partner. ¶ ~을 하다 play 《a part》 opposite (to) 《an actor》.

상도(常道) 《떳떳한 도리》a regular [normal] course.

상도덕(商道德) commercial [business] morality.

상되다(常—) (be) vulgar; low; mean; base; indecent.

상등(上等) ¶ ~의 first-class[-rate]; superior; very good [nice]; fine. ‖ ~품 first-class articles.

상등병(上等兵) ☞ 상병(上兵).

상량(上樑) ~하다 set up the framework (of a house); put up the ridge beam. ‖ ~식 the ceremony of putting up the ridge beam of a new house.

상례(常例) ¶ ~의 regular; customary; usual; …을 ~로 하다 be in the habit of 《doing》;

상록(常綠) ¶ ~의 evergreen. ‖ ~수 an evergreen (tree).

상론(詳論) ~하다 state (treat) in detail; dwell 《upon》.

상류(上流) 《강의》 the upper stream (reaches); 《사회에서의》 the higher (upper) classes. ¶ ~의 《상류》 upstream; upriver. ‖ ~계급 the upper classes / 사회 high society / ~생활 high (fashionable) life.

상륙(上陸) landing. ~하다 land 《at》; go on shore. ‖ ~부대 (지점) a landing force (place) / ~작전 landing operations.

상말(常-) vulgar words; vulgarism; four-letter words.

상면(相面) ~하다 meet 《a person》 for the first time; have an interview 《with》.

상무(尙武) ¶ ~의 기상 martial (militaristic) spirit.

상무(常務) 《업무》 regular business; 《회사 간부》 a managing director.

상무(商務) commercial affairs. ‖ ~관 a commercial *attaché*.

상미(上米) first-class (top-grade) rice; rice of the best quality.

상미(賞味) ~하다 relish; appreciate.

상민(常民) the common people; 「a commoner.

상박(上膊) 【解】 the upper arm.

상반(相反) ~되다 be contrary (run counter) to 《each other》; conflict (disagree) with 《each other》.

상반기(上半期) the first half of the year.

상반신(上半身) the upper half of the body. ¶ ~을 벗고 stripped to the waist / ~을 내밀다 lean forward. 「vidual table.

상밥(床-) a meal sold on an indi-
상배(賞杯) a prize cup; a trophy.

상벌(賞罰) rewards and punishments. ¶ ~ 없음 (이력서에서) No reward and no punishment.

상법(商法) the commercial law

상병(上兵) a corporal. 「(code).

상병(傷兵) a wounded soldier; a disabled veteran (제대한); the wounded (총칭).

상보(床褓) a tablecloth.

상보(詳報) a detailed (full) report. ~하다 report in detail (full).

상복(喪服) a mourning dress; mourning clothes. ¶ ~을 입고 있다 be in mourning (black).

상봉(相逢) ~하다 meet each other.

상부(上部) the upper part (위쪽) the upside; 《기관·직위》 superior offices; a superior post. ‖ ~구조 the superstructure.

상부상조(相扶相助) mutual help (aid); interdependence.

상비(常備) ~하다 reserve 《something》 for; have 《something》 ready (on hand); be provided with. ¶ ~의 standing; permanent; regular. ‖ ~군 a standing army / ~약 a household medicine. 「geant.

상사(上士) a Master (First) Ser-
상사(上司) superior authorities; 《상관》 one's superior. 「like.

상사(相似) ¶ ~의 similar 《figures》.

상사(相思) mutual love. ‖ ~병 lovesickness 《~병에 걸린 lovesick / ~병을 앓다 languish for love》.

상사(商事) a (commercial) firm; a trading concern (company).

상사(商社) business affairs; commercial matters. ‖ ~회사 a commercial firm.

상사람(常-) a commoner; the common people (전체).

상상(想像) (an) imagination; (a) fancy (공상); (a) supposition (가정); (a) guess (추측). ~하다 imagine; fancy; suppose; guess; surmise. ¶ ~의 imaginary; imaginative / ~할 수 있는 (~도 못지) (un) imaginable; (un) thinkable / ~의 로 이 맞다 guess right. / ~력 imaginative power / ~임신 imaginary (false) pregnancy.

상상봉(上上峰) the highest peak.

상서(上書) 《웃어른께》 a letter to one's senior (superior). ~하다 send (write) a letter to one's superior.

상서(祥瑞) a good omen. ¶ ~로운 auspicious; propitious.

상석(上席) 《서열의》 seniority; 《상좌》 an upper (the top) seat; 《주빈석》 the seat (place) of honor.

상석(床石) the stone table in front of a tomb.

상선(商船) a merchant (trading) vessel; a merchantman; the mercantile marine (총칭). ‖ ~대 a merchant fleet.

상설(常設) ~하다 establish permanently. ¶ ~의 standing 《commitees》; permanent 《facilities》.

상설(詳說) ~하다 explain in detail; state in full (at length).

상세(詳細) ¶ ~한 full; detailed; minute / ~히 in full (detail); minutely; fully.

상소(上疏) ~하다 present (send up) a memorial to the Throne.

상소(上訴) an appeal. ~하다 appeal to 《a higher court》. ¶ ~를 포기 (취하) 하다 waive (withdraw) an appeal. ‖ ~권 the right of appeal.

상소리(常-) four-letter words; vulgar language; indecent talk. ~하다 use vulgar (coarse) language.

상속(相續) succession; inheritance. ~하다 succeed (*to*); inherit. ‖ ~세에 an inheritance tax / ~인 a successor; an heir(남자); an heiress(여자) / ~재산 an inheritance.

상쇄(相殺) ~하다 offset [cancel] each other; set (*the advantages*) off. ‖ ~계정 an offset account / ~관세 countervailing duties.

상수(上手) a better hand; a superior. ¶ ~이다 be no (*more than a*) match (*for a person*).

상수(常數) [數] a constant; an invariable (*number*).

상수도(上水道) (물) tap water; 《설비》 waterworks; water service [supply].

상수리나무 [植] an oak (tree).

상순(上旬) the first ten days of a month. ¶ 5월 ~에 early in May; at the beginning of May.

상술(上述) ☞ 상기(上記).

상술(商術) a knack of the trade (요령); a business policy(정책); business ability(상채).

상술(詳述) ~하다 explain [state] in full [detail].

상스럽다(常-) (be) vulgar; mean; low; base; indecent.

상습(常習) ¶ ~적인 customary; habitual; regular. ‖ ~범 a habitual crime(범죄); a habitual [confirmed] criminal(범인).

상승(上昇) ~하다 rise; ascend; climb; go up; soar (up). ¶ ~기류(氣流) a rising current of air.

상승(相乘) ~하다 multiply. ¶ ~비 a geometrical ratio / ~작용 synergism《*defeated*》.

상승(常勝) ¶ ~의 invincible; un-

상시(常時) ① ☞ 평상시(平常時). ② ☞ 항시(恒時).

상식(常食) staple food; daily food. ~하다 live on (*rice*).

상식(常識) common [practical] sense. ¶ ~인 commonsense; sensible; practical / ~을 벗어난 eccentric; senseless / ~적으로 생각하여 in the name of common sense.

상신(上申) ~하다 report [state] (*to a superior official*). ‖ ~서 a written report.

상실(喪失) ~하다 lose; be deprived (*of*); forfeit.

상심(傷心) ~하다 be down-hearted; be heartbroken; be distressed.

상심(喪心) stupor; stupefaction. ~하다 be dazed [stunned] (*by*).

상아(象牙) ivory. ‖ ~세공 ivory work / ~질 《치아의》 a dentin / ~탑 an ivory tower.

상악(上顎) [解] the upper jaw.

상어 a shark. ‖ ~가죽 sharkskin; sea leather.

상업(商業) commerce; trade; business. ¶ ~의 commercial; business / ~화하다 commercialize / ~에 종사하다 engage in business. ‖ ~고교 a commercial high school / ~미술 commercial art / ~어음 a commercial bill / ~영어 business [commercial] English.

상업방송(商業放送) commercial broadcasting. ~하다 begin broadcasting on a commercial basis. ‖ ~국 a commercial radio [TV] station.

상여(喪輿) a bier. ¶ ~를 메다 take [carry] a bier on the shoulders. ‖ ~꾼 a bier carrier.

상여금(賞與金) a bonus; a reward; a prize(상금). ¶ 연말 ~을 타다 get a year-end bonus.

상연(上演) presentation; performance. ~하다 put (*a play*) on the stage; stage [present] (*a drama*).

상영(上映) ~하다 show; put (*a film*) on the screen; run. ¶ ~중으로 be on (show) (*at*) / 곧 ~될 영화 the forthcoming film. ‖ ~시간 the running time (*of a movie*).

상오(上午) the forenoon. ☞ 오전.

상온(常溫) a normal temperature.

상용(商用) ~으로 on business / ~으로 방문하다 pay a business call [visit] (*to*). ‖ ~문 commercial correspondence; a business letter / ~어 a commercial term.

상용(常用) common [everyday] use. ~하다 use habitually; make regular use (*of*). ‖ ~어 common [everyday] words / ~영어 everyday English / ~자 a habitual user.

상원(上院) the Upper House; the Senate 《美》. ‖ ~의원 a member of the Upper House; a Senator 《美》.

상위(上位) a high rank. ¶ ~에 있다 be higher in rank (*than*) / ~를 차지하다 rank high.

상위(相違) (a) difference; (a) variation; (a) disparity. ~하다 differ (*from*); vary; disagree (*with*). ‖ ~점 a point of difference.

상응(相應) ① 《호응》 ~하다 act in concert (*with*); respond to (*a request*). ② 《대응》 ~하다 correspond (*to*); answer (*to*). ③ 《합당》 ~하다 be suitable; fit; be suited (*to*); be proper; be due.

상의(上衣) a coat; a jacket; an upper garment.

상의(上意) ¶ ~를 하달하다 convey the will and ideas of those

상의(相議) (a) consultation; (a) conference. ~하다 consult (confer) 《with》; talk over 《a matter with》; negotiate.

상이(傷痍) ¶ ~의 disabled; wounded. ‖ ~군인 a disabled veteran; a wounded soldier.

상인(商人) a merchant; a tradesman; a shopkeeper. ‖ ~근성 a mercenary spirit.

상인방(上引枋) 【建】 a lintel.

상일 manual (rough) work; odd jobs. ‖ ~꾼 a manual laborer.

상임(常任) ¶ ~의 standing; regular. ‖ ~위원(회) (a member of) the standing committee / ~지휘자 a regular conductor.

상자(箱子) a box 《of apples》; a case; a packing case (포장용). ‖ 포도주 한 ~ a case of wine.

상자성(常磁性) paramagnetism.

상잔(相殘) ~하다 struggle (fight) with each other. ‖ 동족~ an internecine (internal) feud (strife).

상장(上場) a list 《of stocks》. ‖ ~되다 be listed 《on the Stock Exchange》. ‖ ~폐지 delisting / ~회사 a listed company / (비)~주 (un)listed stocks (shares) / 제1부~회사 a company listed on the first section (of the Stock Exchange); 【crape.

상장(喪章) a mourning badge; a

상장(賞狀) a certificate of merit; an honorary certificate.

상재(商才) business ability.

상쟁(相爭) ~하다 be at feud with each other; struggle against each other.

상적(商敵) a commercial (trade) rival; a rival in trade.

상전(上典) one's master (employer).

상전(相傳) ~하다 《대대로》 inherit; hand down 《to》; transmit.

상전(桑田) a mulberry field. ‖ ~벽해 convulsions of nature; changes in nature.

상점(商店) a shop; a store 《美》. ‖ ~가 a shopping street; an arcade.

상접(相接) 【數】 contact. ~하다 come in contact with each other; touch each other.

상정(上程) ~하다 place (put) 《a bill》 on the agenda; lay 《a bill》 before the House (의회에); bring 《a bill》 up for discussion (토의에). 【ture [feeling].

상정(常情) (ordinary) human na-

상정(想定) ~하다 suppose; imagine; estimate. ¶ ~한 hypothetic; imaginary; estimated (어림의).

상제(上帝) ☞ 하느님.

상제(喪制) a person in mourning;

a mourner (사람) of mourning (제도).

상조(尙早) ¶ ~의 too early; premature / ~시기 ~ 다 It is too early yet 《to do》.

상조(相助) mutual aid. ~하다 help each other (one another); be interdependent; cooperate. ¶ ~적인 cooperative; friendly.

상종(相從) ~하다 associate (keep company) 《with》; mingle 《with》.

상종가(上終價) 《증권》 (hit) the daily permissible ceiling.

상좌(上座) the top seat; an upper seat; the seat of honor.

상주(上奏) ~하다 report to the Throne. 【lation.

상주(常住) ¶ ~인구 a settled popu-

상주(常駐) ~하다 be stationed 《at》.

상주(喪主) the chief mourner.

상주(詳註) copious notes. 【ing.

상중(喪中) ¶ ~이다 be in mourn-

상중하(上中下) the first, the second and the third classes (grades); the three grades of quality—good, fair and poor.

상지상(上之上) the very best.

상징(象徵) a symbol; an emblem. ~하다 symbolize; be symbolic 《of》. ¶ ~적인 symbolic(al). ‖ ~주의 symbolism.

상찬(賞讚) admiration. ~하다 admire; praise; laud. ¶ ~할 만한 admirable; praiseworthy.

상찰(詳察) ~하다 observe carefully (closely); consider in full.

상책(上策) a capital plan; the best policy.

상처(喪妻) ~하다 lose one's wife; be bereaved of one's wife.

상처(傷處) a wound; an injury; a hurt; a cut; a bruise (타박상); a scar (흉터). ¶ ~를 입히다 inflict a wound 《on》 / ~가 나다 leave a scar. 【body.

상체(上體) the upper part of the

상추 【植】 a lettuce.

상춘(賞春) enjoying spring. ‖ ~객 springtime picnickers.

상층(上層) the upper layer (stratum); 《하늘》 the upper air; 《건물의》 the upper stories; 《사회》 the upper classes. ‖ ~기류 the upper air current(s).

상충(相衝) a conflict. ~하다 be in discord 《with》; collide 《with》.

상쾌(爽快) ¶ ~한 refreshing; fresh; crisp.

상태(狀態) a state 《of things》; a condition; a situation. ¶ 현~는 under the present circumstances / 건강 ~ the state of health / 생활 ~ living conditions / 위험한 ~ a critical condition; a crisis / 정신 ~ one's mental state.

상통(相通) ① 《연락》 ~하다 communicate [be in touch] 《with》. ② 《의사소통》 ~하다 be mutually understood. ¶ 의사가 ~하다 understand each other; come to mutual understanding. ③ 《공통》 ~하다 have something in common 《with》.
상투 a topknot. ¶ ~를 틀다 do one's hair up into a topknot.
상투(常套) ¶ ~적(인) commonplace; conventional; hackneyed. ~수단 an old trick; a well-worn device / ~어 a hackneyed expression. 「[a carefree] life.
상팔자(上八字) a happy lot; an easy
상패(賞牌) a medal.
상편(上篇) the first volume [piece].
상표(商標) a trademark; a brand; a label(라벨). ¶ ~를 도용하다 pirate the trademark 《of》. ∥ ~권 the trademark right / ~도용 trademark piracy / ~명 a brand name.
상품(上品) first-grade articles; an article of superior quality.
상품(商品) a commodity; goods; merchandise(총칭). ¶ ~화하다 produce 《something》 on a commercial basis; commercialize. ∥ ~가치 commercial value / ~견본 a trade sample / ~견본시 a trade fair / ~권 a gift certificate [token] / ~목록 a catalog(ue) / ~이미지 the brand image / ~진열실[진열장] a showroom [showcase] / ~학 the study of merchandize.
상품(賞品) 《win》 a prize.
상피(上皮) 《生》 the epithelium.
상피병(象皮病) 《醫》 elephantiasis.
상피붙다(相避──) commit incest.
상하(上下) ① 《위와 아래》 up and down; upper and lower sides; top and bottom. ② 《귀천》 the upper and lower classes: high and low; superiors and inferiors. ③ 《책》 the first and second volumes.
상하(常夏) ¶ ~의 나라 a land of everlasting [eternal] summer.
상하다(傷──) ① 《다치다》 get hurt [injured]; be damaged [spoiled] (손상); (썩다) rot; go bad; turn sour(우유 따위). ② 《마음이》 be hurt; be worried 《about》. ¶ 《야위다》 get thin [emaciated].
상학(商學) commercial science.
상한(象限) 《數》 a quadrant. ☞ 사분면.
상한선(上限線) a ceiling; the maximum. ¶ ~을 두다 [정하다] put a ceiling on; fix limits.
상항(商港) a commercial harbor.
상해(傷害) (bodily) harm; (a) bodily injury. ~하다 injure; do 《a person》 an injury. ∥ ~보험 accident [casualty] insurance / ~죄 mayhem / ~치사 (a) bodily injury resulting in death.
상해(詳解) ~하다 explain minutely; give a detailed explanation 《of》.
상해(霜害) frost damage. ¶ ~를 입다 suffer from frost.
상행(上行) ∥ ~선[열차] an upline [-train]. 「action.
상행위(商行爲) a business trans-
상현(上弦) ∥ ~달 a young [an early crescent] moon.
상형문자(象形文字) a hieroglyph.
상호(相互) 《부사적》 mutually; each other; one another. ¶ ~의 mutual; reciprocal / ~의 합의로 by mutual consent. ∥ ~관계[작용] reciprocal relation [action] / ~부조[협조] mutual aid [help] / ~의존 interdependence.
상호(商號) a firm [trade] name.
상혼(商魂) a commercial spirit [enthusiasm]. ¶ ~이 악착 같다 be shrewd in business; be very business-minded [-conscious].
상환(相換) ~하다 exchange 《a thing for another》. ¶ …과 ~으로 in exchange for…. / ~권 an exchange ticket; a coupon.
상환(償還) repayment; redemption. ~하다 repay; redeem 《loans》. ∥ ~금 money repaid; a repayment / ~기한 the term of redemption; maturity (만기).
상황(狀況) the state of things; a situation; circumstances. ¶ 현 ~으로는 under the present conditions. / ~판단 circumstantial judgment.
상황(商況) the condition of the market. ¶ ~이 부진[활발]하다 The trade [market] is dull [brisk].
상회(上廻) ~하다 be more than; be over [above]; exceed 《the average crop》.
상회(商會) a firm; a company.
샅 the crotch; the groin. 「band.
샅바 《씨름의》 a wrestler's thigh
샅샅이 all over; in every nook and corner.
새(動物) a bird; a fowl; poultry(家禽). ¶ ~소리 bird cries; birdsong / ~를 기르다 keep a (cage) bird.
새¹ new(새로운); novel(신기한); fresh(신선한); recent(최근의).
새가슴 pigeon breast [chest]. ¶ ~의 pigeon-breasted.
새겨듣다 listen attentively to; give ear to; 《참뜻을》 catch 《a person's》 meaning. 「[bones].
새골(鰓骨) 《魚》 branchial skeleton
새근거리다 《뼈마디가》 feel a slight

pain (*in one's joints*); 《솟음》 gasp; be out of breath.

새근새근 ¶ ~ 잠자다 sleep peacefully (calmly); sleep a sound sleep.

새기다 ① 《파다》 carve (*an image*); engrave; chisel; incise; inscribe. ¶ 도장을 ~ engrave a seal. ② 《마음에》 bear (keep) (*a thing*) in mind; take (*a thing*) to heart; engrave (*an image*) on one's mind. ③ 《해석함》 interpret; construe; translate(번역). ④ 《반추》 ruminate; chew the cud.

새김 《뜻의》 interpretation; explanation; 《조각》 engraving. ∥ ~칼 a carving knife.

새김질 《조각》 carving; engraving; sculpture; 《반추》 rumination.

새까맣다 (be) deep-(jet-)black.

새끼 《끈》 a (coarse) straw rope. ¶ ~를 꼬다 make (twist) a rope.

새끼 ① 《동물의》 the young (총칭); a cub (맹수·여우의); a litter (한 배의); a calf (소의); a colt(말, 사슴의); a puppy(개의); a kitten (고양이의); a lamb(양의); 《뒤에 동물 명을 붙여》 a baby (*monkey*). ¶ ~를 낳다 bring forth (*its*) young / ~를 배다 be with young / 고양이 ~ 두 마리를 낳다 have a litter of two kittens. ② 《자식》 a child; a son(사내); a daughter (딸). ③ 《욕》 a fellow; a guy. ¶ 저 ~ that fellow.

새끼발가락 the little toe.

새끼손가락 the little finger.

새나다 《비밀이》 get (slip) out; leak out; be disclosed. ¶ 비밀이 ~ a secret leaks out.

새너토리엄 a sanatorium; a sanitarium (美).

새다 《날이》 ¶ ~ 날이 샐 녘에 at the crack (peep) of dawn / 날이 샌다 The day breaks. *or* It dawns. ② 《기체·액체 따위가》 leak (out); run out; escape; 《불빛 따위가》 come through; 《말소리가》 be heard outside. ¶ 새는 곳 a leak / 새는 곳을 막다 stop a leak. ③ 《비밀이》 get (slip) out; leak out; be disclosed.

새달 《다음 달》 next month; the coming month.

새댁 ☞ 새색시. [maker.]

새들다 act as go-between (match-

새들다 ¶ ~하다 be somewhat withered. [neat and clean.]

새뜻하다 (be) fresh and bright;

새로 new(ly); freshly; afresh; anew; (over) again.

새롭다 (be) new; fresh; novel; 《최근의》 (be) recent; latest; modern; up-to-date. ¶ 새롭게 newly; afresh / 새롭게 하다 renew; reno-

vate / 기억에 ~ be fresh in one's memory / 다시 한 번 새롭게 시작하자 Let's start it anew (afresh).

새마을 a *Saemaul*; a new community. ∥ ~금고(사업) a New Community [*Saemaul*] fund [project] / ~운동 the *Saemaul* movement / ~정신 *Saemaul* (New Community) spirit.

새매 《鳥》 a sparrow-hawk.

새물 ① 《과일·생선 따위》 the first product of the season. ② 《옷》 clothes fresh from washing.

새벽 《아침》 dawn; the break of the day; daybreak. ¶ ~같이 early in the morning / ~에 at dawn; at break of day.

새봄 early spring.

새빨갛다 (be) deep-red; crimson; downright (거짓말). ¶ 새빨간 거짓말 a downright lie / 새빨개지다 turn red; 《얼굴이》 flush; blush.

새사람 ① 《신인》 a new figure (face). ② 《신부》 a new bride. ③ 《갱생된》 another man. ¶ ~이 되다 start life anew; turn over a new leaf.

새삼 《植》 a dodder.

새삼스럽다 (be) abrupt; new; fresh. ¶ 새삼스럽게 anew; afresh; specially(특히); formally(형식적으로); now(이제서야).

새색시 a bride.

새알 a bird's egg.

새암 jealousy; envy. ☞ 샘².

새앙 《植》 ginger (나무, 근경).

새옹지마 (塞翁之馬) the irony of fate. ¶ 인간만사 ~ Inscrutable are the ways of Heaven.

새우 《動》 a shrimp (작은); a prawn (보리새우); a lobster (바닷가재). ¶ ~로 잉어를 낚다 《俗談》 throw a sprat to catch a mackerel. ∥ ~젓 pickled shrimp.

새우다 《밤을》 sit (stay) up all night; keep vigil. ¶ 밤을 새워 일하다 sit up all night working; work all night.

새우등 a stoop hunchback. ¶ ~의 stooped; round-shouldered.

새우잠 ~ 자다 lie (sleep) curled up in bed.

새장 (-欌) a bird cage. ¶ ~에 갇힌 새 a bird in the cage; a caged bird.

새조개 《貝》 a cockle.

새집¹ 《one's》 new house; a newly built house(신축의).

새집² 《가옥》 a bird's nest.

새총 (-銃) an air gun (rifle) (공기총); a slingshot (고무줄의).

새출발 (-出發) a fresh start. ¶ ~하다 make a fresh start; set out anew.

새치 prematurely gray hair. ¶ ~

가 have gray hair though *one* is still young.
새치기 cutting [breaking] into the line. ~하다 break into [the line]; push in front of others.
새침하다 (be) cold; prim; look prim; assume a prim air.
새침데기 a prim-looking girl; a smug-looking person; a prude.
새카맣다 (be) pitch-dark; jet-black.
새큼하다 (be) sour; acid.
새털 a feather; a plume; down (솜털). ‖ ~구름 a cirrus.
새파랗다 (be) deep blue; 《안색이》 (be) deadly pale. ¶새파랗게 질리다 turn deadly pale.
새하얗다 (be) pure-[snow-]white.
새해 a new year; the New Year. ¶ ~ 복 많이 받으세요 (I wish you a) Happy New Year! ‖ ~문안 a New Year's greeting.
색 a color; a shade (농담); a complexion (얼굴); 《색사(色事)》 sensual pleasure; female charms; a mistress (여색). ¶ 진한 [흐린] ~ a deep [light] color.
색 a sack; 《피임구》 a condom.
색감(色感) the color sense.
색골(色骨) a sensualist; a lewd person; a lecher.
색광(色狂) an erotomaniac; a sexual maniac. ‖ ~증 sex mania; erotomania.
색다르다(色-) (be) fresh; new; 《기이》 (be) unusual; uncommon.
색도(色度) chromaticity; 《조명》 chroma. ‖ ~측정 colorimetry.
색동(色-) stripes of many colors. ¶ ~저고리 a jacket with sleeves of many-colored stripes.
색마(色魔) a sex maniac.
색맹(色盲) color blindness. ¶ 적 ~ 의 color-blind / 적 ~ 의 red-blind / 적록 ~ red-green color blindness / 전(색) ~ total color blindness.
색상(色相) the tone of color; a color tone; color quality. ¶ 그림의 부드러운 녹색 ~ the soft green tone of a painting.
색색 ¶ ~거리다 breathe lightly / ~ 잠을 자다 sleep peacefully.
색소(色素) a coloring matter; a pigment. ‖ ~체(生) a plastid.
색소폰(樂) a saxophone.
색시(新婦) a bride; 《아내》 a wife; 《처녀》 a maiden; a girl; 《술집의》 a barmaid.
색실(色-) dyed [colored] thread.
색쓰다(色-) have sex; sex up; ejaculate (사정하다).
색안경(色眼鏡) (a pair of) colored glasses; sunglasses. ¶ ~으로 보다 look on 《things》 from a biased viewpoint [with a jaundiced eye].

색연필(色鉛筆) a colored pencil.
색욕(色慾) lust; sexual [carnal] desire.
색유리(色琉璃) stained glass.
색인(索引) an index. ¶ ~을 달다 index 《a book》; provide 《a book》 with an index.
색정(色情) sexual [carnal] passion [desire]; lust. ‖ ~광(狂) 색광.
색조(色調) a tone of color; a color tone; shade; 《美術》 tonality. ¶ 갖가지 푸른 ~ various shades of blue.
색종이(色-) (a) colored paper.
색주가(色酒家) a shady bar; a bar-whorehouse.
색채(色彩) a color; a hue; a tint; a tinge. ¶ ~를 띤 with a tinge [tint] of... / 종교적 ~를 띠다 have a religious color. ‖ ~감각 a color sense.
색출(索出) ~하다 search (out); hunt up; seek (out). ¶ 간첩 ~작전 a search operation against an espionage agent.
색칠(色漆) coloring; painting. ~하다 color; paint.
샌님 a meek person; a weak-kneed and bigoted person.
샌드위치 a sandwich. ‖ ~맨 a sandwich man.
샌들 sandals.
샐러드 a salad. ‖ ~유 salad oil.
샐러리 a salary. ‖ ~맨 a salaried man.
샘¹(泉) a spring; a fountain.
샘² 《시샘을》 jealousy; envy. ~내다 be jealous [envious] 《of》; envy.
샘물 spring [fountain] water.
샘바르다 (be) jealous; envious.
샘솟다 《물이》 rise in a fountain; gush [spring] out [forth]. ¶ 눈물이 ~ tears well up in *one's* eyes.
샘터 a fountain place [site].
샘플 a sample.
샛강(-江) a tributary; a feeder.
샛길 a byway; a narrow path; a bypath; a byroad.
샛노랗다 (be) bright [vivid] yellow.
샛밥 snack for farmhands.
샛별 the morning star; Lucifer.
샛서방(-書房) a secret lover; a paramour.
생(生) life (생명); living (삶). ¶ ~을 받다 be born; live.
생… 《조리하지 않은》 raw; uncooked; 《자연 대로의》 crude; 《신선한》 fresh; 《익지 않은》 green; 《덜 요리된》 underdone; half-boiled; 《살아있는》 live; green. ¶ ~고무 crude [raw] rubber / ~밥 half-boiled rice / ~우타리 hedge / ~우유 raw milk.
생가(生家) the house of *one's* birth; *one's* parents' home.

생가죽(生一) 《무두질하지 않은》 a rawhide; an untanned skin.
생각 ① 《사고》 thinking; feeling(느낌); 《상상》 (a) thought; 《관념》 an idea; a notion; a conception. ② 《의견》 one's opinion [view]; 《신념》 a belief. ¶ 내 ~으로는 in my opinion. ③ 《의도·의향》 mind; an idea; an intention; an aim; 《방책》 a plan; 《동기》 a motive; a view. ¶ 좋은 ~ a good idea / 그렇게 할 ~ 없다 have no mind to do so. ④ 《기대》 expectation; hope; 《소원》 wish; desire. ¶ ~밖의 unexpected; unforeseen / ~이 어긋나다 be disappointed of one's expectations. ⑤ 《판단》 judgment; 《사려》 prudence; sense; discretion. ¶ ~있는 prudent; discreet; thoughtful. ⑥ 《상상》 imagination; fancy; supposition. ¶ ~도 못할 unimaginable; unthinkable. ⑦ 《고려》 consideration; regard; thought; 《참작》 allowance. ¶ ~에 넣다 [안 넣다] take [leave] 《a matter》 into [out of] consideration. ⑧ 《추억》 retrospection; recollection; 《명상》 meditation; reverie(공상). ⑨ 《각오》 a resolution.
생각건대 It seems to me that…; I believe [think]….
생각나다 《사물이 주어》 come to mind; occur to one; be reminded of; 《사람이 주어》 call [bring] 《something》 to mind; recall; remember; 《생각이 떠오르다》 think of 《something》; hit on 《a plan》; take [get] it into one's head 《to do》. ¶ 생각나게 하다 remind 《a person》 of 《something》; suggest 《an idea》 to 《a person》 / 갑자기 ~ it strikes one 《to do》 / 너를 보면 내 동생이 생각난다 You put me in mind [remind me] of my brother.
생각하다 ① 《사고·고려》 think 《of, about》; consider. ¶ 다시 ~ think over; reconsider. ② 《믿다》 believe; hold; 《판단》 judge. ¶ 옳다고 ~ believe 《it》 to be right. ③ 《간주》 take 《a thing》 as [for]; regard [consider] 《as》. ¶ 명예로 ~ regard 《it》 as an honor. ④ 《의도》 intend; plan; be going to; think of 《doing》. ⑤ 《예기》 expect; hope; anticipate. ¶ 생각한 대로 as 《one》 expected / 생각했던 대로 되다 turn out just as one wanted. ⑥ 《상상》 suppose; imagine; fancy; guess. ¶ 생각할 수 없는 unimaginable; unthinkable / 네가 생각하는 바와 같이 as you suppose. ⑦ 《기억·회상》 recall; remember; look back 《upon》; recollect. ¶ 그를 어디서 만났던 것으로 생각한다 I remember seeing him somewhere. ⑧ 《염두에 두다》 think of; be interested in; care for; yearn after [for]. ¶ 고향을 ~ yearn for one's home / 아무렇지도 않게 ~ do not care a bit 《about》.

생각해내다 think out 《a plan》; work out 《a scheme》; invent; contrive; 《상기하다》 recall; remember; call to mind.
생강(生薑) 〔植〕 a ginger.
생것(生一) ☞ 날것.
생견(生絹) raw silk.
생경(生硬) ~하다 (be) raw; crude; unrefined; stiff.
생계(生計) livelihood; living. ¶ ~를 세우다 make a living 《by》. ‖ ~비 the cost of living.
생과부(生寡婦) a neglected wife; a grass widow.
생과(실)(生果(實)) (raw) green fruits.
생과자(生菓子) a pastry; a cake.
생굴(生一) a raw [fresh] oyster.
생글거리다 smile (affably).
생기(生氣) life; vitality; vigor; verve. ¶ ~있는 vital; lively; animated / ~없는 lifeless; dull; anemic / ~를 되찾다 come to life; be revitalized / ~를 발휘하다 be vigorous; be full of life / ~를 주다 enliven.
생기다 《발생》 happen; occur; take place; come into being(존재); 《야기함》 give rise to; cause; bring about; 《유래함》 originate 《from, in》; result 《from》; 《산출》 yield; produce; 《얻다》 obtain; get; 《낳다》 be born; 《얼굴이》 have looks.
생김새 looks; personal appearance.
생나무(生一) a live tree; green wood.
생남(生男) the birth (begetting) of a son; delivery of a boy. ~하다 give birth to a son; be delivered of a boy. ‖ ~턱 celebration of the birth of one's son; "handing out cigars".
생녀(生女) the birth (begetting) of a daughter. ~하다 give birth to a daughter; be delivered of a daughter.
생년(生年) ‖ ~월일(시) the date (and hour) of one's birth.
생니(生一) a healthy tooth.
생담배(生一) a lighted cigaret(te); a live butt.
생도(生徒) ‖ 사관~ a cadet; a midshipman(해군의). 〔purpose.
생돈(生一) money spent to no
생동(生動) ~하다 move lively; be full of life; be vivid(lifelike).
생득(生得) ¶ ~의 natural; inborn; innate. ‖ ~권 one's birthright.

생때(거리) ¶ ~ 쓰다 persist; stick to 《it》 doggedly; be obstinate.

생략(省略) omission; abbreviation. ¶ ~하다 omit; abbreviate. / ~한 〔된〕 omitted; abridged / 이하 ~ The rest is omitted. ¶ ~법 ellipsis / ~부호 an apostrophe.

생력(省力) labor saving. ¶ ~에 도움이 되는 기계 work-〔labor-〕saving machines. ‖ ~장치 a labor-saving device.

생령(生靈) souls; lives; people.

생리(生理) physiology.《월경》menstruation; one's period. ¶ ~적인 physical; physiological / ~적 요구 the needs of the body / ~중에 있다 be having one's period. ‖ ~대 a sanitary napkin 〔towel, belt〕 / ~위생 physiology and hygiene / ~일 one's menstrual period; one's monthly day / ~통 period pains / ~학 physiology / ~학자 a physiologist / ~현상 a physiological phenomenon / ~휴가 a women's holiday.

생매장(生埋葬) ~하다 bury 《a person》 alive.

생맥주(生麥酒) draft 〔draught《英》〕 beer; beer on draft 〔tap〕.

생면(生面) ~하다 see 〔meet〕《a person》 for the first time. ‖ ~부지 an utter stranger.

생명(生命) life; existence; the soul 《of thing》. ¶ ~을 걸다 risk one's life / 많은 ~을 희생하여 at the cost of many lives / ~이 걸려 있는 fatal 《disease》; mortal 《wounds》 / 그의 정치적 ~도 이제 끝이다 His political life 〔career〕 is over 〔finished〕. / ~ 력이 연설의 ~이다 Clarity is the life 〔soul〕 of a speech. ‖ ~감 a feeling of vitality / ~공학 biotechnology / ~과학 life science / ~력 life force; survival power 〔ability〕 / ~보험 life insurance 《~보험에 들다 have one's life insured》 / ~선 a life line / ~수 life-giving water / ~유지 장치 a life-giving support system.

생모(生母) one's real mother.

생목숨(生一) ①《산》 life. ②《죄없는》 an innocent 《person》's life.

생무지 a novice; a green hand.

생물(生物) a living thing; a creature; life 《총칭》. ‖ ~계 animals and plants / ~학 biology / ~학자 a biologist / ~학적 산소요구량 the biological oxygen demand 《생략 BOD》 / ~화학 biochemistry.

생방송(生放送) a live broadcast; live broadcasting. ~하다 broadcast 《a drama》 live; cover 〔carry〕《an event》 live on radio 〔television〕.

생벼락(生—) an unreasonable 〔undeserved〕 scolding; a sudden 〔an unexpected〕 calamity.

생부(生父) one's real father.

생불(生佛) a living Buddha.

생사(生死) life and 〔or〕 death; one's safety 《안부》. ¶ ~에 관한 문제 a matter of life and death; a vital question / ~를 같이하다 share one's fate 《with》 / ~지경을 헤매다 hover between life and death / 그의 ~는 아직 불명이다 He is still missing.

생사(生絲) raw silk.

생사람(生—) an innocent 〔unrelated〕 person. ¶ ~ 잡다 kill an innocent person 《살해》; inflict injury upon an innocent person 《피해》.

생산(生産) production. ~하다 produce; make; turn 〔put〕 out. ¶ ~을 개시하다 bring 〔put〕《something》 into production / 국내 ~ domestic production. ‖ ~고〔액〕 an output / ~파일 overproduction / ~관리 production control / ~력 productive capacity / ~목표 〔attain〕 a goal of production / ~물 a product / ~비 production cost / ~성 productivity 《~성을 높이다 increase 〔raise〕 the productivity 《of》》 / ~자 a producer; a maker / ~자 가격 the producer('s) price / ~제한 restriction of output / ~지 a producing district.

생살여탈(生殺與奪) ¶ ~권을 쥐다 hold the power of life and death 《over a person》.

생색(生色) ¶ ~이 나다 reflect credit on 《a person》; do 《a person》 credit / ~을 내다 pose as a benefactor 《to》; try to gain 《a person's》 gratitude.

생생하다(生生—) (be) fresh; vivid; lively; full of life. ¶생생히 vividly; true to life.

생석회(生石灰) quicklime.

생선(生鮮) (a) fish; fresh 〔raw〕 fish. ¶ ~가게 a fish shop / ~구이 baked 〔broiled〕 fish / ~장수 a fishmonger / ~회 slices of raw fish.

생성(生成) ~하다 create; form; generate; be created 〔formed〕.

생소(生疎) ¶ ~한 unfamiliar; strange; inexperienced 《in》.

생소리(生—)《엉뚱한》 an absurdity; a nonsense;《근거가 없는》 a groundless remark.

생수(生水) natural 〔spring〕 water.

생시(生時) ①《난 시간》 the time 〔hour〕 of one's birth. ②《깨어 있을 때》 one's waking hours;《생전》 one's lifetime.

생식(生食) ~하다 eat 《fish》 raw; eat uncooked food.

생식(生殖) reproduction; generation. ~하다 reproduce; procreate; generate. ‖ ~기 sexual organs / ~기능 reproductive function / ~력 generative power; fecundity / ~세포 a germ cell.
생신(生辰) ☞ 생일. [a lifetime.
생애(生涯) a 《happy》 life; a career;
생약(生藥) a herb medicine; a crude drug. ‖ ~학 pharmacognosy.
생억지(生一) ¶ ~ 쓰다 say extremely unreasonable things; stick to one's unjust opinion.
생업(生業) an occupation; a calling. ¶ …을 ~으로 하다 live by 《doing》. ‖ ~자금 a rehabilitation fund.
생육(生肉) raw [uncooked] meat.
생육(生育) ~하다 grow; raise.
생으로(生一) ① 《날로》 raw. ~먹다 eat raw. ② 《억지로》 forcibly; willy-nilly; by force; 《까닭없이》 unreasonably; without any reason; causelessly.
생이별(生離別) ~하다 be separated from 《one's spouse》 by adverse circumstances; part from 《one's spouse》 and lose contact with him [her].
생인손 a sore finger.
생일(生日) one's birthday. ‖ ~케이크 a birthday cake.
생장(生長) growth. ¶ ~성장.
생전(生前) one's life(time). ¶ ~에 in [during] one's life(time); before one's death.
생존(生存) existence; survival. ~하다 exist; live; survive(살아남다). ¶ ~경쟁 a struggle for existence / ~권 the right to live / ~자 a survivor.
생죽음(生一) ~하다 die an accidental death; die by violence.
생쥐 〖動〗 a mouse [pl. mice].
생지옥(生地獄) a hell on earth.
생질(甥姪) one's sister's son; a nephew. ‖ ~녀 one's sister's daughter; a niece.
생짜(生一) 《날것》 something raw; uncooked food; 《익지 아위》 an unripe [green] fruit(과실).
생채(生菜) a vegetable salad.
생채기 a scratch.
생체(生體) a living body. ‖ ~공학 bionics / ~반응 the reaction of a living body / ~실험 medical experimentation [a medical experiment] on living person / ~해부 vivisection.
생태(生態) a mode of life. ‖ ~계 an ecosystem / ~변화 ecological adaptation / ~학 ecology.
생트집(生一) a false charge. ~하다 find fault 《with a person》;

accuse 《a person》 falsely.
생판(生板) completely; utterly; quite. ¶ ~ 다르다 be utterly different.
생포(生捕) capture. ~하다 take 《a person》 prisoner; capture; catch 《an animal》 alive.
생화(生花) a natural [fresh] flower.
생화학(生化學) biochemistry. ‖ ~자 a biochemist.
생환(生還) ~하다 return alive; 〖野〗 reach the home plate; score home. ¶ ~시키다 《야구에서》 bring home 《the runner》 ‖ ~자 a survivor.
생활(生活) life; living; livelihood (생계). ~하다 live; lead a 《lonely》 life; support oneself; make a living. ¶ ~이 안정되다 secure one's living / ~이 어렵다 be unable to make a living; be badly off. ¶ ~개선 the improvement of living condition / ~고 hardships of life / ~곤궁자 a needy people; the needy [poor] / ~난 hard living [life] / ~력 vitality; one's capacity for living / ~방식 the mode of living / ~보호 livelihood protection(~~비 the cost of living / ~상태 the condition of living / ~설계 a plan for one's life; life planning / ~설계사 a life planner / ~수준 the standard of living / ~양식 a mode of living; a way of life / ~연령 one's chronological age / ~지도 《교육상의》 educational guidance / ~체험 experience in actual life / ~필수품 necessaries of life / ~환경 life environment.
생후(生後) after [since] one's birth. ¶ ~ 3개월된 아이 a three-month-old baby.
샤워 《have, take》 a shower (bath).
샴페인 (술) champagne.
샴푸 《have》 a shampoo.
샹들리에 a chandelier.
샹송 a *chanson* 《프》.
서(西) (the) west.
서(書) ① ☞ 관서. ② 《글씨》 경찰.
서가(書架) a bookcase; a bookshelf; a bookstack (도서관의).
서가(書家) a calligrapher.
서간(書簡) a letter; a note. ‖ ~문 an epistolary style.
서거(逝去) death. ~하다 pass away; die.
서경(西經) the west longitude. ¶ ~ 20도 longitude 20 degrees west; long. 20 W.
서고(書庫) a library.
서곡(序曲) an overture; a prelude.
서관(書館) 《서점》 a bookstore; 《출판사》 a publisher.

서광(曙光) the first streak of daylight; dawn; 《희망》 hope. ¶ 평화의 ~ the dawn of peace.
서구(西歐) West(ern) Europe; the West(서양). ‖ ~문명 Western civilization.
서글서글하다 (be) free and easy; open-hearted; magnanimous; sociable; affable. 「some.
서글프다 (be) sad; plaintive; lone-
서기(西紀) the Christian Era; *Anno Domini* (생략 A. D.).
서기(書記) a clerk; a secretary. ‖ ~국 a secretariat / ~장 the head clerk; a chief secretary / 《일등》 ~관 a (first) secretary *(of the embassy)*.
서기(瑞氣) an auspicious sign; a good omen.
서까래 a rafter. 「good omen.
서남(西南) the southwest. ‖ ~의 southwestern; southwesterly. / ~풍 a southwester; a southwesterly wind.
서낭 a tutelar(y) deity. ‖ ~당 the shrine of a tutelary deity.
서너 three or four; a few.
서너너덧 three or four; a few *(of)*.
서늘하다 ① 《날씨가》 (be) cool; refreshing; chilly 《차갑다》. ② 《마음이》 have a chill; be chilled.
서다 ① 《기립》 stand (up); rise (to *one's* feet); get up. ② 《정지》 stop; (make a) halt; come to stop; draw up 《말 따위가》; run down《시계가》; 「갑자기 ~ stop short. ③ 《건립》 be built (erected); be established; be set up. ④ 《장이》 be opened (held). ⑤ 《칼날이》 be sharpened (edged). ⑥ 《명령이》 be obeyed; be followed; be carried out; 《질서가》 be orderly; be in good order. ⑦ 《조리가》 hold good; be made good; 《이유가》 pass; be admissible. ⑧ 《계획이》 be formed (established); be worked out. ⑨ 《위신·체면이》 save 《*one's* face》. ⑩ 《잉태함》 ¶ 아이가 ~ become pregnant. ⑪ 《결심이》 make up *one's* mind.
서당(書堂) a village schoolhouse.
서도(書道) calligraphy.
서두르다 《급히》 be in a hurry; hasten; make haste; 《재촉》 press; urge. ¶ 서둘러서 in haste (a hurry); hastily / 일을 ~ speed
서랍 a drawer. [up] *one's* work.
서러워하다 grieve 《at, over》; sorrow 《at, over》; be sorrowful.
서럽다 (be) sad; sorrowful; mournful; grievous.
서력(西曆) ☞ 서기(西紀).
서로 mutually; (help) each other 《one another 《셋 이상》》.
서론(序論) an introduction; introductory remarks; a preface.

서류(書類) 《shipping》 documents; 《important》 papers. ¶ 관계 ~ related documents. / ~가방 a briefcase / ~전형(銓衡) selection (screening) of candidates by examining their papers / ~함 a filing cabinet.
서른 thirty.
서름~하다 ① 《익숙잖다》 (be) unacquainted (unfamiliar) 《with》; inexperienced. ② 《태도가》 (be) reserved; distant; quite estranged (alienated) 《from》.
서리¹ frost. ¶ ~가 내리다 it frosts. ~된 heavy frost / 첫 ~ the first frost of the season.
서리² 《훔치기》 stealing 《fruits, chickens, etc.》 in a band (out of a mischievous motive).
서리(署理) administering as an acting director《일》; an acting director, a deputy 《official》《사람》. ~하다 administer 《affairs》 as a deputy (acting director); stand proxy for. ¶ 국무총리 ~ an acting premier.
서리다 ① 《김이》 rise; be clouded (up) 《with》; steam up. ② 《기가》 get dejected; be disheartened.
서리맞다 ① 《내리다》 be frosted 《over》; be nipped (shriveled) by frost. ② 《기운이》 be dispirited; 《타격》 be hard hit; receive a setback.
서막(序幕) 《극에서》 the opening (first) scene; 《시초》 a prelude 《to》; the beginning.
서머타임 daylight saving time; summer time 《英》.
서먹(서먹)하다 feel awkward (nervous) 《before an audience》; feel small (embarassed) 《in company》; feel ill at ease.
서면(書面) a letter; 《문서》 writing; a document. ¶ ~으로 by letter; in writing.
서명(書名) the title (name) of a book.
서명(署名) a signature. ~하다 sign *one's* name 《to》; affix *one's* signature to; autograph. ¶ ~ 날인을 하다 sign and seal. ‖ ~국 a signatory / ~운동 a signature-collecting campaign / ~자 a signer; the undersigned (oversigned) 《서면에서》. 「bine.
서모(庶母) *one's* father's concu-
서몽(瑞夢) an auspicious dream.
서무(庶務) general affairs 《section》.
서문(序文) a foreword; a preface.
서민(庶民) the 《common》 people; common (ordinary) folks《美》; the masses. ¶ ~적(인) popular; common; unpretentious 《tastes》.

¶ ~금융 petty loans for the people.　「sphere.
서반구(西半球) the Western Hemi-
서방(西方) the west. ¶ ~의 western / ~에 to the west 《of》. ¶ ~세계 the Western world / ~정토 〔宗〕 the Western Paradise; the Buddhist Elysium.
서방(書房) ① 《남편》 one's husband (man). ¶ ~을 맞다 get married to a man. ② 《호칭》 Mr. 《Kim》; ~ 《한인의이》 Old....
서방질(書房―) adultery. ~하다 cuckold one's husband; misconduct oneself 《with a man》.
서법(書法) penmanship.
서부(西部) the western part; the West 《미국의》. ¶ ~의 western. ¶ ~극 a western; a cowboy picture.
서북(西北) ① 《서와 북》 north and west. ② 《서북간》 the northwest. ¶ ~의 northwestern; northwesterly. ¶ ~풍 a northwestern 〔northwesterly〕 wind.
서브 〔테니스〕 a serve; a service. ~하다 serve.
서비스 service. ¶ ~가 좋다 〔나쁘다〕 give good 〔bad〕 service. ¶ ~료 a service charge; a cover charge 《식당의》 / ~업 a service industry.
서사(敍事) (a) description of deeds 〔incidents〕. ¶ ~적(인) descriptive; narrative. ¶ ~시 an epic.
서산(西山) the western mountain. ¶ ~에 지는 해 the sun setting behind the hill(s).
서생(書生) a student; 《남의 집의》 a student houseboy.
서서히(徐徐―) slow(ly); gradually; by degrees.
서설(瑞雪) propitious snow.
서성거리다 walk up and down restlessly; go back and forth uneasily.
서수(序數) an ordinal (number).
서술(敍述) description; depiction. ~하다 describe; narrate; depict. ¶ ~적(인) descriptive; narrative. ¶ ~어 the predicative.
서스펜스 suspense. ¶ ~가 넘치는 suspenseful.
서슬 ① 《칼날》 a burnished blade; a sharp edge. ② 《기세 따위》 the brunt 《of an attack, argument》; impetuosity.
서슴다 hesitate 《to do》; waver. ¶ 서슴지 않고 without hesitation.
서슴없다 (be) unhesitating; 《《서술적》》 be not hesitant.
서식(書式) a (fixed, prescribed) form. ¶ ~에 따라 in due form.
서식(棲息) ~하다 live 《in water》; inhabit 《a forest》. ¶ ~에 적합한 inhabitable. ¶ ~동물 an inhabitant 《of》 / ~지 a habitat.
서신(書信) 〔편지 왕래〕 correspondence; 〔편지〕 a letter.
서약(誓約) an oath; a pledge, a vow. ~하다 (make a) pledge, vow; swear; take an oath. ¶ ~을 지키다 〔어기다〕 keep 〔break〕 one's pledge. ¶ ~서 a written pledge.
서양(西洋) the West; the Occident. ¶ ~의 Western; Occidental / ~화하다 Westernize; Europeanize. ¶ ~문명 〔사상〕 Western civilization 〔ideas〕 / ~사 European history / ~사람 a Westerner; a European / ~식 the Western style; the Western way 《of thinking》.
서언(序言·緖言) a foreword; an introduction; a preface.
서열(序列) rank; order; grade.
서예(書藝) calligraphy.
서운하다 (be) sorry; regrettable; disappointing. ¶ 서운해 하다 be sorry 《for》; regret; be disappointed; miss.
서울 Seoul; 《수도》 the capital; the metropolis. ¶ ~내기 a Seoulite.
서원(書院) ① a traditional lecture-hall. ② a memorial hall for the great scholars of the past.
서원(署員) (a member of the 《police》) staff. ¶ 세무~ a tax office clerk.　　　　　〔Indies.
서인도제도(西印度諸島) the West
서임(敍任) appointment. ~하다 appoint.
서자(庶子) an illegitimate child.
서장(署長) the head 〔chief〕 《of》; a marshal. ¶ 경찰~ the chief of police station.
서재(書齋) a study; a library.
서적(書籍) books; publications 《출판》. ¶ ~상 a bookseller 《사람》; a bookstore 《가게》.
서점(書店) a bookstore; a bookshop; a bookseller's.
서정(敍情·抒情) lyricism. ¶ ~적(인) lyric(al). ¶ ~시 lyric poetry 《총칭》; a lyric / ~시인 a lyrist.
서정(庶政) all administrative affairs; civil services. ¶ ~쇄신 purification 〔renovation〕 of officialdom.
서지(書誌) a bibliography. ¶ ~학 bibliography / ~학자 a bibliographer.
서진(書鎭) a (paper)weight.
서쪽(西―) the west. ¶ ~의 west; western / ~으로 westward.
서책(書冊) a book; 《저작》 a work.
서체(書體) a style of handwriting; a calligraphic style.

서출(庶出) ¶ ~의 bastard; born out of wedlock.
서치라이트 a searchlight 《on》.
서캐 a nit.
서커스 《run》 a circus.
서투르다 (be) unskillful; clumsy; poor; awkward. ¶ …이 ~ be bad[not good] at…; be a poor hand at 《doing》….
서평(書評) a book review.
서표(書標) a bookmark(er).
서푼(一分) three *p'un*; 《형용사적》 of little worth.
서품(敍品) [가톨릭] ordination. ~하다 ordain.
서풍(西風) the west [westerly] 〔wind〕.
서해(西海) the western sea; 《황해》 the Yellow Sea.
서해안(西海岸) the west coast. ‖ ~ 간선도로 the west coast highway.
서행(徐行) ~하다 go slow(ly); slow down. ¶ ~ 《게시》 Slow down. *or* Go 《Drive》 slow.
서향(西向) a western exposure.
서혜(鼠蹊) [解] the groin. ‖ ~ 부 the inguinal region.
서화(書畵) paintings and writings [calligraphic works].
서훈(敍勳) (conferment of a) decoration. ~하다 confer a decoration 《on a person》.
석(石) ① 《시계 등의》 a jewel. ¶ 15~의 시계 a 15-jewel watch. ② 《섬》 a *sŏk*(=4.9629 bushels).
석 ~ 세. ¶ ~ 달 three months.
석가(釋迦) 석가모니.
석가모니(釋迦牟尼) S(h)akyamuni; Buddha.
석가산(石假山) an artificial [a miniature] hill; a rockery.
석각(石刻) stone carving; a carved stone. ~하다 carve in stone.
석간(夕刊) an evening paper; the evening edition 《of》.
석고(石膏) gypsum; plaster (of Paris). ‖ ~ 세공 plasterwork.
석공(石工) 석수(石手).
석굴(石窟) a rocky cavern; a stone cave.
석권(席卷·席捲) ~하다 overwhelm; carry everything before 《one》; conquer; sweep 《over》.
석기(石器) stoneware; stonework [考古]. ¶ ~ 시대 the Stone Age. / ~ 시대 the Early [New] Stone Age.
석남(石南) [植] a rhododendron.
석류(石榴) [植] a pomegranate (tree). ‖ ~석(石) [鑛] garnet.
석면(石綿) [鑛] asbestos.
석명(釋明) ~하다 explain; give an explanation 《of》; vindicate 《oneself》.
석방(釋放) release; acquittal. ~하다 set 《a person》 free; release.

석벽(石壁) ① 《절벽》 a cliff; a rockwall. ② 《벽》 a stone wall.
석별(惜別) ~하다 be loath to part 《from》; express regret at parting. ¶ ~의 정을 나누다 express *one's* sorrow at parting.
석부(石斧) a stone ax.
석불(石佛) a stone (image of) Buddha.
석비(石碑) a stone monument.
석사(碩士) master. ‖ ~ 과정[학위] a master's course [degree] / 이학~ a master of science; Master of Science(생략 M.S.).
석상(石像) a stone image [statue].
석상(席上) ~에서 at the meeting.
석쇠 a grill; a gridiron. 〔ing.
석수(石手) a stonemason; a stonecutter.
석수(汐水) the evening tide.
석순(石筍) [鑛] stalagmite. 〔sun.
석양(夕陽) the setting 〔evening〕
석연(釋然) ~하다 (be) satisfied 《with》; satisfactory. ¶ ~치 않다 be not satisfied 《with》.
석영(石英) [鑛] quartz. ‖ ~암(岩) quartzite.
석유(石油) oil; petroleum; kerosene(등유). ¶ ~갱 an oil well / ~난로 an oil stove / ~생산국 an oil producing country / ~시추 oil drilling / ~시추업자 an oil driller / ~위기 an oil crisis / ~풍로 an oil stove for cooking.
석유수출국기구(石油輸出國機構) the Organization of Petroleum Exporting Countries(생략 OPEC).
석유안정기금(石油安定基金) the Petroleum Stability [Stabilization] Fund.
석유자원(石油資源) petroleum resources; oil riches. ¶ ~을 개발하다 develop [exploit] petroleum resources. 〔products.
석유제품(石油製品) petroleum [oil]
석유화학(石油化學) petrochemistry. ‖ ~ 공업 the petrochemical industry / ~제품 petrochemicals / ~콤비나트 a petrochemical complex.
석재(石材) (building) stone.
석전(釋奠) the rite observed in memory of Confucius.
석조(石造) ~의 (built of) stone. ¶ ~건물 a stone building.
석존(釋尊) Buddha; Sakyamuni.
석종유(石鐘乳) [鑛] stalactite.
석주(石柱) a stone pillar.
석차(席次) 《자리의》 the order of seats [places]; 《학교의》 standing; ranking; the class order. ¶ ~가 5등 오르다[내리다] go up [down] five places in the class standing / 그는 반에서 ~가 3등이다 He ranks third in his class.
석창포(石菖蒲) [植] a sweet rush.

석탄(石炭) coal. ¶ ~을 캐다 mine coal. ∥ ~가스 coal gas / ~갱(坑) a coal pit [mine] / ~갱부 a coal miner / ~산 carbolic acid / ~액화(장치) coal liquefaction (equipment) / ~층 a coal bed / ~통 a coal box.

석탑(石塔) a stone pagoda (tower).

석판(石板) a slate.

석판(石版) [印] lithography.

석패(惜敗) ~하다 be defeated by a narrow margin.

석필(石筆) a slate pencil.

석학(碩學) a man of erudition.

석화(石火) a flint spark (불꽃); a flash (빠름).

석회(石灰) lime. ¶ ~질의 calcic. ∥ ~석 limestone / ~수 limewater.

섞갈리다 get confused [mixed, tangled, complicated].

섞다 mix; mingle; blend; admix; adulterate 《with》.

섞바꾸다 take the wrong one; mistake one for the other.

섞바뀌다 be mistaken for.

섞이다 be mixed [mingled] 《with》; mix [mingle] 《with》.

선(혼인의) an interview [a meeting] with a view to marriage. ¶ ~보다 be formally introduced [meet each other] with a view to marriage; have an interview with a prospective bride [bridegroom]. [game].

선(先) the first move 《in a chess

선(善) (do) good; goodness; (practice) virtue. / ~과 악 good

선(腺) [解] a gland. Land evil.

선(線) (draw) a line; a route (항로); a track (역의); a wire (전선). ¶ 경부~ the Gyeong-bu [Seoul and Busan] line / ···을 따라 along the line 《of》; in line with / ~을 이루어 in a line. / 38도~ the 38th Parallel.

선(選) selection; choice. ¶ ~에 (못)들다 be (not) chosen.

선(禪) Zen (Buddhism); religious meditation (contemplation).

선가(禪家) a Seon temple [priest]; a Zen temple [priest].

선각자(先覺者) a pioneer; a pathfinder; a leading spirit.

선객(船客) a passenger. ∥ ~명부 a passenger list / 1(2)등 ~ a first-(second-)class passenger.

선거(船渠) a dock.

선거(選擧) (an) election. ~하다 elect; vote for. ¶ ~를 실시하다 hold an election / ~에 압승하다 win a landslide victory in an election / ~에 지다 lose [be defeated in] an election. ∥ ~관리 위원회 the Election Administration Committee / ~구 a constituency; an electoral district; / ~권 the right to vote; suffrage / ~방해 (an) election obstruction / ~사무소 an election campaign office / ~연설 a campaign speech / ~운동 an election campaign / ~위반 election irregularities / ~유세 a canvassing [campaign] tour / ~인 a voter; a constituent; the electorate(총칭) / ~인 명부 a pollbook; a voter's list: a register of electors 《美》 / ~일 the election [polling] day / ~자금 an election campaign fund / ~참관인 a referee of an election / 공제 a fair election / 대(소)~구제 the major [minor] electorate system / 보궐~ a special election 《美》 a by-election 《英》 / 중간~ an off-year election 《美》.

선거법(選擧法) election (electoral) law. ∥ ~개정 (an) electoral reform / ~위반 (a) violation of election law / ~위반자 an election law breaker [violator].

선견(先見) foresight. ¶ ~지명 the wisdom and power to see into the future / ~지명이 있는 far-sighted; farseeing; foresighted / ~지명이 있다[없다] have [lack] foresight.

선결(先決) ~하다 settle 《something》 beforehand. ¶ ~장소의 확보가 ~이다 We must get the place first of all. ∥ ~문제 the first consideration; a matter that must be settled first.

선경(仙境) a fairyland; an enchanted land.

선고(先考) one's deceased father.

선고(宣告) (a) sentence; (a) verdict(평결); (a) judgment(심판). ~하다 (pass) a sentence 《on》; condemn [pronounce] 《a person to death》. ¶ 사형의 ~ a sentence of death / 파산 ~ a decree in bankruptcy. 「go to bat first.

선공(先攻) ~하다 attack first; [野]

선광(選鑛) ore dressing. ~하다 ore dress. ∥ ~부 an ore dresser.

선교(宣敎) missionary work. ¶ ~사 a missionary.

선교(船橋) ① ~적 배다리, ② bridge (갑판의).

선구(先驅) ~적 pioneering 《works》; pioneer 《physicist》. ∥ ~자 a pioneer; a pathfinder.

선구(船具) ship's fittings; rigging.

선구안(選球眼) (야구의) (have) a 《sharp》 batting eye.

선글라스 (a pair of) sunglasses.

선금(先金) an advance; a prepayment. ¶ ~을 치르다 pay in advance.

선급(先給) (돈의) payment in

선급 advance.: 《상품 따위의》 delivery in advance. ¶ 《상품을》 ~으로 사다 〔팔다〕 buy 〔sell〕 《goods》 for forward delivery.
선급(船級) (ship's) classification 〔class〕. ‖ ~증서 a classification certificate / ~협회 a classification society.
선남선녀(善男善女) pious people.
선납(先納) payment in advance. ~하다 pay in advance; prepay.
선녀(仙女) a fairy; a nymph.
선다형(選多型) a multiple choice system 〔format〕. ‖ ~문제 a multiple-choice question.
선단(船團) a fleet of vessels.
선대(先代) one's predecessor.
선도(先渡) forward delivery.
선도(先導) ~하다 guide; 〔take the〕 lead. ‖ ~자 a guide; a leader.
선도(善導) proper guidance. ~하다 lead properly; guide aright.
선도(鮮度) freshness. ¶ ~가 높은〔낮은〕 very〔not very〕 fresh / ~가 떨어지다 become less fresh.
선돌 〔史〕 a menhir.
선동(煽動) instigation; agitation. ~하다 instigate; stir up; agitate. ¶ ~적인 inflammatory; seditious; incendiary. ‖ ~자 an agitator; an instigator.
선두(先頭) the lead; the head; the top; 〔軍〕 the van. ¶ ~에 서다 take the lead 《in doing》; be at the head. ‖ ~타자 〔野〕 a lead-off man; the first batter.
선두(船頭) the bow; the prow.
선두르다 put a border 《on》; border; fringe; hem.
선들거리다 《cool breezes》 blow gently; be rather cool 〔chilly〕.
선뜩하다 chilly; 《서술적》 feel a chill; feel 〔be〕 chilled; feel a thrill, shudder 《at, to think of》.
선뜻 《가볍게》 lightly; 《쾌히》 readily; willingly; with a good grace; offhand 《즉석에서》.
선량(善良) ~하다 《be》 good; virtuous; honest. ¶ ~한 사람 a good-natured man / ~한 시민 a good (law-abiding) citizen.
선량(選良) a representative of the people; a member of the Congress.
선령(船齡) the age of a vessel.
선례(先例) a precedent. ☞ 전례.
선로(線路) (lay) a (railway) line; a (railroad) track 《美》. ‖ ~공사 railroad construction.
선류(蘚類) 〔植〕 mosses.
선린(善隣) neighborly friendship. ‖ ~관계 good neighborly relations 《with》 / ~우호정책 〔외교〕 a good-neighbor policy.

선망(羨望) envy. ~하다 envy 《something, somebody》; feel envy 《at》; be envious 《of》.
선매(先賣) an advance sale.
선매권(先買權) (the right of) preemption.
선머슴 a naughty boy; an urchin.
선명(宣明) ~하다 announce; proclaim.
선명(鮮明) clearness; vividness; distinctness. ~하다 〔be〕 clear; distinct; vivid; clear-cut. ¶ ~한 영상《TV의》 a clear 〔distinct〕 picture / 기치를 ~히 하다 define 〔clarify〕 one's attitude. ‖ ~도 《TV의》 distinction, definition.
선무(宣撫) placation; pacification. ‖ ~공작 pacification activity 〔work〕 / ~반 a placation squad.
선물(先物) 〔buy, deal in〕 futures. ‖ ~거래 trading in futures / ~매입 purchase of futures / ~시장 a future market.
선물(膳物) a gift; a present; a souvenir (기념품).
선민(選民) the chosen (people); the elect. ‖ ~의식 elitism.
선박(船舶) a vessel; a ship; shipping (총칭). ‖ ~사용료 charterage / ~업 the shipping industry / ~업자〔회사〕 a shipping man〔company〕.
선반(一盤) a shelf; a rack(그물의). ¶ ~에 얹다 put 《a thing》 on a shelf.
선반(旋盤) a lathe. ‖ ~공 a latheman / ~공장 a turnery.
선발(先發) ~하다 start first; start〔go〕 in advance 《of others》; go ahead. ¶ ~대 an advance party / ~투수 a starting pitcher.
선발(選拔) selection; choice. ~하다 select; choose; pick 〔single〕 out. ‖ ~시험 a selective examination / ~팀 a picked 〔selected〕 team; an all-star team.
선배(先輩) a senior; an elder. ¶ 3년 ~이다 be one's senior by three years / ~티를 내다 pose 〔give oneself〕 airs as a senior. ‖ ~대 a big senior.
선별(選別) sorting; selection. ~하다 sort (out); select. ¶ ~기 a sorting machine / ~융자 selective lending. 《constitution》.
선병(腺病) ¶ ~질〔質〕 lymphatic 《선박》 (Korean) bottoms; shipping(총칭); 《적재량》 tonnage; 〔freight〕 space. ‖ ~부족 a shortage 〔scarcity〕 of bottoms.
선봉(先鋒) 〔lead〕 the van(guard); the spearhead. ¶ ~이 되다 be in the van 《of the attack》; spear

선분 (線分) 〖數〗 a line segment.
선불 (先拂) payment in advance. ~하다 pay in advance; prepay. ¶ 운임을 ~로 보내다 send (*goods*) freight prepaid.
선비 a (gentleman) scholar; a classical scholar; a learned gentleman.
선사 (선물을 줌) ~하다 give (make) (*a person*) a present; send (*a person's*) a gift.
선사 (先史) ¶ ~의 prehistoric(al). ‖ ~시대 the prehistoric age.
선사 (禪師) a Zen priest. 〔yard.
선산 (先山) one's ancestral grave-
선생 (先生) (교사) a teacher; an instructor; a master; a doctor (의사); (호칭) Mr.; Sir; Madam. ¶ 음악 (수학) ~ a teacher of music (mathematics).
선서 (宣誓) an oath. ~하다 swear; take an oath. ¶ ~시키다 put (*a person*) on his oath. ‖ ~문 a written oath / ~식 the administration of an oath; a swearing-in ceremony (취임의).
선선하다 ① (날씨가) (be) cool; refreshing. ¶ 선선해지다 become (get) cool. ② (사람·태도가) (be) candid; frank; open-hearted; free and easy. ¶ 선선히 with a good grace (선뜻).
선셈 (先-) payment in advance.
선소리 nonsense; silly talk.
선손 (先-) ¶ ~ 쓰다 take the initiative; get the start; forestall (*another*) / ~ 걸다 strike the first blow.
선수 (先手) ¶ ~를 쓰다 forestall (*another*); get the start of; have the first move (바둑).
선수 (船首) ☞ 이물.
선수 (選手) a (*tennis*) player; an athlete; a representative player (대표 선수). ¶ 후보 ~ a substitute (player) / 최우수 ~ the most valuable player (생략 MVP). ‖ ~ 교체를 change (switch) of players / ~권 (win, lose, defend) a championship; a title / ~권 보유자 a championship holder; a titleholder / ~권 시합 a title match / ~촌 an athletic village.
선술집 a (stand) bar; a pub; a tavern. 〔game.
선승 (先勝) ~하다 win the first
선실 (船室) a (*first-class*) cabin. ¶ 2등 ~ a second-class cabin / 3등 ~ the steerage / ~을 예약하다 book a berth.
선심 (善心) ① (착한 마음) virtue; moral sense. ② (큰 마음) generosity; benevolence. ¶ ~ 쓰다 do a kindness (*for a person*); show one's generosity. ‖ ~공세 〈선거시

의〉 pork-barrelling (promises).
선심 (線審) 〖蹴〗 a linesman.
선악 (善惡) good and evil; right and wrong. ¶ ~을 가릴 줄 알다 know right from wrong.
선약 (仙藥) the elixir of life.
선약 (先約) (have) a previous engagement (appointment).
선양 (宣揚) ~하다 raise; enhance; promote.
선언 (宣言) declaration; proclamation. ~하다 declare; proclaim. ‖ ~서 (draw up) a declaration.
선열 (先烈) patriotic forefathers. ¶ 순국 ~ the martyred patriots.
선외 (選外) ¶ ~의 (be) left out of selection (choice). ‖ ~가작 a good work left out of the final selection.
선용 (善用) ~하다 make good use of (*one's knowledge*); employ (*time*) well (wisely).
선웃음 a forced (an affected) smile. ¶ ~ 치다 force (feign) a smile.
선원 (船員) a seaman; a crew (총칭). ‖ ~수첩 a seaman's pocket ledger / ~실 the crew's quarters / 고급 ~ an officer (of a ship) / 하급 ~ a sailor.
선유 (船遊) boating; rowing.
선율 (旋律) a melody. ¶ ~적 melodious.
선의 (船醫) a ship's doctor.
선의 (善意) a favorable sense (미); good intentions (의도); 〖法〗 good faith; bona fide. ¶ ~의 well-intentioned; bona-fide / ~로 in good faith / ~로 해석하다 take (*a person's words*) in a favorable sense.
선의권 (先議權) the right to prior consideration (*of the budget*).
선인 (仙人) a hermit (은자); a fairy (선녀) an unworldly being.
선인 (先人) ① ☞ 선친. ② (전대 사람) one's predecessors.
선인 (善人) a good (virtuous) man.
선인선과 (善因善果) the fruit of good deeds.
선인장 (仙人掌) 〖植〗 a cactus.
선임 (先任) seniority. ¶ ~의 senior. ‖ ~순 (in) the order of seniority / ~자 a senior member.
선임 (船賃) ☞ 뱃삯. 〔nominate.
선임 (選任) ~하다 elect; appoint;
선입견 (先入見) preconception; a preconceived idea; a prejudice (편견). ¶ ~을 품다 have a preconceived idea (opinion) / ~을 버리다 get rid of one's prejudice. ‖ ~관 (先入觀) ☞ 선입견.
선잠 (have) a light (dog, short) sleep; (take) a nap.
선장 (船長) a captain; a commander; a skipper.

선적(船積) (발송) shipping; shipment; (적재) loading; lading. ~하다 ship (*a cargo*); load (*a boat with*). ¶ ~송장 a shipping invoice / ~항 a port of shipment (loading).

선적(船籍) the nationality (registration) of a ship. ¶ 그리스~의 화물선 a cargo ship sailing under the flag of Greece. ‖ ~명세서 shipping specifications / ~항 a port of registry.

선전(宣傳) (through) propaganda; publicity; advertisement; (광고). ~하다 propagandize; give publicity (*to*); advertise. ¶ 자기를 하다 advertise *oneself*. ‖ ~가치 the propaganda (promotional) value / ~공세 a propaganda offensive / ~공작 propaganda efforts (maneuvers) / ~기관 (정부의) a propaganda organ (machine) / ~문구 an advertising statement; a catch phrase; a copy / ~부 the publicity department / ~비 publicity (advertising) expenses / ~삐라 a handbill / ~업자 a publicity agent / ~원 a publicity man; a public relations man / ~차 an advertising van; a sound truck (美) / ~효과 (a) propaganda effect.

선전(宣戰) ~하다 declare war (*upon, against*). ¶ ~포고 a proclamation of war.

선전(善戰) ~하다 put up a good fight; fight (play) well.

선점(先占) prior occupation. ‖ ~취득 an acquisition by occupancy.

선정(善政) good government (administration); just rule. ¶ ~을 베풀다 govern well (wisely).

선정(煽情) ¶ ~적인 sensational; suggestive.

선제(先制) a head start. ¶ ~점을 올리다 score first point; be (the) first to score.

선제공격(先制攻擊) a preemptive strike (attack). ~하다 strike《*the enemy*》first; take the initiative in an attack.

선조(先祖) an ancestor; a forefather.

선종(禪宗) the Zen sect; Zen Buddhism.

선주(船主) a shipowner.

선지 blood from a slaughtered animal.

선진(先陣) (lead) the van (of an army).

선진(先進) ¶ ~된 advanced (*techniques*). ‖ ~국 an advanced nation / ~국수뇌회의 the Summit Conference of the Leading Industrialized Nations.

선집(選集) a selection 《*of*》; an anthology.

선착(先着) ¶ ~순으로 in order of arrival; on a first-come-first-served basis.

선창(先唱) ~하다 lead the song (chorus); take the lead (*in*); (비유적) advocate; advance.

선창(船窓) a porthole.

선창(船艙) (부두의) a (landing) pier; a wharf; a quay; (배의) a hatch. ¶ ~에 대다 bring a boat alongside the pier. ‖ ~정책 policy.

선책(善策) a capital plan; a good policy.

선처(善處) ~하다 take the appropriate (*in a matter*); deal adequately (*with*); make the best of (*a good bargain*).

선천(先天) ¶ ~적인 (성의) inherent; native; inborn; hereditary; inherited (*character*) / ~적으로 by nature; inherently. ‖ ~성 매독 congenital syphilis / ~적 결함 a congenital defect.

선철(銑鐵) pig iron.

선체(船體) a hull; a ship(배).

선출(船出) election. ~하다 elect.

선취(先取) preoccupancy. ~하다 take first; preoccupy. ¶ ~득점을 올리다 (野) score (*two runs*) first. ‖ ~특권 (法) (the right of) priority; a preferential right.

선측(船側) the side of a ship. ¶ ~인도 free alongside ship (생략 f.a.s.).

선친(先親) my deceased (late) father.

선태(蘚苔) (植) moss(es).

선택(選擇) selection; choice; (an) option. ~하다 select; choose. ¶ ~의 자유 freedom of choice / ~을 망설이다 be at a loss which to choose / ~을 그르치다 (잘 하다) make a bad (good) choice. ‖ ~과목 an optional (elective) (美) course / ~권 (have) the option; (the right of) choice.

선팽창(線膨脹) (理) linear expansion.

선편(船便) shipping service. ¶ ~으로 by ship (steamer, water).

선포(宣布) proclamation. ~하다 promulgate; proclaim. ¶ 계엄령을 ~하다 proclaim martial law.

선폭(船幅) the beam. ¶ ~이 넓다 be broad in the beam / ~이 넓은 배 a broad-beamed ship.

선표(船票) a (ship) passenger ticket.

선풍(旋風) a whirlwind; a cyclone. ¶ ~을 일으키다 (비유적) create a great sensation; make a splash. ‖ ~기 an electric fan.

선풍기(扇風機) (turn on, turn off) an electric fan.

선하다(鮮─) (be) vivid (fresh) (*before one's eyes*); live vividly in *one's* memory. ¶ 그 광경이 눈에 ~ The

sight still haunts me.
선행(先行) ~하다 precede; go [be ahead (of)]. ‖ ~권 (도로에서의) (have) (the) right of way / ~법규 established regulations / ~사 [文] an antecedent / ~조건 a condition precedent; an essential prerequisite / ~투자 prior investment.
선행(善行) (do) a good deed; good conduct.
선향(仙鄕) a fairyland.
선향(線香) (offer) an incense stick.
선험(先驗) ¶ ~적인 [哲] transcendental; *a priori* (라).
선혜엄 treading water. ‖ ~ 치다 tread water.
선현(先賢) ancient sages.
선혈(鮮血) (fresh) blood. ¶ ~이 낭자하다 be covered with blood.
선형(扇形) a fan shape; a sector (기하의). ¶ ~의 fan-shaped.
선호(選好) preference. ~하다 prefer (*to*). ¶ 남아 ~사상 a notion of preferring a son to a daughter.
선화(線畫) a line drawing.
선화(船貨) a cargo; freight. ¶ ~증권 a bill of lading (생략 B/L).
선화지(仙花紙) reclaimed paper.
선회(旋回) revolution; circling; a turn. ~하다 revolve; circle; revolve; rotate. ‖ ~비행 a circular flight / ~운동 a rotating movement.
선후(先後) (앞과 뒤) front and rear; (순서) order; sequence.
선후책(善後策) a remedial [relief] measure. ¶ ~을 강구하다 devise [work out] remedial measures.
설달 the twelfth month of the lunar calendar; December.
설불리 awkwardly; tactlessly; clumsily; 《부주의하게》 unwisely; carelessly; thoughtlessly.
설(새해) New Year's Day. ¶ ~(을) 쇠다 observe [celebrate] the New Year's Day.
설(說) (의견) an opinion; a view; (학설) a theory; a doctrine; (풍설) a rumor. ¶ 다른 ~에 의하면 according to another theory.
설거지 dishwashing. ~하다 wash [do] dishes; wash up.
설경(雪景) a snow scene.
설계(設計) (기계·건물의) a plan; a design; (생활의) planning. ~하다 plan; design; make a plan (*for*); draw up (*a plan*). ‖ ~도 a plan; a blueprint / ~변경 design changes / ~자 a designer.
설교(說敎) a sermon; preaching. ~하다 preach (a sermon); (훈계) lecture (*a child*); give (*a person*) a lecture. ‖ ~단 a pulpit / ~사 a preacher.

설기(떡) steamed rice cake (in layers).
설날 New Year's Day.
설다 ① (서투르다) (be) unfamiliar; unskilled. ② (덜 익다) (be) half-done; underdone (음식이); be not fully pickled (김치가); be unripe (과일 따위가). ¶ 선밥 half-cooked rice.
설다루다 handle carelessly; do a poor [halfway] job.
설대 a bamboo pipestem.
설득(說得) persuasion. ~하다 persuade; prevail on (*a person*); talk (*a person*) into *doing*. ¶ 일을 말도록 ~하다 persuade (*a person*) to take [into taking] the job; talk (*a person*) into taking the job / 그녀에게 ~되어 담배를 끊었다 She talked me out of smoking. ‖ ~력 persuasive [convincing] power / ~력이 있다 [없다] (be) [be not] persuasive.
설렁탕(-湯) beef bone and tripe [internals] soup (and rice); *seolleongtang*.
설렁하다 be a bit chilly.
설레다 (가슴이) (*one's heart*) throbs [beats] fast; feel uneasy; have a presentiment (움직이다) move about uneasily; be restless. ¶ ~는 고개를 ~흔들다 shake *one's* head.
설령(設令) even if; even though; (al)though. ¶ ~ 어떤 일이 있더라도 whatever may happen.
설립(設立) establishment; foundation. ~하다 establish; found; set up; organize. ‖ ~발기인 a promoter / ~자 a founder / ~취지서 a prospectus.
설마 surely (*not*); (not) possibly; That's impossible.; You don't say (so)!
설맞다 receive a flesh wound; (매를) have just a taste of the beating *one* deserves.
설맹(雪盲) snow blindness; [醫] niphablepsia.
설명(說明) (an) explanation. ~하다 explain; illustrate; describe. ¶ ~적 explanatory. ‖ ~도 a diagram / ~서 instructions (사용설명서) / ~자 an explainer / ~회 a briefing session.
설문(設問) a question. ~하다 pose a question.
설법(說法) a Buddhist sermon; preaching. ~하다 preach.
설봉(舌鋒) ¶ 날카로운 ~으로 with an incisive tongue; in most cutting terms.
설비(設備) facilities; equipment; conveniences; accommodations (수용 시설). ~하다 equip [furnish, fit, provide] (*with*); accommodate. ¶ ~가 좋은 well-equipped

설빈 [-furnished] / …의 ~가 되어 있다 be equipped [provided, furnished] with / 방화 ~ fire prevention devices / 숙박 ~ sleeping accommodations. ‖ ~비 the cost of equipment / ~ 투자 investment in plant and equipment.

설빔 the New Year's garment; a fine (gala) dress worn on the New Year's Day.

설사 (泄瀉) loose bowels; diarrhea. ~하다 have loose bowels; suffer from diarrhea. ‖ ~약 a binding medicine.

설사 (設使) ☞ 설령 (設令).

설산 (雪山) a snow(-covered) mountain.

설상가상 (雪上加霜) ~으로 to make things (matters) worse; to add to one's troubles (miseries).

설선 (雪線) a snow line.

설설 (boil) temperately; (warm) comfortably. ‖ 물이 ~ 끓다 water simmers.

설설기다 keep one's head low 《before a person》; be under 《a person's》 thumb; be awe-stricken.

설암 (舌癌) cancer on the tongue.

설염 (舌炎) [醫] glossitis.

설왕설래 (設往說來) ~하다 argue back and forth; bandy (cross) words 《with》.

설욕 (雪辱) ~하다 vindicate one's honor; wipe out a shame; get even 《with》(경기에서). ‖ ~전 a return match (game).

설움 sorrow; grief; sadness.

설원 (雪原) a snowfield; the frozen waste.

설원 (雪寃) ~하다 clear oneself of a false charge.

설음 (舌音) a lingual (sound).

설익다 (과실) become half-ripe; (음식) get half-done [-boiled].

설전 (舌戰) a wordy war (fare). ~하다 have a wordy (verbal) war 《with a person》.

설정 (設定) ~하다 establish; create 《a right》; set up 《a fund》. ‖ 저당권 ~ settlement of mortgage.

설중 (雪中) ~에 in the snow. ‖ ~ 행군 snow march.

설치 (設置) establishment. ~하다 establish; institute; set up.

설치다 (못 마침) leave 《something》 half-done; do 《a thing》 by halves; (날뜀) rampage; run riot [amuck].

설치류 (齧齒類) [動] rodents.

설탕 (雪糖) sugar. ‖ ~물 sugared water / 정제 ~ refined sugar / 흑 ~ raw sugar.

설태 (舌苔) [醫] fur. ¶ ~가 낀 혀 a coated (furred) tongue.

설파 (說破) ① (명시) ~하다 state clearly; elucidate. ②(논박) ~하다 argue against; refute; confute.

설피다 (be) loose-woven; coarse.

설핏하다 (be) somewhat coarse; rather loose-woven.

설하선 (舌下腺) [解] the sublingual gland.

설해 (雪害) damage from (by) snow; snow damage.

설형 (楔形) ¶ ~의 cuneiform. ‖ ~ 문자 a cuneiform (character).

설화 (舌禍) an unfortunate slip of the tongue.

설화 (雪花) ① (눈송이) snowflakes. ② (나뭇가지의) silver thaw.

설화 (說話) a story; a tale; narrative. ¶ ~적 narrative. ‖ ~문학 narrative (legendary) literature.

섬¹ (용기) a straw-bag; a bale; (용량) a sŏm (=5.12 U.S. bushels).

섬² (산) an isle; an islet; (작은 섬). ¶ ~의 insular / 외딴 ~ an isolated island. ‖ ~사람 an islander.

섬광 (閃光) a flash; a glint of light. ‖ ~전구 a flash bulb.

섬기다 serve; be in 《a person's》 service; work under; wait on.

섬나라 an island (insular) country. ¶ ~ 근성 an insular spirit; insularism.

섬돌 a stone step; (a flight of) stone steps.

섬뜩하다 (be) startled; frightened; alarmed; be taken aback.

섬망 (譫妄) [醫] delirium.

섬멸 (殲滅) ~하다 annihilate; wipe out; exterminate. ¶ ~전 a war of extermination.

섬섬옥수 (纖纖玉手) slender (delicate) hands.

섬세 (纖細) ~한 delicate; slender; exquisite.

섬약 (纖弱) ~한 weak; feeble; delicate.

섬유 (纖維) a fiber. ¶ ~질의 fibrous / ~로 된 fibroid / ~ 모양의 fibriform / 인조 (자연) ~ a staple (natural) fiber / 합성 (화학) ~ a synthetic (chemical) fiber. ‖ ~ 공업 the textile industry / ~ 소 cellulose / [動] fibrin / ~ 유리 fiber glass / ~제품 textile goods.

섬금류 (涉禽類) [鳥] wading birds.

섭렵 (涉獵) ~하다 (책을) read extensively (widely); range extensively over 《the literature》.

섭리 (攝理) (divine) providence. ¶ 하늘의 ~ the wise providence of Heaven / ~에 맡기다 trust in providence.

섭생 (攝生) care of health. ~하다 take care of one's health. ‖ ~법 hygiene.

섭섭하다 (서운하다) (be) sorry; sad; disappointed; heartbreaking; miss; (유감) be regrettable; sorry. ¶ 섭섭한 뜻을 표하다 express one's regret / 헤어지기가 ~ be sorry to part 《with a person》.

섭씨(攝氏) Celsius 《생략 C.》. ¶ ~ 온도계 a centigrade thermometer / ~ 15도 《at》 fifteen degrees centigrade; 15℃.

섭외(涉外) public relations. ‖ ~계원 a public-relations man 〔clerk〕 / ~ 관계 public relations.

섭정(攝政) 〔appoint〕 a regent 《사람》; 〔set up〕 regency 《직》. ~하다 attend to the affairs of state as a regent.

섭취(攝取) ~하다 take 〔in〕; absorb; ingest; adopt; assimilate. ¶ 영양을 ~하다 take nourishment / 외국 문화를 ~하다 adopt 〔assimilate〕 foreign cultures. ‖ ~량 an intake 《of vitamins》.

성(姓) a family name; a surname.

성(性) sex(남녀의); gender(문법의); nature(성질). ¶ ~의 sexual / ~적인 충동 a sexual urge / ~에 눈뜨다 be sexually awakened. ‖ ~교육 〔give〕 sex education / ~도덕 sex(ual) morality / ~도착 sexual perversion / ~도착자 a sexual pervert / ~문제 a sex problem / ~차별 sexism; sex discrimination / ~행위 sexual intercourse.

성(省) 〔내각〕 a department; a ministry; 〔행정 구역〕 a province. ¶ 국무~ the Department of State / 산동~ Shantung province.

성(城) a castle; a fort(ress); a citadel (성채).

성(聖) ¶ ~스러운 holy; sacred; saint ~ 바울 St. Paul.

성가(聖歌) a sacred song; a hymn. ‖ ~대 a choir / ~집 a hymnal; a hymnbook.

성가(聲價) 〔a〕 reputation; fame. ¶ ~를 높이다 〔얻다〕 enhance 〔lose〕 one's popularity.

성가시다 (be) troublesome; annoying; bothersome. ¶ 성가시게 하다 trouble 《a person》; give 《a person》 trouble.

성감(性感) sexual feeling. ¶ ~을 높이다 promote 〔work up〕 one's sexual feeling. ‖ ~대 an erogenous zone.

성게 〔動〕 a sea urchin.

성격(性格) character; personality; individuality (개성). ¶ ~이 강한 사람 a man of strong character. ‖ ~묘사 character description.

성결(聖潔) ~한 holy and pure. ‖ ~교 the Holiness Church.

성경(聖經) the 〔Holy〕 Bible; the Scriptures; the Book. ¶ 구약〔신약〕~ the Old 〔New〕 Testament.

성공(成功) (a) success 《in life》; achievement. ~하다 succeed 《in》; be successful; get on in life. ¶ ~한 사람 a successful man / ~할 가망 the chance of success.

성공회(聖公會) 〔宗〕 the Anglican Church 《英》; the 〔Protestant〕 Episcopal Church 《美》.

성과(成果) a result; the fruit; an outcome. ¶ ~를 올리다 obtain good results.

성곽(城郭) 〈성〉 a castle; a citadel; 〈성벽〉 a castle wall; 〈성채〉 a fortress; a stronghold.

성교(性交) sexual intercourse. ~하다 have sexual intercourse 《with》. ‖ ~불능 impotence.

성구(成句) a set phrase; an idiomatic phrase.〔cluster of stars.

성군(星群) 〔天〕 an asterism;

성금(誠金) a contribution; a donation; a subscription. ¶ 방위 ~ a contribution to the national defense fund.

성급(性急) ~한 hasty; quick-〔short-〕tempered; impatient.

성기(性器) genitals; genital organs.

성기다 (be) thin; sparse; loose.

성깔(性―) a sharp temper. ¶ ~을 부리다 lose one's temper 《with a person》.

성나다 get angry 《with a person, at a thing》; lose one's temper; get excited; get mad 《with, at》.

성냥 a match. ¶ ~을 긋다〔켜다〕 strike 〔light〕 a match. ‖ ~갑 matchbox / ~개비 a matchstick / 종이~ a matchbook.

성년(成年) 〔legal〕 majority; full 〔adult〕 age. ¶ ~이 되다 come of age; attain one's majority. ‖ ~자 an adult.

성능(性能) ability; capacity; efficiency; performance. ¶ ~이 좋은 efficient. ‖ ~검사 a performance 〔an efficiency, an ability〕 test.

성단(星團) 〔天〕 a star cluster.

성단(聖壇) an altar; a pulpit.

성당(聖堂) a 〔Catholic〕 church; a sanctuary.

성대 〔魚〕 a gurnard; a gurnet.

성대(盛大) ~한 prosperous; flourishing; thriving; 〈당당한〉 grand; magnificent / ~히 splendidly; on a grand scale.

성대(聲帶) the vocal cords. ‖ ~모사 vocal mimicry(~ 모사를 하다 mimic 《a person's》 voice).

성도(聖徒) a saint; a disciple; an apostle(제자).

성량(聲量) the volume of one's voice. ¶ ~이 풍부하다 have a rich voice.

성령(聖靈) the Holy Ghost 〔Spirit〕. ‖ ~강림절 Whitsunday.

성례(成禮) ~하다 hold a matrimonial ceremony.

성루(城樓) a castle turret; a tur-

성루(城樓) a fort(ress); a rampart.

성립(成立) ① 《실현》 materialization; realization. ~하다 come into existence (being); be materialized (realized, effected). ②《조성》 formation; organization. ~하다 be formed (organized). ③《체결》 conclusion; completion. ~하다 be completed (concluded).

성마르다(性─) (be) short-(quick-)tempered; intolerant.

성망(聲望) reputation; popularity. ¶ ~이 있는 popular 《with》; of high reputation.

성명(姓名) (give) one's (full) name. ¶ ~ 미상의 unidentified.

성명(聲明) a declaration; a statement. ~하다 declare; proclaim; announce. ∥ ~서(를 발표하다) (issue) a statement.

성모(聖母) the Holy Mother. ∥ ~ 마리아 the Holy Mother; the Virgin Mary.

성묘(省墓) ~하다 visit one's ancestor's grave. ∥ ~객 a visitor to one's ancestor's grave.

성문(成文) ~의 written / ~화하다 codify; put in statutory form. ∥ ~법 a statute; a written law.

성문(城門) a castle gate.

성문(聲門)〖解〗 the glottis. ∥ ~폐쇄음 a glottal stop.

성문(聲紋) a voiceprint.

성미(性味) nature; disposition; temperament. ¶ ~가 급한 (quick-, short-)tempered / ~가 못된 ill-natured; wicked / ~에 맞는 congenial 《work》.

성범죄(性犯罪) a sex offense; a sexual crime.

성벽(性癖) one's natural disposition; a mental habit; a propensity.

성벽(城壁) a castle wall. [sity.

성별(性別) sex (distinction).

성병(性病) a venereal disease (생략 VD); a social disease (美).

성복(成服) ~하다 wear mourning; go into mourning 《for》.

성부(聖父) 〖聖〗 the Father.

성분(成分) an ingredient;《조직의》 a component; a constituent; an element.

성불(成佛) ~하다 attain Buddhahood; enter Nirvana.

성불성(成不成) success or failure; 《결과》 the result; the issue.

성사(成事) success; attainment (of an end); achievement. ~하다 accomplish; achieve; succeed 《in》.

성산(成算) confidence (chances) of success. ¶ ~이 있다 (없다) be confident (have little hope) of success. [ten year's time.

성상(星霜) years; time. ¶ 십 개 ~

성상(聖上) (His Majesty) the King.

성상(聖像) a sacred image.

성상학(性相學) physiognomy.

성서(聖書) ⇒ 성경(聖經). [gonad.

성선(性腺) 〖解〗 a sex gland; a

성선설(性善說) the ethical doctrine that man's inborn nature is good.

성성이(猩猩─)〖動〗 an orangutan.

성성하다(星星─) (be) hoar(y); gray; gray-streaked.

성쇠(盛衰) ups and downs; rise and fall; vicissitudes.

성수(星宿)〖天〗 constellations.

성수(聖水) holy water. ¶ ~반 a font for holy water.

성수기(盛需期) a high-demand season. ¶ ~를 맞다 be in great demand.

성숙(成熟) ~하다 ripen; mature; attain full growth; reach maturity. ¶ ~한 ripe; mature. ∥ ~기 the age of puberty (maturity). [divine.

성스럽다(聖─) (be) holy; sacred;

성시(成市) opening a fair (market).

성시(城市) a castle town; a walled town (city).

성신(星辰) stars; heavenly bodies. ∥ ~숭배 astrolatry.

성신(聖神) 〖聖〗 성령(聖靈).

성실(誠實) sincerity; fidelity; faithfulness; honesty. ¶ ~한 sincere; faithful; honest; truthful.

성심(誠心) sincerity; a single heart; devotion. ¶ ~껏 sincerely; in all sincerity; 《work》 heart and soul.

성싶다 be likely 《to do》; look; seem; appear. ¶ 비가 올 ~ It looks like rain. or It is likely to rain.

성악(聖樂) sacred music.

성악(聲樂) vocal music. ∥ ~가 a vocalist / ~과 a vocal music course.

성악설(性惡說) the ethical view that human nature is evil.

성안(成案) (have) a definite plan.

성애(性愛) sexual love; eros.

성야(星夜) a starry (starlit) night.

성어(成魚) an adult fish. [idiom.

성어(成語) 《숙어》 a phrase; an

성업(成業) the completion of one's work (studies).

성업(盛業) ~중이다 drive a thriving (booming) trade; have a large practice (병원 따위).

성에 (a layer of) frost; 《영엣장》 a drift ice; a floe. ¶ 냉장고의 ~를 없애다 defrost a refrigerator.

성역(聖域) sacred (holy) precincts.

성역(聲域) 〖樂〗 a range of voice; a register.

성연(盛宴) a grand feast.

성욕(性慾) sexual desire; sex drive.

¶ ~이 강한 highly-sexed.
성우(聲優) a radio actor [actress]; a dubbing artist.
성운(星雲) a nebula [*pl.* -lae]. ¶ ~ (모양)의 nebular.
성원(成員) a member 《*of society*》; 《회 성립의》 a quorum; a constituent (member). ¶ ~이 되다 constitute [make] a quorum. ‖ ~ 미달 lack of a quorum.
성원(聲援) encouragement; (moral) support; cheering 《경기에서의》. ~하다 encourage; support; 《경기에서》 cheer; root for 《*a team*》.
성은(聖恩) Royal favor [grace].
성음(聲音) a vocal sound. ‖ ~학 phonetics.
성의(誠意) sincerity; (in) good faith. ¶ ~ 있는 sincere; honest; faithful / ~ 없는 insincere; dishonest / ~를 보이다 show *one's* good faith.
성인(成人) an adult; a grown-up. ¶ ~교육 adult education / ~병 geriatric diseases / ~영화 adults movies.
성인(聖人) a sage; a saint.
성자(聖者) a saint.
성장(成長) growth. ~하다 grow (up). ¶ ~한 full-grown / 연차적인 경제 ~ 목표 an annual economic growth target. ‖ ~과정 a growth process / ~기간 a growth period; the growing season《식물의》 / ~률 a growth rate / ~산업 a growth industry / ~주 a growth stock / ~호르몬 a growth hormone.
성장(盛裝) ~하다 be dressed up; be in full dress; be dressed in *one's* best.
성적(成績) result; record; grade; marks《점수》. ¶ ~순으로 앉다 sit in the order of merit / ~이 좋다 [나쁘다] do well [poorly] at school; show good [poor] business result. ‖ ~표 a report card; a grade transcript / 학교 ~ *one's* school record.
성적(性的) sexual. ‖ ~ 매력 a sex appeal / ~ 충동 a sex impulse
성전(聖典) ☞ 성경. [urge, drive).
성전(聖殿) a sacred shrine [hall]; a sanctuary.
성전(聖戰) a holy war.
성전환(性轉換) sex change. ‖ ~수술 a transsexual operation.
성정(性情) *one's* nature.
성조기(星條旗) 《미국기》 the Stars and Stripes.
성좌(星座) a constellation. ‖ ~도 a planisphere; a star chart.
성주[民俗] the guardian deity of a house.
성주(城主) the lord of a castle.
성지(聖地) a sacred ground; the Holy Land. ‖ ~순례 a pilgrimage to the Holy Land.
성직(聖職) 《take》 holy orders; the ministry; the clergy. ‖ ~자 a churchman; a clergyman.
성질(性質) 《기질》 (a) disposition; temper; 《특질》 a property; 《소질》 a quality. ¶ ~이 좋은 [못된] 사람 a good-[ill-]natured man / 문제의 ~상 from the nature of the matter.
성찬(盛饌) a sumptuous dinner; a good table.
성찬(식) (聖餐(式)) Holy Communion; the Lord's Supper. ¶ ~을 영(領)하다 take [receive] the Sacrament / ~용의 빵 [포도주] the sacramental wafer [wine].
성찰(省察) self-reflection; introspection.
성채(城砦) a fort; a fortress.
성상(成像) [動] an imago. 「an.
성취(成娶) ~하다 marry a wom-
성취(成就) 《달성》 accomplishment; achievement. ~하다 accomplish; achieve 《*an end*》; realize 《*one's wishes*》; succeed 《*in doing*》.
성층(成層) ‖ ~광맥 a bedded vein / ~권 (fly through) the stratosphere / ~권 비행기 a stratoplane / ~암 a stratified rock / ~화산 a stratovolcano.
성큼성큼 with big [long] strides.
성탄(聖誕) the birth of a saint [king]. ¶ ~목(木) a Christmas tree / ~절 ☞ 크리스마스.
성토(聲討) ~하다 censure; denounce; impeach. ‖ ~대회 an indignation meeting. [failure.
성패(成敗) hit or miss; success or
성폭행(性暴行) (a) sexual assault [violence]; a sexual harassment.
성품(性品) *one's* nature [disposition; character); *one's* temper.
성하(盛夏) midsummer; high summer.
성하다 ① 《온전하다》 (be) intact; unimpaired; undamaged. ② 《탈없다》 (be) healthy; in good health.
성하다(盛—) ① 《초목이》 (be) dense; thick; luxuriant; rampant. ②《사회·국가 따위가》 (be) prosperous; flourishing; thriving; 《기운이》 (be) vigorous; extensive 《광범위하다》. 「name.
성함(姓銜) your [his] esteemed
성행(盛行) ~하다 prevail; be prevalent (rampant).
성향(性向) an inclination; a disposition. ‖ 소비[저축] ~ the propensity to consume [save].
성현(聖賢) saints; sages. ¶ ~의 가르침 the teaching of the sages; the words of wise.
성형(成形) [醫] correction of de-

성혼 (成婚) a marriage; a wedding.
성홍열 (猩紅熱) scarlet fever.
성화 (成火) worry; annoyance; irritation; vexation; a bother; a trouble. ¶ ~나다 be irritated 《vexed》.
성화 (星火) ① 유성 (流星). ② 《불빛》 the light of a shooting star. ③ 《급한 일》 (be) urgent; pressing; importunate; press. ¶ ~같다 urge 《importune, press》《a person for...》; press 《a person》 hard 《for》.
성화 (聖火) sacred fire; the Olympic Torch. ‖ ~대 a flame-holder / ~주자 a flame-bearer.
성화 (聖畵) a holy 〔sacred, religious〕 picture.
성황 (盛況) ¶ ~을 이루다 《모임이》 be a success; be well attended.
성희롱 (性戱弄) sexual harassment.
섶 (버팀) a support; a prop.
섶 (웃옷) outer collar of a coat.
섶, 섶나무 brushwood. ¶ 섶을 지고 불로 뛰어들다 jump from the frying pan into the fire.
세 (稅) a tax; taxes; a duty 《물품세》; taxation 《과세》 / ~ 폐지 ~ abolition / ~를 거두다 collect taxes / ~를 부과하다 impose a tax 《on》.
세 (貰) 《임대 · 임차》 lease; tenancy; hire; 《임대료》 (a) rent; hire. ¶ ~놓다 rent 〔lease (out)〕 《a house》; let 《a room》; let 《a thing》 out on hire / ~ 들다 take 〔hold〕 《a house》 by 〔on〕 lease; rent 《a room》.
세 (세) three.
…세 (世) 《대 · 시대》 a generation; an age; 《지질》 an epoch. ¶ 헨리 5~ Henry V 〔the Fifth〕 / 한국계 3~의 미국인 a third-generation Korean American.
세간 household effects 《goods, stuffs》; household furniture. ¶ ~ 나다 set up housekeeping on one's own / ~를 내다 set up a separate home 《for》.
세간 (世間) the world; (a) society.
세계 (世界) the world; the earth; the globe; 《특수 사회 · 분야》 a world; circles; a realm. ¶ ~의 world / ~적 worldwide; universal; international; global 《affairs, war》 / 온 ~에〔의〕 all over the world / 각지에서 from all parts of the world / 이상의 ~ an ideal world / 음악의 ~ the world of music; music circles /

~적인 불경기 a worldwide depression / ~적으로 유명한 world-famous; of worldwide 〔global〕 fame / ~를 일주하다 go round the world / 오존층의 파괴는 이제 ~적인 문제이다 The destruction of the ozone layer is now a global problem. ‖ ~관 one's outlook in the world / ~기록 《establish》a world record / ~ 보건기구 the World Health Organization 《생략 WHO》 / ~사 world history / ~시 (時) universal time 《생략 UT》 / ~어 a universal language / ~연방 the World Federation / ~은행 the World Bank / ~인권선언 the Universal Declaration of Human Rights / ~ 일주여행 a round-the-world trip / ~정세 the world situation; world affairs / ~주의 cosmopolitanism / ~지도 a world map / ~평화 world peace.
세계무역기구 (世界貿易機構) the World Trade Organization 《생략 WTO》.
세계화 (世界化) globalization; Segyehwa. ¶ ~ 구상 (the) globalization vision / ~의 성취는 선언만으로는 오지 않는다 The achievement of globalization never comes only through a mere declaration.
세공 (細工) work; workmanship; 《세공품》 a piece of work. ~하다 work 《on bamboo》. ¶ 금속 ~ metalwork / 조개 ~ shellwork. ‖ ~인 an artisan.
세관 (稅關) a customhouse 《장소》; the customs 《기관》. ¶ ~을 통과하다 pass 〔get through〕 customs / 나는 ~에 걸려 짐 검사를 당했다 I was caught and got my baggage examined at customs. ‖ ~검사 customs inspection / ~수속 customs preceedures / ~신고서 customs declaration / ~원 a customs officer / 부산~ the Pusan Customhouse.
세광 (洗鑛) ore washing. ~하다 wash 《ore》; scrub 《ore》.
세균 (細菌) a bacillus; a bacterium; a germ. ¶ ~의 bacterial. ‖ ~검사 a bacteriological examination / ~배양 germ culture / ~병기 a bacteriological weapon / ~성질환 a germ disease / ~전 germ warfare / ~학 bacteriology.
세금 (稅金) a tax; a duty 《on foreign goods》. ‖ ~공제급료 take-home pay; pay after tax / ~ 납부 tax payment / ~징수 the collection of a tax / ~체납 tax arrears / ~체납자 a tax delinquent / ~포탈 tax evasion / ~ 포탈자 a tax evader / ~포함가격 the price with taxes included.

세기(世紀) a century. ¶ 20 ~ the twentieth century / ~ 말 the end of a century / 기원전 3 ~ the third century B.C.

세나다 〖잘 팔리다〗 sell well; sell like hot cakes; be in great demand.

세납(稅納) payment of tax. ☞ 납세(納稅).

세내다(貰 —) hire 《a boat》; rent 《a house》.

세네갈 Senegal. ¶ ~의 Senegalese / ~사람 a Senegalese.

세뇌(洗腦) brainwashing. ~하다 brainwash.

세다¹ ① 〖힘이〗 (be) strong; powerful; mighty; 〖마음이〗 (be) tough; firm; stubborn; 〖정도·세력이〗 (be) strong; violent; intense 《heat》; hard; severe. ¶ 세게 hard; severely; strongly; powerfully / 힘이 센 사람 a strong 〔powerful〕 man / 고집이 ~ be stubborn / 센 바람 a strong 〔violent〕 wind / 세게 때리다 strike hard. ② 〖팔자가〗 (be) ill-starred; unlucky. ¶ 팔자가 세게 태어나다 be born under an unlucky star.

세다² 〖머리털이〗 《one's hair》 turns gray 〔grey 《英》〕; be gray-haired.

세다³ 〖계산〗 count; number; calculate. ¶ 잘못 ~ miscalculate; miscount.

세대(世代) a generation. ¶ 젊은 ~ the rising 〔younger〕 generation / ~ 간의 intergenerational 《conflict》. ‖ ~ 교체 shift 〔transfer〕 in generation; generational change; the change of generations / ~ 차 a generation gap.

세대(世帶) a household. ‖ ~ 수 the number of households / ~ 주 the head of the household 〔family〕; a householder.

세도(勢道) power; (political) influence 〔authority〕. ~하다 seize political power. ¶ ~ 부리다 exercise 〔wield〕 one's authority 〔power〕 《over》. ‖ ~ 싸움〔다툼〕 a struggle for power; a power struggle.

세라믹스 ceramics.

세레나데 〖樂〗 a serenade.

세력(勢力) influence; power; 《물리적》 force; energy. ¶ ~ 있는 influential; powerful / ~ 없는 powerless; uninfluential / ~이 강해지다 increase in power / ~을 부리다 wield power / ~을 펴다 establish one's influence. ‖ ~가 a man of influence / ~권 one's sphere of influence / ~균형 the balance of power.

세련(洗鍊) ~하다 polish up; refine. ¶ ~된 polished; refined; elegant / ~되지 않은 unpolished; coarse.

세례(洗禮) baptism; christening 《유아의》. ¶ ~를 받다 be baptized 〔christened〕. ‖ ~명 one's Christian 〔baptismal〕 name / ~식 (a) baptism.

세로 (길이) height (높이); 《부사적으로》 vertically; lengthwise; lengthways. ¶ ~ 2 피트 가로 30피트 two feet by thirty.

세론(世論) (public) opinion; general sentiment. ☞ 여론.

세류(細流) a streamlet; a brooklet.

세륨 〖化〗 cerium. ¶ ~금속 cerium metals.

세리(稅吏) a tax collector; a revenue officer.

세립(細粒) a granule; infinitesimal grains.

세말(歲末) ☞ 세밑.

세면(洗面) ~하다 wash one's face. ‖ ~기 a washbowl; a wash basin 《英》/ ~대 a washstand / ~장 a lavatory; a washroom.

세모(歲暮) ☞ 세밑.

세목(細目) details; particulars. ¶ ~ 으로 나누다 itemize; specify.

세목(稅目) items of taxation.

세무(稅務) taxation business. ‖ ~ 사 a licensed tax accountant / ~ 서 a tax 〔revenue〕 office / ~서 원 a tax office clerk / ~서장 the superintendent of a revenue office.

세물(貰物) object for rent. ‖ ~ 전 a renter's store.

세미나 a seminar.

세미다큐멘터리 semidocumentary 《film》.

세미콜론 a semicolon (기호 ;).

세밀(細密) ¶ ~한 minute; close; detailed; elaborate / ~히 minutely; in detail; closely / ~한 검사 a close 〔minute〕 examination / ~히 조사하다 inquire minutely into 《a matter》; examine closely.

세밑(歲—) the year-end; the end of the year.

세발(洗髮) a shampoo. ~하다 wash one's hair. ‖ ~제 shampoo.

세배(歲拜) a formal bow of respect to one's elders on New Year's day; a New Year's greeting 〔call〕. ~하다 perform a New Year's bow.

세버들(細—) a weeping willow.

세법(稅法) the tax〔ation〕 law.

세별(細別) ~하다 subdivide 《into》; break 《into parts》.

세부(細部) details.

세부득이(勢不得已) by force of circumstances; by an unavoidable circumstances. ☞ itemize.

세분(細分) ~하다 subdivide 《into》.

세비(歲費) annual expenditure; 《수당》 yearly pay; an annual allowance.

세상(世上) the world; life; society. ¶ ~에 in the world / ~일 worldly affairs; the way of the

세상살이 / ~일에 훤하다 know much of the world; see much of life / ~을 모르다 know nothing (little) of the world / ~에 나가다 go out into the world; start in life / ~에 알리다 bring to light; make public / ~에 알려지다 be known to the world / ~을 떠나다 die; leave this world / 제 ~이라고 판치다 have *one's* own way; be *one's* own master; be without a rival.

세상살이(世上-) living. ~하다 live; get on in the world.

세상없어도(世上-) under (in) any circumstances; whatever may happen; by all means.

세세하다(細細-) (be) minute; detailed. ¶ 세세히 minutely; in detail; closely.

세속(世俗) the world; popular customs (세상 풍습). ¶ ~의 (적인) worldly; mundane / ~을 떠난 unworldly / ~을 초월하다 stand aloof from the world.

세수(洗手) ~하다 wash *one's* face and hands; wash *oneself*; have a wash. ¶ ~수건 a (face) towel / 세숫대야 a washbowl / 세숫물 wash(ing) water.

세수(稅收) the revenue.

세슘(化) cesium (기호 Cs).

세습(世襲) ¶ ~의 hereditary; patrimonial. ‖ ~재산 hereditary property (estate); a patrimony.

세심(細心) ~하다 (be) prudent; circumspect; scrupulous; careful. ¶ ~한 주의를 기울이다 pay close attention (*to*).

세쌍둥이(-雙-) triplets; a triplet (그 중의 하나). ¶ ~을 낳다 have three at a birth.

세안(洗眼) ~하다 wash *one's* eyes. ‖ ~약 a collyrium; eyewash.

세안(歲-) ¶ ~에 within the present year; before the current year is out.

세액(稅額) the amount of a tax. ¶ ~을 정하다 assess.

세우(細雨) a fine rain; a drizzle.

세우다 ① 《일으키다》 stand; raise; set (put) up; erect; turn up 《*one's collar*》. ② 《정지》 stop; hold up. ③ 《건조》 build; construct; set up. ④ 《설립》 establish; found; create; set up. ⑤ 《조직》 organize; institute; constitute. ⑥ 《정하다》 establish; lay down (regulations); enact 《*a law*》; form (make) 《*a plan*》. ⑦ 《공훈 따위를》 render 《*a service*》; perform 《*meritorious deeds*》. ⑧ 《날을》 sharpen; set 《*the teeth of a saw*》. ⑨ 《체면을》 save 《*one's face*》. ⑩ 《생계를》 earn 《*one's living*》.

세원(稅源) a source of taxation.

세월(歲月) time; time and tide; years. ¶ ~이 감에 따라 with the lapse of time; as time passes by; as days go by / ~없다 《Business》 is dull (bad).

세율(稅率) tax rates; a tariff (관세의). ¶ ~을 올리다 (내리다) raise (lower) the tax rate.

세이프(野) (declare) safe. ¶ 1루에서 ~되다 be safe on first base.

세이프티번트(野) a safety bunt.

세인(世人) people; the public.

세일러복(-服) (a girl in) a sailor (middy) blouse.

세일즈맨 a salesman.

세입(稅入) tax revenue (yields).

세입(歲入) an annual revenue (income). ‖ ~세출 revenue and expenditure.

세자(世子) the Crown Prince.

세정(洗淨) washing; cleaning. ~하다 wash; rinse; clean.

세정(稅政) tax administration.

세제(洗劑) (a) cleanser; (a) detergent. ¶ 합성(중성) ~ (a) synthetic (neutral) detergent.

세제(稅制) a tax(ation) system.

세제곱(數) cube. ~하다 cube. ‖ ~근 a cube root.

세존(世尊) Buddha; Sakyamuni.

세주다 (貰-) rent 《*a room to a person*》; let (집 따위); 《英》 lease (땅을); hire out (임대).

세차(洗車) car washing. ~하다 wash a car. ¶ ~장 a car wash.

세차(歲差)《天》 precession.

세차다 (be) strong; violent; fierce; hard. ¶ 세찬 물결 rough waves / 세차게 불다 blow hard (furiously).

세찬(歲饌)《선물》 a year-end present (gift);《음식》 food for serving New Year's guests.

세척(洗滌) ~하다 wash; rinse; clean. ¶ 위를 ~하다 carry out a lavage of 《*a person's*》 stomach. ‖ ~기 a washer; a syringe / ~약 a wash; a lotion.

세출(歲出) annual expenditure.

세칙(細則) detailed rules (regulations); bylaws. ¶ 시행~ rules for operation.

세탁(洗濯) wash(ing); laundry. ~하다 wash; launder; do washing. ‖ ~기 a washing machine / ~물 the laundry; (have a lot of) washing / ~비누 laundry (washing) soap / ~소 a laundry / ~솔 a scrub(bing) brush / ~업자 a laundryman; a washerman.

세태(世態) social conditions; aspects (phases) of life; the world. ¶ ~의 일단을 보이다 show an aspect of life / 흐트러진 ~를 반영하다 reflect disturbed social conditions.

세트 ① 《한 벌》 a set. ¶응접 ~ a drawing-room suite / 커피 ~ a coffee set. ② 《영화의》 a set. ¶ ~ 를 《build》 a set. ③ 《수신기》 a receiving set. ④ 《퍼머의》 a set. ¶머리를 ~ 하다 have one's hair cut. ⑤ 《테니스 따위의》 《play》 a set.

세파 (世波) the storms (rough-and-tumble) of life. ¶ ~ 에 시달리다 be buffeted about in the world.

세평 (世評) public opinion; (a) reputation; rumor. ¶ ~ 에 오르 다 be talked about / ~ 에 무관심 하다 do not care what people say about one.

세포 (細胞) ① 《생물의》 a cell. ¶ ~ 의 cellular. ‖ ~ 막 cell membrane / ~ 분열 cell division / ~ 조직 cellular tissue / ~ 질 cytoplasm / ~ 학 cytology. ② 《조직 의》 《organize》 a communist cell 《fraction》 (공산당의).

섹스 (남녀) (a) sex; 《성교》 《have》 sex 《with》.

센물 hard water. [sex 《with》.

센세이션 a sensation. ¶ ~ 을 일으 키다 cause 《create》 a sensation.

센스 a sense. ¶ ~ 있는 sensible / ~ 가 없다 have no sense 《of》.

센터 ① 《野》 the center field; a center fielder (사람). ② 《시설》 a center. ¶ 쇼핑 ~ a shopping center.

센트 《미국 화폐의》 a cent. [center.

센티 《미터법의》 centi-; 《센티미터》 a centimeter (기호 cm).

셀러리 《植》 celery.

셀로판 cellophane 《paper》.

셀룰로이드 celluloid 《toy》.

셀프서비스 self-service 《store》.

셀프타이머 《寫》 a self-timer.

셈 ① 《계산》 calculation; counting (《셈하기》). ¶ ~ 이 빠르다 (느리다) be quick (slow) at figures. ② 《지 불》 settlement of accounts; payment of bills (☞ 셈하다). ③ 《분 별》 discretion; prudence; good sense. ¶ ~ 이 나다 grow sensible; mature. ④ 《의도》 intention; idea. ¶ ~ 할 ~ 으로 with the intention 《idea》 of 《doing》; in the hope of 《doing》.

셈속 (속 내용) the real state of affairs (things); 《속마음》 the mind; one's inmost thoughts.

셈치다 (가정) suppose; assume; grant (that...); 《요량》 think of 《doing》; expect (that...). ¶ 다시 팔 셈치고 사다 buy 《something》 intending to resell it.

셈판 ① 《사정》 circumstances; conditions; the situation; 《원인》 reason. ¶ ~ 을 모르다 do not know how the matter stands. ② ☞ 주판 (籌板).

셈하다 (계산) count; reckon; calculate; 《지불》 pay [make out] a bill; settle one's accounts.

셋 three; Ⅲ 《로마 숫자》. [☞ 셈.

셋돈 (貰-) rent 《money》.

셋방 (貰房) a room to let [for rent]; a rented room. ¶ ~ 살이 하다 live in a rented room / ~ 을 얻다 rent a room.

셋집 (貰-) a house to let [for rent]; a rented house. ¶ ~ 을 얻다 rent a house.

셋째 the third.

셔츠 an undershirt; a shirt (와이 셔츠). ¶ ~ 바람으로 《work》 in one's shirt sleeves.

셔터 《카메라·문의》 a shutter. ¶ ~ 를 누르다 release 《click》 the shutter / ~ 를 내리다 pull down a shutter.

셰이커 《cocktail》 shaker.

셰퍼드 《動》 a German shepherd.

소¹ 《動》 a cow (암소); a bull (황소); an ox (거세한 소); cattle (총칭).

소² (떡의) dressing; stuffing. ¶ 팥 ~ red bean jam.

소 (小) little; small; minor; lesser; miniature (소형).

소 (少) little; few; young (젊은).

소각 (燒却) ~ 하다 burn (up); destroy by fire.

소간 (所幹), **소간사** (所幹事) business; affairs; 《일》 work; things to do.

소갈머리 ¶ ~ 없는 thoughtless; imprudent; shallow-minded.

소감 (所感) 《give》 one's impressions 《of》; 《express》 one's opinions.

소강 (小康) ¶ ~ 상태가 되다 come to a 《state of》 lull.

소개 (紹介) (an) introduction; presentation; recommendation (추천). ~ 하다 introduce 《a person to another》; present 《to》; recommend. ¶ 자기를 ~ 하다 introduce oneself 《to》. ‖ ~ 자 an introducer / ~ 장 a letter of introduction / 직업 ~ 소 a public employment agency 《exchange》.

소개 (疎開) dispersal; evacuation. ~ 하다 disperse; evacuate; thin out 《houses》. ¶ 전시에 시골로 ~ 되 다 be evacuated to the country during the war / 강제 ~ compulsory evacuation / 집단 ~ an evacuation in a group. ‖ ~ 자 an evacuee.

소거 (消去) ~ 하다 eliminate. ‖ ~ 법 《數》 elimination.

소견 (所見) 《give, express》 one's views 《opinions》 《on》. ¶ 진단 ~ one's diagnosis and observations 《entered on a patient's clinical record card》.

소경 a blind person; the blind (총칭). ☞ 장님.

소계 (小計) a subtotal. ¶ ~ 가 되 다 It subtotals....

소고(小鼓) a small hand drum.
소곡(小曲) a short piece of music.
소곤거리다 whisper; talk in whispers.
소관(所管) jurisdiction; competency(권한). ‖ ~사항 matters under the jurisdiction 《of》 / ~청 the competent authorities; the authorities concerned.
소관(所關) what is concerned. ‖ ~사 one's business 〔concern〕; matters concerned.
소국(小國) a small country; a minor power.
소굴(巢窟) a den; a nest; a haunt; a hide-out. ¶ 범죄의 ~ a hotbed of crime.
소권(訴權)〔法〕 the right to bring an action in a court.
소규모(小規模) a small scale. ¶ ~의 small-scale / ~로 on a small scale; in a small way.
소극(消極) ~적(으로) negative(ly); passive(ly); not active(ly) enough / ~적인 성격 a negative character. ‖ ~성 passivity.
소금 salt. ¶ ~으로 간을 맞추다 season with salt / ~에 절이다 salt 《fish》; pickle 〔preserve〕 《vegetables》 with salt. ‖ ~기 a salty taste; saltiness / ~물 salt water; brine.
소금쟁이〔蟲〕 a water strider.
소급(遡及) ~하다 trace〔go〕 back to;〔法〕 be retroactive 《to》; be effective 《to》. ¶ 이 법은 1998년 4월 5일로 ~한다 This law is effective retroactively to April 5, 1998. ‖ ~력 retroactivity / ~법 a retroactive law.
소기(期期) ¶ ~의 《as was》 expected; anticipated / ~의 목적을 이루다 achieve the expected results 〔desired end〕.
소꿉동무 a childhood playmate; a friend of one's early childhood.
소꿉질 playing house. ~하다 play (at keeping) house.
소나기 a shower; a passing rain. ¶ ~를 만나다 be caught in a shower. ‖ ~구름 a shower cloud; a cumulonimbus.
소나무 a pine (tree).
소나타〔樂〕 a 《violin》 sonata.
소네트 a sonnet.
소녀(少女) a girl; a maiden. ¶ ~시절에 one's girl-hood / ~같은 girlish.
소년(少年) a boy; a lad. ¶ ~시절에 one's boyhood〔childhood〕; when a boy / ~들이여, 큰 뜻을 품어라 Boys, be ambitious. ¶ 이로학난성(易老學難成)이라 The day is short and the work is much. ‖ ~단 the Boy Scouts / ~단원 a boy scout / ~범죄 a juvenile crime; juvenile delinquency / ~소녀 가장 a young family head / ~원 a reformatory; a reform school / 비행~ a juvenile delinquent.
소농(小農) a small farmer; a
소농가(小農家) a petty farmer.
소뇌(小腦)〔解〕 the cerebellum.
소다 soda. ¶ 세탁용 ~ washing soda. ‖ ~공업 alkali manufacture / ~수 soda water.
소담하다 look nice and rich; be tasty.
소대(小隊) a platoon. ‖ ~장 a platoon leader (commander).
소독(消毒) disinfection; sterilization;《우유 등의》 pasteurization. ~하다 disinfect; sterilize; pasteurize. ¶ 일광〔끓는 물〕 ~ disinfection by sunlight 〔boiling〕 / 상처를 ~하다 disinfect the wound / ~이 된 disinfected; sterilized / 이 타월은 ~이 다 됐다 This towel has already been sterilized. ‖ ~기 a sterilizer / ~액 an antiseptic solution / ~약〔제〕 a sanitizer; a disinfectant / ~저(箸) sanitary 〔disposable〕 chopsticks.
소동(騷動) (a) disturbance;《쟁의》 a dispute;《분쟁》 a trouble;《혼란》 confusion;《폭동》 a riot. ¶ ~을 일으키다 raise a disturbance; give rise to confusion; make a trouble.
소두(小斗) a half-mal measure.
소득(所得) (an) income;《수익》 earnings. ¶ 고액〔저액〕 ~층 high 〔low〕 income group / 순(純)~ net income / 실질~ real income / 종합~세 the composite income tax. ‖ ~격차 income differentials 〔disparities〕 / ~공제액 a (tax) deduction; an amount deducted from one's income / ~세 income tax / ~수준 income standard / ~자 an income earner / ~정책 an incomes policy.
소등(消燈) ~하다 put out lights.
소라〔貝〕 a turban〔wreath〕 shell. ‖ ~게〔動〕 a hermit crab / ~고둥〔貝〕 a trumpet shell.
소란(騷亂) a disturbance; a disorder;《commotion》 a trouble; a riot. ‖ ~소동. ¶ ~을 일으키다 create 〔raise〕 a disturbance / ~을 진압하다 quiet〔put down〕 the disorder. ‖ ~죄 the crime of riot.
소량(少量) a small quantity 《of》; a little. ¶ ~의 a little; a small quantity 〔amount, dose〕 of.
소련(蘇聯) the Soviet Union; Soviet Russia.
소령(少領) a major(육군, 공군); a lieutenant commander(해군).

소로(小路) a narrow path; a lane.
소름 gooseflesh; goose pimples. ¶ ~이 끼치는 hair-raising; horrible / ~이 끼치다 get [have] gooseflesh (all over); (무서워서) shudder《at》; make one's hair stand on end《at》.
소리 ① (음향) (a) sound; a noise (소음); a roar (굉음). ¶ ~를 내다 make a noise [sound] / 뒤뜰에서 이상한 ~가 났다 I heard a strange noise in the backyard. / 아무 ~도 안 들렸다 Not a sound was heard. ② (음성) a voice; a cry; a shout. ¶ 맑은 ~로 in a clear [silvery, ringing] voice / 큰 [작은] ~로 in a loud [low] voice / 새 ~ the notes [singing] of a bird / 벌레 ~ the song [chirping] of an insect. ③ (말) a talk; words. ¶ 이상한 ~ 같지만 it may sound strange, but… / (소문) a rumor; a report. ¶ 터무니없는 ~ an unfounded rumor. ⑤ (노래) a song; singing. ~하다 sing (a song).
소리(小利) a small profit. ¶ 눈앞의 ~에 눈이 어두워지다 be blinded by a small immediate profit.
소리개〖鳥〗 a kite.
소리지르다 shout; cry (call (out)); scream; roar; yell; (요란하게) clamor; bawl.
소립자(素粒子) an elementary particle.
소망(所望) a wish: (a) desire. ~하다 desire; wish for; ask for; hope for; expect. ¶ 간절한 ~ an ardent desire / ~을 이루다 realize one's wishes (desire).
소매 a sleeve; an arm (양복의). ¶ ~가 긴 long-sleeved / ~가 없는 sleeveless / ~를 걷어올리다 roll up one's sleeves / ~를 끌다 pull 《a person》 by the sleeve. ‖ ~통 the breadth of a sleeve / 소맷부리 a cuff.
소매(小賣) retailing; retail sale. ~하다 retail; sell at retail. ¶ ~로 at (by) retail. ‖ ~가격 a retail price / ~물가지수 a retail price index / ~상인 a retailer / ~업 retail trade / ~점 a retail store.
소매치기 pocket-picking; a pickpocket (사람). ~하다 pick 《a person's》 pocket. ¶ ~ 당하다 have one's pocket picked.
소맥(小麥) ☞ 밀.
소멸(消滅) ~하다 disappear; vanish; cease to exist; go out of existence; become null and void (실효). ¶ 권리의 ~ the lapse of one's right / ~시키다 extinguish; nullify 《a right》 / 자연 ~하다 die out in course of time. ‖ ~시효 extinctive prescription; 〖형법상의〗 the statute of limitations (소취를 위한).
소명(召命) a royal summons.
소모(消耗) 〘소비〙 consumption; 〘마손〙 wear and tear. ~하다 consume; use up; exhaust; waste (낭비하다). ¶ 일에 정력을 ~하다 exhaust one's energy on the work; be worn out by the work. ‖ ~전 a war of attrition / ~품 articles for consumption; an expendable.
소목장이(小木匠–) a cabinet maker; a joiner.
소몰이 a cattle droving (일); a cowboy (사람). [dessin 프].
소묘(素描) a (rough) sketch;
소문(所聞) (a) rumor; (a) gossip; a report; talk; hearsay. ¶ 사실 무근한 ~ a groundless report / ~을 퍼뜨리다 spread a rumor / ~을 내다 set (start) a rumor afloat / ~에 듣다 hear a rumor 《that…》 / …라는 ~이다 it is rumored that…; there is a rumor going around that….
소문자(小文字) a small letter.
소박(疎薄) ill treatment to one's wife. ~하다 ill-treat one's wife; give the cold shoulder to one's wife; desert. ¶ ~ 맞다 be neglected (deserted) by one's husband. ‖ ~데기 a deserted (neglected) wife.   「naive.
소박(素朴) ¶ ~한 simple; artless;
소반(小盤) a small dining table.
소방(消防) fire service; fire fighting (美). ¶ ~용 사다리 a fire ladder; an extension ladder. ‖ ~관 (사) a fireman; a fire fighter / ~대 a fire brigade / ~서 a fire (brigade) station / ~연습 a fire drill / ~자동차 a fire engine.
소변(小便) urine; piss 《俗》; pee (소아어). ~보다 urinate; pass [make] water; have [take] a pee (口); piss [俗] / ~을 참다 retain [hold] one's urine. ‖ ~금지 (게시) No Urinating: Commit no nuisance / ~소 a urinal.
소복(素服) 〘wear〙 white (mourning) clothes.
소비(消費) consumption. ~하다 consume; spend; expend. ¶ 시간을 ~하다 expend [spend] time / 건전한 ~풍토를 해치다 hamper the sound consumption climate. ‖ ~경제 consumption economy / ~량 (the amount of) consumption / ~세 a consumption tax / ~자 a consumer; the consuming public (일반소비자) / ~자 가격 a consumer's price / ~자 단체 a consumer's group (organization) / ~자 물가(지수) the consumer's price (index) / ~자

소비에트 421 **소요**

보호(운동) consumerism / ~자 신뢰지수 the index of consumer confidence / ~자 심리 consumer sentiment / ~자 조합 a consumers' cooperative union / ~재 consumer goods.
소비에트 Soviet. ‖ ~연방 the Union of Soviet Socialist Republics《생략 U.S.S.R.》.
소사(掃射) machine-gunning. ~하다 machine-gun; mow 《the enemy》 down; sweep [rake] 《the enemy's position》 with fire.
소사(燒死) ~하다 be burnt to death; die [be killed] in the fire. ‖ ~자 a person burnt to death / ~한 시체 a charred body.
소산(所産) a product; fruit(s); an outcome.
소산(消散) ~하다 disappear; vanish; disperse; lift《안개가》.
소상(小祥) the first anniversary of 《a person's》 death.
소상(塑像) a plastic image; a clay figure [statue].
소상하다(昭詳—) (be) detailed; full; minute; circumstantial. ¶ ~히 minutely; in detail.
소생(小生) I; me; myself. [dren].
소생(所生) one's offspring [chil-
소생(蘇生) revival; resuscitation; reanimation. ~하다 revive; come to 《oneself》; be restored to life.
소석고(燒石膏) plaster of Paris.
소석회(燒石灰) slaked lime.
소선거구(小選擧區) a small electoral district. ‖ ~제(制) the single-member constituency system.
소설(小說) a story; a novel; fiction《총칭》; a romance《공상적》. ¶ ~적인 romantic; fictitious. ‖ ~가 a novelist; a story [fiction] writer.
소성(塑性)《理》plasticity. ¶ ~이 있다 be plastic.
소소하다(小小—)《자질구레함》 (be) minor; trifling; insignificant.
소속(所屬) belong [be attached] 《to》. ¶ ~의 belonging [attached] 《to》 / ~시키다 attach; assign.
소송(訴訟) a (law)suit; an action. ~하다 sue 《a person》; bring a lawsuit [an action] 《against》. ¶ …에 대해 ~을 일으키다 go to court against [with] 《a person》; raise [start] a lawsuit 《against》 / ~에 이기다 [지다] win [lose] a lawsuit / 이혼 ~을 하다 sue for divorce. ‖ ~대리인 a counsel; an attorney / ~사건 a legal case / ~의뢰인 a client / ~의 원고 a plaintiff(원고) / ~절차(를 밟다) (take) legal proceedings.
소수(小數)《數》a decimal (fraction). ¶ ~점 a decimal point《소수점 이하 3자리까지 계산하다 calcu-

late down to three places of decimals》.
소수(少數) a minority; a few. ¶ ~당[파] a minority (party) / ~민족 a minority race / ~의견 the opinion of the minority.
소수(素數)《數》a prime number.
소스 《Worcester》sauce. ¶ ~를 치다 pour sauce 《over food》.
소승(小乘) Hinayana; the Lesser Vehicle. ¶ ~적인 shortsighted 《view》.
소시민(小市民) ‖ ~계급 the petite bourgeoisie. 「one's youth.
소시(적)(少時—) one's early days;
소시지 a sausage.
소식(小食) ~하다 do not eat much. ¶ ~가 a light eater. 「fare.
소식(素食) meatless meal; plain
소식(消息) news; tidings; information. ¶ ~이 있다 [없다] hear [hear nothing] 《from》 / ~을 전하여 주다 bring news 《of》. ‖ ~통 well-informed circles [sources]; a well-informed person《사람》.
소식자(消息子)《醫》a probe; a sound.
소신(所信) one's belief [conviction]; one's opinions [views]. ¶ ~을 밝히다 express one's opinions [beliefs].
소실(小室) ~하다 keep a mistress.
소실(消失) ~하다 vanish; disappear.
소실(燒失) ~하다 be burnt down; be destroyed by fire. ‖ ~가옥 houses burnt down.
소심(小心) ¶ ~한 timid; fainthearted; cautious.
소아(小我)《哲》the ego.
소아(小兒) an infant; a little child. ‖ ~마비 《suffer from》 infantile paralysis / ~병 infantile disease.
소아과(小兒科) pediatrics. ‖ ~의사 a pediatrician; a children's doctor / ~의원 a children's hospital.
소아시아(小—) Asia Minor. 「tal.
소액(少額) a small sum [amount] 《of money》.
소야곡(小夜曲) a serenade.
소양(素養) knowledge; a grounding; training. ¶ ~이 있는 cultured; educated / 경제학에 ~이 없는 학생 students untrained in economics / …의 ~이 있다 have some knowledge of….
소연(騷然) ¶ ~한 noisy; confused; disturbed; agitated; troubled.
소염제(消炎劑) an antiphlogistic.
소외(疏外) ¶ ~당하다 be shunned [neglected]. ‖ ~감 a sense of alienation.
소요(所要) ¶ ~의 《the time》 required; necessary; needed.

소요(逍遙) ~하다 stroll; ramble; take a walk.

소용(所用) need; want; demand; necessity; use. ¶ ~되는 necessary; needful; wanted / ~ 없다 be useless [needless].

소용돌이 (be drawn into) a whirlpool; a swirl. ¶ ~ 치다 whirl around; swirl.

소원(所願) one's desire [wish]. ¶ ~이 성취되다 have one's wishes realized / ~을 들어 주다 grant [meet] 《a person's》 wishes.

소원(訴願) a petition; an appeal. ~하다 petition; appeal 《to》.

소원(疎遠) ~하다 (be) estranged [alienated]. ¶ ~해지다 become estranged; drift apart.

소위(少尉) 《육군》 a second lieutenant 《美·英》; 《해군》 an acting sublieutenant 《英》; an ensign 《美》; 《공군》 a second lieutenant 《美》; a pilot officer. 「work」.

소위(所為) a deed; one's 'doing

소위(所謂) 《이른바》 so-called; what is called; what you call. 「tee.

소위원회(小委員會) a subcommit-

소유(所有) possession. ~하다 have; possess; own; hold. ¶ ~에 속하다 belonging to...; owned by.... ¶ ~격 the possessive [case] / ~권 the right of ownership; a right [title] 《to a thing》 / ~물 one's property [possessions] / ~욕 a desire to possess / ~자 an owner; a proprietor.

소음(騒音) (a) noise. ¶ ~방지의 antinoise / 거리의 ~ the din and bustle of a town; city sounds; street noises. ¶ ~공해 noise damage [pollution] / ~방지 prevention of noise; sound supression / ~측정기 a noise [soundlevel] meter.

소음기(消音器) a sound arrester; a muffler; a silencer.

소이(所以) (the reason) why.

소이탄(燒夷彈) an incendiary bomb [shell].

소인(小人) 《난쟁이》 a dwarf; a pigmy; 《어린이》 a child; a minor; 《소인물》 a small-minded person; 《나》 I, me, myself.

소인(消印) a postmark; a date stamp. ¶ ~이 찍힌 postmarked 《from London on May 1》.

소인(素因) a primary cause.

소인수(素因數) a prime factor.

소일(消日) ~하다 while away [kill] one's time. ¶ ~거리 a time killer; a pastime.

소임(所任) one's duty [task]. ¶ ~을 다하다 fulfill [discharge] one's duty / ~을 맡다 take a duty [job] on oneself.

소자(素子) 『電子』 an element. ¶ 발광 ~ a light-emitting diode 《생략 LED》.

소작(小作) tenant farming. ~하다 tenant a farm. ¶ ~농 tenant farming(농사); a tenant farmer (농민) / ~료 farm rent / ~인 a tenant (farmer). 「ine.

소장(小腸) 『解』 the small intest-

소장(少壯) ¶ ~의 young; youthful. ¶ ~파 the young group.

소장(少將) 《육군》 a major general 《美·英》; 《해군》 a rear admiral 《美·英》; 《공군》 a major general 《美》; an air vice-marshal 《英》.

소장(所長) the head [chief] 《of an office, a factory》.

소장(所藏) ¶ ~의 in one's possession / Y씨 ~의 《a book》 owned by [in the possession of] Mr. Y.

소장(訴狀) 『法』 a (written) complaint; a petition (청원장).

소재(所在) one's whereabouts; the position [location] (위치). ¶ ~를 감추다 conceal one's whereabouts; disappear; hide oneself / ~불명이다 be missing / 책임의 ~를 밝히다 find out 'who is responsible [where the responsibility lies]. ¶ ~지 the seat 《of》.

소재(素材) (a) material; subject matter.

소전(小傳) a biographical sketch; a brief biography. 「mise.

소전제(小前提) 『論』 a minor pre-

소정(所定) ¶ ~의 fixed; established; prescribed; appointed / ~의 절차를 밟다 go through the regular course [the prescribed formalities].

소조(塑造) modeling; molding.

소주(燒酒) distilled spirits; soju.

소중(所重) ¶ ~한 important; valuable; precious / ~히 carefully; with care / ~히 여기다 (존중) value; make much of 《a person, a thing》; treasure / ~히 하다 take good care of.

소지(所持) possession. ~하다 have (in one's possession); possess; carry. ¶ ~금 money in hand [one's pocket] / ~자 a holder; a possessor; an owner (면허증 ~자 a license holder) / ~품 one's belongings; one's personal effects.

소지(素地) 《요인이 되는 바탕》 a foundation; a groundwork; an aptitude 《for》; the makings. ¶ 배우가 될 ~가 있다 have the makings of an actor / 우호 관계의 ~를 만들다 lay the foundation for friendly relations 《between》.

소지(燒紙) 『民俗』 sacrificial paper (burned to departed spirits).

소진(消盡) ~하다 exhaust; use up; consume; vanish; disappear.

소진(燒盡) ~하다 be burnt down (to the ground); be totally destroyed by fire.
소질(素質) 《자질》 the making(s); qualities; talent; genius; 《체질》 a constitution; predisposition (병의); 《경향》 a tendency 《to》. ¶ 문학적 ~이 있는 사람 a person with a literary talent 〔turn〕 / 어학에 ~이 있다 have linguistic genius; have a natural aptitude for languages / 유전적 범죄 ~ inherited criminal tendencies.
소집(召集) a call; a summons; convocation(의회 따위의); mobilization(동원). ~하다 《회의를》 call; convene; summon; 《군대를》 muster; call up; 《군대의》 call 《a person》 into the army; draft 《a person》 for service (美). ¶ ~해제가 되다 be demobilized. ‖ ~ 영장 a draft call; a call-up paper; a draft notice [card] (美).
소쩍새 [鳥] a (common) cuckoo.
소차(小差) a small difference; a narrow margin.
소찬(素饌) a plain dish [dinner].
소채(蔬菜) vegetables; greens.
소책자(小冊子) a pamphlet; a booklet; a brochure.
소철(蘇鐵) [植] a sago palm.
소청(所請) a request. ¶ ~을 들어주다 grant 《a person's》 request.
소총(小銃) a rifle; small arms(총칭). ¶ ~탄 a bullet / 엠 16 자동 ~ an M-16 automatic rifle.
소추(訴追) prosecution; indictment. ~하다 prosecute [indict] 《a person for a crime》.
소출(所出) crops; yield(s); products. ¶ ~이 많은 heavily [highly] productive 《farm》.
소치(所致) 《결과》 consequences; result; 《영향》 effect. ¶ …의 ~이다 be caused by; be due to.
소켓 [電] a socket. ¶ ~에 끼우다 socket. ‖ 쌍~ a two-way socket.
소쿠리 a bamboo [wicker] basket.
소탈(疏脫) ~하다 (be) informal; unconventional; free and easy.
소탐대실(小貪大失) ~하다 suffer a big loss in going after a small gain.
소탕(掃蕩) ~하다 wipe [stamp] out; sweep away; mop up. ‖ ~작전 a mopping-up operation.
소태 [植] 《나무》 a kind of sumac; 《껍질》 sumac bark.
소택(沼澤) a marsh; a swamp. ‖ ~지 marshland; swampy areas.
소통(疏通) 《의사의》 ~하다 come to understand each other; come to a mutual understanding.
소파(搔爬) [醫] curettage. ¶ ~수술을 받다 undergo curetting.

소파 《긴 의자》 a sofa.
소포(小包) a parcel; a package; a packet. ‖ ~우편 (by) parcel post.
소품(小品) 《문예의》 a short piece 《of music, writing》; a 《literary》 sketch; 《물건》 a trifle article; 《무대의》 (stage) properties. ‖ ~담당원 a property man [master].
소풍(逍風) 《산책》 a walk; a stroll; an outing; 《행락》 an excursion; a picnic. ~하다 go for a walk; go on a picnic. ¶ 학교의 ~ a school picnic [excursion]. ‖ ~객 an excursionist; a holidaymaker.
소프라노 [樂] soprano; a soprano (가수).
소프트 soft. ‖ ~드링크 (have) a soft drink / ~볼 (play) softball / ~웨어 [컴] software / ~ 칼라 a soft collar.
소피(所避) ~보다 pass [make] water; urinate.
소하다(素─) stick to a vegetarian diet.
소한(小寒) the 23rd of the 24 seasonal divisions; the beginning of the coldest season.
소해(掃海) sea clearing. ~하다 clear the sea; sweep the sea for mines. ‖ ~작업 minesweeping [sea-clearing] operation / ~정 a minesweeper.
소행(所行) an act; a deed; one's doing.
소행(素行) conduct; behavior. ¶ ~이 못되다 be dissolute in conduct; be a person of loose morals.
소형(小型·小形) a small size. ¶ ~의 small (-sized); tiny; pocket(size). ‖ ~자동차 a small (-sized) car; a minicar / ~카메라 a miniature camera; a minicam / ~화 miniaturization; microminiaturization; ~하다 miniaturize; 초~화 microminiaturization. 〔Office〕.
소호 SoHo (◀ Small Office, Home
소홀(疏忽) ~하다 (be) negligent; neglectful; careless; rash. ‖ ~히 하다 neglect; 《경시》 make light of; slight.
소화(消火) ~하다 extinguish [put out, fight] a fire. ‖ ~기 (fire) extinguisher / ~전 (栓) a fireplug; a hydrant / ~호스 a fire hose.
소화(消化) digestion(음식의); consumption(상품의). ~하다 digest; consume; absorb. ¶ ~하기 쉬운 [어려운] be easy [hard] to digest; be digestible [indigestible] / ~를 돕다 help [promote] one's digestion / 국내 시장으로는 이들 제품을 ~시킬 수 없다 The home market alone cannot absorb all these goods. ‖ ~계통 the digestive system / ~기관 digestive organs /

소화물 (小貨物) a parcel; a package; a packet. ¶ ~로 부치다 send (forward) (*something*) by mail (우편); consign (*something*) as a parcel (철도편). ‖ ~취급소 a parcel-office.

소환 (召喚) 〖法〗 a summons. ~하다 summon; call; subpoena. ¶ ~되다 be summoned (called). ‖ ~장 (writ of summons); a subpoena.

소환 (召還) the recall. ~하다 recall; call (*a person*) back. ¶ 본국에 ~되다 be summoned (ordered) home.

속 ① (내부·안) the interior (inside); the inner part; (깊숙한) the inmost recesses (*of*). ¶ ~에(서) within; in; inside / ~에서 문을 잠그다 lock the door on the inside / 문은 ~에서 열렸다 The door opened from within. ② (속에 든 것) contents (내용); substance (실질); stuffing (박제품 등의); pad (ding) (의자 등의); wad (-ding) (이불속 따위). ¶ 요에 ~을 넣다 stuff the mattress. ③ (중심·핵) the heart (core). ¶ ~까지 썩다 be rotten to the core. ④ (마음) the heart; the depth (bottom). ¶ ~검은 wicked; malicious / ~으로(는) at heart / ~을 떠보다 sound (*a person*). ⑤ (뱃속) insides; stomach. ¶ ~이 비다 get hungry / ~이 거북하다 feel heavy in the stomach.

속 (屬) 〖生〗 a genus. ¶ ~의 generic.

속 (續) (계속) continuance; continuation; a sequel (이야기의); a series; 〖song〗 a ballad.

속가 (俗歌) a popular song; a folk song.

속간 (續刊) ~하다 continue (*its*) publication.

속개 (續開) resumption. ~하다 continue; resume (재개).

속겨 (곡식의) bran.

속격 (屬格) 〖文〗 the genitive (case).

속결 (速決) 즉결.

속계 (俗界) the workaday world; the earthly (secular) life.

속곳 a slip; a petticoat; underwear. ¶ ~ 바람으로 with nothing on but a slip.

속공 (速攻) a swift attack. ~하다 launch a swift attack (*against*).

속구 (速球) 〖野〗 a speed (fast) ball. ¶ ~투수 a fast-ball pitcher; a speedballer (美俗).

속국 (屬國) a dependency; a vassal (subject) state (country).

속기 (速記) (速記法) shorthand (writing); stenography. ~하다 write (do) shorthand; take down in shorthand. ‖ ~록 a stenographic (shorthand) records / ~사 a stenographer; a shorthand writer / ~술 stenography; shorthand.

속념 (俗念) worldly considerations (thoughts); vulgar (secular) thoughts. 〖false eyelashes.

속눈썹 the eyelashes. 〖인조~

속다 be cheated (deceived, taken in, imposed upon, fooled). ¶ 속기 쉬운 credulous; gullible.

속단 (速斷) ~하다 decide hastily; jump to a conclusion.

속달 (速達) express (special (美)) delivery. ~하다 send (*a letter*) by express; express (*a parcel*). ‖ ~료 a special delivery fee / ~우편 express delivery post; special delivery mail (美).

속달다 be anxious (worry *oneself*) (*about*); be eager (impatient, mad) (*for, to do*).

속담 (俗談) a proverb; (common) saying. ¶ ~에도 있듯이 as the proverb says (goes).

속대 the heart of vegetable. ‖ ~쌈 boiled rice wrapped in cabbage hearts.

속도 (速度) speed; velocity; (a) rate; 〖樂〗 a tempo. ¶ ~를 내다 speed up / ~를 빠르게 하다 gather (increase) speed / ~를 줄이다 slow down; reduce the speed / 매시 600마일의 ~로 at the rate of 600 miles an hour. ¶ ~계 a speedometer; a speed indicator / ~위반 speeding / ~위반에 걸리다 be charged with (speeding) / ~제한 (set) a speed limit / 경제~ an economic speed.

속독 (速讀) rapid (fast) reading. ~하다 read (*a book*) fast.

속돌 〖鑛〗 (a) pumice (stone).

속되다 (俗-) (비속) (be) vulgar; (통속) be common; popular; (세속적) be worldly; earthly; mundane. ¶ 속된 욕망 worldly desires (ambitions).

속등 (續騰) a continued advance (rise) (*in stock prices*). ~하다 continue to rise (advance).

속락 (續落) a continued fall (drop) (*in prices*). ~하다 continue to fall (drop).

속력 (速力) ~ 속도. ¶ ~이 빠른(느린) fast (slow) in speed / 전~으로 (at) full speed / 최대~ the greatest (maximum) speed.

속령 (屬領) a possession; a dependency (속국). ‖ ~지 a dominion.

속론 (俗論) a popular opinion; conventional views.

속마음 one's inmost heart; real inward feeling; one's right mind. ¶ ~을 꿰뚫어 보다 see through (*a

속말 a confidential (private, frank) talk.

속명(俗名) ① 《통속적인》 a common (popular) name. ②《佛》 a secular name.

속명(屬名) 〖生〗 a generic name.

속문학(俗文學) vulgar (popular) literature.

속물(俗物) a worldly man; a snob; a man of vulgar (low) taste. ‖ ~근성 Philistinism; snobbery.

속박(束縛) (a) restraint; (a) restriction; fetters; a yoke. ~하다 restrict; restrain; shackle; bind; fetter. ¶ ~을 받다 be placed under restraint / ~을 벗어나다 shake off the yoke 《of》/ 언론의 자유를 ~하다 place a gag on freedom of speech.

속발(續發) successive (frequent) occurrence. ~하다 occur (happen) in succession; crop up one after another. [sease.

속병(-病) a chronic internal di-

속보(速步) a quick pace.

속보(速報) 《뉴스》 a prompt (quick) report; a (news) flash. ~하다 report promptly; make a quick report 《on》. ‖ ~판 a bulletin (flash) board; a newsboard 《주로 英》.

속보(續報) further news (particulars); a continued report; a follow-up.

속보이다 betray (reveal) one's heart; be seen through.

속사(速射) quick firing (fire). ~하다 fire quickly. ¶ ~포 a quick-firing gun; a quick-firer.

속사(速寫) 《사진의》 a snapshot. ~하다 (take) a snapshot 《of》. ‖ ~카메라 a snapshot camera.

속삭이다 whisper; murmur; speak under one's breath; talk in whispers. ¶ 속삭이는 (듯한) whispery; whisperous / 사랑의 속 삭임 sweet whispers of love / 귀에 대고 ~ whisper in 《a person's》 ear.

속산(速算) 《do》 a rapid calculation.

속살 (옷속의) the part of the skin covered by clothes.

속상하다(-傷-) feel distressed; be annoyed (irritated, troubled); be vexed (chagrined) 《at》.

속새 〖植〗 a scouring rush.

속설(俗說) a common saying; a popular view; (전설) folklore.

속성(速成) rapid completion; quick mastery. ~하다 complete rapidly; give a rapid training. ‖ ~과 a short (an intensive) course / ~법 a quick-mastery method.

속성(屬性) 〖論〗 an attribute.

속세(俗世) this world; earthly life; the mundane world. ¶ ~를 떠난 unworldly; supermundane / ~를 버리다 renounce the world.

속셈 ① inner thoughts; what one has in mind; an ulterior motive; a secret intention. ② 암산.

속속(續續) successively; one after another; in (rapid) succession.

속속들이 wholly; thoroughly; to the core (속까지). ¶ ~ 썩다 be rotten to the core / ~ 젖다 get wet to the skin.

속손톱 a half-moon (of the fingernail); a lunula.

속수무책(束手無策) ¶ ~이다 be at the end of one's tether; nothing can be done.

속아넘어가다 be deceived (fooled). ¶ 감쪽같이 ~ be nicely taken in.

속악(俗惡) ~하다 (be) vulgar; low; coarse; gross.

속병. [coarse; gross.

속어(俗語) 《총칭》 colloquial language; slang; 《개별》 a colloquial expression; a slang word.

속림 one's guess. ¶ ~으로 one's estimate; by guess.

속옷 an underwear; an undergarment; underclothes.

속요(俗謠) a popular (folk) song.

속음(俗音) the popular pronunciation of a Chinese character.

속이다 deceive; cheat; fool; swindle (금품을); impose on; play 《a person》 false; play a trick 《on》; falsify; (tell a) lie (거짓말); feign (가장). ¶ 이름을 속이고 under a false name / 사람을 감언으로 ~ delude 《a person》 / 감언으로 ~ impose upon 《a person》 by honeyed words / 나이를 ~ misrepresent one's age / 대학생이라고 ~ feign (pretend to be) a university student.

속인(俗人) 《세속인》 a worldling; a worldly man; the common crowd; 《중이 아닌》 a layman.

속인(屬人) ~의 individual; personal. ¶ ~주의 〖法〗 the personal principle / ~특권 personal privileges.

속임수(-數) (a) deception; trickery. ¶ ~를 쓰다 cheat; play a trick on 《a person》; take 《a person》 in.

속잎 the inner leaves.

속자(俗字) the popular (simplified) form of a Chinese character. [paper}.

속장 the inside pages 《of a news-

속전(贖錢) a ransom.

속전속결(速戰速決) an intensive (all-out) surprise attack (offensive);

a *blitzkrieg* (獨). ¶ ~로 행하다 act decisively on the basis of a quick decision. ‖ ~전법 blitz tactics.

속절없다 (be) helpless; hopeless; futile; unavailing. ¶ 속절없이 helplessly; unavoidably; inevitably; in vain.

속죄(贖罪) atonement; expiation; redemption. ~하다 atone for [expiate] *one's* sin(s). ¶ ~할 수 없는 inexpiable (*offense*) / 죽음으로써 ~하다 expiate a crime with death.

속주다 take (*a person*) into *one's* confidence; open *one's* heart (*to*).

속지(屬地) a possession; a dependency; a territory; a dominion. ‖ ~주의 [法] the territorial principle.

속진(俗塵) the world; earthly affairs. ~을 씻다 disengage [disentangle] *one's* mind from all worldly cares.

속출(續出) successive occurrence. ~하다 appear [occur] in succession (one after another).

속치마 an underskirt; a petticoat; a slip.

속칭(俗稱) a popular (common) name. ~하다 call commonly; be popularly known as…

속타다 be distressed (*about, by*); be worried (*about*); be vexed [irritated] (*at*); be [get] harassed [annoyed].

속탈(─頉) a stomach trouble (upset); stomach disorder.

속태우다 ① (남을) vex; fret; worry; irritate; annoy; trouble. ② 《스스로》 worry (*oneself*) (*about*); fret (*about*); be distressed [bothered, harassed].

속편(續篇·續編) a sequel (*of, to*); a second volume.

속필(速筆) quick (rapid) writing.

속하다(速─) ⓐ be quick; fast; swift; rapid; speedy (☞ 빠르다). ¶ 속히 fast; rapidly; quickly; hastily.

속하다(屬─) belong (*to*); come [fall] (*under*); be subject (*to*).

속행(續行) ~하다 continue; resume; go on (proceed) (*with*); keep on (*doing*).

속화(俗化) vulgarization. ~하다 vulgarize; be vulgarized.

속회(續會) ~하다 resume (*a meeting*). ¶ ~ 속개(續開).

솎다 thin (out) (*plants*).

손¹ ① 《사지의》 a hand; an arm (팔). 오른~ right hand / ~을 마주 잡고 hand in hand; arm in arm / ~으로 만든 hand-made; manual / ~을 들다 raise *one's* hand; give up (단념) / ~을 잡다 grasp *a person's* hands / ~을 불에 쬐다 warm *one's* hand over the fire / ~을 뻗치다 stretch *one's* hand; (사업 등에) extend *one's* business (확장하다). / (일손) a hand; a help. ¶ ~을 빌리다 give a hand; lend a (helping) hand / ~이 비다 be free; have no work on hand / ~이 모자라다 be short-handed; be short of hands. ③ (솜씨) hand; skill. ¶ ~에 익다 be at home (*in*); know *one's* game. ④ (손질) trouble; care(돌봄); troublesome; elaborate; ~을 덜다 save trouble. ⑤ (소유) the hands (*of*); possession. ¶ ~에 넣다 get; obtain; win / ~에 들어오다 come into *one's* possession / ~에 넘어가다 pass (fall) into another's hands. ⑥ (관계) ~을 대다 ①. 남의 일에 ~을 대다 meddle in other people's affairs / ~을 떼다 wash *one's* hands of (*the business*) / …와 ~을 끊다 break with (*a woman*). ⑦ (경유) ~을 거쳐서 through (the medium of) / 아무의 ~을 거쳐 ~사 사다 buy (*a thing*) through *a person*.

손² ☞ 손님.

손(損) loss(손실); disadvantage(불리); damage(손해).

손가락 a finger. ¶ ~에 끼다 put (wear) (*a ring*) on a finger / 엄지~ the thumb / 집게 〔가운뎃, 약, 새끼〕~ the index 〔middle, ring, little〕 finger.

손가락질 ~하다 point at (to); indicate (지탄); shun; scorn. ¶ ~을 받다 be pointed at with scorn; be an object of social contempt.

손가방 a briefcase; a handbag; a valise; a gripsack (俗).

손거스러미 an agnail; a hangnail.

손거울 a hand glass (mirror).

손겪다 (도벽) light-fingered; thievish; (서술치) have sticky fingers.

손겪다(待接하다) entertain a guest; play host (*to*).

손곱다 (*one's* hands are) stiff [benumbed] with cold.

손금 the lines of the palm. ¶ ~을 보다 read (*a person's*) palm; have *one's* palm read(남에게 보게 하다); practice palmistry(영업). ‖ ~쟁이 a palmist.

손금(損金) pecuniary loss.

손길 ① hands; *one's* hands(뻗은); a (helping) hand (구원의). ¶ 따뜻한 구원의 ~ (extend) a warm helping hand (*to*) / ~이 닿는 곳 within *one's* reach.

손꼽다 ① (셈하다) count on *one's* fingers. ¶ 손꼽아 기다리다 look forward to (*a person's arrival*). ②

손꼽아치다 《굴지》 ¶ 손꼽는 leading; outstanding.

손꼽아치다 count (for) much; be leading(prominent, outstanding).

손끝 a finger tip; manual dexterity(솜씨). ¶ ~(이) 여물다 be clever with *one's* hands.

손끝맵다 《서술적으로》 have an ill-starred touch; have an unlucky touch.

손끝맺다 remain idle; stand by with *one's* arms folded.

손넘기다 ① 《시기를 놓치다》 lose (miss) an opportunity; let a chance go (slip). ② 《잘못 세다》 skip numbers in counting; miscalculate; count wrong.

손녀(孫女) a granddaughter.

손놓다 《일을》 leave (lay) off *one's work*.

손님 ① 《내객》 a caller; a visitor; a guest(초대객). ¶ 사업상의 ~ a business visitor / ~을 대접하다 entertain a guest / ~을 맞다 receive a visitor(caller) / ~이 있다 have a visitor; have company / ~접대가 좋다 (나쁘다) be a good(poor) host(ess). ② 《고객》 a customer; a patron; an audience(극장의); a guest(여관·의사의); a client(변호사·의사의). ¶ 단골 ~ a customer; a frequenter / 고정 ~ a regular customer / ~이 없다 have no customer / ~이 늘다(줄다) gain (lose) customers / ~을 끌다 attract (draw) customers / ~ 서비스가 좋다(나쁘다) give good (poor) service(호텔 등에서) / ~은 왕이다 The customer is King (is always right). ③ 《승객》 a passenger; a fare.

손대다 ① 《건드리다》 touch; lay (put) *one's* hands (on); 《남의 것에》 make free with *another's money*. ¶ 음식에 손도 안 대다 leave food untouched / 손대지 마시오 Hands off. ② 《착수》 put (turn, set) *one's* hand (to); take (up). ¶ 《관계》 have a hand (in). ¶ 정치에 ~ dabble in politics / 여자에게 ~ become intimate with a woman. ③ 《손지검》 beat; strike.

손대중 measuring (weighing) by hand. ¶ ~으로 by hand measure.

손도끼 a hand ax(e); a hatchet.

손도장(一圖章) a thumb-mark; a thumbprint. ¶ ~ 찍다 seal with the thumb.

손독(一毒) ¶ ~이 오르다 be infected by touching; become worse by fingering *it*.

손들다 raise (lift, hold up) *one's* hand; show *one's* hand(찬성); be defeated (beaten)(지다); yield (to)(항복); give up(단념). ¶ 손들어! Hands (Hold) up!

손등 the back of the hand.

손때 dirt from the hands; finger marks; soiling by hand. ¶ ~ 묻은 finger-marked; hand-stained.

손떼다 《…에서》 get 《*something*》 off *one's* hands; wash *one's* hands of; break with; withdraw *oneself from*.

손맑다 ① 《생기는 것이 없다》 have hard luck in making money(서술적). ② 《다랍다》 (be) stingy.

손목 a wrist. ¶ ~을 잡다 take 《*a person*》 by the wrist. [work.

손바느질 sewing by hand; needle-

손바닥 the palm (of the hand). ¶ ~을 뒤집듯이 without the least trouble / ~으로 때리다 (give a) slap.

손발 hands and feet; the limbs.

손버릇 ¶ ~(이) 나쁘다 (be) light-fingered; thievish; larcenous.

손보다 《돌보다》 care for; take care of; 《수리》 repair; mend; put 《*something*》 in repair; 《원고를》 touch up; retouch.

손부축 《공구》 clap (*one's* hands).

손보주다 《빌려주다》 give (lend) a helping hand; 《고쳐주다》 repair (fix) 《*a thing*》 for 《*a person*》.

손빌리다 get help; get (receive) the aid 《*of*》.

손뼉치다 clap (*one's* hands).

손상(損傷) injury; damage. ~ 하다 injure; damage; impair. ¶ ~을 입다 be injured (damaged); suffer a loss.

손색(遜色) inferiority. ¶ ~없다 bear (stand) comparison 《*with*》; be equal (to); be by no means inferior 《*to*》.

손서투르다 (be) unskil(l)ful; poor; clumsy; 《서술적》 be a poor hand 《*at*》.

손속 gambler's luck; the golden touch. ¶ ~이 좋다 be a lucky gambler / ~이 나쁘다 have a wretched hand.

손수 with *one's* own hands; in person, personally(몸소).

손수건(一手巾) a handkerchief.

손수레 a handcart; a barrow.

손쉽다 《용이함》 (be) easy; simple. ¶ 손쉬운 일 an easy job (task) / 손쉽게 이기다 win easily; get a walkover / 손쉽게 생각하는 것 《*things*》 easy / 돈을 손쉽게 벌다 make an easy gain.

손실(損失) a loss. ¶ 국가적인 ~ a national loss / ~을 주다 (입다) inflict (suffer) a loss.

손심부름 a petty errand.

손싸다 (be) dexterous; quick-handed; nimble-fingered.

손쓰다 take (resort to) a measure; take steps; do some-

손아귀 ¶ ~에 넣다 get (*something*) in one's hands; 《사람을》 have (*a person*) in one's hands (*control*) / ~에 들다 fall into (*a person's*) hands (*power*); be under (*a person's*) thumb.

손아래 ~의 younger; junior 《의 아랫사람》 one's junior (*inferior*) / 세 살 ~다 be one's junior by three years.

손어림 hand measure. ~하다 (make a rough) estimate by the hand.

손위 ~의 older; elder / 손윗사람 one's elder; one's senior.

손익(損益) profit and loss; gains and loss. ¶ ~계산서 a statement of profit and loss / ~분기점 the break-even point.

손익다 (be) accustomed; familiar; 《서술적》 get accustomed to; be (quite) at home (*in*, *on*).

손일 handwork; manual work; handicraft. [son.

손자(孫子) a grandchild; a grand-

손잡이 a handle; 《문의》 a knob; a catch. ¶ ~끈 a strap.

손장난 ~하다 finger (*a doll*); fumble (*with*, *at*); play (*toy*) (*with*).

손장단(-長短) ~을 치다 beat time with the hand; keep time with hand-clapping.

손재주(-才―) ~ 있는 clever-fingered; deft-handed; dexterous.

손전등(-電燈) a flashlight; an electric torch.

손질 repair(s); care. ¶ ~(을) 하다 take care of; trim (*a tree*); repair (*a house*); mend (*shoes*); maintain (*a car*); improve (*one's essay*) / ~이 잘 되어 있다 [있지 않다] be in good [poor] repair; be well-kept [ill-kept] / 집을 ~해야 한다 My house needs repairing.

손짓 a gesture; signs; a hand signal. ~하다 (make) a gesture; make signs; beckon (*to*).

손찌검하다 beat; slap; strike.

손치다 《여관에서》 take in (*lodgers*); put up (*a person*).

손치르다 entertain one's guests; play host (*to*).

손크다 《후하다》 (be) liberal; free-handed; generous. ¶ 손(이) 큰 사람 a liberal giver; an open-handed man.

손톱 a (finger) nail. ¶ ~을 깎다 cut (trim) one's nails / ~으로 할 퀴다 scratch with one's nails; claw / 빨갛게 물들인 ~ red polished nails. ‖ ~가위 nail scissors / ~깎이 a nail clipper /

~자국 a nail mark; a scratch (상처).

손풍금(一風琴) an accordion.

손해(損害) damage; (an) injury; (a) loss. ¶ ~을 주다 damage; injure; do [cause] damage [losses] (*to*) / (큰) ~을 입다 be (greatly) damaged (*by*); suffer a (heavy) loss / ~을 배상하다 pay for damage; repair the loss [damage]; compensate (*a person*) for his loss. ‖ ~배상 (a) compensation for damage [the loss]; damages (~배상을 청구하다 claim [demand] damages) / ~배상금 damages / ~보험 property damage [liability] insurance; insurance against loss / ~액 the amount of damages.

솔¹ (터는) a brush. ¶ ~로 털다 brush off (*dust*).

솔² (나무) a pine (tree). ‖ ~가지 a pine branch (twig) / ~방울 a pine cone / ~밭 a pine grove (wood) / ~잎 a pine needle.

솔개 [鳥] a (black-eared) kite.

솔기 a seam. ¶ ~없는 seamless.

솔깃하다 《서술적》 be interested (*in*); be enthusiastic (*about*); feel inclined to do. ¶ 이야기에 귀 가 ~ be interested in (*a person's*) talk / 그거 귀가 솔깃해지는 제안이로군 That's a tempting offer.

솔다¹ (귀가) be [get] sick [tired] of hearing; hear more than enough of.

솔다² ① ☞ 좁다. ② 《서술적》 be itchy and too sore to scratch.

솔로(樂) (sing) a solo. ¶ ~가수 a soloist / 피아노 ~ a piano solo.

솔선(率先) ~하다 take the lead (initiative) (*in*); set an example (*to others*). ¶ ~해서 …하다 be the first to do.

솔솔 soft-flowing; gently; softly.

솔직(率直) ~한 [히] plain(ly); frank(ly); candid(ly) / ~한 대답 a straight answer / ~한 사람 a straightforward [an open-hearted] person / ~히 말하면 frankly speaking; to be frank (*with you*).

솔질 brushing. ~하다 brush.

솜 cotton; wadding (옷의). ¶ ~타 기 cotton beating / ~을 두다 stuff (*a cushion*) with cotton; wad (*a gown*) (옷에) / ~을 틀다 gin [fluff] cotton.

솜사탕(-砂糖) cotton candy; spun sugar; candy fluff.

솜씨 《손재주》 skill; dexterity; finesse; workmanship; craftsmanship; 《능력》 ability. ¶ ~ 있는 skillful; clever; dexterous; able (유능한) / ~가 좋다 be a good

솜옷 wadded (padded) clothes.
솜털 downy (fine, soft) hair; down.
솜틀 a cotton gin; a willow(er); a willowing machine.
솜화약(一火藥) guncotton; cotton powder.
솟구다 jump up; leap (to one's feet).
솟구치다 leap (jump, spring) up; 《불길이》 blaze (flame) up; 《물가가》 rise suddenly; make a jump.
솟다 ① 《높이》 rise; tower; soar. ¶ 구름 위로 (치) ~ rise above the clouds. ② 《샘 등이》 gush out; spring out; well. ③ 《불길이》 flame (blaze) up.
솟아나다 ① 《샘이》 gush (out); well 《up, out, forth》. ② 《여럿 중에서》 (be) conspicuous; 《서술적》 cut a figure.
솟을대문(一大門) a lofty (tall) gate.
송가(頌歌) an anthem; a hymn of praise.
송골매(松鶻一) 〔鳥〕 a peregrine falcon.
송곳 a gimlet (도래송곳); a drill (금속·돌을 뚫는); ~으로 구멍을 뚫다 bore a hole with a gimlet.
송곳니 an eyetooth; a canine tooth; a dogtooth; a cuspid.
송곳칼 a combination knife-drill.
송구(送球) ① 〔=핸드볼〕. ② 《던지다》 ~하다 throw a ball 《to》.
송구(悚懼) ¶ ~스럽다 《죄송하다》 be very sorry 《for》; be abashed; feel small; 《감사하면》 be much obliged 《to》; 《어찌할 바를 모르다》 be (feel) embarrassed 《by, at》; be floored 《by》.
송구영신(送舊迎新) ~하다 see the old year out and the new year in.
송금(送金) (a) remittance; ~하다 remit (send) money 《to》. ¶ 은행 〔우편〕환으로 ~하다 remit (send) money by bank draft (postal money order). ∥ ~수수료 a remittance charge / ~수취인 the remittee; the payee / ~수표 a remittance check / ~액 the amount of remittance / ~인 the remitter.
송년(送年) (bidding) the old year out.
송달(送達) delivery; dispatch. ~하다 send; deliver; dispatch; serve(교부). ¶ 영장을 ~하다 serve a writ on 《a person》. ∥ ~부 a delivery book.
송당송당 ¶ ~ 자르다 cut to pieces; chop up; hash.
송덕(頌德) eulogy. ∥ ~비 a monument in honor of 《a person》.
송두리째 《뿌리째》 root and branch; 《몽땅》 all; completely; entirely;

thoroughly. ¶ ~ 없애다 uproot; root 《something》 out; eradicate 《the drug traffic》 / 노름으로 재산을 ~ 날리다 gamble away all one's property.
송로(松露) ① 〔植〕 a truffle; a mushroom. ② 《이슬》 dew on pine needles.
송료(送料) the carriage 《on a parcel》(운임); the postage 《of a book》. ¶ ~ 선불 carriage prepaid / ~ 포함 1,000원. 1,000 won postage included.
송림(松林) a pine wood (forest).
송별(送別) farewell; send-off. ∥ ~사(辭) a farewell speech (address) / ~회 a farewell meeting (party).
송부(送付) ~하다 send; forward; remit(송금).
송사(訟事) a lawsuit; a suit; legal proceedings (steps).
송사(頌辭) a laudatory address; a eulogy; a panegyric.
송사리 〔魚〕 a killifish. ② 《사람》 small fry.
송송 ¶ ~ 썰다 chop into small pieces.
송수(送水) water supply (conveyance). ~하다 supply 《the town》 with water. ∥ ~관 a water pipe; a water main(본관).
송수신기(送受信機) 〔라디오〕 transceiver.
송수화기(送受話機) 〔전화의〕 a handset.
송신(送信) transmission 《of a message》. ~하다 transmit (dispatch) a message. ∥ ~국(탑) a transmitting station (tower) / ~기 a transmitter.
송아지 a calf. ¶ ~를 낳다 calve. ∥ ~ 가죽 calfskin / ~ 고기 veal.
송알송알 ¶ ~ 땀이 나다 perspire profusely.
송어(松魚) 〔魚〕 a trout.
송영(送迎) greeting and farewell; welcome and send-off. ~하다 welcome and send off.
송영(誦詠) ~하다 recite 《a poem》.
송유(送油) oil supply; sending oil. ~하다 supply oil; send oil. ∥ ~관 an oil pipe(line).
송이 《과실의》 a bunch; a cluster; 《꽃의》 a cluster; 《눈의》 a flake (of snow). ¶ 포도 한 ~ a bunch (cluster) of grapes.
송이(松珥) a song-i mushroom.
송장 a (dead) body; a corpse. ¶ 산 ~ a living corpse.
송장(送狀) an invoice; a dispatch note. ¶ ~을 작성하다 invoice 《a shipment of goods》; make out an invoice / 내국 〔수출, 수입〕 ~ an inland (export, import) invoice.
송전(送電) transmission of electricity; electric supply. ~하다 transmit electricity 《from ... to》;

송죽 (松竹) pine and bamboo.

송진 (松津) (pine) resin.

송청 (送廳) ~ 하다 turn (*a culprit*) over to the public prosecutor's office; send (*the papers*) to the public procurator's office.

송축 (頌祝) ~ 하다 praise and bless; bless; eulogize.

송충이 (松蟲-) a pine caterpillar. ¶인간 ~ a human caterpillar.

송치 (送致) ~ 하다 send; forward; dispatch; remand. ¶ 용의자를 ~ 하다 remand a suspect.

송판 (松板) a pine board.

송편 (松-) *songpyeon*; a half-moon-shaped rice cake steamed on a layer of pine needles.

송풍 (送風) ventilation. ~ 하다 ventilate (*a room*); send air (*to*). ‖ ~ 관 a blastpipe / ~ 기 a ventilator; a blower / ~ 기 a fan.

송화 (松花) pine flowers (pollen).

송화 (送話) transmission. ~ 하다 transmit. ‖ ~ 기 a transmitter; 《전화기의》 a mouthpiece.

송환 (送還) sending back (home); repatriation (포로 따위). ~ 하다 send back (home); repatriate; deport (국외로). ¶ ~ 되다 be sent back home / 강제 ~ compulsory repatriation; deportation. ‖ ~ 자 a repatriate (본국으로의 송환자); a deportee (피 (被) 추방자).

솥 an iron pot; a kettle (물 끓이는); a cauldron (가마솥). ¶ 한 ~ 밥을 먹다 live under the same roof (*with*). ‖ ~ 뚜껑 the lid of a kettle.

쇄 《소리》 rustlingly; noisily; briskly. 「stopping.

솰솰 ¶ ~ 흐르다 flow without

쇄골 (鎖骨) [解] the collarbone; the clavicle. 「a crusher.

쇄광기 (碎鑛機) a crushing machine;

쇄국 (鎖國) national isolation. ~ 하다 close the country (*to*); close the door (to foreigners). ‖ ~ 시 대 the isolation period / ~ 정책 an isolation policy; a policy of seclusion (from the outside world); a closed-door policy / ~ 주의 (national) isolationalism.

쇄도 (殺到) a rush; a flood. ~ 하다 rush[pour] (*in*); throng (*a place*); swoop down on (*the enemy*). ¶ 주문이 ~ 하다 have a rush [flood] of orders.

쇄빙선 (碎氷船) an icebreaker.

쇄신 (刷新) reform; renovation. ~ 하다 (make a) reform; renovate; innovate. ¶ 정계의 ~ a political reform [cleanup] / 일대 ~ 을 단행 하다 carry out a radical reform.

쇠 ① 《철》 iron; steel (강철); a metal (금속). ¶ ~ 로 만든 iron; (made) of iron. ‖ ~ 갈고리 an iron hook / 쇳빛 iron-blue. ② 《열쇠》 a key; 《자물쇠》 a lock. ¶ ~ 채우다 turn a key on; lock.

쇠가죽 oxhide; cowhide.

쇠고랑 (a pair of) handcuffs; cuffs (口). ¶ ~ 채우다 handcuff (*a person*); put handcuffs on (*a person*). 「hoop; a clasp.

쇠고리 an iron ring; a metal

쇠공이 an iron pestle (pounder).

쇠귀 cow's ears. ¶ ~ 에 경읽기 preaching to deaf ears.

쇠귀나물 [植] an arrowhead.

쇠기름 beef tallow.

쇠꼬리 a cow's tail; (an) oxtail. ¶ 닭벼슬이 될 망정 ~ 는 되지마라 《俗談》 Better be the head of an ass than the tail of a horse.

쇠꼬챙이 an iron skewer.

쇠다 ① 《생일·명절을》 keep (*one's birthday*); celebrate; observe. ¶ 명절을 ~ celebrate [observe] a festival day / 설을 ~ keep the New Year's Day. ② 《채소가》 become tough (and stringy). ③ 《병이 덧나다》 get worse; grow chronic.

쇠똥¹ 《소의 똥》 cattle-dung; ox-droppings; ox-manure (거름).

쇠똥² 《쇳부스러기》 slag; scoria.

쇠망 (衰亡) ~ 하다 fall; decline; go to ruin; be ruined.

쇠망치 an iron hammer.

쇠몽둥이 an iron bar [rod]; a metal rod (bar).

쇠뭉치 a mass of iron.

쇠미 (衰微) ~ 하다 《서술적》 be on the decline (wane).

쇠버짐 a kind of ringworm.

쇠붙이 metal things; ironware.

쇠비름 [植] a purslane.

쇠뼈 cow (ox) bones.

쇠뿔 a cow's horn. ¶ ~ 도 단김에 빼랬다 《俗談》 Strike the iron while it is hot.

쇠사슬 a chain; a tether (개의). ¶ ~ 로 매다 enchain; chain up (*a dog*); put (*a person*) in chains / ~ 을 풀다 unchain; undo the chain.

쇠새 [鳥] a kingfisher; a halcyon.

쇠스랑 a rake; a forked rake.

쇠약 (衰弱) weakening; emaciation. ~ 한 weak; weakened; emaciated (야윈); debilitated / 병 으로 ~ 해지다 grow weak from illness. ¶ 전신 ~ general weakening (prostration).

쇠운 (衰運) declining fortune. ¶ ~ 에 접어들다 begin to decline;

쇠잔(衰殘) ~하다 《쇠약》 become emaciated; lose vigor; 《쇠퇴》 fall off; 《기운이》 sink; wane.
쇠줄 iron wire; a cable; a chain.
쇠진(衰盡) decay; exhaustion. ~하다 decay; be exhausted.
쇠코뚜레 a cow's nose ring.
쇠톱 a hacksaw.
쇠퇴(衰退·衰頹) ~하다 decline; decay; wane.
쇠파리 a warble fly.
쇠푼 a small [petty] sum of money.
쇠하다(衰一) 《쇠약》 become weak; lose vigor; be emaciated; 《위축》 wither; 《쇠망》 decline; wane; 《감퇴》 fall off.
쇳내 a metallic taste. ¶ ~가 나다 taste iron [metallic].
쇳물(녹물) a rust stain; 《녹인 쇠》 melted iron.
쇳소리 a metallic sound.
쇳조각 a piece [scrap] of iron.
쇳줄(鑛脈) a mineral vein; a vein of ore.
쇼 a show. ¶ ~를 보러 가다 go to see a show / 퀴즈 ~ a (TV) quiz show. ∥ ~걸 a show girl.
쇼룸 a showroom.
쇼맨 a showman. ∥ ~십(기질) showmanship.
쇼비니즘 chauvinism.
쇼윈도 a show [display] window; a showwindow. ¶ ~를 장식하다 dress a show window.
쇼크(☞ 충격) a shock. ¶ ~를 받다 be shocked (at) / ~를 주다 give (a person) a shock.
쇼핑 shopping. ~하다 shop. ¶ ~가다 go shopping. ∥ ~백 a shopping bag / ~센터 a shopping center [district].
숄 a shawl. ¶ ~을 걸치다 wear [put on] a shawl.
숄더백 a shoulder(-strap) bag.
수(手) ① 《바둑·장기의》 a move. ¶ 나쁜 ~ a bad move (at) / 두 번 make a move. ② 《수법·피》 a trick; wiles. ¶ ~에 넘어가다 fall into a trap; be taken in.
수(壽) 《나이》 age; one's natural life; 《장수》 longevity; long life. ¶ ~를 누리다 enjoy a long life; live to be 《90 years old》 / ~를 다하다 die a natural death.
수(數) ① (수) a number; a figure (숫자). ¶ ~가 많은 numerous; (a great) many; a large number of / ~ 없는 countless; innumerable / ~를 세다 count; take count of / ~에 넣다 count in the number (of); include in the number. ② ☞ 운수, 행운. ¶ ~사납다 be unlucky.
수(繡) embroidery. ¶ ~실 embroidery thread / ~ 놓다 embroider (a figure on).
수 ① 《수단·방법》 a means; a way; a resource; help; a device (방안). ¶ 가장 좋은 ~ the best way [method] / 무슨 ~를 써서라도 by all means; at any cost; at all risks [costs] / …하는 ~밖에 없다 cannot help (doing); have no choice but (to do) / 별 ~ 없다 There is no help for it. ② 《가능성·능력》 possibility; likelihood; ability. ¶ ~ 있다, 수 없다.
수(首) a poem; a piece.
수…(수컷) a male; a he (俗).
수…(凸面) convex; external; protruding. [al [a few] days.
수…(數) (몇) several; a few; sever-
…수(囚) 미결~ an unconvicted prisoner / 사형~ a condemned criminal; a death-row convict.
수가(酬價) a medical charge [fee].
수감(收監) imprisonment; confinement. ~하다 put in jail; confine in prison; imprison.
수갑(手匣) (a pair of) handcuffs; manacles; cuffs (俗). ¶ ~을 채우다 handcuff; put [slip] handcuffs on (a person).
수강(受講) ~하다 take lectures; attend a lecture. ∥ ~생 a member (of a class); a trainee.
수개(數個) ~의 several.
수갱(竪坑) a shaft; a pit.
수건(手巾) a towel. ¶ ~걸이 a towel rack / ~으로 얼굴을 닦다 dry one's face on a towel.
수검(受檢) ~하다 undergo inspection. ∥ ~자 an examinee.
수결(手決) a signature. ¶ ~(을) 두다 sign; affix one's signature.
수경(水耕) ~재배 hydroponics; water culture; tray agriculture; aquiculture.
수고 trouble; hardship; difficulty; labor; toil; pains; efforts. ~하다 take pains [trouble]; work [labor] hard; go through hardships. ¶ ~스러운 troublesome; hard; laborious; painful / ~를 아끼지 않다 spare no efforts [pains] (to do); do not mind work / ~를 끼치다 (시키다) give (a person) trouble; trouble (another); put (a person) to trouble / ~를 덜다 save (a person) trouble / ~스럽지만 I am sorry to trouble you, but….
수고양이 a tomcat; a he-cat.
수공(手工) manual arts [work]; handiwork; handicraft. ∥ ~업 handicraft; manual industry / ~업자 a handicraftsman / ~(예)품 a piece of handicraft [handiwork].
수괴(首魁) the ringleader.

수교(手交) ~하다 hand over; deliver 《*something*》 personally 《*to*》. ¶ 각서를 ~하다 hand a memorandum; deliver a note.

수교(修交) amity; friendship(수호(修好)). ¶ ~훈장 the Distinguished Order of Diplomatic Service.

수구(水球) [競] water polo.

수국(水菊) [植] a hydrangea.

수군거리다 talk in whispers; speak under *one*'s breath.

수군수군 in whispers; in an undertone; secretly.

수굿하다 (be) somewhat drooping; hanging down a little.

수그러지다 ① (머리 등이) become low; lower; droop; drop; sink; respect (존경). ② (바람 따위가) go [die, calm] down; subside; abate. ③ (병세가) be suppressed [subdued]; (분노 등이) be appeased.

수그리다 ☞ 숙이다.

수금(收金) collection of money; bill collection. ~하다 collect money [bills]. ¶ ~원 a bill [money] collector.

수급(需給) demand and supply. ¶ ~관계 the relation between supply and demand / ~의 균형을 유지하다 keep [maintain] the balance of supply and demand. ¶ ~계획 a demand-supply program 《*of*》 / ~조절 adjustment of demand and supply.

수긍(首肯) assent; consent; a nod. ~하다 agree [consent] 《*to*》; assent to; be convinced 《*of, that*》(납득하다).

수기(手記) a note; memoirs; a memorandum [*pl.* -da, -dums].

수기(手旗) a flag. ¶ ~신호 flag signaling.

수꽃 [植] a male flower.

수난(水難) a disaster by water.

수난(受難) sufferings; ordeals. ¶ ~을 겪다 suffer; undergo hardships [trials]. ¶ ~일 [聖] Good Friday. 「¶ ~인 a receiver.

수납(收納) receipt. ~하다 receive.

수납(受納) ~하다 accept; receive. ¶ ~자 a recipient.

수녀(修女) a nun; a sister. ¶ ~가 되다 enter a convent. ¶ ~원 a nunnery; a convent.

수년(數年) (for) several years.

수뇌(首腦) a head; a leader. ¶ ~부 (정부의) the leading members of the government; (회사의) the top-level executives (of a company) / ~회담 a summit [top-level] conference [meeting]; a talk [conference] at the highest level.

수뇨관(輸尿管) [解] the ureter.

수다 chattering; idle talk; chat; gossip; a talk. ¶ ~스럽다 (be) talkative; chatty; gossipy / ~떨다 chat; talk idly; chatter; gossip 《*with*》. ¶ ~쟁이 a chatterbox; a nonstop talker; a gossip.

수단(手段) a means; a way; a step; a measure; a shift(편법). ¶ 목적을 위한 ~ a means to an end / 일시적인 ~ a makeshift; an expedient / 부정한 ~ a foul means / ~을 안 가리고 by any means / 최후의 ~으로 as a last resort / ~이 다하다 be at *one*'s wit's end / ~을 그르치다 take a wrong step / 비상 ~을 쓰다 take drastic measures / 온갖 ~을 다 쓰다 try every possible means.

수달(水獺) [動] an otter. ¶ ~피 an otter skin (fur).

수당(手當) an allowance; a bonus (상여금). ¶ ~을 주다 pay [give, get] an allowance / 가족 [특별, 퇴직] ~ a family [special, retiring] allowance / 연말 ~ a year-end bonus / 출산 ~ a maternity benefit. 「unsophisticated.

수더분하다 (be) simple(-hearted).

수도(水道) waterworks; water service [supply]; (물) tap [city, piped] water. ¶ ~를 틀다 [잠그다] turn on [off] the tap / ~를 놓다 have water supplied. ¶ ~공사 water works / ~관 a water pipe / ~국 the Waterworks Bureau / ~꼭지 a tap / ~료 [요금] water rates [charges].

수도(首都) a capital (city); a metropolis. ¶ ~의 metropolitan / ~경찰 the Metropolitan Police.

수도(修道) ~하다 practice asceticism; search for truth. ¶ ~생활 [lead] monastic life / ~승 a monk / ~원 a religious house; a monastery(남자의); a convent (여자의).

수도권(首都圈) the Metropolitan area. ¶ ~방위 the defense of the Metropolitan area / ~전철화 electrification of Metropolitan railroads.

수동(手動) ¶ ~의 hand-operated; hand-worked. ¶ ~펌프 a hand [manual] pump.

수동(受動) ¶ ~적(으로) passive(ly). ¶ ~태 [文] the passive voice.

수두(水痘) [醫] chicken pox.

수두룩하다 (많다) (be) abundant; plentiful; (흔하다) be common. ¶ 수두룩이 plentifully; abundantly; commonly / 할 일이 ~ have a heap of work to do; have much [a lot] to do.

수득수득 ¶ ~한 dried-up; shriveled; withered.

수들수들 ☞ 수득수득.

수라(水剌) a royal meal.
수라장(修羅場) a scene of bloodshed (carnage). ¶ ~이 되다 be turned into a shambles.
수락(受諾) acceptance. ~하다 accept; agree (to).
수란관(輸卵管) [解] the oviduct.
수랭식(水冷式) ¶ ~의 water-cooled (engine).
수량(水量) the volume of water. ‖ ~계 a water gauge.
수량(數量) quantity; volume. ¶ ~이 늘다 increase in quantity.
수렁 a (quag)mire; a morass; a bog. ¶ [도로가] ~처럼 되다 turn into a morass / ~에 빠지다 (비유적) bog down; get bogged down / ~에서 빠져나오다 find a way out of the swamp. ‖ ~논 a swampy rice field. 〔field.
수렁배미 a strip of swampy rice
수레 a wagon; a cart. ¶ ~에 싣다 load a cart. ‖ ~바퀴 a (wagon) wheel. 〔beautiful; fine.
수려하다(秀麗―) (be) graceful;
수력(水力) (by) water (hydraulic) power. ¶ ~으로 움직이는 waterpowered; hydraulic. ‖ ~발전 hydroelectric power generation; water-power generation / ~발전소 a hydroelectric power plant (station) / ~전기 hydroelectricity / ~터빈 a hydraulic turbine.
수련(修鍊) training; practice. ~하다 train; practice; discipline. ¶ ~의 an intern(e); an apprentice doctor.
수련(睡蓮) [植] a water lily.
수렴(收斂) ① [돈을 거둠] levying and collecting of taxes; exaction. ~하다 collect strictly; exact taxes. ② [理] convergence; [醫] astriction. ~하다 be astringent; be constricted; converge. ③ [여론 등의] collecting; (a) reflection. ~하다 collect. ¶ 민의를 ~하다 collect the public opinions.
수렴청정(垂簾聽政) administering state affairs from behind the veil.
수렵(狩獵) hunting; shooting. ‖ ~가 a hunter / ~금지기 the closed season / ~기 the shooting (hunting) season / ~지 a hunting ground / ~해금일 the first day of the hunting (shooting) season / ~허가증 a hunting license. 〔governor.
수령(守令) a magistrate; a local
수령(受領) accept; receive. ‖ ~인 a receiver; a recipient.
수령(首領) a leader; a head; a chief; a boss (俗).
수령(樹齡) the age of a tree.
수로(水路) a waterway; a water course; a channel; a line (항로). ¶ ~로 가다 go by water (sea). ‖ ~도 a hydrographic map.
수로안내(水路案內) pilotage; piloting; (사람) a pilot. ~하다 pilot (a boat). ‖ ~료 pilotage (dues) / ~선 a pilot boat.
수록(收錄) recording; mention. ~하다 put (somebody's letters) (together) in a book; mention; contain; (기록) record; tape (녹음). ¶ 회합에 모인 사람들의 의견을 테이프에 ~하다 tape (record) the opinions of those who attended the meeting / 이 사전에는 일상 생활에 필요한 표현이 모두 ~되어 있다 This dictionary contains all the necessary expressions for daily life.
수뢰(水雷) a torpedo; a naval mine. ‖ ~정 a torpedo boat.
수료(修了) completion (of a course). ~하다 complete; finish. ¶ 3년의 (과정)을 ~하다 finish the third-year course. ‖ ~증서 a certificate (of completion of a course). 〔flow.
수류(水流) a (water) current; a
수류탄(手榴彈) 《throw》 a hand grenade (at); a pineapple 《軍俗》.
수륙(水陸) land and water. ‖ ~양용(양용)의 amphibious. ‖ ~양서동물 an amphibian (animal) / ~양용 비행기(자동차, 전차) an amphibian plane (vehicle, tank).
수리 [鳥] an eagle.
수리(水利) water supply (급수); irrigation (관개); water carriage (수운). ‖ ~권 water (irrigation) rights / ~시설 (사업) irrigation facilities (works, projects).
수리(受理) ~하다 accept; receive. ¶ 원서(사표)를 ~하다 receive an application (a person's resignation).
수리(修理) repair(s); mending. ~하다 repair; mend; fix; make repairs on (a house). ¶ ~ 중이다 be under repair / ~할 수 없다 be beyond repair / 차 ~에 5만원 들었다 It cost fifty thousand won to have my car repaired (fixed). ‖ ~공 a repairman(자동차 ~공 an auto repairman) / ~공장 a repair shop(자동차 ~공장 an auto repair shop) / ~비 repairing charges.
수리(數理) a mathematical principle. ¶ ~적(으로) mathematical(ly). ‖ ~경제학 mathematical economics.
수림(樹林) a wood; a forest.
수립(樹立) ~하다 establish; found; set up.
수마(水魔) a disastrous flood.
수마(睡魔) sleepiness. ¶ ~와 싸우다 try not to fall asleep.

수만(數萬) tens of thousands.
수매(收買) (a) purchase; buying; procurement(정부의). ～하다 purchase; buy (out). ¶정부의 쌀 ～ 가격 the Government's purchasing price of rice.
수맥(水脈) (strike) a vein of water.
수면(水面) the surface of the water. ¶～에 떠오르다 rise (come up) to the surface.
수면(睡眠) sleep. ¶～을 충분히 취하다 sleep well; have [take] a good sleep /～을 방해하다 disturb 《*a person's*》 sleep. ‖～부족 lack [want] of sleep /～시간 *one's* sleeping hours /～제 a sleeping drug [pill, tablet].
수명(壽命) life; life span. ¶자동차 [전지]의 ～ the life of a car [battery] /～이 길다[짧다] be long- [short-]lived; have a long [short] life /～을 연장[단축]하다 prolong [shorten] *one's* life.
수모(受侮) insult; contempt. ～하다 be insulted; suffer insult.
수목(樹木) trees (and shrubs). ¶～이 울창한 wooded 《*hills*》; tree-covered 《*mountains*》; woody.
수몰(水沒) ～하다 be submerged; go under water. ¶그 마을은 홍수로 ～되었다 The village was submerged by the flood. ‖～지역 submerged districts.
수묵(水墨) India ink. ‖～화 a painting in India ink.
수문(水門) a sluice (gate); a flood-gate; a water gate.
수미(首尾) beginning and end; alpha and omega.
수밀도(水蜜桃) a peach.
수박 a watermelon. ¶～ 겉 핥기 a superficial [half] knowledge; a smattering.
수반(首班) the head; the chief. ¶내각 ～ the head of a Cabinet; a premier.
수반(隨伴) ～하다 accompany; follow. ¶행정 개혁에 ～되는 여러 문제 the problems accompanying administrative reform.
수방(水防) flood control; prevention of floods; defense against flood. ‖～대책 an anti-flood measure; measures to prevent floods /～훈련 a flood-fighting drill.
수배(手配) ～하다 arrange [prepare] 《*for*》; take necessary steps 《*for, to do*》; 《경찰이》 begin (institute) a search 《*for*》; cast a dragnet 《*for*》. ¶경찰은 그 사내를 강도 용의자로 전국에 지명 ～했다 The police put the man on the wanted list throughout the country. ‖～사진 a photo of a wanted criminal; a mug shot 《俗》/～서 《경찰의》 search instructions.
수배(數倍) ¶～의 several times as 《*many, much, fast, good*》 as.
수백(數百) ～의 several hundred; hundreds of /～마일 a few hundred miles.
수법(手法) a technique; a style; a way; a trick. ¶새 ～의 사기 a swindle of a new type.
수병(水兵) a sailor; a seaman. ‖～복 a sailor suit.
수복(收復) reclamation; recovery. ～하다 recover; reclaim. ‖～지구 a reclaimed area.
수복(修復) restoration (to the original state). ～하다 restore 《*a thing*》 to *its* former condition [state].
수복(壽福) long life and happiness. ‖～강녕 longevity, happiness, healthiness and peace.
수부(水夫) a sailor; a seaman. ¶～장 a boatswain (갑판장).
수북하다 be heaped up. ¶수북이 full(y); in a heap.
수분(水分) moisture; juice (액즙). ¶～이 많은 watery; juicy 《*fruit*》; water-laden 《*winds*》/～을 흡수하다 absorb 《suck up》 water 《*from*》. 「～하다 pollinate.
수분(受粉·授粉) 〔植〕 pollination.
수비(守備) defense; 〔野〕 fielding. ～하다 defend; guard; garrison 《*a fort*》; 〔野〕 field. ¶철벽 같은 [어설픈] ～ 《야구에서》 airtight [poor] fielding /～를 강화하다 strengthen the defenses. ‖～대 a garrison; guards /～범 a guard; a garrison(총칭) /～율 〔野〕 *one's* fielding average.
수사(手寫) copying by hand. ～하다 copy (by hand).
수사(修士) a monk; a friar.
수사(修辭) figures of speech. ‖～학 rhetoric /～학자 a rhetorician.
수사(搜查) (a) criminal investigation; a search. ～하다 investigate 《*a case*》; search 《*for*》. ¶～에 착수하다 institute a search 《*for*》. ‖～과 the criminal investigation section /～망 the (police) dragnet /～본부 the investigation headquarters /～합동～반 the joint investigation team.
수사(數詞) 〔文〕 a numeral.
수사납다(數―) (be) unlucky; unfortunate; be out of luck.
수산(水産) marine products. ‖～가공품 processed marine products /～대학 a fisheries college /～물 marine [aquatic] products /～업 the marine products industry; fisheris /～업 동조합중앙회 the National Federation of Fisheries Coperatives /

수산화(水酸化) 〖化〗 hydration. ¶ 나트륨 sodium hydroxide / ~물 a hydroxide.
수삼(水蔘) undried [fresh] ginseng.
수상(水上) ¶ ~의 aquatic; on the water. ‖ ~경기 water [aquatic] sports / ~경찰 the marine (harbor, river) police / ~비행기 a seaplane; a hydroplane / ~스키 water-skiing; water skis (도구).
수상(手相) ☞ 손금. ¶ ~술 palmistry; chiromancy.
수상(受像) ~하다 receive (television) pictures. ‖ ~기 a television [TV] set.
수상(受賞) ~하다 get [receive] a prize [an award]; win [be awarded] a prize. ‖ ~자 a prize winner / ~작가 a award-winning writer / ~작품 a prize-winning work (novel).
수상(首相) the Prime Minister; the premier. ‖ ~의 관저 the prime minister's official residence / ~서리 the acting prime minister / ~직 premiership.
수상(殊常) ~하다 (be) suspicious; dubious; doubtful; questionable. ¶ ~하게 여기다 suspect; feel suspicious 《about》.
수상(授賞) ~하다 award [give] a prize 《to》. ‖ ~식 a prize-giving ceremony.
수상(隨想) occasional [stray, random] thoughts. ‖ ~록 essays; stray notes.
수색(搜索) a search; an investigation; a manhunt 《美》. ~하다 look [hunt, search] for; rummage. ‖ ~대 a search party / ~영장 a search warrant / ~원 an application to the police to search for a missing person.
수색(愁色) a worried look; melancholy [gloomy] air.
수생(水生) ¶ ~의 aquatic. ‖ ~식물 an aquatic plant.
수서(手書) an autograph letter.
수서(水棲) ¶ ~의 aquatic. ‖ ~동물 an aquatic animal.
수석(首席) 《사람》 the head [chief]; 《석차》 the top [head] seat. ¶ ~의 leading; head / ~을 차지하다 be at the top [head] 《of a class》 / ~으로 졸업하다 graduate first 《on the list》. ‖ ~대표 the chief delegate.
수선 fuss; ado; bustle. ¶ ~스럽다 (be) noisy; unquiet; clamorous; bustling / ~ 떨다 make a (great) fuss [make much ado] about nothing. ‖ ~쟁이 a fussbudget [-box].

수선(修繕) repair(s); mending. ~하다 repair; mend; fix (up). ¶ ~ 중 be under repair / ~이 되다 be beyond [past] repair. ‖ ~비 repairing expenses; repair costs.
수선화(水仙花) 〖植〗 a narcissus; a daffodil.
수성(水性) ¶ ~의 aqueous. ‖ ~도료 emulsion (paint); water paint / ~유제(乳劑) an aqueous emulsion.
수성(水星) Mercury.
수성(獸性) animality; beastliness; brutality.
수성암(水成岩) an aqueous rock.
수세(水洗) flushing; rinsing. ‖ ~식 변소 a flush toilet.
수세(水勢) the force of water [a current].
수세(守勢) 〖take, assume〗 the defensive. ¶ ~적인 defensive.
수세공(手細工) hand(i)work; handicraft. ¶ ~의 handmade. ‖ ~품 handmade goods.
수세미 a scrubber made from a sponge gourd. ‖ ~외 〖植〗 a sponge gourd; a loofa(h).
수소 a bull; an ox.
수소(水素) hydrogen(기호 H). ¶ ~의 하이드릭 hydrogenous. ‖ ~가스 hydrogen gas / ~산 hydracid / ~폭탄 a hydrogen bomb; an H-bomb.
수소문(搜所聞) ~하다 ask around; trace rumors.
수속(手續) ☞ 절차.
수송(輸送) transport(ation). ~하다 transport; convey. ¶ 국내[해외] inland [overseas] transport / 육상 [해상] / 철도 [항공] ~ transport by land [sea] / railway [air] transport. ‖ ~기(선) a transport plane [ship] / ~량 volume of transportation.
수쇠 (맷돌의) a pivot.
수수 〖植〗 Indian millet; kaoliang.
수수(授受) delivery. ~하다 give [deliver] and receive.
수수께끼 a riddle; a puzzle; a mystery. ¶ ~ 같은 enigmatic; mysterious / ~의 인물 a mysterious person / ~를 내다 [풀다] ask [guess] a riddle.
수수료(手數料) a fee; (take) a commission 《of 5%》; brokerage.
수수방관(袖手傍觀) ~하다 look on with folded arms; be an idle spectator (onlooker).
수수하다 (be) plain; quiet; sober; simple; modest. ¶ 수수한 무늬 a plain pattern / 수수한 빛깔 a sober color.
수술 〖植〗 a stamen.
수술(手術) an (a surgical) operation 《for appendicitis》. ~하다 operate 《on》; perform an operation. ¶ 위 ~을 받다 undergo [have] an operation on one's stomach / ~중에 죽다 die on the operating

수습 table / 외과의는 환자를 ~ 했다 The surgeon performed an operation on the patient. ¶ ~실〔대, 복〕 an operating room (table, gown).

수습(收拾) control; settlement. ~하다 settle; control; get 《*something*》 under control; save; manage; cope 《*with*》. ¶ 난국을 ~ 하다 save 〔settle〕 a difficult situation / ~ 못 하게 되다 get out of hand 〔control〕.

수습(修習) apprenticeship; probation. ~하다 receive training; practice *oneself* 《*at*》. ¶ ~ 간호사 a student nurse / ~ 기간 the period of apprenticeship; the probationary period / ~ 기자 a cub 〔junior〕 reporter / ~ 사원 a probationary employee / ~ 생 a trainee; a probationer / ~ 제도 apprenticeship training system.

수시(隨時) ¶ ~로 at any time; at all times; on demand; as occasion calls.

수식(水飾)〔地〕 erosion.

수식(修飾) ~하다 embellish; ornament; 〔文〕 modify 《*a noun*》. ¶ ~어 a modifier.

수신(水神) a naiad(여신); the god of water; a water nymph.

수신(受信) the receipt of a message; reception. ~하다 receive 《*a message*》. ¶ ~국〔안테나〕 a receiving station (antenna) / ~ 기 a receiver; a receiving set / ~ 인 an addressee; a recipient / ~ 회로 a receiving circuit.

수신(修身) moral training. ¶ ~ 제가하다 order *one's* life and manage *one's* household.

수심(水深) (sound) the depth of water. ¶ ~계 a hydrobarometer.

수심(垂心)〔數〕 an orthocenter.

수심(愁心) worry; anxiety; apprehension(s). ¶ ~에 잠기다 be lost in apprehension; be sunk in grief.

수십(數十) scores 〔dozens〕 《*of*》. ¶ ~ 년 for several decades.

수압(水壓) water 〔hydraulic〕 pressure. ¶ ~계 a water-pressure gauge / ~ 시험 a hydraulic test.

수액(樹液) sap. ¶ ~을 채취하다 sap 《*a tree*》.

수양(收養) adoption. ~하다 adopt. ¶ ~ 부모 foster parents / ~ 아들〔딸〕 an adopted 〔a foster〕 son 〔daughter〕.

수양(修養) moral 〔mental〕 culture; cultivation of the mind. ~하다 cultivate *one's* mind; improve *oneself*. ¶ ~을 쌓은 사람 a well-cultivated mind.

수양버들(垂楊–) a weeping willow.

수업(修業) study. ~하다 study; make a study 《*of*》; get *one's* education 《*from*》. ¶ ~ 연한 the years required for graduation.

수업(授業) teaching; school (work); (school) lessons; a class; instruction. ~하다 teach; give lessons (classes). ¶ ~을 받다 take lessons 《*in*》; attend school (class) / ~을 받지 않다 do not attend class; miss a lesson / ~이 없다 We have (There is) no school. ¶ ~료 a school (tuition) fee / ~ 시간 school hours / ~ 일수 the number of school days.

수없다(–不可能) have no way to 《*do*》; cannot *do* 《*it*》; be unable to 《*do*》; 〔힘겹다〕 be too much for 《*one*》; cannot afford to 《*do*》.

수없다(數—) (be) countless; numberless; innumerable. ¶ 수없이 innumerably; countlessly.

수에즈운하(–運河) the Suez Canal.

수여(授與) ~하다 give; confer; award. ¶ 학위를 ~ 하다 confer a degree on *a person* / 상품을 ~ 하다 award a prize to *a person* / 훈장을 ~ 하다 decorate 《*a person*》 with a medal. ¶ ~식 (노벨상 따위의) an awarding ceremony.

수역(水域) the water area 《*of*》; (in Korean) waters. ¶ 200해리 어업~ the 200 mile fishing zone / 배타적 어업전관~ the exclusive fishing zone (waters). ¶ 경제~ an economic zone (off the coast) / 공동규제~ a jointly controlled waters / 중립~ neutral waters.

수역(獸疫) a livestock disease; an epizootic. 〔old man.

수연(壽宴) a birthday feast for an

수염(鬚髥) a mustache; 〔콧수염〕 (구레나룻) whiskers; 〔턱수염〕 a beard. ¶ ~이 있는 〔난〕 bearded / ~이 덥수룩한 bushy bearded / ~을 깎다 shave / ~을 기르다 grow a beard (mustache). ¶ 가짜 ~ (wear) a false mustache 〔beard〕 / 옥수수~ corn silk.

수영(水泳) swimming; a swim. ~하다 (have a) swim. ¶ ~ 하러 가다 go swimming; go for a swim / ~을 잘 하다 be a good swimmer. ¶ ~ 대회〔대회, 복〕 swimming class 〔meet, suit〕 / ~ 선수 a swimmer / ~ 장 a swimming pool 〔place〕 / ~ 팬츠 swimming trunks.

수예(手藝) manual arts; a handicraft. ¶ ~품 a piece of fancywork; handicraft articles.

수온(水溫) water temperature.

수완(手腕) ability; capability; talent. ¶ ~ 있는 (cap)able; talented; competent / ~이 없는 incompetent / ~을 발휘하다 show 〔display, exercise〕 *one's* ability. ¶ ~가 a man of ability; an

able man / 외교(적) ~ diplomatic ability.
수요(需要) (a) demand. ¶ 가~ imaginary demand; speculative demand / ~가 있다 be in demand; be wanted / ~를 채우가 meet a demand. ‖ ~공급 demand and supply / ~파다 (감소)~ an excessive (a reduced) demand / ~파임인플레 demand-pull (inflation) / ~자 a consumer. 〔Wed.〕
수요일(水曜日) Wednesday (생략 Wed.).
수욕(獸慾) animal (carnal) desire.
수용(水溶) ¶ ~성의 water-soluble. ‖ ~액 a solution.
수용(收用) expropriation. ~하다 expropriate 《*estates*》 from 《*a person*》. 토지~ expropriation of land / 토지~권 [法] (the right of) eminent domain / 토지~법 the Compulsory Land Purchase Law.
수용(收容) accommodation. ~하다 receive; accommodate; take to 《*a hospital*》; intern. ¶ 수재민을 ~하다 house flood victims (*in schools*) / 부상자는 인근 병원에~되었다 The injured were taken to the nearby hospital. ‖ ~력 seating capacity (극장의); sleeping accomodation (호텔의) / ~소 an asylum; a concentration (refugee) camp.
수용(受容) reception. ~하다 accept; receive. ‖ ~태세 preparations to receive.
수운(水運) water transport(ation).
수원(水源) the head (source) of a river; a riverhead; a source of water supply (수도의). ‖ ~지 a reservoir.
수원(受援) ‖ ~국 a recipient country.
수월찮다 (be) not easy (simple); hard.
수월하다 (be) easy; simple; light. ¶ 하기가 ~ it is no trouble to do / ~하게 easily; with ease.
수위(水位) a water level. ‖ ~표 a watermark / 위험~ the dangerous water level.
수위(守衛) a guard; a doorkeeper; a gatekeeper. ‖ ~실 a guard office; a (porter's) lodge / ~장 the chief guard.
수위(首位) the head (leading) position; the first place. ¶ ~를 차지하다 be at the top (head) 《*of*》; stand (rank) first 《*in*》. ‖ ~다툼 a struggle for priority / ~타자 [野] the leading hitter.
수유(授乳) ~하다 breast-feed; suckle; give the breast to 《*a baby*》. ‖ ~기 the lactation period. 〔duct.〕
수유관(輸乳管) [解] the lactiferous
수유자(受遺者) [法] a legatee (동산

의); a devisee (부동산의).
수육 boiled beef.
수육(獸肉) meat.
수은(水銀) mercury; quicksilver (기호 Hg). ‖ ~등 a mercury-vapor lamp / ~전지 a mercury cell / ~주 a mercurial column / ~중독 mercury poisoning.
수음(手淫) (practice) masturbation (onanism).
수의(壽衣) graveclothes; a shroud.
수의(隨意) ¶ ~의 voluntary; optional; free / ~로 freely; at will; voluntarily. ‖ ~계약 a private (free) contract / ~근 a voluntary muscle / ~선택 free choice.
수의(獸醫) a veterinary surgeon; a veterinarian (美). ‖ ~과 대학 a veterinary college / ~학 veterinary science (medicine).
수익(收益) earnings; profits; gains; 《투자의》 returns. ¶ ~을 올리다 make profits. ‖ ~률 an earning rate / ~세 profit tax.
수익(受益) ~하다 benefit 《*by*》; receive benefits. ‖ ~자 a beneficiary / ~증권 a beneficiary certificate.
수인(囚人) a convict; a prisoner.
수인성(水因性) ¶ ~의 waterborne. ‖ ~질병 waterborne diseases.
수임(受任) ~하다 accept an appointment; be nominated. ‖ ~자 an appointee; a nominee.
수입(收入) 《소득》 an income; earnings; 《세입》 revenue; 《입금》 receipts; 《매상고》 proceeds. ¶ ~과 지출 income and outgo / ~이 많다 (적다) have a large (small) income / ~의 길이 막히다 lose sources of *one's* income. ‖ ~인 지 a revenue stamp / ~실 a net (actual) income / 월~ a monthly income.
수입(輸入) import(ation); 《문물의》 introduction. ~하다 import; introduce. ¶ 인도에서 한국으로 면화를 ~하다 import cotton into Korea from India / 원료를 ~해서 완제품으로 수출하다 import the raw materials and export the finished product. ‖ ~가격 an import price / ~감시품목 the import surveillance items / ~결제어음 an import settlement bill / ~계약 an import contract / ~과징금 import surcharge / ~국 an importing country / ~규제 import restraints (curbs, restrictions) / ~금지 an import prohibition / ~담보율 the import deposite (mortgage) rate / ~대리점 an import agent / ~대체산업 import substitute (replacing, saving) industry / ~량 import volume / ~면장 an import

license / ~무역 import trade / ~상[업자] an importer; an import trader / ~상사 an import firm [house] / ~성향(性向) the propensity of import / ~세[관세] import duties / ~쇠고기 the imported beef / ~수속 an import procedure; importation formalities / ~신고(서) a declaration of importation; an import declaration / ~신용장 an import letter of credit / ~액 the amount of imports / ~어음 an import bill / ~억제[금지] 품목 import-restricted [-banned] items / ~의존도 the rate of dependence on imports / ~자유화 the import liberalization / ~절차 the process of import; import procedure / ~제한 import restrictions / ~초과 an excess of imports (over exports); an unfavorable balance of trade / ~품 imports; imported articles / ~할당 an import (allotment) quota / ~할당제도 the import quota system / ~항 an import port / ~허가 an import permit / ~허가제 the import licensing system / 직접[간접] ~ direct [indirect] import.

수있다 (능력) can (do); be able to (do); be capable of (doing); be equal (to); (사물이 주어) be in one's power; be possible; (무방) may; be entitled to. ¶ 될 수 있는 대로 as (much) as one can; (as much) as possible / 할 [될] 수 있으면 if you can; if possible.

수자원(水資源) water resources. ‖ ~개발 the development of water resources / 한국 ~공사 the Korea Water Resources Corporation.

수작(秀作) an excellent [outstanding] work (of art).

수작(授爵) ennoblement. ~하다 ennoble; confer a peerage on (a person).

수작(酬酌) ~하다 (말을) exchange words; (술잔을) exchange cups (of wine). ¶ 허튼 ~을 하다 talk nonsense.

수장(水葬) (a) burial at sea. ~하다 bury at sea. [up; collect.

수장(收藏) ~하다 garner; store

수재(水災) a flood (disaster). ‖ 이재 民 flood victims / ~의연금 a relief fund for flood victims.

수재(秀才) a genius; a talented person; a bright student. ‖ ~교육 education of gifted children.

수저 a spoon; spoon and chopsticks.

수저(水底) (at) the bottom of the water. ‖ ~어 a ground fish.

수전(水田) a paddy [rice] field.

수전(水戰) a sea fight. ☞ 해전.

수전노(守錢奴) a miser; a niggard.

수전증(手顫症)【韓醫】palsy in the arm; tremor of the hand.

수절(守節) ~하다 (정조) preserve one's chastity (virtue); (절조) be true to one's principles.

수정(水晶) (a) (rock) crystal. ¶ ~ 같은 crystal(line). ¶ ~시계 a quartz watch (clock) / ~체 the crystalline lens (눈의).

수정(受精)【生】fecundation; fertilization;【植】pollination. ~하다 be fertilized (fecundated, pollinated). ~시키다 fertilize; pollinate. ¶ ~란 a fertilized egg / 인공 ~ artificial fertilization / 체외 ~ external fertilization.

수정(修正) (an) amendment; (a) modification; (a) revision. ~하다 amend; modify; revise. ¶ ~신고 a revised return [report] / ~안 an amended bill; an amendment / ~예산 a revised budget / ~자본주의 modified capitalism / ~주의 revisionism.

수정과(水正果) cinnamon flavored persimmon punch.

수정관(輸精管)【解】the spermatic cord [duct].

수제(手製) ¶ ~의 handmade; homemade. ¶ ~품 a handmade article; handiwork.

수제비 flour dumplings served in soup. ¶ ~국 (of).

수제자(首弟子) the best pupil (dis-

수조(水槽) a (water) tank; a cistern; a fish [glass] tank (완상용 물고기의).

수조(水藻) duckweed; seaweed.

수족(手足) hands and feet; the limbs (사지). ¶ (남의) ~처럼 일하다 serve a person like a tool; move [act] at another's beck and call.

수족관(水族館) an aquarium. ‖ 해양 ~ an oceanarium.

수주(受注) ~하다 accept [receive] an order (from). ‖ ~액 the amount of orders received.

수준(水準) the water level; (a) level [standard] (표준). ¶ 지적 ~ an intellectual level / ~에 달하다 [을 높이다] reach [raise] the level / ~ 이상[이하]이다 be above [below] the (common) level / 문화 ~이 높다 have a high level of culture. ‖ ~기 a (water) level / 최고 ~ the highest level.

수줍다 (be) shy; bashful; timid. ¶ 수줍어 하다 be [feel] shy.

수중(水中) ¶ ~의 underwater / ~에 under [in the] water. ‖ ~동물[식물] an aquatic animal

수중 [plant] / ~보(洑) sluice gates under a bridge / ~속력《잠수함의》an underwater speed / ~안경 a water [swimming] glass; diving goggles《잠수용의》; hydroscope(관측용의) / ~익선(翼船) a hydrofoil / ~작업원 an aquanaut / ~청음기 a hydrophone / ~촬영 underwater photography / ~TV카메라 an underwater TV camera.

수중(手中) ¶ ~에 들어가다 fall into 《*a person's*》hands / ~에 넣다 take possession 《*of*》; secure.

수증기(水蒸氣) vapor; steam.

수지(收支) 《균형》income and costs; revenue and expenditure; 《채산》profits. ¶ ~ 맞는 paying; profitable / ~가 맞다 make even; 《채산》pay; be profitable / ~가 안 맞다 income does not cover the expenses; 《채산》do not pay; be unprofitable / ~를 맞추다 make both ends meet; balance the budget; make 《*it*》pay / ~를 결산하다 strike a balance.

수지(樹脂) resin《유동체》; rosin《고체》. / ~《질의》resinous / ~모양의 resinoid. ¶ ~가공 plasticization; resin treatment (~가공의 resin-treated 《*textiles*》).

수지(獸脂) grease; animal fat.

수직(手織) ¶ ~의 handwoven; homespun. ¶ ~기 a handloom.

수직(垂直) ¶ ~의 perpendicular; vertical / ~으로 perpendicularly; vertically; at right angles; upright. ‖ ~선 a vertical line / ~이착륙기 a vertical takeoff and landing craft《생략 VTOL》.

수질(水質) the quality [purity] of water. ‖ ~검사 water analysis [examination] / ~오염 water pollution.

수집(蒐集) collection. ~하다 collect; gather. ‖ ~가 a collector / ~벽 collection mania.

수차(水車) a water mill [wheel].

수차(收差) 〔理〕 aberration. ‖ 구면 (球面)~ spherical aberration.

수채 a sewer; a drain. ¶ 수챗구멍 a drainage vent [outlet].

수채화(水彩畫) a watercolor painting. ¶ ~가 a watercolor painter; a watercolorist / ~물감 watercolors.

수척하다(瘦瘠—) (be) emaciated; wornout; worn; gaunt; haggard.

수천(數千) thousands 《*of people*》.

수첩(手帖) a (pocket) notebook; a pocketbook.

수초(水草) a water [an aquatic] plant.

수축(收縮) shrinking; contraction. ~하다 contract; shrink. ‖ 통화의 ~ deflation. ‖ ~근 〔解〕a contractile muscle / ~력 contractile force [power] / ~성 contractibility.

수축(修築) ~하다 repair; rebuild.

수출(輸出) export(ation). ~하다 export; ship abroad. ¶ ~을 금하다 ban [prohibit] the export 《*of*》 / ~을 증가시키다 increase the amount of export 《*of cars*》 / ~주도의 경제 an export-oriented economy. ‖ ~가격 [면장, 장려금] an export price [permit, subsidy] / ~공업단지 the export industrial complex / ~국 an exporting country / ~산업 an export industry / ~세 [관세] export duties 《*on*》 / ~수속 export formalities / ~시장다변화 a diversification of export markets / ~업 the export business [trade] / ~업자 an export trader; an exporter / ~자주규제 voluntary export restrictions / ~초과 an excess of exports (over imports) / ~품 an export; exported goods / ~항 an export port; an outport.

수출경쟁력(輸出競爭力) competitiveness in exports.

수출금융(輸出金融) export financing.

수출금지(輸出禁止) an export ban; an embargo. ~하다 put [place, lay] an embargo 《*on*》.

수출송장(輸出送狀) an export invoice.

수출신용보험(輸出信用保險) [credit insurance].

수출신용장(輸出信用狀) an export letter of credit.

수출실적(輸出實績) the export performance; the actual exports.

수출액(輸出額) exports; the amount of export (in terms of money). ¶ ~총 the total export.

수출입(輸出入) import and export; exportation and importation. ‖ ~의 차액 the balance of trade. ‖ ~금지품 a contraband / ~은행 an export-import bank.

수취(受取) receipt. ~하다 receive. ‖ ~인 a receiver; a recipient; a payee《어음의》; a remittee (송금의).

수치(羞恥) shame; disgrace; dishonor; humiliation. ¶ ~스런 shameful; disgraceful / ~하다 be put to shame; be humiliated.

수치(數値) the numerical value. ¶ ~를 구하다 evaluate.

수캉아지 a he-puppy; a male pup.

수캐 a he-dog; a male dog.

수컷 a male; a cock《새의》. ¶ ~의 male 《*dog*》; cock; he-.

수탁(受託) trust. ~하다 be given 《*something*》in trust; be entrusted with 《*a thing*》; take charge

수탈 (收奪) exploitation. ~하다 exploit; plunder.

수탉 a rooster 《주로 美》; a cock.

수태 (受胎) conception. ~하다 conceive; become pregnant. ¶ ~고지(告知) the Annunciation / ~조절 birth control.

수통 (水筒) a (water) flask; a canteen.

수퇘지 a boar.

수틀 (繡─) an embroidery frame.

수평 (水平) horizontality. ¶ ~의 level; horizontal / ~으로 horizontally; at a level 《with》 / ~으로 하다 level / ~면 a horizontal plane; a level surface / ~비행 a level flight / ~선 a horizontal line; the horizon.

수포 (水泡) foam; a bubble. ¶ ~로 돌아가다 end in smoke 〔(a) failure〕; come 〔be brought〕 to nothing 〔naught〕.

수포 (水疱) 〖醫〗 a blister.

수폭 (水爆) ☞ 수소폭탄. ¶ ~실험 a thermonuclear 〔an H-bomb〕 test.

수표 (手票) a check 《美》; a cheque 《英》. ¶ 10만 원짜리 ~ a check for 100,000 *won* / ~로 지불하다 pay by check / ~를 떼다 draw a check / ~를 현찰로 바꾸다 cash a check / ~장 a checkbook / 분실〔위조〕 ~ a lost 〔forged〕 check / 자기앞 ~ 《은행의》 a cashier's check.

수풀 a forest; a wood; a bush; a thicket.

수프 (eat) soup. ¶ ~접시 a soup plate.

수피 (樹皮) bark; rind. ¶ ~를 벗기다 bark 《a tree》.

수피 (獸皮) a hide; a (an animal) skin; a fell; a fur《로》.

수필 (隨筆) an essay; stray notes. ¶ ~가 an essayist / ~집 a collection of 《a person's》 essays.

수하 (手下) a subordinate; an underling; one's men《총칭》.

수하 (受荷) receipt of goods. ¶ ~인 a consignee.

수하 (誰何) ① 〔검문〕 a challenge. ~하다 challenge 《a person》. ② 〔누구〕 ¶ ~를 막론하고 anyone; regardless of who it may be.

수하다 (壽─) live long; enjoy a long life.

수학 (修學) ~하다 learn; study. ¶ ~여행 (go on) a school excursion 〔trip〕 《to》; a study tour.

수학 (數學) 《applied》 mathematics. ¶ ~의 mathematic《al》. ¶ ~자 a mathematician / 고등 ~ higher mathematics.

수학능력시험 (修學能力試驗) a scholastic aptitude test.

수해 (水害) damage by a flood; a flood disaster. ¶ ~를 입다 suffer from a flood. ~대책 a flood-control measure 《예방》; a flood-relief measure 《구조》 / ~지〔가옥〕 a flooded district 《house》.

수행 (修行) 《수련》 training; practice; 《종교상의》 ascetic practices. ~하다 receive one's training; train oneself 《in》; practice asceticism.

수행 (遂行) ~하다 accomplish; carry out 《a plan》; execute; perform.

수행 (隨行) ~하다 attend; accompany; follow. ¶ ~원 a (member of a person's) suite; an attendant; a retinue《총칭》.

수험 (受驗) ~하다 take 《undergo, sit for》 an examination. ¶ ~준비를 하다 prepare 《oneself》 for an examination. ¶ ~과목 subjects of examination / ~료 an examination fee / ~번호 an examinee's seat number / ~생 a candidate for examination; an examinee / ~자격 qualifications for an examination / ~지옥 the hell of examination ordeal / ~표 an admission ticket for an examination.

수혈 (輸血) (a) blood transfusion. ~하다 give a blood transfusion 《to》; transfuse blood. ¶ ~을 받다 receive a blood transfusion.

수형 (受刑) ~하다 serve time 《for murder》. ¶ ~자 a convict.

수호 (守護) ~하다 protect; guard; watch over. ¶ ~신 a guardian deity; a tutelary god.

수호 (修好) friendship; amity. ¶ ~조약 《conclude》 a treaty of amity 〔friendship〕 《with》.

수화 (水化)〔化〕 hydration. ¶ ~물 a hydrate.

수화 (手話) sign language. ¶ ~로 말하다 talk with the hands; use 〔talk in〕 sign language.

수화기 (受話器) a receiver; an earphone. ¶ ~를 놓다〔들다〕 hang up 〔take off〕 the receiver.

수화물 (手貨物) (a piece of) baggage 〔luggage 《英》〕; personal effects 《휴대품》. ¶ ~를 맡기다 have one's baggage checked. ¶ ~일시보관소 a cloakroom 《美》— 취급소 a baggage 〔luggage〕 office / ~표《공항의》 a baggage-claim check 〔tag〕.

수확 (收穫) a harvest; a crop; the fruits《성과》. ~하다 harvest;

수회(收賄) bribery; graft. ~하다 take [accept] a bribe; take graft 《美》. ¶ ~ 공무원 a corrupt official / ~ 혐의로 on the charge of taking a bribe. ∥ ~ 사건 a bribery case; a graft scandal 《美》/ ~자 a bribe-taker; a bribee; a grafter.

수효(數爻) a number.　　　Ler《美》.

수훈(垂訓) a precept; teachings. ∥ 산상(山上) ~ the Sermon on the Mount.

수훈(殊勳) distinguished services; meritorious deeds. ¶ ~을 세우다 render distinguished services. / ~타 [野] a winning hit / 최고 ~ 선수 the most valuable player《생략 MVP》.

숙고(熟考) (mature) consideration; deliberation. ~하다 think over; consider (carefully). ¶ ~한 후 after due consideration / 충분히 ~된 계획 a well-thought-out plan.

숙군(肅軍) 《effect》 a purge in the army; restoration of military discipline.

숙녀(淑女) a lady; a gentlewoman. ¶ ~다운 ladylike.

숙달(熟達) ~하다 become proficient《*in*》; get a mastery《*of*》. ¶ ~되어 있다 be proficient 《*in*》; be a master 《*of*》.

숙당(肅黨) a purge of disloyal elements from a party.

숙덕(淑德) feminine virtues.

숙덕거리다 talk in whispers; talk in a subdued tone. ¶ 숙덕숙덕 in whispers [an undertone]; secretly.

숙덕공론(─公論) exchanges of subdued remarks; secret counsel.

숙독(熟讀) (a) perusal. ~하다 read carefully [thoroughly]; peruse.

숙련(熟練) skill; dexterity. ¶ ~된 skillful; trained; expert / 미 ~의 unskilled; inexperienced / ~되다 become skilled [skillful, proficient]. ∥ ~공 a skilled worker; skilled labor 《총칭》/ ~자 an expert. 　　[ished desire.

숙망(宿望) 《attain》 one's long-cher-

숙맥(菽麥) a fool; an ass; a simpleton.

숙면(熟眠) a deep [sound] sleep. ~하다 sleep well [soundly]; have a good sleep.

숙명(宿命) fate; destiny; 【佛】 karma. ¶ ~적인 fatal; predestined. ∥ ~론 fatalism / ~론자 a fatalist.

숙모(叔母) an aunt.

숙박(宿泊) lodging. ~하다 put up [stay]《*at*》; lodge《*in, at*》; take up one's lodgings. ∥ ~료 hotel [lodging] charges; a hotel bill / ~부 a hotel register [book] / ~ 설비 accommodations / ~소 one's lodgings; one's quarters《군인의》/ ~인 a lodger; a guest; a boarder.

숙변(宿便) feces contained for a long time in the intestines; 《suffer from》 retention of feces.

숙부(叔父) an uncle.

숙사(宿舍) lodgings; quarters; a billet《군대》. ¶ ~를 마련하다 provide accommodation 《*for*》.

숙성(熟成) ripening; maturing. ~하다 ripen; mature; get mellow.

숙성하다(夙成―) (be) precocious; premature. ¶ 숙성한 아이 a precocious child.

숙소(宿所) a place of abode; one's quarters [address]. ¶ ~를 잡다 stay [put up] at 《*a hotel*》.

숙식(宿食) ~하다 board and lodge. ∥ ~비 the charge for board and lodging.

숙어(熟語) an idiom; an idiomatic phrase.

숙연(肅然) ¶ ~한 solemn《엄숙》; quiet; ~히 solemnly; quietly; silently / ~해지다 be struck with reverence [into silence].

숙영(宿營) ~하다 be billeted; be quartered; camp. ∥ ~지 a billeting area.

숙원(宿怨) an old [a deep-rooted] grudge《*against*》; (a) long-harbored enmity [resentment]. ¶ ~을 풀다 pay off one's old scores 《*with*》.

숙원(宿願) 《realize》 one's long-cherished desire [ambition].

숙의(熟議) ~하다 deliberate 《*on*》; discuss (fully); talk 《*a matter*》 over. ¶ ~(한) 끝에 after careful discussion.

숙이다(고개를) hang [bow, droop, bend] one's head. ¶ 고개를 숙이고 걷다 walk with one's head slightly drooping / 부끄러워 얼굴을 ~ hang [bend] down one's head for shame.

숙적(宿敵) an old enemy [foe].

숙정(肅正) (바로잡음) regulation; enforcement; a cleanup. ¶ 관기를 ~하다 enforce official discipline / 공무원 ~ 작업 a cleanup drive in officialdom.

숙제(宿題) 《do one's》 homework; a home task; an assignment; a pending [unsolved] question《미해결의》. ¶ 오랜 ~ a question of long standing / ~를 내다 give 《*students*》 homework / ~를 봐주다 help a person with his homework / ~로 남기다 leave 《*a problem*》 for future solution.

숙주(宿主) 【生】 a host. ¶ …의

숙주(나물) 442 **순수**

가 되다 play host to... / 중간 an intermediary host.

숙주(菽―)나물 green-bean sprouts.

숙지(熟知) ~하다 know well; be well aware 《of》; be familiar 《with》; have a thorough [full, detailed] knowledge 《of》.

숙직(宿直) night duty [watch]. ~하다 be on night duty; keep [do] night watch. ‖ ~실 a night-duty room / ~원 a night guard.

숙질(叔姪) uncle and nephew.

숙청(肅淸) a purge; a cleanup. ~하다 clean up; purge. ‖ ~운동 a purge campaign.

숙취(宿醉) a hangover. ¶ ~에 시달리다 suffer from [have] a hangover.

숙환(宿患) a long [protracted, lingering] illness. ¶ 그는 오랜 ~으로 죽었다 He died after a long illness.

순(旬) 《10일》 (a period of) ten days; 《10년》 ten years; a decade.

순(筍) 《싹》 a sprout; a bud.

순(純) 《순수한》 pure; genuine; unmixed; true 〈진정한〉; net 〈이익의〉. ¶ ~ 거짓말 a pure fabrication; real lie / ~ 서울 사람 a trueborn Seoulite / ~ 수입 net income / ~ 한국식 정원 a garden in a purely Korean style.

…순(順) turn. ¶ 가나다 〈번호〉 〈in〉 alphabetical 〈numerical〉 order / 성적 〈나이〉 〈in〉 order of merit 〈age〉.

순간(瞬間) (in) a moment; an instant; a second. ¶ ~을 목격하다 witness [see] the very moment / 그를 본 ~ the moment [instant] (that) I saw him. ‖ ~최대풍속 the maximum instantaneous wind velocity. [section.

순검(巡檢) (make) a tour of in-

순견(純絹) pure silk; all-silk.

순결(純潔) purity; chastity. ¶ ~한 clean; chaste / ~한 사랑 platonic [pure] love / ~한 처녀 a chaste maiden / 마음이 ~한 사람 a pure-hearted person / ~을 빼앗기다 be deprived of *one's* virginal purity. / ~교육 education in sexual morality.

순경(巡警) a policeman; a police officer; a constable 《英》; a cop 《美口》.

순교(殉敎) martyrdom. ~하다 die a martyr (for *one's* faith); be martyred. ‖ ~자 a martyr.

순국(殉國) ~하다 die for *one's* country. ‖ ~선열 a (patriotic) martyr / ~정신 the spirit of martyrdom; patriotism.

순금(純金) pure [solid] gold.

순대 *sundae*, a Korean sausage made of pig's blood, bean curd and green bean sprouts stuffed in pig intestine. ‖ 순댓국 pork soup mixed with sliced *sundae*.

순도(純度) purity.

순라(巡邏) a patrol; a round. ¶ ~돌다 go *one's* rounds. ‖ ~꾼 a patrolman.

순력(巡歷) ~하다 make a tour 《of, round》; tour (round) 《Europe》.

순례(巡禮) a pilgrimage. ~하다 make [go on] a pilgrimage 《to》. ‖ ~자 a pilgrim; a palmer / ~지 a place of pilgrimage.

순록(馴鹿) [動] a reindeer.

순리(純理) pure reason; logic. ‖ ~적(인) rational; logical. ‖ ~론 rationalism.

순리(順理) ~적(인) reasonable; rational; right; proper / ~적으로 reasonably; rationally.

순면(純綿) pure [all] cotton. ‖ ~의 pure-cotton; all-cotton.

순모(純毛) pure wool. ‖ ~의 all-wool; pure-wool. ‖ ~제품 all-wool goods [fabrics].

순무(蕪) a turnip.

순박(淳朴) ~한 simple and honest; naive; homely.

순방(巡訪) a round of calls [visits]. ~하다 make a round of calls. ¶ 각국을 ~하다 visit many countries one after another.

순배(巡杯) ~하다 pass the wine cup around.

순백(純白) ¶ ~의 pure-[snow=] white / ~의 웨딩드레스 a snow-white wedding dress.

순번(順番) order; turn〈교대〉. ¶ ~으로 in (due, regular) order; in turn; by turns [rotation] / ~을 기다리다 await [wait (for)] *one's* turn.

순사(殉死) self-immolation. ~하다 immolate *oneself* at the funeral of *one's* lord [master].

순산(順産) an easy delivery [birth]. ~하다 have an easy delivery.

순서(順序) order; sequence; 〈절차〉 procedure; formalities. ¶ ~바르게 in good order; in regular sequence / ~가 틀리다 be in wrong order; be out of order / ~를 바로잡다 put 《something》 in the correct [proper] order / ~을 밟다 go through due formalities.

순수(純粹) purity. ¶ ~한 pure; genuine; real; unmixed / ~한 동기 pure motives / ~한 미국사람 a trueborn American / ~한 페르시아 고양이 a pure-blooded Persian cat. ‖ ~과학 [시] pure science [poetry] / ~문학 pure [polite] literature.

순순하다(順順―) 《성질이》 (be) gentle; docile; obedient; submissive. ¶ 순순히 tamely; meekly; obediently; smoothly.

순시(巡視) ~하다 make a tour of inspection; inspect; patrol. ¶ 공장 안을 ~하다 inspect [go over] a factory. ‖ ~선 a patrol boat / ~인 a patrolman / 연두 ~ the new year inspection tour.

순식간(瞬息間) ~에 in an instant; in a moment; in a twinkling.

순양(巡洋) ~하다 cruise; sail about. ¶ ~전함 a battle cruiser / ~함 a cruiser.

순연(順延) ~하다 postpone; put [off].

순위(順位) order; grade; ranking. ¶ ~를 정하다 rank; decide ranking / ~를 다투다 compete for precedence / 전보다 학급에서의 ~가 올라갔다 I ranked higher in the class than before. ‖ ~결정 a play-off (동점자간의).

순음(脣音) {音聲} a labial.

순응(順應) ~하다 adapt (accommodate, adjust) oneself (to circumstances). ¶ ~시대에 ~하다 go with the tide (times). ‖ ~성(性) adaptability.

순(이)익(純(利)益) net [clear] profit (gain). ¶ 연간 1만 달러의 ~을 올리다 net [clear] (a profit of) 10,000 dollars a year.

순장(殉葬) 〔古制〕 burial of the living with the dead. ~하다 bury someone alive with the dead.

순전(純全) ¶ ~한 pure (and simple); absolute; perfect; sheer; utter / ~히 purely; perfectly; totally; utterly / ~한 개인 문제 a purely personal matter.

순정(純情) a pure heart. ¶ ~의 purehearted / ~을 바치다 give all one's love (to). ‖ ~소설 a boy-meets-girl story.

순조(順調) ¶ ~롭다 (be) favorable; satisfactory; fine; smooth; seasonable (날씨) / ~롭게 (progress) favorably; 《go》 very smoothly [well].

순종(純種) a pure blood; a thoroughbred. ¶ ~의 full-blooded; thoroughbred.

순종(順從) ~하다 obey without objection; submit tamely.

순직(殉職) ~하다 die at one's post; die on duty. ¶ ~경찰관 a policeman who died on duty. ‖ ~자 a victim to one's post of duty.

순직(純直) ¶ ~한 pure and honest; simple and upright.

순진(純眞) ¶ ~한 naive; pure; innocent; ingenuous / ~한 어린 아이 an innocent child / ~한 소녀 a girl pure in heart.

순차(順次) order; turn. ¶ ~적으로 in order; successively. ☞ 순서.

순찰(巡察) a patrol. ~하다 patrol; go one's rounds. ‖ ~대 a patrol party / ~대원 a patrolman / ~차 a (police) patrol car; a squad car.

순치(順治) 《길들임》 ~하다 tame; domesticate.

순탄하다(順坦―) 《길이》 (be) even; flat; smooth; 《일이》 (be) favorable; uneventful; 《성질이》 (be) gentle; mild. ¶ 순탄한 길 a (broad-)level road / 순탄하게 자라다 be bred in favorable circumstances.

순풍(順風) a favorable [fair] wind. ¶ ~에 돛을 달다 sail before [with] the wind.

순하다(順―) ① 《성질이》 (be) obedient; gentle; docile; meek; submissive. ② 《맛이》 (be) mild; light 《wine》; weak. ¶ ~한 담배 mild cigarettes. ③ 《일이》 (be) easy; smooth.

순항(巡航) a cruise. ~하다 sail (about); cruise. ‖ ~미사일 a cruise missile / ~선 a cruiser / ~속도 (at full) cruising speed.

순행(巡行) ~하다 go round. ☞ 순회.

순화(醇化) ~하다 purify; refine; sublimate. ¶ 국어 ~운동 (launch) a campaign to refine the Korean language.

순환(循環) circulation; rotation; a cycle. ~하다 circulate; rotate; go in cycles (circles). ¶ 혈액 ~을 좋게 하다 improve the circulation of the blood. ‖ ~곡선 a recurring curve / ~기(계) {醫} the circulatory organs (system) / ~도로 a circular road / ~버스 a loop-(belt-)line bus / ~선 a belt (loop) line; a circular railway / ~경기 a business cycle / 경기 ~설 the cycle theory.

순회(巡廻) a round; a patrol; a tour (of inspection). ~하다 go (walk) round; go one's rounds; patrol. ¶ ~강연 a lecturing tour / ~공연 a road show; a show on tour / ~구역 one's beat (round) / ~대사 a roving ambassador / ~도서관 (진료소) a traveling library (clinic) / ~재판소 a circuit court.

순후하다(淳厚―) (be) pure-minded; warm-hearted.

숟가락 a spoon. ¶ ~으로 뜨다 spoon up / 한 ~의 설탕 a spoonful of sugar.

술 《음료》 liquor (독한 술); wine(포도주); alcohol; spirits; alcoholic drink (beverage)(알코올 음료); 《

술 국술) rice wine; sul. ¶ 독한 [약한] ~ a strong [weak] wine / ~김에 under the influence of liquor / ~김에 하는 싸움 a drunken brawl / ~ 버릇이 나쁘다 be a bad drunk / ~로 시름을 달래다 drown care in wine bowl; drink down one's cares / ~에 물을 타다 mix [dilute] (whisky) with water; water wine (down) / ~을 만들다 brew rice wine [liquor] / ~을 마시다 drink (alcohol, sul) / ~을 끊다 give up drinking; abstain from drinking / ~에 취하다 get drunk; become intoxicated / ~이 세다 [약하다] be a heavy [poor] drinker. / ~값 drink money / ~고래 [꾼] a heavy drinker; a drunkard / ~주정뱅이 a sot; a drunkard / ~친구 a drinking pal. 「fringe.
술² (장식용의) a tassel; a tuft; a
술 (戌) the zodiacal sign of the dog. ‖ ~년 the Year of the Dog. 「on sul.
술구더기 a grain of rice floating
술래 a tagger; a hoodman (눈을 가린); (You are) it. 「seek.
술래잡기 (play) tag; hide-and-
술렁거리다 be disturbed [noisy]; be astir; be in commotion.
술망나니 a (confirmed) drunkard; a sot.
술법 steamed-rice for brewing.
술법 (術法) magic; witchcraft; con-
술병 (一甁) a liquor bottle. 「jury.
술상 (一床) a drinking table; a table for drink. ¶ ~을 차리다 prepare dishes for drink; set a drinking table.
술수 (術數) ① ☞ 술법. ② ☞ 술책.
술술 (순조롭게) smoothly; without a hitch; (유창하게) (speak) fluently; facilely; (쉽게) easily; readily; (바람이) gently; softly. ¶ 어려운 문제를 ~ 풀다 solve a hard question easily.
술어 (述語) [文] a predicate.
술어 (術語) a technical term. ¶ 의학상의 ~ medical terms.
술자리 (give) a drinking party; (hold) a banquet.
술잔 (一盞) a wine cup; a wineglass. ¶ ~을 돌리다 pass the wine cup round / ~을 비우다 drain (drink off) one's cup / ~을 주고받다 exchange cups of wine (with).
술집 a bar; a tavern; a saloon (美); a public house (英). ‖ ~여자 a bar girl / ~주인 a barkeeper.
술책 (術策) a trick; an artifice; a stratagem; tactics. ¶ ~을 부리다 use a cunning trick; resort to tricks / ~에 걸리다 fall into the trap (of the enemy); be entrapped (by).

술추렴하다 share the expense of drinking; club the expense together to pay for drinking.
술타령 (一打令) ¶ ~하다 indulge in drinking; ask for nothing but liquor.
술통 (一桶) a wine cask [barrel].
술파제 (一劑) a sulfa drug; sulfas.
술회 (述懷) ~하다 speak reminiscently; relate one's thoughts [reminiscences]; reminisce.
숨 a breath; breathing (호흡). ¶ ~을 헐떡이며 out of breath; breathlessly / ~을 거두다 breathe one's last / ~을 죽이다 hold one's breath / ~을 돌리다 take breath; take a pause (쉬다).
숨결 breathing. ¶ ~이 가쁘다 breathe hard; be short of breath (환자가) / 봄의 ~을 느끼다 feel a breath of spring.
숨구멍 (숨통) the trachea; the windpipe.
숨기다 (모습·사물) hide; conceal; cover (up); put (something) out of sight; (비밀로) keep (a matter) secret [back] (from). ¶ 나이를 ~ conceal one's age / 잘못을 ~ cover one's mistake / 문 뒤에 몸을 ~ hide oneself behind the door / 감정을 ~ conceal [hide] one's feelings / 본색을 ~ wear [put on] a mask. 「reserve.
숨김없이 frankly; openly; without
숨다 (안 보이게) hide [conceal] oneself; disappear; (피신) take [seek] refuge (in). ¶ 숨은 hidden (meaning); unknown (genius) / 숨어서 out of sight; in secret (몰래) / 숨은 재주 one's hidden talents / 숨은 자선가 an anonymous philanthropist / 침대 밑에 ~ hide oneself under the bed.
숨막히다 be suffocated; be choked. ¶ 숨막히는 stuffy; stifling; suffocating; breath-taking (game).
숨바꼭질 (play) hide-and-seek; I spy; hy-spy. 「☞ 숨.
숨소리 the sound of breathing.
숨숨하다 be pockmarked.
숨쉬다 breathe; take [draw] a breath.
숨지다 breathe one's last; die.
숨차다 pant; be out [short] of breath; be breathless.
숨통 (一筒) the windpipe.
숫기 (一氣) ¶ ~없는 shy; coy; self-conscious / ~좋은 unabashed; unashamed; bold.
숫돌 (sharpen on) a whetstone; a grindstone. 「minded; naive.
숫되다 (be) innocent; simple-

숫자(數字) a figure; a numeral. ¶세자리 ~ three figures / 천문학적 ~ astronomical figures / ~적으로 numerically / ~상의 착오 a numerical error / ~로 나타내다 express in figures.

숫제(차라리) rather (than); preferably; from the first. 〔naive.

숫지다 (be) simple and honest;

숫처녀(─處女) a maiden; a maid.

숫총각(─總角) an innocent bachelor; a (male) virgin.

숭고(崇高) ¶ ~한 lofty; noble; sublime / ~한 이상 a lofty idea.

숭굴숭굴하다(생김새가) (be) chubby; plump; (성질이) (be) well-rounded; bland; suave; affable; amiable. ¶숭굴숭굴한 얼굴 a chubby face / 숭굴숭굴한 태도 smooth (bland) manners.

숭늉 water boiled with scorched rice.

숭덩숭덩 ¶ ~ 자르다 chop thickly (in large parts).

숭배(崇拜) worship; adoration. ~ 하다 worship; admire; adore; idolize. ‖ ~자 a worshipper; an adorer / 영웅 (조상) ~ hero (ancestor) worship.

숭상(崇尙) ~하다 respect; esteem; venerate; revere.

숭숭 ① ☞ 숭덩숭덩. ② (바느질) with large stitches; coarsely.

숭어(魚) a gray mullet.

숭엄(崇嚴) ~한 solemn; majestic; sublime.

숯 charcoal. ¶ ~을 굽다 burn (make) charcoal / ~불을 피우다 make fire with charcoal / ~내를 맡다 inhale carbonic gas. ‖ ~가마 a charcoal kiln (oven) / ~등걸 charcoal cinders / ~머리 a headache caused by carbonic gas / ~불 (검정) charcoal fire (soot) / ~장수 a charcoal dealer / (얼굴이 검은 사람) a dark-faced person.

숱 thickness; density. ¶ ~이 많은 머리 thick hair / 머리 ~이 적다 have thin hair.

숱하다 (be) many; much; numerous; plentiful.

숲 ☞ 수풀. ¶소나무 ~ a pine grove. / ~길 a forest path.

쉬¹(파리 알) a flyblow. ¶ ~슬다 flyblow.

쉬²(미구에) soon; shortly; before long; (쉽게) easily; readily.

쉬³(조용히) Hush!; Sh! (=Be quiet!)

쉬다¹(상하다) spoil; go bad; turn sour (우유 따위가). ¶쉰내 a stale (sourish) smell / 쉰 밥 spoiled rice.

쉬다²(목이) get (grow) hoarse; become husky; hoarsen. ¶쉰 목소리 (in) a hoarse (husky) voice.

쉬다³(휴식·휴양하다) rest; take (have) a rest; relax. ¶ ~ 잠시 ~ take a rest (break) from *one's* work / 쉬지 않고 아침부터 밤까지 일하다 work without rest from morning till night / 바빠서 쉴 틈이 없다 I'm so busy (that) I have no time to rest. ‖ 열중 쉬어 (구령) Stand at ease!; (결근·결석하다) be absent from (*school*); cut (*a class*); take a day off; absent *oneself* (*from*); stay away from (*work*). ¶일요일에는 쉰다 We get Sunday off. / 그녀는 3일간이나 일을 쉬고 있다 She has stayed away from work for three days. ③ (중단하다) suspend; pause. ¶ 불경기로 장사를 ~ suspend business due to the recession. ④ (잠자다) sleep; go to bed. ¶이제 늦었으니 쉬도록 하자 It's getting late. Let's go to bed.

쉬다⁴(숨을) breathe; take breath.

쉬쉬하다 (숨기다) keep (*a matter*) secret; cover (*a fact*); hide (*from*); hush up (*a scandal*).

쉬엄쉬엄 with frequent rests; (do a job) at an easy (slow) pace. ¶ ~ 일하다 work taking frequent breaks; do a job in easygoing manners.

쉬지근하다 (음식이) (be) quite stale-smelling; smells like rotten.

쉬파리 a blowfly; a bluebottle.

쉬하다 (오줌 누다) piddle; piss.

쉰 fifty.

쉴새없이 incessantly; continuously; continually; unceasingly; without a break.

쉼표(─標) (樂) a rest; a pause. ‖ 온 (2분, 4분) ~ a whole (half, quarter) rest.

쉽다 ① (용이) (be) easy; simple; light; plain. ¶쉽게 easily; simply / 쉬운 일 an easy task; easy (light) work / 쉬운 영어 (write in) easy (plain) English / 아주 쉬운 as easy as ABC / 쉽게 말하면 in plain language (words) / 깨지기 ~ break easily; be apt to break. ② (경향) (be) apt (liable, prone) to; tend to (*do*). ¶잘못을 저지르기 ~ be apt to make an err / 감기 들기 ~ be liable to catch cold; be susceptible to a cold. 〔ficulty.

쉽사리 easily; readily; without dif-

슈미즈 a chemise. 「*crème* (프).

슈크림 a cream puff; *chou à la*

슈퍼마켓 a supermarket.

슛 (구기에) shooting; a shot. ~하다 shoot (*a ball*).

스낵 (have, eat) a snack. ‖ ~바 a snack bar.

스냅사진 (—寫眞) a snap(shot). ¶ ~을 찍다 take a snapshot 《of》.

스님 (중) a Buddhist priest (monk); a bonze; 《경칭》 the Reverend.

스라소니 〖動〗 a lynx; a bobcat.

…스럽다 (be) like; seem; -(a)ble; -ous; -ish. ¶ 바보~ be foolish / 촌~ be boorish; looks awkward.

스르르 smoothly; easily; softly.

스리랑카 Sri Lanka.

스릴 thrill. ¶ ~을 느끼다 have a thrill from 《a game》.

스마트 ~한 smart; stylish.

스매싱 〖테니스·탁구〗 smashing; a smash. ~하다 smash. 〖creepy〗.

스멀거리다 itch; be itchy; feel

스모그 smog. ¶ ~가 심한 smoggy; smog-laden 《city》.

스무 twenty; the twentieth.

스물 twenty; a score.

스미다 soak (penetrate, infiltrate) 《into》; permeate through. ¶ 스며 나오다 ooze 〔seep〕 out / 물이 바닥으로 스며들었다 The water soaked through the floor.

스스럼 ~ 없이 unreservedly; freely; without reserve 〔constraint〕; without ceremony 〔~ 없이 이야기하다 talk in a familiar way; speak without restraint〕.

스스럽다 ① 《조심스럽다》 be ill at ease, feel constrained 〔awkward〕. ② 《부끄럽다》 (be) shy; coy.

스스로 (for) oneself; in person. ¶ ~의 one's own; personal / ~ 결정하다 decide 《a matter》 for oneself.

스승 a teacher; a master. ¶ ~의 은혜 the favors of one's teacher / ~으로 받들다 look up to 《a person》 as a teacher.

스웨덴 Sweden. ¶ ~의〔말〕 Swedish / ~ 사람 a Swede.

스웨터 (knit) a sweater.

스위스 Switzerland. ¶ ~의 Swiss / ~ 제의 《a watch》 of Swiss make; Swiss-made / ~ 사람 a Swiss.

스위치 a switch. ¶ ~를 켜다 (끄다) switch on (off).

스윙 ① 〖樂〗 swing (music). ② 〖스포츠〗 a swing. ~하다 swing 《a club》.

스쳐보다 cast a sidelong glance at; glance sidewise at.

스치다 graze; skim; flit(생각 등이); 《살짝 닿다》 touch; feel; 《서로 스쳐지나가다》 pass each other; meet 《on the road》; brush past. ¶ 수면을 스칠 듯이 날다 skim the surface of the water / 총알이 그의 오른팔을 스쳤다 A bullet grazed his right arm. / 소녀는 스쳐지나며 나에게 미소를 지었다 The girl smiled at me as we passed each other. / 의심스런 생각이 그의 뇌리를 스쳤다 A suspicion flitted across his mind.

스카우트 a scout. ~하다 scout 《a promising player》; recruit 《new members》.

스카이다이빙 skydiving. ¶ ~(을) 하다 skydive.

스카치 ~ 〔위스키〕 Scotch (whisky) / ~테이프 Scotch tape.

스카프 a scarf.

스칸디나비아 Scandinavia. ¶ ~의 Scandinavian / ~ 사람 a Scandinavian.

스캔들 a scandal.

스커트 a skirt. ¶ ~를 입다 (벗다) put on 〔take off〕 one's skirt. ‖ 롱~ a long skirt.

스컹크 a skunk.

스케이트 〖動〗 a skate.

스케이트 skating; 《구두》 (a pair of) skates. ¶ ~ 타다 skate; do skating / ~ 타러 가다 go skating. ‖ ~장 (skating) rink; an ice rink / 스피드 ~ speed skating.

스케일 《규모》 a scale. ¶ ~이 큰 〔작은〕 large-(small-)scaled / ~이 큰 〔작은〕 사람 a man of large (small) scale.

스케줄 (make) a schedule 〔plan, program〕. ¶ ~대로 as scheduled; on schedule / 꽉 짜인 a crowded 〔tight〕 schedule / ~을 짜다 make (map, lay) out a schedule 《for, of》.

스케치 a sketch; sketching. ~하다 sketch; make a sketch of 《a thing》. ‖ ~북 a sketchbook.

스코어 a score. ¶ 2대 1의 ~로 by (a score of) 2 to 1. ‖ ~보드 a scoreboard.

스코틀랜드 Scotland. ¶ ~의 〔말〕 Scotch; Scottish / ~사람 a Scotchman; a Scot; the Scotch (총칭).

스콜 〖열대 지방의〗 a squall.

스콜라철학 (—哲學) Scholasticism.

스쿠버 a scuba. ¶ ~다이빙 scuba diving / 스킨~ skin scuba.

스쿠터 a (motor) scooter.

스쿠프 《특종》 a scoop; a beat 《英》. ~ 하다 scoop 《the piece of news》; get a scoop.

스쿨 a school. ¶ ~버스 a school bus.

스쿼시 (lemon) squash.

스퀴즈 〖野〗 a squeeze play.

스크랩북 a scrapbook.

스크럼 a scrum(mage); a scrimmage. ¶ ~을 짜다 form 〔line up for〕 a scrummage; scrimmage.

스크린 a screen; the screen 《영화계》. ‖ ~테스트 a screen test.

스키 skiing; 《a pair of》 skis. ~ 타다 ski. / ~ 타러 가다 go skiing. ‖ ~복 〔화〕 a ski suit 〔boots〕 / ~장 a skiing ground.

스킨다이빙 skin diving.

스타 a star; a cinema 〔film〕 star.

스타디움 ¶~가 되다 become a star; enter stardom. ‖ 일류~ a star of the first class.

스타디움 [first class.

스타일 (옷의) a style; (모습) one's figure (form); (방식) one's style. ¶ ~이 좋다 [나쁘다] have a good [poor] figure / 최신 ~ the latest style. ‖ ~북 a stylebook.

스타카토 [樂] staccato.

스타킹 (nylon) stockings. ¶ 올이 풀리지 않는 ~ runproof (ladderproof) stockings.

스타트 a start. ~하다 (make a) start. ¶ ~가 좋다 [나쁘다] start well [ill]; make a good [bad] start. ‖ ~라인 a starting line.

스태미나 stamina. ¶ ~를 기르다 develop (build up) one's stamina.

스탠드 ① (관람석) the stands; bleachers (美) (지붕 없는). ② (전등) a desk (floor) lamp.

스탬프 a stamp; a datemark (일부인); a postmark (소인). ¶ ~를 찍다 stamp (a card).

스턴트 stunt. ¶ ~맨 a stunt man.

스테레오 a stereo. ¶ ~의 stereo (-phonic) ‖ ~로 듣다 listen on the stereo. ‖ ~녹음 stereo(phonic) recording / ~레코드 (디스크, 테이프) a stereo (phonic) record (disc, tape) / ~방송 stereo (-phonic) broadcasting / ~전축 a stereo (phonograph).

스테로이드 steroid.

스테이지 the stage.

스테이크 a (beef) steak.

스테인리스스틸 stainless steel.

스텐실 a stencil. [step; dance.

스텝 (춤의) a step. ¶ ~을 밟다

스토리 story. ¶ ~가 별로 없는 소설 a novel with not much of a plot

스토브 a stove (heater). [story.

스토아 ‖ ~주의 Stoicism / ~학파 the Stoic school.

스톡 (재고) a stock.

스톱 stop. ‖ ~사인 a stop sign / ~워치 a stop-watch.

스튜디오 a studio. [air) hostess.

스튜어디스 a stewardess; a (an

스트라이크 ① (파업) a strike; a walkout. ¶ ~중이다 be on strike / ~를 중지하다 call off a strike. ② (野) a strike.

스트레스 (dispel) a stress. ¶ ~가 많은 stressful (situations) / ~에 의한 궤양 a stress ulcer / ~가 쌓이다 stress builds up / ~를 풀다 'get rid of (ease) stress (by playing tennis).

스트레이트 straight. ¶ ~로 이기다 win a straight victory (over) / 오른쪽 ~을 얻어 맞다 take a right straight (to the jaw) / ~로 위스키를 마시다 drink whisky straight.

스트렙토마이신 [藥] streptomycin.

스트로 (suck through) a straw.

스트리킹 streaking.

스트립쇼 a strip show.

스틸 (강철) steel; (영화의) a still (photograph).

스팀 steam; (난방) steam heating. ¶ ~을 넣은 steam-heated

스파게티 spaghetti (이). [room).

스파르타 Sparta. ‖ ~식의 Spartan (training).

스파링 [拳] sparring. ‖ ~파트너 one's sparring partner.

스파이 a spy; a secret agent. ¶ ~노릇을 하다 (act as) spy / 산업 ~ an industrial spy / 이중 ~ a double agent. ‖ ~망 an espionage chain / ~비행 aerial spying / ~활동 (행위) spying; espionage.

스파이크 a spike; (구두) spiked shoes; (배구의) spiking; a spike.

스파크 a spark. ~하다 spark. ‖ ~플러그 a spark plug.

스패너 a wrench; a spanner.

스펀지 (a) sponge. ‖ ~고무 sponge rubber. [tire.

스페어 a spare. ‖ ~타이어 a spare

스페인 Spain. ¶ ~의 [말] Spanish / ~사람 a Spaniard; the Spanish (총칭).

스펙터클 a spectacle. ‖ ~영화 a spectacular film.

스펙트럼 a spectrum. ‖ ~분석 spectrum analysis.

스펠(링) (철자) spelling.

스포츠 sports. ¶ ~를 좋아하는 sports-minded (youth). ‖ ~계 the sporting world / ~난 a sports section / ~맨 a sportsman / ~방송 sportscasting; a sportscast (1회) / ~지 a sports paper / ~웨어 sportswear / ~의학 sports medicine / ~정신 sportsmanship / ~카 a sports car. [(on).

스포트라이트 (focus) a spotlight

스폰서 a sponsor. ¶ ~가 되다 sponsor (a concert).

스폿 spot. ‖ ~뉴스 (방송) spot news (broadcasting).

스프링 (용수철) a spring. ‖ ~보드 a springboard.

스프링코트 a topcoat.

스프링클러 a sprinkler.

스피드 speed. ‖ ~광 a speed maniac / ~시대 the age of

스피츠 [動] a spitz (dog). [speed.

스피커 (확성기) a (loud) speaker; (라디오의) a radio speaker.

스핑크스 a sphinx. [the kneecap.

슬개골 (膝蓋骨) [解] the kneepan;

슬그머니 stealthily; secretly; by stealth. ¶ ~나가다 (들어가다) steal out of (into) (a room).

슬금슬금 stealthily; sneakingly.

슬기 wisdom; intelligence; sagacity; resources. ¶ ~롭다 (be)

wise; intelligent; intellectual; sagacious.
슬다 ① 《알을》 oviposit《곤충이》; blow《파리가》; spawn《물고기가》. ② 《녹이》 gather《form》 rust; be rusted; get rusty; rust.
슬라브 Slav. ¶ ~말 Slavic / ~민족 the Slavs / ~사람 a Slav.
슬라이드 《환등》 a (lantern) slide. ¶칼라 ~ a color slide.
슬라이딩 [野] sliding.
슬랙스 (a girl in) slacks.
슬랭 slang; a slang word.
슬럼 a slum. ¶대도시의 ~가 화하다 the slums of a big city / ~화하다 turn into slums.
슬럼프 a slump. ¶ ~에 빠지다 《에서 벗어나다》 get into (out of) a slump.
슬레이트 [建字] a slate. ¶ ~ 지붕 이다 slate a roof. ¶ ~로 지은 slate a roof.
슬로 slow. ¶ ~ 모션 (영화·TV의) a slow motion (picture).
슬로건 a slogan; a motto. ¶ …하는 ~으로 under the slogan of….
슬로바키아 the Slovak Republic.
슬로프 a slope.
슬리퍼 (a pair of) slippers.
슬며시 secretly; quietly; stealthily.
슬슬 ① 《가볍게》 softly; gently; lightly. ② 《온건히》 cajolingly. ¶ ~ 달래다 soothe 《a person》; appease.
슬쩍 ① 《몰래》 secretly; stealthily. ② 《쉽게》 lightly; easily; readily.
슬퍼하다 feel sad (unhappy); feel sorry (sorrow) 《for》; grieve; 《죽음을》 mourn 《for, over》; 《한탄하다》 lament. ¶ 아무의 불행을 ~ feel sorry for a person's misfortune / …은 슬퍼할 일이다 It is a pity that… / 아무의 죽음을 ~ grieve (mourn) over a person's death.
슬프다 (be) sad; sorrowful; pathetic. ¶ 슬프도다 Alas!; Woe is (to) me!
슬픔 sorrow; sadness; grief. ¶ ~에 잠기다 be in deep grief.
슬피 sadly; sorrowfully; mournfully. ¶ ~ 울다 cry sadly.
슬하(膝下) the parental care. ¶부모 ~에서 자라다 grow up under one's parental roof (care) / 부모 ~를 떠나다 leave one's paternal roof; live away from one's parents.
습격(襲擊) an attack; an assault. ~하다 attack; assault.
습관(習慣) habit (습성); practice (습성인); usage (관용); custom (풍속); a convention (인습). ¶ ~적인 customary; habitual; conventional / 평소의 ~ one's habitual ways / ~을 들이다 form a (good) habit / …하는 ~이 있다 have (be in) the habit of doing. ¶ ~성 의약품 habit-forming drugs.

습기(濕氣) damp(ness); moisture; humidity.
습도(濕度) humidity. ¶ ~는 현재 80퍼센트이다 The humidity is 80 percent at present. ¶ ~계 a hygrometer.
습득(拾得) ~하다 pick up; find. ¶ ~물을 하다 find; a found article / ~자 a finder.
습득(習得) ~하다 learn 《French》; acquire 《an art》.
습득(習得) a habit; one's way.
습성(濕性) wet. ¶ ~ 늑막염 [醫] moist (wet) pleurisy.
습자(習字) (practice) penmanship; calligraphy (붓씨). ¶ ~책 a writing (copy) book.
습작(習作) a study; étude (프).
습작하다(襲爵―) succeed to the title (peerage).
습전지(濕電池) a galvanic battery.
습지(濕地) damp ground; marsh; swampland. [濕] (humid) tetter.
습진(濕疹) [醫] eczema; moist
습하다(濕―) (be) damp; humid; moist; wet.
승(勝) a victory. ¶ 3－1패, 3. victories (wins) and (against) 1 defeat.
…승(乘) -seater. ¶ 5인~ 비행기 a 5-seater (air)plane / 9인 ~ 자동차 a nine-passenger car.
승강(昇降) ~하다 go up and down; ascend and descend. ¶ ~구 an entrance; a hatch (-way) / ~기 an elevator 《美》; a lift 《英》.
승강이(昇降－) 《티격태격》 (have) a petty quarrel; wrangling. ~하다 wrangle 《with》.
승객(乘客) a passenger. ¶ 100명 이상의 ~을 태운 비행기가 산 속에 추락했다 A plane carrying over one hundred passengers crashed into the mountain. ¶ ~명부 a passenger list.
승격(昇格) ~하다 be promoted (raised) to a higher status.
승계(承繼) succession. ☞ 계승.
승급(昇級) promotion. ~하다 be promoted 《to》. ☞ 승진.
승급(昇給) a raise (rise) in salary; a raise 《美》. ¶ ~시키다 increase a person's salary.
승낙(承諾) consent; assent; agreement. ~하다 say yes; consent (agree, assent) 《to》; comply 《with》.
승냥이 [動] a Korean wolf; a coyote.
승단(昇段) promotion. ~하다 be promoted 《to a higher grade》.
승려(僧侶) 중.
승률(勝率) the percentage of victories; the chance of success.
승리(勝利) a victory; a triumph. ~하다 win; win (gain) a victo-

ry. ¶ 최후의 ~를 얻다 gain the final victory. ∥ ~자 a victor; a winner(경기의) / ~투수 the winning pitcher.
승마(乘馬) horse riding. ~하다 ride (mount) a horse. ∥ ~바지 (화) riding breeches (boots) / ~복 a riding suit / ~술 horsemanship / ~클럽 a riding club.
승무(僧舞) a Buddhist dance.
승무원(乘務員) a crew member; a crewman; the crew(총칭). ¶ 비행기의 여자 ~ a stewardess; an air hostess.
승방(僧房) a Buddhist nunnery.
승복(承服) ~하다 《동의하다》 agree (consent) 《to》; 《받아들이다》 accept. ¶ ~할 수 없는 조건 unacceptable terms (conditions).
승복(僧服) a clerical (priest's) robe.
승부(勝負) victory or defeat;《경기》 a 《tennis》 match; a game. ¶ 단판 ~ a game of single round / ~를 짓다 fight to the finish / ~에 이기다 (지다) win (lose) a game / ~는 끝났다 The game is over (up). ∥ ~차기 a shoot-out.
승산(勝算) prospects of victory; chances of success. ¶ ~ 없는 hopeless to win / ~이 있다 (없다) have a (no) chance of success.
승상(丞相) ☞ 정승(政丞). 〔cess.
승선(乘船) embarkation; boarding. ~하다 embark; go aboard; get on board (a ship). 〔(case).
승소(勝訴) ~하다 win a suit
승수(乘數) 《數》《곱수》 a multiplier.
승승장구(乘勝長驅) ~하다 keep on winning.
승압기(昇壓器) a step-up (boosting) transformer; a booster.
승용차(乘用車) a (passenger) car. ¶ 4인승 ~ a four-seater car / 고급 ~ a delux car.
승원(僧院) a Buddhist monastery; a cloister; a temple.
승인(承認) recognition; acknowledgment; admission; approval (인가). ~하다 recognize; admit; approve. ¶ ~을 얻다 obtain approval / 자동 ~ 품목 immediate import liberal items. ∥ ~서 a written acknowledgment.
승자(勝者) a winner; a victor.
승적(僧籍) (enter) the priesthood; the holy orders.
승전(勝戰) ~하다 win a war (battle). ∥ ~고(鼓) the drum of victory. 〔division.
승제(乘除) 《數》 multiplication and
승직(僧職) the priesthood; the clerical profession.
승진(昇進) promotion; advancement. ~하다 rise (in rank); be promoted (advanced). ¶ ~시키다 promote; raise.
승차(乘車) ~하다 take a train (taxi); get on a train (bus); get in a car. ¶ ~거부를 하다 refuse to accept passengers. ∥ ~구 the entrance to a platform; the gate; a way-in / ~권 a ticket / ~권 매표소 a ticket window / 할인 ~권 a reduced-rate ticket.
승천(昇天) ascension to heaven; 《그리스도의》 the Ascension. ~하다 go (ascend) to heaven. ∥ ~축일 the Ascension Day.
승패(勝敗) victory or defeat. ¶ ~를 다투다 contend for victory.
승하(昇遐) demise. ~하다 die; pass away. 〔다 sublimate.
승화(昇華) 《化》 sublimation. ~하
시(市) a city; a town; a municipality (행정구획). ¶ ~의 municipal; city. ∥ ~당국 the city (municipal) authorities.
시(時) 《시각》 hour; 《시각》 o'clock; time. ¶ 8~ eight o'clock / 3~ 15분 a quarter past three / 2~ 20분이다 It is twenty minutes past (after) two. / 5~ 5분 전이다 It is five minutes to (of) five.
시(詩) poetry (총칭); verse (운문); 《write, compose》 a poem.
시가(市街) the streets; a city. ∥ ~전 street fighting / ~지 a city (an urban) area / ~지도 a city map.
시가(市價) the market price. ∥ ~변동 market fluctuations.
시가(時價) the current price. ¶ ~로 팔다 sell 《something》 at the current (market) price.
시가(媤家) 시집 同一.
시가(詩歌) poetry; poems and songs. ∥ ~선집 an anthology.
시가 a cigar.
시각(時刻) time; hour.
시각(視角) the visual angle.
시각(視覺) (the sense of) sight; vision; eyesight. ∥ ~교육(교재) visual education (aids) / ~기관 an organ of vision / ~언어 (a) visual language / ~예술 visual arts.
시간(時間) time; 《학교의》 a lesson; a class. ¶ ~과 공간 time and space / 영어 ~ an English lesson (class) / 제~에 on time / ~에 늦다 be late; be behind time / ~을 벌다 buy (gain) time; use delaying tactics / ~을 지키다 be punctual / ~제로 일하다 work by the hour / ~이 (많이) 걸리다 take (much) time / ~에 쫓기다 be pressed for time. ∥ ~강사 a part-time lecturer / ~급 hourly wages;

시경(詩經) the Book of Odes.
시경찰서(市警察署) 지방경찰서.
시계(時計) a watch; a clock (괘종, 탁상시계) / ~ 로 ones watch 《by the time signal》 / ~ 방향으로 돌리다 turn clockwise / ~ 반대방향으로 counterclockwise. ‖ ~ 탑 a clock tower / ~ 포 a watch store 《美》; a watchmaker's 《英》 / 시곗바늘 the hands of a watch / 시곗소리 the ticking of a clock / 시곗줄 a watchband (목시계) / ~ 팔찌 a wrist watch / 자동 ~ a self-winding watch.
시계(視界) the field [range] of vision; the visual field. ¶ ~ 에서 사라지다 go out of sight [view] / ~ 에 들어오다 come into sight [view]. ‖ ~ 비행 ☞ 유시계 비행.
시골 the country(side); a rural district (고향) one's home [native] village. ¶ ~ 의 country; rural / ~ 에서 자란 country-bred; rustic / ~ 로 은퇴하다 retire into the country. ‖ ~ 구석 a remote village; a secluded place / ~ 길 a country lane [road] / ~ 뜨기 a rustic; a country bumpkin / ~ 말 (사투리) a provincial dialect / ~ 사람 a countryman; a countryfolk / ~ 생활 (a) country life / ~ 풍경 rural scenery.
시공(施工) execution (of works). ~ 하다 undertake construction; construct 《a building》; carry out 《building works》. ‖ ~ 도 a drawing / ~ 자 a (main) constructor.
시구(始球) ~ 하다 throw [pitch] the first ball. ¶ …의 ~ 로 with the first ball pitched by…
시구(詩句) a verse; a stanza.
시국(時局) the situation; the state of things (affairs). ¶ ~ 의 추이 the development of the situation / 어려운 ~ 을 수습하다 settle [straighten out] a difficult situation / ~ 에 대처하다 deal [cope] with the situation. ‖ 중대 ~ a critical juncture.
시굴(試掘) 《鑛》 prospecting; (a) trial digging (boring). ~ 하다 prospect 《a mine》; bore (drill) for 《oil》. ‖ ~ 권 prospecting rights / ~ 자 a (mine) prospector; a wildcater 《美》 / ~ 정(井) 《석유의》 a test (trial) well. 「a sewer.
시궁창 a ditch; a gutter; a drain;
시그널 a 《traffic》 signal.
시극(詩劇) a poetical drama (play).

시근거리다 《숨을》 pant; gasp; 《뼈마디가》 twinge; tingle; smart.
시글시글 in swarms. 「ache.
시금떨떨하다 (be) sourish and astringent. 「test.
시금석(試金石) a touchstone; a
시금치 spinach.
시급(時給) hourly wages (pay).
시급(時急) ¶ ~ 한 urgent; imminent.
시기(時期) time; a period; season (계절). ¶ 이 중대한 ~ 에 at this crucial period / 매년 이 ~ 에 at this time of (the) year.
시기(時機) a chance; (miss) an opportunity; an occasion (경우). ¶ ~ 에 적합한 opportune; timely; appropriate; well-timed / ~ 를 기다리다 wait for an opportunity / ~ 를 포착하다 take (seize) an opportunity / ~ 를 놓치다 lose an opportunity; miss one's chance / 아직은 그 ~ 가 아니다 The time is not quite ripe for it.
시기(猜忌) jealousy; green envy. ~ 하다 be jealous (envious) 《of》; envy. 「black.
시꺼멓다 (be) deep black; jet-
시끄럽다 ① 《소란함》 (be) noisy; clamorous; boisterous. ¶ 시끄럽게 noisily; clamorously / 시끄러워 Be quiet!; Silence! / 시끄러운 이 be much discussed. ② 《세론이》 be much discussed. ¶ 시끄러운 세상 the troublous world / 시끄러운 문제가 되다 become a subject of much discussion.
시나리오 a scenario; a screenplay. ‖ ~ 작가 a scenario writer; a scenarist; a scriptwriter.
시내 a brook(let); a rivulet; a stream(let). ‖ ~ 가 the edge (bank) of a stream / 시냇물 the waters of a brook.
시내(市內) ¶ ~ 에(서) in the city; within the city limits. ‖ ~ 거주자 a city resident / ~ 관광 sightseeing in the city / ~ 버스 an urban bus / ~ 통화 a local (city) call / ~ 판 a city edition.
시네라마 a Cinerama (상표명).
시네마 a cinema. ‖ ~ 스코프 a CinemaScope (상표명).
시녀(侍女) a waiting maid [woman]; a lady-in-waiting (궁녀).
시누이(-님) one's husband's sister; a sister-in-law.
시늉(흉내) mimicry; imitation (모방); 《체함》 pretense. ~ 하다 mimic; imitate; copy (체하다) feign; pretend. ¶ 어른 ~ 을 하다 imitate adults / 죽은 ~ 을 하다 pretend to be dead.
시다 ① 《맛이》 (be) sour; acid; tart. ¶ 시어지다 turn sour / 신맛이 나다 taste sour. ② 《뼈마디가》

시단 (詩壇) poetical circles.
시달 (示達) ~하다 instruct; give directions.
시달리다 be troubled (annoyed, harassed, vexed, tormented) 《with, by》; be ill-treated; suffer 《from》. ¶ 가난에 ~ be distressed by poverty / 압제에 ~ groan under oppression / 밤새도록 기침에 ~ be troubled with a bad cough all through the night / 갈증에 ~ be tormented by thirst / 빚에 ~ be harassed with debts / 아이들에게 ~ be worn to a frazzle by one's children.
시대 (時代) 《시기》 a period; an epoch; an age; an era; 《시절》 one's day(s); 《시세》 the times. ¶ 우주 여행의 ~ the age of space travel / 봉건 ~ the era of feudalism / 빙하 ~ the glacial period (age) / 아버지 ~에는 in my father's days / ~에 뒤떨어진 behind the times; out-of-date / ~에 역행하다 swim against the current / ~의 요구에 부응하다 meet the needs of the times / 이제 그의 ~도 끝났다 He has had his day. ‖ ~감각 a sense of the times / ~상(相) 〔정신〕 the phases (spirit) of the times / ~착오 an anachronism.
시도 (試圖) an attempt. ~하다 attempt; make an attempt. ¶ 새로운 ~ a new attempt.
시동 (始動) 《기계의》 starting. ~하다 start. ¶ ~을 걸다 set 〔start〕 a machine. ‖ ~장치 a starting device 〔gear, system〕.
시동생 (媤同生) one's husband's younger brother; a brother-in-law.
시들다 ① 《초목이》 wither; droop; fade; be shriveled up; dried-up. ② 《기운이》 weaken; wane. ¶ 인기가 ~ lose popularity.
시들하다 《마음에》 (be) unsatisfactory; 《마음에 없다》 (be) half-hearted; uninterested; 《시시하다》 (be) trivial. ¶ 삶이 시들해지다 lose interest in life.
시래기 dried radish leaves. ‖ 시래깃국 soup cooked with dried radish leaves.
시럽 syrup; sirup 《美》.
시렁 a shelf; a rack 《그물꼴의》.
시력 (視力) (eye)sight; vision. ¶ ~이 좋다 〔약하다〕 have good 〔poor〕 eyesight / ~을 잃다 〔회복하다〕 lose 〔recover〕 one's sight. ‖ ~감퇴 amblyopia / ~검사 an eyesight test / ~(검사)표 an eye-test chart.
시련 (試鍊) a trial; a test; an ordeal. ¶ 가혹한 ~ severe 〔bitter〕 trials / ~을 겪다 be tried 《by》; be tested / ~에 견디다 endure 〔stand〕 the trials 《of life》.
시론 (時論) comments on current events; a current view; public opinion 《of the day》 〔여론〕.
시론 (詩論) poetics; an essay on poetry; a criticism of poems.
시료 (施療) free medical treatment. ~하다 treat 《a person》 free 《of charge》. ‖ ~원 a free clinic; a charity hospital / ~환자 a free patient.
시루 an earthenware steamer. ‖ ~떡 steamed rice cake.
시류 (時流) 《풍조》 the current 〔trend〕 of the times; 《유행》 the fashion of the day. ¶ ~에 따르다 follow the fashion of the day / ~에 순응 〔역행〕하다 go with 〔against〕 the current of the times.
시름 trouble; anxiety; worry; cares. ¶ ~을 놓다 be relieved from worry.
시름없다 ① 《걱정되다》 (be) worried; anxious. ② 《멍하다》 (be) absent-minded; blank. ¶ 시름없이 carelessly; unintentionally; vacantly; absent-mindedly. 〔be cold.
시리다 《손발이》 feel cold 〔freezing〕.
시리아 Syria. ‖ ~사람 a Syrian.
시리즈 a series. ¶ ~로 출판하다 publish in a serial form. ‖ ~물 a serial / 월드~ the World Series.
시립 (市立) ¶ ~의 city; municipal. ‖ ~도서관 a city library / ~병원 a municipal hospital.
시말서 (始末書) a written apology.
시멘트 cement. ¶ ~를 바르다 cement. ‖ ~공장 〔기와, 벽돌〕 a cement factory 〔tile, brick〕.
시무룩하다 (be) sullen; sulky; glum; ill-humored. ¶ 시무룩한 얼굴 a sullen 〔long〕 face.
시무식 (始務式) the opening ceremony of (government) offices (for the year).
시민 (市民) a citizen; the citizens (총칭). ‖ ~권 citizenship / ~대회 a mass meeting of citizens.
시발 (始發) the first departure; the start. ‖ ~역 the starting station.
시범 (示範) a model for others. ~하다 set an example 《to》; show 〔give〕 a good example 《of》. ‖ ~경기 〔play〕 an exhibition game / ~농장 a model farm.
시베리아 Siberia. ‖ ~의 Siberian.
시보 (時報) ① 《시간의 알림》 a time signal. ¶ 시계를 정오 ~에 맞추다 set one's watch by the time signal at noon. ② 《보도》 current news.

시보(試補) a probationer. ¶ 사법관 ~ a judiciary probationer.
시부렁거리다 say useless [pointless] things; prattle.
시부모(媤父母) one's husband's parents; parents-in-law.
시비(市費) municipal expenses; city expenditure(경비).
시비(是非) right and [or] wrong; the propriety (of). ¶ ~를 가리다[논하다] tell right from wrong; discuss the rights and wrongs (of). ∥ ~론 a question of right or wrong.
시비(詩碑) a monument inscribed [with a poem].
시뻘겋다 (be) deep red; crimson. ¶ 시뻘겋게 단 난로 a red-glowing stove.
시사(示唆) suggestion; hint. ~하다 hint; suggest. ¶ ~적인 suggestive / 그 제안은 ~하는 바가 많다 The proposal is full of suggestions.
시사(時事) current events [news]. ∥ ~문제[영어] current topics [English] / ~해설 news commentary; comments on current topics / ~해설가 a news commentator.
시사(試寫) a (film) preview. ~하다 preview. ¶ 영화의 ~회를 개최하다 hold a preview of a motion picture.
시산(試算) (make) a trial calculation. ∥ ~표 a trial balance (sheet).
시삼촌(媤三寸) one's husband's uncle.
시상(施賞) ~하다 award a prize. ∥ ~식 a ceremony of awarding prizes.
시상(詩想) a poetical imagination [sentiment].
시새(우)다 be terribly jealous (of); be green with envy (of).
시선(視線) one's eyes; a glance. ¶ ~을 ~에 돌리다 turn one's eyes upon a person / 아무의 ~을 피하다 avoid a person's gaze / 그들의 ~이 마주쳤다 Their eyes met.
시선(詩選) an anthology; a selection of poems.
시설(施設) an establishment; (특히, 공공의) an institution; (설비) equipment; facilities. ~하다 establish; institute. ¶ 공공 ~ a public facilities / 교육 ~ an educational institution / 군사 ~ military installations / 산업[항만] ~ industrial [port] facilities. ∥ ~투자 investment in equipment.
시성(詩聖) a great poet.
시세(時世) the times.
시세(時勢) ① 〈시대〉 the times; the age; 《시류》 the current [trend] of the times. ② 〈시가〉 the current price; the market (price). ¶ ~의 변동 fluctuations in the mar-

ket / ~가 오르다[내리다] rise [fall] in price. ∥ 개장[폐장] ~ [證] an opening [a closing] quotation / 달러 ~ the exchange rate of the dollar / 쌀 ~ the price of rice; the rice market / 증권 ~ stock quotations [prices] / 최고[최저] ~ the ceiling [bottom] price.
시소 a seesaw. ¶ ~를 타고 놀다 play (at) seesaw. ∥ ~게임 a seesaw game. ∥ ~(times).
시속(時俗) the customs of the age [times].
시속(時速) speed per hour. ¶ ~ 24마일, 24 miles an [per] hour (약호 24 m.p.h.).
시숙(媤叔) one's husband's brother; a brother-in-law.
시술(施術) ~하다 operate; perform an operation. [engineering].
시스템 a system. ∥ ~공학 system **시승**(試乘) a trial ride. ~하다 have a trial ride (in); test (a new plane).
시시(時時) ~로 often; frequently; many [lots of] times.
시시각각(時時刻刻) ~으로 hourly; (in) every hour [moment]; momentarily. [flirt (with).
시시덕거리다 chat and giggle; **시시부지하다** drop into oblivion; drift into obscurity; go up in smoke. ¶ 일을 시시부지 내버려두다 leave a matter unsettled (and do nothing definite about it).
시시비비(是是非非) ~하다 call a spade a spade; call what is right right, and wrong wrong. ∥ ~주의 a free and unbiased policy.
시시콜콜 inquisitively. ¶ ~ 캐묻다 inquire of (a person) about every detail of (a matter); be inquisitive about (a matter).
시시하다 《흥미 없다》 (be) dull and flat; uninteresting; 《사소하다》 (be) trifling; trivial; petty; (be) of little importance; (가치 없다) (be) worthless. ¶ 시시한 것[일] a matter of no importance; a trifling [trivial] thing / 시시한 책 a worthless book / 시시한 녀석 a good-for-nothing / 시시한 말을 하다 talk nonsense.
시식(試食) sampling. ~하다 try; taste; sample (a cake). ∥ ~회 a sampling party.
시신(屍身) a dead body; a corpse.
시신경(視神經) [解] the optic nerve.
시아버지(媤—) a father-in-law; one's husband's father.
시아주버니(媤—) a brother-in-law; one's husband's elder brother.
시안(試案) a tentative plan.
시앗 one's husband's concubine.
시야(視野) a visual field; sight; one's view. ¶ ~에 들어오다 come

시약(試藥) 〖化〗 a (chemical) reagent.

시어(詩語) a poetic word.

시어머니(媤—) a mother-in-law; one's husband's mother.

시업(始業) ~하다 begin (commence) (work). ‖ ~식 an opening ceremony.

시여(施與) ~하다 give (in charity); contribute; give free.

시역(市域) the municipal area; the city limits.

시역(弑逆) the murder of one's lord (parent). ~하다 murder 《one's lord》.

시연(試演) (give) a trial performance; a rehearsal; a preview. ~하다 preview.

시정(市政) municipal management. ¶ ~의 municipal / ~으로 하다 municipalize. ‖ ~버스 a city bus / ~주택 a municipal dwelling house.

시오니즘 Zionism.

시외(市外) the suburbs; the outskirts. ¶ ~의 suburban; out of town. ‖ ~거주자 an out-of-towner / ~국번 an area code / ~전화 (make) a long-distance call 《美》; a trunk call 《英》.

시용(試用) trial. ~하다 try; make a trial 《of》.

시운(時運) the tendency (luck) of the times.

시운전(試運轉) (make) a trial run (trip); a test drive (자동차 등의).

시원섭섭하다 have mixed emotions of joy and sorrow.

시원스럽다 (성격이) frank; unreserved; open-hearted; (동작이) be brisk; lively; active.

시원시원하다 ☞ 시원스럽다.

시원찮다 ① (기분이) (be) not refreshing; dull; heavy. ② (언행 따위가) (be) reserved; not agreeable (cheerful, sprightly). ③ (형세) (be) not satisfactory; unfavorable.

시원하다 ① (선선하다) feel cool (refreshing). ¶ 시원해지다 become cool. ② (후련하다) feel good (relieved); feel a sense of relief (freedom).

시월(十月) October.

시위(활의) a bowstring.

시위(示威) a demonstration. ~하다 demonstrate; hold (stage) a demonstration. ‖ ~적인 demonstrative; threatening. ‖ ~자 a demonstrator.

시유(市有) ¶ ~의 municipal; city-owned / ~화하다 municipalize. ‖ ~재산 municipal property / ~지 city land.

시음(試飮) ~하다 sample 《wine》; try 《a glass of bourbon》. ‖ ~회 a sampling party; a wine-testing. (villages; municipalities.)

시읍면(市邑面) cities, towns and

시의(時宜) ¶ ~에 맞는 timely; opportune / ~에 맞다 be opportune.

시의(猜疑) suspicion (의심); jealousy(질투). ~하다 be suspicious of; distrust; suspect.

시의회(市議會) a municipal (city) assembly. ‖ ~의사당 a municipal assembly hall / ~의원 선거 a municipal election.

시인(是認) approval. ~하다 approve of; admit. (자).

시인(詩人) a poet; a poetess (여

시일(時日) time; (날짜) the date 《of, for》; the days 《of》. ¶ ~ 문제 a question of time / ~을 정하다 fix (set) the date / ~의 경과에 따라 as time passes / ~이 걸리다 require (take) (much) time.

시작(始作) the start; the beginning. ~하다 begin; start; commence. ¶ 사업을 ~하다 start (go into) business / ~하다 begin to do.

시작(試作) trial manufacture (production). ~하다 manufacture (produce) as an experiment. ‖ ~품 a trial product. (a poem.)

시작(詩作) ~하다 write (compose)

시장 ~하다 (be) hungry. ¶ ~기 hungriness (~기를 느끼다 feel empty (hungry)).

시장(市長) a mayor. ¶ 서울 ~ the Mayor of Seoul / ~선거 a mayoral election. ‖ ~직 〔임기〕 mayoralty; mayorship.

시장(市場) a market. ¶ 국내 ~ the home (domestic) market / 외국 〔해외〕 ~ a foreign (overseas) market / 중앙 도매 ~ the central wholesale market / 주식 ~ the stock exchange (market) / 금융 ~ the financial market / 현물 ~ a spot market / 침체된 ~ sick (dull) market / ~에 나오다 (나와 있다) come into (be on) the market / ~에 내다 (put (place)) 《goods》 on the market / ~을 개척하다 cultivate (open up) a market 《for》. ‖ ~가격 a market price (rate) / ~가치 market value / ~개발 market development / ~개방 opening 《Korea's》 markets 《to the world》 / ~개방 정책 market-opening policies (measures) / ~경제 the market economy / ~분석 〔점유율〕 market analysis (share) / ~성 marketability (~성이 없는 unmarketable) / ~조사 market research / ~조작 market operations (manipulation).

시재(詩才) a poetic talent.

시재(詩材) verse material.

시적(詩的) poetic(al). ¶ ~ 감정 a poetic sentiment.

시적거리다 do half-heartedly.

시절(時節) a season; 《시기》 one's time; a chance; 《시세(時世)》 the times. ¶ ~에 맞지 않는 out of season; unseasonable / 그 ~에(는) at that time; in those days / 젊은 ~에 while (one is) young / 학생~에 in one's school days.

시점(時點) a point of [in] time. ¶ 오늘의 ~에서 as of today.

시점(視點) a visual point; 《관점》 a point of view; a viewpoint.

시정(市政) municipal government; city administration.

시정(是正) correction. ~하다 correct; put to right; improve.

시정(施政) government; administration. ‖ ~방침 《decide upon》 an administrative policy / ~연설 a speech on one's administrative policies.　　　[ment].

시정(詩情) poetic feeling 〔sentiment〕.

시정아치(市井—) a market tradesman.　　　[nization].

시제(市制) municipal system 〔orga-

시제(時制) 〖文〗 the tense.

시조(始祖) the founder; the originator; the father 《of》; 《인류의》 ~ the progenitor of the human race.　　　[verse; a shijo.

시조(時調) a Korean ode; Korean

시종(始終) 《부사적》 from beginning to end; all the time; constantly.　　　[in waiting.

시종(侍從) a chamberlain; a lord

시주(施主) 《일》 offering; oblation; almsgiving; 《물건》 an offering; 《사람》 an offerer; a donor. ~하다 offer; donate.

시준(視準) collimation. ‖ ~기 a mercury collimator.

시중 service; attendance; nursing《간호》. ~하다 《들다》 serve; attend; nurse. ‖ ~꾼 an attendant; a nurse《간호인》.

시중(市中) 《in》 the open city 〔streets〕. ‖ ~금리 the open market (interest) rate / ~은행 a city (commercial) bank.

시즌 a season. ¶ ~이 아닌 off-season; out of season / 야구 ~ the baseball season.

시진(視診) an ocular inspection.

시집(媤—) one's husband's home〔family〕. ¶ ~ 가다 be 〔get〕 married 《to》 / ~(을) 보내다 marry 《one's daughter》 off 《to》.

시집(詩集) a collection of poems.

시차(時差) time difference; difference in time. ¶ 8시간의 ~ a eight-hour time difference 《be- tween》 / ~로 인한 피로에 시달리다 suffer from jet lag. ‖《출근》~제 staggered office hours.

시차(視差) 〖天〗 (a) parallax.

시찰(視察) (an) inspection. ~하다 inspect; visit; make an inspection 《of》. ‖ ~단 《send》 an inspecting party / ~여행 an observation trip 《go on》 a tour of inspection.　　　[bond].

시채(市債) a municipal loan

시책(施策) a measure; a policy. ¶ ~을 강구하다 take measures to meet 《the situation》.

시척지근하다 (be) sourish.

시청(市廳) a city 〔municipal〕 office; a city hall.

시청(視聽) seeing and hearing. ‖ ~각 the visual and auditory senses / ~각 교육 〔교재〕 audio-visual education 〔aids〕 / ~료 TV subscription fee / ~률 an audience rating / ~자 a TV viewer; the TV audience《총칭》.

시청(試聽) an audition 《room》.

시체(屍體) a corpse; a dead body; 《동물의》 a carcass. ¶ ~로 발견되다 be found dead. ‖ ~부검《剖檢》 an autopsy; a post-mortem (examination).

시체(詩體) a style of a poem.

시초(始初) the beginning; the start; 《발단》 the outset.

시추(試錐) a trial drilling 〔boring〕; prospecting《시굴》. ‖ ~선 an oil prospecting rig / 해저 석유 ~ offshore oil drilling.

시치다 baste; tack. ‖ 시침질 basting; a fitting.

시치미떼다 pretend not to know; feign 〔affect〕 ignorance; play innocent.　　　[watch].

시침(時針) the hour hand 《of a

시커멓다 (be) jet-black.

시큼하다 (be) sourish.

시키다 《하게 하다》 make 〔let, get〕 《a person》 do; 《주문》 order. ¶ 잡채를 ~ order chop suey.

시트 《침대의》 a 〔bed〕 sheet. ¶ ~를 바꾸다 change the sheets / 침대에 ~를 깔다 put a sheet on the bed.

시판(市販) marketing. ~하다 market; put 〔place〕 《goods》 on the market. ¶ ~되고 있다 be on the market. ‖ ~품 goods on the market / ~공동~ joint marketing.

시퍼렇다 《색깔이》 (be) deep blue; 《서슬이》 (be) sharp; sharp-edged. ¶ 서슬이 시퍼런 날 a sharp-edged blade / 서슬이 ~ 《사람이》 put on fearful airs.　　　[Psalms.

시편(詩篇) 〖聖〗 the Book of

시평(時評) comments on current events; 《신문의》 editorial comments. ‖ ~란《欄》 editorial col-

시하(侍下) 〖부사적〗 with *one's* grandparents〔parents〕living.
시학(詩學) poetics; poetry.
시한(時限) a time limit; a deadline; a period(수업 등의). ¶ 1 ~ 은 50분이다 One period is 50 minutes long. ‖ ~부 파업 a time-limited strike / ~입법 legislation of specified duration / ~폭탄 a time bomb / 법적 ~ the legal deadline.
시할머니(媤—) *one's* husband's grandmother. 「grandfather.
시할아버지(媤—) *one's* husband's
시합(試合) ☞ 경기(競技).
시해(弑害) ☞ 시역(弑逆).
시행(施行) enforcement. ~하다 《법률을》 enforce; put 《*a law*》 into operation〔effect〕. ¶ ~되고 있다 be in force. ‖ ~령 an enforcement ordinance / ~세칙 detailed enforcement regulations.
시행착오(試行錯誤) trial and error.
시험(試驗) an examination; an exam《口》; a test; 《실험》 an experiment; a trial. ~하다 examine; test; put to the test; experiment. ¶ 학기말〔중간〕~ a term-end〔midterm〕examination / 국가〔검정〕~ a state〔certificate, license〕examination / ~삼아 tentatively; on trial / ~에 합격〔실패〕하다 pass〔fail in〕an examination / ~을 치다 take an examination. ‖ ~공부 study for an examination / ~과목 an examination subject / ~관〔管〕a test tube / ~관 아기 a test-tube baby / ~기간《새 방식 등의》a testing period / ~단계 the testing stage / ~답안지 an examination 〔a test〕paper / ~대〔臺〕a test board〔desk〕/ ~문제 exam questions / ~발사〔비행〕a test fire〔flight〕/ ~지옥 the ordeal of examinations. 「fest.
시현(示現) ~하다 reveal; mani-
시호(諡號) a posthumous name〔title〕. 「‖ ~법 visible speech.
시화(視話) lip reading〔language〕.
시화(詩畫) a poem and a picture. ‖ ~전 an exhibition of illustrated poems《by》.
시황(市況)〔the tone of〕the market. ‖ ~보고 a market report.
시효(時效)〖法〗acquisitive prescription(민법상의); the statute of limitations(형법상의). ¶ ~에 걸리다 be barred by prescription / 소멸〔취득〕~ negative〔positive〕prescription / ~기간 the period of prescription / ~정지

〔중단〕suspension〔interruption〕of prescription. 「er; climate.
시후(時候) the season; 《일기》 weath-
시흥(詩興) poetical inspiration.
식(式) ① 《식전》〔hold〕a ceremony; rites; rituals. ② 《양식》form; 《형》type; style; model; fashion; 《방법》a method. ¶ 한국~ 〔식〕 (of) Korean style〔fashion〕. ③ 〖數〗an expression; 〖化〗a formula. ¶ ~으로 나타내다 formularize.
식간(食間) ~에 between meals.
식객(食客) a dependent; a free-loader; a hanger-on. ¶ ~노릇을 하다 be a dependent《*on*》; freeload《*on*》. ‖ ~생활 freeloading.
식견(識見) discernment; insight; judgment; 《견해》view; opinion.
식곤증(食困症) languor〔drowsiness〕after a meal.
식구(食口) a family; members of a family. ¶ 많은〔적은〕~ a large〔small〕family.
식권(食券) a food〔meal〕ticket.
식기(食器) tableware; a dinner set; a table service.
식다 ① 《냉각》become cool; get cold. ② 《감퇴》cool down; flag; subside; be chilled(흥, 몸이). ¶ 열의가 ~ lose interest《*in*》; grow less enthusiastic.
식단(食單) a menu(식단표).
식당(食堂) a dining room; a mess hall (군대 등); 《음식점》a restaurant; a cafeteria(셀프서비스의); 《간이식당》a lunchroom. ¶ ~차 a dining car.
식대(食代) the charge for food; food expenses.
식도(食刀) ☞ 식칼.
식도(食道)〖解〗the gullet. ‖ ~암〖醫〗cancer of the esophagus / ~염〖醫〗esophagitis.
식도락(食道樂) epicurism. ‖ ~가 an epicure; a gourmet.
식량(食糧) food; provisions; food supplies. ¶ 하루분의 ~ a day's rations / ~의 자급자족 self-sufficiency in food. ‖ ~관리제도 the food control system / ~난 the difficulty of obtaining food / ~부족 a food shortage / ~사정〔문제〕the food situation〔problem〕/ ~위기 a food crisis / 세계~계획 the World Food Program(생략 WFP).
식료(食料) food. ‖ ~품 an article of food; provisions; foodstuffs / ~품상 a dealer in foodstuffs; a grocer / ~품점 a grocery〔store〕.
식림(植林) afforestation. ~하다 afforest; plant trees.
식모(食母)〔keep〕a kitchenmaid. ‖ ~살이(하다)(be in) domestic

식목(植木) tree planting. ~하다 do planting; plant trees. ‖ ~일 Arbor Day 《美》.

식물(植物) a plant; vegetation (총칭). ‖ ~(성)의 vegetable 《oil》. ~계 the vegetable kingdom / ~성 기름 vegetable oil / ~성 단백질 vegetable albumin / ~원 a botanical garden / ~인간 a (human) vegetable / ~(誌) a flora; a herbal / ~채집 (go) plant collecting / ~학 botany / ~학자 a botanist.

식민(植民) colonization; settlement. ~하다 colonize; plant a colony 《in》. ‖ ~지 a colony 《~지화하다 colonialize》 / ~지 정책 a colonial policy / 해외~지 an overseas colony / (반)~지주의 (anti-)colonialism.

식별(識別) discrimination; discernment. ~하다 discriminate (distinguish) 《between A and B, A from B》; tell 《A from B》. ¶ ~할 수 있는 〔없는〕 (in)distinguishable. 「with things to eat.」

식복(食福) ¶ ~이 있다 be blessed

식비(食費) food cost (expenses); (하숙의) (charges for) board.

식빵(食─) bread. ¶ ~ 한 개 〔조각〕 a loaf 〔slice〕 of bread.

식사(式辭) (read, give) an address 《at a ceremony》.

식사(食事) a meal; a diet. ~하다 〔have〕 a meal; dine. ¶ 가벼운 ~ a light meal / ~ 중이다 be at table / ~ 대접을 〔준비를〕 하다 serve 〔prepare〕 a meal. ‖ ~시간 mealtime; dinner time / ~예법 table manners.

식상(食傷) ~하다 〔물리다〕 be surfeited 〔fed up〕 《with》; be sick 《of》 《口》; (식중독) get food poisoning.

식생활(食生活) dietary life; eating habits. ¶ ~을 개선하다 improve one's diet 〔eating habits〕.

식성(食性) likes and dislikes in food / 《one's》 taste. ¶ ~에 맞다 suit one's taste / ~이 까다롭다 be particular about food.

식수(食水) drinking water.

식순(式順) the order 〔program〕 of a ceremony.

식식거리다 gasp; pant.

식언(食言) ~하다 eat one's words; break one's promise.

식염(食鹽) salt. ‖ ~수 a solution of salt / ~주사 a saline 〔salt〕 injection.

식욕(食慾) (an) appetite. ¶ ~이 있다 〔없다〕 have a good 〔poor〕 appetite / ~을 잃다 lose one's appetite. ‖ ~감퇴 〔증진〕 loss 〔promotion〕 of appetite / ~증진제

an appetizer.

식용(食用) ¶ ~의 edible; eatable / ~으로 하다 use 《a thing》 for food. ‖ ~개구리 an edible frog / ~유 cooking oil / ~품 eatables.

식육(食肉) (edible) meat. ¶ ~용 소 beef cattle. ‖ ~가공업자 a meat processor.

식은땀 a cold sweat. ¶ ~을 흘리다 be in a cold sweat.

식음(食飮) ¶ ~을 전폐하다 give up eating and drinking.

식이요법(食餌療法) a dietary cure. ¶ ~을 하다 go on a diet.

식인종(食人種) a cannibal race; cannibals.

식자(植字) 〔印〕 typesetting. ~하다 set (up) type. ‖ ~공 a typesetter.

식자(識者) intelligent people.

식자우환(識字憂患) Ignorance is bliss.

식장(式場) the hall of ceremony; a ceremonial hall. 「uals.」

식전(式典) a ceremony; rites; rit-

식전(食前) ¶ ~에 before meals / ~ 30분에 To be taken 30 minutes before meals. ‖ ~주(酒) an aperitif.

식중독(食中毒) food poisoning. ¶ ~에 걸리다 be poisoned by food.

식체(食滯) indigestion; dyspepsia.

식초(食醋) vinegar.

식충(食蟲) ~동물〔식물〕 an insectivore; an insectivorous animal 〔plant〕 / ~이 〔사람〕 a glutton.

식칼(食─) a kitchen knife.

식탁(食卓) a (dining) table. ¶ ~에 앉다 sit at table. ‖ ~보 a cloth; a tablecloth.

식탈(食頉) sickness caused by overeating; food poisoning.

품(品) food(stuffs); groceries. ‖ ~가공업 the food industry / ~위생 food hygiene / 불량~ unsanitary 〔illegal〕 foodstuff.

식피(植皮) 〔醫〕 (skin) grafting. ~하다 graft skin 《to》.

식혜(食醯) a sweet drink made from fermented rice.

식후(食後) ¶ ~에 after meal / 매 ~ 30분에 To be taken 30 minutes after each meal.

식히다 cool; let 《a thing》 cool; bring down 《the fever》. ¶ 식힌 cooled / 머리를 ~ cool one's head.

신[1]《신발》footgear; footwear; shoes. ¶ ~을 신은 채로 with one's shoes on / ~을 신다 〔벗다〕 put on 〔take off〕 one's shoes.

신[2]《신이지》enthusiasm; excitement; interest; fervor. ¶ ~이 나다 become enthusiastic. 「of the ape.」

신(申)《십이지》the zodiacal sign

신(神) God (일신교의); the Lord (주님); a god (다신교의); a goddess

(여신). ¶ ~의 divine; godly; ~의 가호[은총] divine protection [blessing]. 「love scene.
신 a 《dramatic》 scene. ¶ 러브 ~
신…(新) new; latest; modern. ~발명 a new invention.
신간(新刊) a new publication. ¶ ~의 newly-published. ‖ ~서적 a new book (publication) / ~소개 a book review.
신개발지(新開發地) 《도시 등의》 a newly-opened [-developed] land [area]. 「[Lenin]. ~하다 deify.
신격화(神格化) deification 《of
신경(神經) a nerve. ¶ ~의 nervous; nerve; ~이 예민한 nervous; sensitive / ~이 둔한 insensitive; thick-skinned / ~이 굵은 be bold; have a lot of nerve / ~을 건드리다 jar [get] on one's nerves. ‖ ~가스 [軍] nerve gas / ~계통 the nervous system / ~과민 nervousness; oversensitiveness / ~과의사 a neurologist / ~병 a nervous disease; neurosis / ~세포 a nerve cell / ~쇠약 (suffer from) a nervous breakdown / ~염 neuritis / ~전 a nerve war; psychological warfare / ~조직 nervous tissues / ~질 nervous temperament / ~통 neuralgia. 「[trend].
신경향(新傾向) a new tendency
신고(申告) a report; a statement; a declaration (세관에서의); ~하다 state; report; declare; make [file] a return. ¶ 소득 ~을 속이다 make a false return / 전입 [전출] ~ a moving-in [-out] notification / 출생 ~ a register [notification] of birth / 확정 [예정] ~ a final [provisional] return / ~할 것 없읍니까 《세관에서》 (Do you have) anything to declare ? / ~납세 tax payment by self-assessment / ~서 a statement; a report; a return; a declaration / ~용지 a return form / ~자 a reporter / ~제 a report system / 소득세 ~ an income-tax return.
신고(辛苦) hardships; trials; toil; pains. ~하다 suffer hardships; take pains.
신곡(新曲) a new song [tune].
신곡(新曲) 《단테의》 the Divine Comedy.
신관(信管) a fuse. ¶ ~을 분리하다 [장치하다] cut [set] a fuse. ‖ 시한 ~ a time fuse.
신관(新館) a new building.
신교(新敎) Protestantism. ‖ ~도 a Protestant.
신구(新舊) ¶ ~의 old and new / ~사상의 충돌 a collision between old and new ideas.

신국면(新局面) a new phase [aspect]. 「정치」 theocracy.
신권(神權) the divine right. ‖ ~
신규(新規) ¶ ~의 new; fresh / ~로 anew; afresh; newly / ~로 채용하다 hire [employ] a new hand. ‖ ~사업 [예금] a new enterprise [deposit].
신극(新劇) 《파》 a new school of acting. ‖ ~운동 a new-drama movement. 「marvelous] skill.
신기(神技) superhuman [exquisite,
신기(神奇) ¶ ~한 marvelous; mysterious; miraculous / ~하게 marvelously; mysteriously.
신기(新奇) ¶ ~의 novel; original.
신기다 put 《shoes》 on 《a person》; get 《a person》 to put on 《shoes》.
신기록(新記錄) (establish, make) a new 《world》 record.
신기루(蜃氣樓) a mirage.
신기원(新紀元) a new era [epoch]. ¶ ~을 이루는 사건 an epoch-making event / ~을 이룩하다 make [mark] an epoch 《in》.
신나 a thinner.
신나다 get in high spirits; get elated; feel on top of the world.
신남(信男) 【佛】 a male believer.
신녀(信女) 【佛】 a female believer.
신년(新年) a new year ☞ 새해. ¶ 근하 ~ (I wish you a) Happy New Year !
신념(信念) belief; faith; conviction(확신). ¶ ~이 강한 [약한] 사람 a man of strong [weak] faith / ~이 없다 lack faith 《in》 / ~을 굳히다 strengthen one's faith.
신다 wear; put [have] on. ¶ 구두를 [양말을] ~ put on one's shoes [socks]. 「tical party.
신당(新黨) 《organize》 a new poli-
신대륙(新大陸) a new continent; the New World.
신도(信徒) a believer; a follower.
신동(神童) an infant prodigy; a shoe heel. 「wonder child.
신뒤축을 the back of 「a syndicate.
신디케이트 《form》 a syndicate.
신랄(辛辣) ¶ ~한 sharp; severe; bitter; cutting / ~한 비평 a severe [sharp] criticism.
신랑(新郞) a bridegroom. ‖ ~감 a likely [suitable] bridegroom / ~신부 the bride and bridegroom, a new couple.
신령(神靈) divine power. 「dar.
신력(新曆) the new [solar] calen-
신령(神靈) 《신》 divine spirits; the gods. ‖ ~산 a mountain god.
신록(新綠) fresh green [verdure].
신뢰(信賴) trust; confidence; reliance. ~하다 trust; rely on; put confidence 《in》 / ~할 수 있는 reliable; trustworthy / ~를 저버리다 betray 《a person's》 trust.
신망(信望) confidence; popularity.

신명 ¶ ~을 잃다 lose the confidence 《of》/ 사람들의 ~을 얻다 win public confidence 《of》/ ~이 있다 enjoy the confidence 《of》; be popular 《with》. ‖ ~ 하다 lay down one's life.
신명(身命) one's life.
신명(神明) God; gods. ¶ ~의 가호 (by) God's 〔divine〕 protection.
신묘(神妙) 신기(神奇).
신문(訊問) a questioning; an examination; an interrogation. ‖ ~하다 question; examine; interrogate. ¶ ~조서 〔法〕 interrogatory 〔法〕 a cross-question.
신문(新聞) a (news)paper; the press(총칭). ¶ 헌 ~ an old newspaper / ~에 나다 appear 〔be reported〕 in the paper / ~에서 얻어맞다 be attacked in the press / ~ 배달(을) 하다 deliver newspapers / ~을 편집〔발행〕하다 edit〔issue〕 a paper. ¶ ~가판대 a newsstand / ~광고 a newspaper advertisement / ~구독료 the subscription / ~구독자 a (newspaper) reader〔subscriber〕/ ~기사 a newspaper article〔report〕/ ~기자 a newspaper man; a (newspaper) reporter; a journalist / ~기자단 a press corps / ~기자석 the press box / ~사 〔보급소〕 a newspaper company〔agency〕/ ~소설 a serial novel in a newspaper / ~스크랩 newspaper clipping〔美〕/ ~용지 newsprint / ~팔이〔배달인〕 a newsboy / 일간〔주간〕~ a daily〔weekly〕(paper) / 조간〔석간〕~ a morning〔an evening〕paper.
신물 ¶ ~이 나다 (비유적) get sick and tired 《of》; have had enough.
신바닥 a shoe sole. ¶ ~《of》.
신바람 exulted〔high〕spirits; elation.
신발 footwear; footgear; shoes.
신발명(新發明) a new invention. ¶ ~의 newly-invented.
신방(新房) a bridal room; the bridal bed; a bride-chamber.
신벌(神罰) divine punishment〔retribution〕.
신변(身邊) one's body; 《처지》 one's circumstances. ¶ ~의 위험 one's personal danger / ~을 걱정하다 be anxious about one's personal safety / ~을 정리하다 put one's affairs in order. ‖ ~경호 personal protection / ~잡기 memoirs on one's private life.
신병(身柄) one's person. ¶ ~을 인수하러 가다 go to claim〔receive〕《a person》/ ~을 인도하다 hand 《an offender》over 《to》.
신병(身病) sickness; illness.
신병(新兵) a new conscript; a recruit. ‖ ~훈련 recruit training / ~훈련소 a recruit training center.
신봉(信奉) ~하다 believe〔have faith〕in; embrace. ¶ 기독교를 ~하다 embrace〔profess〕 Christianity. ‖ ~자 a believer; a follower. ┌father.
신부(神父) a (Catholic) priest; a
신부(新婦) a bride. ¶ ~의상 a bridal costume / ~학교 a finishing school. ┌kidney failure.
신부전(腎不全) renal insufficiency;
신분(身分) 《사회적 지위》 one's status〔rank〕;《신원》one's identity; origin; 《one's》birth. ¶ ~이 다르다 differ in social standing / ~이 높은 사람 a person of high rank / ~을 밝히다 〔숨기다〕 disclose〔conceal〕one's identity〔origins〕/ ~에 알맞게〔지나치게〕 살다 live within〔beyond〕one's means. ‖ ~증(명서) an identity〔identification〕card; an ID card.
신불(神佛) gods and Buddha. ¶ ~의 가호 divine protection.
신비(神秘) (a) mystery. ¶ ~한 mystic; mysterious / ~에 싸여 있다 be shrouded〔wrapped〕in mystery. ‖ ~경 a land of mystery / ~주의 mysticism.
신빙성(信憑性) authenticity; credibility; reliability. ¶ ~이 있다〔없다〕 be authentic〔unauthentic〕; be reliable〔unreliable〕.
신사(紳士) a gentleman; ~적인 gentlemanly; gentlemanlike / 비~적인 ungentlemanly / 세련된 ~ a finished gentleman / ~연하다 play the gentleman. ‖ ~도 the code of a gentleman / ~록 a Who's Who; a social register〔美〕/ ~복 a men's suit / ~협정 a gentleman's agreement.
신상(身上) 《몸》one's body;《처지》 one's circumstances. ¶ ~을 조사하다 examine a person's history〔family〕. ‖ ~문제 one's personal affairs / ~상담란 a personal advice column / ~조사서〔명세서〕 a report card on one's family.
신색 looks; countenance.
신생(新生) a new birth; (a) rebirth. ‖ ~국(가) a newly emerging nation / ~대 the Cenozoic era.
신생아(新生兒) a newborn baby.
신서(信書) a letter; correspondence《with》.
신석기(新石器) a neolith. ‖ ~시대 the Neolithic era; the New Stone Age.
신선(神仙) a supernatural being. ¶ ~경 a fairyland; an enchanted place.
신선(新鮮) ¶ ~한 new; fresh / ~하게 하다 make fresh; freshen /

신선로 (神仙爐) 《그릇》 a brass chafing dish; 《요리》 various ingredients in a chafing dish; *shinsŏllo*.

신설 (新設) ~하다 establish; found. ¶ 위원회를 ~하다 establish [set up] a committee / ~의 〔된〕 newly-established. ‖ ~학교 (공장) a newly-founded school (factory).

신성 (神性) divinity; divine nature.

신성 (神聖) sacredness; sanctity. ¶ ~한 sacred; holy; divine / ~불가침이다 be sacred and inviolable. ‖ ~로마제국 the Holy Roman Empire.

신세 a debt of gratitude. ¶ ~를 지다 be indebted (obliged) 〔to〕; owe 《a person》 a debt of gratitude; receive assistance / ~를 갚다 repay 《a person's》 kindness.

신세 (身世) one's lot 〔circumstances, condition〕. ¶ 가련한 ~ a miserable 〔wretched〕 life / ~ 타령을 하다 express grievances about *one's* own lot.

신세계 (新世界) a new world; the New World 〔대륙〕.

신세대 (新世代) the new generation.

신소리 a pun; a play on words.

신속 (迅速) ¶ ~한 rapid; swift; quick; prompt; speedy / ~히 rapidly; swiftly; quickly; promptly.

신수 (身手) *one's* appearance; looks. ¶ ~가 훤하다 have a fine appearance.

신수 (身數) *one's* star; fortune; luck. ¶ ~를 보다 have *one's* fortune told.

신시대 (新時代) a new age 〔epoch, era〕. ¶ ~를 이루는 epoch-making; epochal.

신식 (新式) a new style 〔pattern, type, method〕. ¶ ~의 new; new-style〔-type〕; modern.

신신부탁 (申申付託) ~하다 request earnestly 〔repeatedly〕; solicit.

신실 (信實) sincerity; faithfulness. ~하다 (be) sincere; true; faithful.

신심 (信心) faith; piety; devotion.

신안 (新案) a new idea 〔design, mode〕. ¶ ~특허를 신청하다 apply for a patent on a new design.

신앙 (信仰) faith; belief. ¶ ~이 두터운 devout; pious; godly / ~이 없는 unbelieving; impious / ~의 자유 religious liberty; freedom of religion 〔faith〕 / ~을 깊게 하다 〔버리다〕 deepen 〔forsake〕 *one's* faith. ‖ ~ 생활 〔lead〕 a religious life / ~요법 the faith cure / ~인 a believer.

신약 (新藥) a new drug 〔medicament〕.

신약성서 (新約聖書) the New Testament.

신어 (新語) 〔coin〕 a new word; a newly-coined word; a neologism.

신열 (身熱) 〔have〕 fever; 〔body〕 temperature.

신예 (新銳) ¶ ~의 new and powerful 《weapons》 / 최~의 전자 장비 the state-of-the-art electronics. ‖ ~기 a newly produced airplane; an up-to-date aircraft.

신용 (信用) 〔신임〕 confidence; trust; faith; 〔신뢰〕 reliance; 〔명망〕 reputation; 〔경제상의〕 credit. ~하다 trust; place 〔put〕 confidence in; give credit to. ¶ ~ 있는 trustworthy; creditable; reliable / ~ 없는 untrustworthy; discreditable / ~으로 돈을 꾸다 borrow money on credit / ~을 얻다 〔잃다〕 gain 〔lose〕 *one's* credit 《with a person》. ‖ ~거래 sales on credit; credit transaction / ~거래선 a charge customer / ~금고 a credit bank 〔association〕 / ~대부 a credit loan / ~도 credit rating / ~보험 credit insurance 〔대손의〕; fidelity insurance 〔대인의〕 / ~상태 *one's* financial 〔credit〕 standing / ~장 a letter of credit 〔생략 L/C〕 / ~조사 credit research / ~조합 a credit union / ~조회 a credit inquiry / ~증권 credit paper / ~카드 a credit card / ~한도 a credit limit.

신우 (腎盂) 〔解〕 the pelvis of the kidney. ‖ ~염 〔醫〕 pyelitis.

신원 (身元) *one's* identity; *one's* background. ¶ ~불명의 시체 an unidentified body / ~을 조사하다 inquire into 《a person's》 background / ~을 증명하다 prove *one's* identity. ‖ ~보증 personal reference / ~보증인 a surety; a reference / ~인수인 a guarantee.

신음 (呻吟) ~하다 groan; moan. ¶ 고통으로 ~하다 moan with pain.

신의 (信義) faith; fidelity. ¶ ~ 있는 faithful / ~을 지키다 〔저버리다〕 keep 〔break〕 faith 《with a person》.

신의 (神意) God's will; providence.

신의 (神醫) a wonderful physician.

신인 (新人) a new figure 〔member〕; a new face 〔star〕 〔연예계의〕; a newcomer 〔신참자〕; a rookie 〔야구 등의〕. ¶ ~가수 a new singer / ~상 《예술인의》 the award for Best New Artist / ~왕 〔野〕 the rookie king.

신임 (信任) trust; confidence. ~하다 trust; confide 《in》. ¶ ~의 두

신임 터운 trusted / ~을 얻다 win the confidence 《of》; be trusted 《by》. ‖ ~장 《present one's》 credentials / ~ 투표 a vote of confidence.

신임(新任) ¶ ~의 newly-appointed. ‖ ~자 a new appointee.

신입(新入) ¶ ~의 new; newly-joined. ‖ ~생 a new student; a freshman (대학의) / ~자 a newcomer.

신자(信者) 《종교의》a believer 《in Buddhism》; an adherent; a devotee; the faithful(총칭). ¶ 기독교로 ~가 되다 become 〔turn〕 a Christian.

신작(新作) a new work (production, composition(작곡)). ‖ ~ 소설 a newly-written novel.

신작로(新作路) a new road; a highway(큰길).

신장(一欌) a shoe chest.

신장(身長) stature; height. ¶ ~이 5피트 6인치다 stand five feet six inches.

신장(伸張) ~하다 extend; expand; elongate. ‖ ~성 expansibility.

신장(新裝) ~하다 give a new look 《to》; refurbish. ¶ 5월 1일 ~ 개업(게시) Completely remodeled. Reopening May 1 / ~된 빌딩 a newly-finished (refurbished) building / 그 책은 ~으로 출시되었다 The book appeared in a new binding.

신장(腎臟) the kidney. ‖ ~결석 a renal calculus / ~병 a renal disease; kidney trouble / ~염 nephritis / 인공~ a kidney machine. ‖ ~ 《publication》(신간서).

신저(新著) one's new work; a new publication.

신전(神前) ¶ ~에 before God.

신전(神殿) a shrine; a sanctuary.

신접살이(新接一) life in a new home. ‖ ~하다 make a new home; set up house.

신정(神政) theocracy; thearchy.

신정(新正) the New Year.

신제(新製) ¶ ~의 newly-made. ‖ ~품 a new product.

신조(信條) a creed; an article of faith; a principle(신념). ¶ 생활~ one's principles of life.

신조(神助) divine grace 〔aid〕; providence.

신조(新造) ¶ ~의 new; newly-made〔-built〕. ‖ ~선 a newly-built ship / ~어 a newly-coined word.

신종(新種) 《종류》a new species 《variety》; 《수법》a new type. ‖ ~ 사기 a new type of swindling.

신주(神主) an ancestral tablet. ¶ ~를 모시다 enshrine one's ancestral tablet.

신주(新株) 《allot》new stocks 《美》 〔shares 《英》〕. ¶ ~를 공모하다 offer new stocks for public subscription.

신중(愼重) ¶ ~한 careful; cautious; prudent; deliberate / ~한 태도를 취하다 take a prudent attitude 《in》.

신지식(新知識) new 〔advanced〕 ideas; new 〔up-to-date〕 knowledge.

신진(新進) ¶ ~의 rising; new / ~ 기예의 young and energetic. ‖ ~ 작가 a rising writer.

신진대사(新陳代謝) 《生》metabolism; 《비유적》renewal; regeneration. ~하다 metabolize; be renewed; be regenerated; replace the old with the new.

신착(新着) ¶ ~의 newly-arrived 《books》. ‖ ~품 new arrivals.

신참(新參) ¶ ~의 new; green. ‖ ~자 a newcomer; a new hand.

신창 a shoe sole. La novice.

신천옹(信天翁) 《鳥》 an albatross.

신천지(新天地) a new world. ‖ ~를 개척하다 open up a new field of activity.

신청(申請) (an) application; (a) petition. ~하다 apply for 《a thing》; petition 《for》. ¶ 허가를 ~하다 apply for a permit 〔patent〕. ‖ ~기한 《마감》the deadline for making application; a time limit for application / ~서 an 〔a written〕 application / ~인 an applicant.

신체(身體) the body; the person. ¶ ~의 bodily; physical / ~의 결함 a physical defect / ~의 자유 personal liberty. ‖ ~각부 the parts of the body / ~ 검사 《undergo》a physical 〔medical〕 examination; a body search(경찰에 의한) / ~장애자 a disabled person; the (physically) handicapped.

신체시(新體詩) the new-style poetry; a new-style poem (한 편).

신체제(新體制) a new structure 〔order, system〕.

신축(伸縮) ~하다 expand and contract; be elastic. ‖ ~자재의 elastic; flexible. ‖ ~성 elasticity.

신축(新築) ~하다 build; construct. ¶ ~의 newly-built / ~중 인 집 a house under construction.

신춘(新春) 《신년》the New Year; 《새봄》early spring. ‖ ~문예 a literary contest in spring.

신출귀몰(神出鬼沒) ~하다 (be) elusive; protean. ¶ 저 사내는 ~한다 That man is really elusive.

신출내기(新出一) a novice; a greenhorn; a tenderfoot; a beginner.

신코 a toecap.
신탁(信託) trust; ~하다 entrust; trust 《a person》 with 《a thing》. ‖ ~기금 a trust fund / ~예금 a trust deposit / ~업 the trust business / ~은행 a trust bank / ~자 a truster / ~재산 an estate in trust / ~증서[회사] a trust deed [company] / ~통치 trusteeship / ~통치령토 a trust territory / 금전 [투자] ~ money [investment] trust / 대부~ a loan trust / 수익~ a beneficial trust / 피~자 a trustee.
신탁(神託) an oracle; a divine revelation [message].
신토불이(身土不二) one's body and soil are inseparable each other; The domestic farm products are the best.
신통(神通) ‖ ~한 mysterious; wonderworking; miraculous; wonderful. ‖ ~력 a divine [an occult] power.
신트림 belch(ing).
신파(新派) 《form》 a new school; a new faction(정당의). ‖ ~극[배우] a new-school play [actor].
신판(新版) a new publication [edition]. ‖ ~의 newly-published.
신품(新品) ‖ ~의 new; brand-new / 거의 ~과 같다 look brand-new; be as good as new.
신하(臣下) a subject; a vassal.
신학(神學) theology. ‖ ~교 a theological [divinity] school / ~자 a theologian.
신형(新型) a new style [fashion]; the latest model [design].
신호(信號) a signal; signaling. ~하다 (make a) signal. ¶ ~를 지키다 observe a (traffic) signal / ~를 잘못 보다 fail to notice a signal / 경계 [위험] ~ a caution [danger] signal / 적색 [청색] ~ a red [green] light. ‖ ~기(旗)[등] a signal flag [lamp] / ~수 a signal man.
신혼(新婚) ¶ ~의 newly-married. ‖ ~부부 [생활] a newly-married [=wedded] couple [life] / ~여행 (set out on) a honeymoon / ~여행자 honeymooners.
신화(神話) a myth; mythology(총칭). ¶ ~적인 mythical. ‖ ~시대 the mythological age / 건국 ~ the birth-myth of a nation.
신흥(新興) ¶ ~의 new; rising. ‖ ~계급 a newly-risen class / ~국가 a rising nation / ~도시 a boom town / ~산업 a new [burgeoning] industry / ~아프리카 제국 the emergent African countries / ~종교 a new religion.
싣다 ① 《적재》 load; take on; put 《goods》 on board, ship(배에); 《배가 주어》 take 《a cargo》 on board.
② 《기재》 record; publish; insert. ¶ 신문에 소설을 ~ publish a novel in a newspaper.
실 yarn(방사(紡絲)); thread(재봉용). ¶ 바늘귀에 ~을 꿰다 thread a needle / ~을 실패에 감다 spool; reel / ~을 잣다 spin thread [yarn] / ~오라기 하나 걸치지 않고 stark-naked.
실(實) 《진실》 truth; reality; 《사실》 a fact; 《실질》 substance. ¶ ~은 really; in fact; as a matter of fact; to tell the truth. ‖ ~중량 net weight.
실가(實價) ① 《진가》 intrinsic value. ② 《원가》 the cost (price).
실각(失脚) ¶ ~한 downfall; a fall. ~하다 fall from power; lose one's position. ‖ ~한 정치가 a fallen politician.
실감(實感) actual feeling; realization(체득). ~하다 feel actually; realize. ¶ ~이 나다 be true to nature.
실개 a spool; a reel; a bobbin.
실개천 a spool; a reel.
실개천 a brooklet; a streamlet.
실격(失格) ~하다 be disqualified 《for a post》. ‖ ~자 a disqualified person.
실경(實景) the actual view [scene].
실고추 threaded [shredded] red pepper.
실과(實果) 과실(果實).
실과(實科) a practical course.
실국수 thin [thread-like] noodles.
실권(失權) ~하다 lose one's rights; forfeit one's power.
실권(實權) real power. ¶ ~을 쥐다 seize [hold] real power / ~이 없는 사장 a president in name only / 정치의 ~을 쥐고 있다 hold the reins of the government. ‖ ~파 people in authority.
실기(失期) ~하다 fail to keep an appointed time.
실기(失機) ~하다 miss [lose] an opportunity [a chance].
실기(實技) practical talent. ‖ ~시험 practical (talent) examination.
실꾸리 a ball of thread [yarn].
실날 a thread; a strand; a ply.
실내(室內) ¶ ~의 indoor / ~에서 indoors; in a room / ~를 장식하다 decorate a room. ‖ ~게임 a parlor game / ~악 chamber music / ~운동 indoor exercise / ~장식 interior decoration.
실농(失農) ~하다 miss the season for farming.
실눈 narrow eyes.
실뜨기 (play) cat's cradle.
실랑이(질) ~하다 bother people.
실력(實力) real power 《ability》; capability; 《진가》 merit; 《힘》 force; arms. ¶ 어학 ~ one's linguistic ability / ~ 있는 able;

실례 capable; talented; efficient; / ~을 기르다 improve 《*one's English*》; improve oneself 《*in*》. ¶ ~자 a 《*political*》strong man; a powerful [dominant] figure 《*in politics*》 / ~주의 the merit system / ~ 행사 use of force.

실례(失禮) rudeness; discourtesy; 《무례》 a breach of etiquette; bad manners. ¶ ~되는 하다 impolite / ~되는 말을 하다 say rude things / ~되는 짓을 하다 behave rudely / ~지만 Excuse me, but.... / ~했습니다 I beg your pardon.

실례(實例) (give) an example; an instance; a precedent (선례).

실로(實一) truly; really; indeed; surely; to be sure.

실로폰 [樂] a xylophone.

실록(實錄) an authentic record (history).

실론 Ceylon. ¶ ~의 Ceylonese / ~ 말(~語) (a) Ceylonese.

실루엣 a silhouette.

실룩거리다 quiver convulsively; twitch 《*one's eyes*》.

실리(實利) an actual profit (gain); utility. ¶ ~적인 utilitarian; practical. ‖ ~외교 utilitarian diplomacy / ~주의 utilitarianism / ~주의자 a utilitarian; a materialist.

실리다 《기재됨》 appear; be printed [reported] (신문에); be recorded (기록); 《싣게 하다》 get 《*goods*》 loaded; have 《*a person*》 load 《*a car, goods*》.

실리콘 [化] silicone. ☞ 규소.

실린더 a cylinder. 《생각 s.》.

실링 《영국 옛 화폐단위》 a shilling.

실마리 《시작》 a beginning; 《단서》 a clue 《*to*》. ¶ ~를 찾다 find a clue to....

실망(失望) (a) disappointment; discouragement; despair (절망). ~ 하다 be disappointed 《*at, in, of*》; be disheartened; despair 《*of*》. ¶ ~하여 in despair / ~시키다 disappoint; discourage.

실명(失名) ¶ ~의 anonymous. ‖ ~ 씨 an anonymous person.

실명(失明) ~하다 become [go] blind; lose *one's* (eye-)sight. ‖ ~자 a blind person.

실명(實名) *one's* real-name. ‖ ~계좌 *one's* real-name bank accounts / 《금융거래》 ~제 the real-name financial transaction system.

실무(實務) (practical) business [affairs]. ¶ ~적인 practical; businesslike / ~에 종사하다 go into business / ~에 어둡다 be not familiar with office routine / ~를 배우다 get a training in the practice of business. ‖ ~가 a man of business / ~자(급) 회담 working-level talks.

실물(實物) the (real) thing; an (actual) object; a genuine article (진짜); an original (원형). ¶ ~ 크기의 life-size(d); full-size(d). ‖ ~거래 a spot transaction / ~교육 practical teaching.

실밥 ① 《솔기》 a seam. ② 《뜯은 보무라지》 waste thread (ripped out of seams).

실백(實柏) a pine-nut kernel.

실버들 a weeping willow.

실보무라지 waste thread (yarn).

실비(實費) actual expenses; 《원가》 cost price; prime cost. ¶ ~로 팔다 《제공하다》 sell (offer) 《*a thing*》 at cost. ‖ ~제공 a cost sale. / ~ly; survey.

실사(實査) ~하다 inspect actually.

실사(實寫) a photograph taken from life (on the spot).

실사회(實社會) the everyday (actual) world. ¶ ~에 나가다 go into the world; get a start in life.

실상(實狀) the actual [real] state of affairs; the actual condition.

실상(實相) real facts 《*of a case*》; real aspects. ¶ 사회의 ~ a true picture of life.

실상(實像) a real image. 「pale.

실색(失色) ~하다 lose color; turn

실생활(實生活) (a) real [(an) actual] life; the realities of life.

실선(實線) a solid (full) line.

실성(失性) ~하다 become insane; go [run] mad; lose *one's* mind.

실소(失笑) ~하다 burst out laughing; burst into laughter. ¶ ~를 금치 못하다 cannot help laughing 《*at*》.

실속(實一) substance; contents (내용). ¶ ~ 있는 substantial; solid / ~ 없는 unsubstantial; empty; poor / 겉보다 ~을 취하다 prefer substance to appearance.

실수(失手) a mistake; 《과실》 a blunder; a fault; 《사소한》 a slip. ~ 하다 make a mistake (slip); commit a blunder; a gross mistake; a (serious) blunder.

실수(實收) 《수입》 an actual [a net, a real] income; 《수확》 an actual yield.

실수(實數) the actual number; [數] a real number (quantity).

실수요(實需要) actual demand. ‖ ~자 an end user / ~자 증명 a certificate of an end user.

실습(實習) practice 《*in cooking*》; (practical) exercise; drill. ~ 하다 practice; have (practical) training. ‖ ~생 a trainee; an

실시(實施) enforcement; operation. ~하다 enforce 《*a law*》; carry 《*a law*》 into effect; put 《*a system*》 in operation [force].
intern(의학의); a student teacher (선생의) / ~시간 practice hours.

실신(失神) ~하다 swoon; faint; lose consciousness.

실액(實額) an actual amount of money.

실어증(失語症) aphasia. ∥ ~환자 an aphasiac.

실언(失言) (make) a slip of the tongue; an improper [indiscreet] remark. ¶ ~을 사과하다 apologize for *one's* slip of the tongue / ~을 취소하다 retract [take back] *one's* improper remark.

실업(失業) 《실직》 unemployment. ~하다 lose *one's* job [work]; be thrown out of work [job]. ¶ ~구제 [보험] unemployment relief [insurance] / ~대책 a measure against unemployment; a relief measure for the unemployed / ~률 the unemployment rate / ~문제 the unemployment problem / ~수당 an unemployment allowance / ~자 an unemployed person; 《총칭》 the unemployed; the jobless / 계절적 ~ seasonal unemployment / 잠재 ~ latent unemployment.

실업(實業) business 《상업》; industry 《산업》. ~에 종사하다 go into [be engaged in] business. ¶ ~가 a businessman / ~계 the business world / ~교육 vocational (industrial) education / ~(고등)학교 a vocational [business] (high) school.

실없다 (be) insincere; faithless; unreliable. ¶ 실없이 frivolously; nonsensically; uselessly / 실없는 소리 silly [idle] talk.

실연(失戀) disappointed [unrequited] love; a broken heart. ~하다 be disappointed [crossed] in love 《*for a person*》. ¶ ~한 lovelorn; broken-hearted.

실연(實演) acting; a stage performance [show]; a demonstration. ~하다 act [perform] on the stage.

실오리 a piece of thread.

실온(室溫) the temperature of a room; room temperature.

실외(室外) ¶ ~의 outdoor / ~에서 outdoors; out of doors.

실용(實用) practical use; utility. ¶ ~적인 practical; utilitarian; serviceable / ~화하다 make 《*a process*》 practicable; put *a thing* to practical use / ~성이 있는 useful; of practical use / ~본위의 functional. ∥ ~신안 a utility model / ~영어 practical English / ~주의 『哲』 pragmatism / ~품 utility goods; daily necessities(일용품).

실의(失意) disappointment; despair(절망); a broken heart; loss of hope. ¶ ~에 빠져 있다 be in the depths of despair.

실익(實益) 《실수입》 an actual [net] profit; 《실리》 practical benefit; utility. ¶ ~이 있다 be profitable.

실인(實印) *one's* registered [legal] seal.

실재(實在) reality; real existence. ~하다 exist (really); be real; actual. ∥ ~론 〔哲〕 realism.

실적(實績) (actual) results. ¶ 영업 ~ business results [performance] 《*for last year*》 / ~을 올리다 give satisfactory results. ∥ ~제 a merit system.

실전(實戰) actual fighting [warfare]; active service. ¶ ~에 참가하다 take part in actual fighting.

실정(失政) misgovernment; maladministration; misrule.

실정(實情) the actual circumstances [condition]; the real [actual] state of affairs; the real situation. ¶ ~을 모르다 don't know how things stand. ∥ ~조사 a fact-finding inquiry.

실제(實際) 《사실》 the truth; a fact; 《실지》 practice; 《실정》 the actual condition [state]; 《현실》 reality. ¶ ~의 true; real; actual; ~적인 practical / ~로 really; in fact; actually / 이론과 ~ theory and practice / ~로 일어난 an actual occurrence.

실족(失足) ~하다 miss *one's* foot [step]; slip; take a false step.

실존(實存) existence. ¶ ~주의 existentialism / ~주의자 an existentialist.

실종(失踪) disappearance; missing. ~하다 disappear 《*from*》; be missing. ¶ ~신고 a report of 《*a person's*》 disappearance / ~자 a missing person.

실증(實證) an actual proof. ~하다 prove; corroborate 《*a proof*》. ¶ ~적(으로) positive(ly). ∥ ~론 〔주의〕 positivism.

실지(失地) a lost territory; ¶ ~를 회복하다 recover the lost territory.

실지(實地) practice; actuality; reality. ¶ ~의 practical; actual; real / ~로 in practice; practically. ∥ ~검증 an on-the-spot investigation / ~경험 practical experience / ~조사 an actual [on-the-spot] survey / ~훈련 on-the-job training.

실직(失職) ☞ 실업(失業).

실질(實質) substance; essence;

실쭉하다

quality. ¶ ~적(으로) substantial(·ly); essential(ly); virtual(ly) / 비~적 unsubstantial; empty / ~적인 합의 substantial agreement. ‖ ~소득 (임금) real income (wages).

실쭉하다 (be) sullen; petulant. ¶ 실쭉하여 sullenly; with a sullen look.

실책(失策) an error; a mistake; a blunder. ~하다 make a mistake; commit a blunder (an error).

실천(實踐) practice. ~하다 practice; put *(a theory)* into practice (action). ¶ ~적인(으로) practical(ly). ‖ ~도덕 practical morality.

실체(實體) substance; essence; entity. ¶ ~의 substantial; solid. ‖ ~론 substantialism / ~화 substantialization.

실추(失墜) loss. ~하다 lose *(one's credit)*; fall; sink. ¶ 위신의 ~ loss of prestige.

실측(實測) an actual survey (measurement). ~하다 survey; measure. ‖ ~도 a surveyed map.

실컷 to *one's* heart's content; as much as *one* wishes. ¶ ~ 먹다 (울다) (cry, weep) *one's* fill.

실크로드 the Silk Road.

실탄(實彈) 《소총》 a live cartridge; 《포탄》 a live (loaded) shell. ¶ ~을 발사하다 fire live cartridges. ‖ ~사격 firing with live ammunition / 《소총의》 ball firing.

실태(失態) a blunder; a fault; disgrace (면목없음). ¶ ~를 부리다 commit a blunder.

실태(實態) the realities; the actual condition (state). ‖ ~조사 research on the actual condition / ~조사위원회 a fact-finding committee.

실토(實吐) ~하다 confess; tell the whole truth.

실팍지다 (be) solid; strong.

실패 a spool; a bobbin; a reel. ¶ ~에 감다 spool; reel.

실패(失敗) (end in) failure; a blunder (대실패). ~하다 fail *(in)*; be unsuccessful; go wrong (계획 등에). ¶ 사업 (시험)에 ~하다 fail in *one's* business (an examination) / ~는 성공의 어머니 Failure is the foundation of success. ‖ ~자 a 《낙오자》a social failure (사회의).

실하다(實一) ① 《실팍》 (be) strong; stout; robust. ② 《재산 등이》 (be) wealthy; well-to-do. ③ 《내용이》 (be) full; substantial.

실학(實學) practical science. ¶ ~파 a realistic school.

실행(實行) 《실천》 practice; action; **464** **실증**

《수행》 execution; fulfil(l)ment. ~하다 practice; execute; carry out; put *(a plan)* in(to) practice. ¶ ~상의 practical; executable; unworkable / 계약을 ~ 하다 execute a contract / 약속을 ~하다 fulfill (keep) *one's* promise. ‖ ~기관 an executive organ / ~력 executive ability / ~예산 the working budget.

실험(實驗) an experiment; a test; experimentation. ~하다 (do an) experiment *(on, in)*. ¶ ~적(으로) experimental(ly). ‖ ~에 성공하다 carry out the experiment successfully. ‖ ~극장 an experimental theater / ~단계 the experimental stage / ~대 a testing bench / ~식(化) an empirical formula / ~실 a laboratory; a lab / ~장치 an experimental device / ~주의 《哲》 experimentalism / ~주의자 an experimentalist / 핵~ a nuclear test / 핵~금지 a ban on nuclear tests.

실현(實現) realization. ~하다 realize *(one's ideal)*; materialize; come true (예언 등이). ¶ ~(불)가 (불)realizable.

실형(實刑) imprisonment.

실화(失火) an accidental fire.

실화(實話) a true (real-life) story.

실황(實況) the actual state of things; the actual scene. ‖ ~녹음 a live recording / ~녹화 a live TV recording / ~방송 on-the-spot (play-by-play 《스포츠의》) broadcasting; a running commentary *(on)* (~방송을 하다 broadcast on the spot) / ~방송 아나운서 《스포츠의》 a sports commentator.

실효(失效) ~하다 lapse; lose effect; become null and void.

실효(實效) actual effect. ¶ ~ 있는 effective / ~ 없는 ineffective.

싫다 (be) disagreeable; unpleasant; disgusting; distasteful; unwilling; reluctant (내키지 않다). ¶ 싫은 글 distasteful (unpleasant) work / 싫어지다 become disgusted *(with)*; be sick (tired) *(of)*; get (be) bored *(with)* / 싫은 얼굴을 하다 make a (wry) face; look displeased.

싫어하다 dislike; hate; loathe; be unwilling (reluctant) *(to do)*. ¶ 남이 하기 싫어하는 일을 하다 do what (things) others hate to do.

싫증(一症) weariness; satiety; tiresomeness. ¶ ~이 나다 grow (get) tired *(of)*; lose interest *(in)*; become weary *(of)* / ~나 게 하다 weary *(a person)* with (an idle talk); bore (with); make (a person) sick of / 이 음악에는 이제 ~이 났다 I'm sick and tired of this music.

심(心) ① 〔핵심〕 a core; 《나무의》 the heart; the pith. ② 〔촛의〕 a wick; 《연필의》 lead; 《양복의》 padding; 《상처에 박는》 a wick sponge. 〔널〕 sense.

…심 〔心〕 heart; mind;

심각(深刻) seriousness; ~하다 (be) serious; grave. ¶ ~해지다 get [become] serious [worse] / ~한 얼굴을 하다 look serious [grave] ~하게 생각하다 think deeply [seriously] / 북한은 ~한 식량 부족에 시달리고 있다 North Korea is suffering from a serious food shortage.

심경(心境) a state [frame] of mind; mental state. ¶ ~의 변화를 가져오다 undergo a change of mind / ~을 토로하다 speak one's mind (to).

심계항진(心悸亢進) 〔醫〕 tachycardia; accelerated heartbeat; palpitations.

심근(心筋) 〔解〕 the heart muscle; the myocardium. ¶ ~경색 〔醫〕 myocardial infraction.

심금(心琴) heartstrings. ¶ ~을 울리다 touch (a person's) heartstrings. 〔timent.

심기(心氣) the mind; mood; sentiment;

심기(心機) ¶ ~일전하다 change one's mind; become a new man; turn over a new leaf.

심낭(心囊) 〔解〕 the pericardium.

심다 plant (trees); sow (barley); 《재배》 grow; raise.

심대(甚大) ~하다 (be) enormous; immense; great; heavy.

심덕(心德) virtue.

심도(深度) depth. ¶ ~를 재다 measure the depth (of); sound (the sea). ¶ ~계 a depth gauge.

심드렁하다 (일이) (be) not urgent; 《마음에》 (be) rather unwilling (to); take no interest (in); 《병이》 be lingering.

심란(心亂) ~하다 feel uneasy; be in a state of agitation; (be) upset; disturbed.

심려(心慮) worry; anxiety; care. ~하다 be anxious [concerned] (about); be troubled [worried] (about, that); care; worry. ¶ 여러가지로 ~를 끼쳐 죄송합니다 I'm sorry to have troubled you [so].

심력(心力) mental power; [much].

심령(心靈) spirit. ¶ ~술 spiritualism / ~학 psychics / ~학자 a psychicist / ~현상 a spiritual phenomenon.

심로(心勞) worry; care; anxiety.

심리(心理) psychology; a mental state; mentality. ¶ ~적(으로) mental(ly); psychological(ly) / 이상 〔군중, 아동〕 ~ abnormal (mass, child) psychology / ~적으로 나쁜 영향을 주다 have a bad effect on the mind of (a child); have a psychological influence on (a child) / ~소설 〔현상〕 a psychological novel [phenomenon] / ~요법 psychotherapy / ~작용 a mental process / ~전 〔묘사〕 psychological warfare [description] / ~학 psychology / ~학자 a psychologist.

심리(審理) (a) trial; (an) examination. ~하다 try (a case); examine; inquire into. ¶ ~중이다 be under [on] trial.

심마니 a digger of wild ginseng.

심문(審問) (a) trial; (give) a hearing (to). ~하다 hear (a case); examine; try; interrogate. ¶ ~을 받다 be given a hearing; be tried [examined].

심미(審美) ~적인 (a)esthetic(al). ¶ ~안 (have) an eye for the beautiful / ~주의 estheticism / ~학 esthetics.

심방(心房) 〔解〕 an atrium [pl. -ria].

심방(尋訪) ~하다 visit. ¶ ~ 방문.

심벌 a symbol (of peace).

심벌즈 〔樂〕 (a pair of) cymbals.

심보(心-) ☞ 마음보.

심복(心服) ~하다 be devoted (to); hold (a person) in high esteem.

심복(心腹) a confidant(남자); a confidante(여자). ¶ ~의 devoted; trusted; confidential. ¶ ~부하 one's confidential subordinate; one's right-hand man.

심부름 an errand. ~하다 go on an errand; do [run] an errand (for a person). ¶ ~ 보내다 send (a person) on an errand / ~꾼 an errand [office] boy; a messenger. 〔ciency; heart failure.

심부전(心不全) 〔醫〕 cardiac insufficiency;

심사(心思) a ill-natured (crossgrained) disposition. ¶ ~ 부리다 thwart; disturb; get in the way; put a spoke in another's wheel / ~ 사나운 malicious; illnatured; cross-grained; cantankerous.

심사(深謝) ~하다 thank heartily. 《사죄》 make a sincere apology.

심사(審査) 〔검사〕 (an) inspection; (an) examination; 〔판정〕 judging. ~하다 examine; judge; investigate. ¶ ~에 합격하다 pass the examination; be accepted. ¶ ~관 an examiner; a judge / ~위원회 a judging committee / ~제도 the screening system.

심사숙고(深思熟考) ~하다 consider

carefully; ponder 《on, over》. ¶ ~ 끝에 after long deliberation.
심산(心算) an intention; designs; calculation. 《~…할 ~으로》 with the intention of *doing* / 무슨 ~인지 모르겠다 I can't quite see *his* idea 〔intention〕.
심산(深山) the mountain recesses; remote mountains. ‖ ~유곡 steep mountains and deep valleys.
심상(心象)〔心〕 an image.
심상(尋常) ¶ ~ 한 common; ordinary; usual / ~ 치 않은 uncommon; unusual; serious.
심성(心性) mind; nature; disposition.
심술(心術) a cross temper; perverseness; maliciousness. ¶ ~ 궂은 ill-tempered〔-natured〕; perverse; cross〔-grained〕; cantankerous / ~ 부리다 be cross with 《a person》 / ~ 궂게 웃다 laugh maliciously. ‖ ~꾸러기 a cross-grained〔an ill-natured〕 person.
심신(心身) mind and body; body and soul. ¶ ~의 피로 mental and physical exhaustion / ~을 단련하다 train both bodies and spirits. ‖ ~장애자〔장애아〕 a mentally and physically handicapped person〔child〕.
심실(心室)〔解〕 the 《right, left》 ventricle 〔of the heart〕.
심심(深甚) ¶ ~ 한 deep; cordial; profound 《gratitude》/ ~한 사의를 표하다 express *one's* deepest gratitude 《to》/ 《사과의 뜻》 beg 《a person》 a thousand pardons.
심심풀이 killing time. ~ 하다 kill time; while away the tedium. ¶ ~로 《read a book》 to kill time; to pass the tedious hours.
심심하다(《일 없이》) be bored; feel ennui; have a dull time.
심심하다(《싱겁다》) be 〔taste〕 slightly flat 〔watery〕.
심안(心眼) the mind's eye; mental perception 〔vision〕. ¶ ~을 뜨다 open *one's* mind's eye.
심야(深夜) the dead of night. ¶ ~에 late at night; in the dead of night / 저 상점은 ~ 영업을 하고 있다 That store is open till late at night. ‖ ~방송 late-night〔all-night〕 broadcasting / ~영업 late-night operation / ~요금 late-night rate / ~작업 late-night work〔labor〕.
심약(心弱) ~ 하다 《be》 timid; feeble-minded; weak-minded.
심연(深淵) an abyss; a gulf.
심오(深奧) ~ 한 profound; abstruse / ~한 뜻 a profound meaning.
심원(深遠) ~ 하다 《be》 deep; profound; abstruse; recondite.
심의(審議) consideration; discussion; deliberation. ~ 하다 consider; discuss; deliberate 《on》. ¶ ~ 중이다 be under deliberation〔consideration〕/ ~에 부치다 refer 《a matter》 to 《a committee》. ‖ ~회 a 〔deliberative〕 council; an inquiry commission / 교육〔경제〕~회 an educational〔economic〕 council.
심장(心臟)〔解〕 the heart; 《뱃심》 《a》 cheek; a nerve; guts. ¶ ~의 고동 the beating〔throbbing〕 of the heart; a heartbeat / ~이 튼튼하다 have a strong〔stout〕 heart / ~이 약하다 have a weak〔bad〕 heart / ~이 강하다 《뱃심이 있다》 be cheeky; be brazen-faced; be bold / ~이 약하다 《뱃심이 없다》 be timid; be shy / 그 광경에 ~이 멎을 것 같았다 My heart stood still when I saw the scene. / 생명 유지 장치로 그의 ~은 고동을 이어갔다 A life-support system kept his heart beating. ‖ ~마비 a heart attack; heart failure / ~병 a heart disease〔trouble〕/ ~외과 heart〔cardiac〕 surgery / ~외과의 a heart〔cardiac〕 surgeon / ~이식 a heart transplant / ~장해 heart trouble / ~판막증 a valvular disease of the heart.
심장(深長) ¶ ~ 한 deep; profound / ~의미 ~하다 have a deep meaning; be 〔deeply〕 significant.
심적(心的) mental. ¶ ~ 현상〔작용〕 a mental phenomenon〔action〕.
심전계(心電計)〔醫〕 an electrocardiograph.
심전도(心電圖)〔醫〕 an electrocardiogram〔생략 ECG〕.
심정(心情) *one's* heart〔feelings〕. ¶ ~을 헤아리다 〔이해하다〕 enter into 《a person's》 feelings; sympathize with 《a person》.
심줄 a tendon; a sinew.
심중(心中) ¶ ~에 at heart; in *one's* heart; inwardly / ~을 털어놓다 unburden 《unbosom》 *oneself* 《to》/ ~을 헤아리다 share 〔appreciate〕 《a person's》 feelings; sympathize with 《a person》.
심증(心證)〔法〕 a conviction; 《인상》 an impression. ¶ ~을 얻다 gain a confident belief / ~을 굳히다 be confirmed in *one's* belief that… / ~을 나쁘게 주다 give 《a person》 an unfavorable impression.
심지(心―) a wick. ¶ ~를 돋우다〔내리다〕 turn up〔down〕 the wick.
심지(心地) disposition; nature; temper〔ament〕; character.
심지어(甚至於) what is worse; on

심취(心醉) ―하다 be fascinated [charmed] 《*with*》; be devoted 《*to*》; adore. ¶ ~자 a devoted admirer; an adorer.
심판(審判) judgment; trial. ~하다 judge; (act as) umpire [referee]. ¶ 최후의 ~ the Last Judgment. ‖ ~관 an umpire; a referee; a judge.
심포니 a symphony.
심포지엄 a symposium.
심하다(甚一) (be) severe; intense; extreme; excessive; heavy. ¶ 심한 경쟁 a keen competition / 심한 더위 intense heat / 심한 부상 a serious wound / 심한 추위 severe [bitter, intense] cold / 심해지다 become violent [severe] / get worse [serious] (악화).
심해(深海) the deep sea. ‖ ~어 a deep-sea fish / ~어업 deep-sea fishing.
심혈(心血) ¶ ~을 기울여 with all one's heart / ~을 기울인 작품 one's most laborious work / ~을 기울이다 put one's heart and soul 《*into*》; do one's energies to 《*one's studies*》.
심호흡(深呼吸) deep breath; deep breathing. ~하다 breathe deeply; take a deep breath. 「심장」
심혼(心魂) one's heart [soul]. ☞
심홍(深紅) deep red; crimson.
심화(心火) fire of anger.
심화(深化) ―하다 deepen.
심황(深黃) deep yellow; saffron (color). 「the mind.」
심회(心懷) thoughts of the heart;
심히(甚一) severely; exceedingly; intensely; terribly; intently.
십(十) ten; the tenth(열째).
십각형(十角形) a decagon. ¶ ~의 decagonal.
십간(十干) the ten calendar signs; the ten celestial stems.
십계명(十誡命) 〖聖〗 the Ten Commandments; the Decalog(ue).
십년(十年) ten years; a decade. ¶ ~간의 decennary / ~을 하루같이 day in and day out; without a break for (ten) long years.
십대(十代) one's teens. ¶ ~의 아이 a teen-ager; a teen-age boy [girl] / 그는 ~이다 He is in his teens.
십만(十萬) a hundred thousand.
십면체(十面體) 〖幾〗 a decahedron.
십분(十分) ① (시간) ten minutes. ② (충분히) enough; sufficiently; fully. ③ (십등분) division in ten. ¶ ~의 일 one-tenth.
십상 all right; just the (just the) thing; admirable; perfect(ly).
십억(十億) a billion《米》; a thousand million《英》.
십오(十五) fifteen. ¶ ~ the fifteenth / ~분 a quarter 《of an hour》.
십육(十六) sixteen; the sixteenth. ¶ ~밀리영화필름 a 16mm movie film / ~분음표 a semiquaver; a sixteenth note.
십이(十二) twelve; a dozen. ¶ 제 ~ the twelfth. 「Dec.》.」
십이월(十二月) December(생략
십이지(十二支) the twelve Earth's Branches; the twelve horary signs.
십이지장(十二指腸) 〖解〗 the duodenum. ‖ ~궤양 a duodenal ulcer / ~충 a hookworm.
십인십색(十人十色) So many men, so many minds.
십일월(十一月) November(생략 Nov.).
십자(十字) a cross. ¶ ~형의 crossshaped; crossed; cruciform / ~를 긋다 cross *oneself*. ‖ ~가 a cross; a crucifix(상) / ~군 a crusade / ~로 a crossroads / ~포화 a cross fire.
십자매(十姉妹) 〖鳥〗 a Bengalee; a society finch. 「foreman.」
십장(什長) the chief workman;
십종경기(十種競技) decathlon.
십중팔구(十中八九) ten to one; in nine cases out of ten; most probably.
십진(十進) ¶ ~의 decimal; denary. ‖ ~법 the decimal system.
십팔(十八) eighteen; the eighteenth(제18). ¶ ~금 18-carat gold / ~번 《자랑거리》 one's forte (specialty).
싱겁다 ① (맛이) (be) insipid; tasteless; be not properly salted; taste flat. ¶ 맛이 ~ be not well salted. ② (언행이) (be) flat; dull; silly. ¶ 싱거운 사람 a wishy-washy (dull-witted) person / 싱겁게 굴지 마라 Don't be silly. 「smile; grin.」
싱긋 ―웃다 smile a gentle
싱그레 ―웃다 smile a gentle
싱글 (침대) a single bed; 《양복》 a single-breasted coat; 《테니스 등의》 a singles (match).
싱글거리다 grin; be grinning
싱글벙글 ―하다 grin; beam 《*upon a person*》; be all smiles.
싱긋 ―웃다 smile 《*at a person*》.
싱숭생숭하다 (be) restless; unset; fidgety.
싱싱하다 (be) fresh; lively; full of life; fresh-looking. ¶ 싱싱한 생선 a fresh fish.
싱크대(一臺) 《부엌의》 a sink.
싱크로트론 〖理〗 a synchrotron.
싶다 (욕구) want 《wish, hope, desire》 to 《*do*》; would 《should》 like to 《*do*》; be eager to 《*do*》; 《기분이》 feel like 《*doing*》; be 《feel》 inclined to 《*do*》. ¶ 싶어 하다

싸개 a cover; a wrapper; a packing sheet.
싸고돌다 〔두둔하다〕 shield; protect; stand by; cover up for. ¶아들을 ~ shield one's son 《from her father's anger》.
싸구려 a cheap 〔low-priced〕 article; 〔hunt for〕 a bargain.
싸늘하다 ☞ 써늘하다.
싸다¹ wrap 〔up〕; pack 《goods》; bundle 《clothes》; 〔덮다〕 cover 《with》; envelop 《in》. ¶종이에 ~ wrap 〔do〕 *something* up in paper / 한데 ~ put 《*things*》 into one parcel / 화염에 싸이다 be enveloped 〔engulfed〕 in flames.
싸다² 〔대소변을〕 discharge; excrete 《*urine, feces*》; void. ¶바지에 오줌을 ~ wet *one's* pants.
싸다³ ①〔입이〕(be) talkative; voluble. ②〔걸음이〕(be) quick; fast. ③〔불이〕burn fast 《briskly》.
싸다⁴ 〔값이〕(be) cheap; inexpensive; low-priced; of a moderate price. ¶싸게 팔다〔사다〕 sell〔buy〕 cheap 〔at a low price〕 / 아주 ~ be dirtcheap. ¶〔마땅〕 deserve, merit; be well deserved. ¶벌받아 ~ deserve to be punished / 그래 ~ It serves you right!
싸다니다 run 《gad, bustle》 about.
싸라기 broken rice. ¶~ 눈 hail.
싸리(나무) 〔植〕 a bush clover.
싸매다 wrap and tie up.
싸우다 fight 《with, against》; fight a battle; make war 《with》; 〔have a〕 quarrel, wrangle 《말다툼》; contend 《with》 (다투다).
싸움 a war〔전쟁〕; a battle〔전투〕; 〔투쟁〕 a fight; a strife; a struggle; 〔말다툼〕 a quarrel. ~하다 (☞ 싸우다). ¶~에 나가다 go to war 〔the front〕 / ~에 이기다〔지다〕 win 〔lose〕 a battle.
싸움꾼 a quarrelsome person; a fire-eater. 〔ground.
싸움터 a battlefield; a battle=
싸이다(一牌) hoodlums; (a gang of) hooligans.
싸이다 be wrapped (covered). ¶수수께끼에 ~ be shrouded in mystery.
싸전(一廛) a rice store. 〔tery.
싸하다 (be) pungent; acrid; sharp; mentholated.
싹¹ ①〔씨앗〕 a bud; a sprout; a shoot. ¶~트다 sprout; put forth buds 〔shoots〕; 〔기회가〕 begin to develop; bud. ② ☞ 싹수.
싹² 〔베는 소리〕 at a stroke; 〔모두〕 completely; all; thoroughly. ¶~ 베다 cut at a stroke / ~ 변하다 change completely / ~ 쓸어

다 sweep out.
싹둑거리다 snip continuously 《off》.
싹수 a good omen; promise. ¶~가 노랗다 be hopeless; have no prospect of.
싹싹 ¶~ 빌다 supplicate 〔beg〕 《a King》 for pardon 〔mercy〕 with joined hands.
싹싹하다 (be) affable; amiable.
싼값 a cheap 〔low〕 price.
쌀 rice. ¶~고장 a rice-producing district / ~의 자급자족 rice self-sufficiency. ¶~ 가게 a rice store / ~ 가루 rice flour / ~ 가마니 a straw rice bag / ~ 겨 rice bran / ~ 농사 rice growing / ~ 밥 boiled rice / ~ 벌레 a rice weevil / ~ 시장개방 the opening of the domestic rice market to foreign suppliers / ~ 알 a grain of rice / ~ 장수 a rice dealer.
쌀보리 〔植〕 rye; naked barley.
쌀쌀하다 〔냉정〕(be) cool; coldhearted; unfriendly; inhospitable. ¶쌀쌀하게 coldly; in a chilly manner. ¶〔일기가〕(be) chilly; cold; wintry.
쌈 rice wrapped in leaves 《of lettuce》; stuffed leaves. ¶상추 ~ lettuce-wrapped rice.
쌈지 a tobacco pouch.
쌉쌀하다 〔서술적〕 taste bitterish.
쌍(雙) a pair; a couple; twins. ¶잘 어울리는 한 ~의 부부 a well=matched couple 〔pair〕 / ~을 만들다 pair; make a pair of 《*two things*》.
쌍겹눈(雙—) a double eyelid eye.
쌍곡선(雙曲線) 〔數〕 a hyperbola.
쌍극자(雙極子) 〔理〕 a dipole.
쌍꺼풀(雙—) a double eyelid.
쌍동기(雙胴機) a twin-fuselage plane.
쌍동밤(雙童—) twin chestnuts.
쌍동선(雙胴船) a twin-hulled ship; a catamaran.
쌍두(雙頭) ¶~ 의 double-headed. ¶~ 마차 a carriage-and-pair.
쌍둥이(雙—) twins; twin brothers 〔sisters〕; a twin(그 중 한 사람). ¶~를 낳다 give birth to triplets.
쌍무(雙務) ¶~적인 bilateral; reciprocal. ¶~계약 a bilateral 〔reciprocal〕 contract / ~조약 a bilateral treaty.
쌍무지개(雙—) a double rainbow.
쌍바라지(雙—) double doors.
쌍발(雙發) ¶~의 bimotored. ¶~ 비행기 a twin-engine plane.
쌍방(雙方) both parties 〔sides〕. ¶~의 both; mutual / ~의 이익을 위하여 in the interest of both parties; in 《*our*》 mutual interests.
쌍벽(雙璧) the two greatest au-

쌍생(雙生) ¶ ~의 twin; [植] binate. ‖ ~아 twins; a twin (한쪽).
쌍수(雙手) (raise) both hands. ¶ ~를 들어 찬성하다 support 《a person's plan》 whole-heartedly.
쌍시류(雙翅類) [蟲] a dipteron.
쌍심지(心─) a double wicks. ¶ 눈에 ~를 켜다 《비유적》 raise one's angry eyebrows; glare at.
쌍십절(雙十節) the Double Tenth Festival.
쌍쌍(雙雙─) by twos; in pairs; [in couples.
쌍안(雙眼) ¶ ~의 binocular. ‖ ~경 (a pair of) binoculars; field glasses (야전용).
쌍태(雙胎) a twin fetus.
쌓다 ① 《포개다》 pile [heap] (up); stack 《boxes》; lay 《bricks》. ② 《구축》 build; construct; lay. ¶ 성을 ~ build 〔construct〕 a castle / 토대를 ~ lay a foundation. ③ 《축적》 accumulate 〔gain〕 《experience》; store; amass 《a big fortune》; practice (연습을).
쌓이다 be piled up; be accumulated. ¶ 쌓이는 원한 growing hatred / 책상 위에 책이 ~ books are piled up on the desk.
쌔비다 《훔치다》 pilfer; filch; snitch.
써넣다 write in; 《서식에》 fill out 《the blank》 《美》; fill up 〔in〕 《the form》 《英》.
써다 《조수가》 ebb; flow back.
써레 a harrow. ¶ ~질하다 harrow a field.
썩 ① 《빨리》 right away; at once. ¶ ~ 물러나라 Get out at once. ② 《대단히》 very (much); exceedingly; greatly. ¶ ~ 좋은 기회 a very lucky opportunity.
썩다 ① 《부패》 go bad 〔rotten〕; rot; decay; spoil; decompose; corrupt (타락). ¶ 썩은 이빨 a decayed tooth / 썩은 과일 spoiled fruit / 썩은 생선 stale 〔rotten〕 fish / 썩은 정치인 a corrupt politician. ② 《활용으로》 gather dust; get rusty. ③ 《마음이》 become heavy; feel depressed; break.
썩이다 ① 《부패》 let rot 〔decay〕; corrupt. ② 《속을》 worry; annoy; eat one's heart out 《with》. ¶ 남의 속을 ~ give 《a person》 trouble; worry another's heart.
썰다 chop (up); mince; dice; slice; cut up; hash (잘게).
썰렁하다 (be) chilly; rather cold.
썰매 a sled; a sledge; a sleigh (대형의). ¶ ~를 타다 ride on a sled 〔in a sledge〕; sled. ‖ ~타기 sledding; sleigh riding.
썰물 an ebb tide; a low tide.
쏘가리 [魚] a mandarin fish.
쏘다 ① 《발사》 fire; shoot; discharge. ¶ 쏘아 죽이다 shoot 《a person》 dead 〔to death〕. ② 《말로》 criticize; censure; attack. ③ 《벌레가》 bite; sting.
쏘다니다 roam 〔wander, gad〕 about; run around.
쏘삭거리다 instigate; incite; stir up 《a fight》. [《at》.
쏘아보다 glare 《at》; look fiercely
쏘아올리다 shoot 〔fire, let, set〕 off; launch (인공 위성을). ¶ 인공 위성을 ~ launch an artificial satellite into the sky.
쏘이다 be stung. ¶ 벌에게 ~ get stung by a bee.
쏜살같다 be as swift as an arrow. ¶ 쏜살같이 like an arrow; at full speed.
쏟다 ① 《물건을》 pour 《into, out》; spill; empty 《a box》. ② 《집중》 devote 《to》; concentrate 《on》. ¶ 마음을 ~ give one's mind 《to》; devote oneself 《to》; concentrate one's thought 《on》.
쏟아지다 pour 《out, down》; 《물 따위가》 gush out; spout; spurt; be spilt. ¶ 비가 ~ it rains hard.
쏠리다 ① 《기울다》 incline 〔lean〕 《to, toward》. ② 《경향이 있다》 be inclined 〔disposed〕 to; tend to; lean toward.
쐐기¹ a wedge; a chock. ¶ ~를 박다 drive in a wedge.
쐐기² [蟲] a caterpillar.
쐐기풀 [植] a nettle (hemp).
쐬다 ① 《바람 따위를》 expose oneself to; be exposed to. ② 《벌레 따위에》 be stung 《by a bee》.
쑤다 cook 《gruel》; prepare; make 《paste》.
쑤석거리다 ① 《쑤시다》 poke about. ② 《선동》 instigate; urge; egg 〔set〕 《a person》 on 《to do》.
쑤셔넣다 stuff 〔pack〕 into; shove in〔to〕; poke into.
쑤시개 a pick.
쑤시다¹ 《구멍 따위를》 pick; poke. ¶ 이를 ~ pick one's teeth.
쑤시다² 《아프다》 throb with pain; tingle; twinge; smart; ache.
쑥¹ [植] a mugwort.
쑥² 《바보》 a fool; a simpleton; an ass; a dupe.
쑥³ 《부사》 ¶ ~ 뽑다 draw 〔pull〕 out 《a thing》 with a jerk / 쑥 들어가다 sink; cave in (땅이); give in / ~ 내밀다 project; thrust 〔jut〕 out.
쑥갓 [植] a crown daisy. 「hair.
쑥대같이 disheveled 〔unkempt〕
쑥대밭 ¶ ~이 되다 be reduced to complete ruin.
쑥덕공론(─公論) secret talks; a secret conference; a talk in whispers. ~하다 discuss things

쑥스럽다 (be) unseemly: improper; embarrassed; awkward.

쓰다¹ 《글씨를》 write 《a letter, a story》; spell《철자하다》; put《write, note》 down《적다》; compose 《a poem》. ¶ 잉크로 ~ write in ink / 연필로 ~ write with a pencil / 수필을 ~ write an essay / 영수증을 ~ write (make) out a receipt / 편지에 …라고 쓰여 있다 the letter says that….

쓰다² ① 《사용》 use 《as, for》; make use of: utilize; put to use; 《취급》 work 《a machine》; handle 《a tool》; 《채택》 adopt. ¶ 쓰기에 편한 handy; convenient 《to handle》 / …을 써서 by means of / 너무 ~ overuse; overwork; use too much / 수단을 ~ take a measure. ② 《고용》 engage; employ; take 《a person》 into one's service; keep; hire. ¶ 시험삼아 써 보다 give 《a person》 a trial. ③ 《소비品》 use; spend 《in, on》. ¶ 돈을 ~ spend money / ~ use up: exhaust; consume; deplete; go through. ④ 《술법 따위》 practice 《magic》. ⑤ 《약을》 administer 《medicine》 to 《a person》; dose. ⑥ 《힘을》 exert; exercise; use. ¶ 머리를 ~ use one's head (brains) / 폭력을 ~ apply force. ⑦ 《행사》 circulate; pass; utter. ¶ 가짜돈을 ~ pass a counterfeit coin. ⑧ 《색을》 have sex. ⑨ 《말하》 speak. ¶ 영어를 ~ speak English.

쓰다³ ① 《머리에》 put on 《모자를》; cover 《수건 따위를》; wear《착용》. ② 《안경을》 put on 《spectacles》. ③ 《물·먼지 따위를》 pour 《water》 upon oneself; be covered with 《dust》. ④ 《우산을》 hold 《put up》 《an umbrella》; hold 《an umbrella》 over one's head. ⑤ 《이불을》 draw (pull) 《the quilt》 over one's head. ⑥ 《누명 등을》 be falsely accused 《of》.

쓰다⁴ 《맛이》 (be) bitter. ¶ 쓴 약을 bitter medicine. ~ bury in 《at》.

쓰다⁵ 《뫼를》 set up a grave.

쓰다듬다 stroke 《one's beard》; pass one's hand 《over, across》; smooth 《one's hair》; pat.

쓰디쓰다 (be) very bitter.

쓰라리다 (be) smart; sore; 《괴롭다》 (be) painful; hard; bitter. ¶ 쓰라린 경험 a bitter experience.

쓰러뜨리다 throw down; knock down; overthrow 《전복》; blow down《바람이》; fell 《a tree》; pull down; 《죽이다》 kill.

쓰러지다 ① 《전도·도괴》 collapse; fall (down); be overturned《전복》. ② 《죽다》 fall dead; die; meet one's death; be killed. ③ 《도산·몰락》 be ruined; go to ruin; go bankrupt; fail. ¶ 쓰러져 가는 회사 a company on the verge of bankruptcy.

쓰레기 rubbish; refuse; garbage; trash. ¶ ~더미 a rubbish heap / ~를 버리다 throw garbage away; throw away household waste / ~를 버리지 마시오 《게시》 No dumping 《here》. ∥ ~ 분리수거 separate garbage collection / ~ 수거인 a garbage collector; 《美》 a dustman 《英》 / ~ 종량제 the volume-rate garbage disposal system / ~차 a dust cart; a garbage truck 《美》 / ~ 처리 waste (rubbish) disposal / ~처리장 a garbage dump; a dumping ground / ~통 a dustbin; an ash can 《美》 / 재활용 ~ recyclable (recurrent) wastes.

쓰레받기 a dustpan.

쓰레질 ~하다 sweep (and clean).

쓰르라미 《蟲》 a clear-toned cicada.

쓰리다 (be) smarting; tingling; 《공복》 (be) hungry. ¶ 가슴이 ~ have a heartburn.

쓰이다¹ 《글씨가 써지다》 write 《well》; 《쓰여 있다》 be written; 《쓰게 하다》 let 《a person》 write. ¶ 이 펜은 글씨가 잘 쓰인다 This pen writes well. / 그녀에게 편지를 ~ have her write a letter.

쓰이다² ① 《사용》 be used; be in use; be utilized. ¶ 항상 쓰이는 말 a word in general use. ② 《소용》 be spent; be consumed; need; take; cost.

쓱 quickly and quietly; stealthily.

쓱싹하다 《해먹다》 pocket; embezzle. ¶ 공금을 ~ embezzle public money. ② 《잘못 따위를》 hush (cover) up. ¶ 스캔들을 쓱싹하려 하다 try to hush up the scandal. ③ 《셈을》 cancel 《out》; write off; cross out. ¶ 계산을 ~ cancel the accounts; consider the accounts settled.

쓴맛 a bitter taste; bitterness. ¶ 인생의 ~ 단맛을 다 보다 taste the sweets and bitters of life.

쓴웃음 a bitter (wry) smile. ¶ ~을 짓다 smile grimly.

쓸개 the gall (bladder). ¶ ~ 빠진 사람 a spiritless man.

쓸다¹ 《쓰레기》 sweep 《up, away, off》. ¶ 쓸어내다 sweep out 《with a broom》; sweep up 《a room》 / 쓸어 모으다 sweep into a heap.

쓸다² 《줄로》 file; rasp.

쓸데없다 《불필요》 (be) needless; unnecessary; 《무용》 be of no use《서술적》; (be) useless; worthless; 《달갑지 않다》 (be) unwant-

쓸리다¹ 《비로》 be swept(쓸어지다); let (a person) sweep (쓸게 하다).
쓸리다² 《줄에》 get rasped (filed).
쓸리다³ 《살갗이》 be skinned (grazed, chafed). ¶쓸말갗이 쓸렸다 I skinned my elbow.
쓸 만하다 (be) useful; serviceable; valuable (가치 있다).
쓸 use; usage. ¶~가 있다 be useful; be serviceable; be of use (service); serve the purpose; be usable (utilizable) (as) / ~없다 be of no use (service); be useless / ~가 많이 있다 be of wide (extensive) use / 그는 ~없는 사내다 He is a good-for-nothing fellow.
쓸쓸하다 (be) lonely; lonesome; desolate; deserted; solitary (고독). ¶쓸쓸하게 lonesomely; solitarily / 쓸쓸하게 지내다 lead a solitary life / 쓸쓸해지다 feel lonely.
슭다 polish (grain); refine. ‖-ly.
씀바귀 [植] a lettuce.
씀씀이 ¶~가 헤프다 spend money wastefully; be free with one's money.
씁쓸하다 (be) bitterish.
씌우다 ① (머리에) put (a thing) on; (덮다) cover (a thing) with. ② (죄를) pin (a fault) on (a person); lay (a blame) at another's door; charge (fix) a person with a blame).
씨¹ ①《씨앗》 a seed; a stone (열매 속의 단단한 씨); a kernel (핵); a pip (사과, 배 따위의). ¶~뿌릴 때 seedtime / ~없는 seedless / 밭에 ~를 뿌리다 sow seeds in the field / ~를 받다 gather the seeds. ②《마소의》 a breed; a stock. ¶~받이 있는 bull / ~가 좋다 be of a good stock. ③《사람의》 paternal blood. ¶불의의 ~ a child born in sin. ④《근원》 the source; the cause. ¶불평의

~ a source of complaint.
씨² 《피륙의》 the woof (weft). ¶~와 날 woof and warp.
씨(氏) 《경칭》 Mr. (남자); Miss. (미혼 여성); Mrs. (기혼 여성).
씨닭 a breeding chicken.
씨름 wrestling; a wrestling match. ~하다 wrestle (have a wrestling match) with (a person); (비유) tackle (a difficult problem). ‖~꾼 a wrestler.
씨아 a cotton gin. ‖~질 gin-[ning.
씨암탉 a brood hen.
씨앗 a seed. ☞ 씨¹ ①.
씨족(氏族) a clan; a family. ‖ ~정치 clan politics / ~제도 the family (clan) system.
씨줄 (a line of) latitude.
씩 ¶~웃다 grin.
…씩 ¶조금~ little by little; bit by bit / 하나~ one at a time; one by one / 1주 2회~ twice a week.
씩씩하다 (be) manly; manful; courageous; brave.
씹 ①《음부》 the vulva; a cunt (卑). ②《성교》 sexual intercourse; fuck (卑).
씹다 chew; masticate.
씹히다 be chewed; 《씹게 하다》 let (a person) chew (on). ¶잘 씹히지 않다 be hard to chew.
씻기다 《씻어지다》 be washed; 《씻게 하다》 let (a person) wash.
씻다 ①《물로》 wash; wash away (씻어버리다); wash off (out) (씻어내다); cleanse (세정); bathe (상처 따위를). ¶먼지를 씻어버리다 wash off the dirt. ②《죄·누명 따위를》 clear; blot out; clear oneself. ¶씻을 수 없는 치욕 an indelible disgrace / 누명을 ~ clear one's honor. ③《닦아내다》 wipe (off); mop (up). ¶이마의 땀을 ~ wipe the sweat off one's brow.
씻은듯이 clean(ly); completely; thoroughly.
씽 《바람》 whistling. ¶바람이 ~ 불다 the wind is singing.

사과의 표현

1. 사소한 실수 따위로 상대방에게 "미안합니다", "실례했습니다", "죄송합니다"라고 사과할 때

   Excuse me. / I'm sorry.
   or Sorry. / Pardon me.

   미국에서는 Excuse me.가 흔히 쓰이고, I'm sorry.는 사과의 정도가 좀 깊은 느낌을 주려고 할 때 쓰인다. 그러나 영국에서는 I'm sorry.가 더 일반적이며, I'm을 생략하여 Sorry.라고 하는 경우가 더 많다. Pardon me.는 영미 공

히 자주 쓰이지만, 앞서의 두 표현보다 사과의 정도가 좀 더 깊은 느낌을 주는 표현이다.

2. 자신의 잘못이 없더라도 상대방에게 불편을 주게 되는 경우, 예를 들면 좌석에서 중간에 자리를 뜨게 되거나, 남의 앞을 지나게 될 때 또는 남에게 질문 따위를 하게 되었을 때

   Excuse me. / Pardon me.

   위의 두 표현은 영미 공히 가장 흔하게 쓰이는 표현이다.

ㅇ

아 《감동》 Ah!; Oh!; 《놀람》 O dear!; O!; Dear me!; Good gracious!; (Good) Heavens!: God bless me!
아(亞) Asia. ¶ ~주(洲) Asian.
아(阿) Africa. ¶ ~아(亞) 블록 the Afro-Asian bloc.
아…(亞) sub-; near-. ¶ ~열대 subtropics.
아가 ☞ 아기.
아가미 the gill(s) (of a fish).
아가씨 a young lady; a girl; 《호칭》 Miss; *Mademoiselle* (프).
아가위 a haw. ‖ ~나무 〔植〕 a hawthorn; a May tree.
아교(阿膠) glue. ¶ ~질의 gluey; glutinous; colloid / ~로 붙이다 glue.
아국(我國) our country. ¶ ~의 our.
아군(我軍) our forces (troops).
아궁이 a fuel hole; a fire door (of a furnace).
아귀 ① 《갈라진》 a fork; a crotch. ② 《싹트는》 ¶ 씨가 ~트다 a seed sprouts open. ③ 《옷의 터놓은 것》 side slits (on an overcoat).
아귀(餓鬼) 〔佛〕 a hungry ghost; a famished devil (demon); 《사람》 a greedy person; a person of voracious appetite. ‖ ~다툼 a quarrel; a dispute.
아귀세다 (be) tough; firm; strong-minded; unyielding.
아귀아귀 greedily; ravenously.
아그레망 *agrément* (프). approval; acceptance.
아기 ① 《어린애》 a baby; a babe; an infant. ② 《딸·며느리》 a young daughter; a daughter-in-law.
아기 서다 become pregnant; conceive. ¶ 임신.
아기자기하다 《예쁘다》 (be) sweet; charming; fascinating; 《재미있다》 (be) juicy; be full of interest 〔delight〕《서술적》.
아기작거리다 toddle 〔waddle〕 along (about). ¶ 아기작아기작 toddlingly; waddlingly. [*pl.* -ri].
아기집 〔解〕 the womb; the uterus
아까 some time (a little while) ago. ¶ ~부터 for some time.
아깝다 ① 《애석하다》 (be) pitiful; regrettable. ¶ 아깝게도 …하다 〔이다〕 It is a pity (regrettable) that…; It is to be regretted that…. ¶ 아깝게도 그녀는 젊어서 죽었다 It's too bad that she died young. ② 《귀중하다》 (be) dear; precious; valuable. ¶ 나라를 위해 아까운 사람이 죽었다 His death is a great loss to the nation. ③ 《과분하다》 (be) too good (to do); worthy of a better cause. ¶ 아까운 듯이 unwillingly; grudgingly / 버리기엔 너무 ~ It is too good to be thrown away.
아끼다 ① 《함부로 안 쓰다》 grudge; spare; be not generous (with); be frugal of (with). ¶ 수고를 아끼지 않다 spare no efforts (pains) / 비용을 ~ spare expense / 돈을 아끼지 않고 쓰다 be liberal with *one's* purse. ② 《소중히 여기다》 value; hold (*a thing*) dear. ¶ 시간을 ~ value time / 목숨을 ~ hold *one's* life dear.
아낌없이 ungrudgingly; unsparingly; generously; freely; lavishly(부하). ¶ 자선을 위해 많은 돈을 ~ 내놓다 give a lot of money freely to charities.
아나운서 an announcer; a radio (TV) announcer.
아낙(내간) a boudoir; woman's quarters; 《아낙네》 a woman; a wife. ¶ ~네들 the womenfolk. / ~군수 a stay-at-home.
아내 a wife; *one's* better half; a spouse(雅우자). ¶ ~를 얻다 take a wife; get married / 훌륭한 ~가 되다 make a fine wife.
아네모네 〔植〕 an anemone. 「en.
아녀자(兒女子) children and wom-
아뇨 no 《대답이 부정일 때》; yes 《대답이 긍정일 때》. ¶ 「이 책은 네 것이냐?」—「~, 아닙니다.」 "Is this book yours?" — "No, it isn't." / 「과자를 싫어하느냐?」—「~, 좋아합니다.」 "Don't you like sweets?" — "Yes, I do."
아늑하다 (be) snug; cozy.
아는 체하다 pretend to know; pretend as if *one* knew; speak in a knowing manner. ¶ 아는 체하는 사람 a knowing fellow.
아니 ① 《부정의 대답》 no; nay; not at all. ¶ ~라고 대답하다 say no; answer in the negative. ② 《놀람·의아함》 why; what; dear me; good heavens. ¶ ~ 이게 웬 일이냐 Why, what happened? / ~ 또 늦었니 What! Are you late again?
아니 《부사》 not. ~하다 do not. ¶ ~ 가다 do not go.
아니꼽다 《불쾌》 (be) sickening; revolting; disgusting; provoking; detestable. ¶ 아니꼬운 자식 a disgustful fellow; a snob.
아니나다를까 as *one* expected; as

아니다 was expected; sure enough. ¶ ~ 그는 나타나지 않았다 As was expected, he failed to turn up.
아니다 (be) not. ¶ 그는 바보가 ~ He is not foolish.
아니면 either 《you》 or 《I》.
아니게아니라 indeed; really.
아닌 밤중 ¶ ~에 홍두깨 내미는 격으로 all of a sudden; unexpected.
아다지오 [樂] adagio 《이》.
아담(雅淡)하다 ¶ ~한 refined; elegant; neat; tidy; dainty.
아동(兒童) a child; children(총칭); boys and girls. ¶ ~용의 책 a book for children; juvenile books / 취학 전의 ~ a preschool child / 초등학교 ~ a primary- [grade-]schoolchild. ‖ ~ 교육 the education of children / ~ 문학 juvenile literature; literature for children / ~ 복지법 the Juvenile [Child] Welfare Law / ~ 심리학 child psychology.
아둔하다 (be) dull(-witted); slow; stupid; dim-witted.
아득하다 《거리》(be) far; far away [off]; in the distance; 《시간》(be) long ago [before]; a long time ago. ¶ 아득히 한라산이 보인다 see Mt. Halla in the distance / 아득한 옛날을 생각하다 think of the days long ago / 갈 길이 ~ have a long way to go.
아들 a son; a boy.
아따 Gosh!; (Oh) Boy! ¶ ~ 걱정도 팔자 Oh! Don't worry so much.
아득(아뜩)하다 (be) dizzy; giddy; dazed; stunned.
아라비아 Arabia. ¶ ~ (사람)의 Arabian; Arabic / ~ 사람 an Arab (-ian) / ~ 숫자 Arabic figures [numerals].
아랍 Arab. ‖ ~국가 the Arab states / ~ 어(語) Arabic.
아랑곳 ¶ ~ 없다 be no concern of; have nothing to do with / 그가 어찌 되든 내가 ~ 할 바 아니다 I don't give [care] a damn what becomes of him.
아래 ① 《하부·바닥》 the low part; the foot; the bottom. ¶ 맨 ~ 서랍을 열다 open the bottom drawer / 층계 ~ 에서 기다리다 wait at the foot of the stairs. ② 《위치·아래쪽》 ¶ ~ 의 under 《…의 밑》; below 《…보다 낮은 위치》; down 《아래쪽》; lower 《…보다 낮은》; following 《다음의》 / ~ 로 내려가다 [내려오다] go [come] down; go [come] downstairs / ~ 와 같다 be as follows / 나무 ~ 로 피신하다 take shelter under a tree / 지평선 ~ 로 가라 앉다 sink [go down] below the horizon. ③ 《하위》 ¶ ~ 의 lower; subordinate; below, under; younger (나이가) / 아랫사람 one's subordinates / …의 지휘 ~ under a person's command / 남의 ~ 에서 일하다 work under a person / 형보다 5세 ~ 다 be five years younger than one's brother.
아래위 up and down; above and below; upper and lower sides; top and bottom.
아래윗벌 upper and lower garments; a suit 《of clothes》.
아래채 the outer-wing house; an annex.
아래층 (一層) downstairs.
아래턱 the lower [under] jaw.
아랫니 the lower teeth.
아랫도리 the lower part 《of the body》.
아랫목 the part of a Korean room nearest the fireplace.
아랫방 (一房) a detached room.
아랫배 the belly; the abdomen.
아랫사람 one's junior(손 아래); an underling; a subordinate(부하).
아랫수염 (一鬚髥) a beard.
아랫입술 the lower [under] lip.
아량 (雅量) generosity; tolerance; magnanimity. ¶ ~ 있는 generous; broad-minded; magnanimous.
아련하다 (be) dim; vague; faint; hazy; obscure; misty.
아령 (啞鈴) a dumbbell.
아로새기다 engrave [carve] elaborately. ¶ 마음에 ~ engrave in [upon] one's mind.
아롱거리다 《사물이》 flicker; flit; 《눈이》 be dazzled. ¶ 등불이 ~ The lamp flickers. / 그녀 얼굴이 눈 앞에 아롱거린다 The memory of her face still haunts me.
아뢰다 tell [inform] a superior.
아류 (亞流) an adherent; a follower; a bad second.
아르바이트 a side job; a part-time job.
아르헨티나 Argentina. ¶ ~의 Argentine / ~ 사람 an Argentine.
아름 an armful 《of firewood》.
아름답다 (be) beautiful; pretty; lovely; 《용모》 (be) good-looking; handsome; 《경치》 (be) picturesque; 《목소리》 (be) sweet; 《마음이》 (be) noble-minded. ¶ 아름답게 beautifully / 아름다운 목소리 a sweet [charming] voice / 아름다운 음악 a lovely music / 아름다운 풍경 picturesque scenery / 아름다운 소녀 a beautiful [lovely] girl.
아름드리 ‖ ~ 나무 a tree measuring more than an arm's span around.
아리다 ① 《맛이》 (be) pungent; acrid; sharp. ② 《상처 따위》 (be) smarting; tingling; burning.
아리땁다 (be) lovely; sweet; pretty; charming. ¶ 아리따운 처녀 a charming young lady.
아리송하다 (be) indistinct; dim;

아리아 [樂] aria.
아리안 Aryan. ‖ ~ 족 [인종] Aryan races.
아마 [亞麻] [植] flax. ¶ ~의 flaxen. ‖ ~씨(기름) flax yarn / ~유 linseed oil / ~천 linen.
아마 (대개) probably; perhaps; maybe; possibly; presumably.
아마존강 (一江) the Amazon.
아마추어 an amateur; a nonprofessional; (초심자) a beginner; a novice. ¶ ~의 amateur; nonprofessional. / ~정신 the spirit of amateurism.
아말감 [化] amalgam.
아메리카 America. ¶ ~의 American. ☞ 미국. ‖ ~대륙 the American continent.
아메바 [動] an amoeba.
아멘 Amen!
아명 (兒名) one's childhood name.
아무 ① (긍정·부정 (不定)) anyone; anybody; any; whoever; (every) one; all; everybody. ¶ ~도 할 수 있다 Anyone can do it. ② (부정 (否定)) no one; no body; none; anyone; anybody. ¶ ~도 …이라는 것은 의심할 수 없다 No one can doubt that….
아무개 Mr. so-and-so; a certain person. ¶ ~김 a certain Mr. Kim; one Kim.
아무것 anything; (부정) nothing. ¶ ~이나 좋아하는 것 anything one likes / ~할 일이 ~도 없다 have nothing to do.
아무데 somewhere; a certain place; anywhere (부정·의문). ¶ ~나 in every place; everywhere; all over / ~도 nowhere.
아무때 ¶ ~나 (at) any time; (항상) always; all the time; (…할 때는 언제나) whenever.
아무래도 ① (어떻든) anyhow; anyway. ¶ ~ 그것은 해야 한다 I must do it anyhow. ② (결국) after all; in the long run; in the end. ③ (모든 점에서) to all appearance; in all respects. ¶ ~ 부라고 밖에 볼 수 없다 They are, to all appearance, man and wife. ④ (싫던 좋던) whether one likes it or not; willy-nilly. ⑤ (결코) by any means; on any account. ⑥ (무관) ¶ 그까것 일은 ~ 좋다 That does not matter.
아무러면 (no matter, it makes no difference) whatever (however) it is; whoever says it is. ¶ 옷이나 ~ 어떠냐 It doesn't matter how your clothes look.
아무런 (부정) any; no. ¶ ~ 사고 없이 without any accident.
아무렇거나 anyhow; anyway; at any rate; in any case. ¶ ~ 해 보세 Anyhow, let us try.

아무렇게나 at random; carelessly; indifferently; half-heartedly; in a slovenly way. ¶ ~ 말하다 talk at random.
아무렇게도 (어떻게도) in any (no) way; (무관심) nothing; not at all; not a bit. ¶ ~ 생각 안 하다 make little (nothing) of (에사); do not hesitate (주저 않다); do not care about (고려 않다).
아무렇든지 anyhow; in any event (way); at any rate.
아무렴 Surely.; To be sure.; Of course!; Certainly!
아무리 ¶ ~ …해도 however much; no matter how / ~ 돈이 많아도 no matter how rich a man may be; however rich a man may be.
아무 말 (not) any word. ¶ ~ 없이 without saying a word.
아무 일 something; anything; (부정) nothing. ¶ ~ 없이 without accident; in safety; quietly.
아무짝 ¶ ~에도 못 쓰겠다 It is of no use whatsoever.
아무쪼록 as much as one can; to the best of one's ability; (꼭) by all means; (부디) (if you) please; I beg. ¶ ~ 몸조심하십시오 Take the best possible care of yourself.
아무튼 anyway; anyhow; in any case; at any rate. ¶ ~ 해 보겠다 At any rate I'll try. / ~ 즐거웠다 I enjoyed myself very much, anyway.
아물거리다 (깜박이다) flicker; (희미하다) be dim (hazy); (눈앞이) be dizzy. ¶ 아물아물하게 flickeringly; dimly; vaguely.
아물다 heal (up); be healed.
아미 (蛾眉) arched eyebrows; eyebrows of a beautiful woman.
아미노산 (一酸) [化] an amino acid.
아미타불 (阿彌陀佛) Amitabha [梵].
아버지 a father. ¶ ~다운 fatherly; fatherlike; paternal / ~를 닮다 take after one's father / ~를 잃다 be left fatherless.
아베마리아 Ave Maria.
아베크 (남녀의 쌍) avec (프); a young man with his girl friend; a girl with her boy friend; lovers on a date. ~하다 have a date 《with》.
아부 (阿附) flattery. ~하다 flatter; curry favor 《with a person》; butter 《a person》 up.
아비규환 (阿鼻叫喚) agonizing cries. ¶ ~의 참상 an agonizing (a heartrending) scene.
아비산 (亞砒酸) [化] arsenious acid. ‖ ~염 arsenite.
아빠 papa; daddy; dad; pa.
아사 (餓死) death from hunger (by

아삭아삭 씹다 crunch.
아서라 (Oh.) no!; Quit!; Stop!; Don't!
아성(牙城) inner citadel; the stronghold; the bastion.
아성(亞聖) a sage (saint) of second order.
아성층권(亞成層圈) the substratosphere.
아세테이트(化) acetate.
아세톤(化) acetone.
아세틸렌(化) acetylene.
아수라(阿修羅) Asura (梵). ¶ ~ 같이 싸우다 fight like a demon.
아쉬워하다 feel that something is missing; feel the lack of; (서운해하다) be unwilling; be reluctant. ¶ 이별을 ~ be unwilling (reluctant) to part from (a person).
아쉰대로 inconvenient though it is; though it is not enough; as a temporary makeshift (임시변통으로).
아쉽다 be not quite satisfactory; be inconvenienced by not having. ¶ 아쉬운 것 없이 지내다 live in comfort; be comfortably off / 그의 설명만으로는 좀 아쉬운 데가 있다 His explanation is not entirely satisfactory.
아스파라거스(植) an asparagus.
아스팍 ASPAC. (◀ Asian and Pacific Council)
아스팔트 asphalt. ¶ ~ 길 an asphalt(ed) road / ~를 깔다 pave (streets) with asphalt; asphalt (streets).
아스피린(藥) aspirin.
아슬아슬 ¶ ~ 한 dangerous; risky; thrilling; exciting; critical / ~하게 narrowly; by hairbreadth / ~한 승부 a close game / ~한 때에 at the critical moment / ~하게 이기다 win by a narrow margin / (아무를) ~하게 하다 make (a person) nervous (uneasy).
아시아 Asia. ¶ ~ 의 Asian; Asiatic. ‖ ~ 개발은행 the Asian Development Bank (생략 ADB) / ~ 경기대회 the Asian Games / ~ 대륙 the Asian Continent / ~ 사람 an Asian / ~ 인종 the Asian race.
아씨(호칭) your lady(ship); Mrs; (한인의) mistress; madam.
아아(阿亞) Africa and Asia. ‖ ~ 블록 the Afro-Asian block.
아아 ① (감동) Ah!; Oh!; Alas! (비탄, 실망); ¶ ~ 기쁘다 Oh, how glad I am! / ~ 그렇군 Oh, I see. / (가벼운 감정) Well, ... / ~ 이제 다 왔군 Well, here we are at last.
아악(雅樂) (classical) court (ceremonial) music.
아야 Ouch!
아양 coquetry; flattery. ¶ ~ 떨다 (부리다) play the coquette; flirt; flatter.
아어(雅語) an elegant word; a polite expression; refined diction.
아역(兒役)(劇) a child's part (in a play); (사람) a child actor.
아연(亞鉛) zinc (기호 Zn). ¶ ~ 을 입힌 galvanized. ‖ ~ 도금 galvanizing / ~ 판(板) a zinc plate / ~ 화 연고 zinc ointment.
아연(俄然) suddenly; all of a sudden. ¶ ~ 활기를 띠다 begin to show signs of activity suddenly.
아연(啞然)(부사적) agape (with wonder); aghast; in utter amazement. ¶ ~ 케 하다 strike (a person) dumb; dumbfound.
아열대(亞熱帶) the subtropics; the subtropical zone. ¶ ~ 의 subtropic(al); near-tropical. ‖ ~ 식물 a subtropical plant.
아예 from the beginning; (절대로) entirely; altogether; never.
아옹다옹하다 bicker; quarrel (dispute) (with).
아우 a younger brother (sister).
아우르다 put (join) together; unite; combine. ¶ 힘을 아울러서 by united effort; in cooperation (with).
아우성 a shout; a clamor; a hubbub. ¶ ~ 을 치다 shout; raise a hubbub.
아욱(植) a mallow.
아웃(野) 이 되다 be (put) out / ~시키다 put out.
아웃라인 an outline.
아이 a child; a boy; a girl; a son; a daughter. / ~ 보는 사람 a (dry) nurse; a nursemaid; a baby-sitter / ~를 배다 be with (conceive a) child / ~를 보다 look after a baby; baby-sit.
아이 Oh!; Oh dear!; Ah!; Dear me!
아이누 an Ainu; an Aino; the Ainus (종속). ‖ ~ 어 Aino.
아이디어 an idea. ¶ ~를 모집하다 invite (ask for) new ideas. ‖ ~ 맨 an idea man / ~ 상품 a novelty.
아이러니 (an) irony.
아이론 a flatiron; an iron.
아이스 ice. ‖ ~ 링크 an ice rink / ~ 캔디 a Popsicle (상표명, (美)) / ~ 하키 ice hockey.
아이스크림 (an) ice cream. ‖ ~ 제조기 an ice-cream freezer.
아이슬란드 Iceland. ¶ ~ 의 Icelandic. ‖ ~ 사람 an Icelander.
아이시 an IC. (◀ Integrated Circuit)
아이에스비엔 《국제 표준 도서 번호》 ISBN. (◀ the International Stand-

아이엠에프 IMF. (◀ the international Monetary Fund (국제 통화 기금)) ¶ ~가 부과한 요구사항에 부응하기 위해 강력한 금융 개혁안을 통과시키다 pass a strong financial-reform package to meet demands imposed by the International Monetary Fund / ~ 사태로 인해 유발된 긴축 운동이 효과를 나타내어 사회 모든 계층으로 확산되고 있다 The IMF-induced frugality campaigns are taking effect, spreading into every corner of society.

아이오시 IOC. (◀ the International Olympic Committee)

아이젠 climbing irons; crampons (등산용).

아이큐 IQ. (◀ Intelligence Quotient)

아일랜드 Ireland. ¶ ~ 말 Irish / ~ 사람 an Irishman.

아장거리다 toddle. ¶ 아장아장 toddlingly.

아전(衙前) a petty town official (of former days).

아전인수(我田引水) turning *something* to *one's* own advantage. ¶ ~ 격인 견해 a selfish view.

아주(전혀) quite; utterly; completely; entirely; thoroughly; altogether; (몹시) exceedingly; extremely; (조금도 …않다) (not) at all; (not) in the least. ¶ ~ 곤하다 be dead tired; be utterly exhausted / 관계를 ~ 끊다 break off entirely (with).

아주(亞洲) the Continent of Asia.

아주(阿洲) the Continent of Africa.

아주까리(植) a castor-oil plant; a castor bean(씨). ¶ ~ 기름 castor oil.

아주머니 (숙모) an aunt; (일반 부인) a lady.

아주버니 *one's* husband's brother; a brother-in-law.

아지랑이 heat haze. ¶ ~가 끼었다 The air is shimmering.

아지작거리다 munch; crunch.

아지트 a hiding place; a hide-out; (거점) a secret base of operation (for Communists).

아직(아직 …않다) (not) yet; still (지금도); so far(현재까지는); (더) still; more. ¶ ~ 모자란다 This isn't enough yet. / ~ 3일 남았다 We still have three more miles to go / …한 지 ~ 3년밖에 안 된다 It is only three years since….

아질산(亞窒酸)(化) nitrous acid. ¶ ~염 nitrite.

아집(我執) egoistic attachment; egotism.

아찔하다 feel dizzy; be giddy.

아차 O my!; Gosh!; Hang it! ¶ ~ 속았구나 O my! I have been fooled!

아첨(阿諂) flattery; adulation. ~하다 flatter; curry favor with (*a person*); fawn (*on*). ¶ ~꾼 a flatterer; a toady; an ass kisser.

아치(雅致) good taste; elegance; tastefulness. ¶ ~ 있는 tasteful; elegant; graceful; refined.

아치 an arch; a green arch (녹엽의). ¶ ~형의 arched.

아침 ① (때) (a) morning. ¶ ~에 in the morning / ~나절 the forenoon / ~ 안개 morning mist / 오늘 ~ this morning / 일찍 early in the morning / 3일날 ~ on the morning of the 3rd / ~부터 밤까지 from morning till night (evening). ②《식사》 breakfast. ¶ ~을 먹다 take (have) breakfast.

아카데미 an academy. ¶ ~상 the Academy Award; the Oscar.

아카시아(植) an acacia.

아케이드 an arcade.

아코디언 an accordion.

아크등(一燈) an arc light (lamp).

아킬레스건(一腱)(解) Achilles' tendon. 「paper(美).

아트지(一紙) art paper; coated

아틀리에 an *atelier* (프) a studio.

아파트(건물) an apartment house (美); a block of flats (英); 《한 세대분》 an apartment (美); a flat (英). ¶ 고층 ~ a multistory apartment building / ~에 살다 live in an apartment (a flat). ¶ ~군(群) an apartment block / ~단지 an apartment complex.

아편(阿片) (smoke, eat) opium. ¶ ~굴(상용자) an opium den (eater, smoker) / ~전쟁 [史] the Opium War / ~중독 opium poisoning. 「Apollo Project.

아폴로 [그神] Apollo. ¶ ~계획

아프가니스탄 Afghanistan. ¶ ~인 Afghan / ~ 사람 an Afghan.

아프다 (be) painful; sore; have (feel) a pain (서술적). ¶ 이 [머리] 가 ~ have a toothache (headache) / 배가 ~ (비유적) be green with envy; be jealous.

아프리카 Africa. ¶ ~의 African / ~ 사람 an African.

아픔 (pain; an ache; a sore; (마음의) (mental) pain; (슬픔) grief. ¶ 상처의 ~ the smart of a wound / 이별의 ~ the pain of parting / 격심한 ~ a severe (sharp, bad) pain / ~을 참다 stand (bear) pain.

아하 Ha!; Aha!; Oh! ¶ ~ 이제 생각이 나는군 Oh! I remember it now.

아한대(亞寒帶) the subarctic zone (북반구의); the subantarctic zone (남반구의).

아호(雅號) a pen name; a (literary) pseudonym.
아홉 nine. ¶ ~째 the ninth.
아흐레 ① (아홉옛날) the ninth day (of the month). ② (아홉 날) nine days.
아흔 ninety.
악 ① (큰소리) a shout; a cry. ¶ ~쓰다 shout; cry; shriek. ② (모질음) excitement; desperation. ¶ ~이 바치다 become [grow] desperate; be excited.
악' (놀랄 때) Oh!; Dear me!
악(惡) badness; evil; wrong (그름); vice (악덕); wickedness (사악). ☞ ~하다. ¶ ~에 물들다 be steeped in vice / ~을 선으로 갚다 return good for evil.
악감(惡感) ill [bad] feeling; an unfavorable impression. ¶ ~을 품다 have [harbor] bad [ill] feeling (*toward*); be ill disposed (*toward*).
악곡(樂曲) a musical composition; a piece of music.
악공(樂工) a (court) musician.
악귀(惡鬼) a demon; an evil spirit; a devil.
악극(樂劇) an opera; a musical [music] drama [play]. ‖ ~단 a musical troupe.
악기(樂器) [play on] a musical instrument. ¶ ~점 a musical instrument store.
악녀(惡女) a wicked woman.
악다구니하다 brawl; engage in mud-flinging at each other; throw mud (*at*).
악단(樂團) an orchestra; a band. ‖ 교향~ a symphony orchestra.
악단(樂壇) the musical world; musical circles.
악담(惡談) an abuse; a curse. ~하다 say bitterly; abuse; curse; revile; speak ill of.
악대(樂隊) a band; a brass band. ‖ ~원 a bandsman.
악덕(惡德) vice; corruption. ‖ ~기업주 a vicious *entrepreneur* (프) / ~기자 [정치인] a corrupt journalist (politician) / ~상인 [업자] wicked dealers [traders].
악독(惡毒) ~하다 (be) villainous; atrocious; brutal; infernal.
악랄하다(惡辣—) (be) mean; nasty; knavish; villainous.
악력(握力) grip; grasping power. ¶ ~계 a hand dynamometer.
악례(惡例) a bad example; a bad precedent.
악마(惡魔) an evil spirit; a devil; a fiend; Satan. ¶ ~ 같은 devilish; fiendish / ~주의 Satanism.
악명(惡名) an evil reputation; a bad name; notoriety. ¶ ~ 높은 infamous; notorious.

악몽(惡夢) a bad [an evil] dream; (suffer from) a nightmare. ¶ ~ 같은 nightmarish / ~에서 깨어나다 awake from a nightmare; (비유적) come to one's senses.
악물다 (이를) gnash [set, clench] (*one's teeth*); shut (*one's teeth*) hard; compress (*one's lips*). ¶ 이를 악물고 with *one's* teeth set.
악바리 a hard tough person.
악보(樂譜) a sheet music; a (*piano*) score (총보); music (집합적). ¶ ~를 보고 [안 보고] 연주하다 play at sight [by ear].
악사(樂士) a band(s)man; a musician.
악서(惡書) a bad [vicious] book; a harmful book. ¶ ~를 추방하다 put harmful books out of circulation.
악선전(惡宣傳) vile [false] propaganda; a sinister rumor. ~하다 launch false propaganda (*about*); spread a bad rumor (*about*).
악성(惡性) ~의 bad; malignant; virulent; vicious (*inflation*). ‖ ~감기 a bad cold / ~빈혈 pernicious anemia / ~종양 a malignant tumor.
악성(樂聖) a celebrated [master] musician. ¶ ~ 모차르트 Mozart, the great master of music.
악센트 an accent; a stress. ¶ ~를 붙이다 accent (*a word*); stress.
악송구(惡送球) 【野】 a bad throw. ~하다 make a bad throw.
악수(握手) a handshake; handshaking. ~하다 shake hands (*with*); (제휴) join hands; (화해) make peace. ¶ 굳은 ~ a firm handshake / ~를 청하다 offer *one's* hand.
악순환(惡循環) a vicious circle. ¶ 물가와 임금의 ~ a vicious circle of prices and wages.
악습(惡習) a bad habit (custom). ¶ ~에 물들다 fall into a bad habit / ~을 극복하다 get rid of a bad habit.
악식(惡食) (음식) coarse [gross] food; plain food; (먹기) gross feeding. ~하다 live [feed] low; live on plain food.
악어(鰐魚) 【動】 a crocodile (아프리카산); an alligator (북아메리카산). ¶ ~ 가죽 crocodile skin; alligator leather / ~핸드백 an alligator handbag.
악역(惡役) 【劇】 a villain's part. ¶ ~을 맡다 play [act] the villain.
악연(惡緣) (나쁜 운명) an evil destiny [fate, connection]; (끊을 수 없는) a fatal bonds; an inseparable unhappy relation; (부부간의) a mismated marriage.

악영향(惡影響) a bad [harmful] influence; ill effects. ¶ ~을 미치다 [받다] have [receive] a bad influence (on; from).

악용(惡用) (a) misuse; (an) abuse; (an) improper use. ~하다 abuse; use for the wrong purpose; make a bad use (of). ¶ ~하다 abuse *one's* authority.

악우(惡友) a bad companion [friend]. ¶ ~와 사귀다 keep bad company. 「ill luck [fate].」
악운(惡運) bad [adverse] fortune;

악의(惡意) an evil intention; ill will; malice. ¶ ~ 있는 ill-intentioned; malicious 「 ~ 없는 innocent / ~에서 out of spite; from malice / ~를 품다 bear ill will (against); harbor malice (to, toward).

악의악식(惡衣惡食) ~하다 be ill-clad and poorly fed.

악인(惡人) a bad [wicked] man; a rogue; a villain; a scoundrel.

악장(樂長) a bandmaster; a conductor of a band.

악장(樂章)〔樂〕 a movement. ¶ 제 1 ~ the first movement (of a symphony).

악장치다 brawl; quarrel [wrangle] with each other.

악전고투(惡戰苦鬪) hard fighting; a desperate fight. ~하다 fight desperately; fight against heavy odds; struggle hard (against).

악정(惡政) ☞ 비정(批政).

악조건(惡條件) adverse [unfavorable] conditions; a handicap. ¶ ~을 극복하다 get over a handicap.

악종(惡種) a wicked fellow; a rogue; a villain; a rascal.

악질(惡疾) a malignant disease.

악질(惡質) ¶ ~의 vicious (fraud); wicked (lies); malicious (businessmen); malignant (tumors); bad / ~ 적인 장난 malicious [wicked] mischief; / ~ 분자 bad [malicious] elements.

악착(齷齪) ¶ ~같이 hard; perseveringly; desperately; 《필사적으로》 ~같이 일하다 toil and moil; work hard / ~같이 돈을 벌다 be all eagerness to make money; be engrossed in moneymaking.

악처(惡妻) a bad wife.

악천후(惡天候) bad [nasty; unfavorable] weather. ¶ ~를 무릅쓰고 in spite of bad [rough] weather.

악취(惡臭) an offensive odor; a bad [nasty] smell; a stink. ¶ ~가 나는 ill-[bad-]smelling; stinking; foul-smelling.

악취미(惡趣味) bad [vulgar] taste.

악평(惡評) a bad reputation; ill repute;《비난》an adverse [unfavorable] criticism. ~하다 speak ill of; make malicious remarks;《신문 따위에서》criticize unfavorably [severely].

악폐(惡弊) an evil; an abuse; evil practices. ¶ ~를 일소하다 stamp [wipe] out evils; uproot evil practices.

악풍(惡風) a bad custom [habit]; evil manners; a vicious practice.

악필(惡筆) bad [poor] handwriting; a poor hand. ¶ ~이다 write a poor hand. ∥ ~가 a bad penman.

악하다(惡—) (be) bad; evil; wrong; wicked; vicious. ¶ 악한 짓 an evil deed; a misdeed; a vice; a crime, a sin(죄악).

악한(惡漢) a rascal; a villain; a rogue; a scoundrel.

악행(惡行) bad conduct; wrong [evil] doing; an evil deed; a misdeed. 「ment; torture.」
악형(惡刑) a severe [cruel] punish-

악화(惡化) a change for the worse. ~하다 get [become] worse; go from bad to worse; deteriorate; take a turn for the worse(병세가). ¶ ~시키다 make (something) worse; aggravate.

악화(惡貨) bad coins (money). ¶ ~는 양화를 구축한다 Bad money drives out good.

안 ① 《내부》 the inside; the interior. ¶ ~에 within; inside; in; indoors(집의) / ~으로부터 from the inside; from within. ② 《이내》 ¶ ~에 [으로] in; within; inside of; less than; not more than; during(…중에) / 그 날 ~으로 in the course of the day / 기한 ~에 within the time limit. ③ (옷의) the lining. ¶ ~을 대다 line (clothes). ④ (내실) the woman's quarters; the inner room. ⑤ (아내) one's wife. ⑥ (여자) a mother.

안(案) 《의안》 a bill; a measure; 《제안》 a proposal;《고안》 an idea; a conception;《계획》 a plan; a project;《초안》 a draft.

안간힘(을) 쓰다 do *one's* best; do what *one* can; make desperate efforts (to do); try [work] hard (to do); strain (*one's* muscle) to (lift a stone). ¶ 어려움에서 벗어나려고 ~ try hard to wriggle out of a difficult situation / ~ 이번 밧줄을 풀려고 ~ struggle desperately to get free of the rope / 이제 와서 안간힘 써봐야 헛수고다 It is too late to do anything about it. 「lining.」
안감 lining (material); cloth for

안개 (a) fog; (a) mist. ¶ 짙은 ~ a dense [thick] fog / ~가 짙은 foggy / ~에 싸이다 be shrouded in fog / ~가 끼다 [짙히다] The fog gathers [lifts].

안건 (案件) a matter; an item; a bill (의안). ¶ 주요 ~ an important matter (on the agenda).

안경 (眼鏡) (a pair of) spectacles; glasses; (보안경) goggles. ¶ ~을 쓰다 [벗다] put on [take off] one's glasses / ~을 쓰고 with spectacles on. ‖ ~가게 an optician / ~다리 the bow / ~알(집) a spectacle lens [case] / ~테 a rim; a spectacle frame / 흐림방지 ~ non-fogging glasses.

안고나다 assume another's responsibility; hold oneself responsible for another's (actions).

안고지다 be entrapped by one's own trick.

안공 (眼孔) an eyehole; an orbit of an eye; the eye socket.

안과 (眼科) [醫] ophthalmology. ‖ ~병원 an ophthalmic hospital / ~의사 an eye doctor [specialist]; an oculist.

안광 (眼光) (눈빛) the glitter of one's eye; (통찰력) penetration. ¶ ~이 날카롭다 be sharp-eyed.

안구 (眼球) an eyeball. ‖ ~은행 an eye bank.

안기다¹ ① (팔에) be embraced; be in (a person's) arms; (안게 하다) let [have] (someone) hold in the arms. ¶ 아기가 엄마 품에 안겨 자고 있다 The baby is sleeping in its mother's arms. ② (알을 닭에) set (a hen) on eggs.

안기다² ① (책임을) fix responsibility upon; charge (a person with a duty); lay (the blame) on. ¶ 빚을 ~ hold (a person) liable for the debt. ② (치다) throw a punch; strike. ¶ 한 대 ~ give (a person) a blow.

안내 (案內) guidance; leading. ~하다 guide; conduct; show; lead (the way); usher (좌석으로). ¶ 응접실로 ~ show (a person) into the drawing room / 그의 ~로 연구소를 견학하다 go around the research institute under the guidance of him. ‖ ~도 a guide (information) map / ~소 an information bureau (desk) / ~인(자) a guide (관광 등의); an usher (극장 등의) / ~장 a letter of invitation / ~판 a guideboard; a direction board.

안녕 (安寧) ① (평온) public peace; tranquility; welfare; well-being (복지). ‖ ~질서 (maintain, disturb) peace and order. ② (건강) good health. ~하다 (be) well; be in good health; (평안) (be) uneventful; live in peace. ¶ ~하십니까 How are you?; (초면) How do you do? ③ (작별인사) good-by(e); bye-bye; farewell (멀리 갈 때). ¶ ~히 가십시요 Good-by!

안다 ① (팔에) hold [carry] in one's arm(s); embrace; hug. ¶ 안고 있다 have (a baby) in one's arms. ② (새가 알을) sit (brood) on (eggs). ③ (떠맡다) undertake (another's responsibility); shoulder; answer for. ¶ 남의 부채를 ~ shoulder another's debt.

안단테 [樂] andante (이).

안달뱅이 a fretful person; a worry-wart.

안달하다 worry (about, over); fret (over); be anxious about; be impatient (nervous). ¶ 가지 못해 ~ be anxious to go.

안대 (眼帶) an eyepatch; an eye bandage.

안데스산맥 (—山脈) the Andes.

안도 (安堵) relief. ~하다 be [feel] relieved; feel at ease. ¶ ~의 한숨을 쉬다 heave [give] a sigh of relief.

안되다 ① (금지) must not; ought not to; shall not; don't. ¶ 떠들면 안 된다 Do not make any noise. / 들어가면 안 됩니까 May I not come in? ② (잘 안 되다) go wrong (amiss); fail. ③ (조심) …하면 안 되느니 lest…; for fear that…; so as not to. ④ (유감) be [feel] sorry (for, to hear that…), be a pity; be regrettable. ¶ 보기에 안됐다 be pitiful to see.

안뜰 a courtyard. ☞ 안마당.

안락 (安樂) ease; comfort. ~한 comfortable; easy; cozy. ¶ ~하게 지내다 live in comfort. ‖ ~사(死) euthanasia; mercy killing / ~의자 an easy chair; an armchair.

안력 (眼力) eyesight; visual power (acuity).

안료 (顔料) colors; paints; pigments.

안마 (按摩) massage. ~하다 give (a person) a massage; massage (a person). ¶ 어깨를 ~해 했다 I had my shoulder massaged. ‖ ~사 a massagist / ~시술소 massage parlor.

안마 (鞍馬) [體操] a pommel horse.

안마당 an inner court (garden).

안면 (安眠) a peaceful (quiet) sleep. ¶ ~히 sleep well (soundly). ‖ ~방해 disturbance of sleep (~방해하다 disturb (a person's) sleep).

안면 (顔面) (얼굴) the face. ¶ ~의 facial / ~이 창백해지다 turn pale. ‖ ~경련 a facial tic / ~마

비 facial paralysis / ~신경 facial nerves / ~신경통 facial neuralgia. ② 《연식·친분》 acquaintance. ¶ ~이 있는 사람 an acquaintance / ~이 없는 사람 a stranger / ~이 있다 know 《a person》; be acquainted with 《a person》.

안목(眼目) a discerning (critical) eye; discernment; an eye. ¶ ~이 있다 have an eye (for).

안방(一房) the inner (main) living room; the women's quarters. 〔bute〕 assign.

안배(按排) ~하다 arrange; distri-

안벽(岸壁) a quay (wall).

안보(安保) ☞ 안전보장. ¶한미 ~조약 the Korea-U.S. Security Treaty.

안부(安否) one's state of health; safety; welfare; health. ¶ ~를 묻다 inquire after 《a person's》 health / ~를 염려(걱정)하다 worry about 《a person's》 safety / ~에게 ~ 전해 주십시오 Give my 《best, kind》 regards 《to》.

안색(顔色) ① 《얼굴빛》 a complexion. ¶ ~이 좋다 (나쁘다) look well (pale) / ~ 소식을 듣고 ~이 변하다 change color (turn pale) at the news. ② 《표정》 a look; an expression. ¶ ~에 나타내다 betray 《one's emotions》; show.

안성맞춤(安城一) ¶ ~의 suitable (fit) 《for》; well-suited; ideal / ~의 사람 (물건) the right person (thing) 《for》; just the person (thing) 《for》.

안섶 an in-turned jeogori collar.

안손님 a lady visitor.

안수(按手) 〔基〕 the imposition of hands. ~하다 impose hands on 《a person》. ~례(禮) the (order of) confirmation (신도의); the ordination (성직의).

안식(安息) ~하다 rest; repose. ¶ 종교에서 ~을 찾다 find relief in religion. ‖ ~교회 the Seventh Day Adventist Church / ~일 the Sabbath (day) / ~처 a place for peaceful living.

안식(眼識) discernment; a critical eye. ¶ ~ 있는 사람 a discerning person; a man of insight.

안심(安心) 《안도》 relief; 《근심·걱정 없음》 peace of mind; freedom from care. ~하다 be at ease; feel easy 《about》; feel (be) relieved. ¶ ~시키다 ease 《a person's》 mind; set 《a person》 at ease / ~찮다 be ill at ease; feel uneasy; be anxious / 그 소식을 듣고 ~했다 I was (felt) relieved at the news.

안심부름 errands around the house.

안약(眼藥) eyewater; eye lotion. ¶ ~을 넣다 apply eye lotion.

안염(眼炎) 〔醫〕 ophthalmia.

안온(安穩) peace. ¶ ~한(히) peaceful(ly); quiet(ly); calm(ly).

안위(安危) fate; safety; welfare. ¶ 국가 ~의 시기 a national crisis / 국가 ~에 관한 문제 a matter affecting the security of the nation.

안이(安易) ¶ ~한 easy (going) / ~하게 easily; with ease / ~하게 생각하다 take 《a thing》 too easy.

안일(安逸) ease; idleness; indolence. ~하다 (be) easy; idle; indolent. ¶ ~하게 살다 lead an idle life.

안장(安葬) ~하다 bury; lay to rest. ‖ ~지 a burial ground.

안장(鞍裝) a saddle. ¶ ~을 지우 다 saddle 《a horse》.

안전(安全) safety; security. ¶ ~ 한 safe; secure; free from danger / ~히 safely; securely / 몸의 ~을 도모하다 look to one's own safety / ~책을 강구하다 take precautions (safety measures). ‖ ~ 감 a sense of security / ~계수 a factor of safety / ~규칙 safety regulations / ~기준 safety standards / ~등(燈) 《면도, 장치, 판, 핀》 a safety lamp 《razor, device, valve, pin》 / ~성 safety / ~운전 safe (careful) driving / ~ 운전을 하다 drive safely (carefully) / ~율 a safety factor (of 99%) / ~점검 a safety check-up / ~제일 Safety First / ~조업 safety operation / ~지대 a safety zone / 《도로상의》 a safety (traffic 〔?〕) island.

안전(眼前) ¶ ~에서 under one's very nose.

안전벨트 a safety belt. ¶좌석의 ~를 매어 주십시오 Please fasten your seat belt.

안전보장(安全保障) security. ¶ 《유엔》 ~이사회 the Security Council. ☞ 안보(安保).

안절부절못하다 be restless (nervous); flutter; be in a fidget; be irritated; grow impatient.

안정(安定) stability; steadiness; 《economic》 stabilization. ~하다 be stabilized; become stable. ¶ ~을 유지하다 (잃다) keep (lose) balance (equilibrium) / 통화를 ~ 시키다 stabilize currency. ‖ ~ 감 a sense of stability / ~도 (성) stability / ~성장 the stable growth / ~세력 a stabilizing power (force) / ~제(劑) a stabilizer.

안정(安靜) rest; repose. ¶ ~절대~ an absolute rest / ~을 유지하다 keep quiet; lie quietly. ‖ ~요법 a rest cure.

안주(安住) ¶ ~할 곳을 찾다 seek a peaceful place to live / 이곳에

안주 ~하기로 결정했다 I decided to settle down here.
안주(按酒) a relish (tidbit) taken with wine; a side side; a snack (eaten with wine). ¶ 이것은 술~로 아주 좋다 This goes very well with wine.
안주머니 an inside (an inner, a breast) pocket.
안주인(一主人) the lady of the house; the mistress; the hostess.
안중(眼中) ¶ ~에 없다 be out of one's account (consideration); 《사람이 주위》 think nothing of.
안중문(一中門) the inner gate.
안질(眼疾) an eye disease (trouble); sore eyes. ¶ ~을 앓다 be afflicted with an eye disease.
안쪽 ① (이내) ¶ ~의 within; less than; not more than / 만원~의 수입 an income short of ten thousand *won*. ② (굽귀의) the first line (of a couplet).
안짱다리 a pigeon-toed person. ¶ ~로 걷다 walk intoed (pigeon-toed).
안쪽 the inside; the inner part. ¶ ~의 inside; inner / ~에서 from within; on the inside.
안차다 (be) bold; daring; fearless.
안착(安着) ~하다 arrive safe (and sound); arrive safely; arrive in good condition (물품이).
안창(구두의) an inner sole.
안채 the main building (of a house).
안출(案出) ~하다 contrive; invent; originate; think (work) out.
안치(安置) ~하다 enshrine; install; lay 《a person's remains》 in state(유해를). 「cooking (boiling).
안치다 (밥을) prepare rice for
안타(安打) 〖野〗 a (safe) hit. ¶ ~를 치다 hit; make (get) a hit.
안타깝다 (be) impatient; irritated; frustrating; 〖애처롭다〗 be pitiful; pitiable; poor. ¶ 안타까워 하다 be (feel) impatient (frustrating).
안테나 an antenna; an aerial. ¶ 실내~ an indoor antenna / ~를 세우다 set up (stretch) an antenna.
안티몬 〖化〗 antimony (기호 Sb).
안티피린 〖藥〗 antipyrin(e).
안팎 ① (안과 밖) the interior and exterior; the inside and outside. ¶ ~으로〖에〗 within and without; inside and outside 《the house》. ② (표리) the right and the wrong side; both sides. ③ (대략) ...or so; about; around 《美》. ¶ 열을 ~ 10 days or so.
안표(眼標) a sign; a mark. ~하

다 mark; put a mark 《on》.
안하(眼下) ¶ ~에 right beneath the eye; under one's eyes.
안하무인(眼下無人) ¶ ~의 outrageous; arrogant; audacious / ~으로 행동하다 behave outrageously; conduct *oneself* recklessly.
앉다 ① 〖자리에〗 sit down; take a seat; be seated. ¶ 의자에 ~ sit on (in) a chair / 편히 ~ sit at one's ease / 바로 ~ sit up; sit erect / 책상다리하고 ~ sit cross-legged. ② 〖지위에〗 take up 《a post》; engage in; be installed. ③ 〖새 따위가〗 perch (alight, sit, settle) on; roost(홰에).
앉은뱅이 a cripple.
앉은일 sedentary work.
앉은자리 ¶ ~에서 immediately; on the spot.
앉은장사 keeping a shop (as contrasted with an itinerant trade). ¶ ~를 하다 keep a shop.
앉은키 one's sitting height.
앉히다 ① 〖앉게 하다〗 have 《a person》 sit down; seat 《a person》. ② 〖추대〗 place 《a person in a position》; install 《a person in a place》.
않다 be (do) not....
않을 수 없다 be compelled (forced, obliged) to 《do》; cannot help 《doing》. ¶ 가지 ~ be forced to go / 쓴 웃음을 짓지 ~ cannot help smiling a bitter smile; cannot but smile a bitter smile.
알[1] 〖동물의〗 an egg; spawn (물고기 따위의). ¶ ~을 낳다 lay an egg; spawn(물고기가).
알[2] ① 〖낱알〗 a grain; a berry. ② 〖작고 둥근 것을〗 a ball; a bead. ¶ 눈~ an eyeball.
알~ bare; naked; stripped; uncovered. ¶ ~몸 a naked body.
알갱이 a kernel; a grain; a berry.
알거지 a man with no property but his own body; a person as poor as a crow.
알겨먹다 cheat (wheedle) 《a person》 out of 《something》.
알곡(一穀) 〖곡물〗 cereals; grain; corn 《英》; 《껍질을 벗긴》 husked grain.
알다 ① 〖일반적으로〗 know; can tell; learn; be informed of 《about》. ¶ 알면서 deliberately; intentionally; knowingly / 알지 못하고 without knowing it; ignorantly / 아시는 바와 같이 as you (must) know; as you are aware / 안다는 듯 knowingly; with a knowing look / 내가 아는 한에서는 so far as I know / ...으로 알 수 있다 pretend to know / 알 수 없다 be unable to know / 알고 있다 know; have

a knowledge of; be acquainted with / 신문을 보고 ~ learn of it in a newspaper / …이오니 그리 아십시오 We beg to inform you that. ② (이해) understand; comprehend; see; grasp 《the meaning》; appreciate; know. ¶ 알기 쉽게 simply; plainly / 알기 쉬운 말로 plain language / 알면한다 be understandable; be easy to understand / 잘못 ~ mistake 《for》/ 음악을 ~ appreciate music; have an ear for music. ③ (인식) recognize; know; be aware of; find out. ¶ 알아볼 수 없을 만큼 자라다 grow out of recognition / 그가 거짓말하고 있음을 안다 I know 《am aware》 that he is telling a lie. ④ (낯이 익다) know; become 《get》 acquainted with. ¶ 아는 사람 an acquaintance / 약간 아는 사이 a casual acquaintance / 잘 아는 well-acquainted; familiar. ⑤ (깨닫다) find; realize; sense; perceive. ¶ 위험을 ~ sense the danger. ⑥ (기억) remember; keep 《have》 in mind. ¶ 똑똑히 〔어렴풋이〕 알고 있다 remember clearly 《vaguely》. ⑦ (관여) have to do with; be concerned with. ¶ 그것은 내가 알 바가 아니다 That's none of my business. ⑧ (경험) experience; feel. ¶ 여자를 ~ know woman.

알뚝배기 a small earthen bowl.
알뜰하다 (be) thrifty; frugal; economical. ¶ 알뜰(살뜰)히 frugally; economically.
알라 《이슬람교의 신》 Allah.
알랑거리다 flatter; curry favor with; toady 《to》; fawn on. ¶ 윗사람에게 ~ curry favor with one's superior.
알랑쇠 a flatterer; a sycophant; a toady; a bootlicker 《口》.
알랑알랑 with flattery.
알래스카 Alaska. ¶ ~의 Alaskan.
알량하다 (be) insignificant; of no account; trivial. ¶ 알량한 일 trifles / 알량한 인간 a person who is not worth bothering about.
알레그로 《樂》 allegro.
알레르기 《醫》 allergy. ¶ ~성의 allergic / 抗 ~ antiallergic 《drugs》. ‖ ~성질환 allergic diseases.
알려지다 be 《become》 known 《to》; make oneself known; 《유명해지다》 become famous 《well-known》. ¶ 널리 알려진 well-known; famous / 알려지지 않게 하다 keep 《a matter》 secret.
알력 (軋轢) friction; discord; a clash; a conflict; strife. ¶ ~을 초래하다 〔피하다〕 produce 〔avoid〕 friction.

알로하셔츠 an aloha shirt.
알루미늄 aluminum (기호 Al). ¶ ~새시 an aluminum sash 〔window-frame〕 / ~제품 aluminum ware.
알리다 let 《a person》 know; tell; inform 《a person》 《of, that…》; report; publish (공표). ¶ 넌지시 ~ suggest; hint 《at》.
알리바이 an alibi. ¶ ~를 입증하다 prove an alibi / ~를 깨다 〔꾸미다〕 break 〔fake〕 an alibi.
알맞다 (적도) (be) modest; moderate; (적량) (be) fit; right; proper; adequate; suitable; appropriate; (합당) (be) reasonable; fair. ¶ 알맞게 properly; rightly; reasonably; suitably; appropriately / 알맞은 값으로 at a reasonable price / 알맞은 조건으로 on fair 〔reasonable〕 terms.
알맹이 a kernel; (실질) substance; contents (내용). ¶ ~ 없는 unsubstantial; empty.
알몸 ¶ ~이 되다 stark-naked; nude / ~으로 (go) stark-naked in one's bare skin / ~이 되다 strip oneself bare.
알밤 a (shelled) chestnut.
알배기 a fish full of roe.
알부랑자 (一浮浪者) a barefaced rascal (scoundrel).
알부민 〔生化〕 albumin.
알선 (斡旋) good offices; mediation; services. ¶ ~하다 act as (an) intermediary between 《A and B》; use one's good offices; do 《a person》 a service. ¶ …의 ~으로 by 〔through〕 the good offices of 《Mr. Kim》. ‖ ~자 a mediator. 〔spawn(물고기가)〕
알슬다 lay 〔deposit〕 eggs; shoot
알싸하다 (be) acrid; pungent; hot; have a spicy taste 〔smell〕.
알쏭달쏭하다 (be) vague; ambiguous; obscure; doubtful. ¶ 알쏭달쏭한 말을 하다 evade the point.
알아내다 find out; detect; locate (소재를); trace 《the origin of a rumor》.
알아듣다 understand; catch 《a person's words》. ¶ 알아들을 수 없다 be inaudible; cannot catch.
알아맞히다 guess right; make a good guess.
알아보다 (문의·조사) inquire 《of a person, about a matter》; look into; investigate; examine. ¶ 원인을 ~ inquire into the cause.
알아주다 ① (인정) acknowledge; recognize; appreciate. ¶ 진가를 ~ appreciate the real worth. ② (이해) understand; sympathize 《with》; feel 《for》.
알아차리다 realize in advance;

알아채다 anticipate 《in one's mind》.
알아채다 become aware [conscious] of; realize; sense. ¶ 적은 우리의 행동을 알아채고 있었다 The enemy was aware of our action.
알아하다 do at one's discretion; do as one thinks fit.
알은체 《남의 일에》 meddling; ~하다 interfere 《in a matter, with a person》; meddle in 〔with〕. ② 《사람을 보고》 recognition. ~하다 recognize; notice.
알음알음 《아는 관계》 mutual acquaintance; 《친분》 shared intimacy.
알젓 seasoned [salted] roe.
알짜 the best thing [part]; the cream; the essence; the choice; the quintessence.
알칼리 [化] alkali.
알코올 alcohol. ¶ ~성의 alcoholic. ‖ ~음료 an alcoholic drink / ~중독 alcoholism / ~중독자 an alcoholic.
알토 [樂] alto. ‖ ~가수 an alto.
알파 alpha; α. ‖ ~선 [입자] alpha rays (particles).
알파벳 the alphabet. ¶ ~순의 [으로] alphabetical(ly).
알파카 [動] an alpaca.
알프스 Alps. ‖ ~산맥 the Alps.
알피니스트 an alpinist.
알현(謁見) an (imperial) audience. ~하다 be received in audience 《by》; have an audience 《with》.
앓는소리하다 moan; groan; complain 《of illness》.
앓다 ① 《병을》 be ill [sick, afflicted] 《with》; suffer from 《cold》. ② 《비유적》 worry about; worry oneself; be distressed [troubled] 《with》. ¶ 골치를 ~ puzzle [cudgel] one's head [brains] 《about, over》.
암(癌) ① [醫] cancer. ¶ ~의 cancerous / 위 [폐] ~ stomach [lung] cancer. ② ~세포 a cancer cell. ③ 《화근》 a cancer; a curse; the bad apple. ¶ 범죄의 증가는 사회의 ~이다 Growing crime is a cancer on society.
암 《감탄사》 Of course!; To be sure!; Certainly!; Why not?
암… 《암컷》 female 《animal, bird, flower》; she.
암거(暗渠) an underdrain; a culvert. ‖ ~배수 drainage by a culvert.
암거래(暗去來) 《매매》 black-market dealings. 《비밀교섭》 secret dealings. ~하다 buy [sell] 《goods》 on the black market; black-marketeer; black-market 《goods》.
암굴(岩窟) a cave; a (rocky) cavern.
암기(暗記) ~하다 learn [get] 《something》 by heart; commit 《something》 to memory; memorize 《책》. ¶ ~하고 있다 know 《the poem》 by heart. ‖ ~과목 a memory subjects / ~력 memory 《~력이 좋다 [나쁘다] have a good [bad] memory.
암꽃 [植] a female flower. 「ory.
암나사 《一螺絲》 a nut.
암내 ① 《겨드랑이의》 underarm odor; the smell of one's armpits; 《체취》 body odor 《생략 B.O.》. ② 《발정》 the odor of a female animal in heat. ¶ ~가 나다 go in [on] heat.
암달러(暗一) a black-market dollar 《transaction》. ‖ ~상인 an illegal dollar currency dealer.
암담(暗澹) the gloom. ~하다 (be) dark; gloomy; dismal.
암류(暗流) an undercurrent.
암매상(暗賣商) a black-marketeer; a black-market dealer.
암매장(暗埋葬) ☞ 암장(暗葬).
암모늄 [化] ammonium.
암모니아 [化] ammonia. ‖ ~비료 ammonite / ~수 liquid ammonia.
암묵(暗默) ¶ ~리에 tacitly / ~의 양해 a tacit understanding; an unspoken agreement. 「bed.
암반(岩盤) a base rock; a rock bed.
암벌 a female bee; a queen (bee).
암범 a tigress.
암벽(岩壁) a rock cliff; a rock face [wall]. ¶ ~등반 rock-climbing.
암산(暗算) mental arithmetic. ~하다 do sums in one's head; do mental arithmetic.
암살(暗殺) assassination. ~하다 assassinate. ¶ ~을 기도하다 make an attempt on 《a person's》 life. ¶ ~계획 an assassination plot against 《a person》 / ~자 an assassin. 「ousy.
암상부리다 show [burn with] jealousy.
암석(岩石) (a) rock. ¶ ~층 a rock layer [stratum].
암소 a cow.
암송(暗誦) recitation; recital. ~하다 recite; repeat from memory.
암수 male and female. 「ory.
암수(暗數) ☞ 속임수. ¶ ~에 걸리다 fall into a trick.
암술 [植] a pistil.
암시(暗示) a hint; a suggestion. ~하다 hint 《at》; suggest. ¶ ~적인 suggestive / ~을 주다 give 《a person》 a hint / 자기 ~ an auto-suggestion. 「price.
암시세(暗時勢) 《값》 a black-market price.
암시장(暗市場) a black market.
암실(暗室) a darkroom.
암암리(暗暗裡) ¶ ~에 tacitly; implicitly; secretly.
암야(暗夜) a (pitch-)dark night.

암약(暗躍) ~하다 be active behind the scenes.
암염(岩塩) [鑛] rock salt.
암영(暗影) a shadow; a gloom. ¶ …의 전도에 ~을 던지다 cast a shadow over the future of ….
암운(暗雲) dark clouds. ¶ ~이 감돌고 있다 Dark clouds are hanging 《over the political world》.
암자(庵子) a hermitage; a hut; a cottage; 《작은 절》 a small temple.
암자색(暗紫色) dark purple.
암장(暗葬) ~하다 bury 《a body》 secretly.
암죽(-粥) thin (rice-)gruel.
암중모색(暗中摸索) groping in the dark. ~하다 grope (blindly) in the dark.
암초(暗礁) a reef; a (sunken) rock. ¶ ~에 걸리다 run aground; strike (run on) a rock.
암치질(-痔疾) internal hemorrhoids.
암캐 a she-dog; a bitch.
암컷 a female (animal); a she.
암키와 a concave roof-tile.
암탉 a hen; a pullet (햇닭의).
암톨쩌귀 a gudgeon.
암퇘지 a sow.
암투(暗鬪) a veiled enmity. a secret strife (feud).
암팡스럽다 《다부지다》 (be) bold; daring; plucky.
암펄 ☞ 암벌.
암펌 ☞ 암범.
암페어 an ampere. ¶ 20~의 전류 a current of 20 amperes.
암평아리 a she-chick; a pullet.
암표상(暗票商) an illegal ticket broker; a speculator; a scalper.
암행(暗行) ~하다 travel incognito. ¶ ~어사 a secret royal inspector.
암호(暗號) a code; a cipher; 《군호》 a password. ¶ 전신 ~ a cable code / ~를 풀다 decode (decipher) 《a message》 / ~로 쓰다 write in cipher (code). ‖ ~문 a coded message / ~장 a code book / ~전보 (send) a code telegram / ~통신 cryptography / ~해독 codebreaking.
암흑(暗黑) darkness. ¶ ~의 dark; black. ‖ ~가 a gangland; the underworld / ~시대 a dark age; a black period.
압권(壓卷) the best; the masterpiece; the best part 《of a book》.
압도(壓倒) overwhelm; overpower. ¶ ~적인 overwhelming; sweeping / ~적인 승리를 얻다 win an overwhelming (a sweeping) victory 《over》 / ~적 다수로 당선되다 be elected by an overwhelming majority.
압력(壓力) pressure. ¶ ~을 가하다

press; give pressure 《to》. ‖ ~계 a pressure gauge / ~단체 a pressure group / ~솥(냄비) a pressure cooker.
압록강(鴨緑江) the Yalu River.
압류(押留) attachment; seizure; distraint(동산의). ~하다 attach; seize. ¶ ~당하다 have one's property attached. ‖ ~영장 a writ of attachment / ~품 seized goods.
압박(壓迫) pressure; oppression. ~하다 oppress; suppress(단압); press(억압). ¶ 정신적인 ~ mental pressure / 재정상의 ~ financial pressure / 언론의 자유을 ~ suppress the freedom of speech / …에 ~을 가하다 put (exert) pressure on…. ‖ ~감 an oppressive feeling; a sense of being oppressed / 피 ~민족 an oppressed people.
압사(壓死) 《눌려서 죽음》 ~하다 be crushed (pressed) to death.
압송(押送) ~하다 escort 《a criminal》; send 《a person》 in custody.
압수(押收) seizure; confiscation. ~하다 seize 《smuggled goods》; confiscate; take legal possession of. ‖ ~물 a confiscated article / ~수색영장 a seizure and search warrant.
압승(壓勝) an overwhelming victory. ~하다 win an overwhelming victory 《over》.
압연(壓延) rolling. ~하다 roll. ‖ ~공장 a rolling mill / 열간 ~ hot rolling.
압정(押釘) a push pin; a (thumb) tack.
압제(壓制) oppression; tyranny(횡정). ~하다 oppress; tyrannize 《over》. ¶ 국민을 ~하다 oppress (tyrannize) the people / 왕의 ~에 시달리다 groan under the tyranny of the king. ‖ ~자 a tyrant; an oppressor.
압지(壓紙) blotting paper.
압착(壓搾) compression. ~하다 press; compress. ¶ ~공기 compressed air / ~기 a compressor / ~펌프 a compressor pump.
압축(壓縮) compression. ~하다 compress 《air》; condense 《a treatise》.
앗다 ① ~ 빼앗다. ② 《씨 빼다》 gin 《cotton》. ③ 《품을》 pay for labor in kind.
앗아가다 snatch 《a thing》 away 《from a person》.
앙가슴 the middle of the chest.
앙감질하다 hop on one leg.
앙갚음 revenge. ~하다 give (pay) tit for tat; revenge oneself; get one's revenge 《on》.
앙금 dregs; sediment; lees(술의); grounds(커피의); refuse(찌꺼기).

앙금앙금 ¶ ~ 기다 crawl; go on all fours.
앙등(昻騰) a sudden (steep) rise (*in prices*). ~하다 rise (suddenly); go up; soar; jump. ¶ ~하는 생활비 the rising cost of living / 집세의 ~ the rise of the house rent.
앙망(仰望) ~하다 beg; entreat; hope; wish.
앙모(仰慕) ~하다 admire; adore.
앙상굳다 (be) terribly gaunt.
앙상블 ensemble (프).
앙상하다 (be) gaunt; haggard; thin; spare; sparse (☞ 엉성하다). ¶ 말라서 뼈만 ~ be wasted [reduced] to a skeleton; be reduced to skin and bones.
앙숙(怏宿) be on bad terms (*with*); (특히 부부가) lead a cat-and-dog life.
앙심(怏心) malice; grudge; ill will; hatred(증오); hostility(적의). ¶ ~을 품다 have a grudge, feel a grudge (*against*); bear malice (*toward*).
앙앙하다(怏怏—) (be) discontented [dissatisfied(*with*)]; grumble (*at, about*).
앙양(昻揚) ~하다 exalt; raise; enhance; uplift (*the national spirit*).
앙증스럽다 (be) very small; tiny.
앙천대소(仰天大笑) ~하다 have a good laugh; laugh loudly.
앙칼스럽다, 앙칼지다 (be) fierce; sharp; aggressive; furious; tenacious. ¶ 앙칼스러운 여자 an aggressive woman.
앙케트 a questionnaire; an opinionnaire; enquête (프).
앙코르 an encore. ¶ ~를 청하다 [받다] call for [receive, get] an encore.
앙탈하다 scheme to disobey; try to avoid what is right; grumble angrily; fuss about [over]. ¶ 공연히 ~ make a big fuss about nothing.
앙화(殃禍) (응보) divine wrath; (재난) disaster; calamity; woe; (불행) misfortune; evil.
앞 ① (미래) the future. ¶ ~을 내다보다 look ahead into the future / 총선거는 두 달 ~이다 The general election is two months away. / ~일을 생각하여라 Think of the future. ② (전방·전면) the front. ¶ ~의 front / ~자리 a front seat / ~에 앉다 take a front seat / ~에서 세 번째 차 the third car from the front (*of the train*) / ~으로 나(아)가다 go ahead; go[step] forward. ③ (면전) presence. ¶ (아무가 있는) ~에서 in (*a person's*) presence.
④ (선두) the head; the foremost; the first. ¶ ~에 서다 be at the head; take the lead. ⑤ (…보다 이전에) ~의 former; last; previous / ~에 prior (*to*); before; earlier than. ⑥ (몫) a share; a portion. ¶ 한 사람 ~에 2개 two (*pencils*) each; two (*pencils*) to each person.
앞(「…에게, …께」) ~내 a letter addressed to me; a letter for me / 홍씨 ~으로 어음을 발행하다 draw a bill for [in favor of] Mr. Hong.
앞가림하다 have just enough education to get by; have the ability to manage *one's* (*duties*).
앞가슴 the breast; the chest.
앞길 (갈길) the road ahead; the way yet to go; (전도) *one's* future; prospects. ¶ 아직 ~이 멀다 have a long way to go / 그의 ~은 암담하다 His prospects are gloomy.
앞날 future (career); remaining years [days]; (여생) the remainder [rest] of *one's* life. ¶ ~을 염려하다 feel anxious about *one's* future.
앞니 a front tooth; an incisor.
앞다리 (짐승의) forelegs; fore limbs.
앞당기다 (시일을) advance; move [carry] up. ¶ 이틀을 ~ advance [move up] (*the date*) by two days.
앞두다 (*a period, a distance*) ahead. ¶ 열흘을 ~ have ten days to go / 시험을 목전에 앞두고 있다 The examination is near at hand.
앞뒤 ① (위치) before and behind; in front and in the rear; before or after; (시간) before and after. ¶ ~로 움직이다 move (*a thing*) back and forth / ~로 적의 공격을 받다 be attacked both in front and in the rear. ② (순서·사리) order; sequence; consequence. ¶ 이야기의 ~가 바뀌다 get things out of sequence / 순서의 ~가 뒤바뀌어 있다 The order is inverted. / ~ 분별도 없이 recklessly / ~ 생각 없이 행동하는 것은 안 된다 Don't behave without considering the consequences.
앞뒷집 the neighboring houses; the neighbors.
앞뜰 a front garden [yard].
앞못보다 (소경) be blind; (무식) be ignorant.
앞문(—門) a front gate [door].
앞바다 the offing; the open sea.
앞바퀴 a front wheel.
앞발 a forefoot; a paw(짐승의).
앞서 ① (이전에) previously; be-

앞서다 fore. ¶ 말한 바와 같이 as previously stated. ② 《먼저》 ahead 《of》; in advance 《of》; earlier (than); prior to. ¶ 정한 시간보다 ~ 떠나다 start before [prior to] a designated hour.

앞서다 go before [ahead of]; go in advance of; precede; head; lead 《others》; take the lead. ¶ 앞서거니 뒤서거니 now ahead and now behind.

앞세우다 make 《a person》 go ahead. ¶ …을 앞세우고 headed [led, preceded] by….

앞이마 the forehead.

앞일 things to come; the future (앞날). ¶ ~을 생각하다 think of the future 《of》.

앞자락 the front hem 《of a garment》.

앞잡이 《주구》 an agent; a tool; a cat's-paw. ¶ 경찰의 ~ a police agent [spy] / ~로 쓰다 make a cat's-paw of 《a person》; use 《a person》 as a tool.

앞장 the head 《선도》; the first; the front 《선도》; the lead 《선도》. ¶ ~서다 be at the head 《of》; take the lead 《in》; be in the front 《of the parade》; spearhead 《a campaign》 / ~서서 걷다 walk at the head 《of a procession》.

앞지르다 get ahead of 《a person》; pass; leave 《a person》 behind; outrun; outstrip; overtake; 《능가하다》 outdo; surpass. ¶ 훨씬 ~ get far ahead of 《a person》; outdistance.

앞집 the house in front; 《길건너의》 the opposite house.

앞차(─車) 《앞에 있는》 the car ahead; 《앞서 떠난》 an earlier departing car (train).

앞채 the front building [wing].

앞치마 an apron.

애¹ 《수고》 pains; trouble; effort; 《걱정》 worry; anxiety.

애² 《아이》. [plaintive song.

애가(哀歌) an elegy; a dirge; a

애개(개) 《아प्री》 My!; Gosh!; Golly!; 《몹시 작을 때》 How skimpy [puny, little]!

애걸(哀乞) implore; plead [beg for. ¶ ~복걸하다 beg earnestly.

애견(愛犬) one's pet dog. ‖ ~가 a dog fancier [lover].

애교(愛嬌) charm; attractiveness. ¶ ~ 있는 attractive; charming; amiable / ~가 넘쳐 흐르는 be overflowing with smiles / ~를 떨다 《부리다》 make oneself pleasant to 《everybody》; try to please 《everybody》.

애교심(愛校心) love of (attachment to) one's school [Alma Mater].

애국(愛國) love of one's country; patriotism. ¶ ~적인 patriotic. ‖ ~선열 deceased patriots / ~심 patriotism; patriotic spirit [sentiment] / ~자 a patriot.

애국가(愛國歌) a patriotic song; 《국가》 the (Korean) national anthem.

애꾸(눈이) a one-eyed person.

애꽃다 (be) innocent. ¶ 애꽃은 사람 an innocent person.

애긇다 feel as if one's heart rent [torn] to pieces.

애긇다 fret 《about》; be anxious [worried] 《about》; worry 《about》.

애달프다 (be) heartbreaking; sad and painful; heartrending; trying; pathetic. ¶ 애달픈 느낌이 들다 feel sad and painful.

애도(哀悼) condolence; sympathy. ~하다 mourn; lament; grieve 《over, for》. ¶ ~의 뜻을 표하다 express one's regret 《over the death of…》; 《유족에게》 express one's condolence 《to》 / 부친의 서거에 대해 삼가 ~의 뜻을 표합니다 Please accept my condolence on the death of your father. ‖ ~사 a funeral oration; a eulogy.

애독(愛讀) ~하다 read 《a book》 with pleasure; read and enjoy; read 《a magazine》 regularly. ¶ 이 책은 학생들에게 ~되고 있다 This book is popular with [among] students. ‖ ~서 one's favorite book / ~자 a (regular) reader (신문 따위의); a subscriber (구독자).

애드벌룬 an adballoon; an advertising balloon. ¶ ~을 띄우다 float an advertising balloon.

애련(哀憐) pity; compassion. ~하다 be piteous [pathetic].

애로(隘路) 《좁은 길》 a narrow path; 《장애》 a bottleneck. ¶ ~를 타개하다 break the bottleneck.

애림(愛林) forest conservation.

애매(曖昧) (be) vague 《expression》; ambiguous 《wording》; obscure 《vowels》; indistinct 《pronunciation》; suspicious 《actions》. ¶ ~한 대답 a vague answer / ~한 태도를 취하다 maintain an uncertain attitude 《toward》.

애매하다 be wrongly (unjustly) accused 《of》; be falsely charged 《with》.

애먹다 be greatly perplexed; be in a bad [pretty] fix; be at one's wits' end. ¶ 애먹이다 give 《a person》 much trouble / 그 문제로 크게 애먹고 있다 be completely at a loss what to do about the problem; be in real trouble with the problem.

애모(愛慕) ~하다 love; be attached to; yearn after [for].

애무(愛撫) ~하다 pet; fondle; caress; cherish.
애벌 the first time. ¶ ~같이 the first tilling / ~빨래 rough washing.
애벌레 a larva.
애사(哀史) a sad [pathetic] story [history].
애사(愛社) ~심 devotion to one's company.
애서가(愛書家) a booklover.
애석(愛惜) ~하다 be reluctant [loath] to part [separate] 《with》. ‖ ~상 a consolation prize.
애석하다(哀惜 —) grieve [lament, mourn, sorrow] 《over》; be regrettable (아깝다).
애소(哀訴) ☞ 애원.
애송(愛誦) ~하다 love to recite. ‖ ~시집 a collection of one's favorite poems.
애송이 a stripling; a greenhorn. ¶ ~시절 one's salad days.
애수(哀愁) sorrow; sadness; pathos. ¶ ~를 자아내다 make 《a person》 feel sad.
애쓰다 exert [strain] oneself; make efforts; strive 《for》; endeavor; take pains [trouble].
애연가(愛煙家) a habitual smoker.
애오라지 to some extent [degree]; somewhat.
애완(愛玩) ~하다 love; pet; make a pet of; fondle. ‖ ~동물 one's pet (animal) / ~물 《object》 of 《one's》 passion.
애욕(愛慾) love and lust; 《a slave
애용(愛用) ~하다 use regularly; patronize. ¶ ~의 one's favorite / 국산품을 ~하다 patronize home production. ‖ ~자 a regular user 《of》; a person who favors 《the production of our company》.
애원(哀願) an appeal; (an) entreaty; supplication. ~ 하다 implore; plead [beg] for; appeal; supplicate. ‖ ~자 an implorer; a petitioner.
애인(愛人) a lover(남자); a love(여자); a sweetheart (주로 여자). ¶ 그의 ~ his love / ~이 생기다 get a girl friend (boyfriend).
애자(碍子) 〖電〗 an insulator.
애절하다(哀切 —) (be) pathetic; sorrowful.
애정(愛情) love; affection. ¶ ~이 있는 affectionate; loving; warmhearted / ~이 없는 cold (-hearted); loveless; unfeeling.
애제자(愛弟子) one's favorite disciple (student).
애조(哀調) 〖곡〗 a plaintive (mournful) melody; 〖樂〗 a minor key.
애족(愛族) ~애국 devotion to one's country and to one's people.
애주(愛酒) ~하다 drink 《wine》 regularly; be fond of drinking 《liquor》. ‖ ~가 a regular drinker.
애증(愛憎) love and hatred.

애중지중(愛之重之) ~하다 treasure; prize (value) highly.
애착(愛着) attachment; fondness; love. ¶ ~이 있다 be attached 《to》; be fond of / ···에 ~을 느끼다 become attached 《to》.
애창(愛唱) ~하다 love to sing 《a song》. ‖ ~곡 one's favorite song.
애처(愛妻) one's (beloved) wife. ‖ ~가 a devoted husband.
애처롭다 (be) pitiful; sorrowful; pathetic; touching. ¶ 애처로운 이야기 a sad (touching) story.
애첩(愛妾) one's favorite concubine.
애초 the very first (beginning). ¶ ~에는 at first; at the start (beginning).
애칭(愛稱) a pet name; a nickname; a term of endearment.
애타(愛他) ~적 altruistic. ‖ ~심 (주의) altruism / ~주의자 an altruist.
애타다 be anxious 《about》; be nervous (much worried) 《about》; worry oneself (sick).
애태우다 ① 《스스로》 worry oneself 《about》; feel anxiety. ¶ 그걸 가지고 애태우지 말라 Don't let that worry you. ② 《남을》 bother; worry; vex; tantalize; keep 《a person》 in suspense. ¶ 부모를 ~ worry one's parents.
애통(哀痛) ~하다 lament; grieve; deplore. ¶ ~할 deplorable; lamentable.
애티 ¶ ~가 나다 be childish (puerile).
애프터서비스 after-sales service (英); guarantee (美). ~하다 service 《a motorcar》; do (carry out) after-sales service 《on》. ¶ 이 TV 는 1년간 ~ 됩니다 This TV set has a one-year guarantee of after-sales service.
애향(愛鄕) ‖ ~심 love of (for) one's hometown (birthplace).
애호(愛好) ~하다 love; be a lover of; be fond of; have a liking for. ¶ 우리는 평화를 ~하는 국민이다 We are a peace-loving people. ‖ ~가 a lover 《of music》; a 《movie》 fan.
애호(愛護) protection; loving care. ~하다 protect; love.
애호박 a zucchini; a courgette; a green pumpkin.
애화(哀話) a sad (pathetic) story.
애환(哀歡) joys and sorrows 《of life》.
액(厄) a misfortune; ill luck.
액(液) (액체) liquid; fluid; (향) juice (과실의); sap (나무의).
···액(額) (금액) an amount; a sum. ¶ 생산 (소비) ~ the amount of production (consumed).
액년(厄年) an evil (an unlucky,

액달 an evil [an unlucky] month; a critical month.
액때움, 액땜(厄一)〖액막이〗 exorcism.
액량(液量) liquid measure.
액막이(厄一) exorcism. ~하다 drive away *one's* evils.
액면(額面) face [par] value (가격); a denomination (증권 등의). ~ 이하로 [이상으로] below [above] par; at a discount [premium] / ~대로 받아들이다 take *(a rumor)* at its face value. ∥ ~주 a par-value stock.
액모(腋毛) the hair of the armpit.
액상(液狀) ~의 liquid; liquefied.
액세서리 accessories; accessaries. ¶ ~를 달다 wear accessaries.
액셀러레이터 an accelerator. ¶ ~를 밟다 step on the [accelerator] gas pedal.
액션 action. ∥ ~스타 [드라마] an action star [teleplay].
액수(額數) a sum; an amount.
액운(厄運) misfortune; evil; ill luck; bad luck.
액일(厄日) an evil [unlucky] day.
액자(額子) a (picture) frame.
액정(液晶) liquid crystal.
액체(液體) (a) liquid; (a) fluid. ∥ ~공기 [연료] liquid air [fuel].
액화(液化)〖化〗 liquefaction. ~하다 liquefy (coal); become liquid. ∥ ~가스 liquefied gas / ~석유가스 liquefied petroleum gas (LPG) / ~천연가스 liquefied natural gas (생략 LNG).

앨범 an album.
앰풀(주사액 따위) an ampule.
앰프(증폭기) an amplifier.
앵 ~ 소리를 내다 hum; buzz.
앵글로색슨 Anglo-Saxon. ∥ ~민족 the Anglo-Saxon (race).
앵두 a cherry. ¶ ~같은 입술 lips red as a cherry. ∥ ~나무〖植〗 *Prunus tomentosa*(학명).
앵무새(鸚鵡一) a parrot.
앵속(罌粟) ☞ 양귀비.
앵앵거리다 hum; buzz. 「caster.
앵커맨 an anchor man; a news-
앵히다 feel bitter *(about)*.
야(놀랄 때의) Oh dear!; O my!; Good heavens!;(부를때의) I say (you)!; Hey there!
야(野) ~에 있다 be in private life; be in opposition (야당에).
야간(夜間) a night; nighttime. ¶ ~에 [by] night. ∥ ~경기(비행) a night game [flight] / ~근무 야근 / ~부 the night shift; the evening session *(of a school)* / ~부 학생 a night-school student / ~영업 night business [operation];(게시) Opening at Night. *or* Staying Open.
야경(夜景) a night view [scene].
야경(夜警) night watch. ~하다 keep watch at night. ¶ ~꾼 a night watchman.
야광(夜光) ¶ ~의 noctilucent. ∥ ~도료 a luminous paint / ~시계 a luminous watch / ~충(蟲) a noctiluca.
야구(野球) (play) baseball. ¶ ~ 경기를 하다 have [hold] a baseball game [match] *(with)*. ∥ ~광 a baseball buff / ~선수 [부, 팬] a baseball player [club, fan] / ~장 a baseball ground; a ball-park (美).
야근(夜勤) night duty [work](야업). ¶ ~ a night shift (주야 교대의). ~하다 be on night duty [shift]. ∥ ~수당 a night-work allowance.
야금(冶金) metallurgy. ¶ ~의 metallurgical. ∥ ~학[술] metal-lurgy / ~학자 a metallurgist.
야금(野禽) a wild fowl.
야금야금 little by little; bit by bit; gradually; by degrees.
야기(夜氣) (밤공기) night air; (냉기) the cool [chill] of the night.
야기하다(惹起一) give rise to; lead to; cause; bring about. ¶ 주택 부족은 심각한 사회 문제를 야기한다 The housing shortage gives rise to serious social problems. / 과속은 많은 사고를 야기시킨다 Speeding causes lots of accidents.
야뇨증(夜尿症)〖醫〗 bed-wetting; (nocturnal) enuresis.
야단(惹端) ① (소란) an uproar; a clamor; a row; a fuss; a disturbance. ~하다 make a fuss [row]; raise [make] an uproar. ② (꾸짖음) a scolding; a rebuke. ~하다 scold; rebuke; chide. ¶ ~을 맞다 be scolded [rebuked] roundly. ③ (곤경) a trouble; a predicament; a quandary. ¶ ~나다 be in a quandary [fix dilemma]; be at a loss.
야담(野談) an unofficial historical story [tale]. ∥ ~가 a historical storyteller.
야당(野黨) an Opposition (party). ∥ ~당수 [기관지] an Opposition leader [organ] / 제1 ~ the leading opposition.
야드 a yard (생략 yd.).
야료(惹鬧) ¶ ~를 부리다 provoke *(somebody)* to *(a quarrel, anger)* with unreasonable demands; hoot (boo, jeer) *(at)*.
야릇하다 (be) queer; strange; odd; curious.
야만(野蠻) ~적 savage; barbarous; uncivilized. ∥ ~인 a barbarian; a savage / ~행위 a barbarous [cruel] act.
야망(野望) (an) ambition; (an)

aspiration. ¶ ~이 있는 ambitious / ~을 품다 be ambitious 《of, for, to do》; have an ambition 《for》. ~ness: nyctalopia.
야맹증(夜盲症) 〔醫〕 night blindness.
야멸스럽다 (be) heartless; cold; inhuman; unsympathetic; hard-hearted.
야무지다 (be) firm; strong; solid; hard; tough. ¶ 야무진 사람 a man of firm character / 솜씨가 ~ be deft-handed; be dexterous.
야바위 trickery; swindle. ¶ ~ 치다 play a trick upon 《a person》; cheat; swindle. ‖ ~꾼 a swindler; an impostor; a trickster.
야박하다(野薄—) (be) cold-hearted; heartless; hard; cruel. ¶ 야박한 세상 a hard world.
야반(夜半) ¶ ~에 at midnight / ~도주하다 flee by night.
야비(野卑) ~하다 (be) vulgar; mean; low; boorish; coarse.
야사(野史) an unofficial history.
야산(野山) a hill; a hillock.
야상곡(夜想曲) 〔樂〕 a nocturne.
야생(野生) ~하다 grow (in the) wild. ¶ ~의 wild; uncultivated / ~상태에서는 in the (a) wild state; in the wild. ‖ ~식물〔동물〕 a wild plant (animal).
야성(野性) wild nature. ¶ ~적인 wild; rough / 개도 굶주리면 ~을 나타낸다 Even dogs run wild when they are hungry. ‖ ~미(美) unpolished beauty.
야속하다(野俗—) (be) cold-hearted; heartless; 《섭섭하다》 (be) reproachful; rueful. ¶ 야속해 하는 눈초리 a reproachful look.
야수(野手) 〔野〕 a fielder.
야수(野獸) a wild beast (animal). ¶ ~같은 brutal; beastlike. ‖ ~성 brutality; 〔美術〕 Fauvism; a Fauvist 《사람》.
야습(夜襲) a night attack (raid). ¶ ~하다 make a night attack 《on》.
야시(장)(夜市場) a night market.
야식(夜食) a midnight snack. ¶ ~으로 국수를 먹다 have a midnight snack of noodles.
야심(野心) (an) ambition; 《음모》 a sinister designs. ¶ ~있는 ambitious. ‖ ~가 an ambitious person.
야심하다(夜深—) be late at night.
야영(野營) a camp; camping. ~하다 camp out. ¶ ~지 a camping ground. ¶~mew.
야옹 mew; miaow. ¶ ~하고 울다
야외(野外) ~의 outdoor; out-of-air; out-of-door; field / ~에서 in the open (air); outdoors in the field / ~에 나가다 go out into the field. ¶ ~극장 an open-air theater / ~요리 outdoor cooking; a cookout / ~운동 outdoor sports / ~음악회 an open-air (outdoor) concert / ~작업〔연습〕 field work (exercise) / ~촬영 a location.
야유(野遊) a picnic; an outing. ¶ ~회 a picnic party 《~회를 가다 go on a picnic》.
야유(揶揄) hoots; heckling; jeer. ~하다 hoot; heckle; jeer 《at》. ¶ 연사를 ~하여 하단시키다 hoot a (the) speaker down.
야음(夜陰) ¶ ~을 틈타 under cover of darkness (night).
야인(野人) ① 《시골 사람》 a rustic; a countryman; 《꾸밈없는 사람》 a man with rough and simple tastes. ② 《재야의》 a person out of official position; a private citizen.
야자(椰子) 〔植〕 a coconut tree; a cocopalm. ¶ ~기름 coconut oil / ~열매 a coconut.
야전(野戰) field operations (warfare). ¶ ~군〔병원〕 a field army (hospital).
야채(野菜) vegetables; greens. ¶ ~를 가꾸다 grow (raise) vegetables. ‖ ~가게 a greengrocery / ~밭 《가정의》 a kitchen (vegetable) garden; 《농가의》 a vegetable field / ~샐러드〔수프〕 vegetable salad (soup) / ~요리 a vegetable dish. ¶ ~(low; shallowish.
야트막하다《깊이가》 (be) rather shallow.
야포(野砲) a field gun; field artillery 《총칭》. ¶ ~대 a field battery.
야하다(冶—) ① 《난하다》 (be) gorgeous; showy; gaudy 《clothes》. ② 《속되다》 (be) vulgar; mean; low; coarse.
야학(夜學) a night school. ¶ ~에 다니다 attend (go to) a night school.
야합(野合) 《남녀간의》 an illicit union (relationship); 《정당간의》 an unprincipled coalition between political parties (formed with a sole view to seizing political power). ~하다 form an illicit union (connection).
야행(夜行) ~하다 go (travel) by night. ‖ ~성 〔動〕 the nocturnal habits / ~성 동물 a nocturnal animal.
야회(夜會) (give) an evening party; a ball 《무도회》. ‖ ~복 an evening dress.
약(葯) 〔植〕 an anther.
약(藥) ① 《치료제》 medicine; a drug; a pill 《환약》. ¶ ~을 먹다 〔바르다〕 take (apply) medicine / ~을 주다 〔먹이다〕 administer medi-

약 (約) 《대략》 about; some; nearly; around 《美》; approximately. ¶ ~ 5마일 about [nearly] five miles.

약가심 (藥—) ~하다 take off the aftertaste of the medicine.

약간 (若干) some; (some) quantity of; a little; 《수》 a few; a number of. ¶ ~의 돈 some money.

약값 (藥—) a charge for medicine; a medical fee. 「health.

약골 (弱骨) ~이다 be of delicate

약과 (藥果) ① 《과줄》. ② 《쉬운 일》 an easy thing. ¶ 그것쯤은 ~다 It's an easy task. *or* That's nothing.

약관 (約款) 《협약》 an agreement; 《조항》 a stipulation; an article; a clause.

약관 (弱冠) a youth of twenty; a young man. ¶ ~에 at the age of twenty.

약국 (藥局) a drugstore 《美》; a pharmacy; a chemist's shop 《英》.

약기 (略記) ~하다 make a short [rough] sketch 《of》; outline.

약다 (be) clever; wise; sharp; shrewd; smart. ¶ 약게 굴다 act smartly; be tactful.

약도 (略圖) a (rough) sketch; a sketch [rough] map 《지도의》. ¶ ~를 그리다 draw a rough map.

약동하다 (躍動—) move in a lively way; throb; be in full play. ¶ 생기 ~ be full of life and energy.

약력 (略歷) one's brief personal history; a sketch of one's life.

약리 (藥理) ~작용 medicinal action / ~학 pharmacology.

약물 (藥物) (a) medicine; drugs. ~ 요법 medication; medical therapy / ~의존 drug dependence / ~중독 drug poisoning.

약밥 (藥—) sweet steamed rice flavored with honey, nuts and jujubes.

약방 (藥房) a drugstore. ☞ 약국.

약방문 (藥方文) a prescription (slip); a recipe. ¶ 사후 ~ the doctor after death.

약변화 (弱變化) 《文》 weak conjugation. ¶ ~의 《동사》 weak (verbs).

약병 (藥瓶) a medicine bottle.

약복 (略服) an informal [ordinary, everyday] dress. 「cine.

약봉지 (藥封紙) a packet of medi-

약분 (約分) reduction. ~하다 reduce 《a fraction》. ¶ ~할 수 없는 irreducible.

약사 (藥師) a pharmaceutist; a pharmacist; a dispenser.

약사 (略史) a brief [short] history.

약사발 (藥沙鉢) ~을 내리다 bestow poison 《to a person》 as a death penalty.

약사법 (藥事法) the Pharmaceutical Affairs Law.

약삭빠르다 (be) clever; sharp; shrewd; smart; quick-witted. ¶ 약삭빠르게 굴다 move smartly; act shrewdly.

약석 (藥石) ¶ ~의 보람 없이 in spite of every medical treatment.

약설 (略說) a summary; an outline. ~하다 give an outline 《of》; outline.

약소 (弱小) ~하다 (be) small and weak. ‖ ~국 (家) a lesser (minor) power (nation) / ~민족 the people of a small and weak power.

약소하다 (略少—) (be) scanty; insignificant; a few 《수》; a little 《양》.

약속 (約束) 《실행의》 a promise; an engagement; 《회합의》 an appointment; a date (남녀간의). ~하다 (make a) promise; give one's word; make an appointment (a date 《美》) 《with》. ¶ ~을 지키다 [어기다] keep [break] one's promise [word]. ‖ ~시간 [장소] the appointed time [spot] / ~어음 (issue) a promissory note.

약손가락 (藥—) the third finger; the ring finger.

약솜 (藥—) absorbent [sanitary] cotton; cotton wool [batting].

약수 (約數) 《數》 a divisor; a factor.

약수 (藥水) 《약물》 medicinal (mineral) water. ‖ ~터 a mineral spring resort; a spa.

약술 (略述) ~하다 give an outline (a rough sketch) 《of》.

약시 (弱視) weak (poor) eyesight; 《醫》 amblyopia. ¶ ~의 weak-sighted; amblyopic.

약시중 (藥—) ~하다 serve 《a person》 with a medicinal decoction.

약식 (略式) 《informal; unceremonious / ~으로 informally; without formality. ‖ ~ 명령 a summary order / ~재판 summary trial / ~절차 informal proceedings.

약실 (藥室) 《총의》 a cartridge chamber.

약쑥 (藥—) 《植》 (medicinal) moxa.

약어 (略語) an abbreviation.

약언 (略言) ~하다 summarize. ¶ ~하면 in short [brief]; in a word; to be brief.

약연 (藥碾) a druggist's mortar.

약오르다 fret (and fume) 《about》; become impatient; be irritated.

약올리다 irritate; fret; tantalize;

tease (놀려서).
약용(藥用) medicinal use. ¶ ~의 medicinal / ~에 쓰다 use (*a thing*) for medical purposes. ‖ ~ 비누 a medicated soap / ~식물 a medicinal plant (herb).
약육강식(弱肉強食) the law of the jungle. ¶ ~은 자연의 법칙이다 It is a rule of nature that the strong prey upon the weak.
약음기(弱音器) a mute.
약자(弱者) the weak. ¶ ~의 편을 들다 side with (stand by) the weak.
약자(略字) a simplified (an abbreviated) form (*of a Chinese character*).
약장(略章) a miniature decoration (medal); a service ribbon.
약장(藥欌) a medicine chest.
약재(藥材) medicinal stuffs.
약전(弱電) a weak electric current. ‖ ~기기 light electric appliances.
약전(略傳) a biographical sketch; a short biography (*of*).
약전(藥典) the pharmacopoeia.
약점(弱點) a weakness; a weak (vulnerable) point;《결점》a defect; shortcomings;《아픈데》a sore (tender) spot (급소). ¶ ~을 지니고 있다 have a weakness (*for women*) / ~을 찌르다 touch (*a person*) on a sore spot.
약정(約定) ~하다 agree; contract; promise. ¶ ~기한 a stipulated time / ~서 an agreement; a written contract.
약제(藥劑) drugs; chemicals; (a) medicine. ‖ ~사 ☞ 약사(藥師).
약조(約條) ~하다 promise; pledge. ¶ ~금 a contract deposit.
약종상(藥種商) a drug merchant; a herbalist(한약의); an apothecary.
약주(藥酒) ①《약용》medical liquor. ②《술》refined *sul*; rice wine.
약진(弱震) a weak (minor) shock (of an earthquake).
약진(躍進) ~하다 (make a) rush (dash) (*for*);《진보》make rapid advance (progress).
약질(弱質) a weak person.
약체(弱體) ¶ ~의 weak; effete / ~화하다 become weak (effete). ‖ ~내각 an effete Cabinet.
약초(藥草) medicinal herbs; a medical plant. ‖ ~학 medical botany.
약탈(掠奪) plunder; pillage; loot. ~하다 pillage; plunder; loot. ‖ ~자 a plunderer; a looter / ~품 spoil; plunder; loot.
약탕관(藥湯罐) a clay pot in which medicines are prepared.
약포(藥圃) a herbal garden.

약품(藥品) medicines; drugs; chemicals (화학 약품).
약하다(弱—) ①《체력·능력·기력이》(be) weak; delicate; poor; feeble; frail. ¶ 몸이 ~ be physically weak; have a delicate (frail) constitution / 위장이 ~ have poor (weak) digestion / 의지가 ~ have a weak will. ②《빛·색·소리 따위가》(be) faint; feeble; gentle;《술 따위가》(be) mild;《정도 따위가》(be) slight. ¶ ~ 약한 소리 a faint sound / 약한 빛 a feeble light / 약한 술 (담배) weak (mild) wine (tobacco) / 약한 바람이 불고 있다 A gentle wind is blowing. ③《깨지기 쉬운》(be) weak; flimsy (boxes). ¶ 약한 토대 a weak foundation. ④《저항력이》 ¶ 술에 ~ easily get drunk; cannot hold *one's* drink / 추위에 ~ be sensitive to cold / 열에 ~ be easily affected by heat / 여성에게 ~ be susceptible to feminine charms; easily fall for women. ⑤《서투르다》(be) weak; poor. ¶ 나는 수학이 ~ I'm weak in (poor at) mathematics.
약하다(略—) ☞ 생략(省略).
약학(藥學) pharmacy; pharmacology. ‖ ~과 the pharmaceutical department / ~대학 the college of pharmacy / ~박사 (학위) a Doctor of Pharmacy (생략 Phar. D.) / ~자 a pharmacologist.
약호(略號) a code (cable) address.
약혼(約婚) an engagement; a betrothal. ~하다 get engaged (*to*). ‖ ~반지 an engagement ring / ~선물 [식] an engagement present (ceremony) / ~자 *one's fiancé* (남), *one's fiancée* (여).
약화(弱化) ~하다 weaken.
약효(藥效) the effect (virtue, efficacy) of a medicine. ¶ ~를 나타내다 take effect; work; prove efficacious / ~가 있다 be effective; be good (*for*).
얄궂다 (be) strange; queer; odd; funny; curious. ¶ 얄궂게도 strange enough; by a curious coincidence / 얄궂은 운명의 irony of fate.
얄따랗다 (be) rather thin.
얄밉다(불쾌) be offensive;《주제넘다》be saucy; cheeky; pert; 《밉다》(be) disgusting; hateful; detestable; provoking. ¶ 얄미운 소리를 하다 say pert (spiteful) thing / 얄밉게 굴다 behave meanly.
얄팍하다 (be) thin.
얇다 (be) thin. ¶ 얇게 thinly / 입술이 ~ have thin lips.
얌심 mean jealousy. ¶ ~ 부리다 display jealousy. ‖ ~데기 a mean

얌전하다 ① 《차분·단정》 (be) gentle; well-behaved; modest; polite; graceful. ¶ 얌전한 색시 a modest girl / 몸가짐이 ~ be modest (graceful) in one's manner / 얌전하게 굴다 behave oneself. ② 《솜씨·모양》 (be) nice; neat; good. ¶ 일을 얌전하게 하다 do a nice job.
양(羊) 《動》 a sheep; a lamb (새끼). ¶ 길 잃은 ~ a lost (stray) lamb. ‖ ~ 가죽 sheepskin/《제본용》 roan / ~ 고기 mutton / ~ 떼 a flock of sheep / ~ 떼구름 《氣》 a cumulocirrus / ~ 털 (sheep's) wool.
양(良) good; fine; B.
양(量) ① 《분량》 quantity; amount; volume. ¶ ~ 적으로 quantitatively / ~ 이 적다 (많다) be small (large) in quantity / ~ 보다 질 quality before quantity. ② 《먹는양》 one's capacity for food 《wine, etc.》. ¶ ~ 껏 먹다 (마시다) eat (drink) to one's fill / ~ 이 크다 be a great eater.
양(陽) the positive; 《哲》 "Yang".
양…(兩) 《둘》 a couple; both; two. ¶ ~ 국 both countries / ~ 가 two (both) houses (families) / ~ 군 both armies.
양…(洋) foreign; Western; European. ¶ ~ 식 foreign food; Western dishes.
…양(孃) Miss 《Kim》.
양가(良家) a respectable (good) family. ¶ ~ 태생이다 come from a good family.
양가(養家) an adoptive family.
양각(陽刻) relief: (a) relief sculpture (carving). ¶ ~ 하다 carve in relief. ‖ ~ 세공 relief (raised) work.
양갈보(洋─) a prostitute who caters to foreigners.
양계(養鷄) poultry farming; chicken raising. ¶ ~ 하다 raise poultry (chickens). ‖ ~ 업 a poultry farming / ~ 장 a poultry (chicken) farm.
양곡(糧穀) cereals; corn; grain. ‖ ~ 도입 importation of grains / ~ 수급계획 a plan for demand and supply of grains.
양공주(洋公主) ☞ 양갈보.
양과자(洋菓子) Western confectionery (cakes).
양궁(洋弓) Western-style archery 《궁술》; a Western-style bow 《활》.
양귀비(楊貴妃) 《植》 a poppy.
양극(兩極) the two poles 《지구의》; the positive and negative poles 《전극의》; the opposite poles 《정반대》. ¶ ~ 의 bipolar. ‖ ~ 지방 the polar circles (areas) / ~ 화 bipolarization. 「the anode.
양극(陽極) 《電》 the positive pole
양극단(兩極端) the two extremes.
양기(陽氣) ① 《햇볕》 sunlight; sunshine. ② 《남자의》 vigor; virility; vitality; energy.
양날(兩─) ¶ ~ 의 double-edged; two bladed.
양녀(養女) an adopted daughter.
양념 spices; flavor; seasoning; condiments. ¶ ~ 을 한 spicy; spiced 《food》 / ~ 을 치다 spice 《a dish》; season (flavor) 《a dish》 with spice. ‖ ~ 병 a cruet.
양다리(兩─) ¶ ~ 를 걸치다 try to have (it) both ways; sit on the fence; play double (내통하다) / ~ (를) 걸치는 사람 a double-dealer; a time server; a fence-sitter.
양단(兩端) both ends; either end. ¶ ~ 을 자르다 cut (a thing) at both ends / 좌우간에 at any rate; in any case (way); at all events / ~ 간 해야 할 일이다 I must do it anyhow.
양단(兩斷) bisection. ~ 하다 bisect; split (break) in two; cut 《something》 in two.
양단(洋緞) satin. 「thing》 in two.
양달(陽─) a sunny place (spot). ¶ ~ 쪽 the sunny side.
양담배(洋─) imported (American) cigarettes (tobacco).
양당(兩黨) the two political parties. ¶ ~ 정치 (제도) the two-party politics (system).
양도(糧道) supply of provisions. ¶ ~ 를 끊다 cut off the 《enemy's》 supplies.
양도(讓渡) transfer; conveyancing; negotiation (어음의). ~ 하다 transfer 《a thing》 to; hand (make) over 《a thing》 over 《to》; deed 《a thing》 to 《a person》 《美》. ¶ ~ 할 수 있는 transferable; alienable; negotiable (어음의). ‖ ~ 성예금 a negotiable deposit / ~ 소득 income from the transfer of one's property / ~ 소득세 a transfer income tax / ~ 인 a grantor; a transferrer (피─인 a transferee) / ~ 증서 a conveyance; a deed of transfer. 「《of heat》.
양도체(良導體) a good conductor
양돈(養豚) hog (pig) raising. ~ 하다 raise (rear) hogs. ‖ ~ 가 a hog raiser 《美》; pig breeder (farmer) 《英》 / ~ 장 a pig farm; a swinery.
양동이(洋─) a metal pail.
양동작전(陽動作戰) a feint operation; (make) a sham attack.
양두(兩頭) ¶ ~ 정치 diarchy.
양두구육(羊頭狗肉) Cry up wine, and sell vinegar.
양력(陽曆) the solar calender.
양력(揚力) 《理》 (dynamic) lift. ¶ ~ 을 얻다 obtain lift.

양로(養老) ∥ ~보험 old-age (endowment) insurance / ~연금 an old-age pension / ~원 a home for the aged; an old people's home; a retirement community (노인촌).

양론(兩論) both arguments; both sides of the argument.

양륙(揚陸) unloading 《*of cargo*》; (상륙) landing. ~하다 unload; land; disembark. ∥ ~비 landing charges / ~지〔장〕 a (designated) landing place (stage).

양립(兩立) ~하다 be compatible 《*with*》; stand together. ¶ ~할 수 없다 be incompatible 《*with*》.

양말(洋襪) socks (짧은); stockings (긴). ¶ ~을 신다〔벗다〕 put on 〔take off〕 socks 〔stockings〕.

양면(兩面) both faces. ∥ ~의 double-faced; both-sided. ∥ ~작전 double-sided operations.

양명(揚名) ~하다 gain fame; make *one*'s name; win distinction.

양모(羊毛) sheep's wool. ∥ ~의 woollen.

양모(養母) an adoptive mother; a foster mother.

양모제(養毛劑) a hair tonic.

양미간(兩眉間) ~을 찌푸리다 knit *one*'s brows; frown 《*at, on*》.

양민(良民) law-abiding citizens; good citizenry. ¶ ~학살 massacre 〔slaughter〕 of the innocent people.

양반(兩班) 《동반·서반》 the two upper classes of old Korea; 《계급》 the nobility; the aristocracy; 《사람》 an aristocrat; a nobleman.

양배추(洋―) a cabbage.

양변(兩邊) both sides.

양병(養兵) building up 〔maintaining〕 an army. ~하다 build up 〔maintain〕 an army.

양보(讓步) concession. ~하다 concede 《*to*》; make a concession; give way to. ¶ 서로 ~하다 make mutual concessions / 한 치도 ~하지 않다 do not yield an inch.

양복(洋服) foreign clothes; European (style) clothes; a suit (of clothes) (한 벌). ¶ ~을 맞추다 have 〔get〕 a suit made / ~을 입다〔벗다〕 put on 〔take off〕 *one*'s clothes. ∥ ~감 material for foreign clothes; cloth / ~걸이 a coat hanger / ~장 a wardrobe / ~점 a tailor's (shop).

양봉(養蜂) beekeeping; apiculture. ~하다 keep 〔culture〕 bees. ∥ ~가 a beekeeper / ~업 bee-farming / ~장 a bee farm; an apiary.

양부(良否) good or bad; quality.

양부(養父) an adoptive 〔a foster〕 father.

양부모(養父母) foster 〔adoptive〕 parents.

양분(養分) nutriment; nourishment. ¶ ~이 있다 be nourishing.

양산(陽傘) a parasol.

양산(量産) mass production. ~하다 mass-produce; produce in large quantities. ¶ ~체제로 들어가다 《제품이 주어》 be put into commercial production. ¶ ~계획 a plan for the mass production 《*of*》.

양상(樣相) an aspect; a phase (국면). ¶ 새로운 ~을 나타내다 take on a new aspect; enter upon a new phase.

양상군자(梁上君子) 《도둑》 a robber; a thief.

양생(養生) 《섭생》 care of health; 《보양》 recuperation. ~하다 take care of *one*'s health; recuperate *oneself* (병후의). ∥ ~법 rules of *one*'s health; hygiene.

양서(良書) a good book.

양서(洋書) a foreign book.

양서동물(兩棲動物) an amphibious animal; an amphibian.

양서류(兩棲類) 〔動〕 Amphibia.

양성(兩性) both (the two) sexes. ¶ ~의 bisexual 《*flower*》. ∥ ~생식 gamogenesis.

양성(陽性) positivity. ¶ ~의 positive / ~이다 prove positive. ∥ ~반응 a positive reaction.

양성(養成) training; education. ~하다 educate; cultivate (재능·품성 따위의). ¶ 기술자를 ~하다 train technicians / 연기력을 ~하다 cultivate *one*'s skill of acting. ∥ ~소 a training school 《*for teachers*》.

양성화(陽性化) ¶ 무허가 건물의 ~ licensing unauthorized shacks / 정치 자금을 ~하다 make public the sources of political funds.

양속(良俗) a good 〔fine〕 custom.

양송이(洋松耳) a mushroom; a champignon (유럽 원산). ∥ ~재배 mushroom cultivation.

양수(羊水) 〔醫〕 amniotic fluid.

양수(兩手) both hands. ¶ ~걸이 《장기 등의》 scoring a double point with a single move / ~잡이 an ambidexter.

양수(揚水) pumping up. ∥ ~기 a water pump / ~발전소 a pumping-up power plant / ~장 a pumping station.

양수(讓受) acquisition by transfer; inheritance (계승). ~하다 obtain by transfer; take over; inherit. ∥ ~인 a grantee; a transferee.

양순(良順) ~하다 (be) good and obedient; gentle; meek. ¶ ~한 백성 law-abiding 〔obedient〕 people.

양식(良識) good sense. ¶ ~ 있는 사람 a sensible person.

양식(洋式) ¶ ~의 Western-style; ~ 화장실 a Western-style toilet; a sit-down type toilet / ~ 방 a room furnished in Western style.

양식(洋食) Western food [dishes]; Western cooking. ‖ ~기[器] Western tableware / ~집 a (Western) restaurant.

양식(樣式) a form; a style; a mode; a pattern (방식). ¶ 소정 ~의 원서를 제출하다 submit one's application in the prescribed [proper] form. ‖ 행동~ patterns of behavior.

양식(養殖) culture; breeding. ~하다 raise; cultivate; breed. ¶ ~어 hatchery fish / ~어업 the fish-raising industry / ~장 a nursery; a farm / ~진주 a cultured pearl / 굴~ oyster culture (farming) / 진주~ pearl culture.

양식(糧食) food; provisions. ¶ 마음의 ~ mental pabulum / 3일분의 ~을 휴대하다 take a three-day supply of food.

양심(良心) conscience. ~적(으로) conscientious(ly) / ~이 없는 사람 a man with no conscience / ~적인 작품 a conscientious piece of work / ~에 호소하다 appeal to (a person's) conscience / ~에 어긋나다 betray one's conscience / ~에 따라 행동하다 act according to one's conscience / ~의 가책을 받다 suffer from a guilty conscience; be stung by one's conscience; feel the pricks (stings, pangs) of conscience / ~에 부끄러운 데가 없다 I have a good [clear] conscience / 그것은 네 ~에 맡기겠다 I'll leave it to your conscience. ‖ ~선언 a declaration of conscience / ~수 a conscientious prisoner.

양악(洋樂) Western music.

양안(兩岸) both banks; either bank (side).

양약(良藥) a good medicine. ¶ ~ 은 입에 쓰다 A good medicine tastes bitter.

양약(洋藥) Western medicines.

양양(洋洋) ~하다 (be) vast; broad; boundless; bright (앞길이). ¶ ~한 전도 (have) a bright (great) future.

양양하다(揚揚-) (be) triumphant; exultant.

양어(養魚) fish breeding (farming). ‖ ~장 a fish farm.

양어머니 a foster mother.

양여(讓與) transfer; 《영토의》 cession; alienation (함양); 《이권의》 concession; 《포기》 surrender; 《양도》 assignment. ~하다 transfer; concede 《a privilege to another》.

양옥(洋屋) a Western-style house.

양용(兩用) 《for》 double use. ¶ 수륙 ~ 전차 an amphibian (amphibious) tank.

양원(兩院) both [the two] Houses [Chambers]. ‖ ~제도 a bicameral systems.

양위(讓位) 《임금의》 abdication (of the throne). ~하다 abdicate (the throne).

양육(養育) ~하다 bring up; rear; nurse; foster. ¶ ~비 the expenses for bringing up 《a child》 / ~자 a fosterer; a rearer.

양은(洋銀) nickel (German) silver.

양의(良醫) a good physician.

양의(洋醫) a Western (medical) doctor.

양이(攘夷) antiforeign sentiment; exclusionism. ¶ ~론 the advocacy of exclusion of foreigners / ~론자 an exclusionist.

양이온(陽-) 【理】 a positive ion.

양자(兩者) both; the two; both parties. ¶ ~택일하다 select one alternatively; choose between the two.

양자(陽子) 【理】 a proton.

양자(量子) 【理】 a quantum.

양자(養子) an adopted son; a foster child. ¶ ~로 삼다 adopt 《a child》 / ~로 가다 be adopted into a family.

양자강(揚子江) ☞ 양쯔 강.

양잠(養蠶) sericulture; silkworm culture (breeding). ~하다 raise (breed) silkworms. ¶ ~농가 a silkworm raiser / ~업 the sericultural industry.

양장(洋裝) ① 《옷》 Western-style clothes. ~하다 be dressed in Western style; wear Western clothes. ¶ ~점 a dressmaking shop; a boutique. ② 《제본》 foreign binding.

양재(良材) good timber (재목); a man of ability (인재).

양재(洋裁) dressmaking. ‖ ~사 a dressmaker / ~학원 a dressmaking school.

양잿물(洋-) caustic soda.

양전기(陽電氣) positive electricity.

양전자(陽電子) 【理】 a positron.

양젖 sheep's milk.

양조(釀造) brewing; brewage; distillation. ~하다 brew 《beer》; distill 《whisky》. ¶ ~업자 a brewer; a distiller / ~장 a brewery; a distillery(위스키의) / ~주 a liquor [an alcoholic beverage] made by fermentation / ~학 zymurgy.

양주(洋酒) Western liquors; whisky and wine.

양지(洋紙) Western paper.

양지(陽地) a sunny place. ¶ ~쪽 the sunny side / ~에 in the sun / ~가 음지(陰地)되고 음지가 ~된다 Life is full of ups and downs.

양지(諒知) ~하다 know; understand; be aware of. ¶ ~하시는 바와 같이 as you see [are aware].

양지머리 the brisket of beef.

양진영(兩陣營) both camps [parties]; the two opposing sides.

양질(良質) ¶ ~의 종이 paper of good [superior] quality.

양쪽(兩—) both sides. ¶ ~에 on both sides [either side] (of the street).

양쯔 강(揚子江) the Yangtze (River).

양차(兩次) two times; twice.

양찰(諒察) ~하다 consider; take into consideration.

양책(良策) a good plan; a wise policy.

양처(良妻) a good wife.

양철(洋鐵) tin plate. ǁ ~가위 snips / ~장이 a tinman / ~깡통 a tin (can); a can (美).

양초 a candle.

양측(兩側) ☞ 양쪽.

양치(養齒) ~하다 rinse (out) one's mouth; gargle (the throat).

양치기(羊—) sheep-raising; a shepherd (목동).

양키 a Yankee; a Yank《俗》.

양탄자 a carpet; a rug. ¶ ~를 깔다 spread a carpet; carpet (a floor).

양토(養兎) rabbit raising [rearing]. ~하다 raise [breed] rabbits. ǁ ~장 a rabbitry.

양파(洋—) an onion.

양팔(兩—) two [both] arms.

양편(兩便) either side; both sides.

양푼 a brass basin.

양품(洋品) haberdashery; fancy goods. ǁ ~점 a haberdashery; a fancy-goods) store.

양풍(良風) a good custom. ǁ ~미속 미풍양속.

양풍(洋風) the European [Western] style (manner).

양피(羊皮) sheepskin; roan (제본용). ǁ ~구두 sheepskin shoes / ~지(紙) parchment.

양학(洋學) (西洋 學問) Western [European] learning.

양항(良港) a good harbor.

양해(諒解)《說明》 consent; agreement; (이해) understanding. ~하다 consent to; agree to; understand. ¶ 상호 ~하에 by mutual agreement / ~를 얻다 obtain (a person's) consent / 두 사람 사이에는 암묵의 ~가 있었다 There was a tacit understanding between them. ǁ ~각서 a memorandum of understanding (생략 MOU) / ~사항 agreed items.

양행(洋行) ① 《외국행》 ~하다 go [travel] abroad. ② 《회사》 a foreign business firm.

양형(量刑) assessment of a case.

양호(良好) ~하다 (be) good; excellent; successful; satisfactory.

양호(養護) nursing; protective care. ~하다 nurse; protect. ǁ ~교사 a nurse-teacher / ~시설 a protective institution.

양화(良貨) good money.

양화(洋靴) ~구두. ǁ ~점 a shoe shop [store 美].

양화(洋畫) ① 《서양화》 a Western-style painting. ② 《영화》 a foreign movie (film).

양화(陽畫) a positive (picture).

양회(洋灰) cement.

얕다 (깊이가) (be) shallow. ¶ 얕은 우물[접시] a shallow well [dish] / 물이 얕은 곳 a shoal; a shallow. ② 《생각·지식이》 (be) shallow; superficial; thoughtless. ¶ 얕은 꾀 shallow wit / 얕은 소견 [지식] a superficial view [knowledge]. ③ 《정도가》 (be) light; slight. ¶ 얕은 상처 a slight injury; a light wound / 얕은 잠 a light sleep / 그 회사와의 관계는 아직 ~ Our relations with that company are still not very close.

얕보다 hold (a person) cheap; make light of; look down on; underestimate; despise. ¶ 얕볼 수 없는 적 a formidable enemy / 그를 어린애라고 ~ make light of him as a mere boy / 그들의 능력을 얕보아서는 안 된다 Don't underestimate their ability.

애《호칭》 Sonny!; My boy!; You!; Hey!; 《이 애》 this child.

어《감탄》 Oh!; Well!; Why!; 《대답》 yea!

어간(語幹) the stem of a word.

어감(語感) a linguistic sense; word feeling (말의). ¶ (말의) 미묘한 ~ (a) subtle nuance.

어개(魚介) 《해산물》 marine products.

어거하다(馭車—) drive (a horse) 〔제어〕 manage; control.

어구 words and phrases.

어구(漁具) a fishing implement; fishing gear [tackle] (총칭).

어구(漁區) a fishing ground [area].

어군(魚群) a shoal [school] of fish. ǁ ~탐지기 a fish finder (detector).

어군(語群) 《文》 a word group.

어귀 an entrance (to a village); an entry (to a river); the mouth (of a harbor).

어그러지다 ① (반대로) be contrary to; be against (the rule); depart from. ¶ 기대에 ~ be contrary to one's expectation. ② 《사이가》 become estranged. ¶ 친구와 사이가 ~ be estranged from a friend.

어근(語根) the root of a word.
어근버근 ① (느슨하다) ~ 하다 (be) loose; do not dovetail (서술적). ② (불화) ~ 하다 (서술적) be at variance; be on bad terms.
어금니 a molar (tooth).
어긋나다 ① (길이) pass (cross) each other; miss each other on the road. ② (빗나가다) go amiss; miss; go wrong; fail. ¶ 계획이 ~ be baffled in *one's* design / 나의 예상이 어긋났다 My guess turned out to be wrong. *or* I guessed wrong. ③ (틀리다·위반되다) be against; be contrary to (*the rule*). ④ (뼈 따위가) be dislocated.
어긋매끼다 cross (*two sticks*); place (stack) crosswise; intercross.
어긋물리다 cross (each other).
어긋버긋하다 (서술적) be out of joint (with each other); (be) loose; uneven.
어기(漁期) the fishing season.
어기다 (약속·명령·규칙 따위를) go against; offend against (*the law*); violate (*a rule*); break (*one's* promise). ¶ 부모 뜻을 어기어 against *one's* parents' wishes / 시간을 어기지 않고 punctually; on time / 명령을 ~ go (act) against orders.
어기대다 disobey; oppose; go (act) against.
어기적거리다 waddle; shuffle along.
어기중하다(於其中) be in the middle; (be) medium; average.
어기차다 be sturdy (stouthearted).
어김 ~없는 unerring; infallible / ~없이 without fail; surely; certainly / ~없이 …하다 do not fail (forget) to (*do*).
어깨 the shoulder. ¶ ~가 넓은 (떡벌어진) broad-(square-)shouldered (*man*) / ~에 메다 shoulder (*a thing*) / ~를 으쓱하다 shrug *one's* shoulders / ~를 나란히 하다 stand side by side; ~를 겨누다 can compare (*with*); rank (*with another*) / ~를 겨루다 compete (*with*).
어깨너멋글 picked-up knowledge.
어깨동무 ~ 하다 put arms around each other's shoulders.
어깨뼈 the shoulder blade.
어깨총(一銃) (구령) Shoulder arms!
어깨춤(一춤) ¶ ~을 추다 dance with *one's* shoulders moving up and down.
어깻바람 ¶ ~이 나서 in high spirits.
어깻숨 ¶ ~을 쉬다 pant.
어깻죽지 the shoulder joint.
어느 ① (한) a; one; a certain; some. ¶ ~ 날 one day / ~ 정도 to some (a certain) extent; somewhat. ② (의문) which; what. ¶ ~ 날 (책) which day (book) / ~ 사람 who / ~ 차를 타겠느냐 Which car will you take? ③ (그 중 어느) whichever; any. ¶ ~ ~ 도 any; every; whichever; (부정) none / ~ 모로 보아도 from every point of view / ~ 컵을 사용해도 좋다 You may use any cup. / 이 중에서 어느 계획을 택해도 좋다 You may choose any of these plans.
어느결 (어느새) before *one* knows (is aware); without *one's* knowledge; unnoticed. ¶ ~에 나이 사십이 되었다 Here I am forty years old without quite realizing it.
어느때 when; (at) what time (어느때나) any time; whenever. ¶ ~고 마음이 내킬 때 오시오 Come whenever (any time) you like.
어느새 어느덧.
어느쪽 (의문) which; (무엇이든) whichever; (선택) either…(or); neither…(nor) (부정); (두 쪽 다) both; either; neither; (방향) which direction (side). ¶ ~ 이든 간에 in either case; either way / ~ 이라도 좋다 Either will do.
어두컴컴하다 (be) very dark. ¶ 어두컴컴한 밤 a dark night.
어득(어둑)하다 (be) dim; gloomy; dusky.
어둠 darkness; the dark. ¶ ~속에(서) in the dark / ~ 속으로 사라지다 vanish into the night / ~침침하다 be dim (gloomy, dusky) / ~침침한 방 a dimly-(an ill-lit) room.
어둡다 ① (암흑) (be) dark; dim (희미); gloomy (음침). ¶ 어두워지기 전에 while it is light; before (it gets) dark / 어둡게 하다 darken; dim (*the light*); make (*a light*) dim / 어두워지다 become (get) dark. ② (무지) be ignorant (*of*); be badly (ill-)informed (*of*); be a stranger (*to*). ¶ 세상 일에 ~ know but little of the world / 이 곳 지리에 ~ I am a stranger here. ③ (눈·귀가) 눈이 ~ have dim eyes / 귀가 ~ be hard of hearing. ④ (비유적) 어두운 얼굴 a clouded face / 어두운 전망 a dark view / 그에게는 어두운 과거가 있다 He has a shady past.
어디¹ (장소) where; what place; somewhere. ¶ ~까지 how far (거리); to what extent (정도) / ~에나 anywhere; everywhere / ~에서 from where; whence / 너는 ~까지 가느냐 How far are you going? / 그 남자의 ~가 좋은가 What (good) do you see in him? / 인정은 ~나 마찬가지다 Human nature is the same everywhere.
어디² (감탄사) Well!; (Well) now!; Just!; Let me see. ¶ ~ 산책이나 할까 Let's see now, shall we

어디까지나 to the end (끝까지); persistently (약속같이); in all respects, in every point (어느 모로나); thoroughly, out and out (철저히).

어딘가, 어딘지 somehow; in some way; without knowing why. ¶ ~ 이상하다 Somehow, it seems strange.

어떠한, 어떤 ① (무슨·여하한) what; what sort (kind) of; any (여하한). ¶ ~ 일이 있어도 whatever (no matter what) may happen; under any circumstances; (결코 …아니다) (not) for all the world / 그는 ~ 사람인가 What is he like? or What sort of a man is he? / 너를 위한 일이라면 ~ 일이라도 하겠다 I'd do anything for you. / ~ 일이 일어날지 알 수가 없다 There is no knowing what may happen. ② (어느) a certain; some. ¶ ~ 마을 a certain village / ~ 사람 someone; somebody / ~ 곳에서 at a certain place; somewhere.

어떻게 how; in what way. ¶ ~ 보아도 to all appearance; in every respect / ~ 해서라도 by all (any) means; at any cost / (이 편지를) ~ 할까요 What shall I do (with this letter)? / 요즈음 ~ 지내십니까 How are you getting along these days? / ~ 되겠지 Something will turn up. / ~ 된 것인가 What is the matter (with you)?

어떻든(지) (좌우간) at any rate; anyway; anyhow; in any case. ¶ 그것은 ~ be that as it may; no matter what it may be / ~ 원인을 조사해야 한다 We have to investigate the cause at any rate.

어란(魚卵) spawn; roe; fish eggs.

어레미 a coarse sieve; a riddle.

어련하다 (be) trustworthy; reliable; be natural to be expected. ¶ 그가 하는데 어련하려구 We may trust him. or He knows how to deal with it.

어련히 naturally; surely; infallibly. ¶ 내버려 둬. ~ 알아서 할라구 Let him alone, he will take care of himself.

어렴풋이 dimly; faintly; vaguely.

어렴풋하다 (be) dim; indistinct; faint; vague (애매).

어렵(漁獵) fishing (and hunting).

어렵다 ① (곤란·난해) (be) hard; difficult; tough (口). ¶ 어려운 difficulty / 어려운 ~ a hard (difficult) language to learn / 믿기 ~ be hard to believe; be incredible / 어려운 고비를 당하다 have a hard (trying) time of it. ② (가난) (be) poor; needy; indigent. ¶ 어려운 살림을 하다 be badly off; live in poverty. ③ (거북하다) feel awkward (constraint); be (feel) ill at ease.

어로(漁撈) fishing; fishery. ∥ ~보호구역 the fisheries conservation zone / ~수역 fishing waters; a fishing zone / ~협정 a fisheries agreement.

어록(語錄) analects; sayings. ∥ 처칠 ~ Quotations from Winston Churchill.

어뢰(魚雷) a torpedo. ∥ ~ 발사관 a torpedo tube / ~ 정 a torpedo boat; a PT boat (美).

어루러기 [醫] leucoderma; vitiligo.

어루만지다 ① (쓰다듬다) stroke (one's beard); pat (a dog); pass one's hand (over, across); smooth down (one's hair). ② (위무하다) soothe; appease; console.

어류(魚類) fishes. ∥ ~학 ichthyology / ~학자 an ichthyologist.

어르다 fondle; amuse; humor; try to please.

어른만지다 ① (성인) a man; an adult; a grown-up. / ~의 adult; grown-up / ~답지 않은 childish; unworthy of a grown man (woman) / ~이 되다 grow up; become a man (woman) / ~스럽다 look like a grown-up; be precocious / ~스럽게 말하다 talk like a grown-up. (윗사람) one's senior; one's elder(s). ¶ ~을 공경하라 Respect your elders.

어른거리다 (사물이) flicker; glimmer; flit; (눈이) be dazzled. ¶ 눈 앞에 ~ flit before one's eye / 그 의 모습이 아직도 눈앞에 어른거린다 The memory of his face still haunts me.

어름거리다 ① (언행을) do (say) ambiguously; mumble. ¶ 대답을 ~ give an equivocal (a vague) answer. ② (일을) scamp (slap-dash) (one's work). ¶ 어름어름 slovenly; at random; inattentive.

어리(병아리의) a hencoop. lly.

어리광 ~ 을 부리다 behave like a spoilt child; play the baby (to).

어리굴젓 salted oysters with hot pepper.

어리다¹ (나이) (be) young; infant; juvenile; (유치) (be) childish; infantile; (미숙) (be) green; inexperienced. ¶ 어린 잎 young leaves / 어린 마음 a childish mind / 어릴 때에 (부터) in (from) one's childhood / ~ 생각하는 것이 ~ have a childish idea.

어리다² (눈물이) be wet (moist, dimmed) (with tears). ¶ 그녀 눈에는 눈물이 어려 있었다 Her eyes

어리둥절하다 were filled with tears. ②《엉기다》coagulate; curdle; congeal. ③《정성 등이 담기다》be filled 《with》. ¶ 애정이 어린 말 affectionate words / 정성 어린 선물 a gift with one's best wishes. ④《눈이》be dazzled (glared).

어리둥절하다 (be) dazed; stunned; bewildered; 《서술적》 (get) confused; be puzzled (at a loss).

어리벙벙하다 (be) dumbfounded; bewildered; disconcerted.

어리석다 (be) foolish; silly; dull; stupid. ¶ 어리석은 사람 a foolish person; a fool / 어리석은 짓을 하다 play (act) the fool; act foolishly / 어리석게도 …하다 be foolish enough 《to do》.

어린것 a little (young) one; a kid.

어린애 a child 《pl. children》; an infant; a baby. ¶ ~ 같은 childlike; childish / ~ 장난 a mere child's play / ~ 취급을 하다 treat 《a person》 like a child / 그들에겐 ~가 없다 They have no children, or They are childless. / 그들에게 ~가 생겼다 A baby (child) was born to them.

어린이 a child 《pl. children》 (☞ 어린애). ‖ ~공원 a children's garden (park) / ~ 날 Children's Day / ~ 방 a nursery / ~ 시간 the children's hour (TV 등의) / ~ 헌장 the Children's Charter.

어림 a rough estimate (guess). ~하다 guess; estimate 《at》; make a rough estimate 《of》. ‖ ~셈 a rough calculation (estimate) / ~수 a rough number (figure).

어림없다 be wide of the mark; be far from it; 《당치 않다》 (be) preposterous; nonsensical; 《가능성이》 be hardly possible 《to》; have no chance 《of》. ¶ 어림없는 수작 preposterous remarks / 그녀의 입상은 ~ There is no chance of her winning a prize.

어릿광대 a clown; a buffoon.

어마《놀람》 My!; Oh!; Good heaven(s)!; O dear!

어마어마하다《당당하다》(be) grand; magnificent; imposing; majestic;《엄청나다》(be) tremendous; terrific 《noise》; immense. ¶ 어마어마한 고층 건물 an imposing skyscraper / 어마어마한 비용이 들다 cost a tremendous amount.

어망(漁網) a fishing net.

어머(나)《놀람》Oh!; Why!; Dear me!; O my!; Good gracious!

어머니 ① a mother. ¶ ~의 motherʼs; motherly; maternal / ~의 사랑 motherʼs love (affection) / ~다운 (같은) motherly; maternal. ‖ ~날 Motherʼs Day. ②《근원》origin; source; mother. ¶ 필요는 발명의 ~ Necessity is the mother of invention.

어멈《하녀》a housemaid; an amah; a maid(servant).

어명(御命)《임금의》a Royal command (mandate).

어물(魚物) dried fish; stockfish. ‖ ~전 a dried-fish shop.

어물거리다 ① 《꾸물거리다》①. ② be slow 《at one's work》; be tardy; be inefficient. ¶ 왜 어물거리느냐 Why are you so slow? / 어물거리지 마라 Make it snappy! or Stop dawdling.

어물쩍거리다 ¶ 태도를 ~ take a vague attitude 《to》 / 말을 ~ use vague language. 〔bird.

어미 a mother. ¶ ~ 새 a mother

어미(語尾) the ending of a word. ‖ ~변화 inflection.

어민(漁民) fishermen.

어버이 parents. ¶ ~의 parental.

어법(語法) usage(사용법); wording; diction; grammar(문법).

어부(漁夫) a fisherman. ¶ ~지리를 얻다 fish in troubled waters.

어분(魚紛) fish meal.

어불성설(語不成說) unreasonable talk; lack of logic. ¶ ~이다 be illogical (unreasonable).

어비(魚肥) fish manure (fertilizer).

어사(御史) a Royal secret inspector traveling incognito.

어사리(漁−) fishing with a moored net. ~하다 fish with a moored net.

어살(魚−) a weir; a fish trap.

어색(語塞)~하다《말이 막히다》be stuck for words; be at a loss 《what to say》; 《열없다》(be) awkward (embarrassed); feel ill at ease; 《서투름》(be) awkward; clumsy.

어서 ① 《빨리》quick(ly); without delay. ¶ ~ 들어오십시오 Come right in, please. ② 《환영》 (if you) please; kindly. ¶ ~ 앉으세요 Please sit down, or Sit down, please. 〔a fishing fleet.

어선(漁船) a fishing boat. ¶ ~단

어설프다 ① 《성기다》(be) coarse; rough; loose. ¶ 어설피 coarsely. ② 《탐탁찮다》(be) clumsy; slovenly; 《겉핥기의》(be) superficial; shallow. ¶ 어설피 clumsily / 어설픈 지식 a superficial (shallow) knowledge.

어세(語勢) emphasis; stress.

어수룩하다 (be) naive; unsophisticated; simple-hearted. ¶ 어수룩한 사람 a simple-hearted person / 어수룩하게 보다 hold 《a person》 cheap / 그런 것을 믿다니 너 참 어수룩하구나 It's naive of you to believe that.

어수선하다《난잡·혼란》be in dis-

어순 (語順) [文] word order.
어스레하다 (날이) (be) dusky; dim; gloomy; murky.
어슬렁거리다 prowl; stroll (ramble) about; hang around. ¶ 어슬렁어슬렁 slowly; lazily.
어슴푸레하다 (be) dim; vague; indistinct; misty; hazy.
어슷비슷하다 (be) much (nearly) the same; somewhat alike.
어슷하다 (be) slant; oblique; 《서술적》 be on the tilt (slant).
어시장 魚市場 a fish market.
어안 (魚眼) ‖ ~ 렌즈 (石) a fish-eye lens (stone).
어안이 벙벙하다 《서술적》 be dumbfounded; be struck dumb; be taken aback.
어언간 (於焉間) before one knows (is aware); unawares.
어업 (漁業) fishery; the fishing industry. ‖ ~권 fishing rights / ~ 전관수역 exclusive fishing waters; an exclusive fishery zone / ~ 협동조합 a fishermen's cooperative association / ~ 협정 a fisheries agreement.
어여차 Heave-ho!; Yo-heave-ho!
어엿하다 (be) respectable; decent; good. ¶ 어엿한 집안 a respectable family / 어엿하게 stately; in a dignified manner.
어용 (御用) ‖ ~ 신문 a state-controlled press; a government mouthpiece / ~ 조합 a company (kept) union / ~ 학자 a government-patronized scholar.
어울리다 ① 《조화》 become; match well; suit; befit; go well 《with》; be in keeping 《with》. ¶ 안 어울리는 unbecoming 《to》; unsuitable 《for》; ill-matched / 《옷이》 잘 ~ suit well on 《a person》; fit 《a person》 well. ② 《한데 섞임》 join 《with》; mix (mingle) 《with》. ¶ 불량소년의 무리와 ~ join a band of bad boys.
어원 (語源) the derivation (origin) of a word; an etymology. ¶ ~ 을 찾다 trace a word to its origin. ‖ ~ 학 (學) etymology.
어유 (魚油) fish oil.
어육 (魚肉) fish (meat).
어음 〔商〕 a bill; a draft; a note. ¶ 3개월 불 ~ a bill at three months' sight / ~ 으로 지급하다 pay by draft / ~ 을 현금으로 바꾸다 cash a bill / ~ 을 결제하다 (부도내다) honor (dishonor) a bill. ‖ ~ 교환소 a clearing house / ~ 발행인 〔수취인〕 the drawer (payee) of a bill / ~ 할인 a discount (on a bill) / 약속 ~ a promissory note.
어의 (語義) the meaning of a word.
어이 (호칭) Hey!; Hi!; There!; Here!; I say!
어이구 (놀람) Oh!; Wow!; Ouch!
어이없다 (be) amazing; surprising; absurd; egregious. ¶ 어이없어서 be dumbfounded 《by》; be amazed 《at the news, to see》 / 어이없어 말이 안 나오다 be (struck) dumb with amazement.
어장 (漁場) a fishing ground; a fishery. 「champ.
어적거리다 munch; crunch;
어정거리다 walk leisurely along; stroll (ramble) about.
어정쩡하다 (모호하다) (be) noncommittal; ambiguous; evasive; vague; (의심스럽다) (be) doubtful; dubious.
어제 yesterday. ¶ ~ 아침 yesterday morning / 어젯밤 yesterday evening; last night.
어조 (語調) a tone; an accent. ¶ ~ 을 누그러뜨리다 soften one's voice; tone down.
어조사 (語助辭) [文] a particle in a classical Chinese.
어족 (魚族) fishes; the finny tribe.
어족 (語族) a family of language.
어줍다 (언동이) (be) dull; slow; awkward; (솜씨가) (be) clumsy; awkward; poor. ¶ 어줍은 솜씨 clumsy workmanship.
어중간 (於中間) ~ 하다 be about half way (midway); 《엉거주춤》 (be) uncertain; ambiguous; noncommittal.
어중되다 (於中 —) 《서술적》 be either too small (little, short) or too big (much, long); be unsuitable (insufficient) either way.
어중이떠중이 (anybody and) everybody; every Tom, Dick, and Harry; a mere rabble.
어지간하다 (상당하다) (be) fair; tolerable; passable; considerable. ¶ 어지간히 fairly; passably; tolerably; considerably / 어지간한 미인 quite a beauty / 어지간한 수입 a handsome income.
어지럽다 ① (어질하다) (be) dizzy; feel giddy; swim. ¶ 자주 ~ have frequent dizzy spells / 머리가 ~ My head swims. ② (어수선) (be) disorderly; confused; disturbed; troubled; be in disorder 《서술적》. ¶ 어지러운 세상 troubled (troublous) times.
어지르다 scatter 《things》 (about); leave 《things》 scattered (lying) about; put 《a room》 in disor-

어질다 (be) wise; kindhearted; benevolent; humane. ¶ 어진 임금 a benevolent (gracious) ruler.
어질어질하다 feel *dizzy* (giddy).
어째서 why; for what reason.
어쨌든 anyhow; anyway; at any rate; in any case (event).
어쩌다 《우연히》by chance (accident); casually; 《이따금》once in a while; now and then.
어쩌면 《감탄사적》how; 《아마·혹》possibly; maybe; perhaps.
어쩐지 ① 《웬일인지》somehow; without knowing why. ¶ ~ 무섭게 느껴지다 have an unaccountable fear. ②《그래서》so that's why; (it is) no wonder.
어쩔 수 없다 (be) inevitable; unavoidable; cannot help it; cannot be helped. ¶ 어쩔 수 없는 사정 unavoidable circumstances / 그것은 어쩔 수 없는 일이다 It can't be helped. *or* There's no help for it.
어쭙지않다 (be) pert; fresh; 《가소롭다》(be) laughable; contemptible. ¶ 어쭙지않게 까불다 talk fresh.
어찌나 how; what; too; so. ¶ ~ 기쁜지 in (the excess of) one's joy; be so glad that....
어찌피 《於此彼》anyhow; anyway; in any (either) case; at any rate.
어처구니없다 be taken aback; be dumbfounded; egregious; amazing; absurd. ¶ 어처구니없는 소리 a damned silly remark / 어처구니없어 말문이 막히다 be speechless with amazement.
어촌(漁村) a fishing village.
…어치 worth. ¶ 달걀을 천원 ~ 사다 buy one thousand *won* worth of eggs.
어투(語套) one's way of speaking.
어퍼컷(拳) an uppercut.
어폐(語弊) ¶ ~ 가 있다 be misleading; be liable to be misunderstood.
어포(魚脯) dried slices of fish.
어프로치 (an) approach.
어필 an appeal. ~ 하다 appeal 《to》.
어학(語學) language study; linguistics. ¶ ~ 의 linguistic (talent). / ~ 교육 linguistic (language) education / ~ 실습실 a language laboratory / ~ 자 a linguist.
어항(魚缸) a fish basin (bowl).
어항(漁港) a fishing port.
어험 Hem!; Ahem!
어형(語形) forms of words. ∥ ~ 변화 《文》inflection; declension.
어획(漁獲) fishing. ∥ ~ 고 a catch (haul) (of fish) / ~ 할당량 the amount of fish quotas.
어휘(語彙) (a) vocabulary.

억(億) a (one) hundred million. ¶ 10 ~ a billion; a thousand million(s) 《英》.
억누르다《진압》suppress;《제지》repress; restrain; control;《제재》hold; check; keep under; curb;《압박》oppress. ¶ 억누를 수 없는 uncontrollable; irrepressible; irresistible / 억눌리다 be overpowered; be repressed / 눈물을 ~ repress (keep back) one's tears / 웃음을 ~ stifle a laugh.
억류(抑留) detention; detainment; internment. ~ 하다 detain (keep) by force; seize; hold; apprehend. ∥ ~ 자 a detainee; an internee.
억만(億萬) 《억》a hundred million;《무수》myriads. ∥ ~ 년 countless years / ~ 장자 a billionaire.
억병 hard drinking. ¶ ~ 이 되다 drink heavily / ~ 으로 취하다 be dead (blind) drunk.
억보 an obstinate man; a stubborn fellow.
억설(臆說) 《억측》a conjecture; a surmise; a mere assumption. ~ 하다 make a conjecture 《about》.
억세다 ①《체격이》(be) stout; sturdy; strong;《정신이》(be) strong; tough; stubborn; dogged; tenacious. ②《뻣뻣하다》(be) tough; hard; stiff.
억수 a pouring (heavy, torrential) rain; a downpour 《美》. ¶ ~ 같이 퍼붓다 pour down; rain in torrents.
억압(抑壓) oppression; suppression; repression; restraint《억제》. ~ 하다 oppress 《the people》; suppress 《freedom of speech》. ∥ ~ 된 감정 pent-up feelings / ~ 된 욕망 suppressed desires.
억양(抑揚) 《음조》intonation; modulation. ¶ ~ 있는 modulated; intoned / ~ 이 없는 monotonous / ~ 을 붙이다 modulate; intone.
억울(抑鬱) ~ 하다 《답답하다》feel pent-up (depressed);《원통하다》feel bitter 《about, at》; be chocked with mortification (vexation); feel *oneself* wronged;《누명을 쓰다》be wrongly (falsely, unjustly) accused 《of stealing》. ¶ ~ 한 죄로 on a false charge / ~ 한 책망을 듣다 get an undeserved scolding / 그는 ~ 해서 발을 굴렀다 He stamped his feet in vexation.
억제(抑制) control; restraint; suppression; repression. ~ 하다 control; repress; suppress; restrain; hold back. ¶ ~ 할 수 없는 uncontrollable / 감정을 ~ 하다 suppress (smother) one's feelings / 충동을 ~ 하다 inhibit (resist) an impulse

억조(億兆) ‖ ~창생 the (common) people; the multitude (masses).

억지 unreasonableness; obstinacy; compulsion. ¶ ~ 부리다 (쓰다) insist on having one's own way; persist stubbornly; make an unreasonable demand 《of a person》 / ~ 부리지 마라 Be reasonable. ‖ ~웃음 (laugh) a forced smile.

억지로 by force; forcibly; against one's will (부득이); willy-nilly. ¶ ~ 문을 열다 force the door open / ~ 지나가다 force one's way / 술을 ~ 먹게 하다 press (force) wine upon 《a person》.

억척스럽다 (be) unyielding; unbending; tough.

억측(臆測) a guess; a conjecture. ~하다 guess; conjecture. ¶ 그것은 ~에 지나지 않다 It is only mere a conjecture.

억하심정(抑何心情) It is hard to understand why.... ¶ 무슨 ~으로 …하느냐 Why (How) in the world...? / 무슨 ~으로 그런 짓을 했을까 What made him do such a thing. I wonder?

언감생심(焉敢生心) ¶ ~ …하느냐 How dare you...?

언급(言及) ~하다 refer (make reference) 《to》; mention. ¶ 위 (앞)에 ~한 above-mentioned; as stated above / 그는 그 점에 관해 ~을 피했다 He avoided mentioning that point.

언니 an elder (older) sister.

언더라인 an underline. ¶ ~을 긋다 underline 《a word》.

언더스로(野) an underhand throw; underhand pitching.

언덕 a slope; a hill. ¶ 가파른 ~ a steep slope / (길이) ~이 되어 있다 slope up (down) / ~을 오르다(내리다) go uphill (downhill).

언도(言渡) a sentence. ☞ 선고.

언동(言動) 《be careful in》 one's speech and behavior.

언뜻(잠간) at a glance; 《우연치》 by chance; by accident. ¶ ~ 보다 catch (get) a glimpse of; take a glance at.

언론(言論) speech. ¶ ~의 자유 freedom of speech. ‖ ~계 the press; journalism / ~기관 an organ of expression (public opinion); the (mass) media.

언명(言明) ~하다 declare; state; make a statement.

언문(言文) ¶ ~일치 the unification of the written and spoken language.

언변(言辯) oratorical talent; eloquence. ¶ ~이 좋다 be gifted with eloquence; have a ready tongue.

언사(言辭) words; speech; language; expression (표현).

언성(言聲) a tone (of voice). ¶ ~을 높이다 raise (lift) one's voice.

언약(言約) a (verbal) promise; a pledge; a vow. ¶ ~ 약속.

언어(言語) language; speech. ¶ 사상을 ~로 표현하다 express one's thoughts through language. ‖ ~교육 language education / ~능력 linguistic (language) ability (competence) / ~심리학 psycholinguistics / ~장애 a speech impediment (defect) / ~학 linguistics / ~학자 a linguist.

언어도단(言語道斷) ~의 inexcusable; outrageous; unspeakable; absurd, preposterous.

언쟁(言爭) a dispute; a quarrel. ~하다 dispute (quarrel) 《with》; have words (a quarrel) 《with》.

언저리 the edge (rim); bounds; parts around. ¶ 입 ~에 about one's mouth.

언제 when; (at) what time (hour); how soon; 《일간》 some time (or other); some day. ¶ ~부터 from what time; since when; how long / 그건 ~ 됩니까 How soon I get it ready? / ~ 한번 (놀러) 오너라 Come and see me one of these days.

언제까지 how long; till when; by what time; how soon. ¶ ~고 as long as one likes; forever.

언제나(항상) always; all the time; 《평소》 (습관적으로) habitually; (…할 때마다) whenever; every time.

언제든지 《어느 때라도》 (at) any time; 《항상》 always; all the time; whenever. ¶ ~ 나를 찾아 오너라 Feel free to come to see me any time.

언젠가 some time (or other) (미래의); some day; one of these days (일간); once (과거의); the other day (일전).

언중유골(言中有骨) ¶ ~이다 speak 《it》 up with implicit bitterness.

언중유언(言中有言) ¶ ~이다 imply some other meaning; (what one says) is very suggestive.

언질(言質) a pledge; a commitment. ¶ ~을 주다 give (pledge) one's word 《to do》; commit oneself 《to do》; give a pledge / ~을 잡다 (받다) get (take) 《a person's》 pledge.

언짢다 ① 《기분이》 (be) displeased; bad-tempered; 《서술적》 feel bad (unhappy, sad). ② 《불길》 (be) bad; ill; unlucky. ¶ 언짢은 꿈을

bad (unlucky) dream. ③ (나쁘다) (be) bad; ill; evil; wrong. ¶아무를 언짢게 말하다 speak ill of a person. ④ (해로움) (be) bad; harmful; detrimental. ¶눈에 ~ be bad for the eyes.

언청이 a harelip. ¶ ~의 hare-lipped.

언필칭(言必稱) ¶ ~ 남녀 평등을 외치다 be always harping on the equality of the sexes / ~ 자식 자랑이다 He never opens his mouth without boasting of his son.

언행(言行) speech and action; words and deeds. ¶ ~이 일치하다 act (live) up to one's words / 그의 ~은 일치하지 않다 He says one thing and does another. ¶ ~록 memoirs / ~일치 conformity of one's action to one's word.

얹다 (놓다) put on; place (lay, set) (a thing) on; load (짐을).

얹히다 ① (놓이다) be placed (put, laid) on. ② (좌초) be stranded; run aground. ③ (음식이) sit (lie) heavy on (the stomach). ④ (붙어살다) be a dependant on (a person); sponge on (a person).

얻다 ① (획득) get; gain; obtain; earn; achieve; win; secure; (이득은) profit (gain) (by, from); (배우다) learn (from). ¶지위를 ~ obtain (secure) a position / 인기를 ~ win (gain) popularity. ② (결혼) take (a wife); marry (a woman); get (a husband). ③ (병을) fall (get) ill. ¶병을 얻어 죽다 die of a disease.

얻어듣다 hear from others; learn by hearsay.

얻어맞다 get (receive) a blow; be struck.

얻어먹다 ① (음식을) get treated to (대접받다); beg one's bread (걸식). ② (욕 따위를) get called names; suffer harsh words; be spoken ill of.

얼 ① (흠) a scratch. ¶~이 가다 get scratched. ② (넋) soul; (정신) spirit; mind. ¶한국의 ~ the spirit of Korea.

얼간 (절임간) salting lightly; (얼간이) a half-wit; a dolt; a fool. ‖ ~ 고등어 lightly salted mackerel.

얼근하다 ① (술이) (be) tipsy; slightly intoxicated (drunk). ② (매워서) (be) rather hot (peppery); somewhat pungent.

얼기설기 ¶ ~ 얽히다 get (become) entangled (실 따위가); be intricated; get complicated (문제가).

얼김 ¶ ~에 on the spur of the moment; under the impulse (of) / ~ 말 a casual remark.

얼다 (추위에) freeze; be frozen (over); be benumbed with cold (몸이); (기죽다) cower; feel small (timid); be scared (by); get nervous (on) (무대 등에서). ¶얼음이 언 연못 a frozen pond / 얼어(서) 죽다 be frozen to death / 얼어서 말 한 마디 못 하다 be too scared to speak.

얼떨결 ¶ ~에 in the confusion of the moment.

얼떨떨하다 (be) confused; dazed; bewildered; perplexed; puzzled. ¶얼떨떨하여 in confusion (embarrassment) / 얼떨떨해지다 get confused; be upset; lose one's head; be puzzled (bewildered).

얼뜨기 a stupid; a blockhead.

얼뜨다 (be) slow-witted; silly; (겁이 많다) (be) cowardly.

얼렁거리다 flatter; fawn upon; play the coquette.

얼렁뚱땅 ¶ ~ 하다 (엉너리로) mystify; behave evasively; beat around the bush; (일을) do a slapdash job.

얼레 a reel; a spool.

얼레빗 a coarse comb.

얼룩 (오점) a stain; a spot; a blot; a smear; a smudge. ¶ ~진 spotted; stained; smeared / ~지게 하다 stain; spot; smear / ~지다 become stained (blotted) / ~을 빼다 remove a stain. ‖ ~ 고양이 a tabby (cat) / ~ 말 a zebra.

얼룩덜룩 ¶ ~한 spotted; dappled; speckled; varicolored.

얼른 quickly; rapidly; promptly; fast; at once. ¶ ~ 해라 Make haste!; Hurry up!

얼리다 (얼게 하다) freeze; refrigerate. ¶얼음을 ~ make ice / 생선을 ~ refrigerate fish.

얼마 ① (값) how much; what price. ¶이게 ~요 How much (is this)? ② (수량) how many (수); how much (양); what number (amount). ¶ ~ 든지 원하는 대로 as many (much) as one wants. ③ (다소·정도) some; what; (동안) a while; (거리) how far. ¶ ~ 있다가 after a while / 몸무게가 ~ 냐 What is your weight? / 서울 ~ 부산간은 거리는 ~ 냐 How far is it from Seoul to Pusan? ④ (비율) by; so much. ¶그 회사에서 하루 ~ 에 일하느냐 How much a day do you work for the company?

얼마나 ① 《값·금액》 how much; what; 《수량》 how many 《수》; how much 《양》. ② 《정도》 how 《far, large, deep, high, long, old, etc.》. ③ 《여북》 what; how. ¶ ~ 기쁠까 How glad I should be!

얼마만큼 how many 《much, long, far, high, heavy》.

얼버무리다 《말을》 equivocate; prevaricate; quibble; shuffle.

얼보이다 ① 《흐릿하게》 be seen dimly 《indistinctly》; be blurred. ② 《바로 안 보이다》 be seen distortedly.

얼빠지다 be stunned 《stupefied》; be abstracted; get absent-minded; look blank. ¶ 얼빠진 abstracted; blank; stupid; silly.

얼싸안다 hug; embrace; hold 《a person》 in one's arms. 「rah!

얼씨구 Yippee!; Whoopee!; Hur-
얼씬 ~ 하다 make one's appearance; show up; turn up / ~ 거리다 keep showing up; hang 《hover》 around / ~ (도) 아니하다 do not appear at all / ~ 못 하다 dare not come around 〔show up〕.

얼어붙다 freeze up 〔over〕.

얼얼하다 《상처가》 smart; 《맛이》 taste hot; bite.

얼음 ice. ¶ ~ 같은 icy 〔cold〕 / 이 언 frozen / ~으로 차게 하다 《cool with》 ice / ~에 채우다 pack 《fish》 in ice / ~장 같은 을 as cold as ice / ~ 과자 a popsicle; 《an》 ice cream (아이스크림) / ~덩이 a block 〔cake〕 of ice / ~물 ice water / ~베개 an ice pillow / ~사탕 rock 〔sugar〕 candy / ~주머니 an ice bag 〔pack〕 / ~판 an icy ground / 인조~ artificial ice.

얼음지치다 skate 《on ice》; do skating. ¶ 얼음지치기 skating; sliding / 얼음지치러 가다 go skating.

얼쩍지근하다 《살이》 be smarting, tingling; 《맛이》 (be) somewhat hot 〔pungent〕.

얼추 《거의》 nearly; almost; roughly; approximately.

얼추잡다 make a rough estimate.

얼치기 an in-between; something half-and-half. ¶ ~의 halfway; half-learned 〔-trained〕 / ~로 halfway; by halves.

얼토당토 않다 《당치 않다》 (be) irrelevant; preposterous; absurd; 《뜻밖의》 (be) unheard-of; unbelievable. ¶ 얼토당토 않은 일이 일어났다 An unbelievable thing happened.

얽다¹ ① 《엮다》 bind; tie up. ② 《꾸미다》 fabricate; cook 〔frame〕 up; forge.

얽다² 《얼굴 등이》 get 〔be〕 pock-marked; be pitted with smallpox. 「restrict.

얽매다 tie 〔bind〕 up tight; fetter;
얽매이다 《속박》 be bound; be tied down; be fettered 〔shackled〕; 《분주》 be taken up with 《business》; be busy. ¶ 규칙에 ~ be bound by a rule.

얽히다 《엉키다》 get intertwined; be 〔get〕 entangled; get 〔be〕 complicated (일 등이); 《감기다》 twine round; get coiled round.

엄격(嚴格) ~ 한〔히〕 strict(ly); stern(ly); rigorous(ly); severe(-ly) / ~ 한 부친 a stern father / ~ 한 규칙 rigid regulation.

엄금(嚴禁) strict prohibition. ~ 하다 prohibit 〔forbid〕 strictly.

엄동(嚴冬) a severe winter; the coldest season.

엄두 ¶ ~를 못 내다 cannot even conceive the idea 《of doing》.

엄마 ma; mom; mama; mammy.

엄명(嚴命) a strict order. ~ 하다 give a strict order 《to do》.

엄밀(嚴密) ~ 한〔히〕 strict(ly); close(ly); exact(ly) / ~ 한 의미로 in a strict sense.

엄벌(嚴罰) a severe punishment. ~ 하다 punish 《a person》 severely. ∥ ~ 주의의 severe punishment policy; strict discipline.

엄범부렁 at random; sloppily; slapdash. ~ 하다 act thoughtlessly 〔carelessly〕.

엄부(嚴父) one's stern father.

엄살 pretense; false show; sham. ~ 하다 pretend pain 〔hardship〕; feign 《illness》; assume the appearance 《of》 / ~꾸러기 a cry-baby; a great one to fuss.

엄선(嚴選) careful selection. ~ 하다 select carefully.

엄수(嚴守) ~ 하다 observe 《a rule》 strictly; keep 《one's promise》 strictly. ¶ 시간을 ~ 하다 be punctual. 《serious(ly); grave(ly).

엄숙(嚴肅) ~ 한〔히〕 solemn(ly);
엄습(掩襲) ~ 하다 make a sudden 《surprise》 attack; take 《the enemy》 by surprise.

엄연(儼然) ~ 한 solemn; grave; stern; majestic; authoritative / ~히 solemnly; gravely / ~한 사실 an undeniable fact.

엄정(嚴正) ~ 한〔히〕 strict(ly); exact(ly); rigid(ly); impartial(ly) 《공평》. ∥ ~ 중립 《observe》 strict neutrality.

엄중(嚴重) ¶ ~ 한〔히〕 strict(ly); severe(ly) / ~ 한 경계 a severe 〔close〕 watch.

엄지 the thumb (손가락); the big toe (발가락). ¶ ~ 발톱 the nail of the big toe / ~ 손톱 the nail of the thumb.

엄책(嚴責) ~하다 reprimand harshly.

엄청나다 (be) surprising; extraordinary; exorbitant; absurd; awful; terrible. ¶ 엄청나게 exorbitantly; extraordinarily; absurdly; awfully; terribly / 엄청나게 큰 very big; huge.

엄친(嚴親) one's own father.

엄탐(嚴探) ~하다 search strictly for; be on a sharp lookout for.

엄파이어 an umpire (야구의); a referee (축구, 권투 등의).

엄폐(掩蔽) ~하다 cover up; conceal; mask. ‖ ~호(壕) a covered trench; a bunker.

엄포 a bluff; bluster. ¶ ~ 놓다 bluff; bluster. ¶ ~ 놓지 마라 Stop bluffing. / 그는 나를 죽이겠으나 협했으나 ~에 지나지 않는다 He threatened to kill me, but it's all a bluff.

엄하다(嚴一) (be) strict; severe; stern; rigorous; harsh; bitter.

엄한(嚴寒) intense (severe) cold.

엄호(掩護) ~하다 back (up); (give) support (to); cover; protect. ‖ ~사격 covering fire.

업(業) (직업) a calling; an occupation; a profession (전문의); (상공업) business; trade; industry.

업² [佛] karma (梵).

업계(業界) the industry; the trade. ¶ ~택시 ~의 사람들 people in the taxi trade / ~의 화제가 되다 be the talk of the trade. ‖ ~지(紙) a trade paper / ~출판 publishing circles.

업다 carry on one's back. ¶ 업히다 be carried on (a person's) back.

업무(業務) business; work. ¶ ~용의 for business use (purpose); ~용 차 a car for business use / ~의 확장 expansion of business / ~에 힘쓰다 attend to one's business with diligence. ‖ ~관리 business control (management) / ~명령 a business order / ~방해 interference with (a person's) duties / ~보고 a report on operation(s) / ~상과실 professional negligence (그는 업무 과실 치사 혐의로 체포되었다 He was arrested on the charge of professional negligence resulting in death.) / ~제휴 a business tie-up.

업보(業報) [佛] retribution for the deeds of a former life; karma effects.

업신여기다 despise; hold in contempt; slight; neglect. ¶ 업신여 김을 받다 be held in contempt.

업자(業者) traders; the trade (업계). ¶ 악덕~ a crooked dealer.

업적(業績) (일의) one's 《scientific》 achievements; results.

업종(業種) 《종류》 a type of industry 《business》. ‖ ~별 industrial classification.

업히다 ride 《get》 on 《a person's》 back; be carried on 《a person's》 back.

없다 ① 《존재하지 않다》 There is no...; (아무것도 없다) nothing at all; (보이지 않다) be missing 《gone》; cannot be found. ¶ 이 이야기는 없던 것으로 하자 Let's act as though nothing had been said. or Let's drop this issue. ② 《갖지 않다》 have no...; be free from 《debt》; 《결여》 lack; want; be lacking 《wanting》 《in》; be out of 《money》 (떨어짐). ¶ 없어서 못 쓰다 want of. ③ 《가난하다》 be poor.

없애다 《제거》 take off; remove; get rid of; run through; squander; 《죽이다》 kill; settle; make away with; 《낭비하다》 waste. ¶ 장해물을 ~ remove obstacles / 옷에다 많은 돈을 ~ spend a lot of money on clothes.

없어지다 《잃다》 be 《get》 lost; be missing; be gone; 《바닥이 나다》 be gone 《used up, exhausted》; run out 《short》; 《사라지다》 be gone; disappear; vanish. ¶ 금고 안의 돈이 없어졌다 The money in the safe is gone 《missing》. / 돈이 다 없어졌다 Money has run out. / 통증이 없어졌다 The pain has now passed.

없이살다 live in poverty.

엇가다 deviate 《swerve》 《from》; run counter 《to》; go astray 《wild》.

엇갈리다 《길이》 pass 《cross》 each other; (번갈아 듦) alternate; take turns. ¶ 길이 ~ cross 《each other》 on the way / 희비가 ~ have a mingled feeling of joy and sorrow.

엇걸다 hang 《suspend, hook, put》 《things》 diagonally (alternately).

엇대다 apply 《put, fix》 askew.

엇바꾸다 exchange 《one thing》 for 《to》 《another》.

엇베다 cut aslant 《obliquely》.

엇비슷하다 《서술적》 be about alike; be nearly the same. ¶ 수준이 ~ be on the almost similar level.

엉거주춤하다 ① 《자세》 half-stand half-sit; stoop slightly; lean a bit forward. ¶ 엉거주춤한 자세로 in a half-rising posture. ② 《주저》 falter; waver; hesitate.

엉겅퀴 [植] a thistle.

엉구다 《a plan》 to be accomplished.

엉금엉금 slowly and clumsily; sluggishly. ¶ ~ 기어가다 go on all fours; crawl on hands and knees.

엉기다 《응축》 curdle; congeal;

엉너리치다 try all sorts of tricks to win 《a person's》 favor.
엉덩방아 ¶ ~를 찧다 fall on one's behind; land on one's rear.
엉덩이 the hips; the behind; the buttocks.
엉덩춤 a hip dance; a hula.
엉뚱하다 (be) extraordinary; extravagant; fantastic; out of the common; eccentric; 《무모하다》 (be) reckless; wild. ¶엉뚱한 생각 a wild 〔fantastic〕 idea; an eccentric notion / 엉뚱한 요구 an extravagant demand / 엉뚱한 짓 하지 마라 Don't act recklessly 〔without consideration〕.
엉망(진창) a mess; (in) bad shape. ¶ ~이 되다 be spoiled 〔ruined〕; get out of shape / ~을 만들다 make a mess 《of》; spoil; ruin; upset / 비로 인해 우리 계획은 ~이 되었다 The rain messed up our plan. *or* Our plan was spoiled by the rain.
엉성하다 ① 《페이지 않다》 (be) thin; sparse; loose; coarse. ¶엉성하게 짜다 knit with large stitches / 엉성한 문장 a loose piece of writing. ② 《담탁잖다》 (be) unsatisfactory; slipshod; poor 《솜씨가》. ¶엉성한 작품 a slipshod piece of work.
엉엉거리다 《울다》 cry bitterly; cry one's heart out; 《하소연》 complain of one's hard lot.
엉클다 entangle; tangle.
엉클어지다 be entangled; become 〔get〕 tangled; be snarled.
엉큼하다 (be) wicked 〔and crafty〕; scheming; insidious; 《서슴지》 have some plot in one's mind; have an ulterior motive (in view). ¶저 녀석은 엉큼해서 무엇을 꾸미고 있는지 알 수가 없다 Because he's a wicked and crafty fellow, you never know what he's up to.
엉터리 ① 《내용이 없는 것·사람》 a fake; a sham; a quack; something cheap and shabby. ¶ ~ 의사 a quack doctor / ~ 회사 a bogus concern / ~ 편지 a forged letter. ② 《터무니없는 언행》 nonsense; an irresponsible remark 〔act〕. ¶ ~의 nonsensical; irresponsible; random / ~로 random; irresponsibly without system 〔a plan〕 / ~로 말하다 talk nonsense 〔rubbish〕 / ~로 추측하다 make a haphazard guess / 이 기사는 ~다 This article is all nonsense. / 저 녀석은 ~다 He is an irresponsible man.
엊그저께 《수일 전》 a few days ago; 《그저께》 the day before yesterday.
엊저녁 last night 〔evening〕. └day.
엎다 《뒤집다》 overturn; turn over; 《거꾸로 하다》 turn 《a thing》 upside down; put 〔lay〕 《a thing》 face down; 《타도》 overthrow.
엎드리다 lie flat 《on the ground》; lie on one's stomach.
엎어지다 《넘어지다》 fall on one's face; fall down; 《뒤집히다》 be turned over; be upset; be overthrown 〔toppled〕. ¶ 엎어지면 코 닿을 데에 있다 be within a stone's throw.
엎지르다 spill; slop. ¶ 엎지른 물 spilt water / 잔의 우유를 ~ spill milk from a cup / 엎지른 물은 다시 담지 못한다《俗談》 What is done cannot be undone.
엎치락뒤치락 ~하다 《잠자리에서》 toss about in bed; toss and turn over in one's sleep; 《경기 등에서》 be nip and tuck; be neck and neck. ¶ ~하는 경기 a seesaw game 〔match〕; a nip-and-tuck game.
엎친데덮친다 add to one's troubles; make things worse. ¶ 엎친 데 덮치기로 make matters worse.
에 《때》 at 《시각》; in 《연, 월, 주》; on 《날》. ¶ 2시 5분~ at 5 minutes past 2 o'clock / 1주일에 ~ in a week / 8월 10일 ~ on the 10th of August. 《장소》 at 《지점》; in 《나라, 도, 도시, 가로》; on 《현장, 구내》; 《위치》 in 《속》; on 《표면》. ¶ 50쪽~ on page 50 / 용산~ 있는 학교 a school at 〔in〕 Yongsan / 한국~ in Korea / 10번지 ~ 살다 live at No. 10. ③ 《방향·목적》 in; to; for; on; into one's; at 《향해서》. ¶ 학교~ 가다 go to school. ④ 《가격》 at 《the price of》; for; in. ¶ 백원~ at 〔for〕 100 won. ⑤ 《나이》 in; at. ¶ 20대 ~ in one's twenties / 30~ at (the age of) thirty. ⑥ 《비율·마다》 a; per; for. ¶ 한다스~ 5백 원 500 won per dozen 〔a dozen〕 / 일주일에 한 번 a week / 백 원 ~ 팔다 sell at 100 won 《a yard》. ⑦ 《원인》 at; with; from; of. ¶ 추위~ 떨다 shiver with cold. ⑧ 《수단》 with; on; to. ¶ ~을 담그다 soak in water. ⑨ 《표준》 by; to; at; on. ¶ 시계를 시보~ 맞추다 set a watch by the timecast. ⑩ 《그 밖의 관계》 to; with; on; in; for. ¶ 어떤 일 ~ 관계하다 relate to 〔be concerned with〕 a certain matter.
에게 to; for; with; from; 《피동》 by. ¶ 아무~ 말을 걸다 speak to 《a person》/ 영어를 영국 사람 ~ 배우다 learn English from an Englishman.

에게서 from; through. ¶ 먼 데 있는 친구~ 온 편지 a letter from a friend far away.
에고이즘 egoism.
에끼 Ugh!; Fie!; Phew!; [could you!
에나멜 enamel. ¶ ~ 가죽 [구두] enameled leather [shoes].
에너지 energy. ¶ ~ 보존법칙 the law of the conservation of energy / ~ 수요 the demand for energy / ~원 an energy source / ~위기 an energy crisis / ~ 자원 energy resources / ~절약운동 an energy conservation drive / ~ 혁명 an energy revolution / ~ 효율 an energy efficiency / 열 ~ heat [thermal] energy / 잠재 ~ latent energy.
에누리 ① 《더 부르는 값》 an overcharge. ~ 하다 overcharge; ask a fancy price [two prices]. ② 《깎음》 a cut [reduction] in price; discount. ~ 하다 ask a discount; bid low; knock the price down. ¶ 1,000원으로 ~ 하다 beat down the price to 1,000 *won* / 심하게 ~ 하다 drive a hard bargain *with a merchant*).
에다 《도려내다》 gouge (out); cut [scoop, hollow, slice] out.
에다(가) to; at; in; on. ¶ 5 ~ 6을 보태라 Add 6 to 5. [Eden.
에덴동산 Eden; the Garden of
에멜바이스 [植] an edelweiss.
에도 《까지도》 even; 《…도 또한》 also; too; as well.
에돌다 linger hesitantly; hang around without doing anything; keep [stay] away (*from*).
에두르다 《둘러싸다》 enclose; surround; 《말을》 hint (*at*); suggest; say in a roundabout way; refer indirectly (*to*).
에러 (make) an error.
에로 erotic(ism).
에메랄드 [鑛] emerald.
에보나이트 ebonite.
에볼라바이러스 the Ebola virus.
에서 ① 《곳》 in (*Seoul*); at (*Jongno*); on (*the table*). ¶ 부산~ 서울까지 from Pusan at Seoul Station. ② 《출발점》 from; out of; off; in; over. ¶ 서울~ 부산까지 from Seoul to Pusan. ③ 《동기》 out of; from. ¶ 호기심~ out of curiosity. ④ 《견지·표준》 from; by; according to. ¶ 사회적 견지~ 보면 from a social point of view. ⑤ 《범위》 from. ¶ 대략 2만 원~ 3만 원사이 all the way from 20,000 *won* to 30,000 *won* / 한 시 ~ 네시 사이에 between one and four o'clock.
에세이 an essay.
에스에프 SF. (◀ science fiction)
에스오시 《사회 간접 자본》 SOC. (◀ Social Overhead Capital)
에스오에스 《send out, flash》 an SOS (call). [ing stairway.
에스컬레이터 an escalator; a mov-
에스코트 escort; 《사람》 an escort. ~ 하다 escort (*a singer*). [kimo.
에스키모 an Eskimo. ¶ ~ 의 Es-
에스페란토 [言] Esperanto. ¶ ~ 학자 an Esperantist.
에어로빅스 (do) aerobics.
에어메일 airmail; 우편 airmail.
에어컨 an air conditioner (기계); air conditioning (장치).
에어컴프레서 an air compressor.
에우다 《둘러싸다》 enclose; surround; fence (around); 《지우다》 cross out; strike off.
에움길 a detour.
에워싸다 surround; enclose; 《사람이》 crowd round; 《포위》 besiege; lay siege to.
에이스 an ace (*pitcher*); a leading player; 《카드》 an ace.
에이에프피 《프랑스 통신사》 AFP. (◀ *Agence France Presse*)
에이엠 ‖ ~방송 an AM [amplitude modulation] broadcast.
에이전트 an agent.
에이즈 [醫] 《후천성 면역 결핍증》 AIDS. (◀ Acquired Immune Deficiency Syndrome) ¶ ~환자 an AIDS patient / ~에 감염되다 contract AIDS / ~가 발병되다 develop AIDS.
에이커 an acre. [op AIDS.
에이프런 an apron.
에잇 《감탄》 Pshaw!; O!; Son of a gun! ¶ ~ 빌어먹을 Damn it!
에콰도르 Ecuador. ¶ ~ 사람 an Ecuadorian.
에테르 [化] ether. [Ethiopian.
에티오피아 Ethiopia. ¶ ~ 사람 an
에티켓 etiquette; manners. ¶ 식사시 ~ table manners.
에틸렌 [化] ethylene.
에틸알코올 [化] ethyl alcohol.
에펠탑(一 塔) the Eiffel Tower.
에프비아이 F.B.I. (◀ Federal Bureau of Investigation)
에프엠 ‖ ~방송 an FM [frequency modulation] broadcast.
에프티에이(FTA) 《자유무역협정》 Free Trade Agreement.
에피소드 an episode.
에필로그 an epilog(ue).
에헴 Hem!; Ahem!
엑스¹ 《미지수》 an unknown (quantity). ‖ ~ (광)선 X [X (Roentgen)] rays / ~ 선 사진 (take) an X-ray picture / ~ 선 요법 X-ray therapy.
엑스² an extract [essence] 《*of*》.
엑스트라 (play) an extra 《*of*》.
엔 a yen (기호 ¥). ‖ ~ 고(高) 《시세》 a strong yen; a high exchange rate of the *yen*; 《상승》 a rise in the exchange rate of the *yen* / ~ 고 차익 a profit accruing from

엔간하다 (적당) (be) proper; suitable; (상당) (be) considerable; fair; tolerable; passable. ¶ 엔간히 pretty; fairly; considerably.

엔드 even; also; too. ¶ 필요하다면 어디~ 못 가랴 I would go anyplace if (it is) necessary.

엔지 (映) N.G.(◀ no good) ¶ ~를 내다 spoil (ruin) a sequence.

엔지니어 an engineer.

엔진 (start, stop) an engine.

엔트리 an entry.

엘니뇨 El Niño. ¶ ~현상 an El Nino phenomenon.

엘레지 an elegy.

엘리베이터 (run) an elevator; a lift (英).

엘리트 the elite (of society); a member of the elite. ¶ ~ 의식이 강하다 have a strong sense of being one of the elite / ~ 코스를 밟다 be on course for membership of the elite. / ~사원 an elite employee / ~주의 elitism.

엘엔지 (액화 천연 가스) LNG. (◀ Liquefied Natural Gas)

엘피 (레코드) an LP (a long-playing) record.

엘피지 (액화 석유 가스) LPG. (◀ Liquefied Petroleum Gas); LP gas; bottled gas.

엠티 (MT) (회원훈련) (a) membership training.

엠피 (헌병) M.P.; the military police.

···여 (餘) (이상) above; over; more than; …and over (more). ¶ 3 마일 ~ over three miles.

여가 (餘暇) (틈) spare time; leisure (hours); odd moments. ¶ ~가 없다 have no leisure (time to spare).

여간아니다 (如干—) (be) uncommon; extraordinary; be no easy task (matter). ¶ 아이를 기르기는 ~ 아이 어려운 일이 아니다 It is no easy thing to bring up a child.

여감방 (女監房) a prison ward (cell) for females.

여객 (旅客) a traveler; a passenger (승객). ‖ ~명부 a passenger list / ~열차(기) a passenger train (plane) / ~운임 passenger fares. 「man; an amazon.

여걸 (女傑) a heroine; a brave woman

여겨듣다 listen attentively (to). 「see closely.

여겨보다 (눈여겨) watch carefully;

여계 (女系) the female line.

여공 (女工) a factory girl; a female operative; a woman worker.

여과 (濾過) filtration; filtering. ~하다 filter; filtrate. ‖ ~기 a filter; a percolator / ~성 filterability

/ ~성 병원체 a filterable virus / ~액 filtrate / ~지(池) a filter bed / ~지 filter paper.

여관 (旅館) a Korean-style hotel (inn); a hotel; a motel. ¶ ~에 묵다 stay (put up) at a hotel / ~에서 나가다 check out / ~을 경영하다 run (keep) a hotel. ¶ ~ 손님 a guest (staying) at an inn; a hotel guest / ~주인 a hotelkeeper; innkeeper. 「light.

여광 (餘光) (잔) afterglow; lingering

여교사 (女敎師) a schoolmistress; a female teacher.

여권 (女權) women's rights. ‖ ~신장 extension of women's rights / ~운동 the women's rights movement / ~운동가 a feminist.

여권 (旅券) a passport. ‖ ~을 신청(발부)하다 apply for (issue) a passport / ~을 교부받다 get (obtain) a passport. ¶ ~법 the passport control law / ~사증 a passport visa. 「(술집의).

여급 (女給) a waitress; a bar-maid

여기 this place; here. ¶ ~에(서) here; in (at) this place / ~서부터 from here.

여기다 think; regard (consider) 《a thing》 as; take 《a thing》 for; 《믿다》 believe. ¶ 아무를 귀엽게 ~ hold a person dear / 대수롭게 여기지 않다 think little (nothing) of.

여기자 (女記者) a woman reporter; female journalist; (잡지의) a female magazine writer.

여기저기 here and there; from place to place; in places; in various places.

여난 (女難) (get into) trouble with women. ¶ 그에게는 ~의 상(相)이 있다 He seems to be destined to have trouble with women.

여남은 some ten odd; more than ten. ¶ ~사람 a dozen men.

여념 (餘念) ‖ (…에) ~이 없다 be busy 《with something》; busy oneself 《with》; be lost (absorbed, engrossed) 《in》; devote oneself 《to》. ¶ 독서에 ~이 없다 be absorbed in one's book.

여단 (旅團) (軍) a brigade.

여닫다 open and shut (close).

여담 (餘談) a digression. ¶ ~은 그만두고 to return to the subject. 「party.

여당 (與黨) the Government (ruling)

여대 (女大) a women's college (university). ‖ ~생 a college girl (woman). 「great virtue.

여덕 (餘德) the influence of a

여덟 eight. ¶ ~째 the eighth.

여독 (旅毒) the fatigue of travel. ¶ ~을 풀다 relieve one's fatigue of travel.

여동생 (女同生) a younger sister.

여드레(8일간) eight days;(날짜) the eighth (day of a month).

여드름 a pimple; an acne.

여든 eighty; a fourscore. ¶ ~째 eightieth.

여러 many; several; various. ¶ ~달 (for) several [many] months / ~사람 several [many] people / ~해 (for) many [several] years / ~ 직업 various occupations.

여러가지 all sorts (of); various kinds (of); varieties. ¶ ~의 various; all kinds [sorts] of; a variety of; several / ~ 이유로 for various reasons / ~ 상품 goods of different kinds / ~로 해석되다 It can be construed in many ways.

여러번(一番) many [several] times; often; repeatedly.

여러분 ladies and gentlemen; all of you; everybody.

여러해살이(풀) [植] a perennial (plant).

여럿(사람) many; many people; a crowd (of people); (수) a large number.

여력(餘力) reserve [remaining] power (strength, energy); (돈의) money to spare. ¶ 충분한 ~이 있다 have a great reserve of energy; have much in reserve / 차를 살 만한 ~이 없다 I have no money to spare for a car.

여로(旅路) a journey.

여론(輿論) public opinion; the general (prevailing) opinion. ¶ ~의 일치 the consensus of public opinion / ~에 호소하다 (을 불러 일으키다) appeal to (arouse) public opinion / ~에 귀를 기울이다 pay attention to the trends of public opinion. ‖ ~조사 a public-opinion poll [survey] / ~조사원 a pollster; a polltaker.

여류(女流) ¶ ~의 lady; female; ~작가 a woman [lady] writer.

여름 summer; the summer season(여름철). ¶ ~용의 for summer use. ‖ ~방학 the summer vacation (holidays) / ~옷 summer wear [clothes] / ~장마 summer monsoon.

여름타다 lose weight in summer; suffer from (the) summer heat; get summer sickness.

여리다 (연하다) (be) soft; tender; (약하다) weak; frail; delicate.

여망(輿望) popularity; esteem; trust. ¶ 국민의 ~을 지고 있다 be trusted by the whole nation.

여명(餘命) one's remaining days; the rest of one's life. ¶ ~이 얼마 남지 않다 have but few days [days] to live.

여명(黎明) dawn; daybreak. ¶ ~에 at dawn [daybreak] / 우주 시대의 ~기 the dawn of the Space Age. ‖ hay. ‖ ~통 a manger.

여물 (마소의) fodder; forage; feed;

여물다(열매가) bear fruit; ripen; get [become] ripe; (기회 따위가) be ripe; mature. ¶ 이 옥수수는 아직 여물지 않았다 This corn is not ripe yet. / 때가 여물기를 기다리라 Wait till the time is ripe.

여미다 ¶ 옷을 ~ make oneself tidy (neat); straighten one's clothes; tidy oneself up.

여반장(如反掌) ¶ 그런 일쯤은 ~이다 That's quite an easy task (job).

여배우(女俳優) an actress. ¶ 영화 [TV]의 ~ a film [TV] actress / ~가 되다 become an actress / 지망자 an aspiring actress.

여백(餘白) a space; a blank; a margin (난외). ¶ ~을 남기다 leave a space / ~을 메우다 fill in [up] the blank [space].

여별(餘-) an excess; a spare; an extra. ¶ ~의 옷 a spare suit of clothes / ~이 하나 있다 There is an extra.

여보 ① (他) (I) say; (look) here; hey (there). ② (부부간) baby; (my) dear; (darling); honey.

여보세요 (호칭) Excuse me!; Hallo!; Say!; I say!; (英) (전화에서) Hello!; Are you there? ¶ ~ 누구시죠 (전화에서 받는자가) Hello, who's calling, please?

여부(與否) yes or no; whether or not; if. ¶ 성공 ~ success or failure / ~ 없다 (be) sure; certain; be beyond doubt; be a matter of course.

여복 how (much). ¶ ~ 좋을까 How glad I shall be! / 그걸 보고 ~ 놀랐겠느냐 What was his surprise to see that?

여분(餘分) a surplus; leftovers; remnants; an extra; an excess. ¶ ~의 extra; spare; excessive / ~으로 in surplus / ~의 돈이 없다 have no extra money; have no money to spare.

여비(旅費) traveling expenses; a traveling allowance (지급되는).

여사(女史) Madame; Mrs.; Miss.

여사무원(女事務員) an office girl [lady]; a female clerk.

여색(女色) (미색) a woman's charm (beauty); (색욕) carnal pleasures (desire). ¶ ~에 빠지다 indulge in lewdness.

여생(餘生) (spend) the rest (remainder) of one's life.

여섯 six. ¶ ~째 the sixth.

여성(女性) a woman; a lady; womanhood; the gentle (fair) sex (총칭). ¶ ~의 female / ~용의 for ladies / ~적인 feminine; womanly; effeminate(연약한). / ~관 a view of womanhood /

여세(餘勢) surplus (reserve) energy; momentum. ¶ ~를 몰아 encouraged (emboldened) by *one's* success / 승리의 ~를 몰아 적을 공격하다 follow up *their* victory with a fresh assault on the enemy.
여송연(呂宋煙) 《smoke》 a cigar.
여수(旅愁) melancholy (ennui) felt while on a journey. ¶ ~에 잠기다 be in a pensive mood while on a journey.
여승(女僧) a Buddhist nun.
여식(女息) a daughter.
여신(女神) a goddess. ¶ 미의 ~ the Goddess of Beauty.
여신(與信) credit. ¶ ~을 주다 give (allow, grant) credit. ¶ ~공급량 the amount of a loan / ~관리 credit management / ~규제 credit control / ~상태 credit condition / ~업무 a loan business / ~한도 a credit line (limit); a line of credit.
여신(餘燼) embers; smoldering fire.
여실(如實) ~하다 (be) real; true; lively. ¶ ~히 faithfully; realistically; true to life / ~히 그리다 depict 《*a thing*》 just as it is.
여식(女息) a daughter (딸).
여아(女兒) a girl; a little (baby) girl.
여야(與野) the ruling party and the opposition party.
여염(閻閻) a middle-class community. ¶ ~집 a commoner's home / ~집 여자 a normal housewife.
여왕(女王) a queen; an empress. ¶ ~벌 (개미) a queen bee (ant).
여우 ① 《動》 a fox; a vixen (암컷). ¶ ~굴 a fox burrow / ~목도리 a fox-fur muffler. ② 《비유적》 a sly fellow; an old fox. ¶ ~ 같은 cunning; sly; foxy.
여우비 a sunshine shower.
여운(餘韻) 《잔향》 reverations; echoes; 《음곡의》 a trailing note; 《시문의》 suggestiveness. ¶ ~이 있는 trailing; lingering; suggestive.
여울 a (swift) current; rapids; a torrent. ¶ ~목 the neck of the rapids.
여위다 grow thin; lose flesh (weight); be worn out. ¶ 근심으로 ~ be careworn / 과로로 매우 여위었다 be worn out with overwork.
여유(餘裕) ① 《시간의》 time (to spare); 《공간의》 room; space;

《돈·시간의》 a margin. ¶ 시간 (돈)의 ~가 없다 have no time (money) to spare / 다섯 사람이 들어갈 만한 ~가 있다 There is enough room for five people. ¶ 자동차를 살 ~가 없다 I cannot afford (to buy) a car. ② 《정신적인》 composure; placidity. ¶ ~있는 be very composed; be calm and at ease / 그는 자신의 일로 다른 것을 생각할 ~가 없다 His mind is too occupied with his own affair.
여의(如意) ~하다 turn out as *one* wishes; things go well. ¶ ~치 (가) 않다 go contrary to *one's* wishes; go wrong (amiss).
여의다 ① 《사별》 have 《*a person*》 die; be bereaved (deprived) 《*of a person*》; lose. ¶ 아버지를 ~ lose *one's* father. ② 《떠나보내다》 send 《*a person*》 away. ¶ 딸을 ~ marry *one's* daughter off 《*to*》.
여의사(女醫師) a lady (female, woman) doctor.
여인(女人) a woman. ¶ ~ 출입금지 No Admittance to Women.
여인숙(旅人宿) an inn; a lodge.
여일(如一) ~하다 (be) consistent; changeless; immutable. ¶ ~하게 consistently; invariably.
여자(女子) a woman; a lady; a girl; a female. ¶ ~의 female; women's; ladies'; girls' / ~다운 womanliness / ~다운 여자 a womanly (ladylike) woman / ~답지 않은 unwomanly; unladylike / ~용의 lady's; for ladies' use. ¶ ~고등학교 a girls' senior high school / ~대학 a women's college (university) / ~대학생 a women's college student / 《美口》 a co-ed (남녀 공학의).
여장(女裝) a female dress (attire). ~하다 wear a female dress.
여장(旅裝) a traveling outfit. ¶ ~을 챙기다 equip *oneself* for a journey; prepare for a trip / ~을 풀다 put up (stop) at 《*an inn*》.
여장부(女丈夫) ☞ 여걸(女傑).
여전(如前) ~하다 《서술적》 be as before; be as it used to be; remain unchanged. ¶ ~히 as usual; as … as ever; as before; still.
여점원(女店員) a saleswoman.
여정(旅程) 《거리》 the distance to be covered; 《여행 일정》 an itinerary; a journey.
여존(女尊) respect for woman. ¶ ~남비 putting women above men. ☞ as stated below.
여좌하다(如左─) be as follows; be as stated below.
여죄(餘罪) (inquire into) further crimes; other charges. ¶ 다른 ~도 있을 것 같다 be suspected of some other crimes.

여죄수(女罪囚) a female prisoner.
여지(餘地) room; a space; a scope 〈사고·행동의〉; a blank 〈여백〉. ¶ 개량(발전)의 ～ room for improvement (development) / 입추의 ～도 없이 be packed full / 타협의 ～가 있다(없다) there is room (no room) for compromise / 불풀이 주어) leave room (no room) for compromise / 그의 성공은 의심할 ～가 없다 There is no doubt about his success.
여진(餘震) 〖地〗 an aftershock.
여쭈다〈말하다〉 tell; say; state; inform; 〈묻다〉 ask; inquire. ¶ 그 점에 관해 제가 자세히 여쭈겠습니다 Perhaps you will allow me to explain that point.
여차(如此) be like this; be this way. ¶ ～한 such; such as; like this / ～ ～한 이야기 such and such a story / ～한 이유 for such-and-such a reason.
여차하면 in case 〔time〕 of need 〔emergency〕; if need be; if one has to; if compelled.
여축(餘蓄) saving; stock; reserve; supplies. ～하다 save; stock; reserve; set aside. ¶ ～이 좀 있다 have some savings.
여치 〖蟲〗 a grasshopper.
여탈(與奪) ¶ 생살～권을 쥐다 hold the power of life and death.
여탕(女湯) the women's section of a public bath.
여태〔까지〕 till 〔until〕 now; up to the present; so far. ¶ ～ 없던 사건 an unprecedented incident / ～ 어디 있었느냐 Where have you been all this while?
여파(餘波)〈影響〉 an aftermath; an aftereffect. ¶ 혁명 (태풍)의 ～ the aftermath of the revolution (typhoon).
여편네 ①《아내》 one's wife. ②《기혼녀》 a (married) woman.
여필종부(女必從夫) Wives should be submissive to their husbands.
여하(如何) what; how. ¶ ～이 how; in what way / ～한 이유로 for what reason / ～한 경우에도 in any case / ～한 희생을 내더라도 at any cost 〔price, sacrifice〕 / ～한 일이 있더라도 whatever may happen / 이유～를 막론하고 regardless of the reasons / 사정 ～에 달리다 depend upon circumstances.
여하간(如何間) anyway; anyhow; in any case; at any rate; at all events.
여하튼(如何一) ☞ 여하간.
여학교(女學校) a girls' school.
여학생(女學生) a schoolgirl; a girl 〔woman〕 student.

여한(餘恨) a smoldering 〔lingering〕 grudge.
여한(餘寒) the lingering cold; the cold of late winter.
여행(旅行) travel; a journey; traveling; a tour; an excursion, a trip 〈짧은〉; a voyage 〈항해〉. ～하다 journey; make a journey 〔trip〕; tour. ¶ ～ 준비를 하다 make preparations for a trip / ～을 떠나다 set out 〔start〕 on a journey 〔tour, trip〕 / 업무로 ～하다 make 〔go on〕 a business trip 〔to〕 / 2,3일간의 ～ a two or three day trip / ～에서 돌아오다 return from one's trip 〔to〕 / 미국～중에 during one's travels in the U.S. ; while traveling in America. ‖ ～가방 a traveling bag; a suitcase / ～사 a travel agency; a tourist bureau / ～안내 guidance to travelers / ～일정 an itinerary; one's travel schedule / ～자 a traveler; a tourist.
여행(勵行) rigid enforcement. ～하다 enforce 〔carry out〕 《the rules》 rigidly.
여호와《히브루의 신》 Jehovah. ¶ ～의 증인 Jehovah's Witnesses.
여흥(餘興) an entertainment; a side show.
역(逆) the reverse 〔contrary〕 《of》; the opposite; 〖數〗 converse. ¶ ～의 reverse 〔order〕; opposite 〈direction〉 / ～으로 conversely; inversely; the other way around / ～이 반드시 진(眞)은 아니다 Converses are not always true.
역(驛) a (railroad, railway) station; a (railroad) depot. ¶ 서울～ Seoul Station / ～전 광장 a station square 〔plaza〕.
역(役)〈연극에서〉(play) the part 〔role〕 《of》; a character. ¶ 어린 이～을 하다 a juvenile 〔child〕 role / 햄릿의 ～을 하다 play the role 〔part〕 of Hamlet.
역(譯) (a) translation; (a) version.
역(亦)〈亦是〉 too; also; as well.
역겹다(逆一)〈속이〉 feel sick 〔queasy, nausea〕; 〈혐오〉 be disgusted 《at》; be nauseated.
역경(逆境) adversity; adverse circumstances. ¶ ～에 빠지다 be in 〔fall into〕 adversity / ～을 이겨내다 tide over a difficult situation.
역광선(逆光線) counterlight. ¶ ～으로 〔take a picture〕 against the light. ‖ ～사진 a shadowgraph.
역군(役軍) a wageworker; a laborer; 〈유능한〉 an able worker.
역대(歷代) successive generations 〔reigns〕. ¶ ～의 내각 successive cabinets. 　〔a weight lifter.
역도(力道) weight lifting. ‖ ～선수

역도(逆徒) rebels; traitors.
역량(力量) 《display》 one's ability; capability. ¶ ~ 있는 able; capable; competent / …할 만한 ~이 있다 have the ability to *do*; be competent for 《*the task*》.
역력하다(歷歷 一) (be) clear; vivid; obvious; undeniable. ¶ 역력히 vividly; clearly; obviously.
역류(逆流) a back 《an adverse》 current; (a) backward flow. ~하다 flow backward 《upstream》; surge back.
역마살(驛馬煞) ¶ ~이 끼었다 have itchy feet.
역마차(驛馬車) a stagecoach.
역모(逆謀) a plot of treason. ~하다 conspire to rise in revolt; plot treason 《against》.
역무원(驛務員) a lower-grade station employee; a station porter.
역문(譯文) a translation; a version.
역반응(逆反應) 『理』 an inverse reaction.
역방(歷訪) a round of calls 《visits》. ~하다 make a round of visits 《to》; make a tour of 《Asian countries》.
역병(疫病) a plague; an epidemic.
역부족(力不足) want of ability. ¶ ~이다 be beyond one's capacity; find oneself unequal 《to the task》.
역비례(逆比例) an inverse proportion.
역사(力士) a muscle 《strong》 man.
역사(役事) construction work; public works.
역사(歷史) ① history; a history 《사略》. ~의[적인] historic; historical / ~적인 사건 〔사실, 인물〕 a historical event 〔fact, figure〕 / ~적으로 유명한 장소 a historic spot; a place of historic interest / ~상 미증유의 대전 the greatest battle in history / 한국의 ~ Korean history / ~ 이전의 prehistoric / ~에 남다 remain 〔go down〕 in history / ~를 더듬다 trace the history 《of》. ∥ ~가 a historian / ~박물관 a museum of history / ~소설 a historical novel / ~학 historical science; the study of history. ② 《내력》 history; tradition 〔전통〕.
역사(轢死) ~하다 be 《run over and》 killed by a vehicle.
역산(逆産) ① 『醫』 breech birth. ② 《재산》 the property of a traitor. 〔reckon〕 backward.
역산(逆算) ~하다 count
역서(曆書) an almanac.
역선전(逆宣傳) counterpropaganda. ~하다 conduct 〔carry out, make〕 counterpropaganda.
역설(力說) ~하다 lay 〔put〕 stress 〔emphasize〕 on 《something》; emphasize; stress.
역설(逆說) a paradox. ¶ ~적인 paradoxical / ~으로 말하면 paradoxically speaking.
역성 taking sides with; partiality. ¶ ~ 들다 be partial 《toward》; show partiality 〔favor〕 《to》; take sides with.
역수(逆數) 『數』 a reciprocal (number); inverse number.
역수입(逆輸入) ~하다 reimportation; reimport.
역수출(逆輸出) ~하다 reexportation; reexport.
역습(逆襲) a counterattack. ~하다 《make》 a counterattack; retort 〔말로〕.
역시(亦是) 《또한》 too; also; as well; 《의연히》 still; 《결국》 after all; 《…에도 불구하고》 but; nevertheless; in spite of; 《예상대로》 as 《was》 expected.
역어(譯語) words 〔terms〕 used in a translation; a 《Korean》 equivalent 《of》.
역연하다(歷然 一) (be) clear; manifest; evident; obvious; plain.
역용(逆用) ~하다 turn 《the enemy's propaganda》 to one's own advantage; take advantage of 《a person's kindness》.
역원(驛員) a station employee; the station staff 〔총칭〕.
역임(歷任) ~하다 hold 《various posts》 successively 〔in succession〕. ¶ 여러 관직을 ~하다 fill 〔hold, occupy〕 various Government posts in succession.
역자(譯者) a translator.
역작(力作) one's labored work; a masterpiece. ∥ ~ verse action.
역작용(逆作用) (a) reaction; a reverse action.
역장(驛長) a stationmaster.
역저(力著) a fine literary work; a masterpiece.
역적(逆賊) a rebel; a traitor.
역전(力戰) ~하다 fight hard.
역전(逆轉) reversal; inversion. ~하다 reverse; be reversed. ¶ ~승하다 win a losing game / ~패하다 lose a winning game / 이제 그들의 입장은 ~되었다 Their positions are now reversed.
역전(歷戰) ¶ ~의 용사 a veteran; a battle-tried warrior.
역전마라톤(驛傳 一) a long-distance relay 《marathon》.
역점(力點) emphasis; the point; 『理』 dynamic point. ¶ …에 ~을 두다 lay 〔put〕 stress 〔emphasis〕 《on》; attach importance 《to》.
역조(逆潮) an adverse 《unfavorable》 condition. ¶ 무역의 ~ an adverse balance of trade; import excess.
역주(力走) ~하다 run as hard

역진(力盡) ~하다 be exhausted; be (get) worn out; be dead tired. ¶ ~탄 bituminous coal.

역청(瀝青) [鑛] bitumen; pitch.

역추진(逆推進) ¶ ~로켓 a retrorocket.

역코스(逆一) (follow) the reverse course.

역투(力投) ~하다 [野] pitch hard.

역풍(逆風) an adverse wind.

역하다(逆一) feel sick (nausea); (혐오) (be) disgusting; offensive.

역학(力學) [理] dynamics.

역학(易學) the art of divination.

역할(役割) a part; a role. ¶ ~을 정하다 allot (assign) a part (role) (to); give (an actor) a part (in a play) / 중대한 ~을 하다 play an important role (part) (in).

역행(力行) ~하다 (힘씀) endeavor; make strenuous efforts.

역행(逆行) ~하다 go (move) backward; run counter (to). ¶ 시대에 ~하다 go against the times.

역효과(逆效果) a counter result; a contrary effect. ¶ ~를 내다 produce an opposite effect (result) to what was intended / 그것은 ~였다 It boomeranged.

엮다 ① (엮어서) plait; weave; (묶다) tie (with a rope). ② (편찬) compile; edit.

연(年) a year. ¶ ~ 1회 once a year; annually / ~ 1회의 yearly; annual / ~ 5부의 이자 interest of five percent a year / ~ 2회의 half-yearly; twice-yearly. ∥ ~수입 an annual income.

연(鳶) a kite. ¶ ~을 날리다 fly a kite.

연(鉛) lead. ☞ 납. [lead. |flower.

연(蓮) [植] a lotus. ¶ ~꽃 a lotus

연(連) a ream (of paper).

연(延) the total. ∥ ~시간 the total number of hours; the total man-hours / ~인원 the total number of man-day / ~일수 the total number of days / ~평수 the total floor space in pyŏng.

연가(戀歌) a love song (poem).

연간(年間) ~계획 a one-year plan; a schedule for the year / ~생산량 a yearly output / ~소득 an annual income.

연감(年鑑) a yearbook; an almanac.

연갑(年甲) a contemporary; a person of about one's own age.

연결(連結) connection; coupling. ~하다 connect; join; couple. ¶ 식당차를 ~하다 couple (attach) a dining car to (a train). ∥ ~기(차량의) a coupler.

연고(軟膏) (an) ointment. ¶ ~를 바르다 apply ointment (to).

연고(緣故) ① (사유) a reason; a cause; a ground. ② (관계) relation; connection. ¶ ~를 통해 입사하다 enter a company through one's personal connection. ∥ ~권 preemptive rights / ~자 a relative.

연골(軟骨) [解] a cartilage; gristle.

연공(年功) long service (근속); long experience (경험). ~을 쌓다 have long service (experience). ∥ ~가봉 a long service allowance / ~서열임금 the seniority wage system / ~서열제도 the seniority system.

연관(鉛管) a lead pipe. ∥ ~공 a plumber.

연관(聯關) ☞ 관련.

연구(研究) a study; a research; (an) investigation (조사). ~하다 study; research (into); make a study (of); do (conduct) research (on, in). ¶ ~를 계속하다 pursue one's studies / ~를 발표하다 publish one's research work / 인공 지능의 ~를 맡다 take up the study of artificial intelligence. ¶ ~가(자) a student; an investigator; a research worker / ~개발 research and development (생략 R&D) / ~과제 a research task / ~논문 a research paper (on); a monograph (전공의); a dissertation (학위의); a treatise(학술의) / ~회 a meeting for reading research papers / ~보고 a report of one's research / ~비 research funds (expenses) /~생 a research student / ~소 a laboratory; a research institute / ~실 a laboratory(실험실) ; a seminar(대학의) / ~심 the spirit of inquiry / ~자료 research materials (data) / ~활동 research activities.

연구개(軟口蓋) the soft palate. ∥ ~음 a velar (sound).

연극(演劇) ① (극) a play; drama. ¶ ~을 상연하다 present (put on) a play; perform a play on the stage / ~을 전공하다 major in theater (drama). ∥ ~계 the theatrical world / ~부 a dramatic (drama) club / ~비평가 a drama critic / ~애호가 a playgoer / ~인 a person of the theater. ② (허위) a make-believe; a trick; a sham. ¶ ~을 꾸미다(부리다) put on an act; play a trick; put up a false show.

연근(蓮根) a lotus root.

연금(年金) an annuity; a pension. ¶ 국민~ the National Pension / 노령 [질병, 유족] ~ an old-age (a disability, a survivor) pension / 종신 ~ a life annuity / ~을 받다 receive a pension; draw one's pension / ~으로 생활하

연금 live on a pension / ~을 받고 到직하다 retire on a pension; be pensioned off. ‖ ~수령자 a pensioner / ~제도 a pension system.
연금(軟禁) house arrest. ~하다 put 《a person》 under house arrest; confine 《a person》 in 《a room》.
연금술(鍊金術) alchemy. ‖ ~사 an alchemist.
연기(延期) postponement. ~하다 postpone; put off; defer 《payment》; adjourn 《a meeting》. ‖ ~되다 be postponed; be put off / 기한을 ~하다 extend [prolong] the term.
연기(連記) ~하다 list; write 《three names》 on a ballot.
연기(煙氣) smoke. ¶ 한 가닥의 ~ a wisp of smoke / 자욱한 ~ clouds [volumes] of smoke / ~ 가 나는 smoking; smoky / ~를 (내)뿜다 emit [give out] smoke / ~에 숨이 막히다 be choked [suffocated] by smoke / ~에 휩싸이다 be enveloped [wreathed] in smoke / 아니 땐 굴뚝에 ~ 날까 There is no smoke without fire.
연기(演技) performance; acting. ¶ ~파의 여배우 an actress who relies on her acting skills (rather than on her looks). ‖ ~력 acting ability / ~자 a performer.
연내(年內) ¶ ~에 within [before the end of] the year.
연년(連年) successive years. ¶ ~ 생이다 be brothers [sisters] born in two successive years.
연놈 the man and the woman.
연단(演壇) a platform; a rostrum; a stand. ¶ ~에 오르다 [에서 내려 가다] take [leave] the rostrum.
연달다(連-) continue; keep on; follow one after another. ¶ 연달 은 continued; continuous; successive / 연달아 one after another; successively; in (rapid) succession; continuously.
연대(年代) 《시대》 an age; a period; an epoch; an era(연호). ¶ ~순의 chronological / ~순으 로 in chronological order / ~ 기 a chronicle / ~표 a chronological table.
연대(連帶) solidarity. ¶ ~의 [로] joint(ly). ‖ ~감 the feeling of togetherness [solidarity] / ~보 증 joint and several liability on guarantee / ~보증인 a joint surety / ~채무 joint and several obligation / ~책임 joint responsibility.
연대(聯隊) 〖軍〗 a regiment. ¶ 보병 ~ an infantry regiment. ‖ ~병 력 a regimental force / ~장(본 부, 기) the regimental commander (headquarters, colors).
연도(年度) a year; a term. ¶ 회계 ~ a fiscal year / 사업 ~ the business year / ~초 [말]에 at the beginning [end] of the year.
연도(沿道) ~의 [에] along the road [route]; by [on] the roadside.
연독(鉛毒) lead poisoning.
연동(聯動) gearing; linkage. ~하 다 be connected [linked, coupled] 《with》. ‖ ~기 a clutch / ~장 치 a coupling [an interlocking] device.
연동(蠕動) peristalsis; vermiculation.
연두(年頭) the beginning of the year. ‖ ~교서 《미국의》 the President's annual State of the Union message [address] to Congress / ~사 the New Year's address [message].
연두(軟豆) ¶ ~빛 yellowish light green.
연락(連絡) 《관계》 (a) connection; 《접촉》 (a) contact; touch; liaison; 《교통·통신상의》 communication; correspondence. ~하다 (be) connect(ed) 《with》; contact; get in touch 《with》; make contact 《with》; communicate 《with》. ¶ ~을 유지하다 keep in touch [contact] 《with》 / 전화 ~을 끊다 cut off telephonic communications 《with》 / 전화로 ~하다 speak to 《a person》 over the telephone / 출발 후 한 시간 만에 ~이 끊기다 《비행기가》 go out of communication an hour after its takeoff. ‖ ~사무소 a liaison office / ~선 a ferry(boat) / ~역 a junction / ~장교 a liaison officer.
연래(年來) for years; over the years. ¶ ~의 숙원 one's long-cherished desire [wish] / ~의 계획 a plan of long standing / ~의 대설 the heaviest snowfall in many years.
연령(年齡) age; years. ¶ ~에 비 해 for one's age / ~을 불문하고 regardless of age. ‖ ~제한 the age limit.
연례(年例) ~의 yearly; annual. ‖ ~보고 an annual report / ~ 행사 an annual event.
연로(年老) ~하다 be old; aged.
연료(燃料) fuel. ¶ ~가 충분하다 have enough fuel / ~가 떨어져 가 고 있다 be running short of gas [fuel]. ‖ ~공급 refueling / ~봉 a (nuclear) fuel rod / ~비 the cost of fuel; fuel expense / 고 체〖기체, 액체〗 ~ solid〖gaseous, liquid〗 fuel.
연루(連累) ~하다 be involved 《in》; be connected 《with》. ‖ ~ 자 an accomplice; a confeder-

연륜(年輪) an annual ring; growth ring. 《*of 6%*》

연리(年利) 〖at〗 an annual interest

연립(聯立) alliance; union; coalition. ‖ ~내각 a coalition cabinet / ~방정식 simultaneous equations / ~주택 a tenement house.

연마(研磨·練磨) ~하다 《갈고 닦다》polish; grind; whet; 《도야하다》drill; train; practice; improve. ¶ 기술을 ~하다 improve 〔practice〕 one's skill. ‖ ~기(機) a grinder; a grinding machine.

연막(烟幕) a smoke screen. ¶ ~을 치다 lay 〔down〕 a smoke screen.

연말(年末) the end of the year; the year-end. ¶ ~의 year-end / ~에 at the end 〔close〕 of the year. ‖ ~대매출 a year-end sale / ~보너스 the year-end bonus / ~정산 《세금의》 the year-end tax adjustment.

연맹(聯盟) a league; a federation; a union; a confederation. ¶ ~에 가입하다 join a league.

연면(連綿) ~하다 (be) continuous; uninterrupted; unbroken. ¶ ~히 continuously; consecutively.

연명(延命) ~하다 barely manage to live; eke out a scanty livelihood. ¶ 내각의 ~을 시도하다 try to prolong the life of the cabinet.

연명(連名·聯名) joint signature. ~하다 sign jointly. ¶ ~으로 in our joint names; under the joint signature of.... ‖ ~진정서 a joint petition.

연모 tools and supplies; instruments; equipments; materials.

연목구어(緣木求魚) seeking the impossible. ~하다 go to a tree for fish.

연못(蓮-) a (lotus) pond. ‖ ~가 the margin of a pond.

연무(烟霧) smoke and fog; mist and fog; smog《도시 등의》.

연무(演武) military exercise. ~하다 practice military exercises. ‖ ~장 a military exercise hall.

연무(鍊武) (a) military drill. ~하다 practice a military drill.

연문(戀文) a love letter.

연미복(燕尾服) a tailcoat; an evening coat.

연민(憐憫) compassion; pity; mercy. ¶ ~의 정을 느끼다 feel pity 〔compassion〕 (for).

연발(延發) ~하다 delayed departure; 하다 start late.

연발(連發) ~하다 fire in rapid succession; fire in volley. ¶ 6 ~의 권총 a six-chambered revolver; a six-shooter / ~식의 quick-firing 《gun》 / 질문을 ~하다 fire questions at 《a person》 in succession; ask one question after another. ‖ ~총 a quick-firing rifle 《gun》; an automatic pistol.

연방(聯邦) a (federal) union; a federation; a federal state. ‖ ~ 정부 the Federal Government / ~제도 a federal system; federalism.

연변(沿邊) the area along 《a river, a road, a rail line》.

연병(練兵) (a) military drill. ~하다 (have) a drill; parade. ‖ ~장 a parade 〔drill〕 ground.

연보(年報) an annual report.

연보(年譜) a chronological history; a biographical note.

연보(捐補) contribution; church offerings. ~하다 donate; subscribe.

연봉(年俸) an annual salary.

연봉(連峯) a chain of mountains; a mountain range.

연부(年賦), **연불**(年拂) annual installments. ¶ 5년 ~로 지불하다 pay by 〔in〕 yearly installments over a period of five years. ‖ ~상환 redemption by annual installments.

연분(緣分) a preordained tie; a predestined bond; fate; connection.

연분홍(軟粉紅) light 〔soft〕 pink.

연불(延拂) deferred payment. ¶ ~방식으로 on a deferred payment basis. ‖ ~수출 deferred-payment export; exporting on a deferred payment basis.

연비(連比) 〖數〗 a continued ratio.

연비(燃比) (gas) mileage; fuel-efficiency. ¶ ~시험 a mileage test / 1리터당 40km라는 효율적인 ~ the efficient mileage of 40km/1ℓ / 고~의 엔진 a fuel-efficient engine / ~가 낮은 차 a gas-guzzler 《美》 / 내 차는 ~가 높다 My car gives very high mileage.

연비(費費) fuel expense(연료비). ¶ 저 ~의 차 an economical car.

연비례(連比例) 〖數〗 continued proportion.《speaker》.

연사(演士) a lecturer; a (public)

연산(年産) an annual output.

연산(演算) 〖數〗 operation; calculation. ~하다 calculate; carry out an operation. ¶ ~을 잘 하다 be good at calculation 〔figures〕.

연상(年上) ~의 older; elder; senior / ~의 사람 one's senior / 3년 ~이다 be three years older than 《a person》; be three years 《his》 senior.

연상(聯想) association (of idea). ~하다 associate 《A》 with 《B》; be reminded of 《something》. ¶

…을 ~시키다 remind 《a person》 of 《something》; suggest 《something》 to 《a person》.
연서(連署) joint signature. ~하다 sign jointly. ¶ ~로 under the joint signature of…. ∥ ~인 사람 a joint signer; a cosignatory.
연석(宴席) a dinner party. ~을 베풀다 hold a banquet; give a dinner party.
연설(演說) a speech; an address (공식의); public speaking (행위). ~하다 make 〔deliver〕 a speech 〔an address〕; address 《an audience》. ~조로 in an oratorical tone / ~을 잘 하다 〔이 서투르다〕 be a good 〔poor〕 speaker / TV 에서 ~하다 make a television speech / 자연 보호에 관해 ~하다 speak on the conservation of nature. ∥ ~자 a speaker / ~회 a speech meeting / 즉석 ~ an impromptu speech. 「cre.
연성하갑(軟性下疳) 〖醫〗 soft chan-
연세(年歲) age; years. 「나이.
연소(年少) ~하다 (be) young; juvenile. ∥ ~자 a youth; one's junior (연하자); a minor (미성년자).
연소(延燒) ~하다 spread 《to》(불이); catch fire (건물이). ∥ ~를 막다 check the spread of the fire / ~를 면하다 escape the fire.
연소(燃燒) burning; combustion. ~하다 burn. ∥ ~성의 combustible; flammable / 완전 ~ complete combustion / 불완전 ~ imperfect combustion. ∥ ~물 combustibles.
연속(連續) continuity; (a) succession; a series 《of》. ~하다 continue; go on; last. ¶ ~적(으로) continuous(ly); consecutive(ly); successive(ly) / ~ 3주간 for three weeks running; for three consecutive weeks / ~적으로 일어난 이상한 사건 a series of strange events. ∥ ~극 a serial radio 〔TV〕 drama; soap (opera) / ~사진 sequence photographs / ~상영 consecutive showing of a film.
연쇄(連鎖) a chain; links; 〖生〗 a linkage. ∥ ~구균 a streptococcus / ~반응 a chain reaction (~반응을 일으키다 cause 〔start, trigger〕 a chain reaction) / ~점(店) a chain store / ~충돌 a chain collision.
연수(年收) an annual income.
연수(年數) (the number of) years.
연수(軟水) soft water.
연수(研修) (in-service) training; an induction course (신입 사원 동의). ~하다 study; train. ∥ ~생 a trainee / ~원 a training institute.

연습(演習) (익힘) (a) practice; an exercise; (a) drill; 《기동 훈련》 maneuvers. ~하다 practice; hold maneuvers. ¶ 야외 ~ field exercises / 예행 ~ a rehearsal / ~장 《군대의》 maneuvering ground.
연습(練習) practice; training; (an) exercise; (a) rehearsal 〔극의〕; a warming-up (경기 전의). ~하다 practice; train; drill; exercise; rehearse. ¶ 피아노를 ~하다 practice the piano / 라디오를 들으며 영어 회화를 ~하다 practice English conversation by listening to the radio / 영어 발음을 ~시키다 drill (practice) 《students》 the sounds of English 〔in English pronunciation〕 / 방과 후에 연극을 ~하다 rehearse the play after school. ¶ ~곡 an étude (프) / ~기(선) a training plane 〔ship〕 / ~문제 exercises 《in grammar》 / ~생 a trainee / ~경기 a practice (tune-up) game.
연승(連勝) consecutive (successive) victories. ~하다 win 《three》 successive 〔straight〕 victories. 「year.
연시(年始) the beginning of the
연시(軟柿) a fair 〔soft〕 persimmon.
연식(軟式) ¶ ~야구 rubber-ball baseball / ~정구 softball tennis.
연안(沿岸) the coast; the shore. ¶ ~의 on 〔along〕 the coast. ∥ ~경비대 the coastal guard / ~무역 coastal trade / ~어업 coastal 〔inshore〕 fishery / ~지방 a coastal region / ~항로 a coastal 〔coastwise〕 route 〔line〕.
연애(戀愛) love; affection. ~하다 be 〔fall〕 in love 《with》. ¶ 정신적 ~ platonic love / ~결혼을 하다 marry for love. ∥ ~결혼 a love match 〔marriage〕 / ~사건 a love affair / ~소설 a love story; a romance.
연액(年額) an annual sum 《of》.
연약(軟弱) weakness. ~하다 (be) weak; soft; 《약한 태도》 weak-kneed; feeble. ¶ ~한 지반 soft ground / ~해지다 weaken; grow effeminate / 나는 ~한 녀석은 질색이다 I have a weak fellow. ∥ ~외교 weak-kneed diplomacy.
연어(鰱魚) 〖魚〗 a salmon.
연역(演繹) deduction. ~하다 deduce; evolve. ¶ ~적(으로) deductive(ly).
연연하다(戀戀—) 《서술적》 be ardently attached 《to》; cling to 《one's position》.
연예(演藝) entertainment; a performance. ¶ ~란 the entertainment column / ~인 a public entertainer; a performer.
연옥(煉獄) purgatory.
연와(煉瓦) a brick. ☞ 벽돌.

연원(淵源) an origin; a source. ~하다 originate (in); take its rise (in). ¶ ~의 …을 더듬다 trace the origin of….

연월일(年月日) a date.

연유(緣由)《유래》(a) reason; a ground. ~하다 originate (from); be derived (from); be due to.

연유(煉乳) condensed milk.

연인(戀人) a lover (남자); a love, a sweetheart (여자). ¶ 한쌍의 ~ a pair of lovers.

연일(連日) every day; day after day. ¶ ~ 연야 day(s) and night(s). [reelected].

연임(連任) ~하다 be reappointed

연잇다(連一)《연결》 join (A) to (B); piece together; 《계속》 continue; be continuous. ¶ 연이어 one after another; continuously; successively.

연자매(研子一) a large millstone worked by ox (horse). [tool.

연장 a utensil; an instrument; a

연장(年長) ~의 older; elder; senior. ¶ ~자 an elder; a senior.

연장(延長) extension; elongation; renewal(계약 따위의). ~하다 prolong; extend; lengthen. ¶ 계약 기간을 ~하다 renew one's contract / 체재를 며칠간 ~하다 extend one's stay for a few days. ¶ ~선 an extension (line) / ~전《野》 extra innings; 《축구의》 extra time.

연재(連載) serial publication. ~하다 publish a series of (articles, stories). ¶ ~되다 appear (be published) serially (in a newspaper). ¶ ~만화 a comic strip; a serial comic / ~소설 a serial story.

연적(硯滴) an ink-water container; a water-holder.

연적(戀敵) a rival in love.

연전(年前) ¶ ~에 some years ago; formerly.

연전(連戰) ~하다 fight a series of battles. ¶ ~연승하다 win battle after battle; win (gain) a series of victories / ~연패하다 lose battle after battle; suffer a series of defeats.

연정(戀情) love; attachment. ¶ ~을 느끼다 feel attached to (a girl). [dress].

연제(演題) the subject (of an address).

연좌(連坐) ~하다 be implicated (involved) in (an affair). ¶ ~데 모 a sit-down (sit-in) demonstration.

연주(演奏) a musical performance; a recital (독주). ~하다 play; give a performance (recital) of. ¶ 피아노로 베토벤을 ~하다 play Beethoven on the piano. ¶ ~곡목 a (musical) program / ~여행 a concert tour / ~자 a performer; a player / ~회 a concert; a recital.

연주창(連珠瘡)《韓醫》 scrofula.

연줄(緣一) connections; (a) pull. ¶ ~을 찾다 hunt up personal connections / 그 회사에 좋은 ~이 있다 have good connections with the company / …의 ~로 through the good offices (influence) of… / ~을 통해 입사하다 enter a company through one's personal connection.

연중(年中) the whole year; (all) the year round; throughout the year. ¶ ~무휴《게시》 Open throughout the year / ~행사 an annual event.

연지(臙脂) (cheek) rouge; lipstick (입술의). ¶ 빰에 ~를 찍다〔바르다〕 rouge one's cheek; put rouge on one's cheek.

연차(年次) ¶ ~의 annual; yearly. ¶ ~계획 a yearly plan / ~보고 an annual report / ~유급휴가 an annual paid holiday / ~총회 an annual convention / ~휴가 an annual leave.

연착(延着) late arrival; delay. ~하다 arrive late; be delayed. ¶ ~될 예정이다 be expected to arrive (one hour) late.

연착(軟着) soft landing. ¶ 달에 ~하다 make a soft landing on the moon; soft-land on the moon.

연창(一窓) an outer window.

연천하다(年淺一) be short in years (time, age).

연철(鍊鐵) wrought iron.

연체(延滯)《지연》 (a) delay; 《체납》 arrears. ~하다 be delayed; be in arrears. ¶ 집세를 ~하고 있다 be in arrears with the rent. ¶ ~금 money in arrears / ~이자 overdue interest.

연체동물(軟體動物)《動》 a mollusk.

연출(演出) production; direction. ~하다 produce; direct. ¶ A씨의 「오셀로」 Othello produced (directed) by Mr. A. / ~가 a producer; a director / 《美》 ~효과 stage effects.

연충(蠕蟲) a worm; vermin.

연탄(煉炭) briquet(te). ¶ ~가스 중독 briquet gas poisoning / ~공장 a briquet manufactory / ~난로 a briquet stove / ~불 briquet fire / ~재 a used briquet.

연통(煙筒) a chimney; a stovepipe.

연투(連投) ~하다《野》 take the (pitcher's) mound in (two) consecutive games.

연판(連判) joint signature (seal). ~하다 sign (seal) jointly. ¶ ~장

a covenant (compact) under joint signature.
연판(鉛版) a (lead) plate; 〖印〗 a stereotype. ¶ ~을 뜨다 make a stereotype 《of》. ‖ ~공 a stereotyper / ~인쇄 stereotypography.
연패(連敗) a series of defeats; successive defeats. ~하다 suffer a series of defeats; lose 《three》 games straight (in succession).
연표(年表) a chronological table.
연필(鉛筆) a (lead) pencil. ¶ ~로 쓰다 write in (with a) pencil / ~을 깎다 sharpen a pencil. ‖ ~깎이 a pencil sharpener / ~심 the lead of a pencil.
연하(年下) ¶ ~의 younger; junior / ~의 사람 one's junior / 3살 ~이다 be three years younger than 《one》; be 《a person's》 junior by three years.
연하(年賀) the New Year's greetings. ¶ ~장 a New Year's card.
연하다(軟一) ① (안질기다) (be) tender; soft. ¶ 연한 고기 tender meat / 연하게 하다 soften; tenderize / 연해지다 become soft (tender). ② (빛이) (be) soft; mild; light. ¶ 연한 빛 a light color / 연한 차 weak tea.
연하다(連一) adjoin; be connected (linked) 《with, to》.
연한(年限) a period; a term. ¶ ~을 채우다 serve one's term. ‖ 재직~ a term of office.
연합(聯合) ~하다 combine; join; be combined (united); form a union. ¶ ~국 the Allied Powers; the Allies / ~군 the Allied Forces / ~작전 combined (joint) operations.
연해(沿海) the sea along the coast (바다); the coast (육지). ☞ 연안. ¶ ~의 coastal. ‖ ~어업 inshore (coastal) fishery.
연해주(沿海州) 《러시아의》 the Maritime Province of Siberia.
연행(連行) ~하다 take 《a person》 to 《a police station》.
연혁(沿革) 《역사》 the history 《of》; 《발달》 the development 《of》; 《변천》 changes.
연호(年號) the name of an era.
연화(軟化) ~하다 become soft; soften.
연화(軟貨) soft money (currency).
연회(宴會) 《give, have》 a dinner party; a banquet.
연후(然後) ¶ ~에 after 《that》; afterwards; (and) then.
연휴(連休) 《two》 consecutive holidays.
열 ten; the tenth (열째). 〖days.
열(列) 《일반적인》 a line; a row; 《세로의》 a file; a column; 《가로의》 a rank; 《차례를 기다리는 줄》 a queue; a line. ¶ ~을 짓다 form a line (row); line (queue) up / 2~ 종대(횡대) a double file (line).
열(熱) ① 《물리적인》 heat. ¶ ~의 thermic; thermal / ~을 가하다 (apply) heat 《to》 / ~을 발생하다 generate heat / ~을 발산하다 radiate (give off) heat / ~을 전하다 (흡수하다) conduct (absorb) heat. ‖ ~교환기 a heat exchanger / ~기관 a heat engine / ~기구 a hot-air balloon / ~오염 thermal pollution / ~용량 heat (thermal) capacity / ~원(源) a source of heat / ~전도율 thermal conductivity / ~처리 heat treatment (~처리하다 heat-treat) / ~팽창 (전도) thermal expansion (conduction) / ~효율 thermal efficiency. ② 《체온》 temperature; 《병으로 인한》 fever. ¶ ~을 재다 take 《a person's》 temperature / ~이 있다 have a fever; be feverish / ~이 내리다 one's fever subsides (goes down). ③ 《열의·열광》 enthusiasm; passion(열정); fever; craze(열광). ¶ 문학~ a craze for literature / 야구~ 을 올리다 be enthusiastic about baseball / ~을 식히다 dampen (chill) one's enthusiasm / ~이 없다 have no enthusiasm 《for》. ‖ 야구~ baseball fever; enthusiasm for baseball.
열가소성(熱可塑性) 〖理〗 thermoplasticity. ¶ ~의 thermoplastic. ‖ ~재료 thermoplastic material(s).
열강(列強) the (world) Powers.
열거(列擧) enumeration. ~하다 enumerate; list.
열경화성(熱硬化性) 〖理〗 a thermosetting property. ¶ ~의 thermosetting. ‖ ~수지 thermosetting resin.
열광(熱狂) (wild) enthusiasm; excitement. ~하다 go wild with excitement; be enthusiastic 《over》. ¶ ~적 (으로) enthusiastic (-ally); frantic(ally).
열기(熱氣) heat; hot air; 《열린 분위기》 a heated atmosphere; 《신열》 fever.
열나다(熱一) ① 《신열이》 develop fever; become feverish. ② 《열중·열심》 become enthusiastic 《about》. ③ 《화나다》 get angry; be enraged. ¶ 열 나서 out of resentment.
열녀(烈女) a virtuous woman.
열다 ① 《닫힌 것을》 open; unfold (펴다); undo (꾸러미를); unlock (열쇠로). ¶ 비틀어 (부숴, 억지로) ~ wrench (break, force) open / 열어 놓다 leave 《a door》 open. ② 《개설》 open; start. ¶ 가게를 ~ open (start) a store. ③ 《개최

hold; give 《a party》. ¶ 운동회를 ~ hold an athletic meeting. ④ 《개척》 clear 《land》; develop; open (up). ¶ 후진국에 길을 열어주다 open a path for the young; giving young people a chance.

열다² (열매가) bear (fruit); fruit.

열대 (熱帶) [地] the tropics. ¶ ~tropical. ‖ ~병 a tropical disease / ~성 저기압 a tropical cyclone / ~식물 a tropical plants / ~야(夜) a sweltering night / 어 a tropical fish.

열댓 about fifteen.

열도 (列島) a chain of islands; archipelago.

열등 (劣等) inferiority. ~하다 (be) inferior. ¶ ~한 inferior; poor. ‖ ~감 inferiority complex / ~생 a backward (poor) student.

열람 (閱覽) reading; perusal. ~하다 read; peruse. ¶ 일반에 ~토록 하다 provide 《books》for public reading. ‖ ~권 a library admission ticket / ~실 a reading room.

열량 (熱量) the quantity of heat; 《단위》 (a) calorie; 《발열량》 calorific value. ‖ ~계 a calorimeter.

열렬 (熱烈) ~한[히] ardent(ly); fervent(ly); passionate(ly). ¶ ~한 연애 passionate love / ~한 환영을 하다 give 《a person》 an enthusiastic welcome.

열리다 ① 《닫힌 것이》 open; be opened; be unlocked. ② 《모임·행사가》 be held; take place; 《개시》 begin; start. ¶ ~주최로 ~ be held under the auspices of…. ③ 《길이》 open; be open(ed). ④ 《승진의 길이》 be given a chance to rise 《in rank》. ④ 《열매가》 bear (fruit); (be in) fruit. ¶ 열매가 많이 열린 나무 a tree laden with fruits.

열망 (熱望) an ardent wish [desire]. ~하다 be eager 《anxious》 for 《after, to do》; long for. ¶ 우리는 평화를 ~하고 있다 We long 《are eager》 for peace.

열매 (a) fruit; a nut 《견과》. ¶ ~를 맺다 bear fruit; 《비유적》 produce a result; come to fruition.

열무 a young radish. ¶ ~김치 young radish kimchi.

열반 (涅槃) Nirvana 《梵》. [speech.

열변 (熱辯) 《make》 an impassioned

열병 (閱兵) a parade; a review. ~하다 review 《inspect》troops. ¶ ~식 a military parade; a review 《of troops》.

열병 (熱病) a fever. ¶ ~에 걸리다 catch 《suffer from》 a fever.

열분해 (熱分解) [化] pyrolysis. ~하다 pyrolyze.

열사 (烈士) a man of fervid loyalty; a patriot.

열사병 (熱射病) [醫] heatstroke.

열상 (裂傷) a laceration; a lacerated wound.

열석 (列席) ~하다 attend; be present 《at》. ‖ ~자 those present.

열선 (熱線) thermic [heat] rays.

열성 (列聖) successive kings; 《성인》 a number of saints.

열성 (熱誠) earnestness; enthusiasm; devotion 《헌신》. ¶ ~적인 earnest; enthusiastic; hearty. ‖ ~가 an enthusiast; a zealot 《열광자》 / ~분자 earnest [devoted] elements.

열세 (劣勢) inferiority. ¶ …보다 ~에 있다 be inferior in numbers [strength].

열쇠 a key. ¶ 사건의 ~ the key to the affair / ~로 열다 unlock with a key. ‖ ~구멍 a keyhole.

열심 (熱心) enthusiasm; eagerness. ¶ ~인 eager; enthusiastic; earnest / ~히 eagerly; earnestly; enthusiastically; hard / ~히 공부하다 be earnest about one's studies.

열십자 (一十字) a cross. ¶ ~의 cross-shaped / ~로 crosswise.

열악 (劣惡) ¶ ~한 inferior; poor / ~한 환경에서 일하고 있다 work under poor surroundings.

열애 (熱愛) ardent love. ~하다 love 《a person》passionately; be devoted 《to》.

열어젖히다 swing 《throw, fling》 open; 《열어 놓다》 leave [keep] 《a door》open.

열없다 ① 《열적다》(be) awkward; shy; self-conscious. ② 《성질이》 be timid; faint-hearted.

열역학 (熱力學) thermodynamics.

열연 (熱演) an enthusiastic performance. ~하다 perform [play] enthusiastically; put spirit into one's part.

열의 (熱意) zeal; enthusiasm. ¶ ~ 있는 eager; zealous; enthusiastic / ~없는 unenthusiastic; halfhearted / ~를 보이다 show zeal 《for》.

열이온 (熱—) [理] thermion.

열자기 (熱磁氣) thermomagnetism.

열전 (列傳) a series of biographies.

열전 (熱戰) a fierce fight; 《경기》 a hot contest; a close game.

열전기 (熱電氣) thermoelectricity.

열전류 (熱電流) a thermocurrent.

열정 (熱情) passion; ardor; fervor. ¶ ~적인 ardent; passionate; fervent. ‖ ~가 an ardent person; a hot-blood.

열중 (熱中) ~하다 become [get] enthusiastic 《about, over》; be absorbed 《in》; be crazy 《about》.

열차 (列車) a train. ¶ ~자동 정지 장치 an automatic train stop (생

열탕(熱湯) hot (boiling) water. ¶ ~ 소독을 하다 scald *a thing*; wash (disinfect) 《*a dish*》 in boiling water. ⌊ish﹞ rough.
열퉁적다 (be) rude; gawky; boorish.
열파(熱波) a heat wave.
열풍(烈風) a violent wind.
열풍(熱風) a hot wind.
열학(熱學) 【理】 thermotics.
열핵(熱核) 【理】 ¶ ~ 반응〔융합〕 thermonuclear reaction〔fusion〕 / ~전쟁 a thermonuclear war.
열혈(熱血) hot blood; ardor. ¶ ~한(漢) a hot-blooded man.
열화(烈火) a blazing fire. ¶ ~ 같이 노하다 be red with anger; be furious.
열화학(熱化學) thermochemistry.
열흘(열날) ten days; 〔십일째〕 the tenth (day).
엷다 ① 〔두께가〕 (be) thin. ☞ 얇다. ② 〔빛이〕 (be) light; pale; faint. ¶ 엷은 빛(깔)의 light-colored.
염(念) ☞ 염불(念佛).
염가(廉價) a low〔moderate〕 price; a bargain rate. ¶ ~의 cheap; low-priced / ~로 팔다 sell 《*things*》 cheap〔at low prices〕. ‖ ~판(版) a cheap〔popular〕 edition / ~품 low-priced goods.
염갱(鹽坑) a salt mine. ⌊abhor.
염기(厭忌) ~하다 dislike; detest⌉
염기(鹽基) 【化】 a base. ¶ ~성의 basic.
염도(鹽度) salinity. ⌊basic.
염두(念頭) ¶ ~에 두다 bear〔keep〕 《*a thing*》 in mind / ~에 두지 않다 do not care 《*about*》 / ~에서 떠나지 않다 〔사람이 주어〕 be unable to forget; cannot put *something* out of one's mind; 《사물이 주어》 be always in one's mind.
염라대왕(閻羅大王) *Yama* 【梵】: the King of Hell.
염려(念慮) anxiety; worry; apprehension; care; concern. ~하다 worry; be concerned〔worried〕; feel anxious〔concern〕 《*about*》; have apprehension 《*of*》. ¶ 아이들의 안전을 ~하다 be anxious 〔concerned〕 about *one's* children's safety.
염료(染料) dyes; dyestuffs; coloring material. ‖ ~공업 the dye industry / 질산염 ~ nitro dyes.
염매(廉賣) a low〔bargain〕 price sale. ~하다 sell cheap; sell at a bargain.

염모제(染毛劑) a hair-dye.
염문(艶聞) a love affair; a romance.
염병(染病) ① ☞ 장티푸스. ¶ ~할 Damn (Hang) it! ② ☞ 전염병.
염복(艶福) good fortune in love. ¶ ~가 a ladies' man.
염분(鹽分) salt; salinity. ¶ ~있는 saline; salty / ~을 없애다 desalt; desalinate.
염불(念佛) a Buddhist invocation. ~하다 pray (offer prayers) to *Amitabba*.
염산(鹽酸) 【化】 hydrochloric acid.
염색(染色) dyeing. ~하다 dye. ‖ ~공장 a dye works / ~체 【生】 a chromosome.
염서(炎暑) intense heat.
염세(厭世) pessimism; weariness of life. ¶ ~적인 pessimistic. / ~자살하다 kill *oneself* in despair; despair of life and kill *oneself* / ~주의 pessimism / ~주의자 a pessimist.
염소 a goat. ¶ 암 ~ a she-goat / 숫 ~ a he-goat / 새끼 ~ a kid; a young goat / ~가 울다 A Goat bleats. ‖ ~가죽 goatskin / ~수염 a goatee / ~자리 【天】 the Goat; the Capricorn.
염소(鹽素) 【化】 chlorine (기호 Cl).
염소(鹽素)산 chloric acid.
염수(鹽水) salt water; brine.
염습(殮襲) ~하다 wash and dress the deceased.
염오(厭惡) loathing; abhorrence. ~하다 detest; loathe; abhor.
염원(念願) *one's* heart's desire. ~하다 desire; wish 《*for*》.
염전(鹽田) a saltpan.
염좌(捻挫) a sprain. ☞ 삐다.
염주(念珠) a rosary; (a string of) beads. ¶ ~알 a bead(한 개); the beads of a rosary.
염증(炎症) inflammation. ¶ ~을 일으키다 be (become) inflamed.
염증(厭症) an aversion; a dislike; disgust; a repugnance. ¶ ~이 나다 be weary (sick) 《*of*》; be fed up 《*with*》.
염직(染織) ~하다 dye and weave.
염천(炎天) hot weather; the burning sun.
염출(捻出) 〔비용 등을〕 ~하다 (manage to) raise 《*money*》; scrape up.
염치(廉恥) a sense of honor 〔shame〕. ¶ ~없는 사람 a shameless fellow / ~가 없다 be shameless; have no sense of honor.
염탐(廉探) ~하다 spy upon 《*the enemy's movement*》; feel (smell) out 《*a plot*》. ‖ ~꾼 a spy; ⌊secret agent.
염통 the heart.⌉
염화(鹽化) chloridation. ~하다 chloridize. ‖ ~나트륨 sodium chloride / ~물 a chloride /

비닐 vinyl chloride. 「dog.
엽견(獵犬) a hound; a hunting
엽관운동(獵官運動) office hunting (seeking). ¶ ~하다 run (hunt) for office.
엽궐련(葉―) a cigar. 「office.
엽기(獵奇) ¶ ~적인 bizarre; macabre. ‖ ~소설 a bizarre story.
엽록소(葉綠素) 〖植〗chlorophyl(l).
엽맥(葉脈) 〖植〗the veins of a leaf.
엽색(獵色) debauchery. ‖ ~가 a debauchee; a lecher.
엽서(葉書) a postal card (관제); a postcard (사제); a postcard (英).
엽전(葉錢) a brass coin.
엽초(葉草) leaf tobacco. 「gun.
엽총(獵銃) a hunting (sporting)
엿 wheat gluten; taffy; (a) candy. ¶ ~가락 a stick of taffy (wheat gluten) / ~장수 a wheat gluten vendor.
엿² 〖여섯〗 six.
엿기름 malt; wheat germ.
엿듣다 overhear; listen secretly; eavesdrop; 《도청》 tap 《wires》; bug.
엿보다 〖기회를〗 look (watch, wait) for 《a chance》; 〖상대를〗 see; spy on; 〖안을〗 peep into (through); 〖슬쩍〗 steal a glance at.
엿새 〖엿샛날〗 the sixth day (of a month); 〖여섯날〗 six days.
영(令) 〖명령〗 an order; a command; 〖법령〗 an ordinance; a law; a decree; an act. ¶ ~을 내리다 command; order / ~을 어기다 disobey an order; act contrary to 《a person's》 order.
영(零) a zero; a nought; a cipher. ¶ 106번 one-o(-zero, -nought)-six (전화) / ~점을 맞다 get a zero 《in an examination》.
영(靈) the soul (spirit); the ghost 《of a dead person》. ¶ ~적인 spiritual.
영감(令監) 〖존칭〗 lord; sir; 〖노인〗 an old (elderly) man; 〖남편〗 one's husband.
영감(靈感) (an) inspiration. ¶ ~을 받다 be inspired 《by》; get inspiration 《from》 / ~이 솟다 have a sudden inspiration.
영걸(英傑) a great man; a hero.
영겁(靈―) miraculous virtue (efficacy).
영겁(永劫) eternity. 「cacy).
영결(永訣) the last (final) parting; separation by death. ¶ ~하다 part forever; bid one's last farewell 《to》. ‖ ~식 a funeral ceremony (service).
영계(―鷄) a (spring) chicken. ‖ ~백숙 a boiled chicken with rice.
영계(靈界) the spiritual world; 〖종교계〗 the religious world.
영고(榮枯) rise and fall; vicissitudes. ‖ ~성쇠=영고.

영공(領空) territorial air (sky); airspace. ¶ ~을 날다 fly over 《Korean》 territory. ‖ ~침범 the violation of the territorial sky.
영관(領官) a field officer(육군); a captain, a commander(해군). ‖ ~급 장관 field grade officers.
영관(榮冠) the crown; 《win》 the laurels (월계관).
영광(榮光) honor; glory. ¶ ~스러운 glorious; honorable; honored; …의 ~을 가지다 have the honor of 《doing》.
영교(靈交) spiritual communion 《with》. ‖ ~술 spiritualism.
영구(永久) ☞ 영원(永遠). ¶ ~히 for good; forever; permanently / ~불변의 everlasting / 반~적인 semipermanent. ‖ ~성 permanency / ~자석 a permanent magnet / ~치(齒) a permanent tooth.
영구(靈柩) a coffin; a hearse; a casket (美). ‖ ~차 a (motor) hearse; a funeral car.
영국(英國) England; (Great) Britain; the United Kingdom (약칭 U.K.). ¶ ~의 English; British. ‖ ~국기 the Union Jack / ~사람 an Englishman; an Englishwoman (여자); the English (British) (총칭) / ~연방 the British Commonwealth of Nations.
영내(營內) ¶ ~의 within (in) barracks. ‖ ~거주 living in barracks / ~근무 service in barracks / ~생활 a barrack life.
영농(營農) farming. ~하다 farm; work on a farm; be engaged in farming. ‖ ~기계화 agricultural mechanization / ~인구 the farming population / ~자금 a farming fund.
영단(英斷) a wise decision. ¶ ~을 내리다 take a decisive step (drastic measures).
영단(營團) a corporation; a management foundation. ‖ 주택~ the Housing Corporation.
영달(榮達) advancement (in life); distinction. ¶ ~을 바라다 hanker after distinction; aspire to high honor. 「freezing point.
영도(零度) zero (degrees); the
영도(領導) leadership. ~하다 take the lead; lead 《a party》; head. ¶ …의 ~하에 under the leadership (direction) of…. ‖ ~자 a leader.
영락(零落) ruin; downfall. ~하다 fall low; be ruined; sink in the world; be reduced to poverty.
영락없다(零落―) be invariably right; (be) infallible; unfailing. ¶ 영락없이 without any slip; without fail; infallibly; for sure.

영령(英靈) the spirit of the departed (war heroes). ¶ ~이여 고이 잠드소서 May your noble soul rest in peace.

영롱(玲瓏) ~하다 (be) brilliant; clear and bright.

영리(怜悧) ¶ ~한 wise; clever; bright; intelligent; smart.

영리(營利) moneymaking; profit; gain. ¶ ~적(인) profit-making; commercial / ~에 급급하다 be intent on gain. ‖ ~사업 a commercial (profit-making) enterprise / ~주의 commercialism.

영림(營林) forestry. ‖ ~서 a local forestry office.

영매(靈媒) a medium.

영면(永眠) death. ~하다 die; pass away; go to one's long rest.

영명하다(英明 —) (be) clever; bright; intelligent.

영묘하다(靈妙 —) (be) miraculous; mysterious; marvelous.

영문 ①《영편》 the situation; circumstances. ¶ 무슨 ~인지 모르다 be unable to make out what it's all about; do not know what's what. ②《까닭》 (a) reason; a cause(원인); the matter. ¶ ~도 없이 without (any) reason (cause).

영문(英文) English; an English sentence. ¶ ~으로(의) in English / ~을 잘 쓰다 write good English. ‖ ~법 English grammar / ~타자기 an English typewriter / ~편지 a letter in English / ~학 English literature / ~(학)과 the department of English language and literature / ~학자 a scholar of English literature / ~한역 translation from English into Korean / ~해석 interpreting an English text.

영문(營門) the gate of military facilities (barracks).

영물(靈物) a spiritual being.

영미(英美) Britain and America. ¶ ~의 English and American; Anglo-American.

영민(英敏) ~하다 (be) bright; intelligent; clever; sagacious; acute.

영별(永別) ~하다 part forever.

영봉(靈峰) a sacred mountain.

영부인(令夫人) your (his) esteemed wife; Mrs. 《Lee》.

영사(映寫) projection. ~하다 project; screen 《a film》. ‖ ~기 a projector / ~막 a screen / ~시간 the running time 《of a film》 / ~실 a projection room.

영사(領事) a consul. ¶ 마닐라 주재 한국 ~ the Korean consul at Manila. ‖ ~관 a consulate / ~관원 a consular officer; the staff of a consulate (총칭) / ~재판권 consular jurisdiction.

영상(映像) 《마음의》 an image; 《TV의》 a picture; 《거울·수면 위의》 a reflection. ¶ 레이더에 비치는 ~ a blip on the radar screen / 선명한 (흐릿한) ~ a clear (blurred) picture.

영생(永生) eternal life; immortality. ~하다 live eternally.

영선(營繕) building and repairs. ‖ ~과(課) a building and repairs section / ~비 building and repairing expenses.

영성(靈性) spirituality; divinity.

영세(永世) all ages; eternity. ‖ ~중립 permanent neutrality / ~중립국 a permanently neutral state.

영세(零細) ~하다 (be) small; petty; trifling. ‖ ~기업 a small business / ~농 a petty farmer / ~민 《총칭》 the destitute; the poor / ~업자 a small-scale businessman.

영속(永續) ~하다 last long; remain permanently. ¶ ~적인 lasting; permanent / ~성 permanence.

영송(迎送) ~하다 welcome and send off; meet and see off.

영수(領收) receipt. ~하다 receive. ¶ 일금 1만원정 확실히 ~함 I certainly received the sum of ₩ 10,000. ‖ ~증 a receipt / ~필 Paid.

영수(領袖) a leader; a head. ¶ 파벌의 ~ the leader of a political faction.

영시(英詩) English poetry(총칭); an English poem(시편).

영시(零時) twelve o'clock; noon (정오); midnight(자정).

영식(令息) your (his, her) son.

영아(嬰兒) an infant; a baby. ¶ ~살해 infanticide.

영악하다 (be) smart; shrewd.

영악하다(獰惡 —) fierce; ferocious.

영안실(靈安室) a mortuary (of a hospital). ¶ ~에 안치하다 place a dead body in a mortuary of a hospital.

영애(令愛) your (his, her) daughter.

영약(靈藥) a miraculous medicine; a miracle drug.

영양(羚羊) an antelope; a goral.

영양(營養) nourishment; nutrition. ¶ ~ 상태가 좋은 (나쁜) well-(ill-) nourished / ~식품 nourishing food / ~이 없는 식품 food lacking in nutrition. ‖ ~가 nutritive value / ~물 nutriments; nutritious food / ~불량 undernourishment / ~불량의 undernourished; ill-fed / ~사 a dietitian (dietician) / ~소 a nutrient /

영어 ~실조 malnutrition / ~장애 nutrition disorder [lesion] / ~학 dietetics.

영어(囹圄) a prison. ¶ ~의 몸이 되다 be put in prison [jail]; be incarcerated.

영어(英語) English; the English language. ¶ ~의 English / ~(speak) in English / ~의 실력 one's knowledge of English / ~를 말하다 speak English / ~를 잘하다 (가 서투르다) be good [poor] at English / ~로 쓰다 write in English / ~로 번역하다 translate [put] into English. ‖ ~ 교사 an English teacher / ~ 교육 the teaching of English; English teaching / ~권 the English-speaking world [community] / ~학 English linguistics.

영어(營漁) fishing; fishery. ‖ ~자금 a fishery fund.

영업(營業) business; trade. ~하다 do [carry on, run] business. ¶ ~용의 for business / ~하고 있다 be in business; be open for business / ~상의 비밀 a trade secret / ~중 (게시) Open. ‖ ~방식 business methods / ~방침 a business policy / ~방해 obstruction of business / ~보고 [부, 세] a business report (department, tax) / ~성적 business (trading) results (performance) / ~소 a business office / ~시간 business hours / ~안내 a business guide; a catalog / ~정지 suspension of business / ~품목 a line of business / ~활동 business activities.

영업권(營業權) right of trade [business]; goodwill. ¶ ~상점의 ~을 넘기다 transfer the goodwill of one's store / ~을 팔다 sell out one's business; sell the goodwill (of a shop).

영역(英譯) (an) English translation. ~하다 translate [put] into English.

영역(領域) ① ☞ 영토. ② 《학문·활동의》 a sphere; a field; a realm; a line. ¶ 과학의 ~ the realm of science / 그것은 내 ~이 아니다 That is not my field. or That is not in my line. or That's outside my sphere [field].

영역(靈域) a sacred ground; holy precincts.

영영(永永) forever; eternally; for good (and all).

영예(榮譽) honor; glory. ¶ ~로운 honorable; glorious.

영웅(英雄) a hero. ¶ ~적인 heroic.

영원(永遠) eternity; perpetuity. ¶ ~한 [히] eternal(ly); perpetual(ly); everlasting; permanent(ly). ‖ ~성 permanen-

영탄 cy; timelessness.

영위(營爲) ~하다 run; carry on; operate. ¶ ~삶을 ~하다 lead a life.

영유(領有) ~하다 possess; get (be in) possession (of).

영육(靈肉) soul and body. ‖ ~일치 the unity of body and soul.

영일(寧日) ¶ ~이 없다 Not a single day passes quietly.

영자(英字) English letters. ‖ ~신문 an English(-language) newspaper.

영장(令狀) a warrant; a writ; a written order. ¶ ~을 발부하다 [집행하다] issue [execute] a warrant.

영장(靈長) ¶ 만물의 ~ the lord of all creation. ‖ ~류 《動》 the primates.

영재(英才) (a) genius; (a) talent; a gifted person. ‖ ~ 교육 special education for the gifted.

영전(榮轉) ~하다 be promoted (and transferred) to (a higher post); be transferred on promotion.

영전(靈前) ¶ ~에 before the spirit of the departed [dead] / ~에 바치다 offer 《flowers》 to the spirit of a dead person.

영점(零點) 《무득점》 (a) zero; the zero point; no points. ¶ 시험에서 ~을 받다 get (a) zero [no points] on the examination.

영접(迎接) ~하다 welcome; receive 《company》; (go out to) meet.

영정(影幀) a (scroll of) portrait.

영제(令弟) your (his, her, etc.) esteemed younger brother.

영존(永存) ~하다 remain forever; exist permanently.

영주(永住) permanent residence. ~하다 reside [live] permanently; settle down (for good). ‖ ~권 the right of permanent residence; denizenship / ~자 a permanent resident / ~지 a place of permanent residence; one's permanent home.

영주(英主) a wise ruler.

영주(領主) a feudal lord.

영지(領地) 《봉토》 a fief; a feud; feudal territory. ¶ ~cred place.

영지(靈地) a holy ground; a sacred place.

영진(榮進) ~하다 achieve promotion.

영차 《이영차》 Yo-heave-ho! Yo-ho!

영창(詠唱) 《樂》 an aria.

영창(營倉) a guardhouse; detention barracks; a military jail.

영치(領置) ~하다 detain; deposit 《something》 in custody 《of the prison officer》. ‖ ~물 money and personal belongings deposited by inmates.

영탄(詠嘆) 《읊조림》 recitation; re-

영토(領土) (a) territory; (a) possession; (a) domain. ‖ ~권(權) territorial rights / ~ 확장 expansion of territory; territorial expansion.

영특하다(英特—) (be) wise; sagacious; outstanding.

영판 ① (맞힘) true (accurate) fortunetelling. ② (꼭) just like; (아주) very; awfully.

영패(零敗) ~하다 be shut out; fail to score. ¶ 가까스로 ~를 면하다 barely miss being shut out.

영하(零下) below zero; sub-zero. ¶ ~의 기온 a sub-zero temperature.

영한(英韓) English-Korean. ‖ ~ 사전 an English-Korean dictionary.

영합(迎合) flattery. ~하다 flatter; fawn upon; curry favor with.

영해(領海) territorial waters. ¶ 한국 ~ 내에서 within (inside) the territorial waters of Korea. ‖ ~선 territorial limits (12마일 ~선 the 12-mile limit of territorial waters) / ~침범 violation of territorial waters.

영향(影響) influence; effect (효과); an impact (충격); consequence (파급효과). ¶ 좋은 (나쁜) ~ a good (bad) influence / …에 ~을 주다 [미치다] influence…; affect…; have an influence (effect) (on) / …의 ~으로 under the influence of…; owing to / 정계에 큰 ~력을 가지다 have a big influence in politics.

영험(靈驗) ☞ 영검. ¶ ~이 있는 wonder-working; miraculous (amulets) / 그 신은 ~이 있다는 소문이다 The god is renowned for his ability to response the wishes of worshipers.

영혼(靈魂) a soul; a spirit. ‖ ~ 불멸(설) (the doctrine of) the immortality of the soul.

영화(映畵) a movie; a (motion) picture; a film; (총칭) the movies; the cinema (英). ¶ ~ 보러 가다 go to the movies (cinema) / ~를 개봉 (상영)하다 release (show) a film (movie) / ~화하다 film (a story); make a movie of. ‖ ~각본 a scenario / ~감독 a movie (film) director / ~검열 film censorship / ~관 a cinema theater; a movie house / ~배우 a movie (film) actor (actress) / ~제 a film festival / ~촬영소 a movie studio / ~팬 a film (movie) fan.

영화(榮華) prosperity; (번영) splendor; luxury. ¶ ~를 누리다 live in splendor; be at the height of one's prosperity / ~롭게 살다 live in luxury.

옆 the flank; the side. ¶ ~ side; next / ~에 (서) by the side (of); beside; at one's side; by; aside / ~방 a side (adjoining) room; the next room / ~모습 a profile; a side face / ~길 ~의 집 a house by the road / ~을 지나가다 pass by / ~으로 비키다 step aside / ~으로 눕혀 놓다 lay (a thing) on its side. (chest).

옆구리 the flank; the side (of the 옆바람 a side wind.

옆질 rolling. ~하다 《배가》 roll (from side to side).

옆집 (the) next door; the adjacent house. ¶ ~사람 one's (next door) neighbor.

옆찌르다 give a nudge in (someone's) side (with one's elbow).

예¹ (옛적) ancient (old) times; old days; former years. ¶ ~나 지금이나 in all ages.

예² ① (대답) yes; certainly; all right; no (부정의문에서); (출석) Yes, sir (madam, ma'am (美))!; (교실에서) Here (sir)!; Present, (sir)! / ~ 알았습니다 I see. / 기꺼이 해드리죠 Yes, with pleasure. ② (반문) Eh?, What?

예(例) ① (실례) an instance; an example; an illustration. ¶ ~를 들면 for instance (example) / ~를 들다 cite (give) an instance. ② (경우) a case. ¶ 유사한 ~ a similar case. ③ (관례) a custom; a usage; a precedent (전례). ¶ ~의 건 the affairs you know of.

예(禮) ① (경례) a salute; a bow. ¶ ~를 올리다 make a bow. ② (예법) etiquette; propriety; courtesy. ¶ ~를 다하다 show (a person) every courtesy.

예각(銳角) 【數】 an acute angle.

예감(豫感) a premonition; a presentiment; a hunch. ~하다 have a presentiment (of death); have a hunch. ¶ 불길한 ~ an ominous foreboding.

예견(豫見) foresight. ~하다 foresee.

예고(豫告) a (previous) notice; a previous announcement; a warning (경고). ~하다 give an advance notice; announce (notify, inform) beforehand (in advance); warn (a person) of. ¶ ~ 없이 without (previous) notice / 신간의 ~ an announcement of forthcoming books. ‖ ~편 (영화의) a trailer; a preview.

예과(豫科) a preparatory course (class, department) (for college). ‖ ~생 a preparatory (course) student.

예광탄(曳光彈) [軍] a tracer shell.
예규(例規) an established rule (regulation).
예금(預金) a deposit; a bank account; money on deposit. ~하다 make a deposit 《money in a bank》; place money on deposit. ¶ ~을 찾다 draw one's deposit 《savings》 《from the bank》. ∥ ~액 the deposited amount / ~이자 interest on a deposit / ~통장 a (deposit) passbook; a bankbook.
예기(銳氣) (animated) spirit; dash. ¶ ~를 꺾다 break (shake) one's spirits.
예기(豫期) 《기대》 expectation; anticipation; 《희망》 hope; 《선견》 foresight. ~하다 expect; anticipate; hope for; look forward to. ¶ ~치 않은 unexpected; unlooked for / ~한 대로 as was expected; as one expected.
예납(豫納) advance payment. ~하다 pay in advance; prepay.
예년(例年) an average 《a normal, an ordinary》 year 《평년》; every year 《매년》. ¶ ~의 annual; usual / ~보다 2할 감, 20 percent below normal / ~대로 as usual; as in other years / ~의 행사 an annual event.
예능(藝能) art; artistic accomplishments; 《연예의》 public entertainments; the performing arts. ¶ 향토 (민속) ~ folk entertainment. ∥ ~계(界) the world of show business; the entertainment world / ~과(科) art course / ~인 an artiste; an entertainer.
예니레 six or seven days.
예닐곱 six or seven.
예라 (비켜라) Get away!; Be off!; (그만뒤라) Stop!; (체념) Well then!. ¶ ~ 모르겠다 Well then, I'll have nothing more to do with it.
예리(銳利) ~하다 (be) sharp; acute; keen; sharp-edged.
예매(豫買) advance purchasing. ~하다 buy in advance.
예매(豫賣) advance sale; sale in advance. ~하다 sell 《tickets》 in advance. ∥ ~권 an advance ticket; a ticket sold in advance.
예명(藝名) a stage (professional) name; a screen name.
예문(例文) an illustrative sentence; an example.
예물(禮物) a gift; a present. ¶ 결혼 ~을 교환하다 exchange wedding presents.
예민(銳敏) ~하다 《감각이》 (be) sharp; keen; acute; sensitive; 《지적으로》 (be) quick-witted; shrewd. ¶ ~한 감각 keen (quick) senses / ~한 두뇌의 소유자 a sharp-witted person.
예바르다(禮一) (be) courteous; decorous; polite; civil.
예방(禮訪) a courtesy call. ~하다 pay a courtesy call on 《a person》.
예방(豫防) 《방지》 prevention 《of》; protection 《from, against》; 《경계》 precaution 《against》. ~하다 prevent; take preventive measures 《against》. ¶ ~의 preventive; precautionary / ~할 수 있는 preventable / ~화재 ~주간 Fire Prevention Week / ~은 치료보다 낫다 Prevention is better than cure. ∥ ~위생 preventive hygiene / ~의학 preventive medicine / ~접종 a vaccination; an inoculation / ~주사 a preventive injection (shot) / ~책 (조치) preventive measures; precautions.
예배(禮拜) worship; 《교회의》 church service. ~하다 worship. ∥ ~당 a church; a chapel / ~자 a worshiper / 아침 ~ morning service.
예법(禮法) courtesy; decorum; etiquette; propriety; manners. ¶ ~에 맞다 〈어긋나다〉 conform to (go against) etiquette.
예보(豫報) a forecast. ~하다 forecast. ¶ ~가 틀렸다 (맞았다) The forecast was wrong (accurate). / ~관 a weatherman; a forecaster.
예복(禮服) 《wear, be in》 full (formal) dress; ceremonial dress; 《군인용》 a dress uniform; 《야회용》 an evening dress.
예봉(銳鋒) a sharp point; the brunt 《of an attack (argument)》. ¶ 공격의 ~을 꺾다 blunt (break) the edge of an attack.
예비(豫備) ~하다 prepare (provide) for; reserve. ¶ ~의 reserve; spare 《여분의》; preparatory 《준비의》; preliminary 《예행의》. ∥ ~공작 spadework; preliminaries / ~교(校) a preparatory (prep) school / ~교섭 a preliminary negotiation / ~군 a reserve army; reserve troops / ~금 (비) a reserve (emergency) fund / ~병력 the effective strength of the reserves / ~역 (service in) the (first) reserve (~역이 되다 go into the reserve(s)) / ~역 대령 a colonel in the reserve(s) / ~조사 (지식) a preliminary investigation (knowledge) / ~타이어 a spare tire / ~회담 a preliminary conference.
예쁘다 (be) pretty; lovely; beautiful; nice.
예쁘장하다(스럽다) (be) rather lovely; comely; pretty.

예사(例事) a common practice; custom; usage; an everyday occurrence; an ordinary affair. ¶ ~롭다 (be) usual; ordinary; commonplace / ~가 아닌 unusual; extraordinary; uncommon.

예산(豫算) a budget; an estimate. ¶ ~을 짜다 make [draw up] a budget / ~을 삭감하다 cut down [reduce] a budget / ~안을 국회에 제출하다 present the budget bill to the National Assembly. ‖ ~ 결산 특별위원회 a special budget-settlement committee / ~편성 compilation of the budget / ~본 an original budget.

예상(豫想) (예기) expectation; anticipation; (예측) forecast; (추산) presumption; (어림) estimate. ~하다 expect; anticipate; forecast; presume; estimate. ¶ ~ 외의 [로] unexpected(ly) / ~ 외로 되다 come up to *one's* expectations / ~ 수확고 the estimated crop (*for this year*) / ~액 an estimated amount.

예선(豫選) (경기·시합 등의) a preliminary match [contest]; an elimination round (contest, heat); a trial heat (game) / (선거의) a provisional election; a pre-election; (美) a primary (election). ~하다 hold a preliminary contest; (선거의) hold a pre-election. ¶ ~을 통과하다 qualify 《*for the semifinal*》; go through the preliminary match / ~에서 떨어지다 be rejected in the preliminary; be eliminated 《*from the tournament*》. ‖ ~통과자 a qualifier.

예속(隷屬) ~하다 be under the control [authority] of; be subordinate [subject] to; belong to. ‖ ~국 a subject nation.

예수 Jesus (Christ). ‖ ~교 Christianity / ~그리스도 Jesus Christ.

예술(藝術) art; the arts(학술). ¶ ~적인 artistic / 비~적인 inartistic / ~을 위한 예술 art for art's sake / ~적 재능 artistic talent / ~은 길고 인생은 짧다 (俗談) Art is long, life is short. ‖ ~가 an artist / ~사진 an artistic photograph / ~영화 an art film / ~원(院) the Korean Academy of Art / ~작품 a work of art / ~제 an art festival.

예습(豫習) preparations (of *one's* lessons). ¶ 내일의 ~을 하다 prepare *one's* lessons for tomorrow.

예시(例示) ☞ 예증(例證).

예시(豫示) ~하다 indicate; adumbrate; foreshadow.

예식(禮式) (예의) etiquette; manners; (의식) a ceremony; a rite. ‖ ~장 a ceremony [wedding] hall.

예심(豫審) [法] a preliminary hearing (trial, examination).

예약(豫約) (좌석·배 따위) booking; reservation; (출판물의) subscription; (상품의) an advance order; (병원 등의) an appointment. ~하다 reserve 《*a seat*》; book 《*a ticket*》; have 《*a room*》 reserved; make an appointment 《*with one's doctor*》; subscribe 《*for*》. ¶ ~취소하다 cancel a reservation / 방의 ~을 해야 합니까 Do I need a reservation of the room? / 호텔에 방을 ~하다 reserve (book) a room at the hotel / 이 테이블은 ~이 되어 있다 This table is reserved. ‖ ~계(係) a reservation desk / ~금 a deposit / ~모집 invitation for subscription / ~석 a reserved seat; (게시) Reserved / ~자 a subscriber / ~출판 publication by subscription.

예언(豫言) a prophecy; a prediction. ~하다 prophesy; foretell; predict; make a prediction. ¶ ~자 a prophet; a prophetess(여자).

예외(例外) an exception. ¶ ~의 exceptional; ~ 없이 without exception / ~를 인정하지 않다 admit of no exception / 올해는 ~적으로 덥다 This year's heat is exceptional.

예우(禮遇) a cordial reception. ~하다 receive 《*a person*》 courteously [cordially]. [assiduously.

예의(銳意) (부사적) in earnest;]

예의(禮儀) courtesy; politeness; civility; manners; etiquette. ¶ ~바른 courteous; polite / ~를 지키다 observe good manners. ‖ ~ 범절 the rules of etiquette.

예인선(曳引船) a tugboat; a towboat. [(appreciation).]

예장(禮狀) A letter of thanks

예장(禮裝) ~하다 wear ceremonial dress; be in full dress.

예전 old days; former days (times). ¶ ~의 old; ancient; former / ~부터 from old times / ~대로 as of old; as usual.

예절(禮節) propriety; decorum; etiquette; manners.

예정(豫定) a plan; a program; a schedule; (그) previous arrangement. ~하다 schedule; expect (예상); arrange in advance; pre-arrange; (계획하다) plan; make a plan; 《…할 계획이다》 intend (plan) *to do*. ¶ ~한 시간에 on scheduled time; at the appointed time / ~대로 as expected (planned); according to schedule. ‖ ~

an estimated amount / ~일 a prearranged date; 《출산의》 the expected date of confinement / ~표 a schedule; a program / 《졸업》~자 an expectant (graduate). 「cise (연습).
예제(例題) an example; an exer-
예증(例證) an illustration; an example; an instance. ~하다 illustrate; exemplify.
예지(豫知) ~하다 foresee; forebode; know beforehand; foretell.
예지(叡智) wisdom; sagacity.
예진(豫診) a preliminary medical examination. ~하다 make a diagnosis in advance.
예진(豫震) a preliminary tremor.
예찬(禮讚) admiration; a high compliment. ~하다 admire; eulogize; speak highly of. ‖ ~자 an adorer; an admirer.
예측(豫測) prediction; forecast; expectation. ~하다 predict; foretell; forecast; estimate.
예치금(預置金) a deposit; [簿] deposits received.
예탁(豫託) ~하다 deposit 《money with a bank》.
예편(豫編) ~하다 transfer to the 《first》 reserve; place on the reserve list. ¶ ~되다 go into the first reserve; be placed (registered) on the reserve list.
예포(禮砲) a salute (gun). ¶ ~를 쏘다 fire a salute 《of 21 guns》.
예항(曳航) ~하다 tow; take 《a ship》 in (on) tow.
예행연습(豫行演習) a rehearsal; a preliminary drill (exercise). ~하다 rehearse; give (have) a rehearsal 《of a graduation ceremony》.
예후(豫後) [醫] prognosis (병세); convalescence (회복). ¶ ~가 좋다 convalesce satisfactorily.
옛 old; ancient. ¶ ~친구 an old friend / 그녀에게서 ~모습을 찾을 수 없다 She is but a shadow of her former self. or She is no longer what she used to be.
옛날 ancient times; old days. ¶ ~에 once upon a time / ~ 이야기 old tales / ~적 days long long ago.
옛말 ①《고어》 an archaic word. ②《격언》 an old proverb (saying).
옛사람 ancient people; men of old; 《죽은이》 the dead.
옛이야기 an old tale (story).
옛일 a past event; the past; a thing of the past; bygones.
옛추억(~追憶) one's old memory.
옜다 Here (it is [they are])!
오(五) five. ¶ ~ the fifth / ~ 배(倍) fivefold; quintuple / ~분

의 일 one fifth.
오(午)《십이지(十二支)의》 the Sign of the Horse. ¶ ~년 the year of the Horse. ¶ ~시 noon.
오(감동) Ah!; Oh!; O!
오가다 come and go. ¶ 오가는 사람들 passersby.
오가리 ①《호박의》 dried slices of pumpkin. ②《나뭇잎의》 curl.
오각형(五角形) a pentagon.
오경(五經) the Five Chinese Classics. 「mandments.
오계(五戒) the five (Buddhist) com-
오곡(五穀) the five cereals; (staple) grains. ‖ ~밥 boiled-rice mixed with four other cereals.
오관(五官) the five organs (of sense).
오구(烏口) a drawing pen.
오그라들다 curl up; shrink; contract; shrivel.
오그라뜨리다 ☞ 오그리다.
오그라지다 ①《오그라들다》 get curled (rolled) up; shrivel; become warped. ②《찌그러지다》 be crushed; be broken (wrecked). ¶ 오그라진 냄비 a broken pan.
오그랑장사 a losing business.
오그리다 ①《몸·발을》 curl 《one's body》 up; crouch; huddle; double up. ¶ 오그리고 자다 sleep curled up. ②《물건을》 bend (squeeze) out of shape; crush; smash; crumple.
오글거리다 ☞ 우글거리다. 「batter.
오금 the crook (hollow) of the knee. 「the move.
오금뜨다 gad about; be always on
오금박다 trap (corner) 《a person》 with his own words. 「(curve).
오금팽이 the inner side of a bend
오굿하다 (be) somewhat curved (crooked); dented.
오기(傲氣) an unyielding spirit. ¶ ~ (를) 부리다 try to rival 《another》; refuse to yield 《to》 / ~가 나서 in a spirit of rivalry.
오기(誤記) a clerical error; a miswriting; a slip of the pen. ~하다 miswrite; make a mistake in writing; write wrong.
오나가나 always; all the time; everywhere; all over; wherever one goes. 「right.
오냐(대답) yea; yes; well; all
오뇌(懊惱) agony; worry; mental anguish. ~하다 be in agony (anguish); have a mental struggle.
오누이, 오뉘 brother and sister.
오뉴월(五六月) May and June. ¶ ~ 긴긴 해 the livelong summer day.
오는《다음의》 next; coming. ¶ ~ 일요일에 on next Sunday; on Sunday next.
오늘 today; this day. ¶ ~부터

오늘날 the present time; these days; today; nowadays. ¶ ~의 한국 the Korea of today.
오늬 the notch 《of an arrow》.
오다 ① (일반적으로) come. ¶ 가지러 〔데리러〕 ~ come for 《a thing, a person》 / 이리 오너라 Come here. or Come this way. / 꼭 오너라 Be sure to come. ② (도착) come; reach; arrive 《at, in》. ¶ 자, 버스가 왔다 Here comes our bus. / 편지가 왔느냐 Has the mail come yet? / 봄이 왔다 Spring has come. or Spring is here. / 보러 ~ come to see; visit. ¶ 그는 종종 놀러 온다 He often comes to see us. / 오늘 밤 집에 오겠느냐 Won't you come over this evening? ④ (비·눈이) come on; drop; rain upon. ¶ 비가 ~ it rains. ⑤ (다가옴) come up; approach; come 〔draw〕 near. ¶ 금년은 겨울이 늦게 온다 Winter is late in coming this year. ⑥ (전래) be introduced 《into》; be brought 《from》. ¶ 미국에서 온 정치 사상 political ideas brought 〔introduced〕 from America. ⑦ (기인) derive from; come of 〔from〕; be caused by. ¶ 많은 영어 단어는 라틴어에서 왔다 Many English words come originally from Latin. / 이 사고는 그의 부주의에서 왔다 This accident comes of his carelessness.
오다가다 (어쩌다가) occasionally; at times; once in a while; now and then; (우연히) by chance; casually. ¶ 그녀와는 ~ 만난다 I see her once in a while.
오달지다 (여무지다) (be) solid; compact; (피륙이) (be) tight and strong; (사람이) (be) solidly built; firm.
오대양(五大洋) the Five Oceans.
오대주(五大洲) the Five Continents. 〔a large order.
오더 (주문) an order; 대양의 ~
오도(悟道) ─하다 (깨침) be spiritually awakened; be disillusioned; attain enlightenment.
오도독 with a crunching sound. ¶ ~ 뼈 cartilage; gristle.
오도방정 a rash act; frivolity. ¶ ~ 떨다 act frivolously; behave in a giddy way.
오독(誤讀) misreading. ~하다 misread; read wrong.
오돌오돌하다 (be) hard and lumpy; somewhat hard to chew; gristly.

오동나무(梧桐─) 〔植〕 a paulownia tree.
오동통하다 (be) (short and) chubby; plump. ¶ 뺨이 오동통한 아기 a baby with plump cheeks.
오두막(─幕) a hut; a shed; a shack; a shanty. ¶ ~을 짓다 put up a shanty.
오들오들 떨다 tremble; shiver; quiver. ¶ 무서워 ~ tremble with fear / 추워서 ~ shiver with cold.
오디 a mulberry. 〔bler.
오뚝이 a tumbling doll; a tumoras (포승) a rope for binding criminals. ¶ ~지다 have one's hands tied behind one's back.
오라기 a piece 〔scrap, bit〕 《of thread, cloth, paper》.
오라비니 a girl's older brother.
오락(娛樂) an amusement; (an) entertainment; (a) recreation; a pastime. ¶ 건전한 실외 ~ a good outdoor recreation / 눈으로 보는 ~ visual entertainment. ‖ ~시설 amusement 〔recreational〕 facilities / ~실 a recreation hall; a game room / ~잡지 a magazine for amusement / ~장 a place of amusement / ~프로 an entertainment program.
오락가락하다 come and go; move 〔go〕 back and forth. ¶ 비가 ~ rain off and on / 생사간을 ~ hover between life and death / 정신이 ~ go 〔become〕 insane 〔crazy〕; lose one's senses.
오랑캐 a barbarian; a savage.
오랑캐꽃 a violet. ☞ 제비꽃.
오래 long; for a long while 〔time〕. ¶ ~전에 long ago / ~된 old; ancient; antique; old-fashioned(시대에 뒤진); stale(음식물이) / 오랫동안 for a long time 〔while〕 / 오랜 습관 an old custom / 오래지 않아 before long / ~ 걸리다 take a long time / ~ 계속되다 last long / ~ 살다 live long / ~ 끌다 drag on; be prolonged; (병이) linger. ¶ 그 환자는 ~ 살지 못할 것 같다 I'm afraid the patient's days are numbered.
오래간만 ¶ ~에 after a long time 〔interval, absence, separation〕 / ~의 좋은 날씨 fine weather after a long spell of 《rain》 / ~일세 It has been a long time since I saw you last.
오래다 be a long time 《since》; be long-continued; (be) long. ¶ 나는 그 일터를 떠난지 오래되었다 A long time has passed since I left the job.
오래오래 for a long time; 《영원히》 forever; eternally.
오렌지 an orange. ‖ ~주스 orange juice.
오려내다 ☞ 오리다.
오로라 an aurora 〔pl. -s, -rae〕.

오로지 alone; only; solely; exclusively; wholly; entirely. ¶ ~ 너 때문에 solely for your sake / 그의 성공은 ~ 아내 덕분이다 His success is due entirely to his wife's support.

오류(誤謬) a mistake; an error; a fallacy. ¶ ~를 범하다 make a mistake; commit an error.

오륜(五倫) the five cardinal articles [principles] of morality.

오륜대회(五輪大會) ☞ 올림픽.

오르간 an organ. ¶ ~을 연주하다 play the organ. ‖ ~연주가[자] an organist.

오르내리다 ① (고저) go up and down; rise and fall; fluctuate (시세 따위가); be intermittent (단속적인). ¶ 오르내리는 열 an intermittent fever. ② (남의 입에서) be talked [gossiped] about.

오르다 ① (높은 곳에) rise; go up; climb; ascend; fly (날아서); soar (하늘 높이). ¶ 산에 ~ climb a mountain / 기세가 ~ be in high spirits / 계단을 ~ go up the stairs. ② (승진・승급) be promoted [elevated, advanced, raised]. ¶ 지위가 ~ be promoted to a higher position / 급료가 ~ get a pay raise. ③ (향상) progress; make progress (in); advance; improve. ¶ 성적이 ~ show a better school record. ④ (성과가) produce; achieve. ¶ 성과가 크게 올랐다 It produced excellent results. ⑤ (의제 등에) be brought up; be placed before; (식탁에) be served. ¶ 인사 문제가 의제에 올랐다 The personnel problem is brought up for discussion at the meeting. / 김치가 상에 올랐다 *Kimchi* is served at our table. ⑥ (화제에) be gossiped [talked] about. ¶ 그의 이상한 행동이 화제에 올랐다 His eccentricities were talked about. ⑦ (물가 따위가) rise; go up; advance (*in price*). ¶ 빵값이 올랐다 Bread has gone up in price. / 물가는 오르기만 한다 Prices go on rising. ⑧ (출발) start; head; (귀로에) leave for home. ⑨ (왕위) ascend (*the throne*). ⑩ (기록) be recorded [entered, registered] (*in, on*). ¶ 공적이 역사에 ~ one's achievement is recorded in history. ⑪ (탈것・탈것에) take; get on [into] (말에); (기차에) ~ get aboard a train / 연단에 ~ get on the platform. ⑫ 《병들이》 be infected [contracted]. ¶ 옴이 ~ be infected with [get] the itch. ⑬ (살이) grow fat; put on weight. ¶ 고기를 먹어 살이 ~ grow fat on meat. ⑭ (연기・김 따위가) rise; go up; 《불길이》 blaze up; go up (in flames).

¶ 굴뚝에서 연기가 ~ smoke rises from a chimney. ⑮ (물이) rise. ⑯ (나무의) ~ the sap rises. ⑯ (약이) ripen to full flavor (고추가); get angry (성이); (때가) get dirty. ⑱ (기세 등이) rise; become highspirited. ¶ 사기가 ~ become full of morale (fighting spirit). ⑲ (신・혼령 등이) possess; be possessed. ¶ 악령이 《사람에 주어》 be possessed by an evil spirit.

오락내리락 rising and falling; going up and down.

오르막 an uprise; an upward slope. ‖ ~길 an ascent [uphill road].

오른손 the right hand.

오름세 an upward tendency (*of the market*).

오리(鳥) a (wild) duck.

오리(汚吏) a corrupt official.

오리나무(植) an alder.

오리너구리(動) a duckbill.

오리다 cut off (out, away); clip (out) (*from*). ¶ 신문 기사를 ~ clip [cut out] an article from a newspaper.

오리목(一木)(建) a lath.

오리무중(五里霧中) ¶ ~이다 be in a fog (*about*); be all at sea.

오리발 a webfoot (물갈퀴).

오리온자리(天) Orion.

오리지널 original; the original book (원본); the original work (원작).

오막살이 (life in) a grass hut. ¶ ~하다 lead a hut life; be a hut-dweller.

오만(五萬) ① (수) fifty thousand. ② (잡다함) ever so much; innumerable. ¶ ~ 걱정 a lot [lots] of worries [troubles]; manifold vexations.

오만(傲慢) ¶ ~하다 (be) haughty; arrogant; overbearing.

오매불망(寤寐不忘) ¶ ~하다 remember when awake or asleep; bear in mind all the time.

오명(汚名) ① a bad name; a disgrace; a stigma. ¶ ~을 남기다 leave a bad name behind (*one*). ② ~ 누명.

오목(五目) a game of *paduk* with five checkers placed in a row.

오목 ‖ ~거울〔렌즈〕 a concave mirror (lens).

오목하다 (be) hollow; dented; sunken; concave. ¶ 오목한 눈 hollow [deep-sunken] eyes.

오묘(奧妙) ~하다 (be) profound; deep; abstruse; recondite.

오물(汚物) filth; dirt; muck; (부엌의) garbage; (주위의) night soil. ‖ ~ 수거인 a night-soil man (분뇨의); a garbage man; an ashman 《美》 / ~차 a

오물거리다

garbage truck / ~처리공장 a sewage purification plant / ~처리시설 sanitation facilities.
오물거리다 ① 《벌레 등이》 swarm; wriggle; squirm. ② 《입을》 mumble; chew on 《one's gum》.
오므라들다 shrink; contract; dwindle; get (grow) narrower; diminish in size.
오므라지다 《닫히다》 be closed; be shut; 《좁아짐》 become narrower.
오므리다 ① 《닫다》 close up; shut; pucker up 《one's mouth》; purse 《one's lips》. ② 《움츠리다》 ¶ 다리를 ~ draw in one's legs / 목을 ~ duck one's head / 몸을 ~ shrink 〖from〗.
오믈렛 an omelet(te). 〔from〕
오밀조밀하다(奧密稠密—) ① 《면밀》 (be) very meticulous; scrupulous. ② 《솜씨가》 (be) elaborate; exquisite.
오발(誤發) 《총기의》 accidental firing. ~하다 fire 《a gun》 by accident.
오버 ① 《외투》 an overcoat. ② 《초과》 ~하다 go over; exceed.
오보(誤報) an incorrect (a false) report; misinformation. ~하다 misreport; misinform; give a false report.
오보에 〖樂〗 an oboe. ∥ ~ 연주자 an oboist.
오불관언(吾不關焉) ~하다 be indifferent 《to the troubles of others》; assume an unconcerned air.
오붓하다 (be) enough; ample; substantial; sufficient. ¶ 오붓한 살림 a comfortable living.
오븐 an oven.
오비 an old boy 《생략 O.B.》; an alumnus 〖pl. -ni〗.
오빠 a girl's elder brother.
오산(誤算) (a) miscalculation. ~하다 make a wrong estimate; miscalculate; miscount.
오색(五色) ¶ ~의 five-colored.
오선지(五線紙) 〖樂〗 music paper.
오세아니아(大洋洲) Oceania.
오소리 〖動〗 a badger.
오손(汚損) stain and damage. ~하다 stain; soil; damage.
오솔길 a narrow path; a (lonely) lane.
오수(午睡) a nap. ☞ 낮잠.
오수(汚水) dirty (filthy) water; polluted water; sewage(하수); slops(구정물). ∥ ~관 a soil (waste) pipe / ~처리 sewage disposal (treatment) / ~처리장 a sewage treatment plant.
오순도순 in amity; on cordial terms; friendly; harmoniously.
오스카상(—賞) an Oscar.
오스트레일리아 Australia. ¶ ~의 (사람) (an) Australian.
오스트리아 Austria. ¶ ~의 Austrian / ~사람 an Austrian.

오자

오슬오슬 ¶ ~하다 feel a chill; feel (be) chilly; be shivery.
오식(誤植) a misprint; a printer's error. ~하다 misprint.
오신(誤信) ~하다 misbelieve; believe erroneously.
오십(五十) fifty. ¶ ~대에 in one's fifties / ~보 백보 There is little difference (not much to choose) between the two.
오싹오싹하다 shiver with cold; be chilly.
오아시스 an oasis.
오얏 a plum (tree).
오언절구(五言絶句) a quatrain with five syllables in each line.
오역(誤譯) (a) mistranslation. ~하다 make a mistake in translation; mistranslate.
오열(五列) the fifth column; secret agents.
오열(嗚咽) choking with sobs, sobbing. ~하다 sob; weep.
오염(汚染) contamination 《of water supplies》; (air) pollution. ~하다 pollute; contaminate; taint. ¶ ~되다 be contaminated (polluted, tainted) / 공장 폐수에 의한 하천의 ~ industrial pollution of a river / ~을 제거하다 decontaminate. ∥ ~도 the degree of contamination / ~물질 a pollutant; a contaminant / ~방지 prevention of 《air》 pollution; pollution control / ~방지장치 antipollution equipment / 수질 ~ water pollution.
오욕(汚辱) disgrace; dishonor.
오용(誤用) a misuse; wrong use; a misapplication. ~하다 use 《a thing》 for a wrong purpose; misapply.
오월(五月) May. 〔use; misapply.
오월동주(吳越同舟) bitter (implacable) enemies in the same boat.
오의(奧義) profound meaning; secrets; the mysteries 《of an art》.
오이 〖植〗 a cucumber. ¶ ~를 거꾸로 먹어도 제멋 《俗談》 Every man to his taste. or Tastes differ. or There is no accounting for tastes. ∥ ~생채 cucumber salad / ~소박이 stuffed cucumber kim-chi / ~지 cucumbers pickled in salt.
오인(吾人) 《나》 I. ② 《우리》 we.
오인(誤認) ~하다 misconceive; mistake 〔take〕 《A》 for 《B》.
오일(五日) five days 《닷새》; the fifth (day of the month).
오일 oil; gasoline. ∥ ~스토브 an oil stove / ~펜스 an oil fence.
오입(誤入) debauchery; dissipation. ~하다 indulge in debauchery; lead a dissolute life; frequent gay quarters. ∥ ~쟁이 a libertine; a debauchee.
오자(誤字) a misused [miswrit-

오장육부(五臟六腑) the Five Vital Organs and the Six Viscera.

오쟁이 a small straw bag. ¶ ~ 지다 be made a cuckold of.

오전(午前) the forenoon (morning); the a.m.

오전(誤傳) ☞ 오보.

오점(汚點) a stain; a blot; a blotch; a blur; a smear; 《결점》 a blemish; a flaw. ¶ ~을 남기다 leave a stain (*upon one's reputation*).

오정(午正) noon; midday.

오존(ozone). ‖ ~계(計) an ozonometer / ~층 an ozone layer (~층의 파괴 disruption (destruction) of the ozone layer).

오종경기(五種競技) pentathlon; five events. ‖ 근대 ~ modern pentathlon.

오죽 very; indeed; how (much). ¶배가 ~ 고프겠느냐 You must be very hungry.

오줌 urine; piss 《卑》; 《兒語》 pee. ¶ ~을 누다 urinate; pass (make) water; empty *one's* bladder; piss / ~을 참다 retain (hold) *one's* urine. ‖ ~싸개 a bedwetter.

오지(奧地) the interior; the hinterland; the back country 《美》.

오지그릇 pottery with a dark brown glaze; glazed earthenware.

오직(汚職) ☞ 독직(瀆職).

오직 《단지》 merely; only; 《오로지》 wholly; solely. ¶ ~ 돈벌이만 생각하다 be solely bent on moneymaking.

오진(誤診) an erroneous diagnosis. ¶ ~하다 make a wrong diagnosis; misdiagnose.

오징어 a cuttlefish; a squid. ‖ ~포 a dried cuttlefish.

오차(誤差) 〖數〗 an (accidental) error. ¶ ~ 허용 ~의 폭 a tolerance; an acceptable error range.

오찬(午餐) a lunch; a luncheon.

오케스트라 an orchestra.

오케이 O.K.; Okay; All right.

오토메이션 automation. ¶ ~화하다 automate (*a factory*).

오토바이 an autocycle; a motorcycle; a motor bicycle.

오톨도톨하다 ☞ 우툴두툴하다.

오트밀 oatmeal; porridge 《英》.

오판(誤判) (a) misjudgment; (a) miscalculation. ¶ ~하다 misjudge; error in judgment; miscalculate.

오팔 〖鑛〗 opal.

오퍼 〖商〗 an offer. ¶ ~를 내다 offer; make an offer (*for goods*) / ~를 갱신[수정, 연기]하다 renew [modify, extend] an offer / ~를 받다 receive an offer. ‖ ~상 a commission agent / 구매[판매] ~ a buying [selling] offer / 확정 ~ a firm offer. 「opera singer.

오페라 an opera. ¶ ~ 가수 an

오페레타 an operetta.

오펙 OPEC. (◀ the Organization of Petroleum Exporting Countries)

오프셋 〖印〗 an offset; a setoff 《英》. ‖ ~ 인쇄 offset printing.

오픈게임 an open game.

오피스 an office. ¶ ~ 걸 an office girl / ~오토메이션 《사무자동화》 office automation (생략 OA).

오한(惡寒) a chill; a cold fit; 〖醫〗 rigor. ¶ ~이 나다 feel (have, catch) a chill.

오합지졸(烏合之卒) 《규율 없는》 a disorderly crowd; a mob.

오해(誤解) a misunderstanding; misconception. ¶ ~하다 misunderstand; misconceive; misconstrue (어구를).

오행(五行) 〖民俗〗 the five primary substance (elements) of the universe (*i.e.* metal, wood, water, fire and earth). 「Okhotsk.

오호츠크해(一海) 〖地〗 the Sea of

오후(午後) the afternoon; the p.m. ¶ 오늘[어제] ~ this [yesterday] afternoon.

오히려 ① 《차라리》 rather (better, sooner) (*than*); preferably. ② 《도리어》 on the contrary; instead.

옥(玉) jade; a precious stone; a gem; a jewel.

옥(獄) ☞ 감옥. ¶ ~에 가두다 put (*a person*) into prison.

옥고(獄苦) the hardships of prison life. ¶ ~를 치르다 groan in prison; serve *one's* term of imprisonment.

옥내(屋內) ¶ ~의 indoor / ~에서 indoors; within doors. ‖ ~ 경기 indoor games / ~ 배선 〖電〗 interior wiring; a service (an indoor) wire.

옥니 an inturned tooth. ‖ ~박이 a person with inturned teeth.

옥다 be turned (curved, bent) inward; 《밑지다》 suffer a loss.

옥답(沃畓) a rich (fertile) paddy field.

옥도(沃度) iodine (기호 I). (☞ 요오드). ¶ ~ 정기 tincture of iodine.

옥돌[一乭] a gem stone; jade.

옥동자(玉童子) a precious son.

옥바라지(獄一) ¶ ~하다 send in private supplies for prisoner.

옥사(獄死) ¶ ~하다 die in prison.

옥상(屋上) the roof; the rooftop 《美》. ‖ ~정원 a roof garden / ~ 주택 a penthouse.

옥새(玉璽) the Royal (Privy) Seal; the Seal of the Emperor.

옥색(玉色) jade green.

옥석(玉石) ① ☞ 옥돌. ②《옥과 돌》 gems and stones;《좋고 나쁜 것》 wheat and tares.《~을 가리다 discriminate "jewels from stones." ∥ ~구분(俱焚) indiscriminate destruction of the good and the bad alike.

옥소(沃素) iodine (기호 I).

옥수(玉手) ①《임금의 손》the king's hands. ②《고운 손》beautiful hands.

옥수수 maize; Indian corn (millet)《英》; corn《美》.

옥시풀【藥】Oxyful (상표명); oxygenated water.

옥신각신하다 wrangle; squabble; argue; have a petty quarrel.

옥안(玉顔) ①《용안》the king's face; the royal visage. ②《미인의》a beautiful (woman's) face.

옥양목(玉洋木) calico.

옥외(屋外) ¶ ~의 outdoor; out-of-door; open-air; outside / ~에서 in the open air; outdoors / out of doors. ¶ ~집회 an open-air meeting.

옥잠화(玉簪花)【植】a plantain lily.

옥좌(玉座) the throne; the Emperor's chair.

옥죄이다 get tightened [cramped]; be too tight for《one》.

옥중(獄中) ¶ ~의[에] in prison [jail]. ¶ ~기 a diary written in prison.

옥체(玉體)《임금의》the king's body; the person of the king;《편지에서》the noble body; your body; you.

옥타브【樂】an octave. ¶ 한 ~을 올리다[내리다] raise [drop]《one's voice》an octave higher [lower].

옥탄가(~價) octane value [number].

옥토(沃土) fertile [fat] land [soil].

옥토끼(玉~) a white rabbit.

옥편(玉篇) a dictionary of Chinese characters; a Chinese-Korean dictionary.

옥황상제(玉皇上帝) the Heaven; the highest of the heavenly gods of Taoism.

온(全部) all; whole; entire. ¶ ~ 세계(에) all (over) the world / ~ 몸 the whole body / 백성 the whole nation; all people.

온갖 all (the); every (possible, available); all sorts [kinds, manner] of; various. ¶ ~ 수단 every possible means; every step / ~ 준비를 갖추다 make every preparation《for》.

온건(穩健) ¶ ~하다 (be) moderate; sound; temperate. ¶ ~주의 moderatism / ~파 the moderate party; the moderates.

온고지신(溫故知新) taking lesson from the past. ¶ ~의 정신으로 임하다 try to find a guide into tomorrow by taking lessons from the past.

온기(溫氣) warmth; warm air.

온난(溫暖) ¶ ~하다 (be) warm; mild; genial; temperate. ¶ ~한 기후 a mild climate / 지구의 ~화 the global warming. ¶ ~전선(氣線) a warm front.

온당하다(穩當—) (be) proper; just; right; reasonable / 온당치 않은 improper; wrong; unreasonable.

온대(溫帶) the temperate zone. ¶ ~성 저기압 an extratropical cyclone. ¶ ~식물[동물] the flora [fauna] of the temperate zone.

온도(溫度) (a) temperature. ¶ ~를 재다 take the temperature. ∥ ~조절 thermostatic control / ~조절차 a thermostat / 실내(평균)~ the room [mean] temperature.

온도계(溫度計) a thermometer. ∥ 섭씨[화씨]~ a centigrade (Fahrenheit) thermometer.

온돌(溫突) *ondol*, the Korean under-floor heating system; a hypocaust.

온라인 ¶ ~의 on-line / ~화되다 go on-line / 은행의 ~이 한 시간이나 불통되었다 The on-line system in the bank was interrupted for an hour. ∥ ~방식 the on-line information processing system.

온면(溫麵) hot noodle soup.

온상(溫床) a hotbed; a warm nursery. ¶ 악[범죄]의 ~ a hotbed of vice [crime].

온수(溫水) warm water.

온순(溫順) ~하다 (be) gentle; meek; obedient; docile; genial.

온스 an ounce (생략 oz.).

온실(溫室) a greenhouse; a hothouse; a glasshouse; a forcing house (속성 재배용의). ¶ ~ 재배하다 grow《plants》under glass / ~재배된 꽃 flowers grown under glass; hothouse flowers / ~에서 자란 아이 (비유적) a boy [girl] brought up with too much tender care / 그는 ~에서 자랐다《비유적》His parents pampered him. *or* He has been overprotected. ∥ ~식물 a hothouse plant / ~효과 the greenhouse effect.

온유(溫柔) ~하다 (be) gentle; mild; tender; sweet; amiable.

온음(—音)【樂】a whole tone. ¶ ~계 the diatonic scale / ~표 a whole note《美》; a semibreve《英》.

온장고(溫藏庫) a heating cabinet.

온전(穩全) ~하다 (be) sound; intact; unimpaired; whole.

온정(溫情) a warm heart; kindly feeling; leniency (관대). ¶ ~ 있는 kindly; warm-hearted; lenient.

온종일(—終日) all day (long); the whole day.
온집안(가족) the whole family; all (members of) the family; (집의) (search) all over the house.
온채 the whole (entire) house.
온천(溫泉) a hot spring; a spa (광천). ¶~에 가다 visit (go to) a hot-spring resort. ∥ ~도시 a hot-spring town / ~요법 hot-spring therapy / ~장 a hot-spring resort; a spa.
온통 all; entirely; wholly; (전면) the whole surface; all over.
온폭(一幅) the overall width.
온혈동물(溫血動物) a warm-blooded animal.
온화(溫和) ¶~한 (인품이) gentle; quiet; mild-tempered; (기후 등이) mild; genial / ~한 성질 good temper; gentle nature / ~한 기후 a mild climate. ⦅mannered.
온후(溫厚) ¶~하다 (be) gentle; mild⦆
올(가닥) ply; strand; (피륙의) the warp. ¶~이 성긴 coarse / ~이 고운 직물 close texture.
올 올해, 금년. ¶~ 여름 this summer / ~해 안에는 before the end of this year.
올가미 ① (올무) a noose; a lasso; the rope. ¶~를 씌우다 put the rope on 《an animal》. ② (함정) a snare; a trap. ¶~를 놓다 lay a snare 《for》 / ~에 걸리다 be caught in a trap; fall into a snare.
올곧다 ① (정직) (be) honest; upright. ② (줄이) (be) straight; direct.
올되다 ① (피륙의 올이) (be) tight; fine; close. ② (조숙하다) (be) precocious; mature young. ③ 《곡식이》 (be) rareripe; ripen early.
올드미스 an old maid; a spinster.
올라가다 ① (높은 곳으로) go up; mount; climb; rise; soar (하늘로). ¶산(나무)에 ~ climb a mountain (tree) / 연단에 ~ mount (step on) the platform / 지붕에 ~ get on the roof. ② (상경) go up (to Seoul). ③ (승진·승급) rise; be promoted (raised) / 봉급이 ~ have one's salary raised. ¶지위가 ~ rise in rank. ④ (진보) advance; make progress 《in》. ¶성적이 ~ show a better school record. ⑤ (물가가) advance in price; go up; rise. ¶값이 ~ the price goes up; rise (advance) in price. ⑥ (강을) go (sail) up 《a river》.
올라서다 (높은 데로) get up a higher place; mount (ascend) 《a platform》; get on.
올라오다 come up 《to Seoul》; step up 《on the stage》.

올리다 ① (위로) raise; lift (up). ¶손을 ~ raise (hold up) one's hand / 기를 ~ lift (hoist, fly) a flag. ② (값·월급·지위·속도·온도 등을) raise; promote; increase. ¶쌀값을 ~ raise the price of rice / 월급을 ~ raise 《a person's》 salary / 아무의 지위를 한 급 ~ promote 《a person》 to a higher class (rank) / 방의 온도를 ~ raise the temperature of the room / 속도를 ~ increase (put on) speed. ③ (바치다) lay (place) 《flowers on a tomb》. ¶기도를 ~ offer a prayer. ④ (기록) put on record; enter 《a name》. ¶명단에 이름을 ~ enter a name on the list. ⑤ (성과·이익 등을) ¶좋은 성과를 ~ (사람이 주어) get good results; (사물이 주어) produce satisfactory results / 이익을 ~ (사물이 주어) bring 《a person》 a profit / 백만 원의 순이익을 ~ (사람이 주어) make a net profit of one million won. ⑥ (소리를) raise 《one's voice》; give (utter) 《a scream》. (기세를) raise (boost) 《a person's》 morale; raise (lift) 《a person's》 spirits. ¶환성을 ~ set up a shout of joy. ⑦ (식을) hold 《a ceremony》; celebrate. ¶결혼식을 ~ hold a wedding.
올리브 an olive. ∥ ~유 olive oil.
올림 (증정) presentation.
올림픽 the Olympic games; the Olympics; the (16th) Olympiad. ¶한국을 대표해서 ~에 나가다 represent Korea in the Olympic games / ~에서 금메달을 따다 win a gold medal at the Olympics / ~ 기록 an Olympic record / ~ 선수 an Olympic sportsman (athlete(육상의), swimmer(수영의)); a member of the Olymic team / ~의 성화 the Olympic torch (fire). ∥ ~경기장 the Olympic stadium / ~촌 the Olympic village / 국제기능~ the International Vocational Training Competition / 국제~위원회 the International Olympic Committee (생략 I.O.C.) / 동계~ the Winter Olympic Games; the Winter Olympics / 프레~ the Pre-Olympics / 한국~위원회 the Korea Olympic Committee (생략 K.O.C.).
올망졸망 in lots of small pieces; in various sizes of small things.
올무 a noose.
올바로 (바르게) right(ly); properly; justly; (정직히) honestly; (정화히) correctly; (곧게) straight.
올밤 an early-ripening chestnut.
올빼미 an owl. ⦅coarse-woven.
올새 texture; weave. ¶~가 거친⦆
올차다 (be) stout; sturdy; solidly

올챙이 a tadpole. [build.
올챙이 robust; be of compact
올케 a girl's sister-in-law; the wife of a girl's brother.
옭다 옭아매다.
옭매다 tie in a knot; tie fast;
옭아매다 ①〈잡아매다〉bind; fasten (up). ¶ 통나무를 옭아매어 뗏목을 만들다 tie〔bind〕 the logs to make a raft. ②〈올가미로〉 put the noose on 《a dog》; tie the rope around 《a dog's neck》. ③〈죄를 씌우다〉entrap 《a person》 by trick *into do*ing; make a false charge against 《a person》.
옭히다 ①〈옭아지다〉be ensnared; be tied up. ②〈얽히다〉be tied in a knot; be tangled. ③〈걸려들다〉be implicated 《involved, entangled》 《in a case》.
옮기다 ①〈이전〉remove 《move》 《to, into》; transfer. ¶ 교외로 ~ move to the suburbs. ¶〈액체 따위를〉transfuse; pour 《empty》 《into》. ¶ 간장을 통에서 병으로 ~ pour soy sauce from the cask into bottles. ②〈이송〉 transfer; carry 《to》. ¶ 사건을 대법원으로 ~ carry a case to the Supreme Court. ④〈전염〉give; infect; pass 《a disease》 on 《to a person》. ¶ 그가 나에게 감기를 옮겼다 He has given me his cold. ⑤〈말을〉pass 《it》 on. ¶ 말을 남에게 ~ pass words on to another. ⑥〈번역〉translate 《English》 into 《Korean》. ⑦〈돌리다〉divert; turn; direct. ¶ 집으로 발을 ~ direct one's steps toward home. ⑧〈상태를 바꾸다〉 계획을 실행에 ~ put 〔carry〕 a plan into effect 〔execution〕.
옮다 ①〈이전〉move 《to, into》. ¶ 부산서 서울로 ~ move from Pusan to Seoul. ②〈감염〉 be infected 《with diphtheria》; catch 《a disease from a person》.
옮아가다 ①〈이사·전근하다〉move away 《to a place》; change quarters. ②〈퍼져가다〉be diffused; spread 《to》. ¶ 불이 옆집으로 옮아갔다 The fire spread to the house next door. ③〈넘어감〉 move 《to, into》; turn 《to》. ¶ 화제는 재정 문제로 옮아갔다 Our talk turned to the financial problems.
옳다 ①〈정당하다〉(be) right; rightful; ②〈옳으시다〉(be) righteous; just; ③〈참되다〉(be) true; truthful; ④〈맞다〉(be) right; correct; accurate; ⑤〈적절하다〉(be) proper; ⑥〈합법적이다〉(be) legal; lawful. ¶ 옳은 대답 the 〔right〕 answer / 옳은 해결 the right solution / 옳은 통계 an accurate statistics / 옳은 일을 하다 do the right thing / 옳은 한국어를 말하다 speak proper Korean.
옳다² 〈감탄사〉Right!; O.K.!; All right!; Right you are! ¶ ~, 됐다 Now I've got it.
옳은길〈바른길〉the right path 〔track〕. ¶ ~로 이끌다 guide 《a person》 into the right path.
옳은말 true 〔right〕 words; righteous remarks.
옳지 Good!; Right!; Yes!
옴¹〔醫〕the itch; scabies.
옴²〔理〕an ohm. ¶ ~의 법칙 the Ohm's law.
옴쭉달싹 ¶ ~ 않다 do not move 〔stir〕 an inch; stand as firm as a rock.
옴츠리다 duck 《one's head》; shrink; huddle *oneself* up. ☞ 움츠리다.
옷〈의복〉clothes; dress; garments; clothing. ¶ ~ 한 벌 a suit of clothes / 가벼운 ~ light clothes for summer wear / ~을 입다〔벗다〕put on〔off〕clothes; dress 〔undress〕 *oneself* / ~의 치수를 재다 measure 《a person》 for *his* clothes.
옷가슴 the breast 《of a garment》.
옷감 cloth; dress 〔suit〕 material; stuff.
옷걸이 a coat 〔dress〕 hanger; a clothes rack 〔suspender〕.
옷고름 a breast-tie; a coat string.
옷깃 the collar 〔neck〕 of a coat.
옷단 a hem; a fly.
옷자락 the hem 《of a skirt》; the bottom 〔lower〕 edge 《of a dress》; the skirt 《of a gown》.
옷장(─欌) a clothes chest; a wardrobe.
옷차림 *one's* attire.
옹(翁) an aged man. ¶ 김 ~ the old Mr. *Kim*.
옹고집(壅固執) stubbornness; obstinacy; 《사람》 an obstinate person. ¶ ~ 부리다 be stiff-necked.
옹골지다 (be) full; substantial; solid; hard.
옹골차다 (be) solid; hard; sturdy.
옹기(甕器) earthenware; pottery. ¶ ~장수〔전〕a pottery 《an earthenware》dealer 〔shop〕 / ~장이 a potter.
옹기종기〔gathered〕 in a small, closely group; in a cluster 〔flock〕. [a small fountain.
옹달… small and hollow. ¶ ~샘
옹립(擁立) back 〔bring〕 up; support; help 《a prince》 to 《the throne》. [wall: a revetment.
옹벽(擁壁)〔土〕 a breast 〔retaining〕
옹색(壅塞) ①〈비좁다〉(be) tight; narrow; cramped. ¶ 옹색한 방 a narrow room. ②〈궁색함〉be hard up; be in straitened circumstances. ¶ 옹색하게 살다 live in poverty.

옹생원(一生員) a narrow-minded (an illiberal) person.
옹이 a node; a knar; a gnarl; a knot. ¶ ~ 있는 gnarled; knotty.
옹졸(壅拙) ~하다 (be) illiberal; intolerant; narrow-minded.
옹주(翁主) a princess; a king's daughter by a concubine.
옹호(擁護)(보호) protection; safeguard;(엄호) cover;(원조) support; assistance. ~하다 support; back up; protect 《A from B》; defend; safeguard. ‖ ~자 a defender; a supporter; a backer.
옻 lacquer. ¶ ~오르다 be poisoned with lacquer / ~칠하다 lacquer. ‖ ~나무 a lacquer tree.
와¹ ①(연결사) and. ¶ 너 ~ 나 You and I. ②(함께)(together) with. ¶ 친구~ 테니스를 치다 play tennis with a friend. ③(대항) with; against. ¶ 친구와 싸우다 quarrel with a friend. ④(접촉) with. ¶ 친구~ 만나다 meet with a friend. ⑤(비교) with. ¶ …와 비교해서 as compared with….
와²(일제히) with a rush; loudly. ¶ ~ 웃음이 터지다 burst into laughter / ~ 밀려가다 advance on with a rush.
와글거리다 (북적거리다) throng; swarm;(떠들다) be clamorous (noisy). ‖ a rush.
와닥닥 suddenly; abruptly; with thumping; boisterously; noisily; clamorously.
와들와들 ¶ ~ 떨다 tremble 《with fear》; quiver, shiver 《with cold》.
와락 suddenly; all of a sudden; all at once; with a rush (jerk).
와르르 ①《사람이》 with a rush. ②《물건이》 clattering down; with a crash. ¶ ~ 무너지다 crumble all in a heap. [sick in bed.
와병(臥病) ~하다 be ill in bed; lie
와삭거리다 rustle.
와신상담(臥薪嘗膽) ~하다 go through unspeakable hardships and privations 《for the sake of vengeance》.
와이더블유시에이 Y.W.C.A. (◀ Young Women's Christian Association)
와이셔츠 a shirt.
와이어로프 a wire rope.
와이엠시에이 Y.M.C.A. (◀ Young Men's Christian Association)
와전(訛傳) a misinformation; a false report. ~하다 misinform; misrepresent.
와중(渦中) a whirlpool; a vortex. ¶ …의 ~에 휩쓸려 들다 be drawn into the vortex of 《war》; be involved in 《a quarrel》.
와지끈 with a crash; snappingly. ~하다 break with a snap; crash; go smash.

와짝(갑자기) all at once; all of a sudden; abruptly;《부쩍》in huge numbers.
와트〖電〗a watt.
와해(瓦解) ~하다 collapse; break up; fall to (in) pieces; become disintegrated.
왁스 wax.
왁자(지껄)**하다** (be) noisy; clamorous; boisterous; uproarious.
완강(頑强) ~하다 (be) stubborn 《resistance》; obstinate; dogged; strong. ¶ ~히 부정하다 deny persistently.
완결(完結) ~하다 complete; conclude; finish. ¶ ~되다 be completed 〔concluded〕/ ~을 짓다 bring the case to a conclusion.
완고(頑固)〔고집〕obstinacy; stubbornness;〔완미〕bigotry. ~하다 (be) obstinate; stubborn; headstrong; bigoted; persistent.
완곡(婉曲) ~하다 (be) indirect; roundabout; euphemistic. ¶ ~히 (say) in a roundabout way; euphemistically; indirectly.
완구(玩具) a toy; a plaything. ‖ ~점 a toyshop.
완급(緩急)〔늦고 빠름〕fast and slow motion; high and low speed. [the whole amount.
완납(完納) ~하다 pay in full; pay
완두(豌豆) a pea.
완력(腕力)(have great) physical (muscular) strength; brawn;(폭력) brutal force. ¶ ~으로 (win) by force; by using one's fist / ~을 쓰다 use (resort to) force.
완료(完了) ~하다 complete; finish. ‖ ~시제 the perfect tense.
완만(緩慢) ~하다 (be) slow (slow-moving); sluggish; dull; inactive. ¶ ~한 경사 a gentle slope.
완미(頑迷) ~하다 (be) bigoted; obstinate.
완벽(完璧) perfection; completeness. ~하다 (be) perfect; faultless; flawless. ¶ ~을 기하다 aim at perfection.
완본(完本) a complete set of books.
완봉하다(完封一)〖野〗shut out.
완비(完備) ¶ ~된 설비가 ~된 병원 a well-equipped hospital / ~되어 있다 be fully equipped 《with》; be well supplied 《with》/ 이 체육관은 운동 설비가 ~되어 있다 This gym has a full range of sports equipment.
완성(完成) completion; accomplishment. ~하다 complete; perfect; finish; accomplish; bring 《a thing》 to perfection; be completed (perfected). ‖ ~품 finished products.
완수(完遂) ~하다 bring 《something》 to a successful completion; complete; carry 《something》 through. ¶ 목적을 ~하다 attain

완승 (完勝) ~하다 win a complete victory.

완역 (完譯) (make) a complete translation.

완연하다 (宛然-) (be) clear; obvious; evident; patent; vivid.

완장 (腕章) an armband; a brassard. ¶ ~을 두르다 wear an armband.

완전 (完全) perfection; completeness. ~하다 (be) perfect; complete. ¶ ~히 perfectly; completely; fully / ~하게 하다 perfect; make 《something》 perfect; bring 《something》 to perfection / ~에 가깝다 be nearly perfect; be near perfection. ‖ ~가동〔조업〕 full operation / ~고용 full employment / ~무결 absolute perfection / ~범죄 a perfect crime / ~시합 a perfect game / ~연소 perfect combustion.

완주하다 (完走-) run the whole distance 《of a marathon race》.

완초 (莞草) a rush. ☞ 왕골.

완충 (緩衝) ‖ ~국 a buffer state / ~기 a shock absorber; a bumper / ~지대 a neutral (buffer) zone.

완치 (完治) ~하다 cure 《a person, a disease》 completely; heal 《a person, a wound》 completely. ~되다 be completely cured (recovered).

완쾌 (完快) 《병이》 ~하다 recover (completely) 《from illness》; be restored to health; get well.

완투하다 (完投-) 【野】 pitch a whole game; go the whole distance.

완행 (緩行) ~하다 go (run) slow. ‖ ~열차 a slow (local) train.

완화 (緩和) 《고통·불안 등의》 relief; alleviation; relaxation; 《국제간 긴장의》 détente. ~하다 ease; relieve; relax. ¶ 제한을 ~하다 relax (ease) restriction 《on trade》 / 규제를 ~하다 deregulate / 교통 정책을 ~하다 ease traffic congestion / 양국간의 긴장은 ~되었다 The tension between the two nations diminished.

알가닥 a tomboy; a hussy.

알가닥거리다 clatter; rattle.

알가왈부 (曰可曰否) ~하다 argue pro and con.

알초 (dance) a waltz. ‖ ~곡 a waltz.

알 all at once; all of a sudden; with a jerk. ¶ ~성내다 flare up.

왔다갔다하다 come and go; walk about; stroll aimlessly.

왕 (王) 《세습적인》 a king; 《군주》 a monarch; 《지배자》 a ruler. ¶ 백수의 ~ the king of beasts / 홈런 ~ a home-run king. ¶ ~가 (家) a royal family.

왕개미 【蟲】 a giant ant.

왕겨 rice bran; chaff.

왕골 【植】 a kind of sedge (plant). ‖ ~자리 a sedge mat.

왕관 (王冠) a crown; a diadem.

왕국 (王國) a kingdom; a palace.

왕궁 (王宮) the king's (a royal) palace.

왕권 (王權) a sovereign right; royal authority (powers). ‖ ~신수설 (the theory of) the divine rights of kings.

왕녀 (王女) a (royal) princess.

왕년 (往年) former years; the years gone by; the past.

왕눈이 (王-) a large-eyed person.

왕대비 (王大妃) the Queen Mother.

왕도 (王都) the royal capital.

왕도 (王道) 【學問】 ~란 없다 There is no royal road to learning.

왕래 (往來) ① 《사람의》 comings and goings; 《차의》 traffic. ~하다 come and go. ¶ ~가 잦은 거리 a busy street 〔thoroughfare〕 / ~를 금하다 block traffic. ② 《교우》 friendly intercourse; 《서신》 correspondence. ~하다 have intercourse (keep company) with; have correspondence with; exchange letters with 《서신 왕래》.

왕릉 (王陵) a royal (king's) tomb.

왕림 (枉臨) ~하다 (come to) visit; honor us with a visit.

왕명 (王命) the king's order; a royal command.

왕방울 (王-) a big bell. ‖ ~눈 big eyes.

왕복 (往復) a round trip; a round-trip flight 《비행기의》. ~하다 go 《to a place》 and come back; 《교통 기관으로》 make a round trip 《to a place》; run between 《two places》. ‖ ~엽서 a return postcard / ~운동 《기계의》 a reciprocating motion / ~차비 the round-trip fare / ~차표 a round-trip ticket 《美》; a return ticket 《英》 / ~편 (便) a shuttle service.

왕비 (王妃) a queen; an empress.

왕새우 (王-) 【動】 a (Yellow Sea) prawn.

왕생극락 (往生極樂) rebirth in paradise; an easy passage into eternity. ~하다 go after death to Nirvana; die a peaceful death. ¶ 어머니는 ~을 바라신다 My mother prays for rebirth in paradise.

왕성 (旺盛) ‖ 원기 ~하다 be full of vigor (health and life) / 식욕이 ~하다 have a good (excellent) appetite.

왕세손 (王世孫) the eldest son of the crown prince.

왕세자 (王世子) the Crown Prince; 《영국의》 the Prince of Wales. ‖ ~비 the Crown Princess.

왕손(王孫) the grandchildren of a king. 〔~family〕

왕실(王室) the royal household

왕왕(往往) 《종종》 often; (every) now and then; more often (than not); frequently; 《때때로》 occasionally; at times.

왕위(王位) the throne; the crown. ‖ ~에 오르다 ascend (accede) to the throne. / ~ 계승 succession to the throne.

왕자(王子) a royal prince.

왕자(王者) 《임금》 a king; 《우승자》 the champion (of).

왕정(王政) imperial rule (reign); (a) king's reign. 〔~tic.

왕조(王朝) a dynasty. ‖ ~의 dynas-

왕족(王族) the royal family; royalty; a member of royalty.

왕좌(王座) 《수위》 the throne; 《수위》 the premier position. 〔pede.

왕지네(王─) 〖動〗 a large centi-

왕진(往診) a doctor's visit to a patient; a house call (visit). ~하다 visit a patient in his home; make a house call to *one's* patient. ‖ ~료 a doctor's fee for a visit / ~시간 hours for visiting patients.

왕통(王統) the royal line.

왕후(王后) an empress; a queen.

왕후(王侯) the king and peers.

왜(어째서) why; for what reason; what...for; with what purpose. ‖ ~나하면 because; for; The reason is.... / ~ 그런지 without knowing why; somehow. 〔how.

왜가리 〖鳥〗 a heron. 〔how.

왜곡(歪曲) distortion. ~하다 distort; pervert; make a false representation of. ‖ ~된 견해 a distorted view / 그 보고는 사실을 ~하고 있다 The report distorts the facts. 〔raiders.

왜구(倭寇) 〖史〗 Japanese pirate

왜색(倭色) Japanese manners and customs. ‖ ~을 일소하다 make a clean sweep of Japanese manners. 〔small; dwarfish.

왜소(矮小) ~하다 (be) short and

왜식(倭食) Japanese food (cuisine).

왜인(倭人) the Japanese 《전부》 a Japanese; 《蔑》 a Jap (한 사람).

왜인(矮人) a dwarf; a pigmy.

왜정(倭政) 〖史〗 Japanese rule. ‖ ~시대 the Japanese administration period in Korea (1910-45).

왱왱(바람의) whistling; 《벌레의》 droning; buzzing.

외(外) ① 《…을 제외하고》 except (for); but; with the exception of; 《…에 더하여》 besides; in addition to. ¶ 목요일 ~에는 모두 집에 있다 I am home every day except Thursday / 그 ~에는 모두 집으로 돌아갔다 Everybody but him went home. / 그녀 ~에도 두 형제가 있다 I have two brothers besides her. ② 《바깥》 outside; out (of); outer; foreign. ¶ 시 ~ outside the city.

외(根) 〖建〗 a lath.

외…(唯) only; one; single; sole. ‖ ~눈이 a one-eyed person / ~아들 an only son. 〔home.

외가(外家) *one's* mother's maiden

외각(外角) 〖幾〗 an exterior (external) angle; 〖野〗 outcorner.

외각(外殼) a shell; a crust.

외견(外見) ⇒ 외관.

외겹 a single layer; one-ply.

외경(畏敬) ~하다 revere; hold (a person) in awe (reverence).

외계(外界) the outside (outer) world. ‖ ~와의 접촉을 끊다 break off contact with the outer world.

외고집(─固執) ~의 obstinate; stubborn; headstrong; pigheaded / ~을 부리다 be (get) obstinate. ‖ ~쟁이 a pigheaded person.

외곬 a singly way (track). ~으로 with a single-mind; singlemindedly / ~의 사람 a singlehearted person / ~으로 생각하다 see things from only one point of view.

외과(外科) surgery; 《병원의》 the surgical department. ‖ ~의 surgical. / ~병원 a surgery / ~수술 (undergo) a surgical operation / ~의사 a surgeon.

외과피(外果皮) 〖植〗 an exocarp; an epicarp.

외곽(外廓) the outline; an outer ring. ‖ ~단체 a fringe (an affiliated) organization; 《관청의》 an extra-departmental body.

외관(外觀) an outside (external) appearance; the exterior; 《표면적 인상》 appearance; the look. ¶ 건물의 ~ the exterior of a building / ~으로 사람을 판단하다 judge people by appearances.

외교(外交) diplomacy; diplomatic relations(관계); foreign policy(외교 정책). ¶ ~상의 diplomatic / ~적 수완을 발휘하다 show diplomatic talent (skill) / ~ 관계를 열다 (단절하다) open (break off) diplomatic relations. ‖ ~관 a diplomat; a diplomatic official / ~교섭 diplomatic negotiations / ~문서 a diplomatic document / ~문제 a diplomatic problem / ~부 the Ministry of Foreign Affairs / ~사령 diplomatic language / ~사절단 a diplomatic mission / ~원 a canvasser / ~특권 diplomatic immunity / ~공개 [비밀] ~ open [secret] diplomacy.

외구(外寇) a foreign invader.

외국(外國) a foreign country [land]. ¶ ~의 foreign; overseas / ~제의 foreign-made; of foreign make / ~ 태생의 born abroad (overseas); foreign-born / ~생활 living abroad; life overseas / ~에 가다 [서 돌아오다] go (return from) abroad. ‖ ~무역 foreign trade / ~상사 a foreign trading company / ~시장 a foreign (an overseas) market / ~어 a foreign language foreign travel; an overseas trip (tour) / ~인 a foreigner; an alien / ~환 foreign exchange / ~환 평형 기금 exchange equalization fund (외환 매입 재원 조달책으로 발행되는 채권) / ~환시장 the foreign exchange market.

외근(外勤) outside duty [service] (보험 따위의) canvassing. ~하다 be on outside duty; work outside; do canvassing. ‖ ~기자 a reporter; a legman (美口) / ~자 a person on outside duty.

외기(外氣) the open air; the air outside. ‖ ~권(圈) exosphere.

외기노조(外機勞組) the Foreign Organizations Employees' Union (생략

외길 a single path. (F.O.E.U.)

외나무다리 a single-log bridge.

외날 a single edge.

외다(암기) recite from memory; learn by heart; memorize.

외도(外道) ① ☞ 오입(誤入). ②《나쁜 길》a wrong (an evil) course. ~하다 go astray; stray from *one's* proper field (*of business*).

외등(外燈) an outdoor lamp.

외따로 (떨어져) all alone; solitarily; in complete isolation.

외딴 isolated; out-of-the-way. ¶ ~집 an isolated house / ~섬 a solitary (lone) island. (lonely.

외딸다 (be) remote; secluded;

외람(猥濫) ~되다 (be) presumptuous; audacious. ¶ ~되지만 제가 설명을 드리겠습니다 With your permission I will explain it.

외래(外來) ¶ ~의 foreign; (coming) from abroad; imported. ‖ ~사상 foreign ideas / ~어 a loanword; a word of foreign origin / ~품 imports; imported goods / ~환자 an outpatient.

외로이 all alone; lonely; solitarily. ¶ ~지내다 lead a lonely life.

외롭다 (be) all alone; lonely; lonesome; solitary.

외륜산(外輪山)(地) the outer rim of a crater. (scream.

외마디소리 an outcry (of pain); an

외면(外面) outward appearance; the exterior.

외면하다(外面一) turn away *one's* face; look away; avert *one's* eyes.

외모(外貌) an (outward) appearance; external features.

외무(外務) foreign affairs. ‖ ~부 [성] the Ministry [Department] of Foreign Affairs / ~부 장관 the Foreign Minister; the Minister of Foreign Affairs / ~사원 a canvasser; a solicitor.

외미(外米) (imported) rice.

외박(外泊) ~하다 stay out overnight; sleep away from home.

외벽(外壁) an outer wall.

외부(外部) the outside (exterior). ¶ ~의 outside; outer; external / ~사람 an outsider / ~로부터 도움을 받다 get outside help / ~와의 접촉을 끊다 break off contact with the outside world / 비밀이 ~로 샜다 The secret has leaked out.

외분비(外分泌)(醫) external secretion. ‖ ~선 an exocrine gland.

외빈(外賓) a (foreign) guest (visitor).

외사(外事) external (foreign) affairs. ‖ ~과 the foreign affairs section.

외사촌(外四寸) a maternal cousin.

외삼촌(外三寸) a maternal uncle.

외상 credit; trust. ¶ ~으로 팔다 [사다] sell (buy) on credit / ~을 주다 give credit. ‖ ~거래 credit transaction / ~사절 (게시) No credit given. / ~판매 credit sale.

외상(外相) the Foreign Minister. ‖ ~회의 a Foreign Minister's conference. (jury); (醫) trauma.

외상(外傷) an external wound (in-

외서(外書) a foreign book.

외설(猥褻) obscenity; indecency. ~하다 (be) obscene; filthy; indecent. ¶ ~ 사진 an obscene (a pornographic) picture. / ~문학 pornography / ~죄 public indecency / ~행위 an indecent behavior.

외세(外勢) 《외국 세력》 outside (foreign) influence (power). ¶ ~에 의존하다 depend on the power of a foreign country. (handed.

외손 ¶ ~의 one-handed; single-

외손(外孫) a child of *one's* daughter; descendants in the daughter's line.

외숙(外叔) an uncle on *one's* mother's side. ¶ ~모(母) the wife of *one's* maternal uncle.

외식(外食) ~하다 eat (dine) out. ¶ ~하는 사람 a diner-out. ‖ ~산업 the food-service industry.

외신(外信) foreign news; a foreign message (telegram). ‖ ~부 (長) (editor of) the foreign news department.

외심(外心)(幾) a circumcenter; an outer center. ‖ ~점(點)(理) the metacenter(경심).

외야(外野) 〖野〗 the outfield. ∥ ~석 outfield bleachers / ~수 an outfielder; a fly-chaser 〖美〗.

외양(外洋) the open sea; the ocean.

외양(外樣) 〖겉모양〗 outward appearance [show]. ¶ ~을 꾸미다 keep up appearances.

외양간(喂養間) a stable(말의); a cowshed (소의). ¶ 소 잃고 ~ 고치는 격이다 be just like locking the stable door after the horse is stolen.

외연기관(外燃機關) 〖機〗 an external combustion engine.

외용(外用) 〖for〗 external use [application]. ~하다 use [apply] externally. ∥ ~약 a medicine for external application [use].

외우(外憂) ☞ 외환(外患).

외유(外遊) ~하다 make a trip abroad; travel [go] abroad.

외유내강(外柔內剛) being gentle in appearance, but sturdy in spirit; an iron hand in the velvet glove.

외이(外耳) 〖解〗 the external [outer] ear. ∥ ~염 〖醫〗 otitis externa.

외인(外人) 〖외국인〗 a foreigner; an alien; 〖타인〗 an outsider; a stranger. ¶ ~부대 the Foreign Legion.

외자(外資) foreign capital [funds]. ∥ ~ 도입 induction [introduction] of foreign capital.

외적(外的) external; outward. ¶ ~ 조건 external conditions. 「er」

외적(外敵) a foreign enemy [invader].

외접(外接) ~하다 〖幾〗 be circumscribed. ∥ ~원 a circumscribed circle.

외제(外製) ¶ ~의 foreign-made; of foreign manufacture [make]. ∥ ~차 a foreign-(made) car / ~품 foreign-made articles; imported goods. 「mother.」

외조모(外祖母) a maternal grand-

외조부(外祖父) a maternal grandfather. 「one's mother's side.」

외종(外從) 〖四寸〗 a cousin on

외주(外注) an outside order. ¶ 기계 부품을 ~ 내다 order the parts of a machine outside the company.

외지(外地) a foreign land [country]. ¶ ~의 overseas; foreign. ∥ ~근무 overseas service / ~(근무)수당 an overseas allowance.

외지다 (be) outlandish; remote; secluded. ¶ 외진 곳 an isolated [out-of-the-way] place.

외채(外債) 〖債權〗 a foreign loan [bond]; 〖負債〗foreign debt. ¶ ~를 모집하다 raise a foreign loan.

외척(外戚) a maternal relative.

외출(外出) going out. ~하다 go out (of doors). ¶ ~ 중 during [in] one's absence / ~ 중이다 be out. ∥ ~ 금지 〖군인의〗 confinement (to the barracks); 〖야간의〗 a curfew / ~날 a leave day / ~복 one's best clothes; outdoor clothes.

외치다 shout; cry [call]; exclaim; shriek; scream; yell. ¶ "도둑이야" 하고 ~ cry "Thief"; ~목청껏 ~ cry at the top of one's voice.

외톨이 a lonely person.

외투(外套) an overcoat.

외판원(外販員) a salesman; a saleswoman; 〖권유원〗 a canvasser; a solicitor.

외풍(外風) ① 〖바람〗 a draft; a draught 〖美〗. ¶ ~이 있는 방 a drafty room / ~을 막다 prevent drafts. ② 〖외국풍〗 foreign ways [fashion, style].

외피(外皮) a skin; a shell(조개의); a husk(과실의); a hull(곡물의); a crust(빵·파이 등의). 「껍질.

외할머니(外一) ☞ 외조모.

외할아버지(外一) ☞ 외조부.

외항(外港) an outer port.

외항선(外航船) an ocean-going ship; an ocean liner. 「seas.」

외해(外海) the open sea; the high

외향성(外向性) 〖心〗 extroversion. ¶ ~의 extrovert; outgoing / ~인 사람 an extrovert.

외형(外形) an external [outward] form [shape]. ¶ ~(상)의 external; outward / ~은 in shape.

외화(外貨) foreign currency [money]. ¶ ~ 가득률 a foreign exchange earning rate / ~보유고 foreign exchange holdings (reserve) / ~어음 a foreign currency bill / ~준비 a reserve in foreign currency / ~획득 the obtaining (acquisition) of foreign currency. 「rency.」

외화(外畫) a foreign film. 「cur-

외환(外換) foreign exchange. ∥ ~은행 a foreign exchange bank.

외환(外患) a foreign (external) threat. ¶ 내우~ domestic troubles and external threats.

왼 left; left-hand. ¶ ~편 the left side / ~팔 the left arm.

왼손 the left hand. ¶ ~잡이 a left-handed person; a left-hander; a southpaw / ~잡이 투수 a southpaw; a lefty 〖美〗.

왼쪽 the left (side). ¶ ~에 앉다 sit on the left side (of).

요(要) 〖요점〗 the point. ¶ ~는 〖컨데〗 what is essential is...; the point is...; in a word; in short.

요 beddings; a mattress. ¶ ~를 깔다 [개다] make [put away] the

bed; lay out 〔stow away〕 the bedding.
요 (얄잡아) this little 〔one〕. ¶ ~ 까지 such a 〔little〕… / ~ 놈 this fellow 〔guy〕. ¶ 〔시간·거리〕 this; these; right near at hand. ¶ ~ 근처에 in this neighborhood; near 〔around〕 here.
요가 yoga. ¶ ~ 수련자 a yogi.
요강 (尿鋼) a chamber pot; a night stool 〔chair〕.
요강 (要綱) the outline; the gist; the general idea.
요건 (要件) 〔필요 조건〕 a necessary condition 〔factor〕; a requirement; 〔중요 용건〕 an important matter. ~ 를 갖추다 fulfill 〔satisfy〕 the necessary 〔required〕 conditions / 건강은 성공의 제일 ~ 이다 Health is the prerequisite for success in life.
요격 (邀擊) ~ 하다 intercept 《raiding bombers》; ambush. ¶ ~ 기 (機) an interceptor / ~ 미사일 an anti-missile 〔interceptor〕 missile.
요괴 (妖怪) an apparition; a specter; 《괴물》a goblin. ¶ ~ 스러운 wicked and mysterious; weird.
요구 (要求) a demand; a claim (권리의); a request (청구); requirement (필요). ~ 하다 demand; request; claim; call upon 《a person to do》; require 《a person to do》. ¶ ~ 에 따라 at 〔by〕 a person's request / ~ 에 응하다 grant 〔comply with〕 a person's request; meet 〔accept〕 the demands 《of the employees》 / ~ 를 물리치다 turn down a person's request / 임금인 상을 ~ 하다 demand 〔call for〕 a raise in one's wages / 손해배상을 ~ 하다 claim 〔make a claim of〕 ($ 10,000) damages 《from a person》. ¶ ~ 불(어음) (a bill) payable on demand / ~ 자 a demandant; a claimant / ~ 조건 the terms desired.
요구르트 yog(h)urt.
요귀 (妖鬼) an apparition; a ghost.
요금 (料金) a charge; a fee (의사·변호사 등의); a fare (탈것의); a toll (유료도로의); a rate (전기·수도 등의). ¶ ~ 징수소 〔유료도로의〕 a tollgate; a tollbooth / ~ 표 a price list; a list of charges.
요기 (妖氣) a weird 〔ghostly〕 air.
요기 (療飢) ~ 하다 satisfy 〔relieve, allay〕 one's hunger; fortify oneself with a meal.
요긴 (要緊) 긴요. ∥ ~ 독 a critical position. 「siren.
요녀 (妖女) an enchantress; a
요다음 next. ¶ ~ 의 next / ~ 에 next time.
요담 (要談) ~ 하다 have a talk with 《a person》 on an important matter 〔business〕.
요도 (尿道) 〔解〕 the urethra. ∥ ~ 관 the urethral canal / ~ 염 (炎) urethritis. 「poisoning.
요독증 (尿毒症) 〔醫〕 uremia; urine
요동 (搖動) ~ 하다 swing; sway; shake; quake; rock; joggle.
요란 (搖亂) ~ 하다, ~ 스럽다 (be) noisy; loud; uproarious; clamorous. ¶ ~ 하게 noisily; boisterously.
요람 (要覽) a survey; an outline; 《안내서》a handbook; a manual.
요람 (搖籃) a swinging cot; a cradle; a nursery. ∥ ~ 기 the cradle; babyhood; infancy / ~ 지 the cradle 《of western civilization》; the cradleland.
요략 (要略) an outline; a summary; an epitome.
요량 (料量) a plan; an intention; an idea. ~ 하다 plan out. ¶ …할 ~ 으로 with the intention of / ~ 없다 have bad judgment; lack common sense.
요런 such; this; like this.
요령 (要領) ① 《요점》 the (main) point; the gist. ¶ ~ 이 없는 pointless / ~ 이 있다 〔없다〕 (be) to 〔off〕 the point / ~ 있게 말하다 talk to the point (purpose). ② 〔비결〕 a knack; an art. ¶ ~ 있는 〔없는〕 사람 a shrewd 〔clumsy〕 fellow / ~ 을 배우다 get 〔learn〕 the knack of 《doing》 / 그는 나에게 ~ 을 가르쳐 주었다 He showed me the knack. / 좀더 ~ 있게 해라 Do it more efficiently.
요로 (要路) 《중요한 길》 an important road; 《요직》 an important position; a high office; 〔당국〕 the authorities. ¶ ~ 에 있는 사람들 those in high authority; the authorities / 교통의 ~ 에 있다 be in the main artery of traffic.
요론 (要論) an important argument.
요리 (料理) ① 〔조리〕 cooking; cookery; cuisine; 〔음식〕 a dish; food. ~ 하다 cook 《food》; dress 《fish》; prepare 《a dish》; do the cooking. ¶ 맛있는 ~ a delicious (tasty) dish; excellent cuisine / ~ 의 명인 a cooking expert / ~ 를 잘 〔못〕하다 be a good 〔poor〕 cook; be a good (poor) hand at cooking. ¶ ~ 기구 cooking utensils / ~ 대 a 〔kitchen〕 counter / ~ 법 a recipe 〔for〕; how to cook / ~ 사 a cook; a chef (프) / ~ 책 a cookbook (美) / ~ 학원 a cooking school (校) / ~ 고기 meat dish / 중국 (서양) ~ Chinese (Western) food. ② 〔일처리〕 management; handling. ~ 하다 manage; handle;

요리조리 deal with. ¶ 그 문제를 간단히 ~ 하다 deal with the problem without any difficulty.

요리조리 here and there; this way and that. ¶ ~ 핑계를 대다 make one excuse after another.

요만(要滿) a so slight (trifling) / ~ 것(일) this small (little) bit; such a trifle.

요만큼 this (little) bit.

요망(妖妄) ¶ ~ 떨다(부리다) behave wickedly; act frivolously (capriciously, flightly).

요망(要望) a desire; a demand (for); a cry (for). ~하다 demand; request; cry (for). ¶ 근무 시간의 단축을 강력히 ~하다 strongly demand that the working hours be shortened.

요면(凹面) concave; concavity. ‖ ~경 a concave mirror.

요목(要目) principal items; the (main) point. ‖ 교수~ a syllabus of lectures.

요물(妖物) (물건) an uncanny thing; (사람) a wicked person; a crafty fellow.

요밀(要密) ~하다 (be) minute; close; detailed. ‖ ~하게 minutely; in detail / ~한 사람 a scrupulous man.

요법(療法) a method of treatment; a remedy; a cure. ‖ 가정~ (try) a home treatment / 민간~ a folk remedy.

요부(妖婦) an enchantress; a vamp; a vampire.

요부(要部) the principal (essential) parts.

요부(腰部) the waist; the hips.

요사(妖邪) ~하다, ~스럽다 (be) capricious; fickle; wicked; wily; crafty. ¶ ~(를) 떨다 behave in a capricious (weird) way.

요산(尿酸) [化] uric acid.

요새(近來) recently; lately; (저번) the other day; a few days ago; (요전부터) these few days; (지금) nowadays; in these days.

요새(要塞) a fortress; a stronghold; fortification. ¶ ~화하다 fortify. ‖ ~지대 a strategic (fortified) zone.

요석(尿石) [醫] a urolith.

요소(尿素) [化] urea.

요소(要所) an important position (point); a key (strategic) point.

요소(要素) an element; a factor; an essential part; a requisite (필요 조건). ¶ …의 ~를 이루다 be essential to.

요술(妖術) (black) magic; witchcraft; sorcery. ¶ ~을 부리다 practice sorcery; use magic. ‖ ~쟁이 a magician; a sorcerer(남자); a sorceress(여자).

요시찰인(要視察人) people on a surveillance (black) list. ¶ ~ 명부에 오르다 be on the black list; be black-listed.

요식(要式) ~의 formal. ‖ ~계약(행위) a formal contract (act).

요식업(料食業) restaurant business. ‖ ~자 a restaurant owner.

요약(要約) a summary; an outline (개요). ~하다 summarize; outline; sum up. ¶ ~해서 말하면 in a word; in brief / 이 구절을 200 단어 이내로 ~하시오 Give a summary of) this passage in less than 200 words.

요양(療養) recuperation; (a) medical treatment. ~하다 recuperate; be under medical treatment. ‖ ~소 a sanitorium (美); a rest (nursing) home.

요업(窯業) the ceramic industry; ceramics. ¶ ~가 a ceramist / ~ 미술 ceramic art / ~소 a pottery / ~제품 a ceramic.

요연(瞭然) ~한 evident; clear; obvious; plain; manifest / 그것은 일목 ~하다 One can see it with half an eye.

요염(妖艶) ~하다 (be) fascinating; bewitching; voluptuous. ¶ ~한 모습 a charming figure.

요오드 iodine. ‖ ~포름 iodoform.

요원(要員) workers required; needed (necessary) personnel. ‖ 기간~ a skeleton staff.

요원(燎原) a prairie on fire. ¶ ~의 불길처럼 퍼지다 spread like wildfire.

요원하다(遙遠一·遼遠一) (be) very far away; distant; remote; far-off. ¶ 전도는 《사람이 주어》 have a long (far) way to go; 《사물이 주어》 be far off.

요인(人) a leading (an important) person; a key figure; a VIP.

요인(要因) a primary factor; a main cause.

요일(曜日) a day of the week. ¶ 오늘 무슨 ~이지 What day (of the week) is it today? or What's today?

요전(一 前) ① (요전날) the other day; not long ago; just recently; lately. ② (전) last; before; last time. ¶ ~ 일요일 last Sunday.

요절(夭折) an early (a premature) death. ~하다 die young (prematurely, before one's time).

요절나다 ① (못쓰게 되다) become useless; (부서지다) break; get broken; be damaged; get out of order (기계 따위가). ② (일이) be spoilt (ruined); come to nothing; fall through.

요절내다 spoil; ruin; make a

요점(要點) the main (essential) point; the gist; the substance. ¶ 전략상의 ~ a strategic point / ~을 파악하다 grasp (get) the point (of) / ~을 말해 주시오 Please get to the point.
요정(妖精) a fairy; a spirit.
요정(料亭) a Korean-style restaurant; a *kisaeng* house.
요조(窈窕) ‖ ~숙녀 a lady of refined manners.
요즈음 recent days; these days; nowadays; just recently; lately. ¶ ~의 today; recent; late / ~ 청년 the young people of today.
요지(要地) an important place; a strategic point. ¶ 상업상의 ~ a place of great commercial importance.
요지(要旨) ① ☞ 요점. ②《취지》 the purport; the keynote.
요지경(瑤池鏡) a magic glass; a toy peep-show.
요지부동(搖之不動) ‖ ~하다 stand as firm as rock; be steadfast (unshakable).
요직(要職) an important post (office); a key (responsible) position. ¶ ~에 있다 be in (hold) an important post.
요처(要處) a strategic (an important) point.
요철(凹凸) ‖ ~있는 uneven; bumpy; rough.
요청(要請) a demand; a request. ~하다 request; demand; ask (*a person*) for; call for. ¶ ~에 응하다 accept *a person's* demand / 시대적 ~에 맞다 meet the demands (needs) of the times / 사태 수습을 위해 군대의 출동을 ~하다 request (ask) for the mobilization of the army to save the situation.
요충(要衝) a strategic point; a key point; an important spot (place). ‖ ~지 요충.
요충(蟯蟲) a threadworm.
요컨대(要 一) in short; in a word; to sum up; after all.
요통(腰痛) lumbago; backache. ¶ ~을 호소하다 complain of lumbago.
요트(~) a *racing* yacht.
요판(凹版) [印] intaglio.
요하다(要一) 《필요로 하다》 need; want; require; take〈시간·노동력을〉; cost〈비용을〉. ¶ 나의 집은 수리를 요한다 My house wants (needs) repairing. / 이 책은 수정을 요한다 This book needs correction. / 이 일은 10일 간을 요한다 It will take ten days to do the work. / 이 일은 긴급을 요하는 일이다 This needs to be done immediately.
요항(要項) essential points; essen-

tials; 《개요》 the gist; an outline. ¶ 모집 ~ a prospectus.
요항(要港) a strategic (naval) port.
요행(僥倖) luck; a piece (stroke) of good luck (chance); a windfall. ¶ ~히 luckily; by luck / ~을 바라다 rely on chance / 나의 시험 합격은 ~이었다 It was pure chance that I passed the exam.
요혈(尿血)[醫] hematuria.
욕(辱) ①《욕설》 abuse; abusive language; slander〈중상〉. ~하다 ☞ 욕하다. ②《치욕》 shame; humiliation; insult; disgrace. ③《고난》 hardships; troubles; pains.
욕(慾)《욕망》(접미사적으로) a desire; a passion. ¶ 금전 ~ love of money; a desire for wealth / 지식 ~ a thirst for knowledge.
욕감태기(辱一) the butt of abuse.
욕구(欲求)《욕망》desire; craving; wants〈필요〉; will〈바람·의지〉. ~하다 desire; want; wish (long) for; crave (*for*). ¶ 생의 ~ the will to live; a craving for life / 성의 ~ sexual desire / ~를 채우다 satisfy *one's* wants. ‖ ~불만 [心] frustration.
욕기부리다(欲氣一) be greedy (*for, after*); be avaricious.
욕되다(辱一)《서술적》be a disgrace (shame, dishonor) (*to*).
욕망(欲望) a desire; wants; lust;《야망》an ambition. ¶ ~을 채우다〔억제하다〕 satisfy (subdue) *one's* desire / ~를 가지다 have an ambition.
욕먹다(辱一) ① 《욕설당하다》 suffer an insult; be abused. ② 《악평을 듣다》 be spoken ill of;《신문 등에서》 be criticized unfavorably; be attacked.
욕보다(辱一) ① 《곤란을 겪다》 have a hard time; go through hardships. ② 《치욕을 당하다》 be put to shame; be humiliated (insulted; abused). ③ 《겁간을 당하다》 be raped (assaulted, violated).
욕보이다(辱一) put to shame; disgrace; dishonor; insult; humiliate;《겁탈》rape; outrage; violate.
욕설(辱說)《욕》 curses; evil-speaking; swearwords; abusive language. ~하다 ☞ 욕하다.
욕실(浴室) a bathroom. ¶ ~이 있다 be furnished (provided) with a bathroom.
욕심(慾心)《탐욕》greed; avarice;《욕망》 a desire; a passion. ¶ ~많은 greedy; avaricious;《소유욕》covetous / ~이 없는 unselfish / 그는 ~이 없는 사람이다 He is a man of few wants. *or* He is far from greedy. / 그는 ~으로 눈이 멀었다 He was blinded by greed. ‖ ~꾸

욕쟁이(욕―) 〈사람〉 a foul-mouthed [-tongued] person.
욕정(欲情) sexual desire; lust. ¶ ~을 자극하다 stimulate sexual desire.
욕조(浴槽) a bathtub.
욕지거리(辱―) abusive [offensive] language; abuse; malicious remarks. ~하다 abuse; call (a person) names; use abusive language; say spiteful things (to). ¶ ~를 마구 퍼붓다 shout [howl] a stream of abuse at (a person).
욕지기 qualm; nausea; queasiness. ¶ ~나다 feel nausea [sick]; feel like vomiting / ~나게 하다 nauseate; cause nausea; turn one's stomach / ~나게 하는 광경 a nauseating [sickening] sight.
욕하다(辱―) abuse; call (a person) names; speak ill of (a person); say bad thing about (a person); bad-mouth (a person).
옷속 batting [cotton wadding] for a mattress.
옷잇 bed sheet [covering]; bed clothes.
용(龍) a dragon. ¶ ~의 눈물 [TV 연속극의] Dragon's Tears.
…용(用) for (the use of). ¶ 남자~ 장갑 gloves for men / 가정~ for home use.
용감(勇敢) bravery; courage. ¶ ~한 brave; courageous / ~히 bravely; courageously / ~에 맞서다 be courageous enough to face….
용건(用件) (a matter of) business. ¶ ~만 간단히 말씀하세요 Come to the point, please.
용골(龍骨) the keel.
용공(容共) ¶ ~의 pro-Communist. ∥ ~정책 a pro-Communist policy.
용광로(鎔鑛爐) a smelting [blast] furnace.
용구(用具) 〈기구〉 a tool; an instrument; implements; gear〈口〉. ¶ 필기~ writing implements / 낚시~ fishing gear.
용궁(龍宮) the Dragon's [Sea God's] Palace.
용기(勇氣) courage; bravery. ¶ ~있는 courageous; brave / ~없는 timid; fainthearted; coward(ly) / ~를 내다 gather [pluck up] one's courage; get up one's nerve / ~를 내게 하다 encourage; cheer up / 자기의 신념을 행할(말할) ~가 있다 have the courage of one's convictions.
용기(容器) a container; a receptacle; a vessel; a case.
용기병(龍騎兵) a dragoon.
용꿈(龍―) ¶ ~을 꾸다 dream (have) a lucky dream; dream about a dragon.

용납(容納) ~하다 tolerate; permit; admit; allow; pardon. ¶ ~할 수 없는 unpardonable.
용뇌(龍腦) 〈향〉 borneol; 〈나무〉 the Borneo (Sumatra) camphor.
용단(勇斷) a courageous decision; a decisive [resolute] step. ¶ ~을 내리다 make a resolute decision (on a matter).
용달(用達) delivery service. ~하다 deliver (goods). ∥ ~사 a delivery agency / ~업 the delivery business / ~차 a delivery van (wagon).
용도(用途) use. ¶ ~가 많다 have many [various] uses; be of wide use.
용돈(用―) pocket [spending] money; an allowance(학생의).
용두레 a scoop bucket.
용두사미(龍頭蛇尾) a good beginning and a dull ending. ¶ ~로 끝나다 end in an anticlimax.
용두질 masturbation; onanism; self-abuse. ~하다 masturbate.
용량(用量) 〈약의〉 a dose; dosage.
용량(容量) (the measure of) capacity; volume(용적). ¶ 물탱크의 ~ (the storage) capacity of a water tank / 열~ heat capacity.
용렬(庸劣) ¶ ~한 mediocre; silly; stupid; awkward; clumsy / ~한 짓 a blunder; a bungle.
용례(用例) an example; an illustration. ¶ ~를 들다 give [show, cite] an example.
용마루 a ridge (of a roof).
용마름 the thatch covering on the ridge of the thatched roof.
용매(溶媒) 〈化〉 a solvent; a menstruum (pl. ~s, -strua).
용맹(勇猛) ¶ ~한, ~스런 intrepid; dauntless; lionhearted. ∥ ~심 an intrepid spirit.
용명(勇名) fame for bravery. ¶ ~을 떨치다 win (gain) fame for bravery.
용모(容貌) looks; (a cast of) features; a face. ¶ ~가 추하다 (아름답다) be ugly (good-looking).
용무(用務) business; a thing to do. ¶ ~를 띠고 on some business / ~를 마치다 finish one's business.
용법(用法) usage; use; the directions (for use) (사용 지시서).
용변(用便) ¶ ~보다 ease nature; go to stool [the restroom].
용병(用兵) tactics; manipulation of troops. ¶ ~술 tactics.
용병(傭兵) a mercenary (soldier); hired troops.
용불용설(用不用說) 〈生〉 Lamarckism.
용사(勇士) a brave man (soldier); a hero; the brave(총칭).
용상(龍床) the (royal) throne;

용서(容恕) pardon; forgiveness. ~하다 pardon; forgive; have mercy on; overlook 《a person's fault》. ¶ ~없이 without mercy; relentlessly; ~할 수 없는 unpardonable; intolerable / ~를 빌다 beg (ask) 《a person's》 pardon; apologize for.

용선(傭船)《행위》chartering; charterage; 《선박》a chartered ship. ~하다 charter (hire) a ship. ‖ ~계약(서) a charter party 《생략 C/P》/ ~료 charterage; charter rates / ~업 chartering business.

용설란(龍舌蘭) an agave; a pita.

용솟음 ¶ ~치다 gush out; spout 《from》; break forth; well up / ~치는 정열 an outpouring of enthusiasm; surging passion.

용수(用水) water (available for use); city water (수도의) 《관개·공업용의》water for irrigation (industrial use). ‖ ~로 《관개용》 an irrigation canal; 《발전소의》 a flume / ~지 (池) a reservoir / ~통 a rainwater barrel (tank).

용수철(龍鬚鐵) a spring.

용신(容身) ¶ ~하다 ① 《몸을 움직임》 narrowly move *one's* body; stir but an inch. ② 《겨우 살아감》 ~하다 eke out a livelihood.

용심부리다 wreak *one's* jealousy [spite] on 《a person》; be nasty to 《a person》.

용쓰다 《기운을》 exert *one's* utmost strength; strain [exert] *oneself*.

용안(龍眼)《植》a longan.

용안(龍顔) the Royal countenance.

용암(鎔岩)《地》molten rock; lava.

용액(溶液) a solution; a solvent.

용약(踊躍) ¶ ~하여 in high spirits; elatedly.

용어(用語)《말씨》wording; diction; phraseology;《술어》a term;《어휘》(a) vocabulary. ‖ ~집 a glossary / 관청 ~ official language / 전문 ~ a technical term.

용언(用言)《문》a declinable word.

용역(用役) service. ¶ 재화와 ~ goods and services. ‖ ~단 (civilian) service corps / ~수출 service export.

용왕(龍王) the Dragon King.

용왕매진(勇往邁進) ~하다 dash [push] on (forward).

용원(傭員) a temporary employee.

용융점(熔融點) the melting point.

용의(用意) readiness; preparedness. ¶ ~주도한 cautious; prudent; 《a plan》 carefully arranged / ~가 있다 be ready [willing] to 《do》.

용의자(容疑者) a suspect; a suspected person. ¶ 유력한 ~ a key suspect / 살인 ~ a murder suspect.

용이(容易) ¶ ~한 easy; simple; plain / ~하지 않은 difficult; serious / ~하게 easily; with ease; without difficulty / 외국어에 숙달하기는 ~한 일이 아니다 It is no easy job to master a foreign language. 〔of; tolerate.

용인(容認) ~하다 admit; approve

용자(容姿) a figure; *one's* looks; *one's* 《an》 appearance.

용장(勇將) a brave general.

용재(用材)《재목》timber; lumber 《美》;《자재》materials. ¶ 건축 ~ building materials.

용적(容積) capacity (용량); volume (체적); bulk (부피). ¶ ~이 큰 capacious; bulky / 물체의 ~ the volume of a body. ‖ ~량 the measure of capacity / ~률 《건축의》floor area ratio / ~톤 a measurement ton.

용전(勇戰) ~하다 fight courageously (bravely).

용점(熔點) ☞ 용융점.

용접(鎔接) welding. ~하다 weld 《to, together》. ¶ 열 군데 ~하다 make ten welds / 용 마스크 a welder's helmet / 철판 ~하다 weld iron sheets. ‖ ~공 a welder / ~기 a welding machine; a welder / ~봉 a welding rod / ~제 a welding agent (flux) / 가스 ~ gas welding.

용제(溶劑) a solvent; a solution.

용지(用地) a lot; a site; land. ¶ 건축 ~ a site for a building; a building lot / 주택 ~ a housing lot / 철도 ~ railroad land.

용지(用紙) paper (to use); a (blank) form; a printed form; stationery. ‖ 시험 ~ an examination paper / 신청 〔주문〕 ~ an application (order) form.

용진(勇進) ~하다 《나아가다》 dash forward bravely; make a dash.

용질(溶質)《化》solute.

용출(湧出) ~하다 gush out 〔forth〕; spurt; well (up); erupt.

용춤 추다 give in 〔yield〕 to flattery.

용퇴(勇退)《물러남》voluntary retirement (resignation). ~하다 retire (resign) voluntarily.

용트림 ~하다 let out a big burp; belch in an affected manner.

용품(用品) an article; supplies. ¶ 가정 ~ domestic articles / 사무실 ~ office supplies / 스포츠 ~ sports equipment / 학 ~ school supplies (things).

용하다 ①《재주가》(be) deft; skillful; dexterous; good 《at》. ¶ 용하게 well; deftly. ②《장하다》(be) admirable; praiseworthy; wonderful. ③《특출》(be) extraordi-

용해(溶解) melting; dissolution; solution. ~하다 melt; dissolve; liquefy. ¶이 가루는 물에 ~ 된다 This powder dissolves in water. ‖ ~도 solubility / ~액 a solution / ~제 a solvent.

용해(鎔解) (s)melt; fusion. ~하다 (s)melt; fuse. ‖ ~로(爐) a (s)melting furnace / ~성 fusibility / ~점 a fusing point.

용호상박(龍虎相搏) a well-matched contest; a Titanic struggle.

우(右) the right. ¶ ~측의 right / ~로 돌다 turn to the right. ‖ ~로 나란히 (구령) Right dress! / ~로 보아 (구령) Eyes right!

우(優) ¶평점에서 수(秀) 다음) B; good; fine. ¶수학에서 ~를 받다 get a B in mathematics.

우 ① (몰려오는 꼴) all at once; with a rush. ¶~ 몰려 나오다 rush (pour) out / 젊은이들이 극장으로 ~ 몰려 왔다 The young people surged on the theater. ② (비·바람이) all at once; suddenly. 「horn.

우각(牛角) a cow's horn; an ox-

우거(寓居) a temporary abode [residence]. ~하다 reside [live] temporarily.

우거지 the outer leaves of Chinese cabbage, white radish, *etc*.

우거지다 (초목이 주어) grow thickly; (장소가 주어) be thickly covered (with (trees)); be overgrown with (trees); be overgrown with (weeds). ¶나무가 우거진 산 a thickly-(heavily-)wooded hill.

우거지상(一相) a frowning [wry] face; a scowl.

우겨대다 cling stubbornly (to one's notions); insist on one's own way; persist (in). ¶그는 무죄라고 우겨댔다 He insisted on his innocence. or He insisted that he was innocent. / 그녀는 거기 가겠다고 우겨댔다 She persisted in going there.

우격다짐 ~하다 resort to high-handed measures; put pressure (on); force; coerce. ¶~으로 high-handedly; forcibly; by force / ~하게 ...하게 하다 compel [force] (a person) to do / 그것은 ~이다 That's forcing things.

우견(愚見) (제 의견) my (humble) opinion (view).

우경(右傾) ~하다 turn [lean] to the right; be rightish. ‖ ~파(派) the Right Wing (Wingers).

우국(憂國) patriotism. ‖ ~지사 a patriot / ~지심 a patriotic spirit / ~충정 one's intense patriotism. 「an allied army.

우군(友軍) friendly forces [army]

우그러뜨리다 crush [bend] out of shape; make a dent (in); dent (a pail). 「shape; be dented.

우그러지다 be crushed out of

우그르르 (벌레가) swarming; in swarms; (물이) simmering.

우그리다 crush; dent.

우글거리다 (벌레 따위가) swarm; be crowded; be alive (with fish); teem (with).

우글쭈글 ~하다 (be) crumpled; rumpled; wrinkled. ¶옷이 ~해졌다 The clothes are all wrinkled.

우금(于今) till now; until now; up to the present. 「ward slightly.

우긋하다 (be) curved [bent] in-

우기(右記) ¶ ~의 the aforesaid; the above-mentioned.

우기(雨氣) threatening to rain; signs of rain.

우기(雨期) the rainy [wet] season. ¶~가 되었다 The rainy season has set in.

우기다 demand *one's* own way; persist (in one's opinion); insist on; impose (one's view upon); assert oneself. ¶하찮은 일에 너무 우기지 마라 Don't be so stubborn about such little things.

우김성(一性) obstinacy; adherence; persistence.

우는소리 (불평) a complaint; a whimper; a grievance; a tale of woes. ~하다 make complaints; complain (of, about); grumble (about, at); whine (about).

우단(羽緞) velvet.

우당탕 a thumping (bumping, clattering, thudding) noise. ~하다 (거리다) go thud.

우대(優待) preferential [warm] treatment; (환대) a warm reception; hospitality. ~하다 give preferential treatment (to); (환대하다) treat (a person) cordially [with hospitality]; receive (a person) warmly. ‖ ~권 a complimentary ticket.

우두(牛痘) cowpox; vaccinia. ¶ ~를 놓다 vaccinate / ~를 맞다 take vaccination; be vaccinated. ‖ ~자국 a vaccination scar.

우두둑 ① (깨무는 소리) crunchingly. ② (부러지는 소리) with a snap; snappishly. ③ (떨어지는 소리) with a clatter (patter); clatteringly.

우두망찰하다 (totally) confused [bewildered]; be at a loss; be in a fix [dilemma].

우두머리 (꼭대기) the top; (사람) the head; the boss; the chief.

우두커니 absent-mindedly; blankly; vacantly; idly; listlessly. ¶ ~ 바라보다 look blankly (at).

우둔(愚鈍) ~한 stupid; silly; dull-witted; thick-headed.

우듬지 a treetop; twigs.
우등(優等) 〔등급〕 the top 〔superior〕 grade; 〔학업의〕 excellency; honors. ¶ ~의 excellent; honor; superior /예일 대학을 ~으로 졸업하다 graduate with honors from Yale University. ∥ ~상〔win〕an honor prize / ~생 an honor student.
우뚝 high; aloft. ~하다 《솟은 모양》(be) high; towering; lofty; 《뛰어남》(be) prominent; conspicuous; outstanding.
우라늄 〔化〕 uranium (기호 U, Ur). ¶ 천연 〔농축〕 ~ natural 〔enriched〕 uranium.
우락부락하다 (be) rude; rough; rowdy; harsh; wild.
우랄 Ural. ¶ ~산맥 the Ural Mountains; the Urals / ~어족 the Uralic.
우람스럽다 (be) imposing; impressive; grand; dignified.
우량(雨量) (a) rainfall; precipitation. ¶ 서울의 평균 ~ the average rainfall in Seoul. ∥ ~계 a rain gauge.
우량(優良) ¶ ~한 superior; excellent; fine / H사는 ~기업이다 Company H is an excellent firm. ∥ ~도서 the best books 《of the year》 / ~아 a healthy child (일반적); a prize-winning child in a health contest / ~주 a superior 〔blue-chip〕 stock / ~품 choice 〔superior〕 goods.
우려나다 soak out; come off; 《차 따위가》 draw. ¶ 짠 맛이 우러나도록 절인 생선을 물에 담그다 put a salted fish in water and leave it until the saltiness soaks out.
우려나오다 spring 〔well〕 up; come from *one's* heart. ¶ 진심에서 우러나오는 감사의 말 words of thanks from the bottom of *one's* heart.
우러러보다 ① 〔쳐다보다〕 look up 《at》. ¶ 하늘을 ~ look up at the sky. ② 〔존경하다〕 look up to. ¶ 우리는 그를 스승으로 우러러본다 We respect 〔look up to〕 him as our teacher.
우러르다 〔쳐들다〕 lift *one's* head up; 〔존경〕 look up to; have respect.
우렁이 a pond 〔mud〕 snail. ¶ ~속 같다 be inscrutable; be a mystery.
우렁차다 (be) sonorous; resonant; resounding; roaring. ¶ 우렁찬 목소리 a ringing 〔resonant〕 voice.
우레 천둥. ¶ ~같은 thunderous; air-splitting / ~와 같은 박수 a storm 〔thunder〕 of applause.
우레탄 〔化〕 urethane.
우려(憂慮) worry; anxiety; concern; fear; apprehensions. ~하다 worry 《over》; be 〔feel〕 anxious 《about》; be apprehensive of. ¶ ~할 만한 serious; grave; alarming /사태를 크게 ~하고 있다 be deeply worried over the situation.
우려내다 wheedle 〔screw〕 《a thing》 out of 《a person》; squeeze 《a thing》 out.
우롱(愚弄) mockery; ridicule. ~하다 mock 《at》; fool; ridicule.
우루과이 Uruguay. ¶ ~의 Uruguayan / ~사람 an Uruguayan. ∥ ~라운드 the Uruguay Round (trade pact).
우르르 ① 〔여럿이 일제히〕 in a crowd. ¶ 방으로 ~ 들어오다 crowd 〔throng〕 into a room / 극장에서 많은 사람들이 ~ 나왔다 Lots of people poured out of the theater. ② 〔우레소리〕 thundering; rolling; rumbling. ③ 〔무너지는 소리〕 clattering; 〔fall〕 all in a heap. ¶ 담이 ~ 무너지다 a wall falls down all in a heap.
우리¹ 〔동물의〕 a cage 《맹수의》; a pen 《가축의》; a fold 《양 따위의》.
우리² we. ¶ ~의 our; our own; my / ~에게 us / ~ 나라 our country 〔nation〕.
우리다 〔물에〕 soak 《out》; steep 《vegetables》 《in water》; infuse.
우마(牛馬) oxen and horses. ∥ ~차 carts.
우매(愚昧) ¶ ~한 stupid; dump 《美》; silly; imbecile; ignorant.
우모(羽毛) feathers; plumage.
우무 agar(-agar). ¶ ~모양의 jellylike.
우묵우묵하다 (be) deeply hollowed; indented here and there.
우묵하다 (be) hollow; sunken.
우문(愚問) a stupid 〔silly〕 question. ¶ ~우답 a silly dialogue / ~현답 a wise answer to a silly question.
우물 a well. ¶ ~ 안 개구리 《비유》 a man of narrow outlook / ~을 쳐내다 clean a well / ~에서 물을 긷다 draw water from a well. ∥ ~가 공론 housewives' gossip / ~물 well water.
우물거리다¹ 〔여럿이〕 squirm in swarm; be alive with 《fish》. ¶ 벌레들이 ~ worms swarm.
우물거리다² 〔씹다·말하다〕 mumble. ¶ 〔입속에서〕 mumblingly ~하다 〔씹다〕 mumble.
우물들다 ① 〔보조개가〕 dimple; turn on the dimples. ② 〔우묵해지다〕 become hollow; form a dimple 《in》.
우물쭈물 indecisively; hesitantly; hesitatingly; half-heartedly. ~

하다 be tardy (slow) in 《*taking action*》; hesitate in 《*coming to a decision*》. ¶ ~하다가 기회를 놓치다 dally away *one's* opportunity. [lon moss.

우룻가사리 [植] an agar-agar; Ceylon moss.
우미(優美) ¶ ~한 graceful; elegant; refined.
우민(愚民) ignorant people. ∥ ~정치 mobocracy.
우박(雨雹) hail; a hailstone (한 알). ¶ ~이 온다 It hails.
우발(偶發) accidental (incidental) occurrence. ¶ ~하다 happen; occur by chance. ¶ ~적(으로) accidental(ly) / 사고는 ~적으로 이어졌다 Unexpectedly accidents happened in succession. ∥ ~사건 an accident; a contingency / ~전쟁 (an) accidental warfare.
우방(友邦) a friendly nation; an ally (맹방).
우범(虞犯) liability to crime. ∥ ~소년 a juvenile liable to committing crime / ~지대 a crime-ridden (crime-prone) area.
우비(雨備) rain-gear; rain things; a raincoat (비옷).
우비다 scoop (gouge) out; bore 《*a hole*》; pick 《*one's ear*》.
우비적거리다 scoop (gouge, bore) repeatedly; keep picking (poking).
우산(雨傘) an umbrella. ¶ ~ 쓰다 put up (raise) an umbrella. ∥ ~살 umbrella ribs.
우상(偶像) an idol. ¶ ~화하다 idolize. ∥ ~ 숭배 idol worship; idolatry / ~ 파괴 iconoclasm.
우생(優生) ¶ ~의 eugenic. ¶ ~ 결혼 a eugenic marriage / ~학 eugenics / ~학자 a eugenist.
우선(于先) ① 《첫째로》 first 《*of all*》; in the first place. ② 《좌우간》 anyway.
우선(優先) priority; preference; precedence. ~하다 take precedence (priority) 《*over*》; be prior 《*to*》. ¶ ~의 preferential; prior / ~적으로 다루다 give 《*a matter*》 priority 《*over*》; give 《*a person*》 preference / 이 임무는 다른 모든 것에 ~한다 This duty takes (has) priority over all others. / 회원은 ~적으로 입장할 수 있다 Members are given admission preference. ∥ ~권 preference; priority / ~ 배당 preference (preferred) dividends / ~순위 the order of priority / ~주 preferred stocks 《美》.
우성(優性) [遺傳] a dominant character; dominance. ¶ ~의 dominant. ∥ ~ 유전 prepotency / ~ 유전인자 a dominant gene / ~ 형질 a dominant trait.
우세 ~하다 be laughed at; be put to shame; be humiliated. ¶ ~스럽다 be shameful (humiliating).
우세(郵稅) postage. [ating).
우세(優勢) superiority; predominance; lead. ~하다 be superior 《*to*》; have an advantage 《*over*》. ¶ ~한 superior; predominant; leading / ~ 하다 gain (get) an advantage 《*over*》; become dominant; lead (경기에서) / 수적으로 ~하다 outnumber 《*the other party*》; be superior in numbers 《*to*》 / 지금 어느 팀이 ~합니까 Which team is leading now?
우송(郵送) ~하다 post; mail; send by post (mail). ∥ ~료 postage / ~ 무료 postage-free 《*goods*》.
우수(右手) the right hand.
우수(憂愁) melancholy; gloom.
우수(優秀) excellence; superiority. ¶ ~한 excellent; superior; superb; distinguished / ~한 학생 an excellent student / ~한 성적으로 with excellent results; with honors. ∥ ~성 excellence.
우수리 ① 《줄 거스름돈》 (the odd) change. ¶ ~를 내주다 (받다) give (get) the change / ~는 네가 가져라 Keep the change. ② 《끝수》 an odd sum; a fraction. ¶ ~를 버리다 omit fractions.
우수수 (fall, scatter) in great masses; in a multitude. ~하다 rustle. ¶ ~ 떨어지다 fall in great masses; rustle down.
우스개 jocularity; drollery. ∥ 우스갯소리 a joke; a jest / 우스갯짓 (a bit of) clowning.
우스꽝스럽다 (be) funny; ridiculous; laughable; comical.
우습게보다 ① look down (up)on 《*a person*》; hold 《*a person*》 in contempt; despise. ② 《경시》 make light (little) of; hold 《*a thing*》 in light esteem; neglect; slight.
우습다 ① 《재미있다》 (be) funny; amusing; 《가소롭다》 (be) laughable; ridiculous; absurd; 《익살맞다》 (be) comic. ② 《하찮다》 (be) trifling; trivial; small; 《쉽다》 (be) easy. ③ 《기이하다》 (be) strange; unusual; queer; funny.
우승(優勝) 《승리》 victory; 《선수권》 championship. ~하다 win; win the victory (championship; pennant 《美》; title). ∥ ~기 (旗) a championship flag; a pennant / ~자 the (first prize) winner; a champion / ~컵 a championship cup; a trophy / ~팀 a winning team / ~후보 the favorite for the championship; the best bet for the title.
우승열패(優勝劣敗) the survival of

우시장(牛市場) a cattle fair; market.
우심하다(尤甚 —) (be) extreme; excessive; severe (추위 등이); heavy (손해 등이). ¶ ~는 세상사다 The survival of the fittest is the way of the world. 〔ket〕.
우아(優雅) elegance. ¶ ~한 elegant; refined; graceful / 몸가짐이 ~하다 have a graceful carriage.
우악(愚惡) ¶ ~스러운〔한〕 uneducated and crude; (harsh and) wild; rough; rude; violent.
우안(右岸) the right bank 《of a river》.
우애(友愛)〔형제간의〕 brotherly 〔sisterly〕 affection; fraternal love;〔친구간의〕 friendship; comradeship. ¶ ~의 정 a friendly spirit of fraternity / ~를 돈독히 하다 promote friendship 《between》.
우어(위) Whoa ! 〔feeling.
우엉(植) a burdock.
우여곡절(迂餘曲折)〔굴곡〕 meandering; twists and turns;〔복잡〕 complications;〔파란〕 vicissitudes 《of life》; ups and downs. ¶ ~ 끝에 두 사람은 결혼했다 They got married after many twists and turns.
우연(偶然) (a singular) chance; accident. ¶ ~한 casual; accidental / ~히 accidentally; casually; by accident; by chance / ~의 일치 a coincidence / ~히 만나다 happen to meet; meet by chance / 그의 성공은 결코 ~이 아니다 Chance has nothing to do with his success. ‖ ~론 accidentalism.
우열(優劣) superiority and〔or〕 inferiority; merits and〔or〕 demerits. ¶ ~을 다투다 contend〔strive〕 for superiority / ~을 두다 discriminate 《between》; make a discrimination 《between》 / ~이 없는 equal; evenly matched.
우왕좌왕(右往左往) ¶ ~하다 go this way and that; run about in confusion.
우울(憂鬱) melancholy; low spirits; gloom; the blues《美口》. ¶ ~한 melancholy; depressed; low-spirited; gloomy / ~해지다 be seized with melancholia. ‖ ~증 melancholia / ~증환자 a melancholiac.
우월(優越) superiority. ¶ ~한 superior; supreme; predominating. ¶ ~감 a superiority complex; a sense of superiority / ~감을 갖다 have a sense of superiority over others》.
우위(優位) predominance; superiority. ¶ ~에 서다 hold a dominant position; get〔gain〕 an advantage over 《a person》; attain superiority 《over》.
우유(牛乳) (cow's) milk. ¶ 상한 ~ sour milk / ~로 기르다 feed 《a baby》 on cow's milk; bring up 《a baby》 on the bottle / ~를 짜다 milk a cow / ~를 배달하다 deliver milk. ‖ ~가게 a dairy / ~배달부 a milkman.
우유부단(優柔不斷) irresolution; indecision. ¶ ~하다 lack decision; be a man of indecision. ¶ ~한 indecisive; irresolute; shilly-shally / ~한 사람 a waverer; a shilly-shallier.
우육(牛肉) beef.
우의(友誼) amity; friendship; fellowship; friendly relations. ¶ ~를 돈독히 하다 promote friendship 《between》.
우의(雨衣) a raincoat.
우이(牛耳) ¶ ~ 잡다 take the lead 《in》; be the leader 《of》. ‖ ~독경(誦經) "preaching to deaf ears."
우익(右翼) ①〔열〕 the right flank〔column〕. ②〔競〕 the right wing;〔野〕 the right field. ¶ ~수 a right fielder. ③〔정치상의〕 the Rightists; the Right Wing. ‖ ~단체 a right-wing organization / ~운동 a Rightist movement.
우자(愚者) a fool; a dunce.
우장(雨裝) a raincoat. ☞ 우비.
우정(友情) friendship; friendly feelings. ¶ ~있는 amicable; friendly / ~을 가지고 with friendship; in a friendly manner / ~을 맺다 form a friendship 《with》; make friends 《with》. 〔istration〕.
우정(郵政) postal service〔admin-
우주(宇宙) the universe; the cosmos; (outer) space. ¶ ~ 적 universal; cosmic / ~의 신비 the mystery of space. ‖ ~개발경쟁 a space race / ~개발계획 a space development project / ~공학 space engineering / ~과학 space science / ~과학자 a space scientist / ~복 a spacesuit / ~비행 a spaceflight / ~비행사 an astronaut; a cosmonaut / ~선(線) the cosmic rays / ~선(船) a spaceship; a spacecraft / ~선기지 a spaceport / ~스테이션 a space (satellite) station / ~시대 the space age / ~여행 space travel (trip) / ~위성 a space satellite / ~유영 a spacewalk / ~인〔외계인〕 a man (being) from outer space; an alien / ~중계 a satellite relay / ~탐사 space exploration / ~협정 a space agreement.
우중(雨中) ¶ ~에 in the rain / ~에도 불구하고 in spite of the rain. 〔dull; dusky; dim.
우중충하다 (be) gloomy; somber;

우지(牛脂) beef fat; (beef) tallow.
우지끈 with a crack (crash). ~하다 crack; snap.
우직(愚直) simple honesty. ¶ ~한 simple (and honest).
우짖다 scream; chirp (새가).
우쭐거리다 ① sway (shake) *oneself* rhythmically; keep swaying; swagger. ② ☞ 우쭐하다.
우쭐하다 become conceited; be puffed up (*by*, *with*); be elated; have a high opinion of *oneself*; have a swelled head 《美》. ¶ 그렇게 우쭐할 것 없다 Don't flatter yourself too much.
우차(牛車) an ox cart.
우천(雨天) rainy (wet) weather (날씨); a rainy (wet) day (날). ∥ ~순연(順延) "To be postponed till the first fine day in case of rain."
우체(郵遞) ∥ ~국 a post office / ~국원 a post-office clerk / ~국장 a postmaster / ~통 a mail-box 《美》; postbox 《英》.
우측(右側) the right side. ∥ ~통행 "Keep to the right."
우툴두툴하다 (be) uneven; rugged; rough.
우편(郵便) mail 《美》; post 《英》; the mail service. ¶ ~으로 보내다 send (*a parcel*) by mail (post) / ~으로 주문하다 order by mail / ~으로 알리다 inform (notify) by mail / ~을 이쪽으로 돌려 주시오 Please forward my mail to this address. ∥ ~낭 a mail bag / ~물 postal matter / ~번호 a zip code 《美》 / ~사서함 a post office box (생략 P.O.B.) / ~요금 postage; postal charges / ~집배원 a postman; a mailman 《美》 / ~함 a mailbox; a letter box / ~환 a (postal) money order / 외국 ~ foreign mail / 제일종 ~ first-class mail.
우표(郵票) a stamp; a postage stamp. ∥ ~수집 stamp collection / ~수집가 a stamp collector.
우피(牛皮) oxhide; cowhide. ⌊tor.
우향(右向) ¶ ~우(右) 《구령》 Right turn (face)! / ~ 앞으로 가 《구령》 Right wheel!
우현(右舷) 〔海〕 starboard.
우호(友好) friendship; amity. ¶ ~적인 friendly; amicable. ∥ ~관계 friendly relations / ~국 a friendly nation / ~조약 a treaty of friendship (amity) / ~협력 조약 a friendship-cooperation treaty.
우화(寓話) a fable; an apologue; an allegory. ∥ ~작가 a fable writer; a fabulist.
우환(憂患) 《병》 illness; 《근심》 troubles; cares; worry; 《불행》 a calamity. ¶ 집안에 ~이 있다 have troubles in *one's* family.
우황(牛黃) 〔韓醫〕 ox (cow) bezoar.
우회(迂廻) a detour. ~하다 take a roundabout course; make a detour; bypass. ∥ ~로 a detour; a bypass; 《게시》 Detour 《美》.
우회전(右回轉) ~하다 turn to the right. ∥ ~금지 《교통표지》 No right-turn.
우후(雨後) after a rainfall. ¶ ~죽순처럼 나오다 spring up like mushrooms after rain.
욱기(—氣) hot (hot-blooded) temper. ¶ 그는 ~가 있다 He is very quick-tempered. *or* He looses his temper easily.
욱다 be dented; get (be) bent in.
욱대기다 ① ☞ 으르다. ② ☞ 우기다.
욱시글득시글 in swarms. ~하다 swarm; be crowded (thronged).
욱신거리다 《쑤시다》 tingle; smart; throb with pain.
욱이다 dent (*in*); batter (bend, turn) (*a thing*) in.
욱일(旭日) the rising (morning) sun. ¶ 그는 ~ 승천의 기세다 His star is rising.
욱적거리다 ☞ 북적거리다.
욱하다 flare up; get impetuous; lose *one's* temper; fly into a sudden rage. ¶ 욱하고 성을 내다 burst into a sudden anger.
운(運) fortune; luck; 《운명》 fate; destiny; 《기회》 chance. ¶ ~ 좋은 lucky; fortunate / ~ 나쁜 unlucky; unfortunate / ~ 좋게 fortunately; luckily; by good fortune (luck) / ~ 나쁘게 unluckily; unfortunately; by ill luck / ~이 좋으면 if fortune smiles upon *one*; if *one* be lucky / ~이 좋아 …하다 be lucky enough to (*do*); have the good fortune to (*do*) / ~이 다하다 *one's* luck runs out / ~에 맡기다 leave (*a matter*) to chance.
운(韻) a rhyme. ¶ ~을 맞추다 rhyme (*with*).
운동(運動) ① 〔理〕 《물체 등의》 motion; movement. ~하다 move; be in motion. ¶ ~의 법칙 the laws of motion. ∥ ~량 momentum / ~에너지 kinetic energy. ② 《몸의》 exercise; 《경기》 sports; athletics; athletic games. ~하다 (take) exercise; get some exercise. ¶ 가벼운(적당한) ~을 하다 do light (moderate) exercise. ∥ ~경기 athletic sports / ~구 sports goods (equipment) / ~복 sports clothes; sportswear / ~부 athletic club / ~부족 lack (shortage) of exercise / ~선수 an athlete; a sportsman / ~신경 the motor nerves; a reflex (action) (반사작용) (~신

운두 〔육상〕 ~ transportation by sea (land).

운수(運數) luck; fortune. ☞ 운(運). ¶ ~가 좋은 (나쁜) lucky (unlucky); fortunate (unfortunate). ∥ ~소관 a matter pertaining to luck (fortune).

운수(運輸) traffic (service). ☞ 운송. ¶ 여객[철도] ~ passenger (railway) traffic. ∥ ~노조(勞組) the Traffic Service Workers Union / ~업 the transportation business.

운신(運身) ~하다 move *one's* body. ¶ ~도 못하다 cannot budge (move) an inch.

운영(運營) management; operation; administration. ~하다 manage; run; operate. ¶호텔을 ~하다 run a hotel. ∥ ~비〔자금〕 working (operating) expenses (funds) / ~위원회 a steering committee.

운용(運用) application; employment. ~하다 apply; employ; use. ¶법률의 ~ the application of the law / 자금을 ~하다 employ funds / 시설을 잘 ~하다 keep the facilities in good working order.

운운(云云) so and so; and so on (forth); et cetera (생략 etc.). ~하다 say something or other (*about*); mention; refer to; criticize (비판하다).

운율(韻律) a rhythm; a meter.

운임(運賃) 〔여객의〕 a fare; 〔화물의〕 a freight (rates); 〔송료〕 shipping expenses. ¶ ~무료〔게시〕 Carriage [Freight] free / ~선불로 짐을 보내다 send goods carriage pre-paid / ~을 환불해 주다 refund the fare / 이 화물의 ~은 얼마입니까 How much would you charge for shipping this parcel? / ~표〔화물의〕 a freight list; 〔여객의〕 a fare table / ~후불 freight to collect.

운전(運轉) ① 〔자동차의〕 driving; 〔기계의〕 operation; working; running. ~하다 〔차·기차를〕 drive; ride (오토바이를); 〔기계를〕 operate; run; set (*a machine*) going. ¶ 자동차를 ~하다 drive a car; take the wheel / 졸음 ~을 하다 doze off at the wheel / 천천히 ~하다 drive slowly / 술마시고 ~해서는 안 된다 You shouldn't drink and drive. / 기계의 ~을 멈추다 suspend the operation of a machine. ∥ ~교습소 a driving school / ~기사 《자동차의》 a driver; a chauffeur (자가용의); a taxi driver; a cabdriver 《美》 (택시의) / ~기술 driving skill / ~석 《차의》 a driver's seat; 〔열차의〕 an engineer's seat / ~면허시험 a driver's li-

경이 발달해 있다〔둔하다〕 have quick (slow) reflexes / ~장 a playground / ~의 〔경기장〕 an athletic field (경기장) / ~화 sports shoes; sneakers《美》 / ~회 a sports meeting; an athletic meeting (meet); a field day 〔날〕 / 옥외 ~ outdoor (field) sports. ③ 〔정치·사회적인〕 a campaign; a drive; a movement 〔집단의〕. ~하다 carry on a campaign; conduct a drive (movement). ¶정치 ~ a political movement / 선거 ~ an election campaign / 노동〔학생〕 ~ a labor (student) movement / 모금 ~ a fund-raising campaign / ~을 지원하다 support a campaign / ~을 일으키다 start (launch) a campaign (drive, movement) (*for, against*) / 유럽에서는 반핵 ~이 한창이다 The anti-nuclear movement has become quite strong in Europe. ∥ ~원 《선거의》 a canvasser; a campaigner / ~자금 campaign funds.

운두 〔키가 높은 (낮은) 신 a high-[low-]cut shoes.

운명(運命) fate; destiny; *one's* lot; doom (나쁜); fortune (좋은). ¶ ~의 장난 a whim 〔an irony〕 of life / ~의 총아 a child of fortune; a fortune's favorite / …과 ~을 같이하다 throw 〔cast〕 in *one's* lot with (*a person*) / ~에 맡기다 leave (*a thing*) to ~ / ~이라고 체념하다 resign *oneself* to *one's* fate / ~할 ~에 있다 be destined (doomed) to…. ∥ ~론 fatalism / ~론자 a fatalist.

운명(殞命) ~하다 die; breathe *one's* last.

운모(雲母) 〔鑛〕 mica.

운무(雲霧) cloud and mist (fog).

운문(韻文) verse; poetry, a poem.

운반(運搬) conveyance; transportation; carriage. ~하다 carry; convey; transport. ∥ ~비 carriage; a portage / ~인 a carrier; a porter (인부) / ~차 a cart; a truck; a wagon.

운산(運算) ☞ 연산(演算).

운석(隕石) 〔鑛〕 a meteorite.

운송(運送) conveyance; transport; transportation; forwarding. ~하다 carry; transport; convey; forward. ¶짐은 내일 트럭으로 ~하겠다 We will send the goods in a truck tomorrow. ∥ ~료 freight (forwarding) charge / ~비 cost of transport; shipping expenses (선편의) / ~업 the express (forwarding) business; the transport (shipping, freight) industry / ~업자 a carrier; a forwarding (shipping) agent / ~점 a forwarding agency / ~회사 a transport (shipping) company / 해상

운지법 (運指法) 〖樂〗 fingering.
운집 (雲集) ~하다 swarm; crowd; throng 《a place》; flock.
운철 (隕鐵) 〖鑛〗 meteoric iron.
운치 (韻致) taste; elegance; refinement. ¶ ~ 있는 tasteful; elegant.
운필 (運筆) strokes of the brush; the use of the brush (법).
운하 (運河) a canal; a waterway. ¶ ~를 파다 dig〔build〕 a canal. ‖ ~통과료 canal tolls.
운항 (運航) navigation; 《shipping》service; airline service (항공기의). ~하다 run; ply 《between》. ¶ 인천과 부산 사이를 ~하는 배들 ships having〔sailing〕 between Inch'ŏn and Pusan.
운행 (運行) 《천체의》 movement; 《교통기관의》 service. ¶ 버스 ~ bus service / 지하철은 러시아워에 3분마다 ~된다 The subways run every three minutes during the rush hour(s). / 임시 열차 ~ extra train service. ‖ ~정지 the suspension of operation 《for 5 days》.
운휴 (運休) suspension of the 《bus》 service.
울¹ (울타리) an enclosure; a fence. ¶ ~을 치다 fence round 《a house》; enclose 《a house》 with a fence.
울² 〖양모〗 wool.
울격거리다 gargle.
울근불근하다 be at odds 《with》; be in discord 《with》; be on bad terms 《with》.
울굿불굿하다 (be) colorful; variegated; colored.
울다① 《사람이》 weep; cry (소리 지르며); sob (흑흑절); wail (통곡); blubber (엉엉하고); shed tears (눈물 흘리며). ¶ 아파서 ~ weep with pain / 비보에 접하여 ~ weep at sad news / 울며 세월을 보내다 spend one's years in tears / 눈이 젖어지도록 ~ cry one's heart out / 감동해서 ~ be moved to tears. ②《동물이》 cry; 《새·벌레 따위가》 sing; chirp; twitter; 《개가》 yelp; 《고양이가》 mew; meow; 《소가》 low; moo; 《말이》 neigh; whinny; 《비둘기가》 coo; 《닭이》 crow (수탉); cluck (암탉). ¶ 매미가 밖에서 울고 있다 There are cicadas singing outside. / 때까치가 죽은 가지 위에서 울고 있다 A shrike is twittering on a dead branch. ③《종이》 ring; have a ringing 《in one's ears》. ④《옷·장판 따위가》 get wrinkled; pucker; cockle.
울대¹ (울타리의) a fence stake.
울대² 《조류의》 the syrinx (of a bird).
울렁거리다 《가슴》 feel one's heart leaping; go pit-a-pat; palpitate; get nervous (메스거림); feel sick (nausea).
울리다 ① 《울게 하다》 make 《a person》 cry; move 〔touch〕 《a person》 to tears (감루); 《슬프게 하다》 grieve; bring sorrow upon 《a person》. ¶ 심금을 울리는 story / 아이를 ~ make a child cry; set a child crying. ②《소리를 내다》 ring; sound; clang (땡그랑 땡그랑); blow (기적); beat (북). ¶ 경적을 ~ sound the horn / 종을 ~ chime (clang, toll) a bell. ③《소리가》 sound; ring; 《반향하다》 resound; echo; reverberate; be echoed; 《천둥 따위가》 roar; thunder; rumble. ¶ 멀리서 천둥이 울렸다 Thunder rumbled in the distance. / 교회의 종이 울렸다 The church bell rang. ④《명성이》 be widely known. ¶ 명성이 전국에 ~ win nationwide fame.
울림 (음향) a sound; (진동) a vibration; 《반향》 an echo; 《굉음》 a roar; a boom (포성의); a peal (종·천둥 따위). ¶ 종의 ~ the peal of a bell.
울먹거리다 be on the verge of tears; be ready to cry; be almost in tears.
울보 a cry-baby.
울부짖다 scream; howl; cry out.
울분 (鬱憤) resentment; pent-up feelings; a grudge; anger. ¶ ~을 풀다 let out〔relieve, vent〕 one's pent-up feelings〔anger〕; let off steam 〖口語〗 / ~을 참다 control one's anger.
울상 (一相) a face about to cry. ¶ ~을 하다 〔짓다〕 wear a tearful face; be ready 〔going〕 to cry.
울새 〖鳥〗 a robin; a redbreast.
울쑥불쑥 toweringly〔ruggedly〕 here and there; soaringly at different quarters; jaggedly.
울음 crying; weeping. ¶ ~소리 a cry; a tearful voice / ~을 터뜨리다 burst out crying / ~을 참다 repress〔gulp down〕 one's tears.
울적 (鬱寂) ~하다 be depressed; be in low spirits; feel gloomy; be cast down. ¶ 울적한 얼굴을 a malancholy look / 날씨가 나쁘면 기분이 ~해진다 Bad weather depresses me.
울창 (鬱蒼) ¶ ~한 〔하게〕 thick(ly); dense(ly); luxuriant(ly) / ~한 숲 a dense forest.
울타리 a fence; a hedge (생울타리); 《장애》 a barrier; one's defences. ¶ 정원에 ~를 치다 fence the yard; put up〔build〕 a fence

울퉁불퉁하다 around the garden / 국제화란 나라 사이를 갈라놓고 있는 ~를 제거하는 것이다 Internationalization means breaking down of barriers separating nations.

울퉁불퉁하다 (be) rugged; rough; uneven. ¶울퉁불퉁한 길 a bumpy road / 울퉁불퉁하면 지면 uneven ground.

울혈(鬱血) 〖醫〗 blood congestion.

울화(鬱火) pent-up resentment (anger). ¶~가 치밀다 feel the surge of anger (resentment) / ~ 터져 burst into a fit of rage; explode with anger. ‖ ~병 a disease caused by frustration (pent-up feelings).

움¹ (싹) sprouts; shoots; buds. ¶~이 돋다 〔트다〕 bud; sprout; put forth shoots.

움² 〈지하 저장고〉 a cellar; a pit. ¶~에 채소를 저장하다 store vegetables in a cellar (pit).

움막(-幕) an underground hut; a dugout. ¶~살이 life in a dugout.

움실거리다 swarm; squirm in a swarm.

움쑥하다 (be) hollow; sunken.

움씰하다 ☞ 움찔하다.

움죽거리다 move; stir.

움죽거리다 keep on moving; stir; twitch; wriggle.

움직이다¹ 〔자동사〕 ① 〈이동하다〉 move. ¶움직이고 있다 be moving; be in motion / 움직이지 않고 있다 keep (remain) still; be at a standstill; stay put / 움직이지 않게 되다 stop moving; come to a standstill / 그는 두려움으로 움직일 수 없었다 Fear rooted him to the ground. / 움직이지 마라 Freeze! / 움직이면 쏜다 If you make a move, I'll shoot. ② 〈기계 따위가〉 work; run; go. ¶전기로 움직이는 기계 a machine run by electricity / 움직일 수 없게 되다 〈고장으로〉 break down; go out of action / 승강기가 움직이지 않는다 The elevator is not working. ③ 〈변동하다〉 change; vary. ¶움직일 수 없는 증거 an indisputable proof; firm (immutable) evidence. ④ 〈마음이〉 be moved (touched, shaken). ¶그녀 이야기에 마음이 움직였다 I was moved by her story. / 신념이 ~ be shaken in one's belief. ⑤ 〈행동하다〉 act; work. ¶상사의 지시로 움직이다 act on one's boss's instructions / 표면이 아닌 뒤에서 ~ work (maneuver) behind the scenes / 곧 당국이 움직일 것이다 Soon the authorities will take action.

움직이다² 〔타동사〕 ① 〈이동시키다〉 move; shift (furniture); stir. ¶다리를 ~ move one's legs / 군대를 ~ move troops / 산들바람이 나뭇잎을 움직였다 A light breeze stirred the leaves. ② 〈기계 따위를〉 work (operate) (a machine); set (a machine) in motion. ¶그는 기계 움직이는 법을 안다 He knows how to operate this machine. ③ 〈마음을〉 move; touch; affect. ¶그녀의 호소는 많은 사람의 마음을 움직였다 Her appeal touched the hearts of many people. ④ 〈기타〉 사회를 움직이고 있는 것은 젊은 이들이다 It is the young that get the society going. / 어떤 것도 그의 마음을 움직일 수 없었다 Nothing could make him change his mind.

움직임 〈운동〉 movement; motion; 〈동향〉 trend; drift; 〈활동〉 activity; 〈행동〉 action. ¶천체의 ~ the movement of heavenly bodies / ~이 둔하다 be slow in one's movement / 세계의 ~에 밝아지다 become well-informed about world trends / 경찰은 그들의 ~을 수사하고 있다 The police are investigating their activities.

움찔하다 shrink (fall, hold) back; flinch; be startled (frightened) 《by, at》; start 〔at〕. ¶권총을 보고 ~ flinch at the sight of the pistol / 갑자기 개가 짖자 그는 움찔했다 He shrank back as the dog suddenly started barking.

움츠리다 shrink (flinch) (at, from); crouch; cower (down, away); draw in (away). ¶목을 ~ duck (pull in) one's head / 손을 ~ draw in (away) one's hand / 어깨를 ~ shrug one's shoulders / 몸을 ~ shrink (flinch, draw back) oneself (from).

움켜잡다 grasp; snatch; seize; grab (at); catch (take) hold of. ¶단단히 ~ grasp tightly / 멱살을 ~ seize (catch) (a person) by the collar / 움켜잡고 놓지 않다 keep a tight grasp (on).

움켜쥐다 hold (a thing) tight in one's hand; clutch; grip (clasp) tightly; clench; squeeze. ¶양손을 단단히 움켜쥐고 일어서다 stand up with one's hands tightly clenched / 손을 꼭 ~ sqeeze (a person's) hand; give (a person's) hand a squeeze.

움큼 a handful (of sand); a fistful.

움트다 〈초목이〉 sprout; bud; shoot; 〈사랑 따위가〉 arise; begin to grow. ¶초목이 움틀 때는 when trees and grasses bud; when new buds begin to appear / 두 사람 사이에 애정이 움텄다 Love began to grow in the hearts of the two.

움패다 become hollow (depressed).

움펑눈 deep-set (sunken) eyes. ¶ ~이 *a person* with sunken eyes; a hollow-eyed person.
움푹하다 (be) sunken; hollow.
웃기다 make (*a person*) laugh; excite (provoke) the laughter of (*the audience*). ¶ 그 농담은 모두를 웃겼다 The joke made everybody laugh (set everybody laughing). / 웃기지 마라 Don't make me laugh!
웃녘 the upper side (part).
웃다 ① laugh (소리 내어); smile (미소짓다); chuckle; giggle (킬낄); grin (빙긋이). ¶ 웃으면서 with a laugh (smile) / 웃지 않을 수 없다 cannot help laughing / 웃어 넘기다 (*a matter*) off (away) / 배를 쥐고 ~ hold *one's* sides with laughter / 함께 ~ join in the laughter / 청중은 그의 익살을 듣고 와 하고 웃었다 The audience burst into laughter at his gag. ② (비웃다) laugh at; ridicule; make fun of (놀리다); sneer at (경멸하다). ¶ 웃을 만한 laughable; ridiculous / 아무의 무식을 ~ laugh at *a person's* ignorance.
웃도리 the upper part of the body; (웃옷) a jacket.
웃돈 a trade-in price; part payment. ¶ ~을 치르고 pay the difference in cash / ~을 주고 헌 차를 새 차와 바꾸다 trade in an old car for a new one.
웃돌다 exceed; be more than; be over (above). ¶ 평년작을 ~ exceed the average crop.
웃목 the place on the floor away from the fireplace.
웃옷 a jacket; a coat; (garment).
웃음 a laugh; laughter; (미소) a smile; a chuckle (킬킬 웃음); a sneer (조소). ¶ ~을 띄우고 with a smile / ~을 터뜨리다 burst into laughter / ~을 사다 be laughed at (by) / ~을 참다 swallow a laugh / 쓴 ~을 짓다 give a bitter smile / 억지 ~을 짓다 give forced smile. ‖ ~소리 laughter; a laughing voice.
웃음거리 a laughingstock; a butt of ridicule. ¶ ~가 되다 make a fool of *oneself*; be the butt of ridicule.
웃자리 (上座) the seat of honor.
웃통 ¶ ~을 벗다 strip (*oneself*) to the waist; take off *one's* jacket. 「*one's* own territory.
웅거 (雄據) ~하다 hold and defend
웅긋쭝긋하다 (be) sticking up here and there.
웅담 (熊膽) [韓醫] bear('s) gall.
웅대 (雄大) ~하다 (be) grand; majestic; magnificent. ¶ ~한 구상 a grand conception.
웅덩이 a pool; a puddle.

웅도 (雄圖) an ambitious enterprise; a great undertaking.
웅변 (雄辯) eloquence; oratory. ¶ ~의 eloquence / ~을 토하며 speak with (great) eloquence. ‖ ~가 an eloquent speaker; an orator / ~대회 an oratorical (a speech) contest / ~술 oratory.
웅비 (雄飛) ~하다 launch out into (politics); start out on (a career). ¶ 해외로 ~하다 go abroad with a great ambition
웅성거리다 be noisy (astir); be in commotion. ¶ 잠시 장내가 웅성거렸다 There was a momentary stir in the hall.
웅숭깊다 (be) deep; profound; inscrutable; broad(-minded).
웅얼거리다 mutter; murmur. ¶ 혼자 ~ mutter to *oneself*.
웅자 (雄姿) a gallant (majestic) figure; a splendid style; an imposing appearance.
웅장 (雄壯) ~하다 (be) grand; magnificent; sublime; majestic. ¶ ~한 경치 a grand sight / ~한 건물 a stately building.
웅크리다 crouch; squat down; huddle (curl) *oneself* up.
워낙 (원래) originally; from the first; (무척) quite; so; very. ¶ 그는 ~ 온순한 사람이다 He is born good-natured. / ~ 사람이 성실해서 채용했다 He was so sincere that I employed him.
워드프로세서 a word processor. ¶ ~로 편지를 쓰다 write a letter on a word prorocessor.
워밍업 warm(ing)-up. ~하다 [warm up.
워석워석 rustling.
워크숍 a workshop.
워키토키 a walkie-talkie.
워터 (물) water. ‖ ~슈트 a water chute / ~탱크 a water tank.
원 (圓) a circle. ‖ ~운동 circular motion.
원 (願) a wish; a desire; (요청) a request; (간원) an entreaty; (청원) a petition. ¶ ~을 이루다 have *one's* wish fulfilled (granted).
원 (화폐 단위) won (생략 ₩). ¶ 천 ~짜리 지폐 a thousand-*won* bill (note) ☞ 원화.
원… (元・原) (원래의) original; first; primary. ¶ ~계획 초안 the first draft of the plan.
원가 (原價) the (prime) cost. ¶ ~로 [이하로] 팔다 sell at (below) cost. / ~견적 an estimate of the cost / ~계산 cost accounting / ~관리 a cost control / ~구성 cost structure / ~절감 cost reduction / ~생산 the cost of production.
원거리 (遠距離) a long distance

[range]. ¶ ~의 long-distance; distant / ~통학 long-distance commuting (to school).
원격(遠隔) (멂) ~하다 (be) distant 《*from*》; far-off; remote. ¶ ~조작 remote control 《*a machine*》 by remote control) / ~지 무역 long-distance trade / ~측정 telemetering.
원경(遠景) a distant view; a perspective.
원고(原告) 〖法〗 an accuser(형사에서); a plaintiff(민사에서).
원고(原稿) a manuscript (생략 MS.); a copy (인쇄·광고의); a contribution (기고문); an article (기사). ¶ ~료 payment for copy; copy money / ~지 copy 〔manuscript〕 paper / 강연 ~ the script for a lecture.
원광(原鑛) a raw ore; an ore.
원광(圓光) a halo; a nimbus.
원교(遠郊) a place remote from a city.
원군(援軍) rescue forces; reinforcements. ¶ ~을 보내주다 send reinforcements 《*to*》; reinforce.
원근(遠近) far and near; distance. ¶ ~을 가리지 않고 regardless 〔irrespective〕 of distance / 그림에 ~감을 주다 give perspective to a painting. ‖ ~법 perspective drawing.
원금(元金) the principal (이자에 대한); the capital (자본).
원급(原級) 〖文〗 the positive degree.
원기(元氣) vigor; energy; vitality; pep. ¶ ~ 왕성한 high-spirited; vigorous; energetic; healthy; spry. ¶ ~부족 lack of vigor.
원내(院內) 〖國會〗 ~의〔에서〕 inside the House 〔National Assembly〕. ‖ ~총무 the floor leader 《美》; the (party) whip 《英》.
원년(元年) the first year.
원단(元旦) (the) New Year's Day.
원당(原糖) raw sugar.
원대(原隊) 〖軍〗 one's (home) unit. ¶ ~복귀하다 return to one's unit.
원대(遠大) ~하다 far-reaching; ambitious; grand. ¶ ~한 계획 a far-reaching 〔grand〕 plan / ~한 포부 a great ambition.
원도(原圖) the original drawing.
원동기(原動機) a motor. ¶ ~를 단 자전거 a motorbike.
원동력(原動力) motive power 〔force〕; driving force (추진력). ¶ 사회의 ~ the driving force of society / 활동의 ~ the mainspring of activity.
원두막(園頭幕) a lookout 〔shed〕 for a melon field. 〖주〗.
원둘레(圓―) circumference. ☞ 원
원래(元來) 〔본래〕 originally; primarily; 〔생래〕 naturally; by nature; 〔본질적으로〕 essentially; 〔사실은〕 really; 〔처음부터〕 from the first. ¶ 이 책은 ~ 아이들용이다 This book is intended primarily for children. / 그는 ~ 내성적이다 He is reserved by nature.
원로(元老) 〖정계의〗 an elder statesman; 〖고참〗 a senior member; an elder; a veteran. ¶ 실업계의 ~ an elder in business circle.
원로(遠路) a long way 〔distance〕. ¶ ~의 여행 a long journey / ~를 무릅쓰고 왕림해 주셔서 고맙습니다 Thank you for coming such a long way.
원론(原論) a theory; the principles 《*of*》. ¶ 경제학 ~ the principles of economics.
원료(原料) raw materials; an ingredient (재료). ¶ 버터의 ~는 무엇이지 What is butter made from?
원룸아파트 a studio (apartment); an efficiency (apartment).
원리(元利), **원리금**(元利金) principal and interest. ‖ ~합계액 the amount with interest added.
원리(原理) a principle; a tenet (사상·신앙의); a law(과학·자연의). ¶ 근본 ~ the fundamental principle / 자연의 ~ a law of nature / ~원칙을 지키다 be faithful to *one's* principles.
원만(圓滿) ~하다 (be) amicable; peaceful; harmonious. ¶ ~한 가정 a happy home / ~한 해결 a peaceful settlement / ~한 인격 a well-rounded personality / 쟁의는 ~히 해결되었다 The dispute has come to a happy compromise.
원망(怨望) a grudge; hatred (증오); ill feeling(악의). ~하다 have 〔harbor, hold〕 a grudge 《*against a person*》; bear 《*a person*》 a grudge. ¶ ~을 사다 incur *a person's* grudge / 하늘을 ~하다 curse Heaven.
원맨쇼 a one-man 〔solo〕 show.
원면(原綿) raw cotton.
원명(原名) an original name; a real name.
원목(原木) raw 〔unprocessed〕 timber. ¶ 펄프 ~ pulpwood.
원무(圓舞) a round 〔circle〕 dance; a waltz. ¶ ~곡 〖樂〗 a waltz.
원문(原文) 〖본문〗 the text; 〖원서〗 the original (text). ¶ ~으로 읽다 read 《*a novel*》 in the original / ~에 충실히 번역하다 make a faithful translation of the original.
원반(圓盤) a disk; a discus (투원반용의). ‖ ~던지기 the discus throw.
원방(遠方) (먼 거리) a distance; 《먼 곳》 a distant place. ¶ ~의 distant; faraway; far-off; remote /

원병(援兵) reinforcement(s). ¶ ~을 보내다 send reinforcements (to). ☞ 원군.

원본(原本) the original; the original copy [text, work]; [法] the script.

원부(怨府) ~가 되다 become the focus of common hatred.

원부(原簿) a ledger; the original register.

원불교(圓佛敎) Won Buddhism. one of the nation's indigenous religions.

원뿔(圓-) a cone(끝); a circular cone(형태). ¶ ~꼴의 conical; conic. ¶ ~곡선 a conic section.

원사(元士) a sergeant major.

원사(寃死) ~하다 die under a false accusation.

원사이드게임 a one-sided game.

원산(原産) ¶동남아 ~의 뱀 a snake native to South-East Asia / 감자는 남미 ~ Potatoes are native to (originally came from) South America. ¶ ~지 the place [country] of origin; the (original) home; the habitat(동식물의) (커피나무의 ~)지 the home of the coffee plant) / ~지증명(서) a certificate of origin / ~지 표지(標識) country-of-origin marks [labels].

원상(原狀) the original state; the former condition; [法] the *status quo ante*[라]. ¶ ~으로 복구하다 return [restore] (*a thing*) to *its* original state.

원색(原色) (기본색) a primary color; (본래의 색) the original color. ¶ 삼 ~ the three primary colors / ~에 충실하라 be faithful to the original colors. ‖ ~사진 a color picture / ~판 (인쇄) a heliotype.

원생(原生) ¶ ~의 primary; primeval. ‖ ~동물 a protozoan [pl. -zoa] / ~식물 a protophyte.

원서(原書) the original. ¶ ~으로 읽다 read (*Byron*) in the original.

원서(願書) an application; (용지) an application form [blank]. ¶ ~를 내다 send [hand] in an application.

원석(原石) (원광) a raw ore; an ore. ¶다이아몬드 ~ a rough diamond. 「plaints [grievances].

원성(怨聲) a murmur of com-

원소(元素) [化] an element. ¶ ~기호 the symbol of a chemical element / ~주기율 the periodic law of the element. 「of state.

원수(元首) a sovereign; the head

원수(元帥) a five-star general (美); (陸軍) a general of the army (美); a field marshal (英); (海軍) a fleet admiral (美); an admiral of the fleet (英).

원수(怨讐) an enemy; a foe. ¶ ~지간 mutual enemies / ~를 갚다 revenge *oneself* upon (*a person*) for (*a matter*) / 은혜를 ~로 갚다 return evil for good.

원수폭(原水爆) atomic and hydrogen bombs.

원숙(圓熟) maturity. ~하다 (be) mature; mellow; fully-developed. ¶ ~한 사상 mature ideas / ~한 경지에 이르다 attain (reach) maturity / 그는 나이가 들면서 ~해졌다 He has mellowed with age.

원숭이 a monkey; an ape.

원시(原始) ~적인 primitive; primeval. ‖ ~림 a virgin (primeval) forest / ~시대 the primitive age / ~인 a primitive man.

원시(遠視) farsightedness (美); longsightedness (英). ¶ ~용의 안경 (a pair of) glasseys for the farsighted / 그녀는 ~이다 She is farsighted [longsighted].

원심(原審) the original (initial) judgment (decision). ¶ ~을 파기하다 reverse [overrule] the original judgment.

원심(遠心) ¶ ~의 centrifugal. ‖ ~력 (use) centrifugal force / ~분리기 a centrifuge; a centrifugal separator / ~탈수기 a centrifugal filter; a hydroextractor.

원아(園兒) kindergarten children.

원안(原案) the original bill (plan, draft).

원앙(鴛鴦) [鳥] a mandarin duck. ¶한 쌍의 ~ a couple of lovebirds. 「(amount).

원액(元額·原額) the original sum

원액(原液) an undiluted solution.

원양(遠洋) the open sea (far from the land). ‖ ~어선 a deep-sea fishing vessel / ~어업 deep-sea [pelagic] fishery / ~항해 ocean navigation [voyage] (~항해에 나가다 set out on a distant voyage).

원어(原語) the original language.

원예(園藝) gardening. ‖ ~가 a gardener / ~식물 a garden plant / ~학교 a horticultural school.

원외(院外) ¶ ~의 outside the House [National Assembly]; non-Congressional (美). ‖ ~세력 an outside pressure group / ~투쟁 an out-of-the-National Assembly struggle / ~활동 lobbying (~을 통하다 lobby).

원용(援用) ~하다 invoke (*a clause*); quote (*an article*); cite (*a precedent*).

원유(原油) crude oil (petroleum). ¶ ~가격 the price of crude oil;

crude oil price / ~생산국 a producer of crude oil.
원유회(園遊會) a garden party.
원음(原音) the original sound (pronunciation). ¶ ~충실 재생 a faithful reproduction of the original sound.
원의(原意) the original intention.
원의(原義) the original meaning.
원의(院議) a decision of the House (National Assembly).
원인(原因) the cause; the origin (발단). ¶ ~과 결과 cause and effect / 불명의 화재 a fire of unknown origin / 사고의 ~을 규명하다 investigate the cause of an accident / …이 ~이다 be caused by…; result from…. / 폭발의 ~은 아직 불명이다 The cause of the explosion is still unknown. ‖ 간접 [직접] ~ mediate [immediate] cause. ∥~cause.
원인(遠因) a remote [distant]
원인(猿人) 〖人類〗 an ape-man. ‖ 자바 ~ the Java man.
원인(願人) an applicant (지원자); a petitioner (청원자).
원일점(遠日點) 〖天〗 the aphelion; the higher apsis.
원자(原子) an atom. ¶ ~의 atomic. ‖ ~가 atomic value / ~구조 atomic structure / ~량 atomic weight / ~로 an atomic reactor / 물리학 nuclear physics / ~번호 atomic number / ~병 radiation sickness / ~병기 an atomic (a nuclear) weapon / ~운 an atomic (mushroom) cloud / ~탄두 an atom(ic) warhead / ~포 an atomic gun / ~폭탄 an atomic bomb; an A-bomb / ~핵 an atomic nucleus.
원자력(原子力) atomic [nuclear] energy. ¶ ~으로 움직이는 nuclear-powered; atomic-powered / ~추진의 nuclear-propelled. ‖ ~국제관리 the international control of atomic energy / ~발전소 an atomic (a nuclear) power plant / ~병원 the Cancer Research Hospital / ~산업 the nuclear industry / ~시대 the atomic age / ~잠수함 a nuclear(-powered) submarine / ~평화이용 peaceful uses of atomic energy / ~기구 the International Atomic Energy Agency (생략 IAEA).
원자재(原資材) raw materials.
원작(原作) the original (work). ‖ ~자 the author.
원장(元帳) the ledger.
원장(院長) the director 《of a hospital》; the president 《of an academy》.
원장(園長) the principal 《of a kindergarten》; the curator 《of a zoo》.
원저(原著) the original work.
원적(原籍) 《원적지》 one's original domicile; one's domicile of origin.
원전(原典) the original (text).
원점(原點) the starting point; the origin (좌표의). ¶ ~으로 되돌아가다 go back to the starting point.
원정(遠征) an expedition; 《선수의》 a visit; a playing tour. ¶ ~하다 make [go on] an expedition; go on a tour 《to the U.S.A.》 (선수의). ‖ ~경기 an away match / ~대 《군대·탐험 등의》 an expedition; an expeditionary team; ~팀 《선수의》 a visiting [an away] team.
원제(原題) the original title.
원조(元祖) 《창시자》 the founder; 《발명자》 the inventor.
원조(援助) help; support; assistance; aid. ~하다 help; support; aid; give assistance 《to》. ¶ ~를 요청하다 ask [appeal to] 《a person》 for help / ~의 손을 뻗치다 stretch out a helping hand 《to》 / 경제 [재정, 식량] ~ economic [financial, food] aid / 해외 ~계획 a foreign aid plan (program) / 피~국 an aid-receiving nation; an aid-recipient country. ‖ ~국 an aid country / ~물자 aid goods / ~자 a supporter; a patron.
원죄(原罪) the original sin.
원죄(冤罪) a false charge (accusation).
원주(圓柱) a column; 〖數〗 a cylinder. ¶ ~상(狀)의 columnar; cylindrical.
원주(圓周) circumference. ‖ ~율 〖數〗 the circular constant; pi (기호 π).
원주민(原住民) a native; an aborigine; indigenous people.
원지(原紙) 《등사용》 a stencil.
원지(遠地) a distant place.
원지점(遠地點) 〖天〗 the apogee.
원천(源泉) a source; the fountainhead. ¶ 힘의 ~ a source of strength / 지식의 ~ a fount of wisdom. ‖ ~과세 taxation at the source (of income); (a) withholding tax (美); pay-as-you-earn (생략 P.A.Y.E) 《英》 / ~소득세 a withholding income tax / ~징수 deducting tax from income at source; withholding / ~징수제도 the withholding system.
원촌(原寸) actual [natural] size. ¶ ~의 full-scale; full-sized; full

size. ¶ ~도 a full-scale drawing.
원추(圓錐) ☞ 뿔대. [Ling.
원추리[植] a day lily.
원칙(原則) a principle; a general rule. ¶ ~적으로 as a (general) rule; in principle / ~을 세우다 establish a principle / ~에 반하다 go against (be contrary to) principle.
원컨대(願~) I hope...; I pray...; I wish...; It is to be hoped (desired) that....
원탁(圓卓) a round table. ¶ ~회의 a roundtable conference.
원통(圓筒) a cylinder.
원통(寃痛) ~하다 (be) resentful; vexing, regrettable; lamentable; grievous. ¶ ~해서 이를 갈다 grind *one's* teeth with vexation / 기회를 놓쳐 ~하다 regret having missed the opportunity.
원판(原版)《사진》 a negative plate.
원폭(原爆) an A-bomb. ¶ ~실험(금지) a nuclear test (ban) / ~희생자 A-bomb victims.
원피스 a one-piece dress.
원하다(願~) desire; wish; hope; want; beg (간원). ¶원하신다면 If you wish / 원하는 대로 as one pleases (wishes) / 누구나 평화를 원하고 있다 Everyone wishes peace. / 내게 무엇을 원하느냐 What do you want with me?
원한(怨恨) a grudge; resentment; spite;《증오》hatred;《적의》enmity;《악의》ill feeling. ¶ ~에 의한 살인 murder from (for) revenge / ~을 품다 cherish, nurse) (*a person*) a grudge / ~을 사다 incur grudge / ~이 뼈에 사무치다 have a deep-rooted grudge (*against a person*).
원항(遠航) ocean navigation; a long cruise. ~하다 set out on ocean navigation.
원행(遠行) a long trip. ~하다 make (go on) a long trip.
원형(原形) the original form. ¶ ~을 보존하다 (잃다) retain (lose) *its* original form. ‖ ~질[生] protoplasm.
원형(原型) an archetype; a prototype; a model;《주물의》a mold. ¶ B는 A의 ~이다 A models after B. *or* B is the original for A.
원형(圓形) a round shape; a circle. ¶ ~의 circular; round / ~으로 in a circle. ‖ ~극장 an amphitheater.
원호(援護) backing; protection; support. ~하다 back (up); support; protect; lend support to. ‖ ~기금[성금] a relief fund (donation) / ~대상자 a relief recipient.
원호(圓弧)[數] a circular arc.
원혼(寃魂) malignant spirits.

원화(一貨) the *won* (currency) / ~예치율 the *won* deposit rate / ~가치의 하락 a fall in the exchange rate of the *won*.
원화(原畫) the original picture.
원활(圓滑) smoothness; harmony. ¶ ~한[히] smooth(ly); harmonious(ly) / ~하게 되어가다 go (on) smoothly (without a hitch).
원흉(元兇) a ringleader; the chief instigator; the prime mover.
월(月)《달》the moon;《달력의》a month;《요일의》Monday. ¶ ~평균 on a monthly average / ~1회의 once a month / ~내에 within this month.
월가(一街)《뉴욕의》Wall Street.
월간(月刊) monthly issue (publication). ¶ ~의 monthly. ‖ ~지 a monthly (magazine).
월경(月經) menstruation; menses; a period. ¶ ~이 있다 (없다) have the (no) menses / ~중이다 have *one's* period / ~기 the menstrual period / ~대 a sanitary belt (napkin) / ~불순 menstrual irregularities / ~폐색기 ☞ 폐경기.
월경(越境) border transgression. ~하다 cross the border (*into*). ‖ ~비행 overflight / ~사건 a border incident.
월계(月計) a monthly account.
월계(月桂)《월계수》[植] a laurel (bay) tree. ¶ ~관 laurels; a laurel crown (wreath) (~관을 쓰다 win *one's* laurels).
월광(月光) moonlight. ¶ ~곡《베토벤의》"The Moonlight Sonata".
월권(越權) arrogation; abuse of authority. ¶ ~(행위를) 하다 exceed (overstep) *one's* power (authority).
월급(月給) a (monthly) salary (pay). ¶ ~높은(낮은) ~ a high (low) salary / ~을 받다 draw (get) a salary / ~이 오르다 (내리다) get a raise (cut) in *one's* salary / 적은 ~으로 살다 live on a small salary. ‖ ~날 the payday / ~봉투 a pay envelope / ~쟁이 a salaried man (worker).
월남(越南)《나라》Viet Nam. ¶ ~의 (사람) (a) Viet-Namese / ~어 Viet-Namese.
월남(越南)《남한으로》 ~하다 come from North Korea (over the 38th parallel); cross the 38th parallel into South Korea.
월동(越冬) ~하다 pass the winter. ¶ ~준비를 하다 prepare for the winter.
월드컵 the World Cup.
월등(越等) ~하다 (be) out of the common; extraordinary; incomparable; unusual; singular. ¶ ~히 out of the common; extra-

월례(月例) ~의 monthly / 경제 동향 보고회의 a monthly economic briefing session. ‖ ~회(보고) a monthly meeting (report).
월리(月利) monthly interest.
월말(月末) ¶ ~(까지) at (by) the end of the month. ‖ ~계산(지불) month-end payment.
월면(月面) the lunar surface; the surface of the moon. ‖ ~도 a selenographic chart / ~보행 a moon (lunar) walk / ~차 a lunar rover; a moon buggy (car) / ~착륙 a landing on the moon.
월변(月邊) a monthly interest.
월보(月報) a monthly report (bulletin).
월부(月賦) payment in (by) monthly installments; monthly payments. ¶ 6개월 ~로 사다 buy 《a thing》 in six months' installments / ~로 5천원씩 지불하다 pay 《for an article》 in monthly installments of 5,000 won 《over a period of 10 months》 / ~판매 installment selling; (방법) the installment plan 《美》.
월북(越北) ~하다 go north over the border; go to North Korea.
월산(月産) a monthly output (production).
월색(月色) moonlight.
월세(月貰) monthly rent. ¶ 그의 집은 ~가 5만 원이다 He is paying 50,000 won a month in rent. *or* His rent comes to 50,000 won a month.
월세계(月世界) the moon. ¶ ~ 여행은 이제 꿈이 아니다 A journey to the moon is no longer a dream.
월수(月收) ① (수입) a monthly income. ¶ ~가 100만 원이다 make one million won a month; have a monthly income of one million won. ② (빛) (make) a monthly installment loan.
월식(月蝕)[天] a lunar eclipse. ‖ 개기[부분]~ a total [partial] eclipse of the moon.
월액(月額) the monthly amount.
월여(月餘) ¶ ~간이나 over a month / ~ 전에 more than a month ago (지금부터); more than a month before (그때까지).
월요병(月曜病) the Monday morning blues.
월요일(月曜日) Monday (생략 Mon.).
월일(月日) the date.
월정(月定) ¶ ~의 monthly. ‖ ~구독료[구독자] a monthly subscription (subscriber).
월초(月初) ¶ ~에 early in [at the beginning of] the month.

월평(月評) a monthly review.
웨딩 wedding. ‖ ~드레스 (마치) a wedding dress (march).
웨이스트볼[野] a waste ball.
웨이터 a waiter.
웨이트리스 a waitress.
웬 what; what sort [manner, kind] of. ¶ ~ 까닭으로 why; 사람이냐 Who is the man? *or* What is he here for? 「Gosh! **웬걸** O my!; Why!; Why no!; **웬만큼** properly, moderately (알맞게); to some extent (어느 정도); fairly (어지간히). ¶ 영어를 ~ 하다 speak English fairly well / ~ 마셔라 Take it easy on the liquor.
웬만하다 (be) passable; serviceable; tolerable; fairly good. 웬만한 집안 a respectable (decent) family / 값이 웬만하면 if the price is reasonable… / 수입이 ~ have a handsome income.
웬셈 ¶ ~인지 나도 모르겠다 I don't know what all this is about.
웬일 what; what matter. ¶ ~인지 for some reason (or other) / ~이냐 What is all this? *or* What is the matter? / ~로 여기에 왔느냐 What brought you here?
웰컴 welcome.
웰터급(一級) the welterweight. ‖ ~선수 a welterweight.
웽그렁웽그렁 clang; clank.
웽웽 noisily; buzzing; humming.
위 ① (상부) the upper part; (표면) the surface. ¶ ~의 upper; up; upward; above / ~에 above; over; upwards; up; upon / ~에 말한 바와 같이 as mentioned above / ~를 쳐다보다 look upward / 머리 ~를 날다 fly over *one's* head / 얼음 ~를 조심스레 걷다 walk carefully on the ice. ② (꼭대기·정상) the top; the summit; the head. ¶ 맨 ~의 the topmost (uppermost) / ~에서 아래까지 from top to bottom / ~에서 다섯째 줄(에) (on) the fifth line from the top. ③ (비교) ~의 higher (높은); more than, above, over (… 이상의); superior (나은); older (연장의) / 제일 ~의 누나 My eldest sister / 훨씬 ~이다 be far better (higher) / 한 학년 ~다 be a class (grade) ahead of 《a person》 / ~를 쳐다보면 한이 없다 Don't compare yourself with those better than you. ④ (신분·지위) ~의 superior; above / ~로부터의 명령 an order from above / 남의 ~에 서다 lead others; be the superior of others.
위 ① (지위·등급) a rank; a place. ¶ 제4~의 the fourth-ranking 《Dodgers》 / 2~가 되다 take (win, gain) second place /

3〜로 떨어지다 drop to third place / 제1〜이다 be (stand) first. ②《위패의》영럼 9〜 nine heroic souls.
위(胃) the stomach. ¶ 〜gastric / 〜가 튼튼하다〔약하다〕 have a strong〔weak〕 stomach; have a good〔weak〕 digestion / 〜가 아프다 have a stomachache; have a pain in one's stomach.
위경(胃鏡)〔醫〕a gastroscope.
위경련(胃痙攣)〔醫〕convulsion of the stomach. ¶ 〜을 일으키다 have the cramps in the stomach.
위계(位階) a (court) rank. ¶ 〜 질서 the order of ranks.
위계(偽計) a deceptive plan. ¶ 〜를 쓰다 use a deceptive scheme.
위관(尉官)〔육군〕officers below the rank of major; a company officer 《美》;〔해군〕officers below the lieutenant commander.
위광(威光) authority; power; influence. ¶ 부모의 〜으로 through the influence of one's parents.
위구(危懼) misgivings; apprehensions. 〜하다 fear; be afraid 《of》. ¶ 〜심을 품다 entertain〔feel〕 misgivings 《about》.
위국(危局) a crisis; a critical situation. 『one's country.
위국(爲國) 〜하다 serve〔benefit〕
위궤양(胃潰瘍)〔醫〕a gastric (stomach) ulcer.
위급(危急) an emergency; a crisis. 〜하다 (be) critical; imminent; crucial / 〜시에 in case of emergency; in time of danger 〔need〕. ∥ 〜존망지추 a time of emergency; a critical moment.
위기(危機) a crisis; a critical moment. ¶ 정치적〔재정적〕인 〜 a political〔financial〕crisis / 〜에 직면하다 face a crisis / 〜에 처하다 be in a critical situation / 〜를 벗어나다 get over a crisis / 〜를 완화하다 ease a crisis / 〜일발로 죽음을 모면하다 escape a death by a hair's breadth. ∥ 〜관리 risk〔crisis〕 management.
위난(危難) danger; peril; distress. ☞ 위험.
위대(偉大) greatness. 〜하다 (be) great; mighty (강대); grand (숭고). ¶ 한 국민 (업적) a great nation (achievement).
위덕(威德) virtue and dignity. ¶ 신의 〜 virtue and dignity of God.
위도(緯度)〔地〕latitude. ¶ 〜의 latitudinal. ∥ 고 〔저〕〜 a high (low) latitude.
위독(危篤) 〜하다 be seriously (dangerously) ill; be in a critical condition. ¶ 〜 상태에 빠지다 fall into a critical condition.

위락시설(慰樂施設) leisure (relaxation) facilities.
위력(威力) (great) power; authority. ¶ 〜 있는 powerful / 그의 펀치는 굉장한 〜이 있다 His punch is very powerful.
위령(慰靈) ∥ 〜제 a memorial service 《for the war dead》; 〜탑 a war memorial; a cenotaph (built in memory of war victims).
위로(慰勞) ①《치사》appreciation of 《a person's》 services (efforts). 〜하다 appreciate 《a person's》 services (efforts). ¶ 〜회를 열다 hold a party in appreciation of services. ∥ 〜금 a bonus; a reward for one's services / 〜회 a 'thank-you' party / 〜휴가 a special holiday given in recognition of one's services. ②《위안》 solace; comfort. ¶ 〜에 solace; comfort. ∥ 〜의 말 comforting words / 노인을 〜하기 위해 병원을 방문하다 visit a hospital to comfort the aged. ∥ 〜여행 a recreational trip. 『ach.
위막(胃膜) the coats of the stom
위명(偽名) a false (an assumed) name; an alias (범죄자의). ¶ …라는 〜으로 under the false name of...
위무(慰撫) 〜하다 pacify; soothe.
위문(慰問)《위안》consolation; (an) expression of sympathy (위로); 《문병》an inquiry after another's health. 〜하다 console; give sympathy 《to》; inquire after another's health. ¶ 〜하러 가다 visit a person (in hospital); pay a sympathy visit 《to》; go and comfort 《a person》. ∥ 〜객 a visitor; an inquirer / 〜금 a gift of money 《for the victims》 / 〜대(袋) a comfort bag for a soldier 《at the front》 / 〜편지 a letter of sympathy (inquiry) / 〜품 comforts; relief goods.
위반(違反) (a) violation; a breach; an offense. 〜하다 violate; offend 《against the rules》; break 《one's promise》; be against 《a law》. ¶ 교통 규칙 〜 traffic violation (offense) / 주차 〜 parking violation / 계약 〜 a breach of contract / 조약을 〜하다 violate a treaty / 법률 〜는 처벌된다 A violation of the law will bring you punishment. or If you break the law, you will be punished. ∥ 〜자 a violator; an offender / 〜행위 an illegal act.
위배(違背) contravention. ☞ 위반. ¶ 올림픽 정신에 〜되다 (it) run counter to the Olympic spirit.
위법(違法) illegality; unlawfulness. ¶ 〜의 unlawful; illegal. ∥ 〜자 a

위벽(胃壁) the walls of the stomach.

위병(胃病) a stomach trouble (disorder).

위병(衛兵) a sentry; a sentinel; a guard. ¶ ~ 근무 sentry (guard) duty / ~소 a guardhouse.

위산(胃散) medicinal powder for the stomach.

위산(胃酸) stomach acids. ¶ ~ 과다의 hyperacid; ~ 과다증 hyperacid dyspepsia. ‖ ~ 과다증 hyperacidity.

위상(位相) 《電》 phase.

위생(衛生) hygiene; sanitation (공중의); health (건강). ¶ ~ 적인〔상의〕 sanitary; hygienic / 공중 ~ public health / 정신 ~ mental hygiene / 저 식당은 별로 ~적이지 않은 것 같다 That restaurant doesn't look very sanitary to me. / 식사 전에 손을 안 씻는 것은 비~적이다 It's unsanitary not to wash your hands before eating. / 그들에겐 ~ 관념이 없다 They have no sense of hygiene (sanitation). ‖ ~ 공학 sanitary engineering / ~ 관리 health control (administration) / ~병 a medical orderly; a medic / ~ 상태 sanitary conditions / ~ 시설〔설비〕 sanitary facilities / ~ 시험소 a hygienic laboratory / ~ 학 hygienics.

위선(胃腺) 《解》 peptic glands.

위선(僞善) hypocrisy. ¶ ~적인 hypocritical; double-faced / ~ 하다 practice hypocrisy; be a hypocrite. ‖ ~자 a hypocrite.

위선(緯線) a parallel (of latitude).

위성(衛星) a satellite. ¶ 그 역사적인 사건은 ~으로 중계되어 전세계로 송신되었다 The historic event was transmitted all over the world by satellite. ‖ ~국 a satellite state (country) / ~ 도시 a satellite city (town) / ~ 방송 satellite broadcasting / ~ 중계 satellite relay / ~ 통신 satellite communications.

위세(威勢) power; influence; authority; (기운) high spirits. ¶ ~를 떨치다 exercise one's authority over (others).

위세척(胃洗滌) 《醫》 gastrolavage. ¶ ~ 하다 carry out a gastric lavage.

위수(衛戍) a garrison. ‖ ~령 the Garrison Decree / ~ 사령관 the commander of the garrison (headquarters) / ~지 a garrison town.

위스키《술》 whisk(e)y. ¶ ~를 스트레이트로 마시다 drink whisky straight (neat). ‖ ~ 소다 a whisky and soda.

위시하다(爲始一) 김 박사를 위시해서 starting with (including) Dr. Kim / 박 씨를 위시하여 다섯명이 선출되었다 Mr. Park and four others were elected 《to the committee》.

위신(威信) dignity; prestige. ¶ ~에 관계되다 affect one's prestige (dignity) / ~을 지키다 maintain one's prestige (dignity) / ~을 떨어뜨리다 lose one's dignity.

위안(慰安) comfort; solace. ¶ ~ 하다 comfort; console. ¶ ~을 주다 give comfort to; afford solace / ~에서 ~을 얻다 find one's comfort in. ‖ ~부 a comfort girl (woman); comfort women (집합적).

위암(胃癌) 《醫》 (a) stomach cancer.

위압(威壓) coercion; overpowering. ¶ ~ 하다 coerce; overpower. ¶ ~ 적(으로) coercive(ly); high-handed(ly) / 무력으로 적을 ~ 하다 overpower an enemy by using armed force / ~ 적인 말투를 쓰다 speak in a high-handed manner.

위액(胃液) 《解》 gastric juice. ‖ ~선(腺) peptic glands.

위약(胃弱) 《醫》 dyspepsia; indigestion.

위약(違約) a breach of promise (contract). ¶ ~ 하다 infringe a contract; break a promise (one's word). ‖ ~금 a penalty; an indemnity.

위엄(威嚴) dignity. ¶ ~ 있는 dignified; majestic / ~ 없는 undignified / ~ 이 있는 사람 a man of dignified appearance / ~을 지키다〔손상하다〕 keep〔impair〕 one's dignity.

위업(偉業) a great undertaking (work, achievement). ¶ ~을 이루다 achieve a great work.

위염(胃炎) gastritis.

위용(偉容·威容) a grand (majestic, imposing) appearance.

위원(委員) a member of 《the Budget Committee》; a committeeman 《美》; a commissioner. ¶ ~의 한 사람이다 be a member of the committee. ‖ ~ 장 be a chairperson; a chairman (남); a chairwoman (여자).

위원회(委員會) 《組織》 a committee; a commission. ¶ 7인 ~ a seven-member committee / ~를 열다 hold a committee meeting / ~ 에 회부되다 be referred to (a) committee / ~를 소집하다 call a meeting of the committee / ~를 조직〔설치〕하다 form〔set up〕 a committee. ‖ 군사정전 ~ the Military Armistice Commission / 소~ a subcommittee.

위의(威儀) dignity; solemnity. ¶

위인(偉人) a great man. ∥ ~전 the biography of a great man.

위인(爲人) one's personality (disposition, nature).

위임(委任) trust; commission. ~하다 entrust (charge) 《a person》 with 《a matter》; leave 《a matter》 to 《a person》. ¶ 권한의 ~ delegation of authority / 나는 그에게 전권을 ~했다 I entrusted him with full powers. ∥ ~권 power(s) of attorney / ~권한 competency of mandate / ~장 a letter of attorney / ~제도 a mandate system / ~통치 mandate.

위자료(慰藉料) consolation money; compensation; [法] alimony (이혼·별거수당). ¶ ~를 청구하다 demand compensation 《for》.

위장(胃腸) [解] the stomach and bowels (intestines). ¶ ~이 튼튼하다 (약하다) have a strong (poor) digestion. ∥ ~병 a gastrointestinal disorder / ~약 a medicine for the stomach and bowels / ~염 gastroenteritis / ~장애 gastroenteric trouble.

위장(僞裝) camouflage. ~하다 camouflage; disguise. ¶ 거지로 ~하다 disguise *oneself* as a beggar. ∥ ~망 a camouflage net / ~평화공세 a disguised peace offensive / ~폭탄 a booby trap (bomb).

위정자(爲政者) a statesman; an administrator.

위조(僞造) forgery (문서 등의); counterfeiting (화폐 등의). ~하다 forge 《a document》; counterfeit 《a coin》. ∥ ~단 a counterfeit ring / ~문서 a forged document / ~자 a forger / ~지폐 a false (counterfeit) note / ~품 a forged article; a counterfeit; a forgery.

위주(爲主) ¶ 자기 ~의 사고 방식 self-centered thinking / 남성 ~의 사회 male-oriented society / 장사는 이득이 ~이다 Profit making is the first consideration in business.

위중하다(危重—) (be) critical.

위증(僞證) false evidence (testimony). ~하다 give false evidence. ∥ ~자 a perjurer / ~죄 《commit》 perjury / ~죄로 기소되다 be accused of perjury).

위촉(委囑) 《위임》 commission; 《의뢰》 request. ~하다 ask 《request, commission》 《a person》 《to do》; entrust 《a person》 with 《a matter》 / ~에 의해 《따라》 at the request of....

위축(萎縮) ~하다 《물건이》 wither; shrink; droop; 《사람이》 be daunted (humbled) 《by》; shrink back; 《기관이》 atrophy. ¶ 근육 ~증 muscular atrophy. ∥ ~증 atrophy.

위층(—層) the upper floor. ¶ ~에 올라가다 go upstairs.

위치(位置) 《상대적인》 a position; 《물리적인》 a location. ~하다 be situated (located); lie; stand. ¶ ~가 좋다 (나쁘다) be in a good (bad) position; be well (ill) situated / ~를 점하다 《차지하다》 take one's position / 새 학교는 도시 중앙에 ~하고 있다 The new school is located (situated) in the center of the town.

위탁(委託) trust; consignment 《상품의》. ~하다 entrust 《a person》 with 《a matter》; place 《a matter》 in 《a person's》 charge. ¶ ~을 받다 be entrusted / 사건을 변호사에게 ~하다 leave the case in the hands of a lawyer / 집의 매각을 부동산업자에게 ~하다 consign one's house (for sale) to a real estate agent. ∥ ~가공 processing on commission / ~금 money in trust; a trust fund / ~수수료 a consignment fee / ~자 a truster; consignor / ~판매 consignment sale / ~판매하다 sell 《goods》 on commission / ~판매인 a commission merchant (agent) / ~품 consignment goods.

위태(危殆) ¶ ~로운 dangerous; perilous; risky / ~롭게 하다 endanger; jeopardize / 생명이 ~롭다 One's life is in danger.

위통(胃痛) stomachache.

위트 wit. ¶ ~ 있는 witty.

위패(位牌) a mortuary tablet.

위폐(僞幣) a counterfeit note (bill). ∥ ~감식기 a counterfeit-bill detector / ~범 a counterfeiter.

위풍(威風) a dignity; a majestic air. ¶ 왕으로 ~ 당당히 행동하다 behave with the dignity of a king.

위필(僞筆) forged handwriting; a forged picture.

위하다(爲—) 《이롭게 하다》 be good for; do 《a person》 good; benefit; 《공경하다》 respect; look up to; 《중시하다》 make much of; take good care of. ¶ …을 ~하여 예술을 위한 예술 art for art's sake / 논쟁을 위한 논쟁을 하다 argue for argument's sake / 일반 학습자를 위한 영어 강좌 an English course for general learners / 부모를 ~ respect (honor) one's parents; take good care of one's parents / 조상을 ~ worship one's ancestors.

위하수(胃下垂) [醫] gastroptosis

위하여(爲—) ① [이익·편의] for; for the sake (benefit) of; in the interests of; for *a person's* sake. ¶ 조국을 ~ for the sake of the fatherland / 장래를 ~ 저축을 하다 save money for *one's* future / 나라를 ~ 죽다 die for *one's* country. ② [목적] for; in order to [that… may] *do*; for the purpose of (*doing*); with a view to (*doing*). ¶ ~하지 않기 ~ lest *one* should; so as not to / 경고하기 ~ by way of warning / 점심을 먹기 위해 귀가하다 come back home to have lunch / 영문학 연구를 위해 영국에 가다 go to England for the purpose of studying English literature.

위해(危害) injury; harm. ¶ ~을 가하다 hurt (*a person*); do (*a person*) harm; inflict an injury on (*a person*).

위헌(違憲) (a) violation of the constitution. ¶ ~이다 be against the constitution; be unconstitutional. ‖ ~성 unconstitutionality / ~입법 unconstitutional legislation.

위험(危險) (a) danger; (a) peril; (a) risk; (a) hazard. ¶ ~한 dangerous; perilous; risky; hazardous / ~한 짓을 하다 run a risk; take risks; run the hazard / ~한 상태에 빠지다 fall into a dangerous situation / 신변에 ~을 느끼다 sense imminent danger / ~에서 벗어나다 escape from (get out of) danger / 생명의 ~을 무릅쓰고 아이를 구하다 save a child at the risk of *one's* own life / 자신을 ~에 노출시키다 expose *oneself* to danger / ~시하다 regard (*something*) as dangerous / ~한 사상 dangerous thoughts (ideas) / ~한 작업 dangerous work; a hazardous job. ‖ ~물 a dangerous object (article) / ~부담 risk bearing / ~상태 dangerous (critical) condition / ~수당 danger money / ~신호(지대) a danger signal (area, zone) / ~인물 a dangerous character (man).

위협(威脅) (a) threat; (a) menace; intimidation. ~하다 threaten; menace; intimidate; browbeat; frighten. ¶ 평화에 대한 ~ a menace (threat) to peace / ~적(으로) threatening(ly); menacing(ly) / ~조로 말하다 speak in a threatening tone / 죽이겠다고 ~하다 threaten (*a person*) with death. ‖ ~사격(射擊) a warning shot / ~수단 an intimidatory measure.

위화감(違和感) (feel) a sense of incongruity (unbelongingness)

/ 그 그룹에 대해 다소 ~을 느끼다 feel somewhat awkward (out of place) with that group.

위확장(胃擴張) [醫] dilation of the stomach; gastric dilation.

윗니 the upper (set of) teeth.

윙[翼] a wing.

윙크 a wink. ~하다 wink (*at*).

유(有) [존재] existence; being. ¶ 무(無)에서 ~는 생기지 않는다 Nothing comes of nothing.

유(類) ① [종류] a kind; a sort; a class; [동식물의] a race (총칭적); an order (목); a family (과); a genus (속); a species (종); a class (강). ¶ 인류의 human race / 파충류 the reptiles. ② [유례] a parallel (case). ¶ 그 ~가 없는 사건 an unprecedented affair.

유가(有價) valuable; negotiable. ‖ ~물 valuables / ~증권 securities; negotiable instruments (papers).

유가(儒家) a Confucian. ‖ ~서(書) Confucian literature.

유가족(遺家族) a bereaved family. ¶ 전몰자(군경) ~ a war-bereaved family.

유감(遺憾) regret. ¶ ~스러운 regrettable; pitiful (안된) / ~으로 생각하다 regret; be sorry (*for*) / 그 사건에 대해 ~의 뜻을 표하다 express *one's* regret over the matter / 그 모임에 참석 못하는 것을 ~으로 생각한다 It is regrettable that we cannot attend the meeting. / ~이지만 이 계획은 보류되었다 I regret to say (To my regret,) this plan has been shelved. / 그는 시험에서 ~없이 실력을 발휘했다 He fully showed his ability in the examination.

유감지진(有感地震) [地] a felt (sensible) earthquake.

유개(有蓋) ~의 covered; closed. ‖ ~화차 a boxcar (美); a covered (roofed) waggon (英).

유개념(類概念) [論] a genus [*pl.* genera].

유격(遊擊) a hit-and-run attack; a raid; an attack by a mobile unit. ¶ ~대 a flying column; mobile forces / ~병(대원) a ranger; a commando; a partisan / ~수[野] a short(stop) / ~전 guerrilla warfare.

유고(有故) ~하다 have an accident (some trouble). ¶ ~시에 in time of an accident.

유고(遺稿) the writings left by the deceased; *one's* posthumous manuscripts.

유고슬라비아 Yugoslavia; Jugoslavia. ¶ ~의 Yugoslav; Yugoslavian / ~사람 a Yugoslav(ian).

유곡(幽谷) a deep valley. ¶ 심산 ~ high mountains and deep valleys.

유골(遺骨) *a person's remains* (ashes). ¶ ~을 줍다 gather *a person's ashes*.

유공(有功) ¶ ~한 meritorious. ‖ ~자 *a person* of merit.

유곽(遊廓) a brothel; a bawdy house; a red-light district.

유괴(誘拐) kidnap(p)ing; abduction. ~하다 abduct; kidnap. ¶ ~범《사람》 a kidnap(p)er; an abductor; 《죄》 kidnap(p)ing; abduction / ~사건 a kidnaping (case). 「Confucian ideas.

유교(儒敎) Confucianism. ‖ ~사상

유구무언(有口無言) ¶ ~이다 have no word to say in excuse.

유구하다(悠久─) (be) eternal; everlasting; permanent.

유권자(有權者) a voter; an elector; the electorate(총칭).

유권해석(有權解釋) an authoritative interpretation.

유급(有給) ¶ ~의 paid; salaried. ‖ ~사원 staff members on the payroll / ~휴가 a paid vacation (holiday); a vacation with (full) pay (1주간의 ~휴가를 받다 take a week off with pay).

유급(留級) ~하다 repeat the same class 《*for another year*》. ‖ ~생 a repeater《美》.

유기(有期) ¶ ~의 terminable; limited; for a definite term. ‖ ~형에 처하다 be sentenced to imprisonment for a definite term. / ~공채 a terminable (fixed-term) bond / ~징역 penal servitude for a definite term.

유기(有機) ¶ ~의 organic; systematic / ~재배된 최고의 야채만을 고르다 select only the finest organically grown vegetables. ‖ ~농업 [농법] organic agriculture (farming) / ~물 organic matter (substance) / ~비료 (an) organic fertilizer / ~체 an organism; an organic body / ~화학 organic chemistry / ~화합물 an organic compound.

유기(遺棄) abandonment; desertion. ~하다 abandon; desert; leave 《*a dead body*》 unattended. ‖ ~물 a left article; a derelict / ~시체 an abandoned corpse.

유기(鍮器) 《놋그릇》 brassware.

유기음(有氣音) an aspirate.

유난스럽다 (be) extraordinary; uncommon; unusual; fastidious. ¶ 유난스럽게 unusually; extraordinarily.

유네스코 UNESCO. (◀the United Nations Educational, Scientific and Cultural Organization)

유년(幼年) infancy; childhood. ¶ ~기 [시대]에 in *one's* childhood.

유념하다(留念─) bear [keep] 《*something*》 in mind; take 《*a matter*》 to heart; mind; give heed to; pay regard to.

유뇨증(遺尿症) 《醫》 enuresis.

유능하다(有能─) (be) able; capable; competent. ¶ 유능한 사람 a man of ability; an able man.

유니버시아드《競》 the Universiade.

유니언(union) ~잭 the Union Jack(영국 국기).

유니폼 a uniform. ¶ ~을 입은《a player》 in uniform.

유다르다(類─) (be) conspicuous; uncommon; unusual. ¶ 유달리 conspicuously; unusually; uncommonly; especially.

유단자(有段者) a grade holder; a black belt. 「tose.

유당(乳糖) 《化》 milk sugar; lac-

유대(紐帶) bonds; ties. ¶ 강한 우정의 ~ a strong bond of friendship 《*between us*》 / 사업상의 ~ a business tie / ~를 끊다 break bonds (the bond) 《*with*》.

유대 Judea. ¶ ~의 Jewish / ~계 학자 a scholar of Jewish origin. ‖ ~교 Judaism / ~민족 the Jews / ~인 a Jew; a Hebrew.

유덕(遺德) posthumous influence.

유덕하다(有德─) (be) virtuous. ¶ 유덕한 사람 a virtuous man.

유도(柔道) *judo*. ‖ ~복 a suit for *judo* practice / ~사범 an instructor of *judo* / ~장 a *judo* hall.

유도(誘導) guidance; inducement; 〔電〕 induction. ~하다 induce; lead; guide. ¶ 아이들을 안전 지대로 ~하다 lead the children to a safe location / 관제탑의 ~에 따라 착륙하다 make a landing following the instructions of the control tower. ‖ ~로《공항의》 a taxiway / ~용 계기 guidance instruments / ~장치 a guidance system (미사일 등의); a talk-down system(관제탑의) / ~전류 an induced current / ~제어 guidance control / ~탄 a guided missile.

유도신문(誘導訊問) a leading question. ~하다 ask 《*a person*》 a leading question.

유독(有毒) ~하다 (be) poisonous; venomous; noxious. ¶ ~성 폐수가 강으로 유출되었다 Poisonous effluents were leaked into the rivers. ‖ ~가스 (a) poisonous gas.

유독(唯獨) only; alone; solely.

유동(流動) a flow. ~하다 flow; run; change. ¶ ~적인 fluid; changeable; unstable / 사태는 아직 ~적이다 Things are still unstable. / 우리의 계획은 아직

유두(乳頭) a nipple; a teat. ¶ ~염(炎) thelitis; acromastitis.

유들유들 ¶ ~한 brazen(-faced); cheeky; brassy.

유람(遊覽) sightseeing. ~을 ~하다 go sightseeing. ¶ ~객 a sightseer / ~선 a pleasure (sightseeing) boat / ~지 a tourist resort.

유랑(流浪) vagrancy; wandering. ~하다 wander about; roam. ¶ ~하는 wandering; vagrant; roaming. ‖ ~민 a nomadic people; nomads / ~생활 a wandering (nomadic) life.

유래(由來) 〔기원〕the origin; 〔내력〕the history; 〔출처〕the source. ~하다 result (stem) 《from》; originate in (from); be derived 《from》 〔언어 등에〕 date (trace) back 《to》. ¶ ~를 조사하다 inquire into the origin of 《a thing》; trace 《a thing》 to its origin. /meter.

유량(流量) 〔理〕flux. ¶ ~계 a flow

유럽 Europe. ¶ ~의 European / ~사람 a European / ~횡단 특급 열차 a Trans-Europe Express (생략 TEE). / ~대륙 the European continent / ~연합 the European Union (생략 EU).

유려하다(流麗—) (be) flowing; fluent; elegant; refined. ¶ 유려한 문장 a flowing and elegant style.

유력(有力) ~하다 (be) powerful; influential; strong; effective; leading. ¶ ~한 후보자 a strong candidate / ~한 신문 a leading newspaper / ~한 용의자 a key (prime) suspect / ~한 증거 strong (convincing) evidence / ~한 정보 reliable information. ‖ ~자 an influential person; a man of influence.

유령(幽靈) a ghost; an apparition; a specter; a phantom. ¶ ~같은 ghostly; ghostlike / ~의 집 a haunted house. ‖ ~도시 a ghost town / ~선 a phantom ship / ~회사 a bogus company.

유례(類例) a similar example (instance); a parallel case. ¶ ~없는 unparalleled; unique.

유로…(유럽의) Euro-. ¶ ~달러 Eurodollars / ~머니 Euromoney / ~시장 Euromarket / ~자금 Eurofund / ~채(債) a Eurobond / ~통화 Eurocurrency.

유료(有料) a charge. ¶ ~의 charged; with charge / 입장은 ~입니까 Is there a charge for the admission? ‖ ~도로 a toll road / ~변소 a pay toilet / 시사회 a (film) preview with an admission fee / ~주차장 a toll parking lot.

유루(遺漏) (an) omission; neglect. ¶ ~없이 without omission (any slip); thoroughly.

유류(油類) oil; all (various) kinds of oil. ¶ ~절약운동 an oil saving drive / ~파동 an oil crisis.

유류품(遺留品) an article left (behind); lost articles (유실물).

유리(有利) ~하다 〔이익〕(be) profitable; paying; 〔좋은〕advantageous; favorable. ¶ ~하게 profitably; advantageously; favorably / ~한 거래 (사업) a profitable deal (enterprise) / 사태는 우리에게 ~하게 전개되었다 Things turned out to be favorable for us. / ~한 조건을 최대로 살리다 make the most of the advantageous conditions.

유리(有理) ~의 rational. ‖ ~식 〔수〕〔數〕a rational expression (number).

유리(琉璃) glass; a window pane (창유리). ¶ ~색 stained (colored) glass / 젖빛 ~ frosted (ground) glass / 망~ wire glass / 판~ plate glass / 광학~ optical glass / 강화~ hardened glass / ~로 덮은 온실 a glass greenhouse / 창문에 ~를 끼우다 glass (glaze) a window / 한 장의 ~ a sheet of glass. ‖ ~가게 a glass store / ~공장 a glassworks / ~구슬 a glass bead / ~문 a glass door / ~섬유 fiberglass / ~세공 glass work / ~제품 glassware / ~창 a glass window / ~칼 a glass cutter.

유리(遊離) isolation; separation (분리). ~하다 isolate; separate.

유린(蹂躪) ~하다 〔짓밟다〕trample (tread) down; trample 《something》 underfoot; devastate; 〔범하다〕 infringe 《on rights》; trample on 《a person's feelings》; violate 《a woman》. ¶ 인권 ~ an infringement upon human rights / 국토를 ~당하다 have one's country trampled underfoot 《by the enemy》.

유림(儒林) Confucian scholars.

유망(有望) ~하다 (be) promising; hopeful; full of promise. ¶ 전도 ~한 청년 a promising youth / 그의 회사는 앞으로 ~하다 His company has bright prospects for the future. ‖ ~주 a hopeful stock(주식); an up-and-coming 《player, politician》 (사람).

유머 humor. ¶ 훌륭한 ~감각이 있다 have a fine sense of humor.

‖ ~소설 a humorous novel / ~작가 a comic writer; a humorist.

유명(有名) ~하다 (be) famous; noted; renowned; well-known; 《악명 높은》 notorious; infamous. ¶세계적으로 ~한 프로 골퍼 a world-famous pro golfer / ~한 고리대금업자 a notorious usurer / ~한 사람들 both humble and famous people; somebodies and nobodies / ~해지다 become famous; win fame; gain notoriety. ‖ ~교(校) a big-name school[university] / ~인 a celebrity; a big name.

유명(幽明) ¶~을 달리하다 pass away; depart this life.

유명무실(有名無實) ~하다 (be) in name only; nominal; titular. ¶~한 사장 a figurehead[nominal] president.

유명세(有名稅) the price of fame; the penalty of popularity. ¶그것은 그에 대한 일종의 ~이다 That's the price he has to pay for being famous.

유모(乳母) a (wet) nurse. ‖ ~차 a baby carriage 《美》; a pram 《英》.

유목(遊牧) ~민 nomads; a nomadic tribe / ~생활 a nomadic life.

유무(有無) existence; presence. ¶재고의 ~를 조사하다 check (as to) whether there is any stock / ~상통하다 supply each other's needs.

유물(唯物) 〖哲〗¶~적인 materialistic. ‖ ~론 materialism / ~사관(史觀) the materialistic view of history / 변증법적 ~론 dialectical materialism.

유물(遺物) a relic; remains. ¶과거의 ~ a relic of the past / 봉건시대의 ~ a holdover from feudal times.

유민(流民) wandering [roaming] people.

유밀과(油蜜菓) oil-and-honey pastry.

유발(乳鉢) a mortar.

유발(誘發) ~하다 lead to; bring about; cause; give rise to; induce. ¶전쟁을 ~하다 touch[set] off a war / 과도한 스케줄은 사고를 ~했다 The overloaded schedule led to the accident.

유방(乳房) the breast(s). ‖ ~암 breast[mammary] cancer; cancer of the breast / ~염 mammitis.

유배(流配) banishment; exile. ~하다 banish[exile] 《a criminal》 (to an island); ¶~지 an exile.

유백색(乳白色) ¶~의 milk-white.

유별(有別) ¶~나다 (be) distinctive; different; special; particular / 남녀 ~하다 There is a distinction between man and woman.

유별(類別) classification; assortment. ~하다 classify; assort.

유보(留保) reservation. ~하다 reserve 《one's decision》; hold over.

유복자(遺腹子) a posthumous son.

유복하다(有福—) (be) blessed; fortunate; lucky.

유복하다(裕福—) (be) wealthy; rich; affluent; well-off; well-to-do. ¶유복한 집안에 태어나다 be born in a rich family.

유부(油腐) 《a piece of》 fried bean curd. ‖ ~국수 noodles with fried bean curd.

유부녀(有夫女) a married woman.

유비무환(有備無患) Be prepared, and you will have no cause for regrets.

유사(有史) ¶~이전의 prehistoric / ~이래의 큰 전쟁 the greatest war in history [since the dawn of history].

유사(類似) (a) resemblance; (a) similarity; (a) likeness. ~하다 resemble; be similiar to; be alike; bear resemblance to. ¶~한 like; similar / 그것들은 빛깔이 거의 ~하다 They are very much alike in color. ‖ ~사건 a similar case / ~점 a (point of) similarity / ~품 an imitation 《~품에 주의하시오》 Beware of imitations》.

유사시(有事時) ¶~에 in an emergency; in case of emergency / ~에 대비하다 provide against emergencies 《a rainy day》.

유산(有産) ¶~의 propertied. ‖ ~계급 the propertied classes / ~자 a man of property.

유산(乳酸) 〖化〗 lactic acid. ‖ ~균 lactic bacilli[ferments]; a lactobacilli / ~(균)음료 a lactic acid drink 《beverage》.

유산(流産) a miscarriage. ~하다 miscarry; have a miscarriage. 그녀는 ~했다 She had a miscarriage. 그의 계획은 모두 ~되었다 All his plans have sadly miscarried.

유산(遺産) an inheritance; property left 《by》; a legacy; a bequest. ¶문화 ~ a cultural heritage / ~을 남기다 leave a fortune[an estate] 《to one's children》 / ~을 상속받다 inherit 《one's father's》 property; succeed to an estate. ‖ ~상속 succession to property.

유산탄(榴散彈) a shrapnel (shell).

유상(有償) ¶~의 〖法〗 onerous / ~으로 for payment / 수리는 ~입니다 You are liable for the cost of repairs. ‖ ~계약 an onerous contract / ~원조 credit assist-

유상 (油狀) ¶ ~의 oily; like oil.
유상 (乳狀) ¶ ~의 milky; emulsified / ~액 milky juice.
유상무상 (有象無象) ① 《이주비띠중이》 the rabble; the mob. ② 《삼라만상》 all things in the universe.
유색 (有色) ¶ ~의 colored; non-white. ‖ ~인종 colored races.
유생 (儒生) a Confucian (scholar); a Confucianist.
유서 (由緖) a (long and honorable) history. ¶ ~ 있는 집안의 《a person》 of good lineage; of noble birth / ~ 있는 건물 a historic building; a building rich in legend.
유서 (遺書) a note left behind by a dead person; a farewell note; a suicide note 《자살자의》; 《유언서》 a will; a testament. ¶ ~를 쓰다 [작성하다] make one's will.
유선 (有線) ¶ ~의 cabled; wired; wire. ‖ ~방송 [전신, 전화] wire broadcasting [telegraph, telephone] / ~의 the wire system / ~중계 cable (wire) relaying / ~텔레비전 cable television [TV]; closed-circuit television 《생략 CCTV》 / ~통신 cable communication.
유선 (乳腺) 〖解〗 the mammary gland. ‖ ~염 〖炎〗〖醫〗 mastitis.
유선형 (流線型) a streamline shape (form). ‖ ~자동차 a streamlined automobile (car).
유성 (有性) ¶ ~의 sexual. ‖ ~생식 sexual reproduction.
유성 (有聲) ¶ ~의 sound; voiced. ‖ ~영화 a sound picture (film) / ~음 a voiced sound.
유성 (油性) ¶ ~의 oily; greasy. ‖ ~페니실린 penicillin oil / ~페인트 an oil paint.
유성 (流星) a shooting star; a meteor. ‖ ~우 (雨) a meteoric shower.
유성 (流星) ☞ 행성.
유세 (有稅) ¶ ~의 taxable; dutiable 《관세》. ‖ ~품 dutiable goods.
유세 (有勢) ① ☞ 유력 (有力). ②《세도부림》 ~하다 wield power (influence) 《over》; lord it over.
유세 (遊說) canvassing; stumping; electioneering (선거 운동). ¶ ~하다 go canvassing (electioneering); canvass; stump 《美》; make an election tour. ¶ ~여행을 떠나다 go on a canvassing tour / 그는 전국을 ~했다 He went about the country canvassing. or He stumped the whole country. ‖ ~자 a canvasser; a stump speaker 《美》.
유속 (流速) the speed of a current. ‖ ~계 a current meter.

유수 (有數) ¶ ~의 prominent; leading; distinguished; eminent / 세계의 ~의 공업국의 하나 one of the world's leading industrial nations.
유수 (流水) flowing (running) water; a stream. ¶ 세월은 ~와 같다 Time flies (like an arrow).
유숙 (留宿) ~하다 lodge 《at》; stay 《at》; stop 《in》. ‖ ~객 숙박.
유순하다 (柔順—) (be) submissive; obedient; mild; meek; gentle.
유스호스텔 a youth hostel.
유습 (遺習) a hereditary custom.
유시 (幼時) childhood; infancy.
유시 (諭示) instruction; admonition; a message. ¶ ~하다 admonish; give an instruction.
유시계비행 (有視界飛行) visual flying; 《make》 a visual flight. ¶ 계기 비행에서 ~으로 바꾸다 shift from instrument to visual flight. ‖ ~규칙 visual flight rules 《생략 VFR》.
유식 (有識) ¶ ~하다 (be) learned; educated; intelligent; well-informed. ¶ ~한 사람 an educated (a learned) person. ‖ ~계급 the learned (intellectual) classes.
유신 (維新) renovation; restoration; the Revitalizing Reforms.
유신 (遺臣) a surviving retainer.
유신론 (有神論) 〖哲〗 theism. ‖ ~자 a theist.
유실 (流失) ~하다 be washed (carried) away 《by a flood》. ‖ ~가옥 houses carried away by the floods.
유실 (遺失) ~하다 lose; leave behind. ‖ ~물 a lost article / ~물 센터 a lost-and-found center / ~물 취급소 a lost-property office 《英》 / ~자 a loser; the owner of a lost property.
유심론 (唯心論) 〖哲〗 spiritualism; idealism. ‖ ~자 a spiritualist; an idealist.
유심하다 (有心—) (be) attentive; careful. ¶ 유심히 듣다 hear attentively; listen 《to》.
유아 (幼兒) a baby; an infant. ‖ ~교육 preschool (infant) education / ~기 babyhood; infancy / ~복 baby wear / ~사망률 the infant mortality rate.
유아 (乳兒) a suckling; a baby. ‖ ~식 baby food.
유아 (唯我) ¶ ~독존 self-conceit; self-righteousness / 천상천하~독존 I am my own Lord 《Holy am I alone》 throughout heaven and earth. ‖ ~론 〖哲〗 solipsism.
유아등 (誘蛾燈) a light trap; a luring lamp.
유안 (硫安) 〖化〗 ammonium sul-

유암 『醫』 ☞ 유방암.
유압(油壓) oil pressure. ¶ ~ 구동의 hydraulically-operated. ∥ ~계 an oil pressure gauge / ~브레이크 a hydraulic [an oil] brake.
유액(乳液) ① 『植』 latex; milky liquid. ② (화장품) milky lotion.
유야무야(有耶無耶) ¶ 대답을 ~하다 give a vague reply; do not commit *oneself* / 일을 ~해 버리다 leave a matter unsettled [undecided] / 그 추문을 ~(로) 덮어버리려 했다 They tried to hush up the scandal.
유약(釉藥) glaze; enamel. ¶ ~을 칠하다 put glaze on 《pottery》.
유약하다(柔弱—) (be) weak; effeminate; fragile.
유어(類語) a synonym.
유언(遺言) a will; *one's* dying wish; *one's* last words. ¶ ~을 express *one's* dying wish; leave [make] a (verbal) will. ¶ …의 ~에 의해 by the will of... / ~ 없이 죽다 die without a will. ∥ ~자 a testator; a testatrix (여자) / ~장 a will; a testament / ~집행자 an executor.
유언비어(流言蜚語) a groundless [wild] rumor; a false report. ¶ ~를 퍼뜨리다 spread a wild rumor; set a false rumor abroad [afloat].
유업(乳業) the dairy industry.
유업(遺業) work left unfinished by someone. ¶ ~을 잇다 take up the work left unfinished by 《*one's* father》.
유에스 U.S. (◀ United States)
유에스에이 U.S.A. (◀ the United States of America)
유에프오 UFO. (◀ an unidentified flying object) ∥ ~연구 ufology.
유엔 UN, U.N. (◀ the United Nations) ¶ ~의 평화 유지 활동 the U.N. Peacekeeping Operation 《in Africa》. ∥ ~군 the UN forces / ~분담금 financial contributions to the United Nations / ~사무총장 the secretary-general of the United Nations / ~안전보장이사회 the United Nations Security Council (생략 UNSC) / ~총회 the UN General Assembly / ~헌장 the United Nations Charter.
유역(流域) a (drainage) basin; a valley(큰 강의). ¶ 한강 ~ the Han River basin / 양자강 ~ the Yangtze valley. ∥ ~면적 the size of a catchment area.
유연탄(有煙炭) bituminous coal.
유연하다(柔軟—) (be) soft; pliable; pliant; elastic; flexible.

유연하다(悠然—) (be) calm; serene; composed. ¶ 유연히 composedly; with an air of perfect composure.
유영(游泳) ~하다 swim. ¶ 우주~을 하다 take [make] a spacewalk.
유예(猶豫) (연기) postponement; deferment; grace (행사 집행 등의) suspension; a respite. ~하다 postpone; put off (delay; 늦추다); give 《a day's》grace(지불을); reprieve; postpone; delay (형 집행을). ¶ 형의 집행을 ~하다 postpone [delay] execution; grant a stay of execution / 지불을 30일간 ~해 주다 give thirty days' grace for payment. ∥ ~기간 the period of grace; an extension of time.
유용(有用) ~하다 (be) useful; of use; valuable; serviceable; good 《for a thing》. ¶ 국가에 ~한 인물 a man useful to the state / 돈을 ~하게 쓰다 make good use of *one's* money; put *one's* money to a good use.
유용(流用) (a) diversion; (an) appropriation. ~하다 divert 《appropriate》《the money》 to 《some other purpose》. ¶ 공금을 ~하다 misappropriate public money.
유원지(遊園地) a pleasure [recreation] ground; an amusement park (美).
유월(六月) June (생략 Jun.).
유월절(逾越節) the Passover.
유위(有爲) ~하다 (be) capable; efficient; promising(유망한).
유유낙낙(唯唯諾諾) readily; quite willingly; at *one's* beck and call.
유유상종(類類相從) ~하다 Birds of a feather flock together.
유유자적(悠悠自適) ~하다 live in quiet [dignified] retirement; live free from worldly cares.
유유하다(悠悠—) (be) calm; composed; easy; leisurely. ¶ 유유히 calmly; composedly; slowly; with an air of perfect composure.
유의(留意) ~하다 take notice 《of》; pay attention 《to》; give heed 《to》. ¶ 건강에 ~하다 take good care of *oneself* / ~해서 듣다 hear attentively / 실업자 증가에 ~하다 take notice of rising unemployment. ∥ ~사항 an important notice.
유익하다(有益—) (be) profitable; beneficial; (교훈적) instructive; (유용) useful; serviceable. ¶ 유익하게 usefully; profitably /젊은이에게 유익한 책 books good for young people / 돈을 유익하게 써라 Make good use of your money.
유인(有人) ¶ ~의 piloted; manned. ∥ ~기(機) a manned [piloted]

유인(誘引) inducement; attraction. ~하다 induce; attract.
유인(誘因) a cause (*of*); a motive; an inducement; an incentive; an occasion. ¶ …의 ~이 되다 cause; bring about; lead (up) to.
유인물(油印物) printed matter. ‖ 불온 ~ subversive printed matter.
유인원(類人猿) 〔動〕 an anthropoid (ape).
유일(唯一) ¶ ~한 the only; the sole; solitary; unique; one and only / 무이한 unique; peerless / ~한 보기 a solitary instance / 남은 ~한 방법 the only measure left.
유임(留任) ~하다 remain (continue) in office. ¶ ~을 권고하다 advise (*the chief*) to stay in office. ‖ ~운동을 하다 movement to retain (*a person*) in *his* office.
유입(流入) an inflow; an influx. ~하다 flow in. ¶ 외자의 ~ an influx (inflow) of foreign capital / 미국 자본의 ~을 장려하다 encourage American capital inflow.
유자(柚子) 〔植〕 a citron.
유자격자(有資格者) a qualified (a competent, an eligible) person.
유자녀(遺子女) a child of the deceased. ¶ K씨의 ~ a child of the late Mr. K.
유자철선(有刺鐵線) barbed wire; barbwire 〔美〕.
유장(悠長) ~하다 (be) long; lengthy; 〔성미가〕 (be) leisurely; slow; easygoing (태평스런).
유저(遺著) a posthumous work. ¶ 김 박사의 ~ writings of the late Dr. Kim.
유적(遺蹟) ruins; remains; relics. ¶ 선사 시대의 ~ a prehistoric site.
유전(油田) an oil field (well). ‖ 해양 ~ an offshore oil field / ~을 개발하다 develop an oil field. ‖ ~지대 an oil (producing) region / ~ 탐사 oil exploration.
유전(流轉) 〔유랑〕 wandering; 〔변천〕 vicissitude. ~하다 wander (*about*); rove; transmigrate. ¶ 만물은 ~한다 Nothing remains the same. *or* Everything changes.
유전(遺傳) heredity; inheritance. ~되다 be inherited; run in the blood (family). ¶ ~성의 hereditary; of hereditary nature / ~적 결함 a genetic defect (flaw) / ~의 법칙 the laws of heredity. ‖ ~공학 genetic engineering / ~병 a hereditary disease / ~인자 a genetic factor / ~자 a gene / ~학 genetics / ~형질 a genetic trait (character).

유정(油井) an oil well.
유제(乳劑) 〔化〕 an emulsion.
유제(油劑) an oily medicine; 〔연고〕 an ointment.
유제동물(有蹄動物) an ungulate (animal); a hoofed animal.
유제품(乳製品) dairy products.
유조(油槽) an oil tank. ¶ ~선 a tanker / ~차 a tank car (열차) / ~ an oil tank truck (트럭).
유족(裕足) ~하다 (be) affluent; rich; well-to-do; well-off.
유족(遺族) a bereaved family; the bereaved(총칭). ¶ 전사자의 ~ the war bereaved.
유종(有終) ¶ ~의 미를 거두다 bring (*a matter*) to a successful conclusion; crown (*a thing*) with perfection; round off (*one's career*).
유종(乳腫) 〔醫〕 mastitis.
유죄(有罪) guilt; guiltiness. ¶ ~의 guilty / ~를 선고하다 declare (sentence) (*a person*) guilty; convict (*a person*) of (*a crime*) / 아무의 ~를 입증하다 prove *a person's* guilt. ‖ ~판결 a guilty verdict; conviction.
유증(遺贈) 〔동의어〕 bequest; 〔부동산의〕 devise. ~하다 bequeath (*one million won to…*); leave (make) a bequest (*of 5,000 dollars to…*); devise (*one's real estate to*). ‖ ~자 the giver of a bequest; a devisor(부동산의).
유지(有志) 〔관심이 있는 사람〕 an interested person; a volunteer (지망자); 〔유력자〕 a leading (an influential) person. ¶ ~일동 all the persons concerned. ‖ 지방 ~ public-spirited men (an influential figure) of the locality.
유지(油紙) oilpaper; oiled paper.
유지(油脂) oils and fats. ‖ ~공업 the oil and fat industry.
유지(維持) maintenance; preservation; upkeep. ~하다 maintain (*peace*); keep (*a club*) going; preserve (*one's health*); support. ¶ 평화 〔치안〕의 ~ the maintenance of peace (public order) / 건강을 ~하다 preserve *one's* health / 집안의 생계를 ~하다 support *one's* family / 현상을 ~하다 maintain the present condition / 체면을 ~하다 keep up appearances. ‖ ~비 maintenance costs; upkeep.
유지(遺志) *one's* dying (last) wishes. ¶ 고인의 ~를 따라야 한다 We should respect the wishes of the deceased.
유지(遺址) an old site; remains; ruins.
유착(癒着) adhesion; conglutination. ~하다 adhere (*to*); conglutinate; have close relation (*to*) (관계 따위가). ¶ 정부와 재계와의

~ a cozy relationship between politics and business.
유창(流暢) fluency. ~하다 (be) fluent; flowing. ¶ ~하게 fluently; with fluency / 영어를 ~하게 말하다 speak English fluently.
유체(有體) ¶ ~의 tangible; 〖法〗 corporeal. ‖ ~동산 〖法〗 corporeal moveables / ~재산 〖法〗 corporeal property. 「fluid mechanics.
유체(流體) 〖理〗 a fluid. / ~역학
유추(類推) analogy; analogical reasoning. ~하다 analogize; know (reason) by analogy; guess. ¶ ~으로 하여 on the analogy of…. ‖ ~해석 analogical interpretation. 「bandry.
유축농업(有畜農業) animal husbandry
유출(流出) an outflow; a drain; spillage. ~하다 flow (run) out; issue; spill. ¶ 기술자의 ~ the outflow of technicians / 두뇌의 ~ a brain drain / 기름의 ~ oil spillage. ‖ ~량 the volume 《of water》 flowing from 《the dam》 / ~물 (an) effluent 《from the mill》. 「기 the larval stage.
유충(幼蟲) a larva 《pl. -vae》. 「~
유취(類聚) ~하다 group in classes; classify.
유치(幼稚) infancy. ~하다 (be) infantile; childish; 《미숙》 immature; crude; primitive. ¶ ~한 생각 a childish idea; a crude opinion / 이 나라의 농업은 아직 ~하다 Agriculture in this country is still primitive (in its infancy). ‖ ~원 a kindergarten.
유치(乳齒) a milk tooth.
유치(留置) ① 〖法〗 (억류) detention; custody. ~하다 detain; keep (hold) 《a person》 in custody; detain. ‖ ~장 a lockup; a police cell; a house of detention. ② 《우편의》 ~하다 leave till called for. ‖ ~우편 a *poste restante* 《프》.
유치(誘致) attraction; invitation. ~하다 attract; lure; invite. ¶ 관광객을 ~하다 try to attract tourists / 마을에 병원을 ~하다 invite hospitals to the town.
유쾌(愉快) pleasure; delight; fun. ~하다 (be) pleasant; happy; delightful; cheerful. ¶ ~히 pleasantly; happily. 「(shell).
유탄(流彈) (be hit by) a stray bullet
유택(幽宅) 《무덤》 a grave; a tomb.
유토피아 ~ Utopia. ¶ ~의 Utopian. / ~문학 Utopian literature.
유통(流通) 《화폐의》 circulation; currency; 《어음의》 negotiation; 《물자의》 distribution; 《공기의》 ventilation. ~하다 circulate; pass current; float 《어음이》; ventilate. ¶ ~되고 있다 be in circulation / 공기의 ~이 좋다 〔나쁘다〕 be well (badly) ventilated. ‖ ~경로 a channel of distribution / ~기구 (구조) the distribution system (structure) / ~산업 the distribution industry / (어음의) ~성 negotiability / ~시스템화(化) the systematization of distribution / ~시장 a circulation market / ~자본 circulating capital / ~증권 a negotiable security (instruments) / ~혁명 a distribution revolution / ~화폐 current money.
유파(流派) a school.
유폐(幽閉) confinement. ~하다 confine 《a person in a place》; shut 《a person》 up.
유포(油布) oilcloth.
유포(流布) circulation; spread. ~하다 circulate; spread; go around; get about. ¶ ~되고 있다 be in circulation / 《소문 등이》 be afloat; be abroad; be in the air.
유품(遺品) relics; an article left by the deceased.
유풍(遺風) old traditions and customs. ¶ 로마의 ~ the old Roman way.
유하다(柔一) 《성격이》 (be) mild; gentle; genial; tender-hearted.
유하다(留一) stay at 《a place》; put up at 《a hotel》; lodge at 《*Mr. Browns*》.
유학(留學) study(ing) abroad. ~하다 study abroad; go abroad to study. ¶ 영어 공부를 위해 L.A.에서 ~하다 go to (stay in) L.A. to study English. ‖ ~생 a student studying abroad / (재미 한국인) ~생 Korean students in the U.S.
유학(儒學) Confucianism. ‖ ~자 a Confucian(ist).
유한(有限) ~하다 (be) limited; finite. ‖ ~급수 a finite series / ~책임 limited liability / ~책임 회사 a limited liability company.
유한(有閑) ¶ ~의 leisure. ‖ ~계급 the leisured class(es) / ~마담 a wealthy leisured woman / ~지(地) unused land.
유한(遺恨) a grudge; (an) enmity. ¶ ~이 있다 have (bear) a grudge 《against》 / ~을 풀다 pay off one's old scores.
유해(有害) ~하다 (be) injurious; harmful; noxious; bad. ¶ ~무익하다 do more harm than good / 흡연은 건강에 ~하다 Smoking is bad for (injurious to) the health. ‖ ~물질 a toxic substance / ~식품 poisonous (contaminated) food (stuff) / ~폐기물 toxic wastes. 「the (dead) body.
유해(遺骸) the (mortal) remains;
유행(流行) ① 《양식·옷 따위의》 (a)

유행 fashion; (a) vogue; a trend; 〔일시적인〕 a craze; a fad. ~하다 come into fashion〔vogue〕; become fashionable. ~하고 있다 be in fashion〔vogue〕; be popular; be fashionable / 파리의 최신 ~ the latest Paris fashion / ~하는 모자 a fashionable hat / 최신 ~형 the lastest fashion style / ~에 뒤진 out of fashion; old-fashioned / ~에 뒤지다 be behind the fashion / ~을 따르다 follow the fashion / 그녀는 ~에 민감하다 She is sensitive to changes in fashion. / 이런 형의 모자는 ~이 지났다 This type of hat is out of fashion. / 스키가 대 ~이다 Skiing is very popular. / 굽이 높은 여성 구두가 ~하고 있다 There is a trend now for very high heels on women's shoes. ② 〔병의〕 prevalence. ~하다 spread; prevail; be prevalent. ¶ 악성 감기가 ~하고 있다 Bad colds are spreading (going around) now. / ~가 a popular song / ~가 가수 a pop singer / ~병 an epidemic / ~색 a fashionable color; a color in fashion / ~성 감기 influenza; flu 〔口〕 / ~성 뇌염 epidemic encephalitis / ~어 a vogue word.

유현(儒賢) the sages of Confucianism. 「profound.

유현하다(幽玄─) (be) subtle and

유혈(流血) bloodshed. ¶ ~의 참극을 빚다 create a scene of bloodshed / ~사태로 번지다 develop into an affair of bloodshed.

유형(有形) ¶ ~의 material; corporeal; tangible; concrete / ~ 무형의 material and immaterial; visible and invisible. ‖ ~문화재 tangible cultural properties / ~물 a concrete object / ~자본 a corporeal capital / ~재산〔자산〕 tangible property〔assets〕.

유형(流刑) exile; banishment. ‖ ~지 a place of exile.

유형(類型) a type; a pattern. ‖ ~학 typology.

유혹(誘惑) temptation; lure; allurement; seduction. ~하다 tempt; entice; lure; seduce (*a girl*) / 대도시의 ~ the allurements of a large city / ~을 이겨내다 overcome〔get the better of〕 temptation / ~에 빠지다 fall into temptation / 돈으로 ~하다 allure (*a person*) with money / ~과 싸우다 resist temptation; fight〔struggle〕against temptation. ‖ ~자 a tempter; a seducer.

유화(乳化) emulsification.

유화(油畵) an oil painting. ‖ ~가 an oil painter.

유화(宥和) appeasement. ~하다 appease; pacify. ‖ ~론자 an appeaser / ~ 정책 an appeasement policy.

유화하다(柔和─) (be) gentle; tender; mild; meek.

유황(硫黄)〔化〕☞ 황(黄). ‖ ~천〔泉〕a sulfur〔sulfurous〕 spring.

유회(流會) an adjournment of a meeting. ~되다 be adjourned; be called off.

유효(有效) 〔법규 따위〕 validity; effectiveness; 〔표 따위〕 availability; 〔약 따위〕 efficiency. ~하다 (be) valid; effective; available; good. ¶ 적절한 effective and well-directed / 이 약은 암에 ~하다 This medicine is effective against cancer. / 이 협약은 아직 ~하다 This agreement still stands. / 이 차표는 2일간 ~하다 This ticket is good for two days. ‖ ~기간 the term of validity / ~사거리 an effective range / ~수요〔경제의〕 (an) effective demand / ~타 a telling blow / ~투표 a valid ballot.

유훈(遺訓) the teachings〔precepts〕of a deceased person.

유휴(遊休) ¶ ~의 idle; unused; unemployed. ‖ ~시설 idle facilities / ~자본 unemployed〔idle〕 capital / ~지 idle land.

유흥(遊興) (worldly) pleasures; merrymaking; amusements. ¶ ~에 빠지다 pursue〔indulge in〕 pleasure. ‖ ~가 an amusement center; gay quarters / ~비 expenses for pleasures〔a spree〕 / ~세 the amusement tax / ~장 a place of amusement.

유희(遊戱) a play; a game; 〔유치원 등의〕 playing and dancing. ~하다 play. ‖ ~실 a playroom.

육(肉) the flesh (육체); meat (식용육); ¶ 영과 ~ flesh and spirit; body and soul.

육(六) six. ¶ 제 ~ the sixth.

육각(六角) a hexagon; a sexangle. ¶ ~의 hexagonal; sexangular. ‖ ~형 a hexagon.

육감(六感) a sixth sense; hunch. ¶ ~으로 알다 know (*a thing*) by intuition (the sixth sense).

육감(肉感) sensuality. ¶ ~적인 sensual; voluptuous / ~적인 미인 a voluptuous beauty.

육개장(肉─) hot shredded beef soup (and rice). 「bark.

육계(肉桂) 〔韓醫〕 cinnamon; cassia

육괴(肉塊) a lump of flesh (meat).

육교(陸橋) a bridge (over a roadway); an overpass 〔美〕.

육군(陸軍) the army. ¶ ~에 입대하다 enter〔enlist in〕 the army. ‖ ~대학 the Military Staff College / ~무

육대주(六大洲) the Six Continents.
육도(陸稻) rice grown in a dry field.
육로(陸路) a land route; ~로 가다 go by land; travel overland.
육류(肉類) various types (kinds) of meat.
육면체(六面體) 〖數〗 a hexahedron. ¶ ~의 hexahedral.
육미(肉味) the taste of meat(맛); meat dishes(음식).
육박(肉薄) ~하다《전쟁에서》press (the enemy) hard; close in upon (the enemy) 《경기에서》run (a competitor) hard(close). ‖ ~전 a hand-to-hand fight.
육배(六倍) six times; sextuple.
육법(六法) the six codes of laws. ‖ ~전서 a compendium of laws; the statute books.
육보(肉補) a meat diet. ~하다 diet (nourish oneself) on meat.
육봉(肉峰) a hump.
육부(六腑) ▷오장육부.
육삼제(六三制) 〖敎〗 the 6-3-3 system of education.
육상(陸上) (on) land; ground; shore. ¶ ~수송하다 transport by land. ‖ ~경기 athletic sports; track-and-field events / ~근무 shore duty(선상에 대한); ground duty(항공에 대한); ~수송 land transportation.
육성(肉聲) a (natural) voice.
육성(育成) ~하다《키우다》rear; nurture; bring up《조성하다》promote; foster;《교육하다》educate; train. ‖ ~회비 school supporting fees (학교의).〔son.
육손이(六一) a six-fingered per-
육송(陸送) land transportation. ‖ ~화물 overland freight.
육수(肉水) meat juice; gravy.
육순(六旬) ¶ ~의 sixty-year-old; sexagenarian. ‖ ~노인 a sexagenarian.
육식(肉食)《사람의》meat-eating; meat diet;《동물의》flesh-eating. ~하다 eat (live on) meat; eat flesh. ‖ ~가 a meat-eater / ~동물 a carnivorous (flesh-eating) animal / ~조 a bird of prey.
육신(肉身) the body; the flesh.
육십(六十) sixty; threescore; LX (로마 숫자). ¶ ~의 the sixtieth / ~분의 일 a sixtieth (part) / ~대의 사람 a sexagenarian; a person in his sixties.
육아(育兒) child care; nursing. ~하다 bring up (nurse) infants; rear children. ‖ ~법 a method of child-rearing / ~비 childcare expenses / ~서 a book on childcare / ~시설 childcare facilities / ~원 an orphanage (고아원) / ~휴가 childcare leave.
육안(肉眼) the naked (unaided) eye. ¶ ~으로 보이는 (안 보이는) 곳에 within (beyond) eyeshot / ~으로 보다 (보이다) see with (be visible to) the naked eye.
육영(育英) education. ~하다 educate. ‖ ~사업 educational work / ~자금 a scholarship / ~회 a scholarship society.
육욕(肉慾) carnal desire; lust; sexual appetite. ¶ ~을 채우다 gratify one's lust.
육우(肉牛) beef cattle.
육운(陸運) overland transportation.
육전(陸戰) a land battle (war).
육종(肉腫) 〖醫〗 a sarcoma.
육종(育種) (selective) breeding (of animals (plants)).
육중(肉重) ~하다 (be) bulky and heavy; heavily-built (몸집이).
육즙(肉汁) meat juice; broth; gravy.
육지(陸地) land; shore (바다에서). ¶ ~쪽으로 toward the land; landward / ~의 동물 a land animal / ~로 둘러싸이다 be landlocked.
육척(六尺) six feet. ¶ ~장신의 남자 a six-foot man.
육체(肉體) the flesh; the body. ¶ ~의 physical; bodily; fleshly / ~적 쾌락 sensual pleasures / 정신과 ~ body and soul; flesh and spirit / ~적 고통 bodily (physical) pain / 육체파 미인 a glamor girl. ‖ ~관계 (sexual) intercourse / ~노동 physical labor / ~미 physical beauty.
육촌(六寸) a second cousin;《치수》six inches.
육친(肉親) a blood relation (relative); one's flesh and blood.
육탄(肉彈) a human bomb (bullet). ‖ ~십용사 the ten human bombs / ~전 a hand-to-hand battle.〔beef; beef jerky.
육포(肉脯) jerked (dried sliced)
육풍(陸風) a land breeze (wind).
육필(肉筆) an autograph; (in) one's own handwriting.
육해공(陸海空) land, sea and air. ‖ ~군 the army, navy and air forces.
육해군(陸海軍) the army and navy.
육혈포(六穴砲) a six-chambered revolver; a pistol.
육회(肉膾) steak (beef) tartare; tartar steak; a dish of minced raw beef.
윤(潤)《광택》gloss; luster; polish;

sheen; shine. ¶ ~나다 be glossy (lustrous, shiny); be polished / ~내다 gloss; polish (up); put a polish (gloss) on; bring out the luster; make 《*a thing*》 glossy / ~을 없애다 take off the luster (shine).

윤―(閏) ‖ ~년 a leap (intercalary) year / ~달 a leap (intercalary) month / ~일 a leap day.

윤간(輪姦) gang (group) rape. ~하다 violate (rape) 《*a woman*》 by turns (in turn).

윤곽(輪廓) an outline; a contour. ¶ 얼굴의 ~ the contour of *one's* face / 그는 얼굴의 ~이 뚜렷하다 He has clear-cut features. / 그는 그 사건의 ~을 말했다 He gave an outline of the case.

윤기(潤氣) ☞ 윤. ¶ ~ 도는 머리 glossy (sleek) hair / ~가 돌다 (호르다) have fine luster; be (bright, lustrous, shiny).

윤독(輪讀) ~하다 read 《*a book*》 in turn. ‖ ~회 a reading circle.

윤락(淪落) ~하다 fall; ruin *oneself*; be ruined. ‖ ~가 a redlight district 《美》; gay quarters / ~여성 a ruined (fallen) woman; a delinquent girl.

윤리(倫理) ethics; morals. ¶ ~적인 ethical; moral / 실천 ~ practical ethics. ‖ ~규정 an ethical code / ~학 ethics / ~학자 an ethicist; a moral philosopher / 한국 신문 ~위원회 the Korean Press Ethics Commission.

윤번(輪番) turn; rotation. ¶ ~으로 in turn; by turns; on a rotation basis. ‖ ~제 a rotation system.

윤색(潤色) (an) embellishment. ~하다 embellish 《*one's story*》; color 《*a report*》; adorn; ornament. ‖ ~자 an embellisher.

윤생(輪生) [植] verticillation.

윤작(輪作) crop rotation. ~하다 rotate crops.

윤전(輪轉) rotation. ~하다 rotate; revolve. ‖ ~기 a rotary press (machine); a cylinder press.

윤창(輪唱) a troll; a round. ~하다 sing a song by turns.

윤택(潤澤) ① ☞ 윤. ② 〈넉넉함〉 abundance. ¶ ~한 abundant; ample; plentiful / 자금이 ~하다 have ample funds / 살림이 ~하다 be well-off.

윤허(允許) royal permission (sanction). ~하다 grant (royal) sanction.

윤화(輪禍) (be killed in) a traffic accident. ¶ ~를 입다 have (meet with) a traffic accident.

윤활(潤滑) lubrication. ¶ ~한 lubricous; smooth. ‖ ~유 lubricating oil; lubricant.

윤회(輪廻) [佛] *Saṃsāra* 《梵》; the transmigration of the soul; the cycle of reincarnation; metempsychosis.

율(律) ① 〈법〉 a law; a regulation; a statute; 《계율》 a commandment. ② 〈시의〉 rhythm; meter.

율(率) a rate; a ratio; a proportion(비율). ¶ ~의 ~로 at the rate of / 투표 ~ the voting rate / 낮은 출생률 the low birth rate / 사망률 the death rate.

율동(律動) rhythm; rhythmic movement. ¶ ~적인 rhythmic(-al). ‖ ~감 rhythmic sense; a sense of rhythm / ~미 rhythmical beauty / ~체조 rhythmic gymnastics.

율무 [植] adlay; adlai.

율법(律法) (a) law; regulations; 《계율》 commandments.

융(絨) cotton flannel.

융기(隆起) 〈지표의〉 upheaval; a rise; 〈부분적 돌기〉 a bulge; a protrusion. ~하다 upheave; rise; bulge. ¶ 화산성 ~ a volcanic upheaval / 지표의 ~ upheavals on the earth.

융단(絨緞) a carpet; a rug. ¶ ~을 깔다 carpet 《*the floor*》. ‖ ~폭격 a carpet (blanket) bombing.

융비술(隆鼻術) plastic surgery of the nose; rhinoplasty.

융성(隆盛) prosperity. ¶ ~한 prosperous; flourishing; thriving.

융숭하다(隆崇―) (be) kind; cordial; liberal; hearty; hospitable. ¶ 융숭한 대접을 받다 have a cordial (warm) reception; be treated hospitably.

융자(融資) financing; a loan 《융자금》. ~하다 finance 《*an enterprise*》; furnish 《*a company*》 with funds. ¶ ~를 받다 obtain a loan / 은행에 ~를 부탁하다 ask a bank for a loan. ‖ ~신청 a request for a loan / 조건부 ~ conditional financing; a tied loan.

융통(融通) ① 〈금전·물품 등의〉 accommodation; financing. ~하다 accommodate; lend; finance. ¶ 그는 내게 돈을 ~해 주었다 He accommodated me with a loan. *or* He loaned me. / 이백만원을 ~해 줄 수 있겠느냐 Will you please lend me two million *won*? ‖ ~력(力) *one's* financing ability / 어음 ~ an accommodation bill. ② 《순응성》 adaptability; flexibility. ¶ ~성 있는 adaptable; flexible / ~성 없는 unadaptable; inflexible / 그는 ~성이 있는 사내이다 He is an adaptable person.

융합(融合) fusion; harmony (조화); unity; union (결합). ~하다 fuse; harmonize; unite.

융해(融解) fusion; melting; dissolution. ~하다 fuse; melt; dissolve. ‖ ~열[점] the melting heat [point].

융화(融化) deliquescence. ~하다 deliquesce; soften.

융화(融和) harmony; reconciliation. ~하다 harmonize; be reconciled 《with》.

윷(놀이) the "Four-Stick Game"; *yut*. ¶ ~놀이하다 play *yut*.

으깨다 crush; squash; smash; mash 《*potatoes*》.

으드득 《뼈를》 ~ 깨물다 crunch on a bone / ~ 이를 갈다 grind one's teeth.

으뜸 ① (첫째) the first (place); the top; the head. ¶ ~가다 be at the head 《of》; occupy the first place; rank first. ② (근본) the foundation; the root; the basis.

으레 ① (응당) of course; to be sure; naturally; no doubt. ② (어김없이) always; without fail. ③ (관례적) habitually; usually.

으로 (☞ 로) ① (원인·근거) of; from; (이유) because of; due to; owing to. ¶ 암 ~ 죽다 die of cancer / 병 ~ 학교를 쉬다 be absent from school because of illness / 병 ~ 누워 있다 be ill in bed / 안색 ~ 알다 know 《*something*》 from 《*a person's*》 look. ② (수단·도구) by; on; with; by means of; through. ¶ 우편 ~ 소포를 보내다 send the parcel by mail / 텔레비전 ~ 축구를 보다 watch a soccer game on TV / 망원경 ~ 달을 보다 look at the moon through a telescope. ③ (원료·재료) of; out of. ¶ 헌 궤짝 ~ 책상을 만들다 make a table out of an old box. ④ (가격·비용) for, at. ¶ 하나에 100원 ~ 팔다 sell at a hundred *won* a piece / 한 달에 20만원 ~ 살다 live on two hundred thousand *won* a month. ⑤ (기준·단위) by; at. ¶ 일급 ~ 일하다 work by the day. ⑥ (방향) for; to; toward. ¶ 부산 ~ 가는 기차 the train for Busan. ⑦ (변화) into; to. ¶ 바다가 산 ~ 변하더라도 though seas turn to mountains. ⑧ (구성·성립) of. ¶ 국회는 상하 양원 ~ 되어 있다 The Assembly consists of two Houses, upper and lower. ⑨ (내용) of; with. ¶ 설탕 ~ 가득 차다 be full of sugar.

으로서 as; in the capacity of 《자격》 (☞ 로서.) ¶ 통역 ~ as an interpreter.

으르다 threaten 《*to kill a person*》; intimidate; scare. ¶ 으르고 달래다 with threats and coaxing; using the carrot and the stick.

으르렁거리다 《맹수가》 roar; growl; howl; 《개가》 snarl; 《사람끼리》 quarrel 《wrangle》 《*with*》; feud with; be at odds 《*with*》.

으름 《植》 an akebi fruit [berry]. ‖ ~덩굴 an akebi (shrub).

으름장 intimidation; browbeating; a threat; (a) menace. ¶ (을) 놓다 intimidate; browbeat; threaten; menace.

으리으리하다 (be) magnificent; stately; imposing; grand; awe-inspiring. ¶ 으리으리한 저택 a stately mansion.

…으면 if 《…면》. ¶ 천만원 있 ~ If I had ten million *won*, ….

…으면서 …면서》 (동시에) while; as; at the same time; with. ¶ 생긋 웃 ~ with a smile / 음악을 들 ~ 고향을 생각하다 think of home while listening to the music.

으스름달 a hazy moon. ‖ ~밤 a faint (misty) moonlit night.

으슬 ¶ ~한 chilly / ~ 춥다 feel a chill; shiver with cold.

으슥하다 (be) retired and quiet; secluded; lonely; deep.

으슴푸레하다 (be) dusky; hazy; misty; dim.

으쓱거리다 [strut] about; give oneself airs; put on airs.

으쓱하다¹ 《추위·무서움으로》 shudder; shiver; feel a thrill 《*of horror*》. ¶ 듣기〔보기〕만 해도 으쓱해지다 shudder at the mere mention 〔sight〕 《*of*》 / 몸을 으쓱하게 하는 무서운 이야기 a bloodcurdling story.

으쓱하다² (우쭐하다) be elated 〔inflated, exultant〕 《*over, with*》; be puffed up 《*by, with*》; perk 〔draw〕 oneself up.

으악 (놀래줄 때) Boo!; (놀라서) Ugh!; with a sudden outcry.

으크러뜨리다 crush 《*a thing*》 (out of shape); crumble; squash; smash. (bled).

으크러지다 get crushed (crumbled).

윽박지르다¹ snub [shout] 《*a person*》 down; bully; threaten; browbeat; intimidate.

은(銀) silver (기호 Ag). ¶ ~ (제)의 silver / ~ 같은 silvery / ~을 입힌 silver-plated. ‖ ~그릇〔제품〕 silverware / ~본위 《經》 the silver standard / ~붙이 (-ware) / ~수저 silver spoon and chopsticks / ~실 silver thread.

은거(隱居) retirement; seclusion. ~하다 retire from the world; live in seclusion.

은고(恩顧) (a) favor; patronage. ¶ ~를 입다 receive favors 《from》;

은공(恩功) favors and merits.
은광(銀鑛) a silver mine; silver ore〔광석〕.
은괴(銀塊) a silver ingot; silver bullion; bar silver〔막대 모양의〕.
은근(慇懃) ① 〔정중〕 politeness. ¶ ~한(히) polite(ly); civil(ly); courteous(ly); attentive(ly). ② 〔은밀〕 quietness. ¶ ~한(히) private(·ly); secret(ly); quiet(ly); inward(ly); indirect(ly).
은기(銀器) silverware.
은닉(隱匿) concealment; secretion. ~하다 conceal; hide. ¶범인을 ~하다 shelter〔harbor〕 the criminal. ‖ ~물자 concealed goods; goods hidden / ~처 a hiding place.
은덕(恩德) a beneficial influence〔virtue〕. ¶ ~을 베풀다 confer a benefit 《upon》.
은덕(隱德) good done by stealth; a secret act of charity.
은도금(銀鍍金) silver plating. ~하다 plate〔gild〕 with silver.
은둔(隱遁) retirement〔from the world〕. ~하다 retire from the world; live in seclusion. ‖ ~생활〔lead〕 a secluded life.
은막(銀幕) the〔silver〕 screen. ¶ ~의 여왕 the queen of the screen.
은밀(隱密) ~하다 (be) secret; covert; private. ¶ ~히 처리하다 dispose of《a matter》secretly / 몸의 ~한 곳 private parts of one's body. 「silver paper.
은박(銀箔) silver leaf〔foil〕. ‖ ~지
은반(銀盤) ① 〔쟁반〕 a silver plate. ② 〔스케이트장〕 a skating rink. ¶ ~의 여왕 the queen on the ice.
은발(銀髮) silver(y)〔gray〕 hair.
은방(銀房) a silversmith's; a jeweler's〔shop〕〔금은방〕.
은방울꽃(銀—)〔植〕 the lily of the valley.
은배(銀杯) a silver cup.
은백(銀白) ¶ ~ (색)의 silver-white; silver-gray.
은분(銀粉) silver dust. 「silvery.
은빛(銀—) ~의 silver-colored;
은사(恩師) one's〔respected〕 teacher; one's former teacher.
은사(隱士) a hermit scholar (who refuses office).
은세계(銀世界) a silver world; a vast snowy scene.
은세공(銀細工) silverwork. ‖ ~인 a silversmith / ~품 silverware.
은신(隱身) ~하다 hide〔conceal〕 oneself; hide out《口》. ‖ ~처 a hiding place; a hide-out〔변인의〕.
은어(銀魚)〔魚〕 a sweetfish.
은어(隱語) secret language; cant; jargon.
은연(隱然) ~하다 (be) latent; underlying; hidden; secret. ¶은연중에 in secret; without 《a person's》 knowledge; behind the scenes / 친구를 ~중에 help a friend on the 「quiet (q.t.).
은유(隱喩) a metaphor. ¶ ~적(으로) metaphorical(ly).
은은하다(隱隱—) ① 〔아련함〕 (be) dim; vague; indistinct; misty. ¶은은한 향기 a subtle perfume. ② 〔소리가〕 (be) dim; faint; distant (to the ears). ¶은은한 포성 the distant booming of guns.
은인(恩人) a benefactor. ¶그는 내 생명의 ~이다 I owe him my life.
은잔(銀盞) a silver (wine) cup.
은장도(銀粧刀) a silver-decorated knife. 「precious metal.
은저울(銀—) a scale for weighing
은전(恩典) a special favor; (a) privilege. ¶ ~을 입다 receive 〔be granted〕 a special favor.
은전(銀錢) a silver coin.
은종이(銀—) silver paper; tin foil.
은총(恩寵) grace《of God》; favor. ¶신의 ~으로 by the grace of God / 신의 ~을 입다 receive〔enjoy〕 divine favor. 「spectacles.
은테(銀—) ¶ ~안경 silver-rimmed
은퇴(隱退) retirement. ~하다 retire《from business》. ¶건강상의 이유로 ~를 결심하다 decide to retire for reasons of health / ~해서 살다 live in retirement. ‖ ~생활 a retired life / ~선수 a retired player.
은폐(隱蔽) concealment; hiding; cover-up. ~하다 conceal; hide; cover up. ¶사실을 ~하다 cover up a fact.
은하(銀河) the Milky Way; the Galaxy. ‖ ~계(系) the galactic system / ~수 =은하.
은행(銀行) a bank. ¶ ~과 거래를 트다〔끊다〕 open〔close〕 an account with a bank / ~에 예금하다 deposit money in the bank. ‖ ~가(家) a banker / ~감독원 Office of Bank Supervision and Examination / ~강도 a bank robber〔사람〕; bank robbery〔행위〕 / ~구좌 a bank account / ~업 banking; the banking business / ~업무 banking services / ~예금 bank deposits〔savings〕 / ~원 a bank clerk〔employee〕 / ~이율 the bank rate / ~인수어음 a bank acceptance / ~자기앞 수표 a bank check / ~주 bank stocks / ~중앙 the Central Bank / ~지방 a local bank.
은행(銀杏)〔植〕a gingko nut. ‖ ~나무 a gingko (tree).
은혜(恩惠) a benefit; a favor. ¶ ~를 베풀다 do《a person》 a favor; do a favor for《a person》 / ~를 입고 있다 be in《a person's》 debt;

은혼식　　　　　　　　　　574　　　　　　　　　　음속

be indebted 《to》 / ~를 갚다 repay an obligation; requite [repay] 《a person's》 favor [kindness] / ~를 원수로 갚다 return evil for good / 그에게 많은 ~을 지고 있다 I owe him a great debt of gratitude.

은혼식(銀婚式) (celebrate) a silver wedding.
은화(銀貨) a silver (coin).
은회색(銀灰色) silver gray.
을(乙) the second; B.
을씨년스럽다 ① 〖살림이〗 (be) poor; needy; poor-looking. ② 〖외양이〗 look miserable [shabby, wretched]; 〖쓸쓸해 보이다〗 (be) lonely; dreary. ¶ 옷차림이 ~ be shabbily dressed.
을종(乙種) class B; second grade.
읊다(낭송) recite 《a poem》; 〖짓다〗 compose [write] 《a poem》.
음(音) ① 〖소리〗 a sound; a noise 〖잡음〗. ② 〖한자의〗 the pronunciation 《of a Chinese character》.
음(陰) the negative [female] principle in nature; the passive; darkness; a negative [minus] sign. ¶ ~으로 양으로 implicitly and explicitly; in every possible way. ‖ ~이온 a negative ion.
음각(陰刻) intaglio; (depressed) engraving. ~하다 intaglio; engrave in intaglio.
음감(音感) a sense of sound. ¶ ~이 있다 have a good ear 《for》. ‖ ~교육 acoustic training; auditory education.
음경(陰莖) the penis.
음계(音階) 〖樂〗 the (musical) scale. ¶ 온 〖장, 단〗~ the full [major, minor] scale / ~을 연습하다 practice scales 《on the piano》.
음곡(音曲) music; musical performance.
음공(陰功) hidden merits.
음극(陰極) the negative pole; the cathode. ‖ ~관 a cathode tube / ~선 the cathode rays.
음기(陰氣) 〖으스스한〗 a chill; chilliness; dreariness; 〖몸안의〗 negativity; the negative element.
음낭(陰囊) the scrotum.
음녀(淫女) a lewd [wanton] woman.
음담패설(淫談悖說) (make) an obscene [indecent] talk; (tell) a dirty [lewd, rude] story.
음덕(陰德) a secret act of charity. ¶ ~을 베풀다 do good by stealth.
음덕(陰德) the ancestor's virtue. ¶ 〖조상의〗 ~을 입다 be indebted to one's forefathers.
음독(音讀) ~하다 read aloud. ¶ 시를 ~하다 read a poem aloud.
음독(飮毒) ~하다 take poison. ¶ ~ 자살하다 commit suicide by taking poison; poison oneself to death.

음란(淫亂) lewdness. ~하다 (be) lewd; lascivious; obscene. ¶ ~한 여자 a lewd [loose, wanton] woman. ‖ ~비디오테이프 an obscene (sex) video tape.
음랭하다(陰冷一) (be) shady and cold; gloomy and chilly.
음량(音量) the volume 《of the radio music》.
음력(陰曆) the lunar calendar. ¶ ~ 8월 보름 August 15th of the lunar calendar.
음료(飮料) a beverage; a drink. ‖ ~수 drinking water; water to drink.
음률(音律) rhythm; meter.
음매(장소울음소리) a moo. ~하다 moo; low.
음모(陰毛) pubic hair; pubes.
음모(陰謀) a plot; a conspiracy; an intrigue. ¶ ~를 꾸미다 plot secretly; conspire 《against》 / ~에 가담하다 be implicated in a plot. ‖ ~자 a plotter; a conspirator; an intriguer.
음문(陰門) the vulva.
음미(吟味) close examination; appreciation 〖감상〗. ~하다 examine closely; appreciate.
음반(音盤) a (phonograph) record; a disc [disk].
음복(飮福) ~하다 partake of sacrificial food and drink.
음부(陰部) the pubic region; the private [secret] parts.
음산하다(陰散一) (be) gloomy and chilly; cloudy and gloomy; dreary; dismal. ¶ 음산한 날씨 dreary weather / 음산한 묘지 a dreary graveyard.
음색(音色) (a) tone color; (a) timbre. ¶ ~이 좋다 have a good timbre.
음서(淫書) an erotic book; 《총칭》 obscene literature; pornography.
음성(音聲) a voice; a phonetic sound. ‖ ~기관 the vocal organs / ~다중방송 sound multiplex broadcasting / ~다중TV a television set tunable to multiplex broadcasts / ~응답시스템 an audio response system 〖생략 ARS〗 / ~인식 speech recognition / ~테스트 audition / ~학 phonetics / ~합성 speech synthesis / ~합성기술 (an) artificial voice technology.
음성(陰性) ¶ ~의 〖기질이〗 gloomy; 〖반응이〗 negative; 〖병이〗 dormant / 에이즈 검사 결과는 ~이였다 The result of his AIDS test was (proved) negative. ‖ ~수입 a side benefit; a perquisite; spoils / ~콜레라 dormant cholera.
음소(音素) a phoneme.
음속(音速) the speed [velocity] of

음수(陰數) a negative number; a minus.
음순(陰脣) the labium [*pl.* -bia].
음습하다(陰濕一) (be) shady and damp; dampish.
음식(飮食) eating and drinking. ☞ 음식물. ~에 손도 대지 않다 leave the food and drink untouched / ~을 절제하다 eat and drink in moderation. ‖ ~물 food and drink; foodstuffs / ~점 an eating house; a restaurant.
음신(音信) correspondence; (a) communication; a letter(편지).
음심(淫心) a zest for lechery.
음악(音樂) music. ¶ ~적인 musical; melodious / ~을 이해하다 [못하다] have an [no] ear for music. ‖ ~가 a musician / ~ 界 music circles / ~당 a concert hall / ~성 musicianship / ~애호가 a music lover / ~영화 a musical (film) / ~평론가 a music critic / ~회 a concert / 고전 ~ classical music / 교회 ~ church music.
음양(陰陽) the positive and negative, the active and passive; 《남녀》 the male and female principles; 《해와 달》 the sun and the moon; 《빛과 그늘》 light and shade. ‖ ~가 a fortuneteller / ~오행설 the doctrine of the five natural elements of the positive and negative.
음역(音域) 〖樂〗 compass; a (singing) range. ¶ ~이 넓다 have a voice of great compass.
음역(音譯) (a) transliteration. ~하다 transliterate.
음영(陰影) shadow; shade. ¶ ~을 가하다 shade *something* (in); put in the shadings.
음욕(淫慾) carnal desire; lust. ¶ ~을 채우다 gratify *one's* lust.
음용(飮用) ¶ ~의 for drinking / ~에 적합하다 be fit [good] to drink; be drinkable.
음운(音韻) a vocal sound; 《음소》 a phoneme. ¶ ~변화 phonological transition / ~조직 the sound system / ~학 phonology / ~학자 a phonologist.
음울하다(陰鬱一) (be) gloomy; dismal; melancholy.
음위(陰痿) impotence. ¶ ~의 impotent.
음자리표(音一標) 〖樂〗 a clef.
음전(音栓) a stop (knob).
음전기(陰電氣) 〖理〗 negative electricity. 「negative electron.
음전자(陰電子) 〖理〗 a negatron; a

음절(音節) a syllable. ¶ ~의 syllabic / ~로 나누다 syllabicate; divide 《*a word*》 into syllables. ‖ 단 [2, 3]~어 a monosyllable [di-syllable, trisyllable].
음정(音程) an [a musical] interval. ¶ ~이 맞다 [틀리다] be in [out of] tune. 반~ a semitone / 온~ a tone. 「(a) rhythm(운율).
음조(音調) a tune; a tone(음색).
음주(飮酒) drinking. ~하다 drink. ‖ ~가 a drinker / ~검사 a breathalyzer test / ~벽 a drinking habit / ~운전 drunken driving / ~운전 강력 단속 캠페인 an intensive campaign against drunken drivers / ~운전자 a drunken driver / ~탐지기[측정기] a drunkometer 《美》; a breathalyser 《英》.
음지(陰地) 도 양달. ¶ ~도 양지된다 《俗談》 The wheel of fortune turns. *or* After a storm comes a calm.
음질(音質) tone (voice) quality. ‖ ~조정기 a tone controller.
음차(音叉) 〖理〗 a tuning fork.
음치(音痴) tone deafness. ¶ 나는 ~이다 I am tone-deaf. *or* I have no ear for music.
음침하다(陰沈一) (be) gloomy; dismal; somber; dark.
음탕하다(淫蕩一) (be) dissipated; lascivious; obscene; lewd.
음파(音波) a sound wave. ‖ ~탐지기 a sonobuoy; sonar(수중의).
음표(音標) 〖樂〗 a (musical) note. ‖ 온 ~ a whole note 《美》 2 [4, 8, 16, 32]분~ a half [a quarter, an eighth, a sixteenth, a thirty-second] note 《美》.
음표문자(音標文字) a phonetic sign (alphabet, symbol).
음해(陰害) ~하다 do 《*a person*》 harm secretly; stab 《*a person*》 in the back; backbite.
음핵(陰核) 〖解〗 the clitoris.
음향(音響) a sound; a noise(소음); a bang(폭발음). ¶ ~이 좋은 ~ 효과가 좋다 [나쁘다] The acoustics of this hall are good [bad]. ‖ ~조절 sound conditioning / ~측심기 an echo sounder / ~학 acoustics / ~효과 sound effects(TV·영화의); the acoustics(실내의).
음험하다(陰險一) (be) sly; cunning; tricky; crafty; insidious.
음화(陰畫) a negative (picture).
음흉(陰凶) ¶ ~한 crafty (wily) and cruel; tricky and treacherous.
읍(邑) a town. ‖ ~민 the townspeople; the townsfolk / ~사무소 a town office / ~소재지 the seat of a town office.
읍소(泣訴) ~하다 implore [appeal to] 《*a person*》 for mercy with

읍하다 (揖─) bow politely with tears. [joined hands in front.

응 (肯定) yea; yeah; yes; all right; O.K.; (否定) no. ¶ ~ 꼭 갈게 Oh yes. I will come without fail.

응결 (凝結) congelation(액체의); coagulation; condensation(증기의); setting(시멘트의). ~하다 congeal; coagulate; condense; set(시멘트가). ‖ ~기 a freezer; a condenser / ~물 a congelation (of) / ~점 the freezing point.

응고 (凝固) (고체화) solidification; congelation; coagulation(혈액). ~하다 solidify; congeal; coagulate. / ~제 a coagulant.

응급 (應急) ¶ ~의 emergency; makeshift(임시의); temporary (일시적인) / ~책을 취하다 take emergency measures; employ temporary expedient. ‖ ~수리 temporary [emergency] repairs / ~실 a first-aid [an emergency] room / ~조치[수단] (take) emergency (stopgap) measures / ~치료 first aid; first-aid treatment / (부상자에게) ~하다 give the wounded first aid / ~치료환자 a first-aid patient.

응낙 (應諾) consent; assent; acceptance. ~하다 consent [assent] (to); accept; agree to (a plan). ¶ 그녀는 고개를 끄덕이며 ~했다 She nodded her assent.

응달 the shade; the shady place. ¶ ~에서 in the shade / ~이 지다 be shaded (by).

응답 (應答) an answer; a reply; a response. ~하다 answer; reply to; respond. ‖ ~자 a respondent.

응대 (應對) ☞ 응접(應接).

응등그리다 shrink one's body; huddle [curl] oneself up.

응모 (應募) (예약) subscription; (지원) application. ~하다 apply for; subscribe for [to] (주식 등에); enter for (a contest). ¶ 취직 ~ an application for a position / 주식 모집에 ~하다 subscribe to stocks / 기술자 모집에 ~하다 apply for a position as an engineer (in the company) / ~자격 불문의 No special qualifications are needed to apply. ‖ ~액 the amount subscribed / ~자 an applicant(입학·취직 등의); a subscriber(주식의); a contestant(콘테스트의) / 현상 ~원고 manuscripts sent in to compete for the prize.

응보 (應報) retribution; nemesis.

응분 (應分) ¶ ~의 appropriate; due; reasonable; (분수에 맞는) according to one's means [ability] / ~의 대우를 받다 be given proper [due] treatment.

응사 (應射) return fire. ~하다 fire [shoot] back.

응석 ¶ ~부리다 behave like a spoilt child; play the baby (to) / 아이의 ~을 받아주다 pamper a child / 그녀는 늘 어머니께 ~을 부린다 She is always playing the baby to her mother. ‖ ~받이 [동이] a spoilt [pampered] child.

응소 (應召) ~하다 answer the call; be [get] drafted [enrolled]. ‖ ~자 [병] a draftee 《美》.

응수 (應手) ~하다 (바둑 따위에서) (make a) countermove.

응수 (應酬) an answer; a response; (교환) an exchange. ~하다 respond; answer; retort. ¶ 비난에 대해 지지 않으려고 ~하다 respond heatedly to the criticism.

응시 (凝視) a steady gaze; a stare. ~하다 stare [gaze] (at); fix [fasten] one's eyes (on).

응시 (應試) ~하다 apply for an examination. ‖ ~자 a participant in an examination; an examinee.

응애응애 (with a) mewl [whimper]. ¶ ~ 울다 mewl; whimper; whine.

응어리 (근육의) (a) stiffness (in a muscle); (종기) a lump; a tumor; (감정의) bad [ill] feeling. ¶ 젖가슴에 ~가 생기다 feel stiff [have a stiffness] in the breast / 그 사건은 두 사람 사이에 ~를 남게 했다 The event left the two with ill feeling. [plain.

응얼거리다 mutter; grumble; com-

응용 (應用) (practical) application; practice(실용). ~하다 apply; adapt; put in(to) practice. ¶ ~할 수 있는[없는] applicable [inapplicable]; practicable [impracticable] / ~ 범위가 넓다 be widely applicable. ‖ ~과학 applied science / ~문제 an applied question / ~물리학 applied physics.

응원 (應援) (원조) help; aid; assistance; support(선거 등에서); (성원) cheering. ~하다 help; aid; support; (성원하다) cheer (a team); (美凡) root for (a team). ¶ ~가 (歌) a rooters' song [pennant] / ~단 a cheer group / ~단장 a captain of the cheer group.

응전 (應戰) ~하다 fight back; return (the enemy's) fire (포격으로); accept [take up] the challenge (도전에).

응접 (應接) (a) reception. ~하다 receive (a visitor). ¶ 방문객을 ~으

응집 로 바쁘다 be busy with visitors. ∥ ~실 a drawing (reception) room.
응집(凝集) cohesion. ~하다 cohere; condense. ∥ ~력 cohesive power; cohesion.
응징(膺懲) (a) chastisement; (a) punishment. ~하다 chastise; punish.
응축(凝縮) condensation. ~하다 condense. ∥ ~기 a condenser.
응하다(應─) (답하다) answer; respond (to); reply (to); (승낙) comply with; accept; (필요·수요에) meet; satisfy; (모집에) apply (subscribe) (for). ¶ 질문에 ~ answer a question / 요구에 ~ comply with a request / 초대(주문)에 ~ accept an invitation (order) / 시대의 요구에 ~ meet the demand(s) of the times / 회원 모집에 ~ apply for membership in a society.
응혈(凝血) coagulation (of blood); (일) coagulated (clotted) blood (피). ~하다 coagulate.
의 (소유·소속) ⋯'s; of. ¶ 형님 ~책 my brother's book / 돈의 가치 the value of money / 장발의 청년 a young man with long hair; a long-haired young man. ② (소재) at; in; on. ¶ 런던의 겨울 the winter in London / 부산~ 삼촌 one's uncle (who lives) in Pusan. ③ (⋯에 관한) of; on; about. ¶ 고전 문학~ 권위 an authority on classical literature. ④ (⋯을 위한) ⋯'s; for. ¶ 아이들용 책 a book for children; a children's book. ⑤ (기점·출신) from; (작가) ~'s; by. ¶ 친구로부터의 전언 a message from one's friend / 워즈워스~ 시 a poem (written) by Wordsworth; a Wordsworth's poem. ⑥ (상태·재료) in; with. ¶ 하트형~ 초콜릿 a heart-shaped chocolate / 푸른눈~ 소녀 a girl with blue eyes / 청동~ 동상 a statue in bronze / 빨간 옷~ 소녀 a girl in a red dress. ⑦ (시간·기간) of; in; for. ¶ 4시간~ 수면 four hours of sleep / 2주간~ 휴가 a two-week vacation / 그 시절~ 사람들 people in those days. ⑧ (사람의 관계) ¶ 누이~ 친구 my sister's friend. ⑨ (목적관계) of. ¶ 사건~ 수사 the investigation of a case.
의(義) (정의) justice; righteousness; (관계) relationship; ties; bonds; (신의) faith; fidelity. ¶ ~를 위하여 죽다 die in the cause of justice.
의(誼) friendship; a bond between friends. ¶ ~좋게 지내다 live together happily / ~를 맺다 make friends (with); enter into friendly relations (with).

의거(依據) ~하다 (준거하다) follow (a precedent); conform to (a rule); act on (go by) (a principle); (근거에서) be based (founded) (on); be due (to). ¶ 이 규정에 ~하여 in conformity with this regulation / 선례에 ~하여 문제를 처리하다 deal with a matter according to precedent / 이 이야기는 사실에 ~한 것이다 This story is based on facts.
의거(義擧) a worthy (noble) undertaking; a heroic deed.
의견(意見) an opinion; a view; an idea. ¶ ~의 대립(충돌) a split (conflict) of opinion / 다수(소수)의 ~ a majority (minority) opinion / 나의 ~으로는 in my opinion / ~의 일치를 보다 reach (an) agreement; get a consensus of opinion / ~이 같다 (다르다) agree (disagree) with (a person) / ~을 교환하다 exchange views (with a person on a subject). / ~서 one's written opinion.
의결(議決) a resolution; a decision. ~하다 decide; resolve; pass a vote (of). ¶ 예산안이 ~되었다 The budget bill was passed. ∥ ~권 the right to vote / ~기관 a legislative organ.
의고(擬古) ~적인 classical. ∥ ~문 a pseudoclassical style.
의과(醫科) the medical department. ¶ ~대학 a medical college / ~학생 a medical student.
의관(衣冠) gown and hat; attire. ¶ ~을 갖추다 be in full dress.
의구(依舊) ~하다 remain as it was; remain unchanged.
의구심(疑懼心) apprehensions; fear; misgivings. ¶ ~을 품다 entertain (feel) misgivings (about).
의기(意氣) spirits; heart; mind. ¶ ~왕성 (소침)하다 be in high (low) spirits / ~상통하는 사이 of a mind.
의기(義氣) (의협심) chivalrous spirit; (공공심) public spirit. ¶ ~있는 chivalrous; public-spirited.
의논(議論) a consultation; a talk; negotiations (교섭). ~하다 talk (have a talk) (with a person) about (a matter); consult (with a person).
의당(宜當) (as a matter) of course; naturally. ~하다 (be) proper; natural; be a matter of course. ¶ 당연(當然). ¶ 그 재산은 ~ 너의 것이다 The property is of course yours.
의도(意圖) an intention; an aim. ~하다 intend to (do); aim (at). ¶ ~적으로 on purpose; intentionally / 질문의 ~하는 바는 무엇이냐 What is your intention in

의례(依例) ~하다 follow a precedent. ¶ ~에 따라 according to precedent. ‖ ~건(件) a matter of precedent.

의례(儀禮) ceremony; courtesy. ¶ ~적(인) ceremonial; formal / ~적으로 방문하다 pay a courtesy [formal] call (on) / 가정 ~ 준칙 the family rite rules.

의론(議論) argument(논의); discussion(토론); dispute(논쟁). ¶ ~하다 argue (dispute) with (*a person*) over (about) (*a matter*); discuss.

의롱스럽다 (be) insidious; sly; [wily.

의롭다(義一) 《바르다》 (be) just; righteous; 《의기가 있다》 (be) chivalrous; public-spirited.

의뢰(依賴) ① 《부탁》 a request; 《위탁》 trust; commission. ~하다 request; ask; 《위임》 trust; entrust; ¶ 변호사에게 ~하다 leave (*a matter*) to a lawyer / 재산의 관리를 ~하다 trust *a person* with *one's* property. ‖ ~서〔장〕 a written request / ~인 〔변호사 등의〕 a client. ② 《의지》 dependence; reliance. ~하다 depend (rely) (up)on. ‖ ~심 a spirit of dependence; lack of self-reliance (~심이 강하다 rely (depend) too much on others).

의료(醫療) medical treatment [care]. ‖ ~기관 a medical institution / ~기구 medical (surgical) instruments / ~보험 medical insurance / ~비 medical expenses; a doctor's bill / ~사고 medical malpractice / ~수가(酬價) a medical fee / ~시설 medical facilities / ~품 medical supplies / ~혜택 a medical benefit.

의류(衣類) clothing; clothes; garments.

의리(義理) ① 《바른 도리》 justice; righteousness; 《의무》 duty; obligation; 《신의》 faith; loyalty. ¶ ~가 있다 be faithful; be strong in the sense of justice / ~ 없다 have no sense of duty (justice). ② 《인간 관계》 relationship; ties; bonds. ¶ 친구간의 ~ the ties of friendship.

의무(義務) a duty; an obligation. ¶ ~할 ~가 있다 be under an obligation to (*do*); ought to (*do*) / ~를 게을리하다 (다하다) neglect (do, perform) *one's* duty / ~를 지다 owe a duty (to *one's* country). ‖ ~감 a sense of duty (obligation) / ~교육 compulsory education / ~연한 an obligatory term of service.

의무(醫務) medical affairs. ‖ ~실 a dispensary(학교·공장 등의); a medical room.

의문(疑問) a question; a doubt. ¶ ~의 doubtful; questionable / ~을 품다 doubt; be doubtful 《of, about》; have *one's* doubt 《about》 / ~의 여지가 없다 be beyond question; there is no doubt 〔question〕 《about, that...》. ‖ ~문 (대명사) an interrogative sentence (pronoun) / ~부 a question (an interrogation) mark / ~사(詞) an interrogative / ~점 a doubtful point.

의미(意味) (a) meaning; (a) sense; 《취지》 the import; (a) point. ~하다 mean; signify; imply(함축하다). ¶ ~ 있는 meaningful; significant / 말의 ~를 파악하다 grasp the meaning of a word / ~를 잘 못 해석하다 mistake the meaning (of) / 그런 ~로 말한 것이 아니다 I didn't mean that.

의법(依法) ¶ ~ 처리하다 deal with (*a matter*) according to law.

의병(義兵) a loyal soldier; a volunteer troops(의용군).

의복(衣服) clothes; a dress; 《총칭》 clothing.

의분(義憤) righteous indignation. ¶ ~을 느끼다 have [burn with] righteous indignation.

의붓 step. ‖ ~딸 a stepdaughter / ~아들 a stepson / ~아버지 a stepfather / ~어머니 a stepmother / ~자식 a stepchild.

의사(義士) a righteous person; a martyr.

의사(意思) an intention; a wish. ¶ ~ 표시를 하다 express *one's* intentions / 아무의 ~를 존중하다 respect (make sure of) *a person's* intentions / 서로 ~ 소통되다 understand each other / 최종 ~ 결정을 하다 make a final decision 《about, on, over》. ‖ ~능력 mental capacity.

의사(擬似) ¶ 유사(類似).

의사(醫師) a doctor; a physician; a surgeon(외과); a (medical) practitioner(개업의). ¶ ~의 진찰을 받다 consult [see] a doctor / ~를 부르러 보내다 send for a doctor / ~가 되다 be (become) a doctor / ~의 치료를 받고 있다 be under the care of a doctor. ‖ ~ 국가시험 the National Examination for Medical Practitioners / ~면허 a medical license / 단골 ~ *one's* family doctor.

의사(議事) (parliamentary) proceedings. ¶ ~를 진행하다 expedite the proceedings. ‖ ~당 an assembly hall; 《한국의》 the National Assembly Building; the Capitol 《미》 / ~록 the minutes of the proceedings / ~봉 a gavel / ~

의상(衣裳) clothes; dress; costume. ¶ 민속[무대] ~ folk [stage] costume.

의생(醫生) a herb doctor; a herbalist.

의서(醫書) a medical book; a book on medicine.

의석(議席) a seat (in the House). ¶ ~을 보유하다 have a seat (in the House).

의성어(擬聲語) an onomatopoeia.

의수(義手) an artificial (a false) arm [hand].

의술(醫術) medicine; the medical art. ¶ ~의 medical / ~을 업으로 하다 practice medicine.

의식(衣食) food and clothing; a livelihood (생계). ¶ ~주(住) food, clothing and housing [shelter].

의식(意識) consciousness; one's senses. ~하다 be conscious [aware] 《of》. ¶ 사회 [계급] ~ the social (class) consciousness / ~ 적(으로) conscious(ly); deliberate(ly); intentional(ly) / ~을 회복하다 (잃다) recover (lose) consciousness / ~불명의 상태에서 병원으로 운반되다 be taken to (the) hospital unconscious. ‖ ~조사 an attitude survey.

의식(儀式) a ceremony; 《종교상의》 a rite; a ritual; a service.

의심(疑心) 《의혹》 (a) doubt; 《의문》 a question; 《혐의》 (a) suspicion. ~하다 doubt; be doubtful 《of, about》; suspect; be suspicious 《of, about》. ¶ ~을 품다 have [feel] doubts about 《a thing》 / 그것은 ~없는 사실이다 It is an unquestionable fact. / 나는 그의 성공을 ~치 않는다 I have no doubt of his success. / 그는 가짜 의사가 아닌가 ~받고 있다 He is suspected of being a bogus doctor.

의아(疑訝) ~하다 [스럽다] (be) dubious; suspicious; doubtful. ¶ ~스런 얼굴을 하다 look suspicious / ~스럽게 여기다 feel doubtful. 《eye.

의안(義眼) an artificial [a false〉

의안(議案) a bill; a measure. ¶ ~에 찬성 [반대]하다 support [oppose] a bill / ~을 국회에 제출하다 present a bill to the Congress.

의약(醫藥) a medicine; a drug. ‖ ~분업 separation of dispensary from medical practice / ~제도 medical and pharmaceutical systems / ~품 medical supplies; medicines.

의업(醫業) the medical profession.

의역(意譯) a free translation. ~하다 translate freely; give [make] a free translation.

의연(依然) ¶ ~히 as before; as it was; as ever; yet, still (아직) / 구태~하다 remain unchanged.

의연(義捐) ‖ ~금 a contribution; a donation; 《raise》 a subscription 《for》.

의연히(毅然─) resolutely; firmly; boldly; in a dauntless manner.

의예과(醫豫科) the premedical course; premed 《美》.

의옥(疑獄) a public scandal; a graft (case) 《美》.

의외(意外) 《의 뜻밖》 unexpected; unforeseen; unlooked-for; 《우연》 accidental; 《놀라운》 surprising / ~로 unexpectedly; contrary [beyond] to one's expectation / ~의 일 a surprise / ~로 빨리 earlier than expected / ~로 여기다 be surprised 《at》.

의욕(意欲) (a) will; volition; eagerness. ¶ ~적인 작품 an ambitious work / …하려는 ~이 대단하다 be eager to do; have a strong will (desire) to do / ~적으로 일에 달려들다 set to work with a will.

의용(義勇) loyalty and courage. ‖ ~병 [군] a volunteer soldier [army].

의원(依願) ¶ ~퇴직 [면직]하다 resign at one's own request.

의원(醫院) a doctor's [physician's] office 《美》; a clinic. ¶ 김 (Y) ~ Dr. Kim's (Y's) office.

의원(醫員) a physician; a doctor.

의원(議院) the House; the Parliament. ☞ 의회. ¶ ~내각제 the parliamentary system of government.

의원(議員) a member of an assembly; an assemblyman; 《국회의》 a member of the National Assembly; a member of Parliament (생략 M.P.) 《英》; a member of Congress (생략 M.C.) 《美》; a Congressman; a Representative (하원의원); a Senator (상원의원). ¶ 김 ~ Rep. Kim / ~으로 당선되다 be elected a member 《of Congress》.

의의(意義) meaning. ¶ ~ 있는 meaningful / 인생의 ~을 찾다 search for the meaning of life / 나는 ~ 있는 인생을 살고 싶다 I want to lead a life worth living.

의인(擬人) personification. ¶ ~화하다 personify.

의자(椅子) a chair. ¶ 긴 ~ a sofa; a lounge; a couch / ~에 앉다 sit on [in] a chair; take a chair (착석) / ~을 권하다 offer 《a person》 a chair.

의장(意匠) a design. ¶ ~을 고안하다 think (work) out a design. ∥ ~가 a designer / ~권 a design right; the right to a design / ~등록 registration of a design.

의장(議長) the chairperson; the chairman(남) the chairwoman(여). ¶ ~으로 선출되다 be chosen chairperson. ∥ ~대리 the deputy chairman / ~직권 the authority as chairman.

의장(議場) an assembly hall; a chamber; the floor(의회).

의장대(儀仗隊) a guard (guards) of honor; an honor guard.

의적(義賊) a chivalrous robber.

의전(儀典) protocol. ¶ ~비서 a protocol secretary / ~실 the Office of Protocol.

의절(義絶) ~하다 break off one's friendship (relationship) with; be through with; have (be) done with. ¶ 그녀와 ~했다 I broke off my relation with her. or I'm through with her.

의젓하다 (be) dignified; imposing; sober. ¶ 의젓하게 처신하다 behave with dignity.　〔a protocol.

의정(議定) an agreement. ¶ ~서

의제(議題) a subject (topic) for discussion; the agenda(전체). ¶ ~가 되다 come (be brought) up for discussion / ~에 포함되다 be on the agenda.　〔wooden〕 leg.

의족(義足) an artificial (a

의존(依存) dependence; reliance. ~하다 depend (rely) (on); be dependent (on). ∥ ~상호 ~ interdependence. ∥ ~도 dependence (on); reliance (on) / ~증 (drug) dependence.

의중(意中) one's mind (heart). ¶ ~의 인물 the choice of one's heart; a man closest to one's heart / ~을 떠보다 sound (a person's) views / ~을 밝히다 speak one's mind.

의지(依支) ~하다 《벽·기둥 따위에》 lean on (against); rest against; 《사람·도움 등에》 rely (depend) on; be dependent on; look to (a person) for help. ¶ 벽에 ~하여 앉다 sit with one's back against the wall / 난간에 ~하다 lean over the rail / 아들에게 ~하다 depend on one's son for support; lean on one's son / ~할 곳이 없는 helpless; forlorn / ~가 되다 become a support; be dependable.

의지(意志) will; volition. ¶ ~가 약한 사람 a weak-willed person / 자신의 ~로 of one's own will / ~에 반하여 against one's will / ~가 강(약)하다 He has a strong (weak) will. ¶ 그는 ~의 힘으로 그 장애를 극복했다 He overcame the obstacle by the strength of will.

의지(義肢) an artificial limb.

의지가지없다 have no person to rely on; (be) helpless.

의처증(疑妻症) a morbid suspicion of one's wife's chastity.

의치(義齒) an artificial (a false) tooth; dentures(한 벌의).

의탁(依託) ~하다 depend (rely) upon; lean on: entrust oneself to. ¶ ~할 곳 없다 be helpless; have no place to go to.

의태(擬態) 〔生〕 mimesis; mimicry. ¶ ~어(言) a mimetic word.

의표(意表) ~를 찌르다 take (a person) by surprise; do something unexpected.

의하다(依一) ① 《의거·근거하다》 depend (turn, rely) on; be based (founded) on. ¶ 최근 실시된 조사에 의하면 according to the latest investigation / 그것에 관한 정보를 신문에 의해 얻는다 We depend on the newspapers for information about it. / 이 소설은 실제 있었던 사건에 의한 것이다 This novel is based (founded) on an actual occurrence. / 조약 제3조에 의해 by (the terms of) Article 3 of the Treaty / 명령에 의해 by (a person's) order. ② 《원인·이유》 be caused by; be due to; 《수단·방법》 by means of; ¶ 사고는 그의 부주의에 의한 것이었다 The accident was due to (caused by) his carelessness. / 그녀의 병은 과로에 의한 것이었다 She fell ill from overwork. / 그의 성공은 내조의 공에 의한 것이다 He owes his success to his wife's assistance.

의학(醫學) medical science; medicine. ¶ ~적(으로) medical(ly). ∥ ~계 medical circles / ~생 a medical student / ~박사 Doctor of Medicine (생략 D.M., M.D.) / ~부(部) the medical department / ~사 a Bachelor of Medicine (생략 B.M., M.B.) / ~지(誌) a medical journal

의향(意向) an intention; one's idea (mind). ¶ ~할 ~이 있다 have a mind to (do); intend to (do) / ~을 비치다 disclose one's intention / 아무의 ~을 타진하다 sound out (a person's) intentions.

의협(義俠) chivalry. ∥ ~심 a chivalrous spirit.

의형제(義兄弟) a sworn brother. ¶ ~를 맺다 swear to be brothers.

의혹(疑惑) doubt; suspicion. ¶ ~의 눈으로 보다 eye (a person) with suspicion / ~을 풀다 clear one's doubts.

의회(議會) the National Assembly (한국); Parliament (영국, 캐나다); Congress(미국); the Diet(덴마크,

스웨덴, 일본. ¶ ~를 해산[소집]하다 dissolve [convoke] the Assembly. ‖ ~민주주의 parliamentary democracy / ~정치 parliamentary government; Congressional government《美》.

이¹ (사람·동물·톱 따위의) a tooth [pl. teeth]; 《톱니바퀴의》 a cog. ~의 dental / ~ 없는 toothless / ~를 닦다 [clean] one's teeth / ~를 갈다 grind one's teeth / ~를 뽑다 draw [extract, pull out] a tooth; have a tooth pulled out (빼게 하다) / ~를 쑤시다 pick one's teeth / ~가 좋다 [나쁘다] have good [bad] teeth / ~가 아프다 have a toothache / 아픔을 참느라 ~를 악물다 clench one's teeth to bear the pain / 우리 아기에게 ~가 나오고 있다 Our baby is cutting his [her] teeth. / 이 아이는 곧 ~를 갈게 될 것이다 This child will soon begin to cut his second [permanent] teeth. / 나는 ~를 치료받고 있다 I'm having dental treatment.

이² [蝨] a louse [pl. lice]. ¶ ~가 끼다 become lousy; be infested with lice / ~ 잡듯 하다 comb《a place》for《a thing》; make a thorough search.

이(利) ① 《이윤》 a profit; a gain; 《유리》 (an) advantage. ¶ ~가 있다 be profitable; be advantageous / ~를 보다 make [gain] a profit; profit《from the sale》/ 이 상점은 위치가 좋다는 ~로운 점이 있다 This store has a geographical advantage. ② 《이자》 interest.

이(里) 《행정구역》 ri; a village.

이(理) 《도리》 (a) reason; 《이치》 a principle. ¶ 음양의 ~ the principles of the negative and positive / ~에 닿지 않는 말을 하다 speak against all reason.

이³ 《지시사》 this; these; present. ¶ ~ 달 this month / ~ 같이 thus; so; like this.

이(二) two; the second(제2).

이가(二價) 《化》 bivalent; diatomic. ‖ ~원소 a dyad.

이간(離間) alienation; estrangement. ~하다 alienate [estrange]《A from B》; separate《a person》from. ‖ ~책 an alienating measure.

이것 ① 《지시》 this [pl. these]; this one. ¶ ~으로 with this; now; here. ② 《부를 때》 ¶ ~ 좀 봐 I say. or Look here.

이것저것 this and [or] that; one thing or another; something or other. ¶ ~ 생각한 끝에 after a great deal of thinking / ~ 생각하다 think of this and that.

이견(異見) a different [dissenting] view [opinion]; an objection.

이겹실 two-ply thread.

이경(二更) the second watch of the night; about 10 at night.

이골나다 《익숙해지다》 become [get] used [accustomed] to; 《경험이 쌓이다》 be richly experienced 《in》; become skilled 《in》. ¶ 일에 ~ be at one's ease on the job / 그녀는 교정이라면 이골이 나 있다 She is an old hand at proofreading.

이곳 this place; here. ¶ ~에(서) in [at] this place; here / ~으로 here; to this place / ~으로부터 from here; from this place.

이공(理工) science and engineering. ‖ ~계(系) science and engineering / ~과(학부) a department of science and engineering.

이과(理科) science; the science course [department]. ‖ ~대학 a college of science.

이관(移管) a transfer of jurisdiction [authority]. ~하다 place 《a matter》 under the authority [control] of another department; transfer 《a matter》 to another department.

이교(異教) paganism; heathenism. ¶ ~적 pagan; heathen. ‖ ~도 a pagan; a heathen.

이구동성(異口同聲) ¶ ~으로 with one voice; unanimously / ~으로 '예'라고 소리쳤다 They all cried 'Yes' with one voice (in chorus).

이국(異國) a foreign country; a strange land. ¶ ~의 foreign; exotic(이국풍의). ‖ ~인 a foreigner / ~정취 an exotic mood; exoticism.

이군(二軍) 《일반적으로》 the second team; 《野》 a farm team. ¶ 감독은 그를 ~로 밀어냈다 The general manager farmed him out [sent him down to the minors]. ‖ ~선수 a farmhand.

이궁(離宮) 《별궁》 a detached palace; a Royal villa.

이권(利權) rights and interests; concessions(관허의). ¶ ~을 노리는 사람 a concession hunter / ~을 노리다 hunt for concessions / ~을 얻다 acquire rights [concessions]. ‖ ~운동 hunting for a concession; graft(ing)《美》.

이글거리다 be in flames; be in a blaze; be all aflame; flame up. ¶ 이글이글 타는 불 a blazing fire / 열정으로 이글거리는 눈 eyes burning with passion.

이기(利己) self-interest; selfishness; egoism. ¶ ~적인 selfish; self-centered; egoistic / ~심 없는 unselfish; disinterested. ‖ ~심 egoistic mind / ~주의 self-

이기 (利益) ishness; egoism / ~주의자 an egoist; an egotist.

이기 (利器) a convenience. ¶ 문명의 ~ a modern convenience.

이기다[^1] 〈승리〉 win; gain a victory; defeat (패배시키다); conquer (정복하다); overcome. ¶ 싸움에 ~ win a battle / 적에게 ~ defeat the enemy (경기[경주]에서 ~ win a game(race) / 크게 [겨우] ~ win by a large (narrow) margin / 4점 차로 ~ win by four points (runs) / 어려움을 이겨내다 overcome a difficulty.

이기다[^2] ① 〈반죽〉 knead《flour》; work《mortar》; mix up. ② 〈칼로〉 mince; hash.

이기죽거리다 make invidious (nagging) remarks.

이까짓 such a; so trifling. ¶ ~ 것 such a trifle (as this).

이끌다 guide; conduct; show (usher) in; lead; head《a party》; 〈지휘〉 command《an army》.

이끌리다 be conducted to; be guided; be led; be commanded. ¶ 이끌리어 가다 be led away; be taken along.

이끼 〖植〗 (a) moss; a moss plant; a lichen (바위옷). ¶ ~ 긴 mossy; moss-grown / 구르는 돌엔 ~ 가 안 낀다 〔俗談〕 A rolling stone gathers no moss.

이나 ① 〈그러나〉 but; however; 〈한편〉 while; 〈…하기는 하나〉 though; although. ② 〈정도〉 as many (much, long, far) as. ¶ 다섯 번이 ~ as often as five times. ③ 〈선택〉 or; either...or.

이날 〈오늘〉 today; this day. ¶ 바로 ~ this very day / 이 때 this time on this day. / 〈당일〉 that day; the (very) day.

이날저날 this day and that day; from day to day.

이남 (以南) south《of the Han River》; 〈남한〉 South Korea. ¶ 38선 ~ south of the 38th parallel.

이내 (以內) within; inside of 〈美〉 less (not more) than. ¶ 500원 ~의 금액 a sum not exceeding 500 won.

이내 (곧) soon《after》; at once; immediately; right away.

이냥 as it is; like this. ¶ ~ 내버려 뒤라 leave《a thing》as it (stands).

이네, 이네들 these people; they.

이년 (二年) two years. ¶ ~생(生) a second-year [-grade] pupil; a sophomore (대학, 고교의) 〈美〉.

이념 (理念) an idea; an ideology; a principle. ¶ ~ 적(으로) ideological(y) / 대학 교육의 ~ an idea of what university education ought to be / 비폭력 저항의 ~ the principle of nonviolent resistance. ∥ ~에 의한 an ideological conflict / ~ 분쟁[논쟁] an ideological dispute.

이놈 this fellow (guy) 〈美〉. ¶ ~ 아 You rascal (villain)!

이농 (離農) giving up farming. ~ 하다 give up (abandon) farming; leave the land.

이뇨 (利尿) diuresis; urination. ∥ ~ 작용 a diuretic effect / ~제 a diuretic.

이니셔티브 〈주도권〉 initiative. ¶ ~ 를 잡다 take the initiative (in doing).

이다[^1] 〈머리에〉 carry (put)《a water jar》on one's head.

이다[^2] 〈지붕을〉 roof《with tiles》: tile《a roof》(기와로); thatch (이엉으로); slate (슬레이트로).

이다지 this much; so much; so. ¶ ~도 오래 so long like this.

이단 (異端) heresy; heterodoxy; paganism. ¶ ~적 heretical / ~ 시하다 consider《a person》 (to be) a heretic; regard《a doctrine》 as heresy. ∥ ~자 a heretic.

이달 this (the current) month. ¶ ~ 10일 the 10th (of) this month; the 10th instant (inst.) / ~호 (잡지의) the current number.

이대로 as it is (stands); like this. ¶ ~ 가면 at this rate; if things go on like this.

이데올로기 ☞ 이념.

이도 (吏道) the duty of officials. ~ 쇄신 renovation of officialdom.

이동 (以東) (to the) east《of Seoul》.

이동 (移動) a movement; (a) migration (민족 등의). ~ 하다 move; travel. ¶ ~식의 movable / 인구의 ~ the movement of population / 민족의 ~ racial migration. ∥ ~ 경찰 mobile (railroad) police / ~ 극단 a traveling troupe / ~ 도서관 a traveling library; a bookmobile / ~ 병원 a hospital on wheels / ~성 고기압 a migratory anticyclone / ~(식)주택 a motor (mobile) home / ~우체국 a mobile post office / ~ 전화 a mobile phone (telephone) / ~ 통신 사업 the (nation's) mobile phone project.

이동 (異動) a change; a transfer. ~ 하다 be transferred to. ¶ 본사로 ~ 되다 be transferred to the head office / 인사 ~이 있을 것 같다 There seem to be some personnel changes.

이득 (利得) (a) profit; gains; returns. ¶ 부당한 ~ an undue profit; profiteering (행위) / 부당 ~자 a profiteer / 부당 ~을 얻다 profiteer.

이든(지) if; whether...or; either

이듬 …or. ¶ 정말 ~ 거짓말 ~ whether it is true or not.

이듬 next; the following. ¶ ~ 해 the next (following) year.

이등(二等) the second (순위); the second class (등급). ¶ ~의 second; second-rate(-class); ¶ ~으로 여행하다 travel second class / ~이 되다 be a runner-up. ‖ ~ 병 a second-rate power / ~병 a private / ~상 a second prize (award) / ~승객 (표) a second-class passenger (ticket). [isosceles triangle.

이등변삼각형 (二等邊三角形) 〖數〗

이등분 (二等分) bisection. ¶ ~하다 divide (a thing) into two equal parts; cut in half; bisect (a line). ‖ ~선 a bisector.

이따금 now and then; occasionally; at times; sometimes; from time to time.

이때 (at) this time (moment).

이똥 《치석》 tartar; dental calculus. ¶ ~을 제거하다 scale (a person's) teeth. [~인 an Iraqi.

이라크 Iraq. ¶ ~사람 an Iraqi.

이란 Iran. ¶ ~사람 an Iranian / ~어 Iranian.

이란성 (二卵性) ‖ ~쌍생아 fraternal (biovular) twins.

이랑 (밭의) the ridge and the furrow (of a field). ¶ ~을 짓다 furrow (a field); make furrows; form ridges.

…이랑 《조사》 and; or; what with. ¶ 기쁨 ~ 부끄러움으로 with a mixture of joy and bashfulness.

이래 (以來) since; ever since. ¶ 그 때 ~ since then; after that.

이래라저래라 ¶ ~ 참견이 심하다 He is always poking his nose into people's business and telling them what to do.

이래봐도 such as I am. ¶ ~ 나는 행복하다 Such as I am, I am happy.

이래저래 with this and (or) that. ¶ ~ 바쁘다 I am busy with one thing or another.

이랬다저랬다 this way and that way. ¶ ~ 하다 be fickle (capricious, whimsical) / ~하는 사람 a moody person; a capricious (whimsical) person / ~ 마음이 늘 변하는 be fickle as a cat's eye; be unstable (unpredictable; unreliable) / 그는 말을 ~ 한다 He says first one thing and then the opposite. [dap!

이러 《마소를 몰 때》 Get up!; Gee-

이러구러 somehow or other; meanwhile. ¶ ~ 10년이 지났다 Meanwhile, ten years went by.

이러나저러나 at any rate; at all events; in any case (event); anyway; anyhow. ¶ ~ 해보는 게 좋겠다 At all events you had better try.

이러니저러니 this and that; one thing or another. ¶ ~ 말하다 talk (say things) 《about》; criticize(비평); grumble 《about》(불평) / 남의 일에 ~ 말라 마라 Don't gossip about others so much. / ~ 말고 해라 Do it without complaint.

이러이러하다 (be) so and so; such and such. ¶ 이러이러한 조건으로 for such and such conditions / 그녀는 울면서 ~고 말했다 She said so and so in tears.

이러쿵저러쿵 ☞ 이러니저러니.

이러하다 (be) so; like this; of this sort (kind). ¶ 이러한 일 a thing of this kind / 그의 이야기는 대강 ~ His story runs like this.

이럭저럭 somehow (or other); by some means or other; barely; with difficulty. ¶ ~ 대학을 마치다 get through one's college course somehow or other / 그는 ~ 겨우 지내고 있다 He is barely picking up a livelihood.

이런 ① 《이러한》 such; like this; of this kind. ¶ ~ 책 such a book / ~ 때에 at a time like this. ② 《놀람》 Oh! O dear me! Good gracious!

이렇게 so; (like) this; in this way; as you see. ¶ ~ 많은 so many (much) / ~ 아침 일찍 at this early hour of (the) morning / 나는 ~ 건강하다 I'm quite well, as you see. / 일이 ~ 될 줄은 생각 못했다 I didn't think things would come to this. / ~ 추운 날씨는 처음이다 I've never seen such cold weather as this. / ~ 해라 Do it this way.

이렇다 ☞ 이러하다. ¶ ~할 (a person, a thing) to speak of; worth mentioning / ~할 이유도 없이 without any particular reason / ~저럴다 말없이 떠나다 leave without saying a word / 나는 ~할 그림이란 점도 갖고 있지 않다 I've no paintings worth mentioning (to speak of).

이레 (이렛날) the seventh day (of the month); 《일곱 날》 seven days.

이력 (履歷) one's personal history; one's career; one's past record; one's background(학력·소양). ¶ ~이 좋다 (나쁘다) have a good (poor) record (of service) / 그의 ~은 어떤가 What is his career? ‖ ~서 a résumé 《美》; a personal history; a *curriculum vitae* 《라》 (회사에 ~서를 내다

이례 send *one's* résumé to the company.

이례(異例) an exception; 《전에 없던》 an unprecedented case. ¶ ~적인 exceptional; unprecedented / ~적인 승진이 되다 be given an exceptional promotion.

이론(異論) an objection. ¶ ~없이 unanimously / ~을 제기하다 raise an objection 《to》.

이론(理論) (a) theory. ¶ ~적인 theoretical / ~상의 in theory / ~을 세우다 form a (new) theory / ~화하다 theorize. ∥ ~가 a theorist / ~물리학 theoretical physics.

이롭다(利―) (be) profitable; beneficial; advantageous; be to *one's* benefit; be good 《favorable》 《to》. ¶ 이로운 사업 profitable business / 이로운 조건을 최대로 살리다 make the most of the advantageous conditions / 사태는 우리에게 이로운 방향으로 전개되었다 Things turned out (to be) favorable for us.

이루(二壘) 【野】 the second base. ¶ ~수 the second baseman / ~타 a two-base hit.

이루(耳漏) 【醫】 otorrhea.

이루 《cannot》 possibly; 《not》 at all; 《can》 hardly. ¶ ~ 말할 수 없는 indescribable; beyond description / ~ 헤아릴 수 없는 numberless; countless; innumerable / ~ 형용할 수 없다 can hardly describe it.

이루다 《성취》 accomplish; achieve 《one's purpose》; attain 《one's ambition》; 《형성》 form; make; 《구성》 constitute. ¶ 이루다 못한 소망 an unattainable desire / 큰 일을 ~ accomplish a great task / 무리를 이루어 in crowds 《groups》 / 큰 부를 ~ make a big fortune; amass riches / 물질계를 ~ constitute the material universe / 가정을 ~ make 《start》 a home.

이루어지다 be 《get》 attained 《accomplished, achieved, concluded》; be realized 《실현》; 《구성되다》 be composed of; consist of; be made up of. ¶ 뜻이 ~ *one's* purpose is realized / 두 나라 사이의 통상 조약이 이루어졌다 A treaty of commerce was concluded between the two nations. / 미국은 많은 인종으로 이루어진 나라 The U.S. is a nation made up of many different ethnic groups.

이룩하다 《새로 세우다》 found; establish; set up. ¶ 나라를 ~ found 《establish》 a new state. ② 《성취하다》 ☞ 이루다.

이류(二流) ¶ ~의 second-class; second-rate; 《시시한》 minor. ∥ ~

이름 시인 a minor poet / ~호텔 a second-class hotel.

이륙(離陸) a takeoff; taking off. ~하다 take off; take the air. ¶ ~시에 at 《during》 takeoff / 원활하게 〔멋지게〕 ~하다 make a smooth 〔an excellent〕 takeoff / ~때의 소음 takeoff noise. ∥ ~시간 takeoff time / ~활주 a takeoff roll. 【two-wheeled vehicle.

이륜(二輪) two wheels. ∥ ~차 a

이르다¹ 《때가》 (be) early; premature. ¶ 이른 봄 〔아침〕 early spring 〔morning〕.

이르다² ① 《도달》 reach; arrive 《at, in》; get to; come (up) to. ¶ 같은 결론에 ~ come to 〔arrive at, reach〕 the same conclusion / 《품질이》 표준에 ~ come up to the standard / 나이 80에 ~ reach the age of 80. ② 《미치다》 extend 〔stretch〕 《over, for》; cover; reach. ¶ 산업 시설은 주변 수 마일에 이른다 The industrial complex extends over several miles around. / 그의 지식은 많은 분야에 이른다 His knowledge covers many fields. ③ 《기타》 ¶ 서울에서 부산에 이르는 철도 a railway leading from Seoul to Busan / 오늘에 이르기까지 until now; to this day / 자살하기에 ~ go so far as to commit suicide / 사장에서 사환에 이르기까지 from the president 〔at the top〕 to the office boy 〔at the bottom〕 / 일이 여기에 이르리라고 누가 생각했으랴 Who would have dreamed that things would come to this!

이르다³ ① 《…라고 하다》 say; call. ¶ 진실로 내가 너희에 이르노니… Verily I say unto you…. ② 《알리다》 inform; tell; let 《a person》 know. ¶ 새 주소를 일러 주시오 Let me know your new address. / 그에 관해 선생님에게 ~ tell the teacher on him. ③ 《타이르다》 advice. ¶ 공부를 열심히 하라고 ~ advise 《a person》 to study hard.

이른바 what is called…; so-called; what you 〔they〕 call…. ¶ ~ 보호색이란 것에 의해 by what is called protective coloring.

이를테면 so to speak; as it were; for instance 〔example〕 (예컨대). ¶ 그는 ~ 산 사전이다 He is, so to speak, a walking dictionary.

이름 ① 《성명》 a name; 《성을 뺀》 *one's* given 〔first〕 name; 《성》 *one's* family name; *one's* surname. ¶ 낸시라는 ~의 소녀 a girl called 〔by the name of〕 Nancy / ~을 속이다 assume a false name; give a wrong name / 그의 ~은 알고 있지만, 아직 만난 적은

없다 I know him by name, but I've never met him. / ~을 여쭤봐도 괜찮겠습니까 May I have (ask) your name, please? ② 《명성》 fame; reputation. ‖ 명성(名聲). ¶ ~이 올라가다 rise in fame / 세계적으로 ~이 알려진 사람 a man of worldwide fame / ~을 떨치다 win (gain) a reputation. ③ 《명목》 a pretext. ¶ 그는 ~뿐인 사장이다 He is a president in name only. or He is a figurehead president. ‖ ~표 a nameplate; a name tag.
이리² 《물고기의》 milt; soft roe.
이리² 《짐승》 a wolf.
이리³ ① 《이렇게》 like this. ② 《이곳으로》 this way (direction); here.
이리듐 《化》 iridium (기호 Ir).
이리이리 so and so; such and such; in this way.
이리저리 《이쪽저쪽》 this way and that; here and there; all about; 《이렇게 저렇게》 like this way and that.
이리하다 do like this. ‖ that.
이마 the forehead; the brow.
이마적 recently; lately.
이만 this 《so》 much. ¶ 오늘은 이만 하자 Let us stop here today. or So much for today.
이만저만 ~하지 않은 노력으로 by (through) extraordinary (great, utmost) efforts / ~하지 않은 미모의 여성 a woman of singular beauty.
이만큼 about this (so) much (many, large, long, etc.); to this extent. ¶ ~이면 된다 This much will do.
이만하다 (be) about this (so) much (many, large, wide, long, etc.); (be) to this degree (extent) 《정도》. ¶ 이만한 크기(높이)였다 It was about this big (tall). / 이만한 영문을 쓸 수 있는 사람은 그리 많지 않다 Very few people can write English as well as this.
이맘때 about this time; (at) this time of day (night, year).
이맛살 ¶ ~을 찌푸리다 knit one's brows; frown.
이면(二面) 《두 면》 two faces (sides); 《형용사적》 two-sided; 《신문의》 the second page. ‖ ~기사 items on the second page.
이면(裏面) the back; the reverse (side); the other side; 《내면》 the inside. ¶ 어음의 ~ the back of a bill / 도시 생활의 ~ the dark (seamy) side of urban life / ~에서 behind the scenes; in the background / ~을 보라 《생략 P.T.O.》 Please turn over. / 정계를 ~에서 조종하다 pull the strings in the political world / ~에는 복잡한 사정이 있는 것 같다 There seems to be complicated circumstances behind it. ‖ ~공작 behind-the-scene (backstage) maneuvering / ~사(史) an inside story.
이명(異名) an alias; a nickname.
이명(耳鳴) (have) a ringing in one's ears. ‖ ~증(症) tinnitus.
이모(姨母) one's mother's sister; an aunt (on one's mother's side).
이모부(姨母夫) one's mother's sister's husband; a maternal uncle-by-marriage.
이모작(二毛作) double-cropping. 《raise》 two crops a year.
이모저모 this angle and that; every facet (side, view) of (a matter). ~로 생각하다 view (a matter) from every angle.
이목(耳目) 《귀와 눈》 the ear and the eye; 《주의》 attention. ¶ ~을 끌다 attract public attention / 세인의 ~을 놀라류다 startle the world; create a sensation.
이목구비(耳目口鼻) features; looks. ¶ ~가 반듯한 good-looking; well-shaped; handsome(남성이) / 그녀는 ~가 반듯하다 She is good-looking. or She has good features.
이무기 ① an imugi, a legendary big snake which failed to become a dragon. ② a big snake; a python.
이문(利文) profit; gain. ☞ 이익 ①.
이물 the bow; the prow; the stem. ¶ ~에서 고물까지 from stem to stern.
이미 《벌써》 already; 《의문문에서》 yet. ¶ 그것은 ~ 끝났다 It's already finished. / 수업은 ~ 시작됐나요 Has class begun yet? ② 《앞서》 before; previously. ¶ ~ 언급한 바와 같이 as previously stated.
이미지 an image. ¶ ~를 좋게(나쁘게) 하다 improve (damage) one's image.
이민(移民) 《이주》 emigration 《외국으로》; immigration 《국내로》; 《이주자》 an emigrant(출국자); an immigrant(입국자). ~하다 emigrate 《to》; immigrate 《from》. ‖ ~선(알선자) an emigrant ship (agent).
이바지하다 contribute 《to》; make a contribution 《to》; render services 《to》. ¶ 회사 발전에 크게 ~ make a great contribution to the prosperity of the firm.
이발(理髮) haircut(ting); hairdressing. ~하다 have one's hair cut (trimmed); get (have) a haircut. ‖ ~기 a hair clipper / ~사 a barber; a hairdresser / ~소 a barbershop 《美》; a barber's

이방인 (shop) 《英》.
이방인(異邦人) a foreigner; an alien; a stranger.
이번(一番) 《금번》 this time; now; 《최근》 recently; lately; 《다음》 next time; shortly. ¶ ~ 시험 the recent [last] examination(최근의); the next [coming] examination (다가오는)~에는 잘됐다 I did it well this time. ~에는 네 차례다 It's your turn now. ¶~만은 용서해 주겠다 I'll let you off just this once. 〔ond.
이번(二番) number two; the sec-
이변(異變) 《변고》 something unusual; 《뜻밖의 사고》 an accident. ¶ 정계에 ~이 일어나고 있다 Something unusual is happening in the political circles.
이별(離別) parting; separation; divorce (이혼). ~하다 part [separate] from; divorce. ¶ 어려서 양친과 ~하다 be separated from one's parents when he was a small child. ‖ ~가 a farewell song / ~주 a farewell drink.
이보다 (more, less, better, worse) than this. ¶ ~ 앞서 prior to this; before this / ~좋다 be better than this.
이복(異腹) ~의 born of a different mother. ‖ ~형제(자매) one's half brother (sister).
이부(二部) 《두 부분》 two parts; 《제2부》 the second part; Part Ⅱ; 《두 권》 two copies [volumes]; 《야간부》 a night school [class]. ¶ ~로 나뉘다 be divided into two parts. ‖ ~수업(제) a double-shift school system / ~작 a two-part work / ~합창 a chorus in two parts.
이부(異父) a different father. ‖ ~형제(자매) half brothers (sisters).
이부자리 bedding; bedclothes; a mattress(요); a quilt(누빈 것). ¶ ~ 세 채 three sets of bedding / ~를 펴다 lay out the bedding; make one's bed.
이북(以北) 《북》 north (of Seoul); 《북한》 North Korea. ¶ 그는 ~ 사람이다 He came from North Korea.
이분(二分) ~하다 divide (a thing) in two; halve. ¶ ~의 일 one half. ‖ ~음표 《樂》 a half note.
이분자(異分子) a foreign [an alien] element; an outsider(사람).
이불 a coverlet; a quilt. ¶ ~을 덮다 put a quilt on (over) oneself.
이브닝드레스 an evening dress.
이비인후과(耳鼻咽喉科) otorhinolaryngology. ¶ ~병원 [의사] an ear, nose and throat [ENT] hospital [doctor].
이사(理事) a director; a trustee (대학 등의). ¶ 상무~ a standing director / 그 단체의 ~가 되다 obtain a seat on the board of directors of the organization. ‖ ~장 the director general; the chief [managing] director / ~회 a board of directors [trustees].
이사(移徙) a move; a change of address (주소 이전). ~하다 move (to, into); move one's residence; change one's place of residence. ¶ 새로 ~하는 곳 one's new address. ‖ ~비용 house-moving expenses / 이삿짐 one's furniture to be moved / 이삿짐운반업자 a mover 《美》.
이삭(곡물의) an ear; a head; a spike. ¶ 밀 [벼] 의 ~ the ears of wheat [a rice plant] / ~이 나오다 come into ears.
이산(離散) ~하다 scatter; disperse; be dispersed; be broken up. ¶ 그것으로 인해 그 가족은 ~되었다 It broke up the family. ‖ ~가족 a dispersed [separated] family / ~가족찾기운동 a campaign for reunion of dispersed family members.
이산화(二酸化)《化》 ‖ ~물 a dioxide / ~탄소 carbon dioxide.
이상(以上) ① 《수량・정도》 more than; over; above; beyond(정도). ¶ 2 마일 ~ two miles and over / 6세 ~의 소아 children six years or (and) over / 《제안이》 3분의 2 이상의 다수로 채택되다 be adopted by a majority of two-thirds / 수입 ~의 생활을 하다 live beyond (above) one's income / 상상 ~이다 be more than one can imagine. ② 《상기(上記)》 ¶ ~의 the above-mentioned (items); / ~과 같이 as mentioned above / ~과 같은 이유로 for the reasons stated above. ③ 《…한 바에는》 since...; now that...; so long as.... ¶ 일이 이렇게 된 ~ so now that things have come to such a pass / 살고 있는 ~ 일을 해야 한다 So long as we live, we have to work. ④ 〔끝〕《문서 등에서》 Concluded; The end; 《통신에서》 Over; 《아ნოは 등이》 That's all (it) (for the moment).
이상(異狀) 《기계 등의》 trouble; something wrong; 《신체의》 disorder. ¶ ~이 있다 be abnormal; be out of order (기계 등에); be (slightly) sick [ill](사람) / ~이 없다 be all right; be normal; be in good order (condition) / 실내에는 ~이 없었다 We noticed nothing unusual in the room.
이상(異常) unusualness; abnormality (비정상). ~하다 (be) unusual; abnormal; strange. ¶ ~한 성격의 사람 a man of abnormal

이상 (理想) an ideal. ¶ ~적(으로) ideal(ly) / ~과 현실 남편 reality / ~적인 남편 an ideal husband / 높은 ~을 가지다 entertain (cherish) a lofty ideal / ~적인 남성의 상(像) one's idea of the perfect man. ‖ ~가 idealist ~주의 idealism / ~향 a Utopia / ~형 an ideal type / ~화(化) idealization (~화하다 idealize).

이색 (異色) a different color; (색다름) novelty; uniqueness. ¶ ~있는 unique; novel / ~적인 작곡가 a unique composer / ~적인 수법 a novel technique.

이서 (以西) (to the) west 《of Seoul》.

이서 (裏書) ☞ 배서(背書).

이설 (異說) a different theory (view); (이단) a heresy.

이성 (異性) the other (opposite) sex. ¶ ~간의 intersexual / 처음으로 ~을 알다 have one's first sexual experience; be sexually initiated / ~과 접촉할 기회 opportunities to meet members of the opposite sex. ‖ ~관계 relations with opposite sex.

이성 (理性) reason; rationality. ¶ ~적인 rational; reasonable / ~이 없는 reasonless; irrational / ~적인 행동 rational conduct / ~적인 사람 a man of reason / ~을 잃다 lose one's reason (cool) / 인간에겐 ~이 있다 Man has the power of reason.

이세 (二世) ① (《2대째》 Junior; the second generation. ¶ 헨리 ~ Henry Ⅰ《Ⅱ는 the second로 읽음》/ 존 스미스 ~ John Smith Jr. 《Jr.은 junior로 읽음》 / 미국의 한국인 ~ a second-generation Korean American; an American-born Korean. ② 《佛教》 this and the next world; the present and the future existence.

이솝 ‖ ~우화 Aesop's Fables.

이송 (移送) (a) transfer; (a) removal. ~하다 transfer; remove.

이수 (里數) mileage; distance(거리).

이수 (履修) ~하다 complete (finish) 《a college course》.

이스라엘 Israel. ¶ ~의 Israeli / ~사람 an Israeli.

이스트 (효모) yeast.

이슥하다 (밤이) be (far) advanced; grow late. ¶ 밤이 이슥하도록 till late at night / 밤이 이슥해졌다 It grew late.

이슬 dew; dewdrops (방울). ¶ ~ 친 꽃 dewy flowers; flowers wet with dew / 그녀의 눈은 ~으로 젖었다 Her eyes were bedewed with tears. / 그녀는 20세의 젊은 나이에 교수대의 ~로 사라졌다 (비유적) She died on the scaffold at the early age of twenty.

이슬람 Islam. ¶ ~의 Islamic. ‖ ~교 Islam / ~교도 an Islamite / ~문화 Islamic culture.

이슬비 a drizzle; a misty rain.

이승 this world; this life. ¶ ~의 괴로움 trials of this life.

이식 (利息) ☞ 이자(利子).

이식 (移植) transplantation; grafting (피부 조직의). ~하다 transplant; graft 《skin》. ¶ 정원에 나무를 ~하다 transplant a tree in the garden. ‖ ~수술 (undergo) a 《heart》 transplant operation.

이신론 (理神論) 《哲》 deism.

이심 (二心) ¶ ~있는 double-faced (-dealing); treacherous / ~을 품다 carry two faces (under one hood); play a double game.

이심전심 (以心傳心) telepathy. ¶ ~으로 tacitly; by telepathy (tacit understanding).

이십 (二十) twenty; a score. ¶ ~번째 twentieth / ~대의 여자 a woman in her twenties. ‖ ~세기 the twentieth century.

이수시개 a toothpick.

이악하다 (be) greedy; grasping; avaricious; be keen for gain; bite off more than one can chew.

이앓이 toothache. 〔(일 따위에).

이앙 (移秧) ~하다 transplant (rice seedlings).

이야기 ¶ ~《일반적》(a) talk; (a) conversation; (한담) a chat; (a) gossip; (연설) a speech; an address. ~하다 speak 《to a person; about (of) something》; talk 《to a person; about something》; have a talk (chat) 《with》. / ~를 잘하(못하)다 be a good (poor) talker / 너에게 할 ~가 있다 I have something to talk about with you. / 그의 ~는 지루했다 His speech was boring. / ~가 좀 이상하게 들릴지 모르지만 ~ It may sound strange, but ~. ② (설화) a story; a tale. ~하다 tell a story (tale). ¶ 꾸민 ~ a made-up story / ~를 시작하다 begin to tell a story. ‖ ~꾼 a storyteller / ~책 a storybook. ③ (화제) a topic; a subject. ¶ ~를 바꾸자 Let's change the topic (subject). ④ (소문) (a) rumor. ¶ 그녀가 결혼한다는 ~가 있다 There is a rumor that she is going to get married. / 인근에 사는 사람들 ~에 의하면 ~ Ac-

이야말로 《부사》 this very one (thing); this indeed. ¶ ~ 는 우리에겐 안성맞춤이다 This is the very thing for us.

이야말로² 《조사》 indeed; precisely; exactly; just; the very. ¶ 이것 ~ 내가 원한 것이다 This is the very thing (just the thing) I wanted.

이양하다 (移讓―) transfer; hand over. ¶ 정권을 ~ turn over the reins of government.

이어받다 《사업 따위를》 succeed to; take over; 《재산·권리·성질 따위를》 inherit. ¶ 부친의 사업을 ~ succeed to (take over) one's father's business / 어머니로부터 미모를 ~ inherit good looks from one's mother.

이어(서) 《계속하여》 continuously; in succession; 《다음으로》 subsequently; 《after (that)》 then. ¶ 연 ~ one after another; successively / 축사에 ~ 건배를 했다 Following (After) the congratulations, we drank a toast. ¶ 불가사의한 사건들이 ~ 일어났다 Mysterious events occurred in succession.

이어지다 《연결되다》 be connected (linked) 《with》; 《인도되다》 lead 《to》; 《계속되다》 continue; be continued. ¶ 태평양은 파나마 운하로 이어져 있다 The Pacific and the Atlantic are linked by the Panama Canal. / 전화가 이어졌다 The telephone connected. / 사막은 몇 마일이나 이어져 있다 The desert continues for miles.

이언정 《although; (even) if.

이엉 thatch. ¶ ~으로 지붕을 이다 thatch a roof with straw.

이에 hereupon; thereupon; on this; at this point.

이에서 than this. ¶ ~ 더한 기쁨은 없다 Nothing will give me more pleasure than this.

이에짬 a joint; a juncture; a junction.

이역 (二役) a double role 《part》. ¶ 1인 ~을 하다 play dual role; play the parts 《of A and B》.

이역 (異域) an alien land; a foreign country.

이열 (二列) two rows; a double column 《line》. ¶ ~로 서다 form two rows; be drawn up in two lines.

이열치열 (以熱治熱) Like cures like. or Fight fire with fire.

이염화물 (二鹽化物) bichloride.

이온 《化》 an ion. ¶ ~층 ionosphere. 「다 slacken; relax.

이완 (弛緩) slackness; laxity. ~ 하

이왕 (己往) ① 《명사》 the past; bygones; 《부사》 already; now that; as long as; since. ¶ ~의 일은 묻지 마라 《俗談》 Let bygones be bygones. / ~ 늦었으니 천천히 하자 It is already late, so let's take our time. ② 《…인 이상, …할 바엔》 if; since; now that. ¶ ~ 하려면 큰 일을 하여라 If you do anything at all, do something great. / ~ 일을 시작했으니 다 마치도록 해라 Now that you have started the job, try to finish it. ③ 《이왕이면》 ~ 이면 프랑스 말을 배우겠다 As long as I am about it, I might as well take French. ‖ ~지사 bygones; the past.

이외 (以外) 《제외하고》 except 《for》; but; save; 《그 외에》 besides; in addition to. ¶ 일요일 ~에는 매일 학교에 간다 go to school every day except on Sundays / 그는 이 책 ~에 다섯 권의 책을 썼다 He wrote five books besides this one.

이욕 (利欲) greed; avarice. ¶ ~을 떠나서 regardless of one's gain.

이용 (利用) ① 《이롭게 씀》 use; utilization. ~하다 use; utilize; make 《good》 use of; put… to 《good》 use; make the most 《best》 of. ¶ 원자력의 평화적인 ~ the peaceful use of atomic energy / 여가를 독서에 ~하다 utilize one's leisure time for reading / 기계의 ~ 법을 알려주다 tell how to use 《operate》 the machine. ② 《방편으로 ~하다》 take advantage of; exploit. ¶ 아무의 허영심을 ~하다 exploit 〔take advantage of〕 a person's vanity. ‖ ~ 가치 utility value / ~ 자 a user.

이용 (理容) ‖ ~사 a barber; a hairdresser / ~업 barbers and beauty parlors business / ~학원 a barber's school.

이울다 《시들다》 wither; fade; 《달이》 wane.

이웃 the neighborhood(근처); one's neighbors(사람); the house next door(이웃집). ¶ ~에 살고 있다 live next door to 《a person》 / ~에 사는 도시 a neighboring town / ~ 사촌 《俗談》 A good neighbor is better than a brother far off. ‖ ~돕기운동 a campaign to help needy neighbors.

이원 (二元) 《哲》 duality. ¶ ~적인 dual; dualistic. ‖ ~론 dual-

이원권(以遠權) beyond rights; the right to fly beyond the 《U.S.》 destination into third countries. ¶ ～ 방송 simultaneous broadcast by two stations.

이원제(二院制) a bicameral [two-chamber] system.

이월(二月) February 〈생략 Feb.〉.

이월(移越) a transfer; a carry-over. ～하다 transfer 《to, from》; carry forward [over] 《to》; bring forward [over] 《from》. ¶ 전기에서 ～ 《簿記》 brought forward 〈생략 BF〉 / 차기로 ～ 《簿記》 carried forward 〈생략 CF〉. ‖ ～금 the balance carried forward (to the next account).

이유(理由) a reason; a cause; ground(s) (근거); a pretext; an excuse (구실); a motive (동기). ¶ 충분한 [빈약한] ～ a good [slender] reason / ～있는 well-grounded [-founded] / ～없는 groundless / ～가 서는 justifiable; excusable / ～없이 without reason [cause]; unreasonably (부당하게) / …한 이유로 by reason of …; because of …; for the reason of … / 무슨 ～로 for what reason; on what grounds; why / 결석한 ～를 말하라 Tell me why you were absent from school.

이유(離乳) weaning. ～하다 wean 《a baby》 (from its mother). ‖ ～기 the weaning period / ～식 baby food.

이윤(利潤) profit; gain. ☞ 이익.

이율(利率) the rate of interest. ¶ ～을 올리다 [내리다] raise [reduce] the rate of interest. ‖ 법정 ～ the legal rate of interest.

이윽고 soon; presently; before long; shortly; in no time. ¶ ～ 그의 부친께서 나타나셨다 It was not long before his father showed up.

이음매 a joint; a juncture; a seam (솔기). ¶ ～ 없는 jointless; seamless / ～가 느슨해진다 The joint loosens. / 철판 ～에 금이 생겼다 Cracks appeared at [around] the joint in the steel plate.

이의(異意) a different opinion.

이의(異義) a different meaning.

이의(異議) 《반대》 an objection; a protest (항의); dissent (불찬성). ¶ ～없이 without any objection / ～를 제기하다 object 《to》; raise an objection to; protest / ～ 있읍니까 Does anyone have an objection? / ～있읍니다 Objection! / ～없읍니다 No objection! ‖ ～ 신청 《법정에서의》 a formal objection.

이익(利益) ① 《이윤》 (a) profit; gains; returns. ¶ ～이 있는 profitable; paying / 많은 ～을 올리다 make a large profit. ② 《편익·도움》 benefit; profit; good; interests; advantage (이점). ¶ ～이 되는 advantageous; beneficial / 공공의 ～을 위해 일하다 work for the public good / 그렇게 하는 것이 너에게 ～이 될 것이다 It will be to your benefit [advantage] to do so. ‖ ～ 대표 a person representing the interests of a group / ～률 profitability / ～ 배당 a dividend / ～ 분배제도 a profit-sharing system / ～ 사회 a gesellschaft.

이인(二人) two men [persons]. ¶ ～ 분의 요리를 주문하다 order dinner for two. ‖ ～ 삼각(三脚) a three-legged race / ～ 승(乘) a two-seater / ～ 조 a pair 《of criminals》 / 《口》 a duo; a twosome.

이인(異人) 《다른 이》 a different person; 《비범한》 a prodigy. ‖ ～ (種) an alien; a different race.

이입하다(移入―) import 《into》; bring in; introduce 《into》《문물 등의》.

이자(利子) interest. ¶ 1할의 ～로 at 10 percent interest / 비싼 [싼] ～로 at high [low] interest / 무 ～로 without interest / ～가 붙다 yield [bear] interest / ～를 붙여 돈을 갚다 pay back money with interest. ‖ ～소득 the income from interest. (擇―).

이택일(二者擇―) ☞ 양자택일(兩者擇―)

이장(里長) the head of a village.

이장하다(移葬―) exhume and bury in another place.

이재(理財) moneymaking; economy. ¶ ～에 밝다 [능하다] be clever at making money.

이재(罹災) suffering. ¶ ～ 구호금 a relief fund / ～민 the sufferers; the victims / ～지구 the afflicted [stricken] districts [area].

이적(利敵) ～하다 profit [benefit] the enemy. ‖ ～행위 an act which serves the interests of the enemy.

이적(移籍) the transfer of one's name in the register. ～하다 be transferred 《to》. ¶ 《선수가》 타이거즈로 ～하다 be transferred to the Tigers.

이적하다(離籍―) remove one's name from the family register.

이전(以前) ago; before; once. ¶ ～의 previous; past; one-time; former / ～에는 …이었다 used to be… / ～에 만난 적이 있다 I have seen him before. / 그것은 훨씬 ～에 일어난 일이다 It happened long ago. / 그는 ～의 그로 돌아왔다 He is his former self again. / ～에는 그녀가 싫었다 Once I disliked her.

이전(移轉) a move; (a) removal; (a) transfer(권리의). ~하다 move. ¶ 그는 새 집으로 ~했다 He moved into a new house. / ~하는 곳 *one's* new address. ‖ ~등기 registration of a transfer (*of a person's estate to another*) / ~통지 a notice of *one's* change of address; a removal notice.

이점(利點) (a point of) advantage. ¶ 이 기계는 운반과 작동이 편리하다는 ~이 있다 This machine has the advantage of being easy to carry and operate.

이정(里程) mileage; distance. ‖ ~표(表) a table of distances / ~표(標) a milestone; a milepost.

이제 now; (더 이상) no [not any] longer [more]. ¶ 막 １[now]; a moment ago / ~까지 until now; up to the present / ~까지도 still; even now / ~라도 (at) any moment. 「ty.

이조(李朝) the *Joseon* [*Yi*] dynas-

이종(二種) ‖ ~우편물 the second-class mail (matter).

이종(異種) a different kind [species]. ‖ ~교배 [生] hybridization; crossbreeding.

이종사촌(姨從四寸) a cousin on *one's* mother's side.

이주(移住) migration; emigration (외국으로); immigration (외국에서); a move (전거). ~하다 migrate; emigrate (*to*); immigrate (*into*); move to. / ~민 an emigrant; an immigrant; a settler / ~지(행선지) the place where *one* is going to live; (이주한 곳) the place in which *one* has settled.

이죽거리다 ☞ 이기죽거리다.

이중(二重) ¶ ~의 double; twofold; duplicate / ~으로 double; twice; over again / ~으로 싸다 wrap (*a thing*) double / ~이 되다 double / ~의 의미가 (목적이) 있다 have a double meaning [purpose] / 같은 책을 ~으로 사다 buy the same book twice. ‖ ~가격(제) double price (system) / ~결혼 bigamy / ~곡가제 the double grain price system; the two-tier price system for staple grains / ~과세 double taxation / ~국적 dual nationality / ~국적자 a person with dual nationality / ~모음 [音聲] a diphthong / ~부정(否定) [文] a double negative / ~생활 a double life / ~인격 dual personality / ~인격자 a double-faced person; a Dr. Jekyll / ~장부 a double accounting system; dual bookkeeping for tax evasion / ~창(주) [樂] a duet / ~창(窓) a double-paned window / ~촬영 an overlap / ~턱 a double chin.

이즈음, 이즘[1] ☞ 요즈음.

이즘[2] (주의·설) an ism.

이지(理智) intellect; intelligence. ¶ ~적인 intellectual (*activities*); intelligent (*person*). / ~주의 intellectualism.

이지러지다 break (off); be broken; chip (*off*); wane (달이). ¶ 달이 이지러지기 시작했다 The moon is on the wane.

이직(離職) ~하다 leave [lose] *one's* job. / ~률 the rate of people leaving their jobs; a turnover. / ~자 an unemployed person; (집합적) the jobless; the unemployed.

이질(姨姪) the children of *one's* wife's sister.

이질(異質) ¶ ~적인 of a different nature / ~문화에 접하다 experience a culture of a different nature.

이질(痢疾) [醫] dysentery.

이집트 Egypt. ¶ ~의 Egyptian / ~사람 an Egyptian / ~말 Egyptian.

이쪽 ① (이런) this way [side]; our side. ¶ ~쪽으로 오십시오 This way, please. ② (우리 편) our party; we; us.

이차(二次) ¶ ~의 second / ~적인 secondary. ‖ ~감염 secondary infection / ~공해 secondary pollution / ~방정식 a quadratic equation / ~에너지 the secondary energy / ~제품 secondary products / ~회 a party after a party; an after-feast / 제~세계대전 the Second World War; World War II.

이착(二着) (순위) the second place; (사람) a runner-up.

이착륙(離着陸) takeoff [taking off] and landing.

이채(異彩) ¶ ~를 띠다 be conspicuous; cut a conspicuous figure.

이처럼 like this; in this way (manner); thus; so.

이첩하다(移牒 ─) transmit (*an order*) to the office concerned; notify (*of, that*).

이체(移替) transfer. ~하다 transfer (*to, into*). ¶ 돈이 아직 ~되지 않은 것 같다 The money doesn't seem to have been transferred yet.

이체동심(異體同心) being different in form but same in mind; two bodies but one mind.

이축(移築) ~하다 dismantle (*a building*) and reconstruct (*it*) in a different place.

이층(二層) (美) the second floor [story]; (英) the first floor; the upper storey. ¶ ~에서 upstairs /

이치 ~에 올라가다 go upstairs. ‖ 2층 ~ 버스 a double-decker (bus) / ~집 a two-story house.

이치(理致) 《사리》 reason; 《원리 원칙》 principle. ¶ ~에 맞다 be reasonable; stand to reason.

이칭(異稱) another name; a different title.

이타(利他) ¶ ~적인 altruistic. ‖ ~주의 altruism / ~주의자 an altruist.

이탈(離脫) ~하다 secede from; break away from; leave 《*a party*》. ¶ 직장을 ~하다 desert *one's* post / 국적 ~ the renunciation of *one's* nationality / ~자 a seceder (당·동맹에서의); a bolter (탈영자).

이탈리아 Italy. ¶ ~의 Italian / ~사람 an Italian / ~인 Italian.

이태 two years.

이탤릭(활자) italic type; italics.

이토(泥土) mud.

이토록 so; like this. ¶ ~ 많은 so many 《much》 / ~ 아침 일찍 at this early hour of (the) morning / ~ 부탁을 해도 그 일을 맡아주지 않는다 With all my asking, he still hasn't taken the job.

이튿날 《다음날》 the next (following) day; 《초이틀》 the second (day of the month).

이틀 ① 《초이틀》 the second (day of the month); 《이튿째》 the second day. ② 《두 날》 two days. ¶ ~마다 every two days; every other day.

이틀² (턱뼈) a jawbone; 《의치》 a dental plate; a denture.

이판암(泥板岩) [鑛] shale.

이팔(二八) sixteen. ¶ ~청춘 a sixteen-year-old; sweet sixteen.

이편 ① 《-便》 I; we. ② 《우리 편》 I; we. ② 《이쪽》 this side (way).

이핑계저핑계 ~하여 on some pretext or other.

이하(以下) 《기준을 포함해서》...or under; 《포함 않고》...or fewer; 《불포함》 below; 《아래의》 the following / 10세 ~의 어린이 children of 10 years or under / 10인 ~ ten or fewer people /그의 성적은 평균 점수 ~였다 His marks were below the average. / 사장 ~ 수위에 이르기까지 from the president (down) to the watchman. / ~ 동문 and so on (forth); etc. / ~생략 The rest is omitted.

이학(理學) science. ¶ ~의 scientific. ‖ ~박사 a Doctor of Science (생략 D.Sc.) / ~부 the department of science / ~사 a Bachelor of Science (생략 B.Sc.).

이합집산(離合集散) meeting and parting; 《정당의》 changes in political alignment. ¶ 대통령 선거 운동 기간중 우리나라 정계는 ~이 계속되었다 There has been constant alignment and realignment in our politics during the presidential election campaign.

이항(移項) [數] transposition. ~하다 transpose.

이해(利害) interests; a concern; advantages and disadvantages (득실). ¶ ~의 충돌 a clash (conflict) of interests / ~에 영향을 미치다 affect *one's* interests / ~관계가 있다 have an interest 《in》; be interested 《in》. ‖ ~관계자 the interested parties; the people (parties) concerned / ~득실 advantages and disadvantages; gains and losses.

이해(理解) understanding; comprehension; appreciation. ~하다 understand; grasp (파악); make out; comprehend; appreciate (문학·예술의). ¶ ~할 수 있는 comprehensible; understandable / ~할 수 없는 incomprehensible; ununderstandable / ~가 빠르다 (더디다) be quick (slow) of understanding / 음악을 ~하다 appreciate music; have an ear for music / ~하기 쉽다 (어렵다) be easy (difficult) to understand / ~를 구하다 ask 《*a person*》 to understand / 그녀 남편은 ~심이 많다 She has an understanding husband. / 그의 말을 칭찬으로 ~했다 I took his words as (to be) praise. ‖ ~력 (a power of) understanding; the comprehensive faculty.

이행(移行) a shift. ~하다 move; shift (switch) (over) 《to》. ¶ 새로운 제도로 ~하다 shift to a new system. ‖ ~기간 a period of transition 《from ...to》; a transition period / ~조치 transition measures.

이행(履行) performance; fulfillment. ~하다 fulfill; carry out; perform. ¶ 계약을 ~하다 fulfill (perform) a contract / 약속을 ~하다 fulfill (carry out, keep, make good) *one's* promise / 충실히 의무를 ~하다 be faithful in the performance of *one's* duties. ‖ ~자 a performer.

이향(離鄕) ~하다 leave *one's* home (native place).

이혼(離婚) a divorce. ~하다 divorce 《*one's* wife》; be divorced from 《*one's* husband》. ‖ ~소송 a divorce suit (~소송을 내다 sue for (a) divorce) / ~수당 alimony / ~신고(서) a notice of divorce; a divorce paper / ~율 a divorce rate / ~절차 divorce procedure (formalities).

이화학(理化學) physics and chemistry.

이환(罹患) ~하다 contract a disease; be infected 《*with*》. ¶ ~(병)율 the disease [infection] rate.

이회(二回) twice; two times. ¶ 월 ~ twice a month / 제2회의 the second.

이후(以後) 〔금후〕 after this; from now on; 〔이래〕 after; since. ¶ 그 ~ since then / 4월 8일 ~ on and after April 8 / 오후 10시 ~ 에는 전화하지 마시오 Don't call me up after 10 p.m. 〔after.

익년(翌年) the next year; the year

익다 ① 〔과실 등이〕 ripen; be [get, grow] ripe; mellow. ¶ 익은 ripe; mature; mellow / 익지 않은 green; unripe / 이 복숭아는 아직 익지 않았다 This peach is not ripe yet. ② 〔음식이〕 be boiled [cooked]. ¶ 잘 익은 well-done [cooked] / 이 호박은 빨리 익는다 This pumpkin cooks quickly. ③ 〔익숙〕 get [become] used [accustomed] 《*to*》. ¶ 빨리 일이 손에 익도록 하여라 You must try to accustom yourself to the work. ④ 〔시운·기운〕 be ripe; mature. ¶ 때가 익기를 기다리다 wait till the time is ripe / 정상 회담의 기운이 이제야 익어가고 있다 The time is now ripe for a summit conference. ⑤ 〔술·김치 따위가〕 ripen; mature; be well seasoned [flavored]. ¶ 통 속의 술이 익기를 기다리다 wait for the wine to mature in the cask.

익명(匿名) anonymity. ¶ ~의 anonymous / ~으로 anonymously / ~으로 기고하다 contribute to 《*a magazine*》 anonymously / ~의 편지 an anonymous letter.

익모초(益母草) 〔植〕 a motherwort.

익사(溺死) drowning. ¶ ~하다 be drowned. ¶ ~할 뻔하다 be nearly drowned. ¶ ~자 a drowned person / ~체 a drowned body.

익살 humor; a jest; a joke. ¶ ~스러운 humorous; witty / ~을 떨다 crack [tell] jokes. ¶ ~꾼 a humorist; a joker.

익숙하다 〔친숙〕 (be) familiar 《*with*》; be well acquainted 《*with*》; 〔능숙〕 be skilled [experienced] in; be good hand at. ¶ 익숙한 일 a familiar job / 미국 사정에 익숙한 사람 a man familiar with things American / 익숙한 솜씨로 with a practiced hand / …에 익숙해지다 get used to 《*something, doing*》; grow [be] accustomed to 《*something, doing*》 / 더위에 익숙해지다 get [become] used to the heat 《*in Seoul*》 / 환경에 익숙해지다 be acclimated to *one's* new environment / 익숙하지 못한 손놀림으로 젓

가락을 사용하다 use chopsticks awkwardly; be awkward in using chopsticks / 나는 외국인 여성과의 대화에 익숙지 않다 I'm not used to talking with foreign ladies.

익일(翌日) the next day.

익조(益鳥) a beneficial bird.

익충(益蟲) a beneficial insect.

익히다 ① 〔익숙하게 하다〕 make [get] oneself accustomed [used] to 《*something, doing*》; accustom *oneself* to 《*something, doing*》; train 〔훈련하다〕. ¶ 추위에 몸을 ~ accustom *oneself* to the cold / 영어 뉴스에 귀를 ~ train *one's* ear by listening to news in English. ② 〔음식을〕 boil; cook. ③ 〔과실을〕 mellow; ripen. ④ 〔술·장을〕 brew; ferment; mature. ¶ 술을 ~ brew rice wine / 김치를 ~ get Kimchi seasoned [flavored].

인(仁) 〔인자〕 benevolence; humanity; 〔유교의〕 perfect virtue.

인(印) a seal; a stamp. ▷ 도장.

인(寅) 〔십이지의〕 the Tiger.

인(燐) 〔化〕 phosphorus (기호 P).

인가(人家) a house; a human dwelling. ¶ ~가 많은 [드문] 곳 a densely-[sparsely-]populated place.

인가(認可) approval; permission; authorization 〔행정상의〕. ~하다 approve; permit; authorize. ¶ ~를 얻다 have the permission 《*to do*》; obtain [get] the authorization 《*of*》.

인각하다(印刻―) engrave (a seal).

인간(人間) 〔사람〕 a human being; a human; a man; a mortal〔언젠가는 죽을 운명의〕; 〔만인〕 man; mankind; 〔인물〕 character; personality. ¶ ~의 human; mortal / ~다운 생활 a life worthy of man / ~중심적인 man-centered / ~은 만물의 영장이다 Man is the lord of creation. / 그는 ~미가 없다 He is lacking in human feelings. ¶ ~개조 reform in humanity / ~공학 human engineering / ~관계 human relations / ~독 medical checkup; clinical survey / ~문화재 human cultural assets / ~생태학 human ecology / ~성〔사회, 애(愛)〕 human nature〔society, love〕 / ~쓰레기 the dregs of society〔humanity〕; a junkie / ~자원개발 human resources development / ~존중 respect for man's life and dignity.

인감(印鑑) a (registered personal) seal; 〔찍은〕 a seal impression. ¶ ~를 등록하다 have *one's* seal impression registered. ¶ ~도장 *one's* registered seal / ~증명〔등록〕 a certificate〔the registration

인건비(人件費) labor costs; personnel expenses.

인걸(人傑) a great man; a hero; a great figure.

인격(人格) character; personality (개성). ¶ ~을 함양하다 build up *one's* character / ~을 존중[무시]하다 respect [disregard] *a person's* personality. ‖ ~적인 character building / ~자 a man of noble character / ~형성 character shaping [molding].

인경 a large curfew bell.

인계(引繼) taking over(인수); handing over(인도); succession(계승). ¶ ~하다 hand over [transfer] *one's official duties* to *(a person)* / 전 임자로부터 사무를 ~ 받았다 I took over the duties from my predecessor.

인공(人工) human work(skill, labor); art; artificiality(기교). ¶ ~적인 artificial; man-made; unnatural / ~적인 미 the beauty of art; man-made beauty / ~적으로 artificially. ‖ ~감미료 an artificial sweetener / ~강우 artificial rain(비) / rainmaking(행위) / ~두뇌 a mechanical [an electronic] brain / ~배양 artificial culture / ~부화 artificial incubation / ~수태 [수정] artificial conception [fertilization] / ~심장 a mechanical heart / ~위성 an artificial satellite / ~임신중절[유산] an (induced) abortion / ~잔디 artificial turf / ~장기 an artificial internal organ / ~피임 artificial contraception / ~혈액 artificial blood / ~호흡 artificial respiration.

인과(因果) (원인과 결과) cause and effect; (운명) fate; (불운) misfortune. ¶ ~라 여기고 체념하다 resign *oneself* to *one's* fate [destiny]. ‖ ~관계 causal relation (between two events) / ~율 the law of causality / ~응보 retribution; retributive justice.

인광(燐光) phosphorescence.

인구(人口) population. ¶ ~가 조밀 [희박]한 곳 a thickly-[sparsely-]populated district / ~ 800만의 도시 a city 'of eight million people (with a population of eight million) / 부동(浮動)~ a floating population / 주간[야간] ~ the daytime [nighttime] population / ~의 도시 유입 an influx of people into the cities / ~의 증가[감소] an increase [a decrease] in population / ~가 많다[적다] have a large [small] population. ‖ 과잉~ overpopulation / ~문제 the population problem / ~밀도 (a) population density / ~억제 population control / ~정책 a population policy / ~조사 a census / ~통계 population statistics; vital statistics(동태) / ~폭발 (a) population explosion.

인권(人權) human rights; civil rights(공민권). ¶ 기본적 ~ the fundamental human rights / 서로~을 존중하다 respect each other's human rights. ‖ ~문제 a question of human rights / ~선언 the Declaration of the Rights of Man / ~옹호 the protection of human rights / ~유린[침해] (a) violation of human rights; an infringement on personal rights.

인근(隣近) *one's* neighborhood; the vicinity. ¶ ~의 neighboring; nearby / ~주민들 neighbors.

인기(人氣) popularity; public favor. ¶ ~ 있는 popular / ~ 없는 unpopular / ~를 얻다 become popular; win popularity / ~를 얻기 위한 정책 a claptrap policy / ~를 잃다 lose *one's* popularity; become unpopular / ~절정에 있다 be at the height of *one's* popularity. ‖ ~가수 a popular singer / ~배우 an popular actor [actress] / ~선수 a star player / ~소설 a sensational [best-selling] novel / ~작가 a popular writer / ~주(株) an active stock / ~투표 a popularity vote / ~프로(TV 등의) a hit program.

인기척(人─) ¶ ~이 없는 deserted; empty / 거리에는 전혀 ~이 없었다 The street was completely empty [deserted].

인내(忍耐) patience; perseverance; endurance. ¶ ~하다 bear; endure; put up with. ¶ ~심 강하게 patiently; with patience / 그는 ~심이 강하다 He is very patient. ‖ ~력 powers of endurance.

인대(靭帶) 〖解〗 a ligament.

인덕(人德) *one's* natural virtue; *one's* personal magnetism. ¶ ~이 있다 be blessed with some sort of personal magnetism (which attracts people's favor) / 그것은 그의 ~에 의한 것이다 That depends on his natural virtue.

인덕(仁德) benevolence; humanity.

인덱스 an index [*pl*. -dices, -es].

인도(人道) ① 《도덕》 humanity. ¶ ~적인 humanitarian; humane / ~적 견지에서 from the humanitarian point of view / ~으로 다루다 treat *(a person)* humanely. ‖ ~주의 humanitarianism / ~주의자 a humanitarian. ② 《보도》 a footpath; a sidewalk (美). ‖ ~교 a footbridge.

인도(引渡) handing (turning) over; delivery《물품의》; transfer《재산·권리의》. ~하다 deliver 《goods》; turn 〔hand〕 over 〔to〕 《죄인 등을》; transfer 《property》. ¶ 상품을 내일 오전 중에 ~하다 deliver the goods tomorrow morning / 도둑을 경찰에 ~하다 hand over a thief to the police / 범인 ~ 조약 《국제간의》 an extradition treaty.

인도(引導) guidance《지도》; lead《선도》. ~하다 guide; lead. ∥ ~자 a guide.

인도(印度) India. ¶ ~의 Indian / ~사람 an Indian / ~어 Hindustani. ∥ ~양 the Indian Ocean.

인도네시아 Indonesia. ¶ ~사람 an Indonesian / ~어 Indonesian.

인도차이나 Indo-China. ¶ ~의 Indochinese / ~말 Indochinese / ~사람 a Indochinese.

인동초(忍冬草) 〔植〕 a honeysuckle.

인두《바느질의》 a small heart-shaped iron; 《납땜질의》 a soldering iron.

인두(咽頭) 〔解〕 the pharynx. ¶ ~의 pharyngeal. ∥ ~염 〔醫〕 pharyngitis.

인두겁(人─) human shape (mask). ¶ ~을 쓴 악마 a demon in human shape.

인두세(人頭稅) a poll〔head〕 tax. ¶ ~를 거두다 levy a poll tax.

…인들 granted that it be〔is〕; even though it be〔is〕. ¶세살 먹은 아이 ~ even a little child.

인디언 an 〔a Red〕 Indian.

인력(人力) human power〔strength〕; a manpower《공급의 단위》. ¶ ~이 미치지 못하다는 beyond human power. ∥ ~감사 manpower inspection / ~동원 mobilization of manpower / ~비행기 a man-powered aircraft / ~수급계획 a manpower supply and demand plan / ~수출 export of labor force.

인력(引力) 〔天〕 《천체의》 gravitation; 《자기의》 magnetism; 《물질의》 attraction. ¶ ~이 있는 magnetic / 태양〔지구〕의 ~ solar〔terrestrial〕 gravitation. ∥ ~권 the gravitation field 《of the earth》.

인력거(人力車) a riksha(w). ∥ ~꾼 a rickshaw-man.

인류(人類) the human race; human beings; humanity; humankind; man. ¶ ~의 human. ∥ ~사(史) the history of man / ~사회 human society / ~애 love for humanity / ~학 anthropology / ~학자 an anthropologist.

인륜(人倫) 《도덕》 morality; humanity. ¶ ~에 어긋나다 go against humanity; be immoral. ∥ ~도덕 ethics and morality.

인마(人馬) men and horses.

인망(人望) popularity. ¶ ~이 있는 popular / ~이 없는 unpopular / ~을 얻다 win (gain) popularity / ~을 잃다 lose *one's* popularity.

인맥(人脈) a line of personal contacts; personal connections (relationships).

인면수심(人面獸心) a demon in human shape; a human monster.

인멸(湮滅) ~하다 destroy 《evidences》.

인명(人名) a *person's* name. ∥ ~록 a directory; Who's Who 《in Korea》 / ~사전 a biographical dictionary.

인명(人命) 《human》 life. ¶ ~의 손실 a loss of lives / ~을 구조하다 save 《a life》 / ~을 존중〔경시〕하다 have respect for〔place little value on〕 human life. ∥ ~구조 lifesaving.

인문(人文) humanity; 《문화》 civilization; culture. ¶ ~의 cultural; humanistic. ∥ ~과학 the humanities; cultural sciences / ~주의 humanism / ~지리 human geography / ~학 human studies; humanities.

인물(人物) ① 《사람》 a man〔woman〕; a person; a character 《별난》; a figure《역사상의》; 《인격》 character; personality. ¶ 큰 ~ a great man〔mind〕 / 위험한 ~ a dangerous character〔person〕 / 요주의의 ~ a man on the blacklist / 역사상의 ~ a historical figure / 작중의 ~ a character in a novel / ~을 보다 read *a person's* character / ~ 본위로 생각하다 judge *a person* chiefly by his character. ② 《용모》 a countenance; looks. ¶ ~이 못생긴 사람 an ugly person. ∥ ~가난 a dearth (shortage) of talented men / ~묘사 a character sketch / ~평 comments about a person / ~화 a portrait.

인민(人民) the people; the populace; the public. ¶ ~의 in, of, to the ~을 위한 정치 government of the people, by the people, for the people. ∥ ~공사 《중국의》 a people's commune / ~공화국 a people's republic / ~재판 a people's 〔kangaroo〕 trial〔court〕 / ~전선 the people's front.

인박이다 fall〔get〕 into the habit of 《*doing*》; be addicted to.

인복(人福) the good fortune to have good acquaintances.

인본(印本) a printed book.

인본주의(人本主義) humanism.

인부(人夫) 《일꾼》 a laborer; 《운반부》 a porter; a carrier.

인분(人糞) human feces. ∥ ~비료

인사(人士) a man (men) of society; people; persons. ¶ 지명~ a noted (well-known) person.
인사(人事) ① (인간사) human affairs. ¶ ~를 다하고 천명을 기다리다 Do your best and leave the rest to Providence. ‖ ~고과(考課) (the) assessment of an employee's performance / ~과 the personnel section / ~관리 personnel management / ~국 the personnel bureau / ~란(欄) personnel columns / ~부 the personnel department / ~위원회 a personnel committee / ~이동 personnel changes; a personnel reshuffle / ~행정 personnel administration. ② (사교상의) a greeting; a salutation; (경의) respects; 《축사·식사 따위의》 an address; a speech. ~하다 greet; salute; (make a) bow; pay one's respects; express 《one's gratitude》. ¶ ~를 주고 받다 exchange greetings (bows) / ~시키다 《소개》 introduce / ~성이 밝다 have good manners / ~도와 준 데 대한 고맙다는 ~를 표하다 express one's gratitude to 《a person》 for his help / 그는 손을 흔들며 우리에게 작별 ~를 했다 He waved good-bye to us. / 그녀는 ~도 없이 돌아가 버렸다 She left without even saying good-bye. / 나는 환영의 ~말을 했다 I gave a welcoming address. / 사장님께 ~드리러 왔습니다 I've come to pay my respects to the president. ‖ ~장(狀) a greeting card; a notice 《of one's new address》.
인사교류(人事交流) an interchange of personnel 《between two Ministries》
인사불성(人事不省) unconsciousness; faint. ¶ ~이 되다 become unconscious; lose consciousness; faint.
인산(燐酸) [化] phosphoric acid. ‖ ~비료 phosphatic fertilizer / ~석회 phosphate of lime.
인산인해(人山人海) a crowd of people. ¶ ~를 이루다 lots [a crowd] of people gather.
인삼(人蔘) a ginseng. ‖ ~차 ginseng tea.
인상(人相) looks; facial features; physiognomy. ¶ ~이 좋지 않은 evil-looking; sinister(-looking). ‖ ~서 a description of a man / ~학 physiognomy.
인상(引上) ① (가격·임금의) raise; increase. ~하다 increase; raise. ¶ 운임을 ~을 하다 raise the fare / 5%의 임금 ~을 요구하다 demand a five percent wage increase (raise). ② (끌어올림) pulling up. ~하다 pull (draw) up.
인상(印象) an impression. ¶ ~적인 impressive / 첫 ~ the first impression / 좋은 ~을 주다 impress 《a person》 favorably; give (make) a good impression 《on a person》 / …라는 ~을 받다 get the impression that… / ~을 남기다 leave an impression 《on a person's mind》; leave 《a person》 with an impression 《of》. ‖ ~주의 impressionism / ~파 the impressionist school.
인색하다(吝嗇一) (be) stingy; miserly; close-fisted; niggardly. ¶ 인색한 사람 a miser; a stingy fellow; a niggard.
인생(人生) life. ¶ ~의 목적 the aim in life / ~의 부침 the ups and downs of life / ~의 문턱에 있는 젊은이 a young man on the threshold of life (a career) / ~이란 그런 거다 That's life. / ~은 종종 항해에 비유된다 Life is often compared to a voyage. / 제목이「하숙생」인 한국 노래의 가사는 "~은 나그네길, 어디서 왔다가 어디로 가나," 로 시작된다 A Korean song titled *Hasuksaeng*, whose lyric lines starts as "Life is a vagabonds path. Where do we come from? Where are we heading for?" ‖ ~관 one's view of life; one's outlook on life / ~철학 one's philosophy of life / ~행로 the path of one's life.
인선(人選) the choice (selection) of a suitable person. ~하다 choose (select) a suitable person 《for》.
인성(人性) human nature; humanity. ‖ ~학(學) ethology.
인세(印稅) a royalty 《on a book》. ¶ 정가 5%의 ~를 지불하다 pay a royalty of five percent on the retail price of the book.
인솔(引率) ~하다 lead; be in charge 《of a party》. ¶ …을 ~하여 leading a party of / ~자 a leader.
인쇄(印刷) printing; print. ~하다 print. ¶ ~ 중이다 be in press / 원고를 ~에 넘기다 send an MS. (a manuscript) to (the) press / 이 책은 ~ 상태가 좋다(나쁘다) This book is well (poorly) printed. ‖ ~공(업자) a printer / ~기 a printing machine (press) / ~물 printed matter / ~소 a printing house (shop) / ~술 (the art of) printing; typography.
인수(人數) the number of persons (people).
인수(引受) (부담) undertaking; 《수락》 acceptance (어음의); under-

writing(주식 등의); (보증) guaranty. ~하다 ☞ 인수하다. ¶어음의 ~를 거부하다 dishonor a bill. ‖ ~거절 nonacceptance 《*of*》/ ~어음 an accepted [acceptable] bill / ~은행 an accepting [underwriting] bank / ~인(보증인) a guarantor/ (어음의) an acceptor.

인수(因數)〖數〗a factor. ¶2와 3은 6의 ~다 Two and three are factors of six. ‖ ~분해 factorization(~분해하다 factorize; break up into factors).

인수하다(引受—) (일 따위를) undertake; take on; (계승하여) take over 《*another's business*》; (책임지다) be responsible for; answer for; take charge of; (보증하다) guarantee. ¶어려운 기획을 ~ undertake a difficult project / 네가 손해를 보면 내가 인수하겠다 I'll answer for your possible losses. / 내가 그의 사업을 인수하여 사장이 되었다 I took over his work and became president. / 아무의 신원을 ~ guarantee *a person's* character.

인술(仁術) ¶의술은 ~이다 Medicine is a benevolent art.

인술린〖藥〗insulin.

인스턴트 instant 《*coffee*》. ‖ ~식품 precooked (convenience, fast) food.

인스피레이션 inspiration. ¶…에서 ~을 얻다 get inspiration from…; be inspired by… / ~이 떠오르다 I have had an inspiration.

인습(因襲) convention. ¶~적(으로) conventional(ly) / ~에 따르다 (을 깨다) follow (break) an old custom.

인식(認識)《(인지)(이해) understanding; (자각) awareness. ~하다 recognize; realize; understand; become aware of; be aware 《*of*》. ¶바르게 ~하다 have a correct understanding of / ~을 새롭게 하다 see 《*a thing*》in a new light / 문제의 중요성을 잘 ~하다 be fully aware of the importance of the matter. ‖ ~부족 lack of understanding / ~표(票) (군인의) an identification tag; a dog tag (俗稱).

인신(人身) a human body. ¶~공격을 하다 make a personal attack on 《*a person*》. ‖ ~매매 traffic in human beings; slave trade / ~보호법 the Protection of Personal Liberty Act.

인심(人心) 《(백성의) public feeling(s); (사람의) the sentiment of the people; (사람의) a man's mind [heart]. ¶~이 좋다 [나쁘다] be warm-hearted [cold-hearted]; be humane [heartless] / ~을 얻다 [잃다] win [lose] the hearts of the people / ~을 현혹시키다 mislead the public / ~쓰다 be generous; grant 《*a person a favor*》.

인심(仁心) generosity; humanity.

인애(仁愛) charity; love; humanity.

인양(引揚) pulling (drawing) up; salvage (침몰선의). ~하다 pull (draw) up; salvage; refloat. ¶~작업(배의) salvage work / 침몰선을 ~하다 salvage (pull up) a sunken ship.

인어(人魚) (상상적인) a mermaid; a merman (수컷).

인연(因緣) (인과) cause and occasion; 〖佛〗karma; fate; destiny; (연분) affinity; connection; relation. ~을 맺다 form relations / ~을 끊다 break off relations; cut connection / ~이 깊다 be closely related / ~이 멀다 have little relation / 돈과는 ~이 없다 Money and I are strangers. / 내가 그녀를 프랑스에서 만난 것은 아마 어떤 ~일 것이다 Perhaps I was predestined to meet her in France.

인용(引用) a quotation. ~하다 quote 《*from a book*》; cite 《*an instance*》. ¶밀튼의 한 구절을 ~하다 quote a passage from Milton. ‖ ~문 a quotation / ~부 quotation marks.

인원(人員) (인원수) the number of persons (people); (직원) the staff; the personnel. ¶~이 부족하다 be short of staff (labor); be understaffed (short-handed) / ~을 제한하다 limit the number of persons / ~을 늘리다 (줄이다) increase (reduce) the personnel. ‖ ~감축 (정리) a cut in personnel; a personnel reduction (~감축을 하다 reduce (curtail, cut down) the personnel) / ~점호 a roll call.

인위(人爲) human work; artificiality. ¶~적(으로) artificial(ly) / 그 사고는 ~적인 과오가 누적되어 일어났다 That accident was caused by a series of human errors. ‖ ~도태 〖生物〗artificial selection.

인육(人肉) human flesh. ‖ ~시장 a white slave market.

인의(仁義) humanity and justice.

인자(仁者) a benevolent person.

인자(仁慈) (love and) benevolence. ~하다 (be) benevolent; benign; clement; merciful.

인자(因子) a factor. ¶결정적인 ~ a determining factor / 유전 ~ = 유전자; a gene.

인장(印章) a seal (☞ 도장). ‖ ~위조 forgery of a seal / 위조~ a forged seal.

인재(人材) a talented (an able) person; talent (총칭). ¶ ~를 등용하는 open positions to the talented / ~를 모으다 (구하다) collect (look out for) talented people / ~가 부족하다 be short of talented people. ‖ ~스카우트 headhunting; a headhunter (스카우트하는 사람) / ~은행 a talent (job) bank.

인적(人的) ‖ ~손해 the loss of manpower / ~자원 human (manpower) resources; manpower.

인적(人跡) a trace of human footsteps; human traces. ¶ ~이 드문 산길 an unfrequented mountain path / ~ 미답의 땅 an untrodden region.

인절미 a glutinous rice cake.

인접(隣接) ~하다 adjoin; be adjacent 《to》; be next 《to》. ¶ ~한 도시 a neighboring town. ‖ ~지 adjacent land.

인정(人情) human feelings; human nature; humanity. ¶ ~이 많은 사람 a man of heart; a sympathetic [warm-hearted] person / ~의 따뜻함 the milk of human kindness / ~에 약하다 be easily moved; be tender-hearted / ~에 이끌리다 be touched with pity / ~에 반하다 be against human nature / ~이 없다 be cold-hearted; be inhumane. ‖ ~미 a human touch; human warmth.

인정(仁政) benevolent government [rule].

인정(認定) 《인가》 authorization; 《인지》 acknowledgment; recognition; 《승인》 approval; 《확인》 confirmation; finding. ~하다 recognize; admit; acknowledge; confirm; authorize. ¶ 전염병으로 되다 be recognized as a contagious disease / 사실의 ~을 서두르다 try to make a finding of the facts / 시인으로 ~받다 be acknowledged as a poet. ‖ ~서 a written recognition 《of championship》.

인조(人造) ¶ ~의 artificial; imitative (모조); synthetic (합성). ‖ ~고무 synthetic rubber / ~보석 imitation jewel / ~섬유 synthetic (chemical) fibers / ~염료 artificial dyes / ~인간 a robot; a cyborg / ~진주 an artificial pearl / ~피혁 artificial (imitation) leather / ~호(湖) a man-made (an artificial) lake.

인조견(人造絹) rayon; synthetic (artificial) silk. ‖ ~사 rayon yarn.

인종(人種) a (human) race. ¶ ~적 편견 racial prejudice / ~차별 racial discrimination / ~의 평등 racial equality / ~황(백)색 the yellow (white) races. ‖ ~문제 a racial problem / ~학 ethnology.

인주(印朱) vermilion inkpad; cinnabar seal ink. ‖ ~합 a red-ink pad.

인증(引證) (an) adduction. ~하다 adduce 《evidence》; quote 《a fact》.

인증(認證) attestation; certification. ~하다 certify; authenticate; attest. ‖ ~서 a certificate of attestation.

인지(人智) human intellect [knowledge]. ¶ ~가 미치지 못하는 beyond human knowledge.

인지(印紙) a revenue stamp. ¶ 영수증에 300원짜리 ~를 붙이다 put a 300-*won* revenue stamp on a receipt. ‖ ~세(稅) revenue stamp duty / ~수입 = 인지.

인지(認知) (legal) acknowledgment. ~하다 recognize; acknowledge. ¶ 사생아를 ~하다 acknowledge an illegitimate child as *one's* own. ‖ ~과학 [심리학] cognitive science (psychology).

인지상정(人之常情) human nature; humaneness. ¶ 그런 때는 그렇게 하는 것이 ~이다 It's quite natural to do so on such an occasion.

인질(人質) a hostage. ¶ ~로 잡다 take (hold) 《a person》 as a hostage / ~이 되다 be held (taken) as hostage.

인책(引責) ~하다 take the responsibility on *oneself*; assume the responsibility 《for》. ¶ ~사직하다 take the responsibility 《for something》 on *oneself* and resign.

인척(姻戚) a relative by marriage; *one's* in-law (美). ¶ ~ 관계에 있다 be related by marriage 《to》.

인체(人體) the human body. ¶ ~의 구조 the structure of the human body / ~에 영향을 주다 affect the human body / ~모형 an anatomical model of the human body / ~실험 a living-body test; an experiment on living persons / ~해부(학) human anatomy.

인축(人畜) men and (or) beasts; humans and animals. ‖ ~무해 No harm to man and beast.

인출(引出) 《예금의》 (a) withdrawal; drawing out. ¶ ~하다 draw out; withdraw. ¶ 은행에서 예금을 ~하다 draw *one's* money (deposit) from the bank.

인치(引致) ~하다 take 《a person》 into custody.

인치 an inch (생략 in.).

인칭(人稱) [文] person. ¶ 제1(2, 3) ~ the first (second, third) person. ‖ ~대명사 a personal pronoun.

인커브 〖野〗 an incurve. [noun.
인코너 〖野〗 an inner corner.
인터넷 〖컴퓨터 통신망〗 Internet.
인터뷰 an interview. ¶ ~ 하는 사람 an interviewer / ~ 받는 사람 an interviewee / …와 ~ 하다 (have an) interview with (*a person*).
인터체인지 〖입체 교차로〗 an interchange. ¶ 어느 ~에서 호남 고속도로로 들어가면 좋습니까? Which [What] interchange should we enter the Honam Expressway at?
인터페론 〖生化〗 interferon.
인터폰 an interphone.
인터폴 the Interpol. (◀ International Police)
인턴 〖수련의〗 an intern. ¶ ~ 근무를 하다 intern (*at*); serve *one's* internship (*at a hospital*).
인텔리 〖겐차아〗 the intellegentzia. ¶ 그는 ~다 He is an intellectual.
인토네이션 intonation. [al.
인파(人波) a surging crowd (of people). ¶ ~에 휘말리다 be jostled in the crowd. [someone.
인편(人便) ~에 듣다 hear from
인품(人品) 《風體》 personal appearance; 《風格》 character; personality. ¶ ~이 좋은 사람 a person of respectable appearance / ~이 좋다 have a fine looking (personality). [력(入力).
인풋 〖컴〗 〖入力〗 (an) input. ‖ 입
인플레이션 〖經〗 inflation. ¶ 악성 ~ vicious (unsound) inflation / ~을 초래하다 (억제하다) cause (curb) inflation. ¶ ~경향 an inflationary trend / ~대책 anti-inflation measures / ~정책 an anti-inflationary policy.
인플루엔자 〖醫〗 flu 〖俗〗.
인하(引下) ~ 하다 pull (draw) down; 《가격·정도를》 lower; reduce; 《값을》 cut. ¶ 물가를 (임금을) ~ 하다 reduce (cut, lower) the price (wages).
인하다(因一) be due (owing) to; be caused by. ¶ 사고는 그의 부주의로 인한 것이었다 The accident was due to (caused by) his carelessness.
인해전술(人海戰術) 《adopt, use》 human-wave tactics.
인허(認許) ~ 인가, ~ 하다 approve; authorize; recognize.
인형(人形) a doll; a puppet (꼭두각시). ¶ ~ 같은 doll-like. ‖ ~극 a puppet show.
인형(仁兄) 《편지에서》 Dear Friend.
인화(人和) harmony (peace and amity) among men. ¶ ~를 도모하다 promote the harmony among men.
인화(引火) ignition. ~ 하다 catch (take) fire; ignite. ¶ 매우 ~ 성이 높다 be highly inflammable. ‖ ~물질 the inflammable / ~점 the flash (ignition) point.
인화(印畵) a print. ~ 하다 print; make a print of. ‖ ~지(紙) printing paper.
인화물(燐化物) phosphide.
인회석(燐灰石) 〖鑛〗 apatite.
인후(咽喉) the throat. ‖ ~염(炎) a sore throat.
일 ① 《사항·사물》 a matter; an affair; a thing; something(어떤 일); 《사정·사실·경우》 circumstances; a fact; a case; 《말썽》 trouble. ¶ 좋은 ~ a good thing / 기분 나쁜 ~ an unpleasant matter; something unpleasant / 네가 말하는 ~ what you say / 생사에 관한 ~ a matter of life and death / 부부간의 ~ a private matter between a man and his wife / ~을 저지르다 cause trouble / 무슨 ~이 있어도 약속을 어기지 않다 keep a promise no matter what happens; do not break a promise under any circumstances / 그것은 틀림없는 ~이다 That is a straight fact. / 나는 할 ~이 많다 I have a lot of things to do. / ~의 ~인 만큼 극비를 요한다 The very nature of the affair requires secrecy. ② 《사건·사고》 an incident; an event; an accident; trouble. ¶ 어제의 ~ yesterday's incident; what happened yesterday / 아무 ~ 없이 일주일이 지나다 A week passes without accident (incident). / 무슨 ~ 만 있으면, 그는 신께 기도한다 Whenever he is in trouble, he prays to God for help. ③ 《작업·용무·일거리》 work; business; labor; a job; 《업무·임무》 a business; a task; a duty; 《a》 need(필요). ¶ 하루의 ~ a day's work / ~을 하다 work; do *one's* work (job) / ~에 쫓기다 be pressed (overloaded) with business; be under great pressure in *one's* work / ~이 손에 잡히지 않다 be unable to settle down to work; cannot concentrate on *one's* work / 공부는 학생이 해야 할 ~이다 It's a student's business (duty) to study. / 네 ~이나 잘 해라 Mind your own business. / 서두를 ~이 아니다 There is no need for haste. / 그는 하다가 쓰러졌다 He collapsed on the job (at work). / 그는 회사 ~로 뉴욕에 출장 중이다 He is in New York on the business of the company. ④ 《계획》 a plan; a program; 《음모》 a plot; a trick. ¶ ~을 꾀(도모)하다 make a plan (plot); 《음모를》 conspire (intrigue) (*against*) / ~을 진행시키다 carry a program forward. ⑤ 《경험》 an experience.

¶ 이 책을 읽은 ~이 있느냐 Have you ever read this book? / 그런 것을 들은 ~이 없다 I've never heard of such a thing. / 미국에 갔던 ~이 있다 I've been to America. ⑥ 《업적》 an achievement; merits; services. ¶ 훌륭한 ~을 하다 render distinguished services

일(一) one; the first (첫째). ⌞(to).
일가(一家) ① a household; a family; one's family (가족). ¶ 《친척》 one's relations (relatives). ¶ 김씨 ~ the (whole) Kim family; the Kims / 먼 〔가까운〕 ~ one's distant 〔near〕 relatives / ~의 주인 the master of a house / ~를 이루다 make a home of one's own. ② 《일파》 a school. ¶ ~를 이루다 establish a school of one's own.
일가견(一家見) one's own opinion; a personal view. ⌞family.
일가족(一家族) one 〔the whole〕
일각(一角) a corner; a section. ¶ 빙산의 ~ the tip of an iceberg / 정계의 ~ a section of political circles.
일각(一刻) a minute; a moment; an instant. ¶ ~의 지체도 없이 without a moment's delay; as soon as possible / ~이 여삼추다 feel a moment as if it were three years / ~을 다투다 There isn't a moment to lose.
일간(日刊) daily issue 〔publication〕. ‖ ~신문 a daily (newspaper).
일간(日間) 《부사적》 soon; before long; at any early date; in a few days.
일갈(一喝) ~하다 thunder (out); roar (at a person).
일개(一介) a (mere) 《student》; only 《a salesman》 / 나는 ~ 교사에 지나지 않는다 I'm a mere schoolteacher.
일개(一個) one; a piece. ¶ ~년 one year / ~월 one month / 만 ~년 a full year.
일개인(一個人) an individual; 《사인》 a private person. ☞ 개인.
일거(一擧) ¶ ~에 at 〔one, a single〕 stroke; at one effort 〔swoop〕; all at once / ~에 적을 무찌르다 defeat the enemy by one charge; crush the enemy at a blow / ~ 양득을 노리다 aim to kill two birds with one stone. ‖ ~일동 every movement; every action / ~일동을 지켜보다 watch a person's every movement.
일거리 a piece of work; a job; a task; things to do. ¶ ~가 있다 have work to do / ~가 없다 be out of job; have nothing to do.
일거수일투족(一擧手一投足) everything one does. ☞ 일거일동.

일건(一件) an affair; a case; a matter. ‖ ~서류 all the papers relating to a case.
일격(一擊) a blow; a stroke; a hit. ¶ ~에 at a blow; with one stroke / ~을 가하다 give 〔deal〕 《a person》 a blow.
일견(一見) a sight; a look 〔glance〕. ¶ ~하다 take 〔have〕 a look 〔at〕; give a glance 《at》. ‖ ~하여 at a look 〔glance〕; at first sight / 백문이 불여 ~이다 Seeing is believing.
일계(日計) a daily account; daily expenses. ‖ ~표 a daily trial balance sheet.
일고(一考) ~하다 take 《a matter》 into consideration; give a thought 《to》. ¶ ~할 여지가 있다 leave room for further consideration.
일고(一顧) ¶ ~의 가치도 없다 be quite worthless; be beneath one's notice / ~도 하지 않다 take no notice 《of》; give no heed 《to》.
일곱 seven; the seventh (7번째).
일과(一過) ~성의 temporary; transitory.
일과(日課) 《수업》 a daily lesson; 《일》 a daily task; daily work 〔routine〕. ¶ 합숙 중의 ~를 정하다 plan the daily schedule for the camp. ‖ ~표 a schedule 《of lessons》.
일관(一貫) ~하다 be consistent. ¶ ~하여 consistently; from first to last / 그의 언동은 ~되지 않는다 His statements and his actions are inconsistent. / 그는 시종 일관 암 연구에 전념했다 He was devoted to cancer research throughout his career. ‖ ~성(性) consistency / ~작업 one continuous operation; an integrated production process (생산 설비의); a conveyor system (단위 공정의).
일괄(一括) ~하다 lump together; sum up. ¶ ~하여 in a lump; collectively; in bulk (대량으로); 교재를 ~하여 주문받다 order teaching materials in bulk / 세 개의 법안이 ~ 상정되었다 Three bills were brought up together for discussion. / 이 문제들은 ~ 처리할 수 있다 Those problems can be dealt with collectively. ‖ ~계약 a blanket contract; a package deal / ~구입 a blanket purchase en masse / ~사표 a resignation en masse / ~안(案) a package plan.
일광(日光) sunlight; sunshine; sunbeams (광선); the sun. ¶ 강한 ~ glaring sunlight; the strong sun / ~에 쐬다 expose 《something》 to the sun / ~을 들이다 let in sunlight / ~이 안 들어오게

커튼을 치다 draw the curtains to shut out the sun. ‖ ~소독 disinfection by exposure to the sun / ~욕 a sunbath; sunbathing / ~욕을 하다 sunbathe; bathe in the sun.

일구난설(一口難說) being difficult to explain in a word (briefly).

일구다 cultivate (reclaim) 《*waste land*》; bring 《*waste land*》 under cultivation.

일구월심(日久月深) ¶ ~으로 single-mindedly; earnestly; with all *one's* heart / 그녀는 ~ 남편만을 기다렸다 She waited only for her husband with all her heart.

일구이언(一口二言) being double-tongued. ~ 하다 be double-tongued; go back on *one's* word (promise).

일군(一軍) ①〈전군〉 the whole army (force). ②〈제1군〉 the First Army.

일그러지다 be distorted (contorted). ¶ 고통으로 일그러진 얼굴 a face distorted with pain; a tortured face.

일급(一級) the first class. ¶ ~의 first-class (-rate); 《an article》 of the highest quality / 그의 솜씨는 ~이다 He does an excellent job. ‖ ~품 first-class goods.

일급(日給) daily wages. ‖ ~ 노동자 a day laborer.

일굿거리다 be rickety (shaky).

일기(一期) ①〈기간〉 a term; a period; 〈병의〉 a stage. ¶ 제~생 the first term students / 제~의 결핵 tuberculosis in its first stage. ②〈일생〉 *one's* whole life; *one's* lifetime. ¶ 50세를 ~로 죽다 die at the age of fifty.

일기(一騎) a (single) horseman. ¶ ~당천의 용사 a mighty warrior.

일기(日記) a diary; a journal. ¶ ~를 쓰다 keep (write) *one's* diary / ~에 쓰다 write in a diary. ‖ ~장을 diary.

일기(日氣) weather (☞ 날씨). ¶ ~개황 general weather conditions / ~도 a weather map (chart) / ~예보 a weather forecast (report).

일기죽거리다 sway *one's* hips.

일깨우다〈자는 사람을〉 wake 《*a person*》 up early in the morning; 〈깨닫게 하다〉 make 《*a person*》 realize 《*something*》; open 《*a person's*》 eyes to 《*something*》.

일껏〈애써〉 with much trouble (effort); at great pains.

일꾼 ①〈품꾼〉 a laborer; a workman; a worker; a farm-hand〈농사의〉. ②〈역량있는 사람〉 a competent and efficient man; a man of ability.

일년(一年) a (one) year. ¶ ~의 yearly; annual / ~에 한 번 once a year; annually / ~ 내내 all the year round / ~ 걸러 every other (second) year; biennially.

일년생(一年生) ①〈학생〉 a first-year student; 〈대학·고교의〉 a freshman《美》. ②〈植〉‖ ~식물 an annual plant.

일념(一念) a concentrated mind; an ardent wish. ¶ 어머니를 만나고 싶다는 ~으로 가출하다 run away from home out of an earnest desire to see *one's* mother.

일다 ①〈파도·바람·연기 등이〉 rise; 〈소문·평판이〉 spread. ¶ 어디선가 연기가 일고 있다 Smoke is rising from somewhere. / 파도가 일고 있다 The sea is running high. / 그가 살해당했다는 소문이 일었다 There rose (spread) a rumor that he had been murdered. ②〈번창해지다〉 prosper; flourish. ¶ 호경기로 사운이 크게 일었다 The company has prospered because of a business boom.

일다〈쌀 따위를〉 wash (rinse) 《*rice*》.

일단(一端) one end〈한 끝〉; a part〈일부〉. ¶ 생각의 ~을 말하다 tell something of what *one* thinks 《*about*》 / 계획의 ~을 누설하다 reveal a part of the project.

일단(一團) a party; a group. ¶ ~의 관광객 a party of tourists / ~이 되어 in a group 《*body*》.

일단(一旦)〈한번〉 once; 〈우선〉 for the present. ¶ ~ 유사시엔 in an emergency / ~ 국가적 위기 in a national crisis / ~ 지금은 이것으로 끝내자 Let's stop here for the present.

일단락(一段落) ~ 짓다 settle *a matter* for the time being; complete the first stage 《*of the work*》.

일당(一堂) ~에 모이다 gather in a hall (room).

일당(一黨)〈한 정당〉 a party; 〈한 패〉 a gang 《*of robbers*》. ¶ ~ 일파에 치우치지 않다 be unpartisan 《*in foreign affairs*》; be nonparty / ~ 4명을 체포하다 arrest a group of four men. ‖ ~독재 one-party rule (dictatorship).

일당(日當) daily allowance (pay, wages). ¶ ~으로 일하다 work by the day / ~ 5천 원을 지불하다 pay five thousand *won* a day.

일당백(一當百) being a match for a hundred.

일대(一代) one generation; 〈일생시대〉 *one's* whole life; *one's* lifetime. ¶ ~의 영웅 the great hero of an age. ‖ ~기 a biography; a life / ~잡종 an F₁ hybrid.

일대(一帶)《일원》 the whole area

일대 [district]; the neighborhood 《of》. ¶서울 ~에 throughout [all over] Seoul.

일대 (一大) great; grand; remarkable. ¶국가의 ~사 a matter of great consequence to the nation / (모임이) ~성황을 이루다 be a great success / ~단을 내리다 take a decisive step; make a brave decision.

일더위 early summer heat.

일도 (一刀) ¶~양단하다 《비유적》 take a drastic measure [step]; cut the Gordian knot; do without beating about the bush.

일독 (一讀) ~하다 read 《a book》 through; look 《a report》 over; run one's eyes over 《a paper》.

일동 (一同) all; everyone. ¶가내 ~ all one's family / 회원 ~ all the member / ~을 대표하여 on behalf of everybody.

일되다 mature early; grow [ripen] early.

일득일실 (一得一失) ¶그것은 ~이다 It has its advantages and disadvantages. / ~이 세상사다 Every gain has its loss.

일등 (一等) 《등급》 the first class [grade, rank]; (제1위) the first place (prize). ¶~석으로 여행하다 travel first-class [in a first-class cabin]. ‖ ~ 병 a First-class power / ~병 Private First Class (생략 Pfc.) / ~상 (win) the first prize / ~성 (星) a star of the first magnitude / ~승객 a first-class passenger / ~품 a first-grade article.

일떠나다 《일찍 떠나다》 leave early in the morning.

일란성 (一卵性) ¶~쌍생아 identical twins.

일람 (一覽) ~하다 have [take] a look at; run through; run one's eyes over. ¶~후 30일 불 payable at thirty days after sight / ~하신 후 되돌려 주십시오 Please return it to me after looking through it. ‖ ~ 불 어음 a bill payable at [on] sight; a sight [demand] bill / ~표 a table; a list.

일러두기 introductory remarks; explanatory notes.

일러두다 tell 《a person》《to do》; bid 《a person》《do》. ¶단단히 ~ give strict orders.

일러바치다 inform [tell] on 《a person》; let on 《to your teacher about》. ¶그는 어머니께 내가 한 짓을 일러바쳤다 He told my mother on me.

일러주다 ① 《알려주다》 let 《a person》 know; tell; inform. ② 《가르치다》 teach; instruct; show.

일렁거리다 bob up and down; toss; rock (on the waves).

일렉트론 [理] an electron.

일력 (日曆) a daily pad calendar.

일련 (一連) ~의 a series of 《games》; a chain of 《events》; ~의 살인 사건 a chain of murders. ‖ ~번호 consecutive numbers; serial numbers / ~번호를 붙이다 number 《the cards》 consecutively.

일련탁생 (一蓮托生) a pledge to rise or sink together. ¶~이다 be in the same boat.

일렬 (一列) a row; a line; a rank (가로의); a file (세로의). ¶~로 줄 서다 form [stand in] a line [row, queue (英)].

일례 (一例) an example; an instance. ¶~를 들면 for example [instance] / ~를 들다 give an example.

일로 (一路) ¶~ 서울을 향하다 head straight for Seoul.

일루 (一縷) ¶~의 희망 a ray of hope / ~의 희망을 품다 cling to one's last hope.

일루 (一壘) first base. ¶~에 나가 다 go to first base. ‖ ~수 the first baseman / ~타 a base hit.

일류 (一流) ¶~의 first-class; first rate; top-ranking; top-notch (口). ~ 식당 a first-rate restaurant 《in town》 / ~ 호텔 a first-class hotel / ~의 외교관 a diplomat of the first rank / 당대 ~의 물리학자 one of the most eminent physicians of the day. ‖ ~교 (校) (one of) the best-known schools / ~병 a passion [kick] for top class / ~회사 (one of) the top-ranking companies.

일류미네이션 illumination; 장치등을 illuminated.

일률 (一律) ¶~적으로 《균등히》 evenly; uniformly; 《무차별로》 impartially / 그들 모두를 ~적으로 다룰 수는 없다 We cannot apply the same rule to them all.

일리 (一理) some truth 《reason》. ¶그의 말에도 ~는 있다 There is some truth in what he says.

일리일해 (一利一害) 일득일실.

일말 (一抹) a touch 《of melancholy》; a tinge 《of sadness》. ¶~의 불안을 느끼다 feel slightly uneasy 《about》.

일망타진 (一網打盡) ~하다 make a wholesale arrest 《of》; round up 《a gang of criminals》.

일매지다 (be) even; uniform.

일맥 (一脈) ~ 상통하는 점이 있다 have something in common 《with》.

일면 (一面) ① 《한 면》 one side. ¶성격의 어두운 ~을 보이다 show a dark side of one's character / 너

일면식 는 문제의 ~만을 보고 있다 You see only one side of the matter. / 그녀는 얌전하지만 마음이 강한 ~도 있다 On the one hand she is quiet, but on the other she is determined. ② 《신문의》 the front page. ¶ (신문의) 제 ~에 보도하다 report *something* on the front page.

일면식 (一面識) ¶ 그와는 ~도 없다 He is a complete stranger to me. *or* I have never met him before.

일모작 (一毛作) single-cropping (*of rice*). ¶ 여기는 ~ 지역이다 This is a single-crop area.

일목 (一目) a glance. ¶ ~요연하다 be obvious; be clear at a glance.

일몰 (日沒) sunset; sundown. ¶ ~ 후(前) after (before) sunset / ~에서 ~까지 from sundown to sunrise.

일문 (一門) ① 《일족》 a family; a clan. ② 《집안》 one's kinsfolk; 《종파》 the whole sect.

일문일답 (一問一答) 《a series of》 questions and answers; a dialogue. ~하다 exchange questions and answers.

일미 (一味) a good 〔superb〕 flavor.

일박 (一泊) a night's lodging. ~하다 stay overnight; put up 《*at a hotel*》 for the night; pass a night 《at》. ¶ ~여행 (make) an overnight trip 《to》.

일반 (一般) ¶ ~의 general; 《보편적인》 universal; 《보통의》 common; ordinary; 《대중의》 public / ~적으로 generally (speaking); in general; as a (general) rule; on the whole / ~적인 지식〔교양〕 general knowledge 〔culture〕 / ~사람들〔대중〕 the general public; the public at large / ~ 대중의 의견 public opinion / ~에게 개방되어 있다 be open to the public / ~에 알려지다 become public knowledge; become known to a wide public / ~용의 for popular 〔general〕 use / 이 상품은 ~취향에 맞게 한 것이다 This article is aimed at the popular taste. / 그 작가는 ~ 독자에게는 인기가 없다 The writer is not popular with general readers. / 이 관습은 한국에서 ~적이다 This custom is common in Korea. ‖ ~ 교양과목 liberal arts; a general education subject / ~의(醫) a general practitioner / ~화(化) generalization 《~하다 generalize; popularize》 / ~회계 (의) general account.

일반사면 (一般赦免) an amnesty; a general pardon.

일발 (一發) a shot. ¶ ~의 총성 a gunshot; the sound of a gun.

일방 (一方) 《한 쪽》 one side; the other side 《반 쪽》. ¶ ~적인 unilateral; one-sided / ~적인 견해 a one-sided view of things / ~적으로 떠들어대다 speak one-sidedly / ~적인 승리를 거두다 win a lopsided 〔runaway〕 victory. ‖ ~통행 one-way traffic/《게시》 One Way (Only).

일번 (一番) the first; No. 1. ¶ ~의 문제에 답하이오 Answer Question No. 1 (the first question). ‖ ~타자 《野》 a lead-off man.

일벌 (一벌) a worker bee.

일벌백계 (一罰百戒) One punishment equals a hundred warnings.

일변 (一邊) 《한 변》 a side. ¶ 삼각형의 ~ a side of a triangle.

일변 (一變) a complete change. ~하다 change completely. ¶ 태도를 ~하다 change one's attitude altogether.

일변 (日邊) daily interest.

일변도 (一邊倒) ¶ 그들은 미국 ~이다 They are completely pro-American. *or* They are wholly devoted to American interests. ‖ ~정책 a lean-to-one-side policy.

일별 (一瞥) a glance; a look. ~하다 glance 《at》; cast a glance 《at》.

일병 (一兵) ☞ 일등병.

일보 (一步) a step. ¶ ~ ~ step by step / ~ 전진〔후퇴〕하다 take a step forward 〔backward〕 / ~도 양보하지 않다 do not yield an inch. ‖ ~ 〔daily (newspaper)〕

일보 (日報) a daily report; 《신문》 a daily (newspaper)

일보다 carry on one's business; take charge of a business.

일본 (日本) Japan. ¶ ~의 Japanese. ‖ ~국민 the Japanese (people) / ~말 Japanese; the Japanese language / ~인 a Japanese.

일봉 (一封) 《금일봉》 an enclosure (a gift) of money.

일부 (一夫) a husband. ¶ ~에 종신하다 remain faithful to one's husband to the last. ‖ ~다처 polygamy / ~일처 monogamy.

일부 (一部) 《일부분》 a part; a portion; a section. ¶ ~의 partial; some / ~의 사람들 some people / ~의 ~ 를 이루다 form (a) part of….

일부 (日賦) a daily installment. ‖ ~금 daily installment payment / ~판매 sale on daily-installment terms.

일부러 《고의로》 intentionally; on purpose; deliberately. ¶ 너 ~ 그랬지 You must have done it on purpose. / ~ 오시게 해서 미안합니다 I am sorry to have troubled

일부분(一部分) ☞ 일부(一部).

일사(一死) 〖野〗 one out. ¶ ~만루가 됐다 The bases were loaded with one out.

일사(一事) one thing. ‖ ~부재리(不再理)〖法〗 a prohibition against double jeopardy / ~부재의(不再議) the principle that the same matter should not be debated twice in the same session (of the Assembly).

일사병(日射病) sunstroke. ¶ ~에 걸리다 be sunstruck; have sunstroke.

일사분기(一四分期) the first quarter of the year.

일사불란(一絲不亂) ~하다《서술적》be in perfect (precise) order.

일사천리(一瀉千里) ~로 rapidly; in a hurry; at a stretch / ~로 일을 처리하다 rush through one's work.

일산(日産)《생산고(production)》;《일본산》 Japanese products;(of) Japanese make. ¶ ~ 300대의 자동차를 생산하다 put (turn) out 300 cars a day.

일산화(一酸化) ~물 monoxide / ~질소 nitrogen monoxide / ~탄소 carbon monoxide.

일삼다《일로 삼다》make it one's business (to do);《전심》 devote oneself to (something);《탐닉》 give oneself up to; do nothing but…. ¶ 술마시기를 ~ do nothing but drink; be given to drink.

일상(日常) every day; daily; usually. ¶ ~의 daily; everyday / ~하는 일 daily work (business) / ~ 일어나는 일 everyday affairs; daily happenings. ‖ ~생활 everyday (daily) life / ~업무 daily business; routine work / ~회화 everyday conversation.

일색(一色) ①《한 빛》 one color. ②《미인》 a rare beauty. ③《비유적》~으로 exclusively / 위원회는 공화당 ~이다 The committee seats are exclusively occupied by Republicans.

일생(一生) a lifetime; one's (whole) life. ¶ ~의 사업 one's lifework / ~일대의 좋은 기회 the chance of a lifetime / ~에 한번 once in a lifetime.

일석이조(一石二鳥) ¶ 이 제안을 받아들이면 ~가 된다 If we accept this proposal, we can kill two birds with one stone.

일선(一線) a line;《전선·실무의》 the front (line);《the fighting (first) line. ¶ ~외교관들 the first-line diplomats / 그는 아직 제~에서 활약 중이다 He is still now one of the leading figures. ‖ ~근무 field (active) service.

일설(一說) ¶ ~에 의하면 according to one opinion (theory); someone says….

일세(一世) ①《그 시대》 the time; the age. ¶ ~를 풍미하다 command the world (time). ②《일대》 a generation;《왕조의》 the first. ¶ 헨리 ~ Henry I (the First).

일소(一笑) a laugh. ¶ ~에 부치다 laugh (*a matter*) off (away); dismiss (*a matter*) with a laugh; shrug (*a matter*) off.

일소(一掃) ~하다 sweep (wash) away; clear away (off); wipe (stamp) out. ¶ ~악습을 ~하다 sweep away all the bad customs / 의혹을 ~하다 clear away one's suspicion.

일손 ①《하고 있는 일》 the work in hand. ②《일솜씨》 skill at a job. ¶ ~이 오르다 improve in one's skill. ③《일하는 사람》 a hand; a help; a worker. ¶ ~이 모자라다 be short of hands / ~ 부족으로 고통받다 suffer from a shortage of workers / ~이 필요하다 We need helping hands.

일수(日收) a loan collected by daily installment. ‖ ~쟁이 a moneylender who collects by daily installment.

일수(日數) ①《날수》 the number of days. ②《날의 운수》 the day's luck. ☞ 일진(日辰).

일순간(一瞬間) an instant; a moment. ¶ 그것은 ~에 일어난 일이었다 It all happened in a moment (flash).

일습(一襲) a suit (of clothes); a set (of tools).

일승일패(一勝一敗) one victory and (against) one defeat.

일시(一時) ①《한때》 at one time; once;《잠시》 for a time (while);《임시로》 temporarily / ~적인 momentary; temporary; passing / ~에 at the same time(동시에); all together(한꺼번에); ~적으로 temporarily / ~적인 흥분 momentary excitement / ~적인 현상 a passing phenomenon / ~적인 미봉책 a temporary expedient; a makeshift / 그는 ~ 서울에 살았다 He lived in Seoul at one time. / 그들은 ~에 떠들기 시작했다 They got noisy all at once. / 그런 스타일은 ~적인 유행에 지나지 않는다 Such a style is only a passing fashion. ‖ ~귀휴제(歸休制) a layoff system / ~불(拂) payment in a lump sum / ~차입금 a floating debt; a temporary loan.

일시(日時) the date (and time) [the time.

일시금(一時金) a lump sum. ¶ ~

일식 (日蝕) [天] an eclipse of the sun; a solar eclipse.
일신 (一身) oneself; one's life. ¶ ~을 바치다 devote *oneself to 《the movement》* / ~상의 상담을 하다 consult 《*a person*》 about *one's* personal affairs / ~상의 사정으로 회사를 그만두다 leave the company for personal reasons.
일신 (一新) 하다 renew; renovate; change completely; refresh (기분을). ¶ 면목을 ~하다 assume a new aspect / 학교 건물은 외관을 ~했다 The schoolhouse has been renovated.
일신교 (一神敎) monotheism. ‖ ~도를 a monotheist.
일심 (一心) 《한마음》 one mind; 《전심》 one's whole heart; wholeheartedness. ¶ ~으로 intently; with one's whole heart; wholeheartedly / 부부는 ~동체이다 Husband and wife are one flesh. / 우리는 ~동체이다 We are of one mind.
일심 (一審) the first trial. ¶ ~에서 패소하다 lose a case at the first trial. ‖ 제일 ~법원 a court of the first instance.
일쑤 habitual practice. ¶ 그는 남을 비웃기 ~다 He's always sneering at others.
일약 (一躍) 《부사적》 at a (one) bound; at a jump; with a leap. ¶ ~ 유명해지다 spring (leap) into fame / 평사원에서 ~ 사장이 되었다 From a mere clerk he became a president at a bound.
일어 (日語) Japanese; the Japanese language.
일어나다 ① 《잠자리에서》 rise; get up. ¶ 일찍 일어나는 사람 an early riser / 일어나 있다 be up; be out of bed / 밤늦게까지 일어나 있다 sit up late at night. ② 《일어서다》 get (stand) up; rise (to one's feet); 《기운을 되찾다》 recover; regain one's strength. ¶ 의자에서 ~ rise from one's chair (seat) / 벌떡 ~ jump (spring) to one's feet / 중병을 앓고 ~ recover from one's serious illness / 간신히 ~ scramble to one's feet. ③ 《발생하다》 happen; occur; take place; come about (up); break out (재해 따위가). ¶ 어떤 일이 일어나도 여기서 꼼짝하지 마라 No matter what happens, don't move from here. / 비오는 날에는 사고가 일어나기 쉽다 Accidents are likely to occur (take place) on rainy days. / 화재가 일어난 것은 한밤중이었다 It was about midnight when the fire broke out. ④ 《출현·생겨나다》 spring up; come into existence (being); 《융성해지다》 prosper; rise; flourish. ¶ 새로운 산업이 일어났다 A new industry has sprung up lately. / 그의 사업은 다시 일어나기 시작했다 His business began to prosper again. ⑤ 《기인한다》 be caused (by); result (arise, stem) from; originate (in). ¶ 오해로 일어난 불화 a discord which originate in a misunderstanding / 홍수로 일어난 피해 the damage resulting from the flood / 그 분쟁은 인종적 편견에서 일어났다 The trouble came (resulted) from racial prejudice. ⑥ 《불이》 begin (start) to burn; 《열·전기 등이》 be produced (generated). ¶ 불은 창고에서 일어났다 The fire started in the barn.
일어서다 ① 《기립》 ☞ 일어나다②. 《구령》 Rise!; Stand up! ② 《분기하다》 rise (up) 《*against*》; stand up and take action. ¶ 사람들은 폭정에 항거하여 일어났다 People rose (up) against tyranny.
일언 (一言) a (single) word. ¶ 남자의 ~ a man's word (of honor) / ~반구의 사과도 없이 without a single word of apology / ~지하에 거절하다 refuse flatly; give a flat refusal.
일언이폐지 (一言以蔽之) One sentence can cover the whole. ¶ ~하다 express in a single word.
일없다 (be) needless; useless. ¶ 이렇게 많이는 ~ I don't need so many 《much》.
일엽편주 (一葉片舟) a small boat.
일요 (日曜) ‖ ~예배 Sunday service(s) / ~일 Sunday / ~특집 《신문의》 a Sunday supplement / ~판 《신문의》 a Sunday edition.
일용 (日用) ‖ ~의 for everyday (daily) use. ‖ ~식료품 staple articles of food / ~품 daily necessities.
일원 (一元) ¶ ~적인 unitary. ‖ ~화 unification; ~집중화 centralization; ~화하다 unify.
일원 (一員) a member. ¶ 이제 너는 우리 클럽의 ~이다 Now you are a member of our club.
일원 (一圓) ☞ 일대(一帶). ¶ 경기 ~ throughout (all over) the *Kyŏnggi* region.
일원제 (一院制) the single-chamber (unicameral) system.
일월 (一月) January (생략 Jan.).
일월 (日月) 《해와 달》 the sun and the moon; 《세월》 time; days (and months).
일위 (一位) 《첫째》 the first (foremost) place; the first rank. ¶ ~를 차지하다 stand (rank) first; win (get) first place.
일으키다 ① 《세우다》 raise; set up;

pick (*a child*) up. ¶ 넘어진 노인을 ~ set [help] an old man on his legs / 환자는 천천히 일어 났다 The patient slowly raised himself to H. ② (《깨우다》) wake (up); awake. ③ (《창립·설립하다》) set up; establish; start; found; (《번영케 하다》) make prosperous. ¶ 새로운 사업을 ~ start a new business / 나라를 크게 ~ 일으킨 bring a nation to great prosperity / 나라를 일으킨 영웅 a hero who aroused the nation. ④ (《야기하다》) cause; bring about; lead to; give rise to. ¶ 소동을 ~ raise [cause] a disturbance / 호기심을 ~ arouse [excite] *a person's* curiosity / 버먼혈을 ~ have an attack of cerebral anemia. ⑤ (《기타》) 전기를 ~ generate electricity / 소송을 ~ bring a suit [action] against (*a person*) / 불을 ~ make [build] a fire.

일의대수 (一衣帶水) ¶ 영국과 유럽은 ~를 끼고 있다 Only a narrow strait lies between England and Europe.

일익 (一翼) ¶ ~을 담당하다 play a part (*in the industrialization of the region*); have a share (*in Korea's foreign trade*) / 그는 그 사업의 ~을 담당하고 있다 He is equally responsible for carrying out the project.

일익 (日益) day by day; increasingly; more and more. ¶ 사태는 ~ 악화되는 것 같다 The situation is likely to go from bad to worse.

일인 (一人) one person [man]. ¶ ~ 독재 one-man dictatorship / ~ 이역 (*play*) a double role / ~ 자 the number-one man; the leading figure. 「nese〕(총칭).

일인 (日人) a Japanese; the Japa-

일인당 (一人當) for each person; per *capita* (*head*). ¶ ~ 인구 per head of population / ~ 연간 소득 annual income for each person / ~ 만원씩 모으다 collect a ten thousand *won* for each person.

일일 (一日) a [one] day; (초하루) the first day (of a month).

일일이¹ (일마다) everything; in every thing [case]; all; without exception. ¶ ~ 간섭하다 meddle in everything.

일일이² (하나씩) one by one; point by point; (상세히) in detail; in full. ¶ 계획을 ~ 설명하다 explain the plan point by point / ~ 조사하다 examine (*things*) one by one / ~ 보고하다 report in full.

일임 (一任) leave; entrust. ¶ 만사를 네게 ~ 한다 I will leave everything to you. / 그 일은 너에게 ~ 할 수 없다 I can't let you handle the matter. / 나는 그 공장에서 생산 관리를 ~ 받고 있다 I am entrusted with the production management in the factory.

일자 (日字) ☞ 날자.

일자리 a position; a job; work. ¶ ~를 잃다 lose *one's* job / ~를 주다 give work / ~를 구하다 look [hunt] for a job / ~를 찾았다 I've found a job.

일자무식 (一字無識) (utter) ignorance; illiteracy. ¶ ~꾼 an (utterly) illiterate person.

일잠 자다 go to bed early.

일장 (一場) ① (《연극의》) a scene. ② (《한바탕》) a (one) time; a round. ¶ ~의 연설을 하다 make a speech; deliver an address / ~ 춘몽이 되다 vanish like an empty dream.

일장일단 (一長一短) merits and demerits. ¶ 이들 계획에는 각각 ~이 있다 Each of these plans has its merits and demerits.

일전 (一戰) (싸움) a battle; a fight; (승부) a game; a bout. ¶ 최후의 ~ a last-ditch fight (*against*) / …와 ~을 겨루다 fight a battle with; (경기) have a game [bout] (*of chess, etc.*).

일전 (日前) the other day; some (a few) days ago; recently. ¶ ~에 그와 만났다 I met him recently. / 그는 ~에 라디오를 샀다 He bought a radio set the other day.

일절 (一切) altogether; wholly; entirely. ¶ ~ …하지 않다 never *do*; do not *do* at all / 나는 이 일과 ~ 관계가 없다 I have nothing whatever to do with this affair.

일정 (一定) ~하다 (be) fixed; set; settled; definite; regular(규칙적인); certain(특정의). ¶ ~ 한 기간 내에 within a fixed period / ~ 한 간격을 두고 at regular intervals / ~ 한 비율로 at a fixed rate / ~ 한 장소 a certain place / ~ 한 직업 a regular occupation; a steady job / ~ 불변의 invariable; fixed and unchangeable / ~ 한 수입을 가지다 have a regular income / 물품세는 주에 따라 ~ 하지 않다 The sales tax varies according to the States.

일정 (日程) the day's program [schedule]; (의사 일정) an agenda. ¶ ~을 세우다 [바꾸다] plan [alter] the day's program / (의사) ~에 올라 있는 사항 the items on the day's agenda. ‖ ~표 a schedule; an itinerary(여행의).

일제 (一齊) ~히 all together (다같이); at the same time; all at once(동시에); in a chorus(이구동성으로) / 관객들은 ~히 웃었다 The audience laughed all together.

‖ ~검거 a wholesale arrest; a roundup / ~사격 a volley (of fire) / ~사격하다 fire a volley).

일조(一朝) ¶ ~ 유사시에 in case of emergency / ~일석에 in a day (short time); overnight / 이것은 ~일석에 해결될 문제가 아니다 This is not a problem that can be solved (settled) overnight.

일조(日照) sunshine. ‖ ~권 (法) the right to sunshine / ~시간 hours of sunlight.

일족(一族) (친척) relatives; kinsmen; (가족) the whole family; (씨족) the 《Kim's》 clan.

일종(一種) a kind; a sort; a species; a variety (변종). ¶ ~의 a kind (sort) of / 이것은 장미의 ~이다 This is a kind of rose.

일주(一周) one round. ~하다 go (travel, walk) round; make a round (of). ¶ 세계 ~ 여행을 하다 make a round-the-world trip / 트랙을 ~ 하다 run once around the race track. ~기(期)〔天〕a period / ~기(忌)〔天〕the first anniversary of a person's death / ~년 기념일을 the first anniversary (of the opening).

일주(一週) (일주일) a week. ¶ ~일회로 once a week; weekly.

일지(日誌) a diary; a journal.

일직(日直) day duty. ~하다 be on day duty. ‖ ~장교 an orderly officer; an officer of the day.

일직선(一直線) a straight line. ¶ ~으로 in a straight line.

일진(一陣) (군사의) a military camp; the vanguard (선봉대). ② (바람) ¶ ~의 광풍 a gust of wind.

일진(日辰) (운수) the day's luck. ¶ ~이 좋다(사납다) It is a lucky (an unlucky) day (for).

일진월보(日進月步) ~하다 make rapid progress.

일진일퇴(一進一退) ~하다 advance and retreat. ¶ ~의 접전 a see-saw game / 그의 상태는 ~한다 He's better one minute (day) and worse the one next.

일찌감치 a little early (earlier). ¶ ~ 집을 떠나다 leave home a bit earlier (than usual) / ~ 저녁을 먹다 have an early supper.

일찍이 ① (이르게) early (in the morning); (어려서) early in life; in one's early days. ¶ ~ 부모를 여의다 lose one's parents at an early age. ② (전에) once; (at) one time; before; formerly; ever (의문문에서); never(부정문에서). ¶ 그녀는 ~ 여배우 노릇을 한 일이 있다 She was once (formerly) an actress. / 이러한 일은 ~ 들어본 일이 없다 I have never heard of such a thing.

일차(一次) ¶ ~의 first; primary / 제~ 처칠 내각 the first Churchill Cabinet / 제~ 세계대전 World War I. ‖ ~방정식 a simple (linear) equation / ~산업 (산품) primary industries (products) / ~시험 a primary examination.

일차원(一次元) ~의 one-dimensional; unidimensional.

일착(一着) ① (경주자) (the) first place; the first to arrive (사람). ~ 하다 come in first; win the first place. ② (옷의) a suit (of clothes). ☞ 벌.

일책(一策) a plan; an idea.

일처다부(一妻多夫) polyandry.

일천(日淺) ~하다 (be) short; be not long (서술적). ¶ 아버님께서 사망하신지 아직 ~하다 It's been only a short time since my father died.

일체(一切) ¶ ~의 all; everything. ¶ ~ 다; all; every; whole / ~의 관계를 끊다 cut off all relations (with); wash one's hands of (a matter).

일체(一體) ~가 되어 in a body; as one body / ~가 되어 일하다 work as one body / 부부는 ~다 Man and wife are one flesh. ‖ ~감 a sense of unity / ~화 unification; integration.

일촉즉발(一觸卽發) a touch-and-go situation. ¶ 두 나라는 ~의 위기에 있다 Relations between the two countries are strained to the breaking point.

일축(一蹴) ~하다 (거절하다) refuse (a request); reject (turn down) (a proposal); (경기에서) beat (the team) easily.

일출(日出) sunrise; sunup (美).

일취월장(日就月將) ~하다 make rapid progress. ☞ 일진월보.

일층(一層) ① (건물의) the first floor (美); the ground floor (英). ¶ ~집 a one-story house. ② (한결) more; still more; all the more.

일치(一致) (부합) agreement; accord; coincidence (우연의); (a) harmony (조화). ~하다 agree (accord) (with); coincide (with). ¶ 전원의 의견이 ~하다 reach (a) consensus (on a matter) / 의견의 ~를 보다 come to an agreement / 두 사람의 의견은 완전히 ~하고 있다 The two are in perfect agreement. / 심판들의 의견은 ~하지 않았다 The opinions of the judges did not coincide. / 우리는 우리의 목적을 위해 ~협력하여야 한다 We must cooperate (join forces) to accomplish our purpose. / 만장 ~로 그는 대장에 선출되었다 He was elected captain by a unanimous vote. or They unanimously elected him captain. ‖ ~단결

일컫다　union; solidarity; total cooperation / ~점 a point of agreement.
일컫다 call; name.
일탈(逸脫)　~하다 deviate〔depart〕《from》／권한을 ~하다 overstep *one's* authority.
일터(근무처) *one's* place of work; 《작업장》*one's* workplace; a workshop. ∥ ~로 가다 go to work.
일파(一派) a school; a party; a faction. ∥ 김씨 ~ Kim and his followers. 「crushing defeat.
일패도지(一敗塗地) ~하다 suffer a
일편(一片) a piece; a bit; a scrap. ∥ ~의 양심도 없는 사내 a man without even a trace of conscience. ∥ ~단심 a sincere (devoted) heart.
일편(一片) a piece 《of poetry》.
일폭(一幅) a scroll 《of Oriental painting》.
일품(一品) 《벼슬의》[史] the first rank of office; 《상등품》an article of top quality; 《요리의》a dish; a course. ∥ ~요리의 one dish meal: an *à-la-carte* dish.
일품(逸品) a superb (fine) article. ∥ 전체 수집품 중의 ~ the gem of the whole collection.
일필휘지(一筆揮之) ~하다 write with one stroke of a brush.
일하다 work; labor; do *one's* work; serve 《at》(근무). ∥ 일.
일한(日限) a (fixed) date; a time limit. ∥ ~ 기한.
일할(一割) ten percent; 10%.
일행(一行) ① 《동아리》a party; a company; a troupe(배우 등의), 한씨 ~ Mr. Han and his party / ~에 끼다 join the party. ② 《한 줄》a line; a row; 《시의》a line of verse.
일화(逸話) an anecdote; an episode. ∥ 그에 대한 재미있는 ~ 가 있다 An amusing story (anecdote) is told about him. ∥ ~집 a collection of anecdotes.
일확천금(一攫千金) ~하다 make a fortune at a stroke. ∥ ~을 꿈꾸다 dream of making a fortune at a stroke. ∥ ~주의 an idea of making a fortune at a stroke; a get-rich-quick-idea.
일환(一環) a link. ∥ ~의 한 고리를 이루다 form a link in the chain of 《events》; form a part of 《the campaign》….
일회(一回) once; one time; 《한 번》a round; a game; a bout(권투의); an inning(야구의). ∥ ~주 ~ once a week. ∥ ~분 《약의》a dose / ~전 the first round 〔~말〕[野] the first 〔second〕half of the first inning.
일흔 seventy; threescore and ten.
일희일비(一喜一悲) ~하다 be glad and sad by turns; cannot put *one's* mind at ease. ∥ ~하면서 restlessly; in suspense.
읽다 ① read; 《정독하다》peruse; 《독송하다》recite; 《뜻;경문을》. ∥ 소리내어 ~ read 《a passage》out (aloud) / 몇 줄씩 건너 뛰어 ~ skip over a few lines / 한 자씩 더듬거리며 ~ spell *one's* way through 《a book》/ 대충대충 ~ run (glance) over 《a book》/ 책을 ~가 잠들다 read *oneself* to sleep / 이 잡지에는 읽을거리가 없다 This magazine has little reading matter in it. / 그가 사망한 것을 신문에서 읽었다 I read about his death in the newspaper. ② 《파악·이해하다》read; see; understand. ∥ 행간을 ~ read between the lines / 상대의 수를 ~ read the next move of the opponent / 그의 의도를 읽었다 I saw (understood) his intention. / 그는 사람의 마음을 잘 읽는다 He is good at reading other people's heart.
읽히다 《읽게 하다》get 《a person》to read; have 《a book》read 《by a person》; 《읽혀지다》be widely-read.
잃다 lose; miss. ∥ 아버지를 ~ lose (be bereaved of) *one's* father / 신용을 ~ lose *one's* credit 《with something》/ 도망칠 수 있는 기회를 ~ miss (lose) an opportunity to escape / 자동차 사고로 아들을 ~ lose *one's* son in a car accident / 수학에 흥미를 ~ lose interest in mathmatics / 그는 직장 〔재산〕을 잃었다 He lost his job (fortune). 「sweetheart.
임 《남자》a lover; 《여자》a love; a
임간(林間) ∥ ~학교 an open-air (a camping) school.
임검(臨檢) an official inspection; a search; boarding(배의). ~하다 make an inspection 《of》; (raid) and search 《a house for something》; (board) and search 《a ship》.
임계(臨界) ∥ ~의 critical. ∥ ~각 〔온도, 압력〕the critical angle (temperature, pressure).
임관(任官) an appointment; a commission (장교의). ~하다 be appointed 《to an office》; be commissioned. ∥ 소위로 ~하다 be commissioned a second lieutenant. 「-cocci.
임균(淋菌) a gonococcus 〔*pl.*
임금(군주) a king; a sovereign.
임금(賃金) wages; pay. ∥ 하루 5만원의 ~으로 일하다 work at a wage of 50,000 *won* a day / 기준 ~ the standard (basic) wages / 능률 ~ efficiency wages / 명목 〔실질〕~ nominal (real) wages / 최고〔최저〕

임기 ~ maximum (minimum) wages. ∥ ~격차 a wage differential / ~근로자(생활자) a wageworker (者); a wage earner / ~수준 a wage level (~수준을 억제하다 hold (keep) down the wage level) / ~인상 a rise (an increase) in wages / ~인하 a wage decrease (cut) / ~체계 a wage structure (system) / ~투쟁 a wage struggle.

임기(任期) *one's* term of office (service). ¶ ~를 끝내다 (채우다) serve out *one's* term / 대통령의 ~는 5년이다 The term of the President is five years.

임기응변(臨機應變) ~하다 act according to circumstances. ¶ ~의 expedient; emergency / ~으로 as the occasion demands; according to circumstances / ~의 조치를 취하다 take emergency measures; resort to a temporary expedient.

임대(賃貸) lease; letting out (on hire). ~하다 lease 〈*the land*〉; rent 〈*a house*〉; let out (on hire). ¶ 집을 여름 동안 ~하다 lease *one's* house for the summer. / ~가격 a rental value / ~료 (a) rent; charterage(선박의) / ~아파트 a rental apartment / ~인 a lessor / ~차(借) lease; letting and hiring; charter (선박의) / ~차 계약 a lease contract.

임면(任免) ~하다 appoint and dismiss. ∥ ~권 the power to appoint and dismiss.

임명(任命) appointment. ~하다 appoint 〈*a person*〉 to 〈*a post of mayor*〉; nominate 〈*a person*〉 for 〈*a position*〉. ¶ ~된 사람 an appointee; a person nominated 〈*as a chairperson*〉. ∥ ~권 the power of appointment / ~식 the ceremony of appointment.

임무(任務) a duty; a task; a mission(사명). ¶ ~를 다하다 do *one's* duties / ~(부)를 carry out *one's* task / ~를 받다 take up (on) the task; take over the duties / 특별 ~를 띠고 거기에 가다 go there on a special mission.

임박(臨迫) ~하다 draw near; be imminent; be impending. ¶ ~한 impending; imminent / 죽음이 ~하다 *one's* time is drawing near.

임부(姙婦) a pregnant woman; an expectant mother. ∥ ~복 a maternity dress.

임산물(林産物) forest products.

임산부(姙産婦) expectant and nursing mothers.

임상(臨床) ~의 clinical / ~적으로 clinically. ∥ ~강의 a clinical lecture / ~경험 clinical experience / ~실험 clinical trials (tests) / ~심리학 clinical psychology / ~의(醫) a clinician / ~의학 clinical medicine; clinics / ~일지 a physician's diary.

임석(臨席) ~하다 attend; be present 〈*at*〉. ¶ 아무의 ~하에 with *a person* in attendance. ∥ ~경관 a policeman present.

임시(臨時) ¶ ~의 temporary(일시적인); special(특별한); extraordinary (보통이 아닌) / ~로 temporarily; specially; extraordinarily / ~직 an odd (extra) job; a casual labor / ~로 고용하다 engage *a person* temporarily. ∥ ~고용자 a temporary (extra) employee / ~국회 an extraordinary session of the National Assembly / ~뉴스 a special newscast; news special / ~비 extraordinary expenses(지출); a reserve fund for contingencies(예산) / ~열차 a special train / ~예산 a provisional budget / ~정부 a provisional government / ~증간(增刊) an extra edition / ~총회 an extraordinary general meeting / ~휴교 temporary school closing; a special school holiday / ~휴업 temporary closure 〈*of a shop*〉.

임시변통(臨時變通) a makeshift; a temporary expedient. ~하다 make shift with 〈*a thing*〉; resort to a temporary expedient. ¶ ~의 방책 a stopgap measure / ~으로 이것을 쓰십시오 Use this as a makeshift. / ~으로 백만원이 필요하다 I want a million *won* for the immediate expenses.

임신(姙娠) pregnancy; conception. ~하다 become (get) pregnant; conceive. ¶ ~시키다 make 〈*a girl*〉 pregnant / 그녀는 ~하고 있다 She is pregnant. *or* She is expecting. 《口》 / 그녀는 ~ 6개월이다 She is six months pregnant. ∥ ~기간 a pregnancy period / ~중독 toxemia of pregnancy / ~중절 an abortion.

임야(林野) forests and fields.

임업(林業) forestry. ∥ ~시험장 a forestry experiment station.

임용(任用) appointment. ~하다 appoint 〈*a person*〉 to 〈*a post*〉.

임원(任員) 《회사·위원회의》 an executive 《美》; a director; (총칭) the board. ∥ ~실 an executive office / ~회 the board meeting; a board of directors.

임의(任意) option. ¶ ~의 any; optional(선택 자유의); voluntary (자발적인); arbitrary (제멋대로의) / ~의 장소 any place / 자백의 ~성 the voluntariness of *one's* confession / ~로 optionally; voluntarily; as *one* pleases / 그것

은 ~로 처분해도 괜찮다 You may do with it as you please. / 경찰관은 그녀에게 ~ 동행을 요구했다 The policeman asked her to go voluntarily to the police station with him. ‖ ~단체 a private organization neither controlled nor protected by law / ~선택 option; free choice / ~조정(調停) voluntary arbitration [mediation] / ~추출법(抽出法) [統計] random sampling / ~출석 voluntary appearance.

임자 ①《주인》 the owner; the proprietor. ¶ ~없는 ownerless; (a dog) belonging to nobody. ②《임자님》 you; honey.
임전(臨戰) ~하다 go into action. ‖ ~태세 (a state of) preparedness for war (~태세를 갖추다 be ready [prepared] for war).
임정(臨政) ☞ 임시정부(臨時政府). ‖ ~요인 key figures of the provisional government.
임종(臨終) ①《죽을 때》 one's dying hour; one's last moments; one's deathbed. ¶ ~의 말 one's last [dying] words / 그에게 이제 ~이 다가오고 있다 His end [time] is near. / ~입니다 He [She] is now in his [her] last moments. ②《임종시의 배석》 ~하다 be with [wait upon] one's parent's death. ¶ 나는 아버지 ~에 늦지 않기를 간절히 바랬다 I ardently wished to be in time for the death of my father.
임지(任地) one's post; one's place of duty. ¶ ~로 떠나다 go to [set out for] one's new post.
임질(淋疾) [醫] gonorrhea. ¶ ~에 걸리다 suffer from gonorrhea.
임차(賃借)《부동산의》 lease; 《차·말 등의》 hire; hiring. ~하다 lease (land); rent (a house). ‖ ~료 rent; hire / ~인 a leaseholder; a tenant(토지·가옥의); a hirer(차·수레 따위의).
임파(淋巴) [解] lymph. ‖ ~선(염) (the inflammation of the lymphatic gland / ~액 lymph.
임하다(臨─) ①《마주 서다》 face (on); front (on); look down (upon). ¶ 바다에 임한 집 a house facing [fronting] the sea. ②《당하다》 meet; face (a problem); be confronted (by). ¶ 죽음에 임하여 on one's deathbed / 우리는 단결해서 이 난국에 임해야 한다 We have to face this difficult situation in a body. ③《임석하다》 attend (a meeting); be present at (a ceremony). ④《담당하다》 undertake; take charge of (something). ¶ 변호의 ~ take charge of (a person's) defense / 그 교섭에 ~ take [have] charge of conducting the negotiations.
임학(林學) forestry. ‖ ~자 a dendrologist; a forestry expert.
임해(臨海) ¶ ~의 seaside; coastal; marine / 《도시의》 ~지역 a waterfront. ‖ ~공업지대 a coastal industrial zone [region] / ~도시 a coastal city / ~생물연구소 a marine biological laboratory / ~학교 a seaside school / ~행락지 a seaside resort.
입 ①《사람·동물 등의》 the mouth. ¶ ~이 큰 big-mouthed / 한 ~ 먹다 take [have] a bite of (sandwiches) / ~을 크게 벌리다 open one's mouth wide / ~에서 냄새가 나다 have foul [bad] breath / ~을 다물다 shut one's mouth / 소문이 ~에서 ~으로 전해졌다 The rumor passed from mouth to mouth. / 나는 놀라 ~이 딱 벌어졌다 I was open-mouthed with surprise. ②《말》 speech; words; tongue. ¶ ~이 가볍다 be talkative / ~이 무겁다(뜨다, 걸다) be close-mouthed [slow of speech, foul-mouthed] / ~을 조심하다 be careful of one's speech / ~을 모아 말하다 say in chorus [unison] / ~을 열다 break the silence; utter; disclose / ~을 다물다 stop talking / ~ 밖에 내다 talk [speak] of; mention; reveal; disclose / 남의 ~에 오르다 be gossiped about; be in everyone's mouth. ③《미각》 one's taste; one's palate. ¶ ~에 맞다 be to one's taste / 이 요리는 내 ~에 안 맞는다 This food is not to my liking (taste). ④《부리》 a bill (넓적한); a beak (갈고리 모양의). ⑤《식구》 a mouth to feed; a dependent.
입가 the mouth; lips(입술). ¶ ~에 미소를 띄우고 with a smile about one's mouth [lips].
입가심 ~하다 take away the aftertaste; kill the (bitter) taste / ~으로 take the nasty taste out of one's mouth; to cleanse [refresh] one's palate.
입각(入閣) ~하다 enter [join] the Cabinet.
입각(立脚) ~하다 be based [founded] on; take one's ground on. ¶ 사실에 ~하다 be based on facts.
입감(入監) imprisonment. ¶ ~ 중이다 be in jail [prison].
입거(入渠) ~하다 go into [enter] dock. ‖ ~료(料) dockage.
입건(立件) ~하다 book (a person) on charge (of); 《형사》 ~되다 be criminally booked (on a charge of...). ┌enter the capital.
입경(入京) ~하다 arrive in Seoul;

입고(入庫) warehousing 《*of goods*》; 《차의》 entering the car shed. ~하다 deposit 《*a thing*》 in a warehouse; store; be stocked; 《차의》 enter the car shed.

입관(入棺) 《시체를》 encoffinment. ~하다 place 《*a person's body*》 in a coffin. ‖ ~식 a rite of placing the dead body in the coffin.

입교(入校) entrance [admission] into a school. ☞ 입학.

입교(入敎) ~하다 enter the church [a religious life]; become a (*Christian*) believer.

입구(入口) an entrance; a way in; a doorway. ¶ ~에서 a the entrance [door] / 터널 ~ a tunnel entrance / ~를 막다 block the entrance / 공원 ~에서 너를 기다리겠다 We'll wait for you at the park gate.

입국(入國) entry [entrance] into a country. ~하다 enter into a country; immigrate into a country(이민이). ¶ ~이 허가되다 be admitted into the country / ~을 거절당하다 be denied [refused] entry into the country / 불법 ~ illegal [unlawful] entry / 그는 그 나라에 불법 ~ 했다 He entered the country illegally. ‖ ~관리국 the immigration bureau / ~사증 an entry visa / ~절차 entry formalities / ~허가서 an entry permit.

입궐(入闕) ~하다 proceed [go] to the Royal Court.

입금(入金) 《수령》 receipt of money; 《수령금》 money received [paid in]; receipts; 《받을 돈》 money due. ~하다 receive 《*money*》; pay in part. ¶ 그 돈은 7월 20일까지 ~해야 한다 The payment is due on July 20. ‖ ~전표 a receipt [paying-in] slip / ~통지서 a credit advice.

입길 gossip. ¶ 남의 ~에 오르내리다 be talked about by others; be on everybody's lips.

입김 the steam of breath. ¶ ~이 세다 breathe hard; 《비유적》 be influential 《*with*》; have a big influence 《*in*》.

입내 ① 《구취》 mouth odor; (the smell of) *one's* breath. ② 《남의 흉내》 mimicry. ¶ ~를 내다 mimic another; imitate another's way of speaking. ‖ ~쟁이 a mimic.

입다 ① 《옷을》 put on; slip into 《*a gown*》 《입는 행위》; wear; have on; be dressed 《*in white*》 《입고 있는 상태》. ¶ 멋진 옷을 입고 있다 be finely dressed / 옷을 입은 채로 자다 sleep in *one's* clothes / 코트를 입어보다 try a coat on / 그녀는 빨간 스웨터를 입고 있다 She is wearing a red sweater. ② 《은혜 등을》 receive 《*a person's*》 favors; receive. ¶ 은혜를 ~ receive favors [kindness]; enjoy 《*a person's*》 patronage / 나는 그녀에게 큰 은혜를 입었다 I'm greatly indebted to her. ③ 《손해 등을》 suffer; have; get; sustain. ¶ 상처를 ~ get injured /손해를 ~ sustain [suffer, have] a loss; be damaged. ④ 《거상을》 ~상을 ~ be in [go into] mourning 《*for a person*》.

입단(入團) ~하다 join 《*the Giants*》; enter; enroll in 《*the Boy Scouts*》.

입담 skill at talking; volubility. ¶ ~이 좋다 be good at talking; be a glib talker.

입당(入黨) joining a political party. ~하다 join a (political) party.

입대(入隊) enrollment; enlistment. ~하다 join [enlist in] the army; be drafted into the army(징집되어). ‖ ~자 a recruit.

입덧 (have) morning sickness.

입도(立稻) ~선매(先賣) selling rice before the harvest.

입동(立冬) "onset of winter"; the first day [the beginning] of winter.

입뜨다 (be) taciturn; reticent; be slow to speak. ¶ 입뜬 사람 a man of few words.

입맛 an appetite 《식욕》; *one's* taste 《구미》. ¶ ~이 있다(없다) have a good(poor) appetite / ~을 돋우다 stimulate 《*one's*》 appetite / ~에 맞다 suit *one's* taste.

입맛다시다 《음식에 대해》 smack [lick] *one's* lips; 《낙치하여》 click *one's* tongue. ¶ 입맛다시며 수프를 먹다 eat soup with relish [gusto] / 아무의 짓이 못마땅해 ~ click *one's* tongue at 《*a person's*》 behavior.

입맛쓰다 taste bitter; have a bitter taste; (be) unpleasant [disgusting]; feel wretched [miserable]. ¶ 낙제해서 입맛이 쓰다 feel miserable for failing the examination / 입맛이 쓴 얼굴을 하다 make a sour face.

입맞추다 kiss 《*a person on the cheek*》; give 《*a person*》 a kiss.

입매 ① 《식사》 ~하다 eat [take] a dab of food. ② 《눈가림》 ~하다 do a slapdash job.

입멸(入滅) entering Nirvana; the death of Buddha. ~하다 enter Nirvana; die. 「tree.

입목(立木) a standing [growing]

입문(入門) ① 《제자가 됨》 ~하다 enter a school; become a disciple [pupil] 《*of*》. ② 《입문서》 a guide [an introduction] 《*to*》; a primer 《*of*》. ‖ 문학 ~ an intro-

입바르다 (be) straightforward; outspoken; plainspoken. ¶ 입바른 소리 plain speaking; a straight talk / 입바른 소리를 하다 speak plainly; call a spade a spade.

입방(立方) 【數】 cube. ¶ 1~미터 a cubic meter / 2미터 ~ 2 meters cube / 용적은 10~센티미터이다 This box is 10 cubic sentimeters in volume. ‖ ~체 a cube.

입방아 ¶ ~찧다 (말이 많다) be talkative over trifles; chatter (gossip) 《about》; (잔소리하다) nag 《at》; cavil 《at, about》 / 사람들의 ~에 오르다 be talked about by people / 그녀는 ~를 찧어 남편을 못살게 군다 She nags her husband half to death.

입버릇 a way (habit) of talking (말버릇); one's favorite phrase (상투어). ¶ ~처럼 말하다 always say; keep saying; be never tired of saying /「열심히 공부해라」라는 것이 어머니의 ~이다 My mother's favorite phrase is "Study hard."

입법(立法) legislation. ~하다 legislate; pass a new law. ¶ ~ 정신 the spirit of legislation / …을 규제하는 ~조치를 취하다 legislate against…. ‖ ~권 legislative power / ~기관 a legislative organ / ~부 the legislature / ~자 a legislator.

입사(入社) ~하다 enter (join) a company. ¶ 무역회사에 ~하고 싶다 I would like to join a trading company. ‖ ~시험 an entrance (employment) examination 《for, of》.

입사(入射) 【理】 incidence. ¶ ~의 incident. ‖ ~각 an angle of incidence / ~광선 an incident ray.

입산(入山) 【佛】 retiring to a mountain to enter the priesthood. ~하다 become a Buddhist monk; enter the priesthood.

입상(入賞) winning a prize. ~하다 win (receive) a prize; gain a place 《in a contest》. ‖ ~자 a prize winner. (소영의).

입상(立像) a statue; a statuette
입상(粒狀) ¶ ~의 granular 《starch》; granulous 《sugar》.

입선(入選) ~하다 be accepted (selected) 《for an exhibition》. ‖ ~자 a winner, a winning competitor / ~작 a winning work.

입성(옷) clothes; a dress. ‖ 옷.
입성(入城) ~하다 make a triumphant entry into a fortress (city).
입소(入所) ~하다 enter (be admitted to) 《an institution》; (교도소에) be put into (sent to) prison (jail); be imprisoned.

입수(入手) acquisition. ~하다 come by; get; obtain; receive; procure; come to hand (사물이 주어). ¶ ~하기 어렵다 be hard to obtain.

입술 a lip. ¶ 윗 (아랫) ~ the upper (lower) lip / ~을 깨물다 bite one's lips / ~을 오므리다 purse (up) one's lips / ~을 삐죽 내밀다 pout (out) one's lips / ~을 훔치다 steal a kiss 《from》.

입시(入試) ☞ 입학시험.
입신(立身) ~양명 (출세) a rise in the world; success in life / ~하다 succeed in life / ~출세주의 the cult of success; careerism / ~출세주의자 a (single-minded) careerist.

입심 boldness in words; eloquence. ¶ ~이 좋다 be bold in words; eloquent.

입씨름 a quarrel; a wrangle. ~하다 quarrel; wrangle.

입씻김《입씻이》 pay a person's silence; pay hush-money; put a gold muzzle 《on》.

입씻이 ① (금품) hush money; a gold muzzle. ¶ ~로 그에게 5만원을 주다 give him 50,000 won to keep his mouth shut. ② ~ 입가심.

입아귀 the corner(s) of the mouth.
입안(立案) planning. ~하다 form (make, draw up, map out) a plan. ‖ ~자 a planner.

입양(入養) adoption. ~하다 (양자로 하다) adopt 《a son》; (양자가 되다) be adopted 《into a family》. ¶ 아들을 ~아로 주다 give one's child to 《a person》 as an adopted son.

입어(入漁) ‖ ~권 an entrance right to a piscary / ~료 charges for fishing in another's piscary; a fishing fee.

입영(入營) ~하다 join the army; enlist in (enter) the army.

입욕(入浴) bathing; a bath. ~하다 take (have) a bath; bathe. ¶ ~시키다 give 《a baby》 a bath; bathe 《a baby》.

입원(入院) hospitalization. ~하다 be hospitalized; be sent (taken) to hospital. ¶ ~중이다 be in the hospital / ~시키다 have (get) 《a person》 admitted to hospital (가족이); admit 《a person》 to hospital (의사가). ‖ ~병동 an inpatients' ward / ~비 hospital charges / ~수속 hospitalization procedures / ~환자 an inpatient.

입자(粒子) 【理】 a particle.
입장(入場) entrance; admission; admittance. ~하다 enter; get in; be admitted 《to, into》. ‖ ~권

입장(入場) an admission [a platform (역의)] ticket; ~권매표소 a ticket office (美); a booking office (英); ~금지 [사절] [게시] No Entrance / ~료 an admission fee [charge] / ~식 an opening ceremony / ~자 a visitor; an attendance (총칭) / ~무료 [게시] Admission Free.

입장(立場) [처지] a position; a situation; a standpoint; a point of view; [자기의 위치·장소] one's ground; [사물을 보는 각도] an angle. ¶ 피로운 ~에 있다 be in a painful position / 자기 ~을 밝히다 make one's position clear / 남의 ~이 되어 생각하다 put [place] oneself in another's place / 다른 ~에서 보다 look at (something) from a different standpoint [angle] / 나는 명령을 내릴 ~이 아니다 I am not in a position to issue orders.

입장단(一長短) ¶ ~을 치다 hum [sing] the rhythm.

입적(入寂) ☞ 입멸.

입적(入籍) official registration as a family member. ~하다 have one's name entered in the family register.

입전(入電) a telegram received.

입정(入廷) ~하다 enter [appear in] the courtroom.

입정놀리다 keep one's mouth busy; eat incessantly between meals.

입정사납다 ① [입이 걸다] (be) foul-mouthed; abusive; foul-[evil-]tongued. ② [탐식하다] (be) greedy [ravenous] (for food).

입주(入住) ~하다 move into (an apartment); live in (one's master's house). ‖ ~가정부 a resident maid / ~자 a tenant; an occupant / ~점원 a living-in [resident] clerk.

입증(立證) proof. ~하다 prove; verify; give proof; testify. ¶ 무죄를 ~하다 prove [establish] one's innocence / 이 사실은 그의 무죄를 ~한다 This fact testifies to his innocence.

입지(立地) location. ~하다 be located. ‖ ~조건 conditions of location (~조건이 좋다 [나쁘다] be favorably [unfavorably] situated).

입지(立志) ¶ ~전 a story of one's aim in life. ‖ ~전 a story of a man who achieved success in life; a success story / ~전적인 인물 a self-made man).

입직(入直) one's turn in office. ~하다 take one's turn in office; be on night duty.

입질(낚시에서) a bite; a strike. ~하다 bite; take a bait. ¶ ~을 느끼다 have [feel] a bite.

입짧다 [서숙적] have a small appetite; eat like a bird.

**입찬말 tall (big) talk; a brag.

입찰(入札) a bid; a tender. ~하다 bid [tender] (for); make a bid (for). ¶ ~로 by bid [tender] / ~에 부치다 sell (articles) by tender; put (something) out to tender / ~을 공모하다 invite tenders (for) / 도로 공사의 ~이 행해졌다 Bids were invited for the construction of the road. / ~가격 a bidding price; the price tendered / ~보증금 a bid bond / ~보증금 a security for a bid / ~일 the day of bidding / ~자 a bidder; a tenderer / 경쟁(지명) ~ a public [private] tender / 일반 ~ an open tender.

입천장(一天障) the palate.

입체(立體) a solid (body). ¶ ~적 solid; cubic / ~적으로 고찰하다 consider (something) from many angles. ‖ ~감 a cubic effect; three-dimensional effect / ~교차 (도로의) a two-[multi-]level crossing; a crossing with an overpass or underpass; an overhead crossing / ~기하학 solid geometry / ~방송 a stereophonic broadcast / ~사진 a stereoscopic photograph / ~영화 a three-dimensional [3-D] movie [film] / ~음악 stereophonic music / ~음향 (a) stereophonic sound / ~음향 재생 stereophonic reproduction / ~작전 combined operations (英) / ~전 a three dimensional warfare / ~주차장 a multi-story parking garage / ~파 [美術] cubism; a cubist(화가).

입초(入超) the excess of imports.

입초(立哨) standing watch; sentry duty. ¶ ~서다 stand watch [guard]. ‖ ~병 a sentry.

입추(入秋) the first day [the beginning] of autumn.

입추(立錐) ¶ ~의 여지도 없다 be closely packed; be filled to capacity.

입춘(立春) the first day [the beginning] of spring.

입하(入荷) arrival [receipt] of goods. ~하다 arrive; be received. ¶ 신선한 과일이 ~됐다 Fresh fruits have arrived.

입하(立夏) the first day [the beginning] of summer.

입학(入學) entrance [admission] into a school; matriculation(대학에의). ~하다 enter [be admitted to] a school; go to a university [college]. ¶ ~을 지원하다 apply for admission to a school / 그는 Y대학 ~을 원한다 He wants to get into Y University. ‖ ~금 an

입항 entrance fee / ~수속 entrance formalities / ~시험 an entrance examination / ~식 an entrance ceremony / ~원서 an application (form) / ~자격 qualifications (requirement) for admission / ~지원자 an applicant (for admission).

입항(入港) arrival 《*of a ship*》 in port. ~하다 enter (put into) port; arrive in (a) port; make port. ¶ ~해 있다 be in port (harbor) / 배는 내일 오후 2시, 부산에 ~예정이다 The ship is due at Pusan at 2 p.m. tomorrow. ∥ ~세(稅) port (harbor) dues / ~신고 an entrance notice / ~예정일 the expected time of arrival / ~절차 clearance inwards.

입향순속(入鄕循俗) When you are in Rome, do as the Romans do.

입헌(立憲) ¶ ~ constitutional. ∥ ~군주국 a constitutional monarchy / ~민주정치 constitutional democracy / ~정체 constitutional polity / ~정치 constitutional government.

입회(入會) admission; joining; entrance. ~하다 join(enter) 《*a club*》; become a member 《*of*》. ¶ ~를 신청하다 apply for membership. ∥ ~금 an entrance fee / ~신청자 an applicant for membership / ~자 a new member.

입회(立會) ☞ 참여.

입후보(立候補) candidacy. ~하다 stand (come forward) as a candidate for 《*the Mayoralty*》; run for 《*the Presidency*》《*美*》; stand for 《*Parliament*》《*英*》. ¶ ~를 신청하다 file *one's* candidacy 《*for*》 / 그는 내년 선거에 서울에서 ~할 것이다 He will run for the next year's election in Seoul. ∥ ~(예정)자 a (potential) candidate 《*for*》.

입히다 ① 《옷을》 dress; clothe; put on. ¶ 아이에게 옷을 ~ dress a child / 코트를 입혀 주다 help 《*a person*》 into his coat. ② 《겉면에》 plate; coat; cover. ¶ 금을 입힌 숟가락 a spoon plated with gold / 구리에 은을 ~ coat (plate) copper with silver / 무덤에 떼를 ~ cover a grave with sod. ③ 《손해를》 inflict 《*damage*》 upon; cause 《*damage*》 to; do 《*harm*》. ¶ 아무에게 손해를 ~ inflict losses upon a person.

잇다 ① 《연결》 connect; join; link. ¶ 줄을 ~ link strings together. ② 《계승》 succeed; succeed (come) to 《*the throne*》; inherit 《*the property*》. ¶ 가업을 ~ succeed to the family business. ③ 《목숨을》 maintain (sustain, preserve) 《*life*》. ¶

빵과 물로 목숨을 이어가다 sustain *oneself* on bread and water.

잇달다 ① ☞ 잇대다. ② 《연달다》 잇달아 one after another; in succession / 잇달은 승리 consecutive victories / 관광객이 잇달아 도착했다 Tourists arrived one after another. / 여러 사건이 잇달아 일어났다 Several incidents happened in succession.

잇닿다 border 《*on*》; adjoin; be adjacent (next) to. ¶ 이웃집과 잇닿은 빈 터 vacant land adjacent to the house next door.

잇대다 《이어대다》 connect; join; link; put together. ¶ 두 가닥의 코드선을 ~ join two cords together / 두 책상을 ~ put two desks (together).

잇몸 the gum(s). ∥ together.

잇속 《이의 생긴 모양》 ~이 고르다 〔고르지 않다〕 have regular 〔irregular〕 teeth; *one's* teeth are even 〔uneven〕.

잇속(利~) substantial gain 〔profit〕; self-interest. ¶ ~이 밝다 have a quick eye for gain.

잇자국 a tooth mark; a bite.

있다 ① 《존재하다》 there is (are); be; exist. ¶ 세상에는 이상한 일들이 많이 ~ There are a lot of strange things in the world. / 있는 것이 없는것보다(는) 낫다 Something is better than nothing. ② 《위치하다》 be; be situated 〔located 《*美*》〕; stand; lie; run 〔길, 강이〕. ¶ 한국은 중국의 동쪽에 ~ Korea lies to the east of China. / 우리 집 뒤에는 개울이 ~ A stream runs 〔flows〕 behind my house. ③ 《소유하다》 have; possess 〔능력·특성이〕; own 〔재산이〕. ¶ 음악의 재능이 ~ have 〔possess〕 a gift of music / 막대한 재산이 ~ have 〔own〕 a vast fortune / 그 집에는 넓은 정원이 ~ The house has a large garden. ④ 《설비되어 있다》 be equipped 〔fitted, provided〕 《*with*》. ¶ 그 집에는 목욕탕이 ~ The house is provided with a bathroom. ⑤ 《내재되어 있다》 lie in; consist in. ¶ 이 작품의 매력은 이 점에 ~ The charm of this work lies 〔exists〕 in this point. / 행복은 만족에 ~ Happiness lies in contentment. / 잘못은 나에게 ~ The fault rests with me. ⑥ 《경험이 있다》 ¶ 거기 가 본 일이 있느냐 Have you ever been there? ⑦ 《발생하다》 happen; take place; occur. ¶ 무슨 일이 있어도 whatever happens; come what may / 어젯밤에 지진이 있었다 We had 〔There was〕 an earthquake last night. ⑧ 《행해지다》 be held; take place. ¶ 경기는 언제 있느냐 When will the game be held 〔take place〕? / 그 시험은 3월에

~ We have the examination in March. ⑨ 《유복하다》 (be) rich; wealthy. ¶ 있는 사람 a well-off person / 그는 집에 태어나다 be born rich. ⑩ 《행위의 완료·상태의 계속》 ¶ 그 건은 이미 신고되어 ~ We have already reported the matter. ⑪ 《기타》 ¶ 소나무는 한국 어디에서나 볼 수 ~ Pine trees are found everywhere in Korea. / 그는 은행장으로 ~ He is in office as the president of the bank.

잉걸불 a burning charcoal; embers.
잉꼬 [鳥] a macaw.
잉어 [魚] a carp *sing*. & *pl*.].
잉여 (剩餘) (a) surplus; the remainder; a balance. ‖ ~ 가치(설) (the theory of) surplus value / ~금 a surplus (fund).
잉카 Inca. ‖ ~ 문명 the Incan Civilization / ~족 the Incas.
잉크 (write in) ink. ¶ ~ 병 an ink bottle / ~ 스탠드 an inkstand.
임태 (孕胎) ☞ 임신 (姙娠).
잊다 ① 《무의식적으로》 forget; be forgetful of; 《사물이 주어》 slip *one's* mind [memory]. ¶ 잊을 수 없는 unforgettable; memorable; lasting / 그것은 잊을 수 없는 사건이었다 It was a memorable event. ② 《의식적으로》 dismiss (*a thing*) from *one's* mind; think no more of; put (*a thing*) out of *one's* mind. ¶ 슬픔을 ~ get over *one's* grief / ~로 술을 ~ drown *one's* sorrows in drink. ③ 《놓고 오다》 leave (*a thing*) behind; 《안가져오다》 forget to bring [take] (*a thing*).
잊히다 be forgotten; pass out of mind (*one's* memory). ¶ 그 스캔들은 곧 잊혀졌다 The scandal blew over quickly.
잎 ① a leaf(활엽); a blade(풀잎); a needle(침엽); foliage(총칭). ¶ ~이 나오다 the leaves come out; 《나무가 주어》 come into leaf / ~이 지다 the leaves fall; 《나무가 주어》 be stripped of leaves. ② 《단위》 a piece 《*of brass coin*》.
잎나무 brushwood.
잎담배 leaf tobacco.
잎사귀 a leaf; 《작은》 a leaflet.

해외 여행

국내 공항을 출발하여 외국에 입국할 때까지 사용되는 필요한 낱말들을 순서대로 아래에 열거하였다.

1. **출발전 기본 준비 사항**
   가장 중요한 것은 여권(a passport)이다. 나라에 따라 예방접종 증명서(a vaccination certificate; a yellow card)를 필요로 하는 곳도 있다. 돈은 대개 여행자수표(a traveler's check)로 준비한다.

2. **비행기 탑승 수속**
   공항내 출발 라운지(a departure lounge)에 있는 항공회사(an airline company) 카운터에서 수하물(baggage; luggage)을 맡기고 영수증(a claim bag) 을 받는다. 여권(a passport), 항공권(an air ticket), 출입국카드(an E/D card)를 제시하고, 탑승권(a boarding card [pass]; a flight coupon)을 받는다. 여기서 좌석 배당(a seat assignment)이 이행해진다. 좌석은 퍼스트 클래스(first class), 이코노미 클래스(economy class)로 나뉘며, 통로측 좌석(an aisle seat), 창문가 좌석(a window seat) 등으로 분류된다.

3. **출국수속(embarkation procedure)**
   (1) 세관(Customs) — 고가의 외국 제품을 휴대하고 출국할 때는 휴대출국 증명 신청서(a customs declaration form)를 함께 제시한다.
   (2) 출국심사(Emigration; passport control) — 여권, 출입국 카드, 탑승권을 제시하고 여권에 출국 스탬프를 받는다.
   (3) 검역(Quarantine) — 출국 목적지에 따라 예방접종 증명서(a yellow card)가 필요하다.
   (4) 수하물 검사 — 비행기 납치(hijack)사고 방지를 위한 기내 반입 수하물(hand-carry baggage)의 검사를 한다. 본인은 위험물 검사 통로(a walk-through gate)를 통과하게 된다.
   (5) 탑승(boarding) — 탑승대합실(a waiting lounge)에서 출발시간까지 기다린다. 그동안 면세품점(a tax-free shop)에서 선물 따위를 살 수 있다.

4. **입국지(the port of entry)에 도착** — 입국심사(Immigration)를 받기 위해 여권, 입국카드를 제시한다. 이때 입국 심사관(an immigration officer)은 예정 체류 기간(intended length of stay)에 관해, How long are you going to stay in the United Sates?(미국에서의 체류 기간은?)이라든가 Are you on sightseeing or business? (관광입니까, 상용입니까?) 등을 질문을 하게 된다. 이때는 Two weeks. 또는 Sightseeing. or Business. 라고 간단히 대답한다. 수하물은 턴테이블(a turntable; a carrousel)에서 빙빙 돌고 있는데 거기서 자기 것을 찾아 검사대를 통과한 후 도착로비(an arrival lounge)로 나온다.

자 ① 《단위》 a cha(=30.3cm). ¶ 이 옷감은 꼭 다섯 ~다 This cloth measures five cha exactly. ② 《계기》 a (measuring) rule (rod, stick); a ruler. ¶ ~로 재다 measure with a rule / 삼각 ~ a set square; a triangle / T~ a T-square. ③ 《척도·표준》 a yardstick 《for》; a standard.
자(子) ① 《民俗》 《십이지의》 the Rat. ② 《자식》 a son; a child.
자(字) ① 《글자》 《이름》 a pseudonym; a pen name.
자(者) 《사람》 a person; one; a fellow. ¶ 김이라는 ~ a man called Kim.
자 《감탄사》 there; here; come (now); now (then); well (now). ¶ ~, 빨리 가십시다 Now, let us hurry. / ~, 드시지요 Help yourself, please.
…자¹ 《…하자 곧》 as soon as; no sooner than; when; at. ¶집에 들어가~ (마자) on entering the house / 소식을 듣~ at the news 《of》.
…자² 《권유형 어미》 let (us); let's. ¶이젠 가~ Come, let's go! / 이제 먹~ Let's eat now.
자가(自家) 《집》 one's (own) house (family). ¶ ~용의 for private use; for domestic (family) use; personal / ~용 자동차 a private car; an owner-driven car / 이것은 ~제 포도주다 This is homemade wine. ‖ ~당착 self-contradiction 《~당착하다 contradict *oneself*》 / ~발전시설 (장치) an independent electric power plant / ~수정 《生》 self-fertilization / ~중독 《醫》 autointoxication.
자각(自覺) (self-)consciousness; awakening; (self-)awareness. ~하다 be conscious 《awake》 《of》; awaken 《to》; realize (깨닫다). ¶자신의 입장을 ~하라 Realize your situation. ‖ ~증상 a subjective symptom 《~증상이 없다 have no subjective symptoms of 《*one's disease*》.
자갈 gravel; pebbles. ¶도로에 ~을 깔다 gravel a road / ~을 깐 도로 a graveled road. ‖ ~밭 an open field covered with gravels / ~야적장 a gravel yard / ~채취 gravel digging / ~채취장 a gravel pit.
자갈색(紫褐色) purplish brown.
자개 mother-of-pearl; nacre. ¶ ~를 박다 inlay 《*a wardrobe*》 with mother-of-pearl. ☞ 나전세공.
자객(刺客) an assassin; a killer. ¶ ~의 손에 쓰러지다 be assassinated; fall (a) victim to an assassin.
자격(資格) qualification; capacity; competency (능력); a requirement(필요조건). ¶ ~이 있다 have qualification 《*as, to do*》 / 《능력이 있다》 be competent 《*as, to do*》 / 《권리가 있다》 have a right 《*to*》 / ~을 주다 give 《*a person*》 the qualification 《*to do, as, for*》; qualify 《*a person*》 《*to do, as, for*》 / ~을 잃다 be disqualified 《*from serving on the committee*》 / 그는 교원 ~증을 땄다 He obtained a teacher's license. or He was qualified as a teacher. / 입학 ~ entrance requirements; requirements for admission / 유-[무]~자 a qualified (an unqualified) person. ‖ ~검정시험 a qualifying examination / ~상실 disqualification / ~심사 screening (test) / ~증 a certificate of qualification.
자격지심(自激之心) a guilty conscience; a feeling of self-accusation.
자결(自決) ① 《자기결정》 self-determination. ~하다 determine by *oneself*. ¶민족 ~ racial self-determination. ② ☞ 자살.
자경단(自警團) a vigilante group (corps). ¶ ~원 a vigilante.
자고로(自古—) from old (ancient) times.
자구(字句) words and phrases; terms; wording; expressions(표현); the letter(문면). ¶ ~에 구애되다 adhere to the letter / ~를 수정하다 make some change in the wording.
자국 a mark; traces; an impression; a track (trail); a stain (더럼). ¶긁힌 ~ a scratch / 모기에 물린 ~ a mosquito bite / 손가락 ~ a finger mark / ~이 나다 get marked; leave a mark 《*on, in*》 / ~을 남기다 leave *one's* traces behind *one*.
자국(自國) one's (own) country; one's native land(본국). ‖ ~민 one's fellow countrymen / ~어 one's native language; one's mother tongue.
자궁(子宮) 〖解〗 the womb; 〖解〗 the uterus. ¶ ~의 uterine. ‖ ~증

자귀 (a) uterine disease / ~외임신 extrauterine (ectopic) pregnancy / ~암 uterine cancer.
자귀 《연장》 an adz.
자귀나무 《植》 a silk tree.
자그마치 ① 《적게》 a little; a few; some. ¶ ~ 술을 마셔라 Don't drink too much. ② 《반어적》 not a little; as much [many] as. ¶ ~ 만원이나 손해다 The loss is as much as 10,000 *won*.
자그마하다 (be) smallish; be of a somewhat small size(서술적).
자극(刺戟) a stimulus; an impulse; a spur; an incentive. ~하다 stimulate *(the appetite)*; excite *(one's curiosity)*; spur up; irritate *(the skin)*. ¶ ~적인 stimulative; *(맛·향기가)* pungent(맛·향기가); sensational(선정적인) ∥ ~성 음료 stimulating drink / ~ 이 없는 생활 a dull life / 아무의 신경을 ~하다 get on *a person's* nerves. ∥ ~제 a stimulant.
자극(磁極) 《理》 a magnetic pole.
자금(資金) funds; capital(자본금); a fund(기금). ¶ ~ 이 충분하다 be well funded / ~ 이 부족하다 be short of funds / ~ 을 대다 provide [furnish] funds for; fund *(a project)* / ~ 을 모으다 (조달하다) raise funds *(for)* / 운동 [정치] ~ campaign [political] funds / 운영 [준비] ~ operating [reserve] funds. ∥ ~난 a financial difficulty; lack of funds / ~부족 shortage of funds / ~운용 financing / ~원 a source of funds [money].

자급(自給) self-support. ~하다 support [provide for] *oneself*. ¶ 한국은 식량 ~ 이 되도록 노력해야 한다 Korea should try to become self-sufficient in food production. ∥ ~를 (the degree of) self-sufficiency *(in oil)* / ~자족 self-sufficiency / ~자족하다 be self-sufficient *(in)*.
자긍(自矜) self-praise; 《자부》 self-conceit.
자기(自己) self; ego. ¶ ~의 *one's* own; personal; private / ~를 알다 know *oneself* 우리는 ~를 반성할 필요가 있다 It is necessary to reflect on ourselves. ¶ 그녀는 ~ 과시욕이 강하다 She likes to show off. / 교통비는 ~부담으로 하자 Let's pay *one's* own carfare. ∥ ~기만 self-deception / ~도취 narcissism; self-absorption / ~만족 self-satisfaction / ~모순 self-contradiction / ~방위 self-defense / ~변호 self-justification; an excuse / ~본위(주의) egoism / ~분석 self-analysis / ~비판 self-criticism / ~비평 self-criticize *oneself* / ~선전 self-display; self-advertisement / ~소개 self-introduction / ~소개하다 introduce *oneself* / ~소외 self-alienation / ~암시 autosuggestion / ~의식 a sense of self; self-identification / ~자금 *one's* own money / ~자본 *one's* own owned capital / ~주장 self-assertion / ~주장이 강하다 be very self-assertive / ~중심 self-centeredness / ~중심주의 egocentrism / ~최면 autohypnotism; self-hypnosis / ~최면에 걸린 self-hypnotized / ~혐오 self-hatred; self-hate / ~희생 self-sacrifice.
자기(自記) ~의 self-registering [-recording] *(thermometer)*.
자기(磁氣) magnetism. ¶ ~를 띤, ~의 magnetic / ~를 띠게 하다 magnetize; make a magnet of. ∥ ~감응 (유도) magnetic induction / ~권 the magnetosphere / ~부상열차 a maglev train (◀ magnetically-levitated train) / ~장 a magnetic field / ~저항 (magnetic) reluctance / ~측정 magnetometry / ~테이프 a magnetic tape / ~폭풍 a magnetic storm / ~학 magnetics.
자기(瓷器) porcelain; china(ware); ceramics.
자꾸 《여러 번》 very often; frequently; 《끊임없이》 incessantly; constantly; 《몹시》 eagerly; earnestly; strongly.
자나깨나 waking or sleeping; awake or asleep. ¶ ~ 그것이 마음에 걸린다 Waking or sleeping, it's on my mind.
자낭(子囊) 《植》 an ascus. ∥ ~균 a sac fungus.
자네 you.
자녀(子女) 《아들딸》 children; sons and daughters.
자다 ① 《잠을》 sleep; 《잠들다》 get [go] to sleep; 《잠자리에 들다》 go to bed. 《잘(잘못)》 ~ have a good [bad] sleep / 너무 ~ oversleep / 이제 자야 할 시간이다 It's (about) time for bed. / 잘 자거라 Good night! / Sweet dreams! ② 《결이》 get pressed [smoothed] down; take a set. ¶ 머리가 ~ *one's* hair sets nicely. ③ 《가라앉다》 go (die, calm) down; subside. ¶ 바람이 잤다 The wind died down. ④ 《시계가》 stop; run down.
자단(紫檀) a red sandalwood.
자당(慈堂) your esteemed mother.
자동(自動) automatic action (motion, operation). ¶ ~ (식)의 automatic / ~적으로 automatically / 이 문은 ~적으로 개폐된다 This door opens and closes automatically [by itself]. ∥ ~문 an automatic door / ~번역기 an electronic

자동사 / 617 / 자르다

translator / ~변속장치 an automatic transmission / ~성에제거장치냉장고 a frost-free refrigerator / ~소총 an automatic rifle / ~유도장치 a homing device / ~장치 an automation / ~전화 an automatic telephone / ~점화기 an automatic lighter / ~제어 automatic control / ~제어장치 an automatic controller / ~조작 automatic operation / ~조종장치 《항공기의》 an automatic pilot; an autopilot / ~판매기 a slot 〔vending〕 machine / ~현금지급기 an automated cash dispenser; a cash machine / ~휴회 an automatic 〔a spontaneous〕 recess.

자동사 (自動詞) an intransitive verb (생략 vi.).

자동차 (自動車) a car; a motorcar 《英》; an automobile 《美》; an auto 《口》; a motor vehicle(총칭). ¶ ~로 가다 go 《to a place》 by car / ~를 몰다 〔달리다〕 drive a car / 《남이 운전하는》 ~를 타다 ride in a car / ~에 태워 주다 give 〔offer〕 《a person》 a lift 《口》 / ~에서 내리다 get out of a car / 자가용 ~ a private car / 임대 ~ a rental car / 배달용 ~ a delivery truck / 경주용 ~ a racing car; a racer / 영업용 ~ a car for business use / 자갈을 만재한 화물 ~ a fully loaded gravel truck. ‖ ~경주 an auto race / ~공업〔산업〕 the automobile 〔car〕 industry / ~공해 automobile pollution / ~매매업자 a car 〔motor〕 dealer / ~번호판 a license plate 《美》; a number-plate 《英》 / ~보험 automobile insurance / ~부품 an auto part / ~사고 an automobile 〔a car〕 accident / ~세 the automobile tax / ~쇼 a motor show / ~수리공장 an auto-repair shop / ~여행 a car 〔motor〕 trip / ~운전면허증 a driver's license / ~운전자 a driver; an automobile driver; a chauffeur 《자가용차 운전사》 / ~전용도로 an expressway; a superhighway 《美》; a motorway 《英》 / ~전화 a car 〔tele〕phone / ~정비공 a car mechanic / ~제조업자 a car manufacturer / ~주차장 a parking lot; a carpark 《英》 / ~차고 a garage / ~학원 a driving school.

자두 〔植〕 a plum; a prune(말린 것).

자디잘다 (be) very small. ☞ 잘다.

자라 〔動〕 a snapping (soft-shelled) turtle. ¶ ~보고 놀란 가슴 솥뚜껑 보고 놀란다 《俗談》 The burnt child dreads the fire.

자라다¹ 《성장하다》 grow (up); be bred; be brought up. ¶ 도시 〔시골〕에서 자란 아이 a city- 〔country-〕 bred child / 우유 〔모유〕로 자란 아이 a bottle- 〔breast-〕 fed child / 빨리 ~ grow rapidly.

자라다² ① 《충분》 (be) enough; sufficient. ¶ 이 연료로 겨울내 자랄까 Will this fuel last out the winter? ② 《미치다》 reach; get at 《손이》. ¶ 손이 자라는 〔자라지 않는〕 곳에 within 〔beyond〕 one's reach / 저 선반에 손이 자라느냐 Can you reach 〔touch〕 the shelf?

자락 옷자락. ¶ 바지 ~을 걷어 올리다 tuck up one's trousers.

자랑 pride; boast. ~ 하다 boast 《of》; be proud 《of, that...》; pride oneself 《on》; take pride 《in》. ¶ ~스럽게 proudly; boastfully; with pride / ~은 아니지만 though I say it myself.... / ~을 하다 sing one's praises; blow one's own trumpet / ~을 해 보이다 make a display 〔show〕 of 《a thing》 / 우리 나라로서는 ~할 만한 기록은 아니다 It is not a proud record for our country. / 그는 양친의 ~거리였다 He was the pride of his parents.

자력 (自力) ¶ ~으로 by one's own efforts 〔ability〕; by oneself / ~으로 숙제를 하다 do one's homework by oneself. ‖ ~갱생 regeneration by one's own efforts; self-reliance.

자력 (資力) means; funds; (financial) resources. ¶ 그에겐 ~이 있다 〔없다〕 He is a man of 〔without〕 means.

자력 (磁力) 〔理〕 magnetism; magnetic force. ¶ ~의 magnetic. ‖ ~계 〔計〕 a magnetometer / ~선 lines of magnetic force.

자료 (資料) material; data. ¶ ~를 수집하다 collect 〔hunt up〕 material / 연구 ~ research data / 통계 ~ materials for statistics. ‖ ~실 a reference room; 《신문사의》 a morgue 《口》.

자루¹ 《푸대》 a sack; a bag. ¶ 쌀 ~ a rice bag / ~에 담다 put (rice) into a sack.

자루² 《손잡이》 a handle; a grip(기계 따위의); a hilt; a haft(칼 따위의); a shaft(창 따위의). ¶ 망치 ~ the handle of a hammer / 식칼 ~가 빠졌다 The handle has come off the kitchen knife.

자루³ 《단위》 a piece 《of》; a pair 《of》. ¶ 분필 한 ~ a piece of chalk / 소총 세 ~ three stands of rifles / 연필 다섯 ~ five pencils.

자르다 《끊다》 cut (off); chop; sever; saw (톱으로); shear; clip (가위로). ¶ 사과를 둘로 ~ cut an apple in two / 종이를 가위로 싹둑

자리 ~ snip at the paper / 톱으로 판자를 둘로 ~ saw the board into two.

자리 ① 《좌석》 a seat; one's place. ¶ ~에 앉다 take one's seat; seat oneself; be seated; sit down / ~에서 일어나다 rise up from one's seat / ~를 뜨다 〔양보하다〕 leave 〔offer〕 one's seat / ~를 잡아두다 keep 〔secure〕 a seat; reserve a seat(예약). ② 《공간》 room; space. ¶ ~를 내다 make room 《for》 / ~를 많이 차지하다 take up a lot of space. ③ 《특정한 장소》 a spot; a scene. ¶ 도둑은 그 ~에서 체포되었다 The thief was arrested on the spot. / 화재가 났던 ~ the scene of a fire / 이곳이 사고가 일어났던 ~이다 This is where the accident happened. ④ 《위치》 a position; a location; a site (터) / 《상황·경우》 an occasion. ¶ ~가 좋다 (나쁘다) be well-(ill-)situated / 도서관이 설 ~ the site where the library will stand / ~에 어울리는 복장을 하다 be properly dressed for the occasion / 그런 것은 공석인 ~에서 말할 일이 아니다 You shouldn't say such a thing on a public occasion. ⑤ 《직책·일자리》 a position; a post; a place. ¶ 중요한 ~ an important position / 장관 ~ a cabinet position; a portfolio / 일할 ~ a job; a post. ⑥ 《깔개》 a mat; matting. ⑦ 《잠자리》 a bed; a sickbed(병석). ¶ ~를 깔다 〔펴다〕 make beddings; prepare a bed / ~에 눕다 〔보전하다〕 lie in one's sickbed. ⑧ 《숫자의》 a figure; a unit; a place. ¶ 네 ~수 a number of four figures.

자리끼 bedside drinking water.

자리옷 nightwear; night clothes; pajamas 《美》; a nightgown.

자리잡다 《위치》 be situated 《at, in》; 《정착》 settle (down); establish oneself; 《공간 차지》 take up room.

자립(自立) independence; self-reliance; self-support(자활). ~하다 become independent 《of one's parents》; support oneself. ¶ 우리 집 아이들은 모두 ~하고 있다 All of my children 〔support themselves〔are on their own feet〕〕 / 부모가 과보호하는 아이들은 ~을 잃기 쉽다 Children whose parents are over-protective are prone to lack in self-reliance. ‖ ~경제 self-supporting economy / ~성장 self-sustained growth.

자릿자릿하다 (be) prickly; tingling; (저리다) (be) numb; have pins and needles 《in》; (마음이) (be) thrilling.

자막(字幕)《영화의》 a title; a caption(제목). ¶ ~를 넣다 superimpose subtitles 《on the film》 / 한국어 ~을 넣은 미국 영화 an American film with Korean subtitles.

자만(自慢) self-praise; self-conceit; vanity; boast(큰소리); brag; pride. ~하다 be proud 〔boastful, vain〕 of; brag 〔boast〕 of; pride oneself on. ¶ ~하는 사람 a boaster; a braggart.

자매(姉妹) sisters. ¶ ~의 (같은) sisterly. ¶ ~교 〔도시〕 a sister school〔city〕/ ~편 a companion volume 《to》; a sequel 《to》/ ~회사 an affiliated company.

자매결연(姉妹結緣) establishment of sisterhood 〔sistership〕. ~을 하다 set up 〔establish〕 sisterly relationship 《with》.

자멸(自滅) self-destruction; self-ruin. ~하다 destroy 〔ruin, kill〕 oneself. ¶ ~적인 suicidal 《behavior》; self-defeating 《processes》 / 그들의 행동은 ~을 초래할 것이다 Their acts will lead to self-destruction.

자명(自明) ~하다 (be) obvious; self-evident. ¶ ~한 이치 a self-evident truth; a truism.

자명종(自鳴鐘) an alarm clock.

자모(字母) an alphabet; a letter; 〔활자〕 a matrix; a printing type.

자모(慈母) one's (tender) mother.

자못 very; greatly; highly; quite. ¶ ~ 기뻐보이다 look highly pleased.

자문(自問) ~하다 question 〔ask〕 oneself. ¶ ~자답 (a) soliloquy / ~자답하다 talk to oneself》.

자문(諮問) an inquiry. ~하다 inquire; refer 〔submit〕 《a problem》 to 《a committee for deliberation》; consult. ¶ ~기관 an advisory body / ~위원회 an advisory committee.

자물쇠 a lock; a padlock. ¶ ~를 채우다(열다) lock 〔unlock〕 《a door》.

자바 Java. ¶ ~사람 a Javanese; a Javan.

자반 salted 〔salt-cured〕 fish.

자반병(紫斑病)《醫》 purpura. ‖ 출혈성 ~ purpura hemorrhagica.

자발(自發) ¶ ~적인 spontaneous; voluntary / ~적으로 voluntarily; spontaneously; of one's own accord / ~적으로 공부하다 study of one's free will; study spontaneously.

자방(子房)《植》 an ovary. ☞ 자낭.

자배기 a large and round pottery bowl.

자백(自白) confession. ~하다 confess 《one's crime》. ¶ ~을 강요하다 force a confession 《out of a sus-

pect*).
자벌레 [蟲] a measuring worm.
자본(資本) (a) capital; a fund. ¶ ~의 축적〔집중〕 accumulation 〔concentration〕 of capital / ~의 유입 the influx 〔inflow〕 of capital / ~의 부족 lack of funds / 얼마 안 되는 ~ a small capital / ~을 투자하다 invest capital *(in an enterprise)*; lay out capital *(for an enterprise)* / ~을 놀리다 let capital lie idle / 그는 1천만원의 ~으로 사업을 시작했다 He started business with a capital of ten million *won*. / 외국 ~ foreign capital / 금융 ~ financial capital / 고정〔유동〕 ~ fixed 〔floating〕 capital / 독점〔공칭, 수권〕 ~ monopolistic 〔nominal, authorized〕 capital / 건강이 유일한 나의 ~이다 Health is the only asset I have. ‖ ~가 a capitalist / ~과세 capital levy / ~구성 the capital structure *(of a firm)* / ~금 capital *(~금 10억원의 회사 a company capitalized at one billion won)* / ~력 the capital strength *(of an enterprise)* / ~재 capital goods / ~주 a financier; a capitalist / ~주의 capitalism / ~주의경제 the capitalistic economy / ~투자 capital investment / ~화(化) capitalization.
자부(自負) self-conceit; pride. ~하다 take pride in; be self-conceited; think highly of *oneself*. ¶ 획기적인 제품을 개발했다고 ~하다 take pride in having developed an epoch-making product. ‖ ~심 self-confidence; pride 〔~심이 강하다 be self-confident〕.
자비(自費) at *one's* own expense. ¶ ~로 수필집을 출판하다 publish a book of essays at *one's* own expense. ‖ ~생 a paying student.
자비(慈悲) mercy; pity. ¶ ~로운 merciful; tender-hearted / ~를 베풀다 have mercy *(on)*; do *(a person)* an act of charity / ~를 청원하다 ask for mercy. ‖ ~심 a merciful heart.
자빠뜨리다 make *(a person)* fall on *one's* back; knock 〔throw〕 *(a thing)* down.
자빠지다 ① 〔넘어가다〕 fall on *one's* back; fall backward. ② 〔눕다〕 lie down.
자산(資産) property; a fortune; assets〔회사・법인의〕. ¶ ~가 make *one's* property 〔assets〕 public. ‖ ~가 a man of property; a wealthy person / ~가치 the value of *one's* property 〔assets〕 / ~상태 *one's* financial standing / ~재평가 revaluation 〔reassessment〕 of property / ~주 an income stock / 현금 ~ cash assets.
자살(自殺) suicide. ~하다 kill *oneself*; commit suicide. ¶ ~을 피하다 attempt suicide. ‖ ~미수 (자) (an) attempted suicide / ~자 a suicide / ~행위 a suicidal act.
자상스럽다, 자상하다(仔詳~) (be) careful; detailed; minute; thoughtful *(of)*. ¶ 자상한 배려 attentive consideration.
자색(姿色) good looks; personal beauty (in a woman). ¶ ~이 뛰어나다 surpass others in beauty.
자색(紫色) purple; violet.
자생(自生) spontaneous 〔natural〕 growth. ~하다 grow wild 〔naturally〕. ‖ ~식물 native 〔wild〕 plants.
자서(自序) the author's preface.
자서전(自敍傳) an autobiography. ¶ ~적인 소설 the autobiographical novel. ‖ ~작가 an autobiographer.
자석(磁石) a magnet. ¶ ~의 magnetic. ‖ 막대〔말굽〕 ~ a bar 〔horseshoe〕 magnet.
자석영(紫石英) ⇨ 자수정.
자선(自選) ~하다 select *(the best)* out of *one's* own works. ‖ ~시집 poems selected by the poet himself.
자선(慈善) charity; benevolence. ¶ ~의 charitable; benevolent / 가난한 사람들에게 ~을 베풀다 render aid to the poor in charity. ‖ ~가 a charitable person / ~기금 a charity fund / ~냄비 a charity pot / ~단체 a charitable institution 〔organization〕 / ~바자 a charity bazaar / ~병원 a charity hospital / ~사업 charitable work; charities / ~음악회 a charity concert.
자설(自說) *one's* own view 〔opinion〕. ¶ ~을 굽히지 않다 stick to *one's* opinion.
자성(自省) reflection (反省).
자성(磁性) 〔理〕 magnetism. ¶ ~의 magnetic / ~을 주다 magnetize / ~을 잃다 lose *its* magnetism / ~을 제거하다 demagnetize. ‖ ~체 a magnetic substance 〔body〕.
자세(仔細) ¶ ~한 detailed; minute; full; particular / ~히 in full; minutely; closely.
자세(姿勢) 〔몸의〕 a posture; a pose; 〔태도〕 an attitude; a carriage〔몸가짐〕. ¶ 앉은 ~로 in a sitting posture / 방어 자세를 취하다 take a defensive posture / ~를 바로하다 straighten *oneself* / ~가 좋다〔나쁘다〕 have a fine 〔poor〕 carriage / 차려 ~를 취하다 stand

자속(磁束) 〖理〗 magnetic flux.
자손(子孫) a descendant; posterity; offspring. ¶ ~을 남기다 leave offspring / ~에게 전하다 hand down to *one's* posterity.
자수(自手) ¶ ~로 with *one's* own hands (efforts); without help / ~성가하다 make *one's* fortune by *one's* own efforts.
자수(自首) self-surrender; (voluntary) confession. ~하다 surrender *oneself* 《to the police》; give *oneself* up 《to the police》.
자수(刺繡) embroidery. ~하다 embroider 《*one's* name on...》.
자수정(紫水晶) 〖鑛〗 amethyst; violet quartz.
자숙(自肅) self-imposed control; self-control. ~하다 practice self-control; voluntary refrain 《from》.
자습(自習) private study; self-teaching. ~하다 study by [for] *oneself*. ¶ 물리학을 ~하다 study physics for *oneself*. ‖ ~ 문제 homework; home exercises [task] / ~서 a self-teaching book; a key《문제집 등의 해답집》 / ~시간 study hours / ~실 a study room.
자승자박(自繩自縛) ~하다 be caught in *one's* own trap; lose *one's* freedom of action as a result of *one's* own actions.
자시(子時) the Hour of the Rat; midnight.
자식(子息) 《자녀》 a child; a son; a daughter; offspring 《총칭》; 《욕》a chap; a wretch; a bastard.
자신(自身) *one's* self; *oneself*. ¶ ~의 *one's* own; personal / ~이 《독자적으로》 by [for] *oneself*; in person; personally / 네 ~이 해 보아라 Try it by yourself. / 네 ~의 판단으로 그것을 결정하라 Decide it according to your own judgement.
자신(自信) (self-)confidence; self-assurance. ~하다《자신이 있다》 have confidence in *oneself*; be confident 《of, about》; be sure 《of, that》. ¶ ~이 없다 have no confidence in *oneself*; be diffident 《of, about》 / ~이 있는 confident; self-confident; self-assured / ~만만하게 with complete self-confidence / 나는 성공할 ~이 있다 I am [feel] confident of success. / 그것에 대해 답할 수 있을지 ~이 없다 I'm not sure that I can answer it. / 시험 결과를 알고, 나는 ~을 얻었다 [잃었다] I gained [lost] confidence in myself, having known the result of
자실(自失) ☞ 망연. [examination.
자심(滋甚) ~하다 be getting [grow-

ing] worse 《severe, serious》.
자아(自我) self; ego. ¶ ~가 센 egotistic《자기 중심의》; (egoistical; selfish; self-willed《제멋대로의》/ ~의 발전 self-development / ~에 눈뜨다 awake to *one's* self. ‖ ~의식 self-consciousness.
자아내다 ① 《뽑아냄》 spin; reel off. ¶ 솜에서 실을 ~ spin thread out of cotton. ② 《느낌울》 evoke 《*a laugh, feeling*》; excite 《arouse》 《*curiosity*》; stir up 《*interest*》; tempt, whet 《*one's appetite*》. ¶ 눈물을 ~ move 《*a person*》 to tears; draw tears from 《*a person*》. ③《액체·기체를》 extract 《*gas, liquid*》 by machine; draw; pump.
자애(自愛) ~하다 take (good) care of *oneself*.
자애(慈愛) affection; love. ¶ ~로운 affectionate 《*smiles*》; loving 《*words*》.
자약(自若) ~하다 (be) self-possessed; composed; calm. ¶ 태연 ~하다 remain cool 《calm》.
자양(滋養) nourishment. ☞ 영양.
자업자득(自業自得) the natural consequences of *one's* own deed. ¶ ~이다 You've brought it on yourself. *or* You asked for it. *or* It serves you right.
자연(自然) ①《천연》 nature; Nature《의인화》. ¶ ~의 힘 natural forces 《의인화》 / ~의 법칙 the law(s) of nature / ~을 노래한 시 a nature poem; nature poetry / 우리는 ~을 벗삼아야 한다 We should commune with nature. *or* We should be in close connection with nature. / 과도한 개발로 ~이 파괴되고 있다 Nature is being ruined by excessive development. ②《당연》¶ ~의 natural / ~스러운 결과로서 as a natural result / ~의 추세에 맡기다 let 《*a matter*》 take its own course / 아기가 우는 것은 ~스러운 일이다 It is natural for a baby to cry. ③ 《저절로》 ¶ ~히 by *oneself*; spontaneously; automatically / 문이 ~으로 닫혔다 The door closed by *itself*. / 환성이 관중에서 ~발생적으로 터져 나왔다 Cheers spontaneously rose from the crowd. ‖ ~개조 the remodeling 《reshaping》 of nature / ~계 nature; the natural world / ~공원 a natural park / ~과학 natural science / ~도태 natural selection / ~미 natural beauty / ~발생《발화》 spontaneous generation 《combustion》 / ~보호 conservation of nature / ~보호 구역 a wildlife sanctuary; a nature reserve / ~보호 운동〔단체〕 a conservation movement 《group》 / ~사(死) (a) natural

자영 death / ~색 a natural color / ~식품 natural foods / ~식품점 a natural food store / ~애호가 a nature lover / ~자원(증가) natural resources (increase) / ~재해 a natural disaster / ~주의 naturalism / ~치유 self-healing; spontaneous recovery / ~파괴 the destruction of nature / ~현상 a natural phenomenon / ~환경 the natural environment.

자영(自營) ~하다 do 《*business*》 independently; be self-supporting. ¶ ~의 independent; self-supporting / ~으로 영업하다 do business on *one's* own account; run *one's* own business. ‖ ~업 an independent enterprise.

자오선(子午線) 《天》 the meridian.

자외선(紫外線) ultraviolet rays. ¶ ~요법 ultraviolet light therapy; (an) ultraviolet treatment.

자우(慈雨) a welcome rain; a rain after the drought.

자욱하다 (be) dense; thick; heavy. ¶ 자욱હ게 in thick clouds; thickly; densely / 자욱한 안개 a dense fog / 연기가 ~ The smoke is thick. / 실내는 담배 연기로 자욱했다 The room was heavy with cigarette smoke.

자웅(雌雄) 《암수》 male and female; the two sexes; 《승패》 victory or defeat. ¶ ~을 감별하다 determine the sex 《*of*》; sex 《*a chicken*》 / ~을 겨루다 fight a decisive battle 《*with*》. ‖ ~도태 sexual selection / ~동체 hermaphrodite.

자원(自願) ~하다 volunteer 《*for*》. ¶ ~하여 voluntarily. ‖ ~봉사자 a volunteer worker / ~자 a volunteer.

자원(資源) (natural) resources. 유한(有限)한 ~ finite resources / ~이 풍부한 rich in natural resources / 지하 ~ underground resources / 인적 ~ human resources; manpower / 천연 ~을 개발하다 exploit (develop) natural resources. ‖ ~개발 exploitation of resources / ~공급국 resource-supplying countries / ~문제 the resources problem / ~보호 conservation of resources / ~산출국 resource-producing countries / ~유한(有限)시대 an era of limited natural resources.

자위(自慰) ①《자기 위로》 self-consolation. ~하다 console *oneself*. ②《수음》 masturbation.

자위(自衛) self-defense [-protection]. ~하다 protect (defend) *oneself*. ‖ ~의 self-preserving; self-defense / ~를 위해서 in self-defense / 테러 조직에 대한 ~ 수단을 강구하다 adopt a measure of self-defense against a terrorist organization. ‖ ~권 the right of self-defense / ~본능 the protective instinct.

자위뜨다 《무거운 물건이》 budge; make (show) a slight move (opening) from *its* place.

자유(自由) freedom; liberty. ¶ ~의(로운) free; liberal; unrestrained / ~롭게 freely; at will; liberally / ~로운 시간 free time / ~자재로 at will; freely / 신앙 〔종교〕의 ~ freedom of worship (religion) / 출판 (보도) 의 ~ freedom of the press / ~의 여신상 the Statue of Liberty / ~로운 몸이 되다 be set free (at liberty) / ~를 잃다 be deprived of *one's* liberty / …할 ~가 있지 못하다 be not at liberty to *do*; be not allowed to *do* / ~는 자칫하면 방종이 되기 쉽다 Liberty often degenerates into lawlessness. ‖ ~결혼 free marriage / ~경쟁 free competition / ~경제 〔무역〕 free economy (trade) / ~무역항 a duty-free port / ~방임 noninterference; 《경제상의》 laissez-faire / ~선택 free choice / ~세계 the free world / ~시간 〔단체 여행시〕 free time; time at leisure / ~시장 a free market / ~업 a liberal profession / ~의지 free will / ~재량 (a) discretionary power / ~주의 liberalism / ~주의자 a liberalist / ~항 a free port / ~행동 free (unorganized) activities (~행동을 하다 act for *oneself*; take *one's* own course) / ~형 《수영·레슬링의》 freestyle.

자유화(自由化) liberalization; freeing 《*of trade*》; removal of restrictions 《*on trade*》. ~하다 liberalize; free. ¶ 한국의 무역을 98퍼센트까지 ~하다 liberalize (remove restrictions on) 98 percent of Korea's trade. ‖ ~상품 liberalized goods / ~조처 liberalization measures.

자율(自律) self-control; autonomy. ¶ ~적인 autonomous. ‖ ~신경 an autonomic nerve / ~신경 실조증 autonomic imbalance.

자음(子音) a consonant.

자의(字義) the meaning of a word. ¶ ~대로 literally.

자의(恣意) 《*of*》 *one's* own will.

자의식(自意識) self-consciousness.

자이로스코프 a gyroscope.

자이르 Zaire. ¶ ~의 Zairian / ~사람 a Zairian.

자인(自認) ~하다 acknowledge *oneself* (to be in the wrong); admit.

자일(등산용) (a) (climbing) rope.

자임하다(自任―) consider (fancy) *oneself* (to be) 《*an expert*》; re-

자자손손(子子孫孫) (*one's*) descendants; posterity; offspring. ¶ ~에 이르기까지 hand down to *one's* remotest descendants / ~에게 전하다 hand down to posterity.

자자하다(藉藉—) be widely spread; be the talk of the town. ¶ 명성이 ~ be highly reputed; enjoy a high reputation.

자작(子爵) a viscount. ‖ ~부인 a viscountess.

자작(自作) *one's* own work. ¶ ~의 of *one's* own making; of *one's* writing [composing] (시문의) ‖ ~ 소설 a novel of *one's* (own) writing [pen]. ‖ ~농 an independent [owner] farmer / ~시 *one's* own poem.

자작나무 [植] a white birch.

자작하다(自酌—) pour *one's* own liquor [wine]; pour 《wine》 for *oneself*.

자잘하다 (be) all small [tiny, minute]. ¶ 자잘한 물건 small things.

자장(磁場) ☞ 자기장.

자장가(—歌) a lullaby; a cradle-song. ¶ ~를 불러 아이를 재우다 sing a child to sleep.

자장면(炸醬麵) noodles with bean sauce.

자장자장 rockabye baby; hushabye baby.

자재(資材) materials. ‖ ~과 the material section / 건축~ construction [building] materials.

자적(自適) 유유~한 생활을 보내다 live [by *oneself*] free from worldly cares / 은퇴하여 유유~한 여생을 보내다 spend the rest of *one's* days in quiet [dignified] retirement.

자전(字典) a dictionary for Chinese characters; a lexicon.

자전(自轉) (a) rotation. ~하다 rotate; revolve; turn on *its* axis.

자전거(自轉車) a bicycle; a cycle; a bike (俗); a tricycle(세발의). ¶ ~를 타다 ride a bicycle / ~로 가다 go by bicycle / ~로 통학하다 go to school by bicycle. ‖ ~경기 a bicycle [cycle] race / ~경기장 a cycling bowl [track]; a velodrome / ~여행 a bicycle trip; a cycling tour / ~전용도로 a cycle track; a cycling path [lane].

자정(子正) midnight.

자정(自淨) self-cleansing; self-purification. ¶ 자연의 ~ 작용 the self-cleansing action of nature / 원래 하천에는 상당한 ~력이 있다 Under natural conditions, rivers have very considerable powers of self-cleansing.

자제(子弟) children; sons.

자제(自制) self-control; self-restraint. ~하다 control [restrain] *oneself*. ‖ ~심[력] *one's* self-control; lose control of *oneself*; let *oneself* go.

자제(自製) *one's* own making.

자조(自助) self-help. ~하다 help *oneself*. ‖ ~정신 the spirit of self-help.

자조(自嘲) self-scorn; self-ridicule. ~하다 scorn [ridicule] *oneself*.

자족(自足) self-sufficiency. ~하다 be self-sufficient. ☞ 자급(自給).

자존(自尊) self-importance. ~하다 respect [esteem] *oneself*. ¶ 민족의 ~과 안녕 national self-esteem and public well-being.

자존심(自尊心) self-respect; pride. ¶ ~ 있는 self-respecting; proud / ~을 상하다 hurt *one's* pride / ~을 상하게 하다 hurt [wound] other people's pride / 그런 일을 하는 것은 내 ~이 허락지 않는다 I have too much pride to do such a thing.

자주(自主) independence. ~적인 independent; autonomous(자치의) / ~적으로 independently; of *one's* own will / ~성이 없다 lack *one's* independence of mind. ‖ ~국 an independent state / ~국방 self-reliance of national defense / ~권 autonomy / ~권 (sovereign) independence / ~독립 외교 an autonomous [independent] foreign policy / 관세~권 tariff [customs] autonomy; claret.

자주(紫朱) purplish red; murex.

자주 often; frequently. ¶ ~ 오다 [가다] come [go] often; visit frequently; frequent 《a place》.

자중(自重) prudence. ~하다 take care of *oneself*; be prudent [cautious].

자중지란(自中之亂) a fight among themselves; an internal strife.

자지 a penis; a cock.

자지러뜨리다 shrink; frighten 《a person》 to death; give 《a person》 shudders [the creeps].

자지러지다 ① 《놀랄 따위로》 shrink; cower; crouch; flinch 《from》. ¶ 자지러지게 놀라다 shrink with fright. ② 《웃음 따위로》 자지러지게 웃다 roll about [be convulsed] with laughter; laugh *oneself* inside out.

자진(自進) ~하여 of *one's* own accord [will]; voluntarily / ~입대하다 volunteer for military service / ~하여 모든 책임을 떠맡다 assume full responsibility of *one's* own will. ‖ ~신고 voluntary reporting.

자질(資質) nature; disposition; temperament(기질); a gift(재능). ¶ 공무원의 ~을 향상시키다 improve the quality of government employees.
자질구레하다 be evenly small.
자찬(自讚) ☞ 자화자찬.
자책(自責) self-reproach. ~하다 reproach (blame) *oneself* (*for*). ¶ ~감에 시달리다 suffer from a guilty conscience; have twinges of conscience. ‖ ~점 [野] an earned run.
자처(自處) ① ☞ 자살(自殺). ②《자임》~하다 fancy (consider) *oneself* (*as, to be*); look upon *oneself* (*as*). ¶ 그는 물리학의 대가로 ~한다 He looks upon himself as an authority on physics.
자천(自薦) ~하다 recommend (offer) *oneself* (*for the post*).
자철(磁鐵) 【鑛】 magnetic iron.
자청(自請) ~하다 volunteer. ¶ ~해서 힘든 일을 맡다 volunteer a difficult job.
자체(字體) the form of a character; a type (활자의).
자체(自體) 【그 ~ (in) itself / 사고 ~는 별것 아니었다 The accident itself was a minor one. ‖ ~감사 self-inspection / ~사업 own business / ~조사 an in-house investigation.
자초(自招) ~하다 bring upon *oneself*; court (*danger*). ¶ 화를 ~하다 bring misfortune on *oneself*.
자초지종(自初至終) the whole story; all the details. ¶ 사고의 ~을 상세히 말하다 give a full (detailed) account (story) of the accident. [event] by *oneself*.
자축(自祝) ~하다 celebrate (*an*
자취(행적) traces; vestiges; marks; signs; evidences(증거). ¶ 진보의 ~ signs of progress / ~을 남기다 leave *one's* traces behind ‖ ~를 감추다 cover up *one's* traces.
자취(自炊) ~하다 cook *one's* own food; do *one's* own cooking; board *oneself*. ¶ 형은 ~을 한다 My brother cooks his own meals. ‖ ~설비 (a room with) cooking facilities.
자치(自治) self-government; autonomy. ~하다 govern *oneself*. ¶ ~의 self-governing; autonomous / ~를 요구하는 집회를 열다 hold a meeting to demand *their* autonomy / 지방 ~ local self-government. ‖ ~권 autonomous rights; autonomy / ~능력 autonomous ability / (단)체 ~ a self-governing body / ~령 a dominion / ~회 a student council(학생의); a residents' association(단지 등의).
자치기 tipcat.
자친(慈親) *one's* mother.
자침(磁針) a magnetic needle. ‖ ~검파기 a magnetic detector.
자칫하면 ~ 목숨을 잃을 뻔하다 come near losing *one's* life / ~ 성을 내다 get mad at the drop of a hat / ~하기 쉽다 be apt (liable, prone) *to do*.
자칭(自稱) ~하다 style (call, describe) *oneself*; pretend (*to be*). ¶ ~의 self-styled; would-be ‖ ~ 변호사 (시인)이다 He is a self-styled lawyer (would-be poet). / 그는 ~ 대학교수라고 하였다 He called himself a professor.
자타(自他) *oneself* and others. ¶ ~의 관계 *one's* relations with others / 그는 ~가 인정하는 시인이다 He is generally acknowledged to be a poet. ‖ ~ ~ 인정하는 바이다 It is commonly acknowledged (generally admitted) that…
자탄(自嘆) ~하다 complain (grieve) *to oneself*; feel grief for *oneself*.
자태(姿態) a figure; a shape; a pose. ¶ 요염한(우아한) ~ a bewitching (graceful) figure.
자택(自宅) 〖자기 집〗 *one's* (own) house (home). ¶ ~에 있다 (없다) be (not) at home / ~에서 개인 교수하다 give private lessons at home / ~에서 대기하라는 명을 받다 be told to stand by at home. ‖ ~연금 house arrest; domiciliary confinement / ~요양 home treatment (remedy).
자토(磁土) kaolin; china clay.
자퇴(自退) ~하다 leave (*one's post*) *of one's own accord*; resign voluntarily.
자투리 odd ends of yard goods; waste pieces from cutting cloth. ‖ ~땅 a small piece of land (in downtown areas).
자판(字板) 〖컴퓨터 등의〗 a keyboard.
자폐증(自閉症) 【心】 autism. ¶ ~의 아이 an autistic child.
자포자기(自暴自棄) desperation; despair(절망); self-abandonment. ~하다 become desperate; abandon *oneself* to despair. ¶ ~하여 in desperation.
자폭(自爆) suicidal explosion. ~하다 crash *one's* plane into the target(비행기가); blow up *one's* own ship(배가).
자필(自筆) *one's* own handwriting; an autograph. ¶ ~의 autograph; (a letter) in *one's* own hand writing. ‖ ~이력서 *one's* résumé in *one's* own handwriting.
자학(自虐) self-torture. ~하다 torment (torture) *oneself*. ¶ ~적이

자해 (自慰) ① ~하다 자살. ② 〈자신을 해침〉 ~하다 injure (hurt) *oneself*.
자행 (恣行) ~하다 do as one pleases; have one's own way.
자형 (姉兄) ☞ 매형(妹兄).
자혜 (慈惠) charity; benevolence. ¶ ~병원 a charity hospital.
자화 (磁化) magnetization. ~하다 magnetize.
자화상 (自畫像) a self-portrait.
자화수정 (自花受精) 〖植〗 self-fertilization.
자화자찬 (自畫自讚) self-praise. ~하다 praise *oneself*; sing one's own praises.
자활 (自活) self-support. ~하다 support (maintain) *oneself.* ¶ ~의 길 a means of supporting *oneself.*
자획 (字劃) the number of strokes 《*in a Chinese character*》.
작 (作) 《작품》 a work; 《농작》 a crop; a harvest.
작 (爵) 《작위》 peerage.
작가 (作家) a writer, an author 《소설의》; an artist.
작고 (作故) ~하다 die; pass away. ¶ ~한 the late….
작곡 (作曲) (musical) composition. ~하다 compose; set 《*a song*》 to music; write music 《*to a song*》. ¶ ~가 a composer.
작금 (昨今) recently; lately; of late; these days. ¶ ~의 recent.
작년 (昨年) last year. ¶ ~ 봄 last spring / ~ 오늘 this day last year; a year ago today.
작다 《크기가》 (be) small; little; tiny; 《나이가》 (be) young; little; 《규모·중요도가》 (be) trifling; slight; trivial; 《마음이》 (be) narrow-minded. ¶ 작은 사람 a small man 《체구가》; a narrow-minded person 《마음이》 / 작은 집 a small house / 작은 일 a trifle; a trivial matter / 작은 고추가 맵다 《俗談》 The smaller, the shrewder.
작다리 a person of short stature; a shorty 《美口》.
작달막하다 be rather short (of stature); be stocky.
작당 (作黨) ~하다 form a group (clique, gang). ¶ ~하여 in a group (league).
작대기 ① 《버팀대》 a pole; a rod; a stick (with a forked head). ② 《가위표》 the mark of failure 《*in a test*》; the mark of elimination.
작도 (作圖) drawing. ~하다 draw a figure (chart); 〖數〗 construct 《*a triangle*》.
작동 (作動) ~하다 operate; work; run; function. ¶ 기계를 ~시키다 set (get) a machine going.
작두 (斫-) a straw cutter; a fodder-chopper.
작렬 (炸裂) an explosion; bursting. ~하다 explode; burst.
작명 (作名) naming. ~하다 name.
작문 (作文) (a) composition; writing. ¶ 영~ an English composition / 자유~ a free composition / ~을 짓다 write a composition 《*on*》.
작물 (作物) 《농작물》 crops; farm products 《produce》.
작법 (作法) how to write (make, grow, produce, *etc.*).
작별 (作別) farewell; parting; a goodbye; leave-taking. ¶ ~의 (인사)말 a farewell word / ~을 고하다 say goodbye 《*to*》; bid 《*a person*》 farewell.
작부 (酌婦) a barmaid; a bar girl.
작부면적 (作付面積) acreage under cultivation; a planted area.
작사 (作詞) ~하다 write the words (lyrics) 《*for*》. ¶ K씨 ~ L씨 작곡 words (lyric) by K and music by L. ∥ ~자 a songwriter; a lyric writer.
작살 a harpoon; a (fish) spear.
작성 (作成) ~하다 draw up 《*a plan*》; make out 《*a list*》. ¶ 계약서를 정부 2통 ~하다 draw up a contract in duplicate 》유언장을 비밀리에 ~하다 make (draw up) 《*a person*》's will secretly.
작시 (作詩) ~하다 write a poem. ∥ ~법 the art of versification.
작심 (作心) ~하다 determine; resolve; make up one's mind. ¶ ~삼일 a resolution good for only three days; a short-lived resolve.
작약 (芍藥) 〖植〗 a peony.
작약 (炸藥) an explosive; gunpowder.
작업 (作業) work; operations. ~하다 work; conduct operations. ¶ ~ 중에 부상을 입다 get hurt while at work / ~을 8시에 개시 (중지) 하다 begin (suspend) operations at eight. ∥ ~계획 a work project / ~교대 work shift(s) / ~량 amount of work done / ~반 a work (working) party / ~복 working clothes; overalls / ~시간 working hours / ~실 a workroom / ~장 working place; a workshop; a job site 《공사장》 / ~화 work shoes / ~효율 work efficiency.
작열 (灼熱) ¶ ~하는 scorching; burning; red-hot / ~하는 태양 a scorching (burning) sun.
작용 (作用) action; operation; a function 〈기능〉; effect 〈영향〉. ~하다 act (operate, work) 《*on a thing*》; affect. ¶ ~과 반작용 ac-

작위(爵位) peerage; a (noble) title. ¶ ～이 있는 titled 《ladies》.
작은곰자리 〖天〗 the Little Bear.
작은아버지 one's uncle; one's father's younger brother.
작은어머니 one's aunt; the wife of one's father's younger brother.
작은집 ① (아들·동생의 집) one's son's (younger brother's) house. ② (첩의 집) one's concubine's house; (첩) one's concubine.
작자(作者) ① 《저작자》 an author; a writer. ② 《살 사람》 a buyer; a purchaser. ¶ ～가 없다 be not in demand. ③ 《위인》 a fellow; a guy.
작작 not too much; moderately. ¶ 농담 좀 ～ 해라 Don't go too far with your jokes.
작전(作戰) (military) operations; tactics 《전술》; strategy 《전략》. ¶ ～상의 operational; strategic / ～을 세우다 《짜다》 map out a plan of operations / 공동 ～ combined operations / 경기 전에 ～을 세우다 plan one's tactics before the game. ‖ ～ 계획 [기지] a plan [base] of operations / ～ 회의 a council of war; a tactical planning conference.
작정(作定) 《결정·결심》 a decision; determination; 《의향》 an intention; a plan; a thought; 《목적》 a purpose. ～하다 decide; determine; plan; intend to 《do》. ¶ ～할 ～으로 with a view to [of] 《doing》; with the intention [aim] of 《doing》; in the hope of 《doing》 / 나는 휴가를 서울에서 보낼 ～이다 I am planning to spend the holidays in Seoul.
작폐하다(作弊－) make [cause] trouble [nuisance].
작품(作品) a (piece of) work; a production. ¶ 예술 ～ a work of art / 문학 ～ a literary work.
작풍(作風) a (literary) style. ¶ ～을 모방하다 model one's style on 《a person》.
작황(作況) a harvest; a crop; a yield. ¶ ～ 보고 a crop report / ～이 좋다 [나쁘다] have a good [bad] crop 《of rice》. ‖ ～ 예상 crop [harvest] prospects / ～ 지수 a crop-situation index.
잔(盞) a (wine) cup; a glass. ¶ 포도주 한 ～ a glass of wine / ～을 돌리다 pass the cup round.
잔걸음 ¶ ～치다 walk back and forth within a short distance.
잔고(殘高) the balance. ¶ 은행예금 ～ 를 [one's] balance at the bank / ～를 전액 인출하다 draw the balance to nothing.
잔교(棧橋) a pier. ☞ 선창(船艙).
잔글씨 small characters; fine letters. ¶ ～로 쓰다 write small characters.
잔금 fine wrinkles [lines].
잔금(殘金) money left (over) 《남은 돈》; the remainder 《지불의》; the balance 《예금의》. ¶ ～을 치르다 pay the remainder / ～은 2만원뿐이다 Twenty thousand won is all there is left. or The balance is only twenty thousand won.
잔기(殘期) the remaining time; the remainder of a period [term].
잔기침 a hacking cough.
잔당(殘黨) the remnants of a defeated party.
잔돈 small money; (small) change. ¶ ～으로 바꾸다 change 《a note》 into small money.
잔돈푼 ① 《용돈》 pocket [pin] money; spending money. ② 《소액》 a small sum of money; petty cash.
잔돌 a pebble; a gravel.
잔디 a lawn; (a patch of) grass; turf. ¶ ～를 심다 plant grass [a lawn] / ～ 깎는 기계 a lawn mower. ‖ ～ 밭 a lawn; a grassplot.
잔뜩 ① 《꽉 차게》 (to the) full; fully; to capacity; to the fullest. ¶ ～ 먹다 [마시다] eat [drink] one's fill / 빚을 ～ 지다 be deeply in debt. ② 《몹시》 intently; heavily; firmly. ¶ ～ 찌푸린 날씨 a heavily leaden sky / …을 ～ 믿다 firmly believe that…
잔류(殘留) ～하다 remain behind; stay. ‖ ～물 a residue; remnants; leavings / ～ 부대 remaining forces / ～ 자기(磁氣) residual magnetism.
잔말 useless [idle, small] talk; chatter; a complaint 《불평》. ～ 하다 twaddle; say useless things.
잔망(孱妄) ～하다, ～스럽다 be feeble and narrow-minded; be weak and light-headed.
잔명(殘命) the rest of one's life; one's remaining days. ¶ 그는 ～이 얼마 남지 않았다 His days are numbered.
잔무(殘務) unsettled business; affairs remaining unsettled. ¶ ～을 정리하다 settle [clear up] the remaining [pending] business.
잔물결 ripples. ¶ ～이 일다 ripple.
잔병(一病) constant slight sickness; sickliness. ¶ ～치례 getting sick frequently / ～이 잦다 be sickly.
잔상(殘像) 〖心〗 an afterimage.

잔설(殘雪) the remaining snow.

잔소리 ① ☞ 잔말. ②《꾸중·싫은 소리》scolding; a rebuke; a lecture; a sermon. ~하다 scold; rebuke; lecture; give 《a person》 a lecture 《about》; find fault 《with》; nag 《at a person》; grumble about 《a thing》. ¶ ~을 들어 be scolded 《by》; catch it 《from》《口》/ 그녀는 늘 ~만 한다 She is always grumbling. ‖ ~꾼 a chatterbox; a nagger.

잔속《자세한 내막》 the intimate details; the inside information. ¶ ~을 알다 have an intimate knowledge 《of》.

잔손 elaborate 《fine》 handwork. ¶ ~이 많이 가는 일 laborious 《troublesome》 work; a time-consuming job 《~이 많이 가다 나름 (require) a great deal of time 〔elaborate handwork〕.

잔술집(盞─) a pub that sells draft liquor.

잔심부름 sundry errands 〔jobs〕; miscellaneous services.

잔악(殘惡) ~하다 (be) cruel; atrocious; inhumane.

잔액(殘額) the balance《은행 예금의》; the remainder《지불할》. ☞ 잔고, 잔금.

잔업(殘業) overtime work. ~하다 work extra hours; work overtime. ‖ ~수당 overtime pay; an allowance for overtime work.

잔여(殘餘) the remainder; the remnant; the rest. ¶ ~의 remaining.

잔월(殘月)《달》 a morning moon.

잔인(殘忍) ¶ ~한 cruel; brutal; inhumane; cold-blooded. ¶ ~무도 inhumanity / ~성 one's brutal nature.

잔잔하다《바람·물결·사태 등이》 (be) quiet; still; calm; placid. ¶ 잔잔한 바다 a calm 〔quiet〕 sea / 잔잔히 흐르는 강 a gently flowing river / 잔잔한 목소리로 이야기하다 speak in a quiet voice.

잔재(殘滓)《남은 찌꺼기》 the residue; dregs《액체의》;《지난날의》 a vestige 《of》. ¶ 봉건주의의 ~ (remaining) vestiges of feudalism.

잔재미 ¶ ~있는 사람 a nice person to have around / ~를 보다 make a hit in a small way《성공》; fish up a nice bit of catch《낚시에서》.

잔재주(─才) a petty artifice; a trick; a device. ¶ ~를 부리다 play 〔resort to〕 petty tricks.

잔적(殘敵)《mop up, clean up》 the remnants of shattered enemy troops.

잔존(殘存) survival. ~하다 sur-

vive; remain; be still alive; be left.

잔주름 fine wrinkles 〔lines〕; crow's-feet《눈가의》. ¶ ~이 있는 finely wrinkled 《skin》.

잔챙이 the smallest 〔poorest〕 one; small fish 《물고기》.

잔치 a 〔ceremonial〕 feast《축연》; a banquet《공식의》; a party. ¶ 혼인 ~ a wedding feast / ~를 베풀다 give a party 〔feast〕; hold a banquet / ~에 손님을 초대하다 invite guests to a feast.

잔학(殘虐) cruelty; brutality; atrocity. ¶ ~한 cruel; atrocious; brutal; inhuman. ‖ ~행위 a cruel act; atrocity.

잔해(殘骸) the wreck; the wreckage. ¶ 비행기의 ~ the wreck 〔wreckage〕 of a plane; the remains of a wrecked plane.

잔허리 the narrow part of *one's* back.

잘 ①《능숙하게》 well; skillfully; nicely. ②《바르게》 rightly; correctly. ¶ 피아노를 ~ 치다 play the piano well / 영어를 ~ 말하다 speak English well / ~ 했다 Well done! / 그것을 ~ 발음하기란 어렵다 It is hard to pronounce it clearly 〔correctly〕. ③《만족·충분하게》 well; fully; thoroughly. ¶ ~ 먹다 〔자다, 살다〕 eat 〔sleep, live〕 well / 이 고기는 ~ 익혔다 This meat is well done. / 그녀는 영화에 관해 ~ 알고 있다 She is well-informed about movie. ③《주의 깊게·상세히》 carefully; closely. ¶ ~을 ~ 보다 have a good look at 《something》; look at 《something》 carefully 〔closely〕 / 내말을 ~ 들어라 Listen to me carefully. ④《친절히·호의적으로》 ¶ 남에게 ~ 하도록 하여라 Be good 〔kind〕 to others. / 그는 나에 관해 ~ 말해 주지 않는다 He speaks ill of me. ⑤《걸핏하면》 readily; easily. ¶ ~ 웃다 laugh readily / ~ 성내다 be apt to get angry; get angry easily. ⑥《곧잘》 often; frequently. ¶ 그는 학교를 ~ 쉰다 He is often absent from school. ⑦《기타》 ¶ 옷이 ~ 맞는다 The dress fits nicely. / 마침 ~ 왔다 You've come at just the right moment. / ~ 있거라 Goodbye!

잘그랑 with a clink 〔clang〕.

잘나다 ①《사람됨이》 (be) distinguished; excellent; great. ¶ 잘난 사람 a distinguished 〔great〕 person / 잘난 체하는 사람 a self-important fellow; a braggart / 잘난 체하다 put on 〔assume〕 airs; think *oneself* somebody. ②《생김새》 (be) handsome; cute; beautiful; good-looking.

잘다 ① 《크기가》 (be) small; little; tiny; minute; fine. ¶잔 모래 fine sand / 고기를 잘게 썰다 chop meat into small pieces. ② 《인품이》 (be) small-minded; stingy. ¶잔 사람 a man of small caliber.

잘라먹다 ① 《음식을》 bite off; cut and eat. ② 《계산·채무 등을》 bilk a creditor; do not pay 《*one's* debt》; fail to pay; welsh on 《*one's* debt》.

잘록하다 be constricted (in the middle). ¶허리가 잘록한 여인 a woman with a wasp waist.

잘리다 ① 《절단》 be cut (off); be chopped; be cut down (나무가). ② 《떼어먹히다》 be cheated out of; be welshed (on); become irrecoverable. ③ 《해고》 get fired.

잘못 《과실·과오》 an error; a mistake; a fault; a slip (사소한); a blunder (큰). ~하다 mistake; make a mistake (in); commit (make) an error; err. ¶~된 견해 the wrong view (of) / 중대한 ~을 범하다 commit a grave blunder (serious mistake) / 상황 판단을 ~하다 misjudge the situation / 계산을 ~하다 miscalculate; make a mistake in calculation / 기계 조작을 ~하다 mishandle a machine / ~을 고치시오 Correct errors if any. / 이 책에는 문법상의 ~이 많다 (없다) This book is full of (free from) grammatical mistakes (errors). ② 《부사적으로》 by mistake; mistakenly; wrong; wrongly. ¶~되다 go wrong (amiss) / ~생각하다 misunderstand; misjudge / 모든 일이 ~되었다 Everything went wrong. / 그녀를 남자로 ~보았다 I mistook her for a man.

잘못짚다 guess wrong; make a wrong guess.

잘생기다 ☞ 잘나다 ②.

잘잘 ① 《끓음》 simmering; boiling. ¶물이 ~끓는다 The water is simmering. / 방바닥이 ~끓다 the floor is piping hot. ② 《끌림》 dragging; trailing. ¶치맛자락을 ~끌며 걷다 walk with *one's* skirt trailing.

잘잘못 right and (or) wrong; good and (or) evil. ¶~을 가리다 distinguish between right and wrong; tell right from wrong.

잘하다 ① be skillful (in); be a good hand; be expert (in); 《…하기 쉽다》 be apt (liable) to 《do》; be too ready to 《believe》. ¶말을 ~하다 be a good speaker / 영어를 ~하다 be good at English. ② 《친절하게 하다》 be good (nice, kind) to 《a person》; do 《a person》 well. ¶그들은 내게 아주 잘한다 They are very kind to me.

잠 《수면》 (a) sleep; a slumber. ¶~을 못 이루다 fail to go sleep; be sleepless; lie awake / ~을 험하게 자다 have a disorderly sleeping manner / ~이 쉽게 들다 can easily get to sleep / ~이 부족하다 be short of sleep / ~에서 깨다 awake from *one's* sleep.

잠결 ¶~에 while asleep; in *one's* sleep / ~에 듣다 hear half asleep.

잠귀 ¶~가 밝다 be easily awakened; be a light sleeper / ~가 어둡다 be a sound sleeper.

잠그다[1] 《자물쇠로》 lock 《a door》; fasten 《a lock》; bolt (빗장을); 《수도꼭지 등을》 turn off. ¶서랍을 ~ lock a drawer / 수도를 ~ turn off the water (faucet) / 열쇠를 차 안에 놔둔 채로 문을 잠그고 나왔다 I'm locked out of my car.

잠그다[2] 《물에》 immerse; soak (dip, steep) 《in》. ¶더러운 옷을 물에 ~ soak dirty clothes in water.

잠기다[1] ① 《물 따위에》 be soaked (steeped) 《in》; be submerged 《in》, be flooded 《with》. ② 《생각·슬픔 따위에》 be lost (buried) 《in》; be sunk 《in》. ¶생각에 ~ be lost (indulged) in thought / 비애에 ~ be overwhelmed by (with) sorrow.

잠기다[2] 《자물쇠 등이》 lock; be locked; be fastened. ¶이 문은 자동으로 잠긴다 This door locks automatically. ② 《목이》 become hoarse.

잠깐 a little while; a moment; a minute. ¶~있으면 in a short time (little while) / ~기다리시오 Wait a minute, please.

잠꼬대 talking in *one's* sleep; 《허튼 소리》 silly talk; nonsense. ~하다 talk in *one's* sleep; talk nonsense (rubbish) (헛소리).

잠꾸러기 a sleepyhead; a late riser.

잠두(蠶豆) 【植】 a broad bean.

잠들다 fall asleep; go (drop off) to sleep. ¶잠든 척하다 feign to be asleep / 깊이 ~ fall fast asleep; sleep like a log.

잠망경(潛望鏡) a periscope.

잠바 a jumper.

잠방이 farmer's knee-breeches.

잠복(潛伏) 《숨기》 hiding; ambush; concealment; 《병의》 latency; incubation. ~하다 lie (be) hidden; hide (out); conceal *oneself*; 《병이》 be dormant (latent). ∥ ~기(期) the incubation (latent) period / ~초소 《군대의》 an ambush sentry box.

잠사(蠶絲) silk yarn (thread). ∥

업 silk-reeling (sericultural) industry.
잠수(潛水) diving. ~하다 dive; go under water; submerge. ∥ ~공 작원 a frogman / ~모(帽) a diving helmet / ~모함 a submarine carrier / ~병(病) submarine (caisson) disease / ~복 a diving suit; diving gear / ~부 a diver / ~함 a submarine; a sub (口) / ~함 탐지기 an asdic; a sonar.
잠시(暫時) a moment (minute); a little while. ¶ ~ 동안 for some time; for a while / ~ 후에 after a while.
잠식(蠶食) ~하다 encroach 《on》; make inroads 《into, on》; eat into 〔up〕. ¶ 해외 시장을 ~하다 make inroads into foreign markets. 〔a proverb.
잠언(箴言) an aphorism; a maxim.
잠업(蠶業) sericulture; the sericultural industry.
잠열(潛熱) latent heat; dormant temperature(인체의).
잠입(潛入) ~하다 enter secretly; steal 《sneak》 《into》; smuggle oneself 《into》. ¶ 군사 기지 안으로 ~을 시도하다 try to sneak into the military base.
잠자다 sleep; fall asleep. ☞ 자다.
잠자리[蟲] a dragonfly.
잠자리 《자는 곳》 a bed; a berth (배의). ¶ ~에 들다 go to bed / ~를 펴다 make a bed / ~에서 책을 읽다 read in bed / ~를 같이하다 sleep with; share the bed 《with》.
잠코 without a word; silently; without leave (permission)(무단히); without objection (question) (순순히). ¶ ~ 있다 keep silence; remain silent / ~ 가버리다 go away without a word.
잠잠하다(潛潛―) (be) quiet; still; silent. ¶ ~거리는 ~ All is quiet in the street.
잠재(潛在) ~하다 be (lie) latent; be dormant; lie hidden. ∥ ~적인 latent; potential / ~적 위험 a potential threat. ∥ ~능력 potential capacities / ~세력 potential (latent) power / ~수요 potential demand / ~실업 latent (invisible) unemployment / ~의식 subconsciousness.
잠정(暫定) ¶ ~적(으로) provisional(ly); tentative(ly). ∥ ~안 a tentative plan / ~예산 a provisional budget / ~조치 (take) a temporary step (measure) / ~ 협정 a provisional agreement.
잠투정하다 get peevish (fret) before (after) sleep. ¶ 우리 아기는 졸리면

늘 잠투정한다 Our baby always starts fretting when he is sleepy. 〔caisson method.
잠함(潛函) a caisson. ¶ 공법 the
잠항(潛航) a submarine voyage. ~하다 cruise 《navigate》 underwater. ∥ ~정 a submarine.
잠행(潛行) ~하다 travel in disguise; travel incognito.
잡거(雜居) ~하다 live (reside, dwell) together. ¶ ~지(地) a mixed-residence quarter.
잡건(雜件) miscellaneous matters; sundries.
잡것(雜―) 《물건》 miscellaneous junk; sundries; 《사람》 a man of coarse fiber; a mean (vulgar) fellow.
잡곡(雜穀) cereals; grain (美). ¶ ~밥 boiled rice and cereals / ~상 a dealer in cereals.
잡귀(雜鬼) sundry evil spirits.
잡기장(雜記帳) a notebook.
잡년(雜―) a loose (wanton) woman; a slut; a tramp (美俗).
잡념(雜念) worldly thoughts. ¶ ~을 떨쳐버리다 banish worldly thoughts from one's mind; put all other thoughts out of one's mind. 〔low.
잡놈(雜―) a loose (dissolute) fel-

잡다 ① 《손으로》 take (hold of); hold; catch; seize; 《쥐다》 grasp; clasp; grip. ¶ 손목을 ~ seize 《a person》 by the wrist / 내 손을 꼭 잡았다 She grasped my hand firmly. / 그 계획을 실행하려면 그들과 손을 잡아야 한다 We should join forces with them to put the plan into practice. ② 《체포》 catch; arrest; capture. ¶ 도둑을 ~ catch a thief. ③ 《포획》 catch; take; get. ¶ 쥐를 ~ catch (hunt) rats / 고기를 잡으러 가다 go fishing. ④ 《기회·권력을》 take; seize; assume. ¶ 권력을 ~ take power / 기회를 ~ catch (seize) an opportunity / 그 당은 오랫 동안 정권을 잡고 있다 That party has been in power for a long time. / 회사의 실권은 그녀가 잡고 있다 The real power over the company is in her hands. ⑤ 《증거를》 seize; hold; secure. ¶ 증거를 ~ secure (obtain) proof 《of》. ⑥ 《담보로》 take (receive) 《a thing as security》. ⑦ 《어림을》 estimate 《a thing》 at; value at. ¶ 줄잡아 ~ make a rough estimate / 최대한 (최소한)으로 잡아서 at the highest (lowest) estimate / 지나치게 많이 ~ overestimate. ⑧ 《차지함》 occupy; take (up). ¶ 장소를 ~ occupy (take up) room. ⑨ 《정하다》 fix; decide; choose (골라서); 《예약》 reserve; book. ¶ 날을 ~ fix the date / 방

향을 ~ take *one's* course / 호텔에 방을 ~ reserve a room at a hotel. ⑩ (도살) butcher; slaughter. ¶ 돼지를 ~ butcher a hog. ⑪ (모해) plot against; lay a trap (for); slander. ¶ 사람 잡을 소리 그만해 Stop slandering me. ⑫ (불을) put out; hold (a fire) under control. ⑬ (주름 따위) pleat; fold; make a crease. ⑭ (마음을) get a grip on *oneself*; hold (*one's passion*) under control. ¶ 마음을 잡고 공부하다 study in a settled frame of mind. ⑮ (트집·약점 등을) find. ¶ 탈을 ~ find fault (with); throw cold water (on) / 아무의 약점을 ~ have something on *a person*.

잡다(雜多) ¶ ~한 various; miscellaneous; sundry.

잡담(雜談) gossip; idle talk; a chat. ~하다 (have) a chat (with); gossip (with).

잡동사니 mixture; odds and ends.

잡되다(雜一) (be) loose; obscene; indecent; vulgar; mean.

잡록(雜錄) a miscellany; miscellaneous notes.

잡목(雜木) miscellaneous small trees. ¶ ~숲 a thicket; scrub.

잡무(雜務) odd jobs; trifling things; (일상의) trivial everyday duties; routine work. ¶ ~에 쫓기다 be kept busy with odd jobs.

잡문(雜文) miscellaneous writings. ¶ ~가 a miscellanist.

잡물(雜物) sundries; (불순물) impurities; foreign ingredients.

잡병(雜病) various diseases.

잡보(雜報) general [miscellaneous] news.

잡부금(雜賦金) miscellaneous fees. ¶ ~을 거두다 collect miscellaneous fees.

잡비(雜費) sundry [miscellaneous, insidental] expenses. ¶ ~계정 a petty expenses account.

잡살뱅이 odds and ends; a jumble; *a medley*.

잡상인(雜商人) peddlers; miscellaneous traders. ∥ ~출입금지 (게시) No peddlers.

잡소리(雜一) (상스러운) an obscene [indecent] talk; (잡음) noise.

잡수다, 잡숫다 ☞ 먹다.

잡수입(雜收入) (개인의) miscellaneous income; (공공단체의) miscellaneous revenues (receipts).

잡스럽다(雜一) ☞ 잡되다.

잡식(雜食) ¶ ~의 omnivorous ; ~성동물 an omnivorous animal.

잡신(雜神) sundry evil spirits.

잡아가다 take (*a suspect*) to (*a police station*).

잡아내다 (결점·잘못을) pick at (*flaws*); point out (*mistakes*).

잡아당기다 pull (at); draw; tug (세게). ¶ 귀를 ~ pull (*a person*) by the ear / 홱 ~ give (*a thing*) a jerk / 밧줄을 힘껏 ~ give a strong pull at the rope / 진흙에 빠진 달구지를 ~ tug the cart out of the mire.

잡아들이다 take (*a person*) in; bring (*a person*) in; arrest.

잡아떼다 ① (손으로) pull (*a thing*) apart; take [tear, rip] off. ② (부인) pretend to know nothing (*about*); deny flatly; brazen (face) it out.

잡아매다 (한데 묶다) tie up; bind; fasten; bundle; (잡아 묶다) tie (*a horse*) to (*a post*); bind (*somebody*) to (*a stake*); fasten (*a rope*) to (*a tree*). ¶ 해적들은 그 사내를 돛대에 잡아맸다 The pirates tied the man to the mast.

잡아먹다 ① (사람이 동물을) slaughter [butcher] (*a hog*) and eat; (짐승이 짐승을) prey on (*birds*). ¶ 족제비는 쥐를 잡아 먹는다 Weasels prey on mice. ② (괴롭히다) torture; harass. ¶ 나를 잡아먹을 듯이 야단치다 harass me mercilessly. ③ (시간·경비 등을) ¶ 시간을 많이 ~ take lots of time.

잡역(雜役) odd jobs; chores. ∥ ~부(夫) an odd-job man; a handyman.

잡음(雜音) ① a noise; radio noise (라디오의); surface noise (레코드의). ¶ 도시의 ~ city noises. ② (부당한 간섭) ¶ 외부의 ~에 귀를 기울이지 않다 close *one's* ears to the irresponsible criticism of outsiders.

잡일(雜一) ☞ 잡역, 잡무.

잡종(雜種) a crossbred; a cross (*between*); a hybrid. ¶ ~을 만들다 hybridize; cross one breed with another; interbreed. ∥ ~견 a mongrel (dog).

잡지(雜誌) a magazine; a journal (전문 분야의); a periodical (정기 간행의). ¶ ~를 구독하다 take [subscribe to] a magazine / ~에 기고하다 write for a magazine. ∥ ~기자 a magazine writer [reporter] / ~편집자 a magazine editor / 여성~ a women's magazine.

잡채(雜菜) chop suey (美); a Chinese dish made of bits of vegetables and meat (served with rice).

잡초(雜草) weeds. ¶ ~를 뽑다 weed (*a garden*) / ~가 우거진 정원 a weed-grown garden / ~처럼 생명력이 강하다 have a strong hold on life like weeds.

잡치다 spoil; ruin; make a mess [muddle] of; hurt (기분을). ¶ 일을

잡탕 ~ make a mess [muddle] of *one's* work / 기분을 ~ hurt *a person's* feeling.

잡탕(雜湯) ① 《음식》 a mixed soup [broth]; (a) hotchpotch; 《범벅》 a medley; a hodgepodge 《美》; a jumble.

잡혼(雜婚) intermarriage; a mixed marriage.

잡화(雜貨) miscellaneous [sundry] goods; general merchandise. ‖ ~상＝a grocer; a general dealer / ~점 a grocer's; a variety store.

잡히다 ① 《손에》 be taken [up]; be held [in *one's* hand]; 《포착·포획》 get caught [seized, taken, captured]. ¶ 경찰에 ~ be caught by the police. ② 《영상》 form, ¶ 모양이 ~ take a form. ③ 《불이》 be held [put] under control. ④ 《담보로》 give (a thing) as security; pawn. ¶ 토지를 ~ mortgage *one's* land; give *one's* land as security (*for a ten million won loan*). ⑤ 《기타》 균형이 ~ be well-balanced / 트집을 ~ be found fault with / 주름이 ~ get creased [wrinkled].

잣 pine nuts [seeds]. ‖ ~나무 a big cone pine / ~죽 pine-nut gruel [porridge]; gruel made of rice and pine nuts.

잣다 ① 《물을》 pump [suck, draw] up. ② 《실을》 spin out: make yarn. ¶ 솜에서 실을 ~ spin cotton into yarn.

잣대 yardstick.

잣새 《鳥》 a crossbill.

잣송이 a pine cone.

장(長) ① 《우두머리》 the head; the chief; the leader. ② ☞ 장점. ¶ ~ 일단이 있다 have both advantages and disadvantages.

장(章) 《책의》 a chapter; 《획기적 시대》 an era. ¶ 제 2 ~ the second chapter / 새로운 ~을 열다 open a new era; make an epoch (*in*).

장(場)¹ 《시장》 a market; mart; a fair(정기적인). ¶ 대목 ~ a fair at the very end of the year / ~거리 a market place / ~날 a market day / ~보다 do *one's* shopping / ~보러 가다 go shopping.

장(場)² 《장소》 a place; a site; a ground; 《연극의》 a scene; 《理》 a field.

장(腸) the intestines; the bowels. ¶ ~의 intestinal / ~이 나쁘다 have bowel trouble / ~내 세균 intestinal bacteria. ‖ ~궤양 an intestinal ulcer / ~암 intestinal cancer / ~염 inflammation of the intestine / ~폐색 intestinal obstruction.

장(醬) 《간장》 soy (sauce); 《간장과 된장》 soy and bean paste.

장(欌) a chest of drawers; a chest; a wardrobe(양복장); 《거울이 달린》 a bureau 《美》.

장(張) a sheet; a piece; a leaf. ¶ 종이 두 ~ two sheets of paper.

장갑(掌甲) (a pair of) gloves [mitten(벙어리 장갑)]. ¶ ~을 끼다 [벗다] put on [pull off] *one's* gloves.

장갑(裝甲) armoring. ~하다 armor. ¶ ~한 armored; armorplated; ironclad. ‖ ~부대 an armored corps / ~자동차 an armored car [truck].

장거(壯擧) a heroic undertaking [scheme]; a daring attempt. ¶ 세계 일주 항해의 ~ a grand project of a round-the-world voyage.

장거리(長距離) a long [great] distance; a long range(사격의). ‖ ~경주〔선수〕a long-distance race [runner] / ~버스 a long-way bus / ~비행 a long-range flight / ~전화 a long-distance call [a trunk call 《英》] / ~포〔폭격기〕 a long-range gun [bomber].

장검(長劍) a (long) sword.

장골(壯骨) stout built physique.

장과(漿果) 《植》 a berry.

장관(壯觀) a grand sight [view]; a magnificent spectacle. ¶ ~을 이루다 present a grand sight [spectacle].

장관(長官) 《내각의》 a minister; a Cabinet minister; 《미국 각 부의》 a Secretary; 《지방의 장관》 a governor. ¶ 국무~ the Secretary of State 《美》 / 지방~ a provincial governor.

장관(將官) 《육군》 a general (officer); 《해군》 a flag officer; an admiral.

장광설(長廣舌) (make) a long [longwindded] speech [talk].

장교(將校) an (a commissioned) officer. ¶ 육군〔해군〕 ~ a military [naval] officer.

장구 traditional double-headed drum pinched in at the middle. ‖ ~채 a drumstick.

장구(長久) permanence; eternity; perpetuity. ¶ ~한 eternal; permanent / ~한 시일을 요하다 require a long period of time.

장구(裝具) an outfit; equipment; gear; harness(말의).

장구벌레 a mosquito larva [*pl.* ~vae].

장국(醬―) soup flavored with soy sauce. ‖ ~밥 rice in beef soup flavored with soy sauce.

장군(將軍) a general.

장기(長技) *one's* specialty [speciality] 《美》; *one's* forte; *one's* strong point. ¶ …을 ~로 하다 be good [skillful] at / 그 노래가 그녀의 ~

이다 That song is her specialty〔favorite〕.
장기(長期) a long time〔term〕. ¶ ~의 long; long-term / ~에 걸치다 extend over a long period of time. / ~결석 a long absence / ~계획〔예보〕 a long-range plan〔forecast〕 / ~대부〔거래〕 a long-term loan〔transaction〕 / ~신용 long-term credit / ~전 a long〔protracted〕 war / ~흥행 a long run.
장기(將棋) *changgi*. the game of Korean chess. ¶ ~를 두다 have a game of *changgi*. ‖ ~짝 a chessman / ~판 a chessboard.
장기(臟器) internal organs; (the) viscera. ¶ 인공 ~ artificial internal organs / ~를 기증하다 give〔donate〕 one's internal organs (after death) 《*to a hospital for medical research*》 / ~이식 an internal organ transplant.
장꾼(場一) marketeers; (고객) marketers; market crowds (모인 사람).
장끼 a cock-pheasant. └암.
장난(놀이) a game; play; fun; amusement; a joke (농); (못된) mischief; a prank; a trick. ~하다 play a trick〔prank, joke〕《*on*》; play with 《*fire*》 do mischief (못된). ‖ 못된 ~ malicious mischief; a joke for (mere) fun; in joke. ¶ ~꾸러기 a naughty〔mischievous〕 child〔fellow〕 / ~전화 a nuisance phone call; a prank call.
장난감 a toy; a plaything.
장남(長男) one's eldest son.
장내(場內) ~에서 in〔within〕 the grounds; on the premises; in the hall. ‖ ~방송 (an announcement over) the public address system《*in the stadium*》 / ~정리 crowd control in the hall / ~조명〔극장의〕 the houselights.
장녀(長女) one's eldest daughter.
장년(壯年) (in) the prime of manhood〔life〕. ¶ ~이 되다 reach manhood; attain the prime of manhood.
장님 a blind man; the blind (총칭). ¶ 눈뜬 ~ an unlettered〔illiterate〕 person / ~이 되다 become〔go〕 blind; lose one's sight.
장단(長短) ① (길이의) (relative) length; (장점과 단점) merits and demerits. ¶ ~이 있다 have both merits and demerits. ② (박자) time; a rhythm. ¶ ~을 맞추다 keep time《*to, with*》.
장담(壯談) assurance; guarantee; affirmation. ~하다 assure; guarantee; vouch 《*for*》; affirm.
장대(長一) a (bamboo) pole. ‖ ~높이뛰기 a pole jump; a pole vault《美》.

장대하다(壯大一) (be) big and stout〔strong〕. ¶ 기골이 장대한 사람 a strapping person; a strapper.
장도(壯途) an ambitious course〔departure〕. ¶ 북극 탐험의 ~에 오르다 start on an ambitious polar expedition.
장도(粧刀) an ornamental knife.
장도리 a hammer; (노루발) a claw hammer. ¶ ~로 치다 hammer / ~로 못을 박다 hammer a nail in / ~로 못을 뽑다 pull〔draw〕 out a nail with a claw hammer. └race).
장대대(瓶─壺) a jar stand (ter- **장돌림, 장돌뱅이**(場─) a roving marketer.
장딴지 the calf (of the leg).
장래(將來) (the) future; the time to come; (부사적) in (the) future. ¶ ~의 future; prospective / 가까운〔먼〕 ~에 in the near〔distant〕 future / ~가 있는 promising; with a bright future / ~를 생각〔예언〕하다 look to〔predict〕 the future. ‖ ~성 possibilities; prospect. └nificent; grand.
장려(壯麗) ~한 splendid; mag- **장려**(獎勵) encouragement. ~하다 encourage; promote. ¶ 우리 학교에서는 운동을 ~한다 Our school encourages sports. ‖ ~금 a bounty《*on*》; a subsidy / ~급〔임금〕 incentive wages.
장력(張力) 〔理〕 tension; tensile strength. ¶ 표면 ~ surface tension. / ~계 a tensiometer.
장렬(壯烈) ~한 heroic; brave; gallant / ~한 죽음을 하다 die a heroic death.
장례(葬禮) a funeral〔burial〕(service). ¶ ~행렬 a funeral procession / ~를 거행하다 conduct a funeral / ~에 참석하다 attend a funeral.
장로(長老) 〔선배〕 an elder; a senior; (교회의) a presbyter. ‖ ~교회 the Presbyterian Church.
장롱(欌籠) a chest of drawers; a bureau《美》.
장마 the long spell of rainy weather (in early summer); the rainy〔wet〕 season. ¶ ~지다 the rainy season sets in / ~가 걷히다 the rainy season is over. ‖ ~전선 a seasonal rainfront.
장막(帳幕) a curtain; a hanging; a tent (천막); 〔철의 ~ the iron curtain / ~을 치다 hang (up) curtains.
장만하다 prepare; provide *oneself*《*with*》; raise; get. ¶ 돈을 ~ make〔raise〕 money / 집을 ~ get a house.
장면(場面) a scene; a place; a

spot. ¶ 연애 ~ a love scene.
장모(丈母) one's wife's mother; one's mother-in-law.
장문(長文) a long sentence [passage]. ¶ ~의 편지 a long letter.
장물(贓物) stolen goods [articles]. ‖ ~매매 dealing in stolen goods; fencing《俗》/ ~아비 dealer in stolen goods; a fence《俗》/ ~취득 buying goods with full knowledge that they are stolen goods.
장미(薔薇) a rose;《나무》a rose tree. ¶ 들~ a wild rose; a brier / 장밋빛의 rosy; rose-colored.
장발(長髮) ¶ ~의 long-haired. ‖ ~족 longhairs.
장벽(障壁) a wall; a fence; a barrier. ¶ ~을 쌓다 build a barrier / ~이 되다 be an obstacle 《to》. ‖ 언어~ a language barrier.
장병(將兵) officers and men; soldiers.
장복(長服) ~하다 take 《a medicine》 constantly.
장본인(張本人) the author 《of a plot》; the ringleader; the prime mover.
장부【建】a tenon; a pivot; a cog. ‖ 장붓구멍 a mortise. 「person.
장부(丈夫) a man; a manly [brave]
장부(帳簿) an account book; a book; a ledger(원부). ¶ ~에 기입하다 enter 《an item》 in the book / ~를 매기다 keep books [accounts] / ~를 속이다 falsify accounts; cook up the books. ‖ ~가격 book value / ~계원 a bookkeeper / ~정리 adjustment of accounts / 이중~ double bookkeeping.
장비(裝備) equipment; (an) outfit. ~하다 equip; outfit; mount (대포를). ¶ 중~의 heavily equipped / ~가 좋은 [나쁜] well-[poorly-]equipped / 완전 ~를 갖춘 병사 fully-equipped soldiers / 진지에 대포를 ~하다 equip a position with guns.
장사 trade; business; commerce. ~하다 do [engage in] business; conduct a trade. ¶ ~를 시작하다 [그만두다] start [close] one's business / ~에 솜씨가 있다 [없다] have a good [poor] sense of business / 이것은 수지 맞는 ~다 This is a paying business. / 무슨 ~를 하십니까 What line of business are you in? /「~가 잘 됩니까?」—「예, 아주 잘 됩니다」"How is your business?" "I'm doing pretty good (business)." ‖ ~꾼 a tradesman; a merchant.
장사(壯士) a man of great [physical] strength; a Hercules. ¶ 힘이 ~다 be as strong as Her-

cules.
장사(葬事) a funeral (service). ¶ ~ 지내다 hold a funeral service; perform the burial.
장사진(長蛇陣) a long line [queue]. ¶ ~을 이루다 make [stand in] a long line [queue].
장삼(長衫) a long-sleeved Buddhist monk's robe.
장삿속 a commercial spirit; a profit-making motive. ¶ ~을 떠나서 with no thought of gain; from disinterested motives.
장색(匠色) an artisan; a craftsman.
장서(藏書) a collection of books; one's library. ¶ 3만의 ~가 있다 have a library of 30,000 books. ‖ ~가 a book collector / ~목록 a library catalog / ~인 an ownership stamp [mark].
장성 ~하다 grow (up); grow to maturity.
장성(將星) generals. ¶ 육해군 ~ army and navy celebrities.
장소(場所) ① 《곳》 a place; a spot (지점); a location; a position(위장); a site(소재지); the scene(현장). ¶ 경치 좋은 ~ a scenic spot / 사람의 눈을 끄는 ~ an attractive spot / 약속의 ~ the appointed place / 화재[사고]가 났던 ~ the scene of a fire [an accident] / 그 건물은 편리한 ~에 위치하고 있다 The building is conveniently located [situated]. ② 《자리》 room; space. ¶ ~를 차지하다 take up (much) space.
장손(長孫) the eldest grandson by the first-born son.
장송(長松) a tall pine tree.
장송곡(葬送曲) a funeral march.
장수 a trader; a dealer; a seller; a peddler(도붓장수). ¶ 생선 ~ a fishmonger.
장수(長壽) long life; longevity. ~하다 live long; live to a great age. ‖ ~법 the secret of longevity.
장수(將帥) a commander-in-chief.
장승 a totem pole; 《키다리》a tall person. ¶ ~ 같다 be as tall as a lamppost.
장시세(場市勢) the market price.
장시일(長時日) a long (period of) time; (for) years. ¶ ~에 걸치다 extend over a long period of time.
장식(裝飾) decoration; ornament; (a) dressing(상점 앞의). ~하다 ornament; decorate; adorn. ¶ ~적인 decorative; ornamental / ~용의 for decorative [ornamental] purpose / ~용 전구 a decorative light bulb / 실내 [무대] ~ interior [stage] decoration / 쇼윈도에 크리

스마스 ~을 하다 dress a store window for Christmas. ‖ ~**품** decorations; ornaments.
장신(長身) ¶ ~**의** tall / ~**의 농구 선수** a tall basketball player.
장신구(裝身具) personal ornaments; accessories.
장아찌 sliced vegetables preserved in soy sauce (pepper paste).
장악(掌握) ~하다 command; have a hold on; completely grasp *(the situation)*. ¶ **정권을 ~** take (over) the reins of government; come into power.
장안(長安)의 the capital. ¶ **서울 ~** Seoul, the capital city / **온 ~에** throughout the capital.
장애(障礙·障碍) an obstacle; an impediment. ¶ ~**가 되다** be an obstacle 《to》; hinder; be in the way 《of》 / ~**를 극복하다** surmount (get over) an obstacle. ‖ ~**물** an obstacle; a barrier / ~**물경주** a hurdle race / ~**인** the handicapped.
장어(長魚) [魚] an eel. ‖ ~**구이** a split and broiled eel.
장엄(莊嚴)하다 (be) sublime; majestic; solemn; grand. ¶ ~**한 음악** solemn (sublime) music / **대관식은 ~하게 거행되었다** The coronation was solemnly performed.
장외(場外) ¶ ~**에(서)** outside the hall (grounds). ‖ ~**거래 (시장)** over-the-counter trading (market) / ~**주(株)** a curb stock / ~**집회** an outdoor rally.
장원(壯元) passing the state examination first on the list; 《사람》 the first place winner in a state examination.
장원(莊園) a manor.
장유(長幼) young and old.
장음(長音) a prolonged sound; a long vowel. ‖ ~**계** [樂] the major scale.
장의사(葬儀社) an undertaker's; a funeral parlor 《美》; 《사람》 an undertaker; a mortician 《美》.
…장이 a professional doer of…; -er. ¶ **구두~** a shoemaker.
장인(丈人) one's wife's father; a man's father-in-law.
장인(匠人) an artisan; a craftsman.
장자(長子) the eldest son. ‖ ~**상속권** the right of primogeniture.
장자(長者) ① 《덕망가》 a man of moral influence; 《어른》 an elder; one's senior. ② 《부자》 a rich (wealthy) man.
장작(長斫) firewood. ¶ ~**을 패다** chop wood. ‖ ~**개비** a piece of firewood.
장장추야(長長秋夜) the long nights of autumn.
장장하일(長長夏日) the long days of summer.

장전(裝塡) charge 《of a gun》**; loading. ~하다** load (charge) 《a gun》.
장점(長點) a merit; a strong (good) point; one's forte.
장정(壯丁) a strong young man; 《징병 적령자》 a young man of conscription age.
장정(裝幀) ~하다 bind; design (표지의). ¶ **호화 ~** deluxe binding / **가죽으로 ~되어 있다** be bound in leather.
장조(長調) [樂] a major key.
장조림(醬—) beef boiled down in soy sauce.
장조카(長—) the eldest son of one's eldest brother.
장족(長足)의 진보를 하다 make great (remarkable) progress 《in》.
장죽(長竹) a long (smoking) pipe.
장중(掌中) ¶ ~**에** within one's hands (power, grip).
장중하다(莊重—) 《장중한 느낌의》 solemn; grave; impressive / **장중한 어조로** in a solemn tone.
장지(障—) a paper sliding-door. ‖ ~**틀** a sliding-door frame.
장지(葬地) a burial ground (ground).
장지(長指) the middle finger.
장차(將次) in (the) future; some day.
장창(長槍) a long spear.
장총(長銃) a (long-barreled) rifle.
장치(裝置) (a) device; equipment; a (mechanical) contrivance; an apparatus (특수 목적의); 《무대의》 setting. ~**하다** install; equip (fit) 《with》. ¶ **안전 ~** a safety device / **레이더 ~** radar equipment / ~**되어 있다** be equipped (fitted) 《with》 / **이 승강기에는 안전 ~가 되어 있다** This elevator has a safety catch. / **난방 〔냉방〕 ~를 하다** install the heating (cooling) apparatus.
장쾌(壯快)하다 stirring; exciting; thrilling.
장타(長打) [野] (make) a long hit. ¶ ~**율** one's slugging average / ~**자** a long hitter. 〔gun〕
장탄(裝彈) ~하다 load (charge) 《a**장티푸스(腸—)** typhoid fever. ¶ ~**균** the typhoid bacillus / ~**예방 주사** anti-typhoid inoculation / ~**환자** a typhoid.
장파(長波) a long wave.
장판(壯版) a floor covered with oil-laquered paper. ‖ ~**방** a room with paper-covered floor / ~**지** (a sheet of) oiled floor paper.
장편(長篇) a long piece. ‖ ~**소설** a long story (novel) / ~**영화** a long film (picture).
장하다(壯—) 《훌륭하다》 (be) great; splendid; glorious; 《가륵하다》 (be) praiseworthy; admirable; brave; 《놀랍다》 (be) wonderful; striking.
장학(獎學) ‖ ~**금** a scholarship

장화 (~금을 주다〔받다〕award〔obtain, win〕a scholarship) / ~기금 a scholarship fund / ~사 a school inspector / ~생 a student on a scholarship; a scholarship student.

장화(長靴) high〔long〕boots; top boots (승마용).

잦다¹〔열로 인해 물이〕dry (up); boil down.

잦다²〔빈번〕(be) frequent;〔빠르다〕(be) quick; rapid. ¶ 잦은 걸음으로 걷다 walk〔at a quick pace〔with quick steps〕/ 겨울에는 불이 ~ Fires are frequent in winter.

잦아지다 dry up; be boiled down.

잦혀놓다 ①〔뒤집다〕turn《a thing》over and leave it; lay《a thing》face〔upside〕down. ②〔열다〕leave《a swing door》flung open.

잦히다 ①〔뒤집다〕turn《a plate》upside down; turn over. ②〔열다〕fling open. ¶ 문을 ~ fling a door open. ③〔몸을 뒤로〕pull back《one's shoulders》; bend《oneself》backward. ④〔일 따위를〕put aside《one's work》.

잦히다〔밥을〕let the rice stand on a low flame; stew.

재〔타고 남은〕ash(es). ¶ ~가 되다 be burnt〔reduced〕to ashes / 담뱃 ~를 떨다 knock〔tap〕the ash off *one's* cigarette (into an ashtray).

재²〔고개〕(cross over) a pass.

재(齋) a Buddhist service〔mass〕

재…(再) re-. 〔for the dead.

재가(再嫁) remarriage (of a woman). ~하다 marry again; remarry.

재가(裁可) sanction; approval. ~하다 sanction; approve; give sanction to.

재간(才幹) ability. ☞ 재능.

재간(再刊) republication; reissue. ~하다 republish; reissue.

재갈 a (bridle) bit. ¶ ~ 물리다 bridle《a horse》; gag《a person》.

재갈매기〔鳥〕a herring gull.

재감(在監) ~하다 be in prison〔jail〕. ~자 a prisoner; a prison inmate.

재감염(再感染) reinfection. ☞ 감염.

재개(再開) reopening; resumption. ~하다 reopen; resume《business》.

재개발(再開發) redevelopment. ~하다 redevelop. ∥ ~지역 a redevelopment area〔zone〕.

재건(再建) reconstruction; rebuilding. ~하다 rebuild; reconstruct. ∥ ~ 비용 rebuilding expenses / 산업〔경제〕~ industrial〔economic〕reconstruction.

재검사(再檢査) reexamination. ~

하다 reinspect; reexamine.

재검토(再檢討) reexamination; reappraisal. ~하다 reexamine; reappraise; review; rethink.

재결(裁決) decision; judgment; verdict (배심원의). ~하다 give *one's* decision〔judgment〕(on); decide. ¶ 문제의 ~을 당국에 맡기다 leave the problem to the authorities' judgment.

재결합(再結合) recombination; reunion. ~하다 reunite《with》; recombine; rejoin together.¶이산 가족의 ~ reunion of *one's* dispersed family members.

재경(在京) ~하다 be in Seoul. ∥ ~ 동창생 alumni in Seoul / ~의 외국인 foreign residents in Seoul.

재경기(再競技) a rematch.

재계(財界) the financial〔business〕world; financial〔business〕circles. ¶ ~의 financial / ~의 거물 a leading financier; a business magnate / ~의 안정〔동요〕financial stability〔unrest〕/ ~가 활기를 띠다 The financial world shows signs of activity. ∥ ~인 a financier; a businessman.

재계(齋戒) ~하다 purify *oneself*. ∥ 목욕 ~ a ritual cleaning〔purification〕of mind and body.

재고(再考) reconsideration. ~하다 reconsider; rethink. ¶ ~의 여지가 없다 There is no room for reconsideration.

재고(在庫) stock. ¶ ~의 in store〔stock〕/ ~가 있다〔없다〕be in〔out of〕stock. ∥ ~ 파일 excess stock; over-stocking / ~ 관리 control of goods in stock; inventory control〔美〕/ ~량 the total stock / ~ 정리 inventory adjustment; clearance / ~ 조사 stock-taking; inventory / ~ 조사하다 check the stock / ~품 a stock (of toys); goods in stock / ~품 목록 an inventory; a stock list.

재교부(再交付) reissue. ~하다 reissue; regrant. ¶ 신분 증명서를 ~하다 reissue an ID card.

재교육(再敎育) reeducation. ~하다 reeducate; retrain. ¶ ~ 코스 a refresher course / 현직 교사의 ~ teachers' in-service training.

재구속(再拘束)〔法〕(a) remand. ~하다 remand《a suspect》(in custody).

재귀(再歸) ∥ ~ 대명사〔동사〕a reflexive pronoun〔verb〕/ ~열〔醫〕a relapsing fever.

재기(才氣) a flash of wit; (a) talent. ¶ ~ 있는 clever; witty; talented / ~ 발랄한 full of wit; resourceful.

재기(再起) a comeback (복귀); recovery (회복); a return to popu-

재깍 《소리》 with a click (clack, snap); 《빨리》 promptly; with dispatch.

재깍거리다 make a clicking (snapping) sound; 《시계가》 tick(tack).

재난(災難) a mishap; a misfortune (불행); a calamity; a disaster (재화). ¶ ~을 당하다 have a mishap (an accident); meet with a misfortune / ~을 면하다 escape a disaster.

재능(才能) (a) talent; ability; a gift. ¶ ~ 있는 talented; able; gifted / ~을 발휘하다 show *one's* ability / 음악에 ~이 있다 have a gift [talent] for music.

재다¹ ① 《크기·치수 등을》 measure; gauge (무게를) weigh; 《깊이를》 sound; 《수·눈금·시간을》 take; time(시간). ¶ 강의 수심을 ~ sound [fathom] the depth of a river / 거리를 ~ measure the distance / 체중을 ~ weigh *oneself*(*a person*) / 풍력을 ~ gauge the strength of the wind / 체온을 ~ take *one's* temperature. ② 《장탄하다》 load (*a gun*); charge (*with*). ③ 《헤아리다》 calculate; give careful consideration. ¶ 앞뒤를 ~ look before and after. ④ 《평가하다》 measure; estimate; judge (판단). ¶ 재산으로는 사람의 가치를 잴 수 없다 We cannot measure a person's worth by his wealth. ⑤ 《재우다》 have (*a thing*) pressed. ⑥ 《으스대다》 give *oneself* [put on] airs.

재다² 《재빠르다》 be quick; prompt; nimble. ¶ 재게 quickly; promptly; nimbly. ⑤ 《입이》 (be) talkative; glib-tongued.

재단(財團) a foundation. ¶ ~ 법인 an incorporated foundation; a foundation / 록펠러 ~ the Rockefeller Foundation.

재단(裁斷) ① ~ 재결. ② 《마름질》 cutting. ¶ ~하다 cut; cut out (*a dress*). ∥ ~기 a cutter; a cutting machine / ~사 a (tailor's) cutter; a cloth-cutter.

재담(才談) a witticism; a joke; a jest; a witty talk.

재덕(才德) talents and virtues. ¶ ~ 을 겸비한 virtuous and talented; of [with] virtue and talent.

재동(才童) a clever [talented] child.

재두루미 [鳥] a white-naped crane.

재떨이 an ashtray.

재래(在來) ① 《여느》 usual; common; ordinary; conventional; traditional / ~식 병기 conventional weapons / ~의 기술 traditional technology. ∥ ~식 a conventional type / ~종 a native kind / ~종 딸기 native strawberries.

재래(再來) ☞ 재림(再臨). 「fulness.

재량(才量) resourcefulness; tact-

재량(裁量) discretion; decision. ¶ …의 ~에 맡기다 leave (*a matter*) to (*a person's*) discretion.

재력(財力) financial power (ability); 《재산》 wealth; means. ¶ ~이 있는 사람 a man of means (wealth) / ~을 과시하다 let *one's* money talk.

재롱(才弄) 《아기의》 cute things. ¶ ~을 부리다 act cute; do cute things.

재료(材料) 《물건을 만드는》 material(s); stuff; raw materials (원료); ingredient(성분); 《중권에서, 장세를 움직이게 하는 요소》 a factor. ¶ 건축 ~ building (construction) materials / 낙관적 [비관적] ~ 《중권에서의》 an encouraging (a disheartening) factor / 실험 ~ materials for experiments / 케이크의 주된 ~ the main ingredients of cake. ∥ ~고갈 exhaustion of materials / ~비 the cost of materials / ~시험 material(s) testing.

재류(在留) ~하다 reside; stay.

재림(再臨) a second coming (advent). ~하다 come again. ¶ 그리스도의 ~ the Second Advent (of Christ).

재목(材木) wood; 《제재목》 lumber 《美》; timber 《英》. ¶ ~을 얻기 위해 벌채하다 lumber 《美》; cut down timber 《英》 / ~을 건조시키다 season the wood. ∥ ~상 a lumber dealer / ~적치장 a lumberyard.

재무(財務) financial affairs. ∥ ~감사 financial audit / ~관 a financial commissioner / ~부(성) 《미국의》 the Department of Treasury / ~부장관 《미국의》 the Secretary of Treasury / ~제표 financial statements.

재무장(再武裝) rearmament. ~하다 rearm; remilitarize.

재물(財物) property; means; goods; treasures; a fortune.

재미 ① 《일반적》 interest; amusement; enjoyment; pleasure; fun. ¶ ~ (가) 있다 (나는) be interesting (pleasant) / ~없다 be uninteresting (dull) / ~를 보다 have a good time (of it); have fun; enjoy *oneself* / ~를 붙이다 amuse *oneself* (*with*); be amused (*at*, *with*) / …에 ~를 붙이다 be interested in: find (take) pleasure in. ② 《취미》 a pastime; a hobby; fun; comfort. ¶ 꽃을 ~로 기르다

재미 grow flowers for a hobby / 낚시가 그의 유일한 ~다 Fishing is his sole comfort. ③ 《관용적 표현》¶ …으로 ~를 보다 make (get, gain) a profit on (out of, from) / 요새 장사 ~가 어떻습니까 How is your business getting along? / 결과는 ~없었다 The result was unsatisfactory.

재미(在美) ¶ ~의 in America (the U.S.) / ~중에 during *one's* stay in America. ∥ ~교포 a Korean resident in America.

재민(災民) ⇨ 이재민(罹災民).

재발(再發) a relapse; recurrence. ~하다 《병이 주어》 return; recur; 《사람이 주어》 have a relapse (of); have a second (another) attack (of). ¶ 그는 병이 ~했다 He had a relapse of the disease. / 비슷한 사고의 ~을 방지하기 위한 최선의 대책 the best possible measure to keep similar accidents from happening again. 《*license*》.

재발급(再發給) ~하다 reissue (*a license*》.

재발족(再發足) ~하다 make a fresh start; start afresh.

재방송(再放送) rebroadcasting; a rerun. ~하다 rebroadcast.

재배(再拜) ~하다 bow twice.

재배(栽培) cultivation; culture; growing. ~하다 cultivate; grow; raise. ¶ 과수 ~ fruit growing / 촉성 ~ 한 야채 forced vegetables / 비닐하우스에서 야채를 ~하다 grow vegetables in a plastic greenhouse. ∥ ~기술 cultivation technique / ~식물 a cultivated plant / ~자 a grower; a cultivator.

재배치(再配置) relocation; reassignment. ~하다 reassign; relocate.

재벌(財閥) a *chaebol*; business conglomerates; a financial combine (group); a giant family concern (친족의). ¶ 호남 ~ the *Honam* financial group. ∥ ~해체 the dissolution of the financial combine.

재범(再犯) repetition of an offense; a second offense. ∥ ~자 a second offender.

재보(財寶) riches (부); treasure(s) (귀중품).

재보험(再保險) reinsurance. ~하다 reinsure.

재봉(裁縫) sewing; needlework. ~하다 sew; do needlework. ∥ ~사 a tailor; a seamstress (여).

재봉틀(裁縫─) a sewing machine. ¶ ~로 박다 sew (*a thing*) by (sewing) machine.

재분배(再分配) redistribution. ~하다 redistribute. ¶ 부(富)의 ~ redistribution of wealth.

재빠르다 (be) quick; nimble. ¶ 재빠르게 nimbly; quickly.

재수

재사(才士) a man of talent (wit).

재산(財産) property; a fortune; estate. ¶ 사유 〔공유, 국유〕 ~ private (public, national) property / ~을 모으다 〔없애다〕 make 〔lose〕 *one's* fortune / 그는 ~을 노리고 그녀와 결혼했다 He married her for money (her fortune). / ~가 a man of property / ~권 the right to own property; property rights / ~목록 an inventory (of property) / ~상속 property inheritance / ~세 a property (wealth) tax.

재삼(再三) ¶ ~재사(再四) again and again; over and over again.

재상(宰相) the prime minister.

재상영(再上映) a rerun. ~하다 rerun (*a movie*); show (*a film*) again.

재색(才色) ¶ ~을 겸비한 여인 a lady gifted with both wits (intelligence) and beauty / 그녀는 ~을 겸비하고 있다 She has both brains and beauty.

재생(再生) ① 《생물의》 rebirth (다시 태어남); revival (소생); regeneration (갱생). ¶ 도마뱀의 꼬리는 잘라도 ~한다 The lizard's tail regenerates if cut off. / 시든 꽃은 물을 주면 ~한다 Drooping flowers revive in water. ② 《녹음·녹화의》 playback. ~하다 play back; reproduce. ¶ 야구 방송을 비디오로 ~하다 play back the broadcast of a baseball game on a VTR. ③ 《폐품의》 recycling; reclamation. ⇨ 재활용(再活用). ¶ ~고무 reclaimed rubber / ~능력 《생물의》 regeneration power(s) / ~장치 《녹음·녹화의》 playback equipment / ~지(紙) recycled (reclaimed) paper / ~타이어 a retread; a recap / ~품 made-over (remade) articles.

재생산(再生産) reproduction. ~하다 reproduce. ¶ 확대 ~ reproduction on an enlarged scale; enlarged reproduction.

재선(再選) ~하다 reelect. ~되다 be reelected.

재세(在世) ¶ ~중에 in *one's* lifetime; in life; while *one* lives.

재소자(在所者) 재감자(在監者).

재수(再修) ~하다 study to repeat a college entrance exam. ¶ 나는 2년 ~했다 I have spent two years preparing for the entrance examinations after I left high school. ∥ ~생 a high school graduate who is waiting for another chance to enter a college.

재수(財數) luck; fortune. ¶ ~(가) 있다 〔좋다〕 be lucky; be fortunate / ~없다 be out of luck;

재수입(再輸入) ~하다 reimport. ‖ ~품 reimports.

재수출(再輸出) ~하다 reexport. ‖ ~품 reexports.

재시험(再試驗) (sit for) a reexamination. ~하다 reexamine.

재심(再審) 《재심리사》 review; reexamination; 《재판관》 a retrial; a new trial. ~하다 reexamine; try again. ¶ ~을 청구하다 apply for a new trial / 그 서류는 ~하도록 반려되었다 The papers were sent back to be reexamined.

재앙(災殃) 《재난》 (a) disaster; a calamity; 《불행》 a misfortune. ¶ ~을 초래하다 bring a misfortune 〔on〕; invite 〔cause〕 a disaster.

재야(在野) ¶ ~의 out of power 〔office〕; in opposition. ‖ ~인사 distinguished men out of office.

재연(再演) ~하다 stage 〔present〕 《a play》 again; show 《a performance》 again.

재연(再燃) ~하다 revive; rekindle; flare up again. ¶ 폭력의 ~ a recurrence of violence / 그것이 계기가 되어 헌법 개정 문제가 ~되었다 It revived 〔rekindled〕 the old debate about amending the constitution.

재외(在外) ¶ ~의 overseas 《offices》; abroad. ‖ ~공관 diplomatic establishments abroad / ~교포 Korean residents abroad / ~자산 overseas assets.

재우다 ① 《숙박》 lodge 《a person》; take 《a person》 in; give 《a person》 a bed. ② 《잠을》 make 《a person》 sleep; put 《a child》 to bed 〔sleep〕. ¶ 아기를 달래서 ~ lull a baby to sleep.

재원(才媛) a talented 〔an intelligent〕 woman.

재원(財源) a source of revenue 〔income〕; financial resources; funds. ¶ ~이 풍부 〔빈약〕하다 be rich 〔poor〕 in resources.

재위(在位) ~하다 reign; be on the throne. ¶ ~시에 in 〔during〕 one's reign. ‖ ~기간 the period of 《Queen Victoria's》 reign.

재음미(再吟味) ~하다 reexamine; review.

재인식(再認識) ~하다 have a new understanding 《of》; see 《something》 in a new 〔fresh〕 light. ¶ 이 문제의 중요성을 ~했다 I realized the importance of the matter again.

재일(在日) ~의 (stationed, resident) in Japan. ‖ ~교포 Korean residents in Japan / ~본 대한민국 민단 the Korean Residents Union in Japan.

재임(在任) ~하다 hold office 〔a post〕; be in office. ¶ ~중의 while in office.

재임(再任) reappointment. ~하다 get reappointed.

재입국(再入國) re-entry 《into a country》. ~하다 re-enter 《into a country》.

재입학(再入學) readmission; re-entrance 《to》. ¶ ~을 허락하다 readmit. 〔last.

재작년(再昨年) the year before

재잘거리다 chatter; gabble; prattle; prate 《about》.

재적(在籍) (an) enrollment. ~하다 be on the register 〔roll〕. ¶ ~학생 700명인 학교 a school with an enrollment of 700 students. ‖ ~자〔학생〕 a registered person 〔student〕 / ~증명서 《학교의》 a certificate of enrollment; 《단체의》 a membership certificate.

재정(財政) finances; financial affairs. ¶ ~(상)의 financial / 적자 〔건전〕 ~ deficit 〔sound, balanced〕 finance / 국가 〔지방〕 ~ national 〔local〕 finance / ~이 넉넉하다 be well off; be in good financial circumstances / ~이 어렵다 be badly off; be in financial difficulties 〔국가 등이〕 / 우리 회사의 ~은 건전하다 Our company's finances are sound. ‖ ~경제부 the Ministry of Finance and Economy / ~규모 a fiscal 〔budget〕 scale / ~난 financial difficulties 〔troubles〕 / ~면(面) financial aspects / ~상태 financial status 〔conditions〕 / ~ 원조 financial assistance / ~전문가 a financial expert / ~투자 financial investments / ~학 (public) finance.

재조사(再調査) reexamination. ~하다 reexamine; reinvestigate.

재종(再從) a second cousin.

재주(능) ability; (a) talent; a gift; 《재치》 wit; intelligence 〔솜씨〕; 《수완》 skill; dexterity. ¶ ~있는 able; talented; gifted / 너의 ~가 메주다 You are all thumbs.

재주꾼 a person of high talents.

재주넘기 a somersault. ¶ ~를 하다 make a somersault.

재중(在中) ~의 containing. ¶ 견본 ~ 〔표시〕 Sample(s) / 사진 ~ 〔표시〕 Photos (only).

재즈 〔樂〕 jazz (music). ‖ ~밴드 a jazz band.

재직(在職) ~하다 hold office; be in office. ¶ 그들은 여기서 5년 이상 ~하고 있다 They have worked here for more than five years. / 그와는 ~중에 알게 되었다 I made friends with him while working.

재질(才質) natural gifts 〔endowment]; talent. ¶ ~이 풍부하다 be highly gifted; be richly endowed / ~을 살리다 make the best use of one's talent.

재질(材質) the quality of the material.

재차(再次) 《부사》 twice; again; a second time. ¶ ~ 시도하다 try again; make another (a second) attempt.

재채기 a sneeze. ~하다 sneeze.

재처리(再處理) reprocessing. ‖ ~공장 a (nuclear fuel) reprocessing plant.

재천(在天) ¶ ~의 in Heaven; Heavenly / 인명은 ~이다 Life and death are providential.

재청(再請) a second request; an encore; 《동의에 대한》 seconding. ~하다 request a second time; encore; second 《a motion》.

재촉 pressing; urging; a demand. ~하다 demand; press 《a person for》; press (urge) 《a person to do》. ¶ 그에게 빚의 변제를 ~하다 press him for payment of his debt.

재출발(再出發) ~하다 make a restart; make a fresh (new) start.

재취(再娶) taking one's wife a second time; 《후처》 a second wife. ~하다 remarry (after the death of one's first wife).

재치(才致) wit; cleverness; resources. ¶ ~ 있는 quick-witted; smart; witty.

재침(再侵) a reinvasion. ~하다 reinvade.

재킷 a jacket; a sweater; a pullover.

재탕(再湯) 《다시 달임》 a second brew 《of herb medicine》; 《비유적으로》 a rehash《개작》; repetition 《반복》. ~하다 《다시 달임》 make a second brew (decoction) 《of》; 《비유적으로》 make a rehash; repeat.

재투자(再投資) reinvestment. ~하다 reinvest.

재투표(再投票) revoting. ~하다 take a vote again.

재판(再版) a reprint; a second edition; a second impression 《제2쇄》. ~하다 reprint. ¶ ~이 되다 run into a second impression.

재판(裁判) a trial; a hearing; 《판결》 judgment; decision. ~하다 judge; try; decide (pass judgment) on 《a case》. ¶ 공정한 ~ a fair trial / ~을 열다 hold a court / ~에 부치다 put 《a case》 on trial / ~에 이기다(지다) win (lose) a suit / 살인 혐의로 ~을 받다 stand (face) trial for murder / ~은 원고(피고)의 승소로 끝났다 The case was decided in favor of the plaintiff (defendant). ‖ ~관 a judge; the court / ~권 jurisdiction / ~비용 judicial costs / ~소 ☞ 법원 / ~절차 court procedure / ~장 the chief justice 《美》.

재편성(再編成) reorganization. ~하다 reorganize.

재평가(再評價) revaluation; reassessment. ~하다 revalue; reassess.

재학(在學) ~하다 be in (at) school(college). ¶ ~중(에) while at (in) school / 본교 ~생은 500명이다 There are 500 students at this college. ‖ ~기간 the period of attendance at school; one's school days / ~증명서 a school certificate.

재할인(再割引) ~하다 rediscount 《a bill》. ‖ ~어음 a rediscount bill / ~율 a rediscount rate.

재합성(再合成) resynthesis. ~하다 resynthesize; synthesize again.

재해(災害) a disaster; a calamity 《대규모의》. ¶ ~를 입다 suffer from a disaster. ‖ ~대책 measures against disaster / ~방지 disaster prevention / ~보상 (보험) casualty (accident) compensation (insurance) / ~지 a stricken (disaster) area.

재향군인(在郷軍人) an ex-soldier; a veteran 《美》; a reservist.

재현(再現) ~하다 reappear; appear again; reproduce. ¶ 그 그림은 당시의 생활을 ~하고 있다 The picture reproduces the life of those days.

재혼(再婚) a second marriage; a remarriage. ~하다 marry again. ‖ ~자 a remarried person.

재화(災禍) a disaster; a calamity.

재화(財貨) money and goods; wealth; goods《상품》.

재확인(再確認) reconfirmation. ~하다 reconfirm; reaffirm.

재활용(再活用) recycling; reclamation. ~하다 recycle 《newspaper》; reclaim 《glass from old bottles》.

재회(再會) ~하다 meet again. ¶ ~를 기약하다 promise to meet again. ‖ ~하다 revive; restore.

재흥(再興) revival; restoration. ~

잭나이프 a jackknife.

잼 jam. ‖ ~ 바른 빵 bread and jam.

잽 a jab.

잽싸다 (be) quick; nimble; agile.

잿더미 a lump of ash. ¶ ~가 되다 be reduced (burnt) to ashes / ~에서 일어나다 rise (stand up) from the ashes.

잿물(세탁용) lye; caustic soda; 《유약》 glaze; enamel.

잿밥(齋一) rice offered to Buddha.

잿빛 ash(en) color; gray 《美》.

쟁강, 쟁그랑 with a clank (clink).

~거리다 clank, clink.

쟁기《농기구》 a plow. ¶ ~질하다

쟁론(爭論) a dispute; a controversy. ~하다 dispute; quarrel.
쟁반(錚盤) a tray; a salver.
쟁의(爭議) a (labor) dispute; a controversy; a trouble; a strike. ¶노동~ a labor dispute (trouble) / ~를 일으키다 cause a dispute; go on (a) strike / ~를 해결하다 settle a dispute (strike). ‖ ~권 the right to strike / ~위원회 a dispute committee.
쟁이다 pile (heap) up; pile (lay) 《one thing》 on (top of) 《another》. ¶산처럼 쟁여져 있다 be piled up mountain-high; lie in a huge pile.
쟁쟁하다(錚錚―) 《귀에》 ring (in *one's* ears). ¶그녀의 말이 아직도 귀에 ~ Her words are still ringing in my ears.
쟁쟁하다(錚錚―) 《출중하다》 be prominent; outstanding; conspicuous. ¶쟁쟁한 음악가 a prominent musician.
쟁점(爭點) the point at issue (in dispute); an issue 《of》. ¶~을 벗어난 발언 remarks off the point.
쟁탈(爭奪) ~하다 struggle (scramble, contest) 《for》. ‖ ~전 a scramble; a contest; a competition.
쟁패전(爭覇戰) a struggle for supremacy; a championship game (경기의).
저¹(笛) 《피리》 a flute; a fife.
저(著) a work; 《형용사적》 written by…. ¶김갑동 ~의 소설 a novel written by Kim Kapdong.
저(箸) 《젓가락》 (a pair of) chopsticks.
저² 《나》 I; me. ¶~로서는 for my part; as for me. ② 《자기》 (one)self. ③ 《지칭》 that (over there). ¶ ~ 사람 that person / ~ 따위 such; that kind (of)《[see; say (美)》.
저³ 《감탄사》 well; I say; let me
저간(這間) ① 《그 당시》 that time; then; ② 《요즈음》 these (recent) days. ¶ ~의 사정 the circumstances of the occasion (days).
저개발(低開發) ¶ ~의 underdeveloped. ‖ ~국 an underdeveloped country / ~ 지역 the underdeveloped areas.
저것 that; that one. ¶이것~ this and that / 이것 ~ 생각 끝에 after a great deal of thinking.
저격(狙擊) sniping. ~하다 shoot (fire) 《at》; snipe 《at》. ‖ ~병 a sniper; a marksman. 〔et.
저고리 a coat; a (Korean) clothing.
저공(低空) a low altitude. ¶ ~비행 a low-altitude flight (~비행하다 fly low).

저금(貯金) savings; a deposit (돈); saving (행위). ~하다 save (money); put (deposit) dollars (*in a bank*). ¶우편~ postal savings / 은행에서 ~을 찾다 draw *one's* savings from the bank / 은행에 100만원이 ~되어 있다 have one million *won* (deposited) in a bank / 매월 2만원씩 ~하다 save twenty thousand *won* a month. ‖ ~통 a savings bank (美); a piggy bank / ~통장 a bankbook; a deposit passbook.
저금리(低金利) low interest. ¶ ~의 돈 cheap money. ‖ ~정책 a cheap (an easy) money policy.
저급(低級) ~하다 (be) low-grade (-class); low; vulgar; inferior.
저기 that place; there 《그 곳》; 《부사적》 over there. ¶여기 ~ here and there / ~ 있는 건물 the building over there.
저기압(低氣壓) (a) low (atmospheric) pressure; 《심기의》 a bad temper. ¶그는 오늘 ~이다 He is in a bad temper today.
저널리스트 a journalist.
저널리즘 journalism.
저녁 ① 《때》 evening. ¶ ~에 in the evening. ‖ ~놀 an evening glow; a red sunset. ② 《식사》 dinner(정찬); the evening meal; supper(가벼운). ¶ ~에 초대하다 invite to dinner / ~을 먹다 eat dinner; take supper.
저능(低能) 《저지능》 mental deficiency; feeble-mindedness. ¶ ~한 weak-(feeble-)minded; mentally deficient; imbecile. ‖ ~아 a weak-(feeble-)minded child.
저다지 so; so much; like that; to that extent.
저당(抵當) mortgage; a security (저당물). ~하다 mortgage 《*one's house*》; give 《*a thing*》 as (a) security. ¶ ~ 잡다 take 《*a thing*》 as security 《*for a loan*》 / ~잡고 돈을 빌려 주다 lend money on mortgage (security) / 이 집은 1천만원에 ~잡혀 있다 This house is mortgaged for ten million *won*. ‖ ~권 mortgage / ~권자 a mortgagee / ~물 a collateral; a mortgage (security) / 1번(2번)~ a first (second) mortgage.
저돌(猪突) recklessness; foolhardiness. ¶ ~적으로 돌진하다 rush recklessly; make a headlong rush 《at》.
저따위 a thing (person) of that sort; such a…. ¶ ~ 사람은 처음 본다 I have never seen such a person in all my life.
저러하다, 저렇다 be like that; be that way. ¶저렇게 so; like that; (in) that way.

저러한, 저런¹ such; so; like that; that (sort of). ¶ ~ 책 that sort of book.

저런² 《감탄사》 Oh dear!; Heavens!; Goodness!; Well well!

저력(底力) latent [potential] power [energy]. ¶ ~ 있는 powerful; energetic / 그는 그 경주에서 ~을 보였다 He showed his full potential in the race.

저렴(低廉) ¶ ~한 cheap; low-priced; moderate.

저류(低流) an undercurrent. ¶ 미국 외교 정책의 ~를 이루다 underlie (lie beneath) the U.S. foreign policy.

저리(低利) (at) low interest. ∥ ~ 대부 a low-interest loan / ~자금 low-interest funds.

저리¹ (저쪽으로) there; to that direction; that way. 「that way.

저리² (저렇게) so; like that; (in)

저리다 《마비되다》 be asleep; be numbed; have pins and needles; be paralysed. ¶ 저린 손 benumbed hands / 발이 저려 일어설 수 없었다 My feet went to sleep and I could not stand up.

저마다 each one; everyone.

저만큼 that much; so (much); to that extent.

저만하다 be that much; be so much; be as much (big) as that.

저맘때 about [around] that time; (at) that time of day [night, year]. ¶ 내가 ~ 나이였을 때 when I was *his* age.

저명(著名) ~하다 (be) eminent; prominent; celebrated; famous. ∥ ~인사 a prominent person (figure).

저물가(低物價) low prices. ∥ ~ 정책 a low-price policy; low living cost policy.

저물다 《날이》 get [grow] dark; 《해·계절 등이》 come [draw] to an end. ¶ 해가 저물기 전에 before (it is) dark; before the sun sets / 날이 저문 뒤에 after dark / 이제 일년도 저물어 간다 The year is coming to an end season.

저미다 cut 《*meat*》 thin; slice.

저버리다 《약속 등을》 break (go back on) 《*one's promise*》; 《기대 따위를》 be contrary to 《*one's expectation*》; 《신의·충고 따위를》 betray; disobey 《*one's father*》; 《돌보지 않음》 desert; forsake; abandon. ¶ 그는 나와의 약속을 저버렸다 He went back on his promise (word) with me. / 그는 나의 신뢰를 저버렸다 He betrayed my trust in him. / 그는 그 가족을 저버렸다 He forsook (deserted) his family.

저벅거리다 walk with heavy footsteps; crunch 《*one's way*》.

저번 (the) last time; the other [time.

저산증(低酸症) subacidity.

저서(著書) a book (work) 《on economics》; *one's* writings.

저성(低聲) a low voice.

저소득(低所得) lower income. ¶ ~층 the lower income bracket.

저속(低俗) ¶ ~한 vulgar; lowbrow; low / ~한 취미 low taste.

저속(도)(低速(度)) low speed. ¶ ~(으)로 at a low speed; in low gear / ~로 하다 slow down. ∥ ~기어 low gear.

저수(貯水) ~하다 keep water in store. ∥ ~량 the volume of water kept in store / ~지 a reservoir / ~탱크 a water tank.

저술(著述) ☞ 저작(著作). ∥ ~가 a writer; an author / ~업 the literary profession.

저습(低濕) ¶ ~하다 (be) low and moist. ∥ ~지 a low, swampy place.

저승 the other [next] world; the afterlife. ¶ ~으로 가다 pass away. ∥ ~길 a journey to the other world; *one's* last journey.

저압(低壓) low pressure; 〖電〗 low voltage; low tension. ∥ ~전류 a low-voltage current / ~회로 a low-tension circuit.

저액(低額) small amount. ∥ ~소득층 the low income classes.

저온(低溫) (a) low temperature. ∥ ~살균 (소독) pasteurization at (a) low temperature / ~수송 refrigerated transport / ~전자공학 cryoelectronics / ~진열장 a deep-freezer showcase / ~학 cryogenics.

저울 a balance; (a pair of) scales. ¶ ~에 달다 weigh 《*a thing*》 in the balance / ~을 속이다 give short weight / ~을 넉넉히 하다 give good weight. ∥ ~대 a balance (scale) beam / ~추 a weight / ~판 a scale pan.

저육(猪肉) pork. 「rate; low.

저율(低率) a low rate. ∥ ~의

저음(低音) a low tone (voice); 〖樂〗 bass.

저의(底意) *one's* secret [true] intention; an underlying motive. ¶ 아무 ~ 없이 말하나 speak frankly (without reserve) / ~를 알아채다 see through 《*a person's*》 underlying motive.

저이 that person; he [him]; she [her]. ¶ ~들 they; those people.

저인망(底引網) a dragnet; a trawl-net. ∥ ~어업 trawling (dragnet) fisheries.

저임금(低賃金) low wages. ∥ ~근로자 a low-wage earner.

저자 《시장》 a market. ☞ 장(場)¹.

저자(著者) a writer; an author.
저자세(低姿勢) ¶ ~를 취하다 assume [adopt, take] a low posture [profile]. ‖ ~ 외교 low-profile diplomacy.
저작(咀嚼) ~하다 chew; masticate.
저작(著作) 《저서》 a book; a work; 《저술 행위》 one's writings;《저술 행위》 writing. ~하다 write (a book). ‖ ~권 copyright 《~권을 획득하다 hold [obtain] the copyright *for the book*》 / ~권을 침해하다 infringe (on) the copyright 《*of*》 / ~권(소유)자 a copyright holder / ~권침해 (an) infringement of copyright; (literary) piracy.
저장(貯藏) storage; storing. ~하다 store (*up*); lay [put] (*things*) up [by] / ~할 수 있는 storable (*products*) / ~되어 있다 be held in storage. ‖ ~고 a storehouse / ~미 stored rice / ~실 a storeroom / ~품 stores; stock.
저절로 of [by] itself; spontaneously (자연 발생적으로); automatically (자동적으로).
저조(低調) ¶ ~한 inactive; dull; low; sluggish; weak (약하다) / ~한 기록 a poor record (result) / 시장 경기가 ~하다 The market is sluggish [dull, weak]. / 사업이 ~하다 Business is slowing down.
저조(低潮) (a) low tide.
저주(詛呪) a curse; imprecation. ~하다 curse; imprecate. ¶ ~받은 cursed / 그녀는 ~받고 있다 She is under a curse.
저주파(低周波) low frequency.
저지(低地) low ground (land).
저지르다 do; commit (*an error*); make (*a mistake*).
저지하다(沮止—) obstruct; prevent; hinder; check; block; hamper. ¶ 법안의 통과를 ~ prevent the passage of a bill / 콜레라의 전염을 ~ check the spread of cholera.
저쪽 there; yonder; 《건너편》 the opposite [other] side;《상대》 the other party. ¶ ~에 있는 집 the house over there.
저촉하다(抵觸—) (be in) conflict with; be contrary to. ¶ 법률에 ~ be contrary to the law; be [go] against the law.
저축(貯蓄) saving (행위); savings (저금). ~하다 save (up); store up; lay by [aside]. ¶ ~심이 있는 [없는] thrifty [thriftless]. ‖ ~률 a rate of savings / ~성향 a propensity to save / ~운동 a savings campaign / ~채권 a savings bond.
저탄(貯炭) a stock of coal. ‖ ~장 a coal yard [depot].
저택(邸宅) a mansion; a residence.

저편 ☞ 저쪽.
저하(低下) a fall; a drop; a decline; 《품질의》 deterioration; 《가치의》 depreciation. ~하다 fall; drop; depreciate; deteriorate. ¶ 생활 수준의 ~ a decline in the standard of living / 능률이 ~ 하다 show a drop in efficiency / ~ 시키다 reduce; lower / 원화의 가치가 ~되고 있다 The value of Korean won is depreciating.
저학년(低學年) the lower grades (classes).
저항(抵抗) resistance (반항); opposition (반대). ~하다 resist; oppose; stand [struggle] against. ¶ 최후의 ~ a last [final] stand; last-ditch resistance / ~하기 어려운 irresistible / 완강히 ~하다 make a strong stand (*against*) / …하는 데 ~을 느끼다 (심리적으로) be reluctant to *do*; do not feel like *doing*. ‖ ~기(器) a resistor / ~력 (power of) resistance (병에 대한 ~력이 거의 없다 have little resistance to diseases).
저해하다(沮害—) hinder; check; obstruct; prevent; hamper.
저혈압(低血壓) low blood pressure; hypotension.
저희(들) we(우리); they(저 사람들). ¶ ~의 our; their.
적(敵) an enemy;《적수》 an opponent; a rival (경쟁자); a match. ¶ ~과 싸우다 fight against the enemy / ~에게 등을 보이다 turn one's back to the enemy / 그는 나의 사업상의 ~이다 He is my business rival. / ~은 마침내 격퇴되었다 The enemy was beaten off at last.
적(籍) 《본적》 one's family register; one's domicile;《단체의》 membership. ¶ ~에 넣다 (~에서 빼다) have (*a person's*) name entered in [removed from] the family register / ~을 두다 be a member (*of a society*); be enrolled (*at a university*).
적(때) the time (when); (on) occasion;《경험》 an experience. ¶ 필요할 ~에 in case of need / 내가 파리에 있을 ~ 그 소식이 도착했다 I was in Paris when the news reached me. / 나도 그런 말을 들은 ~이 있다 I've heard such talk too.
…적(的) ¶ 직업 ~ (인) professional / 정치 ~ 인 political / 일반 ~ 으로 in general / 역사 ~ 및 지리 ~ 으로도 both historically and geographically; in terms of history and geography / 한국 ~ 인 사고 방식을 가지고 있다 have a Korean way of thinking.
적갈색(赤褐色) reddish brown.

적개심(敵愾心) a hostile feeling; hostility. ¶ ~을 불러일으키다 excite a feeling of hostility; inflame [stir up] *(a person's)* animosity *(against)*.

적격(適格) ¶ ~의 qualified; competent; adequate ¶ 그는 이 일에 ~이다 He is qualified [eligible] for this job. / 그 일에는 누가 ~ㄴ가 Who'll be the right man for the work? ‖ ~자 a qualified person / ~품 standard [acceptable] goods.

적국(敵國) an enemy [a hostile] country; a hostile power.

적군(敵軍) the enemy (troops).

적극(積極) ¶ ~적(인) positive; active / ~적으로 positively; actively / ~적으로 원조하다 give positive aid *(to)*. ‖ ~성 positiveness; enterprising spirit (그는 ~성이 없다 He doesn't have a positive attitude.).

적금(積金) installment savings. ¶ ~을 붓다 deposit [save up] by installments.

적기(赤旗) a red flag.

적기(適期) a proper time; a good [favorable] chance. ¶ ~에 timely; well-timed / ~를 놓치다 miss a good opportunity / ~를 잃다 lose a chance.

적기(敵機) an enemy plane.

적꼬치(炙—) a spit; a skewer.

적나라(赤裸裸) ¶ ~한 naked; bare; frank (솔직한) / ~한 사실 a naked [bald] fact / ~하게 (솔직히) plainly; frankly; without reserve.

적다¹ (「기입」) write [put down]; record; make [take] a note of.

적다² (「많지 않다」) (be) few (수); little (양); (부족하다) be scanty; scarce; poor. ¶적은 수입 a small income / 적지 않이 not a little [few] / 적어지다 become scarce; run short *(of funds)* / 천연 자원이 매우 ~ be very poor in natural resources / 그는 교사로서의 경험이 ~ He has little experience in teaching.

적당(適當) ¶ ~한 fit *(for)*; suitable *(to, for)*; adequate; competent *(양)*; ~히 suitably; as *one* thinks fit [right] / ~한 값으로 at a reasonable price / 양담은 ~한 조건으로 성립되었다 We concluded negotiations on fair [reasonable] terms. / 자네가 ~히 알아서 해 주게 Please do as you think [see] fit.

적대(敵對) ~하다 be hostile *(to)*; turn [fight] against. ¶ 아무를 ~시하다 regard *a person* with hostility. ‖ ~행위 hostilities; hostile operations (actions).

적도(赤道) the equator. ¶ ~의 equatorial / ~를 횡단하다 cross the equator. ‖ ~무풍 the doldrums / ~의 an equatorial telescope / ~제 Neptune's revel.

적동(赤銅) red copper. ‖ ~광 cuprite; red copper (ore).

적란운(積亂雲) ☞ 소나기구름.

적량(適量) a proper quantity [dose (약)].

적령(適齡) the right age *(for)*. ¶ ~에 이르다 reach [attain] the right age *(for)* / 결혼 ~ marriageable age. ‖ ~징병 ~자 a person old enough for military service.

적례(適例) a good example; a case in point.

적린(赤燐) red phosphorus.

적립(積立) ~하다 save; put [lay] by (aside); reserve. ¶ 노후를 위해 급료의 일부를 ~하다 lay aside a part of *one's* salary for *one's* old age. ‖ ~금 a reserve fund; a deposit / ~배당금 accumulated dividends.

적막(寂寞) ¶ ~한 lonely; lonesome; dreary. ‖ ~감 a lonely feeling.

적바르다 be barely [just] enough.

적바림 a note; a summary. ~하다 make a note of; sum up.

적반하장(賊反荷杖) ¶ ~이란 바로 이를 두고 하는 말이다 This is what they mean by 'the audacity of the thief'.

적발(摘發) disclosure; exposure. ~하다 disclose; expose; uncover; lay bare [open]. ¶ 부정 사건을 ~하다 expose [lay bare] a scandal.

적법(適法) ¶ ~한 legal; legitimate; lawful. ‖ ~행위 a legal act.

적병(敵兵) an enemy (soldier); the enemy (전체).

적부(適否) suitability; fitness (사람의); propriety (사물의). ¶ ~를 결정 [판단]하다 decide [judge] whether *(a thing)* is proper or not.

적분(積分) 【數】 integral calculus. ~하다 integrate. ‖ ~법 integration.

적빈(赤貧) dire poverty.

적산(敵産) enemy property.

적색(赤色) (빛깔) a red color; red; 【상】 communist; Red. ‖ ~분자 a Red; Red elements / ~테러 Red terrorism / ~혁명 (a) Red revolution.

적선(敵船) an enemy ship [vessel].

적선(積善) ~하다 accumulate virtuous deeds; render benevolence.

적설(積雪) (fallen) snow; snow (lying upon the ground). ¶ (교통이) ~로 두절되다 be snowbound; be held up by snow / ~이 120cm 에 달렸다 The snow lay 120cm deep. ‖ ~량 snowfall.

적설초(積雪草) [植] a ground ivy.
적성(適性) fitness; aptitude(재능의). ¶ ~을 보이다 show an aptitude for…. ~검사 an aptitude test / 직업~ vocational aptitude. [try.
적성(敵性) ~국가 a hostile country.
적세(敵勢) the morale of the foe.
적소(適所) the right [proper] place.
적송(赤松) [植] ☞ 소나무.
적송(積送) ~하다 ship; forward; send; consign. ¶ ~인 a shipper; a forwarder / ~품 a shipment; a consignment.
적수(敵手) a match; an opponent; a rival. ¶ ~가 못 [안] 되다 be no match 《for a person》. ¶ 호~ a good match [rival].
적수공권(赤手空拳) empty hands and naked fists; being without any financial support. ¶ ~으로 사업을 시작하다 start a business with no capital. [tack).
적습(敵襲) an enemy's raid(attack).
적시(適時) ~의 timely; opportune. ‖ ~안타 [野] a timely hit.
적시(敵視) ~하다 look upon 《a person》 as an enemy; be hostile 《to each other》.
적시다 moisten; 《담그다》 soak; drench; dip. ¶ 손을 물에 ~ get one's hands wet; dip one's hands into water(담그다).
적신호(赤信號) a red [danger] signal; a red light.
적십자(赤十字) the Red Cross. ‖ ~병원 a Red Cross Hospital / ~사 the Red Cross (Society).
적악(積惡) ~하다 build up wickedness; practice evils.
적약(適藥) the right medicine for a sickness. [least of it).
적어도 at (the) least; not 《the》
적역(適役) 《연극 등》 a well-cast role [part]. ¶ 그 역은 그에게 이었다 He was well cast in the role.
적역(適譯) a good translation; an exact rendering.
적외선(赤外線) infrared [ultrared] rays. ‖ ~사진 an infrared photograph / ~요법 infrared therapy.
적요(摘要) a summary; an outline; an abstract; a synopsis.
적용(適用) application. ~하다 apply 《a rule to a case》. ¶ ~할 수 있는 [없는] applicable (inapplicable) 《to》 / 잘못 ~하다 misapply; make a wrong application 《of the law》.
적운(積雲) ☞ 뭉게구름.
적원(積怨) a deep-seated grudge.
적응(適應) adaptation. ~하다 adjust [adapt] oneself 《to》; fit. ¶ ~시키다 fit [suit, adapt] 《something》 《to》; accommodate / 그는 새로운 환경에 쉽게 ~할 수 없었다 He couldn't easily adapt himself to the new surroundings. ‖ ~성 adaptability; flexibility 《~성이 있는 adaptable; flexible》 / ~증 a disease which is susceptible to treatment 《by a particular medicine》.
적의(適宜) ~한 suitable; proper; appropriate; fit.
적의(敵意) hostile feelings; hostility; enmity. ¶ ~ 있는 hostile; antagonistic / ~를 품다 [나타내다] have [show] hostile feelings 《toward me》.
적임(適任) 적격(適格). ¶ 비서에는 그녀가 ~이다 She is the right person for a secretary. or She is fit as a secretary. ‖ ~자 a well-qualified person.
적자(赤字) red figures; 《결손》 the red; a loss; a deficit. ¶ ~를 내다 show a loss; 품다 go [get] into the red / ~를 내고 있다 be in the red / ~를 메우다 make up (cover) the deficit / ~경영을 하다 operate at a loss (in the red). ¶ ~공채 a deficit bond / ~노선 《철도 등의》 a loss-making (deficit-ridden) railroad line / ~예산 an unbalanced (a deficit) budget / ~재정 "red ink" finances.
적자(嫡子) a legitimate child (son); one's heir.
적자(適者) a fit (suitable) person; the fit. ‖ ~생존 the survival of the fittest. [er.
적장(敵將) the enemy commander.
적재(適材) a person fit for the post; the right man. ‖ ~적소 the right man in the right place.
적재(積載) loading. ~하다 load; carry; 《배에》 have 《cargo》 on board; take 《on, in》. ‖ ~능력 carrying (loading) capacity (power) / ~량 loadage; load capacity / ~톤수 capacity tonnage / ~화물 cargo on board.
적적하다(寂寂一) (be) lonesome; lonely; solitary; desolate; deserted. ¶ 적적한 생활 a lonely (lonesome) life.
적전(敵前) ¶ ~상륙하다 land in the face of the enemy.
적절(適切) ~한 fitting; proper; appropriate / ~히 suitably; to the point; properly; fittingly / ~한 예 an appropriate (apt) example / ~한 조치를 취하다 take a proper measure.
적정(適正) ~한 proper; right; fair; just. ‖ ~가격 a reasonable price / ~이윤 reasonable profit.

적정(敵情) the enemy's movements. ¶ ~을 살피다 reconnoiter the enemy's movements.

적조(赤潮) a red tide. ∥ ~ 경보 a red tide warning.

적중(的中) ~하다 hit the mark (target); be right to the point; (예언 따위가) come (turn out) true; (추측이) guess right. ¶그의 예언이 ~ 했다 His prediction has come true. ∥ ~률 a hitting ratio.

적지(敵地) the enemy's land (territory); the hostile country.

적진(敵陣) the enemy('s) camp; the enemy line. ¶ ~을 돌파하다 break through the enemy line.

적처(嫡妻) a wedded (legitimate) wife.

적철광(赤鐵鑛)〔鑛〕hematite.

적출(摘出) ~하다 pick (take) out; remove; extract.

적출(嫡出) legitimacy (of birth). ∥ ~자 a legitimate child.

적출(積出) shipment; forwarding. ∥ ~항 a port of shipment.

적치(積置) ~하다 pile up; stack. ¶석탄 ~장 a coal yard.

적탄(敵彈) the enemy's bullets (shells).

적평(適評) (an) apt criticism; an appropriate comment.

적하(積荷) (적재) loading; shipping; (짐) a freight; a load; a cargo (배의). ~하다 load (a ship) with cargo; put (goods) on board. ∥ ~량 intakeweight (중량) / ~ 명세서 a freight list / ~ 목록 an invoice / ~ (船) manifest / ~보험 cargo insurance.

적함(敵艦) an enemy ship.

적합(適合) conformity; agreement; adaptation (적응). ~하다 conform; agree; adapt oneself (to); be suitable (for, to); fit. ¶기질에 ~ 하다 be congenial to one's disposition / 목적에 ~ 하다 serve (suit) one's purpose / 채용 조건에 ~ 한 응모자는 없었다 There were no applicants who fitted the requirement of the job.

적혈구(赤血球) a red (blood) corpuscle; a red (blood) cell. ¶ ~ 수 검사 a red cell count.

적화(赤化) ~하다 turn (go) red; go communist. ¶한반도 ~통일의 망상 the fanatic dream of communizing the entire Korean peninsula / ~ 를 방지하다 check the spread of communism. ¶ ~ 운동 the red [Bolshevik] movement.

적히다 be written (noted, put) down; be recorded.

전(前) ① 〔시각의〕 before; to; 〔과거〕 before; ago; since; previous. ¶ ~의 previous; former; last / ~에 before; previously / 오래 ~ 부터 since a long time ago / 10시 15분 ~ a quarter to ten / ~에 말한 바와 같이 as previously stated / 3일 ~의 신문 a newspaper of three days ago / ~ 처럼 as (it was) before. ② 〔…하기 전〕 before; prior to; earlier than. ¶그가 도착하기 ~에 before his arrival / 출발 하기 ~에 before (prior to) one's departure. ③ 〔편지에서〕 Dear; Sir. ¶어머니 ~ 상서 Dear Mother.

전(煎) fried food.

전(廛) a shop; a store.

전(全) all; whole; entire; total; complete; full; pan-. ¶ ~국민 the whole nation / ~세계 the whole world / ~ 생도가 체육관에 모였다 All the pupils gathered in the gym.

전…(前) 〔이전의〕 former; ex-; 〔앞부분의〕 the front; the fore part. ¶ ~ 남편 one's former husband (ex-husband) / 케네디 ~ 대통령 the former President Kennedy / ~ 페이지 the preceding page.

…전(傳) 〔전기〕 a biography; a life. ¶위인 ~ the lives of great men.

전가(傳家) ¶ ~의 보도 a sword treasured in the family for generations.

전가(轉嫁) ~하다 shift onto (a person); throw (lay) onto (a person). ¶죄를 아무에게 ~하다 lay the blame on a person / 남에게 책임을 ~ 하지 마라 Don't shift the responsibility to others.

전각(殿閣) a (royal) palace.

전갈(全蠍)〔蟲〕a scorpion. ∥ ~ 자리〔天〕the Scorpion; Scorpio.

전갈(傳喝) a (verbal) message. ~하다 give (a person) a message; leave a message for (a person); send (a person) word (that). ¶낸 시로부터 너에게 ~이 있다 I have a message for you from Nancy.

전개(展開) development(s). ~하다 develop; unfold; roll out; spread. ¶국면의 ~ 를 기다리다 wait for further developments / 이 사건은 앞으로 어떻게 ~ 될까 What will be the future development of this affair?

전격(電擊) an electric shock; a lightning attack. ¶ ~적인 lightning; electric / ~적인 결혼 a sudden marriage / ~요법 electroshock therapy / ~작전 blitz tactics / ~전 a lightning war; a blitz.

전경(全景) a complete (panoramic) view (of); a panorama (of).

전경(戰警) ☞ 전투 경찰대. 〔dent.

전고(典故) an authentic prece-

전곡(田穀) dry-field crop (grain).
전곡(錢穀) money and grain.
전골 beef with vegetables cooked in casserole.
전공(專攻) a special study; one's major; a specialty; a speciality《英》. 〜하다 major in《美》; specialize in《英》; make a special study (of). ‖ 〜과 a graduate course / 〜과목 a subject of special study; a major《美》/ 〜분야 a major field of study.
전공(電工) an electrician.
전공(戰功) distinguished services in war. ¶ 〜을 세우다 distinguish *oneself* on the field of battle.
전과(全科) the whole (full) curriculum.
전과(前科) a previous conviction (offense); a criminal record. ¶ 〜 3범의 사내 a man with three previous convictions / 〜가 있다 have a criminal record; be an ex-convict. ‖ 〜자 an ex-convict.
전과(戰果) (achieve brilliant) military results.
전과(轉科) 〜하다 be (get) enrolled in another (a different) course.
전관(前官) the predecessor (전임자); one's former post(자기의). ¶ 〜 예우를 받다 be granted the privileges of *one's* former post.
전관(專管) exclusive jurisdiction. ‖ 〜(어업)수역 an exclusive fishing zone.
전광(電光) electric light; (a flash of) lightning. ¶ 〜석화와 같이 as quick as lightning. ‖ 〜판 an electric scoreboard.
전교(全校) the whole school. ‖ 〜생 all the students of a school.
전교(轉交) 《남을 거쳐 줌》 delivery (transfer) through (a person); care of (c/o). ¶ 한국대사관 〜 김선생 귀하 Mr. Kim, c/o the Korean Embassy.
전구(電球) an electric (a light) bulb. ¶ 〜를 소켓에 끼우다 screw a bulb into a socket. ‖ 백열 〜 an incandescent light bulb.
전국(全一) undiluted liquor (soy, sauce, *etc*.). ‖ 〜술 raw spirit.
전국(全國) the whole country. ¶ 〜적(인) national; nationwide / 〜에 걸쳐 throughout (all over) the country / 〜적인 규모로 on a national scale / 경찰은 〜적인 규모로 청소년의 비행 방지 운동을 전개하고 있다 The police are conducting a nationwide campaign to prevent juvenile delinquency. ¶ 〜 경제인연합회 the Federation of Korean Industries (생략 KFI) / 〜 대회 a national conference; 《정당의》 a national convention; 《경기의》 a national athletic meeting / 〜방송 a broadcast on a national network / 〜중계 a nationwide hookup / 〜지 a newspaper with nationwide circulation / 〜평균 the national average.
전국(戰局) the war situation; the progress of the war.
전국구(全國區) 《선거의》 the national constituency; the national constituency under the proportional representation system. ¶ 〜의원 a member of the House elected from the national constituency.
전국민(全國民) the whole (entire) nation. ¶ 〜적 national; nationwide / 그 사건은 〜의 주목을 끌었다 The incident attracted nationwide attention.
전군(全軍) the whole army (military force).
전권(全卷) the whole book; 《영화의》 the whole reel. ¶ 〜을 통독하다 read (*the book*) from cover to cover; read (*the book*) through.
전권(全權) full (plenary) powers; full authority. ¶ 〜을 위임하다 invest (entrust) (*a person*) with full powers. ‖ 〜대리 an alternate delegate; a universal agent(총대리인) / 〜대사 an ambassador plenipotentiary / 〜특명 〜대사 an ambassador extraordinary and plenipotentiary.
전권(專權) an exclusive right; arbitrary power.
전극(電極) an electrode; a pole.
전근(轉勤) a transfer. 〜하다 be transferred (*to*). ¶ 그는 마산 지점으로 〜되었다 He was transferred to the Masan branch.
전기(前記) ¶ 〜의 above; aforesaid; above-mentioned; the said; referred to above / 〜의 장소 the above address.
전기(前期) 《1년의 전반기》 the first half year; the first term; (앞의 기) the last (previous) term. ¶ 이것은 〜에서 이월된 금액이다 This is the sum brought over from the previous account. ¶ 〜결산 settlement for the first half year / 〜이월금 the balance brought forward from the previous (preceding) term.
전기(傳記) a life; a biography. ‖ 〜물 biographical writings / 〜소설 a fictional biography / 〜작가 a biographer.
전기(電氣) electricity; electric current (전류). ¶ 〜의 electric; electrical (전기에 관한) / 〜를 일으키다 generate electricity / 〜를 켜다 [끄다] 《전등을》 switch (turn) on (off)

전기 the light / 이 기계는 ~로 움직인다 This machine works by electricity. / 이 선에는 ~가 통하고 있다 This wire is live with electricity. ‖ ~계통 an electrical system / ~공업 the electric industry / ~공학 electrical engineering / ~기관차 an electric locomotive / ~기구 an electric appliance / ~기구점 an electric(al) goods store 《美》/ ~기사 an electric engineer; an electrician / ~난로 an electric heater / ~냉장고 an electric refrigerator (freezer) / ~다리미(담요, 밥솥) an electric iron (blanket, rice-cooker) / ~도금 electroplating / ~난로 an electric furnace / ~면도기(시계, 풍로) an electric shaver (clock, hot plate) / ~방석 a heating pad / ~배선 electric wiring / ~분해 electrolysis / ~세탁기 an electric washing machine / ~스탠드 a desk lamp (탁상의) / a floor lamp (마루용의) / ~역학 electrodynamics / ~요금 electric charges / ~용접 electric welding / ~의자 an electric chair / ~자동차 an electric car; an electromobile / ~장치 an electric device / ~제품 electric appliances (products) / ~집진기(集塵機) an electric (electrostatic) precipitator / ~철도 an electric railroad / ~청소기 an (electric) vacuum cleaner / ~통신 electric communication / ~회로 an electric circuit.

전기(電機) electrical machinery and appliances. ‖ ~공업 electrical machinery industry.

전기(轉記) 《부기에서》 posting. ~하다 post; transfer. ¶ 일기장에서 하나의 계정을 원장으로 ~하다 post an item from the daybook to a ledger.

전기(轉機) a turning point; a point of change. ¶ ~에 서 있다 be at a turning point / 이것은 내 인생의 일대 ~가 될 것이다 This is going to be a major turning point in my life.

전깃불(電氣—) an electric light.
전깃줄(電氣—) an electric wire (cord).
전나무(-榎) a fir.
전날(前—) the other day, some days (지난날); the previous (preceding) day(그 전날).
전납(全納) ~하다 pay in full.
전납(前納) ☞ 선납.
전년(前年) the previous (preceding) year; the year before.
전념하다(專念—) devote oneself (to); be absorbed (in). ¶ 지금은 학업에만 전념하여라 Devote yourself to studies now.

전뇌(前腦) 〖解〗 the forebrain.
전능(全能) omnipotence. ~한 omnipotent; almighty; all-powerful / ~하신 하느님 Almighty God. 〖(ability)〗
전능력(全能力) *one's* full capacity
전단(專斷) (an) arbitrary decision. ~하다 act arbitrarily. ~적인 arbitrary / ~으로 arbitrarily; at *one's* own discretion.
전단(傳單) a handbill; a leaflet. ¶ ~을 돌리다 distribute (circulate) handbills / ~을 뿌리다 drop leaflets 《from a plane》.
전단(戰端) ¶ ~을 열다 open hostilities 《with》; take up arms 《against》.
전달(前—) 《전의 달》 the previous (preceding) month; 《지난 달》 last month; ultimo (생략 ult).
전달(傳達) delivery; transmission. ~하다 transmit; communicate; notify. ¶ 그 메시지는 잘못 ~되었다 The message was transmitted (conveyed) incorrectly.
전담(全擔) ~하다 take (assume, bear) full charge of.
전담(專擔) ~하다 take exclusive charge (responsibility) 《of》.
전답(田畓) paddies and dry fields.
전당(典當) pawn; pledge. ¶ ~ 잡다 take 《a thing》 in pawn; hold 《a thing》 in pledge / ~ 잡히다 pawn; pledge; give (put) 《a thing》 in pawn. ‖ ~물을 an article in pawn; a pawned article (~물을 찾다 redeem a pawn / ~물이 유질되다 be forfeited) / ~포 a pawnshop; a hock shop 《美口》/ ~표 a pawn ticket.
전당(殿堂) a palace(궁전); a sanctuary (신전·성역). ¶ 학문의 ~ a sanctuary of learning.
전당대회(全黨大會) the national convention of a party.
전대(前代) former ages (generation). ~미문의 unheard-of; unprecedented / ~미문의 대참사 an unheard-of calamity.
전대(戰隊) a battle corps; a (naval) squadron.
전대(轉貸) sublease. ~하다 sublease; sublet. ¶ ~책을 ~하다 lend a borrowed book to another / 방 〔집〕을 ~하다 sublet a room (house) 《to》. ‖ ~인 a sublessor / ~차(借) subletting and subleasing.
전도(前途) *one's* future; prospects; outlook. ¶ ~ 유망하다 have a bright future / ~ 유망한 청년 a promising young man / 철강업의 ~는 어둡다 The prospects for the steel industry are dark. / 우리의 ~는 다단하다 Many difficul-

전도(前渡)《돈의》 payment in advance; 《물품의》 delivery in advance. ‖ ~금 an advance; 〖法〗 an advancement.

전도(傳道) mission(ary) work. ~하다 preach the gospel; engage in mission work. ‖ ~사 an evangelist; a missionary (선교사).

전도(傳導)〖理〗 conduction(열·빛의); transmission(소리·빛의). ~하다 conduct; transmit. ‖ ~력〔율, 성〕 conductivity / ~체 a conductor; a transmitter.

전도(顚倒) ① 《엎드러짐》 a fall; overturn(전복). ~하다 fall 〔tumble〕 down; tumble; overturn. ② 《거꾸로 함》 reverse; inversion. ~하다 reverse; invert. ‖ 상하를 ~하다 turn 《a thing》 upside down / 앞뒤를 ~하다 invert the order / 본말을 ~하다 put the cart before the horse.

전동(電動) ‖ ~의 electromotive; electrically-powered〔-driven〕《machines》. ‖ ~기 an electric motor / ~력 electromotive force / ~ 의수(義手) a motorized artificial arm〔hand〕《arrows》.

전동(箭筒) 《살통》 a quiver (for arrows).

전등(電燈) an electric light〔lamp〕. ‖ ~을 켜다〔끄다〕 turn〔switch〕 a light on〔off〕 / ~을 달다 install electric lights.

전라(全裸) ~의 stark-naked; nude 《pictures》; 《a girl》 in the nude. ‖ ~로 헤엄치다 swim in the nude.

전락(轉落) a fall; a downfall; degradation(타락). ~하다 fall 《down, off》; fall low; degrade; sink 《in the world》. ‖ 창녀로 ~하다 sink 〔be reduced〕 to a prostitute.

전란(戰亂) the disturbances of war. ‖ ~의 도가니 a scene of deadly strife and carnage.

전람(展覽) exhibition; show. ‖ ~중이다 be on show. ‖ ~물 exhibits / ~회 an exhibition; a show(~회를 열다 hold an exhibition) / ~회장 an exhibition gallery〔hall〕.

전래(傳來) ~하다 be transmitted; be handed down 《from》;《외국에서》 be introduced 《into, from》. ‖ 조상 ~의 가보 one's family treasure (handed down from generation to generation) / 불교는 3세기에 한국에 ~되었다 Buddhism was introduced into Korea in the third century.

전략(前略) 《편지에서》 I hasten to inform you that…; Dispensing with the preliminaries, ….

전략(戰略) strategy; stratagem. ‖ ~적인 strategic / ~을 세우다 work 〔map〕 out one's strategy / ~상으로 보아 from the strategical point of view; strategically. ‖ ~가 a strategist / ~공군 a strategic air force / ~공군사령부《美》 the Strategic Air Command (생략 SAC) / ~목표 a strategic target / ~무기 strategic arms〔weaponry〕 / ~무기감축회담 the Strategic Arms Reduction Talks (생략 START) / ~무기제한회담 Strategic Arms Limitation Talks (생략 SALT) / ~무역정책 a strategic trade policy / ~물자 strategic goods〔materials〕 / ~방위구상 the Strategic Defense Initiative (생략 SDI) / ~수출품목 a strategic export item / ~폭격 strategic bombing / ~폭격기 a strategic bomber / ~핵무기 strategic nuclear weapons / ~회의 a strategy meeting / 국제 ~ 연구소 the International Institute for Strategic Studies (생략 IISS).

전략산업(戰略産業) a strategic industry. ‖ ~으로서 집중적으로 육성되다 be intensively fostered as strategic industries.

전량(全量) the whole quantity.

전력(全力) all one's strength〔power, might〕. ‖ ~을 다하다 do one's best〔utmost〕; do everything in one's power / ~을 기울이다 devote all one's energies 《to》 / ~을 다해 그들을 도와야 한다 We should go all out to help them.

전력(前歷) one's past record〔life〕. ‖ 그는 은행에서 일한 ~이 있다 He once served in a bank.

전력(專力) ~하다 concentrate one's energies 《on》; devote oneself 《to》.

전력(電力) electric power. ‖ ~개발 power development / ~계 a wattmeter / ~공급 supply of electric power / ~부족 (electric) power shortage (~부족의 power-short 《areas》) / ~사정 the power condition / ~수요 (the) demand for (electric) power / ~요금 power rates / ~자원 (electric)-power resources / ~제한(소비, 통제) power restrictions〔consumption, control〕.

전력(戰力) war potential; fighting power. ‖ ~증강 the strengthening〔build-up〕 of war potential.

전령(傳令) 《사람》 a messenger; a runner; 〖軍〗 an orderly; 《명령》 an official message.

전례(前例) a precedent. ‖ ~없는 unprecedented; without precedent / ~가 되다 be〔form〕 a precedent / ~를 만들다 create〔set〕 a precedent / ~를 깨뜨리다

전류(電流) an electric current; a flow of electricity. ¶ ~을 통하다 send an electric current (*into a wire*); charge (*a wire*) with electricity / ~를 차단하다 shut (switch) off an electric current / ~가 흐르고 있다 (흐르지 않다) The current is on (off). / ~계 an ammeter / 교류(직류) ~ an alternating (a direct) current.

전리(電離) [理] electrolytic dissociation; ionization. ~하다 ionize. ‖ ~층 the ionosphere.

전리품(戰利品) a (war) trophy; (약탈품) booty, the spoils of war.

전립선(前立腺) [解] the prostate (gland). ‖ ~비대 enlargement of the prostate gland / ~염 prostatitis.

전말(顚末) 《자세한 내용》 the details; the whole story; 《사정》 the whole circumstances. ¶ 사고의 ~을 이야기하다 give a full (detailed) account of the accident. ‖ ~서 an account; a report.

전망(展望) a view; a prospect; an outlook. ~하다 view; survey; have a view of. ¶ 앞으로의 ~ the future prospect / ~이 좋다 have (command) a fine view (*of*); have a bright prospect / 《장래가》 경기의 동향을 ~하다 survey the economic prospects / ~을 방해하다 obstruct the view (*of*). ‖ ~대 an observation platform / ~차 an observation car / ~탑 an observation tower.

전매(專賣) monopoly; monopolization. ~하다 monopolize; have the monopoly (*of, on*). ¶ ~권 monopoly / ~사업 the monopoly enterprise / ~제도 the monopoly system / ~품 monopoly goods.

전매(轉賣) resale. ~하다 resell. ¶ ~할 수 있는 resalable.

전매특허(專賣特許) a patent. ¶ ~을 얻다 get a patent (*on an article*); patent (*a thing*) / ~을 출원하다 apply for a patent.

전면(全面) the whole (entire) surface. ¶ ~의 全 all-out; general; overall; whole; sweeping / ~적으로 generally; wholly; sweepingly / ~적으로 개정하다 make an overall (a sweeping) revision (*of*) / ~적으로 지지하다 give full support to (*a person's proposal*) / 문제를 ~적으로 재조사하다 investigate the problem again from all sides (angles). ‖ ~강화 an overall peace / ~광고 a full-page advertisement / ~전쟁 an all-out (total) war / ~파업 an all-out (total) strike.

전면(前面) the front (*of a building*). ¶ ~의 front; in front; fore / ~에 in front of / ~의 적 the enemy in front.

전멸(全滅) (an) annihilation; complete (total) destruction; extinction. ~하다 be annihilated; be wiped (stamped) out. ¶ ~시키다 annihilate; destroy totally / 많은 야생 동물이 ~의 위기에 처해 있다 Many wild animals are on the verge of extinction.

전모(全貌) the whole aspect. ¶ …의 ~를 밝히다 bring the whole matter to light / 그 ~를 알고 싶다 I want to know all about it.

전몰(戰歿) death on the battlefield. ¶ ~장병 the war dead (총칭); a fallen soldier.

전무(專務) 《사람》 a managing (executive) director. ¶ 여객 ~ a conductor (美).

전무(全無) none; nothing (at all); no (not any) (*doubt*) whatever (whatsoever). ¶ 그의 회복 가능성은 ~하다 There is no hope of his recovery (at all). / 거래가 ~하다 There has been no trading at all. / 나는 법률 지식이 ~하다 I don't have the least knowledge of law.

전무후무(全無後無) ~하다 be the first and (probably) the last; be unprecedented; be unheard-of. ¶ ~한 명화 the greatest film of all time / 이처럼 많은 사람들이 참석한 것은 ~한 일이다 There never was and never will be such a large attendance as this.

전문(全文) the whole sentence (passage); the full text (*of a treaty*). ¶ ~을 인용하다 quote a whole sentence / ~을 우리말로 옮기시오 Put the whole passage into Korean.

전문(前文) the above (passage); the foregoing remark; 《조약의》 the preamble (*to, of*).

전문(專門) a specialty (美); a speciality (英); a special subject of study 《학문에서》; a major 《전공 과목》 (美). ¶ ~으로 연구하다 make a specialty of; specialize (*in*) / ~ 밖이다 be not in *one's* line; be off *one's* beat. ‖ ~가 a specialist (*in*); an expert (*on*) / ~교육 technical (professional) education / ~분야 a specialized field; *one's* field (line) / ~서 a technical book / ~어 a technical term 《의》 / ~어 medical terminology / ~위원 an expert advisor; a technical expert / ~의(醫) a medical specialist / ~점 a specialty store / ~학교 a

전문 professional [technical] school; a college / ~화 specialization 〈~화하다 specialize〉. ‖ [gram.

전문(電文) a telegram; a cable.

전문(傳聞) hearsay; a rumor; a report. ~하다 hear 《*something*》 from other people; know by report. ¶ ~한 바에 의하면 from what I hear; according to a rumor. ‖ ~증거 hearsay evidence.

전반(全般) the whole. ~적으로 generally; on the whole; by and large / ~적인 상황 the overall (all-over) situation / 과학의 ~에 걸치다 cover the whole field of science.

전반(前半) the first half; 《축구의》 the first period. ¶ 그는 40대 ~이다 He is in his early forties. ‖ ~기 the first half year / ~전 the first half of the game.

전반사(全反射) [理] total reflection.

전방(前方) the front (line). ~의 front; in front ~에 in front of; ahead; forward / 100미터 ~에 다리가 있다 There is a bridge a hundred meters ahead. / ~에 무엇이 보이느냐 What can you see in front of you? ‖ ~기지 an advanced base / ~지휘소 a forward command post.

전방위외교(全方位外交) omnidirectional diplomacy.

전번(前番) the other day; sometime ago. ¶ ~의 last; previous; former / ~에 last (time); before this; previously / ~에 널 만났을 때 when I saw him last.

전범(戰犯罪) war crimes; 《사람》 a war criminal. ‖ ~법정 a war crimes court.

전법(戰法) tactics; strategy.

전변(轉變) changeableness; variableness. ¶ 위의 〈有為〉 ~ the vicissitudes of life.

전보(電報) a telegram; a telegraphic message; a wire; 《무전》 a wireless (telegram). ~치다 send a telegram (wire) 《to》; telegraph (wire) 《*a person*》로 by telegraph (telegram, wire, cable) / 외국〈국내〉 ~ a foreign (domestic) telegram / 지급 ~ an urgent telegram. ‖ ~료 a telegram fee (charge) / ~용지 a telegram form / ~환 a telegraphic remittance.

전보(轉補) ~하다 transfer. ¶ ~되다 be transferred 《*to another position*》.

전복(全鰒) [貝] an abalone; an ear shell; a sea-ear.

전복(顚覆) overturning; an overthrow; capsize (선박의). ~하다 overturn; capsize. ¶ 인천역 구내에서 열차가 탈선해서 ~했다 The train derailed and overturned in the Inch'ŏn Station yard. / 정부의 ~을 기도하다 plot to overthrow the government / 배는 강풍으로 ~됐다 The ship was capsized by a strong wind.

전부(全部) 《명사》 all; the whole; 《부사》 in all; altogether; all told; wholly; entirely.

전부인(前婦人) one's ex-wife.

전분(澱粉) starch. ¶ ~질의 starchy / ~질이 많은 식품 starchy foods.

전비(戰費) war expenditure.

전비(戰備) preparations for war. ¶ ~를 갖추다 prepare for war.

전사(戰士) a warrior; a champion 《*of liberty*》. ‖ 산업 ~ an industrial worker.

전사(戰史) a military (war) history. ¶ ~에 남다 be recorded in war history.

전사(戰死) death in battle (action). ~하다 be killed in action; die (fall) in battle. ¶ 명예롭게 ~하다 meet a glorious death in action. ‖ ~자 a fallen soldier; the war dead (총칭).

전사(轉寫) transcription; copying. ~하다 copy; transcribe.

전산(電算) computation (calculation) by computer. ¶ ~조판 시스템 a computer type-setting system. ‖ ~기 a computer / ~화(化) computerization / ~소형 ~기 a minicomputer.

전상(戰傷) a war (battle) wound. ¶ ~을 입다 be wounded in war (action). ‖ ~자 a wounded soldier (veteran); the war wounded (총칭).

전색맹(全色盲) total color-blindness; [醫] achromatopsia.

전생(前生) one's previous (former) life (existence). ¶ ~의 업 predestination; one's karma 《梵》; one's fate.

전생애(全生涯) one's whole life. ~를 통하여 throughout (all through) one's life.

전서(全書) a complete book (collection). ¶ 백과 ~ an encyclopedia / 법률 ~ a compendium of law.

전서구(傳書鳩) a carrier pigeon.

전선(前線) ① 《계일선》 the front (line). ¶ ~에서 싸우다 fight in (on) the front line / ~으로 나가다 go up to the front line. ‖ ~기지 a front-line base / ~전 초 an outpost. ② 《氣》 a front. ¶ 한랭 〈온난〉 ~ a cold (warm) front / 장마 ~이 호남 지방에 머물러 있다 The seasonal rain front is lingering over the Honam district.

전선(電線) 《전화》 a telephone [telegraph] wire; 《전기의》 an electric wire (line, cord). ¶ ～을 가설하다 string [lay] electric wires.

전선(戰線) the battle front; the front line. ¶ 서부 ～에 on the western front / 인민 ～ the popular [people's] front / 통일 [공동] ～을 펴다 form a united line [front] (*against*) / ～을 축소하다 shorten the line.

전설(傳說) a legend; folklore (민간전승의). ¶ ～적인 legendary; traditional / ～적인 영웅 a legendary hero / ～에 의하면 according to legend [tradition].

전성(全盛) the height of prosperity. ¶ ～하다 be at the height of *its*(*one's*) prosperity. ¶ ～기 [시대] the golden age [days] (*of English literature*); one's best days (그의 ～기는 지나갔다 He has seen his best days.).

전성(展性) 〖理〗 malleability.

전성관(傳聲管) a voice [speaking] tube.

전세(前世) ① 〈전생〉 a former life. ② 〈전대〉 the former generations; past ages.

전세(專貰) ～ 내다 make reservation; reserve (美); engage; book; hire; charter / ～낸 chartered [reserved] (예약된). ‖ ～버스 [비행기] a chartered bus [plane].

전세(轉貰) the lease of a house [room] on a deposit basis. ¶ ～놓다 lease a house [room] on a deposit basis. ‖ ～계약 a contract to rent a house [room] with a deposit [key money] (to be repaid on leaving) / ～금 security [key] money for the lease of a house [room] / ～금 융자 loans to pay for house rents / 전셋집 a house for rent on a deposit basis.

전세(戰勢) the progress of a battle; the war situation.

전세계(全世界) the whole [all the] world. ¶ ～에 [걸쳐서] all over [throughout] the world.

전세기(前世紀) the former [last] century.

전소(全燒) total destruction by fire. ¶ ～하다 be burnt down (to the ground); burn out.

전속(專屬) ～하다 belong exclusively (*to*); be attached (*to*). ‖ ～가수 (여배우) a singer [an actress] attached to [under exclusive contract with] (*the KBS*).

전속(轉屬) (a) transfer (*to another section*). ¶ ～되다 되었다 He was transferred from the head office to the branch office in Inch'ŏn.

전속력(全速力) full speed. ¶ ～으로 at full speed / ～을 내다 put forth full speed.

전손(全損) 〖商〗 total loss. ‖ ～담보 security for total loss only (생략 T.L.O.).

전송(傳送) ～하다 transmit; convey; communicate; deliver.

전송(電送) electrical transmission. ～하다 send [transmit] (*a picture*) by wire(less). ‖ ～사진 a telephoto(graph); a facsimile; a fax.

전송(餞送) ～하다 see (*a person*) off; give a send-off.

전송하다(轉送—) send on; forward; transmit; 우편물은 새 주소로 전송하여 주십시오 Please forward mail to my new address.

전수(全數) the whole; the total number.

전수(專修) ～하다 make a special study (*of*); specialize [major] (*in*). ‖ ～과(科) a special course / ～과목 a specialized subject; a major (美) / ～학교 a vocational school.

전수(傳授) instruction; initiation. ～하다 give instruction [initiate (*a person*) into (*the secrets of an art*). ‖ ～를 받다 receive instruction; be instructed.

전술(前述) ～한 aforesaid; above-mentioned; foregoing ¶ 바와 같이 as stated above.

전술(戰術) tactics. ¶ ～상의 요점 a tactical point / 교묘한 ～ a clever piece of tactics / 고등 ～ grand tactics / ～로 …에 이기다 outmaneuver. ‖ ～가 a tactician / ～공군 tactical air forces / ～전환 a change of tactics / ～핵무기 a tactical nuclear weapon.

전승(傳承) ～하다 hand down; transmit from generation to generation. ‖ ～문학 oral literature.

전승(戰勝) a victory; a triumph. ～하다 win (gain) a victory. ¶ ～을 축하하다 celebrate a victory. ‖ ～국 a victorious country (nation) / ～기념일 the anniversary of a victory.

전승하다(全勝—) win (gain) a complete victory (*over*); 〖競〗 win [sweep] all games [matches, bouts]; make a clean record.

전시(全市) the whole city.

전시(展示) exhibition; display. ～하다 exhibit; display; put (*things*) on display. ¶ ～용 견본 a sample for display / ～되어 있다 be on display [show]. ‖ ～물 [品] an exhibit; exhibition (총칭) / ～장 an exhibition hall [room, area] / ～회 an exhibition; a display / ～효과 a demon-

전시(戰時) wartime; time of war. ¶ ~ 중에 during the war; in wartime. ‖ ~ 경제 wartime economy / ~ 내각 a war Cabinet / ~ 산업 industry in wartime / ~ 상태 a state of war; belligerency / ~ 재정 wartime finance / ~ 체제 the wartime structure.

전시대(前時代) former ages (times).

전신(全身) the whole body. ¶ ~ 에 all over the body / ~ 의 힘을 다하여 with all *one's* strength (might) / 수영은 ~ 운동이 된다 Swimming gives exercise to every part of your body. ‖ ~ 마비 total paralysis / ~ 마취 general anesthesia / ~ 사진 a full-length portrait.

전신(前身) *one's* former self; the predecessor 《*of a school*》.

전신(電信) telegraph; telegraphic communication; 《해외전신》 cable. ¶ ~ 의 telegraphic (cable). ‖ ~ 국 a telegraph office / ~ 부호 a telegraphic cord / ~ 주 a telegraph pole; a utility pole 《美》 / ~ 환 a telegraphic transfer (remittance).

전실(前室) *one's* ex-wife (former wife) ‖ ~ 자식 a child of *one's* former wife.

전심(全心) *one's* whole heart (soul). ¶ ~ 전력을 다하여 put *one's* whole heart and strength into 《*one's* work》.

전심(專心) ~ 하다 devote (apply, bend) *oneself* 《*to*》; be devoted 《*to*》; concentrate 《*on*》; give all *one's* mind 《*to*》. ¶ 연구에 ~ 하다 concentrate on *one's* researches.

전아(典雅) ¶ ~ 한 graceful; refined.

전압(電壓) voltage. ¶ ~ 이 높다 [낮다] be high [low] in voltage / ~ 을 높이다 [낮추다] increase [drop] voltage. ‖ ~ 계 a voltmeter.

전액(全額) the total (full) amount; the sum total. ¶ ~ 을 지불[지급, 납입]하다 pay in full / ~ 을 부담하다 cover all the expenses. ‖ ~ 담보 full coverage / ~ 보험 full insurance.

전야(前夜) the previous night; the night before; the eve 《전야제 따위》; last night 《간밤》. ‖ 크리스마스 ~ Christmas Eve.

전언(前言) *one's* previous remarks (words, statement).

전언(傳言) a (verbal) message. ~ 하다 send 《*a person*》 word; send a message that...; leave 《*a person*》 a message. ¶ ~ 을 부탁하다 leave a message with 《*a person*》.

전업(專業) a special [principal] occupation. ¶ 그는 꽃재배를 ~ 으로 하고 있다 He specializes in growing flowers. ‖ ~ 농가 a full-time farmer / ~ 주부 a (full-time) housewife.

전업(電業) the electrical industry.

전업(轉業) ~ 하다 change *one's* occupation (business). ‖ ~ 자금 funds for occupational change.

전역(全域) all the (whole) area 《*of Seoul*》.

전역(全譯) a complete translation 《*of the Bible*》. ~ 하다 translate 《*a book*》 completely 《*into Korean*》.

전역(戰役) a war; warfare.

전역(戰域) a war area; a theater of war. ‖ ~ 핵병기 a theater nuclear weapon (생략 TNW).

전역(轉役) ~ 하다 discharge from service; transfer 《*to the first reserve*》.

전연(全然) ☞ 전혀.

전열(電熱) electric heat. ‖ ~ 기 an electric heater (난방용) ; (요리용) an electric range (stove); a hotplate.

전열(前列) the front rank (row).

전열(戰列) a battle line. ¶ ~ 에 참가하다 join the battle line.

전염(傳染) (병의) infection (공기에 의한); contagion (접촉에 의한). ~ 하다 (병이) be contagious (infectious, catching); 《사람이》 be infected with 《*a disease*》. ~ 성의 contagious; infectious / 콜레라는 ~ 된다 Cholera is contagious (infectious). / 그의 병은 아이에게서 ~ 되었다 He caught (contracted) the disease from his child. ‖ ~ 경로 a route of infection / ~ 력 virulence / ~ 원(源) a source of infection.

전염병(傳染病) an infectious (a contagious) disease; an epidemic. ‖ ~ 환자 an infectious (a contagious) case.

전와(轉訛) corruption (of a word). ~ 하다 corrupt into; be corrupted from (into).

전용(專用) private use; exclusive use. ~ 하다 use exclusively (solely). ¶ ~ 의 exclusive; for private / 외국인 ~ 의 나이트클럽 a night club reserved only for foreign customers / 야간 ~ 의 전화 a telephone for night use only / 자동차 ~ 도로 a driveway / 한글 ~ the exclusive use of *hangeul*. ‖ ~ 기 a plane for *one's* personal use (대통령 ~ 기 a presidential plane) / ~ 차 a private car (사장 ~ 차 the president's private car).

전용(轉用) diversion. ~ 하다 use 《*a thing*》 for another purposes; divert 《*fund*》 to 《*some other purposes*》.

전우(戰友) a comrade; a war buddy; a fellow soldier.

전운(戰雲) war clouds. ¶ 중동에 ~이 감돌다 War clouds hang over the Middle East.

전원(田園) 《시골》 the country (side); rural districts; 《교외》 suburbs. ∥ ~도시 a garden [rural] city / ~생활 a rural [country] life / ~시(詩) an idyl; a pastoral / ~시인 a pastoral poet; an idyllist / ~주택 a house for rural life / ~풍경 a rural landscape.

전원(全員) all the members; the entire staff. ¶ ~일치의 unanimous / ~일치로 unanimously / 우리 학급 ~이 게임에 참가했다 All the class took part in the game.

전원(電源) a power source. ∥ ~개발 development of power resources.

전월(前月) last month.

전위(前衛) an advanced guard(군의); a forward player(테니스); a forward(축구). ¶ ~을 맡아보다 play forward. / ~음악 [미술] avant-garde music [art].

전위(電位) electric potential. ∥ ~계 an electrometer / ~차 a potential difference(생략 p. d.).

전유(專有) exclusive possession. ~하다 take sole possession of; monopolize 《a right》; have 《a thing》 to oneself. ∥ ~권 an exclusive right; monopoly / ~자 a sole owner.

전율(戰慄) a shiver; a shudder. ~하다 shudder; shiver; tremble with fear. ¶ ~할 (만한) terrible; horrible; shocking; bloodcurdling / ~케 하다 make 《a person》 shudder [shiver]; freeze 《a person's》 blood.

전음(顫音) a trill.

전의(戰意) the will to fight; a fighting spirit. ¶ ~를 잃다 lose the will to fight; lose one's fighting spirit / ~를 북돋우다 whip up war sentiment.

전의(轉義) a transferred [figurative] meaning.

전이(轉移) 《변화》 (a) change; 《암 따위》 spread 《of a disease》 from its original site to another part of the body; 〖醫〗 metastasis. ~하다 metastasize; spread by metastasis. ¶ 위암이 간장으로 ~된 것 같다 It seems that the stomach cancer has spread to the liver.

전인(全人) ¶ ~교육 education for the whole man.

전인(前人) a predecessor. ¶ ~미답의 untrod(den); unexplored; virgin 《forests》 / ~의 영역 a region no man has ever explored.

전일(前日) the previous day; the day before.

전임(前任) ¶ ~의 former; preceeding. ∥ ~자 one's predecessor / ~지 one's former [last] post.

전임(專任) ¶ ~의 full-time. ∥ ~교사 [강사] a full-time teacher [lecturer].

전임(轉任) change of post [assignment]. ~하다 be transferred to another post. ∥ ~지 one's new post.

전입(轉入) ~하다 move in[into]; be transferred to. ∥ ~생 a transfer student / ~신고 a moving-in notification.

전자(前者) the former; that (this 에 대해); the one (the other 에 대해).

전자(電子) an electron. ¶ ~의 electronic. ∥ ~계산기 [두뇌] an electronic computer [brain] / ~공업 [산업] electronic industry / ~공학 electronics / ~레인지 a microwave oven / ~볼트 an electron volt (생략 EV) / ~ 상거래 e-commerce (transactions); ~수첩 an electronic notebook / ~오락실 an electronic game [amusement] room; a video game room / ~오락업 electronic amusement business / ~오르간 an electronic organ / ~우편 electronic mail; E mail / ~음악 electronic music / ~전(戰) electronic warfare / ~전기제품 상가 an electronic and electric products (sales) center / ~정보처리 시스템 an electronic data processing system (생략 EDPS) / ~주민카드 an electronic resident card / ~파일 an electronic file / ~핵공학 nucleonics / ~현미경 an electron microscope.

전자(電磁) ☞ 전자기(電磁氣).

전자기(電磁氣) electromagnetism. ¶ ~의 electromagnetic. ∥ ~단위 an electromagnetic unit(생략 EMU) / ~유도 electromagnetic induction / ~자물쇠 an electromagnetic door lock / ~장(場) an electromagnetic field / ~조리기 an electromagnetic cooker / ~파 an electromagnetic wave; a radio wave / ~학 electromagnetics.

전자(篆字) a seal character.

전작(前酌) ~이 있다 have already taken some liquor.

전장(全長) the total [full] length. ∥ ~백 피트인 ~ have an overall length of 100 feet.

전장(前章) the preceding chapter.

전장(前場) 〖證〗 the first [morning] session.

전장(電場) 〖理〗 an electric field.

전장(戰場) a battlefield; a battleground. ¶ ~의 이슬로 사라지다 die

전재(戰災) war damage (devastation). ¶ ~를 입다 (당하다) suffer (escape) war damage. ∥ ~ 지구 war-damaged areas.

전재(轉載) ~하다 reprint (reproduce) 《an article》 from 《the Life》. ¶ B씨의 승낙을 얻고 ~함 Reprinted by courtesy of Mr. B. ∥ ~불허 All rights (Copyright) reserved.

전쟁(戰爭) (전란) (a) war; warfare. ~과 go to war 《with, against》; war 《with, against》; wage war 《against》. ¶ ~의 참화 war calamities / ~중이다 be at war 《with》 / ~에 이기다(지다) win(lose) a war / ~을 일으키다 provoke (bring on) war. ∥ ~경기 a wartime boom / ~고아 a war orphan / ~기념관 the War Memorial 《in Yongsan》 / ~도발자 a warmonger; a warmaker / ~ 미망인 a war widow / ~범죄 a war crime / ~범죄자 a war criminal / ~상태 (enter into) a state of war / ~이재민 war refugees / ~지역 a war area 《zone》 / ~터 a battlefield; the seat (theater) of war.

전적(全的) total; complete; whole; entire; the full. ~으로 entirely; utterly / ~인 협력 wholehearted cooperation.

전적(戰跡) (visit) the trace of battle; an old battlefield.

전적(戰績) military achievements; a war record; 《경기의》 results; a record; a score.

전적(轉籍) ~하다 transfer one's domicile (family register) 《from, to》.

전전(戰前) ¶ ~의 prewar; before the war; ante-bellum. ∥ ~파 the prewar generation.

전전하다(轉轉—) change 《one's address》 frequently; pass from hand to hand 《임자가 바뀌다》; wander from place to place 《헤매다》.

전전긍긍(戰戰兢兢) ~하다 be in great fear; be trembling with fear. ¶ 그는 추문이 드러나지 않을까 ~하였다 He was in constant fear that the scandal would come to light.

전전일(前前日) two days ago; 《그저께》 the day before yesterday.

전정(剪定) ~하다 prune; trim. ∥ ~ 가위 (a pair of) pruning shears.

전제(前提) 【論】 a premise. ¶ …을 ~로 하여 on the assumption (premise) that…; on condition that… / 우리는 결혼을 ~로 교제하고 있다 We are dating with marriage in mind. ∥ ~조건 a precondition.

전제(專制) despotism; autocracy. ¶ ~적인 despotic; autocratic; absolute. ∥ ~국 an absolute monarchy / ~군주 an autocrat; a despot / ~정치 despotic government; autocracy / ~주의 absolutism; despotism.

전조(前兆) an omen; a sign; foreboding (불길한); a symptom (병 따위의 징후). ¶ 좋은(나쁜) ~ a good (bad) omen / ~가 되다 bode; forebode (불길한) be ominous of / 이 검은 구름은 폭풍의 ~다 This black cloud is a sign of a storm.

전조(轉調) 【樂】 modulation; transition.

전조등(前照燈) a headlight.

전족(纏足) foot-binding. ~하다 bind one's feet.

전죄(前罪) a former crime (sin).

전주(前奏) 【樂】 a prelude; an introduction. ∥ ~곡 an overture 《to》; a prelude 《to》.

전주(前週) last week (지난 주일); the preceding week; the week before (그 전주). ¶ ~의 오늘 this day last week.

전주(電柱) a telegraph (an electric, a telephone) pole.

전주(錢主) a financial backer (supporter). ¶ ~가 되다 finance 《an enterprise》; give 《a person》 financial support.

전중이 a prisoner; a convict; a jailbird 《俗》.

전지(全知) ¶ ~의 all-knowing; omniscient / ~전능하신 하느님 Almighty God; the Almighty.

전지(全紙) the whole sheet of paper.

전지(電池) a battery; a dry cell (건전지). ¶ ~로 작동되다 work on (by) batteries / ~를 충전하다 charge a battery / ~를 교환하다 replace a battery with a new one / 이 ~는 다 소모 되었다 This battery is dead.

전지(轉地) ~하다 move (go) to 《a place》 for a change of air. ∥ ~요법 treatment by change of air / ~을 하다 (take) a change of air for one's health.

전지일(剪枝—) lop; trim; prune.

전직(前職) one's former occupation (office). ∥ ~장관 an ex-minister; an ex-secretary.

전직(轉職) a job-change. ~하다 change one's occupation (employment); switch jobs 《to》.

전진(前進) an advance; a forward movement; progress. ~하다 advance; go (move) forward. ∥ ~기지 an advanced base; an outpost / ~명령 (give) orders for an advance; marching orders.

전질(全帙) 《질로 된 책》 a complete set 《of books》.

전집(全集) the complete works 《of Shakespeare》. ¶ ~물 a complete works series.

전차(電車) a streetcar 《美》; a trolley car 《美》; a tram(car) 《英》.

전차(戰車) a (war) tank. ¶ ~병 a tankman; tank crew(총칭) / ~부대 a tank corps(unit) / ~전 tank warfare / ~포 a tank gun / ~호(壕) an antitank trench; a tank trap / 중[경]~ a heavy [light] tank.

전차(轉借) ~하다 borrow at second hand. ¶ ~인 a sublessee; a subtenant.

전채(前菜) 《料理》 an *hors d'oeuvre* 《프》, an appetizer.

전처(前妻) one's ex-wife 《former wife》.

전천후(全天候) ¶ ~의 all-weather / ~용 테니스 코트 an all-weather tennis court. ‖ ~기 (전천기) an all-weather plane (fighter) / ~농업 all-weather agriculture / ~비행 all-weather flying.

전철(前轍) wheel tracks left by vehicles that have passed before. ¶ ~을 밟다 tread in 《a person's》 steps; make the same mistake [error] as one's predecessors.

전철(電鐵) an electric railroad.

전철(轉轍) (railroad) switching. ‖ ~기 (a) (railroad) switch 《美》; points 《英》 / ~수(手) a switchman; a pointsman.

전체(全體) (전부) the whole. ¶ ~의 whole; entire; general / ~적으로 wholly; entirely; generally; on the whole / ~적인 문제 an overall problem / 학급 ~의 의견 을 요약하면 다음과 같다 The summary (general) opinion of the whole class is as follows. ‖ ~주의 totalitarianism / ~주의 국가 a totalitarian state / ~회의 a general meeting.

전초(前哨) an advanced post; an outpost. ‖ ~부대 outpost troops / ~전 a (preliminary) skirmish; (비유적으로) a prelude 《to the coming election》.

전축(電蓄) 《美》 an electric phonograph; a radiogram (라디오 겸의). ¶ 스테레오(하이파이)~ a stereophonic (high-fidelity) phonograph.

전출(轉出) ~하다 move out 《to》; (직원이) be transferred 《to a new post》. ‖ ~신고 a moving-out notification.

전치(全治) ~되다 be completely cured (healed) 《of》; recover completely from 《a wound》. ¶ ~ 3주의 부상 an injury which will take 3 weeks to recover completely.

전치사(前置詞) 《文》 a preposition.

전통(傳統) a tradition. ¶ ~적(으로) traditional(ly); conventional(ly) / ~적인 한국의 축제 a traditional Korean festival / ~을 자랑하는 학교 a school with a proud history / ~을 중히 여기다 [cherish] tradition / ~을 깨뜨리다 break with tradition / 오랜 ~을 굳게 지키다 stick (adhere) to time-honored traditions. ‖ ~문화 a cultural heritage.

전퇴직률(轉退職率) the separation [turn over] rate.

전투(戰鬪) a battle; a fight; a combat; an action (교전). ¶ ~중인 병사 a soldier in combat / ~에 참가하다 take part in a battle / ~을 개시하다 go into battle; open hostilities / ~를 중지하다 break off a battle; cease hostilities. ‖ ~경찰대 a combatant police unit / ~기 a fighter (plane) / ~대형 (a) battle formation / ~력 fighting strength(power) / ~부대 a combat unit (corps) / ~상태 a state of war / ~상태에 들어가다 enter a state of war; go to war with each other / ~원 a combatant (비)~원 a noncombatant / ~준비 preparation for action / ~지역 a battle zone (area) / ~태세 (be in) combat readiness / ~행위 an act of hostilities / ~훈련 combat drill; field training / 차세대 ~기 the next-generation fighter (plane).

전파(全破) complete destruction. ~하다 destroy completely; demolish. ~되다 be completely destroyed (demolished, ruined). ‖ ~가옥 a completely destroyed house.

전파(電波) an electric [a radio] wave. ¶ ~를 통해 over the air / ~을 타다 be broadcast; go on the air. ‖ ~관리 radio regulation / ~망원경 a radio telescope / ~방해 jamming / ~장해 radio interference / ~탐지기 a radar.

전파(傳播) propagation 《of sound》; spread 《of disease》. ~하다 spread; propagate. ¶ 문명의 ~ the spread of civilization.

전패(全敗) a complete [total] defeat [lost]. ~하다 lose all one's games (every game). 〔ume〕.

전편(全編) the whole book [volume〕.

전편(前篇) the first volume.

전폐(全廢) total abolition. ~하다 abolish (totally); do away with.

전폭(全幅) ~적인 full; utmost; all; wholehearted 《sympathy》 / ~적으로 신뢰하다 trust 《a person》 completely; place full confidence in 《a person》.

전폭기(戰爆機) a fighter-bomber.
전표(傳票) a (payment) slip. ¶ ~를 떼다 issue a slip. / 수납 (지급) ~ a receiving (payment) slip.
전하(電荷) (an) electric charge.
전하(殿下) His (Her, Your) Highness. ¶ 왕세자 ~ the Prince of Wales《英》; the Crown Prince.
전하다(傳一) ① 〈전달〉 tell; inform; report; convey; communicate. ¶ 가족에게 비보를 ~ break the sad news to the family / 내가 도우셨다고 너의 아버지께 전해다오 Please tell your father that I have arrived. / 대통령은 자신의 생각을 국민에게 전했다 The President communicated his ideas to the people. / 신문이 전하는 바에 의하면 according to the newspaper reports; it says in the newspaper that…. ② 〈전수〉 teach; impart; initiate(비전); 〈소개·도입〉 introduce. ¶ 지식을 ~ impart knowledge to (a person) / 비법을 제자에게 ~ teach one's pupil the mysteries of art / 그는 기독교를 한국에 전했다 He introduced Christianity into Korea. ③ 〈남겨주다〉 hand down; leave; transmit; bequeath. ¶ 후세에 ~ hand down to posterity / 대대로 ~ transmit from father to son 〔generation to generation〕.

전학(轉學) ~하다 change one's school; remove from one school to another; transfer to another school. ‖ ~생 a transfer student.
전함(戰艦) a battleship.
전항(前項) the preceding 〔foregoing〕 clause 〔paragraph〕; the antecedent.
전해(電解) electrolysis. ~하다 electrolyze.
전향(轉向) conversion. ~하다 switch (A from B); turn; be converted (to). ¶ 180도로 ~하다 do a complete about-face; make a complete volte-face / 그는 급진에서 보수로 ~했다 He turned 〔switched〕 from Radical to Conservative. ‖ ~자 a convert.
전혀(全一) quite; totally; completely; utterly; wholly; entirely; altogether; 〈조금도 …않다〉 (not) at all; (not) in the least; (not) a bit. ¶ ~ 모르는 사람 a total stranger / 그와는 ~ 아무런 관계도 없다 I have absolutely nothing to do with him.
전형(典型) a type; a model; a pattern. ¶ ~적인 typical; model; ideal / ~적인 한국인 a typical Korean.
전형(銓衡) choice; selection; screening. ~하다 screen; select. ¶ ~에서 빠지다 be not chosen; be rejected; fail to be selected. ‖ ~기준 a criterion for selection / ~시험 a screening test / ~위원 a member of a selection committee / ~위원회 a selection committee. [number 〔issue〕.
전호(前號) the preceding 〔last
전화(電話) a (tele)phone. ¶ ~를 걸다 telephone; phone; call; make a phone call; call 〔ring〕 up《美》/ ~를 끊다 hang up (the receiver); ring off / ~를 받다 answer the phone / 나에게 ~가 걸려 왔다 I was called up. / ~가 혼선 되었다 The lines are crossed. / ~가 잘 안 들리는군요. 좀더 크게 말씀해 주십시오 I can't hear you. Speak a little louder, please. ‖ ~가입자 a telephone subscriber / ~교환대 a telephone switchboard / ~교환원 a telephone operator / ~국 a telephone office / ~번호 a (tele)phone number / ~번호부 a telephone directory; a phone book《美》/ 구내 ~ an extension phone / 장거리 ~ a long-distance call《美》; a trunk call《英》. [war.
전화(戰火) the flames 〔fires〕 of
전화(戰禍) war damage; the disasters of war; war(전쟁). ¶ ~를 입은 war-torn 〔war-shattered〕(countries) / ~에서 구하다 save (Asia) from war. [transformed.
전화(轉化) ~하다 change; be
전화위복(轉禍爲福) ~하다 a misfortune turns into a blessing. ¶ 이것은 good 보기라고 할 수 있다 This is a case of good coming out of evil.
전환(轉換) conversion; diversion 〈기분의〉. ~하다 convert; change. ¶ 성 ~ a change of sex / 방향을 ~하다 change one's direction / 기분 ~에는 운동이 제일이다 Sport is the best diversion. ‖ ~기(期) a turning point / ~사채(社債) a convertible bond.
전황(戰況) the progress of a battle; the war situation. ¶ ~에 관한 뉴스 war news / ~을 보고하다 report on the military situation / ~이 바람직하지 않다 The war is not going on in our favor.
전회(前回) the last time 〔occasion〕. ¶ ~의 last; previous; preceding / ~까지의 줄거리 a synopsis of the story up to the last installment; the story so far.
전횡(專橫) arbitrariness; despotism; high-handedness. ~하다 be despotic; have one's own way; manage (a matter) arbitrarily.
전후(前後) ① 〈위치·장소〉 before and behind; in front and in the rear. ¶ ~에서 적의 공격을 받다 be

attacked both in front and in the rear / 나는 ~ 좌우를 주의깊게 살폈다 I looked about (around) me carefully. ② (시간) before and after. ¶ 식사 ~에 과격한 운동을 피하다 avoid hard exercise before or after a meal / 식사 ~에 기도하다 say grace before and after each meal. ③ (대략) about; around; or so. ¶ 그는 20세 ~이다 He is about (around) twenty. / 한달에 40만원 ~의 수입 an income of 400,000 won or so a month / 12시 ~ about (around) twelve o'clock. ¶ ~ 관계 the context (모르는 낱말의 뜻을 ~ 관계로 추측하다 guess the meaning of unknown words from the context).

전후(戰後) ~의 postwar; after the war / ~ 최대의 위기 the worst crisis since the war / ~의 경제 발전 post-bellum (postwar) economic development. ¶ ~파 the postwar (apres guerre) generation.

절¹ (사찰) a Buddhist temple. ¶ ~에 불공 드리러 가다 go to a temple to offer a Buddhist mass; visit a temple for worship.

절² (인사) a deep bow; a kowtow. ¶ 공손히 ~하다 bow politely; make a deep bow / 큰 ~을 하다 a ceremonial deep bow / 서로 맞 ~을 하다 salute each other with a bow.

절¹ (節) [文] a clause; (문장의) a paragraph; (시의) a stanza; (성경의) a verse.

-절(折) (종이의) folding. ¶ 12~ duodecimo; a 12 mo.

-절(節) (절기) a season; (명절) the (independence) day; a festival. ¶ 성탄~ Christmas.

절감(節減) reduction; curtailment. ¶ ~하다 reduce; curtail; cut down. ¶ 경비를 ~하다 cut down expenses.

절감하다(切感―) feel keenly (acutely) (the necessity of linguistic knowledge).

절개(切開) incision. ¶ ~하다 cut open (out); operate on; [醫] incise. ¶ 환부를 ~하다 cut out an affected part. ¶ ~수술 a surgical operation.

절개(節槪) fidelity and spirit (절의와 기개); integrity; honor. ¶ ~가 있는 사람 a man of integrity / ~를 지키다 remain faithful to one's cause; keep one's chastity.

절경(絶景) a superb (marvelous) view; picturesque scenery; a grand sight.

절교(絶交) ~하다 break off one's friendship (relationship) (with); break with; be done (through)

with (a person) (美). ¶ 나는 그 남자와 ~했다 I broke off all relations with the man. ¶ ~장 a letter breaking off one's relationship (with a person); a Dear John letter (여성이 남성에 보내는) (美).

절구 a mortar. ¶ ~에 쌀을 1 pound (grain) in a mortar. ¶ ~의 몸통 the body of a mortar / 절굿공이 a (wooden) pestle. [train.

절구(絶句) (한시의) a Chinese qua-

절규(絶叫) ~하다 a shout (exclaim) at the top of one's voice; cry out loudly.

절그렁거리다 clink; clank; jingle; rattle (one's keys). [sions.

절기(節氣) the 24 seasonal divi-

절꺼덕, 절꺼덕 with a snap (click, flop). ¶ ~하다 make a snap.

절다¹ (소금에) get (well) salted.

절다² (발을) walk lame; limp (along). ¶ 발을 저는 lame; crippled; limping.

절단(切斷·截斷) cutting; amputation (손·발이); disconnection (전선 등의). ¶ ~하다 cut (off); amputate (a leg); disconnect. ¶ 그는 한쪽 다리를 ~했다 He had one of his legs amputated. ¶ ~기 a cutting machine; a cutter / ~면 a section / ~환자 an amputee.

절대(絶對) absoluteness. ¶ ~의 (적) absolute / ~로 absolutely / ~진리 absolute (incontrovertive) truth / 의사에게서 ~ 안정하라는 지시를 받다 be ordered by the doctor to take an absolute (a complete) rest / 그 계획에 ~ 반대하다 be positively (dead) against the plan / 과학을 ~시하는 것은 위험하다 It is dangerous to place absolute trust in science. ¶ ~군주제 an absolute monarchy / ~권력 absolute authority (power) / ~다수 an absolute majority / ~빈곤 absolute poverty / ~온도 absolute temperature / ~음감 absolute (perfect) pitch / ~주의 absolutism / ~평가 an absolute evaluation.

절도(節度) ¶ ~가 없는 uncontrolled; unrestrained; loose. ¶ ~를 지키다 be moderate; exercise moderation (in).

절도(竊盜) (행위) [法] larceny; (사람) a thief. ¶ [法] larceny; (사람) a thief. ¶ ~ 습관성 ~ kleptomania / 상습~ a habitual thief; a larcenist.

절뚝거리다 limp (hobble) (along). ¶ 절뚝절뚝 limping; hobbling.

절량(絶糧) ~농가 a food-short farm household / ~농가의 구호 대책을 세우다 work out relief measures for food-short farmers.

절렁거리다 clink; clank.

절레절레 shaking one's head.

절륜(絶倫) ¶ ~한 matchless; unequaled / 정력이 ~한 사람 a man of unequaled (boundless) energy.

절름거리다 limp slightly. ‖ 절름절름 limping; hobbling.

절름발이 a lame person.

절망(絶望) ~하다 despair (of); give up hope. ¶ ~적인 hopeless; desperate / ~에 빠지다 be in the depths of despair / ~한 나머지 자살하려 하다 try to kill *oneself* in despair / 사태 수습은 ~적인 상태이다 Settling the matters is in a hopeless condition.

절명(絶命) 《죽음》 ~하다 expire; die; breathe *one*'s last.

절묘(絶妙) ~한 superb; exquisite / ~한 필치 an exquisite touch / ~한 기예에 superb performance.

절무하다(絶無—) be none at all.

절미(節米) rice saving. ~하다 economize on rice. ‖ ~계획 a rice-saving program / ~운동 a movement for rice saving.

절박(切迫) ~하다 ① 《급박》 be imminent; draw near; be impending. ¶ ~은 urgent 《problems》; imminent 《dangers》; impending 《doom》 / 시간이 ~하다 Time presses. *or* The time is drawing near. / 우리는 ~한 상황에 있다 We are in an urgent condition. ② 《긴박》 be 〔grow, become〕 tense 〔strained〕. ¶ ~한 tense; acute; urgent / 사태가 ~해졌다 The situation suddenly became tense. ‖ ~감 a sense of urgency.

절반(折半) (a) half. ¶ ~으로 나누다 divide 《a thing》 into halves; cut in halves.

절벅거리다 splash 《about》; dabble in the water; splash water.

절벽(絶壁) 《낭떠러지》 a precipice; (a sheer) cliff; a bluff.

절삭(切削) cutting. ‖ ~공구 a cutting tool.

절색(絶色) a woman of matchless 〔peerless〕 beauty.

절세(絶世) ~의 peerless; matchless. ¶ ~의 미인 a rare beauty.

절손(絶孫) letting *one*'s family line die out. ~하다 leave 〔have〕 no posterity.

절수(節水) water saving. ~하다 save water; make frugal use of water.

절식(絶食) fasting. ☞ 단식(斷食).

절식(節食) ~하다 be temperate 〔moderate〕 in eating; be on a diet. ¶ 그녀는 건강을 위해 ~하고 있다 She's on a diet for her health.

절실(切實) ¶ ~한 urgent (긴급한);

serious (중대한); earnest (간절한) / 물 부족은 이제 ~한 문제이다 Lack of water is an urgent problem. / 평상시의 노력이 중요하다는 것을 ~히 느꼈다 I keenly 〔acutely〕 felt that everyday efforts are important.

절약(節約) saving; economy; frugality; thrift. ~하다 save; economize (*on*); be economical (thrifty, frugal); cut down (절감하다). ¶ ~해 thrifty with money / 시간의 ~ the saving of time / 비용의 ~ economy in expenditure / 시간과 정력을 ~하다 economize (on) time and energy. ‖ ~가 an economist.

절연(絶緣) ① 〔電〕 isolation; insulation. ~하다 isolate; insulate. ¶ ~기 an insulator / ~선 an insulated wire / ~체 an insulator / ~테이프 〔전선에 감는〕 friction tape. ② 《관계의》 ~하다 break 《with》; break off relations 《with》; cut 〔sever〕 *one*'s connections 《with》.

절이다 pickle. salt 《*vegetables*》.

절전(節電) power saving. ~하다 save electricity (electric) power / ~의 효과가 나타나기 시작했다 The effects of conserving electricity are beginning to be seen.

절절 ① 《끓는 모양》 물이 ~ 끓는다 The water is simmering. ② 《흔드는 모양》 shaking slowly.

절절이(節節—) each word; phrase by phrase.

절정(絶頂) the top; the summit; the height; the peak. ¶ 인기 ~에 있다 be at the height of *one*'s popularity / 그녀는 행복의 ~에서 불행의 나락으로 내동댕이 쳐졌다 She was knocked down from the height 〔apex〕 of happiness into the depths of misery.

절제(切除) 〔醫〕 resection; (a) surgical removal. ~하다 cut off; excise; resect. ‖ 위~ gastrectomy.

절제(節制) moderation; temperance; self-restraint; abstinence 《from alcohol》. ~하다 be temperate 〔moderate〕 (*in*); (끊다) abstain from 《drinking》. ‖ ~품 pod.

절지동물(節肢動物) 〔動〕 an arthropod.

절차(節次) formalities; procedures; steps (조치). ¶ ~를 밟다 go through the formalities; follow the 《*usual*》 procedures; take proceedings 《*for divorce*》; take steps 《*to do*》 / 복잡한 〔번거로운〕 ~ complicated formalities; annoying red tape. ‖ ~법 an adjective law.

절찬(絶讚) ~하다 praise highly; admire greatly. ¶ ~을 받다 win

절충(折衷) a compromise. ~하다 work out (make, arrange) a compromise (*between*). ‖ ~안 a compromise (plan) / ~주의 eclecticism.

절충(折衝) (a) negotiation. ~하다 negotiate (parley) (*with*). ¶임금 인상에 관한 ~이 진행 중이다 Negotiations are going on about our wage hike. [fer: embezzle.

절취(竊取) theft. ~하다 steal; pil-
절취선(切取線) a perforated line; the line along which to cut (*a section*) off.

절친하다(切親―) be close friends with; be on good terms with. ¶그녀는 나의 절친한 친구다 She is a good friend of mine.

절토하다(切土―) cut the ground.

절통하다(切痛―) (be) extremely regrettable.

절판(絶版) ~된 책 an out-of-print book / ~이 되다 go (be) out of print.

절품(絶品) a unique article; a rarity; a nonpareil.

절필(絶筆)《작품》one's last writing (working); 《행위》putting down one's pen. ~하다 stop (give up) writing.

절하(切下) reduction; devaluation (*of the won*). ~하다 reduce; lower; cut down; devalue (*the U.S. dollar*). ¶또 한 차례 원화 ~가 행해졌다 There's been a further devaluation of the won.

절해(絶海) ¶~의 고도(孤島) a lonely (solitary) island (in the far-off sea).

절호(絶好) ¶~의 best; capital; splendid; golden (*opportunity*).

절후(節侯) → 절기.

젊다 (be) young; youthful. ¶젊었을 때에는 in one's youth; when young / 젊어서 보이다 look young / 나이에 비해 ~ look younger for one's age. 「(총칭).

젊은이 a young man; the young

점(占) divination; fortune-telling. ¶~을 치다《쳐주다》tell (*a person's*) fortune; divine (*the future*) /《치게 하다》have one's fortune told (*by*); consult a fortune-teller (*about a thing*). ‖ ~쟁이 a fortuneteller.

점(點) ① 《작은 표시》a dot; a point; 《반점》a spot; a speck. ¶태양의 흑~ a sunspot /흰 ~ 박힌 검은 개 a black dog with white spots / ~을 찍다 put a dot; dot / 하늘에는 한 ~의 구름도 없었다 There was not a speck of cloud in the sky. ② 《성적의》a grade《美》; a mark; 《경기의》a point; a score; a run

《야구의》. ¶ 60 ~으로 합격하다 pass an exam with 60 marks / 영어에서 80 ~을 받다 get a grade of 80 in English / 야구에서 5~이 나다 score 5 runs at baseball. ③ 《문제가 되는 개소》a point; a respect; 《관점》a standpoint; a point of view. ¶모든 ~에서 in all respects; in every respect / 상업적인 ~에서 보면 from a commercial point of view / 이 ~에서 그녀와 의견을 달리했다 I disagreed with her on this point. ④ 《물품의 수》a piece; an item. ¶의류 10 ~ ten pieces (items) of clothing /가구 2 ~ two articles (pieces) of furniture. ⑤ 《지점》a point. ¶출발 ~ a starting point.

점감(漸減) ~하다 diminish (decrease) gradually.

점거(占據) occupation. ~하다 occupy (*a place*); take; hold. ¶불법 ~ illegal occupation.

점검(點檢) an inspection; a check. ~하다 inspect; check; examine. ¶가스 기구를 ~하다 inspect (check) gas fittings / 자동차를 ~하게 하다 have one's car checked (examined).

점괘(占卦) a divination sign.

점도(粘度) viscosity.

점두(店頭) a store; a storefront 《美》; a show window《영국판》. ¶물품을 ~에 진열하다 display articles in the show window / ~에 내놓다 put (*goods*) on sale. ‖ ~거래 [매매]《證》over-the-counter transactions (sales).

점등(點燈) ~하다 light a lamp; switch (turn) on a light. ‖ ~시간 the lighting hour.

점등(漸騰) a gradual rise (*of price*). ~하다 rise gradually.

점락(漸落) a gradual fall (*of prices*). ~하다 fall gradually.

점령(占領) occupation; capture (공략). ~하다 occupy; take possession of; seize; capture. ¶~하에 있다 be under occupation. ‖ ~군 an occupation forces (army) / ~지 an occupied territory (area).

점막(粘膜)《生》a mucous membrane.

점멸(點滅) ~하다 switch (turn, blink) (*lights*) on and off. ‖ ~기 a switch / ~신호 a blinking signal.

점묘(點描) ¶~화가 a pointillist / ~화법 pointillism.

점박이(點―)《사람》a person with a birthmark; 《짐승》a brindled

점선(點線) a dotted line. [animal.

점성(占星) a horoscope. ‖ ~가 an astrologer; a horoscopist / ~술 astrology.

점성(粘性) viscosity; viscidity. ‖

점수(點數)《평점》a mark; a grade (성적)《美》;《경기의》a score; point.《美》¶ 좋은 ~를 얻다(주다) get(give) a good mark / ~를 따다(비유적으로) ingratiate *oneself* (*with somebody*); curry favor (*with somebody*) / ~가 후하다(짜다) be generous (severe, harsh) in marking.

점술(占術) the art of divination.

점심(點心) lunch; a midday meal. ¶ ~을 먹다 have (take) lunch / ~ 시간에 at lunchtime.

점안(點眼) ~하다 apply eyewash (*to*). ‖ ~기(器) an eyedropper / ~수 eyewash; eye drops.

점액(粘液) mucus; viscous liquid. ¶ ~성(性)의 mucous; viscous; sticky.

점원(店員) a (store) clerk; a salesclerk《美》.

점유(占有) occupancy; possession. ~하다 occupy; possess. ‖ ~권 the right of possession / ~율《시장의》a (market) share / ~자 an occupant; a possessor.

점입가경(漸入佳境) ¶ 이야기는 ~이었다 We've reached (got into) the most interesting part of the story.

점자(點字)《맹인용》Braille; braille. ¶ ~를 읽다 read Braille / ~로 옮기다(를 치다) put (translate) into braille/ braille. ‖ ~기 a braillewriter / ~본 a book in Braille (type) / ~ 읽기 finger-reading.

점잔빼다 assume (take on) an air of importance; put on (superior) airs. ¶ 점잔빼며 이야기하다 speak with an air of importance.

점잖다 (be) dignified; well-behaved; genteel; decent. ¶ 점잖게 굴다 behave *oneself*; behave like a gentleman.

점재하다(點在─) be dotted (scattered, studded, interspersed) with 《houses》. ¶ 섬들이 점재한 바다 an island-studded (-dotted) sea.

점점(漸漸) by degrees; little by little; gradually; more and more (많이); less and less (적게). ¶ 일이 ~ 익숙해지다 become more and more accustomed to the work / ~ 나빠지다 go from bad to worse.

점점이(點點─) here and there; in places; sporadically.

점주(店主) a storekeeper《美》; a shopkeeper《英》.

점증(漸增) a steady (gradual) increase. ~하다 increase gradually.

점진(漸進) ~하다 progress (advance) gradually; move step by step. ¶ ~적인 gradual; moderate (의견 따위). ‖ ~주의 moderatism; gradualism.

점차(漸次) gradually; by degrees.

점착(粘着) adhesion. ~하다 stick (adhere, be glued) (*to*). ‖ ~력 adhesive force / ~성 adhesiveness / ~성의 sticky; adhesive.

점철(點綴) interspersion. ~하다 intersperse; dot 《*with*》; stud.

점토(粘土) clay. ¶ ~질의 clayey. ‖ ~ 세공 clay works.

점판암(粘板岩)《地》(clay) slate.

점포(店鋪) a shop; a store《美》.

점호(點呼) a roll call. ~하다 call the roll; take the roll call 《*of workers*》. ‖ 조(일석)~《軍》the morning (evening) roll call.

점화(點火) ignition. ~하다 ignite (엔진 따위); light (fire) (up); kindle; set off (로켓 따위). ¶ 다이너마이트를 ~하다 detonate (set off) a charge of dynamite. ‖ ~약 an ignition charge; a detonator / ~장치 an ignition system; a firing mechanism; the ignition (엔진의) / ~플러그 a spark plug.

접《과일·채소 등의 단위》a hundred. ¶ 감 한 ~ a hundred persimmons.

접객(接客) ~하다 wait on customers. ¶ ~용의 for customers / 저 식당은 ~ 태도가 좋다는 평판이다 That restaurant has a reputation for offering good service. ‖ ~담당자 a receptionist / ~업(업자) a service trade; hotel and restaurant business (businessmen).

접견(接見) an interview (a reception) 《*with the Queen*》. ~하다 receive 《*a person*》 in audience; give an interview 《*to*》. ‖ ~실 an audience chamber; a reception room.

접경(接境) a borderline; a borderland. ~하다 share borders (*with*); border (*on*). ¶ 프랑스는 이탈리아와 ~하고 있다 France borders on Italy.

접골(接骨) bonesetting. ~하다 set a bone. ‖ ~사 a bonesetter.

접근(接近) approach; access. ~하다 approach; draw (come, go) near / ~해 있다 be near; be close together; be close (*to*) / ~하기 쉽다(어렵다) be easy (difficult) to approach; be easy (difficult) of access. ‖ ~로 an access route / ~전 close combat (fighting); infighting (권투등).

접다 fold (up); furl. ¶ 우산을 ~ fold up (furl, close) an umbrella / 종이를 네 겹으로 ~ fold a sheet of paper into four / 색종이로 종이학을 ~ fold a square

접대(接待) reception; entertainment. ~하다 receive; entertain; attend to 《a guest》. ¶손님 ~에 바쁘다 be busy receiving one's guests / 다과 ~를 받다 be entertained with refreshments. ‖ ~계원 a receptionist; a reception committee《총칭》/ ~부 a waitress; a barmaid / ~비 reception [entertainment] expenses / ~실 a reception room.
접두사(接頭辭)〖文〗a prefix.
접때 a few days ago; not long ago《before》.
접목(接木) grafting; a grafted tree 《나무》. ~하다 graft 《a tree on another》; put a graft in [on] 《a stock》.
접미사(接尾辭)〖文〗a suffix.
접본(接本) 〈바탕나무〉 a stock.
접선(接線) ①〖幾〗a tangent (line). ②〈접속〉 a contact. ~하다 contact; make contact 《with》.
접속(接續) joining; connection; link. ~하다 connect; join; link. ¶스피커를 앰프에 ~하다 connect the speaker to the amplifier. ‖ ~곡〖樂〗a medley / ~사〖文〗a conjunction / ~역 a junction (station).
접수(接收) requisitioning; seizure. ~하다 requisition; take over. ¶토지의 ~ the requisitioning of land. ‖ ~가옥 a requisitioned house / ~해제 derequisition.
접수(接受) receipt; acceptance. ~하다 receive; accept 《application》; take up 《an appeal》. ¶여기 ~인을 찍어 주시오 Stamp here and acknowledge receipt, please. ‖ ~계원 an information clerk; a receptionist / ~구 a reception counter / ~번호 a receipt number / ~처 a reception [information] office.
접시 a plate; a dish; a platter《美》. ¶수프용 ~ a soup plate / 고기용 ~ a meat dish / 콩 한 ~ a dish of beans / 음식을 ~에 담아 내놓다 serve food in a ~ on a plate》. ‖ ~닦이《행위》dishwashing;《사람》a dishwasher / ~돌리기 a dish-spinning trick.
접시꽃〖植〗a hollyhock.
접안(接岸) ~하다 come alongside the pier 《quay, berth》. ‖ ~동시 ~능력 the simultaneous berthing capacity.
접안경(接眼鏡) an eyepiece; an ocular; an eye lens.
접어넣다 fold [tuck] in.
접어들다 enter; set in; approach. ¶선거전이 종반전에 ~ The election campaign enters its last days. / 장마철에 접어들었다 The rainy season has set in.
접어주다〈봐주다〉give《a person》vantage ground; make due allowances 《for a person》;〈바둑·장기 등에서〉give a head start of; give an edge [advantage, a handicap] of. ¶다섯 점 ~ give a 5-point handicap 《in playing baduk》.
접의자(摺椅子) a collapsible chair.
접자(摺─) a folding scale.
접전(接戰)〈근접전〉a close [tight] battle; close combat;〈경기의〉a close game [match]. ~하다 fight at close quarters; have a close contest [game]. ¶~ 끝에 B 후보가 승리했다 Mr. B won in a close contest.
접점(接點)〖幾〗a point of contact.
접종(接種)〖醫〗(an) inoculation; (a) vaccination. ~하다 inoculate; vaccinate. ¶~백신을 ~하다 inoculate 《a person》with a vaccine / 나는 독감 예방 ~을 받았다 I was inoculated against influenza. ‖ ~요법 a vaccine cure.
접지(接地)〖電〗a ground《美》; an earth《英》. ~하다 ground; earth. ‖ ~선 a ground [an earth] wire.
접지(接枝) a slip; a graft; a scion.
접지(摺紙) paper folding. ~하다 fold paper 《to bind a book》. ‖ ~기 a folder.
접질리다 sprain; get sprained.
접착(接着) glueing. ~하다 glue; bond. ‖ ~제 an adhesive (agent) / ~테이프 adhesive tape.
접촉(接觸) contact; touch. ~하다 touch;〈연락을 취하다〉contact; get in touch with; come into [in] contact 《with》. ¶~시키다 bring ─ into contact with / 그는 외국인과 ~할 기회가 많다 He has a lot of chances to come into contact with foreigners. ‖ ~감염 contagion / ~면 a contact surface / ~반응〖化〗a catalysis / ~사고 a minor [near] collision.
접칼(摺─) a folding knife.
접하다(接─) ①〈접속〉touch;〈대면·교제〉come [be] in contact 《with》;〈만나다〉see;〈맞닿아 있다〉. ¶이 원은 점 C에서 선 A와 접한다 The circle touches line A at point C. / 나는 기자들과 접할 기회가 자주 있다 I often come into contact with journalists. ②〈인접〉adjoin; border 《on》; be adjacent [next] 《to》. ¶이웃집에 접한 공터 vacant land adjacent to the house next door / 프랑스와 스위스는 서로 국경을 접하고 있다 France and Switzerland border on each other. ③〈받다〉receive; get. ¶그가 죽었다는 비보에 ~ receive the sad news of his death. ④〈경

접합 형・조우하다) meet with; encounter. ¶ 사고를 ~ meet with an accident.

접합(接合) union; connection. ~하다 unite; join; connect. ‖ ~재(材) a binder / ~제(劑) a glue.

접히다 ① 〈종이 등이〉 be (get) folded. ¶ 세 겹으로 ~ be folded in three. ② 〈바둑 등에서〉 take odds 〈of two points〉.

젓 pickled (salted) fish (guts). ¶ 새우 〔조개〕 ~ pickled shrimps (clams). 「use chopsticks.」

젓가락 chopsticks. ¶ ~을 사용하다

젓다 ① 〈배를〉 row 〈a boat〉; pull the oar. ② 〈휘젓다〉 stir; churn; beat 〈eggs〉; whip. ③ 〈손을〉 wave; 〈머리를〉 shake 〈one's head〉.

정(연장) a chisel; a burin.

정(情) 〈감정〉 (a) feeling; (a) sentiment; 〈정서〉 (an) emotion; 〈애정〉 love; affection; heart; 〈동정〉 sympathy. ¶ 부모 자식간〔부부간〕의 ~ love between〔parents and children〔husband and wife〕/ 어머니는 ~에 무르다 My mother is tender-hearted (soft-hearted). / 숙부는 ~이 많은 사람이다 My uncle is a warm-hearted person. / ~이 없는 사람 a cold-hearted person / …의〔불륜의〕 ~을 통하다 have an affair〔a liaison〕with 〈a person〉.

정(정말로). really; indeed; quite. ¶ ~ 그렇다면 if you really meant it…; if you insist upon it.

정…(正) 〈부(副)에 대한〉 the original. ¶ ~ 2통 the original and copy. ② 〈자격의〉 regular; full. ‖ ~ 회원 a regular (full) member.

…정(錠) 〈금액〉 ¶ 5만 원 ~ a clear 50,000 *won*.

…정(錠) a tablet; a tabloid.

정가(正價) a (net) price.

정가(定價) a fixed (set, regular, tag, list) price. ¶ ~를 올리다 〔내리다〕 raise (reduce, lower) the price〈of〉/ 시계를 ~에서 3할 할인하여 사다 buy a watch at thirty percent discount off the list price. ‖ ~표(表) a price list / ~표(票) a price tag.

정가극(正歌劇) a grand opera.

정각(正刻) the exact time. ¶ ~에 just; sharp; punctually / ~ 5시에 just at five; at five sharp.

정각(定刻) the fixed time. ¶ ~에 도착하다 〔기차 따위가〕 arrive on (scheduled) time; arrive duly.

정간(停刊) suspension of publication. ~하다 suspend publication 〈of〉; stop issue.

정갈하다 (be) neat and clean. ¶ 방 안은 정갈하게 정돈되어 있었다 The room was clean and tidy.

정강(政綱) a political principle; a party platform.

정강마루 the ridge of the shin.

정강이 the shin; the shank. ¶ ~를 차다 kick 〈a person〉 on the shin. ¶ ~뼈 the shinbone〔tibia〕.

정객(政客) a politician.

정거(停車) a stop; stoppage. ~하다 stop〔halt〕〈at a station〉; make a stop; come to a halt. ¶ 5분간 ~ a five minutes' stop / 사고로 ~하다 be held up by an accident. ‖ ~장 a〔railway〕station; a〔railroad〕depot 〖美〗.

정견(定見) a definite〔fixed〕view (opinion). ¶ ~이 없다 have no definite opinion of *one's* own.

정견(政見) *one's* political views (opinions). ¶ ~을 발표하다 state〔set forth〕*one's* political views.

정결하다(貞潔 —) (be) chaste and pure; faithful.「neat; pure.」

정결하다(淨潔 —) (be) clean and

정경(政經) politics and economics. ‖ ~ 분리정책 a policy separating economy from politics / ~ 유착 politics-business collusion / ~ 학부 the political and economic〔politico-economic〕faculty.

정경(情景) a scene; a sight; a view; a pathetic (touching) scene. ¶ 참담한 ~이다 be (present) in a frightful sight.

정계(正系) a legitimate line.

정계(政界) the political world; political circles (quarters). ¶ ~의 거물 a great political figure / ~의 움직임 a political trend / ~로 진출하다 go into politics.

정곡(正鵠) the main point; the mark; the bull's-eye. ¶ ~을 찌르다 hit the mark (bull's-eye) / ~을 찔리다 be spotted right.

정공법(正攻法) a frontal attack; the regular tactics for attack.

정과(正果) fruits or roots preserved in honey or sugar.

정관(定款) the articles of an association (incorporation).

정관(精管) 〖解〗 the spermatic duct (cord). ‖ ~ 절제술 vasectomy.

정관(靜觀) ~하다 watch 〈*the situation*〉 calmly; wait and see. ¶ 사태의 추이를 ~하다 calmly watch the development of the situation. 「article.」

정관사(定冠詞) 〖文〗 the definite

정광(精鑛) 〖鑛〗 concentrate.

정교(正敎) 《사교에 대한》 orthodoxy. ‖ ~회 the Greek Church; the Orthodox Church.

정교(政敎) ① 〈정치와 종교〉 religion and politics. ¶ ~ 일치〔분리〕 the union (separation) of Church and State. ② 〈정치와 교육〉 politics and education.

정교(情交) ① 〈친교〉 friendship. ¶

정교사(正敎師) a certificated (regular) teacher.

정교하다(精巧—) (be) elaborate; exquisite; delicate. ¶ 정교한 기계 a delicate machine; a machine of mechanical excellence.

정구(庭球) (play) tennis. ∥ ~장 a tennis court.

정국(政局) the political situation. ¶ ~의 위기 a political crisis / ~을 수습하다 (안정시키다) bring stability to the political situation / ~을 타개하다 break a political deadlock / 현재의 ~은 불안정하다 The present political situation is unstable.

정권(政權) (political) power. ¶ ~을 잡다 (얻다) come into (take) power; take (lose) office. ∥ ~쟁탈(전) a scramble for political power / 피뢰 ~ a dummy government; a puppet regime.

정규(正規) ~의 (정식의) regular; formal; proper; (합법의) legitimate; legal / ~교육을 받다 have regular school education. ∥ ~군 a regular army (생략 RA) / ~병 regulars.

정근(精勤) (근면) diligence; (무결근) regular attendance. ~하다 (be) diligent; industrious; attend 《school》 regularly. ¶ ~상 gym.

정글 a jungle. ∥ ~짐 a jungle gym.

정금(正金) ① (금은화) specie. ¶ ~은행 a specie bank. ② (순금) pure gold.

정기(定期) a fixed period. ¶ ~의 fixed; regular; periodical / ~적으로 regularly; periodically; at regular intervals. ∥ ~간행물 a periodical / ~검사 a periodical inspection / ~검진 a periodic medical check-up / ~승차권 a commutation (season) ticket / ~ 예금 a fixed deposit / ~총회 a regular general meeting / ~항공기 an airliner / ~항공로 a regular air route (line); an airway / ~항로 a regular line (service) / ~휴업일 a regular holiday.

정기(精氣) spirit and energy; (만물의 기) the spirit of all creation; (기력) energy; vigor.

정나미(情—) ¶ ~(가) 떨어지다 be disgusted 《with, at, by》; be disaffected 《toward》; fall out of love 《with》.

정남(正南) due south.

정낭(精囊) [解] a seminal vesicle; a spermatic sac.

정년(丁年) full (adult) age. ¶ 20세로 ~에 이르다 come of age (reach adulthood) at twenty. ∥ ~자 an adult; a person of full age.

정년(停年) retiring age; the (compulsory) retirement age. ¶ ~으로 퇴직하다 retire (at the retirement age); leave *one's* job on reaching retiring age / 그는 금년에 ~이다 He is due to retire this year. / 우리 회사는 60세가 ~이다 Sixty is (the) retirement age in our company. ∥ ~제 the age-limit system / ~퇴직 (compulsory) retirement 《*on reaching the age of 60*》 / ~퇴직자 a retired person (worker).

정녕(丁寧) certainly; surely; for sure; without fail. ¶ ~(코) 그러냐 Are you sure?

정다각형(正多角形) a regular (an equilateral) polygon. [hedron.

정다면체(正多面體) a regular poly-

정담(政談) a political talk (chat).

정담(情談) a friendly talk; a lover's talk.

정답다(情—) (be) affectionate; loving; harmonious; on good (friendly) terms 《with》. ¶ 정답게 affectionately; harmoniously; happily / 그 부부는 정답게 살고 있다 The couple live happily. / 두 사람 사이는 매우 ~ They are a really affectionate (loving) couple.

정당(正當) ~하다 (be) just; right; proper; fair and proper; (합법적) legal; lawful; legitimate. ¶ ~한 행동 right conduct / ~한 근거 legitimate grounds 《for》 / ~한 이유 없이 without good (sufficient) reason / ~한 수단으로 by fair means / ~한 법적 절차를 밟지 않고 without due process of law / ~하게 평가하다 do 《*a person*》 justice; do justice to 《*a thing*》; duly appreciate 《*a person's achievement*》 / ~화하다 justify / 목적은 수단을 ~화한다 The end justifies the means. ∥ ~방위 [法] self-defense 《~의 행위로 살인하다 kill a man in self-defense》.

정당(政黨) a political party. ¶ 2대 (二大) ~ two major political parties / 2대(二大) ~제(制) a two-party system / 새로운 ~을 결성하다 form (organize) a new political party / ~에 참여하다 join a political party / ~간의 협력 inter-party cooperation / ~정치 party politics (government).

정당(精糖) sugar refining; (정제당) refined sugar. ∥ ~공장 a sugar refinery (mill).

정도(正道) the right path; the path of righteousness. ¶ ~에서 벗어나다 stray from the right path / ~를 밟다 tread on the

정도(程度) (a) degree; (an) extent (범위); 《표준》 a standard; a grade; 《한계》 a limit. ¶~가 높은 [낮은] of a high [low] standard / 손해의 ~를 높이다[낮추다] raise [lower] the standard / 그것은 ~ 문제이다 It is a matter of degree. / 어느 ~까지 그의 말을 믿어야 하는가 To what extent can I believe him? / 5달러 ~의 좋은 선물이 없겠습니까 Do you have a nice gift for about $5? ‖ 지능~ an intellectual standard.

정도(精度) ☞ 정밀도(精密度).

정독(精讀) perusal; careful [close] reading. ~하다 peruse; read 《a book》 carefully.

정돈(整頓) (good) order; tidying (up). ~하다 put 《something》 in order; tidy up; keep 《a thing》 tidy. ¶~된 neat and tidy 《room》; in order; orderly / 대열을 ~하다 dress the ranks; dress 《the men》 in line / 그녀는 항상 방을 ~해 놓는다 She always keeps her room tidy.

정동(正東) due east.

정동(精銅) refined copper.

정동사(定動詞)《文》 a finite verb.

정들다(情—) become attached 《to》; become familiar [friendly, acquainted] 《with》; get used to 《a place》. ¶정든 님 one's beloved lover / 정들던 여자 a girl that one has come to love.

정떨어지다(情—) be disgusted 《at, with》; be sick 《of》; despair 《of》. ¶정떨어지는 소리를 하다 say spiteful [unkind] things 《to》.

정략(政略) political tactics; a political maneuver [move]. ~적 political; ~을 꾸미다 plan political tactics. ¶~가 a political tactician / ~결혼 a marriage of convenience.

정량(定量) a fixed quantity; a dose (내복약의). ¶~의 quantitative / ~을 정하다 determine the quantity 《of》. ‖ ~분석 quantitative analysis.

정력(精力) energy; vigor; vitality; 《성적인》 one's sexual capacity; potency; virility. ¶~이 왕성한 energetic; vigorous / ~이 다하다 have one's energy exhausted; run out of steam / ~을 쏟다 put [throw] all one's energies 《into》 / ~이 매우 두드러진 사람 a man of unbounded potency 《virility》. ‖ ~가 an energetic man; a ball of fire (口).

정련(精鍊) ~하다 refine 《metals》; smelt 《copper》. ‖ ~소 a refinery.

정렬(整列) ~하다 stand in a row; form a line; line up; 〖軍〗 Fall in! (구령). ¶3열로 ~하다 be drawn up in three lines / ~시키다 dress 《the men》.

정령(政令) a government ordinance.

정령(精靈) the soul; the spirit.

정례(定例) the ordinary; regular; ~에 따라 according to usage. ‖ ~의 [閣議] (기자회견) a regular cabinet meeting [press conference] / ~회의 a regular meeting. [ment.

정론(正論) a sound [just] argu-

정론(定論) a settled view [opinion]; an established theory.

정론(政論) political argument [discussion].

정류(停留) ~하다 stop; halt; come to a stop. ‖ ~소 a stopping place; a 《train, bus》 stop.

정류(精溜) rectification; refinement. ~하다 rectify; purify; refine. ‖ ~주정 rectified spirit.

정류(整流) 〖電〗 rectification; commutation. ~하다 rectify. ‖ ~기 a rectifier.

정률(定率) a fixed rate. ‖ ~세 proportional taxation. [ory.

정리(定理) 〖幾〗 a theorem; a the-

정리(整理) ① 《정돈》 arrangement. ~하다 arrange; put 《a thing》 in order; straighten 《out》; keep 《a thing》 tidy. ¶서랍을 ~하다 put the drawer in order / 소지품을 ~하다 arrange one's belongings / 말하기 전에 생각을 ~할 필요가 있다 It is necessary to put our thoughts in order before we speak. / 오늘의 회의 기록을 ~해 놓아라 Please keep the records of today's conference straight. ② ~하다 《회사 등을》 reorganize; liquidate; 《교통 등을》 regulate; control; 《행정·구획·장부 등을》 adjust; readjust. ¶~구획 land readjustment; replanning of streets / 행정 ~ administrative readjustment [reorganization] / 회사를 ~하다 liquidate [reorganize] a company / 교통을 ~하다 regulate [control] traffic / 재정 관계의 일을 ~하다 sort out [adjust] one's financial affairs. ③ 《줄이다·없애다》 ~하다 cut down 《on》; reduce; dispose 《of》. ¶잔품을 ~하다 clear off the unsold goods / 가제도구를 ~하다 dispose of one's household goods and furniture / 인원을 ~하다 reduce [cut down] the personnel; cut the number of employees. ‖ ~해고 ~해고(解雇). ④ 《부채를》 ¶부채를 ~하다 pay off [clear away] one's debt.

정립하다(鼎立—) stand in a trio.
정말(正—) 《부사적》 really; quite; indeed; truly; actually; in real earnest (진정으로). ¶ ~ 같은 거짓말 a plausible lie / ~로 여기다 accept 《a story》 as true / take 《a word》 seriously.
정맥(靜脈) a vein. ¶ ~의. ‖ ~류(瘤) a varix / ~주사 an intravenous injection.
정면(正面) the front; the facade (건물의). ¶ ~의 front; frontal / ~에서 본 얼굴 a full face / ~으로 공격하다 make a frontal attack / 우체국은 정거장의 ~에 있다 The post office is right in front of the station. ‖ ~공격 a frontal attack / ~도 a front view / ~입구 a front entrance / ~충돌 a head-on collision; a frontal clash.
정모(正帽) a full-dress hat.
정무(政務) affairs of state; state 〔political〕 affairs. ‖ ~차관 a parliamentary vice-minister.
정문(正門) the front 〔main〕 gate; the main entrance.
정물(靜物) still life. ‖ ~화〔사진〕 a still life 〔photo〕.
정미(正味) ¶ ~의 net; clear / ~중량 a net weight.
정미(精米) rice polishing; 《쌀》 polished rice. ¶ ~하다 polish 〔clean〕 rice. ‖ ~소 a rice mill.
정밀(精密) minuteness; precision. ¶ ~하다 (be) minute; precise; detailed. ¶ ~히 minutely; in detail; precisely / ~하게 조사하다 investigate closely / ~한 지도를 만들다 make a detailed map. ‖ ~검사 a close examination / ~공업 the precision industry / ~과학 an exact science / ~기계〔기기〕 a precision machine 〔instrument〕 / ~조사 a close investigation.
정밀도(精密度) precision; accuracy. ¶ ~가 높다 be extremely precise 〔accurate〕 / ~를 높이다 improve the precision of 《a thing》 / 상당히 높은 ~의 기계 a machine with considerable precision.
정박(碇泊) anchorage; mooring. ¶ ~하다 (cast, come to) anchor; moor. ‖ ~기간 lay days / ~료 anchorage 〔dues〕 / ~지〔항〕 an anchorage 〔harbor〕.
정박아(精薄兒) a mentally-handicapped〔-retarded〕 child. ‖ ~수용시설 a home for retarded children.
정반대(正反對) direct opposition; the exact reverse. ¶ ~의 directly opposite / 그는 너의 의견과 ~다 His opinion is directly opposite of yours. / 나는 ~방향으로 갔다 I went in the opposite direction.
정백(精白) ¶ ~당(糖) refined sugar / ~미 polished 〔cleaned〕 rice.
정벌(征伐) conquest; subjugation. ¶ ~하다 conquer the enemy.
정범(正犯) 《法》 the principal offense 〔offender(사람)〕.
정변(政變) a political change; a change of government; a coup d'état. ¶ 페루에서 ~이 일어났다 A coup d'état took place in Peru.
정병(精兵) a crack 〔an elite〕 troop. ¶ ~3천 a crack troop of 3,000 strong.
정보(情報) 《a piece of》 information; intelligence(비밀의); news. ¶ ~를 얻다 〔입수하다〕 obtain 〔get〕 information 《on, about》 / ~를 누설하다 leak information / ~를 수집하다 collect information / …라는 ~가 있다 It is reported that… / ~를 처리하다 process information / ~에 어둡다 be not well informed 《about》. ‖ ~검색 information retrieval(생략 IR) / ~공개 information disclosure / ~공해 (오염) information pollution / ~과학 information science / ~국 《미국의 중앙정보국》 the Central Intelligence Agency (생략 CIA) / ~기관 a secret 〔an intelligence〕 service / ~루트 a pipeline; a 《secret》 channel of information / ~망 an intelligence network / ~산업 the information 〔communication〕 industry / ~수집 information gathering / ~시대 the information age / ~원(員) an informer(경찰의); an intelligence agent(정보기관의) / ~원(源) information sources / ~처리 〔컴〕 data 〔information〕 processing / ~처리산업 the data processing industry / ~처리시스템 the information processing system / ~통신부 the Ministry of Information-Communication / ~혁명 information revolution / ~화 사회 an information-oriented society / ~활동 intelligence activities / 국가~원 the National Intelligence Service.
정복(正服) a formal dress; a full uniform. ‖ ~경찰관 a police officer.
정복(征服) conquest. ~하다 conquer; gain mastery over 《the environment》; overcome. ¶ 산정을 ~하다 conquer the summit. / ~욕 lust for conquest / ~자 a conqueror.
정본(正本) the original 《copy, text》.
정부(正否) right or wrong.
정부(正副) 《서두의》 the original and a duplicate 〔copy〕. ¶ ~2통

을 작성하다 prepare [make out] 《a document》 in duplicate. ‖ ~의장 the speaker and deputy speaker; the chairperson and vice-chairperson.

정부(政府) a government; the Government(한 나라의); the Administration(美). ¶ ~의 government(al) / 현 ~ the present Government / 한국 ~ the Korean Government / 클린턴 ~ the Clinton Administration / ~의 소재지 [수반] the seat [head] of government / ~를 수립하다 establish [set up] a government / ~를 지지[타도]하다 support [overthrow] the Government. ‖ ~ 고관 a high-ranking government official / ~기관 a government body [agency] / ~당국 the government authorities / ~보조금 government subsidies / ~안 a government bill [measure] / ~종합청사 an integrated government building / ~특혜 government's favors.

정부(情夫) a lover; a paramour.

정부(情婦) a mistress; a paramour.

정북(正北) due north.

정분(情分) a cordial friendship; intimacy; affection. ¶ ~이 두텁다 be on terms of intimacy.

정비(整備) 《장비·시설 등의 유지·수리》 maintenance; service; 《조정》 adjustment. ¶ ~하다 put 《the facilities》 in good condition; service 《an airplane》; fix 《a car》. ¶ ~가 잘 되어 있는 차 a car kept in good repair / 도로를 ~하다 repair a road / 기업을 ~하다 consolidate an enterprise. ‖ ~공 a (car) mechanic; a repairman(기계의) / ~공장 a repair [service] shop; a garage(자동차의) / ~사 a maintenance man; a ground man; the ground crew(총칭).

정비례(正比例) 〖數〗 direct proportion [ratio]. ¶ ~하다 be in direct proportion 《to》.

정사(正史) an authentic history.

정사(正邪) right and wrong.

정사(政事) political affairs.

정사(情死) 《바둑의》 a lovers' [double] suicide. ¶ ~하다 commit a double suicide; die together for love.

정사(情事) 《남녀간의》 a love affair. ¶ 혼외 ~ extramarital intercourse.

정사각형(正四角形) a (regular) square. 〖hedron.

정사면체(正四面體) a regular tetra-

정사원(正社員) a regular member; a staff member 《of a company》.

정산(精算) exact calculation; 《결산》 settlement of accounts; adjustment. ~하다 settle up; keep an accurate account. ¶ 운임을 ~하다 pay the difference on one's ticket; adjust the fare. ‖ ~서 a settlement of accounts. 〖gle.

정삼각형(正三角形) a regular trian-

정상(正常) normalcy(美); normality. ¶ ~의 normal / ~이 아닌 abnormal / ~으로 normally / ~으로 돌아오다 return [get back] to normal; be restored to normal(ly). ‖ ~상태 the normal state / ~화 normalization(~화하다 normalize).

정상(頂上) the top; the summit; the peak 《of》. ¶ 산의 ~을 정복하다 attain the summit of the mountain. ‖ ~회담 a summit meeting [conference, talk].

정상(情狀) conditions; circumstances. ¶ ~을 참작하다 take the circumstances into consideration / ~ 참작을 요구하다 plead extenuating circumstances.

정상배(政商輩) a businessman with political affiliations [influence].

정색(正色) ¹《안색》 a serious countenance [look]; a solemn look. ~하다 put on a serious look; wear a sober look. ¶ ~으로 with a serious look ~을 하고 농담을 하다 tell a joke with a straight face.

정색(正色) ² 〖理〗 a primary color.

정서(正西) due west.

정서(正書) 《또박또박 쓰기》 ~하다 write in the square style.

정서(淨書) ~하다 make a fair [clean] copy 《of》.

정서(情緖) 《감정》 emotion; feeling; (a) sentiment; 《분위기》 a mood; an atmosphere. ¶ 그녀는 ~가 불안정하다 She is emotionally unstable. / 그 도시에는 이국 ~가 있다 There is an exotic atmosphere in the city. ‖ ~교육 cultivation of sentiments / ~장애 an emotional disorder (~장애로 고통받다 suffer from emotional disorder).

정석(定石) 《바둑의》 the standard moves (in the game of baduk); a formula; 《원칙》 the cardinal [first] principle. ¶ ~대로 두다 play by the book / 그것은 범죄 수사의 ~이다 It's the ABC of a criminal investigation.

정선(停船) stoppage of a vessel. ~하다 stop; heave to. ¶ ~을 명하다 stop 《a ship》; order 《a ship》 to stop / 안개로 인해 ~하다 be held up in a fog.

정선(精選) ~하다 select [sort out] carefully. ¶ ~된 choice; select / 여름옷의 ~품 a fine selection of

정설(定說) 〖학계의〗 an established theory; 〖일반의〗 an accepted opinion. ¶ ~을 뒤엎다 overthrow an established theory / ...라는 것이 ~로 되다 It is the accepted view that....

정성(精誠) a true heart; sincerity; earnestness; devotion. ¶ ~껏 with one's utmost sincerity; wholeheartedly; devotedly / ~들이다 devote oneself 《to》; put the whole mind to.

정세(情勢) the state of things (affairs); a situation; conditions. ¶ 국내〔국제〕 ~ the domestic (international) situation / ~ 변화에 대응하다 correspond to the change in the situation.

정수(正數) 〖양수〗 〖數〗 a positive number.

정수(定數) ① 〖일정 수〗 a fixed number. ② 〖상수〗 〖數〗 a constant; an invariable. ③ 〖운수〗 fate; destiny.

정수(淨水) clean water. ¶ ~장 a filtration (purification) plant / ~장치 a water-purifying device; a cleaning (filter) pad.

정수(精粹) pureness; purity.

정수(精髓) ① 〖뼛속의〗 marrow. ② 〖사물의〗 the essence; the pith.

정수(整數) 〖數〗 an integral number; an integer.

정수리(頂─) 〖이마〗 the crown of the head; the pate 〖口〗.

정숙(貞淑) chastity; (female) virtue. ~하다 (be) chaste; virtuous. ¶ 그녀는 한 아내다 She is a virtuous (chaste) wife.

정숙(靜肅) silence. ~하다 (be) silent; still; quiet. ¶ ~하여라 Be silent. *or* Keep silent.

정승(政丞) 〖史〗 a minister of State; a prime minister (in the Kingdom of Korea).

정시(正視) ~하다 look 《a person》 in the face; look straight (squarely) 《at a fact》.

정시(定時) a fixed time; regular hours; a scheduled period. ¶ ~의〔에〕 regular(ly); periodical(ly) / 열차는 ~에 도착하였다 The train arrived on schedule (time). / ~ 퇴근〔게시〕 No overtime.

정식(正式) formality; due form. ¶ ~의 formal; regular; due; official (공식의) 〔~으로〕 formally; regularly; officially / ~으로 신청하다 make a formal application for / ~으로 결혼하다 be legally married. ¶ ~ 결혼 legal marriage / ~ 멤버 a regular (card-carrying) member / ~ 승인 (a) de jure recognition / ~ 절차 due formalities.

정식(定式) a formula. ¶ ~의 formal; regular. ‖ ~화(化) formularization.

정식(定食) a regular (set) meal; 《요리점의》 a *table d'hôte* (프). 〖점심으로 ~을 먹다 have a set lunch (lunch special).

정신(艇身) a boat's length. ¶ 3~의 차로 이기다 win by three boat's lengths.

정신(精神) mind; spirit; soul (영혼); will (의지); 〖근본적 의의〗 the spirit. ¶ ~적인 mental; spiritual; moral; emotional (감정적인) / ~적인 사랑 platonic love / ~적인 타격 a mental blow; a shock / 법의 ~ the spirit of the law / 비판 ~ a critical spirit / ~적인 지지 (암박) moral support (pressure) / ~적으로 동요하다 be emotionally disturbed (upset) / ~적으로 자립하다 achieve emotional autonomy / ~을 집중하다 concentrate one's attention on 《a thing》 / ~이 이상해지다 be mentally deranged (unbalanced); have a mental breakdown / ~ 일도 하사 불성 Where there is a will, there is a way. ‖ ~감정 a psychiatric test / ~교육 moral education / ~근로자 a mental (brain) worker / ~력 mental power / ~문명 spiritual civilization / ~ 박약아 a weak-(feeble-)minded child / ~병 a mental disease (illness) / ~병원 a mental hospital / ~병 전문의 a psychiatrist / ~병 (환)자 a mental (psychiatric) patient; a psychopath / ~분석 psychoanalysis / ~분열증 split personality; 〖醫〗 schizophrenia / ~분열증 환자 a schizophrenic / ~상태 a mental condition / ~신경과 neuropsychiatry / ~안정제 a tranquilizer / ~연령 mental age / ~요법 psychotherapy / ~위생 mental health / ~의학 psychiatry / ~이상 mental derangement / ~작용 mental function / ~장애아 a mentally handicapped child.

정신기능(精神機能) a psychic (mental) function. ¶ ~의 쇠퇴 failure of a psychic function.

정실(正室) a lawful (legal) wife.

정실(情實) private circumstances; personal considerations; favoritism (편애). ¶ ~에 흐르다 be influenced by personal considerations / ~을 배제하다 disregard any private consideration. ‖ ~인사 (the appointment 《of a person》 to a position through) favoritism.

정액(定額) 〖일정액〗 a fixed amount (sum). ¶ ~에 달하다 come up to

정액(精液) ① [生] semen; sperm. ‖ ～사출 seminal emission / ～은행 a sperm bank. ②《엑스》an extract; an essence.
정양(靜養) (a) rest; recuperation (병후의). ～하다 take a rest; recuperate *oneself*.
정어리 [魚] a sardine.
정언적(定言的) [論] categorical.
정업(定業) a fixed occupation; a regular employment.
정역학(靜力學) [理] statics.
정연(整然) orderly; systematic; ～히 in good [perfect] order; systematically.
정열(情熱) passion; enthusiasm; zeal. ¶ ～적인 passionate; enthusiastic; ardent / ～적인 사랑 a passionate love / ～을 쏟다 put *one's* heart (and soul) into 《*one's work*》. ⌈flame of love.
정염(情炎) the fire of passion; the
정예(精銳) the pick [best] 《*of*》. ¶ ～ 오천 a troop 5,000 strong / 팀의 ～ the best player of the team. ‖ ～부대 an elite [a crack] unit.
정오(正午) (high) noon; midday. ¶ ～에 at noon; at midday.
정오(正誤) (a) correction 《*of errors*》. ‖ ～문제 a true-false question / ～표 a list of errata.
정온(定溫) (a) fixed temperature. ‖ ～동물 a homoiothermic animal.
정욕(情慾) sexual desire; lust; a passion. ¶ ～의 노예 a slave of *one's* lust / ～을 북돋우다 arouse [stimulate] *one's* sexual desire.
정원(定員) the fixed number; 《수용력》 the (*seating*) capacity. ¶ ～ 500명의 극장 a theater with a seating capacity of 500 / 신청자는 아직 ～ 미달이다 The application has not reached the fixed number. / 이 버스는 ～ 이상 의 손님을 태우고 있다 This bus is overloaded.
정원(庭園) a garden. ¶ 옥상 ～ a roof garden. ‖ ～사 a gardener / ～수(樹) a garden tree.
정월(正月) January. ⌈tion.
정위치(定位置) *one's* regular posi-
정유(精油) oil refining; refined oil(기름). ‖ ～공장 an oil refinery.
정육(精肉) fresh meat; dressed meat(적당 크기로 잘라 포장된). ～ 업자 a butcher / ～점 a butcher [meat] shop.
정육면체(正六面體) a regular hexahedron; a cube.
정은(正銀) pure [solid] silver.
정의(正義) justice; right. ¶ ～의 투 사 a champion of right / ～로운 싸움 a just [righteous] war / ～ 를 위해 싸우다 fight in the cause of justice / ～는 우리 편에 있다 Right and justice are on our side. ‖ ～감 a sense of justice (～감이 강하다 have a strong sense of justice).
정의(定義) a definition. ～하다 define 《*something as...*》. ¶ ～를 내 리다 define 《*words*》; give a definition 《*to*》.
정의(情意) emotion and will; feelings. ¶ ～ 상통하다 enjoy mutual understanding [affection].
정의(情誼) friendly feelings; ties of friendship; affections. ¶ ～가 두텁다 be very friendly; be cordial 《*to a friend*》.
정자(正字) a correct [an unsimplified] character.
정자(亭子) an arbor; a pavilion; a summerhouse; a bower. ¶ ～ 나무 a big tree serving as a shady resting place in a village.
정자(精子) spermatozoon; a sperm.
정자형(丁字形) a T-shape.
정작《부사격》 actually; indeed; really; practically. ¶ ～ 사려고 하 면 살 수 없다 When you actually try to buy one, it is not to be had.
정장(正裝) full dress [uniform]. ～ 하다 be in full dress [uniform].
정장석(正長石) [鑛] orthoclase.
정쟁(政爭) political strife. ¶ ～의 도구로 삼다 make a political issue 《*of*》.
정적(政敵) a political opponent [rival, enemy, adversary].
정적(靜的) static; statical.
정적(靜寂) silence; quiet; stillness. ¶ ～을 깨뜨리다 break the silence / 무거운 ～이 방안에 감돌았 다 A gloomy silence hung over the room. ⌈chamber.
정전(正殿) the royal audience
정전(停電) (a) power failure [cut, stoppage]; a blackout (전등의). ～하다 cut off the electricity [power]. ¶ ～이 되다 The power supply is cut off. / 예고 없이 ～ 이 되었다 The electricity was cut off without warning. / 아, ～이 다 Oh, the lights went out.
정전(停戰) a cease-fire; a truce (협정에 의한). ～하다 cease fire; have a truce. ～협정 a cease-fire agreement / ～회담 a cease-fire conference.
정전기(靜電氣) [電] static electricity. ¶ ～의 electrostatic.

정절(貞節) fidelity; chastity; virtue; faithfulness. ¶ ~을 지키다 lead a chaste life.

정점(定點) a definite (fixed) point.

정점(頂點) the top; the peak; 〖절정〗 the climax; the height; the apex 《of a triangle》. ¶ ~에 이르다 reach the peak (summit) 《of》.

정정(訂正) (a) correction; (a) revision 〖개정〗. ~하다 correct 《errors》; revise 《books》. ¶ A를 B로 ~하다 correct A to B. / 〖증보〗판 a revised (and enlarged) edition.

정정(政情) political conditions (affairs). ¶ ~의 안정〖불안정〗 political stability (instability) / ~에 밝다 be familiar with political conditions 《in Korea》.

정정당당(正正堂堂) ¶ ~한 fair and square; open and aboveboard / 두 팀은 ~히 싸웠다 Both teams played fair with each other.

정정하다(亭亭-) 〖노익장〗 (be) hale and hearty; healthy. ¶ 아버님은 80을 넘으셨지만, 아직 정정하시다 My father has turned eighty, but he is still in very good health.

정제(精製) refining. ~하다 refine. ∥ ~공장 a refinery / ~당〖염〗 refined sugar (salt) / ~법 a refining process.

정제(整除) 〖數〗 divisibility. ¶ ~되는 (exactly) divisible 《number》. ∥ ~수 exact divisor.

정제(錠劑) a tablet; a pill.

정조(貞操) chastity; (feminine) virtue. ¶ ~를 바치다 give *oneself* to 《a man》 / ~를 잃다 lose *one's* chastity (virtue) / ~를 지키다 keep *one's* virtue; remain faithful to 《*one's* husband》. ∥ ~관념 a sense of virtue / ~대 a chastity belt / ~유린 a violation of chastity.

정족수(定足數) a quorum. ¶ ~에 달하다 form 〖be enough for〗 a quorum / ~ 미달로 유회되다 be adjourned for lack of a quorum.

정좌하다(正坐-) sit straight (upright); sit square 《on *one's* seat》.

정주(定住) settlement. ~하다 settle down 《in》; reside permanently. ¶ 앞으로 캐나다에 ~하고 싶다 I want to settle down in Canada in the future. ∥ ~자 a permanent resident.

정중(鄭重) ¶ ~한 polite; courteous; respectful / ~한 말로 in courteous (respectful) words / ~히 모시다 treat 《a person》 courteously / 그들의 제의를 ~히 받아들였다 〖거절하였다〗 I respectfully accepted (politely declined) their offer 《to help》.

정지(停止) a stop; suspension 〖중지〗. ~하다 stop; 〖일시적〗 halt; suspend. ¶영업〖지불〗 ~ a suspension of business (payment) / 차를 ~시키다 stop a car / 집 앞에서 차가 ~했다 The car stopped in front of my house. / 그는 한 달 간 운전 면허가 ~되었다 He had his driver's license suspended for a month. ∥ ~선 a stop line / ~신호 a stop signal; a stoplight.

정지(靜止) rest; standstill. ~하다 rest; stand still; be at a standstill. ¶ 그 물체는 공중에 가만히 ~해 있다 The object is remaining still in the air. ∥ ~궤도 (put a satellite in) a geostationary (geosynchronous) orbit / ~상태 (in) a state of rest / ~상태의 stationary; static / ~위성 a stationary satellite.

정지(整地) 〖건축을 위한〗 leveling of ground; site preparation; 〖경작을 위한〗 soil preparation. ~하다 level the land 《for construction》; prepare the soil 《for planting》.

정직(正直) honesty; frankness 〖솔직〗. ¶ ~한 honest; frank; straightforward / ~히 honestly; frankly / ~한 소녀 an honest girl / 그것에 대해 숨기지 말고 ~하게 말해라 Be honest and tell me everything about it. / ~은 최선의 방책 〖俗談〗 Honesty is the best policy.

정직(停職) suspension from duty (office). ¶ ~되다 be suspended from *one's* duties.

정진(精進) ① 〖열심히 노력함〗 close application; devotion. ~하다 devote *oneself* 《to the study》; apply *oneself* 《to》. ② 〖종교적 수행〗 devotion to the pursuit of *one's* faith. ~하다 devote *one's* life to the pursuit of *one's* faith.

정차(停車) ☞ 정거(停車). ∥ ~시간 stoppage time.

정착(定着) fixation; fixing 〖사진의〗. ~하다 fix; take root 《사상·생각 등이》. ∥ ~금 (수당) resettlement funds (allowance) / ~액 a fixing solution / ~제 a fixing agent.

정찬(正餐) a dinner.

정찰(正札) a price tag. ¶ ~을 붙이다 mark (put) a price on 《an article》. ∥ ~가격 a marked (fixed) price / ~제 a price-tag (fixed price) system.

정찰(偵察) reconnaissance; scouting. ~하다 reconnoiter; scout. ¶ ~ 나가다 go scouting / 적정을 ~하다 spy on the enemy. ∥ ~기 a reconnaissance plane / ~대 a reconnaissance party / ~비행 a reconnaissance flight / ~위성 a spy satellite.

정책(政策) a policy. ¶ 경제 ~을 세우다 shape an economic policy / ~을 실행에 옮기다 carry out a policy / ~을 전환하다 change one's policy / 전 내각의 ~을 답습하다 take over 〔make no change in〕 the policy of the previous cabinet. ‖ ~ 노선 party line 《美》 / ~심의회 the Policy Board / ~입안자 a policy maker.

정처(定處) ~ 없이 떠돌다 wander from place to place.

정체(正體) one's true character 〔colors〕. ¶ ~를 알 수 없는 unidentifiable 《objects》 / ~를 드러내다 show 〔reveal〕 one's true colors.

정체(政體) a form 〔system〕 of government. ¶ 공화〔입헌〕 ~ the republican 〔constitutional〕 system of government.

정체(停滯) 〔침체〕《자금의》 a tie-up;《화물의》 accumulation. ~하다 be stagnant; pile up; accumulate. ¶ 교통의 ~ the congestion of traffic / 우편물의 ~ the pile-up of mail / 경기가 ~되다 The economy is stagnant.

정초(正初) the first ten days of January. ¶ ~에 early in January.

정초(定礎) ~하다 lay the cornerstone 〔of a building〕.

정취(情趣) 〔기분·느낌〕 mood; sentiment; 〔아취〕 artistic flavor 〔taste〕; 〔분위기〕《an》 atmosphere. ¶ ~가 있는 rich in artistic flavor; tasteful; charming / ~를 맛보다 experience 《a》 mood 〔atmosphere〕.

정치(定置) ~하다 fix; be fixed. ¶ ~의 fixed; stationary. ‖ ~망 a fixed 〔shore〕 net / ~망어업 fixed-net fishing.

정치(政治) politics; government〔통치〕; administration〔시정〕. ~하다 govern 〔the country〕; administer 〔conduct〕 the affairs of state. ¶ ~적인 political / ~적 수완 political skill 〔skill〕 / ~를 말하다 talk 〔discuss〕 politics / 밝은〔깨끗한〕 ~ clean politics / ~에 대한 불신감을 갖다 have a distrust of politics / ~적인 자유를 요구하다 demand political freedom 〔liberties〕 / 지금 필요한 것은 강력한 ~이다 What is needed at present is strong government. ‖ ~가 a statesman; a politician / ~결사 a political organization / ~공작 political maneuvering / ~문제 a political structure / ~기구 a political problem / ~범 (罪) a political offense;《사람》 a political offender / ~사찰 political surveillance / ~운동 a political campaign / ~의식 political awareness / ~자금 political funds / ~적 망명 political asylum / ~적 무관심 political apathy / ~적 책임 《one's》 administrative responsibilities / ~지리학 political geography / ~학 politics; political science / ~헌금 a political contribution 〔donation〕.

정치깡패(政治-) political hoodlums; a political henchman.

정치력(政治力) political power 〔influence〕. ¶ ~의 빈곤 lack of political ability; poor statesmanship.

정치풍토(政治風土) the political climate. ‖ ~쇄신 the renovation of the political climate.

정치활동(政治活動) political activities. ~을 하다 engage in politics 〔political activities〕. ‖ ~정화법 the Political Purification Law.

정크(중국배) a junk. 〔같은〕.

정크본드〔證〕 a junk bond 〈쓰는〉

정탐(偵探) ~하다 spy 〔on〕. ~꾼 a spy; a scout.

정태(靜態) ~의 static(al) / ~경제학 static economics.

정토(淨土) 〔佛〕 the Pure Land; Paradise. ¶ 서방 ~ the Pure Land in the West.

정통(正統) legitimacy; orthodoxy. ¶ ~의 legitimate; orthodox / ~적인 견해 an orthodox point of view / ~정부 a legitimate government. ‖ ~파 an orthodox school.

정통(精通) ~하다 be well「versed in〔informed about〕; have a thorough knowledge 《of》; be familiar 〔well acquainted〕 with. ¶ ~한 소식통 a well-informed source.

정판(整版) 〔印〕 recomposition; justification. ~하다 recompose; justify. ‖ ~공 a justifier.

정평(定評) an established reputation. ¶ ~ 있는 acknowledged; recognized;《a novelist》 with an established reputation / 그는 실력 있는 변호사로 ~이 나 있다 He enjoys an established reputation for his ability as a lawyer.

정표(情表) a love token; a keepsake; a memento. ¶ 애정의 ~ a token of one's love and affection / 감사의 ~로서 as a token of one's gratitude.

정풍(整風) ‖ ~운동 the rectification campaign.

정하다(定一) 〔결정하다〕 fix; settle; decide; 〔규정하다〕 establish; provide. ¶법이 정하는 바에 따라 as provided by law / 방침을 ~ decide on one's policy / 날〔값〕을 ~ fix a date 〔the price〕 / 국경일은

정하다 으로 정해져 있다 The national holidays are established by law. / 이 도로의 제한 속도는 40Km/h로 정해져 있다 The speed limit on this road is fixed at 40 kilometers an hour.

정하다(淨—) (be) clear; clean; pure.

정학(停學) suspension (from school). ¶ 7일 간 ~ 당하다 be suspended from school for a week.

정해(正解) a correct answer. ~하다 give a correct answer. ‖ ~자 a person who gives a correct answer.

정해(精解) full [detailed] explanation. ~하다 explain minutely [in detail].

정형(定型, 定形) a fixed [regular] form [type]. ~ 화 하다 standardize; conventionalize. ‖ ~시(詩) a fixed form of verse.

정형(整形) ‖ ~ 수술 orthopedic surgery / ~외과 orthopedics / ~외과병원 an orthopedic hospital / ~외과의 an orthopedist.

정혼(定婚) ~하다 arrange a marriage; betroth.

정화(正貨) specie. ‖ ~ 보유고 specie holdings / ~ 준비 specie [gold] reserve.

정화(淨化) purification; a cleanup. ~하다 purify; purge; clean up 《the political world》. ¶ 선거 ~운동 a 'clean election' campaign. ‖ ~실비 [하수의] sewage disposal facilities; a sewage treatment plant / ~장치 a purifier / ~조 [하수의] a septic tank.

정화수(井華水) 〖民俗〗 clear water drawn from the well at daybreak.

정확(正確) correctness; exactness; accuracy; precision. ¶ ~한 [히] exact(ly); correct(ly); accurate(ly) / ~ 한 발음 correct pronunciation / 이 시계는 ~ 하다 This clock is correct [keeps good time]. / 그는 계산이 빠르고 ~ 하다 He is quick and accurate at figures. / 그녀는 시간을 ~ 히 지킨다 She is punctual. / ~ 히 말하면 이것은 시가 아니다 Properly speaking, this is not a poem.

정황(情況) ☞ 상황. ‖ ~증거 〖法〗 circumstantial [indirect, presumptive] evidence.

정회(停會) adjournment; prorogation (의회). ~하다 suspend; adjourn; prorogue. ¶ 회의는 2시에 ~ 되었다 The meeting was suspended at two.

정회원(正會員) a regular member. ¶ ~의 자격 full membership.

정훈(政訓) troop information and education.

정휴일(定休日) a regular holiday.

정히(正一) 《確》 surely; certainly; no doubt; really.

젖 《乳房》 a breast; 《乳汁》 milk; mother's milk (모유). ‖ ~ 같은, milky / ~을 짜다 milk 《a cow》 / ~을 달라고 울다 cry for milk / 아기가 어머니 ~ 을 빨고 있다 A baby is sucking its mother's breast. / 어머니가 ~ 을 먹이고 있다 The mother is nursing her baby. / 아기를 어머니 ~ 으로 기르다 nurse a baby on mother's milk / ~이 나오지 않게 되다 one's breasts have run dry. / ~가슴 the breast / ~꼭지 the teat(s); the nipple(s) / ~니 a milk tooth / ~먹이 a suckling; a baby / ~병 a nursing bottle / ~소 a milch [milking] cow.

젖내 the smell of milk. ¶ 그는 아직 ~ 가 난다 He is still green. or He still smells of his mother's milk.

젖다 get wet; be soaked [drenched] 《흠뻑》. ¶ 비[이슬]에 ~ get [be] wet with rain [dew] / 땀에 ~ be wet with perspiration / 젖은 옷을 갈아입다 change one's wet clothes / 그녀의 얼굴은 눈물로 젖어 있었다 Her cheeks were wet with tears. / 그는 소나기를 맞아 흠뻑 젖었다 He was drenched to the skin in the shower.

젖몸살 mastitis. ¶ ~을 앓다 suffer from mastitis; have inflamed mammary glands.

젖히다 bend... backward; curve. ¶ 몸을 뒤로 ~ bend oneself backward / 가슴을 ~ straighten [pull] oneself up; stick one's chest out.

제 ① 《나의》 I, myself; 《나의》 my; my own. ¶ ~ 모자 my hat / ~가 이 회사 사장입니다 I am the president of this company. / 잘못은 ~ 게 있습니다 It is I who am to blame. / ~ 딴엔 [입장으로는] for my part; as for me [myself]. ② 《자기의》 one's; one's own. ¶ ~ 일은 one's own business / ~ 이익만 생각하다 look to one's own interest.

제(祭) 《제사》 a memorial service 《for one's ancestors》; 《축제》 a festival; a fête. ¶ 기념 ~ a commemoration / 50년 ~ a jubilee / 백년 ~ a centennial.

제(諸) many; several; various; all sorts of. ¶ ~ 문제 various problems / ~ 경비 charges; expenses / 아시아 ~ 국 the Asian nations.

제—(第) No.; number...; -th. ¶ ~ 4조 2항 the second clause of Article IV [Four].

—제(制) a system; an institu-

…제 tion. ¶ 8시간~ the eight-hour system.
…제(製) make; manufacture. ¶ 외물건 articles of foreign manufacture (make) / X회사~ 사진기 a camera made (manufactured) by X Company.
…제(劑) a medicine; a drug.
제각기(―各其) each; individually; respectively. ¶ ~는 그 책을 한 권씩 갖고 있다 We each have (Each of us has) a copy of the book.
제강(製鋼) steel manufacture. ‖ ~소 a steel mill; a steelworks / ~업 the steel industry / ~업자 a steelmaker; a steelman.
제거(除去) removal; elimination. ~하다 get rid of; do away with; remove; eliminate; weed out. ¶ 바람직하지 않은 것들은 ~되었다 Undesirable things were weeded out (eliminated).
제것 one's own property; one's possession (belongings). ¶ ~으로 만들다 make (things) one's own; have (a thing) for one's own / ~이 되다 fall into one's hands.
제격(―格) becoming (being suitable) to one's status. ¶ 그 자리에 그가 ~이다 He is the right man for the post.
제고(提高) ~하다 raise; uplift; heighten; improve; enhance. ¶ 가치를 ~하다 enhance (heighten) the value (of) / 생산성 ~ the heightening of productivity.
제곱 a square. ~하다 square (multiply) (a number). ‖ ~근 a square root.
제공(提供) an offer. ~하다 (make an) offer; supply; furnish; provide; sponsor (a TV program). ¶ 그는 믿을 만한 시장 정보를 ~했다 He provided me with reliable market tips. / 이 프로는 A회사 ~으로 보내드렸습니다 This program has been sponsored by A Corporation. ‖ ~가격 the price offered.
제공권(制空權) (the) mastery (command) of the air; air supremacy. ¶ ~을 장악하다 (잃다) secure (lose) the mastery of the air / ~을 장악하고 있다 have (hold) the command of the air; command the air.
제과(製菓) confectionery. ‖ ~업자 a confectioner / ~점 a confectionery / ~회사 a confectionery company.
제관(製罐) can manufacturing; canning (美). ‖ ~공장 a cannery; a canning factory / ~업자 a canner.
제구(祭具) → 제기(祭器).
제구력(制球力) 『野』 one's (pitching) control. ¶ ~이 있다 (없다) have good (poor) ball control.
제구실 one's duty (function, role); one's share (part). ~하다 perform one's function (part, duty); do one's duties; play one's role. ¶ 그는 ~을 훌륭히 해냈다 He performed his part most effectively.
제국(帝國) an empire. ‖ ~의 imperial. ‖ ~주의 imperialism (~주의의 imperialistic) / ~주의자 an imperialist.
제국(諸國) all (many) countries.
제기¹(―器) a Korean shuttlecock game played with the feet.
제기²(提起) Shucks!; Hell!; Damn (it)!; Hang it!
제기(祭器) a ritual utensil.
제기(提起) ~하다 present; bring up (forward) (a proposal); raise (a question); propose (a plan); pose (a problem). ¶ 중요한 문제를 ~하다 bring up a very important question / 이의를 ~하다 raise an objection (to).
제깐에 in one's own estimation (opinion); to one's own thinking. ¶ ~는 잘 한 줄 안다 He fancies himself to have done it well.
제너레이션(世代) a generation. ‖ ~갭 a generation gap.
제네바 Geneva.
제단(祭壇) an altar.
제당(製糖) sugar manufacture. ‖ ~공장 a sugar mill / ~업 the sugar-manufacturing industry.
제대(除隊) discharge from military service. ~하다 be discharged from military service. ‖ ~병 a discharged soldier / 의가사~ a discharge from service by family hardships / 의병~ a medical discharge (의병~하다 get a medical discharge).
제대(梯隊) 『軍』 an echelon.
제대로 (잘·순조로이) well; smoothly; (변변히) properly; fully; enough. ¶ 일이 ~되면 내달에는 끝난다 If all goes well, this job will be finished next month. / ~ 읽지도 않고 without reading (a book) properly.
제도(制度) a system; an institution. ‖ ~상의 institutional / 현행 ~ the existing system / 교육(사회) ~ an educational (a social) system / 구~ 하에서는 under the old system / ~화하다 systematize / 새로운 ~를 만들다 establish a new system / ~를 폐지하다 abolish a system / 그 지방에는 독특한 가족 ~가 남아 있다 An unusual family system remains in that area.

제도(製陶) pottery manufacture; porcelain making. ∥ ~술 ceramics; pottery.

제도(製圖) drafting; drawing. ~하다 draw; draft. ∥ ~가 a draftsman / ~기 a drawing instruments / ~실 a drafting room / ~판 a drafting [drawing] board.

제도(諸島) a group of islands; an archipelago.

제도(濟度) salvation; redemption. ~하다 save; redeem. ¶ 중생 ~ salvation of the world.

제독(提督) an admiral; a commodore.

제독하다(制毒─) neutralize a poison; rid of noxious influence.

제동(制動) braking; 〖電〗 damping. ~ 을 걸다 put on the brake. ∥ ~기 a brake / ~레버 a safety lever / ~수 (철도의) a brakeman / ~장치 (美) a braking system (이중~장치 a dual braking system) / ~회전 (스키의) a stem turn.

제등(提燈) a (paper) lantern.

제때 an appointed [a scheduled, a proper] time.

제라늄 〖植〗 a geranium.

제련(製鍊) refining; smelting. ~하다 refine 《*metals*》; smelt 《*copper*》. ∥ ~소 a refinery; a smelting plant.

제례(祭禮) religious ceremonies.

제로 (a) zero; (a) nought; nothing. ¶ 나의 영문학 지식은 ~다 I know nothing about English literature. / ~게임 〖테니스의〗 a love game / ~성장 〖인구·경제의〗 zero (economic, population) growth.

제록스 〖상표명〗 Xerox. ¶ ~로 복사하다 xerox a copy.

제막(除幕) ~하다 unveil 《*a statue*》. ∥ ~식 an unveiling ceremony [exercise (美)].

제멋 one's own taste [way, fancy, style]. ¶ ~ 을 거부로 먹어도 ~ 《俗談》 There is no accounting for tastes.

제멋대로 as one pleases [likes]; at will; willfully; waywardly. ¶ ~ 굴다 have one's own way; act willfully.

제면(製綿) ~하다 gin cotton.

제면(製麵) noodle making. ~하다 make noodles. ∥ ~기 a noodle-making machine.

제명(除名) expulsion; dismissal from membership. ~하다 expel 《*a person*》《*from a club*》; strike [take] 《*a person's*》 name off the list [roll]. ¶ 당에서 ~ 처분을 당하다 be expelled from the party.

제명(題名) a title.

제모(制帽) a regulation [uniform, school] cap.

제목(題目) a subject; a theme; a title(표제). ¶ 「자유」라는 ~의 논문 an essay entitled "Liberty" / ~을 붙이다 give a title 《*to*》.

제문(祭文) a funeral oration.

제물(祭物) an offering; a sacrifice(산 제물).

제물낚시 a fly fishing.

제물로[에] of its own accord; by [of] itself; spontaneously. ¶ 불이 ~ 꺼졌다 The fire went out all by itself.

제반(諸般) all sorts. ¶ 이런 ~ 사정 때문에 for these reasons; under these circumstances / ~ 사정을 고려하다 take all the circumstances into consideration.

제발 if you please; please; kindly; by all means; for mercy's (God's) sake. ¶ ~ 용서해 주십시오 Please forgive me. / ~ 내 말좀 들어봐라 Will you please listen to what I have to say?

제방(堤防) a bank; an embankment; a dike. ¶ ~을 쌓다 construct [build] a bank. / ~공사 bank revetment.

제번(除煩) ~하옵고 《편지 첫머리에》 I hasten to inform you that....

제법 quite; pretty; rather; considerably. ¶ ~ 오랫동안 for quite a long time / ~ 큰 집 rather a [a rather] large house / 오늘 아침에 눈이 ~ 많이 내렸다 Quite a bit of snow fell this morning. / ~ 어렵다 be more difficult than one (had) expected.

제법(製法) a method [process] of manufacture; a process; 《요리의》 a recipe. ¶ 케이크 ~을 가르치다 teach 《*a person*》 how to make a cake / ~을 보고 만들다 make 《*something*》 from a formular [recipe].

제복(制服) a uniform.

제복(祭服) ceremonial robes.

제본(製本) bookbinding. ~하다 bind 《*a book*》. ¶ ~ 중이다 be at the binder's. ∥ ~소 a (book) bindery.

제분(製粉) milling. ~하다 grind 《*corn*》 to flour. ∥ ~기, (a flour) mill / ~업 the milling industry / ~업자 a miller.

제비¹ 《추첨》 a lot; lottery(뽑기). ¶ ~를 뽑다 draw lots / ~ 뽑아 결정하다 decide by lot.

제비² 〖鳥〗 a swallow.

제비꽃 〖植〗 a violet.

제비족(─族) a gigolo.

제비추리 beef from the inside ribs.

제빙(製氷) ice manufacture. ∥ ~공장 an ice plant / ~기 an ice machine; an ice-maker.

제사(第四) the fourth. ∥ ~계급 the proletariat / ~세대항생제 the

4th-generation antibiotic.

제사(祭祀) a religious service [ceremony]. ¶ ~를 지내다 hold a memorial service (for).

제사(製絲) spinning; (견사의) silk reeling. ~하다 reel; draw silk. ‖ ~공장 a spinning mill; a silk mill / ~기계 reeling machine / ~업 the silk-reeling industry.

제살붙이 one's own people; one's relatives (kinfolk).

제삼(第三) the third. ¶ ~계급 the bourgeoisie / (평민) the third estate / ~국 the third power / ~세계 the Third World / ~세력 the third force / ~자 the third person (party); an outsider / ~차 산업 (의) the tertiary industries.

제상(祭床) a table used in a religious [memorial] service.

제설(除雪) ~하다 clear [remove] the snow. ¶ ~작업 snow removing / ~차 a snowplow.

제세(濟世) salvation of the world. ~하다 save the world.

제소(提訴) ~하다 sue; bring a case before (the court); file a suit (in the court against a person).

제수(弟嫂) a younger brother's wife; one's sister-in-law.

제수(除數) 【數】 the divisor.

제수(祭需) ① things used in the memorial services. ② ☞ 제물.

제스처 (make) a gesture. ¶ ~에 불과하다 be a mere gesture / 그에게 거절한다는 ~를 나타내다 make a gesture of refusal at him.

제습(除濕) ~하다 dehumidify. ‖ ~기 a dehumidifier / ~제 a dehumidifying agent.

제시(提示) presentation. ~하다 present; show.

제시간(一時間) the appropriate [proper, scheduled] time. ¶ ~에 on time.

제씨(諸氏) gentlemen; Messrs.

제안(提案) a proposal; a proposition; a suggestion; an offer. ~하다 propose; make a proposal [an offer]; suggest. ¶ 반대 ~ a counterproposal / 나의 ~이 가결 [부결]되었다 My proposal (motion) was adopted [rejected]. ‖ ~설명 enunciation of a proposal / ~이유 the reason for a proposal / ~자 a proposer.

제암(制癌) cancer prevention [inhibition]. ¶ ~의 anticancer. ‖ ~제 an anticancer drug [medicine].

제압(制壓) ~하다 control; bring... under control; gain supremacy over (the enemy). ¶ 군대는 데모대를 ~했다 The army controlled the demonstrators.

제야(除夜) (on) New Year's Eve.

제약(制約) a restriction; a limitation. ~하다 restrict; limit. ¶ 시간 ~으로 하고 싶은 말을 반밖에 못했다 I said only half as much as I wanted to say because of limited time.

제약(製藥) 《제조》 medicine manufacture; pharmacy; 《약》 a manufactured medicine [drug]. ‖ ~공장 [회사] a pharmaceutical factory [company].

제어(制御) control. ~하다 control; govern; manage. ¶ ~하기 쉬운 [어려운] easy [hard] to control / ~할 수 없는 uncontrollable / 자동 ~장치 an automatic control system [device] / 본능을 ~하기란 매우 어렵다 It is pretty hard to have control over instinct.

제염(製鹽) salt manufacture. ‖ ~소 a saltern; a saltworks.

제오(第五) the fifth. ¶ ~공화국 the Fifth Republic / ~열 the fifth column.

제왕(帝王) an emperor; a monarch; a sovereign. ‖ ~절개 (수)술 【醫】 a Caesarean operation.

제외(除外) ~하다 except; exclude; make an exception of; exempt (a person from taxes) (면제). ¶ 인원수에서 ~ 하다 exclude (a person) from the number. ‖ ~조항 an escape clause.

제우스 【그神】 Zeus.

제위(諸位) gentlemen; my friends.

제유법(提喩法) 【修】 synecdoche.

제육(돼지고기) pork.

제육감(第六感) the sixth sense; a hunch. ¶ ~으로 그것을 알다 feel it by intuition [the sixth sense].

제의(提議) 제안. ¶ 새로운 계획의 변경을 ~하고 싶다 I want to propose an amendment to the new plan.

제이(第二) number two; the second. ¶ ~의 second; secondary / 습관은 ~의 천성이다 Habit is second nature. ‖ ~국민역 disqualified conscription status / ~인칭 the second person / ~차 산업 a [the] secondary industry / ~차 세계대전 the Second World War; World War Ⅱ / ~차 집단 【社】 a secondary group.

제일(第一) the first; number one. ¶ ~의 first; primary; foremost / ~과 the first lesson; Lesson One / 건강이 ~이다 Health is above everything else. / 안전 ~ 《게시》 Safety First. / 그는 심장 외과의 ~인자다 He is the foremost [leading] authority on heart surgery. / 우리는 목표를 향해 ~보를 내딛었다 We took [made] the first step toward our goal. ‖

성(聲) one's first speech (새 대통령의 ~) 성 the inauguration speech of the President) / ~인칭 [文] the first person / ~차 산업 primary industries / ~차 제품 primary products (produce).

제일선(第一線) 《최전선》 the forefront; the front(전선). ¶ ~의 병사 a front-line soldier / 그는 ~에서 물러났다 He has retired from active life.

제자(弟子) a pupil; a disciple; an apprentice(도제). ¶ ~애 one's favorite pupil / 그는 ~를 두지 않는다 He doesn't take pupils. / 그녀는 유명한 도예가의 ~가 되었다 She apprenticed herself [was apprenticed] to a famous ceramist.

제자(諸子) 《중국의》 sages; masters. ¶ ~백가 all philosophers and literary scholars.

제자(字字) the title letters.

제자리걸음 ~하다 step; stamp; mark time; be at a standstill (정체). ¶ 발이 시려워 ~하며 기차를 기다렸다 I stamped my cold feet as I waited for the train. / 실험은 ~을 하고 있다 The experiment is at a standstill.

제작(製作) ~하다 manufacture; make; produce. ¶영화 ~에 2년이 걸리다 take two years to make the movie. ‖ ~비 production costs / ~소 a plant; a factory; a works / ~자 a maker; a manufacturer; producer (영화의).

제재(制裁) punishment; sanctions (against). ¶ 군사적 ~ military sanctions / 경제적 ~를 가하다 take [apply] economic sanctions.

제재(製材) sawing; lumbering. ~하다 lumber; do lumbering; saw up (logs). ‖ ~소 a sawmill; a lumbermill. / ~테마 theme.

제재(題材) subject matter; a theme.

제적(除籍) ~하다 remove (a person's name) from the register; expel (a person from school).

제전(祭典) (hold) a festival. ¶ 스포츠 ~ a sports festival.

제절(諸節) all the family; all of you. ¶ 댁내 ~이 무고하신지요 How is your family?

제정(制定) ~하다 enact (laws); establish. ¶ 새로운 세법이 지난달 ~되었다 The new tax laws were enacted last month.

제정(帝政) imperial government [rule]. ‖ ~러시아 Czarist Russia / ~시대 the monarchical days [periods].

제정(祭政) ~일치 the unity of church and state.

제정신(一精神) 《기절에 대해》 consciousness; senses; 《미친 정신에 대해》 sanity; right mind; 《취하지 않은》 soberness. ¶ ~의 sane; sober / 는 ~을 잃다 lose consciousness(의식); go mad(발광) / ~이 아니다 be out of one's senses / ~이 들다 come to oneself; recover consciousness / ~이 들게하다 bring (a person) to his senses / 그녀는 너무나 두려워 ~을 잃었다 He was terrified out of her wits.

제조(製造) manufacture; production. ~하다 manufacture; make; produce; turn out. ‖ ~공장 a manufactory; a factory / ~공정 a manufacturing process / ~능력 manufacturing capacity / ~번호 the (manufacture) serial number (on a camera) / ~법 a mode of preparation / ~업 the manufacturing industry / ~업자 [원(元)] a manufacturer; a maker; a producer / ~원가 manufacturing [production] cost / ~일자 the date of manufacture.

제주(祭主) the chief mourner; the master of religious rites.

제주(祭酒) sacred wine; wine offered before the altar.

제주도(濟州島) Jeju Island.

제지(制止) control; restraint. ~하다 restrain; check; hold back; stop. ¶ ~할 수 없다 be beyond one's control / ~할 수 없게 되다 (대상이 주어) get out of one's control; (사람이 주어) lose control (of).

제지(製紙) paper making (manufacture). ¶ ~용 펄프 paper pulp. ‖ ~공장[업자] a paper mill (manufacturer) / ~업 the paper industry / ~회사 a paper manufacturing company.

제차(諸車) ¶ ~ 통행 금지 《게시》 Closed to all vehicles.

제창(提唱) (a) proposal. ~하다 propose; bring forward; advocate. ¶ 새로운 안을 ~하다 bring forward a new proposal. ‖ ~자 an advocate; an exponent.

제창(齊唱) a unison. ~하다 sing (the national anthem) in unison.

제철 the season (for apples); suitable time.

제철(製鐵) iron manufacture. ‖ ~소 an ironworks / ~업 the iron industry / ~회사 an iron-manufacturing company / ~종합공장 an integrated steelworks.

제쳐놓다 lay (put) aside; set apart [aside]. ¶ 모든 일을 제쳐놓고 before anything (else); first of all / 그는 하던 일을 제쳐놓고 여행을 떠났다 He left his job half done and went on a trip.

제초(除草) ~하다 weed (a garden). ‖ ~기 a weeder / ~제

제출 (提出) presentation. ~하다 present; introduce 《*a bill*》; submit; bring forward; advance 《*an opinion*》; hand (send) in (답안·원서 등을); lodge (이의 등을); tender 《*one's resignation*》. ∥ ~기한 a deadline / ~자 a presenter; a proposer. ¶ the Seventh Fleet.
제칠 (第七) the seventh.
제트 (a) jet. ¶ ~기 조종사 a jet pilot. ¶ ~기류 a jet stream / ~수송기 a jet transport (plane) / ~엔진 a jet engine / ~여객 [전투, 폭격]기 a jet airliner (fighter, bomber) / ~정보기 a jumbo jet plane.
제판 (製版) [印] plate-making; make-up. ∥ ~하다 make a plate; make up. ∥ ~소 a plate-maker's shop / ~업자 a plate-maker / ~사진 photoengraving.
제패 (制覇) conquest; domination. ~하다 conquer; dominate. ¶ 세계 ~ domination of the world; world hegemony / 그는 세계 ~를 꿈꾸었다 He dreamed of conquering the world. / 그녀는 그 대회에서 전 종목을 ~했다 She won all the events at that meet.
제품 ¶ ~로 [에] of itself; of its own accord; spontaneously.
제품 (製品) manufactured goods; a product; a manufacture. ¶ 유리 ~ glassware / 미국 ~ articles of American make / 외국 [국내] ~ foreign (domestic) products / 이 사진기들은 당사 ~이다 These cameras are the products of our company. ∥ ~광고 a product advertisement / ~생산량별 임금제 the piece rate pay system.
제하다 (除一) ① 《제외》 leave out; exclude; except; 《빼다》 take away (off); deduct; subtract. ¶ 달리 특별한 규정이 있는 경우를 제하고 unless otherwise provided / 급료에서 ~ deduct 《*a sum*》 from one's pay; take 《*a sum*》 off one's salary. ② 《나누다》 divide.
제한 (制限) restriction; limitation; a limit. ~하다 restrict; limit; put (impose, place) restrictions 《on》. ¶ ~적인 restrictive / ~ 없이 without limit (restriction); freely; unrestrictedly / 한자 사용의 ~ a limitation (restriction) on the use of Chinese characters / 산아 ~ birth control / 수입 ~ import restriction / 수에 ~이 있다 be limited in number; there is a limit to the number 《of》 / ~을 완화하다 relax the restrictions 《on trade》 / ~을 철폐하다 remove (lift) restrictions / 수량 ~ quantitative restrictions / 전력의 소비 ~ restriction on power consumption / 회원 자격에는 남녀 및 연령의 ~이 없다 Membership is open to persons of either sex and of any age. ¶ ~속도 a speed limit; the regulation speed / ~시간 a time limit / ~전쟁 a limited war.
제해권 (制海權) the command of the sea; naval supremacy. ¶ ~을 장악하다 [잃다] have (lose) the command of the sea.
제헌 (制憲) ∥ ~국회 the Constitutional Assembly / ~절 Constitution Day.
제혁 (製革) tanning; leather manufacture. ∥ ~소 a tannery / ~업자 a tanner.
제현 (諸賢) (Ladies and Gentle)men.
제형 (梯形) [幾] a trapezoid; [軍] an echelon formation.
제형 (蹄形) 《말굽 형상》 ¶ ~의 hoof-shaped; U-shaped.
제호 (題號) a title 《*of a book*》.
제화 (製靴) shoemaking. ∥ ~공장 a shoemaking factory / ~업 the shoe(making) industry.
제휴 (提携) cooperation; a tie-up. ~하다 cooperate 《with》; join hands; tie up 《with》. ¶ …와 ~하여 in cooperation with / ~하여 공동의 적에 대항하다 be leagued together against the common enemy / 기술 ~ a technical tie-up (도) (an agreement for) technical cooperation. ∥ ~회사 an affiliated concern.
젠장 Hang (Damn) it!; Hell!
젠체하다 put on airs; assume an air of importance.
젠틀맨 a gentleman.
젤라틴 [化] gelatin(e).
젯밥 (祭一) food for ceremonial service.
조 (粟) [植] a grain of millet.
조 (條) an article; a clause; an item. ¶ 제 5 ~ Article 5.
조 (組) 《무리》 a group; a party; a gang (악한의); a team (경기의). ¶ 3인 ~ 강도 a gang of three burglars / 일곱 사람씩 ~를 짜라 Form groups of seven. / 우리는 두 사람씩 ~를 이루어 출발했다 We set off in groups of two.
조 (調) ① 《곡조》 a tune; meter. ¶ 장 [단] ~ major [minor] key. ② 《말투》 an air (attitude) 《*of*》. ¶ 비난 ~로 with an air of censure.
조 (朝) a dynasty. ¶ 청 ~ the Ching dynasty.
조 (兆) a trillion 《美》; a billion 《英》.
조² that little 《*thing over there*》. ¶ ~ 놈 that little guy.
조가 (弔歌) a dirge; an elegy.
조가비 a shell. ∥ ~세공 shellwork.
조각 a fragment; a (broken)

piece; a scrap; a chip; a splinter(날카로운). ¶ 깨진 접시 ~ a fragment of a broken dish / 유리 ~ a piece of broken glass ‖ ~(이)나다 break into pieces (fragments). ‖ ~달 a crescent (moon) / ~ 보 a patchwork wrapping-cloth.

조각(彫刻) (a) sculpture; (a) carving; (an) engraving(「조각물」의 뜻일 때는 (C)). ~하다 sculpture; sculpt; carve(나무에); engrave(금속·돌에). ¶ ~ 코끼리 / 나무로 상을 ~하다 carve an image in wood. ‖ ~가 an engraver; a carver; a sculptor.

조각(組閣) formation of a cabinet. ~하다 form (organize) a cabinet.

조간(朝刊) a morning paper. ¶ 오늘 아침 ~의 일면 기사는 무엇이냐 What is the front-page article of today's morning paper?

조갈(燥渴) thirst. ¶ ~이 나다 feel thirsty.

조감도(鳥瞰圖) a bird's-eye-view; an airscape.

조강(粗鋼) crude steel.

조강지처(糟糠之妻) one's good old wife; one's wife married in poverty.

조개 a shellfish; a clam. ‖ ~젓 salted clam meat / ~탄 oval briquets / ~껍질 clam meat.

조객(弔客) a caller for condolence; a condoler.

조건(條件) a condition; terms(계약·지불 등의); a requirement(필수의); a qualification(제한적인). ¶ 계약의 ~ the terms of a contract / 열악한 노동 ~ poor working conditions / 제 1 ~ the first condition / 회원이 될 수 있는 ~ a membership requirement ‖ ~을 달다 make (impose) conditions (on) / ~을 채우다 meet (a person's) conditions (requirements) / …라는 ~으로 on the condition that…; provided that…; under the condition that… / 정부는 미국 측의 제안을 ~부로 승낙하였다 The government accepted the proposal from the U.S. with some reservations. ‖ ~문 [文] a conditional sentence / ~반사 [生] conditional reflex (response) / ~부 채용 conditional appointment(임용) (employment (고용)).

조건표(早見表) a chart; a table. ‖ 계산~ a ready reckoner / 전화 번호~ telephone numbers at a glance.

조경(造景) landscape architecture. ‖ ~사 a landscape architect (gardener) / ~술(術) landscape architecture (gardening). 「ment.

조계(租界) a concession; a settle-

조공(朝貢) ~하다 bring a tribute 《to a country》. ‖ ~국 a tributary state. 「concession.

조광권(租鑛權) a mineral right; a

조교(弔橋) a suspension bridge.

조교(助敎) an assistant teacher; an assistant(조수). 「fessor.

조교수(助敎授) an assistant pro-

조국(祖國) one's fatherland (motherland); one's mother country. ‖ ~애 love of one's country; patriotism.

조그마하다 (be) smallish; be of a somewhat small size (서술적).

조그만큼 just a little; 《수》 just a few; 《정도》 slightly; a little.

조금 《수·양》 a few(수); a little (양); some(수·양); 《정도》 a little; a bit; 《시간》 a moment; a minute; a while; 《거리》 a little way. ¶ ~씩 little by little; bit by bit / ~ 더 a little (few) more / ~ 전에 a little while ago / ~ 떨어져서 a little (way) off / ~도 …하지 않다 not… at all; not… in the least; not… a bit / 달걀이라면 냉장고에 ~ 있다 There are a few (some) eggs in the refrigerator. / 소금이 ~ 밖에 없다 There is not much salt left. / 나는 영어를 ~ 말할 수 있다 I can speak English a little. / ~ 만 기다려 주십시오 Wait a moment (minute), please. / ~ 쉬도록 하자 Let's take a rest for a while. / 이 강을 따라 ~ 만 가십시오 Go a little way along this river. / 그녀는 ~도 놀라지 않았다 She was not surprised at all (in the least). / 그는 복장 따위에는 ~도 신경을 쓰지 않는다 He doesn't care a bit about his clothes.

조금(潮─) [地] the neap tide.

조급(躁急) ~하다 (be) impatient; impetuous; hasty. ¶ ~한 사람 a hothead; a man of impetuous disposition / 그렇게 ~히 굴지 마라 Don't be so impatient.

조기[魚] a yellow corvina.

조기(弔旗) 《hang》 a flag at half-mast (-staff); a mourning flag.

조기(早起) getting up early 《in the morning》. ‖ ~회 an early risers' club (meeting).

조기(早期) an early stage. ¶ 암은 ~ 발견하면 고칠 수 있다 Cancer can be cured if detected in its early stages. ‖ ~경보체제 the early warning system / ~발견 early detection 《of cancer》 (~진단(치료) early diagnosis (treatment) (~진단을 받다 be diagnosed in an early stage).

조깅 jogging; a jog. ¶ ~을 하다 jog; take a (*morning*) jog / ~하는 사람 a jogger.
조끼¹ a vest; 《美》 a waistcoat.
조끼² (beer) mug; a tankard (큰). ¶ 맥주 한 ~ a mug of beer.
조난(遭難) a disaster; an accident; a shipwreck(배의). ~하다 meet with a disaster [an accident]; be in distress; be wrecked (파선되다). ‖ ~구조대 a rescue party / ~구조선 a rescue boat / ~선 a ship in distress; a wrecked ship / ~신호 a distress signal; (call) Mayday / ~자 a victim; a survivor (생존자).
조달(調達) 《물자 등의》 supply; procurement; 《자금의》 raising; 《일용품 등의》 provision. ~하다 supply [furnish] (*a person with things*); procure; raise (*capital*). ¶ 해외 ~ off-shore procurement. ‖ ~처 the procurement [supply] section / ~기관 a procurement agency / ~청 the Supply Administration.
조당(粗糖) raw [unrefined] sugar.
조도(照度) intensity of illumination. ‖ ~계 an illuminometer.
조동사(助動詞) 〖文〗 an auxiliary verb.
조락(凋落) 《나뭇잎의》 withering; 《영락》 a decline; a decay. ~하다 《시들다》 wither; fade; 《영락하다》 decline; go downhill. ¶ ~의 길을 걷다 head for ruin[downfall].
조력(助力) help; aid; assistance; cooperation(협력). ~하다 help; aid [assist] (*in*); give aid [assistance] (*to*); cooperate (*with*). ¶ 아무의 ~을 구하다 ask for *a person's* help. ‖ ~자 a helper; an assistant.
조력(潮力) tidal energy [power]. ¶ ~발전 tidal power generation / ~발전소 a tidal-powered electric plant.
조령모개(朝令暮改) lack of principle; an inconsistent policy. ¶ ~의 정책 a fickle [an inconsistent] policy. 「(manners).
조례(弔禮) condolatory etiquette 」
조례(條例) regulations; an ordinance; a law. ¶ 시의 ~ a municipal ordinance / ~를 반포하다 issue regulations [an ordinance].
조례(朝禮) a morning gathering [meeting, assembly]. ¶ 매주 월요일에 ~가 있다 We have the morning meeting every Monday.
조로(早老) premature senility. ~하다 《prematurely aged. ‖ ~현상 symptoms of premature old age.
조로아스터교(—敎) Zoroastrianism.
조롱(嘲弄) ridicule; derision; mockery. ~하다 ridicule; deride; mock; make a fool of; laugh at.
조롱박 ① 〖植〗 a bottle gourd. ② 《바가지》 a water dipper made of gourd. 「tion.
조루(早漏) 〖醫〗 premature ejaculation.」
조류(鳥類) birds; fowls. ‖ ~보호 bird protection / ~학 ornithology / ~학자 an ornithologist.
조류(潮流) 《예수의 흐름》 a (tidal) current; a tide; 《시세의 동향》 a trend; a tendency; a current. ¶ ~는 저쪽에서 방향을 바꾸고 있다 The tide runs in a different direction over there. / 시대의 ~에 따르다 [역행하다] swim with [against] the current of the times.
조류(藻類) 〖植〗 (the) algae; seaweeds. ¶ ~의 algoid. ‖ ~학 algology.
조르다 ① 《죄다》 tighten; wring; strangle(목을). ¶ 목을 졸라 죽이다 strangle (*a person*) (to death). ② 《졸라대다》 ask [press, pester, importune] (*a person for a thing, to do*). ¶ 그는 자전거를 사달라고 어머니를 졸랐다 He pestered his mother to buy him a bicycle.
조르르 《물 따위가》 trickling; dribbling; running; 《구르듯·미끄러지듯》 slipping (rolling, sliding) down; 《뒤따름》 tagging along. ¶ 물이 ~ 나오다 water dribbles from (*the faucet*) / ~ 따라가다 tag at (*a person's*) heels.
조르륵 bubblingly; droppingly.
조리(笊籬) a (bamboo) strainer; a (bamboo) mesh dipper. ¶ ~로 쌀을 일다 rinse rice using a (bamboo) strainer.
조리(條理) logical sequence; logic; reason. ¶ ~가 서는 reasonable; logical; consistent / ~가 안 서는 unreasonable; absurd; illogical / ~가 맞다 stand to reason; be reasonable.
조리(調理) ① 《조섭》 care of health. ~하다 take care of *one's* health. ② 《요리》 cooking; cookery. ~하다 cook; prepare (*a dish*). ‖ ~대 a dresser; a kitchen table / ~법 the art of cooking; cookery; cuisine / ~사 a licensed cook.
조리개 ① 《끈》 a tightening string (cord). ② 《사진기의》 an iris; a diaphragm; a stop. ¶ ~를 열다[닫다] open[shut] the diaphragm.
조리다 boil (*fish*) down. ¶ 생선을 간장에 ~ boil fish with soy sauce / 생선을 은근한 불에 ~ let fish simmer gently.
조림 boiled food. ¶ 고등어 ~ mackerel boiled with soy sauce.

조림(造林) afforestation. ~하다 afforest 《a mountain》; plant trees. ‖ ~학 forestry.

조립(組立) assembling(기계의); fabrication; construction. ~하다 put 《things》 together; assemble; construct; build; fabricate. ¶기계를 ~하다 build (frame, construct) a machine; assemble (put together) a machine (부품을 조립하여). ‖ ~공 an assembler / ~공장 an assembly plant / ~(식) 주택 a prefabricated house; a prefab (house) / ~(식) 책장 a sectional bookcase.

조마(調馬) horse training (breaking). ‖ ~사 a horse trainer.

조마조마하다 (be) fidgety; edgy; agitated; feel nervous (uneasy, anxious)(서술적).

조막손이 a claw-handed person.

조만간(早晩間) sooner or later.

조망(眺望) a view; a prospect; a lookout(전망). ~하다 command a view of; look out over 《upon》 《the sea》. ¶그 산정은 ~이 좋다 The view from the top of the mountain is superb. ‖ ~권 the right to a view.

조명(照明) lighting; illumination. ~하다 light (up); illuminate. ¶직접(간접) ~ direct (indirect) lighting / 무대 ~ stage lighting / 이 방은 ~이 나쁘다 This room is badly (dimly) lit (lighted). ‖ ~기구 an illuminator; lighting fixtures / ~탄 a flare bomb / ~효과 lighting effects.

조모(祖母) a grandmother.

조목(條目) an article; a clause; an item.

조무래기 《물건》 petty goods; odds and ends; sundries; 《아이》 little kids; kiddies.

조문(弔文) a message of condolence; a memorial (funeral) address.

조문(弔問) a call of condolence. ~하다 call on 《a person》 to express one's condolence / ~을 받다 receive callers for condolence. ‖ ~객 a caller for condolence / ~사절(使節) a 《U.S.》 delegation to memorial service; a condolence delegation.

조문(條文) the text 《of regulations》; 《조항》 provisions.

조물주(造物主) the Creator; the Maker; God.

조미(調味) ~하다 season 《with salt》; give flavor 《to》; flavor 《with onions》. ‖ ~료 a seasoning; a condiment; a flavor enhancer.

조밀(稠密) density. ¶인구가 ~한 지역 a densely (thickly) populated area; an area of dense population / 인구가 ~하다 be densely populated; have a high population density.

조바심하다 be anxious (cautious) 《about》; be nervous; feel impatient (restless).

조반(朝飯) breakfast. ¶~을 먹다 take (have) breakfast.

조밥 boiled millet (and rice).

조방농업(粗放農業) extensive agriculture.

조변석개(朝變夕改) ☞ 조령모개.

조병창(造兵廠) an arsenal; an armory《美》.

조복(朝服) a court dress.

조부(祖父) a grandfather.

조부모(祖父母) grandparents. ¶~의 grandparental.

조분(鳥糞) bird droppings. ‖ ~석(石) guano.

조붓하다 be a bit narrow.

조사(早死) an early 《a premature, an untimely》 death. ~하다 die young (before one's time, at an early age).

조사(弔辭) a letter (message) of condolence; 《give》 a funeral address. 《particle.

조사(助詞)《文》 a postpositional

조사(照射) irradiation. ¶X선을 ~하다 apply X-rays to 《a person's neck》.

조사(調査) (an) investigation; (an) examination; an inquiry(질문 등에 의한); a survey (측량 등에 의한); (a) census (인구의); a research (학술상의). ~하다 investigate; examine; survey; look (inquire) into. ¶고대 유적을 ~하다 survey the remains of ancient times / 철저히 ~하다 make a thorough (an intensive) investigation 《into》; investigate 《a thing》 thoroughly / 그 사건은 지금 ~중이다 The matter is under investigation. / 당국은 사고의 원인을 ~하기 시작했다 The authorities have started to investigate the cause of the accident. / ~결과 엔진에 이상이 있음이 판명되었다 On investigation it was found that the engine was out of order. ‖ ~결과 findings (위원회 등의) / ~관 an examiner; an investigator / ~보고 a report of an investigation / ~부(과) an investigation division (section) / ~위원회 an investigation (a fact-finding) committee / ~자료 data for investigation / ~표 a questionnaire.

조산(早産) a premature birth. ~하다 give birth to a baby prematurely. ‖ ~아 a prematurely born baby.

조산(助産) midwifery. ‖ ~사 a

조산(助産) midwife / ~학 obstetrics.
조산(造山) an artificial [a miniature] hill; a rockery. ¶ ~운동 [작용] [地] mountain-building [-making] activity [movements]; orogeny.
조상(弔喪) condolence. ~하다 condole with a mourner 《on *his wife's death*》. 「ther.
조상(祖上) an ancestor; a forefa-
조상(彫像) a (carved) statue.
조색(調色) mixing colors.
조생종(早生種) a precocious species; an early-ripening lots.
조서(書) a royal edict (rescript).
조서(調書) [法] a record; written evidence. ¶ ~를 꾸미다 put 《*a deposition*》 on record.
조석(朝夕) morning and evening.
조선(造船) shipbuilding. ~하다 build a ship. ¶ ~공학 marine engineering / ~기사 a naval [marine] engineer; a shipbuilder / ~능력 shipbuilding capacity / ~대 a shipway; a slip / ~소 a shipyard; a dockyard / ~업 the shipbuilding industry / ~학 naval architecture.
조성(助成) ~하다 《보조하다》 assist; aid; 《촉진하다》 further; promote; 《후원하다》 support; sponsor; subsidize(정부가). ¶ ~금 a subsidy; a grant-in-aid.
조성(造成) 《토지의》 development; reclamation 《매립》; preparation 《*of a housing site*》 ~하다 make 《*a new land*》; develop 《*an area of land*》; prepare 《*the ground for housing*》. ¶ 택지를 ~하다 develop land for housing lots.
조성(組成) formation; composition. ~하다 form; make up; compose. ¶ ~물 a composite.
조세(租稅) taxes; taxation(과세). ¶ ~를 부과하다 impose a tax 《*on*》.
조소(彫塑) carvings and sculptures; the plastic arts 《조형미술》.
조소(嘲笑) ridicule; derision; a sneer; a scornful (derisive) laughter. ~하다 laugh (jeer) at 《*a person*》; ridicule. ¶ ~거리가 되다 become a laughingstock; be ridiculed / 세인의 ~를 사다 incur the public ridicule; draw ridicule upon *oneself*.
조속(早速) ~히 as soon as possible; at your earliest convenience.
조수(助手) an assistant; a helper. ¶ ~ 노릇을 하다 serve as assistant 《*to a person*》; assist / 운전 ~ an assistant driver. / ~석 《자동차의》 the passenger seat; the assistant driver's seat.
조수(鳥獸) birds and beasts; fur and feather.
조수(潮水) tidal (tide) water; the tides. ¶ ~의 간만 the ebb and flow of the tide.
조숙(早熟) precocity; premature growth. ~하다 be precocious; grow (mature) early. ¶ ~한 premature; precocious. / ~아 a precocious child.
조식(粗食) poor food; a plain(simple) diet. ~하다 live on poor food (a frugal diet).
조신(操身) carefulness of conduct (behavior). ~하다 be careful of *oneself*; be discreet.
조실부모(早失父母) ~하다 lose *one's* parents early in life.
조심(操心) 《주의》 caution; heed; care; 《신중》 prudence; circumspection; 《경계》 precaution; vigilance. ~하다 take care (be careful 《*of*》; beware 《*of*》; be cautious (careful) 《*about*》; look out 《*for*》. ¶ 말을 ~하다 be careful in one's speech / 몸을 ~하다 be careful about *one's* health / 발 밑을 ~해라 Watch your step. / ~해서 걷다 walk with care / 앞으로는 ~하겠습니다 I will be more cautious in the future.
조심성(操心性) cautiousness; carefulness. ¶ ~이 없이 be careless (thoughtless); be heedless (imprudent). 「erence」; kowtow.
조아리다 give a deep bow 《in rev-
조아팔다 sell in small lots 《*of*》.
조악(粗惡) ¶ ~한 bad; coarse; crude. / ~품 a poor-quality goods; goods of inferior quality. 「minerals.
조암광물(造岩鑛物) rock-forming
조야(粗野) ¶ ~한 coarse; rough; unrefined; rude; rustic.
조야(朝野) the government and the people; the whole nation. ¶ ~의 명사들 men of distinction both in and out of the government.
조약(條約) a treaty; an agreement; a pact. ¶ ~을 맺다 conclude (enter into) a treaty 《*with*》 / ~을 개정 (파기)하다 revise (denounce) a treaty / 통상 (평화) ~ a commercial (peace) treaty / 북대서양~기구 the North Atlantic Treaty Organization 《생략 NATO》 / ~의 비준 the ratification of a treaty. ∥ ~가맹국 the members of a treaty; signatory countries / ~규정 the treaty provisions (stipulations, terms).
조약돌 a pebble; a gravel.
조어(造語) 《말》 a coined word; 《만들기》 coinage. ¶ 한자가 가지고 있는 높은 ~력 the high word-forming ability of Chinese characters.

조언(助言) (a piece of) advice; counsel; a hint; a suggestion. ∥ ~하다 advise; counsel; give 《a person》 advice 《counsel》; suggest. ¶ ~을 구하다 ask 《a person》 for advice; seek 《a person's》 advice 《about》 / 나는 그의 ~에 따르겠다 I'll follow 〔take〕 his advice. ∥ ~자 an adviser; a counselor.

조업(操業) operation; work. ∥ ~하다 run 《a factory》; work 《a mill》; operate 《a mine》. ¶ ~을 재개하다 get back in operation; resume operation / ~을 단축하다 cut down 〔reduce〕 operations / 완전 ~ full operation. ∥ ~단축 a reduction of operation 〔work hours〕 / ~시간 operating hours.

조역(助役) an assistant; a helper. 《조역자》 《철도 역장의》 an assistant stationmaster.

조연(助演) ~하다 play a supporting role 《in》; support 〔assist〕 《the leading actor》; act with. ∥ ~배우 a supporting actor 《actress》.

조예(造詣) knowledge. ¶ 그는 그리스 신화에 ~가 깊다 He has a profound 〔deep〕 knowledge of Greek mythology. or He is well-informed in Greek mythology.

조용하다〔잠잠하다〕 (be) quiet; silent; still; 〔안온〕 (be) calm; placid; tranquil; serene; peaceful; gentle; soft. ¶ 조용히 quietly; calmly; peacefully / 조용한 공원 a quiet park / 조용한 밤 a silent 〔still〕 night / 조용한 발소리 quiet 〔silent〕 footsteps / 그는 조용한 소리로 이야기했다 He spoke in a soft 〔gentle〕 voice. / 조용히 해라 Be quiet!; Quiet down!; Keep still! / 조용히 하고 들어라 Be quiet and listen.

조우(遭遇) ~하다 come across; encounter 《the enemy》; meet with 《an accident》. ¶ 근접 ~ a close encounter / ~전 an encounter 〔battle〕.

조울병(躁鬱病) [醫] manic-depressive psychosis. ∥ ~환자 a manic-depressive.

조위금(弔慰金) condolence money.

조율(調律) tuning. ∥ ~하다 tune 《a piano》; put 《a piano》 in tune. ∥ ~사 《a piano》 tuner.

조의(弔意) condolence; mourning. ¶ 충심으로 ~를 표하다 express 〔offer, tender〕 one's sincere condolences 《to》 / ~를 표해 반기(半旗)를 달다 hang out a flag at half-mast.

조인(鳥人) an airman. 〔halfmast.

조인(調印) signature; signing. ~하다 sign 《a treaty》; affix one's seal 《to a document》. ¶ 서명 ~하다 sign and seal / 가 ~하다 initial 《an agreement》. ∥ ~국 a signatory (power) / ~식 the signing ceremony / ~자 a signer; a signatory.

조작(造作) invention; fabrication. ~하다 fabricate; invent; forge; make 〔cook〕 up. ¶ 그의 증언은 모두 ~된 것이었다 His whole testimony had been faked 《concocted》.

조작(操作) (an) operation; (a) handling. ~하다 operate 《a machine》; manipulate 《the market》; handle. ¶ 원격 ~ remote control / 시장 ~ market manipulation / 가격의 인위적 ~ artificial manipulation of prices / 금융 ~ monetary manipulation / 기계를 잘못 다루다 mishandle a machine / 이 컴퓨터는 ~하기 쉽다 This computer is easy to operate. 〔crude.

조잡(粗雜) ~한 rough; coarse;

조장(助長) ~하다 encourage; promote; foster; further. ¶ 국제간의 친선을 ~하다 promote international friendship / 악폐를 ~하다 aggravate evils.

조장(組長) a head; a foreman 《직공 등의》.

조장(鳥葬) sky burial.

조전(弔電) (send) a telegram of condolence 〔sympathy〕.

조절(調節) regulation; control; adjustment. ~하다 regulate 《prices》; control 《a mechanism》; adjust 《a telescope》. ¶ 라디오의 다이얼을 ~하다 tune in the radio / 실내 온도를 25도로 ~하다 regulate the temperature of the room to 25°C / 의자를 당신 몸에 맞도록 하시오 Adjust the seat to fit you. ∥ ~기 a regulator; an adjustor; a modulator 《라디오의》 / ~판 a control valve.

조정(朝廷) the (Royal) court.

조정(漕艇) rowing; boating. ∥ ~ 경기 a boat race.

조정(調停) mediation; arbitration; intervention; 〔法〕 reconciliation. ~하다 mediate 《a labor dispute》; arbitrate 《in a case》; reconcile; settle 《a dispute》. ¶ ~에 부치다 refer 〔submit〕 《a dispute》 to arbitration / 유엔은 양국 간의 분쟁에 ~에 나섰다 The United Nations set about 〔to〕 the mediation of the dispute between the two countries. ∥ ~안 a mediation plan; an arbitration proposal / ~위원회 a mediation committee / ~자 an arbitrator; a mediator.

조정(調整) regulation; adjustment; coordination. ~하다 regulate; adjust 《the price of》; coordinate. ¶ 속도를 ~하다 adjust the speed / 스테레오의 소리를 ~하다 adjust

조제 the stereo sounds / 우리의 서로 다른 의견을 ~을 시도하다 try to coordinate our different views / 세금의 연말 ~ the year-end tax adjustment.
조제(粗製) coarse [crude] manufacture. ‖ ~품 a crude [coarse] article; coarse manufactures.
조제(調製) preparation; manufacture. ~하다 make; prepare.
조제(調劑) preparation of medicines. ~하다 prepare a medicine; fill [make up] a prescription. ‖ ~실 a dispensary.
조조(早朝) early morning.
조종(弔鐘) a funeral bell; a knell.
조종(祖宗) ancestors of a king.
조종(操縱) handling; operation; control; steering. ~하다 work; manage; handle; control; operate; manipulate; pilot (비행기); steer (배를). ¶ ~할 수 없게 되다 lose control of 《an airplane》 / ~하다 work [operate] a machine / 그는 경비행기를 ~할 수 있다 He can fly a lightplane. / ~하기 쉽다[어렵다] be easy [hard] to control [manage] / 그녀는 남편을 제 마음대로 ~하고 있다 She turns [twists] her husband around her little finger. or She makes her husband do whatever she wants. ‖ ~간 a control stick [lever] / ~사 a pilot (부~사 a copilot) / ~석 a cockpit; the pilot's seat.
조준(照準) aim; aiming; sight. ~하다 aim 《at》; take aim 《at》; set one's sight 《on》. ‖ ~기 a sight / ~선 a line of sight / ~수(대표的) a gunlayer.
조지다 ① (단단히 맞춤) fix tightly; tighten [screw] up. ② (단속함) control strictly; exercise strict control 《over》. ③ (호되게 때리다) give 《a person》 a good beating.
조직(組織) an organization; formation; 《집단》 a structure; 《체계》 a system; 《생물의》 tissue. ~하다 organize; form; compose. ¶ ~적인 systematic / ~적으로 systematically / 사회의 ~ the structure of society / 정당[노동조합]을 ~하다 organize a political party [labor union] / 내각을 [회사를] ~하다 form a cabinet [company] / 그는 그 ~의 우두머리이다 He is the leader of the organization. / 근육 [신경] ~ muscle [nervous] tissue / 위원회는 5명의 위원으로 ~되어 있다 The committee is composed of five members. ‖ ~망 the network of a system / ~책(責) a chief organizer / ~학 [生] histology / ~화 organization; systematization (~화하다 organize; systematize / 고도로 ~화된 사회 a highly structured society).
조짐(兆朕) (질병의) symptoms; (일반적인) a sign; an indication; (전조) an omen. ¶ 성공의 ~ an omen of success / 폐렴의 ~을 보이다 develop symptoms of pneumonia / 경기 회복의 ~이 나타났다 We've had encouraging signs for economic recovery.
조차(租借) lease 《of territory》. ~하다 lease; hold 《land》 by [on] lease. ‖ ~권 a 《99 years'》 lease; leasehold / ~지 a leased territory.
조차(潮差) tidal range.
조차(操車) [鐵] marshaling. ‖ ~원 a train dispatcher / ~장 a marshaling yard; a switchyard (美).
조차 even; so much as; (게다가) besides; on top of; ¶ 자신의 이름 ~ 못 쓰다 cannot even [so much as] write one's own name / 비가 오는데 우박~ 쏟아진다 Hail began to fall on top of rain.
조찬(朝餐) breakfast. ‖ ~기도회 a breakfast prayer meeting.
조처(措處) a step; a measure; disposal. ~하다 take a step; take measures; take action. ¶ 적절한 ~를 취하다 take appropriate measures / 잘못 ~하다 take a wrong step / 강경한 ~를 취하다 take strong action 《against》.
조청(造淸) grain syrup.
조촐하다 (be) neat; nice; tidy; (아담함) (be) cozy; snug; little; small. ¶ 조촐하고 아늑한 방 a cozy [snug] room; a compact little apartment / 조촐하게 살다 live in a small way.
조총(弔銃) (fire) a (rifle) volley for the dead.
조총련(朝總聯) the pro-North Korean residents' league in Japan.
조처 ☞ 조치. ¶ 보완 ~ complementary measures / 후속 ~ follow-up measures / 강력한 ~를 취하다 take strong [decisive] measures [steps] 《against outlaws》.
조카 a nephew. ‖ ~딸 a niece.
조타(操舵) steering; steerage. ~하다 steer. ‖ ~기 [실] a steering gear [house] / ~수 a steersman.
조탁(彫琢) 《보석 따위의》 carving and chiseling; 《문장 따위의》 elaboration. ~하다 carve and chisel; elaborate.
조탄(粗炭) low-grade coal.
조퇴(早退) ~하다 leave work [the office, school] early.
조판(組版) typesetting; composition. ~하다 set [up] type; put 《a manuscript》 in type.
조폐(造幣) coinage; minting. ‖ ~

국 the Mint (Bureau) / ~국장 《美》the Treasurer of the Mint (Bureau) / ~공사 the Korea Minting, Printing & ID Card Operating Corp.

조포(弔砲) 《fire》(a salute of minute guns.

조합(組合) an association; a guild (동업자의); a union (노동자의). ¶ ~을 만들다 form an association (a union) / ~에 가입하다 join an association; become a union member. ‖ ~비 union dues / ~원 a member of an association (a union); a union member / ~활동 union activities.

조항(條項) articles; clauses (법률·조약의); 《法》provisions; stipulations (계약·약정의).

조혈(造血) blood formation; hematosis. ‖ ~기관 a blood-forming organ / ~기능(조직) hematogenous (blood-forming) functions (tissues) / ~제 a blood-forming medicine.

조형(造形) molding, modeling. ‖ ~미술 formative (the plastic) arts.

조혼(早婚) an early marriage. ~하다 marry young.

조화(弔花) funeral flowers; a funeral wreath (화환).

조화(造化) creation; nature. ‖ ~의 묘 the wonders of nature / ~의 장난 a freak of nature.

조화(造花) an artificial (imitation) flower.

조화(調和) harmony. ~하다 harmonize (be in harmony) 《with》; go 《with》; match. ¶ ~된 harmonious 《colors》; well-matched / ~시키다 harmonize; adjust / 이 카펫의 색은 방과 ~ 을 이룬다 [~가 안 된다] The color of this carpet [is in harmony with (doesn't match) the room. / 이 두 색은 ~가 되지 않는다 These two colors do not go well together.

조회(朝會) ☞ 조례(朝禮).

조회(照會) (an) inquiry; (a) reference. ~하다 inquire 《of a person about something》; make inquiries 《as to》; apply (write, refer) 《to a person for information》. ¶ 서신으로 ~하다 send a letter of inquiry / ~중이다 be under inquiry / 그 상품에 관하여 제조회사에 ~했다 We 「made inquiry (inquired of) the maker about the goods. / 본사에 직접 ~해 주십시오 Please refer directly to our main office. / 저의 신원에 관하여는 김 교수님께 ~해 주십시오 Please refer me to Professor Kim. ‖ ~서신 a letter of inquiry / ~선(先) a reference.

족(足) ① 《소·돼지의》 beef or pork hock. ② 《켤레》 a pair 《of socks》.

…족(族) a tribe; a clan; a family. ¶ 티베트~ the Tibet tribe.

족두리 a headpiece worn by a bride at marriage.

족발(足―) 《돼지의》 pork hock.

족벌(族閥) a clan. ‖ ~정치 clan government / ~주의 nepotism.

족보(族譜) a genealogical record (table); a genealogy; a family pedigree; a family tree.

족생(簇生) ~하다 grow in clusters. ‖ ~식물 a social plant.

족속(族屬) relatives; clansmen.

족쇄(足鎖) fetters; shackles (for the feet). ¶ ~를 채우다 fetter; shackle.

족자(簇子) a hanging roll (scroll).

족장(族長) a tribal head; a patriarch.

족적(足跡) a footprint; footmarks. ¶ ~을 남기다 leave one's footmarks.

족제비 《動》 a weasel.

족쪽¹ 《옛는 모양》 (tear) to pieces (shreds); into shreds.

족쪽² 《마다》 every time; whenever; 《모두》 everything. ¶ 오는 ~ whenever one comes / 하는 ~ 모든 일이 잘 안 되었다 Whatever I tried was a failure.

족집게 (a pair of hair) tweezers.

족치다 ① 《줄여 작게 하다》 shorten; shrink; reduce the scale 《of》; 《쭈그러지게 하다》 squeeze to hollow. ② 《몹시 족대기다》 censure (reproach, torture) 《a person》 severely; question 《a person》 closely; grill; urge (press) 《a person to do》. ¶ 아무를 족쳐서 실토하게 하다 squeeze (extort) a confession from a person.

족친(族親) (distant) relatives.

족하다(足―) ① 《충분》 (be) enough; sufficient; 《동사적 용법》 suffice; will do; serve. ¶ 열 사람에게 족한 음식 sufficient food for ten / 생활하기에 족한 월급 enough salary to live on / 2천원이면 ~ Two thousand won will do. ② 《만족》 be satisfied (content) 《with》. ¶ 마음에 ~ be satisfactory.

족히(足―) enough; sufficiently; fully; well (worth). ¶ ~ 2마일 good 2 miles / ~ 볼만하다 be well worth seeing.

존 a zone. ‖ ~디펜스 zone defense / 스트라이크 ~ 《野》 a strike zone.

존경(尊敬) respect; esteem; reverence. ~하다 respect; honor; esteem; hold 《a person》 in respect; think highly (much) of; look up to. ¶ 나는 선생님을 매우 ~하고 있다 I deeply respect my teacher. / 그는 모두로부터 ~ 받고 있다 He is highly respected by everybody. / 내가 가장 ~하는 사

존귀 람은 나의 아버지이다 The person I have the highest regard for is my father. / 그는 ～할 만한 사람이다 He is an honorable man. *or* He deserves to be respected.

존귀(尊貴) nobility. ～하다 (be) high and noble.

존대(尊待) ～하다 treat with respect; hold 《*a person*》 in esteem. ¶ ～를 받다 be esteemed (respected). ‖ ～어 honorific words; a term of respect.

존득존득하다 (be) chewy; gummy; elastic; sticky; glutinous.

존망(存亡) life or death; existence; destiny; fate. ¶ 국가 ～지추에 in this time of national crisis / 그것은 국가 ～에 관한 문제였다 It was a life-or-death question for the nation.

존비(尊卑) the high and the low; the aristocrats and the plebeians. ‖ ～귀천 high and low; noble and mean.

존속(存續) continuance. ～하다 continue (to exist); last. ¶ ～시키다 continue; maintain; keep up. ‖ ～기간 a term of existence.

존속(尊屬) 【法】 an ascendant. ¶ 직계〔방계〕～ a lineal (collateral) ascendant. ‖ ～살해 parricide; the killing (murder) of a close relative.

존안(尊顔) your esteemed self. ¶ ～을 뵙다 have the honor of seeing you.

존엄(尊嚴) dignity; majesty. ¶ 법의 ～(성)을 지키다 protect the dignity of law / 인간의 ～을 지키다 protect the dignity of man. ‖ ～사 death with dignity.

존장(尊長) an elder; a senior.

존재(存在) existence; being; presence (어떤 장소에 있는 것). ～하다 exist; be in existence. ¶ 나는 신의 ～를 믿는다 I believe in (the existence of) God. / 그는 ～감이 있는 인물이다 He is a person who makes his presence felt. / 그는 이 분야에서 귀중한 ～이다 He is a valuable figure in this world. ‖ ～론 ontology / ～이유 the *raison d'être* (프); one's (it's) reason for existing (being).

존절하다 be frugal (thrifty). ¶ 돈을 존절히 쓰다 be economical of money. 「fine (close) weave.

존존하다 be finely woven; be of

존중(尊重) respect; esteem. ～하다 respect; esteem; value; have a high regard (for); estimable / 여론을 ～하다 have a high regard for public opinion / 법률을 ～하다 show respect for the law.

존체(尊體) your health.

존칭(尊稱) a title of honor; an honorific (title).

존폐(存廢) (the question of) maintenance (or abolition); existence. ¶ 우리 조직의 ～에 관해 토의하다 discuss whether we should maintain our organization or not.

존함(尊銜) your name.

졸(卒) 《장기의》 a Korean-chess pawn. ¶ ～을 잡다 take a pawn.

졸경치(르)다(卒更-) have bitter experiences; have a hard time of it. 「gummy.

졸깃졸깃하다 (be) chewy; sticky;

졸다¹ 《졸려서》 doze (off); fall into a doze; drowse. ¶ 신문을 읽으면서 ～ be dozing over the newspaper / 졸면서 열차가 움직이기 시작하는 것을 느꼈다 Half asleep, I felt the train start moving.

졸다² 《줄다》 shrink; contract; 《끓어서》 be boiled dry; get boiled down.

졸도(卒倒) a faint; a swoon; fainting. ～하다 faint; swoon; fall unconscious.

졸때기 ① 《작은 일》 a small-scale affair; a petty job. ②《사람》 a petty person; a small fry. ¶ ～공무원 a petty official.

졸라매다 fasten tight(ly); tie (bind) 《*something*》 fast; tighten (up). ¶ 허리띠를 ～ tighten up one's belt.

졸렬(拙劣) ～한 poor; clumsy; unskillful / ～한 방법 a poor method / ～한 문장 a crude style of writing.

졸리다 《남에게》 get pestered (importuned) 《by》; be teased (urged, pressed) 《by》. 「(fastened).

졸리다 《매어지다》 be tightened

졸리다 《잠오다》 feel (be) sleepy (drowsy). ¶ 졸린 강의 a dull lecture / 졸린 눈을 비비다 rub one's drowsy eyes / 그 음악을 들으면 졸립다 I become sleepy as I listen to the music. 「sizes.

졸막졸막하다 be of various small

졸망졸망 ① 《울퉁불퉁》 ～한 uneven; rough. ②《자잘한》 ～한 물건들 things small and irregular in size / 한 떼의 ～한 아이들 a bunch of different-aged children.

졸문(拙文) a poor writing; 《자기의 글》 my (unworthy) writing (경손의 뜻으로). 「private.

졸병(卒兵) a (common) soldier;

졸부(猝富) an upstart; the newly rich (집합적). ¶ ～가 되다 suddenly get (become) rich / 전쟁으로 〔토지 거래로〕 된 ～ a war (land) profiteer (millionaire).

졸속(拙速) ～의 rough-and-ready; knocked-up; hasty / ～ 공사의

관행 the faster-the-better construction practices. ¶ ~주의 a rough-and-ready method (rule).
졸아들다 shrink; contract; 〔끓어서〕 be boiled down (dry).
졸업(卒業) graduation. ~하다 graduate (be graduated) 《from》; complete a course. ¶ 남자〔여자〕대학~생 a male (female) university graduate / 고교~생 a senior high school graduate / 대학을 갓~한 청년 a young man fresh from college / 중학교를 ~ 하다 complete the junior high school course / K대학을 우등으로 ~하다 graduate from K University with honors. / ~논문 a graduation thesis / ~시험 a graduation examination / ~식 the commencement (exercises) 〔美〕 / ~장〔증서〕a diploma 〔美〕 / ~정원제 the graduation quota system.
졸음(-) drowsiness; sleepiness. ¶ ~이 오다 feel drowsy (sleepy) / ~을 쫓으려고 진한 커피를 마시다 drink strong coffee in order to "keep awake (banish sleep).
졸이다 ① 〔마음을〕 worry *oneself*; be nervous (uneasy, anxious) about. ② 〔끓여서〕 boil down (hard).
졸작(拙作) ① 〔졸렬한〕 a poor work; trash. ② ☞ 졸저(拙著).
졸장부(拙丈夫) a man of small caliber; an illiberal fellow.
졸저(拙著) my humble work; my book.
졸졸(-) murmuring; tricklingly; 〔따라다님〕 (follow *a person*) persistently; tagging along. ¶ 물이 ~ 흐른다 Water trickles. / 그녀는 나를 ~ 따라다녔다 She followed me about (tagged along with me) persistently.
졸중(卒中) 〔醫〕 apoplexy.
졸지에(猝地-) suddenly; all of a sudden; unexpectedly. ¶ ~ 사고를 당하다 have an accident all of a sudden.
졸책(拙策) a poor plan (policy).
졸필(拙筆) bad (poor) handwriting; a poor hand. ¶ 그는 ~이다 He has bad handwriting.
좀¹ 〔蟲〕 a clothes moth; a bookworm; a silverfish. ¶ ~이 먹은 책 a worm-eaten book / …하고 싶어 ~이 쑤시다 〔비유적으로〕 itch (have an itch) 《for action》 / 소년은 영어를 써먹고 싶어 ~이 쑤셨다 The boy was itching to use his English.
좀² ① 〔조금〕 a bit; a little; a few; some; somewhat. ¶ 피로하다 be somewhat weary / 달걀이 냉장고에 ~ 있다 There are a few

〔some〕 eggs in the refrigerator. / 나는 영어를 ~ 말할 수 있다 I can speak English a little. ② 〔제발〕 just; please. ¶ 내일 ~ 오너라 Please come tomorrow.
좀³ 〔사람〕 a small mind; a petty person. ② 〔물건〕 small things; trifles.
좀더 〔양〕 a little more; 〔수〕 a few more; 〔시간〕 a little longer.
좀도둑 〔사람〕 a sneak (petty) thief; a pilferer. ¶ ~질하다 pilfer; filch; snitch 〔美口〕.
좀먹다 ① 〔벌레가〕 be (get) motheaten. ② 〔서서히 나쁘게 하다〕 undermine; spoil; affect. ¶ 동심을 ~ spoil the child's mind / 수면 부족은 건강을 좀먹는다 Lack of sleep affects (ruins) your health. / 부패 (행위)가 나라의 심장부를 좀먹고 있다 Corruption is eating at the heart of the country.
좀스럽다 〔마음이〕 (be) small-minded; petty. ¶ 좀스럽게 굴다 be too meticulous. ② 〔규모가〕 (be) small; trifling.
좀약 a mothball.
좀처럼 rarely; seldom; hardly; scarcely. ¶ 그는 ~ 앓지 않는다 He is seldom ill. / ~ 그를 만나지 않는다 I rarely meet him. / 이런 기회는 ~ 오지 않는다 Such opportunities "do not occur every day 〔seldom occur〕. / ~ 여행할 기회가 없다 I hardly get a chance to take a trip. / 「버스는 ~ 오지 않는군 그래.」—「그렇군, 택시라도 잡을까」 "The bus is long (in coming, isn't it?" — "Yes, shall we catch a taxi?"
좀팽이 a petty little person.
좁다 〔폭·범위가〕 (be) narrow; 〔면적이〕 (be) small; limited 〔한정된〕; 〔갑갑하게〕 (be) tight; 〔도량 따위가〕 (be) narrow-minded; illiberal. ¶ 좁은 복도 a narrow corridor / 좁은 집 a small house / 좁은 바지 tight trousers / 그는 시야가 ~ He has a narrow view of things. *or* He is short-sighted. / 나는 교제 범위가 ~ I have a small circle of acquaintances. / 국제 정세에 관한 그의 지식은 ~ His knowledge about the international situation is quite limited. / 세상은 ~ It is a small world. / 그는 도량이 ~ He is narrow-minded.
좁다랗다 (be) narrow and close; rather narrow; narrowish.
좁쌀 hulled millet; 〔비유적〕 petty. ¶ ~뱅이 a petty person / ~영감 a petty old man.
좁쌀풀 〔植〕 a loosestrife.
좁히다 〔줄게〕 narrow; reduce 《the width》.
종 (奴婢) a servant; a slave.

종(種) ① [生] a species. ¶ ~의 기원 the Origin of Species. ② ☞ 종류. ¶ 3종 우편 third-class mail. ③ 〔품종〕 a breed, a stock (소·말의); 《종자》 a seed. ¶ 몽골종의 말 a horse of Mongolian breed. ‖ ~견(犬)〔돈(豚)〕 a breeding dog(pig).

종(鐘) a bell; a handbell(손 종); a gong (징); a doorbell (현관의). ¶ ~을 울리다〔치다〕 ring〔strike, toll〕 a bell. ‖ ~각(閣) a bell house; a belfry / ~소리 a sound of a bell / ~지기 a bell ringer.

종가(宗家) the head family (house).

종가세(從價稅) an ad valorem duty.

종결(終結) a conclusion; an end; a close. ~하다 end; terminate; come to an end〔a close〕; be concluded. ¶ 전쟁 ~의 교섭을 개시하다 begin negotiations for an end to the war / 소유권에 관한 쟁의가 ~됐다 The dispute over ownership came to an end.

종곡(終曲) [樂] the finale.

종교(宗敎) (a) religion; (a) religious faith. ¶ ~상의 religious / ~를 믿다 believe in a religion / ~적 의식 a religious ceremony / 신흥 ~ a new religion / 기존의 ~ the established religions / 나는 무 ~다 I don't have any particular religion. ¶ ~가 a man of religion / ~개혁 the Reformation / ~계 the religious world / ~단체 a religious body〔organization〕/ ~법인 a religious corporation / ~음악 sacred music / ~재판 [史] the Inquisition / ~학 the science of religion; theology (신학) / ~화(畵) a religious picture.

종국(終局) an end; a close; a final; a conclusion. ¶ ~의 final; ultimate; eventual / ~에 가서는 ultimately; in the long run / ~을 고하다 come to an end.

종군(從軍) ~하다 join the army; go to the front. ‖ ~간호사 a (Red Cross) nurse attached to the army / ~기자 a war correspondent / ~기장(記章) a war medal / ~위안부 "comfort women" (attached to the army).

종굴박 a small gourd.

종국(終極) finality. ¶ ~의 final; ultimate. ☞ 마침내.

종기(終期) the end (of a term); the close; the termination.

종기(腫氣) a boil; a tumor; a blotch; a swell. ¶ 발에 ~가 났다 I have got a boil on my foot.

종내(終乃) at last〔length〕; finally; in the end. ☞ 마침내.

종다래끼 a small fishing basket.

종단(宗團) the religious order.

종단(縱斷) ~하다 cut〔divide〕《a thing》 vertically; 〔장소를〕 run through; traverse. ¶ 그 철도는 대평원을 ~하고 있다 The railroad runs through the prairie. / 그녀는 한국 ~ 여행을 계획하고 있다 She is planning to travel through Korea from North to South. ‖ ~면 a longitudinal〔vertical〕 section.

종달새 a skylark; a lark.

종답(宗畓) paddy fields set apart as provision for sacrificial purposes.

종대(縱隊) a column; a file. ¶ 4열 ~로 in column of fours / 2열 ~로 행진하다 march in file.

종래(從來) ~의 old; former; usual; customary / ~에는 up to now〔this time〕; so far / 대로 as usual; as in the past / ~의 판매 방법으로는 이 매상 목표를 달성할 수 없다 It is impossible to reach this sales goal with our customary sales methods. / 이것은 ~의 모델보다 사용하기가 훨씬 편하다 This is much easier to use than previous models.

종량세(從量稅) a specific duty.

종려(棕櫚) [植] a hemp palm. ‖ ~나무 a palm tree / ~유 palm oil.

종렬(縱列) a column; a file.

종료(終了) an end; a close; a conclusion. ~하다 (come to an) end; close; be over (concluded). ¶ 회의는 ~됐다 The conference came to an end.

종루(鐘樓) a bell tower; a belfry.

종류(種類) a kind; a sort; a class; a type; a variety. ¶ 이런 ~의 사람 a man of this type / 이런 ~의 범죄 crimes of this nature / 온갖 ~의 것 all kinds〔sorts〕 of things; things of every kind / 그는 여러가지 ~의 진귀한 우표를 내게 보여 주었다 He showed me rare varieties of stamps. / 나는 그 서류를 세 ~로 나눴다 I divided the papers in three classes. / 이것은 저것과 ~가 다르다 This is different from that in type.

종마(種馬) a breeding horse; a stallion.

종막(終幕) 〔연극의〕 the final act 《of a play》; 〔종말〕 an end; a close.

종말(終末) an end; a close; a conclusion. ¶ ~을 고하다 come〔be brought〕 to an end / ~이 다가오다 draw to a close〔an end〕.

종매(從妹) a younger female cousin.

종목(種目) items; 〔경기의〕 an event. ¶ 영업 ~ items of business / 수영 경기의 2 ~에서 우승하다 win two events at the swimming meet.

종묘(宗廟) the royal ancestors' shrine.

종묘(種苗) seeds and saplings; seedlings. ‖ ~장 a nursery (garden) / ~회사 a nursery company.

종물(從物)〖法〗an accessory 〔thing〕.

종반전(終盤戰)〖바둑 등의〗the end game;〖선거 등의〗the last stage 〔phase〕*(of an election campaign)*.

종범(從犯)〖法〗participation in a crime. ¶ 사전〔사후〕~ an accessory before 〔after〕 the fact. ‖ ~자 an accessory *(to a crime)*; an accomplice.

종별(種別) (a) classification. ~하다 classify; assort.

종복(從僕) a servant; an attendant.

종사(宗嗣) the heir of a main family.

종사(從死) ~하다 die in attendance on *(a person)*; follow *(a person)* to the grave.

종사(從事) ~하다 engage in 《business》; attend to 《one's work》; pursue 《a calling》; follow 《a profession》. ¶ ~하고 있다 be engaged in 《atomic research》; be at work 《on a new book》/ 그는 흥행업에 ~하고 있다 He is engaged in the show business.

종산(宗山) a family cemetery.

종서(縱書) ~하다 write vertically.

종선(縱線) a vertical line;〖樂〗a bar.

종속(從屬) subordination. ~하다 be subordinate 〔subject〕 *(to)*; be dependent *(on)*. ‖ ~적인 subordinate / 그 당시 대영 제국은 많은 나라들을 ~시켰다 The British Empire subordinated many countries at that time. ‖ ~구〔절〕 a subordinate phrase 〔clause〕/ ~국 a dependency.

종손(宗孫) the eldest grandson of the main family.

종손(從孫) a grandnephew.

종손녀(從孫女) a grandniece.

종시속(從時俗) ~하다 follow the customs of the day.

종식(終熄) cessation; an end. ~하다 cease; come to an end; end. ¶ ~시키다 put an end 〔a stop〕 to *(a war)*.

종신(終身) ①《한평생》 all one's life. ¶ ~의 lifelong; for life. ‖ ~ 제도 the lifetime 〔lifelong〕 employment system / ~연금 a life pension / ~직 a life office; an office for life / ~형 life imprisonment 〔sentence〕/ ~ 회원 a life member. ②《임종》~하다 be at *(one's parent's)* deathbed.

종실(宗室) a Royal family.

종심(終審) the final trial.

종씨(宗氏) a clansman (of the same surname).

종씨(從氏) my 〔your〕 elder cousin;

a paternal cousin of *a person*.

종아리 the calf (of the leg). ¶ ~를 맞다 get whipped on the calf / ~를 때리다 lash 〔whip〕 *(a person)* on the calf. 〔*to oneself*〕.

종알거리다 murmur *(at)*; mutter to oneself.

종양(腫瘍)〖醫〗a tumor. ¶ 뇌~ a cerebral tumor / 악성〔양성〕~ a malignant 〔benign〕 tumor.

종언(終焉) an end; a close. ¶ ~을 고하다 end; come to an end.

종업(從業) ~하다 be employed; be in the service. ‖ ~시간 working hours / ~원 a worker; an employee / ~원 교육 the training of employees; employee education 〔training〕/ ~원 전용입구 a staff 〔an employees'〕 entrance.

종업(終業)《일의》finishing 〔the end of〕 work;《학교의》the close of school 〔term〕. ~하다 end 〔finish〕 one's work. ‖ ~시간 the closing hour / ~식 the closing ceremony.

종연(終演) the end of a show. ~하다 end; finish; close 〔*the theater, the performance*〕. ¶ 오후 10시 ~ The curtain falls at 10 p.m.

종요롭다 (be) important; essential.

종용(慫慂) ~하다 advise; persuade; suggest. ¶ 아무의 ~으로 at *(a person's)* suggestion / 경찰에 자수할 것을 ~하다 advise *(a person)* to surrender *oneself* to the police.

종우(種牛) a (seed) bull.

종유동(鍾乳洞) a stalactite grotto 〔cavern〕.

종유석(鍾乳石)〖鑛〗stalactite.

종이 paper. ¶ ~ 한 장〔연〕 a sheet 〔ream〕 of paper / 면이 거친〔매끄러운〕 ~ rough 〔slick〕 paper / 얇은〔두꺼운〕~ thin 〔thick〕 paper / ~에 싸다 wrap in thin 〔thick〕 paper / ~에 쓰다 write 《something》on paper / ~처럼 얇게 자르다 slice 《a thing》paper thin / ~를 접다〔펼치다〕 fold 〔unfold〕 paper / 양자의 차이는 한 장 차이다 The difference between them is very slight. ‖ ~기저귀 a disposable diaper / ~꾸러미 a paper parcel / ~냅킨 a paper napkin / ~봉지 a paper bag 〔sack〕/ ~부스러기 waste paper / ~컵 a paper cup / ~테이프 a paper tape; a paper streamer 〔환영·환송용의〕/ ~표지 a paper cover / ~호랑이 a paper tiger.

종일(終日) all day (long); the whole day; throughout the day; from morning till 〔to〕 night.

종자(宗子) the eldest son of the head family.

종자(從者) an attendant; a follower; a retinue (수행자).

종자(種子) a seed. ☞ 씨.
종자매(從姉妹) female cousins.
종작없다 (be) desultory; rambling; pointless; absurd. ¶ 종작없는 생각에 잠기다 indulge in wandering speculation / 종작없는 말을 하다 talk in a rambling way.
종잡다 get the gist 《of》; get a rough idea 《of》; get the point 《of》; roughly understand. ¶ 종잡을 수 없다 cannot get the gist [grasp the point] of; be unable to figure 《it》 out.
종장(終場) 〖證〗 closing. ‖ ~ 가격[시세] the closing price [quotations].
종적(蹤跡) ¶ ~을 감추다 disappear; cover one's tracks; leave no trace behind.
종전(從前) ¶ ~과 의 관계 one's past relations 《to a person》 / ~과 같다 be the same as before.
종전(終戰) the end of the war. ¶ ~ 후의 postwar / ~이 되다 the war comes to an end. ‖ ~일 the anniversary of the end of the Pacific War.
종점(終點) 〖철도 등의〗 the terminal (station); 〖美〗 the end of the line; 〖버스의〗 the bus terminal; the last stop. ¶ 여기가 ~입니다 This is the last stop. / 이 선의 ~은 부산이다 The terminal on this line is Pusan.
종제(從弟) a (younger) cousin.
종조모(從祖母) a grandaunt.
종조부(從祖父) a granduncle.
종족(宗族) a family; a clan.
종족(種族) 〖인종〗 a race; a tribe; 《동식물의》 a family; a species. ¶ ~ 간의 intertribal; interracial 《민족간의》 / ~ 보존의 본능 the instinct of preservation of the species / ~을 퍼뜨리다 spread 《their》 kind.
종종(種種) ① 《가지가지》 various [different] kinds. ② 《가끔》 《every》 now and then; occasionally; often; frequently. ¶ ~ 친구를 찾다 visit a friend now and then / ~ 놀러 오십시오 Please come and see us often.
종종걸음 short and quick steps; a quick pace; hurried [mincing] steps. ¶ ~ 치다 walk with hurried steps.
종주(宗主) a suzerain. ‖ ~국 a suzerain state / ~권 suzerainty.
종중(宗中) the families of the [same clan].
종지 a small cup (bowl).
종지(宗旨) the fundamental meaning; the main purport; a tenet; principles.
종지부(終止符) ☞ 마침표. ¶ ~를 찍다 put an end [a period] 《to》.
종지뼈 the kneecap; the patella.
종질(從姪) a cousin's son. [ter.
종질녀(從姪女) a cousin's daugh-
종착역(終着驛) a terminal (station); a terminus 《pl. -ni, -es》. ¶ 인생의 ~ the terminus of one's life.
종축(種畜) breeding stock. ‖ ~장 a breeding stock farm.
종친(宗親) the royal family.
종탑(鐘塔) a bell tower; a belfry.
종파(宗派) 《종교상의》 a 《religious》 sect; a denomination. 《종가의 계통》 the main branch of a family [clan]. ¶ 당신은 무슨 ~입니까 What denomination are you? ‖ ~심 sectarianism / ~싸움 a sectarian strife.
종합(綜合) synthesis; generalization. ~하다 synthesize; generalize. ¶ ~적인 synthetic; general; all-round / ~적으로 synthetically; generally / ~해서 생각하다 think collectively / ~적으로 검토한 결과, 당 위원회는 그의 제안을 받아들이기로 했다 Taking every factor into consideration, this committee decided to accept his proposal. ‖ ~경기 combined exercise; all-round games / ~계획 an overall plan / 과세 consolidated taxation / ~대학 a university / ~병원 a general hospital / ~상사 a general trading company / ~생활기록부 comprehensive high school records / ~소득세 a composite income tax / ~예술 a synthetic art / ~잡지 a general (interest) [all-round] magazine.
종형(從兄) an elder cousin.
종형제(從兄弟) cousins.
종횡(縱橫) ~으로 lengthwise and crosswise; 《사방팔방으로》 in all directions; in every direction / 그는 ~무진으로 활약하고 있다 He is acting vigorously. / 많은 도로가 도시 중심로부터 ~으로 뻗어 있다 Many roads extend out from the center of the town.
좇다 ① 《뒤를》 follow; go with; accompany 《동반》. ¶ 그를 좇아가다 follow [accompany] him / 시대 흐름을 ~ go with the tide. ② 《따르다》 follow; conform oneself to; act on. ¶ 유행을 〔선례를〕 ~ follow the fashion 〔a precedent〕 / 관습을 좇아서 행동하다 act in conformity with custom / 원칙을 좇아 행하다 act on a principle. ③ 《복종》 obey; be obedient to 《a person》; give in to 《a person's view》. ¶ 부모님 말씀을 ~ obey (be obedient to) one's parents.
좋다 ① 《양호》 (be) good (비교급 better; 최상급 best); fine; nice.

¶**좋은 집[책]** a good house [book] / **좋은 날씨** good [fine, nice] weather / **좋든 나쁘든** for better or (for) worse / **좋은 소식을 주실 것을 기대하고 있습니다** I'm looking forward to hearing good news from you. / **한국 자동차는 품질이 ~** Korean cars are of good quality. / **네 차는 내 것보다 ~** Your car is better than mine. / **이 문제를 해결하는 가장 좋은 방법은 무엇이냐** What is the best way to solve this problem? / **그는 건강이 좋아 보인다** He looks fine. / **이 수프는 맛이 참 ~** This soup tastes very nice. ② (적당) (be) right; good; fit; proper; suitable. ¶**좋은 기회** a good opportunity / **마침 좋은 때에** just at the right time / **네가 영어를 사용할 좋은 기회이다** It's a good opportunity to use your English. ③ (귀중) (be) precious; valuable. ¶**좋은 자료** valuable material. ④ (운) (be) lucky; fortunate. ¶**좋은 징조는** a good omen / **운이 ~ 는** be lucky. ⑤ (효용) (be) good; beneficial; efficacious ¶**몸에 ~** be good for the health. ⑥ (용이) (be) easy. ¶**읽기 좋은** easy to read. ⑦ (친밀) (be) intimate; friendly. ¶**사이가 ~** be on good [intimate] terms 《*with*》; be good friends 《*with*》 / **김군과 남군은 사이가 ~** Kim and Nam are good friends. ⑧ (…해도 괜찮다) may; can. ¶**가도 ~** You may go. / **이것 가져도 좋습니까** Can I have this? ⑨ (…이 낫다) had better 《*do*》. ¶**그런 짓은 하지 않는 것이 ~** You had better not do such a thing. ⑩ (소원) ¶**…이면 좋겠다** I wish though….
좋다 (느낌) Good!; Well!; All right!; (O.K.); (환성) Whoopee!; Oh boy!; Whee!
좋아지다 ① (상태가) improve; become [get] better; take a turn for the better. (날씨가) clear up. ¶**그의 병은 곧 좋아질 것이다** He will get well [better] soon. / **날씨는 차차 좋아지고 있다** The weather is improving. / **대미 수출도 서서히 좋아질 것으로 예상됩니다** Exports to the U.S. are expected to pick up by degrees. ② (좋아하게 되다) get [come] to like 《*a thing*》; become [grow] fond of; take a fancy [liking] to. ¶**나는 수학이 점점 좋아졌다** I've come to like math.
좋아하다 ① (기뻐하다) be pleased [amused, delighted, glad]. ¶**뛰며 ~** dance with joy / **그녀는 그 소식을 듣고 좋아했다** She was glad to hear the news. ② (사랑) love; 《기호》like; 《선택》prefer. ¶**좋아하는 책** *one's* favorite book / **나는 맥주보다 와인을 좋아한다** I prefer wine to beer. *or* I like wine better than beer.
좋이 well; good; full(y); enough. ¶**~ 10마일** a good ten miles / **~ 70은 넘다** be well over seventy.
좋지 않다 ① (불량) (be) inferior; foul. ~ **날씨** bad weather / **품질이 ~** be of inferior quality / **머리가 ~** be dull [stupid]. ② (도덕상) (be) bad; evil; wrong. ¶**좋지 않은 행위** a wrong; an evil deed / **그는 좋은 일과 좋지 않은 일을 구별하지 못한다** He doesn't know what is right and what is wrong. *or* He can't tell right from wrong. ③ (악하다) (be) bad; evil; wicked. ¶**좋지 않은 사람** a wicked man; a rascal. ④ (해롭다) (be) bad; harmful; detrimental; unadvisable. ¶**눈에 ~** be bad for the eyes. (기분·건강 등이) (be) ill; unwell. ¶**위가 ~** have a weak stomach / **기분이 ~** feel unwell. (불길) (be) ill; unlucky. ¶**좋지 않은 징조** ill omen. ¶**~** turn [face]!
좌(左) (the) left. ¶**~ 향** ~ Left
좌(座) a seat.
좌경(左傾) an inclination to the left; radicalization. **~ 하다** incline to the left; turn leftish. **~ (인)** leftist(-leaning); radical; Red. ‖ **~ 문학** leftist literature / **~ 분자** a radical [leftist] element / **~ 사상** leftist [radical] thoughts.
좌고우면(左顧右眄) **~ 하다** be irresolute; vacillate; waver; sit on the fence.
좌골(坐骨) 《解》 the hipbone; the ischium. ‖ **~ 신경** the sciatic nerves / **~ 신경통** hip gout; sciatica.
좌기(左記) ¶**~ 의** undermentioned; the following / **~ 와 같이** as follows.
좌담(座談) a (table) talk; a conversation. **~ 하다** converse with; exchange a talk. ‖ **~ 회** a round-table talk; a discussion meeting.
좌르르 with a rush [splash]. ¶**물이 ~ 쏟아진다** Water comes rushing out.
좌변기(坐便器) 《양변기》 a stool-type flush toilet.
좌불안석(坐不安席) **~ 하다** be ill at ease; be unable to sit comfortably 《*from anxiety*》.
좌상(坐像) a seated figure [image].
좌상(座上) the elder in a company.
좌석(座席) 《자리》 a seat. ¶**앞[뒤] ~** a front [back, rear] seat / **창가[통로 쪽의] ~** a window [an

aisle seat / ~을 예약하다 book (reserve) a seat (*in a theater*) / ~을 양보하다 offer (give) one's seat to (*an old man*). ‖ ~권 a reserved-seat ticket / 만원 (게시) Standing Room Only (생략 SRO). / ~ 배치도 the (theater) seat-plan / 버스 a seat bus / ~번호 the seat number / ~수 seating capacity / ~조절용 레버 a seat adjustment lever.

좌선 (坐禪) Zen meditation. ~하다 sit in Zen meditation.

좌시 (坐視) ~하다 remain an idle spectator; look on idly (unconcernedly). ¶ 차마 ~할 수 없다 cannot remain an idle spectator

좌안 (左岸) the left bank. └(*of*).

좌약 (坐藥) 〖醫〗 a suppository; a bougie. 「(pitcher); a lefty.

좌완투수 (左腕投手) 〖野〗 a southpaw

좌우 (左右) right and left. ~하다 control; dominate; sway (지배); influence (영향); decide (결정). ¶ 도로의 ~에 on 「either side (both sides) of the road / 길을 건너기 전에 ~를 잘 살펴라 Look 「right and left (both ways) carefully before you cross the street. / 인간은 환경에 ~되기 쉽다 Man is easily influenced by his surroundings. / 단 한 번의 체험이 사람의 일생을 ~하는 경우도 있다 Only one experience may decide a person's fate. ‖ at any rate.

좌우간 (左右間) anyhow; anyway;

좌우명 (座右銘) a favorite maxim (motto). 「wings.

좌우익 (左右翼) the left and right

좌익 (左翼) the left wing; (사람) the leftists. ‖ ~ 분자 a left-wing element / ~수 〖野〗 a left fielder / ~운동 a left movement.

좌절 (挫折) a setback; frustration; a breakdown; collapse; failure. ~하다 fail; be frustrated; break down; collapse. ¶ 계획이 ~되었다 Our plan 「broke down (collapsed). / 계획의 ~로 그는 자신감을 잃었다 The collapse of his plan caused him to lose confidence. ‖ ~감 (a sense of) frustration.

좌정 (坐定) ~하다 sit; be seated.

좌지우지 (左之右之) ~하다 have (*a person*) at one's beck and call; twist (*a person*) round one's little finger.

좌천 (左遷) (a) demotion; (a) relegation. ~하다 demote (*to*); relegate (*to*). ¶ ~되다 be demoted (relegated) / 그는 지방의 지점으로 ~되었다 He was demoted to a post in a local branch.

좌초 (坐礁) ~하다 run on a rock; run aground; strand. ¶ ~한 배 a stranded ship.

좌충우돌 (左衝右突) ~하다 dash this way and rush that; plunge forward on this side and dash in on that.

좌측 (左側) the left (side). ‖ ~통행 《게시》 Keep to the left.

좌파 (左派) the left wing; the left faction (*of a party*); (사람) the left wingers; the leftists. ¶ ~의 leftist; left-wing.

좌판 (坐板) a board to sit on.

좌편 (左便) the left side.

좌표 (座標) 〖數〗 coordinates.

좌향 (左向) ¶ ~ 좌 《구령》 Left turn (face)! / ~ 앞으로 가 《구령》 Left wheel!

좌현 (左舷) (on the) port (side). ¶ ~으로 기울다 list to port.

좌회전 (左廻轉) a turn to the left. ~하다 turn (to the) left; make a left (*at*). ¶ ~금지 《교통 표지》 No left turn.

좍 broadly; extensively. ¶ 소문이 ~ 퍼지다 a rumor runs abroad.

좍좍 ① (쏟아짐) (it rains) in torrents; heavily. ¶ 비가 ~ 퍼붓는다 It's raining cats and dogs. *or* The rain is pouring down. ② (글을) with ease; fluently. ¶ 글을 ~ 읽다 read 「with ease (eloquently).

좔좔 with a gush (rush); (flow) freely. ¶ 물이 ~ 흐르다 water runs

좽이 a casting net. └freely.

죄 (罪) 〖형법상의〗 a crime; an offense (가벼운); guilt; 〖종교·도덕상의〗 a sin; guilt; 〖형벌〗 a punishment; 〖책임〗 blame. ¶ ~의식에 시달리고 있는 사람 guilt-ridden people / ~ (가) 있는 guilty; blamable; sinful / ~ 없는 not guilty; blameless; innocent / ~를 범하다 commit a crime / ~를 자백하다 confess one's crime (guilt) / ~가 없음이 판명되다 turn out to be innocent (not guilty) / 〖정신적인〗 ~의 값을 치르다 atone for one's sin / ~를 면하다 escape (elude) punishment; be acquitted of the charge (법정에서) / 그 사고는 그의 ~가 아니다 He is not to be blamed for the accident. / ~를 짓을 하다 do a cruel (wicked) thing.

죄과 (罪科) an offense; a crime.

죄과 (罪過) an offense; a sin(죄악); a fault(과오).

죄다[1] ① (바짝) tighten (up); strain; stretch. ¶ 나사를 ~ tighten up a bolt. ② (마음을) feel anxious (uneasy, nervous, tense). ¶ 결과가 어찌 될까 마음을 ~ be worried over the result.

죄다[2] (모두) all; entirely; every-

죄명(罪名) a charge. ¶…으로 기소되다 be on a charge of 《fraud》 / 그는 사기 ~으로 기소되었다 He was indicted on a charge of fraud. or He was charged with fraud.

죄받다(罪-) suffer [incur] punishment; be [get] punished.

죄상(罪狀) the nature of a crime; guilt. ¶ ~을 조사하다 inquire into 《a person's》 guilt / ~의 정도에 따라 according to the degree of culpability / ~을 인정[부인]하다 plead guilty[not guilty] to a criminal charge.

죄송(罪悚) 《~하다》 be sorry 《for》; regret. ¶ ~합니다 I beg your pardon. or I am sorry.

죄수(罪囚) a prisoner; a jailbird.

죄악(罪惡) 《종교상》 a sin; a vice; 《법률상》 a crime. ¶ ~시하다 consider 《a thing》 as a sin / 시간의 낭비는 일종의 ~이다 Waste of time is a sort of sin. /~감 the sense of sin [guilt].

죄어들다 get tightened [drawn up]. ¶ 피부가 ~ one's skin is drawn up / 수사망이 ~ the dragnet moves in.

죄어치다 《바짝》 tighten; 《재촉》 press; urge; rush; dun.

죄업(罪業) 《佛》 sins. ¶ ~을 쌓다 commit many sins.

죄의식(罪意識) be anxious [uneasy].

죄인(罪人) a criminal; an offender; a culprit; a sinner;《종교상》.

죄증(罪證) proofs [evidence] of a crime. 〔교상〕 commit a sin.

죄짓다(罪-) commit a crime; 《종**죄책**(罪責) liability for a crime [an offense]. ¶ ~감을 느끼다 feel guilty; feel a sense of guilt.

죔쇠 a clamp; a clasp; a vise; **죔틀** a vise. 　　　　　　 a buckle.

주(主) ① 《천주》 the Lord. ② 《주장·근본》 the main [chief] part; the principal part. ¶ ~가 되는《주된》 main; chief; principle / ~로 ☞ 주로.

주(州) 《행정 구획》 a province; 《미국의》 a State. ¶ ~립 (대학) 《주》주 《大陸》 a continent. 　　　[립.

주(株) ① 《주식》 a share; a stock;《美》. 성장주 a growth stock / 우량~ gilt-edged stocks / 우선~ preferred stocks / ~에 손을 대다 speculate in stocks / 안전한 ~에 투자하다 invest one's money in a safe stock / 그는 ~《증권》매매로 큰 돈을 벌었다 [잃었다] He made [lost] a lot of money on the stock market. ② 《그루》 ¶ 나무 한 ~ a tree.

주(註) annotations; explanatory notes. ¶ ~을 달다 annotate.
                                    [make note on.
주(週) a week.

주가(株價) stock prices. ¶ ~가 오르다 《주식의》 rise in stock price; stocks rise in price;《사람의》 rise in public estimation; gain in 《a person's》 estimation / ~를 조작하다 manipulate stock prices. /~지수 the price index of stocks /종합~지수 the composite stock exchange index / 평균~ stock price average.　　　　[editor.

주간(主幹) the chief [managing]

주간(週刊) weekly publication. ¶ ~의 weekly. /~지 a weekly (magazine).

주간(週間) a week. ¶ 교통 안전 ~ Traffic Safety Week / 3~에 걸쳐 over [for] three weeks / 지금부터 2~ 후에 two weeks from today. ¶ ~일기예보 a weather forecast for the coming week.

주간(晝間) daytime; day. ¶ ~에 in the daytime / ~의 더위 the heat of the daytime.

주객(主客) 《주인과 손》 host and guest; 《사물》 principal and subsidiary [auxiliary]. ¶ ~이 전도되다 put the cart before the horse.

주객(酒客) a drinker; a tippler.

주거(住居) a 《dwelling》 house; a residence. ¶ ~를 서울로 옮기다 remove one's residence to Seoul / ~를 정하다 settle down 《in》; fix one's residence 《in the country》. / ~면적 living space / ~비 housing expenses / ~지역 a residential area [district] / ~침입 homebreaking; violation of domicile.

주걱 a large wooden spoon; a rice scoop.

주검 (屍體) a dead body; a corpse.

주격(主格) 《文》 the nominative [subjective] case.

주견(主見) 《의견》 one's own opinion [view]; a fixed view.

주경야독(晝耕夜讀) 《~하다》 spend the days in the fields and the nights at one's books.

주고받다 give and take; exchange. ¶ 편지를 ~ exchange letters.

주공(住公) 《주택공사》. ¶ ~ 아파트 the KNHC-built apartment.

주공(鑄工) a cast-iron worker.

주관(主管) 《~하다》 manage; be in charge 《of》; superintend; supervise. ¶ ~사항 matters in one's charge.

주관(主觀) subjectivity. ¶ ~적(으로) subjective(ly) / ~을 쉽지 말고 설명하시오 Explain it without being subjective. /~적인 판단을 해서는 안 된다 We should not judge things subjectively. ¶ ~론·주관주의 subjectivism / ~식 문제 a subjective question / ~화 subjecti-

주광색(晝光色) ∥ ~전구 a daylight lamp.
주교(主敎)《성직자》 a bishop. ¶ ~ an archbishop.
대교(大敎) a pontoon bridge.
주구(走狗)《앞잡이》 a tool; a cat's-paw. ¶공산당의 ~ a mere tool of communists.
주권(主權) sovereignty. ¶ ~ 재민(在民) The Sovereignty rests with the people. / ~을 침해《존중》하다 violate《respect》the sovereignty《of》. ∥ ~국 a sovereign state / ~자 the sovereign; the ruler.
주권(株券) a share《stock》certificate. ¶기명 ~ a registered share / 무기명 ~ a share certificate to bearer.
주근깨 freckles; flecks.
주금(鑄金) casting. 「sorial birds.
주금류(走禽類)［鳥］runners; cur-
주급(週給) weekly wage(s)《pay》. ¶ ~이 200달러이다 get 200 dollars a week in wages; get wages of 200 dollars a week.
주기(酒氣) the smell of alcohol《liquor》. ¶ ~가 있다 be under the influence of liquor; be intoxicated.
주기(週期) a periodic; a cycle. ¶ ~적인 cyclical; periodic(al) / ~적으로 periodically / 경기의 ~ a business cycle / ~적으로 증감을 되풀이하다 have cyclic ups and downs. ∥ ~성 periodicity / ~율 the periodic law / ~율표［化］the periodic table (of the elements).
주기도문(主祈禱文)［基］the Lord's Prayer.
주년(周年) an anniversary. ¶5 ~ the fifth anniversary. 「timid.
주눅들다 lose one's nerve; feel
주눅좋다(be) shameless; unabashed; brazen-faced.
주니어 a junior.
주다 ①《일반적으로》give; present《수여》; award《상을》; feed《먹이를》. ¶환자에게 약을 ~ give medicine to a patient / 닭에게 모이를 ~ feed the chickens / 그녀에게 금메달이 주어졌다 She was presented《with》a gold medal. / 그 학생에게 장학금이 주어졌다 The student was awarded a scholarship. ②《공급·제공하다》supply; provide. ¶주어진 시간 안에 일을 ~ provide work《for a person》/ 그에겐 연구를 위한 온갖 편의가 주어지고 있다 He was supplied with all sorts of facilities for his research. ③《효과·손해·영향 따위를》. ¶영향을 ~ affect; influence; have an effect《on》/ 그녀는 나에게 좋은 인상을 주었다 She made a good impression on me. / 그녀의 죽음은 나에게 큰 쇼크를 주었다 His death was a shock to me. / 태풍은 그 지방에 큰 피해를 주었다 The typhoon caused a lot of damage in the district. ④《할당하다》allot; assign. ¶숙제를 ~ assign homework《to students》/ 몫을 ~ allot a share《to a person》. ⑤《기타》¶5천 원을 주고 고기 한 파운드를 사다 pay 5,000 won for a pound of meat / 힘주어 말하다 emphasize one's words / 책을 사 ~ buy《a person》a book.
주단(綢緞) silks and satins.
주도(主導) ~하다 lead; assume leadership《of》. ¶민간 ~의 경제 private-initiated economy / ~적 역할을 하다 play a leading role《for》; play a leading part《in》. ∥ ~권 the initiative (~권을 잡다 take the initiative《leadership》《in》) / ~산업 a leading industry / ~자 the leader《of a movement》; the prime mover《in a revolt》.
주도하다(周到―) (be) careful; thorough; scrupulous; elaborate. ¶그는 무슨 일에나 용의 ~ He is scrupulously careful about everything.
주독(酒毒)《suffer from》alcohol poisoning.
주동(主動) leadership. ~하다 take the lead. ∥ ~자 the prime mover; the leader (~자가 되다 take the lead).
주둔(駐屯) stationing. ~하다 be stationed. ∥ ~군 stationary troops; a garrison《수비의》; an army of occupation《점령군》.
주둥이《입》the mouth;《부리》a bill; a beak;《물건의》a mouth-piece.
주란사(― 紗) cloth woven from gassed cotton thread.
주량(酒量) one's drinking capacity. ¶ ~이 크다 be a heavy drinker; drink much.
주렁주렁 in clusters. ¶《열매가》~ 달리다 hang in clusters.
주력(主力) the main force《body, strength》. ¶ ~을 집중하다 concentrate the main force《on》. ∥ ~부대 main-force units / ~산업 (the) key《major》industries / ~상품 key commodities / ~업종 a core《main》business / ~주 leading《key》stocks《shares》/ ~함대 the main fleet《squadron》.
주력하다(注力―) exert oneself《for》; concentrate one's effort《on》; devote oneself《to》.
주렴(珠簾) a bead curtain; a bead screen.
주례(主禮)《일》officiating at a wedding ceremony;《사람》an officiator. ∥ ~목사 an officiating

주로(主-) mainly; chiefly; principally; 《대개》 generally; mostly. ¶ ~ 여자에 의해 행해지다 be done mainly [chiefly] by women.

주로(走路) a track; a course.

주룩주룩 《비가》 ¶ ~ 오는 비 pouring rain.

주류(主流) the main current; the mainstream. ‖ ~ 파 the leading faction / 반 ~ 파 an anti-mainstream group.

주류(酒類) liquors; alcoholic beverages [drinks]. ‖ ~ 판매점 a liquor store.

주르륵 trickling; dribbling; running.

주름 《피부의》 wrinkles; lines; furrows; 《물건의》 creases; rumples; 《옷의》 a fold. ¶ ~ 진 얼굴 a wrinkled face / 이마에 ~ 을 짓다 crease one's forehead; knit one's brows; frown / ~ 을 펴다 smooth out / 그녀는 눈가에 ~이 생기기 시작하다 She is beginning to get crow's feet. / 이 옷감은 ~이 지지 않는다 This fabric won't wrinkle, or This fabric is wrinkle-free. ‖ ~ 상자 bellows.

주름잡다 ① pleat; crease; fold. ☞ 주름. ② 《지배》 wield power; dominate; gain control of (the market). ¶ 금융계를 ~ have a firm grip on the banking business.

주리다 《배를》 be [go] hungry; starve; be famished; 《갈망》 be hungry [thirsty] for [after]. ¶ 배를 주린 늑대의 무리 a pack of hungry wolves / 지식에 주려 있다 have a thirst for knowledge.

주리틀다 《형벌》 impose leg-screw torture; torture on the rack.

주립(州立) ‖ ~ 의 state(-established); provincial. ‖ ~ 대학 a state [provincial] university.

주마가편(走馬加鞭) ~ 하다 whip [lash] one's galloping horse; 《사람을》 inspire [urge] (a person) to further efforts.

주마간산(走馬看山) ~ 하다 take a cursory view (of); give a hurried glance (to, over).

주마등(走馬燈) a revolving lantern; a kaleidoscope. ¶ ~ 같은 ever changing [shifting]; kaleidoscopic / 여러가지 생각이 ~ 처럼 뇌리를 스쳤다 Many images came and went in my mind's eye.

주막(酒幕) an inn; a tavern.

주말(週末) the weekend. ‖ ~ 여행 a weekend trip / ~ 여행자 a weekender.

주머니 a bag; a sack; a pouch 《작은》; a pocket 《호주머니》. ¶ ~ 에 넣다 put (a thing) into one's pocket / ~ 에서 꺼내다 take (a thing) out of one's pocket.

주머니칼 a pocketknife.

주먹 a fist. ¶ ~ 을 쥐다 clench one's fist. / ~ 밥 a rice ball.

주먹구구(一九九) 《어림》 rule of thumb; a rough calculation.

주먹다짐 ~ 하다 strike (a person) with one's fist.

주먹질하다 exchange blows.

주명곡(奏鳴曲) 《樂》 a sonata.

주모(主謀) ~ 하다 take the lead; mastermind. ‖ ~ 자 a prime mover; a ringleader.

주모(酒母) 《술밑》 yeast; ferment; 《작부》 a barmaid.

주목(朱木) 《植》 a yew (tree).

주목(注目) attention; notice; observation. ~ 하다 pay attention to; watch; observe; take note [notice] of. ¶ ~ 할 만한 noteworthy; remarkable; significant / 세인의 ~ 을 끌다 attract public attention; hold the public eye.

주무(主務) ‖ ~ 관청 the competent authorities.

주무르다 ① 《물건을》 finger; fumble with; 《몸을》 massage. ¶ 어머니의 젖을 ~ finger one's mother's breast / 어깨를 ~ massage one's shoulder. ② 《농락》 have (a person) under one's thumb.

주문(主文) the text; 〔文〕 the principal clause.

주문(注文) ① ~ 하다 order 《new books from England》; give an order (for machines to America). ¶ ~ 을 받다 take [accept] orders / ~ 에 따라 만들다 make (a thing) to order / …의 ~ 이 많다 have a large order (for) / 이 상품의 ~ 이 점점 늘고 〔줄고〕 있다 Orders for this article have been increasing [falling off]. ‖ ~ 서 an order sheet / ~ 자 상표 부착생산 original equipment manufacturing 《생산 OEM》 / ~ 품 an article made to order; an article on order; an order. ② 《요구》 a request; a demand. ¶ 까다로운 ~ a delicate request / 그것은 무리이다 That's too much to ask, or That's a tall order.

주문(呪文) an incantation; a spell; a magic formula. ¶ ~ 을 외다 utter an incantation / ~ 을 걸다 chant a spell.

주물(鑄物) a casting; an article of cast metal. ‖ ~ 공장 a foundry.

주물럭거리다 finger; fumble with.

주미(駐美) ‖ ~ 의 stationed [resident] in America. ‖ ~ 한국대사 the Korean Ambassador to [in] the United States.

주민(住民) inhabitants; residents. ‖ ~ 등록 resident registration / ~ 등록번호 a resident registration number / ~ 등록증 a certifi-

주발(周鉢) a brass bowl.
주방(廚房) a kitchen; a cookroom; a cookery; a cuisine(호텔 등의). ‖ ~장 a head (chief) cook; a chef(프).
주번(週番) weekly duty. ‖ ~사관 an officer of the week.
주범(主犯) the main offender.
주법(走法) (a) form of running.
주법(奏法) 〖樂〗 a style of playing; execution.
주벽(酒癖) ¶ ~이 있다 turn nasty when drunk; be quarrelsome in one's cups.
주변 resourcefulness; versatility (융통성). ¶ ~이 있는 사람 a versatile person.
주변(周邊) (주위) a circumference; (도시 따위의) environs; outskirts. ¶ 도시 ~에 on (at, in) the outskirts of a city / 서울 및 그 ~에 in and around Seoul; in Seoul and its vicinity. ‖ ~기기(機器) (컴퓨터의) peripherals / ~단말장치(컴퓨터의) peripheral and terminal equipment.
주보(週報) (신문) a weekly (paper); (보고) a weekly report; (공보) a weekly bulletin.
주봉(主峰) the highest peak.
주부(主部) 〖文〗 the subject.
주부(主婦) a housewife.
주부코 a red bulbous nose.
주빈(主賓) the guest of honor; a principal guest.
주사(主事) (관리) a junior official; the clerical staff (총칭).
주사(朱砂) 〖鑛〗 cinnabar.
주사(走査) 〖TV〗 scanning. ‖ ~면 a scanning area / ~선 scanning lines.
주사(注射) (an) injection; a shot 《美俗》. ~하다 inject; give (a person) an injection. ¶ ~ 바늘 자국 a needle mark / 의사는 내 팔에 진통제 ~를 놨다 The doctor injected a pain-killing drug into my arm. ‖ ~기 a syringe; an injector / ~약 an injection.
주사(酒邪) ¶ ~가 있다 be a vicious drinker; be quarrelsome in one's cups.
주사위 a die 〔pl. dice〕. ¶ ~를 던지다 throw (cast) dice. ‖ ~놀이 a diceplay.
주산(珠算) abacus calculation; calculation on the abacus. ‖ ~경기 an abacus contest.
주산물(主産物) the principal (main, chief) products.
주산지(主産地) a chief producing district 《of》.
주상(主上) (임금) the Sovereign; His Majesty.
주색(酒色) ¶ ~에 빠지다 be addicted to sensual pleasures. ‖ ~잡기(雜技) wine, women and gambling. 〔ink〕; rubricate.
주서(朱書) ~하다 write in red
주석(主席) the head; the chief; the Chairman (중국의). ‖ ~국가 the head of a state.
주석(朱錫) tin. ‖ ~ 도금 tin plating / ~의 tin. / ~박(箔) tin foil / ~ 제품 tinware. 「산 tartaric acid.
주석(酒石) 〖化〗 crude tartar. ‖ ~
주석(酒席) (give) a feast; a banquet; a drinking party. ¶ ~을 베풀다 give a banquet.
주석(註釋) an annotation; notes. ¶ ~을 달다 annotate; write notes 《on a book》. ‖ ~자 an annotator.
주선(周旋) (알선) good (kind) offices; (중개) agency; mediation. ~하다 use one's influence 《on a person's behalf》; exercise one's good offices; act as an intermediary. ¶ …의 ~으로 through one's good offices / 그의 ~으로 집을 샀다 I bought a house through his agency. / 그녀가 대학 강사 자리를 ~해 주었다 She found (got) me a position as a college lecturer. / 그는 내게 좋은 땅을 ~해 주었다 He exercised (used) his influence in getting me some good land. ‖ ~인 an agent; an intermediary.
주선(酒仙) a son of Bacchus.
주섬주섬 ¶ ~ 줍다 〔입다〕 pick up (put on) one by one.
주성분(主成分) the chief ingredients; the principal elements.
주세(酒稅) the liquor tax.
주소(住所) one's address; one's residence (abode); one's dwelling (place); 〖法〗 a domicile. ¶ ~가 일정치 않은 사람 a man of no permanent address; a vagrant / 그는 ~ 부정이다 He has no fixed abode. / ~가 바뀌면 알려 주십시오 Let me know if you change your address. / ~ 성명을 말하시오(쓰시오) Give (Write) your name and address. ‖ ~록 an address book / ~ 불명(표시) Address unknown / 현 ~ the present address.
주스 《orange》 juice.
주시(注視) close observation; a steady gaze. ~하다 gaze steadily; observe (a person) closely; watch (a thing) carefully. ¶ ~의 표적이 되다 become the center of attention.
주식(主食) the principal (staple)

food; a (diet) staple. ¶ 쌀을 ~으로 하다 live on rice.
주식(株式) shares; stocks. ¶ ~을 발행하다 issue shares / ~을 모집하다 offer shares for subscription. ‖ ~거래 stock trading / ~공개 offering of stock to the public; going public / ~배당 a stock dividend / ~시세 stock prices / ~시장 the stock market / ~청약서 an application for stocks / ~회사 a joint-stock company; a stock company (corporation) 《美》(생략... Inc. 《美》; ... Co., Ltd. 《英》).
주심(主審) 〖野〗 the chief umpire; 《축구·권투 따위》 the chief referee.
주악(奏樂) ~하다 play (perform) music.
주안(主眼) the principal object; the chief aim. ¶ …에 ~을 두다 aim at...; have an eye to... / 이 법안의 ~(점)은 영세 기업 구제에 있다 The chief aim of this law is to give aid to small businesses. ‖ ~점 the essential (main) point.
주야(晝夜) day and night. ¶ ~ 교대로 in day and night shifts. ‖ ~장천 day and night ever passing; unceasingly.
주어(主語) 〖文〗 the subject.
주역(主役) (play) the leading part (role); 《배우》 the leading actor (actress); the star. ¶ ~을 맡다 play (take) the leading part (role) (in).
주역(周易) the Book of Changes.
주연(主演) ~하다 play the leading part (role) (in); star (in a play). ‖ ~배우 a leading actor (actress); a star.
주연(酒宴) (give) a banquet; a drinking party (bout).
주영(駐英) ¶ ~의 resident (stationed) in England. ‖ ~한국대사 the Korean Ambassador to the Court of St. James's.
주옥(珠玉) a gem; a jewel. ¶ ~같은 문학 작품 a literary gem.
주요(主要) ~하다 (be) main; chief; leading; principal; important. ¶ ~한 점 the main points (of) / ~인물 the leading characters (극·소설의); the key figures (사건 등의). ‖ ~도시 principal (major) cities / ~산물 staple products / ~산업 major (key) industries / ~수입품 the staple for import / ~수출품 chief (principal) exports / ~식품 staple article of food / ~원인 main cause.
주워담다 pick up and put in.
주워대다 enumerate glibly; cite this and that.
주워듣다 learn by hearsay. ¶ 주워들은 지식 knowledge picked up from others.
주워모으다 collect; gather.
주워섬기다 say all sorts of things one heard of and saw. ¶ 윗사람들의 결점을 ~ run (go) through a list of one's superiors' faults.
주위(周圍) 《언저리》 circumference; 《환경》 surroundings; environment; 《부근》 the neighborhood. ¶ ~의 surrounding; neighboring / ~사람들 those around a person / ~ 상황 circumstances; all the surrounding things and conditions / ~을 둘러보다 look around.
주유(注油) oiling; lubrication; oil supply (급유). ~하다 oil (an engine); lubricate; fill; feed. ‖ ~소 an oil (a service, a gas 《美》) station. 〈excursion.〉
주유(周遊) ~하다 tour; make an
주은(主恩) 《임금의》 royal benevolence; the favors of one's lord; 《주인의》 one's master's favor; 《천주의》 the grace of God.
주음(主音) 〖樂〗 a tonic; a keynote.
주의(主意) the main meaning (idea).
주의(主義) a principle; a doctrine; an ism; a cause; 《방침》 a line; a rule; a basis. ¶ ~를 지키다 live (act) up to one's principles; stick (hold fast) to one's principles / 현금 ~로 장사하다 do business on a cash basis / 그는 ~ 주장이 없는 사내야 He has no principles nor opinions.
주의(注意) ① 《주목·유의》 attention; observation; notice; heed. ~하다 pay attention (to); take notice (of); pay (give) heed (to). ¶ ~할 점 a point to notice / ~할 만한 사실 a noteworthy fact / ~을 촉구하다 call a person's attention (to) / ~를 딴데로 돌리다 divert one's attention from (a matter) / ~를 환기시키다 provoke (arouse) a person's attention / ~를 끌다 attract a person's attention / 그는 내 경고에 전혀 ~를 기울이지 않았다 He paid no attention to my warning. or He took no notice of my warning. / ~력 attentiveness / ~사항 matters to be attended to / ~서 instructions; directions / ~요~인물 a person on the black list; a suspicious character. ② 《조심》 care; precaution; (a) caution. ~하다 take care (be careful) (of); beware (of); be cautious (about); look out (for). ‖ 깊은 careful; cautious; watchful / ~하여 carefully; with care; cautiously / 전강에 ~하다 take care of oneself;

주의 be careful about *one's* health / ~가 부족하다[를 태만히 하다] be careless; be negligent / ~에 …하십시오 Beware of pickpockets. 「an airplane〕.
주익(主翼) the main wings 《*of*
주인(主人) 《가장》 the head (master) 《*of the family*》; 《남편》 *one's* husband; 《손님에 대하여》 the host; the hostess (여자); 《여관 등의》 the landlord; the landlady (여자); 《상점의》 the proprietor; the shopkeeper; 《고용주》 an employer; the master; 《임자》 the owner 《*of goods*》. ‖ ~공 《소설·영화의》 a hero; a heroine (여자); the leading character / ~역 을 하다; a hostess (여자) 《~역을 맡아 하다 act as host; play the host》 / ~집 *one's* master's house.

주인(主因) a principal cause; the prime factor; the main reason.

주일(主日) the Lord's day; Sunday. ‖ ~학교 a Sunday school.

주일(週日) a week(day). ‖ 이번[지난, 오는] ~ this [last, next] week.

주일(駐日) ¶ ~의 resident [stationed] in Japan. ‖ ~한국대사관 the Embassy of the Republic of Korea to Japan.

주임(主任) the person in charge; the head; the chief; the manager. ‖ ~교수 the head professor 《*of*》 / ~기사 a chief engineer / ~변호사 the chief counsel.

주입(注入) ~하다 《액체·활력 따위를》 pour [put, pump] into; 《주사약 따위를》 inject into; 《생각 등을》 instill 《infuse》 《*an idea*》 into 《*a person's mind*》; 《공부 따위를》 cram. ¶ 침체된 경제에 활기를 ~하다 pump new life into the stagnant economy. ‖ ~식 교육 the cramming system of education.

주자(走者) 《野》 a (base) runner.

주자(鑄字) a metal printing type. ‖ ~소 a type foundry.

주장(主張) assertion; a claim; 《고집》 insistence; 《의견》 an opinion. ~하다 insist 《*on*》; assert; maintain; hold; claim. ¶ 권리를 ~하다 assert *one's* rights / 판권을 ~하다 lay claim to the copyright / ~을 굽히지 않다 stick [hold firm] to *one's* convictions [opinions]. ‖ ~자 an assertor; an advocate(주의의); a claimant(권리의).

주장(主將) the captain. ¶ 야구팀 ~ the captain of a baseball team.

주장(主掌) ~하다 take charge of; have 《*a matter*》 in charge.

주재 ~하다 superintend; supervise; preside 《*over the meeting*》. ‖ ~자 the president; the chairman.

주재(駐在) ~하다 reside 《*at, in*》; be stationed 《*at, in*》. ¶ ~의 resident / 파리 ~ 외교관 a diplomat residing in Paris / 내 형은 신문 기자로 L.A.에 ~하고 있다 My (big) brother is stationed in L.A. as a newspaper reporter. ‖ ~관 a resident officer / ~국 the country of residence / ~원 an employee assigned to the 《*San Francisco*》 office.

주저(躊躇) hesitation; indecision. ~하다 hesitate; waver; have scruples 《*about doing*》. ¶ ~하면서 hesitatingly / ~없이 without hesitation.

주저앉다 sit [plump] down; plant *oneself* down; 《함몰》 fall; sink; cave in; 《머물다》 stay on; settle down. ¶ 의자에 털석 ~ drop [plump down] into a chair / 지붕이 ~ a roof caves [falls] in.

주저앉히다 force 《*a person*》 to sit down; 《못 떠나게》 make 《*a person*》 stay on.

주전(主戰) ¶ ~론 the advocacy of war; a pro-war argument; jingoism / ~론자 a war advocate; a jingoist / 〔野〕 ~투수 an ace pitcher.

주전부리 snack. ~하다 take snacks (between meals).

주전자(酒煎子) a (copper, brass) kettle. ¶ 물~ a (water) jug; a pitcher.

주절(主節) 〔文〕 the principal clause. 「《美俗》.

주점(酒店) a bar; a tavern; a pub

주접들다 be stunted [blighted]; be in poor shape.

주접스럽다 《음식에 대하여》 (be) avaricious; greedy.

주정(酒酊) drunken frenzy. ~하다 act in a drunken and disorderly way; be a bad drunk. ‖ ~꾼 a drunken brawler; a bad drunk.

주정(酒精) alcohol; spirits. ‖ ~계 an alcoholometer / ~음료 alcoholic beverages [drinks].

주제 《몰골》 seedy appearance; shabby looks. ¶ 돈도 없는 ~에 사납다 have a shabby appearance.

주제(主題) 《주제목》 the main subject; 《작품의 중심점》 the theme; the motif. ¶ ~가 a theme song.

주제넘다 (be) impertinent; presumptuous; impudent; cheeky. ¶ 주제넘게 / 주제넘은 impudently / 주제넘은 녀석 an impertinent [insolent] fellow; a smart aleck / 주제넘게 …하다 have the

주조(主調) 〖樂〗 the keynote.
주조(酒造) brewing (맥주 따위); distilling (소주 따위). ~하다 brew.
주조(鑄造) casting; founding; (화폐의) coinage; minting. ~하다 cast; found 《*a bell*》; (화폐를) mint; coin. ¶ 활자를 ~하다 cast metal types. ‖ ~소 a foundry.
주종(主從) master and servant; lord and vassal (retainer). ‖ ~관계 the relation between master and servant.
주주(株主) a stockholder 《美》; a shareholder 《英》. ¶ 대[소] ~ a large [small] shareholder. ‖ ~배당금 dividends to stockholders / ~총회 a general meeting of stockholders.
주지(主旨) the general purport; the gist; the point.
주지(住持) the chief priest of a Buddhist temple.
주지(周知) ¶ ~의 well-known; known to everybody / ~하는 바와 같이 as is generally known / ~의 사실 a matter of common knowledge; a well-known fact.
주지육림(酒池肉林)〖술잔치〗a sumptuous feast (banquet).
주차(駐車) parking. ~하다 park 《*a car*》. ¶ 거리에는 ~할 장소가 없었다 There was no parking place (space) along the street. ‖ ~금지 〖게시〗 No parking. / ~금지구역 a no-parking zone / ~난 parking difficulties / ~요금 a parking fee / ~위반 (a) parking violation / ~장 a parking lot 《美》; a car park 《英》.
주창(主唱) advocacy. ~하다 advocate; promote. ¶ …의 ~으로 at the instance of …; on the suggestion of …. ‖ ~자 an advocate; a promoter.
주책 a definite (fixed) opinion (view). ¶ ~없다 have no definite opinion (view) of *one's* own; be wishy-washy; be spineless / ~없이 말하다 talk senselessly.
주철(鑄鐵) cast iron; iron casting (주철하기). ‖ ~소 an iron foundry.
주청(奏請) ~하다 petition the Emperor (King) 《*for*》.
주체 ~하다 cope with (take care of) *one's* troubles. ¶ 그는 ~ 못할 만큼 돈이 많다 He has more money than he knows what to do with.
주체(主體) the subject; the main body; (중심) the core. ¶ ~적인 independent / 권리의 ~ the subject of rights / 북한의 ~ 사상 the North Korea's *"juche"*(self-reliance) ideology / 대학생으로 ~로 하는 단체 a group (an organization) mainly composed of college students. ¶ ~ 독립하다 establish *one's* independence / ~의식을 확립하다 establish a sense of independence.
주체(酒滯) indigestion caused by drinking.
주체스럽다 (be) troublesome; unmanageable; unwieldy; be hard to handle.
주최(主催) auspices; sponsorship. ¶ …의 ~로 under the auspices (sponsorship) of …; with the support of …; sponsored 《*by*》 / 자선 바자는 한 신문사 ~로 열렸다 The charity bazaar was 「held under the sponsorship of (sponsored by)」 a newspaper company. ‖ ~국 the host country / ~자 the sponsor; the promoter.
주춧(柱一)〖주춧돌〗a foundation stone; (lay) a cornerstone.
주축(主軸) the principal axis.
주춤거리다 (주저) hesitate; waver; hold back. ¶ 결단을 내리지 못하고 ~ be hesitant to make a decision.
주춤주춤 hesitantly; hesitatingly; falteringly; waveringly.
주치(主治) ~하다 take charge of 《*a case*》. ‖ ~의 a physician in charge 《*of*》; *one's* family doctor (가정의).
주택(住宅) a house; a residence; housing(집합적). ¶ 그 건물은 ~으로 알맞지 않다 The building is not fit to live in. / 공영 ~ a city-built (-owned) house / 임대 ~ houses for rent / 호화 ~ a luxurious (deluxe) house. ‖ ~가(街) a residential street / ~난 a housing shortage / ~문제 the housing problem / ~비 housing costs (expenses) / ~수당 a housing allowance / ~융자 a housing loan / ~조합(제도) a housing cooperative (system) / ~지구 residential quarters (areas) / ~청약 예금 an apartment-application deposit / ~행정 (정책) the housing administration (policy) / 대한~공사 the Korea National Housing Corporation.
주파(走破) ~하다 run (cover) the whole distance 《*between*》.
주파(周波) a cycle. ‖ ~수 frequency / ~수변조 frequency modulation (생략 FM).
주판(籌板·珠板) an abacus. ¶ ~을 놓다 reckon (count) on an abacus. ‖ ~알 a counter.

주피터(羅神) Jupiter.
주필(主筆) the chief editor; an editor in chief.
주필(朱筆) ¶ ~을 가하다 correct; revise.
주한(駐韓) ¶ ~의 resident (stationed) in Korea. ¶ ~미군 U.S. armed forces in Korea / ~외교 사절단 the diplomatic corps in Korea.
주항(周航) circumnavigation. ~하다 sail (cruise) round 《the world》; circumnavigate.
주해(註解) (explanatory) notes; (an) annotation. ~하다 comment (make notes) upon; annotate. ‖ ~서 an annotated edition; a horse 《俗》.
주행(走行) ~하다 travel 《from A to B》; cover 《100 miles in an hour》. ‖ ~거리 the distance covered 《in a given time》; mileage / ~거리계 an odometer / ~선 a driving lane / ~시간 time taken in traveling 《from A to B》.
주형(鑄型) a mold; a cast; a matrix. ¶ ~을 뜨다 cast a mold.
주호(酒豪) a heavy drinker; a man who drinks like a fish.
주홍(朱紅) scarlet; bright orange color.
주화(鑄貨) coinage; 《낱의》 a coin. ¶ 불량 ~를 넣지 마시오 《게시》 Do not use odd coins. ‖ 기념 ~ commemorative coins.
주화론(主和論) advocacy of peace. ‖ ~자 an advocate of peace; a pacifist.
주황(朱黃) orange color.
주효(奏效) ~하다 be effective; be effectual; bear fruit; take effect 《약이》. [food].
주효(酒肴) wine and refreshments
주흥(酒興) (drunken) merrymaking; conviviality. ¶ ~에 겨워 heated by wine / ~을 돋우 (깨리다) heighten (dampen) conviviality.
죽(粥) (rice) gruel; porridge; hot cereal. ¶ ~을 끓이다 cook hot cereal / 식은 ~ 먹기다 be an easy task. [etc.].
죽¹ (열 벌) ten pieces; ten 《plates,
죽² ① 《늘어선 모양》 in a row (line). ¶ ~ 늘어놓다 make an array of; display. ② 《내내》 all through; throughout. ¶ 아침부터 ~ all through the morning / 일년 동안 ~ all the year round. ③ 《대강》 ¶ ~ 훑어보다 run through; look over. ④ 《물·기운 따위가》 (recede) utterly; all down the line. ¶ 기운이 ~ 빠졌다 I am utterly exhausted. ⑤ 《찢는 모양》 with a rip. ¶ 손수건을 ~ 찢다 rip a handkerchief.
죽기(竹器) bamboo ware.

죽는소리 ① 《엄살》 talking (making a) poor mouth. ~하다 talk poor mouth. ¶ ~ 좀 그만해라 Stop talking poor mouth. ② 《비명》 a shriek; a scream. ¶ ~를 지르다 utter a shriek.
죽다 ① 《사망》 die; pass away; 《숨지다》 expire; breathe one's last; 《목숨을 잃다》 be killed; lose one's life. ¶ 죽은… dead; deceased; the late 《Mr. Kim》 / 죽은 사람은 the dead / 죽느냐 사느냐의 문제 a matter of life and (or) death / 죽음 각오로 at the risk of one's life / 병으로 ~ die of a disease / 철도 사고로 ~ be killed in a railway accident / 그녀가 죽은 지 5년이 되었다 She has been dead for five years. / 지루해서 죽을 지경이다 I'm dying of boredom. or I'm bored to death. / 더위서 죽을 것 같다 The heat is killing me. / 인간은 죽게 마련이다 Man is mortal. ② 《초목이》 die; be dead. ③ 《기(氣)가》 be downhearted (depressed); be dejected (dispirited); be in the blues. ¶ 이 그림은 죽어 있다 This painting is lifeless. ④ 《풀기가》 lose its starch. ⑤ 《정지》 run down; stop. ¶ 시계가 죽었다 The clock has stopped. ⑥ 《불이》 go out; die out. ¶ 불이 거의 죽었다 The fire is nearly out. ⑦ 《野》 be (put) out; 《장기·바둑 등》 be captured (lost).
죽도(竹刀) a bamboo sword.
죽도화(一花) 《植》 a yellow rose; a kerria.
죽림(竹林) a bamboo thicket (grove). ¶ ~칠현 the seven wise men in a bamboo grove fabled in a Chinese classic.
죽마(竹馬) stilts. ‖ ~ 고우(故友) a childhood (bosom) friend; an old playmate.
죽세공(竹細工) bamboo ware (work).
죽순(竹筍) a bamboo shoot (sprout). ¶ 우후~처럼 나오다 shoot (spring) up like mushrooms after a rain; increase rapidly in number.
죽지내다 live under oppression; live a life of subjugation. ¶ 그는 아내 앞에 죽어 지낸다 He lives under his wife's thumb.
죽음등살룸 desperately; frantically; life and death; tooth and nail.
죽을병(一病) a fatal disease.
죽을상(一相) an agonized look; a frantic (desperate) look.
죽을힘 ¶ ~을 다하여 desperately; frantically; with all one's might; for one's life / ~을 다해 헤엄치다 swim for one's life.
죽음 death; decease; demise 《영

죽이다 온 사람의). ¶ ~의 재 radioactive ashes; fall-out / ~에 대한 공포 the terror of death / ~에 대한 각오를 하다 be prepared for death; be ready to die / ~을 애도하다 mourn (over) the death of... / 그녀는 가까스로 ~을 면했다 She narrowly missed death.

죽이다 ① (살해) kill; murder; put (*a person*) to death; take (*a person's*) life / (도살) butcher (*a cow*). ¶ 때려 ~ beat to death / 독약을 먹여 ~ dose (*a person*) to death / 죽이겠다고 협박하다 threaten to kill [murder] (*a person*); threaten (*a person's*) life / 아무를 죽이려고 하다 make an attempt on (*a person's*) life. ② (잃다) lose (*a son, a chessman*). ③ (억압) suppress; stifle; smother; hold back. ¶ 숨을 ~ hold *one's* breath / 감정을 ~ suppress *one's* feelings. ④ (기타) ¶ 맛을 ~ spoil the flavor; kill the taste / 재능을 ~ destroy [suppress] *one's* talent.

죽일놈 a rascal. ¶ 이 ~야 Damn you! *or* Be damned to you.

죽자꾸나하고 at the risk of *one's* life; for all *one's* life; desperately; frantically.

죽장(竹杖) a bamboo stick.

죽죽 ☞ 쭉쭉.

죽지 ① (날갯~) the joint of a wing / 어깻~ the shoulder joint.

죽창(竹槍) a bamboo spear.

죽책(竹栅) a bamboo fence.

죽치다 confine [shut] *oneself* in *one's* house; keep *oneself* indoors.

준-(準) quasi-; semi-; associate. ¶ ~여당 a quasi-government party / ~회원 an associate member.

준거(準據) ~하다 base (*a decision*) on; conform to; follow. ¶ ~에 준하여 in conformity to...; in accordance with....

준결승(準決勝) a semifinal (game). ¶ ~에 진출하다 go on to the semifinals.

준공(竣工) completion. ~하다 be finished [completed]. ¶ ~도(圖) 《건물의》 a drawing showing how a building will look when completed / ~식 a ceremony to celebrate the completion (*of a bridge*).

준교사(準敎師) an assistant teacher.

준동(蠢動) wriggling; squirming; activities. ~하다 《벌레가》 crawl; wriggle; 《무리가》 be active; move; infest.

준령(峻嶺) a steep mountain pass.

준마(駿馬) a swift (gallant) horse.

준말 an abbreviation.

준법(遵法) ¶ ~의 law-abiding / ~정신 a law-abiding spirit / ~투쟁 (쟁의 행위) a work-to-rule; a slow-down / ~투쟁을 하다 work to rule.

준봉(峻峰) steep [lofty] peak.

준비(準備) preparation(s); arrangements; readiness. ~하다 prepare; get ready; make preparations [arrangements]. ¶ 식사를 하다 get dinner ready; cook dinner / ~중에 있다 《사람이 주어》 be getting ready (*for*); 《사물이 주어》 be in (course of) preparation / 시험 ~는 되었느냐 Are you prepared to take the test? / ~는 다 됐다 Everything is ready now. *or* We are all set now. ¶ ~단계 a preparatory stage / ~운동 warming-up exercises / ~운동을 하다 warm up / ~은행 《美》 a reserve bank / ~절차 【法】 preparatory proceedings / ~통화 a reserve currency / 법정~금 a legal reserve fund.

준사관(準士官) a warrant officer.

준사원(準社員) a junior employee.

준설(浚渫) dredging. ~하다 dredge (*a river*). ¶ ~선 a dredger; a dredging vessel / 대한 ~공사 the Korea Dredging Corporation.

준수(遵守) observance. ~하다 observe (*rules*); conform to; follow; obey.

준수하다(俊秀―) (be) outstanding; prominent; excel in talent and elegance.

준엄하다(峻嚴―) (be) severe; strict; rigid; stern; stringent.

준열하다(峻烈―) (be) rigorous; stern; severe; sharp; relentless. ¶ 준열한 비판 sharp criticism.

준용(準用) ~하다 apply (*a rule*) correspondingly (*to other cases*).

준우승(準優勝) a victory in the semifinals. ¶ ~자 a winner of the semifinals. 「WO」

준위(準尉) a warrant officer 《생략 **준장**(准將) 《美》 a brigadier general / 《해군》 a commodore 《해군》.

준족(駿足) ① (말) a swift horse. ② (사람) a swift runner.

준준결승(準準決勝) a quarterfinal (game).

준치 【魚】 a kind of herring. ¶ 썩어도 ~ 《俗談》 An old eagle is better than a young crow.

준칙(準則) a standing [working] rule; (기준) a standard; a criterion.

준평원(準平原) 【地】 a peneplain.

준하다(準―) be proportionate (*to*); 《운동》 apply correspondingly to; follow; be based on. ¶ ...에 준해서 in accordance with; in proportion to / 대우는 정사원에 준한다 We treat you the same

way as a regular employee. / 작업에 준하여 보수를 지불하겠다 We'll pay you in proportion to the amount of work you do. 「ber.
준회원(準會員) an associate mem-
줄¹ ① 《끈붙이》 a rope; a cord; a string 《연, 악기 등의》. ¶ ~을 치다 (stretch a) rope / ~에 걸리다 《발이》 be caught in the ropes. ② 《선》 a line; a stripe. ¶ ~을 긋다 draw a line. ③ 《열》 a row; a line. ¶ ~을 지어 서다 line up. ④ 《행》 a line. ¶ ~을 바꾸다 begin a new line.
줄² 《쇠를 깎는》 a file; a rasp. ¶ ~질하다 file (*the wood smooth*).
줄³ ① 《방법》 how to (*do*). ¶ 사진 찍을 ~(을) 모르다 do not know how to take a photograph. ② 《하게 됨》 (the fact) that…. ¶ 《셈》 너와 만날 ~ 몰랐다 This is the last place where I expected to meet you. / 그가 간첩인 ~ 누가 알았으랴 Who ever suspected that he was a spy?
줄거리 ① 《가지》 a stalk; a stem; a caulis. ② 《얘기의》 an outline; a plot; a story; a summary. ¶ 이야기의 ~를 말하다 outline a plot.
줄곧 all along; all the way (*time*); all through; throughout; constantly; continually.
줄기 ① 《식물의》 a trunk; a stem 《화초의》; a stalk 《벼, 보리 따위의》; a cane 《등, 대 따위의》. ② 《빛 따위의》 ray; a streak. ¶ 한 ~의 광선 a ray (streak) of light. ③ 《물 등의》 a stream; a current; a vein 《혈관의》. ④ 《산의》 a range. ⑤ 《비 따위의》 a shower; a downpour.
줄기세포(-細胞) stem cell.
줄기차다 (be) strong; vigorous. ¶ 줄기차게 strongly; vigorously.
줄넘기 《뛰놀려》 rope skipping; rope jumping. ~하다 skip. ¶ ~의 줄을 돌리다 turn the skipping rope (*for the girls*).
줄다 ① 《감소》 decrease; lessen; diminish 《점차로》; fall off 《수량이》; get fewer [less, smaller]. ¶ 체중이 ~ lose weight / 흡연자의 수가 줄고 있다 The number of smokers (*in Korea*) has fallen [decreased]. / 생사의 수요가 줄고 있다 The demand for silk is diminishing [on the decrease]. ② 《축소》 contract; diminish in size; be shortened; shrink. ¶ 《빨아도》 줄지 않다 be unshrinkable.
줄다리기 《play at》 a tug-of-war.
줄달다 follow one after another. ¶ 줄달아서 continuously; successively.
줄둠읗질 dashing. ~하다 [치다] run hard; rush; dash. ¶ 거리로 ~쳐 나가다 dash out into the street.
줄담배 ¶ ~를 피우다 chainsmoke / ~ 피우는 사람 a chainsmoker.
줄대다 continue; go on; keep on. ¶ 줄대어 continuously; in succession; in a row.
줄무늬 stripes. ¶ ~의 striped.
줄사닥다리 a rope ladder.
줄어들다 ① 《감소》 decrease; diminish; lessen; dwindle 《차차로》. ② 《축소》 become smaller; dwindle; shrink.
줄이다 《감소》 reduce; decrease; lessen; 《단축·축소》 shorten; cut down; curtail. ¶ 3분의 2를 [로] ~ reduce by [to] two-third / 경비를 ~ cut down expenses / 체중을 ~ reduce one's weight / 석유의 소비량을 줄여야 한다 We've got to cut down (on) our consumption of petroleum. / 육식을 줄이고 채식을 더 해라 I advise you to eat less meat and more vegetables. 「line.
줄자 a tape measure; a tape-
줄잡다 make a moderate estimate (*of*); estimate low; underestimate. ¶ 줄잡아서 at a moderate estimate.
줄줄 ☞ 졸졸. ¶ ~ 흐르다 flow (gush) out; stream down / 땀을 ~ 흘리다 swelter.
줄줄² 《막힘없이》 smoothly; without a hitch; fluently.
줄짓다 form a line [queue]; line [queue] up; 《정렬》 be in a row; stand in 〈in〉 line.
줄치다 draw lines; mark with lines; stretch a rope 《새끼줄》.
줄타다 walk on a (tight) rope. ¶ 줄타기하는 사람 a ropewalker.
줄행랑(-行廊) 《도망》 flight; running away. ¶ ~을 치다 run away; take 〈to〉 flight.
줌 《분량》 a handful; a grip; a grasp. ¶ 소금 한 ~ a handful of salt.
줍다 pick up; gather (up) (*shells*); find (*a purse on the road*); glean (*ears of rice*). ¶ 주워 모으다 gather; collect.
줏대(主-) a fixed principle; a definite opinion; moral fiber; backbone. ¶ ~가 있는 사람 a man of principle / ~가 없다 lack backbone [moral fiber].
중 a Buddhist priest; a monk. ¶ ~의 제머리 못 깎는다 《俗談》 You cannot scratch your own back.
중(中) ① 《정도》 the medium; the average. ¶ ~키의 사람 a man of medium height / ~ 이상 [이하] 이다 be above [below] the average. ② 《중앙부》 the center; the middle. ③ 《동안에》 during; with-

…중 in; while. ¶전시 ~ during the war. ④(진행중) under; in process of; in progress. ¶건축 ~ under (in course of) construction / 식사 ~이다 be at table. ⑤(…중에서) among; in; out of; within. ¶십 ~ 팔구 nine out of ten. ⑥(내내) throughout; all over.

…중 (重) ① (겹) fold. ¶ 2~의 two-fold; double. ② (무게) weight.

중간 (中間) the middle; the midway. ¶~의 middle; midway; intermediate; interim (기한의). ¶…의 ~쯤에 in (about) the middle of; halfway between 《*A and B*》. ‖~결산 interim closing / ~관리 (직) the middle management / ~배당 interim dividends / ~보고 an interim report / ~상인 a middle man; a broker / ~색 a neutral tint (color) / ~선거 an off-year election (미국의) / ~시험 (고사) a midterm examination / ~업자 a middleman / ~역 an intermediate station / ~착취 intermediary exploitation / ~층 a middle class / ~파 a neutral party; the neutrals; the middle-of-the-roaders.

중간자 (中間子) 【理】 a meson.
중간치 (中間─) an article of medium size 《price, quality, *etc*.》.
중간하다 (重刊─) republish; reprint; reissue.
중갑판 (中甲板) the middle deck.
중개 (仲介) mediation; agency. ~하다 mediate; act as a go-between. ¶그의 ~로 그들은 타협했다 They compromised 《*on these terms*》 by (through) his agency. ‖~업 the brokerage business / ~자 a mediator; a go-between; 《중개상》 an agent.

중거리 (中距離) ¶~경주 (선수) a middle-distance race (runner) / ~탄도탄 an intermediate-range ballistic missile (생략 IRBM) / 핵병기 intermediate-range nuclear forces (생략 INF).
중견 (中堅) a backbone; a mainstay. ¶회사의 ~이 되다 form (prove *oneself*) the backbone of a company. ‖~수 【野】 a center fielder / ~작가 a writer of middle (medium) standing.
중계 (中繼) relay; a hookup 《美》. ~하다 relay; 《라디오·TV로》 broadcast. ¶전국에 ~방송하다 broadcast over a nationwide network / 위성 ~ a transmission via satellite / 실황 ~ on-the-spot broadcasting / 무대 ~ a stage relay broadcast. ‖~국 (局) a relay station / ~무역 intermediate trade / ~방송 a relay broadcast; ~항 an intermediate port; a port of transit.

중고 (中古) ¶~의 used; secondhand / 나는 ~피아노를 샀다 I bought a used piano. ‖~차 a used car / ~품 a used article; secondhand goods.
중공업 (重工業) heavy industries.
중과 (衆寡) ¶~ 부적이다 be outnumbered.
중구 (衆口) ¶~난방이다 It is difficult to stop the voice of the people.
중국 (中國) China. ¶~의 Chinese. ‖~어 Chinese / ~통 (通) an authority on Chinese affairs; a person versed in things Chinese.
중궁 (中宮) (中宮殿) 《왕후의 높임말》 the Queen.
중금속 (重金屬) a heavy metal.
중급 (中級) an intermediate grade. ¶~의 intermediate; of the middle class. ‖~품 an article of medium (average) quality.
중기 (中期) the middle period. ¶~에 in the middle (years) 《*of the Koryo era*》. ‖~계획 a medium-range plan.
── chine gun.
중기관총 (重機關銃) a heavy machine gun.
중길 (中─) 《물건》 a product of medium quality; medium goods.
중남미 (中南美) South and Central America. ¶~ 라틴 아메리카.
중년 (中年) middle age. ¶~의 사람 a middle-aged person / ~이 지난 사람 an elderly person / ~이 되어 살이 찌다 develop middle-aged flab (spread). ‖~기 the middle years of *one's* life.
중노동 (重勞動) heavy (hard) labor.
중농 (中農) a middle-class farmer.
중농 (重農) ‖~정책 an agriculture-first policy / ~주의 physiocracy / ~주의자 a physiocrat.
중뇌 (中腦) the midbrain; 【解】 mesencephalon.
중늙은이 (中─) an elderly person.
중단 (中斷) interruption; stoppage. ~하다 discontinue; interrupt. ¶경기는 소나기로 인해 10분간 ~되었다 The game was interrupted for ten minutes by a shower.
중대 (中隊) a company (보병, 공병); a battery (포병); a squadron (비행중대). ‖~장 a company commander.
중대 (重大) ~하다 (be) important; serious; grave. ¶~한 과실 the grave (a gross) mistake / ~해지다 become serious (worse) / 사태는 ~하다 The situation is serious. / 나는 그녀의 행동을 ~시 하고 있다 I am taking a grave view of her conduct. ‖~문제 a matter of great concern; a question of

중도(中途) ¶ ~에서 halfway; midway; in the middle/일을 ~서 그만두다 leave (*a matter*) half-done; give up halfway.
중도(中道) ¶ ~를 걷다 take (choose) a moderate course; take the golden mean. ∥ ~정당 a centrist party / ~파 the middle-of-the-roaders. 「mediate) payment.
중도금(中渡金) a midterm (inter-
중독(中毒) poisoning; 《마약 등의》 addiction; toxication (중독증). ¶ ~성의 poisonous; toxic / ~되다 get (become) addicted (*to*); get hooked (*on heroin*) / ~증상을 나타내다 develop (present) symptoms of poisoning / ~을 일으키다 be (get) poisoned / 그는 식~에 걸렸다 He suffered from food poisoning.
중동(中東) the Middle East. ∥ ~전쟁 the Middle East War.
중동무이(中一) ~하다 do 《*things*》 by halves; leave 《*a thing*》 half-done.
중등(中等) ¶ ~의 middle; medium; average. ∥ ~교육 secondary education / ~품 medium-grade articles; middlings / ~학교 a secondary school.
중략(中略) an omission; an ellipsis(생략); 《표시로서》 "omitted". ~하다 omit; skip.
중량(重量) weight. ¶ 총~ gross weight / ~감이 있다 be massive; look solid / ~이 4톤이다 It weighs four tons. ∥ ~급 the heavyweight class / ~급 권투 선수 a heavyweight boxer / 부족~ short weight / ~제 classification by weight / ~제한 weight (load) limits / ~초과 overweight / ~톤 a deadweight tonnage.
중력(重力) 【理】 gravity; gravitation. ¶ ~의 법칙(중심) the law (center) of gravity / 〖인공위성 내의〗 인공~ artificial gravity / 무~ 상태 weightlessness.
중령(中領) 《육군》 a lieutenant colonel; 《해군》 a commander; 《공군》 a lieutenant colonel 《美》; a wing commander 《英》.
중론(衆論) general consultation; public opinion.
중류(中流) ① 《강의》 the middle of the river; midstream. ② 《사회의》 the middle class. ∥ ~가정 a middle-class family / ~계급 the middle classes.
중립(中立) neutrality. ¶ ~적인 neutral / 비무장 ~주의 unarmed neutralism / ~의 입장에서 on neutral ground / ~을 지키다 observe neutrality. ∥ ~국 a neutral power (country) / ~내각 a neutral cabinet / ~노선 neutral policy / ~주의 neutralism / ~주의 정책 a neutralist policy / ~지대 a neutral zone / ~화 neutralization.
중매(仲買) brokerage. ~하다 act as (a) broker. ¶ ~구전 a broker's commission / ~인 a broker.
중매(仲媒) matchmaking. ~하다 arrange a (marriage) match 《*between*》; act as a go-between. ¶ ~결혼 a marriage arranged by a go-between / ~인 〖젊은이〗 a matchmaker; a go-between.
중문(中門) an inner gate.
중문(重文) 【文】 a compound sentence.
중미(中美) Central America. ¶ ~의 Central American.
중반전(中盤戰) 《바둑 등의》 the middle game; 《선거전 등의》 the middle phase. ¶ ~에 들어〔가〕다 get into the middle stage (*of the game*).
중벌(重罰) a heavy [severe] punishment. ¶ ~에 처하다 sentence 《*a person*》 to a severe punishment. 「felon.
중범(重犯) 《중죄》 felony; 《중범인》 a
중병(重病) a serious illness. ¶ ~에 걸리다 fall (get) seriously ill. / ~환자 a serious case.
중복(中伏) the middle period of dog days.
중복(重複) repetition; duplication; redundancy. ~하다 overlap; be repeated; duplicate. ¶ ~된 duplicate; overlapping; repeated.
중부(中部) the central (middle) part. ¶ ~지방 the central districts; the midland.
중뿔나다(中一) be nosy (intrusive, meddlesome, officious, pert). ~중뿔나게 말하다 make uncalled-for (impertinent) remarks.
중사(中士) a sergeant first class.
중산계급(中産階級) the middle classes; middle-class people.
중산모(中山帽) a derby (hat) 《美》.
중상(中傷) (a) slander; defamation (명예훼손); mudslinging(선거 운동 등에서의). ~하다 slander; speak ill of; defame. ¶ ~적 defamatory; calumnious; slanderous / ~적인 보도 a slanderous report / 친구로부터 ~을 당하다 be defamed by *one's* friend / 그것은 지독한 ~이다 It's a gross slander. ∥ ~자 a slanderer; a scandalmonger.

중상(重傷) a serious wound (injury). ¶ ~을 입다 get badly (be seriously) wounded. / ~자 a seriously wounded (injured) person. / ~자 a mercantilist.

중상주의(重商主義) mercantilism.

중생(衆生) living things; all creatures; human beings.

중생대(中生代) the Mesozoic (Era).

중서부(中西部) the Middle West; the Midwest. ¶ ~의 Middle Western. 「ite.

중석(重石) [鑛] tungsten; scheel-

중선거구(中選擧區) 〈선거의〉 a medium(-sized) electoral district.

중성(中性) ① [文] the neuter gender. ¶ ~의 neuter. ② [化] neutrality. ¶ ~의 neutral. / ~반응 a neutral reaction / ~자 a neutron / ~자폭탄 a neutron bomb.

중세(中世) the Middle Ages; medieval times. ¶ ~사(史) the medieval history. 「taxation (과세).

중세(重稅) a heavy tax; heavy

중소(中蘇) Sino-Soviet. ¶ ~논쟁 Sino-Soviet dispute.

중소기업(中小企業) small and medium-sized enterprises; smaller businesses. ¶ 부친께서 ~을 경영하고 계시다 My father runs a small business. ‖ ~청 the Small & Medium Business Administration (생략 SMBA).

중수(重水) [化] heavy water.

중수(重修) restoration; remodeling. ~하다 repair; remodel; restore. 「gen; deuterium.

중수소(重水素) [化] heavy hydro-

중순(中旬) the middle (second) ten days of a month. ¶ 4월 ~에 in mid-April; about (in) the middle of April.

중시하다(重視—) attach importance 《to》; make (think) much of; lay stress on; regard... as important; take... seriously. ¶ 나는 그녀의 충고를 중시한다 I attach importance to her advice.

중신(重臣) a chief (senior) vassal (retainer).

중심(中心) 《한복판》 the middle; the heart; 《중핵》 the core. ¶ ~의 central; middle / ~의 ~이 되다 take a leading part 《in a project》; play a central role 《in a movement》 / ~을 벗어나다 be out of center; be wide of the mark: be off the mark. ¶ ~인물 a central figure / ~점 the central point / ~지 a center 《공업 ~지 an industrial center》.

중심(重心) [理] the center of gravity. ¶ 몸의 ~을 잡다 [잃다] keep [lose] one's balance.

중압(重壓) (heavy) pressure. ¶ ~을 가하다 put pressure on 《a person》 to do / 경제적인 ~을 받다 undergo (be under) economic stress. ‖ ~감 an oppressive feeling.

중앙(中央) the center; the heart; the middle. ¶ ~의 central; middle / …의 ~에 in (at) the center (heart) of... / 도시의 ~에 있다 be (situated) in the center of the town. ¶ ~관청 central government agencies / ~냉난방 central airconditioning and heating / ~돌파 a frontal breakthrough / ~부 the central part; the midsection / 《도로상의》 a median strip / ~선 the central line of the highway; 《철도의》 the Central Line / ~선거관리위원회 the Central Election Management Committee / ~아시아 [아메리카] Central Asia (America) / ~우체국 the Central Post Office / ~정보부 《美》 the Central Intelligence Agency (생략 CIA) / ~정부 central government / ~집권 centralization (of administrative power) / ~집행위원회 a central executive committee.

중언부언(重言復言) ~하다 reiterate; say over again; repeat.

중얼거리다 mutter; murmur; grumble (불평을). ¶ 중얼중얼 muttering / 무어라고 혼자 ~ mutter something to oneself.

중역(重役) a director. ‖ ~회 a board of directors / ~회의 a meeting of directors.

중역(重譯) (a) retranslation. ~하다 retranslate.

중엽(中葉) the middle part (of a period). ¶ 19세기 ~ the mid-nineteenth century.

중외(中外) ¶ ~에 at home and abroad.

중요(重要) ~하다 (be) important; of importance; essential; vital; valuable (귀중한); principal. ¶ 그것은 우리에게 매우 ~한 문제이다 That is a matter of great importance to us. / 그는 그 팀의 ~한 멤버이다 He is a valuable member of the team. / 심장과 폐는 ~한 기관이다 The heart and lungs are vital organs. ¶ ~무형문화재 an important intangible cultural asset / ~문화재 an important cultural asset / ~사항 an important matter / ~서류 important papers / ~성 importance / ~인물 an important person; a very important person (생략 VIP).

중요시하다(重要視—) ☞ 중시하다.

중용(中庸) moderation; a middle course; the golden mean. ¶ ~의 moderate / ~을 지키다 take

중용(中庸) the golden mean; be moderate 《in》.
중용(重用) ~하다 promote 《a person》 to a responsible post. ¶ ~되다 be taken into confidence.
중우(衆愚) ‖ ~정치 mobocracy; mob rule.
중위(中位) 〔정도〕 medium; average. 〔평균〕 〔등급〕 second rate.
중위(中尉) 〔육군〕 a first lieutenant 〔美〕; a lieutenant 〔英〕; 〔해군〕 a lieutenant junior grade 〔美〕; a sublieutenant 〔英〕; 〔공군〕 a first lieutenant 〔美〕; a flying officer 〔英〕. 〔leum.
중유(重油) heavy oil; crude petro-
중음(中音) 〔樂〕 alto; baritone (남성); contralto (여성).
중의(衆意) public (popular, general) opinion.
중의(衆議) public discussion; general consultation. ¶ ~에 의하여 결정하다 decide by majority of votes.
중이(中耳) the middle ear; the tympanum. ‖ ~염 tympanitis.
중임(重任) ① 〔책임〕 a heavy responsibility; 〔지위〕 a responsible post; 〔임무〕 an important duty. ¶ ~을 맡다 take upon *oneself* an important task; shoulder a heavy responsibility. ② 〔재임〕 reappointment; reelection (재선). ¶ ~하다 be reappointed; be reelected.
중장(中將) 〔육군〕 a lieutenant general; 〔해군〕 a vice admiral; 〔공군〕 a lieutenant general 〔美〕; an air marshal 〔英〕.
중장비(重裝備) heavy equipment.
중재(仲裁) mediation; arbitration. ¶ ~하다 mediate; arbitrate 《between》. ¶ ~를 부탁하다 ask for arbitration / 그 쟁의는 그의 ~로 해결되었다 The dispute was settled through his mediation. ‖ ~인 a mediator; an arbitrator / ~재판 arbitration / ~재판소 a court of arbitration.
중절(中絶) interruption. ~하다 interrupt.
중절모(中折帽) a soft (felt) hat.
중점(中點) 〔數〕 the middle point; the median (point).
중점(重點) 〔강조〕 emphasis; stress; 〔중요〕 importance. ¶ ~적으로 in priority / ~을 두다 lay emphasis (stress) on 《something》. ‖ ~주의〔생산〕 priority policy (production).
중조(重曹) 〔化〕 bicarbonate of soda; baking soda (俗).
중졸자(中卒者) a junior high school
중죄(重罪) (a) felony; a grave offense (crime). ‖ ~인 a felon.
중증(重症) a serious illness.
중지(中止) stoppage; suspension; ~하다 stop; give up (단념); pend; call off. ¶ 경기는 ~되었다 / Our match was called off. / 우리는 그 실험의 ~를 요구했다 We called for the discontinuation of the experiment.
중지(中指) the middle finger.
중지(衆智) ~를 모으다 seek (ask) the counsel of many people.
중진(重鎭) 〔사람〕 a prominent (leading) figure; a person of influence (authority); an authority (학계의). 〔country.
중진국(中進國) a semideveloped
중창(中 一) 〔구두의〕 an insole.
중책(重責) a heavy responsibility; an important mission (duty). ¶ ~을 맡다 assume a heavy responsibility. 〔the zenith.
중천(中天) midair; the midheaven
중첩(重疊) ~하다 lie one upon another; overlap each other; pile up.
중추(中樞) the center; the pivot; the backbone. ¶ ~적인 central; leading; pivotal / ~적인 인물 the central (pivotal) figure. ‖ ~산업 a pivotal industry / ~신경 the central nerve / ~신경계통 the central nervous system.
중추(仲秋) midautumn. ¶ ~명월 the harvest moon.
중축(中軸) the axis; the pivot.
중층구조(重層構造) 〔經〕 a multilayer structure.
중크롬산(重 一酸) 〔化〕 bichromic acid. ‖ ~염 bichromate.
중키(中 一) medium height (size, stature).
중탄산(重炭酸) 〔化〕 bicarbonate. ¶ ~소다 bicarbonate of soda / ~염 bicarbonate.
중태(重態) a serious (critical, grave) condition. ¶ ~이다 be in a serious condition; be seriously ill 《*with cancer*》 / 그는 ~에 빠졌다 He fell into a critical condition.
중턱(中 一) 〔산의〕 the mountainside; the mid-slope of a mountain. ¶ 산 ~에서 좀 쉬도록 하자 Let's take a short rest halfway up (down) the mountain.
중퇴(中退) ~하다 leave school without completing the course; leave (college) before graduation; drop out. ¶ 그는 배우가 되고 싶어 대학을 ~했다 He quit the university out of his desire to be an actor. ‖ ~자 a (school) dropout / 고교 ~자 a high school dropout.
중파(中波) 〔無電〕 a medium wave.
중판(重版) an another (a second) impression (edition).
중편(中篇) 〔제2 권〕 the second part (volume). ‖ ~소설 a medium-length story; a short novel.

중평(衆評) public opinion (criticism).

중포(重砲) a heavy gun; heavy artillery (총칭). ~er.

중폭격기(重爆擊機) a heavy bomber.

중품(中品) medium quality (goods).

중풍(中風) 〔韓醫〕 palsy; paralysis. ¶ ~에 걸린 paralytic / ~에 걸리다 be stricken with paralysis; have a stroke of paralysis / 그녀는 ~에 걸려 있다 She is suffering from palsy. *or* She is paralyzed. ‖ ~환자 a paralytic.

중하(重荷) a heavy burden (load).

중하다(重一) (be) serious; critical; 《죄가》(be) grave; 《병이》(be) heavy; 《책임이》(be) important.

중학교(中學校) a middle school; a junior high school 〔美〕.

중학생(中學生) a middle (junior high 〔美〕) school student (boy, girl).

중합(重合) 〔化〕 polymerization. ~하다 polymerize. ‖ ~체 a polymer.

중핵(中核) the kernel; the core. ¶ 그는 그 당의 ~이다 He belongs to the central core of the party.

중형(中形·中型) a medium (middle) size. ¶ ~의 middle-sized.

중형(重刑) a heavy penalty; a severe punishment.

중혼(重婚) double marriage; bigamy. ~하다 commit bigamy. ‖ ~자 a bigamist / ~죄 bigamy.

중화(中和) 〔化〕 neutralization; 《독의》counteraction. ~하다 neutralize; counteract. ¶ 산은 알칼리로 ~된다 An acid is neutralized with (an) alkali. ‖ ~제 a neutralizer; a counteractive; an antidote (독에 대한).

중화(中華) ‖ ~사상 Sinocentrism / ~요리 Chinese dishes (cuisine) / ~요리점 a Chinese restaurant / ~인민공화국 the People's Republic of China.

중화기(重火器) heavy firearms.

중화학공업(重化學工業) the heavy and chemical industries.

중환(重患) a serious illness; 《환자》a serious case.

중후(重厚) ~하다 (be) grave and generous; profound; imposing; deep. ¶ 그는 ~한 느낌을 주는 사람이다 He is a grave-looking man. *or* He impresses one as being a man of depth.

중흥(中興) restoration; revival. ~하다 revive; be restored. ¶ 민족 ~의 아버지 the father of the national restoration.

중히(重一) 소중하다. ¶ ~ 여기다 attach importance to; take a serious view of.

쥐[1] 〔動〕 a rat; a mouse 〔*pl.* mice〕 (새앙쥐). ¶ ~ 잡기 운동 an anti-rat drive / 독 안에 든 ~와 같다 be like a rat in a trap. / ~덫 a mousetrap; a rattrap / ~약 rat poison.

쥐[2] (경련) a cramp. ¶ 다리에 ~가 나다 have a cramp in the leg.

쥐구멍 a rathole. ¶ ~이라도 찾고 싶은 심정이다 I'm so embarrassed (that) I could dig a hole and crawl into it. *or* I wish I could sink through the floor. / ~에도 별들 날이 있다 〔俗談〕 Fortune knocks at our door by turns.

쥐꼬리 a rattail. ¶ ~만한 월급 a low (small) salary.

쥐다 ① 《물건 따위를》grip; grasp; clasp; take hold of; hold; seize; clench. ¶ 단단히 (꼭) ~ take fast (firm) hold of 《a person's hand》; clasp (grip) 《something》tightly; 주먹을 ~ clench *one's* fist / 이 막대기를 오른손으로 쥐시오 Please hold this stick in your right hand. ② 《권력 따위를》아무의 약점을 쥐고 있다 have something on *a person* / 회사의 실권은 그가 쥐고 있다 The real power over the company is in his hands.

쥐똥나무 〔植〕 a wax tree; privet.

쥐라기(一紀) 〔地質〕 the Jurassic.

쥐며느리 〔蟲〕 a sow bug.

쥐뿔같다 (be) worthless; useless.

쥐뜯다 tear (pluck) (off); pinch.

쥐어박다 strike with *one's* fist; deal a blow.

쥐어주다 《돈을》 slip 《money》 into 《a person's》hand; put 《a thing》 in *one's* hand; 《뇌물을》grease 《a person's》palm; bribe 《a person》; 《팁을》tip. "squeeze."

쥐어짜다 press (out); wring (out);

쥐어흔들다 grab and shake. ¶ 어깨를 ~ shake 《a person》 by the shoulder.

쥐여지내다 be placed under 《a person's》control; live under 《a person's》thumb; live in the grips (of). ¶ 마누라에게 ~ 든 be henpecked; be under the petticoat government.

쥐잡듯(이) (one and) all; without exception; one by one; thoroughly. ¶ 도망자를 잡기 위해 한 집 한 집 ~ 수색하다 search thoroughly for the runaway from door to door.

쥐젖 a small wart.

쥐죽은듯 ~하다 (be) deathly quiet; be silent as the grave.

쥐치 〔魚〕 a filefish.

즈음 the time (when). ¶ ~하여 when; at the time (of); in case (of); on the occasion (of) / 출발에 ~하여 at the time of *one's* departure / 어려운 때에 ~하여 in

즈크 case of emergency.
즈크 duck; canvas. ‖ ~신 〔화〕 canvas shoes.
즉(卽) 〔관〕 namely; that is (to say); in other words: *id est* 〔생략 i.e.〕; 〔바로〕 just; exactly. ¶ 그녀는 2주일 전, ~ 5월 20일에 미국으로 떠났다 She left for the U.S. two weeks ago, that is, on May 20. / 그 일을 할 수 있는 사람은 오직 한사람, ~ 자네지 Only one person can do the work, namely you. / 그것이 ~ 내가 바라는 바이다 That's just (exactly) the thing I want.
즉각(卽刻) instantly; immediately; at once; on the spot.
즉결(卽決) an immediate decision; 〔法〕 summary judgment (decision). ~하다 decide promptly (immediately, on the spot). ‖ ~재판 a summary trial (decision) / ~처분 summary punishment.
즉답(卽答) a prompt (an immediate) answer. ~하다 answer promptly; give an immediate answer. ¶ 질문에 대해 ~을 피하다 avoid giving a prompt answer to *a person's* question.
즉사(卽死) an instant death. ~하다 die on the spot; be killed instantly. ¶ 그 사고로 운전사는 ~했다 The driver was killed instantly in that accident.
즉석(卽席) ¶ ~의 impromptu; extempore; offhand; instant 〔*meal*〕 / ~에서 offhand; on the spot; immediately / ~에서 …하다 *do* offhand (on the spot); improvise 〔*a poem*〕. ‖ ~복권 an instant lottery ticket / ~연설 an offhand speech / ~요리 a quickly prepared dish; an instant meal.
즉시(卽時) at once; immediately; instantly; without delay. ‖ ~불 spot (immediate) payment.
즉위(卽位) 〔등극〕 accession to the throne. ~하다 come (accede) to the throne. ‖ ~식 a coronation (ceremony).
즉응(卽應) prompt conformity. ~하다 conform immediately (to); adapt *oneself* 〔*to*〕.
즉일(卽日) 〔on〕 the same 〔very〕 day.
즉효(卽效) (have, produce) an immediate effect 〔*on*〕. ‖ ~약 a quick 〔an immediate〕 remedy 〔*for*〕.
즉흥(卽興) ¶ ~으로 impromptu; extempore; ad-lib; extemporaneously / ~적으로 시 한 수를 짓다 compose a poem extemporaneously. ‖ ~곡 〔樂〕 an impromptu / ~시 an impromptu poem.

즐거움 pleasure; joy; delight; enjoyment; amusement 〔오락〕; happiness 〔행복〕. ¶ ~의 the pleasure of reading / …하는 것을 ~으로 여기다 take pleasure 〔delight〕 in *doing*.
즐거이 happily; pleasantly; joyfully; with delight. ¶ 친구를 ~ 맞다 receive a friend with pleasure.
즐겁다 (be) pleasant; happy; delightful; merry; cheerful; joyful. ¶ 즐거운 우리집 *one's* happy 〔sweet〕 home / 즐거운 한 때를 보내다 have a good (happy) time / 결혼 생활은 즐겁기만 한 것이 아니다 Married life isn't rose all the way.
즐기다 enjoy; take pleasure 〔delight〕 in; get pleasure 〔*from*〕; enjoy *oneself* 〔*over*〕; have fun 〔*doing, with*〕. ¶ 인생을 〔자연을〕 ~ enjoy life (nature) / 꽃을 보고 ~ enjoy 〔feast *one's* eyes on〕 the flowers.
즐비하다(櫛比—) stand closely together; stand in a (continuous) row; be lined 〔*with shops*〕.
즙(汁) juice 〔과실의〕; sap 〔초목의〕. ¶ ~이 많은 juicy / ~을 내다 extract (squeeze) juice 〔*from a lemon*〕.
증(症) 〔증세〕 symptoms. ¶ 허기 ~이 나다 feel hungry.
증(證) 〔증거〕 (a) proof; evidence; 〔증서〕 a certificate. ¶ 학생 ~ a certificate of student; a student's card.
증가(增加) (an) increase; (a) gain; (a) rise. ~하다 increase; grow. ¶ ~되고 있다 be on the increase / 수〔인구〕가 ~하다 increase in number (population) / 자연 ~ a natural increase / 실업자의 수가 ~하고 있다 Unemployment is 〔up〕 (on the rise). / ~액 the amount increased / ~율 the rate of increase.
증간(增刊) a special 〔an extra〕 number (issue). ‖ ~춘기 ~호 a special spring issue.
증감(增減) ~하다 increase and 〔or〕 decrease; fluctuate; vary 〔*in quantity*〕. ¶ 수입은 달에 따라 ~이 있다 The income varies (fluctuates) with the month.
증강(增強) reinforcement. ~하다 reinforce; strengthen 〔강화〕; increase 〔수량을 늘리다〕. ¶ 군사력을 ~하다 reinforce the country's military strength / 수송력을 ~다 increase the carrying capacity 〔*of the railroad*〕.
증거(證據) evidence; (a) proof; 〔法〕 (a) testimony. ¶ 결정적인 〔확실한〕 ~ decisive (positive) evi-

증권(證券) a bill; a bond (공사채); securities (유가증권). ¶ 선화(船貨) ~ a bill of lading (생략 BL) / ~ 화하다 convert 《funds》 into securities / ~에 손을 대다 speculate in stocks. ‖ ~거래소 a stock exchange / ~시세 stock prices / ~시장 a securities market / ~ 투자 investment in securities / ~ 회사 a securities (stock) company.

증기(蒸氣) steam; vapor. ¶ 이 기계는 ~ 로 움직인다 This machine is driven by steam. ‖ 기관 steam engine / ~기관차 a steam locomotive / ~난방(장치) steam-heating (system) / ~선 a steamship / ~소독 steam disinfection; autoclaving.

증대(增大) ~ 하다 enlarge; increase; get (grow) larger (bigger). ¶ ~ 하는 세계 위기 a mounting world crisis / 인구의 ~ an increase in population. ‖ ~호 (잡지의) an enlarged number.

증류(蒸溜) distillation. ~ 하다 distill. ¶ ~기 a distiller / ~수 distilled water / ~주 distilled liquor; spirits; liquors 《美》/ ~장치 distillation apparatus.

증명(證明) a proof; evidence; 《증언》 testimony. ~ 하다 prove (실증하다); testify 《to》 (증언하다); certify (문서로); verify (입증하다); identify (신원을). ¶ 잘못임을 ~ 하다 prove that 《something》 is wrong / 이에 ~ 임을 한다 《증명서의 문구》 This is to certify that…; I hereby certify that… / 그 약은 효력이 있다는 것이 ~ 되었다 The drug has been proved (to be) effective. ¶ 「신분을 ~ 할 수 있는 것을 가지고 계십니까?」 / 「운전 면허증이 있습니다.」"Do you have anything to identify yourself?" — "I have a driver's license." ‖ ~ 서 a certificate; a testimonial (신분 ~서 an identification card).

증모(增募) ~ 하다 《군인 등을》 recruit larger enlistment; 《학생 등을》 receive larger enrollment.

증발(蒸發) evaporation; vaporization. ~ 하다 evaporate; vaporize; 《사람이》 disappear. ¶ ~성의 evaporative / 물이 모두 ~ 했다 The water entirely evaporated. / 휘발유는 ~ 하기 쉽다 Gasoline is volatile. / 그녀는 큰 돈을 가지고 ~ 했다 She disappeared without a trace taking (carrying) a lot of money. ‖ ~열 the heat of evaporation; evaporation heat.

증발(增發) 《통화의》 an increased issue 《of notes》; 《열차의》 operation of an extra train. ¶ 적자공채의 ~ a further issue of "red-ink" bonds / 지폐를 ~ 하다 issue additional paper money / 열차를 ~ 하다 increase the number of trains 《between》.

증배(增配) an increased ration (배당); an increased ration (배급). ~ 하다 pay an increased dividend; increase the (rice) ration.

증보(增補) ~ 하다 enlarge; supplement; make an addition 《to a book》. ¶ ~ 개정 ~ 판 a revised and enlarged edition 《of》.

증빙(證憑) evidence; proof; testimony. ‖ ~ 서류 documentary evidence.

증산(增産) increased production (output); 《농산물의》 an increased yield 《of rice》. ~ 하다 increase (boost, step up) production; increase the yield. ¶ 강철의 ~ 계획 a plan for increasing steel output / 목재의 장기 ~ 계획 a long-range program for increasing the output of lumber. ‖ ~ 운동 a production increase campaign / ~ 의욕 《farmers'》 willingness to produce more.

증상(症狀) symptoms (징후); the condition of illness (병세).

증서(證書) a deed (양도 따위의); a bond (채무의); a certificate (증명서); a diploma (졸업증서). ¶ 예금 ~ a certificate of deposit / 차용 ~ an IOU (=I owe you) / ~ 를 작성하다 prepare (draw out, write out) a deed.

증설(增設) ~ 하다 increase; establish more 《schools》; install more 《telephones》. ¶ 지점을 2개소 ~ 하다 set up (establish) two more branches.

증세(症勢) symptoms 《of》; the condition of a patient 《for》; …의 ~ 를 나타내다 show (develop) symptoms 《of measles》.

증세(增稅) a tax increase. ~ 하다 increase (raise) taxes. ‖ ~ 안(案) a proposed tax increase (제안) ; a tax increase bill (법안).

증손(曾孫) a great-grandchild. ‖ ~자 a great-grandson / ~녀 a great-granddaughter.

증수(增水) the rise (rising) of a

river; flooding. ~하다 〈강이〉 rise; swell. ‖ ~기 the annual flooding period.

증수(增收) increase of revenue [receipts, income] (수입); an increased yield (농산물). ~하다 increase revenue [income, receipts]. ¶ 1할의 ~ an increase of ten percent in income.

증수회(贈收賄) corruption; bribery. ¶ ~사건 a bribery case.

증식(增殖) ~하다 increase; multiply; propagate. ¶ 자기 ~ self-reproduction. ‖ ~로〈원자로의〉 a breeder reactor.

증액(增額) (an) increase. ~하다 increase; raise. ¶ 가족 수당을 ~하다 raise the level of the family allowance / 예산의 ~을 요구하다 demand an increase in *one's* budget allocation. ‖ ~분(分) the increased amount.

증언(證言) testimony; witness; (verbal) evidence. ~하다 give evidence; testify 〈to〉; bear witness〈to〉. ¶ 목격자의 ~ the testimony of an eyewitness / ~을 하다 testify 「in favor of [against] the accused」. ‖ ~대 [take] the witness stand.

증여(贈與) donation; presentation. ~하다 give; present; donate 《*money*》: make a present of 《*a thing*》. ‖ ~세 a donation [gift] tax / ~자 a giver; a donor / ~재산 a donated property.

증오(憎惡) hatred; abhorrence. ~하다 hate; abhor; detest. ¶ ~할 만한 hateful; detestable / ~하는 마음을 품다 have [bear] a hatred 〈*for*〉; feel animosity 〈*toward*〉.

증원(增員) ~하다 increase the number of staff [personnel].

증원(增援) ~하다 reinforce. ‖ ~부대 reinforcements.

증인(人) a witness; an attestor. ¶ ~이 되다 bear witness [testimony] 〈to〉; testify 〈to〉 / ~으로서 출두하다 present *oneself* as a witness / ~으로 법정에 소환되다 be summoned to the court as a witness. ‖ ~석 [대] the witness stand.

증자(增資) an increase of capital; a capital increase. ~하다 increase the capital. ‖ ~주 additional stocks [shares] / 무상 ~ free issue of new shares / 유상 ~ issue of new shares to be purchased.

증정(贈呈) presentation; 《책에 저자가 서명할 때의》 With the compliments of the author. ~하다 present; make a present 《of a thing》. ¶ 우리는 선생님께 손목시계를 ~했다 We presented our teacher with a wristwatch. ‖ ~본 a presentation copy 〈*of*〉 / ~식 the ceremony of the presentation 〈*of*〉 / ~자 a giver; a donor / ~품 a present; a gift.

증조모(曾祖母) a great-grandmother.

증조부(曾祖父) a great-grandfather.

증진(增進) ~하다 increase; promote; further; advance. ¶ 사회 복지의 ~ promotion of social welfare.

증축(增築) extension of a building. ~하다 extend [enlarge] a building; build an annex. ¶ 집에 작업실로 별채를 ~하다 build an annex to my house to use as a workshop. ‖ ~공사 extension work.

증파(增派) ~하다 dispatch more 《*troops, warships*》.

증폭(增幅) amplification. ~하다 amplify. ‖ ~기 an amplifier.

증표(證標) a voucher.

증험(證驗) verification. ~하다 verify; bear witness to.

증회(贈賄) ~하다 bribe; give a bribe; grease [oil, tickle] 《*a person's*》palm. ¶ ~사건 a bribery [graft] case / ~자 a briber / ~죄 bribery. ‖ ~ syndrome.

증후(症候) 증세(症勢). ‖ ~군

지(後) since; from; after. ¶ 떠난 지 두 시간 후 two hours after the departure.

지…(至) 〈까지〉to…; till….

…지 ① 〈의문〉 어떻게 하는 것인 ~ 가르쳐 주세요 Tell me how to do it. ② 〈말끝〉 오늘은 누가 오겠 ~ Someone may come to see me today. ③ 〈부정〉 저 배엔 사람이 타고 있 ~ 않다 The boat has no passengers on board.

지가(地價) the price [value] of land; land prices [values]. ¶ 공시 ~ the assessed value of land / ~가 일년만에 배가 되었다 Land prices have doubled over the past year.

지각(地殼) 〖地〗 the earth's crust; the lithosphere. ‖ ~운동 [변동] crustal activity [movements].

지각(知覺) ① 〖心〗 perception; sensation. ~하다 perceive; feel; be conscious 〈*of*〉. ¶ ~기관 the organs of perception / ~력 perceptibility / ~신경 sensory nerves. ② 〈분별〉 discretion; judgment; (good) sense. ¶ ~있는 sensible; discreet; prudent.

지각(遲刻) being late. ~하다 be [come] late; be behind time. ¶ 학교에 ~하다 be late for school. ‖ ~자〖생〗 a late-comer.

지갑(紙匣) a purse; a pocket-book; a wallet.

지게 an A-frame (carrier). ¶ ~를 지다 carry the A-frame on *one's* back. / ~꾼 an A-frame coolie; a burden carrier / ~차 a fork-lift (truck).

지게미(술의) wine lees.

지겹다(넌더리나다) (be) tedious; wearisome; tiresome; 《지긋지긋하다》(be) loathsome; detestable; disgusting; repulsive.

지경(地境) ①《경계》a boundary; a border. ②《형편》a situation; circumstances. ¶ …할 ~에 있다 be on the point (verge, brink) of; be about to / ~에 이르다 be in a bad fix / 파멸될 ~이다 stand on the brink of ruin.

지계(地階) the basement.

지고(至高) supremacy. ~하다 (be) highest; supreme.

지관(地官) a geomancer.

지구(地球) the earth; the globe. ¶ ~의 terrestrial; earthly / ~상의 모든 생물 all life on the earth / ~의 인력 the earth's gravitation / ~ 반대편의 half the globe away / ~는 태양의 주위를 돈다 The earth goes around the sun. ‖ ~물리학 geophysics / ~온난화 global warming / ~의(儀) a globe / ~인 an earthling; an earthman / ~자원관측(탐사)위성 an earth resources observation (technology) satellite / ~촌 a global village.

지구(地區) 《지역》 a district; a zone; a region; an area; a section 《美》. ¶ 경인~ the Seoul-Inch'on district (area) / 상업 (주택) ~ the business (residence) zone. ‖ ~당 a (electoral) district party chapter.

지구(地溝) 〔地〕 a rift valley.

지구(持久) ¶ ~력 endurance; staying power; tenacity / ~전 a long-drawn-out struggle (war).

지국(支局) a branch (office).

지그시 ①《슬며시》softly; quietly; gently. ¶ 눈을 ~ 감다 close *one's* eyes gently. ②《참는 모양》 patiently; perseveringly.

지극(至極) ~하다 (be) utmost; extreme; 《대단하다》 (be) excessive; enormous; tremendous; 《극진하다》 (be) most faithful; utterly sincere. ¶ ~히 very; most; quite; exceedingly.

지근거리다 ①《귀찮게 굴다》annoy; bother; tease; 《졸라대다》 importune. ②《머리가》have a shooting pain (in *one's* head). ③《씹다》 chew softly.

지글거리다 sizzle; simmer; bubble up; seethe.

지글지글 sizzling; simmering; bubbling up; seething. ¶ ~ 끓다 sizzle.

지금(只今) ①《현재》the present; the present time (day); this time (moment); now. ¶ ~의 present; of today (the present day) / ~까지 till now; up to the present; hitherto / ~부터 from now (on); after this; hence / ~ 그것을 생각해 보니 when I think of it now / ~까지 나는 그녀를 사랑하고 있다 I still love her. / ~이 5년 전보다 훨씬 살기가 좋다 We are much better off now than five years ago. ②《지금 막》just; just now; a moment ago. ¶ 삼촌은 ~ 도착했다 My uncle has just arrived (came just now). ③《지금 곧》soon; at once; (just) in a moment; immediately. ¶ ~ 그 것을 해라 Do it 「at once (immediately).

지금(地金) ingot gold(세공하지 않은); ground metal (세공품의 재료); bullion (화폐용의).

지금거리다 chew gritty; be gritty to the teeth.

지급(支給) provision; supply; payment(지불). ~하다 give; provide (supply, furnish) *a person* with 《*a thing*》; allow; pay. ¶ 이재민에게 식량을 ~하다 provide food to the victims; provide (supply) the victims with food / 여비를 ~하다 allow (pay) 《*a person*》 traveling expenses; pay 《*a person*》 a travel allowance / ~을 정지하다 stop (suspend) payment. ‖ ~기일 the due date; the date of payment / ~능력 solvency; ability to pay / ~보증 (bank's) payment guarantees / ~보증수표 a certified check / ~불능 insolvency / ~액 an allowance; the amount supplied / ~어음 a bill (note) payable / ~유예 postponement of payment; [法] moratorium / ~인 a payer; a drawee(어음의) / ~전표 a payment slip / ~준비금 a reserve fund for payment / ~지 the place of payment / ~청구 a demand for payment / ~품 articles supplied; supplies.

지급(至急) ¶ ~한 urgent; pressing; immediate / ~으로 urgently; immediately; at once; without delay / ~편으로 보내다 send 《*a package*》 by express. ‖ ~전보 (전화) an urgent telegram (call).

지긋지긋하다 ①《넌더리나다》 (be) tedious; wearisome; tiresome. ②《지겹다》 (be) loathsome; detestable; tedious; repulsive; horrible. ¶ 생각만해도 ~ It makes me sick even to think of it.

지긋하다 be advanced in years; be well up in years. ¶ 나이가 지긋한 사람 an elderly person; a person well 「on [advanced] in years.

지기(知己) a bosom friend(친한 친구); an acquaintance(아는 사람). ¶ ~지우(之友) an appreciative friend.

…지기¹ 《논밭의》 an area 〔a measure〕 of land. ¶ 닷마~ a plot of land that will take 5 *mal* of seed / 두 섬~ a stretch of land requiring 2 *sŏm* of seed.

…지기² 《사람》 a keeper; a guard. ¶ 문~ a gatekeeper.

지껄거리다 ☞ **지껄이다**.

지껄이다 talk garrulously; chat; chatter; gabble(빨리).

지끈지끈 ① 《부러지는 소리》 with a snap. ② 《아프다》 끌치가 ~ 아프다 have a splitting headache.

지나가다 ☞ **지나다** ②, ③.

지나다 ① 《기한이》 expire; terminate; be out. ¶ 기한이 지났다 The time limit has expired. ② 《통과》 pass (by); go past; pass through. ¶ 대구를 지났습니까 Have we passed Taegu yet? / 숲속을 ~ pass through a wood. ③ 《경과》 pass (away); elapse; go on (by). ¶ 10년이 지나 after ten years / 시간이 지남에 따라 as time goes on (by) / 지난 일은 되돌릴 수 없다 What is done cannot be undone. *or* Let bygones be bygones.

지나새나 always; all the time.

지나오다 pass (by); come along (by, through); 《겪다》 go through; undergo. ¶ 숲을~ come through a forest / 많은 어려움을~ go through hardships.

지나치다 ① 《과도》 exceed; go too far. ¶ 지나친 excessive; immoderate / 지나치게 excessively; immoderately / 그녀의 농담은 정도가 지나쳤다 Her joke went too far. ② 《통과》 ☞ **지나다**②. ☞ 과유불급.

지난날 old days 〔times〕; bygone days. ¶ ~의 추억 the memory of old days.

지난한(至難—) (be) most 〔extremely〕 difficult.

지날결 ~에 as one passes; on the way / ~에는 when you happen to come this way / ~에 잠시 들렀다 As I was passing this way, I've just dropped in to say hello.

지남철(指南鐵) 《자석》 a magnet.

지내다 ① 《세월을》 spend 〔pass〕 *one's* time; get along; 《생활》 live; make a living. ¶ 독서로~ spend *one's* time in reading / 행복하게~ live happily / 바쁘게~ live 〔lead〕 a busy life / 빈둥거리며 놀고~ idle *one's* time away; loaf. ② 《치름》 hold; observe. ¶ 장례를~ hold a funeral (ceremony). ③ 《겪다》 follow a career; serve; go through; experience.

지내보다 사람은 지내봐야 안다 It takes time to really get to know a person.

지네 〖動〗 a centipede.

지노(紙—) a paper string.

지느러미 a fin. ¶ 등 〔가슴, 꼬리〕~ a dorsal 〔pectoral, caudal〕 fin.

지능(知能) intelligence; intellect; mental 〔intellectual〕 faculties. ¶ ~적인 intellectual; mental / ~의 발달 intellectual growth / ~이 낮은 아이 a mentally retarded child / ~이 뛰어난 아이 an intellectually gifted child. ‖ ~검사 an intelligence test / ~로봇 an intelligent 〔industrial〕 robot / ~범 an intellectual offense 〔crime〕 / ~지수 intelligence quotient(생략 I.Q.).

지니다 《보전》 keep; preserve; retain; 《가지다》 have; carry; 《품다》 hold; entertain; cherish. ¶ 비밀을~ cherish a secret / 몸에 권총을~ carry a pistol with *one*.

지다¹ ① 《패배》 be defeated; be beaten; be outdone; lose 《a game》. ¶ 경주에~ lose a race / 선거에~ be defeated in the election / 소송에~ lose a lawsuit / 지는 것이 이기는 것이 되는 경우도 있다 Sometimes it pays to lose. *or* Sometimes defeat means victory. ② 《굴복》 give in 〔to〕; be overcome with; yield 〔to〕. ¶ 유혹에~ yield 〔give way〕 to temptation. ③ 《뒤지어》 be second to; be inferior to; fall behind. ¶ 누구에도 지지 않다 be second to none / 이것은 질에 있어서 일본 제품에 지지 않는다 This is not inferior to Japanese products in quality.

지다² ① 《짐을》 shoulder 《a burden》; carry 《*something*》 on *one's* back. ¶ 그녀는 보따리를 지고 있었다 She had 〔was carrying〕 a bundle on her back. ② 《빚을》 get into 《*debt*》; be saddled with 《a *debt*》; owe (money). ¶ 그에게 돈을 얼마나 졌느냐 How much money do you owe him? ③ 《책임을》 hold; bear 〔assume〕 《a responsibility of》; be burdened with 《an important duty》. ④ 《신세 따위를》

지다 owe; be indebted to; be under an obligation to. ¶ ~신세를 많이 졌습니다 I am indebted to you for kindness.

지다³ ① 〈해·달이〉 set; sink; go down. ② 〈잎·꽃이〉 fall; be strewn 〔to the ground〕; be gone. ③ 〈때 따위가〉 come off 〔out〕; be removed; be taken out. ④ 〈숨이〉 breathe one's last 〔breath〕; die.

지다⁴ ① 〈그늘·얼룩이 생기다〉 ¶ 그늘이 ~ be shaded; get shady / 얼룩이 ~ become stained 〔soiled〕. ② 〈장마가〉 set in. ¶ 장마가 ~ The rainy season has set in.

지다⁵ 〈되어가다〉 become; get; grow. ¶ 좋아 〔나빠, 추워, 더워〕 ~ get better 〔worse, colder, warmer〕.

지당하다(至當一) 〔be〕 proper; right; fair; just; reasonable.

지대(支隊) a detachment; detached troops.

지대(地代) a ground 〔land〕 rent.

지대(地帶) a zone; an area; a region; a belt. ¶ 공장 ~ an industrial area / 녹 ~ a green belt / 면화 ~ 《미국 남부의》 the Cotton Belt / 비무장 ~ a demilitarized zone / 안전 〔위험, 중립〕 ~ a safety 〔danger, neutral〕 zone.

지대공(地對空) ¶ ~미사일 a ground-to-air missile.

지대지(地對地) ¶ ~미사일 a ground-to-ground missile.

지대하다(至大一) 〔be〕 〔very〕 great; vital; vast; ¶ 지대한 관심사 a matter of great concerns.

지덕(智德) knowledge and virtue.

지도(地圖) a map; a chart 〈해도〉; an atlas 〈지도책〉. ¶ 벽걸이 ~ a wall map / 한국 〔세계〕 ~ a map of Korea 〔the world〕 / 도로 ~ a road map / 5만 분의 1 ~ a map on a scale of 1 to 50,000 / ~를 그리다 〔보다〕 draw 〔consult〕 a map / ~에서 찾다 look up 《a place》 on a map / 이 도로는 ~에 나와 있지 않다 This road is not shown on the map.

지도(指導) guidance; directions; leadership; instruction. ~하다 guide; direct; coach; lead; instruct. ¶ ~적인 leading / ~적인 입장에 있다 be in a position of leadership / 잘 ~해 주십시오 I look to you for guidance. ∥ ~교사 a guidance teacher / ~력 leadership / ~방침 〔원리〕 a guiding principle; guidelines / ~자 a leader; a director; a coach; an instructor.

지독하다(至毒一) ① 〈독하다〉 〔be〕 vicious; vitriolic; spiteful; atrocious. ¶ 지독한 짓 an atrocious act. ② 〈모질다〉 〔be〕 severe; terrible; awful. ¶ 지독한 추위 the severe cold / 지독한 구두쇠 an awful miser. 「theory.

지동(地動) ∥ ~설 the Copernican

지라 〔解〕 the spleen; the milt.

지랄 ① 〈잠스런 언행〉 an outburst 《of temper》; a fit 《of hysteria》. ~하다 go crazy; get out of line; behave rampageously; get hysterical. ② 〈간질〉 ~하다 have an epileptic fit. ∥ ~병 간질.

지략(智略) resources; artifice. ¶ ~이 풍부하다 be resourceful; be full of resources / ~이 풍부한 사람 a man of resources.

지렁이 〔動〕 an earthworm. ¶ ~도 밟으면 꿈틀한다 《俗談》 Even a worm will turn.

지레¹ 〈지렛대〉 a lever; a handspike. ¶ ~로 들어올리다 lever 《something》 up; raise 《something》 with a lever.

지레² 《미리》 in advance; beforehand. ¶ ~짐작하다 jump to a conclusion; draw 〔form〕 a hasty conclusion.

지력(地力) fertility 〔of soil〕.

지력(智力) mental capacity; intellectual power; intellect; mentality. ¶ 12세 어린이의 ~ a mentality of 12-year-old boy.

지령(指令) an order; an instruction. ~하다 order; direct; give instructions. ¶ 비밀 ~ a secret order / 무전으로 ~을 받다 receive radio instructions. ∥ ~서 written instructions 〔orders〕.

지령(紙齡) the issue number of a newspaper.

지론(持論) a cherished opinion; one's pet theory; a stock argument. ¶ ~을 굽히지 않다 stick 〔hold fast〕 to one's opinion.

지뢰(地雷) a 〔land〕 mine. ¶ ~를 묻다 lay a mine; mine 《a field》. ∥ ~밭 〔지대〕 a mine field / ~탐지기 a mine detector / 국제대인~금지운동 the International Campaign to Ban Landmines 《생략 ICBL》.

지루하다 〔be〕 tedious; boring; wearisome; dull; tiresome. ¶ 지루한 강연 a tedious lecture.

지류(支流) a tributary; a branch 〔stream〕.

지르다 ① 〈차다〉 kick hard; 〈치다〉 beat; hit; strike. ② 〈꽂아 넣다〉 insert; thrust 〔stick, put〕 in. ¶ 빗장을 ~ bolt 〔bar〕 a door. ③ 〈불을〉 불을 ~ set fire to; set 《a house》 on fire. ④ 〈자르다, 끊다〉 ¶ 순을 ~ cut 〔nip〕 off the buds. ⑤ 〈질러가다〉 take a shorter way; cut across 《a field》;

지르르 take a short cut. ⑥《돈을 태우다》 stake; wager. ¶ (노름)판에 돈을 ~ 놓다 lay (down) a bet 《*on the gambling table*》. ⑦《소리를》 yell; scream; cry aloud. ¶ 고함을 ~ yell; shout; holler.

지르르 ①《물기·기름기가》 glossy with grease. ②《뼈마디가》 with a dull pain 《*in the joint*》.

지르코늄 [化] zirconium (기호 Zr).

지르콘 [鑛] zircon.

지르퉁하다 (be) sulky; sullen; pouting. ¶ 그는 지르퉁하여 말이 없었다 He was in a sulky mood and wouldn't say a word.

지름 a diameter.

지름길 a short cut; a shorter road. ¶ ~로 가다 take a short cut. 「graphical advantage.

지리(地利) (gain, have) a geo-

지리(地理) 《지세》 geographical features; topography; 《지리학》 geography. ¶ ~적인 geographical / ~적 조건 geographical conditions / 그는 이 부근 ~에 밝다 He is well acquainted (quite familiar) with this place. ‖ ~책 a geography book / ~학자 a geographer.

지리다¹ 《냄새가》 smell of urine.

지리다² 《오줌을》 wet (soil) one's pants.

지리멸렬(支離滅裂) ~하다 be incoherent; 《사분오열》 be disrupted; be torn asunder; break up; come to pieces. ¶ ~이 되다 go to pieces; be thrown into confusion.

지린내 the smell of urine.

지망(志望) a wish; a desire; choice; 《선택》 an aspiration. ~하다 wish; desire; aspire 《*to*》; choose; prefer. ¶ 외교관을 ~하다 want to be a diplomat; aspire to a diplomatic career. ‖ ~자 an applicant; a candidate 《*for*》 / ~ 학과 the desired course / 제1[제2] ~ one's first [second] preference [choice].

지맥(支脈) a branch of a mountain range(산맥의).

지맥(地脈) a stratum [*pl*. strata]; a layer; a vein.

지면(地面) 《지표》 the surface of land [the earth]; 《지상》 the ground; the earth.

지면(紙面) 《신문의》 (paper) space. ¶ ~ 관계로 for want of space; on account of limited space / ~에 ~을 할당하다 give space to 《*a subject*》 / 많은 ~을 차지하다 take up a lot of space.

지명(地名) a place name; the name of a place. ‖ ~사전 a geographical dictionary; a gazetteer.

지명(知名) ~의 noted; well-known / 이 나라에서 우리 회사의 ~ 도는 아직 낮다 Our company is not well-known in this country. ‖ ~도 name value; notoriety (악명의) / ~인사 a noted (well-known) person; a notable.

지명(指名) nomination. ~하다 nominate; name; designate. ¶ ~된 사람 a nominee / 의장으로 ~되다 be nominated (as) chairman / 그는 아들을 후계자로 ~했다 He designated his son as his successor. ‖ ~수배 a search for the named suspect (under an arrest warrant) / ~수배자 a wanted criminal (man) / ~자 a nominator / ~타자 [野] a designated hitter. 「ness.

지모(知謀) ingenuity; resourceful-

지목(地目) the classification of land category. ‖ ~변경 re-classification of land; a change in the category of land.

지목(指目) ~하다 point out; spot; indicate; put the finger on.

지문(指紋) a fingerprint. ¶ ~을 남기다 leave one's fingerprints 《*on*》 / ~을 채취하다 take 《*a person's*》 fingerprints.

지문학(地文學) physiography.

지물(紙物) paper goods. ‖ ~포 a paper goods store.

지반(地盤) ①《토대》 the base; the foundation; 《지면》 the ground. 단단한 ~ firm (solid) ground / 약한 ~ soft (flimsy) ground / ~을 굳히다 strengthen (solidify) the foundation. ②《기반》 footing; foothold. ¶ 확실한 ~ a sure foothold / ~을 닦다 establish one's foothold. ③《세력범위》 a sphere of influence; a constituency(선거구). ¶ 《선거의》 ~을 닦다 nurse one's constituency.

지방(地方) 《지역》 a locality; a district; a region; an area; 《시골》 the country; the province. ¶ ~의 local; regional; provincial / 서울 ~ Seoul and its neighboring districts / 서북 ~ north-western districts / 이 ~에서는 in this part of the country; in these parts / ~의 중심 도시 a district (provincial) capital / ~에 가다 go into the country / ~에서 올라오다 come up from the country. ‖ ~검사 the district attorney / ~검찰청 the district public prosecutor's office / ~공무원 a local public service worker; a provincial government official / ~관청 a local government / ~기사 local news / ~도시 a provincial city / ~법원

지방 a district court / ~분권 (the) decentralization of power / ~사투리 a local accent (dialect) / ~색 local color / ~선거법 local autonomy election laws / ~신문 a local paper / ~은행 a local bank / ~의회 (의원) a local assembly (assemblyman) / ~자치 local self-government (autonomy) / ~자치단체 a self-governing body / ~주의 regionalism / ~채 (債) a local bond / ~판 (版) a local (provincial) edition / ~행정 local administration.

지방 (脂肪) fat; grease; lard (돼지의); suet (소·양의). ¶ ~이 많은 고기 fat meat. ~간 (肝) a fatty liver / ~과다 excess of fat; obesity / ~산 a fatty acid / ~조직 adipose tissue / ~질 fat; sebaceous constitution.

지배 (支配) 《관리》 control; 《통치》 rule; government. ~하다 control; rule; govern; dominate. ¶ …의 ~를 받다 be [put] under the control (rule) of… / ~하에 두다 keep (place) 《somebody, something》 under *one's* control. / ~계급 the ruling classes / ~권 control; management; supremacy / ~자 a ruler.

지배인 (支配人) a manager; an executive; a superintendent. ¶ 부~ an assistant manager / 총 ~ a general manager.

지벅거리다 stumble along.

지번 (地番) a lot number.

지변 (地變) 『천재 ~ a natural disaster (calamity).

지병 (持病) a chronic disease; an old complaint. ¶ 두통이 나의 ~이다 Headaches are chronic to me.

지보 (至寶) the most valuable treasure. 〖beatitude.

지복 (至福) the supreme bliss.

지부 (支部) a branch (office); a chapter. ‖ ~장 the manager of a branch. 〖make fun of.

지부럭거리다 annoy; pester; tease;

지분 (脂粉) rouge and powder.

지분거리다 ☞ 지부럭거리다.

지불 (支拂) payment; defrayment. ~하다 pay (out); clear 《*one's debts*》; honor 《*a check*》. ☞ 지급. ¶ ~을 거절하다 refuse payment / ~을 청구하다 ask 《*a person*》 to pay; ask for payment / ~을 연기하다 postpone (put off, delay) payment / 식사 대금을 신용 카드로 ~했다 I paid for our meal by credit card.

지붕 a roof. ¶ ~을 이다 roof. 《*a house with slate*》 / 기와~ a tiled roof / 둥근~ a dome / 초가~ a thatched roof / 평~ a flat roof. ‖ ~널 a (roof) shingle.

지사 (支社) a branch (office).

지사 (志士) ¶ 우국~ a patriot; a public-spirited man.

지사 (知事) a (prefectural) governor.

지상 (地上) ¶ ~에(서) on the ground; on (the) earth / 5층 지하 2층의 빌딩 a building with five stories above ground and two below / ~의 낙원 an earthly paradise; a paradise on earth / 80피트 eighty feet above the ground. ‖ ~관제센터 a ground control center / ~군 ground forces / ~권 〖法〗 surface right; superficies / ~근무 ground service / ~부대 a ground unit / ~시설 ground facilities / 유도착륙 방식 〖항공의〗 ground control approach (생략 GCA) / ~전 ground warfare; land war / ~정비사 a ground crew / ~포화 ground fire.

지상 (至上) ¶ ~의 highest; supreme. ‖ ~권 supreme power / ~명령 a supreme order / 〖哲〗 a categorical imperative / 예술~주의 the art-for-art principle.

지상 (紙上) ¶ ~에 on paper; in the newspaper. ‖ ~상담란 a personal advice column.

지새는달 a wan morning moon.

지새다 the day breaks; it dawns.

지새우다 awake (sit up, stay up) all (through) night; pass a night without sleep.

지서 (支署) a branch office; a substation / 〖경찰의〗 a police substation (box).

지선 (支線) a branch line.

지성 (至誠) 《absolute》 sincerity. ¶ ~이면 감천이라 Sincerity moves heaven.

지성 (知性) intellect; intelligence. ¶ ~적인 intellectual. ‖ ~인 an intellectual; a highbrow.

지세 (地貰) (ground) rent.

지세 (地稅) a land tax.

지세 (地勢) topography; geographical features.

지속 (持續) ~하다 continue; last; maintain; keep up. ¶ ~적인 lasting; continuous. ‖ ~기간 a duration period / ~력 sustaining (staying) power / ~성 durability / ~성이 있는 durable.

지수 (指數) an index (number); 〖數〗 an exponent. ¶ 물가 (불쾌) ~ a price (discomfort) index.

지스러기 waste; trash; odds and ends.

지시 (指示) directions; instructions. ~하다 direct; instruct. ¶ ~대로 하여라 Do it as indicated. or Follow my instructions. ‖ ~

대명사 〖文〗 a demonstrative pronoun / ~서 directions; an order / ~약 〖化〗 an indicator.

지식 (知識) knowledge; information (정보); learning (학문). ¶ 전문적 ~ an expert [a professional] knowledge / 해박한 ~ an extensive knowledge / ~의 보고 treasure house of knowledge; a thesaurus / ~을 활용하다 put *one's* knowledge to practical use. ‖ ~계급 the intellectuals / ~욕 a desire to learn; a thirst for knowledge / ~인 an intellectual; an educated person / ~(집약형)산업 a knowledge(-intensive) industry.

지아비 (남편) *one's* husband.
지압요법 (指壓療法) finger-pressure therapy (cure).
지양 (止揚) 〖哲·論〗 *Aufheben* 〖獨〗; sublation. ¶ ~하다 sublate.
지어내다 make up; invent; fabricate. ¶ 지어낸 얘기 a made-up story.
지어미 (아내) *one's* wife.
지엄 (至嚴) ~하다 (be) extremely strict (stern).
지엔피 the G.N.P. (◀ Gross National Product)
지역 (地域) an area; a zone; a region. ¶ ~적인 local; regional / ~적으로 locally; regionally / ~별로 by regional groups / ~에 따라 다르다 differ from place to place; vary in different localities. ‖ ~구 a local district / ~단체 a local organization / ~대표 local union delegates / ~사회 a community; a local society / ~연구 area studies / ~이기주의 regional selfishness / ~차(差) regional differences.

지연 (遲延) (a) delay. ~하다 delay; be delayed; be late. ¶ 오래 ~된 long-deferred. ‖ ~작전 stalling (delaying) tactics.
지연 (地緣) ¶ ~사회 a territorial society / ~과 혈연의 덕을 보려 했으나 허사였다 I tried to get help from my relatives and people in the local community, but it was useless.
지열 (地熱) terrestrial heat; the heat of the earth. ‖ ~발전 geothermal power generation.
지엽 (枝葉) ① (가지와 잎) branches and leaves. ② (이야기에서) side issues (*of a story*); a digression. ¶ 주제에서 ~으로 흐르다 turn aside from the main subject.
지옥 (地獄) hell; Hades; the inferno. ¶ ~에 떨어지다 go to hell. ‖ 입시~ an ordeal of entrance examinations.
지용 (智勇) wisdom and courage.
지우개 an eraser; a chalk [black-

board] eraser (칠판의).
지우다¹ ① (짐을) put 《something》 on 《*a person's*》 back; make 《*a person*》 shoulder 《*a burden*》. ¶ 무거운 짐을 ~ burden 《*a person*》; lay [put] a burden upon 《*a person*》. ② (부담) charge 《*a person with a duty*》; lay 《*a duty upon a person*》.
지우다² (없어지게) erase; rub out; wipe out; strike out.
지우다³ (그늘 따위를) form; 《눈물 따위를》 shed; spill. ¶ 그늘을 ~ form shade / 눈물을 ~ shed tears. ‖ ~ the better of.
지우다⁴ (이기다) beat; defeat; get
지우산 (아이를) have a miscarriage; (숨을) die; expire. ‖ 라~ (雨傘) an oil-paper umbrella.
지원 (支援) support; assistance. ~하다 support; assist; back (up). ¶ 적극적인 ~ active (positive) support / …의 ~을 구하다 seek support from…. ‖ ~부대 backup (support) forces.
지원 (志願) application; volunteering (자진). ~하다 apply (*for*); volunteer (*for*); desire (*for*). ¶ 군대에 ~하다 volunteer to be a soldier / 그 대학에 입학을 ~하다 apply for admission to that university. ‖ ~병 a volunteer / ~서 a written application / ~자 an applicant; a volunteer.
지위 (地位) (신분) position; status; (social) standing; (직위) a position; (계급) a rank. ¶ 사회적 ~ *one's* social position (status) / ~가 높다 (낮다) be high (low) in position / 좋은 ~을 얻다 get (obtain) a good position / 그녀는 여성의 사회적 ~ 향상을 위해 힘썼다 She has made great efforts to improve the status of women.
지육 (知育) intellectual training; mental culture (education).
지은이 ◀ 저자 (著者).
지인 (知人) an acquaintance.
지자 (知者) a man of intelligence; a man of knowledge and experience. ‖~ism.
지자기 (地磁氣) terrestrial magnetism.
지장 (支障) hindrance; an obstacle; a difficulty; a hitch (장애). ¶ ~을 초래하다 hinder; obstruct; be an obstacle (*to*) / ~이 없으면 if it is convenient to you / ~없이 (의)식을 끝마치다 finish the ceremony without a hitch.
지장 (指章) a thumbprint; a thumb impression. ¶ ~을 찍다 seal 《*a document*》 with the thumb.
지저귀다 sing; chirp; twitter.
지저분하다 (be) dirty; filthy; unclean; (난잡) (be) untidy; disordered; messy. ¶ 지저분한 거리 a

지적(地積) acreage.
지적(地籍) a land register. ‖ ~도 a land registration map / ~측량 a cadastral survey.
지적(知的) intellectual; mental. ‖ ~기준 an intellectual level / ~능력 one's intellectual powers; one's mental faculties / ~생활 an intellectual life / ~소유권 보호 protection of intellectual property / ~재산권 intellectual property rights / ~직업 an intellectual occupation.
지적(指摘) indication. ~하다 point out; indicate. ¶위에서 ~한 바와 같이 as pointed out above / 논문에서 잘못된 곳을 몇 군데 ~하다 point out some mistakes in the essay.
지전(紙錢) a (bank) note; paper money.
지점(支店) a branch (office). ¶해외 ~ an overseas branch / ~을 열다 open (establish) a (new) branch (office). ‖ ~장 a branch manager.
지점(支點) ① 【理】 a fulcrum (지래 받침). ② 【建】 a bearing.
지점(地點) a spot; a point; a place. ¶유리한 ~ a vantage point.
지정(指定) appointment; designation. ~하다 appoint; designate; name; specify. ¶~된 appointed; specified; designated / ~한 대로 as specified / 별도 ~이 없는 한 unless otherwise specified / 만날 장소를 ~하다 appoint (designate) the place / 그녀는 ~된 시간에 ~된 장소로 갔다 She went to the appointed place at the appointed hour. ‖ ~권 a reserved ticket / ~석 a reserved seat / ~일 a specified (designated) date.
지정학(地政學) geopolitics. ‖ ~자 a geopolitician.
지조(志操) a man of ~; 《절조》 constancy. ¶~를 굳게 지키다 stick to (be faithful to) one's principles.
지존(至尊) His Majesty (the King).
지주(支柱) a support; a prop; a stay; a strut. ¶한 집안의 ~ the prop and stay of a family.
지주(地主) a landowner; a land-lord. ‖ ~계급 the landed class.
지주(持株) one's (stock) holdings; one's shares. ‖ ~회사 a holding company / 종업원 ~제도 a stock-sharing plan for the employees (of a company).
지중(地中) ¶~의 underground / ~에 in the ground (earth).
지중해(地中海) the Mediterranean (Sea). ¶~의 Mediterranean.

지지 (支持) support; backing. ~하다 support; back (up); stand by. ¶국민의 ~를 얻다 be supported by the people; have (get) the support of the people / 여론의 ~를 얻다 have the backing of public opinion. ‖ ~율 the approval rate / ~자 a supporter; a backer.
지지(地誌) a topography; a geographical description.
지지난달 the month before last.
지지난밤 the night before last.
지지난번 the time before last.
지지난해 the year before last.
지지다 《끓이다》 stew; 《지짐질》 pan-fry; sauté; 《머리를》 frizzle; curl; wave.
지지르다 ① 《내리 누르다》 press (hold, pin) down; weight (down). ② 《기세를》 dispirit; dampen one's enthusiasm; 《기를》 overawe; overbear.
지지리 very; awfully; terribly. ¶~ 못나다 《얼굴이》 be awfully ugly-looking / 《태도가》 be downright stupid / ~(도) 고생하다 go through terrible hardships.
지지부진(遲遲不進) ~하다 make little (slow) progress.
지지하다 (be) trifling; trivial; poor; worthless.
지진(地震) an earthquake; a quake (口). ¶~의 seismic; seismal / ~의 중심 the epicenter (진원지); the seismic center / ~이 잦다 be subject to frequent earthquake / 약한 ~ a weak (slight) earthquake / 어젯밤에 강한 ~이 있었다 We had a strong (severe) earthquake last night. ‖ ~계 a seismograph; a seismometer / ~관측 seismography / ~대(帶) an earthquake zone / ~설계기준 (Japanese) earthquake-design standards / ~파(波) a seismic wave / ~학 seismology / ~학자 a seismologist.
지진아(遲進兒) a (mentally) retarded child.
지질(地質) the geology; the nature of the soil (土質). ‖ ~분석 a soil analysis / ~연구소 the Geological Survey Office / ~조사 a geological survey / ~학 geology / ~학자 a geologist.
지질리다 《무게로》 get pressed down; 《기가》 get overawed; be dispirited.
지질하다 ① 《싫증나다》 (be) boresome; tiresome; tedious. ② 《변변찮다》 (be) worthless; good-for-nothing; poor; wretched; trashy.
지짐이 (a) stew. ¶고기 ~ meat stew. 「grill.
지짐질 pan-frying. ~하다 pan-fry;
지참(持參) ~하다 《가져오다》 bring (a thing) with one; 《가져가다》 take

지참 (持參) 〜하다 carry; (a thing) with one. ¶ 〜금 a dowry / 〜인 a bearer.

지참 (遲參) 〜하다 come (arrive) late. 〜자 a latecomer.

지척 (咫尺) a very short distance. ¶ 〜에 있다 be very close; be within a foot.

지청 (支廳) a branch office.

지체 lineage; birth. ¶ 〜가 높다 (낮다) be of noble (humble) birth.

지체 (肢體) the limbs and the body. ¶ 〜부자유아 a physically handicapped child.

지체 (遲滯) delay; deferment. 〜하다 delay; be retarded; be in arrears. 〜 없이 without delay; immediately.

지축 (地軸) the earth's axis. ¶ 〜을 뒤흔드는 듯한 굉음 a deep, earth-shaking rumble.

지출 (支出) expenditure; expenses; outlay. 〜하다 pay; spend; disburse; expend. ¶ 수입과 〜 revenues and expenditures; income and outgo / 군비를 위한 다액의 지출 heavy expenditure(s) for military preparation / 총(경상, 임시) 〜 total (ordinary, extraordinary) expenditure. ∥ 〜액 the sum expended; an expenditure.

지층 (地層) a (geologic) stratum; a layer. ¶ 〜도 a strata map.

지치 [植] a gromwell.

지치다¹ (피로하다) be (get) tired; be exhausted (fatigued); be worn out. ¶ 일에 〜 be tired from one's work / 나는 몹시 지쳤다 I am dead tired.

지치다² (미끄럽을) skate; slide; glide. ¶ 얼음을 〜 skate (slide) on the ice.

지치다³ (문을) close (a door) without locking.

지친 (至親) close relatives.

지침 (指針) a compass needle; (계기의) an indicator; (길잡이) a guide. ¶ 인생의 〜을 주다 give a guiding principle of (a person's) life. ∥ 〜서 a guide (book). 〜ignate.

지침 (指鍼) 〜하다 call; name; designate.

지키다 ① (수호하다) defend (방어); protect (보호); guard (경호; 막다). ¶ 나라를 〜 defend one's country / 몸을 〜 guard oneself (against) / 눈을 지키기 위해 색안경을 쓰다 put on sunglasses to protect one's eyes (from, against) / 친구를 부당한 비난으로부터 〜 shield one's friend from unjust censure. ② (살피다) watch; keep a watch (on, for, against). ¶ 엄중히 〜 watch closely. ③ (준수하다) keep; observe; follow; obey; (고수) cling to (a cause); adhere (stick) to. ¶ 약속을 〜 keep one's word (promise) / 아버지 말씀을 충실히 〜 follow one's father's lessons faithfully / 신념을 굳게 〜 stick to one's belief firmly / 법을 〜 observe the law. ④ (수절) remain faithful to. ⑤ (보존) keep; preserve; 《유지》 maintain. ¶ 신용을 〜 keep up one's credit / 그는 그 사건에 대해 침묵을 지키고 있다 He keeps silence about the incident.

지탄 (指彈) 〜하다 censure; blame; condemn; denounce; criticize. ¶ 〜을 받다 be blamed (censured) (for).

지탱하다 (支撑—) keep (up); preserve; maintain; support. ¶ 건강을 지탱해 나가다 preserve one's health / 집안을 〜 maintain one's family.

지파 (支派) a branch family; a branch; a sect.

지팡이 (walking) stick; a cane. ¶ 대 〜 a bamboo cane / 〜를 짚고 걷다 walk with a stick.

지퍼 a zipper. ¶ 〜를 채우다 zip (up) (a coat) / 〜를 열다 unzip (a coat).

지평선 (地平線) the horizon. ¶ 〜 상에 above (on) the horizon.

지폐 (紙幣) (issue) paper money; a bill (美); (bank) note (英). ¶ 위조 〜 a counterfeit (forged) note / 태환 〜 a convertible note / 10달러짜리 〜 a ten-dollar bill / 10만원 one hundred thousand won in notes. ∥ 〜발행 issue of paper money.

지표 (地表) the earth's surface.

지표 (指標) an index; an indicator; a pointer; [數] a characteristic. ¶ 경제 번영의 〜 an index of (a country's) economic prosperity.

지푸라기 a straw.

지피다 put (fuel) into a fire; make a fire. ¶ 난로에 불을 〜 make a fire in the stove.

지필묵 (紙筆墨) paper, brushes (pens) and ink.

지하 (地下) 〜의(에) under the ground; underground / 〜 이층 the second basement / 〜 20 미터 되는 곳에 at twenty meters underground (below ground) / 〜 100미터까지 파다 dig (in the ground) to a depth of 100 meters / 〜에 잠들다 sleep in one's grave / 〜로 잠입하다 go underground. ∥ 〜 경제 underground economy / 〜 공작 underground operations / 〜도 an underpass (美); a subway (英) / 〜상가 an underground shopping center (arcade, complex) / 〜수 (under-)ground (subterranean) water / 〜실 a basement / 〜운동 under-

지학 (地學) physical geography.

지핵 (地核) the earth's nucleus.

지향 (志向) intention; aim; inclination. ~하다 intend (aspire) (to do); aim (at, to do). ¶ 미래 ~형 future-oriented.

지향 (指向) ~하다 point (to); head (for, toward). ¶ ~성 안테나 a directional antenna.

지혈 (止血) arrest (stopping) of bleeding; [醫] hemostasis. ~하다 stop (check, arrest) bleeding. ‖ ~대 a tourniquet / ~제 a hemostatic (agent); a styptic.

지협 (地峽) an isthmus; a neck of land.

지형 (地形) the lay of the land; geographical features. ‖ ~도 a topographical map / ~학 topography.

지형 (紙型) a *papier-mâché* mold; a matrix. ~ ~을 뜨다 make (take) a *papier-mâché* mold (of).

지혜 (智慧) wisdom; intelligence; sense; wit(s). ¶ ~있는 wise; sagacious; intelligent / ~가 생기다 grow wise (intelligent) / ~를 짜내다 cudgel (rack) one's brains.

지화 (指話) (use) finger (hand) language. ‖ ~법 dactylology.

지휘 (指揮) command; direction; supervision(감독). ~하다 command; lead; conduct(악단을). ¶ ~ 감독하다 direct and supervise / …의 ~를 받다 be under the command (direction) of (*a person*); 그의 ~하에 30명의 부하가 있다 He has thirty men under his command. ‖ ~계통 a chain of command / ~관 a commander / ~ 권 the right to command / ~봉 (棒) a baton / ~자 a leader; a commander; a conductor (악단의).

직(職) (일자리) employment; work; a job; (직무) one's duties; (직업) a calling; an occupation; a trade; an office; a post; a position(지위). ‖ ~에서 과장 ~을 얻다(잃다) get (lose) a position as the chief of a section in the company / 나는 컴퓨터 관련 ~을 찾고 있다 I am looking for a job in computers.

직각 (直角) a right angle. ¶ ~의 right-angled / …과 ~으로 show 이루다 make a right angle (with). ‖ ~ 삼각형 a right triangle.

직간 (直諫) ~하다 reprove (*a person*) to his face.

직감 (直感) intuition; a hunch (口). ~하다 know by intuition; sense; perceive; feel (*something*) in one's bones. ¶ ~적으로 intuitively; by intuition / 내 ~이 맞았다 I guessed right. / 나는 위험을 ~했다 I sensed danger. / 나는 ~적으로 그가 수상하다고 느꼈다 I suspected intuitively that he was guilty.

직거래 (直去來) direct (spot) transactions (dealings). ~하다 make a direct deal (*with*); do (transact) business directly (*with*). ¶ 그 회사와 ~하게 되었다 We have started dealings directly with the firm.

직격 (直擊) a direct hit. ¶ ~당하다 take a direct hit; be hard hit (*by*) (비유적). ‖ ~탄 a direct hit.

직결 (直結) direct connection. ~하다 connect (link) (*a thing*) directly (*with*). ¶ …와 ~되다 be connected directly with… / 그 문제는 국민 생활과 ~된다 The problem is directly connected with national life.

직경 (直徑) a diameter. ¶ ~1미터 one meter in diameter.

직계 (直系) a direct line (of descent). ¶ ~의 직손 a direct descendant. ‖ ~가족 family members in a direct line / ~존속 (尊屬) a lineal ascendant (descendant) / ~회사 a directly affiliated concern; a subsidiary company(자회사).

직계 (職階) the class of position. ‖ ~제(制) a job-ranking (job classification) system.

직고 (直告) ~하다 inform (tell) truthfully.

직공 (職工) a worker; 《공장의》 a (factory, mill) hand.

직교역 (直交易) direct barter trade.

직구 (直球) [野] a straight ball.

직권 (職權) authority; official power. ¶ ~으로써 in virtue of *one's* office / ~을 행사〔남용〕하다 exercise (abuse) *one's* authority (*on*). ‖ ~남용 abuse of *one's* authority / ~조정 mediation by virtue of *one's* authority (*as chairman*).

직녀성 (織女星) [天] Vega.

직능 (職能) a function. ‖ ~급 wages based on job evaluation / ~대표(제) (the system of) vocational representation.

직답 (直答) (즉답) a prompt answer; a ready reply; 《직접하는 답변》 a direct answer.

직렬 (直列) [電] ~로 잇다 connect (join up) (*batteries*) in series. ‖ ~회로 〔변압기〕 a series circuit [transformer].

직류(直流) [電] direct current (생략 D.C.). ‖ ~전동기 [발전기] a D.C. motor (dynamo) / ~회로 a direct current circuit.

직립(直立) ~하다 stand erect (straight; upright). ¶ ~의 straight; erect; upright / ~보행하다 walk erect (upright). ‖ ~원인(猿人) Pithecanthropus erectus.

직매(直賣) direct sales. ~하다 sell direct(ly) 《to》. ¶ 산지 ~의 사과 apples sold directly by the producers. ‖ ~소 [점] a direct sales store.

직면(直面) ~하다 face; confront; be faced (confronted) with 《by》. ¶ 회사는 경영 위기에 ~해 있다 The firm is in a financial crisis.

직무(職務) a duty; an office. ¶ ~상의 official / ~을 수행하다 do one's duty; perform (discharge) one's duties / ~를 게을리하다 neglect one's duties. ‖ ~규정 office regulations / ~수당 a service allowance / ~태만 neglect of duty.

직물(織物) textiles; textile fabrics; cloth (천). ‖ ~공업 the textile industry / ~공장 a textile factory / ~류 woven (dry) goods / ~상 a textile (dry goods) dealer / ~업 《제조》 textile manufacture; 《판매》 the textile (dry goods) business.

직분(職分) one's duty (job). ¶ ~을 다하다 do (fulfill) one's duty.

직사(直射) 《포화의》 direct (frontal) fire; 《일광의》 direct rays. ~하다 fire direct 《upon》; shine directly 《upon》. ¶ 태양의 ~광선을 받다 be exposed to the direct rays of the sun. ‖ ~포 a direct-firing gun.

직사각형(直四角形) a rectangle; an oblong. [triangle.]

직삼각형(直三角形) a right-angled

직선(直線) a straight line. ¶ ~의 straight / ~을 긋다 draw a straight line 《on a paper》 / 집에서 학교까지는 ~거리로 2km이다 It is two kilometers from my home to the school, as the crow flies. ‖ ~거리 a lineal distance / ~미(美) lineal beauty / ~운동 a straight-line (rectilineal) motion / ~코스 a straight course.

직설법(直說法) [文] the indicative mood.

직성(直星) ¶ ~이 풀리다 feel satisfied (gratified); be appeased / ~이 안 풀리다 be not satisfied; feel unsatisfied 《for》.

직소(直訴) (make) a direct appeal (petition) 《to》.

direct control 《of》. ‖ ~부하 a subordinate under one's direct control / ~상관 one's immediate superior.

직송(直送) direct delivery. ~하다 send direct(ly) 《to》. ¶ ~산지 ~의 과실 fruit sent directly from the growing district.

직수굿하다 (be) submissive; obedient; docile.

직수입(直輸入) direct importation. ~하다 import 《goods》 direct(ly) 《from》. ‖ ~상 direct importer / ~품 direct imports.

직수출(直輸出) direct exportation. ~하다 export 《goods》 direct(ly) 《to》. ‖ ~품 direct exports.

직시(直視) ~하다 look 《a person》 in the face; face 《the fact》 squarely.

직언(直言) ~하다 speak plainly (frankly); speak without reserve. ¶ ~직행하다 speak plainly and act immediately.

직업(職業) an occupation; a profession; a calling; a trade; a vocation. ¶ ~적(인) professional / ~상의 비밀 a trade secret / ~을 ~으로 삼다 be 《a doctor》 by profession; be 《a printer》 by trade / ~을 바꾸다 change one's occupation; switch jobs / …을 ~으로 선정하다 choose 《farming》 as one's occupation; take up 《dancing》 professionally. ‖ ~경력 one's business (professional) career / ~교육 vocational education / ~군인 a professional (career) soldier / ~별 전화번호부 a classified telephone directory; the yellow pages / ~별 조합 a craft union / ~별 an occupational disease / ~보도(補導) vocational guidance / ~선수 a professional player; a pro / ~소개소 an employment agency (office) / ~안내란 a 'Help Wanted' column / ~야구 professional baseball / ~여성 a working (career) woman / ~의식 occupational consciousness; professional sense / ~학교 a vocational school / ~훈련 [윤리] vocational training (ethics).

직역(直譯) (a) literal (word-for-word) translation. ~하다 translate 《a passage》 literally (word-for-word).

직영(直營) ~하다 manage (operate) directly. ¶ ~의 under the direct management 《of》 / 정부의 ~사업 an enterprise under government management / 호텔 ~의 식당 a restaurant managed by the hotel in which it is housed.

직원(職員) a staff member; 《총칭》 the staff; the personnel. ¶ 그는

직유 시청의 ~이다 He is on the staff of the city office. / 이 회사의 ~은 50명이다 This company has a staff of 50. ‖ ~명부 a staff list / ~실 a faculty(teachers') room / ~회의 a staff meeting; a teachers'(faculty) conference.

직유(直喩) a simile.

직인(職印) an official seal; a government seal (정부의).

직임(職任) one's office duties.

직장(直腸) 〖解〗 the rectum. ‖ ~암 rectal cancer.

직장(職場) one's place of work; one's workplace(post, office). ¶ ~을 지키다 stick to one's post / ~을 떠나다(버리다) quit(walk out 《美》) one's job. ‖ ~내 결혼 marriage between people who work in the same place / ~대표 (노동 쟁의의) a shop steward(deputy) / ~연수 on-the-job training.

직전(直前) ¶ …에 just (immediately) before… / 시험 ~에 just before the examination.

직접(直接) ¶ ~의 direct; immediate (대리 없이 본인의); personal; firsthand(매개자 없이) / ~으로 directly; immediately; in person; firsthand; at first hand / 사고의 ~적인 원인 the immediate cause of the accident / 그를 ~ 만나는 것이 좋겠다 You had better see him in person. / 나는 본인에게서 ~ 들었다 I got the news firsthand (at first hand). / 나는 그 건에 관해 사장과 ~ 교섭했다 I negotiated directly with the president on that matter. ‖ ~교섭 (have) direct negotiations 《with》 / ~배달 direct delivery / ~비(費) direct cost / ~선거 a direct election / ~세 a direct tax / ~행동 direct action / ~화법 〖文〗 direct narration.

직제(職制) the organization (set-up) of an office. ¶ ~를 개편하다 reorganize an office.

직조(織造) weaving. ¶ ~하다 weave.

직종(職種) a type(sort) of occupation; an occupational category. ¶ ~별로 (arrange) by (the) occupation.

직직거리다 (신발을) keep dragging (scuffing) one's shoes.

직진(直進) ¶ ~하다 go straight on (ahead). ¶ 빛은 ~한다 Light travels in a straight line.

직책(職責) the responsibilities of one's work(job); one's duty. ¶ ~을 다하다 perform(fulfill) one's duties.

직통(直通) ¶ ~하다 communicate directly 《with》; 《버스 따위가》 go directly 《to》; 《도로가》 lead directly 《to》. ‖ ~열차 a through(nonstop) train / ~전화 a direct telephone line; a hot line.

직필(直筆) ¶ ~하다 write plainly 《on a matter》.

직할(直轄) direct control (jurisdiction). ¶ ~하다 control directly; hold under direct jurisdiction.

직함(職銜) one's official title.

직항(直航) 《배가》 sail direct (straight) 《to》; 《비행기가》 fly direct 《to》; make a nonstop flight 《to》. ¶ 그는 런던으로 ~했다 He flew straight to London. ‖ ~로 a direct line; a direct air route (항공기의).

직행(直行) ¶ ~하다 go straight (direct); run through 《to》. ¶ …에 ~으로 가다 go by(take a) through train to. ‖ ~버스 a nonstop bus / ~열차 a through (nonstop) train / ~편 (비행기의) a direct (nonstop) flight 《to》.

직활강(直滑降) 《스키의》 (make) a straight descent.

직후(直後) ¶ …의 (에) immediately (right) after; 《장소》 just behind(at the back of)… / 종전 ~에 just (directly, immediately) after the end of the war.

진(辰) 《십이지의》 the Dragon. ¶ ~년(시) the Year(Hour) of the Dragon.

진(津) 《나무의》 resin; gum; 《담배의》 nicotine; tar.

진(陣) 《진형》 a battle array (formation); 《진지》 a camp; 《전지》 a position; 《구성원》 a staff; a group. ¶ 교수 ~ a teaching staff / 보도 ~ a group of pressmen; a press corps / ~을 치다 take up a position; pitch a camp; encamp.

진(숲) gin. ‖ ~피즈 gin fizz.

진가(眞價) true(real) value(worth). ¶ ~를 발휘하다 display one's real ability(worth).

진갑(進甲) the sixty-first birthday.

진개(塵芥) dust; dirt; rubbish.

진객(珍客) a least-expected visitor; a welcome guest.

진걸레 a wet floorcloth(dust-cloth).

진격(進擊) 《전진》 an advance; 《공격》 an attack; 《돌격》 a charge. ¶ ~하다 advance 《on》; make an attack 《on》; charge 《at》. ‖ ~령 an order to advance / ~부대 a storming party; an attacking force.

진공(眞空) a vacuum. ¶ ~이 된 evacuated 《vessels》 / ~으로 하다 evacuate 《a flask》; form a vacuum. ‖ ~관 a vacuum tube / ~방전 vacuum discharge / ~청소기 a vacuum cleaner / ~포장 vacuum packing (~포장하다 vacuum-seal 《frankfurters in a plas-

진구렁 a mud hole. ¶ ~에 빠지다 fall in a mud hole.
진국(眞-) ① 《사람》 a man of sincerity. ② 진국(-酒).
진군(進軍) march; advance. ~하다 march; advance 《on》. ¶ ~ 중이다 be on the march.
진귀(珍貴) ~ 하다 (be) rare and precious; valuable.
진급(進級) (a) promotion. ~하다 be (get) promoted 《to》; be moved up 《to》. ¶ ~시키다 promote 《a person》 to a higher grade [position] / ~이 빠르다[늦다] be rapid [slow] in promotion. ‖ ~시험 [상신] an examination [a recommendation] for promotion.
진기(珍奇) ~ 하다 (be) rare; novel; curious; queer; strange.
진날 a rainy [wet] day.
진노(震怒) wrath; rage. ~하다 burst with rage; be enraged.
진눈 bleary [sore] eyes. 「sleets.
진눈깨비 sleet. ¶ ~가 내린다 It
진단(診斷) diagnosis. ~하다 diagnose; make a diagnosis 《of》. ¶ ~을 받다 consult [see] a doctor / ~을 잘못하다 make a wrong diagnosis / 의사는 내 병을 늑막염이라고 했다 The doctor diagnosed my illness as pleurisy. / 조기 ~ an early checkup / 종합 ~ a comprehensive medical checkup / 건강 ~ a medical examination / 신체 ~ a physical checkup 《美》. ‖ ~서 a medical certificate.
진달래 [植] an azalea.
진담(眞談) a serious talk. ¶ ~으로 듣다 take 《a person's》 story seriously.　　　　　　「《a person》.
진대붙이다 annoy [harass, pester]
진도(進度) progress. ¶ 학과의 ~ the progress of classwork. ‖ ~표 a teaching schedule; a progress chart(일반의).
진도(震度) seismic intensity.
진동(振動) vibration; oscillation. ~하다 vibrate; oscillate. ¶ 공기의 ~ air vibration. ‖ ~계 a vibrometer / ~공해 a vibration hazard / ~수 the number (frequency) of vibrations / ~자 a vibrator / ~주파수 an oscillation frequency / ~파 an oscillating wave / ~판 a trembler; a diaphragm.
진동(震動) a shock; a tremor; a quake. ~하다 shake; quake; tremble; vibrate. ¶ ~시키다 shake; (몹시) ~하다(적다) This car [shakes horribly (runs smoothly)]. ‖ ~수 the number of vibrations / ~시간

the duration of the shock (지진의) / ~파 an earthquake wave.
진두(陣頭) ~에 서다 be at the head 《of an army》; take the lead 《in doing》 / 그는 신제품의 판매 촉진을 ~지휘했다 He took the lead in promotion of the new products.　　　　　「acarid.
진드기 [動] a tick; a mite; an
진득거리다 [들러붙다] (be) sticky; glutinous; (검질기다) (be) stubborn; unyielding; tough.
진득하다 be staid; sedate; patient. ¶ 진득한 성격 a staid character.
진디 [蟲] a plant louse; an aphid.
진땀(津-) sticky [greasy] sweat; cold sweat(식은땀). ¶ ~ 나다 be in a greasy [cold] sweat; sweat hard / ~빼다 have a hard time; have bitter experiences.
진력(盡力) ~하다 endeavor; strive; make efforts; exert *oneself*; try hard to *do*; do *one*'s best 《for》. ¶ …의 ~으로 through the efforts [good offices] of…; thanks to *a person*'s efforts.　　　　　「《of》.
진력나다 be (get) sick (tired, weary)
진로(進路) a course; a way. ¶ ~를 열어 주다 make way 《for one's juniors》 / ~를 뚫다 cut [cleave] *one*'s way 《through》 / 졸업후의 ~를 결정하다 decide on 「the course to take (the career to pursue) after graduation.
진료(診療) medical examination and treatment(☞ 진찰, 치료). ‖ ~소 a clinic / ~시간 consultation hours / ~실 a consultation room.
진리(眞理) (a) truth. ¶ 영구불변의 ~ eternal truth / 보편적 ~ a universal truth / 과학적 ~ a truths of science; the scientific truths / ~의 탐구 a search for truth / ~를 탐구하다 seek after truth / 그의 말에도 어느 정도이는 있다 There is some truth in what he says.
진맥(診脈) ~하다 feel (examine) 《a person's》 pulse.
진면목(眞面目) *one*'s true character(self). ¶ ~을 발휘하다 show (exhibit) *one*'s true character (ability, worth).
진무르다 be sore; be inflamed (blistered). ¶ 빨갛게 진무른 살 an inflamed raw skin.
진문(珍聞) rare news; an interesting (a curious) story.
진문진답(珍問珍答) an incomprehensible question and a garbled reply.
진물 ooze from a sore. ¶ ~이 나다 a sore oozes.
진미(珍味) 《식품》 a dainty; a deli-

진미(珍味) a delicate flavor〔taste〕. ¶ 산해~ all sorts of delicacies.

진미(眞味) true〔real〕 taste; genuine appreciation. ¶ 동양화의 ~를 알다 appreciate what oriental painting is all about.

진배없다 be as good as; be equal〔to〕; be on a level〔with〕; be no worse than. ¶ 새것이~ be as good as new.

진버짐 eczema; watery ringworm.

진범(眞犯) the real〔true〕 culprit.

진보(進步) progress; (an) advance; improvement(개선). ~하다 (make) progress; improve; advance. ¶ ~적(인) advanced; progressive / 과학의 ~ the progress of science / 장족의 ~을 이루다 make remarkable progress; make a marked advance / 학문이 ~하다 make progress in *one's* studies. ‖ ~주의 progressivism / ~주의자 a progressivist / ~파 the progressive group〔faction〕.

진본(珍本) a rare〔old〕 book.

진본(眞本) an authentic book〔copy〕; a genuine piece of writing〔painting〕(서화의).

진부(眞否) truth (or otherwise). ¶ ~를 확인하다 check〔find out〕 whether 《a thing》 is true or not; check the truth 《of》.

진부하다(陳腐—) (be) commonplace; trite; stale; hackneyed. ¶ 진부한 생각 a commonplace idea / 진부한 문구 a hackneyed phrase.

진사(陳謝) an apology. ~하다 apologize 《to a person》《for》; express *one's* regret 《for》.

진상(眞相) the truth; the actual facts; what's what. ¶ ~을 규명하다 inquire into the real state of affairs / 사건의 ~을 알다 get at the truth / ~을 밝히다 reveal the real facts of the case. ‖ ~조사단 a fact-finding mission〔committee〕.

진상하다(進上—) 《一 바침》 offer a local product to the king.

진선미(眞善美) the true, the good and the beautiful.

진성(眞性) 〔醫〕 ¶ ~의 true; genuine. ‖ ~콜레라 (a case of) true〔genuine〕 cholera〔world〕.

진세(塵世) this dirty world!

진솔《새 옷》 brand-new clothes; 《진솔옷》 ramie-cloth garments made in spring or fall.

진수(珍羞) rare dainties; delicacies. ¶ ~성찬 rich viand and sumptuous meal.

진수(眞髓) the essence; the quintessence; the gist; the pith; the soul.

진수(進水) launching. ~하다 be launched; launch 《a ship》. ‖ ~대 the launching platform〔ways〕 / ~식 a launching〔ceremony〕.

진술(陳述) a statement. ~하다 state; set forth; declare. ¶ 자기 입장을 ~하다 state *one's* case / 허위 ~을 하다 make a false statement. ‖ ~서 a (written) statement.

진실(眞實) truth. ~의 true; real; sincere / ~로 really; truly; in reality / ~을 말하면 to tell the truth / ~을 왜곡하다 distort the truth / ~을 말하다 tell〔speak〕 the truth / 그 증언은 ~임이 증명되었다 The testimony was proved true.

진실성(眞實性) the truth〔authenticity〕《of a report》; credibility. ¶ ~을 의심하다 doubt the truth of 《a statement》.

진심(眞心) *one's* true heart; sincerity(성심); earnest. ¶ ~으로 heartily; sincerely; from the bottom of *one's* heart.

진압(鎭壓) repression. ~하다 repress; suppress; subdue; put down. ¶ 폭동을 ~하다 quell〔put down〕 a riot.

진앙(震央) the epicenter.

진액(津液) resin; gum; sap.

진언(進言) advice; counsel. ~하다 advise; counsel; suggest.

진열(陳列) a display; an exhibition; a show. ~하다 display; exhibit; place〔put〕《things》 on exhibition. ¶ ~되어 있다 be placed on show; be exhibited. ‖ ~대 a display stand / ~실 a showroom / ~장 a showcase / ~창 a show window / ~품 an exhibit; articles on display.

진영(眞影) a true image; a portrait; a picture.

진영(陣營) a camp; quarters. ¶ 동서 양 ~ the East and the West camps / 보수 ~ the conservative camp / 공화당 ~ the Republican camp.

진용(陣容) 《군대의》 battle array〔formation〕; 《야구팀·당의 등의》 a lineup; 《구성 인원》 staff. ¶ ~을 갖추다 《군대의》 array 《troops》 for battle; put 《troops》 in battle formation; 《팀의》 arrange〔organize〕 *one's* line-up〔team〕《for the game》 / 내각의 ~을 바꾸다 carry out a cabinet reshuffle.

진원(震源) the seismic center; the epicenter. ‖ ~지=진원.

진위(眞僞) truth (or falsehood); genuineness. ¶ 보고의 ~를 확인하다 ascertain the truth of a report.

진의(眞意) *one's* real intention;

진인(眞因) the real (true) cause.
진일 wet housework; chores in which one's hands get wet.
진입(進入) 〔들어섬〕 ~하다 enter; go (advance) into; make one's way 《*into*》. ¶ ~궤도로 ~하다 go into orbit / 고속도로로 ~하다 enter the express way. ‖ ~등 〔항공·철도의〕 an approach light / ~로 〔자동차 도로의〕 an approach ramp / 〔비행기의〕 an approach.
진자(振子) 〔理〕 a pendulum.
진작(振作) ~하다 promote; brace 〔stir, shake〕 up. ¶ 사기를 ~시키다 stir up the morale 《of troops》.
진작 〔그 때에〕 then and there; on that occasion; 〔좀더 일찍〕 earlier. ~ 갔어야 했다 You should have gone earlier.
진재(震災) an earthquake disaster. ¶ ~지 a quake-stricken district 〔area〕.
진저리 ~나다 be 〔get〕 sick 《of》; be disgusted 《with, at》; be fed up 《with》 / ~치다 shudder 《at》; shiver 《with cold》; tremble 《for fear》.
진저에일 ginger ale.
진전(進展) development; progress. ~하다 develop; progress. ¶ 계획은 잘 ~되고 있다 The plan is shaping up 〔going on〕 well. / 교섭은 예상 밖의 방향으로 ~되었다 The negotiation has progressed in an unexpected direction.
진절머리 ☞ 진저리.
진정(眞正) ¶ ~한 true; real; genuine / ~한 사람 true love / ~한 의미에서 in the true sense of the word.
진정(眞情) one's true heart 〔feeling〕; true 〔genuine〕 sentiments. ¶ ~의 true; sincere; earnest / ~으로 truthfully; sincerely; from one's heart / ~을 토로하다 express one's true sentiments; reveal one's true feeling.
진정(陳情) a petition; an appeal. ~하다 make a petition 《*to*》; petition; appeal. ¶ ~을 받아들이다 grant a petition. / ~서 〔submit〕 a petition / ~자 a petitioner.
진정(進呈) ☞ 증정(贈呈).
진정(鎭定) ~하다, ~시키다 〔감정을〕 soften; appease; pacify; calm 〔cool〕 down; 〔고통을〕 relieve; lessen; ease; alleviate. ¶ 노여움을 ~시키다 calm 〔soften〕 one's anger / 그 약이 그녀의 통증을 ~시켰다 The medicine eased 〔lessened, relieved〕 her pain. ‖ ~제 a sedative; a tranquilizer.
진종일(盡終日) all day 〔long〕; the whole day.
진주(眞珠) a pearl. ¶ ~의 pearly /

인조〔양식〕 ~ an artificial 〔a cultured〕 pearl / 모조 ~ an imitation pearl / 목걸이 a pearl necklace / 진줏빛 pearl gray. ‖ ~양식 pearl culture / ~양식장 a pearl farm / ~조개 a pearl oyster / ~채취 pearl fishery; pearling / ~채취자 a pearl diver.
진주(進駐) ~하다 be stationed 《*at*》; advance 《*into*》. ‖ ~군 the occupation forces 〔army〕.
진중(珍重) ~하다 〔보중함〕 value highly; treasure 《*a thing*》; 〔귀중함〕 be precious; valuable.
진중(陣中) 〔부사적〕 at the front; on the field 〔of battle〕. ‖ ~일기 a field 〔war〕 diary.
진중(鎭重) ~하다 (be) reserved; dignified; sedate; grave.
진지 a meal; dinner.
진지(陣地) a position; an encampment. ¶ ~포 an artillery position / ~를 구축하다 build up a strong point / ~를 고수하다 hold a position / ~를 탈환하다 recover a position.
진지(眞摯) ~하다 serious; sincere; sober; earnest. ¶ ~하게 in earnest; seriously; gravely / ~한 표정을 짓다 look grave 〔serious〕 / ~하게 생각하다 take things seriously.
진진하다(津津 ─) be very interesting; be of immense interest / 이 이야기가 어떻게 전개될지 ~ It'll be very interesting to see how this story develops.
진짜 a genuine article; a real thing. ¶ ~의 real; genuine; true / 고려자기 ~ a genuine piece of Koryŏ pottery / ~와 가짜를 구별하다 tell the difference between the real thing and a fake / ~처럼 흉내내다〔만들다〕 imitate to the life / 이 조화는 ~처럼 보인다 These artificial roses are quite lifelike.
진찰(診察) a medical examination. ~하다 examine 〔see〕 《*a patient*》. ¶ 의사의 ~을 받다 see 〔consult〕 a doctor. ‖ ~권 a consultation ticket / ~료 a medical 〔doctor's〕 fee / ~시간 consulting 〔surgery 《英》〕 hours / ~실 a consulting 〔consultation〕 room.
진창 mud; mire. ¶ ~에 빠지다 get 〔stuck〕 in the mud. ‖ ~길 a muddy road.
진척(進陟) progress; advance. ~시키다 speed up; hasten; expedite / 공사는 ~중에 있다 The construction is 「in progress 〔under way〕.
진출(進出) advance. ~하다 advance; find one's way 《*into*》; go 〔launch〕 《*into*》. ¶ 정계〔영화계〕에 ~하다 go into politics 〔the

movies) / 해외 시장에서 ~하다 make inroads into foreign markets / 우리나라의 자동차 산업은 해외 여러나라에 ~해 있다 The car industry of Korea is making its way into various foreign countries.

진취(進取) ¶ ~적(인) progressive; pushing; enterprising / ~의 기상 a go-ahead (an enterprising) spirit / ~적인 기상이 있는 사람 a man of great enterprise.

진탕(震盪) shock; concussion. ¶ 뇌~(腦) concussion of the brain.

진탕(―껏) to one's heart's content; to the full. ¶ ~ 먹다(마시다) eat (drink) one's fill.

진통(陣痛) labor (pains); the pains of childbirth. ¶ ~이 시작되었다 Her labor started. or She felt the beginnings of labor.

진통(鎭痛) alleviation of pain; soothing. ¶ ~에 즉효가 있다 bring quick relief from pain. ¶ ~제 an anodyne; an analgesic; a painkiller (口).

진퇴(進退) advance or retreat (움직임); one's course of action (행동); one's attitude (태도). ¶ ~를 같이하다 share in one's lot with another / ~를 결정하다 decide on one's course of action; define one's attitude / ~양난에 빠지다 be left with nowhere to turn; be driven into a corner.

진폐증(塵肺症) [醫] pneumoconiosis.　　　　　　　　[tion).

진폭(振幅) an amplitude (of vibration).

진품(珍品) a rare (priceless) article; a rarity.　　　[real) article.

진품(眞品) a genuine (sterling,

진필(眞筆) an autograph.

진하다 ① (색이) be dark; deep. ¶ 진한 청색 deep blue / 진한 색은 나에겐 어울리지 않는다 Dark colors don't suit me. ② (농도·맛이) (be) thick; strong. ¶진한 차 strong tea (coffee) / 이 수프는 너무 ~ This soup is too thick.

진하다(盡―) (다하다) be exhausted; be used up; run out.

진학(進學) ~하다 proceed to (enter, go on to) a school of a higher grade; go on to (college). ¶ 우리 학교 학생의 3분의 1이 대학에 ~한다 One-third of the students of our school go on to college.

진항(進航) ~하다 sail (out); steam ahead.

진해제(鎭咳劑) a cough remedy.

진행(進行) progress; advance. ~하다 (make) progress; make headway; advance. ¶ 예정대로 계획을 ~시키다 progress with the program as arranged / 의사를 ~시키다 expedite the proceedings / ~이 빠르다(느리다) make rapid (slow) progress / ~중이다 be on progress; be going on; be under way / (병의) ~을 막다 arrest (tuberculosis). ¶ ~(계) a program director; master of ceremonies (사회자) / ~형 [文] the progressive form.　　　　　　　　　[tle array.

진형(陣形) (battle) formation; bat-

진혼(鎭魂) repose of souls. ¶ ~곡 a requiem / ~제 a service for the repose of the deceased.

진홍(眞紅) scarlet; crimson. ¶ ~의 crimson; cardinal.

진화(進化) 〈생물학적인〉 evolution; 〈발달〉 development. ~하다 evolve (develop) (from... into...). ¶ ~적인 evolutional. ¶ ~론 the theory of evolution / ~론자 an evolutionist.

진화(鎭火) ~하다 be extinguished; be put out; be brought under control. ¶ 화재는 곧 ~되었다 The fire was soon brought under control.

진흙 〈질척질척한〉 mud; 〈차진〉 clay. ¶ ~의, ~투성이의 muddy / ~투성이가 되다 get muddy; be covered with mud.

진흥(振興) promotion. ~하다 promote; encourage; further. ¶ 해외 무역을 ~하다 promote (develop) foreign trade. ¶ ~책 a measure for the promotion (of) / 대한 무역 투자 ~공사 the Korea Trade-Investment Promotion Agency (생략 KOTRA).

질(帙) a set of books.

질(質) 〈품질〉 quality; 〈성질〉 nature; character. ¶ ~이 좋은(나쁜) superior (inferior) in quality; 〈성질〉 good-(ill-)natured; of good (bad) character / ~을 높이다(낮추다) improve (lower) the quality / 양보다 ~이 중요하다 Quality matters more than quantity.

질(膣) the vagina. ¶ ~구 (벽) the vaginal opening (wall) / ~염 [醫] vaginitis.

질겁하다 get appalled (astounded); be frightened (out of one's wits); be taken aback.

질경이 [植] a plantain.

질곡(桎梏) ¶ ~에서 벗어나다 shake off the fetters (of); throw off the yoke (of).

질권(質權) [法] the right of pledge. ¶ ~설정자 a pledger / ~자 a pledgee.　　　　　　　　　[clayware.

질그릇 unglazed earthenware;

질금거리다 trickle; dribble; fall (run down) off and on.

질기다 〈고기 따위가〉 (be) tough; 〈천 따위가〉 〈성질이〉 tenacious. ¶ 질긴 고기(종이) tough meat (paper) / 질긴 옷감 durable cloth / 성질이 ~ be tenacious by

nature / 이 옷감은 ~ This cloth wears well.
질기와 an unglazed roof tile.
질끈 tight(ly); fast; closely.
질녀(姪女) a niece.
질다 《반죽·밥이》 (be) soft; watery; 《땅이》 (be) muddy; slushy.
질량(質量) 〖理〗 mass; 《물과 양》 quality and quantity. ¶ ~ 보존의 법칙 the law of the conservation of mass / 저것은 이것보다 ~ 이 우수하다 That is better in quality and quantity than this.
질러 ~가다 take a shorter way [short cut] / ~오다 come by a short cut.
질리다 ① 《기가》 be amazed [stunned, aghast, dumbfounded] 《at》; be overawed; 《파랗게》 turn pale; lose color. ¶ 질려서 말도 안 나오다 be stuck dumb with amazement / 두려움으로 파랗게 ~ turn deadly pale with horror. ② 《싫증남》 be [get] sick [weary] 《of》; be fed up 《with》. ¶ 이 음악은 이제 질렸다 I'm sick and tired of this music. ③ 《채이다》 be [get] kicked; get struck(맞다).
질문(質問) a question; an inquiry (문의). ~하다 question; put a question 《to》; ask 《a person》 a question. ¶ ~에 답하다 answer a question / 잇달아 ~하다 fire [shoot] question after question 《at》 / ~을 받아 넘기다 turn a question aside; parry a question / ~공세를 받다 face a barrage of questions. ‖ ~서 a written inquiry; a questionnaire / ~자 a questioner.
질박하다(質朴-) (be) simple(-minded); unsophisticated.
질병(疾病) a disease; a malady.
질빵 a shoulder-pack strap; a backstrap.
질산(窒酸) 〖化〗 nitric acid. ‖ ~염 a nitrate.
질색하다(窒塞-) 《아주 싫어하다》 disgust; abhor; hate; detest; have an abhorrence 《of》; be appalled [shocked] 《at, by》. ¶ 질색할 노릇은 나의 disgust / 나는 양고기는 질색이라서 절대로 먹지 않는다 I hate mutton and never eat it.
질서(秩序) order; discipline (규율); system (체계). ¶ ~있는 orderly; well-ordered; systematic / ~없는 disorderly; unsystematic / 사회~를 문란케 하다 disturb public order / ~정연하다 be in good [perfect] order / 집단 생활에서 ~를 지키는 것이 중요하다 It is important to keep [maintain, preserve] order in a group life.
질소(窒素) nitrogen (기호 N). ‖ ~공해 nitrogen pollution / ~비료 nitrogenous fertilizer / ~산화물 nitrogen oxide.
질솥 an earthen pot.
질시(嫉視) ~하다 regard 《a person》 with jealousy; be jealous of 《a person》.
질식(窒息) suffocation. ~하다 be suffocated; be choked [smothered]. ~시키다 suffocate; choke; smother. ¶ ~사 death from [by] choke (그는 ~사 했다 He was choked to death.).
질의(質疑) a question; an inquiry; an interpellation(국회의). ~하다 question; inquire of; interpellate. ‖ ~응답 questions and answers.
질적(質的) qualitative. ¶ ~으로 우수하다 be superior in quality.
질주하다(疾走-) run at full speed; run fast; dash.
질질 ① 《끄는 모양》 ¶ ~끌다 drag 《a heavy thing》 / 치마를 ~ 끌며 걷다 walk with one's skirt trailing / 무거운 발을 ~끌며 걷다 drag oneself along; shuffle one's feet along / 회의를 몇시간이나 ~끌다 drag a talk out for hours. ② 《눈물 따위를》 ¶ 눈물을 ~ 흘리다 shed tears; 침을 ~ 흘리다 let saliva dribble from one's mouth.
질책(叱責) a reproof; a reproach. ~하다 reprove 《a person》; scold; take 《a person》 to task; reproach.
질척거리다 be muddy; be slushy; be sloppy. ‖ 질척질척한 muddy; slushy.
질타(叱咤) (a) scolding(꾸짖음); encouragement(격려). ~하다 scold; encourage [spur] 《a person to do》.
질투(嫉妬) jealousy. ~하다 be jealous 《of》; envy 《a person》. ¶ ~한 나머지 out of jealousy / ~가 많은 jealous; envious. ‖ ~심 jealousy.
질퍼거리다 ☞ 질척거리다.
질펀하다 ① 《넓다》 (be) broad and level. ¶ 질펀한 들 a broad expanse of fields. ② 《게으르다》 (be) sluggish; idle.
질풍(疾風) a violent wind; a gale. ¶ ~같이 swiftly; like a whirlwind.
질항아리 an earthenware jar.
질환(疾患) a disease; an ailment; 《가벼운》 a 《heart》 complaint; 《chest》 trouble; a disorder.
질흙 ① 《진흙》 mud. ② 《질그릇 만드는》 potter's clay.
짊어지다 ① 《짐을》 bear; carry (have) 《something》 on one's back; shoulder 《a heavy burden》. ② 《책임·빚 따위를》 be burdened with 《an important duty》; be saddled with 《a debt》. ¶ 골치 아픈 일을

짐 be burdened with a troublesome task / 아무의 빚을 ~ shoulder *a person's* debt.

짐 ① (화물) a load; a cargo (뱃짐); freight (기차의); baggage [luggage 《英》] (수하물). ¶ ~을 싣다 load (*a ship*); pack (*a horse*) / ~을 부리다 unload (*a ship*); unpack (*a horse*) / (배가 주어) discharge *its* cargo. ② (마음의) a burden. ¶ ~이 되다 be a burden (*to one*) / 일을 무사히 끝내니 ~을 벗은 기분이었다 I felt relieved since I finished the work without any problem.

짐꾸리기 packing; package.

짐꾼 a porter; a carrier; a red cap 《美》 (역의).

짐마차 (一馬車) a wagon; a cart.

짐바리 a load on the packsaddle; a pack load.

짐스럽다 (be) burdensome; troublesome. ¶ 짐스럽게 여기다 find (*it*) burdensome.

짐승 a beast (네발 짐승); a brute (맹수); an animal (동물).

짐작 a guess; guesswork; a conjecture; (a) surmise. ~하다 guess; conjecture; surmise; suppose. ¶ 그것은 단순이 ~이다 It's a mere guess. *or* It's pure conjecture. / 내 ~이 맞았다[틀렸다] I guessed right [wrong].

짐짓 intentionally; deliberately.

짐짝 a pack(age); a parcel; a piece of baggage [luggage].

집 ① a house; a home (가정); a family (가족); a household (가구). ¶ ~없는 사람은 homeless people / ~~마다 in [at] every house / ~에 있다 stay [be] at home / ~에 없다 stay away from home; be not at home / 살 ~이 없다 have no house to live in / 가난한 ~에서 태어나다 be born poor; be born into a poor family / 같은 ~에서 살다 live in the same house. ② (동물의) (build) a nest, a den, a lie. ③ (물건의) a sheath; a case. ④ (바둑의) an eye; a point. ¶ 열 ~ 이기다 [지다] win [lose] by ten points [eyes].

집게 (a pair of) tongs; pincers; nippers (소형의); pliers.

집게발 claws.

집게손가락 the forefinger; the [index finger.

집결 (集結) ~하다 concentrate; gather; assemble; mass (*its troops*). ¶ 대군이 국경 부근에 ~하고 있다 A large army is gathering near the border. ‖ ~지 an assembly place [area].

집계 (集計) a total. ~하다 add [sum] up; total. ¶ 비용을 ~하니 300달러가 되었다 The costs totaled [added up to] $ 300. ‖ ~표 a tabulation; a summary sheet.

집권 (執權) grasping political power. ~하다 come into power; take the reins (of the government). ¶ 한 사람에 의한 장기 ~을 막다 prevent long-term seizure of power by one man. ‖ ~당 the party in power; the ruling party.

집권 (集權) centralization of power (authority). ¶ 중앙 ~제 centralized administration.

집기 (什器) a utensil; an article of furniture; a fixture (비치된). ¶ 사무(실) ~ office fixtures.

집념 (執念) a deep attachment (*to*); tenacity of purpose. ¶ ~이 강한 (too) persistent; tenacious / 그는 그 일에 강한 ~을 가지고 있다 He is deeply attached to the work.

집다 take [pick] up. ¶ 집게로 ~ pick up with tongs.

집단 (集團) a group; a mass. ¶ ~적인 collective / ~으로 (act) in a group; en masse / ~적으로 collectively; as a group / ~을 이루다 form a group. ‖ ~검진 (檢診) a mass examination [checkup] (*for cancer*) / ~결근 mass absenteeism / ~결혼 a group marriage / ~경기 a mass game / ~농장 a collective farm; a kolkhoz (러); a kibbutz (이스라엘) / ~린치 group bullying [violence] / ~반응 (a) mass reaction / ~발생 a mass outbreak (*of cholera*) / ~생활 living in a group; communal living [life] / ~소송 (bring) a class action [suit] / ~수용소 a concentration camp / ~식중독 mass food poisoning / ~심리 mass [group] psychology / ~안전보장 collective security / ~의식 group consciousness / ~이민 지도로 (be under) collective leadership / ~폭행 mob violence.

집달관 (執達官) a (court) bailiff.

집대성 (集大成) ~하다 compile (*all the available data*) into one book. ¶ 각종 자료를 ~하여 책을 만들다 compile various materials and make them into a book.

집도 (執刀) the performance of an operation. ~하다 perform an operation (*on*).

집들이 (give) a housewarming (party). ‖ ~선물 a housewarming gift.

집무 (執務) ~하다 work; attend to *one's* business. ¶ 그는 지금 ~중이다 He is on duty now. ‖ ~시간 business [office] hours.

집문서 (一文書) a house deed; deed papers. ¶ ~를 잡히고 돈을 차용하

집배(集配) collection and delivery. ~하다 collect and deliver. ¶ 우편~원 a postman; a mailman 《美》.

집비둘기 a dove; a house pigeon.

집사(執事) a steward; a manager; a deacon(교회의).

집산(集散) ~하다 gather (collect) and distribute. ¶ ~지 a collecting and distributing center / 이 도시는 과일의 ~지이다 This town is a trading center for fruit.

집성하다(集成―) collect; compile.

집세(―貰) a (house) rent. ¶ ~가 밀리다 be behind with one's rent / ~를 올리다 (내리다) raise (lower) the rent / 이 아파트는 ~가 비싸다 (싸다) The rent on this apartment is high (low).

집시 ①《서양의》 a Gypsy; a Gipsy 《英》. ②《방랑자》 a gypsy; a vagabond.

집안 ①《가족》 a family; a household; 《일가》 one's kin (clan); one's relatives; 《가문》 the (social) standing of a family; lineage(가계). ¶ ~식구 the family members / 김씨 ~ the Kim's clan (family) / ~의 큰 일 a matter of great concern to the family / 그는 훌륭한 ~ 출신이다 He comes from a good family. ‖ ~싸움 a family trouble; domestic discord. ②《옥내》 the inside of a house. ¶ ~에(서) indoors; within doors.

집약(集約) ~하다 put 《all one's ideas》 together; condense 《the reports》; summarize 《the report》. ¶ ~적인 intensive / 자본 (노동) ~적인 capital- (labor-)intensive 《industries》 / 나는 우리 모임에서 토의된 것을 ~했다 I summarized what we discussed in our group. ‖ ~농업 intensive agriculture (farming).

집어넣다 ①☞ 넣다. ②《투옥》 throw 《a person》 into prison; imprison.

집어먹다 ①《음식을》 pick up and eat. ¶ 손으로 ~ eat with one's fingers / 젓가락으로 ~ eat with chopsticks. ②《착복하다》 pocket 《money》; embezzle.

집어삼키다 ①《음식을》 pick up and swallow. ②《남의 것을》 usurp; embezzle; appropriate 《public money》.

집어주다 ①《주다》 pick up 《a thing》 and hand it over; pass. ②《뇌물을》 bribe; grease 《a person's》 palm.

집어치우다 put away; stow away; lay aside; quit; leave (lay) off. ¶ 일을 ~ leave off work / 장사를 ~ quit one's business.

집요(執拗) ~하다 (be) obstinate; stubborn; persistent; tenacious. ¶ ~하게 항의하다 make an obstinate protest 《against》.

집장사 housing business. ¶ ~의 집 a ready-built house; a house built for sale.

집적(集積) accumulation. ~하다 accumulate; be heaped (piled) up. ¶ ~회로 an integrated circuit (생략 IC) / 대규모 ~회로 a large-scale integrated circuit (생략 LSI).

집적거리다 ①《손대다》 turn (put) one's hand to; 《관계》 meddle with 《in》; have a hand (finger) in. ②《건드리다》 tease; needle; provoke; vex. ¶ 아무를 ~ needle a person.

집주름 a rental agent; a real-estate agent.

집주인(―主人) ①《임자》 the owner of a house. ②《가장》 the head of a family (house).

집중(集中) concentration. ~하다 concentrate 《on》; center 《on》. ¶ ~주의를 ~하다 concentrate one's attention on 《one's work》 / 이 일에는 ~력이 필요하다 This job requires concentration. / 의론은 한 논점으로 ~됐다 The discussion centered around one point. / 나는 그 문제를 ~적으로 연구했다 I made an intensive study of the subject. ‖ ~강의 a closely-packed series of lectures; an intensive course 《in Korean literature》 / ~공격 (launch) a concentrated attack 《on》 / ~데이터처리시스템 the centralized data processing system / ~력 (power of) concentration; ability to concentrate / ~안타 《野》 a rally of hits / ~치료실 an intensive care unit (생략 ICU) / ~포화 a concentrated fire / ~호우 a localized torrential downpour.

집진기(集塵機) a dust collector.

집착(執着) attachment; 《고집》 tenacity; persistence. ~하다 stick (cling) 《to》; be attached 《to》. ¶ 인생에 대한 ~ tenacity for life / 낡은 관습에 ~하다 cling to an old custom. ‖ ~력 tenacity / ~심 attachment.

집채 (the bulk of) a house. ¶ ~만하다 be as large as a house; be massive.

집치장(―治粧) (the interior) decoration of a house. ~하다 decorate a house.

집터 a house (building) site (lot). ¶ ~를 닦다 level a site for a house.

집필(執筆) writing. ~하다 write 《for a magazine》. ¶ ~을 의뢰하다 ask 《a person》 to write 《for a magazine》. ‖ ~료 payment for

집하(集荷) collection of cargo. ~하다 collect (pick up) cargo. ¶ ~장 a cargo-picking point.

집합(集合) (a) gathering; (a) meeting; an assembly; 《數》 a set. ~하다 gather; meet; assemble. ¶ 1시에 공원에서 ~하다 gather (meet) in the park at one / ~시간과 장소를 확실히 모른다 I'm not sure where and when to meet. ¶ ~명사 《文》 a collective noun / ~장소[시간] the meeting place [time] / ~체 an aggregate.

집행(執行) execution; performance (수행). ~하다 execute; carry out; perform. ¶ 형을 ~하다 execute a sentence / 형의 ~을 유예하다 place *a person* on probation. ¶ ~기관 an executive organ / ~명령[영장] an order [a writ] of execution / ~부 an executive / ~위원회 an executive committee / ~유예 a stay [suspension] of execution; probation. / ~관 a bailiff.

집행관(執行官) an executor; 《法》 a bailiff.

집회(集會) a meeting; a gathering; an assembly. ~하다 meet together; gather; hold a meeting. ¶ ~의 자유 freedom of assembly [meeting] / 옥외 ~ an open-air meeting / ~에 참석하다 attend a meeting. ¶ ~신고 a notice of an assembly.

짓(행위) an act; *one's* doing; a deed; behavior. ¶ 못된 ~을 하다 do wrong; commit an evil act.

짓궂다 (be) ill-natured; spiteful; nasty; malicious; mischievous. ¶ 짓궂게 illnaturedly; spitefully / 짓궂은 노인 a nasty old man / 그는 여자애들에게 짓궂게 굴었다 He was always nasty to girls.

짓다¹ ①(집을) build; erect; construct. ¶ 집을 ~ build a house. ②(만들다) make; manufacture; tailor(옷을). ¶ 구두를 ~ make shoes(구둣가게에서) / 새옷을 ~ have a new suit made. ③(글을) write; compose; make. ¶ 작문을 ~ write a composition. ④(밥을) boil; cook; prepare. ¶ 밥을 ~ cook [boil] rice. ⑤(약을) prepare; fill a prescription. ⑥(편성) form; make. ¶ 줄을 ~ form in line; form a line (queue); line up. ⑦(농사를) grow; raise; rear. ¶ 보리농사를 ~ raise [grow] barley. ⑧(죄를) commit. ¶ 죄를 ~ commit a crime. ⑨(꾸며냄) make up; invent; fabricate. ¶ 지어낸 이야기 a made-up story. ⑩《표정》 show; express; look 《glad, sad》. ¶ 미소를 ~ smile. ⑪《결정·결말을》 decide 《on》; settle.

짓다² 《유산》 miscarry; abort.

짓밟다 trample 《*on*》; trample 《*a thing*》 underfoot; devastate; infringe 《*upon rights*》.

짓밟히다 be trampled down; be trodden down; get trampled underfoot.

짓부수다 batter; smash down; crush 《down》.

짓이기다 mash; knead to (a) mash. ¶ 감자를 ~ mash potatoes.

짓찧다 《빻다》 pound; crush down; smash; 《부딪치다》 strike 〔hit, bump〕 hard. ¶ 벽에 이마를 ~ bump *one's* head against the wall.

징¹ 《악기》 a gong.

징² 《구두의》 a hobnail; a clout (nail). ¶ ~을 박다 have *one's* shoes clouted.

징건하다 feel heavy on the stomach.

징검다리 a stepping-stone.

징계(懲戒) an official reprimand; a disciplinary punishment. ~하다 discipline; reprimand; reprove. ¶ ~위원회 a disciplinary committee / ~위원회에 회부하다 refer 《*a case*》 to the Disciplinary Committee) / ~처분 (take) disciplinary action / ~처분을 받다 be subjected to disciplinary action) / ~파면 a disciplinary dismissal [discharge] (~파면되다 be dismissed in disgrace).

징그럽다 (be) disgusting; odious; creepy; uncanny; weird. ¶ 징그러운 벌레 creepy insects / 징그러운 느낌 a creepy sensation / 이런 징그러운 것을 어떻게 먹나 I wouldn't eat odious stuff like this.

징발(徵發) ~하다 commandeer; press 《*a thing*》 into service; requisition. ¶ ~되다 be placed under requisition; be pressed into service / ~된 토지 commandeered land / 말을 군용으로 ~하다 requisition horses for troops. ¶ ~대 a foraging party / ~령 a requisition order.

징벌(懲罰) discipline; (a) punishment; chastisement. ~하다 punish; discipline; chastise. ¶ ~위원회 a disciplinary committee.

징병(徵兵) conscription; draft 《美》; call-up 《英》. ~ 되다 be drafted [conscripted]; be called up for military service / ~을 기피하다 evade the draft. ¶ ~검사 an examination for conscription / ~기피자 a draft evader [dodger 《美》] / ~적령 conscription age / ~제도 the conscription system.

징세(徵稅) tax collection. ~하다 collect taxes 《*from*》.

징수(徵收) collection; levy. ~하다 collect [levy] 《*taxes*》; charge 《*a fee*》. ¶1인당 5천원씩 회비를 ~하다 collect a fee of five thousand *won* per person. ‖ ~액(額) the collected amount.

징악(懲惡) ~하다 chastise vice; punish the wicked.

징역(懲役) penal servitude; imprisonment. ~에 처해지다 be sentenced to imprisonment with hard labor / 2년간 ~살이 하다 serve a two-year prison term.

징용(徵用) drafting; commandeering. ~하다 draft; commandeer. ¶중년의 남성들도 군에 ~되었다 Even middle-aged men were drafted into the army. ‖ ~자 a drafted worker; a draftee.

징조(兆兆) a sign; an indication; a symptom; an omen. ¶좋은[나쁜] ~ a good [an evil] omen / …의 ~가 있다 show signs of.

징집(徵集) enlistment; enrollment; recruiting. ~하다 levy 《*troops*》; enlist; enroll; conscript 《*young men*》; call out; mobilize. ¶~되다 be conscripted [drafted, enlisted] (for military service). ‖ ~령 a mobilization order / ~면제 exemption from enlistment / ~연기 postponement of enlistment.

징크스 (break, smash) a jinx.

징후(徵候) 《병의》 a symptom; 《일반의》 a sign; an indication. ¶폐렴의 ~를 나타내다 develop symptoms of pneumonia / 경기 회복의 ~가 나타났다 We've had encouraging signs for economic recovery.

짖다 bark 《*at*》 《개가》; howl, roar 《맹수가》; caw, croak 《까막까치가》.

짙다 《색이》 (be) dark; deep 《blue》; 《안개가》 (be) thick; dense; 《조밀》 (be) thick; heavy. ¶짙은 안개 a thick fog / 짙은 눈썹 thick eyebrows.

짚 a straw. ¶~으로 싸다 wrap up in straw / ~을 깔다 spread straw; litter straw. ‖ ~단[뭇] a sheaf of straw 《~단 뭇을 만들다 tie up straw in sheaves》 / ~부티기 waste straw in a heap / ~신 straw sandals.

짚가리 a rick; a stack of straw. ¶~를 쌓다 heap up in rick.

짚다 ① 《맥을》 feel; take; examine. ¶맥을 ~ take [feel, examine] the pulse. ② 《지팡이·손을》 rest [lean] 《*on*》; place [put] *one's* hand on 《*something*》; support. ¶지팡이를 짚고 걷다 walk with a stick [cane]. ③ 《미지의 것을》 guess; give [make] a guess. ¶잘못 ~ make a wrong guess.

짚이다 《마음에》 (happen to) know of; have in mind. ¶짚이는 데가 있다 a likely place / 전혀 짚이는 데가 없다 have no faintest [slightest] idea 《*of*》.

짜개다 split; cleave; rip.

짜다¹ ① 《피륙을》 weave; 《뜨개질》 knit; crochet. ② 《상투를》 tip up [wear] (a topknot).

짜다² ① 《제작》 make; construct; 《조립》 put [fit] 《*a machine*》 together; assemble. ¶나무로 책상을 ~ make a desk of wood. ② 《편성》 form; organize; compose. ¶클럽을 ~ organize a club. ③ 《활자로 판을》 compose; set up (in type). ④ 《계획》 form 《*a plan*》; prepare; make 《*a program*》. ¶장래의 계획을 ~ form a plan for *one's* future. ⑤ 《공모》 conspire with; plot together; work together; act in concert [collusion] with. ¶…와 서로 짜고 있다 be in collusion [league] with. ⑥ 《물기를》 wring; squeeze; 《기름 따위를》 squeeze; press; extract. ¶수건을 ~ wring a towel; squeeze out water from a towel / 오렌지의 즙을 ~ squeeze juice from oranges. ⑦ 《머리를》 rack [cudgel] *one's* brains.

짜다³ ① 《맛이》 (be) salty; briny. ¶너무 ~ be too salty. ② 《점수가》 be severe [strict] in marking. ¶저 선생님은 점수가 ~ The teacher is a hard [strict] grader.

짜르르 ☞ 지르르.

…짜리 ① 《가치》 worth; value. ¶천원 ~ 지폐 a 1,000-*won* bill / 만원 ~ 물건 an article worth 10,000 *won*. ② 《용량》 3리터 ~ 병 a three-liter bottle / 이 병은 2리터 ~이다 This bottle holds two liters. ③ 《나이 뒤에 붙어》 ¶다섯살 ~ 소년 a five-year-old boy.

짜임새 《구성》 making; make-up; structure; composition; 《피륙의》 texture. ¶문장의 ~ sentence structure / ~가 거친[고운] 천 coarse-[close-]woven cloth; cloth with a coarse [close] texture.

짜증 fret; irritation; vexation. ¶~을 내다, ~이 나다 show temper; get irritated; be vexed / ~나게 하다 irritate; make 《*a person*》 irritated; get [jar] on 《*a person's*》 nerve.

짜하다 《소문이》 be widespread; be abroad 《about》.

짝 ① 《쌍을 이루는》 one of a pair [couple]; the mate [partner] 《*to*》; a counterpart. ¶~이 맞다 match with another; make a pair [set] / ~이 맞지 않는 odd / ~을 맞추다 make a pair of 《*two*

짝 *things*); make match.
짝 ① (갈비의) a side of beef (pork) ribs. ② (아무곳) 아무에도 쓸모가 없다 be quite useless; be good for nothing.
짝 (찢는 소리) ripping; tearing.
짝사랑 one-sided love; a crush. ¶ ~하다 love (*a girl*) secretly; worship (*a girl*) at a distance. ¶ 너 학교 다닐 때 ~한 선생님이 있었는가 Did you have a crush on one of the teachers when you were at school?
짝수(-數) an even number. ¶ ~ 날 even-numbered days.
짝없다 ① (비길바없다) (be) matchless; incomparable. ¶ 기쁘기 ~ be happy without measure. ② (대중없다) (be) preposterous; incongruous.
짝짓다 pair; make a match; mate. ¶ 새를 ~ mate a bird / 둘 셋씩 짝지어 오다 come by twos and threes.
짝짜꿍 a baby's hand-clapping.
짝짝 ① (입맛을) ~ smack *one's* lips; lick *one's* chops ② 달라붙다 stick fast to / ~ 찢다 rip up; tear up.
짝짝이 an odd (unmatched) pair (*of socks*); a wrongly matched pair. ¶ ~가 되다 become an odd pair / 이 구두는 ~다 These shoes are wrongly paired.
짝채우다 make a match (set); match.
짝패 (*one's*) mate (partner).
짝하다 become a partner (mate); mate (*with*).
짠물 salt water; brine.
짤그랑거리다 clink; chink; rattle; jingle-jangle.
짤끔거리다 ☞ 찔끔거리다.
짤랑거리다 절그렁거리다.
짤막하다 (be) shortish; brief. ¶ 짤 막한 인사말 a brief address.
짧다 (be) short; brief. ¶ 짧은 여행 a short trip / 짧게 말하면 in short / 짧게 하다 shorten; cut (make) short / 2미터 ~ be two meters shorter.
짬 (여가) spare time; leisure (hours). ¶ ~름.
짭짤하다 ① (맛이) be nice and salty; be quite tasty. ¶ 짭짤한 고 기 반찬 a nicely salted meat dish. ② (꽤 좋다) be quite good (nice); be fairly good. ¶ 짭짤한 부자 a quite well-to-do person / 솜씨가 ~ be quite good at.
짱구머리 (a person with) a bulging head.
…째 (통째로·그대로) and all; altogether with; whole. ¶ 배를 통 ~ 먹다 eat a pear, peel and all / 나무를 뿌리 ~ 뽑다 pull up a tree by the roots. ② (차례를 나 타내어) ¶ 두번 ~ 결혼 *one's* second marriage / 닷새 ~에 on the fifth day. ¶lance; incise.
째다¹ (칼로) cut open (*a boil*).
째다² (꼭 끼다) (be) tight; be too small to wear comfortably.
째다³ (부족하다) be short (in want, in need) (*of*). ¶ 살림이 ~ be in want; be needy / 일손이 ~ be short of hands.
찢(이)다 split; tear; rend; rip.
짹소리 ☞ 찍소리.
짹짹거리다 chirp; twitter.
쨍 ring with a clink (clank).
쨍쨍 blazing(ly); bright(ly); glaring(ly). ¶ ~ 쬐다 shine (blaze) (down) (*on*) / ~ 내리 쬐는 태양 (under) a burning (scorching) sun.
쩔절 ☞ 절절 ②.
쩔쩔매다 (박두한 어려움에) be confused; be flustered; lose *one's* head; be at a loss; (바빠서) be tremendously busy in *doing*; be rushed off *one's* feet; never stop moving.
쩡쩡 ① (세력이) ~ 울리다 enjoy wide reputation (이름이); enjoy resounding influence (권세가). ② (갈라지는 소리) cracking.
쩨쩨하다 (인색하다) (be) stingy; close-fisted; tight-fisted; misery; (다랍다) (be) mean; humble; (시시하다) (be) worthless. ¶ 쩨쩨한 사람 a miser; a stingy person / 쩨쩨한 생각 a narrow-minded idea.
쪼개다 split (*a bamboo*); crack (*a nut*); ¶ ~ 가르다) divide (*into*); cut (*into*).
쪼그리다 ☞ 쭈그리다.
쪼글쪼글 ☞ 쭈글쭈글.
쪼다 (부리 따위로) peck (pick) (*at*); (정 따위로) chisel; carve.
쪼들리다 be hard pressed; be in narrow (needy) circumstances. ¶ 돈에 ~ be pressed for money / 빚 에 ~ be harassed with debts / 생 활에 ~ be hard up for living.
쪼아먹다 peck at and eat.
쪽¹ [植] an indigo plant. ¶ ~빛 indigo; deep blue.
쪽² (방향) a direction; a way; (편) a side. ¶ 서 ~ 에 (to the) west (*of Seoul*) / 이(저) ~ this (that) way / 우리 ~ our side / 맞은 ~ 에 on the other side.
쪽³ (여자의) a chignon. ¶ ~ (을) 찌다 do *one's* hair up in a chignon.
쪽⁴ (조각) a piece; a slice (cut). ¶ 참외 한 ~ a slice of melon.
쪽 (가지런한 모양) ~ 고르다 be even (equal, uniform).
쪽마루 a narrow wooden veranda.
쪽매붙임 mosaic (work); parquetry.
쪽박 a small gourd dipper.

쪽지 a slip of paper; a tag.
쫀득쫀득 ~한 glutinous; sticky; elastic; tough《질긴》.
쫄깃쫄깃 ~한 chewy; sticky.
쫄딱 totally; completely; utterly. ¶ ~ 망하다 be completely ruined; go to ruin 〔pieces〕.
쫓기다 ① 《일에》 be pressed 《by business》; be overtasked 《with》. ② 《뒤쫓기다》 be pursued 〔chased〕. ③ 《내쫓기다》 be driven out; get dismissed 〔fired〕.
쫓다 ① 《물리치다》 drive away 〔out〕. ¶ 파리를 ~ drive flies away. ② 《뒤쫓다》 pursue; chase; run after; 《따르다》 follow 《the fashion》.
쫓아가다 ① go in pursuit; follow; run after. ② 《따라 가다》 follow; accompany; go with. ③ 《따라잡다》 catch up with.
쫓아내다 drive 〔turn, send〕 out; expel; oust 《지위에서》; 《피거주집》 evict; 《해고》 dismiss; fire.
쫓아오다 《바싹 뒤따르다》 come in pursuit; follow 《a person》; 《뛰어서》 run after 《a person》.
쫙 《소문이》 widely; far and wide.
쬐다 《빛이》 shine on 〔over〕; shed light on; 《별·볕에》 warm *oneself*; bask 〔bath〕 《in the sun》. ¶ 불을 ~ warm oneself at the fire.
쭈그러뜨리다 press 〔squeeze〕 out of shape; crush.
쭈그러지다 《우그러지다》 get pressed 〔squeezed〕 out of shape; be crushed; 《쪼글쪼글해지다》 get lean; grow gaunt; wither; shrivel.
쭈그렁이 ① 《늙은이》 a withered old person. ② 《물건》 a thing crushed out of shape.
쭈그리다 ☞ 쭈그러뜨리다. ② 《몸을》 crouch; squat 〔down〕; bend low; stoop.
쭈글쭈글 ~하다 (be) withered, wrinkled; crumpled. ¶ ~한 거리어진 옷 crumpled clothes / ~한 얼굴 a wrinkled face.
쭈르륵 gurgling; trickling.
쭈뼛쭈뼛 hesitatingly; hesitantly; in a hesitating way.
쭈뼛하다 (be) bloodcurdling; horrible; 《서술적》 one's hair stands on end; feel a thrill; be horrified. ¶ 쭈뼛하게 하다 make 《a person》 shudder; curdle 《a person's》 blood.
쭉 ① 《늘어선 모양》 ☞ 죽¹ ①. ② 《내내》 ☞ 죽². ③ 《곧장》 direct(ly); straight. ④ 《숨·기운이》 (recede) utterly; completely. ¶ 기운이 ~ 빠지다 be utterly exhausted / 물이 ~ 빠졌다 The water sank completely. ⑤ 《벗는 모양》 with a rip.
쭉정이 a blasted ear; an empty husk of grain.
쭉쭉 ① 《줄이이》 in rows 〔lines〕.

row after row; in streaks. ¶ 줄을 ~ 긋다 draw line after line. ② 《비가》 in sheets 《showers》. ③ 《거침없이》 briskly; vigorously; rapidly; 《대충》 roughly. ¶ ~ 나가다 go ahead at a rapid pace / 나뭇잎을 ~ 훑다 strip off leaves briskly. ④ 《찢다》 into shreds; in 〔to〕 pieces.
쭝긋거리다 ① 《입을》 move the lips; purse 〔up〕 one's lips. ② 《귀를》 prick 〔cock〕 up 《its ears》.
…쯤 about; around; some; …or so. ¶ 네 시 ~에 at about four o'clock / …의 중간 ~에 at 〔about〕 the middle of; halfway between 《A and B》. ...... pot stew.
찌개 a pot stew. ¶ 생선 ~ a fish
찌그러… ☞ 쭈그러….
찌긋거리다 ① 《눈을》 wink (an eye) at 《a person》. ② 《당기다》 pull 《a person》 by the sleeve.
찌꺼기, 찌끼 《술·커피의》 dregs; the lees; scum《떠는는 것》; 《남은 것》 left overs; remnants; scraps.
찌다¹ 《살이》 grow fat; gain weight; put on flesh.
찌다² (be) sultry; be steaming hot. ¶ 찌는 듯한 더위 the sweltering heat.
찌다³ 《음식을》 steam; 《식은 것을》 steam over again. ¶ 찐 감자 steamed potatoes.
찌드럭거리다 pester; harass.
찌들다 ① 《물건이》 be stained 〔tarnished〕; become dirty. ② 《고생으로》 be careworn.
찌르다 ① 《날붙이로》 pierce; stab; thrust; prick《바늘로》; poke《막대기로》. ② 《비밀을》 inform 《on, against》; tell 〔report〕 《on a person》. ③ 《냄새가》 be pungent; stink. ④ 《마음 속을》 strike; come home to 《a person》. ⑤ 《공격》 attack. ¶ 적의 배후를 ~ take the enemy in the rear.
찌부러뜨리다 crush; smash; squash. ¶ 찌부러지다 be crushed 〔out of shape〕; be squashed 〔battered〕.
찌뿌드드하다 feel unwell 〔out of sorts〕; be indisposed 《with a slight fever》.
찌푸리다 ① 《얼굴을》 grimace 《at》; frown 〔scowl〕 《at, on》; knit the brows. ② 《날씨》 be gloomy 〔overcast〕; cloud over.
찍다¹ 《도끼 따위로》 cut 〔down〕; chop 《with an axe》; hew 《표 위》 punch; clip.
찍다² ① 《도장을》 stamp; seal; impress; set 〔affix〕 a seal 《to》. ② 《인쇄》 (put into) print. ③ 《들에》 stamp out; cast in a mold. ④ 《점을》 mark 《with a dot》; dot; point. ⑤ 《뾰족한 것으로》 thrust; pierce;

spear.
찍다³ ① 《사진을》 (take a) photograph《자기가》; have one's photograph taken 《남이 자기를》. ② 《묻히다》 dip 《a pen into the ink》.
찍소리 ¶ ~ 못하다 be silenced; be beaten hollow / ~ 못하게 하다 put 《a person》 to silence / ~ 없이 in silence; without a whimper.
찐빵 steamed bread.
찔끔거리다 trickle; overflow 《run down》 off and on; 《조금씩》 in driblets.
찔끔하다 get struck with fear; be startled.
찔레나무 《植》 a brier; a wild rose.
찔름 ~ 거리다 《넘치다》 brim over 《with》; run over the brim; 《조금씩 주다》 give in driblets.
찔름찔름 《액체가》 dribbling》; ~ 거리다 《넘치다》 little by little; bit by bit; by 《in》 driblets.
찔리다 《가시·날붙이에》 stick; be stuck 《thrust, pierced, pricked》; 《가슴에》 go home to one's heart.

찜 a steamed 〔smothered〕 dish.
찜질 fomentation; applying a poultice 《compress》; ~ 하다 foment; apply a poultice 《to》; pack.
찜찜하다 《마음이》 (it) weigh on one's mind; feel awkward 〔embarrassed〕. ¶ 말하기가 ~ find it awkward to say 《that…》.
찝찔하다 (be) saltish.
찡그리다 frown; make a wry face.
찡긋거리다 《눈을》 contract one's eyebrows; frown at; wink at.
찡얼거리다 ① 《불평을》 grumble; murmur. ② 《애가》 fret; be peevish.
찡찡거리다 grumble; murmur.
찡찡하다 ☞ 찜찜하다.
찢기다 get torn 《rent. ripped》.
찢다 tear; rend; rip. ¶ 갈가리 ~ tear to pieces.
찢어발기다 tear to threads.
찢어지다 tear; get torn; rend; rip.
찧다 pound 《rice》; hull; 《부딪다》 ram 《against》.

자동차
1. 크기에 의한 분류 대형차 a large-size 〔full-sized〕 car / 중형차 a medium-sized car / 보통차 a standard-sized car / 소형차 a compact 〔pony〕 car / 준소형차 a subcompact car. 2. 구조에 의한 승용차의 분류 일반 승용차 a car; a passenger car / 4도어 세단차 a four-door sedan / 하드탑 (금속제 지붕, center pillar가 없는 차) a hardtop / 쿠페 (2도어 하드탑의 차) a coupe; a two-door sedan 〔hardtop〕 / 리무진 (운전석과 객석 사이가 막혀 있는 대형 고급승용차) a limousine; a limo / 《미》 스테이션왜건 (후부 시트가 접게 되어 있는 화물 겸용차) a station wagon / 컨버터블 (헝겊 지붕을 접을 수 있는 차) a convertible. 3. 용도에 의한 승용차의 분류 자가용차 a private car / 택시 a taxi; a cab / 경주용차 a racing car; a racer / 순찰차 a patrol 〔police〕 car; a cruiser 《美》 / 구급차 an ambulance / 소방차 a fire engine / 영구차 a hearse. 4. 버스의 분류 일반버스 a bus; a coach / 2층버스 a double-decker / 시영버스 a municipal bus / 장거리 버스 a long-distance bus / 관광버스 a sightseeing bus / 스쿨버스 a school bus / 순환버스 a shuttle bus / 마이크로버스 a microbus / 미니버스 a minibus 5. 기타 신형차 a new model car / 중고차 a used car / 1997년형의 차 a 1997 model car / 개조차 a hot rod / 높은 연료비의 차 a gas guzzler; a gas eater / 낮은 연료비의 차 a gas-snipper; a fuel economy car / 고성능차 a high-performance car / 결함차 (口) a lemon / 스포츠카 a sports car / 해치백 자동차 a hatchback / 전기 자동차 an electric 〔a battery〕 car / 전륜구동차 a front-wheel-drive car / 후륜자동차 a rear-wheel-drive car / 4륜구동차 a four-wheel-drive car. 6. 교통사고(a traffic accident) 충돌 a collision / 정면충돌 a head-on collision / 연쇄충돌 a multiple collision 〔pile-up〕 / 펑크 a flat tire; a puncture / 자동차책임보험 compulsory insurance for one's car. 7. 교통규칙위반 주차위반 illegal parking / 신호무시 ignoring a traffic light; driving through the red light / 속도위반 speeding / 음주운전 driving while intoxicated (D.M.I.) / 음주테스트 a balloon test.

차(車) 《일반적으로》 a vehicle; 《자동차》 a (motor)car; an auto(-mobile); 《차량》 a (railway) carriage; a freight car(화물); 《한 차분 화물》 a carload. ¶ ~를 타다 take [get into] a car; take a taxi(택시에) / ~로 가다 go by car / ~에서 내리다 get out of a car / 이 ~는 다섯명이 탈 수 있다 This car holds [seats] five people.

차(茶) tea; green tea(녹차); black tea(홍차); a tea plant(나무); tea leaf(잎). ¶ 진한 [묽은] ~ strong [weak] tea / ~를 (새로) 끓이다 make (fresh) tea / ~를 대접하다 serve [offer] 《a person》 tea / ~를 마시며 이야기하다 talk over tea. 찻숟갈 a teaspoon(찻숟갈로 하나 a teaspoonful of…).

차(差) a difference; 《격차》 a gap; a disparity; a margin(이윤의). ¶ A와 B의 품질의 ~ the difference in quality between A and B / 연령의 ~ an age difference 《of two years》 / 큰 ~가 있다 there is a great difference 《between》; differ greatly 《from》 / 빈부의 ~가 심하다 There is a big gap between the rich and the poor. / 우리는 세대~를 느낀다 We feel a generation gap between us.

차(次) ① 《순서》 order; sequence; 《횟수》 times. ② 《다음의》 next; the following; 《하위》 sub-. ③ 《…김에》 while; when; by the way. ¶ 서울 가는 ~에 on the way to Seoul / 찾아가려던 ~에 마침 그가 왔다 He came at the very moment when I was going to see him.

…차(次) ① 《하기 위하여》 with the purpose of; with the intention of; by way of. ¶ 연구~ for the purpose of studying. ② 《순서》 order; 《數》 degree. ¶ 제2~ 세계대전 the Second World War / 제 3~ 산업 (the) tertiary industries / 일~ 방정식 a first-degree [linear] equation.

차갈다 carry off; snatch 《off, away》. ¶ 그는 그녀의 핸드백을 차갔다 He snatched her purse away.

차감(差減) ~하다 take (off); deduct; subtract; strike a balance 《between the debts and credits》. ǁ ~잔액 a balance.

차갑다 《온도가》 (be) cold; chill(y); 《냉담하다》 (be) cold; unfriendly. ¶ 차가운 날씨 cold [chilly] weather / 차가운 태도 a cold [unfriendly] attitude / 그녀는 차가운 여자이다 She is a cold-hearted woman.

차고(車庫) 《자동차의》 a garage; 《전차의》 a car shed. ¶ ~에 넣다 put a car into the garage.

차곡차곡 in a neat pile; neatly; one by one; one after another.

차관(次官) a vice-minister; an undersecretary 《英》; a deputy secretary 《美》. ǁ ~보 an assistant secretary 《美》.

차관(借款) a loan. ¶ ~을 신청하다 ask [apply] for a loan / ~을 얻다 obtain a loan / ~을 주다 〔공여하다〕 grant [give] credit 《to》 / 단기〔장기〕 ~ a short-〔long-〕term loan / 상업〔민간〕 ~ a commercial 〔private〕 payment loan / 연불 ~ a delayed payment loan / 현금 ~ cash loan. ǁ ~협정 a loan agreement.

차광(遮光) ~하다 shield [shade] 《a light》. ǁ ~막 a shade; a blackout curtain / ~장치 shading.

차근차근 step by step; methodically; carefully; scrupulously.

차기(次期) the next term [period]. ¶ ~ 대통령 the President for the next term / 집권을 노리다 aspire to take over the reins of government. ǁ ~정권 the next Administration.

차꼬 shackles; fetters(발의).

차내(車內) the inside of a car. ¶ ~에서 in the car [train] / ~에서는 금연이다 Smoking is prohibited in the car. ǁ ~광고 advertising posters (displayed) in the train / ~등 an interior light.

차녀(次女) one's second daughter.

차다¹ 《충만》 be full 《of》; be filled 《with》; 《달이》 be wax; 《조수가》 rise; flow; 《기한이》 expire(임기가); mature(어음 등이); 《흡족하다》 be satisfied 〔contented〕 《with》. ¶ 꽉 〔빽빽이〕 들어~ be jammed; be tightly packed / 며느리가 마음에 ~ be satisfied with one's daughter-in-law / 달이 ~ The moon is full. / 학장의 임기가 찼다 The dean's term of office has expired. / 어음 기한이 ~ a bill matures.

차다² ① 《발로》 kick; give 《a per-

차다 son) a kick. ¶ 차이다 get kicked. ② 《거절》 reject; 《애인 등을》 jilt 《one's lover》. ③ 《혀를》 click. ¶ 혀를 ~ click one's tongue.

차다 《패용》 carry; wear. ¶ 훈장을 ~ wear a decoration.

차다 《온도·날씨가》 (be) cold; chilly; 《냉담》 (be) cold; cold-hearted. ¶ 찬바람 a chilly (cold) wind / 찬물 cold water / 얼음 같이 ~ be ice-cold; be as cold as ice / 차가워지다 become (get) cold; cool of 《태도》.

차단(遮斷) ~하다 intercept; isolate; cut (shut) off; stop; hold up 《traffic》. ¶ 도로를 ~하다 block up 《a street》 / 퇴로를 ~하다 cut off (intercept) 《the enemy's》 retreat / 그 도로는 1시간 동안 교통이 ~되었다 Traffic on the street was stopped (held up) for an hour. ¶ ~기 a (circuit) breaker / 《전널목의》 a crossing gate.

차대(車臺) a chassis.

차도(車道) a roadway; a carriageway; a traffic lane; a driveway.

차도(差度) improvement 《of illness》; convalescence. ¶ ~가 있다 get better; improve; take a turn for the better 《병이 주어》.

차돌 quartz; silicates. ¶ ~ 같은 사람 a man of firm and straight character.

차등(差等) grade; gradation; difference. ¶ ~을 두다 grade; graduate; discriminate. ¶ ~세율 a graded tariff.

차디차다 (be) ice-cold; icy; frigid; 《서술적》 be ever so cold.

차라리 rather (sooner, better) 《than》; if anything; preferably. ¶ 이런 고통 속에서 사느니 ~ 죽는 편이 낫겠다 I would rather die than live in this agony.

차량(車輛) vehicles; cars; a (railroad) coach 《객차》; 《화차·객차》 rolling stock 《총칭》. ¶ 대형 ~ large vehicles / 이 도로는 ~ 통행이 금지되어 있다 This road is closed to vehicular traffic. ¶ ~ 검사 vehicle (maintenance, safety) inspection / ~ 고장 a car trouble; a breakdown / ~ 등록 vehicle registration / ~ 번호판 《자동차의》 a (license) plate / ~ 십부제 운행 제도 the '10th-day-no-driving' system / ~ 정비 vehicle maintenance / ~ 통행금지 《게시》 No Thoroughfare for Vehicles.

차례 ①《순서》 order; turn 《순번》. ¶ ~로 (arrange) in order; (go) by (in) turns; one by one 《하나씩》 / ~를 기다리다 wait for one's turn / ~가 뒤바뀌다 be out of order. ②《횟수》 a time. ¶ 한 ~ once / 여러 ~ several times.

차례(茶禮) 《정초·추석의》 ancestor-memorial rites. ¶ ~를 지내다 observe a memorial rite for one's ancestors on 《New year's day》.

차례차례 in due (regular) order.

차륜(車輪) a wheel. ¶ ~ 제동기 a wheel brake.

차리다 ① 《장만·갖춤》 prepare; make (get) 《something》 ready; arrange; set up / 음식을 ~ prepare food / 가게를 ~ start (set up) a store / 밥상을 ~ set the table 《for dinner》. ② 《정신을》 keep; come to 《one's senses》; collect 《oneself》. ¶ 정신을 차리게 하다 bring 《a person》 to himself 《his senses》. ③ 《예의·체면을》 keep up; save; observe. ¶ 인사를 ~ observe decorum / 체면을 ~ keep up appearances. ④ 《외관을》 equip oneself 《for》; deck 《oneself》 up; deck out. ¶ 옷을 차려 입다 dress up; deck out / 잘 차려 입다 be in one's best clothes.

차림새 《복색의》 one's clothing (dress); 《one's (personal) appearance. ¶ ~가 좋다 (나쁘다) be well (badly) dressed / ~를 단정히 하다 tidy (up) oneself / ~에 신경을 쓰다 《무관심하다》 be careful (careless) about one's appearance. ② 《살림의》 the setup; arrangements. ¶ 살림 ~가 훌륭하다 be a nice setup for living.

차림표 《식단》 a menu.

차마 ~ 그대로 볼 수 없어서 (being) unable to stand (idly) by any longer / ~ 볼 수 없다 cannot look on with indifference; cannot be indifferent 《to》 / ~ ……을 못 하다 do not have the heart to do.

차멀미(車-) carsickness. ~하다 get carsick.

차명(借名) ~하다 borrow (use) 《another's》 name. ¶ ~ 계좌 a false-name bank account.

차반(茶盤) a tea tray.

차변(借邊) the debtor (생략 dr.); the debit side. ¶ ~에 기입하다 debit 《a sum of money》 against 《a person》; enter 《an item》 on the debit side 《to a person's debt》.

차별(差別) distinction; discrimination. ~하다 be partial; discriminate. ¶ 인종 ~ racial discrimination; racialism / 무 ~ 폭격 indiscriminate bombing / ~ 없이 without distinction 《of sex》; indiscriminately / 그 회사는 사원을 고용할 때 외국인을 ~한다 That company discriminates against foreigners in its hiring. ¶ ~ 관세 a discriminatory tariffs / ~ 대우 discriminative treatment 《-

대우를 하다 treat 《persons》 with discrimination.
차분하다 (be) calm; composed; quiet; sober.
차비(車費) carfare; railway fare.
차석(次席) 〔관리 등의〕 an official next in rank; a deputy; 《수석의 다음》 the second winner.
차선(車線) a (traffic) lane. ¶ 편도 2~의 도로 a four-lane road (highway) / ~구분선 a (painted) lane marking / 6~ 도로 a six-lane expressway. ‖ ~분리대 a divisional strip (island).
차압(差押) ☞ 압류.
차액(差額) the difference (balance). ¶ ~을 지불하다 pay the difference (balance) / 무역 ~ the balance of trade.
차양(遮陽) 〔모자의〕 a visor; a peak; 〔건물의〕 an awning 《around the eaves》; a pent roof; 〔창의〕 a blind.
차용(借用) ~하다 borrow; have the loan 《of》. ‖ ~어 a loan-word / ~증 a bond of debt (loan); an I.O.U.
차원(次元) 〔數〕 dimension. ¶ 3~의 three-dimensional / 다~의 multi-dimensional 그녀의 연구는 나의 것과는 ~이 다르다 Her study belongs to a different level from mine.
차월(借越) an outstanding debt; an overdraft 〔당좌예금의〕. ~하다 overdraw.
차위(次位) the second rank (place); the second position.
차이(差異) a difference; (a) disparity; (a) distinction 〔구별〕. ¶ 연령(신분)의 ~ disparity of age (in social standing) / ~가 있다 there is a difference; differ 《from》; vary 《with》.
차익(差益) marginal profits.
차일(遮日) a sunshade; an awning; a tent.
차일피일(此日彼日) ~하다 put off from day to day. ¶ 빚을 ~ 미루고 갚지 않다 defer payment on the debt time and again.
차입(差入) 〔감옥에〕 ~하다 send in 《a thing》 to a prisoner. ‖ ~물 a thing sent in to a prisoner.
차자(次子) one's second son.
차장(次長) a deputy manager (of a department) 《英》.
차장(車掌) a conductor; a guard (기차의) 《英》.
차점(次點) the second highest mark (number of points); 〔표수〕 the second largest number 《of votes》. ¶ ~이 되다 rank second. ‖ ~자 the second winner; the runner-up 〔선거의〕.
차조 〔植〕 glutinous millet.

차조기 〔植〕 a perilla; a beefsteak plant.
차주(借主) a borrower; a debtor (돈의); a renter (집의); a lessee (토지의).
차지(借地) rented ground; leased land. ‖ ~권 a lease; a leasehold / ~료 (a) (land) rent 〔~인 a leaseholder; a tenant.
차지다 (be) sticky; glutinous.
차지하다 occupy 《a position》; hold 《a seat》; take (up). ¶ 수급에서 수석을 ~ sit at the top of one's class / 과반수를 ~ have the majority (in) / 제2위를 ~ rank second / 높은 지위를 ~ secure (occupy) a high position.
차질(蹉跌) a failure; a setback. ¶ ~일에 ~이 생기다 fail in one's attempt; things go wrong 《with one》 / 그 계획은 사소한 잘못으로 ~을 가져왔다 The project received a setback because of a slight error.
차차(次次) 〔점점〕 gradually; little by little; by degrees; step by step; 〔그 동안에〕 by and by; in (due) time.
차창(車窓) a car (train) window.
차체(車體) the (car) body; 《자전거의》 the frame.
차축(車軸) an axle.
차치(且置) ~하다 set (put) apart (aside); let alone. ¶ 농담은 ~하고 본론으로 들어가자 Joking aside (apart), let's have a main subject.
차트 〔도표〕 a chart. ¶ ~로 만들다 make a chart 《of》; chart.
차폐(遮蔽) a hood cover; shelter; shade 《a light》. ‖ ~막 a blackout curtain / ~물 a cover; a shelter / ~진지 a covered position.
차표(車票) a 《railroad, bus》 ticket; a coupon (ticket) 〔회수권의〕. ¶ ~파는 데 a ticket office; a ticket window (counter) 〔매표구〕 / ~를 끊다 get (buy, take) a ticket / 편도 ~ a one-way ticket / 왕복 ~ a round-trip ticket / 10일간 유효한 ~ a ticket valid for ten days. ‖ ~자동판매기 a ticket (vending) machine.

차호(次號) the next number (issue).
차회(次回) next time. 〔issue〕.
차후(此後) 〔금후〕 after this; hence (forth); hereafter; from now on; 〔장래〕 in (the) future. ¶ ~로는 조심해라 Be careful after this.
착(붙음) closely; fast; tight(ly). ‖ ~ 붙다 stick to (on); cling to.
착각(錯覺) an (optical) illusion; (a) misapprehension. ~하다 have (be under) an illusion. ¶ 몸이 공중에 떠 있는 것 같은 ~을 일

착공(着工) ~하다 start (construction) work. ¶ 이 공사는 내주에 ~된다 This work will be started next week. ∥ ~식 a ground-breaking ceremony.

착란(錯亂) ~하다 be distracted [deranged]. ¶ 정신을 일으키다 go mad [distracted]. ∥ ~상태 a state of dementia / 정신 ~ dementia; distraction; (a state of) mental derangement; insanity.

착륙(着陸) landing. ~하다 land; make a landing. ¶ 무~ 비행 a non-stop flight / 불시 ~ (비상) ~ a forced [an emergency] landing / ~ 소프트 한 an emergency] landing / 동체 ~ (a) belly landing / 비행기가 비행장에 무사히 ~ The airplane landed safely at the airfield. ∥ ~선 (우주탐사용) a landing module / ~장 a landing ground [field, strip] / ~장치 a landing gear / ~지역 a landing zone / ~지점 a touchdown point [spot].

착복(着服) ① (착의) clothing. ~하다 dress [clothe] *oneself*; put on clothes. ② (횡령) embezzlement; misappropriation. ~하다 embezzle; pocket (secretly) (口). ¶ 회사의 돈을 ~하다 embezzle money from *one's* company.

착살스럽다 ① (인색) (be) stingy; petty. ② (짓이) (be) mean; indecent; base.

착상(着想) an idea; a conception. ~하다 conceive; hit upon. ¶ ~이 떠오르다 an idea occurs to *one*; hit on an idea (사람이 ~어) / 그것 참 좋은 ~이다 It is a clever idea.

착색(着色) ~하다 color; paint; stain. ¶ 이 식품은 인공 ~되어 있다 This food is artificially colored. / 인공~제 함유 [표시] Contains artificial colorants. ∥ ~유리 stained [colored] glass / ~제 a coloring agent; colorant.

착석(着席) ~하다 take a seat; sit down; be seated. ¶ ~시키다 seat (*a person*).

착수(着水) ~하다 land on the water; splash down (우주캡슐이). ¶ 우주선은 태평양에 무사히 ~했다 The spaceship made a safe splashdown in the Pacific.

착수(着手) ~하다 start (*the work*); get started (*on the work*); set to work. ¶ 그 공사는 아직 ~되지 않았다 No start has been made with the work yet. / ~ 금으로 5백만원이 필요합니다 We want five million *won* to start the work with.

착실(着實) ~하다 (be) steady; sound; trustworthy (믿을 만한); faithful. ∥ ~히 steadily; faithfully.

착안(着眼) ~하다 aim (*at*); pay attention to; turn *one's* attention to (유의). ¶ 자네 ~을 잘 했네 Your aim is right. ∥ ~점 the point aimed at; a viewpoint.

착암기(鑿巖機) a rock drill.

착오(錯誤) (make) a mistake; (fall into) an error.

착용(着用) ~하다 wear; be in (*uniform*); have (*a coat*) on.

착유기(搾油機) an oil press.

착유기(搾乳機) a milking machine.

착잡하다(錯雜─) be complicated; intricate; be mixed up. ¶ 착잡한 표정 an expression of mixed feelings.

착착(着着) steadily; step by step. ¶ ~ 진척되다 make steady progress; be well under way.

착취(搾取) exploitation. ~하다 exploit; squeeze. ¶ 가난한 사람을 ~하다 exploit [bleed] the poor.

착탄(着彈) ∥ ~거리 the range (*of a gun*) / ~지점 an impact area.

착하(着荷) arrival of goods. ∥ ~인도(불) delivery [payment] on arrival.

착하다 (마음이) (be) good; nice; kind-hearted. ¶ 착한 사람 [행동] a good person [deed].

찬(饌) ∥ ~거리 materials for side dishes / ~이 많다 have many side dishes / ~이라곤 김치뿐이다 We have nothing but *kimchi* to eat along with rice.

찬가(讚歌) a paean; a poem [song] in praise (*of*).

찬동(贊同) approval; support. ~하다 approve of; support; give *one's* approval (*to*). ¶ ~을 얻다 obtain *a person's* approval / ~을 얻어 with *a person's* approval.

찬란하다(燦爛─) (be) brilliant; radiant; bright; glittering. ¶ 찬란한 다이아몬드 a brilliant diamond / 찬란한 별 bright [glittering] stars.

찬미(讚美) praise; glorification. ~하다 praise; glorify; extol. ∥ ~자 an admirer; an adorer.

찬반(贊反), **찬부**(贊否) approval or disapproval; for and against; yes or no. ¶ ~을 [을] 묻다 put (*a matter*) to the [을] vote (투표로). ∥ ~양론 pros and cons.

찬사(讚辭) a eulogy; a praise. ¶ ~를 보내다 eulogize; pay (*one's*) tribute of praise (*to*).

찬성(贊成) approval; support. ~하다 《동의》 approve of (*a plan*); agree with (*an opinion*); agree to 《*a plan*》;《지지》 support 《*a bill*》; second 《*a motion*》; be in favor 《*of*》. ¶ ~을 구하다 ask 《*a person's*》 approval / ~을 표명하다 express one's approval / ~을 얻다 gain〔win〕the approval 《*of*》 / 의안은 ~ 50, 반대 20으로 통과되었다 The bill was passed with fifty in favor to twenty against. ¶ ~연설 a speech in support 《*of a motion*》 / ~자 a supporter / ~투표 a vote in favor 《*of*》 (~투표하다 vote for a bill).

찬송(讚頌) ☞ 찬미. ‖ ~가(sing) a hymn;(chant)a psalm.

찬스 a chance; an opportunity. ¶ ~를 잡다〔놓치다, 만들다, 얻다〕 seize〔lose, make, get〕 a chance〔an opportunity〕《*to do, of doing*》.

찬양(讚揚) ~하다 praise; admire; commend. ¶ ~할 만한 admirable; laudable; praiseworthy / 용기를 ~하다 praise 《*a person*》 for *his* courage.

찬의(贊意) express 《*one's*》 approval 《*to, toward*》;(give one's)assent 《*to*》.

찬장(饌欌) a cupboard; a pantry〔chest〕.

찬조(贊助) support; patronage. ~하다 support; back up; patronize. ¶ ~을 얻다〔청하다〕 obtain〔solicit〕*a person's* support. ¶ ~금 a contribution / ~연설 a supporting speech; a campaign speech 《*for a candidate*》 / ~자 a supporter; a patron / ~출연 appearance 《*in the play*》 as a guest / ~회원 a supporting member.

찬찬하다《꼼꼼》(be) attentive; meticulous; cautious; careful;《침착》(be) staid; self-possessed. ¶ 찬찬히 carefully; cautiously; meticulously.〔praise.

찬탄(讚嘆·贊嘆) ~하다 admire;

찬탈(簒奪)《왕위를》 usurp 《*the throne*》. ‖ ~자 a usurper.

찬합(饌盒) a nest of food boxes; a picnic box.

찰… glutinous.

찰가난 dire poverty; indigence.

찰거머리〔動〕 a leech. ¶ ~ 같다 cling to 《*a person*》 like a leech.

찰과상(擦過傷)(sustain) a scratch 《*on*》; an abrasion.

찰깍 ①《붙음》 sticking tight(ly); close; fast. ②《소리》 with a snap (click, crack, slap).

찰나(刹那) a moment; an instant. ¶ ~적(인) momentary / ~적인 쾌락에 빠지다 be addicted to momentary pleasures. ‖ ~주의 impulsiveness; momentalism.

찰떡 a glutinous rice cake.

찰랑 splash. ¶ 찰랑찰랑 to the brim; brimfully; splashing.

찰밥 boiled glutinous rice.

찰벼 a glutinous rice plant.

찰흙(粘土) clay.

참[1]《사실·진실》 a fact; truth;《성실》 sincerity; a true heart(진정). ¶ ~된 the true picture 《*of*》 / ~ 사람 a true〔honest〕man / ~된 용기 true courage.

참(站)《역참》 a post; a stage; a station;《쉬는 곳》 a stop;《휴식》 a short rest;《…하려는 때》(the) time;(the) moment. ¶ 저녁 ~에 at dinner time / 막 귀가하려는 ~이다 be about to go home.

참[2]《참으로》 really; truly; indeed; very. ¶ ~ 좋다 be quite good.

참가(參加) participation. ~하다 participate〔take part〕《*in*》; join; enter 《*a contest*》. ¶ ~를 신청하다 send an entry. ‖ ~국 a participating nation / ~자 a participant.

참견(參見) meddling; interference. ~하다 meddle〔interfere〕《*in*》; poke *one's* nose 《*into another's affair*》. ¶ ~ 잘하는 officious; meddlesome / ~ 마라 Mind your own business.

참고(參考) reference. ~하다 refer 《*to*》; consult 《*a book*》. ¶ ~로 for reference〔*one's* information〕 / ~가 되다 be instructive (helpful). ¶ ~서(書) a reference book / ~서목(書目) a bibliography / ~인 a witness / ~자료 reference materials.

참관(參觀) ~하다 visit; inspect. ¶ ~이 허용되다〔되지 않다〕 be open (closed) to visitors. ‖ ~인 a visitor; a witness (선거).

참극(慘劇) a tragedy; a tragic event. ¶ ~의 현장 the scene of the tragedy.

참기름 sesame oil.

참깨〔植〕 sesame; sesame seeds

참나무 an oak (tree). 〔(씨).

참다《견디다》 bear; endure; tolerate; stand 《*heat*》; put up with;《인내하다》 persevere; be patient;《억제하다》 control; suppress; keep〔hold〕 back. ¶ 참을 수 있는〔없는〕 bearable (unbearable) / 웃음을 꾹 ~ stifle (suppress) *one's* laughter / 배고픔을 ~ put up with hunger / 참을 수 없는 모욕 an intolerable insult / 나오는 눈물을 ~ hold〔keep〕back *one's* tears / 나는 노여움을 참을 수 없었다 I couldn't control my temper.

참담(慘憺) ~하다 (be) tragic; miserable; horrible;《가련》(be) pitiful; piteous. ¶ ~한 상태에 있다 be in a very sorry

참답다 (be) true; real; honest; faithful; sincere; upright.

참뜻 the true meaning; *one's real intention*.

참말 a true story [remark]; the truth; a (real) fact. ¶ ~로 truly; really; indeed / ~로 여기다 believe *what a person says*; take *(a person's word)* seriously.

참모(參謀) the staff(총칭); a staff officer; (상담역) an adviser *(to)*. ‖ ~본부 the General Staff Office / ~장 the chief of staff / ~총장 the Chief of the General Staff / ~회의 a staff conference / 합동~본부 the Joint Chiefs of Staff.

참배(參拜) ~하다 visit a temple [shrine]; worship *(at)*.

참변(慘變) a tragic incident; a disaster. ¶ ~을 당하다 suffer a disastrous accident.

참빗 a fine-toothed bamboo comb.

참사(參事) a secretary; a councilor. ‖ ~관 (대사관의) a councilor of an embassy.

참사(慘死) a tragic death. ~하다 meet with (a tragic) death; be killed *(in an accident)*.

참사(慘事) a disaster; a disastrous accident; a tragedy.

참살(慘殺) slaughter; murder. ~하다 cruelly murder; slaughter; butcher. ‖ ~(시)체 a mangled body [corpse].

참상(慘狀) a horrible [dreadful] scene [sight]; a miserable condition [state]. ¶ ~을 드러내다 present a horrible spectacle [sight].

참새 a sparrow.

참석(參席) attendance. ~하다 attend; be present *(at)*; present oneself *(at)*; take part in.

참선(參禪) ~하다 practice Zen meditation *(in a temple)*. ‖ ~자 a Zen practicer.

참수(斬首) ~하다 behead; decapitate. ¶ ~를 당하다 be beheaded.

참신하다(斬新 ─) (be) new; novel; original; up-to-date. ¶ 참신하고 기발한 디자인 a novel and quite unconventional design.

참여(參與) participation; presence (입회). ~하다 participate (take part) *(in)*; (have a) share *(in)*; (회) attend; be present *(at)*; ¶ 증인 ~하에 in the presence of a witness. ‖ ~정부 the participatory government.

참외 a melon.

참으로 really; truly; indeed.

참을성(─性) (인내심) patience; endurance; perseverance; staying power (지구력). ¶ ~ 있는 patient; persevering / ~ 있게 patiently / 요즘 젊은이들은 ~이 없어서 너무 쉽게 단념해 버린다 Young men nowadays have no staying power, they give up too easily.

참의원(參議院) ☞ 상원(上院).

참작(參酌) ~하다 take into consideration; make allowances (for); consult; refer to. ¶정상 ~하다 take the circumstances into consideration.

참전(參戰) ~하다 participate in [enter, join] a war.

참정(參政) ~하다 participate in government. ‖ ~권 suffrage; the franchise; the right to vote (~권을 주다 give [extend] the franchise *(to)*).

참조(參照) ☞ 참고.

참참이 at intervals; once in a while; after a short interval. ¶ ~ 아프다 ache by fits and starts.

참패(慘敗) a crushing defeat. ~하다 suffer [sustain] a crushing defeat; be routed [crushed].

참하다 (얌전함) (be) nice and pretty; quiet; calm; modest; good-tempered. (말쑥함) (be) neat; tidy.

참해(慘害) heavy damage; havoc; disaster; ravages. ¶ ~를 주다 wreak havoc on *(the city)* / ~를 입다 suffer heavily from *(a storm)*.

참형(慘刑) a cruel punishment; a merciless penalty.

참호(塹壕) (dig) a trench; a dugout. ¶ ~를 파다 dig a trench. ‖ ~생활 [전] a trench life [warfare].

참혹하다(慘酷 ─) (be) miserable; wretched; tragic(al); (잔인) cruel; brutal.

참화(慘禍) a terrible [dire] disaster; a crushing calamity. ¶ 전쟁의 ~ the revages [horrors] of war.

참회(懺悔) (a) confession; (회오) repentance; penitence. ~하다 confess; repent. ¶ ~의 눈물 penitential tears / ~생활 a penitent's life. ‖ ~자 a penitent.

찹쌀 glutinous rice.

찻길(車─) a roadway; a carriageway; a track(궤도).

찻삯(車─) (car)fare; carriage (운반료).

찻잔(茶盞), **찻종**(茶鍾) a teacup.

찻집(茶─) a teahouse; a tearoom; a coffeehouse.

창 (구두의) the sole (of shoes). ¶ ~을 갈다 put a new sole (on); resole / ~을 대다 sole (shoes).

창(窓) a window. ¶ ~ 밖을 보다

창 look out of the window / ~ 밖으로 얼굴을 내밀지 마시오 Please don't put your head out of the window. ‖ ~유리 a window glass; a windowpane(끼워넣은) / ~틀 a window frame.

창(槍) a spear; a lance(기병의). ¶ ~ 끝 a spearhead / ~으로 찌르다 spear. ‖ ~던지기 javelin; a javelin-throwing.

창가(唱歌) singing; a song.

창간(創刊) ~하다 found (start) 《a periodical》. ¶ 1920년 ~ founded (started, first published) in 1920. ‖ ~호 the first issue (number) 《of a magazine》.

창건(創建) foundation; establishment. ~하다 ☞ 창립. ~하다 establish; found.

창고(倉庫) a storehouse; a warehouse. ¶ ~에 넣다 store; warehouse; put (deposit) 《goods》 in storage. ‖ ~계원 a storekeeper; a warehouseman / ~료 warehouse charges; storage 《charges》 / ~업 warehousing business / ~증권 a warehouse bond / ~회사 a warehouse (storage) company.

창공(蒼空) the blue sky; the azure.

창구(窓口) a window. ¶ 매표~ a ticket window / 출납~ a cashier's (teller's(은행)) window.

창궐(猖獗) ~하다 rage; be rampant.

창극(唱劇) a Korean classical opera.

창기병(槍騎兵) a lancer.

창녀(娼女) a prostitute; a whore.

창달(暢達) ¶언론 ~에 공헌하다 contribute to the promotion of the freedom of speech.

창당(創黨) ~하다 form (organize) a political party. ‖ ~정신 the spirit underlying the formation of the party.

창도(唱導) advocacy. ~하다 advocate; advance. ‖ ~자 an advocate; a proponent.

창립(創立) foundation; establishment. ~하다 found; establish; set up; organize. ¶ ~30주년(celebrate) the 30th anniversary of the foundation 《of the school》. ‖ ~기념일 the anniversary of the founding 《of the school》 / ~기념식 a ceremony marking the 《group's 50th》 founding anniversary / ~자 a founder / ~총회 an inaugural meeting.

창문(窓門) a window. ☞ 창(窓).

창백(蒼白) ~하다 (be) pale; pallid. ¶ ~해지다 turn pale (white).

창살(窓-) a lattice; a latticework; iron bars (감옥의). ¶ ~이 달린 latticed 《door》 / ~ 없는 감옥 a prison without bars.

창상(創傷) a cut; a wound.

창설(創設) ☞ 창립(創立).

창성(昌盛) a prosperity. ~하다 prosper; thrive; flourish.

창세(創世) 〔聖〕 the creation of the world. ‖ ~기(記) Genesis.

창시(創始) origination; foundation. ~하다 originate; create; found. ‖ ~자 an originator; a founder.

창안(創案) an original idea. ~하다 originate; devise; invent. ‖ ~자 the originator.

창업(創業) the foundation (founding) of an enterprise. ~하다 start 《business》; establish; found. ¶ ~ 이래 since the foundation / ~ 40주년을 기념하다 celebrate the 40th anniversary of the founding 《of a business》. ‖ ~비 starting expenses / ~자 the founder.

창연(蒼鉛) bismuth (기호 Bi).

창의(創意) an original idea; originality (독창성). ¶ ~성이 있는 original; creative; inventive / ~성이 없다 lack originality / ~성 (창의력) creative power / ~성을 발휘하다 use one's originality; exert one's ingenuity / 그 방법은 순전히 그녀가 ~한 것이다 The method is entirely original with her.

창자 the intestines; the bowels; the entrails. ¶ ~를 빼다 gut 《a fish》.

창작(創作) an original work; creation. ~하다 create; originate; write 《a novel》. ¶ ~적인 creative; original. ‖ ~력 creative power; originality / ~활동 creative activity.

창조(創造) creation. ~하다 create; make. ¶ ~적인 creative; original / 천지~ the Creation / 새로운 문화를 ~하다 create a new culture. ‖ ~력 creative power; ~물 a creature; a creation(예술・패션 등) / ~자 a creator; the Creator(하느님).

창졸(倉卒) ¶ ~간에 suddenly; all of a sudden; in the midst of great hurry.

창창(蒼蒼) ~하다 (be) deep blue (green); (멀다) be far off (away); (밝다) be bright; rosy. ¶ ~한 장래 a bright (rosy) future / 갈 길이 아직도 ~하다 still have a long way to go / 앞길이 ~한 청년 a young man who has a bright future.

창파(滄波) big (sea) waves.

창포(菖蒲) 〔植〕 an iris; a (sweet) flag.

창피(猖披) shame; humiliation(굴욕); disgrace(불명예). ~하다, ~

스럽다 be a shame; (be) shameful; humiliating. ¶ ~를 당하다 be put to shame; be [feel] humiliated; disgrace *oneself* / ~를 주다 put (*a person*) to shame; humiliate / ~를 알다 have a sense of shame [honor] / ~를 모르다 be shameless; have no shame / ~해서 얼굴을 붉히다 blush with shame / 헌 옷을 입는 것은 창피한 일이 아니다 There is no reason for shame in wearing old clothes. 〔the bucket.

창해(滄海) ‖ ~일속(一粟) a drop in
창호(窓戶) windows and doors. ¶ ~지 window (door) paper.
찾다 ① (사람·무엇을) search [hunt, look] for; seek for; hunt. ¶일자리를 ~ hunt [look] for a job / 거리를 샅샅이 ~ comb the streets / 찾아다니다 search [look] about for (*a thing*) / 지도에서 그 도시를 ~ look up the town on the map / 사전에서 그 단어를 ~ look up the word in the dictionary / 무엇을 찾느냐 What are you looking for? ② (찾아내다) find (out); locate (*a person*); discover. ¶아무의 거처를 ~ locate [find out] *a person's* whereabouts. ③ (저금을) draw (out) (*money from a bank*). ④ (되돌려 오다) take [get] back; have (*it*) back; (잡힌 것을) redeem (*a pawned watch*). ¶ 빌려준 돈을 다시 ~ get back the money which had been lent. ⑤ (방문) call on (*a person*); call at (*a house*); (pay *a*) visit; (들르다) drop in; stop at; 찾아온 사람 a caller; a visitor / 이 군을 ~ call on [visit] Mr. Lee / 사무소를 ~ call at [visit] an office. ⑥ (원리·근원을) trace. ¶근원을 ~ trace (*something*) to its original.
채¹ (북·장구의) a drumstick; a pick (현악기의).
채² a shaft (우마차의); a (palanquin) pole (가마의).
채³ (야채의) shredding vegetables; vegetable shreds (썬 것).
채⁴ (집의) a building; a wing. ¶ 큰 ~ the main house (building).
채⁵ (그대로 곧) (just) as it is. ¶신을 신은 ~ with *one's* shoes on / 손을 안 댄 ~ 두다 leave just as it is / 불을 켠 ~ 자다 sleep with the light on.
채⁶ (아직) (not) yet; as yet; only. ¶날이 ~ 밝기도 전에 before light / 3분도 ~ 못 되어 in less than three minutes.
채결(採決) ‖ ~하다 take (a) vote (*on*). ¶ ~에 들어가다 come to a vote / ~에 부치다 put (*a matter*) to the vote.

채광(採光) lighting. ¶ ~이 잘 된 [잘 안 된] 방 a well-(poorly-)lit room. / ~창(窓) a skylight.
채광(採鑛) ~하다 mine. ‖ ~권 mining rights / ~기계 mining machinery.
채굴(採掘) ☞ 채광(採鑛).
채권(債券) a debenture; a (loan) bond. ¶ ~을 발행 [상환] 하다 issue (redeem) bonds. / ~시장 the bond market.
채권(債權) credit; a claim. ~이 있다 have a claim (*against a person*); be (*a person's*) creditor. ‖ ~국 a creditor nation / ~순위 the order of credit / ~양도 cession (assignment) of an obligation / ~자 a creditor.
채그릇 a wicker; wickerware.
채널 (TV의) a channel. ¶ ~ 4로 돌리다 turn on channel 4 / 아이들이 텔레비전 ~권을 쥐고 있다 Our children hold a monopoly of the TV channels. ‖ ~다툼 a dispute over which TV program (*they*) should watch.
채다 (알아채다) perceive; notice; get wind [scent] of; suspect (*a danger*); smell out (*the secret*).
채다 (당기다) pull with a jerk; snatch off [away] (*from*) (빼앗다).
채다 ☞ 채우다.
채도(彩度) saturation.
채독(菜毒) a vegetable-borne disease. ¶ ~에 걸리다 get [suffer from] a vegetable-borne disease.
채료(彩料) colors; paints.
채마(菜麻) ‖ ~밭 a vegetable garden.
채무(債務) a debt; an obligation; liabilities. ¶ ~가 있다 be liable for debts; owe / ~를 청산하다 settle *one's* debt / ~를 보증하다 stand surety for loans. ‖ ~국 a debtor nation / ~불이행 default on financial obligations / ~상환 redemption of a debt / ~소멸 expiration of an obligation / ~자 a debtor / ~증서 a bond; an obligation.
채반(-盤) a wicker disk.
채비(-備) preparations; arrangements. ~하다 prepare (*for*); make arrangements (*for*); get ready (*for, to do*). ¶길 떠날 ~를 하다 make preparations for a journey; fit *oneself* out for a trip.
채산(採算) (commercial) profit. ¶ ~이 맞다 [맞지 않다] pay (do not pay); be profitable (unprofitable) / ~을 무시하고 with no thought of profit. ‖ ~가격 a remunerative price / ~성 payability.
채색(彩色) coloring; painting. ~하다 color; paint. ‖ ~화 a

채색 (彩色) ~하다 quarry 《marble》. ‖ ~장 a quarry; a stone pit.
채소 (菜蔬) ☞ 야채, 푸성귀.
채송화 (菜松花) [植] a rose moss.
채식 (菜食) a vegetarian diet. ~하다 live on vegetables. ‖ ~동물 herbivorous (grass-eating) animals / ~주의 vegetarianism / ~주의자 a vegetarian.
채용 (採用) ① (채택) adoption (= 채택). ~하다 adopt; use. ¶ 미터법을 ~하다 adopt the metric system. ② (임용) employment; appointment. ~하다 employ; take into service. ¶ 임시로 ~하다 employ on trial / 우리는 그녀를 타자수로 ~했다 We employed her as a typist. / ~시험 an examination for service / ~조건 hiring requirements / ~통지 a notification of appointment.
채우다¹ ① (자물쇠를) lock; fasten. ② (단추 따위) button (up).
채우다² (물에) keep 《something》 in cold water; (얼음에) cool on ice; refrigerate (냉동).
채우다³ (충만) fill (up) 《a cup with water》; (잔뜩) pack (stuff) 《a bag with books》; (충족) satisfy; meet 《a demand》; (보충) make up; (기한을) complete 《a period, term》; see 《it》 through. ¶ 사복을 ~ fill (stuff) one's pocket / 욕망을 ~ satisfy one's desire / 계약 기한을 ~ see one's contract through; fulfill the period (term) of a contract.
채유 (採油) drilling for oil. ~하다 drill for oil; extract oil. ‖ ~권 oil concessions (rights).
채자 (採字) [印] type picking. ~하다 pick type.
채잡다 take the lead (in); take charge of. ¶ 일을 채잡아 하다 take charge of matters.
채점 (採點) marking; scoring (경기의). ~하다 give marks; mark (look over) 《examination papers》; score. ‖ ~자 a marker; a scorer / ~표 a list of marks.
채집 (採集) ~하다 collect; gather. ¶ 곤충 ~ insect collecting / 약초 ~ gathering medicinal herbs.
채찍 a whip; a lash; a rod. ¶ ~질하다 whip; lash; flog; (격려) spur (urge) 《a person to do》.
채취 (採取) ~하다 pick; gather; collect; fish 《pearls》; extract 《alcohol》. ¶ 진주~ pearl fishery; pearling.
채치다¹ (재촉) urge 《on, a person to do》; press 《a person for payment》.
채치다² (썰다) cut 《a radish》 into fine strips; chop up.
채칼 a knife for shredding vegetables; a chef's knife.
채탄 (採炭) coal mining. ~하다 mine coal. ‖ ~량 the output of coal / ~부 a pitman.
채택 (採擇) adoption; choice. ~하다 adopt; select. ¶ 새 방법을 ~하다 adopt a new method.
채필 (彩筆) a paintbrush; a brush.
채혈 (採血) drawing (collecting) blood. ~하다 gather (collect) blood 《from a donor》; draw blood 《from a vein》 (검사용).
책 (冊) a book; a volume. ¶ ~을 많이 읽다 read much (many books) / ~을 읽어주다 read to 《children》 / ~으로 출판하다 have 《one's papers》 published in book form / ~을 통해 얻은 지식 knowledge gained from books. / ~가위 a (dust) jacket / ~꽂이 a bookshelf / ~뚜껑 a (book) cover / ~받침 a pad to rest writing paper on; a celluloid board.
책 (責) ① ~책임. ② ~책망.
책갑 (冊匣) a bookcase.
책동 (策動) maneuvers; machination. ~하다 maneuver 《behind the scenes》; scheme 《for power》; pull the strings. ¶ ~하는 사람 a schemer; a wire-puller.
책략 (策略) a stratagem; a trick; an artifice. ¶ ~을 꾸미다 devise a stratagem / ~을 쓰다 resort to an artifice; play a (mean) trick on 《a person》. ‖ ~가 a strategist; a schemer.
책력 (冊曆) an almanac; a book calendar.
책망 (責望) (비난) blame; censure; reproach. ~하다 blame; reprimand; reproach; call (take) 《a person》 to task.
책무 (責務) duty; obligation; responsibility.
책방 (冊房) ☞ 서점.
책보 (冊褓) 《책 싸는》 a book wrapper.
책사 (策士) a schemer; a tactician.
책상 (冊床) a desk; a writing table; a bureau (서랍 달린). ¶ ~에 앉다 sit (be) at a desk.
책상다리 (冊床—) (책상의) a leg of a desk (table); (앉음새) sitting cross-legged.
책상물림 (冊床—) a novice from the ivory tower; a naive academic inexperienced in the ways of the world.
책임 (責任) responsibility; liability (지불의); (의무) obligation; duty. ¶ ~ 있는 자리 a responsible post; a position of trust / ~의 분담 the division of responsibili-

ty / ~을 묻다 take (*a person*) to task (*for*); call (*a person*) to account / ~을 다하다 fulfill *one's* responsibility [duty] / ~을 전가하다 shift *one's* responsibility [to *another*] / ~을 지다 take [bear] the responsibility / ~을 회피하다 evade *one's* responsibility / ~이 있다 be responsible [answerable] (*for*); be to blame (*for*); must answer (*to a person, for one's action*) / 나는 지금의 무거운 ~으로부터 벗어나고 싶다 I want to be free from the heavy responsibilities I bear now. ¶ ~감 (관념) (have a strong) sense of responsibility / ~자 a responsible person; a person in charge (*of*) / ~회피 evasion of responsibility.

책자 (冊子) a booklet; a leaflet; a pamphlet.

책장 (冊欌) a bookshelf; a book chest.

책정 (策定) (예산 등의) appropriation; (가격 등의) fixing (*prices*). ~하다 appropriate [apply, assign] (*to*); allot; earmark (*sums of money*) for; fix (up). ¶ 가격을 ~하다 fix a price / 학교 보조금으로 2천만 원을 ~하다 appropriate twenty million *won* for school aid.

챔피언 a champion; a champ (俗). ¶ 헤비급 세계 ~ the heavy-weight champion of the world. ‖ ~십 (a) championship.

챙기다 (정리) put [set] (*things*) in order; (치우다) put (*a thing*) away; (꾸리다) pack; (한데 모으다) gather all together; collect.

처 (妻) a wife. ☞ 아내.

…처 (處) a place; (정부 기구) an office. ¶ 근무~ *one's* place of employment; *one's* office.

처가 (妻家) the home of *one's* wife's parents. ¶ ~살이하다 live in *one's* wife's home with her parents.

처결 (處決) ~하다 settle; dispose of; decide.

처남 (妻男) *one's* wife's brother; *one's* brother-in-law.

처넣다 cram (*things*) into (*a drawer*); stuff; jam; squeeze; pack; (사람을) crowd (*people*) into (*a room*). ¶ 가방에 책들을 ~ pack books into *one's* bag / 모든 옷을 여행 가방에 ~ cram [jam] all *one's* clothes into the suitcase.

처녀 (處女) a maiden; a young girl; a virgin. ¶ ~의 virgin; maiden / ~다운 maidenly; maidenlike / ~답게 like a maiden; in a maidenlike manner / ~이다 be still [remain] a virgin / ~성을 잃다 lose *one's* virginity. ‖ ~막 the hymen; the maidenhead / ~작 [항해] a maiden work [voyage] / ~지 [림] virgin soil [forests].

처단 (處斷) disposal; punishment. ~하다 dispose (*of*); do [deal] with; punish. ¶ 엄중히 ~하다 punish [deal with] (*an offender*) severely.

처덕거리다 (빨래를) (keep beating with a) paddle; (바르다) daub [paste] all over; paint [powder] (*one's face*) thickly (粗).

처량하다 (凄凉—) (황량하다) (be) desolate; dreary; bleak; (구슬프다) (be) sad; piteous: miserable, wretched (비참). ¶ 처량한 생각이 들어 feel miserable.

처럼 as; like; as… as; so… as. ¶ 여느 때~ as usual / 아무 일도 없었던 것~ as if nothing had happened.

처리 (處理) disposition; management; treatment (약품 등의). ~하다 manage; deal with; handle; transact; dispose (*of*); treat. ¶ 사무 ~ the transaction of business / 열 ~ heat treatment / 문제를 ~하다 deal with a problem / 그 서류들은 아직 ~되지 않았다 Those papers haven't been processed yet. / 이 문제는 신중히 ~해야 한다 We must handle [treat] this problem carefully. ‖ ~장 a processing plant; (하수 따위의) a treatment plant.

처마 the eaves. ¶ ~ 밑에 under the eaves.

처먹다 eat greedily; shovel [shove] down; dig [tuck] in.

처방 (處方) a (medical) prescription. ~하다 prescribe. ¶ ~대로 as prescribed. ‖ ~전 (箋) (write out) a prescription.

처벌 (處罰) punishment; penalty. ~하다 punish. ¶ ~을 면하다 escape punishment / 증거 불충분으로 ~을 면하다 be set free because of lack of evidence.

처분 (處分) disposal; management; dealing; a measure (조치). ~하다 dispose (*of*); deal with; do away with; get rid of. ¶ 매각~ disposal by sale / 토지를 ~하다 dispose of *one's* land / 허드레 물건들을 ~ get rid of junk.

처사 (處事) management; disposal; a measure (조치); (행위) conduct; an action. ¶ ~를 잘하다 deal with (*a matter*) properly.

처세 (處世) conduct of life. ~하다 get on [make *one's* way] through the world. ¶ ~를 잘하다 do [make] a good job of life; know how to get on in the world. ‖ ~술 how to get on in

처소(處所) 〖장소〗 a place; 〖거처〗 a living place; one's residence.
처시하다(妻侍下) a wife-ridden man; a henpecked husband.
처신(處身) conduct; behavior. ~하다 bear〔behave〕 oneself; act. ¶점잖게 ~하다 behave oneself gracefully〔well〕; move with grace.
처우(處遇) treatment. ~하다 treat; deal with. ¶근로자의 ~개선 the improvement of labor conditions / 공평하게 ~하다 treat 《a person》 fairly / K씨 ~ 문제로 애를 먹다 have a lot of trouble working out how to treat Mr. K.
처음(개시) the beginning; the opening; the commencement; 〖발단〗 the start; the outset; 〖기원〗 the origin. ¶~의 first; original; early (초기의); ~으로 first; for the first time / ~에는 at first; originally / ~부터 끝까지 from beginning to end; from start to finish; from first to last / ~부터 다시 하다 do all over again; make a fresh start / 모든 일은 ~이 어렵다 Everything is hard at the beginning. / 나는 ~부터 그 제안에 반대했다 I have been against the proposal from the beginning. / 나는 생전 ~으로 바다를 보았다 I saw the sea for the first time in my life. / ~계획에서는 학교 건물을 여기에 세우도록 되어 있었다 According to the original plan, a school building was to be built here.
처자(妻子) one's wife and children; one's family (가족).
처절하다(悽絶—) (be) extremely lurid 〔gruesome, miserable〕.
처제(妻弟) one's wife's younger sister; one's sister-in-law.
처지(處地) a situation; circumstances. ¶곤란한 ~ a difficult 〔an awkward〕 situation; a fix / 지금 ~로는 in the present circumstances / 남의 ~가 되어 보다 put 〔place〕 oneself in another's place.
처지다 ①〖늘어지다〗 hang down; droop; become loose (팽팽하지 않다). ¶귀가 처진 개 a dog with drooped ears. ②〖뒤처지다〗 fall 〔remain, stay〕 behind; drop 〔behind〕. ¶혼자만 뒤에 ~ remain behind all alone. ③〖못하다〗 be inferior 《to》; be not so good 《as》; 질에 있어서 많이 ~ be far inferior in quality 《to》.
처지르다 stuff; pack; cram; squeeze.
처참하다(悽慘—) (be) ghastly; grim; miserable; wretched.
처처(處處) everywhere; 〖in〗 every quarter. ¶~에 here and there; everywhere.
처치(處置) ①〖처리〗 disposition; disposal; 〖조치〗 a measure; a step. ~하다 deal with; dispose of; take measures 〔steps, action〕. ¶어떻게 ~할지 모르다 do not know what to do with…; be at a loss how to deal with…. ②〖제거〗 ~하다 remove; take 〔move〕 away; get rid of; do away with. ③〖상처 등의〗 treatment. ~하다 treat; give medical treatment. ¶응급 ~를 하다 give first aid to 《the wounded》.
처하다(處—) ①〖놓이다〗 be placed 《in》; get faced 《with》. ¶위기에 ~ face 〔rise to〕 a crisis / 곤란한 처지에 ~ be in a fix (quandary). ②〖처벌하다〗 condemn; sentence. ¶벌금형에 처해지다 be fined / 사형에 ~ sentence 《a criminal》 to death.
처형(妻兄) one's wife's elder sister; one's sister-in-law.
처형(處刑) punishment; execution(사형의). ~하다 punish; execute. ¶~되다 be executed. / ~장 an execution ground.
척(尺) 〖길이의 단위〗 a ch'ŏk(= 0.994 ft.).
척(隻) 〖두 ~의 배〗 two ships 《vessels》.
척 ①〖단단히 붙는 모양〗 (sticking) fast; close; tight. ¶~ 들러붙다 stick fast 《to one's hand》. ②〖선뜻〗 without hesitation (서슴지 않고); readily; 〖즉각〗 quickly; right away (off).
척결(剔抉) ~하다 〖긁어내다〗 gouge; scrape out; 〖들춰내다〗 expose 《a crime》.
척도(尺度) 〖계측 도구〗 a (measuring) rule; a scale; 〖표준〗 a standard; a yardstick; a criterion. ¶선악의 ~ standards of morality / …의 ~가 되다 be a measure of…; be a yardstick for….

척살(刺殺) ~하다 stab 《a person》 to death; 〖野〗 put 〔touch〕 《a runner》 out.
척수(脊髓) 〖解〗 the spinal cord. ‖ ~마비 spinal paralysis / ~병 a spinal disease / ~신경 spinal nerves / ~염 myelitis.
척식(拓殖) colonization.
척주(脊柱) 〖解〗 the spinal column; the spine; the backbone. ‖ ~만곡 spinal curvature.
척척 ①〖거침없이〗 quickly; promptly; readily; efficiently 〔능률 있게〕; without delay (지체 없이). ¶~ 일을 하다 work quickly; do one's work with dispatch / ~ 대답하

척척하다 742 **천명**

다 give a ready answer. ②《들러붙다》 tight(ly); fast; close(ly). ¶ ~ 붙다 stick fast 《to》; cling tightly 《to》. ③《차곡차곡》 fold by fold; heap by heap 《쌓다》; neatly; tidily. ¶ ~ 개키다 fold up the bedding / ~ 쌓다 pile up in a heap.

척척하다 (be) wet; damp.

척추(脊椎) [瘠] the backbone. ~ 동물 a vertebrate / ~염 spondylitis / ~카리에스 vertebra caries. [grenade launcher.

척탄(擲彈) a grenade. ‖ ~ 통(筒) a

척후(斥候) 《임무》 reconnaissance; patrol duty;《사람》a scout; a patrol. ~ 하다 reconnoiter 《the area》. ¶ ~를 내보내다 send out scouts / ~ 나가다 go out scouting. ‖ ~ 대 a reconnoitering party / ~ 병 a scouting soldier.

천(피륙) cloth; texture.

천(千) a thousand. ¶ ~ 배의 a thousandfold / ~ 분의 일 a [one] thousandth / 몇 ~ 씩 in thousands; by the thousand / 수~ thousands of.

천거(薦擧) recommendation. ~ 하다 recommend; put in a good word for 《a person》. ¶ …의 ~ 로 on the recommendation of….

천격(賤格) 《性格》 ~ 스럽다 (be) mean; humble; low.

천견(淺見) a shallow view.

천계(天界) the heavens; the skies.

천고마비(天高馬肥) ~의 계절 autumn with the sky clear and blue, and horses growing stout.

천공(穿孔) boring; punching. ~ 하다 bore; punch. ‖ ~기 a boring (drilling) machine.

천구(天球) [天] the celestial sphere. ‖ ~의(儀) a celestial globe.

천국(天國) ☞ 천당. 지상 ~ a terrestrial [an earthly] paradise; a heaven on earth / ~의 문 Heaven's Gate [Door].

천군만마(千軍萬馬) a great multitude of troops and horses.

천궁도(天宮圖) a horoscope.

천금(千金) ¶ ~으로도 바꿀 수 없는 priceless / 일확 ~ 을 꿈꾸다 dream of making a fortune at a stroke; plan to get rich at a single bound.

천기(天機) the profound secrets of Nature; the hidden plans of Providence.

천당(天堂) Heaven; Paradise; the Kingdom of Heaven. ¶ ~에 가다 go to glory [Heaven]; die《죽다》.

천대(賤待) contemptuous treatment. ~ 하다 treat 《a person》 contemptuously [with contempt]. ¶ ~ 받다 be treated contemptuously.

천더기(賤 —), **천더꾸러기**(賤 —) a despised person; a poor wretch; a child of scorn.

천도(遷都) ~ 하다 move [transfer] the capital 《to》.

천동설(天動說) the Ptolemaic theory.

천둥(~ 의) a roll of thunder.

천둥벌거숭이 a man of reckless valor; a reckless simpleton.

천둥지기 rain-dependent farmland.

천랑성(天狼星) [天] Sirius.

천량 money and food; wealth.

천렵(川獵) river fishing. ~ 하다 fish in a river.

천륜(天倫) moral laws; morals. ¶ ~ 에 어긋리다 transgress [violate] moral laws.

천리(千里) a thousand *ri*; a long distance. ¶ ~ 만리 떨어진 곳 a place far far away. / ~ 마 a swift [an excellent] horse / ~ 안 clairvoyance; a clairvoyant 《사람》.

천막(天幕) a tent. ¶ ~ 을 치다 pitch [set up, put up] a tent / ~ 을 걷다 strike [pull down] a tent. ‖ ~ 생활 camping (life) 《~생활을 하다》 camp 《out》.

천만(千萬) 《수효》 ten million; a myriad 《무수》;《매우》 exceedingly; very much; indeed. ¶ 몇 ~이나 되는 tens of millions of / 유감 ~ 이다 It is really regrettable that…. / ~의 말씀입니다 Not at all. *or* Don't mention it.

천만년(千萬年) ten million years; a long long time.

천만다행(千萬多幸) being very lucky; a piece of luck; a godsend. ¶ ~으로 luckily; fortunately; by good luck / ~ 이다 be extremely fortunate; be very lucky.

천만뜻밖(千萬 —) being quite unexpected [unanticipated]. ¶ ~의 quite unexpected; least expected; unlooked-for / ~에 quite unexpectedly; contrary to *one*'s expectation / ~에 그를 거리에서 만났다 I met him quite unexpectedly on the street.

천만부당(千萬不當) being utterly unjust; being unreasonable. ~ 하다 (be) utterly unjust [absolutely, entirely] unjust [unfair, unreasonable, absurd]. ¶ ~한 말 an absolutely unreasonable remark.

천명(天命) ① 《수명》 *one*'s life. ② 《하늘 뜻》 God's will; Heaven's decree; Providence; 《운명》 fate; destiny. ¶ ~으로 알다 resign *oneself* to *one*'s fate / ~을 다하다 come to the end of *one*'s jour-

천명(闡明) ~하다 make clear; explicate.
천문(天文) 《현상》 astronomical phenomena; 《천문학》 astronomy; 《점성술》 astrology. ¶ ~학적인 숫자에 이르다 reach astronomical figures. ‖ ~관측위성 an (orbiting) astronomical satellite / ~대 an astronomical observatory / ~학자 an astronomer.
천민(賤民) the humble; the lowly (people); the poor.
천박(淺薄) ~하다 (be) shallow; superficial; half-baked. ¶ ~한 사람 a shallow-minded fellow / ~한 이론 half-baked theories / ~한 생각 a superficial way of thinking / ~한 지식 superficial knowledge.
천방지축(天方地軸)《부사적》 recklessly; foolhardily; in a stupid flurry; hurry-scurry. ¶ ~으로 덤비다 (서두르다) rush recklessly; make a headlong rush.
천벌(天罰) ¶ ~을 받다 be punished by Heaven / 그런 짓을 하면 ~을 받는다 Heaven will punish you for it.
천변(川邊) a riverside; a streamside; a riverbank. ¶ ~에 (on) a river (stream) / ~에서 at the riverside (streamside).
천변(天變) a natural disaster (calamity). ~지이(地異) = 천변(天變).
천변만화(千變萬化) innumerable changes. ~하다 change endlessly. ¶ ~의 kaleidoscopic; ever-changing.
천복(天福) a heavenly blessing; benediction. ¶ ~을 받다 be blessed by Heaven.
천부(天賦) ¶ ~의 natural; inborn; inherent; innate / ~의 재능 a natural gift (endowment); an innate talent.
천분(天分) one's natural gifts (talents); one's talent. ¶ ~이 있는 talented / ~이 많은 사람 a highly-gifted person; a person richly endowed by nature / …의 ~을 갖추고 있다 have an aptitude for….
천사(天使) an angel.
천생(天生) ¶ ~의 natural; born; designed by nature. ‖ ~배필 a predestined couple; a well-matched pair / ~연분 marriage ties preordained by Providence.
천성(天性) one's nature; one's innate character; disposition(성질); temperament(기질). ¶ ~의 natural; born; innate / 습관은 제2의 ~이다 Habit is (a) second nature.
천성나다 be much in demand; become scarce; run short.
천수(天水) rainwater. ‖ ~답(畓) 천둥의기.
천수(天壽) one's natural term of existence; one's natural span of life. ¶ ~를 다하다 die of old age; complete the natural span of one's life / ~를 누리지 못하고 죽다 die before one's time.
천시(天時) 《때》 a good (heaven-sent) opportunity. ¶ ~를 기다리다 wait one's time.
천시(賤視) ~하다 take a disdainful view (of); contempt; despise; look down on.
천식(喘息) 《醫》 asthma. ‖ ~환자 an asthmatic (patient).
천신(天神) the heavenly gods.
천신만고(千辛萬苦) ~하다 undergo (go through) all sorts of hardships.
천심(天心) ①《하늘의 뜻》 the divine will; Providence. ¶ ~ 민심은 ~이다 The voice of people (is) the voice of God. ②《하늘 복판》 the zenith.
천애(天涯) ①《하늘 끝》 the sky-line; the horizon. ②《먼 곳》 a far-off country; a distant land. ¶ ~ 고아 a lonely orphan.
천양지차(天壤之差) a great (wide) difference(between); all the difference in the world. ¶ ~이다 be entirely different; be as different as light from darkness.
천언만어(千言萬語) innumerable words; endless arguments.
천업(賤業) a mean (discreditable) occupation; a dirty job.
천역(賤役) a mean task (job).
천연(天然) nature. ¶ ~의〔적인〕 natural; unartificial; spontaneous(자생의) / ~적으로 naturally; spontaneously. ‖ ~가스 natural gas / ~기념물 a natural monument / ~자원 natural resources / ~액화 ~가스 liquefied natural gas(생략 LNG).
천연(遷延) delay; procrastination. ~하다 delay; procrastinate; put off.
천연두(天然痘) smallpox.
천연색(天然色) natural color. ‖ ~사진 a color photograph / ~영화 a (Techni)color film.
천연스럽다(天然─) (be) natural; unartificial; unaffected; 《대연》 (be) calm; unmoved; indifferent (to); 《서슴직이》 do not care (about). ¶ 천연스럽게 calmly; coolly; unconcernedly; as if nothing had happened; with indifference; without scruple.
천왕성(天王星) 『天』 Uranus.

천우신조(天佑神助) 《by》 the grace of Heaven 〔God〕; the providence of God.

천운(天運) fate; destiny 《운명》; fortune 《행운》.

천은(天恩) the blessing of Heaven; the grace of Heaven.

천의(天意) the divine will.

천인(天人) 《하늘과 사람》 God 〔Heaven〕 and man. ¶ ~공노할 죄 a sin against Heaven and man; a heinous atrocity 〔offence〕.

천인(賤人) a man of humble origin; a lowly man.

천일염(天日塩) bay 〔sun-dried〕 salt.

천자(千字) 1,000 characters. ‖ ~문 the Thousand-Character Text; a primer of Chinese characters.

천자(天子) 《황제》 the Emperor.

천자만홍(千紫萬紅) a resplendent variety of flowers.

천장(天障) the ceiling. ¶ 반자~ a boarded ceiling / ~이 높은 〔낮은〕 방 a high-〔low-〕ceilinged room / ~에 파리가 붙어 있다 There is a fly on the ceiling. ‖ ~널 a ceiling board / ~등 〔터널·차의〕 a ceiling lamp 〔light〕.

천재(千載) ~일우의 호기 《throw away》 a golden opportunity.

천재(天才) 《재능》 genius; a natural talents; 《사람》 a genius. ¶ ~적인 gifted; talented / 그녀는 음악의 ~이다 She has a genius for music. or She is a born musician. / 그에게는 ~적인 데가 있다 He has a touch of genius. ‖ ~교육 (the) education of gifted children / ~아(兒) an infant prodigy; a child genius.

천재(天災) a natural calamity 〔disaster〕. ¶ ~을 당하다 be struck by a natural calamity / 그것은 ~가 아니라 인재(人災)였다 It was not a natural disaster but a man-made one. ‖ ~지변 ☞ 천재 〔天災〕.

천적(天敵) a natural enemy.

천정(天井) 천장. ¶ ~부지의 soaring; skyrocketing / 물가는 ~부지로 치솟고 있다 Prices are skyrocketing. ‖ ~시세 the ceiling 〔top〕 price.

천주(天主) the Lord (of Heaven); God. ‖ ~경(經) the Lord's Prayer / ~삼위(三位) the Trinity.

천주교(天主教) 가톨릭.

천지(天地) ① 《하늘과 땅》 heaven and earth; 《우주》 the universe 《세계》 the world. ~개벽 이래 ever since the beginning of the world. / ~만물 the whole creation / ~창조 the Creation. ② 《장소》 a land; a world. ¶ 자유 ~ a free land; the land of freedom / 신~ a new world / 별~ a different world. ③ 《많음》 being full 《of》. ¶ 그 책은 오자 ~다 The book is full of misprints.

천지신명(天地神明) gods of heaven and earth; divinity. ¶ ~께 맹세하다 swear by; call heaven to witness.

천직(天職) mission; a calling; a vocation. ¶ 이 일이 나의 ~이다 I have a vocation for this work. / 나는 교직을 ~으로 여기고 있다 I believe that teaching is my true vocation. or I believe that I was born to be a teacher.

천진난만(天眞爛漫) ~하다 《be》 naive; artless; innocent; simple. ¶ ~한 아이 a simple and innocent child.

천진하다(天眞—) be innocent; artless; naive.

천차만별(千差萬別) innumerable changes; infinite variety. ¶ ~의 multifarious; 《insects》 of infinite 〔endless〕 variety.

천천히 slowly; without hurry 〔haste〕; leisurely. ¶ ~하다 take one's time 《in doing》 / ~ 생각하다 take time to think; ponder over 《a matter》.

천체(天體) a heavenly 〔celestial〕 body. ‖ ~관측 astronomical observation / ~도 a celestial map / ~망원경 an astronomical telescope / ~물리학 astrophysics / ~역학 celestial mechanics; dynamical astronomy.

천추(千秋) 《천년》 a thousand years; 《긴 세월》 many 〔long〕 years. ¶ ~의 한이 되는 일 a matter of great regret / 하루를 ~같이 기다리다 wait impatiently 《for a person》.

천치(天痴) an idiot; an imbecile.

천태만상(千態萬象) ☞ 천차만별.

천편일률(千篇一律) ~적(인) monotonous; stereotyped.

천품(天稟) nature; character; 《재질》 a natural endowment; natural talents.

천하(天下) 《세계》 the world; 《나라》 the whole country. ¶ ~에 under the sun; in the world / ~를 잡다 《정권을》 hold 〔assume〕 reins of government; come into power / 《정복하다》 conquer the country / ~무적이다 be unrivaled 〔peerless〕 in the world / ~를 통일하다 unify a country; bring the whole country under one's rule / 자네 부인의 요리 솜씨는 ~일품이네 Your wife's cooking is out of this world. ‖ ~명창 one of the most excellent singers in the country / ~일

천하다(賤一) ①《신분이》(be) humble; low(ly); ignoble. ¶ 천한 사람 a lowly man. ②《상스럽다》(be) vulgar; mean; base. ¶ 말씨가 ~ be vulgar in *one's* speech / 천한 말을 쓰다 use vulgar (coarse) language. ③《흔하다》(be) superfluous; plenty; cheap (값싸미). ¶ 요즘 천한 것이 사과다 Apples are very cheap these days.

천행(天幸) the blessing (grace) of Heaven; a godsend. ¶ ~으로 살아나다 have a narrow escape by good luck.

천혜(天惠) (a) blessing; a gift of nature; natural advantage.

철¹(계절) a season. ¶ 여름~ the summer season / 제~이 아닌 unseasonable; out of the season / ~지난 behind the season.

철²(분별) (good) sense; discretion; prudence; wisdom. ¶ ~이 들 나이의 age of discretion / ~이 들다 (나다) become sensible; attain (reach) the age of discretion / ~이 든 이래로 ever since *one* could remember / ~이 있다 have sense (discretion) / ~이 없다 have no sense (discretion); be indiscreet (thoughtless).

철(鐵) iron; steel. ~의 iron; ferrous / ~의 장막 the Iron Curtain / ~제의 iron; (made) of iron.

…철(綴) file. ☞ 철하다. ¶ 서류~ a file of papers / 신문~ a newspaper file.

철갑(鐵甲) an iron armor (갑옷); 《형용사적》ironclad. ‖ ~선 an ironclad ship.

철강(鐵鋼) steel. ¶ ~제의 (made) of steel; steel. ‖ ~업 the iron and steel industry / ~제품 steel manufactures.

철거(撤去) withdrawal; removal (제거). ~하다 withdraw; remove; take (clear) away; pull down. ¶ 무허가 판잣집의 ~ removal of illegally built shacks / 장애물을 ~하다 remove the obstacles; clear 《*the passage*》.

철골(鐵骨) an iron (a steel) frame. ¶ 저 공장은 ~슬레이트 지붕이다 The factory has a slate roof on iron frames. (an ironworks).

철공(鐵工) an ironworker. ‖ ~소

철관(鐵管) an iron pipe.

철광(鐵鑛) an iron ore (광석); an iron mine (광산).

철교(鐵橋) an iron bridge; a railway bridge (철도의).

철군(撤軍) withdrawal of troops. ~하다 withdraw troops 《*from*》; evacuate 《*a place*》. ¶ ~의 규모와 일정 the size and timetable of the pullout of the troops / ~을 요구하다 demand troop withdrawal(s).

철권(鐵拳) an iron fist. ¶ ~을 휘두르다 shake *one's* fist at 《*a person*》.

철근(鐵筋) a reinforcing bar (rod). ‖ ~콘크리트 ferroconcrete; reinforced concrete / ~콘크리트 건물 a ferroconcrete (reinforced concrete) building.

철기(鐵器) ironware; hardware. ‖ ~시대 the Iron Age.

철도(鐵道) a railroad; a railway 《英》. ¶ ~를 놓다 lay (construct, build) a railway / ~를 이용하다 take the train 《*to get there*》; go 《*to a place*》 by train / ~로 운반되는 화물 rail-borne good / ~로 연결되어 있다 be linked by rail 《*with*》 / 교외 ~ a suburban railroad / 단선 (복선) ~ a single-track (double-track) railroad / 고속 ~ a high-speed railroad. ‖ ~공사 railroad construction / ~국 the Railway Bureau / ~망 a network of railroads / ~사고 (be killed in) a railway accident / ~선로 a railroad line (track) / ~안내소 a railroad information bureau / ~운임 railroad fare (여객의); freight rates (화물의) / ~종업원(공안원) a railroad worker (security officer) / ~청 《한국의》the National Railroad Administration.

철두철미(徹頭徹尾) 《부사적》from beginning to end; every inch; out-and-out; thoroughly.

철떡거리다 keep clinging (sticking)

철렁거리다 ☞ 찰랑거리다. 〔*to*〕.

철리(哲理) philosophy.

철망(鐵網) ① wire netting (총칭); a wire net (gauze(촘촘한)). ¶ ~을 치다 cover 《*the window*》 with wire netting. ② ~ 철조망.

철면(凸面) a convex surface.

철면피(鐵面皮) a brazen face; impudence. ¶ ~한 brazen-faced; shameless; cheeky; impudent / ~처럼 …하다 have the cheek (gall, face, impudence) to 《*do*》.

철모(鐵帽) a (steel) helmet.

철모르다(鐵一) (be) indiscreet; thoughtless; imprudent; simpleminded. ¶ 철모르는 애 a thoughtless child.

철문(鐵門) an iron door (gate).

철물(鐵物) hardware; ironware; metal fittings. ‖ ~상 an ironmonger 《英》; a dealer in hardware / 《가게》 a hardware store; an ironmonger's 《英》.

철바람 a seasonal wind.
철버덕거리다 《철벅거리다》 splash; dabble in (*water*).
철벽(鐵壁) an iron wall. ¶ ~ 같은 진지 an impregnable fortress.
철병(撤兵) military withdrawals. ▫ 철군(撤軍).
철봉(鐵棒) an iron bar [rod]; 《체조용》 a horizontal bar; the horizontal bar.
철부지(-不知) a person of indiscretion; a thoughtless person; 《어린애》 a mere child; just a child.
철분(鐵分) iron (content). ¶ 많은 ~을 포함하다 contain a lot of iron.
철사(鐵絲) (a) wire; wiring; 《총칭》. ¶ 가시 ~ barbed wire / ~로 묶다 wire together.
철삭(鐵索) a cable; a wire rope.
철새 a bird of passage; a migratory bird.
철석(鐵石) 《몹시 굳음》 ¶ ~ 같은 adamant; firm; strong / ~ 같은 마음 an iron will; a firm [steadfast] resolution / ~ 같은 언약 a solemn promise.
철선(鐵線) iron wire.
철수(撤收) withdrawal; removal. ~ 하다 withdraw (*from*); pull (*troops*) out of (*a region*). ¶ 캠프를 ~하다 strike camp / 군대를 ~하다 withdraw the troops.
철시(撤市) ~하다 close the market; close up shops [stores]; suspend business.
철썩 ① 《물소리》 with splashes [spattering noise]. ~하다 splash; swash. ② 《때림》 with a slap [spank, crack]. ~하다 slap. ¶ 뺨을 ~ 때리다 slap (*a person*) in the face.
철야(徹夜) ~하다 sit [stay] up all night. ¶ ~로 회의를 하다 have an all-night conference / ~로 간호하다 sit up all night with (*an invalid*); keep an all-night vigil over (*a sick child*). ‖ ~작업 all-night work.
철옹성(鐵甕城) an impregnable fortress. ¶ ~ 같다 be impregnable.
철인(哲人) a man of wisdom; a philosopher.
철자(綴字) spelling; orthography. ~하다 spell. ‖ ~법 the system of spelling.
철재(鐵材) iron (material); steel.
철저(徹底) ¶ ~한 thorough; thoroughgoing; exhaustive; complete; out-and-out 《口》 ~히 thoroughly; exhaustively / ~한 이기주의자 an out-and-out egoist / ~한 연구 an exhaustic study / ~한 변혁 a sweeping [complete]

change / 병원에서 ~한 검사를 받다 have a thorough medical examination at the hospital / 나는 무슨 일이나 ~히 한다 I do everything thoroughly.
철제(鐵製) ¶ ~ (made of) iron; steel / ~ 공구 an iron tool.
철조망(鐵條網) barbed-wire entanglements. ¶ ~을 치다 set [stretch] barbed-wire around (*a place*) / ~을 둘러친 건물 a building with barbed-wire entanglements.
철쭉(植) a royal azalea; a rhododendron.
철창(鐵窓) a steel-barred window; 《감옥》 prison bars; a prison. ¶ ~ 생활 life behind (the) bars / ~에 갇히다 be imprisoned.
철책(鐵柵) an iron fence. ¶ ~을 두르다 stretch an iron fence (*around*).
철천지한(徹天之恨) a lasting regret (유감); deep-rooted enmity (원한). ¶ ~을 품다 bear a lasting regret; have [nurse] (*a person*) a deep-rooted enmity.
철철 (넘치는 모양) ¶ ~ 넘치도록 잔에 술을 따르다 fill a glass to the brim with wine / 물이 ~ 넘치다 be brimming over with water.
철칙(鐵則) an iron rule.
철통(鐵桶) an iron (a steel) tub. ¶ ~ 같은 방어의 an impenetrable defense position / ~ 같은 경계망을 펴다 lay a tight cordon (*around*).
철퇴(撤退) (a) withdrawal; a pullout. ~하다 withdraw (*troops*); pull out (*of a place*).
철퇴(鐵槌) an iron hammer. ¶ ~를 내리다 give a crushing blow (*to*).
철판(凸板) ‖ ~인쇄 relief printing.
철판(鐵板) an iron plate; a sheet iron.
철편(鐵片) a piece of iron.
철폐(撤廢) abolition; removal. ~하다 abolish; remove; do away with. ¶ 악법은 ~ 되어야 한다 Bad laws must be abolished.
철필(鐵筆) a (steel) pen.
철하다(綴-) file (*papers*); bind (*a book*). ¶ 서류를 ~해놓다 keep papers on file.
철학(哲學) philosophy. ¶ ~적(으로) philosophical(ly) / 인생 ~ a philosophy of life. ‖ ~박사 a doctor of philosophy; Doctor of Philosophy(학위) (생략 Ph.D.) / ~자 a philosopher.
철혈(鐵血) blood and iron. ¶ ~정책 a blood-and-iron policy.
철회(撤回) withdrawal. ~하다 withdraw; take back. ¶ 사표를 ~하다 withdraw one's resignation / 앞서 말을 ~하다 take

첨가(添加) annexing; addition. ~를 하다 add 《to》 《식품에 방부제를》 ~를 하다 add preservative to food. ‖ ~물 an additive.

첨단(尖端) ① 《뾰족한 끝》 the point; the tip; a pointed end [head]. ② 《선두》 the spearhead. ¶ ~의 ultramodern; up-to-date; ultrafashionable《유행의》/시대《유행》의 ~을 걷는 사람 a trendsetter / 시대의 ~을 걷다 be in the van of the new era / 유행의 ~을 걷다 lead the fashion. ‖ ~기기 high [up-to-date] technology.

첨병(尖兵) a spearhead.

첨부(添附) attach 《A to B》; append; annex. ¶ …이 ~이 되다 be accompanied by… / …을 ~하여 together with…. ‖ ~서류 attached papers.

첨삭(添削) correction. ~하다 correct; touch up.

첨예(尖銳) ¶ ~한 radical / ~화하다 become acute; be radicalized. ‖ ~분자 radicals; the extreme 〔radical〕 elements.

첨탑(尖塔) a steeple; a spire.

첩(妾) a concubine; a mistress. ¶ ~을 두다 keep a mistress.

첩(貼) a pack of herb-medicine; a dose.

…첩(帖) 《note》book; an album.

첩경(捷徑) 《지름길》 a shortcut; 《쉬운 방법》 a short 〔quick, easy〕 way.

첩보(捷報) news of a victory.

첩보(諜報) intelligence. ‖ ~기관 an intelligence office 〔agency〕; a secret agency / ~망 an intelligence 〔espionage〕 network / ~부 an intelligence bureau / ~원 a secret agent; a spy / ~활동 espionage.

첩부하다(貼付하다) ☞ 붙이다 ①.

첩약(貼藥) a pack 〔dose〕 of prepared herb-medicine.

첩첩(疊疊) ¶ ~산중에 in the depths of mountains.

첫 first; new; maiden. ¶ ~공연 the first performance 《of a play》/ ~글자 an initial 〔letter〕/ ~서리 the first frost of the season / ~아이 one's first 〔-born〕 child / ~항해 a maiden voyage.

첫걸음 the first step 《to》; an initial step; a start; 《초보·기본》 the rudiments 《of》; the ABC 《of》. ¶ 성공에의 ~ the first step to success / 영어의 ~ the first step in English.

첫길(초행길) an unaccustomed course; one's first trip 《to》; 《신행길》 the way to one's wedding.

첫날 the first 〔opening〕 day.

첫날밤 the bridal night; the first night of a married couple.

첫눈(일견) the first sight 《look》. ¶ ~에 반하다 fall in love with 《a person》 at first sight.

첫눈²(초설) the first snow of the season.

첫돌 the first birthday 《of a baby》.

첫마디, 첫말 the first word; an opening remark.

첫머리 the beginning; the start; the outset.

첫무대(一舞臺) one's debut. ¶ ~를 밟다 make one's debut.

첫물 ① 《우외》 first wearing; 옷 clothes that have never been laundered. ② ☞ 맏물.

첫배(새끼) the first litter 〔brood〕.

첫사랑 one's first love.

첫새벽 early dawn 〔morning〕; daybreak. ¶ ~에 at daybreak 〔dawn〕.

첫선 the first appearance; a debut; the first public presentation. ¶ ~을 보이다 《make a》 debut.

첫술 the first spoonful 《of food》. ¶ ~에 배부르랴 《俗談》 You must not expect too much at your first attempt.

첫여름 early summer.

첫인상(一印象) one's first impression 《of》. ¶ ~이 좋다 make 〔give〕 a good 〔favorable〕 first impression. 〔ment〕.

첫정(一情) one's first love 〔attach-

첫째 the first 〔place〕; No. 1; the top. ¶ ~의 first; primary; foremost; top / ~로 first 《of all》; in the first place; to begin with / ~가 되다 come out 〔at the〕 top / ~를 차지하다 stand first; be at the forefront 〔head〕 of 《a class》. 〔weather.

첫추위(一出) the first spell of cold

첫출발(一出發) a start; a beginning. ¶ 인생의 ~ one's start in life.

첫판(경기) the first round.

첫판(初版) the first edition.

첫해 the first year.

첫행보 one's first visit.

청(請) 《a》 request; a favor; one's wishes; 《간청》 an entreaty. ¶ 간절한 ~ an earnest request / ~에 의하여 at 《a person's》 request / ~을 넣다 make a request through 《another》 / ~을 들어주다 grant 〔comply with〕 《a person's》 request / ~이 있다 have a favor to ask of 《a person》.

청가뢰 〖蟲〗 a green blister beetle.

청각(聽覺) the auditory sense; 〔the sense of〕 hearing. ‖ 시~교육 audio-visual education. ‖ ~기관 a hearing organ / ~신경

the auditory nerve / ~장애 hearing difficulties.

청강(聽講) attendance (at a lecture). ~하다 attend 《*a lecture*》; audit 《*a course at a university*》(美). ¶ ~료 an admission (fee) / ~무료 《게시》 Attendance Free / ~생 an auditor (美) / ~자 a listener; attendance(총칭).

청개구리(青一) 《動》 a tree frog.

청결(清潔) cleanliness; neatness. ~하다 (be) clean; neat; pure. ¶ ~히 하다 make clean / ~히 해 두다 keep 《*a thing*》 clean.

청과(青果) vegetables and fruits. ¶ ~ greens; fruits / ~물상 greengrocery / ~ 시장 a vegetable and fruit market.

청교도(清教徒) a Puritan. ‖ 청교(도주)의 Puritanism.

청구(請求) a demand; a claim(당연한 권리로); a request(요청). ~하다 claim; charge(요금을); ask[apply] 《for》; demand 《*payment*》. ¶ 손해 배상의 ~ a claim for damages / ~하는 대로 on demand [request] / ~에 응하다 meet [comply with] 《*a person's*》 demand [request] / 그는 내 차의 수리비로 200달러를 ~했다 He charged me $200 for repairing my car. ‖ ~권 a 〔right of〕 claim(~권을 포기하다 give up *one's* claim) / ~서 a bill; an account / ~액 the amount claimed / ~인 an applicant; a claimant.

청기와(青一) a blue tile.

청년(青年) a young man; a youth; (총칭) the young people; the younger generation. ¶ ~시절 *one's* younger days. ‖ ~단 a young men's association.

청대(青) 《植》 a short-jointed variety of bamboo.

청대콩(青一) green 〔unripe〕 bean.

청동(青銅) bronze. ¶ ~기 bronze ware / ~기 시대 the Bronze Age.

청둥오리 〔鳥〕 a wild duck; a mallard 〔duck〕.

청량(清涼) ¶ ~한 cool; refreshing. ‖ ~음료 a soft drink; a refreshing drink; soda 〔pop〕(美).

청력(聽力) 〔the power of〕 hearing; hearing ability. ¶ ~을 잃다 lose *one's* hearing. ‖ ~검사 a hearing test / ~계 an audiometer / ~측정 audiometry.

청렴(清廉) ¶ ~한 honest; upright; cleanhanded / ~결백 absolute honesty; unsullied integrity / ~결백한 사람 a man of integrity; a man of pure heart and clean hands.

청루(青樓) a brothel; a whorehouse.

청류(清流) a 〔clear〕 limpid stream.

청맹과니(青盲一) amaurosis; an amaurotic person(사람).

청명하다(清明一) (be) clear (and bright); fine; fair. ¶ 청명한 하늘 a clear sky.

청바지(青一) (blue) jeans. ¶ ~를 입은 소년 a boy in blue jeans.

청백(青白) blue and white. ¶ ~전 a contest between the blue and white groups.

청백하다(清白一) (be) upright; honest; cleanhanded.

청병(請兵) requesting the dispatch of troops. ~하다 request 〔the dispatch of〕 troops.

청부(請負) a contract 《*for work*》. ☞ 도급(都給). ‖ ~살인 a contract murder / ~업 contracting business / ~인〔업자〕 a contractor.

청빈(清貧) honest poverty. ~하다 be poor but honest. ¶ ~한 생활을 하다 live a poor but honest life.

청사(青史) history; annals. ¶ ~에 길이 남다 live 〔remain long〕 in history.

청사(廳舍) a Government office building.

청사진(青寫眞) a blueprint. ¶ ~을 만들다 make a blueprint of 《*a plan*》; blueprint 《*a plan*》 / ~을 제시하다 present a blueprint for 《*the future*》.

청산(青酸) 〔化〕 hydrocyanic 〔prussic〕 acid. ‖ ~가스 hydrocyanic acid gas / ~염 a prussiate; a cyanide / ~칼리 potassium cyanide.

청산(清算) clearance; liquidation. ~하다 liquidate 〔wind up〕 《*a company*》; clear up 《*one's debts*》; balance〔settle〕《*one's accounts*》. ¶ 과거를 ~하다 bury the past / 그녀와 관계를 ~하다 separate from 〔break up with〕 her / 마침내 밀린 집세를 ~했다 I finally settled my back rent. ‖ ~서 a statement of liquidation / ~인 a liquidator / ~회사 a company in liquidation.

청산(青山) green mountains 〔hills〕. ¶ 인간 도처 유 ~ 〔人間到處有青山〕 Fortune can be found everywhere. *or* There's room for us all in the world. ‖ ~유수 eloquence; fluency(말이 ~유수다 be very eloquent).

청상과부(青孀寡婦) a young widow.

청색(青色) blue (color); green.

청서(清書) 정서(淨書).

청소(清掃) cleaning; sweeping(쓸기). ~하다 clean; sweep. ¶ 방을 깨끗이 ~하다 clean up the room.

청소년 (青少年) young people; the younger generation; youth. ‖ ~범죄 juvenile delinquency.

청순 (清純) purity. ~하다 (be) pure (and innocent). ¶ ~한 처녀 a pure girl.

청승 a miserable (wretched) way of gesture. ~떨다 act like fortune's orphan; try to work on 《*another's*》 compassion.

청승맞다, **청승스럽다** (be) sad; pitiful: miserable; poor; have the way of being plaintive.

청신 (清新) ¶ ~한 fresh; new.

청신경 (聽神經) the auditory nerve.

청신호 (青信號) a green (traffic) signal; a green light; a go signal. ¶ 계획을 실행하라는 ~가 떨어지다 get (be given) the green light to go ahead with the project.

청아 (清雅) elegance. ¶ ~한 elegant; graceful; refined; clear / ~한 목소리 a clear ringing voice.

청약 (請約) (a) subscription 《*for stocks*》. ~하다 subscribe 《*for*》. ¶ ~순으로 in order of subscription / ~이 쏟아져 들어오다 be deluged with subscriptions. ‖ ~금 subscription money / ~인 a subscriber.

청어 (青魚) 〖魚〗 a herring.

청옥 (青玉) 〖鑛〗 sapphire.

청와대 (青瓦臺) the Blue House; the Presidential residence(한국의).

청우계 (晴雨計) a barometer; a 〔weatherglass〕.

청운 (青雲) ¶ ~의 뜻을 품다 have a great ambition; entertain (have) a high ambition.

청원 (請援) ~하다 ask for 〔seek〕 《*a person's*》 assistance; call (ask) for help.

청원 (請願) a petition. ~하다 petition; present 〔submit〕 a petition 《*to*》. ‖ ~경찰(관) a policeman on special guard assignment / ~서 a (written) petition / ~자 a petitioner.

청음기 (聽音機) a sound detector; 《수중의》 a hydrophone.

청일 (清日) ‖ ~전쟁 the Sino-Japanese War.

청자 (青瓷) celadon (porcelain). ‖ 고려 ~ Koryŏ celadon (porcelain) / ~색의 celadon (green).

청정 (清淨) purity; cleanness. ¶ ~한 pure; clean. ‖ ~야채 clean vegetables / ~재배 sanitary 〔germ-free〕 culture.

청주 (清酒) clear, refined rice wine. ‖ 특급 ~ special-grade rice wine.

청중 (聽衆) an audience; an attendance. ¶ 많은(적은) ~ a large (small) audience (attendance). ‖ ~석 audience seats; an auditorium.

청지기 (廳─) a steward; a manager of the household.

청진 (聽診) 〖醫〗 auscultation. ~하다 auscultate. ‖ ~기 a stethoscope 《~기를 대다 apply a stethoscope 《*to*》》.

청천 (青天) the blue sky. ‖ ~백일 a bright blue sky / ~벽력 a thunder bolt from a clear sky.

청천 (晴天) fine (fair) weather.

청첩(장) (請牒)(狀) a letter of invitation; an invitation (card). ¶ 결혼 ~ a wedding invitation (card).

청청하다 (青青─) (be) freshly (vividly) green; fresh and green.

청초 (清楚) ¶ ~한 neat and clean.

청춘 (青春) youth; the springtime of life. ¶ ~의 youthful / 꽃다운 ~ the bloom of 《*one's*》 youth / ~의 정열 the passion of youth / 나의 몸에는 ~의 피가 끓고 있다 Young blood is stirring in me. ‖ ~기 adolescence / ~시대 *one's* youth; *one's* youthful days.

청출어람 (青出於藍) outshining *one's* master.

청취 (聽取) ~하다 listen to; hear. ¶ 라디오 ~자 a (radio) listener / B.B.C.의 ~자 a listener to the B.B.C. / 증언을 ~하다 hear 《*a person's*》 testimony. ‖ ~율 an audience rating.

청컨대 (請─) (if you) please; I pray (beg); It is to be hoped that….

청탁 (清濁) ¶ 그는 ~을 가리지 않는 사람이다 He can accept all kinds, the good and the evil.

청탁 (請託) 《부탁》 asking; begging; a request. ~하다 ask 〔beg〕 《*a person*》 to exercise *his* influence 《*in favor of*》; solicit 《*a person*》 for *his* good offices. ‖ ~을 받다 be asked 〔solicited〕 《*to do*》; receive a request.

청태 (青苔) 《이끼》 (green) moss; 《김》 green laver.

청풍 (清風) a cool breeze. ¶ ~명월 a cool breeze and a bright moon.

청하다 (請─) ① 《부탁》 ask 〔request〕 《*a person to do*》; beg; entreat. ② 《달라다》 ask 〔request〕 《*for a thing*》; beg. ③ 《초빙》 invite; ask.

청허 (聽許) ~하다 give assent to; grant; sanction; approve.

청혼(請婚) a proposal 《of marriage》. ~하다 propose 《to a person》. 구혼. ¶ ~을 승낙 [거절]하다 accept [decline] 《a person's》 proposal.
청훈(請訓) a request for instructions. ¶ 본국 정부에 ~하다 ask the home government for instructions.
체 a sieve; a sifter; a (mesh) strainer. ¶ ~로 치다 put [pass] 《something》 through a sieve; sieve; screen / 모래를 ~로 쳐서 자갈을 골라내다 sift (out) the pebbles from the sand; sieve the sand to get the pebbles out. ~ing. 체하는.
체 《짐짓 꾸밈》 pretense; pretend.
체 《아니꼬울 때》 pshaw!; shucks!
체(滯) 《먹은 것의》 indigestion; dyspepsia.
체(體) the body; a style.
체감(遞減) successive diminution. ~하다 decrease in order; diminish successively. ¶ 수확 체감의 법칙 the law of diminishing returns. ‖ ~속도 slowdown speed.
체감(體感) bodily sensation; somesthesia. ‖ ~온도 effective temperature.
체격(體格) physique; build; a constitution. ¶ ~이 좋다 [나쁘다] have a good [weak] constitution; be of strong [weak] build.
체결(締結) conclusion. ~하다 conclude 《a treaty》; enter into 《a contract》. ¶ 평화 조약을 ~하고 동맹국이 되다 conclude a peace treaty and become allies.
체경(體鏡) a full-length mirror.
체계(體系) a system. ¶ ~적(으로) systematic(ally) / ~화하다 systematize / ~를 세우다 develop [formulate] a system 《of》.

체공(滯空) ~하다 stay [remain] in the air. ‖ ~비행[기록] an endurance flight [record] / ~시간 the duration of flight.
체구(體軀) ¶ 체격.
체기(滯氣) a touch of indigestion.
체납(滯納) nonpayment; arrears 《of taxes》; delinquency in (making) payment. ~하다 fail to pay; be in arrears. ¶ 나는 세금을 ~한 일이 없다 I have never let my taxes get in arrears. ‖ ~금 arrears / ~액 an amount in arrears / ~자 a delinquent / ~처분 disposition for the recovery of taxes in arrears; coercive collection.
체내(體內) the interior of the body. ¶ ~의[에] in the body; internal.
체념(諦念) ① 〖佛〗〖諦觀〗 apprehension of the truth. ~하다 apprehend the truth. ② 《단념》 resignation. ~하다 give up 《an idea》; abandon; resign oneself 《to》. ¶ 없어진 것으로 ~하다 give up for lost / ~하다 resign oneself to one's fate [lot].
체능(體能) physical aptitude (ability). ‖ ~검사 a physical aptitude test.
체득하다(體得一) learn from experience; master; acquire.
체력(體力) physical strength. ¶ ~을 기르다 develop [build up] one's physical strength / ~이 떨어지다 one's strength declines. ‖ ~검정 an examination of physical strength.
체류(滯留) a stay; a visit; a sojourn. ¶ 체재(滯在). ~하다 stay [stop] 《at a place》; make a stay 《at》. ¶ 런던 ~중 during one's stay in London / 3일간의 ~ 예정으로 〈arrive in Seoul〉 on a three-day visit 《to Korea》 / 파리 ~중에 당신 신세를 졌습니다 You were a great help to me during my stay in Paris. ‖ ~객 a guest; a visitor / ~기간 the length of one's stay / ~지 the place one is staying [will stay].
체르니 Czerny.
체리 《서양 앵도》 a cherry.
체머리 a shaky head. ¶ ~를 흔들다 have a shaky head.
체면(體面) honor(명예); reputation(명성); face(면목); dignity(위신); appearance(외관). ¶ ~상 for appearance' sake; to save one's face / ~에서 save one's face / ~을 세우다 [차리다] save appearances; save 《one's》 face / ~을 유지하다 keep up appearances [face] / ~에 관계되다 affect one's honor / ~을 손상하다 impair one's dignity; bring disgrace 《on》 / 이것은 나의 ~에 관한 일이다 This is my point of honor.
체모(體毛) hair.
체면(體面) 체면.
체벌(體罰) corporal punishment.
체불(滯拂) a delay in payment; payment in arrears. ¶ ~임금 wages in arrears.
체비지(替費地) lands secured by the authorities in recompense of development outlay.
체스 《서양 장기》 chess.
체신(遞信) communications. ‖ ~업무 post and telegraphic service.
체언(體言) 〖文〗 the substantive.
체온(體溫) temperature. ¶ ~을 재다 take one's temperature / ~이 높다 [낮다] have a high [low] temperature / ~이 오르다 [내리다]

One's temperature rises (falls). ¶ ~계 a (clinical) thermometer.

체위(體位) 《체육》 physique ; 《자세》 a posture. ¶ ~를 향상시키다 improve the physique.

체육(體育) 《학과》 physical education ; gym 《美》. ¶ 오늘은 ~시간이 있다 I have a gym class today. ‖ ~과 the course of physical education / ~관 a gym(nasium) / ~특기자 an athletic meritocrat / 대한 ~회 the Korea Amateur Athletic Association.

체재(滯在) ☞ 체류(滯留). ‖ ~비 the living expenses during *one's* stay ; hotel expenses 〈숙박비〉.

체재(體裁) 《일정한 형식》 (a) form ; a style ; a format ; 《겉모양》 an appearance ; show ; 《만듦새》 a get-up. ¶ ~가 좋은 presentable ; seemly / ~가 나쁜 unseemly ; awkward / 이 논문은 일정한 ~로 짜여 있다 This paper has a fixed format. 「contents.

체적(體積) (cubic) volume ; cubic

체제(體制) 《조직》 an organization ; a system ; a structure ; 《권력·정치의》 the establishment. ¶ 경제~ an economic structure / 기성~ the Establishment / 신(구)~ a new (an old) order / 정치~ a political system / 반~운동 an anti-establishment movement / 현~를 타파하다 destroy the existing establishment.

체조(體操) physical (gymnastic) exercises ; gymnastics. ¶ ~를 하다 do gymnastics / 기계~ apparatus gymnastics / 라디오 (TV) ~ radio (TV) exercise program / 유연(柔軟)~ stretching (limbering) exercises ; shape-up. ¶ 경기~ gymnastics / ~기구 gymnastic apparatus / ~선수 a gymnast.

체중(體重) *one's* weight. ¶ ~이 늘다(줄다) gain (lose) weight / ~을 달다 weigh *oneself* / 나는 ~이 50킬로그램이다 I weigh 50 kilograms. ‖ ~계 the scales.

체증(滯症) indigestion. ¶ 교통~ traffic congestion (jam) / ~기(氣)가 있다 suffer from indigestion.

체질 sifting ; sieving ; screening. ¶ ~하다 sift (out) ; screen.

체질(體質) constitution. ¶ ~적(으로) constitutional(ly) / 허약~의 사람 a man of delicate (weak) constitution / 기업의 ~ the nature of enterprise / ~이 약한 다 (강하다) have a weak (strong) constitution / 내 ~에 맞지는 않는다 It does not agree with me.

체취(體臭) body odor.

체코 Czech Republic.

체크 ① 《무늬》 checks ; checkers. ¶ ~무늬의 블라우스 a checkered blouse. ② 《대조·검사》 a check. ~하다 check ; check (*something*) up ; mark (off). / 입구에서 사진과 본인을 ~하다 check the person against the entrance / 문장에서 잘못된 곳을 ~하다 mark a mistake in the sentence. ¶ ~아웃 a check-out (~아웃하다 check out (*of the hotel*)) / ~인 a check-in (~인하다 check in (*at a hotel*)) / ~포인트(검문소) a check point.

체통(體統) (an official's) dignity ; honor ; face. ¶ ~을 잃다 lose (*one's*) face. / ~ 세면.

체포(逮捕) (an) arrest ; capture. ~하다 arrest ; capture ; catch. ‖ ~영장 an arrest warrant.

체하다(滯─) have a digestive upset ; lie heavy on the stomach.

체하다 pretend ⟨*sickness, to be asleep*⟩ ; affect ⟨*not to hear*⟩ ; feign ⟨*surprise*⟩ ; pose ⟨*as*⟩ ; assume an air of. ¶ 모르는 ~ pretend to be ignorant ; feign ignorance.

체험(體驗) ~하다 (have an) experience ; go through. ‖ ~담 a story of *one's* experience.

체형(體刑) penal servitude ; corporal punishment ; a jail sentence. ¶ ~을 과하다 inflict corporal punishment ⟨*on a person*⟩ ; impose a jail sentence.

체화(滯貨) accumulation of cargoes (freights, stocks, goods) ; freight congestion.

첼로 〖樂〗 a cello. ‖ ~연주가 a cellist.

쳄발로 〖樂〗 a cembalo. 「list.

쳐가다 collect and take (carry) away ⟨*garbage*⟩ ; empty (dip up) and carry away.

쳐내다 take (clear, sweep) away ; clear off (out) ; remove. 「⟨*at*⟩.

쳐다보다 look at ; stare (gaze)

쳐들다 ① 《올리다》 lift (up) ; raise ; hold up. ② 《초들다》 point out ; (make) mention ⟨*of*⟩ ; refer ⟨*to*⟩.

쳐들어가다 invade ; make an inroad ⟨*on*⟩ ; penetrate ⟨*into*⟩ ; break in ; raid.

쳐주다 ① 《값을》 estimate (value, rate) ⟨*a thing*⟩ at ; set (put) a price ⟨*on*⟩. ② 《인정》 recognize ; acknowledge ; think highly of ⟨*a person*⟩. / 정직한 사람으로 ~ give ⟨*a person*⟩ credit for being an honest man.

초 a candle. ¶ ~를 켜다 (끄다) light (put out) a candle. / ~심지 a candlewick / 대 a candlestick.

초(草) 《초안》 a rough copy. ¶ ~를 잡다 draft.

초(醋) vinegar. ¶ ~간장 soy

sause mixed with vinegar / ~를 치다 flavor [season] 《food》 with vinegar.

초(秒) a second. ¶ 천분의 1~ a millisecond.

초…(初) the beginning; (the) first [stage]; the early part. ¶ ~가을 early autumn / ~하루 the 1st of the month.

초…(超) super-; ultra-. ¶ ~자연적 supernatural / ~음속의 supersonic / ~단파의 ultrashort wave.

초가(草家)〖집〗 a (straw-)thatched house. ¶ 삼간 ~ a three-room thatched house; a small cottage.

초강대국(超强大國) a superpower; the superpowers〖집합적〗.

초개(草芥) bits of straw; a worthless thing. ¶ ~ 죽음을 ~ 같이 여기다 hold one's life as nothing.

초계(哨戒) a patrol. ‖ ~하다 patrol. ‖ ~기〖집〗a patrol plane [boat].

초고(草稿) a (rough) draft〖초안〗; a manuscript〖원고〗. ¶ ~를 작성하다 make a draft; draft (out).

초고속(超高速) superhigh [ultrahigh] speed. ‖ ~도로 a superhighway / ~정보통신망 the Information Superhighway Network / ~도촬영기 an ultrahigh-[super high-]speed camera.

초고주파(超高周波) superhigh [ultrahigh] frequency 〖생략 SHF, UHF〗. ‖ ~트랜지스터 an ultrahigh-frequency transistor.

초과(超過) (an) excess; surplus 〖잉여〗. ~하다 exceed; be in excess (of); be more than. ¶ 6만원의 ~ an excess of sixty thousand won / 수입의 ~ an excess of imports over exports / 이 버스는 정원을 ~했다 This bus is overloaded. ‖ ~근무 수당 overtime allowance / ~액 a surplus; an excess.

초국가주의(超國家主義) ultranationalism. ‖ ~자 an ultranationalist.

초근목피(草根木皮) the roots of grass and the barks of trees; coarse and miserable food. ¶ ~로 연명하다 barely manage to stay alive with the aid of roots and bark.

초급(初級) the beginner's class; the junior course 〖in〗. ‖ ~대학 a junior college / ~영문법 English Grammar for Beginners.

초기(初期) the first stage [period]; the early days [years]; the beginning. ¶ 19세기 ~에 in the early years [part] of the 19th century / ~단계에 in the first stage (of).

초년(初年) 《첫해》 the first year; 《초기》 the early years; 《인생의》 one's youth; one's earlier years. ¶ ~에 과거하다 pass the State examination in one's youth. ‖ ~병 a recruit / ~생 a (mere) beginner.

초능력(超能力) a supernatural power; extrasensory perception 〖초감각적 지각〗; psychokinesis〖염력〗. ¶ ~의 psychokinetic. ‖ ~보유자 a supernatural power holder.

초단(初段) the first grade; a first grade expert 《in Taekwondo》〖사람〗.

초단파(超短波) ultrashort waves.

초당파(超黨派) ¶ ~의 nonpartisan 《policies》 / ~적으로 의안을 통과시켰다 All the parties agreed to pass the bill through Congress. ‖ ~외교 nonpartisan diplomacy.

초대(初代) the founder; the first generation〖제1대〗. ¶ ~의 the first / ~ 대통령 the first President.

초대(招待) an invitation. ~하다 invite; ask. ¶ ~에 응하다[를 사절하다] accept [decline] an invitation / 그는 이따금 친구들을 다과에 ~한다 He occasionally invites his friends for tea. or He sometimes asks his friends to come for tea. ‖ ~객 an invited guest / ~권 an invitation card; a complimentary ticket 《흥행의》 / ~석 a reserved seat / ~일〖전시회 따위의〗a preview 《美》; a private view / ~작가 the invited artist / ~장 an invitation (card); a letter of invitation.

초대작(超大作) a super-production; 《영화의》 a superfilm; a super-feature film.

초대형(超大型) ¶ ~의 extra-large; outsized. ‖ ~여객기 a superliner.

초동(樵童) a boy woodcutter. 〖er.

초두(初頭) the beginning; the outset; the first; the start.

초들다 mention; refer to; enumerate; cite.

초등(初等) ¶ ~의 elementary; primary. ‖ ~과 an elementary course / ~교육 elementary (primary) education / ~학교 an elementary [a primary] school / ~학생 a primary schoolboy [schoolgirl].

초라하다 (be) shabby; miserable; poor-looking; wretched. ¶ 옷이 ~ be shabbily [poorly] dressed.

초래(招來) ~하다 cause; bring about; give rise to; lead to. ¶ 뜻밖의 결과를 ~하다 bring about [lead to] an unexpected result / 불황이 물가 등귀를 ~했다 The depression caused a rise in

초로(初老) ¶ ~의 elderly; middle-aged / 저 ~의 신사는 유명한 학자이다 That elderly gentleman is a famous scholar.
초로(草露) dew on the grass. ¶ ~ 같은 인생 transient life / 인생은 ~와 같다 Life is but a span.
초록(抄錄) an abstract; an extract; a selection. ¶ ~하다 make an abstract (extract) of.
초록(草綠), **초록색**(草綠色) green. ¶ ~의 green / ~을 띤 greenish; greeny.
초롱(동) a tin 《英》; a can 《美》. ¶ 석유~ a kerosene can (tin).
초롱(一籠)(등불) a hand lantern.
초롱꽃(一籠一)(植) a dotted bellflower.
초름하다 ① (넉넉지 못하다) be not abundant. ② (모자라다) be a bit short of.
초립(草笠) a straw hat. ‖ ~동(童) a young man who wears a straw hat.
초막(草幕) a straw-thatched hut.
초만원(超滿員) ¶ ~이다 be filled to overflowing; be crowded beyond capacity.
초면(初面) ¶ ~의 meet 《a person》 for the first time / ~인사람 a stranger. ‖ ~인사 greetings on the first meeting.
초목(草木) trees and plants; vegetation. ¶ ~산천 ~ nature.
초미(焦眉) ¶ ~의 urgent; impending; pressing / ~의 관심사 an issue of burning concern. ‖ ~지급(之急) an urgent need.
초반(初盤) the opening part 《of a game》.
초밥(醋一) *sushi*; a Japanese dish consisting of pieces of raw fish on top of cooked rice.
초배(初褙) the first coat of wallpaper.
초벌(初一) 애벌. ¶ ~그림 a rough sketch; a draft.
초범(初犯) the first offense; a first offender(사람).
초법적(超法的) ¶ ~의 extrajudicial; extralegal / ~ 행동을 취하다 take extralegal (extralegal) action / ~인 조치를 취하다 go beyond (above) the law; take extralegal measures.
초벽(初壁) (벽) a rough-coated wall(벽) / (일) a rough coat of plaster 《on a wall》.
초병(哨兵) a sentinel; a sentry. ‖ ~근무 sentry duty.
초보(初步) the first stage; the rudiments; the ABC 《of》. ¶ ~의 elementary; rudimentary / 수학의 ~ the rudiments of arith-

metic; the ABC of arithmetic. ¶ ~자 a beginner; a green hand. 「dog days.」
초복(初伏) the beginning of the
초본(抄本) an abstract; an extract. ¶ 호적 ~ an abstract of one's family register.
초본(草本) herbs. ¶ ~의 herbal.
초봄(初一) early spring.
초봉(初俸) a starting (an initial) pay (salary); a starter 《美俗》.
초부(樵夫) a woodcutter.
초빙(招聘) an invitation. ~하다 invite; extend a call 《to》. ¶ ~에 응하다 accept a call 《from Mr. Kim》; accept the invitation 《to give a lecture》; accept the offer of a position / 《…의》 ~으로 오다 invite a lecturer. ‖ ~국 a host country. 「*self* 《about》.」
초사(焦思) ¶ ~하다 worry *one-*
초사흗날(初一) the third (day) of a month.
초산(初産) one's first childbirth (delivery). ‖ ~부 a primipara; a woman bearing (expecting) her first child.
초산(醋酸) 《化》 acetic acid. ‖ ~염(塩) acetate.
초상(初喪) (a period of) mourning. ¶ 아버지의 ~을 당하다 be in mourning for one's father / ~을 치르다 observe mourning. / ~집 a house (family) in mourning.
초상(肖像) a portrait. ¶ 등신대의 ~ a life-sized portrait / ~을 그리게 하다 have one's portrait painted; sit for one's portrait. ‖ ~화 a portrait 《in oils》 / ~화가 a portrait painter.
초서(草書) the cursive style of writing Chinese characters; 《글씨》 cursive characters.
초석(硝石) 《鑛石》 niter; saltpeter.
초석(礎石) (lay) a foundation stone; a cornerstone.
초선(初選) ¶ ~의 newly-elected. ‖ ~의원 a newly-elected member of the National Assembly.
초성(初聲) an initial sound.
초속(初速) 《理》 initial velocity.
초속(秒速) a speed per second. ¶ ~ 20미터로 at a speed of 20 meters per (a) second.
초고속(超高速) superhigh (ultrahigh) speed; supervelocity.
초순(初旬), **초승**(初一) (달의) the early part 《of the month》. ¶ 초승달 a new (young) moon; a crescent / 이 책은 4월 ~에 출간된다 This book will be published early in April.
초식(草食) ¶ ~의 grass-eating; herbivorous. ‖ ~동물 a grass-eating (herbivorous) animal.

초심(初心) ① 《처음 먹은 마음》 one's original intention [aim]. ☞ 초지(初志). ② 《초심자》 a beginner; a novice; a greenhorn (美口). ¶ ~의 inexperienced / ~자를 위한 (books) for beginners.

초심(初審) the first trial [hearing].

초안(草案) a (rough) draft. ¶ 민법 ~ a draft civil code / ~을 기초하다 draft 《a bill》; make a draft.

초야(草野) an out-of-the-way place. ¶ ~에 묻혀 살다 lead a humble [a quiet country] life.

초여름(初─) early summer.

초역(抄譯) ~하다 make an abridged translation 《of》; translate selected passages 《from》.

초연(初演) the first (public) performance; the *première* (프).

초연(超然) ~하다 stand [hold, keep] aloof 《from》; be transcendental [aloof]. ¶ ~히 with a detached air.

초연(硝煙) the smoke of powder.

초열흘날(初─) the tenth (day) of a month.

초엽(初葉) the early years [days]; the beginning. ¶ 20세기 ~에 in the early part of the 20th century.

초옥(草屋) a thatched hut.

초원(草原) a grass-covered plan; a grassland; a prairie(북아메리카의); pampas(남아메리카의); a steppe(중앙아시아의).

초월(超越) ~하다 transcend; stand aloof; rise above. ¶ 그녀는 세속을 ~해 있다 She keeps herself aloof from the world.

초유(初有) ~의 first; initial; original / 사상 ~의 unprecedented in history.

초음속(超音速) supersonic speed. ‖ ~비행 (make) a supersonic flight / ~제트기 a supersonic jet plane.

초음파(超音波) supersonic waves.

초이렛날(初─) ① 《아기의》 the seventh day after birth. ② 《달의》 the seventh (day) of a month. 〔a month.

초이튿날(初─) the second (day) of

초인(超人) a superman. ¶ ~적인 노력 a superhuman effort.

초인종(招人鐘) a call bell; a doorbell; a buzzer.

초일(初日) the first [opening] day; an opening; the *première* (프) (연극의).

초읽기(秒─) a countdown. ~하다 count down.

초임(初任) the first appointment. ‖ ~급(給) a starting [an initial] salary.

초입(初入) ① 《어귀》 an entrance; a way in. ② 《처음 들어감》 the first entrance.

초자연(超自然) ¶ ~적(인) supernatural. ‖ ~주의 supernaturalism.

초잡다(草─) make a draft 《of》; draft 《a speech》.

초장(初章) the first movement(음악의); the first chapter(글의).

초장(醋醬) soy sauce mixed with vinegar.

초저녁(初─) ¶ ~에 early in the evening / ~에 잠들다 fall asleep early in the evening.

초전도(超電導) superconductivity. ‖ ~물질(체) a superconductor; a superconductive substance (matter) / ~선재(線材) a superconductive wire rod / ~자석 a superconductive magnet.

초점(焦點) a focus; the focal point. ¶ ~을 맞추다 (take the) focus; adjust the focus of / 새에게 사진기의 ~을 맞추다 focus the camera on the bird. ¶ ~거리 the focal distance (length) 《of a lens》.

초조(焦燥) impatience; irritation. ~하다 (be) fretful; impatient; irritated. ¶ ~해하다 fret; get irritated; feel restless / 일 진행이 제대로 안 되어 ~감을 느꼈다 I felt impatient (got irritated) as my work was not going as smoothly as I expected.

초주검되다(初─) be half-dead; be more dead than alive; 《남의 손에》 be half-killed.

초지(初志) one's original intention (purpose). ¶ ~를 관철하다 accomplish (carry out) one's original intention.

초진(初診) the first medical examination. ¶ ~료 the fee charged for a patient's first visit / ~환자 a new patient.

초창(草創) ‖ ~기 an early stage; the pioneer days(인류의 ~기 the early days of mankind).

초청(招請) (an) invitation. ~하다 invite (ask) 《a person》 to. ¶ ~받다 be invited; be asked 《to a dinner》. ¶ ~경기 an invitation game / ~국 inviting country; a host nation / ~장 a letter of invitation; (send) an invitation 《to》.

초췌(憔悴) ~하다 haggard; emaciated; thin. ¶ ~한 모습 a haggard figure.

초치(招致) ~하다 summon; invite; 《유치》 attract 《tourists》.

초판(抄本) a second hand.

초콜릿 a chocolate.

초토(焦土) ¶ ~화하다 get reduced to ashes; be burnt to the ground / 전쟁으로 온 나라가 ~화되었다 The whole country was

초특급(超特急) a superexpress 〔train〕.

초특작(超特作) a super production; a superfilm (영화의).

초판(初版) the first edition.

초피나무 a Chinese pepper tree.

초하룻날(初一) the first (day) of a month.

초학자(初學者) a beginner; a beginning student; a novice. ¶~용 책 a book for beginners.

초행(初行) one's first trip [journey]. ¶~길 road new to one / ~로 온 ~이다 This is my first trip to Seoul.

초현실주의(超現實主義) surrealism. ∥~자 a surrealist.

초호(礁湖) a lagoon.

초혼(初婚) one's first marriage.

초혼(招魂) invocation of the spirits of the dead [deceased]. ~하다 invoke. ∥~제(祭) a memorial service for the dead [deceased].

초회(初回) the first round.

촉(鏃) 《살촉》 an arrowhead; 《뾰족한 끝》 a point; a tip; a nib (of a pen).

촉(燭) ☞ 촉광(燭光). ¶ 60~짜리 전구 a 60 candle power bulb.

촉각(觸角) [蟲] a feeler; an antenna; a tentacle.

촉각(觸覺) the sense of touch; (a) tactile sensation; (a) feeling. ¶~기관 a tactile [touch] organ.

촉감(觸感) the sense of touch; the feel. ¶~이 좋다 be soft to the touch; feel soft.

촉광(燭光) [電] candle power.

촉구(促求) ~하다 urge [press] 《a person to do》; encourage 《a person to do》; quicken; stimulate (자극). ¶~세심한 주의를 ~하다 call 《a person's》 good attention 《to the handling of the machine》; urge 《one's men》 to utmost caution.

촉망(囑望) expectation. ~하다 put one's hopes 《on》; expect much 《from》; hold expectation 《for》. ¶~되는 청년 a promising youth.

촉매(觸媒) [化] a catalyst; a catalyzer. ¶~반응 catalytic reaction; catalysis ∥~법 the contact [catalytic] process / ~작용 catalytic action.

촉모(觸毛) 《동물의》 a tactile hair; a feeler; an antenna.

촉박(促迫) ~하다 (be) urgent; imminent; pressing. ¶시간이 ~하다 be pressed for time / 기일이 ~하다 A set date is near at hand.

촉발(觸發) contact detonation. ~하다 《기뢰 따위가》 detonate on contact; 《사태 따위가》 touch off; trigger (off); provoke 《a crisis》. ¶지역 감정을 ~시키다 touch off the regional emotion 《of》. ∥~장치 a contact-detonating device.

촉성재배(促成栽培) forcing culture. ~하다 force 《strawberries》. ¶~용 온실(온상) a forcing house [bed] / ~한 야채 forced vegetables.

촉수(觸手) ① [動] a feeler; a tentacle. ② 《손을 댐》 touching. ¶~엄금 《게시》 Hands off.

촉수(觸鬚) a palp(us); a feeler; a tentacle.

촉진(促進) ~하다 quicken; promote; accelerate; speed up; facilitate; expedite. ¶식물의 생장을 ~하다 hasten [accelerate] the growth of a plant / 판매 ~를 위해 더 많은 돈을 광고에 쓰다 spend more money on advertising to promote sales. ∥~제 an accelerator.

촉진(觸診) [醫] palpation. ~하다 palpate; examine by the hand [touch].

촉촉하다 (be) dampish.

촉탁(囑託) 《일》 part-time service [engagement]; 《사람》 a nonregular member (of the staff); a part-time employee. ¶~교사 a part-time instructor [teacher].

촌(寸) ① 《단위》 a 치. ② 《촌수》 a degree of kinship. ¶삼~ an uncle / 사~ a cousin.

촌(村) 《마을》 a village; 《시골》 the country(side); a rural district.

촌가(寸暇) a moment's leisure; a spare moment.

촌각(寸刻) a moment. ¶~을 다투다 call for prompt treatment (병 따위); need a speedy solution (문제 따위).

촌극(寸劇) a skit; a short (comic) play; a tabloid play.

촌놈(村─) a country fellow; a rustic; 《놀림조》 a bumpkin; a boor.

촌락(村落) a village; a hamlet.

촌민(村民) village folk; the villagers.

촌보(寸步) a few steps.

촌부(村婦) a country woman.

촌사람(村─) a countryman.

촌수(寸數) the degree of kinship.

촌스럽다(村─) (be) rustic; boorish; countrified; farmlike.

촌음(寸陰) ☞ 촌각. ¶~을 아끼다 be careful of every minute.

촌지(寸志) a little token of one's gratitude; a small present.

촌충(寸蟲) a tapeworm.

촌토(寸土) an inch of land [territory].

촌평(寸評) a brief review 《of》; a brief comment 《on》.

촐랑거리다 ① 《물이》 찰랑거리다. ② 《행동을》 act frivolously; be flippant.

촐랑이 a frivolous person.

촐랑촐랑 《경박하게》 frivolously; flippantly; irresponsibly. ¶ ~ 돌아다니다 gad 《flit》 about.

촐싹거리다 ① 《가볍다》 act frivolously 《flippantly》. ② 《부추기다》 agitate; stir up; instigate.

촘촘 ~ 하다 be somewhat hungry; feel a bit empty. ¶ ~ 굶다 starve.

촘촘하다 《be》 close; dense; thick. ¶ 촘촘한 박음새 close stitching.

촛대(一臺) a candlestick; a candlestand; a candle holder. ¶ ~ 에 초를 꽂다 fix a candle in a candlestick.

촛불 candlelight. ¶ ~ 을 켜다《끄다》 light 《put out》 a candle.

총(銃) a gun; a rifle; a pistol《권총》; a shotgun《산탄총》. ¶ 22구경의 ~ a 22-caliber gun / 연발 ~ a magazine rifle / 2연발 ~ a double barreled gun《rifle》/ ~ 을 겨누다 aim a gun 《at a bear》. ‖ ~ 개머리 the stock; the butt of rifle.

총…(總) whole; all; entire; total; general. ¶ ~ 소득 gross income / ~ 예산 the total budget.

총가(銃架) a rifle stand; an arm rack.

총각(總角) a bachelor; an unmarried man; a bach《美俗》. ¶ ~ 처녀 unmarried 《young》 men and women.

총각김치(總角一) young radish kimchi.

총검(銃劍) 《총과 검》 rifles and swords; 《무기》 arms; 《총에 꽂는 칼》 a bayonet. ¶ ~ 을 꽂다 fix bayonet 《to a rifle》 / ~ 을 들이대고 at the point of the bayonet / ~ 으로 찌르다 bayonet 《a person》; stab 《a person》 with a bayonet. ‖ ~ 술 bayonet exercises《fencing》.

총격(銃擊) rifle shooting. ¶ ~ 을 가하다 fire; shoot a rifle 《at an enemy》. ‖ ~ 전 a gunfight.

총결산(總決算) the final settlement of accounts. ~ 하다 make final settlement of accounts; settle 《balance》 accounts.

총감(總監) a senior superintendent 《略 sen. supt.》.

총계(總計) the total 《amount》; the sum total. ~ 하다 total; sum 《add》 up. ¶ ~ 로 in all 《total》; all told; ~ 이 되다 total 《one million won》; amount to 《$1,000》.

총공격(總攻擊) an all-out attack; a full-scale offensive. ~ 하다 launch 《make, start》 an all-out attack 《on, against》; attack 《the enemy》 in full force. ¶ 미국 공군은 적의 탱크 부대를 ~ 했다 The U.S. Air Force launched an all-out attack against the enemy tank forces.

총괄(總括) ~ 하다 summarize; sum up; generalize. ¶ ~ 적인 summary; general; all-inclusive / ~ 해서 말하면 generally speaking; to sum up / ~ 적으로 as a whole; summarily; *en masse* / ~ 적 조항 a blanket clause / ~ 적 의안 an omnibus 《a blanket》 bill / 그는 몇 마디로 상황을 ~ 말했다 He summed up the situation in a few words.

총구(銃口) the muzzle 《of a gun》. ¶ ~ 를 들이대고 《threat 《a person》》 at the point of a gun.

총기(銃器) small 《fire》 arms. ‖ ~ 고《실》 an armory.

총기(聰氣) brightness; intelligence; sagacity. ¶ ~ 가 있다 be bright 《intelligent》.

총대(銃一) a gunstock.

총독(總督) a governor-general; a viceroy. ‖ ~ 부 the government-general.

총동원(總動員) general mobilization. ¶ 국가 ~ the national mobilization / 마을 사람들은 ~ 하여 산불을 껐다 All the villagers were mobilized to extinguish the forest fire. ‖ ~ 령 orders for the mobilization of the entire army.

총득점(總得點) the total score.

총답(總一) superintendence. ~ 하다 superintend; preside over; control.

총량(總量) the total amount; the gross weight 《volume》.

총력(總力) all one's energy 《strength》. ¶ ~ 을 다하여 with all one's strength 《might》; with concerted efforts. ‖ ~ 안보《태세》 an all-out national security 《posture》 / ~ 외교 a total diplomacy / ~ 전 a total war; an all-out war.

총렵(銃獵) hunting; shooting 《美》. ~ 하다 shoot; hunt.

총론(總論) general remarks; an introduction 《to》; an outline 《of》.

총리(總理) 《내각의》 the Premier; the Prime Minister. ¶ 부 ~ the Deputy Prime Minister / ~ 직《위》 the premiership.

총망(忽忙) ~ 하다 be in a hurry; 《be》 hurried; flurried; rushed.

총명(聰明) ¶ ~ 한 wise; sagacious; intelligent.

총무(總務) general affairs; 《사람》 a manager; a director. ¶ 원내 ~ a floor leader 《美》; a whipper-in 《英》. ‖ ~ 부 《과》

총반격(總反擊) an all-out counterattack. ~하다 mount a general counteroffensive.

총복습(總復習) a general review of one's lessons. ~하다 make a general review of one's lessons; go over all one's lessons.

총부리(銃—) the muzzle. ¶ ~를 들이대다 point (aim) 《a pistol》.

총사령관(總司令官) a supreme commander; the commander in chief.

총사령부(總司令部)《軍》the General Headquarters《생략 GHQ》.

총사직(總辭職) general resignation; resignation in a body (en masse). ~하다 resign in a body (en masse). ¶ 내각 ~ the general resignation of the Cabinet.

총살(銃殺) shooting (to death). ~하다 shoot 《a person》 dead; execute 《a criminal》 by shooting.　　　　　　　　［wound.

총상(銃傷) a bullet (gunshot)

총생(叢生)《植》fasciculation. ~하다 grow dense (in clusters); form fascicles.

총서(叢書) a series (of books); a library. ¶ 국문학 ~ a series of Korean literature.

총선거(總選擧) a general election. ~하다 hold a general election.

총설(總說) ⇨ 총론(總論).

총성(銃聲), **총소리**(銃—) the report of a gun; the sound of gunfire; a (gun) shot.

총수(總帥) the supreme leader; the commander in chief.

총수(總數) the total (aggregate) (number); 《부사적》 in all; all told. ¶ ~ 500이 되다 amount to five hundred (in all).

총수입(總收入) the total income.

총신(銃身) ⇨ 총열(銃—).

총아(寵兒) a favorite; a popular person; a beloved child 《사랑하는 애》; a pet. ¶ 문단의 ~ a popular writer / 시대의 ~ a hero of the times / 운명의 ~ a fortune's favorite.

총안(銃眼) a loophole; a crenel.

총알(銃—) a bullet. ¶ ~ 자국 a bullet hole / ~에 맞다 be hit by a bullet.

총애(寵愛) love; patronage. ~하다 favor; make a favorite of; love 《a person》 tenderly. ¶ ~를 받다 win 《a person's》 favor; be in 《a person's》 favor.

총액(總額) the total amount; the sum (grand) total. ¶ ~으로 in total (all) / 비용은 ~ 10만원에 달했다 The expenses reached a total of 100,000 won.

총열(統—) a gun barrel.

총영사(總領事) a consul general. ¶ ~관 a consulate general.

총원(總員) the (entire) personnel; the entire strength (force). ¶ ~ 50명 fifty people in all (all told).

총의(總意) consensus; the general opinion (will). ¶ 국민의 ~ the consensus (will) of the people (the whole nation).

총장(總長) ①《대학의》the president;《美》the chancellor;《英》.②《사무총장》the secretary-general. ③《군대의》the Chief 《of the General Staff》.

총재(總裁) a president; a governor《관청·은행의》. ¶ 부~ a vice-president.

총점(總點)《시험의》the (sum) total of one's marks;《경기의》the total score.　　　　　　　　　　［ager.

총지배인(總支配人) a general man-

총지출(總支出) gross (total) expenditure.

총지휘(總指揮) the high (supreme) command. ~하다 take the supreme command of 《an army》.

총질(銃—) shooting. ~하다 shoot (fire) a gun.

총채 a duster (of horsehairs). ¶ ~질하다 dust 《a thing》.

총총(忽忽) hurriedly; hastily / ~히 떠나다 leave in haste / ~ 걸음으로 with hurried (hasty) steps; at a quick pace.

총총하다(悤悤—) (be) thick; dense; close. ¶ 산에 나무가 ~ a mountain is densely wooded.

총총하다(叢叢—) (be) dense; crowded; numerous. ¶ 별이 총총한 밤 a bright starry night.

총출동(總出動) general (full) mobilization. ~하다 be all mobilized (called out).

총칙(總則) general rules (provisions). ¶ 민법 ~ general provisions of the civil code.

총칭(總稱) a general (generic) term (name). ~하다 name generically; give a generic name 《to》.

총칼(銃—) a gun and a sword; firearms. ¶ ~로 다스리다 rule over with guns and swords (by force).

총탄(銃彈) a bullet; a shot.

총톤수(總—數) gross tonnage.

총통(總統) a president; a generalissimo 《of》.

총파업(總罷業) a general strike. ¶ ~으로 돌입하다 go on a general strike.

총판(總販) an exclusive sale; sole agency (trade). ~하다 make an exclusive sale 《of》. ¶ ~점 a (the) sole agency / ~인 the

총평(總評) a general survey (review).

총포(銃砲) guns; firearms.

총괄(總括) general control (supervision). ~하다 supervise; have a general control 《over》.

총화(總和) general harmony. ¶ 정치 ~ politics of integration / 국민~ national fusion.

총회(總會) a general meeting (assembly). ¶ ~에 회부하다 submit 《a matter》 to the general meeting for discussion / 정기[임시] ~ an ordinary (extraordinary) general meeting / 주주 ~ a general meeting of stockholders / 유엔 ~ the United Nations General Assembly. ¶ ~꾼 a professional troublemaker at stockholders' meeting.

촬영(撮影) photographing. ~하다 take a photograph (picture) of; photograph (picture); shoot 《a scene》. ¶ ~이 끝난 필름 an exposed film / ~ 중이다 They are on location. / 기념~ 《take》 a souvenir picture / 야간 ~ night photography / 고속 ~ high-speed photography / ~금지《게시》 No photos. ¶ ~기 a (movie) camera / ~기사 a (movie) cameraman / ~기술 camera work / ~소 a 《film, movie》 studio.

최…(最) the most; the extreme. ¶ ~남단의 the southernmost / ~첨단의 ultramodern / ~하등의 the worst.

최강(最強) ¶ ~의 the strongest; the most powerful / ~팀 the strongest team.

최고(最高) ¶ ~의 the highest; the best; supreme; the maximum / ~에 뒤어에 있는 사람들은 the top men 《in the world》 / 지금 나는 ~의 기분이다 I've never felt better. / 물가 지수는 ~에 달했다 The price index hit (reached) a new high. / 그녀는 차의 속도를 ~로 냈다 She increased the speed of the car to the maximum. ¶ ~가격 the top (ceiling) price / ~권위 the supreme authority / ~기관 the highest organ / ~기록 the best (highest) record / ~도 the highest degree / ~사령관 the supreme commander; the commander in chief / ~속도 the maximum (top) speed / 수뇌회담 a summit (top-level) conference / ~임금제 the maximum wage system / ~점 the highest point (mark(s) 《시험의》, score 《시합의》, vote 《투표의》) / ~조 the highest watermark; the climax; the zenith / ~학부 the highest seat of learning; the top educational institution / ~한도 the maximum.

최고(催告) notice; demand; a call (납입의). ~하다 call upon 《a person to do》; notify; demand payment 《of》. ¶ ~공시 《法》a public summons / ~서 a call notice.

최고봉(最高峰) the highest peak.

최근(最近) ¶ ~의 the latest 《news》; late; recent / ~에 recently; lately; of late / ~5년에 in the last five years / 그녀를 만난 것은 언제지 When did you see her last? / 나는 ~의 유행을 따를 수 없다 I can't keep up with the latest fashion.

최다수(最多數) the greatest number 《of》; the largest majority.

최단(最短) ¶ ~의 the shortest / ~코스를 가다 take the shortest route 《to》. ¶ ~거리 [시일] the shortest distance [time].

최대(最大) ¶ ~의 the greatest 《number》; the biggest (largest) 《territory》; 《최대한의》 the maximum / ~ 다수의 ~ 행복 the greatest happiness of the greatest number / 세계 ~의 배 the biggest ship in the world / 우리는 최소의 노력으로 ~의 능률을 올리려고 한다 We are trying to find the maximum of efficiency with the minimum of labor. ¶ ~공약수 《數》the greatest common measure (생략 G.C.M.) / ~량 the largest quantity / ~속력 the greatest (maximum) speed / ~지속생산량 the maximum sustainable yield (생략 MSY) / ~한(도) the maximum (limit) / ~허용량 a maximum permissible dosage (약, 방사능의).

최루(催淚) ¶ ~가스 tear gas / ~탄 a tear bomb; a lachrymatory shell.

최면(催眠) hypnosis. ¶ ~을 걸다 hypnotize 《a person》 / 자기~ self-hypnotism. ¶ ~상태 a hypnotic state; hypnotism / ~술 hypnotism / ~술사 a hypnotist / ~요법 a hypnotic treatment [cure]; hypnotherapy.

최상(最上) ¶ ~의 the best; the finest; the highest 《quality》; supreme; superlative / 이것이 우리가 할 수 있는 ~의 것이라 생각한다 I don't think we could do better. / ~의 방법은 선생님의 조언을 구하는 것이다 The best way is to consult your teacher. ¶ ~급 《文》 the superlative degree / ~품 an article of the best quality.

최상층(最上層) the uppermost lay-

최선(最善) the best; the highest good. ¶ ~의 노력 the utmost effort / ~을 다하다 do *one's* best.
최성기(最盛期) the golden age (days); the peak period; the prime;《한창 때》the best time; the season. ¶ 고딕 미술은 13세기에 그 ~를 맞았다 Gothic art reached its zenith in the 13th century.
최소(最小) the smallest; the minimum. ¶ ~의 minimum; the smallest; the least. ∥ ~공배수 【數】 the least common multiple(생략 L.C.M.) / ~공분모 【數】 the least common denominator (생략 L.C.D.) / ~한(도) the (a) minimum(비용을 ~한으로 줄이다 reduce the expenses to the minimum).
최소(最少) ¶ ~의 the least; the fewest / ~의 시간밖에 남지 않았다 We have the least time left. ∥ ~량 the minimum quantity.
최신(最新) the newest; the latest; up-to-date / ~ 기술 the newest technology / ~ 유행의 of the latest fashion / ~ 뉴스가 방금 들어왔다 The latest news has just arrived. ∥ ~형(식) the latest (newest) model (type) 《*of a machine*》(~형 차 the latest model car).
최악(最惡) ¶ ~의 (the) worst / ~의 경우에는 at the worst / ~의 경우를 대비하다 prepare (provide) for the worst.
최우수(最優秀) ¶ ~의 (the) most excellent; superior; first-rate. ∥ ~상 the first prize / ~선수 the most valuable player 《*of the year*》 / ~품 a choice《*of article*》; A1 goods.　　　　　　　「(medicine)
최음제(催淫劑)　an aphrodisiac
최장(最長) ¶ ~의 the longest. ∥ ~거리 the greatest distance.
최저(最低) ¶ ~의 the lowest; the lowermost; the minimum / ~로 견적하다 give the lowest possible estimate; estimate 《*a repair job*》 at 《₩ 20,000》 at the minimum. ∥ ~가격 the lowest price / ~생활 the minimum standard of living / ~생활비 the minimum cost of living / ~임금 the minimum wages / ~임금제 the minimum wage system / ~필요조건 the minimum requirements.
최적(最適) ¶ ~의 the most suitable (suited); ideal; the fittest / 여기가 낚시하는에는 ~의 장소다 This is the most suitable place for fishing. / ~온도 the optimum temperature / ~조건 【生】

the optimum (conditions).
최전선(最前線) the front; the first line.
최종(最終) ¶ ~의 the last; the final; the closing; ultimate. ¶ ~결과 an end result / ~결정(안) the final decision (program, plan) / ~기한 the deadline / ~열차 the last train.
최초(最初) ¶ ~의 the first; the beginning. ¶ ~의 the first; the original 《*purpose*》; the initial 《*stages*》; the opening 《*games*》 / ~에 in the first place; (at) first; at the start; originally / ~의 2년간 the first two years / 그녀가 ~에 왔다 She came first. *or* She was the first to come.
최하(最下) ¶ ~의 the lowest; the worst(최악의). ∥ ~급 the lowest grade / ~등 the lowest class (grade, stratum) / ~위 the lowest rank / ~품 an article of the worst (lowest) quality.
최혜국(最惠國) a most favored nation. ∥ ~대우 most-favored-nation treatment (~대우를 하다 treat 《*Korea*》 as a most favored nation) / ~조항 the most-favored-nation clause.
최후(最後) ¶ ~의 the last; the end. ① 《맨 뒤》 ~의 last; final; ultimate / ~로 last(ly); finally; in conclusion (결론적으로); in the end(끝); at last(기어이) / ~의 한 사람까지 to the last man / ~까지 싸우다 fight it out; fight to a finish / ~의 승리 the final (ultimate) victory / ~의 점검 a last-minute checkup / ~의 저항 (a) last-ditch resistance / ~의 승리를 얻다 win in the long run. ② 《끝장》 *one's* last moment; *one's* end (death). ¶ ~의 말 *one's* dying words / 비참한 ~를 마치다 meet (die) a tragic end; die a sad death.
최후수단(最後手段) the last resort (resource). ¶ ~을 취하다 take the ultimate step; resort to a drastic measure.
최후통첩(最後通牒) an ultimatum. ¶ ~을 보내다 send (deliver) an ultimatum.
추(錘)《겨울의》a weight;《낚싯줄의》a bob; a sinker;《먹줄의》a plumb;《시계의》a bob. / ~를 달다 weight 《*a thing*》.
추가(追加) an addition; supplement. ¶ ~하다 add 《*A to B*》; supplement. ¶ ~의 additional; supplementary / 1인분 식사를 ~하다 order a dish for one more person. ∥ ~비용 additional expenses / ~시험 a supplementary examination / ~예산 a sup-

추격(追擊) pursuit; a chase. ~하다 pursue; chase; give chase to 《*an enemy*》. ‖ ~기 a pursuit plane / ~전 a running fight.

추경(秋耕) 가을갈이.

추경예산(追更豫算) (the) supplementary (extra) budget.

추계(秋季) autumn; fall. ‖ ~운동회 an autumn athletic meeting.

추계(推計) estimation. ~하다 estimate. ‖ ~학 inductive statistics; stochastics.

추곡(秋穀) autumn-harvested grains (rice). ‖ ~수매(가격) the government purchase (buying) (price) of rice.

추구(追求) pursuit. ~하다 pursue; seek after. ¶ 행복의 ~ the pursuit of happiness / 이윤을 ~하다 pursue profits.

추구(追究) ~하다 inquire 《*a matter*》 closely; investigate 《*a matter*》 thoroughly. ¶ 진리를 ~하다 inquire into truth.

추궁(追窮) ~하다 press 《*a person*》 hard 《*for an answer*》; question 《*a person*》; investigate; check up on. ¶ 사고의 원인을 ~하다 investigate the cause of an accident / 그의 책임을 엄하게 ~하다 severely criticize him for his irresponsibility / 그는 그녀의 과거를 ~하려 했다 He tried to check up on her past.

추근추근 persistently; doggedly; 《귀찮게》 importunately. ¶ ~한 persistent; tenacious; importunate; inquisitive / ~조르다 ask 《*a person*》 importunately 《*for*》 / 그렇게 ~ 캐묻지 마라 Don't be so inquisitive.

추기(追記) 《추신》 a postscript《생략 P. S.》; an addendum. ~하다 add a postscript 《*to*》; add 《*to*》.

추기경(樞機卿) a cardinal. ‖ ~회의 the consistory.

추기다 부추기다.

추남(醜男) a bad-looking 〔an ugly〕 man. 「woman.

추녀(醜女) a homely 〔an ugly〕

추념(追念) ~하다 cherish the memory for the deceased. ‖ ~사 a memorial address 〔tribute〕.

추다 《춤을》 dance.

추단(推斷) 《추론》 inference; deduction; 《판단·처벌》 judgment; meting out punishment. ~하다 infer 《*from*》; deduce 《*from*》; render judgment on; mete out punishment 《*for*》.

추대(推戴) ~하다 have 《*a person as the president of*》; set up 《*a person as chairman*》; have 《*a person*》 over 《*a society*》; be presided by.

추도(追悼) mourning. ~하다 mourn 《*for the dead*》; lament 《*over, for a person's death*》. ¶ ~가《歌》 a dirge / ~사 a memorial address 〔ceremony〕 / ~식 a memorial service 〔ceremony〕.

추돌(追突) a rear-end collision. ~하다 collide with 〔run into〕 《*a car*》 from behind; strike the rear of 《*a car*》.

추락(墜落) a fall; a crash《비행기의》. ~하다 fall; drop; crash; plunge. ¶ 지면에 거꾸로 ~하다 fall to the ground head over heels. ‖ ~사 death from a fall.

추레하다 be shabby; dirty; untidy; slovenly. 「weed out.

추려내다 pick 〔single, sort〕 out;

추렴(各欽) collection of money; 《각자 부담》 a Dutch treat; going Dutch. ~하다 collect 〔raise〕 money; pool; contribute jointly; each contributes *his* own share; 《비용 부담》 share the expenses 《*with*》; split cost. ¶ 소풍 가는 비용을 ~하다 pool the expenses for a picnic / 술 ~ a drinking party that goes Dutch.

추록(追錄) a supplement; an addition. ~하다 add; supplement.

추론(推論) reasoning; inference. ~하다 reason; infer 《*from*》. ¶ 그의 ~은 약간 무리가 있는 것 같다 His reasoning seems a little unnatural. ‖ ~식(式) 〔論〕 syllogism.

추리(推理) reasoning; inference. ~하다 reason; infer 《*from*》. ¶ ~의 과정 a reasoning process / 귀납〔연역〕 ~ inductive 〔deductive〕 inference. ‖ ~력 reasoning powers / ~소설 a detective 〔mystery〕 story / ~작가 a mystery writer.

추리다 pick 〔out〕; choose; select; assort. ¶ 다 추리고 난 나머지 the leftovers after all the best things have been picked out.

추맥(秋麥) autumn-sown barley.

추명(醜名) an ill name; bad repute.

추모(追慕) ~하다 cherish 《*a person's*》 memory. ¶ 선친을 ~하다 cherish the memory of *one's* late father.

추문(醜聞) a scandal; ill fame. ¶ ~이 돌다 a scandal gets around.

추물(醜物) 《물건》 an ugly 〔a dirty〕 object; 《사람》 an ugly person 《못생긴》; a dirty 〔filthy〕 fellow《더러운》.

추밀원(樞密院) the Privy Council.

추방(追放) expulsion; deportation; banishment; ouster 《美》; purge

(공직에서) ~하다 expel; banish; deport; exile; 《공직에서》 purge. ¶ 국외로 ~하다 banish (deport, expel) 《a person》 from the country / 공직 ~ a purge from public service. ¶ ~령 a deportation order; an expulsion decree / ~자 an exile(국외로의); a purgee(공직에서의) / 국외~ deportation.
추분(秋分) the autumnal equinox.
추비(追肥) additional fertilizer.
추산(推算) calculation; estimate (어림). ~하다 estimate; calculate. ¶ 2만으로 ~되다 be estimated at 20,000.
추상(抽象) abstraction. ~하다 abstract 《from》. ~적(으로) abstract(ly). ¶ ~론 an abstract argument [opinion] / ~론에 빠지다 fall into an abstract argument) / ~명사 an abstract noun / ~예술 abstract art / ~파 abstractionism / ~화 an abstract painting.
추상(秋霜) ① 《가을 서리》 autumn frost(s). ② 《비유》 sternness. ¶ ~같은 severe; rigorous; stern.
추상(追想) retrospection; recollection; reminiscence. ~하다 recollect; look over; recall. ¶ ~록(錄) reminiscences.
추상(推想) ~하다 guess; conjecture; infer 《from》; imagine.
추색(秋色) autumnal scenery (tints); a sign of autumn.
추서(追書) a postscript (略 P.S.).
추서(追敍) ~하다 give posthumous honors on 《a person》.
추서다 (회복) get well again; recover from illness).
추석(秋夕) Harvest Moon Festival [Day]; *Chuseok*, the Korean Thanksgiving Day. ¶ ~성묘 a visit to *one's* ancestral graves on the occasion of *Chuseok*.
추세(趨勢) a tendency; a drift; a trend; a current. ¶ 증가~에 있다 be on the increasing trend / 시대의 ~에 따르다 [역행하다] go with [against] the current / 시대의 ~에 역행하려 해도 헛수고다 It is no use trying to resist the trend [tendency] of the times.
추수(秋收) a harvest. ~하다 harvest. ¶ ~감사절 Thanksgiving Day.
추스르다 (매만지다) pick and trim; 《일 따위를》 set in order; put into shape; straighten up (out). ¶ 짚을 ~ pick straws and trim them / 일을 ~ straighten matters out.
추신(追伸) a postscript (생략 P.S.).
추심(推尋) collection. ~하다 collect. ¶ 수표를 ~에 돌리다 put a check through for collection.

¶ ~료 collection charge / ~어음 a collection bill / ~위임배서 endorsement for collection / ~은행 a collection bank.
추썩거리다 keep shrugging [raising] 《one's shoulders》; keep pulling up 《one's coat》.
추악(醜惡) ~하다 《얼굴 따위가》 (be) ugly; unsightly; abominable; mean; hideous; disgusting.
추앙(推仰) ~하다 adore; worship; revere; look up to. ¶ ~받다 be held in high esteem.
추어올리다 ① 《위로》 pull up; lift up; hoist. ② ☞ 추어주다.
추어주다 praise; applaud; extol; compliment; sing the praise 《of》.
추어탕(鰍魚湯) loach soup.
추억(追憶) remembrance; recollection; memory; reminiscence. ~하다 recollect; reminisce 《about》; look back upon; recall. ¶ 즐거운 ~ pleasant memories / ~을 더듬다 recall [recollect] the past / ~에 잠기다 indulge [be lost] in retrospection.
추위하다 feel cold; be sensitive to the cold; complain of the cold.
추월(追越) ~하다 pass; overtake; outstrip; get ahead of. ¶ 내 차는 트럭을 ~했다 My car got ahead of a truck. ¶ ~금지 No Passing / ~금지 구역 a no-passing zone / ~(차)선 a passing lane; an overtaking lane (英).
추위 cold(ness). ¶ 심한 ~ intense [bitter] cold / 살을 에는 듯한 ~ biting [piercing] cold / ~를 타다 be sensitive to the cold / ~를 참다 stand [bear] the cold / ~를 막다 keep out [off] the cold.
추이(推移) (a) change; (a) transition; (a) shift. ~하다 change; undergo a change; shift. ¶ 시대의 ~와 함께 with the change of the times / 사태의 ~를 지켜보자 We'll see how things change.
추인(追認) confirmation; ratification. ~하다 ratify; confirm 《a telegraphic order》. ¶ ~자 a ratifier; a confirmer.
추잡(醜雜) ~하다 (be) filthy; foul; indecent; obscene. ¶ ~한 말 a foul [filthy] talk.
추장(酋長) a chieftain; a chief.
추장(推獎) recommendation.
추저분하다 (醜-) (be) dirty; messy.
추적(追跡) chase; pursuit; tracking. ~하다 chase; pursue; give chase 《to》; run after. ¶ ~중이다 be in pursuit [chase] of; be on the track of 《a criminal》. ¶ ~기지 《인공위성 등에 대한》 a tracking station / ~자 a pursuer; a chaser / ~장치 a tracking

device / ~조사 a follow-up [tracing] survey(~조사를 하다 conduct a follow-up survey *(of)*).

추접스럽다 (be) dirty; mean; sordid; low-down. ¶ 추접스럽게 굴다 behave in a mean [low-down] fashion.

추정(推定) (a) presumption; (an) inference; (an) estimation. ~하다 presume; infer; assume; estimate. ¶ 피해 총액은 약 5억원에 이를 것으로 ~된다 The sum total of damage is estimated to be about five hundred million *won*. / 그것은 단순한 ~에 지나지 않는다 It's a mere presumption. ‖ ~가격 estimated [presumed] value *(of an article)* / ~량 an estimated volume / ~상속인 an heir presumptive / ~연령 the estimated [probable] age.

추종(追從) ~하다 follow; follow suit; be servile to. ¶ ~을 불허하다 have no equal [parallel, second]; be second to none; be unrivaled.

추증(追贈) ~하다 confer [give] honors posthumously.

추진(推進) propulsion. ~하다 propel; drive [push] forward; (촉진하다) step up; promote. ¶ 자연보호 운동을 ~하다 promote a conservation movement. ‖ ~기 a propeller; a screw(배의) / ~력 the driving force; propulsive energy / ~모체 a nucleus / ~용 연료 propellant.

추징(追徵) ~하다 make an additional collection *(of)*; (별로로) fine; impose a penalty *(of $100)* on *(a person)*. ¶ 그녀는 200만원의 소득세를 ~당했다 She was charged an additional two million *won* for income tax. ‖ ~금 money collected in addition / ~세 a penalty tax.

추천(推薦) recommendation. ~하다 recommend *(for, as)*; nominate *(for, as)* (지명); propose; say [put in] a good word for *(a person)*. ¶ 적극적으로 ~하다 give *one's* hearty recommendation *(to)* / …의 ~으로 by [through] the recommendation of... / 김교수님이 이 책을 ~해 주셨다 *Professor Kim* recommended this book to me. ‖ ~자 a recommender; a proposer; a nominator / ~장 a letter of recommendation / ~후보 a recommended candidate.

추첨(抽籤) drawing; lots a lottery. ~하다 draw lots; hold a lottery. ¶ ~으로 결정하다 decide by lot / ~에 뽑히다 win a prize in a lottery. ‖ ~권 a lottery ticket.

추축(樞軸) 《중추》 a pivot; an axis; 《중심》 a central point; the center (of power). ‖ ~국 〖史〗 the Axis powers.

추출(抽出) abstraction; 〖化〗 extraction. ~하다 draw; abstract; extract. ‖ ~물 an extract; an extraction / 임의~법 a random sampling method.

추측(推測) (a) guess; conjecture. ~하다 guess; suppose; conjecture. ¶ ~대로 as conjectured [supposed] / ~이 맞다 [어긋나다] guess right [wrong]. ‖ ~기사 a speculative news story [article].

추켜들다 raise; lift; hold up.

추켜잡다 lift (up); hold up.

추태(醜態) disgraceful behavior; an unseemly sight. ¶ ~를 부리다 behave *oneself* disgracefully; make a scene; cut a sorry figure / ~를 드러내다 make a spectacle of *oneself*.

추파(秋波) an amorous glance; an ogle. ¶ ~을 던지다 cast an amorous glance at; make (sheep's) eyes at; wink (ogle *(at a girl)*.

추하다(醜—) ① (못생김) (be) ugly; bad-looking; ill-favored. ② (더러움) (be) dirty; filthy; unseemly, indecent, obscene(추잡); (수치스러움) (be) ignominious. ③ (비루) (be) mean; base; sordid; dirty(美). ¶ (마음이) 추한 사람 a mean-spirited person.

추해당(秋海棠) 〖植〗 a begonia.

추행(醜行) disgraceful [scandalous] conduct; misconduct; immoral relations(남녀간의).

추호(秋毫) ¶ ~도 (not) in the least; (not) at all; (not) a bit; (not) in the slightest degree / 남을 해칠 생각은 ~도 없다 I don't have the slightest intention to harm others.

추후(追後) ¶ ~에 later on; afterwards; by and by / ~ 통고가 있을 때까지 until further notice.

축(丑) the zodiacal sign of the ox. ~시 the Year [Hour] of the Ox.

축(軸) (굴대) an axis; an axle(차의); a pivot(선회축); a shaft(기계의). ¶ 지~ the earth's axis / 댄서는 발뒤꿈치를 ~으로 해서 바퀴 돌았다 The dancer pivoted sharply on her heel.

축 《무리》 a group; a company; a circle; a party.

축 《맥없이》 sluggishly; languidly; droopingly. ¶ ~ 늘어지다 dangle; hang.

축가(祝歌) a festive song. ¶ 결혼 ~ a nuptial song.

축객(逐客) ¶문전 ~하다 refuse to see; turn 《a person》 away.

축구(蹴球) soccer; (association) football 《英》. ¶ ~경기 a soccer [football] game / ~계 the world of soccer [football] / ~공 a soccer [football] ball / ~선수[팀] a soccer [football] player [team] / ~장 a soccer [football] field [ground] / 국제 ~연맹 the Fédération Internationale de Football Association(생략 FIFA) / 대한 ~협회 the Korea Football Association / 2002년(도) ~ the 2002 World Cup Soccer.

축나다(縮—) ¶물건이 ~ lessen; decrease; suffer a deficit [loss]; 《몸이》 become [get] lean [thin]; lose weight [flesh].

축내다(縮—) reduce a sum by 《a certain amount》; spend part of a sum; take a bit of a sum.

축농증(蓄膿症) 〖醫〗 empyema.

축대(築臺) a terrace; an elevation; (erect) an embankment. ¶위험한 ~ an embankment in dangerous conditions.

축도(縮圖) a reduced-size drawing; an epitome; a miniature copy. ¶인생의 ~ an epitome of life / 사회의 ~ society in miniature. / ~기 a pantograph; an eidograph.

축도(祝禱) a benediction [blessing]. ¶ ~를 하다 give the benediction.

축문(祝文) a written prayer (offered at ancestor memorial service).

축배(祝杯) a toast. ¶ ~를 들다 drink a toast 《for, to》; drink in celebration 《of》; toast.

축복(祝福) a blessing. ~하다 bless. ¶ ~받은 blessed.

축사(畜舍) a stall; a cattle shed.

축사(祝辭) a congratulatory address; greetings. ¶결혼 ~ wedding congratulations / ~를 하다 deliver a congratulatory address 《at a ceremony》; offer [extend] one's congratulations 《to a person》.

축사(縮寫) ~하다 draw on a smaller scale; make a reduced copy. ¶ ~도 a reduced drawing.

축산(畜産) livestock breeding [raising]; stockbreeding 《축산업》 a livestock industry. ¶ ~공해 stockbreeding pollution / ~물 stock farm product / ~시험장 the Livestock Experiment Station / ~업자 a livestock raiser / ~진흥사업단 〖심의회〗 the Livestock Industry Promotion Corporation [Council] / ~학 animal husbandry.

축성(築城) castle construction [building]. ~하다 construct a castle; fortify 《a hill》.

축소(縮小·縮小) (a) reduction; a cut; (a) curtailment. ~하다 reduce; cut [scale] down; curtail. ¶ 군비 ~ reduction of armaments / ~하다 reduce [cut (down)] armaments / 나는 불경기 때문에 사업을 ~해야 했다 I had to make cutbacks in my business because of the depression.

축쇄(縮刷) ~하다 print in reduced size. ¶ ~판 a reduced-[smaller-]size edition.

축수(祝手) ~하다 pray with one's hands pressed together.

축수(祝壽) ~하다 wish 《a person》 a long life.

축어(逐語) ~적(으로) word for word; verbatim; literal(ly). ¶ ~역 a literal (word-for-word) translation.

축연(祝宴) a feast; a banquet. ¶ ~을 베풀다 give a feast in honor of 《a person》; hold a banquet in celebration of 《an event》.

축우(畜牛) a domestic cow [ox]; cattle (총칭).

축원(祝願) (a) prayer; (a) wish. ~하다 pray for; supplicate; wish. ¶ ~문 a written prayer.

축음기(蓄音機) a gramophone; a phonograph 《美》. ¶ ~를 듣다 play a phonograph.

축의(祝意) congratulations (사람에 대한); celebration (일에 대한). ¶ ~를 표하다 express one's congratulations 《on》; congratulate 《a person on》 / ···에 ~를 표하여 in honor of 《a person》; in celebration of 《an event》.

축이다 wet; moisten; dampen; damp. ¶목을 ~ moisten one's throat / 수건을 ~ wet [damp] a towel.

축일(祝日) a public holiday; a festival.

축재(蓄財) 《행위》 accumulation of wealth; 《모은 재산》 accumulated wealth. ~하다 amass [accumulate] wealth. ¶ ~자 a money-maker / 부정~자 an illicit fortune maker.

축적(蓄積) accumulation; storage; hoard. ~하다 accumulate [amass] 《wealth》; store (up) 《energy》; hoard (up). ¶ 부[자본의] ~ accumulation of wealth [capital] / 장기간에 걸친 농약의 체내 ~ a long-term accumulation [build-up] of agricultural chemicals in the body.

축전(祝典) (hold) a celebration; a festival. ¶기념 ~ a commemorative festival.

축전(祝電) 《send》 a congratulato-

축전기(蓄電器) an electric condenser.

축전지(蓄電池) a storage battery.

축제(祝祭) a festival; a fête; a gala. ¶ ~를 열다 hold a festival / ~ 기분이다 be in a festive mood. ‖ ~일 a festival (day); a gala (fête) day.

축제(築堤) embankment; banking. ~하다 embank (a river); construct an embankment. ‖ ~공사 embankment works.

축조(逐條) ~ 심의하다 discuss (a bill) article by article.

축조(築造) building; construction. ~하다 build; construct; erect.

축지다(縮一) ① (사람 가치가) discredit oneself; fall into discredit; bring discredit on oneself. ② (몸이) become weaker; get (grow) thin; get run-down.

축척(縮尺) a reduced scale. ¶ ~ 천 분의 일의 지도 a map on the scale of one to one thousand.

축첩(蓄妾) ~하다 keep a concubine.

축축(늘어진 모양) drooping; hanging down.

축축하다 (be) damp(ish); moist; wet; humid. ¶ 축축한 땅 moist ground / 축축한 옷 wet clothes / 축축한 날씨 damp weather.

축출(逐出) expulsion. ~하다 drive (turn, send) out; expel; oust (지위에서); (퇴거) eject; (해고) fire. ¶ ~당하다 get driven (kicked) out; be expelled / 당에서 ~하다 oust (expel) (a person) from the party.

축포(祝砲) a cannon salute; a salute of guns. ¶ 21발의 ~를 쏘다 give (fire) a twenty-one gun salute.

축하(祝賀) congratulations; (a) celebration; one's good wishes. ~하다 congratulate (a person on); celebrate (Xmas). ¶ ~의 말씀 congratulatory remarks; congratulations / …을 ~하여 in celebration of / ~ 인사를 하다 offer congratulations / ~객 a congratulator / ~선물 a congratulatory gift / ~연 (hold) a celebration; (hold) a congratulatory banquet / ~퍼레이드 a celebration parade.

축항(築港) ~하다 construct a harbor. ‖ ~공사 harbor works.

춘경(春耕) spring plowing.

춘경(春景) spring scenery.

춘계(春季) spring(time); spring season. ¶ ~운동회 a spring athletic meet.

춘곤(春困) the lassitude of spring; spring fever.

춘궁(春宮) the Crown Prince.

춘궁기(春窮期) 《보릿고개》 the spring lean (food-short) season.

춘기발동기(春機發動期) (the age of) puberty (adolescence).

춘몽(春夢) spring dreams; visionary fancies; a springtime fantasy. ¶ 인생은 일장 ~ Life is but an empty dream.

춘부장(春府丈) your august father.

춘분(春分) the vernal equinox.

춘사(椿事) an accident; a disaster; a tragedy (비극).

춘삼월(春三月) March of the lunar month. ¶ ~ 호시절 the pleasant days of spring.

춘색(春色) spring scenery.

춘설(春雪) spring snow.

춘신(春信) signs of spring; news of flowers (화신).

춘양(春陽) 《햇빛》 spring sunshine; 《철》 the spring season. 「worms.

춘잠(春蠶) a spring breed of silk

춘정(春情) sexual (carnal) desire (passion). ¶ ~을 느끼다 be seized with low passions; feel the sex urge.

춘추(春秋) 《봄과 가을》 spring and autumn; 《연령》 age; years. ¶ ~ 80의 노인 a man of eighty winters. ‖ ~복 a suit for spring (autumn) wear; spring-and-autumn wear.

춘풍(春風) the spring breeze.

춘하(春夏) ¶ ~추동 the four seasons; all the year round; throughout the year.

춘화도(春畫圖) an obscene picture; pornography.

춘흥(春興) the delights of spring.

출가(出家) ~하다 leave home (집을 떠나가다); become a priest (승려가 되다).

출가(出嫁) ~하다 be (get) married to (a man). ¶ 딸을 ~시키다 marry one's daughter off; get a daughter married.

출간(出刊) ☞ 출판.

출감(出監) release from prison. ~하다 be set free; be released (discharged) from prison. ‖ ~자 a released convict.

출강(出講) ~하다 (give a) lecture (at); teach (at); be a part-time teacher (at).

출격(出擊) a sally; a sortie. ~하다 sally forth; make a sortie. ¶ 100회의 ~ 기록을 보유하다 have a record of 100 sorties.

출고(出庫) delivery of goods from a warehouse. ~하다 take (goods) out of warehouse. ¶ 갓 ~된 소주 soju fresh from the brewery. ‖ ~가격 a factory (store) price / ~지시 a delivery order.

출구(出口) a way out; an exit; an outlet; a gateway.

출국(出國) ~하다 depart from the

출근(出勤) attendance (at work). ~하다 go (come) to (the office); go on duty. ¶ ~해 있다 be at work; be present / 이늦을 be late for the office / 사원은 9시에 ~하도록 되어 있다 Workers are expected to come to their office at 9:00 am. / 그는 아직 ~하지 않았다 He is not at the office yet. ‖ ~부 an attendance book / ~시간 the hour for going to work; the office-going hour.

출금(出金) (지불) payment; (출자) (an) investment. ~하다 pay; invest. ‖ ~전표 a paying-out slip.

출납(出納) receipts and disbursements. ~계원 a cashier; (은행의) a teller / ~부 a cashbook; an account book / ~책임자 a chief accountant.

출동(出動) (동원) mobilization; (파견) dispatch. ~하다 be mobilized; be sent; be called out; put to sea(함대가). ¶ 기동대를 ~시키다 mobilize the riot police / 미국은 제7함대를 인도양에 ~시켰다 The United States moved the Seventh Fleet to the Indian Ocean. ‖ ~명령 an order for moving (turning out) / ~준비 readiness to move.

출두(出頭) an appearance. ~하다 appear to; present oneself at; report (oneself) to. ¶ 몸소 ~하다 appear in person / 법정에 ~를 요구받다 be ordered to appear in court / 자진 (임의) ~형식으로 in the form of voluntary appearance. ‖ ~명령 a summons.

출렁거리다 surge; roll; wave; undulate.

출력(出力) generating power; output. ¶ ~ 200마력의 엔진 a motor that has a capacity of 200 hp / 이 엔진의 ~은 600마력이다 This is a 600 horsepower engine.

출루(出壘) ~하다 get (get) to first base. ¶ ~해 있다 be on (first) base.

출마(出馬) ~하다 put oneself as a candidate; run (stand)(英) for (election).

출몰(出沒) ~하다 make frequent appearance; frequent; haunt.

출발(出發) a start; departure. ~하다 start (depart) (from); set out (from); leave (Seoul); leave (for); set out (for); start (for); embark (for)(배로).

출범(出帆) sailing. ~하다 (set) sail (for); sail away; leave (for).

출병(出兵) ~하다 send (dispatch) troops (to); send an expeditionary force.

출비(出費) expenses; expenditure; (make) an outlay (for).

출사(出仕) ~하다 go into government service.

출산(出産) a birth; childbirth; delivery. ~하다 give birth (to); be delivered (of); have a baby. ¶ 그녀는 사내애를 ~했다 She gave birth to a baby boy. ‖ ~예정일 the expected date of birth / ~율 the birth rate / ~휴가 maternity leave.

출생(出生) a birth. ~하다 be born. ¶ ~의 비밀을 캐다 spy out the secret of (a person's) birth. ‖ ~률 the birth rate / ~신고 the report (register) of a birth / ~지 one's birthplace.

출석(出席) attendance; presence. ~하다 attend; be present at. ¶ ~을 부르다 call the roll (names). ‖ ~부 a roll book / ~자 a person present; an attendance; those present(총칭).

출세(出世) success in life. ~하다 rise in the world; succeed (in life); attain distinction; be promoted. ¶ ~한 사람 a successful man / 입신 ~ advancement in life / 그는 ~가 빨랐다 (회사 등에서) He won quick promotion. / 그는 꼭 ~할 것이다 He is bound to succeed in life. or I'm sure he'll get on in life. ‖ ~작 the work which has made the author famous.

출신(出身) ¶ 대학 ~자 a university graduate / …의 ~이다 be a graduate of (a university); come from (Masan) / 우리 사장은 농가 ~이다 The president of our company comes from a peasant family. ¶ ~교 one's alma mater / ~지 one's birthplace; one's home town.

출애굽기(出─記)【聖】The Book of Exodus; Exodus(Exod.).

출어(出漁) ~하다 go (sail) out fishing. ‖ ~구역 a fishing area / ~권 the fishing right.

출연(出捐) ~하다 donate; contribute. ‖ ~금 a donation; a contribution.

출연(出演) one's appearance (on the stage); one's performance. ~하다 appear on the stage; play; perform. ¶ 처음으로 ~하다 make one's debut (on the stage) / 그녀는 지난 주 TV 토크쇼에 ~했다 She appeared on a TV talk show last week. ‖ ~계약 (a) booking / ~료 a performance fee / ~자 a performer.

출영(出迎) meeting; reception(영

출옥(出獄) ~하다 be discharged [released] from prison; leave prison. ¶ ~자 a released convict.

출원(出願) (an) application. ~하다 make an application (to the government for an official sanction); file an application (with the Patent Office for a patent). ¶ ~ 수속은 끝났느냐 Have you already made an application? / 특허 ~ 중 (표시) Patent applied for. ‖ ~기일 the deadline for application(s) / ~자 an applicant.

출입(出入) coming and going; entrance and exit. ~하다 go in and out; enter and leave; frequent(자주 가다). ¶ ~자유롭게 하다 have free access to (a house) / ~하는 선박 incoming and outgoing vessels / 차량(사람) ~이 많은 곳 a place with a lot of traffic (people coming and going). ‖ ~구 an entrance; a doorway; a gateway / ~국 entry into, and departure from the country / ~국 관리국 the Immigration Bureau / ~금지 (게시) No trespassing; Off limits; Keep out.

출자(出資) investment. ~하다 invest (money in); finance (an enterprise). ¶ 사업에 많은 돈을 ~하다 invest a lot of money in the enterprise. ‖ ~금 money invested; a capital / ~액 the amount of investment / ~자 an investor.

출장(出張) an official (a business) trip. ~하다 make an official (a business) trip; travel on business. ‖ ~소 an agency; a branch office / ~여비 a travelling allowance; travel expenses.

출장(出場) ~하다 appear; be present (at); participate (take part) (in). ¶ 대회에의 ~을 취소하다 cancel one's entry for the contest. ‖ ~자 a participant; a contestant (컨테스트의) ; the entry (총칭) / ~정지 suspension.

출전(出典) the source. ¶ ~을 밝히다 give (name, indicate) the source (of).

출전(出戰) ~하다 (출정) depart for the front; (참가) participate (take part) (in); enter.

출정(出廷) ~하다 appear in (at-tend) court.

출정(出征) ~하다 depart for the front; go to the front. ‖ ~군인 a soldier in active service (at the front).

출제(出題) making questions (for an examination). ~하다 set (a person) a problem (in English); make questions (for an examination in English) out of (a textbook). ‖ ~경향 a tendency of questions / ~범위 a range of possible questions.

출중(出衆) ~하다 (be) uncommon; extraordinary; outstanding; distinguish oneself (in).

출찰(出札) issue of a ticket. ‖ ~계원 a ticket clerk (英); a booking clerk (英) / ~구 a ticket (booking 英) window.

출처(出處) the source; the origin. ¶ 뉴스의 ~ the source of the news.

출초(出超) an excess of exports (over imports); an exports surplus. ¶ 50억 달러의 ~ an excess of exports amounting to five billion dollars.

출출하다 feel a bit hungry.

출타(出他) ~하다 leave the house (office); go out (on a visit). ¶ ~중에는 in one's absence; while one is away (out).

출토(出土) ~하다 be excavated (unearthed) (at a site; from the ruin of...). ‖ ~지 the site (location) at which (an artifact) was found; the find site / ~품 an excavated article.

출판(出版) publication; publishing. ~하다 publish; put (bring) out (a book); issue. ¶ 그의 새로운 저서가 ~되었다 His new book is out. / 나는 그 책을 자비로 ~했다 I published the book at my own expense. ‖ ~계 the publishing world / ~기념회 a party in honor of the publication (of a person's book) / ~목록 a catalog of publication / ~물 a publication / ~사 a publisher; a publishing company / ~업 publishing business.

출품(出品) ~하다 exhibit; display; show; put on exhibition (display). ‖ ~목록 a catalog(ue) of exhibits / ~물 an exhibit.

출하(出荷) shipment; forwarding. ~하다 forward (goods); ship. ¶ 생선을 트럭으로 서울에 ~하다 ship fish by truck to Seoul. ‖ ~선(先) (목적지) the destination; / ~자 a forwarder; a shipper.

출항(出航) ~하다 start on voyage; leave (port); set sail (from).

출항(出港) departure (from a

출현 (出帆) port). ～하다 leave port; set sail 《from》; clear (a port). ¶ 악천후로 배는 ～할 수 없었다 Bad weather kept the boat in port. ∥ ～선 an outgoing vessel / ～절차 clearance formalities / ～정지 an embargo / ～정지를 풀다 lift an embargo) / ～허가 (get) clearance for leaving port.

출현 (出現) an appearance; an advent. ～하다 appear; make one's appearance; turn [show] up. ¶ 제트기의 ～ the advent of jet aircraft / 서울 빌딩가 상공에 비행접시가 ～했다 A flying saucer appeared above the buildings in Seoul.

출혈 (出血) ① 《피가 남》 bleeding; 〔醫〕 hemorrhage. ～하다 bleed; hemorrhage. ¶ ～과다로 from excessive bleeding / ～을 멈추게 하다 stop the bleeding / 내～ internal hemorrhage. ② 《희생・결손》 sacrifices; deficit; loss. ¶ ～ 수주하다 take orders below cost (at a sacrifice) / ～대매출 a sacrifice [below-cost] sale; a clearance sale / 새로운 사업을 하려면 얼마간의 ～은 각오해야 한다 We must be prepared for some losses to run a new business. ∥ ～경쟁 (업계의) a cutthroat competition / ～수출 a below-cost export; dumping.

출회 (出廻) supply 《of goods》; arrival on the market. ～하다 appear [arrive] on the market. ¶ 요즈음은 감자의 ～기이다 The potato is in season.

춤[1] 《무용》 dancing; a dance. ～추다 dance; ～을 잘 추다 be a good dancer. ∥ ～상대 (선생) a dancing partner [master, mistress(여자)].

춤[2] 《우두》 height.

춥다 (be) cold; chilly. ¶ 추운 날씨 cold weather; a freezing day / 추워 보이다 look cold / 추워지다 get [grow] cold / 추워서 떨다 shiver with cold / 나이가 들수록 더 추위한다 be more sensitive to the cold as one grows older.

충 (蟲) ① ☞ 벌레. ② ☞ 회충.

충격 (衝擊) an impact; a shock. ¶ ～적인 뉴스 shocking news / 폭발의 ～ the shock [impact] of the explosion / ～에 견디는 shock-resistant; shockproof 《watches》 / ～을 받다 be shocked 《at》 / ～을 주다 give (a person) a shock / 나는 그 소식에 ～을 받았다 I was shocked by the news. ∥ ～사 (死) (a) death from shock / ～요법 shock therapy / ～파 (波) a shock wave.

충견 (忠犬) a faithful dog.

충고 (忠告) 《a piece of》 advice; admonition (간언); a warning (경고). ～하다 advise; warn; give warning. ¶ ～에 따르다 follow [take] 《a person's》 advice / ～를 무시하다 take no notice of (pay no heed to) 《a person's》 advice. ∥ ～자 an adviser.

충당 (充當) appropriation. ～하다 allot 《money》 《to》; appropriate (a sum of money for a purpose). ¶ 그 돈은 난민 구제에 ～하여야 한다 The money should be alloted for the relief of the destitute.

충돌 (衝突) a collision; a conflict; a clash. ～하다 collide (conflict) 《with》; run (bump) 《against, into》; clash 《with》. ¶ 의견 (이해)의 ～ a clash (conflict) of views (interests) / 이중 (삼중) ～ a double (three-way) collision / 정면(공중) ～ a head-on (mid-air) collision.

충동 (衝動) ① 《의식》 (an) impulse; (an) impetus; a drive; an urge. ¶ 성적 ～ sexual urges / ～적인 impulsive / ～적으로 행동하다 act impulsively / ～을 억누르다 resist the impulse [urge] 《to do》 / ～ 구매를 하다 buy a thing on impulse / ～에 이끌리다 be driven by an impulse / …하고 싶은 ～을 느끼다 feel the urge to 《do》 / ～구매 impulse buying. ② 《교사・선동》 instigation; incitement. ～하다 instigate; set 《a person》 on; spur on.

충만 (充滿) ～하다 be full 《of》; be filled 《replete》 《with》.

충복 (忠僕) a faithful servant.

충분 (充分) ～(be) sufficient; enough; full; plenty; thorough. ¶ ～한 시간 plenty of time 《for》 / ～히 enough; well; fully; thoroughly; sufficiently / 이 식사는 3인분으로 ～하다 This meal is enough for three.

충성 (忠誠) loyalty; devotion; allegiance; fidelity. ¶ ～스러운 loyal; devoted; sincere; faithful / 여왕에게 ～을 맹세하다 make a pledge of allegiance to the Queen.

충신 (忠臣) a loyal subject; a faithful retainer.

충실 (充實) ～하다 (be) full; complete; substantial. ¶ 내용이 ～한 작품 a substantial work / ～한 생활을 하다 lead a full life / 그녀의 책은 내용이 ～하다 Her book is substantial (rich in content).

충실 (忠實) ～하다 (be) faithful; honest; devoted; true; loyal. ¶ ～한 하인 a faithful [loyal] servant / ～히 faithfully; devotedly; truly; honestly.

충심 (衷心) one's true heart. ¶ ～으로 from the bottom of one's

충언(忠言) good (honest) advice; counsel. ~하다 give good advice (counsel); advise.

충원(充員) supplement of the personnel; recruitment(보충). ~하다 supplement the personnel; call up (recruit) personnel. ‖ ~계획 a levy plan.

충의(忠義) loyalty; fidelity.

충일(充溢) ~하다 overflow; be full (of); be overflowing (with).

충적(沖積) 〖地〗 ¶ ~의 alluvial. ‖ ~기 the alluvial epoch.

충전(充電) charging. ~하다 charge (a battery) (with electricity); electrify. ‖ ~기 a charger.

충전(充塡) filling up. ~하다 fill (plug up; stop (up)); replenish. ¶ 충치를 금으로 ~하다 have one's tooth filled (plugged) with gold. ‖ ~물 fillers.

충절(忠節) loyalty; allegiance. ¶ ~을 다하다 serve with loyalty.

충정(衷情) one's true heart. ¶ ~을 털어놓다 open one's heart (to).

충족(充足) ~하다 fill up; be sufficient; full; make up (for). ¶ ~되지 않은 욕구 an unfilled desire / 욕망을 ~시키다 satisfy one's desire / 조건을 ~시키다 meet the requirements; satisfy the conditions.

충직(忠直) ~한 faithful; honest; upright; true.

충천(衝天) ~하다 rise (soar) high up to the sky; go sky-high. ¶ 의기가 ~하다 one's spirit soars (to the skies); be in high spirits.

충충하다 be dark; gloomy; somber; dusky; dim.

충치(蟲齒) a decayed tooth; a dental caries. ¶ ~가 생기다 get a decayed tooth; have a tooth decay.

충해(蟲害) insect pests; damage from insects. ¶ ~를 입다 be damaged by insects.

충혈(充血) ~하다 be congested (with blood); be bloodshot (눈이). ¶ ~된 눈 bloodshot eyes.

충혼(忠魂) the loyal dead; a loyal soul. ‖ ~비 a monument dedicated to the loyal (war) dead.

충효(忠孝) loyalty and filial piety. ¶ ~의 길은 둘이 아니요 하나다 Loyalty and filial duty are one and the same.

췌액(膵液) 〖動〗 pancreatic juice.

췌언(贅言) superfluous words; pleonasm.

췌장(膵臟) 〖解〗 the pancreas. ‖ ~암 〖醫〗 cancer of the pancreas / ~염 pancreatitis / ~절개(술) pancreatotomy.

취객(醉客) a drunkard; a drunken man; a drunk.

취관(吹管) a blowpipe; a blast pipe.

취급(取扱) 《사람 등의》 treatment; dealing; 《물건의》 handling; 《사무의》 management. ~하다 treat; deal (with) (문제, 사람을); handle (물건을); manage (사무를); carry on. ¶ ~어린애처럼 ~하다 treat (a person) like a child / (사람을) 공평히 ~하다 treat (a person) fairly; deal fairly with (a person) / 사무를 ~하다 manage affairs; carry on (conduct) business / 소년 범죄 문제를 ~한 책 a book concerned (dealing) with the problems of juvenile delinquency / 유리 그릇을 조심하여서 ~하다 handle glasses with care. ‖ ~소 an office; an agent / ~시간 service hour / ~요령 설명이 an instruction manual / ~인 an agent.

취기(醉氣) (signs of) intoxication; tipsiness. ¶ ~가 돌다 become (get) tipsy; get drunk.

취담(醉談) drunken words. ~하다 talk under the influence of liquor. ¶ ~이 진담이다 People tell the truth when they are drunk.

취득(取得) (an) acquisition. ~하다 acquire; obtain. ¶ 소유권을 ~하다 acquire the ownership (of). ‖ ~가격 acquisition cost / ~물 an acquisition / ~세 the acquisition tax / ~시효 acquisitive prescription / ~자 an acquisitor / 부동산 ~세 the real property acquisition tax.

취락(聚落) a settlement; a community; a village; a colony.

취로(就勞) ~하다 find work; go to work. ‖ ~사업 a job-producing project / ~시간 (일수) working hours (days).

취미(趣味) (a) taste; an interest. ¶ 고상한 〔세련된〕 ~ a noble (refined) taste / ~가 있는 tasteful; interesting / ~가 없는 tasteless; dry / ~를 갖다 take (an) interest (in); have a taste (for) / ~에 맞다 meet one's taste / 골동품 〔독서, 우표 수집, 음악〕에 대한 ~ an interest in antiques (reading, stamp collection, music) / 문학에 대한 ~ literary taste. ‖ ~생활 a dilettante('s) life.

취사(炊事) cooking; kitchen work. ~하다 cook; do (the) cooking. ‖ ~당번 the cook's duty; a kitchen police (병사의) / ~도구 cooking utensils / ~장 a kitchen.

취사 (取捨) selection; sorting out. ¶ ~ 선택하다 choose; sort out; make *one's* choice / 너는 자유롭게 ~ 선택할 수 있다 You can have a free choice.

취생몽사 (醉生夢死) ~하다 dream 〔drone〕 *one's* life away.

취소 (取消) cancellation; retraction; annulment (계약 등의); withdrawal (철회). ~하다 cancel; take back; retract; withdraw; revoke 《*a command*》; 〔法〕 repeal. ¶ ~할 수 있는 revocable; retractable / ~할 수 없는 irrevocable; beyond recall (revoke) / ~ the revocation of a license / 약속을 ~하다 withdraw *one's* promise / 주문 (예약)을 ~하다 cancel an order (a reservation) / 약혼을 ~하다 break off *one's* engagement / 그는 내 발언의 ~을 요구했다 He demanded that I should withdraw my words. / 그는 앞서 한 말을 ~하였다 He took back his words. ‖ ~권 〔法〕 right of rescission; the right to rescind / ~명령 a countermand.

취안 (醉眼) drunken eyes.

취약 (脆弱) ~하다 be weak; fragile; frail. ‖ ~지역 〔지점〕 〔軍〕 a vulnerable area (point).

취업 (就業) ~하다 begin 〔start, go to〕 work. ¶ ~ 중이다 be at work; be on duty / ~ 계약을 하다 sign on with a company. ‖ ~규칙 office 〔shop〕 regulations / ~률 the percentage of employment / ~시간 (the) working 〔business〕 hours / ~인구 the working population / ~일수 days worked.

취역 (就役) ~하다 be commissioned; go 〔come〕 into commission 〔service〕. ¶ 유럽 항로에 ~하다 go into service on the European line. 「transliterate.

취음 (取音) transliteration. ~하다

취임 (就任) inauguration; assumption of office. ~하다 take office 《*as*》; be installed (inaugurated) 《*as*》. ¶ 대통령직에 ~하다 be inaugurated as President / ~을 수락하다 accept an appointment / ~ 선서를 하다 take the oath of office. ‖ ~식 an inauguration; an inaugural ceremony (대통령~식 날 《美》 Inauguration Day) / ~연설 an inaugural address.

취입 (吹入) recording. ~하다 put 《*a song*》 on a record; have 《*one's song*》 recorded; make a record 《*of*》.

취재 (取材) ~하다 collect 〔gather〕 (news) data 〔materials〕 《*on, for*》; 〔기자가〕 cover 《*a meeting*》. ¶ 그녀는 그 사고를 ~하러 나갔다 She went out to cover the accident. ‖ ~경쟁 a competition in coverage / ~기자 a reporter; a legman 《美》 / ~원 〔源〕 a news source / ~활동 coverage activities; legwork 《美》.

취조 (取調) ☞ 문초(問招).

취주 (吹奏) ~하다 blow 《*the trumpet*》; play (on) 《*the flute*》. ‖ ~악 wind instrument music / ~악기 a wind instrument / ~악대 〔악단〕 a brass band / ~자 a player.

취중 (醉中) ~에 in a drunken state; under the influence of liquor. ‖ ~운전 drunken driving.

취지 (趣旨) 〔생각〕 an opinion; an idea; 〔목적〕 an object; a purpose; an aim; 〔뜻·요지〕 a purport; the effect. ¶ 질문의 ~ the purport of a question / …의 ~의 〔letter〕 to the effect that … / ~를 그녀에게 전하겠다 I will tell her to that effect. / 이 운동의 ~를 설명하겠다 Let me explain the object of this movement. ‖ ~서 a prospectus.

취직 (就職) getting employment; taking a job. ~하다 get 〔find〕 employment 〔work〕; get a position 〔job〕. ¶ ~의 기회 employment 〔job〕 opportunities / ~을 신청하다 apply for a position 〔job〕 / 그는 은행에 ~했다 He got a position in the bank. / ~시켜 주다 find 《*a person*》 a job 〔position, place〕. ‖ ~난 an employment shortage; the difficulty of finding employment 〔getting a job〕 / ~률 an employment rate / ~시험 an employment examination / ~알선 job placement / ~자리 employment; a position; an opening / ~정보지 a job-placement journal 〔magazine〕 / ~처 *one's* place of employment 〔work〕 / ~활동 job hunting.

취침 (就寢) ~하다 go to bed; retire (to bed, to rest). ¶ ~ 중 while 《*one is*》 asleep 〔sleeping〕; in bed. ‖ ~나팔 taps / ~시각 bedtime; time to go to bed.

취태 (醉態) drunkenness; drunken behavior. ¶ ~를 부리다 put on a drunken display.

취하 (取下) withdrawal. ~하다 withdraw; drop. ¶ 소송을 ~하다 withdraw (drop) a legal action.

취하다 (取―) ① 〔채택〕 adopt; take. ¶ 강경한 태도를 ~ assume 〔take〕 a firm attitude. ② 〔선택하다〕 prefer; choose; pick; take. ¶ 여럿 가운데서 하나를 ~ choose 〔pick〕 one out of many. ③ 〔섭취하다〕 take; have. ¶ 영양식을

취하다 take nourishing food. ④ (꾸다) borrow; lend. ¶돈을 ~ borrow money.

취하다 (醉―) ① (술에) get drunk; become intoxicated (tipsy). ¶취하여 under the influence of liquor (drink) / 곤드레만드레 ~ be dead drunk / 거나하게 ~ be a bit tipsy. ② (중독) be poisoned. ¶담배에 ~ become sick from smoking. ③ (도취) be intoxicated; be exalted. ¶성공에 ~ be elated (intoxicated) with success.

취학 (就學) ~하다 enter (go to) school. ¶~시키다 put (send) (a boy) to school. ‖~률 the percentage of school attendance / ~아동 a school child / ~연령 the school age / ~전 교육 preschool education / 미~아동 a preschool child.

취한 (醉漢) a drunken fellow; a drunkard.

취항 (就航) ~하다 enter service; go into commission. ¶유럽 항로에 ~하다 be put on the European line.

취향 (趣向) (기호) taste; liking; fondness; (경향) bent. ¶예술가~의 사람 a man with an artistic bent / 옷에 대한 ~ one's taste in dress / ~에 맞다 suit (be to) one's taste.

취흥 (醉興) (drunken) merrymaking. ¶~을 돋우다 heighten the merriment; add life to the party / ~에 겨워 춤을 추다 dance in drunken delight.

…측 (側) a side; a part. ¶양~ both sides / 유엔~ the UN side / 노동자~의 요구 the demands on the part of the workers.

측거의 (測距儀) a range finder.

측근 (側近) one's closest associates. ¶~에 around; near by; close to / 총리 ~ those close to the Premier / 대통령 ~ aides of the President; Presidential aides.

측량 (測量) measurement; (토지의) a survey; (물 깊이의) sounding. ~하다 measure; survey; sound. ¶토지를 ~하다 survey an area of land / 토지 ~ land surveying / 사진 ~ a photo survey / 공중 ~ an aerial survey / 새로운 도로 건설을 위해 ~을 시작하다 start surveying for the construction of a new road. ‖~기계 surveying instruments / ~기사 a surveyor / ~반 a surveying corps (squad) / ~선 a surveying ship / ~술 surveying.

측면 (側面) the side; the flank. ¶적을 ~에서 공격하다 attack the enemy on its flank / 사태를 다른 ~에서 보다 look at the situation from a different angle. ‖~공격 a flank attack / ~도 a side view.

측백나무 (側柏―) 【植】 an oriental arborvitae; a thuja.

측선 (側線) ① 〖철도의〗 a sidetrack; a siding. ¶~에 넣다 sidetrack. ② 〖어류의〗 the lateral line.

측심 (測深) sounding. ~하다 sound (the sea); fathom. ¶~기 a (depth) sounder; a depth finder.

측연 (測鉛) a plumb; a sounding lead; a plummet. ‖~선 a sounding (plummet) line.

측우기 (測雨器) a rain gauge.

측은 (惻隱) ~하다 commiserate; sympathize; (be) compassionate; pitiful. ¶~히 여기다 ~ commiserate with / ~한 마음이 들다 be overwhelmed with pity (for); feel compassion (pity) (for).

측점 (測點) (측량의) a measuring point; a surveying station.

측정 (測定) measurement. ~하다 measure. ¶정확히 ~하다 take an accurate measurement of / 거리를 ~하다 measure the distance. ‖~기 a measuring instrument / ~기술 measurement techniques / ~장치 a measuring device / ~치 a measured value.

측지 (測地) land surveying. ~하다 survey land; make a geodetic survey (of). ‖~위성 a geodetic satellite / ~학 geodesy.

측후 (測候) a meteorological observation. ~하다 make a meteorological observation. ‖~소 a meteorological observatory (station).

층 (層) (계층) a class; (건물의) a story; (美) a floor; (지층) a layer; a stratum. ¶근로자~ the working class / 석탄 ~ a coal bed / 2~ the second floor (story) / 사회 중간~ the middle classes of society / 고(저)소득~ a higher-(lower-)income group / 이~ 두껍다 be thick-layered; (인재·선수층 따위가) have a large stock (of players) to draw on / ~을 이루다 be in layers (strata); be stratified / ~상(狀)의 stratiform; stratified.

층계 (層階) stairs; a staircase; a stairway; a flight of steps. ¶~를 오르다 go up the stairs. ‖~참 a landing (place).

층나다 (層―) be stratified into classes (grades); stratify; show disparity (in). ¶연령이 ~ there

is disparity in age.
층등(層等) gradation; grade.
층면(層面) [地] the stratification plane.　　　　　[(a rocky) cliff.
층암절벽(層岩絶壁) an overhanging
층애(層崖) a stratal precipice (cliff).
층운(層雲) a stratus [*pl.* -ti].
층적운(層積雲) a roll cumulus; a stratocumulus.
층지다(層 —) ☞ 층나다.
층층다리(層層 —) a staircase; stairs; a stairway; a flight of
층층대(層層臺) ☞ 층층다리. [steps.
층층시하(層層侍下) serving both parents and grandparents alive.
치(値) [數] numerical value.
치¹ (殺) a share; a part; a portion. ¶ 이틀~ 식량 food for two days. ②《사람》 a fellow; a guy. ¶ 그 ~ that fellow (guy).
치² 《길이의 단위》 a Korean inch; a *chi* (=3.0303 cm).
치가(治家) home management. ¶ ~하다 manage a home (well).
치가 떨리다(齒 —) grind *one's* teeth with vexation (indignation); be tense with indignation.
치감(齒疳) [韓醫] bleeding gums.
치경(齒莖) gums; [醫] the gingiva. ¶ ~ 잇몸.
치고 ¶ 그것은 그렇다 ~ be that as it may; apart from that / 학생 ~ 영어 못 읽는 사람이 없다 There is no student who cannot read English.
치골(恥骨) [解] the pubis; the pubic bones.
치과(齒科) dentistry; dental surgery. ¶ ~용 설비 dental equipment / ~용 기계 dentist's instruments. ǁ ~기공사 a dental technician / ~대학 a dental college / ~의(사) a dentist; a dental surgeon / ~의원 a dental clinic; a dentist's (office).
치국(治國) ruling a nation. ǁ ~책(策) statecraft; statesmanship.
치근(齒根) the root of a tooth.
치근거리다 tease; annoy; pester; bother. ¶ 치근치근 teasingly; importunately.
치기(稚氣) childishness; puerility. ¶ ~넘친 childish; puerile.
치기배(— 輩) a snatcher; a sneak thief; a shoplifter.
치다¹ ①《때리다》 strike; beat; give a blow. ¶ 머리를 ~ hit (strike) (*a person*) on the head / 볼기를 ~ flog (*a person*) on the buttocks. ②《두드리다》 beat (북을); ring (종을); play (on) (금풍 따위); drive (hammer) in (못을); clap (박을) / 피아노를 ~ play (on) the piano / 손뼉을 ~ clap *one's* hands. ③《맞히다》 (make a good) hit; strike. ¶ 배트로 ~ hit with a bat. ④《떡을》 pound. ¶ 떡을 ~ pound steamed rice into dough. ⑤《벼락 따위》 fall; strike.
치다² ①《공격·토벌》 attack; assault; strike. ¶ 적을 불시에 ~ make a sudden (surprise) attack on the enemy. ②《베어내다》 prune; trim. ¶ 가지를 ~ prune (trim) a tree; prune (trim) the branches off. ③《채를》 cut (*a cucumber*) into fine strips.
치다³ ①《깨끗이》 clean (out); tidy (*something*) up; put in order; (쓰레기》 remove; carry away; get rid of; dredge (*a river*). ¶ 방을 ~ tidy a room; put a room in order / 눈을 ~ clear away (off) snow.
치다⁴ ①《체로》 sieve; sift. ¶ 가루를 체에 ~ put (pass) flour through a sieve. ②《장난을》 do; play. ¶ 불을 가지고 장난을 ~ play with fire. ③《소리를》 shout; cry; yell. ¶ 살려달라고 소리 ~ scream (cry) for help.
치다⁵ ①《셈》 value; appraise; estimate; count. ¶ 집값을 4천만원으로 ~ value the house at forty million *won*. ②《…로 보다》 consider; regard as; think of (as). ¶ 그를 위대한 학자로 쳐준다 He is regarded as (considered to be) a great scholar.
치다⁶ 《액체·가루를》 add (*sauce*); put; pour (붓을); sprinkle (가루를). ¶ 샐러드에 소스를 ~ put sauce on the salad.
치다⁷ ①《매다》 tie; wear; put on; attach. ¶ 각반을 ~ wear gaiters. ②《장막 따위를》 hang (*a curtain*); put up (*a mosquito net*); pitch (*a tent*); draw (*a line*) (줄을).
치다⁸ 《차에》 run over (*a man*); knock (*a person*) down. ☞ 치이다.
치다⁹ ①《사육》 keep; raise; rear; breed. ¶ 누에를 ~ rear (raise) silkworms / 닭을 ~ breed (raise) chickens. ②《꿀을》 ¶ 벌이 꿀을 ~ bees store honey. ③《손님을》 keep a lodger (roomer). ④《가지가 뻗다》 spread; shoot out. ¶ 나무가 가지를 ~ a tree shoot out (spreads) branches.
치다¹⁰ 《그물 등을》 cast (*a net*); (끈을) braid; (휘갑을》 hem (*the edges*).
치다¹¹ ①《전보를》 send (*a telegraph, cable*). ②《시험을》 take; sit for; undergo (*an examination*).
치다¹² 《화투를》 shuffle (섞다); play (놀다).
치다꺼리 ①《일처리》 management; control; taking care of. ¶ ~하다 manage; deal with. ¶ 손님 ~를

치닫다 run up; go up.

치대다 put (stick, fix) on the upper part. ¶판자를 ~ fix a piece of board on the upper part 《of a wall》.

치도곤(治盜棍) a club (for the lash). ¶~ 을 안기다 club (cudgel) 《a criminal》; (비유적) teach 《a person》 a lesson; give 《a person》 a 「raw deal (hard time)」.

치둔(痴鈍) ¶~ 한 dull-witted; stupid.

치뜨다 raise; lift 《one's eyes》.

치뜨리다 toss up; throw up.

치런치런 ① (넘칠락말락) full to the brim; brimfully. ② (스칠락말락) ¶치맛자락을 ~ 늘어뜨리고 걷다 walk dragging one's skirt along.

치렁거리다 ① (드린 물건이) hang down; droop; dangle. ② (시일이) be put off from day to day; be prolonged; drag on.

치레 embellishment; adornment; decorating. ~하다 embellish; adorn; decorate; dress (smarten) up. ¶겉 ~ 로만은 for mere form's sake / 옷 ~ 를 하다 dress 《oneself》 up; be gaily dressed; be in one's (Sunday) best.

치료(治療) medical treatment; (a) cure. ~하다 treat; cure. ¶~를 받다 be treated 《for cancer》; undergo medical treatment / 눈을 ~ 받다 have one's eyes treated / ~ 받으러 다니다 go to 《a doctor》 for treatment / ~ 중이다 be under medical treatment / 물리 ~ physical therapy / 재 ~ retreatment / ~ 법 a remedy; a cure / ~비 a doctor's fee (bill) / ~ 효과 remedial (therapeutic) value; (a medicine with) a curative effect.

치루(痔瘻) 〖醫〗 an anal fistula.

치르다 ① (돈을) pay (off). ¶값을 ~ pay the price 《for an article》 / 계산을 ~ pay a bill / 어떤 대가를 치르고서라도 at any price (cost). ② (겪다) undergo; go through; experience; suffer. ¶시험을 ~ undergo an examination / 감기를 ~ suffer a cold / 홍역을 ~ (비유적) have a bitter experience; have a hard time of it. ③ (큰 일을) carry out; go through; have; observe; entertain 《guests》. ¶생일 잔치를 ~ hold (give) a birthday party / 화학 실험은 어디에서 치러지느냐 Where are chemical experiments carried out? / 결혼식을 ~ have a wedding ceremony.

치름 떨다(齒―) ① (인색) grudge; be awfully stingy. ② (격분) grit one's teeth; grind one's teeth with indignation.

치마 a skirt. ¶치맛바람 the swish of a skirt; the influence of women's power / 치맛자락 the edge (end, tail) of the skirt / ~의 주름을 pleat (gather) on a skirt / ~를 입다 put on (wear) a skirt.

치매(痴呆) 〖醫〗 dementia; imbecility. 노인성 ~ senile dementia. ‖ ~ 노인 a dotard; an old man (woman) in one's dotage.

치명(致命) ¶~ 적인 fatal; mortal; deadly / 그것은 한국의 대미 수출에 ~ 적인 타격을 주었다 It dealt a deathblow (fatal blow) to Korean exports to America. / 나는 ~ 적인 실수를 저질렀다 I made a fatal blunder. ‖ ~ 상 a mortal (fatal) wound; a fatal blow / ~ 상을 입다 be mortally wounded; receive a fatal blow.

치밀(緻密) ¶~ 한 precise; minute; fine; close; elaborate / ~ 한 계획 a careful (an elaborate) plan.

치밀다 (위로 밀다) push (shove, thrust) up; (감정이) surge; swell well up. ¶분노가 ~ feel the surge of anger; flare up; fly into a rage.

치받이 an upward slope; an ascent. ¶~ 를 올라가다 breast (struggle with) an ascent.

치받치다 (감정이) surge; swell; well up; (밀을) prop; bolster (prop) up; support.

치부(致富) ~하다 make money; become rich; amass a fortune.

치부(恥部) (남녀의) the private (intimate) parts (of the body); (창피한 부분) a disgrace; a shameful part 《of the city》.

치부(置簿) ~하다 keep books; keep accounts; enter 《an item》 in a book. ¶…앞으로 ~ 하다 charge (put) 《a sum》 to 《a person's》 account. ‖ ~ 책 an account book.

치사(致死) ¶~ 의 fatal; mortal; deadly / 과실 ~ 〖法〗 homicide (death) by misadventure / 상해 ~ (a) bodily injury resulting in death. ‖ ~ 량 a fatal dose.

치사(致謝) ~하다 thank 《a person》 for 《his kindness》; express one's gratitude.

치사스럽다(恥事―) be disgraceful; shameful; dishonorable; (인열) (be) mean; dirty. ¶치사스러운 꼴을 당하다 be put to shame;

치산 bring disgrace upon *oneself* / 치사스럽게 굴다 behave meanly (shamefully).

치산(治山) afforestation. ~하다 reserve (protect) forest; afforest. ‖ ~치수 antiflood (flood control) afforestation; conservation of rivers and forests / ~치수 사업 anti-erosion project.

치산(治産) management of one's property.

치살리다 praise (*a person*) to the skies; speak highly of. 「ing.

치석(齒石) tartar. ~ 제거 scal-

치성(致誠) 《정성을 다함》 devotion; loyal service; 《신불에의》 sacrificial service 《to spirits》. ¶ ~을 드리다 offer a devout prayer.

치세(治世) a reign; a rule; a regime. ¶ 엘리자베스 2세의 ~ 중에 in (during) the reign of Elizabeth II.

치수(一數) measure; dimensions; size. ¶ ~대로 according to the measurements / ~를 재다 measure; take the measurements (*of*).

치수(治水) flood control; river improvement. ~하다 embank a river; control floods. ‖ ~공사 embankment works; levee works; flood prevention works.

치수(齒髓) 〔解〕 the dental pulp. ‖ ~염 pulpitis.

치술(治術) 《치료술》 the medical (healing) art; 《정치술》 administrative skill; statecraft.

치신(위신) prestige; dignity. ¶ ~을 잃다 lose (impair) one's dignity; degrade *oneself*. 「nerve.

치신경(齒神經) 〔解〕 the dental

치신사납다 (be) shameful; indecent; outrageous; unseemly. ¶ 치신사납게 굴다 behave indecently (unseemly).

치신없다 (be) undignified; unbecoming; ungentlemanly. ¶ 치신없는 짓 an undignified act / 치신없이 굴다 behave unseemly; act disho-

치아(齒牙) ☞ 이. 「norably.

치안(治安) public peace and order; public security. ¶ ~을 유지하다 (혼란케 하다) maintain (disturb) public order. ‖ ~감 Senior Superintendent General / ~경찰 the peace (security) police / ~당국 law enforcement authorities / ~방해 the disturbance of public peace / ~방해자 a peace-breaker / ~유지 the maintenance of public peace / ~정감 Chief Superintendent General / ~총감 Commissioner General.

치약(齒藥) toothpaste; dental

치열(齒列) a row (set) of teeth. ¶ ~이 고르다 (고르지 않다) have a regular (an irregular) set of teeth. ‖ ~교정 straightening of irregular teeth.

치열(熾烈) ~하다 (be) severe; keen; intense. ¶ ~한 경쟁 a keen (sharp) competition / ~한 논쟁 a heated argument.

치외법권(治外法權) extraterritorial rights; extraterritoriality.

치욕(恥辱) disgrace; shame; dishonor; insult(모욕). ¶ 국가의 ~ a disgrace to the country / ~을 참다 pocket an insult; bear insult / …을 ~이라고 생각하다 feel shame at 《*doing*》; be ashamed of 《*doing*》.

치우다 ① 《정리》 put 《*things*》 in order; set (put) 《*a room*》 to rights; tidy (up); 《제거》 take away; remove; get rid of; clear away (off). ¶ 방을 ~ straighten *one's* room up / 길에 있는 돌을 ~ remove stones from the road / 식탁 위에 있는 접시들을 ~ clear away dishes on the table. ② 《딸을》 give 《*one's daughter*》 in marriage; marry 《*one's daughter*》 off.

치우치다 《기울다》 lean (incline) 《*to, toward*》; 《편파적》 be partial 《*to*》; be biased (one-sided); have a partiality 《*for*》; be prejudiced. ¶ 치우친 생각 a biased (one-sided) view / 《김 따위가》 한 쪽으로 치우쳐 있다 be leaning to one side.

치유(治癒) healing; cure. ~하다 cure; heal; recover. ¶ 상처는 곧 ~될 것이다 The wound will soon heal up. ‖ ~기(期) convalescence / ~력 healing power / ~을 a cure rate.

치음(齒音) a dental sound.

치이다¹ ① 《덫에》 get trapped (entrapped); be caught in a trap. ¶ 곰이 덫에 ~ a bear is trapped. ② 《피륙의 올이》 lose (*its*) weave; 《솜이》 form into a lump; lump up to one side.

치이다² 《차바퀴에》 run over (down); knock down; be hit. ¶ 차에 ~ be hit (run over, knocked down) by a car.

치이다³ 《값이》 cost; amount to; be worth. ¶ 비싸게 (싸게) ~ come expensive (cheap) / 그것들은 개당 400원씩 쳐였다 They cost four hundred *won* apiece.

치자(治者) the sovereign; the ruler; a person in power.

치자(梔子) 〔植〕 gardenia seeds. ¶ ~나무 a Cape jasmine; a gardenia.

치장(治粧) decoration; adornment; embellishment; 《화장》 *one's* make-up. ~하다 decorate; adorn; pret-

치적(治績) 〖업적〗 (the results of an) administration; administrative achievements. ¶그의 ~을 기념하여 in commemoration of his remarkable executive services….
치정(癡情) foolish [blind] love [passion]; illicit love [affair]; lust. ‖ ~에 의한 범죄 a crime of passion. ‖ ~살인 a sex [scandalous] murder (case).
치조(齒槽) 〖解〗 an alveolus. ¶~농루〖膿漏〗〖醫〗 pyorrhea alveolaris.
치죄(治罪) punishment of crime. ~하다 punish; penalize (for).
치중(置重) ~하다 put [lay] emphasis (stress) on (a matter); emphasize; attach importance to (something); give priority to (something). ¶문법에 ~하다 lay stress [emphasis] on grammar.
치즈 cheese. ¶~ 덩어리 a chunk of cheese. ‖ ~버거 a cheeseburger / ~케이크 (a) cheesecake.
치질(痔疾) 〖醫〗 hemorrhoids; piles. ¶수〔암〕~ external [internal] hemorrhoids.
치켜세우다 extol [praise] (a person) to the skies; sing the praises of (a person); speak highly of; pay a tribute to.
치키다 raise; lift; heave; boost; pull [draw] up. ¶눈을 치켜 뜨다 lift [up] one's eyes; cast an upward glance / 치맛자락을 치켜올리다 tuck up the skirt.
치킨(닭고기) chicken. ‖ ~수프 〔라이스〕 chicken soup (and rice) / ~프라이 a fried chicken.
치통(齒痛) (a) toothache. ¶~이 나다 have a toothache; suffer from a toothache.
치하(治下) ~의 under the rule [reign] (of). ‖ 엘리자베스 여왕의 영국 England under the reign of Queen Elizabeth.
치하(致賀) congratulations; compliments. ~하다 congratulate a person (on something); celebrate (an event). ¶~하는 글 a congratulatory address / …을 ~하기 위하여 in honor [celebration] of… / 노고를 ~하다 show appreciation of (a person) for his services / 대학 졸업을 ~하다 congratulate (a person) on his graduation from college.
치한(癡漢) 〖호색한〗 a molester of women; a wolf; a masher 〖俗〗.
치환(置換) 〖數·化〗 metathesis; substitution; replacement; transposition. ~하다 metathesize; substitute; replace; transpose.
칙령(勅令), **칙명**(勅命) a Royal command [order].
칙사(勅使) a Royal messenger [envoy]. ¶~ 대접을 하다 treat (a person) very courteously; give (a person) a red carpet treatment 〖美〗.
칙칙하다 (be) somber; dull; dark. ¶칙칙한 빛깔 a dark color / 칙칙한 청색 sordid blue / 칙칙해 보이다 look dark and dull.
친(親) ① 〖혈육〗 one's own; one's blood. ¶~형제 one's blood brothers. ② 〖친일〗 pro-. ¶~미의 pro-American / ~여 후보 a pro-government candidate.
친가(親家) 〖=〗 친정(親庭).
친고(親告) ‖ ~죄 an offense subject to prosecution only upon complaint (from the victim).
친교(親交) friendship; friendly relations. ¶~를 맺다 form a close friendship (with) / ~를 도모하다 promote friendly relations (with, between) / 우리는 서로 오랜 ~가 있다 We have been friendly with each other for many years.
친구(親舊) a friend; a companion; company 〖교우〗; a pal 〖口〗. ¶학교 ~ a schoolmate / 낚시 ~ a fishing companion / 술~ a drinking pal / 여자 ~ a girlfriend / 평생(平生) ~ a lifelong friend / …와 ~가 되다 make friends with… / 좋은 〔나쁜〕 ~ 사귀다 keep good [bad] company.
친권(親權) 〖法〗 parental authority [prerogatives]. ‖ ~을 행사하다 exercise parental power. / ~자 a person in parental authority.
친근(親近) ~하다 (be) close; familiar; friendly. ¶~한 사이다 be on good [familiar] terms with… / 두 사람은 매우 ~한 사이다 They are very friendly with each other. ‖ ~감 a sense of closeness [affinity] (~감을 느끼다 feel very close to (her)).
친기(親忌) a memorial service for one's parent.
친남매(親男妹) one's real [blood] brothers and sisters.
친목(親睦) friendship; amity; friendliness. ¶서로의 ~을 도모하다 cultivate [promote] mutual friendship. ‖ ~회 a social [get-together] meeting 〖美〗.
친밀(親密) ¶~한 friendly; close; intimate / ~한 벗 a close friend / ~한 사이다 be on friendly terms (with); be very good

친부모(親父母) one's real parents.
친분(親分) acquaintanceship; friendship. ¶ ~이 있다 be acquainted 〔familiar〕 《with》 / ~이 생기다 become acquainted 〔familiar〕 《with》 / ~이 두터워지다 get more closely acquainted.
친상(親喪) mourning for a parent. ¶ ~을 당하다 have a parent die; mourn be bereaved of a parent.
친서(親書) an autograph letter; a personal letter.
친선(親善) friendly relations; friendship; goodwill. ¶ 국제적 ~ international goodwill / ~을 도모하다 promote friendly relations 《between》; strengthen the ties of friendship 《between》. ‖ ~ 경기 a friendly 〔goodwill〕 match / ~ 방문 a goodwill visit / ~사절 a goodwill mission 〔envoy〕.
친손자(親孫子) one's real 〔blood〕 grandchild.
친숙(親熟) 〔익숙함〕 ~하다 be familiar 《with》; be well acquainted 《with》.
친아버지(親―) one's real father.
친애(親愛) ~하는 dear; beloved; darling / ~하는 김군〔편지 서두에서〕My dear (Mr.) Kim / ~하는 형으로부터〔편지 끝에〕Your affectionate brother.
친어머니(親―) one's real mother.
친영(親英) ¶ ~의 pro-British 《policies》. ~주의 Anglophilism.
친위대(親衛隊) the Royal guards; the bodyguards 《to the King》.
친일(親日) ¶ ~의 pro-Japanese. ‖ ~파 a pro-Japanese (group).
친자식(親子息) one's real 〔blood〕 children.
친전(親展)〔서신에서〕Confidential; Personal; To be opened by addressee only.
친절(親切) (a) kindness; goodwill; a favor. ¶ ~한 kind; good; kind-hearted; obliging; friendly / …에게 ~히 대하다 be kind to; show kindness to; treat 《a person》 with kindness / ~하게도 … 하다 be kind 〔good〕 enough to do; have the kindness to do; be so kind as to do / ~해 보이는 kind(ly)-looking / 여러 가지로 ~히 해 주셔서 감사합니다 Thank you for all you've done for me. / 그 남자는 ~하게도 나에게 자리를 양보해 주었다 The man was kind enough to offer his seat to me.
친정(親政) royal governing in person. ~하다 《the King》 govern in person.
친정(親庭) the house of one's wife's parents; one's maiden home. ¶ 아내는 ~에 가 있다 My wife has been staying with her parents.
친족(親族) a relative; a relation; kinfolk. ¶ 직계 ~ lineal 〔close〕 relatives / 방계 ~ collateral 〔distant〕 relatives. ‖ ~ 관계 kinship / ~법 the Domestic Relations Law / ~ 회의 a family council.
친지(親知) an acquaintance; a friend.
친척(親戚) a relative; a relation; a kinsman; kinfolk(복수). ¶ 먼〔가까운〕~ a distant 〔near〕 relation〔relative〕. ‖ ~ 관계 relationship; kinship / 일가 ~ one's kith and kin; relatives in blood and law.
친필(親筆) an autograph; one's own handwriting;〔法〕 a holograph. ¶ ~의 autographic.
친하다(親―) ① 〔가깝다〕 (be) friendly; familiar; close. ¶ 친한 벗 a great 〔close〕 friend / 친한 사이다 be on good 〔friendly〕 terms with. ② 〔사귀다〕 become friendly 〔familiar〕 《with》.
친할머니(親―) one's real 〔blood〕 grandmother. 〔grandfather.
친할아버지(親―) one's real 〔blood〕
친형(親兄) one's real elder brother.
친화(親和) harmony. ‖ ~력 〔化〕 affinity 《for》.
친히(親―) ① 〔친하게〕 intimately; familiarily; in a friendly way. ¶ ~ 사귀다 be in close association with. ② 〔몸소〕 personally; in person; directly(직접). ¶ ~ 방문하다 pay a visit in person / ~ 보다 see 《a thing》 with one's own eyes. 〔enth.
칠(七) seven. ¶ 제 ~ (의) the seventh.
칠(漆)〔재료〕paints; lacquer (옻);〔칠하기〕coating; painting; lacquering (옻칠). ¶ ~ 조심〔게시〕Wet Paint.
칠각형(七角形) a heptagon.
칠기(漆器) lacquer(ed) ware; lacquer(work).
칠떡거리다 drag; draggle; trail. ¶ 칠떡칠떡 trailing; dragging.
칠렁거리다 overflow; slop 〔spill〕 over.
칠렁하다 be full to the brim.
칠레 Chile. ¶ ~의 Chilian; Chilian. ‖ ~사람 a Chilean; a Chilian / ~초석〔鑛石〕〔鑛〕 Chile saltpeter; cubic niter.
칠면조(七面鳥) a turkey; a turkey cock (수컷); 〔hen〕(암컷). ¶ 크리스마스에 ~ 요리를 하다 roast a turkey on Christmas day.
칠보(七寶)〔佛〕 the Seven Treasures (*i.e.* gold, silver, lapis,

crystal, coral, agate, and pearls. ‖ ~自己 *cloisonné*《프》.
칠석(七夕) the seventh day of the seventh lunar month.
칠순(七旬) ① 《70일》 seventy days. ② 《70살》 seventy years of age.
칠십(七十) seventy. ¶ 제~(의) the seventieth.
칠야(漆夜) a pitch-dark night.
칠월(七月) July 《생략 Jul.》. 「er」.
칠장이(漆-) a painter 《lacqu-
칠전팔기(七顚八起) not giving in to adversity; standing firm in difficult matters. ~하다 never give in to adversity.
칠칠하다 ¶ 칠칠치 못하다 be untidy 《slovenly》; be careless 《loose》 ¶ 칠칠치 못한 계집 a draggle-tailed woman; a slattern.
칠판(漆板) a blackboard. ¶ ~을 지우다 wipe 《clean》 a blackboard. ‖ ~을 지우는 솔 a chalk 〔blackboard〕 eraser.
칠하다(漆-) 《페인트를》 paint; 《니스를》 varnish; 《벽을》 plaster; 《옷을》 lacquer. ¶ 갓 칠한 freshly-painted 〔-varnished〕 / 벽을 희게 ~ paint a wall white.
칠현금(七絃琴) a seven-stringed harp; a heptachord.
칠흑(漆黑) ¶ ~ 같은 pitch-black; jet-black; coal-black / ~ 같은 밤 a jet-black 〔pitch-dark〕 night.
칡〔植〕 an arrowroot. ¶ ~덩굴 arrowroot vines 〔runners〕.
칡소 a striped cow 〔ox〕.
침 spittle; saliva 《타액》. ¶ ~을 뱉다 spit; salivate / 아무의 얼굴에 ~을 뱉다 spit in *a person's* face.
침(針) ①《가시》a thorn. ②《바늘》a needle; 《시계의》 a hand.
침(鍼) a needle 《도구》; acupuncture 《침술》. ¶ ~을 놓다 treat 《*a person*》 with acupuncture / ~은 뻔 허리나 뻣뻣해진 어깨 치료에 이용된다 Acupuncture is used in the treatment for a strained back or stiff shoulders. ‖ ~술 마취 anesthesia by acupuncture / ~의(醫) an acupuncturist.
침강(沈降) sedimentation. ~하다 precipitate. ‖ ~속도 sedimentation rate 《혈액의》.
침공(侵攻) an attack; an invasion. ~하다 attack; invade.
침구(寢具) bedding; bedclothes.
침구(鍼灸) acupuncture and moxibustion. ¶ ~술 the practice of acupuncture and moxibustion / ~술사(師) a practitioner in acupuncture and moxibustion.
침낭(寢囊) a sleeping bag.
침노하다(侵擄-) invade; encroach 《on》; make inroads 《on, into》. ¶ 이웃 나라를

~ make inroads into the neighboring country.
침다그다(沈-) cure 《a persimmon》 in salt water.
침대(寢臺) a bed; 《열차·배의》 a 〔sleeping〕 berth; a bunk 《미》. ¶ 나는 상단 〔하단〕 을 좋아합니다 《침대권을 살 때》 I prefer an upper 〔a lower〕 berth, please. ‖ ~권 a berth ticket / ~요금 a berth charge / ~차 a sleeping car; a sleeper.
침략(侵略) aggression; invasion. ~하다 invade; make a raid 《upon》. ¶ 직접〔간접〕 ~ a direct 〔an indirect〕 invasion / 이웃 나라들을 여러 차례에 걸쳐 ~하다 invade the neighboring countries several times. ‖ ~국 an aggressor nation / ~군 an invading army / ~자 an aggressor; an invader / ~전쟁 an aggressive war; a war of aggression / ~주의 an aggressive policy / ~행위 an act of aggression.
침례(浸禮) 〔宗〕 baptism by immersion. ‖ ~교도 a Baptist / ~교회 the Baptist Church.
침로(針路) 《나침반에 의한》 a course; 《항공기의》 a flight path. ¶ ~를 〔잘못〕 잡다 take a 〔wrong〕 course / ~를 바꾸다 change 〔alter, turn〕 *one's* course / ~에서 벗어나다 swerve 〔deviate〕 from *one's* course / ~을 …으로 향하게 하다 direct 〔set〕 *one's* course toward 〔for〕… / ~을 남서로 잡다 take 〔beat〕 a southwesterly course.
침모(針母) a seamstress; a needlewoman.
침목(枕木) 《철도의》 a 〔railroad〕 tie 《미》; a crosstie; a sleeper 《영》.
침몰(沈沒) sinking; foundering. ~하다 sink; go down; founder《승객에서》. ¶ ~시키다 sink 《a ship》 / 승객 40명을 태우고 ~하다 sink with forty passengers on board. ‖ ~선 a sunken ship.
침묵(沈默) silence. ~하다 become 〔fall〕 silent; say nothing. ¶ ~시키다 silence; put 《*a person*》 to silence / ~을 지키다 remain 〔keep〕 silent; hold *one's* tongue / ~을 깨다 break silence / 웅변은 은, 침묵은 금이다 《俗談》 Speech is silver, silence is golden.
침범(侵犯) 《영토의》 invasion; 《권리의》 violation, infringement. ~하다 invade; violate. ¶ 영공~ a violation of another country's territorial air / 국경 ~ a border violation / 어선들이 영해를 ~했다 Fishing boats invaded the country's territorial waters.
침삼키다(-침을) swallow saliva; 《먹고 싶어》 *one's* mouth waters

《at》; 《욕정으로》 lust 《after, for》; 《부러워》 be envious 《of》.
침상(針狀) 《바늘모양》 ~의 needle-shaped; pointed. ‖ ~엽(葉) a needle (leaf).
침상(寢狀) a bed-floor. ☞ 침대.
침소(寢所) a bedchamber; a bedroom.
침소봉대(針小棒大) (an) exaggeration. ~하다 exaggerate; overstate 《one's case》. ‖ ~의 exaggerated; high-flown; bombastic.
침수(浸水) inundation; flood. ~하다 be flooded; be inundated; be under water. ¶ 50호 이상의 가옥이 마루 위까지 ~되었다 Over a fifty houses were flooded above the floors. ¶ ~가옥 flooded houses; houses under water / ~지역 the flooded (inundated) area.
침술(鍼術) acupuncture. ‖ ~사 an acupuncturist.
침식(侵蝕) erosion; corrosion. ~하다 erode 《the cliff》; eat away 《at the bank》; gain 《encroach》 on 《the land》 (바닷가). ¶ 파도에 ~되어 동굴이 되었다 Eroded by waves, it formed a cave. ‖ ~작용 erosion; erosive action.
침식(寢食) ¶ ~을 같이 하다 live under the same roof / ~을 잊고 간호하다 nurse 《a sick person》 devotedly / ~을 잊고 공부에 ~을 absorbed in one's studies.
침실(寢室) a bedroom; a bedchamber.
침엽(針葉) 〖植〗 a needle (leaf). ‖ ~수 a needle-leaf tree; a conifer.
침울(沈鬱) melancholy; gloom. ¶ ~한 melancholy; gloomy; dismal; depressed / ~한 얼굴 a gloomy face; a dismal look / ~해 지다 feel (be) depressed.
침윤(浸潤) ~하다 be saturated 《with》; permeate 《through》; infiltrate 《into》.
침입(侵入) 《적국 따위에》 (an) invasion; inroad; 《급습》 a raid; 《남의 땅에》 trespass; intrusion. ~하다 invade; make an inroads 《into enemy country》; raid; 《남의 집에》 break into; force one's way into. ¶ 적군은 서부 지방에 ~했다 The enemy has invaded the western provinces. / 어젯밤 그녀의 집에 도둑이 ~했다 A burglar broke into her house last night. ‖ ~군 an invasion force / ~자 an invader; an intruder; a trespasser.
침쟁이(鍼一) ① ☞ 침술사. ② 《아편쟁이》 an opium addict.
침전(沈澱) precipitation; deposition. ~하다 settle; precipitate; be deposited. ‖ ~농도 precipitation density / ~물 a precipitate; a sediment; a deposit / ~조(槽) a settling tank / ~지(池) a settling basin.
침착(沈着) self-possession; composure. ~한 self-possessed; calm; cool; composed / ~한 태도 a calm attitude / ~하게 행동하다 act with coolness; play it cool.
침체(沈滯) stagnation; dullness. ¶ ~된 a dull (slack) market / ~된 분위기 stagnant atmosphere / ~해 있다 be stagnant; be slack (dull, inactive) / 경기가 ~되었다 The market is stagnant (dull).
침침하다(沈沈 —) 《장소 따위가》 (be) gloomy; dim; dark; dimly-lit / 《날씨가》 (be) cloudy; dull / 《눈이》 (be) misty; dim; obscure. ¶ 침침청한 방 a dimly-lit room / 침침한 날 a gloomy (cloudy) day / 나이를 먹으면 눈이 침침해진다 Our sight grows dim with age.
침통(沈痛) ¶ ~한 grave; sad; serious / ~한 어조로 in a sad (serious, grave) tone / 그녀는 ~한 얼굴로 방에서 나왔다 She came out of the room with a grave look.
침투(浸透) penetration; infiltration. ~하다 penetrate (infiltrate) 《into, through》. ¶ 무장 간첩의 ~ infiltration of armed agents. ‖ ~성(性) 〖化〗 osmosis; permeability / ~작용(압) osmotic action (pressure) / ~작전 an infiltration operation.
침팬지 〖動〗 a chimpanzee.
침하(沈下) sinking; subsidence. ~하다 subside; sink. ¶ 도로의 지반이 약 10센티 ~했다 The road subsided (sank) about 10 centimeters.
침해(侵害) infringement; violation; encroachment 《무단 침입》. ~하다 violate; infringe 《upon》; encroach 《trespass》 upon. ¶ 저작권의 ~ infringement of copyright / 사생활에 ~에 화를 내다 get angry at one's privacy being violated / 나는 나의 기득권을 ~당하고 싶지 않다 I don't want my vested interests to be trespassed upon. ‖ ~자 a trespasser; an invader.
침향(沈香) 〖植〗 aloes wood.
침흘리개 a slobberer; a driveler.
칩거(蟄居) ~하다 keep indoors; live in seclusion; confine oneself in one's house.
칫솔(齒 —) a toothbrush.
칭병(稱病) ~하다 pretend to be ill.
칭송(稱頌) praise; laudation. ~하다 admire; praise highly.
칭얼거리다 fret; whine; be pee-

칭찬(稱讚) praise; admiration 《of》. ~하다 praise; admire; speak highly of. ¶ ~의 말 words of praise; a compliment / ~할 만한 admirable; praiseworthy; laudable / ~을 받다 be praised; win〔receive, enjoy〕praise / 장군은 부하들의 용기를 ~했다 The general praised his men for their bravery.

칭탁(稱託) ~하다 make a pretext of; use 《*a traffic accident*》 as a pretext. ¶ …을 ~하여 under the pretext of….

칭하다(稱—) 《부르다》 call; name; designate. ¶ 남궁이라 칭하는 사람 a man named Namgung; a Mr. Namgung.

칭호(稱號) a name; a title; a degree. ¶ 아무에게 ~를 수여하다 confer a title on *a person* / 그에게 명예 교수의 ~가 주어졌다 He was given〔granted〕the title of professor emeritus.

친인척 계보표 (family tree)

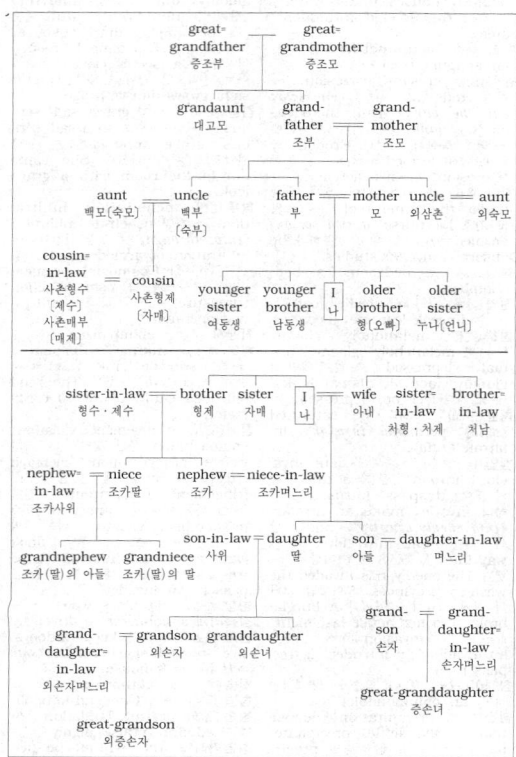

ㅋ

카 a car. ☞ 차, 자동차. ¶ ~스테레오 a car stereo (system) / ~페리 a car ferry / ~ 레이스 a car (motor) race / ~섹스 (have) sex in the car.

카나리아 [鳥] a canary (bird).

카네이션 [植] a carnation.

카누 a canoe. ¶ ~를 젓다 paddle a canoe / ~로 강을 내려가다 go down a river by canoe. ‖ ~경조(競漕) a canoe race.

카니발 [사육제] a carnival.

카드 a card; a slip (of paper); (트럼프) (playing) cards; (크레디트카드 따위의) a (credit) card. ¶ 전화[버스, 현금] ~ a telephone (bus, cash) card / ~에 의한 분류 classification by cards / ~에써 넣다 note [put] down 《something》 on a card / 트럼프 ~를 나눠주다 [뒤섞어] deal [shuffle] the cards / 이 ~로 지불이 가능합니까 Do you accept this (credit) card? ‖ ~목록 a card catalog / ~색인 a card index / ~케이스 a card case.

카드놀이 card playing; a card game. ¶ ~를 하다 play cards / ~를 하는 사람 a cardplayer / ~에서 지다 [이기다] win (lose) at cards.

카드뮴 [化] cadmium (기호 Cd). ¶ ~에 중독되다 be poisoned by cadmium.

카디건 [스웨터] a cardigan.

카라반 a caravan. ¶ ~슈즈 (a pair of) hiking boots.

카랑카랑하다 (날씨가) (be) clear and cold; (목소리가) (be) clear and high-pitched.

카레 curry. ¶ ~가루 curry powder / ~라이스 curry and rice / ~요리를 하다 curry; curried food.

카르테 [醫] a (clinical) chart; a Karte.

카르텔 [經] a cartel. ¶ ~을 결성하다 form a cartel; cartelize / ~을 해체하다 dissolve (break up) a cartel 《of steel companies》 / 불황 ~ a (business) recession cartel. ‖ ~협정 a cartel agreement.

카리스마 charisma. ¶ ~적인 charismatic / 그 정치가는 매우 ~적이다 The politician is very charismatic.

카리에스 [醫] caries. ¶ 척추 ~ [醫] spinal caries.

카메라 a camera. ¶ 수중 ~ an underwater camera / 아무에게 ~를 겨냥하다 point (aim) one's camera at 《a person》/ 풍경을 ~에 담다 take a photograph of the scenery / ~에 필름을 넣다 load a camera / ~ 플래시 세례를 받다 be bathed in camera flashes. ‖ ~맨 a cameraman / ~앵글 a camera angle.

카메룬 〈아프리카의〉 Cameroon; Cameroun.

카멜레온 [動] a chameleon.

카무플라주 a camouflage; 〈비유적〉 a smoke screen. ~하다 camouflage 《a military vehicle》; disguise 《one's real intentions》.

카바레 a cabaret.

카바이드 [化] (calcium) carbide.

카본 carbon. ‖ ~복사 a carbon copy / ~지(紙) carbon paper.

카빈총(—銃) a carbine.

카세트 a cassette. ¶ 라디오 프로를 ~에 녹음하다 tape-record the radio program on a cassette. ‖ ~녹음기 a cassette tape recorder / ~테이프 a cassette tape.

카스텔라 sponge cake.

카우보이 a cowboy.

카운슬링 counseling.

카운터 (service) counter.

카운트 a count; counting. ~하다 count. ¶ 그는 ~ 나인에 일어섰다 He got up at the count of nine.

카이로 〈이집트의 수도〉 Cairo.

카이저수염(—鬚髥) a Kaiser (an upturned) mustache.

카지노 a casino.

카키색(—色) khaki color.

카타르[1] 〈나라이름〉 (the State) of Qatar.

카타르[2] [醫] catarrh. ¶ ~성의 catarrhal.

카탈로그 a catalog(ue). ¶ ~에 올리다 put (place) 《an item》 on (in) a catalog / 상품의 가격을 기재한 ~ a priced catalog / ~의 게재된 값 the list price.

카테고리 [論] a category. ¶ …의 ~에 들다 belong to (fall under) the category of.

카투사 KATUSA. (◀ Korean Augmentation Troops to the United States Army)

카트리지 a cartridge. ¶ ~를 갈아 끼우다 replace the cartridge.

카페 a café (프); a coffee house (shop); a bar.

카페인 [化] caffeine. ¶ ~을 뺀 커피 caffeine-free coffee.

카페테리아 (셀프서비스의) a cafeteria.

카펫 a carpet. ¶ ~을 깔다 lay (spread) a carpet; carpet 《a

카피 《복사》 a copy. ¶ 이 서류를 두 장 ~해 주시오 Please make two copies of this document. / ~라이터 《광고 등의》 a copywriter / ~라이트 《저작권》 a copyright.

칵칵거리다 keep coughing (to clear one's throat).

칵테일 a cocktail. ‖ ~ 드레스 a cocktail dress / ~ 파티 a cocktail party.

칸 ① 《면적》 *kan*(=36 square feet); a room. ¶ 두 ~ 방 a two-*k'an* room. ② 《방을 세는 단위》 a room. ¶ 네 ~ 집 a four-room house. ③ 《칸막이》 a partition. ¶ ~을 막다 partition 《a room》. ④ 《빈 곳》 a blank (space). ¶ 빈 ~에 알맞은 전치사를 써 넣으시오 Fill (in) the blanks with appropriate prepositions.

칸나 《植》 a canna.

칸막이 《막음》 partitioning; screening; 《막은 것》 a partition; a screen; ~하다 partition 《a room》; partition off 《with a screen》. ¶ ~벽 a partition wall.

칸초네 *canzone* (이).

칸타빌레 《樂》 cantabile.

칸타타 《樂》 cantata.

칸트 Kant. ¶ ~의 Kantian. ¶ ~ 철학 Kantism / ~ 학파 the Kantists.

칼 《썰거나 자르는》 a knife; a kitchen knife(식칼); a table knife(식탁용); a cleaver(토막을 내는); 《무기용의》 a sword; a saber (군도); a dagger (단검); 《날이 시퍼렇게 선》 a well-sharpened knife / ~이 잘 들다〔안 들다〕 the knife cuts well〔won't cut〕/ ~을 뽑다 draw a sword / ~을 휘두르다 brandish a sword / ~을 차다 wear〔carry〕 a sword (at one's side). ‖ ~ 날 the blade〔edge〕 of a knife〔sword〕/ ~등 the back of a sword / ~집 a sheath.

칼[2] 《형구》 a cangue; a pillory. ¶ ~ 씌우다 put 《a person》 in the pillory / ~을 쓰다 wear a cangue.

칼국수 noodles cut out with a kitchen knife.

칼깃 a flight feather; the pinion.

칼라 《옷깃》 a (shirt) collar.

칼로리 a calorie; a calory. ¶ ~가 높은〔낮은〕 식품 food of high〔low〕 caloric content / ~가 (價)가 높다 have a high calorific value / 하루 3,000 ~의 식사를 섭취하다 take a 3,000 caloric diet per day. ‖ ~ 계산 calorie counting (~계산을 하다 count calories) / ~ 섭취량 (a) caloric intake / ~원(源) a caloric source / ~함유량 caloric [calory] content.

칼륨 《化》 potassium (기호 K).

칼리 《化》 *kali*; kalium: potassium.

칼리지 a college.

칼맞다 be stabbed; suffer a sword-.

칼부림 wielding a knife〔sword〕; bloodshed(유혈극). ~하다 wield a knife; stab〔cut〕 at 《a person》. ¶ ~으로 번지다 develop into bloodshed; shed blood.

칼슘 calcium (기호 Ca). 「(sword).

칼자국 a scar from a knife

칼자루 the handle 《of a knife》; the haft 《of a dagger》; the hilt 《of a sword》.

칼잡이 a butcher(고깃간의); a swordsman(검객). 「ting.

칼슙 cutting; ~하다 cut: do cut-

칼춤 (perform) a sword dance.

칼질하다 ☞ 칼질하다.

칼코등이 a sword-guard.

칼판 《一板》 a chopping〔kitchen〕 board.

캄캄하다 《어둡다》 (be) utterly dark; pitch-dark; (as) dark as pitch; 《암담하다》 (be) dark; gloomy; 《사물에》 be ignorant 〔uninformed〕 of; be poorly〔badly〕 informed; be a stranger 《to》. ¶ 캄캄한 밤 a pitch-dark night / 시국에 대해 ~ be ignorant of the current situation / 앞날이 ~ The future looks gloomy. / 나는 이 부근 지리에 ~ I am a stranger here.

캉캉 《춤》 *cancan* (프).

캐나다 Canada. ¶ ~의 Canadian. ‖ ~사람 a Canadian.

캐다 ① 《파내다》 dig up〔out〕; unearth. ¶ 금을 ~ dig gold. ② 《묻다》 inquire 〔probe〕 into; dig 〔pry, delve〕 into; poke and pry. ¶ 철저히 ~ probe 《a matter》 to the bottom / 비밀을 ~ probe into a secret.

캐디 《골프》 a caddy. ¶ ~ 노릇을 하다 caddy 《for a golfer》.

캐러멜 a caramel.

캐럴 a Christmas carol.

캐럿 a carat; a karat. ¶ 18~의 금 18 karats fine / 5~의 다이아몬드 a 5-carat diamond.

캐묻다 ask inquisitively; be inquisitive 《about》; make a searching inquiry. ¶ 시시콜콜이 ~ inquire of 《a person》 about every detail of 《a matter》.

캐비닛 a (steel) cabinet.

캐비아 caviar(e).

캐비지 《양배추》 a cabbage.

캐빈 a cabin.

캐스터네츠 《樂》 castanets.

캐스트 《배역》 the cast (of a play).

캐스팅보트 the casting vote.

캐시미어 kashmir; cashmere.

캐처 [野] a catcher. 「catch.
캐치 a catch. ¶ ~볼을 하다 play
캐치프레이즈 a catch phrase.
캐터펄트 a catapult.
캐터필러 a caterpillar.
캐피털리즘 capitalism.
캔디 a candy.
캔버스 《화포》 a canvas. ‖ ~ 틀 a stretcher.
캔슬 《취소》 cancellation. ~ 하다 cancel. ¶ 예약을 ~ 하고 싶습니다 I'd like to cancel my reservation.
캘린더 a calendar. ¶ ~를 한 장 떼어내다 tear a sheet off the calendar. 「phor injection.
캠퍼 camphor. ‖ ~ 주사 a camphor injection.
캠퍼스 a campus. ¶ 대학 ~ a college campus / 그 교수님은 ~에서 거주하신다 The professor lives on campus.
캠페인 a campaign. ¶ 판매 촉진 ~ 을 벌이다 conduct a campaign for sales promotion.
캠프 a camp. ¶ 우리는 그 숲에서 ~ 를 했다 We camped (out) in the woods. ‖ ~ 생활 a camp life / ~ 파이어 a campfire.
캠핑 camping. ¶ 산으로 ~ 가다 go camping in the mountains. ‖ ~ 용품 a camping outfit; camping equipment(장비 전체) / ~ 장 a camping ground / ~ 촌 a camping village.
캡 a cap.
캡슐 a capsule. ¶ 타임 ~ a time capsule / 우주 ~ a space capsule.
캡틴 a captain (of a team).
캥거루 [動] a kangaroo.
커녕 far from 《doing》; anything but; not at all; aside (apart) from; (…은 말할 것도 없고); to say nothing of; not to mention; not to speak of. ¶ 즐겁기는~ 불쾌하다 Is it anything but pleasant. / 저축은 ~ 그날그날 살아가기 바쁘다 Far from saving money, I can hardly make my living. / 그는 영어는 ~ 한국어도 모른다 He does not know Korean, to say nothing of English.
커닝 cribbing; cheating in an examination. ~ 하다 cheat in (on) an examination; crib. ‖ ~ 페이퍼 a crib.
커다랗다 (be) very big(large, great); huge; enormous. ¶ 커다란 손실을 입다 a great loss / 커다란 잘못을 짓다 make a big (huge) mistake / 커다란 집을 짓다 build an enormous house.
커다래지다 ☞ 커지다.
커리큘럼 《교과과정》 a curriculum; a course of study. ¶ 그 학교는 ~ 의 범위가 넓다 The school has a wide curriculum.
커머셜 메시지 《라디오・TV의》 a commercial message. ¶ 약품의 ~ a commercial for a drug / TV의 ~ a TV commercial.
커뮤니케이션 (a) communication. ¶ 매스~ mass communication / ~의 단절 a breakdown in communication; a communication gap / 노사간의 ~ 향상을 도모하다 encourage (try to develop) better communication between management and workers.
커미션 a commission. ¶ 매상에 대해 10%의 ~ 을 받다 get a commission of 10 percent on the sales made.
커버 《덮개》 a cover; a jacket(책 따위의); 《경기에서》 covering. ‖ ~ 의 자 a chair cover.
커버하다 《경기에서》 cover 《3rd base》; back up; 《보충》 cover 《a loss》; make up for 《a loss》. ¶ 회사는 자산의 일부를 매각하여 손실을 커버하려 했다 The company tried to make up its losses by selling some of its assets.
커브 《곡선》 a curve; a curved line; 《도로의》 a bend; a curve; [野] a curve ball. ¶ 아웃~ an out-curve / 인~ an incurve / 이 도로는 급~ 가 많다 This road has a lot of sharp curves (turns). / (차가) 급~ 를 돌다 make a sharp turn / 길은 우측으로 완만한 ~를 이루고 있다 The road curves gently to the right. / 그는 날카로운 ~ 볼을 던졌다 He pitched a sharply breaking curve.
커스터드 custard.
커지다 《크기・부피 따위가》 get bigger; grow larger; increase in size; expand; 《성장하다》 grow (up); 《키가》 get (become) taller; 《중대해지다》 get (become) serious; assume serious proportions. ¶ 너무 커진 도시 an overgrown city / 담이 ~ become emboldened / 세력이 ~ increase in power; gain in influence / 부피가 ~ increase in volume / 이 도시는 지난 2, 3년 동안에 커졌다 This town has grown large (big) during the past few years. / 사건이 커질 것 같다 The affair threatens to become serious.
커트 《테니스・탁구 등에서》 a cut. ~ 하다 cut 《a ball》.
커튼 a curtain; drapes 《美》. ¶ 창 ~ a window curtain / ~ 을 치다 [닫다] close (draw) the curtains / ~ 을 젖히다 [열다] pull (draw) the curtains back (aside); open the curtains. ‖ ~ 콜 을 받다 take a curtain call).
커틀릿 a cutlet. ¶ 닭고기 [돼지고기] ~ a chicken (pork) cutlet.
커프스 cuffs. ¶ ~ 버튼 cuff (sleeve)

커피 coffee. ¶ ~를 끓이다 make coffee / ~을 블랙으로 마시다 drink coffee black. ‖ ~세트 a coffee set / ~숍 a coffee shop / ~포트 a coffeepot.

컨덕터 a conductor.

컨디션 condition. ¶ ~이 좋다(나쁘다) be in(out of) condition.

컨베이어 a conveyor; a conveyer. ‖ ~시스템 a conveyor system.

컨설턴트 a consultant. ¶ 경영 ~ a management consultant.

컨테이너 a container. ‖ ~트럭(열차) a container truck(train) / ~선 a container ship(vessel).

컨트롤 control. ¶ ~하다 control. ‖ ~이 좋다(나쁘다) 《야구에서》 have good(poor) control. / ~타워 a control tower.

컬 a curl (of hair). ¶ ~이 풀리다 go out of curl.

컬러 (a) color. ¶ ~방송 《텔레비전의》 colorcasting; a colorcast / ~사진 a color photo / ~텔레비전 color television; 《수상기》 a color television (set) / ~필름 a color film.

컬컬하다 (be) thirsty.

컴컴하다 《어둡다》 (be) dark; black; somber; gloomy; dim; 《마음이》 (be) dark; secretive; blackhearted; insidious.

컴퍼스 《제도용의》 (a pair of) compasses; 《나침의》 the mariner's compass.

컴퓨터 a computer. ¶ ~화(化)하다 computerize / 데이터를 ~에 입력하다 put(feed) data into a computer / 정보를 ~로 처리하다 process information with a computer / 이 기계는 ~로 제어되고 있다 This machine is controlled by computer. / ~로 제어되는 기계 a machine under computer control; a computer-controlled machine. ‖ ~게임 a computer game / ~그래픽스 computer graphics / ~기술 computer technology / ~바이러스 a computer virus; a bug / ~백신(왁친) a computer vaccine / ~범죄 a computer crime / ~언어 a computer language / ~제어장치 a computer-control system / ~칩 a computer chip / ~통신(망) a computer network / ~해커 a (computer) hacker.

컴프레서 a compressor.

컵 a cup; a trophy(우승컵); 《잔》 a glass; a drinking cup. ¶ 물 한 ~ a glass of water / 우승~을 주다 honor 《a winner》 with a trophy / 종이 ~ a paper cup.

컷 《판화》 a (wood)cut; an illustration; a picture; 《영화에서의》 cutting; a cut; 《삭제》 a cut; 《머리의》 a cut. ~하다 cut; cross out; strike off. ¶ ~을 넣다 fill 《the space》 with a cut / 몇몇 장면을 ~하다 cut some scenes from the film / 임금을 5% ~하다 cut the wages by five percent / 머리를 짧게 ~하다 have one's hair cut short.

케이블 a cable. ¶ 해저 ~ a submarine cable / 지하 ~ an underground cable. ‖ ~카 a cable car / ~텔레비전 cable television.

케이스 《상자·사례》 a case. ¶ 유리 ~ a glass case / 드문 ~ a rare case / 긴급을 요하는 ~에는 in case of emergency / ~ 바이~로 according to the case; depending on the case. ‖ ~스터디 a case study.

케이에스 KS. (◀Korean Standards). ‖ ~마크 a KS mark / ~상품 KS goods.

케이오 K.O. (◀knock-out)

케이크 a cake. ¶ ~ 한 조각 a piece(slice) of cake / 생일 ~ a birthday cake.

케임브리지 Cambridge.

케첩 ketchup; catsup; catchup. ¶ 토마토 ~ tomato ketchup.

케케묵다 《낡다》 (be) old; antiquated; 《구식》 (be) old-fashioned: out of date; 《진부하다》 (be) hackneyed; timeworn. ¶ 케케묵은 이야기 an old story / 케케묵은 생각 old-fashioned(outdated) ideas.

켕기다 ① 《팽팽해짐》 be stretched tightly; be strained; become tense(taut). ¶ 힘줄이 ~ have a strain on the sinew; feel a sinew taut. ② 《마음이》 feel a strain; feel ill at ease; have something on one's conscience. ③ 《팽팽하게 함》 strain; stretch; draw tight; make taut.

켜 a layer; a ply. ¶ 여러 ~를 쌓다 heap up in several layers.

켜다 ① 《불을》 light; kindle; turn (switch) on 《an electric lamp》. ② 《성냥을 ~ strike a match. ③ 《들이켜다》 finish off 《one's drink》; drink up 《one's beer》; drain 《a cup》. ③ 《톱으로》 saw. ¶ 통나무를 켜서 판자를 만들다 saw a log into planks. ④ 《누에고치를》 spin 《threads》 off 《a cocoon》. ⑤ 《거지개를》 stretch 《oneself》. ⑥ 《악기를》 play (on) 《the violin》.

켤레 a pair. ¶ 양말 두 ~ two pairs of socks.

코[1] 《일반적》 a nose; a trunk (코끼리의); a muzzle(개, 말 따위의); a snout (돼지의). ¶ ~가 막히다 one's nose is stuffed (stopped) up / ~를 후비다 pick one's nose / ~가 높다(낮다) have a

long [flat] nose. ② 〈콧물〉 (nasal) mucus; snivel; snot. ¶ ~를 흘리고 있는 아이 a child with a running nose / ~를 훌쩍이다 snivel / ~를 흘리다 one's nose runs; run (at) the nose / ~를 풀다 blow one's nose. 　[a knot.
코*〈편물(編物)의〉 a stitch; 〈그물의〉
코감기(一感氣) (have) a cold in the head [nose]; snore loudly.
코골다 snore. ¶ 드르렁드르렁
코끝 the tip of the nose. ¶ ~에 칼을 들이대다 present [thrust] a knife under one's nose.
코끼리 an elephant. ¶ 수[암] ~ a bull [cow] elephant.
코냑 〈술〉 cognac.
코너 a corner.
코넷 〈樂〉 a cornet.
코대답(一對答) ~하다 answer indifferently [nonchalantly].
코드 ① 〈줄〉 〈전깃줄〉 an electric cord. ¶ 연장 ~ an extension cord / TV의 ~ 를 꽂다 [빼다] plug in [unplug] the TV. ② 〈암호〉 a code. ¶ 자동검사 ~ 〈컴퓨터의〉 a self-checking code / ~화하다 code. ‖ ~네임 a code name / ~북 a code book.
코딱지 nose dirt [wax]; dried nasal mucus.
코떼다 get snubbed [humbled, rejected]; be put to shame.
코뚜레 a nose ring [duroy suit.
코르덴 corduroy. ¶ ~ 양복 a cor-
코르셋 a corset; stays 〈英〉.
코르크 (a) cork. ¶ ~ 마개 a cork stopper.
코뮈니케 a communiqué 〈프〉. ¶ 공동 ~ a joint communiqué / ~ 를 발표하다 issue [read] a communiqué.
코뮤니스트 a communist.
코뮤니즘 communism.
코미디 a comedy.
코미디언 a comedian.
코믹 a comic 〈희극〉; comics 〈만화〉.
코바늘 a crochet hook [needle].
코발트 〈化〉 cobalt 〈기호 Co〉. ¶ ~〈색〉의 cobaltic. ‖ ~폭탄 a cobalt bomb.
코방귀 뀌다 pooh-pooh; snort [sniff] at; treat 〈a person〉 with contempt.
코방아 찧다 fall flat on one's face.
코브라 〈動〉 a cobra.
코사인 〈數〉 a cosine 〈생략 cos〉.
코사크 a Cossack; the Cossacks 〈민족〉. ¶ ~기(一旗)병 a Cossack.
코세다 (be) stubborn; headstrong.
코스 a course〈과정·과정〉; a route; a lane〈경주 등의〉. ¶ 골프 ~ a golf course / 제1 ~ Lane No. 1〈수영 등의〉 / 대학 진학 〈취직〉 ~ a college [vocational] course / 프랑스 요리의 풀 ~ a full-course meal of French cuisine.
코스닥 〈證〉 Korea Securities Dealers Automated Quotations〈생략 KOSDAQ〉〈한국의 벤처 기업 육성을 위해 미국의 나스닥(NASDAQ)을 본떠 1996년에 설립된 주식 시장〉.
코스모스 〈植〉 a cosmos.
코스트 〈원가·가격〉 cost. ¶ ~를 다운하다 reduce [cut] costs; bring about a reduction in costs / 우리들 생산 ~를 줄였다 We reduced the cost of production. ‖ ~업 an increase in costs / ~인플레이션 cost-push inflation.
코웃음 치다 sneer.
코일 a coil. 　[citizen of the world.
코즈머폴리턴 a cosmopolitan; a
코즈메틱 a cosmetic.
코치 〈훈련〉 coaching; 〈사람〉 a coach. ~하다 coach 〈a team〉.
코카서스 Caucasus; Caucasia. ¶ ~ 사람 a Caucasian.
코카인 〈化〉 cocain(e). ‖ ~중독 cocainism.
코카콜라 Coca-Cola; Coke 〈俗〉.
코코넛 〈植〉 a coconut.
코코아 〈음료〉 cocoa. ¶ ~를 마시다 drink [have] cocoa.
코크 coke. 　[cot].
코탄젠트 〈數〉 a cotangent〈생략 cot〉.
코털 hairs in the nostrils. ¶ ~을 뽑다 pull hairs out of one's nostrils.
코트 ① 〈양복 상의〉 a coat; a jacket; an overcoat〈외투〉. ¶ ~를 입다 [벗다] put on [take off] a coat. ② 〈테니스 따위의〉 a 〈tennis〉 court. 　[hagen.
코펜하겐 〈덴마크의 수도〉 Copen-
코프라 〈야자유의 원료〉 copra.
코피 (a) nosebleed. ¶ ~를 흘리다 bleed at [from] the nose; one's nose bleeds. 　[sniveler.
코흘리개 a snotty-nosed kid; a
콕 stinging [thrusting, poking, pricking] hard [sharply, fast]. ¶ ~ 바늘로 ~ 찌르다 prick with a needle.
콘덴서 〈電〉 a condenser.
콘덴스트밀크 condensed milk.
콘도미니엄 a condominium.
콘돔 a condom; a rubber 〈俗〉.
콘비프 corn[ed] beef.
콘서트 a concert.
콘센트 〈電〉 an (a wall) outlet.
콘체르토 〈樂〉 a concerto.
콘크리트 concrete. ¶ ~ 벽 a concrete wall / 도로를 ~로 포장하다 concrete the road / 이것은 철근 ~ 건물이다 This is a ferroconcrete [reinforced concrete] building. ‖ ~ 믹서 a cement mixer / ~블록 a concrete block / ~포장 concrete pavement.
콘택트렌즈 〈wear〉 a contact lens.
콘트라베이스 〈樂〉 a contrabass.
콘트라스트 a contrast.

콜걸 a call girl《美俗》.
콜드게임〔野〕a called game.
콜드크림 cold cream.
콜레라 cholera. ¶ 진성~ malignant cholera. ‖ ~예방주사 (an) anticholera injection.
콜로이드〔化〕colloid.
콜로타이프 a collotype. 〔loidal.
콜록거리다 keep coughing(hacking).
콜론〔經〕a colon.
콜론〔이중점〕a colon(기호 :).
콜타르 coal tar; tar. ¶ ~를 칠하다 tar.
콜호스〔집단농장〕a *kolkhoz*〔러〕; a collective farm.
콤마 a comma(기호 ,); 〔數〕a decimal point. 〔vester〕.
콤바인〔탈곡기〕a combine(har-
콤비 a combination. ¶ ~와 ~가 되다 (form a) pair with… / 두 사람은 명~다 They are good partners for each other.
콤비나트 an industrial complex; *kombinat*〔러〕. ¶ 석유 화학 ~ a petrochemical complex.
콤팩트 a compact. ‖ ~디스크 a compact disk(생략 CD).
콤플렉스〔心〕a complex;《열등감》an inferiority complex. ¶ 그는 대학 출신자에게 ~를 느낀다 He feels inferior to university graduates.
콧구멍 the nostrils; the nares.
콧김 the breath from the nose.
콧날 ¶ ~이 선 (a person) with a shapely (clear-cut) nose. 〔tune〕.
콧노래 ¶ ~를 부르다 hum a song
콧대 ¶ ~가 높다 be conceited; be puffed up《*with pride*》/ ~가 세다 be haughty / ~가 세다 be self-assertive; be defiant / ~를 꺾다 humble 《*a person's*》pride; snub《*a person*》down; take《*a person*》down a peg (or two) 〔nose.
콧등 the ridge(bridge) of the
콧물 snivel. ¶ ~을 흘리다 snivel; have a running nose / 그 애는 ~을 흘리고 있다 The boy's nose is running.
콧소리 a nasal (tone of) voice; a (nasal) twang. ¶ ~로 말하다 speak 「through *one's* nose」《with a twang》.
콧수염 a moustache; a mustache《美》. ¶ ~을 기르다 grow a mustache.
콩〔植〕beans; a pea《완두》; a soybean《대두》. ¶ ~과의 식물 a legume / ~을 볶는 듯한 기관총 소리가 들렸다 A cracking(rattle) of machine guns was heard. / ~밭에서 꽃이 나랴 An onion will not produce a rose. / ~심은 데 ~나고 팥 심은 데 팥 난다《俗談》Don't expect the extraordinary. *or* Like father, like son. ‖ ~가루 soybean flour / ~기름 (soy)bean oil / ~깍지 bean chaff / ~깻묵 bean cake; soybean (oil) meal / ~꼬투리 a bean pod.
콩국 soybean soup.
콩국수 soybean noodle.
콩나물 bean sprouts. ¶ ~교실 an overcrowded classroom / ~국 bean sprout soup / ~밥 rice cooked with bean sprouts.
콩밥 bean-mixed rice. ¶ ~(을) 먹다《비유적 표현》be put to prison.
콩비지 bean-mixed rice cake.
콩새〔鳥〕a Korean hawfinch.
콩자반 beans boiled in soysauce.
콩쿠르 a *concours*〔프〕; a contest. ¶ 음악 ~ a musical contest.
콩튀듯하다 jump up with anger; be hopping mad. ¶ 분해서 ~ stamp *one's* feet with frustration《vexation》.
콩트 a *conte*〔프〕; a short story.
콩팥 the kidney. ☞ 신장.
콰르텟〔樂〕a quartet.
쾅 strongly; hard; violently. ¶ ~밀다 push with a sudden jerk / 단검을 ~ 찌르다 thrust a dagger《*into*》/ 숨이 ~ 막히다 be choked; be stiffed / 이상한 냄새가 코를 ~ 찔렀다 An offensive smell assailed *one's* nostrils.
쾈쾈 gushingly. ¶ ~ 흘러나오다 gush out.
쾅 boom; bang; thud. ¶ 문을 ~ 닫다 shut a door with a bang / ~하고 떨어지다 fall with a thud.
쾌 ¶ 북어 한 ~ a string of twenty dried pollacks.
쾌감(快感) a pleasant sensation; an agreeable feeling; ecstasy. ¶ ~을 느끼다 feel good: have a good《nice》feeling / 말할 수 없는 ~을 느끼다 feel an indescribable pleasure.
쾌거(快擧) a brilliant《spectacular》achievement《feat》.
쾌남아(快男兒) a jolly good fellow.
쾌도(快刀) a sharp knife《sword》. ¶ ~난마하다 cut the Gordian knot; solve a knotty problem readily.
쾌락(快樂) pleasure; enjoyment. ¶ 육체적 ~ carnal pleasure / ~을 쫓다 seek pleasure / ~에 빠지다 be given to pleasure. ‖ ~주의 epicureanism; hedonism / ~주의자 a hedonist; an epicurean.
쾌보(快報) good news; glad tidings; a joyful report. 〔event.
쾌사(快事) a pleasant《joyful》
쾌속(快速) high speed. ¶ ~의 high-speed; fast; speedy; swift. ‖ ~선 a fast boat《ship》.
쾌승(快勝) ~하다 win a sweeping《an overwhelming》victory《over》; win easily.
쾌유(快癒) complete recovery《from

illness); ~하다 recover completely 《from》; make a complete recovery 《from》; get [be] quite well again; be completely restored to health.
쾌재(快哉) ¶ ~를 부르다 shout for joy (delight); cry out "bravo".
쾌적(快適) ~하다 (be) agreeable; pleasant; comfortable. ¶ ~한 버스 a comfortable bus / ~한 여행 a pleasant trip / 따뜻하고 ~한 작은 방 a warm and cozy little room.
쾌조(快調) an excellent condition. ¶ ~이다 be in top [the best] condition; be in good shape / ~로 나아가다 make good (steady) headway; progress steadily.
쾌차(快差) ☞ 쾌유.
쾌척(快擲) ~하다 give 《a fund》 willingly; make a generous contribution.
쾌청(快晴) fine [fair and clear] weather.
쾌활(快活) ~하다 (be) cheerful; merry; lively; jolly. ¶ ~하게 cheerfully; merrily; livelily; with a light heart.
쾌히(快―) 《즐거이》 pleasantly; cheerfully; delightfully; agreeably; 《기꺼이》 willingly; gladly; readily. ¶ ~ 승낙하다 agree (consent) willingly [readily].
쾨쾨하다 ☞ 퀴퀴하다.
쿠냥 a Chinese girl.
쿠데타 a coup d'état《프》; a coup. ¶ 군부~ a military coup / 무혈 ~ a bloodless coup / ~를 일으키다 carry out a coup d'état.
쿨렁쿨렁하다 be not full.
쿠바 Cuba. ¶ ~의 Cuban / ~사람 a Cuban.
쿠션 a cushion. ¶ ~이 좋은 의자 a soft, comfortable chair / ~ 역할을 하다 cushion; act as a buffer.
쿠페 《승합차》 a coupé; a coupe.
쿠폰 a coupon; a voucher (식권 따위). ‖ ~권(제) a coupon ticket [a cook.
쿡 《요리인》 a cook.
쿨롬 [電] a coulomb. [system).
쿨룸 [電] a coulomb.
쿨룩거리다 keep coughing (hacking).
쿨리 a coolie; a cooly.
쿨쿨 z-z-z; snoring. ¶ ~ 자다 sleep snoring.
쿵 with a thud (bang, bump, plump). ¶ ~하고 떨어지다 fall plump (heavily) / 벽에 ~하고 부딪다 bump against the wall.
퀀셋 [建] a Quonset hut 《美》.
퀘스천마크 a question mark.
퀭하다 《눈이》 (be) hollow. ¶ 퀭한 눈 hollow eyes.
퀴닌 [藥] quinine.
퀴즈 a quiz. ¶ ~쇼(프로) a quiz show [program].
퀴퀴하다 (be) musty; fusty; stale;

fetid; stinking. ¶ 퀴퀴한 냄새 a musty [an offensive] smell.
큐 《당구의》 a cue.
큐비즘 [美術] cubism.
큐피드 Cupid.
크기 size; dimensions; magnitude (덩치); volume(용적).
크나크다 (be) very big; huge.
크낙새 [鳥] a Korean redheaded woodpecker.
크다¹ 《모양이》 (be) big; large; 《부피가》 (be) bulky; massive; 《소리가》 (be) loud; 《위대》 (be) great; grand; 《강대》 (be) mighty; powerful; 《거대》 (be) gigantic; huge; 《광대》 (be) vast; extensive; spacious; 《심하다》 (be) severe; heavy; 《마음이》 (be) generous; liberal. ¶ 큰 잘못 a big [great] mistake; a grave error / 큰 인물을 a great man / 큰 손해 heavy loss / 큰 목소리로 in a loud voice / 야망이 ~ have a great ambition / 마음이 ~ be broad-minded / 《돈에 대해》 손이 크다 be liberal with one's money / 서울은 세계에서 가장 큰 도시 중의 하나다 Seoul is one of the biggest (largest) cities in the world. / A는 B보다 어느만큼 큰가 How much larger is A than B?
크다² 《자라다》 grow (up). ¶ 다 큰 아이 a grown-up child.
크라운 a crown.
크래커 《비스킷》 a cracker.
크랭크 a crank. ¶ ~를 돌리다 crank 《an engine》; turn a crank. ‖ ~축 a crankshaft.
크랭크업 [映] ~하다 finish filming.
크랭크인 [映] ~하다 start filming.
크레디트 a credit. ¶ ~를 설정하다 establish [set up, open] a credit. ‖ ~카드 a credit card (~ 카드로 ⋯을 사다 buy something on credit).
크레오소트 creosote.
크레용 《a picture in》 crayon.
크레인 a crane; a derrick (배의).
크레졸 cresol. ¶ ~ 비눗물 saponated solution of cresol.
크레파스 crayon pastel.
크렘린 the Kremlin.
크로켓 a croquétte《프》.
크롤 [水泳] crawl. ¶ ~ 해엄을 치다 swim the crawl.
크롬 chrome; chromium (기호 Cr).
크리스마스 Christmas; Xmas. ¶ ~를 축하하다 celebrate Christmas / ~ 선물을 하다 give [present] a Christmas gift. ‖ ~이브 Christmas Eve / ~카드(선물) a Christmas card [present] / ~트리 a Christmas tree.
크리스천 a Christian.
크리켓 cricket.
크림 《식품》 cream; 《화장품》 (face, hand) cream. ¶ ~모양의 creamy;

큰곰자리

큰곰자리 [天] the Great Bear.

큰기침하다 clear one's throat loudly; say a big 'ahem'.

큰길 a main street (road); a highway; a thoroughfare.

큰누이 one's eldest sister.

큰달 a long month.

큰대 (一大) ☞ 큰집.

큰돈 a large sum (of money); a lot of money; a great cost (경비). ¶ ~을 벌다 make a lot of money / ~을 들여 그 집을 샀다 He bought the house at a great cost.

큰딸 the eldest daughter.

큰마음 ① (대망) great ambition; great hopes (expectations). ¶ ~이 되려는 ~을 먹다 be ambitious to become…. ② (아량) broad-mindedness; generosity; liberality. ¶ ~ 쓰다 act generously. ③ (어려운 결심을 하고) ¶ ~ 먹고 daringly; boldly; resolutely / ~ 먹고 …하다 venture (dare) to do; take the plunge and do; make so bold as to do / ~ 먹고 저의 마음을 털어 놓겠습니다. 나는 당신을 사랑합니다 I dare to express my feelings. I love you.

큰물 a flood; an inundation. ¶ ~ 나다 be in flood; be flooded.

큰불 a big (great) fire; a conflagration.

큰비 a heavy rain(fall). ☞ 호우.

큰사랑 (一舍廊) (넓은) a large guest room; (웃어른의) the living room of one's elders.

큰상 (一床) (잔치의) a reception table (offered bride or groom); (커다란) a large dinner table.

큰소리 ① (큰소리) a loud voice. ¶ ~로 in a loud voice; loudly. ② (야단침) a shout; a yell; a roar; a bawl; a brawl. ¶ 아무에게 ~치다 shout (roar, rave) at a person. ③ (허풍) talk big (tall); bragging. ¶ ~치다 talk big (tall); brag.

큰솥 a cauldron; a big kettle.

큰아기 (맏딸) one's eldest daughter; (처녀) a (grown-up) girl.

큰아버지 (백부) one's father's elder brother; one's uncle.

큰어머니 the wife of one's father's elder brother; one's aunt.

큰언니 one's eldest sister.

큰오빠 one's eldest brother.

큰일 ① (큰 사업) a big enterprise (business, plan). ¶ ~을 계획하다 plan a big enterprise. ② (중대사) a matter of grave concern; a serious matter; a great trouble; a disaster; a crisis (위기). ¶ ~ 나다 a serious thing happens; a serious problem pops up / ~이 되다 get (become) serious; assume serious proportions / ~이다 This is serious! ③ (예식·잔치 따위) a big ceremony (banquet); a wedding. ¶ ~을 치르다 go through (carry out) a wedding.

큰절 (여자의) a formal deep bow. ¶ ~하다 make a formal deep bow.

큰집 ① (종가) the head family (house). ② (맏형의) the house of one's eldest brother. ③ (형무소) pillory.

큰칼 (형구) a big cangue; a large pillory.

코코다치다 have bitter experiences; have a hard time of it; pay dearly (for). ¶ 못 믿을 사람을 믿었다가 코코다쳤다 I made a bitter mistake of putting my faith in someone who couldn't be trusted.

큰형 a man's eldest brother.

클라리넷 [樂] a clarinet. ‖ ~주자 (奏者) a clarinetist.

클라이맥스 the climax. ¶ 연극은 ~에 이르렀다 The play has reached its climax.

클라이밍 (등산) climbing.

클래식 a classic; (the) classics. ¶ ~음악 classical music.

클랙슨 a horn; a klaxon. ¶ ~을 울리다 sound one's klaxon; honk.

클러치 [機] a clutch. ¶ ~를 밟다 step on the clutch / ~를 넣다 put in the clutch / ~를 늦추다 release the clutch.

클럽 (단체) a club; a clubhouse (건물). ¶ ~에 들다 join a club. ‖ ~활동 club (extracurricular) activities (학교의) / ~회비 club dues / ~회원 a member (of a club).

클레임 [經] a claim (for damages). ¶ ~을 제기하다 make (bring forward) a claim (for compensation) / ~에 응하다 meet a claim for damages.

클로로다인 [藥] chlorodyne. 「tin.

클로로마이세틴 [藥] chloromyce-

클로로포름 [藥] chloroform.

클로르 [化] chlorine; *Chlor* (獨) (기호 Cl). ← 염소(塩素).

클로버 (four-leaf) clover.

클로즈업 [映] a close-up. ¶ 배우의 얼굴을 ~하다 take a close-up of an actor's face / 그 문제가 크게 ~ 되었다 The problem was highlighted.

클리닝 cleaning; laundering. ¶ 드라이 ~ dry cleaning / 코트를 ~ 하러 보냈다 I sent my coat to the laundry (cleaner's).

클립 a (paper) clip; (머리의) a curling pin; a curler. ¶ 서류를

~으로 끼우다 clip the papers together.
큼직하다 (be) quite big. ¶큼직한 집 quite a big house / 큼직한 글씨로 쓰다 write large / 신문에 큼직한 광고를 내다 run a large ad in the newspaper. [winnow.
키¹ a winnow. ~ 질하다
키² 《배의》 a rudder (키판); a helm (키자루); a (steering) wheel. ~를 잡다 steer; be at the wheel.
키³ 《신장》 stature; height. ¶ ~ 가 크다 (작다) be tall (short) / ~ 가 자라다 grow in height; grow taller / ~ 가 180센티가 되다 attain a stature of 180 centimeters tall / ~를 재다 measure *one's* height.
키⁴ a key. ¶자동차의 ~ a car key; a key to *one's* car. ‖ ~ 보드 a keyboard / ~스테이션 a key station 《美》 / ~펀처 a keypuncher / ~포인트 a main point / ~홀더 a key ring (둥근형의).
키다리 a tall fellow.
키순《-順》 ¶ ~ 으로 서다 stand [line up] in order of [according to] height.

키스 a kiss; a smack (쪽소리 내는). ~하다 kiss. ¶손에 ~하다 kiss (*a person's*) hand / 이마에 [입에] ~하다 kiss (*a person*) on the forehead (mouth).
키우다 ① 《양육하다》 bring up; rear; raise; foster; nurse;《동·식물을》 breed; raise. ¶아이를 우유[모유]로 ~ raise a child on the bottle (at the breast). ②《양성·육성하다》 train; bring up; promote; cultivate. ¶외교관으로 ~ train (*a person*) for the diplomatic service / 담력을 ~ cultivate courage / 국내 산업을 ~ promote domestic industry / 재능을 ~ cultivate *one's* talent.
키잡이《조타수》 a helmsman; a steersman.
키퍼 a keeper. ¶골 ~ a goalkeeper.
킥《蹴》 a kick.
킥오프《蹴》 a kickoff.
킥킥거리다 giggle; titter; chuckle.
킬로 a kilo. ¶ ~ 그램 a kilogram / ~리터 a kiloliter / ~ 미터 a kilometer.
킬킬거리다 ☞ 킥킥거리다.
킹사이즈 ~의 king-size(d).
킹킹거리다 whine; whimper.

컴퓨터

1. **여러 형태의 컴퓨터**
   슈퍼컴퓨터 a supercomputer / 대형컴퓨터 a mainframe / 미니컴퓨터 a minicomputer / 워크스테이션 a workstation / 개인용 컴퓨터 a personal computer / 포터블 컴퓨터 a portable computer / 랩톱 컴퓨터 a laptop computer / 탁상용 컴퓨터 a desktop computer / 마이크로컴퓨터 a microcomputer.

2. **하드웨어 (hardware) 관련 용어**
   아이씨《집적회로》 IC; an integrated circuit / 엘시디《액정 디스플레이》 LCD; a liquid crystal display / 엘에스아이《대규모 집적회로》 LSI; a large-scale integration / 카드 판독기 a card reader / 주변 장치 a peripheral (device) / 단말기 a terminal / 바코드 판독기 a barcode reader / 하드디스크 a hard (fixed) disk / 광디스크 an optical disk / 플라즈마 디스플레이 a plasma display / 마이크로프로세서 a microprocessor / 모뎀 a modem / 라이트 펜 a light pen.

3. **소프트웨어 (software) 관련 용어**
   응용프로그램 an application (program) / 전문가 시스템 an expert system / 운영 체제 OS; an operating system / 인공지능 시스템 AI system; an Artificial Intelligence system / 디스크 운영체제 DOS; a disk operating system / 버그《잘못》 a bug / 공개 소프트웨어 public-domain software / 프로그래밍 언어 a programming language.

4. **대표적인 소프트웨어의 종류**
   게임 프로그램 a game (entertainment) program / 통신 프로그램 a communications program / 데이터베이스 관리자 a database manager / 탁상 출판 프로그램 a desktop publishing program / 스프레드시트 a spreadsheet / 워드 프로세서 a word processor.

5. **기타, 일반적인 용어**
   출력 output / 액세스《접근》 access / 아스키 ASCII《◀ American Standard Code for Information Interchange》 / 어셈블러 an assembler / 아날로그 analog / 접속《인터페이스》 interface / 온라인 on-line / 입력 input / 기계어 a machine language / 문자 a character / 행 a line / 부호《코드》 a code / 명령 a command / 컴파일러 a compiler / 호환의 compatible / 서브루틴 a subroutine / 순차 액세스 sequential access / 시뮬레이션 simulation / 문자열 a string / 데이터베이스 a database / 바코드 bar code / 로드《적재》 load / 화일 a file / 하드 카피 a hard copy.

타(他) the rest; the other; others; another (thing). ‖ ~가(家) another house (family) / ~도(道) other provinces / ~의 추종을 불허하다 be peerless (unrivaled); be without a peer; have no equal; be second to none.

타(打) a dozen. ☞ 다스.

타개(打開) ~하다 break through (a deadlock); get (tide) over (a difficult situation); overcome; find a way out of (the difficulties). ‖ 난국 ~를 위해 의논하다 discuss how to overcome difficulties / 정부는 재정위기에 대한 ~책을 찾아야 한다 The government has to find a way out of the financial crisis. ‖ ~책 a way out (of depression); a countermeasure.

타격(打擊) a blow; a hit; a shock (충격); a damage (손해); 〔野〕 batting. ‖ 치명적 ~ a fatal (mortal) blow / ~을 주다 deal a blow (at, to); give a blow (to) / ~을 받다 (입다) be hit; suffer a blow; be shocked (at, by). ‖ ~상〔野〕 the batting award / ~순〔野〕 the batting order / ~연습 batting practice / ~왕〔野〕 the batting champion; the leading hitter / ~전〔野〕 a game with many hits; slugfest 《美口》.

타결(妥結) a (compromise) settlement; an agreement (협정). ~하다 come to terms (with); reach an compromise agreement (with); make a compromise agreement (with); settle (with). ‖ ~의 조건 terms of agreement / 교섭은 원만히 ~되었다 The negotiations reached a peaceful and satisfactory settlement. ‖ ~점 a point of agreement.

타계(他界) ~하다 ☞ 죽다①.

타고나다 be born (with, into); be gifted (endowed) (with). ‖ 타고난 born; inborn; natural; inherent / 타고난 시인(노름꾼) a born poet (gambler) / 타고난 권리 one's birthright. 〔vince〕.

타고장(他─) another place (province).

타관(他─) a foreign land; a place away from home; another place. ‖ ~사람 a stranger.

타구(打球) 〔野〕 batting (치기); a batted ball.

타구(唾具) a spittoon; a cuspidor.

타국(他國) a foreign country; an alien [a strange] land; another country. ‖ ~의 foreign; alien. ‖ ~인 a foreigner; an alien.

타기(唾棄) ~하다 throw away in disgust. ‖ ~할 detestable; disgusting; abominable.

타내다 get (from one's elders); obtain. ‖ 아버지께 용돈을 ~ get pocket money from one's father.

타닌(化) tannin (acid).

타다¹ ① 《불에》 burn; be burnt; blaze. ‖ 활활 타고 있는 불 a blazing fire; roaring flames (소리를 내며) / 새빨갛게 타고 있는 석탄 burning (live) coals / 불꽃을 내며 ~ burn with a flame / 잘 ~ burn easily; catch fire easily; be (in)flammable / 잘 안 ~ do not burn easily / 타고 있다 be burning; be on fire; be in flame / 다 타버리다 be burnt out; burn itself out. ② 《눋다》 scorch; be (get) scorched (charred, burned). ‖ 밥이 ~ the rice is scorched. ③ 《볕에》 be sunburnt; be tanned with the sun. ‖ 햇볕에 탄 얼굴 a suntanned face. ④ 《마음·정열 등이》 burn; blaze; glow; 《애가》 be agonized (anxious, anguished). ‖ 타오르는 정열 burning passion / 애타게 기다리다 wait anxiously. ⑤ 《목이》 be parched with thirst.

타다² 《액체에》 put in; add; 《섞다》 mix; blend; dilute; 《분순물을》 dissolve (용해시키다). ‖ 위스키에 물을 ~ mix (dilute) whisky with water / 커피에 브랜디를 ~ lace one's coffee with brandy / 물에 소금을 ~ dissolve salt in water.

타다³ ① 《달것에》 ride (a horse, a bicycle); take (a bus, a plane); get into (a car); board (a bus); get on board (a ship). ‖ ~ ride (take a ride) in an automobile / 차를 타고 가다 go (to) in a car, a train) / 열차(버스)를 타고 가다 go (to Masan) by rail (bus) / 비행기를 타고 가다 go (travel) (to London) by air; fly (to Hawaii) / 승강기를 타고 오르내리다 go up and down in an elevator. ② 《기타》 줄을 ~ walk on a rope / 산을 ~ climb a mountain / 기회를 ~ seize the opportunity / 얼음을 지치고 놀다 have a slide on the ice.

타다⁴ 《받다》 get (receive) 《a prize, an award》; win (be awarded) 《a prize》; be given. ‖ 노벨상을

be awarded a Nobel prize.
타다[5] ① 《맷돌로》 grind. ¶ 탄 보리 ground barley. ② 《가르다》 divide; part 《one's hair》.
타다[6] ① 《잘 느끼다》 be apt to feel; be sensitive to. ¶ 부끄럼을 ～ be bashful 〔shy〕 / 간지럼을 ～ be ticklish. ② 《영향을》 be susceptible 〔sensitive〕 to; be allergic to; suffer easily from; be affected. ¶ 옻을 ～ be allergic to lacquer / 추위를 ～ be sensitive to cold.
타다[7] ① 《연주》 play (on). ¶ 가야금을 ～ play on a *gayageum* (Korean harp). ② 《솜을》 beat (*cotton*) out; 《틀다》 willow 〔whip〕 (*a cotton*).
타당거리다 《빨래를》 beat pat-pat-pat. ¶ 빨래를 방망이로 ～ paddle the laundry pat-pat-pat.
타당(安當) ¶ ～한 proper; adequate; appropriate; pertinent / ～하지 않은 improper; inappropriate; inadequate / 그의 의견은 ～하다 His opinion is proper. ‖ ～성 appropriateness; suitability; validity.
타도(打倒) ～하다 overthrow; strike down. ¶ 정부를 ～하다 overthrow a government / ～ 식민주의 (植民主義) Down with colonialism !
타도(他道) another province.
타동사(他動詞) a transitive verb.
타락(墮落) degradation; corruption; depravity. ～하다 go wrong 〔astray〕; be corrupted; become depraved; go to the bad; degenerate; fall low. ¶ 예술의 ～ decadence of art / ～한 학생 a depraved student / ～한 정치인 a corrupt politician / ～한 여자 a fallen 〔ruined〕 woman / ～시키다 degrade; deprave; lead (*a person*) astray / 그녀가 저렇게까지 ～할 줄은 몰랐다 I never thought she would fall so low. / 그는 술 때문에 ～했다 Drink led him astray.
타락줄 a rope made of human hair.
타래 a bunch; a skein; a coil. ¶ 실한 ～ a skein of thread / 새끼를 ～～ 감다〔사리다〕 coil the rope up.
타래송곳 a gimlet; a corkscrew.
타력(他力) the power of another; outside help; 《종교의》 salvation from outside.
타력(打力) 〖野〗 batting (power).
타력(惰力) inertia; momentum.
타령(打令) 《곡조의 하나》 a kind of tune; 《민요》 a ballad.
타륜(舵輪) 〖海〗 a steering wheel; the helm.
타르 tar. ¶ ～을 칠하다 tar.
타면(打綿) cotton beating. ‖ ～기 a cotton gin.
타면(他面) the other side. ¶ ～으로는 on the other hand; while; whereas.
타박 ～하다 find fault with; pick flaws with; grumble at. ¶ 음식 ～ grumbling at 〔about, over〕 the food / ～꾼 a grumbler.
타박(打撲) a blow. ‖ ～상 a bruise; a contusion 《다리에 ～상을 입다 get a bruise on the leg》.
타박거리다 trudge (trod) along.
타박타박하다 《음식이》 be dry and hard to eat.
타방(他方) the other side.
타봉(打棒) 〖野〗 batting.
탄분하다 (be) stale; moldy; musty. ¶ 타분한 생선 stale fish / 타분한 생각 a musty idea.
타블로이드 a tabloid.
타사(他事) other matters. ¶ ～를 돌볼 겨를이 없다 have no time to think about other things.
타산(打算) calculation. ～하다 calculate; reckon; consider 〔consult〕 one's own interests. ¶ ～적인 calculating; selfish / ～적인 생각 a selfish 〔an egocentric〕 idea / 그는 무슨 일에나 ～적이다 He always has his own interests in mind. *or* He always has an eye to the main chance.
타산지석(他山之石) an object lesson. ¶ 그의 실패를 ～으로 삼아라 Let his failure be a good lesson to you.
타살(他殺) homicide; murder. ¶ ～ 시체 the body of a murder victim.
타살(打殺) ～하다 beat 〔club〕 (*a person*) to death.
타석(打席) 〖野〗 the batter's box. ¶ ～에 들어가다 walk 〔step〕 into (the batter's) box; go to bat / ～에 서 있다 be at bat.
타선(打線) 〖野〗 the batting line-up. ¶ ～에 불이 붙다 make many hits; pump out hits / 상대 팀의 ～을 침묵시키다 keep the opposing team's bats silent.
타선(唾腺) 〖解〗 ☞ 타액선.
타성(惰性) 〖理〗《관성》 inertia; momentum; 《버릇》 force of habit. ¶ 공이 ～으로 굴렀다 The ball rolled on by the force of momentum. / 그는 단지 ～으로 그 일을 계속한다 He continues with the work just out of habit.
타수(打數) 〖野〗 at-bats; times at bat; 《골프》 the number of strokes. ¶ 5～ 3안타를 치다 make three hits in five at bats.
타수(舵手) a steersman; a helmsman; 《보트의》 a cox; coxswain.
타순(打順) 〖野〗 a batting order 〔line-up〕. ¶ ～을 바꾸다 reshuffle

타악기(打樂器) a percussion instrument.
타액(唾液) saliva; sputum. ¶ ~분비 salivation / ~선 the salivary gland.
타원(楕圓) an ellipse; an oval. ¶ ~의 elliptic; oval. ‖ ~ 궤도 an elliptic orbit / ~ 운동 elliptic motion / ~체 an ellipsoid / ~형 an oval.
타월 a towel. 〖an oval.
타율(他律) heteronomy. ¶ ~적인 행동 heteronomous behavior.
타율(打率) 〖野〗 one's batting average (생략 bat. avg.). ¶ ~이 높다 [낮다] have a high [low] batting average / 그의 ~은 3할 2푼이다 He has a batting average of .320.
타의(他意) 〖남의 뜻〗 another's will; 〖다른 의도〗 any other intention [purpose]. ¶ ~는 없다 I have no other purpose. or That's all there is to it.
타이¹ Thailand. ¶ ~의 Thai. ‖ ~말 Thai / ~사람 a Thai; a Thailander.
타이² ① 〖넥타이〗 a (neck)tie. ② 〖동점〗 a tie; a draw. ¶ 세계 기록을 세우다 tie the world record / 양 팀은 2대 2 가 되었다 The two teams tied 2-2. / 경기는 2대 2로 끝났다 The game ended in a 2-2 tie. ‖ ~스코어 a tie score.
타이르다 reason (*with*); remonstrate; admonish; advise; persuade. ¶ 잘못을 ~ reason with (*a person*) on his mistake / 타일러서 ~시키다 persuade (*a person to do, into doing*).
타이밍 timing. ¶ ~이 좋다 [나쁘다] be timely [untimely].
타이어 a tire 〖美〗; a tyre 〖英〗.
타이츠 (a girl in) tights.
타이트스커트 a tight skirt.
타이틀 a title; a championship 〖선수권〗. ¶ ~을 차지하다 [얻다] gain [lose] a title / ~방어에 성공하다 defend the title successfully; retain the title / ~매치 a title match / ~보유자 the holder of the title; the champion.
타이프 ① 〖형(型)〗 type. ② 〖활자〗 a type. ③ ~타이프라이터. ‖ ~용지 typewriting paper.
타이프라이터 a typewriter. ¶ ~로 찍은 typewritten; typed / ~를 치다 typewrite. ‖ ~인쇄물 typescript.
타이피스트 a typist. ¶ 영문 ~ an English typist.
타인(他人) 〖다른 사람〗 others; another person; 〖남〗 an unrelated person; a stranger; an outsider. ~앞에서 in the presence of others; before other people / 그녀는 나를 낯모르는 ~취급을 했다 She treated me like a stranger.
타일 a tile. ¶ ~을 붙인 바닥 a tiled floor / 현관 계단에 ~을 붙이다 tile the front steps.
타임 time〖(경기 중의)〗 a time-out. ¶ ~을 재다 time / ~을 선언하다 〖(심판이)〗 call the time. ‖ ~리코더 a time recorder [clock] / ~머신 a time machine / ~카드 a time card / ~캡슐 a time capsule.
타자(打者) 〖野〗 a batter; a batsman; a hitter. ¶ 강~ a slugger; a heavy [hard] hitter / 대(代)~ a pinch hitter.
타자기(打字機) a typewriter.
타자수(打字手) a typist.
타작(打作) threshing. ~하다 thresh. ¶ 벼를 ~하다 thresh rice / ~마당 a threshing ground.
타전(打電) ~하다 telegraph (*a message to*); send a telegram (wire) (*to*); 〖(특히 해외로)〗 wire (*to*); cable.
타점(打點) ① 〖(붓으로)〗 ~하다 dot; point. ② 〖(마음 속으로)〗 ~하다 fix one's choice on. ③ 〖野〗 a run batted in (생략 rbi.). ¶ 그는 3 ~을 올렸다 He knocked in three runs.
타조(駝鳥) 〖鳥〗 an ostrich.
타종(打鐘) ~하다 strike [toll, ring] a bell; sound [ring] a gong. ¶ ~식 [hold] a trial tolling ceremony.
타진(打診) ① 〖醫〗 percussion. ~하다 percuss; tap; sound; examine. ¶ 폐렴의 징후는 없는지를 보려고 흉부를 ~하다 percuss [sound] one's chest for sign of pneumonia. ‖ ~기 a plexor. ② 〖(남의 뜻을)〗 ~하다 sound (out); feel (*a person*) out; tap. ¶ 의향을 ~하다 tap [sound] (*a person's*) opinion / 그 자리를 맡아주겠는지 그의 생각을 ~해 주겠느냐 Will you sound him out to see if he will accept the post?
타처(他處) another [some other] place; somewhere else. ¶ ~에 [서] from [in [at] another [some other] place / ~에서 온 사람들 people from other places.
타파(打破) ~하다 break down; do away with; abolish; overthrow. ¶ 계급 ~ abolition of class distinctions / 인습을 ~하다 do away with conventionalities.
타합(打合) a previous arrangement. ~하다 make arrangements (*with a person for a matter*); arrange (*a matter with a person that...*).
타향(他鄕) a place away from

타협 791 **탄력**

home; a foreign land. ¶ ~에서 죽다 die far from home; die in a foreign (strange) land.

타협(妥協) (a) compromise; mutual concession. ~하다 (make a) compromise 《with a person》; come to terms [an understanding] 《with》; reach a compromise 《with》. ¶ ~적인 태도를 보이다 (not) show a (no) willingness to compromise / ~의 여지가 없다 There is no room for compromise. ‖ ~안 a compromise plan [proposal] 《~안을 만들다 work out a compromise》 / ~점 (find) a point of compromise; common (a meeting) ground.

탁 ① 《치거나 부딪는 소리》 with a bang (pop, slam); with a crack. ¶ 문을 ~ 닫다 slam [bang] the door; shut the door with a bang. ② 《부러지거나 끊어지는 소리》 with a snap. ¶ ~ 꺾이다 break with a snap (click) / ~ 부러지다 break off with a snap. ③ 《트이어 시원한 모양》 widely; extensively; vastly. ¶ 시야가 ~ 트이다 command extensive views.

탁견(卓見) a fine idea; foresight; an excellent idea [view] (명안). ¶ ~이 있는 clear-sighted; long-headed.

탁구(卓球) 《play》 ping-pong; table tennis. ¶ ~대 a ping-pong table / ~선수 a ping-pong player.

탁류(濁流) a muddy stream; a turbid current.

탁마(琢磨) 《연마》 polishing; cultivation (학덕을). ~하다 polish; improve 《one's virtue》; cultivate 《one's mind》.

탁발(托鉢) religious mendicancy. ~하다 go about asking for alms. ‖ ~승 a mendicant [begging] monk; a friar.

탁본(拓本) ☞ 탑본(搨本).

탁상(卓上) ~의 (에) on the table [desk]. ‖ ~ 사전 a desk dictionary 《dictionaries》. ‖ ~계획 [공론] a desk plan [theory] / ~시계 a table clock / ~전화 a desk telephone.

탁선(託宣) an oracle; the Revelation.

탁설(卓說) an excellent view [opinion].

탁성(濁聲) a thick [hoarse] voice.

탁송(託送) consignment. ~하다 consign 《a thing to a person》; send 《a thing》 by 《through》 《a person》. ¶ 공항에서 짐을 운송업자에게 ~ 했다 At the airport I sent my baggage on through a forwarding agency. ‖ ~품 a consignment.

탁아소(託兒所) a day [public] nursery; a day-care center (美). ¶ ~에 아이를 맡기다 leave one's child at a day-care center.

탁월(卓越) excellent; eminent; prominent; distinguished / ~한 학자 a prominent scholar / ~한 업적 an outstanding [a brilliant] achievement. ‖ ~풍 [氣] the prevailing wind.

탁자(卓子) a table; a desk. ¶ ~에 둘러 앉다 sit around a table.

탁주(濁酒) ☞ 막걸리.

탁탁 ① 《쓰러짐》 ~ 쓰러지다 fall one after another. ② 《숨이》 ¶ 숨이 ~ 막히다 be choky; be stifled. ③ 《침을》 ~ 뱉다 spit 《on》; go spit-spit. ④ 《두드리다·부딪다》 ¶ 먼지를 ~ 털다 beat the dust off; beat the dust out of.... ⑤ 《일을 해치우는 모양》 briskly; promptly; quickly; in business-like way. ¶ 일을 ~ 해치우다 do one's work briskly; be prompt in one's work.

탁탁거리다 keep cracking [popping, flapping].

탁탁하다 ① 《천이》 (be) close-woven; thick and strong. ② 《살림이》 (be) abundant; be well-off.

탁하다(濁一) 《물 따위가》 (be) muddy; turbid; 《불순한》 impure; 《공기 따위가》 (be) cloudy; 《공기 따위가》 foul; 《목소리가》 (be) thick. ¶ 탁한 공기 foul [impure] air / 탁한 목소리 a thick voice / 탁한 색깔 a dull [somber] color.

탄갱(炭坑) a coal pit [mine]. ‖ ~부(夫) a coal miner; a collier (英).

탄고(炭庫) a coal cellar; a coal bin; a (coal) bunker.

탄광(炭鑛) a coal mine; a colliery (英). ‖ ~근로자 a coal miner / ~업 the coal-mining industry / ~지대 a mining region / ~회사 a colliery company.

탄내(炭—) scorched smell. ¶ ~(가) 나다 smell something scorching [smoldering, burning].

탄내(炭—) (char)coal fumes.

탄도(彈道) a trajectory; a line of fire. ¶ ~를 그리며 날다 follow a ballistic course. ‖ ~계수 the coefficient of a trajectory / ~곡선 a ballistic curve / ~비행 a trajectory (suborbital) flight.

탄도탄(彈道彈) a ballistic missile. ‖ 대륙간 [중거리] ~ an intercontinental [a medium range] ballistic missile 《생략 ICBM [MRBM]》.

탄두(彈頭) a warhead. ¶ 핵 ~ an atomic [a nuclear] warhead / 핵 ~ 미사일 a nuclear-tipped missile; a nuclear missile.

탄띠(彈—) a cartridge belt.

탄력(彈力) elasticity; 《융통성》 flexibility. ¶ ~ 있는 elastic; flexible; springy / ~이 없어지다 lose

탄로(綻露) ¶ ~나다 be found out; come to light; come (be) out; be discovered / 음모가 ~ 났다 The plot came to light. / 비밀이 곧 ~ 났다 The secret soon came out (leaked out).

탄막(彈幕) a barrage. ¶ ~을 치다 put up a barrage / 엄호 ~ a covering barrage. ‖ ~포화 curtain fire.

탄복(歎服) ~하다 admire. ¶ ~할 만한 admirable; praiseworthy / 그녀의 아름다움에 ~했다 I was struck by her beauty.

탄산(炭酸) carbonic acid. ‖ ~가스 carbon dioxide; carbonic acid gas / ~나트륨[칼슘, 칼륨] sodium (calcium, potassium) carbonate / ~수 〔음료〕 carbonated water (drinks) / ~천 (泉) a carburetted spring.

탄생(誕生) (a) birth. ~하다 be born; come into the world. ¶ 우리는 새 회사의 ~을 축하했다 We celebrated the birth of the new company. / ~일 a birthday / ~지 the birthplace (of a noble person).

탄성(彈性) elasticity. ‖ ~고무 elastic gum / ~체 an elastic body.

탄성(歎聲) (단식) a sigh; a groan; (감탄) a cry of admiration. ¶ ~을 발하며 heave a sigh of grief; sigh (over); (감탄하다) let out (utter) a cry of admiration.

탄소(炭素) 〔化〕 carbon (기호 C). ‖ ~강 carbon steel / ~강화 콘크리트 carbon fiber reinforced concrete / ~봉 a carbon rod / ~섬유 a carbon fiber.

탄수화물(炭水化物) 〔化〕 a carbohydrate. ¶ ~이 적은 식사 a low-carbohydrate diet; a diet low in carbohydrate.

탄식(歎息) a sigh; grief. ~하다 heave a sigh of grief; (비탄) lament; grieve over.

탄신(誕辰) a birthday. 「shell(포탄).

탄알(彈─) a shot; a bullet; a

탄압(彈壓) oppression; suppression. ~하다 oppress (the people); suppress (a strike). ¶ ~적인 oppressive; high-handed / 언론의 자유를 ~하다 suppress freedom of speech / 군사 정권은 좌익 정당을 심하게 ~했다 The military government cracked down ruthlessly on the left-wing political parties.

탄약(彈藥) ammunition; munitions. ‖ ~고 a (powder) magazine / ~상자 an ammunition box / ~저장소 an ammunition dump (storage area).

탄우(彈雨) a rain (shower, hail) of bullets (shells).

탄원(歎願) (an) entreaty; (a) supplication; a petition; an appeal. ~하다 entreat; appeal (to); petition. ¶ 그는 장관에게 아내의 석방을 ~했다 He entreated the minister to release his wife. ‖ ~서 a (written) petition / ~자 a petitioner; a supplicant.

탄저병(炭疽病) 〔醫〕 (an) anthrax.

탄전(炭田) a coalfield.

탄젠트(數) a tangent (생략 tan).

탄주(炭柱) 〔鑛〕 a post.

탄주(彈奏) ~하다 play (the piano); perform. ‖ ~자 a player; a performer.

탄진(炭塵) coal dust.

탄질(炭質) the quality of coal. ¶ ~이 좋다 [나쁘다] The coal is good (poor) quality.

탄차(炭車) a coal wagon.

탄착(彈着) the fall (hit, impact) of a shot (bullet, shell). ‖ ~거리 the range of a gun; (within) gunshot / ~관측 spotting / ~짐 point of the impact (of a shell) / ~지역 the area within (rifle, mortar, etc.) range; the possible target area (of a missile).

탄창(彈倉) 〔軍〕 a magazine.

탄층(炭層) a coal seam (bed).

탄탄(坦坦) ‖ ~대로 a broad and level highway.

탄탄하다 (be) firm; strong; solid; stout; sturdy; durable (내구성). ¶ 탄탄한 집 a solidly-built house / 탄탄하게 만들어져 있다 be strongly built (made).

탄폐(炭肺) 〔醫〕 anthracosis.

탄피(彈皮) a cartridge case; shell.

탄핵(彈劾) impeachment; accusation. ~하다 impeach (a person for taking a bribe); accuse; censure. ¶ ~안 an impeachment motion / ~재판 an impeachment trial / ~재판소 the Impeachment Court.

탄화(炭化) carbonization. ~하다 carbonize. ‖ ~물 a carbide / ~수소 hydrocarbon.

탄환(彈丸) a shot; a ball; a bullet(소총의); a shell(대포의). ¶ ~열차 a bullet-like train.

탄흔(彈痕) a bullet mark; a hole made by a shot.

탈 (가면) a mask. ¶ ~을 쓰다 wear (put on) a mask; mask one's face / ~을 벗다 pull (throw) off one's mask / ~을 벗기다 unmask (a villain); expose (an imposter).

탈(頉) ① 《사고·고장》 a hitch; a

트러블; a failure. ¶ ~없이 without a hitch [trouble]; smoothly. ② 《병》 sickness; illness. ¶ ~ 이 in good health. ③ 《흠》 a fault; a defect; a flaw. ☞ 탈잡다.

탈…(脫) ~공업 사회 the postindustrial society. ¶ ~ 하려는 a wish to quit [extricate *oneself* from] the life of a white-collar worker / ~ 이온화 deionization.

탈각(脫却) ~하다 get rid [clear] of; free *oneself* from. ¶ 구습에서 ~ 하다 shake *oneself* free from the old custom.

탈각(脫殼) ~하다 exuviate; cast off a skin [shell].

탈것 a vehicle; a conveyance.

탈고(脫稿) ~하다 finish writing 《an article》; complete 《a novel》.

탈곡(脫穀) threshing. ~하다 thresh; thrash. ¶ ~기 a threshing [thrashing] machine.

탈구(脫臼) 《醫》 dislocation. ~ 하다 be dislocated; be put out of joint.

탈나다(頉─) 《사고》 an accident happens; have a hitch [mishap]; develop [run into] trouble; 《고장》 get out of order; go wrong; break [down]; 《병》 fall [be taken] ill.

탈당(脫黨) withdrawal (from a party); defection. ~ 하다 leave [withdraw from, secede from] a party. ‖ ~ 성명(서) a (written) statement of *one's* secession from the party / ~ 자 a seceder; a bolter 《美》.

탈락(脫落) ~하다 be left out; fall off; drop out 《of》. ¶ 전열[戰列]에서 ~ 하다 drop out of the line. ‖ ~ 자 a dropout.

탈락거리다 keep dangling.

탈루(脫漏) an omission. ~하다 be omitted; be left out; be missing.

탈모(脫毛) loss [falling out] of hair. ~하다 lose *one's* hair. ‖ ~ 제 depilatory / ~ 증 alopecia / 원형~증 alopecia areata.

탈모(脫帽) 《구령》 Hats off! ~ 하다 take off *one's* hat. ¶ 선생님에게 ~ 하고 절을 하다 take off *one's* hat and bow to the teacher.

탈법행위(脫法行爲) an evasion of the law; a slip from the grip of the law.

탈산(脫酸) 《化》 ~하다 deoxidize.

탈상(脫喪) ~하다 finish [come out of] mourning; leave off [get over] mourning.

탈색(脫色) decoloration; bleach (표백). ~하다 remove (the) color 《from》; bleach; decolorize. ‖ ~ 제 a decolorant; a bleaching agent; a bleach.

탈선(脫線) 《철도의》 derailment; 《이야기의》 digression. ~ 하다 derail; run off the rails; 《이야기에서》 digress from the subject; get sidetracked. ¶ 열차가 ~ 했다 The train derailed (ran off the rails). / 우리는 자주 토론의 주제에서 ~ 한다 We are apt to 'digress (get sidetracked) from the main subject of our discussion.

탈세(脫稅) tax evasion. ~하다 evade (dodge) taxes. ¶ ~ 를 고발 하다 accuse 《a person》 of tax evasion. ‖ ~ 액 the amount of the tax evasion / ~ 자 a tax dodger (evader) / ~ 품 smuggled goods(밀수 등으로 인한).

탈속(脫俗) ~하다 rise above the world. ¶ ~ 적인 detached from worldly things; unworldly.

탈수(脫水) 《化》 dehydration. ~하다 dehydrate; dry; 《세탁기로》 spin-dry 《laundry》; spin 《clothes》 dry. ‖ ~ 기 a dryer; a dehydrator / ~ 제 a dehydrating agent / ~ 증상 dehydration.

탈습(脫濕) dehumidification. ~ 하다 dehumidify.

탈싹 flop; with a thud. 「desalt.

탈염(脫鹽) ~하다 desalinize.

탈영(脫營) desertion from barracks; decampment. ~하다 run away (desert) from barracks; go AWOL 《美》. ‖ ~ 병 a deserter; a runaway soldier.

탈옥(脫獄) prison-breaking; a jailbreak 《美》. ~하다 break (out of) prison; escape (from) prison. ‖ ~ 수 a prison breaker; an escaped convict.

탈의(脫衣) ~하다 undress *oneself*; take off *one's* clothes. ‖ ~ 장 (실) a dressing (changing) room.

탈자(脫字) an omission of a letter (word); a missing letter.

탈잡다(頉─) find fault with 《a person, a thing》; pick flaws with; cavil at; criticize 《a person》 for one thing or another.

탈장(脫腸) 《醫》 a rupture; (a) hernia. ¶ ~ 이 되다 be affected with hernia. ‖ ~ 대 (帶) a hernia band; a truss. 「tification.

탈적(脫籍) 《韓籍》 gangrene; mortification. ~하다 have *one's* name removed (deleted) from the 《family》 register.

탈주(脫走) escape; (a) flight; desertion(군대에서). ~ 하다 escape; run away; flee; desert 《barracks》. ‖ ~ 병 a deserter / ~ 자 a runaway; an escapee.

탈지(脫脂) ~하다 remove grease (fat) 《from》. ‖ ~ 면 absorbent (sanitary) cotton / ~ 분유 nonfat

탈출 (脫出) escape; get out of. ¶침몰하는 배에서 ~하다 escape from the sinking ship. ‖ ~속도 《인력권에서의》 escape velocity.

탈춤 a masque (masked) dance.

탈취 (脫臭) ~하다 deodorize. ‖ ~제 a deodorant.

탈취 (奪取) ~하다 capture; seize; grab; usurp(권력·지위 등을). ¶군사적 수단으로 권력을 ~한 자들 those who capture (usurp) power by military means.

탈퇴 (脫退) withdrawal; secession. ~하다 withdraw (secede) from; leave. ¶그 회에서 ~하다 withdraw (secede) from the society. ‖ ~자 a seceder; a bolter 《美》.

탈피 (脫皮) ① 《동물의》 molting; a molt; 《動》 ecdysis. ~하다 shed (slough, cast off) its skin. ② 《옛것으로부터의》 ~하다 grow out of; outgrow. ¶구태에서 ~하다 break with convention; grow out of one's former self. 〖anus.

탈항 (脫肛) 《醫》 prolapse of the

탈환 (奪還) ~하다 recapture; recover; regain; take (win) back 《the pennant》.

탈황 (脫黃) 《化》 desulfurization. ~하다 desulfurize; desulfur; purify. ‖ ~장치 desulfurization equipment.

탈회 (脫會) ~하다 leave (resign from) an association (a society, a club).

탐관오리 (貪官汚吏) a corrupt official; a graft-happy official.

탐광 (探鑛) prospect. ~하다 prospect (for gold). ‖ ~자 a prospector.

탐구 (探究) search; research(연구); a study; investigation(조사). ~하다 search for; investigate; do research. ¶미의 ~ the search for beauty / 인간의 ~ the study of man / 철학자는 진리를 ~한다 Philosophers seek for (after) the truth. ¶~심 the spirit of inquiry / ~자 an investigator; a pursuer (of truth).

탐나다 (貪-) be desirable; be desirous (covetous) of 《money》. 탐나는 여자 a desirable woman / 탐나는 음식 appetizing food.

탐내다 (貪-) want; desire; wish (long, care) for; covet. ¶남의 것을 ~ covet what belongs to others.

탐닉 (耽溺) addiction; indulgence. ~하다 indulge in; be addicted to; give oneself up (abandon oneself) to. ¶주색에 ~하다 abandon oneself to liquor and sex.

탐독 (耽讀) ~하다 be absorbed (engrossed) in reading.

탐문 (探聞) ~하다 inquire about indirectly; detect; pick up information.

탐문 (探問) ~하다 obtain information (by inquiry); get wind of (소문 등을); snoop for information(형사가).

탐미 (耽美) ☞ 심미(審美).

탐방 (探訪) (an) inquiry. ~하다 (visit a place and) inquire (make inquiries) into 《a matter》. ¶사회 ~ an inquiry (a fact-finding survey) on community life. ‖ ~기(사) a report of; a reportage 《프》 / ~기자 a (newspaper) reporter; an interviewer.

탐사 (探査) (an) inquiry; (an) investigation. ~하다 investigate; inquire (look) into.

탐색 (探索) a search; (an) inquiry; (an) investigation. ~하다 look (seek, search) (for); hunt up(범인을); investigate. ‖ ~전 an engagement in reconnaissance.

탐스럽다 look nice (attractive); (be) nice-looking; tempting; desirable; charming.

탐승 (探勝) sightseeing. ~하다 explore the beauties 《of》; go sightseeing. ¶~길을 떠나다 go on a sightseeing trip.

탐식 (貪食) ~하다 eat greedily; devour.

탐욕 (貪慾) greed; avarice. ¶~스런 greedy; avaricious; covetous / 돈과 권력에 ~스러운 greedy for money and power.

탐정 (探偵) 《일》 detective work(service); 《사람》 a detective; an investigator. ~하다 investigate (inquire into) 《a matter》 secretly; spy 《on a person》. ¶사설 ~ a private detective / 사설 ~ 사(社) a private detective agency(firm) / ~을 붙이다 set (put) a detective on 《a person》 / ~에게 뒤밟히다 be shadowed by a detective. ‖ ~소설 a detective story.

탐조 (探鳥) bird watching. ¶~하러 가다 go out for bird-watching. ‖ ~자 a bird watcher.

탐조등 (探照燈) a searchlight.

탐지 (探知) detection. ~하다 find out; detect; spy (smell) out. ‖ ~기 a detector.

탐측 (探測) sounding; probing. ‖ ~기(機) a probe; a prober / ~기구(氣球) a pilot balloon / ~로켓 a sounding rocket(기상용).

탐탁하다 (be) desirable; satisfactory; be to one's satisfaction (liking). ¶탐탁하지 않은 undesir-

탐폰 [醫] 《생리·지혈용》 a tampon.

탐하다 (貪—) be greedy 《of, for》; be covetous 《of》; covet; crave. ¶ 명리(名利)를 ~ covet fame and fortune.

탐험 (探險) exploration; expedition. ~하다 explore. ¶ 미지의 섬을 ~하다 explore an unknown island / 우주는 이제 꿈이 아니다 Space exploration is no longer a dream. ∥ ~가 an explorer / ~대 an expeditionary party / ~대장 the leader [chief] of an expedition team / ~비행 an exploratory flight.

탑 (塔) a tower; a pagoda 《사찰 의》; a steeple 《뾰족탑》; a monument (기념탑). ¶ 5층~ a five-storied pagoda / 에펠 ~ the Eiffel Tower.

탑본 (搨本) a rubbed copy. ¶ 비문의 ~을 뜨다 make [do] a rubbing of a monumental inscription.

탑삭 with a snap [snatch]; with a dash. ¶ ~ 움켜쥐다 snatch [grasp] at / 《물고기가》 미끼를 ~ 물다 rise to [snap at] the bait.

탑삭부리 a man with a shaggy beard. ☞ 텁석부리.

탑승 (搭乘) boarding; embarkation (승선). ~하다 board [get on] 《a plane》; go [get] on board 《the aircraft》. ¶ 그 추락한 비행기에는 한국인 ~객이 없었다고 한다 It is reported that there were no Koreans on board the crashed plane. ∥ ~권 a boarding card [pass] / ~대합실 [공항의] a departure lounge / ~수속 boarding procedures / ~자 (승객) a passenger.

탑재 (搭載) ~하다 load; carry. ¶ ~되어 있다 be loaded [laden] with 《goods》; be equipped with 《heavy guns》 / 그 군함은 12인치포 12문이 ~되어 있다 The warship carries twelve 12-inch guns. ∥ ~량 loading [carrying] capacity; 《공군에서》 the bomb load (폭탄의).

탑파 (塔婆) a stupa 《梵》.

탓 (원인) reason; 《잘못》 fault; blame; 《영향》 influence; effect. ¶ 나이 ~으로 because of [owing to] one's age; on account of age / 기후(의) ~으로 under the influence of the weather / …의 ~이다 be caused by; be due to / 남의 ~으로 돌리다 put the blame on another.

탓하다 put [lay] blame upon; lay the fault to; attach blame to; blame [reproach] 《a person》 for 《something》. ¶ 자신을 ~ reproach oneself 《for》 / 나만 잘못한다고 탓하지 마시오 Don't lay the blame on me alone.

탕 (소리) a bang; boom. ~하다 bang; (go) boom. ¶ 문을 ~ 닫다 bang a door.

탕 (湯) ① [국] soup; broth; 《한약》 a medicinal (herb) broth. ② [목욕] a hot bath; 《공중목욕탕》 a public bath. ¶ 남[여] ~ a bath for men [women].

탕감 (蕩減) ~하다 write off 《a debt》; cancel (out). ¶ 빚을 ~해 주다 forgive 《a person》 a debt.

탕아 (蕩兒) a prodigal; a libertine. 〔an infusion.

탕약 (湯藥) a medicinal decoction.

탕진 (蕩盡) ~하다 squander; waste; run through 《one's fortune》; dissipate.

탕치 (湯治) a hot-spring cure. ~하다 take a hot-spring baths for medical purposes. ∥ ~요법 a hot-spring cure; spa treatment.

탕치다 (蕩—) ① 《재산을》 squander one's fortune; ~ 탕진하다. ② 《탕감하다》 write off; let off; cancel.

탕탕 (쏘거나 치는 소리) booming [banging] repeatedly; (두드리는 소리) rapping [pounding] repeatedly; (큰소리 치는 모양) with loud boasts [big talk]. ¶ ~ 총을 쏘다 fire a gun in rapid succession / 문을 ~ 두드리다 rap [pound] at the door / ~ 큰소리 치다 talk big [boastfully] 《about》; make a great brag [boast] 《about, of》.

탕파 (湯婆) a hot-water bottle [bag]; a foot warmer.

태 (胎) the umbilical cord and the placenta; the womb. ¶ ~를 가르다 cut the navel cord.

태고 (太古) ancient times. ¶ 태곳적부터 from time immemorial.

태공망 (太公望) an angler. ☞ 강태공(姜太公).

태교 (胎敎) prenatal care [training] of an unborn child through the attention of a pregnant woman to her own mental health. ¶ ~에 좋은 [나쁜] ~ have a good [bad] prenatal influence on 《one's child》.

태권도 (跆拳道) the Korean martial arts of empty-handed self-defense; taekwondo.

태극기 (太極旗) the national flag of Korea; the Taegeukgi.

태극선 (太極扇) 《부채》 a fan with a Taegeuk design.

태기 (胎氣) signs [indications] of pregnancy.

태깔 (態—) ① 《태와 빛깔》 form and

태껸 kicking and tripping art (as a self-defense art).

태내(胎內) the interior of the womb. ∥ ~의 (에) (a child) in the womb. ∥ ~전염 antenatal [prenatal] infection.

태도(態度) an attitude; behavior; bearing; a manner. ¶ ~가 좋다 [나쁘다] have good [bad] manners / 강경한 ~를 취하다 assume [take] a firm (strong) attitude (*toward*) / 우호적인 ~로 in a friendly manner / 침착한 ~를 잃지 않도록 하라 Try to preserve a calm demeanor.

태독(胎毒) 【醫】 the baby's eczema (traceable to congenital syphilis).

태동(胎動) 〈태아의〉 quickening; fetal movement; 〈비유적〉 a sign (an indication) (*of*). ~하다 quicken; show signs of. ∥ ~기 the quickening period.

태두(泰斗) a leading scholar; an authority (*on*). ¶ 영문학의 ~ an authority on English literature.

태만(怠慢) negligence; neglect; (a) default. ¶ ~한 neglectful; inattentive; negligent; careless / 직무 ~으로 해고당하다 be fired [dismissed] for neglect of duty.

태몽(胎夢) a dream of forthcoming conception.

태무(殆無) ~하다 (be) very scarce; very few (rare). ¶ 나는 소득이 ~했다 I scarcely gained anything.

태반(太半) the greater [most, best] part; the majority. ¶ ~은 대개 mostly; for the most part / 응모자의 ~은 남성이었다 The applicants were mostly men.

태반(胎盤) 【解】 the placenta.

태부리다(態―) strike an attitude; assume affected manners; give *oneself* airs.

태부족(太不足) ~하다 be in great want [shortage] (*of*).

태블릿 a tablet.

태산(泰山) 〈큰 산〉 a great mountain; 〈크고 많음〉 a huge amount; a mountain (*of*). ¶ ~같이 믿다 place great trust (*on, in*) / 명 동에 서일패 《俗談》 Much ado about nothing. *or* Much cry *and little* wool. ∥ ~준령 high mountains and steep passes.

태생(胎生) ① 〈출생〉 birth; origin; 〈출생지〉 one's birthplace. ¶ ~ ~이다 come from (*Seoul*); be of (*foreign*) birth. ② 【生】 viviparity. ∥ ~의 viviparous. ∥ 동물 viviparous animals.

태서(泰西) the West; the Occident. ¶ ~의 Western; Occidental. ∥ ~문명 Occidental civilization.

태선(苔癬) 【醫】 lichen.

태세(態勢) an attitude; a setup. ¶ ~를 갖추다 get ready (*for*); be prepared (*for, to do*) / 회원을 받아들일 ~를 갖추다 make preparations to receive (*members*).

태수(太守) a viceroy; a governor.

태아(胎兒) a fetus (8주 이후); an embryo (8주까지); an unborn baby (일반적). ¶ ~의 embryonic; fetal / ~의 성감별 fetal sex-identification.

태양(太陽) the sun. ¶ ~의 solar / ~의 빛 sunlight / ~광선 the rays of the sun; sunbeams / 당신은 나의 ~이다 〈상징적 표현〉 You are the light of my life. ∥ ~계 the solar system / ~등(燈) a sun (-ray) lamp / ~력(曆) the solar calendar / ~열 solar heat / ~열 발전 solar heat power generation / ~열 자동차 a solar vehicle (car) / ~열 주택 a solar house / ~열 집열기 a solar heat collector / ~전지 a solar battery (cell) / ~풍 solar wind.

태어나다 be born; come into the world. ¶ 부자로 [가난하게] ~ be born rich [poor]; be born of rich [poor] parents / 다시 ~ be born again; be reborn; become a new man (새사람이 되다).

태업(怠業) a slowdown (strike) (美); a go-slow (英). ~하다 start [go on] a slowdown (strike).

태연하다(泰然―) (be) humble; modest; unaffected.

태연자약(泰然自若) ~하다 (be) calm and self-possessed; remain cool [calm, composed].

태연하다(泰然―) (be) cool; calm; composed; self-possessed. ¶ 태연히 coolly; calmly; with composure / 태연히 죽음에 임하다 face death calmly.

태열(胎熱) 【醫】 congenital fever.

태엽(胎葉) a spring. ¶ 시계의 ~을 감다 wind the spring of a watch / ~이 풀리다 a spring runs down, ∥ ~장치 clockwork / 장난감은 ~장치로 움직인다 The toy moves (works) by clockwork.).

태우다 ① 〈연소·소각하다〉 burn (*a thing*) (up); commit (*something*) to the flames; incinerate. ¶ 불에 태워 없애다 destroy (*a thing*) by fire / 정원의 낙엽을 긁어모아 ~ rake the garden leaves together and burn them. ② 〈그슬리다〉 scorch; parch; 〈살갗을〉 tan. ¶ 밥을 ~ scorch [burn] the rice / 해변에서 살갗을 ~ tan *oneself* on the beach. ③ 〈애를〉 burn (*one's soul*); agonize; 〈정열을〉 burn (*with passion*). ¶ 속을 ~ be wor-

ried〔anxious, agonized〕; burn with anxiety / 그녀는 교육에 정열을 불태우고 있다 She is burning with the passion for teaching.
태우다²〔탈것에〕 carry; take in; pick up; take 《passengers》 on board(승선). ¶ 태워 주다 give 《a person》 a lift(자기 차에); help 《a person》 into 《a car》(부축해서) / 내 새 차에 너를 한번 태워주겠다 I will give you a ride in my new car.
태우다³〔상금 등을〕 award 《a price》;〔몫 등을〕 give 《a person his share》;〔노름·내기에〕 bet; stake. ¶ 돈을 ~ lay a wager 《on the table》.
태음(太陰) the moon. ‖ ~력 the lunar calendar.
태자(太子) 황태자. 〔dynasty〕.
태조(太祖) the first king 《of》
태질치다〔벼타작〕 thresh 《grain》;〔메어침〕 throw 《a person》 down.
태초(太初) the beginning of the world.
태코그래프 a tachograph.
태코미터 a tachometer.
태클 a tackle. ~하다 tackle.
태평(太平·泰平) ① 〔세상·가정의〕 (perfect) peace; tranquility. ¶ ~한 peaceful; tranquil; quiet / ~을 구가하다 enjoy the blessings of peace / 천하~이다 All the world is at peace. ‖ ~가 a song of peace / ~성대 a peaceful reign. ② 〔마음이〕 ~한 easygoing; carefree / 마음이 ~한 사람 an easygoing〔happy-go-lucky〕 person.
태평양(太平洋) the Pacific (Ocean). ¶ 북〔남〕~ the north〔south〕 Pacific. ‖ ~ 안전보장조약 the Pacific Security Pact / ~ 연안 the Pacific coast; the Western Coast(미국의) / ~ 전쟁 the Pacific War / ~ 제주(諸州) 《미국의》 the Pacific states / ~ 함대 the Pacific Fleet / ~ 횡단 비행 a transpacific flight.
태풍(颱風) a typhoon. ¶ ~의 눈 the eye of a typhoon / ~에 타격을 입다 be hit 〔struck〕 by a typhoon. ‖ ~경보 a typhoon warning / ~권 the typhoon area / ~진로예보 a typhoon route forecast.
태형(笞刑) flogging. ~을 가하다 punish 《a person》 by flogging.
태환(兌換) conversion. ‖ ~권(券) ☞ 태환지폐 / ~은행 a bank of issue / ~지폐 convertible notes.
태후(太后) ☞ 황태후.
택배(宅配) home (door-to-door) delivery (service). ~하다 deliver 《a thing》 to 《a person's house》. ¶ 소화물을 ~편으로 보내다 send a parcel by home delivery service. ‖ ~취급소 a home delivery service agent.
택시 a taxi; a cab; a taxicab. ¶ 개인 ~ an owner-driven taxi; a driver-owned taxi / ~를 타다〔에서 내리다〕 get in〔out of〕 a cab / ~로 가다 go by taxi / ~를 잡다 take〔pick up〕 a taxi / ~를 부르다 call a taxi. ‖ ~강도 a taxi holdup / ~승차장 a taxi stand / ~요금 taxi fare / ~운전사 a taxi driver; a cabman.
택일(擇日) ~하다 choose an auspicious day; fix the date.
택지(宅地) building land; a housing 《building》 lot 《site》. ¶ ~를 조성하다 turn 《the land》 into housing lots / ~ 분양 sale of building lots / ~조성 development of residential sites. 〔for〕.
택지(擇地) ~하다 select a site
택하다(擇―) choose; make choice 《of》; select; pick 《a thing》 out 《from》. ¶ 날을 ~ select〔choose〕 a day / 어느 것이든 좋아하는 것을 택하시오 Choose whatever you like.
탤런트 a pop star;《TV의》a TV personality; a TV talent. ¶ 그녀는 유명한 TV ~이다 She is a well-known TV personality.
탬버린〔樂〕 a tambourine.
탭댄스 a tap dance.
탯줄 the navel string; the umbilical cord.
탱고〔樂〕 (dance) the tango.
탱자〔植〕 a fruit of the trifoliate orange.
탱커〔유조선〕 a tanker (boat). ¶ 초대형 ~ a supertanker / 오일 ~ an oil tanker.
탱크(전차) a tank;《가스·기름 등의》a tank. ¶ 석유〔가스〕~ an oil〔a gas〕 tank / 고압 ~ a high-pressure tank (vessel); ~로리 a tank lorry〔truck〕; a tanker.
탱탱하다 be swollen (puffed) up; tight; tense; taut.
탱화(幀畵)〔佛〕 a picture of Buddha to hang on the wall.
터¹ ① 〔집터〕 a (building) site〔lot〕; a plot of ground; a place. ¶ 빈 ~ a vacant land〔lot〕 / ~를 찾다〔고르다〕 look for〔choose, select〕 a site 《for》. ② 〔기초〕 the ground; the foundation; footing; groundwork. ¶ ~를 닦다 prepare the ground 《for》; build up a site 《for》 / ~가 잡히다 be well-grounded; have a firm foothold.
터²〔예정〕 a plan; a schedule;〔의도〕 an intention. ¶ …고 ~이다 intend to 《do》; have the intention of …ing; think of …ing.

터널 a tunnel. ¶ ~을 뚫다 build (cut, bore) a tunnel 《through》 / ~에서 나오다 come out of a tunnel / (열차가) ~로 들어 가다(을 나다) go into (through) a tunnel.

터놓다 ① (막힌 것을) open (it) up; put (a thing) out of the way; undam (a river); lift (a ban). ¶ 물꼬를 ~ open a paddle sluice / 봉쇄를 ~ lift (raise) the blockade. ② (마음을) open one's heart to. (마음을) 터놓고 without reserve; unreservedly; frankly / 터놓고 말하면 to be frank with you.

터다지다 consolidate the foundation 《of a building》; level the ground 《for》.

터덕거리다 ① (걸음을) walk wearily; walk heavily over (along); plod (on, along). ② (살림을) make a bare living. ③ (일을) struggle with hard work.

터덜거리다 ① (걸음을) walk wearily; trudge (along). ¶ 터덜터덜 trudgingly; wearily. ② (소리가) jolt; rattle along 《a stony road》.

터득 (攄得) ~하다 understand; grasp; comprehend; master 《the art of...》. ¶ 그 일의 요령을 ~하다 get the hang (knack) of the job; learn how to do the job.

터뜨리다 (폭발) explode; detonate; blast; (갇힌 것을) break; burst. ¶ 종기를 ~ have one's boil break / 풍선을 ~ burst a balloon / 폭탄을 ~ explode a bomb / 노염을 ~ let loose one's anger.

터럭 hair. ☞ 털.

터무니없다 (부당) (be) unreasonable; absurd; extraordinary; exorbitant; (과도) excessive; (근거 없음) groundless; wild. ¶ 터무니없이 unreasonably; excessively; absurdly / 터무니없는 거짓말을 하다 tell a whopping (damned) lie / 터무니없는 계획을 세우다 a wild (an absurd) project (scheme) / 그녀는 터무니없는 값을 불렀다 She asked an exorbitant price.

터미널 (終點) a terminal (station); a terminus (英); (컴) (단말기) a terminal. ¶ 버스 ~ a bus terminal / 에어 ~ an air terminal.

터벅터벅 ploddingly; trudgingly; totteringly. ¶ ~ 걷다 plod (trudge) along.

터부 (a) taboo; (a) tabu. ¶ ~시 (視)하다 taboo; (place) a taboo on 《something》 / ~시되다 be taboo; be under (a) taboo.

터분하다 (be) unpleasant-(muddy-)tasting. ¶ 입이 ~ have a muddy taste in one's mouth.

터빈 a 《gas, steam》 turbine.

터세다 (집터가) (be) unlucky; ill-omened; ill-fated; haunted.

터수 ① (처지) one's status; lot; financial (social) standing. ② (관계) relationship; terms.

터울 (나이) the age gap (among siblings); the disparity of ages between siblings. ¶ ~이 잦다 be frequent in having a baby.

터전 a (residential) site; the grounds; a basis. ¶ 이것이 우리들의 생활 ~을 이루고 있다 This forms the basis of our livelihood.

터주 (一主) 【民俗】 the tutelary spirit of a house site. ¶ 터줏대감 a senior member; an old-timer.

터주다 lift (remove) the ban (on); clear 《a thing》 out of one's way. ¶ 후진들을 위해 길을 ~ give the young people a chance; open the way for 《the promotion》 of one's juniors.

터지다 ① (폭발) explode; burst; blow up; (발발) break out. ¶ 터지기 직전에 있다 be close to the explosion point / 내란이 터졌다 A civil war broke out. / 굉장한 소리를 내며 터졌다 It blew up with a terrible bang. / (과일·갈라짐) explode; burst; tear; crack (split) open; (피부가) get chapped; (무너져서) break down; collapse. ¶ 터진 손은 chapped hands / 옷솔기가 ~ come apart at the seams / 둑이 ~ a dike collapses / 추위로 수도관이 터졌다 The water pipe burst because of the cold weather. / 보일러가 터져서 세 사람이 부상당했다 The boiler burst, injuring three people. ③ (탄로) be brought to light; be disclosed; be exposed. ④ ~ 얻어맞다.

터치다운 (蹴) touchdown.

터키 Turkey. ¶ ~의 Turkish. ‖ ~말 Turkish / ~사람 a Turk.

터프 ~한 tough; hardy; firm ¶ ~ 가이 a tough guy.

턱¹ the jaw; the chin (아래턱). ¶ ~이 나온 (늘어진) with prominent (drooping) jaws / ~을 쓰다듬다 rub one's chin / ~을 내밀다 stick out one's chin / ~이 빠지다 one's jaws get out of joint. ‖ ~뼈 a jawbone / 위(아래) ~ the upper (lower) jaw.

턱² (조금 높이 된 곳) a projection; a rise; a raised spot. ¶ ~이 지다 rise; swell.

턱³ (대접) a treat. ¶ ~을 내다 treat 《a person》 to 《a drink》 / 오늘은 내가 한 ~ 내겠다 It is my treat today.

턱⁴ (까닭) reason; grounds. ¶ 내가 알 ~이 있나 How should I

턱 ① 《안심》¶ ~ 놓이다 be relieved; feel reassured. ② 《잡는 꼴》 남의 손을 ~ 잡다 hold *a person's* hand passionately. ③ 《의젓이》 with a grand air; composedly. ¶ 의자에 ~ 앉다 sit at ease in a chair.
턱걸이 《붙봉의》 chinning; a chin-up. ~하다 chin *oneself* (up); do chinning exercises.
턱받이 a pinafore; a bib.
턱수염 (一鬚髥) a beard.
턱시도 a tuxedo.
턱없다 (be) groundless; unreasonable; exorbitant; excessive. ¶ 턱없이 unreasonably; exorbitantly / 턱없는 요구 an exorbitant (unconscionable) demand.
턱짓하다 make a gesture with *one's* chin.
턱찌끼 the leftovers.
턴테이블 a turntable.
털 《세모·머발》 (a) hair; 《짐승의》 fur; 《것》 feather. ¶ 돼지 ~ a hog bristle / 양 ~ wool / 겨드랑이 ~ underarm hair / 안에 ~을 댄 코트 a fur-lined coat / ~이 있는 haired; hairy / ~이 나다 hair grows (on one's legs) / ~이 빠지다 hair falls (comes) out; 《사람이 주어》 lose *one's* hair / 닭의 ~을 뽑다 pluck a chicken / 개는 ~이 탐스럽다 This dog has thick fur. ∥ ~내의 woolen underwear / ~셔츠 a woolen shirt / ~옷 woolen clothing; a fur (woolen) garment / ~외투 a fur (over)coat.
털가죽 a fur; a pelt (소, 양 따위의). ☞ 모피(毛皮).
털갈이 《새의》 molting; 《짐승의》 coat-shedding; shedding hair. ~하다 molt (the feathers); shed (the hair). ¶ 그 새는 ~를 다 했다 The bird has molted.
털끝 the end of a hair; 《조금》 a bit; a jot; a trifle. ¶ ~ 만큼도 (not) in the least; (not) a bit of; (not) a particle of / 그에게는 너에 대한 동정심이 ~만큼도 없다 He does not have a particle (grain) of sympathy for you.
털다 ① 《붙은 것을》 shake off (dust); throw off (먼지를) dust; brush up (솔로). ② 《가진 것을》 empty (one's pocket). ¶ 가진 돈을 몽땅 ~ empty *one's* purse to the last penny. ③ 《도둑이》 rob (a bank); rob (strip) (a person's).
털럭거리다 keep jogging (jolting); keep slapping; flap.
털버덕거리다 keep splashing.
털벙 with a plop (splash). ¶ ~거리다 plop.
털보 a hairy (shaggy) man.
털복숭이 a hairy person (thing).
털붙이 《모피》 a fur; 《털로 만든 물건》 woolen stuff; fur goods; 《털옷》 fur clothes.
털실 woolen yarn; knitting wool (편물용). ¶ ~양말 woolen socks / ~로 뜨다 knit (a sweater) out of wool; knit wool into (socks).
털썩 flop; with a thud. ¶ 의자에 ~ 앉다 flop (plump (oneself)) down in a chair / ~ 떨어뜨리다 bump (something) down.
털어놓다 《마음 속을》 confide; unbosom *oneself* (to); speak *one's* mind; unburden *oneself* (of *one's* secrets). ¶ 비밀을 아내에게 ~ confide a secret to *one's* wife / 털어놓고 이야기를 하면 ~ to be frank (candid) with you; frankly speaking.
털털거리다 ☞ 덜덜거리다.
털털이 ① 《사람》 a free and easy person. ② 《차량》 a rattling thing; a rattletrap; a jalopy 《美俗》.
털털하다 《사람이》 (be) unaffected; free and easy.
텀벙 with a plump (splash, plop). ¶ ~거리다 keep splashing.
텁석 with a snatch (snap). ¶ ~움켜쥐다 snatch.
텁석나룻 shaggy whiskers.
텁석부리 a bushy-whiskered man.
텁수룩하다 (be) unkempt; shaggy; bushy. ¶ 텁수룩한 머리 long unkempt hair / 수염이 ~ have a thick (bushy) beard.
텁텁하다 ① 《음식》 (be) thick and tasteless; 《입 속》 (be) unpleasant; disagreeable. ② 《눈이》 (be) vague; dim; bleary; obscure. ③ 《성미가》 (be) easy; broad-minded.
텃밭 a field attached to a home site; a kitchen garden.
텃세 (一貫) rent for a (house) site; site rent.
텃세 (一勢) ~하다 lord it over a newcomer; play cock-of-the-walk.
텅 ¶ ~비다 empty; vacant; hollow / 집은 ~ 비어 있었다 The house was found empty.
텅스텐 《化》 tungsten (기호 W). ∥ ~전구 a tungsten light bulb.
텅팅 《빈 모양》 all hollow; quite empty. ¶ 방이 ~ 비다 a room is all empty.
테 《둘린 언저리》 a frame (틀의); a band; a brim (모자의); a rim (안경 따위의); a hoop (둥근 통 따위의); a frill (장식한). ¶ 통에 ~를 두르다 hoop (a barrel). ☞ 테두리.
테너 《樂》 a tenor.
테니스 (play) (lawn) tennis. ∥ ~코트 a tennis court.

테두리 ① 《윤곽》 an outline; a contour. ¶계획의 ~ an outline of a scheme. ②《범위》 a framework; a limit. ¶~ 안에서 within the limits (framework) 《of the budget》 / ~를 정하다 fix the limit; set limits (bounds) 《to》.
테라마이신 〔藥〕 Terramycin.
테라스 《on》 a terrace.
테러 terror(ism). ¶~에 희생이 되다 fall a victim to terrorism. / ~ 전술 terrorist tactics / 조직 ~ a terrorist organization / 집단 ~ a gang of terrorists / ~행위 《an act of》 terrorism.
테러리스트 a terrorist.
테레빈유 (一油) turpentine.
테마 a theme; a subject matter. ¶연구 ~ a subject of study (research). ‖ ~ 음악 theme music.
테리어 〔犬〕 a terrier.
테스트 a test; a tryout. ~하다 test; give 《something》 a test; put 《a thing》 to the test. ¶실력 ~ an ability test / 학력 ~ an achievement test / 성능 ~ a performance (an efficiency) test. ‖ ~케이스 a test case / ~코스 a test course.
테이블 a table; a desk. ‖ ~ 매너 table manners / ~보 a tablecloth; a table cover / ~스피치 (make) an after-dinner speech; a speech at a dinner.
테이프 a tape; a paper streamer (축하용의). ¶녹음하지 않은 ~ a blank tape / ~를 끊다 (경주자가 골인할 때) break 《breast》 the tape / ~를 던지다 throw a (paper) streamer / ~에 녹음하다 record 《music》 on tape; tape; put 《the speech》 on tape / ~로 붙이다 tape 《A to B》 / 도지사가 개회식 ~을 끊었다 The governor cut the tape at the opening ceremony. / 모든 데이터는 ~에 저장된다 All data goes on tape for storage. ‖ ~ 녹음 tape recording / ~ 리코더 a tape recorder.
테일라이트 a taillight.
테제 〔哲〕 a thesis; a These 〔獨〕.
테크노크라트 〔기술관료〕 a technocrat.
테크놀러지 《과학기술》 technology.
테크니션 〔기술자〕 a technician.
테크니컬녹아웃 〔권투에서〕 a technical knockout; a T.K.O.
테크닉 (a) technique. ¶~이 뛰어나다 be superior in technique; play an excellent technique.
텍스트 a text; a textbook.
텐트 a tent. ¶~를 치다 (건다) pitch (strike) a tent / ~생활을 하다 camp (out); lodge in a tent. ‖ ~촌 a tent village.

텔레비전 television 《생략 TV》;《수상기》 a television (TV) set. ¶TV를 장시간 보는 사람 a heavy TV watcher / ~을 켜다 〔끄다〕 turn the television on 〔off〕 / ~을 보다 watch 《a drama on》 television / ~에 출연하다 appear on television / 이 ~은 영상이 선명하다 This TV set gives a clear picture. ‖ ~뉴스 television (TV) news / ~드라마 a television (TV) drama; a teledrama / ~방송 a television broadcast; a telecast / ~방송국 a television station / ~시청자 a television (TV) viewer; the audience (전체) / ~영화 a television (TV) movie; a telefilm / ~음성다중방송 a TV multiplex sound broadcast / ~전화 a TV phone; a videophone / ~탤런트 a TV personality; a TV star / 고화질 ~ a high-definition television 《생략 HDTV》 / 교육 ~ educational television.
텔레타이프 a teletype(writer). ¶~로 송신하다 teletype a message; send a message by teletype.
텔레파시 (communicate by) telepathy. ¶~를 행하는 사람 a telepathist.
텔렉스 Telex. (◀ teleprinter-exchange)
템포 a tempo; speed. ¶~가 빠른 speedy; rapid; fast-moving / ~가 느린 slow-moving / 빠른 ~로 in quick tempo; rapidly / …와 ~를 맞추다 keep pace with the tempo of….
토 〔조사〕 a particle.
토건 (土建) civil engineering and construction. ‖ ~업 civil engineering and construction business / ~업자 a civil engineering constructor / ~회사 a construction firm (company).
토관 (土管) (lay) an earthen pipe; a drainpipe.
토굴 (土窟) a cave; a dugout [den].
토기 (土器) earthenware (총칭); an earthen vessel.
토끼 a rabbit(집토끼); a hare(산토끼). ‖ ~ 굴 (play) a rabbit burrow / ~뜀 (play) leapfrog / ~장 a rabbit hutch.
토너먼트 (win) a tournament.
토닉 a tonic. ¶헤어 ~ hair tonic.
토닥거리다 keep patting (tapping); beat lightly.
토담 (土 ー) a dirt (mud) wall. ¶~집 a mud-wall hut.
토대 (土臺) 《건축물의》 a foundation; 《사물의 기초》 a foundation; a base; a basis; ground work. ¶《건물의》 ~를 앉히다 lay the foundation(s) / 이 집은 ~가 튼튼하다 This house is built on firm foun-

토라지다 get (become) sulky (peevish); pout; sulk. ¶ 토라져서 말도 안 하다 be sullen and silent; 토라지지 마라 Don't be sulky (sullen).

토란(土卵) 【植】 a taro. ‖ ~국 taro soup.

토렴하다 warm up 《rice, noodles》 by pouring hot broth over a little at a time.

토로(吐露) ~하다 lay bare 《one's heart》; express 《one's view》; speak 《one's mind》.

토론(討論) (a) debate; (a) discussion. ~하다 discuss 《a problem》; argue; debate; dispute. ¶ 활발한 ~ a lively discussion; a hot debate / 자주 ~ 되는 문제 a much-debated question / 공개 ~회 an open forum; a panel discussion / ~에 부치다 put 《a matter》 to debate. ‖ ~자 a debater; ~회 a debate; a forum; a panel discussion (공개의).

토륨 【化】 thorium (기호 Th).

토르소 a torso.

토리 a ball (spool) of string (thread). ‖ ~실 balled string (thread).

토마토 a tomato. ‖ ~주스 tomato juice / ~케첩 tomato ketchup

토막 a piece; a bit; a block. ¶ ~난 시체 a dismembered body / 나무 한 ~ a piece of wood / ~내다 (치다) cut (chop) into pieces. ‖ ~살인사건 a mutilation murder case.

토멸(討滅) ~하다 conquer; exterminate; destroy. ¶ 적을 ~ 하다 destroy the enemy.

토목(土木) engineering work; public works (토목공사). ‖ ~건축업 토건업 (土建業) / ~공사 engineering works / ~공학 civil engineering / ~기사 a civil engineer / ~장비 an earth-moving machine.

토박이(土─) a native; an aborigine. ¶ ~의 native-born; native 《to》; 서울~ born and bred; trueborn 《a》 Seoulite to the backbone; a trueborn Seoulite.

토박하다(土薄─) (be) sterile; barren; poor. ¶ 토박한 땅 sterile (barren, poor) land (soil).

토벌(討伐) subjugation. ~하다 put down; subjugate; suppress. ¶ 반란군을 ~ 하다 suppress a rebellion. ‖ ~대 a punitive force.

토벽(土壁) a mud (dirt) wall.

토사(土沙) earth and sand. ‖ ~붕괴 a landslide; a washout 《美》.

토사(吐瀉) vomiting and diarrhea. ~하다 suffer from diarrhea and vomiting. ‖ ~곽란(癨亂) acute gastroenteric trouble / ~물 vomit and excreta.

토산물(土産物) local products; native produce. ¶ ~인 수박 locally grown watermelons.

토색(討索) (an) extortion; blackmail(ing). ~하다 extort 《money from a person》; practice extortion; blackmail.

토스 a toss. ~하다 toss 《a ball》. ‖ ~배팅 【野】 a toss batting.

토스트 (a piece of) toast.

토시 wristlets.

토신(土神) a deity of the soil.

토실토실 ~하다 (be) plump; chubby; rotund; fat. ¶ ~한 아기 a chubby baby; a roly-poly little baby.

토악질(吐─) ① ~하다 vomit; throw up. ② 《부정 소득의》 repaying ill-gotten money. ~하다 repay ill-gotten money; disgorge.

토양(土壤) soil. ¶ 기름진 (비옥한) ~ rich (fertile) soil / 메마른 ~ poor (sterile) soil / 벼농사에 알맞은 ~ the soil suitable for growing rice / ~의 산성화 acidification of soil. ‖ ~오염 soil pollution / ~조사 agronomical survey / ~학 pedology.

토역(土役) (do) earth (mud) work. ¶ ~꾼 a navvy; a construction laborer. 「Sat.」.

토요일(土曜日) Saturday (생략)

토욕(土浴) 《새·짐승의》 a dust bath; wallowing in mud (dirt). ~하다 have (take) a dust bath; wallow in mud (dirt).

토우(土雨) 《흙비》 a rain of dust; a dust storm.

토의(討議) (a) discussion; (a) debate; (a) deliberation. ~하다 discuss; have a discussion 《about》; debate 《on》. ¶ ~에 부치다 take (bring) up 《a matter》 for discussion / ~중이다 be under discussion / ~를 시작하다 begin (open) a discussion (debate) 《on》. ‖ ~안 a subject for debate.

토인(土人) a native; an aboriginal 《원주민》; the aborigines (총칭); a savage (미개인).

토일릿 a toilet room 《美》. ‖ ~페이퍼 (a roll of) toilet paper (tissue).

토장(土葬) burial; interment. ~하다 inter; bury in the ground.

토장(土醬) 《된장》 bean paste.

토제(吐劑) 【藥】 an emetic.

토지(土地) 《땅·흙·대지》 land; soil; ground; 《한 구획》 a lot; a plot; a piece of land; 《부동산》 a real estate. 《영토》 (a) territory. ¶ ~에 투자하다 invest 《money》 in land / 그는 텍사스에 광대한 ~를 갖고 있다 He owns a large tract of land in Texas. / 이 토지는 멜론 재배에 적합하다 This soil is suited to the cultivation of melons. / ~가격 the price 〔value〕 of land / ~개량 land improvement / ~개발 land 〔estate〕 development / ~개혁 land reform / ~구획정리 land adjustment / ~대장 a land ledger 〔register〕; a cadaster / ~매매 dealing in land 〔real estate〕 / ~면적 land area / ~소유권 landownership / ~소유자 a landowner / ~수용 expropriation of land / ~전매 "land-rolling"; selling land from one person to another (when one has chances to earn money) / ~제도 the land system / ~초과이득세 a land profit tax; a tax for the excessively increased value of land.
토질(土疾) an endemic disease.
토질(土質) the nature of the soil. ¶ ~분석 soil analysis.
토착(土着) ¶ ~의 native(-born); indigenous. ¶ ~민 a native; the natives《총칭》.
토치카 a pillbox; a *tochka* 《러》.
토큰(代用貨幣) a token 《coin》. ¶ 버스 ~ a bus token.
토키 a talkie; a talking film [picture]; talkies《총칭》.
토탄(土炭) peat; turf.
토템 a totem. ¶ ~숭배 totemism / ~기둥 a totem pole.
토플 TOEFL. (◀Test of English as a Foreign Language)
토픽 a topic; a subject 《of conversation》.
토하다(吐─) ① 《뱉다》 spew; spit (out); 《게우다》 vomit; throw up; disgorge. ¶ ~ vomit what one have eaten / 피를 ~ spit [vomit] blood / 토할 것 같다 feel sick 《nausea》. ② 《토로》 express 《one's view》; speak 《one's mind》; give vent to 《one's feelings》.
토현삼(土玄蔘)〔植〕 a figwort.
토혈(吐血) vomiting 〔spitting〕 of blood. ~하다 vomit 〔bring up〕 blood; spit blood.
톡탁 beating 《each other》. ¶ ~거리다 exchange blow after blow; beat each other up. ¶ ~톡탁거리다.
톡톡하다 ① 《두껍다》 (be) thick; rich. ② 《피륙이》 (be) close; thick; close-woven.

톡톡히 ① 《많이》 a lot; a great deal. ¶ ~ 벌다 make a big profit / 돈을 ~ 모으다 make quite a lot of money. ② 《엄하게》 severely; harshly; scathingly. ¶ ~ 꾸짖다 scold 《a person》 scathingly.
톤 a ton; tonnage. ¶ 미터 ~ a metric ton / ~ 수《배수, 적재, 중량》 ~수 gross 〔displacement, freight, dead weight〕 tonnage / 5천 ~의 배 a ship of 5,000 tons / 적재량 10 ~ 트럭 a ten-ton truck / ~베는 몇 ~이냐 What is the tonnage of this ship?
톨 a grain 《of rice》; a nut.
톨게이트 《고속도로 등의》 a tollgate.
톱¹ 《나무 자르는》 a saw. ¶ 손~ a handsaw. ¶ 내릴~ a ripsaw / 동가리~ a crosscut saw / ~으로 통나무를 자르다 saw up a log; cut a log with a saw / ~질하다 saw 《wood》. ¶ ~날 the teeth of a saw; a saw blade 〔tooth〕 《~ 날을 세우다》 set a saw / ~밥 sawdust.
톱² a top; 《클래스의》 first-rate; top-class; top-notch; top-ranking / 그는 학급에서 ~이다 He is at the top of his class. *or* He stands first in his class. / 조간 신문의 ~을 장식하는 be treated as the main 〔top〕 story in the morning paper. ¶ ~기사 a front-page story; a banner head; the lead (story) / ~뉴스 top news.
톱니 ¶ 톱날. ¶ ~ 모양의 sawlike; serrated; jagged.
톱니바퀴 a toothed wheel; a cogwheel; a gear wheel. ¶ ~가 서로 물리다 〔안 물리다〕 be in 〔out of〕 gear / 나는 이 조직의 한 ~에 지나지 않는다 I am only a cog in this organization.
톱상어〔魚〕 a saw shark.
톱톱하다 《국물이》 (be) thick; rich; heavy. ¶ 톱톱한 국물 thick soup.
톳 a bundle 《of laver》.
통¹ ① 《배추 따위의 몸피》 the bulk 《of a cabbage》; a head 《of cabbage》《셀 때》. ¶ 배추 세 ~ three heads of cabbage. ② 《피륙의》 a roll. ③ 《동아리》 a gang; a group; cahoots. ¶ 한 ~이 되다 be in cahoots with; be in league with.
통² 《소매·바지의》 the width of crotch part 《of trousers》; breadth. ¶ 소매~이 좁다 a sleeve is rather tight. ② 《도량·씀씀이》 caliber; scale 《of doing things》. ¶ ~이 큰 사람 a man who does things in a big way / 사람이 ~이 작다 be a person of small caliber.
통³ 《복잡한 둘레·상황》 ¶ … ~에

amidst; in the midst 《of》; in the bustle 〔confusion〕 《of》 / 싸움~에 휘말리다 be involved in the turmoil of a fight / 북새~에 한몫 보다 fish in troubled waters; gain an advantage from the confused state of affairs.

통⁴ ① ☞ 온통. ② 〈전혀〉 quite; entirely; 〈전혀 …않다〉 (not) at all; (not) in the least. ¶그녀는 요즘 ~ 오지 않는다 She does not come here at all these days.

통 (筒) a tube; a pipe; a gun barrel; a sleeve〔기계의〕; a can 〈깡통〉. ¶대~ a bamboo / 마분지 ~ a cardboard tube.

통 (桶) a tub; a pail; a (wooden) bucket; a barrel; a can. ¶술~ a wine barrel〔cask〕 / 석유~ a kerosene can; an oil can.

통 (―) 〈동네의〉 a neighborhood unit; a *t'ong*; a subdivision of a *dong*. ‖ ~장 the head of a *t'ong*.

통 (通) 〈서류의〉 a copy 《of documents》. ¶편지 세 ~ three letters / 서류 네 ~ four documents; four copies of a document 〈동일한 것〉 / 계약서를 두 ~ 작성하다 make two copies of the contract / 정부 (正副) 2 ~ 을 제출하다 present in duplicate.

…통 (通) 〈전문가〉 an authority 〔expert〕 《on a subject》; a well-informed person. ¶경제~ an economics expert / 그는 중국~이다 He knows everything about China. *or* He is an authority on Chinese affairs.

통가리 (桶―) a rick〔stack〕of grain.

통각 (痛覺) sense〔sensation〕of pain.

통감 (痛感) ~하다 feel keenly 〔acutely〕; fully〔keenly〕realize. ¶사람들은 환경 보호의 필요를 ~하기 시작했다 People are beginning to feel keenly the need to protect the environment.

통겨주다 let 《a person》 know stealthily; disclose; let out 《a secret》.

통겨지다 ☞ 튕겨지다.

통격 (痛擊) a severe〔hard〕blow; a severe attack. ¶~을 가하다 attack 《a person》 severely; deal a hard blow to 《a person》.

통계 (統計) statistics. ¶~ (상의) statistical / ~를 내다 take〔collect, gather, prepare〕statistics 《of》. ‖ ~연감〔표〕 a statistical yearbook〔table〕 / ~청 the National Statistical Office / ~학 statistics / ~학자 a statistician.

통고 (通告) notification; notice; announcement. ~하다 notify 《a person of a matter》; give 《a person》 notice 《of》. ¶물러날 것을 ~하다 give notice to quit / 사전에 ~하다 give 《a person》 previous notice. ‖ ~서 a (written) notice / ~처분 a noticed disposition.

통곡 (痛哭) lamentation; wailing. ~하다 lament; wail; weep bitterly (loudly).

통과 (通過) passage; transit. ~하다 pass 《along, by, over, through》; go 〔get〕 through. ¶역을 ~하다 pass a station without stopping / 터널을 ~하다 pass through a tunnel / 서울 상공을 ~하다 pass over 〔fly over, overfly〕 Seoul / 의안을 ~시키다 pass 〔get〕 a bill through the National Assembly. ‖ ~관세 a transit tariff / ~무역 transit trade / ~사증 a transit visa / ~세 (稅) transit duties / ~의례 a rite of passage.

통관 (通關) customs clearance 《of goods》; clearance 《of goods》 through the customs. ~하다 pass 〔clear〕 the customs; clear 《a bill》; clear 《goods》 through the customs. ‖ ~베이스 the customs basis / ~사무소 a customs-clearance office / ~수수료 a clearance fee〔출항 수수료〕 / ~절차〔go through〕 customs formalities〔entry〕; clearance〔출항의〕 / ~허가서 a goods clearance permit.

통괄 (統括) ~하다 generalize.

통권 (通卷) the consecutive number of volumes.

통근 (通勤) ~하다 attend〔go to〕 the office; live out〔입주 근무의 반대 개념으로〕; 《승차권 등을 사용해서》 commute 《from Inch'ŏn to Seoul》《美》. ¶매일 버스로 ~하다 take the bus daily to work; go to the office every day by bus / 매일 지하철로 ~하다 commute daily by subway. ‖ ~거리 commuting distance / ~수당 a commutation allowance / ~시간 〈소요 시간〉 time required to get to the office; 《시간대》 commuter time / ~열차〔버스〕 a commuter train〔bus〕 / ~자 a commuter.

통금 (通禁) 〈야간의〉 a curfew. ¶~을 실시하다 impose〔order〕a curfew. ‖ ~시간 curfew hour / ~위반 a curfew violation / ~해제 the removal〔lifting〕of curfew.

통김치 *kimchi* made of whole cabbages.

통나무 a (whole) log. ¶~ 다리 a log bridge.

통념 (通念) a common〔generally accepted〕idea. ¶그러한 사회

은 타파되어야 한다 Such a commonly accepted idea should be shattered.

통달하다(通達—) be well versed (*in*); have a thorough knowledge (*of*); be conversant (*with*).

통닭구이 a roast chicken; a chicken roasted whole.

통독(通讀) ~하다 read through (over) (*a book*); read (*a book*) from cover to cover.

통렬(痛烈) ¶ ~한 severe; sharp; bitter; fierce / ~히 severely; bitterly / 그의 소설은 ~한 비판을 받았다 His novel received severe criticism.

통례(通例) a common (an ordinary) practice. ¶ ~로 usually; customarily; ordinarily; as a rule.

통로(通路) a path; a passage; a way; a passageway; an aisle (극장·열차 등의). ¶ ~측 좌석 an aisle seat / ~에서 standin the path (way) / ~를 막다 obstruct the passage.

통론(通論) an outline (*of law*); an introduction (*to*). ¶ 한국 문학 ~ an introduction to Korean literature.

통매(痛罵) a bitter criticism; violent abuse. ~하다 criticize severely; abuse (*a person*) bitterly.

통발[植] a bladderwort (plant).

통발(筒—) 〔고기 잡는〕 a weir; a fish trap.

통보(通報) a report. ~하다 report; inform. ¶ 기상 ~ a weather report / 경찰에 ~하다 report to the police. ‖ ~자 an informer; an informant.

통분(通分)〖數〗 ~하다 reduce (*fractions*) to a common denominator.

통사정(通事情) ~하다 《사정함》 speak *one's* mind; tell frankly (*about*); make an appeal (*to*). ¶ 어려운 사정을 친구에게 ~하다 tell a friend quite frankly about *one's* difficulties.

통산(通算) the (sum) total. ~하다 total; sum up; add up.

통상(通常) 〔부사적〕 ordinarily; commonly; usually; generally. ¶ ~의〔적인〕 usual; ordinary; common; customary; regular. ‖ ~복 everyday (ordinary) clothes; casual wear.

통상(通商) commerce; trade; commercial relations. ~하다 trade (*with a country*). ¶ ~을 시작하다 open trade (commerce) (*with a country*). ‖ ~대표부 the Office of Trade Representative / ~사절단 a trade mission (delegation) / ~조약 a commercial treaty.

통설(通說) a popular (commonly accepted) view; a common opinion. ¶ …라는 것이 ~이다 It is a commonly accepted view that….

통성명(通姓名) exchanging names. ~하다 exchange names; introduce (*themselves*) to each other.

통속(通俗) ~적인 popular; common; ~적으로 (explain) in plain language; (write) in a popular style / ~화하다 popularize; vulgarize. ‖ ~문학 popular literature / ~소설 a popular (lowbrow) novel / ~화 popularization.

통솔(統率) command; leadership. ~하다 command; lead; assume leadership; take the lead of. ¶ …의 ~하에 있다 be under the command of…. / 그는 ~력이 있다 He has good leadership. ‖ ~자 a leader; a commander.

통송곳 a drill with a crescent blade.

통수(統帥) the supreme command. ‖ ~권 the prerogative of supreme command / ~권자 a leader; a supreme commander.

통신(通信) correspondence; communication; 〔보도〕 news; 〔정보〕 information. ~하다 correspond (communicate) (*with*); report (*for a paper*). ¶ 런던발 ~에 의하면 according to a dispatch from London / ~을 시작〔계속〕하다 get into (keep in) communication (*with*). ‖ ~강좌 a correspondence course / ~공학 communication engineering / ~교육 correspondence education / ~기관 communications media / ~대(隊) a signal corps / ~두절 a communication blackout / ~망 a communications (news service) network (system) / ~사(士) a telegraph operator / ~사(社) a news agency (service) / ~사업 a communication service / ~수단 a means of communication / ~원 a correspondent; a reporter / ~위성 a communications satellite / ~판매 mail order; mail-order selling / ~판매하다 sell (*goods*) by mail).

통심정(通心情) ~하다 open *one's* heart (*to*).

통어(統御) ~하다 reign (rule) over; govern; control; manage.

통역(通譯) 〔일〕 interpretation; 《사람》 an interpreter. ~하다 interpret; act (serve) as (an) interpreter (*for*). ¶ ~를 통해 말하다 speak through an interpreter / 나는 동시~사 자격증을 가지고

통용 I have a license as a simultaneous interpreter. ∥ ~관 an official interpreter.

통용(通用) popular (common) use; circulation; currency. ~하다 pass; circulate; be good (available); be accepted; hold good (규칙 등이). ¶미국 달러가 유럽에서도 ~되느냐 Are U.S. dollars accepted in Europe? / 그 규칙은 지금도 ~된다 The rule still holds good. ¶ ~기간 the term of validity / ~문 a side gate; 《사원 등의》 a service entrance / ~어 a current word / ~화폐 current coins; a currency.

통운(通運) transportation; forwarding. ¶ ~회사 a transportation (an express 《美》) company; a forwarding agent.

통원(通院) ~하다 attend a hospital (as an outpatient); go to hospital (for treatment).

통으로 for all; wholly; all together; in the lump.

통음(痛飮) ~하다 drink heavily; have a booze (口).

통일(統一) unification; uniformity; unity. ~하다 unify; unite 《a nation》; 《표준화》 standardize; 《집중》 concentrate. ¶남북 ~ unification of North and South (Korea) / 정신 ~ mental concentration / 평화 ~ peaceful unification / 정신을 ~하다 concentrate one's mind / 그가 나라를 ~한 것은 언제였지 When did he unify the nation (country)? ¶ ~국가 a unified nation / ~부 the Ministry of Unification / ~전선을 펴다 form a united front to 《against》.

통장(通帳) 《예금의》 a passbook; a bankbook; 《외상의》 a chit book.

통절(痛切) ~한 keen; acute; poignant; severe ¶ ~히 (feel) keenly; acutely; severely.

통정(通情) 《간통》 adultery. ~하다 have an illicit affair 《with》; commit adultery 《with》.

통제(統制) control; regulation. ~하다 control; regulate. ¶물가 ~ price control / 정부는 ~를 강화〔완화, 해제〕했다 The government tightened [loosened, removed] the controls. / 그 나라는 군의 ~하에 있다 The country is under the control of the army. ¶ ~가격 controlled prices / ~경제 controlled economy / ~품 controlled goods (articles).

통제부(統制府) 《해군의》 a naval yard (station).

통조림(桶—) canned (tinned 《英》) food (goods). ¶ ~한 canned; tinned / 쇠고기〔연어〕 ~ canned beef (salmon) / ~으로 만들다 can 《beef》; pack 《meat》 in a can. ∥ ~공업 the canning industry / ~공장 a cannery; a canning factory (plant) / ~식품 canned food / ~업자 a canner.

통증(痛症) a pain; (an) ache. ¶위에 격렬한 ~을 느끼다 feel a sharp pain in the stomach / 가슴의 ~을 호소하다 complain of a pain in the chest.

통지(通知) (a) notice; (a) notification; information; an advice (상업상의). ~하다 inform (notify) 《a person》 of 《a matter》; give notice of 《a matter》; let 《a person》 know. ¶입시 합격의 ~를 받았다 I got [received] (a) notice that I had passed the entrance examination. / 다음 ~가 있을 때까지 기다리시오 Wait till further notice. ∥ ~서 a notice.

통짜다 ① 《맞추다》 frame; assemble; put together. ② 《동아리가 되다》 form a gang (group); band (club) together.

통째 all (together); wholly. ¶ ~로 먹다 eat 《something》 whole.

통찰(洞察) penetration; insight; discernment. ~하다 penetrate into; see through. ¶ ~력 insight / ~력이 있는 사람 a man of keen insight.

통첩(通牒) a notice; a notification. ~하다 notify; give notice to; send (issue) a notification. ¶최후 ~ an ultimatum.

통촉(洞燭) ~하다 (deign to) see; understand; judge.

통치(統治) rule; reign; government. ~하다 reign (rule) 《over》; govern. ¶ ~권 sovereignty; the supreme power / ~기관 government organs (machinery) / ~자 the sovereign; the ruler / ~ 행위 an act of the state.

통치마 a pleatless skirt.

통칙(通則) general rules (provisions).

통칭(通稱) a popular (common) name; an alias. ¶ ~ …이라고 부르다 go by the name of….

통쾌(痛快) ~하다 (be) extremely delightful (pleasant); exciting; thrilling. ¶ ~하게 (be) thrilled (delighted) 《to hear that…》 / 그날 저녁에는 ~히 마셨다 That night I drank to my heart's content.

통탄(痛嘆) ~하다 lament (regret, grieve) deeply; deplore. ¶ ~할 deplorable; lamentable / ~할 일이다 It is deplorable that….

통통거리다 pound; resound.

통통하다 (be) portly; plump;

통틀어 (all) in all; all told; all taken together; altogether; in total. ¶ ~ 얼마요 How much is it altogether (in all)?

통폐(通弊) a common abuse (evil). ¶ 중수회는 우리나라 정계의 ~이다 Bribery is an evil practice prevalent in our political circles.

통풍(痛風) 〖醫〗 the gout.

통하다(通-) ① (길·통로·교통) run 《to》; go (lead) 《to》(…에 이르다); open 《into, upon》; be opened 《to》(개통). ¶ 모든 길은 로마로 통한다 All roads lead to Rome. ② (잘 알다) be well informed 《about》; be familiar (well acquainted) 《with》; have a good knowledge 《of》. ¶ 중국 문제에 ~ be well informed about the Chinese affairs. ③ 《말·의사가》 be understood; be spoken; make *oneself* understood. ¶ 영어가 ~ be able to speak English; make *oneself* understood in English / 서로 기맥이 ~ have a tacit understanding with each other. ④ (…로 알려지다) pass 《for, as》; be known 《as》. ¶ ~란 이름으로 ~ be known by the name of…; circulate; be available (valid); hold good. ⑤ (유효하다) pass; circulate; be available (valid); hold good. ¶ 이 돈은 어디서나 통한다 This money passes (can be used) freely everywhere. ⑥ (연락·관계) communicate (be in touch) 《with》; betray (적에게) ; have intimacy (become intimate) 《with》 (사동). ¶ 정을 ~ have an affair (illicit intercourse) 《with》. ⑦ (전기 등이) circulate; transmit; 《공기 등이》 ventilate; flow; circulate; pass through; penetrate(빛·열이). ¶ 공기가 잘 ~ have a good ventilation. ⑧ (경유·경과·매개) go (pass) through. ¶ 김씨를 통해서 ~ through (the good office of) Mr. Kim / 시베리아를 통해서 파리에 가다 go to Paris via (by way of) Siberia.

통학(通學) ~하다 attend (go to) school. ¶ 버스〔자전거〕로 ~하다 go to school by bus (bicycle) / 걸어서 ~하다 walk to school. ‖ ~버스 a school bus / ~생 (기숙생과 대비해서) a day student.

통한(痛恨) deep (bitter) regret.

통할(統轄) supervision; (general) control. ~하다 supervise; control; exercise general control 《over》. ‖ ~구역 the area under the direct control 《of》.

통합(統合) unity; unification; integration. ~하다 unify; unite; integrate; put together. ¶ 몇 개의 정부 기관을 하나로 ~하다 integrate some government agencies into one. ‖ ~참모본부 the Joint Chiefs of Staff (생략 J.C.S.) 《美》/ ~참모본부 의장 the Chairman of the Joint Chiefs of Staff 《美》.

통행(通行) passing; transit; traffic. ~하다 pass (through); go through (along); be allowed to pass; 《갈 수 없다》 be impassable / ~량이 많은 도로 a road with heavy (busy) traffic / ~을 금지하다 close the street to traffic; close up a road / ~을 방해하다 obstruct traffic; bar the way. ‖ ~권 the right of way / ~금지 the suspension of traffic; 〔게시〕 No thoroughfare; Closed to traffic. / ~료 〔요금〕 a toll / ~세 〔화물의〕 a transit tax / ~인 a passer-by; a pedestrian (보행자) / ~(허가)증 a pass / 우측 〔게시〕 Keep right. / 일방 〔게시〕 One way.

통혼(通婚) ~하다 make a proposal of marriage; intermarry 《with》.

통화(通貨) currency; money. ¶ 관리 ~ the managed (controlled) currency / ~의 안정 stabilization of currency / ~안정을 흔들리다 disturb the stability of the currency. ‖ ~정책〔위기〕a monetary policy (crisis) / ~제도 a monetary system / ~팽창〔수축〕 inflation (deflation).

통화(通話) a (tele)phone call. ~하다 talk over the telephone 《with》. ¶ ~ one (telephone) call / ~ 3분 간의 요금은 200원이다 The charge is 200 won for a three-minute call. / ~ 중입니다 〔교환원의 말〕 Line's busy. *or* Number's engaged 《美》. ‖ ~료 a telephone charge.

퇴각(退却) retreat; withdrawal. ~하다 (make a) retreat 《from, to》; withdraw 《from》. ¶ 그들은 총 ~ 중이었다 They were in full retreat. ‖ ~명령 an order to retreat.

퇴거(退去) 〔이전〕 leaving; removal; 〔철수〕 evacuation; withdrawal. ~하다 leave; depart; evacuate; withdraw; remove. ¶ ~을 명하다 order 《a person》 out of 《a place》. ‖ ~령 an expulsion order.

퇴고(推敲) ~하다 work on *one's* manuscript to improve 〔revise〕 the wording; polish; elaborate. ¶ ~를 거듭하여 기사를 쓰다 work hard to polish the article.

퇴골(腿骨) 〖解〗 a leg bone.

퇴교(退校) ⇨ 퇴학.

퇴근(退勤) ~하다 leave *one's* office; go home from work. ‖ ~시간 the closing hour.

퇴락(頹落) dilapidation. ~하다 dilapidate; go to ruin; fall into decay.

퇴로(退路) the (path of) retreat. ¶적의 ~를 차단하다 intercept [cut off] the (*enemy's*) retreat.

퇴물(退物) ① 《물려받은》 a hand-me-down; a used article. ② 《거절된》 a thing rejected [refused] (*from*). ③ 《사람》 a retired person. ¶기생 ~ an ex-*kisaeng*.

퇴박맞다(退─) be refused [rejected].

퇴박하다(退─) refuse; reject; turn down.

퇴보(退步) retrogression; a setback. ~하다 retrograde; go back(ward). ¶~적인 retrogressive.

퇴비(堆肥) compost; barnyard manure. ¶밭에 ~를 주다 compost the field. ‖ ~더미 a compost pile [heap].

퇴사(退社) ① 《퇴직》 ~하다 retire from [leave] the company; 《口》 quit. ¶그는 3년 전에 ~했다 He quit three years ago. ② → 퇴근.

퇴색(退色) ~하다 fade; be discolored; lose color; be faded.

퇴석(堆石) ① 《돌무더기》 a pile of stones. ② 〖地〗 a moraine.

퇴세(頹勢) a decline; a downward tendency.

퇴역(退役) retirement (from service). ~하다 retire from service; leave the army. ¶~군인 an ex-serviceman; 《美》 a veteran / ~장교 a retired officer.

퇴영(退嬰) ¶~적인 retrogressive, conservative.

퇴원(退院) ~하다 leave (the) hospital; be discharged from hospital. ¶~해 있다 be out of hospital.

퇴위(退位) (an) abdication. ~하다 abdicate (*the throne*); step down from the throne. ¶~시키다 dethrone [depose] (*a king*).

퇴임(退任) retirement. ~하다 retire [resign] from *one's* office [post]. ¶임기만료로 ~하다 retire from office upon completing *one's* term of office.

퇴장(退場) ~하다 leave (*a place*); walk out (*of*); go away (*from*); (make *one's*) exit (*from*) (무대에서). ¶~을 명하다 order (*a person*) out of (*the hall*).

퇴적(堆積) (an) accumulation; a heap; a pile. ~하다 accumulate; be piled [heaped] up. ‖ ~암 sedimentary rocks.

퇴정(退廷) ~하다 leave (the) court; withdraw from the court.

퇴직(退職) 《정년의》 retirement; 《사직》 resignation. ~하다 retire; resign (*one's position*); leave [retire from] office (공직 등에서). ¶자진 ~ voluntary retirement [resignation] / ~하도록 압력을 가하다 put pressure on (*a person*) 「to resign to leave the job」. ‖ ~공무원〔자〕 a retired official [employee] / ~권고 advice to resign / ~금〔수당〕 retirement allowance / ~금〔수당〕 a severance allowance [pay] / ~연금 a retirement annuity [pension] / 명예〔조기〕 ~ voluntary (early, downsizing) retirement.

퇴진(退陣) ~하다 《진지에서》 decamp; withdraw; 《지위에서》 retire (from a position); step down; give up *one's* position; go out of office; resign. ¶곧 ~할 수상 the outgoing premier.

퇴짜(退─) ~놓다 refuse; reject; rebuff; turn down / ~(를) 맞다 get rejected; meet a rebuff; be turned down / 월급을 올려 달랬다가 ~ 맞았다 I asked for a raise but got turned down.

퇴청(退廳) ~하다 leave the office.

퇴치(退治) 《박멸》 extermination. ~하다 exterminate; wipe [stamp, root] out; get rid of (*rats*). ¶문맹 ~ 운동 a crusade against illiteracy.

퇴침(退枕) a wooden [box] pillow.

퇴폐(頹廢) corruption; decadence. ~하다 be corrupted; 《…의》 decadent / 도의의 ~ moral decay; decadence / ~한 세상 the decadent world. ‖ ~주의 decadence.

퇴학(退學) withdrawal from school. ~하다 leave [quit, give up] school. ¶~시키다 expel [dismiss] (*a student*) from school / ~당하다 be dismissed [expelled] from school. ‖ ~생 a dropout / ~처분 expulsion [dismissal] from school.

퇴화(退化) retrogression; degeneration. ~하다 degenerate; retrogress. ¶~한 degenerate(d) / 근육은 쓰지 않으면 ~한다 Muscles, if not used, degenerate. ‖ ~기관〖生〗 a rudiment; a rudimentary organ.

툇마루(退─) a narrow porch.

투(套) 《버릇》 a manner; a habit; a way; 《양식》 a form; a style. ¶~의 *one's* way of talking / 농담 ~로 말하다 say just for fun [said in jest].

투견(鬪犬) 《싸움》 a dogfight; 《개》 a fighting dog.

투계(鬪鷄) 《싸움》 a cockfight; 《닭》

투고(投稿) a contribution; ~하다 contribute (*an article to*); write (*to the Times*); write (*for*). ‖ ~란 the readers'(contributors') columns / ~자 a contributor.

투과(透過) permeation; penetration; 〖化〗 transmission. ~하다 permeate (*through*); penetrate; filter (out). ‖ ~성 permeability (~성막 a permeable membrane) / ~율 transmissivity / ~인자 a transmission factor / ~형 전자망원경 a transmission electron microscope.

투광기(投光器) a floodlight.

투구 a helmet; a headpiece.

투구(投球) 〖野〗 pitching (투수의); throwing (야구의). ~하다 pitch (throw, hurl) a ball; make a throw (*to second*). ‖ ~동작 a windup / ~연습 a warming up for pitching.

투기(妬忌) jealousy; envy. ~하다 be jealous (*of, over*); be envious (*of*).

투기(投機) speculation; a flier (美口). ~하다 speculate (*in*); gamble (*in stocks*). ¶ ~적인 speculative; risky / ~에 손을 대다 dabble in speculation. ‖ ~꾼 a speculator; a stockjobber (주식거래인) / ~사업 a speculative business (enterprise) / a venture / ~심 speculative spirit (streak) / ~열 a speculative craze; a craze (mania) for speculation / ~자본 venture capital (美).

투기(鬪技) a contest; a match.

투덕거리다 tap. ¶ 토닥거리다.

투덜거리다 grumble (*about, at*); complain (*about, of*); murmur with discontent. ¶ 투덜투덜 grumblingly; complainingly.

투망(投網) a casting net.

투매(投賣) a sacrifice sale; dumping. ~하다 sell (*goods*) at a loss (sacrifice); dump (*goods abroad*). ‖ ~상품 sacrifice goods.

투명(透明) ~하다 (be) transparent; lucid; clear; limpid. ‖ ~도 the degree of transparency / ~인간 an invisible man / ~체 a transparent body.

투묘(投錨) anchoring; anchorage. ~하다 anchor; cast anchor.

투미하다 (be) stupid; silly; dull.

투박하다 《사람이》 crude; vulgar; boorish; 《물건이》 (be) crude; coarse; rough; unshapely. ¶ 투박한 구두 heavy unshapely shoes.

투베르쿨린 〖醫〗 tuberculin. ‖ ~ 반응(검사) a tuberculin reaction (test).

투병(鬪病) a fight (struggle) against a disease. ¶ ~생활 one's life under medical treatment / 2년간의 ~생활 끝에 이전 직무로 복귀하다 return to one's former job after two years of struggling with illness.

투사(投射) 〖數〗 projection; 〖理〗 incidence. ~하다 project (*on*). ‖ ~각 the angle of incidence.

투사(透寫) tracing. ~하다 trace (*a drawing*). ‖ ~지(紙) tracing paper.

투사(鬪士) a fighter; a champion. ¶ 자유(노동 운동)의 ~ a fighter for freedom (labor) / 혁명 ~ a champion of revolution.

투서(投書) a contribution; an anonymous letter(밀고). ~하다 send (*a note*) anonymously; contribute an article (*to*) (투고). ‖ ~함 a suggestion (complaints) box.

투석(投石) ~하다 throw (hurl) a stone (rock) (*at*).

…투성이 (온통 …으로 덮인) covered (smeared) all over with; (…이 많은) full of; filled with. ¶ 오자의 ~ 의 책 a book full of misprint / 먼지(흙) ~가 되다 be covered with dust (mud).

투수(投手) a pitcher; a hurler. ¶ 이기고 (지고) 있는 ~ a winning (losing) pitcher / 주전 ~ an ace pitcher / 구원 ~ a relief pitcher / 우완 (좌완) ~ a right-hand (left-handed) pitcher. ‖ ~전 a pitchers' battle; a pitching duel / ~진 the pitching staff / ~판 a pitcher's plate; a mound.

투숙(投宿) ~하다 put up at (*a hotel*); check into (*a hotel*); lodge (*at a hotel; with a family*). ‖ ~객 a guest; a lodger.

투시(透視) 〖천리안〗 clairvoyance; second sight. ~하다 see through; look at (*a person's chest*) through the fluoroscope (X선으로). ‖ ~검사 (X선의) fluoroscopy / ~도 a perspective drawing / ~자 a clairvoyant.

투신(投身) ① 《자살》 ~하다 drown oneself; throw (hurl) oneself (*into the water, from a cliff*); leap to one's death. ② 《종사》 ~하다 engage (take part) (*in*). ¶ 정계에 ~하다 enter the political world.

투약(投藥) medication; prescription (of medicine); dosage. ~하다 prescribe (*for a patient*); prescribe (give) a medicine; medicate.

투영(投影) 《그림자》 a (cast) shadow; 《그림》 a projection. ~하다 reflect; cast a reflection. ‖ ~도 a projection chart / ~도법 the method of projections.

투옥(投獄) imprisonment. ~하다 put 《a person》 in prison 〔jail〕; throw 《a person》 into prison; imprison. ¶ 무고죄로 ~되다 be put into prison on a false charge.

투우(鬪牛) 《싸움》 a bullfight; 《소》 a fighting bull; 《~사 a bullfighter; a matador / ~장 a bullring.

투원반(投圓盤) the discus throw. ‖ ~선수 a discus thrower.

투입(投入) ① 《자본을》 ~하다 invest 《capital》. ¶ ~ 자본 an investment. ② 《던져 넣기》 a throw 〔cast〕 《a thing》 into. ¶ 전투에 3개 사단을 ~하다 commit three divisions to the battle.

투자(投資) (an) investment. ~하다 invest 《in》; put 〔lay out〕 《money in an enterprise》. ¶ 공공 ~ public investment / 시설 ~ investment in plant and equipment / 확실한 ~ a sound investment / 전재산을 토지에 ~하다 invest all one's money in land. ‖ ~상담소 an investment counsel office / ~신탁 investment trust / ~가 〔가〕 an investor 《기관 ~ an institutional investor / 일반 ~가 the investing public》.

투쟁(鬪爭) a fight; a struggle; a conflict; strife. ~하다 fight 《for, against》. ¶ 계급〔권력〕 ~ a class 〔power〕 struggle / 노사간의 ~ strife between labor and management / 인종간의 ~ racial conflicts 〔strife〕. ‖ ~위원회 a strike 〔struggle〕 committee / ~자금 strike 〔struggle〕 funds.

투전(鬪錢) gambling(도박). ‖ ~꾼 a gambler.

투정 grumbling; complaining. ~하다 grumble 《at, for, over》; growl; complain 《about, of》. ¶ 밥~ grumbling over 〔at〕 one's food.

투지(鬪志) fighting spirit; fight. ¶ ~ 만만하다 be full of fight 〔fighting spirit〕 / ~가 없다 lack in fight; have no fighting spirit.

투창(投槍) javelin throw(ing). ~하다 throw a javelin. ‖ ~선수 a javelin thrower.

투척(投擲) throwing; a throw. ~하다 throw 《a hand grenade》. ‖ ~경기 a throwing event.

투철(透徹) ~하다 be penetrating; lucid; clear; clear-cut. ¶ ~한 이론 an intelligible 〔a clear-cut〕 theory / ~한 두뇌 clear brains.

투포환(投砲丸) the shot put; shot putting. ‖ ~선수 a shot-putter.

투표(投票) 《투표하기》 poll; voting; ballot; 《표》 a vote; a ballot《무기명》. ~하다 vote 《for, against》; cast a vote 《ballot》; give a vote 《to a person》; ballot. ¶ ~에 부치다 put 《a matter》 to the vote / ~하러 가다 go to the poll / ~로 결정하다 decide by vote. ‖ ~권 the right to vote; voting rights / ~소〔장〕 a polling place (station); 《go to》 the polls 《美》 / ~용지 a voting paper; a ballot (paper) / ~용지 기입소 a ballot booth / ~율 a voting rate 《높은〔낮은〕 ~율 a heavy〔light〕 poll》 / ~일 a voting day / ~자 a voter / ~참관인 a voting witness / ~함 a ballot box.

투피스 a two-piece suit 《dress》.

투하(投下) ~하다 throw 《a thing》 down; drop 《a bomb》; 《자본을》 invest 《in》. ¶ 비행기가 구호 물자를 ~했다 The plane dropped relief supplies. / ~자본 invested 〔investment〕 capital.

투함(投函) ~하다 mail 〔post 《英》〕 《a letter》; put 《a letter》 in a mailbox.

투항(投降) surrender. ~하다 surrender 《to》; capitulate; lay down 〔give up〕 one's arms. ¶ 조건부로 ~하다 surrender to the enemy under certain terms. ‖ ~자 a surrenderer.

투해머(投―) 〔競〕 the hammer throw.

투혼(鬪魂) a fighting spirit.

툭 ① 《튀어나온 모양》 protruding; protuberant; bulging; 《불거짐·비어짐》 popping out; bulging out 《of a pocket》. ② 《치는 소리》 with a pat 《rap》. ¶ 어깨를 ~ 치다 tap 《a person》 on the shoulder. ③ 《끊어지는 소리》 with a snap. ¶ 《실이》 ~ 끊어지다 snap off. ④ 《쏘는 모양》 sharply; prickingly.

툭탁거리다 exchange blows; beat each other up.

툭툭하다 (be) thick; close.

툭하면 without any reason; be apt to 《do》; always; ready to. ¶ ~ 사람을 치다 ready to punch 《a person》; punch 《a person》 at the slightest provocation.

툰드라 〔地〕 a tundra.

툴툴거리다 grumble 《at, over, about》; growl.

퉁겨지다 ① 《쑥 드러나다》 get disclosed; be revealed 〔exposed〕; come out; transpire. ② 《어긋나서》 come apart; get out of the place 〔joint〕. ¶ 책상다리가 ~ the leg of a table gets disjointed.

퉁기다 ① 《버틴 것을》 get 《it》 out of place; take 《it》 apart; slip 《a stay》. ② 《기회를》 let 《it》 slip;

miss (*a chance*). ③ 〔관절을〕 put (*in*) out of the joint. ④ 〔현악기를〕 pluck the strings (*of*); pick (thrum on) (*a guitar*).
퉁명스럽다 (be) blunt; curt; brusque. ¶ 퉁명스럽게 말하다 talk bluntly; be blunt in *one's* speech / 그는 누구에게나 ~ He is brusque with everyone.
퉁방울 〔방울〕 a brass bell.
퉁방울이 a popeyed person.
퉁소(-簫) a bamboo flute.
퉁탕 ① 〔발소리〕 keep pounding; stamp (*along*). ② 〔총성〕 ~거리다 keep banging away.
퉁퉁 〔부은 꼴〕 swell up.
퉁퉁하다 〔살찐 꼴〕 (be) plump; full.
튀각 fried kelp (tangle).
튀기 〔잡종·혼혈아〕 a hybrid; a crossbreed; a half-breed; a half-blood. ¶ ~의 hybrid.
튀기다¹ 〔손가락으로〕 flip; fillip; snap; 〔물 따위를〕 splash; spatter.
튀기다² 〔기름에〕 fry; 〔뛰밥을〕 pop (*rice*).
튀김 deep-fried food. ¶ 새우 ~ a deep-fried shrimp.
튀다 ① 〔뛰어오르다〕 spring; 〔공이〕 bound; rebound; bounce. ② 〔침·물이〕 spatter; splash; splatter. ¶ 얼굴에 침이 ~ *one's* face is spattered with saliva. ③ 〔불꽃이〕 spark; sputter; 〔나무·장작이〕 snap; crack; crackle. ¶ 불똥이 ~ emit (give off) sparks; sparks shoot up in the air. ④ 〔달아나다〕 run away; make off; take to flight; flee. ¶ 도둑이 ~ a robber takes to flight.
튀밥 popped rice.
튀하다 scald (*a pig in hot water*).
튜너 a tuner.
튜닝 〔조율〕 tuning. ~하다 tune [up].
튜바 〔樂〕 a tuba.
튜브 a tube; an inner tube (자전거 따위의). ¶ ~에 든 치약 a tube of toothpaste.
튤립 〔植〕 a tulip.
트다¹ ① 〔싹이〕 bud out; sprout. ② 〔먼동이〕 dawn; break (*open*); turn grey. ③ 〔피부가〕 crack; be (get) chapped.
트다² 〔길을〕 clear the way (*for*); make way (*for another*). ¶ 거래를 ~ enter into a business relation (*with*); open an account (*with*).
트라이앵글 〔樂〕 a triangle.
트라코마, 트라홈 〔醫〕 trachoma.
트랙 a track. ∥ ~경기 track events (athletics).
트랙터 a tractor.
트랜스 〔電〕 a transformer.
트랜지스터 〔電〕 a transistor (*radio*).
트랩 〔비행기의〕 a ramp; landing steps; 〔배의〕 a gangway (ladder). ¶ ~을 올라〔내려〕가다 go (step) (down) the ladder (ramp).
트러블 a (*family*) trouble. ¶ ~을 일으키다 make (stir up) trouble.
트러스 〔建〕 a truss.
트러스트 〔經〕 a trust. ∥ ~금지법 an antitrust law.
트럭 a truck; a lorry 〔英〕. ¶ ~ 3 대 분의 짐 three truckloads of goods / ~ 운전사 a truck driver / ~으로 수송하다 transport (*goods*) by truck. ∥ ~운송 trucking.
트럼펫 a trumpet. ¶ ~을 연습을 하다 practice the trumpet. ∥ ~ (연)주자 a trumpeter.
트럼프 a deck (pack) of cards. ¶ ~를 하다 play cards / ~ 속임수 card tricks / ~로 점을 보다 tell *one's* fortune from (with) cards.
트렁크 〔대형의〕 a trunk; 〔소형의〕 a suitcase; 〔자동차의〕 a trunk.
트레몰로 〔樂〕 a tremolo (이).
트레이너 a trainer.
트레이닝 training. ¶ 하드 ~ hard training / 〔선수가〕 ~을 받고 있다 be (in) training (*for the coming Olympics*); ∥ ~셔츠 a training jacket; a sweat shirt / ~캠프 a training camp / ~팬츠 sweat pants.
트레이드 〔거래〕 a trade. ¶ 그 투수는 자이언트에 ~되었다 The pitcher was traded to the Giants. ∥ ~마크 a trademark / ~머니 money paid for a (*baseball*) player.
트레일러 a trailer. ∥ ~버스 a trailer bus / ~하우스 a house trailer.
트로이 Troy. ¶ ~의 목마 the Trojan Horse. ¶ ~전쟁 the Trojan War.
트로이카 a troika.
트로피 (win) a trophy.
트롤 a trawl. ¶ ~망〔그물〕 a trawl(net) / ~선 a trawlboat; a trawler / ~어업 trawling.
트롤리 a trolley (*bus*).
트롬본 〔樂〕 a trombone. ∥ ~ (연)주자 a trombonist.
트리밍 〔寫〕 trimming. ~하다 trim.
트리오 〔樂〕 a trio.
트리코 〔옷감〕 tricot 〔프〕.
트릭 a trick. ¶ ~을 쓰다 resort to tricks / 감쪽같이 ~에 걸려들다 be nicely tricked (taken in). ∥ ~촬영 a trick shot.
트림 a belch; belching; a burp (아기의). ~하다 belch; burp.
트릿하다 〔속이〕 feel heavy on the stomach; 〔의심함〕 (be) dubious; vague; lukewarm.
트위스트 (dance) the twist.
트이다 ① 《막혔던 것이》 get cleared;

트적지근하다 feel uncomfortable in the stomach; be belchy.

트집(닭) a fault; blemish; (틈) a split; a gap. ¶ ~ 잡다 find fault with ⟪a person⟫; pick flaws (holes) in⟫ / ~나다 get cracked; have a split. ‖ ~쟁이 a faultfinder; a nitpicker.

특가(特價) (sell at) a special [bargain] price. ‖ ~판매 a bargain sale / ~품 an article offered at a special price.

특검법(特檢法) the independent [special] counsel bill (to investigate the scandals).

특공대(特攻隊) a special attack corps; a commando; a suicide squad. ‖ ~ a technical corps.

특과(特科) a special course; 〖軍〗

특권(特權) a prerogative; special rights. ¶ ~을 주다 give ⟪a person⟫ a privilege / ~을 행사하다 exercise one's privilege / ~을 누리다 enjoy privileges ⟪of⟫ / ~층 the privileged few [minority]. ‖ ~계급 the privileged classes.

특근(特勤) overtime work. ~하다 work overtime; do ⟪one hour⟫ overtime. ‖ ~수당 overtime allowance.

특급(特急) a special [limited] express (train). ¶ ~ 새마을호를 타다 take the limited express Saemaul.

특급(特級) a special grade; the highest quality. ¶ ~주 the highest quality wine / ~품 the highest quality item [article, goods, brand].

특기(特技) special ability [talent, skill]; one's speciality.

특기(特記) ~하다 mention specially. ¶ ~할 만한 remarkable; striking; noteworthy / ~할 만한 것은 없다 There is nothing to make special mention of.

특대(特大) ¶ ~의 extra-large; outsize(d); king-size(d) 〖美〗. ‖ ~호 an enlarged special edition(잡지의).

특대(特待) ~하다 treat specially; give a special treatment ⟪to⟫. ‖ ~생 a scholarship [an honor] student (~되다 get [be given] a scholarship).

특등(特等) a special class [grade]. ‖ ~석 a special seat; a box (seat) (극장의) / ~실 a special room; a stateroom(여객선의) /

~품 an extra-fine article; a choice article.

특례(特例) ⟪case⟫; a particular case; ⟪예외⟫ an exception. ¶ ~로서 as an exception(예외로) / ~를 만들다 make an exception ⟪in favor of⟫ / ~법 the Exception Law.

특매(特賣) a special [bargain] sale. ~하다 sell at a special price; conduct a special sale. ¶ ~장 a bargain counter / ~품 an article offered at a bargain (price).

특명(特命) special command [appointment, order]. ¶ ~을 띠고 on a special mission. ‖ ~전권 대사 an ambassador extraordinary and plenipotentiary.

특무(特務) special duty [service]. ‖ ~기관 the Special Service Agency [Organization]; the secret (military) agency [service].

특배(特配) an extra ration; special distribution. ~하다 distribute [ration] specially.

특별(特別) ~한 (e)special; ⟪특정의⟫ particular; ⟪고유의⟫ peculiar; ⟪여분의⟫ extra; ⟪비정상의⟫ extraordinary; ⟪예외⟫ exceptional / ~히 (e)specially; particularly / ~취급하다 give ⟪a person⟫ special treatment. ¶ ~교서 a special message / ~기 a special airplane / ~배당 a special [bonus] dividend / ~보좌관 President's Special Adviser; Special Adviser ⟪to⟫ / ~사찰 a special inspection / ~석 a special seat / ~수당 a special [an extra] allowance (~수당을 타는 be paid extra) / ~승급 a special raise in salary / ~열차 a special train / ~예산 [회계] a special budget [account] / ~위원회 a special [an ad hoc] committee / ~치료 a special (medical) treatment / ~프로 a special program / ~호 a special (an extra) (임시) number (잡지 등의) / ~회원 a special member.

특보(特報) a (news) flash; a special news. ¶ 개표 결과를 ~하다 flash the ballot counting results.

특사(特使) a special envoy [messenger]. ¶ 대통령 ~ a presidential personal envoy / ~를 파견하다 dispatch a special envoy.

특사(特赦) (an) amnesty(일반); a special pardon(개인). ~하다 grant [give] an amnesty ⟪to⟫. ¶ ~로 출감하다 be released from prison on amnesty / ~를 받다 be granted amnesty. ‖ ~령 an act of grace [amnesty]; a

특산(물)(特産物) a special product; a speciality. ¶ 이 지방의 주요 ~ the principal products of this district. ‖ 특산지 special production localities.

특상(特上) ¶ ~의 the finest; the choicest; superfine. ‖ ~품 an extra-fine brand; choice goods.

특상(特賞) a special prize [reward].

특색(特色) a (special) feature; a characteristic; a distinctive character. ¶ ~(이) 있는 characteristic; distinctive / ~(이) 없는 featureless; common / ~ 있게 하다 characterize (a thing).

특선(特選) special selection [choice]; 〈상에서〉 the highest honor. ¶ ~품 choice goods.

특설(特設) ―하다 set up [establish] specially. ¶ ~의 specially installed. ‖ ~링 a specially prepared ring / ~전화 a specially installed telephone.

특성(特性) a special character [quality]; a characteristic; a trait; a property. ¶ 인간의 ~ a characteristic of man / 국민적 ~ national traits / ~을 살리다 make the most of (its) characteristics; turn (its) peculiar quality to account.

특수(特殊) ¶ ~한 (특별) special; particular; specific; 〈특이〉 peculiar; unique / ~화하다 specialize; differentiate. ‖ ~강 special steel / ~교육 special education; education for the handicapped / ~법인 a corporation (judicial person) having special status / ~부대 special forces / ~사정 special circumstances [situations] / ~성 peculiarity; specific characteristics / ~은행 a special [chartered] bank / ~촬영 〈영화에서〉 shooting for special effects; trick shooting / ~취급 special [preferential] treatment [handling] / ~층 a privileged class / ~효과 special effects.

특수경기(特需景氣) a special procurement boom.

특약(特約) a special contract [agreement]. ~하다 make a special contract. ¶ …과 ~이 있다 have a special contract with …. ‖ ~점 a special agent; a chain store(미국식의) / ~조항 a clause containing special policy conditions.

특용(特用) ‖ ~작물 a crop for a special use; a cash crop.

특유(特有) ¶ ~의 special; peculiar (to); characteristic (of) / 이것은 한국인 ~의 습관이다 This custom is unique [peculiar] to the Korean. ‖ ~성 a peculiarity.

특이(特異) ¶ ~한 singular; peculiar; unique; unusual / ~한 예 a peculiar case / ~한 재능의 소유자 a person with a unique talent / ~한 형상〈전례가 없는〉 an unprecedented phenomenon. ‖ ~성 singularity; peculiarity / ~체질 an idiosyncrasy; an allergy.

특작(特作) a special production; 〈영화의〉 a special [feature] film.

특장(特長) a strong point; a merit; a forte.

특전(特典) (grant) a privilege (to); a special favor.

특전(特電) a special dispatch [telegram].

특정(特定) ―하다 specify; pin (something) down. ¶ ~의 specially fixed; specific; special / 그 돈은 ~ 목적에 쓰기로 되어 있다 The money is to be used for a specific purpose. ‖ ~인 a specific person / ~품 specialty goods.

특제(特製) special make [manufacture]. ¶ ~의 specially made [manufactured]; of special make / ~빵 the bread of special make. ‖ ~품 a specially-made article.

특종(特種) ① 〈종류〉 a special kind. ② 〈기사의〉 exclusive news; a scoop; a news beat (美). ¶ ~으로 타사를 앞지르다 scoop other papers.

특지(特旨) a special Royal order; a special directive from the Throne.

특진(特進) a special promotion of rank. ¶ 2계급 ~ a double promotion of rank. 〔characteristic.

특질(特質) a special quality; a

특집(特輯) a special edition. ~하다 make up a special edition. ‖ ~기사 a feature article[story] / ~부록 a special supplement / ~호 a special number [issue].

특징(特徵) a characteristic; a peculiarity; a special [distinctive] feature; a trait〈성격상의〉. ¶ ~ 있는〈적인〉 characteristic; peculiar; distinctive / ~ 없는 featureless; common / ~ 짓다 characterize; mark; distinguish / 아무런 ~이 없는 얼굴 a face without any character.

특채(特採) special appointment. ―하다 employ specially.

특출(特出) ~하다 (be) preeminent; distinguished; outstanding; conspicuous; remarkable. ¶ ~한 인물 an outstanding figure.

특칭(特稱) special designation; [論] a particular.
특파(特派) dispatch; special assignment. ~하다 dispatch (*a person*) specially. ¶ 사원을 뉴욕에 ~하다 dispatch (send) an employee to New York for special purposes. ∥ ~대사 an ambassador extraordinary / ~사절(使節) a special envoy; an envoy extraordinary / ~원 (신문사의) a (special) correspondent (*at Washington*).
특필(特筆) special mention. ~하다 mention specially; make special mention of: give prominence to. ¶ ~할 만한 worthy of special mention; remarkable; striking / 대서 ~하다 write in golden (large) letters.
특허(特許) 〖발명·고안의〗 a patent; 〖특별 허가〗 a special permission; a licence (면허); 〖채굴·부설권 등의〗 a concession. ~하다 apply for a patent; file a patent (*for*) / ~출원 중 〖표기〗 Patent pending (applied for). ∥ ~권(료) a patent right (fee) / ~자 a patentee / ~권 침해 a patent infringement / ~법 the patent law / ~청 the Patent Office / ~품 a patent; a patented article.
특혜(特惠) a special (preferential) treatment (benefit). ~의 preferential / ~를 받다 receive preferential treatment / ~를 주다 offer (afford) a preference. ¶ ~관세 a preferential tariff / ~융자 a privileged (preferential) loan.
특효(特效) (have) special virtue (efficacy). ¶ ~약 a special remedy; a specific (medicine) (*for*); a wonder drug.
특히(特-) (e)specially; in particular; particularly; expressly. ¶ ~ 이럴다 할 이유도 없이 for no particular reason.
튼튼하다 ① 〖건강〗 (be) strong; robust; healthy. ¶ 튼튼한 몸을 a strong body / 튼튼해지다 become healthy; grow strong / 튼튼하게 하다 make strong; build up (improve) *one's* health. ② 〖견고〗 (be) solid; strong; firm; durable (오래가다). ¶ 튼튼한 상자 a solid box / 튼튼하게 하다 〖만들다〗 strengthen; make firm (solid); solidify / 이 천은 ~ This cloth wears well.
틀 ① 〖모형〗 a mold; a cast; a matrix. ¶ ~에 부어 만들다 cast in a mold. ② 〖엄격한 격식·형식〗 formality; formula; a limit (범위). ¶ ~에 박힌 conventional; stereotyped / …의 ~ 안에서 within the limit (framework) of…. ③ 〖테〗 a frame; framework (창문·액자 따위의); a tambour (둥근 수틀). ¶ 사진을 ~에 끼우다 frame a picture; set (put) a picture in frame. ④ 〖기계〗 a machine; a device; a gadget. ¶ 재봉~ a sewing machine. ⑤ 〖인간의〗 caliber; capacity. ¶ 사람의 ~이 크다 be a person of large caliber.
틀니 an artificial tooth; a denture.
틀다 ① 〖돌리다〗 wind; turn. ¶ 라디오(수도꼭지)를 ~ turn on the radio (tap). ② 〖비틀〗 twist; wrench; screw (나사를); 〖방향을〗 change; shift; turn. ¶ 방향을 ~ change (shift) *one's* course. ③ 〖일을〗 thwart (*a plan*); cross. ④ 〖상투·머리를〗 tie (do) up (*one's hair*). ⑤ 〖솜을〗 gin (willow) (*cotton*).
틀리다 ① 〖비틀림〗 be distorted; get twisted (wrenched, warped). ② 〖잘못되다〗 go wrong (amiss, awry); be wrong (mistaken, erroneous, incorrect). ¶ 틀린 생각 the wrong idea; a mistaken notion. ③ 〖불화〗 ☞ 틀어지다 ②. ④ 〖끝장나다〗 be done for; be ruined; fail. ¶ 그 환자는 이제 틀렸다 The patient is hopeless. / 그는 교사로서는 틀렸다 As a teacher, he is a failure.
틀림 an error; a mistake; a fault; 〖다름〗 being different. ¶ ~없는 correct; exact; ¶ ~없이 correctly; surely; certainly; no doubt; without fail (꼭) / 그것은 ~없다 There's no doubt about it. / 그는 ~없이 약속시간에 올 것이다 Surely (Certainly) he will come by the appointed time. *or* He will come by the appointed time without fail.
틀어넣다 push (thrust, squeeze) (*a thing*) in; stuff (jam, pack, cram) (*a thing*) into.
틀어막다 ① 〖구멍을〗 stop (*it*) up; stuff; fill; plug. ¶ 구멍을 흙으로 ~ fill a hole with earth. ② 〖입을〗 stop (*a person's mouth*); muzzle; gag; 〖행동을〗 curb (*a person's free action*); check; put a stop to.
틀어박히다 be isolated (*from society*); 〖집에〗 keep (be confined) indoors; shut *oneself* up (*in a room*). ¶ 하루종일 방에 ~ shut (lock) *oneself* up in *one's* room all day.
틀어지다 ① 〖일이〗 go wrong (amiss); fail; be a fiasco. ② 〖사이가〗 fall out (be on bad terms) (*with a person*); be estranged

틀지다 (be) dignified; have dignity.
톱톱 a pit saw.
틈 ① 《벌어진 사이》 an opening; an aperture; a gap; a crevice; a crack; 《불화》 an estrangement; a breach 《of friendship》. ¶ 문~ a chink in the door / 바위~ a crack in a rock / ~이 생기다 crack; cleave; 《불화》 be estranged from 《each other》 / 벽 ~을 메우다 stop 〔fill〕 up the crevice in the wall. ② 《빈 여지》 room; space; 《간격》 interval. ¶ ~이 없다 there is no room…. ③ 《기회》 a chance; 〔seize〕 an opportunity. ¶ ~을 노리다 watch for a chance. ⇨ 틈타다. ④ 《방심》 unpreparedness; an unguarded moment; a blind side. ¶ 빈~이 없다 be thoroughly on guard. ⑤ 《짬》 leisure 〔hours〕; spare time. ¶ ~이 있다 have time to spare; be free / ~을 내다 make 〔find〕 time 《to do》.
틈새기 a chink; a crack. ¶ ~ 바람 a draft 〔美〕; a draught 〔英〕.
틈타다 take advantage of; avail oneself of. ¶ ~을 틈타서 under favor 〔cover〕 of 《the night》; taking advantage of 《the confusion》.
틈틈이 ① 《틈날 때마다》 at odd 〔spare〕 moments; in one's spare moments. ② 《구멍마다》 in every opening.
티¹ ① 《이질물》 dust; a mote; a particle; a grit. ② 《흠》 a defect; a flaw; a speck; a blemish. ¶ 옥에 ~ a flaw in a gem.

티² 《기색·색태》 a touch 〔smack, taste〕 of…; an air of…. ¶ 군인 ~ be soldierly; soldierlike.
티³ ① 《차》 tea. ¶ ~룸 a tea-room / ~ 파티 a tea party. ② 《글자》 the letter "T". ¶ ~셔츠 a T-shirt / ~자 a T square. ③ 《골프의》 a (golf) tee. ¶ ~ 〔with〕.
티격나다 break up 《with》; fall out
티격태격하다 dispute 〔quarrel〕 《with》; bicker with each other.
티끌 dust; a mote. ¶ 양심이라곤 ~ 만큼도 없다 He hasn't an ounce of conscience in him. / ~ 모아 태산 《俗談》 Many a little makes a mickle.
티눈 a corn. ¶ 발에 ~이 박이다 have a corn on one's foot.
티뜯다 《흠잡기》 find faults with.
티베트 Tibet. ¶ ~의 Tibetan. ¶ ~말 Tibetan / ~사람 a Tibetan.
티켓 a ticket.
티크 a teak 《목재》 teak(wood).
티탄 〔化〕 titanium (기호 Ti).
티티새 〔鳥〕 a dusky thrush.
티푸스 typhoid fever; typhus.
팀 a team. ¶ 야구~ a baseball team; the nine / 축구~ a football 〔soccer〕 team; the eleven. ¶ ~워크 teamwork 《~워크가 좋다 have fine teamwork》 / ~을 컬러 the characteristics of a team / ~플레이 the play for one's team.
팀파니 〔樂〕 timpani.
팁 a tip; a gratuity. ¶ ~을 후하게 주는 손님 a high-tipping customer; a good 〔generous〕 tipper / ~을 주다 give 〔offer〕 a tip; tip 《the waiter 5,000 won》 / ~을 받다 accept a tip / ~을 놓자 leave a tip 《on the plate》.

만화에 나오는 의성어·의음어

1. 의성어 (擬聲語)
(개의 성난 소리) 으르렁 GRRRR! / (위급시 놀라 지르는 소리) 이크! EEEK! / (코고는 소리) 쿨쿨 ZZZ; Z-Z-Z / (기침소리) 콜록콜록 COUGH COUGH / (재채기 소리) 에취! AAHHCHOOO! / (울음소리) 엉엉 WAA WAA / (불만의 소리) 투덜투덜 GRUMBLE GRUMBLE / (재잘거리는 소리) 재잘재잘 YAK YAK / (중얼거리는 소리) 중얼중얼 MUMBLE MUMBLE

2. 의음어 (擬音語)
(쇠붙이가 맞닿아 울리는 소리) 쩔그렁 CLANK / (부딪거나 깨지는 요란한 소리) 쿵, 쾅, 쨍그렁 CRASH! ; KRASH! / (차의 급브레이크 등을 밟을 때 나는 소리) 끼익! SCREECH! / (머리 따위를 쥐어박는 소리) 콩! CONK! / (문 따위를 세게 닫는 소리) 쾅! SLAM! / (입맞추는 소리) 쪽! SMACK! ; SMAK! / (버저 소리) 부-! BUZZ!

3. 만화에서 볼 수 있는 구어적 표현
I'm 이나 You're 따위 단축형은 만화 뿐 아니라 일반적으로도 흔하게 쓰이는데, 특히 만화에서는 그림에 현실감을 주기 위해 소리대로 표현하는 경우가 많다. 다음은 그 보기이다.

I'm going to → I'm gonna
I want to → I wanna
I don't know → I dunno
You're looking good → You're lookin' good
Give me… → Gimmie.
That fellow → That fella
I'm glad to know you → Glad to know ya
Come on, you guys! → C'mon, you guys!
Put them out → Put'em out

프

파 [植] a Welsh (green) onion; a leek.
파(派) 《족벌》 a branch of a family (clan); 《학파》 a school; 《당파》 a party; a faction; a clique (파벌); 《종파》 a sect; a denomination; a group(분파).
파격(破格) ¶ ~적인 special; exceptional; unprecedented; irregular (변칙의) ¶ ~적인 대우를 받다 receive exceptionally good treatment.
파견(派遣) dispatch. ~하다 dispatch; send. ¶ 중국에 사절을 ~하다 dispatch (send) an envoy to China. ‖ ~군 an expeditionary army (force) / ~대 a contingent; a detachment.
파경(破鏡) 《이혼》 divorce; separation. ¶ ~에 이르다 be divorced.
파계(破戒) ~하다 break (violate) the 《Buddhist》 commandment. ‖ ~승 a depraved (fallen) monk.
파고(波高) the height of a wave; wave height.
파고다 a pagoda.
파고들다 ① 《조사·규명》 dig (delve, probe) into 《a problem》; examine (look into) 《a matter》 closely (minutely). ¶ 문제에 대해 좀 더 깊이 ~ dig a bit deeper into the matter / 사건의 진상을 ~ get at the truth (to the bottom) of an affair. ② 《비집고 들어가다》 encroach 《upon》; cut into. ¶ 남의 선거 기반에 ~ encroach upon another candidates constituency / 유럽 시장에 ~ make inroads into European markets. ③ 《마음에 스며들다》 be deeply ingrained (in one's mind); eat into; be imbued 《with》. ¶ 사회주의 사상이 ~ 《사람이 주어》 be imbued with socialism / 그 말은 내 마음 속에 파고들었다 The remark sank (eat) into my mind.
파괴(破壞) destruction; demolition. ~하다 break (down); destroy; demolish; wreck; ruin. ¶ ~적인 destructive. ‖ ~공작 subversive activities / ~력 destructive power / ~분자 a subversive (element) / ~자 a destroyer / 대량 ~ 병기 a weapon of mass destruction.
파국(破局) a catastrophe; a collapse; an end(파멸). ¶ ~적인 catastrophic / ~으로 몰고 가다 drive into catastrophe / 우리들의

결혼은 3년 만에 ~을 맞이했다 Our marriage broke down (collapsed) in the third year.
파급(波及) ~하다 spread (extend) 《to, over》; influence; affect. ¶ ~효과 the ripple effect.
파기(破棄) 《찢어버리다》 tear up; destroy; 《무효로 하다》 annul 《an agreement》; cancel 《a contract》; break 《a promise》. ¶ 그 계약은 일방적으로 ~되었다 The contract was canceled one-sidedly.
파김치 pickled scallion (leek). ¶ ~가 되다 《비유적》 get dead tired.
파나다(破—) get broken (damaged); become defective.
파나마 Panama. ‖ ~운하 the Panama Canal.
파내다 dig out; unearth.
파노라마 a panorama. ¶ ~같은 풍경 a panoramic view.
파다 ① 《땅·구멍을》 dig; excavate; bore(뚫어서). ¶ 우물을 ~ dig a well / 산에 터널을 ~ dig (bore) a tunnel through the mountain / 참호를 ~ excavate a trench. ② 《새기다》 carve 《in, on, from》; engrave; 《이름 따위를》 cut; inscribe. ¶ 목판에(으로) 멋진 조각상을 ~ carve a wonderful image on (from) a piece of wood / 돌에 자기 이름을 ~ cut one's name on the stone. ③ 《진상·문제 따위를》 study (investigate) 《something》 thoroughly; 《공부를》 study (work) hard. ¶ 영어를 들이 ~ study English very hard in earnest.
파다하다(播多—) (be) widely rumored (known); be rife.
파닥거리다 ☞ 퍼덕거리다.
파도(波濤) waves; billows; surges. ¶ ~소리 the sound (roar) of the waves / ~타기 surfing.
파동(波動) a wave motion; an undulation. ¶ 빛의 ~설 the wave theory of light. ‖ 가격~ fluctuations in prices / 경제~ an economic crisis / 정치~ a political upheaval / 증권~ wild fluctuations of the stock market; a stock market crisis.
파라과이 Paraguay. ¶ ~의 Paraguayan. ‖ ~사람 a Paraguayan.
파라솔 (hold) a parasol. ‖ 비치 ~ a beach umbrella.
파라슈트 (para)chute.
파라티온 《농약》 parathion.
파라핀 paraffin(e). ‖ ~지 (유) paraffin paper (oil).

파란(波瀾) 《풍파》 disturbance; troubles; a storm; 《성쇠》 ups and downs (of life); vicissitudes. ¶ ~ 많은 eventful / ~을 일으키다 cause troubles. [billed roller.
파랑 [鳥] ~새 [鳥] a broad-
파랗다 (be) blue; green(초록); 《창백》 pale. ¶ 파랗게 질린 얼굴 빛 a pale complexion.
파래 a green laver.
파래지다 become green[blue]; 《얼굴이》 turn pale.
파렴치(破廉恥) ~한 shameless; infamous / 그는 ~하다 He has no sense of decency. ¶ ~ 범 an infamous crime [offense] (죄); an infamous criminal(범인).
파르르 ① ~ 끓다 be hissing hot / ~ 화를 내다 simmer with rage / ~ 떨다 tremble.
파릇파릇하다 (be) freshly blue; vividly green.
파리¹ a fly. ¶ 파리채로 ~를 잡다 flap [swat] a fly / ~가 윙윙거린다 Flies are buzzing around. / 여름에는 장사가 ~를 날린다 《비유적》 Business is slack [dull] in summer. ‖ ~ 목숨 an ephemeral [a cheap] life / ~ 약 fly poison / ~ 채 a flyflap; a fly swatter.
파리² Paris. ¶ ~의 Parisian. ‖ ~ 사람 a Parisian [Parisienne(여자)].
파리하다 (be) thin and pale; look thin and pale [unwell].
파먹다 ① 《수박 따위를》 scoop [dig] (a watermelon) out and eat (it); 《벌레 따위가》 eat [bore] into (an apple). ¶ 벌레가 파먹은 목재 worm-eaten timber. ② 《재산 따위를》 eat away what one has; 《무위도식하다》 eat idle bread; live in idleness.
파면(罷免) dismissal; discharge. ~하다 dismiss; discharge; 《美口》 fire. ¶ 수회 사건으로 ~되다 be dismissed for one's involvement in the bribery case. ‖ ~권 the right to remove (a person) from office; the right of dismissal.
파멸(破滅) ruin; destruction; downfall. ~하다 be ruined [wrecked]; go to ruin. ¶ ~을 초래하다 bring ruin (upon oneself).
파문(波紋) a ripple; a water ring. ¶ ~을 일으키다 ripple; start a water ring / 《비유적》 cause a stir [cause a sensation] (in the political world).
파문(破門) 《종교상의》 excommunication; 《사제간의》 expulsion. ~하다 excommunicate; expel(제자를).
파묻다 ① 《…속에》 bury (in, under). ¶ 눈에 파묻히다 be buried under snow / 시체를 땅에 ~ burry the body in the ground / 그녀는 어머니 무릎에 머리를 파묻었다 She buried her head in her mother's lap. ② 《마음 속에》 keep [bear] (a matter) in mind; 《목살하다》 shelve [kill, table] (a bill); hush up; smother. ¶ 그 건은 어둠 속에 파묻혔다 The case has been covered [hushed] up.
파묻다 《꼬치꼬치 묻다》 be so inquisitive (about).
파미르고원(一高原) the Pamirs.
파벌(派閥) a clique; a faction. ¶ ~을 없애다 disband [dissolve] the factions. ‖ ~싸움 a factional dispute [strife] / ~주의 factionalism.
파병(派兵) ~하다 dispatch [send] troops (to). ¶ 해외 ~하다 send troops overseas.
파삭파삭 ¶ ~ 한 crisp; fragile.
파산(破産) bankruptcy; insolvency. ~하다 go [become] bankrupt. ¶ ~ 선고를 받다 be declared bankrupt / 사업 실패로 ~하다 fail in one's business and go bankrupt / ~관재인 a trustee in bankruptcy / ~자 a bankrupt; an insolvent.
파상(波狀) ~적인 wavelike; undulating. ¶ ~공격 an attack in waves.
파상품(破傷風) [醫] tetanus.
파생(派生) derivation. ~하다 derive (be derived) (from). ¶ ~ 적인 derivative; secondary(이차적). ‖ ~어 a derivative.
파선(破船) shipwreck. ~하다 be shipwrecked.
파손(破損) damage; breakage. ~하다 be damaged; be broken (down); be destroyed. ‖ ~부분 a damaged part / ~품(品) damaged goods.
파쇄(破碎) ~하다 break (a thing) (to pieces); smash; crush (up, down).
파쇠(破一) scrap iron.
파쇼 Fascism《주의》; a Fascist(사람). ¶ ~의 Fascist (movement) / ~화하다 Fascistize.
파수(把守) watch; lookout; guard. ¶ ~ 보다 (keep) watch; stand guard; stand on sentry (파수병이). ‖ ~꾼 a watchman; a guard / ~병 a sentry; a sentinel; a guard. [cylic acid)
파스 [藥] PAS. (◀para-aminosali-
파스너 a slide [zip] fastener; a zipper. ¶ ~를 잠그다 [열다] close [open] the zipper.
파스텔 [美術] pastel.
파시즘 Fascism.
파악(把握) grasp; understanding. ~하다 grasp; catch; hold of; understand. ¶ 뜻을 ~하다 grasp the meaning (of) / 실정을 잘 ~

하고 있다 have a good grasp of the situation. ┌broad smile.
파안대소(破顔大笑) ~하다 give a
파약(破約) a breach of contract [promise]. ~하다 break an agreement [a contract, a promise]. ¶협약은 ~되었다 The agreement was broken off.
파업(罷業) a strike; a walkout. ~하다 strike; go on strike; walk out. ¶~중이다 be on strike / ~을 중지하다 call off a strike. ∥~권 the right to strike / ~파괴자 a strikebreaker / 동정~ a sympathetic strike.
파열(破裂) ~하다 explode; burst (up); rupture; blow up. ∥~음 a plosive (sound).
파운드(화폐단위) a pound (기호 £); (무게) a pound (기호 lb. [*pl.* lbs.]). ∥~지역 the (pound) sterling area.
파울 [競] a foul (ball). ~하다 foul (off); commit a foul.
파이 a pie. ∥애플~ an apple pie.
파이프 ① (관) a pipe. ~오르간 a pipe organ. ② (담배 피는) a (tobacco) pipe; a cigarette holder(물부리).
파인애플 a pineapple.
파일 a file. ~하다 file. ¶ ~해두다 keep 《something》 on file; file 《something》 away / ~용 카드 a filing card / ~용 폴더 a file folder / ~처리 file processing.
파일럿 a pilot.
파자마 pajamas.
파장(波長) (a) wavelength. ¶~이 맞다 be on the same wavelength. ∥~계(計) a cymometer / ~조정기 a tuner.
파장(罷場) the close of a marketplace. ~하다 close (the marketplace). ∥~시세 the closing quotation [price] 《거래소의》.
파쟁(派爭) a factional strife.
파종(播種) seeding; sowing; planting. ~하다 sow seeds 《in》; plant 《a garden》. ¶봄에 ~하다 sow seeds in spring. ∥~기(期) the seedtime; the sowing season / ~기(機) a sowing machine; a sower.
파죽지세(破竹之勢) irresistible [crushing] force. ∥~로 나아가다 carry [sweep] all [everything] before one; advance unresisted [unopposed]. ┌paper.
파지(破紙) wastepaper; scraps of
파초(芭蕉) [植] a banana plant.
파출(派出) ~하다 send (out); dispatch. ∥~부 a visiting housekeeper [housemaid] / ~소 a police substation 《경찰의》.
파충(爬蟲) [動] a reptile. ∥~류 the reptiles.
파치(破—) a waster; a defective article; unsalable goods.
파키스탄 Pakistan. ¶ ~의 Pakistani. ∥~사람 a Pakistani.
파킨슨 ~법칙 the Parkinson's law. ∥~병 Parkinson's disease.
파탄(破綻) (결렬) (a) rupture; (실패) failure; (파산) bankruptcy; (사업 따위의 붕괴) a breakdown. ¶ ~되다 come to rupture; fail; break down; become 《go》 bankrupt; be ruined / 교섭은 ~에 이르렀다 The negotiation came to rupture.
파트너 a partner.
파티 《give, hold》 a party.
파파야 [植] a papaya.
파편(破片) a broken piece; a fragment; a splinter. ¶포탄 ~ a shell splinter / 도자기 ~ a fragment of a chinaware.
파하다(罷—) close 《at six》; finish; stop; end; break off; bring to an end; be over (out); quit; put an end to. ¶일을 ~ leave (off) work / 학교(회사)가 파한 뒤에 after school [office hours].
파행(跛行) ~하다 limp (along).
파헤치다 (속의 것을) open 《a grave》; (폭로하다) expose 《a secret plan》; unmask 《a deception》; uncover 《a plot》; bring 《a secret》 to light.
파혼(破婚) ~하다 break off one's engagement 《to》; cancel the engagement.
파흥(破興) ~하다 spoil one's pleasure (fun); throw a wet blanket 《on, over》; put a damper 《on the party》. ∥~꾼 a killjoy; a spoilsport. ┌crisp.
팍팍하다 (물기가 없어) (be) dry and
판 ① (장소) a place; a spot; a scene. ¶난장~ a scene of utter confusion / 노름~ a gambling place. ② (판국) (the) state of affairs; the situation; 《때의 moment; 《경우》 the occasion; the case. ¶막~에 at the last moment / 위급한 ~에 in the moment of danger; at critical moment. ③ (승부의) a game; a round; a match. ¶두 ~ (내리) 이기다 [지다] win (lose) two games (straight).
판(板) a board; a plank; a plate; a disk (disc) 《원반》. ∥~유리 plate glass.
판(判) size; format 《of a book》. ¶사륙~ 《판형》 duodecimo; crown octavo / 이 책은 B5 ~이다 This is a B5-sized book. ∥~에 박은 듯한 대답을 하다 make a stereotyped [cut-and-dried] answer 《to》; give exactly the same answer 《to》.
판(版) (책의) an edition; an impression. ¶《책이》 ~을 거듭하다 run into [go through] several im-

pressions / (신문의) 지방 ~ the local (provincial) edition. ‖ 개정 ~ a revised edition / 3~ the third edition.

판(瓣) a petal (꽃잎); a valve (기계·심장의); a ventil (악기의).

판가름 ~하다 judge 《a competition》; pass judgment 《on》; give a decision 《for, against》. ¶ ~ 나다 be decided; turn out (prove) to be…; be settled.

판각(版刻) wood engraving. ~ 하다 engrave (letters) on wood; make a print from a wood block. ‖ ~ 본 a block-printed book.

판검사(判檢事) judges and public prosecutors; judicial officers.

판결(判決) a judgment; a (judicial) decision; a ruling. ~하다 decide 《on a case》; give decision [pass judgment] 《on a case》. ¶ ~ 을 내리다 deliver a decision [ruling]; sentence 《on the accused》. ‖ ~ 문 the (text of a) decision / ~ 사례 a judicial precedent / ~ 이유 reasons for judgment.

판공비(辦公費) expediency fund; (접대비) expense account; (예비비) extra expenses; (기밀비) confidential money (expenses).

판국(一局) the situation; the state of affairs. ☞ 판 ②.

판권(版權) copyright. ¶ ~ 저작권. ‖ ~ 소유 (表示) All rights reserved. or Copyrighted. / ~ 소유자 a copyright holder / ~ 침해 (an) infringement of copyright; literary piracy.

판금(板金) a (metal) plate; sheet metal. ‖ ~ 공 a sheet metal worker.

판단(判斷) judgment; decision(결정); conclusion(결론). ~ 하다 judge; decide; conclude. ¶ 나의 ~ 으로는 in my judgment; it is my judgment that… / ~ 을 잘못 하다 misjudge; make an error of judgment. ‖ ~ 력 judgment; discernment.

판도(版圖) (expand) (a) territory; a dominion. ¶ ~ 를 넓히다 expand the territory.

판독(判讀) ~하다 read; make out; decipher (암호를). ¶ ~ 하기 어려운 illegible; undecipherable; hard to make out.

판돈 a wager; stakes; a bet. ¶ 400달러의 ~ a wager of four hundred dollars.

판례(判例) a judicial precedent. ¶ ~ 를 인용하다 cite (refer to) a precedent / 새로운 ~ 를 만들다 set (establish) a new precedent. ‖ ~ 법 case law / ~ 집 a (judicial) report.

판로(販路) (find) a market 《for goods》; an outlet. ¶ ~ 를 열다 find (open) a (larger) market 《for》.

판막(瓣膜) [解] a valve. ‖ ~증 [醫] mitral disease.

판매(販賣) sale; selling; marketing. ~ 하다 sell; deal (trade) (in silk). ¶ ~ 중이다 be on sale; be on the market. / ~ 가격 the selling price / ~ 과(課) [망] a sales department (network) / ~ 대리점 a selling agent; a distributor / ~ 루트 a distribution channel; a marketing route / ~ 원 a sales (wo)man / ~ 전 (a) sales war / ~ 점 a store; a shop / ~ 정책 a sales policy / ~ 촉진 sales promotion / ~ 통신 selling by mail / 호별 방문 ~ 원 a bell ringer; a door-to-door salesman.

판명(判明) ¶ ~ 되다 be identified 《as…》; prove (turn out) (to be) 《false》/ 시체의 신원이 옷으로 ~ 되었다 The corpse was identified by its clothing. / 소문은 사실로 ~ 되었다 The rumor turned out to be true.

판목(版木) a printing block.

판물이 sweep the board.

판사(判事) a judge; a justice. ¶ 예비 ~ a reserve judge / 부장 ~ a senior judge / 주심 ~ the presiding judge.

판설다 (be) unfamiliar 《with》; unaccustomed 《to》.

판세(一勢) (形勢) the situation; the state of affairs (things); a prospect.

판소리 a traditional Korean narrative song; a Korean (classical) solo opera drama; p'ansori.

판수 (점쟁이 소경) a blind fortuneteller.

판연하다(判然 —) (be) clear; distinct; evident. ¶ 판연히 distinctly; clearly.

판유리(板琉璃) plate (sheet) glass.

판이하다(判異 —) (be) entirely (quite) different 《from》; differ entirely 《from》.

판자(子) a board; a plank(두꺼운). ¶ ~ 를 대다 (깔다) board 《over》; lay boards 《on》; plank (a floor) 《with》. ‖ ~ 집 a makeshift hut; a shack.

판장(板墻) a wooden wall; a board fence.

판정(判定) a judgment; a decision. ~ 하다 judge; decide. ¶ ~ 으로 이기다(지다) win (lose) by a decision / 심판 ~ 에 따르다 accept (abide by) the umpire's decision. ‖ ~ 승 (패) a win (loss) on a decision.

판지(板紙) cardboard; pasteboard.
판치다 have a great deal of influence 《with, over》; be influential; lord it over. ¶ 그는 정계, 재계에서 판치는 실력자다 He is a man of influence both in the financial and the political world.
판판이 at every round; every time. ¶ ∼ 지다 get defeated every time.
판판하다 (be) even; flat; level. ¶ 판판히 smoothly; evenly.
판화(版畫) a print, an engraving; 〔목판의〕 a woodcut (print); 〔동판의〕 an etching.
팔 an arm. ¶ 애인의 ∼을 끼고 걷다 walk arm in arm with one's lover / ∼을 걷어붙이다 roll [tuck] up one's sleeves / ∼이 부러지다 have one's arm broken; break one's arm.
팔(八) eight; the eighth (여덟째).
팔각(八角) ¶ ∼의 octagonal. ‖ ∼정 an octagonal pavilion / ∼형 an octagon. ┌armchair.
팔걸이 an armrest. ‖ ∼의자 an
팔꿈치 an elbow. ¶ ∼의 관절을 elbow joint / ∼를 펴다 spread out one's elbows.
팔난봉 a libertine; a debauchee.
팔다 ① 〔판매를〕 sell; offer (a thing) for sale; put on sale; deal in 〔goods〕; dispose of 〔처분〕. ¶ 팔 수 있는 salable / 파는 사람 a seller / 팔 물건 an article for sale / 싸게 〔비싸게〕 ∼ sell (a thing) cheap 〔dear〕 / 이익을〔손해를〕 보고 ∼ sell 〔goods〕 at a profit 〔loss〕 / 정조를 ∼ sell one's chastity; prostitute oneself / 팔아치우다 sell 〔off, out〕; dispose of. ② 〔배반〕 betray; sell 〔out〕. ¶ 나라를 ∼ betray 〔sell〕 one's country. ③ 〔시선·주의를 딴 데로〕 turn one's eyes away 《from》; divert one's attention 《from》. ¶ 한눈(을) ∼ look away 〔aside, off〕; take one's eyes off (a thing) / 한눈 팔지 마라 Don't look 〔turn your eyes〕 away! / 운전하면서 한눈 팔지 마라 Don't divert your attention from driving a car. ④ 〔이름을〕 take advantage of; trade on 《another's name》. ¶ 아버지의 이름을 팔아 장사하다 do business by taking advantage of one's father's reputation. ⑤ 〔곡식을〕 buy 〔purchase〕 〔grain〕.
팔다리 the limbs; the legs and arms.
팔도강산(八道江山) the land of Korea; the scenery of all parts of Korea.
팔등신(八等身) ¶ ∼미인 a beautiful well-proportioned 〔well-shaped〕 woman.
팔딱거리다 《맥박이》 pulsate; palpitate; throb; beat; 《뛰다》 hop; leap; spring (up). ¶ 가슴이 ∼ feel the heart pulsating / 그 광경에 가슴이 심하게 팔딱거렸다 My heart beat fast at the scene.
팔뚝 the forearm.
팔랑개비 a pinwheel.
팔랑거리다 해방기구
팔레스타인 Palestine. ‖ ∼해방기구 ┌팔레오.
팔레트 〔美術〕 a palette.
팔리다 ① 〔물건이〕 sell; be sold; be in demand; be marketable 〔salable〕 (시장성이 있다). ¶ 잘 ∼ sell well; be in great demand; have 〔enjoy〕 a good 〔large〕 sale / 날개 돋친 듯 잘 ∼ sell like hot cakes / 잘 안 ∼ do not sell well; be not in much demand; have a poor sale. ② 〔눈·마음이 딴 데로〕 get turned away; be diverted 〔distracted〕; 《눈·마음이 한쪽으로》 be fascinated 〔attracted〕; be absorbed 《in》; lose one's head 《over》. ¶ 눈이 딴 데 ∼ look at something else / 정신이 딴 데 ∼ one's attention is diverted 〔wanders〕 / 마음이 여자에게 ∼ be attracted by a woman / 노는 데 정신이 팔려 공부는 뒷전이다 be too much absorbed in play to think of one's study. ③ 〔얼굴·이름이〕 become well-known 〔popular, famous〕 《as》.
팔림새 ∼가 좋다 sell well; have a good 〔large〕 sale / ∼가 나쁘다 do not sell well; be in poor demand.
팔만대장경(八萬大藏經) the *Tripitaka Koreana*.
팔매질하다 throw; hurl 〔stones〕.
팔면(八面) eight sides; 〔여러 방면〕 all sides; 〔형용사적〕 8-sided. ‖ ∼부지 a complete stranger / ∼체 an octahedron.
팔목 the wrist.
팔방(八方) 〔in〕 all directions; 〔on〕 every side; 〔on〕 all sides. ‖ ∼미인 a person who is affable to everybody; everybody's friend (그는 ∼미인이다 He tries to please everybody.).
팔베개 ∼를 베다 make a pillow of one's arm.
팔불출(八不出) a good-for-nothing.
팔삭둥이(八朔–) 〔조산아〕 a prematurely-born infant; 〔바보〕 a half-witted person; a stupid.
팔심 the muscular strength of one's arm.
팔십(八十) eighty; the eightieth (제팔십). ¶ ∼ (대) 노인 an octogenarian.
팔씨름 arm 〔Indian〕 wrestling. ∼하다 arm-wrestle.
팔월(八月) August. ‖ ∼한가위

15th day of the eighth lunar month.
팔이 a peddler; a vendor. ¶ 신문~ a newsboy.
팔자(八字) destiny; fate; *one's* lot. ¶ ~가 좋다 be blessed with good fortune / ~가 사납다 be ill-fated / ~를 잘 타고 나다 be born under a lucky star / ~를 고치다 (출세하다) rise suddenly in the world; (부자가 되다) gain sudden wealth; (개가하다) remarry.
팔자걸음(八字—) ¶ ~으로 걷다 walk with *one's* toes turned out.
팔죽지 the upper arm.
팔짓하다 swing (wave) *one's* arms; make gestures with *one's* arms.
팔짱 ¶ ~ 끼다 《혼자》 fold *one's* arms; (남과) lock arms (with); ~을 끼고 있다 with *one's* arms folded / 서로 ~을 끼고 《walk》 arm in arm (with).
팔찌 a bracelet; a bangle.
팔촌(八寸) a third cousin. ¶ 사돈의 ~ an unrelated person.
팔팔하다 (성질이) (be) quick-(hot-)tempered; impatient; (발랄한) (be) active; lively; sprightly.
팡파르 a fanfare.
팥 a red (an Indian) bean.
팥고물 mashed red bean (used to coat rice cake).
팥밥 rice boiled with red beans.
팥죽 rice and red bean porridge.
패(牌) ① (표조각) a tag; a tablet; a plate. ¶ 나무~ a wooden tag. ② (화투 따위의) a (playing) card; a piece (마작, 골패의). ③ (무리) a group; a company; a gang; a set. ¶ 못된 (시시한) ~리 a gang of punks / ~거리를 짓다 form a gang.
패가(敗家) ~ 하다 ruin *one's* family; become bankrupt. ‖ ~망신 ruining both *oneself* and *one's* family.   [sword.
패검(佩劍) ~ 하다 wear (carry) a
패군(敗軍) a defeated army.
패권(覇權) ① (지배권) supremacy; domination; hegemony (국가간의). ¶ ~을 다투다 struggle for supremacy / ~을 잡다 hold supremacy (*of*) ; gain the hegemony (*of*) / 해상의 ~을 잡다 dominate (rule) the sea. ② (선수권) a championship. ¶ ~을 잡다 win a championship. ‖ ~주의 hegemonism / ~반대 조항 the anti-hegemony clause.
패기(覇氣) an ambitious spirit; ambition; aspiration. ¶ ~ 있는 full of spirit; ambitious / ~ 있는 사람 a man of spirit 《with ambition》.
패널 (建) a panel.   [tion).
패다 ① (장작) chop (*wood*); split (*firewood*). ② (때리다) beat (strike) hard. ¶ 멍이 들도록 ~ beat (*a person*) black and blue.
패다[2] (이삭이) come into ears. ¶ 벼 이삭이 팼다(패어 있다) Rice plants have come into ears (are in (the) ears).
패다[3] (우묵하게) become dented (hollow); sink; be hollowed out. ¶ 비에 도로가 팼다 The road is hollowed out by the rain.
패담(悖談) improper (indecent) talk; an unreasonable remark.
패덕(悖德) immorality; a lapse from virtue. ‖ ~한(漢) an immoral person / ~행위 immoral conduct (act).
패도(覇道) the rule of might.
패러다이스 a paradise.
패러독스 a paradox. 「chology.
패류(貝類) shellfish. ‖ ~학 con-
패륜(悖倫) immorality. ¶ ~적 immoral; sinful. ‖ ~아 an immoral person / ~행위 immoral conduct (behavior).
패리티 (經) (동등·등가) parity. ‖ ~계산 (가격, 지수) a parity account (price, index).
패망(敗亡) defeat; ruin. ~하다 get defeated (ruined).
패모(貝母) (植) a checkered lily.
패물(佩物) personal ornaments.
패배(敗北) (a) defeat. ~하다 be defeated (beaten); suffer a defeat; lose a game (battle). ‖ ~선언 a declaration of defeat; a public concession of defeat / ~주의 defeatism.
패보(敗報) the news of defeat.
패색(敗色) signs of defeat. ¶ ~이 짙다 Defeat seems certain.
패석(貝石) a fossil shell.
패설(悖說) ☞ 패담.
패세(敗勢) a losing situation; the reverse tide of war; unfavorable signs in battle.
패션 a fashion (show, model).
패소(敗訴) a lost case. ~하다 lose *one's* suit (case).
패스 ① (무료입장·승차권) a pass; a free ticket; (정기권) a commutation ticket (정기); (여권) a passport. ② (합격) passing. ~하다 pass. ¶ 시험에 ~하다 pass (succeed in) an examination. ③ (球技) a pass; passwork. ~하다 pass (*a ball to another*).
패싸움(牌—) (have) a gang fight.
패쓰다(覇—) (위기모면) use a trick; (바둑) make a no-man's point.
패용(佩用) ~하다 wear (*a medal*).
패인(敗因) the cause of defeat.
패자(敗者) a loser; the conquered (defeated) (복수취급). ~부활전 a *repêchage* (프); a consolation match (game).

패자(霸者) a supreme ruler; a champion (경기의).

패잔(敗殘) ¶ ~된 defeated. ∥ ~병 remnants of a defeated troop; stragglers.

패잡다《牌一》《물주가 되다》deal; become the dealer.

패장(敗將) a defeated general.

패적(敗敵) a defeated enemy.

패전(敗戰) a defeat; a lost battle. ~하다 be defeated; lose a battle[war]. ¶ ~國 a defeated nation / ~투수〔野〕a losing pitcher.

패주(敗走) (a) rout; flight. ~하다 be routed; take to flight. ¶ 적을 ~시키다 put the enemy to rout.

패총(貝塚) a shell mound[heap].

패퇴(敗退) defeat; retreat. ~하다 《퇴각》 retreat; 《패함》 be defeated; be beaten. 「자」.

패트런 a patron; a patroness〔─

패트롤 (go on) patrol. ∥ ~카 a patrol car.

패하다(敗一)《지다》be defeated 〔beaten〕; lose (a game, battle). ¶ 선거에 ~ be defeated in the election / 소송에 ~ lose the lawsuit / 큰 차이로 ~ be beaten by a large score.

패혈증(敗血症) 〔醫〕septicemia; blood poisoning.

팩스¹ a fax. ∥ ~ 팩시밀리로 보내다 send (the data) by fax / ~로부터 ~를 한 통 받다 get a fax from him / ~ 번호 a fax number.

팩스² pax. ∥ ~아메리카나 Pax Americana (미국 지배에 의한 평화).

팩시밀리 (a) facsimile.

팬 a fan; an enthusiast. ¶ ~레터 fan letters〔mail〕 / ~클럽 a fan club / 영화 ~ a movie fan.

팬츠《속옷》underpants; shorts 《美》; pants 《英》; panties (여성용); 《운동용》athletic shorts; trunks.

팬케이크 a pancake; a griddlecake.

팬터마임 a pantomime. ∥ ~배우 a pantomimist.

팬티 panties. ∥ ~스타킹 a panty hose; (a pair of) tights 《英》.

팸플릿 a pamphlet; a brochure.

팽¶ ~~ 돌다 turn〔go〕round and round; twirl; spin / 눈이 ~ 돈다 be〔feel〕dizzy; My eyes swim. / 머리가 ~ 돌았다 My head went round. or My head reeled 〔swam〕.

팽개치다 ¶ ~ 《던지다》throw〔cast〕(away); fling (at); hurl (at). ② 《일을》give up; neglect (one's work); lay aside. 「smoothly.

팽그르르 ¶ ~ 돌다 turn〔go〕round

팽글팽글 (turn, spin) round and round.

팽나무 〔植〕a (Chinese) nettle tree.

팽대(膨大) ~하다 swell; expand.

팽배(澎湃) ~하다 overflow; surge; rise like a flood tide. ¶ ~하는 정치적 개혁의 요청 the surging tide of people's request for political reform.

팽이《spin》a top.

팽창(膨脹) swelling; expansion; (an) increase(증대); growth(발전). ~하다 swell; expand; increase. ¶ 열 ~ thermal expansion / 도시의 ~ urban growth / 예산의 ~ an increase in the budget / 인구의 급격한 ~ a rapid increase in population / 금속은 열을 가하면 ~한다 Metals expand when they are heated. ∥ ~계수〔률〕 the coefficient〔rate〕of expansion / ~력(力) expansive power.

팽팽하다 ① 《켕기어서》(be) taut; tight; tense. ¶ 팽팽하게 closely; tensely / 줄을 팽팽하게 당기다 stretch a rope tight; tighten a rope. ② 《대등하다》 be equal 《to》; be on a par 《with》; be evenly matched. ¶ 팽팽한 경기 a close contest; an even match / 세력이 (서로) ~ be equally balanced in power.

팍팍 《대드는 모양》unyieldingly; firmly; 《날카롭게》sharply. ¶ ~ 대들다 stand up to (a person) firmly / ~ 쏘다 make cutting remarks. 「quick-tempered.

팍하다(愎─) be peevish; touchy;

퍼내다 bail 〔dip, ladle〕out (water); dip〔scoop〕up; pump (out). ¶ 배에서 물을 ~ bail water out of a boat.

퍼덕거리다 ① 《새가》flap 〔clap, beat〕the wings; flutter. ② 《물고기가》leap; flop; splash.

퍼뜨리다 《소문 등을》spread (a story) (around); set (a rumor) afloat; circulate (a rumor); 《종교·사상 등을》spread; propagate (a religion).

퍼뜩 suddenly; in a flash. ¶ ~ 생각 나다 suddenly occur to one; flash into one's mind / 좋은 생각이 떠올랐다 Suddenly I had a good idea.

퍼렇다 (be) deep blue〔green〕.

퍼레이드 a parade.

퍼머《펀트》a permanent (wave); a perm (口). ~하다 get〔have〕a perm; have one's hair permed 〔permanently waved〕.

퍼먹다 ① 《퍼서》scoop〔dip〕and eat. ② 《게걸스레》shovel (food) into one's mouth; eat greedily.

퍼붓다 ① 《비·눈이》pour on; rain 〔snow〕hard. ¶ ~는 듯한 thick 〔heavy〕snow / 퍼붓는 비를 무릎쓰고 in spite of the pouring rain. ② 《퍼서 붓다》dip〔scoop〕(water)

퍼석퍼석하다 and pour (it) into (a jar); (끓이다) pour [shower] (water) on (a person); (욕을) pour [shower, rain] (abuses) upon; lay [blame] on; (포화를) rain fire (on).

퍼석퍼석하다 be dried out; be crumbling.

퍼센트 a per cent; a percent (기호 %). ¶ 5∼의 증가 an increase by five percent / 30∼의 가격 인하 a 30 percent discount / 개혁안에 대한 찬성자는 약 40∼이다 Some 40% are in favor of the reform plan.

퍼센티지 (a) percentage.

퍼지다 ① (벌어지다) spread out; get broader. ② (소문 등이) spread; get around (about); be propagated (circulated, diffused); (유행이) come into fashion; become popular. ③ (자손·초목이) grow thick (wild); flourish. ¶ 자손이 ∼ have a flourishing progeny. ④ (삶은 것이) be properly steamed; swell. ⑤ (병이) be prevalent; prevail. ⑥ (구김살이) get [become] smooth. ⑦ (술·약기운이) take effect. ¶ 독이 전신에 퍼졌다 The poison has passed into his system.

퍼펙트게임 [野] a perfect game.

퍽¹ ① (힘있게) forcefully; with a thrust. ¶ 칼로 ∼ 찌르다 thrust with a knife. ② (넘어지는 꼴) (fall) with a thud; plump; flop.

퍽² (매우) very much; quite; awfully; terribly; highly. ¶ ∼ 재미있다 be quite interesting.

퍽석 (앉는 꼴) heavily; plump; flop; (깨지는 꼴) fragilely; easily. ¶ 의자에 ∼ 주저앉다 sit limply on a chair; plump down on a chair / ∼ 깨지다 break easily.

펀치 ① (구멍 뚫는) a punch. ② (타격) a punch. ¶ ∼을 맞다 get a punch (on the nose) / ∼를 먹이다 land a punch (on); punch (a person on the chin).

편편하다 be even; flat; level.

펄떡거리다 ☞ 팔딱거리다.

펄럭거리다 flutter; flap; stream; wave. ¶ 바람에 ∼ flutter [flap] in the wind / 펄럭펄럭 with a flutter [flap]; flutteringly.

펄썩 ① (먼지 따위가) rising in a puff. ¶ 먼지가 ∼ 나다 a cloud of dust rises in a puff. ② (앉는 모양) heavily; plump (down). ¶ 그는 의자에 ∼ 앉았다 He sank into [plumped down on] a chair.

펄쩍뛰다 jump up suddenly; leap [start] to one's feet; (어떤 부당한 말에) hear something undeserved [ungrounded]. ¶ 놀라서 ∼ jump up with surprise / 성나서 ∼ leap up with anger.

펄펄 ¶ 물이 ∼ 끓다 The water is boiling hard. or The water has come to a rolling boil. / 몸이 ∼ 끓다 have a high [violent] fever; be burning up with fever / 눈이 ∼ 날리다 snow flutters about.

펄프 펄프를 만들다 reduce (wood) to pulp; pulp. ∥ ∼ 공장 a pulp mill / ∼재(材) pulpwood / ∼ 인견 a rayon pulp.

펌프 a pump. ¶ ∼질(을) 하다 work a pump / ∼로 퍼올리다 [내다] pump up [out] (water). ∥ ∼ 우물을 a pump well / 공기 ∼ an air pump / 증기 (압력, 흡입) ∼ a steam [pressure, suction] pump.

펑 pop; bang. ∼ 하다 pop; bang. ¶ ∼ 하고 with a pop [bang].

펑퍼짐하다 (be) broad and roundish. ¶ 펑퍼짐한 엉덩이 well-rounded hips.

펑펑 ① (폭음 소리) bang! bang!; pop, pop; popping. ② (쏟아지는 모양) in continuous gushes; gushingly; profusely; copiously. ¶ ∼ 흐르다 flow in streams; gush out; stream down / ∼ 나오다 gush [stream] out / 눈이 ∼ 내리다 snow falls thick and fast.

페넌트 a pennant.

페널티 (스포츠) a penalty. ∥ ∼에어리어 a penalty area / ∼킥 a penalty kick.

페니 (화폐 단위) a penny; pence (금액의 복수); pennies (화폐의 복수).

페니실린 [藥] penicillin. ∥ ∼연고 [주사] a penicillin ointment [shot, injection].   「(one's bicycle).

페달 a pedal. ¶ ∼을 밟다 pedal

페더급(一級) the featherweight. ∥ ∼선수 a featherweight (boxer).

페루 Peru. ∥ ∼의 Peruvian. ∥ ∼사람 a Peruvian.

페르시아 Persia. ¶ ∼의 Persian. ∥ ∼사람 a Persian.

페리보트 a ferry (boat).

페미니스트 a feminist.

페미니즘 feminism.

페소 (화폐 단위) a peso (기호 $, P).

페스트 a pest; the black plaque.

페이스 (a) pace. ¶ 자기 ∼를 지키다 do not overpace oneself; keep within one's speed.

페이지 a page; a leaf. ¶ 5∼에 on page 5 / ∼를 넘기다 turn (over) the pages (of a book) / ∼를 매기다 page (a book) / 교과서의 10∼를 여시오 Open your textbook to [at] page 10. / 역사에 새로운 ∼를 장식하다 add a new page to the history (of...).

페이퍼 paper; (사포) sandpaper.

페인트 paint. ¶ ∼를 칠하다 paint (a room white). ∥ ∼장이 a paint-

페티코트 er / ~주의〔게시〕 Wet paint. or Fresh paint. / 수성～ water paint.
페티코트 a petticoat.
펜 (write with) a pen. ‖ ～네임 a pen name / ～대 a penholder / ～촉 a pen point / ～팔 a pen pal / ～화(畵) a pen sketch 〔drawing〕.
펜스 pence. ☞ 페니.
펜싱 fencing. ‖ ～선수 a fencer.
펜클럽 the P.E.N. (◀the International Association of Poets, Playwrights, Editors, Essayists, and Novelists) ‖ 한국～ the Korea P.E.N. club.
펜타곤 《미국 국방부》 the Pentagon.
펨프 《뚜쟁이》 a pimp; a pander.
펭귄 〖鳥〗 a penguin.
펴내다 《발행하다》 publish; issue. ¶ 펴낸이 a publisher.
펴다 ① 《펼치다》 spread; open 《a book》; unfold 《a newspaper》; unroll 《a scroll》. ¶ 이부자리를 ～ spread 〔prepare, make〕 a bed / 날개를 ～ spread the wings. ② 《몸을》 stretch 《one's back》; 《가슴을》 stick 〔throw〕 out 《one's chest》. ¶ 가슴을 펴고 걷다 walk with one's chest out / 팔을 ～ stretch 〔hold out〕 one's arm. ③ 《구김살을》 smooth out 《creases》; iron out (다리미로); 《굽은 것을》 straighten; unbend; uncoil (말린 것을). ¶ 구부러진 철사를 ～ straighten out a crooked wire / 다리미로 구겨진 식탁보를 ～ smooth out the tablecloth by ironing it. ④ 《기를》 ease 《one's mind》; relieve. ¶ 기를 못 ～ feel ill at ease; feel constrained. ⑤ 《살림을》 ease; alleviate; improve. ¶ 궁색한 살림을 ～ improve one's meager livelihood. ⑥ 《공포하다》 issue; declare; 《경계망을》 form; set up; spread. ¶ 계엄령을 ～ enforce 〔declare〕 martial law / 경계망을 ～ form 〔throw〕 a police cordon 《around an area》 / 수사망을 ～ spread 〔set up〕 a dragnet. ⑦ 《세력 등을》 extend 《one's power》; establish 《one's influence》.
펴이다 《형편이》 get better; improve; be eased; 《일 따위가》 get straightened out: be smoothed (down). ¶ 셈이 ～ become better off / 일이 ～ a matter gets straightened out; an affair is smoothed down.
펴지다 ①《펼쳐지다》 get unfolded 〔unrolled, spread〕; get out 〔spread〕. ② 《주름이》 get smoothed; be flattened; 《굽은 것이》 get straightened.
편(便) ①《쪽》 a side; 《방향》 a direction; a way. ¶ 왼～ the left (-hand) side / 서～에 on the west side / 이〔저〕 ～(으)로 this 〔that〕 way. ②《교통편》 service; facilities; 《편의》 convenience. ¶ 철도〔버스〕～ a railroad (bus) service / 이 곳은 교통 ～이 좋다 There are good transportation facilities here. / 우리 집은 버스 ～이 좋은〔나쁜〕 곳에 있다 My house is conveniently 〔inconveniently〕 located near the bus stop. ③《상대편·한패》 a side; a part; a party; a faction. ¶ 우리 ～ our side; our party 〔team〕; our friends / 근로자 ～의 요구 the demands on the part of the workers / 그녀는 내 ～이다 She is on my side. or She takes sides with me. ④ 《인편》. ⑤《…하는 쪽》 ¶ 자네는 바로 가는 ～이 좋겠네 You had better go at once. / 그는 나이에 비해 늙어 보이는 ～이다 He is rather old for his age. / 그는 말이 많은 ～이다 He is more talkative than anything else.
편(編) 《편찬》 compilation; editing. ¶ 김 박사 ～ edited by Dr. Kim.
편(篇) 《권》 a volume; 《장·절》 a chapter; a section; a piece. ¶ 《시·영화의 수》 상〔중·하〕 ～ the first 〔second, third〕 volume / 제2 ～ the second chapter / 시 한 ～ a piece of poetry.
편가르다(便一) divide 〔separate〕 《pupils》 into groups 〔classes〕.
편각(偏角) 〖地〗 declination; 〖數〗 amplitude.
편견(偏見) (a) prejudice; a bias; a prejudiced view. ¶ ～ 있는 prejudiced; biased / ～을 가지다 be prejudiced 〔have a prejudice〕 《against》.
편곡(編曲) 〖樂〗 arrangement. ～하다 arrange 《music》 for 《the piano》.
편광(偏光) 〖理〗 polarized light. ‖ ～ 렌즈〔필터〕 a polarizing lens 〔filter〕.
편년(編年) ～사 a chronicle; annals / ～체(體) (in) a chronological form 〔order〕.
편달(鞭撻) 《격려》 ～하다 urge (encourage, excite) 《a person to do》; spur on.
편대(編隊) (in) a formation. ¶ 폭격기의 대～ a large formation of bombers. ‖ ～비행 a formation flight.
편도(片道) one way. ¶ 부산행 ～ 한 장 주십시오 A one-way ticket to Pusan, please. ‖ ～ 승차권 a one-way ticket 《美》; a single (ticket) 《英》 / ～ 요금 a single (one-way) fare.
편두통(偏頭痛) 〖醫〗 a megrim.
편들다(便一) 《지지》 side 〔take

편람 sides 《with》; take 《a person's》 part [side]; support; back up. ¶ 아들은 ~ side with 《one's son》 / 그를 편들기만 하지 마라 Don't always take sides with him.

편람(便覽) a handbook; a manual.

편력(遍歷) wandering; a travel; a pilgrimage. ~하다 travel [tour, wander] about; make a tour of 《the country》~ 각지를 ~하다 wander from place to place / 여성 ~이 많은 남자 a man having a number of love affairs.

편리(便利) convenience; handiness (알맞음); facilities (설비의). ¶ ~ 한 convenient; handy; useful / 상거래를 위해 convenience' sake / 편리한 도구 a handy gadget / ~하게 하다 facilitate / 한 곳에 있다 be conveniently located / 교통이 ~하다 be convenient for transportation.

편린(片鱗) a part; a glimpse. ¶ 그것으로 그의 성격의 ~을 엿볼 수 있다 It enables us to get a glimpse of his personality.

편모(偏母) one's lone [widowed] mother. ¶ ~ 슬하에서 자라다 grow [be brought up] under widowed mother's care.

편무(片務) ¶ ~적인 unilateral; one-sided. ¶ ~계약 a unilateral [one-sided] contract.

편물(編物) ☞ 뜨개질. ¶ ~기계 a knitting machine.

편발(辮髮·編髮) a pigtail; a queue.

편법(便法) (편한 방법) an easier [a handy] method; an expedient. ¶ ~을 강구하다 resort to [devise] an expedient / 그의 행위는 일시적 ~에 불과하다 His act is only a temporary expedient.

편복(便服) casual wear; ordinary dress [clothes]; informal dress. ¶ ~으로 외출하다 go out in one's casual wear.

편상화(編上靴) lace boots.

편서풍(偏西風) the prevailing westerlies.

편성(編成) organization; formation. ~하다 organize 《a corps》; form 《a class》; make up 《a budget》; draw up 《a program》; compose 《a train》. ¶ ~ …으로 되어 있다 consist of…; be made up of… / 10량 ~의 열차 a train of ten cars.

편수(編修) ~하다 edit; compile. ¶ ~관 an editorial officer; an (official) editor.

편승(便乘) ~하다 ① 《차에》 get a lift in 《a person's car》. ¶ 나는 그녀의 차에 ~했다 I got a lift in her car. or She gave me a lift in her car. ② 《기회에》 take advantage of 《the trend of public opinion》; avail oneself of 《an opportunity》; jump on the bandwagon 《口》.

편식(偏食) 《have》 an unbalanced diet.

편심(偏心) a one-sided mind; 【機】 eccentricity.

편싸움(便) a gang fight; a fight between two groups. ~하다 have a gang fight; fight in groups.

편안(便安) 《무사》 safety; 《평온》 peace; tranquility; 《건강》 good health; being well; 《편함》 ease; comfort. ~하다 (be) safe; peaceful; well; comfortable; easy. ¶ ~히 지내다 live in peace 《comfort》/ 마음이 ~할 때가 없다 have no moment of ease.

편애(偏愛) partiality 《for》; favoritism 《to》. ~하다 be partial 《to》; show favoritism 《to》. ¶ 어머니는 그를 ~했다 The mother was partial to him.

편육(片肉) slices of boiled meat.

편의(便宜) a convenience; facilities (설비의); advantage (이익). ¶ ~상, ~를 위해 for convenience' sake; for (the sake of) convenience / 모든 ~를 제공하다 afford [accord] every facility 《for》/ 가능한 모든 ~를 도모하겠습니다 I will give you every convenience [facility] for it. ¶ ~주의 opportunism / ~주의자 an opportunist.

편의점(便宜店) a convenience store.

편익(便益) benefit; advantage; convenience. ¶ ~을 주다 provide facility; give [offer] advantage.

편입(編入) admission; incorporation(합병). ~하다 include in; transfer; 《학급 등에》 put [admit] 《a person》 into; 《합병하여》 incorporate 《into》. ¶ 고교 2학년에 ~하다 be admitted in the second year of the high school / 예비역에 ~되다 be transferred to the reserve / 그 도시는 서울에 ~되었다 The town was incorporated into the city of Seoul. ¶ ~생 an enrolled student / ~시험 a transfer admission test.

편자(말굽의) a horseshoe. ¶ ~를 박다 shoe 《a horse》.

편자(編者) an editor; a compiler.

편재(偏在) uneven distribution; maldistribution. ~하다 be unevenly distributed 《among》. ¶ 부(富)의 ~ the maldistribution [uneven distribution] of wealth.

편재(遍在) omnipresence. ~하다 be omnipresent (ubiquitous).

편제(編制) 【軍】 organization. ¶ ~ 표 the table of organization.

편주(片舟·扁舟) a small [light]

boat; a skiff. ¶ 일엽 ~ a light skiff.
편중(偏重) ~하다 attach too much importance 《to》; make too much of; overemphasize 《*intellectual training*》. ¶ 학력에 ~하다 make too much of school (academic) careers.
편지(便紙) a letter; a note (짧은); mail (집합적). ¶ ~의 사연 the contents of a letter / ~를 내다 send a letter; write (to) 《*a person*》 / ~를 부치다 mail (美)(post (英)) a letter / 보내신 ~ 잘 받았습니다 Thank you very much for your letter. ∥ ~봉투 an envelope / ~지 letter paper.
편집(偏執) bigotry; obstinacy. ∥ ~광(狂)(상태) monomania; (사람) a monomaniac / ~병 환자 a paranoiac.
편집(編輯) editing; compilation. ~하다 edit 《*a magazine*》; compile 《*a dictionary*》. ∥ ~국 the editorial office (board) / ~자 an editor; a (film) cutter (필름의) / ~장(주간) the chief editor; an editor in chief / ~회의 an editorial meeting / ~후기 the editor's comment.
편짜다(便—) form a team (party).
편쪽(便—) a (one) side. ¶ 이 (저) ~ this (the other) side.
편차(偏差)(理) deflection; variation; (포탄의) windage; (統計) deviation. ∥ ~값 the deviation (value).
편찬(編纂) compilation; editing. ~하다 compile; edit. ∥ ~자 a compiler; an editor.
편찮다(便—)(불편) (be) inconvenient; uncomfortable; (병으로) (be) ill; unwell; indisposed. ¶ 몸이 ~ feel unwell 《*with a cold*》.
편취(騙取) ~하다 swindle 《*money*》 out of 《*a person*》; cheat (swindle) 《*a person*》 out of 《*one's money*》. ¶ 전재산을 ~당하다 be swindled out of *one's* whole fortune.
편친(偏親) one parent. ¶ ~의 아이 a child with only one parent living; a fatherless (motherless) child.
편파(偏頗) partiality; favoritism; (unfair) discrimination. ¶ ~적인 partial; one-sided; unfair; biased / ~적인 판단 an unfair judgment.
편평(扁平) ¶ ~한 flat; even; level.
편하다(便—) ① (원리) (be) convenient; handy; expedient. ② (편안) (be) comfortable; easy; free from care (걱정없다). ¶ 편히 comfortably; at 《*one's*》 ease; in comfort / 마음이 ~ carefree; have

nothing to worry. ③ (수월함) (be) easy; light; simple. ¶ 편한 일 an easy (a soft) job.
편향(偏向) a tendency 《*toward, to*》; an inclination 《*toward, to*》. ~하다 tend 《*toward, to*》; be inclined. ¶ ~된 biased; prejudiced. ∥ ~교육 deflected education; ideologically prejudiced education.
편협(偏狹) (be) narrow-minded; illiberal; intolerant. ¶ 편협한 생각을 갖다 have a narrow-minded view 《*of*》.
편형동물(扁形動物)(動) a flatworm.
펼치다 spread; lay out; unfold; open. ¶ 모포를 ~ spread (lay out) a blanket / 책을 ~ open a book. ∥ ~ 기: abuse.
폄하다(貶—) disparage; speak ill 《*of*》.
평(坪) a p'yŏng (=약 3.3m²). ¶ ~수 (면적) area; acreage; 《건평》 floor space.
평(評) criticism; (a) comment; (a) review 《*of movies*》; a remark. ~하다 criticize; review; comment 《*on*》. ¶ 신문~ a newspaper comment / ~이 좋다(나쁘다) have a good (bad) reputation.
평…(平) (보통의) common; ordinary; plain; (단순한) mere. ¶ ~교사 a common teacher / ~당원 a rank-and-file member / ~사원 a plain clerk / ~신도 a layman.
평가(平價)(經) par; parity. ¶ ~를 절상하다 revalue the currency 〔won, dollar, *etc.*〕 / ~를 절하하다 devalue the currency. ∥ ~절상 (upward) revaluation / ~절하 devaluation.
평가(評價) evaluation; valuation; (an) estimation (견적); (an) appraisal (매각을 위한); assessment (과세를 위한); grading (성적의). ~하다 evaluate; value; estimate; appraise; assess; grade. ¶ ~ 높이 ~하다 set a high value on 《*a person's abilities*》; rate 《*something*》 highly. ∥ ~교수단 a group of professors assigned to evaluate the government policies / ~기준 a valuation basis; an appraisal standard / ~액 the estimated (appraised) value / an assessment / ~이익(손실) a valuation profit (loss) / ~전 a tryout match.
평각(平角)(數) a straight angle.
평결(評決) a decision; a verdict (배심원의). ~하다 decide.
평교(平交) friends of about the same age.
평균(平均) ① (보통) an average; (數) the mean. ~하다 average. ¶ ~의 average; mean / ~

평년 on (an, the) average / ~이상(이하)이다 be above (below) the average / ~을 잡다 take (get) the average / ~을 내다 calculate (strike) the average (of); average out (the cost) / 그들은 하루 ~ 8시간 일한다 They work 8 hours a day on average. ‖ ~수명 the average life span (of the Koreans) / ~연령 the average age / ~점 the average mark / ~치 the mean (average) value / 연(월)~ the yearly (monthly) mean. ② (평형) balance; equilibrium. ‖ ~이 잡힌 well-balanced. ‖ ~대 (臺) a balance beam.

평년(平年) a common year (윤년이 아닌); a normal (an average) year (예년). ‖ ~작 a normal (an average) crop / ~작 이상(이하) above (below) the average crop).

평등(平等) equality; 《공평》 impartiality. ‖ ~한(히) equal(ly); even(ly); impartial(ly). ‖ ~한 권리를 요구하다 demand (call for) equal rights / 사람은 모두 ~하게 태어났다 All men are created equal. / ~주의 the principle of equality / ~화(化) equalization.

평론(評論) criticism; 《비평》 a comment; a review (저작물의). ~하다 criticize; review; comment (on). ‖ 영화의 ~을 하다 make a critical remark on the movie. ‖ ~가 a critic; a reviewer; a commentator (정치·스포츠 등의).

평면(平面) a plane; a level. ‖ ~의 plane; level; flat. ‖ ~교차 grade (level) crossing / ~기하 plane geometry / ~도 a plane figure (수학의) ; a ground plan (건축의).

평민(平民) a commoner; the common people (총칭).

평방(平方) ☞ 제곱.

평범(平凡) ~한 common; ordinary; mediocre; commonplace / ~한 일 an everyday affair; a commonplace / ~한 인간 an ordinary man / ~한 얼굴 a face without any character.

평복(平服) ordinary dress (clothes) ; (제복이 아닌) plain (civilian) clothes.

평상(平床) a flat wooden bed.

평상(平常) ~의 usual; ~ 상태 the normal condition / ~시 ordinarily / ~시와 같이 as usual.

평생(平生) one's whole life (일생). ‖ ~을 두고 for all one's life / ~에 한 번 있는 기회 the chance of a lifetime / ~을 독신으로 지내다 stay (remain) single all one's life. / ~소원 one's lifelong desire.

평소(平素) ordinary times. ‖ ~에 usually, ordinarily; at ordinary (normal) times / ~의 ordinary; usual; everyday / ~대로 as usual / ~와는 달리 unusually / ~의 행실 one's everyday conduct.

평시(平時) (평상시) normal times. (평화시) peacetime. ‖ ~에는 in normal times. ‖ ~산업 peace-time industry.

평안(平安) peace. ‖ 마음의 ~ peace of mind / ~한 peaceful; tranquil / ~히 in peace; peacefully.

평야(平野) a plain; plains. ‖ 호남 ~ the Honam plains. [ture.

평열(平熱) the normal tempera-

평영(平泳) the breaststroke. ~하다 swim on one's chest. ‖ ~선수 a breaststroker.

평온(平溫) ① (평균 온도) an average temperature. ② ~ 평열.

평온(平穩) calmness; quietness; peace. ‖ ~한 quiet; peaceful; tranquil; untroubled / ~해지다 become (get) quiet; quiet down / ~무사 ~하게 지내다 live in peace and quiet.

평원(平原) a plain; a prairie (美).

평의(評議) conference; discussion. ~하다 confer; consult (with); discuss (a matter). ‖ ~원(員) a councilor / ~회 a council.

평이(平易) ~한 easy; plain; simple.

평일(平日) ① (일요일 이외의) a weekday; weekdays. ‖ ~에는 on weekdays. ② (평상시) ordinary days. ‖ ~에는 on ordinary days.

평점(評點) examination (evaluation) marks; a grade.

평정(平定) ~하다 suppress; subdue. ‖ 반란을 ~하다 suppress a revolt.

평정(平靜) calm; tranquility; composure; peace. ‖ ~한 calm; quiet; composed; peaceful / 마음의 ~ peace of mind / composure / (마음의) ~을 되찾다 remain calm / ~을 잃다 lose one's composure (head).

평정(評定) rating; evaluation. ~하다 rate; evaluate.

평준(平準) level (수준); equality (평균). ‖ ~점 a level point / ~화 equalization (~화하다 level; make equal; equalize).

평지(平地) flatlands; level land (ground); the plains (평원). ‖ ~풍파를 일으키다 raise unnecessary troubles; cause a flutter in the dovecotes.

평직(平織) plain weave.

평탄(平坦) ~한 even; flat; level / ~한 인생 an uneventful life / ~하게 하다 level (a road).

평토(平土) ~하다 level off a grave (after burying the body). ‖ ~

평판(葬) burying without making a mound on the grave.
평판 a lithograph. ¶ ~의 lithographic. ‖ ~인쇄 lithography; lithoprinting 《美》.
평판(評判) 《명성》 fame; reputation; popularity 《인기》; 《세평》 the public estimation 〔opinion〕; a rumor 《소문》. ¶ ~이 난 reputed; famed / ~이 좋다〔나쁘다〕 be well〔ill〕 spoken of; have a good〔bad〕 reputation; be popular〔unpopular〕/ 좋은 ~을 잃다 lose *one's* good reputation; fall into disrepute.
평평하다(平平—) (be) flat; even; level.
평행(平行) ~하다 run 〔be〕 parallel to 〔with〕. ¶ …과 ~으로 선을 긋다 draw a line parallel to / 철도와 ~ 으로 도로가 나 있다 A highway runs parallel to the railroad. ‖ ~봉〔선〕 parallel bars 〔lines〕/ ~사변형 a parallelogram / ~운동 a parallel motion.
평형(平衡) balance; equilibrium. ¶ ~을 유지하다〔잃다〕 keep 〔lose〕 *one's* balance. ‖ ~감각 the sense of balance.
평화(平和) peace; harmony 《화합》. ¶ ~스럽다 (be) peaceful; tranquil / ~적인 peaceful; peace-loving / ~적으로 peacefully; in peace / ~적 해결 a peaceful settlement 《of a dispute》/ ~를 유지〔회복, 회복〕하다 keep 〔disturb, restore〕 peace / 항구적인 ~를 확립하다 establish (an) everlasting peace. ‖ ~공세 a peace offensive / ~공존 (노선) peaceful coexistence (line) / ~봉사단 the Peace Corps / ~애호국 a peace-loving nation / ~운동 a peace movement / ~유지군 《유엔의》 the Peace Keeping Forces 《생략 PKF》/ ~유지활동 the Peace Keeping Operations 《생략 PKO》/ ~주의 pacifism / ~주의자 a pacifist / ~협상 peace talks 〔negotiations〕/ ~회의〔조약〕 a peace conference 〔treaty〕.
평활근(平滑筋) 〖解〗 a smooth muscle.
폐(肺) the lungs. ¶ ~가 나쁘다 have a weak chest. ‖ ~기종 〖醫〗 pulmonary emphysema / ~동맥〔정맥〕 the pulmonary artery 〔vein〕 / ~암 lung cancer.
폐(弊) ① ☞ 폐단. ② 《괴로움》 (a) trouble; a bother 《to》; a nuisance. ¶ ~를 끼치다 trouble 〔bother〕 《a person with》; give 〔cause〕 《a person》 trouble; bother.
폐가(廢家) ① 《버려진 집》 a deserted house. ② 《절손》 an extinct family.
폐간(廢刊) discontinuance 《of publication》. ~하다 discontinue 〔cease to publish〕 《the magazine》. ~ ~이 되다 be discontinued / ~시키다 ban the publication 《of》.
폐결핵(肺結核) (pulmonary) tuberculosis; consumption. ¶ ~에 걸리다 suffer from tuberculosis of the lungs. ‖ ~환자 a consumptive (patient).
폐경기(閉經期) 《a woman at》 the menopause.
폐관(閉館) ~하다 close. ¶ 도서관은 5시에 ~한다 The library closes at five. / 오늘 ~ 《게시》 Closed Today.
폐광(廢鑛) 「(pit)」 an abandoned mine
폐교(廢校) ¶ 저 학교는 작년에 ~되었다 That school was closed last year.
폐기(廢棄) ① 《불필요한 물건의》 abandonment; abolition. ~하다 abolish; abandon; scrap; do away with. ¶ 헌 서류들을 ~하다 scrap old documents / 쓰레기를 ~ 처분하다 dispose of junk. ‖ ~물 waste / ~물 처리장 a garbage 〔refuse〕 dump / 방사성 ~물 처리 disposal of radioactive waste. ② 《법령 등의》 abrogation; repeal. ~하다 abrogate 《a treaty》; repeal 《a law》; scrap 《a plan》.
폐농(廢農) ~하다 give up farming.
폐단(弊端) an evil; an abuse. ¶ ~을 시정하다 remedy an evil.
폐렴(肺炎) 〖醫〗 pneumonia.
폐롭다(弊—) ① 《귀찮다》 (be) troublesome; annoying; be a nuisance. ¶ 폐롭게 굴다 cause a nuisance. ② 《성질이》 (be) particular; fussy; fastidious. ¶ 폐로운 할머니 a difficult old lady.
폐막(閉幕) a curtainfall; a close; the end 《of an event》. ~하다 end; come to a close.
폐문(肺門) 〖解〗 the hilum of a lung.
폐물(廢物) a useless article; waste (materials); refuse; trash 《美》; a scrap. ¶ ~이 되다 become useless. ‖ ~이용 the utilization of waste materials; the reuse of discarded articles.
폐백(幣帛) 《신부의》 presents to her parents-in-law.
폐병(肺病) ① 〖醫〗 a lung trouble (disease). ② ☞ 폐결핵.
폐부(肺腑) ① ☞ 폐문. ② 《마음 속》 *one's* inmost heart. ¶ ~를 찌르는 듯한 이야기 a heart-breaking story / ~를 찌르다 give 《a person》 a deep thrust; touch *one's* heart deeply.
폐사(弊社) our company 〔firm〕.
폐색(閉塞) (a) blockade; blocking; (a) stoppage. ~하다 blockade

폐선(廢船) a scrapped ship (vessel); a ship that is out of service. ~하다 scrap a ship.

폐쇄(閉鎖) closing; a lockout. ~하다 close (down); lock out. ¶ ~적인 사회 a closed society / 공장을 ~하다 close down a factory. ‖ ~회로(電) a closed circuit / ~회로 텔레비전 closed-circuit television (생략 CCTV).

폐수(廢水) wastewater. ¶ 공장~ liquid waste from a factory / 생활~ domestic wastewater. ‖ ~처리 wastewater treatment / ~처리장 a wastewater disposal plant.

폐습(弊習) a bad habit; bad practices (customs).

폐어(廢語) an obsolete word.

폐업(廢業) ~하다 give up (close) one's business; shut up one's shop; give up one's practice (의사, 변호사 등).

폐위(廢位) ~하다 dethrone; depose (a sovereign); (clots (덩어리).

폐유(廢油) waste oil; waste oil.

폐인(廢人) a crippled (disabled) person. ¶ ~이나 다름없이 되다 become as good as a living dead.

폐일언하고(蔽一言—) In a word…; To sum up….

폐장(閉場) closing of a place. ~하다 close (a place); be closed.

폐점(閉店) ~하다 close the shop; close one's doors; 《예일》 shut up shop; wind up one's business. ¶ ~시간 (the) closing time.

폐점(弊店) our shop.

폐정(閉廷) 《법원이》 ~하다 adjourn (dismiss) the court.

폐지(廢止) stoppage. ~하다 stop; close; cease.

폐지(廢止) abolition; disuse; repeal (법률 등의). ~하다 abolish; do away with; discontinue; phase out (법률 따위); abrogate; repeal. ¶ ~되다 be abolished; go out of use.

폐질(廢疾) an incurable disease. ‖ ~자 a person with an incurable disease.

폐차(廢車) a disused (scrapped) car; a car out of service. ¶ ~처분하다 scrap a car; put a car out of service. ‖ ~장 an auto junkyard.

폐품(廢品) useless (discarded) articles; waste materials. ¶ ~을 회수하다 collect scraps. ‖ ~이용 the reuse (utilization) of waste materials / ~회수 collection of waste articles / ~회수업자 a ragman; a junk dealer.

폐하(陛下) His [Her] Majesty (3인칭); Your Majesty (2인칭).

폐하다(廢—) 《그만두다》 give up (one's studies); discontinue (《철폐》 abolish (군주를) dethrone. ¶ 허례를 ~ do away with formalities.

폐함(廢艦) ~하다 put (a warship) out of commission.

폐합(廢合) ~하다 abolish and amalgamate; reorganize. ¶ 국과(局課)를 ~하다 rearrange (reorganize) bureaus and sections.

폐해(弊害) an evil; abuses; an ill (a bad) effect; an evil influence. ¶ ~가 따르다 be attended by an evil / ~를 끼치다 exert an evil influence upon; be a cause of damage to.

폐허(廢墟) ruins; remains. ¶ ~가 되다 be ruined; fall into ruins / ~가 되어 있다 be (lie) in ruins.

폐활량(肺活量) breathing (lung) capacity. ‖ ~계(計) a spirometer.

폐회(閉會) the closing (of a meeting). ~하다 close (a meeting); come to a close; be closed. ‖ ~사 (give) a closing address / ~식 a closing ceremony.

포(苞) 〔植〕 a bract.

포(砲) 《대포》 (fire) a gun; an artillery gun; a cannon (구식의).

포(脯) 포육(脯肉).

포가(砲架) (set) a gun carriage.

포개다 put (lay) one upon another; pile (heap) up. ¶ 포개지다 be (lie) heaped (piled) up; be piled on top of one another.

포격(砲擊) (artillery) bombardment; fire; cannonade (연속적인). ~하다 bombard; fire; shell. ¶ ~을 받다 be under fire; be shelled (bombarded) (by).

포경(包莖) phimosis.

포경(捕鯨) whaling; whale fishing. ¶ ~산업 the whaling industry / ~선(船) a whaler.

포고(布告) proclamation. ~하다 proclaim; declare; decree. ¶ 선전~ a declaration of war / ~를 내다 issue (make) a proclamation. ‖ ~령〔문〕 a decree; an edict; a proclamation.

포괄(包括) inclusion. ~하다 include; comprehend; contain; cover. ¶ ~적(으로) inclusive(ly); comprehensive(ly) / ~적인 군축계획 the Comprehensive Program on Disarmament. ‖ ~사항 a blanket clause / ~요금 an inclusive charge.

포교(布敎) propagation (of religion); missionary work. ~하다 preach (propagate) (a religion).

포구(浦口) an inlet; an estuary.

포구(砲口) a muzzle (of a gun).

포구(捕球) 〔野〕 catching; (a) catch.

포근하다 ① 《푹신》 (be) soft and

포기 a head; a root; a plant. ¶배추 두 ~ two heads of Chinese cabbage.

포기(抛棄) abandonment; renunciation. ~하다 give up; abandon; renounce; relinquish. ¶권리를 ~하다 give up (relinquish) one's right ((to)) / 상속권을 ~하다 renounce the right of succession.

포대(布袋) ☞ 부대(負袋).

포대(砲臺) a battery; a fort (요새).

포대기 a baby's quilt; a wadded baby wrapper.

포도(葡萄) a grape; a (grape) vine (덩굴 나무). ‖ ~당 grape sugar; 《化》 glucose / ~밭 a vineyard / ~송이 a bunch (cluster) of grapes / ~주 (red, white) wine / ~즙 grape juice.

포도(鋪道) a pavement; a paved (road).

포동포동하다 (be) chubby; plump.

포로(捕虜) a prisoner of war (생략 POW); a captive. ¶~가 되다 be taken prisoner / ~로 하다 take (make) ((a person)) prisoner. ‖ ~교환 an exchange of war prisoners / ~송환 the repatriation of prisoners of war / ~수용소 a prison (POW) camp.

포르노 pornography; porno. ¶~영화 a pornographic (blue) film.

포르말린 《化》 formalin. ‖ ~소독 formalin disinfection.

포르투갈 Portugal. ¶~의 Portuguese. ¶~말 Portuguese / ~사람 a Portuguese.

포름아미드 《化》 formamide.

포마드 pomade. ¶~를 바르다 pomade ((one's hair)).

포만(飽滿) satiety. ~하다 be satiated (full) ((with)).

포말(泡沫) a bubble; foam. ‖ ~경기 an ephemeral boom / ~회사 a bubble company.

포목(布木) linen and cotton; dry goods 《美》; drapery 《英》. ‖ ~상 a dry-goods store; a draper's.

포문(砲門) the muzzle of a gun; a porthole (군함의). ¶~을 열다 open fire ((on)).

포물선(物物線) 《數》 a parabola. ¶~을 그리다 draw (describe) a parabola.

포박(捕縛) ~하다 arrest; apprehend.

포병(砲兵) an artilleryman (군인); artillery (총칭). ‖ ~기지 an artillery base / ~대 an artillery unit (corps) / ~사령관 an artillery commander / ~전 an artillery duel.

포복(匍匐) ~하다 creep (crawl) flat on the ground; walk on ((one's)) hands and knees.

포복절도(抱腹絶倒) convulsions of laughter. ~하다 hold ((one's)) sides (roll about) with laughter; be convulsed with laughter. ¶그는 우리들을 ~케 했다 He set us roaring with laughter. or He had us all in fits of laughter.

포부(抱負) (an) ambition; (an) aspiration. ¶~를 품다 have an ambition ((to do)).

포상(褒賞) a prize; a reward. ~하다 give a prize. ¶~을 받다 be rewarded ((for)).

포석(布石) (바둑의) the strategic placing of (paduk-)stones; (비유적) (take) preparatory steps (for doing); (lay) the groundwork (for). ~하다 make a strategic move; make strategic arrangements. ¶장래 발전을 위한 ~을 하다 lay the foundations for future development.

포석(鋪石) a paving stone.

포섭(包攝) 《論》 subsumption. ~하다 win (gain) ((a person)) over ((to one's side)); subsume. ¶~공작을 하다 contrive to win ((a person)) over to one's side.

포성(砲聲) the sound of gunfire; the roaring boom of guns.

포수(砲手) a gunner;《포경선의》a harpooner;《사냥꾼》a hunter.

포수(捕手) 《野》 a catcher.

포술(砲術) gunnery; artillery.

포스터 a poster (bill). ¶~를 붙이다 (떼다) put up (tear off) a poster.

포슬포슬 ~하다 (be) crumbly.

포승(捕繩) a policeman's rope.

포식(飽食) ~하다 eat ((one's)) fill; satiate oneself.

포신(砲身) a gun barrel.

포악(暴惡) ¶~한 atrocious; outrageous; ruthless.

포안(砲眼) (함선·성벽 등의) an embrasure.

포연(砲煙) the smoke of cannon; powder (artillery) smoke.

포열(砲列) a battery.

포옹(抱擁) an embrace; a hug. ~하다 embrace; hug. ¶양팔을 크게 벌려 ~하다 give ((a person)) a big hug.

포용(包容) tolerance. ~하다 tolerate. ¶~력이 있는 사람 a broad-minded person / 갖가지 다른 의견을 ~하다 tolerate different opinions. ‖ ~력 broad-mindedness; tolerance.

포위(包圍) encirclement; 《軍》 (a) siege. ~하다 close in; surround; besiege; encircle. ¶적을 ~하다 lay siege to the enemy / 적의 ~를 돌파하다 break through the besieging enemy forces / ~를

다 raise [lift] the siege 《of》 / 경찰은 그들의 은신처를 ~했다 The police closed in on their hideout. ∥ ~공격 a siege / ~군 the besieging army / ~망 an encircling net / ~작전 an encircling [enveloping] operation.

포유(哺乳) suckling; nursing. ∥ ~동물 a mammal / ~류 the Mammalia.

포육(脯肉) jerky 《美》; jerked meat.

포인트 ① (소수점) a decimal point. ② (전철기) a (railroad) switch 《美》. ③ (활자 크기의 단위) point. ¶ 9~활자 a 9-point type. ④ (득점) a point; a score. ¶ ~를 올리다 gain (get, score) a point. ⑤ (요점·지점) the point 《of a story》. ¶ 설명의 ~를 잡다 get the point of 《a person's》 explanation / 인생의 터닝 ~ the turning point in one's life.

포자(胞子) [植] spore. ∥ ~낭(囊) a spore case / ~식물 sporophyte.

포장(布帳) a linen awning [screen]; a curtain; (마차의) a hood; (차의) a top. ¶ ~을 씌우다 [걷다] pull up [down] the hood [top]. ∥ ~마차 [술파는] a covered cart bar; a small wheeled snack bar with a tent; [美史] a prairie schooner [wagon]; a covered wagon.

포장(包裝) packing; packaging; wrapping. ~하다 pack; package; wrap (up). ¶ ~끈 wrapping string / ~을 풀다 unpack 《a box》; unwrap 《a package》 / 이 시계를 선물용으로 ~해 주시오 Please gift-wrap this clock. / 과잉 ~은 자원의 낭비다 Overpackaging wastes resources. ∥ ~비 packing charges / ~재료 packing materials / ~지(紙) packing [wrapping, brown] paper.

포장(鋪裝) pavement; paving. ~하다 pave 《a road》. ¶ ~이 안 [잘] 된 도로 an unpaved [a well-paved] road. ∥ ~공사 pavement works; paving / ~도로 a paved road.

포장(褒章) a medal 《for merit》.

포좌(砲座) [軍] a gun platform.

포주(抱主) a keeper of brothel; a whore-master; a bawd(여자).

포즈 a pose. ¶ ~를 취하다 take one's pose.

포진(布陣) the lineup. ~하다 line up; take up one's position; array troops for battle(군대를).

포진(疱疹) [醫] herpes. ∥ ~성 herpetic. ¶ ~환자 a herpetic / 대상 ~ herpes zoster (라); shingles.

포착(捕捉) capture. ~하다 capture; take hold of; seize and hold. ¶ 기회를 ~하다 seize an opportunity.

포커 《play》 poker. ∥ ~페이스 a poker face; a dead pan 《美俗》.

포켓 a pocket. ¶ ~에 들어가는 pocketable 《books》 / ~에 넣다 pocket 《a thing》; put 《a thing》 in one's pocket. ∥ ~머니 pocket money / ~판(版) a pocket edition.

포크¹ (용구) a fork.
포크² (돼지고기) pork.

포크댄스 a folk dance.

포크송 a folk song.

포탄(砲彈) a shell; an artillery shell; a cannonball. ¶ ~의 폭발 a shell burst / ~연기 shell smoke / 적에게 ~을 퍼붓다 fire shells over the enemy; rain artillery fire on the enemy.

포탈(逋脫) evasion of tax《☞ 탈세》.

포탑(砲塔) a (gun) turret. ¶ 회전 ~ a revolving turret.

포터블 portable 《radio》.

포트와인 port 《wine》.

포플러 [植] a poplar(미루나무).

포플린(포류) poplin; broadcloth 《美》.

포피(包皮) [解] the foreskin; the prepuce.

포학(暴虐) (an) atrocity; cruelty; tyranny(폭정). ¶ ~한 군주 a tyrant; a cruel [bloody] ruler.

포함(包含) inclusion. ~하다 contain; hold; include; imply(의미를). ¶ ~된 비용을 ~ 해서 including all expenses 《of》 / 다량의 탄산가스를 ~한 공기 air loaded with carbonic acid gas / 그 값에는 세금이 ~되어 있지 않다 The price is not inclusive of tax.

포함(砲艦) a gunboat.

포화(砲火) gunfire; artillery fire. ¶ 맹렬한 ~ heavy fire / ~의 섬광 a gunflash / ~세례를 받다 be under fire / ~를 주고받다 exchange fire / ~를 퍼붓다 rain fire on 《the enemy》.

포화(飽和) saturation. ¶ ~상태에 있다 be saturated 《with》 / ~상태가 되다 《become》 saturated 《with》 / 이 도시의 인구는 ~상태에 이르다 The population of this city is at its peak of congestion. ∥ ~용액 a saturated solution / ~점 a saturation point.

포획(捕獲) capture; seizure. ~하다 capture; catch; seize. ∥ ~고 a catch 《of whales》 / ~물 a booty.

포효(咆哮) 《맹수의》 roaring; 《늑대의》 howling. ~하다 roar; howl.

폭(幅) ① (너비) width; breadth. ¶ ~이 넓은 wide; broad / ~이 좁은 narrow / ~을 넓히다 widen; broaden. ② (행동·사고의) latitude; a range; (값·이익의) a difference (between two prices); a margin 《of profit》. ¶교제의 ~이 넓다 have a wide circle of friends／가격의 ~이 크다 The price range is large.／선택의 ~이 매우 넓다 There is much latitude of choice.

폭거(暴擧) a reckless attempt; (an) outrage; a riot(폭동). ¶인간의 존엄을 해하는 ~ an outrage against human dignity.

폭격(爆擊) bombing. ~하다 bomb 《a town》. ¶~기 a bomber／융단 ~ carpet〔blanket〕 bombing.

폭군(暴君) a tyrant.

폭도(暴徒) 〔put down〕 a mob; rioters. ¶~의 무리 a mob of rioters／~에게 습격당하다 be mobbed／~를 선동하다 stir up a mob／~화하다 turn into a mob.

폭동(暴動) a riot; an uprising; a disturbance. ¶인종 ~ a race riot／~을 일으키다 raise〔start〕a riot／~을 진압〔선동〕하다 suppress〔instigate〕a riot. ‖무장 ~ armed revolt.

폭등(暴騰) a sudden rise; a jump. ~하다 rise suddenly; jump; soar. ¶물가가 ~하고 있다 Prices are skyrocketing.

폭락(暴落) a sudden〔heavy〕fall; a slump. ~하다 decline heavily; slump; fall suddenly. ¶주가의 ~ a heavy fall〔steep decline〕in stock prices.

폭력(暴力) force; violence. ¶~으로 by force／~에 호소하다 appeal〔resort〕to force／~을 휘두르다 use〔employ〕violence《on》／~으로 위협하다 threaten《a person》with force. ‖~교실 a classroom ruled by violence／~단 an organized group of gangsters／~단원 a gangster／~범죄 a crime of violence／~혁명 a violent〔an armed〕revolution／학교~ school violence.

폭로(暴露) exposure; disclosure. ~하다 expose; disclose; reveal; bring 《a matter》 to light. ¶~되다 be disclosed〔exposed〕／~되어 밝혀지다 be brought to light／비밀을 ~하다 disclose〔reveal〕《a person's》secret／정체를 ~하다 reveal《a person's》true character／무지를 ~하다 betray one's ignorance.‖~기사 an exposé〔프〕／~전술 exposure〔muckraking《미ㅁ》〕tactics.

폭뢰(爆雷) a depth bomb〔charge〕.

폭리(暴利) an excessive〔undue〕profit; profiteering(부당이득). ¶~를 단속하다 control profiteering／~를 취하다 make undue profits.

폭발(爆發) explosion; eruption(화산의). ~하다 explode; blow up; burst out; erupt(화산이). ¶~(으로) explosive(ly)／~적인 인기 tremendous popularity／인구의 ~적인 증가 a population explosion／분노가 ~하다 explode with anger. ‖~가스 explosive gas／~력 explosive power／~물 an explosive／~물 처리반 a bomb disposal unit／~성(性) explosiveness／~음 a blast.

폭사(爆死) ~하다 be killed by a bomb; be bombed to death.

폭서(暴暑) intense〔severe〕heat.

폭설(暴雪) a heavy snowfall.

폭소(爆笑) ~하다 burst into laughter; burst out laughing.

폭식(暴食) gluttony; voracious eating. ~하다 overeat《oneself》; eat too much.

폭신폭신하다 (be) soft; spongy; fluffy.

폭약(爆藥) an explosive; a blasting powder. ‖고성능 ~ a high explosive.

폭양(曝陽) the burning sun.

폭언(暴言) violent〔rude〕language; harsh〔wild〕words. ~하다 use offensive〔violent〕language; speak with wild words. 〔intense heat.〕

폭염(暴炎) scorching summer heat;

폭우(暴雨) 〔be damaged by〕 a heavy rain; a downpour.

폭음(暴飮) heavy drinking. ~하다 drink heavily〔too much〕／~폭식하다 eat and drink immoderately〔to excess〕.

폭음(爆音) an explosion; a roar《of an engine》; a whir(기계의). ¶제트기의 ~ the noisy roar of jet planes.

폭정(暴政) tyranny; despotism. ¶~을 펴다 tyrannize over a country／~에 시달리다 groan under tyranny.

폭주(輻輳) overcrowding; congestion. ~하다 be congested〔crowded〕《with》. ¶교통의 ~ a traffic congestion／주문의 ~ a pressure〔a flood〕of orders.

폭주(暴走) ~하다 run〔drive〕recklessly. ¶~운전 reckless driving／~족 reckless〔crazy〕drivers; a motorcycle gang; 《口》bikers; hell's angels.

폭죽(爆竹) 〔set off〕 a firecracker.

폭탄(爆彈) a bomb〔shell〕. ¶시한 ~을 장치하다 set〔plant〕a time bomb／~을 투하하다 drop〔throw〕bombs 《on a town》. ‖~선언 a bombshell declaration／~테러 a bomb terrorism／~투하 bombing.

폭투(暴投) 《野》 a wild pitch〔throw〕. ~하다 pitch〔throw〕wild.

폭파(爆破) blast; blowing up.

폭포 (瀑布) a waterfall; falls; a cascade(작은); cataract(큰). ∥ 나이아가라 ~ (the) Niagara Falls.

폭풍 (暴風) a storm; a wild〔violent〕 wind. ¶ ~을 만나다 encounter a storm; be overtaken by a storm. / ~경보〔주의보〕 a storm warning〔alert〕 / ~권 a storm zone.

폭풍우 (暴風雨) a rainstorm; a storm; a tempest. ¶ ~로 고립된 마을 a stormbound village / 동해 연안에 ~가 엄습했다 A violent storm raged along the East Coast.

폭한 (暴漢) a ruffian; a rowdy.

폭행 (an act of) violence; an outrage; an assault; a rape (여자에 대한). ~하다 behave violently; commit an outrage; do〔use〕 violence to 《a person》; rape 《a woman》. ∥ ~자 an outrager; an assaulter; a rapist(여자에 대한).

폴라로이드 ∥ ~카메라 《상표명》 a Polaroid (Land) camera.

폴라리스 a Polaris (missile). ∥ ~잠수함 a Polaris(-armed) submarine.

폴란드 Poland. ¶ ~의 Polish. ∥ ~말 Polish / ~사람 a Pole; the Poles(총칭).

폴리에스테르 《化》 polyester.

폴리에틸렌 《化》 polyethylene.

폴카 《春·무곡》 polka.

푄 《氣》 foehn; *Föhn* 《獨》. ∥ ~현상 a foehn phenomenon.

표 (表) a table; a list; a chart. ¶ 정가~ a price list / 시간~ a timetable / 일람~ a catalog / ~를 만들다 tabulate; make a list 《of》.

표 (票) ① 《차표·입장권 따위》 a ticket; a coupon(하나씩 떼는); 《꼬찰》 a card; a label(레테르); a tag(꼬표). ¶ ~ 파는 곳 a ticket office / ~를 찍다 punch a ticket(검표) / ~를 달다 put a tag 《on》 / ~를 붙이다 paste a card〔label〕; label 《a thing》. ∥ 번호~ a number plate〔ticket〕. ② 《투표의》 a vote. ¶ ~ 모으기 vote-catching 〔-getting〕 / 깨끗한 ~를 던지다 cast an honest vote / ~ 모으기 운동을 하다 canvass for votes. / ~수 (數) 〔득표수〕 the number of votes polled; a vote; 〔획득 가능수〕 voting strength.

표 (標) 《부호·푯말》 a sign; a mark; 《표시》 a token; 《휘장》 a badge; 《증거》 proof; evidence; 《상표》 a brand; trademark (☞ 표하다). ¶ 물음 ~ an interrogation mark / ~를 하다 mark 《a thing》; put a mark 《on》.

표결 (表決) ☞ 의결 (議決).

표결 (票決) a vote; voting. ~하다 take a vote 《on》; vote 《on》. ¶ ~에 부치다 put 《a bill》 to a vote 〔ballot〕.

표고 (桶) 《버섯》 a p'yogo mushroom; *Lentinus edodes*(학명).

표고 (標高) ☞ 해발 (海拔).

표구 (表具) mounting. ~하다 mount 《a picture》. ∥ ~사 a paper hanger; a mounter.

표기 (表記) ~의 (금액) (the sum) inscribed on the face / ~된 주소 the address mentioned on the outside(face). / ~가격 the declared value / ~법 notation.

표기 (標記) marking; a mark.

표독 (慓毒) ~하다 (be) fierce; ferocious; venomous.

표류 (漂流) drifting. ~하다 drift 《about》. ∥ ~물 a drift; floating wreckage / ~선 (船) a drifting ship / ~자 a person adrift on the sea; a castaway 《on an island》.

표리 (表裏) 《겉과 속》 the front and (the) back; inside and outside; 《양면》 both sides 《of a thing》. ¶ ~가 있는 two-faced; double-dealing; treacherous / ~가 없는 straight; single-hearted; honest; faithful / 그는 ~가 있는 사람이다 He is a double-dealer. *or* He is two-faced.

표면 (表面) 《겉면》 the surface; the face; 《외부》 the outside; the exterior; 《외견》 (an) appearance. ¶ ~적인 superficial; outward, external(외면의) / 거친〔매끈한〕 ~ a rough〔smooth〕 surface / 건물의 ~ the outside of a building / ~상의 이유 an ostensible reason / ~상의 친절 surface kindness / ~화하다 come to the surface; come into the open / …을 ~적으로 이해하다 have only a superficial understanding of.... ∥ ~금리 a coupon rate / ~예금 a nominal gross deposit 《at a bank》 / ~장력(張力) 《理》 surface tension.

표면적 (表面積) surface area.

표명 (表明) (an) expression; (a) manifestation. ~하다 express; manifest; declare. ¶ 감사〔유감〕의 뜻을 ~하다 express *one's* gratitude〔regret〕 《to》.

표방 (標榜) ~하다 profess 《*oneself* to be》; stand for 《democracy》; advocate. ¶ 인도주의를 ~하다 claim to stand for humanitarian principles.

표밭 (票―) a reliable source of

표백(漂白) bleaching; ~하다 bleach. ‖ ~제 a bleach; a bleaching agent; a decolorant.
표범(豹~) [動] a leopard; a panther.
표변(豹變) a sudden change. ~하다 change suddenly; do a complete turn around; turn one's coat(변절).
표본(標本) a specimen; a sample(견본); (전형) a type; an example. ¶ ~학자의 a typical scholar. ‖ ~조사 a sample survey / ~추출 sampling / 동물(식물) ~ a zoological (botanical) specimen / 박제 ~ a stuffed (mounted) specimen (of a tiger) / 임의 ~ a random sample.
표상(表象) (상징) a symbol (of); an emblem; [哲] an idea; a representation; [心] an image.
표시(表示) indication; expression. ~하다 express; indicate; show. ¶ 감사의 ~로 as a token of one's gratitude. ‖ ~기 an indicator / 의사~ expression of one's intention. [catchword.
표어(標語) a motto; a slogan; a
표연(飄然) ¶ ~히 aimlessly; casually; abruptly.
표음문자(表音文字) a phonogram; a phonetic alphabet.
표의문자(表意文字) an ideogram; an ideograph.
표적(表迹) a sign; a mark; a token; a proof(증표); (혼적) a trace(지나간). ¶ ~을 남기지 않다 leave no trace behind.
표적(標的) a target; a mark. ¶ ~을 벗어나다 fall beside the mark / 비난의 ~이 되다 be exposed to censure; / ~사격 target shooting / ~지역 a target area.
표절(剽竊) plagiarism; literary piracy. ~하다 pirate; plagiarize. ‖ ~자 a plagiarist / ~판 a pirated edition.
표정(表情) (an) expression; a look. ¶ 무표정한 expressive / ~없는 얼굴 an expressionless face / ~을 굳히다 harden one's face; look grim (stern) / ~을 살피다 read (a person's) face / 곤혹스런 ~을 짓다 wear a puzzled expression.
표제(表題·標題) (책의) a title; (논설 등의) a heading; a head; (사전·만화의) a caption. ¶ 작은 ~ a subtitle / ~를 달다 give a title (to a book); entitle. ‖ ~어 an entry; a headword / ~음악 program music.

표주(標註) a marginal note.
표주박(瓢~) a small gourd vessel; a dipper.
표준(標準) a standard; a norm(작업용 등의); a level(수준); average (평균). ¶ ~적인 standard; normal; average / 정해진 ~ a fixed standard / ~에 달(미달)하다 come up to (fall short of) the standard / ~이상(이하)이다 be above (below) the standard. ‖ ~가격 the standard price / ~생활비 the standard (average) cost of living / ~어(시) the standard language (time) / ~편차 a standard deviation / ~형 a standard type (size) / ~화 standardization / ~화하다 standardize.
표지(表紙) a cover. ¶ 종이 (가죽, 형겊) ~ a paper (leather, cloth) cover / 앞(뒤) ~ a front (back) cover / 책에 ~를 씌우다 cover a book; put the cover on a book.
표지(標識) a sign; a mark; a landmark (경계의); a beacon (항공의). ¶ ~를 세우다 put up a sign. ‖ ~등 a beacon light.
표징(表徵) a sign; a symbol.
표착(漂着) ~하다 drift ashore.
표창(表彰) (official) commendation; citation. ~하다 commend a person (for a thing) officially; honor (a person). ¶ 구조대에 협력하여 ~받다 receive an official commendation for helping the rescue party. ‖ ~대(臺) a honor platform / ~식 a commendation (an awarding) ceremony / ~장 a citation (美); a testimonial.
표토(表土) topsoil; surface soil.
표피(表皮) [解] the cuticle; the epidermis. ‖ ~조직 (세포) the epidermal tissue (cell).
표하다(表~) express; show. ¶ 경의를 ~ pay one's respects (to) / 감사의 뜻을 ~ express (show) one's gratitude (for) / 축의(조의)를 ~ offer one's congratulations (condolences) (to).
표현(表現) (an) expression. ~하다 express; represent. ¶ ~의 자유 freedom of expression. ‖ ~력 power of expression / ~주의 expressionism. [post.
푯말(標~) (set up) a signpost; a
푸념(불평) an idle complaint; a grumble. ~하다 complain (of, about); grumble (whine) (about).
푸다(물을) draw (water from a well); dip (scoop) up; pump(펌프로). ¶ 버킷의 물을 ~ dip water from a bucket / 우물물을 펌프로 ~ pump water up (out) from a well.
푸닥거리 a shamanistic exorcism;

a service of exorcism. ~하다 exorcize; drive out an evil spirit performing an exorcism.

푸대접(一待接) inhospitality; a cold treatment (reception). ~하다 treat (receive) (a person) coldly; give (show) (a person) the cold shoulder. ¶ ~ 받다 get a cold reception; be left out in the cold.

푸드덕거리다 flap; flutter.

푸들(개) a poodle.

푸딩 a pudding.

푸르다 ① (색이) (be) blue; azure; green (초록). ¶ 푸른 잎 green leaves (foliage). ② (서슬이) (be) sharp(-edged).

푸르스름하다 (be) bluish; greenish.

푸른곰팡이[植] green mold.

푸릇푸릇 ¶ ~한 fresh and green here and there.

푸석돌 a crumbly stone.

푸석이 (물건) a crumbly thing; friable stuff; (사람) a fragile (frail) person.

푸석푸석 ¶ ~한 fragile; crumbly.

푸성귀 greens; vegetables.

푸주(一廚) a butcher's (shop). ‖ ~한(漢) a butcher.

푸짐하다 (be) abundant; profuse; generous. ¶ 푸짐히 plentifully; in plenty (abundance) / 푸짐하게 돈을 쓰다 lavish money (on).

푹 ① (쑥 빠지는 모양) ¶ ~ 가라앉다 sink deep / 수렁에 ~ 빠지다 stick in the mud. ② (찌르는 모양) ¶ 단검으로 ~ 찌르다 thrust a dagger home. ③ (덮거나 싸는 모양) ¶ 모자를 ~ 눌러 쓰다 pull (draw) one's hat over one's eyes / 담요로 ~ 싸다 wrap (it) in a blanket. ④ (잠자는 모양) fast; soundly. ¶ ~ 자다 sleep soundly. ⑤ (흠씬) well; thoroughly. ¶ 고기를 ~ 삶다 do (boil) meat well (thoroughly). ⑥ (쓰러지는 모양) ¶ ~ 쓰러지다 fall (on the floor) with a flop.

푹신하다 (be) soft; downy; spongy; cushiony; flossy; 푹신푹신한 all soft; downy; fluffy; spongy.

푹푹 ¶ ~ 쓰다 spend (money) freely / 찌르다 thrust repeatedly / ~ 썩다 grow rotten fast / ~ 쑤시다 prickle; tingle (날씨가) ~ 찌다 be sultry (muggy) / 발이 눈에 ~ 빠지다 one's feet sink deep in the snow.

푼 ① (돈 한 닢) a p'un(한 개 Korean penny(=1/10 don). ¶ 돈 ~이나 모으다 make a pretty penny. ② (백분율) percentage; percent(%). ¶ 3~ 이자 3% interest. ③ (길이) a tenth of a Korean inch(=ch'i). ④ (무게) a Korean penny-weight(=0.375 gram).

푼더분하다 ① (얼굴이) (be) plump; fleshy. ② (넉넉하다) (be) plentiful; ample; rich. 「petty cash.

푼돈 a small sum (of money).

푼푼이 (money saved) penny by penny (little by little).

풀¹ grass; a weed (잡초); a herb (약초). ¶ ~ 베는 기계 a mowing machine; a mower / ~을 뽑다 weed (a garden) / ~을 뜯다 (마소가) feed on grass; graze.

풀² paste (붙이는); starch (풀먹이는). ¶ ~ 먹이다 starch (clothes) / ~ 먹인 옷 a starched cloth / ~을 쑤다 ☞ 풀쑤다 / ~으로 붙이다 paste; fasten (stick) (a thing) with paste.

풀³ (수영장) a swimming pool.

풀⁴ ¶ ~ 스피드로 (run) (at) full speed. ¶ ~ 가동 full operation.

풀기(一氣) starchiness. ¶ ~ 있는 starchy.

풀다 ① (끄르다) untie (a knot); loosen (one's hair); undo (a bundle); untwist (꼰 것을); disentangle (얽힌 것을); unpack (짐 등을); unfasten (a rope). ② (문제를) solve (a problem); answer; work out (an equation). ¶ 수수께끼를 ~ solve (guess) a riddle / 암호를 ~ decipher. ③ (의심·오해를) dispel; remove; clear up (doubts); (울적함을) dissipate; chase (one's gloom away). ¶ 오해를 ~ remove a misunderstanding. ④ (용해) melt; dissolve (salt in water). ⑤ (코를) blow (one's nose). ⑥ (사람을) send out; call out. ¶ 사람을 풀어 범인을 찾다 send out men in search of a criminal. ⑦ (논을) convert (a farm) into (a paddy field). ⑧ (해제하다) remove (a prohibition); lift (a ban); release (a man). ¶ 봉쇄를 ~ lift the blockade / 포위를 ~ raise a siege / 자금의 동결을 ~ thaw the frozen assets / 마침내 그들은 인질을 풀어 주었다 At last they released the hostages. ⑨ (소원·성취) realize. ¶ 소원을 ~ have one's desire fulfilled. ⑩ (긴장·피로) relieve (the tension, one's fatigue). ⑪ (화 따위) appease; calm. ¶ 노염을 ~ quell (appease) one's anger / 갈증을 ~ quench one's thirst.

풀리다 ① (매듭이) get loose; come untied (undone); (솔기가) come apart; (소매 끝 따위가) fray; (얽힌 것이) come (get) disentangled; (짐이) come (get) unpacked. ② (감정이 누그러지다) be softened; calm (cool) down; be allayed (appeased). ¶ 그녀의 미소로 나의 마음이 풀렸다 Her smiles disarmed me. ③ 《문제가》 be solved; be worked out. ④ 《의혹·오해가》

풀무 835 품평

resolved〔dispelled〕; be cleared away. ⑤ (피로가) recover from; be relieved of 《one's fatigue》. ⑥ (추위가) abate; thaw. ¶ 추위가 ~ Cold weather turns warm. ⑦ (해제) be removed〔lifted〕. ⑧ (용해) dissolve; melt. ⑨ (돈이) get circulated. ¶ 은행 돈이 ~ Money in the bank is released.

풀무 a (pair of) bellows. ¶ ~질하다 blow with the bellows.

풀밭 a grass field; a meadow.

풀뿌리 grass roots. ‖ ~ 민주주의 grass-roots democracy / ~ 운동 a grass roots movement (일반 대중의 운동).

풀솜 floss〔silk〕.

풀숲 a bush; a thicket.

풀썩 먼지가 ~ 나다 A cloud of dust rises lightly. / 땅 위에 ~ 주저앉다 flop down on the ground.

풀쐐기 [蟲] a (hairy) caterpillar.

풀쑤다 ① (풀을) make paste. ② (재산을) squander; dissipate 《a fortune》.

풀어놓다 ① (놓아줌) (set) free; release; let〔cast〕 loose. ② (개를 풀어서) Let the dog loose. ② (끄나풀을) put; send; dispatch. ¶ 형사를 ~ set〔put〕 detectives upon 《a person》.

풀어지다 ① (국수·죽이) (noodles) turn soft. ② (눈이) 《one's eyes》 become bleared. 「(of grass).

풀잎 a blade of grass; a leaf

풀죽다 be dejected; be cast down; be dispirited; lose 《one's》 heart.

풀칠 (칠하기) ~ 하다 paste. ② (생계) ~ 하다 make 《one's》 bare living; eke out a living.

풀풀 ¶ ~ 날다 fly〔run〕 swiftly

풀피리 a reed. 「(nimbly).

품[1] ① (옷의) width 《of a coat》; 앞 ~ the breast width. ② (가슴) the breast; the bosom. ¶ ~ 속에 in 《one's》 bosom; to 《one's》 breast / 자연의 ~ 에 안기어 in the bosom of nature.

품[2] (수고·힘) labor; work. ¶ 하루 ~ a day's work / ~ 이 들다 require (much) labor / ~ 을 덜다 save labor / ~ 을 팔다 work for (daily) wages.

품[3] (외양) appearance; (모양) a way. ¶ 사람된 ~ (a) personal character; personality / 말하는 ~ one's way of talking.

품갚음하다 do return service to 《a person's》 help; work in return.

품격(品格) elegance; refinement; grace; dignity(품위). ¶ ~ 있는 refined; elegant.

품계(品階) rank; grade.

품귀(品貴) a scarcity〔shortage〕 of goods〔stock〕. ¶ ~ 상태다 be scarce; be in short supply / ~ 되다 run short; get〔become〕 scarce.

품다 ① (가슴에) hold 《a child》 in one's bosom; put 《a thing》 in one's bosom; embrace; hug. ② (마음에) hold; entertain 《a hope》; cherish 《an ambition》; harbor 《suspicion》; bear 《malice》. ③ (알을) sit (brood) 《on eggs》.

품명(品名) names of goods.

품목(品目) a list of articles; an item(한 종목). ¶ ~ 별로 item by item. ‖ 영업 ~ business items / 주요 수출 ~ the chief items of export.

품사(品詞) [文] a part of speech. ‖ 팔 ~ the eight parts of speech.

품삯 charge (pay, wages) for labor. ¶ ~ 을 치르다 pay 《a person》 for his labor.

품성(品性) character. ¶ ~ 이 훌륭한(비열한) 사람 a man of fine (low) character.

품앗이 exchange of services (labor). ‖ ~ 하다 exchange services; work in turn for each other.

품위(品位) ① (품격) dignity; grace. ¶ ~ 있는 dignified; noble; graceful / ~ 를 지키다(떨어뜨리다) keep (lose) one's dignity. ② (금속의) standard; fineness(순도); carat (금의).

품의(稟議) the process of obtaining sanction 《from senior executives》 for a plan by circulating a draft proposal. ~ 하다 consult (confer) 《with a superior》. ‖ ~ 서 a round robin; a draft prepared and circulated by a person in charge to obtain the sanction to a plan.

품절(品切) absence of stock; (게시) All Sold. or Sold Out. ‖ ~ 되다 be (run) out of stock; be sold out.

품종(品種) ① (종류) a kind; a sort; (변종) a variety; (가축의) a breed; [生] species. ¶ ~ 개량 improvement of breed (가축); plant breeding(식물); selective breeding 《of cattle, rice plants》.

품질(品質) quality. ¶ ~ 이 좋다(나쁘다) be good (poor) in quality / ~ 을 개량하다 improve 《a thing》 in quality; improve the quality of 《a thing》. ‖ ~ 관리 quality control / ~ 보증(본위) (게시) Quality Guaranteed (First). / ~ 저하 deterioration / ~ 증명 a hallmark.

품팔이 work for (daily) wages.

품팔이꾼 a day laborer; a wage worker.

품평(品評) ~ 하다 evaluate. ‖ ~ 회

품하다 a competitive (prize) show; an exhibition; a fair 《美》.

품하다(稟一) proffer 《*something*》 to a superior for approval; submit 《*a plan*》 to a superior.

품행(品行) conduct; behavior. ¶ ~이 좋은 [나쁜] 사람 a well-behaved [an ill-behaved] person.

풋… new; fresh; young; early (일찍 나온); green, unripe (덜 익은).

풋것 the first product 《*of fruits, vegetables*》 of the season.

풋곡식(一穀一) unripe grain.

풋과실(一果實) green fruits.

풋김치 *kimchi* prepared with young vegetables. 〔herbs.

풋나물 (a dish of) seasoned young

풋내 smell of fresh young greens. ¶ ~나다 smell of greens: (비유적) be green (unfledged, inexperienced).

풋내기 a greenhorn; a green (new) hand; a novice; a beginner. ¶ ~의 new; green; raw. ∥ ~기자 a cub reporter 《美》.

풋바심하다 harvest 《*rice*》 too early (before *it* is ripe).

풋사랑 calf (puppy) love.

풍(風) [허풍] a boast; a brag; a tall talk. ¶ ~을 떨다 (치다) boast; brag; talk big (tall).

풍(風) ⇨ 풍병(風病).

…풍(風) [외양] (an) appearance; a look; an air; [양식] a style; a fashion. ¶ 미국—의 American-style / 상인—의 남자 a man looking like a merchant.

풍각쟁이(風角一) a street singer (musician).

풍경(風景) [경치] a landscape; a scenery. ¶ 거리의 ~ a street scene. ∥ ~화(畵) a landscape (painter).

풍경(風磬) a wind-bell.

풍광(風光) scenery; (scenic) beauty. ¶ ~명미(明媚) beautiful scenery. 〔play the organ.

풍금(風琴) an organ. ¶ ~을 치다

풍기(風紀) public morals (decency); discipline. ¶ ~를 단속하다 enforce discipline / ~를 문란케 하다 corrupt public morals / 요즘 ~이 문란해졌다 Public decency has recently become corrupt (loose).

풍기다 ① [냄새 등을] give out (off) an odor (a scent) 《*of*》; [냄새가] smell 《*of*》; [향기가] be fragrant; [악취가] stink 《*of oil*》; reek 《*of garlic*》. ② [암시하다] hint 《*at*》; give (drop) a hint; suggest. ¶ 내가 사직할지도 모른다는 인상을 ~ drop 《*him*》 a hint that I might resign.

풍년(豊年) a year of abundance; a fruitful (bumper) year. ¶ ~이다 have a rich harvest (crop) 《*of rice*》. ∥ ~잔치 a harvest festival.

풍덩 plop; with a plop. ¶ ~거리다 keep plopping (splashing).

풍덩이 a goldbug; a May beetle.

풍랑(風浪) (battle with the) wind and waves; heavy seas.

풍력(風力) the force (velocity) of the wind. ∥ ~계(計) a wind gauge. 〔stove.

풍로(風爐) a (portable) cooking

풍류(風流) ① [멋] elegance; refinement; taste. ¶ ~있는 refined; elegant; tasteful / ~를 알다 have a love of the poetical / ~를 모르다 be out of taste. ∥ ~가(客) a man of refined taste. ② [음악] music.

풍만(豊滿) ¶ ~한 plump; buxom (여성이); voluptuous (관능적으로); ~한 가슴 well-developed breast / ~한 자태 a voluptuous figure.

풍매(風媒) ¶ ~의 wind-pollinated. ∥ ~화 an anemophilous flower.

풍모(風貌) features; countenance; looks; appearance.

풍문(風聞) [세평] a rumor; hearsay; [소문] (a) gossip. ¶ 항간의 ~ the rumor (talk) of the town / ~을 퍼뜨리다 spread a rumor / …라는 ~이다 There is a rumor that…, or It is said that….

풍물(風物) ① [경치] scenery; [풍속 사물] things; scenes and manners. ¶ 자연의 ~ natural features / 한국의 ~ things Korean. ② [악기] instruments for folk music.

풍미(風味) flavor; taste; savor; relish. ¶ ~가 있다 (없다) taste good (bad); be nice (nasty).

풍미(風靡) ¶ ~하다 sway; dominate. ¶ 문단을 ~하다 dominate the literary world / 일세를 ~하다 sway the whole nation.

풍병(風病) nervous disorders believed to be caused by wind; palsy.

풍부(豊富) ¶ ~한 rich 《*in*》; abundant; wealthy; ample / ~한 지식 a great store of knowledge / 내용이 ~한 substantial / 경험이 ~하다 have much experience 《*in*》 / ~하게 하다 enrich 《*the contents*》.

풍비박산(風飛雹散) ~하다 scatter (disperse) in all directions.

풍상(風霜) wind and frost; 《시련》 hardships. ¶ ~을 겪다 undergo (go through) hardships.

풍선(風船) a balloon. ¶ ~을 불다 [띄우다] inflate (fly) a balloon. ∥ ~껌 a bubble gum / 고무~ a rubber balloon. 〔snow.

풍설(風雪) a snowstorm; wind and

풍성(豊盛) ~하다 (be) rich; abundant; plentiful.

풍속(風俗) manners; customs. 《사회 도덕》 public morals. ¶ ~을 어지럽히다 corrupt [offend] public morals [decency]. / ~도[화] a genre picture / ~(사)범 an offense against public morals; a morals offense.

풍속(風速) the velocity of the wind. ¶ ~ 30미터의 태풍 a typhoon blowing at thirty meters per second. ‖ ~계 an anemometer; a wind gauge / 순간 최대 ~ the maximum instantaneous wind speed.

풍수(風水) 《학설》 fengshui; 《지관》 a practitioner of fengshui. ‖ ~설 the theory of fengshui.

풍수해(風水害) damage from storm and flood.

풍습(風習) customs; manners; practices. ¶ 시골 ~ rural customs / ~에 따르다 observe a custom.

풍식(風蝕) wind erosion; weathering. ¶ ~된 weather-worn.

풍신(風神) ① the god of the wind(s). ② 🔾 풍채.

풍악(風樂) music. ¶ ~을 잡히다 have music played.

풍압(風壓) wind pressure. ‖ ~계(計) a pressure anemometer.

풍어(豊漁) a big [large, good] catch 《of》; a big haul (of fish).

풍요(豊饒) ~하다 (be) rich; affluent; abundant. ¶ ~한 사회 an affluent society / ~의 땅 《聖》 a land flowing with milk and honey.　　　　[storm. ◇ 비바람.

풍우(風雨) wind and rain; a rain-

풍운(風雲) winds and clouds; 《형세》 the state of affairs; the situation. ‖ ~아 a hero [adventurer] of the troubled times; a whiz kid (口).

풍월(風月) the beauties of nature; poetry(시). ¶ 들은 ~ a smattering (of knowledge) / ~을 벗삼아 converse (commune) with nature.

풍유(諷諭) an allegory.

풍자(諷刺) (a) satire; (a) sarcasm; an irony. ~하다 satirize. ¶ ~적인 satirical; ironical; sarcastic. ‖ ~가 a satirist / ~문학 a satire / ~시 a satirical poem / ~화 a caricature.

풍작(豊作) a good [rich] harvest; a heavy [bumper] crop.　　[ial].

풍장(風葬) aerial sepulture [bur-

풍재(風災) damage from wind.

풍전등화(風前燈火) ~이다 be in an extremely precarious position / 그녀의 운명은 ~였다 Her life hung by a thread.

풍조(風潮) a tendency; a trend; a drift; the current. ¶ 세상 ~를

따르다 [거스르다] go with [against] the stream of the times.

풍족(豊足) ~한 abundant; plentiful; ample; rich(부유) / ~하게 살다 be well off.

풍차(風車) a windmill.

풍채(風采) one's (personal) appearance; presence. ¶ ~가 당당한 사람 a man of imposing appearance / ~가 좋다 have a fine presence.

풍치(風致) scenic beauty. ¶ ~를 더하다 add charm to the view. ¶ ~림 a forest grown for scenic beauty / ~지구 a scenic zone.

풍토(風土) climate; natural features 《of a region》. ¶ 문화[정신]적 ~ the cultural [spiritual] climate 《of a country》. ‖ ~병 an endemic disease; a local disease.

풍파(風波) ① 《파도와 바람》 wind and waves; a storm; 《거친 파도》 rough seas. ② 《불화》 discord; a trouble; 《어려움》 hardships; a storm. ¶ ~를 겪다 suffer hardships / ~를 일으키다 create [raise] a disturbance; cause trouble. ¶ ~ 많은 family troubles.

풍해(風害) wind damage.

풍향(風向) the direction of the wind.

풍화(風化) 《地》 weathering. ~하다 weather. ‖ ~작용 weathering.

퓨리턴 a Puritan. 　　[tanism.

퓨리터니즘 Puritanism.

퓨즈 a fuse. ¶ 안전 ~ a safety fuse / ~를 갈다 replace a fuse / ~를 끼우다 put [fit] a fuse 《to》 / ~가 끊어졌다 The fuse has blown (burnt out).

퓰리처상(─賞) the Pulitzer Prize.

프라우다 《러시아 신문》 the Pravda.

프라이 a fry. ~하다 fry. ¶ ~한 fried 《eggs》. ‖ ~팬 a frying pan.

프라이드 pride. ¶ ~가 있는 be proud; self-respecting.

프라이버시 (infringe upon *a person's*) privacy.

프라임레이트 《經》 the prime rate.

프랑 《프랑스 화폐》 a franc.

프랑스 France. ¶ ~의 French. ‖ ~요리 French dishes / ~인 a Frenchman; the French (국민).

프래그머티즘 pragmatism.

프러포즈 a proposal. ~하다 propose 《to》.

프런트 《호텔의》 the front [reception] desk. ‖ ~유리 《자동차의》 a windshield 《英》.

프레스 ① 《누르기》 press. ② 《신문》 the press. ‖ ~박스 the press box(기자석).

프레젠트 (give) a present 《to》.

프로 ① 《~ 프로그램》. ¶ ~를 짜다 make up a program / ~에 올리다 put 《*a play*》 on the program.

프로그래머 838 피다

② ☞ 프롤레타리아. ‖ ~문학 proletarian literature. ③ ☞ 프로페셔널. ‖ ~선수[야구] a pro(fessional) player [baseball]. ④ (퍼센트) percent.
프로그래머 a program(m)er.
프로그래밍 program(m)ing.
프로그램 a program; a playbill(연극의).
프로덕션 (영화의) a movie studio; a film production.
프로듀서 a producer.
프로모터 a promoter.
프로세스 a process.
프로젝트 a project 《team》.
프로카인 [化] procaine.
프로테스탄트 a Protestant(신자).
프로파간다 propaganda; publicity.
프로판가스 propane gas.
프로페셔널 professional.
프로펠러 (spin) a propeller.
프로필 a profile.
프록코트 a frock coat.
프롤레타리아 the proletariat(총칭); a proletarian (한 사람). ‖ ~독재 proletarian dictatorship / ~혁명 a proletarian revolution.
프롤로그 a prolog(ue) 《to》.
프리마돈나 a prima donna 《이》.
프리미엄 a premium. ¶ ~을 붙이다 [place] a premium 《on》.
프리즘 [理] a prism.
프리패브 [조립식] ¶ ~주택 a prefab; a prefabricated house.
프린트 (인쇄) a print; a copy; (옷감) print. ~하다 print. ¶강의의 ~ a printed synopsis of a lecture. / ~배선 a printed circuit / ~합판 printed plywood.
프토마인 [化] ptomaine 《poisoning》.
플라스마 plasma.
플라스크 [化] a flask.
플라스틱 plastic(s). ‖ ~공업 the plastics industry / ~용기 a plastic container / ~제품 plastic goods / ~폭탄 plastic explosive.
플라이급 (一級) the flyweight.
플라타너스 [植] a plane (tree); a sycamore 《美》.
플라토닉러브 platonic love.
플란넬 flannel.
플랑크톤 plankton.
플래시 a flash. ¶ ~를 터뜨리다 light a flash bulb / ~세례를 받다 be in a flood of flashlights.
플래카드 a placard.
플래티나 platina; platinum(기호 Pt).
플랜 a plan 《for》; a scheme. ¶ ~을 짜다 make a plan.
플랜트 a [an industrial] plant. ‖ ~수출 export of (industrial) plants 《to》.
플랫폼 a platform.
플러그 [電] a plug. ¶ ~를 꽂다 [뽑다] put the plug in [pull the plug out of] the socket.

플러스 plus. ~하다 add 《two》 to 《six》. ¶ 3－5는 8, Three plus five is eight. ‖ ~기호 a plus (sign) / ~알파 plus something.
플레어스커트 a flared skirt.
플레이트 a plate; [野] a pitcher's plate. ¶ ~를 밟다 take the plate [mound].
플루토늄 [化] plutonium(기호 Pu).
피¹ ① (혈액) blood. ¶ ~의 순환 blood circulation / ~바다 a sea of blood / ~묻은 blood-stained / ~를 흘리다 spill [shed] blood / ~를 뽑다 draw blood / ~를 토하다 vomit blood(토혈); spit blood (객혈) / ~를 멎게 하다 stop bleeding / ~를 보다 result [end] in bloodshed. ② (혈연) blood (relation). ¶ ~를 나눈 형제 one's blood brother / ~를 이어 받다 be descended 《from》 / ~는 물보다 진하다 Blood is thicker than water. / ~는 속이지 못한다 Blood will tell. ③ (비유적으로) ¶ ~에 굶주린 bloodthirsty / ~가 끓다 one's blood boils / ~로 맺어진 우의 the friendship sealed in blood / 그는 ~도 눈물도 없는 인간이다 He is a cold-blooded person.
피² [植] a barnyard grass.
피³ (소리) pooh!; pshaw!
피…(被) ~지배자 the ruled(총칭) / ~선거인 a person eligible for election / ~압박 민족 an oppressed race.
피검(被檢) ~되다 be arrested. ‖ ~자 the arrested; a person in custody. 〔선수 ☞ a figurer.〕
피겨스케이팅 figure skating. ‖
피격(被擊) ~당하다 be attacked [assaulted; assaulted] 《by》.
피고 (被告) a defendant (민사의); the accused(형사의). ‖ ~석 the dock; the bar / ~측 변호인 the counsel for the defense [accused].
피고름 bloody pus.
피고용자(被雇傭者) an employee; the employed(총칭).
피곤(疲困) tiredness; fatigue; weariness. ~하다 (be) tired; weary; exhausted.
피골(皮骨) ¶ ~이 상접하다 be all skin and bones; be worn to a shadow.
피나무 [植] a lime tree; a linden.
피난(避難) refuge; shelter. ~하다 take refuge [shelter] 《in, from》. ‖ ~명령 an evacuation order / ~민 a refugee / ~살이 refugee life / ~처 a shelter; a (place of) refuge.
피날레 a finale; the end.
피눈물 (shed) bitter tears; tears of agony; salt tears.
피닉스 (불사조) the phoenix.
피다 ① (꽃이) bloom; blossom;

피대(帶) a (leather) belt.
피동(動) passivity. ¶ ~적(으로) passive(ly). ‖ ~사(詞) a passive verb.
피둥피둥 ① (몸이) ¶ ~한 plump; fat; healthy / ~ 살찌다 be fat. ② (불복종) ¶ ~한 disobedient; stubborn / ~ 말을 안 듣다 refuse to listen to 《a person》.
피땀 blood and sweat; greasy sweat. ¶ ~ 흘려 번 돈 money earned by the sweat of one's brows / ~ 흘리며 일하다 sweat blood; toil and moil.
피똥 bloody excrement.
피라미 [魚] a minnow.
피라미드 a pyramid. ¶ ~형의 pyramidal / 역(逆)~ an inverted pyramid.
피란(避亂) refuge; shelter. ~하다 take refuge 《in》; get away from war; flee 《to a place》 for safety. ‖ ~민 refugees; evacuees.
피랍(被拉) ◁ 납치(拉致).
피력(披瀝) ~하다 express 《one's opinion, oneself》.
피로(披露) (an) announcement. ~하다 announce; introduce. ‖ ~연 a reception; a banquet.
피로(疲勞) fatigue; exhaustion. ¶ ~하다 tired; weary / 눈의 ~ eye strain / ~를 풀다 rest oneself; take a rest / ~를 느끼다 feel fatigue (tired, weary). ‖ ~감 tired feeling.
피로침(避雷針) [理] a lightning rod (conductor).
피륙 dry goods (美); drapery (英); (직물) cloth; (textile) fabrics.
피리 a pipe (세로로 부는); a flute (옆으로 부는). ¶ ~를 불다 play the flute (pipe).
피리새 [鳥] a bullfinch.
피리어드 (put) a period 《to》; a full stop.
피마자(萞麻子) ◁ 아주까리.
피막(皮膜) a film; [解] a tapetum.
피멍들이다 be (get) bruised.
피보증인(被保證人) a warrantee.
피보험물(被保險物) an insured article; insured property.
피보험자(被保險者) a person insured (보험의) (충지).
피보호자(被保護者) [法] a ward; a protégé(남), a protégée(여) 《프》.
피복(被服) clothing; clothes. ¶ ~비(費) clothing expenses / ~수당 a clothing allowance.

피복(被覆) covering; coating. ¶ ~선(線) covered (coated) wire ‖ ~재료 covering material.
피부(皮膚) the skin. ¶ ~가 거칠다 (약하다) have a rough (delicate) skin. / ~과 의사 a dermatologist / ~병 a skin disease / ~암 skin cutaneous cancer / ~염 dermatitis / ~이식 skin grafting / ~호흡 skin respiration. 「Tower of Pisa.
피사(披) ¶ ~의 사탑 the Leaning
피살(被殺) ¶ ~되다 get killed (murdered) / ~체 the body of a murdered person.
피상(皮相) ¶ ~적인 견해 (관찰자) a superficial view (observer).
피상속인(被相續人) [法] an ancestor; a predecessor.
피서(避暑) summering. ~하다 (pass the) summer 《at, in》; ~가다 go to 《a place》 for summering. ‖ ~객(지) a summer visitor (resort).
피선(被選) ¶ ~되다 be elected.
피선거권(被選擧權) eligibility for election. ¶ ~이 있다 be eligible for election.
피선거인(被選擧人) a person eligible for election.
피스톤 a piston.
피스톨 a pistol; a revolver.
피습(被襲) ¶ ~당하다 be attacked.
피승수(被乘數) [數] a multiplicand.
피신(避身) ~하다 escape (secretly); flee to 《a place of safety》; hide (conceal) oneself; take refuge (shelter) 《in a place》. ‖ ~처 a refuge; shelter.
피아(彼我) he and I; they and we; both sides. ¶ ~간의 세력이 백중하다 Both sides are nearly equal in strength.
피아노 a (grand) piano. ¶ ~를 치다 play on the piano / ~를 배우다 take piano lessons 《from》. ‖ ~독주곡 a piano solo / ~협주곡 a piano concerto.
피아니스트 a pianist.
피아르 P.R. (◁ public relations) ~하다 publicize; advertise. ¶ ~가 잘 되다 be well publicized. ‖ ~영화(담당자) a PR film(man) / ~활동 public relations activities. 「② 대안(對岸).
피안(彼岸) ① [佛] Paramita (梵).
피앙세 a fiancé(남자) 《프》, a fiancée(여자) 《프》.
피어나다 ① (불이) burn up again. ② (소생) revive; come to oneself (life again). ③ (꽃이) come into bloom. ④ (형편이) get better; improve.
피에로 a pierrot; a clown.
피엘오 P.L.O. (◁ Palestine Libera-

피우다 ① 《불을》 make a fire 《in the stove》. ② 《담배·향을》 smoke; puff 《at a pipe》; burn 《incense》. ¶ 한 대 ~ have a smoke. ③ 《재주를》 use; play 〔do〕 《tricks》. 《바람을》 have an affair 《with》. ¶ 그녀는 바람을 피우고 있다 She is having an affair. ④ 《냄새를》 emit 《a scent》; give out 〔off〕 《an odor》.

피의자(被疑者) a suspect; a suspected person.

피임(被任) ¶ ~ 되다 be appointed. ¶ ~자 an appointee; an appointed person.

피임(避姙) contraception. ~하다 prevent conception. ¶ ~ 법《구·수술》a contraceptive method 〔device, operation〕/ ~약 a contraceptive.

피장파장 ¶ ~이다 be all square; be quits 《with a person》.

피제수(被除數) 〖數〗 a dividend.

피진(疲疹) 〖醫〗 an efflorescence; an exanthema.

피차(彼此) 《이것과 저것》 this and that; 《서로》 you and I; both; each other. ¶ ~의 mutual / ~ 간 between you and me; between both sides / ~ 일반이다 be mutually the same.

피처 〖野〗 《play as》 a pitcher. ¶ ~플레이트 the pitcher's plate.

피천 ¶ ~ 한 닢 없다 (be) penniless.

피천(被薦) ¶ ~ 되다 be recommended 《for, to》. 「demandeur.

피청구인(被請求人) a claimee; a

피치 ① 《소리의》 a pitch. ¶ 높은 ~의 소리 a high-pitched voice. ② 《漕艇》 a stroke. ¶ 20~로 노를 젓다 row 20 strokes to the minute. ③ 《아스팔트》 pitch. ④ 《능률·속도》 a pace. ¶ ~로 at a high pace / ~를 올리다〔늦추다〕 quicken〔slacken〕 one's pace; speed up〔slow down〕.

피치자(被治者) the governed〔ruled〕.

피침(被侵) ¶ ~ 되다 be invaded 《침략》; be violated《침범》.

피칭 〖野〗 pitching.

피켈 《登山》 pickel; an ice ax.

피켓 a picket. ¶ ~을 들다 put 〔place〕 pickets 《in front of a factory》; 《~라인》 break through a picket line.

피콜로 〖樂〗 a piccolo.

피크 a peak. ¶ ~시에 at peak hours / ~시 전력량 on-peak energy / ~출력 peaking capacity.

피크닉 《go on》 a picnic.

피크르산(一酸) 〖化〗 picric acid.

피타고라스 Pythagoras. ¶ ~의 정리 the Pythagorean theorem.

피탈(被奪) ¶ ~ 당하다 be robbed of 《a thing》; have 《something》 taken〔snatched〕 away.

피투성이 ¶ ~의 bloody; bloodstained / ~가 되다 be smeared〔covered〕 with blood.

피트 feet ft; a foot《단수》. ¶ 1 ~ one foot / 2 ~ two feet / 10 ~ 짜리 장대 a ten-foot 〔long〕 pole.

피폐(疲弊) ~하다 become〔be〕 exhausted〔impoverished〕.

피폭(被爆) ¶ ~ 되다 be bombed / 원폭의 ~자 an A-bomb victim. ¶ ~지구 a bombed block〔area〕.

피피엠(백만분율) ppm; PPM. 《◀ parts per million》

피하(皮下) ¶ ~의 hypodermic. ¶ ~주사 a hypodermic injection /~지방 subcutaneous fat / ~출혈 hypodermal bleeding.

피하다(避一)《비키다》 avoid; avert; dodge (duck)《a blow》; 《멀리하다》 keep away from《danger》; 《책임·의무를》 shirk (sidestep)《one's responsibility》; 《도피하다》 get away《from》; 《모면하다》 escape. ¶ 피치 못할 inevitable; unavoidable / 잘 ~ avoid《something》 neatly / 나쁜 친구를 ~ avoid《keep away from》 bad company / 재난을 ~ escape a disaster / 남의 눈을 ~ avert people's eyes / 난을 ~ flee from the war.

피한(避寒) wintering. ~하다 spend〔pass〕 the winter《at, in》. ¶ ~지 a winter resort.

피해(被害) damage; harm;《상해》 injury. ¶ ~를 입다 be damaged 《by》; suffer damage / ~를 주다 damage; do damage〔harm〕《to》. ¶ ~망상 〖醫〗 persecution mania / ~액 the amount〔extent〕 of damage / ~자 《재해·범죄의》 sufferer; a victim; 《부상자》 the injured / ~지구 the affected area; the stricken district. 「testee.

피험자(被驗者)《실험의》 a subject; a

피혁(皮革) hides; leather《무두질한》. ¶ ~공업 the leather industry / ~상 a leather dealer / ~제품 a leather article; leather goods 《총칭》.

피후견인(被後見人) 〖法〗 a ward.

픽 ¶ ~하는 a hiss; a swish / ~ 쓰러지다 fall down feebly / ~ 웃다 grin; sneer 《비웃다》.

픽션 fiction.

픽업(전축의) a pickup; a stylus bar;《자동차》 a pickup〔truck〕. ¶ a pin; a hairpin《머리의》. ¶ ~을 낳다 fasten with a pin; pin 〔up〕《on, to》.

핀란드 Finland. ¶ ~의 Finnish. ¶ ~사람 a Finn / ~어 Finnish.

핀셋 《a pair of》 tweezers; a pincette《프》.

핀잔 a 《personal》 reprimand〔reproof〕. ¶ ~ 주다 reprove《a person》

핀치 a pinch; a crisis; a fix (옛 미다). ¶ ~에 몰리다 be thrown into a fix; get *oneself* in a fix / ~를 벗어나다 get out of a pinch / ~ 러너(히터) a pinch runner (hitter).

핀트 ① (초점) (a) focus. ¶ ~가 맞다(안 맞다) be in (out of) focus / …에 ~를 맞추다 focus *one's* camera on (*an object*). ② (요점) ~가 어긋나다 be off the point.

필(匹) 《마소의》 a head. ¶ 세 ~의 말 three head of horses.

필(疋) a bolt (roll) of cloth.

…필(畢) finished; O.K. (필하다). 「지불 (支拂) ~ "Paid."

필경(畢竟) after all; in the end.

필경(筆耕) copying; stencil-paper writing.

필공(筆工) a writing-brush maker.

필기(筆記) taking notes. ~하다 take notes (*of*); write (note) down. ‖ ~시험 written examination / ~장 a notebook.

필담(筆談) ~하다 talk by means of writing.

필답(筆答) a written answer (reply). ~하다 answer in writing.

필독(必讀) a must to read. ¶ ~서 a must book (for students) / 이 책은 모든 사람의 ~서이다 This book is a must.

필두(筆頭) the first on the list. ¶ …의 ~에 at the head of / 사장 A를 ~로 from president A.

필라멘트(電) a filament.

필력(筆力) the power (strength) of the brush stroke(s).

필름 a film. ¶ ~ 한 통 a roll (spool) of film /(영화의) a reel of film / 36매짜리 ~ a 36-exposure (roll of) film / ~에 담다 film (*a scene*); get (*a scene*) on film.

필리핀 the Philippines. ~의 Philippine. ‖ ~사람 a Filipino.

필마(匹馬) a single horse.

필멸(必滅) being fated to perish. ~의 perishable; mortal. ‖ 생 ~ All living things must die.

필명(名名) a pen name.

필묵(筆墨) brush and Chinese ink; stationery (문방구).

필법(筆法) (운필법) a style of penmanship; (문체) a style of writing. ¶ 힘이 있는 ~ a powerful stroke of the brush.

필봉(筆鋒) the power of the pen. ¶ ~이 날카롭다 have a sharp style of writing / 날카로운 ~으로

논하다 be sharp in *one's* argument.

필부(匹夫) a man of humble position.

필사(必死) ~의 frantic; desperate / ~적으로 frantically; desperately; for *one's* life / ~적으로 노력하다 make desperate efforts.

필산(筆算) calculation with figures. ~하다 cipher; do sums on a piece of paper.

필살(必殺) ~의 일격을 가하다 deliver a deadly (death) blow.

필생(畢生) ~의 lifelong / ~의 사업 *one's* lifework.

필설(筆舌) ~로 다할 수 없다 be beyond description; be indescribable (unspeakable).

필수(必須) ~의 indispensable (to); necessary; essential (to); required. ‖ ~과목 a required (compulsory) subject / ~조건 an indispensable condition / ~조항 a mandatory clause.

필수품(必需品) necessary articles; necessaries; necessities. ‖ 생활 ~ daily necessaries; the necessities of life.

필승(必勝) ~의 신념 faith in *one's* certain success; a conviction of sure victory / ~을 기하다 be sure of victory (success) / ~의 신념을 가지고 싸우다 fight with firm assurance of victory.

필시(必是) certainly; no doubt; presumably.

필연(必然) inevitability; necessity. ¶ ~의 necessary; inevitable / ~적으로 necessarily; inevitably; naturally / ~의 결과로서 as a logical consequence. ‖ ~성 necessity; inevitability.

필요(必要) necessity; need. ¶ ~한 necessary; indispensable; essential. ¶ ~한 경우에는 in case of need; if necessary; if need be / …할 ~가 있다 it is necessary to do; must do / …할 ~가 없다 it is not necessary to do; there is no need to do / …이 ~하다 be in need (of money); need… / ~에 의해서 out of necessity; driven by necessity / 서두를 ~는 없다 There is no need to hurry. / ~는 발명의 어머니 Necessity is the mother of invention. / 사업 성공에는 충분한 자금이 절대로 ~하다 Enough funds are essential to (for) the success of the business. ‖ ~경비 necessary expenses / ~성(性) necessity / ~악 a necessary evil / ~조건 a necessary (an essential) condition; a requirement / ~품 a necessity; a requisite.

필유곡절(必有曲折) There must be some reason for it.

필자(筆者) a writer; an author;

필적 this writer(자신).

필적(匹敵) ~하다 be equal 《to》; be a match 《for》; rival. ¶ ~할 만한 사람[것]이 없다 have no equal [match]; be unrivaled.

필적(筆跡) 《글씨》 handwriting; a hand. ¶ 판별하기 쉬운 ~ a clear [legible] hand [writing] / 남자 [여자]의 ~ a masculine [feminine] hand / ~을 감정하다 analyze handwriting. ‖ ~감정 handwriting analysis / ~감정인 a handwriting analyst.

필주(筆誅) ¶ ~를 가하다 denounce 《a person》 in writing.

필지(必至) inevitability. ~하다 be sure to come; be inevitable. ¶ ~의 inevitable.

필지(必知) a must to know; indispensable information. ¶ ~사항 matter everyone must know.

필지(筆地) a lot [plot] of land.

필진(筆陣) the writing [editorial] staff.

필치(筆致) 《필세》 a stroke of the brush; 《화면의》 a touch; 《문체》 a literary style. ¶ 가벼운 ~로 with a light touch / 경묘하고 원숙한 ~ an easy and well-mellowed style.

필터 a filter; a filter tip 《담배의》. ¶ ~ 담배 a filter-tipped cigarette.

필통(筆筒) a pencil [brush] case.

필하다(畢-) finish; end; get 《go》 through; complete. ¶ 대학원 과정을 ~ complete the postgraduate course.

필화(筆禍) ¶ ~를 입다 be indicted for one's article [writing] / ~를 입게 되다 get into trouble because

of one's article 《in a magazine》.

필휴(必携) ¶ ~의 《a book》 indispensable 《to students》.

핍박(逼迫) ① 《재정이》 ~하다 be tight; get stringent. ¶ 재정의 ~ pressure for [tightness of] money. ② 《박해》 ~하다 molest; persecute.

핏기 ☞ 혈색(血色). ¶ ~ 없는 as white as a sheet; pale (and bloodless) / ~가 가시다 turn white [pale] 《with》.

핏대 a (blue) vein. ¶ ~를 올리다 boil with rage; turn blue with anger.

핏덩어리 《피의 덩이》 a clot of blood; 《갓난아이》 a newborn baby.

핏발서다 be bloodshot; be congested 《with blood》.

핏줄 ① ☞ 혈관. ② 《혈족》 blood (relationship); 《가계》 lineage. ¶ ~이 같은 blood-related.

핑 ① 《도는 꼴》 《turn》 round. ② 《어질한 꼴》 《feel》 dizzy 《giddy》.

핑계 a pretext; an excuse (☞ 구실). ¶ ~를 대다 make [find] an excuse; use 《a traffic accident》 as a pretext.

핑그르르 (spinning, whirling, turning) around 《smoothly》. ¶ 공을 ~ 돌리다 spin a ball round.

핑크 ¶ ~색의 pink. ‖ ~무드 an amorous mood.

핑퐁 《play》 ping-pong. ☞ 탁구.

핑핑 round and round. ¶ ~ 돌다 turn [revolve] rapidly; spin; 《눈이》 feel dizzy 《giddy》.

핑핑하다 ① 《켕기다》 (be) taut; tense. ② 《어슷비슷함》 (be) even; equal; be evenly matched.

병명(病名)·병원(病院)

1. 병명(the name of diseases)

간질환 liver disorder / 결핵 tuberculosis / 꽃가룻병 hay fever / 눈병 eye disease / 디프테리아 diphtheria / 백일해 whooping cough / 백혈병 leukemia / 변비 constipation / 설사 diarrhea / 성홍열 scarlet fever / 신경증 neurosis / 신경통 neuralgia / 알레르기 allergy / 암 cancer(위암 stomach cancer) / 영양실조 malnutrition / 위장병 stomach disease [trouble] / 이질 dysentery / 인플루엔자 influenza / 일사병 sunstroke / 장티푸스 typhoid / 천식 asthma / 천연두 smallpox / 충수염 appendicitis / 치질 hemorrhoids; piles / 카타르 catarrh / 콜레라 cholera / 폐렴 pneumonia / 폐병 lung disease / 피부병 skin disease / 홍역 measles.

2. 의학의 전문 분야 및 전문의

내과 internal medicine / 내과 의사 a physician / 외과 surgery / 외과 의사 a surgeon / 소아과 pediatrics / 소아과 의사 a pediatrician / 안과 ophthalmology / 안과 의사 an ophthalmologist; an eye doctor / 이비인후과 otolaryngology / 이비인후과 의사 an otolaryngologist / 피부과 dermatology / 피부과 의사 a dermatologist; skin doctor / 신경과 neurology / 신경과 의사 a neurologist / 정신과 psychiatry / 정신과 의사 a psychiatrist / 산과 obstetrics / 산과 의사 an obstetrician / 부인과 gynecology / 부인과 의사 a gynecologist / 산부인과 obstetrics and gynecology / 정형외과 orthopedics / 정형외과 의사 an orthopedist / 방사선과 radiology / 방사선과 의사 a radiologist / 마취과 anesthesiology / 마취과 의사 an anesthetist / 비뇨기과 urology / 비뇨기과 의사 a urologist / 항문과 proctology / 항문과 의사 a proctologist / 치과 dentistry / 치과 의사 a dentist.

하(下) ① 《하급》 the low class (grade). ¶ ~치 an inferior article; low grade goods. ②《아래·밑》 ~ 반신 the lower half of the body / ~악(顎) the lower jaw; the underjaw. ③《한자로 된 명사 아래 붙어》 below; under. ¶ 아무의 감독~에 under the supervision of *a person*.

하강(下降) a fall; a drop; a descent; 《경기 등의》(a) decline; a downturn. ─하다 descend; fall; go (come) down. ¶ 경기가 ~하고 있다 The economy is on the decline. / 비행기가 서서히 ~하고 있다 The airplane is gradually descending (coming down).

하객(賀客) a congratulator; a well-wisher. ¶ 신년~ a New Year's caller (visitor).

하계(下界) 《현세》 this world; 《지상》 the earth. ¶ 하늘에서 ~를 내려다보다 look down on the earth from the sky.

하계(夏季) ☞ 하기(夏期).

하고 《및》 and; 《함께》 with; along (together) with. ¶ 너~ 나 you and I / 그녀~ 가다 go with her.

하고많다 (be) numerous; innumerable; countless; plentiful. ¶ 하고많은 네 주변의 미인들 중에서 왜 그녀를 파트너로 골랐느냐 Why did you choose her for your partner among so many pretty girls around you.

하곡(夏穀) summer crops; wheat and barley.

하관(下棺) ~하다 lower a coffin into the grave.

하관(下顴) the lower part of the face; the jaw (area). ¶ ~이 빨다 have a pointed jaw.

하교(下敎) 《왕의 명령》 a royal command; 《명령·지시》 an instruction (order) from a superior.

하교(下校) ~하다 leave school 《at the end of the day》. ¶ ~길에 아무를 만나다 meet *a person* on *one's* way home from school.

하구(河口) the mouth of a river; a river mouth.

하권(下卷) the last volume; the second volume.

하극상(下剋上) the lower (juniors) dominating the upper (seniors).

하급(下級) a low(-er) class (grade). ¶ ~의 low (-class); lower; junior; inferior. ∥ ~공무원 a petty (lower, junior) official; a lower-level (government) officials (총칭) / ~ 관청 a subordinate office / ~ 법 원 a lower court / ~ 생 a student in a lower class (grade); an underclassman 《美》 / ~ 장교 a junior officer / ~ 품 lower-grade goods.

하기(下記) ¶ ~의 the following; mentioned below / ~ 사항 the following items / 내용은 ~ 와 같다 The contents are as follows.

하기(夏期) summer(time); the summer season. ∥ ~강습회 a summer school / ~휴가(방학) the summer vacation (holidays).

하기는 《실상은》 in fact (truth); indeed. ¶ ~ 네 말이 옳다 Indeed, you are right.

하기식(下旗式) a flag-lowering ceremony; 《軍》 the retreat.

하나 《1, 한 개》 one; single; a unity 《단일체》; 《동일》 the same; (the) identical. ¶ ~의 one; single; only / ~씩 one by one / ~ 걸러 alternately / ~도 남김 없이 all; entirely; without exception; to the last / ~에서 열까지 from beginning to end; in everything / 그녀의 단 ~의 꿈 her one and only dream / 그것들은 ~에 1,000원이다 They are a thousand *won* each (a piece). / ~도 남아 있지 않다 There are none left. / 여러 회사가 합병하여 ~이 되었다 Several firms united into one. / 그녀의 작품에는 잘못된 곳이 ~도 없다 There is not a single mistake in her composition.

하나님 ☞ 하느님.

하녀(下女) a maid (servant).

하느님 God; the Lord; the Father; Heaven. ¶ ~의 섭리 (devine) Providence / ~께 기도 하다 pray to God 《for》 / 당신은 ~을 믿습니까 Do you believe in God? / 그것은 ~의 뜻이다 It is the will of God.

하늘 ① 《천공》 the sky; the air; the heavens. ¶ ~빛(색)의 sky-blue; azure / 갠(흐린) ~ a clear (cloudy) sky / ~의 용사 an air hero / ~높이 high up in the sky / ~을 찌를 듯한 skyscraping / ~을 날다 fly in the air (sky) / ~에서 별따기 (be) not easier than picking a star out of the sky. ② 《하늘의 섭리》 Heaven; Providence; 《하느님》 Heaven; God. ¶ ~이 주신 god-given / ~을 두려워하다 fear god / ~은 스스로 돕는 자를 돕는다 Heaven helps those who help themselves.

하늘거리다 swing; sway; tremble.
하늘다람쥐 [動] a flying squirrel.
하늘소 [蟲] a long-horned beetle.
하늘지기 [植] a kind of sedge.
하다 ①《행하다》 do; perform; make; try(시도); play(games); act(행동); (시행) carry on; practice; (착수) set about; go in for. ¶ 하고 있는 일 the work in hand / 하라는 대로 (do) as (a person) says (likes) / 일을 ~ do one's work / 연설을 ~ make a speech / 할 일이 많다(없다) have much(nothing) to do / 해보다 try to do; have a try / 해치우다 get through (a task); finish / 잘 ~ do well; make a success of /…하기 일쑤다 be apt (liable) to (do) / ~ 말고 그만두다 leave (a thing) half-done / 문학을 ~ go in for literature / 되는 일 없이 지내다 idle away one's time / 과학 실험을 ~ perform a scientific experiment. ② 《배우다》 study; learn; 《알다》 know. ¶ 불어를 ~ know French. ③ 《연기》 perform; act (the part of Hamlet); play. ④ 《먹다》 take; help oneself to; have; eat; drink; 《피우다》 smoke. ¶ 한 잔 더 ~ have another glass. ⑤ 《경험하다》 experience; go through. ¶ 고생을 ~ undergo hardships. ⑥ 《종사》 act as; serve as (a maid); engage (be engaged) (in); 《경영》 keep; run (a business); work; operate. ¶ 책방을 ~ run (keep) a bookstore / 중매장이 노릇을 ~ act as a matchmaker. ⑦ 《값이》 cost (1,000 won); be worth. ¶ 그는 3만원 하는 라이터를 내게 주었다 He gave me a lighter worth 30,000 won. ⑧ 《착용》 wear (earrings). ⑨ 《칭하다》 call; name. ¶ X라고 하는 사나이 a man named (called) X / 그것은 영어로 뭐라고 합니까 What is the English for it?
하다못해 at least (most); 《심지어》 so far as; to the extent of. ¶ 못된 짓을 ~ 나중에는 도둑질까지 했다 He went so far as to commit theft in the end. / ~ 만원이라도 주었으면 좋겠다 At least you can let me have 10,000 won.
하단 (下段) ① 《글의》 the lower column. ② 《제단의》 the lowest step (tier).
하달 (下達) ~ 하다 ¶ 명령을 ~ 하다 issue an order; give orders.
하대 (下待) ~ 하다 treat with disrespect; be inhospitable toward;

《말을》 call (a person) by name impolitely; do not mister (a person).
하도 too (much); so (much); to excess. ¶ ~ 기뻐서 in the excess of one's joy / ~ 바빠서 잠도 제대로 잘 수 없다 be too busy to get enough sleep.
하도급 (下都給) a subcontract. ~ 하다 subcontract. ¶ ~을 주다 sublet; underlet; subcontract (one's work) to (a person) / ~을 맡다 take on (a job) as subcontractor; be a subcontractor (on the construction work) / 우리는 A 회사의 ~ 일을 하고 있다 We get subcontracted work from A company. ¶ ~업자 a subcontractor.
하도롱지 (下都籠紙) 《종이》 sulfate (kraft) paper; brown paper.
하드웨어 [컴] hardware.
하등 (下等) ~ 의 low; inferior; coarse; vulgar. ‖ ~ 동물(식물) the lower animals (plants) / ~ 품 an inferior article.
하등 (何等) (not) any; whatever; the least; (not) in any way. ¶ ~ 의 위험도 없이 without the least danger / ~ 관계가 없다 be not in any way related (to, with); have nothing to do (with) / 그는 ~ 의 이유도 없이 결근했다 He was absent from his job without any reason.
하락 (下落) a fall (drop, decline) (in price). ~ 하다 fall (off); decline; drop; depreciate; come (go) down. ¶ 급격한 ~ a sharp drop / 주가가 ~ 하고 있다 Stock prices are on the decline. / 달러에 대한 원화 가치가 절정 ~ 하고 있다 The value of the won is falling steadily against the dollar. ‖ ~ 세(勢) a downward (falling) tendency; a downtrend.
하략 (下略) the rest omitted. ~ 하다 omit the rest.
하렘 (회교국의) a harem.
하례 (賀禮) 《예식》 a congratulatory ceremony; a celebration; 《축하》 congratulation; greetings. ~ 하다 congratulate (a person on); celebrate. ¶ 신년 ~ the New Year's ceremony.
하롱거리다 act rashly (carelessly); be flippant.
하루 ① 《초하루》 the first day of a month. ② 《날수》 a (single) day; one day. ¶ ~ 종일 all day (long); the whole day / ~ 일 a day's work / ~ 이틀(에) (in) a day or two / ~ 걸러 every other (second) day / ~ 에 세 번 (8시간) three times (eight hours) a day / 내일 ~ 쉬겠습니다 I'm going to have

하루거리 [醫] a malarial fever.
하루빨리 without a day's delay; as soon as possible. ¶ ~ 회복하시기를 바랍니다 I wish you earliest possible recovery.
하루살이 [蟲] a dayfly; a mayfly; 《덧없는 것》 an ephemera. ¶ ~ 같은 인생 this ephemeral life (existence).
하루아침 one morning. ¶ ~에 in a morning (day); overnight; suddenly / ~에 유명해지다 leap (spring at a bound) into fame / 로마는 ~에 이루어진 것이 아니다 Rome was not built in a day.
하루하루 by (after) day. ¶ ~ 연기하다 put off (*a matter*) from day to day / ~ 나아지다 get better day by day.
하룻강아지 a (one-day-old) puppy. ¶ ~ 날뛰듯 하다 act naughtily / ~ 범 무서운 줄 모른다 《俗談》 Fools rush in where angels fear to tread.
하룻밤 one [a] night. ¶ ~ 사이에 in a single night / 묵다 stay [stop] overnight / ~을 지내다 pass a night (*in, at*).
하류 (下流) ① 《하천의》 the downstream; the lower course [reaches] (*of a river*). ¶ 한강 ~에 가는 Han River / ~로 가다 go down the river / 여기서부터 3km ~ three kilometers downstream from here. ② 《사회의》 the lower classes; the people of the lower class. ¶ ~의 lower-class. ‖ ~사회 the lower strata of society / ~의 a day off tomorrow. ③ 《어느 날》 one day. ¶ ~는 그녀가 산책을 나갔다 One day she went out for a walk.
하르르하다 (be) thin; flimsy (life.
하리놀다 slander; defame.
하릴없다 (be) unavoidable; inevitable; cannot be helped(서술적); 《하릴없이 …하다》 be obliged to 《(do)》 / 바보라는 말을 들어도 ~ I can't help being called a fool.
하마 (下馬) ~ 하다 dismount (from a horse). ‖ ~비(~碑) a notice stone requiring riders to dismount / ~석 a horse block; a step(-stone) / ~평(~評) an outsider's irresponsible talk; common gossip (about the man who will be appointed to a high official). (hippo (口).
하마 (河馬) [動] a hippopotamus;
하마터면 《거의》 nearly; almost; 《자칫하면》 barely; narrowly; ¶ ~ 익사할[죽을] 뻔했다 I came near drowning (being killed).
하명 (下命) 《명령》 a command; an order. ~ 하다 command; order; make an order. ¶ ~을 바랍니다 We solicit your orders.
하모니카 a harmonica.
하문 (下問) ~ 하다 ask; inquire.
하물며 《긍정》 much [still] more; 《부정》 much [still] less. ¶ 그는 영어도 못 읽는데 ~ 독일어를 어찌 읽겠는가 He cannot read English, much less German.
하박 (下膊) [解] the forearm. ‖ ~골 forearm bones.
하반 (下半) the lower half. ‖ ~기(~期) the latter [second] half of the year / ~신 the lower half of body.
하복 (夏服) summer clothes [wear, uniform]; a summer suit.
하복부 (下腹部) the abdomen; the abdominal region.
하부 (下部) the lower part. ‖ ~구조 《건물의》 a substructure; 《단체 등의》 infrastructure / ~기관 subordinate offices [agencies] / ~조직 a subordinate organization; a substructure.
하비다 ① 《할퀴다》 scratch; claw. ② ~ 후비다.
하사 (下士) a staff sergeant. ‖ ~관 《육군》 a noncommissioned officer 《생략 N.C.O.》; 《해군》 a petty officer 《생략 P.O.》.
하사 (下賜) ~ 하다 grant; bestow; confer; donate(금전을). ¶ 금일봉을 ~ 하다 grant (*a person*) money. ‖ ~품 [금] an Royal [an Imperial] gift (grant, bounty).
하산 (下山) ~ 하다 ① 《산에서》 descend (go down) a mountain. ② 《절에서》 leave a temple.
하상 (河床) a riverbed; the bottom of a river.
하선 (下船) leaving [getting off] a ship. ~ 하다 get off a ship; leave a ship; go ashore.
하선 (下線) an underline. ¶ ~을 긋다 underline (*a word*).
하소연 an appeal; a petition; a complaint. ~ 하다 (make an) appeal (*to*); supplicate; complain of (about). ¶ 동정해 달라고 ~ 하다 appeal to (*a person*) for *his* sympathy / 불공평하다고 ~ 하다 complain of the injustice.
하수 (下水) sewage; waste [foul] water. ¶ ~구가 막혔다 The drain is stopped [blocked]. ‖ ~관 a sewer pipe; a drainpipe / ~구 a drain; a sewer; a gutter(도로의) / ~도 a sewer; a drain / ~도 공사 drainage [sewerage] works / ~설비 sewerage [drainage] system / ~처리 sewage disposal / ~처리장 a sewage disposal [treatment] plant.
하수 (下手) 《낮은 솜씨》 lack of talent; unskillfulness; 《사람》 a

poor hand; 《바둑·장기의》 a lower grader; a lower-grade player.
하수(下手)² 《살인》 ～하다 murder. ‖ ～인 the murderer.
하숙(下宿) lodging; boarding. ～하다 take in (keep) lodgers (英) 《at a place, with a person》/ ～을 치다 take in (keep) lodgers / 나는 숙부댁에서 ～하고 있다 I am boarding with my uncle (at my uncle's). ‖ ～비 the charge for room and board / ～생 a student boarder / ～인 a lodger; a boarder; a roomer 《美》/ ～집 (run) a boarding house (식사 제공의); a rooming house (방만 쓰는); a lodging house 《英》.
하순(下旬) the latter part (the last ten days) of a month. ¶ 5월 ～경에 toward the end of May; late in May.
하야(下野) ～하다 resign (step down) from *one's* public post.
하얗다 (be) pure white; snow-white.
하얘지다 become white; turn white (gray). ¶ 머리가 ～ *one's* hair turns gray.
하여금 ¶ 그로 ～ 책을 읽게 하다 make him read a book / 나로 ～ 우리 팀을 대표하게 하라 Let me represent our team.
하여간(何如間) ☞ **하여튼**.
하여튼(何如—) anyhow; anyway; in any case; at all events. ¶ ～ 출발하도록 하자 Let's get started, anyway.
하역(荷役) loading and unloading. ～하다 load and unload. ¶ 석탄을 ～하다 load (unload) coal. ‖ ～시설 loading facilities / ～인부 a stevedore; a longshoreman.
하염없다 ① 《아무 생각이 없다》 (be) absent-minded; vacant; blank; empty. ② 《끝맺는 데가 없다》 endless. ～이 endlessly; ceaselessly / 눈물이 하염없이 흘러내다 Tears kept pouring out. *or* Tears streamed endlessly down *one's* cheek.
하오(下午) p. m.; 오후.
하옥(下獄) ～하다 put 《a person》in prison; imprison.
하와이 Hawaii. ¶ ～의 Hawaiian / ～사람 a Hawaiian.
하원(下院) the Lower House; the House of Representatives 《美》; the House of Commons 《英》. ‖ ～의원 a member of the House of Representatives; a Congressman; a Congresswoman; a Congressperson 《美》; a Member of Parliament (the House of Commons) 《英》/ ～의장 the Speaker of the House of Representatives 《美》; the Speaker (of the House of Commons) 《英》.
하위(下位) a low(er) rank; a low grade. ¶ ～의 low-ranking 《teams》; subordinate 《officers》.
하의(下衣) (a pair of) trousers; pants 《美》.
하이 high. ¶ ～다이빙 high diving / ～다이빙선수 a high diver / ～허들 the high hurdles.
하이라이트 a highlight. ¶ 오늘 뉴스의 ～ the highlights of today's news / 다음은 스포츠 뉴스의 ～입니다 Coming next are the sports highlights.
하이볼(알코올 음료) a highball 《美》; a whisky and soda 《英》.
하이브리드 컴퓨터 a hybrid computer.
하이잭(a plane) hijacking. ～하다 hijack 《an airplane》. ～범인 a hijacker.
하이킹 hiking; a hike. ¶ ～하는 사람 a hiker / ～가다 go hiking; go on a hike.
하이테크 high-tech; high technology. ‖ ～산업 a high-tech industry.
하이틴 ～의 소년소녀 boys and girls in their late teens ('high teen'은 우리식 영어임).
하이파이(고충실도) hi-fi; high fidelity. ¶ ～의 hi-fi; high-fidelity. ‖ ～ 음향 재생 장치 a high-fidelity sound reproduction system.
하이픈 a hyphen. ¶ 두 단어를 ～으로 연결하다 hyphen (hyphenate) two words.
하이힐 high-heeled shoes.
하인(下人) a servant.
하인(何人) ～을 막론하고 whoever it may be; no matter who he may be.
하인방(下引枋) 〖建〗 a lower lintel.
하자(瑕疵) 《결점》〖法〗 a flaw; a blemish; a defect. ¶ ～ 없는 flawless; all-perfect.
하자마자 as soon as; no sooner… than; immediately (on). ¶ 한국에 도착 ～ 나에게 알려 주십시오 As soon as you arrive in Korea, please let me know.
하잘것없다 (be) insignificant; trifling; negligible. ¶ 하잘것없는 일 trifles / 하잘것없는 사람 a person of no importance; a person who is not worth bothering about; a nobody / 그의 의견은 ～ *His opinion* is not worth serious consideration.
하저(河底) a riverbed; the bed (bottom) of a river. ‖ ～터널 a riverbed tunnel.
하전(荷電)〖理〗electric charge.
하제(下劑)〖醫〗a purgative (medicine); a laxative (완하제). ¶ ～를 먹다 take a laxative.
하주(荷主) a shipper (선적인); a consignor (하송인); an owner of

하중 (荷重) load. ¶ 안전~ safe load. ‖ ~시험 a load test.
하지 (下肢) the lower limbs; the legs.
하지 (夏至) the summer solstice.
하지만 but; however; though. ¶ 그렇기는 ~ It is true…, but… / ~ 그것은 너무 심한 요구가 아닌가 But it is asking too much, isn't it?
…하지 않을 수 없다 cannot help but *do*; cannot but *do*; cannot help *doing*; be compelled (obliged) to *do*. ¶ 웃지 않을 수 없다 I cannot help laughing. / 그를 동정하지 않을 수 없다 I cannot help but feel sorry for him. / 그는 술을 삼가하지 않을 수 없었다 He obliged himself to refrain from drinking.
하직 leave-taking. ~하다 say good-by(e) (*to*); take *one's* leave (*of*); bid farewell (*to*). ¶ ~하러 가다 make a farewell call (*on a person*); pay a farewell call (*to a person*).
하차 (下車) ~하다 leave (get off) (*the train*); get out of (*the car*); alight from (*the car*).
하찮다 (be) worthless; trifling; trivial; insignificant; of little importance. ¶ 하찮은 일에 성내다 get angry about a trifle.
하천 (河川) rivers. ¶ 1급 ~ A-class rivers. ‖ ~개수 river improvement / ~공사 river conservation work / ~부지 a dry riverbed / ~수질 기준치 criteria for measuring river water quality / ~오염 the river contamination; pollution of a river.
하청 (下請) a subcontract. ~을 맡다 subcontract / ~을 주다 sublet. ‖ ~공사 subcontracted work / ~공장 a subcontract factory / ~인 a subcontractor.
하체 (下體) the lower part of the body. ¶ ~의 waist-down.
하층 (下層) a lower layer (stratum); an underlayer; a substratum. ¶ ~계급 the lower classes / ~사회 the lower strata of society / ~생활 (a) low life.
하치 (下一) an inferior article; low-grade goods; goods of inferior quality.
하치장 (荷置場) a yard; a storage space; a depository; a repository. ¶ 노천 ~ an open storage yard (*for coal*).
하키 (英) (play) hockey. ¶ ~선수 a hockey player.
하퇴 (下腿) the lower leg; the crus. ‖ ~골 the leg bones / ~동맥 the crural artery.
하편 (下篇) ☞ 하권 (下卷).
하품 a yawn; a gape. ~하다 (give a) yawn. ¶ ~을 참다 stifle a yawn / 손으로 가리고 ~하다 hide a yawn behind *one's* hand.
하프 [樂] a harp.
하필 (何必) of all occasion (places, persons, *etc.*). ¶ ~이면 그날에 on that day of all days / 너 나 왜, of all persons, you? / ~이면 그(런) 남자와 결혼하다니 Fancy her marrying him out of all boys! 〔loudly.
하하 Ha-ha! ¶ ~웃다 laugh
하학 (下學) the end of the school day. ~하다 leave school (*at the end of the day*). ‖ ~시간 the time *one* gets out of school; the time school is over (out).
하한 (下限) the lowest limit.
하항 (河港) a river port.
하행 (下行) ~하다 go down; go away from Seoul. ‖ ~열차 a down train.
하향 (下向) looking downward (시선의); a downward trend (시세의). ¶ (물가 따위가) ~세를 나타낸다 show a downward tendency / (자동차의) 라이트를 ~시키다 lower a light. ‖ ~조정 a downward adjustment.
하향 (下鄕) ~하다 go to *one's* country home.
하현 (下弦) the last phase of the moon. ¶ ~달 a waning moon.
하혈 (下血) ~하다 discharge blood through the vulva (anus); flux.
하회 (下廻) ~하다 be less (lower) than (*something*); be (fall) below (*the average*). ☞ 밑돌다.
학 (鶴) [鳥] a crane.
학감 (學監) a school superintendent; a dean (대학의).
학계 (學界) academic circles.
학과 (學科) a subject of study; (과정) a course of study; a school course; (전공의) department. ¶ 심리 ~ the department of psychology / 좋아하는 ~는 무엇이냐 What are your favorite subjects at school? / 전공은 무슨 ~이냐 Which department are you in? ‖ ~시험 examination in academic subjects.
학과 (學課) a lesson; schoolwork. ¶ ~를 복습(예습)하다 review (prepare) *one's* lessons.
학교 (學校) a school; a college (대학). ¶ ~가 파한 후 after school (is over) / ~에 들어가다 enter a school / ~에 다니다 attend (go to) school / ~를 쉬다 (빼먹다) stay away (play truant) from school.

‖ ~급식 school lunch [meal] / ~당국 the school authorities / ~대항(의) interschool; intercollegiate (game) / ~방송 school broadcast(ing) / ~법인 an (a legally) incorporated educational institution / ~생활 school life / ~성적 one's school record / ~차(差) (a) disparity (in academic standards) among schools / ~친구 a schoolmate; a school fellow.

학교교육(學校教育) school education; schooling. ¶ 정규~ regular [formal] schooling / ~을 받다 have school education; have schooling.

학구(學究) ¶ ~적인 scholarly; scholastic; academic / ~적인 정신 a scholastic spirit / ~적인 생활 a scholarly [an academic] life.

학구(學區) a school district.

학군(學群) a school group. ‖ ~제 the school group system.

학급(學級) a class. ¶ 그가 담임하는 ~ the class in his charge / 성적별로 ~을 편성하다 make up [organize] classes according to pupils' performance. ‖ ~위원 a class representative / ~회 a class meeting.

학기(學期) a (school) term; a session (美); a semester(1년 2학기제). ¶ 제1~ the first term. / ~말 the end of (the) term / ~말시험 a final examination; a final; the finals (美).

학년(學年) a school [an academic] year; (학급) a year; a grade. ¶ 제1[2, 3, 4]~생도 a first-[second-, third-, fourth-]year student(초·중등교); a freshman [sophomore, junior, senior](고교·대학생). ‖ ~말 the end of a school year / ~말 시험 an annual (a final) examination.

학당(學堂) ① ~ 글방. ② ~ 학교.

학대(虐待) cruelty; ill-treatment; maltreatment. ~하다 ill-treat; treat (a person) cruelly; maltreat. ¶ 정신적인 ~ mental cruelty / ~에 못이겨 being unable to endure the severity of the treatment / 동물을 ~하지 마라 Don't be cruel to animals.

학덕(學德) learning and virtue. ¶ 그는 ~을 겸비한 사람이다 He excels both in virtue and scholarship.

학도(學徒) a student; a scholar. ‖ ~병 a student soldier / ~호국단 the Student Defense Corps.

학동(學童) school children; a schoolboy [schoolgirl]; a grade school pupil (美).

학력(學力) academic ability; scholastic achievement (attainment). ¶ ~이 있다[없다] be a good [poor] scholar [learner] / 그는 고교 졸업 이상의 ~이 있다 His level of school achievement is higher than that of a high school graduate. / 최근 고등학생의 ~이 저하되고 있다 The grades of senior high school students in scholastic achievements have declined recently. ‖ ~고사 a scholastic achievement test.

학력(學歷) educational [academic] background. ¶ ~이 없는 사람 a person who has had no regular schooling / ~을 불문하고 regardless [irrespective] of educational background / 한국은 자주 ~을 중시하는 사회라는 말을 듣고 있다 Korea is often called an academic credentials society. ‖ ~편중 overemphasis of educational qualifications; excessive valuing of academic background.

학령(學齡) (reach) school age. ‖ ~아동 children of school age.

학리(學理) a theory; a scientific principle. ¶ ~적인 theoretical / ~를 실지로 응용하다 put a theory into practice.

학명(學名) a scientific name [term]. ¶ ~을 붙이다 give a scientific name (to).

학무(學務) educational [school] affairs.

학문(學問) learning; study; scholarship(학식); knowledge(지식). ¶ ~을 하다 study; pursue one's studies [learning] / ~이 있는 사람 a man of learning; a learned man / ~이 없는 사람 a man without learning; an uneducated man / ~의 자유 academic freedom / ~에 전념하다 be devoted to one's studies / ~적(인) 업적 an academic achievement.

학벌(學閥) (form) an academic clique.

학부(學府) an academic institution center. ¶ 최고 ~ an institution of highest learning / 그녀는 최고 ~를 나왔다 She is a graduate of an institution of higher learning, or She is a college graduate.

학부(學部) a college; a department (美); a faculty (英). ¶ 경제~ the School [College] of Economics / 법~ the School of Law / 사회과학~ the School of Social Sciences / ~의 학생 an undergraduate. ‖ ~장 a dean.

학부모(學父母) parents of students.

학비(學費) school expenses. ¶ ~를 벌다 earn money to pay one's school expenses / ~에 곤란을 받다 be hard up for school expenses.

학사(學士) a university (college) graduate; a bachelor; a bachelor's degree (학위). ¶ 문(공)~ Bachelor of Arts (Engineering).

학사(學事) school affairs. ¶ ~보고 a report on education (al) matters.

학살(虐殺) slaughter; massacre (대량의). ~하다 slaughter; massacre; butcher. ¶ 집단 ~ mass slaughter; genocide. ‖ ~자 a slaughterer.

학생(學生) a student. ¶ ~ 소요 student riot (disturbances) / ~ 시절 one's student (school) days / ~증 a student's (identification) card / ~회 a student council / ~회관 a students' hall / ~회장 a student president.

학설(學說) a theory; a doctrine. ¶ 새로운 ~을 세우다 set forth (formulate) a new theory / 새로운 ~을 발표하다 publish (put forward) a new theory.

학수고대(鶴首苦待) ~하다 eagerly look forward to; await with impatience. ¶ 네가 상경하기를 ~하고 있다 I am eagerly looking forward to your coming up to Seoul.

학술(學術) arts and sciences (학예); learning; science (과학). ¶ ~상의 scientific; academic / ~적 연구 scientific research. / ~강연 a scientific lecture / ~논문 (잡지) a scientific treatise (journal) / ~능력 learning ability / ~용어 a technical term / ~원 (회원) (a member of) the (Korean) Academy of Arts and Sciences / 한국~회의 the Science Council of Korea.

학습(學習) learning; study. ~하다 study; learn. ‖ ~서 a handbook for students / ~장 a workbook / ~지도요령 the government curriculum guidelines.

학식(學識) learning; scholarship. ¶ ~이 있다 be learned (an erudite) scholar.

학업(學業) one's studies (school-work). ¶ ~에 힘쓰다 work hard (at one's lessons) / ~을 게을리하다 neglect one's schoolwork / ~을 중도에서 포기하다 abandon one's studies. / ~성적 school record; grades.

학연(學緣) school ties. ¶ ~이 있는 사람들 those who related by school ties (bonds) / 우리 사회에서 ~은 때때로 귀중한 자산이 된다 School ties would sometimes be a valuable asset in our society.

학예(學藝) arts and literature. ‖ ~란(欄) the fine arts and literature columns; a culture page (신문의) / ~부 the fine arts and literary department / ~회 literary exercises (plies).

학용품(學用品) school things (supplies).

학우(學友) a schoolmate; a schoolfellow; a fellow student. ‖ ~회 (재학생의) a students' society (association); (졸업생의) an alumni (alumnae) association (美); an old boys' (girls') association (英).

학원(學院) an educational institute; an academy; a school. ¶ 외국어~ a foreign language institute / 입시~ a preparatory school (for examinees) / 자동차 ~ a driver's school.

학원(學園) an educational institution; a school; a campus (구내). ‖ ~도시 a university (college) town / ~분쟁 a campus dispute / ~사찰 inspection on campus activities / ~생활 school (campus) life / ~축제 a school festival.

학위(學位) an academic degree. ¶ 박사~ a doctoral degree / ~을 획득하다 get (take) a degree (from Havard University) / ~를 수여하다 grant (award) (a person) a degree. ‖ ~논문 a thesis for a degree / ~수여식 a degree ceremony.

학자(學者) a scholar; a learned man; a savant (석학). ¶ ~다운 scholarly / ~연(然)하는 pedantic / 탁월한 영어 ~ an eminent English scholar / 그는 자신이 ~인 체한다 He sets himself up as a scholar.

학자금(學資金) ☞ 학비.

학장(學長) a president; a dean (부학장).

학적(부)(學籍簿) the school (college) register. ¶ 학적부에서 이름을 삭제하다 strike (a person's) name off the school register.

학점(學點) a point; a credit. ¶ ~이 모자라다 do not have sufficient credits.

학정(虐政) tyranny; despotism. ¶ ~에 신음하다 groan under tyranny.

학제(學制) an educational system. ¶ ~개혁 a reform of the educational system.

학질(瘧疾) malaria. ¶ ~에 걸리다 catch (contract) malaria / ~에서 회복하다 recover from malaria; 《비유적》 get rid of a nuisance. ‖ ~환자 a malaria patient.

학창(學窓) ☞ 학교. ¶ ~을 떠나다

leave [graduate from] school. ¶ ~생활 school [student] life.
학칙(學則) (observe, break) school regulations.
학파(學派) a school; a sect. ¶ 헤겔~ the Hegelian school.
학풍(學風) academic traditions(전통); a method of study(연구법); the character [atmosphere] of a college [school](학교 기풍). ¶ ~을 세우다 establish academic traditions.
학회(學會) a learned [scientific] society; an academic meeting(회합). ¶ 영문~ the English Literature [Literary] Society / 한글~ the Korean Language (Research) Society.
한(恨) ①(원한) a bitter [disgruntled] feeling; a grudge; rancour; hatred. ¶ ~을 품다 have [harbor, feel] a grudge (against); bear malice (toward); ~을 풀다 pay off old scores (with a person); square accounts (with a person); vent one's grudge (on a person). ②(한탄) regret; a matter for regret; an unsatisfied desire. ¶ ~ 많은 regrettable; deplorable / 천추의 ~ a lasting regret; a matter for great regret; ~이 없다 have nothing to regret; ~ 많은 인생을 보내다 lead a life full of tears and regrets.
한(限) ①(한도) a limit; limits; bounds. ¶ 인간의 욕망은 ~이 없다 Human desire knows no limits. ②(…하는 한) as [so] far as; 될 수 있는 ~ as far [much, soon] as possible; as much as one can / 내가 아는 ~ so far as I know / 따로 규정이 없는 ~ unless otherwise provided. ③(기한) not later than. ¶ 이달 15일 ~ not later than the 15th of this month.
한 ①(하나) a; one; a single. ~ 사람 a [one] man / ~ 마디 a [one] word; some; nearly. ③(같은) the same. ¶ ~ 집에 in the same house.
한··· ①(큰) large; broad. ~ 길 a (main) street. ②(가장·한창) the most; the very. ¶ ~ 밤중에 in the middle of the night; at dead of night.
한가운데 the middle [center, midst]. ¶ 방 ~ 눕다 lie in the middle of the room.
한가위 August 15th of the lunar month; the Harvest Moon festival.
한가을 the depth of autumn [fall]; the busy harvest time.

한가지 ①(일종) a kind [sort] (of); ②(동일) (one and) the same thing. ¶ 그녀에겐 ~ 독특한 매력같은 것이 있다 She has a kind of peculiar charms. / 그녀는 죽은 거나 (매)~다 She is as good as dead.
한가하다(閑暇—) (be) free; not busy; be at leisure. ¶ 한가할 때 그는 낚시하러 간다 He goes fishing in his leisure time.
한갓 simply; merely; only; no more than. ¶ 그것은 ~ 모방에 불과하다 It is no more than an imitation. or It's merely an imitation.
한갓지다 (be) quiet; peaceful and leisurely. ¶ 한갓진 시골 생활 leisurely country life.
한강(漢江) the Han River. ¶ ~ 대교 the Grand Han River Bridge / ~ 종합 개발 계획 the integrated Han River development project.
한가(閑暇) (lead) a quiet [retired] life. ¶ 소인이 ~ 하면 나쁜 짓을 한다 The devil makes work for idle hands.
한걱정 great cares [worries]. ¶ ~ 생기다 have (something) to worry about / ~ 놓다 be relieved of a great anxiety.
한걸음 a step; a pace. ¶ ~에 at a stride / ~ ~ step by step / ~ 앞으로 나오다 take a step forward.
한겨울 midwinter; the depth of winter.
한결 (눈에 띄게) remarkably; conspicuously; (한층 더) all the more; much [still] more; (특히) especially; particularly. ¶ 바꾸니까 ~ 보기가 낫다 The change makes it look much nicer.
한결같다 (be) uniform; even; (변함없다) (be) constant; never-changing. ¶ 한결같이 uniformly; constantly; as ever / 한결같은 태도 a consistent attitude.
한계(限界) a limit; bounds. ¶ ~를 정하다 set limits (to); limit / 자기 능력의 ~를 알다 know the limit of one's ability / 체력의 ~에 달하다 reach the limit of one's physical strength / ~ 가격 a ceiling price / ~생산력 marginal productivity / ~ 속도 critical speed / ~점 the critical point; the uppermost limit / ~효용(설) (the theory of) marginal utility.
한고비 the serious [critical] moment; a crisis; the peak. ¶ ~ 넘기다 pass the crisis [peak]; turn the corner(병 따위가) / 교섭은 이제 ~에 이르렀다 The negociations reached the critical stage at last.
한교(韓僑) Korean residents [nationals] abroad; overseas Kore-

한구석 a corner; a nook. ¶ 방 ~에 in a corner of a room.
한국(韓國) the Republic of Korea (생략 R.O.K.). ¶ ~의 Korean / ~화하다 Koreanize. ∥ ~계 미국인 an American of Korean descent; a Korean American / ~ 국민 the Korean (people) / ~요리 Korean dishes / ~육군 the Republic of Korea Army (생략 ROKA) / ~은행 the Bank of Korea / ~인 a Korean / ~학 Koreanology.
한군데 one place; the same place [spot](같은 데). ¶ ~ 쌓다 pile (the books) up in one place [spot] / ~ 살다 live in the same place.
한글 Hangeul; the Korean alphabet. ¶ ~로 in Hangeul. ∥ ~날 Hangeul Proclamation Day / ~ 맞춤법 the rules of Korean spelling [orthography] / ~ 전용 exclusive use of Hangeul.
한기(寒氣) (the) cold; (chill・기) a chill. ¶ ~를 막다 [피하다] keep off [out] the cold / ~를 느끼다 feel a chill; have a cold fit.
한길 a (main) street; a thoroughfare; a highway.
한꺼번에 [한번에] at a time; at once; at a stretch [breath]; (동시에) at the same time; (다) 같이 all together. ¶ ~ 두 가지 일을 하지 마라 Don't attempt to do two things at a time.
한껏(限-) ① [할 수 있는 데까지] to the utmost limit; to the best of one's ability; with all one's might. ¶ ~ 잡아당기다 draw (a string) out to its (full) length / ~ 싸게 팔다 sell at the lowest possible price / ~ 최선을 다해 일하다 work to the best of one's ability. ② [실컷] to one's heart's content; as much as one likes; to the full. ¶ ~ 먹다 eat one's fill / ~ 즐기다 enjoy oneself to one's heart's content.
한끼 a [one] meal. ¶ ~를 거르다 miss a meal.
한나절 half a day; a half day.
한낮 (at) midday; noontide; high noon; (in) broad daylight (백주).
한낱 only; mere(ly); nothing but. ¶ 그것은 ~ 구실에 불과하다 It's merely an excuse. or It's a mere excuse.
한눈 팔다 look away [aside]; take one's eyes off (one's book). ¶ 한눈 팔며 걷다 walk along gazing around / 한눈 팔지 말고 운전해라 Keep your eyes on the road!
한다한 eminent; influential; distinguished. ¶ ~ 집안 a respectable family / ~ 선비 an eminent scholar.
한담(閑談) a chat; an idle talk. ~하다 chat (with); have a chat [casual talk] (with); gossip. ¶ ~으로 시간을 보내다 chat the time away.
한대(寒帶) the Frigid Zone; the arctic regions. ∥ ~ 동물 [식물] a polar [an arctic] animal [plant].
한댕거리다 dangle; sway [swing] lightly.
한더위 fierce heat; the midsummer heat.
한데 [노천] the open (air); outdoors. ¶ ~의 open-air; outdoor / ~에서 자다 sleep (pass the night) in the open (air).
한도(限度) a limit; bounds. ¶ 신용 ~ a credit limit / 최대 [최소] ~ the maximum (minimum) / ~를 정하다 limit; set limits [bounds] (to) / …의 ~ 내에서 within the limits of… / ~에 달하다 [를 넘다] reach [exceed] the limit.
한동안 for a good while; for a long time; for quite some time; at one time (한때). ¶ ~에서 머물다 stay there for a good while.
한되다(恨-) be regretted; be a regret; be a matter for regret.
한두 one or two. ¶ ~ 번 once or twice.
한때 [잠시] a short time [while]; for a time [while](부사적); [전에] once; (at) one time. ¶ 즐거운 ~를 보내다 have a good time《at the party》.
한랭(寒冷) ~하다 (be) cold; chilly. ¶ ~ 전선 [氣] a cold front / ~ 전선이 남하했다 The cold front pushed southward.
한량(限量) a limit; limits; bounds. ¶ ~없는 unlimited; boundless; endless / ~없이 귀중한 교훈 a lesson of incalculable value.
한량(閑良) a prodigal; a debauchee; a libertine; a playboy.
한련(旱蓮) [植] a tropaeolum; a garden nasturtium.
한류(韓流) 'Korean Wave', the ongoing frenzy of Korean pop culture that is sweeping across the vast regions of East Asia.
한류(寒流) a cold current.
한마디 a (single) word. ~하다 speak briefly [say a word] 《about》; say a (good) word [for a person](충고조로). ¶ ~로 말하면 in a word; to sum up / ~도 없이 without (saying) a single word / ~도 없다 be silent; do not speak a word.
한마음 one mind. ¶ ~으로 with one accord / ~이 되어 일하다 work in close cooperation; act in concert 《with》.
한 모금 a draft [draught] 《of

한목 all at one time; in the (a) lump; in one [a] lot. ¶ 일년치 봉급을 ~에 타다 receive a year's pay in a lump.

한몫 a share; a portion; a quota. ¶ ~ 끼다 have a share in; share (participate) in (*the profits*).

한문(漢文) Chinese writing; Chinese classics(한학). ¶ ~으로 쓴 책 a book written in classical Chinese.

한물 (the (best) season; the best time (*for*); (최성기) the prime. ¶ ~ 가다 be past (*its*) season; be out of season; (사람이) be past *one's* prime / ~ 지다 be (come) in season.

한미(韓美) ¶ ~의 Korean-American (*relations*). ¶ ~ 공동성명 a Korea-U.S. Joint Statement / ~ 무역마찰 Korea-U.S. trade friction / ~ 상호 방위협정 the ROK-U.S. Mutual Defense Agreement / ~ 연합군 사령부 the ROK-U.S. Combined Forces Command / ~ 통상협의 the Korea-U.S. Commercial Conference / ~ 행정협정 the ROK-U.S. Status of Forces Agreement.

한밑천 a sizable amount of capital. ¶ ~ 잡다 amass (make) a sizable fortune.

한바닥 the busiest quarters; the heart; the center. ¶ 시장 ~ the center of a market place.

한바퀴 a turn; a round. ¶ ~ 다 돌다 take a turn; go round; go *one's* rounds (담당 구역을).

한바탕 for a time (while); for a spell. ¶ ~ 울다 cry for a spell / ~ 소나기가 오더니 개었다 After a short shower it cleared up. / 우리는 ~ 이야기 꽃을 피웠다 We enjoyed chatting for a while.

한반도(韓半島) the Korean peninsula. ¶ ~ 에서의 평화와 안정의 유지 the maintenance of peace and stability on the Korean Peninsula. ¶ ~ 에너지개발기구 the Korean Peninsula Energy Development Organization (생략 KEDO).

한발(旱魃) a drought; a long spell of dry weather. ¶ ~의 피해 drought damage / ~ 지역 a drought-stricken area.

한 발짝 a step. ¶ 한걸음.

한밤중(-中) (at) midnight; (at) dead of night. ¶ ~까지 far into the night.

한방(漢方, 韓方) Chinese medicine (漢方); Korean herb medicine(韓方). ¶ ~약 a herbal medicine / ~의(醫) a herb doctor.

한방울 a drop (*of water*). ¶ ~씩 drop by drop.

한배 ① (동물의) a litter; a brood. ¶ ~ 병아리 a brood of chickens / ~ 세 마리의 강아지 three puppies at a litter. ② (사람의) ~ 형제 (자매) brothers (sisters) of the same mother; uterine brothers (sisters).

한번 once; one time. ¶ ~에 at once; at a time; at the same time(동시에) / 다시 ~ once more (again) / 1년에 ~ once a year.

한 벌 a suit (*of clothes*); a set (*of furniture*). ¶ 여름옷 ~ a suit of summer wear.

한복(韓服) traditional Korean clothes (costume). ¶ ~으로 갈아 입다 change into traditional Korean clothes.

한복판 the middle; the center; the heart (*of Seoul*).

한 사람 one person. ¶ ~ ~ one by one; one at a time; one after another / ~도 남김없이 every one (*of them*); (be killed) to the last man / ~당 for each person; per head.

한사리 the flood tide.

한사코(限死-) persistently; desperately; by all (possible) means; at any cost. ¶ ~ 반대하다 persist in *one's* opposition; oppose persistently (stoutly) / 그녀는 ~ 자기가 간다고 우겼다 She insisted on going in person. / ~ 무력개입은 피해야 한다 We must avoid military intervention at any cost.

한산(閑散) ~하다 《경기가》 (be) dull; inactive; slack. ¶ ~ 한 시장 a dull (flat) market / 피서지는 매우 ~ 했다 The summer resort was almost desserted. / 불황으로 주식시장은 ~ 하다 Due to the recession, business in the stock market is slack. 「ature(온도).

한서(寒暑) heat and cold; temper-

한서(漢書) a Chinese book; Chinese classics (고전).

한선(汗腺) a sweat gland.

한세상(-世上) ① (한평생) a lifetime; *one's* (whole) life. ¶ 이렇게 살아도 ~ 저렇게 살아도 ~ 이다 Life is one and the same no matter how you spend it. ② (한창때) the best time in *one's* life.

한센병(-病) Hansen's disease: leprosy.

한속 one mind. ¶ ~이다 be of one mind (뜻이 같다) / 그는 일당과 ~ 이 되어 은행 강도를 기도했다 He was in cahoots with the gang in their attempt to rob the bank.

한 수(-手) 《바둑・장기의》 a move; a skill. ¶ ~ 두다 make a move / ~ 위다 (아래다) be a cut above

[below] (*a person*).
한숨 ① 《잠》 a wink of sleep. ¶ ~ 자다 take [have] a nap; sleep a wink. ② 《탄식》 a (deep) sigh; a long breath. ¶ ~ 쉬다 〔것뇌〕 (heave a) sigh; draw a long breath. ③ 《호흡·휴식》 a breath; a rest. ¶ ~ 돌리다 take a (short) break [rest].
한시(一時) ¶ ~ 도 even for a moment. / ~ 도 잊지 않다 do not forget (*it*) even for a moment.
한시(漢詩) a Chinese poem; Chinese poetry(총칭).
한시름 a big worry. ¶ ~ 놓다 be relieved of a great anxiety.
한식(韓式) a Korean-style. / ~ 집 a Korean-style house.
한심하다《스럽다》(寒心—) (be) pitiable; miserable; wretched; sorry; lamentable; shameful (부끄럽다). ¶ 한심한 녀석으로군 What a miserable guy! / 네가 그걸 모르다니 It is a pity that you don't know it. / 한심한 짓을 하다 do a shameful thing.
한 쌍(一雙) a pair; a couple. ¶ ~ 의 a pair [couple, brace] of / 좋은 ~ 을 이루다 make [form] a good pair; be a good match (*for*).
한 아름 an armful (*of firewood*).
한약(韓藥. 漢藥) a herbal(herb) medicine. ‖ ~ 방(局) a dispensary of Chinese medicine; a herb shop / ~ 재상(材商) a herb dealer.
한없다(限一) (be) unlimited; boundless; endless; limitless. ¶ 한없이 without end (limit); endlessly / 한없는 사랑 eternal love / 한없는 기쁨 a limitless (an everlasting) joy.
한여름 (in) midsummer. ¶ ~ 더위 the midsummer heat.
한역(漢譯) a Chinese translation. ~ 하다 translate into Chinese.
한역(韓譯) a Korean translation. ~ 하다 translate into Korean. ¶ '죄와 벌'을 ~ 본을 읽다 read a Korean version of *Crime and Punishment*.
한영(韓英) ¶ ~ 의 Korean-English. ‖ ~ 사전 a Korean-English dictionary.
한옥(韓屋) a Korean-style house.
한외(限外) out of bounds; beyond the limit. ¶ ~ 발행 excess issue; an overissue (of paper money).
한 움큼 a handful (*of rice*).
한일(韓日) Korea and Japan. ¶ ~ 의 Korean-Japanese / ~ 무역의 불균형 the trade imbalance between Korea and Japan. ‖ ~ 공동규제 수역 the Korean-Japanese Joint Regulation Water Basin / ~ 대륙붕협정 the Korean-Japanese Continental Shelf Agreement / ~ 회담 〔각료 회담〕 the Korea-Japan talks (Ministerial Conference).
한입 a mouthful; a bite. ¶ 사과를 ~ 먹다 take a bite out of an apple.
한자(漢字) a Chinese character. ¶ 상용(常用) ~ Chinese characters in common use / ~ 로 쓰다 write in Chinese characters. ‖ ~ 제한 restriction on the use of Chinese characters.
한잔 ① 《분량》 a cup (*of tea*); a glass (*of beer*); a shot (*of whisky*); a cupful; a glassful. ② 《음주》 a drink. ~ 하다 have a drink. ¶ 맥주라도 ~ 하면서 이야기하자 Let's talk over a glass of beer. / "오늘 일 끝나 ~ 하지 않겠나」「좋고말고」 "How about a drink after work today?" "Sounds great."
한잠 a sleep; a nap; 《깊은 잠》 a deep (sound) sleep. ~ 자다 get [have] a sleep; take a nap / ~ 도 못 자다 can not get a wink of sleep; do not sleep a wink.
한재(旱災) drought damage. ¶ ~ 를 입다 suffer from a drought. ‖ ~ 지구 a drought-stricken district (area).
한적하다(閑寂—) (be) quiet; secluded. ¶ 한적한 곳 a retired (quiet) place.
한정(限定) limitation. ~ 하다 limit; restrict; set limits to; qualify(의미 등을). ¶ ~ 된 지면 limited space. ‖ ~ 치산(治産) quasi-incompetence / ~ 치산자 a quasi-incompetent (person) / ~ 판 a limited edition.
한줄기 ① 《한 가닥》 a line; a streak (*of light*). ¶ ~ 의 눈물 a trickle of tears / ~ 의 희망 a ray of hope. ② 《같은 줄기》 the same lineage. (*of straw*).
한줌 a handful (*of rice*); a lock
한중(寒中) midwinter. ¶ ~ 의 during the cold season / ~ 훈련 midwinter training; winter exercises.
한중(韓中) ¶ ~ 의 Korean-Chinese; Sino-Korean / ~ 관계 Sino-Korean relations; relations between Korea and China / ~ 무역 trade between Korea and China.
한증(汗蒸) a steam (sweating) bath. ~ 하다 take steam bath. ‖ ~ 막 a sweating bathroom; a sauna; a sudatorium.
한지(寒地) a cold region (district).

¶ ~ 식물 a psychrophyte.

한직(閑職) a sinecure; a leisurely post; an unimportant post. ¶ ~으로 쫓겨나다 be downgraded to a trifling job.

한집안 one's family; one's people 〔folk〕; 《친척》 one's relatives.

한쪽 one side; the other side 《party》; one of a pair.

한참 for some time; for a time 〔while〕; for a spell. ¶ ~ 만에 after a good while.

한창 《가장 성할 때》 the height 〔peak〕; the climax; the zenith; the prime (of time). ¶ ~이다 be in full swing; be at its height; be in the prime (of)《사랑이》; be in full bloom 《glory》, be at 〔their〕 best《꽃이》/ 식목하기에 ~ 좋은 때 the prime time for planting / 지금 벚꽃이 ~이다 The cherry blossoms are now at their best. / 우리는 지금 기말시험이 ~이다 We are in the midst of the term examination now. / 지금 토론이 ~ 진행 중이다 The argument is now in full swing.

한창때 《최성기》 the peak period; the prime; the golden age 《days》; 《청춘》 the prime of life; the bloom of youth; 《청과물 따위》 the best time (for); the season. ¶ ~이다 be at its peak; be at the height of one's 〔its〕 prosperity; 《사람이》 be in the prime of 〔in〕 manhood, womanhood》; 《청과물 따위가》 be in season / ~를 지나다 《사람이》 be past one's prime; be on the wane 〔decline〕.

한천(寒天) ☞ 우무.

한촌(寒村) a poor and lonely village.

한추위 severe 〔intense〕 cold.

한층(一層) more; still 〔even〕 more; all the more. ¶ ~ 더 노력하다 make even greater efforts; work harder than ever / 2월에는 ~ 더 추위질 것이다 It will get much colder in February.

한치 an inch. ¶ ~도 물러서지 않다 will not budge 〔yield〕 an inch.

한칼 a single stroke of the sword. ¶ ~에 목을 베다 cut down (a person's) head at a single stroke of the sword.

한탄(恨歎) a sigh; deploration. ~하다 lament; deplore; sigh; regret. ¶ 자기의 불운을 ~하다 lament one's misfortune.

한턱 a treat. ~하다 《내다》 stand treat (for a person); treat (a person) to (a dinner); give (a person) a treat.

한테 ~에게. 〔son) a treat.

한통속 an accomplice. ¶ ~이 되다 act 〔be〕 in league 〔collusion〕 《with》; plot together; conspire 《with》/ 정치가 중에는 군부와 ~이 된 자도 있었다 Some politicians were hand in glove with the military.

한파(寒波) a cold wave.

한판 a round; a game; a bout. ¶ 바둑을 ~ 두다 have a game of paduk. ‖ ~승부 a contest of single round.

한패(一牌) one of the (same) party; a confederate; a circle; a company. ¶ 그도 ~임에 틀림없다 He must be one of the gang.

한편 ① 《한쪽》 one side; one way; one direction. ¶ ~으로 치우치다 be one-sided. ② 《자기편》 an ally; a supporter; a friend; one's side. ③ 《부사적》 meanwhile; besides; 《한편으로는》 on the other hand …; in the meantime.

한평생(一平生) one's whole life; 《부사적》 all 〔throughout〕 one's life. ¶ ~을 독신으로 지내다 remain single all one's life.

한푼 a coin; a penny. ¶ ~ 없다 be penniless.

한풀 겪이다 be dispirited 〔disheartened, discouraged〕.

한풀다(恨—) have one's will: realize one's desire; gratify one's wishes.

한풀이하다(恨—) vent one's spite; satisfy 〔work off〕 one's grudge.

한풍(寒風) a cold 〔an icy〕 wind.

한하다(限—) limit; restrict. ¶ 지원자는 여성에 한한다 Only women applicants are accepted. / 정당한 이유가 있는 경우에 한해서 provided there is just reason for it.

한학(漢學) Chinese literature (classics). ‖ ~자 a scholar of Chinese classics.

한해(旱害) damage from 〔caused by〕 a drought. ‖ ~지구 a drought-stricken area.

한해(寒害) cold-weather damage.

한화(韓貨) Korean money.

할(割) 《백분의》 percentage; percent. ¶ 연 1~의 이자로 돈을 빌리다 borrow money at an interest of ten percent per annum.

할거(割據) ~하다 each holds his own sphere of influence; hold one's own ground. ¶ 군웅~ rivalry between warlords / 군웅~의 시대 the age of rival chiefs 〔warlords〕.

할당(割當) allotment; assignment; a quota《할당량》. ~하다 assign; allot; allocate; apportion. ¶ ~된 일을 끝내다 finish 〔one's assignment〕 the work assigned to one / 몫을 ~하다 allot shares / 예산의 20%를 그 기획에 ~했다 We allocated twenty percent of our budget to the project. ‖ ~량

할듯할듯하다 look as if *one* is going (ready) to (*do*).
할듯말듯하다 hesitate to (*do*); be half-hearted.
할례(割禮) [宗] circumcision.
할말 (하고 싶은 말) what *one* has (got) to say; *one's* say; *one's* claim (주장); a complaint (불평); an objection (이의). ¶ 네게 ~ 있다 I have something to tell you. / ~ 있으면 해라 Tell me what you have to say. / ~ 은 다 했다 I have had my say.
할머니 (조모) a grandmother; (노파) an old lady (woman).
할멈 an old woman; a granny.
할미꽃 [植] a pasqueflower.
할미새 [鳥] a wagtail.
할복(割腹) disembowelment; *harakiri* (일). ~ 하다 disembowel *oneself*; commit harakiri. ‖ ~ 자살 (commit) suicide by disembowelment.
할부(割賦) [分割 지급] payment in [by] installments. ¶ 차를 ~로 팔다 [사다] sell [buy] a car on the installment plan. / ~ 납입금 an installment (money) / ~ 상환 [經] amortization / ~제(制) the installment plan [system] / ~판매 selling on an installment basis.
할선(割線) [數] a secant.
할아버지 ① (조부) a grandfather. ② (노인) an old man.
할아범 an old [aged] man.
할애(割愛) (나누다) share (*a thing*) with (*a person*); part with; spare. ¶ 지면을 ~ 하다 give [allow] space to (*a subject*).
할양(割讓) (a) cession. ~ 하다 cede; [法] alienate. ¶ 영토를 ~ 하다 cede territory to (*a country*) / 토지를 남에게 ~ 하다 alienate lands to (*a person*).
할인(割引) (a) discount; (a) reduction. ~ 하다 (make a) discount; reduce (*the price*); take [cut] off. ¶ 단체 ~ a discount (special rates) for a group / 단체 ~ 요금 a group rate / 2할 ~ 하여 팔다 [사다] sell [buy] (*a thing*) at a discount (reduction) of 20 percent. ‖ ~ 가격 a reduced price / ~권 a discount coupon / ~ 차권 a reduced fare ticket / ~ 어음 a discounted bill / ~율 a discount rate / ~ 채권 a discounted (*loan*) bond.
할인(割印) a tally impression. ¶ ~ 을 찍다 affix [put] a seal at the joining of two leaves (*of a deed*).
할일 things to do. ¶ ~ 이 많다 have lots to do; be busy / ~ 이 없다 have nothing to do.

할증금(割增金) [賃金의] an extra pay (요금의) an extra fare (charge); a surcharge; (주식 따위의) a premium; a bonus. ‖ ~ 부(付) 채권 a bond with a premium; a premium-bearing debenture.
할짝거리다 lick; lap.
할퀴다 scratch; claw. ¶ 할퀸 상처 a scratch; a nail mark / 얼굴을 ~ scratch (*a person's*) face.
핥다 lick; lap. ¶ 그릇을 핥은 듯 깨끗이 먹다 lick the bowl clean / 고양이가 접시의 우유를 핥아 먹었다 The cat lapped the milk from the saucer. / 개가 내 손을 핥았다 The dog licked my hand.
함(函) a box; a case; a chest.
함교(艦橋) a bridge (of a warship).
함구(緘口) ~ 하다 hold *one's* tongue; keep *one's* mouth shut; keep silent. ¶ ~ 령을 내리다 order (*a person*) to keep silent (*about*); order (*a person*) not to mention (*something*); gag (*the press*).
함께 (같이) together; (…와 함께) with…; together (along) with; in company with. ¶ 모두 ~ all together / ~ 살다 live with (*a person*); live under the same roof / ~ 가다 go with (*somebody*).
함대(艦隊) [큰] a squadron; (작은) a combined fleet / 연습 ~ a training squadron / ~ 근무를 하다 do *one's* sea time. ‖ ~ 사령관 the commander of a fleet.
함락(陷落) ~ 하다 (땅이) sink; fall; (성·진지 등이) fall; surrender. ¶ 수도가 마침내 반란군에게 ~ 되었다 The capital fell to the rebels at last.
함량(含量) content. ‖ 알코올 ~ alcohol content.
함몰(陷沒) a cave-in; sinking; subsidence; collapse. ~ 하다 sink; cave (fall) in; subside; collapse. ¶ 도로의 ~ 장소 a cave-in in the road / 도로가 지진으로 ~ 됐다 The road sank (caved in) by the earthquake.
함미(艦尾) the stern (of a warship). ‖ ~ 닻 the stern anchor / ~ 포 a stern chaser; a tail gun.
함박꽃 [植] a peony.
함박눈 large snowflakes.
함부로 (허가·이유 없이) without permission [good reason]; (마구) at random; recklessly; indiscriminately; thoughtlessly; roughly; carelessly; (무례하게) rudely. ¶ ~ 들어오지 마시오 (게시) No entry without permission. / ~ 돈을 쓰다 spend money recklessly / 말을 ~ 하다 talk at random; have a careless manner of

함상(艦上) ¶ ~의[에] aboard; on board.

함석(函石) tin; a galvanized tin. ¶ ~지붕 a zinc [tin] roof / 골 ~ a sheet of corrugated iron [zinc]. ∥ ~판 sheet zinc; galvanized iron sheet.

함선(艦船) 《군함·배》 warships and other ships; vessels (선박).

함성(喊聲) a battle [war] cry; shouting. ¶ 승리의 ~ a shout of victory [triumph] / ~을 지르다 give [raise] a war cry.

함수(含水) ¶ ~의 《化》 hydrous; hydrated. ∥ ~량 the water content 《of a substance》 / ~탄소 carbohydrate / ~화합물 a hydrated compound.

함수(函數) 《數》 a (mathematical) function. ∥ ~ 관계 functional relation / ~방정식 a functional equation.

함수(艦首) the bow. ∥ ~포(砲) a bow gun (chaser).

함수초(含羞草) 《植》 a sensitive plant; a mimosa.

함양(涵養) ~하다 cultivate; develop; foster; build up. ¶ 덕성을 ~ 하다 cultivate moral character; foster one's moral sentiment.

함유(含有) ~하다 contain; have (in); hold. ∥ ~량 content / ~ 성분 a component / ~율 content by percentage.

함자(銜字) your [his, etc.] name.

함장(艦長) the commander [captain] of a warship.

함재기(艦載機) a deck [carrier-based] (air)plane; carrier-borne [-based] aircraft (총칭).

함정(陷穽) a pitfall; a pit; a trap. ¶ ~에 빠뜨리다 ensnare; entrap / ~에 빠지다 fall in a pit; fall into a snare [trap, pitfall].

함정(艦艇) a naval vessel.

함지 a large wooden vessel. ∥ ~박 a large round bowl.

함축(含蓄) ~하다 imply; signify; suggest. ¶ ~성 있는 significant; suggestive; pregnant; implicit / 그녀의 말에는 ~성이 있다 What she says is full of significance [suggestions].

함포사격(艦砲射擊) bombardment from a warship.

함흥차사(咸興差使) a messenger sent out on an errand who never returns.

합(合) 《합계》 the sum; the total (amount). ¶ 2와 2의 ~은 4다 Two and two make four.

합(盒) a brass bowl with a lid.

합격(合格) success in an examination; passing an exam. ~하다 《시험에서》 pass [succeed in] an examination; 《입사 시험 등에서》 be accepted; 《검사 등에서》 come up to the standard(표준에). ¶ 검사에 ~하다 pass inspection; pass the test / 그는 X대학 입시에 ~했다 He succeeded in the entrance examination to X University. / ~을 축하한다 Congratulations on your success in the examination. ∥ ~라인 the passing mark [grade] / ~률 the ratio of successful applicants; the pass rate / ~자 a successful candidate [applicant] / ~점 a passing mark / ~통지 a notice of 《a person's》 success in the examination.

합계(合計) the sum total; a total (amount). ~하다 sum [add] up; total; foot up 《美》. ¶ ~하여 all in all [total]; all told / ~ 되다 come [amount] to... (in all).

합금(合金) an alloy. ¶ 초(超) ~ a superalloy / 형상 기억 ~ shape memory alloy / 구리와 아연을 ~ 하다 alloy copper with zinc.

합당(合當) ~하다 (be) adequate; suitable; proper; fit; appropriate; right. ¶ ~한 사람 a competent person / ~한 가격으로 at a reasonable price / ~하지 않다 be improper [unsuitable].

합당(合黨) the merger [fusion] of political parties. ~하다 merge the parties.

합동(合同) (a) combination; (a) union; 《기억·조직 등의》 merger; amalgamation. ~하다 combine; unite; incorporate. ¶ ~의 joint; united; combined / ~해서 사태 수습에 임하다 make a joint effort to save the situation. ∥ ~결혼 a mass [group] wedding / ~관리 joint control [management] / ~ 사업 a joint undertaking [venture] / ~위령제 a joint memorial service 《for the war dead》 / ~위원회 a joint committee / ~참모회의 the Conference of the Joint Chief of Staff / ~회의 a joint session [convention].

합력(合力) 《理》 a resultant (force). ~하다 join forces; make a united effort; cooperate with.

합류(合流) ~하다 join; meet; unite with(합세). ¶ 그 강은 여기서 한강과 ~한다 The river joins the Han river here. / 우리는 그들과 마산역 에서 ~했다 We joined them at Masan Station. ∥ ~점 the junction 《of two rivers》.

합리(合理) ¶ ~적인 rational; reasonable; logical / 그의 사고방식은 ~적이다 His way of thinking

합리화(合理化) rationalization. ~하다 rationalize. ¶산업의 ~ rationalization of industry; industrial rationalization / 경영을 ~하다 streamline the management ¶공장에서는 조립 공정을 ~로 대폭적인 원가 절감을 실현했다 A major cost reduction was realized at this plant through rationalization of the assembly process.

합명회사(合名會社) an unlimited partnership.

합반(合班) a combined class. ¶~ 수업 combined classwork.

합방(合邦) ~하다 annex a country 《to》.

합법(合法) legality; lawfulness. ¶~적인 lawful; legal; legitimate / ~적으로 lawfully; legally; legitimately / ~으로 자네가 그렇게 하는 것은 ~적이다 It is lawful for you to do so. / ~적인 수단으로 그에게 대항해 나가겠다 I will challenge him by lawful means. ‖ ~성 lawfulness / ~정부 the legitimate government / ~화 legalization (~화하다 legalize).

합병(合併) union; combination 《병합》; merge 《회사 따위의》; annexation. ~하다 combine; merge; annex. ¶인수 ~ 《기업의》 mergers and acquisitions 《생략 M & A》 / 작은 상사들이 ~하여 큰 조직이 되었다 Some small business firms were merged into a large organization. ‖ ~증 〔醫〕 a complication.

합본(合本) the bound volume 《of the magazines》. ~하다 bind 《magazines》 in one volume.

합산(合算) ☞ 합계(合計).

합석(合席) ~하다 sit with 《a person》; sit in company with 《a person》.

합성(合成) 〔化〕 synthesis; 〔理〕 composition. ~하다 compound; synthesize. ¶~의 compound; mixed; synthetic. ‖ ~고무 〔주〕 synthetic rubber / ~물 ~물 a compound / ~물질 a synthetic substance 《liquor》 / ~사진 a composite photograph 《of wartime scenes》 / ~섬유 synthetic fiber / ~세제 synthetic detergents / ~수지 plastics; synthetic resin / ~어 a compound (word) / ~염료 synthetic dyes / ~음 a synthetic sound.

합세(合勢) ~하다 join forces. ¶~하여 괴롭히다 join in bullying 《a person》.

합숙(合宿) ~하다 lodge together; stay in a camp for training 《운동 선수가》. ‖ ~소 a lodging (boarding) house; a training camp 《운동선수의》 / ~훈련 camp training (~훈련하다 train at a camp).

합승(合乘) ~하다 ride together; ride in the same car 《with》. ¶나는 그녀와 택시를 ~했다 I shared a taxi with her. ‖ ~객 a fellow passenger.

합심(合心) ~하다 be united; be of one accord (mind).

합의(合意) mutual agreement; mutual 《common》 consent. ~하다 be agreed; reach 《come》 to an agreement. ¶~에 의해 by mutual agreement (consent) / 양자는 그 점에 관해 ~하였다 The two agreed on that point, or They reached an agreement on that point. ‖ ~서 a written agreement; a statement of mutual agreement / ~이혼 a divorce by mutual agreement.

합의(合議) consultation; conference. ~하다 consult together; confer 《with》. ‖ ~사항 an agreed item; items of understanding / ~재판 collegiate judgment / ~제 a council system.

합일(合一) union; oneness; unity. ~하다 unite; be united.

합자(合資) partnership. ~하다 join stocks; enter into partnership 《with》. ‖ ~회사 a limited partnership (남산 ~ 회사 Namsan & Co., Ltd.).

합작(合作) collaboration; a joint work. ~하다 collaborate 《with》; cooperate 《with》; write 《a book》 jointly 《with》. ¶한미 ~ 영화 a Korean-American joint-product film. ‖ ~자 a collaborator; a coauthor / ~회사 a joint corporation (concern).

합장(合掌) ~하다 join one's hands in prayer.

합장(合葬) ~하다 bury together. ¶부부를 ~하다 bury the wife's remains with her husband's.

합주(合奏) a concert; an ensemble. ~하다 play in concert. ‖ ~단 an ensemble.

합죽거리다 mumble with 《a toothless mouth》. 〔pursed lips.

합죽이 a toothless person with

합중국(合衆國) the United States (of America); a federal states.

합창(合唱) chorus. ~하다 sing together (in chorus). ¶남성 〔여성〕 ~ a male 〔female〕 chorus / 혼성 ~ a mixed chorus / 2부 〔3부〕 ~ a chorus of two 〔three〕 parts. ‖ ~대 〔단〕 a chorus; a choir 《교회의》.

합치(合致) ~하다 agree 〔accord〕 《with》; be in accord 《with》;

합치다 (合一) ① [하나로] put together; unite; combine; join together; [병합] merge; amalgamate; annex. ② [섞다] mix; compound. ③ [셈을] add up; sum up; total.

합판 (合板) a veneer board; (a sheet of) plywood. ¶ 프린트 ~ printed plywood.

합판화 (合瓣花) [植] a gamopetalous (compound) flower.

합하다 (合一) ① [하나로 하다] add (put, join) together; combine; unite. ② [하나가 되다] be put together; be combined; be united.

합헌 (合憲) ¶ ~적 constitutional. ~성 constitutionality.

합환주 (合歡酒) the wedding drink. ¶ ~를 나누다 exchange nuptial cups.

핫 hot. ‖ ~뉴스 hot news / ~도그 a hot dog / ~라인 the hot line 《*between Washington and Moscow*》 / ~케이크 a hot cake; a pancake 《英》.

핫바지 (솜바지) (a pair of) padded trousers; 《존칭기》 a bumpkin.

항 (項) [조항] a clause; an item; [글의] a paragraph; [数] a term. ¶ 제3조 제2항에 해당되다 come under Article 1, Clause 2.

항간 (巷間) ¶ ~에 in the world (city, streets) / ~에 떠도는 얘기 the talk of the town / ~에 떠도는 소문에 의하면 a rumor has it that…; people say that…; it is rumored that….

항거 (抗拒) ~하다 resist; defy; oppose. ¶ 독재 정치에 ~하다 resist dictatorial government.

항고 (抗告) [法] a complaint; an appeal; a protest. ~하다 complain 《*against a decision*》; file a protest 《*against*》. ¶ 판결에 대해 즉시 ~하다 make an immediate appeal against the sentence. ‖ ~기간 the term for complaint / ~심 hearing of a complaint / ~인 a complainant; a complainer / ~장 a bill of complaint.

항공 (航空) aviation; flying. ¶ ~의 aeronautic(al); aerial / 민간 ~ civil aviation / 국제〔국내〕 ~ international (domestic) aviation. ‖ ~공학 aeronautical engineering / ~관제관 an airtraffic controller / ~관제탑 a control tower / ~권(표) an air ticket / ~기 an airplane; aircraft (총칭) / ~기지 an air base / ~대학 a college of aviation / ~등(燈) a navigation light / ~로(線) an air route (line) / ~모함 a (an aircraft) carrier / ~봉합엽서 an aerogram / ~사(士) an aerial navigator / ~사진 an air photo / ~수송 air transportation / ~술 aeronautics; airmanship / ~요금 an air fare / ~우주산업 the aerospace industry / ~우편 air mail / ~표지(標識) an air [aerial] beacon / ~회사 an aviation company / 대한 ~ the Korean Air (생략 KA).

항구 (恒久) ¶ ~적 permanent; perpetual; (ever)lasting; eternal / ~적 평화 permanent peace. ‖ ~화(化) perpetuation 《~화하다 perpetuate》.

항구 (港口) a harbor; a port. ‖ ~도시 a port city (town).

항균성 (抗菌性) antibiosis. ¶ ~성 antibiotic. ‖ ~물질 antibiotics.

항내 (港內) ¶ ~에 in (within) the harbor. ‖ ~설비 harbor facilities.

항독소 (抗毒素) an antitoxin; an antivenom. ‖ ~요법 antitoxin treatment.

항등식 (恒等式) [数] an identical equation; an identity.

항렬 (行列) degree (distance) of kin relationship.

항례 (恒例) ☞ 상례 (常例).

항로 (航路) [배의] a (sea) route; a course; a shipping lane; 《항공기의》 an air route. ¶ 정기 ~ a regular line (service) / 부정기 ~ an occasional line / 외국 ~선(船) an ocean liner / 국내 ~선(船) a steamer on the domestic line (course). ‖ ~표지 a beacon.

항만 (港灣) harbors. ‖ ~공사 harbor construction work / ~노동자 a stevedore; a longshoreman 《美》 / ~시설 harbor facilities.

항명 (抗命) disobedience. ~하다 disobey 《*a person's*》 order.

항목 (項目) a head; a heading; an item. ¶ ~으로 나누다 itemize / ~별로 item by item / 문제를 네 ~으로 나누다 divide the problem under four headings. ‖ ~별 표 an itemized list.

항문 (肛門) [解] the anus. ‖ ~과 proctology / ~과 의사 proctologist.

항법 (航法) navigation. ¶ 무선 ~ radio navigation.

항변 (抗辯) a protest; [法] a refutation; 《피고의》 a plea. ~하다 refute; protest; make a plea 《*for, against*》.

항복 (降伏·降服) (a) surrender; capitulation. ~하다 surrender 《*to*》; capitulate 《*to the enemy*》; submit 《*to*》. ‖ ~문서 an instrument of surrender / 무조건〔조건부〕 ~ an unconditional (a conditional) surrender.

항상(恒常) always; at all times; as a rule; constantly; habitually (습관적으로).

항생물질(抗生物質) an antibiotic (substance). ∥ ~학 antibiotics.

항설(巷說) gossip; a town talk; a rumor.

항성(恒星) a fixed star. ∥ ~시〔일, 년〕 sidereal time〔day, year〕.

항소(抗訴) 〖法〗 the appeal suit; an appeal 《to a higher court》. ~하다 appeal; lodge an appeal 《against》. ∥ ~심 a trial on an appeal case / ~인 an appellant / ~장 a petition of appeal.

항속(航續) 《배의》 cruising; 《비행기의》 flying; flight. ∥ ~거리 a cruising〔flying〕 range / ~시간 the duration of a cruise〔flight〕; maximum flying time.

항시(恒時) ☞ 항상(恒常).

항아리(缸—) a jar; a pot.

항암(抗癌) ¶ ~의 anti-cancer. ∥ ~제 an anti-cancer drug〔agent〕.

항원(抗原·抗元) 〖生〗 antigen.

항의(抗議) an objection; a protest. ~하다 protest 《against》; make〔lodge〕 a protest 《against》; object 《to》. ¶그들은 원자력 발전소 건설에 ~하고 있다 They are protesting against the building of the atomic power plant. ∥ ~데모 a protest demonstration / ~문 a note of protest / ~집회 a protest rally.

항일(抗日) anti-Japan; 《형용사적》 anti-Japanese. ∥ ~감정 anti-Japanese sentiment / ~운동 an anti-Japanese movement.

항쟁(抗爭) (a) dispute; contention; resistance(저항); a struggle(투쟁). ~하다 contend; dispute; struggle 《against》.

항적(航跡) a wake〔behind a sailing ship〕; a furrow; a track; 《항공기의》 a flight path; a vapor trail.

항전(抗戰) resistance. ~하다 offer resistance; resist.

항정(航程) the distance covered〔by a ship〕; a ship's run; 《항공기의》 a flight; a leg〔장거리 비행 의 한 행정〕.

항진(亢進) 〔heart〕 acceleration. ~하다 accelerate; grow worse (병세가).

항체(抗體) 〖生〗 an antibody.

항해(航海) navigation; a voyage; a cruise(순항). ~하다 navigate; make a voyage 《to》; cruise. ¶ ~ 중이다 be on a voyage(사람이); be at sea(선박이). ∥ ~ 중인 배 a ship at sea / ~도 a chart / ~사 a mate; a navigation officer(1등〔2등〕 ~사 chief〔second〕 mate〕 / ~술 (the art of) navigation / ~일지 a logbook; a ship's journal〔log〕 / ~자 a mariner; a navigator / 처녀 ~ a maiden trip〔voyage〕.

항행(航行) navigation; sailing; a cruise(순항). ~하다 navigate; sail; cruise.

항히스타민제(抗—) 〖藥〗 (an) antihistamine; an antihistaminic agent〔medicine〕.

해¹〔태양〕 the sun. ¶ ~가 뜨다 the sun rises / ~가 지기 전에 before the sun sets / ~가 진 후 after dark.

해² ① 〔일년〕 a year. ¶지난 ~ last year. ② 〔낮 동안〕 the daytime; a day. ¶여름에는 ~가 길다 In summer (the) days are long.

해(亥) 〖십이지지〗 the Boar. ∥ ~년(年) the year of the Boar.

해(害) harm; injury; damage. ¶ …에 ~를 주다 do harm to / ~를 입다 suffer damage〔loss〕; be damaged; be killed.

해…(該) that; the very; the said; the 《matter》 in question.

해갈하다(解渴—) 〔갈증을〕 appease 〔quench〕 one's thirst; 《가뭄을》 wet dry weather; be relieved from drought.

해결(解決) solution; settlement. ~하다 solve; settle. ¶원만한 ~ an amicable settlement / 외교로 국제 분쟁을 ~하다 settle an international dispute by diplomacy. ∥ ~법 a solution; a way out(~법을 찾다 find〔work out〕 a solution 《to》) / ~조건 terms of settlement / ~책 the means of solving 《a problem》.

해고(解雇) discharge; dismissal; a layoff(일시적인). ~하다 dismiss; discharge; fire; lay 《a person》 off. ¶ ~당하다 be 〔get〕 dismissed 〔discharged〕; be fired; be laid off. ∥ ~수당 a dismissal allowance; severance pay / ~통지 a dismissal notice / 정리 ~ forced 〔mandatory〕 retirement / 집단 ~ a mass dismissal.

해골(骸骨) ① 〔전신〕 a skeleton. ② 〔머리〕 a skull; the cranium.

해괴(駭怪) ¶ ~한 strange; queer; outrageous; monstrous; scandalous / ~망측하다 be extremely outrageous〔scandalous〕.

해구(海狗) ☞ 물개. ∥ ~신 the penis of a sea bear.

해구(海溝) 〖地〗 a deep; an oceanic trench〔deep〕.

해군(海軍) the navy; the naval forces. ¶ ~의 naval. ∥ ~기지 a naval base / ~사관학교 the Naval Academy / ~성(省) 〔미〕

해금 the Department of the Navy; the Navy Department / ~ 참모총장 the Chief of Naval Operations (생략 C.N.O.).

해금(奚琴) a Korean fiddle.

해금(解禁) lifting of the ban; the opening 《of the shooting〔fishing〕 season》. ‖ ~기(期) an open season.

해기(海技) ‖ ~사 면허증 a certificate of competency in seamanship.

해낙낙하다 (be) satisfied; pleased; contented.

해난(海難) a disaster at sea; a shipwreck; a shipping casualty. ‖ ~ 구조 sea rescue; salvage / ~구조선 a salvage boat / ~사고 a marine accident / ~심판 a marine accident inquiry.

해내다 ① 《수행·성취》 carry out 〔through〕; accomplish; achieve; perform. ¶ 맡은 일을 ~ perform the work assigned one / 우리는 해냈다 We made it ! ② 《이겨내다》 get the better of 《a person》; put 〔talk〕 《a person》 down.

해넘이 sunset; sundown 《美》.

해녀(海女) a woman diver. ¶ 진주 캐는 ~ a woman pearl diver.

해단(解團) disbanding. ~ 하다 disband. ‖ ~식 the ceremony of disbanding.

해달(海獺) [動] a sea otter.

해답(解答) an answer 〔a solution〕 《to a problem》. ~ 하다 answer; solve. ¶ 모범 ~ a model answer / 시험 문제의 ~ answers to examination questions. ‖ ~용지 an answer sheet / ~자 a solver; an answerer.

해당(該當) ~ 하다 come 〔fall〕 under 《Article 7》; be applicable to; correspond 《to》; fulfill. ¶ 조건에 ~ 하다 meet 〔fit, satisfy〕 the requirements / 이 경우에 ~ 되는 규칙은 없다 This case comes under no rule. or There's no rule that applies to this case.

해당화(海棠花) [植] a sweetbrier.

해대다 attack; go at.

해도(海圖) a chart.

해독(害毒) evil; poison; harm. ¶ ~을 끼치다 poison 〔corrupt〕 《society》; exert a harmful influence 《on society》.

해독(解毒) ~ 하다 counteract 〔neutralize〕 the poison. ‖ ~제(劑) an antidote; a toxicide; a counterpoison.

해독(解讀) decipherment. ~ 하다 decipher; make out. ¶ 암호를 ~ 하다 decode a code.

해돋이 sunrise; sunup 《美》.

해동(解凍) thawing. ~ 하다 thaw.

해독(解得) ~ 하다 understand; comprehend; grasp 《the meaning》.

해드리다 ☞ 해어드리다.

해로(海路) a sea route; a seaway. ¶ ~로 by sea 〔water〕.

해로(偕老) ~ 하다 grow old together. ¶ 백년의 가약을 맺다 be united as husband and wife for weal or woe.

해롭다(害─) (be) injurious; harmful; bad. ¶ 건강에 해로운 bad for the health; injurious to health.

해류(海流) a current; an ocean current. ‖ ~도(圖) a current chart.

해륙(海陸) land and sea. ¶ ~ 양면 작전 amphibious operations / ~ 양서 동물 an amphibian.

해리(海里) a nautical 〔sea〕 mile (1,852m).

해리(海狸) [動] a beaver.

해리(解離) [化] dissociation. ~ 하다 dissociate. ‖ ~압(壓) dissociation pressure.

해마(海馬) [魚] a sea horse; [動] a walrus.

해마다 every year; annually; yearly; year after year.

해머 a hammer. ‖ ~ 던지기 hammer throwing.

해먹 a hammock; a hanging bed.

해먹다 《횡령하다》 take unjust possession of 《something》; embezzle. ¶ 은행의 돈을 ~ embezzle money from a bank.

해면(海面) the surface of the sea; the sea level. ‖ ~온도 (a) sea-surface temperature.

해면(海綿) a sponge. ¶ ~질 〔모양〕의 spongy. ‖ ~동물 the Poriferan / ~조직 spongy tissue / ~체 spongy body.

해명(解明) ~ 하다 make 《a mystery》 clear; elucidate 《the meaning》. ¶ 진상 ~ 에 나서다 set about uncovering the truth.

해몽(解夢) ~ 하다 interpret a dream. ‖ ~가 a dream reader.

해무(海霧) a sea fog; a fog on the sea.

해묵다 《물건이》 get a year old; age a year; 《일이》 drag on for a year. ¶ 〔해〕묵은 쌀 rice of the previous year's crop.

해묵히다 《물건을》 let 《a thing》 get to be a year old; 《일을》 let work drag on for a year without getting finished.

해물(海物) ☞ 해산물.

해미 a thick sea fog.

해바라기 [植] a sunflower.

해박(該博) ~ 하다 (be) profound; erudite; extensive. ¶ ~한 지식 profound 〔extensive〕 knowledge.

해발(海拔) (300 meters) (height) above the sea (level).

해방(解放) liberation; emancipation. ~하다 liberate; emancipate; set free; release (*a person from*). ¶ 빈곤으로부터의 ~ freedom from poverty / 노예의 ~을 선언하다 proclaim the release of the slaves. ‖ ~감 a sense (feeling) of freedom (liberation) / ~전쟁(운동) a liberation war (movement).

해법(解法) a (key to) solution.

해변(海邊) the beach; the seashore; the coast.

해병(海兵) a marine. ‖ ~대 a marine corps / ~대원 a marine; a leatherneck 《美俗》.

해보다 try; have (make) a try (*at*); attempt (*to do*); make an attempt (*to do*). ¶ 다시 한번 ~ try again; make another attempt / 도망치려고 ~ make an attempt to run away.

해부(解剖) anatomy; 〔생물체의〕 dissection; 〔시체의〕 autopsy; 〔분석〕 analysis. ~하다 dissect; hold an autopsy (*on*); 〔분석하다〕 analyze. ¶ 유체를 ~하도록 내놓다 submit a dead body for an autopsy / 아무의 심리를 ~하다 analyze *a person's* psychology. ‖ ~도(圖) an anatomical chart / ~실(臺) a dissecting room (table) / ~학 anatomy / ~학자 an anatomist.

해빙(解氷) thawing. ~하다 thaw. ‖ ~기 the thawing season.

해사(海事) maritime affairs (matters).

해사하다 (be) clean and fair.

해산(海産), 해산물(海産物) marine products. ¶ ~물 상인 a dealer in marine products.

해산(解産) childbirth; delivery. ~하다 give birth to (*a child*); be delivered of (*a baby*).

해산(解散) 〔회합의〕 breakup; dispersion; 〔군대의〕 disbandment; 〔의회 따위의〕 dissolution. ~하다 break up; disperse; disband; dissolve. ¶ 강제 ~ compulsory winding-up / ~을 명하다 order (*a crowd*) to break up; order (*an organization*) to be disbanded. ‖ ~권(의회에 대한) the right to dissolve (*the House*).

해삼(海蔘) 〔動〕 a trepang; a sea cucumber (slug).

해상(海上) ~의 marine; maritime; on the sea / ~에서 폭풍을 만나다 be overtaken by a storm at sea. ‖ ~근무 sea service; sea duty / ~법 the maritime law / ~보급로 a maritime supply route / ~보험 marine insurance / ~봉쇄 blockade at sea / ~생활 a seafaring life / ~수송(운송) marine transportation / ~징찰기 a maritime patrol aircraft (생략 MPA).

해상(海床) the sea floor.

해상력(解像力) resolution; resolving power. ¶ ~이 높은 렌즈 a high resolution lens.

해서(楷書) the square style of writing (Chinese characters).

해석(解析) analysis. ~하다 analyze. ‖ ~기하학 analytic geometry.

해석(解釋) (an) interpretation;〔법률 어구 등의〕 a construction;〔설명〕 (an) explanation. ~하다 interpret; construe; explain. ¶ ~의 차이 discrepancies of interpretation / ~을 잘못하다 misinterpret / 선의(악의)로 ~하다 put a good (bad) interpretation on (*what one has said*); take (*a person's words*) in good (bad) faith; interpret (*a person's action*) favorably (unfavorably).

해설(解說) (an) explanation; (a) commentary; (an) interpretation. ~하다 comment on (*the news*); interpret; explain. ¶ 뉴스 ~ a news commentary. ‖ ~자 a commentator / 뉴스~자 a news commentator.

해소(解消) dissolution; cancellation. ~하다 dissolve; cancel; annul; break off. ¶ 불만을 〔스트레스를〕 ~하다 get rid of discontent (stress) / 교통 정체를 ~시키다 solve the (problem of) traffic congestion.

해손(海損) sea damage;〔保險〕 an average. ‖ ~계약(계약서) an average agreement (bond) / ~정산(정산서, 정산인) an average adjustment (statement, adjuster) / ~조합 an average clause.

해수(咳嗽) a cough. ☞ 기침.

해수(海水) sea (salt) water.

해수욕(海水浴) sea bathing. ~하다 bathe in the sea. ‖ ~객 a sea bather / ~장 a swimming beach; a (sea) bathing resort.

해시계(-計) a sundial.

해식(海蝕) erosion by seawater.

해신(海神) the sea-god;〔로신〕 Neptune;〔그신〕 Poseidon.

해쓱하다 (be) pale; pallid; wan. ¶ 해쓱해지다 turn pale (white).

해악(害惡) evil; harm;〔악영향〕 an evil influence (effect). ¶ ~을 끼치다 have a harmful influence (*on*).

해안(海岸) the seashore; the coast; the seaside; the beach. ¶ ~에(서) on the shore; by (at) the seaside / ~의 별장 a

seaside villa; a villa by the seaside / ~을 산책하다 take a walk along the beach [seashore]. ∥ ~경비 coast defense / ~경비대 the coast guard / ~선 a coastline / ~포대 shore [coast] batteries.

해약(解約) cancellation of a contract. ~하다 cancel [break] a contract. ¶ ~ 보험을 ~하다 cancel an insurance contract / 정기예금을 ~하다 cancel a time deposit. ∥ ~금 a cancellation fee.

해양(海洋) the ocean; the sea(s). ∥ ~경찰청 the National Maritime Police Agency / ~관측위성 a marine observation satellite / ~목장 a marine ranch / ~성기후 oceanic climate / ~소설 a sea story / ~수산부 the Ministry of Oceans and Fisheries / ~식물 an oceanophyte / ~오염 sea contamination; marine pollution / ~온도차 발전(power generation by) ocean thermal energy conversion / ~자원 resources of the sea; marine resources / ~학 oceanography.

해어드리다 wear away (down).

해어지다 wear (be worn) out; become threadbare. ¶ 다 해어진 worn-out; threadbare; frayed / 너덜너덜 ~ be worn to rags.

해역(海域) a sea [an ocean] area.

해연(海淵) [地] an abyss.

해열(解熱) ~하다 alleviate fever; bring down one's fever. ∥ ~제 an antifebrile; a febrifuge; an antipyretic.

해오라기, 해오리 [鳥] a white heron.

해왕성(海王星) [天] Neptune.

해외(海外) foreign [overseas] countries. ¶ ~의 overseas; foreign / ~로 abroad; overseas / ~로 나가다 go abroad / ~에서 돌아오다 return from abroad / 군대를 ~로 파견하다 send an army abroad [overseas] / ~공관 a diplomatic office in the foreign country / ~근무 overseas service / ~무역 foreign trade / ~방송 overseas [international] broadcasting / ~시장 overseas [foreign] markets / ~여행 an overseas trip; foreign travel / ~이민 emigration / ~지점 an overseas office / ~진출 the advance (of Korean exports) into overseas markets; starting up overseas activities (by Korean firms) / ~투자 foreign investment.

해우(海牛) [動] a sea cow; a manatee; a dugong.

해운(海運) shipping; marine transportation. ∥ ~업 the shipping industry [business] / ~업자 a shipping agent; shipping interests(총칭).

해원(海員) a seaman; a sailor; a crew(총칭). ∥ ~숙박소 a sailor's [seamen's] home.

해이(解弛) relaxation; slackening. ~하다 relax; get loose; slacken; grow lax. ¶ 기강이 ~하다 discipline slackens [grows lax].

해일(海溢) a 「tidal wave(tsunami).

해임(解任) dismissal; discharge. ~하다 release (a person) from office; relieve (a person) of his post; dismiss. ¶ 대통령은 교육부 장관을 ~했다 The President dismissed the Education Minister.

해자(垓子) a moat.

해장 ~하다 chase a hangover with a drink. ¶ ~국 a broth to chase a hangover / ~술 alcohol used as a hangover chaser.

해저(海底) the bottom [bed] of the sea; the ocean floor [bed]. ¶ ~에 가라앉다 sink [go down] to the bottom of the sea. ∥ ~유전 a submarine oil field / ~자원 sea bottom resources / ~전선 [화산] a submarine cable [volcano] / ~터널 a submarine [undersea] tunnel.

해적(海賊) a pirate. ¶ ~질을 하다 commit piracy. ∥ ~선 a pirate ship / ~판 a pirate edition(책의) / ~행위 (an act of) piracy.

해전(海戰) a naval battle; a sea fight; naval warfare(총칭).

해제(解除) cancellation; lifting; release. ~하다 cancel; remove; lift; release (a person) from. ¶ 금지령을 ~하다 lift [remove] a ban (on) / 책임을 ~하다 release (a person) from his responsibility / 계약을 ~하다 cancel [annul] a contract.

해제(解題) a bibliographical introduction [explanation]. ∥ ~자 a bibliographer.

해조(害鳥) an injurious bird.

해조(海鳥) a sea bird; a seafowl.

해조(海藻) [植] seaweeds; marine plants; seaware(비료용).

해주다 do (something) for another; do as a favor. ¶ 편지를 번역 ~ translate a letter (for a person).

해중(海中) ¶ ~의 submarine; in the sea / ~공원 an undersea park.

해지다 ☞ 해어지다.

해직(解職) dismissal; discharge. ~하다 dismiss [release] (a person) from office; relieve (a person) of his post. ¶ ~당하다 be dismissed; be removed from

해질녘 (at) sunset; (toward) sundown. ¶ ~에 toward nightfall (evening).

해체 (解體) ~하다 take (pull) 《*a thing*》 to pieces; dismantle 《*an engine*》; pull down 《*a building*》; scrap 《*a ship*》; 《조직을》 dissolve; disorganize; disband. ¶ 거대 재벌을 ~하다 dissolve (break up) a great financial conglomerate.

해초 (海草) ☞ 해조 (海藻).

해충 (害蟲) a harmful (an injurious) insect; vermin (총칭).

해치다 (害一) harm; hurt; impair; damage. ¶ 건강을 ~ injure *one's* health.

해치우다 finish up; get 《*it*》 done; 《죽이다》 kill; finish off.

해커 a (computer) hacker.

해탈 (解脫) deliverance (of *one's* soul); (Buddhistic) salvation. ~하다 be delivered from 《*worldly passions*》; emancipate *oneself* from all worldly desires and worries.

해태 (海苔) laver.

해파리 〔動〕 a jellyfish; a medusa.

해하다 (害一) ☞ 해치다.

해학 (諧謔) a joke; a jest; humor. ¶ ~적인 humorous; witty. ∥ ~가 a humorist; a joker / ~소설 a humorous story.

해해거리다 keep laughing playfully (in fun).

해협 (海峽) a strait; a channel. ¶ ~을 건너다 cross a strait (channel). ∥ 대한 ~ the Straits of Korea / 도버 ~ the Straits of Dover.

해후 (邂逅) ~하다 meet by chance; chance to meet; come across 《*a person*》.

핵 (核) ① a kernel; a core; a stone (과실의). ② a nucleus (원자핵). ~의 nuclear 《*umbrella*》. ∥ ~가족 a nuclear family / ~공격 a nuclear attack / ~군축 〔동결〕 nuclear disarmament (freeze) / ~균형 nuclear parity / ~대피소 a fallout (nuclear) shelter; a nuclear bomb shelter / ~무기 a nuclear weapon / ~무장 nuclear armament 《~무장하다 be armed with nuclear weapons》 / ~미사일 a nuclear missile / ~반응 nuclear reaction / ~보유국 a nuclear power 《state》 / ~분열〔융합〕 nuclear fission (fusion) / ~시설 nuclear facilities / ~실험 (금지협정) a nuclear test (ban agreement) / ~안전협정 the nuclear safeguard accord / ~연료 nuclear fuel / ~의학 nuclear medicine / ~전략 nuclear strategy / ~전쟁 a nuclear war / ~탄두 a nuclear warhead / ~폭발 (실험) a nuclear explosion (test) / ~폭탄 a nuclear bomb / ~협정 a nuclear accord / ~확산 방지 조약 the nuclear nonproliferation treaty (pact) / 비~무장 지대 a nuclear(-)free zone.

핵과 (核果) a stone fruit; a drupe.

핵산 (核酸) 〔生〕 nucleic acid. ¶ 리보~ ribonucleic acid (생략 RNA).

핵심 (核心) the core; a kernel. ¶ 문제의 ~ the heart (kernel) of a question.

핵우산 (核雨傘) the 《*U.S.*》 nuclear umbrella.

핵질 (核質) 〔生〕 nucleoplasm; karyoplasm.

핵폐기물 (核廢棄物) nuclear waste. ∥ ~처리 nuclear waste disposal / ~처리장 a nuclear waste dump site.

핸드백 a handbag; a vanity bag.

핸드볼 〔競〕 handball. ¶ ~을 하다 play handball.

핸들 a handle; a wheel (자동차의); a handle bar (자전거의); a knob (도어의).

핸디캡 a handicap. ¶ ~을 주다 handicap.

핼쑥하다 have a bad complexion; look pale (unwell).

햄 《고기》 ham. ∥ ~샐러드 ham and salad.

햄버거 a hamburger.

햄버그스테이크 a hamburg(er) steak.

햅쌀 new rice; the year's new crop of rice. ¶ ~밥 rice cooked from the new crop.

햇‥‥ new. ¶ ~곡식 a new crop of the year.

햇무리 the halo of the sun. ∥ ~구름 a cirrostratus.

햇볕 the heat of the sunlight (sunbeams); the sun. ¶ ~에 타다 get sunburnt / ~에 말리다 dry 《*a thing*》 in the sun.

햇빛 sunshine; sunlight. ¶ ~에 쬐다 expose 《*a thing*》 to the sun.

햇살 sunbeams; sunlight.

햇수 (-數) the number of years.

행 (幸) happiness. ¶ ~인지 불행인지 for good or for evil.

‥‥행 (行) 《가는 곳》 bound for; for 《*Seoul*》 / 수원~ a train for Suwon.

행각 (行脚) 《돌아다님》 traveling on foot; 〔佛〕 a pilgrimage. ~하다 travel on foot; go on a pilgrimage. ¶ 사기 ~을 하다 commit a fraud; practice a deception.

행간 (行間) (leave) space between lines.

행군 (行軍) a march. ~하다 march. ¶ 강~ a forced march.

행글라이더 a hang glider. ¶ ~로 날다 hang-glide.

행낭(行囊) a mail bag (sack) 《美》; a postbag 《英》.

행동(行動) (an) action; conduct; (a) movement; behavior. ~ 하다 act; behave (*oneself*); conduct (*oneself*); take action; make a ~. ¶ 직접(자유) ~ direct (free) action / ~ 을 같이하다 act in concert (*with*) / ~에 옮기다 carry out / ~ 적인 사람 an active person; a man of action. ‖ ~방침 a course of action / ~주의 behaviorism.

행동거지(行動擧止) bearing; manner.

행동대(行動隊) an action corps (group). ¶ 청년 ~ a youth's action group.

행락(行樂) an excursion; a picnic; an outing; pleasure-(holiday)making. ¶ ~객(客) a holidaymaker; a hiker / ~지(地) a holiday (pleasure, picnic) resort.

행렬(行列) 《행진》 a procession; a parade; a queue (차례를 기다리는 사람의); 《數》 matrix. ¶ 장의 ~ a funeral procession / 제등 ~ a lantern procession. ‖ ~식《數》 determinant.

행로(行路) a path; a road; a course. ¶ 인생 ~ the course (path) of life.

행방(行方) the place (where) one has gone; *one's* whereabouts; *one's* traces. ¶ ~을 감추다 disappear; cover *one's* traces.

행방불명(行方不明) ~ 이 되다 be missing; be lost / 그는 아직도 ~이다 He is still missing. ‖ ~자 the missing.

행복(幸福) happiness; 《행운》 good luck (fortune). ¶ ~한 happy; fortunate; blissful / 더없이 ~한 as happy as a king; as happy as can be / ~하게 살다 lead (live) a happy life; live happily.

행불행(幸不幸) happiness or misery. ¶ 인생의 ~ the lights (ups) and shadows (downs) of life.

행사(行使) ~ 하다 use; make use of; exercise (*one's rights*). ¶ 묵비권을 ~ 하다 use *one's* right to keep silent / 무력을 ~ 하다 use force; take military action; resort to arms.

행사(行事) an event; a function. ¶ 연례 ~ the year's regular function; an annual event.

행상(行商) 《행위》 peddling; hawking; 《사람》 a peddler 《美》; a pedlar 《英》. ~ 하다 peddle; hawk.

행색(行色) 《차림새》 appearance; 《태도》 demeanor; attitude. ¶ ~이 초라하다 look shabby.

행서(行書) 《서체》 a cursive style of writing (Chinese characters).

행선지(行先地) *one's* destination; the place where *one* is going.

행성(行星) 【天】 a planet. ¶ ~의 planetary / 대 ~ a major planet / 소 ~ a minor planet.

행세(行世) ~ 하다 conduct *oneself*; behave; 《가장》 assume (put on) an air (*of*). ¶ 백만장자 ~를 하다 pose as a millionaire.

행세(行勢) ~ 하다 wield (exercise) power (influence). ¶ ~ 하는 집안 a distinguished (an influential) family.

행수(行數) the number of lines.

행실(行實) behavior; conduct; manners. ¶ ~이 나쁜 사람 a man of bad conduct.

행여(幸-), **행여나**(幸-) by chance; possibly.

행운(幸運) good fortune (luck). ¶ ~의 fortunate; lucky / ~을 빕니다 I wish you the best of luck. *or* Good luck! ‖ ~아 a lucky person; a fortune's favorite.

행원(行員) a bank clerk (employee).

행위(行爲) 《행동》 an act; an action; a deed; 《처신》 behavior; conduct. ¶ 불법 ~ an illegal (unlawful) act / 법률 ~ a juristic act. ‖ ~ 능력 legal capacity / ~자 a doer; a performer (*of a deed*).

행인(行人) a passer-by; a passer. ¶ 거리엔 ~의 발길이 끊어졌다 The street is deserted. *or* There is not a soul to be seen on the street.

행장(行裝) a traveling suit (outfit). ¶ ~을 챙기다 prepare (outfit) *oneself* for a journey / ~을 풀다 take off *one's* traveling attire; 《숙박하다》 check in at a hotel 《美》.

행적(行蹟) the achievements of *one's* lifetime; *one's* work (contributions).

행정(行政) administration. ¶ 그는 ~적 수완이 있다 He has administrative ability. ‖ ~개혁 (an) administrative reform / ~관 an executive officer; an administrative official; ~관청 a government (an administrative) office / ~구역 an administrative district (section) / ~기관 an administrative organ (body) / ~명령 an administrative (executive) order / ~법 administrative law / ~서사 an administrative scrivener / ~소송 administrative litigation / ~지도 administrative guidance / ~처분 administra-

행정 (行政) a journey; distance(거리); an itinerary(여정).
행주 a dishcloth; a dishtowel. ¶ ~(를) 치다 wipe with a dishcloth. ‖ ~치마 an apron.
행진 (行進) a march; a parade. ~하다 march; parade; proceed. ‖ ~곡 a march / 결혼(장송)~곡 a wedding(funeral) march.
행차 (行次) ~하다 go; come; visit.
행패 (行悖) misconduct; misbehavior. ¶ ~를 부리다 resort to violence; commit an outrage.
행하 (行下) a tip; gratuity.
행하다 (行一) 《行》 act; do; 《처신》behave 〈conduct, carry〉 oneself; 《실행》 carry out; perform; practice; execute(명령대로); fulfill (약속 따위); commit(나쁜 짓을); 《거행》 observe; celebrate.
향 (香) (an) incense. ¶ ~을 피우다 burn incense.
향교 (鄕校) a local Confucian school.
향군 (鄕軍) ① ☞ 재향 군인. ② ☞ 향토 예비군.
향긋하다 (be) somewhat fragrant; have a faint sweet odor.
향기 (香氣) (a) scent; a sweet odor; fragrance; an aroma; a perfume. ‖ 국화의 ~ the scent of chrysanthemums.
향기롭다 (香氣一) (be) sweet; sweetsmelling〔-scented〕; fragrant; aromatic. ¶ 향기로운 냄새 a sweet〔fragrant〕 odor.
향나무 (香一) a Chinese juniper.
향내 (香一) ☞ 향기. ¶ ~ 나는 sweet; fragrant; sweet-scented.
향년 (享年) one's age at death. ¶ ~ 칠십 세다 He died at the age of 70.
향도 (嚮導) 《사람》 a guide(leader).
향락 (享樂) enjoyment. ~하다 enjoy; seek pleasure (in). ¶ ~적인 pleasure-seeking. ‖ ~주의 epicurism; hedonism / ~주의자 an epicurean; a hedonist.
향로 (香爐) an incense burner; a (bronze) censer.
향료 (香料) ① 《식품의》 (a) spice; spicery. ② 《화장품 따위의》 (a) perfume; perfumery; (총칭) an aromatic.
향리 (鄕里) one's (old) home; one's birthplace (native town).
향미 (香味) flavor. ‖ ~료 spices; seasoning.
향방 (向方) a direction(방위); a course; one's destination (목적지).
향배 (向背) for or against; pro or con.
향불 (香一) an incense fire; burning incense. ¶ ~을 피우다 burn incense.

향사 (向斜) 〔地〕 a syncline.
향상 (向上) elevation; rise; improvement. ~하다 rise; be elevated; become higher; progress; improve; advance. ¶ 여성의 사회적 지위 ~ the rise in women's social status / 젊은이들의 체위 ~ improvement in the physique of young people. ‖ ~심 aspiration; ambition.
향수 (享受) enjoyment. ~하다 enjoy.
향수 (享壽) ~하다 enjoy old age; live to a ripe old age.
향수 (香水) a perfume; a scent; scented water. ¶ 몸에 ~를 뿌리다 perfume oneself. ‖ ~뿌리개 a scent sprayer; a perfume atomizer.
향수 (鄕愁) homesickness; nostalgia. ¶ ~를 느끼다 feel homesick.
향습성 (向濕性) 〔植〕 positive hydrotropism.
향연 (饗宴) a feast; a banquet. ¶ ~을 베풀다 hold a banquet.
향유 (享有) ~하다 enjoy; possess; participate (in). ¶ 자유를 ~할 권리 the right to enjoy liberty.
향유 (香油) 《참기름》 sesame oil.
향유고래 (香油一) 〔動〕 a sperm whale; a cachalot.
향응 (饗應) an entertainment; a banquet; a treat. ~하다 entertain 〈a person at〔to〕 dinner〉; treat 〈a person to〉; give〔hold〕 a party 〈for a person〉.
향일성 (向日性) 〔植〕 (positive) heliotropism.
향지성 (向地性) 〔植〕 (positive) geotropism.
향토 (鄕土) one's native place (district); one's birthplace(hometown). ‖ ~문학〔음악〕 folk literature〔music〕 / ~색 local color 〈~색 짙은 rich in local color〉 / ~예비군 the homeland reserve forces / ~예술 folk art.
향하다 (向一) ① 《대하다》 face; front; look(out) on. ¶ 바다를 ~〔집이〕 look out on the sea. ② 《지향해 가다》 go to〔toward〕; leave〔start〕 for; head for. ¶ 향하여 for; toward; in the direction of / 한국을 떠나 미국으로 ~ leave Korea for America / 승리를 향하여 전진하다 go ahead to victory.
향학심 (向學心) desire for learning; love of learning; a desire to learn; intellectual appetite. ¶ ~에 불타다 burn with the desire for learning.
향후 (向後) hereafter; henceforth; from now on; in future.
허 (虛) an unguarded position (moment); unpreparedness; a

허가 weak point. ¶ 적의 ~를 찌르다 make a surprise attack on the enemy; take the enemy unawares / ~를 찔리다 be caught off (one's) guard / ~를 틈타다 take advantage of (a person's) unpreparedness.

허가(許可) permission; leave; approval(인가); licence (면허); admission(입학·입장). ~하다 permit; give leave; license, allow (면허); admit(입장을). ¶ ~를 얻어 by permission of / ~ 없이 without permission / 외출 ~를 얻다 get leave (permission) to go out / ~를 얻어 영업하다 do business under license. ‖ ~제(制) a license system / ~증(證) a permit; a written permission: a

허겁지겁 ☞ 허둥지둥.

허공(虛空) the empty air; empty space; (공중) the air; the sky.

허구(虛構) a lie; a fabrication; a fiction; a falsehood; an invention. ¶ ~의 made-up; false; fabricated; invented; fictitious / 그 이야기는 순전히 ~이다 The story is pure fiction.

허구렁 an empty hollow; a pit.

허구하다(許久―) be very long; be a very long time. ¶ 허구한 세월을 덧없이 보내다 spend many long years in vain.

허기(虛飢) an empty stomach; hunger. ¶ ~를 느끼다 feel hungry / ~를 달래다 appease (alleviate) one's hunger.

허깨비 《환영》 a phantom; a ghost; 《환상》 a vision; an illusion.

허니문 a honeymoon.

허다하다(許多―) (be) numerous; many; innumerable; frequent; common. ¶ 허다한 학생 중에 among so many students.

허덕거리다 ① (숨이 차) pant; gasp for breath; (지쳐서) be exhausted; be tired out. ② (애쓰다) struggle; make frantic efforts; strive wildly.

허두(虛頭) (첫머리) the beginning; the opening (of a speech).

허둥거리다 fluster oneself; be all in a flurry; be confused.

허둥지둥 in a flurry; in hot haste; helter-skelter; hurry-scurry. ¶ ~ 달아나다 run away in a flurry.

허드레 odds and ends. ¶ ~꾼 an odd(-job) man; an odd-jobber / 허드렛물 water for sundry uses / 허드렛일 odd jobs; a trifling job.

허들 a hurdle. ‖ ~레이스 a hurdle race.

허락(許諾) (승인) consent; assent; approval; sanction; (허가) per-

허물었다 mission; permit; leave. ~하다 consent to; give consent to; approve; permit; allow; admit (입학 따위를). ¶ ~를 얻어 with a person's permission / ~ 없이 without a person's permission).

허랑방탕(虛浪放蕩) ~하다 (be) loose; profligate; dissolute.

허례(虛禮) formalities; formal courtesy; empty forms. ¶ ~를 없애다 dispense with formalities. ‖ ~허식 (虛飾) (formalities and) vanity.

허룩하다 (be) almost empty.

허름하다 ① (낡아서) (be) old; shabby. ¶ 허름한 옷 a shabby clothes. ② (값이) (be) cheap; low-priced; inexpensive.

허리 ① the waist; the loin. ¶ ~가 날씬하다 have a supple [slender] waist. ② (옷의) the waist.

허리띠 a belt; a girdle; a (waist) band; belting (총칭). ¶ ~를 매다 (풀다) tie (untie) a belt.

허리춤 inside the waist of one's trousers.

허리케인 《氣》 a hurricane.

허리자 a waist measure.

허릿매 the waistline.

허망(虛妄) ~하다 (be) vain; false; untrue; groundless.

허무(虛無) nothingness; nihility. ~하다 (be) empty; vain; nonexistent. ¶ ~하게 to no purpose; in vain. ‖ ~감 a sense of futility / ~주의 nihilism / ~주의자 a nihilist.

허무맹랑하다(虛無孟浪―) (be) fabulous; empty; groundless; false; unreliable. ¶ 허무맹랑한 소문 a groundless rumor.

허물[1] (살가죽) the skin; a slough (뱀 따위의).

허물[2] (잘못) a fault; a mistake; an error; a misdeed; a blame. ¶ ~을 용서하다 forgive (a person) for his fault / ~을 뉘우치다 repent one's error.

허물다 demolish; pull (take, tear) down; destroy. ¶ 오래된 집들을 ~ demolish (pull down) old houses.

허물 벗다[1] (뱀 따위가) cast off the skin; slough (off, away); exuviate.

허물 벗다[2] (누명 벗다) clear oneself of a false charge.

허물어지다 collapse; fall (break) down; crumble (벽 따위); give way (다리 따위); be destroyed. ¶ 허물어져 가는 낡은 성 a crumbling old castle / 담의 일부가 허물어졌다 Part of the wall broke down.

허물없다 be on familiar [friendly] terms; (be) unceremonious;

허밍 humming.
허방짚다 miscalculate.
허벅다리 a thigh.
허벅지 the inside of the thigh.
허비(虛費) waste. ~하다 waste; cast (throw) away. ¶ 시간을 ~하다 waste *one's* time; idle away *one's* time.
허사(虛事) a vain attempt; a failure. ¶ ~로 돌아가다 come to nothing (naught); end in failure.
허상(虛像) 【理】 a virtual image.
허섭스레기 odd ends (bits); trash.
허세(虛勢) a bluff; bluster; a false show of power (strength, courage). ¶ ~를 부리다 bluff; make a show of power / ~를 부리는 사람 a bluffer; a swaggerer.
허송세월(虛送歲月) ~하다 waste time; idle *one's* time away.
허수(虛數) 【數】 an imaginary number.
허수아비 a scarecrow; 《사람》 a dummy; a puppet.
허술하다 ① 《초라하다》 (be) shabby; poor-looking; worn-out. ¶ 허술한 옷 shabby clothes. ② 《허점이 있다》 (be) lax; loose; careless.
허스키 (in) a husky voice.
허식(虛飾) show; display; ostentation; affectation; vanity. ¶ ~적인 showy; ostentatious / ~ 없는 unaffected; plain / ~을 좋아하다 love stand play; be fond of display.
허실(虛實) truth and falsehood.
허심탄회(虛心坦懷) ~하다 (be) open-minded; frank; candid. ¶ ~하게 with an open mind; candidly; frankly; without reserve.
허약(虛弱) ~하다 (be) weak; sickly; frail; feeble. ¶ 몸이 ~하다 have a weak constitution. ‖ ~자 a weakly (an infirm) person.
허언(虛言) a lie; a falsehood.
허여멀겋다, 허여멀쑥하다 (be) nice and fair; have a fair complexion.
허영(虛榮) vanity; vainglory. ¶ ~ 때문에 for vanity's sake. ‖ ~심 vanity / ~심이 강한 vain; vainglorious).
허옇다 (be) very white. ☞ 하얗다.
허욕(虛慾) vain ambitions; false desires; avarice; greed. ¶ ~ 많은 greedy; avaricious.
허용(許容) permission; allowance; tolerance; ¶ ~하다 permit; allow; tolerate. ¶ 방사능의 최대 ~ 선량(線量) the maximum permissible dose of radiation. ‖ ~량 a permissible (tolerable) amount / ~범위 a permissible range / ~오차 an allowable (a permissible) error / ~한도 a tolerance (an acceptable) limit.
허우대 a fine tall figure.
허울 (a nice) appearance; exterior. ¶ ~만 좋은 물건 a gimcrack / ~뿐이다 be not so good as *it* looks; be deceptive.
허위(虛僞) a lie; a falsehood. ¶ ~의 false; sham; fictitious; feigned. ¶ ~보고 (신고) a false report (return) / ~진술 misrepresentation.
허위단심 making strenuous efforts. ¶ ~으로 with great efforts.
허위적거리다 struggle; wriggle; flounder; squirm.
허장성세(虛張聲勢) bravado and bluster. ¶ ~하다 indulge in bravado and bluster.
허전하다 feel empty; miss 《something》; feel lonesome.
허점(虛點) a blind point (spot); a weak point. ¶ ~을 노리다 watch for an unguarded moment; try to catch 《a person》 napping; 《법의》 find a loophole in the law.
허청거리다 be unsteady on *one's* feet; feel weak at *one's* knees.
허탈(虛脫) 【醫】 (physical) collapse; lethargy (무기력). ¶ ~하다 collapse; be atrophied (prostrated). ‖ ~감 despondency / ~상태 a state of lethargy (stupor).
허탕 lost (fruitless) labor; vain effort. ¶ ~ 치다 labor (work) in vain; come to nothing; make vain efforts.
허투루 carelessly; roughly; negligently; in a slovenly way. ¶ ~ 보다 hold 《a person, a matter》 cheap; make light of; think little (nothing) of / ~ 물건을 다루다 handle things roughly.
허튼계집 a loose woman; a slut.
허튼맹세 an idle pledge (vow); an irresponsible oath.
허튼소리, 허튼수작(—酬酌) idle talk (remarks); irresponsible utterance. ¶ ~로 시간을 보내다 pass time in idle talk.
허파 the lungs; lights(소, 양, 돼지의). ¶ ~에 바람이 들다 be giggly (gigglesome); giddy).
허풍(虛風) a brag; a big (tall) talk; exaggeration. ¶ ~(을) 떨다

boast; talk big; brag; exaggerate. ¶ ~선이 a boaster; a braggart; a gasbag.

허하다(虛―) (속이 빔) (be) hollow; empty; vacant; void; (허약) (be) weak; feeble; delicate; frail. ¶ 몸이 ~ be weak in body.

허행(虛行) ~하다 헛걸음하다.

허허벌판 a vast expanse of plains; a wide field.

허혼(許婚) ~하다 consent to (a person's) marriage.

허황(虛荒) ~하다 (be) false; wild; unbelievable; ungrounded; unreliable. ¶ ~된 생각 a fantastic (wild) idea.

헌 old; shabby; worn-out; used; secondhand. ¶ 물건 an old (a used) article / ~ 옷 worn-out clothes.

헌걸차다 《몸이》 (be) strong and sturdy; vigorous and plucky; 《의기가》 (be) in high spirits.

헌것 old (worn-out, secondhand, used) things.

헌계집 a divorced woman; a divorcee; a deflowered girl.

헌금(獻金) a gift of money; a contribution; a donation; 《교회에 하는》 an offering; a collection. ~하다 contribute; donate. ¶ 정치 ~ a political donation. ‖ ~자 a contributor; a donor / ~함 a contribution (collection) box.

헌납(獻納) contribution. ~하다 contribute; donate; offer. ‖ ~자 a contributor; a donor / ~품 an offering; a present; a gift.

헌데 a swelling; a boil; an abscess; an eruption.

헌법(憲法) the constitution. ¶ ~ (상의) constitutional / ~상으로 constitutionally / ~을 제정(개정)하다 establish (revise) a constitution / 대한 민국 ~ the Constitution of the Republic of Korea /성문 (불문) ~ a written (an unwritten) constitution / ~ 제7조 Article 7 of the constitution. / ~위반 a breach of the constitution.

헌병(憲兵) 《육군》 a military policeman; the military police(총칭) (생략 MP); 《해군》 a shore patrolman; the shore patrol(총칭) (생략 SP). ‖ ~대《육군》 the Military Police; 《해군》 the Shore Patrol / ~ 사령관 a provost marshal / ~ 파견대 a detachment of the military police.

헌상(獻上) an offering to a superior. ~하다 offer (present) (a thing) to a superior. ‖ ~품 an offering; a gift.

헌신(獻身) devotion. ~하다 devote (dedicate) oneself (to). ¶ ~적인 devotional / ~적으로 devotedly / 일생을 빈민 구제에 ~하다 devote one's whole life to helping the poor.

헌신짝 a worn-out (an old) shoe. ¶ ~ 처럼 버리다 throw (cast) (a thing) away like an old shoe.

헌옷 old (worn-out, secondhand) clothes.

헌장(憲章) the constitution; the charter. ¶ 대서양 ~ the Atlantic Charter / 대~ 《영국의》 the Magna Carta; the Great Charter / 어린이 ~ the Children's Charter.

헌정(憲政) constitutional government; constitutionalism. ¶ ~의 위기 a constitutional crisis.

헌정(獻呈) ~하다 present (a copy) to (a person); dedicate. ‖ ~본 a presentation (complimentary) copy.

헌책(一冊) a secondhand (used) book. ‖ ~방 a secondhand bookstore.

헌칠하다 (be) tall and handsome; have a well-proportioned figure.

헌혈(獻血) blood donation; donation of blood. ~하다 donate (give) blood. ‖ ~운동 a blood donation campaign / ~자 a blood donor.

헐값(歇―) a giveaway (dirt-cheap, low) price.

헐겁다 (be) loose; loose-fitting. ¶ 이 신발은 좀 ~ These shoes are a little loose.

헐다¹《물건이》get old; become shabby; wear out; be worn-out; 《피부가》get (have) a boil (on); develop a boil.

헐다² ① 《쌓은 것 등을》 destroy; pull (break) down; demolish. ¶ 오래된 건물을 ~ pull down old buildings. ② 《남을》 speak ill of; slander. ③ 《돈을》 break; change.

헐떡거리다 pant; gasp; breathe hard. ¶ 헐떡거리며 between gasps / 그 여인은 가파른 언덕을 헐떡거리며 달려 올라갔다 The lady ran up the steep slope panting.

헐뜯다 slander; defame; pick on (a person) pantingly; speak ill (of). ¶ 뒤에서 남을 ~ speak ill of (a person) behind his back.

헐렁거리다 be loose (-fitting); fit loose. ¶ 헐렁거리는 볼트 a loose bolt. ② 《행동을》 act rashly; be frivolous.

헐렁이 a frivolous person; an unreliable person.

헐렁하다 (be) loose; loose-fitting. ¶ 헐렁한 바지 loose trousers.
헐레벌떡 panting and puffing; out of breath. ¶ ~ 달려가다 run along panting and puffing.
헐리다 be pulled (torn) down; be demolished (destroyed).
헐벗다 be in rags; be poorly (shabbily) clothed; (나무·산이) be bared (stripped). ¶ 헐벗은 아이들 children in rags / 헐벗은 산 a bare (bald) mountain.
헐하다 (歇一) ① (값이) (be) cheap; inexpensive. ¶ 헐하게 사다 buy cheap; buy at a bargain. ② (쉽다) (be) easy; simple; light. ¶ 헐한 일 light work. ③ (벌이) (be) light; lenient. ¶ 헐한 벌 a light (lenient) punishment.
험구 (險口) an evil tongue; slander. ~하다 make blistering remarks; use abusive language; slander; abuse. ‖ ~가 a foul-mouthed person; a slanderer.
험난 (險難) ~하다 (be) rough and difficult; rugged; be full of danger.
험담 (險談) slander; calumny. ~하다 slander; speak ill of; talk scandal (about); backbite. ¶ ~ 잘 하는 사람 a scandalmonger; a backbiter.
험상궂다. 험상스럽다 (險狀一) (be) sinister; rugged, grim, savage-looking. ¶ 험상스러운 얼굴 a grim face; a sinister countenance.
험악하다 (險惡一) ① (위험) (be) dangerous; perilous; (사태가) (be) serious; critical; grave; (날씨가) (be) threatening; stormy; (험준) (be) rugged. ¶ 험악한 표정 a grim (stern) expression / 날씨가 매우 ~ The sky looks very threatening. / 사태가 매우 험악해 졌다 The situation has become serious.
험준하다 (險峻一) (be) steep; precipitous; rugged. ¶ 험준한 산길 a steep (rugged) mountain road.
험하다 (險一) ① (산길 따위가) (be) rugged; steep; perilous. ② (날씨 따위) (be) foul; stormy; rough. ③ (표정 따위) (be) sinister; grim; savage-looking. ④ (상태가) (be) critical; serious. ⑤ (생태가) grave; grim.
헙수룩하다 (머리털이) (be) shaggy; (옷차림이) (be) shabby; poor-looking; seedy. ¶ 헙수룩한 옷 shabby clothes.
헙합다 ① (사람됨이) (be) generous; liberal; broad-minded. ② (씀씀이가) (be) wasteful; lavish.
헛간 (一間) a barn; a shed.
헛걸음하다 go on a fool's errand; make a trip in vain.
헛구역 (一嘔逆) queasiness; a queasy feeling. ¶ ~질이 나다 have a queasy feeling; be queasy.
헛기침하다 clear one's throat (to attract attention); ahem.
헛다리짚다 make a wrong guess (estimate); miscalculate; shoot at a wrong mark.
헛되다 (보람없다) (be) idle; vain; futile; unavailing; empty; (무근) (be) groundless; false; untrue. ¶ 헛된 노력 vain efforts / 헛된 소문 groundless rumor / 헛되이 uselessly; in vain; aimlessly; idly / 하루하루를 헛되이 보내다 spend one's days idly.
헛듣다 hear (something) wrong (amiss); mishear. ¶ 아무의 말을 ~ mishear a person's remark / 내가 헛듣는 것이나 아닌지 의심됐다 I could hardly believe my ears.
헛디디다 miss one's step; take a false step.
헛물켜다 make vain efforts.
헛배부르다 have a false sense of satiety.
헛소리하다 talk in delirium (정신 없이); talk nonsense (rubbish).
헛소문 (一所聞) a false rumor.
헛손질하다 paw the air.
헛수 (一手) a wrong move.
헛수고 fruitless (vain) effort; lost labor. ~하다 make vain efforts; work in vain; waste time and labor. ¶ ~가 되다 one's labor comes to nothing (naught).
헛웃음 a feigned (pretended) smile; a simper; a smirk. ¶ ~(을) 치다 simper; smirk.
헛일 useless work; vain effort; lost (fruitless) labor. ~하다 do useless work; make vain efforts; try in vain.
헛헛증 (一症) hungriness; a chronic hunger. ¶ ~이 있다 suffer from chronic hunger.
헛헛하다 feel (be) hungry.
헝겊 a piece of cloth; a rag.
헝클다 tangle; entangle; dishevel.
헝클어지다 be (get) tangled (entangled); be in a tangle.
헤게모니 hegemony.
헤드라이트 a headlight.
헤딩 heading. ~하다 head.
헤뜨리다 scatter; strew; disperse. ¶닭이 모이를 ~ chickens scatter their feed.
헤로인 (여주인공) a heroine; 《마약의 일종》 heroin.
헤르니아 [醫] hernia (탈장).
헤매다 ① (돌아다니다) wander (roam) about; rove. ¶ 숲 속을 ~ wander (roam) about in the woods / 생사경을 ~ hover between life and death. ②(마음이) be embarrassed (perplexed);

헤먹다 puzzled); be at a loss. ¶ 어쩔줄 몰라 ~ be at a loss what to do.
헤먹다 get loose; become loose-fitting.
헤모글로빈 〖生〗 hemoglobin.
헤벌쭉 하다 wide open. ¶ ~ 웃다 smile a broad smile.
헤브라이 Hebrew. ‖ ~어 Hebrew.
헤비급(一級) the heavyweight. ‖ ~선수 a heavyweight (*boxer*).
헤살 hindrance; slander(중상). ~ 놓다 thwart; hinder; interfere with. ‖ ~꾼 slanderer; a malicious interferer.
헤식다 (be) brittle; fragile; weak.
헤실바실 frittering away; inadvertently running away of. ¶ ~ 가진 돈을 ~ 다 써버리다 fritter away all the money *one* has.
헤아리다 ① 《요량하다》 consider; weigh; ponder. ¶ 일을 헤아려 하다 undertake a plan with due consideration. ② 《가늠·짐작》 fathom; sound; plumb; surmise; conjecture. ③ 《셈》 count; calculate; estimate. ¶ 헤아릴 수 없는 incalculable; innumerable.
헤어나다 cut (fight) *one's* way through; ride over 《*a crisis*》; get out of 《*a difficulty*》.
헤어네트 a hairnet.
헤어브러시 a hairbrush.
헤어스타일 a hair style.
헤어지다 ① 《이별》 part from (with); separate from; part company 《*with*》; divorce *oneself* 《*from*》. ¶ 헤어진 아내 a separated (divorced) wife / 친구와 ~ part from a friend. ② 《흩어지다》 get scattered (strewn, dispersed). ¶ 삼삼오오 헤어지다 가다 disperse by twos and threes.
헤어핀 a hairpin.
헤엄 swimming; a swim. ¶ ~ 치다 swim; have a swim / ~ 치러 가다 go swimming.
헤적이다 rummage 《*about, through, among*》; ransack.
헤집다 dig up and scatter; tear up; turn up.
헤치다 ① 《파헤치다》 dig (turn) up. ② 《흩뜨리다》 scatter; disperse. ③ 《좌우로》 push aside; make *one's* way 《*through*》; elbow *one's* way 《*through*》. ¶ 군중을 헤치고 나아가다 elbow (cut) *one's* way through a crowd.
헤프다 ① 《쓰기에》 be not durable; be easy to wear out; be soon used up. ② 《씀씀이가》 (be) uneconomical; wasteful. ¶ 돈을 헤프게 쓰다 spend money lavishly [wastefully]. ③ 《입이》 (be) talkative; glib(-tongued). ④ 《몸가짐이》 (be) loose; dissipated; dissolute.
헥타르 a hectare.
헬레니즘 〖史〗 Hellenism.
헬륨 〖化〗 helium (기호 He).
헬리콥터 a helicopter; a chopper
헬리포트 a heliport. 〔〖美俗〗
헬멧 a helmet.
헷갈리다 ① 《마음이》 be confused; *one's* attention is distracted. ② 《뜻이》 be confused; be hard to distinguish.
헹가래 ¶ ~ 치다 toss (*a person*) 〔into the air〕〔shoulder-high〕.
헹구다 wash out; rinse out (away). ¶ 빨래를 ~ rinse laundry in fresh water after washing.
혀 a tongue; 《악기의》 a reed. ¶ ~를 내밀다 put (stick) out *one's* tongue / ~를 차다 tut; clack the tongue. ¶ ~끝 the tip of the tongue.
혁대(革帶) a leather belt.
혁명(革命) a revolution. ¶ ~적인 revolutionary / ~을 일으키다 start (raise) a revolution / 산업 ~ an industrial revolution / 무혈(無血) ~ an armed (a bloodless) revolution / 반~세력 antirevolutionary group(force). ‖ ~가 a revolutionist / ~군 [정부] a revolutionary army (government) / ~운동 a revolutionary movement.
혁신(革新) (a) reform; (a) renovation; (an) innovation. ~하다 (make a) reform; renovate 《*in, on*》. ¶ ~적인 innovative; progressive / 기술의 ~ innovation in techniques. ‖ ~운동 a renovation movement / ~정당 a reformist (progressive) (political) party / ~파 a reformist group.
혁혁하다(赫赫一) (be) bright; brilliant; glorious; distinguished.
현(弦) ① 《활시위》 a bowstring. ② 〖數〗 a chord. ③ 〖天〗 a quarter (moon). ④ 《줄》 a string; a chord.
현(現) present; existing; actual. ¶ ~내각 the present Cabinet.
현격(懸隔) 하다 (be) different; wide apart. ¶ ~한 차이 a great disparity; a wide difference.
현관(玄關) the (front) door; the porch; the entrance hall. ¶ 자동차를 ~에 대다 drive a car up to the door.
현군(賢君) a wise king.
현금(現今) ¶ ~의 present time (day); nowadays; of today / ~에는 at present; now; nowadays; in these days.
현금(現金) cash; ready money.

¶ ~으로 치르다 pay in cash / ~으로 팔다[사다] sell [buy] for cash / 수표로 ~ 으로 바꾸다 cash a check. ‖ ~가격 a cash price / ~거래 cash transactions / ~상환 cash redemption / ~수송차 (美) an armored car / ~자동현금입출기 an automatic teller machine (생략 ATM) / ~자동지급기 a cash dispenser / ~의 pay-as-you-go policy; no-credit policy / ~지급 cash payment / ~출납원 a cashier.

현기(眩氣), **현기증**(眩氣症) giddiness; dizziness; [醫] vertigo. ¶ 현기증이 나다 be dizzy; get [feel] giddy.

현대(現代) the present age [day]; today. ¶ ~의 current; present-day; modern; up-to-date. ‖ ~극 a modern play / ~문학 current literature / ~성(性) modernity / ~어 a living [modern] language / ~영어 present-day English / ~음악 modern music / ~인 a modern; men of today (총칭) / ~작가 a contemporary writer / ~화(化) modernization (~화하다 modernize).

현란(絢爛) ~하다 (be) gorgeous; brilliant; dazzling; flowery.

현명(賢明) wisdom. ¶ ~한 wise; sensible: sagacious.

현모양처(賢母良妻) a wise mother and good wife.

현몽하다(現夢—) appear in one's dream; come to one in a dream.

현물(現物) the actual thing [goods]. ¶ ~을 보지 않고 사다 buy an article without seeing it / ~로 지급하다 pay in kind. ‖ ~가격 a spot price / ~거래 a spot transactions / ~급여 an allowance [wages] in kind / ~출자 (make) investment in kind. rice.

현미(玄米) unpolished [unmilled]

현미경(顯微鏡) a microscope. ‖ ~배율 백배의 ~ a microscope of 100 magnifications / ~전자 ~ an electron microscope.

현상(現狀) the present [existing] state; the present condition [situation]; the *status quo*. ¶ ~으로는 in [under] the present [existing] circumstances / ~대로 놔두다 leave 《*the matter*》 as it is. / ~유지 maintenance of the *status quo*.

현상(現象) a phenomenon. ¶ 자연 ~ natural phenomena / 일시적 ~ a passing phenomenon.

현상(現像) [寫] developing; development. ~하다 develop. ¶ 필름을 ~하다 have one's film developed. ‖ ~액 a developer.

현상(懸賞) a prize; a reward. ¶ ~을 걸다 offer a prize [reward] 《*for*》/ 《범인 등에》 set a prize 《*on an offender's head*》/ ~에 응모하다 participate in a prize competition. ‖ ~금 prize money; a reward / ~당선자 a prize winner / ~소설 a prize novel.

현세(現世) this world. ☞ 이승.

현손(玄孫) a grandson's grandson.

현수(懸垂) suspension. ‖ ~교(橋) a suspension bridge / ~막 a hanging banner [placard].

현숙(賢淑) ¶ ~한 아내 a wise and virtuous wife.

현시(現時) the present time; today.

현시(顯示) ~하다 show; reveal.

현실(現實) reality; actuality. ¶ ~의 actual; real / ~로 actually / ~화하다 realize / 인생의 혹독한 ~ the stern [hard] realities of life / ~을 직시하다 face (up to) reality / ~에서 도피하다 escape from reality / ~적으로 생각하다 think realistically. ‖ ~성 reality / ~주의 realism.

현악(絃樂) string music. ‖ ~기 a stringed instrument / ~사중주 a string quartet.

현안(懸案) a pending [an outstanding] question [problem].

현역(現役) active service. ‖ ~의 군함 a warship in commission [active service]. ‖ ~군인 a soldier in active service / ~선수 a player on the active list / ~장교 an officer in [on] active service.

현인(賢人) a wise man; a sage.

현임(現任) the present office. ‖ ~자 the present holder of the office.

현장(現場) the spot; the scene (of action). ¶ ~에서 on the spot / ~에서 잡히다 be caught in the act 《*of stealing*》. ‖ ~감독 a foreman; a field supervisor / ~검증 an on-the-spot inspection / ~부재증명 an alibi / ~연수(研修) on-the-job training [experience] / ~중계 TV coverage of the scene / ~취재 news-gathering of the scene 《*of*》.

현재(現在) the present (time). ¶ ~의 present; existing / ~까지 up to now; to date / 중동의 ~정세 the present state of the Middle East / 1998년 4월 1일 ~의 서울 인구 the population of Seoul as of April 1, 1998 / ~의 일에 만족하다 be content with one's present job. ‖ ~시제 the present (tense).

현저(顯著) ¶ ~한 remarkable; marked; outstanding; striking /

인구의 ~한 증가 a marked increase in population / 의견의 ~한 차이 a remarkable (striking) difference between the opinions.

현존(現存) ~하다 exist; be in existence. ¶ ~의 living; existing. ¶ ~작가 living writers.

현주(現住) ① 《현재 삶》 actual residence. ¶ ~민 the present inhabitants (residents). ② 《주소》 one's present address.

현지(現地) the spot; the field. ¶ ~로부터 보고를 받다 receive a report from the spot. ¶ ~보고 an on-the-spot report / ~생산 local production / ~시간 local time / ~인 a native; a local people / ~조사 field investigations.

현직(現職) the present office (post). ¶ ~의 serving 《officials》; incumbent / ~에 머물다 remain (stay) in one's present office / ~교육부 장관 the incumbent Minister of Education.

현찰(現札) cash; ready money.
현처(賢妻) a wise wife.
현충일(顯忠日) the Memorial Day.
현충탑(顯忠塔) a memorial monument.
현판(懸板) a hanging board (plate).
현품(現品) the (actual) goods. ¶ 물품.
현행(現行) ¶ ~가격 the going price / ~교과서 the textbooks now in use / ~제도는 시대에 안 맞는다 The present system is behind the time. ¶ ~범 a crime committed in the presence of a policeman (~범으로 잡다 catch 《a thief》 red-handed) / ~법규 the existing laws.

현혹(眩惑) dazzlement. ~하다 dazzle; enchant; mesmerize; take 《a person》 in. ¶ 달콤한 말에 ~되지 마라 Don't be taken in by seductive words.

현황(現況) ☞ 현상(現狀).

혈거(穴居) ~하다 dwell in a cave. ¶ ~시대 the cave age.

혈관(血管) a blood vessel. ¶ ~파열 the rupture of a blood vessel.
혈구(血球) a blood corpuscle (cell).
혈기(血氣) hot blood; youthful vigor. ¶ ~ 왕성한 passionate; hot-blooded / ~가 왕성하다 be full of youthful vigor / ~에 이끌리다 be driven by youthful ardor. 「hematuria.
혈뇨(血尿) bloody urine; 〖醫〗〈증상〉
혈담(血痰) bloody phlegm.
혈당(血糖) 〖生理〗 blood sugar; glucose (포도당). ¶ ~검사를 받다 have one's blood sugar tested. ¶ ~치 a blood sugar level (~치를

내리다 lower one's blood sugar level).

혈로(血路) ¶ ~를 열다 find a perilous way out; cut one's way 《through the enemy》.
혈맥(血脈) 〈혈관〉 a blood vessel; 〈혈통〉 lineage; blood; pedigree.
혈반(血斑) a blood spot.
혈변(血便) bloody stool.
혈색(血色) a complexion. ¶ ~이 좋다 (나쁘다) look well (pale); have a ruddy (bad) complexion / ~이 좋아(나빠)지다 gain (lose) color. ¶ ~소 hemoglobin.
혈서(血書) ¶ ~를 쓰다 write in blood. 「tax.
혈세(血稅) an unbearable heavy
혈안(血眼) a bloodshot eye. ¶ ~이 되어 찾다 make a desperate effort to find; make a frantic search 《for》.
혈압(血壓) blood pressure. ¶ ~을 재다 (내리다) measure (reduce) one's blood pressure / ~이 높다 (낮다) have high (low) blood pressure. ¶ ~강하제 a hypotensive drug / ~계 a tonometer.
혈액(血液) blood. ¶ ~순환을 좋게 하다 improve blood circulation. ¶ ~검사 (형) a blood test (type) / ~암 leukemia / ~은행 a blood bank.
혈연(血緣) blood relation (ties); family connection(s). ¶ ~관계 consanguinity; blood relationship (~ 관계에 있다 be related by blood (birth)) / ~단체 a kinship society. 「hemophilia.
혈우병(血友病) bleeder's disease;
혈육(血肉) 〈피와 살〉 blood and flesh; 〈자식〉 one's offspring. ¶ ~ 하나 없다 be childless.
혈장(血漿) blood plasma.
혈전(血戰) a bloody battle; a desperate fight.
혈족(血族) 〈관계〉 blood relationship (ties); 〈사람〉 a blood relative (relation). ¶ ~결혼 an intermarriage.
혈청(血淸) 〖醫〗 (blood) serum. ¶ ~간염 serum hepatitis / ~주사 a serum injection.
혈통(血統) blood; lineage; pedigree; a family line. ¶ ~은 속이지 못한다 Blood will tell. ¶ ~서 a pedigree (~서가 있는 개 a pedigreed dog).
혈투(血鬪) a bloody fight.
혈판(血判) ~하다 seal with one's blood. ¶ ~서 a petition sealed with blood.
혈행(血行) circulation of the blood.
혈혈단신(孑孑單身) all alone in the world. ¶ ~이다 be all alone.
혈흔(血痕) a bloodstain.
혐연(嫌煙) a hatred of smoking.

‖ ~권(權) non-smoker's rights; the right to be free from other's smoking.
혐오(嫌惡) hatred; dislike. ~하다 hate; dislike; detest. ¶ ~할 hateful; detestable / ~감을 갖다 have a hatred 《for》; feel an aversion 《to》.
혐의(嫌疑) (a) suspicion; a charge. ¶ …의 ~로 on suspicion 〔a charge〕 of… / ~를 두다 suspect 《a person》《of》/ ~를 받다 be suspected 《of》. ‖ ~자 a suspected person; a suspect.
협객(俠客) a chivalrous person.
협곡(峽谷) a gorge; a ravine; a canyon.
협공(挾攻) ~하다 attack 《the enemy》 from both sides. ‖ ~작전 a pincer operation.
협기(俠氣) a chivalrous spirit.
협동(協同) cooperation; collaboration; partnership. ~하다 cooperate 《collaborate》《with》; work together. ¶ ~하여 jointly; in cooperation 〔collaboration〕 《with》. ‖ ~기업 a cooperative enterprise / ~정신 cooperative spirit / ~조합 a cooperative society 〔association〕.
협력(協力) cooperation; joint efforts. ~하다 cooperate 〔join forces〕 《with》; work together 《with》. ¶ 경제 ~ economic cooperation / …와 ~하여 in cooperation 〔collaboration〕 with. ‖ ~자 a collaborator; a cooperator.
협박(脅迫) a threat; intimidation; a menace. ~하다 threaten; menace; intimidate. ‖ ~자 an intimidator / ~장〔전화〕 a threatening letter 〔call〕 / ~죄 intimidation.
협살(挾殺) 〖野〗 a rundown. ~하다 run down 〔touch out〕 《a runner between second base and third》.
협상(協商) negotiations; an *entente* (프.). ~하다 negotiate 《with》. ¶ ~을 맺다 conclude an *entente* 《with》.
협소하다(狹小—) (be) narrow and small; limited. ¶ 협소한 방 a small room.
협심(協心) unison. ~하다 unite; be united. ¶ ~하여 일하다 work in unison.
협심증(狹心症) 〖醫〗 stricture of the heart; angina (pectoris).
협약(協約) ☞ 협정. ‖ 노동〔단체〕 ~ a labor 〔collective〕 agreement.
협의(協議) (a) conference; (a) consultation; discussion. ~하다 talk 《with a person》 over 《a matter》; discuss 《a matter with a person》; confer 《with》. ¶ ~ 결과 다음과 같이 결정하였다 As a result of the conference the following decision was made. ‖ ~사항 a subject of discussion / ~회 a conference.
협의(狹義) (in) a narrow sense.
협잡(挾雜) cheating; trickery; swindle; fraud. ~하다 cheat; swindle; commit a fraud; juggle. ‖ ~꾼 an swindler; an impostor; a cheat / ~선거 a fraudulent election.
협정(協定) an agreement; an arrangement; a pact. ~하다 agree 《on》; arrange 《with》. ¶ ~을 맺다 〔폐기하다〕 conclude 〔abrogate〕 an agreement 《with》 / ~을 이행하다 fulfill 〔carry out〕 an agreement. ‖ ~가격 an agreed price / ~서 a written agreement 《~서를 교환하다 exchange copies of an agreement 《with》》 / ~위반 a breach of an agreement.
협조(協調) cooperation; harmony 〔조화〕; conciliation 〔타협〕. ~하다 cooperate 《with》; act in concert 《with》. ¶ ~적 cooperative; conciliatory 《attitude》 / 그는 ~적이다 〔~적이 아니다〕 He is 〔is not〕 cooperative. ‖ ~성 cooperativeness; cooperation / ~심 a spirit of cooperation / ~자 a cooperator.
협주곡(協奏曲) a concerto.
협착(狹窄) 〖醫〗 a stricture; contraction. ¶ 요도~ stricture of the urethra.
협찬(協贊) approval 〔찬성〕; support 〔지지〕; cooperation 〔협력〕; co-sponsorship 〔후원〕. ~하다 approve 《a plan》; support 《a campaign》; cosponsor 《a contest》.
협화음(協和音) a consonance.
협회(協會) an association; a society. ‖ 대한축구~ the Korea Football Association.
혓바늘 fur. ¶ ~이 돋다 have fur on one's tongue.
혓소리 〔音聲〕 a lingual 〔sound〕.
혓바닥 (the flat of) the tongue.
형(兄) ① 〔동기간〕 an elder brother; 〔부를 때〕 Brother! ② 〔친구간〕 you; Mr. 《Kim》.
형(刑) a punishment; a penalty; a sentence.
형(型) a size.
형(形) 〔형태〕 form; shape; 〔대소〕
형(型) 〔모형〕 a model; 《주물》 a mold; a matrix; 〔양식〕 a style; a type; a model; a pattern. ¶ 1998년 ~ 자동차 an auto of 1998 model.
형광(螢光) 〖理〗 fluorescence. ‖ ~도료〔도료〕 a luminous 〔fluorescent〕 paint / ~등〔판〕 a fluores-

형구(刑具) an implement of punishment.

형극(荊棘) brambles; thorns. ¶ ~의 길 (tread) a thorny path.

형기(刑期) a prison term. ¶ ~를 마치다 complete (serve out) one's term.

형무소(刑務所) ☞ 교도소.

형벌(刑罰) a punishment; a penalty. ¶ ~을 과하다 punish; inflict (impose) a punishment 《on》.

형법(刑法) the criminal law (code). ¶ ~상의 죄 a criminal (penal) offense.

형부(兄夫) a brother-in-law; one's elder sister's husband.

형사(刑事) 《사람》 a (police) detective; a plainclothes man(사복). ¶ ~의 criminal; penal. ‖ ~ 문제 [사건] a criminal case / ~ 범 (죄) a criminal (penal) offense / 《사람》 a criminal offender / ~ 소송 a criminal action (suit) / ~ 소송법 the Criminal Procedure Code / ~ 책임 criminal liability (~ 책임을 묻다 hold 《a person》 liable (for a case)).

형상(形狀) (a) shape; (a) form.

형석(螢石) 〖鑛〗 fluor(ite).

형설(螢雪) ¶ ~의 공을 쌓다 devote (apply) oneself to one's studies; study diligently.

형성(形成) formation; shaping. ~하다 form; shape. ‖ ~기(期) the formative period.

형세(形勢) the situation; the state of things (affairs); 《watch》 the development 《of affairs》. ¶ ~를 보다 watch the situation; sit on the fence / ~가 좋다 (나쁘다) The situation is favorable (unfavorable). / ~가 유리(불리)해졌다 The tide turned to (against) us.

형수(兄嫂) an elder brother's wife; a sister-in-law.

형식(形式) (a) form; formality. ~ 적인 formal; conventional / ~적으로 formally / ~을 차린 표현 a formal expression / 소나타 ~의 곡 a piece of music in sonata form / ~을 차리지 않고 without ceremony (formality) / ~에 구애되다 stick (adhere) to formality. ‖ ~ 논리 formal logic / ~ 주의 formalism / ~ 주의자 a formalist.

형안(炯眼) insight; a quick (keen) eye. ¶ ~의 quick-sighted.

형언(形言) ~하다 describe; express. ¶ ~할 수 없는 be beyond description.

형용(形容) 《비유》 a metaphor; 《서술》 description. ~하다 express; describe. ¶ 그 그림의 아름다움은 ~할 수가 없다 The beauty of the picture is beyond description. ‖ ~ 사 〖文〗 an adjective.

형이상(形而上) ¶ ~의 metaphysical. ‖ ~학 metaphysics.

형이하(形而下) ¶ ~의 physical; concrete. ‖ ~학 concrete (physical) science.

형장(刑場) a place of execution. ¶ ~의 이슬로 사라지다 die on the scaffold; be executed.

형적(形跡) 《흔적》 marks; traces; 《증거》 signs; evidences.

형정(刑政) penal administration.

형제(兄弟) a brother; 《자매》 a sister; 《신도》 brethren. ¶ ~의 brotherly; sisterly / ~의 사랑 brotherly (sisterly) affection. ‖ ~ 자매 brothers and sisters; brethren (신도).

형질(形質) characteristic form and quality.

형태(形態) (a) form; (a) shape. ¶ 정부의 한 ~ a form of government. ‖ ~학 〖生〗 morphology.

형통(亨通) ~하다 go well; turn out well; prove successful. ¶ 만사가 ~하다 Everything goes well.

형편(形便) ① 《경과》 the course 《of events》; the development 《of an affair》; 《형세·사정》 the situation; the state 《of things》; the condition 《of affairs》; circumstances; reasons; 《편익》 convenience. ¶ ~에 의해 for certain reasons; owing to circumstances / ~을 보다 watch the development 《of》 / 되어 가는 ~대로 놔두다 leave 《a thing》 to take its own course / ~이 좋으면 if it is convenient for you / 잠시 돌아가는 ~을 지켜보도록 하자 For the time being let's wait and see how things turn out. ‖ 재정 (財政) ~ financial condition. ② 《살림의》 one's livelihood; one's living condition. 생계.

형편없다(形便−) 《지독함》 (be) terrible; awful; 《터무니없음》 exorbitant. ¶ ~없이 severely; terribly; awfully; exorbitantly / 형편 없는 연극 (바보) a terrible play (fool) / 형편없이 고생하다 suffer terribly. ‖ ~ple of equity.

형평(衡平) ¶ ~의 원칙 the principle of equity.

형형색색(形形色色) ¶ ~의 various; all sorts and kinds; diverse.

혜서(惠書) your (esteemed) letter.

혜성(彗星) a comet. ¶ ~과 같이 나타나다 make a sudden rise from obscurity.

혜안(慧眼) keen insight; a keen (sharp) eye. ¶ ~의 keen-(sharp-) eyed; insightful 《comments》.

혜존(惠存) 《증정본에》 "With the compliments 《of the author》."

혜택(惠澤) a favor; benefit; a blessing(신의). ¶ 자연의 the

호 blessing of nature / ~을 입다 be benefited; receive a favor 《*from*》; be indebted 《*to*》 / 전국민이 고루 ~을 누릴 수 있도록 하다 enable all citizens to receive equal benefits.

호(戶) a house; a door.

호(號) 〖명칭〗 a title; a pen name 〖아호〗; 〖번호〗 a number; an issue; 〖크기〗 a size.

호가(呼價) a nominal price 〖quotation〗; the price asked; 《경매의》 a bidding. ~하다 ask 〖bid, offer〗 a price 《*for*》. ¶ ~하는 대로 치르고 사다 buy 《*a thing*》 for the asking price.

호각(號角) 〖blow〗 a whistle.

호감(好感) good feeling; a favorable 〖good〗 impression. ¶ ~을 주다 make a good impression 《*on a person*》 / ~을 가지다 feel friendly 《*toward*》 / ~을 사다 win 《*a person's*》 favor.

호강 comfort; luxury. ~하다 live in luxury 〖comfort〗.

호객(呼客) touting. ~하다 tout 《*for customers*》. ‖ ~꾼 a tout; a barker 〖구경거리의〗.

호걸(豪傑) a hero; a gallant 〖bold〗 man. ¶ ~풍의 heroic; gallant.

호경기(好景氣) prosperity; good times; a boom. ¶ ~의 흐름을 타다 take advantage of a boom.

호구(戶口) the number of houses and families. ‖ ~조사 a census; census taking / ~조사를 하다 take a census 《*of*》.

호구(虎口) ¶ ~을 벗어나다 get out of danger; escape with bare life.

호구(糊口) (a) bare subsistence. ¶ 겨우 ~하다 earn enough to keep body and soul together; live from hand to mouth.

호국(護國) defense of the fatherland. ¶ ~ 영령 a guardian spirit of the country.

호기(好機) a good 〖golden〗 opportunity; a good chance. ¶ ~를 잡다 seize 〖take〗 an opportunity / ~를 놓치다 miss 〖lose〗 a chance.

호기(豪氣) 〖기상〗 a heroic temper; an intrepid spirit. ¶ ~롭다 be heroic 〖intrepid; gallant〗 / ~(를) 부리다 display bravery; display *one's* liberality.

호기심(好奇心) curiosity. ¶ ~이 많은 〖강한〗 curious; inquisitive / ~으로 out of curiosity.

호남(湖南) the *Honam* district.

호남아(好男兒) a fine 〖good〗 fellow; 〖미남〗 a handsome man.

호놀룰루 Honolulu.

호농(豪農) a rich 〖wealthy〗 farmer.

호다 sew 《*a quilt*》 with large stitches; make long stitches.

호담(豪膽) ¶ ~한 stout-hearted; daring; dauntless.

호도(糊塗) ~하다 gloss over 《*one's mistakes*》; patch up. ¶ ~지책 a temporary expedient.

호되다 (be) severe; stern; hard; harsh. ¶ ~호된 비평 a severe criticism / 호되게 꾸짖다 scold severely.

호두(胡-) 〖植〗 a walnut. ¶ ~를 깨다 crack a walnut.

호들갑떨다 say extravagantly; act frivolously; be bubbling over; make too much of 《*a matter*》.

호들갑스럽다 (be) abrupt and frivolous; flippant; rash.

호떡(胡-) a Chinese stuffed pancake.

호락호락 readily; easily. ~하다 (be) ready; easily manageable; tractable. ¶ ~ 속아넘어가다 be deceived easily.

호랑나비 a swallowtail 〖butterfly〗.

호랑이 〖動〗 a tiger. ¶ ~도 제 말하면 온다 〖俗談〗 Talk of the devil, and he will appear. ② 《사람》 a fierce 〖formidable〗 person.

호령(號令) a word of command; an order. ~하다 (give an) order; 〖꾸짖다〗 reprimand 《*a person*》 severely. ¶ 천하를 ~하다 hold sway over the country.

호르몬 hormone.

호리다 seduce; allure; entice; 〖정신을〗 bewitch; enchant; fascinate.

호리병(胡-瓶) a gourd. ¶ ~모양의 gourd-shaped.

호리호리하다 (be) tall and slender; slim.

호명(呼名) ~하다 call 《*a person*》 by name; make a roll call.

호미 a weeding hoe.

호밀(胡-) 〖植〗 rye.

호박 〖植〗 a pumpkin. ¶ ~이 굴렀다 〖뜻밖의 행운〗 have a windfall. ‖ ~고지 dried slices of pumpkin / ~씨 pumpkin seeds.

호박(琥珀) 〖鑛〗 amber. ¶ ~색의 amber(-colored).

호반(湖畔) a lakeside. ¶ ~의 호텔 a lakeside hotel / ~을 산책하다 walk along the lake.

호방(豪放) ¶ ~한 manly and openhearted / ~한 사람 an openhearted person.

호배추(胡-) a Chinese cabbage.

호별(戶別) ¶ ~로 from house 〖door〗 to house 〖door〗 / ~ 방문하다 make a house-to-house visit.

호봉(號俸) serial 〖pay〗 step; salary step 〖class〗.

호부(好否) ¶ ~간에 whether *one* likes it or not.

호사(豪奢) extravagance; luxury. ~하다 live in luxury 〖clover〗. ~스러운 luxurious; sumptuous; extravagant.

호사(好事) a happy event. ∥ ~가 a dilettante; a person with fantastic taste; ~다마 Lights are usually followed by shadows.

호상(好喪) a propitious mourning (of *a person* dying old and rich).

호상(豪商) a wealthy merchant.

호상(護喪) taking charge of a funeral. ∥ ~소 the office in charge of a funeral.

호색(好色) ¶ ~의 lustful; lewd. ∥ ~가 a lewd man; a sensualist.

호생(互生) 〔植〕 ¶ ~의 alternate.

호선(互先) 〔바둑에서〕 ~으로 have the first move in alternate games; play on an equal footing.

호선(互選) mutual election. ~하다 elect by mutual vote.

호선(弧線) an arc (of a circle).

호소(呼訴) a complaint; an appeal; a petition. ~하다 complain of; appeal to; resort to 《*violence*》 (폭력에). ¶법 〔대중〕에 ~하다 appeal to the law 〔public〕/ 아픔을 ~하다 complain of a pain.

호소(湖沼) lakes and marshes.

호송(護送) escort; convoy. ~하다 escort; convoy; send 《*a person*》 under guard (병인을). ¶ ~선 an escorted convoy / ~차 a patrol wagon 《美》; a prison van.

호스 a hose. ¶소망~ a fire hose.

호스텔 a 《*youth*》 hostel.

호스티스 a hostess; 《여급》 a barmaid; a waitress. 《*son*》

호시절(好時節) a good 〔nice〕 season.

호시탐탐(虎視眈眈) ~하다 watch for an opportunity 〔a chance〕; keep a vigilant eye 《*on*》.

호신(護身) self-protection. ¶ ~용의 《*a pistol*》 for self-protection. ∥ ~술 the art of self-defense.

호심(湖心) the center of a lake.

호안공사(護岸工事) embankment works; riparian works (하천의).

호양(互讓) ~하다 make a mutual concession; compromise. ¶ ~정신으로 in a give-and-take 〔conciliatory〕 spirit.

호언(豪言) big 〔tall〕 talk; boasting. ~하다 talk big 〔tall〕; boast; brag. 《~〔of a play〕》

호연(好演) a good performance

호연지기(浩然之氣) ¶ ~를 기르다 refresh *oneself* 《*with*》; enliven *one's* spirits.

호외(戶外) the open air; the outdoor. ¶ ~의 open-air; outdoor / ~에서 일하다 work outdoors.

호외(號外) 《*issue*》 an extra.

호우(豪雨) a heavy rain; a downpour. ¶집중~ a heavy rain that swept the area. ∥ ~주의보 (a) torrential 〔heavy〕 rain warning.

호위(護衛) guard; escort; convoy. ~하다 guard; escort; convoy. ¶ ~구축함에 ~된 선단 a convoy with a destroyer escort. ∥ ~병 a guard. 《*agant spree*》

호유(豪遊) ~하다 go on an extrav-

호응(呼應) ① 〔기맥상통〕 ~하다 act in concert 〔unison〕 《*with*》. ¶ ~에 ~하여 in response to; in concert with. ② 〔文〕 concord.

호의(好意) goodwill; good wishes; favor; kindness. ¶ ~적인 kind; friendly / ~적인 제안 a kind offer / ~적인 충고 well-meant advice / ~적으로 out of goodwill / ~로 through the kindness of *a person* / ~를 가지다 be favorably disposed 《*towards*》; be friendly 《*to*》.

호의호식(好衣好食) ~하다 dress well and fare richly; live well 〔in clover〕.

호인(好人) a good-natured man.

호적(戶籍) census registration; a census 〔family〕 register (개인의 부). ¶ ~에 올리다 have 《*a person's*》 name entered in the census register. ∥ ~등〔초〕본 a copy of *one's* family register.

호적수(好敵手) a good match 〔rival〕. ¶그는 나의 ~다 He's a good match for me. 〔*ted*〕

호적하다(好適—) (be) suitable; fitting. 《*hostess*》

호전적(好戰的) ¶ ~인 warlike / ~적인 민족 a warlike race.

호전(好轉) ~하다 take a favorable turn; change for the better; improve; pick up 〔口〕. ¶그의 병은 ~되었다 His illness took a turn for the better.

호젓하다 (be) quiet; lonely; deserted. ¶호젓한 산길 a lonely mountain path / 호젓한 생활을 하다 lead a lonely life.

호조(好調) ¶ ~의 favorable; satisfactory; in good condition 〔shape〕 / 만사가 ~를 보이고 있다 Everything is going well.

호주(戶主) the head of a family. ¶ ~와의 관계 *one's* relation to the head of the family. ∥ ~제 the head of family system.

호주(濠洲) Australia. ¶ ~의 (사람) (an) Australian.

호주머니 a pocket. ¶ ~에 넣다 put 《*a thing*》 in *one's* pocket / ~를 뒤지다 fish around in *one's* pocket.

호출(呼出) a call; calling out; a summons(소환). ~하다 call 《*a person*》 up(전화로); summon. ¶ ~에 응하다[응하지 않다] answer [ignore] a summons 《*from the police*》. ‖ ~부호[신호] a call sign[signal].

호치키스 a stapler.

호칭(呼稱) 《이름》 a name; designation(칭호); 《통칭》 an alias; a popular[common] name. ~하다 call; name; designate.

호크 a hook. ¶ 옷의 ~를 채우다[풀다] hook up[unhook] a dress.

호탕(豪宕) ~하다 (be) magnanimous; large-minded; open-hearted.

호텔 a hotel. ¶ 정부에 등록된 국제 관광 ~ a government-registered international tourist hotel / 일류[호화, 최고급] ~ a first-rate [delux, five-star] hotel / ~에 묵다 stay[put up] at a hotel / ~에 방을 예약하다 reserve 《*a room at a hotel*》 / ~에 체크인 [~을 체크아웃]하다 checkin[checkout] at a hotel. ‖ ~보이 a bellboy.

호통치다 roar 《*at*》; thunder 《*at, against*》; storm 《*at*》.

호투(好投) 《野》 nice[fine] pitching. ~하다 pitch well[cleanly].

호평(好評) a favorable criticism [comment]; public favor. ¶ ~을 받다 be well received; win [enjoy] popularity.

호프 a hope; a youth of promise.

호프만 방식 the Hoffmann method.

호피(虎皮) a tiger skin.

호헌운동(護憲運動) a constitution protection movement.

호형(弧形) an arc.

호형호제(呼兄呼弟) ~하다 call each other brother; be good friends each other.

호혜(互惠) reciprocity; mutual benefits. ¶ ~의 reciprocal. ‖ ~무역 reciprocal trading / ~조약[관세율] a reciprocal treaty [tariff] / ~주의 the principle of reciprocity.

호호백발(皓皓白髮) hoary hair.

호화(豪華) ~스러운[로운] splendid; gorgeous; luxurious; deluxe; luxury. ‖ ~생활 an extravagant life / ~선 a luxury [deluxe] liner / ~주택 a palatial mansion / ~판(版) a deluxe edition.

호황(好況) (a wave of) prosperity; prosperous conditions; a boom. ¶ ~이다 be booming [flourishing, thriving] / ~의 기미를 보이다 show signs of prosperity / ~과 불황의 순환 the cycle of boom and bust. ‖ ~산업 a booming industry / ~시대 prosperous days; boom days.

호흡(呼吸) 《숨》 breath; breathing; respiration. ~하다 breathe; respire. ¶ 심~하다 breathe deeply; take a deep breath / 인공~ artificial respiration. ‖ ~곤란 (have) difficulty in breathing / ~기 the respiratory organs / ~기 질환 a respiratory disease.

혹(或) ①《더러》 occasionally; sometimes. ②《혹시》 perhaps; maybe; by any chance.

혹(瘤) ① 《살혹》 a wen; a lump; a hump(낙타의). ¶ 얻어 맞아서 머리에 ~이 생겼다 I was beaten so hard that I got a lump on my head.

혹(마시는 모양) sipping. 《마시는 소리》 with a whiff [puff];

혹간(或間) ☞ 혹시.

혹독(酷毒) ~한 severe; harsh; cruel; stern; merciless / ~한 비평 a severe criticism.

혹부리 a person who has a wen (on his face).

혹사(酷使) ~하다 work [drive] 《*a person*》 hard; sweat 《*one's workers*》. ¶ 몸을 ~하다 overwork; drive *oneself* relentlessly.

혹서(酷暑) intense[severe] heat.

혹성(惑星) 《天》 a planet. ¶ ~대[소] ~ a major[minor] planet.

혹세무민(惑世誣民) ~하다 delude the world and deceive the people.

혹시(或是) ①《만일》 if; by any chance; in case 《*of*》; provided [supposing] 《*that*》. ¶ ~비가 오면 if it rains; in case of rain. ②《아마》 maybe; perhaps; possibly. ¶ ~그가 올지도 모른다 He may possibly come.

혹심(酷甚) ~한 severe; extreme.

혹자(或者) some(one); a certain person.

혹평(酷評) severe[harsh] criticism. ~하다 criticize severely; speak bitterly[badly] 《*of*》.

혹하다(惑−) ①《반함》 be charmed; be bewitched; be fascinated; be captivated. ②《빠지다》 indulge 《*in*》; give *oneself* up 《*to*》. 《미혹됨》 be deluded.

혹한(酷寒) severe[intense] cold.

혹형(酷刑) a severe punishment.

혼(魂) a soul《정신》; a spirit《정신》.

혼기(婚期) marriageable age. ¶ ~가 되다 be of a marriageable age / ~를 놓치다 lose [miss] a chance of marriage; become an old maid.

혼나다(魂−) ①《놀라다》 be frightened; be startled (horrified). ②《된통 겪다》 have bitter experiences; have a hard time of it.

혼내다(魂−) ①《놀래다》 surprise; startle; frighten; horrify; scare. ②《따끔한 맛》 give 《*a person*》 a

**hard [an awful] time; teach 《*a person*》 a lesson.
혼담**(婚談) an offer of marriage. ¶ ~이 있다 have a proposal of marriage / ~에 응하다 [을 거절하다] accept [decline] an offer of marriage.
혼돈(混沌) chaos; confusion(혼란). ~의 chaotic / ~ 상태에 있다 be in a chaotic state.
혼동(混同) ~하다 confuse [mix up] 《*one thing with another*》; mistake 《*A*》 for 《*B*》. ¶ 공사(公私)를 ~하다 confuse public and private matters.
혼란(混亂) confusion; disorder; chaos. ~하다 (be) confused; disorderly; chaotic; be in confusion. ¶ ~시키다 confuse; disorder; throw into confusion.
혼령(魂靈) ☞ 영혼.
혼례(婚禮) a marriage ceremony 「a wedding.
혼미(昏迷) ~하다 (be) stupefied; confused. ¶ ~해지다 (정신이) lose *one's* consciousness.
혼방(混紡) mixed [blended] spinning. ¶ ~사(絲) mixed [blended] yarn.
혼백(魂魄) the soul; the spirit.
혼비백산(魂飛魄散) ~하다 get [be] frightened out of *one's* senses.
혼사(婚事) marriage (matters).
혼색(混色) a compound [mixed] color.
혼선(混線) entanglement of wires; confusion(혼란). ~하다 get entangled [mixed up]; get crossed (전화가) / ¶ 전화가 ~되었다 The lines were crossed.
혼성(混成) ¶ ~하다 compose. ¶ ~물 a mixture(혼합물); a compound(합성물) / ~어 a hybrid word / ~팀 a combined team.
혼성(混聲) mixed voices. ¶ ~합창 a mixed chorus.
혼솔 broad-stitched seams.
혼수(昏睡) a coma; a trance. ¶ ~상태에 빠지다 fall into a coma.
혼수(婚需) articles [expenses] essential to a marriage.
혼식(混食) (eat) food; mixed cereal meals.
혼신(渾身) the whole body. ¶ ~의 힘을 다하여 with all *one's* might.
혼신(混信)〔電〕 jamming; (an) interference; crosstalk.
혼연(渾然) ~일체가 되다 be joined [united] together; form a complete [harmonious] whole.
혼욕(混浴) mixed bathing. ~하다 《men and women》 bathe together.
혼용하다(混用-) use 《*A*》 together with 《*B*》; mix 《*A and B*》.
혼인(婚姻) a marriage (☞ 결혼). ¶ ~신고 registration of *one's* marriage / ~신고를 하다 register *one's* marriage.
혼자 alone; by *oneself*(단독); for *oneself*(혼자 힘으로). ¶ ~ 살다 live alone; (독신으로) live [stay, remain] single / 다시 ~되다 return to single status / ~ 남다 be left alone / ~웃다 smile (chuckle) to *oneself*.
혼자말 a monologue. ~하다 talk [mutter] to *oneself*.
혼작(混作) mixed cultivation. ~하다 grow mixed crops together; raise [cultivate] together.
혼잡(混雜)(혼란) confusion; disorder; (붐빔) congestion; a jam. ~하다 (be) confused; congested; crowded; be in confusion [disorder]. ¶ ~교통~을 완화하~ relieve [ease] traffic congestion; ease a traffic jam.
혼잣손 ¶ ~으로 (do) single-handed; by [for] *oneself*; unaided.
혼전(婚前) ¶ ~의 premarital / ~ 관계 premarital relations 《*with*》; premarital sex.
혼전(混戰) a confused [mixed] fight; a melee. ~하다 fight in confusion.
혼처 a marriageable family or person; a prospective marriage partner.
혼천의(渾天儀)〔天〕 an armillary sphere.
혼탁(混濁) ¶ ~한 turbid; cloudy; thick; muddy / ~해지다 get [become] muddy.
혼합(混合) mixing; mixture. ~하다 mix; mingle; blend. ¶ (테니스·탁구 등의) ~복식 mixed doubles. ¶ ~기(機) a mixer / ~물 a mixture; a blend / ~비료 (a) compound fertilizer / ~색 a mixed color / ~주 a mixed drink; cocktail.
혼혈(混血) mixed blood [breed]. ¶ ~의 《a person》 of mixed blood; half-breed; racially mixed. ¶ ~아 a child of mixed parentage; a half-breed; a hybrid.
홀 a hall. ¶ 댄스 ~ a dance (dancing) hall.
홀… single.
홀가분하다 (가뿐·거든함) (be) light; free and easy; feel relieved; unencumbered. ¶ 홀가분한 기분으로 with a light heart / 옷차림이 ~ be lightly dressed / 기분이 ~ feel free and easy.
홀딱 ① ~ 올떡. ② (반한 꼴) ¶ ~ 반하다 be deeply in love 《*with*》; lose *one's* heart 《*to*》. ③ (속는 꼴) ¶ ~ 속아 넘어가다 be nicely [completely] taken in.
홀랑 all naked. ¶ 옷을 ~ 벗다 strip *oneself* all naked.

홀로 alone; by *oneself*(단신). ¶ ~ 살다 live alone; remain single. / ~ 외출하다 go out by *oneself*.

홀리다 ① (이성에게) be charmed; be fascinated; be bewitched; (현혹되다) be tempted [deluded]. ② (여우·귀신 따위에) be possessed; be obsessed; be bewitched (*by*).

홀몸 a single [an unmarried] person.

홀소리 ☞ 모음(母音).

홀수 (一數) an odd [uneven] number.

홀시 (忽視) ~하다 neglect; disregard; pay no attention (*to*).

홀씨 (植) a spore. ¶ ~ 포자(胞子).

홀아비 a widower. ¶ ~ 살림 a single [bachelor] life; a bachelor.

홀어미 a widow. ¶ ~lor's home.

홀연 (忽然) suddenly; all of a sudden; in a moment [an instant].

홀쭉하다 (be) long and slender; slim; thin; lean; (뾰족하다) (be) pointed; tapering.

홀태바지 skin-tight trousers.

홀태질하다 hackle; thresh; thrash.

홈 a groove; a flute(기둥의). ¶ ~을 파다 groove; cut a groove.

홈런 (野) a home run; a homer. ¶ 만루 ~ a grand-slam (homer).

홈스펀 (옷감) homespun.

홈인 ~하다 (野) get home.

홈통 (一桶) ① (물 끄는) an eaves trough; a gutter; a downspout (美). ② (창틀·장지의) a groove.

홉¹ (植) a hop.

홉² a hob (=0.18 liter).

훗훗하다 (be) unencumbered; carefree; have no encumbrances.

홍당무 (紅唐一) a red radish; a carrot (당근). ¶ 얼굴이 ~가 되다 turn red; blush; be flushed (*with shame*).

홍두깨 a wooden roller used for smoothing cloth (by wrapping and beating on it). ¶ 아닌 밤중에 ~ a bolt from the blue.

홍등가 (紅燈街) gay quarters; a red light district (美).

홍보 (弘報) public information; publicity. ¶ ~실 a public relations section / ~ 활동 publicity [information] activities; public relations.

홍보석 (紅寶石) a ruby.

홍삼 (紅蔘) red ginseng.

홍색 (紅色) red; (홍색짜리) a bride (dressed in a red skirt).

홍소 (哄笑) ~하다 laugh loudly.

홍수 (洪水) a flood; an inundation; a deluge. ¶ ~가 나다 [지다] have a flood; be flooded. / ~ 경보 flood warnings / ~ 지역 a flooded area (district).

홍시 (紅柿) a mellowed persimmon.

홍안 (紅顔) ¶ ~의 rosy-cheeked;

ruddy-faced / ~의 미소년 a handsome [fair] youth; an Adonis.

홍어 (洪魚) (魚) a skate; a thornback.

홍역 (紅疫) (醫) measles. ¶ ~을 앓다 catch [have, get] (the) measles. 「autumnal tints.

홍엽 (紅葉) (단풍 든 잎) red leaves;

홍옥 (紅玉) (鑛) ruby; carbuncle; (사과) a Jonathan (apple).

홍익인간 (弘益人間) devotion to the welfare of mankind.

홍인종 (紅人種) the red race; the Red Indian.

홍일점 (紅一點) the only woman in the company [group].

홍적세 (洪積世) (地) the Pleistocene [diluvial] epoch.

홍조 (紅潮) a flush(얼굴의); a glow. ¶ ~를 띠다 flush; blush.

홍차 (紅茶) (black) tea. 「iritis.

홍채 (虹彩) (解) the iris. ¶ ~염

홍콩 Hong Kong.

홍합 (紅蛤) (貝) a (hard-shelled) mussel.

홍해 (紅海) the Red Sea.

홑… single; onefold(한겹). ¶ ~겹 a single layer / ~벽 a single partition; a thin wall / ~실 a single-ply thread.

홑몸 ① 단신(單身). ② (임신하지 않은) a woman who is not pregnant.

홑옷 unlined clothes. 「nant.

홑이불 a single-layer quilt; a (bed) sheet.

홑치마 (한겹의) an unlined skirt; (속치마 없이 입는) a skirt worn without an underskirt.

화(火) ① (불) fire. ② (노염) anger; wrath. ¶ 홧김에 in a fit of anger / ~를 잘 내는 사람 a hot-tempered [touchy] person.

화(禍) (재난) a disaster; a calamity; a woe; (불행) (a) misfortune; an evil. ¶ ~를 당하다 meet with a calamity [misfortune] / ~를 부르다 bring an evil (*on oneself*); invite [cause] a disaster (*by one's misconduct*).

화가 (畵家) a painter; an artist. ¶ 동양 ~ an Oriental painter / 서양 ~ an artist of Western painting.

화간 (和姦) (法) fornication. ~하다 fornicate (*with a woman*).

화강암 (花崗岩) granite. 「ship.

화객선 (貨客船) a cargo-passenger

화공 (畵工) a painter; an artist.

화공 (化工) ☞ 화학공업. ¶ ~과 (科) (대학의) the department of Chemical Engineering.

화관 (花冠) ① (植) a corolla. ② ornamental. ¶ ~무(舞) a flower crown dance.

화광 (火光) the light of fire [flames].

화교 (華僑) Chinese residents

화구(火口) ① (아궁이) a fuel hole. ② (화산의) a crater. ‖ ~원(原) a crater basin.

화근(禍根) the root of evil; the source(s) of trouble. ¶ ~을 없애다 eliminate the root of evil; remove the source(s) of trouble.

화급(火急) urgency. ¶ ~한 urgent; pressing; exigent.

화기(火氣) (불기) fire. ‖ ~엄금 (게시) Caution: Inflammable.

화기(火器) firearms. ‖ 소(중)~ light (heavy) firearms / 자동~ automatic firearms.

화기(和氣) harmony; peacefulness. ¶ ~애애하게 harmoniously; peacefully / ~애애한 분위기 a very friendly atmosphere.

화끈 with a sudden flush (glow, flash of heat). ~하다 get a hot flash; get a glow (flush). ¶ ~달다 get enraged; fly into a passion (sudden rage) / 부끄러워서 얼굴이 ~~했다 My face burned (was flushed) in embarrassment.

화끈거리다 feel hot (warm); glow; burn; flush. ¶ 화끈거리는 얼굴로 with flushed face / 위스키 한 잔에 온몸이 ~ one's body is all in a glow after drinking a glass of whisky.

화나다(火一) get angry (enraged, indignant, infuriated); get mad. ¶ 화나게 하다 enrage; exasperate; provoke.

화내다(火一) get angry 《at, with》; fly into a passion; get into a rage; lose one's temper.

화냥년 a wanton (dissolute) woman; a whore.

화냥질 ☞ 서방질.

화농(化膿) 【醫】 suppuration; the formation of pus. ~하다 suppurate; fester; come to a head (종기 따위가). ¶ ~성의 suppurative. / ~균 a suppurative germ.

화단(花壇) a flower bed (garden).

화대(花代) (기생의) a charge for kisaeng's service.

화덕(火德) (charcoal) brazier; (솥 거는 ~) a (cooking) stove.

화동(和同) (be in) harmony.

화드득거리다 keep crackling (banging, whizzing).

화락(和樂) harmony; unity; peace. ~하다 (be) harmonious; peaceful; be at peace with each other.

화랑(畫廊) a picture (an art) gallery.

화려(華麗) ~한 splendid; magnificent; gorgeous; brilliant ¶ ~한 옷 gorgeous clothing / ~한 발레 공연 a splendid performance of ballet.

화력(火力) heat; heating (thermal) power; 〖軍〗 firepower. ¶ ~(난로의) ~을 낮추다 damp down 《a furnace》 / ~이 우세하다 surpass 《the enemy》 in firepower. ¶ ~발전 steam (thermal) power generation / ~발전소 a thermal power station (plant) / ~지원 fire support.

화로(火爐) a brazier; a fire pot.

화룡점정(畫龍點晴) giving a finishing touch.

화류계(花柳界) the gay quarters (world); a red-light district ¶ ~의 여자 a woman of the gay world. 「(생략 V.D)

화류병(花柳病) venereal diseases

화면(畫面) 《TV·영화의》 a screen; (영상) a picture. ¶ 넓은 ~ a wide screen / ~에 들어오다 enter (get into) the picture (screen) / ~에서 사라지다 go (get out) of the picture (screen).

화목(和睦) peace; harmony; reconciliation (화해). ~하다 (be) harmonious; peaceful; be at peace with each other; be in harmony.

화문(花紋) floral designs. ‖ ~석 a mat woven with flower designs.

화물(貨物) freight (美); goods (英); (ship's) cargo (뱃짐). ¶ ~을 나르다 carry freight. ‖ ~선 a cargoship; a freighter (美) / ~수송기 a cargo plane; an air freighter / ~역 a freight depot (美) / ~열차 a freight (goods 英) train / ~운임 carriage; freight (rates); freightage / ~자동차 a truck; a lorry 《英》 / ~적재량 cargo capacity / ~취급소 a freight (goods 《英》) office / 철도 ~ rail freight.

화방수(一水) a whirlpool; an eddy.

화백(畫伯) a (master, great) painter; 〖軍〗 Painter Kim.

화법(話法) 〖文〗 (direct, indirect) narration. 「(drawing).

화법(畫法) the art of painting

화병(花瓶) a (flower) vase.

화보(畫報) a pictorial; a graphic; pictorial news. ¶ 시사 ~ news in pictures; a pictorial record of current events.

화복(禍福) fortune and misfortune; good or evil.

화부(火夫) a stoker; a fireman.

화분(花盆) a flowerpot.

화분(花粉) pollen. ‖ ~열(熱) hay fever; pollinosis.

화불단행(禍不單行) Misfortunes never come single.

화사(華奢) ~한 luxurious; pompous; splendid.

화산(火山) a volcano. ‖ ~대(帶) a

화산 volcanic belt (zone) / ~맥 a volcanic chain / ~학 volcanology / ~학자 a volcanist 《재》 volcanic ashes 《활[휴, 사]~ an active (a dormant, an extinct) volcano.

화살 an arrow. ¶ ~을 먹이다 fix an arrow (to the bow) / ~을 쏘다 shoot an arrow / ~처럼 빠르다 be as swift as an arrow. ‖ ~대 a shaft of an arrow / ~촉 an arrowhead / ~표 an arrow.

화상(火床) a fire grate.

화상(火傷) a burn; a scald (끓는 물에). ¶ ~을 입다 get (be) burnt; suffer burns; get (be) scalded.

화상(和尙)〖佛〗 a Buddhist priest.

화상(華商) a Chinese merchant abroad.

화상(畫商) a picture (an art) dealer.

화상(畫像)《TV의》 a picture; 《초상》 a portrait. ¶ 선명한 a clear picture / ~이 찌그러졌다 The picture is distorted (fuzzy).

화색(和色) a peaceful (ruddy, healthy) countenance; a genial expression.

화생방전(化生放戰)〖軍〗 chemical, biological and radiological warfare; CBR warfare.

화서(花序)〖植〗 inflorescence.

화석(化石)《작용》 fossilization; 《돌》 a fossil 《animal, fish》. ‖ ~학 fossilology / ~학자 a fossilologist.

화섬(化纖) a chemical (synthetic) fiber. ‖ ~직물 synthetic textiles.

화성(化成) transformation. ~하다 transform; change.

화성(火星)〖天〗 Mars. ‖ ~인 a Martian.

화성(和聲)〖樂〗 harmony. ‖ ~학 harmonics.

화성암(火成岩)〖地〗 igneous rocks.

화수분 an inexhaustible fountain of wealth.

화수회(花樹會) a convivial party of the members of a clan; a family reunion.

화술(話術) the art of conversation (narration, talking). ¶ ~에 능한 사람 a good talker (storyteller, conversationalist).

화승(火繩) a fuse; a matchlock (cord). ‖ ~총 a matchlock (gun); a firelock.

화식(火食) ~하다 eat cooked food. ‖ ~조〖鳥〗 a cassowary.

화식도(花式圖)〖植〗 a flower diagram.

화신(化身) (an) incarnation; (a) personification. ¶ 악마의 ~ a devil incarnate; an incarnate fiend.

화신(花信) tidings of flowers. ‖ ~풍(風) spring breezes (presaging blossoms).

화실(畫室) a studio; an atelier《프》.

화씨(華氏)〖理〗 Fahrenheit (略 Fahr., F.). ¶ ~ 75도, 75 degrees Fahrenheit (생략 75°F.). ‖ ~온도계 a Fahrenheit (thermometer).

화약(火藥) (gun) powder. ‖ ~고 a (powder) magazine / ~공장 a powder mill (plant) / ~취급인 a dealer in (handler of) gunpowder.

화염(火焰) a flame; a blaze. ¶ ~에 휩싸이다 be enveloped in flames. ‖ ~방사기 a flame thrower (projector) / ~병 a petrol (fire) bomb; a Molotov cocktail.

화요일(火曜日) Tuesday (생략 Tues.).

화용월태(花容月態) a lovely face and graceful carriage.

화원(花園) a flower garden.

화음(和音) a chord; an accord. ‖ ~기초 the fundamental chord / 5도 ~ the fifth (chord).

화의(和議) ① 《화해교섭》 negotiations for peace; a peace conference; reconciliation. ~하다 negotiate for peace; make reconciliation 《with》. ¶ ~를 맺다 make (conclude) peace 《with》 / ~을 신청하다 sue (make overtures) for peace. ② 〖法〗 composition. ~하다 make a composition 《with》. ¶ 채권자와의 ~가 성립되다 make a composition with one's creditors. ‖ ~법 the Composition Law.

화인(火因) the origin (cause) of a fire. ¶ ~ 불명의 화재 a fire of unknown origin / ~을 조사하다 inquire into the cause of the fire.

화장(一長) the sleeve length.

화장(化粧) (a) make-up; (a) toilet. ~하다 make (oneself) up; put on (one's) make-up; do one's face (口); dress oneself (몸치장). ¶ 엷은 (짙은) ~ heavy (light) make-up / ~을 고치다 adjust (fix) one's make-up / ~을 지우다 remove one's make-up / 그녀는 별로 ~을 하지 않는다 She doesn't wear much make-up. / 그녀는 ~을 안 해도 아름답다 She is beautiful with no make-up on. ‖ ~대 a dressing table; a dresser《美》 / ~도구 a make-up (toilet) set / ~실 a dressing room; 《변소》 a rest room / ~지 tissue paper / ~품 cosmetics; toilet articles / ~품 가게 a cosmetic shop.

화장(火葬) cremation. ~하다 burn 《the body》 to ashes; cremate. ‖ ~장(터) a crematory《美》; a

crematorium 《英》.
화재(火災) a fire; a conflagration (큰 불). ¶ 누전으로 인한 ~ a fire caused by the short circuit / ~가 나다 a fire breaks out (occurs, takes place) / ~를 당하다 suffer from a fire. ∥ ~경보기 a fire alarm; a firebox / ~보험 fire insurance / ~보험회사 a fire insurance company / ~예방 주간 Fire Prevention Week.
화재(畵才) artistic genius; talent for art.
화전(火田) fields burnt away for cultivation. ∥ ~민 "fire-field" farmers; slash-and-burn farmers.
화제(畵題) the subject of a picture (painting).
화제(話題) a subject (topic, theme) of conversation. ¶ 오늘의 ~ the topics of the day; current topics / ~에 오르다 become the topic of a conversation; be talked about / ~를 바꿉시다 Let's change the subject.
화주(火酒) strong liquor; spirits; firewater 《美俗》.
화주(貨主) the owner of goods; a shipper.
화중지병(畵中之餠) 「그림의 떡」 a desirable but unattainable object; "pie in the sky".
화차(貨車) a freight car 《美》; a goods wagon (van) 《英》. ¶ 유개 〔무개〕 ~ a freight (flat) car 《美》; a covered (an open) wagon 《英》.
화창(和暢) ~하다 (be) bright; genial; serene; balmy. ¶ ~한 날씨 balmy weather.
화채(花菜) honeyed juice mixed with fruits as a punch.
화첩(畵帖) a picture album.
화초(花草) a flower; a flowering plant. ¶ ~를 화분에 심다 pot flowers; plant flowers in a pot. ∥ ~밭 a flower garden / ~재배(법) floriculture / ~전시회 a flower show.
화촉(華燭) ¶ ~을 밝히다 celebrate a wedding; hold a marriage ceremony. ∥ ~동방 the bridal room for the wedding night.
화친(和親) friendly relations; amity. ~하다 make peace 《with》; enter into friendly relations 《with》. ∥ ~조약 a peace treaty.
화톳불 (make) a bonfire.
화투(花鬪) Korean playing cards; "flower cards". ¶ ~를 치다 play (shuffle) "flower cards".
화판(畵板) a drawing board.
화평(和平) peace. ~하다 (be) peaceful; placid. ¶ ~을 주장하다 advocate peace 《with》. ∥ ~교섭 a peace negotiation.
화폐(貨幣) money; 《통화》 currency; 《경화》 a coin; coinage (총칭). ¶ ~의 구매력 purchasing power of money. / ~의 가치 the value of money 《~ 가치가 올라가다〔내려 가다〕 increase〔decrease〕 in monetary value》 / ~경제 economy / ~단위 a monetary unit / ~본위〔제도〕 a monetary 〔currency〕 standard 〔system〕.
화포(畵布) 【美術】 a canvas.
화폭(畵幅) a picture; a drawing.
화풀이(火―) ~하다 satisfy one's resentment; vent one's wrath 《on》; wreak one's anger 〔wrath〕 《on a person》.
화풍(畵風) a style of painting. ¶ 라파엘의 ~ the brush of Raphael.
화필(畵筆) a paintbrush.
화하다(化하다) 《변화》 change 〔turn〕 《into, to》; 《변형》 transform 《into, to》; be transformed.
화학(化學) chemistry. ¶ ~적(으로) chemical(ly). ∥ ~공업 the chemical industry / ~기호〔식〕, 방정식 a chemical symbol 〔formula, equation〕 / ~무기〔전〕 a chemical weapon 〔warfare〕 / ~변화〔반응〕 a chemical change 〔reaction〕 / ~비료 a chemical fertilizer / ~섬유 a synthetic 〔chemical〕 fiber / ~약품 chemicals / ~자 a chemist / ~작용 (a) chemical action / ~적 산소 요구량 【環境】 a chemical oxygen demand 《생략 COD》 / ~제품 chemical goods 〔products〕 / ~조미료 (a) chemical seasoning / ~처리 (a) chemical treatment.
화환어음(貨換―) a documentary bill 〔draft〕.
화합(化合) (chemical) combination. ~하다 combine 《with》. ∥ ~물 a (chemical) compound.
화합(和合) 《조화》 harmony; 《결합》 unity; union. ~하다 harmonize 《with》; live in harmony 〔peace〕 《with》; get along well 《with》. ¶ 부부 ~의 비결 the secret of harmonizing as man and wife.
화해(和解) (a) reconciliation; an amicable settlement. ~하다 be reconciled 《with》; make peace 《with》; come to terms 《with》; settle out of court (소송하지 않고). ¶ 우리는 (서로) ~했다 We have been reconciled with each other.
화형(火刑) burning at the stake. ¶ ~에 처하다 burn 《a person》 at the stake / ~당하다 be burned at the stake; be burned alive.
화환(花環) a (floral) wreath; a (floral) garland. ¶ ~을 바치다 place 〔lay〕 a wreath 《at the tomb》.

화훼(花卉) a flowering plant. ‖ ~산업 floricultural industry / ~원예 floriculture.

확《순식간에》in a flash;《갑자기》suddenly;《세차게》violently; with a jerk. ¶ 밧줄을 ~ 당기다 pull the rope with a jerk / 타오르다 burst into flames / 개가 ~ 달려들다 a dog suddenly springs 《at a person》.

확고(確固) ~하다 (be) firm; definite; resolute; fixed; steady. ¶ ~한 신념을 갖다 have a firm belief.

확답(確答) a definite answer 〔reply〕. ¶ ~을 하다 answer definitely; give a definite answer / ~을 피하다 give no definite answer.

확대(擴大) magnification; enlargement; expansion; escalation. ~하다《넓히다》magnify;《넓어지다》spread; expand;《전쟁 등이》escalate;《사진 등을》enlarge. ¶ 100배로 ~하다 magnify a thing a hundred times / 전쟁의 ~를 막다 stop the escalation of the war / 사업〔무역〕을 ~하다 expand〔extend〕business〔trade〕 / 생산을 ~하다 increase〔boost〕the production《of》 / ~되는 소프트웨어의 시장 the expanding market for software. ‖ ~경 a magnifying glass; a magnifier / ~기 an enlarger / ~사진 an enlarged photo / ~율〔寫〕 an enlargement ratio / ~재생산 reproduction on an expanded scale.

확론(確論) a solid argument.

확률(確率) probability. ¶ 비가 올 ~ the probability that it will rain.

확립(確立) establishment. ~하다 establish; settle. ¶ 지위를 ~하다 establish one's position《in》.

확보(確保) ~하다 secure; insure. ¶ 좌석을 ~하다 secure〔save〕a seat.

확산(擴散) spread(ing); proliferation; diffusion. ~하다 spread; diffuse. ¶ 핵무기의 ~를 막다 check the spread of nuclear weapons. ‖ 핵~ spread of nuclear arms; nuclear proliferation / 핵~ 금지조약 the nuclear nonproliferation treaty〔생략 NPT〕.

확성기(擴聲器) a (loud)speaker; a megaphone.

확신(確信) a conviction; a firm belief; confidence《자신》. ~하다 be confident 《of》; believe firmly《in》; be sure《of, that》. ¶ ~하여 with confidence; in the firm belief《that…》 / ~을 얻다 gain confidence / 우리는 승리를 ~한다 We are sure 〔certain, confident〕of a victory.

확실(確實) ~하다《틀림없다》(be) sure; certain; secure;《믿을 만하다》(be) reliable; trustworthy; valid;《견실하다》(be) solid. ¶ ~히 certainly; surely; reliably; to a certainty / ~치 ~ 않은 uncertain; unreliable; doubtful / ~한 대답 a definite answer / ~한 증거 a positive proof / ~한 투자 a sound〔solid, safe〕investment / 그것은 100%〔절대〕 ~하다 It's one hundred percent certain. ‖ ~성 certainty; reliability; sureness.

확약(確約) a definite promise. ~하다 make a definite promise; promise definitely; give one's word《to》; commit oneself《to》.

확언(確言) a definite statement. ~하다 say positively; assert; affirm.

확연(確然) ~하다 (be) definite; positive; clear. ¶ ~히 definitely; positively; clearly.

확인(確認) confirmation; affirmation; verification. ~하다 confirm; affirm; verify. ¶ 미~의 unconfirmed / 신원을 ~하다 verify〔check〕one's identity.

확장(擴張) extension; expansion; enlargement. ~하다 extend; expand; enlarge. ¶ 군비~ an expansion of armaments / 도로를 ~하다 widen a street / 사업을〔점포를〕~하다 expand the business〔shop〕.

확전(擴戰) escalation of the war. ~하다 escalate. ¶ ~을 막다 stop the escalation of the war.

확정(確定) decision; settlement. ~하다 decide on《a matter》; settle; fix; confirm. ¶ ~적(으로) definite(ly); decided(ly) / ~된 settled; fixed; decided; definite / 그의 사형이 ~되었다 His death sentence was confirmed. ‖ ~사항 a settled matter / ~신고〔소득세의〕a final income tax return《for the year》 / ~안 a final draft / ~판결 a final decision〔judgment〕.

확증(確證) conclusive evidence; a positive proof. ¶ ~을 잡다 obtain 〔secure〕positive evidence《of》.

확충(擴充) (an) expansion《of productivity》; (an) amplification. ~하다 expand; amplify. ¶ 군비를 ~하다 expand armaments / 시설을 ~하다 expand and improve the facilities.

확확《바람이》with great puffs; with gusts;《불길이》flaring up repeatedly; with flame after flame.

환(丸) a pill. ☞ 환약(丸藥).
환(換) 【經】 a money order; exchange. ¶ 외국 [내국] ~ foreign [domestic] exchange / 우편 ~ a postal money order / 전신 ~ a telegraphic remittance. ¶ ~시세 an exchange rate / ~시세변동 foreign exchange fluctuations / ~어음 a bill of exchange; a draft / ~차손 an exchange loss / ~차익 a foreign exchange profit.
환가(換價) conversion (into money); realization. ~하다 convert into money; realize.
환각(幻覺) 【心】 a hallucination; an illusion. ¶ ~을 일으키다 hallucinate. ¶ ~제 a hallucinogenic drug; a hallucinogen / ~제 중독자 a psychedelic / ~중상 hallucinosis.
환갑(還甲) one's 60th birthday. ¶ ~ 노인 a sexagenarian / ~잔치(를 베풀다) (give) a banquet on one's 60th birthday.
환경(環境) (an) environment; surroundings. ¶ 새로운 ~에 적응하다 adapt oneself to the new environment / 좋은 ~에서 자라다 be brought up in a favorable environment. ¶ ~공학 environmental engineering / ~기준 the environmental standard (for sulfurous acid gas) / ~문제 an environmental problem (issue) / ~보호 environmental conservation (protection) / ~부 the Ministry of Environment / ~오염 [위생] environmental pollution [hygiene] / ~파괴 environmental disruption; the destruction of the environment.
환국(還國) ☞ 귀국(歸國).
환금(換金) ① (현금화) realization. ~하다 realize (one's securities, property); convert (turn) (goods) into money; cash (a check). ② ☞ 환전(換錢).
환급(還給) ~하다 return; restore; give back; retrocede.
환기(喚起) ~하다 awaken; arouse (public opinion); stir up. ¶ 주의를 ~하다 call (a person's) attention (to) / 여론을 ~시키다 arouse public opinion.
환기(換氣) ventilation. ~하다 ventilate. ¶ ~가 잘 (안) 되다 be well-[ill-]ventilated. ¶ ~공 a vent (hole) / ~장치 a ventilator / ~창 a vent; a window for ventilation.
환난(患難) misfortune; hardships; distress. ¶ ~을 겪다 undergo (go through) hardships.
환담(歡談) a pleasant talk. ~하다 have a pleasant talk (chat) (with).
환대(歡待) a warm (cordial) reception. ~하다 give a warm reception; entertain warmly; receive cordially.
환도(還都) ~하다 return to the capital.
환등(幻燈) a magic lantern; a film slide. ¶ ~기 a magic lantern apparatus; a slide projector.
환락(歡樂) pleasure; amusement; mirth. ¶ ~에 빠지다 indulge in pleasure / ~을 쫓다 pursue (seek) pleasure. ¶ ~가 an amusement district.
환류(還流) flowing back; (a) reflux. ~하다 flow back; return; be refluxed.
환매(換買) barter. ~하다 barter.
환매(還買) repurchase; 【證】 short covering. ~하다 buy back; repurchase; redeem; cover short (증권). ¶ ~권 the right of repurchase.
환멸(幻滅) disillusion. ¶ ~을 느끼다 be disillusioned (at, about, with) / ~의 비애를 느끼다 feel the bitterness (sorrow) of disillusion.
환문(喚問) a summons. ~하다 summon (a person) for examination. ¶ ~에 응하다 answer (obey) a summons. [part.
환부(患部) the affected (diseased)
환부(還付) ~하다 return; refund (a tax); pay back. ¶ ~금 refund.
환불(還拂) repayment; refundment. ~하다 pay back; repay; refund.
환산(換算) change; conversion. ~하다 change; convert (into). ¶ 달러를 원으로 ~하다 convert dollars into won / ~율을 the exchange rates / ~표 a conversion table.
환상(幻想) an illusion; a vision; a fantasy; a dream(몽상). ¶ ~적인 fantastic; dreamy / ~을 가지다 have an illusion (about). ¶ ~곡 a fantasia; a fantasy.
환상(幻像) a phantom; a phantasm; an illusion.
환상(環狀) ¶ ~의 ring-shaped; loop; circular; annular. ¶ ~도로 a loop (circular) road / ~선 a loop (circular, belt) line.
환생(還生) ~하다 be born again; be reincarnated.
환성(歡聲) a shout of joy; a cheer. ¶ ~을 올리다 shout for joy; give (send up, raise) a cheer.
환송(還送) ~하다 return; send back.
환송(歡送) a send-off; a farewell. ~하다 give (a person) a hearty send-off. ¶ ~식 [회] a

환시(幻視) [心] a visual hallucination.
환심(歡心) ¶ ~을 사다 win 《a person's》 favor; curry favor with 《a person》; 여자의~ win a girl's heart.
환약(丸藥) a (medical) pill; a globule.
환어음(換─) ☞ 환(換). ¶ 요구불 ~ a draft on demand / 일람불 ~ a bill at sight.
환언(換言) ¶ ~하면 in other words; that is (to say); namely.
환영(幻影) a phantom; a vision; an illusion.
환영(歡迎) a welcome; a reception. ~하다 welcome; give 《a person》 a welcome; bid 《a person》 welcome; receive 《a person》 warmly. ¶ 열렬한 ~을 받다 recieve an enthusiastic (a hearty) welcome. ¶ ~만찬회 a reception dinner / ~사 an address of welcome / ~회 a welcome party.
환원(還元) ① (복귀) restoration. ~하다 restore 《something》 (to its original state). ¶ 이익을 사회에 ~하다 return the profits to society. ② [化] reduction; deoxidization(산화물의). ~하다 be reduced 《to》; reduce 《to its components》; deoxidize. ¶ ~제 a reducing agent.
환율(換率) the exchange rate. ¶ ~은 매일 변동한다 The exchange rates fluctuate every day. ¶ 고정(변동) ~제 the fixed(fluctuating) exchange rate system / 대미 ~ the exchange rate on the U.S. dollar. ∥ ~변동 exchange rate fluctuation / ~인상 a raise in the exchange rates.
환자(患者) a patient; a sufferer 《from a cold》; a victim 《of a disease》; a subject 《of an operation》. ¶ 입원(외래) ~ an inpatient(outpatient) / 콜레라 ~ a case of cholera / ~를 진찰하다 examine (see) a patient. ∥ ~명부 a sick list.
환장(換腸) ~하다 become (go) mad; lose (be out of) one's mind.
환전(換錢) exchange (of money). ~하다 change 《money》; exchange 《dollars into won》. ∥ ~상(상점) an exchange house(shop) / (사람) an exchanger; a money changer / ~수수료 a commission for an exchange.
환절(環節) [動] a segment.
환절기(換節期) the turning point of the season.
환청(幻聽) auditory hallucination.
환초(環礁) a lagoon island; an atoll.
환태평양(環太平洋) ¶ ~의 circum-Pacific; Pan-Pacific / ~국가 the Pacific basin (rim) countries / ~(합동 군사)연습 the RIMPAC (Rim of the Pacific Exercise).
환표(換票) (선거의) ballot switching. ~하다 switch ballots.
환풍기(換風機) a ventilation fan.
환하다 ① (밝다) (be) bright; light. ¶ 달빛이 환한 밤 a bright moonlit night. ② (앞이 탁 띄다) (be) open; clear; unobstructed. ¶ 길이 ~ A road is clear (wide open). ③ (얼굴이) (be) bright; fine-looking; handsome. ④ (정통하다) be familiar 《with》; be well acquainted 《with》; be conversant 《with》. ¶ (그 곳) 지리에 ~ be familiar (well acquainted) with 《a place》.
환형(環形) ¶ ~의 ringshaped; annular; looped / ~동물 Annelida.
환호(歡呼) a cheer; an acclamation; an ovation. ~하다 cheer; give cheers. ¶ ~속에 amid cheers / ~성을 올리다 give cheers; give a shout of joy.
환희(歡喜) (great) joy; delight. ~하다 be delighted; be very glad; rejoice 《at, over》.
활을 a bow; archery (궁술). ¶ ~의 명수 an expert archer / ~을 쏘다 shoot an arrow.
활강(滑降) a descent.
활개(스키의)
활개 ① (사람의 두 팔) one's arms (limbs). ¶ ~치다 swing one's arms / ~치며 걷다 walk swinging one's arms. ② (새의) wings. ¶ ~치다 flap the wings; flutter.
활공(滑空) ~하다 glide. ¶ ~기 a glider; a sailplane.
활극(活劇) a stormy (riotous) scene; (영화의) an action film (picture). ¶ 서부 ~ a Western (film); a cowboy picture.
활기(活氣) activity; life; vigor. ¶ ~있는 active; lively; full of life / ~없는 inactive; dull; lifeless; spiritless / ~를 띠다 become active (lively); show life.
활달(豁達) ~하다 be generous; magnanimous; broad-minded.
활대 the cross-stick at the top of a sail; (a sail) yard.
활동(活動) activity; action. ~하다 act; play (take) an active part 《in》. ¶ ~적인 active; energetic / ~무대 the 「stage for (field of) one's activities」 / ~을 개시하다 go into action; begin operations(군대 등의). ∥ ~가 a man of action; an energetic person; a go-getter 《美俗》 / ~적 activity; vitality / ~범위 the scope (sphere) of activity.

활량 ① an archer; a bowman. ② ☞ 한량.

활력(活力) vital power [force]; vitality; energy. ‖ ~소 a tonic.

활로(活路) ¶ ~를 열다 [찾다] find a way out 《of the difficulty》; cut one's way 《through the enemy》.

활발(活潑) ~하다 (be) active; brisk; vigorous; lively. ¶ ~한 거래 active business / ~히 actively; lively; briskly; vigorously / ~히 동작하다 be brisk (in one's movements).

활보(闊步) ~하다 stride; stalk; strut. ¶ ~거리를 ~하다 stalk (along) the streets.

활석(滑石) talc; talcum. ¶ ~분(粉) talcum powder.

활성(活性) ~의 active; activated / ~화하다 revitalize; activate / 증권 시장의 ~화 revitalization of the securities market. ‖ ~비타민제 an activated vitamin preparation / ~탄(소) 〖化〗 active [activated] carbon.

활수(滑手) ~하다 (be) liberal 《of, with》; generous 《with》; openhanded.

활시위 a bowstring.

활액(滑液) 〖解〗 synovia.

활약(活躍) activity. ~하다 be active 《in》; take [play] an active part 《in》. ¶ 그는 정계에서 ~한다 He is active in politics.

활엽수(闊葉樹) a broad-leaved tree.

활용(活用) ① 《응용》 practical use; application. ~하다 put [turn] 《knowledge》 to practical use; make good use of 《one's ability in a job》; utilize; apply. ¶ 최대한으로 ~하다 make the best use of 《something》 / 여가를 보다 더 잘 ~하다 make better use of one's leisure time / 인재를 ~하다 make the best of talent. ② 〖文〗 inflection (어미의); declension (명사의); conjugation (동사의). ~하다 inflect; decline; conjugate.

활자(活字) a printing type; type (총칭). ¶ 7호~ No. 7 type / 작은[큰] ~로 인쇄하다 print in small [large] type / 큰 ~의 국어 사전 a Korean dictionary in large print. ‖ ~체로 쓰다 write in block letters. ‖ ~체로 이름을 ~로 쓰다 print one's name.

활주(滑走) ~하다 glide (활공); taxi(지상을); fling (스키의). ‖ ~로 a runway; a landing strip.

활짝 ①《열린·트인 모양》 wide(ly); extensively; broad; open. ¶ 트이다 be open / ~ 열다 fling 《the door》 open. ②《날씨》 entirely; 《꽃 따위가》 brightly; radiantly. ¶ ~ 갠 하늘 a clear sky / 꽃이 ~ 피(어 있)다 be in full bloom.

활차(滑車) a pulley; a block.

활촉(一鏃) an arrowhead.

활터 an archery ground [range].

활판(活版) printing; typography. ‖ ~인쇄 type printing.

활화산(活火山) an active volcano.

활활 《불이》 vigorously; in flames; 《부채질》 《fan》 briskly.

활황(活況) activity (in business); briskness. ¶ ~을 보이다 show signs of activity.

홧김(火一) ¶ ~에 in (a fit of) anger; in the heat of passion / ~에 테이블을 탕탕 치다 pound the table in a fit of anger (rage).

홧홧하다 feel hot [warm]; (be) hot; sultry; feverish.

황(黃) ①《색》 yellow (color). ② 〖鑛〗 orpiment(석웅황); 〖化〗 sulfur; sulphur《英》. ¶ ~의 sulfurous.

황갈색(黃褐色) yellowish brown.

황감(惶感) ~하다 be deeply grateful; be much obliged 《to》.

황겁(惶怯) ~하다 (be) awe-stricken; fearful.

황고집(黃固執) stubbornness; 《사람》 a hardheaded person.

황공(惶恐) ~하다 (be) awe-stricken; be overwhelmed (with awe); 《감사로》 (be) gracious.

황국(黃菊) a yellow chrysanthemum.

황금(黃金) gold (금); money (금전). ¶ ~의 gold(en). ‖ ~만능주의 mammonism / ~만능주의자 a mammonist / ~빛 a golden color / ~시대 the golden age.

황급(遑急) ~하다 (be) urgent. ¶ ~히 in (a great) hurry; hastily; in a flurry / ~히 떠나다 leave in a hurry.

황달(黃疸) jaundice; the yellows. ‖ ~환자 an icteric(al).

황당(荒唐) ~하다 (be) absurd; nonsensical; wild. ¶ ~무계한 이야기 an absurd story; a cock-and-bull story / 그 무슨 ~한 소리야 What an absurd suggestion!

황도(黃道) 〖天〗 the ecliptic. ‖ ~대(帶) the zodiac.

황동(黃銅) brass. ‖ ~광 copper pyrites; chalcopyrite / ~색 brass yellow.

황량(荒凉) ~하다 (be) desolate; dreary. ¶ ~한 벌판 a desolate plain; a wilderness.

황린(黃燐) 〖化〗 yellow phosphor.

황마(黃麻) 〖植〗 a jute.

황막(荒漠) ~하다 (be) desolate (waste) and vast. ¶ ~한 벌판 a vast wasteland.

황망(遑忙) ~하다 (be) very busy.

황망(慌忙) ~하다 (be) hurried;

황무지 waste (wild, barren) land; a wilderness.
황사(黃砂) yellow sand. ¶ ~현상 atmospheric phenomena of the wind carrying yellow dusts (sand); the floating yellow-sand phenomena.
황산(黃酸)〖化〗sulfuric acid; vitriol. ¶ ~구리[철, 암모늄] copper (iron, ammonium) sulfate / ~염 a sulfate / ~지 sulfate (parchment) paper.
황새(鳥) a white stork.
황새걸음 the gait of a stork; a long stride.
황색(黃色) yellow. ¶ ~인종 the yellow race.
황석(黃石)〖鑛〗yellow calcite.
황성(皇城) the capital.
황소(黃—) a bull. ¶ ~처럼 일하다 work like a bull; work very hard. ¶ ~걸음 the gait of a bull; a leisurely pace; a slow step.
황송하다(惶悚—)《황공하다》(be) awestricken;《고맙고 죄송하다》(be) grateful; indebted;《분에 넘치다》be too good for one. ¶ 황송하게도 graciously.
황실(皇室) the Imperial (Royal) Household (Family).
황아장수(荒—) a peddler of sundries.
황야(荒野) a wilderness; a waste; a desert land; the wilds.
황열병(黃熱病)〖醫〗yellow fever.
황옥(黃玉)〖鑛〗(a) topaz.
황음(荒淫) carnal excesses; sexual indulgence.
황인종(黃人種) the yellow race.
황제(皇帝) an emperor.
황진(黃塵) dust in the air;〖氣〗~폭풍 a dust storm.
황차(況且) much (still) more (less).
황천(黃泉) Hades; the land of the dead. ‖ ~객 a dead person (~객이 되다 go down to the shades; join the majority) / ~길 the way to Hades (~길을 떠나다 go to one's last home).
황철광(黃鐵鑛)〖鑛〗(iron) pyrites.
황체호르몬(黃體—)〖生〗progesterone; progestin.
황태자(皇太子) the crown prince. ‖ ~비 the crown princess.
황태후(皇太后) the Empress Dowager; the Queen Mother.
황토(黃土) yellow soil; loess.
황통(皇統) the Imperial (Royal) line.
황폐(荒廢) waste; ruin; devastation. ¶ ~하다 go to ruin; be devastated. ¶ ~한 땅 desolate land.
황하(黃河) the Yellow River; the Huang He.
황해(黃海) the Yellow Sea.
황혼(黃昏) dusk; (evening) twilight. ¶ 인생의 ~기 the twilight years of one's life / ~이 지다(깃들다) dusk falls.
황홀(恍惚) ¶ ~한 charming; fascinating; enchanting; bewitching / ~히 in an ecstasy; in raptures; absorbedly / ~해지다 be enraptured (in raptures); be charmed (enchanted). ‖ ~경 a trance; an ecstasy; a dreamy state.
황화(黃化)〖化〗sulfuration. ‖ ~고무 vulcanized rubber / ~물 a sulfide / ~수소[은] hydrogen (silver) sulfide / ~염료 sulphide dyes.
황화(黃禍) the yellow peril.
황후(皇后) an empress; a queen.
홰《새의》(be on) a perch.
홰《햇불의》a torch.
홰치다 flap (clap, beat) the wings; flutter.
홰홰 ¶ ~ 휘두르다 turn round and round; brandish (a stick) / ~ 감기다 coil (twine) (around a pole).
홱 ① with a snap. ¶ 홱홱 ①. ②《갑자기》suddenly;《힘차게》with a jerk; violently;《잽싸게》quickly; nimbly. ¶ ~ 잡아당기다 pull with a jerk / ~ 던지다 jerk / ~ 열다 fling (a door) open.
홱홱 ① 《빠르게》snap-snap; with dispatch; quickly. ¶ 일을 ~ 해 치우다 finish one's job quickly. ② 《던징》flinging repeatedly. ③ 《때리다》with whack after whack.
횃대 a clothes rack; a clotheshorse.
횃불 a torch(light);《봉화》a signal fire. ¶ ~을 들다 carry a torch in one's hand.
횅댕그렁하다 (be) hollow; empty; deserted; feel hollow (empty).
횅하다 ① 《통달하다》(be) well versed (in literature); familiar (with). ¶ 이 곳 지리에 ~ know the lay of the land around here. ② 《공허》(be) empty; vacant; deserted. ¶ 거리는 ~ A street is deserted.
회(灰) ☞ 석회(石灰). ¶ ~를 바르다 plaster; stucco.
회(蛔) a roundworm. ☞ 회충.
회(會)《회합》a meeting; a gathering; a party (사교상의);《단체》a society; a club; an association. ¶ ~를 개최하다 hold a meeting / ~를 조직하다 organize (form) a society / ~에 가입하다 join (become a member of) a society.
회(膾) seasoned raw fish (meat).

회(回) a time; a round; an inning(야구). ¶ 1 ~ once / 2 ~ two times; twice / 3 ~ 초 [말] [野] the first [second] half of the 3rd inning / 토너먼트 등의 제3~ the third round / (복싱 등의) 10~전 a bout [fight] of ten rounds; a ten-round bout.

회갑(回甲) ☞ 환갑. [(fight).

회개(悔改) repentance; penitence. ~하다 repent 《of》; be penitent 《for》; reform *oneself*.

회견(會見) an interview. ~하다 meet; interview; have an interview 《with》. ¶ 공식 [비공식] ~ a formal [an informal] interview / 기자~ a press [news] conference / ~을 요청하다 ask for an interview 《with》 / 총리는 기자~을 했다 The Prime Minister had a press conference. ¶ ~기(記) an interview / ~자 an interviewer.

회계(會計) 〔경리〕 accounting; 〔계산〕 an account; a bill; a check. ~하다 keep accounts(기장); pay the bill(지불). ¶ 그녀의 ~는 엉망이었다 Her accounts were in disorder. / 그는 클럽의 ~를 담당하고 있다 He keeps the club's accounts. / 공인~사 a certified public accountant (생략 C.P.A.) / 일반[특별] ~ the general [special] account. ‖ ~감사 auditing / ~과 the accounting section / ~담당계원 an accountant; a cashier; a treasurer(회사·클럽 등의) / ~보고 a financial report / ~연도 a fiscal year 〔美〕; a financial year 〔英〕 / 〔장〕부 an account book / ~학 accounting.

회고(回顧) reflection; recollection, retrospection, retrospect. ~하다 reflect [look back] 《upon》; retrospect. ‖ ~록 reminiscences; memories.

회고(懷古) reminiscence. ~하다 recall the past (to *one's* mind); look back on the past. ‖ ~담 recollections; reminiscences.

회관(會館) a hall; an assembly hall. ¶ 시민~ the Citizens' Hall / 학생~ a student's hall.

회교(回敎) Muslimism; Islam. ☞ 이슬람. ‖ ~도 a Muslim / ~사원 a mosque.

회군(回軍) ~하다 withdraw troops 《from》.

회귀(回歸) a recurrence. ~하다 recur; return. ‖ ~성(性) recurrence; a tendency to recur / ~열[醫] recurrent fever.

회기(會期) a session; a period; a term(기간). ¶ ~ 중에 during the session 《of the National Assembly》 / ~를 연장하다 extend a session.

회나무[植] a Korean spindle tree.

회담(會談) a talk; a conference. ~하다 have a talk 《with》; talk together; confer 《with》. ¶ 무역 마찰에 관한 예비 ~ preliminary talks on trade friction / 한미 정상 ~이 서울에서 열릴 예정이다 The US-Korea summit talks will be held in Seoul.

회답(回答) an answer; a reply. ~하다 reply 《to》; give a reply; answer. ¶ 문서 또는 구두로 ~하다 reply in writing or verbally / 그는 내 질문에 대해 서신으로 ~했다 He replied to my question by letter.

회당(會堂) 〔예배당〕 a chapel; a church; 〔공회당〕 a hall; an assembly hall; a meeting house.

회독(回讀) ~하다 read 《a book》 in turn.

회동(會同) ~하다 meet together; assemble; get together; have a meeting.

회람(回覽) circulation. ~하다 circulate. ‖ ~잡지 〔판〕 a circulating magazine [bulletin].

회랑(回廊) a corridor; a gallery.

회례(回禮) a round of complementary visits (calls). ¶ 신년 ~를 하다 make [pay] (a round of) New Year's calls.

회로(回路) ① 〔귀로〕 a return trip; *one's* way home (back). ② 〔電〕 a circuit. ¶ 고정[집적] ~ a stationary [an integrated] circuit / 병렬 [직렬] ~ a parallel [series] circuit / ~를 열다 [닫다] open [close] a circuit. ‖ ~차단기 a circuit breaker.

회반죽(灰—) mortar; plaster; stucco. ¶ ~을 바르다 plaster.

회백색(灰白色) light gray; light ash color.

회벽(灰壁) a plastered wall.

회보(回報) a reply; an answer; 〔복명〕 reporting. ~하다 give a reply; send an answer; 〔복명〕 report to 《a person on…》; bring back a report.

회보(會報) a bulletin; assembly [association] reports. ¶ 동창회 ~ an alumni bulletin.

회복(回復·恢復) recovery; restoration(복구). ~하다 recover 《from illness》; regain; restore 《peace》. ¶ 경기의 ~ recovery of economy / 건강 [기력] 을 ~하다 recover *one's* health [strength, spirits] / 의식을 ~하다 regain consciousness / 명예를 ~하다 restore

one's honor (good name). ‖ ~기 a convalescent stage / ~력 recuperative power (병으로부터의) / ~실 a recovery room.
회부(回附) ~하다 transmit (refer) (to); forward (send (over)) (to); pass on (to).
회비(會費) dues (of a member) (정기적인). ¶ ~를 거두다 (내다) collect (pay) dues / 클럽 ~ club dues.
회사(會社) a company (생략 Co.); a corporation (美); a concern; a firm. ¶석유 (보험) ~ an oil (insurance) company / 증권 (출판) ~ a securities (publishing) company / 모 (자) ~ a parent (subsidiary) company / ~를 만들다 establish (form) a company / ~에 근무하다 serve in a company; be employed in the office. ‖ ~사장 a company president / ~원 a company employee; an office worker / ~채 a company bond; a debenture.
회상(回想) recollection; reminiscence. ~하다 recollect; recall 《a fact》 to *one's* mind. ‖ ~록 reminiscences; memoirs.
회색(灰色) ¶ ~ (의) gray; grey (英) / ~을 띤 grayish. ‖ ~분자 a wobbler / ~차일구름 altostratus.
회생(回生) 소생 (蘇生) tus.
회서(回書) a reply; an answer.
회석(會席) a place of meeting.
회전(回轉) rotation. ~하다 rotate; revolve. ‖ ~운동 a rotary motion / ~탑 (유희용의) a swing on) a ring pole.
회선(回線) 〖電〗 a circuit. ¶ ~도 a circuit diagram / 전화 ~ a telephone circuit.
회송(回送) ~하다 (편지를) forward; send on; (화물을) transfer. ¶편지를 이사 간 새 주소로 ~하다 forward (send on) a letter to 《a *person's*》 new address.
회수(回收) collection; withdrawal; recall. ~하다 collect; withdraw; recall. ¶꾸어준 돈을 ~하다 collect (recover) a debt / 폐품을 ~하다 collect waste materials / 결함 상품을 ~하다 recall the defective goods.
회수(回數) the number of times; frequency. ‖ ~권 a commutation ticket (美); a book of tickets (英); a coupon ticket.
회식(會食) ~하다 have a meal together; dine together; dine 《with》.
회신(回信) 회답 (回答). ‖ ~료 return postage / ~용 봉투 a stamped addressed envelope.
회심(會心) ¶ ~의 미소를 짓다 give a smile of satisfaction; smile complacently. ‖ ~작 a work after *one's* (own) heart.
회양목(一楊木) 〖植〗a box tree; (재목) boxwood.
회오(悔悟) repentance; remorse; penitence. ~하다 repent 《of》; feel remorse 《for》. ¶ ~의 눈물을 흘리다 shed tears of remorse.
회오리바람 a whirlwind; a cyclone; a twister (美口).
회원(會員) a member 《of a society》; membership (총칭). ¶ ~이 되다 become a member; join 《a society》 / 정 (준, 특별, 명예, 종신) ~ a full (an associate, a special, an honorary, a life) member. ‖ ~명부 (배지, 증) a membership list (badge, card).
회유(懷柔) appeasement; conciliation. ~하다 appease; conciliate; win 《a *person*》 over to 《to *one's*》 side). ¶ ~책 an appeasement policy; a conciliatory measure.
회음(會陰) 〖解〗the perineum. ‖ ~부 the perineal region.
회의(會議) a meeting; a conference; a session (의회의). ~하다 confer 《with》. ¶군축에 관한 ~ a conference on disarmament / 국제 ~ an international conference / 가족 ~ a family meeting / 국회의 본 ~ a plenary session of the National Assembly / ~를 열다 hold a conference (meeting) / ~를 소집하다 call a conference / ~에 참석하다 attend a meeting (conference) / ~에 참가하다 take part (participate) in a conference / 문제를 ~에 내놓다 bring up (raise) a problem (an issue) at the meeting / 그는 지금 ~중입니다 He is in conference now. ‖ ~록 the minutes / ~실 a conference (council, meeting) room / ~장 a convention (conference) hall.
회의(懷疑) doubt; skepticism. ¶ ~적(인) skeptic(al). ‖ ~론 skepticism / ~론자 a skeptic.
회자(膾炙) ~하다 (되다) be in everybody's mouth; be on everybody's lips; become the talk of all. 「must part.
회자정리(會者定離) Those who meet
회장(回章) a circular letter (note).
회장(回腸) 〖解〗the ileum.
회장(會長) the president 《of a society》; the chairman (of the board of directors). ¶부 ~ the vice-president; the vice-chairman / 본 협회의 ~은 김 박사이다 The president of this society is Dr. Kim.
회장(會場) a meeting place; a hall; 《옥외의》 the grounds (site).

회장(會葬) attendance at a funeral. ~하다 attend (go to) a funeral. ‖ ~자 the mourners.

회전(回電) a reply telegram.

회전(回轉) turning; (a) revolution; (a) rotation. ~하다 revolve; rotate; turn (go) round. ¶ 360°~하다 turn full circle; make a 360° turn / 그는 머리의 ~이 빠르다 He has a quick mind. *or* He is quick on the uptake. / 달은 지구의 주위를 ~한다 The moon revolves around the earth. ‖ ~경기 (스키의) the slalom / ~목마 a merry-go-round / ~무대 a revolving stage / ~문 a revolving door / ~율 《자금 등의》 (the rate of) turnover 《*of capital*》 / ~의자 a swivel chair / ~익(翼) a rotor (헬리콥터의); a wafter (송풍기의) / ~자금 a revolving fund / ~체 a rotating body / ~축 the axis of rotation; a shaft.

회전(會戰) a battle; an encounter; an engagement. ~하다 fight with 《engage》 the enemy.

회절(回折) [理] diffraction.

회중(會衆) people gathered together; an attendance; a congregation (교회의).

회중(懷中) ~시계 a watch / ~전등 a flashlight 《美》; an electric torch 《英》.

회진(回診) (a doctor's) round of visits. ~하다 go the rounds 《*of one's patients*》; do *one's* rounds.

회초리 a whip; a rod; a cane (등·대 따위); a lash(주). ~로 때리다 whip; lash; use the rod 《*on*》 / ~를 맞다 be whipped (caned).

회춘(回春) rejuvenation. ~하다 be rejuvenated (젊어지다). ‖ ~제 [약] a rejuvenating drug (medicine).

회충(蛔蟲) a roundworm; a belly worm. ¶ ~이 생기다 get roundworms. ‖ ~약 a vermifuge; an anthelmintic.

회칙(會則) the rules (regulations) of a society.

회포(懷抱) one's bosom [thoughts]. ¶ ~를 풀다 unbosom *oneself* 《*to a person*》.

회피(回避) evasion; avoidance. ~하다 evade; avoid; dodge; shirk. ¶ ~할 수 없는 unavoidable; inevitable / 책임을 ~하다 evade 《shirk》 *one's* responsibility / 전쟁을 ~하다 avoid war / 취재 기자의 질문을 ~하다 evade 《sidestep》 the reporter's questions / 귀찮은 일을 ~하다 shirk unpleasant tasks.

회한(悔恨) remorse; (a) regret; (a) repentance. ¶ ~의 눈물 tears of remorse.

회합(會合) a meeting; a gathering. ~하다 meet; assemble; gather. ¶ ~장소 a place of meeting.

회항(回航) ~하다 《돌아다니다》 sail about; navigate; 《되돌아오다》 sail back; return from a cruise.

회향(茴香) [植] a fennel.

회향(懷鄕) the longing for home; nostalgic reminiscence. ~하다 long for home; be nostalgic. ¶ ~의 homesick. ‖ ~병 homesickness; nostalgia.

회화(會話) (a) conversation; a dialogue (☞ 대화). ~하다 talk 《speak》 《*to, with*》; have a conversation (talk) 《*with*》. ¶ 영어 ~에 익숙하다 be good at English conversation / ~책 a conversation book / ~체 a colloquial 《conversational》 style.

회화(繪畵) a picture; a painting; a drawing. ¶ ~적인 pictorial; picturesque. ‖ ~전(展) an art exhibition.

획(劃) a stroke. ¶ 5~의 한자(漢字) a Chinese character of five strokes.

획기적(劃期的) epoch-making; epochal. ¶ ~인 발견 an epoch-making discovery / ~인 사건 an epoch-making event; a landmark.

획득(獲得) acquisition. ~하다 acquire; obtain; secure; gain; win; get. ¶ 금메달을 ~하다 win a gold medal / 권리를 ~하다 acquire (secure) rights / 정권을 ~하다 come to power / 캐나다 시민권을 ~하다 obtain Canadian citizenship. ‖ ~물 an acquisition; gainings.

획수(劃數) the number of strokes (in a Chinese character).

획일(劃一) uniformity; standardization. ~하다 make 《*something*》 uniform; standardize. ¶ ~적인 uniform; standardized / ~적인 교육 uniform education. ‖ ~화 standardization 《~화하다 standardize》.

획정(劃定) ~하다 demarcate; mark out. ¶ 경계를 ~하다 mark out (fix) a boundary.

획책(劃策) a plot; a scheme; scheming. ~하다 plan; (lay a) scheme; 《책동》 maneuver; plot. ¶ 경쟁 상대를 내쫓으려고 ~하다 scheme to oust *one's* rival 《*from office*》.

횟돌(灰一) limestone. ☞ 석회석.

횡격막(橫膈膜) [解] the diaphragm; [醫] the phrenic.

횡단(橫斷) crossing. ~하다 cross; go (run) across; traverse. ¶ 거리

를 ~하다 cross a street / 해협을 헤엄쳐 ~하다 swim across the channel / 태평양을 제트기로 ~ 다 fly across the Pacific by jet. ∥ ~면 a cross section / ~보도 a pedestrian crossing; a cross walk (美); a zebra crossing (英).

횡대(橫隊) (in) a line; a rank. ¶ 2열 ~로 정렬하다 be drawn up in a double line / 4열 ~ 되다 form (up) four deep.

횡듣다(橫—) hear (it, him) wrong.

횡령(橫領) (a) usurpation; 《공금의》 embezzlement. ~하다 usurp; embezzle; appropriate 《a person's property》. ¶그녀는 공금을 ~했다 She embezzled public money. ∥ ~죄 embezzlement.

횡보다(橫—) see wrong(ly); (make a) mistake; misread.

횡사(橫死) a violent [an unnatural] death. ~하다 meet a violent death; be killed in an accident.

횡서(橫書) ~하다 write laterally. ☞ 가로쓰기.

횡선(橫線) a horizontal [cross] line. ∥ ~수표 a crossed check.

횡설수설(橫說竪說) incoherent talk; random [idle] talk; nonsense. ~ 하다 talk incoherently; make disjointed remarks; talk 「at random [nonsense]」. ¶ ~하지 마라 Don't talk nonsense !

횡액(橫厄) an unexpected accident; an unforeseen disaster [calamity].

횡재(橫財) unexpected fortune (gains); a windfall. ~하다 come into unexpected fortune; have a windfall; make a lucky find.

횡포(橫暴) tyranny; oppression. ~하다 (be) oppressive; tyrannical; high-handed. ¶그의 발언은 ~다 His speech is high-handed.

횡행(橫行) ~하다 be rampant; overrun 《the town》; 《장소가》 be infested with 《robbers》. ¶건달들이 ~하는 거리 a hooligan-infested street; a town infested [overrun] with hooligans / 큰 도시에는 범죄가 ~하고 있다 Crime is rampant in the big city.

효(孝) filial piety [duty].

효과(效果) (an) effect; efficacy(효력); a result(결과). ¶~적인 effective; fruitful / ~ 없는 ineffective; fruitless / ~가 있다 have an effect 《on》; be (of) no good / ~를 거두다 obtain the desired results / 이 약은 차멀미에 ~가 있다 This medicine is effective for carsickness. / 그녀의 눈물은 그에게 아무런 ~가 없었다 Her tears had no effect on him.

효녀(孝女) a filial daughter.

효능(效能) (an) effect; virtue; efficacy. ¶약의 ~ the virtue of medicine / ~이 있는 effective; efficacious /이 약은 환자에게 ~이 있었다 This medicine worked well on the patient.

효도(孝道) filial piety [duty]. ¶~를 다하다 be dutiful to one's parents.

효력(效力) effect; efficacy(약의); validity; force(법의). ¶~이 있는 effective; efficacious; valid / ~이 없는 ineffective; null and void (법률·계약에) / ~이 생기다 come into effect [force] / ~을 잃다 lose effect [force] / 이 규칙은 아직 ~이 있다 This rule is still in effect [force].

효모(酵母) yeast; ferment. ∥ ~균 yeast fungus.

효부(孝婦) a filial daughter-in-law.

효성(孝誠) filial affection [piety]. ¶ ~스럽다 (be) dutiful; filial / 부모에게 ~을 다하다 discharge one's duties to one's parents / ~이 지극하다 be devoted to one's parents.

효소(酵素) an enzyme; a ferment. ¶ ~의 enzymatic. ∥ ~학 enzymology.

효수(梟首) ~하다 gibbet a head.

효시(嚆矢) the beginning; the first; the first person 《to do》; a pioneer; the first instance.

효심(孝心) filial piety. ¶ ~이 있는 dutiful; filial; devoted.

효용(效用) use; usefulness; utility; 《효력》 effect. ¶ ~이 있다 [없다] be useful [useless]; be of use [no use] / 한계 ~ marginal utility. ∥ ~가치 effective value; utility value.

효율(效率) 〔理〕 efficiency. ¶기계의 ~ mechanical efficiency.

효자(孝子) a dutiful [filial] son.

효행(孝行) filial piety [duty].

효험(效驗) efficacy; (an) effect. ¶ ~이 있다 be efficacious; be effective.

후(後) ① 《나중에》 after; later (on); afterward(s); in future. ¶한 이틀 ~에 in a couple of days(지금부터); a couple of days after [later] (그때부터) / 지금부터 10년 ~에 in ten years; ten years from now / 흐린 ~에 맑음 〔일기 예보〕 Cloudy, fine later. ② 《… 한 뒤에》 after 《doing》; next to; following. ¶그 ~에 since then; after that.

후 blowing; with a puff [whiff]. ¶ ~ 불다 whiff; puff.

후각(嗅覺) the sense of smell. ¶ ~이 예민하다 have a keen nose.

후견(後見) guardianship. ~하다

후계(後繼) succession; ~하다 succeed to; succeed 《*a person in his office*》. ‖ ~내각 the succeeding [incoming] Cabinet / ~자 a successor; an heir (남자); an heiress (여자).

후고(後顧) looking behind; the future outlook 《*for*》. ~하다 look behind; worry over the future. ¶ ~의 염려 anxiety about *one's* future [home].

후골(喉骨) [解] the Adam's apple.
후관(嗅官) the olfactory organ.
후광(後光) a glory; an aureole; 〔광환〕 a halo; a nimbus; a corona.
후굴(後屈) retroflexion. ¶ 자궁~ [醫] retroflexion (of the uterus).
후궁(後宮) a royal harem 〔concubine〕.
후기(後記) a postscript 〔생략 P. S.〕. ¶ 편집~ an editorial postscript.
후기(後期) the latter term (period); the second (last, next) half year. ¶ ~인상〔주의〕파 [美術] the Post-impressionists.
후끈거리다 ☞ 화끈거리다.
후납(後納) 〔우편의〕 subsequent payment 《*of postage*》.
후닥닥 〔후딱〕 with a jump [start]; suddenly; 〔서두름〕 hurriedly; in a hurry; in haste. ¶ ~거리다 keep jumping; scamper; hurry up; rush; make haste.
후대(後代) future generation; the next [coming] generation.
후대(厚待) ~하다 give a warm [hearty] reception 《*to*》; receive warmly; treat hospitably [kindly]. ¶ ~를 받다 be given hospitable treatment.
후덕(厚德) liberal favor; liberality. ~하다 (be) liberal; virtuous.
후두(喉頭) the larynx. ¶ ~암 laryngeal cancer / ~카타르 laryngeal catarrh.
후두부(後頭部) [解] the back (part) of the head; [解] the occipital region; the occiput.
후들거리다 tremble; shake; shiver 《*with cold*》. ¶ 무서움으로 다리가 ~ *one's* legs are trembling with fear.
후딱 quickly; speedily; promptly; instantly. ¶ 일을 ~ 해치우다 get a job done promptly.
후레아들 an ill-bred fellow; a boor; a lout.
후련하다 feel refreshed [relieved]; feel unburdened. ¶ 다 털어놓고 이야기하면 ~ 후련해진다 Make a clean breast of it, and you will feel relieved.

후렴(後斂) a (musical) refrain; a burden.
후루루(호각부는 소리) whistling; blowing; 〔불타는 모양〕 burning up with a flicker. ~하다 whistle; blow; 〔불타다〕 burn up with a flicker.
후루룩〔날짐승이〕 with a flutter; 〔마시는 소리〕 with a slurp. ¶ 새가 ~ 날아가다 a bird flutters away / 죽을 ~ 들이 마시다 slurp down *one's* porridge.
후리다 ① 〔모난 곳을〕 shave off; plane off(대패로); cut off the edge 《*of*》. ② 〔채어가다〕 snatch 《*a thing*》 away 《*from*》; take 《*a thing*》 by force; tear 《*a thing*》 《*from a person*》. ③ 〔뒤돌러서 몰다〕 round up; net; catch 《*with a net*》. ¶ 그물로 물고기를 ~ chase [catch] fish with a net. ④ 〔호리다〕 captivate; charm; bewitch; seduce 《*a woman*》.
후리질 seining. ~하다 seine.
후리후리하다 (be) tall and willowy [slender].
후림(誘·誘) seduction; a seductive trick; a wile. ¶ ~을 당하다 be seduced.
후릿그물 a seine; a dragnet.
후면(後面) the back (side); the rear 《*of*》. ¶ 학교 ~ in the rear of the school.
후무리다 embezzle; pocket. ¶ 많은 공금을 후무려 도망치다 run [fly] away embezzling a lot of public money.
후문(後門) a rear [back] gate.
후문(後聞) an after-talk.
후물거리다 mumble; gum; chew with toothless gums.
후물림(後一) 〔물려받음〕 handing down; a thing handed down; a hand-me-down. ¶ 형의 ~옷 clothes handed down from *one's* brother.
후미 a cove; an inlet.
후미(後尾) 〔뒷쪽〕 the tail (very) end; 〔배의〕 the stern. ¶ ~의 후미 rear; back / ~에 at the rear [back] 《*of*》.
후미지다 ① 〔물가가〕 (get) a bend in; form an inlet. ② 〔장소가〕 (be) secluded; retired; lonely. ¶ 후미진 곳 a secluded spot; an out-of-the-way place.
후반(後半) the latter [second] half 《*of*》. ¶ 20세기 ~ the second half of the 20th century; the latter part of 20th century. ‖ ~기 the latter half of the year / ~전 the second half of a game.
후발(後發) ¶ ~ 중소 기업체들 a group of small enterprises that got into the business later. ‖

~개발도상국 the least developed among developing countries(생략 LDDC).
후방(後方) the rear; the back side. ¶ ~에 in the rear; at the back; behind / 적의 ~을 공격하다 attack the enemy in the rear. ‖ ~ 근무 service [duties] in the rear; rear service (at the base) / ~기지 a rear base / ~부대 troops in the rear / ~사령부 headquarters in the rear.
후배(後輩) one's junior(s); younger men; the younger generation (총칭). ¶학교 ~ one's junior in school / 나는 김씨의 2년 ~다 I am two years Mr. Kim's junior. or I am Mr. Kim's junior by two years.
후배지(後背地) a hinterland.
후보(候補) ① (입후보) candidacy; candidature; (후보자) a candidate. ¶만년 ~ an ever-unsuccessful candidate / ~로 나서다 be a candidate for (the next Presidency); run (as a candidate) (in the coming election). ‖ ~자 명부 a list of (eligible) candidate; (정당의) a slate; a ticket(美) / ~지 a site proposed (for). ② (운동팀의) substitution. ‖ ~선수 a substitute (player); a reserve.
후부(後部) the rear; the back [hind] part.
후분(後分) one's luck [fortune] in the latter part of life. ¶ ~이 좋다 be lucky late in life.
후불(後拂) deferred (post, future) payment. ¶물건을 ~로 사다 buy goods on credit [deferred terms].
후비다 dig (up); (귀·코·이를) pick (one's ears).
후비적거리다 scoop out repeatedly; keep gouging; keep picking (one's nose).
후사(後事) (죽은 뒤의) affairs after one's death; (장래의) future affairs. ¶ ~을 부탁하다 entrust (another) with future affairs.
후사(後嗣) a successor; (상속인) an heir(남자); an heiress(여자).
후사(厚謝) ~하다 reward (a person) handsomely; thank (a person) heartily; express one's hearty thanks.
후산(後産) the afterbirth.
후살이(後一) (재가) remarriage; a second marriage (of a woman).
후생(厚生) social [public] welfare. ‖ ~과(課) the welfare section / ~사업 public welfare enterprises; welfare work / ~시설 welfare facilities.
후생(後生) 《후진》 juniors; younger men; 《내생》 the future life.
후서방(後書房) one's second husband. ¶ ~을 얻다 marry again; remarry.
후세(後世) 《장래》 coming age; 《후대 사람》 future generations; posterity. ¶이름을 ~에 남기다 hand down one's name to posterity.
후속(後續) ~의 succeeding; following. ‖ ~부대 further reinforcements / ~조치 follow-up steps.
후손(後孫) descendants; a scion; offspring; posterity. ¶ ~이 없다 have no descendants / …의 ~이다 be descended from…; be a descendant of….
후송(後送) ~하다 send back (from the) front; evacuate (to the rear). ¶ ~되다 be sent back to the rear; be invalided home (병, 부상으로). ‖ ~병원 an evacuation hospital / ~환자 an evacuated casualty [patient].
후술(後述) ~하다 say [mention, describe] later. ¶상세한 것은 ~하겠다 Full particulars will be mentioned later.
후신(後身) one's later self; one's future being; one's new existence after rebirth.
후신경(嗅神經) 〖生〗 an olfactory nerve.
후실(後室) one's second wife. ¶ ~자식 a child born of the second wife / ~을 맞아들이다 take (a woman) for a second wife.
후안(厚顔) a brazen face. ¶ ~무치 shamelessness; brazen; impudence (~무치하다 be brazenfaced [shameless]).
후열(後列) the rear (rank, row); the back row.
후예(後裔) ⇨후손.
후원(後苑·後園) a rear garden; a backyard(美).
후원(後援) support; backing; patronage. ~하다 give support (to); back (up); aid; help; get behind(美). ¶재정적으로 ~하다 support (a person) financially; give financial support to (a person) / …의 ~하에 with the support of…; 《주최》 sponsored by…; under the auspices of…. ‖ ~자 a supporter; a sponsor; a patron; a booster(美口) / ~회 a supporters' association; a society for the support (of…).
후위(後衛) 〖競〗 a back (player); 〖軍〗 the rear (guard). ¶ ~를 보다 play the back.
후유증(後遺症) 〖醫〗 sequelae; an aftereffect (of a disease); 《여파》 an aftereffect; an aftermath. ¶선거의 ~ the aftermath

of elections / ~이 있을지도 모른다 I am afraid there may be an aftereffect. 〔(kindness)〕.
후은(厚恩) (receive) great favor
후의(厚意) 《호의》 kindness; goodwill; good wishes; kind intentions. ¶ …의 ~로 through the courtesy (good offices) of….
후의(厚誼) close friendship; (your) favor (kindness). ¶ ~를 입다 enjoy your esteemed favor.
후일(後日) later days; the future. ¶ ~에 in (the) future; one of these days; later (on); some (other) day / ~을 위하여 《참고로》 for future reference; 《증거로》 as a future proof of. ¶ ~담 recollections; reminiscences; a sequel 《to an event》.
후임(後任) 《사람》 a successor 《to a post》. ¶ ~의 …으로 in succession to…; as a successor to… / ~이 되다 succeed 《a person in his post》; take 《a person's》 place / 자네 ~을 찾기가 힘드네 You are a hard man who will replace.
후자(後者) the latter. ¶ 전자와 ~ the former and the latter / 전자가 ~보다 낫다 The former is better than the latter.
후작(侯爵) a marquis; a marquess. ¶ ~부인 a marchioness.
후장(後場) 〖證〗 the afternoon session (market, sale).
후정(厚情) ☞ 후의(厚意).
후제(候-) some other day (time).
후조(候鳥) a migratory bird; a bird of passage. ☞ 철새.
후주곡(後奏曲) 〖樂〗 a postlude.
후줄근하다 (be) wet and limp; be a little soggy. ¶ 옷이 이슬에 젖어 ~ one's clothes get wet with dew and lose their starch.
후진(後陣) the rear guard.
후진(後進) ① 《후배》 a junior; a younger man; the younger generation (총칭). ② 《미발달》 backwardness; underdevelopment. ¶ ~의 backward; underdeveloped / ~국 a backward (underdeveloped) nation / ~성 backwardness. ③ 《후퇴》 ~하다 go astern (선박이); move (slip) backward.
후처(後妻) ☞ 후취.
후천성(後天性) (be) postnatal; acquired. ¶ ~면역결핍증 〖醫〗 Acquired Immune Deficiency Syndrome(생략 AIDS).
후천적(後天的) a posteriori 《라》; postnatal; acquired 《생물학적》. ¶ ~ 면역 acquired immunity / 그의 낙천적 성격은 ~인 것이다 He was not born an optimist.
후추(-) (black) pepper. ¶ ~를 치다 sprinkle pepper on 《meat》. ‖ ~

병 a pepper pot; a pepperbox (美).
후취(後娶) remarriage; one's second wife(妻). ¶ ~를 얻다 take a second wife; remarry.
후탈(後-) complications from childbirth(산후의); later complications of a disease(병후의); the troublesome aftermath; an aftereffect. ¶ ~이 없도록 하다 leave no seeds of future trouble.
후텁지근하다 (be) sultry; stuffy; sticky. ¶ 그 방은 후텁지근했다 It was stuffy in the room.
후퇴(後退) (a) retreat (퇴각); (a) recession(경기의); retrogression (퇴보). ~하다 retreat; recede; go (move, fall) back; back. ¶ 경기의 ~ a business recession / 2, 3보 ~하다 take a few steps backward / 국경에서 15마일 ~하다 retreat fifteen miles from the border.
후편(後便) 《뒤쪽》 the back side; 《나중 인편》 a later messenger.
후편(後篇) the second (last) volume; the latter part 《of a book》.
후하다(厚-) ① 《인심이》 (be) cordial; hospitable; warm-hearted. ¶ ~한 대접 a cordial (hospitable) reception. ②《인색하지》 (be) lenient; generous; liberal. ¶ 후하게 generously; liberally / 점수가 ~ be generous in marking; be a lenient marker. ③《두껍다》(be) thick.
후학(後學) a junior; younger students (scholars). ¶ ~을 지도하다 instruct one's juniors.
후항(後項) 〖數〗 the consequent; (다음 조항) the succeeding (following) clause.
후환(後患) later (future) trouble; an evil consequence; later complications. ¶ ~을 남기ف sow seeds of trouble / ~을 없애다 remove the source of evils.
후회(後悔) (a) repentance; penitence; regret; remorse. ~하다 regret; repent 《of》; feel remorse for 《one's crime》; be penitent (sorry) 《for》. ¶ 자기가 한 행동을 ~하다 regret (repent of) one's act / ~는 앞서 소용 없다 It is no use crying over spilt milk. 〔now.
후년(後年) three years from
훅[1] 〖拳〗 a hook. ¶ ~을 넣다 (deliver) a hook. ②《고리단추》 a hook.
훅 with a sip (slurp); with a puff. ¶ 불을 ~ 불어 끄다 blow out light.
훈(訓) the Korean rendering (reading) of a Chinese character.
훈계(訓戒) (an) admonition; ex-

훈공(勳功) merits; distinguished services; meritorious deeds. ¶ ~을 세우다 render distinguished services (*to the state*); distinguish oneself (*in*).

훈기(薰氣) ① 《훈훈한 기운》 warm air; heat; warmth. ② ☞ 훈김 ②.

훈김(薰―) ① ☞ 훈기(薰氣) ② 《세력》 influence; power. ¶ 삼촌의 ~으로 출세하다 rise in the world through *one's* uncle's influence.

훈련(訓練) training; (a) drill. practice. ~하다 train; drill; discipline. ¶ 잘 ~되어 있다 be highly disciplined; be well trained (*in*); be trained (*in*); train (*for*); undergo training (*for*); 맹~ hard [intensive] training. ‖ ~교관 a drillmaster / ~교본 a drill book; a training manual / ~생 a trainee / ~소 a training school [center] / 육군신병~소 an army recruit training center.

훈령(訓令) instruction; an (official) order. ~하다 instruct; give [issue] instructions [orders]. ¶ 정부는 다음과 같은 ~을 발했다 The Government issued the following instructions. / 정부의 ~에 의하여 by instructions from the Government.

훈민정음(訓民正音) ☞ 한글.
훈방(訓放) ~하다 dismiss (*a person*) with a warning (caution).
훈수(訓手) ~하다 give (*a person*) a hint [tip] (*on*).
훈시(訓示) (an address of) instructions; admonition. ~하다 instruct; give instructions.
훈위(勳位) the order of merit.
훈육(訓育) (moral) education; discipline; character building.
훈장(訓長) a teacher; a schoolmaster.
훈장(勳章) a decoration; an order; a medal. ¶ ~을 수여하다 confer [award] a decoration (*on a person*); decorate (*a person*) with a medal.
훈제(燻製) smoke-dried; smoked / ~연어 a kippered [smoked] salmon / 청어를 ~하다 smoke herring.
훈증(燻蒸) fumigation. ~하다 fumigate; smoke. ‖ ~제(劑) a fumigant. [breeze.
훈풍(薰風) a balmy wind; a warm

훈화(訓話) a moral discourse; admonitory lecture.
훈훈하다(薰薰―) 《온도가》 (be) comfortably warm; 《인정이》 (be) warmhearted [kindhearted].
훌닦다 nag [snarl] (*at*); attack [criticize, rebuke] (*a person*) severely; berate.
훌떡 《벗거나 뒤집히는 모양》 all quite; utterly; completely; 《뛰어넘는 모양》 at a bound [jump]; lightly; quickly. ¶ 옷을 ~ 벗다 strip oneself bare [stark-naked] / 신을 ~ 벗다 slip off *one's* shoes / 담을 ~ 뛰어넘다 jump [leap] over a fence nimbly [lightly].
훌라댄스 hula(-hula). ¶ ~를 추다 dance the hula.
훌륭하다 ① 《멋지다》 (be) fine; nice; handsome; excellent; splendid; grand. ¶ 훌륭히 finely; nicely; excellently; splendidly. ② 《존경할 만한》 (be) honorable; respectable; decent. ¶ 훌륭한 직업[인물] a respectable occupation [person]. ③ 《칭찬할 만한》 (be) admirable; praiseworthy; creditable; commendable. ¶ 훌륭한 저작 an admirable writing [work] / 훌륭한 일생을 보내다 live an honorable [a praiseworthy] life. ④ 《고상한》 (be) noble; lofty; high. ¶ 훌륭한 정신 a noble spirit / 훌륭한 인격자 a man of fine [noble] character. ⑤ 《위대한, 뛰어난》 (be) great; prominent; eminent. ¶ 훌륭한 학자 an eminent scholar.
훌부시다 wash clean; rinse out.
훌쩍 ① 《날쌔게》 quickly; with a jump [bound]; nimbly. ② 《마시는 모양》 at a gulp [draught]. ¶ ~ 마시다 gulp down a drink. ③ 《코를》 sniffling; snivelling. ¶ 콧물을 ~ 들이마시다 sniffle; snivel. ④ 《표연히》 aimlessly. ¶ ~ 여행을 떠나다 go on a trip aimlessly.
훌쩍거리다 《액체를》 sip (*hot coffee*); slurp (*one's soup*); suck in (*one's noodles*); 《콧물을》 snivel (sniff) repeatedly; 《울다》 sob; weep silently. ¶ 시끄럽게 코를 ~ sniff noisily / 그녀는 훌쩍거리며 대답했다 She answered with a sob.
훑다 strip; hackle; thresh (*rice*).
훑어보다 ① 《읽다》 read [run] through. ¶ 급히 편지를 ~ run through the letter in a hurry. ② 《눈여겨 보다》 give a searching glance (*at*); look carefully for [at]; scrutinize. ¶ 아무의 위 아래를 ~ look (*a person*) up and down; survey (*a person*) from head to foot.
훑이다 get threshed [hackled].
훔치개질하다 《도둑질》 steal; pilfer;

《닦다》 wipe out; mop; swab.
훔치다 ① 《절도》 steal 《*a thing from a person*》; pilfer 《*a thing from shop*》. ② 《닦다》 wipe 《off, away》; mop. ¶ 먼지를 ～ wipe dust off / 이마의 땀을 손수건으로 ～ wipe (mop) the sweat off *one's* forehead with a handkerchief.
훗날(後—) ☞ 후일.
훗배앓이(後—) afterpains.
훗훗하다 (be) uncomfortably warm; stuffy; sultry.
훤칠하다 (be) strapping; tall and slender; high in stature.
훤하다 ① 《흐릿하게 밝다》 (be) dimly white; slightly light; half-lighted; gray. ¶ 동쪽 하늘이 훤하게 밝았다 The eastern sky has become slightly light. ② ☞ 환하다 ②, ③, ④.
훨씬 《정도》 much bigger; by far; far (and away); (very) much; greatly. ¶ ～ 이전에 a long time ago / 이것이 ～ 낫다 This is much (far) better.
훨훨 ① 《나는 모양》 flutter away. ② 《벗는 모양》 ¶ 옷을 ～ 벗다 take off *one's* clothes briskly.
훼방(毀謗) ① 《비방》 slander; calumny; defamation; vilification. ～하다 slander; defame; vilify; backbite; speak ill of. ② 《방해》 interference; obstruction. ～하다 interfere 《with》; interrupt; thwart; disturb. ¶ 작업을 ～놓다 hinder 《*a person*》 in *his* work; interfere with 《*a person's*》 work.
훼손(毀損) damage; injury; defamation; libel. ～하다 damage; injure; impair; spoil; defame 《명예를》. ¶ 명예 ～ a libel; defamation of character / 발행자를 명예 ～으로 고발하다 accuse a publisher of libel.
행하다 ☞ 행하다.
휘감기다 get wound 《round》; twine 《coil, wind》 *itself* round. ¶ 담쟁이덩굴에 휘감긴 나무 a tree entwined with ivy.
휘감다 wind 《wind, twine》 around; fasten 《tie》 round.
휘갑치다 ① 《수습》 settle 《dispose of》 《*a matter*》; fix 《up》; finish, wind 《clear》 up. ② 《바느질에서》 *border*; hem 《up》; stitch up.
휘날리다 《바람에》 fly; flap; flutter; wave 《in the wind》. ¶ 기가 바람에 휘날리고 있다 A flag is fluttering in the wind.
휘늘어지다 《처져》 hang; dangle; 《가지 따위가》 droop; hang down.
휘다 bend; be 《get》 bent; curve; warp. ¶ 눈의 무게로 나뭇가지가 휘어 있었다 The tree branches have bent under the snow.
휘도(輝度) brightness.
휘돌리다 turn; revolve 《*a thing*》.
휘두르다 《돌리다》 whirl 〔swing〕 《*a thing*》 round; brandish; flourish. ¶ 팔을 ～ swing *one's* arm around / 막대기를 휘둘러 상대방을 위협하다 threaten *one's* opponent flourishing a stick. ¶ 《얼떨하게》 confuse; bewilder. ¶ 《뜻대로》 exercise 〔wield〕 《*authority over*》; have 《*a person*》 under perfect control. ¶ 권력을 ～ wield 〔exercise〕 *one's* power / 폭력을 ～ resort to violence.
휘둥그래지다 《눈이》 open 《*one's eyes*》 wide; be surprised 〔startled〕 《*at*》. ¶ 눈이 휘둥그래져서 with *one's* eyes wide open. 〔*prise*〕.
휘둥그렇다 be wide-eyed 《with surprise》.
휘두루 for general 〔all〕 purposes; for various uses. ¶ ～ 쓰이다 have various uses.
휘뚝거리다 《흔들리다》 rock; shake; be shaky 〔rickety, unsteady〕; 《마음이》 feel nervous 〔jittery〕.
휘말리다 be rolled 〔wrapped〕 《up》 《*in*》; be dragged 《*into*》; be involved 《entangled》 《*in a war*》; get mixed up 《*in a trouble*》.
휘몰다 《차·말을》 drive hard; urge on; 《가축 따위를》 drive; chase; round up; run.
휘발(揮發) ～하다 volatilize. ∥ ～성 volatility 《～성의 volatile 《*matter*》 / ～유 gasoline 《가솔린》; volatile oil.
휘석(輝石) 《鑛》 pyroxene.
휘선(輝線) 《理》 a bright line. ∥ ～ 스펙트럼 a bright-line spectrum.
휘어들다 be forced 〔squeezed, pushed〕 in.
휘어잡다 ① 《잡다》 hold 《*a thing*》 in *one's* hand; grasp; seize; clutch. ② 《사람을》 control; have 《*a person*》 under *one's* control; keep a firm grip 《*on a person*》.
휘어지다 get bent; bend; curve; warp 《제목 등이》.
휘장(揮帳) a curtain.
휘장(徽章) 《wear, put on》 a badge; an insignia. 《*arms*》.
휘적거리다 swagger; swing 《*one's arms*》.
휘젓다 ① 《뒤저어》 stir 《up》; churn 《*milk*》; beat up. ¶ 계란을 휘저어 거품이 일게 하여 beat up eggs well. ② 《어지럽게》 disturb; upset; disarrange. ③ 《팔 등을》 swing 《*one's arms*》.
휘청거리다 yield; be flexible 〔pliant〕; totter; stagger; reel. ¶ 무거운 짐을 지고 ～ totter 〔stagger〕 under a heavy load / 강타를 맞고 ～ reel under a heavy blow.
휘파람 a whistle. ¶ ～을 불다 (give a) whistle; whistle a

tune / ~을 불어 개를 되돌아오게 하다 whistle a dog back.
휘하(麾下) 〖딸린 군사〗 (troops) under *one's* command; *one's* men.
휘호(揮毫) 〖글씨〗 writing; 〖그림〗 painting; drawing. ~하다 write; draw; paint. ‖ ~로 a fee (an honorarium) for the writing.
휘황찬란하다(輝煌燦爛—) (be) resplendent; brilliant; bright.
휘휘 round and round (about). ¶ ~ 감다 wind (*a rope*) round (*a thing*) / 방안을 ~ 둘러보다 run *one's* eyes around the room.
휘휘하다(쓸쓸) (be) dreary; desolate; lonely.
휙 ① 〖돌아가는 꼴〗 swiftly; with a jerk; (a)round. ¶ ~ 돌다 turn (right) around. ② 〖바람이〗 with a sweep; with a whiff; whizzing. ¶ ~ 소리가 나다 whiz(z); whistle / ~ 일진의 강풍이 불었다 There was a gust of strong wind. ③ 《던지는 꼴》 light and nimbly.
휠체어 a wheel chair.
휩싸다 ① 〖싸다〗 wrap (up) (*in paper*); tuck (*a child*) up (*in a blanket*). ② 〖뒤덮다〗 envelope; shroud. ③ 〖비호하다〗 protect; shield.
휩싸이다 be covered (veiled, enveloped, shrouded); get wrapped up; 〖감정 등에〗 be seized (*with a panic*). ¶ 불길에 ~ be enveloped in flames.
휩쓸다 sweep (*away, up, off, over*); make a clean sweep (*of*); 〖설침〗 overwhelm; overrun; rampage. ¶ 휩쓸리다 be swept away (*by the waves*); be involved in (*a war*).
휴가(休暇) holidays; a vacation; a leave (of absence); a (*summer*) recess (대학의); a furlough (장기의). ¶ 겨울 [크리스마스] ~ the winter [Christmas] vacation [holiday] / 유급 ~ a paid vacation (holiday); a vacation (holiday) with pay / ~을 얻다 take a (*week's*) holiday / ~를 주다 grant leave of absence. ‖ ~객 a vacationer / ~여행 a leave vacation trip / ~원 a leave application.
휴간(休刊) suspension of publication. ~하다 suspend publication; stop issuing.
휴강(休講) ~하다 cancel a class [lecture]; give no lecture (*for the day*); absent *oneself* from *one's* lectures.
휴게(休憩) (a) rest; a recess; an interval (intermission) (막간) 〖美〗. ~하다 take a rest (recess). ‖ ~소 a resting place / ~시간 a rest room; a lounge (호텔의); a foyer

(프) 〖극장의〗.
휴경(休耕) ~하다 lay land fallow; leave (*a field*) fallow (idle). ‖ ~기간 a fallow period / ~지 a fallow field; a field lying fallow.
휴관(休館) ~하다 close (*a theater*). ‖ 금일~ 〖게시〗 Closed today.
휴교(休校) a (short) closure of school. ~하다 close (*the school*) temporarily; be closed. ¶ 학교는 3일간 ~다 School is closed for three days.
휴대(携帶) ~하다 carry; bring (take, have) (*a thing*) with (*one*). ~용 portable; handy (to carry) / ~용 라디오 a portable radio. ‖ ~식량 field [combat 〖美〗] ration / ~품 hand baggage 〖美〗 (luggage 〖英〗); personal effects; *one's* belongings / ~품 보관소 a checkroom 〖美〗; a cloakroom 〖英〗.
휴머니스트 a humanist.
휴머니즘 humanism.
휴머니티 humanity.
휴식(休息) (a) rest; repose; recess; 〖일하는 사이의〗 a break. ~하다 (take a) rest; repose; take breath (숨돌림). ¶ 5분간의 ~을 취하다 take a five-minute break. ‖ ~시간 a recess; a break.
휴양(休養) (a) rest; repose; relaxation; recreation; recuperation (병후의). ~하다 (take a) rest; repose; relax; refresh (recreate) *oneself*; recuperate (병후에). ‖ ~시설 recreation facilities / ~지 a recreation center; a rest area.
휴업(休業) closing down (상점의); suspension of business (trade) (영업의); a shutdown (공장의). ~하다 《사람이》 rest from work; 《점포 등이》 close (*an office, a factory*); be closed; suspend business (operations). ¶ 금일 ~ 〖게시〗 Closed today. ‖ 임시~ 〖일〗 a special (an extra) holiday; 〖게시〗 Temporarily closed. / ~일 a (business) holiday; a bank holiday (은행의).
휴일(休日) a holiday; a day off; an off day. ‖ ~수당 non-duty allowance / 법정 [임시]~ a legal (special) holiday.
휴전(休電) suspension of power supply. ‖ ~일 a no-power day.
휴전(休戰) a truce; an armistice; a cease-fire. ~하다 conclude an armistice (*with*); make a truce; stop fighting. ¶ ~기념일 (1차 대전의) the Armistice Day / ~명령 orders to suspend hostilities; a cease-fire (order) (~명령을 내리다 call a cease-fire) / ~선 a truce line; a cease-fire (

휴정(休廷) recess. ~하다 hold no court; adjourn the court. ¶~일 a non-judicial day.

휴지(休止) (a) pause; stoppage. ~하다 stop; pause; cease; suspend.

휴지(休紙) wastepaper; toilet paper (화장지). ¶~통 a wastebasket; a wastepaper basket.

휴직(休職) suspension from office (service, duty); leave of absence. ~하다 retire from office temporarily; be temporarily laid off. ¶1년간 ~하다 have (be given) one year's leave of absence.

휴진(休診) ~하다 see (accept) no patients 《for the day》. ¶금일 〈게시〉 No Consultation Today.

휴학(休學) temporary absence from school. ~하다 absent *oneself* (stay away) from school for a time. ¶동맹~ a students' strike.

휴한지(休閑地) idle (fallow) land.

휴항(休航) suspension of sailing. ~하다 suspend the sailing (flying) 《on a line》; be laid up (배가).

휴화산(休火山) a dormant (inactive) volcano.

휴회(休會) (an) adjournment; a recess. ~하다 adjourn; (go into) recess. ¶~ 중이다 be in recess / ~를 선언하다 call a recess.

흉 ① 〈흉터〉 a scar. ¶~이 있는 얼굴 a scarred face / ~이 남다 have a scar. ② 〈결점〉 a fault; a defect; a flaw (흠). ☞ 흉보다, 흉잡다.

흉가(凶家) a haunted house.

흉계(凶計) a wicked scheme; (devise) an evil (a sinister) plot.

흉골(胸骨) 〖解〗 the sternum; the breastbone.   [rax.

흉곽(胸廓) 〖解〗 the chest; the tho-

흉금(胸襟) ¶~을 터놓다 open *one's* heart 《to》; unbosom *oneself* 《to》 / ~을 털어놓고 이야기하고 싶다 I want to have a heart-to-heart talk with you.

흉기(凶器) a lethal (dangerous) weapon. ¶달리는 ~ a weapon on wheels.

흉내 imitation; mimicry; a take-off 《of》. ~을 내다 imitate; copy; mimic. ‖ ~쟁이 a (clever) mimic; an imitator.

흉년(凶年) a year of famine (bad harvest); a lean year.

흉노(匈奴) 〖史〗 the Huns.

흉몽(凶夢) an ominous (a bad) dream.

흉물(凶物) a snaky person; an insidious (evil) fellow.

흉변(凶變) (a) disaster; a calamity; a tragic accident. ¶~을 당하다 meet with (suffer) a calamity (disaster).

흉보(凶報) bad (ill, sad) news; news of death. ¶갑작스러운 ~에 접하여 놀라다 be surprised at the (sad) news of *a person's* unexpected death.

흉보다 speak ill of; disparage.

흉부(胸部) 〖解〗 the breast; the chest. ‖ ~질환 a chest disease (trouble); a trouble in the chest.

흉사(凶事) an unlucky affair; a misfortune; a disaster; a calamity.

흉상(凶相) a vicious look; an evil countenance (face).

흉상(胸像) a bust.

흉악(凶惡) ~하다 (be) wicked; villainous; atrocious. ¶~한 범죄 a heinous (violent) crime. ‖ ~범 a brutal criminal.

흉어(凶漁) a poor catch (haul).

흉위(胸圍) chest (bust) measurement (여성의 경우는 bust). ¶~를 재다 measure the chest (bust).

흉일(凶日) an evil (unlucky) day.

흉작(凶作) a bad (poor, lean) crop (harvest); a failure of crops.

흉잡다 find fault with; pick at.

흉잡히다 be found fault with; be spoken ill of; be picked on.

흉조(凶兆) an ill (evil) omen.

흉중(胸中) *one's* heart (feelings). ¶~을 밝히다 unbosom *oneself*; open *one's* heart / ~을 헤아리다 read *a person's* mind; enter into *a person's* feelings.

흉측스럽다(凶測—) ☞ 흉측하다.

흉측하다(凶測—) (be) terribly heinous (wicked, villainous); 〈얼굴이〉 (be) very ugly (crude).

흉탄(凶彈) an assassin's bullet. ¶~에 쓰러지다 be killed by an assassin's bullet (shell); be shot to death by an assassin.

흉터 a scar; a seam 《of an old wound》. ¶~를 남기다 leave a scar.

흉포하다(凶暴—) (be) ferocious; brutal; atrocious; violent. ¶흉포한 살인자 a fierce (violent) killer.

흉하다(凶—) ① 〈사악〉 (be) bad; evil; wicked; ill-natured. ② 〈불길함〉 (be) unlucky; ominous; sinister. ③ 〈보기에〉 (be) ugly; unsightly; unseemly.

흉하적 faultfinding. ~하다 find fault with 《a person》; cavil at 《another's》 fault.

흉한(凶漢) a ruffian; a villain; a rascal; 《암살자》 an assassin.

흥행(興行) 《폭행》 violence; (an) outrage/《살인》 (a) murder; (an) assassination《암살》. ¶ ~을 저지르다 do violence to 《a person》.

흠집하다 a fault; a defect. ¶ ~없다 be intimate enough to overlook each other's faults / ~없는 사이다 be on intimate 〔familiar〕 terms with.

흥흥하다(洶洶─) 《인심이》 be panic-stricken; be filled with alarm.

흐느뜨리다 pull 〔take〕 down; demolish; destroy.

흐느지다 collapse; crumble; fall down; get pulled down.

흐느끼다 sob; whimper; be choked with tears. ¶ 흐느껴 울다 sob (convulsively) / 그녀는 흐느끼면서 자기 이야기를 했다 She told her story with tears in her eyes.

흐느적거리다 flutter; sway gently; wave. ¶ 잎이 바람에 ~ leaves flutter in the breeze.

흐늘거리다 ① 《놀고 지내다》 idle 〔dawdle〕 one's time away; fritter away one's time; dawdle. ② 《흔들거리다》 hang loosely; dangle; swing; sway gently.

흐늘흐늘 ~ 하다 (be) soft; pulpy; flabby; mushy; limp. ¶ 더위로 아스팔트 길이 ~해졌다 The asphalt roads became limp in the heat.

흐느갑스럽다 be exaggerated〔overexcited〕 in speech; (be) bombastic; flippant.

흐려지다 ① 《날이》 get 〔become〕 cloudy 〔overcast〕; cloud 《over》. ② 《유리 따위가》 become dim 〔blurred〕; be clouded; get fogged (misted). ¶ 입김에 안경이 흐려졌다 My breath fogged up my glasses. ③ 《마음·얼굴·눈이》 cloud; be clouded.

흐르다 ① 《액체》 flow; stream; run (down); trickle(졸졸). ¶ 물은 낮은 쪽으로 흐른다 Water runs downhill. ② 《세월 등이》 pass (away); flow by. ¶ 몇 년이나는 세월이 흘렀다 Several years passed. ③ 《경향으로》 lapse 〔fall〕 《into》; run (incline) 《to》; be swayed 《by》. ¶ 사치에 ~ lapse into luxury / 감정에 ~ be swayed by sentiment.

흐리다¹ ① 《탁하다》 (be) muddy; turbid; thick; cloudy(술이). ② 《날이》 (be) cloudy; overcast. ¶ 흐린 날씨〔날〕 cloudy weather; a cloudy day / 날이 ~ It is cloudy. ③ 《희미하다》 (be) dim; clouded; blurred; smoked; vague; obscure; indistinct. ④ 《눈이》 (be) dull; bleared; bleary.

흐리다² ① 《흔적을》 blot out; efface. ② 《혼탁하게 함》 make 《water》 muddy (turbid, cloudy); make unclean. ¶ 물을 ~ muddy water. ③ 《불분명하게 함》 make indistinct (vague, obscure, ambiguous). ¶ 대답을 ~ give a vague answer / 말끝을 ~ leave one's statement vague. ④ 《더럽힘》 stain; blemish. ¶ 집안의 명성을 ~ stain the good name of one's family.

흐리멍덩하다 ① 《기억·정신 따위가》 (be) vague; obscure; dim; indistinct; hazy. ¶ 기억이 ~ one's memory is dim (hazy). ② 《불명화》 (be) muddled; indecisive; uncertain; dubious. ¶ 태도가 ~ one's attitude is ambiguous / 대답이 ~ an answer is indecisive.

흐릿분하다 《사물 따위가》 (be) cloudy; hazy; indistinct; obscure. ¶ 흐리터분한 날씨 a cloudy 〔gloomy〕 weather. ② 《사람이》 (be) dark-minded; sluggish; slovenly; be not open. ¶ 흐리터분한 사람 a slovenly person.

흐릿하다 (be) rather cloudy (dim, dull, muddy, indistinct, ambiguous). ¶ 흐릿한 날씨 dull weather / 흐릿한 하늘 a gloomy sky / 흐릿한 목소리 an indistinct (a thick) voice.

흐무러지다 ① 《푹 익어서》 be overripe. ② 《물에 불어서》 be sodden; be swollen.

흐물흐물 ~ 하다 (be) overripe; very soft; flabby. ¶ ~하게 삶다 boil to pulp / ~해지다 be reduced to pulp (jelly).

흐뭇하다 (be) pleasing; satisfied. ¶ 흐뭇해서 웃다 smile with satisfaction.

흐슬부슬 ~ 하다 (be) not sticky; crumbly. ¶ 과자가 ~ 부서지다 cakes crumble.

흐지부지 《어물어물》 ¶ ~ 끝나다 end in smoke; come to nothing / 우리의 계획은 모두 ~ 되고 말았다 All our plans have fizzled out (come to nothing).

흐트러뜨리다 ① 《여기저기》 scatter 《things》 (about); leave 《things》 scattered (lying) about; strew. ¶ 온 방에 장난감을 ~ scatter one's toys all around the room. ② 《군중을》 disperse; break up. ¶ 군중을 ~ disperse (break up) the crowd. ③ 《머리칼 따위를》 dishevel. ¶ 머리를 흐트러뜨리고 with disheveled hair.

흐트러지다 《흩어짐》 disperse; scatter; be dispersed; be scattered; 《정신이》 be distracted 《머리칼·복장 등이》 be disheveled. ¶ 바람에 그녀의 머리가 흐트러졌다 Her hair was 「wind-blown (disheveled by the wind).

흑(黑) ① ☞ 흑색. ②《바둑돌》a black stone. ¶ ~으로 두다 move first.
흑내장(黑內障)《醫》amaurosis.
흑단(黑檀)《植》ebony; black wood.
흑막(黑幕) ①《검은 장막》a black curtain. ②《음흉한 내막》concealed circumstances; the inside. ¶ ~을 벗기려 하다 try to uncover the concealed circumstances.
흑맥주(黑麥酒) black beer; porter《英》.
흑백(黑白) black and white;《시비》right and wrong. ¶ ~을 가리다 discriminate between good and bad (right and wrong); tell good from bad. ¶ ~논리 an all-or-nothing logic [attitude] / ~사진[영화] a black-and-white photograph [picture].
흑빵(黑—) rye [brown] bread.
흑사병(黑死病)《醫》the pest; the (black) plague.
흑색(黑色) black; black color. ¶ ~의 black. ‖ ~인종 the black race.
흑설탕(黑雪糖) raw [unrefined] sugar; muscovado. [bunt.
흑수병(黑穗病) smut; dustbrand
흑수정(黑水晶)《鑛》morion.
흑심(黑心) an evil intention. ¶ ~을 품은 evil-minded; black-hearted. [ite.
흑연(黑鉛)《鑛》black lead; graph-
흑요석(黑曜石)《鑛》obsidian.
흑운모(黑雲母)《鑛》biotite.
흑인(黑人) a black; a black person; an African- (Afro-) American《美》; a Negro. ¶ ~과학자 a black scientist. ‖ ~거주지구 a black neighborhood / ~영가 a Negro spiritual / ~종 the black race.
흑자(黑字) black figures [ink]. ¶ 국제수지 ~국 a balance-of-payments surplus country / ~를 내다 go into the black / 사업이 ~다 The business is in the black.
흑점(黑點) a black spot. ¶ 태양 ~《天》a sunspot; a macula.
흑탄(黑炭) black coal.
흑토(黑土) black soil [earth].
흑판(黑板) a blackboard.
흑해(黑海) the Black Sea.
흑흑 ¶ ~ 느껴 울다 sob; weep convulsively.
흔들다 shake 《one's head》; wave 《a handkerchief》; swing; rock 《a cradle》; wag (꼬리를). ¶ 흔들어 깨우다 shake 《a person》 awake / 흔들어 떨어뜨리다 shake 《fruit》 off 《a tree》.
흔들리다 shake; sway; rock; quake; flicker(불꽃 따위);《마음이》waver;《차가》joggle; jolt(덜컥);《매달린 것이》swing;《배가》roll(옆으로); pitch (앞뒤로). ¶ 이가 ~ a tooth is loose / 결심이 ~ one's resolution shakes.
흔들의자(—椅子) a rocking chair; a rocker.
흔들이《理》a pendulum.
흔들흔들 shake; sway; swing; rock. ¶ 지진으로 집이 흔들흔들했다 The house shook in the earthquake.
흔연(欣然—) joyfully; gladly; cheerfully; willingly.
흔적(痕迹) traces; marks; vestiges; evidences; signs. ¶ ~을 남기지 않다 leave no traces [marks] 《of》. ‖ ~기관《生》a vestigial organ.
흔쾌(欣快) ~하다 (be) pleasant; agreeable; delightful. ¶ ~히 pleasantly; agreeably; delightfully; willingly / 그는 ~히 나의 청을 받아들였다 He willingly accepted my wishes.
흔하다 (be) very common; usual; ordinary; be found [met with] everywhere. ¶ 흔치 않은 uncommon; extraordinary; rare.
흔히 commonly; usually; 《대개》generally. ¶ ~ 쓰이는 말 a frequently used word / ~ 있는 일 a common [an everyday] affair.
흘게늦다 《매듭·사개 따위》(be) loose(-jointed); 《하는 짓이》(be) loose; lax; slovenly; slipshod.
흘겨보다 give [cast] a sharp sidelong glance 《at》.
흘금거리다 cast a sidelong glance [look] 《at》; glare 《at》.
흘굿거리다 ☞ 흘금거리다.
흘기다 glare fiercely at; give a sharp sidelong glance 《at》; cast a reproachful [disapproving] glance 《at》; scowl 《at》.
흘끗 at a glance. ¶ ~ 보다 catch [get] a glimpse 《of》.
흘러들다 flow into; empty [drain] 《itself》 into. ¶ 태평양으로 ~ flow [run, empty] into the Pacific.
흘레(交尾) copulation; coition. ~하다 copulate(동물);pair; mate(새가); cover(씨말이). ¶ ~붙이다 couple; mate.
흘리다 ①《떨어뜨림》spill 《soup》; shed [drop] 《tears》. ②《빠르다》lose; drop. ③《글씨를》write in a cursive hand; scribble 《a letter》. ④《귓전으로》take no notice 《of》; give no heed 《to》.
흘림 the cursive style (☞ 초서). ¶ ~으로 쓰다 write in a cursive hand.
흡수(吃水) draught. ¶ ~가 얕다[깊다, 15피트이다] draw light [deep, 15 feet of water]. ‖ ~선 the

waterline.

흙 《토양》 earth; soil; 《지면》 the ground; 《진흙》 clay. ¶ ~ 을 담다 heap up earth / 외국의 ~을 밟다 step〔set foot〕 on foreign soil / ~으로 돌아가다 return to dust; die.

흙구덩이 a hollow in the ground.
흙덩이 a clod; a lump of earth.
흙먼지 dust; a cloud of dust.
흙더미 a pile 〔heap〕 of earth.
흙받기 ① 《미장이의》 a mortarboard; a hawk. ② 《자동차 등의》 a splashboard; a fender.
흙비 a dust storm; a sandstorm.
흙빛 earth color. ¶ 《안색이》 ~ 의 ashy; deadly〔deathly〕 pale / 얼굴이 ~ 이 되다 turn ashy〔deadly, deathly〕 pale.
흙손 a trowel; a float (마무리하는).
흙손질 ~ 하다 trowel; plaster with a trowel.
흙일 《do》 earthwork.
흙칠 ~ 하다 soil〔smear〕 with mud.
흙탕물 muddy water. ¶ ~ 을 뒤집어 쓰다 get 《one's clothes》 splashed with muddy water.
흙투성이 ~ 가 되다 be covered with mud.
흠 (欠) ① ☞ 흠 ①. ② 《물건의》 a crack; a flaw; 《과일의》 a speck; a bruise. ¶ ~ 이 있는 flawed; cracked; bruised / ~ 없는 flawless; perfect. 《결점》 a fault; a defect; a flaw; a stain (오점). ¶ ~ 이 없는 사람은 없다 There is no man but has some faults. or Nobody is perfect.

흠 (비웃는 소리) humph!
흠내다 (欠—) crack; (make a) flaw.
흠뜯다 (欠—) backbite; whisper against 《a person》.
흠모 (欽慕) ~ 하다 admire; adore.
흠뻑 fully; thoroughly; to the skin (젖은 끝이). ¶ ~ 젖다 be soaked to the skin; be 〔get〕 wet through.
흠씬 enough; sufficiently; to the fullest measure; thoroughly. ¶ ~ 패주다 give 《a person》 a sound thrashing / 고기를 ~ 삶다 boil meat to a pulp 〔soft enough〕.
흠잡다 (欠—) find fault with; cavil at 《a person's》 fault. ¶ 흠잡을 데 가 없다 be faultless 〔flawless〕.
흠정 (欽定) ¶ ~ 의 authorized; compiled by royal order. ‖ ~ 헌법 a constitution granted by the Emperor.
흠지다 (欠—) get scarred (몸에); be damaged; be cracked (금가다).　　　　　　　　　　　　　　〔trice.
흠집 (欠—) 《몸의》 a scar; a cicatrice.
흠치르하다 (be) sleek; glossy.
흠칫 ~ 하다 recoil; shrink; pull back 《one's head, neck, shoulders》 in surprise. ¶ ~ 놀라다 be startled 《at》.　　　　　　　〔ulum.
흡반 (吸盤) a sucker; an acetab-
흡사 (恰似) ~ 하다 resemble closely; be exactly alike. ¶ 아주 ~ 하다 be as like as two peas 〔eggs〕.
흡수 (吸水) suction of water. ‖ ~ 관 (管) a siphon; a suction pipe / ~ 펌프 a suction pump.
흡수 (吸收) absorption. ~ 하다 absorb; imbibe; suck in. ¶ ~ 성 의 〔천 따위〕 absorbent; absorptive. / ~ 력 absorbing power; absorbency / ~ 제(劑) an absorbent / ~ 합병 merger.
흡습 (吸濕) moisture absorption. ‖ ~ 성(性) hygroscopic property; hygroscopicity / ~ 의 hygroscopic; moisture-absorbing / ~ 제 (劑) a desiccant; a moisture absorbent.
흡연 (吸煙) smoking. ~ 하다 smoke 《tobacco, a pipe》. ‖ ~ 실 a smoking room / ~ 자 a smoker / ~ 칸 〔열차의〕 a smoking car (carriage 《英》); a smoker 《英》.
흡음 (吸音) sound absorption. ‖ ~ 재 a sound-absorbing materials.
흡인 (吸引) absorption; suction. ~ 하다 absorb; suck (in). ‖ ~ 력 absorptivity; sucking force.
흡입 (吸入) inhalation. ~ 하다 inhale; breathe in; suck (in). ‖ ~ 기 an inhaler / 산소 ~ 기 an oxygen inhaler.
흡족 (洽足) ~ 하다 (be) sufficient; ample; satisfactory (만족). ¶ ~ 히 enough; sufficiently; fully.
흡착 (吸着) adhesion; 〔化〕 adsorption. ~ 하다 adhere to; 〔化〕 adsorb. ¶ ~ 성의 adsorbent. ‖ ~ 제 an adsorbent.
흡혈 (吸血) bloodsucking. ‖ ~ 귀 (鬼) a vampire; a bloodsucker.
흥 (興) interest; fun; amusement. ¶ ~ 에 겨워서 in the excess of mirth / ~ 이 나다 become interested 《in》; amuse oneself 《by doing》 / ~ 을 돋우다 add to the fun 〔amusement〕 / ~ 을 깨다 spoil the fun 〔pleasure〕.
흥 hum!; humph!; pish!
흥건하다 be full to the brim; be filled up with.
흥겹다 (興—) (be) gay; merry; joyful; cheerful. ¶ 흥겹게 gaily; merrily; joyously; cheerfully; pleasantly.
흥동항동 heedlessly; inattentively; half-heartedly.
흥망 (興亡) rise and fall 《of a nation》 (일국의); ups and downs; vicissitudes. ¶ 로마제국의 ~ the

흥미 **(興味)** (an) interest. ¶ ~ 있는 interesting; amusing; exciting / ~ 없는 uninteresting; dull (따분한) / ~ 본위의 aimed chiefly at amusing / ~ 본위의 out of mere curiosity / ~ 본위의 주간지 a sensational weekly (magazine) / ~를 가지다[느끼다] take [have, feel] (an) interest (in); be interested (in) / ~ 진진하다 be full of interest / ~를 잃다 lose interest.

흥분 **(興奮)** excitement; stimulation. ~하다 be [get] excited [stimulated]. ¶ ~시키다 excite; stimulate / ~(한) 상태 an excited condition [state] / ~을 가라앉히다 calm down *one's* excitement. ¶ ~제 a stimulant / ~제를 먹다[먹이다] take [administer] a stimulant.

흥성하다 **(興盛—)** grow in prosperity; become prosperous; prosper; rise.

흥신소 **(興信所)** a detective agency (美); an inquiry office [agency] 《인사관계의》; 《상업관계의》 a credit bureau; a commercial inquiry agency.

흥얼거리다 hum 《a tune》; sing to *oneself*.

흥업 **(興業)** promotion of industry; an industrial enterprise.

흥이야항이야 ~하다 intermeddle in 《other people's affair》; obtrude *oneself*; thrust *one's* nose into 《another's affair》.

흥정 buying and selling; dealing 《거래》; bargaining; a bargain. ~하다 buy and sell; deal; make a deal 《with》; bargain 《with a person》 over. ¶ 정치적 ~ political compromise / ~(을) 붙이다 act as (a) broker / ~이 많다 have a lot of business / ~이 없다 make few sales; do little business / 값을 ~하다 bargain (haggle) 《with a person》 about the price.

흥청거리다 be on the spree; be highly elated; make lavish [free] use 《of》. ¶ 바,클럽 등을 돌아다니며 ~ paint the town red.

흥청망청 《즐기는 모양》 with elation; merrily; 《혼전만전》 (spend money) in profusion; wastefully. ¶ ~ 돈을 쓰다 lavish money 《on》; spend money in profusion.

흥취 **(興趣)** interest; gusto; taste. ¶ ~가 있다 be of absorbing interest / 아무 ~도 없다 have no attractive features.

흥하다 **(興—)** rise; thrive; flourish; be prosperous; prosper. ¶ 흥하는 집안 a thriving family / 장사가 ~ business flourish.

흥행 **(興行)** show business 《사업》; a show; 《give》 a performance; a run. ~하다 perform; give a performance; show 《a play》; run 《put on》 a show. ¶ 장기 ~ a long run / 그 연극은 10일간 ~되었다 The play ran for ten days. ǁ ~가치 (수입) box-office value [profits] / ~권 right of performance / ~물 a performance; a show / ~사 a showman / ~ 성적을 a box-office record / ~장 a show place / ~주 a promoter.

흥얼거리다 hum; croon; sing to *oneself*; 《부정》 grumble; whimper.

흘날리다 blow 《something》 away [off]; be blown off; fly about [off]. ¶ 꽃이 바람에 ~ the wind sends blossoms flying.

흘다 scatter; strew; disperse 《군중을》; dishevel 《머리털 따위를》.

흘뜨리다 scatter 《things》 《about》; dishevel 《머리칼 따위를》; leave 《things》 scattered 《lying about》. ¶ 방에 종이 조각들을 ~ scatter (litter) the room with scraps of paper.

흘어지다 scatter; be scattered; disperse; be dispersed; be disheveled 《머리가》. ¶ 방 안에 흩어져 있는 장난감 toys scattered all over *one's* room / 가족이 사방으로 ~ a family scatters in all directions.

희가극 **(喜歌劇)** a comic opera.

희곡 **(戱曲)** a drama; a play. ¶ ~화하다 dramatize 《a novel》 / ~작가 a dramatist; a playwright; a playwriter.

희구하다 **(希求—)** desire 《to do》; aspire 《to, after》; long 《for something》. ¶ 쌍방이 다 평화를 희구하고 있다 Both sides are longing for peace.

희귀 **(稀貴)** ~하다 (be) rare. ¶ ~한 우표를 수집하다 collect rare stamps. ǁ ~조 a rare bird.

희극 **(喜劇)** a comedy; a farce. ¶ ~적(인) comic(al); farcical / ~을 연기하다 perform a comedy / ~을 벌이다 《비유적》 make a fool of *oneself* 《웃기다》. ǁ ~배우 a comic actor; a comedian / ~영화 a comic film (movie); a comedy film (picture).

희끄무레하다 (be) whitish.

희끗거리다 be [feel] dizzy; get giddy; reel; whirl.

희끗희끗 ~하다 (be) spotted with white; 《머리털이》 grizzled. ¶ ~한 머리 grizzled (gray) hair / 머리가 ~한 사람 a grizzle-haired man.

희노애락 **(喜怒哀樂)** ~ 희로애락.

희다 (be) white; fair 《피부가》; gray 《머리가》. ¶ 눈같이 흰 snow-

white / 회게 하다 make (a thing) white; whiten; blanch(탈색) / 살빛이 ~ have a fair complexion.
희대(稀代) ¶ ~의 rare; uncommon; extraordinary / ~의 영웅 a unique (peerless) hero / ~의 사기꾼 a notorious swindler.
희디희다 (be) pure (very) white; snow-white; be as white as snow. ¶ 희디흰 웨딩드레스 a snow-white wedding dress.
희떱다 ① (허영) (be) showy; vain; vainglorious. ② (씀씀이가) (be) open-handed; liberal. ③ (언행이) (be) snobbish; conceited.
희뜩거리다 get very dizzy (giddy, shaky); reel.
희뜩희뜩 ~ 하다 (be) dotted with white; grizzly(머리털이). ¶ ~한 신사 a gray-haired gentleman.
희랍(希臘) Greece.
희로애락(喜怒哀樂) joy and anger together with sorrow and pleasure; (감정) emotion; feelings. ¶ ~을 얼굴에 나타내지 않다 do not betray (show) one's feelings.
희롱(戲弄) ridiculing; jesting. ~하다 make fun (sport) of; poke fun at; banter; tease; make a jest of; ridicule; trifle (fool) (with). ¶ ~조로 말하다 say (a thing) in (for) sport.
희롱거리다 joke; jest; frolic; play pranks; play (sport) (with).
희맑다 (be) white and clean.
희망(希望) (a) hope; (a) wish; (a) desire; expectation (기대). ~하다 hope (to do, for); wish; desire; aspire to (after) (a thing). ¶ ~적 관측 one's wishful thinking / ~에 찬 젊은이들 young hopefuls / 절실한 ~ an ardent desire / ~에 살다 live in hope / ~을 걸다 anchor one's hope in (on) / 그는 ~했던 대학에 들어갔다 He got into the university, just as he had hoped. ‖ ~음악회 a request concert / ~자 a person who wants (desires) (to do); (지원자) an applicant; a candidate / ~조건 the terms (conditions) desired.
희망봉(希望峰) [地] the Cape of Good Hope.
희멀겋다 (be) fair; fair-complexioned.
희멀쑥하다 (be) fair and clean.
희미하다(稀微—) (be) faint; dim; vague. ¶ 희미한 소리 a faint sound / 희미한 불빛 a faint (dim) light / 희미하게 faintly; dimly; vaguely / 어렸을 때의 일을 희미하게 기억하다 vaguely remember one's childhood.
희박하다(稀薄—) (be) thin; weak; sparse. ¶ 인구가 희박한 지방 thinly (sparsely) populated district.
희번덕거리다 keep goggling one's eyes.
희번드르르하다 (얼굴이) (be) fair and bright; (말 따위가) (be) specious; glittering.
희보(喜報) ☞ 희소식.
희봄하다 (be) faintly light; half-light.
희비(喜悲) joy and sorrow. ¶ ~가 엇갈리다 have mixed (mingled) feelings of joy and sorrow. ‖ ~극 a tragicomedy.
희사(喜捨) charity; contribution; offering; donation. ~하다 give alms; give in charity; contribute; offer; donate. ¶ ~를 받다 receive alms (donations) / ~를 요청하다 beg for donation (offerings). ‖ ~금 a gift of money; a contribution; a donation; offerings; alms.
희색(喜色) a glad countenance; a joyful look. ¶ ~이 만면하다 be all smiles (with joy); beam with joy (delight).
희생(犧牲) (a) sacrifice; a scapegoat. ~하다 sacrifice; make a victim of (a person). ‖ ~적(인) self-sacrificing (spirit) / …을 ~하여 at the sacrifice (expense, cost) of... / …의 ~이 되다 be sacrificed (fall a victim) to... / 어떠한 ~를 치르더라도 at any cost; at all costs / 가족을 위해 한몸을 ~하다 sacrifice oneself for the sake of one's family. ‖ ~자 a victim; a prey / ~타 [野] a sacrifice hit (bunt, fly).
희서(稀書) a rare book.
희석(稀釋) [化] dilution. ~하다 dilute. ‖ ~액 a diluted solution / ~제 a diluent.
희소(稀少) ~하다 (be) scarce; rare. ‖ ~가치 scarcity (rarity) value / ~물자 scarce materials.
희소식(喜消息) good news; glad news (tidings). ¶ ~을 전하다 convey (bring) good news; give glad tidings.
희열(喜悅) joy; gladness; delight.
희염산(稀鹽酸) [化] dilute hydrochloric acid.
희유원소(稀有元素) [化] a rare element.
희읍스름하다 (be) whitish. [acid.
희질산(稀窒酸) [化] dilute nitric]
희치희치 (천 따위가) worn out here and there; (벗어진 모양) coming (peeling) off here and there.
희한하다(稀罕—) (be) rare; curious; singular; uncommon.
희화(戱畫) a comic picture; a caricature; a cartoon. ¶ ~화 하다 caricature; make a caricature of. [acid.
희황산(稀黃酸) [化] dilute sulphuric]
희희낙락(喜喜樂樂) ~하다 rejoice;

흰개미 be in delight; be glad; jubilate.
흰개미 [蟲] a termite; a white ant.
흰나비 [蟲] a cabbage butterfly.
흰떡 rice cake. ¶ (떡메로) 쳐서 ~을 만들다 pound steamed rice into cake.
흰무리 steamed rice cake.
흰소리 a big[tall] talk; bragging. ~하다 talk big[tall]; brag.
흰자위 ① (눈의) the white of the eye. ② (달걀의) the white of an egg); albumen.
횡하다 feel dizzy[giddy]; (one's head) reel[swim].
횡허케 without delay; swiftly; quickly.
히로뽕 [藥] philopon(상표면에서). ¶ ~환자 a philopon addict.
히말라야산맥 (一山脈) the Himalayas; Himalaya Mountains.
히스타민 [化] histamine.
히스테리 [醫] hysteria; hysterics (발작). ¶ ~를 일으키다 go into hysterics; become hysterical.
히아신스 [植] a hyacinth.
히어링 (학습에서) (practice) hearing; (공청회) a (public) hearing. ¶ ~연습 a drill in hearing.
히죽이 with a grin; with a sweet smile. ¶ ~ 웃다 grin at(a person); smile sweetly.
히터 (turn on[off]) a heater.
히트 [野] (a base) hit. ¶ ~ 치다 (make a) hit. ② (성공) a hit; a great success. ~하다 win a success; be a (big) hit. ‖ ~송 a hit song.
히피 a hippie; (the) hippies(총칭).
힌두교 (一敎) Hinduism. ‖ ~신자 a Hindu.
힌트 a hint. ¶ ~를 주다 give [drop] a hint; ~를 얻다 get a hint (from); pick up an idea.
힐난하다 (詰難―) condemn; blame [rebuke] (a person for); censure.
힐문하다 (詰問―) cross-examine; question [examine] closely.
힐책하다 (詰責―) reproach; rebuke; reprimand; censure.
힘 ① (몸의) (physical) strength; force; might. ¶ ~있는 strong; mighty; powerful / ~ 없는 weak; powerless; feeble / ~껏 with all one's might[strength]; with might and main / ~이 지치다 be exhausted; be tired out / ~을 내다 put forth one's strength. ② (기력) spirit; vigor; energy. ¶ ~없는 low-spirited; downhearted; spiritless(기운 없는) / ~없는 목소리로 in a weak voice. ③ [理] (electric) power; force; energy (of heat). ④ (능력) ability; power; faculty. ¶ ~이 자라는 限(한) as far (much) as one can; to the best of one's abiltiy / …할 ~이 있다 be able (competent) to do; be capable of doing. ⑤ (노력) effort; endeavors; exertions. ¶ 자기 ~으로 by one's own efforts / ~을 합하여 in cooperation (with); with united efforts. ⑥ (효력) effect; efficacy; power; influence. ⑦ (조력) help; (give) assistance (to); support; aid. ¶ …의 ~으로 by the aid (force, help) of; by dint (virtue) of. ⑧ (어세) emphasis; stress; force. ¶ ~을 주어 emphatically(강조); forcibly (힘차게) / ~이 있는 글 a forceful sentence. ⑨ (위력) power; authority; might; influence; sway. ¶ 돈의 ~ the power of money / ~의 정치 power politics; rule by might / 여론의 ~ the force of public opinion / ~의 외교 power diplomacy. ⑩ (작용) agency (of Providence); action. ¶ 눈에 보이지 않는 ~ an invisible agency.
힘겨룸 (have) a strength contest.
힘겹다 ¶ 힘부치다.
힘들다 ① (힘이 들다) (be) tough; laborious; toilsome; painful; (어렵다) (be) hard; difficult; (수고가 되다) be troublesome. ¶ 힘 드는 일 a hard (laborious) work; a tough job.
힘들이다 ① (세력·노력을) make efforts; exert oneself. ¶ 일에 ~ throw oneself into one's work. ② (애쓰다) take pains (trouble); elaborate (on). ¶ 힘들여 번 돈 hard-earned money / 힘들여 계획을 세우다 elaborate upon a plan.
힘부치다 be beyond one's power (ability, reach); be too much for (one). ¶ 그 일은 내 힘에 부치는 일이다 The job is beyond my ability.
힘세다 (be) strong; mighty; powerful. ¶ 힘세어 보이는 strong-looking.
힘쓰다 ① (노력) exert oneself; make efforts; endeavor; try hard. ② (정려) be assiduous; be industrious; be diligent (in). ¶ 학업에 ~ attend to one's studies with diligence. ③ (고심) take pains; be at great pains. ④ (조력) help; aid; assist; give (a person) assistance (in, on). ¶ 김군이 힘써 주어서 through Mr. Kim's aid; by the help (kind assistance) of Mr. Kim.
힘입다 owe; be indebted (to). ¶ 힘입은 바 크다 be greatly indebted to; owe (a person) much.
힘줄 ① (근육) a muscle; a sinew; a tendon(건[腱]); a vein(혈관).

¶ ~ 투성이의 stringy; sinewy. ② 《섬유질의》 a fiber; a string. ¶ 고기~ strings in the meat.

힘차다 (be) powerful; energetic; forceful; vigorous; be full of strength. ¶ 힘찬 연설 [목소리] a powerful speech [voice] / 힘차게 powerfully; energetically; vigorously / 힘차게 일하다 buckle down to a task; gather *oneself* up for an effort; work vigorously.

회사의 조직과 직위의 영어명

1. **회사의 조직·부서명**—회사의 조직은 업종·규모 등에 따라 다양하다. 일반적인 회사 조직을 순서대로 나열해 보면: 이사회(board of directors)—사업본부(division)—부(department)—실(office)—과(section)—계(subsection) 등으로 나뉜다. 그러나 본부제도가 없는 회사 조직에서는 division(부)—department(과)—section(계)의 순서가 된다. 또 본사와 지사가 있는 경우, 동일 부서의 표기 구분은 본사의 것을 corporate account department 처럼 앞에 corporate를 붙인다. 부서명을 실제로 표기할 때는 정관사 the를 붙이며, 고유명사적으로 생각하여 단어 첫자를 대문자로 표기하는 것이 일반적이다. 아래에 쓰인 d.는 department 또는 devision의 약자이다. 다음은 각 부서의 구체적인 일의 내용을 참작하여 영역한 것이다.

감사부 internal auditing d. / 건설부 (development &) construction d./ 경리부 general accounting d.; account d.; budget & accounting d. / 관재부 properties administration d. / 구매부 purchasing d./기술부 engineering d.;technical development d. / 기자재부 machinery & materials d. / 기획부 planning d. / 노무부 labor relations d. / 무역부 import & export d. / 문서부 correspondence d. / 발송부 dispatch d./복지후생부 welfare d./사업부 enterprises d. / 상품개발부 product development d. / 상품관리부 product administration d. / 생산관리부 production control d. / 생산부 production d. / 서무부 general affairs d. / 선전 [광고]부 advertising d. / 섭외부 foreign [public] relations d. / 시설부 administration d. / 연구개발부 R & D d./영업부 sales. d. / 마케팅 d. / 인사부 personnel d. / 자금부 finance processing d. / 자재부 materials d. / 전자 계산부(electronic) information system d. / 조사부 business research d.;information & research d. / 총무부 general affairs d. / 특허부 patent d. / 판매관리부 sales administration d. / 판매촉진부 sales promotion d. / 해외부 overseas d.;international d. / 해외사업부 overseas operations d. / 홍보부 public relations d.; publicity d. / 기획실 corporate planning office / 비서실 secretariat / 사사실(社史室) corporate history office.

2. **회사의 직위명**—회사의 직위명은 직무 권한에 따라 갖가지 호칭이 있을 수 있기 때문에 정해진 영어가 불가능하다. 일반 통념에 따라 아래와 같이 영역하였다. 실제 사용시는 정관사 the를 붙이나 여기서는 생략하였다.

회장 chairman (of the board); board chairman;CEO (=Chief Executive Officer) 《美》/ 부회장 vice-chairman (of the board of directors) / 사장 president; managing director 《英》/ 부사장 executive vice-president / 대표이사 representative director; managing director 《美》/ 전무(이사) executive managing director / 상무(이사) managing director / 이사 director; member of the board / 사외이사 outside director / 감사역 auditor / 고문 adviser; corporate adviser; counselor / 본부장 division director; general manager / 부장 general manager; director; manager/division(department) head / 차장 deputy(assistant (to)) general manager/과장 manager; section head [chief]; section manager / 과장 대리 acting [assistant (to)]manager / 계장 sub-section head[chief]; senior staff / 지점장 director; general manager / 지점장 branch manager; district [regional] manager / 지점 차장 deputy branch manager / 공장장 plant manager/반장 foreman / 부원 (과원)staff/평사원 rank= and-file employee[worker]

부 록

차 례

I. 이력서 쓰기 ·················· 907
II. 편지 쓰기 ·················· 907
III. 기호 읽기 ·················· 909
IV. 수 ························ 909
V. 미·영 철자의 차이 ············ 910
VI. 도량형표 ··················· 911
VII. 국어의 로마자 표기법 ········· 912
VIII. 지방 행정 단위의 영어 표기 ···· 914
IX. 한국 전통 식품의 영어명 표기 방법 ··· 915
X. 우리식 표현의 영어 낱말들 ······ 917
XI. 국제 전화 거는 법 ············ 918
XII. 세계 주요도시 표준시 대조표 ···· 919
XIII. 우리 나라 행정 구역의 로마자 표기 ··· 920
XIV. 미국의 주명(州名) ············ 923
XV. 불규칙동사표 ················ 924

I. 이력서 쓰기

<u>Personal History</u>

Personal History:
- Name in Full: Park Jae-sŏng
- Permanent Domicile: 102 Tangju-dong, Chongno-gu, Seoul Korea

- Present Address: 1-48 Namsan-dong, Chung-gu, Seoul Korea
- Born: August 18, 1955
- Height & Weight: 177cm. — 75.9kg.
- Health: Excellent
- Marital Status: Single
- Education: Hanseong High School, graduated 1973
  Korea University (Faculty of Literature), graduated 1977
  - Major—English Literature
  - Other main courses of study—French, Chinese
- Experience: Employed as translator in Publishing Department, Korea Travel Bureau, Myong-dong, Seoul, April 1977

References:
- Academic: Prof. Kim Bong-han, Korea University, Seoul
- Business: Mr. Han Myong-hwan, the chief of the Publishing Department, Korea Travel Bureau, Myong-dong, Seoul

May 4, 1979

(Signature)
Park Jae-sŏng

《註》 오늘날에는, 이력서도 컴퓨터 따위로 작성하여 맨끝에 서명하는 것이 보통임. 용지의 크기는 23cm×28cm.

II. 편지쓰기

1. 겉봉투 쓰기

```
┌─────────────────────────────────────────────────────────┐
│ Yim Byong-jun                         ①                 │
│ 1—48 Namsan-dong, Chung-gu,       Air Mail      ┌─────┐ │
│ Seoul, Korea                                    │ 우 표 │ │
│                                                 └─────┘ │
│              Miss Edith M. Green                        │
│              312 Greenwood,                             │
│              Ann Arbor, Michigan 59104                  │
│              U.S.A.                                     │
│                                                         │
│ ②                                                       │
└─────────────────────────────────────────────────────────┘
```

《註》 1. ①, ②의 번호는 다음 용어를 쓸 때의 위치를 보인다.

Air Mail (항공편)
Special Delivery (속달)
via... (…경유)   ① 또는 ②
Printed Matter (인쇄물)
Photo only (사진 재중)

Poste Restante... Post Office (…국 유치)
Registered (등기)   ②
Introducing... (…을 소개)

2. …씨방, …씨 전교(轉交)는 c/o Mr....로 씀.
3. 소개장은 봉하지 않음.
4. 수신인명 끝의 다섯 자리 숫자는 ZIP Code임.

2. 편지의 양식

1-48 Namsan-dong
Chung-gu, Seoul Korea
April 2, 1981

Miss Edith M. Green
312 Greenwood
Ann Arbor, Michigan
U.S.A.

Dear Miss Green,

 I read from your last letter you are going to visit this country soon. The news is like a dream to me. To meet you and your family in this country! By the time we meet, I'll make up a wonderful plan to show you this country. Please let me be a guide for you at that time. I am waiting for your arrival.

Sincerely yours,
(Signature)
(Yim Byeong-jun)

《註》 1. 친한 친구간에는 발신자 및 수신자의 주소는 흔히 생략
2. 날짜 영국식 2nd April 1981, 미국식 April 2, 1981
3. 수신자 이름에는 다음과 같은 경칭을 붙인다.
   남성단수 Mr., Sir, Dr., Prof., Rev. (목사), Hon. (시장 등)
   남성복수 Messrs. (상사 앞일 때에는 미국에서는 이 경칭을 안 씀)
   여성단수 Miss, Mrs. (기혼자), Christian name과 남편의 성을 합쳐 Mrs.를 붙임. 미망인도 같음.
   여성복수 Misses (미혼자에만), Mmes. (기혼자에만)
4. 본문 허두의 인사말
   공용통신 Gentlemen, Ladies, Mesdames, Dear Sir(s), Dear Madam, My dear Sir, Madam, 따위
   사　　신 Dear Mr. ...., My dear Mrs. ...., 따위
             이 때 구두점은 (,)을 쓰는데, 미국에서는 흔히 상용문일 때에는 (:)가 쓰임.
5. 맺음말 일반적 Yours very truly, Yours truly 따위
          사　신 Sincerely yours, Cordially yours, Affectionately yours 따위
6. 여성이 서명할 때에는 상대가 회신할 때 편리하도록 (Miss) (Mrs.)를 덧붙여 밝히는 경우도 있다.

III. 기호 읽기

1. 수학

+   plus, and
−   minus, less
±, ∓   plus or minus
×   multiplied by, times
÷   divided by
=   is equal to, equals
≒, ≈   is approximately equal to
≠, ≠   is not equal to
>   is greater than
<   is less than
≧, ≥   is equal to or greater than
≦, ≤   is equal to or less than
{ }   braces
—   vinculum 보기: $\overline{a+b}$
∴   therefore
∵   since, because
∞   infinity
:   is to
::   as, equals
∠   angle
∟   right angle
⊥   (is) perpendicular (to)
∥, ∥   (is) paralleled (to)
△   triangle
□   square
▱   parallelogram
°   degree(s)
′   minute(s)
″   second(s)

2. 참조표

*   asterisk (별표)
†   dagger, obelisk (검표)
‡   double dagger (이중검표)
§   section
∥   parallels (병행표)
¶   paragraph
☞   index, fist (손가락표)
∴·∵   asterism (세별표)

3. 표음부호

´   acute (양음부호) ((é))
`   grave (저음부호) ((à))
ˆ   circumflex (곡절음부호) ((ê))
~   tilde (물결부호) ((ñ))
¯   macron (장음부호) ((ā))
˘   breve (단음부호) ((ă))
¨   dieresis (분음부호) ((ö))
¸   cedilla (시딜라) ((ç))

4. 기타

&   and, ampersand
&c   et cetera; and so forth
/   or, per
number
%   percent
c/o   care of
@   at
©   copyright(ed)

IV. 수

1. 수 읽기

1,000 (천) one thousand
10,000 (만) ten thousand
100,000 (십만) one hundred thousand
1,000,000 (백만) one million
10,000,000 (천만) ten million
100,000,000 (억) one hundred million
1,000,000,000 (십억) one billion
10,000,000,000 (백억) ten billion
100,000,000,000 (천억) one hundred billion
1,000,000,000,000 (조) one trillion; 《英》 one thousand billion

이상 중, 천억까지는 《美》《英》 공통, 조(兆) 및 그 이상의 수는 《美》《英》에서 각기 그 호칭이 다름. 예컨대,

1,000,000,000,000,000 (천조): 《美》 one quadrillion; 《英》 one million billion
1,000,000,000,000,000,000 (백경) one quintillion; 《英》 one trillion

이 밖에,
sextillion= 《美》 10^{21}; 《英》 10^{35}
septillion= 《美》 10^{24}; 《英》 10^{42}
octillion= 《美》 10^{27}; 《英》 10^{48}
nonillion= 《美》 10^{30}; 《英》 10^{54}, *etc.*
처럼 명칭은 《美》《英》 공통이지만 수치는 다름.

2. 로마 숫자

I=1, V=5, L=50, C=100, D=500, M=1,000의 로마자를 써서. 좌에서 우로 수치의 대소순으로 늘어놓거나 (e.g. XVIII=10+5+3=18), 순서가 역이 되면 대소 수치의 차를 나타냄 (e.g. XIX=10+(10−1)=19). 로마자는 소자 (i, v, x, l, c, *etc.*)를 쓸 때도 있음. 문자 위에 ¯를 붙이면 1,000배의 수치가 됨.

I	1	V	5	X	10
III	3	VI	6	XV	15
IV (IIII)	4	IX	9	XL	40

L	50	CM	900
LX	60	M	1000
XC	90	MCD	1400
C	100	MDC	1600
CD	400	MDCCCXCIV	1894
D	500	MCMLXXIX	1979
DC	600	MMM	3000

V̄	5000
X̄	10,000
L̄	50,000
C̄	100,000
D̄	500,000
M̄	1,000,000

Ⅴ. 미・영 철자의 차이

(일반적 경향으로서 다음과 같은 점을 지적할 수 있음)

(美)	(英)	(美)	(英)
-a-	**-au-**	**-ll-**	**-l-**
balk	baulk	skillful	skilful
gantlet	gauntlet	**-m**	**-mme**
-ck-	**-qu-**	gram	gramme
check	cheque	program	programme
checkered	chequered	**-o-**	**-ou-**
-ction	**-xion**	mold	mould
connection	connexion	smolder	smoulder
reflection	reflexion	**-or**	**-our**
-dgment	**-dgement**	color	colour
judgment	judgement	labor	labour
acknowledg-	acknowledge-	**-se**	**-ce**
ment	ment	defense	defence
-e-	**-ae-**	offense	offence
archeology	archaeology	**-y**	**-ey**
esthete	aesthete	story	storey
-er	**-re**	bogy	bogey
center	centre	**-ze**	**-se**
theater	theatre	analyze	analyse
-et	**-ette**	paralyze	paralyse
cigaret	cigarette		
omelet	omelette	악센트부호없음	악센트부호있음
-g-	**-gg-**	cafe	café
fagot	faggot	fete	fête
wagon	waggon		
-i-	**-y-**	기타	
flier	flyer	aluminum	aluminium
tire	tyre	curb	kerb
in-	**en-**	draft	draught; draft
infold	enfold		(도안・어음)
inquire	enquire	gray	grey
-ing	**-eing**	jail	gaol
aging	ageing	maneuver	manoeuvre
eying	eyeing	mustache	moustache
-k-	**-c-**	pajama	pyjama
disk	disc	plow	plough
ankle	ancle	sulfur	sulphur
-l-	**-ll-**	veranda	verandah
councilor	councillor		
traveler	traveller		

Ⅵ. 도량형표(度量衡表)

부	1 홉(合)	0.18039 리터	1.0567 quarts 0.31741 파인트 《英》0.39678 갤런 《美》0.4765 4.9595 부셸
	1 되(升)	1.8039 리터	
	1 석(石)	0.18039 킬로리터	
피	1 액량온스(ounce)	0.15753 홉	28.416 입방센티미터 (cube centimeters)
	1 파인트(pint)	3.1505 홉	0.56823 리터
	1 영(英)갤런(gallon)	2.5204 되	4.5459 리터
	1 부셸(bushel)	20163 석	36.867 리터
	1 리터(liter)	0.55435 되	《英》0.21995 《美》0.26417 264.17 《美》갤런
	1 킬로리터(kiloliter)	5.5435 석	
길	1 치(寸)	3.0303 센티미터	1.1931 인치
	1 자(尺)	0.30303 미터	11.9305 인치 0.99421 피트
	1 간(間)	1.8182 미터	1.9884 야드
	1 정(町)	0.10909 킬로미터	5.423 체인
	1 리(里)	3.9273 킬로미터	2.4403 마일
	1 인치(inch)	0.83818 치	2.5400 센티미터
	1 피트(foot)	1.0058 자	0.30479 미터
	1 야드(yard)	3.0175 자 0.50291 간	0.91438 미터
	1 체인(chain)	11.064 치	20.116 미터
	1 마일(mile)	14 정 45 간 1 자	1.6093 킬로미터
이	1 센티미터(centimeter)	3 분(分) 3 리(厘)	0.39371 인치
	1 미터(meter)	3 자 3 치	39.371 인치 3.2809 피트
	1 킬로미터(kilometer)	555 간 9 정 10 간	49.71 체인 0.62138 마일
넓	1 평(坪)(보(步))	0.000861 에이커	3.9524 평방야드
	1 무(畝)	0.0245 에이커	118.572 평방야드
	1 단(段)	0.245 에이커	1185.72 평방야드
	1 정(町)	2.4509 에이커 9917.335 평방미터	11857.2 평방야드
이	1 에이커(acre)	4 단 24보여(餘) (1224 평여)	4840 평방야드
	1 아르(are) (100평방미터)	약 1무 0보 25	119.6 평방야드
	1 헥타르(hectare) (10,000평방미터)	약 1 정 25보	11960 평방야드 2.471 에이커
무	1 돈	3.75 그램	0.13228 온스
	100 돈	0.375킬로그램	0.82673 파운드
	1 관(貫)	3.75 킬로그램	8.2673 파운드
	1 온스(ounce)	7.5599 돈	28.350 그램
	1 파운드(pound) (=16 ounces)	120.963 돈	0.45359 킬로그램
	1 톤(short[long] ton) 《美》=2000 pounds 《英》=2240 pounds	241.923 관	907.18 킬로그램
게	1 그램(gram)	0.2667 돈	15.432 grains 0.035274 온스
	1 킬로그램 (kilogram)	0.2667 관	2.2046 파운드
	1 톤(metric ton) (=1000 kilograms)	2666.7 관	2204.6 파운드

Ⅶ. 국어의 로마자 표기법

문화관광부고시 제2000-8호, 2000.7.7.

제 1 장 표기의 기본 원칙

제1항 국어의 로마자 표기는 국어의 표준 발음법에 따라 적는 것을 원칙으로 한다.
제2항 로마자 이외의 부호는 되도록 사용하지 않는다.

제 2 장 표기 일람

제1항 모음은 다음 각 호와 같이 적는다.
 1. 단모음

ㅏ	ㅓ	ㅗ	ㅜ	ㅡ	ㅣ	ㅐ	ㅔ	ㅚ	ㅟ
a	eo	o	u	eu	i	ae	e	oe	wi

 2. 이중모음

ㅑ	ㅕ	ㅛ	ㅠ	ㅒ	ㅖ	ㅘ	ㅙ	ㅝ	ㅞ	ㅢ
ya	yeo	yo	yu	yae	ye	wa	wae	wo	we	ui

 (붙임1) 'ㅢ'는 'ㅣ'로 소리 나더라도 'ui'로 적는다.
  [보기] 광희문 Gwanghuimun
 (붙임2) 장모음의 표기는 따로 하지 않는다.

제2항 자음은 다음 각 호와 같이 적는다.
 1. 파열음

ㄱ	ㄲ	ㅋ	ㄷ	ㄸ	ㅌ	ㅂ	ㅃ	ㅍ
g,k	kk	k	d,t	tt	t	b,p	pp	p

 2. 파찰음

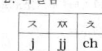

ㅈ	ㅉ	ㅊ
j	jj	ch

 3. 마찰음

ㅅ	ㅆ	ㅎ
s	ss	h

 4. 비음

ㄴ	ㅁ	ㅇ
n	m	ng

 5. 유음

ㄹ
r,l

 (붙임1) 'ㄱ, ㄷ, ㅂ'은 모음 앞에서는 'g, d, b'로, 자음 앞이나 어말에서는 'k, t, p'로 적는다.([ ]안의 발음에 따라 표기함.)
  [보기] 구미 Gumi 영동 Yeongdong 백암 Baegam
   옥천 Okcheon 합덕 Hapdeok 호법 Hobeop
   월곶[월곧] Wolgot 벚꽃[벋꼳] beotkkot 한밭[한받] Hanbat
 (붙임2) 'ㄹ'은 모음 앞에서는 'r'로, 자음 앞이나 어말에서는 'l'로 적는다. 단, 'ㄹㄹ'은 'll'로 적는다.
  [보기] 구리 Guri 설악 Seorak 칠곡 Chilgok
   임실 Imsil 울릉 Ulleung 대관령[대괄령] Daegwallyeong

제 3 장 표기상의 유의점

제1항 음운 변화가 일어날 때에는 변화의 결과에 따라 다음 각 호와 같이 적는다.
 1. 자음 사이에서 동화 작용이 일어나는 경우
  [보기] 백마[뱅마] Baengma 종로[종노] Jongno
   왕십리[왕심니] Wangsimni 별내[별래] Byeollae
   신문로[신문노] Sinmunno 신라[실라] Silla
 2. 'ㄴ, ㄹ'이 덧나는 경우
  [보기] 학여울[항녀울] Hangnyeoul 알약[알략] allyak
 3. 구개음화가 되는 경우

[보기] 해돋이[해도지] haedoji 같이[가치] gachi 맞히다[마치다] machida

4. 'ㄱ, ㄷ, ㅂ, ㅈ'이 'ㅎ'과 합하여 거센소리로 소리 나는 경우

[보기] 좋고[조코] joko   놓다[노타] nota
      잡혀[자펴] japyeo   낳지[나치] nachi

다만, 체언에서 'ㄱ, ㄷ, ㅂ'뒤에 'ㅎ'이 따를 때에는 'ㅎ'을 밝혀 적는다.

[보기] 묵호 Mukho   집현전 Jiphyeonjeon

(붙임) 된소리되기는 표기에 반영하지 않는다.

[보기] 압구정 Apgujeong   낙동강 Nakdonggang   죽변 Jukbyeon
      낙성대 Nakseongdae   합정 Hapjeong   팔당 Paldang
      샛별 saetbyeol   울산 Ulsan

제2항 발음상 혼동의 우려가 있을 때에는 음절 사이에 붙임표(-)를 쓸 수 있다.

[보기] 중앙 Jung-ang   반구대 Ban-gudae
      세운 Se-un   해운대 Hae-undae

제3항 고유 명사는 첫 글자를 대문자로 적는다.

[보기] 부산 Busan   세종 Sejong

제4항 인명은 성과 이름의 순서로 띄어 쓴다. 이름은 붙여 쓰는 것을 원칙으로 하되 음절 사이에 붙임표(-)를 쓰는 것을 허용한다.(( )안의 표기를 허용함.)

[보기] 민용하 Min Yongha (Min Yong-ha)
      송나리 Song Nari (Song Na-ri)

(1) 이름에서 일어나는 음운 변화는 표기에 반영하지 않는다.

[보기] 한복남 Han Boknam (Han Bok-nam)
      홍빛나 Hong Bitna (Hong Bit-na)

(2) 성의 표기는 따로 정한다.

제5항 '도, 시, 군, 구, 읍, 면, 리, 동'의 행정 구역 단위와 '가'는 각각 'do, si, gun, gu, eup, myeon, ri, dong, ga'로 적고, 그 앞에는 붙임표(-)를 넣는다. 붙임표(-) 앞뒤에서 일어나는 음운 변화는 표기에 반영하지 않는다.

[보기] 충청북도 Chungcheongbuk-do   제주도 Jeju-do
      의정부시 Uijeongbu-si   양주군 Yangju-gun
      도봉구 Dobong-gu   신창읍 Sinchang-eup
      삼죽면 Samjuk-myeon   인왕리 Inwang-ri
      당산동 Dangsan-dong   봉천1동 Bongcheon 1(il)-dong
      종로 2가 Jongno 2(i)-ga   퇴계로 3가 Toegyero 3(sam)-ga

(붙임) '시, 군, 읍'의 행정 구역 단위는 생략할 수 있다.

[보기] 청주시 Cheongju   함평군 Hampyeong   순창읍 Sunchang

제6항 자연 지물명, 문화재명, 인공 축조물명은 붙임표(-) 없이 붙여 쓴다.

[보기] 남산 Namsan   속리산 Songnisan
      금강 Geumgang   독도 Dokdo
      경복궁 Gyeongbokgung   무량수전 Muryangsujeon
      연화교 Yeonhwagyo   극락전 Geungnakjeon
      안압지 Anapji   남한산성 Namhansanseong
      화랑대 Hwarangdae   불국사 Bulguksa
      현충사 Hyeonchungsa   독립문 Dongnimmun
      오죽헌 Ojukheon   촉석루 Chokseongnu
      종묘 Jongmyo   다보탑 Dabotap

제7항 인명, 회사명, 단체명 등은 그동안 써 온 표기를 쓸 수 있다.

제8항 학술 연구 논문 등 특수 분야에서 한글 복원을 전제로 표기할 경우에는 한글 표기를 대상으로 적는다. 이때 글자 대응은 제2장을 따르되 'ㄱ, ㄷ, ㅂ, ㄹ'은 'g, d, b, l'로만 적는다. 음가 없는 'ㅇ'은 붙임표(-)로 표기하되 어두에서는 생략하는 것을 원칙으로 한다. 기타 분절의 필요가 있을 때에도 붙임표(-)를 쓴다.

[보기]
집 jib	짚 jip	밖 bakk
값 gabs	붓꽃 buskkoch	먹는 meogneun
독립 doglib	문리 munli	물엿 mul-yeos
굳이 gud-i	좋다 johda	가곡 gagog
조랑말 jolangmal	없었습니다 eobs-eoss-seubnida	

부 칙

① (시행일) 이 규정은 고시한 날부터 시행한다.
② (표지판 등에 대한 경과 조치) 이 표기법 시행 당시 종전의 표기법에 의하여 설치된 표지판(도로, 광고물, 문화재 등의 안내판)은 2005.12.31.까지 이 표기법을 따라야 한다.
③ (출판물 등에 대한 경과 조치) 이 표기법 시행 당시 종전의 표기법에 의하여 발간된 교과서 등 출판물은 2002.2.28.까지 이 표기법을 따라야 한다.

로마자 표기법 조견표

1. 모음

ㅏ	ㅑ	ㅓ	ㅕ	ㅗ	ㅛ	ㅜ	ㅠ	ㅡ	ㅣ	ㅐ	ㅒ	ㅔ	ㅖ	ㅘ	ㅙ	ㅚ	ㅝ	ㅞ
a	ya	eo	yeo	o	yo	u	yu	eu	i	ae	yae	e	ye	wa	wae	oe	wo	we

ㅟ	ㅢ
wi	ui

2. 자음

ㄱ	ㄴ	ㄷ	ㄹ	ㅁ	ㅂ	ㅅ	ㅇ	ㅈ	ㅊ	ㅋ	ㅌ	ㅍ	ㅎ	ㄲ	ㄸ	ㅃ	ㅆ	ㅉ
g,k	n	d,t	r,l	m	b,p	s	ng	j	ch	k	t	p	h	kk	tt	pp	ss	jj

Ⅷ. 지방 행정 단위의 영어 표기

내무부 1995. 2

지방 행정 단위명	사 용 구 분	영 어 표 기	비고
서울 특별시	주소로 사용시	Seoul City (서울 시티)	
	기관 명칭	Seoul Metropolitan City (서울 메트로폴리탄 시티)	
○○광역시	주소로 사용시	○○City(○○시티)	
	기관 명칭	○○Metropolitan City (○○ 메트로폴리탄 시티)	
○○도		○○ Province(○○ 프라빈스)	
○○시		○○ City(○○ 시티)	
○○군		○○ County (○○ 카운티)	
○○구	주소로 사용시 • 특별시·광역시 구별없이	○○ District(○○ 디스트릭트)	
	기관 명칭 • 자치구 • 일반구	○○ Metropolitan District ○○ District	

IX. 한국 전통 식품의 영어명 표기 방법

농림 수산부 1994. 12

부류	식품명	영 어 표 기	비 고
김 치	깍두기김치 나박김치 동치미김치 배추김치 무청김치 유채김치 갓잎김치 갓줄기김치	Kimchi (Radish roots kimchi) Kimchi (Watery kimchi) Kimchi (Watery radish kimchi) Kimchi (Cabbage kimchi) Kimchi (Radish leaf kimchi) Kimchi (Rape leaf kimchi) Kimchi (Mustard leaf kimchi) Kimchi (Mustard stem kimchi)	김치류는 Kimchi로 표기 통일하고 ( ) 안에 품목명을 영어로 병기
장	고추장 간장 된장 청국장	Korean hot pepper paste (Gochujang) Soy sauce Soybean paste (Toenjang) Soybean paste (Ch'ŏnggujang)	외국의 hot sauce, chilli sauce와 구별 표기 ( )에 품목명을 소리나는대로 영어로 표기
죽	호박죽 들깨죽 쌀죽 현미죽 찹쌀죽 율무죽 단팥죽	Pumpkin soup powder Perilla soup powder Rice soup powder Brown rice soup powder Sweet rice soup powder Job's tears soup powder Red bean soup powder	분말죽류: soup powder 죽(물이 포함된 것): soup
국 수	즉석면 (라면) 쑥국수 칡국수 도토리국수 메밀국수 쌀국수 감자국수 메밀냉면	Instant noodles Mugwort noodles Arrowroot noodles Acorn noodles Buckwheat noodles Rice noodles Potato noodles Buckwheat vermicelli	Noodle로 표기 통일하고 메밀냉면만 vermicelli로 구별 표기
묵	메밀묵 도토리묵	Buckwheat curd Acorn curd	묵류는 curd로 통일 표기
미 숫 가 루	쌀미숫가루 찹쌀 〃 보리 〃 쌀보리 〃 수수 〃 조 〃	Parched rice powder Parched sweet rice powder Parched barley powder Parched naked barley powder Parched sorghum powder Parched millet powder	Parched+품목명+powder로 통일 표기
건 채 류	무말랭이 호박고지 가지말랭이 박고지 토란말랭이 도라지말랭이 산채나물 실고추	Dried radish slice Dried squash/pumpkin slice Dried eggplant slice Dried gourd slice Dried taro stem slice Dried bell-flower root slice Edible greens Shredded red pepper	Dried+품목명+slice로 통일 표기

부류	식품명	영어표기	비 고
절임	단무지	Radish pickle	품목+pickle로 통일 표기
	오이지	Cucumber pickle	
	염교	Scallion pickle	염교=부추
	달래지	Wild garlic pickle	
	깻잎지	Perilla leaf pickle	
음료	식혜	Rice nectar (Shikhye)	쌀알이 포함되어 nectar로 표기
	수정과	Sweet cinnamon punch	수정과는 건물이 포함되지 않으므로 punch로 표기
	소주	Soju	
	약주	Rice wine (clear)	
	탁주	Rice wine (cloudy)	
차류	계피차	Cinnamon tea	품목명+tea로 통일 표기
	구기자차	Boxthron tea	
	치커리차	Chicory tea	
	컴프리차	Comfry tea	
	유자차	Citron tea	
	인삼차	Korean ginseng tea	한국 인삼을 강조 표기
	녹차	Green tea	
	감잎차	Persimmon leaf tea	
	홍차	Black tea	
	옥수수차	Corn tea	
해조류	말린김	Dried laver	돌김은 양식이 아닌 자연산 김이므로 stone보다는 natural이 적합
	조미김	Seasoned, roasted laver	
	돌김	Natural laver	
	미역	Sea mustard	
	염장미역	Salted sea mustard	fried+품목명으로 통일 표기
	미역튀각	Fried sea mustard	
	다시마튀각	Fried sea tangle	
	건파래	Dried sea lettuce	
	말린다시마	Dried sea tangle	
	다시말이	Rolled sea tangle	
젓갈류	새우젓	Salted shrimp	젓갈류에는 fermented란 표기없이 Salted+품목명으로 통일 표기
	멸치젓	Salted anchovy	
	명란젓	Salted pollack egg	
	창란젓	Salted viscera	
	밴댕이젓	Salted shad	
	황새기젓	Salted sword fish	
	굴젓	Salted oyster	
	전복젓	Salted abalone	
	조개젓	Salted clam	
	게젓	Salted crab	액젓의 경우 품목명+sauce로 통일 표기
	멸치액젓	Anchovy sauce	
한과류	강정	Korean cracker (Kangjung)	
	유과	Korean cracker (Yoogwa)	
	약과	Korean cracker (Yakgwa)	
	전병	Korean cracker (Junbyung)	
	산자	Korean cracker (Sanja)	
	야채만두	Vegetable dumpling	Dumpling으로 표기

부류	식품명	영어 표기	비 고
만두류	쇠고기만두	Beef dumpling	하되 내용물의 영어명을 그 앞에 표기
	돼지고기만두	Pork dumpling	
	꿩만두	Pheasant dumpling	
	김치만두	Kimchi dumpling	
기타	감식초	Persimmon vinegar	
	죽염	Salt roasted in bamboo	
	물엿	Dextrose syrup	
	삼계탕	Chicken stew with ginseng	
	엿기름	Malt	
	누룽지	Nurungji (Roasted cooking rice)	

Ⅹ. 우리식 표현의 영어 낱말들

우리식으로 꾸며 만들어진 영어의 낱말들을 순수한 영어로 잘못 알고 사용하는 경우가 많다. 대표적인 몇 가지를 열거해 본다.

우리말 표현	우리식 영어 표현	올바른 영어 표현
가솔린 스탠드	gasoline+stand	filling station; gas station; 《英》petrol station
골든 아워	golden+hour	prime (television) time
골인	goal+in	reach the finish (line); get (make, score) a goal; get married
덤프카	dump+car	dump truck; 《英》dump lorry
마이카	my+car	family car (자가용); privately owned car
매스컴	mass+com	mass communication (media)
모닝 서비스	morning+service	special rate in the morning
백미러	back+mirror	rearview mirror; 《英》driving mirror
베드타운	bed+town	bedroom suburbs (communities); exurbs (도시주변의 신흥 주택지)
사인펜	sign+pen	felt-tipped pen; felt pen
샐러리맨	salary+man	office (white-collar) worker
애프터 서비스	after+service	after-sales service; repair service
오더 메이드	order+made	made-to-order; custom-(ready-)made
오피스 레이디	office+lady	(woman) office worker
올드 미스	old+Miss	old maid; unmarried woman
자꾸	jack	zipper; 《英》zip fastener
팬티 스타킹	panty+stocking	(a pair of) panty hose
프런트 글래스	front+glass	《美》windshield; 《英》windscreen
테이블 스피치	table+speech	(after-dinner) speech
헬스 센터	health+center	gym; health club (farm); fitness center

XI. 국제 전화 거는 법

1. 한국에서 외국으로

001
002 } —국가번호—지역번호—전화번호

한국의 국제 전화회사는 한국통신(001), 데이콤(002), 온세통신(008) 등이 있다.

001을 통해 미국, L.A.(지역번호 213)의 전화번호 123-4567에 거는 경우: 001-1-213-123-4567

2. 외국에서 한국으로

서비스번호—국가번호—지역번호(첫번째의 0은 생략한다)—전화번호

미국 L.A.에서 서울의 02-1234-5678에 거는 경우: 011-82-2-1234-5678

3. 통신 수단의 눈부신 발달로, 국제 전화도 국내 전화 못지않게 다양한 서비스를 받을 수 있게 되었다. 한국 직통 자동전화(Auto Korea Direct), 국제통화 신용카드(KT Card Call), 마스터폰 서비스, 다자 통화 서비스 등 국제 전화 회사마다 편리한 서비스를 제공한다. 이러한 서비스를 자유롭게 이용하려면 사전에 전화회사에 문의하여 이용 방법·요령 등을 정확히 알아야 한다.

	국명	서비스번호	국가번호		국명	서비스번호	국가번호
아시아	네팔	00	977	유럽	그리스	00	30
	베트남	00	84		네덜란드	00	31
	말레이시아	007	60		노르웨이	095	47
	스리랑카	00	94		덴마크	00	45
	싱가포르	005	65		독일	00	49
	인도	00	91		러시아	8	7
	인도네시아	001	62		벨기에	00	32
	일본	001	81		스웨덴	009	46
	중국	00	86		스위스	00	41
	타이완	002	886		스페인	07	34
	태국	001	66		아이슬란드	00	353
	파키스탄	00	92		영국	010	44
	필리핀	00	63		오스트리아	00/90	43
	한국	001	82		이탈리아	00	39
	홍콩	001	852		터키	00	90
오세아니아	괌	011	61		포르투갈	00	351
	사이판	011	670		프랑스	19	33
	뉴질랜드	00	64		핀란드	990/999	358
	오스트레일리아	0011	61	중동	사우디아라비아	00	966
	파푸아뉴기니	05	675		아랍에미리트	00	971
	피지	05	679		오만	00	968
남북아메리카	멕시코	98	52		이란	00	98
	미국	011	1		이스라엘	00	972
	브라질	00	55		카타르	0	974
	아르헨티나	00	54		쿠웨이트	00	965
	자메이카	011	1	아프리카	남아프리카	09	27
	캐나다	011	1		모로코	00	212
	코스타리카	00	506		이집트	00	20
	콜롬비아	90	57		케냐	000	254
	페루	00	51		코트디부아르	00	225
					튀니지	00	216

XII. 세계 주요 도시 표준시 대조표

※ 하루를 24시간으로 표시

런던·GMT (A)	베를린·파리 (B)	카이로·아테네 (C)	바그다드 (D)	카라치 (E)	방콕 (F)	홍콩 (G)	서울 (H)	시드니 (I)	호놀룰루 (J)	샌프란시스코 (K)	시카고·달라스 (L)	뉴욕 (M)	리우데자네이루 (N)
15	16	17	18	20	22	23	0	1	5	7	9	10	12
16	17	18	19	21	23	24	1	2	6	8	10	11	13
17	18	19	20	22	24	1	2	3	7	9	11	12	14
18	19	20	21	23	1	2	3	4	8	10	12	13	15
19	20	21	22	24	2	3	4	5	9	11	13	14	16
20	21	22	23	1	3	4	5	6	10	12	14	15	17
21	22	23	24	2	4	5	6	7	11	13	15	16	18
22	23	24	1	3	5	6	7	8	12	14	16	17	19
23	24	1	2	4	6	7	8	9	13	15	17	18	20
24	1	2	3	5	7	8	9	10	14	16	18	19	21
1	2	3	4	6	8	9	10	11	15	17	19	20	22
2	3	4	5	7	9	10	11	12	16	18	20	21	23
3	4	5	6	8	10	11	12	13	17	19	21	22	24
4	5	6	7	9	11	12	13	14	18	20	22	23	1
5	6	7	8	10	12	13	14	15	19	21	23	24	2
6	7	8	9	11	13	14	15	16	20	22	24	1	3
7	8	9	10	12	14	15	16	17	21	23	1	2	4
8	9	10	11	13	15	16	17	18	22	24	2	3	5
9	10	11	12	14	16	17	18	19	23	1	3	4	6
10	11	12	13	15	17	18	19	20	24	2	4	5	7
11	12	13	14	16	18	19	20	21	1	3	5	6	8
12	13	14	15	17	19	20	21	22	2	4	6	7	9
13	14	15	16	18	20	21	22	23	3	5	7	8	10
14	15	16	17	19	21	22	23	24	4	6	8	9	11

(1) 위 표 안의 숫자는 서울(한국 표준시)을 기준으로 한, 각지의 동일 날짜의 시간; 고딕체 숫자는 하루 전 날짜의 시간을 나타낸다. GMT는 그리니치 표준시.

(2) 여름에는 나라에 따라 서머타임을 실시하는 곳이 있으므로 요주의.

(3) 위 표에 없는 도시는 아래 지명을 참조. ( )의 알파벳은 위 표 상단에 명시된 지명과 같다는 뜻. +30, +60은 해당 숫자에 30분 또는 60분을 더한 시간, -30은 30분을 뺀 시간을 나타낸다.

나이로비(D)
뉴델리(E) +30
뉴올리언스(L)
도쿄/동경(H)
디트로이트(M)
로마(B)
로스앤젤레스(K)
리스본(A)
마닐라(G)
마드리드(B)
마이애미(M)
멕시코시티(L)
모스크바(D)
몬트리올(M)
베를린(B)
베이루트(C)

베이징(G)
밴쿠버(M)
보스턴(M)
봄베이(E) +30
부다페스트(B)
부에노스아이레스(N)
브뤼셀(B)
빈(B)
상파울루(N)
상하이(G)
세인트피터즈버그(D)
스톡홀름(B)
시애틀(K)
싱가포르(G)
암스테르담(B)
앙카라(C)

앵커리지(J) +60
양곤(F) -30
오슬로(B)
오타와(M)
와르소(B)
워싱턴(디씨)(M)
자카르타(F)
캔버라(I)
캘커타(E) +30
코펜하겐(B)
콜롬보(E) +30
프라하(B)
하노이(F)
헬싱키(C)

XIII. 우리 나라 행정 구역의 로마자 표기 (도·시·구·군·읍)

Names of Administrative Units

* 문화관광부고시 제2000-8호, 2000.7.7. 국어의 로마자 표기법에 의거.
* 지면 관계로 반복되는 동일한 구명(區名) 및 군명(郡名)과 읍명이 같은 것은 생략하였음.

한글(한자) Hangeul(Chinese Characters)	로마자 표기 Romanization	한글(한자) Hangeul(Chinese Characters)	로마자 표기 Romanization
서울특별시(特別市)	Seoul-teukbyeolsi	수성구(壽城區)	Suseong-gu
종로구(鍾路區)	Jongno-gu	달성군(達城郡)	Dalseong-gun
중구(中區)	Jung-gu	인천광역시 (仁川廣域市)	Incheon-gwangyeoksi
용산구(龍山區)	Yongsan-gu		
성동구(城東區)	Seongdong-gu	연수구(延壽區)	Yeonsu-gu
광진구(廣津區)	Gwangjin-gu	계양구(桂陽區)	Gyeyang-gu
동대문구(東大門區)	Dongdaemun-gu	부평구(富平區)	Bupyeong-gu
중랑구(中浪區)	Jungnang-gu	남동구(南洞區)	Namdong-gu
성북구(城北區)	Seongbuk-gu	강화군(江華郡)	Ganghwa-gun
강북구(江北區)	Gangbuk-gu	옹진군(甕津郡)	Ongjin-gun
도봉구(道峰區)	Dobong-gu	광주광역시 (光州廣域市)	Gwangju-gwangyeoksi
노원구(蘆原區)	Nowon-gu		
은평구(恩平區)	Eunpyeong-gu	광산구(光山區)	Gwangsan-gu
서대문구(西大門區)	Seodaemun-gu	대전광역시 (大田廣域市)	Daejeon-gwangyeoksi
마포구(麻浦區)	Mapo-gu		
강서구(江西區)	Gangseo-gu	유성구(儒城區)	Yuseong-gu
양천구(陽川區)	Yangcheon-gu	대덕구(大德區)	Daedeok-gu
구로구(九老區)	Guro-gu	울산광역시(蔚山廣域市)	Ulsan-gwangyeoksi
금천구(衿川區)	Geumcheon-gu	울주구(蔚州區)	Ulju-gu
영등포구(永登浦區)	Yeongdeungpo-gu	경기도(京畿道)	Gyeonggi-do
동작구(銅雀區)	Dongjak-gu	수원시(水原市)	Suwon-si
관악구(冠岳區)	Gwanak-gu	성남시(城南市)	Seongnam-si
강남구(江南區)	Gangnam-gu	의정부시(議政府市)	Uijeongbu-si
서초구(瑞草區)	Seocho-gu	안양시(安養市)	Anyang-si
강동구(江東區)	Gangdong-gu	부천시(富川市)	Bucheon-si
송파구(松坡區)	Songpa-gu	광명시(光明市)	Gwangmyeong-si
부산광역시(釜山廣域市)	Busan-gwangyeoksi	고양시(高陽市)	Goyang-si
중구(中區)	Jung-gu	동두천시(東豆川市)	Dongducheon-si
동구(東區)	Dong-gu	안산시(安山市)	Ansan-si
서구(西區)	Seo-gu	과천시(果川市)	Gwacheon-si
남구(南區)	Nam-gu	평택시(平澤市)	Pyeongtaek-si
북구(北區)	Buk-gu	오산시(烏山市)	Osan-si
영도구(影島區)	Yeongdo-gu	시흥시(始興市)	Siheung-si
부산진구(釜山鎭區)	Busanjin-gu	군포시(軍浦市)	Gunpo-si
동래구(東萊區)	Dongnae-gu	의왕시(儀旺市)	Uiwang-si
해운대구(海雲臺區)	Haeundae-gu	구리시(九里市)	Guri-si
금정구(金井區)	Geumjeong-gu	용인시(龍仁市)	Yongin-si
사하구(沙下區)	Saha-gu	기흥읍(器興邑)	Giheung-eup
강서구(江西區)	Gangseo-gu	수지읍(水枝邑)	Suji-eup
연제구(蓮堤區)	Yeonje-gu	남양주시(南陽州市)	Namyangju-si
수영구(水營區)	Suyeong-gu	와부읍(瓦阜邑)	Wabu-eup
사상구(沙上區)	Sasang-gu	진접읍(榛接邑)	Jinjeop-eup
기장군(機張郡)	Gijang-gun	화도읍(花道邑)	Hwado-eup
대구광역시(大邱廣域市)	Daegu-gwangyeoksi	하남시(河南市)	Hanam-si
달서구(達西區)	Dalseo-gu	파주시(坡州市)	Paju-si

한글(한자) Hangeul(Chinese Characters)	로마자 표기 Romanization	한글(한자) Hangeul(Chinese Characters)	로마자 표기 Romanization
법원읍(法院邑)	Beobwon-eup	청주시(淸州市)	Cheongju-si
문산읍(汶山邑)	Munsan-eup	상당구(上黨區)	Sangdang-gu
이천시(利川市)	Icheon-si	흥덕구(興德區)	Heungdeok-gu
장호원읍(長湖院邑)	Janghowon-eup	충주시(忠州市)	Chungju-si
부발읍(夫鉢邑)	Bubal-eup	주덕읍(周德邑)	Judeok-eup
안성시(安城市)	Anseong-si	제천시(堤川市)	Jecheon-si
김포시(金浦市)	Gimpo-si	봉양읍(鳳陽邑)	Bongyang-eup
양주군(楊州郡)	Yangju-gun	청원군(淸原郡)	Cheongwon-gun
회천읍(檜泉邑)	Hoecheon-eup	보은군(報恩郡)	Boeun-gun
여주군(驪州郡)	Yeoju-gun	옥천군(沃川郡)	Okcheon-gun
화성군(華城郡)	Hwaseong-gun	영동군(永同郡)	Yeongdong-gun
태안읍(台安邑)	Taean-eup	진천군(鎭川郡)	Jincheon-gun
광주군(廣州郡)	Gwangju-gun	괴산군(槐山郡)	Goesan-gun
연천군(漣川郡)	Yeoncheon-gun	증평읍(曾坪邑)	Jeungpyeong-eup
전곡읍(全谷邑)	Jeongok-eup	음성군(陰城郡)	Eumseong-gun
포천군(抱川郡)	Pocheon-gun	금왕읍(金旺邑)	Geumwang-eup
가평군(加平郡)	Gapyeong-gun	단양군(丹陽郡)	Danyang-gun
양평군(楊平郡)	Yangpyeong-gun	매포읍(梅浦邑)	Maepo-eup
강원도(江原道)	Gangwon-do	충청남도(忠淸南道)	Chungcheongnam-do
춘천시(春川市)	Chuncheon-si	천안시(天安市)	Cheonan-si
신북읍(新北邑)	Sinbuk-eup	성환읍(成歡邑)	Seonghwan-eup
원주시(原州市)	Wonju-si	성거읍(聖居邑)	Seonggeo-eup
문막읍(文幕邑)	Munmak-eup	공주시(公州市)	Gongju-si
강릉시(江陵市)	Gangneung-si	유구읍(維鳩邑)	Yugu-eup
주문진읍 (注文津邑)	Jumunjin-eup	논산시(論山市)	Nonsan-si
동해시(東海市)	Donghae-si	강경읍(江景邑)	Ganggyeong-eup
태백시(太白市)	Taebaek-si	연무읍(鍊武邑)	Yeonmu-eup
속초시(東草市)	Sokcho-si	보령시(保寧市)	Boryeong-si
삼척시(三陟市)	Samcheok-si	웅천읍(熊川邑)	Ungcheon-eup
도계읍(道溪邑)	Dogye-eup	아산시(牙山市)	Asan-si
원덕읍(遠德邑)	Wondeok-eup	염치읍(鹽峙邑)	Yeomchi-eup
홍천군(洪川郡)	Hongcheon-gun	서산시(瑞山市)	Seosan-si
횡성군(横城郡)	Hoengseong-gun	대산읍(大山邑)	Daesan-eup
영월군(寧越郡)	Yeongwol-gun	금산군(錦山郡)	Geumsan-gun
상동읍(上東邑)	Sangdong-eup	연기군(燕岐郡)	Yeongi-gun
평창군(平昌郡)	Pyeongchang-gun	조치원읍 (鳥致院邑)	Jochiwon-eup
정선군(旌善郡)	Jeongseon-gun	부여군(扶餘郡)	Buyeo-gun
사북읍(舍北邑)	Sabuk-eup	서천군(舒川郡)	Seocheon-gun
신동읍(新東邑)	Sindong-eup	장항읍(長項邑)	Janghang-eup
고한읍(古汗邑)	Gohan-eup	청양군(靑陽郡)	Cheongyang-gun
철원군(鐵原郡)	Cheorwon-gun	홍성군(洪城郡)	Hongseong-gun
김화읍(金化邑)	Gimhwa-eup	광천읍(廣川邑)	Gwangcheon-eup
갈말읍(葛末邑)	Galmal-eup	예산군(禮山郡)	Yesan-gun
동송읍(東松邑)	Dongsong-eup	삽교읍(挿橋邑)	Sapgyo-eup
화천군(華川郡)	Hwacheon-gun	태안군(泰安郡)	Taean-gun
양구군(楊口郡)	Yanggu-gun	안면읍(安眠邑)	Anmyeon-eup
인제군(麟蹄郡)	Inje-gun	당진군(唐津郡)	Dangjin-gun
고성군(高城郡)	Goseong-gun	합덕읍(合德邑)	Hapdeok-eup
간성읍(杆城邑)	Ganseong-eup	전라북도(全羅北道)	Jeollabuk-do
거진읍(巨津邑)	Geojin-eup	전주시(全州市)	Jeonju-si
양양군(襄陽郡)	Yangyang-gun	군산시(群山市)	Gunsan-si
충청북도(忠淸北道)	Chungcheongbuk-do	옥구읍(沃溝邑)	Okgu-eup

한글(한자) Hangeul(Chinese Characters)	로마자 표기 Romanization	한글(한자) Hangeul(Chinese Characters)	로마자 표기 Romanization
익산시(益山市)	Iksan-si	신안군(新安郡)	Sinan-gun
함열읍(咸悅邑)	Hamyeol-eup	지도읍(智島邑)	Jido-eup
정읍시(井邑市)	Jeongeup-si	경상북도(慶尙北道)	Gyeongsangbuk-do
신태인읍 (新泰仁邑)	Sintaein-eup	포항시(浦項市)	Pohang-si
남원시(南原市)	Namwon-si	구룡포읍 (九龍浦邑)	Guryongpo-eup
운봉읍(雲峰邑)	Unbong-eup	연일읍(延日邑)	Yeonil-eup
김제시(金堤市)	Gimje-si	조천읍(朝川邑)	Jocheon-eup
만경읍(萬頃邑)	Mangyeong-eup	흥해읍(興海邑)	Heunghae-eup
완주군(完州郡)	Wanju-gun	경주시(慶州市)	Gyeongju-si
삼례읍(參禮邑)	Samnye-eup	감포읍(甘浦邑)	Gampo-eup
봉동읍(鳳東邑)	Bongdong-eup	안강읍(安康邑)	Angang-eup
진안군(鎭安郡)	Jinan-gun	건천읍(乾川邑)	Geoncheon-eup
무주군(茂朱郡)	Muju-gun	외동읍(外東邑)	Oedong-eup
장수군(長水郡)	Jangsu-gun	김천시(金泉市)	Gimcheon-si
임실군(任實郡)	Imsil-gun	아포읍(牙浦邑)	Apo-eup
순창군(淳昌郡)	Sunchang-gun	안동시(安東市)	Andong-si
고창군(高敞郡)	Gochang-gun	풍산읍(豊山邑)	Pungsan-eup
부안군(扶安郡)	Buan-gun	구미시(龜尾市)	Gumi-si
전라남도(全羅南道)	Jeollanam-do	고아읍(高牙邑)	Goa-eup
목포시(木浦市)	Mokpo-si	선산읍(善山邑)	Seonsan-eup
여수시(麗水市)	Yeosu-si	영주시(榮州市)	Yeongju-si
돌산읍(突山邑)	Dolsan-eup	풍기읍(豊基邑)	Punggi-eup
순천시(順天市)	Suncheon-si	영천시(永川市)	Yeongcheon-si
승주읍(昇州邑)	Seungju-eup	금호읍(琴湖邑)	Geumho-eup
나주시(羅州市)	Naju-si	상주시(尙州市)	Sangju-si
남평읍(南平邑)	Nampyeong-eup	함창읍(咸昌邑)	Hamchang-eup
광양시(光陽市)	Gwangyang-si	문경시(聞慶市)	Mungyeong-si
담양군(潭陽郡)	Damyang-gun	가은읍(加恩邑)	Gaeun-eup
곡성군(谷城郡)	Gokseong-gun	경산시(慶山市)	Gyeongsan-si
구례군(求禮郡)	Gurye-gun	하양읍(河陽邑)	Hayang-eup
고흥군(高興郡)	Goheung-gun	군위군(軍威郡)	Gunwi-gun
도양읍(道陽邑)	Doyang-eup	의성군(義城郡)	Uiseong-gun
보성군(寶城郡)	Boseong-gun	청송군(靑松郡)	Cheongsong-gun
벌교읍(筏橋邑)	Beolgyo-eup	영양군(英陽郡)	Yeongyang-gun
화순군(和順郡)	Hwasun-gun	영덕군(盈德郡)	Yeongdeok-gun
장흥군(長興郡)	Jangheung-gun	청도군(淸道郡)	Cheongdo-gun
관산읍(冠山邑)	Gwansan-eup	화양읍(華陽邑)	Hwayang-eup
대덕읍(大德邑)	Daedeok-eup	고령군(高靈郡)	Goryeong-gun
강진군(康津郡)	Gangjin-gun	성주군(星州郡)	Seongju-gun
해남군(海南郡)	Haenam-gun	칠곡군(漆谷郡)	Chilgok-gun
영암군(靈岩郡)	Yeongam-gun	왜관읍(倭館邑)	Waegwan-eup
무안군(務安郡)	Muan-gun	예천군(醴泉郡)	Yecheon-gun
일로읍(一老邑)	Illo-eup	봉화군(奉化郡)	Bonghwa-gun
함평군(咸平郡)	*Hampyeong-gun*	울진군(蔚珍郡)	Uljin-gun
영광군(靈光郡)	Yeonggwang-gun	평해읍(平海邑)	Pyeonghae-eup
백수읍(白岫邑)	Baeksu-eup	울릉읍(鬱陵邑)	Ulleung-eup
홍농읍(弘農邑)	Hongnong-eup	경상남도(慶尙南道)	Gyeongsangnam-do
장성군(長城郡)	Jangseong-gun	마산시(馬山市)	Masan-si
완도군(莞島郡)	Wando-gun	합포구(合浦區)	Happo-gu
금일읍(金日邑)	Geumil-eup	회원구(檜原區)	Hoewon-gu
노화읍(蘆花邑)	Nohwa-eup	내서읍(內西邑)	Naeseo-eup
진도군(珍島郡)	Jindo-gun	진주시(晉州市)	Jinju-si

한글(한자) Hangeul(Chinese Characters)	로마자 표기 Romanization	한글(한자) Hangeul(Chinese Characters)	로마자 표기 Romanization
문산읍(文山邑)	Munsan-eup	창녕군(昌寧郡)	Changnyeong-gun
창원시(昌原市)	Changwon-si	남지읍(南旨邑)	Namji-eup
동읍(東邑)	Dong-eup	고성군(固城郡)	Goseong-gun
진해시(鎭海市)	Jinhae-si	남해군(南海郡)	Namhae-gun
통영시(統營市)	Tongyeong-si	하동군(河東郡)	Hadong-gun
산양읍(山陽邑)	Sanyang-eup	산청군(山淸郡)	Sancheong-gun
사천시(泗川市)	Sacheon-si	함양군(咸陽郡)	Hamyang-gun
양산시(梁山市)	Yangsan-si	거창군(居昌郡)	Geochang-gun
웅상읍(熊上邑)	Ungsang-eup	합천군(陜川郡)	Hapcheon-gun
물금읍(勿禁邑)	Mulgeum-eup	제주도(濟州道)	Jeju-do
김해시(金海市)	Gimhae-si	제주시(濟州市)	Jeju-si
진영읍(進永邑)	Jinyeong-eup	서귀포시(西歸浦市)	Seogwipo-si
밀양시(密陽市)	Miryang-si	북제주군(北濟州郡)	Bukjeju-gun
삼랑진읍(三浪津邑)	Samnangjin-eup	한림읍(翰林邑)	Hallim-eup
		애월읍(涯月邑)	Aewol-eup
하남읍(下南邑)	Hanam-eup	구좌읍(舊左邑)	Gujwa-eup
거제시(巨濟市)	Geoje-si	조천읍(朝天邑)	Jocheon-eup
신현읍(新縣邑)	Sinhyeon-eup	남제주군(南濟州郡)	Namjeju-gun
의령군(宜寧郡)	Uiryeong-gun	대정읍(大靜邑)	Daejeong-eup
함안군(咸安郡)	Haman-gun	남원읍(南元邑)	Namwon-eup
가야읍(伽倻邑)	Gaya-eup	성산읍(城山邑)	Seongsan-eup

XⅣ. 미국의 주명(州名)

네바다 Nevada	(Nev., NV)	아칸소 Arkansas	(Ark., AR)
네브래스카 Nebraska	(Neb., Nebr., NE)	알래스카 Alaska	(Alas., AK)
노스다코타 North Dakota	(N.D., N.Dak., ND)	애리조나 Arizona	(Ariz., AZ)
		앨라배마 Alabama	(Ala., AL)
노스캐롤라이나 North Carolina	(N.C., NC)	오리건 Oregon	(Ore., Oreg., OR)
뉴멕시코 New Mexico	(N.M., N.Mex., NM)	오클라호마 Oklahoma	(Okla., OK)
뉴욕 New York	(N.Y., NY)	오하이오 Ohio	(O., OH)
뉴저지 New Jersey	(N.J., NJ)	와이오밍 Wyoming	(Wyo., WY)
뉴햄프셔 New Hampshire	(N.H., NH)	워싱턴 Washington	(Wash., WA)
델라웨어 Delaware	(Del., DE)	웨스트버지니아 West Virginia	(W. Va., WV)
로드아일랜드 Rhode Island	(R.I., RI)	위스콘신 Wisconsin	(Wis., Wisc., WI)
루이지애나 Louisiana	(La., LA)	유타 Utah	(Ut., UT)
매사추세츠 Massachusetts	(Mass., MA)	인디애나 Indiana	(Ind., IN)
메릴랜드 Maryland	(Md., MD)	일리노이 Illinois	(Ill., IL)
메인 Maine	(Me., ME)	조지아 Georgia	(Ga., GA)
몬태나 Montana	(Mont., MT)	캔자스 Kansas	(Kan., Kans., KS)
미네소타 Minnesota	(Minn., MN)	캘리포니아 California	(Calif., Cal., CA)
미시간 Michigan	(Mich., MI)	켄터키 Kentucky	(Ky., Ken., KY)
미시시피 Mississippi	(Miss., MS)	코네티컷 Connecticut	(Conn., CT)
미주리 Missouri	(Mo., MO)	콜로라도 Colorado	(Colo., CO)
버몬트 Vermont	(Vt., VT)	테네시 Tennessee	(Tenn., TN)
버지니아 Virginia	(Va., VA)	텍사스 Texas	(Tex., TX)
사우스다코타 South Dakota	(S.D., S.Dak., SD)	펜실베이니아 Pennsylvania	(Pa., Penn., Penna., PA)
사우스캐롤라이나 South Carolina	(S.C., SC)	플로리다 Florida	(Fla., FL)
아이다호 Idaho	(Id., Ida., ID)	하와이 Hawaii	(Hi., HI)
아이오와 Iowa	(Ia., IA)		

XV. 불규칙 동사표

이탤릭체는 《古》 또는 《稀》

현 재	과 거	과거분사	현 재	과 거	과거분사
abide	abode; abided	abode; abided	cleave	cleft; cleaved; clove	cleft; cleaved; cloven
arise	arose	arisen	cling	clung	clung
awake	awoke	awoke, awaked	clothe	clothed; *clad*	clothed; *clad*
be(am, is; are)	was, were	been	come	came	come
			cost	cost	cost
bear	bore	borne, born	creep	crept	crept
beat	beat	beaten	crow	crowed, crew	crowed
become	became	become	cut	cut	cut
befall	befell	befallen	dare	dared, *durst*	dared
beget	begot	begotten	deal	dealt	dealt
begin	began	begun	dig	dug	dug
behold	beheld	beheld, *beholden*	do, does	did	done
			draw	drew	drawn
bend	bent	bent, *bended*	dream	dreamed; *dreamt*	dreamed; *dreamt*
bereave	bereaved; bereft	bereaved; bereft	drink	drank	drunk, drunken
beseech	besought	besought	drive	drove	driven
beset	beset	beset	dwell	dwelt	dwelt
bespeak	bespoke	bespoken	eat	ate	eaten
bestride	bestrode	bestridden	fall	fell	fallen
bet	bet; betted	bet; betted	feed	fed	fed
betake	betook	betaken	feel	felt	felt
bethink	bethought	bethought	fight	fought	fought
bid	bade; bid	bidden; bid	find	found	found
bide	bided, bode	bided	flee	fled	fled
bind	bound	bound	fling	flung	flung
bite	bit	bitten, bit	fly	flew	flown
bleed	bled	bled	forbear	forbore	forborne
blend	blended; blent	blended; blent	forbid	forbade, forbad	forbidden
			forecast	forecast; forecasted	forecast; forecasted
bless	blessed; blest	blessed; blest			
blow	blew	blown	forego	forewent	foregone
break	broke	broken	foreknow	foreknew	foreknown
breed	bred	bred	foresee	foresaw	foreseen
bring	brought	brought	foretell	foretold	foretold
broadcast	broadcast; broadcasted	broadcast; broadcasted	forget	forgot	forgotten
			forgive	forgave	forgiven
browbeat	browbeat	browbeaten	forsake	forsook	forsaken
build	built	built	freeze	froze	frozen
burn	burnt; *burned*	burnt; *burned*	gainsay	gainsaid	gainsaid
burst	burst	burst	get	got	got, gotten
buy	bought	bought	gild	gilded; gilt	gilded; gilt
can	could	—	gird	girded; girt	girded; girt
cast	cast	cast	give	gave	given
catch	caught	caught	gnaw	gnawed	gnawed, gnawn
chide	chid; chided	chid, chidden; *chosen*	go	went	gone
choose	chose	chosen	grave	graved	graved,

현재	과거	과거분사	현재	과거	과거분사
		graven	overcome	overcame	overcome
grind	ground	ground	overdo	overdid	overdone
grow	grew	grown	overdraw	overdrew	overdrawn
hang	hung; hanged	hung; hanged	overdrink	overdrank	overdrunk
have, has	had	had	overeat	overate	overeaten
hear	heard	heard	overfeed	overfed	overfed
heave	heaved; hove	heaved; hove	overgrow	overgrew	overgrown
hew	hewed	hewn, hewed	overhang	overhung	overhung
hide	hid	hidden, hid	overhear	overheard	overheard
hit	hit	hit	overlay	overlaid	overlaid
hold	held	held	overpay	overpaid	overpaid
hurt	hurt	hurt	override	overrode	overridden
inlay	inlaid	inlaid	overrun	overran	overrun
inset	inset; insetted	inset; insetted	oversee	oversaw	overseen
			overshoot	overshot	overshot
keep	kept	kept	oversleep	overslept	overslept
kneel	knelt; kneeled	knelt; kneeled	overspread	overspread	overspread
knit	knitted; knit	knitted; knit	overtake	overtook	overtaken
know	knew	known	overthrow	overthrew	overthrown
lay	laid	laid	overwork	overworked	overworked
lead	led	led	partake	partook	partaken
lean	leaned; (英) leant	leaned; (英) leant	pay	paid	paid
			plead	pleaded; plead; pled	pleaded; plead; pled
leap	leaped; leapt	leaped; leapt	prepay	prepaid	prepaid
learn	learned; learnt	learned; learnt	proofread	proofread	proofread
			prove	proved	proved, proven
leave	left	left			
lend	lent	lent	put	put	put
let	let	let	quit	quitted; quit	quitted; quit
let	let; letted	let; letted	read	read	read
lie	lay	lain	rebuild	rebuilt	rebuilt
light	lighted; lit	lighted; lit	recast	recast	recast
list	list; listed	list; listed	remake	remade	remade
lose	lost	lost	relay	relaid	relaid
make	made	made	rend	rent	rent
may	might	—	repay	repaid	repaid
mean	meant	meant	reset	reset	reset
meet	met	met	retell	retold	retold
melt	melted	melted	rewrite	rewrote	rewritten
mislead	misled	misled	rid	rid; ridded	rid; ridded
misunderstand	misunderstood	misunderstood	ride	rode	ridden
			ring	rang	rung
mow	mowed	mowed, mown	rise	rose	risen
			run	ran	run
must	(must)	—	saw	sawed	sawn, (稀) *sawed*
ought	(ought)	—			
outdo	outdid	outdone	say, *saith*	said	said
outgo	outwent	outgone	see	saw	seen
outgrow	outgrew	outgrown	seek	sought	sought
outride	outrode	outridden	sell	sold	sold
outrun	outran	outrun	send	sent	sent
outshine	outshone	outshone	set	set	set
outspread	outspread	outspread	sew	sewed	sewed, sewn
overcast	overcast	overcast	shake	shook	shaken

현 재	과 거	과거분사	현 재	과 거	과거분사
shall, *shalt*	should	—	strike	struck	struck, 《때로》 *stricken*
shave	shaved	shaved, shaven	string	strung	strung
shear	sheared	sheared; shorn	strive	strove	striven
			swear	swore	sworn
shed	shed	shed	sweat	sweat; sweated	sweat, sweated
shine	shone; shined	shone; shined	sweep	swept	swept
shoe	shod	shod	swell	swelled	swollen
shoot	shot	shot	swim	swam	swum
show	showed	shown, 《稀》*showed*	swing	swung	swung
			take	took	taken
shred	shredded	shredden	teach	taught	taught
shrink	shrank	shrunk	tear	tore	torn
shrive	shrived; shrove	shrived; shriven	telecast	telecast; telecasted	telecast; telecasted
shut	shut	shut	tell	told	told
sing	sang	sung	think	thought	thought
sink	sank; sunk	sunk; sunken	thrive	throve; thrived	thriven; thrived
sit	sat	sat	throw	threw	thrown
slay	slew	slain	thrust	thrust	thrust
sleep	slept	slept	toss	tossed	tossed
slide	slid	slid, 《美》slidden	tread	trod	trodden
			typewrite	typewrote	typewritten
sling	slung	slung	unbend	unbent; unbended	unbent; unbended
slink	slunk	slunk			
slip	slipped	slipped	unbind	unbound	unbound
slit	slit; *slitted*	slit; *slitted*	undergo	underwent	undergone
smell	smelled; smelt	smelled; smelt	understand	understood	understood
			undertake	undertook	undertaken
smite	smote	smitten	underwrite	underwrote	underwritten
sow	sowed	sown, sowed	undo	undid	undone
speak	spoke	spoken	uphold	upheld	upheld
speed	sped; speeded	sped; speeded	upset	upset	upset
			wake	waked; woke	waked; woken
spell	spelled; spelt	spelled; spelt			
spend	spent	spent	waylay	waylaid	waylaid
spill	spilled; spilt	spilled; spilt	wear	wore	worn
spin	spun	spun	weave	wove	woven
spit	spat	spat	wed	wedded	wedden, wed
split	split	split	weep	wept	wept
spoil	spoiled; spoilt	spoiled; spoilt	wet	wet; wetted	wet; wetted
spread	spread	spread	will	would	—
spring	sprang	sprung	win	won	won
stand	stood	stood	wind	wound	wound
stave	staved; stove	staved; stove	withdraw	withdrew	withdrawn
stay	stayed	stayed	withhold	withheld	withheld
steal	stole	stolen	withstand	withstood	withstood
stick	stuck	stuck	work	worked; wrought	worked; wrought
sting	stung	stung			
stink	stank, stunk	stunk	wrap	wrapped; wrapt	wrapped; wrapt
strew	strewed	strewn, strewed			
			wring	wrung	wrung
stride	strode	stridden	write	wrote	written

❖ 민중서림의 사전 ❖

사전명	판형/쪽수	사전명	판형/쪽수
• 국 어 대 사 전	4·6배판 4,784쪽	• 리틀자이언트일한·한일소사전	미니판 1,792쪽
• 엣센스 국어사전	4·6판 2,886쪽	• 리틀자이언트일한소사전	미니판 896쪽
• 엣센스 스탠더드영한사전	국 판 3,120쪽	• 독 한 · 한 독 사 전	3·5판 1,264쪽
• 엣센스 영한사전	4·6판 2,968쪽	• 신 일 한 사 전 [예해]	4·6판 1,154쪽
• 엣센스 한영사전	4·6판 2,704쪽	• 신 한 일 사 전 [예해]	4·6판 1,168쪽
• 엣센스 영영한사전	4·6판 2,048쪽	• 엣센스 실용일한사전	4·6판 1,864쪽
• 엣센스 한일사전	4·6판 2,760쪽	• 엣센스 日本語漢字읽기사전	4·6판 2,080쪽
• 엣센스 독한사전	4·6판 2,784쪽	• 일본외래어·カタカナ어사전	4·6판 1,696쪽
• 엣센스 한독사전	4·6판 2,104쪽	• 漢 韓 大 字 典	국 판 2,936쪽
• 엣센스 불한사전	4·6판 2,208쪽	• 漢 韓 大 字 典	크라운판 2,936쪽
• 엣센스 中韓辭典	4·6판 3,344쪽	• 민 중 活 用 玉 篇	3·6판 1,120쪽
• 엣센스 韓中辭典	4·6판 2,640쪽	• 最 新 弘 字 玉 篇	4·6판 960쪽
• 엣센스 스페인어사전	4·6판 1,816쪽	• 엣센스 한자사전	4·6판 2,448쪽
• 엣센스 한서사전	4·6판 2,776쪽	• 엣센스 실용한자사전	3·6판 1,380쪽
• 엣센스 국어사전 [가죽]	4·6판 2,886쪽	• 민 중 실 용 국 어 사 전	4·6판 1,832쪽
• 엣센스 영한사전 [가죽]	4·6판 2,968쪽	• 메 인 영 한 사 전	4·6판 2,846쪽
• 엣센스 한영사전 [가죽]	4·6판 2,704쪽	• 엣센스 칼리지영한사전	4·6판 2,072쪽
• 엣센스 일한사전 [가죽]	4·6판 2,992쪽	• 엣센스 실용영한사전	4·6판 1,888쪽
• 엣센스 국어사전 [특장판]	국 판 3,104쪽	• 엣센스 실용한영사전	4·6판 1,936쪽
• 엣센스 영한사전 [특장판]	국 판 3,296쪽	• 엣센스 실용군사영어사전	4·6판 1,168쪽
• 엣센스 한영사전 [특장판]	국 판 3,032쪽	• 엣센스 실용중한사전	4·6판 2,400쪽
• 포 켓 영 한 사 전	3·6판 976쪽	• 엣센스 韓中활용사전	3·6판 1,184쪽
• 포 켓 한 영 사 전	3·6판 928쪽	• 엣센스 실용영어회화사전	4·6판 1,400쪽
• 포 켓 영한 · 한영사전	3·6판 1,904쪽	• 엣센스 실용일본어회화사전	4·6판 1,240쪽
• 포 켓 한 중 사 전	3·6판 960쪽	• 엣센스 현대중국어회화사전	국 판 1,268쪽
• 포켓중한 · 한중사전	3·6판 1,992쪽	• 고교영어 단축문 총정리	4·6판 1,176쪽
• 포 켓 스 페 인 어 사 전	3·6판 1,184쪽	• 엣센스 수능영어사전	4·6판 960쪽
• 포 켓 한 서 사 전	3·6판 1,096쪽	• 엣센스 중학영어사전	4·6판 1,088쪽
• 엣센스 신일한사전 [포켓판]	3·6판 1,056쪽	• 엣센스 영어입문사전	4·6판 1,104쪽
• 엣센스 신한일사전 [포켓판]	3·6판 1,120쪽	• 엣센스 초등영어사전	크라운판 4,888쪽
• 엣센스 일한·한일사전 [포켓판]	3·6판 2,176쪽	• 스마트 초등영어사전	신국판 1,064쪽
• 핸 디 영 한 사 전	3·5판 976쪽	• 초등학교 으뜸국어사전	4·6판 1,360쪽
• 핸 디 한 영 사 전	3·5판 928쪽	• 초등학교 민중새국어사전	3·6판 1,024쪽
• 핸디 영한 · 한영사전	3·5판 1,904쪽	• 엣센스 한자입문사전	국 판 735쪽
• 리틀자이언트영한·한영사전	미니판 1,776쪽	• 엣센스 기초한자사전	4·6판 608쪽
• 리틀자이언트영한소사전	미니판 880쪽	• 엣센스 초등한자사전	크라운판 424쪽
• 리틀자이언트한영소사전	미니판 896쪽		